P9-CAS-644

### Search through the complete book in PDF.

- ✔ Access the entire *MCSE: Windows 2000 Directory Services Administration Study Guide,* complete with figures and tables, in electronic format.

- ✔ Search the *MCSE: Windows 2000 Directory Services Administration Study Guide* chapters to find information on any topic in seconds.

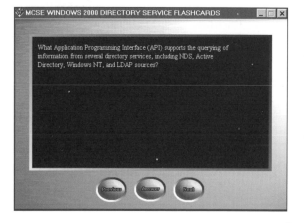

### Use the Electronic Flashcards for PCs or Palm devices to jog your memory and prep last-minute for the exam!

- ✔ Reinforce your understanding of key concepts with these hardcore flashcard-style questions.

- ✔ Download the Flashcards to your Palm device, and go on the road. Now you can study anywhere, any time.

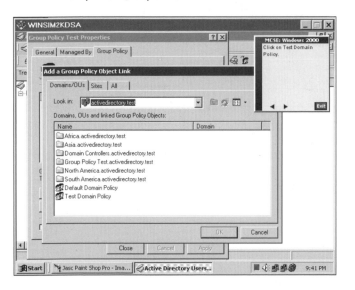

### Prepare for Microsoft's tough simulation questions with the WinSim Windows 2000 program!

- ✓ Use the simulators to guide you through real-world tasks step-by-step, or watch the movies to see the "invisible hand" perform the tasks for you.

SYBEX

# MCSE: Windows 2000 Directory Services Administration Study Guide

SYBEX

## Exam 70-217: Objectives

**MANAGING, MONITORING, AND OPTIMIZING THE COMPONENTS OF ACTIVE DIRECTORY**

**CONFIGURING, MANAGING, MONITORING, AND TROUBLESHOOTING ACTIVE DIRECTORY SECURITY SOLUTIONS**

NOTE Exam objectives are subject to change at any time without prior notice and at Microsoft's sole discretion. Please visit Microsoft's Training & Certification Web site (www.microsoft.com/Train_Cert) for the most current listing of exam objectives.

SYBEX

# MCSE:
# Windows 2000 Directory Services Administration

## Study Guide

### Second Edition

# MCSE:
## Windows® 2000 Directory Services Administration
### Study Guide

**Second Edition**

Anil Desai

with James Chellis

San Francisco • Paris • Düsseldorf • Soest • London

Associate Publisher: Neil Edde
Contracts and Licensing Manager: Kristine O'Callaghan
Acquisitions and Developmental Editor: Jeff Kellum
Editor: Rebecca Rider
Production Editor: Elizabeth Campbell
Technical Editors: Dan Renaud, Mark Kovach
Book Designer: Bill Gibson
Graphic Illustrators: Tony Jonick, Jerry Williams
Electronic Publishing Specialist: Susie Hendrickson
Proofreader: Emily Hsuan, Nelson Kim, Laurie O'Connell, Nancy Riddiough
Indexer: Ted Laux
CD Coordinator: Christine Harris
CD Technician: Kevin Ly
Cover Designer: Archer Design
Cover Photographer: Natural Selection

Library of Congress Card Number:  2001088244

ISBN: 0-7821-2948-X

SYBEX

To Our Valued Readers:

When Sybex published the first editions of the four core Windows® 2000 MCSE Study Guides, Windows® 2000 had been out for only six months, and the MCSE exams had just been released. In writing the Study Guides, the authors brought to the table their experience with Windows® 2000 as well as insights gained from years of classroom teaching. With the official Microsoft exam objectives as their guides, the authors set out to write comprehensive, yet ultimately clear, concise, and practical courseware. And we believe they succeeded.

Over the past year, however, our authors have learned many new things about how Windows® 2000 works and have received significant and useful feedback about how Microsoft is testing individuals on the vast array of topics encompassed by the four core exams. We at Sybex have also received a tremendous amount of invaluable feedback—both praise and criticism—regarding the four core Windows® 2000 Study Guides. The second edition that you hold in your hand is the product of the feedback that readers such as yourself have provided to us.

So what "new and improved" material will you find in this new edition? We have confidence in the core instructional material in the books, so the authors have made only minor modifications to this content. They have, however, made the chapter review questions and bonus exam questions more challenging, to better reflect the type of questions you'll encounter on the actual exasms. We've also added Real World Scenarios throughout the book. This new feature allowed the authors to add critical context and perspective on Windows® 2000 technologies that wasn't available when Microsoft first released the products. Finally, we've added Exam Essentials to the end of each chapter. These re-emphasize those subject areas that are most important for success on the exams.

We believe you'll find this Study Guide to be an indispensable part of your exam prep program. As always, your feedback is important to us. Please send comments, questions, or suggestions to support@sybex.com. At Sybex we're continually striving to meet and exceed the needs of individuals preparing for IT certification exams. Readers like you are critical to these efforts.

Good luck in pursuit of your MCSE!

Neil Edde
Associate Publisher—Certification
Sybex, Inc.

SYBEX Inc. 1151 Marina Village Parkway, Alameda, CA 94501
Tel: 510/523-8233    Fax: 510/523-2373    HTTP://www.sybex.com

# Software License Agreement: Terms and Conditions

*To Monica*

# Acknowledgments

As professionals in the IT industry, many of you have probably learned the value of teamwork. Therefore, it will probably come as no surprise to you that this book is the result of a lot of hard work from several people. In this brief section, I'll try to give credit where it's due.

During the last two years, I've had the pleasure of working with many energetic, enthusiastic, and driven people at QuickArrow, Inc. At first, I was planning to acknowledge some of them specifically. But, it's much more appropriate to thank *all* of them. Just a few short months ago, I could have easily listed the names of everyone in the company on this page. We used to be a small team with big plans. Things have changed, and we're now a large team (with even bigger plans). The company has grown dramatically, without sacrificing focus and dedication, and I've learned a lot in the process.

Next, I'd like to thank the many people at Sybex with whom I have worked on this project. Thanks to Jeff Kellum, Rebecca Rider, Elizabeth Campbell, Susie Hendrickson, and proofreaders Emily Hsuan, Nelson Kim, Laurie O'Connell, and Nancy Riddiough for their assistance in the writing process for the second edition of this book. And, as operating systems and services get more and more complex, it becomes increasingly important to verify the accuracy of technical information. That's why technical input from Dan Renaud and Mark Kovach was so important in the process.

Thanks also to James Chellis and Matthew Sheltz for their work on the WinSim tool and other content that you'll find on the accompanying CD-ROM. I thank all of these people for making my job easier, and you can thank them for making this book a complete, accurate, and valuable resource for IT professionals.

Acknowledgments are difficult to write (at least for me), but the Dedication was an easy choice—my wife, Monica, has always been a great source of support and encouragement, despite the seemingly incessant clicking of my keyboard throughout the night and through long weekends of writing and editing. I want to thank her for her patience and support.

Finally, thanks to you, the reader, for using this book. I'm confident that the information you find here will be an excellent resource as you prepare to work with Windows 2000 and the Active Directory in the real world. For most of you, I suspect that it will be a challenge—large-scale, pervasive changes always are. Add to that political and business issues, and you've got a long climb ahead of you. However, I trust that the challenge will be a personally and professionally rewarding one.

If you have any questions or comments about the contents of the book, please feel free to e-mail me at anil@austin.rr.com. Good luck!

# Contents at a Glance

# Contents

# Table of Exercises

# Introduction

**M**icrosoft's Microsoft Certified Systems Engineer (MCSE) track for Windows 2000 is the premier certification for computer industry professionals. Covering the core technologies around which Microsoft's future will be built, the MCSE Windows 2000 program is a powerful credential for career advancement.

This book has been developed to give you the critical skills and knowledge you need to prepare for one of the core requirements of the new MCSE certification program: *Implementing and Administering a Microsoft Windows 2000 Directory Services Infrastructure* (Exam 70-217).

## The Microsoft Certified Professional Program

Since the inception of its certification program, Microsoft has certified over one million people. As the computer network industry grows in both size and complexity, these numbers are sure to grow—and the need for *proven* ability will also increase. Companies rely on certifications to verify the skills of prospective employees and contractors.

Microsoft has developed its Microsoft Certified Professional (MCP) program to give you credentials that verify your ability to work with Microsoft products effectively and professionally. Obtaining your MCP certification requires that you pass any one Microsoft certification exam. Several levels of certification are available based on specific suites of exams. Depending on your areas of interest or experience, you can obtain any of the following MCP credentials:

**Microsoft Certified System Engineer (MCSE)**   This certification track is designed for network and systems administrators, network and systems analysts, and technical consultants who work with Microsoft Windows 2000 client and server software. You must take and pass seven exams to obtain your MCSE.

Since this book covers one of the Core MCSE exams, we will discuss the MCSE certification in detail in this Introduction.

**Microsoft Certified Solution Developer (MCSD)** This track is designed for software engineers and developers and technical consultants who primarily use Microsoft development tools. Currently, you can take exams on Visual Basic, Visual C++, and Visual FoxPro. However, with Microsoft's pending release of Visual Studio 7, you can expect the requirements for this track to change by the end of 2001. You must take and pass four exams to obtain your MCSD.

**Microsoft Certified Database Administrator (MCDBA)** This track is designed for database administrators, developers, and analysts who work with Microsoft SQL Server. As of this printing, you can take exams on either SQL Server 7 or SQL Server 2000, but Microsoft is expected to announce the retirement of SQL Server 7. You must take and pass four exams to achieve MCDBA status.

**Microsoft Certified Trainer (MCT)** The MCT track is designed for any IT professional who develops and teaches Microsoft-approved courses. To become an MCT, you must first obtain your MCSE, MCSD, or MCDBA; then you must take a class at one of the Certified Technical Training Centers. You will also be required to prove your instructional ability. You can do this in various ways: by taking a skills-building or train-the-trainer class; by achieving certification as a trainer from any of a number vendors; or by becoming a Certified Technical Trainer through the Chauncey Group (www.chauncey.com/ctt.html). Last of all, you will need to complete an MCT application.

As of March 1, 2001, Microsoft no longer offers MCSE NT 4 track. Those who are certified in NT 4 have until December 31, 2001, to upgrade their credentials to Windows 2000. Also, Microsoft has retired three other certification tracks: MCP+Internet, MCSE+Internet, and MCP+Site Builder. The topics and concepts that are tested in these certifications have been incorporated into the MCSE and MCSD exams.

### Windows 2000

Over the next few years, companies around the world will deploy millions of copies of Windows 2000 as the central operating system for their mission-critical networks. This will generate an enormous need for qualified consultants and personnel who can design, deploy, and support Windows 2000 networks.

Because Windows 2000 is such a vast product, its administrators must have a wealth of professional skills. As an example of Windows 2000's complexity, consider it has more than 35 million lines of code as compared with Windows NT 4's 12 million! Much of this code is needed to support the wide range of functionality that Windows 2000 offers.

The Windows 2000 line comprises several versions:

**Windows 2000 Professional**  This is the client edition of Windows 2000, which is comparable to Windows NT Workstation 4 but also includes the best features of Windows 98, as well as many new features.

**Windows 2000 Server/Windows 2000 Advanced Server**  A server edition of Windows 2000, this version is for small to midsized deployments. Advanced Server supports more memory and processors than Server does.

**Windows 2000 Datacenter Server**  This is a server edition of Windows 2000 for large, widescale deployments and computer clusters. Datacenter Server supports the most memory and processors of the three versions.

Companies implementing the expansive Windows 2000 operating system want to be certain that you are the right person for the job being offered. The MCSE track is designed to help you prove that you are.

## How Do You Become an MCSE?

Attaining MCSE certification has always been a challenge. In the past, students have been able to acquire detailed exam information—even most of the exam questions—from online "brain dumps" and third-party "cram" books or software products. For the new MCSE exams, this is simply not the case.

Microsoft has taken strong steps to protect the security and integrity of the new MCSE track. Now, prospective MCSEs must complete a course of study that develops detailed knowledge about a wide range of topics. It supplies them with the true skills needed, derived from working with Windows 2000 and related software products.

The new MCSE program is heavily weighted toward hands-on skills and experience. Microsoft has stated that "nearly half of the core required exams' content demands that the candidate have troubleshooting skills acquired through hands-on experience and working knowledge."

Fortunately, if you are willing to dedicate the time and effort to learn Windows 2000, you can prepare yourself well for the exams by using the proper tools. By working through this book, you can successfully meet the exam requirements.

This book is part of a complete series of Sybex MCSE Study Guides, published by Sybex Inc., that together cover the core Windows 2000 requirements as well as the new Design exams needed to complete your MCSE track. Study Guide titles include the following:

- *MCSE: Windows 2000 Professional Study Guide,* Second Edition, by Lisa Donald with James Chellis (Sybex, 2001)

- *MCSE: Windows 2000 Server Study Guide,* Second Edition, by Lisa Donald with James Chellis (Sybex, 2001)

- *MCSE: Windows 2000 Network Infrastructure Administration Study Guide,* Second Edition, by Paul Robichaux with James Chellis (Sybex, 2001)

- *MCSE: Windows 2000 Directory Services Administration Study Guide,* Second Edition, by Anil Desai with James Chellis (Sybex, 2001)

- *MCSE: Windows 2000 Network Security Design Study Guide,* by Gary Govanus and Robert King (Sybex, 2000)

- *MCSE: Windows 2000 Network Infrastructure Design Study Guide,* by Bill Heldman (Sybex, 2000)

- *MCSE: Windows 2000 Directory Services Design Study Guide,* by Robert King and Gary Govanus (Sybex, 2000)

## Exam Requirements

Candidates for MCSE certification in Windows 2000 must pass seven exams, including four core operating system exams, one design exam, and two electives, as described in the sections that follow.

**Core Requirements**

| Windows 2000 Professional (70-210) |
|---|

| Windows 2000 Server (70-215) |
|---|

| Windows 2000 Network Infrastructure Administration (70-216) |
|---|

| Windows 2000 Directory Services Administration (70-217) |
|---|

**Plus one of the following**

**Design Requirement**

| Designing a Windows 2000 Directory Services Infrastructure (70-219) |
|---|

| Designing Security for a Windows 2000 Network (70-220) |
|---|

| Designing a Windows 2000 Network Infrastructure (70-221) |
|---|

| Designing Web Solutions with Windows 2000 Server Technologies (70-226) |
|---|

**Plus two of the following**

**Electives**

| Any of the Design exams not taken for the Design requirement |
|---|

| Any current Elective exam. Topics include Exchange Server, SQL Server, and ISA Server. |
|---|

For a more detailed description of the Microsoft certification programs, including a list of current and future MCSE electives, check Microsoft's Training and Certification Web site at www.microsoft.com/trainingandservices.

## The *Implementing and Administering a Microsoft Windows 2000 Directory Services Infrastructure* Exam

The *Implementing and Administering a Microsoft Windows 2000 Directory Services Infrastructure* exam covers concepts and skills related to installing, configuring, and managing Active Directory. It emphasizes the following elements of working with Windows 2000 Directory Services:

- Concepts related to the Windows 2000 Directory Services

- Preparing your network environment for Windows 2000 Directory Services

- Installing Active Directory

- Configuring and managing features of Active Directory

- Monitoring and optimizing Active Directory

- Managing Active Directory in distributed network environments

- Managing Active Directory environments through the use of security features, Group Policy settings, and software deployment tools

- Troubleshooting problems with Active Directory

This exam is quite specific regarding what is needed to set up and administer Windows 2000 Directory Services, including knowledge of the requirements and operational settings. The exam is particular about how administrative tasks are performed within the operating system. It also focuses on fundamental concepts of implementing an Active Directory environment. Careful study of this book, along with hands-on experience, will help you to prepare for this exam.

Microsoft provides exam objectives to give you a very general overview of possible areas of coverage on the Microsoft exams. For your convenience, this Study Guide includes objective listings positioned within the text at points where specific Microsoft exam objectives are discussed. Keep in mind, however, that exam objectives are subject to change at any time without prior notice and at Microsoft's sole discretion. Please visit Microsoft's Training and Certification Web site (www.microsoft.com/trainingandservices) for the most current listing of exam objectives.

## Types of Exam Questions

In an effort to both refine the testing process and protect the quality of its certifications, Microsoft has focused its Windows 2000 exams on real experience and hands-on proficiency. There is a higher emphasis on your past working environments and responsibilities, and less emphasis on how well you can memorize. In fact, Microsoft says an MCSE candidate should have at least one year of hands-on experience.

Microsoft will accomplish its goal of protecting the exams' integrity by regularly adding and removing exam questions, limiting the number of questions that any individual sees in a beta exam, limiting the number of questions delivered to an individual by using adaptive testing, and adding new exam elements.

Exam questions may be in a variety of formats: Depending on which exam you take, you'll see multiple-choice questions, as well as select-and-place and prioritize-a-list questions. Simulations and case study–based formats are included, as well. You may also find yourself taking what's called an *adaptive format exam*. Let's take a look at the types of exam questions and examine the adaptive testing technique, so that you'll be prepared for all of the possibilities.

With the release of Windows 2000, Microsoft has stopped providing a detailed score breakdown. This is mostly because of the various and complex question formats. Previously, each question focused on one objective. The Windows 2000 exams, however, contain questions that may be tied to one or more objectives from one or more objective sets. Therefore, grading by objective is almost impossible.

For more information on the various exam question types, go to www.microsoft.com/trainingandservices/default.asp?PageID=mcp&PageCall=tesinn&SubSite=examinfo.

### Multiple-Choice Questions

Multiple-choice questions come in two main forms. One is a straightforward question followed by several possible answers, of which one or more is correct. The other type of multiple-choice question is more complex and based on a specific scenario. The scenario may focus on a number of areas or objectives.

### Select-and-Place Questions

Select-and-place exam questions involve graphical elements that you must manipulate in order to successfully answer the question. For example, you might see a diagram of a computer network, as shown in the following graphic taken from the select-and-place demo downloaded from Microsoft's Web site.

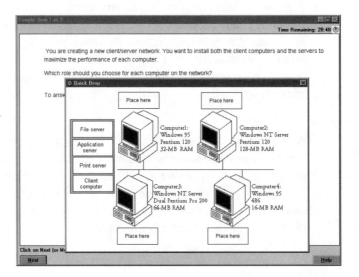

A typical diagram will show computers and other components next to boxes that contain the text "Place here." The labels for the boxes represent various computer roles on a network, such as a print server and a file server. Based on information given for each computer, you are asked to select each label and place it in the correct box. You need to place *all* of the labels correctly. No credit is given for the question if you correctly label only some of the boxes.

In another select-and-place problem you might be asked to put a series of steps in order, by dragging item from boxes on the left to boxes on the right, and placing them in the correct order. One other type requires that you drag an item from the left and place it under an item in a column on the right.

### Simulations

Simulations are the kinds of questions that most closely represent actual situations and test the skills you use while working with Microsoft software interfaces. These exam questions include a mock interface on which you are asked to perform certain actions according to a given scenario. The simulated interfaces look nearly identical to what you see in the actual product, as shown in this example:

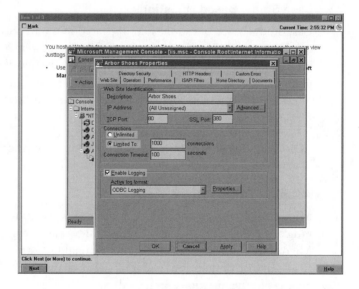

Because of the number of possible errors that can be made on simulations, be sure to consider the following recommendations from Microsoft:

- Do not change any simulation settings that don't pertain to the solution directly.

- When related information has not been provided, assume that the default settings are used.

- Make sure that your entries are spelled correctly.

- Close all the simulation application windows after completing the set of tasks in the simulation.

The best way to prepare for simulation questions is to spend time working with the graphical interface of the product on which you will be tested.

We recommend that you study with the WinSim 2000 product, which is included on the CD that accompanies this study guide. By completing the exercises in this study guide and working with the WinSim 2000 software, you will greatly improve your level of preparation for simulation questions.

### Case Study–Based Questions

Case study–based questions first appeared in the MCSD program. These questions present a scenario with a range of requirements. Based on the information provided, you answer a series of multiple-choice and select-and-place questions. The interface for case study–based questions has a number of tabs, each of which contains information about the scenario.

At present, this type of question appears only in most of the Design exams.

### Adaptive Exam Format

Microsoft presents many of its exams in an *adaptive* format. This format is radically different from the conventional format previously used for Microsoft certification exams. Conventional tests are static, containing a fixed number of questions. Adaptive tests change depending on your answers to the questions presented.

The number of questions presented in your adaptive test will depend on how long it takes the exam to ascertain your level of ability (according to the statistical measurements on which exam questions are ranked). To determine a test-taker's level of ability, the exam presents questions in an increasing or decreasing order of difficulty.

Unlike the earlier test format, the adaptive test does *not* allow you to go back to see a question again. The exam only goes forward. Once you enter your answer, that's it—you cannot change it. Be very careful before entering your answers. There is no time limit for each individual question (only for the exam as a whole). Your exam may be shortened by correct answers (and lengthened by incorrect answers), so there is no advantage to rushing through questions

Microsoft will regularly add and remove questions from the exams. This is called *item seeding*. It is part of the effort to make it more difficult for individuals to merely memorize exam questions that were passed along by previous test-takers.

---

### Exam Question Development

Microsoft follows an exam-development process consisting of eight mandatory phases. The process takes an average of seven months and involves more than 150 specific steps. The MCP exam development consists of the following phases:

**Phase 1: Job Analysis**   Phase 1 is an analysis of all the tasks that make up a specific job function, based on tasks performed by people who are currently performing that job function. This phase also identifies the knowledge, skills, and abilities that relate specifically to the performance area being certified.

**Phase 2: Objective Domain Definition**   The results of the job analysis phase provide the framework used to develop objectives. Development of objectives involves translating the job-function tasks into a comprehensive package of specific and measurable knowledge, skills, and abilities. The resulting list of objectives—the *objective domain*—is the basis for the development of both the certification exams and the training materials.

**Phase 3: Blueprint Survey**   The final objective domain is transformed into a blueprint survey in which contributors are asked to rate each objective. These contributors may be MCP candidates, appropriately skilled exam-development volunteers, or Microsoft employees. Based on the contributors' input, the objectives are prioritized and weighted. The actual exam items are written according to the prioritized objectives. Contributors are queried about how they spend their time on the job. If a contributor doesn't spend an adequate amount of time actually performing the specified job function, his or her data are eliminated from the analysis. The blueprint survey phase helps determine which objectives to measure, as well as the appropriate number and types of items to include on the exam.

**Phase 4: Item Development**   A pool of items is developed to measure the blueprinted objective domain. The number and types of items to be written are based on the results of the blueprint survey.

**Phase 5: Alpha Review and Item Revision**   During this phase, a panel of technical and job-function experts review each item for technical accuracy. The panel then answers each item and reaches a consensus on all technical issues. Once the items have been verified as being technically accurate, they are edited to ensure that they are expressed in the clearest language possible.

**Phase 6: Beta Exam**   The reviewed and edited items are collected into beta exams. Based on the responses of all beta participants, Microsoft performs a statistical analysis to verify the validity of the exam items and to determine which items will be used in the certification exam. Once the analysis has been completed, the items are distributed into multiple parallel forms, or *versions*, of the final certification exam.

**Phase 7: Item Selection and Cut-Score Setting**   The results of the beta exams are analyzed to determine which items will be included in the certification exam. This determination is based on many factors, including item difficulty and relevance. During this phase, a panel of job-function experts determine the *cut score* (minimum passing score) for the exams. The cut score differs from exam to exam because it is based on an item-by-item determination of the percentage of candidates who answered the item correctly and who would be expected to answer the item correctly.

**Phase 8: Live Exam**   In the final phase, the exams are given to candidates. MCP exams are administered by Prometric and Virtual University Enterprises (VUE).

## Tips for Taking the Directory Services Infrastructure Exam

Here are some general tips for achieving success on your certification exam:

- Arrive early at the exam center so that you can relax and review your study materials. During this final review, you can look over tables and lists of exam-related information.

- Read the questions carefully. Don't be tempted to jump to an early conclusion. Make sure you know *exactly* what the question is asking.

- Answer all questions. Remember that the adaptive format does *not* allow you to return to a question. Be very careful before entering your answer. Because your exam may be shortened by correct answers (and lengthened by incorrect answers), there is no advantage to rushing through questions.

- On simulations, do not change settings that are not directly related to the question. Also, assume default settings if the question does not specify or imply which settings are used.

- For questions you're not sure about, use a process of elimination to get rid of the obviously incorrect options first. This improves your odds of selecting the correct answer when you need to make an educated guess.

## Exam Registration

You may take the Microsoft exams at any of more than 1,000 Authorized Prometric Testing Centers (APTCs) and VUE Testing Centers around the world. For the location of a testing center near you, call Prometric at 800-755-EXAM (755-3926), or call VUE at 888-837-8616. Outside the United States and Canada, contact your local Prometric or VUE registration center.

Find out the number of the exam you want to take, and then register with the Prometric or VUE registration center nearest to you. At this point, you will be asked for advance payment for the exam. The exams are $100 each and you must take them within one year of payment. You can schedule exams up to six weeks in advance or as late as one working day prior to the date of the exam. You can cancel or reschedule your exam if you contact the center at least two working days prior to the exam. Same-day registration is available in some locations, subject to space availability. Where same-day registration is available, you must register a minimum of two hours before test time.

You may also register for your exams online at www.prometric.com or www.vue.com.

When you schedule the exam, you will be provided with instructions regarding appointment and cancellation procedures, ID requirements, and information about the testing center location. In addition, you will receive a registration and payment confirmation letter from Prometric or VUE.

Microsoft requires certification candidates to accept the terms of a Non-Disclosure Agreement before taking certification exams.

# Is This Book for You?

If you want to acquire a solid foundation in implementing and administering Windows 2000 Directory Services, and your goal is to prepare for the exam by learning how to use and manage the new operating system, this book is for you. You'll find clear explanations of the fundamental concepts you need to grasp, and plenty of help to achieve the high level of professional competency you need to succeed in your chosen field.

If you want to become certified as an MCSE, this book is definitely for you. However, if you just want to attempt to pass the exam without really understanding Windows 2000, this Study Guide is *not* for you. It is written for people who want to acquire hands-on skills and in-depth knowledge of Windows 2000.

## How to Use This Book

What makes a Sybex Study Guide the book of choice for over 100,000 MCSEs? We took into account not only what you need to know to pass the exam, but what you need to know to take what you've learned and apply it in the real world. Each book contains the following:

**Objective-by-objective coverage of the topics you need to know**   Each chapter lists the objectives covered in that chapter, followed by detailed discussion of each objective.

**Assessment Test**   Directly following this Introduction is an Assessment Test that you should take. It is designed to help you determine how much you already know about Windows 2000. Each question is tied to a topic discussed in the book. Using the results of the Assessment test, you can figure out the areas where you need to focus your study. Of course, we do recommend you read the entire book.

**Exam Essentials**    To highlight what you learn, you'll find a list of Exam Essentials at the end of each chapter. The Exam Essentials section briefly highlights the topics that need your particular attention as you prepare for the exam.

**Key Terms and Glossary**    Throughout each chapter, you will be introduced to important terms and concepts that you will need to know for the exam. These terms appear in italic within the chapters, and a list of the Key Terms appears just after the Exam Essentials. At the end of the book, a detailed Glossary gives definitions for these terms, as well as other general terms you should know.

**Review questions, complete with detailed explanations**    Each chapter is followed by a set of Review Questions that test what you learned in the chapter. The questions are written with the exam in mind, meaning that they are designed to have the same look and feel of what you'll see on the exam. Question types are just like the exam, including multiple choice, exhibits, select-and-place, and prioritize-a-list.

**Hands-on exercises**    In each chapter, you'll find exercises designed to give you the important hands-on experience that is critical for your exam preparation. The exercises support the topics of the chapter, and they walk you through the steps necessary to perform a particular function.

**Real World Scenarios**    Because reading a book isn't enough for you to learn how to apply these topics in your everyday duties, we have provided Real World Scenarios in special sidebars. These explain when and why a particular solution would make sense, in a working environment you'd actually encounter.

**Interactive CD**    Every Sybex Study Guide comes with a CD complete with additional questions, flashcards for use with a palm device, a Windows simulation program, and two complete electronic books. Details are in the following section.

The topics covered in this Study Guide map directly to Microsoft's official exam objectives. Each exam objective is covered completely.

# What's on the CD?

With this new member of our best-selling MCSE Study Guide series, we are including quite an array of training resources. The CD offers numerous simulations, bonus exams, and flashcards to help you study for the exam. We have also included the complete contents of the Study Guide in electronic form. The CD's resources are described here:

**The Sybex E-book for Directory Services Administration**   Many people like the convenience of being able to carry their whole Study Guide on a CD. They also like being able to search the text via computer to find specific information quickly and easily. For these reasons, the entire contents of this Study Guide are supplied on the CD, in PDF format. We've also included Adobe Acrobat Reader, which provides the interface for the PDF contents as well as the search capabilities.

**WinSim 2000**   We developed the WinSim 2000 product to allow you to experience the multimedia and interactive operation of working with Active Directory. WinSim 2000 provides both audio/video files and hands-on experience with key features of the Windows 2000 tools that you use to administer Active Directory. Built around the Study Guide's exercises, WinSim 2000 will help you attain the knowledge and hands-on skills that you must have in order to understand Windows 2000 (and pass the exam). Here is a sample screen from WinSim 2000:

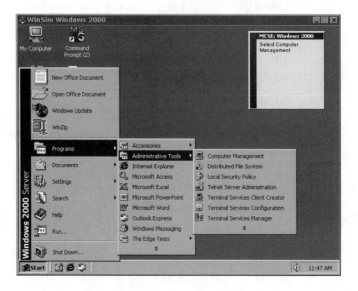

**The Sybex MCSE EdgeTests**   The EdgeTests are a collection of multiple-choice questions that will help you prepare for your exam. The questions are grouped into seven sets:

- The Assessment Test.

- Two bonus exams designed to simulate the actual live exam.

- All the questions from the Study Guide organized by chapter for your review.

- All the questions from the Study Guide, plus the two bonus exams, organized by objective area for your review.

- A random test generator that selects up to 75 questions from all of the questions listed above.

- An adaptive test simulator that will give the feel for how adaptive testing works.

Here is a sample screen from the Sybex MCSE EdgeTests:

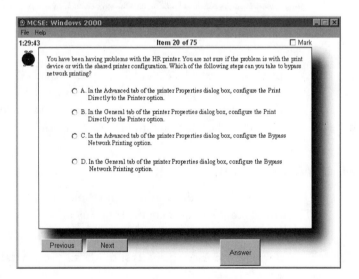

**Sybex MCSE Flashcards for PCs and Palm Devices**   The "flashcard" style of question offers an effective way to quickly and efficiently test your understanding of the fundamental concepts covered in the exam. The Sybex MCSE Flashcards set consists of more than 150 questions presented in a special engine developed specifically for this Study Guide series. Here's what the Sybex MCSE Flashcards interface looks like:

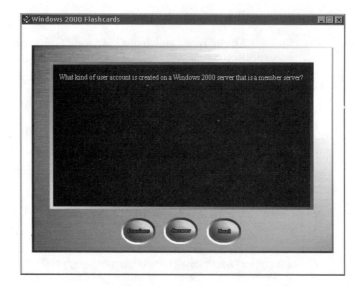

Because of the high demand for a product that will run on palm devices, we have also developed, in conjunction with Land-J Technologies, a version of the flashcard questions that you can take with you on your Palm OS PDA (including the PalmPilot and Handspring's Visor).

## How Do You Use This Book?

This book provides a solid foundation for the serious effort of preparing for the exam. To best benefit from this book, you may wish to use the following study method:

1. Take the Assessment Test to identify your weak areas.

2. Study each chapter carefully. Do your best to fully understand the information.

3. Complete all the hands-on exercises in the chapter, referring back to the text as necessary so that you understand each step you take. If you don't have access to a lab environment in which you can complete the exercises,

install and work with the exercises available in the WinSim 2000 software included with this Study Guide.

 To do the exercises in this book, your hardware should meet the minimum hardware requirements for installing Windows 2000 Server as a domain controller. These requirements are described in Chapter 3, "Installing and Configuring the Active Directory."

4. Read over the Real World Scenarios, to improve your understanding of how to use what you learn in the book.

5. Study the Exam Essentials and Key Terms to make sure you are familiar with the areas you need to focus on.

6. Answer the review questions at the end of each chapter. If you prefer to answer the questions in a timed and graded format, install the Edge-Tests from the book's CD and answer the chapter questions there instead of in the book.

7. Take note of the questions you did not understand, and study the corresponding sections of the book again.

8. Go back over the Exam Essentials and Key Terms.

9. Go through the Study Guide's other training resources, which are included on the book's CD. These include WinSim 2000, electronic flashcards, the electronic version of the chapter review questions (try taking them by objective), and the two bonus exams.

To learn all the material covered in this book, you will need to study regularly and with discipline. Try to set aside the same time every day to study, and select a comfortable and quiet place in which to do it. If you work hard, you will be surprised at how quickly you learn this material. Good luck!

## Contacts and Resources

To find out more about Microsoft Education and Certification materials and programs, to register with Prometric or VUE, or to obtain other useful certification information and additional study resources, check the following resources.

**Microsoft Training and Certification Home Page**
www.microsoft.com/trainingandservices

This Web site provides information about the MCP program and exams. You can also order the latest Microsoft Roadmap to Education and Certification.

**Microsoft TechNet Technical Information Network**
www.microsoft.com/technet

800-344-2121

Use this Web site or phone number to contact support professionals and system administrators. Outside the United States and Canada, contact your local Microsoft subsidiary for information.

**Palm Pilot Training Product Development: Land-J**
www.land-j.com

407-359-2217

Land-J Technologies is a consulting and programming business currently specializing in application development for the 3Com PalmPilot Personal Digital Assistant. Land-J developed the Palm version of the Flashcards, which is included on the CD that accompanies this Study Guide.

**Prometric**
www.prometric.com

800-755-3936

Contact Prometric to register to take an MCP exam at any of more than 800 Prometric Testing Centers around the world.

**Virtual University Enterprises (VUE)**
www.vue.com

888-837-8616

Contact the VUE registration center to register to take an MCP exam at one of the VUE Testing Centers.

### *MCP Magazine Online*
www.mcpmag.com

Microsoft Certified Professional Magazine is a well-respected publication that focuses on Windows certification. This site hosts chats and discussion forums, and tracks news related to the MCSE program. Some of the services cost a fee, but they are well worth it.

### *Windows 2000 Magazine*
www.windows2000mag.com

You can subscribe to this magazine or read free articles at the Web site. The study resource provides general information on Windows 2000.

### *Cramsession on Brainbuzz.com*
cramsession.brainbuzz.com

Cramsession is an online community focusing on all IT certification programs. In addition to discussion boards and job locators, you can download one of a number of free cramsessions, which are nice supplements to any study approach you take.

# Assessment Test

1. Which of the following operations is not supported by the Active Directory?

   A. Assigning applications to users

   B. Assigning applications to computers

   C. Publishing applications to users

   D. Publishing applications to computers

   E. None of the above

2. Which of the following single master operations apply to the entire forest?

   A. Schema Master

   B. Domain Naming Master

   C. Relative ID Master

   D. Infrastructure Master

   E. Both A and B

3. Which of the following is *not* a valid Active Directory object?

   A. User

   B. Group

   C. Organizational unit

   D. Computer

   E. None of the above

4. Which of the following pieces of information should you have before beginning the Active Directory Installation Wizard?

   A. Active Directory domain name

   B. Administrator password for the local computer

   C. NetBIOS name for the server

   D. DNS configuration information

   E. All of the above

5. Which of the following is *not* considered a security principal?

   A. Users

   B. Security groups

   C. Distribution groups

   D. Computers

   E. None of the above

6. All of the following types of network computers can be used with RIS *except*

   A. A laptop with a PCMCIA network card

   B. A laptop attached to a docking station

   C. A desktop computer with a PXE Boot ROM-enabled network adapter

   D. A desktop computer with a PCI network adapter

   E. None of the above

7. Which of the following is a valid role for a Windows 2000 Server computer?

   A. Stand-alone server

   B. Member server

   C. Domain controller

   D. All of the above

**8.** Trust relationships *cannot* be configured as which of the following?

   **A.** One-way and transitive

   **B.** Two-way and transitive

   **C.** One-way and nontransitive

   **D.** Two-way and nontransitive

   **E.** None of the above

**9.** Which of the following should play the *least* significant role in planning an OU structure?

   **A.** Network infrastructure

   **B.** Domain organization

   **C.** Delegation of permissions

   **D.** Group Policy settings

**10.** Which of the following file extensions is used primarily for backward compatibility with non-Windows Installer setup programs?

   **A.** .msi

   **B.** .mst

   **C.** .zap

   **D.** .aas

   **E.** None of the above

**11.** How can the Windows NT 4 file and printer resources be made available from within the Active Directory?

   **A.** A systems administrator can right-click the resource and select Publish.

   **B.** A systems administrator can create Printer and Shared Folder objects that point to these resources.

   **C.** The Active Directory Domains and Trusts tool can be used to make resources available.

   **D.** Only Windows 2000 resources can be accessed from within the Active Directory.

**12.** An Active Directory environment consists of three domains. What is the maximum number of sites that can be created for this environment?

    **A.** 2

    **B.** 3

    **C.** 9

    **D.** None of the above

**13.** Which of the following statements regarding auditing and the Active Directory is false?

    **A.** Auditing prevents users from attempting to guess passwords.

    **B.** Systems administrators should regularly review audit logs for suspicious activity.

    **C.** Auditing information can be generated when users view specific information within the Active Directory.

    **D.** Auditing information can be generated when users modify specific information within the Active Directory.

    **E.** All of the above.

**14.** A systems administrator wants to allow a group of users to add Computer accounts to only a specific OU. What is the easiest way to grant only the required permissions?

    **A.** Delegate control of a User account.

    **B.** Delegate control at the domain level.

    **C.** Delegate control of an OU.

    **D.** Delegate control of a Computer account.

    **E.** None of the above.

**15.** A GPO at the domain level sets a certain option to Disabled, while a GPO at the OU level sets the same option to Enabled. All other settings are left at their default. Which setting will be effective for objects within the OU?

**A.** Enabled

**B.** Disabled

**C.** No effect

**D.** None of the above

**16.** The process by which a higher-level security authority assigns permissions to other administrators is known as?

**A.** Inheritance

**B.** Delegation

**C.** Assignment

**D.** None of the above

**17.** What is the minimum amount of information needed to create a Shared Folder Active Directory object?

**A.** The name of the share

**B.** The name of the server

**C.** The name of the server and the name of the share

**D.** The name of the server, the server's IP address, and the name of the share

**18.** Which of the following is *not* a benefit of using the Active Directory?

**A.** Hierarchical object structure

**B.** Fault-tolerant architecture

**C.** Ability to configure centralized and distributed administration

**D.** Flexible replication

**E.** None of the above

**19.** A systems administrator plans to deploy 50 computers using RIS. There are two RIS servers on the network. They want to assign half of the client computers to receive images from one RIS server and the other half to receive images from the other RIS server. How can they accomplish this?

    **A.** Divide the computers into two different OUs, and use GPOs to specify to which server each client will be directed.

    **B.** Use the Delegation of Control Wizard to assign permissions to half of the computers.

    **C.** Prestage the computers, and assign half of the computers to each RIS server.

    **D.** Nothing—the default behavior of RIS will ensure that load balancing occurs.

    **E.** None of the above—the first RIS server to respond will provide the image files.

**20.** Which of the following features of DNS can be used to improve performance?

    **A.** Caching-only servers

    **B.** DNS forwarding

    **C.** Secondary servers

    **D.** Zone delegation

    **E.** All of the above

**21.** Which of the following tools can be used to create GPO links to the Active Directory?

    **A.** Active Directory Users and Computers

    **B.** Active Directory Domains and Trusts

    **C.** Active Directory Sites and Services

    **D.** Both A and C

**22.** Which of the following tools can be used to automate the creation and management of User accounts?

**A.** LDIFDE

**B.** ADSI

**C.** CSVDE

**D.** WSH

**E.** All of the above

**23.** A systems administrator suspects that the amount of RAM in a domain controller is insufficient and that an upgrade is required. Which of the following System Monitor counters would provide the most useful information regarding the upgrade?

**A.** Network Segment ➤ % Utilization

**B.** Memory ➤ Page faults/sec

**C.** Processor ➤ % Utilization

**D.** System ➤ Processes

**E.** All of the above would be equally useful

**24.** Which of the following tools are considered security principals?

**A.** User accounts and groups

**B.** User accounts, groups, and OUs

**C.** Groups and OUs

**D.** None of the above

**25.** Which of the following single master roles does *not* apply to each domain within an Active Directory forest?

**A.** PDC Emulator Master

**B.** RID Master

**C.** Infrastructure Master

**D.** None of the above

**26.** Which of the following types of server configurations *cannot* be used within a single DNS zone?

**A.** A single primary server with no secondary servers

**B.** Multiple primary servers

**C.** A single primary server with a single secondary server

**D.** A single primary server with multiple secondary servers

**E.** A single primary server and multiple caching-only servers

**27.** A GPO at the domain level sets a certain option to Disabled, while a GPO at the OU level sets the same option to Enabled. No other GPOs have been created. Which option can a systems administrator use to ensure that the effective policy for objects within the OU is Enabled?

**A.** Block Policy Inheritance on the OU

**B.** Block Policy Inheritance on the site

**C.** Set No Override on the OU

**D.** Set No Override on the site

**E.** None of the above

**28.** Which of the following is *not* a type of backup operation that is supported by the Windows 2000 Backup utility?

**A.** Normal

**B.** Daily

**C.** Weekly

**D.** Differential

**E.** All of the above

**29.** Which of the following is generally *not* true regarding the domain controllers within a site?

   **A.** They are generally connected by a high-speed network.

   **B.** They may reside on different subnets.

   **C.** They are generally connected by reliable connections.

   **D.** They may be domain controllers for different domains.

   **E.** None of the above.

**30.** Which of the following types of servers contain a copy of the Active Directory?

   **A.** Member server

   **B.** Stand-alone server

   **C.** Domain controller

   **D.** All of the above

**31.** When running in native mode, which of the following Group scope changes *cannot* be performed?

   **A.** Universal ➢ Global

   **B.** Domain Local ➢ Universal

   **C.** Global ➢ Universal

   **D.** None of the above

**32.** Which of the following protocols may be used for intrasite replication?

   **A.** RPC

   **B.** IP

   **C.** SMTP

   **D.** NNTP

   **E.** All of the above

**33.** Which of the following is *not* a benefit of Windows 2000's DNS?

    **A.** Dynamic updates

    **B.** Integration with WINS

    **C.** Integration with DHCP

    **D.** Integration with Active Directory

    **E.** None of the above

# Answers to Assessment Test

1. D.   Applications cannot be published to computers. See Chapter 11 for more information.

2. E.   There can be only one Domain Naming Master and one Schema Master per Active Directory forest. The remaining roles apply at the domain level. See Chapter 5 for more information.

3. E.   All of the choices are valid types of Active Directory objects and can be created and managed using the Active Directory Users and Computers tool. See Chapter 7 for more information.

4. E.   Before beginning the installation of a domain controller, you should have all of the information listed. See Chapter 3 for more information.

5. C.   Permissions and Security settings cannot be made on Distribution groups. Distribution groups are used only for the purpose of sending e-mail. See Chapter 8 for more information.

6. A.   Windows 2000 RIS does not support the use of PCMCIA or PC Card network adapters. All of the other configurations are supported (although specific drivers from third-party manufacturers may be required). See Chapter 12 for more information.

7. D.   Based on the business needs of an organization, a Windows 2000 Server computer can be configured in any of the above roles. See Chapter 1 for more information.

8. E.   All of the trust configurations listed are possible. See Chapter 5 for more information.

9. A.   In general, you can accommodate your network infrastructure through the use of Active Directory sites. All of the other options should play a significant role when you go to design your OU structure. See Chapter 4 for more information.

10. C.   Initialization ZAP files are used primarily to point to older programs that do not use the Windows Installer. See Chapter 11 for more information.

**11.**  B.   Printer and Shared Folder objects within the Active Directory can point to Windows NT 4 file and printer resources, as well as Windows 2000 resources. See Chapter 7 for more information.

**12.**  D.   The number of sites in an Active Directory environment is independent of the domain organization. An environment that consists of three domains may have one or more sites, based on the physical network setup. See Chapter 6 for more information.

**13.**  A.   The purpose of auditing is to monitor and record actions taken by users. Auditing will not prevent users from attempting to guess passwords (although it might discourage them from trying, if they are aware it is enabled). See Chapter 8 for more information.

**14.**  E.   In order to allow this permission at the OU level, the systems administrator must create a Group Policy object with the appropriate settings and link it to the OU. See Chapter 12 for more information.

**15.**  A.   Assuming that the default settings are left in place, the Group Policy setting at the OU level will take effect. See Chapter 10 for more information.

**16.**  B.   Delegation is the process by which administrators can assign permissions on the objects within an OU. See Chapter 4 for more information.

**17.**  C.   The name of the server and the name of the share make up the UNC information required to create a Shared Folder object. See Chapter 7 for more information.

**18.**  E.   All of the options listed are benefits of using the Active Directory. See Chapter 1 for more information.

**19.**  C.   One of the primary advantages of using prestaging is that systems administrators can distribute the load of installations between multiple RIS servers. See Chapter 12 for more information.

**20.**  E.   One of the major design goals for DNS was support for scalability. All of the features listed can be used to increase the performance of DNS. See Chapter 2 for more information.

**21.** D.   Both the Active Directory Users and Computers tool and the Active Directory Sites and Services tool can be used to create GPO links to the Active Directory. See Chapter 10 for more information.

**22.** E.   All of the above tools and scripting languages can be used to automate common administrative tasks, such as the creation and management of user accounts. See Chapter 7 for more information.

**23.** B.   A page fault occurs when the operating system must retrieve information from disk instead of from RAM. If the number of page faults per second is high, then it is likely that the server would benefit from a RAM upgrade. See Chapter 9 for more information.

**24.** A.   User accounts and groups are used for setting security permissions, while OUs are used for creating the organizational structure within the Active Directory. See Chapter 4 for more information.

**25.** D.   All of the roles listed are configured for each domain within the Active Directory forest. See Chapter 5 for more information.

**26.** B.   DNS does not allow for the use of more than one primary server per zone. See Chapter 2 for more information.

**27.** A.   By blocking policy inheritance on the OU, you can be sure that other settings defined at higher levels do not change the settings at the OU level. However, this will only work if the No Override option is not set at the site level. See Chapter 10 for more information.

**28.** C.   The Windows 2000 Backup utility does not include an operation for weekly backups. Weekly backups can be performed, however, by using the scheduling functionality of the Backup utility. See Chapter 9 for more information.

**29.** E.   All of the descriptions listed are characteristics that are common to domain controllers within a single site. See Chapter 6 for more information.

**30.** C.   Only Windows 2000 Server computers configured as domain controllers contain a copy of the Active Directory database. See Chapter 3 for more information.

**31.** A.   The scope of Universal groups cannot be changed. See Chapter 8 for more information.

**32.** A.   Remote Procedure Calls (RPCs) are used for intrasite replication. See Chapter 6 for more information.

**33.** E.   All of the above are features and benefits of Windows 2000's DNS service. See Chapter 2 for more information.

# Chapter 1

# Overview of the Active Directory

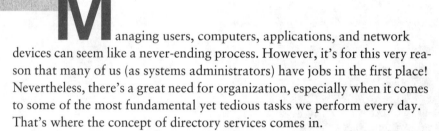

**M**anaging users, computers, applications, and network devices can seem like a never-ending process. However, it's for this very reason that many of us (as systems administrators) have jobs in the first place! Nevertheless, there's a great need for organization, especially when it comes to some of the most fundamental yet tedious tasks we perform every day. That's where the concept of directory services comes in.

To truly appreciate the value of a directory service, let's first look at a real-world example of a situation without organization. Suppose we're trying to find an old friend from college. The first step we would take would probably be to look for their name in the local phone book. If we couldn't find it there, we might try searching in the phone books of a few other cities or on the Internet. If none of those methods were successful, we'd probably resort to calling friends who might have kept in touch with others.

As you can see, this is not an exact science! We could search forever without finding our old friend's telephone number. Part of the problem is due to the lack of a single central repository of phone number information. Without knowing where the information is stored, perseverance and luck are one's strongest tools. Clearly, this is a problem. Yet, it's the way a lot of networks are managed in the real world. That is, information is scattered throughout the organization, and finding what you need may take several phone calls and database searches.

If you've heard about the *Active Directory*, there's a good chance that you already have an idea of its purpose. Microsoft's Active Directory technology is designed to store information about all of the objects within your network environment, including hardware, software, network devices, and users. Furthermore, it is designed to increase capabilities while it decreases administration through the use of a hierarchical structure that mirrors a business's logical organization. In other words, it forms the universal "phone book" we so badly need in the network world!

You've probably also heard that a great deal of planning and training is required to properly implement the Active Directory's many features. We're not talking about a few new administrative tools or check boxes here! In order to reap the true benefits of this new technology, you must be willing to invest the time and effort to get it right. And you'll need buy-in from the entire organization. From end users to executive management, the success of your directory services implementation will be based on input from the entire business. All of these statements about the Active Directory are true.

There's no excuse for poor planning when it comes to the Active Directory. If you're not sure how to configure the directory services for your environment, you'll probably benefit very little from its implementation. In fact, you could make your network more difficult to manage if you improperly implement Windows 2000. It's not a "one size fits all" type of feature. Once you have a good idea for the logical organization of your business and technical environment, however, you will have made much progress toward successfully installing and configuring the Active Directory. That's where the content of this book—and the Microsoft exam for which it will prepare you—come in.

It's a difficult task to cover the various aspects of Windows 2000's most important feature—the Active Directory—even in a whole book. As we briefly mentioned in the introduction, Microsoft's main goal in *Exam 70-217: Implementing and Administering a Microsoft Windows 2000 Directory Services Infrastructure* is to test your ability to *implement* the various features of the Active Directory. The problem is that it doesn't make much sense to begin implementing the Active Directory until you understand the terms, concepts, and goals behind the Active Directory and this big change in the network operating system.

Planning an entire directory services architecture that conforms to your business and technical requirements is beyond the scope of this book. The topic is considerably complex and requires a thorough understanding of all the ramifications for your organization. You must take into account, for example, business concerns, the geographic organization of your company, and its technical infrastructure. In fact, it's such an important topic that Microsoft has decided to test those concepts under a separate exam: *Exam 70-219: Designing a Microsoft Windows 2000 Directory Services Infrastructure*. You can study for that exam using another Sybex book, *MCSE: Windows 2000 Directory Services Design Study Guide*. It would be difficult to overemphasize the importance of planning for Windows 2000 and the Active Directory.

Planning, however, is just one part of the process. Once you have determined exactly *what* your Active Directory should look like, it's time to find out *how* to implement it. And that's what we'll cover throughout this book. Specifically, we'll talk about the various methods for implementing the tools and features of Windows 2000 based on your company's business and technical requirements. Despite the underlying complexity of the Active Directory and all of its features, Microsoft has gone to great lengths to ensure that implementation and management of the Active Directory are intuitive and straightforward, for no technology is useful if no one can figure out how to use it.

In this chapter, we'll take a look at some of the many benefits of using a directory services system and, specifically, Microsoft's Active Directory. We'll cover basic information regarding the various concepts related to Microsoft's Active Directory. The emphasis will be on addressing why the entire idea of directory services came about and how it can be used to improve operations in your environment. We'll then move on to looking at the various logical objects created in the Active Directory and the ways in which you can configure them to work with your network environment. Finally, we'll cover the details related to mapping your organization's physical network infrastructure to the directory services architecture. The goal is to describe the framework on which the Active Directory is based.

With that goal in mind, let's get started!

No specific exam objectives are covered in this chapter, but a basic understanding of how the Active Directory is structured and why it was created are essential for performing well on the exam. If you've had little previous exposure to the Active Directory, or if you want to know how Active Directory is different from NT's domain model, you should definitely read this chapter! Also, be sure to see the appendix, "Planning the Active Directory," for more information on designing a directory services environment.

# The World before the Active Directory

The title of this section hints of a time long past. However, the overwhelming majority of networks today run without any single unified directory service. Almost all companies—from small businesses to global enterprises—store information in various disconnected systems. For example, a company might record data about its employees in a human resources database while network accounts reside on a Windows NT 4 domain controller. Other information—such as security settings for applications—reside within various other systems. And there's always the classic: paper-based forms. The main reason for this disparity is that no single flexible data storage mechanism was available. But implementing and managing many separate systems is a huge challenge for most organizations. Before we look at some potential solutions, let's examine the problem further.

## The Benefits of Windows NT 4

Microsoft designed the Windows 2000 operating system platform to succeed its highly successful Windows NT 4 Workstation and Server products. Therefore, it's important to understand the basics of Windows NT before diving into the new features that are available with the Active Directory, a completely new technology introduced with Windows 2000.

The goal of using a network operating system (NOS) is to bring security, organization, and accessibility to information throughout a company's network. In contrast to a peer-to-peer network, properly configured file and print servers allow users and systems administrators to make the most of their resources.

For many years, the realm of network and systems management was one that was controlled by administrators who often worked with cryptic command-line interfaces. That is, only specialists normally managed information systems. Newer network operating systems, such as Novell NetWare and Windows NT, started bringing ease of administration into the network computing world so that network administration no longer needed to be a task delegated to only a few individuals. For example, by bringing the intuitive graphical user interface (GUI) to the world of systems and network administration, Windows NT 4 opened up the doors to simplifying management while still providing the types of security required by most businesses. With these tools, managers and non-technical staff could perform basic systems management functions.

Windows NT Server and Workstation computers offered many benefits, including reliability, scalability, performance, and flexibility. In many cases, companies saw Windows NT 4 as a much more cost-effective solution than their existing client-server solutions. Other benefits of Windows NT included its compatibility with a large installed base of current software products. Application developers could, with a minimal amount of effort, develop programs that would run properly on various Windows-based platforms.

The purpose of this introduction is to provide an overview of the functionality of Windows NT 4. For more details about the product, see www.microsoft.com/ntserver.

A major design goal for the Windows NT 4 operating system was to provide for a secure yet flexible network infrastructure. A few years ago, few technical and business professionals would have imagined that personal computers would make inroads into corporate server rooms and data centers. For many reasons, including cost-efficiency and price-performance ratios, they have done just that. With these characteristics in mind, we have set the stage for discussing the model used by Windows NT to organize users and secure resources and some of its shortcomings.

## The Domain Model in Windows NT 4

The Windows NT 4 platform has met many of the challenges of the network world. However, like any technical solution, it has its limitations. First and foremost, questions regarding the scalability of its rudimentary directory services prevented some potential inroads into corporate data centers. Windows NT uses the concept of a domain to organize users and secure resources. A Windows NT domain is essentially a centralized database of security information that allows for the management of network resources.

*Domains* are implemented through the use of Windows NT Server computers that function as *domain controllers*. Every domain has exactly one Primary Domain Controller (PDC) and may have one or more Backup Domain Controllers (BDCs). All network security accounts are stored within a central database on the PDC. To improve performance and reliability in distributed environments, this database is replicated to BDCs. Although BDCs can help distribute the load of network logon requests and updates, there can be only one master copy of the accounts database. This primary copy resides on the PDC, and all user and security account changes must be recorded by this machine and transmitted to all other domain controllers. Figure 1.1 provides an example of such a topology.

**FIGURE 1.1**    A Windows NT 4 domain topology using PDCs and BDCs

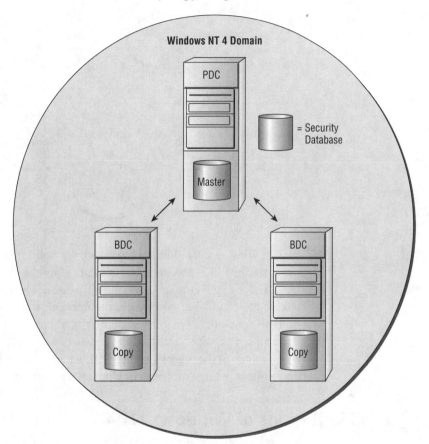

In order to meet some of these design issues, several different Windows NT domain models have been used. Figure 1.2 provides an example of a multiple-master domain topology. In this scenario, user accounts are stored on one or more master domains. The servers in these domains are responsible primarily for managing network accounts. BDCs for these user domains are stored in various locations throughout the organization. Network files, printers, databases, and other resources are placed in resource domains with their own PDC and BDCs. These domains may be created and managed as needed by the organization itself and are often administered separately. In order for resources to be made available to users, each of the resource domains must trust the master domain(s). The overall process places all users from the master domains into global *groups*. These global groups are then granted access to network resources in the resource domains.

**FIGURE 1.2** A multiple-master domain topology

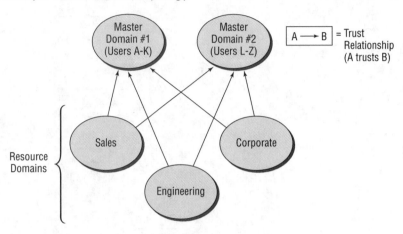

The Windows NT domain model works well for small- to medium-sized organizations. It is able to accommodate several thousands of users fairly well, and a single domain can handle a reasonable number of resources. Above these guidelines, however, the network traffic required to keep domain controllers synchronized and the number of trust relationships to manage can present a challenge to network and systems administrators. As the numbers of users grow, it can get much more difficult for the domains to accommodate large numbers of changes and network logon requests.

## The Limitations of Windows NT 4

The Windows NT 4 domain model has several limitations that hinder its scalability to larger and more complex environments. We already alluded to one earlier—it can't accommodate the number of users supported by large organizations. Although multiple domains can be set up to ease administration and network constraint issues, administering these domains quickly becomes quite complicated and management-intensive. For example, trust relationships between the domains can quickly grow out of control if not managed properly, and providing adequate bandwidth for keeping network accounts synchronized can be a costly burden on the network.

Domains, themselves, are flat entities used to organize and administer security information. They do not take into account the structure of businesses and cannot be organized in a hierarchical fashion (using subdomains for administrative purposes). Therefore, systems administrators are forced to place users into groups. As groups cannot be nested (that is, have subgroups), it is not uncommon for many organizations to manage hundreds of groups within each domain. Setting permissions on resources (such as file and print services) can become an extremely tedious and error-prone process.

As far as security is concerned, administration is often delegated to one or more users of the IT department. These individuals have complete control over the domain controllers and resources within the domain itself. This poses several potential problems—both business and technical. As the distribution of administrator rights is extremely important, it would be best to assign permissions to certain areas of the business. However, the options available in the Windows NT operating system were either difficult to implement or did not provide enough flexibility. All of this leads to a less-than-optimal configuration. For example, security policies are often set to allow users far more permissions than they need to complete their jobs.

If you have worked with Windows NT 4 domains in a medium- to large-sized environment, you are probably familiar with many of the issues related to the domain model. Nevertheless, Windows NT 4 provides an excellent solution for many businesses and offers security, flexibility, and network management features unmatched by many of its competitors. As with almost any technical solution, however, there are areas in which improvements can be made.

Now that we've gone over the basics of Windows NT 4 and its directory structure, let's move on and examine how Windows 2000's Active Directory addresses some of these challenges.

# The Benefits of the Active Directory

**M**ost businesses have created an organizational structure in an attempt to better manage their environments. For example, companies often divide themselves into departments (such as Sales, Marketing, and Engineering), and individuals fill roles within these departments (such as managers and staff). The goal is to add constructs that help coordinate the various functions required for the success of the organization as a whole.

The Information Technology (IT) department in these companies is responsible for maintaining the security of the company's information. In modern businesses, this involves planning for, implementing, and managing various network resources. Servers, workstations, and routers are common tools that are used to connect users with the information they need to do their jobs. In all but the smallest environments, the effort required to manage each of these technological resources can be great.

That's where Windows 2000 and Microsoft's Active Directory come in. In its most basic definition, a directory is a repository that records information and makes it available to users. The overall design goal for the Active Directory was to create a single centralized repository of information that securely manages a company's resources. User account management, security, and applications are just a few of these areas. The Active Directory is a data store that allows administrators to manage various types of information within a single distributed database, thus solving one of the problems we stated earlier. This is no small task, but there are many features of this directory services technology that allow it to meet the needs of organizations of any size. Specifically, the Active Directory's features include the following:

**Hierarchical Organization**   In sharp contrast to the flat structure of the Windows NT 4 domain model, the Active Directory is based on a hierarchical layout. Through the use of various organizational components, a company can create a network management infrastructure that mirrors its business organization. So, if a company has 10 major divisions, each of which has several departments, the directory services model can reflect this structure through the use of various objects within the directory. This structure can efficiently accommodate the physical and logical aspects of information resources, such as databases, users, and computers. In addition to the hierarchical organization of objects within the Active Directory, the integration of network naming services with the *Domain Name System* (*DNS*) provides for the hierarchical naming and location of resources throughout the company and on the public Internet.

**Extensible Schema**   One of the foremost concerns with any type of database is the difficulty encountered when trying to accommodate all types of information in one storage repository. That's why the Active Directory has been designed with extensibility (i.e., the ability to add to and change the schema) in mind. In this case, extensibility means the ability to expand the directory schema. The *schema* is the actual structure of the database in terms of data types and location of the attributes. This is important because it allows applications to know where particular pieces of information reside. You cannot delete any portion of the schema, even the pieces that you may add. The information stored within the structure of the Active Directory can be expanded and customized through the use of various tools. One such tool is the Active Directory Services Interface (ADSI), which is available to Windows developers. ADSI provides objects and interfaces that can be accessed from within common programming languages, such as Visual Basic, Visual C++, and Active Server Pages (ASP). This feature allows the Active Directory to adapt to special applications and to store additional information as needed. It also allows all of the various areas within an organization (or even between them) to share data easily based on the structure of the Active Directory.

**Centralized Data Storage**    All of the information within the Active Directory resides within a single, yet distributed, data repository. This allows users and systems administrators to easily access the information they need from wherever they may be within the company. The benefits of the centralized data storage include reduced administration requirements, less duplication, greater availability, and increased organization of data.

**Replication**    If server performance and reliability were not concerns, it might make sense to store the entire Active Directory on a single server. In the real world, however, accessibility and cost constraints require the database to be replicated throughout the network. The Active Directory provides for this functionality. Through the use of replication technology, the data store can be distributed between many different servers in a network environment. The ability to define sites allows systems and network administrators to limit the amount of traffic between remote sites while still ensuring adequate performance and usability. Reliable data synchronization allows for multimaster replication—that is, all domain controllers can update information stored within the Active Directory and can ensure its consistency at the same time.

**Ease of Administration**    In order to accommodate various business models, the Active Directory can be configured for centralized or decentralized administration. This gives network and systems administrators the ability to delegate authority and responsibilities throughout the organization while still maintaining security. Furthermore, the tools and utilities used to add, remove, and modify Active Directory objects are available from all Windows 2000 domain controllers. They allow for making companywide changes with just a few mouse clicks.

**Network Security**    Through the use of a single logon and various authentication and encryption mechanisms, the Active Directory can facilitate security throughout an entire enterprise. Through the process of *delegation*, higher-level security authorities can grant permissions to other administrators. For ease of administration, objects in the Active Directory tree inherit permissions from their parent objects. Application developers can take advantage of many of these features to ensure that users are identified uniquely and securely. Network administrators can create and update permissions as needed from within a single repository, thereby reducing chances of inaccurate or outdated configuration.

**Client Configuration Management**   One of the biggest struggles for systems administrators comes with maintaining a network of heterogeneous systems and applications. A fairly simple failure—such as a hard disk crash—can cause hours of work in reconfiguring and restoring a workstation or server. Hours of work can also be generated when users are forced to move between computers and they need to have all of their applications reinstalled and the necessary system settings updated. Many IT organizations have found that these types of operations can consume a great deal of IT staffers' time and resources. New technologies integrated with the Active Directory allow for greatly enhanced control and administration of these types of network issues. The overall benefit is decreased downtime, a better end user experience, and reduced administration.

**Scalability and Performance**   Large organizations often have many users and large quantities of information to manage. The Active Directory was designed with scalability in mind. Not only does it allow for storing up to millions of objects within a single domain, it also provides methods for distributing the necessary information between servers and locations. These features relieve much of the burden of designing a directory services infrastructure based on technical instead of business factors.

**Searching Functionality**   One of the most important benefits of having all of your network resources stored in a single repository is the ability to perform accurate searches. Users often see network operating systems as extremely complicated because of the naming and location of resources. But it shouldn't be that complicated. For example, if we need to find a printer, we should not need to know the name of the domain or print server for that object. Using the Active Directory, users can quickly find information about other users or resources, such as printers and servers, through an intuitive querying interface.

We'll cover the technical aspects of how Windows 2000 addresses all of the above within the technical chapters of this book. For now, keep in mind the various challenges that the Active Directory was designed to address. The scope of this chapter is limited to introducing only the technical concepts on which the Active Directory is based. In order to better understand this topic, let's now discuss the various areas that make up the logical and physical structure of the Active Directory.

# The Active Directory's Logical Structure

**D**atabase professionals often use the term schema to describe the structure of data. A schema usually defines the types of information that can be stored within a certain repository and special rules on how the information is to be organized. Within a relational database or Microsoft Excel spreadsheet, for example, we might define tables with columns and rows. Similarly, the Active Directory schema specifies the types of information that are stored within a directory. By default, the schema supports information regarding usernames, passwords, and permissions information. The schema itself also describes the structure of the information stored within the Active Directory data store. The Active Directory data store, in turn, resides on one or more domain controllers that are deployed throughout the enterprise. In this section, we'll take a look at the various concepts that are used to specify how the Active Directory is logically organized.

## Components and Mechanisms of the Active Directory

In order to maintain the types of information required to support an entire organization, the Active Directory must provide for many different types of functionality. These include the following:

**Data Store**   When you envision the Active Directory from a physical point of view, you probably imagine a set of files stored on the hard disk that contain all of the objects within it. The term *data store* is used to refer to the actual structure that contains the information stored within the Active Directory. The data store is implemented as just that—a set of files that reside within the file system of a domain controller. This is the fundamental structure of the Active Directory.

The data store itself has a structure that describes the types of information it can contain. Within the data store, data about objects is recorded and made available to users. For example, configuration information about the domain topology, including trust relationships (which we'll cover later in this chapter), are contained within the Active Directory. Similarly, information about users, groups, and computers that are part of the domain are also recorded.

**Schema**   The Active Directory schema consists of rules on the types of information that can be stored within the directory. The schema is made up of two types of objects: attributes and classes. Attributes define a single granular piece of information stored within the Active Directory. First Name and Last Name, for example, are considered attributes, which may contain the values of Bob and Smith. Classes are objects that are defined as collections of attributes. For example, a class called Employee could include the First Name and Last Name attributes.

It is important to understand that classes and attributes are defined independently and that any number of classes can use the same attributes. For example, if we create an attribute called Nickname, this value could conceivably be used to describe a User class and a Computer class. By default, Microsoft has included several different schema objects. In order to support custom data, however, applications developers can extend the schema by creating their own classes and attributes. As we'll see in Chapter 5, "Installing and Managing Trees and Forests," the entire schema is replicated to all of the domain controllers within the environment to ensure data consistency between them.

The overall result of the schema is a centralized data store that can contain information about many different types of objects—including users, groups, computers, network devices, applications, and more.

**Global Catalog**   The *Global Catalog* is a database that contains all of the information pertaining to objects within all domains in the Active Directory environment. One of the potential problems with working in an environment that contains multiple domains is that users in one domain may want to find objects stored in another domain, but they may not have any additional information about those objects.

The purpose of the Global Catalog is to index information stored in the Active Directory so that it can be more quickly and easily searched. In order to store and replicate all of this information, the Global Catalog can be distributed to servers within the network environment. That is, network and systems administrators must specify which servers within the Active Directory environment should contain copies of the Global Catalog. This decision is usually made based on technical considerations (such as network links) and organizational considerations (such as the number of users at each remote site). You can think of the Global Catalog as a universal phone book. Such an object would be quite large and bulky, but also very useful. Your goal (as a systems administrator) would be to find a balance between maintaining copies of the phone book and making potential users of the book travel long distances to use it.

This distribution of Global Catalog information allows for increased performance during companywide resource searches and can prevent excessive traffic across network links. Since the Global Catalog includes information about objects stored in all domains within the Active Directory environment, its management and location should be an important concern for network and systems administrators.

**Searching Mechanisms**    The best-designed data repository in the world is useless if users can't access the information stored within it. The Active Directory includes a search engine that can be queried by users to find information about objects stored within it. For example, if a member of the Human Resources department is looking for a color printer, they can easily query the Active Directory to find the one located closest to them. Best of all, the query tools are already built into Windows 2000 operating systems and are only a few mouse clicks away.

**Replication**    Although it is theoretically possible to create a directory service that involves only one central computer, there are several problems with this configuration. First, all of the data is stored on one machine. This server would be responsible for processing all of the logon requests and search queries associated with the objects that it contained. Although this scenario might work well for a small network, it would create a tremendous load on servers in larger environments. Furthermore, clients that are located on remote networks would experience slower response times due to the pace of network traffic. Another drawback is that the entire directory would be stored in only one location. If this server became unavailable (due to a failed power supply, for example), network authentication and other vital processes could not be carried out. To solve these problems, the Active Directory has been designed with a replication engine. The purpose of *replication* is to distribute the data stored within the directory throughout the organization for increased availability, performance, and data protection. Systems administrators can tune replication to occur based on their physical network infrastructure and other constraints.

Each of these components must work together to ensure that the Active Directory remains accessible to all of the users that require it and to maintain the accuracy and consistency of its information. Now that we've seen the logical structure and features of the Active Directory, let's move on to looking at organizational concepts.

## An Overview of Active Directory Domains

In Windows 2000 Active Directory, a domain is a logical security boundary that allows for the creation, administration, and management of related resources. You can think of a domain as a logical division, such as a neighborhood within a city. Although each neighborhood is part of a larger group of neighborhoods (the city), it may carry on many of its functions independently of the others. For example, resources such as tennis courts and swimming pools may be made available only to members of the neighborhood, while resources such as electricity and water supplies would probably be shared between neighborhoods. So, think of a domain as a grouping of objects that utilizes resources exclusive to its domain, but keep in mind that those resources can also be shared *between* domains.

Although the names and fundamental features are the same, Active Directory domains vary greatly from those in Windows NT. As we mentioned earlier, an Active Directory domain can store many more objects than a Windows NT domain. Furthermore, Active Directory domains can be combined together into *forests* and *trees* to form hierarchical structures. This is in contrast to Windows NT domains, which treat all domains as peers of each other (that is, they are all on equal footing and cannot be organized into trees and forests). Before going into the details, let's discuss the concept of domains.

Within most business organizations, network and systems administration duties are delegated to certain individuals and departments. For example, a company might have a centralized IT department that is responsible for all implementation, support, and maintenance of network resources throughout the organization. In another example, network support may be largely decentralized—that is, each department, business unit, or office may have its own IT support staff. Both of these models may work well for a company, but implementing such a structure through directory services requires the use of logical objects.

Domains are composed of a collection of computers and resources that share a common security database. An Active Directory domain contains a logical partition of users, groups, and other objects within the environment. Objects within a domain share several characteristics, including the following:

**Group Policy and Security Permissions**   Security for all of the objects within a domain can be administered based on one set of policies. Thus, a domain administrator can make changes to any of the settings within the domain. These settings can apply to all of the users, computers, and objects within the domain. For more granular security settings, however, permissions can be granted on specific objects, thereby distributing administration responsibilities and increasing security. Domains are configured as a single security entity. Objects, permissions, and other settings within a domain do not automatically apply to other domains.

**Hierarchical Object Naming**    All of the objects within an Active Directory container share a common namespace. When domains are combined together, however, the namespace is hierarchical. For example, a user in one department might have an object name called `janedoe@engineering`
`.microsoft.com` while a user in another department might have one called `johndoe@sales.microsoft.com`. The first part of the name is determined by the name of the object within the domain (in these examples, the username). The suffix is determined by the organization of the domains. The hierarchical naming system allows each object within the Active Directory to have a unique name. For more information on naming Active Directory objects, see the appendix.

**Hierarchical Properties**    Containers called *organizational units* (OUs) (described later) can be created within a domain. These units are used for creating a logical grouping of objects within the Active Directory. The specific user settings and permissions that are assigned to these objects can be inherited by lower-level objects. For example, if we have an organizational unit for the North America division within our company, we can set user permissions on this object. All of the objects within the North America object (such as the Sales, Marketing, and Engineering departments) would automatically inherit these settings. This makes administration easier, but inheritance is an important concept to remember when implementing and administering security since it results in the implicit assignment of permissions. The proper use of hierarchical properties allows systems administrators to avoid inconsistent security policies (such as a minimum password length of six characters in one object and a minimum password length of eight characters in another).

**Trust Relationships**    In order to facilitate the sharing of information between domains, trust relationships are automatically created between them. Additionally, the administrator can break and establish trust relationships based on business requirements. A trust relationship allows two domains to share security information and objects, but does not automatically assign permissions to these objects. This allows users who are contained within one domain to be granted access to resources in other domains. To make administering trust relationships easier, Microsoft has made transitive two-way *trusts* the default relationship between domains. As shown in Figure 1.3, if Domain A trusts Domain B and Domain B trusts Domain C, Domain A implicitly trusts Domain C.

**FIGURE 1.3** Transitive two-way trust relationships

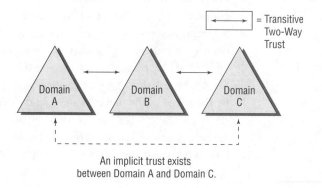

An implicit trust exists
between Domain A and Domain C.

Generally, triangles are used to represent Active Directory domains (thereby indicating their hierarchical structure), and circles are used to represent flat domains (such as those in Windows NT).

Overall, the purpose of domains is to ease administration while providing for a common security and resource database.

## Using Multiple Domains

Although the flexibility and power afforded by the use of an Active Directory domain will meet the needs of many organizations, there are reasons for which companies might want to implement more than one domain. We'll cover these planning issues in the appendix. For now, however, it is important to know that domains can be combined together into domain trees.

Domain trees are hierarchical collections of domains that are designed to meet the organizational needs of a business (see Figure 1.4). Trees are defined by the use of a contiguous namespace. For example, the following domains are all considered part of the same tree:

- microsoft.com
- sales.microsoft.com
- research.microsoft.com
- us.sales.microsoft.com

Notice that all of these domains are part of the `microsoft.com` domain. Domains within trees still maintain separate security and resource databases, but they can be administered together through the use of trust relationships. By default, trust relationships are automatically established between parent and child domains within a tree.

**FIGURE 1.4**   A domain tree

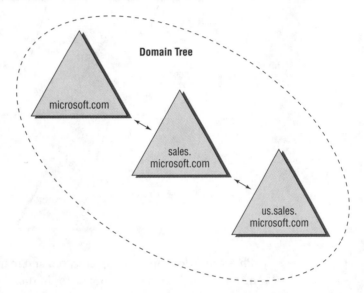

Although single companies will often want to configure domains to fit within a single namespace, noncontiguous namespaces may be used for several reasons. We'll look at several of these reasons in Chapter 5. When domain trees are combined together into noncontiguous groupings, they are known as forests (see Figure 1.5). Forests often contain multiple noncontiguous namespaces consisting of domains that are kept separate for technical or political reasons. Just as trust relationships are created between domains within a tree, trust relationships are also created between trees within a forest so resources can be shared between them.

FIGURE 1.5 An Active Directory forest

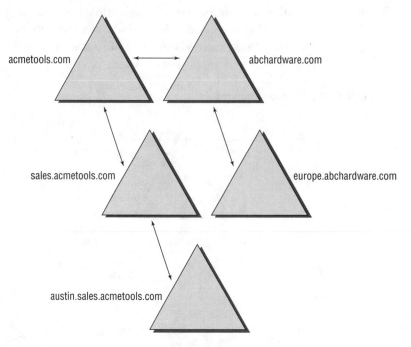

Physically, domains are implemented and managed by the use of domain controllers. We'll cover this topic later in this chapter.

## Creating a Domain Structure with Organizational Units

As we mentioned earlier, one of the fundamental limitations of the Windows NT 4 domain organization is that it consists of a flat structure. All users and groups are stored as part of a single namespace. Real-world organizations, however, often require further organization within domains. For example, we may have three thousand users in one domain. Some of these should be grouped together in an Engineering group. Within the Engineering group, we might also want to further subdivide users into other groups (for example, Development and Testing). The Active Directory supports this kind of hierarchy. Figure 1.6 provides a depiction of the differences between the structure of a Windows NT 4 domain and that of an Active Directory domain.

**FIGURE 1.6** Windows NT 4 vs. Active Directory domains

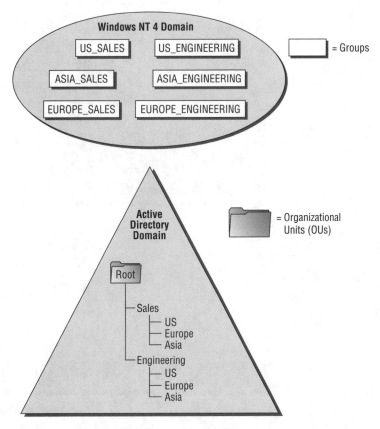

The fundamental unit of organization within an Active Directory domain is the organizational unit (OU). OUs are container objects that can be hierarchically arranged within a domain. Figure 1.7 provides an example of a typical OU setup. OUs can contain other objects such as users, groups, computers, and even other OUs. The proper planning and usage of OUs are important because they are generally the objects to which security permissions and Group Policies are assigned. A well-designed OU structure can greatly ease the administration of Active Directory objects.

OUs can be organized based on various criteria. For example, we might choose to implement an OU organization based on the geographic distribution of our company's business units.

**FIGURE 1.7** Two different OU hierarchy models

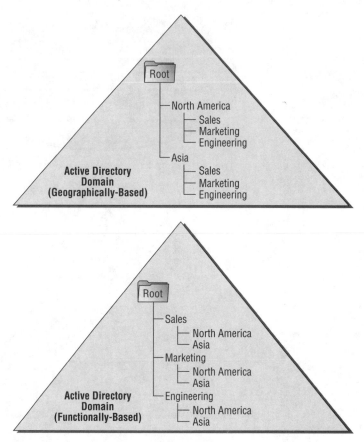

We'll look at various planning issues for OUs in the appendix.

## Active Directory Object Names

A fundamental feature of a directory service is that each object within the directory should contain its own unique name. For example, our organization may have two different users named John Smith (who may or may not be in different departments or locations within the company). There should be some unique way for us to distinguish these users (and their corresponding user objects).

Generally, this unique identifier is called the *distinguished name*. Within the Active Directory, each object can be uniquely identified using a long name that specifies the full path to the object. Following is an example of a distinguished name:

```
/O=Internet/DC=Com/DC=MyCompany/DC=Sales
 /CN=Managers/CN=John Smith
```

In the above name, we have specified the following several different types of objects:

**Organization (O)**    The company or root-level domain. In this case, the root level is the Internet.

**Domain Component (DC)**    A portion of the hierarchical path. DCs are used for organizing objects within the directory service. The DCs specify that the user object is located within the `sales.mycompany.com` domain.

**Common Name (CN)**    Specifies the names of objects in the directory. In this example, the user John Smith is contained within the Managers container.

When used together, the components of the distinguished name uniquely identify where the user object is stored. Instead of specifying the full distinguished name, we might also choose to use a relative distinguished name. This name specifies only part of the path above and is relative to another object. For example, if our current context is already the Managers group within the `sales.mycompany.com` domain, we could simply specify the user as `CN=John Smith`.

Note that if we change the structure of the domain, the distinguished name of this object would also change. A change might happen if we rename one of the containers in the path or move the user object itself. This type of naming system allows for flexibility and the ability to easily identify the potentially millions of objects that might exist in the Active Directory.

## User, Computer, and Group Objects

The real objects that you will want to control and manage with the Active Directory are the users, computers, and groups within your network environment. These are the types of objects that allow for the most granular level of control over permissions and allow you to configure your network to meet business needs.

User accounts are used to enforce the security within the network environment. These accounts define the login information and passwords that are used to receive permissions to network objects. Computer objects allow systems administrators to configure the functions that can be performed on client machines throughout the environment. Both User accounts and Computer objects enable security to be maintained at a granular level.

Although security can be enforced by placing permissions directly on User and Computer objects, it is much more convenient to combine users into *groups*. For example, if there are three users who will require similar permissions within the Accounting department, we could place all of them in one group. If users are removed or added to the department, we could easily make changes to the group without having to make any further changes to security permissions. Figure 1.8 shows how groups can be used to easily administer permissions.

**FIGURE 1.8** Using groups to administer security

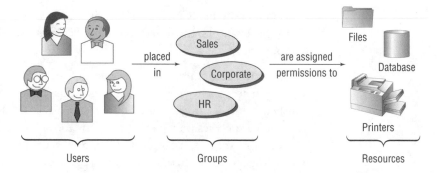

There are two main types of groups within the Active Directory: security groups and distribution groups. *Security groups* are used for the administration of permissions. All members of a security group will receive the same security settings. *Distribution groups*, on the other hand, are used only for sending e-mail and other messages to several different users at once. They do not involve the maintenance of security permissions but can be helpful in handling multiple users.

Overall, the proper use of groups assists greatly in implementing and managing security and permissions within the Active Directory.

# The Active Directory's Physical Structure

**S**o far, we have focused our attention on the logical units that make up the Active Directory. That is, the ideas presented so far are designed to bring organization to the structure of the network. What we haven't discussed is exactly *how* domains, trees, forests, and the Active Directory itself are created and managed. In this section, we'll see how various servers and network devices can be used to implement and manage the components of the Active Directory.

## Server Roles within the Active Directory

The Active Directory data store is stored on one or more computers within an organization's network environment. All editions of the Windows 2000 Server platform are able to participate in Active Directory domains under the following roles:

**Domain Controllers**   The heart of the Active Directory's functionality resides on domain controllers. These machines are responsible for maintaining the Active Directory data store, including all of its objects, and for providing security for the entire domain. Although an Active Directory configuration may involve only one domain controller, it is much more likely that organizations will have more servers in order to increase performance and establish fault-tolerance. All of the information that resides within the Active Directory is synchronized between the domain controllers, and most changes can be made at any of these servers. This functionality is referred to as multimaster replication and is the basis through which Active Directory information is distributed throughout an organization.

**Member Servers**   Often, you will want to have servers that function as part of the domain but are not responsible for containing Active Directory information or authenticating users. Common examples include file/print servers and Web servers. A Windows 2000 Server computer that is a member of a domain but is not a domain controller itself is referred to as a *member server*. By using member servers, systems administrators can take advantage of the centralized security database of the Active Directory without dedicating server processing and storage resources to maintaining the directory information.

**Stand-Alone Servers**   It is possible to run Windows 2000 Server computers in a workgroup environment that does not include Active Directory functionality at all. These machines are known as stand-alone servers. They maintain their own security database and are administered independently of other servers, as no centralized security database exists. Stand-alone servers might be used for functions such as public Web servers or in situations in which only a few users require resources from a machine and the administrative overhead for managing security separately on various machines is acceptable.

A major benefit in the Windows 2000 Server operating system is the ability to easily promote and demote domain controllers after the operating system has been installed. Unlike the situation with Windows NT 4, reinstallation of the entire operating system is no longer required to change the role of a server. Furthermore, by properly promoting and demoting domain controllers, you can effectively move them between domains, trees, and forests.

In addition to the various types of server roles that the Windows 2000 Server platform can take on within the Active Directory domains, the Active Directory requires systems administrators to assign specific functionalities to other servers. In discussing replication, certain servers might be referred to as masters. Masters contain copies of a database and generally allow both read and write operations. Some types of replication may allow multiple masters to exist, while others specify that only a single master is allowed. Certain tasks within the Active Directory work well using multimaster replication. For example, the ability to update information at one or more of the domain controllers can speed up response times while still maintaining data integrity through replication. Other functions, however, better lend themselves to being defined centrally. These operations are referred to as single-master operations because the function only supports modification on a single machine in the environment. These machines are referred to as Operations Masters servers. The role of these servers is to handle operations that are required to ensure consistency within an Active Directory environment. Some of these are unique within a domain, and others are unique within the tree or forest. The changes made on these machines are then propagated to other domain controllers, as necessary. The various roles for Operations Masters servers within the Active Directory include the following:

**Schema Master**    As we mentioned earlier, one of the benefits of the Active Directory schema is that it can be modified. All changes to the schema, however, are propagated to all domain controllers within the forest. In order for the information to stay synchronized and consistent, it is necessary for one machine within the entire tree or forest to be designated as the Schema Master. All changes to the schema must be made on this machine. By default the first domain controller installed in the tree or forest is the Schema Master.

**Domain Naming Master**    When creating, adding, or removing domains, it is necessary for one machine in the tree or forest to serve as a central authority for the Active Directory configuration. The Domain Naming Master ensures that all of the information within the Active Directory forest is kept consistent and is responsible for registering new domains.

Within each Active Directory domain, the following roles can be assigned to domain controllers:

**Relative ID Master**   A fundamental requirement of any directory service is that each object must have a unique identifier. All users, groups, computers, and other objects within the Active Directory, for example, are identified by a unique value. The Relative ID (RID) Master is responsible for creating all of these identifiers within each domain and for ensuring that objects have unique IDs between domains by working with RID Masters in other domains.

**Primary Domain Controller (PDC) Emulator**   In order to support Windows NT, Windows 2000 Server must have the ability to serve as a Windows NT PDC. Microsoft has made a conscious decision to allow networks to work in a mixed mode of Windows NT domains and Active Directory domains in order to facilitate the migration process (and encourage more people to buy Windows 2000!). As long as there are computers in the environment running Windows NT 4, the PDC Emulator will allow for the transmission of security information between domain controllers. This provides for backward compatibility while an organization moves to Windows 2000 and the Active Directory.

**Infrastructure Master**   Managing group memberships is an important role fulfilled manually by systems administrators. In a potentially distributed Active Directory environment, though, it is important to make sure that group and user memberships stay synchronized throughout the network. In order to understand how information might become inconsistent, let's look at an example using two domain controllers named DC1 and DC2. Suppose we make a change to a user's settings on DC1. At the same time, suppose another systems administrator makes a change to the same user account but on DC2. There must be some way to determine which change takes precedence over the other. More important, all domain controllers should be made aware of these changes so that the Active Directory database information remains consistent. The role of the Infrastructure Master is to ensure consistency between users and their group memberships as changes, additions, and deletions are made.

If there is more than one domain controller in the domain, the Global Catalog should not reside on the same server as the Infrastructure Master. This would prevent it from seeing any changes to the data and would result in replication not occurring between the various domain controllers.

It is important to note that the above assignments are *roles* and that a single machine may perform multiple roles. For example, in an environment in which only a single domain controller exists, that server will assume all of the above roles by default. On the other hand, if multiple servers are present, these functions can be distributed between them for business and technical reasons. By properly assigning roles to the servers in your environment, you'll be able to ensure that single-master operations are carried out securely and efficiently.

## Accessing the Active Directory through LDAP

In order to insert, update, and query information from within the Active Directory, Microsoft has chosen to employ the worldwide Internet Engineering Task Force (IETF) standard protocol called the *Lightweight Directory Access Protocol (LDAP)*. LDAP is designed to allow for the transfer of information between domain controllers and to allow users to query information about objects within the directory.

As LDAP is a standard, it also facilitates interoperability between other directory services. Furthermore, communications can be programmed using objects such as the Active Directory Services Interface (ADSI). For data transport, LDAP can be used over TCP/IP, thus making it an excellent choice for communicating over the Internet, as well as private TCP/IP-based networks.

## Managing Replication with Sites

A common mistake made in planning the Active Directory is to base its structure on the technical constraints of a business instead of on business practices. For instance, a systems administrator might recommend that a separate domain be placed at each of a company's three remote sites. The rationale for this decision is understandable—the goal is to reduce network traffic between potentially slow and costly remote links. However, the multidomain structure may not make sense for organizations that have a centralized IT department and require common security settings for each of the three locations.

In order to allow the Active Directory to be based on business and political decisions while still accommodating network infrastructure issues, Windows 2000 supports the concept of *sites*. Active Directory sites are designed to define the physical layout of a company's network by taking into account multiple subnets, remote access links, and other network factors. When performing vital functions between domain controllers, for example, you might want to limit bandwidth usage across a slow link. However, within your local area network (LAN) environment, you will want replication to occur as quickly as possible to keep machines synchronized.

Sites are usually defined as locations in which network access is quick and inexpensive. Windows 2000 uses sites to determine when and how information should be replicated between domain controllers and other machines within the environment. Figure 1.9 provides an example of how a distributed company might choose to implement sites.

**FIGURE  1.9**    A typical site configuration

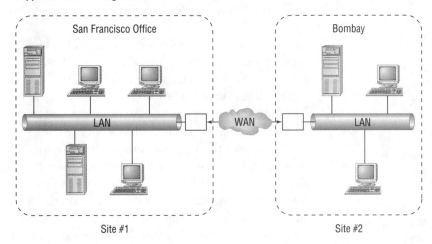

It is important to understand the distinction between logical and physical components of the Active Directory. When planning your objects and domains, you will want to take into account the business requirements of your organization. This will create the logical structure of the directory. In planning for the implementation of the Active Directory, however, you must take into account your network infrastructure—the physical aspects. Sites provide a great way to isolate these two requirements.

# Active Directory Names and DNS

The Domain Name System (DNS) is a distributed database built upon an Internet standard that is used to resolve friendly, hierarchical names to TCP/IP network addresses. Systems administrators who have to remember many server IP addresses will easily recall the need for DNS—it can be quite a difficult and error-prone process to remember all of these numbers. For example, if we have a server on the Internet with an IP address of 24.133.155.7, we may want to give it a friendly name, such as sales.mycompany.com. Instead of typing the IP address every time we need to access the resource, we could specify the fully-qualified name of the machine and leave it to the DNS servers on the Internet to resolve the address.

Understanding TCP/IP is vital to understanding the use of almost any modern network operating system. If you're planning to deploy a Windows 2000 environment, be sure you take the time to learn the details of working with TCP/IP.

The Windows 2000 Active Directory relies on DNS for finding DCs and naming and accessing Active Directory objects. Windows 2000 includes a DNS server service that can be used for automatically updating records that store machine name to IP address mappings. DNS offers many advantages. First, it is the primary name resolution method used on the Internet. Therefore, it has widespread support in all modern operating systems and works well between various operating system platforms.

Second, DNS is designed with fault-tolerance and distributed databases in mind. If a single DNS server does not have the information required to fulfill a request for information, it automatically queries another DNS server for this information. Systems administrators are only responsible for maintaining the DNS entries for their own machines. Through the use of efficient caching, the load of performing worldwide queries on large networks can be minimized.

The various technical details related to DNS are well beyond the scope of this section, but we will cover them later in Chapter 2, "Integrating DNS with the Active Directory."

---

 **Real World Scenario**

### Upgrading Windows NT Domains to Active Directory

You are a consultant doing work for an organization that has decided to move its environment to the Active Directory. However, before the upgrade can begin, you must first design a suitable Active Directory. You have several choices that need to be made and many considerations to take into account. Factors that should affect your decision include the following:

**Political Issues**  How does the current business operate—as single, independent business units, or as a centralized environment? Who will be responsible for administering portions of the network?

**Network Issues**   What types of network connections are present between your remote offices? How reliable are these connections? Also, what are the domain name requirements for this environment?

**Organizational Structure**   How are various areas of the business structured? For example, do the departments operate individually, with separate network administrators for each department? Or is the environment much more centralized?

Based on the answers to these questions, you might choose to implement only a single domain. This method provides for simple administration and should meet most requirements. You may, however, have other concerns (such as the need to support multiple DNS namespaces). In any case, the best solution will be based on the specific needs of the environment.

# Summary

In this chapter, we took a high-level overview of the concepts related to the Active Directory. Specifically, we discussed the following:

- The benefits of implementing the Active Directory
- How the Active Directory compares to Windows NT's domain model
- How and why multiple Active Directory domains can be created
- The logical components of an Active Directory environment
- The naming of Active Directory objects
- The physical components that make up an Active Directory environment

# Exam Essentials

**Understand the problems that Active Directory is designed to solve.** The creation of a single, centralized directory service can make network operations and management much simpler. The Active Directory solves many shortcomings in Windows NT's domain model.

**Understand Active Directory design goals.**   The Active Directory should be structured to mirror an organization's logical structure. Understand the factors that you should take into account, including business units, geographic structure, and future business requirements.

**Understand features of Active Directory.**   Understand how and why Microsoft has included features that allow for extensibility, centralized data storage, replication, ease of administration, security, and scalability.

Remember the Operations Master server roles that are required in an Active Directory environment. Operations Master roles are vital to the proper operations of the Active Directory. Some of these roles must be present in each Active Directory domain while others require only one for the entire Active Directory environment.

**Understand the basic domain structure for an Active Directory environment.**   An Active Directory environment can consist of only a single domain, or it can include multiple domains that form a tree. Multiple trees can be combined into a forest.

# Key Terms

Before you take the exam, be certain you are familiar with the following terms:

| | |
|---|---|
| Active Directory | Lightweight Directory Access Protocol (LDAP) |
| delegation | member server |
| distinguished name | organizational units (OUs) |
| Domain Name Systems (DNS) | replication |
| Distribution group | schema |
| domain | Security group |
| domain controllers | sites |
| forests | trees |
| Global Catalog | trusts |
| groups | |

# Review Questions

1. Which of the following is not a feature of the Active Directory?

   **A.** The use of LDAP for transferring information

   **B.** Reliance on DNS for name resolution

   **C.** A flat domain namespace

   **D.** The ability to extend the schema

2. Domains provide which of the following functions?

   **A.** Creating security boundaries to protect resources and ease of administration

   **B.** Easing the administration of users, groups, computers, and other objects

   **C.** Providing a central database of network objects

   **D.** All of the above

3. Which of the following types of servers contain copies of the Active Directory database?

   **A.** Member servers

   **B.** Domain controllers

   **C.** Stand-alone servers

   **D.** None of the above

4. Which of the following objects are used for creating the logical structure within Active Directory domains?

   **A.** Users

   **B.** Sites

   **C.** Organizational units (OUs)

   **D.** Trees

   **E.** None of the above

**5.** Which of the following is *false* regarding the naming of Active Directory objects?

   **A.** The Active Directory relies on DNS for name resolution.

   **B.** Two objects can have the same relative distinguished name.

   **C.** Two objects can have the same distinguished name.

   **D.** All objects within a domain are based on the name of the domain.

**6.** Which of the following are *true* regarding Active Directory trust relationships?

   **A.** Trusts are transitive.

   **B.** By default, trusts are two-way relationships.

   **C.** Trusts are used to allow the authentication of users between domains.

   **D.** All of the above.

**7.** Which of the following protocols is used to query Active Directory information?

   **A.** LDAP

   **B.** NetBEUI

   **C.** NetBIOS

   **D.** IPX/SPX

**8.** Which of the following is not true regarding the Windows NT domain namespace?

   **A.** Windows NT domains have a hierarchical namespace.

   **B.** Windows NT domains allow thousands of users.

   **C.** Windows NT domains can be implemented as master domains.

   **D.** Windows NT domains can be implemented as resource domains.

   **E.** All of the above.

**9.** Which of the following is a possible role for a Windows 2000 Server?

   **A.** Member server

   **B.** Primary Domain Controller

   **C.** Backup Domain Controller

   **D.** Stand-alone server

   **E.** Both A and D

**10.** Which of the following statements is *true* regarding domain controllers?

   **A.** All Active Directory domain controllers are automatically configured as Windows NT domain controllers.

   **B.** Windows NT domain controllers can host a copy of the Active Directory database.

   **C.** Windows 2000 domain controllers can be configured to provide the functionality of Windows NT domain controllers.

   **D.** None of the above.

**11.** Which of the following is not a characteristic of DNS?

   **A.** Built-in redundancy

   **B.** Reliance on proprietary technologies

   **C.** Scalability

   **D.** Distributed databases

**12.** An organization uses 12 Active Directory domains in a single forest. How many Schema Masters must this environment have?

   **A.** 0

   **B.** 1

   **C.** 12

   **D.** More than 12

   **E.** None of the above

**13.** An organization has three remote offices and one large central one. How many sites should this environment contain?

**A.** 0

**B.** 1

**C.** 3

**D.** 4

**E.** Not enough information

**14.** Which of the following features of the Active Directory allows information between domain controllers to remain synchronized?

**A.** Replication

**B.** The Global Catalog

**C.** The schema

**D.** None of the above

**15.** Jane is a systems administrator for a large, multidomain, geographically distributed network environment. The network consists of a large, central office and many smaller remote offices located throughout the world. Recently, Jane has received complaints about the performance of Active Directory–related operations from remote offices. Users complain that it takes a long time to perform searches for network resources (such as Shared Folders and Printers). Jane wants to improve the performance of these operations. Which of the following components of the Active Directory should she implement at remote sites to improve the performance of searches conducted for objects in *all* domains?

**A.** Data store

**B.** Global Catalog

**C.** Schema

**D.** None of the above

# Answers to Review Questions

1. C. The Active Directory uses a hierarchical namespace for managing objects.

2. D. All of these options are features of domains and are reasons for their usefulness.

3. B. Only domain controllers contain a copy of the Active Directory database. Member servers rely on the Active Directory but do not contain a copy of the database, and stand-alone servers do not participate in the Active Directory at all.

4. C. OUs are used for creating a hierarchical structure within a domain. Users are objects within the directory, sites are used for physical planning, and trees are relationships between domains.

5. C. The distinguished name of each object in the Active Directory must be unique, but the relative distinguished names may be the same. For example, we might have a User object named Jane Doe in two different containers.

6. D. Trusts are designed for facilitating the sharing of information and have all of the above features.

7. A. LDAP is the IETF standard protocol for accessing information from directory services. It is also the standard used by the Active Directory.

8. A. The Windows NT namespace is a flat model because groups cannot contain other groups and there is no hierarchical structure within a domain. The components of Active Directory domains, on the other hand, allow the use of organizational units (OUs) in order to create a manageable hierarchy within a domain.

9. E. Primary Domain Controllers and Backup Domain Controllers are only used in Windows NT domains.

10. C. Through the use of the PDC Emulator functionality, Windows 2000 domain controllers can provide services for Windows NT domains.

**11.** B. DNS is a worldwide standard that is widely supported in all modern operating systems.

**12.** B. Only one Schema Master is allowed in an Active Directory environment, regardless of the number of domains.

**13.** E. The site topology is completely independent from domain architecture—a domain can span many sites, and many domains can be part of the same site. The fact that the organization has four locations does not necessarily mean that it should use a specific number of sites. Rather, this determination should be made based on physical network characteristics.

**14.** A. Replication ensures that information remains synchronized between domain controllers.

**15.** B. The Global Catalog contains information about multiple domains, and additional Global Catalog servers can greatly increase the performance of operations such as searches for shared folders and printers. The other options are features of the Active Directory, but they are not designed for fast searching across multiple domains.

# Chapter

# 2

# Integrating DNS with the Active Directory

## MICROSOFT EXAM OBJECTIVES COVERED IN THIS CHAPTER:

✓ **Install, configure, and troubleshoot DNS for Active Directory.**

- Integrate Active Directory DNS zones with non-Active Directory DNS zones.

- Configure zones for dynamic updates.

✓ **Manage, monitor, and troubleshoot DNS.**

- Manage replication of DNS data.

In the previous chapter, we looked at the things you need to consider before you implement the Active Directory in your own environment. In this chapter on the *Domain Name System (DNS)*, we'll look at the technical details of implementing the Active Directory and DNS.

Understanding DNS is vital to the deployment of the Active Directory and is a prerequisite for installing and configuring domain controllers (which we'll cover in more detail in Chapter 3, "Installing and Configuring the Active Directory"). A common mistake made by systems administrators is underestimating the importance and complexity of DNS. The Active Directory, itself, relies on DNS in order to find clients, servers, and network services that are available throughout your environment. Clients rely on DNS in order to find the file, print, and other resources they require to get their jobs done. Fully understanding DNS is not an easy task, especially for those who have limited experience with *Transmission Control Protocol/Internet Protocol (TCP/IP)*. However, the understanding and proper implementation of DNS is vital to the use of the Active Directory.

# DNS Overview

DNS is a TCP/IP standard that is designed to resolve Internet Protocol (IP) addresses to host names. One of the inherent complexities of working in networked environments involves working with various protocols and network addresses. Thanks largely to the tremendous rise in popularity of the Internet, however, most environments have transitioned to the use of TCP/IP as their primary networking protocol, and Microsoft is no exception when it comes to support for TCP/IP. All current versions of Microsoft operating systems support it, as do almost all other modern operating systems. Since the introduction of Windows NT 4, TCP/IP has been the default protocol installed.

TCP/IP is actually a collection of different technologies that allow computers to function together on a single network. Some of the major advantages of the protocol include widespread support for hardware, software, and network devices, reliance on a system of standards, and scalability.

TCP/IP is not the simplest protocol to understand, however. Because it was designed to support large, heterogeneous networks, there are many issues involved with TCP/IP addressing, the use of subnets, routing, and name resolution. It is beyond the scope of this chapter to fully describe the intricacies of working with TCP/IP. However, we will cover the information required to understand DNS as it relates to Windows 2000 and the Active Directory.

TCP/IP and DNS are based on a series of standards ratified by the Internet Engineering Task Force (IETF), a global standards organization. The job of this committee is to consider submissions for new features to the TCP/IP protocol and other related communications methods. Standards that are approved by the IETF are covered in Requests for Comments (RFCs). If you are looking for in-depth technical information on various Internet protocols and standards, see www.ietf.org.

An IP address is simply a number used to uniquely identify a computer on a TCP/IP network. The address takes the form of four octets (eight binary bits), each of which is represented by a decimal number between 0 and 255. Decimal points logically separate each of the decimally represented numbers. For example, all of the following are valid IP addresses:

- 128.45.23.17

- 230.212.43.100

- 10.1.1.1

Believe it or not, the dotted decimal notated representation was created to make it easier for humans to deal with IP addresses. Obviously, this idea did not go far enough, hence the development of the other abstraction layer of using names to represent the dotted decimal notation. For example, 11000000 10101000 00000001 00010101 maps to 192.168.1.21, which maps to server1.company.org, which is how the address is usually presented to the user or application. First, ASCII flat files, called HOSTS files, were used, but as the number of entries grew, this became unwieldy with all the manual updates that were required. This was the impetus for the development of DNS.

When dealing with large networks, it is vital for both users and network administrators to be able to locate the resources they require with a minimal amount of searching. From a user's standpoint, they don't care about the actual physical or logical network address of the machine. They just want to be able to connect to it using a simple name. From a network administrator's standpoint, however, each machine must have its own logical address that makes it part of the network on which it resides. Therefore, some method for resolving a machine's logical name to an IP address is required. DNS was created to do just that.

DNS is based on an Internet standard defined by the IETF. It is a hierarchical naming system that contains a distributed database of name-to-IP address mappings. A DNS name is much friendlier and easier to remember than an IP address. For example, every time you enter a URL (such as `www.microsoft.com`), your computer makes a query to a DNS server that resolves it to an IP address. From then on, all communications between your computer and Microsoft's Web server take place using the IP address. The beauty of the system is that it's all transparent to users. The scalability and reliability of DNS can easily be seen by its widespread use on the Internet.

From a network and systems administration standpoint, however, things are considerably more complex. The Active Directory itself is designed to use DNS to locate servers and clients. Microsoft has included a DNS server service with the Windows 2000 operating system. As we'll see, Microsoft has also included many advanced features (some of which are not yet part of the IETF-approved standard DNS) in order to reduce the complexity of maintaining DNS databases.

If you're new to DNS, the following sections will provide a lot of useful information on how DNS works. If you're a seasoned DNS veteran, you should still read about Windows 2000's DNS, which includes several additional features and enhancements that will be covered thoroughly in this chapter.

We'll begin this chapter by looking at how DNS works. Then, we'll move on to look at how Microsoft's implementation of DNS can be used for name resolution. Finally, we'll look at the integration between the Active Directory and DNS.

# DNS Namespace

If the world could run on only one flat network, things might be easier. We wouldn't need subnets, routers, and switches to isolate connections from each other. In the real world, however, technological and other limitations force network and systems administrators to create and adhere to their own specific set of names and network addresses. Furthermore, hierarchical names are extremely useful and necessary when participating in a worldwide network such as the Internet. For example, if I have a computer called Workstation 1, there must be some way to distinguish it from another computer with the same name at a different company. Similar to the way the Active Directory uses hierarchical names for objects, DNS allows for the use of a virtually unlimited number of machines. In this section, we'll look at how these friendly names are structured.

## The Anatomy of a DNS Name

We already mentioned that DNS is designed to resolve network addresses with friendly names. DNS names take the form of a series of alphanumeric strings separated by decimal points. Together, the various portions of a DNS name form what is called the *DNS namespace,* and each address within it is unique. All of the following examples are valid DNS names:

- `microsoft.com`

- `www.microsoft.com`

- `sales.microsoft.com`

- `engineering.microsoft.com`

The leftmost portion of the name is called the host name and refers to the actual name of a machine. The remaining portions are part of the domain name and uniquely specify the network on which the host resides. The full name is referred to as the Fully-Qualified Domain Name (FQDN). For example, the host name might be engineering, whereas the FQDN is `engineering.microsoft.com`.

There are several features and limitations to note about a DNS name:

**The name is hierarchical.**   The domains listed at the right-most side of the address are higher-level domains. As you move left, each portion zooms in on the actual host. In other words, as you read from left to right, you are moving from the specific host name to its various containers.

**The name is case-insensitive.**   Although DNS names are sometimes printed in mixed-case for clarity, the case of the characters has no relevance.

**Each FQDN on a given network must be unique.** No two machines on the same network may have the same FQDN. This requirement ensures that each machine can be uniquely identified.

**Only certain characters are allowed.** Each portion of the DNS name may include only standard English characters, decimal numbers, and dashes.

**There are maximum lengths for addresses.** A DNS address can have a maximum length of 255 characters, and each name within the full name can have up to 63 characters.

Figure 2.1 shows an example of a valid hierarchical domain name.

**FIGURE 2.1** A sample DNS namespace

Now that we know the structure of a DNS name, let's move on to look at how the name is actually composed in the real world.

## The Root

In order to be able to resolve friendly names with IP addresses, we must have some starting point. All DNS names originate from one address known as the root. This address typically does not have a name and is represented in the DNS as a ".". Until recently, there were only nine root DNS servers in the world. After the last Internet brownout, this number was increased and their administration policies were modified. Registered in the root servers are the standard top-level domains with which most people are familiar.

Many organizations worldwide require domain names to be resolved starting at the root. That is the purpose of the top-level domains. On the Internet, there are several established top-level domains. Table 2.1 provides a list of the common North American top-level domains. Each domain space is reserved for a particular type of user, also shown in the table.

**TABLE 2.1** North American Top-Level Domain Names

| Top-Level Domain | Typical Users |
|---|---|
| .com | Commercial organizations |
| .edu | Educational institutions |
| .gov | U.S. governmental organizations |
| .int | International organizations |
| .mil | U.S. military organizations |
| .net | Large network providers (such as Internet Service Providers) |
| .org | Nonprofit organizations |

In addition to these top-level domain names, there are many country codes for top-level domains throughout the world. Each is managed by its own authority. For example, a DNS name that is based in the United Kingdom may have a domain name of mycompany.co.uk. If you require a foreign domain name registration, you should inquire with the country's name service provider.

In order for an organization's own domain name to be resolved on the Internet, it must request that a second-level domain name be added to the global top-level DNS servers. Several registrars can perform this function worldwide.

For more information on registering a domain name for your own organization, see www.internic.net. There, you will find a list of common registrars available worldwide. There is a nominal charge for each domain name you register.

The name that is registered on the Internet is known as a second-level domain name. Company1.com, for example, would be considered a second-level domain name. Within an organization, however, all of the domain names would be subdomains of this one. Figure 2.2 provides an example of how the various levels of DNS domain names form a hierarchy.

**FIGURE 2.2** A DNS name hierarchy

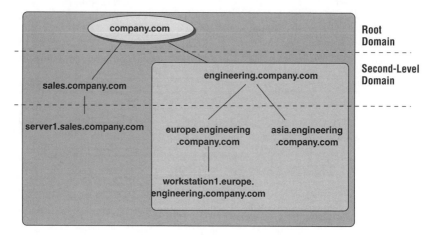

A major consideration of DNS namespace configuration is whether or not you want to trust public Internet Service Providers (ISPs) for name resolution. If not, the alternative is to host your own domain name (which can consist of any top-level domain name you choose), but your servers cannot be made directly accessible on the Internet. For example, I might choose to use the names `sales.mycompany` and `engineering.mycompany`. Although these are perfectly valid DNS names for internal use, Internet users will not be able to access them. On the other hand, I could trust public Internet authorities and use names such as `sales.mycompany.com` and `engineering.mycompany.com` (as long as I am the registered owner of the `mycompany.com` domain name). In this last scenario, you would need to rely on the DNS servers managed by your ISP for external name resolution.

## Parent and Child Names

Once an organization has registered its own domain name, it must list that name on a DNS server. This might be a server controlled by the organization, or it might be one controlled by a third party such as an ISP that hosts the name. In either case, systems and network administrators can start adding names to their DNS servers using this top-level domain name.

If, for example, I have three computers that I want to make available on the Internet, I would first need to register a second-level domain name, such as `mycompany.com`. I could then choose to add my own domain names, such as the following:

- `www.mycompany.com`

- `mail.mycompany.com`

- `computer1.northamerica.sales.mycompany.com`

Each of these domain names must be listed on the DNS server as a *resource record (RR)*. The records themselves consist of a domain name to IP address mapping. When users try to access one of these machines (through a Web browser, for example), the name will be resolved with the appropriate TCP/IP address.

DNS servers themselves are responsible for carrying out various functions related to name resolution. One of its functions is related to fulfilling DNS name mapping requests. If a DNS server has information about the specific host name specified in the request, it simply returns the appropriate information to the client that made the request. If, however, the DNS server does not have information about the specific host name, it must obtain that information from another DNS server. In this case, a process called name resolution is required. In order to resolve names of which it has no knowledge, DNS servers query other DNS servers for that information. As a result, you can see how a worldwide network of names can be formed. Later in this chapter, we'll see the various steps required to ensure that DNS servers are communicating worldwide.

# Planning a DNS Structure

It is extremely important for your organization to choose intuitive and consistent names when planning its DNS infrastructure. These are the names that users throughout the world will use to access your resources. The *root domain* name is especially important since it will be a part of the FQDN of all the machines on your network. For example, many users are accustomed to accessing a company's main Web servers via the host name www, and they may find it difficult to access your main Web servers if you use another host name. In this section, we'll look at several issues related to selecting internal and external DNS names.

## Selecting a DNS Root Name

The first step in establishing a DNS structure for your organization involves selecting a top-level domain name. The most common choice for a top-level domain is .com (for commercial companies). Usually, you would then want to reserve a second-level domain name based on the name of your company. Currently, however, due to the large number of registered domains, it may be difficult to reserve that name. In any case, you should inquire with the Internet Network Information Center (InterNIC) at www.internic.net to find a usable domain name. A good name would be one that is easy to remember and that people will quickly associate with your company. If your company has a long name or its name consists of multiple words, you might want to abbreviate it. For example, users might find ComputerTechnologiesInc.com difficult to type, whereas CompTech.com is much simpler. Some common guidelines for choosing a suitable name include the following:

- Choose a name that is similar to the name of your company.

- Use a name that will not usually change. Department or product names, for example, might change over time, whereas company names will remain relatively static.

- Ensure that you have the approval of your company's management before registering and using a name.

- Consult with your company's legal department (or a legal service) to ensure that the domain name is not currently being used and that a trademark on the name is not currently held by another company.

Once you have found a name, the process of registering it is quite simple and can be carried out entirely online. To start the registration process, connect to rs.internic.net and follow the links for registering a new domain name. You will need to choose from among several official registrars and then follow the instructions provided.

During the rise in popularity of the World Wide Web, many people rushed to reserve domain names based, for example, on the names of popular companies. These people (sometimes affectionately referred to as cyber-squatters) planned to sell the domain names to the companies that owned the copyright for the name. Today, however, organizations exist to prevent third parties from using trademarked names as domain names. To inquire into the process of regaining a domain name to which you may have rights, see rs.internic.net.

In order for your computers to be accessible via the Internet, you will need to have a worldwide-registered domain name. As part of the name registration process, you will be required to provide technical information about the DNS server(s) that will host your domain name. If you have your own DNS servers, you can simply provide their IP addresses. Otherwise, you can receive this service from many commercial ISPs (for a fee). Figure 2.3 shows how DNS names are resolved with company domain names.

**FIGURE 2.3**   How root domain requests are resolved

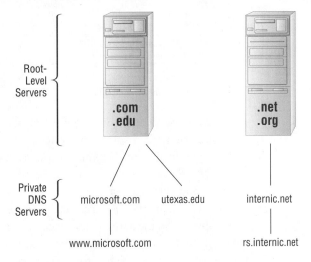

## Choosing Internal and External Names

So far, we have been talking about choosing an Internet root domain name. This external name is designed to make computers accessible publicly on the Internet. You will also need to choose a domain name for your internal network. The internal domain name may be the same as the external one, or it may be different. When you're managing internal names, you can choose any name that meets your own standards. You should, however, ensure that any external domain name you use has been properly registered with the Internet name authorities. Figure 2.4 provides an example of how different internal and external DNS names can be used.

**FIGURE 2.4** Using different internal and external DNS names

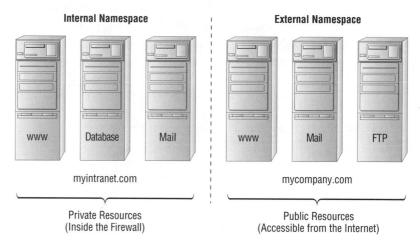

There are several pros and cons to consider when deciding whether or not to use the same domain name for internal and external resources. The advantages of using the same name include consistency between internal and external resources. This means that users will be able to use the same e-mail address for internal and external communications. However, having the same name will require taking great care in naming resources and configuring DNS servers. A small mistake in the naming, for instance, may result in an internal server being made available on the public Internet. Similarly, users must be told which resources are only available from the internal network and which machines are accessible from the public Internet.

If you choose separate internal and external names, you will be able to easily determine which resources are publicly accessible and which ones are restricted to your private network. This also simplifies routing and DNS settings. However, this method requires that you reserve two domain names (which are getting more and more difficult to find!) and that users have two different e-mail addresses (one for internal e-mail and one for e-mail sent by users that are located outside of the private network (such as Internet users).

You should base your decision regarding whether to use separate or identical internal and external namespaces on your organization's business and technical requirements.

# Overview of DNS Zones

DNS servers work together to resolve hierarchical names. If they already have information about a name, they simply fulfill the query for the client; otherwise, they query other DNS servers for the appropriate information.

The system works well as it distributes the authority of separate parts of the DNS structure to specific servers. A DNS *zone* is a portion of the DNS namespace over which a specific DNS server has authority. In this section, we'll see how the concept of zones is used to ensure accurate name resolution on the Internet.

## Purpose and Function of DNS Zones

In order to ensure that naming remains accurate in a distributed network environment, one DNS server must be designated as the master database for a specific set of addresses. It is on this server that updates to host-name–to–IP-address mappings can be updated. Whenever a DNS server is unable to resolve a specific DNS name, it simply queries other servers that can provide the information. Zones are necessary because many different DNS servers could otherwise be caching the same information. If changes are made, this information could become outdated. Therefore, one central DNS server must assume the role of the ultimate authority for a specific subset of domain names.

There is an important distinction to make between DNS zones and Active Directory domains. Although both use hierarchical names and require name resolution, DNS zones do not map directly to DNS domains.

As shown in Figure 2.5, a zone may be an entire domain or represent only part of one.

**FIGURE 2.5** The relationship between DNS domains and zones

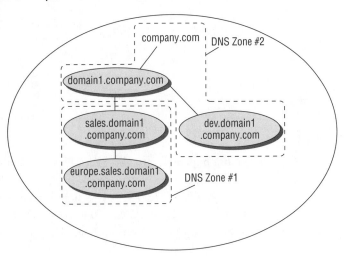

With this information in mind, let's take a more detailed look at the actual process of DNS name resolution.

## DNS Name Resolution

When using the Internet, DNS queries are extremely common. For example, every time you click a link to visit a Web site, a DNS query must be made. In the simplest scenario, the client computer requests a DNS address from its designated DNS server. The DNS server has information about the IP address for the specified host name, it returns that information to the client, and the client then uses the IP address to initiate communications with the host. This process is shown in Figure 2.6.

**FIGURE 2.6** A simple DNS name resolution process

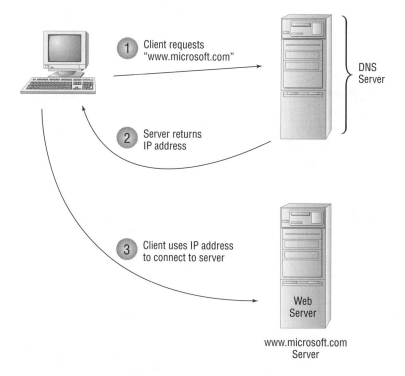

1 Client requests "www.microsoft.com"

DNS Server

2 Server returns IP address

3 Client uses IP address to connect to server

Web Server

www.microsoft.com Server

What happens, though, if the DNS server does not contain information about the specific host requested? In this case, the DNS server itself initiates a query to another DNS server, which thereby assumes responsibility for ultimately resolving the name. If the second DNS server is unable to fulfill the request, it, in turn, queries another. This process is known as *recursion*. In the process of recursion, one DNS server will contact another, which will then contact another, until one of the servers is able to resolve the host name. The name resolution process will usually begin with a query to the top-level DNS servers and continue downward through the domain hierarchy until the resource is reached. If, at this point, the name still cannot be resolved, an error is returned to the client. Figure 2.7 illustrates the process of recursion. Usually, DNS servers include information about the root- and top-level DNS servers. This information is entered in during the initial configuration of the server.

**FIGURE 2.7**    DNS name resolution through recursion

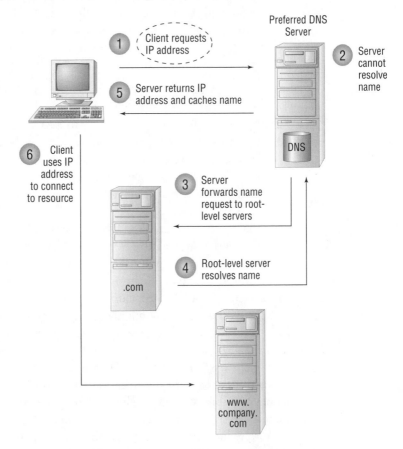

Because recursion is such an important process, let's look at an example. Suppose I want to connect to the DNS name `Computer1.sales.somecompany.com`. The following steps will occur to make this happen:

**1.** The client requests information from its preferred DNS server.

2. The preferred DNS server is unable to find a resource record for this information in its own cache and must therefore query another server. The DNS server first queries a root server and then sends a query to the top-level domain server and requests information about the server that has authority over the `somecompany.com` domain.

3. Once the information is obtained, the preferred DNS server then queries the `somecompany.com` DNS server for information about the computer1 host name within the sales domain.

4. The client's preferred DNS server then returns the IP address of the host name to the client. It can then use the IP address to communicate with the host. The preferred DNS server may choose to cache a copy of the resource record information just in case additional requests for the domain name are made.

A client may also be configured to query multiple DNS servers for names. This process is known as *iteration*. Iteration is normally used when a client queries DNS servers, but instructs them not to use recursion. Alternatively, systems administrators may configure DNS servers, themselves, not to perform recursion. For example, we may configure all DNS servers to forward resolution requests to one DNS server on our network. This will direct all DNS traffic through this one server, thereby reducing network traffic and allowing us to secure DNS requests.

In the iteration process, the DNS server fulfills a request if it is able to do so based on the information in its own database. If it cannot, it will either return an error or will point the client to another DNS server that may be able to resolve the name. Iteration requires the client to remain responsible for ultimately resolving the name request.

Usually, the client is configured with multiple DNS servers that are utilized according to a certain search order. This is useful, for example, if different DNS servers are required to resolve intranet and Internet names. For example, a client may use one DNS server to resolve names for a specific department within the organization and another DNS server to resolve names of public Web sites. This method places the burden of finding the right name server on the client. In certain configurations, though, you may want to reduce network traffic with DNS *forwarding*, which allows you to specify exactly which DNS servers will be used for resolving names. For example, if you have multiple DNS servers located on a fast network (such as a LAN), you may want each of them to request DNS information from only a few specific DNS servers that can then gain information from other

DNS servers on the network. Figure 2.8 provides an example of how DNS forwarding can be used.

**FIGURE 2.8**    Using DNS forwarding to reduce network traffic

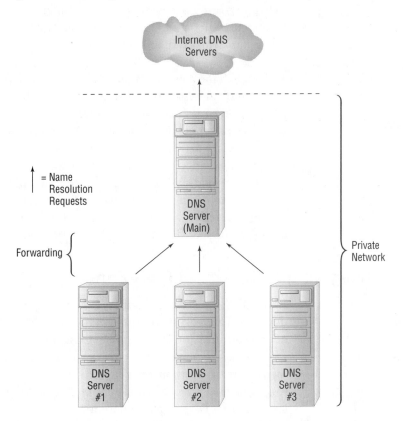

Another feature of DNS servers is their ability to cache information. As you can imagine, going through the recursion process each time a DNS query is initiated can place a significant load on servers worldwide. In order to limit some of this traffic, DNS servers usually save information about mapped domain names in their own local database. If future requests are made for the same host and domain names, this cached information is usually used. To ensure that the cached information is reasonably up-to-date, a Time to Live (TTL) value is attached to each cached DNS record. Typical TTL values range from three to seven days. Once this time limit is exceeded, the cached value is no longer used, and the next request for the information will result in going through the entire recursion process again.

Since DNS names are updated on a pull basis, it can take time for some DNS servers to update their databases. If you are required to make changes to a DNS entry, be sure to allow sufficient time for all of the name servers on the Internet to be updated. Usually, this should take only a few days, but, in some cases, it may take more than a week.

Although the most common DNS functions involve the mapping of DNS names to IP addresses, certain applications might require the opposite functionality—the resolution of an IP address to a DNS name. This is handled through a *reverse lookup zone* in the DNS server. Reverse lookup zones start with a special Internet authority address and allow the DNS server to resolve queries for specific TCP/IP addresses. As we'll see later in this chapter, reverse lookup zones are configured similarly to standard *forward lookup zones*.

In order to determine from which DNS server specific information can be found, zones must be used. Let's now examine the process of establishing authority for specific DNS zones.

## Delegating Authority in DNS Zones

Every DNS server can be configured to be responsible for one or more DNS domains. The DNS server is then known as the authoritative source of address information for that zone. Generally, if you are using only a single DNS domain, you will have only one zone. Remember that there can be a many-to-many relationship between domains (which are used to create a logical naming structure) and zones (which refer primarily to the physical structure of a DNS implementation).

When you add subdomains, however, you have two options. You can allow the original DNS server to continue functioning as the authority for the *parent* and *child domains*. Or, you can choose to create another DNS zone and give a different server authority over it. The process of giving authority for specific domains to other DNS servers is known as *delegation*. Figure 2.9 shows how delegation can be configured.

**FIGURE 2.9**    Delegating DNS authority to multiple DNS servers

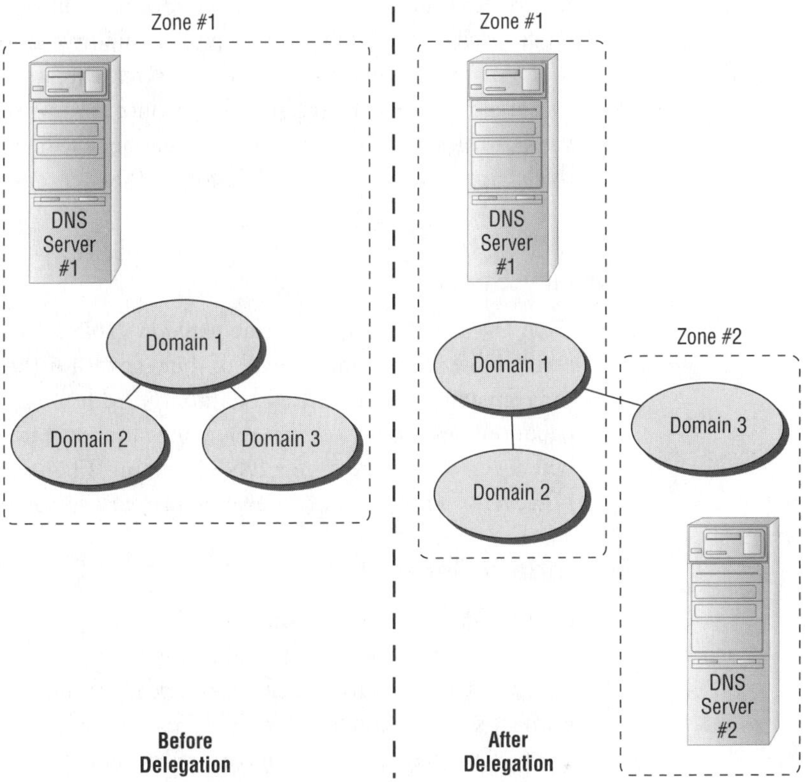

The main reasons for using delegation are performance and administration. Using multiple DNS servers in a large network can help distribute the load involved in resolving names. It can also help in administering security by allowing only certain types of records to be modified by specified systems administrators.

## DNS Server Roles

One of the potential problems with configuring specific DNS servers as authorities for their own domains is fault tolerance. What happens if an authoritative server becomes unavailable? Normally, none of the names for the resources in that zone could be resolved to network addresses. This could be a potentially serious problem for networks of any size. For example, if the primary server for the `sales.mycompany.com` zone becomes unavailable (and there are no secondary servers in that zone), users will not be able to find resources such as `server1.sales.mycompany.com` or `workstation1.sales.mycompany.com`. In order to prevent the potential network problems of a single failed server, the DNS specification allows for supporting multiple servers per zone.

To maintain a distributed and hierarchical naming system, DNS servers can assume several different roles at once. In this section, we'll look at the various roles that DNS servers can assume within a zone. In later sections of this chapter, we'll see how Windows 2000 Server computers can assume these roles.

## Primary Server

Each DNS zone must have one *primary DNS server*. The primary server is responsible for maintaining all of the records for the DNS zone and contains the primary copy of the DNS database. Additionally, all updates of records occur on the primary server. You will want to create and add primary servers whenever you create a new DNS domain. When creating child domains, however, you may want to use the primary server from the parent domain.

## Secondary Server

A *secondary DNS server* contains a database of all of the same information as the primary name server and can be used to resolve DNS requests. The main purpose of a secondary server is to provide for fault tolerance. That is, in case the primary server becomes unavailable, name resolution can still occur using the secondary server. Therefore, it is a good general practice to ensure that each zone has at least one secondary server to protect against failures.

Secondary DNS servers can also increase performance by offloading some of the traffic that would otherwise go to the primary server. Secondary servers are also often located within each location of an organization that has high-speed network access. This prevents DNS queries from having to run across slow wide area network (WAN) connections. For example, if there are two remote offices within the `mycompany.com` organization, we may want to place a secondary DNS server in each remote office. This way, when clients require name resolution, they will contact the nearest server for this IP address information, thus preventing unnecessary WAN traffic.

Although it is a good idea to have secondary servers, having too many of them can cause increases in network traffic due to replication. Therefore, you should always weigh the benefits and drawbacks and properly plan for secondary servers.

## Master Server

*Master DNS servers* are used in the replication of DNS data between primary and secondary servers. Usually, the primary server also serves as the master server, but these tasks can be separated for performance reasons. The master server is responsible for propagating any changes to the DNS database to all secondary servers within a particular zone.

## Caching-Only Server

*Caching-only DNS servers* serve the same function as primary DNS servers in that they assist clients in resolving DNS names to network addresses. The only difference is that caching-only servers are not authoritative for any DNS zones, and they don't contain copies of the zone files. They only contain mappings as a result of resolved queries and, in fact, they will lose all of their mapping information when the server is shut down. Therefore, they are installed only for performance reasons. A caching-only DNS server may be used at sites that have slow connectivity to DNS servers at other sites.

 **Real World Scenario**

### Optimizing DNS Performance

As the DNS administrator for your network environment, you are responsible for ensuring that DNS is working optimally. Recently, you've received several complaints that DNS queries are taking a long time and that sometimes client applications time-out when trying to reach a remote server. The network is fairly large and includes three large offices and 25 remote sites.

So far, you have attempted to keep the DNS infrastructure design as simple as possible to ease administration. The current DNS environment consists of a single forward lookup zone that includes a primary server and two secondary servers. The primary server is located in one large office, and each of the secondary servers is located in the other two large offices. This design is simple and easy to administer, but the performance problem must be solved. So, what's the easiest way to do this?

Fortunately, DNS has been designed from the ground up to offer scalability and high performance for even the most distributed networks. In this example, you could choose to redesign the DNS infrastructure. For example, you could break a single zone down into multiple smaller zones and then implement additional DNS servers for those zones. However, this would require a considerable amount of effort for planning, design, and implementation. It might also be more difficult to administer. Since performance is currently the only complaint, let's look at another solution.

Another option is to create additional secondary servers and place them in areas where users are complaining about the performance of DNS queries. For example, you might decide that you need to deploy DNS servers in several of the larger remote offices and remote offices that are located across slow or unreliable WAN links. There is a potential problem with implementing additional secondary servers: This can increase the amount of network traffic that flows between the DNS servers when updates are made. However, you'll probably find that it's a worthwhile trade-off.

There's one more option that's easy to implement and can help increase performance: caching-only DNS servers. These servers are particularly helpful in environments that consist of multiple DNS zones. They're easy to administer since they don't contain authoritative copies of your DNS databases, and they can improve performance by providing a quicker way to resolve DNS queries for remote clients.

As you can see, DNS is powerful and flexible enough to offer you many different types of solutions to performance problems. Be sure to keep this in mind as you work with DNS in the real world!

## Zone Transfers

Similar to the situation with domain controllers and the Active Directory, it is important to ensure that DNS zone information is consistent between the primary and secondary servers. The process used to keep the servers synchronized is known as a *zone transfer*. When a secondary DNS server is configured for a zone, it first performs a zone transfer during which it obtains a copy of the primary server's address database. This process is known as an all-zone transfer (AXFR).

In order to ensure that information is kept up-to-date after the initial synchronization, incremental zone transfers (IXFRs) are used. Through this process, the changes in the DNS zone databases are communicated between primary and secondary servers. IXFRs use a system of serial numbers to determine which records are new or updated. This system ensures that the newest DNS record is always used, even if changes were made on more than one server.

Not all DNS servers support IXFRs. Windows NT 4's DNS services and earlier implementations of other DNS services require a full-zone transfer of the entire database in order to update their records. This can sometimes cause significant network traffic. As with any software implementation, you should always verify the types of functionality supported before deploying it.

Zone transfers may occur in response to the following different events:

- The zone refresh interval has been exceeded.

- A master server notifies a secondary server of a zone change.

- A secondary DNS server service is started for the zone.

- A DNS zone transfer is manually initiated (by a systems administrator) at the secondary server.

An important factor regarding zone transfers is that secondary servers always initiate them. This type of replication is commonly known as a pull operation. Normally, a zone transfer request is made when a refresh interval is reached on the secondary server. The request is sent to a master server, which then sends any changes to the secondary server. Usually the primary server is also configured as a master server, but this can be changed for performance reasons.

One of the problems with pull replication is that the information stored on secondary servers can sometimes be out-of-date. For example, suppose an IXFR occurs today, but the refresh interval is set to three days. If I make a change on the primary DNS server, this change will not be reflected on the secondary server for at least several days. One potential way to circumvent this problem is to set a very low refresh interval (such as a few hours). However, this can cause a lot of unnecessary network traffic and increased processing overhead.

In order to solve the problems related to keeping resource records up-to-date, a feature known as DNS notify was developed. This method employs push replication to inform secondary servers whenever a change is made.

When secondary servers receive the DNS notify message, they immediately initiate an IXFR request. Figure 2.10 shows how DNS notify is used to keep secondary servers up-to-date. This method ensures that compatible DNS servers are updated immediately whenever changes are made.

**FIGURE 2.10** Using DNS notify to update secondary servers

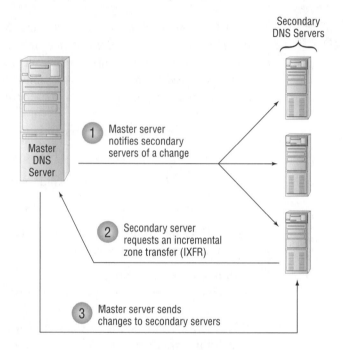

## Managing DNS Resource Records

So far, we have looked at various ways in which DNS servers remain synchronized with each other. Now, it's time to look at the actual types of information stored within the DNS database. Table 2.2 provides a list of the types of records that are used within the DNS database. Each of these records is important for ensuring that the proper type of resource is made available. For example, if a client is attempting to send e-mail, the DNS server should respond with the IP address corresponding to the Mail Exchanger (MX) record of the domain.

**TABLE 2.2** DNS Resource Record Types

| Resource Record Type | Meaning | Notes |
| --- | --- | --- |
| A | Address | Used to map host names to IP addresses. Multiple A records may be used to map to a single IP address. |
| CNAME | Canonical Name | Used as an alias or a nickname for a host (in addition to the A record). |
| MX | Mail Exchanger | Specifies the Simple Mail Transfer Protocol (SMTP) e-mail server address for the domain. |
| NS | Name Server | Specifies the IP address of DNS servers for the domain. |
| PTR | Pointer | Used for reverse lookup operations. |
| RP | Responsible Person | Specifies information about the individual that is responsible for maintaining the DNS information. |
| SOA | Start of Authority | Specifies the authoritative server for a zone. |
| SRV | Service | Specifies server services available on a host; used by the Active Directory to identify domain controllers. The standard for SRV records has not yet been finalized. |

Additionally, certain conventions are often used on the Internet. For example, the host names mail, www, ftp, and news are usually reserved for e-mail, World Wide Web, file transfer protocol, and USENET news servers, respectively.

Now that you have a good understanding of the purpose and methods of DNS, let's move on to looking at how Microsoft's DNS service operates.

# Planning for Microsoft DNS

**S**o far, we've presented a lot of information regarding DNS concepts. By covering the DNS namespace and how DNS servers interact with each other, you should have a good understanding of the name resolution infrastructure required by the Active Directory. If you are still unclear on some of the concepts related to planning a DNS structure for an organization, be sure to review the information presented earlier in this chapter.

One of the major benefits of using Microsoft DNS is the ability to manage and replicate the DNS database as a part of the Active Directory. This allows for automating much of the administration of the DNS service while still keeping information up-to-date.

With respect to your DNS environment, you'll want to plan for the use of various DNS servers. As we mentioned earlier in this chapter, there are several possible roles for DNS servers, including primary, secondary, master, and caching-only servers. With respect to the Active Directory, DNS services are absolutely vital. Without the proper functioning of DNS, Active Directory clients and servers will not be able to locate each other, and network services will be severely impacted.

Let's look at how DNS zones and servers can be planned for use with the Active Directory.

## Planning DNS Zones

The first step in planning for DNS server deployment is to determine the size and layout of your DNS zones. In the simplest configurations, there will be a single Active Directory domain and a single DNS zone. This configuration usually meets the needs of single-domain environments.

When multiple domains are considered, you generally need to make some choices when planning for DNS. In some environments, you might choose to use only a single zone that spans over all of the domains. In other cases, you might want to break zones apart for administrative and performance reasons.

The DNS zone configuration you choose is largely independent of the Active Directory configuration. That is, for any given Active Directory configuration, you could use any setup of zones, as long as all names can be properly resolved. With that said, make no mistake—the proper functioning of DNS zones is critical to the functionality of the Active Directory.

## Planning Server Roles

So far in this section, we've talked about the logical layout of DNS zones in relation to Active Directory domains. Now, it's time to look at how DNS servers should optimally be configured for various environments.

First and foremost, DNS servers are extremely important in the Active Directory environment. In order to provide for fault tolerance for DNS servers, you should ensure that each DNS zone you configure consists of one primary DNS server and at least one secondary server. If the primary DNS computer fails, the secondary server can still carry out name resolution operations, and most operations will continue normally. This is, however, a temporary solution since you will need to restore or replace the primary DNS server in order to make updates to the DNS zone information.

Generally, you will want to make the primary DNS server the master server for the zone. If it is necessary for performance reasons, however, you can choose to use a separate machine for DNS services.

Caching-only servers are generally used when you want to make DNS information available for multiple computers that do not have a fast or reliable connection to the main network. Because they do not have any authority over specific zones, the decision to use caching-only servers is generally based on the physical network layout.

Figure 2.11 shows a representative DNS server configuration for an Active Directory domain.

**FIGURE 2.11** Arranging servers for the Active Directory

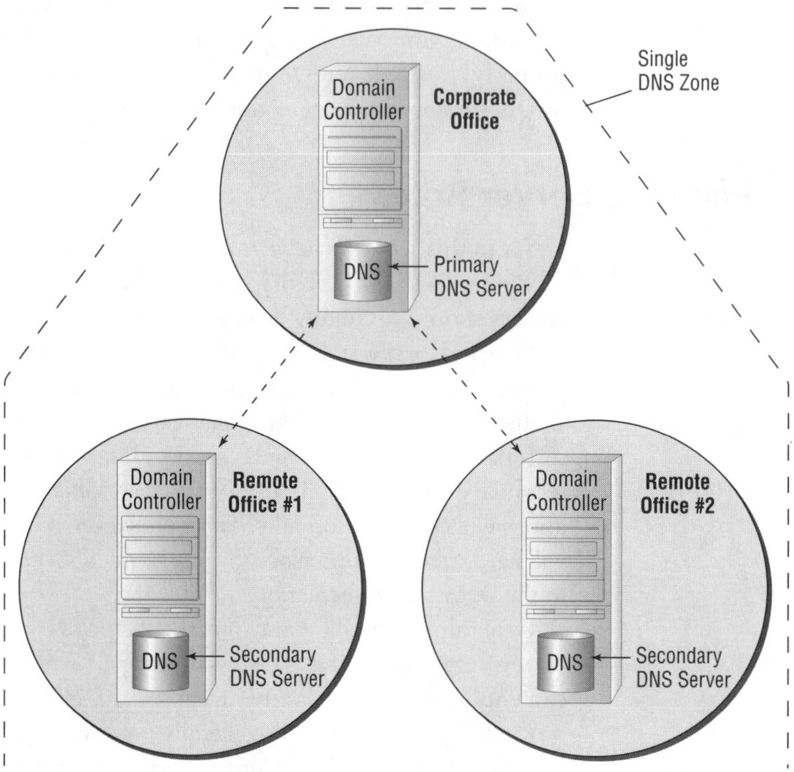

# Installing and Configuring a DNS Server

**M**icrosoft has made the technical steps involved in installing the DNS service extremely simple. This, however, is not an excuse for not thoroughly understanding and planning for a DNS configuration. In this section, we'll cover the actual steps required to install and configure a DNS server for use with Microsoft's Active Directory.

---

*Microsoft* ✓ *Exam* *Objective*

**Install, configure, and troubleshoot DNS for Active Directory.**

- Integrate Active Directory DNS zones with non-Active Directory DNS zones.

- Configure zones for dynamic updates.

See "Managing DNS Interoperability," a section later in this chapter, for coverage of the "Integrate Active Directory DNS zones with non-Active Directory DNS zones" subobjective and "Configuring Zones for Automatic Updates," another section later in this chapter, for coverage of the "Configure zones for dynamic updates" subobjective.

Exercise 2.1 walks you through the steps required to install the DNS service.

**EXERCISE 2.1**

### Installing the DNS Service

This exercise will walk you through the steps required to install the DNS service.

1. Click Start ➢ Settings ➢ Control Panel, and then double-click the Add/Remove Programs icon.

2. Select Add/Remove Windows Components.

3. Click the Components button to access a list of services and options available for installation on Windows 2000.

4. In the Windows 2000 Components Wizard, select Networking Services, and then click Details.

5. Place a check mark next to the option titled Domain Name System (DNS).

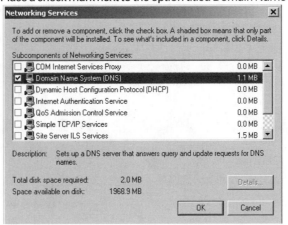

6. Click OK to accept your choice, then click Next to continue with the Wizard.

Once you have installed the DNS service, you are ready to begin configuring the server for the Active Directory.

# Adding DNS Zones

Once you have installed the DNS service, you'll need to configure DNS for your specific environment. The most important aspect of configuring the DNS properly is planning. Based on the information presented in the previous sections, you should be aware of how you plan to configure DNS zones for your Active Directory environment.

The technical implementation process is quite easy, thanks to the Configure DNS Server Wizard. Exercise 2.2 walks you through the process used to configure DNS zones.

---

**EXERCISE 2.2**

### Using the Configure DNS Server Wizard

In this exercise, you will configure basic DNS zones, including a standard primary forward lookup zone. This exercise assumes that you have already installed the DNS service and that no configuration options have been set.

1. Open the DNS snap-in in the Administrative Tools program group.

2. In the DNS administrative tool, right-click the name of your local server and select Configure the Server. The introduction page will inform you that the Configure DNS Server Wizard will help you configure DNS zones for this server. Click Next to begin the process.

3. Create a forward lookup zone by choosing Yes, Create a Forward Lookup Zone, then click Next.

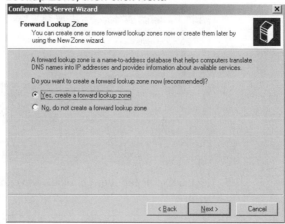

**4.** Select the type of DNS zone you want to create. The available options include Active Directory-integrated (only available if Active Directory is installed), Standard Primary, and Standard Secondary. Select Standard Primary, and click Next.

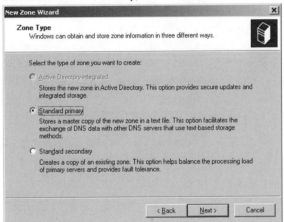

**5.** Enter the zone name by typing in the name of the DNS zone for which you want to record addresses. For example, you might type **test.mycompany.com**. Click Next.

6. Once you have determined the name for the DNS domain, you can choose either to create a new local DNS file or to use an existing DNS file. DNS zone files are standard text files that contain mappings of IP addresses to DNS names. Usually, zone files are named as the name of the domain followed by a .DNS suffix (for example, test.mycompany.com.dns). These files must be stored in the system32/dns subdirectory of your Windows 2000 system root. Leave the default option, and click Next.

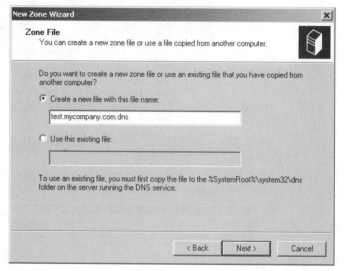

7. Although reverse lookup zones are not required for basic DNS functionality and are, therefore, optional, you will probably want to create one. Reverse lookup zones are used to map IP addresses to DNS names and are required for the proper operation of some TCP/IP applications. Select Yes, Create a Reverse Lookup Zone, and click Next.

8. Choose the reverse lookup zone type. The options are similar to those for the forward lookup zone. Select Standard Primary, and click Next.

9. Specify the reverse lookup zone. In order for reverse lookups to work properly, you must specify the network to which the zone applies. You can specify the value using a network ID or the name of the reverse lookup zone. The value you enter will be based on the subnet(s) for which this DNS server will provide reverse lookup information. Enter **169** for the Network ID, and click Next to continue.

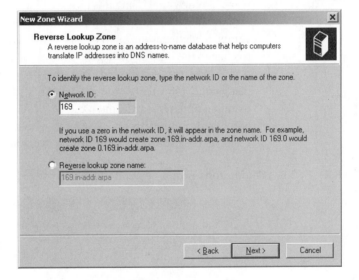

10. Select a reverse lookup zone file. Reverse lookup zone files are created and managed similarly to forward lookup zone files. Choose the default option, and click Next.

11. To finalize the settings made by the Wizard, click Next. The Wizard will automatically create the forward and reverse lookup zones based on the information you specified.

If your network environment will require this DNS server to manage multiple zones, you can run the Configure DNS Server Wizard again. Alternatively, if you are comfortable with the options available, you can right-click the name of your server and select New Zone.

## Configuring DNS Zone Properties

Once you have properly configured forward and reverse lookup zones for your DNS server, you can make additional configuration settings for each zone by right-clicking its name within the DNS administrative tool and selecting Properties. The following tabs and settings are available for forward lookup zones:

**General**   The General tab allows you to set various options for the forward lookup zone. Using this tab (see Figure 2.12), you can pause the DNS service. When the service is paused, it continues to run, but clients cannot complete name resolution requests from this machine. The second option is to change the type of the zone. Choices include primary, secondary, and Active Directory–integrated (available only if the Active Directory is installed). You can also specify the name of the DNS zone file. Allowing dynamic updates is extremely useful for reducing the management and administration headaches associated with creating resource records. Finally, you can specify aging and scavenging properties for this zone.

**FIGURE  2.12**   Setting zone properties with the General tab

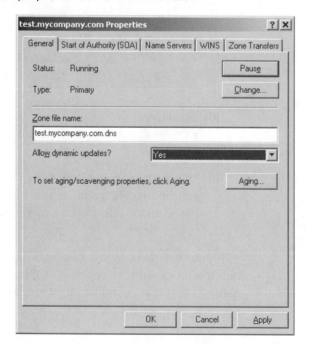

**Start of Authority (SOA)**    The SOA tab allows you to specify information regarding the authority of the DNS server (see Figure 2.13). The Serial Number text box is used to determine whether a zone transfer is needed to keep any secondary servers up-to-date. For example, if a secondary server has a serial number of 7, but the SOA serial number is set to 6, the secondary server will request a zone transfer. The Primary Server text box allows you to designate the primary DNS server for the zone. The Responsible Person text box allows you to specify contact information for the systems administrator of the DNS server. The Refresh Interval text box and drop-down menu are used to specify how often a secondary zone should verify its information. Lower times ensure greater accuracy but can cause increased network traffic. The Retry Interval text box and drop-down menu are used to specify how often zone transfers will be requested. The Expires After text box and drop-down menu allow you to specify how long secondary DNS servers must try to request updated information before resource records expire. The Minimum (default) TTL text box is used to specify how long a resource record will be considered current. If you are working in an environment where many changes are expected, a lower TTL value can help in maintaining the accuracy of information.

**FIGURE 2.13**    Setting zone properties with the SOA tab

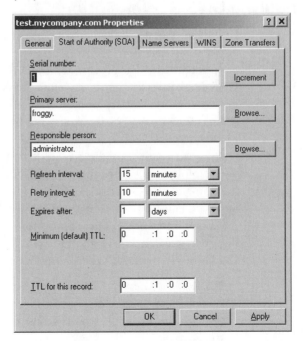

**Name Servers** The Name Servers tab shows a list of DNS servers for the specified domain. You can add specific DNS servers based on the configuration of your network. Generally, the list of name servers will include the primary name server and any secondary name servers for that zone.

**WINS** This tab allows you to set options for allowing *Windows Internet Name Service (WINS)* lookups to resolve DNS names. WINS and DNS issues are covered later in this chapter.

**Zone Transfers** Using the options on this tab, you can select which servers will be allowed to serve as a secondary server for the forward lookup zones specified in the properties for the zone. The default option allows any server to request a zone transfer, but you can restrict this by specifying specific IP addresses or allowing only the name servers listed on the Name Servers tab to request transfers. Setting restrictions on zone transfers can increase security by preventing unauthorized users from copying the entire DNS database.

The ability to set each of these options gives systems administrators the power to control DNS operations and resource record settings for their environment.

## Configuring DNS Server Options

DNS record databases would tend to become disorganized and filled with outdated information if processes that periodically removed unused records were not present. The process of removing inactive or outdated entries in the DNS database is known as scavenging. Systems administrators use scavenging to configure DNS records to require refreshing based on a certain time setting. When the DNS record has not been refreshed for a certain amount of time, the next DNS query forces the record to be updated. By default, the DNS server is not configured to perform this process at all.

To implement scavenging in the DNS snap-in, you should right-click the name of the server or DNS zone for which you want the settings to apply and choose Set Aging/Scavenging. For example, if you right-click the server name and choose this option, the aging and scavenging settings you specify will apply to all of the DNS zones managed by that server. As shown in Figure 2.14, you can specify two different options:

**No-Refresh Interval** This allows you to specify the *minimum* amount of time that must elapse before a DNS record is refreshed. Higher values can reduce network traffic but may cause outdated information to be returned to clients.

**Refresh Interval**   This allows you to specify the amount of time between when the no-refresh interval expires and when the resource record information may be refreshed. Lower values can provide for greater accuracy in information but may increase network traffic.

**FIGURE 2.14**    Setting aging and scavenging options

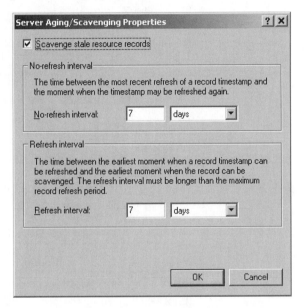

There are also several other DNS server options that can be set to maximize performance functionality in your network environment. To access the properties of the DNS server using the DNS snap-in, right-click the name of the server and choose Properties. The following tabs will be available:

**Interfaces**   On servers that are enabled with multiple network adapters, you might want to provide DNS services on only one of the interfaces. The default option is to allow DNS requests on all interfaces, but you can limit operations to specific adapters by clicking the Only the Following IP Addresses option (see Figure 2.15).

**FIGURE  2.15**   Selecting DNS server interfaces

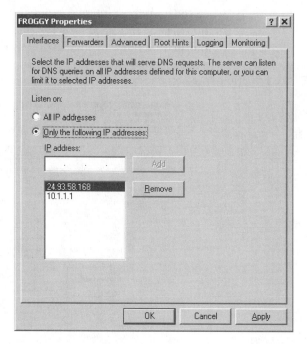

**Forwarders**   DNS forwarding can be configured to relay all DNS requests that cannot be resolved by this server to one or more specific machines. To configure forwarders, check the box and specify the IP address of one or more DNS servers. If you check the Do Not Use Recursion option, name resolution will occur only through the configured forwarders.

**Advanced**   The DNS service has several advanced options (see Figure 2.16). For example, you can disable DNS recursion for the entire server by checking the appropriate box. We'll cover specific options as they pertain to the Active Directory later in this chapter.

**Root Hints**   In order to resolve domain names on the Internet, the local DNS server must know the identities of the worldwide root servers. By default, the Microsoft DNS server is configured with several valid root IP addresses (see Figure 2.17). Additionally, you can add or modify the root hints as needed, but you should only do this if you are sure of the configuration information.

**FIGURE  2.16**    Advanced DNS server configuration options

**FIGURE  2.17**    Viewing default DNS server root hints

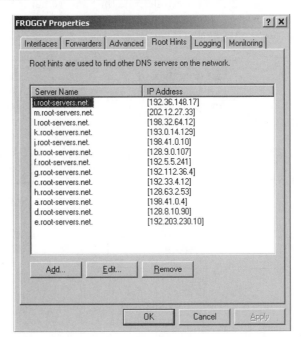

**Logging**   Logging various DNS operations can be useful for monitoring and troubleshooting the DNS service. You can select various different events to monitor using the properties on this tab. We'll cover more details on logging later in this chapter.

**Monitoring**   The Monitoring tab is useful for performing a quick check to ensure that the DNS service is operating properly. Using this tab, you will be able to perform a simple query as well as a recursive request. If both operations are successful, you can be reasonably sure that the DNS server is functioning properly.

Once you are satisfied with the DNS server settings, it's time to look at how resource records can be configured.

## Creating DNS Resource Records

The main functionality of a DNS server is based on the various resource records present within it. During the Active Directory installation process, you have the option of automatically configuring the DNS server for use with the Active Directory. We'll cover the details of this process in Chapter 3. If you choose to create the default records, the resource records listed in Table 2.3 will automatically be created. Each of these records is of the type SRV (Service). The Domain and DomainTree specifiers will be based on the DNS domain name for the local domain controller, and the Site specifier will be based on your site configuration.

**TABLE 2.3**   Default Active Directory DNS Resource Records

| Resource Record | Purpose |
| --- | --- |
| _ldap._tcp.*Domain* | Enumerates the domain controllers for a given domain |
| _ldap._tcp.*Site*.sites.*Domain* | Allows clients to find domain controllers within a specific site |
| _ldap._tcp.pdc.ms-dcs.*Domain* | Provides the address of the server acting as the Windows NT Primary Domain Controller (PDC) for the domain |

**TABLE 2.3**  Default Active Directory DNS Resource Records *(continued)*

| Resource Record | Purpose |
|---|---|
| _ldap._tcp.pdc.ms-dcs.*DomainTree* | Enumerates the Global Catalog servers within a domain |
| _ldap._tcp.*Site*.gc.ms-dcs.*DomainTree* | Allows a client to find a Global Catalog server based on site configuration |
| _ldap._tcp.*GUID*.domains.ms-dcs.*DomainTree* | Used by computers to locate machines based on the Global Unique Identifier (GUID) |
| _ldap._tcp.writable.ms-dcs.*Domain* | Enumerates the domain controller(s) that hold(s) modifiable copies of the Active Directory |
| _ldap._tcp.*site*.sites.writable.ms-dcs.*Domain* | Enumerates domain controller(s) based on sites |

In addition to the default DNS records, you will likely want to create new ones to identify specific servers and clients on your network. Exercise 2.3 provides a walk-through of the creation of a DNS MX record. Although different resource record types require different pieces of information, the process is similar for other types of records.

**EXERCISE 2.3**

**Creating a DNS Mail Exchanger (MX) Record**

In this exercise, you will specify a new DNS MX record. This exercise assumes that you have installed the DNS service and have configured at least one forward lookup zone.

1. Open the DNS snap-in in the Administrative Tools program group.

2. Expand the forward lookup zones folder for the local server.

**3.** Right-click the name of a zone and select New Mail Exchanger.

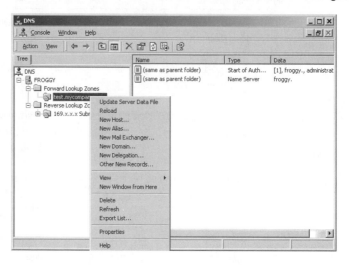

**4.** Specify the MX options. You'll need to configure several options for the MX record. The options are as follows:

- Host or Domain: You will need to type the name of the host that will serve as the mail server for this domain. This is the machine to which clients will connect in order to send e-mail messages using SMTP. Usually, this will be a standard DNS name (such as "mail"), but it can also be left blank if you want the entire domain name itself to be used for mail services. Note that the name must be part of the current domain.

- Mail Server: Here, you will be able to specify the actual DNS name of the mail server. This must be a machine name that has a corresponding Address (A) record already configured. You can either type the name or click Browse to find the specific record within any available DNS server on your network.

- Mail Server Priority: DNS supports the assignment of more than one MX record per domain. In order to specify the order in which the various mail servers will be used, a systems administrator can specify priorities for each server. The priority value must be an integer between 0 and 65,535 (inclusive). The lower the number, the higher the priority will be (0 specifies the highest priority). For example, if you have three MX records in the same domain, clients will prefer to use the lowest number mail server priority first. If this server is unavailable or busy, they can then contact the other mail servers.

5. When you are ready to create the record, click OK. This will add the MX record to the forward lookup zone specified in step 3.

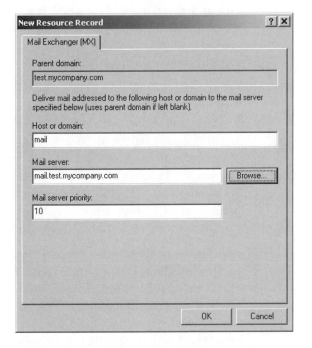

### Real World Scenario

### Implementing DNS for Multiple Mail Servers

You are a systems administrator for a medium-sized organization. One of your responsibilities is managing the DNS configuration for the entire domain. You have already implemented and configured DNS, including forward and reverse lookup zones. Currently, the environment consists of a single e-mail server (called `mail.xyzservices.com`). This mail server (and the corresponding DNS MX record) has been working properly. However, messaging traffic has been increasing, and users commonly report that the mail server is unavailable or that they must sometimes make multiple attempts before messages are sent.

To help alleviate some of the problems, another systems administrator has set up a second mail server. She wants you to create a DNS record for this second mail server, but she wants this server to be contacted only if the primary mail server is unavailable.

The appropriate steps can be taken quite easily using Windows 2000's DNS features. First, you must create a new Address (A) record within the domain. You will need to give this server a DNS name (such as `mail2.xyzservices.com`). Next, you must edit the properties of the domain's MX. Within the MX record, you can add both servers to the list and assign priorities for the servers. Since you want the original mail server to be the primary machine, set its priority to 1. For the second server, set the priority to 2. (Note that only the relative values are important—you could have just as easily chosen numbers such as 50 and 100.)

Now, users should be able to access the second mail server when the first mail server is unavailable. Similar techniques can be used for other types of TCP/IP-based servers. For example, Web servers (but not mail servers) can take advantage of "round-robin" DNS to help distribute load among multiple servers. In this configuration, clients will be directed to different Web servers, although they will always connect to the same DNS name. This technique is used, for example, to allow multiple servers to respond to connection requests for "www.microsoft.com."

Although you can manually specify DNS server records, this process can become quite tedious. In Chapter 3, we'll look at how DNS services can be configured for the Active Directory.

# Managing DNS Servers

**O**nce your DNS server is installed and configured properly, you will need to manage various settings. In the previous section, we looked at the various options and features available within the DNS service. In this section, we'll focus on some specific operations that are required for working with the Active Directory. The exercises should be helpful in learning your way around the various operations.

## Configuring Zones for Automatic Updates

By allowing automatic updates to DNS zones, you will be able to dramatically reduce the administrative burden of managing resource records. Exercise 2.4 shows how to enable this option.

*Microsoft*
✓ *Exam*
*Objective*

**Install, configure, and troubleshoot DNS for Active Directory.**

- Integrate Active Directory DNS zones with non-Active Directory DNS zones.

- Configure zones for dynamic updates.

See "Managing DNS Interoperability," a section that appears later in this chapter, for coverage of the "Integrate Active Directory DNS zones with non-Active Directory DNS zones" subobjective.

### EXERCISE 2.4

**Allowing Automatic Updates**

This exercise assumes that you have properly installed and configured the DNS service and have configured at least one forward lookup zone.

1. Open the DNS snap-in in the Administrative Tools program group.

2. Expand the forward lookup zones folder under the name of the current server.

**EXERCISE 2.4** *(continued)*

3. Right-click the name of a zone and select Properties.

4. Change the Allow Dynamic Updates option to Yes.

5. Click OK to accept and commit the setting.

# Creating Zone Delegations

When you configure a DNS server as a primary server for a zone, that server is responsible for performing name resolution for all of the resources within that zone. In some cases, you might want to delegate authority for a portion of the zone to another DNS server. Exercise 2.5 shows how this can be done.

**EXERCISE 2.5**

**Creating a Zone Delegation**

This exercise will delegate authority for a DNS zone to another DNS server. This exercise assumes that you have already created at least one DNS zone. Additionally, this server must be the primary DNS server for at least one zone.

1. Open the DNS administrative tool and expand the branch for the local server.

2. Right-click the name of a zone for which the machine is the primary server, and select New Delegation.

3. This will open the New Delegation Wizard. Click Next.

**EXERCISE 2.5** *(continued)*

4. Enter the name of the delegated domain. The delegated domain must be a subdomain of the domain you selected in step 2. For example, if the domain name is `activedirectory.test`, the subdomain might be `domain2`. This will make the fully-qualified domain name `domain2.activedirectory.test`. Click Next.

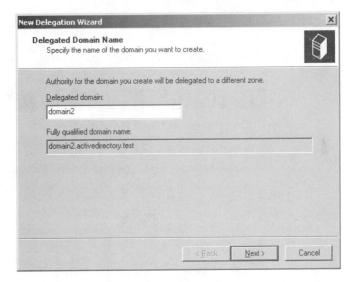

5. Specify the name server(s) to which you want to delegate authority for the domain. To add servers to the list, click Add. You will be able to browse a list of available name servers or specify one by name or IP address. You can also click Edit to change the properties for servers you have already added to the delegation list.

6. Click Next to accept the setting, and then click Finish to create the new delegation.

## Managing DNS Replication

Managing DNS replication is an important concern. If optimal settings are not chosen, you might encounter too much replication traffic. Alternatively, you might have the opposite problem—updates are not occurring frequently enough. Earlier in this chapter, we looked at ways to configure the DNS

Notify properties within a zone. In this section, we'll see what is required to enable DNS replication.

***Microsoft*** ✓ ***Exam*** ***Objective***

**Manage, monitor, and troubleshoot DNS.**

- Manage replication of DNS data.

Exercise 2.6 walks through the steps required to configure DNS replication.

**EXERCISE 2.6**

### Configuring DNS Replication

In this exercise, you will configure various DNS replication options. This exercise assumes that you have already created at least one DNS zone and that the local server is the primary DNS server for at least one zone.

1. Open the DNS administrative tool, and expand the branch for the local server.

2. Right-click the name of a zone for which this machine is the primary server, and select Properties.

3. Select the Zone Transfers tab.

4. Place a check mark in the Allow Zone Transfers box.

5. Choose whether you want to allow zone transfers from any server (the default setting), only servers specified on the Name Servers tab, or specific DNS servers based on their IP addresses. It is recommended that you choose one of the latter two options because these provide greater security.

6. Click the Notify button. Place a check mark in the Automatically Notify box. You can choose to automatically notify the servers listed on the Name Servers tab, or you can specify DNS servers by IP addresses. Each of these servers will be notified automatically whenever a change to the DNS database is made.

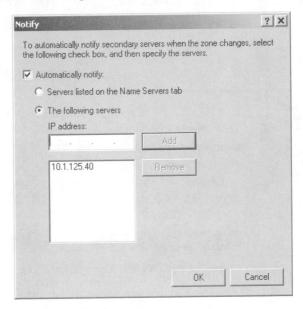

7. Click OK twice to save the settings.

## Managing DNS Interoperability

In a pure Windows 2000 environment, you would probably choose to use only Microsoft's DNS service. However, in the real world (and especially in larger environments), you might require the DNS service to interact with other implementations of DNS. A common Unix implementation of DNS is known as the Berkeley Internet Name Domain (BIND) service. Active Directory mandates the use of SRV records and optionally supports DNS dynamic updates. The minimum version of BIND that supports both is version 8.2.1. When using a BIND server as the DNS server for Active Directory, it must be running version 8.2.1 or greater. Before you can configure various DNS server settings for interoperability, you must know which features are supported by the non-Microsoft DNS system you are using.

---

***Microsoft*** ✓ ***Exam Objective***

**Install, configure, and troubleshoot DNS for Active Directory.**

- Integrate Active Directory DNS zones with non-Active Directory DNS zones.

- Configure zones for dynamic updates.

---

See "Configuring Zones for Automatic Updates," a section that appears earlier in this chapter, for coverage of the "Configure zones for dynamic updates" subobjective.

Exercise 2.7 shows you how to set up a Windows 2000 DNS server to interoperate with non–Windows 2000 DNS servers.

**EXERCISE 2.7**

**Enabling DNS Interoperability**

This exercise assumes that you have properly installed and configured the DNS service and have configured at least one forward lookup zone. It also assumes that you know the various features supported by the types of DNS servers in your environment.

1. Open the DNS snap-in in the Administrative Tools program group.

2. Right-click the name of the local server, and click Properties.

3. Click the Advanced tab. You will see a list of the various settings that can be enabled and disabled. Place a check mark next to a feature to enable it, or remove the check mark to disable it. For more information about the various options, click the Question Mark icon, then click the option.

4. Click OK to save the changes.

# Interoperation with WINS and DHCP

**E**arlier in this chapter, we saw some of the benefits of Microsoft's implementation of DNS. In Windows 2000, DNS was designed to integrate with other services such as WINS and *Dynamic Host Configuration Protocol (DHCP)*. In this section, we'll drill down into the details of how these two services work and how they can further reduce administration headaches by integrating with Microsoft's DNS.

## Overview of DHCP

As we mentioned in the beginning of this chapter, TCP/IP requires a considerable amount of manual configuration. Some of the information that might be required by a TCP/IP client in a Windows environment may include the following pieces of information:

- TCP/IP address

- Subnet mask

- Default gateway

- DNS servers

- DNS domain name

- WINS servers

Additionally, other TCP/IP services must be set. For example, if the network is using the Network Time Protocol (NTP), information on the timeserver address should also be transmitted. It's easy to see how maintaining this information even on small networks can be quite troublesome. For much larger ones, the technical and management issues associated with assigning appropriate information can be overwhelming. DHCP was designed to ease some of these problems. DHCP works by automatically assigning TCP/IP address information to client computers when they are first connected to the network. The general process works as follows:

1. A client computer is initialized on the network. During the boot-up process, a broadcast is sent requesting information from a DHCP server.

2. If a DHCP server is present, it receives the request and generates an IP address from its database of valid assignments. It sends an offer of TCP/IP information to the client that requested it.

3. The client receives the packet and uses the IP address information.

4. The client sends an acknowledgement to the DHCP server that it will accept the offer.

5. The DHCP server sends an acknowledgment to the client, which then configures its IP stack. The DHCP server prevents the address from being used again from its database as long as it is assigned to the client.

Figure 2.18 provides an example of the DHCP process.

**FIGURE 2.18**   Obtaining a DHCP lease

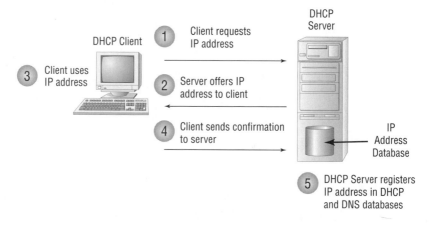

If more than one DHCP server is present on the network, the client would simply take the IP address from the first one to respond. Since IP addresses are a limited resource on most networks, DHCP servers generally assign a lease duration to each IP address they assign to clients. The typical lease duration is approximately three to five days for networks with mobile workstations like laptops and longer for a more static environment. Clients are required to renew their IP address lease within this time frame, or the IP address will be retired and made available for other clients.

The pool of TCP/IP addresses that are available for assignment to clients is called the DHCP scope. A scope consists of a range of IP addresses and a subnet mask. Additionally, scope options can be used to specify other TCP/IP parameters, such as the default gateway, DNS servers, and WINS servers. Figure 2.19 shows the Server Options dialog box within the DHCP administrative tool.

**FIGURE 2.19**   Setting DHCP server options

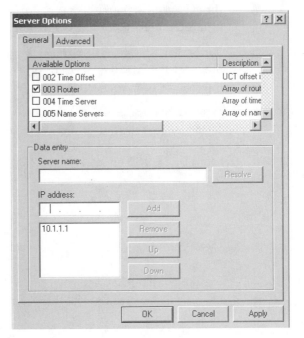

To provide for fault tolerance of DHCP services, a common practice is to place more than one DHCP server on the same network. However, in order to prevent any problems with duplicate IP address assignments, the DHCP servers are configured with non-overlapping scopes.

## Integrating DHCP and DNS

It doesn't take much imagination to see how DHCP information can be used to populate a DNS database. The DHCP service already records all of the IP address assignments within its own database. In order to reduce manual administration of DNS entries for client computers, Windows 2000's DNS implementation can automatically create Address (A) records for hosts based on DHCP information. When Windows 2000 dynamic updates are enabled, the client updates the A record and the DHCP server updates the client's pointer (PTR) record. However, the method in which DHCP information is transmitted to the DNS server varies based on the client. There are two different modes of DHCP/DNS integration based on the client type:

**For Windows 2000 Clients**   Windows 2000 DHCP clients have the ability to automatically send updates to a dynamic DNS server as soon as they receive an IP address. This method places the task of registering the new address on the client. It also allows the client to specify whether or not the update of the DNS database should occur at all.

**For Earlier Clients**   The DHCP client code for Windows 95/98 and Windows NT 4 computers does not support dynamic DNS updates. Therefore, the DHCP server itself must update the DNS A and PTR records.

Figure 2.20 illustrates the two different methods of Dynamic DHCP/DNS updates based on the different client types.

**FIGURE 2.20**   Dynamic DHCP/DNS updates

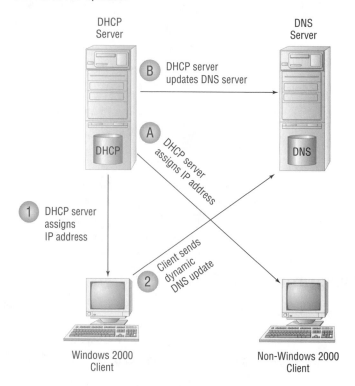

Implementing dynamic updates of DNS using information from DHCP can be done by opening the DHCP administrative tool. By right-clicking the name of the server and choosing Properties, you will have the option to select the DNS tab (see Figure 2.21).

**FIGURE 2.21**    Setting DNS options using the DHCP administrative tool

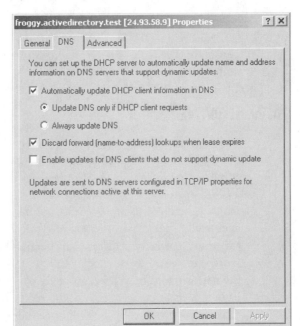

The options on this tab include the following:

**Automatically Update DHCP Client Information in DNS**    This option allows you to enable dynamic DNS updates from the client. This selection applies only to Windows 2000 clients. Systems administrators can choose between two options:

- The client can decide whether or not the update is made.

- DNS is always updated.

**Discard Forward (Name-to-Address) Lookups When Lease Expires**
When this option is checked, DNS entries for clients are automatically removed if a lease is not renewed in time. This is a useful option because it will ensure that outdated entries no longer exist in the DNS database.

**Enable Updates for DNS Clients That Do Not Support Dynamic Update**    If you are using Windows NT 4, Windows 95, or Windows 98 DHCP clients and want dynamic updates of DNS, you should choose this option. When it is set, the DHCP server will be responsible for updating the DNS database whenever a new IP address is assigned.

By using the DHCP/DNS integration features of Windows 2000, you can automate what can be a very tedious process—managing client host name address mappings.

## Overview of WINS

Although TCP/IP has been the default base protocol since Windows NT 4, the NetBIOS protocol is heavily relied upon by versions of Windows before Windows 2000. WINS was designed to allow clients using the NetBIOS over TCP/IP protocols to resolve host names to network addresses. One of the major benefits of using WINS is that it is largely self-configuring and manages itself. That is, names are added automatically to the WINS database as the server learns the addresses of clients. This facilitates browsing on the network. However, WINS has several limitations in larger environments. First, the performance of WINS can begin to degrade when many clients are registered in its database. Second, the replication functionality of the WINS database is not as robust as that of other methods (such as DNS).

With Windows 2000 and the Active Directory, Microsoft has eliminated the need for WINS altogether. However, most networks will still require the use of WINS for down-level clients (including Windows NT 4, Windows 95, and Windows 98 computers). Therefore, Windows 2000 includes an improved version of WINS. To make it easier to manage two different name resolution methods (WINS and DNS), Windows 2000 supports automatic querying of WINS records if a host name is not found within a DNS server's database. This process, called a WINS referral, occurs on the server side and requires no special configuration on the client.

## Integrating WINS and DNS

To enable the automatic update process, right-click the name of a forward lookup zone using the DNS administrative tool and select Properties. Click the WINS tab to set the dynamic update options (see Figure 2.22).

**FIGURE 2.22**    Setting WINS updates

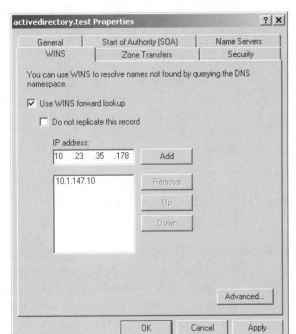

The available options include the following:

**Use WINS Forward Lookup**    Checking this box instructs the DNS server to query one or more WINS servers if it is unable to fulfill a host name request. The DNS server adds a new record type—the WINS record—to its own database.

**Do Not Replicate This Record**    This option prevents the WINS record from being sent as part of a zone transfer request. Therefore, the WINS records are not sent to other secondary DNS servers in the domain. You should enable this option if you are using non–Windows 2000 DNS servers on your network because those servers will not support the WINS record type and might cause errors.

**IP Address**    Here, you can specify the IP address(es) of the server(s) to be contacted for name resolution. If a lookup in the DNS database fails, these servers will be queried for the host name information. Note that the order of the IP addresses matters. That is, WINS server addresses higher in the list will be contacted before those lower on the list. You can re-sort the numbers using the Up and Down buttons.

Once the preceding options are configured, the DNS server will automatically query the specified WINS servers for host names if it is unable to resolve the request within its own database. This allows both WINS and DNS clients to perform name resolution accurately while reducing administrative burdens.

In addition to WINS forward lookups, Windows 2000 DNS servers are able to perform WINS reverse lookups. The configuration options are similar and can be set by right-clicking the name of a reverse lookup zone in the DNS administrative tool and then clicking Properties. The WINS-R tab allows you to set the WINS-R lookup information.

# Troubleshooting DNS

Name resolution problems are extremely common when working with distributed networks. If, for example, we are unable to connect to a specific host name, it could be due to various reasons. First, the host itself may be unavailable. This could occur if a server has gone down or if a client computer is not online. In other cases, we may be receiving an incorrect IP address from a DNS server. Usually, the most common symptom of a DNS configuration problem is the ability to connect to a host using its IP address, but not its host name. In this section, we'll look at some ways in which you can troubleshoot client and server DNS problems.

---

***Microsoft***
✓ ***Exam***
***Objective***

**Manage, monitor, and troubleshoot DNS.**

· Manage replication of DNS data.

---

See "Managing DNS Replication," an earlier section of this chapter, for more coverage of the "Manage replication of DNS data" subobjective.

# Troubleshooting Clients

The most common client-side problem related to DNS is incorrect TCP/IP configuration. For example, if the DNS server values are incorrect or the default gateway is set incorrectly, clients may not be able to contact their DNS server. Consequently, they will be unable to connect to other computers using DNS names.

One of the fundamental troubleshooting steps in diagnosing network problems is to determine whether the problem is occurring on the client side or is the fault of the server side. The most common way to determine this is by testing if other clients are having the same problem. If, on the one hand, a whole subnet is having problems resolving DNS names, it is much more likely that a server or network device is unavailable or improperly configured. On the other hand, if only one or a few clients are having problems, then it is likely that the clients are misconfigured.

In this section, we'll look at ways to diagnose and troubleshoot client-side DNS configuration problems.

## Using the *IPCONFIG* Command

Many times, an error in client configuration can cause computers to be unable to resolve DNS names. The common symptom is that the client computer can connect to a machine if it is using the machine's IP address, but it cannot connect if it is using the DNS name. The first step in troubleshooting such problems is to verify the proper TCP/IP configuration on the client. This can easily be done using the following command in Windows NT 4, Windows 98, or Windows 2000 (note that in Windows 95, you must use the `WINIPCFG` command):

```
IPCONFIG /ALL |More
```

This command will list the TCP/IP configuration information for each of the client's network adapters (as shown in Figure 2.23).

The command-line parameters and output of the IPCONFIG utility are slightly different in various Microsoft operation systems. To get a listing of the exact syntax, just type **IPCONFIG /?**.

If the client computer is using DHCP, you can use the IPCONFIG / RELEASE command to release the current TCP/IP information. Then, you can issue the IPCONFIG /RENEW command to obtain a new IP address lease from a DHCP server.

**FIGURE 2.23**  Viewing TCP/IP configuration information using IPCONFIG

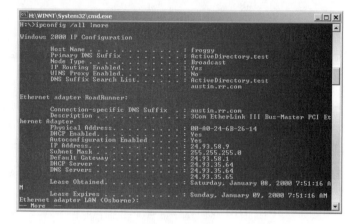

Windows 95/98 clients include a graphical utility for viewing the same information provided by the IPCONFIG utility. The easiest way to access the utility is to click Start ➢ Run, and then type **winipcfg**.

The Windows 2000 version of the IPCONFIG utility also supports several new command-line switches in addition to those already described. These options are shown in Table 2.4.

**TABLE 2.4**  Windows 2000 IPCONFIG Command-Line Switches

| Switch | Function |
| --- | --- |
| /flushdns | Clears all of the entries in the local DNS cache; useful if names are being resolved to incorrect IP addresses |
| /registerdns | Renews all current DHCP leases and updates DNS server information |
| /displaydns | Shows the contents of the current local DNS resolver cache |

**TABLE 2.4**   Windows 2000 IPCONFIG Command-Line Switches *(continued)*

| Switch | Function |
|--------|----------|
| /showclassid | Shows the current DHCP class ID; used when different types of machines require specific DHCP information (for example, a different class might be used for servers and workstations) |
| /setclassid | Allows the current DHCP class ID to be changed |

## Using the *PING* Command

After verifying the client configuration, a good second step when troubleshooting a DNS client problem is to ensure that the server is accessible on the network. The PING command provides a simple way to do this. You can use PING by simply typing **PING** and then an IP address or host name at the command line.

When troubleshooting DNS problems, you should first start by PINGing a machine's TCP/IP address. For example, the command PING 172.16.25.33 should return a response from a server. If no response is received, either the server is down, or there is a problem with the network connectivity (such as a failed router). If, however, a response is received, you should attempt to PING a computer using its machine name. An example is PING server1.mycompany.com. If this test fails (but using PING with an IP address works), then you have a problem with your name resolution services.

## Using the *NSLOOKUP* Command

Sometimes, it is useful to find information about the name servers on the network. The NSLOOKUP command is designed to do just that. A basic test is to run the command with no arguments. This will display the IP address of the current DNS server for this client. For NSLOOKUP to work properly, a PTR record must exist in the server's database.

The NSLOOKUP command is only available on Windows NT 4 and Windows 2000 machines. Windows 95/98 computers do not include the command.

The NSLOOKUP command supports many other functions for determining name resolution paths and testing recursion. For further information, type **HELP** at the NSLOOKUP command prompt. A sample of this display is shown in Figure 2.24.

**FIGURE 2.24**   Viewing NSLOOKUP commands

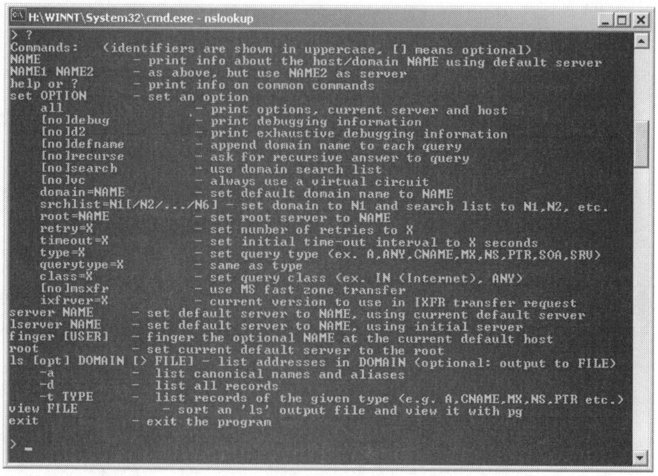

Exercise 2.8 provides an example of how NSLOOKUP can be used to verify the DNS server settings on the local machine.

**EXERCISE 2.8**

## Using the *NSLOOKUP* Command to Verify DNS Configuration

In this exercise, the NSLOOKUP command will be used to verify the proper operation of the DNS server on the local machine. This exercise assumes that you have already installed and configured DNS.

1. Open a command prompt by clicking Start ➢ Programs ➢ Accessories ➢ Command Prompt. Alternatively, you can click Start ➢ Run and type **cmd**.

2. At the command prompt, type **NSLOOKUP** and press Enter. This will run the NSLOOKUP command and present you with a > prompt. This prompt indicates that NSLOOKUP is awaiting a command.

3. To activate the local DNS server, type **Server 127.0.0.1**.

**EXERCISE 2.8** *(continued)*

4. Type **set type = SRV** to filter resource records to only SRV types, and press Enter. If the command is successful, you will receive another > prompt.

5. To verify a resource record, simply type its FQDN. For example, if our domain name is activedirectory.test, we would type _ldap._tcp.activedirectory.test. You should receive information about the host name that is mapped as a domain controller for this domain.

6. If you want to test other resources, simply type the names of the resources. You should receive valid responses. Table 2.3 provided a list of the default resource records that should be present.

7. When you are finished using NSLOOKUP, type **exit** and then press Enter. This will return you to the command prompt. To close the command prompt, type **exit** again and hit Enter.

Unfortunately, the NSLOOKUP command is not as user-friendly as it could be. It requires that you learn several different commands and use them in a specific syntax. Nevertheless, NSLOOKUP command is an invaluable tool for troubleshooting DNS configuration issues.

## Troubleshooting DNS Servers

The symptoms related to DNS server problems generally include the inability to perform accurate name resolution. Provided that the DNS server has been installed, some troubleshooting steps to take include the following:

**Verify that the DNS service has started.**   By using the DNS administrative tool, you can quickly determine the status of the DNS server.

**Check the Event Viewer.**   Especially if you are having intermittent problems with the DNS server or the service has stopped unexpectedly, you can find more information in the Windows NT Event Log.

**Verify that the DNS server is accessible to clients.**   A simple check for network connectivity between clients and the DNS server can eliminate a lot of potential problems. Browsing the network and connecting to clients or using the PING command is the easiest way to do this. Note, however, that if name resolution is not occurring properly, you may not be able to connect to clients.

**Verify operations with the NSLOOKUP command.**   The NSLOOKUP command provides several very powerful options for testing recursion, WINS lookups, and other features of Microsoft's DNS.

**Verify the DNS configuration.**   If the DNS server is providing inaccurate or outdated results, you may need to manually change the server settings or retire individual records. If outdated records are truly the problem, it is likely that users are able to get to many other machines (on the LAN or the Internet) but cannot connect to one or more specific computers.

Additionally, if you're using implementations other than Microsoft DNS, you should consult with the documentation that accompanies that product. Although DNS is an Internet standard, various DNS server software applications function quite differently from one another.

## Monitoring DNS Servers

It's always a good idea to know how your network services are performing at any given moment. Monitoring performance allows you to adequately determine the load on current servers, evaluate resource usage, and plan for any necessary upgrades. After you install the DNS service, you will be able to select the DNS object in the Windows 2000 System Monitor. This object contains many different counters that are related to monitoring DNS server performance and usage.

Using the System Monitor, you can generate statistics on the following types of events:

- AXFR requests (all-zone transfer requests)

- IXFR requests (incremental zone transfer requests)

- DNS server memory usage

- Dynamic updates

- DNS Notify events

- Recursive queries

- TCP and UDP statistics

- WINS statistics

- Zone transfer issues

All of this information can be analyzed easily using the Chart, Histogram, or Report views of the System Monitor. Additionally, you can use the Alerts function to automatically notify you (or other systems administrators) whenever certain performance statistic thresholds are exceeded. For example, if the total number of recursive queries is very high, you might want to be notified so you can examine the situation. Finally, information from Performance logs and Alerts can be stored to a log data file.

The System Monitor application in Windows 2000 is an extremely powerful and useful tool for managing and troubleshooting systems. You should become familiar with its various functions to ensure that system services are operating properly. For more information on using Windows 2000 Performance Monitor, see Chapter 9, "Active Directory Optimization and Reliability."

# Summary

In this chapter, we looked at a very powerful but complicated prerequisite to installing the Active Directory. DNS was designed to be a robust, scalable, high-performance system for resolving friendly names to TCP/IP host addresses. We started by taking an overview of the basics of DNS and how DNS names are generated. We then looked at the many features available in Microsoft's version of DNS and focused on how to install, configure, and manage the necessary services.

Important points to remember include the following:

- DNS is based on a widely accepted standard. It is designed to resolve friendly network names to IP addresses.

- DNS names are hierarchical and are read from left (most-specific) to right (least-specific).

- DNS zones are created to create a database of authoritative information for the hosts in a specific domain.

- Within DNS zones, servers can assume various roles.

- Through the use of replication, multiple DNS servers can remain synchronized.

- Windows 2000's DNS services can integrate with DHCP and WINS.

Understanding DNS is extremely important for using the Active Directory, so if you aren't yet comfortable with the concepts described in this chapter, be sure to review them before going on.

# Exam Essentials

**Understand design goals and features of DNS.**   DNS has been designed as a distributed database that allows for scalability, performance, and maintainability of a large number of records. It is based on a widely accepted standard.

**Be able to identify portions of a DNS name.**   DNS names are hierarchical and include information about the names of various networks resources (such as mail and Web servers), as well as the networks on which they reside.

**Plan for DNS naming based on business requirements.**   Understand the pros and cons of using the same domain for internal and external resources vs. using different names.

**Understand the purpose of DNS zones.**   Be able to decide when multiple DNS zones should be implemented, and how they can be created from existing zones.

**Be able to choose DNS Server Roles.**   A DNS server can be designated as a master, primary, secondary, or caching-only server for a particular zone. DNS servers can assume multiple roles for other DNS zones, as well. Be sure you understand the differences between these roles and how they can be used to optimize DNS performance and reliability. And, be sure you know the advantages of integrating DNS with the Active Directory for simplifying management and for performance reasons.

**Manage DNS replication.**   You should understand how DNS replication (zone transfer) operations works, potential issues that might occur due to network traffic and how to monitor and troubleshoot DNS.

**Decide how to best integrate DNS with WINS and DHCP.**   DNS is a vital part of your Active Directory environment. Therefore, it's important that DNS integrates with other network services. Understand how DNS records can be automatically updated through WINS and DHCP.

**Troubleshoot DNS problems.**   Understand the various tools that are available for isolating and fixing DNS name resolution issues. Various methods are available for troubleshooting client- and server-side issues.

# Key Terms

Before you take the exam, be certain you are familiar with the following terms:

| | |
|---|---|
| caching-only DNS server | primary DNS server |
| child domain | recursion |
| delegation | resource record (RR) |
| DNS namespace | reverse lookup zone |
| Domain Name System (DNS) | root domain |
| Dynamic Host Configuration Protocol (DHCP) | secondary DNS server |
| forward lookup zone | Transmission Control Protocol/ Internet Protocol (TCP/IP) |
| forwarding | Windows Internet Name Service (WINS) |
| iteration | zone |
| master DNS server | zone transfer |
| parent domain | |

# Review Questions

1. A user is reporting a problem with resolving access to various network resources. After walking the user through some basic troubleshooting steps, you determine that the problem is related to DNS. Which of the following tools can be used to troubleshoot the issue?

   **A.** IPCONFIG

   **B.** NSLOOKUP

   **C.** PING

   **D.** All of the above

2. You're the DNS administrator for your organization's network. Thus far, the network has included three different DNS zones:

   - research.mycompany.com

   - development.mycompany.com

   - engineering.mycompany.com

   Recently, the organization has acquired another company. Since the organizations will be operated independently, you must provide DNS support for a new domain called "newcompany.com". Which two of the following steps must you perform?

   **A.** Create a new DNS zone called newcompany.com.

   **B.** Remove all host records from the existing DNS zone.

   **C.** Create resource records (RRs) for the resources that are available in the new domain.

   **D.** Add the new domain to the research.mycompany.com zone.

**3.** A member of your organization's Help Desk reports that a specific client has a TCP/IP configuration problem. However, she notes that she has determined that the TCP/IP protocol has been configured on the client machine. She ran several commands to test for this. If the problem is due to the inability of the client to connect to a DNS server, which of the following commands would fail?

**A.** PING 127.0.0.1

**B.** PING localhost

**C.** PING server1.mycompany.com

**D.** None of the above

**4.** Which of the following is used to automatically assign TCP/IP information to clients?

**A.** WINS

**B.** DNS

**C.** DHCP

**D.** RRAS

**5.** You have just made a change to a resource record in the DNS database on a master server. Which two of the following processes may the server use to alert secondary servers that a change has been made and then copy the data to the secondary server?

**A.** Zone transfer

**B.** Forwarding

**C.** Recursion

**D.** Iteration

**E.** DNS Notify

**6.** A large organization has implemented 12 DNS zones and has configured at least two DNS servers in each zone. Recently, users in one department within the organization have reported intermittent problems connecting to portions of the organization's intranet. A system administrator suspects that there is a problem with the configuration of one of the organization's DNS servers. Which of the following tools can she use to determine the source of the problem?

**A.** Event Viewer

**B.** System Monitor

**C.** DNS administrative tool

**D.** The NSLOOKUP command

**E.** All of the above

**7.** The process that occurs when a DNS server cannot return enough information to fully resolve a DNS name to a TCP/IP addresses is known as

**A.** Recursion

**B.** Iteration

**C.** Zone transfers

**D.** Dynamic DNS updates

**8.** Which of the following is *not* a valid type of resource record (RR)?

**A.** SRV

**B.** PTR

**C.** A

**D.** MX

**E.** PDC

**9.** When using which of the following types of clients is the DHCP server responsible for dynamically updating the DNS database?

   **A.** Windows 95

   **B.** Windows 98

   **C.** Windows NT 4

   **D.** Windows 2000

   **E.** All of the above

**10.** Your organization has implemented several DNS servers in multiple zones, including a master server, a primary server, and two secondary servers. Users are complaining about performance problems related to DNS. You must solve the problem, but you have the following constraints:

   **1.** The new server must improve DNS performance for multiple zones.

   **2.** The new server must not be an authority for any DNS zone.

   **3.** Due to budget constraints, you can only implement one new server.

   You determine that you need to add an additional server to the environment. Which of the following types of DNS servers should you implement?

   **A.** Master server

   **B.** Caching-only server

   **C.** Primary server

   **D.** Secondary server

**11.** The process through which authority for a portion of a DNS zone is assigned to another DNS server is known as

   **A.** Zone transfer

   **B.** Forwarding

   **C.** Delegation

   **D.** Promotion

12. Recently, you've experienced problems in communications between domain controllers. For example, when you log on from some locations throughout the network, you are unable to access a domain controller. Also, when you examine the Directory Services log information through the Event Viewer tool, you see that there have been several failed communication attempts between domain controllers.

   It is likely that this problem is caused by the lack of which of the following types of DNS resource records (RRs)?

   **A.** SRV

   **B.** PTR

   **C.** A

   **D.** MX

   **E.** None of the above

13. The process by which one or more DNS servers use a specified DNS server for all recursive lookups is known as

   **A.** Recursion

   **B.** Iteration

   **C.** DNS Notify

   **D.** Forwarding

14. Which of the following resource records (RRs) indicates the zone(s) for which a DNS server is an authority?

   **A.** SRV

   **B.** PTR

   **C.** SOA

   **D.** MX

**15.** A system administrator for a small network has completed the upgrade of all clients and servers on the network to Windows 2000. Additionally, she has ensured that none of the applications on her network rely on NetBIOS names and that they use DNS names for finding network resources. Which of the following name resolution methods should she disable?

**A.** DNS

**B.** DHCP

**C.** WINS

**D.** IPX/SPX

**16.** You are configuring DNS replication for your zone. You want to notify all of the servers listed on the Name Servers tab of the zone properties dialog box whenever the zone changes. Where would you click in the following exhibit in order to accomplish this?

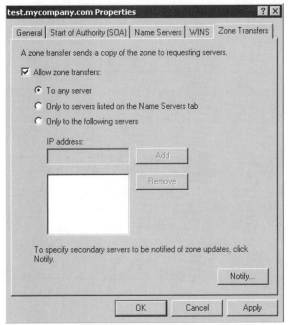

**A.** The To Any Server radio button

**B.** The Only to Servers Listed on the Name Servers Tab radio button

**C.** The Notify... button

**D.** The Only to the Following Servers radio button

**17.** The following diagram outlines DNS name resolution through recursion. Move each item into the correct position so that the flow of DNS traffic is correct.

Choices:

Client uses IP address to connect to www.company.com.
Root-level server resolves name.
Server returns IP address and caches name.
Client requests IP address.
Server cannot resolve name. Forwards request.

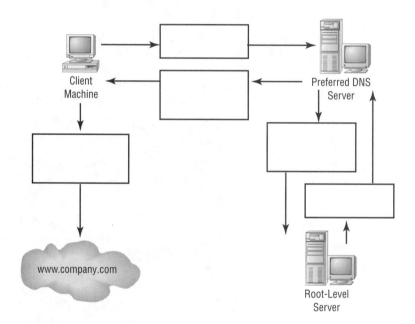

**18.** Your company needs to upgrade all of its Windows NT 4 machines to Windows 2000. You need to maintain the four DNS zones that are currently in place: San Jose, San Francisco, San Diego, and Los Angeles. The Los Angeles zone uses a Unix-based primary DNS server, and the administrator at that site insists that it remains in place in its current role. The other sites all use Windows-based primary and secondary DNS servers. The San Diego zone has a very unreliable WAN connection, so you decide that it will be worthwhile to use this machine to complete name resolution requests. For ease of administration, however, you do not want the San Francisco server to store a copy of the zone file.

You need to configure Windows 2000 servers at each site. Drag the different zone types to their appropriate places within the diagram. Note that each item can be used more than once, and some items might not be used at all.

Choices:

Standard Primary Zone
Standard Secondary Zone
Caching-Only Server
Active Directory–Integrated Zone

**San Francisco**

**San Jose**

**Los Angeles**

**San Diego**

**19.** Which of the following accurately describes which servers *must* be running the DNS service?

**A.** All domain controllers

**B.** At least one Windows 2000 Server in an Active Directory environment

**C.** At least one domain controller per Active Directory site

**D.** None of the above

# Answers to Review Questions

1. D. All of the tools listed here are helpful for resolving TCP/IP connectivity and name resolution issues.

2. A, C. Since the new domain is not part of the namespace of any existing zones, you must create a new zone. Then, you must add information about network resources to this zone.

3. C. If DNS is not configured properly, resolving the name of a remote server will fail. Option A uses an IP address (which is not dependent on DNS), and option B uses a special alias for the localhost.

4. C. The Dynamic Host Configuration Protocol (DHCP) automatically assigns TCP/IP address information to clients. Optionally, DHCP information can be used to automatically update DNS databases.

5. A, E. A DNS Notify message can be sent by a master server to notify secondary servers that changes have been made to the DNS database and that they should request an update. Zone transfers are the process by which information is replicated between master and secondary DNS servers.

6. E. All of the above can be used to view performance or operational information about the DNS service.

7. B. In the process of iteration, a DNS server will return its best guess about a domain name, but the client will be responsible for ultimately resolving the name.

8. E. There is no "PDC" type of resource record. All of the other options are standard DNS RRs.

9. D. When using Windows 2000, the *client* can be responsible for sending dynamic updates to DNS. The legacy clients do not have DNS update capability so the updates are handled with W2K DHCP.

10. B. Of the choices, only a "caching-only" server meets the requirements. All of the other server types contain information about specific DNS zones.

11. C. Delegation is used to break zones apart into smaller units for performance or manageability.

12. A. SRV records are used by Active Directory domain controllers and client computers to find domain controllers for a specific domain. If this record were missing or incorrect, it would cause problems when attempting to communicate with domain controllers.

13. D. Forwarding can be used to route all recursive DNS requests through specific DNS servers. This is often used to reduce network traffic across slow links.

14. C. The Start of Authority (SOA) record indicates that a server is considered an authority for a specific zone.

15. C. Windows 2000's support for WINS is primarily included for backward compatibility with legacy applications that rely on the usage of NetBIOS names. Since this is no longer required, the system administrator can reduce network traffic and increase performance by relying primarily on DNS for name resolution.

16. C. In order to notify any servers of zone updates, you need to click the Notify... button. From the Notify dialog box, you can choose to notify all of the servers listed on the Name Servers tab or only particular servers that you specify.

**17.**

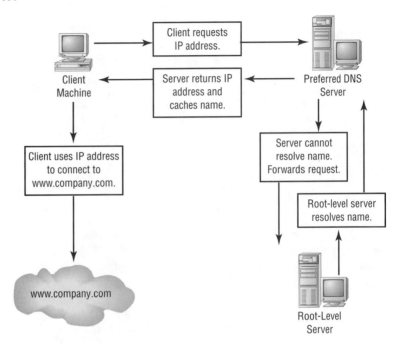

The client machine places its request with its preferred DNS server. If the DNS server doesn't have an entry in its DNS database, then it forwards the request to a root-level server. The root-level server resolves the name and sends it back to the preferred DNS server. The DNS server caches the name so that any future requests don't need to be forwarded, and then it sends the IP address to the client. The client then uses the IP address to reach the intended target.

**18.**

**San Francisco**

| Active Directory–Integrated Zone |
|---|

**San Jose**

| Active Directory–Integrated Zone |
|---|

**Los Angeles**

| Standard Secondary Zone |
|---|

**San Diego**

| Standard Primary Zone |
|---|

Secure DNS updates can only be run on Active Directory-integrated zones. San Diego should use a standard primary server because it won't be reliably available for Active Directory-integrated DNS updates. The Los Angeles site is using a Unix primary DNS server, so the best you can do here is run a standard secondary zone.

**19.** D.   Although DNS is required for the proper operation of the Active Directory, DNS is not required on all domain controllers. While DNS is required to locate a DC it does not have to be running on a Windows 2000 server.

# Chapter

# 3

# Installing and Configuring the Active Directory

## MICROSOFT EXAM OBJECTIVES COVERED IN THIS CHAPTER:

✓ **Install, configure, and troubleshoot the components of Active Directory.**

- Install Active Directory.
- Create sites.
- Create subnets.
- Create site links.
- Create site link bridges.
- Create connection objects.
- Create global catalog servers.
- Move server objects between sites.
- Transfer operations master roles.
- Verify Active Directory installation.
- Implement an organizational unit (OU) structure.

In previous chapters, we looked at the various factors you need to take into account when planning for the Active Directory. Then, we moved on to understand the Domain Name System (DNS) and how it works with the Active Directory. The time you spend understanding these concepts is very important because the success of your Active Directory implementation will depend on them. If you plan to work through the exercises presented in this chapter, be sure that you have either already installed DNS or have at least planned for doing so as part of the process.

With the basic information out of the way, it's time to start looking at exactly how the Active Directory can be implemented. This chapter will walk you through the steps required to prepare for and implement the Active Directory using Windows 2000 domain controllers.

This chapter covers material related to the Active Directory and its installation, for the "Install, configure, and troubleshoot the components of Active Directory" objective. See Chapter 4, "Creating and Managing Organizational Units," for coverage on implementing an OU structure; Chapter 5, "Installing and Managing Trees and Forests," for material on creating Global Catalog servers and transferring operations master roles; and Chapter 6, "Configuring Sites and Managing Replication," for coverage on creating sites, subnets, site links, site link bridges, and connection objects, as well as on moving server objects between sites.

# Preparing for Active Directory Installation

All too often, systems and network administrators implement hardware and software without first taking the time to evaluate the prerequisites. For example, purchasing and installing a tape backup solution will not be possible without first ensuring that the appropriate network connectivity and attachment interface are available on servers. Installation and configuration of the Active Directory is no exception.

The physical components that form the basis of the Active Directory are Windows 2000 domain controllers. Before you begin installing domain controllers to set up your Active Directory environment, you should ensure that you are properly prepared to do so. In this section, we'll examine some of the prerequisites and types of information you'll need to successfully install the Active Directory.

The technical information and exercises in this chapter are based on the assumption that you will be using Microsoft's implementation of DNS (unless otherwise noted). If you are using other types of DNS servers in your environment, you may not be able to take advantage of all the features mentioned in this chapter.

## Install DNS

In Chapter 2, "Integrating DNS with the Active Directory," we described how the Active Directory depends on DNS for name resolution. Therefore, it should come as no surprise that the proper installation and configuration of DNS must be completed before installing an Active Directory domain. If it is not already installed on the system, you can install the DNS service by using the Add/Remove programs icon in the Control Panel. DNS will be used for performing name resolution to other domain controllers or resources on your network (if any).

Technically, if you haven't yet installed DNS, you will be prompted to do so as part of the configuration of a domain controller. In some cases, this provides an easy way to configure DNS with the appropriate options for the Active Directory. It's not the right choice for every environment, however. Unless you are setting up the Active Directory in a test environment or on a network that doesn't yet have DNS services, it can be easier to test and verify DNS configuration before starting the Active Directory installation.

Although the presence of DNS servers on your network is a requirement, you are not forced to use Microsoft's DNS service. If other DNS servers are available on the network, you may choose to use those servers when installing the Active Directory. Note, however, that if you're using other implementations of DNS servers (such as Unix or Windows NT 4), you will not be able to take advantage of all of the features of Windows 2000's DNS and its integration with the Active Directory. In addition, you will be required to enter the proper SRV records manually because most current DNS servers do not support dynamic updates.

For more details on planning for, installing, and configuring DNS, see Chapter 2.

## Verify the DNS Configuration

Once DNS has been installed, you should ensure that it has been configured to allow updates. This option allows the Active Directory to automatically add, modify, and remove resource records (RRs) to the DNS database whenever changes are made in the Active Directory. The Allow Updates option is extremely useful because it reduces the chances for error in manual data entry and greatly reduces the effort required for administration.

You should also verify the proper creation of DNS forward and reverse lookup zones. These zones will be used for resolving names to network addresses and are extremely important for the successful setup of the Active Directory.

For more information on configuring the Allow Updates option and configuring forward and reverse lookup zones for DNS, see Chapter 2.

## Verify the File System

The file system used by an operating system is an important concern for many reasons. First, the file system can provide the ultimate level of security for all of the information stored on the server itself. Second, the file system is responsible for managing and tracking all of this data. Furthermore, certain features are available only on certain file systems. These features include support for encryption, remote file access, remote storage, disk redundancy, and disk quotas.

The Windows 2000 platform allows the use of multiple different file systems, including the following:

- *File Allocation Table (FAT)* file system
- File Allocation Table 32 (FAT32) file system

- *Windows New Technology File System (NTFS)*

- Windows New Technology File System 5 (NTFS 5)

The fundamental difference between FAT and NTFS partitions is that NTFS allows for file-system–level security. Support for FAT and FAT32 are mainly included in Windows 2000 for backward compatibility. Specifically, these file systems are required in order to accommodate multiple boot partitions. For example, if we wanted to configure a single computer to boot into Windows 98 and Windows 2000, we would need to have at least one FAT or FAT32 partition. Although this is a good solution for situations such as training labs and test environments, you should strongly consider using only NTFS partitions on production server machines.

Windows 2000 uses an updated version of the NTFS file system called NTFS 5. There are many other benefits to using the NTFS 5 file system, including support for the following functionality:

**Disk Quotas**   In order to restrict the amount of disk space used by users on the network, systems administrators can establish disk quotas. By default, Windows 2000 supports disk quota restrictions on a volume level. That is, we could restrict the amount of storage space used by a specific user on a single disk volume. Third-party solutions that allow more granular quota settings are also available.

**File System Encryption**   One of the fundamental problems with network operating systems is that systems administrators are often given full permissions to view all files and data stored on hard disks. In some cases, this is necessary. For example, in order to perform backup, recovery, and disk management functions, at least one user must have all permissions. Windows 2000 and NTFS 5 address these issues by allowing for file system encryption. Encryption essentially scrambles all of the data stored within files before they are written to the disk. When an authorized user requests the files, they are transparently decrypted and provided. The use of encryption prevents the usability of data in case it is stolen or intercepted by an unauthorized user.

**Dynamic Volumes**   Protecting against disk failures is an important concern for production servers. Although earlier versions of Windows NT supported various levels of Redundant Array of Independent Disks (RAID) technology, there were shortcomings with software-based solutions. Perhaps the most significant was that server reboots were required in order to change RAID configurations. Some configuration changes could not be made without a complete reinstallation of the operating system. With the support for dynamic volumes in Windows 2000, systems administrators can change RAID and other disk configuration settings without requiring a reboot or reinstallation of the server. The end result is greater protection for data, increased scalability, and increased uptime.

**Mounted Drives**   With the use of mounted drives, systems administrators can map a local disk drive to an NTFS 5 directory name. This is useful for organizing disk space on servers and increasing manageability. By using mounted drives, I could mount the C:\Users directory to an actual physical disk. If that disk became full, I could copy all of the files to another, larger drive without requiring any changes to the directory path name or reconfiguration of applications.

**Remote Storage**   When it comes to disk space, it seems like you can never get enough of it! Systems administrators often notice that as soon as more space is added, the next upgrade must be planned. Moving infrequently used files to tape is one way to recover disk space. However, backing up and restoring these files could be quite difficult and time consuming. Systems administrators can use the Remote Storage features supported by NTFS 5 to automatically off-load seldom-used data to tape or other devices. The files remain available to users. Should they request an archived file, Windows 2000 can automatically restore the file from a remote storage device and make it available. Using remote storage frees up systems administrators' time and allows them to focus on more important tasks (such as installing the Active Directory!).

Although these reasons probably compel most systems administrators to use the NTFS 5 file system, there are reasons that prove its use is mandatory.

The most important reason is that the Active Directory data store must reside on an NTFS 5 partition. Therefore, before you begin the installation process for Active Directory, you should ensure that you have at least one NTFS partition available. Also, be sure you have a reasonable amount of disk space available (1GB). As the size of the Active Directory data store will grow as you add objects to it, be sure you have adequate space for the future. Exercise 3.1 shows how you can use the administrative tools to view and modify disk configuration.

Before you make any disk configuration changes, be sure you completely understand their potential effects. Changing partition sizes and adding and removing partitions can result in a total loss of all information on one or more partitions.

**EXERCISE 3.1**

## Viewing Disk Configuration

In this exercise, you will use the Disk Management functionality in Windows 2000 to view disk configuration information.

1. Open the Computer Management icon in the Administrative Tools program group.

2. Under the Storage branch, click Disk Management.

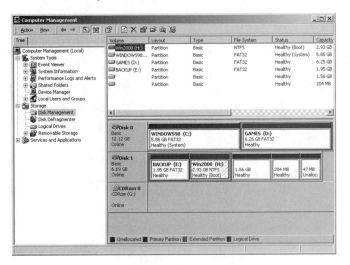

3. The Disk Management program will show you the logical and physical disks that are currently configured on your system. Note that information about the size of each partition is also displayed. By using the View menu, you can choose various depictions of the physical and logical drives in your system.

4. (Optional) To modify partition settings, you can right-click any of the disks or partitions and choose from the available options.

Windows 2000 allows the conversion of existing FAT or FAT32 partitions to NTFS. However, this is a one-way process. You cannot convert an NTFS partition to any other file system without losing data. If this conversion is required, the recommended process is to back up all existing data, delete and reformat the partition, and then restore the data. Needless to say, it's a time-consuming process!

If you want to convert an existing partition from FAT or FAT32 to NTFS, you'll need to use the CONVERT command-line utility. For example, the following command will convert the C: partition from FAT to FAT32:

```
CONVERT c: /fs:ntfs
```

Only the Windows NT and Windows 2000 operating systems can read and write to and from NTFS partitions. Therefore, if you are using other operating systems on the same computer, be sure you fully understand the effects of converting the file system.

If the partition you are trying to convert contains any system files or the Windows 2000 virtual memory page file, a command-line message will inform you that the conversion will take place during the next reboot of the machine. When the computer is rebooted, the conversion process will begin. After the partition is converted to NTFS, the computer will automatically reboot again, and you will be able to continue using the system.

## Verify Network Connectivity

Although a Windows 2000 Server computer can exist on a network by itself (or without a network card at all), you will not be harnessing much of the potential of the operating system without network connectivity. As the fundamental purpose of a network operating system is to provide resources to users, you must verify network connectivity.

Before you begin to install the Active Directory, you should perform several checks of your current configuration to ensure that the server is configured properly on the network. Some general tests include the following:

**Network Adapter** At least one network adapter should be installed and properly configured on your server. A quick way to verify that a network adapter is properly installed is to use the Computer Management administrative tool. Under the Network Adapters branch, you should have at least one network adapter listed. If not, you can use the Add/Remove Hardware icon in the Control Panel to configure hardware.

**TCP/IP Protocol**   The TCP/IP protocol should be installed, configured, and enabled on any necessary network adapters. The server should also be given a valid IP address and subnet mask. Optionally, you may need to configure a default gateway, DNS servers, WINS servers, and other network settings. If you are using the Dynamic Host Configuration Protocol (DHCP), be sure that the assigned information is correct. In general, it is a good idea to use a static IP address for servers because IP address changes can cause network connectivity problems if not handled properly.

Understanding TCP/IP is essential to the use of Windows 2000 and the Active Directory. See *MCSE: Windows 2000 Network Infrastructure Administration Study Guide,* 2nd ed., by Paul Robichaux with James Chellis (Sybex, 2001) to learn more about TCP\IP.

**Internet Access**   If the server should have access to the Internet, you should verify that it is able to connect to external Web servers and other machines outside the LAN. If the server is unable to connect, you might have a problem with the TCP/IP configuration.

**LAN Access**   The server should be able to view other servers and workstations on the network. You can quickly verify this type of connectivity by using the My Network Places icon on the Desktop. If other machines are not visible, ensure that the network and TCP/IP configuration is correct for your environment.

**Client Access**   Network client computers should be able to connect to your server and view any shared resources. A simple way to test connectivity is to create a share and test if other machines are able to see files and folders within it. If clients cannot access the machine, ensure that both the client and server are configured properly.

**WAN Access**   If you're working in a distributed environment, you should ensure that you have access to any remote sites or users that will need to connect to this machine. Usually, this is a simple test that can be performed by a network administrator.

In some cases, verifying network access can be quite simple. You might have some internal and external network resources with which to test. In other cases, it might be more complicated. There are several tools and techniques you can use to verify that your network configuration is correct:

**Using the IPCONFIG Utility**   By typing **IPCONFIG/ALL** at the command prompt, you can view information about the TCP/IP settings of a computer. Figure 3.1 shows the types of information you'll receive.

**FIGURE 3.1**   Viewing TCP/IP information with the IPCONFIG utility

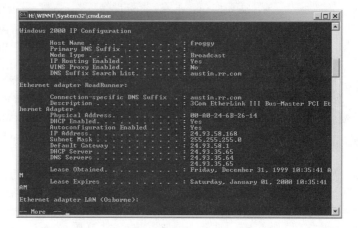

**Using the PING Utility**   The PING command was designed to test connectivity to other computers. You can use PING by simply typing **PING** and then an IP address or host name at the command line. The following are some steps for testing connectivity using the PING command.

**PING Other Computers on the Same Subnet**   You should start by PINGing a known active IP address on the network to check for a response. If one is received, then you have connectivity to the network. Next, check if you can PING another machine using its host name. If this works, then local name resolution works properly.

**PING Other Computers on Different Subnets**   In order to ensure that routing is set up properly, you should attempt to PING computers that are local on other subnets (if any exist) on your network. If this test fails, try PINGing the default gateway. Any errors will indicate a problem in the network configuration or a problem with a router.

Some firewalls, routers, or servers on your network or on the Internet might prevent you from receiving a successful response from a PING command. This is usually done for security reasons because malicious users might attempt to disrupt network traffic using excessive PINGs. Just because you do not receive a response, do not assume that the service is not available. Instead, try to verify connectivity in other ways. For example TRACERT can be used to demonstrate connectivity beyond your subnet even if ICMP responses are ignored by the other routers. Since the display of a second router implies connectivity, the path to an ultimate destination will show success even if it does not display the actual names and addresses.

**Browsing the Network**   To ensure that you have access to other computers on the network, be sure that they can be viewed using the Network Neighborhood icon. This will verify that your name resolution parameters are set up correctly and that other computers are accessible. Also, try connecting to resources (such as file shares or printers) on other machines.

**Browsing the Internet**   You can quickly verify whether your server has access to the Internet by visiting a known Web site, such as www.microsoft.com. This will ensure that you have access outside of your network. If you do not have access to the Web, you might need to verify your proxy server settings (if applicable) and your DNS server settings.

By performing these simple tests, you can ensure that you have a properly configured network connection and that other network resources are available.

## Determine the Domain Controller Mode

When you are installing a Windows 2000 domain controller, you must determine if you will be supporting a *mixed-mode Active Directory domain* or a *native-mode Active Directory domain*. The decision should be quite simple.

Mixed mode is the default option when installing a domain controller. It is designed for allowing backwards compatibility with Windows NT 4 and earlier domain models. If you will need to support Windows NT domain controllers for one or more domains within your environment, you should choose mixed mode for those domains. However, as long as you are using mixed mode, certain Active Directory features (such as universal and nested groups) will be unavailable.

If your environment does not require support for Windows NT domain controllers within any of your domains, then you can choose to implement your domains in native mode. Native mode allows the full functionality of the Active Directory for all domain controllers, but it does not allow for backwards compatibility. Since this means that Windows NT domain controllers can not be used in native-mode Active Directory domains, it's an important decision. Note also that domains cannot be converted from native mode back to mixed mode. We'll cover the details of mixed-mode and native-mode Active Directory domains in later chapters.

## Plan the Domain Structure

Once you have verified the technical configuration of your server for the Active Directory, it's time to verify the Active Directory configuration for your organization. Since the content of this chapter focuses on the installation of the first domain in your environment, you really only need to know the following information prior to beginning setup:

- The DNS name of the domain

- The NetBIOS name of the server (used by previous versions of Windows to access server resources)

- Whether the domain will operate in mixed mode or native mode

- Whether or not other DNS servers are available on the network

However, if you will be installing additional domain controllers in your environment or will be attaching to an existing Active Directory structure, you should also have the following information:

- If this domain controller will join an existing domain, the name of that domain. You will also either require a password for an Enterprise Administrator or have someone with those permissions create a domain account before promotion.

- Whether the new domain will join an existing tree and, if so, the name of the tree it will join.

- The name of a forest to which this domain will connect (if applicable).

For more information on planning domain structure, review the information in Chapter 1, "Overview of the Active Directory." We'll cover the details of working in multidomain Active Directory environments (including the creation of new trees and participating in an existing forest) in Chapter 5, "Installing and Managing Trees and Forests."

# Installing the Active Directory

Installation of the Active Directory is an easy and straightforward process as long as you have performed adequate planning and have made the necessary decisions beforehand. In this chapter, we'll look at the actual steps required to install the first domain controller in a given environment.

---

**Microsoft** ✓ **Exam Objective**

**Install, configure, and troubleshoot the components of Active Directory.**

- Install Active Directory.

---

With previous versions of Windows NT Server, you had to determine the role of your server as it relates to the domain controller or member server during installation. Choices included making the machine a Primary Domain Controller (PDC), a Backup Domain Controller (BDC), or a member server. This was an extremely important decision because, even though a BDC can be promoted to a PDC, any changes to the server's role between a domain controller and a member server required a complete reinstallation of the operating system.

Instead of forcing you to choose whether or not the machine will participate as a domain controller during setup, Windows 2000 allows you to promote servers after installation. Therefore, at the end of the setup process, all Windows 2000 Server computers are configured as either member servers (if they are joined to a domain) or stand-alone servers (if they are part of a workgroup). The process of converting a member server to a domain controller is known as *promotion*. Through the use of a simple and intuitive Wizard, systems administrators can quickly configure servers to be domain controllers after installation.

In this chapter, we'll cover the steps required to use the *Active Directory Installation Wizard (DCPROMO)*. This tool is designed for use after a server has been installed in the environment. As part of the promotion process, the server will create or receive information related to the Active Directory configuration.

# Promoting a Domain Controller

The first step in installing the Active Directory is to configure a domain controller. The first domain controller in an environment will serve as the starting point for the forest, trees, domains, and the Operations Master roles. Exercise 3.2 shows the steps required to promote an existing Windows 2000 Server to a domain controller.

---

**EXERCISE 3.2**

### Promoting a Domain Controller

In this exercise, we will install the first domain controller in the Active Directory environment. In order to complete the steps in this exercise, you must have already installed and configured a Windows 2000 Server computer and a DNS server that supports SRV records.

1. To start the Active Directory Installation Wizard, open the Configure Your Server applet in the Administrative Tools program group. Click the Active Directory option shown below. At the bottom of the page, click the Start the Active Directory Wizard hyperlink. Alternatively, you can click Start ➢ Run and type **dcpromo**.

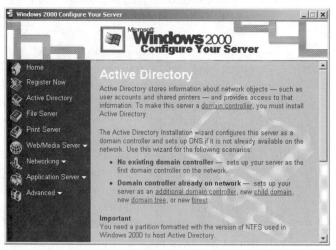

2. Click Next on the first page of the Wizard to begin the process.

**3.** The first option you will need to specify is the type of domain controller this server will be. To choose the domain controller type, select Domain Controller for a New Domain and click Next. Note the warning that proceeding will delete all local accounts on this machine.

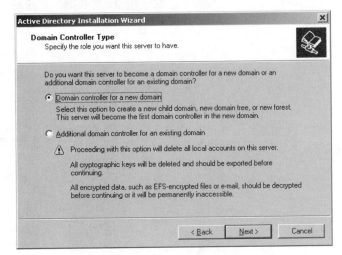

**4.** You will need to specify whether you want to create a new domain tree or make the new domain part of an existing tree. Since this will be the first domain in the Active Directory environment, choose Create a New Domain Tree and click Next.

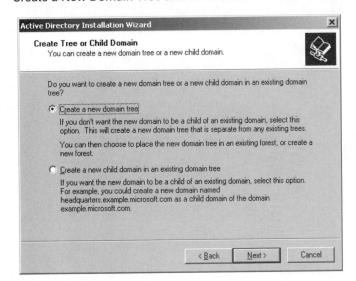

5. Choose whether the new domain tree will be part of an existing forest or a new one that you will create. Since this will be the first tree in the forest, select Create a New Forest of Domain Trees and click Next.

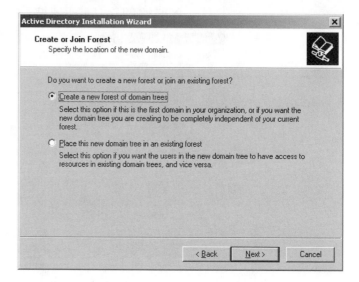

6. Specify a name for the new domain by typing in the full name of the DNS domain. For example, you can type *test.mycompany.com*. If you are not working in a test environment, be sure that you have chosen a root domain name that is consistent for your organization, and doesn't overlap with others. Click Next.

7. In order to preserve backward compatibility with earlier versions of Windows, you must provide a NetBIOS computer name. A NetBIOS name can be up to 15 characters. Although special characters are supported, you should limit yourself to the English alphabet characters and Arabic numbers. Type in the NetBIOS name for this machine and click Next.

8. In the Database and Log Locations dialog box, you should specify the file system locations for the Active Directory database and log file. Microsoft recommends that these files reside on separate physical devices in order to improve performance and to provide for recoverability. The default file system location is in a directory called NTDS located within the system root. However, you can choose any folder located on a FAT, FAT32, or NTFS partition. Click Next.

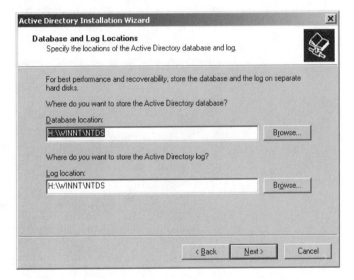

9. You will need to select a shared system volume location. The system volume folder will be used to store domain information that will be replicated to all of the other domain controllers in the domain. This folder must be stored on an NTFS 5 partition. The default location is in a directory called SYSVOL within the system root, but you can change this path based on your server configuration. Click Next.

**10.** As part of the promotion process, Windows 2000 will need you to set permissions on user and group objects. In this step, you can choose to select Permissions Compatible with pre-Windows 2000 servers. This is a good choice if you're running in a mixed environment. If you are sure you will not be supporting non-Windows 2000 machines, however, you should choose Permissions Compatible Only with Windows 2000 Servers. Although this option will not allow compatibility with previous operating systems, it will implement stronger security settings. Once you have made the appropriate selection, click Next.

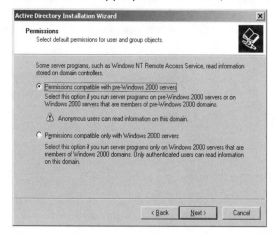

**11.** You will need to provide a Directory Services Restore Mode Administrator password that can be used to restore the Active Directory in the event of the loss or corruption of the Active Directory. Note that this password is not required to correspond with passwords set for any other Windows 2000 account. Type the password, confirm it, and then click Next.

**EXERCISE 3.2** *(continued)*

**12.** Based on the installation options you've selected, the Active Directory Installation Wizard will present a summary of your choices. It
is a good idea to copy and paste this information into a text file for
later reference. Verify the options, and then click Next to begin the
Active Directory installation process. When the necessary operations are complete, the Wizard will prompt you to click Finish.

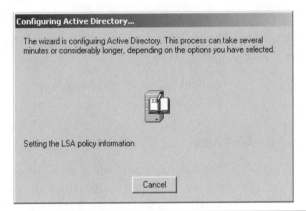

Once the Active Directory has been installed, you will be prompted to
reboot the system. Following the reboot, you will be able to access the
administrative tools that are related to the configuration and management of
the Active Directory.

# Implementing Additional Domain Controllers

The Active Directory Installation Wizard has been designed to make the process of promoting servers to domain controllers as easy as possible. With this
tool, you can easily promote servers to domain controllers and demote them
(that is, convert domain controllers back to member servers or stand-alone
servers) without reinstalling the operating system.

The Wizard allows you to choose whether or not the domain will participate
in an existing forest or tree. This allows systems administrators to easily specify
the options necessary to create new domains and complete the promotion process. Later, in Chapter 5, you'll see how to install additional domain controllers
in your environment.

# Verifying the Active Directory Installation

**O**nce the Active Directory has been configured, you'll want to verify that it is properly installed. There are several good ways to verify the proper installation and configuration of the Active Directory. In this section, we'll look at methods for verifying the proper installation and configuration of the Active Directory.

*Microsoft* ✓ *Exam Objective*

**Install, configure, and troubleshoot the components of Active Directory.**

- Verify Active Directory installation.

## Using Event Viewer

The first (and perhaps most informative) way to verify the operations of the Active Directory is to query information stored in the Windows 2000 event log. This can be done through the Windows 2000 Event Viewer. Exercise 3.3 walks you through this procedure. Entries seen with the Event Viewer include errors, warnings, and informational messages.

**EXERCISE 3.3**

### Viewing the Active Directory Event Log

In order to complete the steps in this exercise, the local machine must be configured as a domain controller.

1. Open the Event Viewer snap-in from the Administrative Tools program group.

2. In the left pane, select Directory Service.

**3.** In the right pane, notice that you can sort information by clicking column headings. For example, you can click on the Source column to sort by the service or process that reported the event.

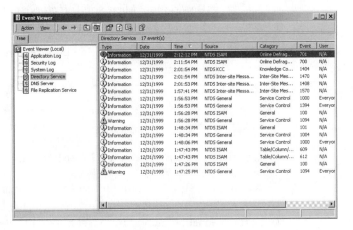

**4.** Double-click an event in the list to see the details for that item. Note that you can click the Copy button to copy the event information to the Clipboard. You can then paste the data into a document for later reference. Also, you can move between items using the Up and Down arrows. Click OK when you are done viewing an event.

**5.** You can filter specific events by right-clicking the Directory Service item in the left pane and selecting the Filter tab. Note that filtering does not remove entries from the event logs—it only restricts their display.

**6.** To verify the Active Directory installation, look for an event with information similar to the following:

Event Type: Information

Event Source: NTDS General

Event Category: Service Control

Event ID: 1000

Date: 04/31/2001

Time: 1:56:53 PM

**EXERCISE 3.3** *(continued)*

User: Everyone

Computer: DC1

Description: Microsoft Directory startup complete, version 5.00.2160.1

**7.** When you're done viewing information in the Event Viewer, close the application.

 **Real World Scenario**

### Gaining Insight through Event Viwer

Although its simple user interface and somewhat limited GUI functionality may make you overlook it, in the real world, the Event View tool can be your best ally in isolating and troubleshooting problems with a Windows 2000 Server. The Event Viewer allows you to view information that is stored in various log files that are maintained by the operating system. This list of logs includes the following:

**Application**  Stores messages that are generated by programs that are running on your system. For example, SQL Server 2000 might report the completion of a database backup job within the Application log.

**Security**  Contains security-related information, as is defined by your auditing settings. For example, you could see when users have logged onto the system or when particularly sensitive files have been accessed.

**System**  Contains operating system-related information and messages. Common messages might include the failure of a service to startup, or information about when the operating system was last rebooted.

**Directory Service**  Stores messages and events related to the functioning of the Active Directory. For example, details related to replication might be found here.

**DNS Server**  Contains details about the operations of the DNS service. This log is useful for troubleshooting replication or name resolution problems.

**Other log files** Various features of Windows 2000 and the applications that may run on this operating system can create additional types of logs. This allows you to view more information about other applications or services through the familiar Event Viewer tool.

Additionally, developers can easily send custom information from their programs to the Application log. Having all of this information in one place really makes it easy to analyze operating system and application messages. There are also many third-party tools and utilities that are available for analyzing log files.

Although the Event Viewer GUI does a reasonably good job of letting you find the information you need, you might want to extract information for analysis in other systems or applications. One especially useful feature of the Event Viewer is the ability to save the log file to various formats. You can access this feature by clicking Action ➤ Save As. You'll be given the option to save to various formats, including tab- and comma-delimited text files. These files can then be opened in other applications (such as Microsoft Excel) for additional data analysis.

Overall, in the real world, the Event Viewer can be your greatest ally in monitoring and troubleshooting your important servers and workstations!

In addition to providing information about the status of events related to the Active Directory, you should make it a habit to routinely visit the Event Viewer to find information about other system services and applications.

# Using the Active Directory Administrative Tools

**F**ollowing the promotion of a server to a domain controller, you will see various tools added to the Administrative Tools program group (see Figure 3.2). These include the following:

**Active Directory Domains and Trusts** This tool is used to view and change information related to the various domains in an Active Directory environment. We'll cover this tool in more detail in Chapter 5.

**Active Directory Sites and Services** This tool is used for creating and managing Active Directory sites and services to map to an organization's physical network infrastructure. We'll cover sites and services in detail in Chapter 6.

**Active Directory Users and Computers** User and computer management is fundamental for an Active Directory environment. The Active Directory Users and Computers tool allows you to set machine- and user-specific settings across the domain.

**FIGURE 3.2** Some of the many Windows 2000 administrative tools

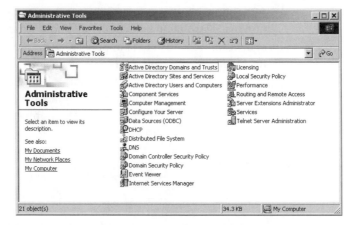

A good way to ensure that the Active Directory is functioning properly and accessible is to run the Active Directory Users and Computers tool. When you open the tool, you should see a configuration similar to that shown in Figure 3.3. Specifically, you should ensure that the name of the domain you created appears in the list. You should also click the Domain Controllers folder and ensure that the name of your local server appears in the right-hand pane. If your configuration passes these two checks, the Active Directory is present and configured.

**FIGURE 3.3**    Viewing Active Directory information

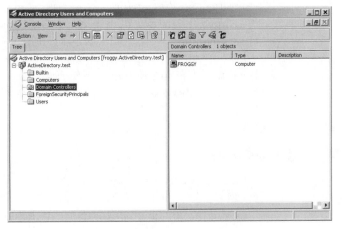

# Testing from Clients

The best test of any solution is to simply verify that it works the way you had intended in your environment. When it comes to the use of the Active Directory, a good test is to ensure that clients can view and access the various resources presented by Windows 2000 domain controllers. In this section, we'll look at several ways to verify that the Active Directory is functioning properly.

## Verifying Client Connectivity

Perhaps the most relevant way to test the Active Directory is by testing operations from clients. Using previous versions of Windows (such as Windows NT 4 or Windows 95/98), you should be able to see your server on the network. Earlier versions of Windows-based clients will recognize the NetBIOS name of the domain controller. Windows 2000 computers should also be able to see resources in the domain, and users can browse for resources using the My Network Places icon.

If you are unable to see the recently promoted server on the network, it is likely due to a network configuration error. If only one or a few clients are unable to see the machine, the problem is probably related to client-side configuration. Ensure that client computers have the appropriate TCP/IP configuration (including DNS server settings) and that they can see other computers on the network.

If, however, the new domain controller is unavailable from any of the other client computers, you should verify the proper startup of the Active Directory using the methods mentioned earlier in this chapter. If the Active Directory has been started, ensure that the DNS settings are correct. Finally, test network connectivity between the server and the clients by accessing the My Network Places icon.

## Joining a Domain

If the Active Directory has been properly configured, clients and other servers should be able to join the domain. Exercise 3.4 provides an example of how you can join another computer to the domain.

### EXERCISE 3.4

#### Joining a Computer to an Active Directory Domain

In order to complete this exercise, you must have already installed and properly configured at least one Active Directory domain controller and a DNS server that supports SRV records in your environment. In addition to the domain controller, you will need at least one other Windows 2000 computer. This computer may be an installation of Windows 2000 Professional or an installation of Windows 2000 Server that is not configured as a domain controller.

1. On the Desktop of the computer that is to be joined to the new domain, right-click the My Computer icon and click Properties. Alternatively, you can right-click My Network Places, and choose Properties. From the Advanced menu, choose Advanced Settings.

2. Select the Network Identification tab. You will see the current name of the local computer as well as information on the workgroup or domain to which it belongs.

3. Click Properties to change the settings for this computer.

4. If you want to change the name of the computer, you can make the change here. This is useful if your domain has a specific naming convention for client computers. Otherwise, continue to the next step.

**EXERCISE 3.4** *(continued)*

5. In the Member Of section, choose the Domain option. Type the name of the Active Directory domain that this computer should join. Click OK.

6. When prompted for the username and password of an account that has permissions to join computers to the domain, enter the information for an administrator of the domain. Click OK to commit the changes. If joining the domain was successful, you will see a dialog box welcoming you to the new domain.

7. You will be notified that you must reboot the computer before the changes take place. Select Yes when prompted to reboot.

Once clients are able to successfully join the domain, they should be able to view Active Directory resources using the My Network Places icon. This test validates the proper functioning of the Active Directory and ensures that you have connectivity with client computers.

# Configuring DNS Integration with Active Directory

In Chapter 2, we looked at the details of the DNS service. We also covered many ways in which the Windows 2000 DNS service can be integrated to work with the Active Directory. There are many benefits to integrating the Active Directory and DNS services.

First, replication can be configured and managed along with other Active Directory components. Second, much of the maintenance of DNS resource records can be automated through the use of dynamic updates. Additionally, you will be able to set specific security options on the various properties of the DNS service. Exercise 3.5 shows the steps that you can take to ensure that these integration features are enabled.

If you instructed the Active Directory Installation Wizard to automatically configure DNS, many of the settings mentioned in this section may already be enabled. However, you should verify the configuration and be familiar with how the options can be set manually.

---

**EXERCISE 3.5**

### Configuring DNS Integration with Active Directory

Before you begin this exercise, ensure that the local machine is configured as an Active Directory domain controller and that DNS services have been properly configured. In this exercise, we'll look at the various DNS functions that are specific to interoperability with the Active Directory.

1. Open the DNS snap-in from the Administrative Tools program group.

2. Right-click the icon for the local DNS Server, and select Properties. Click the Security tab. Notice that you can now specify which users and groups have access to modify the configuration of the DNS Server. Make any necessary changes, and click OK.

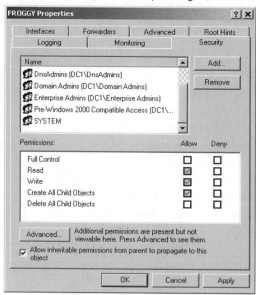

**3.** Expand the local server branch and the forward lookup zones folder.

**4.** Right-click the name of the Active Directory domain you created, and select Properties.

**5.** On the General tab, verify that the DNS server type is set to Active Directory-Integrated and that the message Data Is Stored in Active Directory is displayed. If this option is not currently selected, you can change it by clicking the Change button next to Type.

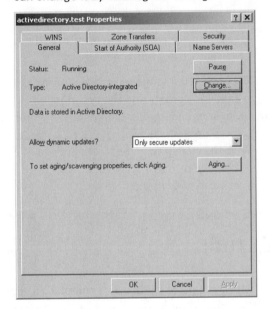

**6.** Verify that the Allow Dynamic Updates? option is set to Only Secure Updates. This will ensure that all updates to the DNS resource records database are made through authenticated Active Directory accounts and processes. The other options are Yes (to allow both secure and nonsecure dynamic updates) and No (to disallow dynamic updates).

**7.** Also, notice that you can define the security permissions at the zone level by clicking the Security tab. Make any necessary changes, and click OK.

Of course, all of the standard options related to configuring DNS are still available. For more information on configuring DNS, refer to Chapter 2.

# Summary

In this chapter, we discussed the following:

- The prerequisites for installing a Windows 2000 domain controller. Considerations include verifying the file system and verifying DNS configuration.

- Domain planning issues (such as the name for the root domain).

- How to use the Active Directory Installation Wizard to create the first domain controller in an Active Directory environment.

- How to verify the configuration of the Active Directory by performing several tests of its functionality.

We limited the scope of this chapter to examining the issues related to installing and configuring the first domain in an Active Directory environment. In later chapters, we'll look at how more complex configurations can be created and managed.

With the installation and configuration of the Active Directory out of the way, it's time to move on to looking at how to establish the organizational unit structure *within* the domain.

# Exam Essentials

**Know the prerequisites for promoting a server to a domain controller.** You should understand the tasks that you must complete before you attempt to upgrade a server to a domain controller.

**Understand the steps of the Active Directory Installation Wizard.** When you run the Active Directory Installation Wizard, you'll be presented with many different choices. You should have a good understanding of the various options provided at each step of the Wizard.

**Be familiar with the tools that are used to administer the Active Directory.** There are three main administrative tools that are installed when you promote a Windows 2000 Server to a domain controller. Be sure you know which tools to use for which types of tasks.

# Key Terms

Before you take the exam, be certain you are familiar with the following terms:

Active Directory Installation Wizard (DCPROMO)

File Allocation Table (FAT)

mixed-mode Active Directory domains

native-mode Active Directory domains

promotion

Windows New Technology File System (NTFS)

# Review Questions

1. A system administrator is trying to determine which file system to use for a server that will become an Active Directory domain controller. Her company's requirements include the following:

   - The file system must allow for file-level security.

   - The file system must make efficient use of space on large partitions.

   - The file system must allow for auditing of logons and access to sensitive files.

   Which of the following file systems meets these requirements?

   **A.** FAT

   **B.** FAT32

   **C.** HPFS

   **D.** NTFS

   **E.** None of the above

2. At any given time, a domain controller may be a member of how many domains?

   **A.** 0

   **B.** 1

   **C.** 2

   **D.** Any number of domains

**3.** In order to support Windows NT backup domain controllers in an Active Directory domain, which of the following modes must be used?

**A.** Native mode

**B.** Mixed mode

**C.** Low-security mode

**D.** Backwards-compatibility mode

**E.** None of the above

**4.** The process of converting a Windows 2000 Server computer to a domain controller is known as

**A.** Advertising

**B.** Reinstallation

**C.** Promotion

**D.** Conversion

**5.** DNS server services can be configured using which of the following tools?

**A.** The DNS administrative tool

**B.** Computer Management

**C.** Network Properties

**D.** None of the above

6. You are the systems administrator for the XYZ Products, Inc. Windows 2000-based network. You are upgrading a Windows 2000 Server computer to an Active Directory domain controller and need to decide the initial domain name. Your business has the following requirements:

   - The domain name must be accessible from the Internet.

   - The domain name must reflect your company's proper name.

   Which two of the following domain names meet these requirements?

   **A.** XYZProducts.com

   **B.** XYZProducts.domain

   **C.** Server1.XYZProducts.com

   **D.** XYZProducts.net

   **E.** All of the above

7. A Windows 2000 Server computer can function as an Active Directory domain controller and can also run which of the following services?

   **A.** DNS

   **B.** DHCP

   **C.** Routing and Remote Access

   **D.** WINS

   **E.** All of the above

8. Recently, you have received several alerts that Server1 is running low on disk space. Server1 primarily stores users' home directories. This problem has occurred several times in the past, and you want to restrict that amount of space that users can use on one of the volumes on the server. Which NTFS 5 feature can you implement to limit the amount of disk space occupied by users?

   **A.** Quotas

   **B.** Encryption

   **C.** Dynamic disks

   **D.** Remote storage

   **E.** Shared Folder Policy Objects

9. Which of the following partition or volume types provides support for RAID?

   **A.** Fixed disks

   **B.** Dynamic disks

   **C.** FAT partitions on fixed disks

   **D.** FAT partitions on dynamic disks

   **E.** Both C and D

**10.** A system administrator is trying to determine which file system to use for a server that will become a Windows 2000 Server. His company's requirements include the following:

- The file system must allow for share-level security from within Windows 2000 Server.

- The file system must make efficient use of space on large partitions.

- For testing purposes, the machine must be able to dual-boot between Windows ME and Windows 2000.

Which of the following file systems meets these requirements?

**A.** FAT

**B.** FAT32

**C.** HPFS

**D.** NTFS

**E.** E. None of the above

**11.** For security reasons, you have decided that you must convert the system partition on your Windows 2000 Server from the FAT32 file system to NTFS. Which two of the following steps must you take in order to convert the file system?

**A.** Run the command CONVERT /FS:NTFS from the command prompt.

**B.** Rerun Windows 2000 Setup and choose to convert the partition to NTFS during the reinstallation.

**C.** Boot Windows 2000 Server Setup from the installation CD-ROM and choose "Rebuild file system."

**D.** Reboot the computer.

**12.** Which of the following file system conversion operations is supported in Windows 2000?

   **A.** FAT/FAT32 to NTFS

   **B.** NTFS to FAT/FAT32

   **C.** Both of the above

   **D.** None of the above

**13.** A novice user is attempting to access a shared folder on the network. Which of the following Desktop icons can he use to view the available computers and resources on the network?

   **A.** My Computer

   **B.** My Network Places

   **C.** Internet Explorer

   **D.** Briefcase

**14.** You are attempting to join various machines on your network to an Active Directory domain. Which of the following will prevent you from adding the machine to the domain?

   **A.** The machine is running Windows 2000 Professional.

   **B.** The machine is a member of another domain.

   **C.** The machine is running Windows 2000 Server.

   **D.** The machine is a member of a workgroup.

   **E.** None of the above.

**15.** Which of the following operations is not supported by the Active Directory Installation Wizard?

   **A.** Promoting a server to a domain controller

   **B.** Demoting a domain controller to a server

   **C.** Moving servers between domains

   **D.** None of the above

**16.** Windows 2000 requires the use of which two of the following protocols in order to support the Active Directory?

  **A.** DHCP

  **B.** TCP/IP

  **C.** NetBEUI

  **D.** IPX/SPX

  **E.** LDAP

**17.** You are promoting a Windows 2000 Server computer to an Active Directory domain controller for test purposes. This server will act alone on the network and does not need to be accessible from other machines. Which of the following domain names is a valid choice for the initial Active Directory domain?

  **A.** `mycompany.com`

  **B.** `test.mycompany.com`

  **C.** `mycompany.org`

  **D.** `activedirectory.test`

  **E.** All of the above

**18.** You are promoting a Windows 2000 Server computer to an Active Directory domain controller for test purposes. The new domain controller will be added to an existing domain. During the use of the Active Directory Installation Wizard, you receive an error message that prevents the server from being promoted. Which of the following might be the cause of the problem? (Choose all that apply.)

  **A.** The system does not contain an NTFS 5 partition on which the SYSVOL directory can be created.

  **B.** You do not have a Windows 2000 DNS server on the network.

  **C.** The TCP/IP configuration on the new server is incorrect.

  **D.** The domain has reached its maximum number of domain controllers.

**19.** You are installing the first domain controller in your Active Directory environment. Where would you click next in the following exhibit in order to begin the Active Directory Installation Wizard?

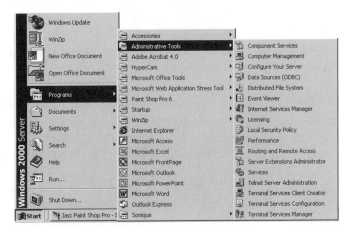

**A.** Component Services

**B.** Configure Your Server

**C.** Server Extensions Administrator

**D.** Services

# Answers to Review Questions

1. D. Only NTFS provides for this level of security and auditing functionality.

2. B. A domain controller can contain Active Directory information for only one domain.

3. B. In order to support Windows NT domain controllers, mixed-mode domains must be used.

4. C. Promotion is the process of creating a new domain controller.

5. A. The DNS administrative tool is designed to configure settings for the DNS server service. DNS zone files can also be manually edited using a standard text file editor.

6. A, D. Both of these domain names are based on the standard DNS top-level domain names and can therefore be made accessible over the Internet.

7. E. Making a server a domain controller still allows the use of all of the same functionality allowed to member and stand-alone servers.

8. A. Quotas allow systems administrators to place restrictions on the amount of disk space used on NTFS volumes.

9. B. Only dynamic disks can be configured for RAID in Windows 2000. Only NTFS is supported on dynamic disks.

10. B. FAT32 partitions are compatible with other versions of Windows (such as Windows 95/98/ME), and makes fairly efficient usage of disk space. If this machine had to be configured as a domain controller, the configuration would have required at least one NTFS partition in order to store the SYSVOL information.

11. A, D. In order to convert the system partition to NTFS, you must first use the CONVERT command-line utility and the reboot the server. During the next boot, the file system will be converted.

**12.** A. FAT/FAT32 partitions can be converted to NTFS using the CON-VERT command-line utility. NTFS partitions cannot be converted to FAT/FAT32 partitions without reformatting and re-creating the partition.

**13.** B. My Network Places is used to view other computers and Active Directory resources located on the network.

**14.** E. All of the above configurations can be joined to a domain.

**15.** C. The only way to move a domain controller between domains is to demote it from its current domain and then promote it into another domain.

**16.** B, E. The use of LDAP and TCP/IP is required to support the Active Directory.

**17.** E. All of the domain names listed may be used. Although it is recommended, a standard domain name is not required for installing the Active Directory.

**18.** A, C. The SYSVOL directory must be created on an NTFS 5 partition. If such a partition is not available, you will not be able to promote the server to a domain controller. An error in the network configuration might prevent the server from connecting to another domain controller in the environment.

**19.** B. You would select the Configure Your Server administrative tool in order to begin the Active Directory Installation Wizard.

# Chapter

# 4

# Creating and Managing Organizational Units

## MICROSOFT EXAM OBJECTIVES COVERED IN THIS CHAPTER:

✓ **Install, configure, and troubleshoot the components of Active Directory.**

- Install Active Directory.
- Create sites.
- Create subnets.
- Create site links.
- Create site link bridges.
- Create connection objects.
- Create global catalog servers.
- Move server objects between sites.
- Transfer operations master roles.
- Verify Active Directory installation.
- Implement an organizational unit (OU) structure.

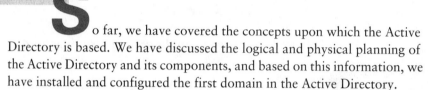

**S**o far, we have covered the concepts upon which the Active Directory is based. We have discussed the logical and physical planning of the Active Directory and its components, and based on this information, we have installed and configured the first domain in the Active Directory.

In order to perform the exercises included in this chapter, you must have already installed the Active Directory. If you are still unsure about the steps and concepts associated with implementing an Active Directory domain, you should review the previous chapters before moving on. If you are working in a real-world environment, you've probably already seen how all of the planning steps mentioned in earlier chapters come into play.

In this chapter, we will begin to look at the structure of the various components *within* a domain. Specifically, we'll see how an organization's business structure can be mirrored within the Active Directory through the use of *organizational units (OUs)*.

Because the concepts related to OUs are quite simple, some systems administrators may underestimate their importance. Make no mistake—one of the fundamental components of a successful Active Directory installation is the proper design and deployment of OUs. With that in mind, let's look at the various steps required to plan for the use of OUs then, based on this information, walk through the steps required to implement and modify an OU structure.

This chapter covers material related to the implementation of an OU structure for the "Install, configure, and troubleshoot the components of Active Directory" objective. See Chapter 3, "Installing and Configuring the Active Directory," for material on the Active Directory and its installation; Chapter 5, "Installing and Managing Trees and Forests," for material on creating Global Catalog servers and transferring operations master roles; and Chapter 6, "Configuring Sites and Managing Replication," for coverage on creating sites, subnets, site links, site link bridges, and connection objects, as well as on moving server objects between sites.

# An Overview of OUs

**B**efore we begin to look at how OUs can be used within an Active Directory domain, we should first take a look at what OUs are and how they can be used to organize an Active Directory structure.

First and foremost, the purpose of OUs is to logically group Active Directory objects, just as their name implies. They serve as containers within which other Active Directory objects can be created. OUs do not form part of the DNS namespace. They are used solely to create organization within a domain.

OUs can contain the following types of Active Directory objects:

**User Objects**   User objects are the fundamental security principals used in an Active Directory environment. A User object includes a username, a password, group membership information, and many customizable fields that can be used to describe the user (e.g., fields for a street address, a telephone number, and other contact information).

**Group Objects**   Group objects are logical collections of users that are used primarily for assigning security permissions to resources. When managing users, the recommended practice is to place users into groups and then assign permissions to the group. This allows for flexible management and prevents systems administrators from having to set permissions for individual users.

**Computer Objects**   Computer objects represent workstations that are part of the Active Directory domain. Every computer within a domain shares the same security database, including user and group information. Computer objects are useful for managing security permissions and enforcing *Group Policy* restrictions.

**Shared Folders**   One of the fundamental functions of servers is to make resources available to users. Often, shared folders are used to give logical names to specific collections of files. For example, systems administrators might create shared folders for common applications, user data, and shared public files. Shared folders can be created and managed within the Active Directory.

**Other Organizational Units**   Perhaps the most useful feature of OUs is that they can contain *other* OUs. This allows systems administrators to hierarchically group resources and other objects in accordance with business practices. The OU structure is extremely flexible and, as we will see later in this chapter, can easily be rearranged to reflect business reorganizations.

Each type of object has its own purpose within the organization of Active Directory domains. We'll look at the specifics of User, Computer, Group, and Shared Folder objects in later chapters. For now, let's focus on the purpose and benefits of using OUs.

## The Purpose of OUs

The main purpose of OUs is to organize the objects within the Active Directory. Before diving into the details of OUs, however, it is very important to understand how OUs, users, and groups interact. Perhaps the most important concept to understand is that OUs are simply containers that are used for logically grouping various objects. They are not, however, groups in the classical sense. That is, they do not contain users, groups, or computers and are not used per se for assigning security permissions. Another way of stating this is that the User accounts, Computer accounts, and Group accounts that are contained in OUs are considered *security principals* while OUs themselves are not.

It is important to understand that OUs do not take the place of standard user and group permissions (a topic we'll cover in Chapter 8, "Active Directory Security"). A good general practice is to assign users to groups and then place the groups within OUs. This enhances the benefits of setting security permissions and of using the OU hierarchy for making settings. Figure 4.1 illustrates this concept.

**FIGURE 4.1** Using Users, Groups, and OUs

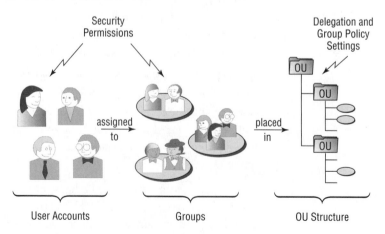

An organizational unit contains objects only from within the domain in which it resides. As we'll see later in this chapter, the OU is the finest level of granularity used for setting Group Policies and other administrative settings.

## Benefits of OUs

There are many benefits to using OUs throughout your network environment:

- OUs are the smallest unit to which you can assign permissions.
- The OU structure can be easily changed, and OU structure is more flexible than domain structure.
- The OU structure can support many different levels of hierarchy.
- OU settings can be inherited by child objects.
- You can set Group Policy settings on OUs.
- Administration of OUs and the objects within them can be easily delegated to the appropriate users and groups.

Now that we have a good idea of why you should use OUs, let's look at some general practices for planning the OU structure.

# Planning the OU Structure

One of the key benefits of the Active Directory is the way in which it can bring organization to complex network environments. Before you can begin to implement OUs in various configurations, you must plan a structure that is compatible with business and technical needs. In this section, we'll look at several factors to consider when planning for the structure of OUs.

## Logical Grouping of Resources

The fundamental purpose of using OUs is to hierarchically group resources that exist within the Active Directory. Fortunately, hierarchical groups are quite intuitive and widely used in most businesses. For example, a typical manufacturing business might divide its various operations into different departments like the ones listed below:

- Sales
- Marketing

- Engineering

- Research and Development

- Support

- Information Technology (IT)

Each of these departments usually has its own goals and missions. In order to make the business competitive, individuals within each of the departments will be assigned to various roles. Some types of roles might include the following:

- Managers

- Clerical Staff

- Technical Staff

- Planners

Each of these roles usually entails specific job responsibilities. For example, managers should be responsible for providing direction to general staff members. Note that the very nature of these roles suggests that employees may fill many different positions. That is, you might be a manager in one department and a member of the technical staff in another. In the modern workplace, such a situation is quite common.

So, how does all of this information help in planning for the use of OUs? First and foremost, the structure of OUs within a given network environment should map well to the needs of the business. This includes the political and logical structure of the organization, as well as its technical needs. Figure 4.2 provides an example of how a business organization might be mapped to the OU structure within an Active Directory domain.

What's in a name? When it comes to designing the Active Directory, the answer is a lot! When naming OUs for your organization, you should keep several considerations and limitations in mind:

**Keep it simple.**   The purpose of OUs is to make administration and usage of resources simple. Therefore, it's always a good idea to keep the names of your objects simple and descriptive. Sometimes, finding a balance between these two goals can be a challenge. For example, although a printer name like "The LaserJet located near Bob's Cube" might seem descriptive, it is certainly difficult to type. Imagine the naming changes that might be required if Bob moves (or leaves the company)!

**FIGURE 4.2** Mapping a business organization to an OU structure

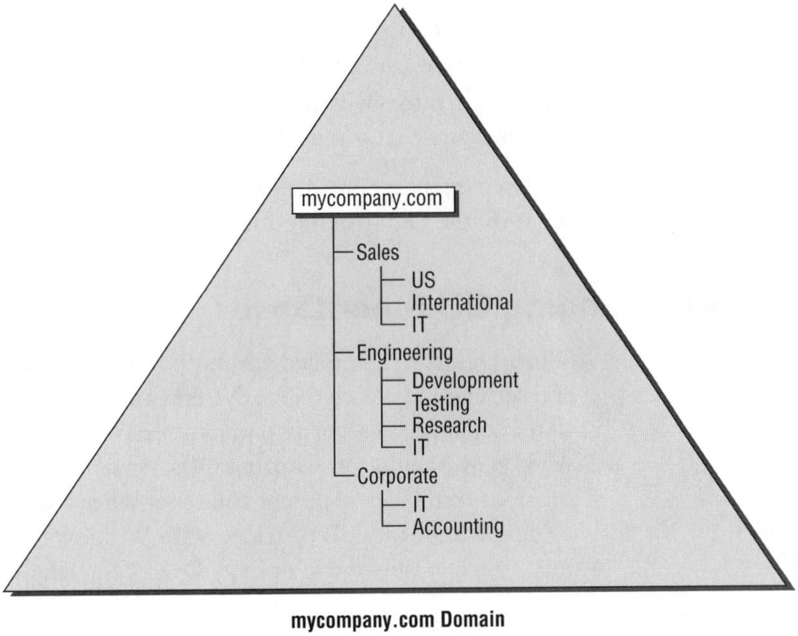

**mycompany.com Domain**

**Pay attention to limitations.** The maximum length for the name of an OU is 65 characters. In most cases, this should be adequate for describing OUs. Remember that the name of an OU object does not have to uniquely describe it because the OU will generally be referenced as part of the overall hierarchy. For example, you can choose to create an IT OU within two different parent OUs. Even though the OUs have the same name, users and administrators will be able to distinguish them based on their complete path name.

**Pay attention to the hierarchical consistency.** The fundamental basis of an OU structure is adherence to a hierarchy. From a design standpoint, this means that you cannot have two OUs with the same name at the same level. However, you can have OUs with the same name at different levels. For example, we could create a Corporate OU within both the North America OU and the South America OU. This is because the fully qualified name includes information about the hierarchy. When an administrator tries to access resources in the Corporate OU, they must specify *which* Corporate OU they mean.

If, for example, you create a North America OU, the Canada OU should logically fit under it. If you decide that you want to separate them into completely different containers, then other names might be more appropriate. For example, North America could be changed to U.S. Users and administrators will depend on the hierarchy of OUs within the domain, so make sure that it remains logically consistent.

Based on these considerations, you should have a good idea of how to best organize the OU structure for your domain.

## Understanding OU Inheritance

When OUs are rearranged within the structure of the Active Directory, several settings may be changed. Systems administrators must pay careful attention to changes in security permissions and other configuration options when moving and reorganizing OUs. By default, OUs will inherit the permissions of their new parent container when they are moved. Note that by using the built-in tools provided with Windows 2000 and the Active Directory, you can only move or copy OUs within the same domain.

If you need to move an entire OU structure between domains, you can use the MOVETREE command available in the Windows 2000 Resource Kit.

## Delegation of Administrative Control

We already mentioned that OUs are the smallest component within a domain to which permissions and Group Policy can be assigned. Now, let's look specifically at how administrative control is set on OUs.

The idea of *delegation* involves a higher security authority that can give permissions to another. As a real-world example, assume that you are the director of IT for a large organization. Instead of doing all of the work yourself (which would result in a very long work day!), you would probably assign roles and responsibilities to other individuals. For example, you might make one systems administrator responsible for all operations within the Sales domain and another responsible for the Engineering domain. Similarly, you could assign the permissions for managing all printers and print queues within the organization to one individual while allowing another to manage all security permissions for users and groups.

In this way, the various roles and responsibilities of the IT staff can be distributed throughout the organization. Businesses generally have a division of labor to handle all of the tasks involved in keeping the company's networks humming along. Network operating systems, however, often make it difficult to assign just the right permissions. Sometimes, the complexity is necessary to ensure that only the right permissions are assigned. A good general rule of thumb is to provide users and administrators the minimum permissions they require to do their jobs. This ensures that accidental, malicious, and otherwise unwanted changes do not occur.

In the world of the Active Directory, the process of delegation is used to define the permissions for administrators of OUs. When considering implementing delegation, there are two main concerns to keep in mind:

**Parent-Child Relationships**   The OU hierarchy you create will be very important when considering the maintainability of security permissions. As we've already mentioned, OUs can exist in a parent-child relationship. When it comes to the delegation of permissions, this is extremely important. You can choose to allow child containers to automatically inherit the permissions set on parent containers. For example, if the North America division of your organization contains 12 other OUs, you could delegate permissions to all of them by placing security permissions on the North America division. This feature can greatly ease administration, especially in larger organizations, but it is also a reminder of the importance of properly planning the OU structure within a domain.

 You can only delegate control at the OU level and not at the object level within the OU.

**Inheritance Settings**   Now that we've seen how parent-child relationships can be useful for administration, we should consider the actual process of inheriting permissions. Logically, the process is known as *inheritance*. When permissions are set on a parent container, all of the child objects are configured to inherit the same permissions. This behavior can be overridden, however, if business rules do not lend themselves well to inheritance.

## Application of Group Policy

One of the strengths of Windows operating systems is that they offer users a great deal of power and flexibility. From installing new software to adding device drivers, users can be given the ability to make many changes to their workstation configurations. This level of flexibility is also a potential problem. Inexperienced users might inadvertently change settings, causing problems that can require many hours to fix.

In many cases (and especially in business environments), users will only require a subset of the complete functionality provided by the operating system. In the past, however, the difficulty associated with implementing and managing security and policy settings has led to lax security policies. Some of the reasons for this are technical—it can be very tedious and difficult to implement and manage security restrictions. Other problems have been political—users and management might feel that they should have full permissions on their local machines, despite the potential problems this might cause.

One of the major design goals for the Windows 2000 platform (and specifically, the Active Directory) was manageability. Although the broad range of features and functionality provided by the operating system can be helpful, being able to lock down types of functionality is very important.

That's where the idea of Group Policies comes in. Simply defined, Group Policies are collections of permissions that can be applied to objects within the Active Directory. Specifically, Group Policy settings are assigned at the Site, Domain, and OU level and can apply to User accounts, Computer accounts, and groups. Examples of settings that a systems administrator can make using Group Policies include the following:

- Restricting access to the Start menu

- Disallowing the use of the Control Panel

- Limiting choices for display and Desktop settings

We'll further cover the technical issues related to Group Policies in Chapter 10, "Managing Group Policy." In the following section, let's focus on how to plan OUs for the efficient use of policy settings.

# Creating OUs

**N**ow that we have looked at several different ways in which OUs can be used to bring organization to the objects within the Active Directory, it's time to look at how OUs can be created and managed. In this section, we'll look at ways to create OUs.

| ***Microsoft*** ✓ ***Exam*** ***Objective*** | **Install, configure, and troubleshoot the components of Active Directory.**<br><br>• Implement an organizational unit (OU) structure. |
| --- | --- |

Through the use of the Active Directory Users and Computers administrative tool, you can quickly and easily add, move, and change OUs. This graphical tool makes it easy to visualize and create the various levels of hierarchy required within an organization.

Figure 4.3 shows a geographically-based OU structure that might be used by a multinational company. Note that the organization is based in North America and has a corporate office located there. In general, all of the other offices are much smaller than those located in North America.

Also, it's important to note that this OU structure could have been designed in several different ways. For example, we could have chosen to group all of the offices located in the United States within a U.S. OU. However, due to the size of the offices, we choose to place these objects at the same level as the Canada and Mexico OUs. This prevents an unnecessarily deep OU hierarchy while still logically grouping the offices.

Exercise 4.1 walks you through the process of creating several OUs for a multinational business. We strongly recommend that you carry out this exercise since we'll be using this OU structure in later exercises within this chapter.

Creating OUs and other Active Directory objects can be a tedious process, especially for large organizations. A good way to speed up the process is to use keyboard shortcuts for creating objects instead of using the mouse. If your keyboard has a right-click key, be sure to use it. Also, learn the shortcuts for the context-sensitive menus. For example, the *n* key automatically chooses the *New* selection and the *o* key will specify that you want to create an OU.

**FIGURE 4.3** A geographically-based OU structure

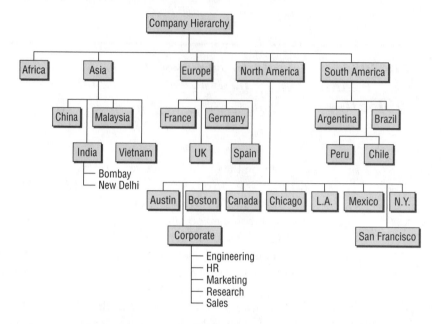

---

**Creating an OU Structure**

In this exercise, we'll create an OU structure for a multinational company. In order to complete this exercise, you must have first installed and configured at least one domain and have permissions to administer the domain.

**1.** Open the Active Directory Users and Computers administrative tool.

**2.** Right-click the name of the local domain, and choose New ➤ Organizational Unit. You will see the dialog box shown in the following graphic. Notice that this box shows you the current context within which the OU will be created. In this case, we're creating a top-level OU, so the full path is simply the name of the domain.

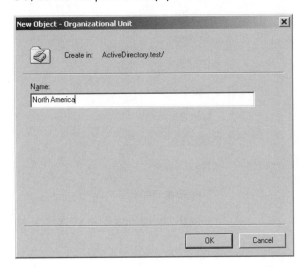

**3.** Type **North America** for the name of the first OU. Click OK to create this object.

**4.** Now, create the following top-level OUs by right-clicking the name of the domain and choosing New ➤ Organizational Unit:

Africa

Asia

Europe

South America

**5.** Note that the order in which OUs are created is not important. In this exercise, we are simply using a method that emphasizes the hierarchical relationship.

**EXERCISE 4.1** *(continued)*

6. Now, create the following second-level OUs within the North America OU by right-clicking the North America OU and selecting New ➤ Organizational Unit:

   Austin

   Boston

   Canada

   Chicago

   Corporate

   Los Angeles

   Mexico

   New York

   San Francisco

7. Create the following OUs under the Asia OU:

   China

   India

   Malaysia

   Vietnam

8. Create the following OUs under the Europe OU:

   France

   Germany

   Spain

   UK

9. Create the following OUs under the South America OU:

   Argentina

   Brazil

   Chile

   Peru

**EXERCISE 4.1** *(continued)*

10. Finally, it's time to create some third-level OUs. Right-click the India OU within the Asia OU, and select New ➤ Organizational Unit. Create the following OUs within this container:

    Bombay

    New Delhi

11. Within the North America Corporate OU, create the following OUs:

    Engineering

    HR

    Marketing

    Research

    Sales

12. When you have completed the creation of the OUs, you should have a structure that looks similar to the one in the following graphic.

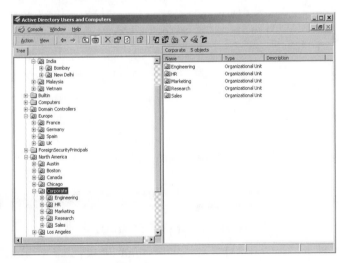

Once you have created a logical OU structure, it's time to look at the various operations that are required to manage OUs.

# Managing OUs

**M**anaging network environments would be challenging enough if things rarely changed. However, in the real world, business units, departments, and employee roles change frequently. As business and technical needs change, so should the structure of the Active Directory.

Fortunately, changing the structure of OUs within a domain is a relatively simple process. In this section, we'll look at ways to delegate control of OUs and make other changes.

## Moving, Deleting, and Renaming OUs

When you delete an OU, the various objects contained within it are deleted along with the OU itself. There are several reasons that you might need to delete OUs. First, changes in the business structure (such as a consolidation of departments) may make a specific OU obsolete. Or, you might choose to make changes to better reflect the changing needs of a business.

The process of moving OUs is an extremely simple one. Exercise 4.2 shows how you can easily change and reorganize OUs to reflect changes in the business organization. The specific scenario covered in this exercise includes the following changes:

- The Research and Engineering departments have been combined together to form a department known as Research and Development (RD).

- The Sales department has been moved from the Corporate office to the New York office.

- The Marketing department has been moved from the Corporate office to the Chicago office.

**EXERCISE 4.2**

### Modifying OU Structure

This exercise assumes that you have already completed the steps in the previous exercise within this chapter. In this exercise, we will make changes to the OUs as described in the text.

**1.** Open the Active Directory Users and Computers administrative tool.

2. To delete an OU, right-click the Engineering OU (located within North America ➤ Corporate) and click Delete. When prompted for confirmation, click Yes. Note that if this OU contained objects, all of the objects within the OU would have been automatically deleted as well.

3. Now, to rename an OU, right-click the Research OU and select Rename. Type **RD** to change the name of the OU and press Enter.

4. To move the Sales OU, right-click the Sales OU and select Move. In the Move dialog box, expand the North America branch and click the New York OU. Click OK to move the OU.

5. To move the Marketing OU, right-click the Marketing OU and select Move. In the Move dialog box, expand the North America branch and click the Chicago OU. Click OK to move the OU.

**EXERCISE 4.2** *(continued)*

6. When you are finished, you should see an OU structure similar to the one shown in the following screen shot. Close the Active Directory Users and Computers administrative tool.

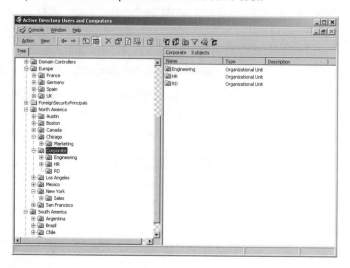

## Administering Properties of OUs

Although OUs are primarily created for the purpose of organization within the Active Directory environment, they have several settings that can be modified. To modify the properties of an OU using the Active Directory Users and Computers administrative tool, you can right-click the name of any OU and select Properties. In the example shown in Figure 4.4, the Corporate Properties dialog box will appear, and you will then see the options on the General tab.

In any organization, it's useful to know who is responsible for the management of an OU. This information can be set on the Managed By tab (see Figure 4.5). The information specified on this tab is very convenient because it will automatically pull the contact information from a user record. You should consider always having a contact for each OU within your organization so that users and other systems administrators will know whom to contact should the need for any changes arise.

**FIGURE 4.4**  Viewing OU general properties

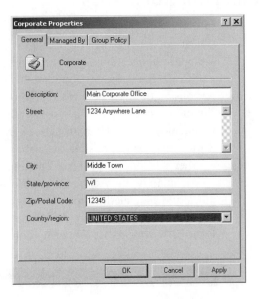

Additionally, you can set Group Policy settings for the OU on the Group Policy tab. We'll cover this topic later in Chapter 10, "Managing Group Policy." We'll also look at several ways to manage all types of objects within the Active Directory in Chapter 7, "Administering the Active Directory."

**FIGURE 4.5**  Setting OU Managed By properties

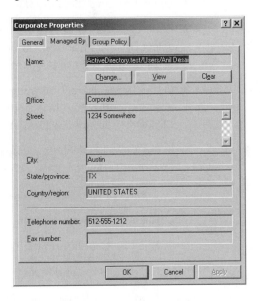

# Delegating Control of OUs

In simple environments, one or a few systems administrators may be responsible for managing all of the settings within the Active Directory. For example, a single systems administrator could be responsible for managing all users within all OUs in the environment. In larger organizations, however, roles and responsibilities may be divided among many different individuals. A typical situation is one in which a systems administrator is responsible for objects within only a few OUs in an Active Directory domain. Or, one systems administrator may be responsible for managing User and Group objects while another is responsible for managing file and print services.

Fortunately, the Active Directory Users and Computers tool provides a quick and easy method for ensuring that specific users receive only the permissions that they require. In Exercise 4.3, we will use the *Delegation of Control Wizard* to assign permissions to individuals.

---

**EXERCISE 4.3**

### Using the Delegation of Control Wizard

In this exercise, we will use the Delegation of Control Wizard to assign permissions to specific users within the Active Directory. In order to successfully complete these steps, you must first have created the objects in the previous exercises of this chapter.

1. Open the Active Directory Users and Computers administrative tool.

2. Right-click the Corporate OU (within the North America OU) and select Delegate Control. This will start the Delegation of Control Wizard. Click Next to begin making security settings.

3. In the Select Users, Computers, or Groups dialog box, select the account for the Built-In Account Operators Group and click Add. Click OK to accept this item, then click Next to continue.

4. In the Tasks to Delegate window, select Delegate the Following Common Tasks and place a check mark next to the following items:

    Create, Delete, and Manage User Accounts

    Reset Passwords on User Accounts

    Read All User Information

    Create, Delete, and Manage Groups

    Modify the Membership of a Group

**5.** Click Next to continue.

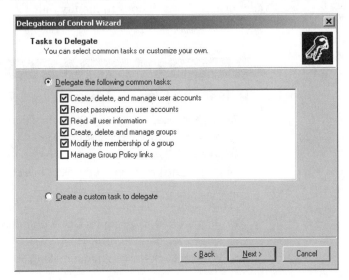

**6.** The Completing the Delegation of Control Wizard dialog box will provide a summary of the operations you have selected. To implement the changes, click Finish.

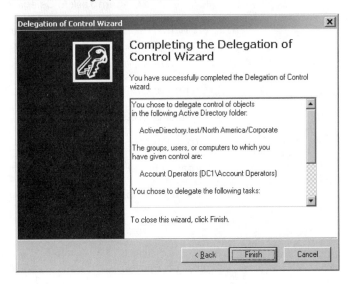

Although the common tasks available through the Wizard will be sufficient for many delegation operations, there might be cases in which you want more control. For example, you might want to give particular systems administrator permissions to modify only Computer objects. Exercise 4.4 uses the Delegation of Control Wizard to assign more granular permissions.

**EXERCISE 4.4**

### Delegating Custom Tasks

In this exercise, we will use the Delegation of Control Wizard to delegate custom tasks to specific users within the Active Directory. In order to successfully complete these steps, you must first have created the objects in the previous exercises of this chapter.

1. Open the Active Directory Users and Computers administrative tool.

2. Right-click the Corporate OU (within the North America OU) and select Delegate Control. This will start the Delegation of Control Wizard. Click Next to begin making security settings.

3. In the Select Users, Computers, or Groups dialog box, select the account for the Built-In Server Operators Group and click Add. Click OK to accept this item, then click Next to continue.

4. Select Create a Custom Task to Delegate, and click Next to continue.

5. In the Active Directory Object Type dialog box, choose Only the Following Objects in the Folder, and place a check mark next to the following items:

    Computer Objects

    Contact Objects

    Group Objects

    Organizational Unit Objects

    Printer Objects

    User Objects

**6.** Click Next to continue.

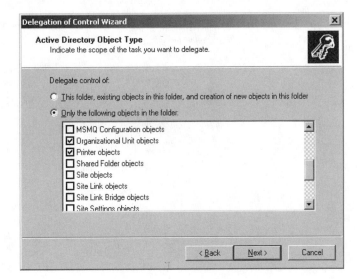

**7.** In the Permissions dialog box, place a check mark next to only the General option. Note that if the various objects within your Active Directory schema had property-specific settings, you would see those options here. Place a check mark next to the following items:

Create All Child Objects

Read All Properties

Write All Properties

8. Click Next to continue.

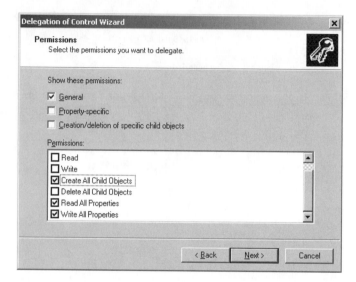

9. This will give the members of the Server Operators group the ability to create new objects within the Corporate OU and the permissions to read and write all properties for these objects. Click Next to continue.

10. The Completing the Delegation of Control Wizard dialog box will provide a summary of the operations you have selected. To implement the changes, click Finish.

In addition to the basic types of security options we set in the exercise, you can create custom tasks and place permissions on specific types of objects within a container. We'll cover security permissions in greater detail in Chapter 8.

### 🌐 Real World Scenario

## Delegation: Who's Responsible for What?

You're the IT Director for a large, multinational organization. You've been with the company for quite a while—since the environment had only a handful of offices and a few network and systems administrators. But, times have changed. Systems administrators must now coordinate the efforts of hundreds of IT staffers in fourteen countries.

When the environment was run under a Windows NT 4.0 domain environment, the network was setup with many domains. For security, performance, and distribution of administration, the computing resources in each major office were placed in their own domain. You have recently decided to move to the Active Directory and have decided to consolidate the numerous Windows NT domains into a single Active Directory domain. However, securely administrating a distributed environment is still an important concern. So, the challenge is in determining how to coordinate the efforts of many different systems administrators.

Fortunately, through the proper use of OUs and delegation, you are given a lot of flexibility in determining how administration will be handled. There are several ways in which this may be structured. First, if you choose to create OUs based on geographic business structure, you could delegate control of these OUs based on the job functions of various systems administrators. For example, one user account may be used for administering the "Europe" OU. Within the Europe OU, this systems administrator could delegate control of offices represented by the "Paris" and "London" OUs. Within these OUs, you could further break down the administrative responsibilities for printer queue operators and security administrators.

Alternatively, the OU structure may create a functional representation of the business. For example, the "Engineering" OU might contain other OUs that are based on office locations such as "New York" and "Paris". A systems administrator of the Engineering domain could delegate permissions based on geography or job functions to the lower OUs.

As with many features of the Active Directory, which model you choose will be based on specific business requirements. However, rest assured that Active Directory OUs are quite flexible and offer many options.

# Troubleshooting OUs

In general, the use of OUs will be a straightforward and relatively painless process. With adequate planning, you'll be able to implement an intuitive and useful structure for OU objects.

The most common problems with OU configuration are related to the OU structure. When troubleshooting OUs, you should pay careful attention to the following factors:

**Inheritance** By default, Group Policy and other settings are transferred automatically from parent OUs to child OUs and objects. This is an important point to consider. Even if a specific OU is not given a set of permissions, objects within that OU might still get them from parent objects.

**Delegation of Administration** If the wrong User accounts or groups are allowed to perform specific tasks on OUs, you might be violating your company's security policy. Be sure to verify the delegations you have made at each OU level.

**Organizational Issues** Sometimes, business practices may not easily map to the structure of the Active Directory. A few misplaced OUs, User accounts, Computer accounts, or groups can make administration difficult or inaccurate. In many cases, it might be beneficial to rearrange the OU structure to accommodate any changes in the business organization. In others, it might make more sense to change business processes.

If you make it a practice to regularly consider each of these issues when troubleshooting problems with OUs, you will be much less likely to make errors in the Active Directory configuration.

# Summary

In this chapter, we covered the following:

- The purpose, function, and benefits of organizational units (OUs)

- Factors to consider when designing an OU structure. Based on this information, we created a sample OU structure for a geographically organized business.

- How to reorganize OUs, which can be a simple and painless process.

- How to use the Delegation of Control Wizard to assign administrative permissions to the objects within an OU.

Through the use of OUs, organizations can quickly and easily group their resources in a hierarchical manner that is logical and consistent with the company's own organization. As we'll see in later chapters, the OUs offer an excellent way to manage Group Policy and administrative functions.

# Exam Essentials

**Understand the purpose of Organizational Units (OUs).**   OUs are used to create a hierarchical, logical organization for objects within an Active Directory domain.

**Know the types of objects that can reside within OUs.**   OUs can contain Active Directory Users, Computers, Shared Folders, and other objects.

**Understand the Delegation of Control Wizard.**   The Delegation of Control Wizard is used to assign specific permissions at the level of OUs.

**Understand the concept of inheritance.**   By default, child OUs will inherit permissions and Group Policy assignments set for parent OUs. However, these settings can be overridden for more granular control of security.

# Key Terms

Before you take the exam, be certain you are familiar with the following terms:

| | |
|---|---|
| delegation | inheritance |
| Delegation of Control Wizard | organizational units (OUs) |
| Group Policy | security principals |

# Review Questions

1. You are a domain administrator for a large domain. Recently, you have been asked to make changes to some of the permissions related to OUs within the domain. In order to further restrict security for the "Texas" OU, you remove some permissions at that level. Later, a junior systems administrator mentions that she is no longer able to make changes to objects within the "Austin" OU (which is located within the Texas OU). Assuming no other changes have been made to Active Directory permissions, which of the following characteristics of OUs might have caused the change in permissions?

   **A.** Inheritance

   **B.** Group Policy

   **C.** Delegation

   **D.** None of the above

2. Which of the following is not a true characteristic of OUs?

   **A.** OUs can contain other Active Directory objects.

   **B.** OUs are security principals.

   **C.** OUs can contain other OUs.

   **D.** OUs can be arranged in a hierarchy.

3. A systems administrator is attempting to rename an OU within a domain for which she is the administrator. Which of the following administrative tools should she use to manage OUs?

   **A.** Active Directory Domains and Trusts

   **B.** Active Directory Users and Computers

   **C.** Active Directory Sites and Services

   **D.** Computer Management

4. Your organization is currently planning a migration from a Windows NT 4 environment that consists of several domains to an Active Directory environment. Your staff consists of 25 systems administrators who are responsible for managing one or more domains. The organization is finalizing a merger with another company.

   John, a technical planner, has recently provided you with a preliminary plan to migrate your environment to several Active Directory domains. He has cited security and administration as major justifications for this plan. Jane, a consultant, has recommended that the Windows NT 4 domains be consolidated into a single Active Directory domain. Which two of the following statements provide a valid justification to support Jane's proposal?

   **A.** In general, OU structure is more flexible than domain structure.

   **B.** In general, domain structure is more flexible than OU structure.

   **C.** It is possible to create a distributed systems administration structure for OUs through the use of delegation.

   **D.** The use of OUs within a single domain can greatly increase the security of the overall environment.

5. Which of the following Active Directory components plays a role in the DNS namespace?

   **A.** Domains

   **B.** Organizational units (OUs)

   **C.** Groups

   **D.** Users

   **E.** All of the above

6. Which of the following operations cannot be performed in a single operation through the use of the Active Directory Users and Computers tool?

   **A.** Moving an OU

   **B.** Renaming an OU

   **C.** Deleting an OU

   **D.** Copying an OU

7. Your organization has recently undergone several changes. As the primary network administrator, you are responsible for reflecting these changes within the Active Directory OU structure. Which two of the following are good reasons for changing the OU structure?

   **A.** A user leaves the company.

   **B.** An IT administrator leaves the company.

   **C.** Business units within the organization are reorganized.

   **D.** The company modifies its line-of-business and eliminates several departments.

   **E.** None of the above.

8. Miguel is a junior-level systems administrator and has basic knowledge about working with the Active Directory. As his supervisor, you have asked Miguel to make several security-related changes to OUs within the company's Active Directory domain. You instruct Miguel to use the basic functionality provided in the Delegation of Control Wizard. Which of the following operations are represented as common tasks within the Delegation of Control Wizard?

   **A.** Reset passwords on user accounts.

   **B.** Manage Group Policy links.

   **C.** Modify the membership of a group.

   **D.** Create, delete, and manage groups.

   **E.** All of the above.

9. Which of the following statements is *false* regarding the naming of OUs (Choose all that apply)?

    **A.** No two OUs within the same domain can have the same name.

    **B.** No two domains can contain OUs with the same name.

    **C.** OUs can contain other OUs.

    **D.** A domain can have multiple top-level OUs.

10. Which of the following operations can be used to move OUs within an Active Directory domain?

    **A.** Dragging and dropping the OU to a new location

    **B.** Right-clicking the OU, and selecting Move

    **C.** Renaming the OU with the fully qualified path to the new location

    **D.** None of the above (OUs cannot be moved)

11. You are creating new OUs within your organization's Active Directory domain. Your manager has provided a list of several department names for which she wants you to create OUs. Which of the following is not a valid name for an OU?

    **A.** Department13

    **B.** Engineering Resources

    **C.** Internal Technical Support for Client Services and Professional Consulting Business Units

    **D.** Temporary

12. The process of inheritance is described by which of the following behaviors?

    **A.** Child OUs may inherit security and other settings from parent OUs.

    **B.** OUs can be copied across domains.

    **C.** OUs can be copied across forests.

    **D.** OUs can be created in Windows NT domains.

    **E.** None of the above.

**13.** You are the primary systems administrator for a large Active Directory domain. Recently, you have hired another systems administrator to offload some of your responsibilities. This systems administrator will be responsible for handling help desk calls and for basic user account management. You want to allow the new employee to have permissions to reset passwords for all users within a specific OU. However, for security, reasons, it's important that the user is not able to make permissions changes for objects within other OUs in the domain. Which of the following is the best way to do this?

**A.** Create a special administration account within the OU and grant it full permissions for all objects within the Active Directory.

**B.** Move the user's login account into the OU that he or she is to administer.

**C.** Move the user's login account to an OU that contains the OU (that is, the parent OU of the one that he or she is to administer).

**D.** Use the Delegation of Control Wizard to assign the necessary permissions on the OU that he or she is to administer.

**E.** None of the above meet the requirements

**14.** You have been hired as a consultant to assist in the design of an organization's Active Directory environment. Specifically, you are instructed to focus on the OU structure (others will be planning for technical issues). You begin by preparing a list of information that you need to create the OU structure for a single domain. Which of the following pieces of information is not vital to your OU design?

**A.** Physical network topology

**B.** Business organizational requirements

**C.** System administration requirements

**D.** Security requirements

**E.** None of the above

**15.** Which of the following operations is allowed when using the Active Directory Users and Computers tool?

   **A.** Moving OUs between domains

   **B.** Copying OUs between domains

   **C.** Merging OUs between domains

   **D.** None of the above

**16.** You want to allow the Super Users group to create and edit new objects within the Corporate OU. Using the Delegation of Control Wizard, you choose the Super Users group, and arrive at the screen shown below. Where would you click in order to add the ability to create and edit new objects in the Corporate OU?

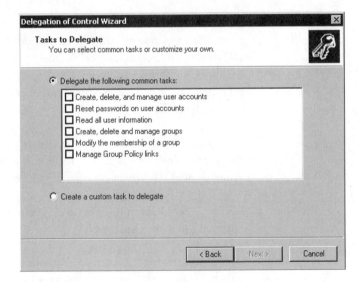

   **A.** Create, Delete, and Manage User Accounts

   **B.** Create, Delete, and Manage Groups

   **C.** Manage Group Policy Links

   **D.** Create a Custom Task to Delegate

# Answers to Review Questions

1. A. Inheritance is the process by which permissions placed on parent OUs affect child OUs. In this example, the permissions change for the higher-level OU ("Texas") automatically caused a change in permissions for the lower-level OU ("Austin").

2. B. While the objects within OUs may be security principals, resource permissions are not assigned to OUs themselves.

3. B. The graphical interface of the Active Directory Users and Computers tool allows systems administrators to easily create, manage, and organize OUs.

4. A, C. OUs can be easily moved and renamed without requiring the promotion of domain controllers and network changes. This makes OU structure much more flexible and a good choice since the company may soon undergo a merger. Since security administration is important, delegation can be used to control administrative permissions at the OU-level.

5. A. Domains form the basis of the DNS namespace in an Active Directory environment. OUs do not form part of the DNS namespace, as domains do. OUs are used primarily for organization *within* a domain.

6. D. The Active Directory Users and Computers tool does not allow for automatically copying an OU.

7. C, D. Business reorganization is a good reason to change the OU structure. The other types of changes listed can be managed easily through the use of the Active Directory Users and Computers tool and the Delegation of Control Wizard rather than through modifications to the OU structure, a more drastic measure than would be necessary.

8. E. All of the options listed are common tasks presented in the Delegation of Control Wizard.

9. A, B. OU naming is hierarchical and must be unique only within the same parent container. Two or more OUs within a domain may have the same name, as long as they are not located within the same parent OU.

**10.** B. The Active Directory Users and Computers tool allows you to move OUs by right-clicking the OU and selecting Move.

**11.** C. The name of an OU can be up to 65 characters. Since this name is so long, it would be a good idea to abbreviate it, anyway, for ease of use. All of the other OU names are valid.

**12.** A. One of the administrative benefits of using OUs is that permissions and other settings can be inherited by child OUs.

**13.** D. The Delegation of Control Wizard is designed to allow administrators to set up permissions on specific Active Directory objects.

**14.** A. OUs are created to reflect a company's logical organization. Since your focus is on the OU structure, you should be primarily concerned with business requirements. Other Active Directory features can be used to accommodate the network topology and technical issues (such as performance and scalability).

**15.** D. None of the operations listed are directly supported. The Active Directory Users and Computers tool only allows moving OUs within the same domain.

**16.** D. When you choose to delegate custom tasks, you have many more options for what you can delegate control of and what permissions you can apply. In this case, you would delegate control of Organizational Unit objects and set the permission to Create All Child Objects, Read All Properties, and Write All Properties.

# Chapter 5

# Installing and Managing Trees and Forests

---

## MICROSOFT EXAM OBJECTIVES COVERED IN THIS CHAPTER:

✓ **Install, configure, and troubleshoot the components of Active Directory.**

- Install Active Directory.
- Create sites.
- Create subnets.
- Create site links.
- Create site link bridges.
- Create connection objects.
- Create global catalog servers.
- Move server objects between sites.
- Transfer operations master roles.
- Verify Active Directory installation.
- Implement an organizational unit (OU) structure.

**S**o far, we have focused on the steps required to plan for the Active Directory and to implement the first Active Directory domain. Although we did briefly cover the concepts related to multidomain Active Directory structures, the focus was on a single domain and the objects within it. Many businesses will find that the use of a single domain will provide an adequate solution to meet their business needs. Through the use of *trees* and *forests*, however, organizations can use multiple domains to better organize their environments.

In this chapter, we'll begin by covering some reasons to create more than one Active Directory domain. Then, we'll move on to look at the exact processes involved in creating a domain tree and joining multiple trees together into a domain forest.

This chapter covers material related to the "Create global catalog servers" and "Transfer operations master roles" subobjectives. See Chapter 3, "Installing and Configuring the Active Directory," for material on the Active Directory and its installation; Chapter 4, "Creating and Managing Organizational Units," for coverage on implementing an OU structure; and Chapter 6, "Configuring Sites and Managing Replication," for coverage on creating sites, subnets, site links, site link bridges, and connection objects, as well as on moving server objects between sites.

# Reasons for Creating Multiple Domains

**B**efore we look at the steps required to create multiple domains, we should cover the reasons why an organization might want to create them. In general, you should always try to reflect your organization's structure within a single domain. Through the use of organizational units (OUs) and other objects, you can usually create an accurate and efficient structure within one domain, and creating and managing a single domain is usually much simpler than managing a more complex environment. With that said, let's look at some real benefits and reasons for creating multiple domains.

## Benefits of Multiple Domains

There are several reasons why you might need to implement multiple domains. These reasons include such considerations as

**Scalability**   Although Microsoft has designed the Active Directory to accommodate millions of objects, this number may not be practical for your current environment. Supporting many thousands of users within a single domain will place higher disk space, CPU (central processing unit), and network burdens on your *domain controllers*. Determining the scalability of the Active Directory is something you will have to test within your own environment.

**Reducing Replication Traffic**   All the domain controllers of a domain must keep an up-to-date copy of the entire Active Directory database. For small- to medium-sized domains, this is not generally a problem. Windows 2000 and the Active Directory data store manage all of the details of transferring data behind the scenes. Other business and technical limitations might, however, affect Active Directory's ability to perform adequate replication. For example, if you have two sites that are connected by a very slow network link (or no link at all), replication will not be practical. In this case, you will probably want to create separate domains to isolate replication traffic.

It is important to realize that the presence of slow network links alone is *not* a good reason to break an organization into multiple domains. Through the use of the Active Directory site configuration, replication traffic can be managed independently of the domain architecture. We'll cover these topics in detail in Chapter 6.

**Political and Organizational Reasons**   There are several business reasons that might justify the creation of multiple domains. One of the organizational reasons to use multiple domains is to avoid potential problems associated with the Domain Administrator account. At least one user will need to have permissions at this level. If your organization is unable or unwilling to place this level of trust with all business units, then multiple domains may be the best answer. Since each domain maintains its own security database, you will be able to keep permissions and resources isolated. Through the use of trusts, however, you will still be able to share resources.

Keep in mind that some types of organizational and political issues might require the use of multiple domains while others do not. If you are considering creating multiple domains for purely political reasons (e.g., so that an IT or business manager can retain control over certain resources), this decision might require some further thinking.

**Many Levels of Hierarchy**    Larger organizations tend to have more complex business structures. Even if the structure itself is not complicated, it is likely that a company that has many departments will have several levels within its structure. As we saw in Chapter 4, OUs can accommodate many of these issues. If, however, you find that many levels of OUs will be required to manage resources (or if there are large numbers of objects within each OU), it might make sense to create additional domains. Each domain would contain its own OU hierarchy and serve as the root of a new set of objects.

**Varying Security Policies**    All of the objects within the domain share many characteristics in common. One of these characteristics is security policy. A domain is designed to be a single security entity. Domains allow settings such as usernames and password restrictions to apply to all objects within the domain. If your organization requires separate security policies for different groups of users, you should consider creating multiple domains.

**Migrating from Windows NT**    Ideally, organizations should store all resources and user information within a single domain. In fact, Microsoft recommends that you try to consolidate multiple domains. In some cases, though, this might not be practical, and the use of multiple domains will be required. If, for instance, you're migrating from an existing multi-domain structure, you will have several choices to make. For more information on planning domain structures, see the appendix, "Planning the Active Directory."

**Decentralized Administration**    There are two main models of administration that are in common use: a centralized administration model and a decentralized administration model. In the centralized administration model, a single IT organization is responsible for managing all of the users, computers, and security permissions for the entire organization. In the decentralized administration model, each department or business unit might have its own IT department. In both cases, the needs of the administration model can play a significant role in the decision to use multiple domains.

Consider, for example, a multinational company that has a separate IT department for offices in each country. Each IT department is responsible for supporting only the users and computers within its own region. Since the administration model is largely decentralized, the creation of a separate domain for each of these major business units might make sense from a security and maintenance standpoint.

**Multiple DNS or Domain Names**    Although it might at first sound like a trivial reason to create additional domains, the use of multiple DNS names or domain names requires the creation of multiple domains. Each domain can have only one Fully-Qualified Domain Name (FQDN). For example, if I require some of my users to be placed within the `sales.mycompany.com` namespace and others to be placed in the `engineering.mycompany.com` namespace, multiple domains will be required. If the domain names are noncontiguous, you will need to create multiple domain trees (a topic we'll cover later in this chapter).

## Drawbacks of Multiple Domains

Although many of these reasons for having multiple domains are compelling, there are also reasons *not* to break an organizational structure into multiple domains. Many of these are related to maintenance and administration.

**Administrative Inconsistency**    One of the fundamental responsibilities of most systems administrators is implementing and managing security. When you are implementing Group Policy and security settings in multiple domains, you must be careful to ensure that the settings are consistent. As we mentioned in the previous section, security policies can be different between domains. If this is what is intended, then it is not a problem. If, however, the organization wishes to make the same settings apply to all users, then similar security settings will be required in each domain.

**More Difficult Management of Resources**    Server, user, and computer management can become a considerable challenge when managing multiple domains since there are many more administrative units required.

In general, you will need to manage all user, group, and computer settings separately for the objects within each domain. The hierarchical structure provided by OUs, on the other hand, provides a much simpler and easier way to manage permissions.

**Decreased Flexibility**   The creation of a domain involves the *promotion* of a domain controller to the new domain. Although the process is quite simple, it is much more difficult to rearrange the domain topology within an Active Directory environment than it is to simply reorganize OUs. When planning domains, you should ensure that the domain structure will not change often.

Now that we have examined the pros and cons related to the creation of multiple domains, let's see how trees and forests can be created.

# Creating Domain Trees and Forests

Now that we've covered some important reasons for using multiple domains in a single network environment, it's time to look at how multi-domain structures can be created. The fundamental structures that we'll be discussing are domain trees and domain forests.

An important fact to remember is that regardless of the number of domains you have in your environment, you always have a tree and a forest. This might come as a surprise to those of you who generally think of domain trees and forests as Active Directory environments that consist of multiple domains. However, when you install the first domain in an Active Directory environment, that domain automatically creates a new forest and a new tree. Of course, there are no other domains that form the tree or forest.

A domain tree is created from multiple domains that share a contiguous namespace. That is, all of the domains within a tree are linked together by a common root domain. For example, all of the following domains make up a single contiguous namespace (and can therefore be combined together to form a single domain tree):

- sales.company.com
- it.company.com
- company.com
- northamerica.sales.company.com

In some cases, you may want to combine Active Directory domains that do not share a contiguous namespace. In other words, you want to merge two or more trees together. Such a structure is known as a forest. The following domains do not share a contiguous namespace:

- `sales.company1.com`

- `sales.company2.com`

- `company3.com`

In order to manage the relationship between these domains, you would need to create three separate domain trees (one for each of the domains), and then combine them into a forest.

If you're unfamiliar with the use of multiple domains, you might be wondering "Why bother to join domains together into a tree or forest?" Well, that's a good question. The main reason to combine domains together is to allow for the sharing of resources. We'll look at how this is done through the use of trust relationships later in this chapter.

All of the domains within a single Active Directory forest have several features in common. Specifically, they share the following features:

**Schema**   The schema is the Active Directory structure that defines how the information within the data store will be structured. In order for the information stored on various domain controllers to remain compatible, all of the domain controllers within the entire Active Directory environment must share the same schema. For example, if I added a field for an employee's benefits plan number, all domain controllers throughout the environment would need to recognize this information before information could be shared between them.

**Global Catalog**   One of the problems associated with working in large network environments is that sharing information across multiple domains can be costly in terms of network and server resources. We already mentioned how the Active Directory schema allows for a standardized set of information to be stored. However, one potential problem with this is realized when users try to search for resources across many domains.

To illustrate this point, consider the question, "Where are all of the color printers in the company?" Clearly, a search throughout all of the domains is intended. So how should this be handled? One possible solution would be to send the query to one domain controller in each domain and then have each respond back with the necessary information. Although this could be done, it would create a large amount of network traffic and generate huge loads on each domain controller. Add in the fact that the nearest domain controller might be thousands of miles (and network hops) away, and you have a network nightmare!

Fortunately, the Active Directory has a better solution: the Global Catalog (GC). The GC serves as a repository for information about a subset of all of the objects within *all* Active Directory domains within a forest. Systems administrators can determine what types of information should be added to the defaults in the GC. Generally, the decision is to store commonly used information, such as a list of all of the printers, users, groups, and computers. Specific domain controllers can be configured to carry a copy of the GC. Now, going back to the question of where all the color printers in the company can be found, all that needs to be done is to contact the nearest GC server. It doesn't take much imagination to see how this could save a lot of time and computing resources!

**Configuration Information**   There are some roles and functions that must be managed for the entire forest. When dealing with multiple domains, this means that you must configure certain domain controllers to perform functions for the entire Active Directory environment. We'll look at some specifics later in this chapter.

The main purpose of allowing multiple domains to exist together is to provide for the sharing of information and other resources. Now that we've covered the basics of domain trees and forests, let's look at how domains are actually created.

## The Promotion Process

A domain tree is created when a new domain is added as the child of an existing domain. This relationship is established during the promotion of a Windows 2000 server to a domain controller. Although the underlying relationships can be quite complicated in larger organizations, the *Active Directory Installation Wizard* makes it easy to create forests and trees.

 Through the use of the Active Directory Installation Wizard, you can quickly and easily create new domains by promoting a Windows 2000 stand-alone server or a member server to a domain controller. When you install a new domain controller, you can choose to make it part of an existing domain, or you can choose to make it the first domain controller in a new domain. In any event, domains are created through the promotion of a server to a domain controller. In the following sections and exercises, we'll look at the exact steps required to create a domain tree and a domain forest when you promote a server to a domain controller.

The promotion process involves many steps and decisions. We covered the details in Chapter 3. If you are unfamiliar with the process and ramifications related to promoting a server to a domain controller, it will be helpful to review that chapter before continuing.

## Creating a Domain Tree

To create a new domain tree, you will need to promote a Windows 2000 Server computer to a domain controller. In so doing, you'll have the option of making this domain controller the first machine in a new domain that is a child of an existing one. The result will be a new domain tree that contains two domains—a parent domain and a child domain.

Before you can create a new child domain, you will need the following information:

- The name of the parent domain
- The name of the child domain (the one you are planning to install)
- The file system locations for the Active Directory database, logs, and shared system volume
- DNS configuration information
- The NetBIOS name for the new server
- A domain administrator username and password

Exercise 5.1 walks you through the process of creating a new child domain using the Active Directory Installation Wizard.

---

**EXERCISE 5.1**

### Creating a New Subdomain

In this exercise, we will create a domain tree by adding a new domain as a subdomain of an existing domain. This exercise assumes that you have already created the parent domain.

1. Open the Configure Your Server tool from the Administrative Tools program group. In the left navigation bar, click Active Directory, then click Start to start the Active Directory Installation Wizard. Alternatively, click Start ➢ Run, and type **dcpromo**. Click Next to begin the Wizard.

2. On the Domain Controller Type page, select Domain Controller for a New Domain. Click Next.

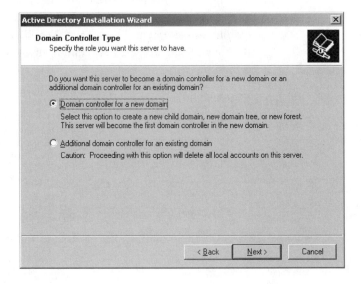

**3.** On the Create Tree or Child Domain page, choose Create a New Child Domain in an Existing Domain Tree. Click Next.

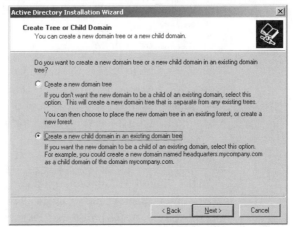

**4.** On the Network Credentials page, enter the username and password for the domain administrator of the domain you wish to join. You will also need to specify the full name of the domain you want to join. After you have entered the appropriate information, click Next.

**5.** If the information you entered was correct, you will see the Child Domain Installation page. Here, you will be able to confirm the name of the parent domain and then enter the domain name for the child domain. If you want to make a change, you can click the Browse button and search for a domain. The Complete DNS Name of New Domain field will show you the fully distinguished domain name for the domain you are creating. Click Next to continue.

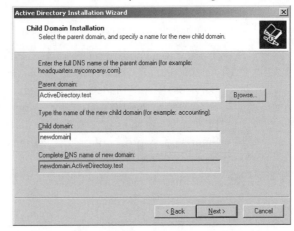

6. Next, you'll be prompted for the NetBIOS name for this domain controller. This is the name that will be used by previous versions of Windows to identify this machine. Choose a name that is up to 15 characters in length and includes only alphanumeric characters. Click Next to continue.

7. Now, it's time to specify the database and log locations. These settings will specify where the Active Directory database will reside on the local machine. As we mentioned previously, it is a good practice to place the log files on a separate physical hard disk because this will increase performance. Enter the path for a local directory, and click Next.

8. On the Shared System Volume page, specify the folder in which the Active Directory public files will reside. This directory must reside on an NTFS 5 partition. Choose the path, and then click Next.

9. If you have not yet installed and configured the DNS service, or if there is an error in the configuration, the Active Directory Installation Wizard will prompt you regarding whether or not the DNS service on the local machine should be configured automatically. Since the Active Directory and client computers will rely on DNS information for finding objects, you will generally want the Wizard to automatically configure DNS. Click Next to continue.

10. On the Permissions page, select whether or not you want to use permissions that are compatible with Windows NT domains. If you will be supporting any Windows NT Server computers or have existing Windows NT domains, you should choose Permissions Compatible with Pre-Windows 2000 Servers. Otherwise, choose Permissions Compatible Only with Windows 2000 Servers. Click Next.

11. In order to be able to recover this server in the event of a loss of Active Directory information, you will need to provide a Directory Services Restore Mode Administrator Password. This password will allow you to use the built-in recovery features of Windows 2000 in the event that the Active Directory database is lost or corrupted. Enter a password, confirm it, and then click Next.

**12.** On the Summary page, you will be given a brief listing of all the choices you made in the previous steps. Click Next to continue on.

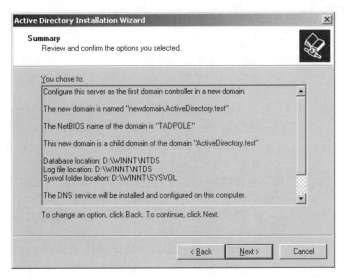

**13.** The Active Directory Installation Wizard will automatically begin performing the steps required to create a new domain in your environment. It's a good idea to copy this information and paste it into a text document for future reference, if needed. Note that you can press Cancel if you want to abort this process. When the process has completed, you will be prompted to reboot the system.

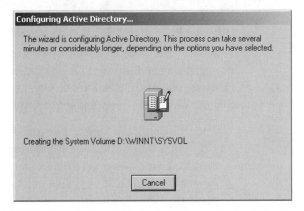

After the system has been rebooted, the local server will be the first domain controller in a new domain. This domain will also be a subdomain of an existing one. Congratulations, you have created a new domain tree!

# Joining a New Domain Tree to a Forest

A forest is formed by joining two or more domains that do not share a contiguous namespace. For example, I could join the `organization1.com` and `organization2.com` domains together to create a single Active Directory environment.

Any two independent domains can be joined together to create a forest, as long as the two domains have non-contiguous namespaces. (If the namespaces were contiguous, you would actually need to create a domain tree.) The process of creating a new tree to form or add to a forest is as simple as promoting a server to a domain controller for a new domain that does *not* share a namespace with an existing Active Directory domain.

In Exercise 5.2, you will use the Active Directory Installation Wizard to create a new domain tree to add to a forest. In order to add a new domain to an existing forest, you must already have at least one other domain. This domain will serve as the root domain for the entire forest. It is important to keep in mind that the entire forest structure will be destroyed if the original root domain is ever entirely removed. Therefore, it is highly recommended that you have at least two domain controllers in the Active Directory root domain. This will provide additional protection for the entire forest in case one of the domain controllers fails.

---

**EXERCISE 5.2**

### Creating a New Domain Tree in the Forest

In this exercise, we will create a new domain tree by adding a new domain as a subdomain of an existing one. In order to complete this exercise, you must have already installed another domain controller that serves as the root domain for a forest.

1. Open the Configure Your Server tool from the Administrative Tools program group. In the left navigation bar, click Active Directory, then click Start to start the Active Directory Installation Wizard. Alternatively, click Start ≻ Run, and type **dcpromo**. Click Next to begin the Wizard.

**2.** On the Domain Controller Type page, select Domain Controller for a New Domain. Click Next.

**3.** On the Create Tree or Child Domain page, choose Create a New Domain Tree. Click Next.

**4.** You'll be given the option of either creating a new forest or joining an existing domain forest. Select Place This New Domain Tree in an Existing Forest, and click Next.

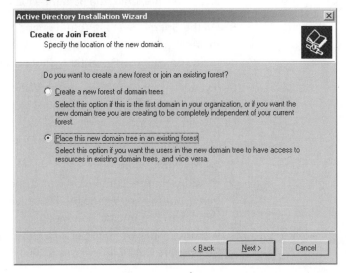

**5.** On the Network Credentials page, enter the username and password for a user account that has permissions to administer the domain you wish to join. You will also need to specify the full name of the domain you want to join. After you have entered the appropriate information, click Next.

**6.** In the New Domain Tree box, you will need to specify the full name of the new domain you wish to create. Note that this domain may not share a contiguous namespace with any other existing domain. Once you have entered the appropriate information, click Next.

**EXERCISE 5.2** *(continued)*

7. You'll be prompted for the NetBIOS name of the domain controller. This is the name that will be used by previous versions of Windows to identify this machine. Choose a name that is up to 15 characters in length and includes only alphanumeric characters. Click Next to continue.

8. You'll need to specify the database and log locations. These settings will specify where the Active Directory database will reside on the local machine. Enter the path for a local directory, and click Next.

9. On the Shared System Volume page, specify the folder in which the Active Directory public files will reside. This directory must reside on an NTFS 5 partition. Choose the path, and then click Next.

10. If you have not yet configured the DNS service, you will be prompted to do so. Since the Active Directory and client computers will rely on DNS information for finding objects, you will generally want the Wizard to automatically configure DNS. Click Next to continue.

11. On the Permissions page, select whether or not you want to use permissions that are compatible with Windows NT domains. If you will be supporting any Windows NT Server computers or have existing Windows NT domains, you should choose Permissions Compatible with Pre-Windows 2000 Servers. Otherwise, choose Permissions Compatible Only with Windows 2000 Servers. Click Next.

12. In order to be able to recover this server in the event of a loss of Active Directory information, you will need to provide a Directory Services Restore Mode Administrator Password. This password will allow you to use the built-in recovery features of Windows 2000 in the event that the Active Directory database is lost or corrupted. Enter a password, confirm it, and then click Next.

**EXERCISE 5.2** *(continued)*

**13.** On the Summary page, you will be given a brief listing of all of the choices you made in the previous steps. Click Next to continue.

**14.** The Active Directory Installation Wizard will automatically begin performing the steps required to create a new domain tree in an existing forest based on the information you provided. Note that you can press Cancel if you want to abort this process. When the setup is complete, you will be prompted to reboot the system.

## Adding Domain Controllers

In addition to the operations we've already performed, you can use the Active Directory Installation Wizard to create additional domain controllers for any of your domains. There are two main reasons to create additional domain controllers:

**Fault Tolerance and Reliability** In organizations that rely upon their network directory services infrastructures, the Active Directory is necessary for providing security and resources for all users. For this reason, downtime and data loss are very costly. Through the use of multiple domain controllers, you can ensure that if one of the servers goes down, another one will be available to perform the necessary tasks. Additionally, data loss (perhaps from the failure of a hard disk) will not result in the loss or unavailability of network security information since you can easily recover the Active Directory information from the remaining domain controller.

**Performance**   The burden of processing login requests and serving as a repository for security permissions and other information can be great, especially in larger businesses. By using multiple domain controllers, you can distribute this load across multiple computers. Additionally, the use of strategically placed domain controllers can greatly increase the response times for common network operations, such as authentication and browsing for resources.

It is recommended that you always have at least two domain controllers per domain. For many organizations, this will provide a good balance between the cost of servers and the level of reliability and performance. For larger or more distributed organizations, however, additional domain controllers will greatly improve performance. We'll cover these issues in detail in Chapter 6.

 **Real World Scenario**

**Planning for Domain Controller Placement**

You're the Senior Systems Administrator for a medium-sized Active Directory environment. Currently, the environment consists of only one Active Directory domain. Your company's network is spread out through 40 different sites within North America. Recently, you've received complaints from users and other system administrators about the performance of Active Directory-related operations. For example, users report that it can take several minutes to log on to their machines in the morning. And, systems administrators complain that updating user information within the OUs for which they are responsible can take a long time.

One network administrator, who has a strong Windows NT domain background but little knowledge about Active Directory design, suggests that you create multiple domains to solve some of the performance problems. However, this would cause a significant change to the environment and could make administration more difficult. Furthermore, the company's business goals are to keep all company resources as unified as possible.

Fortunately, the Active Directory's distributed domain controller architecture allows you to optimize performance for this type of situation without making dramatic changes to your environment. You decide that the quickest and easiest solution is to deploy additional domain controllers throughout the organization. The domain controllers are generally placed within areas of the network that are connected by slow or unreliable links. For example, a small branch office in Des Moines, Iowa receives it's own domain controller. The process is quite simple: You install a new Windows 2000 Server computer and then run the Active Directory Installation Wizard to make the new machine a domain controller for an existing domain. Once the initial directory services data is copied to the new server, it will be ready to service requests and updates of your domain information.

Note that there are potential drawbacks to this solution, including the management of additional domain controllers and the network traffic that is generated from communications between the domain controllers. It's important that you monitor your network links to ensure that you've reached a good balance between replication traffic and overall Active Directory performance. In later chapters, we'll see how you can configure Active Directory sites to better map Active Directory operations to your physical network structure.

# Demoting a Domain Controller

In addition to being able to promote member servers to domain controllers, the Active Directory Installation Wizard can do the exact opposite—demote domain controllers.

You might choose to demote a domain controller for a couple of reasons. First, if you have determined that the role of a server should change (for example, from a domain controller to a Web server), you can easily demote it to effectuate this change. Another reason to demote a domain controller is if you wish to move the machine between domains. Since there is no way to do this in a single process, you will need to first demote the existing domain controller to remove it from the current domain. Then, you can promote it into a new domain. The end result is that the server is now a domain controller for a different domain.

To demote a domain controller, simply access the Active Directory Installation Wizard. The Wizard will automatically notice that the local server is a domain controller. You will be prompted to decide whether or not you really want to remove this machine from the current domain (see Figure 5.1). Note that if the local server is a Global Catalog server, you will be warned that at least one copy of the Global Catalog must remain available in order to perform logon authentication.

**FIGURE 5.1**  Demoting a domain controller using the Active Directory Installation Wizard

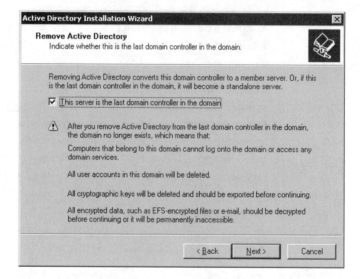

In order for a domain to continue to exist, there must be at least one remaining domain controller in that domain. As noted in the dialog box in Figure 5.1, there are some very important considerations to take into account if you are removing the last domain controller from the domain. Since all of the security accounts and information will be lost, you should ensure that the following steps are taken before removing a domain's last domain controller:

**Computers no longer log on to this domain.**   Ensure that computers that were once a member of this domain have changed domains. If computers are still attempting to log on to this domain, they will not be able to use any of the security features of the domain. This includes any security permissions or logon accounts. Users will, however, still be able to log on to the computer using cached authenticated information.

**No user accounts are needed.** All of the user accounts that resided within the domain (and all of the resources and permissions associated with them) will be lost when the domain is destroyed. Therefore, if you have already set up usernames and passwords, you will need to transfer these accounts to another domain; otherwise, you will lose all of this information.

**All encrypted data is unencrypted.** The security information (including User, Computer, and Group objects) stored within the Active Directory domain database is required to access any encrypted information. Once the domain fails to exist, the security information stored within it will no longer be available, and any encrypted information stored in the file system will become permanently inaccessible. So, unencrypt encrypted data before beginning the demotion process to ensure accessibility to this information afterwards. For example, if you have encrypted files or folders that reside on NTFS volumes, you should choose to decrypt them before continuing with the demotion process.

**Back up all cryptographic keys.** If you are using cryptographic keys for the purpose of authentication and data security, you should export the key information before demoting the last domain controller in a domain. As this information is stored in the Active Directory database, any resources locked with these keys will become inaccessible once the database is lost as a result of the demotion process.

Removing a domain from your environment is not an operation that should be taken lightly. Before you plan to remove a domain, make a list of all the resources dependent on the domain and the reasons why the domain was originally created. If you are sure your organization no longer requires the domain, then you can safely continue. If not, think again!

By now, you've probably noticed a running theme—a lot of information will go away when you demote the last domain controller in a domain. The Active Directory Installation Wizard makes performing potentially disastrous decisions very easy. Be sure that you understand these effects before demoting the last domain controller for a given domain.

By default, at the end of the demotion process, the server will be joined as a member server to the domain for which it was previously a domain controller.

# Managing Multiple Domains

**Y**ou can easily manage most of the operations that must occur *between* domains by using the Active Directory Domains and Trusts administrative tool. If, on the other hand, you want to configure settings *within* a domain, you should use the Active Directory Users and Computers tool. In this section, we'll look at ways to perform two common domain management functions with the tools just mentioned: managing *single master operations* and managing trusts.

## Managing Single Master Operations

For the most part, the Active Directory functions in what is known as multi-master replication. That is, every domain controller within the environment contains a copy of the Active Directory data store that is both readable and writable. This works well for most types of information. For example, if we want to modify the password of a user, we can easily do this on *any* of the domain controllers within a domain. The change will then be automatically propagated to the other domain controllers.

---

*Microsoft* ✔ *Exam Objective*

**Install, configure, and troubleshoot the components of Active Directory.**

- Transfer operations master roles.

---

There are, however, some functions that are not managed in a multimaster fashion. These operations are known as Operations Masters. Single master operations must be performed on specially designated machines within the Active Directory forest. There are five main single master functions: two that apply to an entire Active Directory forest and three that apply to each domain.

Within an Active Directory forest, the following two single master operations apply to the entire forest:

**Schema Master**   Earlier, we mentioned the fact that all of the domain controllers within a single Active Directory environment share the same schema. This is necessary to ensure the consistency of information. Developers and systems administrators can, however, modify the Active Directory schema by adding custom information. An example might be adding a field to employee information that specifies a user's favorite color.

When these types of changes are required, they must be performed on the domain controller that serves as the *Schema Master* for the environment. The Schema Master is then responsible for propagating all of the changes to all of the other domain controllers within the forest.

**Domain Naming Master**   The purpose of the *Domain Naming Master* is to keep track of all the domains within an Active Directory forest. This domain controller is accessed whenever new domains are added to a tree or forest.

*Within* each domain, at least one domain controller must fulfill each of the following roles:

**Relative ID (RID) Master**   It is extremely important that every object within the Active Directory be assigned a unique identifier so that they are distinguishable from other objects. For example, if you have two OUs named IT that reside in different domains, there must be some way to easily distinguish the two objects. Furthermore, if you delete one of the IT OUs and then later re-create it, the system must be able to determine that it is not the same object as the other IT OU. The unique identifier for each object is made up of a domain identifier and a relative identifier (RID). RIDs are always unique within an Active Directory domain and are used for managing security information and authenticating users. The *Relative ID (RID) Master* is responsible for creating these values within a domain whenever new Active Directory objects are created.

**PDC Emulator Master**   Within a domain, the *Primary Domain Controller (PDC) Emulator* is responsible for maintaining backward compatibility with Windows NT domain controllers. When running in mixed-mode domains, the PDC Emulator is able to process authentication requests and serve as a PDC with Windows NT Backup Domain Controllers (BDCs).

When running in native-mode domains (which do not support the use of pre-Windows 2000 domain controllers), the PDC Emulator Master serves as the default domain controller to process authentication requests if another domain controller is unable to do so. The PDC Emulator Master will also receive preferential treatment whenever domain security changes are made.

**Infrastructure Master**   Whenever a user is added to or removed from a group, all of the other domain controllers should be made aware of this change. The role of the domain controller that acts as an *Infrastructure Master* is to ensure that group membership information stays synchronized within an Active Directory domain.

Now that we are familiar with the different types of single master operations, Exercise 5.3 shows how these roles can be assigned to servers within the Active Directory environment.

**EXERCISE 5.3**

## Assigning Single Master Operations

In this exercise, we will assign single master operations roles to various domain controllers within the environment. In order to complete the steps in this exercise, you will require only one Active Directory domain controller.

**1.** Open the Active Directory Domains and Trusts administrative tool.

**2.** Right-click Active Directory Domains and Trusts, and choose Operations Master.

**3.** In the Change Operations Master dialog box, note that you can change the operations master by clicking the Change button. If you want to move this assignment to another computer, you will first need to connect to that computer and then make the change. Click Cancel to continue without making any changes. Close the Active Directory Domains and Trusts administrative tool.

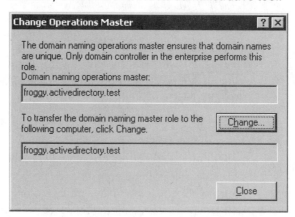

**4.** Open the Active Directory Users and Computers administrative tool.

**5.** Right-click the name of a domain and select Operations Master. This will bring up the RID tab of the Operations Master dialog box. Notice that you can change the computer that is assigned to the role. In order to change the role, you will first need to connect to the appropriate domain controller. Notice also that there are similar tabs for the PDC and Infrastructure roles. Click Cancel to continue without making any changes.

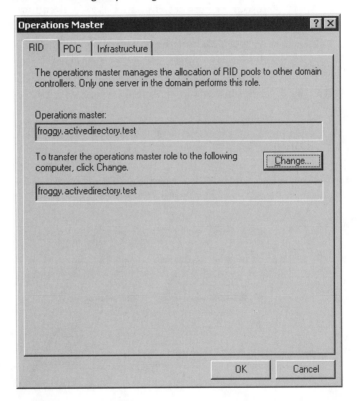

**6.** Click Cancel to exit the Operations Master dialog box without making any changes.

**7.** When finished, close the Active Directory Users and Computers tool.

Note that two different tools are used to manage single master operations. The Active Directory Domains and Trusts snap-in is used to configure forest-wide roles, while the Active Directory Users and Computers snap-in is used to administer roles within a domain. Although this might not seem intuitive at first, it can be helpful when remembering which roles apply to domains and which apply to the whole forest.

## Managing Trusts

When it comes to creating Active Directory domains, the relationships must be based on trusts. OK, so this may be a weak attempt at humor. But, trust relationships facilitate the sharing of security information and network resources between domains. As we already mentioned, standard transitive two-way trusts are automatically created between the domains in a tree and between each of the trees in a forest. Figure 5.2 shows an example of the default trust relationships in an Active Directory forest.

**FIGURE 5.2**   Default trusts in an Active Directory forest

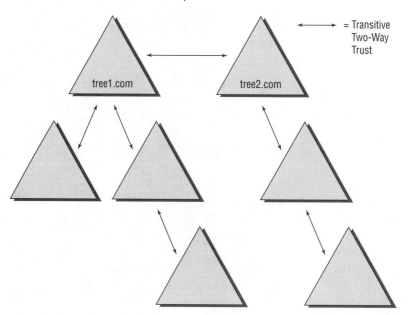

When configuring trusts, there are two main characteristics you'll need to consider. These characteristics are as follows:

**Transitive Trusts**   By default, Active Directory trusts are *transitive trusts*. The simplest way to understand transitive relationships is through an analogy like the following: If Domain A trusts Domain B and Domain B trusts Domain C, then Domain A implicitly trusts Domain C.

Trusts can be configured so that this type of behavior does not occur. That is, transitivity can be disabled.

**One-Way vs. Two-Way**    Trusts can be configured as one-way or two-way relationships. The default operation is to create *two-way trusts*. This facilitates the management of trust relationships by reducing the number of trusts that must be created. In some cases, however, you might decide that two-way trusts are not required. In one-way relationships, the trusting domain allows resources to be shared with the trusted domain.

When domains are added together to form trees and forests, an automatic transitive two-way trust is created between them. Although the default trust relationships will work well for most organizations, there are some possible reasons for managing trusts manually. First, you may want to remove trusts between domains if you are absolutely sure that you do not want resources to be shared between domains. Second, security concerns may require you to keep resources isolated. In some cases, you may actually want to create direct trusts between two domains that implicitly trust each other. Such a trust is sometimes referred to as a shortcut trust and can improve the speed at which resources are accessed across many different domains.

Perhaps the most important aspect to remember regarding trusts is that their creation only *allows* resources to be shared between domains. The trust does not grant any permissions between domains by itself. Once a trust has been established, however, systems administrators can easily assign the necessary permissions. Exercise 5.4 walks through the steps required to manage trusts.

**EXERCISE 5.4**

### Managing Trust Relationships

In this exercise, we will see how trust relationships between domains can be assigned. In order to complete the steps in this exercise, you must have domain administrator access permissions.

**1.** Log on to the domain controller as a domain administrator, and open the Active Directory Domains and Trusts tool.

**2.** Right-click the name of a domain, and select Properties.

**EXERCISE 5.4** *(continued)*

3. Select the Trusts tab. You will see a list of the trusts that are currently configured.

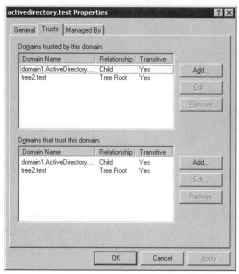

4. To modify the trust properties for an existing trust, highlight that trust and click Edit. Information about the trust's direction, transitivity, and type will be displayed, along with the names of the domains involved in the relationship. Click Cancel to exit without making any changes.

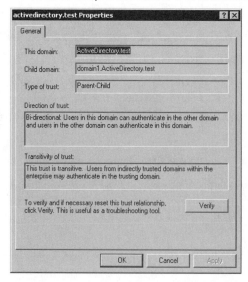

**EXERCISE 5.4 *(continued)***

5. To create a new trust relationship, click Add. You will be prompted for the name of the domain with which the trust should be created. Enter the name of the domain along with a password that should be used to administer the trust. Note that if there is an existing trust relationship between the domains, the passwords must match. Click Cancel to continue without making any changes.

6. Exit the Trust properties for the domain by clicking Cancel.

Once the trust relationships have been established, you will be able to share resources between domains. We'll look at exactly how this is done in Chapter 8, "Active Directory Security."

## Managing Global Catalog Servers

One of the best features of a distributed directory service like the Active Directory is the fact that different pieces of information can be stored throughout an organization. For example, a domain in Japan might store a list of users who operate within a company's Asian Operations business unit, while one in New York would contain a list of users who operate within its North American Operations business unit. This architecture allows systems administrators to place the most frequently accessed information on domain controllers in different domains, thereby reducing disk space requirements and replication traffic.

***Microsoft Exam Objective***

**Install, configure, and troubleshoot the components of Active Directory.**

- Create global catalog servers.

There is, however, a problem in dealing with information that is segmented into multiple domains. The issue involves querying information stored within the Active Directory. What would happen, for example, if a user wanted a list of all of the printers available in all domains within the Active Directory forest? In this case, the search would normally require information from at least one domain controller in each of the domains within the environment. Some of these domain controllers may be located across slow network links or may have unreliable connections. The end result would include an extremely long wait while retrieving the results of the query.

Fortunately, the Active Directory has a mechanism that speeds up such searches. Any number of domain controllers can be configured to host a copy of the Global Catalog. The Global Catalog contains all of the schema information and a subset of the attributes for all domains within the Active Directory environment. Although there is a default set of information that is normally included with the Global Catalog, systems administrators can choose to add additional information to this data store. Servers that contain a copy of the Global Catalog are known as Global Catalog servers. Now, whenever a user executes a query that requires information from multiple domains, they need only contact their nearest Global Catalog server for this information. Similarly, when users are required to authenticate across domains, they will not have to wait for a response from a domain controller that may be located across the world. The end result is increased overall performance of Active Directory queries.

Exercise 5.5 walks through the steps required to configure a domain controller as a Global Catalog server. Generally, Global Catalog servers are only useful in environments that use multiple Active Directory domains. We will cover the details involved with placing Global Catalog servers in a distributed environment in Chapter 6.

---

**EXERCISE 5.5**

### Managing Global Catalog Servers

In this exercise, you will set the option that defines whether a domain controller is a Global Catalog server.

1. Open the Active Directory Sites and Services administrative tool.

2. Find the name of the local domain controller within the list of objects, and expand this object. Right-click NTDS Settings, and select Properties.

**EXERCISE 5.5** *(continued)*

3. In the NTDS Settings Properties dialog box, type **Primary GC Server for Domain** in the Description field. Note that there is a check box that determines whether or not this computer contains a copy of the Global Catalog. If the box is checked, then this domain controller contains a subset of information from all other domains within the Active Directory environment. Select or deselect the Global Catalog check box, and then click OK to continue.

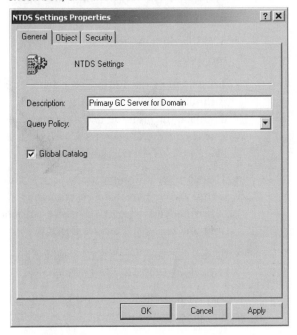

4. When finished, close the Active Directory Sites and Services administrative tool.

# Summary

In this chapter, we discussed the following:

- There are several good reasons for creating multiple domains. By using multiple domains, organizations can retain separate security databases. However, they are also able to share resources between domains.

- The use of multiple domains can provide two major benefits for the network directory services—security and availability. This is made possible through the use of the structure of the Active Directory and the administrative tools that can be used to access it.

- Systems administrators can simplify operations while still ensuring that only authorized users have access to their data.

- Multiple domains can interact to form Active Directory trees and forests.

- The Active Directory Installation Wizard can be used to create new Active Directory trees and forests.

- Multiple domain trees can be combined together into Active Directory forests.

- Trusts can be used to balance security and domain interoperability. Although each domain in the environment retains a separate security database through the use of properly configured trusts, you will be able to enjoy the benefits of separate security domains while still being able to share resources.

- There are several single master operations roles that must be managed within Active Directory environments. Some of these roles must be performed in each Active Directory domain while others must exist on only one server per Active Directory environment.

- Global Catalog servers can be used to greatly improve the performance of cross-domain Active Directory queries.

In Chapter 6, we'll see how the components of the Active Directory can be used to manage replication operations and traffic.

# Exam Essentials

**Understand the purpose of Organizational Units (OUs)**   OUs are used to create a hierarchical, logical organization for objects within an Active Directory domain.

# Key Terms

Before you take the exam, be certain you are familiar with the following terms:

Active Directory Installation Wizard

domain controllers

Domain Naming Master

forests

Infrastructure Master

Primary Domain Controller (PDC) Emulator

promotion

Relative ID (RID) Master

Schema Master

single master operations

transitive trusts

trees

two-way trusts

# Review Questions

1. You are a systems administrator for an environment that consists of two Active Directory domains. Initially, the domains were configured without any trust relationships. However, the business now has a need to share resources between the domains. You decide to create a trust relationship between Domain A and Domain B. Before you take any other actions, which of the following statements is true?

    A. All users in Domain A can access all resources in Domain B.

    B. All users in Domain B can access all resources in Domain A.

    C. Resources cannot be shared between the domains.

    D. All of the above.

    E. None of the above.

2. Jane is a systems administrator for a large Active Directory environment that plans to deploy four Active Directory domains. She is responsible for determining the hardware budget for the deployment of four Active Directory domains. She has the following requirements:

    - The budget should minimize the number of servers to be deployed initially.

    - Each domain must implement enough fault-tolerance to survive the complete failure of one domain controller.

    - In the event of a failure of one domain controller, users in all domains should still have access to Active Directory information.

    In order to meet these requirements, what is the minimum number of domain controllers that Jane can deploy initially?

    A. 0

    B. 1

    C. 2

    D. 4

    E. 8

**3.** Juan is a network administrator for three Active Directory domains that support offices based primarily in South America. His organization has recently decided to open several offices in North America and Asia, and many of the employees will be relocated to staff these offices. As part of the change, several offices in South America will either be closed or reduced in size.

Currently, the environment consists of many Windows 2000 Server computers in different configurations. In order to conserve hardware resources, Juan plans to reassign some of the servers located in South America to support operations in North America and Asia, which will include the creation of new domains. Which of the following server configurations can be directly promoted to become a domain controller for a new domain? (Choose all that apply.)

**A.** Member server

**B.** Stand-alone server

**C.** Domain controller

4. Monica is the systems administrator for a mixed domain environment that consists of Active Directory domain controllers and Windows NT 4 domain controllers. The server roles are as follows:

Server1: Schema Master

Server2: RID Master

Server3: Windows NT 4 Backup Domain Controller

Server4: Infrastructure Master

Server5: PDC Emulator Master

When the business finishes migrating the entire environment to Windows 2000, which of the following machines will no longer be required?

A. Server1

B. Server2

C. Server3

D. Server4

E. Server5

5. Implicit trusts created between domains are known as which of the following?

A. Two-way trusts

B. Transitive trusts

C. Both of the above

D. None of the above

6. You are a developer for a small organization that has deployed a single Active Directory domain. Your organization has begun using the Active Directory schema in order to store important information related to each of the company's 350 employees. Most of the fields of information you plan to support are already included with the basic Active Directory schema. However, one field—a "security clearance level" value—is not supported. You want to take advantage of the extensibility of the Active Directory by adding this field to the properties of a User object. On which of the following servers can the change be made?

   **A.** Any domain controller

   **B.** Any member server

   **C.** The Schema Master

   **D.** None of the above

7. What is a set of Active Directory domains that share a contiguous namespace called?

   **A.** A forest

   **B.** A domain hierarchy

   **C.** A tree

   **D.** A DNS zone

   **E.** None of the above

8. A junior systems administrator who was responsible for administering an Active Directory domain accidentally demoted the last domain controller of your ADTest.com domain. He noticed that after the demotion process was complete, no Active Directory-related operations could be performed. He calls you to ask for advice about recreating the domain. Your solution must meet the following requirements:

   - There can be no loss of Active Directory security information.

   - All objects must be restored.

   - The process must not require the use of Active Directory or server backups because they were not being performed for the ADTest.com domain.

   After the last domain controller in a domain has been demoted, how can the domain be re-created to meet the above requirements?

   **A.** By creating a new domain controller with the same name as the demoted one

   **B.** By creating a new domain with the same name

   **C.** By adding a new member server to the old domain

   **D.** None of the above solutions meets the requirements.

9. Which of the following item(s) does not depend on the DNS namespace? (Choose all that apply.)

   **A.** Organizational units

   **B.** Domains

   **C.** Domain trees

   **D.** Domain forests

   **E.** DNS Zones

   **F.** Active Directory Sites

**10.** Which of the following types of computers contain a copy of the Global Catalog?

   **A.** All Windows NT domain controllers

   **B.** All Active Directory domain controllers

   **C.** Specified Active Directory domain controllers

   **D.** Active Directory workstations

   **E.** All of the above

**11.** Which of the following pieces of information should you have before beginning the Active Directory Installation Wizard?

   **A.** Active Directory domain name

   **B.** NetBIOS name for the server

   **C.** DNS configuration information

   **D.** All of the above

**12.** Which type of trust is automatically created between the domains in a domain tree?

   **A.** Transitive

   **B.** Two-way

   **C.** Transitive two-way

   **D.** None of the above

**13.** The Active Directory Installation Wizard can be accessed by typing which of the following commands?

   **A.** domaininstall

   **B.** domainupgrade

   **C.** dconfig

   **D.** dcinstall

   **E.** None of the above

**14.** If Domain A trusts Domain B and Domain B trusts Domain C, then Domain A trusts Domain C. This is an example of which type of trust?

**A.** Bidirectional

**B.** Transitive

**C.** Cumulative

**D.** Recursive

**15.** A systems administrator wants to remove a domain controller from a domain. Which of the following is the easiest way to perform the task?

**A.** Use the Active Directory Installation Wizard to demote the domain controller.

**B.** Use the DCPROMO /REMOVE command.

**C.** Reinstall the server over the existing installation, and make the machine a member of a workgroup.

**D.** Reinstall the server over the existing installation, and make the machine a member of a domain.

**16.** Which of the following is *true* regarding the sharing of resources between forests?

**A.** All resources are automatically shared between forests.

**B.** A trust relationship must exist before resources can be shared between forests.

**C.** Resources cannot be shared between forests.

**D.** None of the above.

# Answers to Review Questions

**1.** E. A trust relationship only allows the *possibility* for the sharing of resources between domains; it does not explicitly provide any permissions. In order to allow users to access resources in another domain, you must configure the appropriate permissions.

**2.** E. Every domain must have at least one domain controller; therefore, at least four domain controllers would be required in order to create the domains. Furthermore, to meet the requirements for fault-tolerance and the ability to continue operations during the failure of a domain controller, each of the four domains must also have a second domain controller. Therefore, Jane must deploy a minimum of eight servers configured as Active Directory domain controllers.

**3.** A, B. Both member servers and stand-alone servers can be promoted to domain controllers for new Active Directory domains. In order to "move" an existing domain controller to a new domain, it must first be demoted to a non-domain controller. It can then be promoted to a domain controller for a new domain.

**4.** C. The Windows NT Backup Domain Controller will no longer be necessary once the environment moves to a Windows 2000 platform (although it may be upgraded to a Windows 2000 domain controller). The PDC Emulator Master is used primarily for compatibility with Windows NT domains, however, it will still be required for certain domainwide functions in a Windows 2000 environment.

**5.** C. Trusts between domains that have not been explicitly defined are known as transitive trusts.

**6.** C. The Schema Master is the only server within the Active Directory on which changes to the schema can be made.

**7.** C. A domain tree is made up of multiple domains that share the same contiguous namespace.

8. D. Once the last domain controller in an environment has been removed, there is no way to re-create the same domain. If adequate backups had been performed, you may have been able to recover information by rebuilding the server.

9. A, F. OUs do not participate in the DNS namespace—they are used primarily for naming objects within an Active Directory domain. The naming for Active Directory objects, such as sites, does not depend on DNS names either.

10. C. Systems administrators can define which domain controllers in the environment will contain a copy of the Global Catalog (GC). Although the GC does contain information about all domains in the environment, it does not have to reside on all domain controllers. In fact, by default, the GC is only contained on the domain controller that is the root of the forest.

11. D. Before beginning the promotion of a domain controller, you should have all of the information listed.

12. C. A transitive two-way trust is automatically created between the domains in a domain tree.

13. E. The `dcpromo` command can be used to launch the Active Directory Installation Wizard. This Wizard can also be accessed by using the Configure Your Server item in the Administrative Tools folder.

14. B. The above is an example of a transitive trust.

15. A. The Active Directory Installation Wizard allows administrators to remove a domain controller from a domain quickly and easily without requiring the reinstallation of the operating system.

16. B. Through the creation of trust relationships, resources can be shared between domains that are in two different forests. To simplify access to resources (at the expense of security), a systems administrator could enable the Guest account in the domains so that resources would be automatically shared for members of the Everyone group.

# Chapter

# 6

# Configuring Sites and Managing Replication

## MICROSOFT EXAM OBJECTIVES COVERED IN THIS CHAPTER:

✓ **Install, configure, and troubleshoot the components of Active Directory.**

- Install Active Directory.
- Create sites.
- Create subnets.
- Create site links.
- Create site link bridges.
- Create connection objects.
- Create global catalog servers.
- Move server objects between sites.
- Transfer operations master roles.
- Verify Active Directory installation.
- Implement an organizational unit (OU) structure.

✓ **Manage and troubleshoot Active Directory replication**.

- Manage intersite replication.
- Manage intrasite replication.

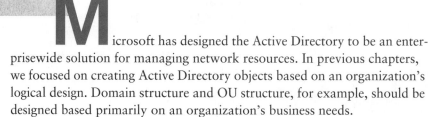

icrosoft has designed the Active Directory to be an enterprisewide solution for managing network resources. In previous chapters, we focused on creating Active Directory objects based on an organization's logical design. Domain structure and OU structure, for example, should be designed based primarily on an organization's business needs.

Now, it's time to talk about how the Active Directory can map to an organization's *physical* requirements. Specifically, we must consider network connectivity between sites and the flow of information between *domain controllers* under less than ideal conditions. These constraints will determine how domain controllers can work together to ensure that the objects within the Active Directory remain synchronized, no matter how large and geographically dispersed the network is.

Fortunately, through the use of the Active Directory Sites and Services administrative tool, you can quickly and easily create the various components of an Active Directory replication topology. This includes the creation of objects called Sites, the placement of servers in sites, and the creation of connections between sites. Once you have configured Active Directory replication to fit your current network environment, you can sit back and allow the Active Directory to make sure that information remains consistent across domain controllers.

In this chapter, we will cover the features of the Active Directory that allow systems administrators to modify the behavior of replication based on their physical network design. Through the use of sites, systems and network administrators will be able to leverage their network infrastructure to best support Windows 2000 and the Active Directory.

This chapter covers material related to creating sites, subnets, site links, site link bridges, and connection objects, as well as on moving server objects between sites, for the "Install, configure, and troubleshoot the components of Active Directory" objective. See Chapter 3, "Installing and Configuring the Active Directory," for material on the Active Directory and its installation; Chapter 4, "Creating and Managing Organizational Units," for coverage on implementing an OU structure; and Chapter 5, "Installing and Managing Trees and Forests," for material on creating Global Catalog servers and transferring operations master roles.

# Overview of Active Directory Physical Components

In an ideal situation, a high-speed network would connect computers and networking devices. In such a situation, you would be able to ensure that, regardless of the location of a network user, they would be able to quickly and easily access resources. When working in the real world, however, there are many other constraints to keep in mind. These include the following:

**Network Bandwidth**    Network bandwidth generally refers to the amount of data that can pass through a specific connection in a given amount of time. For example, a standard analog modem may have a bandwidth of 33.6Kbps (kilobits per second) while an average physical network connection may have a bandwidth of 100Mbps (megabits per second).

**Network Cost**    Cost is perhaps the single biggest factor in determining a network design. If cost were not a constraint, organizations would clearly choose to use high-bandwidth connections for all of their sites. Realistically, trade-offs in performance must be made for the sake of affordability. Some of the factors that can affect the cost of networking include the distance between networks and the types of technology available at certain sites throughout the world. Network designers must keep these factors in mind and often must settle for less than ideal connectivity.

When designing and configuring networks, certain devices can be made to automatically make data transport decisions based on an assigned network cost. In many cases, for example, there may be multiple ways to connect to a remote site. When two or more routes are available, the one with the lower cost is automatically used first.

**Technological Limitations**   In addition to all of the other constraints that have been presented thus far, there's one that we have little control over—the laws of physics! Although newer networking technologies are emerging very quickly, there will always be limits to how quickly and efficiently information can travel throughout the world.

All of these factors will play an important role when you make your decisions related to the implementation of the Active Directory.

When designing networks, systems and network administrators use the following terms to distinguish the types of connectivity between locations and servers:

**Local Area Networks (LANs)**   A *local area network (LAN)* is usually characterized as a high-bandwidth network. Generally, an organization owns all of its LAN network hardware and software. Ethernet is by far the most common networking standard. Ethernet speeds are generally at least 10Mbps and can scale to multiple gigabits per second. Several LAN technologies, including routing and switching, are available to segment LANs and reduce contention for network resources.

**Wide Area Networks (WANs)**   The purpose of a *wide area network (WAN)* is similar to that of a LAN—to connect network devices together. Unlike LANs, however, WANs are usually leased from third-party telecommunications carriers. Although extremely high-speed WAN connections are available, they are generally much too costly for organizations to implement through a distributed environment. Therefore, WAN connections are characterized by lower-speed connections and, sometimes, non-persistent connections.

**The Internet**   You would have to be locked away in a server room (without network access) for a long time to not have heard about the Internet. The Internet is a worldwide public network infrastructure. It is based on the *Internet Protocol (IP)*. Access to the Internet is available through organizations known as Internet Service Providers (ISPs). Because it is a public network, there is no single "owner" of the Internet. Instead, large network and telecommunications providers are constantly upgrading the infrastructure of this network to meet growing demands.

Recently, organizations have started to make use of the Internet for business purposes. For example, it's rare nowadays to see advertisements that don't direct you to one Web site or another. Through the use of technologies such as Virtual Private Networks (VPNs), organizations can use encryption and authentication technology to enable secure communications across the Internet.

Regardless of the issues related to network design and technological constraints, network users will have many different requirements and needs that must be addressed. First and foremost, network resources such as files, printers, and shared directories must be made available for use. Similarly, the resources stored within the Active Directory—and, especially, its security information—are required for many operations that occur within domains.

With these issues in mind, let's look at how you can configure the Active Directory to reach connectivity goals through the use of replication.

The focus of this chapter is on implementing sites. However, in the real world, it won't make much sense to implement sites until you have properly planned for them based on your business needs. You can find more information on planning for sites in the appendix, "Planning the Active Directory."

## Active Directory Replication

The Active Directory was designed as a scalable, distributed database that contains information about an organization's network resources. In previous chapters, we looked at how domains can be created and managed and how domain controllers are used to store Active Directory databases.

Even in the simplest of network environments, there is generally a need to have more than one domain controller. The major reasons for this include fault tolerance (if one domain controller fails, others can still provide network services) and performance (the load can be balanced between multiple domain controllers). Windows 2000 domain controllers have been designed to contain read-write copies of the Active Directory database. However, the domain controllers must also contain knowledge that is created or modified on other domain controllers since a systems administrator may make changes on only one out of many domain controllers. This raises an important point—how is information kept consistent between domain controllers?

The answer is *Active Directory replication*. Replication is the process by which changes to the Active Directory database are transferred between domain controllers. The end result is that all of the domain controllers within an Active Directory domain contain up-to-date information. Keep in mind that domain controllers may be located very near to each other (e.g., within the same server rack) or may be located across the world from each other. Although the goals of replication are quite simple, the real-world constraints of network connections between servers cause many limitations that must be accommodated.

In this chapter, we will look at the technical details of Active Directory replication and how the concept of sites can be used to map the logical structure of the Active Directory to a physical network topology. Let's begin by looking at the fundamental concepts on which the Active Directory is based.

## Active Directory Site Concepts

One of the most important concepts regarding the design and implementation of the Active Directory focuses on the separation of the logical components from the physical components of the directory service. The logical components include the features that map to business requirements. For example, Active Directory domains, organizational units (OUs), users, groups, and computers are all designed to map to political requirements of a business.

Active Directory physical components, on the other hand, are based on technical issues. These issues will crop up, for instance, when we address the question of how the Active Directory can remain synchronized in a distributed network environment. The Active Directory uses the concept of sites to map to an organization's physical network. Stated simply, a *site* is a collection of well-connected computers. We'll define the technical implications of sites later in this chapter.

It is important to understand that there is no specified relationship between Active Directory domains and Active Directory sites. An Active Directory site can contain many domains. Alternatively, a single Active Directory domain can span multiple sites. Figure 6.1 illustrates this very important characteristic of their relationship.

**FIGURE  6.1**    Potential relationships between domains and sites

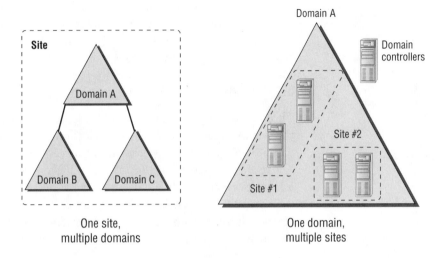

One site,
multiple domains

One domain,
multiple sites

There are two main reasons to use Active Directory sites. These are as follows:

**Service Requests**    Clients often require the network services of a domain controller. One of the most common reasons for this is that they need the domain controller to perform network authentication. Through the use of Active Directory sites, clients can easily connect to the domain controller that is located closest to them. By doing this, they avoid many of the inefficiencies associated with connecting to distant domain controllers or those that are located on the other side of a slow network connection. Other network services include the Licensing service (for tracking licenses associated with Microsoft and other compatible products) and such applications as messaging (such as Exchange Server 2000). All of these functions are dependent on the availability of network services. In the case of the Active Directory, clients should try to connect to the domain controllers that are located closest to them. This reduces network costs and results in increased performance. In order for this to work, however, systems administrators must define which services are available at specific sites.

**Replication**    As we mentioned earlier, the purpose of Active Directory replication is to ensure that the information stored on domain controllers remains synchronized. However, in environments with many domains and domain controllers, there are multiple paths of communication between them, which makes the synchronization process more complicated. One method of transferring updates and other changes to the Active Directory would be for all of the servers to communicate directly with each other as soon as a change occurs. This is not ideal, however, since it places high requirements on network bandwidth and is inefficient for many network environments that use slower and more costly WAN links. So how can we efficiently solve this problem?

Through the use of sites, the Active Directory can automatically determine the best methods for performing replication operations. Sites take into account an organization's network infrastructure and are used by the Active Directory to determine the most efficient method for synchronizing information between domain controllers. Systems administrators can make their physical network design map to Active Directory objects. Based on the creation and configuration of these objects, the Active Directory service can then manage replication traffic in an efficient way.

Whenever a change is made to the Active Directory database on a domain controller, the change is given a logical sequence number. The domain controller can then propagate these changes to other domain controllers based on replication settings. In the event that the same setting (such as a user's last name) has been changed on two different domain controllers (before replication can take place), these sequence numbers are used to resolve the conflict.

# Implementing Sites and Subnets

Now that we have an idea of the goals of replication, let's do a quick overview of the various Active Directory objects that are related to physical network topology.

The basic objects that are used for managing replication include the following:

**Subnets** A *subnet* is a partition of a network. Subnets are usually connected through the use of routers and other network devices. All of the computers that are located on a given subnet are generally well connected.

It is extremely important to understand the concepts of TCP/IP and the routing of network information when designing the topology for Active Directory replication. See *MCSE: Windows 2000 Network Infrastructure Administration Study Guide,* 2nd ed., by Paul Robichaux with James Chellis (Sybex, 2001) for more information on this topic.

**Sites**  An Active Directory site is a logical object that can contain servers and other objects related to Active Directory replication. Specifically, a site is a grouping of related subnets. Sites are created to match the physical network structure of an organization.

**Site Links**  *Site links* are created to define the types of connections that are available between the components of a site. Site links can reflect a relative cost for a network connection and can reflect the bandwidth that is available for communications.

Each of these components works together in determining how information is used to replicate data between domain controllers. Figure 6.2 provides an example of the physical components of the Active Directory.

**FIGURE 6.2**  Active Directory replication objects

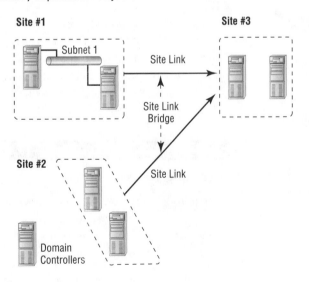

There are many issues related to configuring and managing sites. Rest assured, we'll cover each in turn throughout this chapter. Overall, the use of sites allows you to control the behavior of the Active Directory replication between domain controllers. With this background and goal in mind, let's look at how sites can be implemented to control Active Directory replication.

## Creating Sites

The primary method for creating and managing Active Directory replication components is to utilize the Active Directory Sites and Services tool. Using this administrative component, you can graphically create and manage sites in much the same way as you create and manage organizational units (OUs). Exercise 6.1 walks you through the process of creating Active Directory sites.

***Microsoft Exam Objective***

**Install, configure, and troubleshoot the components of Active Directory.**

- Create sites.

The exercises in this chapter have been designed to work through the use of a single domain controller and single Active Directory domain. Although you can walk through all of the steps required to create sites and related objects without using multiple domain controllers, real-world replication will generally involve the use of multiple domain controllers in multiple physical sites.

**EXERCISE 6.1**

**Creating Sites**

In this exercise, you will create new Active Directory sites. In order to complete this exercise, the local machine must be a domain controller. Also, this exercise assumes that you have not yet changed the default domain site configuration.

1. Open the Active Directory Sites and Services tool from the Administrative Tools program group.

2. Expand the Sites folder.

3. Right-click the Default-First-Site-Name item, and choose Rename. Rename the site to CorporateHQ.

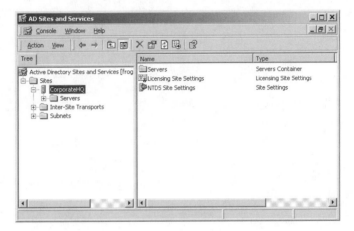

4. To create a new site, right-click the Sites object and select New Site.

5. For the name of the site, type **Austin**. Click the DEFAULTIPSITELINK item, and then click OK to create the site. Note that you cannot include spaces or other special characters in the name of a site.

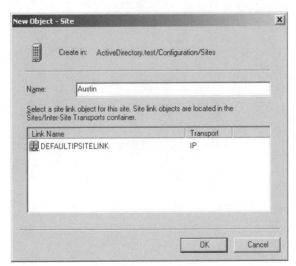

6. You will see a dialog box stating the actions that you should take to finish the configuration of this site. Click OK to continue.

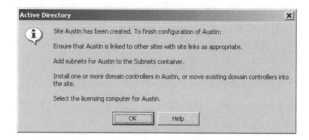

7. Create another new site and name it NewYork. Again, choose the DEFAULTIPSITELINK item.

8. When finished, close the Active Directory Sites and Services tool.

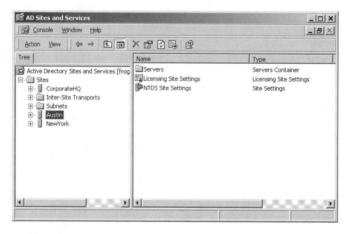

Now that you have created a couple of new sites, it's time to configure them so they can be used to manage replication operations.

# Creating Subnets

Once you have created the sites that map to your network topology, it's time to define the subnets that belong with the site.

***Microsoft*** ✓ ***Exam*** ***Objective***

**Install, configure, and troubleshoot the components of Active Directory.**

- Create subnets.

Subnets are based on TCP/IP address information and take the form of a TCP/IP address and a subnet mask. For example, the TCP/IP address may be 10.120.0.0, and the subnet mask may be 255.255.0.0. This information specifies that all of the TCP/IP addresses that begin with the first two octets are part of the same TCP/IP subnet. All of the following TCP/IP addresses would be within this subnet:

- 10.120.1.5

- 10.120.100.17

- 10.120.120.120

The Active Directory Sites and Services tool expresses these subnets in a somewhat different notation. It uses the provided subnet address and appends a slash followed by the number of bits in the subnet mask. In the example above, the subnet would be defined as 10.120.0.0/16.

Generally, information regarding the definition of subnets for a specific network environment will be available from a network designer. Exercise 6.2 walks you through the steps that are required to create subnets and assign subnets to sites.

### EXERCISE 6.2

### Creating Subnets

In this exercise, you will create subnets and then assign them to sites. In order to complete the steps in this exercise, you must have first completed Exercise 6.1.

1. Open the Active Directory Sites and Services tool from the Administrative Tools program group.

2. Expand the Sites folder. Right-click the Subnets folder, and select New Subnet.

3. You will be prompted for information regarding the TCP/IP information for the new subnet. For the address, type **100.1.1.0,** and for the mask, type **255.255.255.0**. You will see that the Name value has been automatically calculated as 100.1.1.0/24. Click the Austin site, and then click OK to create the subnet.

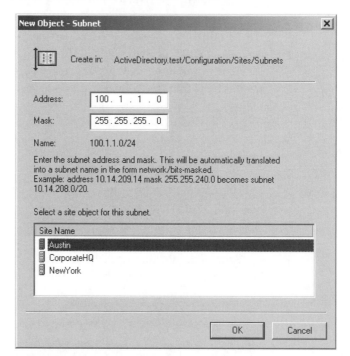

**4.** Right-click the newly created 100.1.1.0/24 subnet object, and select Properties. On the Subnet tab, type **Austin 100Mbit LAN** for the description. Click OK to continue.

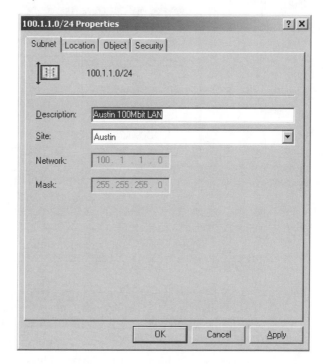

**5.** Create a new subnet using the following information:

Address: 160.25.0.0

Mask: 255.255.0.0

Site: NewYork

Description: NewYork 100Mbit LAN

**6.** Finally, create another subnet using the following information:

Address: 176.33.0.0

Mask: 255.255.0.0

**EXERCISE 6.2** *(continued)*

Site: CorporateHQ

Description: Corporate 100Mbit switched LAN

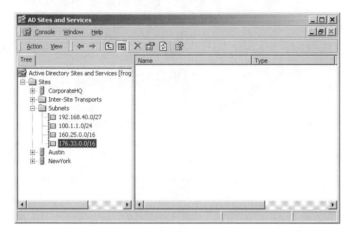

7. When finished, close the Active Directory Sites and Services tool.

So far, we have created the basic components that govern Active Directory sites: sites and subnets. We also linked these two components together by defining which subnets belong in which sites. These two steps—the creation of sites and subnets—form the basis of mapping the physical network infrastructure of an organization to the Active Directory. But wait, there's more! In addition to the basic configuration options we have covered thus far, sites can be further customized. Now, let's look at the various settings that you can make for sites.

## Configuring Sites

Once you have configured Active Directory sites and defined which subnets they contain, it's time to make some additional configurations to the site structure. Specifically, you'll need to assign servers to specific sites and configure the site licensing options. Exercise 6.3 walks you through the steps necessary to accomplish this. Placing servers in sites tells the Active Directory replication services how to replicate information for various types of servers.

Later in this chapter, we'll look at the details of working with replication within sites and replication between sites.

The purpose of the *licensing server* is to track the operating system and Microsoft BackOffice licenses within a domain. This is an important feature because it allows systems administrators to ensure that they have purchased the proper number of licenses for their network environment. Since licensing information must be recorded by servers, you can use the Active Directory Sites and Services tool to specify a License server for a site.

### Configuring Sites

In this exercise, you will add servers to sites and configure site-licensing options. In order to complete the steps in this exercise, you must have first completed Exercises 6.1 and 6.2.

1. Open the Active Directory Sites and Services tool from the Administrative Tools program group.

2. Expand the Sites folder, and click the Austin site.

3. Right-click the Servers container, and select New ➢ Server. Type **AustinDC1** for the name of the server, and then click OK.

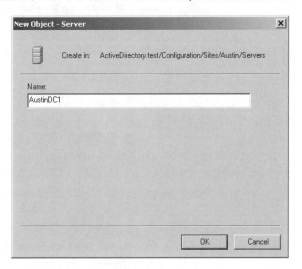

4. Create a new Server object within the CorporateHQ site, and name it CorpDC1. Note that this object will also include the name of the local domain controller.

**EXERCISE 6.3** *(continued)*

5. Create two new Server objects within the NewYork site, and name them NewYorkDC1 and NewYorkDC2.

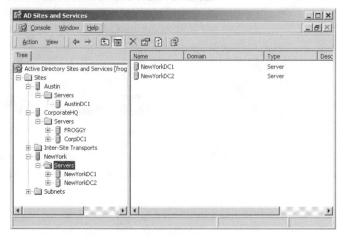

6. Right-click the NewYorkDC1 server object and select Properties. Select the IP item in the Transports Available for Intersite Data Transfer box, and click Add to make this server a preferred IP bridgehead server. Click OK to accept the settings.

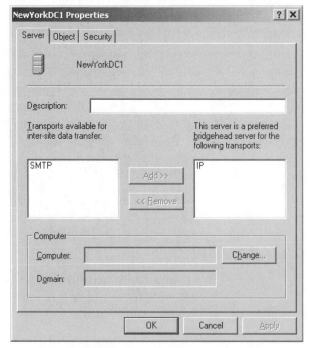

7. To set the Licensing server for the CorporateHQ site, click the Austin container and look in the right windowpane. Right-click the Licensing Site Settings object, and select Properties. To change the computer that will act as the Licensing server for the site, click Change. Select the name of the local domain controller from the list of available computers, and click OK. To save the settings, click OK.

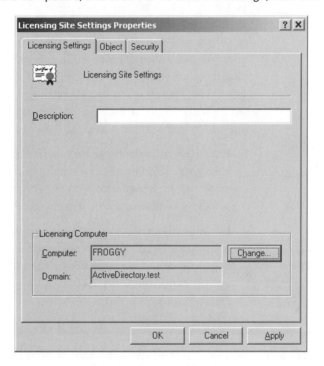

8. When finished, close the Active Directory Sites and Services tool.

With the configuration of the basic settings for sites out of the way, it's time to focus on the real details of the site topology—creating site links and site link bridges.

# Configuring Replication

**S**ites are generally used to define groups of computers that are located within a single geographic location. In most organizations, machines that are located in close physical proximity (for example, within a single building or branch office) are well connected. A typical example is a LAN in a branch office of a company. All of the computers may be connected together using Ethernet, and routing and switching technology may be in place to reduce network congestion.

Often, however, domain controllers are located across various states, countries, and even continents. In such a situation, network connectivity is usually much slower, less reliable, and more costly than that for the equivalent LAN. Therefore, Active Directory replication must accommodate accordingly. When managing replication traffic within Active Directory sites, there are two main areas of synchronization.

**Intrasite** *Intrasite replication* refers to the synchronization of Active Directory information between domain controllers that are located in the same site. In accordance with the concept of sites, these machines are usually well connected by a high-speed LAN.

**Intersite** *Intersite replication* occurs between domain controllers in different sites. Usually, this means that there is a WAN or other type of costly network connection between the various machines. Intersite replication is optimized for minimizing the amount of network traffic that occurs between sites.

---

| *Microsoft* ✓ *Exam* *Objective* | **Manage and troubleshoot Active Directory replication.**<br><br>• Manage intersite replication.<br><br>• Manage intrasite replication. |
| --- | --- |

In this section, we'll look at ways to configure both intrasite and intersite replication. Additionally, we'll look at features of the Active Directory replication architecture that can be used to accommodate the needs of almost any environment.

# Intrasite Replication

Intrasite replication is generally a simple process. One domain controller contacts the others in the same site when changes to its copy of the Active Directory are made. It compares the logical sequence numbers in its own copy of the Active Directory with that of the other domain controllers, then the most current information is chosen, and all domain controllers within the site use this information to make the necessary updates to their database.

Since it is assumed that the domain controllers within an Active Directory site are well connected, less attention to exactly when and how replication takes place is required. Communications between domain controllers occur using the *Remote Procedure Call (RPC) protocol*. This protocol is optimized for transmitting and synchronizing information on fast and reliable network connections. The actual directory synchronizing information is not compressed. Therefore, it provides for fast replication at the expense of network bandwidth.

Intrasite replication works well for domain controllers that are well connected. But what should be done about replication between sites? We'll cover this topic next.

# Intersite Replication

Intersite replication is optimized for low-bandwidth situations and network connections that have less reliability.

Intersite replication offers several specific features that are tailored toward these types of connections. To begin with, there are two different protocols that may be used to transfer information between sites:

**RPC over Internet Protocol (IP)**   When connectivity is fairly reliable, the Internet Protocol is a good choice. IP-based communications require a live connection between two or more domain controllers in different sites and allow for the transfer of Active Directory information. RPC over IP was originally designed for slower WANs in which packet loss and corruption may occur often. As such, it is a good choice for low-quality connections involved in intersite replication.

**Simple Mail Transfer Protocol (SMTP)**   *Simple Mail Transfer Protocol (SMTP)* is perhaps best known as the protocol that is used to send e-mail messages on the Internet. SMTP was designed to use a store-and-forward mechanism through which a server receives a copy of a message, records it to disk, and then attempts to forward it to another mail server. If the destination server is unavailable, it will hold the message and attempt to resend it at periodic intervals.

This type of communication is extremely useful for situations in which network connections are unreliable or not always available. If, for instance, a branch office in Peru is connected to the corporate office by a dial-up connection that is available only during certain hours, SMTP would be a good choice.

SMTP is an inherently insecure network protocol. You must, therefore, take advantage of Windows 2000's Certificate Services functionality if you use SMTP for Active Directory replication.

Other intersite replication characteristics that are designed to address low-bandwidth situations and less reliable network connections include the compression of Active Directory information. This is helpful because changes between domain controllers in remote sites may include a large amount of information and also because network bandwidth tends to be less available and more costly. Intersite replication topology is determined through the use of site links and site link bridges and can occur based on a schedule defined by systems administrators. All of these features provide for a high degree of flexibility in controlling replication configuration.

You can configure intersite replication by using the Active Directory Sites and Services tool. Select the name of the site for which you want to configure settings. Then, right-click the NTDS (Windows NT Directory Services) Site Settings object in the right windowpane, and select Properties. By clicking the Change Schedule button, you'll be able to configure how often replication between sites will occur (see Figure 6.3).

**FIGURE 6.3** Configuring intersite replication schedules

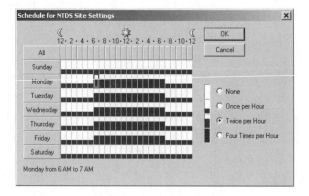

## Creating Site Links and Site Link Bridges

The overall topology of intersite replication is based on the use of site links and site link bridges. Site links are logical connections that define a path between two Active Directory sites. Site links can include several descriptive elements that define their network characteristics. *Site link bridges* are used to connect site links together so that the relationship can be transitive.

**Microsoft
✓Exam
Objective**

**Install, configure, and troubleshoot the components of Active Directory.**

- Create site links.

- Create site link bridges.

Figure 6.4 provides an example of site links and site link bridges.

**FIGURE  6.4**    An example of site links and site link bridges

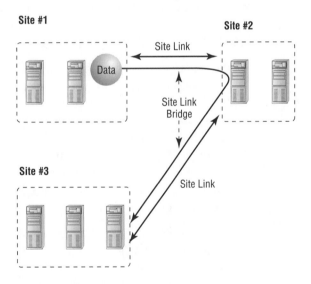

Both of these types of logical connections are used by the Active Directory services to determine how information should be synchronized between

domain controllers in remote sites. So how is this information used? The Knowledge Consistency Checker (KCC) forms a replication topology based on the site topology created. This service is responsible for determining the best way to replicate information within and between sites.

When creating site links for your environment, you'll need to consider the following factors:

**Transport**   You can choose to use either RPC over IP or SMTP for transferring information over a site link. The main determination will be based on your network infrastructure and the reliability of connections between sites.

**Cost**   Multiple site links can be created between sites. Site links can be assigned a cost value based on the type of connection. The systems administrator determines the cost value, and the relative costs of site links are then used to determine the optimal path for replication. The lower the cost, the more likely the link is to be used for replication.

For example, a company may primarily use a T1 link between branch offices, but it may also use a slower dial-up Integrated Services Digital Network (ISDN) connection for redundancy (in case the T1 fails). In this example, a systems administrator may assign a cost of 25 to the T1 line and a cost of 100 to the ISDN line. This will ensure that the more reliable and higher-bandwidth T1 connection is used whenever it's available but that the ISDN line is also available.

**Schedule**   Once you've determined how and through which connections replication will take place, it's time to determine *when* information should be replicated. Replication requires network resources and occupies bandwidth. Therefore, you will need to balance the need for consistent directory information with the need to conserve bandwidth. For example, if you determine that it's reasonable to have a lag time of six hours between when an update is made at one site and when it is replicated to all others, you might schedule replication to occur once in the morning, once during the lunch hour, and more frequently after normal work hours.

Based on these factors, you should be able to devise a strategy that will allow you to configure site links.

Exercise 6.4 walks you through the process of creating site links and site link bridges.

### Creating Site Links and Site Link Bridges

In this exercise, you will create links between sites. In order to complete the steps in this exercise, you must have first completed the steps in Exercises 6.1, 6.2, and 6.3.

1. Open the Active Directory Sites and Services tool from the Administrative Tools program group.

2. Expand Sites ➢ Inter-Site Transports ➢ IP object. Right-click the DEFAULTIPSITELINK item in the right pane, and select Rename. Rename the object to CorporateWAN.

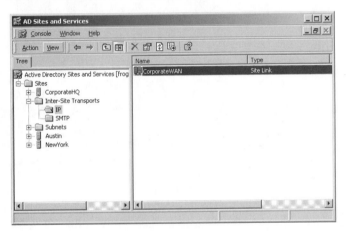

**EXERCISE 6.4** *(continued)*

3. Right-click the CorporateWAN link, and select Properties. For the
   description of the link, type **T1 connecting Corporate and New
   York offices**. Remove the Austin site from the link. For the Cost
   value, type **50**, and specify that replication should occur every 60
   minutes. To create the site link, click OK.

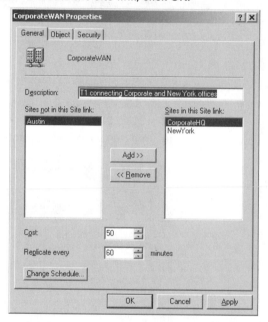

4. Right-click the IP folder, and select New Site Link. For the name of
   the link, type **CorporateDialup**. Add the Austin and CorporateHQ
   sites to the site link, and then click OK.

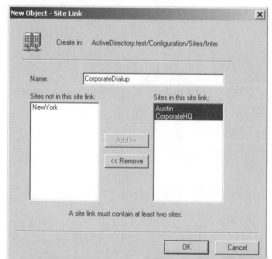

5. Right-click the CorporateDialup link, and select Properties. For the description, type **ISDN Dialup between Corporate and Austin office**. Set the Cost value to 100, and specify that replication should occur every 120 minutes.

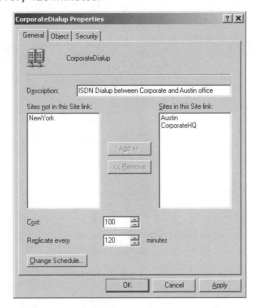

6. To specify that replication should occur only during certain times of the day, click the Change Schedule button. Highlight the area between 8:00 A.M. and 6:00 P.M. for the days Monday through Friday, and click the Replication Not Available option. This will ensure that replication traffic is minimized during normal work hours. Click OK to accept the new schedule, and then OK again to create the site link.

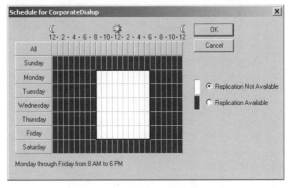

**EXERCISE 6.4** *(continued)*

7. Right-click the IP object, and select New Site Link Bridge. For the name of the site link bridge, type **CorporateBridge**. Note that the CorporateDialup and CorporateWAN site links are already added to the site link bridge. Since there must be at least two site links in each bridge, you will not be able to remove these links. Click OK to create the site link bridge.

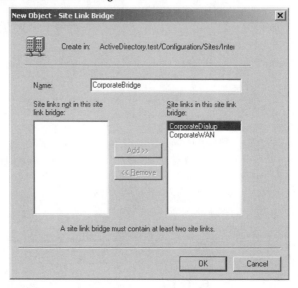

8. When finished, close the Active Directory Sites and Services tool.

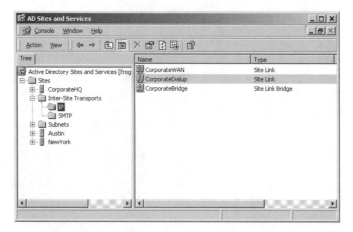

## Creating Connection Objects

Generally, it is a good practice to allow the Active Directory's replication mechanisms to automatically schedule and manage replication functions. In some cases, however, you may want to have additional control over replication. Perhaps you want to replicate changes on demand (when you create new accounts). Or, you may want to specify a custom schedule for certain servers.

---

*Microsoft*
✓ *Exam*
*Objective*

**Install, configure, and troubleshoot the components of Active Directory.**

- Create connection objects.

---

You can set up these different types of replication schedules through the use of *connection objects*. Connection objects can be created with the Active Directory Sites and Services tool by expanding a server object, right-clicking the NTDS Settings object, and selecting New Active Directory Connection (see Figure 6.5). Exercise 6.5 takes you through the steps for creating connection objects in more detail.

**FIGURE 6.5** Creating a new connection object

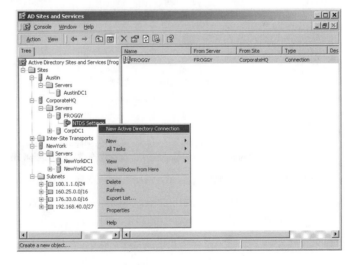

Within the properties of the connection object, which you can see in the right pane, you can specify the type of transport to use for replication (RPC over IP or SMTP), the schedule for replication, and the domain controllers that will participate in the replication (see Figure 6.6). Additionally, you will have the ability to right-click the connection object and select Replicate Now.

**FIGURE 6.6** Viewing the properties of a connection object

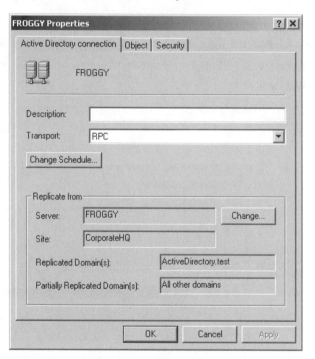

---

**EXERCISE 6.5**

### Creating Connection Objects

In this exercise, you will create and configure a custom connection object to control Active Directory replication.

1. Open the Active Directory Sites and Services tool.

2. Find the site that contains the local domain controller, and expand this object.

**EXERCISE 6.5** *(continued)*

**3.** Expand the name of the local domain controller. Right-click NTDS Settings, and select New Active Directory Connection. The Find Domain Controllers box will appear, showing a list of the servers that are available.

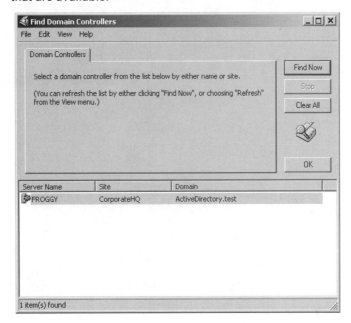

**4.** Highlight the name of the local server, and click OK.

**5.** For the name of the connection object, type **Connection**. Click OK.

**6.** In the right pane of the window, right-click the Connection item, and select Properties.

**EXERCISE 6.5** *(continued)*

7. For the description, type **After-hours synchronization**. For the Transport, choose IP.

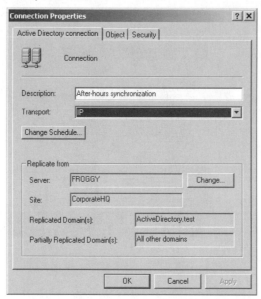

8. When finished, click OK to save the properties of the connection object.

9. To modify the allowed times for replication, click the Change Schedule button. Highlight the area from 8:00 A.M. to 6:00 P.M. for all days, and then click the Once per Hour item. This will reduce the frequency of replication during normal business hours. Click OK to save the schedule.

10. Close the Active Directory Sites and Services tool.

## Moving Server Objects between Sites

Using the Active Directory Sites and Services tool, you can easily move servers between sites. To do this, simply right-click the name of a domain controller,

and select Move. You can then select the site to which you want to move the domain controller object.

---

*Microsoft* ✓ *Exam* *Objective*

**Install, configure, and troubleshoot the components of Active Directory.**

- Move server objects between sites.

---

Figure 6.7 shows the screen that you'll see when you attempt to move a server. After the server is moved, all replication topology settings will be updated automatically. If you want to choose custom replication settings, you'll need to manually create connection objects (as described earlier). See Exercise 6.6 for a detailed explanation of the steps involved in moving server objects between sites.

**FIGURE 6.7** Choosing a new site for a specific server

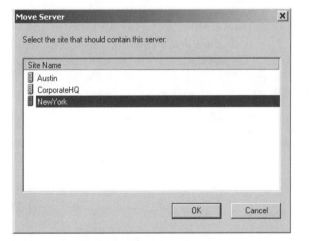

---

**EXERCISE 6.6**

### Moving Server Objects between Sites

In this exercise, you will move a server object between sites. In order to complete the steps in this exercise, you must have first completed the previous exercises in this chapter.

**EXERCISE 6.6**

1. Open the Active Directory Sites and Services administrative tool.

2. Right-click the server named NewYorkDC1, and select Move.

3. Select the Austin site, and then click OK. This will move this server to the Austin site.

4. To move the server back, right-click NewYorkDC1 (now located in the Austin site) and then click Move. Select New York for the destination site.

5. When finished, close the Active Directory Sites and Services administrative tool.

## Creating Bridgehead Servers

By default, all of the servers in one site will communicate with the servers in another site. You can, however, further control replication between sites by using *bridgehead servers*. This method is useful for minimizing replication traffic in larger network environments and allows you to dedicate machines that are better connected to receive replicated data. Figure 6.8 provides an example of how bridgehead servers work.

**FIGURE 6.8** A replication scenario using bridgehead servers

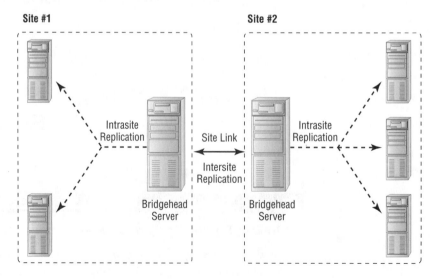

A bridgehead server is used to specify which domain controllers are preferred for transferring replication information between sites. Different bridgehead servers can be selected for RCP over IP and SMTP replication, thus allowing you to balance the load. To create a bridgehead server for a site, simply right-click a domain controller and select Properties (See Figure 6.9).

**FIGURE  6.9**    Specifying a bridgehead server

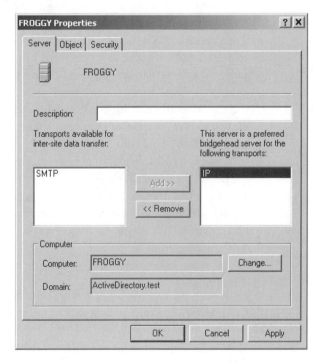

## Configuring Server Topology

In environments that require the use of multiple sites, it is very important to consider the placement of servers. In so doing, you can greatly improve performance and end-user experience by reducing the time required to perform common operations such as authentication or searching the Active Directory.

There are two main issues to consider when designing a distributed Active Directory environment. The first is the placement of domain controllers within the network environment. The second is managing the use of Global Catalog (GC) servers. Finding the right balance between servers, server resources, and performance can be considered an art form for network and systems administrators. In this section, we'll look at some of the important considerations that must be taken into account when designing a replication server topology.

## Placing Domain Controllers

It is highly recommended that you have at least two domain controllers in each domain of your Active Directory environment. As mentioned earlier in this chapter, the use of additional domain controllers allows for additional performance (since the servers can balance the burden of serving client requests) and provides for fault tolerance (in case one domain controller fails, the other still contains a valid and usable copy of the Active Directory database). Furthermore, the proper placement of domain controllers can increase overall network performance since clients can connect to the server closest to them instead of performing authentication and security operations across a slow WAN link.

As we just mentioned, having too few domain controllers can be a problem. However, there is such a thing as *too many* domain controllers. Keep in mind that the more domain controllers you choose to implement, the greater the replication traffic will be. As each domain controller must propagate any changes to all of the others, you can probably see how this can result in a lot of network traffic.

For more information on installing additional domain controllers for a domain, see Chapter 5.

## Placing Global Catalog Servers

A *Global Catalog (GC) server* is a domain controller that contains a copy of all the objects contained in the forestwide domain controllers that compose the Active Directory database. Making a domain controller a GC server is a very simple operation, and you can change this setting quite easily. That brings us to the harder part—determining which domain controllers should also be GC servers.

The placement of domain controllers and GC servers is an important issue. Generally, you will want to make GC servers available in every site that has a slow link. However, there is a trade-off that can make having too many GC servers a bad thing. The main issue is associated with replication traffic—each GC server within your environment must be kept synchronized with the other servers. In a very dynamic environment, the additional network traffic caused by the use of GC servers can be considerable. Therefore, you will want to find a good balance between replication burdens and GC query performance in your own environment.

To create a GC server, simply expand the Server object in the Active Directory Sites and Services tool, right-click NTDS settings, and select Properties. To configure a server as a GC server, simply place a check mark in the Global Catalog box (see Figure 6.10).

**FIGURE 6.10** Enabling the Global Catalog on an Active Directory domain controller

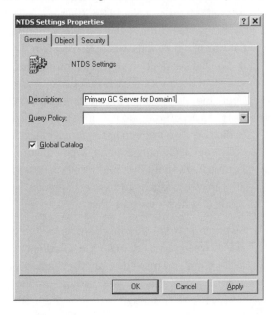

**Real World Scenario**

### Accommodating a Changing Environment

You're a systems administrator for a medium-sized business that consists of many offices located throughout the world. Some of these offices are well connected through the use of high-speed, reliable links, while others are not so fortunate. Overall, things are going well until your CEO announces that the organization will be merging with another large company and that the business will be restructured. The restructuring will involve the opening of new offices, the closing of old ones, and the transfer of employees to different locations. Additionally, changes in the IT budget will affect the types of links that exist between offices. Your job as the systems administrator is to ensure that the network environment and, specifically, the Active Directory, keeps pace with the changes.

An important skill for any technical professional is the ability to quickly and efficiently adapt to a changing organization. When a business grows, restructures, or forms relationships with other businesses, there are often many IT-related changes that must also occur. Fortunately, the Active Directory has been designed with these kinds of challenges in mind. For example, you can use the Active Directory Sites and Services administrative tool to reflect physical network changes in the Active Directory topology. If a site that previously had 64Kbps of bandwidth was upgraded to a T1 connection, you could change those characteristics for the site link objects. Conversely, if a site that was previously well connected was reduced to a slow, unreliable link, you could reconfigure the sites, change the site link transport mechanisms (perhaps from IP to SMTP to accommodate a non-persistent link), and create connection objects (which would allow you to schedule replication traffic to occur during the least busy hours). Or, suppose that many of your operations move overseas to a European division. This might call for designating specific domain controllers as preferred bridgehead servers to reduce the amount of replication traffic over costly and slow overseas links.

Sweeping organizational changes will inevitably require you to move servers between sites. For example, an office may be closed and its domain controllers may be moved to another region of the world. Again, you can accommodate this change through the use of the Active Directory administrative tools. You may change your OU structure to reflect new logical and business-oriented changes, and you can move server objects between sites to reflect physical network changes.

Rarely can the job of mapping a physical infrastructure to the Active Directory "complete." In most environments, it's safe to assume that there will always be changes required based on business needs. Overall, however, you should feel comfortable that the physical components of the Active Directory are at your side to help you accommodate the change.

# Monitoring and Troubleshooting Active Directory Replication

**F**or the most part, domain controllers handle the processes involved with replication automatically. However, systems administrators will still need to monitor the performance of Active Directory replication. Failed network links and incorrect configurations can sometimes prevent the synchronization of information between domain controllers.

*Microsoft* ✓ *Exam Objective*

**Manage and troubleshoot Active Directory replication.**

- Manage intersite replication.
- Manage intrasite replication.

This section covers general information related to troubleshooting replication. See "Configuring Replication," a section that appears earlier in this chapter, for coverage of the "Manage intersite replication" and "Manage intrasite replication" subobjectives.

There are several ways in which you can monitor the behavior of Active Directory replication and troubleshoot the process if problems occur.

## Using System Monitor

The Windows 2000 System Monitor administrative tool was designed to allow you to monitor many performance statistics associated with the use of the Active Directory. Included within the various performance statistics that may be monitored are counters related to Active Directory replication. We'll cover the details of working with the System Monitor tools of Windows 2000 in Chapter 9, "Active Directory Optimization and Reliability."

## Troubleshooting Replication

A common symptom of replication problems is that information is not updated on some or all domain controllers. For example, a systems administrator creates a User account on one domain controller, but the changes are not propagated to other domain controllers. In most environments, this is a potentially serious problem because it affects network security and can prevent authorized users from accessing the resources they require.

There are several steps that you can take to troubleshoot Active Directory replication:

**Verify network connectivity.**   The fundamental requirement for replication to work properly in distributed environments is network connectivity. Although the ideal situation would be that all domain controllers are connected by high-speed LAN links, this is rarely the case for larger organizations. In the real world, dial-up connections and slow connections are common. If you have verified that your replication topology is set up properly, you should confirm that your servers are able to communicate. Problems such as a failed dial-up connection attempt can prevent important Active Directory information from being replicated.

**Verify router and firewall configurations.**   Firewalls are used to restrict the types of traffic that can be transferred between networks. Their main use is to increase security by preventing unauthorized users from transferring information. In some cases, company firewalls may block the types of network access that must be available in order for Active Directory replication to occur. For example, if a specific router or firewall prevents data from being transferred using SMTP, replication that uses this protocol will fail.

**Examine the event logs.**   Whenever an error in the replication configuration occurs, events are written to the Directory Service event log. By using the Event Viewer administrative tool, you can quickly and easily view the details associated with any problems in replication. For example, if one domain controller is not able to communicate with another to transfer changes, a log entry will be created. Figure 6.11 shows an example of the types of events you will see in the Directory Service log, and Figure 6.12 shows an example of a configuration error.

**FIGURE 6.11** Viewing entries in the Directory Service event log

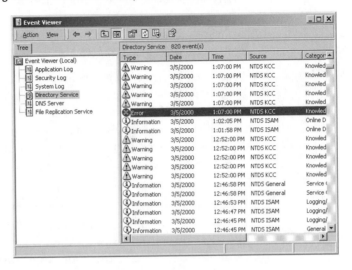

**FIGURE 6.12** Examining the details of an event log entry

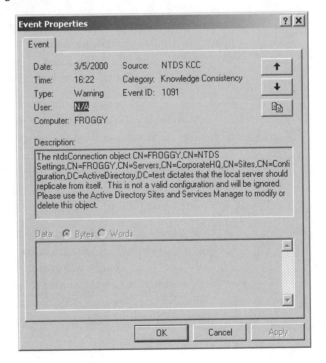

**Verify site links.** Before domain controllers in different sites can communicate with each other, the sites must be connected by site links. If replication between sites is not occurring properly, verify that the proper site links are in place.

**Verify that information is synchronized.** It's often easy to forget to perform manual checks regarding the replication of Active Directory information. One of the reasons for this is that Active Directory domain controllers have their own read/write copies of the Active Directory database. Therefore, you will not encounter failures in creating new objects if connectivity does not exist.

It is important to periodically verify that objects have been synchronized between domain controllers. The process might be as simple as logging on to a different domain controller and looking at the objects within a specific OU. This manual check, although it might be tedious, can prevent inconsistencies in the information stored on domain controllers, which, over time, could become an administration and security nightmare.

**Verify authentication scenarios.** A common replication configuration issue occurs when clients are forced to authenticate across slow network connections. The primary symptom of the problem is that users will complain about the amount of time that it takes to log on to the Active Directory (especially during times of high volume of authentications, such as at the beginning of the workday).

Usually, this problem can be alleviated through the use of additional domain controllers or a reconfiguration of the site topology. A good way to test this is to consider the possible scenarios for the various clients that you support. Often, walking through a configuration, such as "A client in Domain1 is trying to authenticate using a domain controller in Domain2, which is located across a slow WAN connection," can be helpful in pinpointing potential problem areas.

**Verify the replication topology.** The Active Directory Sites and Services tool allows you to verify that a replication topology is logically consistent. You can quickly and easily perform this task by right-clicking the NTDS Settings within a Server object and choosing All Tasks ➢ Check Replication Topology (see Figure 6.13). If any errors are present, a dialog box will alert you to the problem.

**FIGURE 6.13** Verifying the Active Directory topology using the Active Directory Sites and Services tool

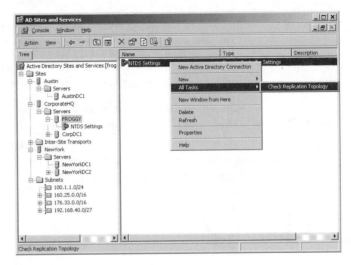

By using the above troubleshooting techniques, you will be able to diagnose and verify any problems with the configuration of your replication topology. This will ensure consistency of data between the various domain controllers in your environment.

# Summary

In this chapter, we covered the very important topic of managing Active Directory replication by discussing the following:

- The purpose of Active Directory replication

- The concepts behind Active Directory sites and how they effect replication and the accessibility of domain services

- Details about various Active Directory features that help optimize replication traffic based on the needs of various network environments. These features include sites, subnets, site links, and site link bridges.

- Connection objects that can be used to define replication behavior at a very granular level

- Bridgehead servers that can be used to reduce replication traffic across slow links

- The importance of domain controller and Global Catalog server placement and how it can affect overall Active Directory performance

- Several tools and methods that are available for monitoring and troubleshooting Active Directory replication

Although replication is a behind-the-scenes type of task, the optimal configuration of sites in distributed network environments will result in better use of bandwidth and faster response by network resources. For these reasons, you should be sure that you thoroughly understand the concepts related to managing replication for the Active Directory.

# Exam Essentials

**Understand the purpose of Active Directory replication.**   Replication is used to keep domain controllers synchronized and is important in Active Directory environments of all sizes.

**Understand the concept of sites and subnets.**   Subnets define physical portions of your network environment. Sites are defined as collections of well-connect IP subnets.

**Understand the differences between intrasite and intersite replication.** Intrasite replication is designed to synchronize Active Directory information to machines that are located in the same site. Intersite replication is used to synchronize information for domain controllers that are located in different sites.

**Implement site links, site link bridges, and connection objects.**   All three of these object types can be used to finely control the behavior of Active Directory replication and to manage replication traffic.

**Determine where to place domain controllers and Global Catalog servers based on a set of requirements.**   The placement of domain controllers and Global Catalog servers can increase the performance of Active Directory operations. However, in order to optimize performance, you should understand where the best places are to put these servers in a network environment that consists of multiple sites.

**Monitor and troubleshoot replication.**   Windows 2000's administrative tools include many methods for troubleshooting and monitoring replication.

# Key Terms

Before you take the exam, be certain you are familiar with the following terms:

| | |
|---|---|
| Active Directory replication | local area network (LAN) |
| bridgehead servers | Remote Procedure Call (RPC) protocol |
| connection objects | Simple Mail Transfer Protocol (SMTP) |
| domain controllers | site |
| Global Catalog (GC) server | site link |
| Internet Protocol (IP) | site link bridge |
| intersite replication | subnet |
| intrasite replication | wide area network (WAN) |
| licensing server | |

# Review Questions

1. Daniel is responsible for managing Active Directory replication traffic for a medium-sized organization that has deployed a single Active Directory domain. Currently, the environment is configured with two sites and the default settings for replication. Each site consists of 15 domain controllers. Recently, network administrators have complained that Active Directory traffic is using a large amount of available network bandwidth between the two sites. Daniel has been asked to meet the following requirements:

   - Reduce the amount of network traffic between domain controllers in the two sites.

   - Minimize the amount of change to the current site topology.

   - Require no changes to the existing physical network infrastructure.

   Daniel decides that it would be most efficient to configure specific domain controllers in each site that will receive the majority of replication traffic from the other site. Which of the following solutions will meet the requirements?

   **A.** Create additional sites that are designed only for replication traffic and move the existing domain controllers to these sites.

   **B.** Create multiple site links between the two sites.

   **C.** Create a site link bridge between the two sites.

   **D.** Configure one server at each site to act as a preferred bridgehead server.

   **E.** None of the above solutions will meet the requirements.

2. Which of the following must not be manually created when setting up a replication scenario involving three domains and three sites?

   **A.** Sites

   **B.** Site links

   **C.** Connection objects

   **D.** Subnets

   **E.** None of the above

3. Which of the following services of the Active Directory is responsible for maintaining the replication topology?

   **A.** File Replication Service

   **B.** Knowledge Consistency Checker

   **C.** Windows Internet Name Service

   **D.** Domain Name System

   **E.** None of the above

4. Matt, a systems administrator for an Active Directory environment that consists of three sites, wants to configure site links to be transitive. Which of the following Active Directory objects is responsible for representing a transitive relationship between sites?

   **A.** Additional sites

   **B.** Additional site links

   **C.** Bridgehead servers

   **D.** Site link bridges

   **E.** None of the above

5. Which of the following is generally *not* true regarding the domain controllers within a site?

   **A.** They are generally connected by a high-speed network.

   **B.** They must reside on the same subnets.

   **C.** They are generally connected by reliable connections.

   **D.** They may be domain controllers for different domains.

   **E.** None of the above.

**6.** Which of the following protocols may be used for intrasite replication? (Choose all that apply.)

**A.** DHCP

**B.** RPC

**C.** IP

**D.** SMTP

**E.** WINS

**7.** You have configured your Active Directory environment with multiple sites and have placed the appropriate resources in each of the sites. You are now trying to choose a protocol for the transfer of replication information between two sites. The connection between the two sites has the following characteristics:

- The link is generally unavailable during certain parts of the day due to an unreliable network provider.

- The replication transmission must be attempted whether the link is available or not. If the link was unavailable during a scheduled replication, the information should automatically be received after the link becomes available again.

- Replication traffic must be able to travel over a standard Internet connection.

Which of the following protocol(s) meets these requirements? (Choose all that apply.)

**A.** IP

**B.** SMTP

**C.** RPC

**D.** DHCP

**E.** None of the above

8. A network administrator has decided that it will be necessary to implement multiple sites in order to efficiently manage your company's large Active Directory environment. Based on her recommendations, you make the following decisions:

   - The best configuration involves the creation of four sites.

   - The sites will be connected with site links and site link bridges.

   - Two small offices must only receive replication traffic during non-business hours.

   - The organization owns a single DNS name: supercompany.com.

   - Administration should be kept as simple as possible, and you want to use the smallest possible number of domains.

   Based on this information, you must plan the Active Directory domain architecture. What is the minimum number of domains that must be created to support this configuration?

   **A.** 0

   **B.** 1

   **C.** 4

   **D.** 8

9. An organization's Active Directory site structure should be primarily based on its

   **A.** Domain structure

   **B.** Political concerns

   **C.** Geographic distribution

   **D.** Physical network infrastructure

   **E.** None of the above

**10.** Andrew is troubleshooting a problem with the Active Directory. He has been told by one systems administrator that she made an update to a user object and that another system administrator reported that he had not seen the changes appear on another domain controller. It has been over a week since the change was made. Andrew further verifies the problem by making a change to another Active Directory object. Within a few hours, the change appears on a few domain controllers, but not on all of them.

Which of the following are possible causes for this problem? (Choose all that apply.)

**A.** Network connectivity is unavailable.

**B.** Connection objects are not properly configured.

**C.** Sites are not properly configured.

**D.** Site links are not properly configured.

**E.** A WAN connection has failed.

**F.** Andrew has configured one of the domain controllers for manual replication updates.

**11.** A systems administrator suspects that there is an error in the replication configuration. How can he look for specific error messages related to replication?

**A.** By using the Active Directory Sites and Services administrative tool

**B.** By using the Computer Management tool

**C.** By going to Event Viewer ➢ System log

**D.** By going to Event Viewer ➢ Directory Service log

**E.** All of the above

**12.** Christina is responsible for managing Active Directory replication traffic for a medium-sized organization. Currently, the environment is configured with a single site and the default settings for replication. The site contains over 50 domain controllers and the system administrators are often making changes to the Active Directory database. Recently, network administrators have complained that Active Directory traffic is consuming a large amount of network bandwidth between portions of the network that are connected by slow links. Ordinarily, the amount of replication traffic is reasonable, but recently users have complained about slow network performance during certain hours of the day.

Christina has been asked to alleviate the problem while meeting the following requirements:

- Be able to control exactly when replication occurs.

- Be able to base Active Directory replication on the physical network infrastructure.

- Perform the changes without creating or removing any domain controllers.

Which two of the following steps can Christina take to meet these requirements? (Choose two.)

**A.** Create and define connection objects that specify the hours during which replication will occur.

**B.** Create multiple site links.

**C.** Create a site link bridge.

**D.** Create new Active Directory sites that reflect the physical network topology.

**E.** Configure one server at each of the new sites to act as a bridgehead server.

13. Jason, a systems administrator, suspects that Active Directory replication traffic is consuming a large amount of network bandwidth. Jason is attempting to determine the amount of network traffic that is generated through replication. He wants to do the following:

    - Determine replication data transfer statistics.

    - Collect information about multiple Active Directory domain controllers at the same time.

    - Measure other performance statistics, such as server CPU utilization.

    Which of the following administrative tools is most useful for meeting these requirements?

    **A.** Active Directory Users and Computers

    **B.** Active Directory Domains and Trusts

    **C.** Active Directory Sites and Services

    **D.** Event Viewer

    **E.** Performance

14. You are the administrator of a large, distributed network environment. Recently, your IT department has decided to add various routers to the environment to limit the amount of traffic going to and from various areas of the network. You need to reconfigure Active Directory replication to reflect the physical network changes. Which of the following Active Directory objects should you modify to define the network boundaries for Active Directory sites?

    **A.** Site links

    **B.** Site link bridges

    **C.** Bridgehead servers

    **D.** Subnets

    **E.** None of the above

**15.** Which of the following are not characteristics of a site link?

    **A.** Transport protocol

    **B.** Cost

    **C.** Route

    **D.** Schedule

**16.** You have recently created a new Active Directory domain by promoting several Windows 2000 Server computers to domain controllers. You then use the Active Directory Sites and Services tool to configure sites for the environment. You soon find that changes that are made on one domain controller may not appear in the Active Directory database on another domain controller. By checking the Directory Services log using the Event Viewer application, you find that one of the domain controllers at a specific site is not receiving Active Directory updates. Which of the following is/are a possible reason(s) for this? (Choose all that apply.)

    **A.** Network connectivity has not been established for this server.

    **B.** A firewall is preventing replication information from being transmitted.

    **C.** There are not enough domain controllers in the environment.

    **D.** There are too many domain controllers in the environment.

    **E.** You chose to disable Active Directory replication during the promotion of the machine to a domain controller.

**17.** You administer a network that consists of one domain that spans three physical locations: San Jose, Chicago, and Austin. All three locations contain domain controllers. You have a T1 line between San Jose and Chicago, with an ISDN for backup. The ISDN line must have the default site link cost assigned to it. You want Austin to always use San Jose for its replication communication, even though a link does exist between Austin and Chicago for other purposes.

In the diagram below, select and place the correct relative costs that should be assigned to the various site links. Each cost can only be used once.

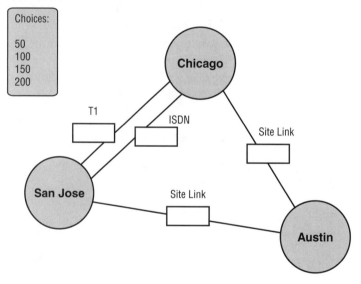

**18.** You need to create a new site named San Diego. Looking at the following screen, what would you do next in order to create the new site?

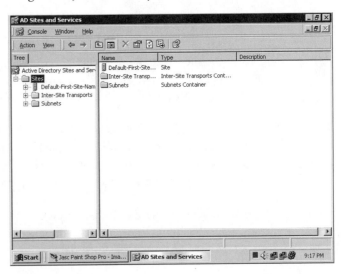

**A.** Right-click Default-First-Site-Name.

**B.** Right-click Sites.

**C.** Double-click Default-First-Site-Name.

**D.** Double-click Sites.

**19.** Which of the following network characteristics does *not* generally apply to LANs?

**A.** High-speed links

**B.** Routing

**C.** Switching

**D.** Non-persistent connections

**E.** All of the above

# Answers to Review Questions

1. D. Preferred bridgehead servers receive replication information for a site and transmit this information to other domain controllers within the site. By doing this, Daniel can ensure that all replication traffic between the two sites is routed through the bridgehead servers and that replication traffic will flow properly between the domain controllers.

2. C. By default, connection objects are automatically created by the Active Directory replication engine. You can, however, choose to override the default behavior of Active Directory replication topology by manually creating connection objects, but this step is not required.

3. B. The Knowledge Consistency Checker (KCC) is respon-sible for establishing the replication topology and ensuring that all domain controllers are kept up-to-date.

4. D. Site link bridges are designed to allow site links to be transitive. That is, they allow site links to use other site links to transfer replication information between sites. By default, all site links are bridged. How-ever, you can turn off transitivity if you want to override this behavior.

5. B. Domain controllers may be located on various different subnets and still be part of the same site.

6. B. Remote Procedure Calls (RPCs) are used to transfer information between domain controllers within an Active Directory site.

7. B. The Simple Mail Transfer Protocol (SMTP) was designed for envi-ronments in which persistent connections may not always be available. SMTP uses the store-and-forward method to ensure that information is not lost if a connection cannot be made.

8. B. Since there is no relationship between domain structure and site structure, only one domain is required. Generally, if there is only one domain, there will be many domain controllers with at least one in each site.

**9.** D. Although all of the choices may play a factor in the ultimate design, the primary consideration for site structure is based on physical network topology.

**10.** A, B, C, D, E. Misconfiguring any of these components of the Active Directory may cause a failure in replication.

**11.** D. The Directory Service event log contains error messages and information related to replication. These details can be useful when troubleshooting replication problems.

**12.** A, D.  By creating new sites, Christina can help define settings for Active Directory replication based on the environment's network connections. She can use connection objects to further define the details of how and when replication traffic will be transmitted between the domain controllers.

**13.** E. Through the use of the Performance administrative tool, systems administrators can measure and record performance values related to Active Directory replication. Jason can also use this tool to monitor multiple servers at the same time and to view other performance-related statistics.

**14.** D. Subnets define the specific network segments that are well connected.

**15.** C. A route is not a characteristic of a site link.

**16.** A, B. Since replication is occurring between most of the domain controllers, it is likely that a network problem is preventing this domain controller from communicating with the rest. A lack of network connectivity or the presence of a firewall can prevent replication from occurring properly. The number of domain controllers in an environment will not prevent the replication of information, nor can replication be disabled during the promotion process.

**17.**

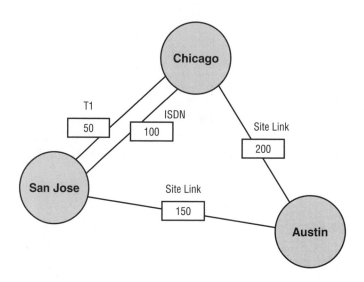

The ISDN line is required to have the default cost of 100. That means that the T1 line's cost must be lower than 100 in order for this connection to be used by preference, and the only choice is 50. That leaves costs of 150 and 200 for the Austin links. Since Austin will never get replication information from Chicago, that link's cost should be 200. That only leaves 150 for the cost of the link between Austin and San Jose.

Chapter: 6

Objective: 1

**18.** B. New sites can be created using the New Site action from the Sites contextual menu.

**19.** D. LAN connections are generally always available. They also share all of the other characteristics mentioned in the choices.

# Chapter

# 7

# Administering the Active Directory

## MICROSOFT EXAM OBJECTIVES COVERED IN THIS CHAPTER:

✓ **Manage Active Directory objects.**

- Move Active Directory objects.
- Publish resources in Active Directory.
- Locate objects in Active Directory.
- Create and manage accounts manually or by scripting.
- Control access to Active Directory objects.
- Delegate administrative control of objects in Active Directory.

**S**o far, we've covered the basic steps required to set up an Active Directory environment. Specifically, we covered the creation of domains, the creation of structures within domains (using organizational units), and the concepts related to Active Directory physical structure (sites). All of this is designed to set the stage for the real purpose of the Active Directory—managing objects.

In this chapter, we'll cover the actual steps required to create common Active Directory objects. Then, we'll see how these objects can be configured and managed. Finally, we'll look at ways to publish resources and methods for automating the creation of User accounts.

Although this chapter covers material related to Active Directory administration for the "Manage Active Directory objects" objective, controlling access to Active Directory objects and delegating administrative control of objects in Active Directory, topics addressed by the last two subobjectives, are covered in Chapter 8, "Active Directory Security."

# Creating and Managing Active Directory Objects

The main tool used to manage the objects within the Active Directory is the *Active Directory Users and Computers tool*. Using this Microsoft Management Console (MMC) snap-in, you will be able to create, manage, and control the use of Active Directory objects.

In Chapter 4, "Creating and Managing Organizational Units," we looked at how a hierarchical structure could be created within a domain. Be sure to review that information if you're unfamiliar with organizational units (OUs). The good news is that if you are familiar with the task of creating OUs, creating other Active Directory objects will be quite simple. Let's look at the details.

## Overview of Active Directory Objects

By default, after you install and configure a domain controller, you will see the following sections of organization within the Active Directory Users and Computers tool:

**Built-In**  The Built-In container includes all of the standard groups that are installed by default when you promote a domain controller. These groups are used for administering the servers in your environment. Examples include the Administrators group, Backup Operators, and Print Operators.

**Computers**  By default, the Computers container contains a list of the workstations in your domain. From here, you can manage all of the computers in your domain.

**Domain Controllers**  This container includes a list of all of the domain controllers for the domain.

**Foreign Security Principals**  *Security principals* are Active Directory objects to which permissions can be applied. They are used for managing permissions within the Active Directory. We'll cover the details of working with security principals in Chapter 8.

Foreign security principals are any objects to which security can be assigned and that are not part of the current domain.

**Users**  The Users container includes all of the security accounts that are part of the domain. When you first install the domain controller, there will be several groups in this container. For example, the Domain Admins group and the Administrator account are created in this container.

There are several different types of Active Directory objects that can be created and managed. The following are specific object types:

**Computer**  *Computer objects* are used for managing workstations in the environment.

**Contact**   Contacts are not security principals like Users, but they are used for specifying information about individuals within the organization. *Contact objects* are usually used in OUs to specify the main administrative contact.

**Group**   Groups are security principals. That is, they are created for assigning and managing permissions. Groups contain User accounts.

**Organizational Unit**   An OU is created to build a hierarchy within the Active Directory domain. It is the smallest unit that can be used to create administrative groupings and can be used for assigning Group Policies. Generally, the OU structure within a domain will reflect a company's business organization.

**Printer**   *Printer objects* map to printers.

**Shared Folder**   *Shared Folder objects* map to server shares. They are used for organizing the various file resources that may be available on file/print servers.

**User**   A *User object* is the fundamental security principal on which the Active Directory is based. User accounts contain information about individuals, as well as password and other permission information.

We'll cover the security aspects related to the use of Active Directory objects in Chapter 8. For now, however, know that these objects are used to represent various items in your network environment. Through the use of these objects, you will be able to manage the content of your Active Directory.

Exercise 7.1 walks through the steps required to create various objects within an Active Directory domain.

**EXERCISE 7.1**

### Creating Active Directory Objects

In this exercise, we will create some basic Active Directory objects. In order to complete this exercise, you must have first installed and configured at least one Active Directory domain.

**1.** Open the Active Directory Users and Computers tool.

2. Expand the current domain to list the objects currently contained within it. You should see folders similar to those shown.

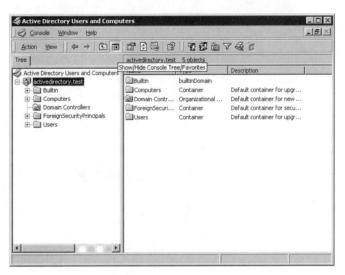

3. Create a new, top-level OU by right-clicking the name of the domain and selecting New ➢ Organizational Unit. When prompted for the name of the OU, type **Corporate** and click OK.

4. Repeat step 3 to create the following top-level OUs:

   Engineering

   HR

   IT

   Marketing

   Sales

**EXERCISE 7.1** *(continued)*

**5.** Right-click the Corporate OU, and select New ➢ User. Fill in the following information:

First Name: Monica

Initials: D

Last Name: President

Full Name: (leave as default)

User Logon Name: mdpresident (leave default domain)

Click Next to continue.

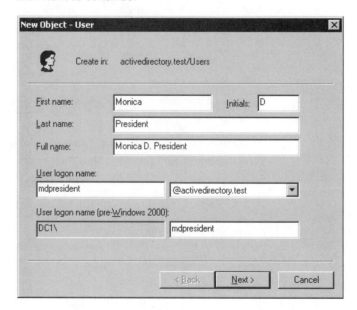

6. Enter in a password for this user, and then confirm it. Note that you can also make changes to password settings here. Click Next. You will see a summary of the user information. Click OK to create the new user.

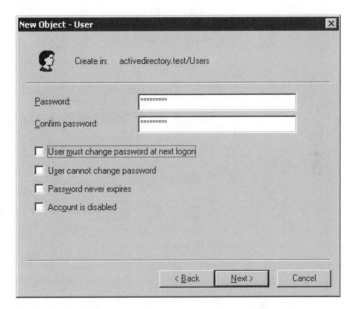

7. Create another user in the IT container with the following information:

   First Name: John

   Initials: Q

   Last Name: Admin

   Full Name: (leave as default)

   User Logon Name: jqadmin (leave default domain)

   Click Next to continue. Assign a password. Click Next, and then click Finish to create the user.

**EXERCISE 7.1** *(continued)*

**8.** Right-click the IT OU, and select New ⮞ Contact. Use the following information to fill in the properties of the Contact object:

First Name: Jane

Initials: R

Last Name: Admin

Display Name: jradmin

Click OK to create the new Contact object.

9. Right-click the IT OU, and select New ➤ Shared Folder. Enter **Software** for the name and **\\server1\applications** for the Network Path. Note that although this resource does not exist, the object can still be created. Click OK to create the Shared Folder object.

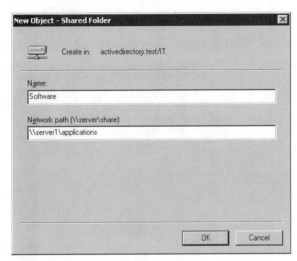

10. Right-click the HR OU, and select New ➤ Group. Type **All Users** for the Group Name [leave the Group Name (Pre-Windows 2000) field with the same value]. For the Group Scope, select Global, and for the Group Type, select Security. To create the group, click OK.

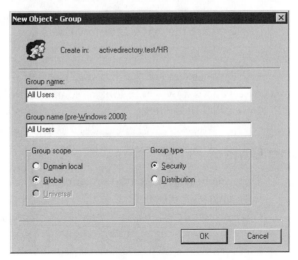

**11.** Right-click the Sales OU and select New ➢ Computer. Type **Workstation1** for the name of the computer. Notice that the pre-Windows 2000 name will automatically be populated and that, by default, the members of the Domain Admins group will be the only ones that will be able to add this computer to the domain. Place a check mark in the Allow Pre-Windows 2000 Computers to Use This Account box, and then click OK to create the Computer object.

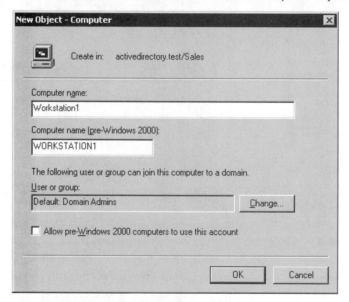

**12.** Close the Active Directory Users and Computers tool.

Now that you are familiar with the process of creating and managing objects, let's move on to look at some additional properties that can be set for each of these items.

## Managing Object Properties

Once the necessary Active Directory objects have been created, you'll probably need to make changes to their default properties. In addition to the settings you made when creating Active Directory objects, there are several more properties that can be configured. Exercise 7.2 walks you through setting various properties for Active Directory objects.

Although it may seem somewhat tedious, it's always a good idea to enter in as much information as you know about Active Directory objects when you create them. Although the name Printer1 may be meaningful to you, users will appreciate the additional information when searching for objects.

### EXERCISE 7.2

## Managing Object Properties

In this exercise, we will modify the properties for Active Directory objects. In order to complete the steps in this exercise, you must have first completed Exercise 7.1.

1. Open the Active Directory Users and Computers tool.

2. Expand the name of the domain, and select the IT container. Right-click the John Q. Admin User account, and select Properties.

3. Here, you will see the various Properties tabs for the User account. The basic tabs include the following:

> General: General account information about this user

> Address: The physical location information about this user

> Account: User logon name and other account restrictions, such as workstation restrictions and logon hours

> Profile: Information about the user's roaming profile settings

> Telephones: Telephone contact information for the user

> Organization: The user's title, department, and company information

> Member Of: Group membership information for the user

> Dial-In: Remote Access Service (RAS) permissions for the user

> Environment: Logon and other network settings for the user

> Sessions: Session limits, including maximum session time and idle session settings

> Remote Control: Remote control options for this user's session

Terminal Services Profile: Information about the user's profile for use with Windows 2000 Terminal Services

Click OK to continue.

**4.** Select the HR OU. Right-click the All Users Group, and click Properties. In this dialog box, you will be able to modify the membership of the group. Click the Members tab, and then click Add. Add the Monica D. President and John Q. Admin User accounts to the Group. Click OK to save the settings and then OK to accept the group modifications.

**5.** Select the Sales OU. Right-click the Workstation1 Computer object. Notice that you can choose to disable the account or reset it (to allow another computer to join the domain under that same name). From the right-click menu, choose Properties. You'll see the properties for the Computer object. The various tabs in this dialog box include the following:

General: Information about the name of the computer, the role of the computer, and its description. Note that you can enable an option to allow the Local System Account of this machine to request services from other servers. This is useful if the machine is a trusted and secure computer.

**EXERCISE 7.2** *(continued)*

Operating System: The name, version, and service pack information for the operating system running on the computer.

Member Of: The Active Directory groups that this Computer object is a member of.

Location: A description of where the computer is physically located.

Managed By: Information about the User or Contact object that is responsible for managing this computer.

After you have examined the available options, click OK to continue.

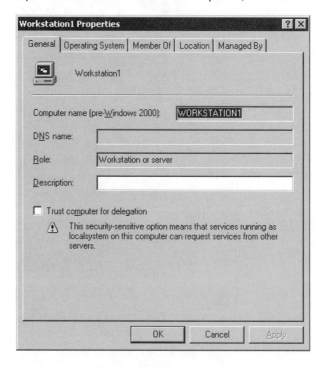

6. Select the Corporate OU. Right-click the Monica D. President User account, and choose Reset Password. You will be prompted to enter a new password and then asked to confirm it. Note that you can also force the user to change this password upon the next logon.

7. Close the Active Directory Users and Computers tool.

By now, you have probably noticed that there are a lot of common options for Active Directory objects. For example, Groups and Computers both have a Managed By tab. As was mentioned earlier, it's always a good idea to enter in as much information as possible about an object. This will help systems administrators and users alike. On the down side, however, it will tell them who is to blame when a printer no longer works!

## More Active Directory Management Features

The Active Directory Users and Computers tool has a couple of other features that come in quite handy when managing many objects. The first is accessed by clicking the View menu in the MMC console and choosing Filter Options. You'll see a dialog box similar to the one shown in Figure 7.1. Here, you can choose to filter objects by their specific types within the display. For example, if you are an administrator who works primarily with User accounts and groups, you can select those specific items by placing a check mark in the list. Additionally, you can create more complex filters by choosing Create Custom Filter. That will provide you with an interface that looks similar to the Find command.

**FIGURE 7.1**   Filtering objects using the Active Directory Users and Computers tool

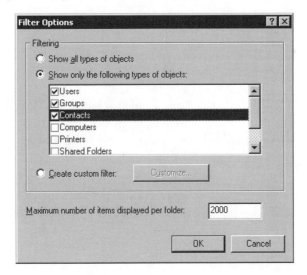

Another option in the Active Directory Users and Computers tool is to view Advanced options. You can enable the Advanced options by clicking Advanced Options in the View menu. This will add two top-level folders to the list under

the name of the domain. The System folder (shown in Figure 7.2) provides a list of some additional features that can be configured to work with the Active Directory. For example, you can configure settings for the Distributed File System (DFS), IP Security policies, the File Replication Service, and more. In addition to the System folder, you'll also see the LostAndFound folder. This folder contains any files that may not have been replicated properly between domain controllers. You should check this folder periodically for any files so that you can decide whether you need to move them or copy them to other locations.

**FIGURE 7.2** Advanced options in the Active Directory Users and Computers tool

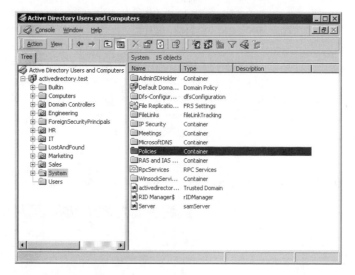

As you can see, managing Active Directory objects is generally a simple task. The Active Directory Users and Computers tool allows you to configure several objects. Let's move on to look at one more common administration function—moving objects.

# Moving Active Directory Objects

One of the extremely useful features of the Active Directory Users and Computers tool is its ability to easily move users and resources.

**Microsoft ✓ Exam Objective**

**Manage Active Directory objects.**

- Move Active Directory objects.

Exercise 7.3 walks through the process of moving Active Directory objects.

### EXERCISE 7.3

## Moving Active Directory Objects

In this exercise, we will make several changes to the organization of Active Directory objects. In order to complete this exercise, you must have first completed Exercise 7.1.

1. Open the Active Directory Users and Computers tool, and expand the name of the domain.

2. Select the Sales OU, right-click Workstation 1, and select Move. A dialog box will appear. Select the IT OU, and click OK to move the Computer object to that container.

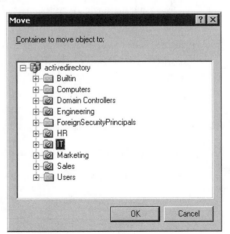

---

**EXERCISE 7.3** *(continued)*

**3.** Click the IT OU, and verify that Workstation1 was moved.

**4.** Close the Active Directory Users and Computers tool.

---

In addition to moving objects within the Active Directory, you can also easily rename them. You can do this by right-clicking an object and selecting Rename. Note that this option does not apply to all objects. For example, in order to prevent security breaches, Computer objects cannot be renamed. Additionally, you can remove objects from the Active Directory by right-clicking them and choosing Delete.

**WARNING** Deleting an Active Directory object is an irreversible action. When an object is destroyed, any security permissions or other settings made for that object are removed as well. Since each object within the Active Directory contains its own security identifier (SID), simply re-creating an object with the same name will not place any permissions on it. Before you delete an Active Directory object, be sure that you will never need it again.

# Publishing Active Directory Objects

One of the main goals of the Active Directory is to make resources easy to find. Two of the most commonly used resources in a networked environment are server file shares and printers. These are so common, in fact, that most organizations will have dedicated File/Print Servers. When it comes to managing these types of resources, the Active Directory makes it easy to determine which files and printers are available to users.

---

*Microsoft*
✓ *Exam*
*Objective*

**Manage Active Directory objects.**

- Publish resources in Active Directory.

- Locate objects in Active Directory.

With that said, let's look at how Active Directory manages the publishing of shared folders and printers.

## Making Active Directory Objects Available to Users

An important aspect of managing Active Directory objects is that a systems administrator can control which objects users can see. The act of making an Active Directory object available is known as *publishing*. The two main publishable objects are Printers and Shared Folders.

The general process for creating server shares and shared printers has remained unchanged from previous versions of Windows. That is, the main method is to create the various objects (a printer or a file system folder) and then to enable it for sharing. To make these resources available via the Active Directory, however, there's an additional step: Resources must be published. Once an object has been published in the Active Directory, it will be available for use by clients.

You can also publish Windows NT 4 resources through the Active Directory by creating Active Directory objects as we did in Exercise 7.3. When publishing objects in the Active Directory, you should know the server name and share name of the resource. The use of Active Directory objects offers systems administrators the ability to change the resource to which the object points without having to reconfigure or even notify clients. For example, if we move a share from one server to another, all we need to do is update the Shared Folder properties to point to the new location. Active Directory clients will still refer to the resource with the same path and name as they used before.

Without the Active Directory, Windows NT 4 shares and printers will only be accessible through the use of NetBIOS. If you're planning to disable the NetBIOS protocol in your environment, you must be sure that these resources have been published, or they will not be accessible.

## Publishing Printers

Printers can be published easily within the Active Directory. Exercise 7.4 walks you through the steps required to share and publish a Printer object.

**EXERCISE 7.4**

## Creating and Publishing a Printer

In this exercise, we will create and share a printer. Specifically, we will install and share a new, text-only printer. In order to complete the installation of the printer, you will require access to the Windows 2000 installation media (via the hard disk, a network share, or the CD-ROM drive).

1. Click Start ➤ Settings ➤ Printers. Double-click Add New Printer. This will start the Add Printer Wizard. Click Next to begin.

2. In the Network or Local Printer box, select Local Printer. Uncheck the Automatically Detect and Install My Plug and Play Printer box. Click Next.

3. In the Select the Printer Port dialog box, select Use the Following Port. From the list below that option, select LPT1: Printer Port. Click Next.

4. For the Manufacturer, select Generic, and for the printer, highlight Generic / Text Only. Click Next.

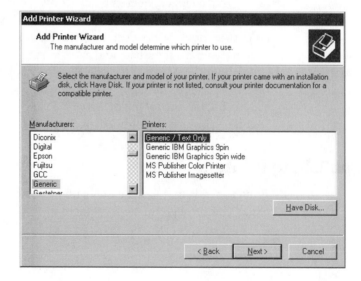

5. When asked for the name of the printer, type **Text Printer**. Click Next.

6. When prompted for the share name, s**elect Share As** and type **Text Printer**. Click Next.

7. For the Location, type **Building 203** and add the comment **This is a text-only printer.** Click Next.

8. When prompted to print a test page, select No. Click Next.

9. You will see a confirmation of the printer options you selected. Click Finish to create the printer.

**EXERCISE 7.4** *(continued)*

**10.** Next, you will need to verify that the printer will be listed in the Active Directory. In the Printers folder, right-click the Text Printer icon and select Properties. Next, select the Sharing tab, and ensure that the List in the Directory box is checked. Note that you can also add additional printer drivers for other operating systems using this tab. Click OK to accept the settings. Close the Printers window.

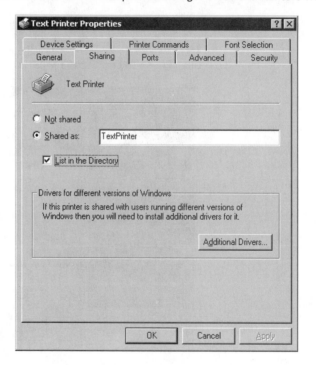

**11.** Now that the printer has been created and shared, we need to verify that it is available for use. To do this, click Start ➢ Search ➢ For Printers. In order to search for all printers, leave all of the options blank. Note that you can use the Features and Advanced tabs to restrict the list of printers to those that match certain requirements. Click Find Now. You should receive results that demonstrate that the printer is available through the Active Directory.

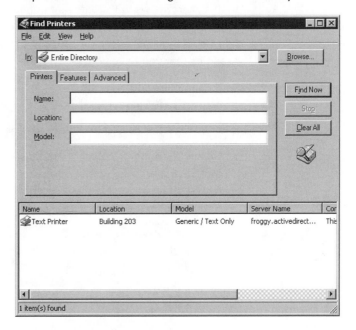

**12.** When finished, exit the Find dialog box.

Note that when you create and share a printer this way, an Active Directory Printer object is not displayed within the Active Directory Users and Computers tool. The printer is actually associated with the Computer object to which it is shared. Printer objects in the Active Directory are manually created for sharing printers from Windows NT 4 and earlier shared printer resources.

## Publishing Shared Folders

Now that we've created and published a printer, let's look at how the same thing can be done to shared folders. Exercise 7.5 walks through the steps required to create a folder, share it, and then publish it in the Active Directory.

**EXERCISE 7.5**

### Creating and Publishing a Shared Folder

In this exercise, we will create and publish a shared folder. This exercise assumes that you will be using the C: partition; however, you may want to change this based on your server configuration. This exercise assumes that you have completed Exercise 7.1.

1. Create a new folder in the root directory of your C: partition, and name it **Test Share**.

2. Right-click the Test Share folder, and select Sharing.

3. On the Sharing tab, select Share This Folder. For the Share Name, type **Test Share,** and for the Comment, enter **Share used for testing Active Directory**. Leave the user limit, permissions, and caching settings as their defaults. Click OK to create the share.

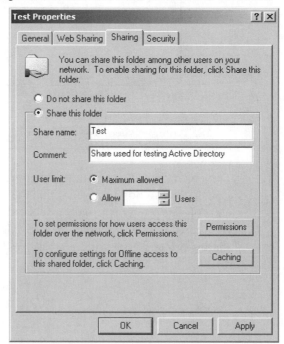

4. To verify that the share has been created, click Start ➢ Run, and type the UNC path for the local server. For instance, if the server was named DC1, you would type **\\dc1**. This will connect you to the local computer where you can view any available network resources. Verify that the Test Share folder exists, and then close the window.

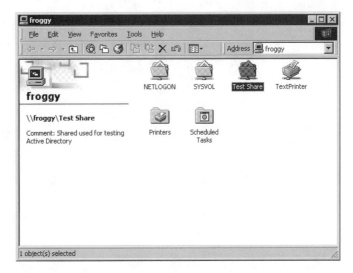

5. Open the Active Directory Users and Computers tool. Expand the current domain, and right-click the IT OU. Select New ➢ Shared Folder.

6. In the dialog box, type **Shared Folder Test** for the name of the folder. Then, type the UNC path to the share (for example, **\\DC1\Test Share**). Click OK to create the share.

7. Now that we have created the shared folder in the Active Directory, it's time to verify that it was created. To do this, right-click the name of the domain and select Find.

**EXERCISE 7.5** *(continued)*

8. On the Find menu, select Shared Folders. Leave the remaining options blank to search for all Active Directory shares. (Notice that you can also use the Advanced tab to further specify information about the share you are searching for.) Click the Find Now button to obtain the results of the search.

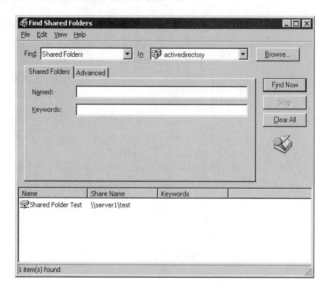

9. Close the Find dialog box, and exit the Active Directory Users and Computers tool.

Once you have created and published the shared folder, clients can use the My Network Places icon to find this object. The shared folder will be organized based on the OU in which you created the Shared Folder object. Through the use of publication, you can see how this makes it easy to manage shared folders.

Although it's beyond the scope of this book to discuss, the Windows 2000 DFS service allows for the use of hierarchical shares. The Active Directory Shared Folders object is completely compatible with this feature.

Once you have created resources, it is likely that you will want to restrict their use to only certain users and groups. We'll cover ways to do this in Chapter 8. In addition to setting permissions for end users, you can also use the Delegation of Control Wizard to assign management permissions to objects. We covered methods for delegating control of OUs in Chapter 4.

## Searching the Active Directory

So far, we've created several Active Directory resources. One of the main benefits of having all of your resource information in the Active Directory is that you should be able to easily find what you're looking for. Remember, when we recommended that you should always enter in as much information as possible when creating Active Directory objects? Well, this is where that extra effort begins to pay off.

Exercise 7.6 walks through the steps required to find objects in the Active Directory.

### EXERCISE 7.6

#### Finding Objects in the Active Directory

In this exercise, we will search for specific objects in the Active Directory. In order to complete this exercise, you must have first completed Exercise 7.1.

1. Open the Active Directory Users and Computers tool.

2. Right-click the name of the domain, and select Find.

3. In the Find field, select Users, Computers, and Groups. For the In setting, choose Entire Directory. This will search the entire Active Directory environment for the criteria you enter. Note that if this is a production domain and if there are many objects, this may be a time-consuming and network-intensive operation.

**EXERCISE 7.6** *(continued)*

4. In the Name field, type **admin** and then click Find Now to obtain the results of the search.

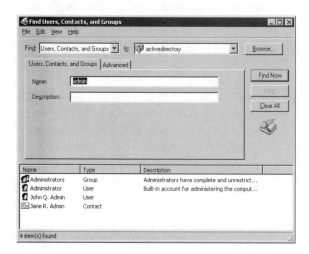

5. Now that we have found several results, let's narrow down the list. Click the Advanced tab. In the Fields drop-down list, select User ➤ Last Name. For the Condition, select Starts With, and for the Value, type **Admin**. Click Add to add this item to the search criteria. Click Find Now. Notice that this time, only the User and Contact that have the last name Admin are shown.

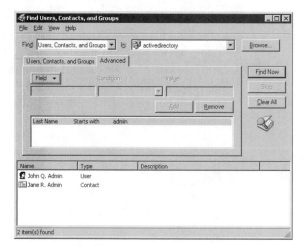

**EXERCISE 7.6** *(continued)*

6. To filter the result set even further, click the View menu and select Filter. The filter is displayed in the row just above the Results windows. In the Name field, type **John** and press Enter. Notice that this filters the list to only the John Q. Admin User object.

7. To view more information about the User object, you can right-click it and select Properties.

8. To quickly view (and filter) more information about multiple objects, select the View menu, and choose Select Columns. By selecting fields and clicking Add, you will be able to view more information about the retrieved objects. Click OK to add the information.

9. When you are finished searching, close the Find box and exit the Active Directory Users and Computers tool.

Using the many options available in the Find dialog box, you can usually narrow down the objects you're searching for quickly and efficiently. Users and systems administrators alike will find this to be useful in environments of any size!

# Creating Accounts through Scripting

**A**lthough the Active Directory Users and Computers tool provides an intuitive way to create and manage objects, sometimes using a GUI tool is not the best solution. Imagine the task facing a systems administrator who must create and populate several hundred User accounts. Clearly, using the point-and-click interface is inefficient. This is especially true if the information already exists in another format—such as a text file or an Excel spreadsheet.

*Microsoft*
✓ *Exam*
*Objective*

**Manage Active Directory objects.**

- Create and manage accounts manually or by scripting.

Fortunately, through the use of scripting and import/export processes, you can make this task much more manageable. In this section, we'll look at several ways to manage import users. The focus will be on an overview of methods. You'll likely need to consult other resources to carry out customizations for your own environment.

Let's start by looking at two command-line tools that can be used to import and export Active Directory objects.

# CSVDE

The *Comma-Separated Value Directory Exchange (CSVDE)* tool is used to import and export Active Directory information to and from comma-separated value (CSV) text files. CSV files are commonly used to transfer information between different types of data storage systems. If we wanted to transfer information between a mainframe application and an Excel spreadsheet, we could use a CSV text file as an intermediate (since both applications can read this format).

Other than serving as a common intermediate, another useful feature of CSV files is that they can be easily edited using any standard text editor (such as the Windows Notepad) or applications that support this format (such as Microsoft Excel).

The CSVDE utility is run from the command line. It offers many options for specifying the exact information you want to import and export. Following are the results of running the CSVDE utility without any arguments:

```
CSV Directory Exchange


General Parameters
==================
-i              Turn on Import Mode (The default is
Export)
-f filename     Input or Output filename
-s servername   The server to bind to (Default to DC of
                    logged in Domain)
-v              Turn on Verbose Mode
-c FromDN ToDN  Replace occurences of FromDN to ToDN
-j              Log File Location
-t              Port Number (default = 389)
-u              Use Unicode format
-?              Help
```

```
Export Specific
===============
-d RootDN        The root of the LDAP search (Default to
                 Naming Context)
-r Filter        LDAP search filter (Default to
                   "(objectClass=*)")
-p SearchScope   Search Scope (Base/OneLevel/Subtree)
-l list          List of attributes (comma separated) to
                   look for in an LDAP search
-o list          List of attributes (comma separated) to
                   omit from input.
-g               Disable Paged Search.
-m               Enable the SAM logic on export.
-n               Do not export binary values
Import
======
-k               The import will go on ignoring 'Constraint
                   Violation' and 'Object Already Exists'
                   errors
Credentials Establishment
=========================
Note that if no credentials are specified, CSVDE will
   bind as the currently logged on user, using SSPI.
-a UserDN [Password | *]          Simple authentication
-b UserName Domain [Password | *]    SSPI bind method
Example: Simple import of current domain
     csvde -i -f INPUT.CSV
Example: Simple export of current domain
     csvde -f OUTPUT.CSV
Example: Export of specific domain with credentials
     csvde -m -f OUTPUT.CSV
             -b USERNAME DOMAINNAME *
             -s SERVERNAME
             -d "cn=users,DC=DOMAINNAME,DC=Microsoft,DC=Com"
             -r "(objectClass=user)"
```

When you are planning to import new User accounts, it's always useful to first perform an export so you can view the structure of the file and the information that you'll need. You can then make changes to this file and import it later. Exercise 7.7 walks through the steps required in order to create User accounts by using the CSVDE.

---

**EXERCISE 7.7**

## Modifying User Accounts Using CSVDE

In this exercise, we will use the CSVDE utility to export a list of User objects from the Active Directory. We will then make changes to this file and then import the changes back into the Active Directory.

1.  Open the Active Directory Users and Computers tool, and expand the name of the Active Directory domain.

2.  Create a new, top-level OU named **Scripting**.

3.  Within the Scripting OU, create four users with the following information (for all other options, use the defaults):

    **a.** User #1

    First Name: Andrew

    Initials: P

    Last Name: Admin

    Logon Name: apadmin

    **b.** User #2

    First Name: Brian

    Initials: C

    Last Name: Manager

    Logon Name: bcmanager

    **c.** User #3

    First Name: Julie

    Initials: A

    Last Name: Finance

**EXERCISE 7.7** *(continued)*

        Logon Name: jafinance

    **d.** User #4

        First Name: Clara

        Initials: D

        Last Name: Manager

        Logon Name: cdmanager

**4.** Click Start ➢ Run, and type **cmd**. This will open up a command prompt. Make a note of the current directory path since this is where we will be creating an export text file for later use.

**5.** Type the following command to export the contents of the Scripting OU (note that you will need to replace the DC= sections to reflect the name of your current domain and that the command should be typed on a single line) and obtain the results shown.

    **Csvde -f export.csv -v -r "(objectclass=user)"**

      **-d "OU=Scripting, DC=DomainName,DC=com" -m**

**6.** Now, open the Active Directory Users and Computers tool. Expand the Scripting OU, and delete all four of the users we created previously.

7. At the command prompt, type the following command:

   **notepad export.csv**

8. In the text file, scroll over to the column that contains the middle initial value. It may be difficult to find the value since the file is not arranged in columns. Change all of the Middle Initial values to X.

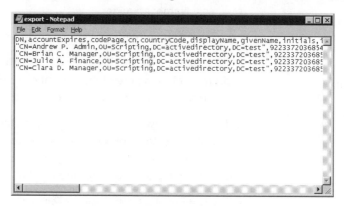

9. To save the file, click File ➢ Save. For the name of the file, type **import.csv**. Make sure that the Save as Type selection is All Files and that the Encoding value is set to ANSI.

10. Now, to import the changed file, return to the command prompt window and type the following:

    **csvde −i −f import.csv -v**

11. Once you receive the results similar to those shown, close the command prompt.

12. To verify that the changes have been imported correctly, open the Active Directory Users and Computers tool. Within the Scripting OU, right-click the name of any of the users. Verify that the middle initials have indeed been changed to X. Notice that the display name and the name displayed in the directory do not change. These are distinct attributes in the directory. When finished, close the Active Directory Users and Computers tool.

This import process can be made much easier if you use an application that can read and properly format CSV files. Microsoft Excel is a good example. You can also cut and paste values from other Microsoft Excel spreadsheets into this same file. When used correctly, the CSVDE utility can save many hours of work (and reduce the chances for errors introduced by manual data entry).

# LDIFDE

In Chapter 1, "Overview of the Active Directory," we mentioned that the main method used to query the Active Directory is through the use of the Lightweight Directory Access Protocol (LDAP). LDAP is commonly used for querying many directory sources, such as X.500-based directories and Novell

Directory Services (NDS). The benefit of using this standard is that systems administrators and application developers can use a common method to access information from different types of directories.

In addition to the LDAP specification, there is a specification called the LDAP Interchange Format (LDIF). The idea behind LDIF is to provide a common data storage and transfer mechanism for working with LDAP-based data. LDIF files can contain the instructions required to create, modify, and delete objects.

The *LDIF Directory Exchange (LDIFDE)* utility works similarly to the CSVDE utility. The primary difference (as you have probably already guessed!) is that the intermediate file is in the LDIF format. Following are the results of running the LDIFDE utility without any commands:

```
LDIF Directory Exchange


General Parameters
==================
-i              Turn on Import Mode (The default is
Export)
-f filename     Input or Output filename
-s servername   The server to bind to (Default to DC
                  of logged in Domain)
-c FromDN ToDN  Replace occurences of FromDN to ToDN
-v              Turn on Verbose Mode
-j              Log File Location
-t              Port Number (default = 389)
-u              Use Unicode format
-?              Help
Export Specific
===============
-d RootDN       The root of the LDAP search (Default to
                  Naming Context)
-r Filter       LDAP search filter (Default to
                  "(objectClass=*)")
-p SearchScope  Search Scope (Base/OneLevel/Subtree)
-l list         List of attributes (comma separated) to
                  look for in an LDAP search
-o list         List of attributes (comma separated) to
                  omit from input.
```

```
-g                    Disable Paged Search.
-m                    Enable the SAM logic on export.
-n                    Do not export binary values
Import
======

-k                    The import will go on ignoring 'Constraint
                         Violation' and 'Object Already Exists'
                         errors
-y                    The import will use lazy commit for better
                         performance
Credentials Establishment
==========================

Note that if no credentials is specified, LDIFDE will bind
   as the currently logged on user, using SSPI.
-a UserDN [Password | *]               Simple authentication
-b UserName Domain [Password | *]    SSPI bind method
Example: Simple import of current domain
     ldifde -i -f INPUT.LDF
Example: Simple export of current domain
     ldifde -f OUTPUT.LDF
Example: Export of specific domain with credentials
     ldifde -m -f OUTPUT.LDF
            -b USERNAME DOMAINNAME *
            -s SERVERNAME
            -d "cn=users,DC=DOMAINNAME,DC=Microsoft,DC=Com"
            -r "(objectClass=user)"
```

Notice that most of these options are the same as those presented for the CSVDE utility. The actual operations are very similar. The major exception is that the LDIF file format is designed for use with specific applications that support this format. It is not optimized for use with Microsoft Excel or Notepad, for example.

## Windows Script Host (WSH)

Although the LDIFDE and CSVDE utilities provide a good way to import and export data, sometimes you need to perform more complicated modifications to data. Suppose you wanted to programmatically change all of your usernames to conform to your company's new naming convention. These types of actions are best performed through scripting methods.

The *Windows Script Host (WSH)* was designed to allow systems administrators to quickly and easily create simple files that automate common functions. Among the various functions that can be performed by WSH are the following:

- Creating Active Directory objects, including users, groups, and printers
- Modifying or deleting Active Directory objects
- Performing network logon functions, such as mapping network drives
- Starting and stopping services
- Accessing Microsoft Office or other applications and performing common tasks

WSH is actually a scripting host, as opposed to a programming language. This means that it allows for the use of many different languages. Specifically, WSH ships with support for VBScript (a simplified version of Visual Basic, optimized for scripting) and JScript (Microsoft's version of JavaScript). Additionally, third-party developers can write interpreters that allow the use of PERL and other types of scripts.

There are two main executables that are used to launch files that are compatible with WSH.

**Cscript**   The command-line version of the scripting host.

**Wscript**   The Windows GUI version of the scripting host.

WSH has a wide array of possible uses and should be a part of any systems administrator's bag of tricks. For more information on obtaining and using WSH, see `msdn.microsoft.com/scripting/`. This site includes the entire object model for WSH, sample script files, tutorials, and VBScript/JScript language references. Figure 7.3 shows an example of the site.

**FIGURE 7.3**    The Microsoft scripting Web site

 **Real World Scenario**

## Scripting to the Rescue!

Recently, your Chief Information Officer (CIO) has decided that the organization will benefit from migrating your large network environment to Windows 2000 and the Active Directory. The current environment is heterogeneous and includes a large number of Novell NetWare servers, as well as many Unix, Windows NT 3.51, and Windows NT 4.0 servers. The majority of information about users and security permissions is scattered throughout hundreds of applications on the network. Based on several technical and business decisions, your IT department has decided to perform the migration by first creating a completely new Active Directory environment from scratch. Then, users will be added to the new domain as soon as possible.

As a systems administrator, you are tasked with creating the user accounts for the new domain. It sounds easy enough, you might think to yourself. However, the environment contains 48,000 users! That's a lot of mouse-clicks and keystrokes for anyone. Clearly, you need a better way. Fortunately, Microsoft saw this potential problem and created two utilities that can be used for transferring information into the Active Directory. You plan to design an automated process for automatically importing the necessary data.

The first step is to find out where the information resides on your network. You might be able to find the majority of the employee-related information that you need from an HR database. You'll likely need to consult other resources for information, as well. For example, each department might maintain its own lists of employees. In some organizations, employee information might already reside in an LDAP-compliant data store.

Once you've located where user information resides in your environment, the next challenge is to obtain the data in a usable format. In order to use the basic CSVDE utilities, you must first translate the data to a comma-separated value file. Most systems are able to export data to this type of format, but in some cases, you might need the help of a developer to get exactly what you need. You could also use the LDIFDE utility to automatically query information from an LDAP-compliant database. Once the data has been collected, you'll need to ensure that all of the information is valid and consistent. It's worth taking the time to make sure that the user accounts are formatted properly (proper case for first and last names, single characters for middle initials, etc.).

Finally, it's time to begin the actual import. You can now simply use the CSVDE or LDIFDE utilities to import the data to an Active Directory domain controller, but also you'll have to specify into which OUs the accounts should be imported. Unless the data is perfect (which is rarely the case in large environments), you'll need to perform multiple attempts for the import. Each time, note any errors that might occur and fix them. For performing other types of functions, you can also take advantage of the Windows Scripting Host (WSH) and the Active Directory Services Interface (ADSI), both of which provide you with an object-oriented way to modify properties and settings in your Active Directory database.

The process of importing data may not be fun, but it sure beats having to key in a large amount of information. It also reduces the chances for the inevitable data entry errors. Overall, scripting can be your best friend when it comes to performing repetitive tasks!

# Active Directory Services Interface

The *Active Directory Services Interface (ADSI)* is designed to allow developers to programmatically view and modify objects within the Active Directory. It is based on a set of Component Object Model (COM) structures that can be used in a variety of environments. The ADSI object model can be accessed from within popular development languages, including Visual Basic, Visual C++, Java, and Active Server Pages (ASP). This makes the use of ADSI very accessible for the vast majority of today's programmers.

In addition to supporting the Active Directory, ADSI also supports the use of the Netware 3.*x* Bindery, NDS, and Windows NT 4 account databases. This broad support makes ADSI an excellent solution for migrating users from other directory services to the Active Directory. For example, a developer could quickly write an ADSI Visual Basic application that takes all of the existing groups and accounts from a Windows NT 4 domain and places them in the appropriate groups and OUs within an Active Directory domain.

It is beyond the scope of this book (and the Microsoft exam for which it prepares you) to cover programming concepts in-depth. For more information on these topics, see Microsoft's Active Directory Services Interface Web site at www.microsoft.com/ADSI and the Windows 2000 Resource Kit.

# Summary

In this chapter, we examined the following topics:

- How to use the Active Directory Users and Computers tool to manage Active Directory objects. If you're responsible for day-to-day systems administration, there's a good chance that you were already familiar with using this tool.

- How to manage Active Directory objects such as users, computers, and groups.

- How to publish network resources (such as printers and shared folders) in the Active Directory.

- How to search the Active Directory for specific types of objects.

- Methods for scripting the import and export of users in bulk.

The concepts and operations we covered in this chapter will be instrumental in understanding the ideas behind other Active Directory topics. A prime example is the topic of Active Directory security, which we'll cover next!

# Exam Essentials

**Understand how Active Directory objects work.**  Active Directory objects represent some piece of information about components within a domain. The objects themselves have attributes that describe details about them.

**Understand how Active Directory objects can be organized.**  Through the use of the Active Directory Users and Computers tool, you can create, move, rename, and delete various objects.

**Learn how resources can be published.**  A design goal for the Active Directory was to make network resources easier for users to find. With that in mind, understand how the use of published printers and shared folders can simplify network resource management.

**Understand how scripting can be used with the Active Directory.**
Tools and utilities such as WSH, ADSI, CSVDE, and LDIFDE can be used to automate repetitive tasks, such as the creation of a large number of user accounts.

# Key Terms

Before you take the exam, be certain you are familiar with the following terms:

| | |
|---|---|
| Active Directory Services Interface (ADSI) | Printer objects |
| Active Directory Users and Computers tool | Publishing |
| Comma-Separated Value Directory Exchange (CSVDE) | security principals |
| Computer objects | Shared Folder objects |
| Contact objects | User object |
| LDIF Directory Exchange (LDIFDE) | Windows Script Host (WSH) |

# Review Questions

1. Gabriel is responsible for administering a small Active Directory domain. Recently, the Engineering Department within his organization has been divided into two departments. He wants to reflect this organizational change within the Active Directory and plans to rename various groups and resources. Which of the following operations *cannot* be performed using the Active Directory Users and Computers tool?

   **A.** Renaming an organizational unit

   **B.** Searching for resources

   **C.** Renaming a group

   **D.** Creating a computer account

   **E.** None of the above

2. Which of the following operations *cannot* be performed using the Active Directory Users and Computers tool?

   **A.** Creating shared folders

   **B.** Creating printers

   **C.** Creating domains

   **D.** Creating organizational units

   **E.** All of the above

**3.** Isabel, a system administrator, has created a new Active Directory domain in an environment that already contains two trees. During the promotion of the domain controller, she chose to create a new Active Directory forest. Isabel is a member of the Enterprise Administrators group and has full permissions over all domains. During the organization's migration to an Active Directory, there have been many updates to the information stored within the domains. Recently, users and other system administrators have complained about not being able to find specific Active Directory objects in one or more domains (although they exist in others).

In order to investigate the problem, Isabel wants to check for any objects that have not been properly replicated between domain controllers. If possible, she would like to restore these objects to their proper place within the relevant Active Directory domains.

Which two of the following actions should she perform to be able to view the relevant information? (Choose all that apply.)

**A.** Change the Active Directory permissions to allow viewing of object information in all domains.

**B.** Select the Advanced Options item in the View menu.

**C.** Promote a member server in each domain to a domain controller.

**D.** Rebuild all domain controllers from the latest backups.

**E.** Examine the contents of the LostandFound folder using the Active Directory Users and Computers tool.

4. You are a consultant hired to evaluate an organization's Active Directory domain. The domain contains over 200,000 objects and hundreds of OUs. You begin examining the objects within the domain, but you find that the loading of the contents of specific OUs takes a very long time. Furthermore, the list of objects can be very large. You want to do the following:

   - You want to avoid the use of any third-party tools or utilities, and you want to use the built-in Active Directory administrative tools.

   - You want to be able to limit the list of objects within an OU to only the type of objects that you're examining (for example, only Computer objects).

   - You want to prevent any changes to the Active Directory domain or any of the objects within it.

   Which of the following actions will meet the above requirements? (Choose all that apply.)

   **A.** Use the Filter option in the Active Directory Users and Computers tool to restrict the display of objects.

   **B.** Use the Delegation of Control Wizard to give yourself permissions over only a certain type of object.

   **C.** Implement a new naming convention for objects within an OU and then sort the results using this new naming convention.

   **D.** Use the Active Directory Domains and Trusts tool to view information from only selected domain controllers.

   **E.** Edit the Domain Group Policy settings to allow yourself to view only the objects of interest.

5. Which of the following default Active Directory containers includes the Print Operators and Server Operators groups?

   **A.** Builtin

   **B.** Users

   **C.** Foreign Security Principals

   **D.** Windows NT

   **E.** None of the above

**6.** Raj is a developer who works for a medium-sized organization. Recently, the company has decided to move to an Active Directory environment. Currently, user information is scattered throughout many different systems in the organization. Raj has been tasked with importing all of this user information from the company's various databases into the Active Directory environment. Raj has been provided with text files that provide the data he needs, separated by commas.

Which of the following utilities can he use to import this file containing employee information into a new Active Directory domain?

**A.** LDIFDE

**B.** CSVDE

**C.** Active Directory Users and Computers

**D.** Active Directory Domains and Trusts

**E.** None of the above

**7.** A systems administrator creates a local printer object, but it doesn't show up in the Active Directory when a user executes a search for all printers. Which of the following is a possible reason for this?

**A.** The printer was not shared.

**B.** The List in Directory option is unchecked.

**C.** The client does not have permissions to view the printer.

**D.** All of the above.

**8.** Shared Folder objects can refer to which of the following types of shares?

**A.** Existing Windows NT shares

**B.** Existing Windows 2000 shares

**C.** Both A and B

**D.** None of the above

9. When searching for printers using the Active Directory Users and Computers tool, which of the following tabs can be used to return a list of only those printers that can print in color?

    **A.** Printer Options

    **B.** Advanced

    **C.** Features

    **D.** General

    **E.** None of the above

10. The Active Directory Users and Computers tool can be used to do all of the following *except*

    **A.** Create a User object

    **B.** Rename a User object

    **C.** Reset a password for a User object

    **D.** Rename a Computer object

    **E.** None of the above

11. Which of the following allows for programmatically transferring information between a Novell Directory Services (NDS) directory and the Active Directory?

    **A.** WSH

    **B.** LDIFDE

    **C.** CSVDE

    **D.** ADSI

    **E.** None of the above

12. A systems administrator can determine the type of operating system a computer is using with which of the following tools?

    **A.** Active Directory Sites and Services

    **B.** Active Directory Domains and Trusts

    **C.** Active Directory Users and Computers

    **D.** DNS

    **E.** None of the above

13. A systems administrator is using the Active Directory Users and Computers tool to view the objects within an OU. He has previously created many users, groups, and computers within this OU, but now only the users are being shown. What is a possible explanation for this?

    **A.** Groups and Computers are not normally shown in the Active Directory Users and Computers tool.

    **B.** Another systems administrator may have locked the group, preventing others from accessing it.

    **C.** Filtering options have been set that specify that only User objects should be shown.

    **D.** The Group and Computer accounts have never been used and are, therefore, not shown.

    **E.** None of the above.

14. A systems administrator wishes to access the System folder within the Active Directory Users and Computers tool, but it does not appear in the utility. What must he do to be able to access this folder (assuming he has the appropriate permissions)?

    **A.** Use the Delegation of Control Wizard.

    **B.** Click View ➢ Advanced Features.

    **C.** Click the Refresh button.

    **D.** Modify the Properties page for the domain.

    **E.** None of the above.

15. A user is having a problem with a Shared Folder located in a specific OU and wants to know who to contact. A good way to find this information is to

    **A.** Right-click the Shared Folder object, select Properties, and select the Managed By tab.

    **B.** Right-click the parent OU, select Properties, and select the Managed By tab.

    **C.** Right-click the Shared Folder object, and choose Notify Operator.

    **D.** Both A and B.

16. You are working in a network environment that currently relies upon an LDAP-compatible data source for storing data about network objects. Recently, the company has decided to migrate to a Windows 2000 Active Directory environment. Since the information is already contained within an LDAP data source, you want to choose a method of importing data that requires the least effort and that ensures the accuracy of data transfers. You also want to maintain the hierarchical structure of the imported objects.

    Which of the following utilities can you use to directly import the LDAP information into a new Active Directory domain? (Choose all that apply.)

    **A.** LDIFDE

    **B.** Active Directory Services Interface (ADSI)

    **C.** Active Directory Users and Computers

    **D.** Active Directory Domains and Trusts

    **E.** CSVDE

17. **Prioritize-a-list:** You work in a team of administrators. One of your superiors is a wiz with editing user accounts using a standard text-editing tool. He asks you to provide him with editable files for some of your Active Directory users. After he is done editing the files, you will need to integrate the changes back into the Active Directory. Place the steps below in the correct order of operations to accomplish this. Note that at least one item will be used more than once.

| | |
|---|---|
| | Run the command:<br>`csvde -f filename.csv -v -r`<br>`↳"(objectclass+user)" -d`<br>`"OU=Scripting,`<br>`↳DC=DomainName, DC=com" -m` |
| | Open a command prompt. |
| | The manager edits `filename.csv`. |
| | Run the command:<br>`csvde -i -f filename.csv -v` |

**18.** You want to publish the printer to the Active Directory. In the following screen, where would you click in order to accomplish this task?

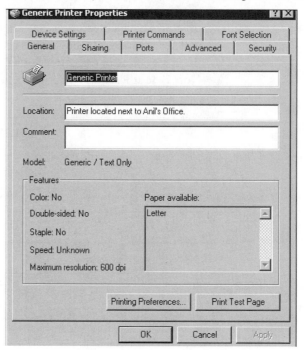

- **A.** The Sharing tab
- **B.** The Advanced tab
- **C.** The Device Settings tab
- **D.** The Printing Preferences button

# Answers to Review Questions

1. E. The Active Directory Users and Computers tool was designed to simplify the administration of Active Directory objects. All of the above operations can be carried out using the Active Directory Users and Computers tool.

2. C. Domains can only be created through the use of the Active Directory Installation Wizard.

3. B, E. The LostAndFound folder contains information about objects that could not be replicated between domain controllers. Enabling the Advanced Options item in the View menu will allow Isabel to see the LostAndFound and System folders.

4. A. Through the use of the Filtering functionality, you can choose which types of objects you want to see using the Active Directory Users and Computers interface. Several of the other choices may work, but they require changes to Active Directory settings or objects.

5. A. The Builtin container contains the default groups that are available within the domain.

6. B. The CSVDE utility can be used to read information from a comma-separated value text file and can then be used to create Active Directory objects based on the information provided.

7. D. All of the reasons listed are explanations for why a printer may not show up within the Active Directory.

8. C. A Shared Folder refers to resources by UNC name and can point to a Windows NT or Windows 2000 share.

9. C. The Features tab can be used to specify the features of a printer object.

10. D. Computer objects can be created and deleted using the Active Directory Users and Computers tool, but they cannot be renamed.

**11.** D. The Active Directory Services Interface (ADSI) presents an object model that can be used to access information from a variety of different directory services.

**12.** C. By right-clicking a Computer object and choosing Properties within the Active Directory Users and Computers tool, a systems administrator can view operating system information about a specific computer that is a member of the domain.

**13.** C. The filtering options would cause other objects to be hidden (although they still exist). Another explanation (but not one of the choices) is that a higher-level systems administrator modified the administrator's permissions using the Delegation of Control Wizard.

**14.** B. The System folder is shown in the Active Directory Users and Computers tool only if the Advanced Features option is enabled.

**15.** D. The Managed By tab is used to specify the individual who is responsible for managing the Active Directory object. In this case, the user will want to determine who manages the Shared Folder and/or the OU in which it is contained.

**16.** A, B. Both ADSI and the LDIFDE utility can be used to import LDAP-related information into the Active Directory. Through the use of either of these tools, you can import LDAP-related information, including the hierarchical structure of the data. Although you can use the CSVDE utility to import information, this method only allows you to import a specific subset of information and would require much more work in order to implement.

**17.**

| |
|---|
| Open a command prompt. |
| Run the command:<br>`csvde -f filename.csv -v -r`<br>↳`"(objectclass=user)" -d "OU=Scripting,`<br>↳`DC=DomainName, DC=com" -m` |
| The manager edits `filename.csv`. |
| Open a command prompt. |
| Run the command:<br>`csvde -i -f filename.csv -v` |

The CSVDE utility is run at the command prompt. The first command exports the user information to the file named `filename.csv`. The manager can then edit this file. When he is done, you need to introduce the changes to the Active Directory by opening the command prompt and running the second command.

**18.** A. The Sharing tab contains a check box that you can use to list the printer in the Active Directory.

# Chapter 8

# Active Directory Security

## MICROSOFT EXAM OBJECTIVES COVERED IN THIS CHAPTER:

✓ **Configure and troubleshoot security in a directory services infrastructure.**

- Apply security policies by using Group Policy.
- Create, analyze, and modify security configurations by using Security Configuration and Analysis and Security Templates.
- Implement an audit policy.

✓ **Monitor and analyze security events.**

✓ **Manage Active Directory objects.**

- Move Active Directory objects.
- Publish resources in Active Directory.
- Locate objects in Active Directory.
- Create and manage accounts manually or by scripting.
- Control access to Active Directory objects.
- Delegate administrative control of objects in Active Directory.

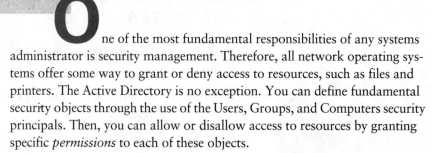

One of the most fundamental responsibilities of any systems administrator is security management. Therefore, all network operating systems offer some way to grant or deny access to resources, such as files and printers. The Active Directory is no exception. You can define fundamental security objects through the use of the Users, Groups, and Computers security principals. Then, you can allow or disallow access to resources by granting specific *permissions* to each of these objects.

In this chapter, you'll learn how to implement security within the Active Directory. Through the use of Active Directory tools, you can quickly and easily configure the settings that you require in order to protect information. Note, however, that proper planning for security permissions is an important prerequisite. If your security settings are too restrictive, users may not be able to perform their job functions. Worse yet, they may try to circumvent security measures. On the other end of the spectrum, if security permissions are too lax, users may be able to access and modify sensitive company resources.

With all of this in mind, let's start looking at how you can manage security within the Active Directory.

With respect to the "Manage Active Directory objects" objective, this chapter covers material related to only the last two subobjectives. See Chapter 7, "Administering the Active Directory," for material on Active Directory administration and the remainder of the subobjectives under the "Manage Active Directory objects" objective.

In order to complete the exercises in this chapter, you should understand the basics of working with Active Directory objects. If you are not familiar with creating and managing users, groups, computers, and organizational units, you should review the information in Chapter 7, before continuing.

# Active Directory Security Overview

**O**ne of the fundamental design goals for the Active Directory is to define a single, centralized repository of users and information resources. The Active Directory records information about all of the users, computers, and resources on your network. Each domain acts as a security boundary, and members of the domain (including workstations, servers, and domain controllers) share information about the objects within them.

The information stored within the Active Directory determines which resources are accessible to which users. Through the use of permissions that are assigned to Active Directory objects, you can control all aspects of network security.

Many security experts state that 20 percent of real-world network security is a technical issue and that 80 percent of it is a process and policy one. Don't make the mistake of trying to solve all security problems through a point-and-click interface. You also need to establish and enforce system usage policies, physically secure your resources, and ensure that users are aware of any restrictions.

In this chapter, we'll cover the details of security as it pertains to the Active Directory. Note, however, that this is only one aspect of true network security. That is, you should always be sure that you have implemented appropriate access control settings for the file system, network devices, and other resources. Let's start by looking at the various components of network security.

# Security Principals

*Security principals* are Active Directory objects that are assigned security identifiers (SIDs). A SID is a unique identifier that is used to manage any object to which permissions can be assigned. Security principals are assigned permissions to perform certain actions and access certain network resources.

The basic types of Active Directory objects that serve as security principals include the following:

**User Accounts**   These objects identify individual users on your network. The User account includes information such as the user's name and their password. User accounts are the fundamental unit of security administration.

**Groups**   There are two main types of groups: *Security groups* and *Distribution groups*. Both types of groups can contain User accounts. Security groups are used for easing the management of security permissions. Distribution groups, on the other hand, are used solely for the purpose of sending e-mail. Distribution groups are *not* considered security principals. We'll cover the details of groups in the next section.

**Computer Accounts**   Computer accounts identify which client computers are members of particular domains. Since these computers participate in the Active Directory database, systems administrators can manage security settings that affect the computer. Computer accounts are used to determine whether a computer can join a domain and for authentication purposes. As we'll see later in this chapter, systems administrators can also place restrictions on certain computer settings to increase security. These settings apply to the computer and, therefore, also apply to any user who is using it (regardless of the permissions granted to the User account).

Security principals can be assigned permissions so that they can access various network resources, be given user rights, and may have their actions tracked (through *auditing*, covered later in this chapter). The three types of security principals—Users, Groups, and Computers—form the basis of the Active Directory security architecture. As a systems administrator, you will likely spend a portion of your time managing permissions for these objects.

It is important to understand that, since a unique SID defines each security principal, deleting a security principal is an irreversible process. For example, if you delete a User account and then later re-create one with the same name, you will need to reassign permissions and group membership settings for the new account.

Note that other objects—such as organizational units (OUs)—do not function as security principals. What this means is that you can apply certain settings (such as Group Policy) on all of the objects within an OU. However, you cannot specifically set permissions with respect to the OU itself. The purpose of OUs is to logically organize other Active Directory objects based on business needs. This distinction is important to remember.

# Understanding Users and Groups

The fundamental security principals that are used for security administration include Users and Groups. In this section, you'll learn how Users and Groups interact and about the different types of Groups that can be created.

## Types of Groups

When dealing with Groups, you should make the distinction between local security principals and domain security principals. Local Users and Groups are used for assigning the permissions necessary to access the local machine. For example, we may assign the permissions necessary to restart a domain controller to a specific local Group. Domain Users and Groups, on the other hand, are used throughout the domain. These objects are available on any of the computers within the Active Directory domain and between domains that have a trust relationship.

There are two main types of Groups used in the Active Directory:

**Security Groups**   Security groups are considered security principals. They can contain User accounts. To make administration simpler, permissions are usually granted to groups. This allows for changing permissions easily at the level of the Active Directory (instead of at the level of the resource on which the permissions are assigned).

Security groups can be used for e-mail purposes—that is, a systems administrator can automatically e-mail all of the User accounts that exist within a group. Of course, the systems administrator must specify the e-mail addresses for these accounts.

Active Directory Contact objects can also be placed within Security groups, but security permissions will not apply to them.

**Distribution Groups**   Distribution groups are not considered security principals and are used only for the purpose of sending e-mail messages.

You can add users to Distribution groups just as you would add them to Security groups. Distribution groups can also be placed within OUs for easier management. They are useful, for example, if you need to send e-mail messages to an entire department or business unit within the Active Directory.

Understanding the differences between Security and Distribution groups is important in an Active Directory environment. For the most part, systems administrators use Security groups for daily administration of permissions. On the other hand, systems administrators who are responsible for maintaining e-mail distribution lists will generally use Distribution groups to logically group members of departments and business units.

When working in native-mode domains (domains that support the use of only Windows 2000 domain controllers), Security groups can be converted to or from Distribution groups. When running in mixed mode (which allows the use of Windows NT domain controllers), Group types cannot be changed.

## Group Scope

In addition to being classified by type, each Group is also given a specific scope. The scope of a Group defines two characteristics. First, it determines the level of security that applies to a Group. Second, it determines which users can be added to the group. Group scope is an important concept in network environments because it ultimately defines which resources users will be able to access.

The three types of Group scope are as follows:

**Domain Local**   The scope of *Domain Local groups* extends as far as the local machine. When you're using the Active Directory Users and Computers tool, Domain Local accounts apply to the computer for which you are viewing information. Domain Local groups are used to assign permissions to local resources, such as files and printers. They can contain *Global groups*, *Universal groups*, and User accounts.

**Global**   The scope of Global groups is limited to a single domain. Global groups may contain any of the users that are a part of the Active Directory domain in which the Global groups reside. Global groups are often used for managing domain security permissions based on job functions. For example, if we need to specify permissions for the Engineering department, we could create one or more Global groups (such as EngineeringManagers and EngineeringDevelopers). We could then assign security permissions to each group for any of the resources within the domain.

**Universal**   Universal groups can contain users from any domains within an Active Directory forest. Therefore, they are used for managing security across domains. Universal groups are only available when you're running the Active Directory in native mode. When managing multiple domains, it is often helpful to group Global groups within Universal groups. For instance, if I have an Engineering Global group in Domain 1 and an Engineering Global group in Domain 2, I could create a universal AllEngineers group that contains both of the Global groups. Now, whenever security permissions must be assigned to all Engineers within the organization, we only need to assign permissions to the AllEngineers Universal group.

In order to process authentication between domains, information about the membership in Universal groups is stored in the Global Catalog (GC). Keep this in mind if you ever plan to place users directly into Universal groups and bypass Global groups because all of the users will be enumerated in the GC, which will impact size and performance.

In addition to the security implications of Group scope, there are also important network replication traffic considerations. This is because domains must communicate information about Global and Universal groups in order to perform authentication. For more information on Active Directory performance, see Chapter 9, "Active Directory Optimization and Reliability."

   As you can see, the main properties for each of these Group types are affected by whether the Active Directory is running in mixed mode or native mode. Each of these scope levels is designed for a specific purpose and will ultimately affect the types of security permissions that can be assigned to them.

There are several limitations on Group functionality when running in mixed-mode domains. Specifically, the following limitations exist:

- Only Distribution groups can have Universal scope.

- Universal security groups are not available in mixed-mode domains.

- Changing the scope of groups is not allowed.

- There are limitations to Group nesting. Specifically, the only nesting allowed is Global groups contained in Domain Local groups.

When running in native-mode domains, you can make the following Group scope changes:

- Domain Local groups can be changed to a Universal group. This change can be made only if the Domain Local group does not contain any other Domain Local groups.

- A Global group can be changed to a Universal group. This change can be made only if the Global group is not a member of any other Global groups.

Universal groups themselves cannot be converted into any other Group scope type. Changing Group scope can be helpful when your security administration or business needs change.

## Built-In Local Groups

Built-in local groups are used to perform administrative functions on the local server. Because they have preassigned permissions and privileges, they allow systems administrators to easily assign common management functions. The list of built-in local groups includes the following:

**Account Operators**    These users are able to create and modify Domain User and Group accounts. Members of this group are generally responsible for the daily administration of the Active Directory.

**Administrators**    Members of the Administrators group are given full permissions to perform any functions within the Active Directory domain and on the local computer. This includes the ability to access all files and resources that reside on any server within the domain. As you can see, this is a very powerful account.

In general, you should restrict the number of users that are included in this group since most common administration functions do not require this level of access.

**Backup Operators**    One of the problems associated with backing up data in a secure network environment is that there must be a way to bypass standard file system security in order to copy files. Although you could place users in the Administrators group, this usually provides more permissions than necessary. Members of the Backup Operators group are able to bypass standard file system security for the purpose of backup and recovery only. They cannot, however, directly access or open files within the file system.

Generally, the permissions assigned to the Backup Operators group are used by backup software applications and data. We'll cover the details of performing backups in Chapter 9.

**Guests**    The Guests group is generally used for providing access to resources that generally do not require security. For example, if you have a network share that provides files that should be made available to all network users, you can assign permissions to allow members of the Guest group to access those files.

**Print Operators**    Members of the Print Operators group are given permissions to administer all of the printers within a domain. This includes common functions such as changing the priority of print jobs and deleting items from the print queue.

**Replicator**    The Replicator group was created to allow the replication of files between the computers in a domain. Accounts that are used for replication-related tasks are added to this group to provide them with the permissions necessary to keep files synchronized across multiple computers.

**Server Operators**    A common administrative task is managing server configuration. Members of the Server Operators group are granted the permissions necessary to manage services, shares, and other system settings.

**Users**    The Users group, as shown in Figure 8.1, is often used as a generic grouping for network accounts. Usually, this group is given minimal permissions and is used for the application of security settings that apply to most employees within an organization.

Additionally, there are two main User accounts that are created during the promotion of a domain controller. The first is the Administrator account. This account is assigned the password that is provided by a systems administrator during the promotion process and has full permissions to perform all actions within the domain. The second account is Guest, which is disabled by default. The purpose of the Guest account is to provide anonymous access to users who do not have an individual logon and password for use within the domain. Although this might be useful in some situations, it is generally recommended that the Guest account be disabled to increase security.

**FIGURE 8.1** Contents of the default Users folder

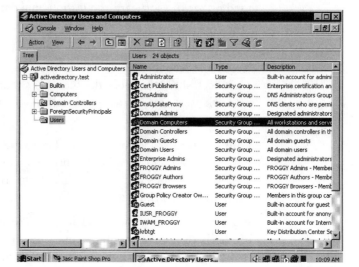

## Predefined Global Groups

As we mentioned earlier in this chapter, Global groups are used for managing permissions at the domain level. The following predefined Global groups are installed in the Users folder:

**Cert Publishers**   Certificates are used to increase security by allowing for strong authentication methods. User accounts are placed within the Cert Publishers group if they require the ability to publish security certificates. Generally, these accounts will be used by Active Directory security services.

**Domain Computers**   All of the computers that are a member of the domain are generally members of the Domain Computers group. This includes any workstations or servers that have joined the domain but does not include the domain controllers.

**Domain Admins**   Members of the Domain Admins group have full permissions to manage all of the Active Directory objects for this domain. This is a powerful account; therefore, membership should be restricted to only those users who require full permissions.

**Domain Controllers**   All of the domain controllers for a given domain are generally included within the Domain Controllers group.

**Domain Guests**    Generally, members of the Domain Guests group are given minimal permissions with respect to resources. Systems administrators may place User accounts in this group if they require only basic access or require temporary permissions within the domain.

**Domain Users**    The Domain Users group usually contains all of the User accounts for the given domain. This group is generally given basic permissions to resources that do not require higher levels of security. A common example is a public file share.

**Enterprise Admins**    Members of the Enterprise Admins group are given full permissions to perform actions within the entire domain forest. This includes functions such as managing trust relationships and adding new domains to trees and forests.

**Group Policy Creator Owners**    Members of the Group Policy Creator Owners group are able to create and modify *Group Policy* settings for objects within the domain. This allows them to enable security settings on OUs (and the objects that they contain).

**Schema Admins**    Members of the Schema Admins group are given permissions to modify the Active Directory schema. This, for example, allows them to create additional fields of information for User accounts. This is a very powerful function since any changes to the schema will be propagated to all of the domains and domain controllers within an Active Directory forest. Furthermore, changes to the schema cannot be undone (although additional options can be disabled).

Members of each of these groups are able to perform specific tasks related to the management of the Active Directory.

In addition to the Groups listed above, new ones might be created for specific services and applications that are installed on the server. Specifically, services that run on domain controllers and servers will be created as Security groups with Domain Local scope. For example, if a domain controller is running the DNS service (described in Chapter 2, "Integrating DNS with the Active Directory"), the DNSAdmins and DNSUpdateProxy groups will be available. Similarly, installing the DHCP service creates the DHCPUsers and DHCPAdministrators groups. The purpose of these groups will vary based on the functionality of the applications being installed.

### Foreign Security Principals

In environments that consist of more than one domain, you may need to grant permissions to users that reside in multiple domains. Generally, this is managed through the use of Active Directory trees and forests. However, in some cases, you may want to provide resources to users that are contained in domains that are not part of the same forest.

The Active Directory uses the concept of *foreign security principals* to allow permissions to be assigned to users that are not part of the same Active Directory forest. This process is automatic and does not require the intervention of systems administrators. The foreign security principals can then be added to Domain Local groups which, in turn, can be granted permissions for resources within the domain. For more information on managing a multiple domain environment, see Chapter 5, "Installing and Managing Trees and Forests."

## Managing Security and Permissions

Now that you have a good understanding of the basic issues, terms, and Active Directory objects that pertain to security, it's time to look at how you can apply this information to secure your network resources. The general practice for managing security is to assign users to groups and then grant permissions to the groups so that they can access certain resources.

For ease of management and to implement a hierarchical structure, you can place groups within OUs. You can also assign Group Policy settings to all of the objects contained within an OU. By using this method, you can combine the benefits of a hierarchical structure (through OUs) and the use of security principals. Figure 8.2 provides a diagram of this process.

**FIGURE 8.2** An overview of security management

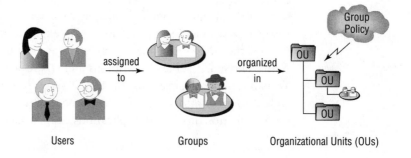

The primary tool used to manage security permissions for Users, Groups, and Computers is the Active Directory Users and Computers snap-in. Using this tool, you can create and manage Active Directory objects and organize them based on your business needs. Common tasks for many systems administrators might include the following:

- Resetting a user's password (for example, in cases where they forget the password)

- Creating new user accounts (when, for instance, a new employee joins the company)

- Modifying group memberships based on changes in job requirements and functions

- Disabling user accounts (when, for example, users will be out of the office for long periods of time and will not require network resource access)

## Permissions

Once you've properly grouped your users, you'll need to set the actual permissions that will affect the objects within the Active Directory. The actual permissions available will vary based on the type of object. The following provides an example of some of the permissions that can be applied to various Active Directory objects and an explanation of what each permission does:

| Permission | Explanation |
| --- | --- |
| Control Access | Changes security permissions on the object |
| Create Child | Creates objects within an OU (such as other OUs) |
| Delete Child | Deletes child objects within an OU |
| Delete Tree | Deletes an OU and the objects within it |
| List Contents | Views objects within an OU |
| List Object | Views a list of the objects within an OU |
| Read | Views properties of an object (such as a user name) |
| Write | Modifies properties of an object |

Now that you have a good idea of the basis of the Active Directory security architecture, let's move on to covering exactly how security is implemented. We'll cover the steps required to set up permissions in the next section.

# Implementing Active Directory Security

**W**ithin the Administrative Tools folder on domain controllers, you will find three useful tools for setting and managing Active Directory and domain controller security.

***Microsoft*** ✓ ***Exam Objective***

**Manage Active Directory objects.**

- Control access to Active Directory objects.

- Delegate administrative control of objects in Active Directory.

The following are the three useful tools just mentioned:

**Local Security Policy**   The Local Security Policy settings pertain to the local computer only. These settings are useful when you have specific computers that require custom security configurations. For example, an intranet Web server may have different settings from a mission-critical database server.

**Domain Security Policy**   The Domain Security Policy utility is used to view security settings that apply to all of the objects within a domain. Using this utility, you can specify settings, such as the audit policy, System Service settings, and other options. These settings will apply to all of the domain controllers within a domain, unless they are specifically overridden.

**Domain Controller Security Policy**   The options presented within the Domain Controller Security Policy are similar to those found in the Domain Security Policy utility. The major difference is that the settings you make using this tool apply only to the local domain controller rather than to all domain controllers within the domain. This tool is useful when you want to specify different settings on different domain controllers.

Figure 8.3 shows an example of the settings available within the Domain Controller Security Policy tool.

**FIGURE  8.3**    The Domain Controller Security Policy tool

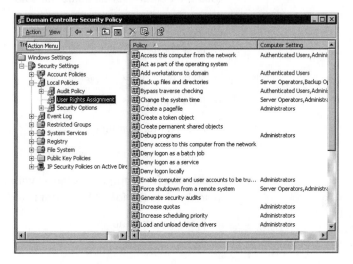

Exercise 8.1 walks you through the steps required to create and manage Users and Groups. If you are unfamiliar with basic Active Directory administration steps, you will find it useful to review Chapter 7.

**EXERCISE 8.1**

### Creating and Managing Users and Groups

In this exercise, you will create Users and Groups within the Active Directory and then place Users into Groups.

**1.** Open the Active Directory Users and Computers tool.

**2.** Create the following top-level OUs:

Sales

Marketing

Engineering

HR

**EXERCISE 8.1** *(continued)*

3. Create the following User objects within the Sales container (use the defaults for all fields not listed):

   **a.** First Name: John

   Last Name: Sales

   User Logon Name: jsales

   **b.** First Name: Linda

   Last Name: Manager

   User Logon Name: lmanager

4. Create the following User objects within the Marketing container (use the defaults for all fields not listed):

   **a.** First Name: Jane

   Last Name: Marketing

   User Logon Name: jmarketing

   **b.** First Name: Monica

   Last Name: Manager

   User Logon Name: mmanager

5. Create the following User object within the Engineering container (use the defaults for all fields not listed):

   **a.** First Name: Bob

   Last Name: Engineer

   User Logon Name: bengineer

6. Right-click the HR container, and select New ➤ Group. Use the name Managers for the Group, and specify Global for the Group scope and Security for the Group type. Click OK to create the Group.

7. To assign Users to the Managers group, right-click the Group object and select Properties. Change to the Members tab, and click Add. From the list, select Linda Manager and Monica Manager, then click OK. You will see the Group membership. Click OK to finish adding the Users to the Group.

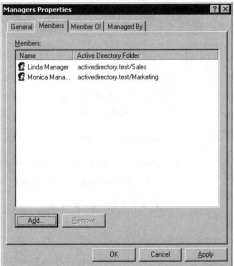

8. When finished creating Users and Groups, close the Active Directory Users and Computers tool.

Notice that you can add Users to Groups regardless of the OU in which they're contained. In Exercise 8.1, for example, we added two User accounts from different OUs into a Group that was created in a third OU. This type of flexibility allows you to easily manage User and Group accounts based on your business organization.

The Active Directory Users and Computers tool also allows you to perform common functions by simply right-clicking an object and selecting actions from the context-sensitive menu. For example, we could right-click a User account and select Add Members to Group to quickly change Group membership.

## Delegating Control of Active Directory Objects

A common administrative function related to the use of the Active Directory involves managing objects. OUs can be used to logically group objects so that they can be easily managed. Once you have placed the appropriate Active Directory objects within OUs, you will be ready to delegate control of these objects.

*Delegation* is the process by which a higher-level security administrator assigns permissions to other users. For example, if Admin A is a member of the Domain Administrators group, they will be able to delegate control of any OU within the domain to Admin B. Exercise 8.2 walks through the steps required to delegate control of OUs.

---

**EXERCISE 8.2**

**Delegating Control of Active Directory Objects**

In this exercise, we will delegate control of Active Directory objects. In order to complete the steps in this exercise, you must have already completed Exercise 8.1.

**1.** Open the Active Directory Users and Computers tool.

**2.** Create a new user within the Engineering OU, using the following information (use the default settings for any fields not specified):

    **a.** First Name: Robert

       Last Name: Admin

       User Logon Name: radmin

**3.** Right-click the Sales OU, and select Delegate Control. This will start the Delegation of Control Wizard. Click Next.

**4.** To add users and groups to which you want to delegate control, click Add. From the list of users, select Robert Admin. Click OK and then Next to continue.

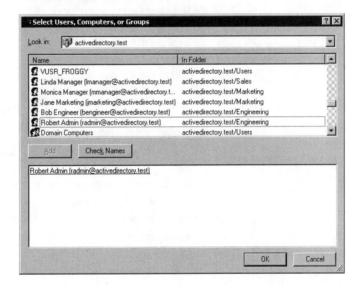

**5.** Select the Delegate the Following Common Tasks option, and place a check mark next to the following options:

Create, Delete, and Manage User Accounts

Reset Passwords on User Accounts

Read all User Information

Create, Delete, and Manage Groups

Modify the Membership of a Group

**EXERCISE 8.2** *(continued)*

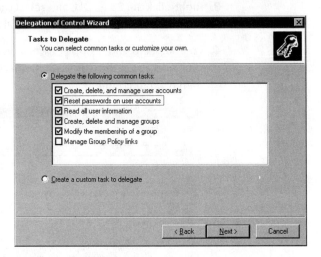

6. Click Next to continue, then click Finish to save the changes. Now, when the user Robert Admin logs on, he will be able to perform common administrative functions for all of the objects contained within the Sales OU.

7. When finished, close the Active Directory Users and Computers tool.

# Using Group Policy for Security

Through the use of the Active Directory, systems administrators can define Group Policy objects and then apply them to OUs. We'll cover the details of creating, assigning, and managing Group Policy settings later in Chapter 10, "Managing Group Policy."

*Microsoft* ✓ *Exam Objective*

**Configure and troubleshoot security in a directory services infrastructure.**

- Apply security policies by using Group Policy.

Exercise 8.3 walks through the steps required to create a basic Group Policy for the purpose of enforcing security settings.

---

**EXERCISE 8.3**

### Applying Security Policies by Using Group Policy

In this exercise, you will assign security permissions by using Group Policy. In order to complete the steps of this exercise, you must have already completed Exercise 8.1.

1. Open the Active Directory Users and Computers tool.

2. Right-click the Engineering OU, and select Properties.

3. Change to the Group Policy tab, and click New. Type **Engineering Security Settings** for the name of the new Group Policy.

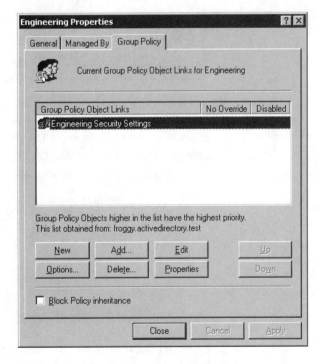

4. To specify the Group Policy settings, click Edit.

**EXERCISE 8.3** *(continued)*

**5.** In the Group Policy window, open Computer Configuration ➢ Windows Settings ➢ Security Settings ➢ Account Policies ➢ Password Policy object.

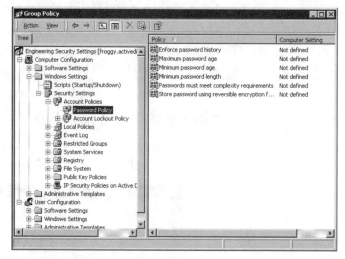

**6.** In the right-hand pane, double-click the Minimum Password Length setting. In the Security Policy Setting dialog box, place a check mark next to the Define This Policy Setting option. Leave the default value of 7 characters. Click OK.

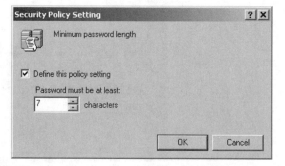

**7.** Open User Configuration ➢ Administrative Templates ➢ Control Panel object. Double-click Disable Control Panel, select Enabled, and then click OK.

8. Close the Group Policy window to save the settings you chose. Click OK and Close to enable the Security Group Policy for the Engineering OU.

9. To view the security permissions for a Group Policy object, right-click the Engineering OU and select Properties. On the Group Policy tab, highlight the Engineering Security Settings Group Policy object, and select Properties.

10. Select the Security tab. Click Add, and select Linda Manager from the list of users. Click Add and OK. Highlight Linda Manager, and allow this user the Read and Write permissions.

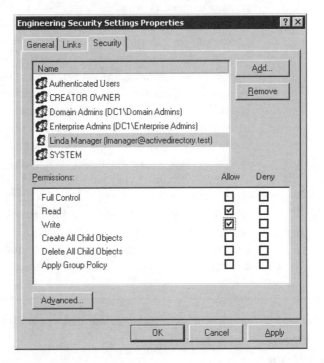

11. Click OK twice to save the changes. Linda Manager will now be able to view and change information for objects in the Sales OU.

12. When finished, close the Active Directory Users and Computers tool.

The settings that you specify will apply to all of the security principals included within the OU to which the Group Policy applies.

# Using the Security Configuration and Analysis Utility

The power and flexibility of Windows-based operating systems is both a benefit and a liability. On the plus side, the many configuration options available allow users and systems administrators to modify and customize settings to their preference. On the negative side, however, the full level of functionality can cause problems. For example, novice users might attempt to delete critical system files or incorrectly uninstall programs to free up disk space. So how can these types of problems be prevented? One method is to strictly enforce the types of actions that users can perform. Since most settings for the Windows 2000 interface can be configured in the Registry, you could edit the appropriate settings using the RegEdit command.

Although you could manage security settings manually through the use of Registry changes, this process can become quite tedious. Furthermore, manually modifying the Registry is a dangerous process and one that is bound to cause problems due to human error. In order to make the creation and application of security settings easier, Microsoft has included the Security Configuration and Analysis tool with Windows 2000. This tool can be used to create, modify, and apply security settings in the Registry through the use of Security Template files. *Security Templates* allow systems administrators to define security settings once and then store this information in a file that can be applied to other computers.

---

*Microsoft* ✓ *Exam* *Objective*

**Configure and troubleshoot security in a directory services infrastructure.**

- Create, analyze, and modify security configurations by using Security Configuration and Analysis and Security Templates.

These Template files offer a user-friendly way of configuring common settings for Windows 2000–based operating systems. For example, instead of searching through the Registry (which is largely undocumented) for specific keys, a systems administrator can choose from a list of common options. The Template file provides a description of the settings, along with information about the Registry key(s) to which the modifications must be made. Templates can be stored and applied to users and computers. For example, we could create three configurations entitled Level 1, Level 2, and Level 3. We may use the Level 3 template for high-level managers and engineers, while the Level 1 and Level 2 templates are used for all other users who require basic functionality.

The overall process for working with the Security Configuration and Analysis tool is as follows:

1. Open or create a Security Database file.

2. Import an existing Template file.

3. Analyze the local computer.

4. Make any setting changes.

5. Save any template changes.

6. Export the new template (optional).

7. Apply the changes to the local computer (optional).

There is no default icon for the *Security Configuration and Analysis utility*. In order to access it, you must manually choose this snap-in from within the Microsoft Management Console (MMC) tool. Exercise 8.4 walks you through the steps required to use the Security Configuration and Analysis utility.

### EXERCISE 8.4

### Using the Security Configuration and Analysis Utility

In this exercise, you will use the Security Configuration and Analysis utility to create and modify security configurations.

1. Click Start ➢ Run, type **mmc**, and press Enter. This will open a blank MMC.

**EXERCISE 8.4** *(continued)*

2. In the Console menu, select Add/Remove Snap-In. Click Add. Select the Security Configuration and Analysis item, and then click Add. Click Close.

3. You will see that the Security Configuration and Analysis snap-in has been added to the configuration. Click OK to continue.

4. Within the MMC, right-click Security Configuration and Analysis, and select Open Database. Change to a local directory on your computer, and create a new Security Database file named SecurityTest.sdb. Note the location of this file, because you'll need it in later steps. Click OK.

**EXERCISE 8.4** *(continued)*

5. Next, you'll be prompted to open a Security Template file. By default, these files are stored within the `Security\Templates` directory of your Windows NT system root. From the list, select DC Security, and place a check mark in the Clear This Database before Importing box. Click Open to load the Template file.

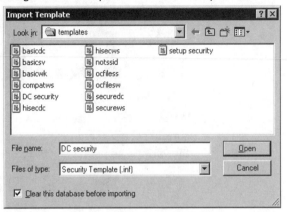

6. Now that we have created a Security Database file and opened a template, we can start performing useful security tasks. Notice that several tasks will be available. To perform an analysis on the security configuration of the local computer, right-click the Security Configuration and Analysis utility, and select Analyze Computer Now. When prompted, enter the path to a local directory with the filename `SecurityTest.log`. Click OK to begin the analysis process.

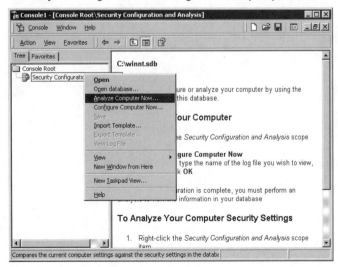

**EXERCISE 8.4** *(continued)*

7. You will see the Security Configuration and Analysis utility begin to analyze your computer.

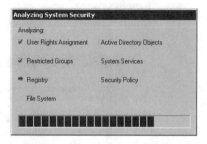

8. When the process has been completed, you will be able to view the current security settings for the local computer. Navigate through the various items to view the current security configuration.

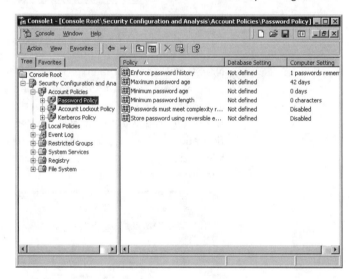

9. To make changes to this template, expand the Password Policy object under the Account Policies object. Double-click the Enforce Password History item. Place a check mark next to the Define This Policy in the Database option, and type **2** for Passwords Remembered. Click OK to make the setting change. Note that this change in setting was not enabled for the local computer—the change was implemented only within the Security Database file.

10. To save the changes to the Security Database file, right-click the Security and Configuration Analysis object, and select Save.

11. To export the current settings to a Template file, right-click the Security and Configuration Analysis object, and select Export Template. You will be prompted for the location and filename to which these settings should be saved. Be sure to choose a meaningful name so that other systems administrators will understand the purpose of this template.

12. So far, the configuration change we made has not yet been applied to any machines. To apply the change to the local computer, right-click the Security and Configuration Analysis object, and select Configure Computer Now. You will be prompted to enter the path for a Log file. Enter any path on the local computer, and specify SecurityTest2.log as the filename. Click OK. You will see the settings being applied to the local computer.

**EXERCISE 8.4** *(continued)*

13. To quickly view the contents of the Log file for the most recent operation, right-click the Security and Configuration Analysis object, and select View Log.

14. When you are finished, exit the Security and Configuration Analysis tool by closing the MMC.

 **Real World Scenario**

**Enforcing Consistent Security Policies**

You are one of 50 systems administrators for a large, multinational organization. As is the case for most of these administrators, you're responsible for all operations related to a portion of an Active Directory domain. Specifically, your job is to manage all of aspects of administration for objects contained within the Austin OU. The Austin office supports nearly 500 employees. Recently, security has become an important concern because the company is growing quickly and new employees are being added almost daily. Additionally, the organization deals with customers' sensitive financial information, and the success of the business is based on this information remaining secure. You've been tasked with creating and implementing an Active Directory security policy for the Austin OU.

At first you start looking into the Group Policy settings that might be appropriate for attaining the desired level of security. You create different "levels" of security based on users' job functions. Specific policy options include restrictions on when users can access network resources and which resources they can access. You also begin to implement settings that "harden" your production servers, especially those that contain sensitive data.

A few days after your analysis has begun, you join the weekly company-wide IT conference call and learn that you're not alone in this task. It seems that systems administrators throughout the company have been given similar tasks. The only difference is that they're all asked to implement policies only for the specific Active Directory objects for which they're responsible. That gets you thinking about pooling resources: That is, although it might make sense to attack this task for just the Austin OU, wouldn't it be great if the entire organization could implement a consistent and uniform security policy? If every systems administrator decided to implement security policies in a different way, this would compromise consistency and ease of administration within the environment. And it's likely that many systems administrators will create useful security policies that the others overlooked. The idea of "think globally, act locally" may apply here.

The Security Configuration and Analysis tool that is included with Windows 2000 Server is designed to solve exactly this type of problem. You find that by using this tool, you can design a set of security configurations and then apply those policies to various computers within the environment. You decide to begin by creating Security Templates based on business needs. Since the environment has many different requirements (and some that are specific only to a few offices), your goal is to minimize the number of different Security Templates that you create while still meeting the needs of the entire organization. Perhaps the best way to proceed in this scenario is to pool resources: Many tech-heads are better than one! Creating the appropriate security policies is unlikely to be an easy task—you'll need to confer with systems administrators throughout the company and you'll need to talk to managers and business leaders, as well. However, it will be worth the effort to ensure that the entire organization has implemented consistent security policies. Overall, a little extra work up-front can save a lot of headaches in the long run.

If any errors occurred during the Security Configuration and Analysis process, the results will be stored in the Log file that was created. Be sure to examine this file for any errors that might be present in your configuration.

# Implementing an Audit Policy

**O**ne of the most important aspects of controlling security in networked environments is ensuring that only authorized users are able to access specific resources. Although systems administrators often spend much time managing security permissions, it is almost always possible for a security problem to occur. Sometimes, the best way to find possible security breaches is to actually record the actions taken by specific users. Then, in the case of a security breach (the unauthorized shutdown of a server, for example), systems administrators can examine the log to find the cause of the problem. The Windows 2000 operating system and the Active Directory offer the ability to audit a wide range of actions. In this section, we'll look at how you can implement auditing for the Active Directory.

| *Microsoft* ✓ *Exam Objective* | **Configure and troubleshoot security in a directory services infrastructure.**<br><br>▪ Implement an audit policy.<br><br>**Monitor and analyze security events.** |
| --- | --- |

## Overview of Auditing

The act of auditing relates to recording specific actions. From a security standpoint, auditing is used to detect any possible misuse of network resources. Although auditing will not necessarily prevent the misuse of resources, it will help determine when security violations occurred (or were attempted). Furthermore, just the fact that others know that you have implemented auditing may prevent them from attempting to circumvent security.

There are several steps that you will need to complete in order to implement auditing using Windows 2000. These steps include the following:

- Configuring the size and storage settings for the audit logs

- Enabling categories of events to audit

- Specifying which objects and actions should be recorded in the audit log

In this section, you'll learn how to complete these steps.

Note that there are trade-offs to implementing auditing. First and foremost, recording auditing information can consume system resources. This can decrease overall system performance and use up valuable disk space. Secondly, auditing many events can make the audit log impractical to view. If too much detail is provided, systems administrators are unlikely to scrutinize all of the recorded events. For these reasons, you should always be sure to find a balance between the level of auditing details provided and the performance management implications of these settings.

## Implementing Auditing

Auditing is not an all-or-none type of process. As is the case with security in general, systems administrators must choose specifically which objects and actions they want to audit.

The main categories for auditing include the following:

- Audit account logon events
- Audit account management
- Audit directory service access
- Audit logon events
- Audit object access
- Audit policy change
- Audit privilege use
- Audit process tracking
- Audit system events

In order to audit access to objects stored within the Active Directory, you must enable the Audit Directory Service Access option. Then, you must specify which objects and actions should be tracked. Exercise 8.5 walks through the steps required to implement auditing of Active Directory objects on domain controllers.

---

### EXERCISE 8.5

### Enabling Auditing of Active Directory Objects

In this exercise, you will enable auditing for an Active Directory domain. In order to complete the steps in this exercise, you must have already completed Exercise 8.1.

**EXERCISE 8.5** *(continued)*

1. Open the Domain Controller Security Policy tool.

2. Expand Security Settings ➢ Local Policies ➢ Audit Policy.

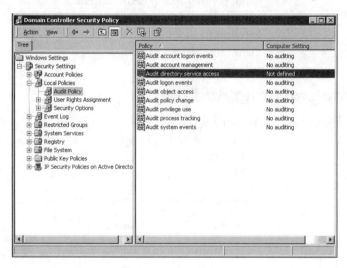

3. Double-click the setting for Audit Directory Service Access. Place a check mark next to the options for Define These Policy Settings, Success, and Failure. Click OK to save the settings.

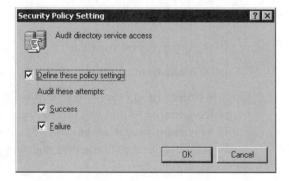

**EXERCISE 8.5** *(continued)*

4. Expand Security Settings ➤ Event Log ➤ Settings for Event Logs to see the options associated with the event logs.

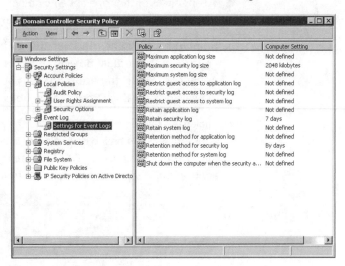

5. Double-click the Maximum Security Log Size item, and set the value to 2048KB. Click OK.

6. Double-click the Retain Security Log item, and specify that events should be overwritten after seven days. Click OK. You will be notified that the Retention Method for Security Log option will also be changed. Click OK to accept the changes.

7. When you are finished enabling auditing options, close the Domain Controller Security Configuration tool.

---

Once you have enabled auditing of Active Directory objects, it's time to specify exactly which actions and objects should be audited. Exercise 8.6 walks through the steps required to enable auditing for a specific OU.

**EXERCISE 8.6**

## Enabling Auditing for a Specific OU

In this exercise, you will enable auditing for a specific OU. In order to complete the steps in this exercise, you must have already completed Exercise 8.1 and Exercise 8.5.

1. Open the Active Directory Users and Computers tool.

2. To enable auditing for a specific object, right-click the Engineering OU, and select Properties. Select the Group Policy tab.

3. Highlight the Engineering Security Settings Group Policy object, and select Properties. Select the Security tab, and then click Advanced. Select the Auditing tab. You will see the current auditing settings for this Group Policy object.

4. Click the View/Edit button. Notice that you can view and change auditing settings based on the objects and/or properties. To retain the current settings, click OK. To exit the configuration for the Engineering object, click OK three more times.

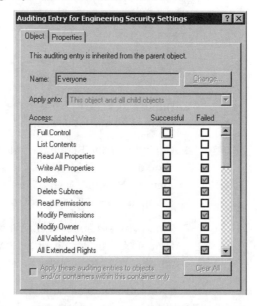

5. When you are finished with the auditing settings, close the Active Directory Users and Computers tool.

## Viewing Auditing Information

One of the most important aspects of auditing is regularly monitoring the audit logs. If this step is ignored (as it often is in poorly managed environments), the act of auditing is useless. Fortunately, Windows 2000 includes the *Event Viewer* tool that allows systems administrators to quickly and easily view audited events. Using the filtering capabilities of the Event Viewer, they can find specific events of interest.

Exercise 8.7 walks through the steps required to generate some auditing events and to examine the data collected for these actions.

---

**EXERCISE 8.7**

### Generating and Viewing Audit Logs

In this exercise, you will perform some actions that will be audited, and then you will view the information recorded within the audit logs. In order to complete this exercise, you must have already completed the steps in Exercise 8.1 and Exercise 8.6.

1. Open the Active Directory Users and Computers tool.

2. Within the Engineering OU, right-click the Bob Engineer User account, and select Properties. Add the middle initial A for this User account, and specify Software Developer in the Description box. Click OK to save the changes.

3. Within the Engineering OU, right-click the Robert Admin User account, and select Properties. Add a description of Engineering IT Admin, and click OK.

4. Close the Active Directory Users and Computers tool.

5. Open the Event Viewer tool from the Administrative Tools program group. Select the Security Log item.

6. You will see a list of audited events categorized under Directory Service Access. Note that you can obtain more details about a specific item by double-clicking it.

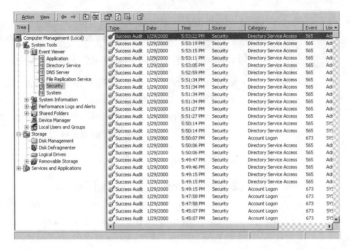

7. To modify the Log file settings, in the right-hand pane of the Computer Management window, right-click the Directory Service Access item, and choose Properties. Change the value for the Maximum Log File Size to 2048KB, and select the Overwrite Events as Needed option. This will allow you to store more audit events in the log and will ensure that events are cleared out of the log as needed. To save the new settings, click OK.

8. When you are finished viewing the security log, close the Computer Management tool.

# Summary

In this chapter, we covered the important topic of security as it pertains to the Active Directory. Specifically, we discussed the following:

- The differences between Security and Distribution groups

- Group scope, including Local, Global, and Universal groups

- Default Groups included in Windows 2000 and the Active Directory that predefine commonly used sets of permissions

- How permissions can be managed

- How the Delegation of Control Wizard can be used to distribute administrative responsibilities

- How Group Policy can be used for security purposes and how the Security Configuration and Analysis utility can ensure consistency

- How any why auditing can be used to increase the security of a networked environment

Thoroughly understanding each of these topics is important when implementing the Active Directory in a business environment (and when you're preparing for the exam)!

# Exam Essentials

**Understand the purpose of security principals.**   Security principals are Active Directory objects that can be assigned permissions. Understanding how they work is vital to creating a secure Active Directory environment.

**Understand group types and group scope.**   The two major types of groups are Security and Distribution groups, and they have different purposes. Groups can be Local, Global, or Universal.

**Understand the purpose and permissions of built-in groups.**   The Active Directory environment includes several built-in Local and Global groups that are designed to simplify common systems administration tasks.

**Understand how to use the Delegation of Control Wizard to allow distributed administration.**   Through the use of this Wizard, you can specify which users can control security for particular objects within the Active Directory.

**Learn how the Security Configuration and Analysis utility can simplify the implementation of security policies.**   Through the use of Security Templates, you can ensure that you are enforcing consistent security policies throughout the environment.

**Understand the purpose and function of auditing.**   Auditing is helpful in determining the cause of security violations and for troubleshooting permissions-related problems.

# Key Terms

Before you take the exam, be certain you are familiar with the following terms:

| | |
|---|---|
| auditing | Group Policy |
| delegation | permissions |
| Distribution groups | Security Configuration and Analysis utility |
| Domain Local groups | Security groups |
| Event Viewer | security principals |
| foreign security principals | Security Templates |
| Global groups | Universal groups |

# Review Questions

1. You are the systems administrator for a medium-sized Active Directory domain. Currently, the environment supports many different domain controllers, some of which are running Windows NT 4 and others that are running Windows 2000. When running in this type of environment, which of the following types of groups *cannot* be used?

   **A.** Universal security groups

   **B.** Global groups

   **C.** Domain Local groups

   **D.** Computer groups

   **E.** None of the above

2. Isabel is a systems administrator for an Active Directory environment that is running in native mode. Recently, several managers have reported suspicions about user activities and have asked her to increase security in the environment. Specifically, the requirements are as follows:

   - The accessing of certain sensitive files must be logged.

   - Modifications to certain sensitive files must be logged.

   - Systems administrators must be able to provide information about which users accessed sensitive files and when they were accessed.

   - All logon attempts for specific shared machines must be recorded.

   Which of the following steps should Isabel take to meet these requirements? (Choose all that apply.)

   **A.** Enable auditing with the Computer Management tool.

   **B.** Enable auditing with the Active Directory Users and Computers tool.

   **C.** Enable auditing with the Active Directory Domains and Trusts tool.

   **D.** Enable auditing with the Event Viewer tool.

   **E.** View the audit log using the Event Viewer tool.

   **F.** View auditing information using the Computer Management tool.

   **G.** Enable failure and success auditing settings for specific files stored on NTFS volumes.

3. A systems administrator wants to allow another user the ability to change User account information for all users within a specific OU. Which of the following tools would allow them to do this most easily?

   **A.** Domain Security Policy

   **B.** Domain Controller Security Policy

   **C.** Computer Management

   **D.** Delegation of Control Wizard

   **E.** None of the above

4. Group Policy can be linked to which of the following Active Directory objects?

   **A.** Organizational units (OUs)

   **B.** Users

   **C.** Computers

   **D.** Groups

   **E.** All of the above

5. Minh, an IT manager, has full permissions over several OUs within a small Active Directory domain. Recently, Minh has hired a junior systems administrator to take over some of the responsibilities of administering the objects within these OUs. She gives the new employee access to modify user accounts within two OUs. This process is known as

   **A.** Inheritance

   **B.** Transfer of control

   **C.** Delegation

   **D.** Transfer of ownership

   **E.** None of the above

6. A systems administrator wants to prevent users from starting or stopping a specific service on domain controllers. Which of the following tools can be used to prevent this from occurring?

   **A.** Active Directory Users and Computers

   **B.** Domain Controller Security Policy

   **C.** Domain Security Policy

   **D.** Local System Policy

   **E.** All of the above

7. Which of the following types of groups can contain users from multiple domains? (Choose all that apply.)

    **A.** Universal groups

    **B.** Domain Local groups

    **C.** Global groups

    **D.** Distribution groups

    **E.** All of the above

8. Raj, a systems administrator, has recently been asked to create a new Active Directory domain in response to the merger of his company with another organization. Formerly, the environment had only a single Active Directory domain running in native mode. As a result of the business restructuring, many employees must be moved to the new domain. Raj decides to create new groups in the original domain and then move these groups to the new domain. Which of the following types of groups should he create in the original domain?

    **A.** Universal groups

    **B.** Domain Local groups

    **C.** Global groups

    **D.** Distribution groups

    **E.** All of the above

9. Which of the following Active Directory objects is not considered a security principal?

    **A.** Users

    **B.** Groups

    **C.** Organizational units (OUs)

    **D.** Computers

**10.** Which of the following folders in the Active Directory Users and Computers tool is used when users from outside the forest are granted access to resources within a domain?

**A.** Users

**B.** Computers

**C.** Domain Controllers

**D.** Foreign Security Principals

**E.** None of the above

**11.** Lance is a systems administrator for an Active Directory environment that contains four domains. Recently, several managers have reported suspicions about user activities and have asked him to increase security in the environment. Specifically, the requirements are as follows:

- Audit changes to user objects that are contained within a specific OU.

- Allow a special user account called "Audit" to view and modify all security-related information about objects in that OU.

Which of the following steps should Lance take to meet these requirements? (Choose all that apply.)

**A.** Convert all volumes on which Active Directory information resides to NTFS.

**B.** Enable auditing with the Active Directory Users and Computers tool.

**C.** Create a new Active Directory domain and create restrictive permissions for the suspected users within this domain.

**D.** Reconfigure trust settings using the Active Directory Domains and Trusts tool.

**E.** Specify auditing options for the OU using the Active Directory Users and Computers tool.

**F.** Use the Delegation of Control Wizard to grant appropriate permissions to view and modify objects within the OU to the "Audit" user account.

12. You are installing a new software application on a Windows 2000 domain controller. After reading the manual and consulting with a security administrator, you find that you have the following requirements:

    - The software must run under an account that has permissions to all files on the server on which it is installed.

    - The software must be able to bypass file system security in order to work properly.

    - The software must be able to read and write sensitive files stored on the local server.

    - Users of the software must not be able to view sensitive data that is stored within the files on the server.

    You decide to create a new user account for the software and then assign the account to a built-in local group. To which of the following groups should you assign the account?

    **A.** Account Operators

    **B.** Backup Operators group

    **C.** Guests

    **D.** Domain Administrators

    **E.** None of the above

13. Members of which of the following groups have permissions to perform actions in multiple domains?

    **A.** Domain Admins

    **B.** Domain Users

    **C.** Administrators

    **D.** Enterprise Admins

    **E.** All of the above

**14.** Which of the following types of groups is/are not considered security principals?

   **A.** Global groups

   **B.** Domain Local groups

   **C.** Distribution groups

   **D.** Universal groups

   **E.** All of the above

**15.** Oscar, a systems administrator, has created a top-level OU called Engineering. Within the Engineering OU, he has created two OUs: Research and Development. Oscar wants to place security permissions on only the Engineering OU. However, when he does so, he finds that the permissions settings automatically applied to the child OUs. Which of the following actions can he take to prevent this from happening?

   **A.** Block the inheritance of properties for the OUs.

   **B.** Rename the parent OU.

   **C.** Delete and re-create the child OUs.

   **D.** None of the above.

16. You are the systems administrator for a small Active Directory domain. Recently, you have hired an intern to assist you with managing user objects within the domain. You want to do the following:

    - Provide the intern with permissions to access the Active Directory using the Active Directory Users and Computers tool.

    - Provide the intern with sufficient permissions to change the properties of user accounts and to create and delete user accounts.

    - Provide the intern with the ability to create groups and computers.

    - Prevent the intern from being able to make any other changes to the Active Directory environment.

    To which of the following groups should you add the user?

    **A.** Backup Operators

    **B.** Account Operators

    **C.** Enterprise Admins

    **D.** Domain Admins

    **E.** Guests

**17.** You want the security log to overwrite events that are more than nine days old. Looking at the following screen, what would you do next in order to accomplish this task?

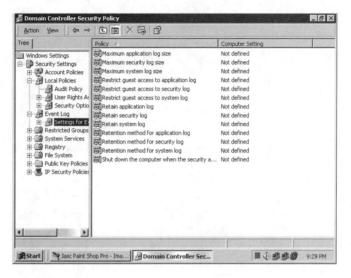

**A.** Double-click Maximum Security Log Size.

**B.** Double-click Retention Method for Security Log.

**C.** Double-click Retain Security Log.

**D.** Right-click Retention Method for Security Log.

# Answers to Review Questions

1. A. Because you are supporting Windows NT 4 and Windows 2000 domain controllers, you must run the environment in mixed mode. Universal security groups are not available when running in mixed-mode Active Directory environments.

2. B, E, G. The Active Directory Users and Computers tool allows systems administrators to change auditing options and to choose which actions are audited. At the file-system level, Isabel can specify exactly which actions are recorded in the audit log. She can then use the Event Viewer to view the recorded information and provide it to the appropriate managers.

3. D. The Delegation of Control Wizard is designed to assist systems administrators in granting specific permissions to other users.

4. A. Group Policy settings are linked at the OU level and may affect other object types within that OU.

5. C. Delegation is the process of granting permissions to other users. Delegation is often used to distribute systems administration responsibilities. Inheritance is the transfer of permissions and other settings from parent OUs to child OUs.

6. B. The settings made in the Domain Controller Security Policy tool apply only to domain controllers.

7. A, B. Universal groups and Domain Local groups can contain members from throughout the forest.

8. A. Universal groups can be moved between domains while all of the other group types must be re-created manually.

9. C. OUs are primarily used to organize objects within the Active Directory and do not function as security principals.

10. D. When resources are made available to users who reside in domains outside of the forest, Foreign Security Principal objects are automatically created.

**11.** B, E, F. The first step is to enable auditing. With auditing enabled, Lance can specify which actions are recorded. To give permissions to the "Audit" user account, he can use the Delegation of Control Wizard.

**12.** B. Members of the Backup Operators group are able to bypass file system security in order to back up and restore files. The requirements provided are similar to those for many popular backup software applications.

**13.** D. Members of the Enterprise Admins group are given full permissions to manage all domains within an Active Directory forest.

**14.** C. Distribution groups are often used to organize users for sending e-mail, but they are not security principals.

**15.** A. This flow of permissions (known as inheritance) can be blocked at any level. By blocking inheritance, the permissions will not flow from the Engineering OU to the Research and Development OUs.

**16.** B. The user should be added to the Account Operators group. Although membership in the Enterprise Admins or Domain Admins group will provide the user with the requisite permissions, these choices will exceed the required functionality.

**17.** C. The Retain Security Log setting allows you to specify how long the security log should be retained before it gets overwritten.

# Chapter

# 9

# Active Directory Optimization and Reliability

## MICROSOFT EXAM OBJECTIVES COVERED IN THIS CHAPTER:

✓ **Manage Active Directory performance.**

- Monitor, maintain, and troubleshoot domain controller performance.

- Monitor, maintain, and troubleshoot Active Directory components.

✓ **Back up and restore Active Directory.**

- Perform an authoritative restore of Active Directory.

- Recover from a system failure.

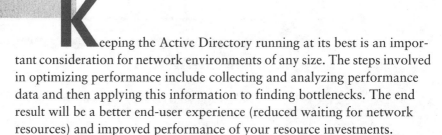

**K**eeping the Active Directory running at its best is an important consideration for network environments of any size. The steps involved in optimizing performance include collecting and analyzing performance data and then applying this information to finding bottlenecks. The end result will be a better end-user experience (reduced waiting for network resources) and improved performance of your resource investments.

Another important consideration when working with the Active Directory is ensuring that your system information is safely backed up. Backups are useful when data is lost due to system failures, file corruptions, or accidental modifications of information.

In this chapter, we'll look at ways in which you can use Windows 2000's performance monitoring and data protection tools to improve network operations.

# Overview of Windows 2000 Performance Monitoring

**W**hen it comes to optimizing performance, a commonly used process is just plain trial and error. Although this can sometimes lead to better results, it depends on the validity of the performance measurements you have made. Does the server just *seem* to be operating faster? If that's your only guideline, it's probably time that you started collecting some hard statistics to back up that feeling! In this chapter, we'll cover tools and methods for measuring performance in Windows 2000. Specifically, we'll focus on domain controllers and the Active Directory. Before we dive into the technical details, however, we should thoroughly understand what we're trying to accomplish and how we'll meet this goal.

---

*Microsoft*
*Exam*
*Objective*

**Manage Active Directory performance.**

- Monitor, maintain, and troubleshoot domain controller performance.

- Monitor, maintain, and troubleshoot Active Directory components.

---

For a more detailed discussion on the topics covered by the "Manage Active Directory performance" subobjectives, see the section "Monitoring Active Directory Components" later in this chapter.

The first step in any performance optimization strategy is to be able to accurately and consistently measure performance. The insight that you'll gain from monitoring factors, such as network utilization, will be extremely useful in measuring the effects of any changes.

The overall process of performance monitoring usually involves the following steps:

1. Establish a baseline of current performance.

2. Identify bottleneck(s).

3. Plan for and implement changes.

4. Measure the effects of the changes.

5. Repeat the process, based on business needs.

Note that the performance optimization process is never really finished since you can always try to tweak more performance out of your machines. Before you get discouraged (or change your job title to Performance Optimizer), realize that you'll reach some level of performance that you consider to be acceptable enough that it's not worth the additional effort it'll take to optimize performance further.

Now that we have an idea of the overall process, let's focus on how changes should be made. Some important ideas to keep in mind when monitoring performance include the following:

**Plan changes carefully.**   When working in an easy-to-use GUI-based operating system like the Windows 2000 platform, it's too easy to just remove a check mark here or there and then retest the performance. You should resist the urge to do this since some changes can cause large decreases in performance or can have an impact on functionality. Before you make haphazard changes (especially on production servers), take the time to learn about, plan for, and test your changes.

**Make only one change at a time.**   The golden rule of scientific experiments is that you should always keep track of as many variables as possible. When the topic is server optimization, this roughly translates into making only one change at a time.

One of the problems with making multiple system changes is that, although you may have improved performance overall, it's hard to determine exactly *which* change created the positive effects. It's also possible, for example, that changing one parameter increased performance greatly while changing another decreased it slightly. While the overall result was an increase in performance, the second, performance-reducing option should be identified so the same mistake is not made again. To reduce the chance of obtaining misleading results, always try to make only one change at a time.

**Ensure consistency in measurements.**   When monitoring performance, consistency in measurements is extremely important. You should strive toward having repeatable and accurate measurements. Controlling variables, such as system load at various times during the day, can help.

Let's assume, for instance, that we want to measure the number of transactions that we can simulate on the accounting database server within an hour. The results would be widely different if we ran the test during the month-end accounting close versus if we ran the test on a Sunday morning. By running the same tests when the server is under a relatively static amount of load, we will be able to get more accurate measurements.

**Utilize a test environment.**   Making haphazard changes in a production environment can cause serious problems. These problems will likely outweigh any benefits you could receive from making performance tweaks. To avoid negative impacts on users, attempt to make as many changes as possible within a test environment. When this isn't possible, be sure to make changes during off-peak hours. After all, the goal is to *improve* performance!

**Maintain a performance history.** Earlier in this chapter, we mentioned that the performance optimization cycle is a continuous improvement process. Since many changes may be made over time, it is important to keep track of the changes that have been made and the results you experienced. Documenting this knowledge will prevent the age-old question, "What did I do to solve this last time?"

As you can see, there are a lot of factors to keep in mind when optimizing performance. Although this might seem like a lot of factors to remember, most systems administrators are probably aware of the "rules." Fortunately, the tools included with Windows 2000 can help in organizing the process and taking measurements. Now that we have a good overview of the process, let's move on to looking at the tools that can be used to set it in motion!

# Using Windows 2000 Performance Tools

**B**ecause performance monitoring and optimization are vital functions in network environments of any size, Windows 2000 includes several performance-related tools. The first and most useful is the Windows 2000 *System Monitor*. The Windows 2000 System Monitor was designed to allow users and systems administrators to monitor performance statistics for various operating system parameters. Specifically, information about CPU, memory, disk, and network resources can be collected, stored, and analyzed using this tool. By collecting and analyzing performance values, systems administrators will be able to identify many potential problems. As we'll see later in this chapter, the System Monitor can also be used to monitor the performance of the Active Directory and its various components.

The Windows 2000 System Monitor itself is an ActiveX control that can be placed within other applications. Examples of applications that can host the System Monitor control include Web browsers and client programs like Microsoft Word or Microsoft Excel. This can make it very easy for applications developers and systems administrators to incorporate the System Monitor into their own tools and applications.

For more common performance monitoring functions, you'll want to use the built-in Microsoft Management Console (MMC) version of the System Monitor. You can easily access the System Monitor by opening the Performance icon in the Administrative Tools program group. This will launch the MMC and will load and initialize the System Monitor.

There are many different methods of monitoring performance when using the System Monitor. One method is to look at a snapshot of current activity for a few of the most important counters. This method allows you to find areas of potential bottlenecks and monitor the load on your servers at a certain point in time. You can also save the information to a log file for historical reporting and later analysis. This type of information is useful, for example, if you want to compare the load on your servers from three months ago to the current load. We'll take a closer look at this method and many others as we examine the System Monitor in more detail.

In this section, we'll cover the basics of working with the Windows 2000 System Monitor and performance tools. Then, in the following section, we'll apply these tools and techniques when monitoring the performance of the Active Directory.

## Choosing Counters

The first step in monitoring performance is to decide *what* you want to monitor. In Windows 2000, the operating system and related services include hundreds of performance statistics that can be tracked easily. All of these performance statistics fall into three main categories that you can choose to measure. These categories are as follows:

**Objects**   An object within the System Monitor is a collection of various performance statistics that you can monitor. Objects are based on various areas of system resources. For example, there are objects for the processor and memory, as well as for specific services such as Web service. Later in this chapter, we'll see how the Windows NT Directory Service (NTDS) object can be used to monitor performance of the Active Directory.

**Counters**   Counters are the actual parameters that are measured by the System Monitor. They are specific items that are grouped within objects. For example, within the Processor object, there is a counter for "% Processor Time." This counter displays one type of detailed information about the Processor object (specifically, the amount of total CPU time that is being used by all of the processes on the system).

**Instances**   Some counters will also have instances. An instance further identifies which performance parameter the counter is measuring. A simple example is a server with two CPUs. If you decide that you want to monitor processor usage (the Processor object) and, specifically, that you're interested in utilization (the "%Total Utilization" counter), you must still specify *which* CPU(s) you want to measure. In this example, you would have the choice of monitoring either of the two CPUs or a total value for both (using the Total instance).

You can specify which objects, counters, and instances you want to monitor by quickly and easily adding them to the System Monitor. Figure 9.1 shows the various options that are available when adding new counters to monitor using the System Monitor.

**FIGURE  9.1**    Adding a new System Monitor counter

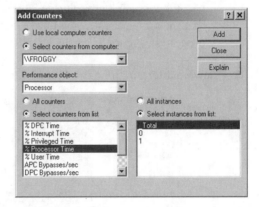

The exact items that you will be able to monitor will be based on your hardware and software configuration. For example, if you have not installed and configured the Internet Information Server (IIS) service, the options available within the Web Server objects will not be available. Or, if you have multiple network adapters or CPUs in the server, you will have the option to view each instance separately or as part of the total value.

We'll cover the details of which counters are generally most useful later in this chapter.

## Viewing Performance Information

The Windows 2000 System Monitor was designed to show information in a clear and easy-to-understand format. Based on the type of performance information you're viewing, however, you might want to change the display.

There are three main views that can be used to review statistics and information on performance. They are as follows:

**Graph View** The Graph view is the default display that is presented when you first access the Windows 2000 System Monitor. The chart displays values using the vertical axis and time using the horizontal axis. It is useful for displaying values over a period of time and for visually seeing the changes in these values over that time period. Each of the points that are plotted on the graph is based on an average value calculated during the sample interval for the measurement being made. For example, you may notice overall CPU utilization starting at a low value at the beginning of the chart and then becoming much higher during later measurements. This would indicate that the server has become busier (specifically, with CPU-intensive processes). Figure 9.2 provides an example of the Graph view.

**FIGURE 9.2** Viewing information in the System Monitor Graph view

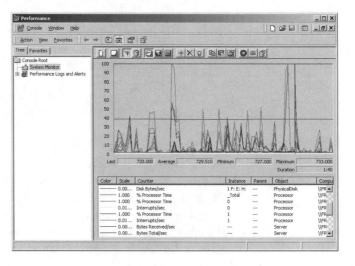

**Histogram View** The Histogram view shows performance statistics and information using a set of relative bar charts. The Histogram is useful for viewing a snapshot of the latest value for a given counter. For example, if we were interested in viewing a snapshot of current system performance statistics during each refresh interval, the length of each of the bars in the display would give us a visual representation of each value. It would also allow us to visually compare each measurement relative to the others. You can also set the histogram to display an average measurement as well as minimum and maximum thresholds. Figure 9.3 shows a typical Histogram view.

**FIGURE 9.3** Viewing information in the System Monitor Histogram view

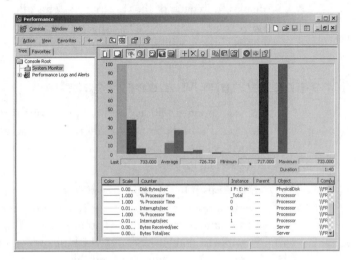

**Report View**   Like the Histogram view, the Report view shows performance statistics based on the latest measurement or displays an average measurement as well as minimum and maximum thresholds. It is most useful for determining exact values since it provides information in numeric terms unlike the Chart and Histogram views, which provide information graphically. Figure 9.4 provides an example of the type of information you'll see in the Report view.

**FIGURE 9.4** Viewing information in the System Monitor Report view

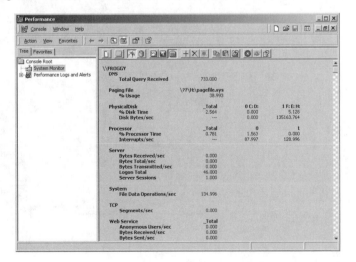

In the System Monitor, the same objects, counters, and instances may be displayed in each of the three views. This allows systems administrators to quickly and easily define the information they want to see once and then choose how it will be displayed based on specific needs.

## Managing System Monitor Properties

You can specify additional settings for viewing performance information within the properties of the System Monitor. You can access these options by clicking the Properties button in the taskbar or by right-clicking the System Monitor display and selecting Properties. The various tabs include the following:

**General**   On the General tab (shown in Figure 9.5), you can specify several options that relate to the System Monitor view. First, you can choose from among the Graph, Histogram, and Report views. Next, you can enable or disable legends (which display information about the various counters), the value bar, and the toolbar.

**FIGURE 9.5**   General System Monitor properties

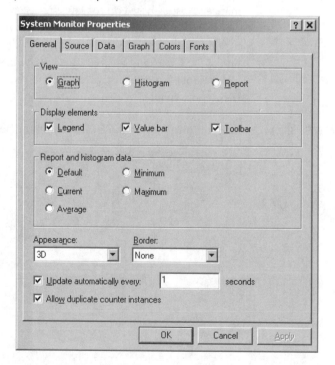

For the Report and Histogram views, you can choose which type of information is displayed. Options include Default, Current, Average, Minimum, and Maximum. It's important to check these settings based on the type of information you're viewing since it will make a big difference in the type of data being collected. These options are not available for the Graph view, since the Graph view displays an average value over a period of time (the sample interval).

With the General tab, you can also choose the appearance (flat or 3-D) and border options for the display. Next, an important setting is the update interval. By default, the display will be set to update every second. If you want the update frequency to decrease, you should increase the number of seconds between updates. The final option on the General tab allows you to specify whether or not you want to allow the same counter to be displayed twice in the same view.

**Source**    On the Source tab, you can specify the source for the performance information you would like to view. Options include current activity (the default setting) or data from a log file. If you choose to analyze information from a log file, you can also specify the time range for which you want to view statistics. We'll cover these selections in the next section.

**Data**    The Data tab (shown in Figure 9.6) displays a list of the counters that have been added to the System Monitor display. These counters apply to the Chart, Histogram, and Report views. Using this interface, you can also add or remove any of the counters and change properties, such as the width and style of the line and the scale used for display.

**Graph**    On the Graph tab, you can specify certain options that will allow you to customize the display of the System Monitor views. Specifically, you can add a title for the graph, specify a label for the vertical axis, choose to display grids, and specify the vertical scale range (see Figure 9.7).

**Colors**    Using the Colors tab, you can specify the colors for the areas of the display, such as the background and foreground.

**Fonts**    On the Fonts tab, you can specify the fonts that are used to display counter values in the System Monitor views. This is a useful option, and you can change settings to find a suitable balance between readability and the amount of information shown on one screen.

Now that we have an idea of the types of information System Monitor tracks and how this data is displayed, let's look at another feature—saving and analyzing performance data.

**FIGURE 9.6** Viewing System Monitor Counter settings

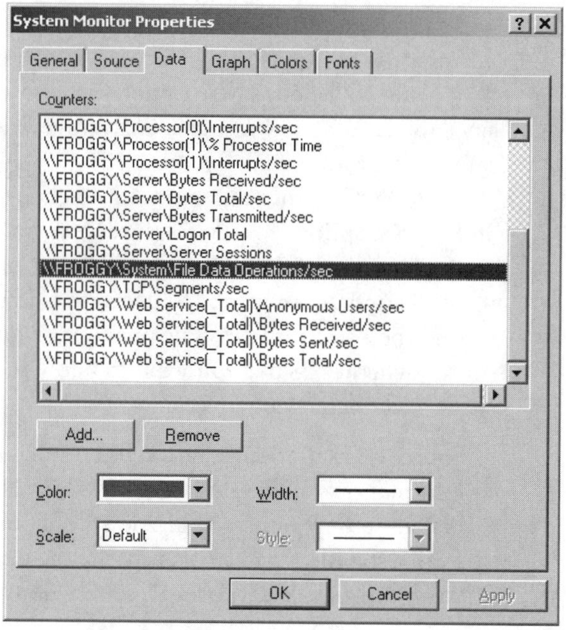

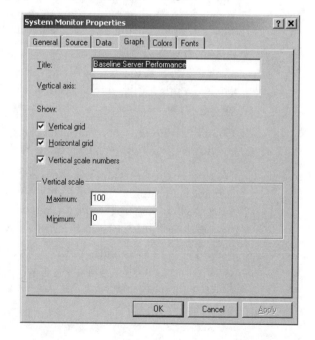

**FIGURE 9.7** Specifying System Monitor Graph settings

# Saving and Analyzing Data with Performance Logs and Alerts

**O**ne of the most important aspects of monitoring performance is that it should be done over a given period of time. So far, we have discussed how the System Monitor can be used to view statistics in real time. We have, however, also alluded to using the System Monitor to save data for later analysis. Now let's take a look at how this is done.

When viewing information in the System Monitor, you have two main options with respect to the data on display. They are as follows:

**View Current Activity**   When you first open the Performance icon from the Administrative Tools folder, the default option is to view data obtained from current system information. This method of viewing measures and displays various real-time statistics on the system's performance.

**View Log File Data**   This option allows you to view information that was previously saved to a log file. Although the objects, counters, and instances may appear to be the same as those viewed using the View Current Activity option, the information itself was actually captured at a previous point in time and stored into a log file.

So how are the log files for the View Log File Data option created? The process is actually very simple. You simply access the Performance Logs and Alerts section of the Windows 2000 Performance tool. Once there, you'll see three types of items available that allow you to customize how the data is collected in the log files. Let's take a look at each type of item in turn:

**Counter Logs**   *Counter logs* record performance statistics based on the various objects, counters, and instances available in the System Monitor. The values are updated based on a time interval setting and are saved to a file for later analysis.

**Trace Logs**   Some types of information are better monitored based on the occurrence of specific events instead of the passage of specified time intervals. *Trace logs* record performance information to files based on system events. There are several trace log types that can be included in this option by default. The following types are included:

- Windows 2000 Kernel Trace Provider

- Active Directory: Netlogon

- Active Directory: SAM
- Active Directory: Kerberos
- Windows NT Active Directory Service
- Local Security Authority (LSA)

Additionally, trace logs can be examined and analyzed through the use of third-party products. These third-party programs can include custom trace log providers for use with the Windows 2000 Performance Monitoring tools. Figure 9.8 shows the types of information that can be recorded using trace logs.

**FIGURE 9.8** The available settings for trace logs

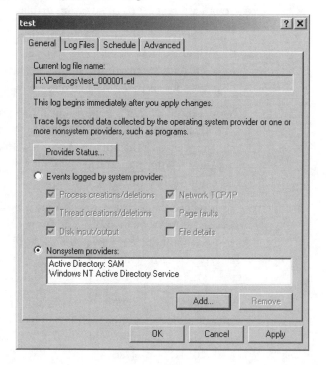

**Alerts**  *Alerts* monitor the standard objects, counters, and instances that are available with the Windows 2000 Performance Monitoring tools. However, they are designed to take specific actions when certain performance statistic thresholds are exceeded. For example, we could create an alert that fires every time the CPU utilization on the local server exceeds 95 percent (as shown in Figure 9.9).

**FIGURE 9.9** Setting an alert on processor utilization

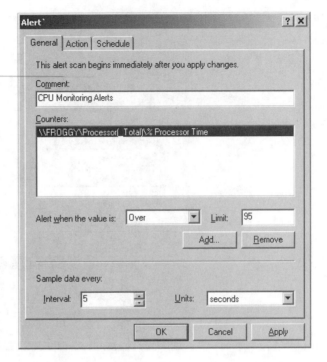

Systems administrators can configure various events to occur when an alert fires. Options include logging an entry in the application event log (which can be viewed using Event Viewer), sending a network message to a specific user or computer, starting a performance data log operation, or running a specific program (see Figure 9.10).

**FIGURE 9.10** Setting alert actions

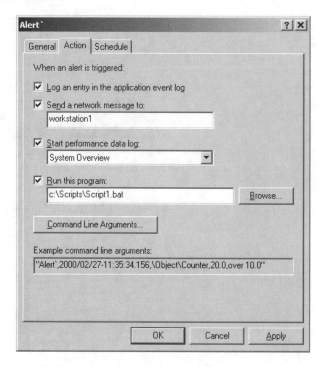

When saving performance information to files, there are two main logging methods that can be used:

**Circular Logging** In circular logging, the data that is stored within a file is overwritten as new data is entered into the log. This is a useful method of logging if you only want to record information for a certain time frame (for example, the last four hours). Circular logging also conserves disk space by ensuring that the performance log file will not continue to grow over certain limits.

**Linear Logging** In linear logging, data is never deleted from the log files, and new information is added to the end of the log file. The result is a log file that continually grows, but the benefit is that historical information is retained.

Now that we have an idea of the types of functions that are supported by the Windows 2000 Performance tool, let's move on to look at how this information can be applied to the task at hand—monitoring and optimizing the Active Directory.

# Monitoring Active Directory Components

The Active Directory utilizes many different types of server resources in order to function properly. For example, it uses memory to increase the speed of accessing data, CPU time to process information, and network resources to communicate with clients and Active Directory domain controllers. Additionally, it uses disk space for storing the Active Directory data store itself and the Global Catalog (GC).

---

**Microsoft** ✓ **Exam Objective**

**Manage Active Directory performance.**

- Monitor, maintain, and troubleshoot domain controller performance.
- Monitor, maintain, and troubleshoot Active Directory components.

---

The types and amount of system resources consumed by the Active Directory is based on many factors. Some of the more obvious factors include the size of the Active Directory data store and how many users are supported in the environment. Other factors include the replication topology and the domain architecture. As you can see, all of the design issues we discussed in earlier chapters of this book will play a role in the overall performance of domain controllers and the Active Directory.

So how do all of these Active Directory requirements impact the server overall? That's a great question that all systems administrators should ask. Although the answer isn't always simple to determine, the System Monitor is usually the right tool for the job. In this section, we'll look at how you can use Windows 2000's performance tools to monitor and optimize the performance of the Active Directory.

## Monitoring Domain Controller Performance

When it comes to performance, domain controllers have the same basic resource requirements as the other machines in your environment. The major areas to monitor for computers include the following:

- Processor (CPU) time
- Memory
- Disk I/O

- Disk space

- Network utilization

When you're deciding to monitor performance, you should carefully determine which statistics will be of most use. For example, if you're measuring the performance of a database server, CPU time and memory may be the most important. However, some applications may have high disk I/O and network requirements. Choosing what to monitor can be difficult since there are so many different options available. Table 9.1 provides an example of some common System Monitor counters and objects you might want to choose.

**TABLE 9.1**  Useful Counters for Monitoring Domain Controller Performance

| Object | Counter | Notes |
|---|---|---|
| Memory | Available MB | Displays the number of megabytes of physical memory (RAM) that is available for use by processes. |
| Memory | Pages/sec | Indicates the number of pages of memory that must be read from or written to disk per second. A high number may indicate that more memory is needed. |
| Network Interface | Bytes Total/Second | Measures the total number of bytes sent to or received by the specified network interface card. |
| Network Interface | Packets Received Errors | Specifies the number of received network packets that contained errors. A high number may indicate that there are problems with the network connection. |

**TABLE 9.1** Useful Counters for Monitoring Domain Controller Performance *(continued)*

| Object | Counter | Notes |
|---|---|---|
| Network Segment | % Net Utilization | Specifies the percentage of total network resources being consumed. A high value may indicate network congestion.* |
| Paging File | % Usage | Indicates the amount of the Windows virtual memory file (paging file) that is in use. If this is a large number, the machine may benefit from a RAM upgrade. |
| Physical Disk | Disk Reads/sec Disk Writes/sec | Indicates the amount of disk activity on the server. |
| Physical Disk | Avg. Disk Queue Length | Indicates the number of disk read or write requests that are waiting in order to access the disk. If this value is high, disk I/O could potentially be a bottleneck. |
| Processor | % Processor Time | Indicates the overall CPU load on the server. High values generally indicate processor-intensive tasks. In machines with multiple processors, each processor can be monitored individually, or a total value can be viewed. |

**TABLE 9.1** Useful Counters for Monitoring Domain Controller Performance *(continued)*

| Object | Counter | Notes |
| --- | --- | --- |
| Server | Bytes Total/sec | Specifies the number of bytes sent by the Server service on the local machine. A high value usually indicates that the server is responsible for fulfilling many outbound data requests (such as a file/print server). |
| Server | Server Sessions | Indicates the number of users that may be accessing the server. |
| System | Processor Queue Length | Specifies the number of threads that are awaiting CPU time. A high number might indicate that a reduction in available CPU resources is creating a potential bottleneck. |
| System | Processes | Indicates the number of processes currently running on the system. |
| Web Service | Bytes Total/sec | Indicates the number of bytes of data that has been transmitted to or from the local Web service. This option is only available if IIS is installed and the Web server is running. |

You must have the Network Monitor installed on the local computer in order to view this computer.

Keep in mind that this list is not by any means a complete list of the items of interest—it's just a good guideline for some of the more common items that you may want to include. The key to determining what to monitor is to first understand the demands imposed by applications or services and then make appropriate choices. When monitored and interpreted properly, these performance values can be extremely useful in providing insight into overall system performance.

Now that we've covered the topic of domain controller performance, let's look at the performance of the Active Directory itself.

## Monitoring Active Directory Performance with System Monitor

As you may have already guessed, the Windows 2000 operating system automatically tracks many performance statistics that are related to the Active Directory. You can easily access these same statistics by using the System Monitor. The specific counters you'll want to monitor are part of the NTDS object and are based on several different functions of the Active Directory, including those that follow:

- The Address Book (AB)
- The Directory Replication Agent (DRA)
- The Directory Service (DS)
- The Key Distribution Center (KDC)
- The Lightweight Directory Access Protocol (LDAP)
- The NTLM Authentications
- The Security Accounts Manager (SAM)
- The Extended Directory Services (XDS)

Each of these objects can be useful when monitoring specific aspects of the Active Directory. The specific counters you choose to monitor will depend on the aspects of Active Directory performance you're planning to examine. For example, if you want to measure performance statistics related to Active Directory replication (covered in Chapter 6, "Configuring Sites and Managing Replication"), you will probably want to monitor the DRA counters. Similarly, if you're interested in performance loads generated by Windows NT computers, you will want to monitor NTLM authentications and the SAM.

Perhaps the best way to learn about the various types of objects, counters, and instances that are related to the Active Directory is by actually measuring these values and saving them for analysis. Exercise 9.1 walks you through the steps of working with various features of the Windows 2000 System Monitor.

---

**EXERCISE 9.1**

### Monitoring Domain Controller and Active Directory Performance with Windows 2000 System Monitor

In this exercise, you will use various features of the Windows 2000 System Monitor to analyze performance information on a Windows 2000 domain controller.

1. Open the Performance tool from the Administrative Tools program group.

2. In the left pane, right-click the System Monitor item and select Rename. Type **Domain Controller Performance**, and press Enter.

3. Click the Add Counter button (the button with the "+" sign). Select Use Local Computer Counters. Choose the Processor object, and then click Select Counters from List. Select the % Processor Time counter and the _Total instance. Note that you can click the Explain button to find more information about the various parameters that are available. Click the Add button to add the counter to the chart.

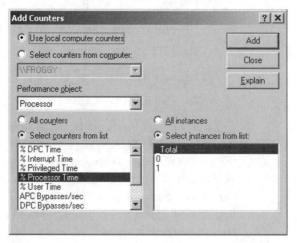

**4.** Add the following counters to the display by using the same process as in step 3.

| Counter | Object | Instance |
| --- | --- | --- |
| Total Query Received | DNS | N/A |
| Packets Sent in Bytes | FileReplicaConn | N/A |
| Pages/sec | Memory | N/A |
| Page Faults/sec | Memory | N/A |
| DRA Inbound Properties Total/sec | NTDS | N/A |
| DRA Outbound Bytes Total/sec | NTDS | N/A |
| DS % Searches from LDAP | NTDS | N/A |
| DS Directory Reads/sec | NTDS | N/A |
| DS Directory Searches/sec | NTDS | N/A |
| LDAP Client Sessions | NTDS | N/A |
| NTLM Authentications | NTDS | N/A |
| % Usage | Paging File | _Total |
| % Disk Time | Physical Disk | _Total |
| Bytes Total/sec | Server | N/A |
| File Data Operations/sec | System | N/A |
| Bytes Total/sec | SMTP Server | _Total |

**5.** When you are finished adding these counters, click the Close button.

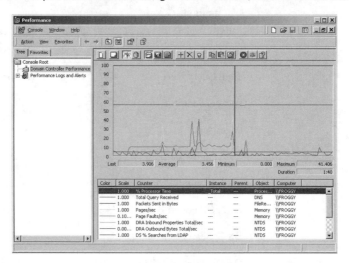

**6.** Click the View Histogram button to view information in the Histogram view. Click the various counters in the bottom pane of the display to view the actual statistical values for last, average, minimum, and maximum.

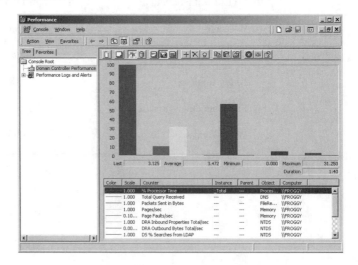

**7.** Click the View Report button to view information in the Report view. Note that you will be shown only the latest values for each of the counters that have been selected.

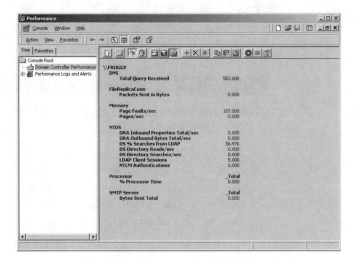

**8.** Click the View Chart button to return to the Graph view. Right-click the chart, and select Save As. Save the chart as a Web page to a folder on the local computer, and name it Domain Controller Performance.htm. You can open this file later if you want to record information for the same counters.

**9.** When finished, close the Windows 2000 System Monitor.

It is useful to have a set of performance monitor counters saved to files so you can quickly and easily monitor the items of interest. For example, you may want to create a System Monitor file that includes statistics related to database services while another focuses on network utilization. In that way, whenever a performance problem occurs, you can quickly determine the cause of the problem (without having to create a System Monitor chart from scratch).

## Monitoring Active Directory Performance Using Performance Logs and Alerts

In addition to using the System Monitor functionality of the Windows 2000 Performance tool, you can also monitor Active Directory performance statistics by using the *Performance Logs and Alerts* functionality. Exercise 9.2 walks you through the steps for using these features to monitor the Active Directory.

---

**EXERCISE 9.2**

### Using Performance Logs and Alerts to Monitor Active Directory Performance

In this exercise, you will use the Performance Logs and Alerts features of the Windows 2000 Performance tool. Specifically, you will create a counter log file, record performance statistics, and then later analyze this information using the System Monitor. In order to complete the steps in this exercise, you must have first completed the steps in Exercise 9.1.

1. Open the Performance tool from the Administrative Tools program group.

2. Under Performance Logs and Alerts, right-click Counter Logs and select New Log Settings From. Select the Domain Controller Performance.htm file that you created in Exercise 9.1.

3. You will see a warning that notifies you that some settings will be set at their defaults. Click OK to continue.

**4.** For the name of the new counter log, type **Domain Controller Log**, and click OK. You will see that the default counters from the System Monitor settings are automatically added to this counter log. On the General tab, set the refresh interval to one second.

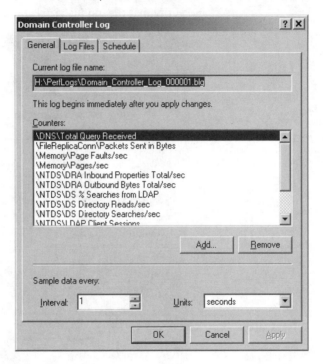

**EXERCISE 9.2** *(continued)*

5. Click the Log Files tab. Verify that the log filename and location are appropriate. Also, note that you have an option to automatically generate log filenames. Leave the default setting at nnnnnn and the start number at 1. Change the log file type to Binary Circular File and verify that the log file size is limited to 1000KB.

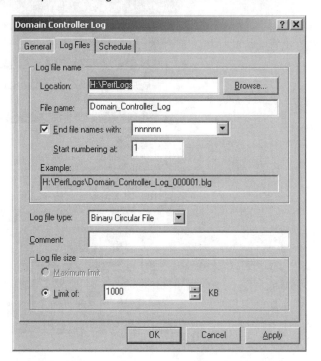

**6.** Click the Schedule tab and select Manually (Using the Shortcut Menu) for both the Start Log and Stop Log options. Leave all other settings at their defaults.

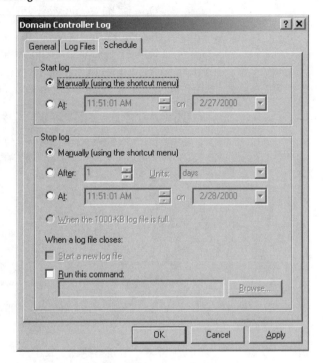

**7.** Click OK to create the counter log.

**8.** To start recording data for the counter log, right-click the Domain Controller Log item in the right windowpane and select Start. You will notice that the icon turns green. If your computer is not actively working (such as one in a test environment), you can simulate activity by running applications and searching the Active Directory.

**9.** Wait at least two minutes for the data collection to occur, and then right-click the Domain Controller Log item and select Stop. The icon will turn red.

10. Click the System Monitor in the left pane, and click the View Log File Data button. Select the file named Domain_Controller_Log_ 000001.log from the directory in which you stored the counter data, and click Open. The Graph view will automatically be populated.

11. To filter the values displayed, right-click the chart and select Properties. On the Source tab, change the Time Range values to view only a specific amount of data. Note that you can only choose times that are within the sampling interval. Click OK to restrict the data.

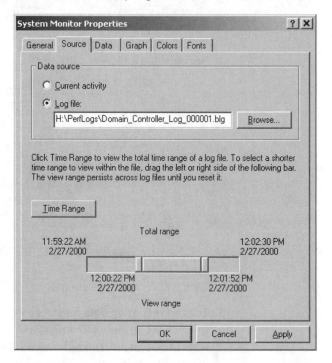

12. Examine the Chart, Histogram, and Report views. When finished, close the System Monitor.

By saving historical performance information, you can get a good idea of how your systems have performed over time. The next time your users complain about slow performance, you'll have some hard statistics to help you to determine the problem!

## Other Performance Monitoring Tools

The System Monitor allows you to monitor various different parameters of the Windows 2000 operating system and associated services and applications. However, there are three other tools that can be used for monitoring performance in Windows 2000. They are the *Network Monitor*, the Event Viewer, and the *Task Manager*. All three of these tools are useful for monitoring different areas of overall system performance and for examining details related to specific system events. In this section, we'll take a quick look at these tools and how they can best be used.

### The Network Monitor

Although the System Monitor is a great tool for viewing overall network performance statistics, it doesn't give you much insight into what types of network traffic are traveling on the wire. That's where the Network Monitor comes in. There are two main components to the Network Monitor: the Network Monitor Agent and the Network Monitor tool itself.

The Network Monitor Agent is available for use with Windows 2000 Professional and Server computers. You can install it by using the Add/Remove Programs Control Panel applet. It allows for the tracking of network packets. When you install the Network Monitor Agent, you will also be able to access the Network Segment System Monitor counter.

On Windows 2000 Server computers, you'll see the Network Monitor icon appear in the Administrative Tools program group. You can use the Network Monitor tool to capture data as it travels on your network (see Figure 9.11).

The version of Network Monitor that is available for free with Windows 2000 Server only allows the capture of information destined to or from the local computer. The full version of Network Monitor is available with Systems Management Server (SMS). This version places the network adapter in promiscuous mode and allows it to capture all data transferred on the network. For more information, see www.microsoft.com/management.

**FIGURE 9.11** Viewing performance statistics using the Network Monitor

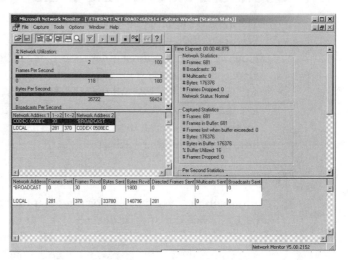

Once you have captured the data of interest, you can save it to a capture file or further analyze it using the Network Monitor. Figure 9.12 shows the level of detail that can be obtained by examining the packets that have been captured. Experienced network and systems administrators can use this information to determine how applications are communicating and the types of data that are being passed via the network.

**FIGURE 9.12** Displaying the details of network packets using the Network Monitor

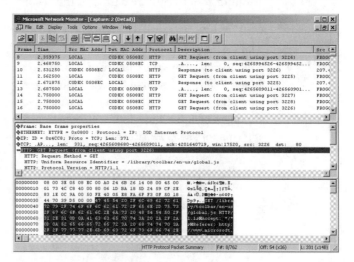

## The Task Manager

The System Monitor is designed to allow you to monitor specific aspects of system performance over time. But what do you do if you want to get a quick snapshot of what the local system is doing? Clearly, creating a System Monitor chart, adding counters, and choosing a view is overkill. Fortunately, the Windows 2000 Task Manager has been designed to provide a quick overview of important system performance statistics without requiring any configuration. Better yet, it's always readily available.

The Task Manager can be easily accessed in several ways, including the following methods:

- Click Start ➤ Run, and type **taskmgr.**

- Right-click the Windows taskbar, and then click Task Manager.

- Press Ctrl+Alt+Del, and then select Task Manager.

- Press Ctrl+Shift+Esc.

Each of these methods makes accessing a snapshot of the current system performance just a few short steps away.

Once you access the Task Manager, you will see the following three tabs:

**Applications** The Applications tab shows you a list of the applications currently running on the local computer. This is a good place to check to determine which programs are running on the system. It is also useful for shutting down any applications that are marked as [Not Responding] (meaning that either the application has crashed or that it is performing operations and not responding to Windows 2000).

**Processes** The Processes tab shows you all of the processes that are currently running on the local computer. By default, you'll be able to view how much CPU time and memory are being used by a particular process. By clicking any of the columns, you can quickly sort by the data values in that particular column. This is useful, for example, if you want to find out which processes are using the most memory on your server.

By accessing the objects in the View menu, you can add additional columns to the Processes tab. Figure 9.13 shows a list of the current processes running on a Windows 2000 Server computer.

**FIGURE 9.13** Viewing process statistics and information using the Task Manager

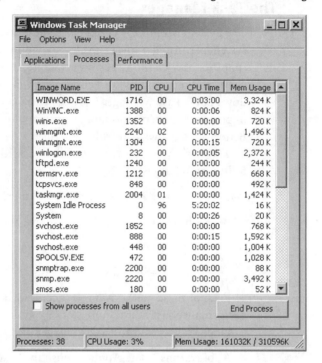

**Performance** One of the problems with using the System Monitor to get a quick snapshot of system performance is that you have to add counters to a chart. Most systems administrators (myself included!) are too busy to take the time to do this when all that is needed is basic CPU and memory information. That's where the Performance tab of the Task Manager comes in. Using the Performance tab, you can view details about how memory is allocated on the computer and how much of the CPU is utilized (see Figure 9.14).

**FIGURE 9.14** Viewing CPU and memory performance information using the Task Manager

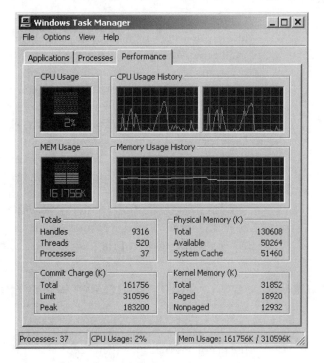

As you can see, the Task Manager is very useful for quickly providing important information about the system. Once you get used to using the Task Manager, you won't be able to get by without it!

## The Event Viewer

The Event Viewer is also useful for monitoring information regarding the Active Directory. Specifically, the Directory Service log can be used to view any information, warnings, or alerts related to the proper functioning of the directory services. For example, if there is an error in the Active Directory configuration that is preventing replication between domain controllers, you will see specific events and information that can help narrow down the problem. Therefore, the Event Viewer is an excellent tool when troubleshooting problems in the behavior of the Active Directory.

In addition to the use of the Directory Service log, you can use the application and system logs to monitor other aspects of the system. In general, you should make it a habit to routinely monitor these logs for any warnings or errors.

## Optimizing the Active Directory

Using the Active Directory performance statistics that you gather, you can identify areas of potential bottlenecks. The specific counters and acceptable values that you use will, however, be based on your specific hardware, software, network, and business requirements. In general, the statistics available via the System Monitor are useful for determining if a hardware upgrade will be useful or if some configuration options should be changed. The specific types of changes that can be made must be evaluated based on an Active Directory subsystem.

Throughout this book, we have included information on optimizing specific Active Directory performance parameters as they pertain to the various topics covered. For example, we covered the details related to monitoring DNS in Chapter 2, "Integrating DNS with the Active Directory," and we'll cover the specifics related to monitoring software deployment in Chapter 11, "Software Deployment through Group Policy."

## Troubleshooting Active Directory Performance Monitoring

Monitoring performance is not always an easy process. As I mentioned earlier, the act of performance monitoring can use up system resources. One of the problems that may then occur is that the System Monitor is not able to obtain performance statistics and information quickly enough. If this occurs, you'll receive an error message similar to that shown in Figure 9.15. In this case, the suggestion is to increase the sample interval. This will reduce the number of statistics System Monitor has to record and display and may prevent the loss of any performance information.

**FIGURE 9.15**   A System Monitor error message

Sometimes, when you're viewing performance information in the Chart or Histogram view, the data is either too small (the bar or line is too close to the baseline) or too large (the bar or line is above the maximum value). In either case, you'll want to adjust the scale for the counter so that you can accurately see information in the display. For example, if the scale for the number of logons is 1 when it displays values from 0–100 and you frequently have more than 100 users per server, you might want to change the scale to a value less than 1. If you choose one-tenth, you will be able to accurately see up to 1,000 user logons in the Chart and Histogram views. You can adjust the scale by right-clicking the properties of the System Monitor display, selecting Properties, and then accessing the Data tab.

### Troubleshooting Reliability

The Windows 2000 operating system platform has been designed to provide high availability and uptime for mission-critical tasks. Occasionally, however, you might experience intermittent server crashes on one or more of the domain controllers or other computers in your environment.

The most common cause of such problems is a hardware configuration issue. Poorly written device drivers and unsupported hardware can cause problems with system stability. Similarly, a failed hardware component (such as system memory) can cause problems, as well. Usually, third-party hardware vendors provide utility disks with their computers that can be used for performing hardware diagnostics on machines. This is a good first step to resolving intermittent server crashes.

When these utility disks are used in combination with the troubleshooting tips provided in this and other chapters of this book, you should be able to pinpoint most Active Directory–related problems that might occur on your network.

# Backup and Recovery of the Active Directory

If you have deployed the Active Directory in your network environment, there's a good chance that your users depend on it to function properly in order to do their jobs. From network authentications to file access to print and Web services, the Active Directory can be a mission-critical component of your business. Therefore, the importance of backing up the Active Directory data store should be evident.

---

*Microsoft* *Exam* *Objective***Back up and restore Active Directory.**

- Perform an authoritative restore of Active Directory.

- Recover from a system failure.

---

See the subsection "Restoring the Active Directory" later in this chapter for coverage of the material related to the "Recover from a system failure" subobjective.

There are several reasons to back up data, including the reasons that follow:

**Protect against hardware failures.**    Computer hardware devices have finite lifetimes, and all hardware will eventually fail. Some types of failures, such as corrupted hard disk drives, can result in significant data loss.

**Protect against accidental deletion or modification of data.**    Although the threat of hardware failures is very real, in most environments, mistakes in modifying or deleting data are much more common. For example, suppose a systems administrator accidentally deletes all of the objects within a specific OU. Clearly, it's very important to be able to retrieve this information from a backup.

**Keep historical information.**    Users and systems administrators sometimes modify files but then later find that they require access to an older version of the file. Or a file is accidentally deleted, but a user does not discover that fact until much later. By keeping backups over time, you can recover information from these prior backups when necessary.

**Protect against malicious deletion or modification of data.**    Even in the most secure environments, it is conceivable that unauthorized users (or authorized ones with malicious intent!) could delete or modify information. In such cases, the loss of data might require valid backups from which to restore critical information.

Windows 2000 includes a Backup utility that is designed to back up operating system files and the Active Directory data store. It allows for basic backup functionality, such as scheduling backup jobs and selecting which files to back up.

Figure 9.16 shows the main screen for the Windows 2000 Backup utility.

**FIGURE  9.16**    The main screen of the Windows 2000 Backup utility

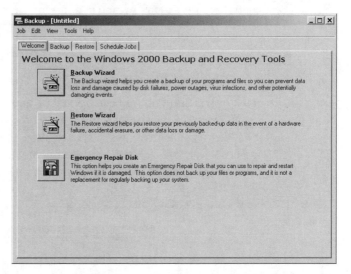

In this section, we'll look at the details of using the Windows 2000 Backup utility and how the Active Directory can be restored when problems do occur.

## Overview of the Windows 2000 Backup Utility

Although the general purpose behind performing backup operations—protecting information—is straightforward, there are many different options that systems administrators must consider when determining the optimal backup and recovery scenario for their environment. Factors include what to back up, how often to back up, and when the backups should be performed.

In this section, we'll look at how the Windows 2000 Backup utility makes it easy to implement a backup plan for many network environments.

Although the Windows 2000 Backup utility provides the basic functionality required to back up your files, you may want to investigate third-party products that provide additional functionality. These applications can provide options for specific types of backups (such as those for Exchange Server and SQL Server), as well as Disaster Recovery options, networking functionality, centralized management, and support for more advanced hardware.

## Backup Types

One of the most important issues when dealing with backups is keeping track of which files have been backed up and which files need to be backed up. Whenever a backup of a file is made, the Archive bit for the file is set. You can view the attributes of system files by right-clicking them, and selecting Properties. By clicking Advanced, you will see the option File Is Ready for Archiving. Figure 9.17 shows an example of the attributes for a file.

**FIGURE 9.17**  Viewing the Archive attributes for a file

Although it is possible to back up all of the files in the file system during each backup operation, it's sometimes more convenient to back up only selected files (such as those that have changed since the last back up operation). There are several types of back ups that can be performed:

**Normal**  *Normal backups* back up all of the selected files and then mark them as backed up. This option is usually used when a full system backup is made.

**Copy** *Copy backups* back up all of the selected files, but do not mark them as backed up. This is useful when you want to make additional backups of files for moving files off-site or making multiple copies of the same data or for archival purposes.

**Incremental** *Incremental backups* copy any selected files that are marked as ready for backup and then mark the files as backed up. When the next incremental backup is run, only the files that are not marked as having been backed up are stored. Incremental backups are used in conjunction with full (normal) backups. The general process is to make a full backup and then to make subsequent incremental backups. The benefit to this method is that only files that have changed since the last full or incremental backup will be stored. This can reduce backup times and disk or tape storage space requirements.

When recovering information from this type of backup method, a systems administrator will be required to first restore the full backup and then to restore each of the incremental backups.

**Differential** *Differential backups* are similar in purpose to incremental backups with one important exception: Differential backups copy all files that are marked for backup but do not mark the files as backed up. When restoring files in a situation that uses normal and differential backups, you only need to restore the normal backup and the latest differential backup.

Figure 9.18 provides an example of the differences between the normal, incremental, and differential backup types.

**Daily** *Daily backups* back up all files that have changed during the current day. This operation uses the file time/date stamps to determine which files should be backed up and does not mark the files as having been backed up.

Note that systems administrators might choose to combine normal, daily, incremental, and differential backup types as part of the same backup plan. In general, however, it is sufficient to use only one or two of these methods (for example, normal backups with incremental backups). If you require a combination of multiple backup types, be sure that you fully understand which types of files are being backed up. Figure 9.19 shows the description of a differential backup type in the "Type of Backup" section of the Backup Wizard.

**FIGURE 9.18** Differences between the normal, incremental, and differential backup types

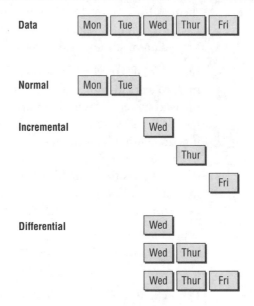

**FIGURE 9.19** Selecting the type of backup to perform

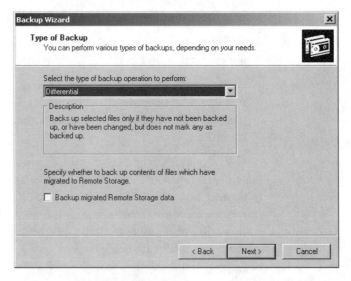

Another option is to create an Emergency Repair Disk (ERD). In the event that boot or configuration information is lost, the ERD and Windows 2000 Repair process can be used to restore a system.

## Backing Up System State Information

When planning to back up and restore the Active Directory, the most important component is known as the *System State*. System State information includes the components that the Windows 2000 operating system relies on for normal operations. The Windows 2000 Backup utility offers the ability to back up the System State to another type of media (such as a hard disk, network share, or tape device). Specifically, it will back up the following components for a Windows 2000 domain controller (see Figure 9.20):

**Active Directory**    The Active Directory data store is at the heart of the Active Directory. It contains all of the information necessary to create and manage network resources, such as users and computers. In most environments that use the Active Directory, users and systems administrators rely on the proper functioning of these services in order to do their jobs.

**Boot Files**    These are the files required for booting the Windows 2000 operating system and can be used in the case of boot file corruption.

**COM+ Class Registration Database**    Applications that run on a Windows 2000 computer might require the registration of various share code components. As part of the System State backup process, Windows 2000 will store all of the information related to Component Object Model+ (COM+) components so that this information can be quickly and easily restored.

**Registry**    The Windows 2000 Registry is a central repository of information related to the operating system configuration (such as desktop and network settings), user settings, and application settings. Therefore, the Registry is absolutely vital to the proper functioning of Windows 2000.

**SysVol**    The SysVol directory includes data and files that are shared between the domain controllers within an Active Directory domain. This information is relied upon by many operating system services for proper functioning.

**FIGURE 9.20**   Backing up the Windows 2000 System State information

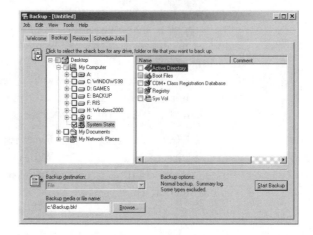

When you back up the System State information, the Windows 2000 Backup utility automatically backs up all of these types of files.

## Scheduling Backups

In addition to the ability to specify which files to back up, you can schedule backup jobs to occur at specific times. Planning *when* to perform backups is just as important as deciding what to back up. Performing backup operations can reduce overall system performance; therefore, you should plan to back up information during times of minimal activity on your servers. Figure 9.21 shows the Schedule functionality of the Window 2000 Backup utility.

**FIGURE 9.21**   Scheduling jobs using the Windows 2000 Backup utility

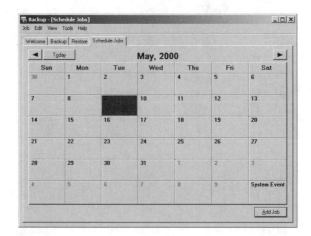

To add a backup operation to the schedule, you can simply click the Add Job button. This will start the Windows 2000 Backup Wizard (which we'll cover later in this chapter).

## Restoring System State Information

In some cases, the Active Directory data store or other System State information may become corrupt or unavailable. This could be due to many different reasons. A hard disk failure might, for example, result in the loss of data. Or the accidental deletion of an OU and all of its objects might require a restore operation to be performed.

The actual steps involved when restoring System State information are based on the details of what has caused the data loss and what effects this data loss has had on the system. In the best case (relatively speaking, of course), the System State information is corrupt or inaccurate, but the operating system can still boot. If this is the case, all that must be done is to boot into a special *Directory Services Restore Mode* and then restore the System State information from a backup. This process will replace the current System State information with that from the backup. Therefore, any changes that have been made since the last backup will be completely lost and must be redone.

In a worst-case scenario, all of the information on a server has been lost or a hardware failure is preventing the machine from properly booting. If this is the case, there are several steps that you must take in order to recover System State information. These steps include the following:

1. Fix any hardware problem that might prevent the computer from booting (for example, replace any failed hard disks).

2. Reinstall the Windows 2000 operating system. This should be performed like a regular installation on a new system.

3. Reinstall any device drivers that may be required by your backup device. If you backed up information to the file system, this will not apply.

4. Restore the System State information using the Windows 2000 Backup utility.

We'll cover the technical details of performing restores later in this section. For now, however, you should understand the importance of backing up information and, whenever possible, testing the validity of backups.

# Backing Up the Active Directory

The Windows 2000 Backup utility makes it easy to back up the System State as part of a normal backup operation. Exercise 9.3 walks you through the process of backing up the Active Directory.

---

**EXERCISE 9.3**

### Backing Up the Active Directory

In this exercise, you will back up the Active Directory. In order to complete this exercise, the local machine must be a domain controller, and you must have sufficient free space to back up the System State (usually at least 300MB).

1. Open the Backup utility by clicking Start ➢ Programs ➢ Accessories ➢ System Tools ➢ Backup.

2. To start the backup process using the Backup Wizard, click the Backup Wizard button.

3. Click Next to start the backup process.

4. In the What to Backup dialog box, select Only Back Up the System State Data. Note that there are also options to back up all files on the computer and to back up only specific information. Click Next to continue.

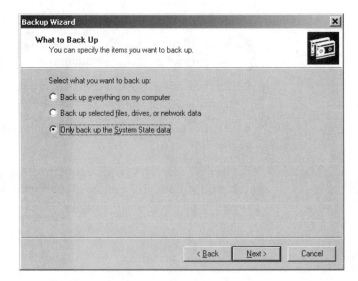

5. Next, you'll need to select where you want to back up this information. If you have a tape drive installed on the local computer, you'll have the option to back up to tape. Otherwise, the option will be disabled, and you can only select File. Select File for the backup media type, and then enter the full path and filename for the backup file. The default file extension for a Windows 2000 Backup file is .bfk. You should ensure that the selected folder has sufficient space to store the System State information (which is usually more than 300MB). Click Next to continue.

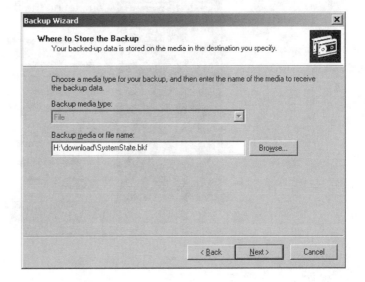

**EXERCISE 9.3** *(continued)*

6. The Windows 2000 Backup Wizard will now display a summary of the options you selected for backup. Verify that the files to be backed up and the location information are correct. Note that by clicking the Advanced button, you can select from among different backup types (such as copy, differential, and incremental) and can choose whether remote storage files will be backed up. Click Finish to begin the backup process.

7. The backup process will begin, and the approximate size of the backup will be calculated. On most systems, the backup operation will take at least several minutes. The exact amount of time required will be based on server load, server hardware configuration, and the size of the System State information. For example, backing up the System State on a busy domain controller for a large Active Directory domain will take much longer than a similar backup for a seldom-used domain controller in a small domain.

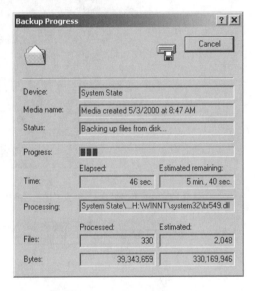

8. When the backup operation has completed, you will see information about the overall backup process. You can click the Report button to see information about the backup process (including any errors that might have occurred). Optionally, you can save this report as a text file to examine the information later.

9. When finished, click Close and then close the Backup application.

Now that we've walked through the steps required to back up the Active Directory, it's time to look at methods for restoring System State information, should the need arise.

## Restoring the Active Directory

The Active Directory has been designed with fault tolerance in mind. For example, it is highly recommended that each domain have at least two domain controllers. Each of these domain controllers contains a copy of the Active Directory data store. Should one of the domain controllers fail, the other one can take over the functionality. When the failed server is repaired, it can then be promoted to a domain controller in the existing environment. This process effectively restores the failed domain controller without incurring any downtime for end users. For more information on promoting domain controllers, see Chapter 3, "Installing and Configuring the Active Directory."

*Microsoft* ✓ *Exam* *Objective*

**Back up and restore Active Directory.**

- Perform an authoritative restore of Active Directory.

- Recover from a system failure.

See the material in the preceding subsections of the "Backup and Recovery of the Active Directory" section for coverage of the material related to the "Perform an authoritative restore of Active Directory" subobjective.

In some cases, you might need to restore the Active Directory from backup media. For example, suppose a systems administrator accidentally deletes several hundred users from the domain. He does not realize this until the change has been propagated to all of the other domain controllers. Manually re-creating the accounts is not an option since the objects' security identifiers will be different (and all permissions must be reset). Clearly, a method for restoring from backup is the best solution.

There are several features in Windows 2000 for solving boot-related problems and for reinstalling the operating system to fix corrupted files. These techniques are beyond the scope of this book (which focuses on restoring the Active Directory). For more information on using the Recovery Console and the Installation Repair options, see *MCSE: Windows 2000 Server Study Guide,* 2nd ed., by Lisa Donald with James Chellis (Sybex, 2001).

## Overview of Authoritative Restore

Restoring the Active Directory and other System State information is an important process should system files or the Active Directory data store become corrupt or otherwise unavailable. Fortunately, the Windows 2000 Backup utility allows for easily restoring the System State information from a backup, should the need arise.

 **Real World Scenario**

**Managing Backups For Large, Active Servers**

You are a systems administrator for a large organization. Your company has experienced dramatic growth in the last six months, and many new servers are being deployed. The existing servers in your environment have also been burdened with more users and data. For example, your most important servers are accessed from users around the world, and they're in use almost 24 hours per day. In order to accommodate the additional needs of users, you have been adding storage to current servers (most of which have plenty of room for expandability). Although this addresses the immediate concern—the need for more storage space—it raises other challenges. One of these is the important issue of performing backups.

Up until now, you have chosen to perform full backups of all of the data on your servers every night. However, the volume of data has grown greatly, and so, too, has the time required to perform the backups. It's clear that you cannot afford to perform full backups every night due to performance and storage considerations. Nevertheless, your business depends heavily on its IT resources, and any loss of data is unacceptable. You're tasked with coming up with a backup methodology. There's one catch, though: Due to budget limitations, you can't purchase larger, faster backup solutions (at least not in the short term). You've got to work with what you already have.

At first, this might seem like a problem: How can you back up a much larger amount of data in the same (or even less) time? There are two main constraints: First, the "backup window" is limited by the increased usage of the servers. The backup window includes the times during which your production servers can sustain the decrease in performance caused by backup operations. Second, your backup hardware can only store a limited amount of data per piece of media, and you're not always available to swap tapes in the middle of the night should the backup operation require more space.

Although this may seem like a difficult problem, you should be able to reduce backup times and storage requirements by using multiple backup types. An efficient design would take advantage of full, differential, and incremental backup types. You can use full backups as the basis of your strategy. Then, you can selectively choose to perform differential and/or incremental backups (instead of full backups) nightly. By examining your business requirements, you decide to implement the following weekly schedule:

Full Backups (est. 8 hours): Sunday afternoons

Differential backups: (est. 2 hours): Tuesday and Thursday nights

Incremental backups: (est. $1/2$–1 hour): Monday, Wednesday, Friday, and Saturday nights

Incremental backups: (est. $1/2$–1 hour): Monday, Wednesday, Friday, and Saturday nights

By using these backup types, you can significantly reduce the amount of time backup operations will take. For example, during the week, you will only be backing up a relatively small subset of all of the data stored on your servers. Therefore, the backups will also use up less space on your backup media (read: fewer required media changes during the week!).

The use of multiple types of backup operations does come at a price, however. One potential issue is that, should you need to restore files, you may need to load data from multiple backup sets. This can be both time-consuming and risky (in the case of the loss or failure of a tape). Also, when you restore data, you must understand how to recover from failures at various times during the week. Overall, though, this solution gives you a good method for continuing to protect your organization's data. And it gives you an opportunity to use ingenuity to stay within budget!

In the real world, coming up with backup plans that meet real-world constraints can be a challenge. Fortunately, you're not alone in this type of problem, and there are many potential solutions. Before you think about investing in larger and faster storage solutions, consider using a combination of backup types to fit within your requirements (and budget). A little bit of planning can save costly upgrades while still providing the data protection your business requires.

We mentioned earlier that in the case of the accidental deletion of information from the Active Directory, you may need to restore the Active Directory data store from a recent backup. But what happens if there is more than one domain controller in the environment? Even if you did perform a restore, the information on this domain controller would be seen as outdated and it would be overwritten by the data from another domain controller (for more information on the replication process, see Chapter 6). And this data from the older domain controller is exactly the information you want to replace.

Fortunately, Windows 2000 and the Active Directory allow you to perform what is called an *authoritative restore*. The authoritative restore process specifies a domain controller as having the authoritative (or master) copy of the Active Directory data store. When other domain controllers communicate with this domain controller, their information will be overwritten with the Active Directory data stored on the local machine.

Now that we have an idea of how an authoritative restore is supposed to work, let's move on to looking at the details of performing the process.

# Performing an Authoritative Restore

**W**hen restoring Active Directory information on a Windows 2000 domain controller, the Active Directory services must not be running. This is because the restore of System State information requires full access to system files and the Active Directory data store. If you attempt to restore System State information while the domain controller is active, you will see the error message shown in Figure 9.22.

When recovering System State information using Windows 2000 Backup, you have the option of restoring data to an alternate location. However, this operation will only copy some components from the System State backup, and it will not restore the Active Directory.

**FIGURE 9.22**   Attempting to restore System State while a domain controller is active

In general, restoring data and operating system files is a straightforward process. It is important to note that restoring a System State backup will replace the existing Registry, SysVol, and Active Directory files. Exercise 9.4 walks you through the process of restoring System State and Active Directory information. This process uses the ntdsutil utility to set the authoritative restore mode for a domain controller after the System State is restored but before the domain controller is rebooted.

Any changes made to the Active Directory since the backup performed in Exercise 9.3 will be lost after the completion of Exercise 9.4.

---

**EXERCISE 9.4**

**Restoring the System State and the Active Directory**

In this exercise, you will restore the Active Directory. In order to complete this process, you must have first completed the steps in Exercise 9.3.

1. Reboot the local machine. During system startup, press the F8 key to enter the Windows 2000 Server boot options.

2. From the boot menu, choose Directory Services Restore Mode "Windows 2000 Domain Controllers Only" and press Enter. The operating system will begin to boot in safe mode.

3. Log on to the computer as a member of the *local* Administrators group. Note that you cannot log on using any Active Directory accounts since network services and the Active Directory have not been started.

4. You will see a message warning you that the machine is running in safe mode and that certain services will not be available. For example, a minimal set of drivers has been loaded, and you will not have access to the network. Click OK to continue.

5. When the operating system has finished booting, open the Backup utility by clicking Start ➤ Programs ➤ Accessories ➤ System Tools ➤ Backup.

6. On the main screen of the Backup utility, click the Restore Wizard icon.

7. Click Next to begin the Restore Wizard.

8. Expand the File item by clicking the plus sign. Expand the Media item, and then click the plus sign next to the System State icon.

**9.** Enter the path and filename of the backup file that you created in Exercise 9.3. The Backup utility will scan the file for the appropriate backup information.

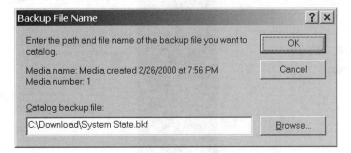

**10.** Place a check mark next to the System State item, and then click Next.

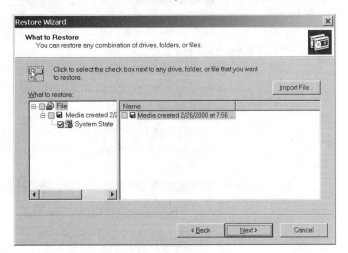

**EXERCISE 9.4** *(continued)*

**11.** The Restore Wizard will display a summary of the recovery options that you selected.

**12.** Click the Advanced button to specify the location for the restored files. The options include the original location, an alternate location, or a single folder. Verify that the original location option is selected, and then click Next.

**13.** You will then be prompted to specify how you want files to be restored. Select the Always Replace the File on the Disk option, and click Next.

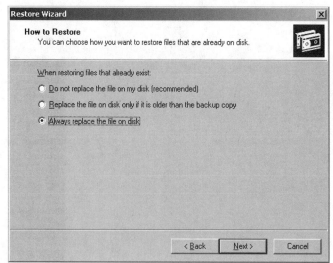

**14.** For the Advanced Restore Options dialog box, use the default settings (none of the boxes checked). Click Next.

**15.** To begin the restore operation, click Finish. Windows 2000 Backup will begin to restore the System State files to the local computer.

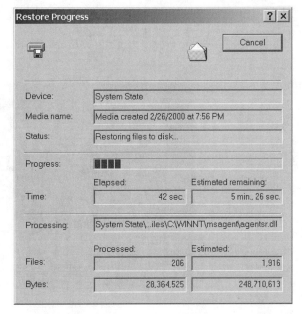

**16.** Once the System State information has been restored, you will see statistics related to the recovery operation. To view detailed information, click the Report button. When you are finished, click Close.

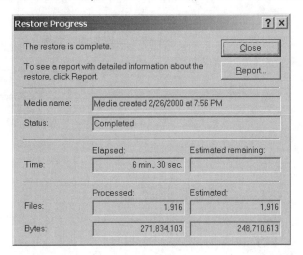

**EXERCISE 9.4** *(continued)*

17. You will be prompted about whether or not you want to restart the computer. Select No. Close the Windows 2000 Backup application.

18. Now, you will need to place the domain controller in authoritative restore mode. To do this, click Start ≻ Run and type **cmd**. At the command prompt, type **ntdsutil** and press Enter. Note that you can type the question mark symbol, "?", and press Enter to view help information for the various commands available with the ntdsutil application.

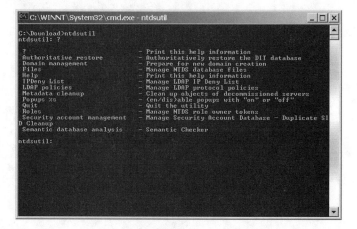

19. At the ntdsutil prompt, type **authoritative restore** and press Enter.

20. At the authoritative restore prompt, type **restore database** and press Enter. You will be asked whether or not you want to perform an authoritative restore. Click Yes.

**EXERCISE 9.4** *(continued)*

**21.** The ntdsutil application will begin the authoritative restore process. When the process has completed, type **quit** twice to exit ntdsutil. Then, close the command prompt by typing **exit**.

```
C:\WINNT\System32\cmd.exe - ntdsutil                              _ □ X
 Help                         - Print this help information
 Quit                         - Return to the prior menu
 Restore database            - Authoritatively restore entire database
 Restore database verinc %d  - ... and override version increase
 Restore subtree %s          - Authoritatively restore a subtree
 Restore subtree %s verinc %d - ... and override version increase

authoritative restore: restore database

Opening DIT database... Done.

The current time is 02-28-00 22:25.03.
Most recent database update occured at 02-26-00 20:01.14.
Increasing attribute version numbers by 300000.

Counting records that need updating...
Records found: 0000001422
Done.

Found 1422 records to update.

Updating records...
Records remaining: 0000000000
Done.

Successfully updated 1422 records.

Authoritative Restore completed successfully.

authoritative restore:
```

**22.** Finally, click Start ➤ Shut Down, and restart the computer. Following a reboot of the operating system, the Active Directory and System State information will be current to the point of the last backup.

In addition to restoring the entire Active Directory database, you can also restore just specific subtrees within the Active Directory using the `restore subtree` command. This allows you to restore specific information and is useful in the case of an accidental deletion of isolated material.

Following the authoritative restore process, the Active Directory should be updated to the time of the last backup. Furthermore, all other domain controllers for this domain will have their Active Directory information overwritten by the results of the restore operation. The end result is an Active Directory environment that has been recovered from media.

# Summary

**A**lthough tasks related to performance optimization and ensuring reliability of Active Directory domain controllers are only two among the seemingly endless tasks performed by systems administrators, they are very important factors in the overall health of a network environment. In this chapter, we covered the following:

- How to monitor the performance of domain controllers.

- How systems administrators can optimize the operations of domain controllers to ensure that end users receive adequate performance.

- How to use the various performance-related tools that are included with Windows 2000. Tools such as the Performance utility, Task Manager, Network Monitor, and Event Viewer can aid in diagnosing and troubleshooting system performance issues.

- How to backup and restore System State information using the Windows 2000 Backup utility. Through the use of Wizards and prompts, this Backup tool can simplify an otherwise tedious process.

- How to restore System State information and the Active Directory database. Using the authoritative restore functionality, you can revert all or part of an Active Directory environment back to an earlier state.

Understanding the issues related to the reliability and performance of the Active Directory and domain controllers is vital to a smoothly running network environment.

# Exam Essentials

**Understand the methodology behind performance monitoring.**   By following a set of steps that involves making measurements and finding bottlenecks, you can perform systematic troubleshooting of performance problems.

**Be familiar with the features and capabilities of the Windows 2000 Performance tool.**   The Performance administrative tool is a very powerful method for collecting data about all areas of system performance. Through the use of objects, counters, and instances, you can choose to collect and record only the data of interest and use this information for pinpointing performance problems.

**Know the importance of common performance counters.**   There are several important performance-related counters that deal with general system performance. Know the importance of monitoring memory, CPU, and network usage on a busy server.

**Understand the role of other performance-related tools.**   The Windows Task Manager, Network Monitor, and Event Viewer can all be used to diagnose and troubleshoot configuration- and performance-related issues.

**Understand common sources of server reliability problems.**   Windows 2000 has been designed to be a stable, robust, and reliable operating system. Should you experience intermittent failures, know how to troubleshoot device drivers and buggy system-level software.

**Understand the various backup types available with the Windows 2000 Backup utility.**   The Windows 2000 Backup utility can perform full, differential, incremental, and daily backup operations. Each of these operations can be used as part of an efficient backup strategy.

**Know how to back up the Active Directory.**   The data within the Active Directory database on a domain controller is part of the System State information. You can back up the System State to a file using the Windows 2000 Backup utility.

**Know how to restore the Active Directory.**   Restoring the Active Directory database is considerably different from other restore operations. In order to restore some or all of the Active Directory database, you must first boot the machine into Directory Services Restore Mode.

**Understand the importance of an authoritative restore process.**   An authoritative restore is used when you want to restore earlier information from an Active Directory backup and you want the older information to be propagated to other domain controllers in the environment.

# Key Terms

Before you take the exam, you should be familiar with the following terms and concepts:

| | |
|---|---|
| alerts | Network Monitor |
| authoritative restore | normal backups |
| Copy backups | Performance Logs and Alerts |
| counter log | System Monitor |
| daily backups | System State |
| differential backups | Task Manager |
| Directory Services Restore Mode | trace logs |
| incremental backups | |

# Review Questions

1. Susan is a systems administrator who is responsible for performing backups on several servers. Recently, she has been asked to take over operations of several new servers. Unfortunately, no information about the standard upkeep and maintenance of those servers is available. Susan wants to begin by making configuration changes to these servers, but she wants to first ensure that she has a full backup of all data on each of these servers.

   Susan decides to use the Windows 2000 Backup utility to perform the backups. She wants to choose a backup type that will back up all files on each of these servers, regardless of when they have last been changed or if they have been previously backed up. Which of the following types of backup operations stores all of the selected files, without regard to the Archive bit setting? (Choose all that apply.)

   **A.** Normal

   **B.** Daily

   **C.** Copy

   **D.** Differential

   **E.** Incremental

2. A systems administrator wants to configure the operating system to generate an item in the Windows 2000 event log whenever the CPU utilization for the server exceeds 95 percent. Which of the following items within the Performance tool can they use to do this?

   **A.** System Monitor

   **B.** Trace logs

   **C.** Counter logs

   **D.** Alerts

   **E.** All of the above

3. Which of the following operations on a domain controller requires the operating system to be booted in Directory Services Repair Mode?

   **A.** Backing up the Active Directory

   **B.** Backing up system files

   **C.** Restoring the Active Directory

   **D.** All of the above

4. A systems administrator boots the operating system using the Directory Services Repair Mode. They attempt to log in using a Domain Administrator account, but are unable to do so. What is the most likely reason for this?

   **A.** The account has been disabled by another domain administrator.

   **B.** The permissions on the domain controller do not allow users to log on locally.

   **C.** The Active Directory service is unavailable, and they must use the local Administrator password.

   **D.** Another domain controller for the domain is not available to authenticate the login.

   **E.** All of the above.

5. Which of the following types of backup operations should be used to back up all of the files that have changed since the last full backup or incremental backup and marks these files as having been backed up?

   **A.** Differential

   **B.** Copy

   **C.** Incremental

   **D.** Normal

   **E.** None of the above

**6.** Following an authoritative restore of the entire Active Directory database, what will happen to the copy of the Active Directory on other domain controllers for the same domain?

   **A.** The copies of the Active Directory on other domain controllers will be overwritten.

   **B.** The information on all domain controllers will be merged.

   **C.** The other domain controllers will be automatically demoted.

   **D.** None of the above.

**7.** Which of the following ntdsutil commands is used to perform an authoritative restore of the entire Active Directory database?

   **A.** `restore active directory`

   **B.** `restore database`

   **C.** `restore subtree`

   **D.** `restore all`

   **E.** None of the above

**8.** You are responsible for managing several Windows 2000 domain controller computers in your environment. Recently, a single hard disk on one of these machines has failed, and the server is now unbootable. You want to perform the following:

- Determine which partitions on the server are still accessible.

- If possible, you want to reinstall the operating system and restore as much of the system configuration (including the Active Directory database) as is possible.

Which of the following could be used to help meet these requirements? (Choose all that apply.)

**A.** The Emergency Repair Disk

**B.** The Windows 2000 installation CD-ROM

**C.** A hard disk from another server that is not configured as a domain controller

**D.** A valid System State backup from the server

**E.** The System Recovery console (access through the Windows 2000 Setup program)

**9.** You have been hired as a consultant to research a network-related problem at a small organization. The environment supports many custom-developed applications that are not well documented. A manager suspects that one or more computers on the network is generating excessive traffic and is bogging down the network. You want to do the following:

- Determine which computer(s) is/are causing the problems.

- Record and examine network packets that are originating to/from specific machines.

- View data related to only specific types of network packets.

Which of the following tools meets these requirements? (Choose all that apply.)

**A.** Task Manager

**B.** System Monitor

**C.** Event Viewer

**D.** Network Monitor

**E.** None of the above

**10.** Which of the following is not backed up as part of the Windows 2000 System State on a domain controller?

**A.** Registry

**B.** COM+ Registration information

**C.** Boot files

**D.** Active Directory database information

**E.** User profiles

**11.** Which of the following System Monitor objects can be used to measure performance statistics related to the Active Directory? (Choose all that apply.)

**A.** Directory Services

**B.** LDAP

**C.** Network

**D.** Replication

**E.** NTDS

**12.** A systems administrator wants to measure performance related to Windows NT 4 logons. Which of the following counters of the NTDS object could provide this information?

**A.** Directory Replication Agent (DRA)

**B.** Directory Service (DS)

**C.** NTLM Authentications

**D.** Lightweight Directory Access Protocols (LDAP)

**E.** None of the above

**13.** Ron is a systems administrator who is responsible for performing backups on several servers. Recently, he has been asked to take over operations of several new servers, including backup operations. He has the following requirements:

- The backup must complete as quickly as possible.

- The backup must use the absolute minimum amount of storage space.

- He must perform backup operations at least daily with a full backup at least weekly.

Ron decides to use the Windows 2000 Backup utility to perform the backups. He wants to choose a set of backup types that will meet all of these requirements. He decides to back up all files on each of these servers every week. Then, he decides to store only the files that have changed since the last backup operation (regardless of type) during the weekdays. Which of the following types of backup operations should he use to implement this solution? (Choose two.)

**A.** Normal

**B.** Daily

**C.** Copy

**D.** Differential

**E.** Incremental

**14.** A systems administrator suspects that a domain controller is not operating properly. Another systems administrator has been monitoring the performance of the server and has found that this is not a likely cause of the problems. Where can the systems administrator look for more information regarding details about any specific problems or errors that may be occurring? (Choose all that apply.)

**A.** Task Manager

**B.** Network Monitor

**C.** System Monitor

**D.** Event Viewer

15. Which of the following System Monitor views displays performance information over a period of time?

    **A.** Chart

    **B.** Histogram

    **C.** Report

    **D.** Current Activity

    **E.** None of the above

16. You are using the Backup Wizard to back up the Active Directory. You want to ensure that the entire Active Directory is backed up while maintaining a minimum backup file size. In the following screen, where would you click in order to accomplish this task?

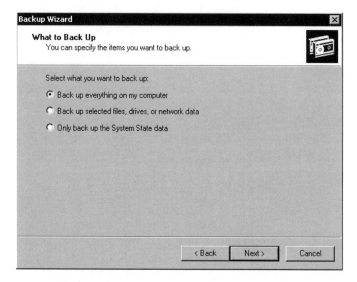

    **A.** Back Up Selected Files, Drives, or Network Data

    **B.** Only Back Up the System State Data

    **C.** Back Up Everything on My Computer

    **D.** The Next button

# Answers to Review Questions

1. A, B, C. Normal and copy backup operations do not use the Archive bit to determine which files to back up, and they will include all files that are selected for backup on the server. The other backup types will store only a subset of files based on their dates or whether or not they have been previously backed up. For this reason, Susan should choose one of these operations to ensure that she performs a valid backup of all files on the servers before she makes any configuration changes.

2. D. Alerts fire in response to certain performance-related parameters, as defined by systems administrators. You can configure an alert to perform several different types of actions, including writing to the Windows 2000 event log.

3. C. Directory Services Repair Mode is only required for restoring System State information, and backups of this information can occur while the operating system is running.

4. C. When booting in Directory Services Repair Mode, the Active Directory is not started, and network services are disabled. Therefore, the systems administrator must use a local account in order to log in.

5. C. Incremental backup operations copy files and mark them as having been backed up. Therefore, they are used when a systems administrator wants to back up only the files that have changed since the last full or incremental backup. Differential backups, although they will backup the same files, will not mark the files as having been backed up.

6. A. In an authoritative restore of the entire Active Directory database, the restored copy will override information stored on other domain controllers.

7. B. The `restore database` command instructs the ntdsutil application to perform an authoritative restore of the entire Active Directory database.

**8.** A, B, D, E. All of these options include various types of backup information that can be used to restore the server to normal configuration. The Emergency Repair Disk contains information that can be used to fix a corrupted Windows 2000 installation, but it is not a bootable floppy. If the system does not boot normally, you must use the Windows 2000 installation floppy disks or CD-ROM in order to repair the installation. During the setup process, you may choose to use the System Recovery console to perform basic diagnostics. Finally, once the server is bootable, you can recover System State information from a backup.

**9.** D. Through the use of the Network Monitor application, you can view all of the network packets that are being sent to or from the local server. Based on this information, you can determine the source of certain types of traffic, such as PINGs. The other types of monitoring can provide useful information, but they do not allow you to drill down into the specific details of a network packet, nor do they allow you to filter the data that has been collected based on details about the packet.

**10.** E. The System State backup includes information that can be used to rebuild a server's basic configuration. All of the information listed, except for user profile data, is backed up as part of a System State backup operation.

**11.** A, B, C, D, E. The various counters that are part of the NTDS object provide information about the performance of various aspects of the Active Directory. By collecting information for each of these objects, you can determine what areas of system performance might be having problems.

**12.** C. Windows NT 4 clients use the NTLM authentication method. By measuring this counter, you can determine how many authentication requests are being generated from non–Windows 2000 computers.

**13.** A, E. In order to meet the requirements, Ron should use the normal backup type to create a full backup every week and the incremental backup type to back up only the data that has been modified since the last full or incremental backup operation.

**14.** D. The Event Viewer is the best tool for viewing information, warnings, and alerts related to Windows 2000 functions.

**15.** A. Using the Graph view, you can view performance information over a period of time (as defined by the sample interval). The Histogram and Report views are designed to show the latest performance statistics and average values.

**16.** B. Backing up the System State data will back up the entire Active Directory. Backing up everything on the computer will require a very large backup file.

# Chapter 10

# Managing Group Policy

## MICROSOFT EXAM OBJECTIVES COVERED IN THIS CHAPTER:

✓ **Implement and troubleshoot Group Policy.**

- Create a Group Policy object (GPO).
- Link an existing GPO.
- Delegate administrative control of Group Policy.
- Modify Group Policy inheritance.
- Filter Group Policy settings by associating security groups to GPOs.
- Modify Group Policy.

✓ **Manage and troubleshoot user environments by using Group Policy.**

- Control user environments by using administrative templates.
- Assign script policies to users and computers.

✓ **Manage network configuration by using Group Policy.**

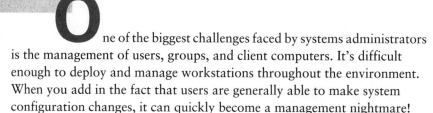

 **O**ne of the biggest challenges faced by systems administrators
is the management of users, groups, and client computers. It's difficult
enough to deploy and manage workstations throughout the environment.
When you add in the fact that users are generally able to make system
configuration changes, it can quickly become a management nightmare!

For example, imagine that a user notices that they do not have enough
disk space to copy a large file. Instead of seeking help from the IT help desk,
they decide to do a little cleanup of their own. Unfortunately, this cleanup
operation involves the deletion of many critical system files! Or, consider the
case of users changing system settings "just to see what they do." Relatively
minor changes, such as modifications of TCP/IP bindings or Desktop settings, can cause hours of support headaches. Now, multiply these problems
by hundreds (or even thousands) of end users. Clearly, there should be a way
for systems administrators to limit the options available to users of client
operating systems.

So how do you prevent small problems like these from occurring in a Windows 2000 environment? Fortunately, there's a solution that's readily available and easy to implement. One of the most important system administration
features in Windows 2000 and the Active Directory is the use of *Group Policy*.
Through the use of *Group Policy objects (GPOs)*, administrators can quickly
and easily define restrictions on common actions and then apply these at the
site, domain, or organizational unit (OU) level. In this chapter, we will examine how Group Policies work and then look at how they can be implemented
within an Active Directory environment.

# An Introduction to Group Policy

 **O**ne of the strengths of Windows-based operating systems is their flexibility. End users and systems administrators can configure many different options to suit the network environment and their personal tastes. However, this flexibility comes at a price—there are many options that generally should not be changed by end users. For example, TCP/IP configuration and security policies should remain consistent for all client computers.

In previous versions of Windows, system policies were available for restricting some functionality at the Desktop level. Settings could be made for users or computers. However, these settings focused primarily on preventing the user from performing such actions as changing their Desktop settings. These changes were managed through the modification of Registry keys. This method made it fairly difficult for systems administrators to create and distribute policy settings. Furthermore, the types of configuration options available in the default templates were not always sufficient, and systems administrators often had to dive through cryptic and poorly documented Registry settings to make the changes they required.

Windows 2000's Group Policies are designed to allow systems administrators to customize end user settings and to place restrictions on the types of actions that users can perform. Group Policies can be easily created by systems administrators and then later applied to one or more users or computers within the environment. Although they ultimately do affect Registry settings, it is much easier to configure and apply settings through the use of Group Policy than it is to manually make changes to the Registry. For ease of management, Group Policy settings can be managed from within the Active Directory environment, utilizing the structure of users, groups, and OUs.

There are several different potential uses for Group Policies. We covered one of them, managing security settings, in Chapter 8, "Active Directory Security." And, we'll cover the use of Group Policies for software deployment in Chapter 11, "Software Deployment through Group Policy." The focus of this chapter will be on the technical background of Group Policies and how they apply to general configuration management.

Let's begin by looking at how Group Policies function.

# Group Policy Settings

Group Policy settings are based on Group Policy *administrative templates*. These templates provide a list of user-friendly configuration options and specify the system settings to which they apply. For example, an option for a user or computer that reads "Require a Specific Desktop Wallpaper Setting" would map to a key in the Registry that that maintains this value. When the option is set, the appropriate change is made in the Registry of the affected user(s) and computer(s).

By default, Windows 2000 comes with several Administrative Template files that can be used for managing common settings. Additionally, systems administrators and application developers can create their own Administrative Template files to set options for specific functionality.

Most Group Policy items have three different settings options:

**Enabled**   Specifies that a setting for this Group Policy object has been configured. Some settings will require values or options to be set.

**Disabled**   Specifies that this option is disabled for client computers. Note that disabling an option *is* a setting. That is, it specifies that the systems administrator wants to disallow certain functionality.

**Not Configured**   Specifies that these settings have been neither enabled nor disabled. Not Configured is the default option for most settings. It simply states that this Group Policy will not specify an option and that settings from other policy settings may take precedence.

The specific options available (and their effects) will depend on the setting. Often, additional information is required. For example, when setting the Account Lockout policy, you must specify how many bad login attempts may be made before the account is locked out. With this in mind, let's look at the types of user and computer settings that can be managed.

## User and Computer Settings

Group Policy settings can apply to two types of Active Directory objects: Users and Computers. Since both Users and Computers can be placed into groups and organized within OUs, this type of configuration simplifies the management of hundreds, or even thousands, of computers.

The main types of settings that can be made within User and Computer Group Policies are as follows:

**Software Settings**   Software settings apply to specific applications and software that might be installed on the computer. Systems administrators can use these settings to make new applications available to end users and control the default configuration for these applications. For more information on configuring software settings using Group Policy, see Chapter 11.

**Windows Settings**   Windows settings options allow systems administrators to customize the behavior of the Windows operating system. The specific options that are available here differ for users and computers. For example, the user-specific settings allow the configuration of Internet Explorer (including the default home page and other settings), while the computer settings include security options, such as account policy and event log options.

**Administrative Templates**   The options available in administrative templates are used to further configure user and computer settings. In addition to the default options available, systems administrators can create their own administrative templates with custom options.

Figure 10.1 provides an example of the types of options that can be configured with Group Policy.

**FIGURE 10.1**   Group Policy configuration options

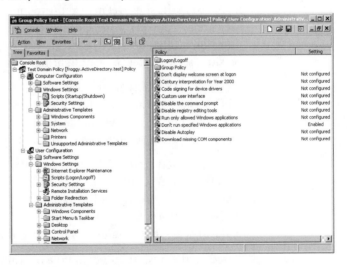

Later in this chapter, we'll look into the various options available in more detail.

# Group Policy Objects

So far, we have been talking about what Group Policies are designed to do. Now, it's time to drill down into determining exactly how they can be set up and configured.

For ease of management, Group Policies may be contained in items called Group Policy objects (GPOs). GPOs act as containers for the settings made within Group Policy files, which simplifies the management of settings. For example, as a systems administrator, you might have different policies for users and computers in different departments. Based on these requirements, you could create a GPO for members of the Sales department and another for members of the Engineering department. Then you could apply the GPOs to the OU for each department.

Another important concept is that Group Policy settings are hierarchical. That is, Group Policy settings can be applied at three different levels:

**Sites**    At the highest level, GPOs can be configured to apply to entire sites within an Active Directory environment. These settings apply to all of the domains and servers that are part of a site. Group Policy settings that are managed at the site level may apply to more than one domain. Therefore, they are useful when you want to make settings that apply to all of the domains within an Active Directory tree or forest. For more information on sites, see Chapter 6, "Configuring Sites and Managing Replication."

**Domains**    Domains are the second level to which GPOs can be assigned. GPO settings that are placed at the domain level will apply to all of the User and Computer objects within the domain. Usually, systems administrators will make master settings at the domain level.

**Organizational Units**    The most granular level of settings for GPOs is at the OU level. By configuring Group Policy options for OUs, systems administrators can take advantage of the hierarchical structure of the Active Directory. If the OU structure is planned well, it will be easy to make logical GPO assignments for various business units at the OU level.

Based on the business need and the organization of the Active Directory environment, systems administrators might decide to set up Group Policy settings at any of these three levels. Since the settings are cumulative by default, a User object might receive policy settings from the site level, from the domain level, and from the organizational units in which it is contained. Group Policy settings can also be applied to the local computer (in which case the Active Directory is not used at all), but this limits the manageability of the Group Policy settings.

## Group Policy Inheritance

In most cases, Group Policy settings will be cumulative. For example, a GPO at the domain level might specify that all users within the domain must change their passwords every 60 days, and a GPO at the OU level might specify the default Desktop background for all users and computers within that OU. In this case, both settings will apply, and users within the OU will be forced to change their password every 60 days and have the default Desktop setting.

So what happens if there's a conflict in the settings? For example, suppose a GPO at the site level specifies that users are to change passwords every 60 days while one at the OU level specifies that they must change passwords every 90 days. This raises an important point about *inheritance*. By default, the settings at the most specific level (in this case, the OU, which contains the User object) will override those at more general levels.

Although the default behavior is for settings to be cumulative and inherited, systems administrators can modify this behavior. There are two main options that can be set at the various levels to which GPOs might apply:

**Block Policy Inheritance** The Block Policy Inheritance option specifies that Group Policy settings for an object are not inherited from its parents. This might be used, for example, when a child OU requires completely different settings from a parent OU. Note, however, that blocking policy inheritance should be managed carefully since this option allows other systems administrators to override the settings made at higher levels.

**Force Policy Inheritance** The Force Policy Inheritance option can be placed on a parent object and ensures that all lower-level objects inherit these settings. In some cases, systems administrators want to ensure that Group Policy inheritance is not blocked at other levels. For example, suppose it is corporate policy that all Network accounts are locked out after five incorrect password attempts. In this case, you would not want lower-level systems administrators to override the option with other settings.

This option is generally used when systems administrators want to globally enforce a specific setting. For example, if a password expiration policy should apply to all users and computers within a domain, a GPO with the Force Policy Inheritance option enabled could be created at the domain level.

One final case must be considered: If there is a conflict between the computer and user settings, the user settings will take effect. If, for instance, there is a default Desktop setting applied for the Computer policy, and there is a different default Desktop setting for the User policy, the one specified in the User object will take effect. This is because the user settings are more specific, and it allows systems administrators to make changes for individual users, regardless of the computer they're using.

# Implementing Group Policy

**N**ow that we've covered the basic layout and structure of Group Policies and how they work, let's look at how they can be implemented in an Active Directory environment. In this section, we'll start by creating GPOs. Then, we'll apply these GPOs to specific Active Directory objects.

---

*Microsoft*
✓ *Exam*
*Objective*

**Implement and troubleshoot Group Policy.**

- Create a Group Policy object (GPO).

- Link an existing GPO.

- Modify Group Policy.

**Manage and troubleshoot user environments by using Group Policy.**

- Control user environments by using administrative templates.

- Assign script policies to users and computers.

---

See the section "Managing Group Policy" later in this chapter for coverage of the material related to the "Assign script policies to users and computers" subobjective.

# Creating GPOs

Although there is only one Group Policy editing application included with Windows 2000, there are several ways to access it. This is because systems administrators may choose to apply the Group Policy settings at different levels within the Active Directory. In order to create GPOs at different levels, you can use the following tools:

**Active Directory Sites and Services**   Used for linking GPOs at the site level.

**Active Directory Users and Computers**   Used for linking GPOs at the domain or OU level.

**MMC Group Policy Snap-In**   By directly configuring the Microsoft Management Console (MMC) Group Policy snap-in, you can access and edit GPOs at any level of the hierarchy. This is also a useful option since it allows you to modify the local Group Policy settings and create a custom console that is saved to the Administrative Tools program group.

Exercise 10.1 walks you through the process of creating a custom MMC snap-in for editing Group Policy settings.

 **WARNING**   You should be careful when making Group Policy settings since certain options might prevent the proper use of systems on your network. Always test Group Policy settings on a small group of users before deploying GPOs throughout your organization. You'll probably find that some settings need to be changed in order to be effective.

---

**EXERCISE 10.1**

### Creating a Group Policy Object Using MMC

In this exercise, we will create a custom Group Policy snap-in for managing user and computer settings.

**1.** Click Start ➢ Run, type **mmc**, and press Enter.

**2.** On the Console menu, click Add/Remove Snap-In.

**EXERCISE 10.1** *(continued)*

3. Click the Add button. Select Group Policy from the list, and click Add.

4. For the Group Policy Object setting, click Browse. Note that you can set the scope to Domains/OUs, Sites, or Computers. On the Domains/OUs tab, click the New Policy button (located to the right of the Look In drop-down list).

5. To name the new object, type **Test Domain Policy**. Click OK to open the Policy object.

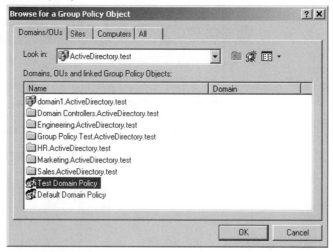

**6.** Place a check mark next to the Allow the Focus of the Group Policy Snap-In to Be Changed When Launching from the Command Line option. This will allow the context of the snap-in to be changed when you launch the MMC item.

**7.** Click Finish to create the Group Policy object. Click Close in the Add Standalone Snap-In dialog box. Finally, click OK to add the new snap-in.

**8.** Next, we'll make some changes to the default settings for this new GPO. Open the following items: Test Domain Policy ➢ Computer Configuration ➢ Windows Settings ➢ Security Settings ➢ Local Policies ➢ Security Options.

**9.** Double-click the Do Not Display Last User Name in Logon Screen option. Place a check mark next to the Define This Policy Setting in the Template option, and then select Enabled. Click OK to save the setting.

**10.** Double-click the Message Title for Users Attempting to Log On option. Place a check mark next to the Define This Policy Setting in the Template option, and then type the following: **By logging onto this domain, you specify that you agree to the usage policies as defined by the IT department**. Click OK to save the setting.

**EXERCISE 10.1** *(continued)*

11. Double-click the Message Title for Users Attempting to Log On option. Place a check mark next to the Define This Policy Setting in the Template option, and then type **Test Policy Logon Message**. Click OK to save the setting.

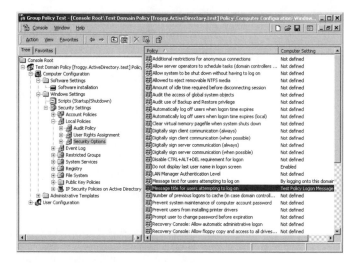

12. Now, to make changes to the user settings, expand the following objects: Test Domain Policy ➢ User Configuration ➢ Administrative Templates ➢ Start Menu & Task Bar.

13. Double-click the Add Logoff to the Start Menu option. Note that you can get a description of the purpose of this setting by clicking the Explain tab. Select Enabled, and then click OK.

14. Expand the following objects: Test Domain Policy ➢ User Configuration ➢ Administrative Templates ➢ System.

**15.** Double-click the Don't Run Specified Windows Applications option. Select Enabled, and then click the Show button. To add to the list of disallowed applications, click the Add button. When prompted to enter the item, type **wordpad.exe**. To save the setting, click OK three times.

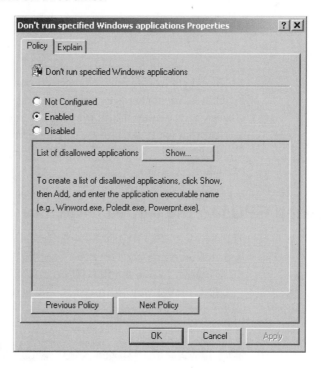

**16.** To change network configuration settings, click Test Domain Policy ➢ User Configuration ➢ Administrative Templates ➢ Network ➢ Offline Files. Note that you can change the default file locations for several different network folders.

**17.** To change script settings (which we will cover later in this chapter), click Test Domain Policy ➢ Computer Configuration ➢ Windows Settings ➢ Scripts (Startup/Shutdown). Note that you can add script settings by double-clicking either the Startup and/or the Shutdown item.

18. The changes you have made for this GPO are automatically saved. You can optionally save this customized MMC console by selecting Save As from the Console menu. Then provide a name for the new MMC snap-in (such as "Group Policy Test"). You will now see this item in the Administrative Tools program group.

19. When you are finished modifying the Group Policy settings, close the MMC tool.

Note that Group Policy changes do not take effect until the next user logs in. That is, users that are currently working on the system will not see the effects of the changes until they log off and log in again.

Now that we've seen how to create a custom MMC snap-in for modifying Group Policy, let's look at how GPOs can be linked to Active Directory objects.

## Linking GPOs to the Active Directory

The creation of a GPO is the first step in assigning Group Policies. The second step is to link the GPO to a specific Active Directory object. As mentioned earlier in this chapter, GPOs can be linked to sites, domains, and OUs.

Exercise 10.2 walks through the steps required to assign a GPO to an OU within the local domain.

**EXERCISE 10.2**

**Linking GPOs to the Active Directory**

In this exercise, we will link the Test Domain Policy GPO to an OU. In order to complete the steps in this exercise, you must have first completed Exercise 10.1.

1. Open the Active Directory Users and Computers tool.

2. Create a new top-level OU called Group Policy Test.

3. Right-click the Group Policy Test OU, and click Properties.

**4.** Select the Group Policy tab. To add a new policy at the OU level, click Add. In the Look In drop-down list, select the name of the local domain. Select the Test Domain Policy GPO, and then click OK.

**5.** Note that you can also add additional GPOs to this OU. When multiple GPOs are assigned, you can also control the order in which they apply by using the Up and Down buttons. Finally, you can edit the GPO by clicking the Edit button, and you can remove the link (or, optionally, delete the GPO entirely) by clicking the Delete button.

**6.** To save the GPO link, click OK. When finished, close the Active Directory Users and Computers tool.

---

Note that the Active Directory Users and Computers tool offers a lot of flexibility in assigning GPOs. We could create new GPOs, add multiple GPOs, edit them directly, change priority settings, remove links, and delete GPOs all from within this interface. In general, creating new GPOs using the Active Directory Sites and Services or the Active Directory Users and Computers tool is the quickest and easiest way to create the settings you need.

To test the Group Policy settings, you can simply create a User or Computer account within the Group Policy Test OU that we created in Exercise 10.2. Then, using another computer that is a member of the same domain, log on as the newly created user. First, you should see the pre-logon message that we set in Exercise 10.1. After logging on, you'll also notice that the other changes have taken effect. For example, you will not be able to run the WordPad.exe program.

When testing Group Policy settings, it is very convenient to use the Terminal Services functionality of Windows 2000. Although it is beyond the scope of this book to describe the use and configuration of Terminal Services in detail, this feature allows you to have multiple simultaneous logon sessions to the same computer. With respect to Group Policy, it is useful when you want to modify Group Policy settings and then quickly log on under another user account to test them. For more information on using Terminal Services, see *MCSE: Windows 2000 Server Study Guide,* 2nd ed., by Lisa Donald with James Chellis (Sybex, 2001).

## Using Administrative Templates

There are many different options that can be modified by Group Policy settings. Microsoft has included some of the most common and useful items by default, and they're made available when you create new GPOs or when you edit existing ones. You can, however, create your own templates and include them in the list of settings.

By default, there are several templates that are included with Windows 2000. These are as follows:

**Common.adm**   Contains the policy options that are common to both Windows 95/98 and Windows NT 4 computers.

**Inetres.adm**   Contains the policy options for configuring Internet Explorer options on Windows 2000 client computers.

**System.adm**    Includes common configuration options and settings for Windows 2000 client computers.

**Windows.adm**    Contains policy options for Windows 95/98 computers.

**Winnt.adm**    Contains policy options that are specific to the use of Windows NT 4.

These Administrative Template files are stored within the `inf` subdirectory of the system root directory. It is important to note that the use of the `Windows.adm`, `Winnt.adm`, and `Common.adm` files is not supported in Windows 2000. These files are primarily provided for backward compatibility with previous versions of Windows.

The `*.adm` files are simple text files that follow a specific format that is recognized by the Group Policy editor. Following is an excerpt from the `system.adm` file:

```
CATEGORY !!WindowsComponents
    CATEGORY !!WindowsExplorer
    KEYNAME "Software\Microsoft\Windows\CurrentVersion
            \Policies\Explorer"

    POLICY !!ClassicShell
       EXPLAIN !!ClassicShell_Help
       VALUENAME "ClassicShell"
    END POLICY



    POLICY !!NoFolderOptions
        EXPLAIN !!NoFolderOptions_Help
        VALUENAME "NoFolderOptions"
    END POLICY

    POLICY !!NoFileMenu
            EXPLAIN !!NoFileMenu_Help
        VALUENAME "NoFileMenu"
        END POLICY

    POLICY !!NoNetConnectDisconnect
```

```
                    EXPLAIN !!NoNetConnectDisconnect_Help
          VALUENAME "NoNetConnectDisconnect"
     END POLICY

     POLICY !!NoShellSearchButton
         EXPLAIN !!NoShellSearchButton_Help
         VALUENAME "NoShellSearchButton"
          END POLICY

     POLICY !!NoViewContextMenu
              EXPLAIN !!NoViewContextMenu_Help
         VALUENAME "NoViewContextMenu"
         END POLICY
```

Notice that the various options that are available for modification are specified within the Administrative Template file. If necessary, systems administrators can create custom Administrative Template files that include more options for configuration.

To add new administrative templates when modifying GPOs, simply right-click the Administrative Templates object and select Add/Remove Templates (see Figure 10.2).

**FIGURE  10.2**   Adding administrative templates when creating GPOs

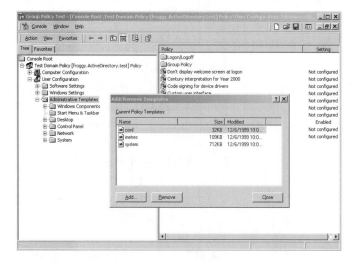

# Managing Group Policy

Once you have implemented GPOs and applied them to sites, domains, and OUs within the Active Directory, it's time to look at some ways to manage them. In this section, we'll look at how multiple GPOs can interact with one another and ways you can provide security for GPO management. These are very important features of working with the Active Directory, and the proper planning of Group Policy can greatly reduce the time the help desk spends troubleshooting common problems.

---

*Microsoft*
✓ *Exam*
*Objective*

**Implement and troubleshoot Group Policy.**

- Delegate administrative control of Group Policy.
- Modify Group Policy inheritance.
- Filter Group Policy settings by associating security groups to GPOs.

**Manage and troubleshoot user environments by using Group Policy.**

- Control user environments by using administrative templates.
- Assign script policies to users and computers.

**Manage network configuration by using Group Policy.**

---

See the section "Implementing Group Policy" earlier in this chapter for coverage of the material related to the "Control user environments by using administrative templates" subobjective.

## Managing GPOs

One of the benefits of GPOs is that they're modular and can apply to many different objects and levels within the Active Directory. This can also be one of the drawbacks of GPOs, if they're not managed properly. A common administrative function related to the use of GPOs is finding all of the Active Directory links for each of these objects. This can be done when viewing the properties of a GPO by clicking the Links tab. As shown in Figure 10.3, clicking the Find Now button will show which objects are using a particular GPO.

**FIGURE 10.3** Viewing GPO links to the Active Directory

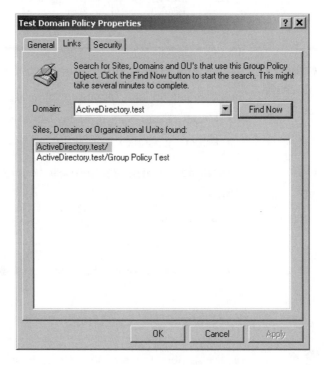

In addition to the common function of delegating permissions on OUs, you can also set permissions regarding the modification of GPOs. One method is to add users to the Group Policy Creator/Owners built-in security group. The members of this group are able to modify security policy.

## Filtering Group Policy

Another method of securing access to GPOs is to set permissions on the GPOs themselves. This is done by selecting the Group Policy tab for an object with the GPO assigned, and then clicking Properties. By clicking the Security tab, you can view the specific permissions that are set on the GPO itself (see Figure 10.4).

**FIGURE 10.4** GPO security settings

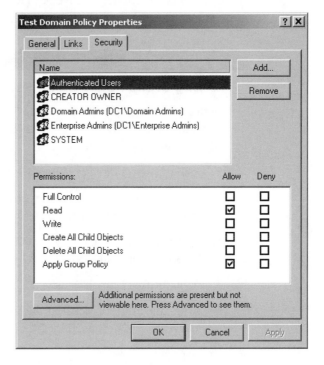

The permissions options include the following:

- Full Control
- Read
- Write
- Create All Child Objects
- Delete All Child Objects
- Apply Group Policy

Of these, the Apply Group Policy setting is particularly important since it is used for filtering the scope of the GPO. *Filtering* is the process by which selected security groups are included or excluded from the effects of the GPOs. To specify that the settings should apply to a GPO, you should grant at least the Apply Group Policy and Read settings. These settings will only be applied if the security group is also contained within a site, domain, or OU to which the GPO is linked. In order to disable GPO access for a group, choose Deny for both of these settings. Finally, if you do not want to specify either Allow or Deny effects, leave both boxes blank. This is effectively the same as having no setting. See Exercise 10.3 for more detailed instructions.

**EXERCISE 10.3**

### Filtering Group Policy Using Security Groups

In this exercise, you will filter Group Policy using security groups. In order to complete the steps in this exercise, you must have first completed Exercises 10.1 and 10.2.

1. Open the Active Directory Users and Computers administrative tool.

2. Create two new Global Security groups within the Group Policy Test OU, and name them PolicyEnabled and PolicyDisabled.

3. Right-click the Group Policy Test OU, and select Properties. Select the Group Policy tab.

4. Highlight Test Domain Policy, and select Properties.

5. On the Security tab, click Add, and select the PolicyEnabled and the PolicyDisabled groups. Click OK.

**6.** Highlight the PolicyDisabled group, and select Deny for the Read and Apply Group Policy permissions. This will prevent users in the PolicyDisabled group from being affected by this policy.

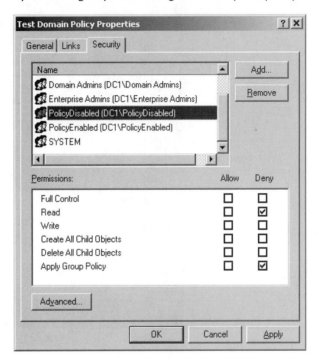

7. Highlight the PolicyEnabled group, and select Allow for the Read and Apply Group Policy permissions. This will ensure that users in the PolicyEnabled group will be affected by this policy.

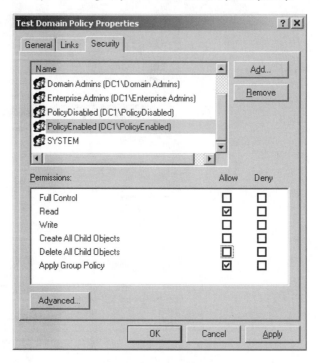

8. Click OK to save the Group Policy settings. You will be warned that Deny takes precedence over any other security settings. Select Yes to continue.

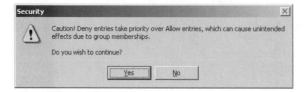

9. Click OK to save the change to the properties of the OU.

10. When finished, close the Active Directory Users and Computers administrative tool.

Through the use of these settings, you can ensure that only the appropriate individuals will be able to modify GPO settings.

# Delegating Administrative Control of GPOs

So far, we have talked about how Group Policy can be used to manage user and computer settings. What we haven't done is determine who can modify GPOs themselves. It's very important to establish the appropriate security on GPOs themselves for two main reasons. First, if the security settings aren't set properly, users and systems administrators can easily override them. This defeats the purpose of having the GPOs in the first place! Second, having many different systems administrators creating and modifying GPOs can become extremely difficult to manage. When problems arise, the hierarchical nature of GPO inheritance can make it difficult to pinpoint the problem.

Fortunately, through the use of the Delegation of Control Wizard, determining security permissions for GPOs is a simple task. We looked at the usefulness of the Delegation of Control Wizard in Chapter 7, "Administering the Active Directory" and in Chapter 8, "Active Directory Security." Exercise 10.4 walks you through the steps required to grant the appropriate permissions to a User account. Specifically, the process involves delegating the ability to manage Group Policy links on an Active Directory object (such as an OU).

---

**EXERCISE 10.4**

### Delegating Administrative Control of Group Policy

In this exercise, you will delegate permissions to manage Group Policies of an OU. In order to complete this exercise, you must have first completed Exercises 10.1 and 10.2.

1. Open the Active Directory Users and Computers tool.

2. Expand the local domain, and create a user named Policy Admin within the Group Policy Test OU.

3. Right-click the Group Policy Test OU, and select Delegate Control.

4. Click Next to start the Delegation of Control Wizard.

**EXERCISE 10.4** *(continued)*

5. On the Users or Groups page, click Add. Select the Policy Admin account, and click OK. Click Next to continue.

6. On the Tasks to Delegate step, select Delegate the Following Common Tasks, and place a check mark next to the Manage Group Policy Links item. Click Next to continue.

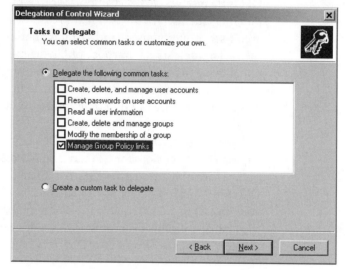

**7.** Finally, click Finish to complete the Delegation of Control Wizard and assign the appropriate permissions. Specifically, this will allow the Policy Admin user to create GPO links to this OU (and, by default, any child OUs).

**8.** When finished, close the Active Directory Users and Computers tool.

## Controlling Inheritance and Filtering Group Policy

Controlling inheritance is an important function when managing GPOs. Earlier in this chapter, we discussed the fact that, by default, GPO settings flow from higher-level Active Directory objects to lower-level ones. For example, the effective set of Group Policy settings for a user might be based on GPOs assigned at the site level, the domain level, and in the OU hierarchy. In general, this is probably the behavior you would want.

In some cases, however, you might want to block Group Policy inheritance. This can be easily accomplished by selecting the properties for the object to which a GPO has been linked. On the Group Policy tab, you will be able to set several useful options regarding inheritance. The first (and most obvious) option is the Block Policy Inheritance check box located at the bottom of the Group Policy tab (see Figure 10.5). By enabling this option, you are effectively specifying that this object starts with a clean slate. That is, no other Group Policy settings will apply to the contents of this Active Directory site, domain, or OU.

**FIGURE 10.5**    Blocking GPO inheritance

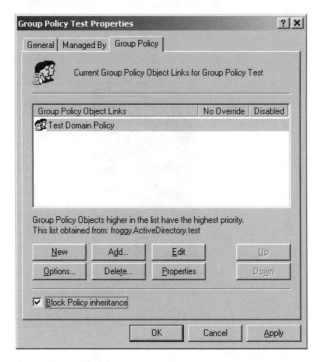

There is, however, a way that systems administrators can force inheritance. This is done using the No Override option and is generally set to prevent other systems administrators from making changes to default policies. You can set the No Override option (shown in Figure 10.6) by clicking the Options button on the Group Policy tab for the object to which the GPO applies. Notice that you can also choose to temporarily disable a GPO. This is useful during troubleshooting and when attempting to determine which GPOs are causing certain behavior.

**FIGURE 10.6**    Setting the No Override GPO option

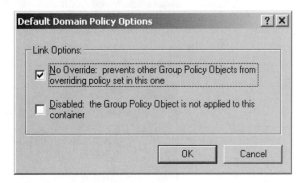

Exercise 10.5 walks through the steps required to manage inheritance and filtering of GPOs.

**EXERCISE 10.5**

## Managing Inheritance and Filtering of GPOs

In this exercise, you will modify the behavior of Group Policy inheritance and filtering.

1. Open the Active Directory Users and Computers administrative tool.

2. Create a top-level OU called Parent.

3. Right-click the Parent OU, and select Properties. Select the Group Policy tab, and click the New button to create a new GPO. Name the new object Master GPO.

4. Click the Options button. Place a check mark next to the No Override... option. This will ensure that administrators of OUs contained within the Parent OU will not be able to override the settings defined in this GPO.

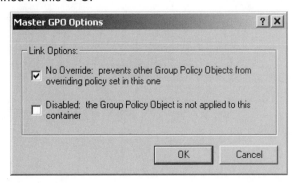

5. To save the settings, click OK. Notice that a check mark appears next to the Master GPO in the No Override column in the list of Group Policy object links.

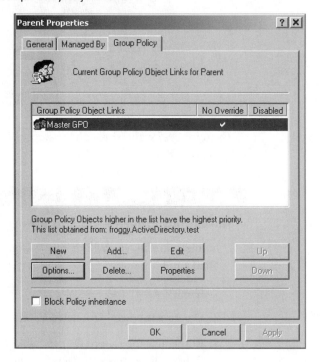

6. Create another GPO for the parent OU, and name it Optional GPO. Click the Apply button to save the changes.

7. Within the parent OU, create another OU called Child.

8. Right-click the Child OU, and select Properties. Select the Group Policy tab, and place a check mark in the Block Policy Inheritance check box. This option will prevent the inheritance of GPO settings from the Parent OU for the Optional GPO settings. Note that since the No Override setting for the Master GPO was enabled on the Parent OU, the settings in the Master GPO will take effect on the Child OU regardless of the setting of the Block Policy Inheritance box.

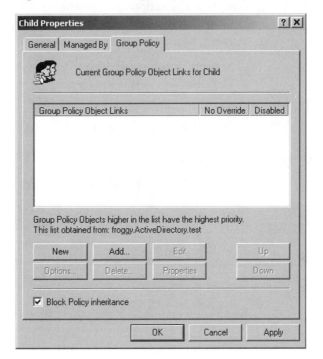

9. When finished, close the Active Directory Users and Computers tool.

# Assigning Script Policies

There are several changes and settings that systems administrators might want to make during the startup of a computer or during the logon for a user. Perhaps the most common operation for logon scripts is mapping network drives. Although users can manually map network drives, providing this functionality within login scripts ensures that mappings stay consistent and that users need only remember the drive letters for their resources.

*Script policies* are specific options that are part of Group Policy settings for users and computers. These settings direct the operating system to the specific files that should be processed during the startup/shutdown or logon/logoff processes. The scripts themselves may be created through the use of the *Windows Script Host (WSH)* or may be standard batch file commands. WSH is a utility included with the Windows 2000 operating system. It allows developers and systems administrators to quickly and easily create scripts using the familiar Visual Basic Scripting Edition (VBScript) or JScript (Microsoft's implementation of JavaScript). Additionally, WSH can be expanded to accommodate other common scripting languages.

To set script policy options, you simply edit the Group Policy settings. As shown in Figure 10.7, there are two main areas for setting script policy settings:

**Startup/Shutdown Scripts** These settings are located within the Computer Configuration ➢ Windows Settings ➢ Scripts (Startup/Shutdown) object.

**Logon/Logoff Scripts** These settings are located within the User Configuration ➢ Windows Settings ➢ Scripts (Logon/Logoff) object.

**FIGURE 10.7** Viewing script policy settings

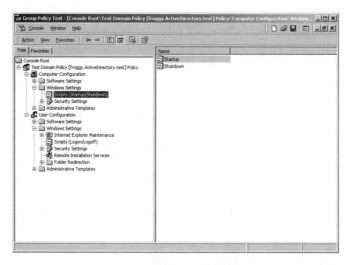

To assign scripts, simply double-click the setting. The Startup Properties dialog box appears, as shown in Figure 10.8. To add a script filename, click the Add button. You will be asked to provide the name of the script file (such as `MapNetworkDrives.vbs` or `ResetEnvironment.bat`). Note that you can change the order in which the scripts are run by using the Up and Down buttons. The Show Files button will open the directory folder in which you should store the Logon files. In order to ensure that the files are replicated to all domain controllers, you should be sure that you place the files within the *SysVol* share.

**FIGURE 10.8** Setting scripting options

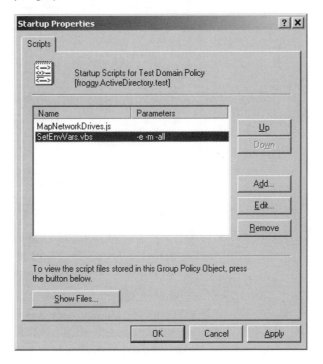

## Managing Network Configuration

Group Policies are also useful in network configuration. Although there are many different methods for handling network settings at the protocol level (such as Dynamic Host Configuration Protocol, or DHCP), Group Policy allows administrators to set which functions and operations are available to users and computers.

Figure 10.9 shows some of the features that are available for managing Group Policy settings. The paths to these settings are as follows:

**Computer Network Options** These settings are located within the Computer Configuration ➤ Administrative Templates ➤ Network folder.

**User Network Options** These settings are located within the User Configuration ➤ Administrative Templates ➤ Network folder.

**FIGURE 10.9** Viewing Group Policy network configuration options

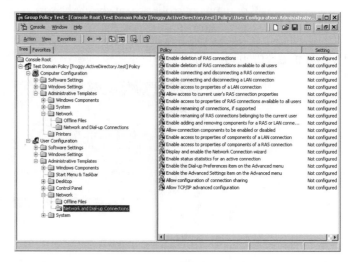

Some examples of the types of settings available include the following:

- The ability to allow or disallow the modification of network settings. In many environments, the improper changing of network configurations and protocol settings is a common cause of help desk calls.

- The ability to allow or disallow the creation of Remote Access Service (RAS) connections. This option is very useful, especially in larger networked environments, since the use of modems and other WAN devices can pose a security threat to the network.

- Setting of Offline files and folders options. This is especially useful for keeping files synchronized for traveling users and is commonly configured for laptops.

Through the use of these configuration options, systems administrators can maintain consistency for users and computers and can avoid many of the most common troubleshooting calls.

# Troubleshooting Group Policy

**D**ue to the wide variety of configurations that are possible when establishing Group Policy, you should be aware of some common troubleshooting methods. These methods will help isolate problems in policy settings or *Group Policy object (GPO) links.*

A possible problem with GPO configuration is that logons and system startups may take a long time. This occurs especially in large environments when the Group Policy settings must be transmitted over the network and, in many cases, slow WAN links. In general, the number of GPOs should be limited because of the processing overhead and network requirements during logon. By default, GPOs are processed in a synchronous manner. This means that the processing of one GPO must be completed before another one is applied (as opposed to asynchronous processing, where they can all execute at the same time).

Other common issues might include unexpected settings of Group Policy options. When this occurs, there are several options that systems administrators should verify.

**Locate Active Directory GPO Links**   To find out where GPOs are being used, you can quickly and easily use the Links tab in the Properties dialog box of the GPOs.

**Verify GPO Configuration**   Since GPOs can be assigned to sites, domains, and OUs, systems administrators should be sure to carefully plan for the inheritance of Group Policy settings. And while careful planning and maintenance of GPOs is important, it's just as important to determine the ramifications of moving and reconfiguring objects of the Active Directory. For example, moving an OU or redefining a site can cause large changes in the effective Group Policy settings.

**Attempt to "Disable" Certain GPOs**   When certain settings are causing problems, it can be difficult to isolate the GPOs from which the settings are being made. One method for troubleshooting GPO problems is to systematically disable and enable various combinations of GPOs. By doing this, you can determine which GPO(s) is causing the problems.

Through the use of these various techniques, you should be able to track down even the most elusive Group Policy problems. Remember, however, that good troubleshooting skills do not replace the need for adequate planning and maintenance of GPO settings!

### Real World Scenario

## Troubleshooting Logon Performance Problems

You are a systems administrator for a medium-sized Active Directory environment. Several weeks ago, you were asked to design and implement the organization's Group Policy security settings. You spent several days designing a working strategy that was easy to maintain. In order to best suit the needs of your users, you also decided to create nine different Group Policy objects. You designed each GPO to contain information about a specific set of permissions. You also had to take into account that the established OU structure within your single Active Directory domain environment consists of a fairly deep hierarchy (for example, many OUs are nested to four levels). In order to work with this system, you linked the nine GPOs you created to these OUs at various levels, which resulted in dozens of links. Before you deployed your solution, you performed several tests to ensure that the resulting policies were what you intended. The settings seemed to work well, and they met the business needs.

Recently, however, you have received several complaints from users throughout the environment; they are complaining about slow performance during login. Based on their reports, the system seems to hang on the Applying Security Settings dialog box, during which time they cannot access their systems. To determine the cause, you examine the network and find no performance problems. Furthermore, the issue seems to have arisen just after you implemented the GPO links. You determine that the problem must be due to the large number of GPO links. After consulting several resources for more information, your opinion seems to be validated—the issue is likely caused by having so many GPO links. You also find out that the GPOs themselves must be processed synchronously (that is, one after the other). You know that this will add significantly to the logon time, regardless of network and other issues.

You can solve this problem by reducing the number of GPO links. For example, if users that are contained in OUs that are four levels deep within the OU structure have many different GPOs that must be applied during login, perhaps you can consolidate the GPOs into a few, more complicated ones. Or, you can take the settings that you have in some GPO's and repeat them in others (so fewer would have to be applied). Overall, you might sacrifice some of the ease with which you could administer features, but your users could save significant time during logon attempts.

Although the initial GPO policy you established above met some of your business requirements (for example, maintaining a good level of security), it failed to meet others (for instance, acceptable performance during logon operations). As is always the case, remember that your technical solutions must meet business goals, and performance issues with GPO links are no exception. Be sure to adequately test logon performance before you begin your GPO rollout.

# Summary

In this chapter, we examined the Active Directory's solution to a common headache for many systems administrators: policy settings. Specifically, we discussed the following:

- Group Policies can restrict and modify the actions that are allowed for users and computers within the Active Directory environment.

- Group Policy objects (GPOs) can be linked to Active Directory objects.

- Group Policy object links can interact through inheritance and filtering to result in an effective set of policies.

- Administrative templates can be used to simplify the creation of Group Policy objects.

- Administrators can delegate control over GPOs in order to distribute administrative responsibilities.

A good understanding of Group Policy is very important for both the exam and for working with the Active Directory in the real world.

# Exam Essentials

**Understand the purpose of Group Policy.** Group Policy is used to enforce granular permissions for users in an Active Directory environment.

**Understand user and computer settings.** Certain Group Policy settings may apply to users, computers, or both. Computer settings affect all users that access the machines to which the policy applies. User settings affect users, regardless of which machines they log on to.

**Know the interactions between Group Policy objects and the Active Directory.** GPOs can be linked to Active Directory objects. This link determines to which objects the policies apply.

**Understand filtering and inheritance interactions between GPOs.** For ease of administration, Group Policy objects can interact via inheritance and filtering. It is important to understand these interactions when implementing and troubleshooting Group Policy.

**Know how Group Policy settings can affect script policies and network settings.** Special sets of Group Policy objects can be used to manage network configuration settings.

**Understand how delegation of administration can be used in an Active Directory environment.** Delegation is an important concept because it allows for distributed administration.

**Know the basic steps for troubleshooting Group Policy.** When implementing Group Policy, it is possible that the set of applied permissions is not what you expected. In such a case, it's important to understand how a particular Active Directory object obtained these settings and at which levels the settings are applied.

# Key Terms

Before you take the exam, you should be familiar with the following terms and concepts:

| | |
|---|---|
| administrative templates | Group Policy object (GPO) link |
| filtering | inheritance |
| Group Policy | script policies |
| Group Policy object (GPO) | Windows Script Host (WSH) |

# Review Questions

1. A systems administrator is planning to implement GPOs in a new Windows 2000 Active Directory environment. In order to meet the needs of the organization, he decides to implement a hierarchical system of Group Policy settings. At which of the following levels is he *not* able to assign Group Policy settings?

   A. Sites

   B. Domains

   C. Organizational units (OUs)

   D. Local system

   E. None of the above

2. Ann is a systems administrator for a medium-sized Active Directory environment. She has determined that several new applications that will be deployed throughout the organization use Registry-based settings. She would like to do the following:

   - Control these Registry settings using Group Policy.

   - Create a standard set of options for these applications and allow other systems administrators to modify them using the standard Active Directory tools.

   Which of the following options can she use to meet these requirements? (Choose all that apply.)

   A. Implement the Inheritance functionality of GPOs.

   B. Implement Delegation of specific objects within the Active Directory.

   C. Implement the No Override functionality of GPOs.

   D. Create Administrative templates.

   E. Provide Administrative templates to the systems administrators that are responsible for creating Group Policy for the applications.

**3.** Script policies can be set for which of the following events?

   **A.** Logon

   **B.** Logoff

   **C.** Startup

   **D.** Shutdown

   **E.** All of the above

**4.** John is developing a standards document for settings that are allowed by systems administrators in an Active Directory environment. He wants to maintain as much flexibility as possible in the area of Group Policy settings. In which of the following languages can script policies be written? (Choose all that apply.)

   **A.** Visual Basic Scripting Edition (VBScript)

   **B.** JScript

   **C.** Other Windows Script Host (WSH) languages

   **D.** Batch files

**5.** The process of assigning permissions to set Group Policy for objects within an OU is known as

   **A.** Promotion

   **B.** Inheritance

   **C.** Delegation

   **D.** Filtering

   **E.** None of the above

6. You are a systems administrator for a medium-sized Active Directory environment. Specifically, you are in charge of administering all objects that are located within the North America OU. The North America OU contains the Corporate OU. You want to do the following:

   - Create a GPO that applies to all users within the North America OU except for those located within the Corporate OU.

   - Be able to easily apply all Group Policy settings to users within the Corporate OU, should the need arise in the future.

   - Accomplish this task with the least amount of administrative effort.

   Which two of the following options meets these requirements? (Choose all that apply.)

   **A.** Enable the Inheritance functionality of GPOs for all OUs within the North America OU.

   **B.** Implement Delegation of all objects within the North America OU to one administrator and then remove permissions for the Corporate OU. Have this administrator link the GPO to the North America OU.

   **C.** Create a GPO link for the new policy at level of the North America OU.

   **D.** Create special Administrative templates for the Corporate OU.

   **E.** Enable the "Block Inheritance" option on the Corporate OU.

7. The process by which lower-level Active Directory objects inherit Group Policy settings from higher-level ones is known as

   **A.** Delegation

   **B.** Inheritance

   **C.** Cascading permissions

   **D.** Overriding

   **E.** None of the above

**8.** To disable GPO settings for a specific security group, which of the following permissions should be applied?

**A.** Deny Write

**B.** Allow Write

**C.** Enable Apply Group Policy

**D.** Disable Apply Group Policy

**9.** Trent is a systems administrator in a medium-sized Active Directory environment. He is responsible for creating and maintaining Group Policy settings. For a specific group of settings, he has the following requirements:

- The settings in the "Basic Users" GPO should remain defined.

- The settings in the "Basic Users" GPO should not apply to any users within the Active Directory environment.

- The amount of administrative effort to apply the "Basic Users" settings to an OU in the future should be minimal.

Which of the following options can Trent use to meet these requirements?

**A.** Enable the No Override option at the domain level.

**B.** Enable the Block Policy Inheritance option at the domain level.

**C.** Remove the link to the "Basic Users" GPO from all Active Directory objects.

**D.** Delete the "Basic Users" GPO.

**E.** Rename the "Basic Users" GPO to break its link with any existing Active Directory objects.

**10.** A systems administrator wants to ensure that certain GPOs applied at the domain level are not overridden at lower levels. Which option can they use to do this?

**A.** The No Override option

**B.** The Block Policy Inheritance option

**C.** The Disable option

**D.** None of the above

11. GPOs assigned at which of the following level(s) will override GPO settings at the domain level?

   **A.** OU

   **B.** Site

   **C.** Domain

   **D.** Both OU and site

   **E.** None of the above

12. A systems administrator wants to ensure that only the GPOs set at the OU level affect the Group Policy settings for objects within the OU. Which option can they use to do this (assuming that all other GPO settings are the defaults)?

   **A.** The No Override option

   **B.** The Block Policy Inheritance option

   **C.** The Disable option

   **D.** None of the above

13. In order to be accessible to other domain controllers, logon/logoff and startup/shutdown scripts should be placed in which of the following shares?

   **A.** Winnt

   **B.** System

   **C.** C$

   **D.** SysVol

   **E.** None of the above

**14.** What is the name of the GPO that is created when a new domain is created?

**A.** Test Group Policy

**B.** Domain Policy

**C.** Temporary Domain Policy

**D.** Default Domain Policy

**E.** None of the above

**15.** Matt, a systems administrator, has recently created a new Active Directory domain. The domain forms a tree with the three other domains in the environment, and all of the domains are configured in a single site. He is planning to implement Group Policy, and has the following requirements:

- Several GPOs must be created to accommodate five different levels of user settings.

- The GPOs may be assigned at any level within the Active Directory environment.

- All users within the "Engineering" domain must receive specific GPO assignments.

At which of the following levels can Matt create a single GPO link in order for it to affect all four domains in the environment?

**A.** Sites

**B.** OUs

**C.** Domains

**D.** Local computer

**E.** Domain Controllers

16. You want to link a GPO to the Group Policy Test OU. You right-click the OU as shown below. In order to accomplish this task, what would you click next?

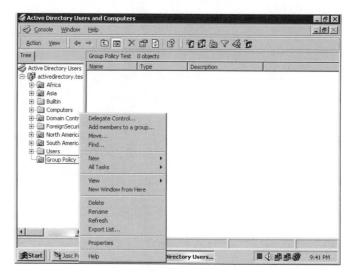

A. Properties

B. Delegate Control

C. All Tasks

D. Add Members to a Group

# Answers to Review Questions

1. E. GPOs can be set at all of the levels listed.

2. D, E. Administrative templates are used to specify the options available for setting Group Policy. By creating new Administrative templates, Ann can specify which options are available for the new applications. She can then distribute these templates to other systems administrators in the environment.

3. E. Script policies can be set for any of the events listed.

4. A, B, C, D. The Windows Script Host (WSH) can be used with any of the above languages. Additionally, standard batch files can also be used.

5. C. The Delegation of Control Wizard can be used to allow other systems administrators permission to add GPO links to an Active Directory object.

6. C, E. The easiest way to accomplish this task is to create GPO links at the level of the parent OU (North America) and disable inheritance at the level of the child OU (Corporate).

7. B. Inheritance is the process by which lower-level Active Directory objects inherit GPO settings from higher-level ones.

8. D. To disable the application of Group Policy on a security group, the Apply Group Policy option should be disabled.

9. C. Systems administrators can disable a GPO without removing its link to Active Directory objects. This prevents the GPO from having any effects on Group Policy but leaves the GPO definition intact so it can be enabled at a later date.

10. A. The No Override option ensures that the Group Policy settings cannot be changed by the settings of lower-level Active Directory objects.

11. A. GPOs at the OU level take precedence over GPOs at the domain level. GPOs at the domain level, in turn, take precedence over GPOs at the site level.

12. B. The Block Policy Inheritance option prevents Group Policies of higher-level Active Directory objects from applying to lower-level objects as long as the No Override option is not set.

13. D. By default, the contents of the SysVol share are made available to all domain controllers. Therefore, scripts should be placed in these directories.

14. D. The Default Domain Policy GPO is created during the creation of a new domain.

15. A. GPO links at the site level affect all of the domains that are part of a site. Therefore, Matt can create a single GPO link at the Site level.

16. A. In order to link a GPO to an OU, you would use the Group Policy tab of the OU Properties dialog box. From there, you can create new GPOs, add GPOs to the OU, and configure each GPO.

# Chapter

# 11

# Software Deployment through Group Policy

## MICROSOFT EXAM OBJECTIVES COVERED IN THIS CHAPTER:

✓ **Manage and troubleshoot software by using Group Policy.**

- Deploy software by using Group Policy.
- Maintain software by using Group Policy.
- Configure deployment options.
- Troubleshoot common problems that occur during software deployment.

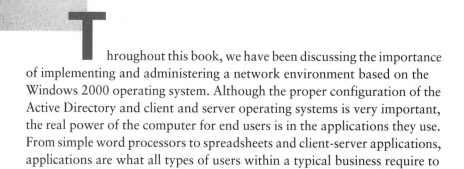

Throughout this book, we have been discussing the importance of implementing and administering a network environment based on the Windows 2000 operating system. Although the proper configuration of the Active Directory and client and server operating systems is very important, the real power of the computer for end users is in the applications they use. From simple word processors to spreadsheets and client-server applications, applications are what all types of users within a typical business require to help them complete their jobs.

From an end user's viewpoint, it's very easy to take software for granted. For example, many of us have come to expect our computers to run messaging applications, productivity applications, and (for people like us) games. However, from the view of systems administrators and help desk staff, deploying and maintaining software can be a troublesome and time-consuming job. Regardless of how much time is spent installing, updating, reinstalling, and removing applications based on users' needs, there seems to be no end to the process!

Fortunately, Windows 2000 and the Active Directory provide many improvements to the process of deploying and managing software. Through the use of Group Policy objects and the Microsoft Installer (MSI), software deployment options can be easily configured. The applications themselves can be made available to any users who are part of the Active Directory environment. Furthermore, systems administrators can automatically assign applications to users and computers and allow programs to be installed automatically when they are needed.

In this chapter, we'll look at how Windows 2000 and the Active Directory can be used to deploy and manage software throughout the network.

# Overview of Software Deployment

It's difficult enough to manage applications on a stand-alone computer. It seems that the process of installing, configuring, and uninstalling applications is never finished! Add in the hassle of computer reboots and reinstalling corrupted applications, and the reduction in productivity can be very real.

When managing software in network environments, there are even more concerns. First and foremost, systems administrators must determine which applications specific users require. Then, IT departments must purchase the appropriate licenses for the software and acquire any necessary media. Next comes the fun part—actually installing the applications on users' machines. This process generally involves help desk staff visiting computers or requiring end users to install the software themselves. Both processes entail several potential problems, including inconsistency in installation and lost productivity from downtime experienced when installing applications. As if this wasn't enough, we haven't even discussed managing software updates and removing unused software!

One of the key design goals for the Active Directory was to reduce some of the headaches involved in managing software and configurations in a networked environment. To that end, Windows 2000 offers several features that can make the task of deploying software easier and less prone to errors. Before we dive into the technical details, though, let's examine the issues related to software deployment.

## The Software Management Life Cycle

Although it may seem that the use of a new application requires only the installation of the necessary software, the overall process of managing applications involves many more steps. When managing software applications, there are three main phases to the life cycle of applications:

**Deploying Software** The first step in using applications is to install them on the appropriate client computers. Generally, some applications are deployed during the initial configuration of a PC, and others are deployed when they are requested. In the latter case, this often used to mean that systems administrators and help desk staff would have to visit client computers and manually walk through the installation process.

It is very important to understand that the ability to easily deploy software does not necessarily mean that you have the right to do so! Before you install software on client computers, you must make sure that you have the appropriate licenses for the software. Furthermore, it's very important to take the time to track application installations. As many systems administrators have discovered, it's much more difficult to inventory software installations after they've been performed.

**Maintaining Software**   Once an application is installed and in use on client computers, there's a need to ensure that the software is maintained. Changes due to bug fixes, enhancements, and other types of updates must be applied in order to ensure that programs are kept up-to-date. As with the initial software deployment, software maintenance can be a tedious process. Some programs require that older versions be uninstalled before updates are added. Others allow for automatically upgrading over existing installations. Managing and deploying software updates can consume a significant amount of time for IT staff.

**Removing Software**   At the end of the life cycle for many software products is the actual removal of unused programs. Removing software is necessary when applications become outdated or when users no longer require their functionality. One of the traditional problems with uninstalling applications is that many of the installed files may not be removed. Furthermore, the removal of shared components can sometimes cause other programs to stop functioning properly. Also, users often forget to uninstall applications that are no longer needed, and these programs continue to occupy disk space and consume valuable system resources.

Each of these three phases of the software maintenance life cycle is managed by the Microsoft Installer application. Now that we have an overview of the process, let's move on to looking at the actual steps involved in deploying software using Group Policy.

# The Windows Installer

If you've installed newer application programs (such as Microsoft Office 2000), you probably noticed the updated setup and installation routines. Applications that comply with the updated standard use the *Windows Installer* specification and software packages for deployment. Each package contains information about various setup options and the files required for installation. Although the benefits may not seem dramatic on the surface, there's a lot of new functionality under the hood!

The Windows Installer was created to solve many of the problems associated with traditional application development. It has several components, including the Installer service (which runs on Windows 2000 Server and Professional computers), the Installer program (`msiexec.exe`) that is responsible for executing the instructions in a *Windows Installer package*, and the specifications for third-party developers to use to create their own packages. Within each installation package file is a relational structure (similar to the structure of tables in databases) that records information about the programs contained within the package.

In order to appreciate the true value of the Windows Installer, let's start by looking at some of the problems with "traditional" software deployment mechanisms. Then we'll move on and look at how the Windows Installer addresses many of these problems.

## Application Installation Issues

Before Windows 2000 and the Windows Installer, applications were installed using a setup program that managed the various operations required for a program to operate. These operations included copying files, changing Registry settings, and managing any other operating system changes that might be required (such as starting or stopping services). However, this method included several problems:

- The setup process was not robust, and aborting the operation often left many unnecessary files in the file system.

- The process of uninstalling an application often left many unnecessary files in the file system and remnants in the Windows Registry and operating system folders. Over time, this would result in reduced overall system performance and wasted disk space.

- There was no standard method for applying upgrades to applications, and installing a new version often required users to uninstall the old application, reboot, and then install the new program.

- Conflicts between different versions of dynamic link libraries (DLLs)—shared program code used across different applications—could cause the installation or removal of one application to break the functionality of another.

## Benefits of the Windows Installer

Because of the many problems associated with traditional software installation, Microsoft has created a new standard known as the Windows Installer. This new system provides for better manageability of the software installation process and, as we'll see later in this chapter, allows systems administrators more control over the deployment process. Specifically, benefits of the Windows Installer include the following:

**Improved Software Removal**   The process of removing software is an important one since remnants left behind during the uninstall process can eventually clutter up the Registry and file system. During the installation process, the Windows Installer keeps track of all of the changes made by a setup package. When it comes time to remove an application, all of these changes can then be rolled back.

**More Robust Installation Routines**   If a typical setup program is aborted during the software installation process, the results are unpredictable. If the actual installation hasn't yet begun, then the Installer generally removes any temporary files that may have been created. If, however, the file copy routine starts before the system encounters an error, it is likely that the files will not be automatically removed from the operating system. In contrast, the Windows Installer allows you to roll back any changes when the application setup process is aborted.

**Ability to Use Elevated Privileges**   Installing applications usually requires the user to have Administrator permissions on the local computer since file system and Registry changes are required. When installing software for network users, systems administrators thus have two options. The first is to log off of the computer before installing the software, then log back on as a user who has Administrator permissions on the local computer. This method is tedious and time-consuming. The second is to temporarily give users Administrator permissions on their own machines. This method could cause security problems and requires the attention of a systems administrator.

Through the use of the Installer service, the Windows Installer is able to use temporarily elevated privileges to install applications. This allows users, regardless of their security settings, to execute the installation of authorized applications. The end result is the saving of time *and* the preservation of security.

**Support for Repairing Corrupted Applications**   Regardless of how well a network environment is managed, critical files are sometimes lost or corrupted. Such problems can prevent applications from running properly and cause crashes. Windows Installer packages support the ability to verify the installation of an application and, if necessary, replace any missing or corrupted files. This saves time and the end-user headaches associated with removing and reinstalling an entire application to replace just a few files.

**Prevention of File Conflicts**   Generally, different versions of the same files should be compatible with each other. In the real world, however, this isn't always the case. A classic problem in the Windows world is the case of one program replacing DLLs that are used by several other programs. Windows Installer accurately tracks which files are used by certain programs and ensures that any shared files are not improperly deleted or overwritten.

**Automated Installations**   A typical application setup process requires end users or systems administrators to respond to several prompts. For example, a user may be able to choose the program group in which icons will be created and the file system location to which the program will be installed. Additionally, they may be required to choose which options are installed. Although this type of flexibility is useful, it can be tedious when rolling out multiple applications. By using features of the Windows Installer, however, users are able to specify setup options before the process begins. This allows systems administrators to ensure consistency in installations and saves time for users.

**Advertising and On-Demand Installations**   One of the most powerful features of the Windows Installer is its ability to perform on-demand installations of software. Prior to Windows Installer, application installation options were quite basic—either a program was installed or it was not.

When setting up a computer, systems administrators would be required to guess which applications the user *might* need and install them all.

The Windows Installer supports a function known as advertising. Advertising makes applications appear to be available via the Start menu. However, the programs themselves may not actually be installed on the system. When a user attempts to access an advertised application, the Windows Installer automatically downloads the necessary files from a server and installs the program. The end result is that applications are installed only when needed, and the process requires no intervention from the end user. We'll cover the details of this process later in this chapter.

To anyone who has had the pleasure of managing many software applications in a network environment, all of these features of the Windows Installer are likely to be welcome ones. They also make life easier for end users and application developers who can focus on the "real work" their jobs demand.

## Windows Installer File Types

When performing software deployment with the Windows Installer in Windows 2000, there are several different file types you may encounter. These are as follows:

**Windows Installer Packages (MSI)**   In order to take full advantage of Windows Installer functionality, applications must include Windows Installer packages. These packages are normally created by third-party application vendors and software developers and include the information required to install and configure the application and any supporting files.

**Transformation Files (MST)**   *Transformation files* are useful when customizing the details of how applications are installed. When a systems administrator chooses to assign or publish an application, they may want to specify additional options for the package. If, for instance, a systems administrator wants to allow users to install only the Microsoft Word and Microsoft PowerPoint components of Office 2000, they could specify these options within a transformation file. Then, when users install the application, they will be provided with only the options related to these components.

**Patches (MSP)**   In order to maintain software, *patches* are often required. Patches may make Registry and/or file system changes. Patch files are used for minor system changes and are subject to certain limitations. Specifically, a patch file cannot remove any installed program components and cannot delete or modify any shortcuts created by the user.

**Initialization Files (ZAP)**   In order to provide support for publishing non–Windows Installer applications, *initialization files* can be used. These files provide links to a standard executable file that is used to install an application. An example might be \\server1\software\program1\setup.exe. These files can then be published and advertised, and users can access the *Add/Remove Programs* icon to install them over the network.

**Application Assignment Scripts (AAS)**   *Application assignment scripts* store information regarding the assignment of programs and any settings that are made by the systems administrator. These files are created when Group Policy is used to create software package assignments for users and computers.

Each of these types of files provides functionality that allows for the customization of software deployment. Windows Installer packages have special properties that can be viewed by right-clicking the file and choosing Properties (see Figure 11.1).

**FIGURE 11.1**   Viewing the properties of a Windows Installer (MSI) package file

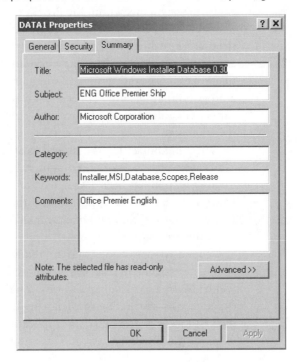

# Deploying Applications

The functionality provided by Windows Installer offers many advantages to end users who install their own software. That, however, is just the tip of the iceberg in a networked environment. As we'll see later in this chapter, the various features of Windows Installer and compatible packages allow systems administrators to centrally determine applications that users will be able to install.

There are two main methods of making programs available to end users using the Active Directory. They are *assigning* and *publishing*. In this section, we'll look at how the processes of assigning and publishing applications can make life easier for IT staff and users alike. The various settings for assigned and published applications are managed through the use of Group Policy objects (GPOs).

## Assigning Applications

Software applications can be assigned to users and computers. Assigning a software package makes the program available for automatic installation. The applications advertise their availability to the affected users or computers by placing icons within the Programs folder of the Start menu.

When applications are assigned to a user, programs will be advertised to the user, regardless of which computer they are using. That is, icons for the advertised program will appear within the Start menu, regardless of whether the program is installed on the computer or not. If the user clicks an icon for a program that has not yet been installed on the local computer, the application will automatically be accessed from a server and will be installed on the computer.

When an application is assigned to a computer, the program is made available to any users of the computer. For example, all users who log on to a computer that has been assigned Microsoft Office 2000 will have access to the components of the application. If the user did not previously install Microsoft Office, they will be prompted for any required setup information when the program is first run.

Generally, applications that are required by the vast majority of users should be assigned to computers. This reduces the amount of network bandwidth required to install applications on demand and improves the end user experience by preventing the delay involved when installing an application the first time it is accessed. Any applications that may be used by only a few users (or those with specific job tasks) should be assigned to users.

### Publishing Applications

When applications are published, the programs are advertised, but no icons are automatically created. Instead, the applications are made available for installation using the Add/Remove Programs icon in the Control Panel. Software can be published only to users (not computers). The list of available applications is stored within the Active Directory, and client computers can query this list when they need to install programs. For ease of organization, applications can be grouped into *categories*.

Both publishing and assigning applications greatly ease the process of deploying and managing applications in a network environment.

# Implementing Software Deployment

**S**o far, we have discussed the issues related to software deployment and management from a high level. Now it's time to drill down into the actual steps required to deploy software using the features of the Active Directory. In this section, we will walk through the steps required to create an application distribution share point, to publish and assign applications, and to verify the installation of applications.

| *Microsoft* ✓ *Exam* *Objective* | **Manage and troubleshoot software by using Group Policy.** |
|---|---|
| | • Deploy software by using Group Policy. |
| | • Troubleshoot common problems that occur during software deployment. |

## Preparing for Software Deployment

Before you can install applications on client computers, you must make sure that the necessary files are available to end users. In many network environments, systems administrators create shares on file servers that include the installation files for many applications. Based on security permissions, either end users or systems administrators can then connect to these shares from a client computer and install the needed software. The efficient organization of these shares can save the help desk from having to carry around a library of CD-ROMs and can allow for installing applications easily on many computers at once.

Exercises 11.1 and 11.2 provide hands-on experience related to the "Manage and troubleshoot software by using Group Policy" objective and its "Troubleshoot common problems that occur during software deployment" subobjective, but see the section "Optimizing and Troubleshooting Software Deployment" later in this chapter for more detailed text coverage of this objective and subobjective.

One of the problems in network environments is that users frequently install applications whether or not they really require them. They may stumble upon applications that are stored on common file servers and install them out of curiosity. These actions can often decrease productivity and may violate software licensing agreements. You can help avoid this by placing all of your application installation files in hidden shares (for example, "software$").

Exercise 11.1 walks you through the process of creating a software distribution share point.

### EXERCISE 11.1

### Creating a Software Deployment Share

In this exercise, you will prepare for software deployment by creating a directory share and placing certain types of files in this directory. In order to complete the steps in this exercise, you must have access to the Microsoft Office 2000 installation files (via CD-ROM or through a network share) and 600MB of free disk space.

1. Using Windows Explorer, create a folder called Software for use with application sharing. Be sure that the volume on which you create this folder has at least 600MB of available disk space.

2. Within the Software folder, create a folder called Admin Tools.

3. Copy the `adminpak.msi` file from the `%systemroot%\system32` folder to the Admin Tools folder that you created in step 2.

4. Within the Software folder, create a folder called Office 2000.

5. Copy all of the installation files for Microsoft Office 2000 from the CD-ROM or network share containing the files to the Office 2000 folder that you created in step 4.

6. Right-click the Software folder (created in step 1), and select the Sharing tab. Choose Share This Folder, and type **Software** in the Share Name text box and **Software Distribution Share Point** in the Comment text box. Leave all other options as the default, and click OK to create the share.

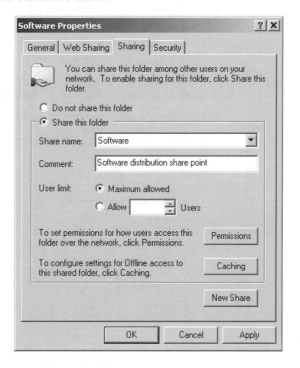

Once you have created an application distribution share, it's time to actually publish and assign the applications. We'll look at that topic next.

# Publishing and Assigning Applications

As we mentioned earlier in this chapter, software packages can be made available to users through the use of publishing and assigning. Both of these operations allow systems administrators to leverage the power of the Active Directory and, specifically, Group Policy objects (GPOs) to determine which applications are available to users. Additionally, the organization provided by OUs can help group users based on their job functions and software requirements.

The general process involves creating a GPO that includes software deployment settings for users and computers and then linking this GPO to Active Directory objects. If you're unfamiliar with creating and linking GPOs, see Chapter 10, "Managing Group Policy." Exercise 11.2 walks you through the steps required to publish and assign applications.

---

**EXERCISE 11.2**

### Publishing and Assigning Applications Using Group Policy

In this exercise, you will create and assign applications to specific Active Directory objects using Group Policy objects. In order to complete the steps in this exercise, you must have first completed Exercise 11.1.

1. Open the Active Directory Users and Computers tool from the Administrative Tools program group.

2. Expand the domain, and create a new top-level OU called Software.

3. Within the Software OU, create a user named Jane User with a login name of juser (choose the defaults for all other options).

4. Right-click the Software OU, and select Properties.

**5.** Select the Group Policy tab, and click New. For the name of the new GPO, type **Software Deployment**.

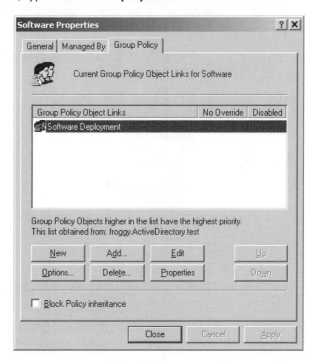

**6.** To edit the Software Deployment GPO, click Edit. Expand the Computer Configuration ➤ Software Settings object.

**EXERCISE 11.2** *(continued)*

7. Right-click the Software Installation item, and select New ≻ Package. Navigate to the Software share that you created in Exercise 11.1. Within the Software share, double-click the Office 2000 folder, and select the Data1 file. Click Open.

8. In the Deploy Software dialog box, choose Advanced Published or Assigned, and click OK. Note that the Published option is unavailable since applications cannot be published to computers.

9. To examine the Deployment options of this package, click the Deployment tab. Accept the default settings by clicking OK.

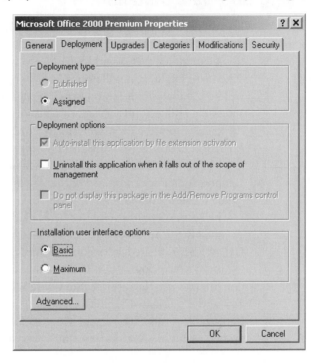

10. Within the Group Policy Editor, expand the User Configuration ➢ Software Settings object.

11. Right-click the Software Installation item, and select New ➢ Package. Navigate to the Software share that you created in Exercise 11.1. Within the Software share, double-click the Admin Tools folder, and select the adminpak.msi file. Click Open.

12. For the Software Deployment option, select Published and click OK.

13. Close the Group Policy Editor, and then click Close to close the Properties of the Software OU.

The overall process involved with deploying software using the Active Directory is quite simple. However, you shouldn't let the intuitive graphical interface fool you—there's a lot of power under the hood of these software deployment features! Once you've properly assigned and published applications, it's time to see the effects of your work.

## Verifying Software Installation

In order to ensure that the settings you made in the GPO for the Software OU have taken place, you can log in to the domain from a Windows 2000 Professional computer that is within the OU to which the software settings apply. When you log in, you will notice two changes. First, Microsoft Office 2000 will be installed on the computer (if it was not installed already). In order to access the Office 2000 applications, all a user would need to do is click one of the icons within the Program group of the Start menu (for example, the Microsoft Word icon). Note also that these applications will be available to any of the users who log on to this machine. Also, the settings apply to any computers that are contained within the Software OU and to any users who log on to these computers.

The second change may not be as evident, but it is equally useful. We assigned the Windows 2000 Administrative Tools program to the Software OU. We also created an account named juser within that OU. When you log on to a Windows 2000 Professional computer that is a member of the domain and use the juser account, you will be able to automatically install any of the published applications. You can do this by accessing the Add/Remove Programs icon in the Control Panel. By clicking Add New Programs, you will see a display similar to that shown in Figure 11.2.

**FIGURE 11.2** Installing published applications in Add/Remove Programs

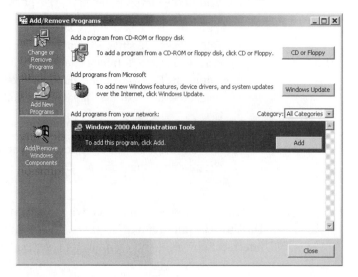

By clicking the Add button, you will automatically begin the installation of the Windows 2000 Administration Tools (see Figure 11.3). This is a useful way of allowing systems administrators to use the Windows 2000 Administration Tools to remotely manage Windows 2000 Server computers.

**FIGURE 11.3** The automatic installation of Windows 2000 Administration Tools

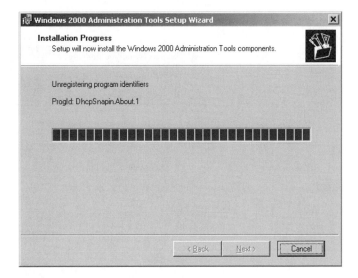

# Configuring Software Deployment Settings

In addition to the basic operations of assigning and publishing applications, there are several other options for specifying the details of how software is deployed. You can access these options from within a GPO by right-clicking the Software Installation item (located within Software Settings in User Configuration or Computer Configuration). In this section, we will examine the various options that are available and their effects on the software installation process.

**Microsoft** ✓ **Exam Objective**

**Manage and troubleshoot software by using Group Policy.**

- Maintain software by using Group Policy.

- Configure deployment options.

## Managing Package Defaults

On the General tab of the Software Installation Properties dialog box, you'll be able to specify some defaults for any packages that you create within this GPO. Figure 11.4 shows the General options for managing software installation settings.

**FIGURE 11.4** General settings for software settings

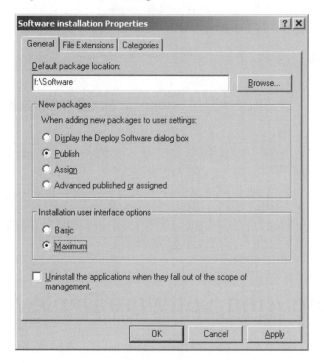

The various options available include the following:

**Default Package Location** This setting specifies the default file system or network location for software installation packages. This is useful if you are already using a specific share on a file server for hosting the necessary installation files.

**New Packages Options** This setting specifies the default type of package assignment that will be used when adding a new package to either the user or computer settings. If you'll be assigning or publishing multiple packages, it may be useful to set a default here.

**Installation User Interface Options**   When an application is being installed, systems administrators may or may not want end users to see all of the advanced installation options. If Basic is chosen, the user will only be able to configure the minimal settings (such as the installation location). If Maximum is chosen, all of the available installation options will be displayed. The specific installation options available will depend on the package itself.

**Uninstall the Applications When They Fall Out of the Scope of Management**   So far, we have discussed how applications can be assigned and published to users or computers. But what happens when effective GPOs change? For example, suppose that User A is currently located within the Sales OU. A GPO that assigns the Microsoft Office 2000 suite of applications is linked to the Sales OU. Now, I decide to move User A to the Engineering OU, which has no software deployment settings. Should the application be uninstalled, or should it remain?

If the Uninstall the Applications When They Fall Out of the Scope of Management option is checked, applications will be removed if they are not specifically assigned or published within GPOs. In our earlier example, this means that Office 2000 would be uninstalled for User A. If, however, the box is left unchecked, the application would remain installed.

Now, let's look at some more options that are available for managing software settings.

## Managing File Extension Mappings

One of the potential problems associated with the use of many different file types is that it's difficult to keep track of which applications work with which files. For example, if I received a file with the extension .abc, I would have no idea which application I would need to view it. And Windows would not be of much help, either!

Fortunately, through software deployment settings, systems administrators can specify mappings for specific *file extensions*. For example, I could specify that whenever users attempt to access a file with the extension .vsd, the operating system should attempt to open the file using the Visio diagramming software. If Visio is not installed on the user's machine, the computer could automatically download and install it (assuming that the application has been properly advertised).

This method allows users to have applications automatically installed when they are needed. The following is an example of the sequence of events that might occur:

- A user receives an e-mail message that contains an Adobe Acrobat file attachment.

- The Windows 2000 computer realizes that Adobe Acrobat, the appropriate viewing application for this type of file, is not installed. However, it also realizes that a file extension mapping is available within the Active Directory software deployment settings.

- The client computer automatically requests the Adobe Acrobat software package from the server and uses the Windows Installer to automatically install the application.

- The Windows 2000 computer opens the attachment for the user.

Notice that all of these steps were carried out without any further interaction with the user! You can manage file extension mappings by viewing the properties for any package that you have defined within the Group Policy settings. Figure 11.5 shows how file extension settings can be managed. By default, the list of file extensions that you'll see is based on the specific software packages you have added to the current GPO.

**FIGURE 11.5** Managing file extensions

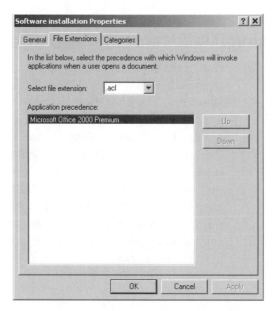

## Creating Application Categories

In many network environments, the list of supported applications can include hundreds of items. For users who are looking for only one specific program, searching through a list of all of these programs can be difficult and time-consuming.

Fortunately, there are methods for categorizing the applications that are available on your network. You can easily manage the application categories for users and computers by right-clicking the Software Installation item, selecting Properties, and then clicking the Categories tab. Figure 11.6 shows you how application categories can be created. It is a good idea to use category names that are meaningful to users because it will make it easier for them to find the programs they're looking for.

**FIGURE 11.6**   Creating application categories

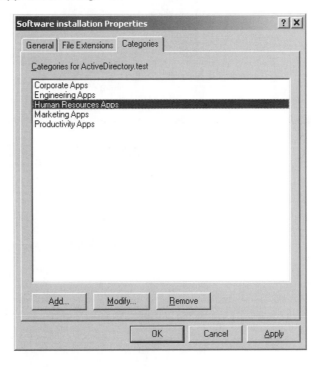

Once the software installation categories have been created, you can view them by opening the Add/Remove Programs item in the Control Panel. When you click Add New Programs, you'll see that there are several options in the Category drop-down list (see Figure 11.7). Now, when you select the properties for a package, you will be able to assign the application to one or more of the categories (as shown in Figure 11.8).

**FIGURE 11.7** Viewing application categories in Add/Remove Programs

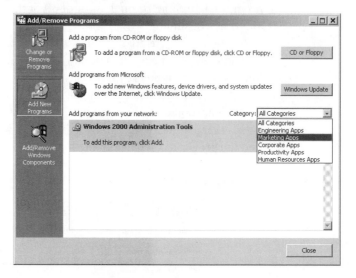

**FIGURE 11.8** Specifying categories for application packages

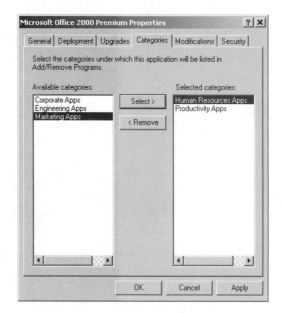

## Removing Programs

As we discussed in the beginning of the chapter, an important phase in the software management life cycle is the removal of applications. Fortunately, using the Active Directory and Windows Installer packages, the process is simple. To remove an application, you can right-click the package within the Group Policy settings and select All Tasks ➢ Remove (see Figure 11.9).

**FIGURE 11.9**   Removing a software package

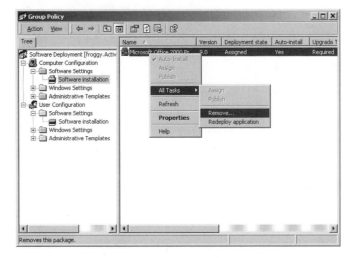

When choosing to remove a software package from a GPO, you have two options:

**Immediately Uninstall the Software from Users and Computers**   Systems administrators can choose this option to ensure that an application is no longer available to users who are affected by the GPO. When this option is selected, the program will be automatically uninstalled from users and/or computers that have the package. This option might be useful, for example, if the licensing for a certain application has expired or if a program is no longer on the approved applications list.

**Allow Users to Continue to Use the Software, but Prevent New Installations**   This option prevents users from making new installations of a package, but it does not remove the software if it has already been installed for users. This is a good option if the company has run out of additional licenses for the software, but the existing licenses are still valid.

Figure 11.10 shows the two removal options that are available.

**FIGURE 11.10** Software removal options

If you no longer require the ability to install or repair an application, you can delete it from your software distribution share point by deleting the appropriate Windows Installer package files. This will free up additional disk space for newer applications.

## Windows Installer Settings

There are several options that influence the behavior of the Windows Installer, that can be set within a GPO. These options are accessed by navigating to User Configuration ➢ Administrative Templates ➢ Windows Components ➢ Windows Installer. The options include the following:

**Always Install with Elevated Privileges** This policy allows users to install applications that require elevated privileges. For example, if a user does not have the permissions necessary to modify the Registry, but the installation program must make Registry changes, this policy will allow the process to succeed.

**Search Order** This setting specifies the order in which the Windows Installer will search for installation files. The options include *n* (for network shares), *m* (for searching removal media), and *u* (for searching the Internet for installation files).

**Disable Rollback** When this option is enabled, the Windows Installer does not store the system state information that's required to roll back the installation of an application. Systems administrators may choose this option to reduce the amount of temporary disk space required during installation and to increase the performance of the installation operation. However, the drawback is that the system cannot roll back to its original state if the installation fails and the application needs to be removed.

**Disable Media Source for Any Install**   This option disallows the installation of software using removable media (such as CD-ROM, DVD, or floppy disks). It is useful for ensuring that users install only approved applications.

With these options, systems administrators can control how the Windows Installer operates for specific users who are affected by the GPO.

# Optimizing and Troubleshooting Software Deployment

**A**lthough the features in Windows 2000 and the Active Directory make software deployment a relatively simple task, there are still many factors that systems administrators should consider when making applications available on the network. In this section, we will discuss some common methods for troubleshooting problems with software deployment in Windows 2000 and optimizing the performance of software deployment.

| *Microsoft*<br>✓ *Exam*<br>*Objective* | **Manage and troubleshoot software by using Group Policy.**<br><br>• Troubleshoot common problems that occur during software deployment. |
| --- | --- |

Specific optimization and troubleshooting methods include those that follow:

**Test packages before deployment.**   The use of the Active Directory and GPOs makes publishing and assigning applications so easy that systems administrators may be tempted to make many applications available to users immediately. However, the success of using the Windows Installer is at least partially based on the quality of the programming of developers and third-party software vendors.

Before unleashing an application on the unsuspecting user population, you should always test the programs within a test environment using a few volunteer users and computers. The information gathered during these tests can be invaluable in helping the help desk, systems administrators, and end users during a large-scale deployment.

**Manage Group Policy scope and links.** One of the most flexible aspects of deploying software with the Active Directory is the ability to assign Group Policy settings to users and computers. Since it is so easy to set up GPOs and link them to Active Directory objects, it might be tempting to modify all of your existing GPOs to meet the current software needs of your users. Note, however, that this can become difficult to manage.

An easier way to manage multiple sets of applications may be to create separate GPOs for specific groups of applications. For example, one GPO could provide all end user productivity applications (such as Microsoft Office 2000 and Adobe Acrobat Reader) while another GPO could provide tools for users in the Engineering department. Now, whenever the software requirements for a group changes, systems administrators can just enable or disable specific GPOs for the OU that contains these users.

**Roll out software in stages.** Installing software packages over the network can involve high bandwidth requirements and reduce the performance of production servers. If you're planning to roll out a new application to several users or computers, it's a good idea to deploy the software in stages. This process involves publishing or assigning applications to a few users at a time, through the use of GPOs and OUs.

**Verify connectivity with the software distribution share.** If clients are unable to communicate with the server that contains the software installation files, the Windows Installer will be unable to automatically copy the required information to the client computer, and installation will fail. You should always ensure that clients are able to communicate with the server and verify the permissions on the software installation share.

**Organize categories.** The list of applications that are available in a typical network environment can quickly grow very large. From standard commercial Desktop applications and utilities to custom client-server applications, it's important to organize programs based on functionality. Be sure to group software packages into categories that end users will clearly recognize and understand when searching for applications.

**Create an installation log file.** By using the `msiexec.exe` command, you can create an installation log file that records the actions attempted during the installation process and any errors that may have been generated.

**Reduce redundancy.** In general, it is better to ensure that applications are not assigned or published to users through multiple GPOs. For example, if a user almost always logs on to the same workstation and requires specific applications to be available, you may consider assigning the applications to both the user and the computer. Although this scenario will work properly, it can increase the amount of time spent during logon and the processing of the GPOs. A better solution would be to assign the applications to only the computer (or, alternatively, to only the user).

**Manage software distribution points.** When users require applications, they will depend on the availability of installation shares. To ensure greater performance and availability of these shares, you can use the Windows 2000 Distributed File System (DFS). The features of DFS allow for fault tolerance and the ability to use multiple servers to share commonly used files from a single logical share point. The end result is increased uptime, better performance, and easier access for end users. Additionally, the underlying complexity of where certain applications are stored is isolated from the end user.

**Encourage developers and vendors to create Microsoft Installer packages.** Many of the benefits of the software deployment features in Windows 2000 rely on the use of MSI packages. To ease the deployment and management of applications, ensure that in-house application developers and third-party independent software vendors use Microsoft Installer packages that were created properly. The use of MSI packages will greatly assist systems administrators and end users in assigning and managing applications throughout the life cycle of the product.

**Enforce consistency using MSI options.** One of the problems with applications and application suites (such as Microsoft Office 2000) is that end users can choose to specify which options are available during installation. While this might be useful for some users, it can cause compatibility and management problems. For example, suppose a manager sends a spreadsheet containing Excel pivot tables to several employees. Some employees are able to access the pivot tables (since they chose the default installation options), but others cannot (since they chose not to install this feature). The users who cannot properly read the spreadsheet will likely generate help desk calls and require assistance to add in the appropriate components.

One way to avoid problems such as these is to enforce standard configurations for applications. For example, we may choose to create a basic and an advanced package for Microsoft Office 2000. The Basic package would include the most-used applications, such as Microsoft Word, Microsoft Outlook, and Microsoft Excel. The advanced package would include these applications, plus Microsoft PowerPoint and Microsoft Access.

**Create Windows Installer files for older applications.**   Although there is no tool included with Windows 2000 to automatically perform this task, it will generally be worth the time to create Windows Installer files for older applications. This is done through the use of third-party applications that are designed to monitor the Registry, file system, and other changes that an application makes during the setup process. These changes can then be combined into a single MSI package for use in software deployment.

By carefully planning for software deployment and using some of the advanced features of Windows 2000, you can make software deployment a smooth and simple process for systems administrators and end users alike.

---

 **Real World Scenario**

**Understanding Application Architecture and Managing Software Rollouts**

The world of computing has moved through various stages and methodologies throughout the past several decades. Real-world business computing began with large, centralized machines called mainframes. In this model, all processing occurred on a central machine and "clients" were little more than keyboards and monitors connected with long extension cords. A potential disadvantage was that client relied solely on these central machines for their functionality, and the mainframe tended to be less flexible.

Then, with the dramatic drop in the cost of personal computers, the computing industry moved more to a client-based model. In this model, the majority of processing occurred on individual computers. The drawback, however, was that is was difficult to share information (even with networking capabilities), and such critical tasks as data management, backup, and security were challenges.

Since then, various technologies have appeared to try to give us good features from both worlds. A new and promising method of delivering application has been through the Application Service Provider (ASP) model. In this method, clients are relatively "thin" (that is, they do not perform much processing, nor do they store data); however, users still have access to the tools they need to do their jobs. The software provider is responsible for maintaining the software (including upgrades, backups, security, performance monitoring, etc.), and your company might engage an ASP through a monthly-fee arrangement.

In some respects, during the past several years, we've moved back toward housing business-critical functionality on relatively large, central servers. However, we've retained powerful client machines that are capable of performing processing for certain types of applications. In a lot of cases, that makes sense. For example, users of Microsoft Office applications have several advantages if they run their applications on their own machines. Other applications, such as a centralized sales-tracking and management tool, might make more sense to reside on a server. However, the fact remains that modern computers are marginally useful without software applications that make practical use of their power and features.

As an IT professional, it's important to understand the business reasons when evaluating an application architecture. Traditionally, the deployment of standard Windows applications was a tedious, error-prone, and inexact process. For example, if a user deleted a critical file, the entire application may have had to be removed and reinstalled. Or, if an application replaced a shared file with one that was incompatible with other applications, you could end up in a situation affectionately referred to as "DLL Hell". Microsoft has attempted to address the sore spot of application deployment and management with the use of the Active Directory and Windows Installer technology. However, it's up to developers and system administrators to take full advantage of these new methods.

As an IT professional, you should urge developers to create installation packages using the Windows Installer architecture. In many ways, it's much simpler to create an Installer package than it is to create the old-style setup programs. On the IT side, be sure that you take advantage of the Active Directory's ability to assign and publish applications. And, when it comes time to update a client-side application, be sure to make use of the Windows Installer's ability to generate patch files that can quickly and easily update an installation with minimal effort. This method can roll out application updates to thousands of computers in just a few days!

All of these features can cut down on a large amount of support effort that's required when, for example, a user needs to install a file viewer for a file that she received via e-mail. And, for applications that just don't make sense on the Desktop, consider the use of Application Service Providers. Outsourced applications can allow you to avoid a lot of these headaches altogether. There's a huge array of options, and it's up to you to make the best choice for your applications!

# Summary

The real reason for deploying and managing networks in the first place is to make the applications that they support available. End users are often much more interested in being able to do their jobs using the tools they require than in worrying about network infrastructure and directory services. In the past, software deployment and management have been troublesome and time-consuming tasks.

In this chapter, we covered the following:

- Ways in which new Windows 2000 features can be used to manage the tasks related to software deployment and the benefits of the Windows Installer technology

- How the Active Directory, Group Policy objects, and the Windows Installer interact to simplify software deployment

- How to publish and assign applications to Active Directory objects

- The tasks associated with deploying, managing, and removing applications using Group Policy

- How to create a network share from which applications can be installed

- How to remotely control software deployment options and configuration through the use of Active Directory administration tools

- How to troubleshoot problems with software deployment

When implemented correctly, the use of the Active Directory software deployment features can save much time, reduce headaches, and improve the end-user experience.

# Exam Essentials

**Identify common problems with the software life cycle.**   IT professionals face many challenges with client applications, including development, deployment, maintenance, and troubleshooting.

**Understand the benefits of the Windows Installer.**   The Windows Installer is an updated way to install applications on Windows-based machines. It offers a more robust method for making the system changes required by applications, and it allows for a cleaner uninstall. Windows Installer–based applications can also take advantage of new Active Directory features.

**Understand the difference between publishing and assigning applications.**   Some applications can be assigned to users and computers so that they are always available. And, they can be published to users so that they may be installed with a minimal amount of effort when a user requires them.

**Know how to prepare for software deployment.**   Before your users can take advantage of automated software installation, you must set up an installation share and provide the appropriate permissions.

**Know how to configure application settings using the Active Directory and Group Policy.**   Using standard Windows 2000 administrative tools, you can create an application policy that meets the needs of your requirements.

Features include automatic, on-demand installation of applications when they're needed.

**Create application categories to simplify the list of published applications.** It's important to group applications by functionality or the users to whom they apply, especially in organizations that support a large number of programs.

**Be able to troubleshoot problems with software deployment.** There are several methods for deploying applications and for testing to make sure that they are working properly. Should you find a problem with a particular installation of software, you can use various methods to repair and/or remove the specific product.

# Key Terms

Before you take the exam, be certain you are familiar with the following terms:

Add/Remove Programs

application assignment scripts

assigning

categories

file extensions

initialization files

patches

publishing

transformation files

Windows Installer

Windows Installer packages

# Review Questions

1. Alicia is a systems administrator for a large organization. Recently, the company has moved most of its workstations and servers to the Windows 2000 platform, and Alicia wants to take advantage of the new software deployment features of the Active Directory. Specifically, she wants to do the following:

   - Make applications available to users through the Add/Remove Programs Control Panel applet.

   - Group applications based on functionality or the types of users who might require them.

   - Avoid the automatic installation of applications for users and computers.

   Which of the following steps should Alicia take to meet these requirements? (Choose all that apply.)

   **A.** Create application categories.

   **B.** Set up a software installation share and assign the appropriate security permissions.

   **C.** Assign applications to users.

   **D.** Assign applications to computers.

   **E.** Create new file extension mappings.

   **F.** Create application definitions using the Active Directory and Group Policy administration tools.

2. A systems administrator has created a Software Deployment GPO. Which tool can they use to link this GPO to an existing OU?

   **A.** Active Directory Users and Computers

   **B.** Active Directory Domains and Trusts

   **C.** Add/Remove Programs Control Panel applet

   **D.** Computer Management

   **E.** All of the above

**3.** Emma wants to make a specific application available on the network. She finds that using Group Policy for software deployment will be the easiest way. She has the following requirements:

- All users of designated workstations should have access to use Microsoft Office 2000.

- If a user moves to other computers on which Microsoft Office 2000 is not installed, they should not have access to this program.

Which of the following options should Emma choose to meet these requirements?

**A.** Assign the application to computers.

**B.** Assign the application to users.

**C.** Publish the application to computers.

**D.** Publish the application to users.

**E.** All of the above.

**4.** A systems administrator wants to ensure that a particular user will have access to Microsoft Office 2000 regardless of the computer to which they log on. Which of the following should they do?

**A.** Assign the application to all computers within the environment and specify that only this user should have access to it.

**B.** Assign the application to the user.

**C.** Publish the application to all computers within the environment and specify that only this user should have access to it.

**D.** Publish the application to the user.

**E.** All of the above.

**5.** A systems administrator wants to ensure that a particular group of users will be able to install Microsoft Office 2000 by using the Add/ Remove Programs applet in the Control Panel. They do not want the applications to be automatically installed. Which of the following should they do?

**A.** Assign the application to their computers.

**B.** Assign the application to the users.

**C.** Publish the application to their computers.

**D.** Publish the application to the users.

**E.** All of the above.

**6.** The files required to install published and assigned applications are stored within

**A.** The Active Directory data store

**B.** File shares

**C.** The Global Catalog

**D.** The System32 directory on all domain controllers

**E.** The System32 directory on specific domain controllers

**F.** None of the above

**7.** In order to install assigned or published applications, a user must have which of the following permissions?

**A.** Ability to modify the Registry

**B.** Local Administrator permissions

**C.** Ability to create directories

**D.** None of the above

8. You are responsible for applications management in your medium-sized network environment. Recently, your organization began deploying a new custom-developed application to your users. On slow client machines, the installation process can take a long time. In some cases, users have chosen to abort the installation process so that they can perform it at a later time. You are now receiving complaints from several users who say that they attempted to cancel the installation process, but the system changes that the application made were not rolled back.

Which of the following Windows Installer settings may be responsible for this?

A. Always Install with Elevated Privileges

B. Disable Rollback

C. Disable Search Order

D. Disallow Uninstall

E. None of the above

9. Which of the following statements is true regarding the actions that occur when a software package is removed from a GPO that is linked to an OU?

A. The application will be automatically uninstalled for all users with the OU.

B. Current application installations will be unaffected by the change.

C. The systems administrator may determine the effect.

D. None of the above.

**10.** You have recently created a new software deployment package for installing a new line-of-business application on many users' systems. You have the following requirements:

- You want to use the features of the Active Directory and Group Policy to automatically deploy the software.

- The software should be installed on specific machines within the environment only.

- The application must be made available with minimal user intervention.

Which of the following steps must be performed in order to meet these requirements? (Choose all that apply.)

**A.** Refresh the Active Directory.

**B.** Synchronize all domain controllers.

**C.** Rebuild the Global Catalog.

**D.** Manually copy the required files to an appropriate file share and set the appropriate permissions on the share.

**E.** Assign the application to the appropriate computers.

**F.** Publish the application to the appropriate computers.

11. Andrew is a Help Desk operator for a large organization. Recently, he has been receiving a large number of calls from users who are attempting to open files for which they do not have viewers. For example, one user wants to open a file named MarketingInfo.ppt, but she does not have the Microsoft PowerPoint viewer installed. Andrew has the following requirements:

   - The appropriate application should automatically be installed when a user clicks specific file types.

   - Applications should not be automatically installed in other circumstances.

   - The installation of applications, when they are needed, should require minimal user intervention.

   Which of the following Group Policy software deployment features should Andrew use? (Choose all that apply.)

   **A.** Categories

   **B.** Publishing options

   **C.** Assignment options

   **D.** File extensions

   **E.** None of the above

12. An applications developer wants to create a patch for an existing application. Which of the following types of files should they create?

   **A.** MSI

   **B.** MSP

   **C.** ZAP

   **D.** AAS

   **E.** None of the above

**13.** How can a systems administrator get more information about a specific Windows Installer setup file?

   **A.** By right-clicking the file and selecting Properties in Windows Explorer

   **B.** By issuing a search within the Active Directory

   **C.** By querying the Global Catalog

   **D.** None of the above

**14.** Jenny is responsible for application deployment in a medium-sized company that is using the Active Directory. She has already configured her Windows 2000 Server computers to deploy new applications (that are packaged using the Windows Installer) automatically. However, she has recently been tasked with the automatic deployment of some applications that use a legacy installation routine.

   How can Jenny create a Windows Installer package from a legacy setup program?

   **A.** By right-clicking the `Setup.exe` file for the application and choosing Migrate

   **B.** By right-clicking the `Setup.exe` file for the application and choosing Upgrade to Windows Installer

   **C.** By adding the application to the Active Directory

   **D.** By placing the application within a Shared Folder object and then assigning the application to the appropriate client computers

   **E.** None of the above

**15.** You want to publish an application by using a GPO. In the GPO shown below, what would you do next in order to publish an application?

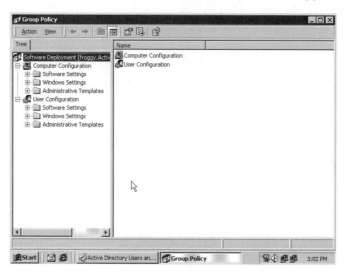

**A.** Right-click Software Settings under Computer Configuration and select New ➤ Package.

**B.** Expand Software Settings under Computer Configuration, right-click Software Installation, and select New ➤ Package.

**C.** Expand Software Settings under User Configuration, right-click Software Installation, and select New ➤ Package.

**D.** Right-click Software Settings under User Configuration and select New ➤ Package.

# Answers to Review Questions

1. A, B, F. Alicia should first create an application share from which programs can be installed. Then, she can define which applications are available on the network. The purpose of application categories is to logically group applications in the Add/Remove Programs Control Panel applet. The other options can result in the automatic installation of applications for users and computers (something that she wants to avoid).

2. A. Group Policy links can be created within the Active Directory Users and Computers tool.

3. A. Assigning the application to the computer will ensure that all users who access the workstation will have access to Microsoft Office 2000.

4. B. Assigning the application to the user ensures that the user will have access to Microsoft Office 2000, regardless of the computer they use.

5. D. When applications are published to users, they can easily install the programs using the Add/Remove Programs icon in the Control Panel.

6. B. Published and assigned applications must be stored within a share on a file server and must be accessible to client computers.

7. D. The Windows Installer is able to use the Installer service to bypass user permissions for installing software. Therefore, the user performing the installation is not required to have any of the permissions listed.

8. B. Disabling rollback can improve performance and reduce disk space requirements, but this option prevents rolling back from a failed installation.

9. C. The systems administrator can specify whether the application will be uninstalled or if future installations will be prevented.

10. D, E. It is the responsibility of the systems administrator to copy installation files to a software deployment share point and ensure that users can access these files. Once this is done, the applications can be assigned to various computers within the environment.

**11.** B, D. Publishing makes the applications available for automatic installation. File extension settings can be used to specify the applications that are installed when specific file types are accessed. This method requires minimal user intervention since it occurs automatically in the background.

**12.** B. Patch (MSP) files are used to update existing applications.

**13.** A. Details about MSI files can be viewed by right-clicking the file and selecting Properties. The other options may be available, but only if software deployment is configured within the Active Directory.

**14.** E. In order to create a Windows Installer package from a legacy setup program, the application must be repackaged, or you must use a third-party utility. These applications and utilities must be obtained from third-party software vendors and are not included as a supported part of the Windows 2000 operating system.

**15.** C. Software can only be published to users, not computers. You can assign software to users or computers.

# Chapter

## 12

# Installing and Configuring RIS

## MICROSOFT EXAM OBJECTIVES COVERED IN THIS CHAPTER:

✓ **Deploy Windows 2000 by using Remote Installation Services (RIS).**

- Install an image on a RIS client computer.
- Create a RIS boot disk.
- Configure remote installation options.
- Troubleshoot RIS problems.
- Manage images for performing remote installations.

✓ **Configure RIS security.**

- Authorize a RIS server.
- Grant computer account creation rights.
- Prestage RIS client computers for added security and load balancing.

If you ask a systems administrator about the most painful parts of their job, you're likely to hear about the pain associated with hardware and software rollouts. Deploying new computers begins with the installation of the operating system. In most environments, this involves having a member of the IT staff sit in front of each new computer for at least an hour choosing the appropriate options. The process may be repeated hundreds or even thousands of times (based on the size of the environment and the number of computers supported).

Apart from the obvious problems—risking death by boredom and allocating potentially productive time to the installation process—manual installations are plagued by inconsistent configurations. It's difficult to remember all of the options that must be configured and to carry out these processes consistently on multiple installations. Clearly, there's a need for a better solution.

Recognizing this problem, Microsoft has included *Remote Installation Services (RIS)* components with Windows 2000 Server. RIS is designed to allow client computers to boot onto a network and immediately begin installing Windows 2000 Professional over the network. This chapter looks at the various technical steps required to install, configure, manage, secure, and troubleshoot RIS. With any luck, you'll never need to sit in front of a Windows 2000 Professional installation progress bar!

# Overview of RIS

One of the dullest and most time-consuming duties of systems administrators is the process of installing and rolling out new PCs. It's a never-ending job because employees are always being added to companies and computers are often upgraded or transferred between users. Worse yet, the process is generally quite repetitive and requires handholding by a systems administrator. Finally, no matter how many times these installations are carried out, it seems that some aspect of the configuration is easily left behind.

Many companies use disk-duplication methods to create an image of a base workstation configuration and then to apply this image to multiple other computers. However, there are several potential problems with this method:

- It can be time consuming to create and generate disk images.

- Workstation images are hardware specific. That is, since the hardware-detection phase of a normal setup process is not carried out, two computers that have, for example, different video adapters must use two completely separate images.

- Images take up large amounts of disk space. Since each different configuration requires the storage of all data from a computer's hard disk, the size and number of the potential files can become quite large.

- Security Identifiers (SIDs) are duplicated between multiple machines. This issue is particularly troublesome in a Windows NT 4 environment. Although there are tools that can consistently change SIDs on imaged computers, this adds an extra step to the process and can be time consuming.

The purpose of RIS is to alleviate the problems and minimize the time associated with installing Windows 2000 Professional on computers, while, at the same time, preserving the benefits of performing individual operating-system installations. RIS works through the creation of images and settings for a remote installation on a RIS server. Clients then connect to the RIS server over the network and install the operating system using settings that are predefined by the systems administrator.

One of the major benefits of using RIS is that the hardware configuration does not have to be an exact match between client machines. The Windows 2000 Plug-and-Play and automatic-hardware-detection features will iron out any differences when the image is applied on client computers. Additionally, RIS is easy to install and configure.

Now that we have an idea of the problems RIS attempts to solve, let's look at the details regarding what you'll need to implement and administer RIS in a Windows 2000 environment!

# Prerequisites for RIS

RIS works only with the Windows 2000 operating system platform. That means that you must be running Windows 2000 Server (which acts as the RIS server) and that you plan to install Windows 2000 Professional on client computers. Based on this information, let's drill down into the details of what's required on the server and client computers.

## RIS Server Requirements

RIS relies upon several different network and operating features and services to function properly. In order to take advantage of RIS, you must have the following services installed, configured, and enabled on your network:

**DNS**   The Domain Name System (DNS) is used for resolving TCP/IP addresses to host names. Active Directory domain controllers and clients rely on DNS services for finding network resources.

**DHCP**   The Dynamic Host Configuration Protocol (DHCP) automatically assigns TCP/IP configuration information to clients. This is especially important for remote boot clients since they must be able to communicate on the network and connect to the RIS server.

**Active Directory**   The Active Directory hosts the Computer accounts used by RIS and allows administrators to control permissions to log on to the domain. Also, the Active Directory's Group Policies are used to specify client options. (These services are required for use by RIS clients.) Finally, security permissions related to which users and computers can be used for a remote installation are stored within the Active Directory.

For more information on DNS and DHCP, see Chapter 2, "Integrating DNS with the Active Directory."

When RIS is installed on a Windows 2000 Server computer, three services are automatically installed and configured:

**Boot Information Negotiation Layer (BINL)**   The *Boot Information Negotiation Layer (BINL)* service is responsible for ensuring that the correct computer is being installed and can be used to create a Computer account within an Active Directory domain.

**Trivial File Transfer Protocol Daemon (TFTPD)**   When a client is first connected to the RIS server computer, it only has the bare minimum information required to communicate. At this stage, the *Trivial File Transfer Protocol Daemon (TFTPD)* service is used to transfer any required files from the server to the client.

**Single Instance Store (SIS)**   *Single Instance Store (SIS)* technology is created to reduce the redundancy of data stored on a RIS server. One of the major problems with creating multiple boot images is that they can take up much disk space. For example, if we were to create six images (with an average size of 300MB each), this would require 1.8GB of disk space. Although this is not a huge amount of space on modern servers, there is a lot of wasted space due to the fact that most files between these images are the same. Consider, for example, that each of the 5,000+ files that reside in the I386 directory would have to be stored six times!

The SIS is designed to eliminate this type of redundant storage by finding duplicate files and then replacing them with a link to one file. For example, suppose the MyProgram.exe file is stored four times on the disk. The SIS notices this and replaces all but one instance of the file with links that point to the real file. Then, whenever a client attempts to access the file, the SIS automatically finds the real copy of the file.

As we'll see later in this chapter, each of these three services is important in the process of automating client installations.

Finally, you should be aware of the following minimum system requirements for a RIS server (as specified by Microsoft):

- Pentium-166 (or equivalent) processor

- 256MB RAM

- 2GB disk drive (reserved for use only by RIS)

- 10MB network adapter

- CD-ROM drive

The disk-space requirement is somewhat unique. The image files created for RIS must be stored on an NTFS volume that does not contain either the Windows 2000 system files or the boot files. The RIS process is resource intensive, especially with respect to disk input/output (I/O). Therefore, it is recommended that your RIS server computers exceed these values for better performance.

Now that we've covered the server side, let's look at the requirements for the client computers.

# RIS Client Requirements

On the client side, you must use a desktop computer with a network interface card or a laptop computer with a port replicator or docking station. Windows 2000 RIS does not support the use of laptop or notebook computers that use PC Card or PCMCIA network adapters for the purpose of connecting to a RIS server.

Client computers may use one of two methods to gain network access and connect to the RIS server:

**Using a PXE Boot ROM**   The *Preboot eXecution Environment (PXE)* specification is designed to allow computers that do not have an operating system to access the network. The PXE Boot Read-Only Memory (ROM) chip is part of a computer's hardware. Its purpose is to allow the computer to initialize the network adapter and to then gain access to the network using DHCP.

Most recent-model computers contain network cards that include a PXE Boot ROM. Computers that meet the Net PC/PC 98 specification must include a PXE Boot ROM. In order to determine whether or not a client computer has a PXE Boot ROM, consult your computer vendor or manufacturer.

**Using a Boot Floppy**   For older computers that do not contain a PXE Boot ROM, there's another option: booting from a floppy disk that contains the bare minimum information to connect to the network and communicate with the RIS server. Windows 2000 Server includes a utility that can be used to create these disks. The utility (which we'll cover in detail later in this chapter) contains drivers for several popular network cards. In order to successfully use a boot floppy for connecting to a RIS server, the client network adapter must be supported.

Regarding the hardware configuration, client computers should meet the following minimum specifications:

- Pentium-166 (or equivalent) processor
- 32MB RAM

- 1.2GB hard disk

- Network adapter

- PXE Boot ROM version .99c or later

As with the server side, it is recommended that a computer have a faster processor, more memory, and a larger hard disk than that specified. A faster network adapter also reduces the required installation time.

# Implementing and Administering a RIS Server

The heart of the RIS system in Windows 2000 Server is the feature that enables it to manage images and provide remote installation shares for clients. Although there are many configuration options, the process of installing and configuring RIS is simplified through the use of various Wizards. This section looks at the exact steps that are required to install a RIS server.

---

*Microsoft*
✓ *Exam*
*Objective*

**Deploy Windows 2000 by using Remote Installation Services (RIS).**

- Configure remote installation options.

- Manage images for performing remote installations.

**Configure RIS security.**

- Authorize a RIS server.

- Grant computer account creation rights.

- Prestage RIS client computers for added security and load balancing.

---

## Installing RIS

Installation of RIS is a straightforward process that involves two main steps. First, you must add the RIS service to a Windows 2000 Server and then reboot the computer. Next, you must configure the RIS server based on the options you require. Exercise 12.1 walks you through the process of installing RIS.

---

**EXERCISE 12.1**

## Installing Remote Installation Services

In this exercise, you will install RIS. In order to complete the steps in this exercise, you must have access to the Windows 2000 Server CD-ROM or a network location that contains the necessary files.

1. Click Start ➤ Settings ➤ Control Panel. Double-click the Add/Remove Programs icon.

2. Click Add/Remove Windows Components.

3. To add a new item, click the Components button.

4. Place a check mark next to the Remote Installation Services item, and then click Next.

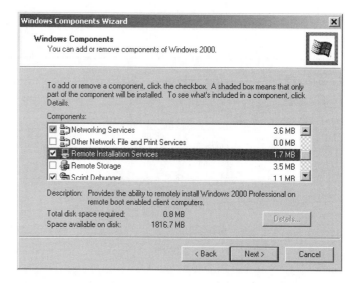

5. If you have installed any optional Windows 2000 components that require additional configuration (such as Terminal Services), you will be prompted to enter the configuration information for these items. The installation process will begin. When it has finished, you will be prompted to restart the computer. Choose Yes to restart the computer.

---

# Configuring a RIS Server

Once RIS has been installed on the server, you need to configure the service to meet the needs of your network environment. There are two main options that can be configured for the RIS server:

**Respond to all clients requesting service.** This option enables the RIS server to respond to remote installation requests from clients. If this option is disabled, clients are not able to access the server for remote installation.

**Do not respond to unknown client computers.** If this option is checked, then a Computer object for the client requesting a remote installation must exist within the Active Directory domain. If a Computer account for the provided *Global Unique Identifier (GUID)* does not exist, the RIS server does not respond to the remote installation request.

You should choose these options carefully since using RIS in an unprotected network environment can be a potential security risk. We'll cover RIS security in detail later in this chapter. For now, let's look at the process involved in creating RIS installation images.

## Creating a CD-Based Image

A RIS server can contain one or more images of operating system installation files. These images contain all of the files necessary to install and configure the Windows 2000 Professional operating system via a remote installation process. There are two main ways to create images for use with RIS. The first involves creating a standard default image through the use of the Windows 2000 Professional CD-ROM; the steps required to do this are shown in Exercise 12.2. The second method (covered in the next section) allows you to create custom images.

---

**EXERCISE 12.2**

### Configuring a CD-Based Image for RIS

In this exercise, you will configure RIS to create a CD-based image of Windows 2000 Professional. In order to complete the steps in this exercise, you must have first completed Exercise 12.1 and have access to the Windows 2000 Professional installation files (located on either a CD-ROM or stored in a network location).

**EXERCISE 12.2** *(continued)*

1. Click Start ➢ Settings Control Panel. Double-click the Add/Remove Windows Components icon.

2. Click Add/Remove Windows Components. Highlight the Configure Remote Installation Services item, and then click the Configure button.

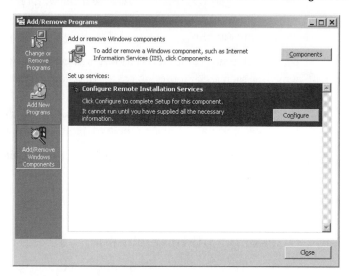

3. You will see the introductory information for the Remote Installation Services Setup Wizard. Click Next to continue.

4. Specify the folder to which the remote installation information will be written. Select a path on a local physical drive that is formatted as an NTFS 5 file system partition and that is neither the boot nor system partition. Ensure that this partition has at least 400MB free (although you will need more if you plan to store many different images). Click Next.

5. On the Initial Settings step, place a check mark next to the Respond to Client Computers Requesting Service option. (This will enable RIS for use by clients.) Click Next.

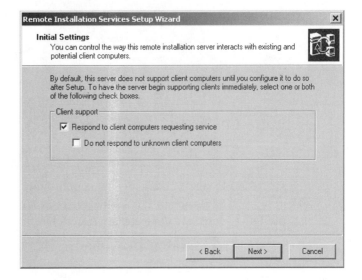

6. Specify the source file location for the Windows installation files. Insert the Windows 2000 Professional CD-ROM, and enter the path to this drive. Alternatively, you can browse for the installation files (which may be on the local system or located on a network drive) by clicking Browse. Once you have selected the appropriate path, click Next to continue.

7. Specify the name of the folder to which the installation files will be copied. The default location will be titled win2000.pro. If you are using multiple images, it is a good idea to use a clear, descriptive name for the image file. Click Next to continue.

**EXERCISE 12.2** *(continued)*

8. Specify a friendly name and a description for this RIS image. This information will be visible to users and systems administrators who are performing remote installations. Therefore, you should make the description as meaningful as possible. Click Next to continue.

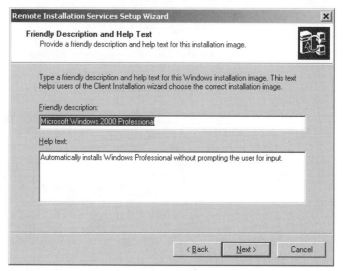

9. Finally, you are given an opportunity to review the settings you have chosen. Ensure that the correct paths have been provided. To complete the installation, click Finish.

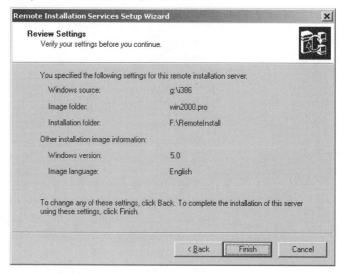

**10.** The RIS Wizard will begin copying the necessary files to the location you specified. This process is likely to take several minutes.

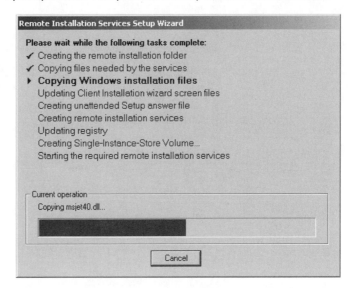

**11.** Once it has finished, you will see a summary of all of the steps performed. To complete the operation, click Done.

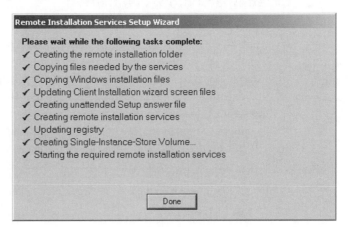

**12.** Close the Add/Remove Programs dialog box and the Control Panel.

Once the Remote Installation Services Setup Wizard has completed, a new share is created on the server. This share, named REMINST, contains all of the files and settings that will be used by clients to access the CD-based image. Figure 12.1 shows the default directories that you will see.

**FIGURE 12.1** Default RIS directories

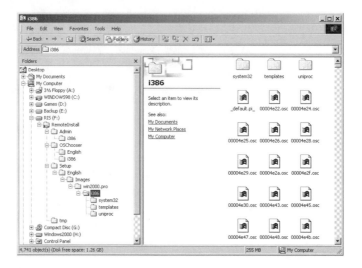

## Creating a Custom Installation

There are usually two main challenges in rolling out new workstation computers. The first involves the installation of the operating system. The second challenge regards configuring the operating system and adding any additional applications that may be required by users of these computers.

Although a CD-based image is sufficient for installing the base operating system, it does not allow you to add any applications or make any other changes to the configuration. The *Remote Installation Preparation (RIPrep) Wizard* is designed to do just that. The process for using RIPrep is as follows:

1. Install Windows 2000 Professional. This can be done using the CD-ROM or by connecting to a network share that contains the necessary files.

2. Configure any operating system settings you want to have copied to client computers. For example, you can change Desktop settings to match your company's default settings. Or you may choose to install optional Windows 2000 components, such as Web services.

3. Install and configure any applications that should be installed as part of the image. (This step is mainly used for installing older applications that do not use the new Microsoft Installer technology, because newer programs can be installed automatically using software deployment. For more information on automating software deployment, see Chapter 11, "Software Deployment through Group Policy.")

4. Close any open applications and then run the RIPrep utility. You will be asked to provide information about the RIS server to which this image will be saved, along with a title and description of the image. The RIPrep utility will collect information about operating system settings and any applications that are installed on the system and then transmit the image to a RIS server.

After using the RIPrep utility, the RIS server will include a new custom image that can be used for installation. Figure 12.2 shows an example of the RIPrep utility screen that allows you to review your settings before you continue with the Wizard. Figure 12.3 shows the screen that allows you to complete the process.

**FIGURE 12.2** Reviewing RIPrep installation settings

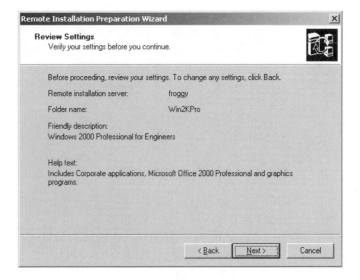

**FIGURE 12.3** Completing the image preparation process

## Using Setup Information Files (SIFs)

Windows 2000 Professional generally requires users or systems administrators to answer many different questions during the setup process. Although this can be done manually, it would be much better to pre-answer the questions and store the settings in a file that can be used by setup.

The specific installation options for the client are specified in a Setup Information File (SIF). These standard text files have the extension .sif and can be edited by systems administrators to specify certain options to be used during the installation process. The following is a portion of the default ristndrd.sif file:

```
[data]
floppyless = "1"
msdosinitiated = "1"
OriSrc = "\\%SERVERNAME%\RemInst\
 %INSTALLPATH%\%MACHINETYPE%"
OriTyp = "4"
LocalSourceOnCD = 1

[SetupData]
OsLoadOptions = "/noguiboot /fastdetect"
```

```
SetupSourceDevice = "\Device\LanmanRedirector\
 %SERVERNAME%\RemInst\%INSTALLPATH%"

[Unattended]
OemPreinstall = no
NoWaitAfterTextMode = 0
FileSystem = LeaveAlone
ExtendOEMPartition = 0
ConfirmHardware = no
NtUpgrade = no
Win31Upgrade = no
TargetPath = \WINNT
OverwriteOemFilesOnUpgrade = no
OemSkipEula = yes
InstallFilesPath = "\\%SERVERNAME%\RemInst\
 A%INSTALLPATH%\%MACHINETYPE%"

[UserData]
FullName = "%USERFULLNAME%"
OrgName = "%ORGNAME%"
ComputerName = %MACHINENAME%

[GuiUnattended]
OemSkipWelcome = 1
OemSkipRegional = 1
TimeZone = %TIMEZONE%
AdminPassword = "*"

[LicenseFilePrintData]
AutoMode = PerSeat

[Display]
ConfigureAtLogon = 0
BitsPerPel = 8
XResolution = 640
YResolution = 480
VRefresh = 60
AutoConfirm = 1
```

```
[Networking]
ProcessPageSections=Yes

[Identification]
JoinDomain = %MACHINEDOMAIN%
CreateComputerAccountInDomain = No
DoOldStyleDomainJoin = Yes

[NetProtocols]
MS_TCPIP=params.MS_TCPIP

[params.MS_TCPIP]
; transport: TC (TCP/IP Protocol)
InfID=MS_TCPIP
DHCP=Yes
```

If you have multiple images on your RIS server, you'll have multiple copies of the `*.sif` files. Each image uses its own SIF, so you can use different sets of installation options. The `*.sif` file can be modified through the use of any standard text editor (such as Windows Notepad).

## Authorizing a RIS Server

Before a RIS server is made available to clients, it must be authorized by a systems administrator. The additional step required to authorize a server adds a measure of security by preventing other individuals from adding new RIS servers to the network.

The authorization process allows clients to gain the services of the DHCP service and the RIS service. Exercise 12.3 walks you through the process of authorizing a RIS server.

### EXERCISE 12.3

**Authorizing a RIS Server**

In this exercise, you will authorize a DHCP server and a RIS server. In order to complete the steps in this exercise, you must have installed and configured RIS (as described in Exercises 12.1 and 12.2) and must not yet have authorized either DHCP or RIS.

1. Log in to the computer as a member of the Domain Admins or Enterprise Admins group.

2. Open the DHCP snap-in from the Administrative Tools program group.

3. Right-click the name of the local computer, and click Authorize.

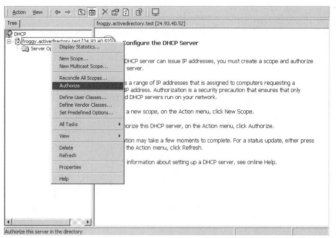

4. When you are finished authorizing the server, close the DHCP administrative tool.

# Managing RIS Server Options

You can change the settings for a RIS server after the service has been configured by opening the Active Directory Users and Computer tool, right-clicking the RIS Server object, and selecting Properties. On the Remote Install tab, you can then change RIS options and settings.

By clicking the Show Clients button, you can automatically find any remote installation clients that are on the network. This is useful when you are trying to determine which computers can be used with RIS.

You can also click the Advanced button to access more options for the RIS server. Here, you'll be able to set options for automatically determining the client computer name. The default options available include the following:

- First initial, last name

- Last name, first initial

- First name, last initial

- Last initial, first name

- Username

- NP Plus MAC (two standard characters followed by the Media Access Card address of the network adapter)

- Custom

By using the Custom option, you can set several different options using variables (see Figure 12.4). This is extremely helpful if you are rolling out several computers, and your organization already has a standard naming convention for client machines.

**FIGURE 12.4**    Setting default client computer name settings

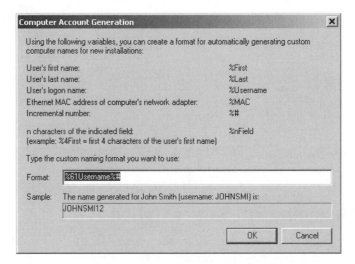

You can also set the location of the Client account within the Active Directory. Options include the following (as shown in Figure 12.5):

**Default Directory Service Location**    This option automatically saves the Computer object to the default location for clients. This is usually the Computers folder.

**Same Location as That of the User Setting Up the Client Computer**
This option saves the Computer account in the Active Directory location in which the user performing the installation process resides. For example, if the user Jane Doe resides within the RIS OU, and this user performs the remote installation, then the Computer object will also reside within the RIS OU.

**The Following Directory Service Location**    Using this option allows systems administrators to specify a single Active Directory location for all new Computer objects. This setting might be useful if, for example, you want to place all Computer objects in a generic container and then manually move them to the appropriate locations later.

**FIGURE 12.5**    Viewing RIS server and Client account location options

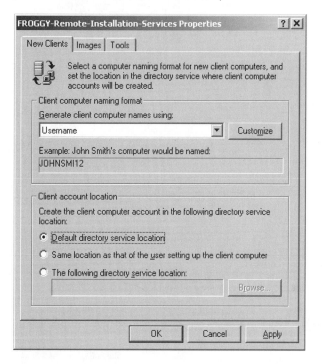

By clicking the Images tab, you will be able to view a list of images that are available on a particular RIS server (see Figure 12.6). You can also add new images, remove images (to make them unavailable for installation), and view the properties of an image (to see the title and description text).

**FIGURE 12.6** Viewing a list of images on a RIS server

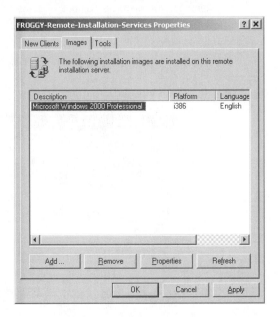

By clicking the Add button, you will access a Wizard that allows you to generate either a new answer file (a SIF, which was described earlier in this chapter) or to generate a new installation image. Figure 12.7 shows the main choices available.

**FIGURE 12.7** The New Answer File or Installation Image Wizard

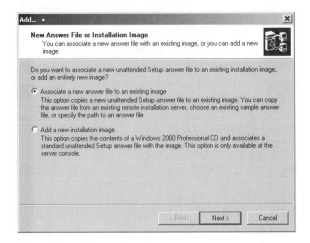

Exercise 12.4 walks you through the detailed steps that are associated with RIS server options.

**Managing RIS Server Options**

In this exercise, you will view the various options that are available when configuring a RIS server. In order to complete the steps in this exercise, you must have first installed RIS on the local computer.

1. Open the Active Directory Users and Computers tool.

2. Find the local domain controller within the Active Directory structure. Right-click the name of this computer, and select Properties.

3. Select the Remote Install tab. Note that you have the option to verify the configuration of the current server. To see any clients that are able to use this RIS server, click the Show Clients button.

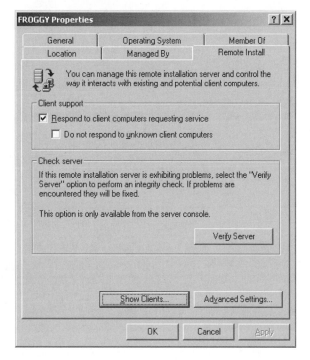

4. Click Advanced Settings to view additional options for the RIS Server.

**EXERCISE 12.4** *(continued)*

5. To manage images, click the Images tab. Note that the list includes any images that are already available for installation. You can find additional information about the images by clicking Properties.

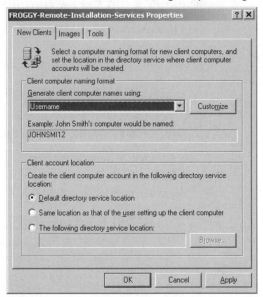

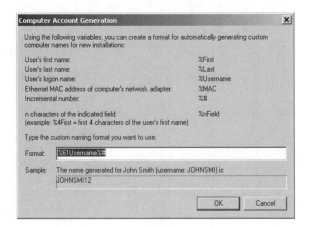

6. Finally, click the Tools tab. By default, this tab will be blank. If, however, you have installed additional Microsoft or third-party tools related to RIS, they will show up here.

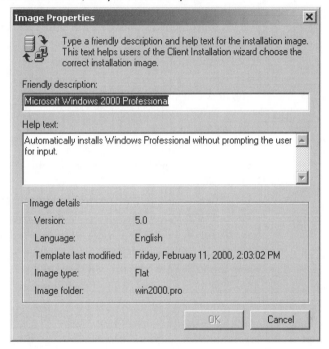

7. Click OK twice to close the settings for the RIS server.

8. When finished, close the Active Directory Users and Computers tool.

By using all of these setting options, you can ensure that your RIS server will behave the way you want it to!

## Prestaging Computer Accounts

Before you install a remote client, you should first create a computer account within a domain. The client computer will use this computer account during installation. When you create the computer account, you will need to set sufficient permissions to allow users to modify the account during installation.

Although you may choose to allow remote clients to request a remote installation from the RIS server, this option reduces security. This is because any valid domain account with the appropriate permissions will be able to install the image to a client computer. Furthermore, you wouldn't be able to control to *which* computer the image will be applied. Certainly, haphazardly installing images to production client machines can cause problems. Another potential problem arises when multiple RIS servers are present in the same network environment. In this case, it would be difficult to tell which RIS server responded to the client first and whether or not it contains the correct images.

So how can systems administrators control the machines that will receive remote installation images? The main method is by *prestaging* client computer accounts within the Active Directory. The process of prestaging involves the creation of a client account, supplying a GUID for the computer, and then specifying the RIS server(s) from which the remote installation can be requested.

In order to uniquely identify computers on the network, there must be some number or value that is dedicated to each machine. For computers that have them, the GUID or *Universally Unique Identifier (UUID)* can be used. This value is set by computer manufacturers and resides in the computers' Basic Input/Output System (BIOS). The BIOS code resides on a chip and is accessed during the startup of the computer. Its purpose is to provide the low-level services and configuration options necessary for system components to interact. For example, the BIOS allows your graphics adapter to use system memory and to communicate with the CPU.

On newer computers, you can find a computer's GUID on a label somewhere on the computer's case. In other cases, the GUID is written inside the computer case. Or you may need to get this value from the system BIOS during the boot process. For specifics, contact your hardware manufacturer or reseller.

A GUID takes the form of a 32-digit hexadecimal (base-16) number. This means that the valid characters for a GUID are the digits zero through nine and the letters A through F (the value is not case sensitive). The format of the number is eight digits, followed by three sets of four digits, followed by 12 digits. For example, the following is a valid GUID:

```
{01234567-ABCD-1234-ABCD-01234567890AB}
```

RIS servers can be configured to respond to specific machine addresses. This adds security to a network environment because it prevents any user from adding a computer to the network and joining the Active Directory. Although it is recommended that this type of security be enabled, the RIS server may also be configured to allow connections from any computer on the network. When this option is chosen, a systems administrator is not required to enter in a GUID when the computer account is created.

Exercise 12.5 walks you through the steps required to prestage a computer account. Using this process, you can ensure that only authorized clients are able to join the domain via RIS, and you can balance the load of remote installations across multiple servers.

---

### EXERCISE 12.5

### Creating a Computer Account

In this exercise, you will create a Computer object within the Active Directory and add the necessary permissions for a user to add the client computer to the Active Directory domain.

1. Open the Active Directory Users and Computers tool.

2. Create a top-level OU called RIS.

3. Within the RIS OU, create a new User object with the name Remote Admin and the logon name remadmin (choose the defaults for all other options).

4. Within the RIS OU, create a Computer object with the name RISClient. Click the Change button to specify the users and groups that will be able to add this computer to a domain. Select Remote Administrator from the list of users, and click OK. Click Next.

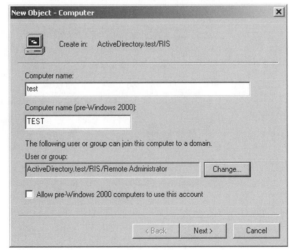

**EXERCISE 12.5** *(continued)*

5. In the Managed dialog box, place a check mark next to the This Is a Managed Computer option. Enter the following (including the {brackets}) for the GUID/UUID value, then click Next:

{123FB937-ED12-11BD-BACD-076A01878937}

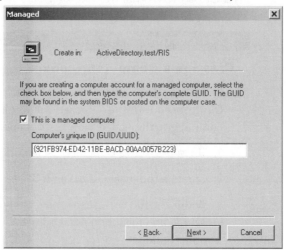

6. In the Host Server dialog box, select the Any Available Remote Installation Server option, and then click Next. Note that you could choose servers from within a specific Active Directory domain if you have multiple RIS servers on the network or if you want the RIS process to be restricted to only one machine.

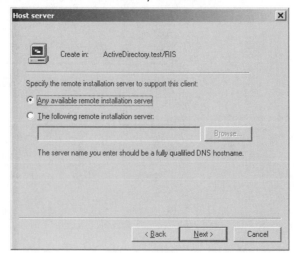

**7.** Click Finish to create the computer account.

**8.** When finished, close the Active Directory Users and Computers tool.

You can also change the RIS settings for an existing computer account by right-clicking a Computer object within the Active Directory and choosing Properties. By clicking the Remote Install tab (as shown in Figure 12.8), you can access the properties of the Computer object.

**FIGURE 12.8** Viewing the Remote Install settings for a Computer object

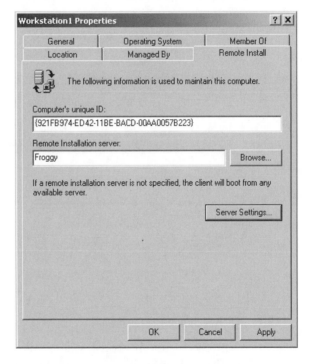

Once a Computer object has been created, you will want to designate which Groups or Users will have permissions to add this computer to the domain using RIS. This can be done by right-clicking a Computer object, choosing Properties, and selecting the Security tab (see Figure 12.9). In order to be able to view this tab, you must ensure that the Advanced Features option is checked within the View menu of the Active Directory Users and Computers console.

**FIGURE 12.9** Viewing the Security settings for a Computer object

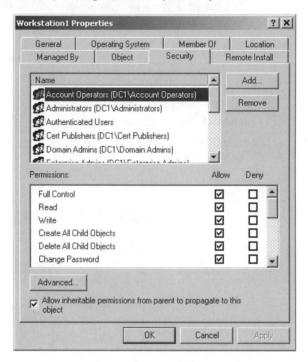

To provide a User or Group with the permissions necessary to add a Computer account to the domain, add the appropriate account(s) and then allow the following permissions:

- Read

- Write

- Reset Password

- Change Password

By clicking on Advanced, you can also set auditing permissions.

Although, in some cases, you may have the appropriate information to create Computer objects before starting the client installation process, you may also want to delegate permissions to create computer accounts within the domain.

## Delegating Permissions to Create Computer Accounts

In addition to setting permissions on specific computer accounts, you can use the Delegation of Control Wizard to allow specific users to create accounts within the domain. This permission must be granted to a user in order to be able to create a new computer account.

The Delegation of Control Wizard within the Active Directory Users and Computers tool is used to assign the appropriate permissions. In the Active Directory Users and Computers tool, right-click the domain name and select Properties. Select Delegate Control. The Wizard will walk you through the steps required to select users and/or groups. As shown in Figure 12.10, you must select the Join a Computer to the Domain permission. For more information on using the Delegation of Control Wizard, see Chapter 7, "Administering the Active Directory," and Chapter 8, "Active Directory Security."

**FIGURE 12.10** Delegating control to join a computer to the domain

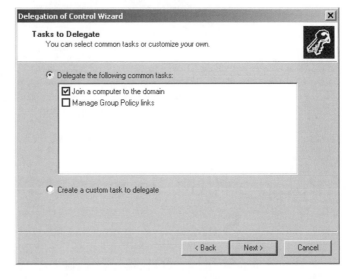

Once you have allowed certain users the permissions to add a computer to the domain, you will not be required to create Computer objects before starting the installation process. Of course, in order for these computers to have access to the RIS server, you must not have set the requirement that computer accounts exist within the domain before the process begins.

In order to allow the creation of Computer objects within an OU, you will need to modify the Group Policy object(s) that apply to the OU. The specific setting you will need to modify can be found in Computer Configuration ➢

Windows Settings ➤ Security Settings ➤ Local Policies ➤ User Rights Assignment. As shown in Figure 12.11, you can add the User and Group objects that will enable you to add computers to the domain by modifying the Add Workstations to Domain option.

**FIGURE 12.11** Setting User Rights to add a computer to the domain

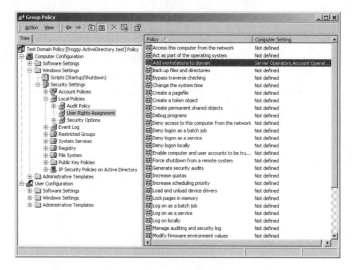

For more information on setting Group Policy, see Chapter 10, "Managing Group Policy."

# Setting Up a RIS Client

So far, we have examined the steps required to set up a RIS server and to configure images. Now, it's time to put this work to use by actually using clients to connect to the server and begin the process. In this section, we'll look at the steps and processes required to install Windows 2000 Professional remotely using RIS.

---

**_Microsoft_** ✓ **_Exam Objective_**

**Deploy Windows 2000 by using Remote Installation Services (RIS).**

- Install an image on a RIS client computer.

- Create a RIS boot disk.

During the client installation process, all information on the hard disk of the client will be lost. Be sure that this is what you want to do before beginning the process. If not, make a backup!

# RIS Installation Process Overview

When performing an automated installation of Windows 2000 using RIS, you will normally be starting with a computer that does not have an operating system installed. Because of this, there are several steps that the client must go through before beginning the actual remote installation process. The following process takes place when a RIS client computer is booted:

1. The computer gains network access through the use of a PXE Boot ROM or a RIS Boot floppy disk.

2. The computer sends a broadcast on the network requesting an IP address; it also sends the computer's GUID.

3. A DHCP server on the computer responds with a valid IP address.

4. The client initiates a remote installation request.

5. The RIS server receives the request and looks in its database for the GUID of the client computer. If the GUID is found, it automatically begins the client installation process. If the GUID is not found, then the client is prompted to authenticate with the server using the Client Installation Wizard prompts.

6. Upon successful negotiation, the RIS server begins transferring files to the client, and the automated installation process proceeds.

All of these steps are performed automatically (with the exception of logging on to the network using the Client Network utility).

**Real World Scenario**

### Planning for a Large Rollout

Recently, you've complete upgrading the majority of your servers to Windows 2000 and have created an Active Directory environment. Now, based on your recommendations, your organization has made the commitment to move all of its 2,000 workstations to the Windows 2000 platform. After thorough testing, it seems that all of the applications that you currently support either work fine on this platform or are being phased out. That's the good news. The not-so-good news is that it's your job to figure out how to upgrade all of these machines and users as soon as possible.

Although Windows 2000 includes many tools for easing the deployment of new machines, no software features can take the place of adequate planning. For example, using the RIS, you know you can set up new machines to install Windows 2000 over the network. But what about users who want to perform an in-place upgrade of their existing operating systems? And what might be the best order in which to upgrade the machines? (You can't expect to do all 2,000 at once.)

When faced with a large-scale Windows 2000 deployment, you should start by first understanding what you have. Be sure you know how many Windows-based machines you have and what version they're running. Although it may not be the first thing that jumps into your mind, it's possible that someone somewhere is still using a DOS-based PC to support some proprietary hardware.

Next, you should understand what hardware your current client machines are running. Windows 2000 has higher system requirements than previous versions of Windows. In an ideal world, you'd be able to deploy all new machines to 2,000 users. In reality, it's more likely that your budget will prevent throwing out all of your existing hardware, so you'll need to decide whether you want to upgrade machines running compatible operating systems (such as Windows NT 4.0 and Windows 95/98), or if you want to wipe the machines and start from scratch. The latter may be a safer and easier method overall, but you'll have to do some up-front work to make sure users' data is backed up and that their applications and settings can be easily migrated.

Once you know *how* you're going to perform the upgrade, it's time to figure out *when* it should be done. For a large number of users, you must come up with some kind of plan for the order in which PCs will be upgraded. In some cases, it might make sense to upgrade entire departments or groups at one time. You could work with managers throughout your organization to determine when downtime would have the least impact on overall productivity. In other cases, it might make sense to create pilot group in each department and then progressively upgrade users as quickly as possible. Note that you might have some support problems in the interim because certain users will be able to take advantage of Windows 2000 functionality earlier than others. The bottom line is that business factors (more than technical ones), will likely drive the decision.

But wait, there's more! You may also have to worry about training users on the features of Windows 2000 Professional. And you'll need to make sure that your own IT staff is adequately trained to answer questions and troubleshoot client-side issues. Finally, you'll need commitment from throughout the company to move to the new platform—you may have to go over a lot of political hurdles if you don't take the time to communicate the benefits to everyone involved. In the real world, doing a large-scale upgrade of clients can be challenge. However, it can go quite smoothly with adequate planning and patience.

# Configuring Client Setup Options

**W**hen the remote installation process is started from the client, you may want to allow or disallow specific options. There are four main options that can be set for clients to choose during the RIS setup procedures:

**Automatic Setup**   When this option is chosen, the systems administrator specifies all of the installation options, and the user is not given any choices when using the Client Installation Wizard.

**Custom Setup**   When this option is chosen, a user or systems administrator is able to specify various options, such as the name of the computer and the Active Directory location for the Computer object.

**Restart Setup**   In some cases, the setup process may terminate before it is finished. This might occur due to a loss of network connectivity or a configuration problem. When the Restart Setup option is enabled, users or systems administrators may choose to restart setup from the point at which it failed.

**Tools**   This option allows users or systems administrators to access various tools that are available when the Client Installation Wizard is running.

For each of these settings just listed, you can choose from among three policies:

**Allow**   This permits users or systems administrators to allow the particular setting during the client setup process.

**Don't Care**   This is the default setting. It specifies that no policy is set at this level and that settings at the parent or higher-level Active Directory objects may specify the Allow or Deny option.

**Deny**   This disallows users or systems administrators from choosing this particular setting during the client setup process.

Figure 12.12 shows where the options are located, and Figure 12.13 shows the various options that are available. You can access these settings by modifying the Group Policy object for an Active Directory object. The Remote Installation Services Choice Options can be accessed by clicking User Configuration ➢ Windows Settings ➢ Security Settings ➢ Remote Installation Services.

**FIGURE  12.12**   Editing Group Policy settings for RIS

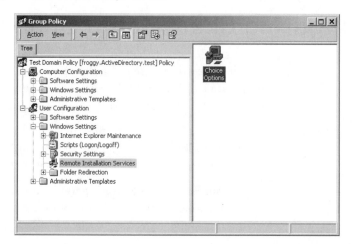

**FIGURE 12.13** Setting RIS Setup Choice Options

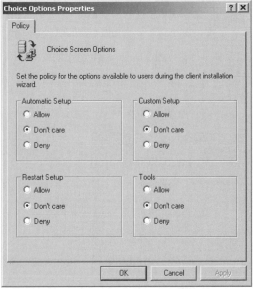

For more information on configuring Group Policy settings, see Chapter 10.

# Using RIS through PXE-Compliant Network Adapters

In order to access the RIS server using the PXE-compliant network adapter, you must configure your computer to access the network during the boot process. Usually, this is done by accessing the system BIOS. The exact procedure should be available from the hardware manufacturer. The remainder of the process is the same as in the next section.

# Using RIS through a RIS Boot Disk

If your computer and network adapter do not support the PXE specification, then you will need to create a boot disk. This disk can be created on a Windows 2000 server that has RIS installed. The purpose of the boot disk is the same as the purpose of the PXE Boot ROM—to load a minimal set of drivers to get the computer on the network. Once the computer has access to the network, the RIS server provides all of the required program code.

By default, the Windows 2000 RIS supports the following network adapters:

| | |
|---|---|
| 3Com 3C900B-Combo | Compaq NetFlex 100 |
| 3Com 3C900B-FL | Compaq NetFlex 110 |
| 3Com 3C900B-TPC | Compaq NetFlex 3 |
| 3Com 3C900B-TPO | DEC DE450 |
| 3Com 3C900-Combo | DEC DE500 |
| 3Com 3C900-TPO | HP DeskDirect 10/100TX |
| 3Com 3C905B-Combo | Intel Pro10+ |
| 3Com 3C905B-FX | Intel Pro100+ |
| 3Com 3C905B-TX | Intel Pro100B |
| 3Com 3C905C-TX | SMC 8432 |
| 3Com 3C905-T4 | SMC 9332 |
| 3Com 3C905-TX | SMC 9432 |
| AMD PCNet Adapters | |

If your network adapter is not included in this list, you will need to contact your computer manufacturer or network card manufacturer in order to obtain the appropriate driver. Note that not all vendors will support remote client installations using RIS. If you are unsure of the network adapter that is installed in the client computer, you should contact your hardware vendor or see the computer manufacturer's Web site. Exercise 12.6 walks you through the process of creating a remote boot disk.

**EXERCISE 12.6**

### Creating a Remote Boot Disk

In this exercise, you will create a remote boot disk. In order to complete this exercise, you must have first installed and configured RIS (see Exercises 12.1 and 12.2). You will also require a single, high-density floppy disk.

**EXERCISE 12.6** *(continued)*

1. Using Windows Explorer, open the folder into which you placed the Remote Installation files.

2. Within this folder, open the Admin\i386 folder.

3. To open the Windows 2000 Remote Boot Disk Generator, double-click the rbfg program.

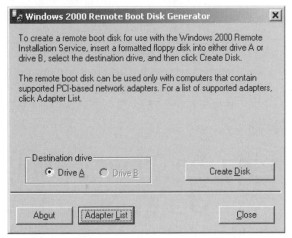

4. To specify the network adapter of the client computer, click the Adapter List button. Select the appropriate network adapter from the list. Click OK.

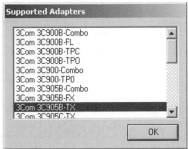

5. To create the boot disk, click Create Disk. The Windows 2000 Remote Boot Disk Generator will begin copying the necessary file(s) to the floppy.

6. When finished, click Close to exit the Windows 2000 Remote Boot Disk Generator.

If you have chosen the wrong network adapter for the boot disk, you will see the following message on the client when you boot the computer:

```
Windows 2000 Remote Installation Boot Floppy

Error: Could not find a supported network card. The boot
floppy currently supports a limited set of PCI based
network cards for use with the Windows 2000 Remote
Installation Service. Ensure this system contains one of
the supported network cards and try the operation again.
For assistance, contact your systems administrator.
```

If this is the case, you will need to re-create the boot disk with the appropriate drivers and/or obtain the name of the proper drivers from your vendor. If you're having problems connecting to the RIS server or are having other problems, see the "Troubleshooting RIS" section later in this chapter.

# Performing the Client Installation

Once you have booted the client (using either a PXE device or a boot floppy), you will be connected to the RIS server. At this point, the text-mode portion of setup will begin. If you chose the Deny settings for all options, then the client will not be provided with any additional choices and setup will automatically start copying files.

If, however, additional information is required (such as authentication information or a computer name), the Client Installation Wizard will appear. The Wizard will ask several questions to gather the required information. Once the information has been provided, the automated remote installation process will begin.

# Optimizing RIS Performance

The actual process required to automatically install an operating system can be bandwidth-intensive. In the case of Windows 2000, the thousands of files required can lead to high network usage. If not managed properly, using RIS can reduce performance for all network users. And the problem is greatly increased if you plan to install multiple clients at the same time!

Fortunately, there are several ways to optimize the performance of RIS in a network environment. They include the following suggestions:

**Use dedicated servers.**   Because of the high disk I/O requirements for the automated client installation process, it is usually a good idea to use a dedicated server for RIS operations. Although using a standard file server might suffice for an occasional installation, the resource usage can add up when rolling out multiple clients.

**Use fast network links.**   Using fast network links between RIS clients and servers can greatly increase performance. Although some of the newest and fastest networking technologies may be too expensive to roll out to every desktop, you may be able to find it in your budget to implement higher-speed networks in a computer rollout lab. The additional bandwidth will make the operation much faster.

For most companies, trying to perform a RIS operation over a WAN link should be out of the question. The high overhead and relatively low-bandwidth situation will greatly reduce performance, increase costs, and possibly prevent other users from doing their jobs!

**Isolate network traffic.**   By placing the RIS server and clients on the same dedicated subnet within your network, you can reduce the impact on performance that results from the load on routers. Additionally, by using a separate subnet, you reduce the chances of affecting other network users.

Another method for isolating network traffic is known as *switching*. Through the use of switches, rather than routers, you can effectively reduce contention for network access. Switching is especially useful if you plan to roll out multiple client machines using RIS at the same time. It is beyond the scope of this book to discuss network design issues in depth. For more information on routing and switching, consult *MCSE: Windows 2000 Network Infrastructure Design Study Guide*, by Bill Heldman (Sybex, 2000).

In general, the methods just listed will be sufficient for increasing RIS performance and minimizing the impact on users. Now that we have some optimization ideas in mind, let's move on and look at what to do when RIS isn't working the way you wanted.

# Troubleshooting RIS

In most cases, the installation and configuration of RIS will be straight-forward. Through the use of the configuration Wizards and Active Directory administration tools, it is usually a simple task to set up RIS the way you want it to work. In some instances, however, you may have problems performing a remote installation. After all, the process involves a client computer that does not have an operating system communicating with a remote server.

---

**_Microsoft_**
**_✓ Exam_**
**_Objective_**

**Deploy Windows 2000 by using Remote Installation Services (RIS).**

- Troubleshoot RIS problems.

---

If you're having trouble performing remote installation options, there are several configuration settings you should verify. Some troubleshooting steps to attempt include the following:

**Verify the server configuration.** Using the Active Directory Users and Computers tool, you can quickly and easily verify the proper functioning of a RIS server. To perform this test, open the Active Directory Users and Computers tool, right-click the name of the RIS server, and choose Properties. On the Remote Install tab, click the Verify Server button. The Check Server Wizard will perform a diagnostic test on the current RIS configuration and then provide information on the configuration in addition to other information (shown in Figure 12.14). If errors in the configuration are found, you should check the System event log for more information.

**Verify the network configuration settings.** Verify the network configuration settings if the client is unable to connect to the RIS server. If the DHCP settings are incorrect, then the remote client may receive unusable TCP/IP address information. If other computers on the same network are using DHCP and are able to connect with the server, then it's likely that there is another problem.

You can ensure that the network interface card on the client is working properly by trying to connect to other resources or servers. Of course, this can only be done after you have installed an operating system (or connected to a terminal server) with this machine.

**Ensure that the RIS server contains the desired images.** Since there is no way for the client to specify to which RIS server it wants to connect, the client may be connecting to the wrong RIS server on the network. This RIS server may not have all of the same images that are available on others.

Although not all vendors support the use of prestaged computers, you may choose to set them up in order to ensure that only the desired RIS server responds to a client. If you want to use multiple RIS servers (for performance and fault-tolerance reasons), you will need to ensure that the appropriate images are available on all servers in your environment.

**FIGURE 12.14** Verifying the configuration of a RIS server

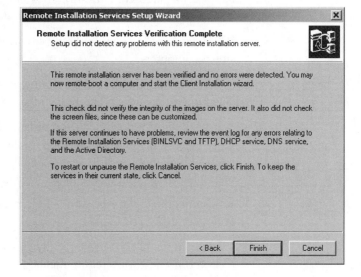

**Verify the PXE Boot ROM version.** In order to be compatible with Windows 2000 Remote Installation Services, the PXE Boot ROM must be version .99c or greater. You may have problems booting and connecting to the RIS server if the client is using an earlier standard.

**Verify that you are using the correct boot disk.** The Windows 2000 Remote Boot disk contains network drivers for only one type of network interface card. If you plan to install the Windows 2000 Professional operating system on multiple computers that have different network adapters, you'll need to create multiple boot disks with different drivers.

**Enable clients to choose options during the RIS setup process.** If the User Configuration Group Policy settings do not allow specific options, clients and systems administrators who are performing installations will be unable to change the settings. To change these settings, simply apply the appropriate Group Policy settings for the Computer object.

# Summary

In this chapter, we covered the details of working with Windows 2000 Remote Installation Services (RIS). RIS was designed to ease the headaches involved with rolling out client operating systems. It accomplishes this by allowing for centralized configuration of standard Windows 2000 Professional images. Specifically, we discussed the following:

- RIS is designed to simplify the deployment of Windows 2000 Professional computers.

- Systems administrators can specify the various setup options for the client operating system before installation begins.

- System administrators can take advantage of various security features of RIS to ensure that only the appropriate client computers can perform a remote installation. Security features include delegation of permissions, prestaging client computers, and managing RIS server permissions.

- RIS is integrated with the Active Directory and makes use of Group Policy settings.

- Client computers can automatically connect to a RIS server if they meet certain hardware requirements.

- Multiple RIS servers can be deployed to optimize the performance of many concurrent installations.

If you're a systems administrator who's facing a large-scale Windows 2000 deployment, we'll bet that this was welcome news! Better yet, the automated remote installation options provided by RIS are extremely easy to configure. And, as long as you're using supported client hardware, the steps should work seamlessly. When you're planning to roll out Windows 2000 Professional computers, be sure to consider using RIS.

# Exam Essentials

**Understand the purpose of Remote Installation Services (RIS)**    RIS can be used to efficiently deploy Windows 2000 Professional to client machines.

**Understand RIS server and client requirements.**    In order to use RIS, your client must meet certain requirements (including the minimum hardware specifications for Windows 2000 Professional), and your server must be configured properly.

**Know how to configure a RIS server.**    In order to use RIS, you must first create the appropriate images from which your operating system will be installed. You must then customize any necessary settings and make the files available on the network.

**Be familiar RIS Security options.**    Windows 2000 includes many options for increasing the security of RIS. You should be familiar with concepts such as authorizing a RIS server, prestaging client computers, and delegating RIS permissions.

**Understand the RIS client setup process.**    In order to take advantage of RIS, client computers must be able to connect to a remote network share and download the necessary files.

**Know how to optimize the performance of RIS.**    Multiple RIS servers can be deployed in order to balance the load of network installation requests.

**Know how to troubleshoot problems with RIS.**    As with any method of installing an operating system, there are several things that can go wrong. Be sure you know how to diagnose and troubleshoot connectivity and configuration problems that may occur when you're attempting an automated install via RIS.

# Key Terms

Before you take the exam, you should be familiar with the following terms and concepts:

Boot Information Negotiation Layer (BINL)

Global Unique Identifier (GUID)

Preboot eXecution Environment (PXE)

prestaging

Remote Installation Services (RIS)

Remote Installation Preparation (RIPrep) Wizard

Single Instance Store (SIS)

switching

Trivial File Transfer Protocol Daemon (TFTPD)

Universally Unique Identifier (UUID)

# Review Questions

1. Gwen is planning to roll out Windows 2000 Professional to 200 new PCs that her organization recently acquired. She has the following requirements:

   - Install the operating systems on new PCs as quickly as possible.

   - Reduce the impact of network traffic caused by the remote installation processes.

   Which of the following methods can she use to meet these requirements? (Choose all that apply.)

   **A.** Place the RIS server(s) on an isolated network.

   **B.** Deploy the OS to all computers at the same time.

   **C.** Deploy the OS to only one computer at a time.

   **D.** Deploy multiple RIS servers.

2. Windows 2000 Remote Installation Services (RIS) can be used to install which of the following operating systems?

   **A.** Windows NT 4 Workstation

   **B.** Windows 2000 Professional

   **C.** Windows 2000 Server

   **D.** Windows 2000 Advanced Server

   **E.** All of the above

3. During the creation of a RIS image, which of the following must a systems administrator have in order to create a CD-based image?

   **A.** The Windows 2000 Server CD-ROM

   **B.** The Windows 2000 Advanced Server CD-ROM

   **C.** The Windows 2000 RIS boot disk

   **D.** The Windows 2000 Professional CD-ROM

   **E.** None of the above

4. A systems administrator is preparing a RIS directory on a new Windows 2000 computer. He is trying to determine which partitions are eligible to store the installation images. Which of the following types of partitions *cannot* be used for the RIS root directory?

   **A.** The boot partition

   **B.** The system partition

   **C.** A FAT partition

   **D.** A FAT32 partition

   **E.** All of the above

5. You are responsible for managing the security of your organization's RIS installations. You want to allow only a select group of help desk staffers to join computers to a domain. What is the easiest way to assign the appropriate permissions for the entire domain?

   **A.** Delegate control of a User account.

   **B.** Delegate control at the domain level.

   **C.** Delegate control of an OU.

   **D.** Delegate control of a Computer account.

   **E.** None of the above.

6. All of the following are minimum system requirements for RIS clients *except*

   **A.** Pentium-166 or faster CPU

   **B.** 32MB RAM

   **C.** 800MB hard disk

   **D.** PXE Boot ROM–equipped network adapter

   **E.** None of the above

**7.** A systems administrator wants to make some changes to the default setup for an existing image. Which file or object should be changed?

   **A.** OU Properties

   **B.** Group Policy Objects (GPOs)

   **C.** Domain policy

   **D.** Setup Information Files (*.SIF)

   **E.** None of the above

**8.** You are planning to deploy Windows 2000 on many of your organization's Windows NT 4.0 Workstation computers. Your company supports three different hardware platforms, each of which has a different network adapter. You want to create a RIS boot disk that contains all of the necessary drivers for each of these three hardware platforms. How can you accomplish this?

   **A.** Create a single RIS boot disk and copy the additional drivers to this disk.

   **B.** Deploy multiple RIS servers, each of which is compatible with one type of client.

   **C.** Create a standard RIS boot disk that contains the "generic" network driver

   **D.** This cannot be done automatically. A RIS boot disk can only contain one network driver.

**9.** Hardware-based Global Unique Identifiers (GUIDs) are used to uniquely identify computers. They are assigned by hardware manufacturers and are hard-coded into which of the following areas of a computer?

   **A.** The hard disk

   **B.** The smart card

   **C.** The BIOS

   **D.** None of the above

10. Which of the following is/are true regarding prestaging of RIS clients, assuming that there is only one RIS server on the network?

    **A.** Increases performance

    **B.** Decreases performance

    **C.** Increases security

    **D.** Decreases security

11. Tara is a systems administrator for a medium-sized organization. She has been placed in charge of network security and is responsible for increasing the security of RIS. She has the following requirements:

    - Since the organization uses a shared network, only authorized clients must be allowed to remotely install Windows 2000.

    - Only features and settings that are available within Windows 2000, the Active Directory, and RIS can be used.

    - Only certain systems administrators should have permissions to perform a remote installation.

    Which of the following features could she use in order to meet these requirements?

    **A.** Prestaged Computer accounts

    **B.** The use of GUIDS to identify clients

    **C.** The assignment of appropriate Active Directory permissions

    **D.** The delegation of permissions to join a computer to the domain to only authorized administrators

    **E.** All of the above

**12.** A systems administrator wants to create an automated installation of the Windows 2000 Server operating system. How can they do this?

**A.** Create a CD-based image using the Windows 2000 Server CD-ROM.

**B.** Copy a Windows 2000 Professional CD-based image and then upgrade it to Windows 2000 Server.

**C.** Modify the setup installation options to specify that the computer should be a server.

**D.** None of the above.

**13.** You are configuring a new Windows 2000 environment to support RIS. As part of the configuration, you are responsible for ensuring that all of the necessary services needed to perform the remote installation of Windows 2000 Professional on 200 new computers have been implemented. For performance reasons, however, you would like to spread these services across multiple machines in the environment. Which of the following services is required by RIS but may be run on a computer separate from the RIS server itself?

**A.** Trivial File Transfer Protocol Daemon (TFTPD)

**B.** Boot Information Negotiation Layer (BINL)

**C.** DNS

**D.** Single Instance Store (SIS)

**E.** None of the above

**14.** Which of the following can be used to create an image that automatically installs applications as part of the RIS process?

**A.** RIPrep

**B.** Prestaging

**C.** CD-based images

**D.** Microsoft Installation Wizard

**E.** All of the above

**15.** A Remote Installation Boot Floppy can be created using programs that are installed on which of the following?

**A.** Any Windows 2000 Server computer

**B.** Any Windows 2000 Professional computer

**C.** Any Windows 2000 RIS server

**D.** None of the above

**16.** You have recently installed and configured the Remote Installation Services on a new Windows 2000 domain controller. You have also created a RIS boot disk for a client computer. You find that the client computer is able to connect to the network but that it does not seem to be able to receive an IP address from the server. You verify that other machines in the environment are able to automatically receive IP addresses. Which of the following is most likely to be the problem?

**A.** The custom setup parameters are not properly configured.

**B.** The client computer does not meet the minimum system requirements.

**C.** The client computer is not running a supported operating system.

**D.** The RIS server has not been authorized for the domain.

**E.** None of the above.

**17.** You need to authorize your RIS server. In the screen shown below, where would you click in order to accomplish this task?

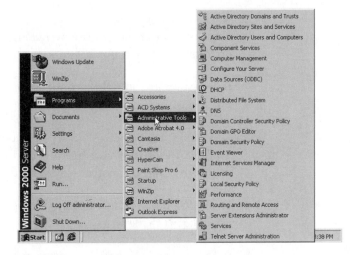

**A.** Active Directory Sites and Services

**B.** Active Directory Users and Computers

**C.** Configure Your Server

**D.** DHCP

# Answers to Review Questions

1. A, D. Using multiple RIS servers and isolating these servers on a separate network segment can increase overall installation performance without impacting the production network.

2. B. RIS supports only the automated installation of Windows 2000 Professional.

3. E. Although the Windows 2000 Professional installation files must be available, they do not have to be provided via CD-ROM. That is, the files may be available on another removable drive or on a network share.

4. E. The RIS root directory must reside on a partition that is formatted using the NTFS file system and is not a system or boot partition.

5. B. Delegating the right to join computers to the domain can most easily be performed using the Delegation of Control Wizard at the domain level.

6. D. A RIS client computer can use a boot floppy if it does not have a PXE Boot ROM–enabled network adapter.

7. D. Setup Information Files specify the basic options used during the automated installation process.

8. D. Each RIS boot disk can contain information for only one type of network adapter.

9. C. GUIDs are used to uniquely identify computers in a networked environment and are assigned by computer manufacturers.

10. C. Prestaging increases security by specifying that only certain computers can perform a remote installation from a RIS server. It does not affect RIS performance.

11. E. All of the options listed are designed to increase the security of RIS in a networked environment.

**12.** D. The version of RIS included with Windows 2000 Server does not support the automated remote installation of the Windows 2000 Server operating system.

**13.** C. DNS must be present in the network environment but does not have to be installed on the RIS server.

**14.** A. The Remote Installation Preparation Wizard (RIPrep) utility can be used to create a RIS image that automatically installs applications during the RIS process.

**15.** C. By default, only a Windows 2000 RIS server will include the `rbfg` executable file (although the file can be copied to or run from other types of computers).

**16.** D. A RIS server must be *authorized* before it can function on the network. This step is necessary to allow clients to receive automatic IP address assignments. If a DHCP server is not available, none of the clients in the environment would be able to receive an IP address. Since the question states that other clients can receive IP addresses, the problem is most likely due to a failure to authorize the RIS server.

**17.** D. You authorize DHCP and RIS servers in the DHCP administrative tool. The procedure for authorizing a RIS server is identical to that for authorizing a DHCP server.

# Appendix A

# Planning the Active Directory

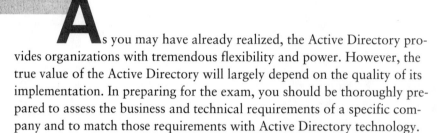

As you may have already realized, the Active Directory provides organizations with tremendous flexibility and power. However, the true value of the Active Directory will largely depend on the quality of its implementation. In preparing for the exam, you should be thoroughly prepared to assess the business and technical requirements of a specific company and to match those requirements with Active Directory technology.

In this appendix, we'll take an overview of the many considerations that are important when determining how best to deploy the Active Directory in a given network environment. The customizability of and configuration options available in the Active Directory make it useful for businesses ranging in size from a few employees to over a hundred thousand. Due to various factors, the Active Directory configuration will vary between (and even within) organizations. The focus of this appendix will be on applying the concepts and features of the Active Directory to real-world environments. Let's start by examining ways to evaluate the current environment.

The purpose of this appendix is to provide an overview of *all* the Active Directory features. Consequently, its coverage includes some features that are covered earlier in the book. However, while the focus of this study guide is implementation and administration, this appendix covers the same technical content from a planning standpoint. This appendix will be especially useful for readers who are not familiar with the Active Directory.

# Evaluating the Current Environment

The specifics of an Active Directory deployment will largely be based on an organization's technical and business environment. Factors such as the network infrastructure, the size of the business, and its organizational layout play large roles in designing a directory services architecture.

Before diving into the technical details of installing and deploying domain controllers, you must take into account your current network and business environment. Sometimes, this is an easy task. In a small business environment, the complexity of the business may be very low. In other cases, however, several months of planning may only scratch the surface of the huge task of planning for the Active Directory. In this section, we'll take a look at several factors you should take into account when evaluating a business environment.

## Number and Types of Users

The very reason to have a network in the first place is to support users by providing them with the information and resources they need. Therefore, a thorough assessment of the number of users you support is very important when planning the deployment of the Active Directory. In some cases, it will be quite easy to measure the number of users. If you're currently using a network operating system, you can simply count the accounts within it. For example, the number of accounts you have in your Windows NT security database may be a good indicator. In other cases, however, you may need to take into account the number of users the network will be supporting at some point in the future. These predictions can be made based on current human resources information as well as hiring and business growth plans. In addition to a simple count of the number of users you'll support, you should be sure to fully understand the needs of these users. Administrative staff will likely have very different requirements from Engineering, for example. Additionally, certain network-enabled applications that take advantage of the Active Directory will have additional requirements. It is important to note that gathering all of this information will require efforts from throughout your organization. For example, you may need to go to the executive managers for an estimate on company growth, while you would probably go to human resources for an accurate count of current employees.

When planning for the Active Directory, you should understand how users are distributed throughout your network environment so that you can design the optimal domain controller distribution, and information on the number and types of users you plan to support will help you to accomplish this.

## Geographic Distribution

IT organizations would have a much easier job if all of their users resided in the same building. In such a scenario, you would be able to rely on fast network connections between all users and the information they need. For most medium- and larger-sized businesses, however, supporting remote sites is a common scenario. Figure A.1 provides an example of a geographically distributed organization and network.

In an ideal world, geographic distribution would not make much of a difference and all sites would enjoy the same high-speed network connectivity. While larger remote sites may be connected by faster (but more costly) connections, technological limitations and costs often require several special considerations to be taken into account when designing a distributed network.

**FIGURE  A.1**   A geographically distributed network

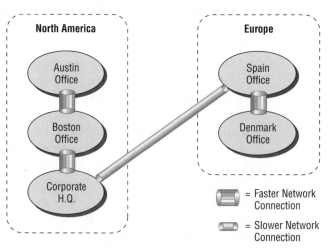

In order to deal with many of the challenges associated with remote sites, companies often implement remote access solutions. This allows telecommuters and traveling users to gain access to network resources. But whatever the case may be, a company's IT group will have to perform support and administrative functions for all of its users. To meet this need, some companies might choose to have an IT department at each location. Others, however, will have a separate IT support staff just for remote offices. In any event, remote access solutions and the means by which IT support is provided to remote access users will help to determine the optimal physical structure of an Active Directory deployment. Keeping the geographic issues in mind, let's now look at the technical issues related to evaluating your network infrastructure.

## Network Infrastructure

The function of a network infrastructure is to connect users to the resources they need to effectively do their jobs. With this goal in mind, IT departments are required to purchase, implement, and manage network connections ranging in speed from analog modems to the fastest local area network (LAN) and wide area network (WAN) connections available. Because of the costs of some of these solutions, however, network administrators often have to make trade-offs. That is, few companies can afford to always invest in the fastest and most efficient network technologies available.

While planning for the deployment of the Active Directory in your organization, you must take into account your network infrastructure. If an accurate and up-to-date network map is available, this is a great place to start. If one is not available, this is a great time to start designing one. Figure A.2 provides an example of a network map that takes into account the number of servers and workstations at each site, along with the network connections between them. Of particular concern will be the bandwidth for each of the network connections and the current amount of traffic between sites.

**FIGURE A.2**   A high-level company network map

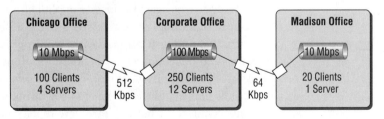

This type of high-level map will be very important when planning for Active Directory sites and domains. In some cases, you might find that upgrades to the current network infrastructure are required once you've examined the map. For example, a remote site may have a slow WAN connection, but, due to changes in the network infrastructure, more servers and other resources are required. In this case, you may choose to deploy domain controllers differently, or you may plan to purchase additional bandwidth for that site.

Also, many IT organizations are constantly upgrading their networks to keep pace with the increasing demand for file sharing, knowledge management, and Internet access. In such environments, it's just as important to take into account future plans for network performance upgrades as it is to consider the current situation. The goal of evaluating the network infrastructure is to ensure that the existing network infrastructure accommodates your organization's replication and administration traffic needs.

## Centralized vs. Decentralized Administration

One of the most common and important functions of the IT department is to administer network resources. This includes planning for, evaluating, deploying, and managing server and workstation computers, as well as supporting end users. Although the fundamental goal is the same, companies might take different approaches to managing IT resources throughout the network.

One common model is that of centralized administration. In such a scenario, a single IT department is responsible for managing all of the resources on the network. This is often chosen for smaller organizations as it allows all of the IT personnel to reside in a single location. Centralized administration can also reduce a lot of redundant work as users, groups, and computers are managed in one place, through the work of a skilled group of individuals. Medium- and large-sized businesses might choose the centralized model, as well, due to economies realized by focusing IT resources in a single location.

Centralized administration may, however, present several problems. First, the need for good network communications between sites can cause problems. For example, what happens when a remote router goes down and no one is available at the other site to provide immediate support for trouble–shooting? Similarly, what if a hardware replacement is required on a client computer? These types of tasks usually require the presence of IT staff at each of an organization's locations. A decentralized administration model takes these factors into account by providing IT departments at each of the company's locations. Figure A.3 provides a comparison of centralized versus decentralized administration models.

**FIGURE A.3**   Centralized vs. decentralized IT administration

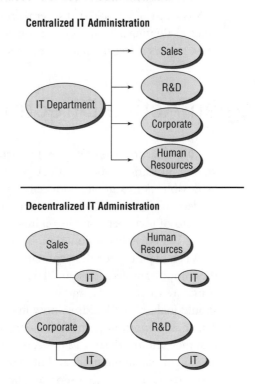

Although technical issues are one factor in determining the type of administration model to implement, political and business issues are also important. A small business might map well to a centralized model if all of the users and resources reside within one administrative unit. Centralized administration fits well in this type of environment as it simplifies the creation and management of users and resources. However, security needs and management structure may influence the creation of multiple administrative units. In some companies, departments might operate as autonomous business units. For example, the Sales department might create and manage its own user account databases and network resources, while Engineering does the same in another completely isolated environment. Each department would have its own administration staff, and the sharing of resources would be based on the cooperation of all the departments. This type of scenario is a good candidate for the decentralized model. The network administration needs of the organization will play a fundamental role in determining the best organization for the Active Directory.

So far, we have looked at several different factors that must be considered when evaluating a business environment. Now, let's take a close look at how these factors affect the planning of the Active Directory.

# Choosing an Active Directory Model

In order to accommodate the various business and technical needs of your organization, Microsoft's Active Directory technology was designed to be flexible. For example, both centralized and decentralized administration models are supported. And, the Active Directory was designed to scale up to millions of users per domain—a huge improvement over the practical limits of the Windows NT 4 domain model.

When planning for the deployment of the Active Directory, one of the most important decisions you'll need to make is related to how you want to configure trees, forests, and domains. In fact, the first major decision you should make should address how many domains your organization needs. The most important point to remember about Active Directory domains is that they are *administrative* units, not technical ones. An administrative unit allows for managing users and network resources within a single shared accounts database with a separate database for security.

In most cases, it is recommended that an organization use as few domains as possible. Fewer domains are simpler to setup and maintain and result in less administrative work overall. In many situations, it is possible to work with only a single domain. This may be true regardless of the size of a business or its geographic distribution. Keeping these ideas in mind, let's look at how domains can be combined together.

# Planning Trees and Forests

**W**e have already mentioned several reasons for requiring multiple domains within a single company. What we haven't yet covered is how multiple domains can be related to each other and how their relationships can translate into domain forests and trees.

A fundamental commonality between the various domains that exist in trees and forests is that they all share the same Active Directory Global Catalog. This means that if we modify the Active Directory schema, the change must be propagated to all of the domain controllers in *all of the domains*. This is an important point because additions and modifications to the structure of information in the Global Catalog can have widespread effects on replication and network traffic.

Every domain within an Active Directory configuration will have its own unique name. For example, even though we might have a sales domain in two different trees, their complete names will be different (such as `sales.company1.com` and `sales.company2.com`). In this section, we'll look at how multiple Active Directory domains can be organized based on business requirements.

## Using a Single Tree

The concept of domain trees was created to preserve the relationship between multiple domains that share a common contiguous namespace. For example, I might have the following DNS domains (based on Internet names):

- `mycompany.com`

- `sales.mycompany.com`

- `engineering.mycompany.com`

- `europe.sales.mycompany.com`

Note that all of these domains fit within a single contiguous namespace. That is, they are all direct or indirect children of the `mycompany.com` domain. In this case, `mycompany.com` is called the *root* domain. All of the direct children (such as `sales.mycompany.com` and `engineering.mycompany.com`) are called *child* domains. Finally, *parent* domains are the domains that are directly above one domain. For example, sales.mycompany.com is the parent domain of `europe.sales.mycompany.com`. Figure A.4 provides an example of a domain tree.

**FIGURE A.4** A domain tree

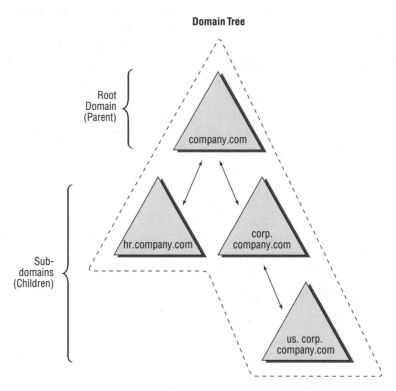

In order to establish a domain tree, the root domain for the tree must be created first. Then, child domains of this root can be added. These child domains can then serve as parents for further subdomains. Each domain must have at least one domain controller, and domain controllers can participate in only one domain at a time. However, domain controllers can be moved between domains. This is done by first demoting a domain controller to a member server and then promoting it to a domain controller in another domain.

Domains are designed to be security boundaries. The domains within a tree are automatically bound together using a two-way trust relationship. This allows users and resources to be shared between domains through the use of the appropriate groups. Since trust relationships are transitive, this means that all of the domains within the tree trust each other. Note, however, that a trust by itself does not grant any security permissions to users or objects between domains. Trusts are designed only to *allow* resources to be shared. Administrators must explicitly assign security settings to resources before users can access resources between domains.

The use of a single tree makes sense when an organization maintains only a single contiguous namespace. Regardless of the number of domains that exist within this environment and how different their security settings are, they are related by a common name. Although domain trees will make sense for many organizations, in some cases the network namespace may be considerably more complicated. Let's look at how forests address those situations next.

## Using a Forest

Active Directory forests are designed to accommodate multiple noncontiguous namespaces. That is, they can combine domain trees together into logical units. An example might be the following tree and domain structure:

- Tree: `Organization1.com`
  - `Sales.Organization1.com`
  - `Marketing.Organization1.com`
  - `Engineering.Organization1.com`
  - `NorthAmerica.Engineering.Organization1.com`
- Tree: `Organization2.com`
  - `Sales.Organization2.com`
  - `Engineering.Organization2.com`

Figure A.5 provides an example of how multiple trees can fit into a single forest. Such a situation might occur in the merger of companies or if a company is logically divided into two or more completely separate and autonomous business units.

**FIGURE A.5** A single forest consisting of multiple trees

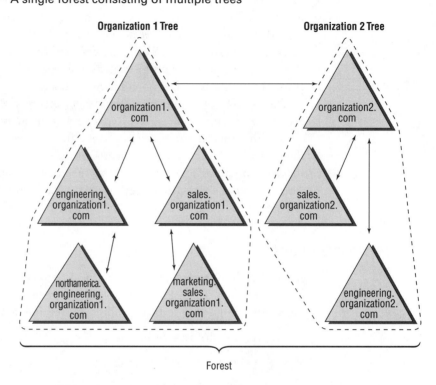

All of the trees within a forest are related through a single forest root domain. This is the first domain that is created in the Active Directory environment. The root domain in each tree creates a transitive trust with the forest root domain. The result is a configuration in which all of the trees within a domain and all of the domains within each tree trust each other. Again, as with domain trees, the presence of a trust relationship does not automatically give any permissions to users between trees and domains. It only allows objects and resources to be shared. Specific permissions must be set up by authorized network administrators.

Through the use of domain trees and forests, a company can easily manage multiple related domains in a single Active Directory configuration.

# Planning Domain Structure

Thus far, we've looked at how domains can be organized within the Active Directory environment through trees and forests. Once you've determined the high-level domain topology, it's time to look into the details of the organization *within* domains themselves. This includes the location and types of servers and domain controllers that might be needed.

The same major considerations described earlier in the "Evaluating the Current Environment" section will apply to the decisions made here. That is, the business and technical requirements of an organization will play a large part in determining the overall domain configuration. In addition, if the company is currently using more than one Windows NT domain, this should be taken into account. Let's start by looking at various types of domains.

## Upgrading from Windows NT 4 Domains

One of Microsoft's major goals in designing the Active Directory was to allow an easy upgrade path for users of Windows NT 4 domains. When you're planning to upgrade from Windows NT 4 domains to the Windows 2000 Active Directory, you'll need to consider the differences between the two types of structures. As we mentioned earlier in this chapter, there are several reasons that businesses might choose to have more than one domain. For reasons of performance, scalability, and administration, the added effort of implementing and managing more than one domain might be worthwhile.

The fundamental structure of Window NT 4 domains is a single flat namespace. Although the product itself does not support the concept of different *types* of domains, multiple configurations and roles for domains were created to accommodate business and technical requirements. These configurations are based on using domains for specific tasks within the network environment. These roles include:

**Master Domains**　In environments that support large numbers of users, one or more master domains may be established. Each master domain is primarily responsible for containing User account information.

**Resource Domains**　Resource domains contain the actual files, printers, and application servers to which users will require access. They generally consist of only a few administrative User accounts. Users receive security permissions in resource domains based on accounts stored in user domains.

In some cases, users and resources might be stored in the same domain. Such domain models fit well with organizations that have independent business units and prefer centralized administration. With master and resource domains, multiple configurations are possible. For example, a multiple-master domain model includes the presence of two or more user domains and any number of resource domains. Each of the resource domains trusts one or more of the master domains. The trusts are generally one-way. Users in the master domains are placed in global groups. These global groups are then given permissions on objects within the resource domains.

Another common Windows NT domain model is the complete trust model. In this system, all of the domains trust each other. Most domains generally consisted of both users and resources, but each domain is administered separately.

Although the Windows NT 4 domain models provide additional scalability and performance, administering more than a few domains can be very cumbersome. For example, since trust relationships are one-way and not transitive, the number of trusts that must be configured can be very large. Additionally, the process issues related to creating and managing users in multiple domains can lead to a less-than-optimal administration system. All of this can lead to political and technical issues that prevent the usability of network resources.

When upgrading a network to the Active Directory, the current Windows NT domain structure must be taken into account. The general practice is to upgrade master domains first and then to upgrade resource domains. Usually, the Windows NT 4 Primary Domain Controller (PDC) is migrated first. Then, other domain controllers, servers, and workstations are upgraded.

With support for backwards-compatibility, Windows 2000 domains can coexist and share resources with Windows NT 4 domains. This mode is called mixed-mode. There are, however, some trade-offs when running in a mixed-mode configuration as some of the more advanced features of Windows 2000 will not be realized until all of the servers have been upgraded to Windows 2000. Once this is done, a systems administrator can convert the domain to native mode.

Although you could translate the existing domain infrastructure into its mirror image using Active Directory domains, it is often beneficial to collapse multiple domains into fewer ones when upgrading. This is especially true for organizations that created multiple Windows NT domains for the purpose of performance and scalability. When domains are collapsed together, the user account databases from master domains and resource domains are combined together. Usually, this can be done while requiring limited re-creation of security permissions.

Overall, by combining real-world business and technical requirements, companies can find a good way to upgrade their Windows NT environments to the Active Directory. With that in mind, let's look at the how you can determine the appropriate number of domains for a given organization.

# Number of Domains

The Active Directory has alleviated many of the technical issues related to working with Windows NT domains. With the Active Directory, domains can span geographic locations, take into account the network infrastructure, and contain more than one million objects. Therefore, it is recommended that, wherever possible, the fewest number of domains should be used.

The use of a single domain provides a good way to manage network resources, security permissions, and users. It also allows network administration to be distributed throughout the organization and accommodates the use of multiple domain controllers. There are, however, several reasons an organization might consider the use of multiple domains. The reasons for using multiple domains may include the following:

**Retaining the Existing Domain Structure** If your current environment uses multiple Windows NT domains for the purpose of sharing and administering network resources, it might make sense to retain this structure for business and technical reasons. On the other hand, several of the reasons for splitting a network into multiple domains had to do with technical limitations in the Windows NT 4 domain model. Scalability of the flat domain model was, for instance, a major reason for using multiple Windows NT domains. In such cases, it is preferable to consolidate multiple existing domains into fewer larger ones.

**Using Extremely Large Numbers of Objects** One of the primary design goals for the Active Directory was to support a large number of objects within a single domain database. Although testing is required to find a practical limit, you can generally count on allowing more than a million objects in one data store. The Active Directory is not without its limits, however. For very large companies, administering many users, groups, computers, and other objects may place technical limitations on scalability and performance. Additionally, replication traffic between domain controllers in very large domains may place a heavy burden on the network infrastructure. In such a scenario, it would be a good idea to break users and resources into multiple domains.

**Using Multiple DNS Names**   Domains are designed to accommodate only a single DNS name for all of the contained users and resources. For various reasons, however, businesses might operate under separate DNS names on the Internet. An example of such a situation is one in which we manage two different organizations, such as `sales.company1.com` and `sales.company2.com`. As the namespace for each of these domains is not contiguous, we would need to create at least two separate domains in order to accurately reflect the DNS names.

**Limiting Replication Traffic**   The need to replicate information between the various domain controllers that are part of a domain can use significant network bandwidth. If fast and reliable network connections are not available for certain sites, it might make sense to create a separate domain. Note, however, that you should not plan to create separate domains solely based on network or geographic distribution. The concept of sites in the Active Directory model might provide a better solution for meeting these network requirements.

**Meeting Decentralized Security Needs**   All of the objects within a single Active Directory domain will inherit similar security permissions. For example, if we set a requirement on the minimum password length, this same setting will apply to all of the users within the domain. If, for any reason, different security and policy information is required for different sets of users, the establishment of multiple domains might be a good solution. However, this will increase the administrative effort required to maintain the domains and might increase the possibility of inconsistencies in the configuration.

**Meeting Decentralized Administration Needs**   All of the information that exists between domains is stored in a single centralized database that is replicated between the domain controllers within that domain. This includes all of the user, group, and computer objects, along with security permissions. If network administration is decentralized, it might make sense to create multiple domains. Each domain would include the objects that are under the control of just one IT organization. For example, if Company A had one department for North American IT support and another for Asian IT support, two domains would allow for autonomous administration of each. However, multiple domains will require more effort to administer overall since many settings must be made independently in each domain.

Under general circumstances, a small number of domains is ideal. And many technical challenges that could hinder the decrease in the number of domains can be addressed through proper planning and use of the features of the Active Directory. However, the preceding reasons can make the use of multiple Active Directory domains the best choice. You'll need to assess the business and technical needs and limitations of your organization to decide what is the appropriate number of domains for your environment.

# Planning Organizational Units

**S**o far, we've looked at reasons why an organization might require multiple domains and ways in which these domains can be combined together to form forests and trees. Now, let's drill-down into the actual logical structure within domains themselves.

The fundamental concept used to hierarchically organize objects within the Active Directory is appropriately named the organizational unit (OU). OUs can contain other OUs (thereby creating a hierarchy), as well as the following types of objects:

- Users

- Groups

- Printers

- Shared Folders

OUs allow systems administrators to create structures that reflect their internal business environment within the domain. In this section, we'll look at several possible uses for OUs and how they can help manage and administer your network environment.

## Using OUs to Manage Resources

Placing information about all of your network resources within the Active Directory allows you to easily manage users, computers, and security permissions from within a single repository. Within a domain, however, you might want to group users into various containers based on your business's organization. Let's look at an example of a hierarchical list of OUs for an

Engineering department. Within the Engineering OU, we could create levels for Engineering Managers and Software Developers. If necessary, we could even break these groups down further (Senior Software Developers could fall under the Software Developers level, for example). Figure A.6 provides an example of such a hierarchy.

**FIGURE A.6**   An OU hierarchy based on business needs

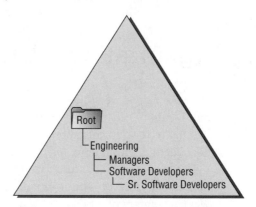

Although you could lump all of the objects within a domain into a single or a few containers, this would make it difficult to administer. If, for example, I wanted to make some settings for only members of the Sales department, I would have to choose each of the users manually. Clearly, this would be a tedious and error-prone process.

Since the concept of an OU will be new to many systems administrators, it's important to make several distinctions about these objects. First, OUs are containers that are designed specifically for administrative purposes. They do not, however, take the place of groups (which are used for administering security and applying permissions). Therefore, OUs do not technically contain members.

The general practice for administration is to place users into groups and then to place the groups into OUs. This arrangement allows for setting security permissions while at the same time making administration of such features as the Group Policy more manageable.

Depending on specific business requirements, you might be able to choose between using OUs or domains when organizing the Active Directory configuration. Earlier in this appendix, we discussed several different reasons for using multiple domains. Many of these issues can also be addressed by properly planning for OUs within a single domain.

The use of OUs instead of multiple domains offers several advantages. First, they allow for administering security and other permissions once for all of the objects within the OU. Second, they allow for flexible containers that can be moved and redesigned much more easily than domains. Finally, OUs allow all objects to use the same namespace while still reflecting the business organization. A good general practice is to use OUs where possible and domains wherever necessary.

The purpose of creating OUs is to provide a means by which to organize and manage users and other objects based on their job functions. With that in mind, let's look at the specific settings you can set with OUs.

## Using OUs to Delegate Administration

When working with the Active Directory, the management and administration of objects are key concerns. *Delegation* is the process by which a systems administrator grants (or delegates) specific permissions to other systems administrators so that they, too, can assist in the management and administration. In a networked environment, you will want to ensure that you delegate administration to only the appropriate individuals.

With a flat domain model like the one used in Windows NT, it was difficult to delegate administration to specific users — either users had specific permissions within the entire domain, or they didn't. For example, if I added Jane Doe to the Print Operators group, she would automatically be able to manage all print jobs on all printers within the domain. In Windows 2000 and the Active Directory, you can still set permissions at the domain- or site-level, if that is what you truly require.

In many environments, however, much more granular security permissions are desirable. The use of OUs supports this. For example, I might want to give one systems administrator full permissions on the Sales and Marketing OU and give another full permissions on the Corporate OU. Or, I might want to give Administrator A permissions to add and delete users for the Corporate OU and Administrator B permissions to manage printers and print jobs. In this way, I can easily distribute administrator permissions while maintaining reasonable security settings.

OUs offer the additional benefit of allowing permissions to be set hierarchically. That is, child OUs and objects can inherit the permissions of parent

OUs, thereby simplifying the most common configurations. Figure A.7 provides an example of how OUs can be used to configure administration permissions.

**FIGURE A.7** Using OUs to delegate administration

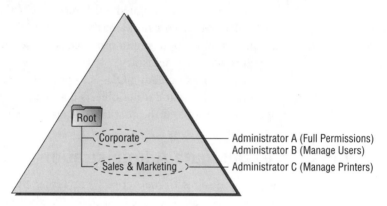

## Using OUs for Group Policy

Managing permissions for systems administrators is an important concern, but maintaining appropriate settings for users and computers can prove to be a much bigger challenge. First, there are many more users and computers than systems administrators in most networked environments. Keeping track of each of these individuals and computers is a difficult task. Ensuring that each has only the required security permissions to perform their jobs makes it even more difficult.

In the past, many systems administrators chose to give all of their users many more permissions than they required. Although this gave them the rights necessary to do their jobs, it wasn't uncommon to hear stories about users accidentally deleting system files or making potentially disastrous driver changes. The main reason for the lax security was the difficulty encountered when configuring and maintaining permissions while trying to ensure that business needs were still met.

Through the use of the Active Directory, Group Policy, and OUs, however, many of these tasks are much simpler. Group Policy is a system of settings that apply to the objects contained within an OU. A Group Policy may apply to users, groups, or other objects. Examples of Group Policy settings might include:

- Logon and Logoff Scripts
- User Policy settings (such as password requirements or workstation logon restrictions)
- Application permissions
- File and printer share information

By making these settings based on OUs, you can get the full benefit of using a hierarchical system while still providing for granular security control. Figure A.8 provides an example of how Group Policies and OUs interact.

**FIGURE  A.8**   Assigning Group Policy settings on OUs

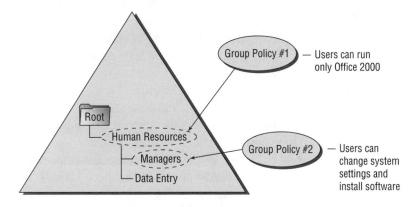

## Using OUs Based on Geography

In addition to using OUs for managing permissions, you can also use them to reflect the geographic distribution of your business and its various business units. Geographically based OUs are useful when distributed administration is supported. They can make it easier to set permissions and delegate authority to specific users who reside at one or more sites within the environment.

Within the geographically based OUs, you can still reflect business structure. For example, in a highly distributed company, each business unit might have it's own Sales, Marketing, and Engineering departments. If they are administered separately, child OUs can be created for each of these administrative units.

Overall, the use of OUs provides for the hierarchical administration and management features required in organizations of almost any size. You should take care in planning OUs and should ensure that they meet your business requirements.

# Planning Your Sites

**M**uch of the challenge in designing the Active Directory is related to mapping a company's business processes to the structure of a hierarchical data store. So far, we've taken into account many of these requirements. But what about the existing network infrastructure? Clearly, when planning for and designing the structure of the Active Directory, you must take into account your LAN and WAN characteristics.

With Windows 2000 and the Active Directory, Microsoft has allowed systems administrators to deal separately with the physical and logical architecture of the Active Directory. That is, the setup of domains, trees, and forests can occur independently of the underlying network infrastructure. Through the use of Sites, systems administrators can define their network topology and limit network communications as necessary. This makes planning much easier and allows the business concerns to be dealt with separately from the technical ones. Let's see how Active Directory Sites can be used to manage replication traffic.

## Planning for Replication Traffic

Synchronization of the Active Directory is extremely important. In order for security permissions and objects within the directory to remain consistent throughout the organization, replication must be used. The Active Directory data store supports multimaster replication. That is, data can be modified at any domain controller within the domain because replication, the process by which changes are transmitted between domain controllers, ensures that information remains consistent throughout the organization.

Ideally, every site within an organization has reliable, high-speed connections with one another. A much more realistic scenario, however, is one in which bandwidth is limited and connections are sometimes unavailable. The term bandwidth refers to the amount of information that can travel through a given network connection per unit of time. For example, a LAN connection might support up to 100 megabits per second (Mbps) while a WAN connection might only support 128 kilobits per second (Kbps).

Through the use of sites, network and systems administrators can define which domain controllers are located on which areas of the network. These settings can be based on the bandwidth available between the areas of the network. Additionally, subnets—logically partitioned areas of the network— can be defined between them. The Windows 2000 Active Directory services will use this information in deciding how and when to replicate data between domain controllers.

Directly replicating information between all domain controllers might be a viable solution for some companies. For others, however, this might result in a lot of traffic traveling over slow links. One way to efficiently synchronize data between sites that are connected with slow connections is to use a bridgehead server. Bridgehead servers are designed to accept traffic between two remote sites and to then forward this information to the appropriate servers. Figure A.9 provides an example of how a bridgehead server can reduce network bandwidth requirements and improve performance. Reduced network bandwidth requirements and improved performance can also be achieved by configuring replication to occur according to a pre-defined schedule if bandwidth usage statistics are available.

**FIGURE A.9**    Using a bridgehead server

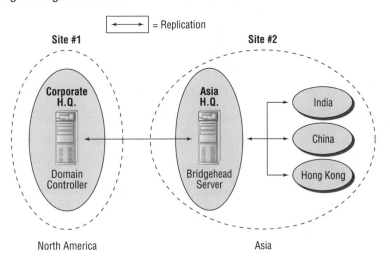

In addition to managing replication traffic, sites also offer the advantage of allowing clients to access the nearest domain controller. This prevents problems with user authentication across slow network connections and can help find the shortest and fastest path to resources such as files and printers. Therefore, it is recommended that at least one domain controller be placed at each site that contains a slow link. Preferably, this domain controller would also contain a copy of the Global Catalog so that logon attempts and resource search queries would not occur across slow links. The drawback, however, is that the deployment of more copies of the Global Catalog to servers will increase replication traffic.

Through proper planning and deployment of sites, organizations can best leverage the capabilities of the their network infrastructure while keeping the Active Directory synchronized.

# Planning Naming Conventions

One of the fundamental reasons for having a directory of any type is to bring organization to your various network accounts and resources. Of course, the value of the Active Directory is only as good as the quality of the information and objects that it contains. When planning to implement the Active Directory, you should take sufficient time to plan for naming conventions. These conventions will apply throughout your network environment.

Specifically, you'll need to decide how to name the following types of resources:

- Users

- Groups

- Computers (workstations and servers)

- Domain controllers

- Printers

- File shares

- Organizational units (OUs)

- Domains

- Sites

These names should be logical and consistent with your current (or planned) business processes. They should accurately reflect the objects to which they refer and the location of these objects within the tree. For example, businesses commonly use the formula first initial + middle initial + last name for network accounts. The fully-qualified name of a user, might be akdesai@northamerica.sales.mycompany.com. Similarly, the name of a printer might be Printer-207A.northamerica.sales.mycompany.com.

Intuitive names will make it easier for users and systems administrators to find the resources they need with minimal searching. Proper planning of naming conventions can go a long way in increasing the organization and usability of your Active Directory configuration.

# Summary

In this appendix, we looked at many factors that must be considered when planning for the Active Directory. We started by examining the current network environment of an organization. Based on the business and technical environments, we then examined how combinations of domains—trees and forests—could be created. Next, we examined several possible reasons for creating more than one domain. Then, we examined the structure within a domain—managing resources and permissions based on OUs. Finally, we considered the importance of proper site planning (to manage network replication traffic) and designing naming conventions (to increase organization and usability). Combined together, the result is a physical and logical structure for deploying directory services.

All of this information is absolutely essential to planning for the Active Directory—a step that will make a significant impact on the usefulness of Windows 2000, in general.

# Glossary

# A

**access control entry (ACE)**   An item used by the operating system to determine resource access. Each access control list (ACL) has an associated ACE that lists the permissions that have been granted or denied to the users and groups listed in the ACL.

**access control list (ACL)**   An item used by the operating system to determine resource access. Each object (such as a folder, network share, or printer) in Windows 2000 has an ACL. The ACL lists the security identifiers (SIDs) contained by objects. Only those identified in the list as having the appropriate permission can activate the services of that object.

**access token**   An object containing the security identifier (SID) of a running process. A process started by another process inherits the starting process's access token. The access token is checked against each object's access control list (ACL) to determine whether or not appropriate permissions are granted to perform any requested service.

**Accessibility Options**   Windows 2000 Professional features used to support users with limited sight, hearing, or mobility. Accessibility Options include special keyboard, sound, display, and mouse configurations.

**Accessibility Wizard**   A Windows 2000 Professional Wizard used to configure a computer based on the user's vision, hearing, and mobility needs.

**account lockout policy**   A Windows 2000 policy used to specify how many invalid logon attempts should be tolerated before a user account is locked out. Account lockout policies are set through account policies.

**account policies**   Windows 2000 policies used to determine password and logon requirements. Account policies are set through the Microsoft Management Console (MMC) Local Computer Policy snap-in.

**ACE**   See *access control entry.*

**ACL**   See *access control list.*

**Active Desktop**   A Windows 2000 feature that makes the Desktop look and work like a Web page.

**Active Directory**   A directory service available with the Windows 2000 Server platform. The Active Directory stores information in a central database and allows users to have a single user account (called a domain user account or Active Directory user account) for the network.

**Active Directory Installation Wizard (DCPROMO)**   The Windows 2000 tool that is used for promoting a Windows 2000 Server computer to a Windows 2000 domain controller. Using the Active Directory Installation Wizard, systems administrators can create trees and forests. See also *promotion.*

**Active Directory replication**   A method by which Active Directory domain controllers synchronize information. See also *replication, intersite* and *replication, intrasite.*

**Active Directory Services Interface (ADSI)**
Code component that can be used for accessing information from various types of Directory Services, such as Active Directory, Windows NT, Novell Directory Services and Lightweight Directory Access Protocol (LDAP) sources. ADSI can be accessed from within various programming languages, including Java, Visual Basic, and Visual C++.

**Active Directory user account**  A user account that is stored in the Windows 2000 Server Active Directory's central database. An Active Directory user account can provide a user with a single user account for a network. Also called a domain user account.

**Active Directory Users and Computers tool**
Windows 2000 administrative tool used for managing objects within the Active Directory.

**adapter**  Any hardware device that allows communications to occur through physically dissimilar systems. This term usually refers to peripheral cards that are permanently mounted inside computers and provide an interface from the computer's bus to another medium, such as a hard disk or a network.

**Add/Remove Programs**  Control Panel applet that allows for installing and uninstalling software applications and components of the Windows 2000 operating system.

**administrative templates**  Templates that specify additional options that can be set using the Group Policy Editor tool.

**Administrator account**  A Windows 2000 special account that has the ultimate set of security permissions and can assign any permission to any user or group.

**Administrators group**  A Windows 2000 built-in group that consists of Administrator accounts.

**ADSI**  See *Active Directory Services Interface (ADSI)*.

**alert**  A system-monitoring feature that is generated when a specific counter exceeds or falls below a specified value. Through the Performance Logs and Alerts utility, administrators can configure alerts so that a message is sent, a program is run, or a more detailed log file is generated.

**Anonymous Logon group**  A Windows 2000 special group that includes users who access the computer through anonymous logons. Anonymous logons occur when users gain access through special accounts, such as the IUSR_computername and TsInternetUser user accounts.

**answer file**  An automated installation script used to respond to configuration prompts that normally occur in a Windows 2000 Professional installation. Administrators can create Windows 2000 answer files with the Setup Manager utility.

**application assignment scripts**  Script files that specify which applications are assigned to users of the Active Directory.

**Application layer**  The seventh (top) layer of the Open Systems Interconnection (OSI) model that interfaces with application programs by providing high-level network services based on lower-level network layers.

**Application log**  A log that tracks events that are related to applications that are running on the computer. The Application log can be viewed in the Event Viewer utility.

**assigned applications** Applications installed with Windows Installer packages. Assigned applications are automatically installed when the user selects the application on the Programs menu or by document invocation (by the document extension).

**assigning** The process by which applications are make available to computers and/or users.

**auditing** The act of recording specific actions that are taken within a secure network operating system. Auditing is often used as a security measure to provide for accountability. Typical audited events include logon and logoff events, as well as accessing files and objects.

**audit policy** A Windows 2000 policy that tracks the success or failure of specified security events. Audit policies are set through Local Computer Policy.

**Authenticated Users group** A Windows 2000 special group that includes users who access the Windows 2000 operating system through a valid username and password.

**authentication** The process required to log on to a computer locally. Authentication requires a valid username and a password that exists in the local accounts database. An access token will be created if the information presented matches the account in the database.

**authoritative restore** See *restore, authoritative.*

**automated installation** The process of installing Windows 2000 using an unattended setup method, such as Remote Installation Services (RIS), unattended installation, or disk images.

# B

**backup** The process of writing all the data contained in online mass-storage devices to offline mass-storage devices for the purpose of safekeeping. Backups are usually performed from hard disk drives to tape drives. Also referred to as archiving.

**backup, copy** A backup operation in which files are backed up but are not marked as having been backed up. A copy backup is often made for archival or redundancy purposes.

**backup, daily** A backup operation in which all of the files that have changed on a certain day are backed up.

**backup, differential** A backup operation in which all files that are marked as not having been backed up are copied. The files are not marked as having been backed up. In most backup plans, a differential backup includes all of the files that have changed since the last full backup.

**backup, incremental** A backup operation in which all files that are marked as not having been backed up are copied. The files are marked as having been backed up. In most backup plans, an incremental backup includes all of the files that have changed since the last full or incremental backup.

**backup, normal** A backup operation in which all of the files in a file system location are backed up and are marked as having been backed up.

**Backup Operators group**   A Windows 2000 built-in group that includes users who can back up and restore the file system, even if the file system is NTFS and they have not been assigned permissions to the file system. The members of the Backup Operators group can only access the file system through the Windows 2000 Backup utility. To be able to directly access the file system, the user must have explicit permissions assigned.

**backup type**   A backup choice that determines which files are backed up during a backup process. Backup types include normal backup, copy backup, incremental backup, differential backup, and daily backup.

**Backup Wizard**   A Wizard used to perform a backup. The Backup Wizard is accessed through the Windows 2000 Backup utility.

**baseline**   A snapshot record of a computer's current performance statistics that can be used for performance analysis and planning purposes.

**Basic Input/Output System (BIOS)**   A set of routines in firmware that provides the most basic software interface drivers for hardware attached to the computer. The BIOS contains the boot routine.

**basic storage**   A disk-storage system supported by Windows 2000 that consists of primary partitions and extended partitions. Drives are configured as basic storage after an operating system has been upgraded from Windows NT.

**Batch group**   A Windows 2000 special group that includes users who log on as a user account that is only used to run a batch job.

**binding**   The process of linking together software components, such as network protocols and network adapters.

**BIOS**   See *Basic Input/Output System.*

**boot**   The process of loading a computer's operating system. Booting usually occurs in multiple phases, each successively more complex until the entire operating system and all its services are running. Also called bootstrap. The computer's BIOS must contain the first level of booting.

**Boot Information Negotiation Layer (BINL)**
A portion of Remote Installation Services (RIS) that allows for connecting clients to a RIS server. See also *Remote Installation Services (RIS).*

**BOOT.INI**   A file accessed during the Windows 2000 boot sequence. The BOOT.INI file is used to build the operating system menu choices that are displayed during the boot process. It is also used to specify the location of the boot partition.

**Boot Normally**   A Windows 2000 Advanced Options menu item used to boot Windows 2000 normally.

**boot partition**   The partition that contains the system files. The system files are located in C:\WINNT by default.

**BOOTSECT.DOS**   An optional file that is loaded if the user chooses to load an operating system other than Windows 2000. This file is only used in dual-boot or multi-boot computers.

**bottleneck**   A system resource that is inefficient compared with the rest of the computer system as a whole. The bottleneck can cause the rest of the system to run slowly.

**bridgehead server** Used in Windows 2000 replication to coordinate the transfer of replicated information between Active Directory sites.

# C

**caching** A speed-optimization technique that keeps a copy of the most recently used data in a fast, high-cost, low-capacity storage device rather than in the device on which the actual data resides. Caching assumes that recently used data is likely to be used again. Fetching data from the cache is faster than fetching data from the slower, larger storage device. Most caching algorithms also copy data that is most likely to be used next and perform write-back caching to further increase speed gains.

**caching-only DNS server** See *DNS server, caching-only*.

**category** A grouping of applications that are available for installation by users through the Add/Remove Programs applet in the Control Panel. Categories are useful for managing large lists of available applications.

**CD-based image** A type of image configured on a Remote Installation Services (RIS) server. A CD-based image contains only the Windows 2000 Professional operating system.

**central processing unit (CPU)** The main processor in a computer.

**Check Disk** A Windows 2000 utility that checks a hard disk for errors. Check Disk (chkdsk) attempts to fix file-system errors and scans for and attempts to recover bad sectors.

**child domain** A relative term that describes a subdomain of another domain.

**CIPHER** A command-line utility that can be used to encrypt files on NTFS volumes.

**cipher text** Encrypted data. Encryption is the process of translating data into code that is not easily accessible. Once data has been encrypted, a user must have a password or key to decrypt the data. Unencrypted data is known as plain text.

**clean install** A method of Windows 2000 Professional installation that puts the operating system into a new folder and uses its default settings the first time the operating system is loaded.

**client** A computer on a network that subscribes to the services provided by a server.

**Comma-Separated Value Directory Exchange (CSVDE)** A Windows 2000 command-line utility for exchanging information between comma-separated-value files and the Active Directory.

**compression** The process of storing data in a form that takes less space than the uncompressed data.

**Computer Management** A consolidated tool for performing common Windows 2000 management tasks. The interface is organized into three main areas of management: System Tools, Storage, and Services and Applications.

**computer name** A NetBIOS name used to uniquely identify a computer on the network. A computer name can be from 1 to 15 characters in length.

**Computer object** An Active Directory object that is a security principal and that identifies a computer that is part of a domain.

**connection object** An object that can be defined as part of the Active Directory's replication topology using the Active Directory Sites and Services tool. Connection objects are automatically created to manage Active Directory replication, and administrators can use them to manually control details about how and when replication operations occur.

**connection-oriented service** A type of connection service in which a connection (a path) is established and acknowledgments are sent. This type of communication is reliable but has a high overhead.

**connectionless service** A type of connection service that does not establish a connection (path) before transmission. This type of communication is fast, but it is not very reliable.

**Contact object** Active Directory objects that store contact information.

**Control Panel** A Windows 2000 utility that allows users to change default settings for operating system services to match their preferences. The Registry contains the Control Panel settings.

**CONVERT** A command-line utility used to convert a partition from FAT16 or FAT32 to the NTFS file system.

**copy backup** A backup type that backs up selected folders and files but does not set the archive bit.

**counter** A performance-measuring tool used to track specific information regarding a system resource, called a performance object. All Windows 2000 system resources are tracked as performance objects, such as Cache, Memory, Paging File, Process, and Processor. Each performance object has an associated set of counters. Counters are set through the System Monitor utility.

**counter log** Files that contain information collected by the Windows Performance tool. Counter logs can be used to track and analyze performance-related statistics over time.

**CPU** See *central processing unit.*

**Creator Group** The Windows 2000 special group that created or took ownership of the object (rather than an individual user). When a regular user creates an object or takes ownership of an object, the username becomes the Creator Owner. When a member of the Administrators group creates or takes ownership of an object, the Administrators group becomes the Creator Group.

**Creator Owner group** The Windows 2000 special group that includes the account that created or took ownership of an object. The account, usually a user account, has the right to modify the object, but cannot modify any other objects that were not created by the user account.

# D

**daily backup** A backup type that backs up all of the files that have been modified on the day that the daily backup is performed. The archive attribute is not set on the files that have been backed up.

**data compression**   The process of storing data in a form that takes less space than the uncompressed data.

**data encryption**   The process of translating data into code that is not easily accessible to increase security. Once data has been encrypted, a user must have a password or key to decrypt the data.

**Data Link layer**   In the Open Systems Interconnection (OSI) model, the layer that provides the digital interconnection of network devices and the software that directly operates these devices, such as network adapters.

**Debugging Mode**   A Windows 2000 Advanced Option menu item that runs the Kernel Debugger, if that utility is installed. The Kernel Debugger is an advanced troubleshooting utility.

**default gateway**   A TCP/IP configuration option that specifies the gateway that will be used if the network contains routers.

**delegation**   The process by which a user who has higher-level security permissions grants certain permissions over Active Directory objects to users who are lower-level security authorities. Delegation is often used to distribute administrative responsibilities in a network environment.

**Delegation of Control Wizard**   A Windows 2000 tool used for delegating permissions over Active Directory objects. See also *delegation*.

**Desktop**   A directory that the background of the Windows Explorer shell represents. By default, the Desktop includes objects that contain the local storage devices and available network shares. Also a key operating part of the Windows 2000 graphical interface.

**device driver**   Software that allows a specific piece of hardware to communicate with the Windows 2000 operating system.

**Device Manager**   A Windows 2000 utility used to provide information about the computer's configuration.

**DHCP**   See *Dynamic Host Configuration Protocol*.

**DHCP server**   A server configured to provide DHCP clients with all of their IP configuration information automatically.

**dial-up networking**   A service that allows remote users to dial into the network or the Internet (such as through a telephone or an ISDN connection).

**Dialup group**   A Windows 2000 special group that includes users who log on to the network from a dial-up connection.

**differential backup**   A backup type that copies only the files that have been changed since the last normal backup (full backup) or incremental backup. A differential backup backs up only those files that have changed since the last full backup, but does not reset the archive bit.

**directory replication**   The process of copying a directory structure from an export computer to an import computer(s). Anytime changes are made to the export computer, the import computer(s) is automatically updated with the changes.

**Directory Services Restore Mode**   A special boot mode for Windows 2000 domain controllers. The Directory Services Restore mode is used to boot a domain controller without starting Active Directory services. This enables systems administrators to log on locally to restore or to troubleshoot any problems with the Active Directory.

**Disk Cleanup**   A Windows 2000 utility used to identify areas of disk space that can be deleted to free additional hard disk space. Disk Cleanup works by identifying temporary files, Internet cache files, and unnecessary program files.

**disk defragmentation**   The process of rearranging the existing files on a disk so that they are stored contiguously, which optimizes access to those files.

**Disk Defragmenter**   A Windows 2000 utility that performs disk defragmentation.

**disk image**   An exact duplicate of a hard disk, used for automated installation. The disk image is copied from a reference computer that is configured in the same manner as the computers on which Windows 2000 Professional will be installed.

**Disk Management**   A Windows 2000 graphical tool for managing disks and volumes.

**disk partitioning**   The process of creating logical partitions on the physical hard drive.

**disk quotas**   A Windows 2000 feature used to specify how much disk space a user is allowed to use on specific NTFS volumes. Disk quotas can be applied for all users or for specific users.

**distinguished name**   The fully qualified name of an object within a hierarchical system. Distinguished names are used for all Active Directory objects and in the Domain Name System (DNS). No two objects in these systems should have the same distinguished name.

**Distribution group**   A collection of Active Directory users that are used primarily for e-mail distribution.

**distribution server**   A network server that contains the Windows 2000 distribution files that have been copied from the distribution CD. Clients can connect to the distribution server and install Windows 2000 over the network.

**DNS**   See *Domain Name System.*

**DNS namespace**   A hierarchical network naming structure that is designed to resolve hostnames to IP addresses. Typical DNS names within a namespace are hierarchical, ranging from most specific on the left to least specific on the right (e.g., `server1.mycompany.com`).

**DNS server**   A server that uses DNS to resolve domain or host names to IP addresses.

**DNS server, caching-only**   A DNS server that is not the authority for any specific zone but can resolve DNS queries. Caching-only DNS servers are used to improve performance.

**DNS server, master**   A DNS server that is responsible as an authority for name resolutions within a DNS zone. Each DNS zone can have only one master DNS server.

**DNS server, primary**   A DNS server that is authoritative for a zone and that is able to receive updates of DNS information.

**DNS server, secondary**   A DNS server that is used to resolve DNS names to TCP/IP addresses. Secondary servers contain a read-only copy of the DNS database.

**domain**   In Microsoft networks, an arrangement of client and server computers referenced by a specific name that shares a single security permissions database. On the Internet, a domain is a named collection of hosts and sub-domains, registered with a unique name by the InterNIC.

**domain controller**   A Windows 2000 Server computer that includes a copy of the Active Directory data store. Domain controllers contain the security information required to perform services related to the Active Directory.

**Domain Local group**   An Active Directory security or distribution group that can contain Universal groups, Global groups, or accounts from anywhere within an Active Directory forest.

**domain name**   The textual identifier of a specific Internet host. Domain names are in the form of server.organization.type (`www.microsoft.com`) and are resolved to Internet addresses by DNS servers.

**domain name server**   An Internet host dedicated to the function of translating fully qualified domain names into IP addresses.

**Domain Name System (DNS)**   The TCP/IP network service that translates textual Internet network addresses into numerical Internet network addresses.

**Domain Naming Master**   The Active Directory domain controller that is responsible for handling the addition and removal of domains within the Active Directory environment.

**domain user account**   A user account that is stored in the Windows 2000 Server Active Directory's central database. A domain user account can provide a user with a single user account for a network. Also called an Active Directory user account.

**drive letter**   A single letter assigned as an abbreviation to a mass-storage volume available to a computer.

**driver**   A program that provides a software interface to a hardware device. Drivers are written for the specific devices they control, but they present a common software interface to the computer's operating system, allowing all devices of a similar type to be controlled as if they were the same.

**dynamic disk**   A Windows 2000 disk-storage technique. A dynamic disk is divided into dynamic volumes. Dynamic volumes cannot contain partitions or logical drives, and they are not accessible through DOS. You can size or resize a dynamic disk without restarting Windows 2000.

**Dynamic Host Configuration Protocol (DHCP)**   A method of automatically assigning IP addresses to client computers on a network.

**dynamic storage**   A Windows 2000 disk-storage system that is configured as volumes. Windows 2000 Professional dynamic storage supports simple volumes, spanned volumes, and striped volumes.

# E

**effective rights**  The rights that a user actually has to a file or folder. To determine a user's effective rights, add all of the permissions that have been allowed through the user's assignments based on that user's username and group associations. Then subtract any permissions that have been denied the user through the username or group associations.

**Emergency Repair Disk (ERD)**  A disk that stores portions of the Registry, the system files, a copy of the partition boot sector, and information that relates to the startup environment. The ERD can be used to repair problems that prevent a computer from starting.

**Enable Boot Logging**  A Windows 2000 Professional Advanced Options menu item that is used to create a log file that tracks the loading of drivers and services.

**Enable VGA Mode**  A Windows 2000 Professional Advanced Options menu item that loads a standard VGA driver without starting the computer in Safe Mode.

**encryption**  The process of translating data into code that is not easily accessible to increase security. Once data has been encrypted, a user must have a password or key to decrypt the data.

**ERD**  See *Emergency Repair Disk*.

**Error event**  An Event Viewer event type that indicates the occurrence of an error, such as a driver failing to load.

**Ethernet**  The most popular Data Link layer standard for local area networking. Ethernet implements the Carrier Sense Multiple Access with Collision Detection (CSMA/CD) method of arbitrating multiple computer access to the same network. This standard supports the use of Ethernet over any type of media, including wireless broadcast. Standard Ethernet operates as 10Mbps. Fast Ethernet operates at 100Mbps.

**Event Viewer**  A Windows 2000 utility that tracks information about the computer's hardware and software, as well as security events. This information is stored in three log files: the Application log, the Security log, and the System log.

**Everyone**  A Windows 2000 special group that includes anyone who could possibly access the computer. The Everyone group includes all of the users (including Guests) who have been defined on the computer.

**extended partition**  In basic storage, a logical drive that allows you to allocate the logical partitions however you wish. Extended partitions are created after the primary partition has been created.

# F

**Failure Audit event**  An Event Viewer event that indicates the occurrence of an event that has been audited for failure, such as a failed logon when someone presents an invalid username and/or password.

**FAT16**  The 16-bit version of the File Allocation System (FAT) system, which was widely used by DOS and Windows 3.*x*. The file system is used to track where files are stored on a disk. Most operating systems support FAT16.

**FAT32**  The 32-bit version of the File Allocation System (FAT) system, which is more efficient and provides more safeguards than FAT16. Windows 9*x* and Windows 2000 support FAT32. Windows NT does not support FAT32.

**fault tolerance**  Any method that prevents system failure by tolerating single faults, usually through hardware redundancy.

**file allocation table (FAT)**  The file system used by MS-DOS and available to other operating systems, such as Windows (all versions), OS/2, and Macintosh. FAT (now known as FAT16) has become something of a standard for mass-storage compatibility because of its simplicity and wide availability. FAT has fewer fault-tolerance features than the NTFS file system and can become corrupted through normal use over time.

**file attributes**  Bits stored along with the name and location of a file in a directory entry. File attributes show the status of a file, such as archived, hidden, and read-only. Different operating systems use different file attributes to implement services such as sharing, compression, and security.

**file extension**  The three-letter suffix that follows the name of a standard file-system file. Using Group Policy and software management functionality, systems administration can specify which applications are associated with which file extensions.

**file system**  A software component that manages the storage of files on a mass-storage device by providing services that can create, read, write, and delete files. File systems impose an ordered database of files on the mass-storage device. Storage is arranged in volumes. File systems use hierarchies of directories to organize files.

**File Transfer Protocol (FTP)**  A simple Internet protocol that transfers complete files from an FTP server to a client running the FTP client. FTP provides a simple, no-overhead method of transferring files between computers but cannot perform browsing functions. Users must know the URL of the FTP server to which they wish to attach.

**filtering**  The process by which permissions on security groups are used to identify which Active Directory objects are affected by Group Policy settings. Through the use of filtering, systems administrators can maintain a fine level of control over Group Policy settings.

**foreign security principals**  Active Directory objects used to give permissions to other security principals that do not exist within an Active Directory domain. Generally, foreign security principals are automatically created by the services of the Active Directory.

**forest**  A collection of Windows 2000 domains that does not necessarily share a common namespace. All of the domains within a forest share a common schema and Global Catalog, and resources can be shared between the domains in a forest.

**format**   The process of preparing a mass-storage device for use with a file system. There are actually two levels of formatting. Low-level formatting writes a structure of sectors and tracks to the disk with bits used by the mass-storage controller hardware. The controller hardware requires this format, and it is independent of the file system. High-level formatting creates file system structures such as an allocation table and a root directory in a partition, thus creating a volume.

**forward lookup zone**   A DNS zone that is used for resolving DNS names to TCP/IP addresses.

**forwarding**   The process by which a DNS server sends a request for name resolution to another DNS server. Forwarding is often used to improve performance and to restrict network traffic over slow connections.

**FTP**   See *File Transfer Protocol.*

# G

**Global Catalog**   A portion of the Active Directory that contains a subset of information about all of the objects within all domains of the Active Directory data store. The Global Catalog is used to improve performance of authentications and for sharing information between domains.

**Global Catalog server**   A Windows 2000 Active Directory domain controller that hosts a copy of the Global Catalog. See also *Global Catalog.*

**Global group**   An Active Directory security group that contains accounts only from its own domain.

**Global Unique Identifier (GUID)**   A special identifier that uniquely identifies an object within the Active Directory.

**GPO**   See *Group Policy object.*

**Graphical User Interface (GUI)**   A computer shell program that represents mass-storage devices, directories, and files as graphical objects on a screen. A cursor driven by a pointing device, such as a mouse, manipulates the objects.

**Group Policy**   Settings that can affect the behavior of, and the functionality available to, users and computers.

**Group Policy object (GPO)**   A collection of settings that control the behavior of users and computers.

**Group Policy object (GPO) link**   A link between a Group Policy object and the Active Directory objects to which it applies. Group Policy objects can be linked to sites, domains, organizational units, and other Active Directory objects.

**groups**   Security entities to which users can be assigned membership for the purpose of applying the broad set of group permissions to the user. By managing permissions for groups and assigning users to groups, rather than assigning permissions to users, administrators can more easily manage security.

**groups, distribution**  Active Directory objects that are used primarily for the purpose of routing e-mail and other electronic communications. Distribution groups are not considered to be security principals.

**Guest account**  A Windows 2000 user account created to provide a mechanism to allow users to access the computer even if they do not have a unique username and password. This account normally has very limited privileges on the computer. This account is disabled by default.

**Guests group**  A Windows 2000 built-in group that has limited access to the computer. This group can access only specific areas. Most administrators do not allow Guest account access because it poses a potential security risk.

# H

**hard disk drive**  A mass-storage device that reads and writes digital information magnetically on discs that spin under moving heads. Hard disk drives are precisely aligned and cannot normally be removed. Hard disk drives are an inexpensive way to store gigabytes of computer data permanently. Hard disk drives also store the software installed on a computer.

**Hardware Compatibility List (HCL)**  A list of all of the hardware devices supported by Windows 2000. Hardware on the HCL has been tested and verified as being compatible with Windows 2000.

**hardware profile**  A file that stores a hardware configuration for a computer. Hardware profiles are useful when a single computer (a laptop that can be docked or undocked) has multiple hardware configurations.

**HCL**  See *Hardware Compatibility List.*

**hibernation**  The storage of anything that is stored in memory on the computer's hard disk. Hibernation ensures that none of the information stored in memory is lost when the computer is shut down. When the computer is taken out of hibernation, it is returned to its previous state.

**home folder**  A folder where users normally store their personal files and information. A home folder can be a local folder or a network folder.

**host**  An Internet server. Hosts are constantly connected to the Internet.

**HTML**  See *Hypertext Markup Language.*

**HTTP**  See *Hypertext Transfer Protocol.*

**hyperlink**  A link within text or graphics that has a Web address embedded in it. By clicking the link, a user can jump to another Web address.

**Hypertext Markup Language (HTML)**  A textual data format that identifies sections of a document, such as headers, lists, hypertext links, and so on. HTML is the data format used on the World Wide Web for the publication of Web pages.

**Hypertext Transfer Protocol (HTTP)**  An Internet protocol that transfers HTML documents over the Internet and responds to context changes that happen when a user clicks a hyperlink.

# I

**IIS**   See *Internet Information Services.*

**incremental backup**   A backup type that backs up only the files that have changed since the last normal or incremental backup. It sets the archive attribute on the files that are backed up.

**Indexing Service**   A Windows 2000 service that creates an index based on the contents and properties of files stored on the computer's local hard drive. A user can then use the Windows 2000 Search function to search or query through the index for specific keywords.

**Information event**   An Event Viewer event that informs you that a specific action has occurred, such as when a system shuts down or starts.

**Infrastructure Master**   The Windows 2000 domain controller that is responsible for managing group memberships and transferring this information to other domain controllers within the Active Directory environment.

**inheritance**   The process by which settings and properties defined on a parent object implicitly apply to a child object.

**inherited permissions**   Parent folder permissions that are applied to (or inherited by) files and subfolders of the parent folder. In Windows 2000 Professional, the default is for parent folder permissions to be applied to any files or subfolders in that folder.

**initialization files**   Files used to specify parameters that are used by an application or a utility. Initialization files are often used by setup programs to determine application installation information.

**initial user account**   The account that uses the name of the registered user and is created only if the computer is installed as a member of a workgroup (not into the Active Directory). By default, the initial user is a member of the Administrators group.

**Integrated Services Digital Network (ISDN)**   A direct, digital, dial-up connection that operates at 64KB per channel over regular twisted-pair cable. ISDN provides twice the data rate of the fastest modems per channel. Up to 24 channels can be multiplexed over two twisted pairs.

**Interactive group**   A Windows 2000 special group that includes all the users who use the computer's resources locally.

**interactive logon**   A logon when the user logs on from the computer where the user account is stored on the computer's local database. Also called a local logon.

**interactive user**   A user who physically logs on to the computer where the user account resides (rather than over the network).

**Internet connection sharing**   A Windows 2000 feature that allows a small network to be connected to the Internet through a single connection. The computer that dials into the Internet provides network address translation, addressing, and name resolution services for all of the computers on the network. Through Internet connection sharing, the other computers on the network can access Internet resources and use Internet applications, such as Internet Explorer and Outlook Express.

**Internet Explorer**   A World Wide Web browser produced by Microsoft and included with Windows 9*x*, Windows NT 4, and now Windows 2000.

**Internet Information Services (IIS)**   Software that serves Internet higher-level protocols like HTTP and FTP to clients using Web browsers. The IIS software that is installed on a Windows 2000 Server computer is a fully functional Web server and is designed to support heavy Internet usage.

**Internet Print Protocol (IPP)**   A Windows 2000 protocol that allows users to print directly to a URL. Printer and job-related information are generated in HTML format.

**Internet printer**   A Windows 2000 feature that allows users to send documents to be printed through the Internet.

**Internet Protocol (IP)**   The Network layer protocol upon which the Internet is based. IP provides a simple connectionless packet exchange. Other protocols such as TCP use IP to perform their connection-oriented (or guaranteed delivery) services.

**Internet Service Provider (ISP)**   A company that provides dial-up connections to the Internet.

**Internet Services Manager**   A Windows 2000 utility used to configure the protocols that are used by Internet Information Services (IIS) and Personal Web Services (PWS).

**internetwork**   A network made up of multiple network segments that are connected with some device, such as a router. Each network segment is assigned a network address. Network layer protocols build routing tables that are used to route packets through the network in the most efficient manner.

**InterNIC**   The agency that is responsible for assigning IP addresses.

**interprocess communications (IPC)**   A generic term describing any manner of client/server communication protocol, specifically those operating in the Application layer. IPC mechanisms provide a method for the client and server to trade information.

**intranet**   A privately owned network based on the TCP/IP protocol suite.

**IP**   See *Internet Protocol*.

**IP address**   A four-byte number that uniquely identifies a computer on an IP internetwork. InterNIC assigns the first bytes of Internet IP addresses and administers them in hierarchies. Huge organizations like the government or top-level ISPs have class A addresses, large organizations and most ISPs have class B addresses, and small companies have class C addresses. In a class A address, InterNIC assigns the first byte, and the owning organization assigns the remaining three bytes. In a class B address, InterNIC or the higher-level ISP assigns the first two bytes, and the organization assigns the remaining two bytes. In a class C address, InterNIC or the higher-level ISP assigns the first three bytes, and the organization assigns the remaining byte. Organizations not attached to the Internet are free to assign IP addresses as they please.

**IPC** See *interprocess communications.*

**IPCONFIG** A command used to display the computer's IP configuration.

**IPP** See *Internet Print Protocol.*

**ISA** See *Industry Standard Architecture.*

**ISDN** See *Integrated Services Digital Network.*

**ISP** See *Internet Service Provider.*

**iteration** The incremental process by which DNS names are resolved to IP addresses.

# K

**kernel** The core process of a preemptive operating system, consisting of a multitasking scheduler and the basic security services. Depending on the operating system, other services, such as virtual memory drivers, may be built into the kernel. The kernel is responsible for managing the scheduling of threads and processes.

# L

**LAN** See *local area network.*

**Last Known Good Configuration** A Windows 2000 Advanced Options menu item used to load the configuration that was used the last time the computer was successfully booted.

**LDAP** See *Lightweight Directory Access Protocol (LDAP).*

**LDIFDE** See *LDIF Directory Exchange (LDIFDE).*

**LDIF Directory Exchange (LDIFDE)** A command-line utility that is used to transfer Active Directory objects between LDIF files and the Active Directory. LDIF files can be read and modified through the use of LDIF-compatible tools.

**licensing server** A Windows 2000 computer that is responsible for managing software licenses. Licensing server properties can be set using the Active Directory Sites and Services tool.

**Lightweight Directory Access Protocol (LDAP)** A protocol used for querying and modifying information stored within directory services. The Active Directory can be queried and modified through the use of LDAP-compatible tools.

**local area network (LAN)** A connection of well-connected computers that usually reside within a single geographic location (such as an office building). An organization typically owns all of the hardware that makes up its LAN.

**Local Computer Policy** A Microsoft Management Console (MMC) snap-in used to implement account policies.

**local group** A group that is stored on the local computer's accounts database. These are the groups that administrators can add users to and manage directly on a Windows 2000 Professional computer.

**Local Group Policy** A Microsoft Management Console (MMC) snap-in used to implement local group policies, which include computer configuration policies and user configuration policies.

**local logon**   A logon when the user logs on from the computer where the user account is stored on the computer's local database. Also called an interactive logon.

**local policies**   Policies that allow administrators to control what a user can do after logging on. Local policies include audit policies, security option policies, and user rights policies. These policies are set through Local Computer Policy.

**local printer**   A printer that uses a physical port and that has not been shared. If a printer is defined as local, the only users who can use the printer are the local users of the computer that the printer is attached to.

**local security**   Security that governs a local or interactive user's ability to access locally stored files. Local security can be set through NTFS permissions.

**local user account**   A user account stored locally in the user accounts database of a computer that is running Windows 2000 Professional.

**local user profile**   A profile created the first time a user logs on, stored in the Documents and Settings folder. The default user profile folder's name matches the user's logon name. This folder contains a file called NTUSER.DAT and subfolders with directory links to the user's Desktop items.

**Local Users and Groups**   A utility that is used to create and manage local user and group accounts on Windows 2000 Professional computers and Windows 2000 member servers.

**locale settings**   Settings for regional items, including numbers, currency, time, date, and input locales.

**logical drive**   An allocation of disk space on a hard drive, using a drive letter. For example, a 5GB hard drive could be partitioned into two logical drives: a C: drive, which might be 2GB, and a D: drive, which might be 3GB.

**Logical Drives**   A Windows 2000 utility used to manage the logical drives on the computer.

**logical port**   A port that connects a device directly to the network. Logical ports are used with printers by installing a network card in the printers.

**logical printer**   The software interface between the physical printer (the print device) and the operating system. Also referred to as just a printer in Windows 2000 terminology.

**logoff**   The process of closing an open session with a Windows 2000 computer or network.

**logon**   The process of opening a session with a Windows 2000 computer or a network by providing a valid authentication consisting of a user account name and a password. After logon, network resources are available to the user according to the user's assigned permissions.

**logon script**   A command file that automates the logon process by performing utility functions such as attaching to additional server resources or automatically running different programs based on the user account that established the logon.

# M

**Magnifier**   A Windows 2000 utility used to create a separate window to magnify a portion of the screen. This option is designed for users who have poor vision.

**mandatory profile**   A user profile created by an administrator and saved with a special extension (.man) so that the user cannot modify the profile in any way. Mandatory profiles can be assigned to a single user or a group of users.

**mapped drive**   A shared network folder associated with a drive letter. Mapped drives appear to users as local connections on their computers and can be accessed through a drive letter using My Computer.

**master DNS server**   See *DNS server, master*.

**member server**   A server that participates in the security of Active Directory domains but does not contain a copy of the Active Directory data store.

**memory**   Any device capable of storing information. This term is usually used to indicate volatile random-access memory (RAM) capable of high-speed access to any portion of the memory space, but incapable of storing information without power.

**Microsoft Installer (MSI)**   A standard that is used to automatically deploy applications with Windows Installer packages.

**Microsoft Management Console (MMC)**
The Windows 2000 console framework for management applications. The MMC provides a common environment for snap-ins.

**mixed-mode Active Directory domains**
An Active Directory mode that allows the use of Windows NT domain controllers.

**MMC**   See *Microsoft Management Console*.

**modem**   Modulator/demodulator. A device used to create an analog signal suitable for transmission over telephone lines from a digital data stream. Modern modems also include a command set for negotiating connections and data rates with remote modems and for setting their default behavior.

**MSI**   See *Microsoft Installer*.

**multi-booting**   The process of allowing a computer to boot multiple operating systems.

**My Computer**   The folder used to view and manage a computer. My Computer provides access to all local and network drives, as well as Control Panel.

**My Documents**   The default storage location for documents that are created. Each user has a unique My Documents folder.

**My Network Places**   The folder that provides access to shared resources, such as local network resources and Web resources.

# N

**native-mode Active Directory domains**
An Active Directory mode that allows the use of only Windows 2000 domain controllers and enhances group capabilities.

**NetBEUI**   See *NetBIOS Extended User Interface*.

**NetBIOS**   See *Network Basic Input/Output System*.

**NetBIOS Extended User Interface (NetBEUI)**
A simple Network layer transport protocol developed to support NetBIOS installations. NetBEUI is not routable, and so it is not appropriate for larger networks. NetBEUI is the fastest transport protocol available for Windows 2000.

**NET USE**   A command-line utility used to map network drives.

**NetWare**   A popular network operating system developed by Novell in the early 1980s. NetWare is a cooperative, multitasking, highly optimized, dedicated-server network operating system that has client support for most major operating systems. Recent versions of NetWare include graphical client tools for management from client stations. At one time, NetWare accounted for more than 70 percent of the network operating system market.

**network adapter**   The hardware used to connect computers (or other devices) to the network. Network adapters function at the Physical layer and the Network layer of the Open System Interconnection (OSI) model.

**Network Basic Input/Output System (NetBIOS)**   A client/server IPC service developed by IBM in the early 1980s. NetBIOS presents a relatively primitive mechanism for communication in client/server applications, but its widespread acceptance and availability across most operating systems makes it a logical choice for simple network applications. Many of the network IPC mechanisms in Windows 2000 are implemented over NetBIOS.

**Network group**   A Windows 2000 special group that includes the users who access a computer's resources over a network connection.

**Network Monitor**   A Windows 2000 utility that can be used for monitoring and decoding packets that are transferred on the network.

**network printer**   A printer that is available to local and network users. A network printer can use a physical port or a logical port.

**New Technology File System (NTFS)**   A secure, transaction-oriented file system developed for Windows NT and Windows 2000. NTFS offers features such as local security on files and folders, data compression, disk quotas, and data encryption.

**normal backup**   A backup type that backs up all selected folders and files and then marks each file that has been backed up as archived.

**NTFS**   See *New Technology File System*.

**NTFS permissions**   Permissions used to control access to NTFS folders and files. Access is configured by allowing or denying NTFS permissions to users and groups.

**NTUSER.DAT**   The file that is created for a local user profile.

**NTUSER.MAN**   The file that is created for a mandatory profile.

**NWLINK IPX/SPX/NetBIOS Compatible Transport**   Microsoft's implementation of the Novell IPX/SPX protocol stack.

# O

**offline files and folders** A Windows 2000 feature that allows network folders and files to be stored on Windows 2000 clients. Users can access network files even if the network location is not available.

**Open Systems Interconnection (OSI) model** A reference model for network component interoperability developed by the International Standards Organization (ISO) to promote cross-vendor compatibility of hardware and software network systems. The OSI model splits the process of networking into seven distinct services, or layers. Each layer uses the services of the layer below to provide its service to the layer above.

**optimization** Any effort to reduce the workload on a hardware component by eliminating, obviating, or reducing the amount of work required of the hardware component through any means. For instance, file caching is an optimization that reduces the workload of a hard disk drive.

**organizational units (OUs)** Used to logically organize the Active Directory objects within a domain.

**OSI model** See *Open Systems Interconnection model.*

**owner** The user associated with an NTFS file or folder who is able to control access and grant permissions to other users.

# P

**packages, Windows Installer** See *Windows Installer packages.*

**page file** Logical memory that exists on the hard drive. If a system is experiencing excessive paging (swapping between the page file and physical RAM), it needs more memory.

**parent domain** A relative term that describes a domain that is a parent of another domain. Parent domains may contain child domains (also called subdomains).

**partition** A section of a hard disk that can contain an independent file system volume. Partitions can be used to keep multiple operating systems and file systems on the same hard disk.

**password policies** Windows 2000 policies used to enforce security requirements on the computer. Password policies are set on a per-computer basis, and they cannot be configured for specific users. Password policies are set through account policies.

**patch** A Windows Installer file that updates application code. Patches can be used to ensure that new features are installed after an application has already completed installation.

**PC Card** A special, credit-card-sized device used to add devices to a laptop computer. Also called a PCMCIA card.

**PCI** See *Peripheral Connection Interface.*

**PCMCIA card** See *Personal Computer Memory Card International Association card.*

**Peer Web Services (PWS)** Software that acts as a small-scale Web server, for use with a small intranet or a small Internet site with limited traffic. Windows 2000 uses PWS to publish resources on the Internet or a private intranet. When you install Internet Information Services (IIS), on a Windows 2000 Professional computer, you are actually installing PWS.

**performance log** Windows 2000 performance information that is stored to a file within the file system for later analysis or for analysis using other applications.

**Performance Logs and Alerts** A Windows 2000 utility used to log performance-related data and generate alerts based on performance-related data.

**permissions** Security constructs used to regulate access to resources by username or group affiliation. Permissions can be assigned by administrators to allow any level of access, such as read-only, read/write, or delete, by controlling the ability of users to initiate object services. Security is implemented by checking the user's security identifier (SID) against each object's access control list (ACL).

**Personal Computer Memory Card International Association (PCMCIA) card** A special, credit-card-sized device used to add devices to a laptop computer. Also called a PC Card.

**Personal Web Manager** A Windows 2000 utility used to configure and manage Peer Web Services (PWS). This utility has options for configuring the location of the home page and stopping the Web site, and displays statistics for monitoring the Web site.

**physical port** A serial (COM) or parallel (LPT) port that connects a device, such as a printer, directly to a computer.

**PING** A command used to send an Internet Control Message Protocol (ICMP) echo request and echo reply to verify that a remote computer is available.

**Plug and Play** A technology that uses a combination of hardware and software to allow the operating system to automatically recognize and configure new hardware without any user intervention.

**policies** General controls that enhance the security of an operating environment. In Windows 2000, policies affect restrictions on password use and rights assignments, and determine which events will be recorded in the Security log.

**POST** See *Power On Self Test*.

**Power On Self Test (POST)** A part of the Windows 2000 boot sequence. The POST detects the computer's processor, how much memory is present, what hardware is recognized, and whether or not the BIOS is standard or has Plug-and-Play capabilities.

**Power Users group** A Windows 2000 built-in group that has fewer rights than the Administrators group, but more rights than the Users groups. Members of the Power Users group can perform tasks such as creating local users and groups and modifying the users and groups that they have created.

**Preboot eXecution Environment (PXE)**   A standard used to boot computers that do not have operating systems installed to connect to a network and transfer information. PXE-enabled computers are supported through the use of the Remote Installation Services (RIS). See also *Remote Installation Services (RIS)*.

**Presentation layer**   The layer of the Open Systems Interconnection (OSI) model that converts and translates (if necessary) information between the Session layer and Application layer.

**prestaging**   The process of identifying computers that are to be installed through the use of Remote Installation Services. Prestaging can increase security by only allowing specific machines to perform a remote installation. See also *Remote Installation Services (RIS)*.

**primary DNS server**   See *DNS server, primary*.

**Primary Domain Controller (PDC) Emulator**   A Windows 2000 domain controller that is used primarily for backward compatibility with Windows NT domain controllers.

**primary partition**   A part of basic storage on a disk. The primary partition is the first partition created on a hard drive. The primary partition uses all of the space that is allocated to the partition. This partition is usually marked as active and is the partition that is used to boot the computer.

**print device**   The actual physical printer or hardware device that generates printed output.

**print driver**   The specific software that understands a print device. Each print device has an associated print driver.

**Printer object**   An Active Directory object that identifies printers that are published within domains.

**print processor**   The process that determines whether or not a print job needs further processing once that job has been sent to the print spooler. The processing (also called rendering) is used to format the print job so that it can print correctly at the print device.

**print queue**   A directory or folder on the print server that stores the print jobs until they can be printed. Also called a printer spooler.

**print server**   The computer on which the printer has been defined. When a user sends a print job to a network printer, it goes to the print server first.

**print spooler**   A directory or folder on the print server that stores the print jobs until they can be printed. Also called a print queue.

**printer**   In Windows 2000 terminology, the software interface between the physical printer (see *print device*) and the operating system.

**printer pool**   A configuration that allows one printer to be used for multiple print devices. A printer pool can be used when multiple printers use the same print driver (and are normally in the same location). With a printer pool, users can send their print jobs to the first available printer.

**priority**   A level of execution importance assigned to a thread. In combination with other factors, the priority level determines how often that thread will get computer time according to a scheduling algorithm.

**process**   A running program containing one or more threads. A process encapsulates the protected memory and environment for its threads.

**processor**   A circuit designed to automatically perform lists of logical and arithmetic operations. Unlike microprocessors, processors may be designed from discrete components rather than be a monolithic integrated circuit.

**processor affinity**   The association of a processor with specific processes that are running on the computer. Processor affinity is used to configure multiple processors.

**promotion**   The act of converting a Windows 2000 Server computer to a domain controller. See also *Active Directory Installation Wizard*.

**protocol**   An established rule of communication adhered to by the parties operating under it. Protocols provide a context in which to interpret communicated information. Computer protocols are rules used by communicating devices and software services to format data in a way that all participants understand.

**published applications**   Applications installed with Windows Installer packages. Users can choose whether or not they will install published applications through the Control Panel Add/Remove Programs icon.

**publishing**   Making applications available for use by users through Group Policy and Software Installation settings. Published applications can be installed on demand or when required by end users through the use of the Add/Remove Programs applet in the Control Panel.

**PWS**   See *Peer Web Services*.

**PXE**   See *Preboot eXecution Environment (PXE)*.

# R

**RAM**   See *random-access memory*.

**random-access memory (RAM)**   Integrated circuits that store digital bits in massive arrays of logical gates or capacitors. RAM is the primary memory store for modern computers, storing all running software processes and contextual data.

**RAS**   See *Remote Access Service*.

**real-time application**   A process that must respond to external events at least as fast as those events can occur. Real-time threads must run at very high priorities to ensure their ability to respond in real time.

**Recovery Console**   A Windows 2000 option for recovering from a failed system. The Recovery Console starts Windows 2000 without the graphical interface and allows the administrator limited capabilities, such as adding or replacing files and starting and stopping services.

**recursion** The process by which DNS servers or clients use other DNS servers to resolve DNS names to TCP/IP address queries.

**Recycle Bin** A folder that holds files and folders that have been deleted. Files can be retrieved or cleared (for permanent deletion) from the Recycle Bin.

**REGEDIT** A Windows program used to edit the Registry. It does not support full editing, as does the REGEDT32 program, but it has better search capabilities than REGEDT32.

**REGEDT32** The primary utility for editing the Windows 2000 Registry.

**Regional Options** A Control Panel utility used to enable and configure multilingual editing and viewing on a localized version of Windows 2000 Professional.

**Registry** A database of settings required and maintained by Windows 2000 and its components. The Registry contains all of the configuration information used by the computer. It is stored as a hierarchical structure and is made up of keys, hives, and value entries.

**Relative ID (RID) Master** The domain controller that is responsible for generating unique identifiers for each of the domains within an Active Directory environment.

**Remote Access Service (RAS)** A service that allows network connections to be established over a modem connection, an Integrated Services Digital Network (ISDN) connection, or a null-modem cable. The computer initiating the connection is called the RAS client; the answering computer is called the RAS server.

**remote installation** Installation of Windows 2000 Professional performed remotely through Remote Installation Services (RIS).

**Remote Installation Preparation (RIPrep) image** A type of image configured on a Remote Installation Services (RIS) server. A RIPrep image can contain the Windows 2000 operating system and applications. This type of image is based on a preconfigured computer.

**Remote Installation Services (RIS)** Windows 2000 service that allows for the installation of the Windows 2000 Professional operating system on remote computers.

**Remote Installation Preparation (RIPrep) Wizard** A remote installation tool used to create "images" of the configuration of a specific workstation. This method increases consistency in workstation rollouts and decreases the administrative effort required.

**Remote Procedure Call (RPC) protocol** A protocol used to allow communications between system processes on remote computers. RPC protocol is used by the Active Directory for intrasite replication. See also *instrasite replication.*

**Removable Storage** A Windows 2000 utility used to track information on removable storage media, which include CDs, DVDs, tapes, and jukeboxes containing optical discs.

**rendering** The process that determines whether or not a print job needs further processing once that job has been sent to the spooler. The processing is used to format the print job so that it can print correctly at the print device.

**replication, intersite** The transfer of information between domain controllers that reside in different Active Directory sites.

**replication, intrasite** The transfer of information between domain controllers that reside within the same Active Directory site.

**Replicator group** A Windows 2000 built-in group that supports directory replication, which is a feature used by domain servers. Only domain user accounts that will be used to start the replication service should be assigned to this group.

**Requests for Comments (RFCs)** The set of standards defining the Internet protocols as determined by the Internet Engineering Task Force and available in the public domain on the Internet. RFCs define the functions and services provided by each of the many Internet protocols. Compliance with the RFCs guarantees cross-vendor compatibility.

**resource** Any useful service, such as a shared folder or a printer.

**resource record (RR)** A DNS entry that specifies the availability of specific DNS services. For example, an MX record specifies the IP address of a mail server, and Host (A) records specify the IP addresses of workstations on the network.

**restore, authoritative** Specifies that the contents of a certain portion of the Active Directory on a domain controller should override any changes on other domain controllers, regardless of their sequence numbers. An authoritative restore is used to restore the contents of the Active Directory to a previous point in time.

**Restore Wizard** A Wizard used to restore data. The Restore Wizard is accessed through the Windows 2000 Backup utility.

**reverse lookup zone** A DNS zone that is used to resolve a TCP/IP address to a DNS name.

**RFC** See *Request For Comments*.

**RIPrep image** See *Remote Installation Preparation image*.

**RIS** See *Remote Installation Services (RIS)*.

**roaming profile** A user profile that is stored and configured to be downloaded from a server. Roaming profiles allow users to access their profiles from any location on the network.

**root domain** In DNS, the name of the top of the Internet domain hierarchy. Although the root domain does not have a name, it is often referred to as ".".

**router** A Network layer device that moves packets between networks. Routers provide internetwork connectivity.

# S

**Safe Mode** A Windows 2000 Advanced Options menu item that loads the absolute minimum of services and drivers that are needed to start Windows 2000. The drivers that are loaded with Safe Mode include basic files and drivers for the mouse (unless a serial mouse is attached to the computer), monitor, keyboard, hard drive, standard video driver, and default system services. Safe Mode is considered a diagnostic mode. It does not include networking capabilities.

**Safe Mode with Command Prompt**   A Windows 2000 Advanced Options menu item that starts Windows 2000 in Safe Mode, but instead of loading the graphical interface, it loads a command prompt.

**Safe Mode with Networking**   A Windows 2000 Advanced Options menu item that starts Windows 2000 in Safe Mode, but it adds networking features.

**schema**   A database structure for all of the types of objects that are supported within the Active Directory, along with the attributes for each of these objects.

**Schema Master**   A Windows 2000 domain controller that is responsible for maintaining the master copy of the Active Directory schema. There is only one Schema Master per Active Directory forest. See also *schema*.

**script policy**   Setting within Group Policy objects that specifies login, logoff, startup, and shutdown script settings.

**SCSI**   See *Small Computer Systems Interface*.

**secondary DNS server**   See *DNS server, secondary*.

**security**   The measures taken to secure a system against accidental or intentional loss, usually in the form of accountability procedures and use restriction, for example through NTFS permissions and share permissions.

**Security Configuration and Analysis utility**   A Windows 2000 utility used for creating security profiles and managing security settings across multiple machines.

**Security groups**   Active Directory objects that can contain users or other groups and that are used for the management and assignment of permissions. Users are placed into Security groups, and then permissions are granted to these groups. Security groups are considered to be security principals.

**security identifier (SID)**   A unique code that identifies a specific user or group to the Windows 2000 security system. SIDs contain a complete set of permissions for that user or group.

**Security log**   A log that tracks events that are related to Windows 2000 auditing. The Security log can be viewed through the Event Viewer utility.

**security option policies**   Policies used to configure security for the computer. Security option policies apply to computers rather than to users or groups. These policies are set through Local Computer Policy.

**security principals**   An Active Directory object that is used for the assignment and maintenance of security settings. The primary security principals are Users, Groups, and Computers.

**Security Templates**   Files used by the Security Configuration and Analysis tool for defining and enforcing security settings across multiple computers.

**separator page**   A page used at the beginning of each document to identify the user who submitted the print job. When users share a printer, separator pages can be useful for distributing print jobs.

**serial**   A method of communication that transfers data across a medium one bit at a time, usually adding stop, start, and check bits to ensure quality transfer.

**service**   A process dedicated to implementing a specific function for another process. Most Windows 2000 components are services used by user-level applications.

**Service group**   A Windows 2000 special group that includes users who log on as a user account that is only used to run a service.

**service pack**   An update to the Windows 2000 operating system that includes bug fixes and enhancements.

**Services**   A Windows 2000 utility used to manage the services installed on the computer.

**Setup Manager (SETUPMGR)**   A Windows 2000 utility used to create automated installation scripts or unattended answer files.

**SETUPMGR**   See *Setup Manager*.

**share**   A resource such as a folder or printer shared over a network.

**Shared Folder object**   An Active Directory object that specifies the name and location of specific shared resources that are available to users of the Active Directory.

**share permissions**   Permissions used to control access to shared folders. Share permissions can only be applied to folders, as opposed to NTFS permissions, which are more complex and can be applied to folders and files.

**shared folder**   A folder on a Windows 2000 computer that network users can access.

**Shared Folders**   A Windows 2000 utility for managing shared folders on the computer.

**shortcut**   A quick link to an item that is accessible from a computer or network, such as a file, program, folder, printer, or computer. Shortcuts can exist in various locations including the Desktop, the Start menu, or within folders.

**SID**   See *security identifier*.

**Simple Mail Transfer Protocol (SMTP)**   A TCP/IP-based protocol that is primarily used for the exchange of Internet e-mail. SMTP can also be used by the Active Directory to manage intersite replication between domain controllers. See also *replication, intersite*.

**simple volume**   A dynamic disk volume that contains space from a single disk. The space from the single drive can be contiguous or noncontiguous. Simple volumes are used when the computer has enough disk space on a single drive to hold an entire volume.

**Single Instance Store (SIS)**   A feature of NTFS 5 that reduces the amount of disk space required to store files by eliminating redundancy of data. The SIS functionality is especially useful for creating images for use with Remote Installation Services (RIS). See also *Remote Installation Services (RIS)*.

**single master operations**   Specific functions that must be managed within an Active Directory environment but are only handled by specific domain controllers. Some single master operations are unique to each domain, and some are unique to the entire Active Directory forest.

**SIS**   See *Single Instance Store (SIS)*.

**site**   A collection of well-connected TCP/IP subnets. Sites are used for defining the topology of Active Directory replication.

**site link**   A link between two or more Active Directory sites. See also *site*.

**site link bridge**   A connection between two or more Active Directory site links. A site link bridge can be used to create a transitive relationship for replication between sites. See also *site* and *site link*.

**Small Computer Systems Interface (SCSI)**

A high-speed, parallel-bus interface that connects hard disk drives, CD-ROM drives, tape drives, and many other peripherals to a computer. SCSI is the mass-storage connection standard among all computers except IBM compatibles, which use SCSI or IDE.

**SMTP**   See *Simple Mail Transfer Protocol*.

**snap-in**   An administrative tool developed by Microsoft or a third-party vendor that can be added to the Microsoft Management Console (MMC) in Windows 2000.

**spanned volume**   A dynamic disk volume that consists of disk space on 2 to 32 dynamic drives. Spanned volume sets are used to dynamically increase the size of a dynamic volume. With spanned volumes, the data is written sequentially, filling space on one physical drive before writing to space on the next physical drive in the spanned volume set.

**special group**   A group used by the system, in which membership is automatic if certain criteria are met. Administrators cannot manage special groups.

**spooler**   A service that buffers output to a low-speed device, such as a printer, so that the software outputting to the device is not tied up waiting for the device to be ready.

**Start menu**   A Windows 2000 Desktop item, located on the Taskbar. The Start menu contains a list of options and programs that can be run.

**stripe set**   A single volume created across multiple hard disk drives and accessed in parallel for the purpose of optimizing disk-access time. NTFS can create stripe sets.

**striped volume**   A dynamic disk volume that stores data in equal stripes between 2 to 32 dynamic drives. Typically, administrators use striped volumes when they want to combine the space of several physical drives into a single logical volume and increase disk performance.

**subnet**   A collection of TCP/IP addresses that define a particular network location. All of the computers within a subnet share the same group of TCP/IP addresses and have the same subnet mask.

**subnet mask**   A number mathematically applied to IP addresses to determine which IP addresses are a part of the same subnetwork as the computer applying the subnet mask.

**Success Audit event**   An Event Viewer event that indicates the occurrence of an event that has been audited for success, such as a successful logon.

**switching**   A network technology that improves performance and manageability by dynamically segmenting network traffic between only those machines that are involved in the communications.

**Sysprep** See *System Preparation Tool*.

**System group** A Windows 2000 special group that contains system processes that access specific functions as a user.

**System Information** A Windows 2000 utility used to collect and display information about the computer's current configuration.

**System log** A log that tracks events that relate to the Windows 2000 operating system. The System log can be viewed through the Event Viewer utility.

**System Monitor** A Windows 2000 tool used for monitoring performance. The System Monitor includes chart, histogram, and report views.

**system partition** The active partition on an Intel-based computer that contains the hardware-specific files used to load the Windows 2000 operating system.

**system policies** Policies used to control what a user can do and the user's environment. System policies can be applied to all users or all computers, or to a specific user, group, or computer. System policies work by overwriting current settings in the Registry with the system policy settings. System policies are created through the System Policy Editor.

**System Policy Editor** A Windows 2000 utility used to create system policies.

**System Preparation Tool (Sysprep)** A Windows 2000 utility used to prepare a disk image for disk duplication.

**System State** Information used to manage the configuration of a Windows 2000 operating system. For Windows 2000 domain controllers, the System State information includes a copy of the Active Directory data store. The Windows 2000 Backup utility can be used to back up and restore the System State.

**System Tools** A Computer Management utility grouping that provides access to utilities for managing common system functions. The System Tools utility includes the Event Viewer, System Information, Performance Logs and Alerts, Shared Folders, Device Manager, and Local Users and Groups utilities.

# T

**Task Manager** A Windows 2000 utility that can be used to quickly and easily obtain a snapshot of current system performance.

**Task Scheduler** A Windows 2000 utility used to schedule tasks to occur at specified intervals.

**Taskbar** A Windows 2000 Desktop item, which appears across the bottom of the screen by default. The Taskbar contains the Start menu and buttons for any programs, documents, or windows that are currently running on the computer. Users can switch between open items by clicking the item in the Taskbar.

**TCP** See *Transmission Control Protocol*.

**TCP/IP** See *Transmission Control Protocol/ Internet Protocol*.

**TCP/IP printer port**  A logical port, used when a printer is attached to the network by installing a network card in the printer. Configuring a TCP/IP port requires the IP address of the network printer.

**Terminal Server User group**  A Windows 2000 special group that includes users who log on through Terminal Services.

**thread**  A list of instructions running in a computer to perform a certain task. Each thread runs in the context of a process, which embodies the protected memory space and the environment of the threads. Multithreaded processes can perform more than one task at the same time.

**trace log**  A log file that can be created through the use of the Windows 2000 Performance tool. Trace logs record specific events and can be analyzed through the use of compatible utilities.

**transformation file**  A type of file used by the Windows Installer to modify the behavior of the application-installation process.

**transitive trust**  A trust relationship that allows for implicit trusts between domains. For example, if Domain A trusts Domain B and Domain B trusts Domain C, then Domain A implicitly trusts Domain C. See also *trust* and *two-way trust*.

**Transmission Control Protocol (TCP)**  A Transport layer protocol that implements guaranteed packet delivery using the IP protocol.

**Transmission Control Protocol/Internet Protocol (TCP/IP)**  A suite of Internet protocols upon which the global Internet is based. TCP/IP is a general term that can refer either to the TCP and IP protocols used together or to the complete set of Internet protocols. TCP/IP is the default protocol for Windows 2000.

**Transport layer**  The Open Systems Interconnection (OSI) model layer responsible for the guaranteed serial delivery of packets between two computers over an internetwork. TCP is the Transport layer protocol in TCP/IP.

**transport protocol**  A service that delivers discreet packets of information between any two computers in a network. Higher-level, connection-oriented services are built on transport protocols.

**tree**  A set of Active Directory domains that share a common namespace and are connected by a transitive two-way trust. Resources can be shared between the domains in an Active Directory tree.

**Trivial File Transfer Protocol Daemon (TFTPD)**  Used by Remote Installation Services (RIS) to transfer data to remote installation clients.

**trust**  A relationship between domains that allows for the sharing of resources.

**two-way trust**  A trust relationship in which two domains trust each other. For example, a two-way trust might involve Domain A trusting Domain B and Domain B trusting Domain A.

# U

**unattended installation**   A method of installing Windows 2000 Professional remotely with little or no user intervention. Unattended installation uses a distribution server to install Windows 2000 Professional on a target computer.

**UNC**   See *Universal Naming Convention.*

**Uniform Resource Locator (URL)**   An Internet standard naming convention for identifying resources available via various TCP/IP application protocols. For example, `http://www.microsoft.com` is the URL for Microsoft's World Wide Web server site, and `ftp://gateway.dec.com` is a popular FTP site. A URL allows easy hypertext references to a particular resource from within a document or mail message.

**Universal group**   An Active Directory Security or Distribution group that can contain members from, and be accessed from, any domain within an Active Directory forest. A domain must be running in native mode to use Universal groups.

**Universally Unique Identifier (UUID)**   A unique number used in newer PCs that can be used to identify a computer. The UUID can be used during the prestaging of clients for use with Remote Installation Services (RIS). See also *prestaging* and *Remote Installation Services (RIS).*

**Universal Naming Convention (UNC)**   A multivendor, multiplatform convention for identifying shared resources on a network. UNC names follow the naming convention `\\computername\sharename`.

**upgrade**   A method for installing Windows 2000 that preserves existing settings and preferences when converting to the newer operating system.

**Upgrade Report**   A report generated by the Setup program that summarizes any known compatibility issues that you might encounter during the upgrade. The Upgrade Report can be saved as a file or printed.

**User object**   An Active Directory object that is a security principal and that identifies individuals that can log on to a domain.

**user profile**   A profile that stores a user's Desktop configuration. A user profile can contain a user's Desktop arrangement, program items, personal program groups, network and printer connections, screen colors, mouse settings, and other personal preferences. Administrators can create mandatory profiles, which cannot be changed by the users, and roaming profiles, which users can access from any computer they log on to.

**user rights policies**   Policies that control the rights that users and groups have to accomplish network tasks. User rights policies are set through Local Computer Policy.

**username**   A user's account name in a logon-authenticated system.

**Users group**   A Windows 2000 built-in group that includes end users who should have very limited system access. After a clean installation of Windows 2000 Professional, the default settings for this group prohibit users from compromising the operating system or program files. By default, all users who have been created on the computer, except Guest, are members of the Users group.

**Utility Manager** A Windows 2000 utility used to manage the three accessibility utilities: Magnifier, Narrator, and On-Screen Keyboard.

# V

**video adapter** The hardware device that outputs the display to the monitor.

**virtual memory** A kernel service that stores memory pages not currently in use on a mass-storage device to free the memory occupied for other uses. Virtual memory hides the memory-swapping process from applications and higher-level services.

**virtual private network (VPN)** A private network that uses links across private or public networks (such as the Internet). When data is sent over the remote link, it is encapsulated, encrypted, and requires authentication services.

**volume** A storage area on a Windows 2000 dynamic disk. Dynamic volumes cannot contain partitions or logical drives, and they are not accessible through DOS. Windows 2000 Professional dynamic storage supports three dynamic volume types: simple volumes, spanned volumes, and striped volumes.

**VPN** See *virtual private network.*

# W

**WAN** See *wide area network.*

**wide area network (WAN)** A distributed network, typically connected through slow, and sometimes unreliable, links. The various sites that make up a WAN are typically connected through leased lines.

**Warning event** An Event Viewer event that indicates that you should be concerned with the event. The event may not be critical in nature, but it is significant and may be indicative of future errors.

**Web browser** An application that makes HTTP requests and formats the resultant HTML documents for the users. Most Web browsers understand all standard Internet protocols.

**Win16** The set of application services provided by the 16-bit versions of Microsoft Windows: Windows 3.1 and Windows for Workgroups 3.11.

**Win32** The set of application services provided by the 32-bit versions of Microsoft Windows: Windows 95, Windows 98, Windows NT, and Windows 2000.

**Windows 9*x*** The 32-bit Windows 95, Windows 98, and Windows ME versions of Microsoft Windows for medium-range, Intel-based personal computers. This system includes peer networking services, Internet support, and strong support for older DOS applications and peripherals.

**Windows 2000 Backup** The Windows 2000 utility used to run the Backup Wizard, the Restore Wizard, and create an Emergency Repair Disk (ERD).

**Windows 2000 boot disk** A disk that can be used to boot to the Windows 2000 Professional operating system in the event of a Windows 2000 Professional boot failure.

**Windows 2000 Multilanguage Version**
The version of Windows 2000 that supports multiple-language user interfaces through a single copy of Windows 2000.

**Windows 2000 Professional** The current version of the Windows operating system for high-end desktop environments. Windows 2000 Professional integrates the best features of Windows 98 and Windows NT 4 Workstation, supports a wide range of hardware, makes the operating system easier to use, and reduces the cost of ownership.

**Windows 2000 Professional Setup Boot Disks** Floppy disks that can used to boot to the Windows 2000 operating system. With these disks, you can use the Recovery Console and the Emergency Repair Disk (ERD).

**Windows Installer** A Windows service that provides for the automatic installation of applications through the use of compatible installation scripts.

**Windows Installer packages** Special files that include the information necessary to install Windows-based applications.

**Windows Internet Name Service (WINS)**
A network service for Microsoft networks that provides Windows computers with Internet numbers for specified NetBIOS computer names, facilitating browsing and intercommunication over TCP/IP networks.

**Windows NT** The predecessor to Windows 2000 that is a 32-bit version of Microsoft Windows for powerful Intel, Alpha, PowerPC, or MIPS-based computers. This operating system includes peer networking services, server networking services, Internet client and server services, and a broad range of utilities.

**Windows NT File System (NTFS)** See *New Technology File System (NTFS)*.

**Windows Script Host (WSH)** A utility for running scripts on Windows-based computers. By default, WSH includes support for the VBScript and JScript languages. Through the use of third-party extensions, scripts can be written in other languages.

**Windows Update** A utility that connects the computer to Microsoft's Web site and checks the files to make sure that they are the most up-to-date versions.

**WINS** See *Windows Internet Name Service*.

**WINS server** The server that runs WINS and is used to resolve NetBIOS names to IP addresses.

**WMI Control** A Windows 2000 utility that provides an interface for monitoring and controlling system resources. WMI stands for Windows Management Instrumentation.

**workgroup** In Microsoft networks, a collection of related computers, such as those used in a department, that do not require the uniform security and coordination of a domain. Workgroups are characterized by decentralized management, as opposed to the centralized management that domains use.

**write-back caching** A caching optimization wherein data written to the slow store is cached until the cache is full or until a subsequent write operation overwrites the cached data. Write-back caching can significantly reduce the write operations to a slow store because many write operations are subsequently obviated by new information. Data in the write-back cache is also available for subsequent reads. If something happens to prevent the cache from writing data to the slow store, the cache data will be lost.

**write-through caching** A caching optimization wherein data written to a slow store is kept in a cache for subsequent rereading. Unlike write-back caching, write-through caching immediately writes the data to the slow store and is therefore less optimal but more secure.

# Z

**ZAP files** Files that can be used with Windows Installer packages instead of Microsoft Installer (MSI) format files. ZAP files are used to install applications using their native Setup program.

**zone** A portion of the DNS namespace that is managed by a specific group of DNS servers.

**zone, forward lookup** See *forward lookup zone*.

**zone, reverse lookup** See *reverse lookup zone*.

**zone transfer** The synchronization of information between DNS servers that are responsible for servicing the same DNS zone.

# Index

**Note to the Reader:** Throughout this index **boldfaced** page numbers indicate primary discussions of a topic. *Italicized* page numbers indicate illustrations.

## B

## J

# N

# O

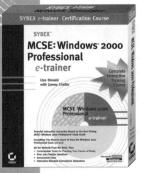

From self-study texts to advanced computer-based training, simulated testing programs to last-minute review guides, Sybex has the most complete MCSE training solution on the market.

# Sybex® Covers
# MCSE
## CERTIFICATION PROGRAMS

## Study Guides

Designed for optimal learning, Sybex Study Guides provide you with comprehensive coverage of all exam objectives. Hands-on exercises and review questions help reinforce your knowledge.

### STUDY

- In-depth coverage of exam objectives
- Hands-on exercises
- CD includes: test engine, flashcards for PCs and Palm devices, PDF version of entire book
- Insights and tips from expert instructors

## Sybex e-trainer™
### software

Based on the content of the Study Guides, Sybex e-trainers offer you advanced computer-based training, complete with animations and customization features. Self-assessment and study planning features put you on the fast track to success.

- Customizable study planning tools
- Narrated instructional animations
- Preliminary assessment tests
- Results reporting

## Virtual Test Center™
### software

Powered by an advanced testing engine, Sybex's new line of *Virtual Test Centers* gives you the opportunity to test your knowledge before sitting for the real exam.

### PRACTICE

- Hundreds of challenging questions
- Computer adaptive testing
- Support for drag-and-drop and hot-spot formats
- Detailed explanations and cross-references

## Exam Notes™

Organized according to the official exam objectives, Sybex *Exam Notes* help reinforce your knowledge of key exam topics and identify potential weak areas requiring further study.

### REVIEW

- Excellent quick review before the exam
- Concise summaries of key exam topics
- Tips and insights from experienced instructors
- Definitions of key terms and concepts

*For a complete listing of MCSE titles, visit us at **www.sybex.com**.*

SYBEX®
www.sybex.com

## 25 Years of Publishing Excellence

# THE ENCYCLOPEDIA OF
# ANIMATED CARTOONS

## THIRD EDITION

# THE ENCYCLOPEDIA OF ANIMATED CARTOONS

## THIRD EDITION

# JEFF LENBURG

## FOREWORD BY CHRIS BAILEY

☑Checkmark Books®
*An imprint of Infobase Publishing*

# THE ENCYCLOPEDIA OF ANIMATED CARTOONS, THIRD EDITION

Checkmark Books
An imprint of Infobase Publishing
132 West 31st Street
New York NY 10001

**Library of Congress Cataloging-in-Publication Data**

Lenburg, Jeff.
The encyclopedia of animated cartoons / Jeff Lenburg.—3rd ed.
p. cm.
Includes bibliographical references and index.
ISBN-13: 978-0-8160-6599-8 (hardcover)
ISBN-10: 0-8160-6599-3 (hardcover)
ISBN-13: 978-0-8160-6600-1 (pbk.)
ISBN-10: 0-8160-6600-0 (pbk.)
1. Animated films—United States—History and criticism. I. Title.
NC1766.U5L46 2008
791.43'34097303—dc22

2007025676

Text design by Cathy Rincon
Cover design by Jooyoung An

Printed in the United States of America

VB Hermitage 10 9 8 7 6 5 4 3 2 1

This book is printed on acid-free paper and contains 30 percent postconsumer recycled content.

All links and Web addresses were checked and verified to be correct at the time of publication. Because of the dynamic nature of the Web, some addresses and links may have changed since publication and may no longer be valid.

*To my wife, Debby,*

*for her love and devotion:*

*This book is for you.*

❀ ❀ ❀ ❀ ❀

# CONTENTS

# FOREWORD

In the beginning (this was the 1960s for me), Saturday mornings existed for the sole purpose of watching cartoons. Before my brother and I were allowed to turn on the TV the only rule was that our beds had to be made, our breakfast eaten (Quisp! cereal) and our teeth brushed. Of course, we were up at the crack of dawn so as to not miss a thing. Luckily, with few exceptions, our taste in cartoons was in sync (except that he liked *Quake*) and the fighting was kept to a minimum. That was good for me since I was the "little" brother by 18 months. Over time, the rules relaxed and our cereal eating overlapped with the TV, but the routine lasted for years. I loved all cartoons; the frosting-colored superjocks, talking animals, new cartoons, old—it didn't matter.

It's funny to look back from 30-plus years at the cartoons that had such a hold on me. Most of them were terrible! Why did I like them so much? Who were the characters and what was the coolness factor that transcended the poor writing and meager production budgets? Maybe it was the inventiveness of the show's concept. Maybe it was the music (I could listen to composer Hoyt Curtin's *Jonny Quest* theme all day long). All I know is that I couldn't get enough. Another favorite of mine was Hanna-Barbera's *Space Ghost,* an outer space, superhero cop designed by the late great, Alex Toth. Brilliant! The music, design and titles were incredible (as in all those classic HB adventure shows). The shows themselves, well . . . not so brilliant. Nonetheless, I watched them religiously. Gary Owens's voice acting didn't hurt either. He could pull off the most ludicrous line with deadly seriousness. Hey, if Space Ghost believed in what he was saying, who was I to argue?

As I got older, my cartoon watching gave way to comic-book reading. Cartoons were on only once a week back then, but there were *always* more comics at the candy store! I still watched cartoons, but the pulp adventures of Spider-Man, Thor, Hulk and countless others had won me over. Comics took the pulp adventure to a new level, just as the animated superheroes on TV were becoming less superheroic and more, well, super*friendly.* As I entered high school, I decided that I would exploit my meager drawing skills in comics, or so I thought.

Although there was never any question in my mind that I would go on to college, the local university didn't seem to be a good fit. A fine arts school didn't seem right either. I wanted to tell stories, to draw guys beating the crap out of giant monsters, not draw pictures to hang in a gallery. It was my junior year in high school and time

was running out. If only there had been a college for comic book artists back then, my problem would have been solved (remember, this was the late '70s before such schools existed)! Fate stepped in (as fate tends to do when one is at a crossroads), and I found the next best thing at CalArts in Valencia, California.

I had recently rediscovered Warner Bros. cartoons on TV after school. They were funny when I was a little kid and seemed funnier to me as a teenager. The Pepe Le Pew cartoon series by the late Chuck Jones particularly grabbed my attention. Even though I had probably seen them a dozen times or so while growing up, watching Pepe's sexually charged shenanigans as a 16-year-old boy was like seeing them for the first time. They cracked me up!

As I said earlier, I was a comic-book kid (or so I thought). Along with my weekly funny book purchases, I often bought a trade magazine called *The Comics Journal* that featured news and interviews about comics and their creators. Literally the same day that I rediscovered the coolness of cartoons in Pepe Le Pew, I read an article in the *Journal* about a Disney-sponsored character animation program at CalArts. My college dilemma was solved. Sure, I knew that they didn't make those great Warner Bros. cartoons anymore and TV animation was a little girl's toyland of *Care Bears* and *My Little Pony,* but I figured that whatever I learned would serve me in the future and, who knew, maybe someday cool cartoons would be made again and I could be a part of them—which they did, and then some.

I spent the next six months educating myself about animation and working on my portfolio. I devoured every animation book I could find. Most focused on the artsy side of independent animation, whereas I wanted to make cartoons. Books like this one were invaluable and I could never get enough of them. Many seemed to cover the same ground, but I read them all in search of any new grain of information. In the spring of my senior year, I was accepted at CalArts.

CalArts was a culture shock. Most of the other students had grown up wanting to be Disney animators just as I had wanted to draw comics. They had seen all the Disney classics, knew the names of the Disney animators and directors, and I was playing catch up. I had seen many of the Disney films growing up and, while I had enjoyed them, I wasn't particularly a fan. For a kid who grew up on comic books and TV action adventure, they didn't deliver the bare-knuckled thrill that I got from a good *Fantastic*

*Four* comic or *Star Trek* episode. Just as the tension would start to build in a Disney cartoon, they would inject some gag to let you know that everything would be "okay." It was a Disney staple, and I hated it. I wanted to believe that the character could die. Otherwise, where was the adventure, the drama? Nonetheless, I was immersed in all things Disney and it was seductive.

Armed with a portfolio of gesture sketches and a short film produced at CalArts, I hit the pavement looking for a job. One of my first jobs was as an animator on the video game *Space Ace* for Don Bluth. His look was akin to a watered-down Milt Kahl design from Disney, but he *moved* like a superhero. I loved it! The studio imploded within the year, but I was fortunate enough to make a smooth transition into another job as a 3-D spaceship animator on the forgettable 2-D/3-D film, *Starchaser: The Legend of Orin*. Why is it "fortunate" to work on a forgettable film? One, it's always good to be working (remember, jobs were scarce before the animation boom of the 1990s), and two, I learned to plot the moves of the Computer Generated Imagery (CGI) spaceships. This put me in the position of being one of the few traditional cartoon animators with experience in 3-D. I had no passion for computer animation; my only goal was to simply become more employable so I wouldn't starve. The opportunity served me well as it has allowed me to jump back and forth from the CGI animation world and the traditional animation world ever since.

My other CGI projects included the Mick Jagger video "Hard Woman," a chrome Spider-Man for Marvel Productions' logo, a Golden Grahams cereal commercial and a few other things for the now defunct Digital Productions. Somewhere between CalArts and Digital, I freelanced some animation for Disney on *The Great Mouse Detective* and *Sport Goofy*. When Digital closed its doors, I went back to Disney as an animator on *Oliver & Company*, *The Little Mermaid* and others.

You'd think one would be content to be an animator at Disney, but I saw the animation world as a shiny red apple and I couldn't take a big enough bite. I was always on the lookout for new freelance challenges, and my first supervisory position was a freelance gig, working on Paula Abdul's video "Opposites Attract," where she danced alongside a 2-D Scat Cat. I did it after-hours and on weekends during a slow time at Disney between *The Little Mermaid* and *The Rescuers Down Under*. I had a pencil test machine set up in the garage and animators would come over to pencil test their shots. After that, I began directing theme park projects for Disney, which included "It's Tough to Be a Bug" in Disney's Wild Kingdom (now known as "Animal Kingdom") and Disney's California Adventure Park and the "It's a Small World" Post Show in Disneyland Resort Paris. My direction on Mickey Mouse's "Runaway Brain" earned an Academy Award nomination in 1995 for best animated short. *Hocus Pocus* was my first film supervising animation for live action and I coordinated the live-action, animatronic and animated cat used in the film.

I left Disney after animating on *Hercules*, but within six months I found myself back at the mouse as a CG animation supervisor on the live-action films *Deep Rising*, *Mighty Joe Young* and *Inspector Gadget*. These films were among the most satisfying experiences I've had to date, especially working with director Ron Underwood on *Mighty Joe Young*. We developed a shorthand communication—he understood that animation was performance and not a post-production effect.

About that time, I wrote and drew a comic book story called *Major Damage* about a little boy who fantasizes about his favorite comic book and video game hero, Major Damage. I expanded the Major Damage comic story into a storyboard with the intent of making a CG short film, but it sat unproduced because the technology didn't exist to produce it as a one-man show. I mentioned Major Damage while I was a guest speaker for the "Women in Animation" group and met independent film producer Kellie-Bea Cooper. She put Damage on the fast track. Kellie-Bea, CG supervisor Doug Cooper and I had the creative, technical and organizational chops to make it happen. The success of the short film led to a few more comics—and I got to scratch my childhood itch to do more in this realm.

In the big red apple of animation, I had taken the Disney feature animation bite, the commercial bite, the CGI bite and the independent filmmaker bite. The only thing left was TV. I had avoided TV for the longest time because TV was, well, just not cool. But now things were different. Kevin Smith asked me to direct his short-lived animated series *Clerks* in 1998, and that led to my producing and directing the first season of *Kim Possible* for the Disney Channel. It had humor, action, a great theme—everything I could want. And if you've ever wondered why Kim's black sweatshirt went only midway down her forearms, look no further than Jonny Quest. As for why her shirt went just midway down her belly, take a wild guess. Kim's creators Mark McCorkle and Bob Schooley and I envisioned her as a female Jonny Quest for the '90s and the signature turtleneck was our homage. I was not only working on a great show, but also scratching that old cartoon itch at the same time.

I'm back in the CG/live action world now, translating 2-D cartoon characters into 3-D for the Garfield films and the Alvin and the Chipmunks movie.

I've never lost touch with the little Saturday morning cartoon fan inside of me, but he fades away from time to time. Luckily there are books like this one to jog my memory and give me an excuse to reminisce about what inspired me to enter this crazy, fun business. To Jeff, a profound *thank you!* To the rest of you, enjoy this book. Reacquaint yourself with old cartoon friends and make some new ones. Our animation history is rich and should be remembered and enjoyed.

Chris Bailey

# PREFACE

Twenty-seven years ago I penned what was intended to be the most complete book on animated cartoon series ever, *The Encyclopedia of Animated Cartoon Series*. The book was born out of the dream that there be a major reference on animated cartoons. This volume became the first to document hundreds of cartoon series—silent cartoons, theatrical cartoons and television cartoons.

In 1991 on the 10th anniversary of the original edition and again in 1999, Facts On File published my updated and expanded versions of the former, retitled *The Encyclopedia of Animated Cartoons*. Unlike my first encyclopedia, each entry was more definitive in scope, chronicling the history of every silent cartoon series, theatrical cartoon series, animated feature, animated television special and animated television series.

In my relentless pursuit to fully document the history of this subject, *The Encyclopedia of Animated Cartoons, Third Edition* again delivers the most comprehensive, authoritative volume on cartoons ever imagined. Designed as the ultimate cartoon fan's guide, it features detailed information on every animated cartoon production, series or program exhibited theatrically or broadcast on television on more than 60 major commercial networks and cable networks, now expanded to cover cartoon programs broadcast on every network from Animal Planet to superstation WGN, in the United States (cartoon imports from Japan, Canada, and elsewhere are included) from 1897 to April 2007—or 110 years' worth of 'toons!

Every attempt has been made to provide the most complete account possible of each cartoon production listed, culling the information from studio production records, motion picture trade paper listings, television program guides, movie and television reviews, film vaults and movie warehouses and, in many cases, from credits listed on the films themselves. This information was then cross-referenced with countless reliable sources to ensure its accuracy.

The book is divided into seven sections: silent cartoon series, theatrical sound cartoon series, full-length animated features, animated television specials, television cartoon series (including Saturday-morning, syndicated and cable-produced programs), Academy Award and Emmy Award listings, featuring winners and nominees in the area of cartoon animation since the honors first began, and Milestones of Animation chronicling the landmark events in animation history for more than a century.

For easy reference, each entry provides the following: series history, voice credits (except silent cartoons, of course), the year produced or broadcast, and complete filmographies (except in the case of animated television specials and animated television series).

Silent cartoon entries include a complete historical account of each series and, where available, director and producer credits, and release dates (month, day and year) of each cartoon in the series. For theatrical sound cartoon series, director credits (overall and for each cartoon), voice credits, release dates (month, day and year), reissue dates (abbreviated as "re"), working titles (original titles of cartoons before they were changed for release), episode costars (example: with Porky Pig), Academy Award nominations (listed as A.A. nominee or A.A. winner) and special film format (i.e., Cinecolor, CinemaScope, Technicolor, etc.) are listed under the respective series.

In the full-length animated feature section, complete summaries have been provided for each entry, as well as technical credits, release dates (month, day and year) and side notes about the production (listed under "PN," for "production notes"). The section contains only feature films that received wide distribution in this country, whether produced domestically or overseas.

For animated television specials and animated television series, program overviews, primary voice credits, premiere dates and rebroadcast dates (in most cases, only primary rebroadcast dates are noted, due to space limitations) have been included wherever possible. In many cases, background information and reminiscences of the animators or producers have been incorporated into the entries to paint a vivid picture of the production and its characters and process. Excluded from this edition are primarily live-action specials with animated sequences and clips or mostly live-action hosted and celebrity-laden programs, retrospectives, tributes and documentaries (see *The Encyclopedia of Animated Cartoons, Second Edition*, for these listings); included are wholly animated and derivative specials aired on networks or in syndication, including original productions, story adaptations and direct-to-DVD movies or specials, sneak preview specials, and series pilots classified as "specials." In the television cartoon series section, personality-hosted children's programs featuring animated cartoons are no longer covered in this edition, devoting their space to fully animated television series (including major network, Saturday-morning and syndicated programs only repackaging original theatrical cartoon series, i.e., *Looney Tunes*, *Merrie Melodies*, etc.) broadcast on major television and cable networks and in syndication.

The following common abbreviations have been used to identify the corresponding networks when listing broadcast dates for television specials and television series entries:

A&E: Arts & Entertainment Network
ABC: American Broadcasting Network
ABC FAM: ABC Family
ANI: Animania VOOM HD
ANIME: Anime Network
AP: Animal Planet
BET: Black Entertainment Television
BFC: Black Family Channel
BOOM: Boomerang
BRAVO: Bravo
CAR: Cartoon Network
CBS: Columbia Broadcasting Company
COM: Comedy Central
COMEDY: The Comedy Channel
CW: The CW Network
DIS: The Disney Channel
DSC: Discovery Channel
DSCK: Discovery Kids
DirecTV: DirecTV
EACTN: Encore Action
EWAM: Encore WAM!
FAM: The Family Channel
FOX: Fox Broadcasting Network
FOX FAM: Fox Family Channel
FX: F/X
G4: G4
HBO: Home Box Office
HBO FAM: Home Box Office Family
HBO KIDS: HBO Kids
HIS: The History Channel
HALMRK: The Hallmark Channel
IFC: Independent Film Channel
ION: ION Network
Kids' WB!: Kids' WB!
MTV: Music Television
MTV2: Music Television 2
N: The N
NBC: National Broadcasting Company
NICK: Nickelodeon

NICK G: Nickelodeon GAS
NICK JR.: Nickelodeon Junior
NICKT: Nicktoons Network
NOG: Noggin
ODY: Odyssey (now Hallmark Channel)
OXY: Oxygen Network
PAX: PAX TV
PBS: Public Broadcasting System
PBS Kids: Public Broadcasting System Kids
PBS Kids Sprout: PBS Kids Sprout
PLYBY: Playboy Channel
Q: qubo
QVC: QVC
SCIFI: Sci Fi Channel
SHO: Showtime
SPEED: Speed Channel
SPIKE: Spike TV
STRZ: Starz!
STRZB: Starz! In Black
STRZF: Starz! Family
STRZK&F: Starz! Kids & Family
STRZK: Starz! Kids
TBS: Turner Broadcasting System
TCM: Turner Classic Movies
TDIS: Toon Disney
TLC: The Learning Channel
TM: Telemundo
TNN: The Nashville Network
TRIO: Trio
TVLND: TV Land
UPN: United Paramount Network
USA: USA Network
VH1: Video Hits One Network
WB: The WB Television Network
WE: Women's Entertainment Network
WGN: WGN Network

In addition, the book has been indexed for each of the following areas of interest: general subject references, voice actors, producers and directors and animated characters.

Enjoy!

Jeff Lenburg
Goodyear, Arizona

# ACKNOWLEDGMENTS

Few people could imagine the intense man-hours involved in compiling a definitive reference with one single purpose: to offer the most informative, nostalgic reference on nearly every animated cartoon since humans first invented the art.

Well, the truth of the matter is that most of the information contained in this volume took more years than I would personally like to remember to research, write and cross-check in order to present the most accurate account possible for each production listed. Studios, distributors, directors, producers, animators, historians, cartoon collectors and even curators of film vaults were consulted in the course of compiling this book. The result was hundreds of letters, phone calls, faxes, emails and other means of correspondence in the United States and abroad to corroborate facts and acquire information necessary to make this wonderful celebration of animated cartoons as complete as possible.

Fortunately, a great many people shared my belief in the importance of documenting the history of this popular medium, and all were willing to offer one more bit of information or render a few more minutes of their precious time to make this "dream book" a reality.

First and foremost, I would like to thank the many producers, directors, animators and voice artists—many of whom I have admired for their ingenuity and talent—who, over the years, supplied information, materials and their personal support to this project. They include Joe Barbera, Jules Bass, Joy Batchelor, Dick Brown, Daws Butler, Fred Calvert, Bob Clampett, Shamus Culhane, David H. DePatie, John R. Dilworth, Friz Freleng, June Foray, John Halas, Bill Hanna, Faith Hubley, Bill Hurtz, Chuck Jones, Fred Ladd, Walter Lantz, Norman Maurer, Bill Melendez, Don Messick, Joe Oriolo, Arthur Rankin, Joe Ruby, Lou Scheimer, Hal Seeger, Ken Spears, Jay Ward and Rudy Zamora.

Much of the information featured in this volume would not have been possible without the generous support of many production companies and their staffs. In this instance, I would like to extend my personal thanks to David R. Smith and Paula Sigman, Walt Disney Archives; Derek Westervelt, Nancy Battele and Nan Kelinson, Walt Disney Productions; Joanna Coletta and Leo Moran, Bill Melendez Productions; William Ruiz, Eric Stein and George Robertson, DIC Enterprises; Trudi Takamatsu, Murakami-Wolf-Swenson Films; Melani Tandon, Nelvana Limited; Steven Gold, Klasky Csupo, Inc.; Henry Saperstein, United Productions

of America (UPA); Jim Graziano, Kelly Irwin and Star Kaplan, Marvel Productions; Stanley Stunell and Jacki Yaro, Lone Ranger Television; Ken Snyder and Tish Gainey, Ken Snyder Productions; Victoria McCollom, Collette Sunderman, Michael Diaz, Hanna-Barbera Productions; Janie Fields and Jan Albright, DePatie-Freleng Enterprises; Dave Bennett, Rick Reinert Pictures; and Jeff Cooke, Ruby-Spears Productions.

I would also like to acknowledge Joanne McQueen, Rankin-Bass Productions; Robert Miller, Walter Lantz Productions; Herbert A. Nusbaum, Metro-Goldwyn-Mayer; Quan Phung, Tod Roberts and Sari DeCesare, National Broadcasting Company (NBC); Jenny Trias and Joyce Loeb, Filmation; Suzy Missirlani, Film Roman Productions; Gloria Foster, ZIV International; Lee Polk and Laurie Tritini, King Features Entertainment; Leon Harvey and Evelyn Johnson, Harvey Films; William Weiss, Charles Tolep, Terrytoons Productions; Ann Pulley, Royal Productions; Deborah Fine, LucasFilm; Janis Diamond, Farmhouse Films; James Stabile and Lee Orgel, Metromedia Producers Corporation; Elizabeth Shaw, MCA; Bart Farber, Virginia Brown and Maury Oken, United Artists; Hal Geer, Ahuva Rabani and Edward A. Hoffman, Warner Brothers; Robert L. Rosen, RLR Associates; Laura Ramsay, Bob Keeshan Enterprises; Loretta Petersohn, Thea Flaum Productions; Dana Booton, Gledye Newman, Amber Santilli and C.J. Grant, Saban International; Stephen Worth, Bagdasarian Productions; Jody Zucker and Howard Barton, Paramount Pictures; Rosalind Goldberg, Larry Harmon Pictures; and Michael Hack, TMS Entertainment.

I would further like to thank Anthony Gentile Sr., Abrams/Gentile Entertainment; Jennifer Thieroff and Julie Hildebrand, Britt Alcroft Incorporated; Marija Miletic Dail, Animation Cottage; Dionne Nosek and Terry Weiss, Children's Television Workshop; Caroline Faucher, CINAR Films; Bob Higgins, Rita Johnstone and Michelle Beber, Columbia/TriStar Television; Chris Greengrove, Curious Pictures; Ralph Edwards, Ralph Edwards Films; Scott Taylor and Russell P. Marleau, Hyperion Animation; Cary Silver, MGM Animation; Becky Mancuso-Winding, Lois Kramer and Dana Coccara, Sony Wonder; Christina Rundbaken and Robin Alcock, Sunbow Productions; Barbara Beasley, Don Barrett, Nest Entertainment, Jerry Reynolds, Perennial Pictures; Liz Topazzio, Active Entertainment; Paola Fantini, Hallmark Entertainment; Jan Nagel, Calico Creations; Michael

Sporn and Christine O'Neill, Michael Sporn Animation; Rick Pack, Kookanooga Toons; Teresa Frisani, Paragon Entertainment (formerly Lacewood Productions); Jay Poynor, AniMagic Entertainment; Paul Marshal, O Entertainment; John Sinclair and Eadie Morley, Playmate Toys; Sara Stern Levin, 4 Kids Entertainment; Christina Rogers, National Film Board of Canada and Fred Schaefer, Sam McKendry, PorchLight Entertainment.

The support of the following individuals and companies was also most appreciated: Tiffany Fegley, Hearst Entertainment; Pam Bobbitt-Daniel, Lightyear Entertainment; Valerie Delafoy, Parafrance Communication; Adrian Woolery, Playhouse Pictures; Keven Reher, Premavision; Liz Foster and Claire Wilmut, Evergreen Productions; Steven Melnick and Joyce Irby, 20th Century-Fox Television; Peggy Ray, Republic Pictures Corporation; Vicki Lowry and Anita Kelso, World Events Productions; Leslie Maryon-LaRose, Scholastic Productions; Allan Migram, Marvel Comics Group; Riaya Aboul Ela, Prism Entertainment; Sallie Smith, Vicki Greenleaf, Family Home Entertainment; Robert Kanner, Buena Vista Home Video; Carol Paskewitz, Just for Kids Home Video; Alex Drosin, Golden Book Home Video; Andy Stern, Celebrity Just For Kids Video; Amy Sprecher, Polygram Home Video, Dirk Van Tilborg, SSA Public Relations; Jeryl Reitzer, Summit Media Group; Linda LePage-Chown, Telegenic; Karen Samfilippo, Jeff Fink and Cindy Anderson, Live Entertainment; Paul J. Newman, Columbia/TriStar Home Video; Aaron Severson, BKN Kids Network (formerly Bohbot Entertainment); Mark Alsbury, Walt Disney Company; Jennifer Erskine, Santa Ventura Studios; Natalie Setton, TV-Loonland; and Michelle Orsi, Three-Sixty Communications.

Television networks, local television stations and television program distributors also played significant roles in contributing material to this book. Among those who helped were Jerry Westfeldt, TV Cinema Sales; Sandy Frank, Sandy Frank Film Syndication; Lonnie D. Halouska, Rex Waggoner and Phyllis Kirk, National Telefilm Associates (NTA); Sandra R. Mueller and Tom Hatten, KTLA-TV; Tim McGowan, KCAL-Channel 9; Carol Martz, KCOP-Channel 13; Casey Garvey, KCET-TV; Lisa Mateas, Dick Connell, Michelle Couch and Walt Ward, Turner Network Television; Mark McCray, Boomerang; Jeff Adams, Joe Swaney, James Anderson, Mike Lazzo and Frederika Brooksfield, Cartoon Network; Peter DeJong, A&E Television Networks; Lee Nash, Worldvision; Barry Kluger, March 5; Caroline Ansell, Viacom International; Robert Ferson, The Right Stuf; Donita J. Delzer, Evangelical Lutheran Church in America; Ann B. Cody, Westchester Films; Nancy Allen, Thames Taffner; Priscilla French, Harmony Gold; Joe Adelman and Elise Sugar, Color Systems Technology; Yvette Bruno and Heather Blanda, Nick Jr.; and Paul Lengyel, and Irene Sherman, Bob Mittenthal, Heather Morgan, Christopher Adams, Kat Fair, Donna Smith; and Robert Salmon, Nicktoons; Lisa Schiraldi and Fran Brochstein, Nickelodeon.

Also Holly Grieve, MG Perin, Inc.; Amy Sauertieg, SFM Entertainment; Daniel Mulholland, Muller Media, Inc.; Yolanda Cortez, Alice Communications; Catherine Korda, ABC; Claudia Cooper, ABC Children's Programming; Josh Van Houdt, ABC Family; Dave Baldwin, Rolande Prince, Carol Rosen, Katherine Pongracz, Jody Stahl, Lisa Fishkind, Mara Mellin, Sara Fitzsimmons, HBO; Carolyn Ceslik and Joyce Nishihira, CBS Entertainment; Jay Postahnick, NBC; Farrell Meisel, WWOR-TV; Jefferi K. Lee and Cindy Mahmoud, Black Entertainment Television; Meryl Alper, Hope Diamond, Katherine Linke, Tracia Ord, The Disney Channel; Carol Sussman, The Disney Channel and Toon Disney; Carol Monroe, Amanda Gumbs and Erik Aronson, FOX Kids Network; Jennifer Gershon, Barry Kluger and Merle Becker, MTV/VH1; Alice Cahn, PBS; Linda Simensky, Katherine Novello, Paul Siefkin, PBS Kids; and David Schwartz, USA Network; Carolyn Miller, Wayne Baker, The Family Channel; Chris Regina, Barry Schulman, Sci-Fi Channel; Steve Albani, Comedy Central; Lainie Tompkins, Discovery Home Channel; Dea Perez, Discovery Kids; Sal Bellissimo, Matt Kalinowski, Playboy TV; Marcia Bartelheim, Starz Entertainment LLC; Emily Mandelbaum, The N; Leisa Rivosecchi and Ken Preister, Italtoons Corporation; Andrea Roy, Cambium Releasing; Chris Lara, Animal Planet; Sal Maniaci, Michele Suite, TV Land; Sally Thoun and Jean Flores, Warner Brothers International; and William Cayton, Radio and Television Packagers.

Many historians, cartoon collectors and buffs (some of them experts in their own field of interest) provided information critical to the successful completion of numerous entries in this book. I would like to pay special tribute to Joe Adamson, Al Bigley, Eric Bolden, Dan Brown, John Cawley, Karl Cohen, Jeff Cook, Greg Duffel, Mark Evanier, James Gauthier, Aaron Handy III, Ronnie James, Mark Kausler, Ken Layton, Mike Lefebvre, Greg Lenburg, Bob Miller, David Moore, Quinn Norman, Brian Pearce, Doug Ranney, Randy Skretvedt, Anthony Specian Jr. and Charles Wagner.

In the area of Japanese cartoons, perhaps the most difficult to document, I would like to thank the following for their time in furnishing vital information and materials to me for the many entries listed: Barbara Edmunds, Meg Evans, Tom Hamilton, James Long, Frederick Patten, Lorraine Savage and Scott Wheeler. My personal thanks as well to Scott McGuire for his invaluable assistance in documenting the airdates for the *Peanuts* television series and specials, and to Scott Oldeman for his kind help in providing much-needed airdates for the FOX Kids Network series and specials and Kids' WB! series.

Naturally, I cannot forget the tremendous support that I received from the following libraries and their staffs in tracking down background information, reviews, production listings, special collections and illustrations to make this project as authoritative as possible. They are: Janet Lorenz, Academy of Motion Pictures Arts & Sciences Margaret Herrick Library; Kristine Krueger and Howard H. Prouty, Academy of Motion Pictures Arts & Sciences Margaret Herrick Library; Museum of Modern Art; Alan Braun, Louis B. Mayer Library of the American Film Institute; the Cerritos Public Library; the Anaheim Public Library; the Arizona State University Fletcher Library; the College of the Desert Library; Estrella Mountain Community College Library and the Rancho Mirage Public Library.

Much of the information contained in this book was dependent not only on studio records and private collections but also on material culled from the pages of a number of major Hollywood motion picture and television journals. To this end, I would like to offer my personal thanks to the men and women of the following publications, whose diligence in recording weekly production logs and other technical information made this book what it is today: *Box Office, Daily Variety, Hollywood Reporter, Motion Picture Herald* and *Motion Picture News*. Also, the following publications were invaluable resources for facts and information contained in this book: *American Film, Animania* (formerly *Mindrot*), *Animation Magazine, Broadcast Information Bureau—TV Series Source Book, Broadcasting Magazine, The Los Angeles Times, Millimeter Magazine, The New York Times, Radio/TV Age, TV Guide* and *USA Today*.

Last but not least, I want to thank God for providing me with the patience and fortitude to cope with the challenges that greeted me at every turn—especially in typing the nearly 3,600-page manuscript—and to complete the task at hand. And, of course, to my wife, Debby, for her love and encouragement every step of the way.

# A NUTSHELL HISTORY OF THE AMERICAN ANIMATED CARTOON

For more than 100 years, the animated cartoon has been entertaining people, young and old, in movie theaters and on television with countless works of art and a virtual cavalcade of cartoon characters that have captured the hearts and imaginations of fans in every corner of the globe. This legion of animated heroes and vast array of cartoon productions still produces wild cheers and uncontrollable laughter, whether it is through television reruns of old favorites or the debut of new, original characters who create enchanting and memorable moments that endure forever.

Why this long-running love affair with cartoons? Why do so many people still watch their favorite cartoon characters in countless television reruns? And why do new characters and new ideas still turn on audiences today? The reason for this amazing phenomenon is simple: Animated cartoons are the embodiment of a fantasy world worth treasuring, worth enjoying and, most of all, worth remembering over and over again, no matter what place in time or what changes have occurred in the real world around it.

It is funny, in a strange sort of way, but animated cartoons were not always held in such high esteem. In the days of silent cartoons, the industry experienced a tremendous backlash of criticism from film critics, movie fans and even studio executives who felt the new medium lacked congruent stories and consistent animation quality to be taken seriously in the world of entertainment. Maybe so. But, like any untested product, it was just a matter of time before the technique of animation would be mastered, creating a visually perfect running machine with plenty of mileage still ahead.

The beginning was 1906, with the debut of the first animated film in this country, *Humorous Phases of Funny Faces*. Released by Vitagraph, cartoonist James Stuart Blackton, who sold his first cartoon to the *New York World* and cofounded Vitagraph, entered the animation business with this first effort six years after his nonanimated triumph, *The Enchanted Drawing*, a stop-motion short Edison film based on the newspaper cartoonist's "chalk-talk" vaudeville act.

By today's standards of animation, Blackton's *Humorous Phases of Funny Faces* is rudimentary at best. The film is composed of a series of scenes featuring letters, words and faces drawn by an "unseen" hand. For the era in which it was made, the simplistically styled one-reel short was an important first step.

The concept of animated cartoons in this country ultimately took root thanks to two other foresighted pioneers: French cartoonist Emil Cohl and American newspaper cartoonist Winsor McCay.

Cohl followed Blackton with a stick-figure animated short presented in a series of comic vignettes entitled *Fantasmagorie* (1908). The film was everything that an animated cartoon was supposed to be—funny, sophisticated and well conceived. McCay surpassed even Cohl's landmark effort with his first entry, *Little Nemo*, the first fully animated cartoon. Based on his own beloved *New York Herald* strip *Little Nemo in Slumberland*, McCay reportedly spent four years animating the production.

While the films of all three men were important to the growth of the cartoon industry, McCay may have done more for the art of animation than his predecessors when he created what many historians consider to be the first genuine American cartoon star in *Gertie the Dinosaur* (1914). The first film to feature frame-by-frame animation and fluid, sophisticated movement, it took McCay approximately 10,000 drawings to animate the five-minute production. The one-reel short was animated on six-by-eight-inch sheets of translucent rice paper, with the drawings lightly penciled first and then detailed in Higgins black ink.

It was a tremendous technical achievement, but surprisingly most critics felt the production lost audiences with its story line. In the film, the animator (McCay) is seen drawing the cartoon, in live action, slowly bringing Gertie into existence and into the real world to then try to tame the beast.

Audiences did not share critics' opinions. Reportedly they were awed by the dinosaur's lifelike movements, unaware that what they had seen would change the course of animation's young history for the better.

The late Paul Terry, the father of Terry-Toons, often credited McCay for arousing his and others' interest in animated cartoons,

1

at a time when most people did not fully grasp the potential of the medium. As he once said, "Together with more than a hundred other artists, I attended a dinner in 1914 at which McCay spoke. He showed us his cartoon *Gertie, the Dinosaur.* It was the first animated cartoon we had ever seen, and as McCay told us his ideas about animation as a great coming medium of expression, we really hardly knew what he was talking about, he was so far ahead of his time."

Four years later McCay further left his mark on animation by producing and directing the first animated re-enactment of a historical event, *The Sinking of the Lusitania* (1918). One of the first films to use cel animation, this landmark film featured an amazing 25,000 inked and drawn celluloid sheets of animation.

McCay's imprint on the cartoon industry was widespread, but another early pioneer was responsible for improving the consistency of animation and the health of the industry overall. John Randolph ("J.R.") Bray was perhaps the country's most prolific producer of cartoon shorts. In June 1913, following a career as an American newspaper cartoonist, Bray produced his first animated short, *The Artist's Dream* (or *The Dachsund and the Sausage*), which quickly established him in the medium.

Bray followed this celluloid feat with his first of many successful cartoon series, *Colonel Heeza Liar*, based on the tale-spinning adventures of Baron Munchausen. (Walter Lantz, the father of Woody Woodpecker, was one of the series' chief animators.) The series spawned other successes for Bray, among them *Bobby Bumps* (1915), *Otto Luck* (1915), *Police Dog* (1915) and *Quacky Doodles* (1917). By 1916 his studio was so successful that he began producing one cartoon per week.

In 1914 Bray revolutionized the business of animation with his patented invention of a labor-saving animation process in which backgrounds were printed on translucent paper to facilitate the positioning of moving objects in successive drawings. (This economy of drawings is evident in many of Bray's early cartoons, including "Col. Heeza Liar, Hobo" (1916), which used only a few more than 100 basic arrangements of the cels in 1,600 frames of footage.) During the next year he would patent two other methods to enhance the quality of animation. The first was a technique that enabled animators to affix solid cutouts to the back of drawings so they were visible from the front of the drawing; the second, a process of cutout animation. Bray also later produced and directed the first color cartoon, *The Debut of Thomas the Cat*, using the then-revolutionary two-color Brewster Color process; it was released to theaters in 1920 as part of the *Goldwyn-Bray-Pictograph* screen magazine series.

Other pioneer animators followed Bray with patented techniques of their own. Earl Hurd patented the first cel animation process, probably one of the most significant of the early animation patents, while Max and Dave Fleischer, of Ko-Ko the Clown and later Betty Boop fame, developed a fascinating process called Rotoscope, which enabled animators to trace figures seen on projected film.

During the teens, Bray was not the only major cartoon studio producing animated films. Two others came into existence: Raoul Barré's and Hearst International. Barré was an established cartoonist whose caricatures of Indians and the lifestyle of French Canadian women were published as *En Rolant Ma Boule*. Turning his energies to animation, he produced several noteworthy animated series. His first was *Animated Grouch Chasers* (1915-16), an intriguing use of live-action openings and animated segues that won him widespread acclaim. He went on to develop one of the most successful comic-strip cartoon adaptations, *Mutt and Jeff* (1918), based on Bud Fisher's popular strip characters.

In 1916 newspaper mogul William Randolph Hearst realized the promise of animation by opening his own studio, International Film Service. Hearst hired talented animators Gregory La Cava, Frank Moser and Bill Nolan away from Raoul Barré's studio to bring many of his newspaper syndicate's cartoon properties to the screen. In short order, Hearst's company produced animated versions of such comic-page favorites as *Krazy Kat* (1916), *The Katzenjammer Kids* (1916) and *Happy Hooligan* (1917).

Other comicstrip artists brought their strip creations to the screen to capitalize on the success of the new medium. Henry ("Hy") Mayer, a prolific illustrator, drew comics on the screen for the Universal Weekly newsreel in 1913. He ultimately produced a series of screen magazines known as *Travelaughs*. Rube Goldberg briefly pursued a career in animation by signing up with Pathé Films to produce a newsreel spoof called *Boob Weekly*. Other animated versions of popular strips included George McManus's *Bringing Up Father* (1918), Walter Hoban's *Jerry on the Job* (1917), Jimmy Swinnerton's *Little Jimmy* (1916) and Tom E. Powers's *Phables* (1916).

Paul Terry, who first started working as an animator for Bray in 1916-17, also became an important figure during this period. After he opened his own studio, Terry became the first to prefigure the visual style of the Hollywood cartoons of the 1930s and 1940s by giving characters more depth and dimension, as is evident in a handful of early titles, including *Farmer Al Falfa's Catastrophe* (1916) and *Farmer Al Falfa's Wayward Pup* (1917).

In general, production staffs for most of these studios were minimal at best. On the average, producers turned out one new cartoon short a week, which was often animated by one person. (Hearst was known to enlist the services of well-known artists who sketched strips for his syndicate to contribute animate ideas to his weekly newsreel.) In most cases the cartoonist was the animator, director, gagman and artist. Toward week's end, the animator's sketchings were collected, photographed and wound onto a single reel before being distributed to theaters throughout the country.

In some cases, the final product was inferior because of such streamlined operations, prompting critics to denounce animated works. As one film critic stated, the major problem inherent in the cartoons was that "the artist was merely sketching his ideas on film."

Walter Lantz, who wrote and directed many cartoons for J. R. Bray, discussed the story-line difficulties he and other animators encountered. "We had a makeshift studio on the top floor of a loft building in Fordham, New York," he recalled. "There weren't enough people in the organization to make the story department of a cartoon studio today. But we didn't bother with stories. Our only object was to turn out 500 to 600 feet of film!"

Because animators overlooked story transitions, the films often confused theater audiences. (Some confusion was due to the inconsistent use of cartoon balloons over the subject's head to describe dialogue or action.) Sometimes when studios churned out 500 to 600 feet of cartoon film, that's exactly what the audience got—just film, with no real story. "Most audiences would rather flee from the theater than sit through a screening of these cartoons," commented one reviewer.

Dick Huemer, who animated *Mutt and Jeff*, had this to say about the reaction of moviegoers to silent cartoons: "They didn't get it. I swear, they didn't get what we were doing. For one thing, our timing was way off or nonexistent. And we didn't have sound. Sound was the great savior of the animated cartoon."

There were at this same time, however, several animators who set new standards for the industry through their unique storytelling ability. Among them were Max and Dave Fleischer, Walt Disney and Walter Lantz. All four men blazed new trails in animation and achieved great success through instinct and imagination, as evidenced by their work.

The Fleischers turned heads with their inventive series, *Out of the Inkwell* (1916), which combined live action and animation and featured the antics of Koko the Clown (later hyphenated as Ko-Ko). The films are technical marvels—beautifully blending animation and live scenes of the animator (Max) bringing Koko to life as well as the entire story on the drawing board at the animator's table. This feat was equaled by Disney and Lantz, who employed the process of live action/animation in similar fashion with successful results. Disney mastered the art with his series of cartoon fables, *Alice Comedies* (1924), shot in Los Angeles at various outdoor locations. The films starred a young girl—played mostly by billboard star-turned-child actor Virginia Davis—who was joined by animated characters in telling each story. The films were extremely popular vehicles, as was Lantz's *Dinky Doodle* (1924), which he wrote and directed for Bray.

Lantz starred as the comic straight man in these films alongside his cartoon counterparts Dinky, a young boy, and his faithful dog, Weakheart, in comical exploits that were often as funny as the best of the era's silent film comedies. (Lantz admitted his source of inspiration was the work of several silent films comedians, including Charlie Chaplin, Harry Langdon and Chester Conklin.)

One reason for Lantz's success may have been his understanding of his role as an animator. In an interview he defined his job thusly: "An animator is like an actor going before the camera, only he has to act out his feelings and interpret the scene with that pencil. Also he has to know how to space characters because the spacing of their movements determines the tempo; he must know expression; he must know feeling; he has to know the character, and make him walk with a funny action."

The ardent process of sound changed the whole method of making animated cartoons and, if anything, enabled the industry to prosper at a time when the silent film industry was stagnating. With the theatrical release of *Mother, Mother Pin a Rose on Me*, the first sound cartoons were produced in 1924 by the Fleischers. *Song Car-Tunes*, a series of "bouncing ball singalongs," were synchronized to popular music by a revolutionary DeForest Phonofilm system. One major disadvantage prevented the concept from flour-

Model sheet for Max and Dave Fleischer's Ko-Ko the Clown.

ishing: Many of the theaters were "unwired" and thus were unable to project the films accompanied by 18-piece orchestrations.

The first "talking" motion picture, Al Jolson's musical feature *The Jazz Singer* (1927), helped popularize the use of sound in the film industry and inspired theaters to accommodate this innovation.

Walt Disney introduced the first widely distributed synchronized sound cartoon in 1928, Mickey Mouse's "Steamboat Willie." With this creation began another chapter in animation history. Sound gave cartoons a dimension that was not possible in silent form. It enabled animators to create better stories, more lifelike characters and fuller animation. The process did not come cheaply, however. Production costs skyrocketed from the normal $6,000 budgets for silent cartoons, yet the all-around quality improved and was worth the price.

During the 1930s, as animators explored the virtues of sound, many new characters burst onto the screen in productions featuring popular musical tunes of the day. Warner Bros. introduced several cartoon stars, many of them influenced by vaudeville and radio. The studio's first real star was Bosko, a Black Sambo-type character, who spoke for the first time in 1930's *Sinkin' in the Bathtub*. Created by former Disney animators Hugh Harman and Rudolf Ising, Bosko became enormously popular and was soon joined by a handful of other characters in the studio's *Looney Tunes* series, among them Foxy, Piggy and Goopy Geer.

Meanwhile, Metro-Goldwyn-Mayer (MGM) contributed its own series of musical cartoons, *Happy Harmonies*, directed by Harman and Ising, who left Warners to open the Metro's cartoon department. Walt Disney continued making his Oscar-winning *Silly Symphony* (1928) series, the forerunner to the musical cartoon concept, while Ub Iwerks, Disney's former protégé, set up shop to produce his musically inclined *Flip the Frog* (1931) series. Van Beuren Studios also joined the competition with its popular *Aesop's Fables* (1928) series, initially released by Pathé and then RKO Radio Pictures.

While many of the early sound cartoons had merit, most of these productions—outside a few that had name stars—lacked distinguishable personalities and featured a myriad of characters appearing in a single setting.

More than any individual, Warner Bros. director Chuck Jones credits Walt Disney for establishing the concept of cartoon "personalities" and inspiring the rest of the industry to develop their own unique characters. As Jones explained: "Anybody who knows anything about animation knows that the things that happened at Disney Studio were the backbone that upheld everything else. Disney created a climate that enabled us all to exist. Everyone in

*The farmer's true identity is unmasked in this scene from Aesop's "Amateur Night on the Ark" (1923).* (COURTESY: BLACKHAWK FILMS)

*Animator Walter Lantz looks on as cartoon star Col. Heeza Liar takes on a menacing bull in a studio publicity still to promote the classic silent cartoon series.* (COURTESY: WALTER LANTZ)

animation considered themselves behind Disney. We all did. Strange thing: That was probably healthy for us all. Perhaps the biggest thing Disney contributed was that he established the idea of individual personality. We would look at his stuff and say 'No matter what we do, Disney is going to be a little ahead of us, particularly in technique.' He created the idea that you could make

*Mickey Mouse starred in the first synchronized sound cartoon, "Steamboat Willie" (1928). © Walt Disney Productions*

an animated cartoon character who had personality and wasn't just leaping in the air like *Terry-Toons*. So without thinking he forced us into evolving our own style."

Thus, from the mid-1930s on, animators began to develop the sound cartoon era's first bona fide stars—characters with heart and soul and mass appeal. Many of the characters people remember today emerged during this period. Walt Disney added to his stable of stars the likes of Donald Duck (1934) and Goofy (1932), while studio rival Warner Bros. introduced several "superstars": Porky Pig (1936), Daffy Duck (1938), and Bugs Bunny (1940). MGM's famed cat-and-mouse tandem Tom and Jerry (1940) won over audiences, as did Walter Lantz's Andy Panda (1940) and Woody Woodpecker (1941). Meanwhile, Paul Terry, of *Terry-Toons* fame, unveiled his most promising creations, Dinky Duck (1939) and Mighty Mouse (1942).

These solidly constructed characterizations together with tightly written scripts captured in animated form the crazy appeal of Laurel and Hardy, the Marx Brothers, Buster Keaton, Abbott and Costello, and Charlie Chaplin, and became important factors in the success of sound cartoons.

One other important element in their success was physical action. Unlike silent cartoons, sound cartoons were fast-paced, full of slapstick and punctuated by violence. Combined, these qualities generated a terrific response from moviegoers whose sides often arched from fits of laughter before the main feature was even introduced. (Cartoons, newsreels and live-action shorts were shown prior to the feature-length attraction, appropriately called "curtain–raisers" in their day.)

In 1932, Walt Disney introduced the first three-strip Technicolor cartoon, "Flowers and Trees," which won an Academy Award. © Walt Disney Productions

Sexy screen star Betty Boop is joined by sidekicks Bimbo and Ko-Ko the Clown in 1932's "A Hunting We Will Go," produced by Max Fleischer.

"We found that you can get terrific laughs out of someone just getting demolished, as long as you clean up and bring him back to life again," the late Tex Avery told biographer Joe Adamson. "It's exaggeration to the point where we hope it's funny."

The successful cartoon formula of transitions, action and sound was further improved in 1932 when Walt Disney produced the first true Technicolor cartoon, a *Silly Symphony* short called "Flowers and Trees." (The production cost $27,500 to make, two-thirds more than black-and-white cartoons.) Disney was not the first to experiment with color by any means. Others toyed with the process as far back as the early 1920s by "tinting" the films. (In 1930 Walter Lantz animated the first two-color Technicolor cartoon, a four-minute opening segment for Paul Whiteman's *King of Jazz*.) Disney's introduction of color to animated cartoons brought a whole new dimension to the screen that had never before been realized. It was a gamble that paid off not only for his studio; it took the cartoon industry into a whole new era of filmmaking.

In the beginning, because of Disney's exclusive contract to use the Technicolor process, several studios were forced to use a less effective two-strip color method, Cinecolor. The results were not as vivid as the three-strip color process, but that did not prevent several rival studios from competing.

Ub Iwerks was among the first to use Cinecolor for his 1933 *ComiColor* cartoon, "Jack and the Beanstalk." Warner Bros. offered two Cinecolor releases in the 1934–35 season, "Honeymoon Hotel" and "Beauty and the Beast," both *Merrie Melodies*. Walter Lantz countered with "Jolly Little Elves" (1934), which received an Oscar nomination the same year Disney's "Flowers and Trees" (1932) won best short subject honors. Max Fleischer also employed the Cinecolor technique in his *Color Classics* series, beginning with "Poor Cinderella" (1934).

The most spectacular use of color was yet to come, however. In 1937 Walt Disney again paved the way when he produced the first full-length feature, *Snow White and the Seven Dwarfs*. It was a monumental undertaking for his studio, costing a tiny fortune to produce (six times more than its original budget of $250,000). Fortunately, it was well worth the price as the film became a tremendous box-office hit, earning $8 million in revenue following its release. With this newfound success, Disney opened many animators' eyes to the full potential of color to animated cartoons, no matter what their length.

In 1940, Disney would further cement his place in history by releasing in "Fantasound" the cinematic jewel *Fantasia*, one of the first films to feature a stereo soundtrack, which only six theaters, equipped with the multi-channel stereo system, could play.

Max Fleischer shared the same vision as Disney. He gave Disney perhaps his strongest competition in the feature-film arena when he produced his studio's first fully animated feature, *Gulliver's Travels* (1939), two years after Disney's Technicolor extravaganza. While the film did compare in quality to Disney's full-length production, unfortunately it never produced the same financial and critical success.

Nonetheless, Fleischer would produce one more feature, *Mr. Bug Goes to Town* (1941), before abandoning the idea of producing cartoon features altogether and leaving the field to his contemporary, Walt Disney, who became the sole producer of feature-length cartoons for the next two decades.

The outbreak of World War II unified the cartoon industry in a patriotic sort of way. Studios showed their allegiance by producing propaganda training films and cartoons satirizing the war, with obvious anti-German and anti-Japanese overtones, to boost the public's morale.

The effort resulted in a number of flag-waving sendups that are still funny today, among them Donald Duck's "Der Fuehrer's Face"

*Max Fleischer's attempt to compete with Walt Disney by producing full-length features ended with the release of his second feature, Mr. Bug Goes to Town (1940).* (COURTESY: REPUBLIC PICTURES)

*Opening title sequence from Ub Iwerks's ComiColor cartoon, "Jack Frost" (1934).* (COURTESY: BLACKHAWK FILMS)

(Disney, 1943), an Oscar-winning short subject; Tex Avery's "Blitz Wolf" (MGM, 1942); and "Daffy's Draftee" (Warner, 1944). Warner Bros. also produced a topical war bond short, "Bugs Bunny's Bond Rally" (1943), with Bugs Bunny, Daffy Duck and Porky Pig urging Americans to buy war bonds, as well as its own share of animated training films, namely *Private Snafu,* first directed by Frank Tashlin, the noted comedy film director, and *Hook,* which dealt with the misadventures of a navy sailor.

While the war proved to be a timely subject, Hollywood animators continued to display their affection for the actors, actresses and comedians of Hollywood's Golden Age. Caricatured versions of many celebrities have made their way to the screen in one cartoon or another since the early 1930s. Some of the most notable appearances by movie stars in animated form include "Hollywood Steps Out" (Warner, 1941), featuring Clark Gable, Harpo Marx, Buster Keaton, Joan Crawford, the Three Stooges and others; "A Tale of Two Mice" (Warner, 1942), depicting Abbott and Costello as mice (*Babbit and Catstello*); "Bacall to Arms" (Warner, 1946), with Humphrey Bogart and Lauren Bacall as cartoon characters; and "Popeye's 25th Anniversary" (Paramount, 1948), with Dean Martin and Jerry Lewis, Bob Hope and Jimmy Durante.

The measure of success that cartoons had attained in the 1930s and 1940s continued into the 1950s. During this decade the cartoon industry experienced several important achievements. In 1953, with 3-D becoming the rage, several studios began turning out three-dimensional feature films and short subjects, to the delight of moviegoing audiences. The technique was used in cartoons as well.

In 1953 Walt Disney's "Melody" and "Working for Peanuts" with Donald Duck, Walter Lantz's "The Hypnotic Hick" starring Woody Woodpecker and Famous Studios' "The Ace of Space" with Popeye were the first cartoons produced and released in 3-D. The following year Warner Bros. added its own 3-D favorite, "Lumber-Jack Rabbit" (1954), starring Bugs Bunny, while Famous Studios' second 3-D cartoon was "Boo Man," with Casper the Friendly Ghost.

Perhaps more important than 3-D was the unveiling of a new style of animation four years earlier, which used fewer cartoon cels to tell a complete story. The method—called "limited anima-

tion"—was the brainchild of United Productions of America (UPA), producers of Mister Magoo and Gerald McBoing Boing cartoons. The concept presented an economical way for producers to animate cartoons while still achieving a wide range of motion and believability on screen. Bill Scott, a former UPA animator, recalls the new process "proved that cartoonists could use fewer drawings and still do an excellent job telling their story."

Economically, the new system of animation made sense, as the cost to produce fully animated cartoons had become more and more prohibitive. As costs rose, many of the major cartoon producers would adopt this method of animation. (Television cartoon producers later employed the same style of animation.) Only through limited animation could theatrical cartoons stay economically feasible.

For years it was believed that television brought about the demise of the animated cartoon short. This is true to some extent. But what actually killed the cartoon short was a 1949 U.S. Supreme Court ruling forcing studios to abandon "block book-

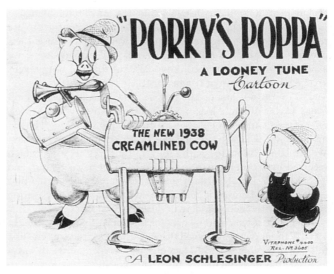

*Lobby card from Bob Clampett's 1938 Looney Tune cartoon, "Porky's Poppa."* © *Warner Bros.*

*MGM animators used this cartoon model sheet for guidelines when drawing Tex Avery's Droopy in "Señor Droopy" (1949). © Turner Entertainment*

ings." Under this method, theater owners were offered hit feature films as long as they agreed to book a cartoon, newsreel or live-action short as part of the package. Usually a percentage of the rental fee helped finance the cartoon production.

After this ruling, theater owners refused to pay more than nominal fees for cartoons. As a result, the animated short couldn't earn back its production costs on its initial release. It often took several rereleases before most cartoons turned a profit, if any. The impact of this ruling and the birth of television ultimately resulted in many Hollywood cartoon studios closing their doors during the late 1950s and early 1960s. Walter Lantz, who was the last to stop production in 1972, said, "We didn't stop producing cartoons because their popularity died out, it was because we couldn't afford to make them."

In essence, television replaced movie theaters as a place to showcase animated productions. The growth of this medium clearly undermined the success of movie theaters in this country, as witnessed in a strong decline in box-office receipts. (The number of television sets in use in 1950 jumped from 1 million at the beginning of the year to 4 million by the end of the year.) With many programs accessible on the "tube" for free, American movie-goers had little incentive to go to the theater.

"People began to care less about going to the movies," remarked Norm Prescott, cofounder of Filmation Studios. "As a consequence, it took four or five years for studios to recoup their cartoon costs."

Viewing television as fertile ground, several film distributors of vintage cartoons kept in well-guarded film vaults took advantage of this new and thriving medium by syndicating the films to local television stations. The first cartoons to appear were black-and-white treasures made by Van Beuren Studios in the 1930s, seen on

*An electrified musician rings out vibrant new sounds on his old harp for the onlooking conductor in a scene from Hugh Harman's "Mad Maestro" (1939). © Turner Entertainment*

*Popeye gets the best of Bluto in the first Popeye two-reeler, "Popeye the Sailor Meets Sindbad the Sailor" (1936).*

*Daffy Duck meets up with Sherlock Holmes in a scene from Bob Clampett's 1946 cartoon, "The Great Piggy Bank Robbery." © Warner Bros.* (COURTESY: BOB CLAMPETT ANIMATION ART)

DuMont's WABD-TV, New York, in 1947 on *Movies for Small Fry*. The program was broadcast Tuesday evenings and inspired *The Small Fry Club*, a network continuation of the show in January 1948, hosted by Big Brother Bob Emery. The latter continued through the 1950-51 season, screening Van Beuren's *Cubby* cartoon series and several early Walter Lantz cartoons before the program was canceled. (The Van Beuren films also appeared on *TV Tots Time* on WENR, Chicago, and on the ABC network between 1950 and 1952.)

This did not mark the first time cartoons were used on television. Chad Grothkopf, a Disney animator in his 20s, went East in 1938 to work for NBC on "the very first animated show on the network." Only 50 television sets were in use at the time when Grothkopf produced "Willie the Worm," a low-budget, eight-minute black-and-white cartoon that aired in April 1938. The film was full of cutout animation, plus a small amount of cel animation, to illustrate the popular children's poem ("Willie Worm has taken a wife, to live and to love the rest of his life").

One year later, in May 1939, when NBC presented its first full schedule of evening programming on experimental station W2XBS (now WNBC), New York, the station previewed Walt Disney's Donald Duck cartoon, "Donald's Cousin," for viewers.

In the early 1950s many classic cartoons that previously had been released to theaters made their way to the tiny screen, shown almost exclusively on children's shows hosted by local television station personalities. Cartoons were the cornerstone of such popular programs as the *Captain Bob Show*, Buffalo, New York; *Uncle Willie's Cartoon Show*, Beaumont, Texas; and scores of others.

In 1953, 20 to 25 stations were regularly broadcasting cartoons throughout the country, garnering high ratings from their predominantly juvenile audience. And by January 1955 more than 400 television stations were programming animated cartoons.

The increase in the number of stations that aired cartoons was due largely to a high number of cartoon packages that became available for the first time. Warner Bros., Paramount-Fleischer-Famous Studios and Terry-Toons all released cartoons to television, joined by MGM's *Tom and Jerry* package and spot broadcasts of various Walt Disney cartoons on ABC's *Disneyland*.

With the availability of new films, television stations throughout the country launched their own afternoon children's shows hosted by a virtual army of "sea captains, space commanders, Western sodbusters and neighborhood policemen." Officer Joe Bolton hosted cartoons and comedy short subjects in New York. In

Los Angeles Tom Hatten entertained youngsters with Popeye cartoons in his *Pier 5 Club* on KTLA-TV Channel 5.

Other stations devised clever titles to inform children when "cartoon time" aired on their local station. Philadelphia's WFIL added *Funny Flickers*, while WGRB in Sche-nectady ran *Kartoon Karnival* to attract young viewers with large doses of cartoon entertainment. CBS was the first network to join the cartoon craze. In 1953, the network added *Barker Bill's Cartoon Show* to its daytime schedule, featuring early Terry-Toons cartoons. Three years later, CBS again segmented an assortment of Terry-Toons cartoons on *The CBS Cartoon Theatre*, a three-month-long prime-time series hosted by newcomer comedian Dick Van Dyke. That same year it also debuted the first half-hour network cartoon show commis-

*Early animated cartoon broadcasts occurred on afternoon children's programs hosted by local television station personalities. Tom Hatten (in sailor outfit) introduced Popeye cartoons on his weekday show, Pier 5 Club, for KTLA-TV, Los Angeles.* (COURTESY: TOM HATTEN)

sioned to include new animation with older cartoons, UPA's *The Gerald McBoing Boing Show.*

These programs only whetted viewers' appetites, however. What was missing from television logs was newly produced cartoon programs to keep viewers interested. Since producers could not afford to produce fully animated, theatrical style cartoons, the medium had to settle for a less expensive process.

"Full animation was very, very expensive," recalled Norm Prescott. "Television, in turn, could not support full animation. The economics just wouldn't jibe unless somebody could come up with a way of doing animation with fewer drawings."

The UPA-style of animation thus came to television. Early animated fare reflected this cost-efficient, or "cookie-cutter," method. The process enabled producers to use a variety of angles, cuts and camera moves to imply motion, while using the fewest number of cels possible to tell their story. For television, the format fit like a glove and audiences never noticed the difference.

The technique was officially introduced to viewers in the first made-for-television series, the cliff-hanging, serialized adventures of *Crusader Rabbit,* co-invented by Rocky and Bullwinkle creator Jay Ward. The series was test marketed in 1949 and made its debut one year later. Ward produced the program expressly for television, animating the series out of his makeshift studio in San Francisco and sending his sketches to Hollywood film producer Jerry Fairbanks to film, edit and add soundtracks to complete each story for broadcast.

"When Jay did *Crusader Rabbit,* it was still axiomatic that no one could produce a cartoon series for television," remembered Bill Scott, who created UPA's Gerald McBoing Boing and was the voice of Bullwinkle J. Moose. "Jay refused to believe that."

As was the case with other cartoon programs that followed, the cost of the *Crusader Rabbit* series is what made it attractive for television sales. One complete 19½-minute story cost approximately $2,500 to produce. "We would simply plan a story so we reused some of the animation with a different background," series producer Jerry Fairbanks recalled.

Ward was followed into the television arena by two veteran animators who were most responsible for giving limited animation its biggest boost: Bill Hanna and Joe Barbera. They perpetuated the art form in a number of highly successful series for television. The seven-time Academy Award-winning directors, who invented the hilarious

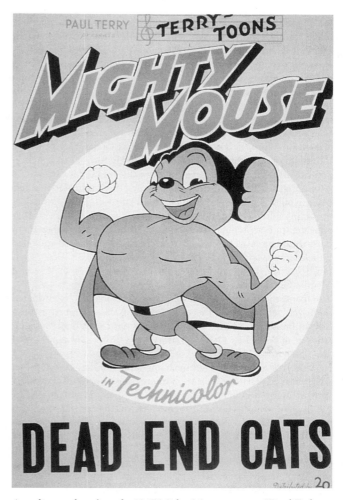

*A studio one-sheet from the 1947 Mighty Mouse cartoon, "Dead End Cats." © 20th Century Fox*

hijinks of MGM's Tom and Jerry, entered television's animated age eight years after Ward with *The Ruff and Reddy Show* (NBC, 1957), the first hosted cartoon series for Saturday morning featuring repackaged older Columbia Pictures cartoon shorts originally released to theaters. (In 1958, Hanna-Barbera produced the first all-new half-hour cartoon show, *The Huckleberry Hound Show,* featuring the cartoon adventures of Huckleberry Hound, Yogi Bear and Pixie and Dixie.) The series used only 12,000 cels to animate 30 minutes of cartoon entertainment (in this case, roughly three cartoons per show).

For television, this style of animation seemed most effective. "When we first started limited animation, it disturbed me," Hanna admitted in an interview. "Then when I saw some of the old cartoons on TV, I saw that actually limited animation came off better on the dimly lit television screen than the old fully animated things."

For Barbera, the biggest adjustment was not conforming to the new style of animation but to the low prices television paid for his and Hanna's animated productions. "We received about $2,700 (per show) and that was after great negotiating and pleading," he once said.

To retain a tidy profit, Hanna and Barbera effectively did away with production items that usually resulted in higher costs. They trimmed most schedule-delaying procedures, eliminated many preliminary sketches and recorded soundtracks in one sitting.

*Walter Lantz reviews the storyboard to a cartoon that is under production.*
(COURTESY: CITIZEN-NEWS)

By producing cartoons at such rock-bottom prices, the marketplace for made-for-television cartoons blossomed overnight. In 1959 Jay Ward returned to television with a new series, the misadventures of a moose and a flying squirrel, better known as *Rocky and His Friends.* (Ward originated the characters years earlier for a never-produced series entitled *The Frostbite Falls Follies.*) Pat Sullivan produced a new litter of *Felix the Cat* cartoons, bearing the trademark limited animation style that had become so suitable for television. (Animator Chuck Jones often has called this style of animation "illustrated radio" because it's like "a radio script with a minimum of drawings in front of it, and if you turn off the picture, you can still tell what's happening because you hear it.")

Consequently, during the next 10 years, the syndicated marketplace would be deluged with other all-cartoon series, aimed at attracting adults and children with characters and situations that appealed to both segments of the population. Other characters to barnstorm the "tube" during its early days of animation included Quick Draw McGraw (1959), Spunky and Tadpole (1960), Q.T. Hush (1960), Lippy the Lion (1962), Wally Gator (1962) and Magilla Gorilla (1964).

Japanese cartoon producers also began to import fully animated fantasy/adventure series that were reedited and redubbed in English for broadcast. Many have cult followings today. Some popular titles were *Astro Boy* (1964), *Eighth Man* (1965), *Gigantor* (1966) and *Speed Racer* (1967).

Many of television's earliest concepts for animated shows were derived from successful characters or formats that worked well in many popular live-action shows. *The Flintstones* (ABC, 1960), featuring television's "modern stone-age family," was actually based on the classic television sitcom *The Honeymooners.* *Top Cat* (ABC, 1961), another Hanna-Barbera Production,

*One of the most popular cartoon shows to appear on prime-time television was* The Flintstones. *The series was a cartoon version of the classic sitcom* The Honeymooners. © *Hanna-Barbera Productions*

mirrored the antics of Sergeant Bilko and his platoon of misfits from *The Phil Silvers Show. Calvin and the Colonel* (ABC, 1961), patterned after radio's *Amos 'n' Andy,* featured the voices of the original radio team, Freeman Gosden and Charles Correll, who created the animated spin-off. Like television sitcoms, several programs even featured studio-recorded laugh tracks to provoke laughter in the home.

Producers later turned to other bankable properties to attract viewers. Comic strips and comics gave television characters with built-in followings. Chester Gould's *Dick Tracy* (1961), caricatured in a series of cheaply produced five-minute cartoons, headed a legion of renowned comic characters in cartoon versions for television. Superheroes were included in this menagerie, flying onto television screens in countless action/adventure shows like *Marvel Superheroes* (1966), featuring the extraordinary feats of Spider-Man, The Incredible Hulk, Captain America and The Mighty Thor; *The New Adventures of Superman* (CBS, 1966) was the first fully animated network show based on a superhero character.

Motion picture and recording stars were also naturals for animated cartoons. Hanna-Barbera was the first to get into the act by producing cartoon versions of Abbott and Costello (1965), featuring the voice of straight man Bud Abbott, and Laurel and Hardy (1966). The Three Stooges (Moe Howard, Larry Fine and Curly Joe DeRita) brought their zany brand of slapstick to animation in *The New Three Stooges,* a live-action/animated series for syndication. Musical artists who gave animation a new beat in cartoon form included Ross Bagdasarian's Alvin and the Chipmunks in *The Alvin Show* (CBS, 1961) and Liverpool's Fab Four in *The Beatles* (ABC, 1965), the last musical group to be given animated life until Motown's *The Jackson 5ive* (ABC, 1971) and teenage rock sensations *The Osmonds* (ABC, 1972) burst onto the musical scene.

With so many programs eventually flooding the market, however, even film and television critics wondered just how long cartoons could last in the medium. In reviewing television animation, Charles Champlin, *Los Angeles Times* critic, wrote: "Operating on the adage 'if it works, copy it,' networks went so cartoon happy there was talk of animating the *Huntley-Brinkley Report.*"

One recurring criticism of television animation was that the work often appeared rushed, thus dramatically undermining the quality. Animators had little control over the quality because "the pressures of television are greater than the pressures of producing films for theatres," Bill Hanna noted. "Back when we made the MGM cartoons, we worked at a more leisurely, almost relaxed pace. There was definitely more care put into the drawing, timing, sound effects and the recording of the music. Much more time was taken to discuss stories and to design characters; pictures were reviewed in pencil test form, and changes were made before they were inked and painted. It was an elaborate process. Every phase of production was handled much more carefully than it is today. We just don't have the time today to put in all that effort."

Friz Freleng, who created several successful cartoon series for television for his company, DePatie-Freleng Enterprises, offered his own perspective of television cartoons. "I used to turn out 11 or 12 theatrical cartoons a year. At six minutes per cartoon, that was a little over an hour's worth. Here, in one week, they'll turn out four shows. They do at least one and a half hours of new animation a week," he said. "The networks go for the numbers (or viewers). They don't care what the quality of the show is—I don't think they even watch the shows. As long as it's got high numbers, it doesn't matter whether the show is good or not."

Former Disney animator Don Bluth, the genius behind such full-length cartoon treasures as *The Secret of NIMH* (1982), *Land*

*Before Time* (1988) and *Anastasia* (1997), shared Freleng's frustration. "They cut corners on Saturday-morning animation and when they cut corners, they kill the product," he said. "The networks say, 'A kid will watch cartoons that cost $90,000 a half hour, so why spend $300,000?'"

While the quality of most cartoons was suspect, most viewers welcomed the glut of animated cartoon fare that infiltrated Saturday mornings and prime-time television. Long before *The Simpsons*, cartoon programs demonstrated they could attract nighttime audiences.

In 1958 CBS pioneered the concept of airing the all-cartoon show in prime-time for the very first time. The network reran that summer *The Gerald McBoing Boing Show*, featuring the first-ever newly produced cartoons for network television. (The series actually debuted two years earlier.)

Networks did not fully pick up on the idea of slotting fully animated cartoons during the family viewing hour until the turn of the decade. ABC did the most with cartoons in prime time. In September 1960 it began airing *The Flintstones* on its nighttime schedule, becoming the first prime-time animated series in television history, followed by *The Bugs Bunny Show* one month later. In 1962 the network also spotted *The Jetsons* on Sunday evenings, with *The Adventures of Johnny Quest* (1964) to make it debut in prime time two years later, also on ABC. CBS ran a distant second in the prime-time cartoon derby. During the 1961–62 season, it aired *Alvin and the Chipmunks* during the evening hours as well as *Calvin and the Colonel*.

In 1962, after networks won big ratings with prime-time cartoon programs, NBC aired the first made-for-television special, sponsored by Timex, *Mister Magoo's Christmas Carol*, starring the nearsighted codger of theatrical cartoon fame. The program, which was also the first animated television musical, was an hour-long adaptation of Charles Dickens's classic holiday story. This program marked the illustrious beginning of the prime-time holiday special and the animated special in general.

Although this charming animated rendering produced explosive ratings, it took three years before television viewers were treated to their second prime-time special, *A Charlie Brown Christmas* (CBS, 1965), based on Charles M. Schulz's beloved *Peanuts* comic-strip characters. (The special remained on the shelf for one year, with no takers, before Coca-Cola agreed to sponsor the show.) The thirty-minute program generated a huge audience—nearly half of the nation's television viewers.

Due to the show's impressive performance, CBS made *Peanuts* an annual attraction on the network; it has since become the longest-running series of cartoon specials in television history. Runner-up Dr. Seuss inspired the first of several specials beginning with 1966's *Dr. Seuss' How The Grinch Stole Christmas*, produced by Chuck Jones and children's book author Ted Geisel. The show also premiered on CBS.

During the 1960s, many other made-for-television cartoon specials were produced, most notably by television innovators Arthur Rankin Jr. and Jules Bass, who presented a string of perennial cartoon classics in prime time. They created such memorable shows as *Rudolph, The Red-Nosed Reindeer* (NBC, 1964); *The Ballad of Smokey the Bear* (NBC, 1964), narrated by James Cagney; *Frosty the Snowman* (CBS, 1969); and *The Little Drummer Boy* (ABC, 1968). The pair's first prime-time entry was the hour-long animated special *Return to Oz*, which debuted on NBC in February 1964.

Not all of these shows used conventional animation, however. Many were filmed using a lifelike stop-motion puppet process created by Rankin and Bass called "Animagic," a technique

*Charlie Brown (left), Lucy and Linus dance around their beagle-topped tree in* A Charlie Brown Christmas *(1965), the first prime-time animated special based on Charles Schulz's popular comic strip.* (**COURTESY: CBS**)

they initiated in their 1961 children's series, *Tales of the Wizard of Oz*.

Until 1963 the Saturday-morning lineup on all three networks was mostly composed of reruns of theatrical cartoons and popular children's programs, including *My Friend Flicka*, *Sky King* and others. For the 1963-64 season, CBS took the first step toward creating an all-cartoon Saturday-morning schedule by offering a two-hour block of cartoons.

Attracting national sponsors like Kellogg's and General Mills, the network's new Saturday-morning lineup included the new *Tennessee Tuxedo and His Tales*, *Quick Draw McGraw*, which had previously premiered in syndication, and network returnees *The Alvin Show* and *Mighty Mouse Playhouse*. (In the following two seasons, CBS expanded the schedule by another hour, adding *Linus the Lionhearted* and *The Tom and Jerry Show*.

CBS daytime programmer Fred Silverman, who was only 26 years old, was responsible for the new Saturday-morning programming. He recognized that adults, like children, love animated cartoons and that cartoons could attract a larger viewing audience. Silverman's assumption proved correct. Ratings skyrocketed and by the 1966–67 season, after restructuring Saturday morning with nine back-to-back half-hour cartoon shows, CBS rocketed into first place in that time slot's ratings derby.

Taking notice of CBS's success, runners-up NBC and ABC soon began their own Saturday-morning cartoon scheduling in earnest. ABC followed CBS in 1964 by adding cartoons to its Saturday-morning schedule, while NBC did the same in 1965. In the late 1960s, Saturday morning became known as "a jungle of competition," and rightfully so. New cartoons were delivering the largest network audience ever, and network bidding for programs became intensely competitive. The average price for a half-hour cartoon show ranged from $48,000 to $62,000, climbing to

*Holiday themes became a popular forum for animated network specials in the 1960s. Here Frosty leads a merry parade in a scene from the animated musical special,* Frosty the Snowman. *© Rankin-Bass Productions*

*Model sheet from Pat Sullivan's syndicated cartoon series,* Felix the Cat. *Pictured: Rock Bottom, the Professor, Felix and Poindexter. © Joe Oriolo Productions*

$70,000 to $100,000 by the 1970s. Financially, these figures were nothing compared to the revenues Saturday-morning cartoons generated. By 1970 the combined network take was $66.8 million in advertising revenue from their respective Saturday-morning lineups.

By 1968, however, the success of television cartoons was somewhat diminished by one factor: the public outcry against television violence. The aftermath of the shocking assassinations of Dr. Martin Luther King and Senator Robert Kennedy brought about tremendous unrest among the public when it came to violence, whether in their neighborhood streets or on television.

In a survey *The Christian Science Monitor* recorded 162 threats or acts of violence on Saturday morning, the majority occurring between 7:30 and 9:30 A.M. when an estimated 26.7 million children, ages 2 to 17, were tuned in. The issue of violence on television was seconded by a report prepared by the National Commission on the Causes and Prevention of Violence (Kerner Commission), which ultimately forced networks to make changes in policy with respect to children's programming.

Network censors were hired to sit in on script meetings, approve storyboards and veto subject matter right up to airtime in an effort to control the violent or suggestive content of cartoons. The policy remains in force today.

In addition to instituting in-house control, the three major networks removed most of the shows and characters that were the subject of parental protests. Action-adventure shows were thus replaced by comedy series that deemphasized violence. The new aim of children's programming would be to "entertain, stimulate and educate." However, not all animators agreed that censorship was the right thing.

"Cartoon characters never die—they never bleed," remarked veteran animator Walter Lantz. "They get blown up or run over and the next scene there they are, hale and hearty. That's part of their magic, their fantasy. These so-called critics say kids can't separate fantasy from reality. They're looking at things they, as adults, consider harmful to the child. The critics don't look at cartoons through the eyes of a child. I always considered our type of humor as being slapstick, not violent."

Director Friz Freleng, of Warner Bros. fame, supported Lantz's theory that home audiences would rather be watching slapstick

comedies. "The adult audience today has been robbed of a certain amount of entertainment," he said. "Kids keep getting it [cartoons] on TV, but you won't find an adult sitting down and watching a kid's show. I believe they miss it, and I believe there's a neglected audience."

Freleng and others had their reason to be concerned. In many instances, the network's decisions on what to censor were questionable. Lou Scheimer, cartoon producer for Filmation Studios, related that he had run into trouble when he was animating *Superboy*. One sequence called for Superboy to stop an oncoming train with his hands. "It was thought that it might tempt kids to try the same," Scheimer said. The scene was changed.

In one episode of CBS's *Josie and the Pussycats* (CBS, 1970), a script called for one of the pussycats to escape from a science-fiction menace by taking refuge in a dish of spaghetti. Former producer and comic-book artist Norman Maurer, who wrote the scene, once recalled, "CBS disallowed it. They said, 'Kids will put their cats in spaghetti.' I was told to rewrite the scene."

*Japanese cartoon offerings were staples of 1960s television. One syndicated favorite was* Kimba, the White Lion. (COURTESY: NBC)

Also frustrating for most animators during this time was the audience response to early screenings of the fall shows. In the late 1970s, during a screening of Filmation's *Fat Albert* and *Space Academy* shows at a Hollywood preview house, more than half the audience walked out, prompting producer Joe Barbera, who was on hand to measure the audience response to his own Hanna-Barbera cartoons, to remark that he yearned for a return to the old days so that "when a cat chases a mouse, he doesn't have to stop and teach him how to blow glass or weave a basket. My wish for Christmas is they would leave education to the schools and entertainment to us."

While many animators might disagree, network censorship, in its earliest form, brought forth stronger values that were necessary in cartoons. The action/adventure shows had their place in history, as much as their replacements, teenage mystery and rock 'n' roll group programs, which served to educate and entertain children in a manner that reflected new attitudes in society and the world.

In the theatrical cartoon marketplace, it was a completely different story. Producers trod forbidden turf by producing animated works that were aimed largely at adults. One principal reason for this was the increase of grown-ups and young adults lining up to see cartoon features.

The one film that changed the visual and commercial style of the cartoon feature more than any single production was *Yellow Submarine* (1968), an animated odyssey featuring The Beatles (John, Paul, George and Ringo) that incorporated images and stylized movement. Audiences were most receptive to the film, proving there was indeed room for animated films that were less Disneyesque.

Another film that revolutionized the cartoon feature industry was Ralph Bakshi's *Fritz the Cat* (1971), the first X-rated full-length cartoon based on Robert Crumb's underground comic strip. Like *Yellow Submarine*, this departure from mainstream animation was full of topical statements—this time about life in the 1960s, including the decade's sexual and political revolution.

The landmark accomplishments of both films marked a new beginning for the animated feature film business that for several years had been stifled by the lack of other innovators in the field taking chances with full-length cartoons in this high-risk area. As a result, more feature-length cartoons were produced than ever before, and, for the first time in years, Disney actually had to compete in an ever-crowded marketplace.

Some of the new and original concepts, from here and abroad, that followed included *A Boy Named Charlie Brown* (1969), *Charlotte's Web* (1972), *Fantastic Planet* (1973), *Hugo the Hippo* (1976), *Raggedy Ann and Andy* (1977) and *Watership Down* (1978).

In the 1980s the success of the animated feature continued, spawning new ideas to meet the increased demand of baby-boomer families. Former Disney animator Don Bluth directed the first independently produced animated feature to successfully challenge Disney's dominance at the box office—*An American Tail* (1986). While other films' characters were mostly based on greeting-card and action-toy figures (this was also true in television animation), another film renewed hope in the animation business that original characters and stories still sold audiences: *Who Framed Roger Rabbit* (1988), a splendidly conceived comedy/mystery produced by Walt Disney whose style harkened back to Hollywood's golden age of animation. The blockbuster film, which grossed more than $100 million, renewed interest in creating quality animated films for adults and children and pumped new life into the cartoon industry.

Further revitalizing animation throughout this period was the introduction of computer animation with Robert Abel & Associates creating the first computer-generated 3-D character animated

television commercial, "Brilliance," featuring the *Sexy Robot* (1984), for the Canned Food Information Council; Pacific Data Images producing the first computer-generated 3-D dinosaurs seen by the public in the animated short *Chromasaurus* (1985); and former Disney animator John Lasseter from Pixar directing the first widely released computer-animated short, *Luxo Jr.* (1986), also the first computer-animated film nominated for an Oscar, following his first computer-animated short for Lucasfilm's computer unit, *Andre and Wally* (1984).

Throughout the 1990s, animated feature films became enduring profit machines, led by Disney with a series of blockbusters: *The Little Mermaid* (1989), *Beauty and the Beast* (1991), *Aladdin* (1992), *The Lion King* (1994, the top-grossing animated feature of all time and first billion-dollar property in history), *Toy Story* (1995, the first fully computer-animated feature), *Pocahontas* (1995) and *The Hunchback of Notre Dame* (1996). Other Hollywood studios rushed onto the scene eager to make animated features. Universal (notably Steven Spielberg's "Amblimation" studios), Warner Bros., Paramount and 20th Century Fox jumped in to compete with Disney, producing animated features aimed at the family market. Also entering the mix around this time was award-winning independent animator Bill Plympton, with his first full-length feature, *The Tune* (1992), becoming the first successful theatrical feature produced, directed and animated by an individual and entirely financed by him. Few came close to having the same box-office success as Disney.

As a ripple effect, theaters witnessed the return of the theatrical cartoon short, absent as a regular program feature in the cinema for almost 20 years. Disney's release of the 1989 Roger Rabbit cartoon short, "Tummy Trouble," ushered in a new era for animated theatrical shorts. The studio began producing new cartoon shorts for theaters, including the first new Mickey Mouse cartoon in 37 years, *The Prince and the Pauper*, a 35-minute featurette released to theaters. In 1991 Warner Bros. produced its first new cartoon short since closing down its animation department in the 1960s: *Box-Office Bunny*, starring Bugs Bunny. More new *Looney Tunes* followed, featuring Bugs and his Looney Tunes pals, and in 1994 legendary animator Chuck Jones returned to Warner Bros. to produce and direct a series of new *Looney Tunes*, beginning with the Road Runner and Coyote cartoon, "Chariots of Fur."

With animation short subjects back in favor with studios to a degree not seen perhaps since animation's heyday, other studios, such Hanna-Barbera, MGM and MCA/Universal got into the act. In 1995 Hanna-Barbera, which had become active in producing cartoon shorts for the Cartoon Network's *World Premiere Toons* program, released several cartoon shorts to movie theaters overseas. That same year MGM issued an all-new Pink Panther cartoon, while Universal distributed its first theatrical cartoon starring Earthworm Jim, star of the popular series of the same name on the WB Television Network. *The Ren & Stimpy Show* creator John Kricfalusi tried to join the already crowded field by producing a series of "Brik Blastoff" and "Jimmy the Idiot Boy" cartoon shorts for theaters, but the films were never released theatrically. In 1997 Kricfalusi instead released them on the Internet under his Spumco company Web page under the series title *The Goddamn George Liquor Program*, becoming the first Internet-produced cartoon series.

Television experienced the largest growth and expansion of cartoon programming in its long and illustrious history. In 1990 the FOX Kids Network premiered, changing the face of kids' TV forever, while Disney unveiled *The Disney Afternoon Block*, a two-hour daily programming service featuring original made-for-syndication cartoon series. The FOX Kids Network, headed by Margaret Loesch, became a force with which to reckon, producing fresh, original and highly rated cartoon series following the network's launching, including *Bobby's World, Tiny Toon Adventures* and *Taz-Mania*. Not to be outdone, media mogul Ted Turner launched another network two years later: Cartoon Network, the first cable network to feature cartoons exclusively around the clock. Turner started the network—his company's fifth—after acquiring the Hanna-Barbera cartoon library for $320 million. Combined with his company's existing stockpile of MGM, Paramount and Warner Bros. cartoons, Cartoon Network—whose audience would be adults and children—had a backlog of 8,500 cartoon titles to broadcast.

Once again FOX Network took a revolutionary approach in programming, and in 1990 it debuted a cartoon series that would become the single most popular animated program of the decade: *The Simpsons*, which matured into a megahit for the network. The success of *The Simpsons* marked the return of animated cartoons to prime time, and other networks attempted to capitalize on Fox's good fortune.

In 1991 MTV aired the first animated series created for a cable broadcaster, *Liquid Television*, featuring the work of independent animators, including Mike Judge, whose *Beavis and Butt-head* attracted immediate attention and premiered as its own series in 1993. Meanwhile, Nickelodeon entered the animation business, introducing three original cartoon series on the network (under the name of Nicktoons): *Rugrats, Ren and Stimpy* and *Doug*, each major hits for the network.

The major networks soon followed with their own prime-time fare. In 1992 ABC added as a midseason replacement, *Capitol Critters*, produced by Steven Bochco and Hanna-Barbera, while CBS premiered another prime-time cartoon series, *Fish Police*, also produced by Hanna-Barbera. Neither was a ratings success, and both were quickly canceled. Other series premiered in prime time but didn't fare any better. Steven Spielberg's long-awaited *Family Dog* was launched on CBS in 1993, but poor reviews and bad ratings brought a swift end to the show. In 1994 ABC tried to succeed where CBS failed by unveiling *The Critic*, an animated spoof of Hollywood and the movies hosted by cable-TV movie critic Jay Sherman (voiced by *Saturday Night Live*'s Jon Lovitz). Despite the program's biting satire of the movie business, the show did not generate ratings to stay in prime time on ABC. It was revived on FOX but its run was short.

In general, cable networks outshined the competition in the prime-time cartoon derby. The same year *The Critic* premiered,

USA Network launched its first prime-time cartoon show, *Duckman*, the adventures of an irritable, web-footed detective. The series, starring the voice of Jason Alexander of TV's *Seinfeld*, proceeded to become USA's signature show, much as *The Simpsons* did for FOX. Cartoon Network also debuted its first series of original programs: in 1994, *Space Ghost Coast to Coast*, the first talk show hosted by an animated cartoon superhero, and in 1995 *What a Cartoon!* a joint project with Hanna-Barbera featuring 48 cartoon shorts created by a pool of well-known cartoon directors. Comedy Central joined the growing list of networks to produce prime-time cartoon series, introducing *Dr. Katz, Professional Therapist*, presented in a process called "Squigglevision."

As in the past, children's advocates turned up the heat over the level of violence in cartoons on television. Networks found themselves on the losing end as Congress ordered an inquiry to determine whether stations had in fact been complying with the Children's Television Act of 1990, a law that limits advertising time in children's programming and requires stations to make a serious effort to serve kids' educational and informational needs. In three years since the law passed, little had changed. Faced with threats from Washington lawmakers, in the fall of 1994 networks unveiled their fall lineups, offering a variety of educational and informational shows, including *Beakman's World, The Spacewatch Club, Mad Scientist Toon Club* and *Real News for Kids*.

For a variety of reasons, economic and otherwise, NBC became the first major network to drop animated cartoons from its Saturday morning lineup. The network's new lineup would feature educational and informational shows for kids instead. NBC's decision to bow out left ABC, CBS and Fox to compete for the $300 million-plus in kids advertising.

Beginning in the fall of 1997, the Federal Communications Commission made it mandatory that television stations air three hours a week of educational programming for children. ABC endorsed the concept and worked with educators, who read scripts for upcoming shows and made suggestions to producers. CBS bowed out altogether, joining NBC in its decision to drop animated cartoons from its Saturday morning lineup and replace them with live-action shows, such as *Wheel of Fortune 2000* and *Sports Illustrated for Kids*.

Strengthening NBC's and later CBS's decision was Disney's $19 billion acquisition of ABC/Capital Cities and the emergence of the KidsWB in 1995. Disney revitalized ABC's Saturday morning programming, turning it into a powerhouse once again, while the Kids' WB Television Network would find its own niche with original programming—some of which first began on FOX—attracting a mix of adults and children as viewers.

Throughout the decade, animation's boom times resulted in a merchandise explosion of epic proportions. Baby boomers principally fueled the growth in cartoon merchandise that for the first time in history saw total licensing revenue top the $100 million mark. The home video market enjoyed record sales and rentals of cartoon videos, capturing lovers of cartoons, young and old. Celebrations of Hollywood's glory days of animation were held the world over. Film festivals honored legendary animators from animation's "golden age"—Warner Bros. animators Chuck Jones, Friz Freleng, and Tex Avery as well as former MGM greats Bill Hanna and Joe Barbera.

The popularity of Saturday-morning and syndicated cartoon series continued throughout this period spurred by the success of such Emmy Award–winning shows as FOX's *Animaniacs* and *Tiny Toon Adventures*, and the WB's *Pinky & the Brain*, all produced by Steven Spielberg and Warner Bros. Television Animation, and

*The dark comedy feature* Beetlejuice *made its way to television as a hit Saturday morning series in 1989. © Warner Bros.* (COURTESY: NELVANA LIMITED)

*In a world divided into four nations, a young boy harnesses his inborn skills combining martial arts and elemental magic to defeat the Fire Lord in Nickelodeon's first fantasy action series targeting boys,* Avatar: The Last Airbender. © *Viacom International.* ALL RIGHTS RESERVED.

CBS's *Garfield and Friends,* as well as a number of video-game adapted shows, including NBC's *Super Mario Brothers Super Show!* and ABC's *Sonic the Hedgehog.*

Meanwhile, animated sitcoms, cartoons aimed at adults, gained traction on the tube. Among the most successful were FOX's *The Simpsons* (1989–  ); *King of the Hill* (1997–  ); *Family Guy* (1999–  ), which was cancelled once in 2000 and again in 2002, but reinstated due to incredible DVD sales and its large viewership of reruns (It is the first cancelled show brought back by DVD sales, and it happened twice!); MTV's *Ren & Stimpy* (1991–96); *Beavis and Butt-head* (1993–97); and Comedy Central's *South Park* (1997–  ), which caused the network's viewership to nearly double. Original cartoon fare for children resulted in several smash hits becoming highly successful franchises spun off into specials and feature films. Leading the pack were Nickelodeon's highly rated, Emmy Award–winning Klasky-Csupo series *The Rugrats* (1991–2004), *The Wild Thornberrys* (1998–2001), John A. Davis's *The Adventures of Jimmy Neutron, Boy Genius* (2002), Stephen Hillenburg's *SpongeBob SquarePants* (1999–  ), and Nick Jr.'s popular preschool series, *Dora the Explorer* (2000–  ).

From the mid-1990s on, anime became a huge hit in America and a staple of children's programming, along with more adult Japanese cartoons, striking a chord with fans of all ages, including such syndicated favorites as *Sailor Moon* (1995–2000), *Pokémon* (1997–2002), *Dragon Ball Z* (1989–2003) and Cartoon Network's *Cowboy Bebop* (1998) and *The Animatrix* (2004), airing on its Adult Swim programming block.

In the meantime, one alarming trend in the new millennium was the disappearance of Saturday-morning cartoon lineups on most of the major networks—ABC, NBC and CBS—where cartoons once reigned with ratings of more than 20 million viewers weekly and dominated the airwaves throughout the 1970s and 1980s. In the fall of 2000, CBS replaced its Saturday-morning lineup with children's programming from Nick Jr. called *Nick Jr. on CBS* (replaced in 2006 by the three-hour *KOL Slumber Party on CBS*). NBC did the same in 2002, replacing its traditional Saturday-morning schedule with live-action and animated programming in partnership with Discovery Kids, which changed again in 2006 to the new E/I weekend programming called qubo. By 2003, traditional Saturday-morning cartoons existed on only three networks, ABC Kids, FOX Kids and Kids' WB!, with all three networks attracting a meager 2 million viewers with its current programming. Throughout the 2000s, branded programming blocks would become the norm not only on major networks, but also on cable networks, including Cartoon Network with its popular late-night Adult Swim animation block and weekday Tickle-U preschool block; the Disney Channel with Playhouse Disney for pee-wee audiences and Toon Disney with the Jetix action block (which also aired on ABC Family); MTV and Spike TV with their own competing nighttime blocks with Cartoon Network's Adult Swim, including Sic'Emation and The Strip, respectively, to name a few.

From the end of the decade through the new millennium, animated features continued to enjoy widespread success while also achieving new heights and new lows. Aside from the premiere of the first animated feature on 70 millimeter IMAX theater screens, Disney's visual and musical masterpiece, *Fantasia/2000* (1999), and *Pokémon: The Movie* (1999) becoming the most successful foreign animated film in American history, grossing more than $85 million at the box office, computer animation virtually surpassed the traditional ink-and-draw technique as the method of choice in making full-length animated features. Studios like Pixar Animation set the standard with the success of seven films, in partnership with Disney, that set new box-office records and new all-time highs—and consecutively opened number-one—including *Toy Story 2* (1999), *Monsters Inc.* (2001), *Finding Nemo* (2003), *The Incredibles* (2004) and *Cars* (2006).

Closely mirroring their success were rivals DreamWorks Animation and 20th Century Fox's Blue Sky Studios, commanding a considerable share of the box-office with hits such as *Antz* (1998), *Shrek* (2001), *Ice Age* (2002), *Shrek 2* (2004), *Shark Tale* (2004), *Madagascar* (2005), *Robots* (2005), *Over the Hedge* (2006) and *Ice Age: The Meltdown* (2006) respectively.

One serious casualty with the new wave of successful computer-animated films was Walt Disney Studios. Following such costly hand-drawn flops as *Treasure Planet* (2002), *Brother Bear* (2003) and, finally, *Home on the Range* (2004), in 2004 the studio shut down its main animation facility in Orlando, Florida, putting approximately 250 animators, technicians and other personnel out of work, followed by its DisneyToon Studios in Sydney, Australia, the company's last studio producing hand-drawn animated features. Turning its attention toward producing more competitive, fully computer-animated productions, a year later it went on to produce its first home-grown computer-animated feature, *Chicken Little* (2005).

With such remarkable interest in this lively art, the future of animated cartoons is in good hands. As it proceeds into the years and decades ahead, the force behind animation's success will be the same underlying element as in the past: its commitment to quality. That said, the animated cartoon will last as long as people thirst for the flicker of action, the ingenious blend of characters and well-conceived original stories that only cartoons can offer. If this holds true, the next 100 years should be worth watching.

# Silent Cartoon Series

## ◎ ABIE THE AGENT

Based on the popular comic strip by Harry Hershfield. *Directed by Gregory La Cava. An International Film Service Production.*

**1917:** "Iska Worreh" (Aug. 5); and "Abie Kabibble Outwitting His Rival" (Sept. 23).

## ◎ AESOP'S FILM FABLES

After forming his own studio near the end of World War I, pioneer animator Paul Terry brought this series of popular fables to the screen in 1920, using animal characters in the roles of humans to depict their improprieties without offending audiences. (The series was later known simply as *Aesop's Fables*.) An Aesop-type moral concluded each picture. While most of the films were enacted by animals, others starred Farmer Al Falfa, Terry's best-known character at the time.

During the first nine years of the series' run, Terry's staff wrote, animated and produced one complete Aesop's cartoon a week. Besides Terry who directed many early films, five other animators shared the workload—men like Frank Moser, Harry D. Bailey, John Foster, Fred Anderson and Jerry Shields each were instrumental in the series' success. Mannie Davis and Bill Tytla, two other animation veterans, joined Terry's team of animators in the late 1920s.

Terry devised the basic stories for most of the films, borrowing many of his "morals" from a short-subject series entitled "Topics of the Day," in addition to others he dreamed up himself.

The Keith-Albee Theatre circuit, one of the largest vaudeville/movie theater chains in the country, bankrolled the series, setting up Terry in business as Fable Pictures Inc. (The name was later changed to Fables Studio.) His deal with Keith-Albee guaranteed that his cartoons played in each of the chain's theaters throughout the country, earning him the distinction of becoming "the first [animator] to really make money in the business," as animator Dick Huemer, who worked on the rival *Mutt and Jeff* series, remarked.

In 1928, following the arrival of sound, Fable Studios was taken over by Amadee J. Van Beuren, who purchased the studio from Keith-Albee. As Van Beuren Productions, the company success-fully revived the series by adding soundtracks. Van Beuren had actually served as president of Fables Studios prior to buying the studio, so he was already familiar with the series. Terry went on to start his famed Terry-Toons studio, where he created such cartoon notables as Mighty Mouse and Heckle and Jeckle. *Directed by Paul Terry, John Foster, Hugh M. Shields, Frank Moser, Harry D. Bailey and Mannie Davis. A Fable Pictures, Inc. Fables Studio Keith-Albee Theatres Production released by Pathé Film Exchange, Inc.*

**1920:** "The Animal Aviators"; "A Cat's Life"; "On the Air"; "Wedding Bells"; and "Wonders of the Deep."

**1921:** "The Goose That Laid the Golden Egg" (May 13); "Mice Council" (May 13); "The Rooster and the Eagle" (May 13); "The Ants and the Grasshopper" (May 13); "Cats at Law" (May 13); "The Lioness and the Eggs" (May 13); "The Country Mouse and City Mouse" (May 13); "The Cat and the Canary" (May 13); "The Fox and the Crow" (May 13); "The Donkey in the Lion's Skin" (May 13); "Mice at War" (May 13); "The Hare and Frogs" (May 13); "The Fashionable Fox" (May 13); "The Hermit and the Bear" (May 13); "The Hare and the Tortoise" (May 13) "The Wolf and the Crane" (May 13); "The Fox and the Goat" (May 13); "Venus and the Cat" (Oct. 15); "The Frog and the Ox" (Oct. 15); "The Dog and the Bone" (Oct. 15); "The Cat and the Monkey" (Oct. 15); "The Owl and the Grasshopper" (Oct. 15); "The Fly and the Ant" (Oct. 15); "The Frogs That Wanted a King" (Nov. 27); "The Conceited Donkey" (Dec. 6); "The Wolf and the Kid" (Dec. 6); "The Wayward Dog" (Dec. 10); "The Cat and the Mice" (Dec. 31); and "The Dog and the Flea" (Dec. 31).

**1922:** "The Bear and the Bees" (Jan. 26); "The Miller and His Donkey" (Jan. 26); "The Fox and the Grapes" (Jan. 26); "The Villain in Disguise" (Jan. 26); "The Dog and the Thief" (Jan. 26); "The Cat and the Swordfish" (Jan. 26); "The Tiger and the Donkey" (Jan. 26); "The Spendthrift" (Jan. 26); "The Farmer and the Ostrich" (Jan. 26); "The Dissatisfied Cobbler" (Feb. 8); "The Lion and the Mouse" (Feb. 21); "The Rich Cat and the Poor Cat" (Feb. 21): "The Wolf in Sheep's Clothing" (Mar. 4); "The Wicked Cat" (Mar. 4); "The Boy and the Dog" (Apr. 3); "The Eternal Triangle" (Apr. 3); "The Model Dairy" (Apr. 11); "Love at First

Sight" (Apr. 11); "The Hunter and His Dog" (Apr. 27); "The Dog and the Wolves" (Apr. 27); "The Maid and the Millionaire" (Apr. 27); "The Farmer and His Cat" (May 17); "The Cat and the Pig" (May 17); "Crime in a Big City" (May 29); "Brewing Trouble" (June 22): "The Dog and the Fish" (June 22); "The Mischievous Cat" (June 22); "The Worm That Turned" (June 22); "The Boastful Cat" (June 22); "The Country Mouse and the City Cat" (June 26); "The Farmer and the Mice" (June 26); "Fearless Fido" (July 20); "The Mechanical Horse" (Aug. 9); "The Boy and the Bear" (Aug. 9); "The Two Explorers" (Aug. 12); "The Two Slick Traders" (Aug. 12); "Two of a Trade" (Sept. 27); "The Big Flood" (Sept. 27); "The Romantic Mouse" (Sept. 27); "Henpecked Harry" (Sept. 27); "The Hated Rivals" (Sept. 27); "The Elephant's Trunk" (Sept. 27); "The Enchanted Fiddle" (Sept. 27); "The Rolling Stone" (Oct. 9); "Friday the Thirteenth" (Nov. 11); "The Fortune Hunters" (Nov. 11) "The Man Who Laughs" (Nov. 11); "Henry's Busted Romance" (Nov. 11); "The Two Trappers" (Dec. 1); "The Dog's Paradise" (Dec. 1); "The Frog and the Catfish" (Dec. 1); "Cheating the Cheaters" (Dec. 14); and "A Stone Age Romeo."

**1923:** "A Fisherman's Jinx" (Jan. 27); "A Raisin and a Cake of Yeast" (Feb. 3); "The Gliders" (Feb. 10); "Troubles on the Ark" (Feb. 17); "The Mysterious Hat" (Feb. 17); "The Traveling Salesman" (Feb. 17); "The Spider and the Fly" (Feb. 17); "The Sheik" (Feb. 17); "The Alley Cat" (Feb. 17); "Farmer Al Falfa's Bride" (Feb. 23); "Day by Day in Every Way" (Mar. 22); "One Hard Pull" (Mar. 22); "The Gamblers" (Mar. 22); "The Jolly Rounders" (Mar. 22); "Pharoah's Tomb" (Apr. 27); "The Mouse Catcher" (Apr. 27); "A Fishy Story" (Apr. 27); "Spooks" (Apr. 27); "Amateur Night on the Ark" (Apr. 27); "The Stork's Mistake" (May 12); "Springtime" (May 12); "The Burglar Alarm" (June 6); "The Covered Pushcart" (June 6); "The Pace That Kills" (June 7); "Mysteries of the Sea" (July 19); "The Marathon Dancers" (July 19); "The Pearl Divers" (July 19); "The Bad Bandit" (July 19); "The Great Explorers" (July 19); "The Nine of Spades" (Aug. 2); "The Cat that Failed" (Aug. 7); "The Walrus Hunters" (Aug. 11); "The Cat's Revenge" (Aug. 11); "Love in a Cottage" (Sept. 1); "Derby Day" (Sept. 1); "The Cat's Whiskers" (Sept. 1); "Aged in the Wood" (Sept. 29); "The High Flyers" (Sept. 29); "The Circus" (Sept. 29); "A Barnyard Romeo" (Sept. 29); "Do Women Pay?" (Nov. 9); "Farmer Al Falfa's Pet Cat" (Nov. 9); "Happy Go Luckies" (Nov. 9); "The Five Fifteen" (Nov. 9); "The Best Man Wins" (Nov. 9); "The Cat Came Back" (Nov. 16); "The Morning After" (Nov. 16); "A Dark Horse" (Nov. 23); "Five Orphans of the Storm" (Dec. 22); "The Good Old Days" (Dec. 24); and "The Animals' Fair" (Dec. 14).

**1924:** "The Black Sheep" (Jan. 9); "Good Old College Days" (Jan. 26); "The Rat's Revenge" (Jan. 26); "A Rural Romance" (Jan. 26); "Captain's Kidder" (Feb. 20); "Herman the Great Mouse" (Feb. 20); "The All Star Cast" (Feb. 20); "Why Mice Leave Home" (Feb. 20); "From Rags to Riches and Back Again" (Feb. 20); "The Champion" (Mar. 20); "Runnin' Wild" (Mar. 20); "If Noah Lived Today" (Apr. 22); "A Trip to the Pole" (Apr. 22); "An Ideal Farm" (Apr. 22); "Homeless Pups" (Apr. 22); "When Winter Comes" (Apr. 22); "The Jealous Fisherman" (Apr. 22); "The Jolly Jailbird" (May 12); "The Flying Carpet" (May 28); "The Organ Grinder" (May 29); "One Good Turn Deserves Another" (May 31); "That Old Can of Mine" (June 14); "Home Talent" (June 28); "The Body in the Bag" (July 5); "Desert Sheiks" (July 12); "A Woman's Honor" (July 19); "The Sport of Kings" (July 26); "Flying Fever" (Aug. 2); "Amelia Comes Back" (Aug. 2); "The Prodigal Pup" (Aug. 2); "House Cleaning" (Aug. 2); "The Barnyard Olympics" (Sept. 5); "A Message from

the Sea" (Sept. 5); "In the Good Old Summer Time" (Sept. 13); "The Mouse That Turned" (Sept. 20); "A Lighthouse by the Sea" (Sept. 25); "Hawks of the Sea" (Sept. 25); "Noah's Outing" (Sept. 25); "Black Magic" (Oct. 18); "The Cat and the Magnet" (Oct. 29); "Monkey Business" (Oct. 29); "She Knew Her Man" (Oct. 29); "Good Old Circus Days" (Nov. 22); "Noah's Athletic Club" (Dec. 3); "Mysteries of Old Chinatown" (Dec. 3); "Down on the Farm" (Dec. 3); "On the Ice" (Dec. 3); "Sharp Shooters" (Dec. 3); "She's in Again" (Dec. 3); "One Game Pup" (Dec. 11); "African Huntsmen" (Dec. 11); "Hold That Thought" (Dec. 26); and "Biting the Dust" (Dec. 31).

**1925:** "A Transatlantic Flight" (Jan. 19); "Bigger and Better Jails" (Jan. 19); "Fisherman's Luck" (Jan. 19); "Clean Up Week" (Jan. 19); "In Dutch" (Feb. 13); "Jungle Bike Riders" (Feb. 13); "The Pie Man" (Feb. 13); "At the Zoo" (Mar. 5); "The Housing Shortage" (Mar. 26); "S.O.S." (Mar. 26); "The Adventures of Adenoid" (Apr. 10); "Permanent Waves" (Apr. 10); "Deep Stuff" (Apr. 25); "House Cleaning" (May 4); "Darkest Africa" (May 4); "A Fast Worker" (May 4); "Echoes from the Alps" (May 4); "Hot Times in Iceland" (May 4); "The Runt" (May 4); "The End of the World" (May 8); "The Runaway Balloon" (May 8); "Wine, Women and Song" (May 18), "When Men Were Men" (May 18); "Bugville Field Day" (June 11); "Office Help" (June 11); "Over the Plate" (June 23); "A Yarn about a Yarn" (July 6); "Bubbles" (July 6); "Soap" (July 6); "For the Love of a Gal" (July 20); "Window Washers" (July 20); "Barnyard Follies" (July 20); "The Ugly Duckling" (Aug. 28); "Hungry Hounds" (Aug. 28); "Nuts and Squirrels" (Aug. 28); "The Lion and the Monkey" (Aug. 28); "The Hero Wins" (Sept. 28); "Air Cooled" (Sept. 28); "Closer than a Brother" (Sept. 28); "Wild Cats of Paris" (Sept. 28); "The Honor System" (Sept. 28); "The Great Open Spaces" (Nov. 6); "More Mice than Brains" (Nov. 21); "A Day's Outing" (Nov. 28); "The Bonehead Age" (Dec. 5); "The Haunted House" (Dec. 12); "The English Channel Swim" (Dec. 17); and "Noah Had His Troubles" (Dec. 17/a.k.a. "Noah and His Trousers").

**1926:** "The Gold Push" (Jan. 23); "Three Blind Mice" (Jan. 23); "Lighter Than Air" (Jan. 23); "Little Brown Jug" (Jan. 23); "The June Bride" (Jan. 23); "The Wind Jammers" (Jan. 23); "The Wicked City" (Jan. 23); "Hunting in 1950" (Jan. 23); "The Mail Coach" (Feb. 6); "Spanish Love" (Feb. 6); "The Fire Fighters" (Mar. 6); "Up in the Air" (Mar. 6); "Fly Time" (Mar. 6); "The Merry Blacksmith" (Mar. 12); "The Big-hearted Fish" (Apr. 20); "The Shootin' Fool" (Apr. 20); "Rough and Ready Romeo" (Apr. 20); "An Alpine Flapper" (May 17); "Liquid Dynamite" (May 17); "A Bumper Crop" (May 26); "The Big Retreat" (May 26); "The Land Boom" (July 6); "A Plumber's Life" (July 6); "Chop Suey and Noodles" (July 6); "Jungle Sports" (July 6); "Red Hot Sands" (July 8); "Pirates Bold" (July 22); "Venus of Venice" (July 22); "Her Ben" (July 22); "Dough Boys" (July 22); "The Little Parade" (July 26); "Scrambled Eggs" (Aug. 22); "A Knight Out" (Aug. 28); "A Buggy Ride" (Sept. 11); "Pests" (Sept. 17); "Watered Stock" (Sept. 17); "The Charleston Queen" (Sept. 17); "Why Argue" (Sept. 17); "The Road House" (Sept. 29); "Gun Shy" (Oct. 22); "Home Sweet Home" (Oct. 26); "The Phoney Express" (Oct. 22); "Thru Thick and Thin" (Oct. 26); "In Vaudeville" (Oct. 26); "Buck Fever" (Oct. 26); "Radio Controlled" (Oct. 26); "Hitting the Rails" (Oct. 26); "Sink or Swim" (Dec. 6); "Bars and Stripes" (Dec. 31); "School Days" (Dec. 31); "The Musical Parrot" (Dec. 31); and "Where Friendship Ceases" (Dec. 31).

**1927:** "The Plowboy's Revenge" (Jan. 13); "Chasing Rainbows" (Jan. 13); "In the Rough" (Jan. 22); "Tit for Tat" (Jan. 22); "The Mail Pilot" (Feb. 14); "Cracked Ice" (Feb. 19); "Taking the Air"

(Mar. 4); "All for a Bride" (Mar. 4); "The Magician" (Mar. 12); "The Crawl Stroke Kid" (Mar. 12); "The Medicine Man" (Apr. 1); "Keep off the Grass" (Apr. 1); "Anti-Fat" (Apr. 1); "The Honor Man" (Apr. 1); "The Pie-Eyed Piper" (May 6); "Bubbling Over" (May 6); "A Fair Exchange" (May 6); "When the Snow Flies" (May 6); "A Dog's Day" (May 12); "Horse, Horses, Horses" (May 12); "Hard Cider" (May 12); "Digging for Gold" (May 12); "Died in the Wool" (May 12); "A One-Man Dog" (May 12); "The Big Reward" (May 12); "Riding High" (May 12); "The Love Nest" (June 7); "The Bully" (June 20); "Subway Sally" (June 20); "Ant Life as It Isn't" (June 20); "The Baby Show" (June 26); "Jungle Sports" (July 6); "Red Hot Sands" (July 8); "A Hole in One" (July 8); "Hook, Line and Sinker" (July 22); "A Small Town Sheriff" (July 22); "Cutting a Melon" (July 22); "The Human Fly" (Aug. 16); "The River of Doubt" (Aug. 16); "In Again, Out Again" (Aug. 16); "All Bull and a Yard Wide" (Aug. 16); "The Big Tent" (Sept. 2); "Lindy's Cat" (Sept. 2); "A Brave Heart" (Sept. 17); "Signs of Spring" (Sept. 29); "The Fox Hunt" (Oct. 13); "Flying Fishers" (Oct. 26); "Carnival Week" (Foster/Nov. 19); "Rats in His Garret" (Shields/Nov. 19); "The Junk Man" (Davis/Nov. 28); "High Stakes" (Shields/Dec. 12); "The Home Agent" (Dec.); and "A Horse's Tale" (Dec.).

**1928:** "The Wandering Minstrel" (Bailey/Jan. 4); "The Good Ship Nellie" (Moser/Jan. 6); "Everybody's Flying" (Foster/Jan. 17); "The Spider's Lair" (Davis/Jan. 24); "A Blaze of Glory" (Davis/Jan. 28); "The County Fair" (Jan. 28); "On the Ice" (Moser/Feb. 8); "The Sea Shower" (Feb.); "Jungle Days" (Foster/Mar. 19); "Scaling the Alps" (Davis/Mar. 21); "Barnyard Lodge Number One" (Moser/Apr. 2); "A Battling Duet" (Apr. 2); "Barnyard Artists" (Shields/Apr. 8); "A Jungle Triangle" (Davis/Apr. 14); "Coast to Coast" (Moser/Apr. 18); "The War Bride" (Bailey/Apr. 20); "The Flying Age" (Apr. 30); "The Flight That Failed" (Shields/May 7); "Happy Days" (May 9); "Puppy Love" (Davis/May 10); "City Slickers" (Bailey/June 12); "The Huntsman" (Moser/June 26); "The Baby Show" (Davis/June 26); "The Early Bird" (Foster/June 26); "Our Little Nell" (Moser/July 2); "Outnumbered" (Shields/July 9); "Sunny Italy" (Davis/July 26); "A Cross Country Run" (Bailey/July 26); "Static" (Aug. 14); "Sunday on the Farm" (Foster/Aug. 16); "Alaska or Bust" (Moser/Aug. 16); "High Seas" (Davis/Sept. 10); "The Magnetic Bat" (Sept. 17); "Kill or Cure" (Shields/Sept. 20); "Monkey Love" (Davis/Sept. 24); "The Big Game" (Bailey/Oct. 2); "Grid Iron Demons" (Moser/Oct. 4); "The Laundry Man" (Oct. 26); "On the Links" (Nov. 10); "A Day Off" (Foster/Nov. 24); "Barnyard Politics" (Shields/Nov. 26); "Flying Hoofs" (Bailey/Dec. 3); "Dinner Time" (Foster/Dec. 17/first *Aesop's Fables* cartoon with sound; also released silent).

**1929:** "Break of Day" (Davis/Jan. 2); "Snapping the Whip" (Bailey/Jan. 6); "Wooden Money" (Foster/Jan. 6); "Sweet Adeline" (Moser/Jan. 8); "The Queen Bee" (Shields/Jan. 30); "Grandma's House" (Feb. 11); "Back to the Soil" (Feb. 12) "The Black Duck" (Mar. 1); "A Lad and His Lamp" (Mar. 2); "The Big Burg" (Mar. 11); "The Under Dog" (Mar. 13); "The Cop's Bride" (Mar. 17); "The Big Shot" (Apr. 12); "The Fight Game" (Apr. 26); "Homeless Cats" (Apr. 26); "The Little Game Hunter" (Apr. 29); "The Ball Park" (May 4); "Concentrate" (May 4); "The Faithful Pup" (May 4); "The Jail Breakers" (May 4); "Fish Day" (May 8); "Custard Pies" (May 9); "The Wood Choppers" (May 9); "Presto Change-o" (May 20); "The Polo Match" (May 20); "Snow Birds" (May 24); "Skating Hounds" (May 27); "Kidnapped" (June 2); "April Showers" (June 14); "The Farmer's Goat" (Foster/June 19); "Cold Steel" (June 23); "In His Cups" (June 25); "By Land and Air" (Foster/July 8); "The Enchanted Flute" (Moser/July 29);

*The farmer conspires to rid himself of a pesky cat in a scene from the Aesop's Fable, "The Farmer and His Cat" (1922).* (COURTESY: BLACKHAWK FILMS)

"Wash Day" (Davis/July 29); "Cabaret" (Moser/Aug. 14); "The Big Scare" (Aug. 15); and "Fruitful Farm" (Aug. 22/last silent *Aesop's Fables* cartoon; series becomes theatrical sound series).

## ◎ ALICE COMEDIES

Walt Disney produced this series featuring animated characters and a live-action girl, employing techniques similar to those popularized earlier by Max Fleischer in his *Out of the Inkwell* series. Alice was portrayed by several girls, primarily Virginia Davis and Margie Gay, who interacted with animated friends on screen in various episodes.

Distributor M.J. Winkler financed the series, which was Disney's second, and enabled the mustached animator to establish a studio in Los Angeles (near the corner of Vermont and Hollywood Boulevard) to animate these imaginative productions. Along with animators Ub Iwerks, Rudolf Ising and Hugh Harman, Disney turned out these films at a rate of one every two or three weeks. For the era in which these were made, the productions were clearly ingenious, with the interplay between the live and cartoon figures proving to be magical on screen.

"We'd film in a vacant lot," said Virginia "Gini" McGhee, formerly Virginia Davis, who remembered her days playing Alice with fondness. "Walt would drape a white tarpaulin over the back of a billboard and along the ground, and I'd have to work in pantomime. They would add the animation around me later. It was such fun. Kids in the neighborhood would act as extras, and Walt paid them fifty cents apiece."

As Disney's first star, Davis appeared in 14 Alice shorts, featured in roles ranging from cowgirl to big-game hunter. Disney brought Davis with him from Kansas to star in the pictures. He selected her for the part after spotting her face on a billboard advertisement for Warneker's bread.

How Disney got the series off the ground is noteworthy. When a bankrupt distributor forced him to shut down his Laugh-O-Grams studio, laying off his entire staff, he raised fare to travel to Los Angeles and, with the financial support of brother Roy, finished the sample reel for what became the series pilot. After relentless attempts to find a distributor, he nearly gave up until noted film distributor M. J. Winkler offered him $1,500 a reel to produce the Alice series. (The venture became quite profitable for Walt since the first film cost him only $750.)

In 1927 Disney dropped the series when his distributor encouraged him to start a new series. It starred a floppy-eared character, dubbed Oswald the Rabbit, which was immediately successful with moviegoing audiences. *Directed by Walt Disney. A Walt Disney Production released by M.J. Winkler.*

**1924:** "Alice's Day at Sea" (Mar. 1); "Alice's Spooky Adventure" (Apr. 1); "Alice's Wild West Show" (May 1); "Alice's Fishy Story" (June 1); "Alice and the Dog Catcher" (July 1); "Alice the Peacemaker" (Aug. 1); "Alice Gets in Dutch" (Nov. 1); "Alice Hunting in Africa" (Nov. 15); "Alice and the Three Bears" (Dec. 1); and "Alice the Piper" (Dec. 15).

**1925:** "Alice Cans the Cannibals" (Jan. 1); "Alice the Toreador" (Jan. 15); "Alice Gets Stung" (Feb. 1); "Alice Solves the Puzzle" (Feb. 15); "Alice's Egg Plant," "Alice Loses Out," "Alice Stage Struck," "Alice Wins the Derby," "Alice Picks the Champ," "Alice's Tin Pony," "Alice Chops the Suey," "Alice the Jail Bird" (Sept. 15); "Alice Plays Cupid" (Oct. 15); "Alice Rattled by Rats" (Nov. 15); and "Alice in the Jungle" (Dec. 15).

**1926:** "Alice on the Farm" (Jan. 1); "Alice's Balloon Race" (Jan. 15); "Alice's Ornery Orphan," "Alice's Little Parade" (Feb. 1); "Alice's Mysterious Mystery" (Feb. 15); "Alice Charms the Fish" (Sept. 6); "Alice's Monkey Business" (Sept. 20); "Alice in the Wooly West" (Oct. 4); "Alice the Fire Fighter" (Oct. 18); "Alice Cuts the Ice" (Nov. 1); "Alice Helps the Romance" (Nov. 15); "Alice's Spanish Guitar" (Nov. 29); "Alice's Brown Derby" (Dec. 13); and "Alice the Lumber Jack" (Dec. 27).

**1927:** "Alice the Golf Bug" (Jan. 10); "Alice Foils the Pirates" (Jan. 24); "Alice at the Carnival" (Feb. 7); "Alice at the Rodeo" (Feb. 21/originally "Alice's Rodeo"); "Alice the Collegiate" (Mar. 7); "Alice in the Alps" (Mar. 21); "Alice's Auto Race" (Apr. 4); "Alice's Circus Daze" (Apr 18); "Alice's Knaughty Knight" (May 2); "Alice's Three Bad Eggs" (May 16); "Alice's Picnic" (May 30); "Alice's Channel Swim" (June 13); "Alice in the Klondike" (June 27); "Alice's Medicine Show" (July 11); "Alice the Whaler" (July 25); "Alice the Beach Nut" (Aug. 8); and "Alice in the Big League" (Aug. 22).

### ◉ AMERICAN PICTURE BOOK

This early 1920s black-and-white silent cartoon series of which little information is known was billed as "a series of decidedly novel animated drawings." *An Aywon Film Corporation Production.*

**1922:** "The American Picture Book" (Mar. 11).

### ◉ ANIMATED CROSSWORDS

Animator Bert Green, who served as animator, writer and director, created this series of cartoon crosswords that debuted in 1925 and was produced by C.H. Ferrell. Additional titles in the series are unknown. *A Banner Production.*

**1925:** "Animated Crosswords No. 1" (Jan. 27).

### ◉ THE ANIMATED GROUCH CHASERS

French Canadian cartoonist Raoul Barré directed this series of thematically related films produced and animated by Gregory La Cava and Frank Moser for Edison Company in New York. Employing the technique of animation on paper, the films featured a burlesque introduction by live actors followed by a comic book

title, *The Grouch Chasers,* signaling the beginning of the animation program.

The series starred a group of insects—the most notable being Ferdinand the fly and his "flyancee"—and three of Barré's other prized creations: Kid Kelly and his larcenous sidekick dog, Jip; Hercule Hicks, a henpecked little man who escaped his overbearing wife by means of dreaming; and Silas Bunkum, a potbellied teller of tales. *A Gaumont Company/Barré Studios release.*

**1915:** "The Animated Grouch Chaser" (Mar. 4); "Cartoons in the Kitchen" (Apr. 21); "Cartoons in the Barber Shop" (May 22); "Cartoons in the Parlor" (June 5); "Cartoons in the Hotel" (June 21); "Cartoons in the Laundry" (July 8); "Cartoons on Tour" (Aug. 6); "Cartoons on the Beach" (Aug. 25); "Cartoons in a Seminary" (Sept. 9); "Cartoons in the Country" (Oct. 9); "Cartoons on a Yacht" (Oct. 29); "Cartoons in a Sanitarium" (Nov. 12); "Black's Mysterious Box" (Dec. 4) and "Hicks in Nightmareland" (Dec. 14).

### ◉ ANIMATED HAIR

Celebrity caricatures evolved (out of "a strand of hair") in this series of line-drawn cartoons by noted caricaturist Marcus, a former *Life* magazine cartoonist. The series ran from November 1924 to 1927 and was distributed by Max Fleischer's Red Seal Pictures and then by Paramount. *A Red Seal Pictures Production released by Red Seal Pictures and Paramount Pictures.*

**1924:** "No. AA" (Oct. 1) and "No. BB" (Nov. 22).

**1925:** "No. CC" (Feb. 2); "No. DD" (Mar. 2); "No. EE" (Apr. 2); "No. FF" (Apr. 9); "No. GG" (Apr. 16); "No. HH" (Apr. 25); "No. II" (May 9); "No. JJ" (May 17); "No. KK" (May 24); "No. LL" (May 30); "No. MM" (June 6); "No. NN" (June 13); "No. OO" (June 20); "No. PP" (June 27); "No. QQ" (July 4); "No. RR" (July 11); "No. SS" (July 18); "No. TT" (July 25); "No. UU" (Aug. 1); "No. VV" (Aug. 8); "No. WW" (Aug. 15); "No. XX" (Aug. 22); "No. YY" (Aug. 29); "No. ZZ" (Sept. 5); "No. 1" (Oct. 15); "No. 2" (Nov. 15); and "No. 3" (Dec. 15).

**1926:** "No. 4" (Jan. 15); "No. 5" (Feb. 15); "No. 6" (Mar. 15); "No. 7" (Apr. 10); "No. 8" (May 1); "No. 9" (June 12); "No. 10" (June 25); "No. 11" (July 17); "No. 12" (July 31); "No. 13" (Aug. 14); "No. 14" (Aug. 28); "No. 15" (Sept. 11); "No. 16" (Sept. 25); "No. 17" (Oct. 16); "No. 18" (Nov. 15); "No. 19" (Dec. 1); and "No. 20" (Dec. 15).

**1927:** "No. 21" (Jan. 1); "No. 22" (Jan. 15); "No. 23" (Feb. 15); "No. 24" (Mar. 15); and "No. 25" (Apr. 15).

### ◉ ANIMATED TECHNICAL DRAWINGS

E. Dean Parmelee directed this series of hand-drawn cartoons for the *Paramount-Bray-Pictographs* magazine series produced by John R. Bray's New York cartoon studio. *A Bray Production released by Paramount.*

**1918:** "Animated Technical Drawings" (July 1) and "Animated Technical Drawing" (July 29).

### ◉ B.D.F. CARTOONS

Paul Felton produced, directed and animated this series of advertising cartoons. *A B.D.F. Cartoons/B.D.F. Company and Felton Films Production.*

**1918:** "Old Tire Man Diamond Cartoon Film" (July 13) and "W.S.S. Thrifteltes."

**1919:** "Re-Blazing the '49 Trail in a Motor Car Train" (Sept. 10); "Tire Injury" (Sept. 13); and "Paradental Anesthesia" (Sept. 13).

**1921:** "A Movie Trip Through Film Land" (Dec. 17).

**1922:** "For Any Occasion" (Nov. 20) and "In Hot Weather" (Nov. 20).

**1923:** "The Champion" (Sept. 30) and "Land of the Unborn Children" (Nov. 1).

**1924:** "Some Impressions on the Subject of Thrift."

**1925:** "Live and Help Live" (May 22).

**1926:** "The Carriage Awaits" (June 15); "Family Album" (June 15); "What Price Noise" (June 16); and "For Dear Life" (Dec. 30).

## ⊚ BERTLEVYETTES

This series combined live action and animation and was produced and written by Bert Levy and directed by Sidney Olcott. A *World Film Corporation Production.*

**1915:** "Great Americans Past and Present" (Jan. 4); "Famous Men of Today" (Jan. 11); "Famous Rulers of the World" (Jan. 18); and "New York and Its People" (Jan. 25).

## ⊚ BLACKTON CARTOONS

Pioneer animator James Stuart Blackton, later credited with producing the first American animated cartoon, *Humorous Phases of Funny Faces,* released on April 6, 1906, starred in this series of live-action shorts for Thomas A. Edison's New York studio in which he performed his "lightning cartoonist" act on film, drawing cartoon characters before audiences' very eyes. In 1898, after Blackton went into business establishing Vitagraph Company of America with Albert E. Smith, he continued producing short subjects for the studio's *Vitagraph Cartoons* series (see entry for details). A *Thomas A. Edison Kinetoscope Production.*

**1897:** "Humorous Cartoon" (Apr.); "Political Cartoon" (Apr.); and "Sketching Mr. Edison" (Apr.).

## ⊚ BOBBY BUMPS

Pioneer animator Earl Hurd created this mischievous little boy, inspired by R.F. Outcault's well-known comic strip character Buster Brown. (Like Buster, Bobby was given a bulldog companion, only named Fido.) These humorous and delightfully sympathetic adventures of a boy's life were first produced in 1915 by J.R. Bray's studio following the success of his *Colonel Heeza Liar* series. The idea of producing a figure "out of the inkwell" was a key element in the films—Bumps was introduced by Hurd's hand—foreshadowing Max Fleischer's technique by several years. Early stories were shaped around Bobby's pranks, often played on his parents or friends. *Directed by Earl Hurd. A Bray Studios Production released by Paramount Pictures.*

**1915:** "Bobby Bumps Gets Pa's Goat" (July 3) and "Bobby Bumps Adventures" (Aug. 18).

**1916:** "Bobby Bumps and His Pointer Pup" (Feb. 24); "Bobby Bumps Gets a Substitute" (Mar. 30); "Bobby Bumps and His Goatmobile" (Apr. 30); "Bobby Bumps Goes Fishing" (June 1); "Bobby Bumps' Fly Swatter" (June 29); "Bobby Bumps and the Detective Story" (July 27); "Bobby Bumps Loses His Pup" (Aug. 17); "Bobby Bumps and the Stork" (Sept. 7); "Bobby Bumps Starts a Lodge" (Sept. 21); "Bobby Bumps Helps Out a Book Agent" (Oct. 23); "Bobby Bumps Queers a Choir" (Oct. 26); and "Bobby Bumps at the Circus" (Nov. 11).

**1917:** "Bobby Bumps in the Great Divide" (Feb. 5); "Bobby Bumps Adopts a Turtle" (Mar. 5); "Bobby Bumps, Office Boy" (Mar. 26); "Bobby Bumps Outwits the Dogsnatcher" (Apr. 16); "Bobby Bumps Volunteers" (May 7); "Bobby Bumps Daylight Camper" (May 28); "Bobby Bumps Submarine Chaser" (June 18); "Bobby Bumps' Fourth" (July 9); "Bobby Bumps' Amusement Park" (Aug. 6); "Bobby Bumps, Surf Rider" (Aug. 27); "Bobby Bumps Starts for School" (Sept. 17); "Bobby Bumps' World Serious" (Oct. 8); "Bobby Bumps, Chef" (Oct. 29); "Bobby Bumps Fido's Birthday" (Nov. 18); "Bobby Bumps Early Shopper" (Dec. 9); and "Bobby Bumps' Tank" (Dec. 30).

**1918:** "Bobby Bumps' Disappearing Gun" (Jan. 21); "Bobby Bumps at the Dentist" (Feb. 25); "Bobby Bumps' Fight" (Mar. 25); "Bobby Bumps on the Road" (Apr. 15); "Bobby Bumps Caught in the Jamb" (May 13); "Bobby Bumps Out West" (June 10); "Bobby Bumps Films a Fire" (June 24); "Bobby Bumps Becomes an Ace" (July 15); "Bobby Bumps on the Doughnut Trail" (Aug. 19); "Bobby Bumps and the Speckled Death" (Sept. 30); "Bobby Bumps Incubator" (Oct. 8); "Bobby Bumps in Before and After" (Nov. 20); and "Bobby Bumps Puts a Beanery on the Bum" (Dec. 4).

**1919:** "Bobby Bumps Last Smoke" (Jan. 24); "Bobby Bumps' Lucky Day" (Mar. 19); "Bobby Bumps' Night Out with Some Night Owls" (Apr. 16); "Bobby Bumps' Pup Gets the Flea-enza" (Apr. 23); "Bobby Bumps Eel-ectric Launch" (Apr. 30); "Bobby Bumps and the Sand Lizard" (May 21); "Bobby Bumps and the Hypnotic Eye" (June 25); and "Bobby Bumps Throwing the Bull" (July 16).

*Paramount Magazine*

**1920:** "Bobby Bumps the Cave Man" (Aug. 8) and "Bobby Bumps' Orchestra" (Dec. 19).

**1921:** "Bobby Bumps Checkmated" (Mar. 20).

*Paramount Cartoons*

**1921:** "Bobby Bumps Working on an Idea" (May 8); "Bobby Bumps in Shadow Boxing" (July 9); and "Bobby Bumps in Hunting and Fishing" (Aug. 21).

**1922:** "Bobby Bumps at School" (Dec. 16/*Bray Magazine*) and "Railroading" (Dec. 2/Earl Hurd Comedies).

**1923:** "The Movie Daredevil" (Apr. 1/Earl Hurd Comedies); and "Their Love Growed Cold" (June 2/Earl Hurd Comedies).

*Educational Pictures release*

**1925:** "Bobby Bumps and Company" (Sept. 22/Pen and Ink Vaudeville).

## ⊚ THE BOOB WEEKLY

Rube Goldberg wrote and directed this series of newsreel spoofs, which were animated by pioneer animators Raoul Barré, Gregory La Cava, Bill Nolan and George Stallings at Barré Studios in 1916. Goldberg was actually contracted by Pathé Films to produce the series as part of a lucrative contract that netted him $75,000 a year for his efforts. A *Rube Goldberg/Barré Studios Production released by Pathé Films.*

**1916:** "The Boob Weekly" (May 8); "Leap Year" (May 22); "The Fatal Pie" (June 5); "From Kitchen Mechanic to Movie Star" (June 19); "Nutty News" (July 3); "Home Sweet Home" (July 17); and "Losing Weight" (July 31).

## ◎ BOOMER BILL

Along with his series of Felix the Cat and Charlie Chaplin cartoons, pioneer animator Pat Sullivan also produced and directed this series of comic misadventures. Unfortunately, no records could be found to describe the character or the films at length. *A Pat Sullivan Cartoon released through Universal Pictures.*

**1917:** "Boomer Bill's Awakening" (Jan. 28); and "Boomer Bill Goes to Sea" (Apr. 15).

## ◎ BOX CAR BILL

Following his widely acclaimed two-reel comic short, "Twenty Thousand Laughs Under the Sea," a spoof of Jules Verne's classic novel *Twenty Thousand Leagues Under the Sea,* Pat Sullivan produced and directed this short-lived series for Universal in 1917. Little else is known about the production and content of the films. *A Pat Sullivan Cartoon released through Universal Pictures.*

**1917:** "Box Car Bill Falls in Luck" (July 16).

## ◎ BRAY CARTOONS

Pioneer cartoon producer and animator John Randolph Bray produced and animated this short-lived series of black-and-white cartoon shorts, along with animators Raoul Barré and L. M. Glackens, at his New York cartoon studio. The series commenced production in June of 1913 and lasted only one year. *A Bray Production released by Pathé-Eclectic.*

**1913:** "The Artist's Dream" (June 7/re: "The Dachshund and the Sausage"); "A Jungle Flirtation" (Sept. 6/re: "Jocko the Lovesick Monk"); and "A Wall Street Wail" (Oct. 4/re: "Exploring Ephraim's Exploit").

**1914:** "The Grafters" (Apr. 25/re: "When Mice Make Merry") and "Rastus' Rabid Rabbit Hunt" (Dec. 26).

**1915:** "Romiet and Julio" (Jan. 9/animated by Raoul Barré); "A Stone Age Adventure" (May 9/animated and written by L. M. Glackens); and "When Knights Were Bold" (June 19/animated and written by L. M. Glackens).

## ◎ BRINGING UP FATHER

Most early silent cartoon series were comic-strip adaptations. This series was based on a long-running weekly strip, featuring henpecked Jiggs and his society wife, Maggie, created by cartoonist George McManus in 1912 and animated by supervising animator Frank Moser. *An International Films Production released by Pathé Film Exchange.*

**1916:** "Father Gets into the Movies" (Nov. 21); and "Just Like a Woman" (Dec. 14).

**1917:** "The Great Hansom Cab Mystery" (Apr. 26); "A Hot Time in the Gym" (Apr. 26); "Music Hath Charms" (June 7); and "He Tried His Hand at Hypnotism" (Aug. 8).

**1918:** "Second, The Stimulating Mrs. Barton" (Apr. 16); "Second, Father's Close Shave" (May 16); and "Third, Jiggs and the Social Lion" (June 27).

## ◎ BUD AND SUSIE

Frank Moser, who supervised George McManus's *Bringing Up Father* series, animated this series of husband-and-wife stories shaped around the madcap adventures of henpecked husband, Bud, and his overbearing wife, Susie. The films were released by Paramount in 1919, the year they were produced. *A Bray Production released by Famous Players-Lasky Corporation.*
(Filmography lists known titles only.)

**1920:** "Handy Mandy's Goat" (Mar. 21); "The Kids Find Candy's Catching" (Apr. 11); "Bud Takes the Cake" (May 2); "The New Cook's Debut" (May 23); "Mice and Money" (June 13); "Down the Mississippi" (July 25); "Play Ball" (Aug. 15); "Romance and Rheumatism" (Aug. 29); "Bud and Tommy Take a Day Off" (Sept. 5); "The North Pole" (Oct. 3); "The Great Clean Up" (Oct. 31); "Bud and Susie Join the Tecs" (Nov. 28); and "Fifty-Fifty" (Dec. 5).

**1921:** "Getting Theirs" (Jan. 2); "Ma's Wipe Your Feet Campaign" (Feb. 27); "Circumstancial Evidence" (Apr. 3); "By the Sea" (May 29); "$10,000 Under a Pillow" (June 26); "Dashing North" (July 31); "Kitchen Bedroom and Bath" (Aug. 28); and "The Wars of Mice and Men" (Sept.).

## ◎ CAMERA MYSTERIES

Known in Great Britain as *Screen Revelations,* Louis Seel wrote, directed and animated this black-and-white silent cartoon series, produced by George D. Swartz. *A Swartz Pictures Production.*

**1926:** "Finding the Lost World"; "Rushing the Gold Rush"; "The Flying Carpet"; "Safety Not Last"; "Motoring"; and "Pirates Bold."

## ◎ CANIMATED NOOZ PICTORIAL

Wallace A. Carlson, of *Goodrich Dirt* fame, unveiled this innovative series of caricatured drawings described as "photographic heads on pen and ink bodies." Premiering on October 13, 1915, Carlson directed this series of 28 split-reel films produced by Pat A. Powers, featuring his famed comic-strip characters Joe Boko and Dreamy Dud, for Essanay Film Manufacturing Company until April 28, 1917, when he left the studio to pursue other interests. *An Essanay Film Manufacturing Company Production released by General Film.*
(Listed are known titles and release dates)

**1916:** "No. 4" (Jan. 12); "No. 5" (Feb. 22); "No. 6" (Mar. 3); "No. 7" (Mar. 23); "No. 8" (Apr. 4); "No. 9" (Apr. 19); "No. 10" (May 24); "No. 11" (June 7); "No. 12" (July 5); "No. 13" (July 26), "No. 14" (Aug. 16); "No. 15" (Sept. 6); "No. 16" (Sept. 20); "No. 17" (Oct. 11); "No. 18" (Oct. 25); "No. 19" (Nov. 15); "No. 20" (Dec. 13); and "No. 21" (Dec. 27).

**1917:** "No. 22" (Jan. 10); "No. 23" (Jan. 24); "No. 24" (Feb. 10); "No. 25" (Mar. 3); "No. 26" (Mar. 17); "No. 27" (Mar. 31); and "No. 28" (Apr. 28).

## ◎ CHARLIE/CHARLEY CARTOONS

Comedian Charlie Chaplin's Little Tramp character inspired several animated cartoon series based on his comical film exploits. As early as 1915, European filmgoers were treated to animated adventures released by Gaumont. In July of that year, Kinema Exchange launched its own series of Chaplin cartoons—known as *Charlot*—which supposedly were authorized by the great comedian himself. Otto Messmer, who animated *Felix the Cat,* animated another series for American release, *Charlie et l'éléphant blanc,* for Beaumont Films.

One year after these series were made, Pat Sullivan contracted with Chaplin to produce a new animated series simply titled *Charlie.* In all, 12 films were made in 1916, each drawing ideas from films and photographs supplied by Chaplin and drawn by Otto Messmer. That same year, S. J. Sangretti produced another series of films that were animated by John Colman Terry, G. A. Bonstrup and Hugh M. Shields and distributed to theaters by the *New York Herald*'s Herald Film Corp. After the armistice following World War I, in 1918, Sullivan and Messmer resumed producing a second series—alternately known as Charlie and Charley cartoons—featuring Chaplin's character for the Keen Cartoon Corporation, which Messmer directed, under the Nestor Comedies banner for Universal Pictures. *A Gaumont Kinema Exchange Beaumont Films/ Pat Sullivan Cartoon/Movca Film Service and Keen Cartoon Corporation Production released by Gaumont, Monopole-Fred, Paramount Studios, Herald Film Corp. and Universal Pictures.*

***Herald Film Corp.***

**1916:** "Charlie in Carmen" (May 15); "Charlie's White Elephant" (June 1); "Charlie Has Some Wonderful Adventures in India" (June 1); "Charlie in Cuckoo Land" (June 1); "Charlie the Blacksmith" (June 1); "Charlie's Busted Romance" (June 1); "Charlie Across the Rio Grande" (June 1); "The Rooster's Nightmare" (June 1); "Charlie's Barnyard Pets" (June 1); and "Charlie Throws the Bull" (June 1).
(The titles listed above are from the Pat Sullivan series.)

***Universal Pictures***

**1918:** "How Charlie Captured the Kaiser" (Messmer/Sept. 3) and "Over the Rhine with Charlie" (Messmer/Dec. 21).

**1919:** "Charlie in Turkey" (Jan. 29); "Charlie Treats 'Em Rough" (Mar. 2); "Charley at the Circus"; "Charley on the Farm"; "Charley at the Beach"; "Charley in the West"; "Charley in Russia"; and "Charley's African Quest" (Oct.).

## ◎ CINEMA LUKE

This live-action and animated series was produced for the *Universal Screen Magazine*. Leslie Elton served as writer, animator and director of the series, which Carl Laemmle produced. *A Universal Pictures Production.*

**1919:** "Cinema Luke" (Dec. 6).

**1920:** "Cinema Luke" (Mar. 11); and "Cinema Luke" (May 28).

## ◎ COLONEL HEEZA LIAR

After working on Mutt and Jeff at Barré/Bowers Studios for a year, Walter Lantz joined the J.R. Bray Studios. His first assignment was to animate this series of misadventures starring a short, middle-age, fibbing army colonel created by J.R. Bray himself.

Bray had created the character 10 years earlier to illustrate gags in magazines. The colonel is said to have been a lampoon of Teddy Roosevelt, noted for telling stories that seemed like "tall tales." (The character also was modeled after Baron von Munchausen, another teller of tales.)

As with most Bray cartoons, the early *Colonel Heeza Liar* films illustrate a remarkable sense of economy in both animation and production values. Only 100 basic arrangements of cels were used for each film, so animation was quite limited. In several episodes, the colonel's small stature was played for laughs, pitting him against his domineering wife, who was three times his size!

In the 1920s Bray assigned Vernon Stallings to direct the series. *A Bray Company Production released by Pathé Film Exchange and W.W. Hodkinson Corporation, Standard Cinema Corporation and Selznick Pictures.*

**1913:** "Col. Heeza Liar In Africa" (Nov. 29).

**1914:** "Col. Heeza Liar's African Hunt" (Jan. 10); "Col. Heeza Liar Shipwrecked" (Mar. 14); "Col. Heeza Liar in Mexico" (Apr. 18); "Col. Heeza Liar, Farmer" (May 18); "Col. Heeza Liar, Explorer" (Aug. 15); "Col. Heeza Liar in the Wilderness" (Sept. 26); and "Col. Heeza Liar, Naturalist" (Oct. 24).

*Producer J. R. Bray and animator Walter Lantz introduced the accomplished liar, Colonel Heeza Liar, in 1915.* (COURTESY: MUSEUM OF MODERN ART/FILM STILLS ARCHIVE)

**1915:** "Col. Heeza Liar, Ghost Breaker" (Feb. 6); "Col. Heeza Liar in the Haunted Castle" (Feb. 20); "Col. Heeza Liar Runs the Blockade" (Mar. 20); "Col. Heeza Liar and the Torpedo" (Apr. 3); "Col. Heeza Liar and the Zeppelin" (Apr. 10); "Col. Heeza Liar Signs the Pledge" (May 8); "Col. Heeza Liar in the Trenches" (May 13); "Col. Heeza Liar at the Front" (May 16); "Col. Heeza Liar, Aviator" (May 22); "Col. Heeza Liar Invents a New King of Shell" (June 5); "Col. Heeza Liar, Dog Fancier" (July 10); "Col. Heeza Liar Foils the Enemy" (July 31); "Col. Heeza Liar, War Dog" (Aug. 21); "Col. Heeza Liar at the Bat" (Sept. 4); "Col. Heeza Liar, Nature Faker" (Dec. 28).

**1916:** "Col. Heeza Liar's Waterloo" (Jan. 6); "Col. Heeza Liar and the Pirates" (Mar. 5); "Col. Heeza Liar Wins the Pennant" (Apr. 27); "Col. Heeza Liar Captures Villa" (May 25); "Col. Heeza Liar and the Bandits" (June 22); "Col. Heeza Liar's Courtship" (July 20); "Col. Heeza Liar on Strike" (Aug. 17); "Col. Heeza Liar Plays Hamlet" (Aug. 24); "Col. Heeza Liar Bachelor Quarters" (Sept. 14); "Col. Heeza Liar Gets Married" (Oct. 11); "Col. Heeza Liar, Hobo" (Nov. 15); and "Col. Heeza Liar at the Vaudeville Show" (Dec. 21).

**1917:** "Col. Heeza Liar on the Jump" (Feb. 4); "Col. Heeza Liar, Detective" (Feb. 25); "Col. Heeza Liar, Spy Dodger" (Mar. 19); and "Col. Heeza Liar's Temperance Lecture" (Aug. 20).

***W.W. Hodkinson Corporation***

**1922:** "Col. Heeza Liar's Treasure Island" (Stallings/Dec. 17).

**1923:** "Col. Heeza Liar and the Ghost" (Stallings/Jan. 14); "Col. Heeza Liar, Detective" (Stallings/Feb. 1); "Col. Heeza Liar's Burglar" (Stallings/Mar. 11); "Col. Heeza Liar in the African Jungles" (Stallings/June 3); "Col. Heeza Liar's Vacation" (Stallings/Aug. 5); "Col. Heeza Liar's Forbidden Fruit" (Stallings/ Nov. 1); and "Col. Heeza Liar, Strikebreaker" (Stallings/Dec. 1).

***Standard Cinema Corp./Selznick Pictures***

**1924:** "Col. Heeza Liar, Nature Faker" (Stallings/Jan. 1); "Col. Heeza Liar's Mysterious Case" (Feb. 1); "Col. Heeza Liar's Ancestors" (Stallings/Mar. 1); "Col. Heeza Liar's Knighthood" (Stallings/Apr. 1); "Col. Heeza Liar, Sky Pilot" (Stallings/May 1); "Col. Heeza Liar, Daredevil" (Stallings/June 1); "Col. Heeza

Liar's Horseplay" (Stallings/July 1); "Col. Heeza Liar, Cave Man" (Stallings/Aug. 1); "Col. Heeza Liar, Bull Thrower" (Stallings/Sept. 1); "Col. Heeza Liar the Lyin' Tamer" (Stallings/Oct. 1); and "Col. Heeza Liar's Romance" (Stallings/Nov. 1).

## ◎ COLORED CARTOON COMICS

This series of 26 black-and-white silent cartoons, made in 1925, was the brainchild of pioneer animator Charles Bowers, the titles of which remain unknown. *A Charles Bowers Cartoons Production released by Short Film Syndicate.*

## ◎ DINKY DOODLE

Walter Lantz, best known for creating Woody Woodpecker, was writer, animator and director of this live-action/animated series for J.R. Bray Studios featuring the adventures of a young button-eyed boy named Dinky and his faithful dog, Weakheart.

Like Max Fleischer's *Out of the Inkwell* series, this production placed a live character (Lantz) in situations with the animated stars. However, several differences existed between the two series. Lantz used an entirely different process from that of Fleischer to blend the live-action sequences with animation.

After filming the scenes, he took the negative and made 8-by-10 stills of every frame—3,000 to 4,000 of them. The stills were then punched like animation paper and rephotographed with each cel of character animation overlapping the live-action scenes. (Character drawings were done on onionskin paper then inked and painted on cels before being shot in combination with the live-action enlargements).

Lantz's job of acting in the live-action scenes was difficult; he had to act without knowing how the characters were going to appear opposite him in each scene. "If Walt was supposed to duel a cartoon villain, he would first duel a live person, like Clyde Geronimi, one of his chief animators," recalled James "Shamus" Culhane, an assistant on the series. "The cartoon characters were added later and the final result was Walt dueling merrily with an animated cartoon."

Lantz took many of his live-action sequences outside the studio to be filmed in a variety of locations, unlike Fleischer, who always opened his Inkwell cartoons seated behind an animator's table. "We never opened a cartoon with the same setting," Lantz remembered in an interview. "We went outside to do our stories. We went to a large field, or to the beach or to Buckhill Falls in upstate New York. We went all over."

As the live actor in these films, Lantz's aim wasn't to upstage his cartoon contemporaries. "I was short and not especially funny

*Animator Walter Lantz is joined at the animator's table by cartoon stars Dinky-Doodle and Weakheart the Dog.* (COURTESY: WALTER LANTZ)

looking, so I imitated Harold Lloyd's prop eyeglasses. All the comedians in those days used something—Chaplin had his tramp outfit; Conklin a walrus mustache; Langdon that ill-fitting peaked cap. The glasses weren't too good of a trademark for me, but then I wasn't aiming to be a full-time comedian."

Even so, Lantz's comic moments placed heavy emphasis on chase scenes, and he had to do more than merely resemble a comedian to make the segments work in each cartoon.

Incredibly, Lantz completed a cartoon for release about every two weeks, at a cost of $1,800 apiece for 700 feet of live-action and animated film. "I had no idea what the cartoons were costing," he admitted, "so this figure didn't frighten me."

Most stories were based on classic fairy tales and standard everyday situations. For Lantz, his personal series favorites were "Cinderella" and "Little Red Riding Hood," both based on popular children's fairy tales. Unfortunately, few examples of this great series remain; most of the films were destroyed in a warehouse fire.

In addition to Lantz, the series' chief animators were Clyde Geronimi and David Hand, who both became key animators at Walt Disney Studios in the 1930s. *A Bray Production and Standard Cinema Corporation release.*

**1924:** "The Magic Lamp" (Sept. 15); "The Giant Killer" (Oct. 15); and "The Pied Piper" (Dec. 1).

**1925:** "Little Red Riding Hood" (Jan. 4); "The House That Dinky Built" (Feb. 1); "Cinderella" (Mar. 1); "Peter Pan Handled" (Apr. 26); "Magic Carpet" (May 24); "Robinson Crusoe" (June 21); "Three Bears" (July 19); "Just Spooks" (Sept. 13); "Dinky Doodle and the Bad Man" (Sept. 20); "Dinky Doodle in the Hunt" (Nov. 1); "Dinky Doodle in the Circus" (Nov. 29); and "Dinky Doodle in the Restaurant" (Dec. 27).

**1926:** "Dinky Doodle in Lost and Found" (Feb. 19); "Dinky Doodle in Uncle Tom's Cabin" (Feb. 21); "Dinky Doodle in the Arctic" (Mar. 21); "Dinky Doodle in Egypt" (Apr. 8); "Dinky Doodle in the Wild West" (May 12); "Dinky Doodle's Bed Time Story" (June 6); "Dinky Doodle and the Little Orphan" (July 4); and "Dinky Doodle in the Army" (Aug. 29).

## ◎ DOC YAK

Created by newspaper cartoonist Sidney Smith, Doc Yak originally ran as a regular strip in the *Chicago Herald* and *New York Daily News* newspapers. Like so many other cartoonists, Smith adapted this middle-age character to the screen in a series of cartoon calamities. Smith produced a few experimental reels that were released by Selig-Polyscope in July 1913. In May 1914 he launched a second series, which was as successful as the first. *A Sidney Smith Production released by Selig-Polyscope.*

**1913:** "Old Doc Yak" (July 11); "Old Doc Yak and the Artist's Dream" (Oct. 29); and "Old Doc Yak's Christmas" (Dec. 30).

**1914:** "Doc Yak, Moving Picture Artist" (Jan. 22); "Doc Yak Cartoonist" (Mar. 14); "Doc Yak the Poultryman" (Apr. 11); "Doc Yak's Temperance Lecture" (May 2); "Doc Yak the Marksman" (May 9); "Doc Yak Bowling" (May 23); "Doc Yak's Zoo" (May 30); "Doc Yak and the Limited Train" (June 6); "Doc Yak's Wishes" (June 11); "Doc Yak's Bottle" (Sept. 16); "Doc Yak's Cats" (Oct. 15); "Doc Yak Plays Golf" (Oct. 24); and "Doc Yak and Santa Claus" (Dec. 8).

### *Chicago Tribune Animated Weekly*

**1915:** "Doc in the Ring" (Sept. 18); and "Doc the Ham Actor" (Oct. 16).

## ◎ DRA-KO CARTOONS

Artist Frank A. Nankivel animated this series of advertising films, the titles of which remain unknown, produced in 1916. *A Dra-Ko Film Company Production.*

## ◎ DREAMS OF A RAREBIT FIEND

Winsor McCay wrote, produced, directed and co-animated this series based on his popular comic strip. *A Rialto Production.*

**1921:** "Bug Vaudeville" (Sept. 26); "The Pet" (Sept. 26); "The Flying House" (Sept. 26); "The Centaurs" (Sept.); "Flip's Circus"; and "Gertie on Tour."

## ◎ DREAMY DUD

Essanay Studios commissioned renowned animator Wallace A. Carlson to direct and animate this series of tall tales starring a Walter Mittyish lad whose daydreams—often a result of boredom and loneliness—lead him into trouble. Carlson projected Dreamy into all kinds of heroic situations and other feats of valor that often included his loyal dog, Wag. *An Essanay Film Manufacturing Company Production release.*

**1915:** "A Visit to the Zoo" (May 15); "An Alley Romance" (May 15); "Lost in the Jungle" (June 1); "Dreamy Dud in the Swim" (June 7); "Dreamy Dud Resolves Not to Smoke" (June 22); "Dreamy Dud in King Koo Koo's Kingdom" (June 30); "He Goes Bear Hunting" (July 17); "A Visit to Uncle Dudley's Farm" (July 26); "Dreamy Dud Sees Charlie Chaplin" (Aug. 9); "Dreamy Dud Cowboy" (Aug. 31); "Dreamy Dud at the Old Swimmin' Hole" (Sept. 17); "Dreamy Dud in the Air" (Oct. 14); and "Dreamy Dud in Love" (Nov. 29).

**1916:** "Dreamy Dud Lost at Sea" (Jan. 22); "Dreamy Dud Has a Laugh on the Boss" (Sept. 20); "Dreamy Dud in the African War Zone" (Oct. 13); and "Dreamy Dud Joyriding with Princess Zlim" (Nov. 21).

## ◎ EARL HURD CARTOONS

After patenting the concept of cel animation in 1915, the process of inking and painting cartoon characters on individual celluloid sheets and then filming one frame at a time, animation legend Earl Hurd used this remarkable discovery to write, produce and direct this series of black-and-white silent cartoons released by different distributors to theaters. *An Earl Hurd Production released by Universal-Joker, Paramount and Pathé Exchange.*

### Universal-Joker

**1915:** "Ski-Hi the Cartoon Chinaman" (July 10).

### Paramount

**1915:** "The Troubles of Mr. Munk" (Aug. 21).

### Pathé Exchange

**1916:** "Teddy and the Angel Cake" (Apr. 15).

## ◎ EARL HURD COMEDIES

After forming his own company, legendary animator Earl Hurd wrote, produced, directed and animated this series of amusing live-action/animated shorts that debuted in theaters in August of 1922 with the premiere episode, "One Ol' Cat," distributed by Mastodon Cartoons. Educational Pictures released the remaining one-reel shorts in the series through June of 1923. Afterward he went on to write, produce and direct another innovative series, *Pen and Ink Vaudeville*, bringing his outlandish drawings and editorial cartoons to the screen from 1924 through 1925. *An Earl Hurd Production released by Mastodon Cartoons and Educational Pictures.*

**1922:** "One Ol' Cat" (Aug. 5); "Fresh Fish" (Aug. 26); and "Railroading" (Dec. 2).

**1923:** "The Message of Emile Coue" (Feb. 18); "Chicken Dressing" (Feb. 24); "The Movie Daredevil" (Apr. 1); and "Their Love Growed Cold" (June 2).

## ◎ EBENEZER EBONY

*A Sering D. Wilson & Company Production.*

**1925:** "The Flying Elephant" (Apr. 22); "An Ice Boy" (May 22); "Gypping the Gypsies" (June 22); "Fire in a Brimstone" (July 1); "High Moon" (Aug. 1); "Love Honor and Oh Boy" (Sept. 1); "Foam Sweet Foam" (Oct. 1); and "Fisherman's Luck" (Oct. 31).

## ◎ ÉCLAIR JOURNAL

Pioneer animator Emile Cohl wrote, directed and animated this series of animated cartoon items for a weekly newsreel. *An Éclair Company Production.*

**1913:** "Bewitched Matches"; "War in Turkey" (Jan.); "Castro in New York" (Jan.); "Rockefeller" (Jan.); "Confidence" (Jan.); "Milk" (Feb.); "Coal" (Feb.); "The Subway" (Feb.); "Graft" (Feb.); "The Two Presidents" (Mar.); "The Auto" (Mar.); "Wilson and the Broom" (Mar.); "The Police Women" (Mar.); "Wilson and the Hats" (Mar.); "Poker" (Mar.); "Gaynor and the Night Clubs" (Mar.); "Universal Trade Marks" (Mar.); "Wilson and the Tariffs" (Apr.); "The Masquerade" (Apr.); "The Brand of California" (Apr.); "The Safety Pin" (May); "The Two Suffragettes" (May); "The Mosquito" (May); "The Red Balloons" (May); "The Cubists" (June); "Uncle Sam and His Suit" (June); "The Polo Boat" (June); "The Artist" (June); "Wilson's Row Row" (July); "The Hat" (Aug.); "Thaw and the Lasso" (Aug.); "Bryant and the Speeches" (Aug.); "Thaw and the Spider" (Sept.); "Exhibition of Caricatures" (Nov.); and "Pickup Is a Sportsman" (Dec.).

**1914:** "The Bath" (Jan.); "The Future Revealed by the Lines of the Feet" (Jan.); "The Social Group" (Nov.); "The Greedy Neighbor"; "What They Eat"; "The Anti-Neurasthenic Trumpet"; "His Ancestors"; "Serbia's Card"; and "The Terrible Scrap of Paper."

## ◎ ESSANAY CARTOONS

Venturing into the field of animation and competing against much larger New York cartoon studios, including Bray and William Randolph Hearst's International Film Service, Essanay produced this series consisting of animators Wallace Carlson's *Joe Boko* and Leon Searl's *Mile-a-Minute Monty* cartoons, also directed by them. *An Essanay Film Manufacturing Company Production.*

**1915:** "Introducing Charlie Chaplin" (Mar. 13/Carlson); "Joe Boko in a Close Shave" (June 1/Carlson); "Joe Boko in Saved By Gasoline" (Aug. 27/Carlson); and "Mile-a-Minute Monty" (Dec. 22/Searl).

## ◎ FARMER AL FALFA

Animator Paul Terry developed this bald, white-bearded farmer shortly after becoming a staff animator for J.R. Bray Studios and first brought him to the screen in 1916. Most of the early films cast this popular hayseed in barnyard skirmishes with animals. The series later focused on his attempts to make "modern improvements" to the farm.

After being inducted into the army in 1917, Terry had to interrupt work on the series briefly. At the end of the war, he returned to New York and formed a company with fellow animators Earl Hurd, Frank Moser, Hugh (Jerry) Shields, Leighton Budd and brother John Terry, but it lasted only for a short time. He continued making Farmer Al Falfa cartoons for release through Paramount until 1923, and later revived the character when sound was introduced. *Paul Terry produced and directed the series. A Paul Terry cartoon released by J. R. Bray, Thomas Edison Inc. and Pathé Film Exchange.*

**1916:** "Farmer Al Falfa's Catastrophe" (Feb. 3); "Farmer Al Falfa Invents a New Kite" (Mar. 12); "Farmer Al Falfa's Scientific Diary" (Apr. 14); "Farmer Al Falfa and His Tentless Circus" (June 3); "Farmer Al Falfa's Watermelon Patch" (June 29); "Farmer Al Falfa's Egg-Citement" (Aug. 4); "Farmer Al Falfa's Revenge" (Aug. 25); "Farmer Al Falfa's Wolfhound" (Sept. 16); "Farmer Al Falfa Sees New York" (Oct. 9); "Farmer Al Falfa's Prune Plantation" (Nov. 3); and "Farmer Al Falfa's Blind Pig" (Dec. 1).

*Thomas Edison, Inc.*

**1917:** "Farmer Al Falfa's Wayward Pup" (May 7).

*Paramount Magazine*

**1920:** "The Bone of Contention" (Mar. 14).

*Pathé Film Exchange*

**1922:** "The Farmer and the Ostrich" (Jan. 26); and "The Farmer and His Cat" (May 17).

**1923:** "Farmer Al Falfa's Bride" (Feb. 23); and "Farmer Al Falfa's Pet Cat" (Nov. 9).

## ◎ FELIX THE CAT

The public loved this clever feline long before the 1960s syndicated cartoon revival. Australian-born artist Pat Sullivan (b. 1887; d. February 15, 1933), serving as producer and director, first introduced this character, created by animator Otto Messmer, in September 1919 in the animated one-reeler, "Feline Follies," released to theaters by Famous Players-Lasky as part of the *Paramount Screen Magazine* series. The devil-eared cat went on to star in possibly 30 or more cartoon shorts produced between 1919 and 1921, and an estimated 150 to 175 cartoons made by him and Messmer through 1930 and into the sound era. He had no bag of tricks as in the television-made cartoons, but through intelligent, spontaneous gags he overcame obstacles and awkward situations. In these early cartoons, Felix was known to transform his "tail" into assorted objects to help him out of jams.

Felix's name came from the word "felicity," meaning "great happiness," and he was made black for practical reasons. "It saves making a lot of outlines, and the solid black moves better," explained pioneer animator Otto Messmer in a published interview.

Oddly, Felix was more popular overseas than in the United States, resulting in assorted merchandise bearing his name. In this country, adoration of the character took a different form. In 1922, Felix appeared as the New York Yankees' lucky mascot. Three years later, a song was written in his honor called, "Felix Kept Walking." By 1927, a Felix doll became aviator Charles Lindbergh's companion on his famed flight across the Atlantic. The following year, Felix became the first image ever to appear on television when the first experimental television broadcast took place and included a Felix doll. To this day in the United Kingdom, a popular pet food is affectionately named after the sly cat.

Sullivan refused to add sound to his pictures following the birth of "talkies." Consequently, series revenues fell off dramatically, and he was forced to lay off his staff. After the silent cartoon series ended in 1928, Sullivan relented and went to California to set up a new studio where he hoped to produce a new Felix the Cat cartoon series in sound and in color. Suffering from various medical

problems at the time, he never completed all he had hoped to accomplish. Instead, a few previously released silent cartoons that Sullivan had produced and directed were reissued with sound tracks added in 1930 by Copley Pictures Corporation. In 1936, RKO-Van Beuren revived Felix in a short-lived series of sound cartoons, *Rainbow Parades. Directed by Pat Sullivan. A Pat Sullivan Production released by Famous Players-Lasky and Educational Pictures and M. J. Winkler.*

*A Pat Sullivan Comics/Paramount Screen Magazine*

**1919:** "Feline Follies" (Sept. 1); "The Musical Mews" (Nov. 16); and "The Adventures of Felix" (Dec. 14).

**1920:** "Felix the Landlord" (Oct. 24) and "My Hero" (Dec. 26).

*M. J. Winkler*

**1922:** "Felix Saves the Day" (Feb. 1); Felix at the Fair" (Mar. 1); "Felix Makes Good" (Apr. 1); "Felix All at Sea" (May 1); "Felix in Love" (June 1); "Felix in the Swim" (July 1); "Felix Finds a Way" (Aug. 1); "Felix Gets Revenge" (Sept. 1); "Felix Wakes Up" (Sept. 15); "Felix Minds the Kid" (Oct. 1); "Felix Turns the Tide" (Oct. 15); "Fifty-Fifty," "Felix on the Trail" (Nov. 1); "Felix Lends a Hand" (Nov. 15); "Felix Gets Left" (Dec. 1); and "Felix in the Bone Age" (Dec. 15).

**1923:** "Felix the Ghost Breaker" (Jan. 1); "Felix Wins Out" (Jan. 15); "Felix Tries for Treasure" (Apr. 15); "Felix Revolts" (May 1); "Felix Calms His Conscience" (May 15); "Felix the Globe Trotter" (June 1); "Felix Gets Broadcasted" (June 15); "Felix Strikes It Rich" (July 1); "Felix in Hollywood" (July 15); "Felix in Fairyland" (Aug. 1); "Felix Laughs Last" (Aug. 15); "Felix and the Radio," "Felix Fills a Shortage" (Nov. 15); "Felix the Goat Getter" (Dec. 1); and "Felix Goes A-Hunting" (Dec. 15).

*Otto Messmer created Pat Sullivan's malicious, inventive adventures of Felix the Cat. The character was one of the most popular cartoon stars of the silent film era.* (COURTESY: MUSEUM OF MODERN ART/FILM STILLS ARCHIVE)

**1924:** "Felix Out of Luck" (Jan. 1); "Felix Loses Out" (Jan. 15); "Felix Hyps the Hippos" (Feb. 1); "Felix Crosses the Crooks" (Feb. 15); "Felix Tries to Rest" (Feb. 29); "Felix Goes West" (Mar. 1); "Felix Doubles for Darwin" (Mar. 15); "Felix Finds Out" (Apr. 1); "Felix Cashes In," "Felix Fairy Tales," "Felix Grabs His Grub," "Felix Pinches the Pole" (May 1); "Felix Puts It Over" (May 15); "A Friend in Need" (June 1); "Felix Finds 'Em Fickle" (June 15); "Felix Baffled by Banjos" (June 15); "Felix All Balled Up" (July 1); "Felix Brings Home the Bacon" (Nov. 15); "Felix Finishes First" (Dec. 1); and "Felix Goes Hungry" (Dec. 15).

**1925:** "Felix Wins and Loses" (Jan. 1); "Felix All Puzzled" (Jan. 15); "Felix Follows the Swallows" (Feb. 1); "Felix Rests in Peace" (Feb. 15); "Felix Gets His Fill" (Mar. 1); "Felix Full o' Fight" (Apr. 13); "Felix Outwits Cupid" (Apr. 27); "Felix Monkeys with Magic" (May 8); "Felix Cops the Prize" (May 25); "Felix Gets the Can" (June 8); and "Felix Dopes It Out" (Aug. 15).

*Educational Pictures*

**1925:** "Felix Trifles with Time" (Aug. 23); "Felix Busts Into Business" (Sept. 6); "Felix Trips Through Toyland" (Sept. 20); "Felix on the Farm" (Oct. 4); "Felix on the Job" (Oct. 18); "The Cold Rush" (Nov. 1); "Eats Are West" (Nov. 15); "Felix Tries the Trades" (Nov. 29); "Felix at the Rainbow's End" (Dec. 13); and "Felix Kept on Walking" (Dec. 27).

**1926:** "Felix Spots the Spooks" (Jan. 10); "Felix Flirts with Fate" (Jan. 24); "Felix in Blunderland" (Feb. 7); "Felix Fans the Flames" (Feb. 21); "Felix Laughs It Off" (Mar. 7); "Felix Weathers the Weather" (Mar. 21); "Felix Uses His Head" (Apr. 4); "Felix Misses the Cue" (Apr. 18); "Felix Braves the Briny" (May 2); "A Tale of Two Kitties" (May 16); "Felix Scoots Through Scotland" (May 30); "Felix Rings the Ringer" (June 13); "School Daze" (June 27); "Felix Seeks Solitude" (July 11); "Felix Misses His Swiss" (July 25); "Gym Gems" (Aug. 8); "Two-Lip Time" (Aug. 22); "Scrambled Eggs" (Sept. 5); "Felix Shatters the Sheik" (Sept. 19); "Felix Hunts the Hunter" (Oct. 3); "Land O'Fancy" (Oct. 17); "Felix Busts a Bubble" (Oct. 31); "Reverse English" (Nov. 14); "Felix Trumps the Ace" (Nov. 28); "Felix Collars the Button" (Dec. 12); and "Zoo Logic" (Dec. 26).

**1927:** "Felix Dines and Pines" (Jan. 9); "Pedigreedy" (Jan. 23); "Icy Eyes" (Feb. 6); "Stars and Stripes" (Feb. 20); "Felix Sees 'Em in Season" (Mar. 6); "Barn Yarns" (Mar. 20); "Germ Mania" (Apr. 3); "Sax Appeal" (Apr. 27); "Eye Jinks" (May 1); "Roameo" (May 15); "Felix Ducks His Duty" (May 29); "Dough-Nutty" (June 12); "'Loco' Motive" (June 26); "Art for Heart's Sake" (July 10); "The Travel-Hog" (July 14); "Jack from All Trades" (Aug. 7); "The Non-Stop Fright" (Aug. 21); "Wise Guise" (Sept. 4); "Flim Flam Films" (Sept. 18); "Switches Witches" (Oct. 2); "No Fuelin'" (Oct. 16); "Daze and Knights" (Oct. 30); "Uncle Tom's Crabbin'" (Nov. 13); "Whys and Other Whys" (Nov. 27); "Felix Hits the Deck" (Dec. 11); and "Felix Behind in Front" (Dec. 25).

**1928:** "The Smoke Scream" (Jan. 8); "Draggin' the Dragon" (Jan. 22); "The Oily Bird" (Feb. 5); "Ohm Sweet Ohm" (Feb. 19); "Japanicky" (Mar. 4); "Polly-Tics" (May 18); "Comicalamities" (Apr. 1); "Sure-Locked Homes" (Apr. 15); "Eskimotive" (Apr. 19); "Arabiantics" (May 13); "In and Out-Laws" (May 27); "Outdoor Indore" (June 10); "Futuritzy" (June 24); "Astronomeows" (July 8); "Jungle Bungles" (July 22); and "The Last Life" (Aug. 5).

## ◎ FULLER PEP

Pat Powers introduced this series of animated films about a benign farmer, Fuller Pep, similar to Paul Terry's Farmer Al Falfa charac-ter. It was drawn by F.M. Follett in 1916–17. The series was listed in some Hollywood trade paper listings as "Mr. Fuller Pep." *A Pat Powers Production released through Universal.*

**1916:** "He Tries Mesmerism" (May 11); "He Dabbles in the Pond" (May 17); and "He Breaks for the Beach" (May 31).

**1917:** "He Celebrates His Wedding Anniversary" (Jan. 14); "He Goes to the Country" (Jan. 21); "He Wife Goes for a Rest" (Feb. 4); "He Does Some Quick Moving" (Feb. 18); "An Old Bird Pays Him a Visit" (Mar. 14); and "His Day of Rest" (Mar. 11).

## ◎ FUN FROM THE PRESS

In 1923 Max Fleischer produced this series of animated sequences adapted from *The Literary Digest*. The series was directed by Max's brother, Dave Fleischer. *An Out of the Inkwell Films Production.*

**1923:** "No. 1" (Apr. 28); "No. 2" (May); and "No. 3" (June).

## ◎ GAUMONT REEL LIFE

This series of technical cartoons appeared in weekly magazine film series in 1917. *A Gaumont Company Production released by Mutual Film Corporation.*

**1917:** "A One Man Submarine" (Apr. 5); "A Flying Torpedo" (Apr. 12); "Cargo Boats of Tomorrow" (Apr. 26); and "The Liberty Loan" (June 7).

## ◎ THE GAUMONT WEEKLY

Launched in 1912, this early black-and-white, weekly newsreel series featured a topical cartoon sequence in each production until it was discontinued in 1913. *A Gaumont Company Production.*

**1912:** "No. 36: Waiting for the Robert E. Lee" (Nov. 13); "No. 38: The War News in Constantinople" (Nov. 27); "No. 39: The Struggle Between Producer and Consumer" (Dec. 4); and "No. 41: The Fate of the Foxes" (Dec. 18).

**1913:** "No. 45: What a Fall, Oh My Countrymen" (Jan. 15).

## ◎ GINGER SNAPS

Short-lived series of cartoons written and directed by famed cartoonist Milt Gross based on his original newspaper comic strip; produced by John R. Bray and released to theaters as part of the *Goldwyn-Bray Pictographs* magazine series in 1920. *A Bray Studios Production released by Goldwyn Pictures Corporation.*

**1920:** "Ginger Snaps" (Apr. 30); "How My Vacation Spent Me" (June 19); and "Ginger Snaps" (Sept. 27).

## ◎ GLACKENS CARTOONS

Famed painter/illustrator L.M. Glackens animated and directed this series of beautifully executed humorous drawings comparing modern customs with those of bygone days. *A Bray Production.* Glackens's first film in this series was *The Stone Age Roost Robber*, which he directed and was released to theaters in April of 1916 under the Paramount-Bray Cartoons banner. That same year, he wrote and animated two additional shorts following the same theme as his predecessor for the Bray Cartoons series, "A Stone Age Adventure" and "When Knights Were Bold," which were distributed by Pathé-Eclectic. From 1915 to 1920 Glackens also directed and animated various cartoons for Bray Productions, all part of existing theatrical cartoon series, including *Pathé News*, *Bray Cartoons*, *Paramount-Bray Pictographs*, *Paramount-Bray Cartoons*, and *Goldwyn-Bray Pictographs*. (See individual series for information and titles.) *A Bray Production released by Paramount and Pathé-Eclectic.*

**1916:** "The Stone Age Roost Robber" (Apr. 9); "A Stone Age Adventure" (May 29); and "When Knights Were Bold" (June 29).

## ◉ GOLDWYN-BRAY COMIC

Umbrella title for this animated cartoon series based mostly on popular newspaper comic strips—*Happy Hooligan, Judge Rummy* and *The Shenanigan Kids*—produced by New York's Bray Studios and International Film Service in 1920. Series directors included Gregory La Cava (*Happy Hooligan* and *The Shenanigan Kids*), Burt Gillett and Grim Natwick (*Judge Rummy* and *The Shenanigan Kids*), and Max Fleischer. *A Bray Studios and International Film Service Production released by Goldwyn Pictures Corporation.*

**1920:** "The Great Umbrella Mystery" (La Cava/Apr. 17/*Happy Hooligan* cartoon); "Knock on the Window, The Door Is a Jamb" (Apr. 17/*Shenanigan Kids* cartoon); "Shimmie Shivers" (Apr. 21/*Judge Rummy* cartoon); "The First Man to the Moon" (Fleischer/Apr. 21); "A Fitting Gift" (May 7/*Judge Rummy* cartoon); "Turn to the Right Leg" (June 2/*Happy Hooligan* cartoon); "Smokey Smokes" (June 6/*Judge Rummy* cartoon); "One Good Turn Deserves Another" (June 17/*Shenanigan Kids* cartoon); "All for the Love of a Girl" (June 18/*Happy Hooligan* cartoon); "Doctors Should Have Patience" (June 19/*Judge Rummy* cartoon); "The Dummy" (June 27/*Shenanigan Kids* cartoon); "His Country Cousin" (July 3/*Happy Hooligan* cartoon); "A Fish Story" (July 3/*Judge Rummy* cartoon); "Lampoons" (Gillett/July 10); "The Last Rose of Summer" (July 17/*Judge Rummy* cartoon); "The Rotisserie Brothers" (Natwick/July 24/*Shenanigan Kids* cartoon); "The Fly Guy" (Aug. 26/*Judge Rummy* cartoon); "Shedding the Professor" (Sept. 5/*Judge Rummy* cartoon); "Cupid's Advice" (Sept. 11/*Happy Hooligan* cartoon); "Happy Houdini" (Sept. 11/*Happy Hooligan* cartoon); "Apollo" (Sept. 18/*Happy Hooligan* cartoon); "The Sponge Man" (Sept. 22/*Judge Rummy* cartoon); "The Prize Dance" (Oct. 3/*Judge Rummy* cartoon); and "Hunting Big Game" (Oct. 9/*Shenanigan Kids* cartoon).

## ◉ GOLDWYN-BRAY PICTOGRAPHS

Distributed to theaters from August of 1919 through March of 1921, this successor to the *Paramount-Bray Pictographs* magazine series featured many popular silent cartoons and silent cartoon series produced by New York's Bray Studios and International Film Service (IFS)—including *Jerry on the Job, Krazy Kat, Us Fellers* and others—animated and directed by Raoul Barré, John R. Bray, Leighton Budd, Wallace A. Carlson, R.D. Crandall, Max and Dave Fleischer, Jean Gic, L.M. Glackens, F. Lyle Goldman, Milt Gross, Gregory La Cava, J.D. Leventhal, Vernon Stallings and Pat Sullivan. *A Bray Production and International Film Service Production released by Goldwyn Pictures Corporation.*

**1919:** "The Clown's Pup" (Fleischer/Aug. 30); "How Animated Cartoons Are Made" (Bray/Sept. 6); "Where Has My Little Coal Bin" (La Cava/Sept. 6/IFS, *Jerry on the Job* cartoon); "The High Cost of Living" (Barré/Sept. 13/IFS cartoon); "Dud's Home Run" (Carlson/Sept. 26/*Us Fellers* cartoon); "Getting a Story or the Origin of the Shimmy" (Sullivan/Sept. 27); "Useless Hints by Fuller Prunes" (Gross/Oct. 4); "The Tantalizing Fly" (Max Fleischer/Oct. 4); "Dud Leaves Home" (Oct. 9/*Us Fellers* cartoon); "My How Times Have Changed" (Budd/Oct. 25); "We'll Say They Do" (Gross/Nov. 7); "Pigs in Clover" (La Cava/Nov. 10/IFS cartoon); "Dud's Geography Lesson" (Carlson/Nov. 17/*Us Fellers* cartoon); "How Could William Tell" (La Cava/Nov. 26/IFS cartoon); "Slides" (Max Fleischer/Dec. 3); "Sauce for the Goose" (Stallings/Dec. 9/IFS cartoon); "Tumult in Toy Town" (Gross/Dec. 16); "Sufficiency" (Stallings/Dec. 23/IFS cartoon); and "A Chip Off the Old Block" (Carlson/Dec. 31/*Us Fellers* cartoon).

**1920:** "The Chinese Question" (Stallings/Jan. 6/IFS cartoon); "The Great Cheese Robbery" (Jan. 16/IFS, *Krazy Kat* cartoon); "Behind the Signs on Broadway" (Leventhal/Jan. 16); "The Debut of Thomas Kat" (Jan. 26/Bray/the first cartoon produced in Brewster Color); "Love's Labor Lost" (Stallings/Jan. 30/IFS, *Krazy Kat* cartoon); "The Boxing Kangaroo" (Max Fleischer/Feb. 2); "A Warm Reception" (Feb. 10/IFS, *Jerry on the Job* cartoon); "All Aboard for the Trip to the Moon" (Max Fleischer/Feb. 10); "Dud's Haircut" (Carlson/Feb. 16/*Us Fellers* cartoon); "How You See" (Leventhal/Feb. 16); "The Wrong Track" (Feb. 27/IFS, *Jerry on the Job* cartoon); "Wireless Telephony" (Goldman/Feb. 27); "The Best Mouse Loses" (Stallings/Mar. 3/IFS, *Krazy Kat* cartoon); "Hello Mars" (Max Fleischer/Mar. 3); "The Tale of the Wag" (Mar. 9/IFS, *Jerry on the Job* cartoon); "Professor B. Flat" (Leventhal, Crandall/Mar. 9); "The Chinaman" (Max Fleischer/Mar. 9); "A Very Busy Day" (La Cava/Mar. 23/IFS cartoon); "Frenchy Discovers America" (Gross/Apr. 3); "A Tax from the Rear" (Apr. 14/IFS, *Krazy Kat* cartoon); "The Ear" (Goldman/Apr. 14); "Spring Fever" (La Cava/Apr. 30/IFS, *Jerry on the Job* cartoon); "Ginger Snaps" (Gross/Apr. 30/first *Ginger Snaps* cartoon); "The Circus" (Dave Fleischer/May 6); "Swinging His Vacation" (La Cava/May 14/IFS, *Jerry on the Job* cartoon); "Here's Your Eyesight" (Leventhal/May 14); "Yes Times Have Changed" (Glackens/May 19); "The Mysterious Vamp" (La Cava/May 29/IFS, *Jerry on the Job* cartoon); "Katz Is Katz" (Stallings/June 4/IFS, *Krazy Kat* cartoon); "The Ouija Board" (Dave Fleischer/June 4); "A Punk Piper" (Stallings/June 12/IFS *Jerry on the Job* cartoon); "Breathing" (Leventhal/June 12); How My Vacation Spent Me (Gross/June 19/*Ginger Snaps* cartoon); "Quick Change" (Stallings/June 26/IFS, *Jerry on the Job* cartoon); "The Chinese Honeymoon" (July 3/IFS, *Krazy Kat* cartoon); "The Clown's Little Helper" (Dave Fleischer/July 6); "The Rhyme That Went Wrong" (Stallings/July 16/IFS, *Jerry on the Job* cartoon); "Dots And Dashes" (Stallings/Aug. 26/IFS, *Jerry on the Job* cartoon); "The Train Robber" (Stallings/Aug. 26/IFS, *Jerry on the Job* cartoon); "If You Could Shrink" (Dave Fleischer/Aug. 26); "Dud the Lion Tamer" (Carlson/Sept. 4/*Us Fellers* cartoon); "Water Water Everywhere" (Stallings/Sept. 11/IFS, *Jerry on the Job* cartoon); "Ze American Girl" (Gic/Sept. 18); "Ginger Snaps" (Gross/Sept. 25/*Ginger Snaps* cartoon); "If We Went to the Moon" (Leventhal/Sept. 25); "Poker" (Dave Fleischer/Oct. 2); "Jerry and the Five Fifteen Train" (Stallings/Oct. 2/IFS, *Jerry on the Job* cartoon); "Lightning" (Leventhal/Oct. 2); "Perpetual Motion" (Dave Fleischer/Oct. 2); "Beaten by a Hare" (Stallings/Oct. 7/IFS, *Jerry on the Job* cartoon); "A Tough Pull" (Stallings/Oct. 7/IFS, *Jerry on the Job* cartoon); "Stories in Lines" (Gic/Oct. 21); "A Family Affair" (Oct. 25/IFS, *Krazy Kat* cartoon); "A Continuous Line of Thought" (Gic/Nov. 2); "The Bomb Idea" (Stallings/Nov. 6/IFS, *Jerry on the Job* cartoon); "The Restaurant" (Dave Fleischer/Nov. 16); and "A Thrilling Drill" (Stallings/Dec. 14/IFS, *Jerry on the Job* cartoon).

**1921:** "The Hinges on the Bar Room Door" (Stallings/Jan. 8/IFS cartoon); "Without Coal" (Stallings/Jan. 8/IFS, *Jerry on the Job* cartoon); "The Automatic Riveter" (Leventhal/Jan. 8); "A Tragedy in One Line" (Gic/Jan. 15); "The Awful Spook" (Jan. 21/IFS cartoon); "How I Became Krazy" (Stallings/Jan. 26/IFS, *Krazy Kat* cartoon); "Scrambled Eagles" (Stallings/Jan. 28/IFS, *Krazy Kat* cartoon); "Cartoonland" (Dave Fleischer/Feb. 2); "The Automobile Ride" (Dave Fleischer/Feb. 12); "Izzy Able the Detective" (Gross/Feb. 16); "The Wireless Wire Walkers" (Feb. 26/IFS, *Krazy Kat* cartoon); and "Othello Sapp's Wonderful Invention" (Gross/Mar. 19/re: *The Cow Milker*).

## ⓦ GOODRICH DIRT

In the tradition of legendary film tramp Charlie Chaplin, Wallace A. Carlson animated and directed these skillfully drawn adventures of a cheerful hobo and his optimistic dog in pursuit of a good meal or a dishonest buck. Carlson, who started in animation in 1915, ended the series two years after its debut. He went on to direct an animated version of *The Gumps. A Bray Production released by Famous Players-Lasky.*

**1917:** "Goodrich Dirt at the Seashore" (Sept. 3); "Goodrich Dirt Lunch Detective" (Oct. 1); "Goodrich Dirt at the Training Camp" (Nov. 5); "Goodrich Dirt's Amateur Night" (Dec. 2); and "Goodrich Dirt and the $1000 Reward" (Dec. 23).

**1918:** "Goodrich Dirt and the Duke De Whatanob" (Jan. 6); "Goodrich Dirt's Bear Hunt" (Feb. 11); "Goodrich Dirt in the Barber Business" (Mar. 18); "Goodrich Dirt Mat Artist" (Apr. 6); "Goodrich Dirt Bad Man Tamer" (May 6); "Goodrich Dirt in Darkest Africa" (May 27); "Goodrich Dirt King of Spades" (June 17); "Goodrich Dirt the Cop" (July 8); "Goodrich Dirt in the Dark and Stormy Knight" (Aug. 5); "Goodrich Dirt Coin Collector" (Aug. 26); "Goodrich Dirt Millionaire" (Sept. 30); "Goodrich Dirt When Wishes Come True" (Oct. 29); and "Goodrich Dirt Cowpuncher" (Dec. 4).

**1919:** "Goodrich Dirt in Spot Goes Romeoing" (Jan. 6); "Goodrich Dirt in a Difficult Delivery" (Jan. 22); and "Goodrich Dirt Hypnotist" (Feb. 26).

## ⓦ THE GUMPS

Harry Grossman of Celebrated Players contracted this series of 13 episodes based on cartoonist Sidney Smith's nationally syndicated strip. Mostly composed of live action, the films also featured animated sequences by Wallace Carlson, who previously animated and directed the *Dreamy Dud* series for Essanay. *A Celebrated Film Players Corp. release.*

**1920:** "Andy's Dancing Lesson" (June 5); "Flat Hunting" (June 5); "Andy Visits His Mamma-in-Law" (June 5); "Andy Spends a Quiet Day at Home" (June 26); "Andy Plays Golf" (June 26); "Andy's Wash Day" (June 26); "Andy on Skates" (June 26); "Andy's Mother-in-Law Pays Him a Visit" (June 26); "Andy on a Diet" (July 3); "Andy's Night Out" (July 3); "Andy and Min at the Theatre" (Aug. 14); "Andy Visits the Osteopath" (Aug. 14); "Andy's Inter-Ruben Guest" (Oct. 23); "Andy Redecorates His Flat" (Oct. 23); "Andy the Model" (Oct. 23); "Accidents Will Happen" (Oct. 23); "Andy Fights the High Cost of Living" (Oct. 23); "Militant Min" (Oct. 23); "Ice Box Episodes" (Oct. 23); "Wim and Wigor" (Oct. 23); "Equestrian Andy" (Oct. 23); "Andy the Hero" (Oct. 23); "Andy's Picnic" (Oct. 23); "Andy the Chicken Farmer" (Oct. 23); "Andy the Actor" (Oct. 23); "Andy at Shady Rest" (Oct. 23); "Andy on the Beach" (Oct. 23); "Andy on Pleasure Bent" (Oct. 23); "Howdy Partner" (Oct. 23); "There's a Reason" (Nov. 27); "Ship Ahoy" (Nov. 27); "The Toreador" (Nov. 27); "The Broilers" (Nov. 27); "Flicker Flicker Little Star" (Nov. 27); "Mixing Business with Pleasure" (Nov. 27); "Up She Goes" (Nov. 27); "A-Hunting We Will Go" (Nov. 27); and "Get to Work" (Nov. 27).

**1921:** "The Best of Luck" (Feb. 12); "The Promoters" (Feb. 12); "The Masked Ball" (Feb. 12); "Giver 'er the Gas" (Feb. 12); "Chester's Cat" (Feb. 12); "Rolling Around" (Feb. 12); "Andy's Holiday" (Feb. 12); "Andy Has a Caller" (Feb. 12); "Le Cuspidoree" (Feb. 12); "Andy's Cow" (Feb. 26); "Jilted and Jolted" (Mar. 19); "A Terrible Time" (Mar. 19); "A Quiet Little Game" (May 14); "Andy's Dog Day" (May 14); "Fatherly Love" (June); and "The Chicken Thief" (June).

## ⓦ HAMMON EGGS

Released as an entry in the *Powers Animated Cartoons* series by Universal Pictures, Pat Sullivan produced this series following the adventures of retired actor Hammon Eggs, who starred in two films, both released in 1917. *A Pat Sullivan Cartoon/Powers Production released by Universal Pictures.*

**1917:** "A Barnyard Hamlet" (July 28); and "Hammon Eggs' Reminiscences" (Aug. 4).

## ⓦ HANS AND FRITZ

Hans and Fritz, the mischievous brothers from Rudolph Dirks' celebrated comic strip *The Katzenjammer Kids*, appeared on screen in this series of cartoons produced by Harry "Bud" Fisher, creator of the *Mutt and Jeff* newspaper comic strip, and animated by Charles Bowers at his Mount Vernon, New York, studio. *A Celebrated Film Corporation and Mutt and Jeff, Inc. Production.*

**1916:** "The Chinese Cook" (Aug. 12).

## ⓦ HAPPY HOOLIGAN

Once a week the Hearst newspaper syndicate produced new installments of its ever popular *Hearst-Vitagraph News Pictorial*, which highlighted the week's news and were screened before the main feature at movie theaters across the country. At the end of each production were alternating adventures based on many of Hearst's comic-strip favorites: Judge Rummy, Maud the Mule, Jerry on the Job, the Katzenjammer Kids and Tad's Daffydils.

*Happy Hooligan* was another Hearst strip to gain national exposure via these weekly productions. Like the strip, Jiggs and Miggs appeared as supporting characters in the film series. Episodes generally ran three minutes in length.

Gregory La Cava, who later graduated to the rank of feature film director, directed the series until William C. Nolan and Ben Sharpsteen assumed this responsibility in 1920. *An International Film Service Production released by Hearst-Vitagraph, Educational Film Corp. and Goldwyn-Bray.*

### *Hearst-Vitagraph News Pictorial*

**1916:** "He Tries the Movies Again" (Oct. 9).

**1917:** "Happy Hooligan in A Trip to the Moon"; "Ananias Has Nothing on Hooligan" (Jan. 20); "Happy Hooligan, Double-Cross Nurse" (Mar. 25); "The New Recruit" (Apr. 8); "Three Strikes You're Out" (Apr. 26); "Around the World in Half an Hour" (June 9); "The Great Offensive" (July 1); "The White Hope" (July 29); "Happy Gets the Razoo" (Sept. 2); "Happy Hooligan in the Zoo" (Sept. 9); "The Tanks" (Sept. 16); "Happy Hooligan in Soft" (Oct. 7); "Happy Hooligan at the Picnic" (Oct. 16); "The Tale of a Fish" (Oct. 16); "The Tale of a Monkey" (Nov. 25); "Happy Hooligan at the Circus" (Dec. 8); and "Bullets and Bull" (Dec. 16).

**1918:** "Hearts and Horses" (Jan. 13); and "All for the Ladies" (Feb. 10).

### *Educational Film Corp.*

**1918:** "Doing His Bit" (Apr. 19); "Throwing the Bull" (June 17); "Mopping Up a Million" (July 22); "His Dark Past" (Aug. 5); "Tramp Tramp Tramp" (Aug. 12); "A Bold Bad Man" (Sept.); "The Latest in Underwear" (Oct.); and "Where Are the Papers" (Dec.).

**1919:** "Der Wash on Der Line" (Jan.); "Knocking the 'H' Out of Heinie" (Feb.); "A Smash-Up in China" (Mar. 22); "The Tale of a Shirt" (June 22); "A Wee Bit o' Scotch" (June 29); "Transatlantic Flight" (July 20); "The Great Handicap" (Aug. 24); "Jungle

Jumble" (Sept. 7); "After the Ball" (Sept. 28); and "Business Is Business" (Nov. 23).

### Goldwyn-Bray Comic

**1920:** "The Great Umbrella Mystery" (Apr. 17); "Turn to the Right Leg" (June 2); "All for the Love of a Girl" (June 18); "His Country Cousin" (July 3); "Cupid's Advice" (Aug.); "Happy Hooldini" (Sept. 11); "Apollo" (Sept. 18); "A Doity Deed" (Nolan/Oct. 25); "The Village Blacksmith" (Sharpsteen/Oct. 27); "A Romance of '76" (Nov. 22); "Dr. Jekyll and Mr. Zip" (Dec. 8); and "Happy Hooligan in Oil" (Nolan/Dec. 23).

**1921:** "Fatherly Love" (Nolan/Jan. 3); "Roll Your Own" (Nolan/Jan. 3); and "A Close Shave" (Nolan/Apr. 29).

## ◉ HARDROCK DOME

Assorted calamities were the end result for this eccentric detective, who appeared briefly in this series produced by J. R. Bray and released as a segment of the *Paramount-Bray Pictographs* series. *Directed by Pat Sullivan. A Bray Production released by Famous Players-Lasky Corp.*

**1917:** "Hardrock Dome, The Great Detective" (Jan. 29); "The Adventures of Hardrock Dome" (Feb. 5); "Further Adventures of Hardrock Dome" (Feb. 12).

## ◉ HEARST-INTERNATIONAL NEWS PICTORIAL

Legendary newspaper mogul-turned cartoon producer William Randolph Hearst produced this newsreel series featuring cartoons written by Tom Powers. From 1917 through 1918, the series continued under a new name, the *Hearst-Pathé News. An International Film Service Production.*

**1916:** "Tom Powers Cartoon" (June 13); "On Again Off Again" (May 22); and "Stripes and Patches" (Aug. 4).

## ◉ HEARST-PATHÉ NEWS

This popular newsreel series, featuring animated items and topical news of the day, was a retitled version of International Film Service's former newsreel series, the *Hearst International News Pictorial.* Directors included animators Leighton Budd, Hal Coffman, F.M. Follett and Gregory La Cava. *An International Film Service Production.*

**1917:** "Help Wanted" (Follett/Jan. 3); "A Hard Cold Winter" (Jan. 10); "Oh Girls What Next" (Budd/Jan. 13); "The Mexican Crisis" (Follett/Jan. 20); "Billy Sunday's Tabernacle" (Follett/Jan. 27); "Up a Stump" (Feb. 14); "Freedom of the Seas" (Mar. 10); "Adventures of Mr. Common People" (Mar. 21); "Solid Comfort" (Mar. 24); "Mr. Common People's Busy Day" (Mar. 28); "Peace Insurance" (Mar. 31); "Cartoon" (Apr. 11); "Heroes of the Past" (Apr. 21); "The Great Offensive" (Apr. 28); "Mr. Slacker" (May 2); "Potato Is King" (May 5); "Her Crowning Achievement" (May 16); "Have You Bought Your Liberty Bond" (May 23); "Both Good Soldiers" (May 26); "When Will He Throw Off This Burden" (May 30); "In the Garden Trenches" (June 2); "Ten Million Men from Uncle Sam" (June 9); "Liberty Loan of 1917" (June 13); "A Regular Man" (July 4); "The Awakening" (Coffman/July 14); "America Does Not Forget" (July 18); "They All Look Alike to Me" (Aug. 4); "Growing Fast" (Aug. 15); "Hoch the Kaiser" (Sept. 5); "Fall Styles for Men" (Sept. 12); "Buy a Liberty Bond" (Oct. 13); "It Has Come At Last" (Nov. 4); "Which?" (Nov. 28); and "The Handwriting in the Sky" (Dec. 1).

**1918:** "Dropping the Mask" (Jan. 19); "Every Little Bit Helps" (Jan. 30); "A New Shadow Haunts Autocracy" (Feb. 9); "Progress" (Feb. 12); "The Heritage" (Feb. 15); "The Threatening Storm" (Feb. 20); "The Glutton" (Feb. 23); "Cartoon" (Mar. 2); "Making an Example of Him" (Mar. 13); "Join the Land Army" (Apr. 6); "Cartoon" (Apr. 13); and "Give Him a Helping Hand" (Apr. 20).

## ◉ HEARST-VITAGRAPH NEWS PICTORIAL

Famed newspaper mogul-turned film producer William Randolph Hearst, through his International Film Service, joined Vitagraph in December 1917 to produce this short-lived newsreel series that also included many famous animated cartoon series produced between 1915 and 1916 and animated by Raoul Barré, Frank Moser, Bill Nolan, and Leon Searl for Hearst. Among them were Barré's *Phables* and *Joys and Gloom* and director Gregory La Cava and animator Frank Moser's *Parcel Post Pete* series, respectively based on Tom E. Powers' enormously entertaining comic drawings and newspaper strips; and Moser, Nolan and Searl's *Krazy Kat* series, based on George Herriman's famed comic strip (who also received story credit in the series on many films). Powers served as a writer on each series. *An International Film Service Production released by Vitagraph.*

**1915:** "Phable of Sam and Bill" (Barré/Dec. 17); "Phable of a Busted Romance" (Barré/Dec. 24); and "Feet Is Feet: A Phable" (Barré/Dec. 31).

**1916:** "A Newlywed Phable" (Barré/Jan. 7); "Phable of a Phat Woman" (Barré/Jan. 14); "Who Said They Never Come Back" (Jan. 18); "Cooks Versus Chefs: The Phable of Olaf and Louie" (Jan. 21); "Bang Go the Rifles" (Jan. 24); "'Twas But a Dream" (Jan. 28); "Mr. Nobody Holme Buys a Jitney" (Searl/Jan. 31); "Poor Si Keeler" (Feb. 4); "Never Again! The Story of a Speeder Cup" (Barré/Feb. 4); "Parcel Post Pete's Nightmare" (La Cava/Feb. 7); "Old Doc Gloom" (Moser/Feb. 11); "Parcel Post Pete: Not All His Troubles Are Little Ones" (La Cava/Feb. 14); "Introducing Krazy Kat and Ignatz Mouse" (Moser/Feb. 18); "Ignatz Believes in Signs" (Moser, Searl/Feb. 21); "Krazy Kat and Ignatz Discuss the Letter 'G'" (Moser, Searl/Feb. 25); "Krazy Kat Goes A-Wooing" (Searl/Feb. 29); "Krazy Kat and Ignatz the Mouse: A Duet" (Moser, Searl/Mar. 3); "He Made Me Love Him" (Moser, Searl/Mar. 3); "Krazy Kat and Ignatz in Their One Act Tragedy" (Moser, Searl/Mar. 6); "The Tale of the Nude Tail" (Moser, Searl/Mar. 6); "The Joys Elope" (Barré/Mar. 10); "Krazy Kat, Bugologist" (Moser, Searl/Mar. 13); "Krazy Kat and Ignatz at the Circus" (Searl/Mar. 17); "Krazy Kat Demi-Tasse" (Moser, Searl/Mar. 20); "Krazy Kat Invalid" (Moser, Searl/Mar. 27); "Do You Know This Man" (Barré/Mar. 31); "Krazy Kat at the Switchboard" (Apr. 3); "Krazy Kat the Hero" (Apr. 14); "Krazy Kat to the Rescue" (Nolan/Apr. 14); and "A Tale That Is Knot" (Moser, Searl/Apr. 14).

## ◉ HESANUT

*A Kalem Company Production.*

**1914:** "Hesanut Hunts Wild Game" (Sept. 25); "Hesanut Buys an Auto" (Oct. 10); "Hesanut Builds a Skyscraper" (Nov.); and "Hesanut at a Vaudeville Show" (Dec.).

**1915:** "A Night in New Jersey" (Jan. 16).

## ◉ HISTORICAL CARTOONS

This timely series mostly propagandized World War I through related stories that were both topical and political in nature. Cartoons were originally released as part of the *Paramount Pictographs* series and then its successor, *Paramount-Bray Pictographs*, beginning with "The Bronco Buster" in 1916. *Produced by J. R. Bray and directed by Bray Leighton Budd, L.M. Glackens, and Santry. A Bray Production released by Paramount.*

**1916:** "The Bronco Buster" (Bray/Feb. 26) and "The Long Arm of Law and Order" (Bray/Apr. 9).

**1917:** "The Awakening of America" (Bray/May 21); "Evolution of the Dachsund" (Budd/June 11); "Sic 'Em Cat" (Budd/July 23); and "Uncle Sam's Dinner Party" (Budd/Aug. 20).

**1918:** "The Peril of Prussianism" (Budd/Jan. 28); "Putting Fritz on the Water Wagon" (Budd/Feb. 4); "Von Loon's 25,000 Mile Gun" (Glackens/July 22); "The Kaiser's Surprise Party" (Aug. 12); "A Watched Pot" (Sept. 9); "Von Loon's Non-Capturable Gun" (Glackens/Oct. 1); "The Greased Pole" (Budd/Oct. 22); "A German Trick That Failed" (Budd/Nov. 6); "Uncle Sam's Coming Problem" (Budd/Nov. 27); and "Pictures in the Fire" (Santry/Dec. 8).

**1919:** "Private Bass His Pass" (Glackens/Jan. 15).

## ◉ HISTORIETS

A series of animated cartoons in color. *A Reel Color Inc. Production.*

**1924:** "The Teapot Dome" (May); "Famous Sayings of Famous Americans" (May); "Witty Sayings of Witty Frenchmen" (May); and "Witty Naughty Thoughts" (May).

## ◉ HODGE PODGE

No main characters starred in this series of animated sequences based on specific themes, such as pioneering the movie business, which was distributed with live-action magazine films. *Produced by Lyman H. Howe. A Lyman H. Howe Films Company Production released by Educational Films Corporation.*

**1922:** "King Winter" (Oct. 8); "Sea Elephants" (Nov. 1); and "The Garden of Geysers" (Dec. 8).

**1923:** "Mrs. Hippo" (Jan. 6); "Hot Shots" (Jan. 23); "Fishing for Tarpon" (Mar. 14); "Speed Demons" (May 2); "Shooting the Earth" (May 17); "A Flivver Elopement" (July 18); "The Cat and the Fiddle" (July 18); "Dipping in the Deep" (Aug. 11); "Why the Globe Trotter Trots" (Sept. 29); "Speedville" (Oct. 16); "The Bottom of the Sea" (Nov. 19); and "Liquid Love" (Dec. 17).

**1924:** "A Sailor's Life" (Jan. 16); "Movie Pioneer" (Feb. 9); "Jumping Jacks" (Mar. 13); "The Realm of Sport" (Apr. 19); "A Tiny Tour of the U.S.A." (May 1); "Snapshots of the Universe" (June 12); "Frozen Water" (July 26); "Hazardous Hunting" (Aug. 29); "A Crazy Quilt of Travel" (Sept. 18); "Whirligigs" (Oct. 16); "Earth's Oddities" (Nov. 28); and "Hi-Flyers" (Dec. 28).

**1925:** "Topsy Turvy Travel" (Jan. 25); "Lots of Knots" (Feb. 16); "Movie Morsels" (Mar. 27); "The Village School" (Apr. 19); "Earth's Other Half" (May 26); "Mexican Melody" (June 16); "Travel Treasures" (June 30); "Pictorial Proverbs" (Aug. 1); "The Story Teller" (Aug. 22); "Knicknacks of Knowledge" (Oct. 18); "Magical Movies" (Nov. 16); and "A Mythical Monster" (Dec. 21).

**1926:** "Mother Goose's Movies" (Jan. 20); "Criss Cross Cruise" (Feb. 16); "Congress of Celebrities" (Mar. 20); "Neptune's Domain" (Apr. 12); "From A to Z Thru Filmdom" (May 23); "Peeking at the Planets" (June 22); "Chips off the Old Block" (July 25); "Alligator's Paradise" (Aug. 22); "A Merrygoround of Travel"

(Sept. 19); "Figures of Fancy" (Nov. 28); and "Movie Medley" (Dec. 26).

**1927:** "A Cluster of Kings" (Jan. 6); "The Wise Old Owl" (Feb. 13); "Climbing into Cloudland" (Mar. 13); "A Bird of Flight" (Apr. 17); "A Scenic Treasure Chest" (May 22); "Tales of a Traveler" (June 16); "Capers of a Camera" (July 17); "Bubbles of Geography" (Aug. 8); "Delving into the Dictionary" (Aug. 30); "Here and There in Travel Land" (Oct. 16); "Models in Mud" (Nov. 13); and "A Whirl of Activity" (Dec. 11).

**1928:** "Recollections of a Rover" (Jan. 8); "Star Shots" (Jan. 28); "How to Please the Public" (Mar. 31); "Nicknames" (Apr. 8); "The Wandering Toy" (May 19); "Pictorial Tidbits" (June 19); "Conquering the Colorado" (July 3); "The Peep Show" (Aug. 7); "On the Move" (Sept. 28); "Glorious Adventure" (Nov. 2); and "A Patchwork of Pictures" (Nov. 30).

**1929:** "Shifting Scenes" (Jan. 11); "Question Marks" (Jan. 25); and "A Dominion of Diversity" (Mar. 15).

## ◉ HY MAYER CARTOONS

Celebrated cartoonist-animator Henry "Hy" Mayer, an established caricaturist and author, illustrated stories for several New York humor magazines and wrote, directed and inked, along with pioneer animator Otto Messmer, this popular series of black-and-white one-reel cartoons, sketched entirely freehand and produced by his company, Imp Films, for Universal Pictures. Mayer's cartoons also appeared in two other popular magazine series: *Universal Weekly*, from June 1913 through November 1916, and its successor, *Universal Screen Magazine*, until 1920. Afterward, he went on to produce a new live-action animated series for Pathé, *Travelaughs. A Universal Pictures and Imp Films Production.*

**1913:** "A Study in Crayon" (March); "Hy Mayer: His Magic Hand" (May 3); "Hy Mayer: His Magic Hand" (May 31); "Pen Talks by Hy Mayer" (June 7); "Hy Mayer's Cartoons" (June 14); "Filmograph Cartoons" (June 21); "Fun in Film by Hy Mayer" (June 28); "Sketches from Life by Hy Mayer" (July 5); "Lightning Sketches by Hy Mayer" (July 12); "In Cartoonland by Hy Mayer" (July 19); "Summer Caricatures" (July 26); "Funny Fancies by Hy Mayer" (Aug. 2); "The Adventures of Mr. Phiffles" (Aug. 9); "In Laughland with Hy Mayer" (Aug. 16); "Pen Talks by Hy Mayer" (Aug. 23); "Hy Mayer: His Merry Pen" (Aug. 30); "Humors of Summer" (Sept. 6); "Hy Mayer Cartoons" (Sept. 13); "Antics in Ink by Hy Mayer" (Sept. 20); "Jolly Jottings by Hy Mayer" (Sept. 27); "Whimsicalities by Hy Mayer" (Oct. 4); "Hilarities by Hy Mayer" (Oct. 11); and "Leaves from Hy Mayer's Sketchbook" (Oct. 18).

**1914:** "Pen Laughs"; "Topical Topics"; "Topical War Cartoons" (Sept.); "Topical War Cartoons No. 2" (Oct.); and "War Cartoons by Hy Mayer" (Nov.).

**1923:** A Movie Fantasy (Dec. 8).

## ◉ INBAD THE SAILOR

Pat Sullivan, who later produced and directed his most famous series, *Felix the Cat*, also produced these adventures of a seafaring sailor with C. Allan Gilbert and J. R. Bray originally for the silent cartoon series *Silhouette Fantasies* in 1916. A year later, the first cartoon, "Inbad the Sailor," was reissued to theaters as part of producer Patrick A. Powers's *Powers Animated Cartoon* series by Universal Pictures. *A Powers/Bray-Gilbert Film Production released by Universal Pictures and Famous Players-Lasky Corp.*

**1916:** "Inbad the Sailor" (Apr. 1/*Powers Animated Cartoon/* originally released Jan. 20 as *Silouette Fantasy*) and "Inbad the Sailor Gets into Deep Water" (Apr. 8).

### ◎ INKLINGS
Max Fleischer produced this series featuring different types of animation between 1924 and 1925. The films were not released until three years later. *Directed by Dave Fleischer. A Red Seal Pictures Production.*

### ◎ INK-RAVINGS
Milt Gross wrote, animated and directed this brief series of cartoons for the *Bray Magazine. A Bray Production.*

**1922:** "Scrap Hangers" (Dec. 16); and "Taxes" (Dec. 30).

**1923:** "If We Reversed" (Jan.).

### ◎ INKWELL IMPS
Ko-Ko the Clown, who first starred in Max Fleischer's *Out of the Inkwell* series, reappeared in this 1927 Paramount series produced by Alfred Weiss and Out of the Inkwell Films. Weiss was removed from the role of producer after his company went bankrupt and Paramount contracted the Fleischer Studios to take over production of the series. (Due to copyright changes, the character's name was hyphenated for the series.) In 1929 the series was converted to sound and became known as *Talkartoons. An Out of the Inkwell Films, Inc. and Fleischer Studios Production released by Paramount Pictures.*

**1927:** (Dates listed are copyright dates.) "Ko-Ko Makes 'Em Laugh" (Aug. 6); "Ko-Ko Plays Pool" (Aug. 6); "Ko-Ko's Kane" (Aug. 20); "Ko-Ko the Knight" (Sept. 3); "Ko-Ko Hops Off" (Sept. 17); "Ko-Ko the Kop" (Oct. 1); "Ko-Ko Explores" (Oct. 15); "Ko-Ko Chops Suey" (Oct. 29); "Ko-Ko's Klock" (Nov. 26); "Ko-Ko's Quest" (Dec. 10); "Ko-Ko the Kid" (Dec. 24); "Ko-Ko Back Tracks"; and "Ko-Ko Needles the Boss."

**1928:** "Ko-Ko's Kink" (Jan. 7); "Ko-Ko's Kozy Korner" (Jan. 21); "Ko-Ko's Germ Jam" (Feb. 4); "Ko-Ko's Bawth" (Feb. 18); "Ko-Ko Smokes" (Mar. 3); "Ko-Ko's Tattoo" (Mar. 17); "Ko-Ko's Earth Control" (Mar. 31); "Ko-Ko's Hot Dog" (Apr. 14); "Ko-Ko's

*Max and Dave Fleischer's most popular silent cartoon character, Ko-Ko the Clown, ardently watches his musical note-eating friend co-orchestrate the melody in "In the Good Old Summertime" (1929).* (COURTESY: BLACKHAWK FILMS)

Haunted House" (Apr. 28); "Ko-Ko's Lamps Aladdin" (May 12); "Ko-Ko Squeals" (May 26); "KoKo's Field Daze" (June 9); "Ko-Ko Goes Over" (June 23); "Ko-Ko's Catch" (July 7); "Ko-Ko's War Dogs" (July 21); "Ko-Ko's Chase" (Aug. 11); "Ko-Ko Heaves Ho" (Aug. 25); "Ko-Ko's Big Pull" (Sept. 7); "Ko-Ko Cleans Up" (Sept. 21); "Ko-Ko's Parade" (Oct. 8); "Ko-Ko's Dog Gone" (Oct. 22); "Ko-Ko in the Rough" (Nov. 3); "Ko-Ko's Magic" (Nov. 16); "Ko-Ko on the Track" (Dec. 4); "Ko-Ko's Act" (Dec. 17); and "Ko-Ko's Courtship" (Dec. 28).

**1929:** "No Eyes Today" (Jan. 11); "Noise Annoys Ko-Ko" (Jan. 25); "Ko-Ko Beats Time" (Feb. 8); "Ko-Ko's Reward" (Feb. 23); "Ko-Ko's Hot Ink" (Mar. 8); "Ko-Ko's Crib" (Mar. 23); "Ko-Ko's Saxophonies" (Apr. 5); "Ko-Ko's Knock Down" (Apr. 19); "Ko-Ko's Signals" (May 3); "Ko-Ko's Conquest" (May 31); "Ko-Ko's Focus" (May 17); "Ko-Ko's Harem Scarum" (June 14); "Ko-Ko's Big Sale" (June 28); "Ko-Ko's Hypnotism" (July 12); and "Chemical Ko-Ko" (July 26).

### ◎ INTERNATIONAL NEWS
Briefly produced weekly newsreel series, shown in movie theaters between 1919 and 1920, which also showcased the work of such celebrated cartoonists as Hal Coffman, Thomas (Tad) Dorgan, Winsor McCay, Harry Murphy, Frederick Opper and Tom Powers. Titles are unknown. *An International Film Service Production released by Universal Pictures.*

### ◎ JERRY ON THE JOB
At the ripe age of 18, Walter Lantz was assigned to animate this series, spotlighting the adventures of a diminutive but exceedingly active and resourceful office boy named Jerry. Created by Walter Hoban, *Jerry on the Job* originated as a daily strip in the *New York Journal.* Like other Hearst cartoons, this animated version appeared at the tail end of weekly *Hearst-Vitagraph News Pictorials.*

In the animated episodes, stories often revolved around Jerry's ineptitude. (In one film, his attempt to soothe his boss's aching tooth results in his successfully uprooting the tooth—and the train station—after stringing the tooth to the outbound train.) Two supporting characters rounded out the series: Fred Blink, a young rival for Jerry's job, and his younger brother, Herman. *Directed by Vernon Stallings and Gregory La Cava. A Bray Production released by International Film Service.*

**1916:** "Jerry Ships a Circus" (Nov. 13); and "On the Cannibal Isle" (Dec. 18).

**1917:** "A Tankless Job" (Jan. 21); "Jerry Saves the Navy" (Feb. 18); "Quinine" (May 20); "Love and Lunch" (July 5); and "On the Border" (Aug. 19).

*Goldwyn-Bray Pictographs*

**1919:** "Where Has My Little Coal Bin" (La Cava/Sept. 6); "Pigs in Clover" (La Cava/Nov. 10); "How Could William Tell" (La Cava/Nov. 26); "Sauce for the Goose" (Stallings/Dec. 9); and "Sufficiency" (Stallings/Dec. 23).

**1920:** "The Chinese Question" (Jan. 6); "A Warm Reception" (Feb. 10); "The Wrong Track" (Feb. 27); "The Tale of a Wag" (Mar. 9); "A Very Busy Day" (La Cava/Mar. 23); "Spring Fever" (La Cava/Apr. 21); "Swinging His Vacation" (La Cava/May 29); "A Punk Piper" (Stallings/June 12); "A Quick Change" (Stallings/July 16); "The Trained Horse" (Stallings/July 27); "Dots and Dashes" (Stallings/Aug. 26); "Water Water Everywhere" (Stallings/Sept. 14); "Jerry and the Five Fifteen Train" (Stallings/Oct. 2); "Beated by a Hare" (Stallings/Oct. 7); "A Tough

Pull" (Stallings/Oct. 7); "The Bomb Idea" (Stallings/Nov. 6); "A Thrilling Drill" (Stallings/Dec. 14); and "Without Coal" (Stallings/Dec. 28).

## ◉ JOE BOKO

Wallace Carlson wrote, produced and directed this short-lived series. *A Historic Feature Film Co./Essanay Film Manufacturing Company Production released by Powers-Universal release.*

**1914:** "Joe Boko Breaking into the Big League" (Oct. 10).

**1915:** "Joe Boko in a Close Shave" (June 1); and "Joe Boko in Saved by Gasoline" (Aug. 27).

**1916:** "Joe Boko" (Apr. 4/Canimated Nooz Pictorial); and "Joe Boko's Adventures" (Feb. 9).

## ◉ JOYS AND GLOOM

Cartoonist Tom E. Powers's characters, Hawkshaw Gloom and The Joys, from his popular newspaper comic strip, were featured in this series of further animated adventures for Hearst's International Film Service issued to theaters as its own series. Most of the cartoons in the series originally debuted under the *Hearst-Vitagraph News Pictorial*, including three cartoons produced in 1915— "Phable of Sam and Bill," "Phable of a Busted Romance" and "Feet Is Feet: A Phable"—that were re-issued to theaters as part of this new series along with other cartoons from the former starring Powers's other popular newspaper strip characters, Mr. Nobody Holme, Parcel Post Pete and Doctor Soakem, adapted for the screen and animated by Frank Moser, Raoul Barré, who quit after only seven films to direct a cartoon series version of Bud Fisher's *Mutt and Jeff* comic strip and later returned, and Leon Searl. *Directed by Gregory La Cava, Raoul Barré and John C. Terry. An International Film Service Production released by Hearst-Vitagraph.*

**1916:** "Bang Go the Rifles" (La Cava/Jan. 4); "Phable of a Busted Romance" (La Cava/Jan. 16); "Phable of a Phat Woman" (with Hawkshaw Gloom, The Joys/La Cava/Jan. 18); "Mr. Nobody Holme: He Buys a Jitney" (with Mr. Nobody Holme/La Cava/Feb. 1); "Never Again! The Story of a Speeder Cop" (with Officer Heeler/La Cava/Feb. 4); "Old Doc Gloom" (with Hawkshaw Gloom, The Joys/La Cava/Feb. 11); "The Joys Elope" (with Hawkshaw Gloom, The Joys/La Cava/Mar. 10); "Adventures of Mr. Nobody Holme" (with Mr. Nobody Holme/La Cava/Mar. 20); "Cooks Versus Chefs: The Phable of Olaf and Louie" (with Hawkshaw Gloom, The Joys/La Cava/Apr. 8); "Feet Is Feet: A Phable" (with Hawkshaw Gloom, The Joys/La Cava/Apr. 27); "A Newlywed Phable" (with Hawkshaw Gloom, The Joys/La Cava/June 4); "Parcel Post Pete: Not All His Troubles Are Little Ones" (with Parcel Post Pete/La Cava/Feb. 14); "Parcel Pete's Nightmare" (with Parcel Post Pete/La Cava/July 12); Phable of Sam and Bill" (with Hawkshaw Gloom, The Joys/La Cava/Sept. 7); "Twas But a Dream" (Barré/Sept. 26); and "Who Said They Never Come Back?" (with Red Smith/La Cava/Oct. 15).

**1919:** "Doctor Soakem" (Terry).

## ◉ JUDGE RUMMY

Created as a Hearst comic strip by Tad Dorgan, orginator of the term *hot dog*, this series featured the misadventures of a dog court justice, whose passion for upholding the law was equaled by his love for cigars. The series was one of several to utilize strip characters originally syndicated by the Hearst newspaper syndicate and transformed into animated series. *Directed by Gregory La Cava, Jack King, Burt Gillett and Grim Natwick. An International Film Service Production released by Goldwyn-Bray.*

**1918:** "Judge Rummy's Off Day" (Aug. 19); "Hash and Hypnotism" (Oct. 1); and "Twinkle Twinkle" (Dec. 1).

**1919:** "Snappy Cheese" (Mar. 22); "The Sawdust Trail" (June 22); "The Breath of a Nation" (June 29); "Good Night Nurse" (Aug. 24); "Judge Rummy's Miscue" (Sept. 1); "Rubbing It In" (Oct. 1); and "A Sweet Pickle" (Nov. 1).

### Goldwyn-Bray Comic

**1920:** "A Joy Ride" (Natwick); "His Country Cousin"; "Judge Rummy on with the Dance" (King); "Shimmie Shivers" (Apr. 21); "A Fitting Gift" (May 7); "His Last Legs" (May 25); "Smokey Smokes" (La Cava/June 6); "Doctors Should Have Patience" (June 19); "A Fish Story" (July 3); "The Last Rose of Summer" (July 17); "The Fly Guy" (Aug. 26); "Shedding the Profiteer" (Sept. 5); "The Sponge Man" (Sept. 22); and "The Prize Dance" (Oct. 3).

### International Cartoons

**1920:** "Hypnotice Hooch" (Oct. 26); "The Hooch Ball" (Nov. 3); "Kiss Me" (King/Nov. 3); "Snap Judgement" (Gillett/Nov. 22); "Why Change Your Husband" (King/Nov. 22); "Bear Facts" (La Cava/Dec. 10); and "Yes Dear" (Natwick/Dec. 12).

**1921:** "Too Much Pep" (King/Jan. 4); "The Chicken Thief" (Natwick/Jan. 17); and "The Skating Fool" (Mar. 15).

## ◉ JUDGE'S CROSSWORD PUZZLES

John Colman Terry produced, directed and animated this series of animated crossword puzzles for Educational Pictures. *A Crossword Film Company Production released by Educational Pictures Corporation.*

**1925:** "No. 1" (Jan. 31); "No. 2" (Mar. 8); "No. 3" (Mar. 15); "No. 4" (Mar. 22); "No. 5" (Mar. 29); "No. 6" (Apr. 5); "No. 7" (Apr. 12); "No. 8" (Apr. 19); "No. 9" (Apr. 26); and "No. 10" (May 3).

## ◉ KARTOON KOMICS

This series of animated creations was produced, written and directed by Harry S. Palmer. *A Gaumont Company Production released by Mutual Pictures.*

**1916:** "Our National Vaudeville" (Mar. 4); "The Trials of Thoughtless Thaddeus" (Mar. 12); "Signs of Spring" (Mar. 26); "Nosey Ned" (Apr. 2); "The Greatest Show on Earth" (Apr. 5); "Watchful Waiting" (Apr. 12); "Nosey Ned" (Apr. 26); "Estelle and the Movie Hero" (May 3); "The Escapes of Estelle" (May 10); "As an Umpire Nosey Ned Is an Onion" (May 17); "Nosey Ned and His New Straw Lid" (May 24); "The Gnat Gets Estelle's Goat" (May 31); "The Escapades of Estelle" (June 7); "Johnny's Stepmother and the Cat" (June 14); "Johnny's Romeo" (June 28); "Scrambled Events" (July 5); "Weary's Dog Dream" (July 12); "Old Pfool Pfancy at the Beach" (July 26); "Music as a Hair Restorer" (Aug. 2); "Kuring Korpulent Karrie" (Aug. 16); "Mr. Jocko from Jungletown" (Aug. 23); "The Tale of a Whale" (Sept. 6); "Nosey Ned Commandeers an Army Mule" (Sept. 13); "Pigs" (Sept. 20); "Golf" (Sept. 27); "Abraham and the Oppossum" (Oct. 4); "Babbling Bess" (Oct. 11); "Inspiration" (Oct. 18); "I'm Insured" (Oct. 25); "Babbling Bess" (Nov. 8); "Haystack Horace" (Nov. 15); "What's Home Without a Dog" (Nov. 22); "Diary of a Murderer" (Nov. 29); "Our Forefathers" (Dec. 6); "Curfew Shall Not Ring" (Dec. 13); "Twas Ever Thus" (Dec. 20); and "Mr. Bonehead Gets Wrecked" (Dec. 27).

**1917:** "Miss Catnip Goes to the Movies" (Jan. 3); "The Gourmand" (Jan. 1); "Mr. Common Peepful Investigates" (Jan. 17); "Absent Minded Willie" (Jan. 24); "Never Again" (Jan.

31); "The Old Roue Visualizes" (Feb. 7); "Taming Tony" (Feb. 14); "Polly's Day at Home" (Feb. 21); "The Elusive Idea" (Feb. 28); "Ratus Runs Amuck" (Mar. 7); and "They Say Pigs Is Pigs" (July 14).

## ◎ THE KATZENJAMMER KIDS

Cartoonist Rudolph Dirks first developed this well-known newspaper strip about the life of a German family in 1897, later adapting it into an animated cartoon series of its own. Spaghetti-bearded Captain, who spoke broken English, commanded this cartoon troupe comprised of the Inspector, Mamma and squat, wavy-haired sons, Hans and Fritz.

Filmmaker Gregory La Cava produced and directed the series under the International Film Service banner. Production was halted because of anti-German feelings that spread throughout the United States during World War I. The series was later revived in sound shorts at MGM in 1938 but renamed *The Captain and the Kids. An International Film Service Production released by Pathé Film Exchange Inc. and Educational Pictures.*

### Pathé Film Exchange

**1916:** "The Captain Goes 'A-Swimming" (Dec. 11).

**1917:** "Der Great Bear Hunt" (Jan. 8); "Der Captain Is Examined for Insurance" (Feb. 11); "Der Captain Goes A-Flivvering" (Apr. 1); "Robbers and Thieves" (Apr. 12); "Sharks Is Sharks" (Apr. 26); "Down Where the Limburger Blows" (June 9); "20,000 Legs Under the Sea" (June 9); "Der Captain Discovers the North Pole" (July 8); "Der Captain's Valet" (Aug. 25); "Der End of Der Limit" (Oct. 14); "By the Sad Sea Waves" (Oct. 16); "The Mysterious Yarn" (Nov. 11); "Der Last Straw" (Nov. 18); "A Tempest in a Paint Pot" (Dec. 8); "Fat and Furious" (Dec. 23); and "Peace and Quiet" (Dec. 30).

**1918:** "Der Captain's Birthday" (Jan. 6); "Rub-a-Dud-Dud" (Jan. 20); "Rheumatics" (Jan. 27); "Policy and Pie" (Feb. 10); "Burglars" (Feb. 24); "Too Many Cooks" (Mar. 3); and "Spirits" (Mar. 10).

### Educational Pictures

**1918:** "Vanity and Vengeance" (Apr. 22); "The Two Twins" (May 6); "His Last Will" (May 13); "Der Black Mitt" (May 20); "Fisherman's Luck" (May 27); "Up in the Air" (June 3); "Swat the Fly" (June 10); "The Best Man Loses" (June 24); "Crabs Iss Crabs" (July 1); "A Picnic for Two" (July 8); "A Heathen Benefit" (July 15); "Pep" (July 19); and "War Gardens" (Aug.).

## ◎ KEEN CARTOONS

Henry W. Zippy and Jerry McDub were central characters in this animated series written, animated and directed by Charles F. Howell, Lee Connor and H.M. Freck. *A Keen Cartoon Corporation Production.*

**1916:** "Henry W. Zippy buys a Motor Boat" (Howell/Oct. 1); "Slinky the Yegg" (Connor/Oct. 1/re: "Slick and Tricky"); "Jerry McDub Collects Some Accident Insurance" (Freck/Oct. 1/re: "Zippy's Insurance"); "Henry W. Zippy Buys a Pet Pup" (Howell/Dec. 1/re: "Zippy Buys a Pet Pup"); and "Dr. Zippy Opens a Sanatorium" (Howell/Dec. 1/re: "Zippy in a Sanatorium").

**1917:** "Mose Is Cured" (Jan. 1); "The Old Forty-niner" (Jan. 8); "Jeb Jenkins the Village Genius" (Jan. 15); "Zoo-illogical Studies" (Feb. 5/re: "Dr. Bunny's Zoo"); "A Dangerous Girl" (Feb. 12/re: "She Was a Dangerous Girl"); "The Fighting Blood of Jerry McDub" (Freck/Feb. 28); "Mr. Coon" (Mar.); and "When Does a Hen Lay" (Howell/May 9).

## ◎ KEEPING UP WITH THE JONESES

A series of cartoons based on the comic strip by Arthur "Pop" Momand. *Directed by Harry S. Palmer. A Gaumont Company Production.*

**1915:** "The Dancing Lesson" (Sept. 13); "Cartoon" (title unknown/Sept. 22); "Cartoon" (title unknown/Sept. 29); "The Reelem Moving Picture Co." (Oct. 6); "The Family Adopt a Camel" (Oct. 13); "Pa Feigns Sickness" (Oct. 20); "The Family's Taste in Modern Furniture" (Oct. 27); "Moving Day" (Nov. 3); "The Family in Mexico" (Nov. 10); "Pa Takes a Flier in Stocks" (Nov. 17); "Pa Buys a Flivver" (Nov. 24); "Pa Lectures on the War" (Dec. 1); "The Skating Craze" (Dec. 7); "Pa Sees Some New Styles" (Dec. 14); "Ma Tries to Reduce" (Dec. 21); and "Pa Dreams He Wins the War" (Dec. 28).

**1916:** "The Pet Parrot" (Jan. 4); "Ma Drives a Car" (Jan. 11); "The Family Visits Florida" (Jan. 23); "Pa Fishes in an Alligator Pond" (Jan. 30); "Pa Tries to Write" (Feb. 6); "Pa Dreams He Is Lost" (Feb. 13); "Pa and Ma Have Their Fortunes Told" (Feb. 20); and "Pa Rides a Goat" (Feb. 27).

## ◎ KID KELLY

Legendary animator Frank Moser inked this series of cartoons for Gaumont Studios originally released to movie theaters in the mid-1900s and as part of the *Animated Grouch Chasers* (see entry for further details). *A Thomas A. Edison/Gaumont Studios Production.*

## ◎ KRAZY KAT

Originally conceived as a daily syndicated Hearst newspaper strip, lovesick Krazy Kat and pesky Ignatz the Mouse headlined their own animated series under the guidance of their creator, George Herriman. Like Pat Sullivan's Felix the Cat, Krazy's onscreen trials and tribulations centered around intellectual fantasies.

In transferring the strip to the screen, however, the Hearst animators were not completely faithful to its original concept. Krazy Kat bore no resemblance to Herriman's drawing, and Offisa Bull Pup, a primary character in the comic panel, was rarely used. Even the humor was diluted. Animator James "Shamus" Culhane, a series inker, once wrote: "The stories were heavy-handed chases and primitive acting. Every gag was automatically repeated three times."

Small budgets played a major factor in the poor production values of these cartoons. Most films were ground out at a cost of $900, so "the animation department was obliged to bat out animation footage at breakneck speed . . . time only for breathing," noted series animator I. Klein.

The series might have benefited greatly if Herriman had been more involved. He nominally supervised the series, and instead the animation was chiefly produced by Klein, Leon Searl, William C. Nolan, Bert Green, Frank Moser, Art Davis, Al Rose and Sid Marcus, all top-notch animators, with little creative input from him. As a result, the series was given a different direction by directors H.E. Hancock, William C. Nolan, Manny Gould and Ben Harrison, who supervised the cartoons.

Initial production of the series was performed in conjunction with Hearst's International Film Service. After a short-lived association with International, the series was later distributed by R-C Pictures and the Paramount-Famous Lasky Corporation. *An International Film Service/Bray Productions/Winkler Pictures/Paramount-Famous Lasky Production released by Hearst-Vitagraph/Famous Players-Lasky and R-C Pictures Corp.*

*Hearst-Vitagraph News Pictorial*

**1916:** "Introducing Krazy Kat and Ignatz Mouse" (Feb. 18); "Krazy Kat and Ignatz Mouse Believe in Signs" (Feb. 21); "Krazy Kat and Ignatz Mouse Discuss the Letter G" (Feb. 25); "Krazy Goes a-Wooing" (Feb. 29); "Krazy Kat and Ignatz Mouse: A Duet, He Made Me Love Him" (Mar. 3); "Krazy Kat and Ignatz Mouse in Their One-Act Tragedy, The Tale of the Nude Tail" (Mar. 6); "Krazy Kat, Bugologist" (Mar. 13); "Krazy Kat and Ignatz Mouse at the Circus" (Mar. 17); "Krazy Kat Demi-tasse" (Mar. 21); "Krazy Kat to the Rescue" (Mar. 24); "Krazy Kat Invalid" (Mar. 27); "Krazy Kat at the Switchboard" (Apr. 3); "Krazy Kat the Hero" (Apr. 7); and "A Tale That Is Knot" (Apr. 14).

*International Film Service Cartoons*

**1916:** "Krazy Kat at Looney Park" (June 17); "A Tempest in a Paint Pot" (July 3); "A Grid-iron Hero" (Oct. 9); "The Missing One" (Nov. 27); and "Krazy Kat Takes Little Katrina for an Airing" (Dec. 23).

**1917:** "Throwing the Bull" (Feb. 4); "Roses and Thorns" (Mar. 11); "Robbers and Thieves" (Apr. 12); "The Cook" (Apr. 29); "Moving Day" (May 27); "All Is Not Gold That Glitters" (June 24); and "A Krazy Katastrophe" (Aug. 5).

*Bray Productions/Goldwyn-Bray Pictographs (released by Famous Players-Lasky)*

**1920:** "The Great Cheese Robbery" (Jan. 16); "Love's Labor Lost" (Stallings/Jan. 30); "The Best Mouse Loses" (Stallings/Mar. 3); "A Tax from the Rear" (Stallings/Apr. 14); "Kats Is Kats" (Stallings/June 4); "The Chinese Honeymoon" (July 3); and "A Family Affair" (Oct. 25).

**1921:** "The Hinges on the Bar Room Door" (Stallings/Jan. 8); "How I Became Krazy" (Stallings/Jan. 26); "The Awful Spook" (Jan. 21); "Scrambled Eagles" (Stallings/Jan. 28); and "The Wireless Wire-Walkers" (Stallings/Feb. 26).

*Winkler Pictures (released by R-C Pictures Corp.)*

**1925:** "Hot Dogs" (Oct. 1); "The Smoke Eater" (Oct. 15); "A Uke-Calamity" (Nov. 1); "The Flight That Failed" (Nov. 15); "Hair Raiser" (Nov. 15); "The New Champ" (Nov. 30); "James and Gems" (Dec. 1); and "Monkey Business" (Dec. 15).

**1926:** "Battling for Barleycorn" (Jan. 1); "A Picked Romance" (Jan. 15); "The Ghost Fakir" (Feb. 1); "Sucker Game" (Feb. 15); "Back to Backing" (Mar. 1); "Double Crossed" (Mar. 15); "Invalid" (Mar. 28); "Scents and Nonsense" (Apr. 1); "Feather Pushers" (Apr. 15); "Cops Suey" (May 1); "The Chicken Chaser" (Nolan/Sept. 2); "East Is Best" (Nolan/Sept. 22); "Shore Enough" (Nolan/Oct. 11); "Watery Gravey" (Nolan/Oct. 25); "Cheese It" (Nov. 8); "Dots and Dashes" (Nov. 22); and "Gold Struck" (Dec. 10).

**1927:** "Horse Play" (Jan. 3); "Busy Birds" (Jan. 17); "Sharp Flats" (Jan. 31); "Kiss Crossed" (Feb. 14); "A Fool's Errand" (Feb. 28); "Stomach Trouble" (Mar. 14); "The Rug Fiend" (Mar. 28); "Hire a Hall" (Apr. 11); "Don Go On" (Apr. 23); "Burnt Up" (May 9); "Night Owl" (May 23); "On the Trail" (June 6); "Passing the Hat" (June 20); "Best Wishes" (July 4); "Black and White" (July 10); and "Wild Rivals" (July 18).

*Paramount-Famous-Lasky*

**1927:** "Sealing Whacks" (Aug. 1); "Tired Wheels" (Aug. 13); "Bee Cause" (Aug. 15); "Web Feet" (Aug. 27); "Skinny" (Aug. 29); "School Daze" (Sept. 10); "Rail Rode" (Sept. 24); "Aero Nuts" (Oct. 8); "Topsy Turvy" (Oct. 22); "Pie Curs" (Nov. 5); "For Crime's Sake" (Harrison, Gould/Nov. 19); "Milk Made" (Dec. 3); "Stork Exchange" (Dec. 17); and "Grid Ironed" (Harrison, Gould/Dec. 31).

**1928:** "Pig Styles" (Jan. 14); "Shadow Theory" (Jan. 28); "Ice Boxed" (Feb. 11); "A Hunger Stroke" (Feb. 25); "Wire and Fired" (Mar. 10); "Love Sunk" (Mar. 24); "Tong Tied" (Apr. 7); "A Bum Steer" (Apr. 21); "Gold Bricks" (May 5); "The Long Count" (May 19); "The Patent Medicine Kid" (June 2); "Stage Coached" (June 16); "The Rain Dropper" (June 30); "A Companionate Mirage" (July 14); "News Reeling" (Aug. 4); "Baby Feud" (Aug. 16); "Sea Sword" (Sept. 5); "The Show Vote" (Sept. 15); "The Phantom Trail" (Sept. 29); "Come Easy, Go Slow" (Oct. 15); "Beaches and Scream" (Oct. 29); "Nicked Nags" (Nov. 9); "Liar Bird" (Nov. 23); "Still Waters" (Dec. 7); and "Night Owls" (Dec. 22).

**1929:** "Cow Belles" (Jan. 5); "Hospitalities" (Jan. 18); "Reduced Weights" (Feb. 1); "Flying Yeast" (Feb. 15); "Vanishing Screams" (Mar. 1); "A Joint Affair" (Mar. 15); "Sheep Skinned" (Mar. 19); "The Lone Shark" (Apr. 12); "Golf Socks" (May 10); "Petting Larceny" (May 24); "Hat Aches" (June 7); "A Fur Peace" (June 22); "Auto Suggestion" (July 6); and "Sleepy Holler" (July 19).

## ◎ KRITERION KOMIC KARTOONS
Harry S. Palmer wrote, produced, directed and animated this series of comic drawn cartoons. *A Pyramid Film Company Production.*

**1915:** "No. 1" (Taft Playing Golf/Feb. 12); "No. 2" (Professor Dabbler/Feb. 15); "No. 3" (Hotel de Gink/Feb. 26); "No. 4" (Industrial Investigation/Mar. 5); "No. 5" (Mar. 19); and "No. 6" (Mar. 26).

## ◎ LAMPOONS
Burt Gillett animated and directed this series of 23 joke cartoons, redrawn from the magazines *Judge* and *Leslie's Weekly* and distributed to theaters from April 17 to October 9, 1920, for producer J.R. Bray. *A Bray Production released by Goldwyn Pictures.*

## ◎ LAUGH-O-GRAMS
Walt Disney, at age 18, produced a series of short films satirizing topics of the day. Subjects ranged from police corruption to ladies' fashions.

The first batch of cartoons were made while Disney worked days for the Kansas City Film Ad Company, which produced advertisements for local businesses that were shown in motion picture theaters in the area. The animation was primitive and crude in its style—figures were cut out of paper and animated—yet the short films were so successful that local theater owners clamored for more.

Disney sold the series to the owner of the Newman Theatre, located in town. (The series was appropriately renamed *Newman Laugh-O-Grams.*) Figuring demand for commercials was great enough in the Kansas City area, he then quit his job and set up his own company, Laugh-O-Grams Films, retaining the series' original name.

After raising enough capital, Disney proceeded to animate six cartoons, each modernized versions of standard fairy tales. In the process, he expanded his staff to include several animators, namely Hugh Harman and Walker Harman, Rudolf Ising, Carman "Max" Maxwell, Lorey Tague and Otto Walliman, in addition to Ub Iwerks, who served as Disney's partner on the early ad company Laugh-O-Grams.

While the first Newman Laugh-O-Grams were produced in 1920, when Walt was a member of the Kansas City Film Ad Company, titles and release dates of these cartoons do not exist. Titles are available only for films made after 1922.

*A scene from the Walt Disney Laugh-O-Grams adventures, "Puss in Boots" (1922).*

Bankruptcy forced Disney to close his Laugh-O-Grams Films studio, after which he moved to California and began anew, forming a new studio named after him. In 1926, he produced a brand-new Laugh-O-Grams cartoon, "Clara Cleans Her Teeth," combining live-action and animation, featuring the character Clara on the subject of dental hygiene. Released to theaters in 1927, Disney produced and directed the black-and-white cartoon, which Ub Iwerks animated, for Dr. Thomas B. McCrum. *Produced and directed by Walt Disney. A Laugh-O-Grams Film Production released by Leslie B. Mace and Walt Disney Studios.*

**Leslie B. Mace**

**1922:** "Little Red Riding Hood" (July 29); "The Four Musicians of Bremen" (Aug. 1); "Jack and the Beanstalk" (Sept. 4); "Goldie Locks and the Three Bears" (Oct. 5); "Puss In Boots" (Nov. 3); "Cinderella" (Dec. 6); "Tommy Tuckers Tooth" (Dec. 6).

(Note: Non-fairy-tale cartoons made during this period were "Tommy Tuckers Tooth" and, in 1923, "Martha" [A Song-O-Reel] and "Alice's Wonderland," a pilot for the Alice Comedies.)

**Walt Disney Studios**

**1927:** "Clara Cleans Her Teeth."

## ◎ LEAVES FROM LIFE

This series featured cartoons from *Life* magazine produced as animated sequences for magazine film series. *A Gaumont Company Production.*

**1917:** "No. 62" (July 5); "No. 63" (July 12/A Hasty Pudding); "No. 64" (July 19); "No. 65" (July 26); "No. 66" (Aug. 2); "No. 67" (Aug. 9/Not a Shadow of Doubt); "No. 68" (Aug. 16/The Absent Minded Dentist); "No. 69" (Aug. 23); "No. 70" (Aug. 30/The March of Science); "No. 71"; (Sept. 6/Fresh Advances); "No. 73" (Sept. 20/When a Big Car Goes By); "No. 74" (Sept. 27/So Easy); "No. 75" (Oct. 4); "No. 77" (Oct. 18); "No. 78" (Oct. 25); "No. 79" (Oct. 31/Had Your Missing Stock Panned Out); and "No. 80" (Nov. 8/It Was Not the Colic).

## ◎ LEDERER CARTOONS

Carl Francis Lederer wrote, produced, directed and animated this short-lived series of cartoons. *A Lubin/Vitagraph release.*

**1915:** "Bunny In Bunnyland" (May 1); "When They Were 21"; (May 27); "Ping Pong Woo" (June 26); and "Wandering Bill" (Sept. 9).

## ◎ LIFE CARTOON COMEDIES

Technical credits and production information could not be found for this series. *A Sherwood-Wadsworth Pictures Production released by Educational Pictures.*

**1926:** "Red Hot Rails" (Sept. 18); "Flaming Ice" (Sept. 25); "Missing Links" (Sept. 25); "The Yellow Pirate" (Oct. 5); "Cut Price Glory" (Oct. 11); "The Mighty Smithy" (Nov. 7); "Barnum Was Right" (Nov. 21); "Balloon Tried" (Dec. 5); and "Why Women Pay" (Dec. 16).

**1927:** "The Peaceful City" (Jan. 2); "Mike Wins a Medal" (Jan. 18); "Soft Soap" (Jan. 30); "A Heavy Date" (Feb. 8); "Hitting the Trail" (Feb. 23); "Local Talent" (Mar. 8); "Ruling the Rooster" (Mar. 27); "The Prince of Whales" (Apr. 10); "Racing Fever" (Apr. 24); and "North of Nowhere" (May 8).

## ◎ LITTLE EBONY

*An L.B. Cornwell Inc. Production.*

**1925:** "Ebony Cleans Up" (Oct. 15); "The Stowaway" (Nov. 1); and "A Drop in the Bucket" (Dec. 30).

**1926:** (An additional 23 cartoons in the series, the titles of which are unknown.)

## ◎ LITTLE JIMMY

Since its inception in mid-December 1915, Hearst's International Film Service planned to produce animated subjects for its weekly newsreel, the *Hearst-Vitagraph News Pictorial.* Animated cartoons based on Tom Powers's and George Herriman's characters were featured until April 1916, when other comic-strip artists joined the studio's lineup. One of the new faces who later joined the roster was star cartoonist Jimmy Swinnerton, who contributed this animated series shaped around the comic misadventures of a mischievous little boy. The series was based on Swinnerton's popular weekday strip, which he developed in 1905. *An International Films Production released by Hearst-Vitagraph.*

## ◎ MACDONO CARTOONS

J.J. MacManus and R.E. Donahue served as producers, directors, animators and writers of this animated series. *A MacDono Cartoons Inc. Production released by Affiliated Distributors and Mastodon Films.*

**Affiliated Distributors**

**1921:** "Mr. Ima Jonah's Home Brew" (June 4); and "Skipping the Pen" (June 4).

**Mastodon Films**

**1922:** "Burr's Novelty Review No. 1" (Mar. 1); "Burr's Novelty Review No. 2" (Apr. 1); "Burr's Novelty Review No. 3" (May 1); "Burr's Novelty Review No. 4" (June 1); "Burr's Novelty Review No. 5" (July 1); and "Burr's Novelty Review No. 6" (Aug. 1).

## ◎ MAUD THE MULE

William Randolph Hearst produced this series based on the original comic strip "And Her Name Was Maud" by Frederick Burr Opper for the *Hearst-Vitagraph News Pictorial. Directed by Gregory La Cava. An International Film Service Production released by Hearst Vitagraph.*

**1916:** "Poor Si Keeler" (Feb. 4); "A Quiet Day in the Country" (June 5); "Maud the Educated Mule" (July 3); and "Round and Round Again" (Oct. 2).

## ◎ MERKEL CARTOONS
Topical issues of the day were turned into animated commentaries in this series produced by Arno Merkel. Kenneth M. Anderson wrote, directed and animated the series. *A Merkel Film Company Production.*

**1918:** "Me and Gott" (Feb. 1); "Power Pro and Con" (Feb. 1); "The Girth of a Nation" (Apr. 1); "Truths on the War on Slang" (Apr. 1); "Oh What a Beautiful Dream" (Apr. 1); and "Hocking the Kaiser" (Apr. 1).

## ◎ MICKEY MOUSE
Loved by generations of fans the world over, Walt Disney's signature character, Mickey Mouse, was originally created by Disney as a silent cartoon star and he cast the likeable character in two black-and-white cartoon shorts, "Plane Crazy" and "The Gallopin' Gaucho," that Disney never released. Directed in 1928 by Disney's star animator, Ub Iwerks, and drawn by animators John Cannon, Les Clark, Norman Ferguson, Burton Gillett, Jack King, Ben Sharpsteen and Iwerks, in 1928, Disney instead made history by introducing Mickey in the first sound cartoon, "Steamboat Willie." He then added sound to both unreleased titles and distributed them to theaters almost a year later. *A Walt Disney Production released by Celebrity Productions.*

**1928:** "Plane Crazy" (Iwerks/May 15/released with sound in May 1929) and "The Gallopin' Gaucho" (Iwerks/Aug. 7/released with sound in May 1929).

## ◎ MILE-A-MINUTE MONTY
Animator Leon Searl wrote, produced and directed this series. *A Lubin Company Production released by Essanay Film Manufacturing Company.*

**1915:** "Mile-a-Minute Monty" (Aug. 25); "Monty the Missionary" (Sept. 14); and "Mile-a-Minute Monty" (Dec. 22).

## ◎ MILT GROSS
Along with George McManus and Sidney Smith, Milt Gross was another famous comic-strip artist who tried his hand at animation. In 1920, following his stint at Barré-Bowers Studios, where he animated the *Mutt and Jeff* series, Gross animated this short-lived series for J.R. Bray. The films burlesqued the foibles and frailties of people. *A Bray Productions released by Famous Players-Lasky Corporation.*

**1920:** "We'll Say They Do"; "Tumult in Toy Town"; "Frenchy Discovers America"; "Ginger Snaps"; and "The Cow Milker."

## ◎ M-IN-A CARTOONS
This series of cartoons featuring different themes was written, animated and directed by Harry S. Palmer and produced by David S. Horley. *An M-in-A Films (Made in America Films) Production.*

**1915:** "The Siege of Liege" (Jan. 9); "Great Americans" (Feb. 6); "The Dove of Peace" (Mar. 6); and "Doctor Monko" (May 29).

## ◎ MISS NANNY GOAT
An overzealous goat starred in this series produced by J.R. Bray. *A J.R. Bray Production released by Famous Players-Lasky Corporation.*

**1916:** "Miss Nanny Goat Becomes an Aviator" (Feb. 17); and "Miss Nanny Goat on the Rampage" (May 14).

**1917:** "Miss Nanny Goat at the Circus" (Apr. 6).

## ◎ MR. NOBODY HOLME
Former American newspaper cartoonist-turned animator Leon Searl, known for his work on the Krazy Kat silent cartoon series for William Randolph Hearst's International Film Service, animated this series based on Tom E. Powers's original comic strip of an everyday man dealing with everyday situations by using unusual methods, like starting a sluggish automobile with a stick of dynamite, for the *Hearst-Vitagraph News Pictorial* series. *Directed by Gregory La Cava. An International Film Service Production released by Hearst-Vitagraph.*

**1916:** "Mr. Nobody Holme in He Buys a Jitney" (Jan. 31) and "Adventures of Mr. Nobody Holme" (Mar. 20).

## ◎ MUTT AND JEFF
Archibald J. Mutt was first sketched by newspaper cartoonist Bud Fisher in 1907. Within a year partner Edgar Horace Jeff appeared. Mutt, a tall, lanky, mustachioed man, and Jeff, his short, wide-bristle-mustachioed, bald-headed partner replete with tuxedo hat and attire, entered films in 1916.

The series reached the screen thanks in part to Raoul Barré, a French Canadian artist who turned to animation following a successful career as a newspaper cartoonist. Barré joined forces with another cartoonist, Charles Bowers, who had acquired the screen rights to the Mutt and Jeff strip. Bowers was in charge of the Mutt and Jeff Company, which Fisher launched to handle production of the cartoon shorts. Distribution of these early films was handled by Fox Films.

Oddly, neither Barré's nor Bowers's name was ever mentioned in the screen credits of these films. Fisher denied them credit, wanting only his name to appear in connection with the characters.

World War I served as a primary backdrop for early series' story lines, pairing off the characters in spy invasions and other entanglements with the Germans. Additional stories dealt with typical daily situations—working as hospital orderlies to running a pawn shop—but with catastrophic results.

Staff animators completed these films at a rate of one a week. So, consequently, not every cartoon made its mark. Animator Dick Huemer remarked in an interview: "Very often they [theater managers] didn't even run the cartoons. If the exhibitor hated them, he didn't run them. That's how interested they were."

Gag development suffered with cartoons being cranked out so quickly. "We used to look at our own work and laugh like hell. We thought it was great. But in the theaters they didn't," said Huemer.

In 1921, production of the series was continued under the Jefferson Film Corporation banner, headed by animator Dick Friel. At that time, Bowers left the series, only to rejoin it four years later to direct a new series of cartoon shorts for Associated Animators, founded by pioneer animator Burt Gillett, Dick Huemer, Ben Harrison and Manny Gould, who revived the series, producing 13 films a year. Short Films Syndicate reportedly distributed the series through 1928, ending production before the arrival of sound and becoming the longest running theatrical silent cartoon series second only to *Krazy Kat*. Known titles listed below are through 1926. *Directed by Bud Fisher. A Pathé Freres/Mutt and Jeff Films/Bud Fisher Film Corporation/Jefferson Film Corporation/Associated Animators production released by Pathé Film Exchange, Celebrated Players, Fox Film Corporation and Short Film Syndicate.*

*Pathé Film Exchange*

**1913:** "Mutt and Jeff" (Feb. 10); "Mutt and Jeff" (Feb. 17); "Mutt and Jeff" (Feb. 24); "Mutt and Jeff at Sea" (Part 1) (Mar. 3); "Mutt and Jeff at Sea" (Part 2) (Mar. 10); "Mutt and Jeff in

Constantinople" (Mar. 17); "The Matrimonial Agency" (Mar. 24); "Mutt and Jeff in Turkey" (Mar. 31); "Mutt's Moneymaking Scheme" (Apr. 7); "The Sultan's Harem" (Apr. 14); "Mutt and Jeff in Mexico" (Apr. 21); "The Sandstorm" (Apr. 28); "Mutt Puts One Over" (May 5); "Mutt and Jeff" (May 12); "Mutt and Jeff" (May 19); "Pickaninni's G-String" (May 26); "Mutt and Jeff" (June 2); "Baseball" (June 9); "The California Alien Land Law" (June 23); "The Merry Milkmaid" (June 30); "The Ball Game" (July 7); "Mutt and Jeff" (July 24); "Mutt's Marriage" (Aug. 4); "Johnny Reb's Wooden Leg" (Aug. 11); "A Substitute for Peroxide" (Aug. 18); "Mutt and Jeff" (Aug. 25); "The Hypnotist" (Sept. 1); "The Mexican Problem" (Sept. 8); "Mutt and Jeff" (Sept. 29); "Mutt and Jeff" (Oct. 13); "Mutt and Jeff" (Oct. 20); "Mutt and Jeff" (Oct. 27); "Mutt and Jeff" (Oct. 30); "Mutt and Jeff" (Nov. 13); "Whadya Mean You're Contended" (Nov. 20); and "Mutt and Jeff" (Dec. 4).

### Celebrated Players

**1916:** "Jeff's Toothache" (Apr. 1); "Mutt and Jeff in the Submarine" (Apr. 8); "The Indestructible Hats" (Aug. 12); "Cramps"; "The Promoters"; "Two for Hire"; "The Dog Pound"; "The Hock Shop"; and "Wall Street."

**1917:** "The Submarine Chasers" (July 9); "The Cheese Tamers"; "Cows and Caws"; "The Janitors"; "A Chemical Calamity"; "The Prospectors"; "The Bell Hops"; "In the Theatrical Business"; "The Boarding House"; "The Chamber of Horrors"; "A Day in Camp"; "A Dog's Life"; "The Interpreters"; "Preparedness"; and "Revenge Is Sweet."

### Fox Film Corporation

**1918:** "The Decoy" (Mar. 24); "Back to the Balkans" (Mar. 31); "The Leak" (Apr. 7); "Freight Investigation" (Apr. 14); "On Ice" (Apr. 21); "Helping McAdoo" (Apr. 28); "A Fisherless Cartoon" (May 5); "Occultism" (May 12); "Superintendents" (May 19); "Tonsorial Artists" (May 26); "The Tale of a Pig" (June 2); "Hospital Orderlies" (June 9); "Life Savers" (June 16); "Meeting Theda Bara" (June 23); "The Seventy-Mile Gun" (June 30); "The Burglar Alarm" (July 7); "The Extra-Quick Lunch" (July 14); "Hunting the U-Boats" (July 21); "Hotel De Mutt" (July 28); "Joining the Tanks" (Aug. 4); "An Ace and a Joker" (Aug. 11); "Landing a Spy" (Aug. 18); "Efficiency" (Aug. 25); "The Accident Attorney" (Sept. 1); "At the Front" (Sept. 8); "To the Rescue" (Sept. 15); "The Kaiser's New Dentist" (Sept. 22); "Bulling the Bolshevik" (Sept. 29); "Our Four Days in Germany" (Oct. 6); "The Side Show" (Oct. 13); "A Lot of Bull" (Nov. 10); "The Doughboy" (Nov. 17); "Around the World in Nine Minutes" (Nov. 24); "Pot Luck in the Army" (Dec. 1); "Hitting the High Sports" (Dec. 15); "The Draft Board" (Dec. 22); and "Throwing the Bull" (Dec. 29).

**1919:** "The Lion Tamers" (Jan. 5); "Here and There" (Jan. 19); "The Hula Hula Cabaret" (Jan. 19); "Dog-Gone Tough Luck" (Jan. 26); "Landing an Heiress" (Feb. 2); "The Bearded Lady" (Feb. 9); "500 Miles on a Gallon of Gas" (Feb. 16); "The Pousse Cafe" (Feb. 25); "Fireman Save My Child" (Mar. 2); "Wild Waves and Angry Woman" (Mar. 9); "William Hohenzollern Sausage Maker" (Mar. 16); "Out an' in Again" (Mar. 23); "The Cow's Husband" (Mar. 30); "Mutt the Mutt Trainer" (Apr. 6); "Subbing for Tom Mix" (Apr. 13); "Pigtails and Peaches" (Apr. 20); "Seeing Things" (Apr. 27); "The Cave Man's Bride" (May 4); "Sir Sidney" (May 11); "Left at the Post" (May 18); "The Shell Game" (May 25); "Oh Teacher" (June 1); "Hands Up" (June 15); "Sweet Papa" (June 15); "Pets and Pests" (June 22); "A Prize Fight" (June 29);

"Look Pleasant Please" (July 6); "Downstairs and Up" (July 13); "A Tropical Eggs-pedition" (July 20); "West Is East" (July 27); "Sound Your 'A'" (Aug. 24); "Hard Lions" (Aug. 31); "Mutt and Jeff in Paris" (Sept. 7); "Mutt and Jeff in Switzerland" (Sept. 7); "All That Glitters Is Not Goldfish" (Sept. 14); "Everybody's Doing It" (Sept. 21); "Mutt and Jeff in Spain" (Sept. 28); "The Honest Book Agent" (Oct. 5); "Bound in Spaghetti" (Oct. 19); "In the Money" (Oct. 26); "The Window Cleaners" (Nov. 2); "Confessions of a Telephone Girl" (Nov. 9); "The Plumbers" (Nov. 16); "The Chambermaid's Revenge" (Nov. 23); "Why Mutt Left the Village" (Nov. 30); "Cutting Out His Nonsense" (Dec. 7); "For Bitter or for Verse" (Dec. 14); "He Ain't Done Right by Our Nell" (Dec. 21); and "Another Man's Wife" (Dec. 28).

**1920:** "A Glutton for Punishment" (Jan.); "His Musical Soup" (Jan.); "A Rose by Any Other Name" (Jan.); "Mutt and Jeff in Iceland" (Jan.); "Fisherman's Luck" (Jan.); "The Latest in Underwear" (Jan.); "On Strike" (Jan.); "Shaking the Shimmy" (Jan.); "The Rum Runners" (Jan.); "The Berth of a Nation" (Jan.); "Mutt and Jeff's Nooze Weekly" (Jan.); "Pretzel Farming" (Jan.); "I'm Ringing Your Party" (Feb.); "Fishing" (Feb.); "Dead Eye Jeff" (Feb.); "The Soul Violin" (Feb.); "The Mint Spy" (Feb.); "The Pawnbrokers" (Feb.); "The Chemists" (Feb.); "Putting on the Dog" (Feb.); "The Plumbers" (Feb.); "The Great Pickle Robbery" (Mar.); "The Price of a Good Sneeze" (Mar.); "The Chewing Gum Industry" (Mar.); "Hula Hula Town" (Mar.); "The Beautiful Model" (Mar.); "The Honest Jockey" (Mar.); "The Bicycle Race" (Apr.); "The Bowling Alley" (Apr.); "Nothing But Girls" (Apr.); "The Private Detectives" (Apr.); "The Wrestlers" (Apr.); "The Paper Hangers" (Apr.); "The Toy Makers" (May); "The Tango Dancers" (May); "One Round Jeff" (May); "A Trip to Mars" (May); "Three Raisins and a Cake of Yeast" (June); "Departed Spirits" (June); "The Mystery of Galvanized Iron Ash Can" (June); "The Breakfast Food Industry" (June); "The Bare Idea" (July); "The Merry Cafe" (Aug.); "In Wrong" (Aug.); "Hot Dogs" (Aug.); "The Politicians" (Aug.); "The Yacht Race" (Aug.); "The Cowpunchers" (Sept.); "Home Sweet Home" (Sept.); "Napoleon" (Sept.); "The Song Birds" (Sept.); "The Tailor Shop" (Oct.); "The Brave Toreador" (Oct.); "The High Cost of Living" (Oct.); "Flapjacks" (Oct.); "The League of Nations" (Oct.); "A Tightrope Romance" (Oct.); "Farm Efficiency" (Nov.); "The Medicine Man" (Nov.); "Home Brew" (Nov.); "Gum Shoe Work" (Nov.); "A Hard Luck Santa Claus" (Nov.); "All Stuck Up" (Nov.); "Sherlock Hawkshaw and Company" (Dec.); "The North Woods" (Dec.); "On the Hop" (Dec.); "The Papoose" (Dec.); "The Hypnotist" (Dec.); "Cleopatra" (Dec.); and "The Parlor Bolshevist" (Dec.).

**1921:** "The Lion Hunters" (Feb. 26); "The Ventriloquist" (Feb. 27); "Dr. Killjoy" (Mar. 18); "Factory to Consumer" (Mar. 20); "A Crazy Idea" (Apr.); "The Naturalists" (Apr. 17); "Mademoiselle Fifi" (May 7); "Gathering Coconuts" (May 7); "It's a Bear" (May 7); "The Far North" (May 7); "The Vacuum Cleaner" (May 7); "A Hard Shell Game" (May 14); "A Rare Bird" (May 21); "Flivvering" (May 21); "The Lion Hunters" (June 11); "The Glue Factory" (June 11); "Cold Tea" (June 11); "The Gusher" (June 12); "Watering the Elephants" (June 26); "A Crazy Idea" (July); "The Far East" (July); "Training Woodpeckers" (Aug.); "A Shocking Idea" (Aug.); "Touring" (Aug.); "Darkest Africa" (Sept. 17); "Not Wedded But A Wife" (Sept. 17); "Crows and Scarecrows" (Sept. 17); "The Painter's Frolic" (Sept. 17); "The Stampede" (Sept. 17); "The Tong Sandwich" (Sept. 17); "Shadowed" (Oct. 18); "The Turkish Bath" (Oct. 18); "The Village Cutups" (Nov. 26); "A Messy Christmas" (Nov. 26); "Fast Freight" (Nov. 26); "The

Stolen Snooze" (Dec. 11); "Getting Ahead" (Dec. 18); and "Bony Parts" (Dec. 25).

**1922:** "A Ghostly Wallop" (Jan.); "Beside the Cider" (Jan.); "Long Live the King" (Jan.); "The Last Laugh" (Jan.); "The Hole Cheese" (Feb.); "The Phoney Focus" (Feb.); "The Crystal Gazer" (Feb.); "Stuck in the Mud" (Feb.); "The Last Shot" (Feb. 27); "The Cashier" (Mar.); "Any Ice Today" (Mar.); "Too Much Soap" (Mar. 12); "Hoot Mon" (Apr.); "Golfing" (Apr.); "Tin Foiled" (Apr.); "Around the Pyramids" (Apr.); "Getting Even" (Apr.); "Hop, Skip and Jump" (May 15); "Modern Fishing" (May); "Hither and Thither" (May); "Court Plastered" (Aug.); "Falls Ahead" (Aug.); "Riding the Goat" (Sept. 17); "The Fallen Archers" (Oct. 1); "Cold Turkey" (Oct. 8); "The Wishing Duck" (Nov. 12); "Bumps and Things" (Nov. 26); "Nearing the End" (Dec. 10); "The Chewing Gum Industry" (Dec. 23); and "Gym Jams" (Dec. 30).

**1923:** "Down in Dixie" (Feb. 4).

***Short Film Syndicate***

**1925:** "Accidents Won't Happen" (Aug.); "Soda Clerks" (Aug.); "Invisible Revenge" (Sept.); "Where Am I?" (Sept.); "The Bear Facts" (Oct.); "Mixing in Mexico" (Oct. 17); "All at Sea" (Nov. 14); "Oceans of Trouble" (Nov.); "Thou Shalt Not Pass" (Dec. 5); and "A Link Missing" (Dec. 12).

**1926:** "Bombs and Boobs" (Jan.); "On Thin Ice" (Feb. 20); "When Hell Froze Over" (Mar. 6); "Westward Whoa!" (Apr.); "Skating Instructors"; "Slick Sleuths" (Aug. 1); "Ups and Downs" (Aug. 15); "Playing with Fire" (Sept. 1); "Dog Gone" (Sept. 15); "The Big Swim" (Oct. 1); "Mummy o' Mine" (Oct. 15); "A Roman Scandal" (Nov. 1); "Alona of the South Seas" (Nov. 15); and "The Globe Trotters" (Dec. 1).

## ◎ NERVY NAT

Animator Pat Sullivan of *Felix the Cat* fame produced and animated this 1916 screen adaptation of American cartoonist/illustrator James Montgomery Flagg's bulbous-nosed tramp who first appeared as a comic strip in national magazines. Not as innocent as Happy Hooligan or Charlie Chaplin, Nat's adventures involved frequent encounters with the law and others who fell prey to his well-planned schemes. *A Pat Sullivan Cartoon release.*

**1916:** "Nervy Nat Has His Fortune Told" (Dec. 24).

## ◎ THE NEWLYWEDS

French pioneer animator Emile Cohl animated and directed this series—the first with a recurring cast of characters and Cohl's only American cartoon series—based on the popular comic strip by George McManus. While completing production of each film between March 1913 and January 1914, the films were released irregularly through July 1915. *An Éclair Films Production.*

**1913:** "When He Wants a Dog, He Wants a Dog" (Mar. 16).

**1914:** "He Does Not Care to Be Photographed" (Jan. 17); "He Never Objects to Noise" (Feb.); and "He Only Wanted to Play with Dodo" (Feb.).

**1915:** "Business Must Not Interfere" (Mar. 15); "He Wants What He Wants When He Wants It" (Mar. 29); "Poor Little Chap He Was Only Dreaming" (Apr. 20); "He Loves to Watch the Flight of Time" (May 18); "He Ruins His Family's Reputation" (June 1); "He Slept Well" (June 15); "He Was Not Ill, Only Unhappy" (June 19); "It Is Hard to Please Him but It Is Worth It" (July 13); and "He Poses for His Portrait" (July 27).

## ◎ NEWSLAFFS

William C. Nolan, who was head animator of the *Felix the Cat* series, wrote, produced, directed and animated this series of humorous news commentaries between 1927 and 1928. *A Film Booking Offices release.*

**1927:** "No. 1"; (Sept. 4); "No. 2" (Sept. 18); "No. 3" (Oct. 16); "No. 5" (Oct. 30); "No. 6" (Nov. 13); "No. 7" (Nov. 27); "No. 8" (Dec. 11); and "No. 9" (Dec. 25).

**1928:** "No. 10" (Jan. 8); "No. 11" (Jan.); "No. 12" (Feb. 5); "No. 13" (Feb. 19); "No. 14" (Mar. 2); "No. 15" (Mar. 2); "No. 16" (Mar. 5); "No. 17" (Apr. 17); "No. 18" (Apr. 30); "No. 19" (May 14); "No. 20" (May 28); "No. 21"; (June 11); "No. 22" (June 25); "No. 23" (July 9); and "No. 24" (July 23).

## ◎ NORBIG CARTOONS

Joseph Cammer served as producer and animator of this series, which premiered in 1915. *A Norbig Company Production released by Powers-Universal.*

**1915:** "Professor Wiseguy's Trip to the Moon" (June 6).

## ◎ OSWALD THE LUCKY RABBIT

The floppy-eared rabbit resembled Walt Disney's Mickey Mouse in attire, wearing short pants. Disney took on the series when his distributor suggested dropping the Alice series and launching something new instead.

The Oswald series became an immediate success, with producer Charles Mintz and his brother-in-law, George Winkler, releasing the cartoons through Universal. The films paid big dividends for Disney, too. He earned as much as $2,500 a short.

Ub Iwerks assisted Walt on the animation, along with several other young animation stalwarts, including Isadore "Friz" Freleng, who replaced Rollin "Ham" Hamilton, later a prominent Warner Bros. animator. Story ideas were derived from "bull sessions" convened by Disney, during which time members of his animation staff made suggestions for gags and ideas to integrate into story lines.

After the second year of production, Disney felt certain he could negotiate a raise during contract negotiations with Mintz. Much to his surprise, Mintz had something else in mind. He wanted to reduce Disney's box-office share from each short to

*Walt Disney's Oswald the Rabbit (right) gallops ahead in a scene from "Ride 'Em Plowboy" (1928). © Walt Disney Productions*

$1,800 a reel! He too realized the tremendous profit potential of the series and was determined to keep a larger percentage for himself. As it turned out, Disney found Mintz's offer completely unacceptable and rejected the proposal even though Mintz threatened to take the series away from him.

Mintz kept his word. He eventually hired animator Walter Lantz to supervise a new Oswald series. Dejected, Disney returned with an even bigger hit—a cartoon series featuring a lovable mouse named Mickey. *Directed by Walt Disney. A Walt Disney Production released by Universal Pictures.*

**1927:** "Poor Papa" (June 11); "Trolley Troubles" (July 4); "Oh, Teacher!" (Sept. 19); "The Mechanical Cow" (Oct. 3); "Great Guns" (Oct. 17); "All Wet" (Oct. 31); "The Ocean Hop" (Nov. 14); "The Banker's Daughter" (Nov. 28); "Empty Socks" (Dec. 12); and "Rickety Gin" (Dec. 26).

**1928:** "Harem Scarem" (Jan. 9); "Neck 'n Neck" (Jan. 23); "The Ol' Swimmin' 'Ole" (Feb. 6); "Africa Before Dark" (Feb. 20); "Rival Romeos" (Mar. 5); "Bright Lights" (Mar. 19); "Sagebrush Sadie" (Apr. 2); "Ride 'Em Plow Boy" (Apr. 16); "Ozzie of the Mounted" (Apr. 30); "Hungry Hoboes" (May 14); "Sky Scrappers" (May 14); "Oh, What a Knight" (May 28); "The Fox Chase" (June 25) and "Tall Timber" (July 9).

## ◎ OTTO LUCK

J. R. Bray produced this short-lived series following the adventures of a romantic young man who persistently creates the impression that there is a screw loose in his mental machinery. *Written, directed and animated by Wallace A. Carlson. A Bray Production released by Famous Players-Lasky Corporation.*

**1915:** "Otto Luck in the Movies" (June 4); "Otto Luck to the Rescue" (June 25); "Otto Luck and the Ruby of Razmataz" (July 16); and "Otto Luck's Flivvered Romance" (Aug. 13).

## ◎ OUT OF THE INKWELL

Animator Max Fleischer created this series starring Koko the Clown (the name was not hyphenated at this time), one of the first to combine live action and animation. The technique was accomplished through a process called Rotoscope, which Max and brother Dave Fleischer developed for the screen.

The Fleischers invented the technique after being unsatisfied with the results of other cartoonists' animated films. They first employed this new technical marvel in the pilot film that launched the series. Rotoscope was simply a drawing board and film projector combined, enabling animators to retrace frame by frame projected film images of human characters to achieve lifelike animation.

The pilot resulted in the birth of Koko, actually Dave Fleischer dressed in a puffy-sleeved clown suit with large white buttons. He performed somersaults and other acrobatics before the camera, then exaggerated them in the final animation.

This initial film, appropriately called *Out of the Inkwell,* was so well received that Max Fleischer decided to produce additional films right away. He sold cartoon magnate J. R. Bray on the idea of handling distribution, and he animated one Inkwell cartoon a month. The films appeared as part of Bray's *Paramount-Bray Pictograph* screen magazine.

Response to the cartoons was overwhelming to say the least. As one critic for the *New York Times* noted: "One's first reflection after seeing this bit of work is, 'Why doesn't Mr. Fleischer do more?'"

Such raves were not uncommon for the series. Koko enthralled audiences with his fluid movement, and the novelty of blending live footage with animation saved these films. The stock opening

*Animator Dave Fleischer, dressed in a clown suit, was actually Koko the Clown, filmed live and transposed into animated sketchings for the Fleischer's* Out of the Inkwell *series.*

had Koko materialize out of a cartoonist's inkwell or pen point, only to harrass the animator before being placed in some type of animated situation. The animator seen in the opening sequence was Max Fleischer, who played both Koko's master and nemesis.

By 1923 Max Fleischer stopped animating the series and brother Dave took over the series direction. Some of the animators who worked on the series included Burt Gillett, Dick Huemer, Mannie Davis, Ben Sharpensteen and Roland "Doc" Crandall. Between Inkwell films, Koko also starred in sing-a-long cartoons called *Koko Songs,* animated versions using a bouncing ball set to popular tunes of the day. "My Bonnie September" was the first production under this series banner in 1925. *A Bray and Out of the Inkwell Films Production released by Warner Bros., Paramount, Rodner Productions, Winkler Pictures and Red Seal Pictures.*

***Paramount-Bray Pictographs***

**1916:** "Out of the Inkwell."

**1918:** "Experiment No. 1 (June 10)."

*Goldwyn-Bray Pictographs*

**1919:** "Experiment No. 2" (Mar. 5); "Experiment No. 3" (Apr. 2); "The Clown's Pup" (Aug. 30); "The Tantalizing Fly" (Oct. 4); and "Slides" (Dec. 3).

**1920:** "The Boxing Kangaroo" (Feb. 2); "The Chinaman" (Mar. 19); "The Circus" (May 6); "The Ouija Board" (June 4); "The Clown's Little Brother" (July 6); "Poker" (Oct. 2); "Perpetual Motion" (Oct. 2); and "The Restaurant" (Nov. 6).

**1921:** "Cartoonland" (Feb. 2); and "The Automobile Ride" (June 20).

*Out of the Inkwell Films Inc.*

**1921:** "Modelling" (Oct.); "Fishing" (Nov. 21); and "Invisible Ink" (Dec. 3).

**1922:** (released by Warner Brothers); "The Fish" (Jan. 7); "The Dresden Doll" (Feb. 7); and "The Mosquito" (Mar. 6).

**1922:** (released by Winkler Pictures): "Bubbles" (Apr. 20); "Flies" (May); "Pay Day" (July 8); "The Hypnotist" (July 26); "The Challenge" (Aug. 29); "The Show" (Sept. 21); "The Reunion" (Oct. 27); "The Birthday" (Nov. 4); and "Jumping Beans" (Dec. 15).

**1923:** (released by Rodner Productions): "Modeling" (Feb. 3); "Surprise" (Mar. 15); "The Puzzle" (Apr. 15); "Trapped" (May 15); "The Battle" (July 1); "False Alarm" (Aug. 1); "Balloons" (Sept. 1); "The Fortune Teller" (Oct. 1); "Shadows" (Nov. 1); and "Bed Time" (Dec. 1).

**1924:** (released by Red Seal Pictures): "The Laundry" (Jan. 1); "Masquerade" (Feb. 1); "The Cartoon Factory" (Feb. 21); "Mother Gooseland" (Mar. 21); "A Trip to Mars" (Apr. 1); "A Stitch in Time" (May 1); "Clay Town" (May 28); "The Runaway" (June 25); "Vacation" (July 23); "Vaudeville" (Aug. 20); "League of Nations" (Sept. 17); "Sparring Partners" (Oct.); and "The Cure" (Dec. 13).

**1925:** "Koko the Hot Shot" (Jan.); "Koko the Barber" (Feb. 25); "Big Chief Koko" (Mar. 2); "The Storm" (Mar. 21); "Koko Trains 'Em" (May 9); "Koko Sees Spooks" (June 13); "Koko Celebrates the Fourth" (July 4); "Koko Nuts" (Sept. 5); "Koko on the Run" (Sept. 26); "Koko Packs 'Em" (Oct. 17); "Koko Eats" (Nov. 15); "Koko's Thanksgiving" (Nov. 21); "Koko Steps Out" (Nov. 21); and "Koko in Toyland" (Dec. 12).

**1926:** "Koko's Paradise" (Feb. 27); "Koko Baffles the Bulls" (Mar. 6); "It's the Cats" (May 1); "Koko at the Circus" (May 1); "Toot Toot" (June 5); "Koko Hot After It" (June 12); "The Fadeaway" (Sept. 1); "Koko's Queen" (Oct. 1); "Koko Kidnapped" (Oct.); "Koko the Convict" (Nov. 1); and "Koko Gets Egg-Cited" (Dec. 1).

**1927:** "Koko Back Tracks" (Jan. 1); "Koko Makes 'em Laugh" (Feb. 10); "Koko in 1999" (Mar. 10); "Koko the Kavalier" (Apr. 10); and "Koko Needles the Boss" (May 10).

## ◎ PARAMOUNT-BRAY CARTOONS

In association with Paramount, which served as its distributor, J.R. Bray produced various popular silent cartoons under the *Paramount-Bray Cartoons* banner, including Bray's acclaimed *Colonel Heeza Liar* series, which he also directed, and many other cartoon favorites of the mid-1900s. Among them were C.T. Anderson's *Police Dog,* Earl Hurd's Bobby Bumps, C. Allen Gilbert's *Inbad the Sailor,* Frank Moser's *Kid Casey the Champion,* Frank Moser and Raoul Barre's *Joy and Glooms,* Clarence Rigby's *Miss Nanny Goat,*

Paul Terry's *Farmer Al Falfa,* plus numerous others directed by animators Leighton Budd, L.M. Glackens and A.D. Reed. *A Bray Production released by Paramount Pictures.*

**1916:** "Col. Heeza Liar's Waterloo" (Bray/Jan. 6); "Haddem Baad's Elopement" (Glackens/Jan. 13); "Inbad the Sailor" (Gilbert/Jan. 20); "The Police Dog on the Wire" (Anderson/Jan. 27); "Farmer Al Falfa's Catastrophe" (Terry/Feb. 3); "Haunts for Rent" (Gilbert/Feb. 10); "Miss Nanny Goat Becomes an Aviator" (Rigby/Feb. 17); "Bobby Bumps and His Pointer Pup" (Hurd/Feb. 24); "How Dizzy Joe Go to Heaven" (Glackens/Mar. 3); "Col. Heeza Liar and the Pirates" (Bray/Mar. 3); "Farmer Al Falfa Invents a New Kite" (Terry/Mar. 13); "The Chess Queen" (Gilbert/Mar. 10); "Inbad the Sailor Gets into Deep Water" (Gilbert/Mar. 26); "The Police Dog Turns Nurse" (Anderson/Apr. 2); "The Stone Age Roost Robber" (Glackens/Apr. 9); "Farmer Al Falfa's Scientific Diary" (Terry/Apr. 16); "Col. Heeza Liar Wins the Pennant" (Bray/Apr. 23); "Bobby Bumps and His Goatmobile" (Hurd/Apr. 30); "The Police Dog in the Park" (Anderson/May 6); "Miss Nanny Goat on the Rampage" (Rigby/May 14); "Col. Heeza Liar Captures Villa" (Bray/May 20); "Bobby Bumps Goes Fishing" (Hurd/May 26); "Kid Casey the Champion" (Moser/June 10); "Col. Heeza Liar and the Bandits" (Bray/June 17); "Bobby Bumps and the Fly Swatter" (Hurd/June 26); "Farmer Al Falfa's Watermelon Patch" (June 29); "The Wild and Woolly West" (Reed/July 7); "Col. Heeza Liar's Courtship" (Bray/July 17); "Bobby Bumps' Detective Story" (Hurd/July 22); "In Lunyland" (Budd/July 28); "Farmer Al Falfa's Egg-Citement" (Terry/Aug. 4); "Bobby Bumps Loses His Pup" (Hurd/Aug. 11); "Col. Heeza Liar Plays Hamlet" (Bray/Aug. 18); "Farmer Al Falfa's Revenge" (Terry/Aug. 25); "Bobby Bumps and the Stork" (Hurd/Sept. 1); "Col. Heeza Liar's Bachelor Quarters" (Bray/Sept. 9); "Farmer Al Falfa's Wolfhound" (Terry/Sept. 16); "Bobby Bumps Starts a Lodge" (Hurd/Sept. 21); "O.U. Rooster" (Bray/Sept. 27); "Farmer Al Falfa Sees New York" (Terry/Oct. 9); "Col. Heeza Liar Gets Married" (Bray/Oct. 17); "Bobby Bumps Queers the Choir" (Hurd/Oct. 23); "Greenland's Icy Mountains" (Bray/Oct. 27); "Farmer Al Falfa's Prune Plantation" (Terry/Nov. 3); "Bobby Bumps at the Circus" (Hurd/Nov. 11); "Col. Heeza Liar Hobo" (Bray/Nov. 17); "What Happened to Willie" (Glackens/Nov. 25); "Farmer Al Falfa's Blind Pig" (Terry/Dec. 1); "Bobby Bumps Helps Out a Book Agent" (Hurd/Dec. 11); "Percy Brains He Has Nix" (Greening/Dec. 18); and "Jack the Giant Killer" (Glackens/Dec. 23).

## ◎ PARAMOUNT-BRAY PICTOGRAPHS

Producer-director John R. Bray launched this popular magazine series in 1917 in association with Paramount, which distributed it to theaters. The series included many animated favorites of the silent era, among them Bray's *Colonel Heeza Liar,* Wallace Carlson's *Dreamy Dud, Goodrich Dirt* and *Otto Luck,* Max Fleischer's *Out of the Inkwell,* F.M. Follet's *Quacky Doodles,* L.M. Glackens's *Von Loon,* Earl Hurd's *Bobby Bumps,* Clarence Rigby's *Miss Nanny Goat* and Sam Lloyd's *Picto Puzzles* cartoons, many of whose creators also directed them as well. The series continued under the new title of *Goldwyn-Bray Pictograph. A Bray Production released by Paramount.*

**1917:** "Col. Heeza Liar on the Jump" (Bray/Feb. 4); "Bobby Bumps in the Great Divide" (Hurd/Feb. 11); "Quacky Doodles' Picnic" (Follett/Feb. 18); "Col. Heeza Liar Detective" (Bray/Feb. 25); "Bobby Bumps Adopts a Turtle" (Hurd/Mar. 5); "Quacky Doodles' Food Crisis" (Follett/Mar. 12); "Col. Heeza Liar Spy Dodger" (Bray/Mar. 19); "Bobby Bumps Office Boy" (Hurd/Mar. 26); "Quacky Doodles as the Early Bird" (Mar. 28); "Picto Puzzles

No. 1" (Lloyd/Apr. 2); "Miss Nanny Goat at the Circus" (Rigby/Apr. 9); "Bobby Bumps Outwits the Dog Catcher" (Hurd/Apr. 16); "Picto Puzzles No. 2" (Lloyd/Apr. 16); "Quacky Doodles Soldiering for Fair" (Follett/Apr. 23); Stung (Budd/Apr. 30); "Bobby Bumps Volunteers" (Hurd/May 7); "The Submarine Mine-Layer" (Leventhal/May 14); "Picto Puzzles No. 3" (Lloyd/May 14); "The Awakening of America" (May 21); "Picto Puzzles No. 4" (Lloyd/May 21); "Bobby Bumps Daylight Camper" (Hurd/May 28); "Otto Luck in the Movies" (Carlson/June 4); "Traveling Forts" (Leventhal/June 11); "Evolution of the Dachshund" (Budd/June 11); "Bobby Bumps Submarine Chaser" (Hurd/June 18); "Otto Luck to the Rescue" (Carlson/June 25); "Mechanical Operation of British Tanks" (Leventhal/July 2); "Picto Puzzles No. 5" (Lloyd/July 2); "Bobby Bumps' Fourth" (Hurd/July 9); "Otto Luck and Ruby Razmataz" (Carlson/July 16); "Sic 'Em Cat" (Budd/July 23); "Fiske Torpedo Plane" (Leventhal/July 30); "Picto Puzzles No. 6" (Lloyd/July 30); "Bobby Bumps' Amusement Park" (Hurd/Aug. 6); "Otto Luck's Flivvered Romance" (Carlson/Aug. 13); "Uncle Sam's Dinner Party" (Budd/Aug. 20); "Bobby Bumps Surf Rider" (Hurd/Aug. 27); "Picto Puzzles No. 7" (Lloyd/Aug. 27); "Goodrich Dirt among the Beach Nuts" (Carlson/Sept. 13); "Quacky Doodles Signs the Pledge" (Follett/Sept. 10); "Bobby Bumps Starts for School" (Hurd/Sept. 17); "A Submarine Destroyer" (Leventhal/Sept. 24); "Goodrich Dirt Lunch Detective" (Carlson/Oct. 1); "Bobby Bumps' World Series" (Hurd/Oct. 8); "Quacky Doodles the Cheater" (Follett/Oct. 15); "The Aeroplane Machine Gun" (Leventhal/Oct. 22); "Bobby Bumps, Chef" (Hurd/Oct. 29); "Goodrich Dirt at the Training Camp" (Carlson/Nov. 5); "Putting Volcanoes to Work" (Leventhal/Nov. 12); "Bobby Bumps and Fido's Birthday Party" (Hurd/Nov. 19); "The Gasoline Engine" (Leventhal/Nov. 26); "Goodrich Dirt at the Amateur Show" (Carlson/Dec. 3); "Bobby Bumps Early Shopper" (Hurd/Dec. 10); "Freak Parents: The Balloon R.R." (Leventhal/Dec. 17); and "Goodrich Dirt and the $1,000 Reward" (Carlson/Dec. 24).

**1918:** "Goodrich Dirt and the Duke De Whatanob" (Carlson/Jan. 7); "The Panama Canal" (Leventhal/Jan. 14); "Bobby Bumps' Disappearing Gun" (Hurd/Jan. 21); "The Peril of Prussianism" (Budd/Jan. 28); "Putting Fritz on the Water Wagon" (Budd/Feb. 4); "Goodrich Dirt's Bear Facts" (Carlson/Feb. 11); "The Rudiments of Flying" (Leventhal/Feb. 18); "Bobby Bumps at the Dentist" (Hurd/Feb. 25); "The Pinkerton Pup's Portrait" (Anderson/Mar. 4); "The Torpedo, Hornet of the Sea" (Leventhal/Mar. 11); "Goodrich Dirt in the Barber Business" (Carlson/Mar. 18); "Bobby Bumps' Fight" (Hurd/Mar. 24); "Me Und Gott" (Glackens/Apr. 1); "Goodrich Dirt Mat Artist" (Carlson/Apr. 8); "Bobby Bumps on the Road" (Hurd/Apr. 15); "A Tonsorial Slot Machine" (Budd/Apr. 22); "The Third Liberty Loan Bomb" (Budd/Apr. 29); "Goodrich Dirt Bad Man Tamer" (Carlson/May 6); "Bobby Bumps Caught in the Jamb" (Hurd/May 13); "The Depth Bomb" (Parmelee/May 20); "Goodrich Dirt in Darkest Africa" (Carlson/May 27); "Bobby Bumps Out West" (Hurd/June 3); "Out of the Inkwell" (Fleischer/June 10); "Goodrich Dirt King of Spades" (Carlson/June 17); "Bobby Bumps Films a Fire" (Hurd/June 24); "The First Flyer" (Glackens/July 1); "Animated Technical Drawings" (Parmelee/July 1); "Goodrich Dirt the Cop" (Carlson/July 8); "Bobby Bumps Becomes an Ace" (Hurd/July 15); "Von Loon's 25,000 Mile Gun" (Glackens/July 22); "Animated Technical Drawing" (Parmelee/July 29); "Goodrich Dirt the Dark and Stormy Knight" (Carlson/Aug. 5); "The Kaiser's Surprise Party" (Budd/Aug. 12); "Bobby Bumps on the Doughnut Trail" (Hurd/Aug. 19); "Goodrich Dirt Coin Collector" (Carlson/Aug. 26); "Aerial Warfare" (Parmelee/Sept. 2); "A Watched Pot" (Santry/Sept. 9); "Cartoon" (Sept. 16/title unknown); "Bobby Bumps and the Speckled Death"

(Hurd/Sept. 23); "Goodrich Dirt Millionaire" (Carlson/Sept. 30); "Von Loon's Non-Capturable Aeroplane" (Glackens/Oct. 1); "Bobby Bumps Incubator" (Oct. 8); "Cartoon" (Oct. 15/title unknown); "The Greased Pole" (Budd/Oct. 22); "Goodrich Dirt When Wishes Come True" (Carlson/Oct. 29); "A German Trick That Failed" (Budd/Nov. 6); "Cartoon" (Nov. 13/title unknown); "Bobby Bumps in Before and After" (Hurd/Nov. 20); "Uncle Sam's Coming Problem" (Budd/Nov. 27); "Bobby Bumps Puts a Beanery on the Bum" (Hurd/Dec. 4); "Goodrich Dirt Cowpuncher" (Carlson/Dec. 11); "Pictures in the Fire" (Santry/Dec. 18/a.k.a.: "Faces in the Fire"); and "Goodrich Dirt in Spot Goes Romeoing" (Carlson/Dec. 25).

**1919:** "Cartoon" (Jan. 1/title unknown); "Bobby Bumps' Last Smoke" (Hurd/Jan. 8); "Private Bass His Pass" (Glackens/Jan. 15); "Goodrich Dirt in a Difficult Delivery" (Carlson/Jan. 22); "The Adventures of Hardrock Dome" (Sullivan/Jan. 29); "The Adventures of Hardrock Dome No. 2" (Sullivan/Feb. 5); "The Further Adventures of Hardrock Dome" (Sullivan/Feb. 12); "Theory of the Long Range Shell" (Parmelee/Feb. 19); "Goodrich Dirt Hypnotist" (Carlson/Feb. 26); "Out of the Inkwell" (Fleischer/Mar. 5); "Theory of the Hand Grenade" (Parmelee/Mar. 13); "Bobby Bumps' Lucky Day" (Hurd/Mar. 19); "Dud Perkins Gets Mortified" (Carlson/Mar. 26); "Out of the Inkwell" (Fleischer/Apr. 2); "Bobby Bumps' Night Out with Some Night Owls" (Hurd/Apr. 16); "Bobby Bumps' Eel-lectric Launch" (Hurd/Apr. 30); "Wounded by the Beauty" (Carlson/May 7); "Dud the Circus Performer" (Carlson/May 14); "Bobby Bumps and the Sand Lizard" (Hurd/May 21); "In 1998 A.D.: The Automatic Reducing Machine" (Budd/May 28); "Dud's Greatest Cirkus on Earth" (Carlson/June 4); "The Biography of Madame Fashion" (Glackens/June 11); "Cartoon" (June 18/title unknown); "Bobby Bumps and the Hypnotic Eye" (Hurd/June 25); "Cartoon" (July 2/title unknown); "At the Ol' Swimmin' Hole" (Carlson/July 9); "Bobby Bumps Throwing The Bull" (Hurd/July 16); "Cartoon" (July 23/title unknown); and "Tying the Nuptial Knot" (Glackens/July 30).

## PARAMOUNT CARTOONS

Like its popular predecessor, the *Paramount Magazine*, this series was comprised of vintage silent cartoon favorites released to theaters by Paramount Pictures from May through August of 1921. They included Earl Hurd's *Bobby Bumps*, Frank Moser's *Bud and Susie*, Pat Sullivan's *Felix the Cat*, Harry D. Bailey's *Silly Hoots* and others directed by Harry D. Leonard. *A Bray Production and Pat Sullivan Production released by Paramount Pictures.*

**1921:** "Bobby Bumps Working on an Idea" (Hurd/May 8); "Spaghetti for Two" (Leonard/May 15); "Felix Goes on Strike" (Sullivan/May 15); "Padding the Bill" (Bailey/May 22); "By the Sea" (Moser/May 29); "In Old Madrid" (Leonard/June 5); "Felix in the Love Punch" (Sullivan/June 5); "Shootin' Fish" (Hurd/June 12); "The Chicken Fancier" (Bailey/June 19); "$10,000 Under a Pillow" (Moser/June 26); "Felix Out of Luck" (Sullivan/July 3); "Bobby Bumps in Shadow Boxing" (Hurd/July 9); "Felix Left at Home" (Sullivan/July 17); "No Tickee No Shirtee" (Bailey/July 24); "Dashing North" (Moser/July 31); "School Days" (Leonard/Aug. 8.); "Black Magic" (Bailey/Aug. 14); "Bobby Bumps in Hunting and Fishing" (Hurd/Aug. 21); and "Kitchen Bedroom and Bath" (Moser/Aug. 28).

## PARAMOUNT MAGAZINE

This early 1920s magazine film series was among many others of its kind that included a package of silent cartoon shorts shown in movie theaters. Featured were Henry D. Bailey's *Silly Hoots*, Earl

Hurd's *Bobby Bumps*, Frank Moser's *Bud and Susie*, Pat Sullivan's *Felix the Cat* and Paul Terry's *Farmer Al Falfa* cartoons, which they directed, and others helmed by Harry D. Leonard. In May 1921, the series resumed under a new name, *Paramount Cartoons*. *A Bray/Pat Sullivan/Paul Terry Production released by Paramount Pictures.*

**1920:** "The Bone of Contention" (Terry/Mar.); "Handy Mandy's Goat" (Moser/Mar. 21); "Feline Follies" (Sullivan/Mar. 28); "Bobby Bumps" (Hurd/Apr. 4); "The Kids Find Candy's Catching" (Moser/Apr. 11); "Felix the Cat" (Sullivan/Apr. 18); "Bobby Bumps" (Hurd/Apr. 25); "Bud Takes the Cake" (Moser/May 2); "Felix the Cat" (Sullivan/May 9); "Bobby Bumps" (Hurd/May 15); "The New Cook's Debut" (Moser/May 23); "Felix the Cat" (Sullivan/May 30); "Bobby Bumps" (Hurd/June 6); "Mice and Money" (Moser/June 13); "Felix the Cat" (Sullivan/June 20); "Silly Hoots" (Bailey/June 27); "The Transatlantic Night Express" (Leonard/July 4); "Bobby Bumps" (Hurd/July 11); "Felix the Cat" (July 18); "Down the Mississippi" (Moser/July 25); "Bobby Bumps the Cave Man" (Hurd/Aug. 8); "Play Ball" (Moser/Aug. 15); "Romance and Rheumatism" (Moser/Aug. 22); "Felix the Cat" (Sullivan/Aug. 29); "Bud and Tommy Take a Day Off" (Moser/Sept. 5); "Silly Hoots" (Bailey/Sept. 12); "Bobby Bumps" (Hurd/Sept. 19); "Felix the Cat" (Sullivan/Sept. 26); "The North Pole" (Moser/Oct. 3); "Silly Hoots" (Bailey/Oct. 10); "Bobby Bumps" (Hurd/Oct. 27); "Felix the Landlord" (Sullivan/Oct. 24); "The Great Clean-Up" (Moser/Oct. 31); "A Double Life" (Bailey/Nov. 7/*Silly Hoots* cartoon); "Bobby Bumps" (Hurd/Nov. 14); "Felix the Cat" (Sullivan/Nov. 21); "One Hundred Percent Proof" (Leonard/Nov. 21); "Bud and Susie Join the Tecs" (Moser/Nov. 28); "Fifty-Fifty" (Moser/Dec. 5); "Are You Married" (Bailey/Dec. 12/*Silly Hoots* cartoon); "Bobby Bumps' Orchestra" (Hurd/Dec. 19); and "My Hero" (Sullivan/Dec. 26).

**1921:** "Getting Theirs" (Moser/Jan. 2); "Some Sayings of Benjamin Franklin" (Leonard/Jan. 2); "Silly Hoots" (Bailey/Jan. 9); "Bobby Bumps" (Hurd/Jan. 16); "Felix the Cat" (Sullivan/Jan. 23); "Bud and Susie" (Moser/Jan. 30); "Hootch and Mootch in Steak at Stake" (Hurd/Feb. 6); "Shimmy Geography" (Feb. 6); "Felix the Cat" (Sullivan/Feb. 13); "Bobby Bumps" (Hurd/Feb. 20); "Clean Your Feet" (Moser/Feb. 27); "Cabaret Courtesy" (Bailey/Mar. 6/*Silly Hoots* cartoon); "Bobby Bumps" (Hurd/Mar. 13); "Bobby Bumps Checkmated" (Hurd/Mar. 20); "Felix the Hypnotist" (Sullivan/Mar. 20); "The Sheriff" (Leonard/Mar. 20); "Silly Hoots" (Bailey/Mar. 27); "Circumstantial Evidence" (Moser/Apr. 3); "Bobby Bumps" (Hurd/Apr. 10); "Felix the Cat: Free Lunch" (Sullivan/Apr. 17); "In Greenwich Village" (Apr. 17); "Silly Hoots" (Bailey/Apr. 24); and "Bud and Susie" (Moser/May 1).

## ◎ PARAMOUNT PICTOGRAPHS

This mid-1900s film magazine series featured animated sequences produced by J.R. Bray, who also directed most of the one-reel shorts, along with C. Allen Gilbert. Also produced as part of the *Paramount Pictograph* series was a second series, animated and directed by Ashley Miller using stop-motion animated plaster models—*Plastiques* (see entry for details) also was produced as part of the series by Bray. *A Bray Production released by Paramount Pictures.*

**1916:** "Our Watch Dog" (Bray/Feb. 20); "The Bronco Buster" (Bray/Feb. 26); "The Struggle" (Bray/Mar. 12); "In the Shadows" (Gilbert/Mar. 12); "The House in Which They Live" (Bray/Mar. 19); "Watchful Waiting" (Bray/Mar. 26); "Found a Big Stick" (Bray/Mar. 26); "Why?" (Bray/Apr. 2); "The Long Arm of Law and Order" (Bray/Apr. 9); "Miss Nomination" (Bray/Apr. 30); and "Fisherman's Luck" (Bray/May 14).

## ◎ PARCEL POST PETE

Short-lived series of comical adventures featuring a curious mailman written by Tom E. Powers and based on his popular comic strip, animated by Frank Moser and directed by Gregory La Cava for New York's International Film Service. The series was released to theaters as part of the *Hearst-Vitagraph News Pictorial* newsreel series. *An International Film Service released by Hearst-Vitagraph.*

**1916:** "Parcel Post Pete's Nightmare" (Feb. 7/La Cava) and "Parcel Post Pete: Not All His Troubles Are Little Ones" (Feb. 14/La Cava).

## ◎ PATHÉ NEWS

New York animator-producer-director John R. Bray, along with animators Vincent Colby, Flohri, J.D. Leventhal, W.C. Morris and Charles Wilhelm, initially produced, directed and animated a series of black-and-white silent cartoons as part of this popular weekly newsreel. Besides producing single-shot cartoons and others dealing with timely issues of the day, one of the series' most popular entries was Bray's *Colonel Heeza Liar*, featured in many animated one-reelers released to theaters during its first year.

In the fall of 1916, Pathé News founded its own cartoon department, hiring former Bray animators Leighton Budd, F.M. Follett, Louis M. Glackens and Hugh M. Shields—joining a year later, A.D. Reed and John C. Terry—duly licensed by Bray to animate and direct topical cartoons for Pathé's newsreel series. In 1917, the *Pathé News* series continued production under the name of *Hearst-Pathé News*. *A Bray Production released by Pathé Exchange.*

**1915:** "The Boomerang" (Feb. 17); "Our Defenses" (Feb. 24); "Hands Across the Sea" (Mar. 3); "The Presidential Chair" (Mar. 10); "Patriotism" (Mar. 17/Flohri); "Col. Heeza Liar Runs the Blockade" (Mar. 20/Bray); "A New Method of Fighting Submarines" (Mar. 31); "Col. Heeza Liar and the Torpedo" (Apr. 3/Bray); "Some Feathers Fly in Turkey (Teasing the Eagle)" (Apr. 7); "Col. Heeza Liar and the Zeppelin" (Apr. 10/Bray); "The Wily Jap" (Apr. 14/Flohri); "The Resourceful Dachshund" (Apr. 24); "The Reward of Patience" (May 8); "Col. Heeza Liar in the Trenches" (May 13/Bray); "Col. Heeza Liar at the Front" (May 20/Bray); "Col. Heeza Liar War Aviator" (May 23/Bray); "Another Fallen Idol" (May 28/Glackens); "Col. Heeza Liar Invents a New Kind of Shell" (June 5/Bray); "When Kitty Spilled the Ink" (June 26); The Dove of Peace (July 31/Morris); "Uncle Same Gets Wise at Last" (Aug. 7); "The Pilot of Peace" (Aug. 14/Morris); "Grandmothers of Yesterday, Today and Tomorrow" (Sept. 4); "Some Presidential Possibilities" (Sept. 11/Morris); "Dr. Worsen Plummer" (Oct. 2); "Dumba's Departure" (Oct. 23); "Dr. Worsen Plummer Starts a Drug Store" (Oct. 30); "I Should Worry" (Nov. 6/Colby); "Wilson Surrenders" (Nov. 13/Morris); "Bubbling Bill" (Dec. 18); and "Troubles of a Pacifist" (Dec. 22).

**1916:** "At It Again" (Mar. 8/Wilhelm); "Patience Is a Virtue" (May 13); "The Black List" (Sept. 2/Morris); "An Engineering Problem" (Sept. 20/Leventhal); "Responsibility for the War" (Sept. 23/Morris); "What Next" (Sept. 30/Glackens); "Misadventures of the Bull Moose" (Oct. 7/Terry); "Hands Across the Sea" (Oct. 14/Terry); "Are We Prepared for the International Trade Hunt" (Oct. 21/Reed); "The Courtship of Miss Vote" (Oct. 28/Budd); "The Pen Is Mightier than the Sword" (Nov. 4/Glackens); "Somewhere in America" (Nov. 11/Terry); "Now You See It Now You Don't" (Nov. 25/Terry); "Our Merchant Marine" (Dec. 2/Terry); "The Mexican Border" (Dec. 9/Budd); "Uncle Sam's Christmas" (Dec. 16/Budd); "Independent Poland" (Dec. 23/Glackens); and "In Verdun Forests" (Dec. 30/Shields).

## PATHÉ REVIEW

Weekly magazine series produced by New York's Pathé Exchange that featured animated cartoons as well, such as Henry "Hy" Mayer's *Such Is Life* series offering humorous perspectives of New York and Europe, and *Travelaughs* live-action/animated travelogue series and Herbert M. Dawley's animated silhouette series, *Silliettes*. *A Hy Mayer/Keen Cartoon/Herbert M. Dawley Production released by Pathé Exchange.*

**1920:** "Such Is Life Among the Dogs" (Mayer/Oct. 2); "Such Life at the Zoo" (Mayer/Oct. 16); "Such Is Life at Coney Island" (Mayer/Oct. 6); "Such Is Sporting Life" (Mayer/Nov. 13); "Such Is Life in Greenwich Village" (Mayer/Dec. 4); and "Such Is Life in East Side New York" (Mayer/Dec. 18).

**1921:** "Behind the Scenes of the Circus" (Mayer/Jan. 15/*Travelaughs* cartoon); "Travelaugh" (Feb. 5/Mayer); "Such Is Life at a County Fair" (Mayer/Feb. 19); "Such Is Life in Summer" (Mayer/Mar. 12); "Spring Hats" (Mayer/Apr. 9/*Travelaughs* cartoon); "All the Merry Bow-Wows" (Mayer/Apr. 30/*Travelaughs* cartoon); "In the Silly Summertime" (Mayer/May 29/*Travelaughs* cartoon); "The Door That Has No Lock" (Mayer/June 26/*Travelaughs* cartoon); "Such Is Life at the Race Track" (Mayer/July 3); "Such Is Life at the Zoo" (Mayer/July 17); "A Ramble Through Provincetown" (Mayer/July 31/*Travelaughs* cartoon); "The Little City of Dreams" (Mayer/Sept. 4/*Travelaughs* cartoon); "Day Dreams" (Mayer/Sept. 18/*Travelaughs* cartoon); "Down to the Fair" (Mayer/Oct. 2/*Travelaughs* cartoon); "Summer Scenes" (Mayer/Oct. 16/*Travelaughs* cartoon); "All Aboard" (Mayer/Oct. 30/*Travelaughs* cartoon); "Such Is Life in New York" (Mayer/Nov. 20); and "Puppies" (Mayer/Dec. 25/*Travelaughs* cartoon).

**1922:** "How It Feels" (Mayer/Sept. 24/*Travelaughs* cartoon); "In the Dear Old Summer Time" (Mayer/Oct. 14/*Travelaughs* cartoon) and "Sporting Scenes" (Mayer/Nov. 25/*Travelaughs* cartoon).

**1923:** "Faces" (Mayer/Jan. 6/*Travelaughs* cartoon); "Silliettes" (Dawley/Mar. 24); "The Lobster Nightmare" (Dawley/Apr. 7); "The Absent Minded Poet" (Dawley/June 9); and "The Classic Centaur" (Dawley/July 7).

**1924:** "Pan the Piper" (Dawley/Feb. 9); "Fable of the Future: The Proxy Letter" (Fleischer/Aug. 9); "The Makin's of an Artist" (Mayer/Sept. 13); "Thumbelina" (Dawley/Sept. 27); "Jack and the Beanstalk" (Dawley); "Cinderella" (Dawley); "Sleeping Beauty" (Dawley); "Beauty and the Beast" (Dawley); "Tattercoats" (Dawley); and "Aladdin and the Wonderful Lamp" (Dawley).

## PAUL TERRY CARTOONS

Pioneer cartoon animator, producer and director Paul Terry officially launched his professional animation career in 1915, producing and animating the first cel-animated cartoon for theatrical release, *Little Herman*, an animated takeoff of famed magician, Herman the Great, for Edwin Thanhouser's company, Thanhouser Film Corporation. A few months later, he produced a second cel-animated cartoon short, "Down on the Phoney Farm," released that October.

Afterwards, Terry approached other New York animation studios to finance additional films, including J.R. Bray's studio. Since Bray owned the patents to the process of cel animation, Terry's efforts to forge a partnership with him were met with resistance and Bray offered him two choices: Either license his patented process or join his studio as an animator. He accepted the second option. At Bray's New York cartoon studio, Terry would go on to create perhaps his most famous cartoon character of the silent era,

Farmer Al Falfa. *A Paul Terry Production released by Thanhouser Film Corporation.*

**1915:** "Little Herman" (June 19) and "Down on the Phoney Farm" (Oct. 16).

## ◉ PAUL TERRY FEATURE BURLESQUES

Paul Terry, who became famous during the silent era for his creation of the hayseed character, Farmer Al Falfa, and as the founder of the Terry-Toons cartoon studio in New York, wrote, produced and directed this series of animated burlesque shorts for theaters. *A Paul Terry Production released by A. Kay Company.*

**1917:** "20,000 Feats Under the Sea" (Apr. 23); "Golden Spoon Mary" (Apr. 30); "Some Barrier" (July); and "His Trial" (July).

## ◉ PEANUT COMEDIES

Produced as part of the *Paramount Magazine*, this series combined live action and animation. The series was produced, directed, written and animated by Harry D. Leonard. *A Famous Players-Lasky Corporation release.*

**1920:** "One Hundred Per Cent Proof" (Nov. 21).

**1921:** "Some Sayings of Benjamin Franklin" (Jan. 9); and "The Sheriff" (Mar. 20).

**1921:** "Spaghetti for Two" (May 15); "In Old Madrid" (June 5); and "School Days" (Aug. 8).

## ◉ PEN AND INK VAUDEVILLE

These absurd cartoons feature an animator on a vaudeville stage sketching various outlandish drawings and editorial cartoons that miraculously come to life onscreen. *An Earl Hurd Production released by Educational Film Corp.*

**1924:** "Boneyard Blues" (Aug. 31); "The Hoboken Nightingale" (Oct. 5); "The Sawmill Four" (Nov. 2); "The Artist's Model" (Nov. 15); and "Broadcasting" (Dec. 20).

**1925:** "He Who Gets Socked" (Feb. 7); "Two Cats and a Bird" (Mar. 7); "The Mellow Quartette" (Apr. 4); "Monkey Business" (May 2); "Two Poor Fish" (May 30); "Props' Dash for Cash" (June 20); "Bobby Bumps and Company" (July 4); and "Props and the Spirits" (Sept. 5).

## ◉ PETE THE PUP

This series starred one of Walter Lantz's last silent cartoon characters, a lovable but pesky pup and his jocular tramp sidekick. Each cartoon was shaped around live segments of Lantz at his animator's table, à la Max Fleischer's *Out of the Inkwell*, while his star characters looked on. The series was also billed as *Hot Dog Cartoons*, for obvious reasons.

Lantz animated and directed the series. It lasted two years. *A Bray Production released by Pathé Film Exchange Inc.*

**1926:** "For the Love o' Pete" (Oct. 2); "Pete's Haunted House" (Oct. 5); and "Pete's Party" (Oct. 26).

**1927:** "Dog Gone It" (Jan. 4); "Along Came Fido" (Jan. 31); "The Puppy Express" (Feb. 4); "Petering Out" (Feb. 16); "S'matter, Pete?" (Mar. 15); "Lunch Hound" (Apr. 8); "Jingle Bells" (Apr. 26); "Bone Dry" (May 14); and "The Farm Hand" (May 27).

## ◉ PHABLES

Raoul Barré, who was associated with William Randolph Hearst's International Film Service, produced this series of films directed by Gregory La Cava and based on Tom E. Powers's clever newspaper comic drawings and short satires of contemporary life starring the stick figures, The Joys and Hawkshaw Gloom. Barré quit after making only seven films to accept an offer to adapt the Mutt and Jeff strip into a series. The films were reissued in 1916 under the series title, "Joys and Glooms," featuring Barré's original cartoons and many new entries reprising the characters animated by Frank Moser and directed by La Cava. In late January of 1916, the series became known as *Joys and Gloom*. (See entry for details.) *A Bray Production released by Hearst-Vitagraph.*

**1915:** "The Phable of Sam and Bill" (Dec. 17/with Hawkshaw Gloom, The Joys); "The Phable of a Busted Romance" (Dec. 24/with Hawkshaw Gloom, The Joys); and "Feet Is Feet: A Phable" (Dec. 31/with Hawkshaw Gloom, The Joys).

**1916:** "A Newlywed Phable" (Jan. 7/with Hawkshaw Gloom, The Joys); "The Phable of a Phat Woman" (Jan. 14/with Hawkshaw Gloom, The Joys); and "Cooks vs. Chefs: The Phable of Olaf and Louie" (Jan. 21/with Hawkshaw Gloom, The Joys).

### ◎ PICTO PUZZLES
Sam Lloyd wrote, directed and animated this brief series of black-and-white silent cartoon puzzles for J.R. Bray's New York cartoon studio. The films were released to theaters as part of the *Paramount-Bray Pictographs* magazine series. *A Bray Production released by Paramount.*

**1917:** "No. 1" (Apr. 2); "No. 2" (Apr. 16); "No. 3" (May 14); "No. 4" (May 21); "No. 5" (July 2); "No. 6" (July 30); and "No. 7" (Aug. 27).

### ◎ PLASTIQUES
Animator Ashley Miller directed this series of stop-motion animated one-reelers using plaster models for the *Paramount Pictograph* series, produced by legendary animator, director and producer John R. Bray's New York cartoon studio. *A Bray Production released by Paramount Pictures.*

**1916:** "Priscilla and the Pesky Fly" (Feb.); "The Law of Gravitation" (Feb.); "Fifty-Fifty" (Mar.); "The High Cost of Living" (Apr.); "Did Sherman Say Law or War" (May); and "Why the Sphinx Laughed" (July 9).

### ◎ POLICE DOG
Extremely funny stories of the amazing achievements of a friendly and most precocious dog who has attached himself to the policeman on the beat. Drawn by gifted comic-strip artist Carl Anderson (who also directed), it was one of three animal series to emerge from the J.R. Bray Studios. *A Bray Production released by Pathé Film Exchange.*

**1914:** "The Police Dog" (Nov. 21).

**1915:** "The Police Dog Gets Piffles in Bad" (July 24); and "The Police Dog to the Rescue" (Sept. 25).

**1916:** "Police Dog on the Wire" (Jan. 27); "Police Dog Turns Nurse" (Apr. 2); "Police Dog in the Park" (May 7); and "Working Out with the Police Dog" (June 6).

### ◎ POPULAR SONG PARODIES
Like Max Fleischer's *Song Car-Tunes* series, this series used popular music as the basis for story lines. *Produced by Louis Weiss. An Artclass Pictures Production released by Film Booking Offices.*

**1926:** "Alexander's Ragtime Band" (May 1); "Annie Laurie" (May 1); "The Sheik of Araby" (May 1); "In My Harem" (May 1); "When I Lost You" (May 1); "Margie" (May 1); "When That Midnight Choochoo Leaves for Alabam" (May 1); "Oh What a Pal Was Mary" (May 1); "Everybody's Doing It" (May 1); "My Wife's Gone to the Country" (May 1); "Oh How I Hate to Get Up in the Morning" (May 1); "Just Try to Picture Me" (May 1); "I Love to Fall Asleep" (May 1); "For Me and My Gal" (May 1); "Yak-a-Hula-Hick-a-Doola" (May 1); "My Sweetie" (May 1); "Old Pal" (May 1); "Tumbledown Shack in Athlone" (May 1); "The Rocky Road to Dublin" (May 1); "When I Leave This World Behind" (May 1): "Finculee Finicula" (May 1); "When the Angelus Was Ringing" (May 1); "Beautiful Eyes" (May 1); "Call Me Up Some Rainy Afternoon" (May 1); "Micky" (May 1); and "Oh I Wish I Was in Michigan" (May 1).

### ◎ POWERS ANIMATED CARTOONS
This long-running series, produced by Patrick A. Powers, showcased the talents of many pioneer animators during the silent era, including Will Anderson, Joseph Cammer, Wallace Carlson, Bill Cause, George Clardy, Vincent Colby, Jay Evans, F.M. Follett, Milt Gross, Joseph Harwitz, Hy (Henry) Mayer, Winsor McCay, Otto Messmer, Charles Saxon, Ernest Smythe, W.E. Stark, Pat Sullivan and John Coleman Terry. Featured were assorted black-and-white animated cartoons written, directed and animated by them.

Several popular cartoon series were released under the *Power Cartoons* banner in their own right; among them Pat Sullivan's *Sammie Johnsin* and *Boomer Bill*, F.M. Follett's *Mr. Fuller Pep* and Hy Mayer's *Travelaughs*. In addition, the series featured the work of legendary animator Otto Messmer, the creator of *Felix the Cat*, including *Motor Mat and His Fliv* (1916) and *20,000 Laughs under the Sea* (1917). *A Powers Production released by Universal Pictures.*

**1915:** "Hunting in Crazyland" (Jan. 2) and "To Frisco by the Cartoon Route" (Aug. 9/Mayer).

**1916:** "Chestnut"; "Sammie Johnsin, Hunter" (Sullivan/Jan. 27); "Joe Boko's Adventures" (Carlson/Feb. 9); "Sammie Johnsin, Strong Man" (Sullivan/Mar. 3); "Globe Trotting with Hy Mayer" (Mayer/Apr. 14); "Mr. Fuller Pep Tries Mesmerism" (Follett/May 3); "Mr. Fuller Pep Dabbles in the Pond" (Follett/May 17); "Mr. Fuller Pep Breaks for the Beach" (Follett/May 31); "Professor Wiseguy's Trip to the Moon" (Cammer/June 6); "Such Is Life in China" (Mayer/June 22); "Sammie Johnsin, Magician" (Sullivan/June 9); "Sammie Johnsin Gets a Job" (Sullivan/July 13); "Jitney Jack and Gasolena" (Evans/July 20); "Sammie Johnsin in Mexico" (Sullivan/Aug. 25); "Pen and Inklings Around Jerusalem" (Mayer/Oct. 5); "Winsor McCay and His Jersey Skeeters" (Mayer/Oct. 5); "Sammie Johnsin Minds the Baby" (Nov. 2); "High Life on a Farm" (Mayer/Nov. 9); "A Pen Trip to Palestine" (Mayer/Nov. 9); "Motor Mat and His Fliv" (Nov. 18); "Sammie Johnsin at the Seaside" (Sullivan/Nov. 26); "The Trials of a Movie Cartoonist" (Sullivan/Dec. 10); "Sammie Johnsin and His Wonderful Lamp" (Sullivan/Dec. 17); "Nervy Nat Has His Fortune Told" (Sullivan/Dec. 24); and "Sammie Johnsin Slumbers Not" (Sullivan/Dec. 31).

**1917:** "Mr. Fuller Pep Goes to the Country" (Follett/Jan 21); "The Trials of Willie Winks" (with Sammie Johnsin/Jan. 22/produced by Pat Sullivan); "Boomer Bill's Awakening" (Clardy/Jan. 28/produced by Pat Sullivan); "Mr. Fuller Pep Celebrates His Wedding Anniversary" (Follett/Jan. 14); "Mr. Fuller Pep Goes for a Rest" (Follett/Feb. 4); "Fearless Freddie in the Woolly West" (Feb. 11/produced by Pat Sullivan); "Mr. Fuller Pep Does Some Quick Moving" (Follett/Feb./ 18); "A Day in the Life of a Dog" (with Sammie Johnsin/Anderson/Feb. 25/produced by Pat Sullivan); "Mr. Fuller Pep: An Old Bird Pays Him a Visit" (Follett/Mar. 4); "Mr. Fuller Pep's Day of Rest" (Follett/Mar. 11); "The Tail of Thomas Kat" (Mar. 18/produced by Pat Sullivan); "The Love Affair of Ima Knut" (Messmer/Mar. 25/produced by Pat Sullivan); "The Ups and Downs of Mr. Phool Phan" (Gross/Mar. 27); "Inbad the Sailor" (Apr. 1/produced by Pat Sullivan); "Boomer Bill Goes to Sea" (Apr. 15/produced by Pat Sullivan); "A Good Story About a Bad Egg" (Apr. 22/produced by Pat Sullivan); "Such Is Life in Algeria" (Mayer/Apr. 28); "A Barnyard Nightmare" (May 6/produced by Pat Sullivan); "20,000 Laughs Under the Sea" (Messmer/May 14/produced by Pat Sullivan); "When Noah's Ark Embarked" (Terry/May 19); "Cupid Gets Some New Dope" (with Sammie Johnsin/May 27/produced by Pat Sullivan); Thim Were Happy Days" (Messmer/June 10/produced by Pat Sullivan); "A Pesky Pup" (Harwitz/June 17/produced by Pat Sullivan); "Young Nick Carter, Detectiff" (Anderson/June 24/produced by Pat Sullivan); "China Awakened" (Mayer/June 26); "Duke Dolittle's Jungle Fizzle" (Saxon/July 1/produced by Pat Sullivan); "Seven Cutey Pups" (Colby/July 7); "Monkey Love" (Smythe/July 15/produced by Pat Sullivan); "Box Car Bill Falls in Luck" (Cause/July 16/produced by Pat Sullivan); "A Barnyard Hamlet" (with Hammon Eggs/Stark/July 28/produced by Pat Sullivan); "A Good Liar" (Messmer/Aug. 4/produced by Pat Sullivan); "Hammon Eggs' Reminiscences" (with Hammon Eggs/Aug. 4/produced by Pat Sullivan); "Colonel Pepper's Mobilized Farm" (Aug. 4/produced by Pat Sullivan); "Seeing Ceylon" (Mayer/Aug. 6); "Doing His Bit" (Aug.4/produced by Pat Sullivan); and "Seeing New York" (Mayer/Oct. 15).

**1918:** "New York by Heck" (Mayer/May 1).

## ◎ QUACKY DOODLES

Cartoonist Johnny B. Gruelle, founder of the *Raggedy Ann* comic strip among others, created this series showcasing a family of ducks: Quacky Doodles, the mother; Danny Doodles, the father; and the little Doodles. They appeared at regular intervals with J.R. Bray's Colonel Heeza Liar, Bobby Bumps and his dog Fido as part of Bray's weekly *Paramount Pictograph* screen magazine. *A Bray Production released by Famous Players-Lasky Corporation.*

**1917:** "Quacky Doodles Picnic" (Feb. 18); "Quacky Doodles' Food Crisis" (Mar. 12); "Quacky Doodles The Early Bird" (Apr. 1); "Quacky Doodles Soldiering for Fair" (Apr. 23); "Quacky Doodles Sings the Pledge" (Sept. 10); and "Quacky Doodles the Cheater" (Oct. 15).

## ◎ RED HEAD COMEDIES

This series of cartoons, which spoofed noted figures in world history, was produced in color. The series was written, produced, directed and animated by Frank A. Nankivell, Richard M. Friel, "Hutch" and W.E. Stark. *A Lee-Bradford Corporation Production.*

**1923:** "Robinson Crusoe Returns on Friday" (Sept. 1); "Cleopatra and Her Easy Mark" (Sept. 1); "Napoleon Not So Great" (Sept. 1); "Kidding Captain Kidd" (Sept. 1); "Rip Without a Wink" (Sept. 1); "Columbus Discovers a New Whirl" (Sept. 1); "Why Sitting Bull Stood Up" (Dec. 1); "What Did William Tell" (Dec. 1); "A Whale of a Story" (Dec. 1); "How Troy Was Collared" (Dec. 1); and "The Jones Boys' Sister" (Dec. 1).

## ◎ RHYME REELS

Walt Mason wrote, produced and directed this series, which combined live action with animated sequences. *A Filmcraft Corporation Production.*

**1917:** "Bunked and Paid For" (Aug. 18); "The Dipper" (Aug. 18); "True Love and Fake Money" (Aug. 18); and "Hash" (Aug. 18).

## ◎ ROVING THOMAS

This series of adventures, featuring a cat named Roving Thomas, combined live action and animation. *Produced by Charles Urban. A Kineto Films Production released by Vitagraph.*

**1922:** Roving Thomas Sees New York" (Sept. 17); "Roving Thomas on an Aeroplane" (Oct. 22); and "Roving Thomas on a Fishing Trip" (Dec. 10).

**1923:** "Roving Thomas at the Winter Carnival" (Feb. 1); and "Roving Thomas in Chicago" (Oct. 27).

## ◎ RUBE GOLDBERG CARTOONS

Famed newspaper cartoonist Rube Goldberg wrote this short-lived series of entertaining, black-and-white cartoon shorts, animated by pioneer animators Raoul Barré, Gregory La Cava, Bill Nolan and George Stallings. *A Rube Goldberg/Barré Studios Production released by Pathé Films.*

**1916:** "The Boob Weekly" (May 8); "Leap Year" (May 22); "The Fatal Pie" (June 5); "From Kitchen Mechanic to Movie Star" (June 19); "Nutty News" (July 3); "Home Sweet Home" (July 17); and "Losing Weight" (July 31).

## ◎ SAMMIE JOHNSIN

Inheriting the rights to comic strips penned by the great William F. Marriner, Pat Sullivan turned one of them, *Sambo and his Funny Noses*, into an animated cartoon series in 1916 called, *Sammie Johnsin*. The films centered around the adventures of this Little Black Sambo character. Sullivan reportedly photographed the films at Universal's studio in Fort Lee, New Jersey, and were released under Patrick A. Powers *Powers Animated Cartoons* series. Additional titles were also produced in 1917. *Produced by Pat Sullivan. Directed by Pat Sullivan and Will Anderson. A Pat Sullivan Cartoon released through Universal Pictures.*

**1916:** "Sammie Johnsin, Hunter" (Jan. 27); "Sammie Johnsin, Strong Man" (Mar. 3); "Sammie Johnsin, Magician" (June 29); "Sammie Johnsin Gets a Job" (July 13); "Sammie Johnsin in Mexico" (Aug. 25); "Sammie Johnsin Minds the Baby" (Nov. 2); "Sammie Johnsin at the Seaside" (Nov. 26); "Sammie Johnsin's Love Affair" (Dec. 3); "Sammie Johnsin and His Wonderful Lamp" (Dec. 17); and "Sammie Johnsin Slumbers Not" (Dec. 3).

**1917:** "The Trials of Willie Winks" (Jan. 7); and "A Day in the Life of a Dog" (Anderson/Feb. 14).

## ◎ SCAT CAT

The success of Pat Sullivan's Felix the Cat inspired several other animators to create cat characters of their own. Frank Moser's series followed the exploits of Scat Cat, which alternated with Sullivan's Felix the Cat on Paramount's *Paramount Magazine* newsreel. The series was produced in 1920. *A Paramount Pictures release.*

## ◎ SCENIC SKETCHOGRAPHS

Following the success of his *Travelaughs* series, Henry "Hy" Mayer wrote, produced, directed and animated this series for Pathé Exchange. *A Mayer Production released by Pathé Film Exchange Inc.*

**1926:** "The Family Album" (July 26); "Tripping the Rhine" (July 26); "A Pup's Tale" (July 26); and "Nurenberg the Toy City" (July 26).

## ◎ SCREEN FOLLIES

Animators Luis Seel and F.A. Dahne wrote, produced, directed and animated this series for which little else is known. *A Capital Film Company.*

**1920:** "No. 1" (Jan. 4); and "No. 2" (Jan. 4).

## ◎ THE SHENANIGAN KIDS

Based on the comic strip by Rudolph Dirks, this series continued the adventures of Dirks's *The Katzenjammer Kids. Directed by Gregory La Cava, Burt Gillett and Grim Natwick. An International Film Service/Goldwyn-Bray Comics Production.*

**1920:** "Knock on the Window, The Door Is a Jamb" (Apr. 17); "One Good Turn Deserves Another" (June 17); "The Dummy" (June 27); "The Rotisserie Brothers" (Natwick/July 24); and "Hunting Big Game" (Gillett/Oct. 9).

## ◎ SILHOUETTE FANTASIES

In the mid-1900s, movie-shadow plays were part of popular entertainment. J.R. Bray teamed up with his associate C. Allan Gilbert to produce a series of animated films based on this archaic art form. The films turned out to be "serious" adaptations of Greek myths, staged in art nouveau arabesque tableaux. Bray had plans to create a five-reel feature using the same technique. However, Gilbert left the studio in 1916 and the series was abandoned. *A Bray-Gilbert Films Production released by Famous Players-Lasky Corporation.*

**1916:** "Inbad the Sailor" (Jan. 20); "Haunts for Rent" (Feb. 10); "The Chess Queen" (Mar. 7); "In the Shadows" (Mar. 15); "Inbad the Sailor Gets into Deep Water" (Apr. 8); and "The Toyland Paper Chase" (May 10).

## ◎ SILLIETTES

Issued as part of film magazine series, this series consisted of animated silhouettes to tell a story. Herbert M. Dawley produced, directed and animated the series. *A Herbert M. Dawley Production released by Pathé Film Exchange Inc.*

**1923:** "Silliettes" (Mar. 24); "The Lobster Nightmare" (Apr. 7); "The Absent Minded Poet" (June 9); and "The Classic Centaur" (July 7).

**1924:** "Pan the Piper" (Feb. 9); "Thumbelina" (Sept. 27); "Jack and the Beanstalk"; "Cinderella"; "Sleeping Beauty"; "Tattercoats"; and "Aladdin and the Wonderful Lamp."

**1925:** "Jack the Giant Killer" (May 9).

## ◎ SILLY HOOTS

Former Bray animator Harry D. Bailey, who worked as the first camera operator on Bray's *Bobby Bumps* cartoon series in 1915 and left Bray's New York cartoon studio in September 1920, wrote, produced, directed and animated this series, initially for the *Paramount Magazine* and then its successor, *Paramount Cartoons. A Paramount Pictures release.*

### Paramount Magazine

**1920:** "Silly Hoots" (June 17); "Silly Hoots" (Aug. 1); "Silly Hoots" (Sept. 12); "Silly Hoots" (Oct. 10); "A Double Life" (Nov. 17); and "Are You Married" (Dec. 12).

**1921:** "Silly Hoots" (Jan. 9); "Cabaret Courtesy" (Mar. 6); "Silly Hoots" (Mar. 27); and "Silly Hoots" (Apr. 24).

### Paramount Cartoons

**1921:** "Padding the Bill" (May 22); "The Chicken Fancier" (June 19); "No Tickee No Shirtee" (July 24); and "Black Magic" (Aug. 14).

## ◎ SKETCHOGRAFS

Social and topical issues were among the themes covered in this series, which was included in a weekly magazine film series. It was written, produced, directed and animated by Julian Ollendorff. *An Ollendorff Production released by Educational Pictures, Pathé Film Exchange Inc. and Cranfield and Clarke.*

### Educational Pictures

**1921:** "Play Ball" (Aug. 7); "Just for Fun" (Sept. 16); "Eve's Leaves" (Oct.); "Seeing Greenwich Village" (Nov.); and "What's the Limit" (Dec. 24).

### Pathé Film Exchange

**1921:** "Jiggin' on the Old Sod" (Sept. 18).

### Educational Pictures

**1922:** "Famous Men" (Oct. 21); "Athletics and Women" (Oct. 28); "Champions" (Nov. 4); "Animals and Humans" (Nov. 11); "Mackerel Fishing" (Dec. 2); and "The Coast-guard" (Dec. 16).

**1923:** "Family Album" (Jan. 8).

### Cranfield and Clarke

**1926:** "Beauty and the Beach" (Sept. 1); "Everybody Rides" (Sept. 15); "Fair Weather" (Oct. 1); "The Big Show" (Oct. 15); "Watch Your Step" (Nov. 1); "Revolution of the Sexes" (Nov. 15); and "Tin Pan Alley" (Dec. 1).

## ◎ SONG CAR-TUNES

Before the advent of sound, theaters were known to project song slides onto the movie screen showing lyrics of well-known tunes, often accompanied by a live singer or musician, to commit audiences into singing along. Animator Max Fleischer took this simple concept and illustrated lyrics with drawings and live-action footage in a series of cartoons, first shown in 1924, called, *Song Car-Tunes.*

In the beginning of most films, on-camera talent—usually a Fleischer employee—highlighted the lyrics using a long stick with a luminescent white ball at the end. Films then often cut away to Fleischer cartoon stars—Koko the Clown, Fritz the dog and others—in ingenious visual gags to lead the second or third chorus of the song.

Some sing-a-long cartoons were synchronized using Dr. Lee DeForest's Phonofilm sound process, but theaters were ill-equipped to project these musical novelties employing what was then a revolutionary technique. *An Out of the Inkwell Film Production released by Arrow Film Corp. and Red Seal Pictures.*

### Arrow Film Corp.

**1924:** "Mother Pin a Rose on Me" (Mar. 9/released in sound in June); "Come Take a Trip in My Airship" (Mar. 9/released in sound in June); and "Goodbye My Lady Love" (Mar. 9/released with sound in June).

### Red Seal Pictures

**1925:** "Come Take a Trip in My Airship" (Jan. 15); "The Old Folks at Home" (Feb. 1); "Mother, Mother Pin a Rose on Me" (Mar. 1); "I Love a Lassie" (Mar. 20); "The Swanee River" (Apr.

25); "Daisy Bell" (May 30); "Nutcracker Suite" (Sept./unconfirmed title); "My Bonnie Lies Over the Ocean" (Sept. 15/first "bouncing ball" cartoon); "Ta-Ra-Ra-Boom-De-A" (Oct. 15); "Dixie" (Nov. 15); and "Sailing, Sailing" (Dec. 15).

**1926:** "Dolly Gray" (Feb. 6); "Has Anybody Here Seen Kelly" (Feb. 21/released with sound); "My Old Kentucky Home" (Mar. 13/released with sound); "Sweet Adeline" (May 1); "Tramp, Tramp, Tramp the Boys Are Marching" (May 8); "Goodbye My Lady Love" (May 22); "Coming Through the Rye" (June 1); "Pack Up Your Troubles" (July 17); "The Trail of the Lonesome Pine" (July 17/released with sound); "By the Light of the Silvery Moon" (Aug. 21/released with sound); "In the Good Old Summer Time" (Sept./released with sound); "Oh You Beautiful Doll" (Sept./released with sound); and "Old Black Joe" (Nov. 1/released with sound).

**1927:** "Jingle Bells" (Apr. 1) and "Waiting for the Robert E. Lee" (Apr. 15).

**1924–1926:** (Following are undated titles from the series): "Dear Old Pal"; "When the Midnight Choo-Choo Comes to Alabama"; "Yaka-Hula-Hickla-Ooola"; "When I Lost You"; "Oh, Suzanna"; "My Wife's Gone to the Country"; "Margie"; "Annie Laurie"; "Oh, How I Hate to Get Up in the Morning"; and "East Side, West Side."

## SUCH IS LIFE

Henry "Hy" Mayer created—he also wrote, produced, directed, and animated—this series of humorous perspectives on life in New York and in Europe, originally part of Pathé Film Exchange's *Pathé Review* series from 1920 to 1922. *A Hy Mayer Production released by Pathé Film Exchange, R.C. Pictures and Film Booking Offices.*

### Pathé Exchange

**1920:** "Such Is Life Among the Dogs" (Oct. 2); "Such Is Life at the Zoo" (Oct. 16); "Such Is Life at Coney Island" (Nov. 6); "Such Is Sporting Life" (Nov. 13); "Such Is Life in Greenwich Village" (Dec. 4); and "Such Is Life in East Side New York."

**1921:** "Such Is Life in the Land of Fancy" (Jan. 30); "Such Is Life at a County Fair" (Feb. 19); "Such Is Life in Summer" (Mar. 12); "Such Is Life in Ramblerville" (Apr. 10); "Such Is Life at the Race Track" (July 3); "Such Is Life at the Zoo" (July 17); and "Such Is Life in New York" (Nov. 20).

**1922:** "Such Is Life" (Feb. 27).

### R.C. Pictures/Film Booking Offices

**1922:** "Such Is Life in London's West End" (Apr. 15); "Such Is Life in Vollendam" (May 7); "Such Is Life in Monte Carlo" (May 31); "Such Is Life in Mon Petit Paris" (June 4); "Such Is Life Among the Children of France" (June 18); "Such Is Life in Munich" (July 22); "Such Is Life in Montemartre" (July 22); "Such Is Life on the Riviera" (Aug. 12); "Such Is Life Among the Paris Shoppers" (Aug. 12); "Such Is Life Near London" (Aug. 19); "Such Is Life in Amsterdam and Alkmaar" (Aug. 27); "Such Is Life Among the Idlers of Paris" (Oct.); "Such Is Life in Busy London" (Nov. 4); "Such Is Life in a Dutch County Fair" (Nov.); and "Such Is Life in Italy" (Dec.).

## TAD CARTOONS

Animated and directed by Walter Lantz and William "Bill" Nolan and produced by William Randolph Hearst, this series of outrageous cartoons shorts was based on the newspaper comics of car-

toonist Thomas "Tad" Dorgan. Introduced to moviegoers in 1918, after the first two cartoons were released, the series was distributed to theaters as an item in the *International News* weekly newsreel. *An International Film Service Production.*

**1918:** "Tad's Little Daffydills" (Nolan) and "Tad's Indoor Sports" (Nolan, Lantz).

### International News

**1919:** "Tad Cartoon" (Apr. 23).

**1920:** "Indoor Sports by Tad" (Feb. 21).

## TAD'S CAT

In 1919 two films may have been made for this Universal cartoon series, produced and animated by popular American newspaper cartoonist Tad Dorgan. The films starred a tall, lanky cat whose creation was spurred by the success of Pat Sullivan's own cat series, *Felix the Cat. A Universal Picture release.*

## TECHNICAL ROMANCES

Produced by J.R. Bray, this series was written, directed and animated by J.A. Norling, Ashley Miller and F. Lyle Goldman. *A Bray Production released by Hodkinson.*

**1922:** "The Mystery Box" (Nov. 25); and "The Sky Splitter" (Dec. 9).

**1923:** "Gambling with the Gulf Stream" (Feb. 4); "The Romance of Life" (Mar. 1); "The Immortal Voice" (June 10); and "Black Sunlight" (Dec. 1).

## TERRY FEATURE BURLESQUES

Paul Terry wrote, produced and directed this series of witty satires. *A Paul Terry Production released by A. Kay Company.*

**1917:** "20,000 Feats Under the Sea" (Apr. 23); "Golden Spoon Mary" (Apr. 30); "Some Barrier" (July 1); and "His Trial" (July 1).

## TERRY HUMAN INTEREST REELS

This series shaped story lines around human characteristics. *Produced and directed by Paul Terry. A Paul Terry Production released by A. Kay Company.*

**1917:** "Character as Revealed by the Nose" (June 1); "Character as Revealed by the Eye" (July 1); "Character as Revealed by the Mouth" (Aug. 1); and "Character as Revealed by the Ear" (Sept. 1).

## TOM AND JERRY

No information could be found for this series—its starring characters or production staff. *An Arrow Film Corporation Production.*

**1923:** "The Gasoline Trail" (Aug. 1); and "Tom's First Flivver" (Sept. 1).

## TONY SARG'S ALMANAC

Famed illustrator Tony Sarg, who toured vaudeville with a marionette routine, wrote and animated this series of animated marionette sequences (called *Shadowgraphs*). The series was cowritten and co-animated by Herbert M. Dawley, who also produced. *A Herbert M. Dawley Production released by Rialto Productions and Educational Pictures.*

### Rialto Productions

**1921:** "The First Circus" (May 21); "The First Dentist" (June); "Why They Love Cave Men" (July 2); "When the Whale Was Jonahed" (Aug. 20); and "Fireman Save My Child" (Sept. 10).

**1922:** "The Original Golfer" (Jan. 7); "Why Adam Walked the Floor" (Feb. 5); "The Original Movie" (Apr. 9); "The First Earful" (May 29); and "Noah Put the Cat Out" (July 9).

*Educational Pictures*

**1922:** "The First Flivver" (July 29); "The First Degree" (July 29); "The First Barber" (Aug. 19); "Baron Bragg and the Devilish Dragon" (Sept. 9); "The Ogling Ogre" (Nov. 19) and "Baron Bragg and the Haunted Castle" (Dec. 17).

**1923:** "The Terrible Tree" (Jan. 6).

### ◎ TOYLAND

This series featured animated dolls and toys and was produced by the team of R.F Taylor and W.W. Wheatley. *Directed by Horace Taylor. A Taylor and Wheatley Production released by Pat Powers.*

**1916:** "A Romance of Toyland" (Mar. 9); "A Toyland Mystery" (Mar. 15); "The Toyland Villain" (Apr. 12); and "A Toyland Robbery" (May 10).

### ◎ TRAVELAUGHS

Henry "Hy" Mayer, a prolific caricaturist and illustrator, was the mastermind behind this series of tastefully done satires on travelogues, combining drawings with live footage. Films appeared as part of screen magazines and were distributed to theaters nationwide. Otto Messmer, who later created *Felix the Cat*, served as Mayer's assistant on the series. In 1920, the series shifted to Pathé. Episodes that appear in the filmography are the only titles available through research. *A Keen Cartoon Corporation Production released by Universal Pictures and Pathé Exchange.*

**1913:** "A Study in Crayon" (Mar.).

**1915:** "To 'Frisco by the Cartoon Route" (Aug. 9).

**1916:** "Globe Trotting with Hy Mayer" (Apr. 14); "Such Is Life in China" (June 22); "Pen and Inklings in and around Jerusalem" (Oct. 5); "High Life on a Farm" (Nov. 9); "A Pen Trip to Palestine" (Nov. 9); and "Such Is Life in Alaska" (Dec. 19).

**1917:** "Such Is Life in South Algeria" (Apr. 28); "China Awakened" (June 26); "Seeing Ceylon with Hy Mayer" (Aug. 6); and "Seeing New York with Hy Mayer" (Oct. 15).

**1918:** "New York by Heck" (May 1).

*Pathé Review*

**1921:** "Behind the Scenes of the Circus" (Jan. 15); "Water Stuff" (Mar. 5); "Spring Hats" (Mar. 26); "All the Merry Bow-Wows" (Apr. 30); "In the Silly Summertime" (May 29); "The Door That Has No Lock" (June 26); "A Ramble Through Provincetown" (July 31); "The Little City of Dreams" (Sept. 4); "Day Dreams" (Sept. 18); "Down to the Fair" (Oct. 2); "Summer Scenes" (Oct. 16); "All Aboard" (Oct. 30); and "Puppies" (Dec. 25).

**1922:** "How It Feels" (Sept. 24); "In the Dear Old Summertime" (Oct. 14); and "Sporting Scenes" (Nov. 25).

**1923:** "Faces" (Jan. 6).

### ◎ THE TRICK KIDS

J.R. Bray produced this series of films, consisting of animated dolls and toys, for the *Paramount Pictographs. A Bray Studios Production released by Famous Players-Lasky Corporation.*

**1916:** "The Birth of the Trick Kids" (Feb. 20); "The Strange Adventures of the Lamb's Tail" (Mar. 12); "Happifat's New Playmate" (Mar. 19); "The Magic Pail" (Apr. 19); "Happifat Does Some Spring Planting" (Apr. 23); "Happifat and Flossy Fisher's Unexpected Buggy Ride" (Apr. 30); "Happifat's Fishing Trip" (May 7); "Happifat's Interrupted Meal" (May 21); "Happifat Becomes an Artist and Draws a Bear" (May 28); and "Everybody's Uncle Sam" (June 1).

### ◎ UNIVERSAL ANIMATED WEEKLY

Animator Henry "Hy" Mayer, who wrote, directed and animated his own series of cartoon shorts for Universal beginning in 1913, and others wrote, animated and directed untitled cartoon sequences dealing with timely issues of the day for this weekly newsreel that enjoyed a near-six-year run from October 1, 1913 to December 1, 1918. *Produced by Carl Laemmle. A Universal Pictures Production released by Universal Pictures.*

### ◎ UNIVERSAL CURRENT EVENTS

Assorted cartoon adaptations of popular newspaper comics were featured in this weekly newsreel series animated by Leslie Elton, Arthur Lewis and others, and produced by Carl Laemmle of Universal Pictures. *A Universal Pictures Production released by Universal Pictures.*

**1917:** "Cartoons: On the Way" by Siebel; "Test of Patriotism" by Brown; and "Hoch der Sedition" by Greene (Oct. 13).

**1918:** "Hoch de Kaiser" (Elton); "Liberty on Guard" (Elton); "Doing Their Bit" (Elton); and "Cartoon" (Lewis/Sept. 28/title unknown).

### ◎ UNIVERSAL SCREEN MAGAZINE

Called the *Universal Weekly* from June 1913 through November 1916, Universal Pictures producer Carl Laemmle launched this popular successor in November 1916. It initially featured animated shorts by J.R. Williams, then Henry "Hy" Mayer, and Willie Hopkins's *Animated Sculptures* cartoons (titles and release dates are unknown) as part of this weekly newsreel series. In 1919, former Bray staffer and animator-director Leslie Elton joined the series, featuring his animated work and live-action/animated series, *Cinema Luke*, until May 1920. *A Universal Pictures Production released by Universal Pictures.*

**1917:** "Trench Warfare in the Sahara" (Williams/Apr. 20).

**1918:** "Hy Mayer Cartoon" (June 29); "Hy Mayer Cartoon" (July 27); "Hy Mayer Cartoon" (Aug. 3); "Hy Mayer Cartoon" (Sept. 1); "Hy Mayer Cartoon" (Oct. 12); "Hy Mayer Cartoon" (Oct. 19); and "Hy Mayer Cartoon" (Oct. 26).

**1919:** "Hy Mayer Cartoon" (Jan. 18); "The Praying Mantis" (Elton); "War in the Air" (Elton); "Won't You Walk into My Parlor" (Elton); "Nightmare Experiences after a Heavy Supper" (Elton); "How Many Bars in a Beetle's Beat" (Elton); "The Sea Serpent and the Flying Dragon" (Elton); "The Courteous Cries of a Cricket" (Elton); "The Lays of an Ostrich Eggstrawdinary" (Elton); "Aphides the Animated Ant's Avarice" (Elton); "The Heart Bug" (Elton); "The Male Mosquito" (Elton); "Ginger for Pluck" (Elton); "Leading Him a Dance" (Elton); and "Cinema Luke" (Dec. 6/Elton).

**1920:** "Cinema Luke" (Mar. 11/Elton); "It's A Bear" (May. 6/Elton); and "Cinema Luke" (May 28/Elton).

### ◎ UN-NATURAL HISTORY

In true Aesopian style, Walter Lantz introduced this series of outlandish history fables, his fourth series for J. R. Bray Studios. Beginning in 1925, the series alternated with *Dinky Doodles* and was distributed by FBO until September 1926, at which time Bray resumed distribution of the series himself.

Two former Disney directors, Dave Hand and Clyde Geronimi, later supervised and helped animate the series, which used child actors to play opposite animal characters in stories that told some deep moral. Actress Anita Louis, later a contract player at 20th Century-Fox, was one of the actors to appear in the series.

Like earlier productions, Lantz's staff was limited to seven people—including the inker, painter, background artist and cameraman—to produce each new installment. He therefore wrote, directed and animated almost every cartoon. Along with *Pete the Pup*, the series marked the end for the Bray Studios, which closed its doors in 1927. *A Bray Production released by Standard Cinema Corporation and Film Booking Offices.*

**1925:** "How the Elephant Got His Trunk" (Lantz/Oct. 4); "How the Bear Got His Short Tail" (Lantz/Oct. 18); "How the Camel Got His Hump" (Geronimi/Nov. 15); and "The Leopard's Spots" (Lantz/Dec. 13).

**1926:** "The Goat's Whiskers" (Lantz/Jan. 10); "How the Giraffe Got His Long Neck" (Lantz/Feb. 7); "The Stork Brought It" (Lantz/Mar. 7); "The King of the Beasts" (Lantz/Apr. 4); "The Ostrich's Plumes" (Apr. 19); "The Pelican's Bill" (Lantz/May 30); "The Cat's Whiskers" (Lantz/June 20); "The Mule's Disposition" (Lantz/July 18); "The Pig's Curly Tail" (Lantz/Aug. 15); and "The Tail of the Monkey" (Lantz, Hand/Dec. 29).

**1927:** "The Cat's Nine Lives" (Lantz, Hand, Geronimi/Jan. 15); and "The Hyena's Laugh" (Lantz, Geronimi/Jan. 18).

## ◎ US FELLERS

Cartoonist Wallace A. Carlson wrote and directed these cartoon reminiscences seen through the eyes of a young lad who dreams about events and mishaps of his boyhood days. *A Bray Production released by Famous Players-Lasky Corporation.*

### *Paramount-Bray Pictographs*

**1919:** "Dud Perkins Gets Mortified" (Apr. 12); "The Parson" (Apr. 26); "Wounded by the Beauty" (Apr. 26); "Dud the Circus Performer" (May 29); "Dud's Greatest Circus on Earth" (June 21); and "At the 'Ol Swimmin' Hole" (Aug. 7).

### *Goldwyn-Bray Pictographs*

**1919:** "Dud's Home Run" (Sept. 23); "Dud Leaves Home" (Oct. 9); "Dud's Geography Lesson" (Nov. 17); and "A Chip Off the Old Block" (Dec. 31).

**1920:** "Dud's Haircut" (Feb. 16); and "Dud the Lion Tamer" (Sept. 9).

## ◎ VERNON HOWE BAILEY'S SKETCHBOOK

This sketchbook travel series was written, produced and directed by Vernon Howe Bailey. *An Essanay Film Manufacturing Company Production.*

**1915:** "Vernon Howe Bailey's Sketchbook" (Nov. 13).

**1916:** ". . . of Chicago" (Jan. 29); ". . . of London" (Mar. 1); ". . . of Philadelphia" (Mar. 14); ". . . of Paris" (Mar. 27); ". . . of Boston" (Apr. 14); ". . . of Rome" (Apr. 26); ". . . of San Francisco" (May 20); ". . . of Berlin" (June 9); ". . . of St. Louis" (June 19); ". . . of New Orleans" (July 10); ". . . of Petrograd" (July 27); and ". . . of Washington."

## ◎ VINCENT WHITMAN CARTOONS

Vincent Whitman served as writer, director and animator of this animated series. *Produced by Sigmund Lubin. A Lubin Manufacturing Company Production.*

**1914:** "A Trip to the Moon" (Mar. 14); "The Bottom of the Sea" (Mar. 21); "A Strenuous Ride" (Apr. 11); "Another Tale" (Apr. 25); "A Hunting Absurdity" (Oct. 3); "An Interrupted Nap" (Oct. 23); and "The Troublesome Cat" (Dec. 15).

**1915:** "Curses Jack Dalton" (Apr. 24); "A Hot Time in Punkville" (May 3); "His Pipe Dreams" (May 21); "Studies in Clay" (July 6); "A Barnyard Mixup" (July 12); "An African Hunt" (July 15); "A One Reel Feature" (July 26); "Relentless Dalton" (Aug. 2); and "The Victorious Jockey" (Aug. 16).

## ◎ VITAGRAPH CARTOONS

After drawing and starring in a series of live-action shorts called *Blackton Cartoons* for Thomas A. Edison in 1897, pioneer animator James Stuart Blackton wrote, produced and directed a second series of animated and non-animated one-reelers for a New York studio he had co-founded with Albert E. Smith called the Vitagraph Corporation of America.

In 1898, Blackton and Smith produced the first stop-motion animated film using inanimate objects, "The Humpty Dumpty Circus," which Smith directed, featuring toy circus animals and acrobats advanced one frame at time. Smith and Blackton each claimed in published interviews that they conceived the idea for the film by borrowing their daughter's wooden circus characters. Two years later, combining live-action and animation, Blackton was featured in black-and-white short, "The Enchanted Drawing" (1900). Reportedly produced earlier than the year it was copyrighted, the film, based on Blackton's popular "chalk-talk" vaudeville act, brought to life a series of letters, words and faces drawn by an "unseen" hand.

On April 6, 1906, Blackton made animation history when he produced the first American animated cartoon released to theaters, "Humorous Phases of Funny Faces." Following this success, Blackton produced and directed four more shorts in the series: "Lightning Sketches" (1907); "Princess Nicotine: Or, a Smokey Fairy" (1909), a film that employed trick photography featuring a woman and her assistant fiddle and a man's pipe and matchbox; "The Magic Fountain Pen," released that July; and "Chew Chew Land; Or the Adventures of Dolly and Jim" (1910), combining live-action and clay animation.

In 1917, Blackton resigned from Vitagraph and went on to work for an independent production company in England, where he was promoted to an executive position in 1923. He remained on board until 1925 when Warner Bros. bought the company. *A Vitagraph Corporation of America Production.*

**1898:** "The Humpty Dumpty Circus" (Smith).

**1900:** "The Enchanted Drawing" (Nov. 16).

**1906:** "Humorous Phases of Funny Faces" (Apr. 6).

**1907:** "Lightning Sketches" (July 15).

**1909:** "The Magic Fountain Pen" (July 17) and "Princess Nicotine: Or, a Smokey Fair" (Aug. 10).

**1910:** "Chew Chew Land; Or the Adventures of Dolly and Jim" (Sept. 6).

## ◎ VON LOON

Legendary cartoonist L.M. Glackens created, animated and directed this short-lived, World War I propaganda series originally released to theaters as part of the *Paramount-Bray Pictograph* magazine series. *A Bray Production released by Paramount.*

**1918:** "Von Loon's 25,000 Mile Gun" (July 22) and "Von Loon's Non-Capturable Aeroplane" (Oct. 1).

## ◎ THE WHOZIT WEEKLY

This series of burlesque cartoon items was produced for the *Universal Screen Magazine*, written, directed and animated by Leslie Elton. *Produced by Carl Laemmle. A Universal Pictures Production released by Universal Pictures.*

**1918:** "No. 100" (Dec. 8); "No. 101" (Dec. 15); "No. 102" (Dec. 22); and "No. 103" (Dec. 29).

**1919:** "No. 104" (Jan. 5); "No. 105" (Jan. 12); "No. 106" (Jan. 19); "No. 107" (Jan. 26); "No. 108" (Feb. 2); "No. 109" (Feb. 9); "No. 110" (Feb. 16); "No. 111" (Feb. 23); "No. 112" (Mar. 2); "No. 113" (Mar. 9); "No. 114" (Mar. 16);

**1919:** "No. 115" (Mar. 23); "No. 123" (May 18); "No. 124" (May 25); "No. 126" (June 8); "No. 129" (June 29); "No. 131" (July 13); "No. 134" (Aug. 3); "No. 137" (Aug. 24); "No. 143" (Oct. 4); and "No. 144" (Oct. 11).

**1920:** "No. 164" (Feb. 28).

## ◎ WINSOR MCCAY CARTOONS

In 1911, Winsor McCay released his first animated cartoon based on his popular syndicated strip, *Little Nemo*. The film was masterful in more ways than style and craftsmanship. It did so much with so little, using only 4,000 penciled drawings to animate five minutes of film. In recalling his work, the famed animator once said, "Not until I drew Gertie the Dinosaur did the audience understand that I was making drawings move."

McCay drew praise from moviegoers and critics with his second fully animated cartoon a year later, "The Story of Mosquito" (also known as "How a Mosquito Operates"), this time using 6,000 drawings.

McCay finally achieved real success in 1914 with "Gertie the Dinosaur" (also called "Gertie the Trained Dinosaur"), generally regarded as the first "cartoon star." Utilizing more than 10,000 drawings (including backgrounds) drawn with ink on rice paper, the cartoon became quite a novelty for McCay, who built on his success and continued making animated films for seven more years.

In addition to taking his act to theaters, combining lectures and demonstrations with screenings of his films, McCay made a huge splash with his biggest undertaking yet, "The Sinking of *Lusitania*" (1918), one of his first cel-animated films drawn on clear celluloid sheets and requiring 25,000 frames of animation to fully animate the nine-minute production. (McCay later expanded the film to 20 minutes, adding live and stock footage.)

In 1921, with the help of his son Robert McCay, he also produced and animated a series of cartoons based on his comic strip, "Dream of the Rarebit Fiend," producing three cartoon shorts overall—"The Pet" (1921), "The Flying House" (1921), and "Bug Vaudeville" (1921)—and three others: "The Centaurs," "Flip's

*Winsor McCay's Gertie the Dinosaur (1914). The cartoon used only 10,000 pencil sketches to produce the action.* (COURTESY: MUSEUM OF MODERN ART/FILM STILLS ARCHIVE)

Circus" and "Gertie on Tour," his second Gertie the Dinosaur cartoon, before producing his last cartoon, "The Midsummer's Nightmare" (1922). *A Winsor McCay and Rialto Production released by Vitagraph Film Corp., Box Office Attractions and Jewel Productions/Universal.*

### Vitagraph Film Corp.

**1911:** "Winsor McCay" (Apr. 8/a.k.a.: "Winsor McCay and His Animated Comics," "Winsor McCay Makes His Cartoons Move," "Winsor McCay Explains His Moving Cartoons to Johnny Bunny" and "Little Nemo")

**1912:** "The Story of Mosquito" (Jan./a.k.a.: "How a Mosquito Operates"/re: "Winsor McCay and His Jersey Skeeters"/based on the comic strip, "Dream of the Rarebit Fiend.")

### Box Office Attractions

**1914:** "Gertie" (Sept. 14/a.k.a.: "Gertie the Dinosaurus," "Gertie the Dinosaur" and "Gertie the Trained Dinosaur")

**1916:** "Winsor McCay and His Jersey Skeeters" (re-issue of "The Story of Mosquito").

### Jewel Productions/Universal

**1918:** "The Sinking of the *Lusitania*" (May 18).

### Rialto Productions

**1921:** "Bug Vaudeville" (Sept. 26); "The Pet" (Sept. 26); "The Flying House" (Sept. 26); "The Centaurs"; "Flip's Circus"; and "Gertie on Tour."

**1922:** "The Midsummer's Nightmare."

# Theatrical Sound Cartoon Series

## ◎ AESOP'S FABLES

After Walt Disney released the first synchronized sound cartoon in 1928, Paul Terry made the conversion to sound with his *Aesop's Fables* series, first popular during the silent era.

Terry directed the series for his new boss, Amadee J. Van Beuren of Van Beuren Productions. The series was announced November 1928. The first sound release was "Dinner Time," featuring synchronized soundtracks—music but no voices—added to the silent product.

Terry directed most of the films until 1929, when he left Van Beuren to form his own studio. Other animators directed the series from then on: John Foster, Harry Bailey, J.J. McManus, George Stallings and George Rufle.

In 1945, under the *Terry-Toons* banner, Terry produced his first new *Aesop's Fables* in 12 years: "Aesop Fables: The Mosquito" starring *Terry-Toons* star Gandy Goose. The cartoon was the first in a new series of Aesop's produced by Terry. By the late 1950s, ushering in the beginning of a new period of Terry-Toons cartoons under the leadership of animator Gene Deitch, who was named creative director in 1956, the Terrytoons name was no longer hyphenated in the credits of the films that were released. *Series directors were Terry-Toons veterans Connie Rasinski and Eddie Donnelly. Black-and-white. Technicolor. CinemaScope. A Pathé Film released by RKO Van Beuren and RKO Pathe Film Exchange. A Terry-Toon Cartoons and Terrytoons CBS Films, Inc. Production released by 20th Century Fox.*

### RKO Van Beuren releases
(Copyright dates are marked by ©.)

**1928:** "Dinner Time" (Terry/© Dec. 17).

**1929:** "The Big Burg"; "The Faithful Pup" (Terry/May 4); "Concentrate" (Terry/May 4); "The Jail Breakers" (Terry/May 6); "Wood-choppers" (Terry/May 9); "Presto Chango" (Terry/May 20); "Skating Hounds" (Terry/May 27); "Stage Struck" (Terry/June 25); "House Cleaning Time" (Foster/July 23); "A Stone Age Romance" (Aug. 1); "The Big Scare" (Terry/Aug. 15); "Jungle Fool" (Foster, Davis/Sept. 15); "Fly's Bride" (Foster/Sept. 21); "Summer Time" (Foster/Oct. 11); "Mill Pond" (Foster/Oct. 18);

"Barnyard Melody" (Foster/Nov. 1); "Tuning In" (Nov. 7); "Night Club" (Foster, Davis/Dec. 1); and "Close Call" (Bailey/Dec. 1).

**1930:** "The Iron Man" (Foster/Jan. 4); "Ship Ahoy" (Foster/Jan. 7); "Singing Saps" (Foster, Davis/Feb. 7); "Sky Skippers" (Foster, Bailey/Feb. 14); "Good Old Schooldays" (Foster, Davis/Mar. 7); "Foolish Follies" (Foster, Bailey/Mar. 7); "Dixie Days" (Foster, Davis/Apr. 8); "Western Whoopee" (Foster, Bailey/Apr. 10); "The Haunted Ship" (Foster, Davis/Apr. 27); "Noah Knew His Ark" (Foster, Davis/May 25); "Oom Pah Pah" (Foster, Bailey/May 30); "A Romeo Robin" (Foster, Davis/June 22); "Jungle Jazz" (Foster, Bailey/July 6); "Snow Time" (Foster, Davis/July 20); "Hot Tamale" (Foster/Aug. 3); "Laundry Blues" (Foster, Davis/Aug. 17); "Frozen Frolics" (Foster, Bailey/Aug. 31); "Farm Foolery" (Foster/Sept. 14); "Circus Capers" (Foster, Bailey/Sept. 28); "Midnight" (Foster, Davis/Oct. 12); "The Big Cheeze" (Foster/Oct. 26); "Gypped in Egypt" (Foster, Davis/Nov. 9); "The Office Boy" (Foster, Bailey/Nov. 23); "Stone Age Stunts" (Foster/Dec. 7); and "King of the Bugs" (Foster, Bailey/Dec. 21).

### RKO Pathé Film Exchange releases

**1931:** "Toy Town Tales" (Foster, Davis/Jan. 4/a.k.a. "Toyland Adventure"); "Red Riding Hood" (Foster, Bailey/Jan. 18); "The Animal Fair" (Foster, Davis/Feb. 1); "Cowboy Blues" (Foster, Bailey/Feb. 15); "Radio Racket" (Foster/Mar. 1); "College Capers" (Foster, Bailey/Mar. 15); "Old Hokum Bucket" (Mar. 29); "Cinderella Blues" (Foster, Bailey/Apr. 12); "Mad Melody" (Foster, Davis/Apr. 26); "The Fly Guy" (Foster, Bailey/May 10); "Play Ball" (Foster, Davis/May 24); "Fisherman's Luck" (Foster, Bailey/June 13); "Pale Face Pup" (Foster, Davis/June 22); "Making 'em Move" (Foster, Bailey/July 5/a.k.a. "In A Cartoon Studio"); "Fun on the Ice" (Foster, Davis/July 19); "Big Game" (Aug. 3); "Love in a Pond" (Foster, Davis/Aug. 17); "Fly Hi" (Foster, Bailey/Aug. 31); "The Family Shoe" (Foster, Davis/Sept. 14); "Fairyland Follies" (Foster, Bailey/Sept. 28). "Horse Cops" (Foster, McManus/Oct. 12); "Cowboy Cabaret" (Foster, Davis/Oct. 26); "In Dutch" (Foster, Bailey/Nov. 9); and "The Last Dance" (Nov. 23).

**1932:** "Toy Time" (Foster, Bailey/Jan. 27); "A Romeo Monk" (Foster, Davis/Feb. 20); "Fly Frolic" (Foster, Bailey/Mar. 5); "The Cat's Canary" (Foster, Davis/Mar. 26); "Magic Art" (Foster, Bailey/Apr. 25); "Happy Polo" (May 14); "Spring Antics" (Foster, Davis/May 21); "Farmerette" (June 11); "Circus Romance" (Foster, Bailey/June 25); "Stone Age Error" (Foster, Davis/July 9); "Chinese Jinks" (Foster, Davis/July 23); "The Ball Game" (Foster, Rufle/July 30); "Wild Goose Chase" (Foster, Davis/Aug. 12); "Nursery Scandal" (Foster, Bailey/Aug. 26); "Bring 'Em Back Half-Shot" (Foster, Davis/Sept. 9); "Down in Dixie" (Foster, Bailey/Sept. 23); "Catfish Romance" (Foster, Davis/Oct. 7); "Feathered Follies" (Oct. 21); "Venice Vamp" (Foster, Davis/Nov. 4); "Hokum Hotel" (Foster, Bailey/Nov. 18); "Pickaninny Blues" (Foster, Davis/© Dec. 12); "A Yarn of Wool" (Foster, Bailey/© Dec. 16); and "Bugs and Books" (Foster, Davis/© Dec. 30).

**1933:** "Silvery Moon" (Foster, Davis/© Jan. 13); "A.M. to P.M." (© Jan. 20); "Tumble Down Town" (Foster, Bailey/© Jan. 27); "Love's Labor Won" (Foster, Davis/© Mar. 10); "A Dizzy Day" (Bailey/© May 5); "Barking Dogs" (Davis/© May 18); "The Bully's End" (Bailey/© June 16); "Indian Whoopie" (Davis/© July 7); "Fresh Ham" (Davis/© July 12); and "Rough on Rats" (Bailey/© July 14).

### 20th Century Fox releases

**1945:** "Aesop's Fables: The Mosquito" (with Gandy Goose/Davis/June 29).

**1950:** Foiling the Fox" (Raskinski/Apr. 1).

**1951:** Golden Egg Goosie" (Donnelly/Aug. 1).

**1952:** "Happy Valley" (Donnelly/Sept. 1).

**1953:** "Sparky the Firefly" (Rasinski/Sept. 1).

**1955:** "The First Flying Fish" (Rasinski/Feb. 1).

**1960:** "The Tiger King" (Rasinski/Mar. 1/CinemaScope).

### ◎ AMOS 'N' ANDY

Van Beuren Studios, creators of the Little King and Cubby cartoon series, attempt to bolster its roster of stars by signing actors Freeman Gosden and Charles Correll to reprise the roles of Amos Jones and Andy Brown, characters from their popular radio program, in a series of cartoon shorts. Unfortunately, the series never caught on with moviegoers. *Directed by George Stallings. Black-and-white. A Van Beuren Studios Production released by RKO Radio Pictures.*

### Voices
**Amos:** Freeman Gosden; **Andy:** Charles Correll

**1934:** "The Rassling Match" (Jan. 5); and "The Lion Tamer" (Feb. 2).

### ◎ ANDY PANDA

Created by Walter Lantz, the cuddly cartoon panda made his film debut in 1939 and proved so successful that Lantz contracted for four or five one-reelers a year. Lantz originated the idea for the character following a national news story he read about a panda being donated to the Chicago Zoo. The series opener was called "Life Begins for Andy Panda," a play on words on the title of a popular Andy Hardy feature of the same name. Three cartoons later Andy Panda marked another historical event in his young career—the first appearance of Lantz's wood-beating bird, Woody Woodpecker, in "Knock Knock" (1940). During the character's 11-year run on the screen, two cartoons in which he appeared

*Andy Panda in a scene from the 1948 Dick Lundy–directed Walter Lantz cartoon short "Playful Pelican." © Walter Lantz Productions*

were nominated for Academy Awards under the "Best Short Subject" category: 1944's "Fish Fry," directed by James Culhane, and "The Poet and Peasant," a 1946 "Musical Miniature" directed by Dick Lundy.

Sarah Berner, who was better known as the switchboard operator on the Jack Benny radio program, was the second actor to voice the character until Bernice Hansen assumed that role for the balance of the series. *Directors were Walter Lantz, Dick Lundy, Alex Lovy and James "Shamus" Culhane. Technicolor. A Walter Lantz Production released through Universal Pictures and United Artists.*

### Voices
**Andy Panda:** Bernice Hansen, Sarah Berner, Walter Tetley

### Universal Pictures releases

**1939:** "Life Begins for Andy Panda" (Lovy/Sept. 9).

**1940:** "Andy Panda Goes Fishing" (Gillett, Lovy [uncredited]/Jan. 22); "100 Pigmies and Andy Panda" (Lovy/Apr. 22); "Crazy House" (Lantz/Sept. 2); and "Knock Knock" (Woody Woodpecker's debut/Lantz/Nov. 25).

**1941:** "Mouse Trappers" (Lantz/Jan. 27); "Dizzy Kitty" (Lantz/May 26); and "Andy Panda's Pop" (Lovy/July 28).

**1942:** "Under the Spreading Blacksmith Shop" (Lovy/Jan. 12); "Good-Bye Mr. Moth" (Lantz/May 11/Andy Panda's first solo cartoon); "Nutty Pine Cabin" (Lovy/June 1); "Andy Panda's Victory" (Lovy/Sept. 9); and "Air Raid Warden" (Lovy/Dec. 21).

**1943:** "Meatless Tuesday" (Culhane/Oct. 25).

**1944:** "Fish Fry" (Culhane/June 19/A.A. nominee); and "The Painter and the Pointer" (Culhane/Dec. 18).

**1945:** "Crow Crazy" (Lundy/July 9).

**1946:** "The Poet & Peasant" (Lundy/Mar. 18/first Musical Miniature/A.A. nominee); "Mousie Come Home" (Culhane/Apr. 15); "Apple Andy" (Lundy/May 20); and "The Wacky Weed" (Lundy/Dec. 16).

### United Artists releases

**1947:** "Musical Moments from Chopin" (with Woody Woodpecker/Lundy/Feb. 24/Musical Miniature/A.A. nominee); and "The Band Master" (Lundy/Dec.).

**1948:** "Banquet Busters" (with Woody Woodpecker/Lundy/Mar. 2/Woody Woodpecker cartoon); "Playful Pelican" (Lundy/Oct. 8); and "Dog Tax Dodgers" (Lundy/Nov. 26).

**1949:** "Scrappy Birthday" (Lundy/Feb. 11).

## ANIMANIACS

Known for their trademark style of zany, physical comedy, nonstop wordplay and rousing music, television's Animaniacs—Yakko, Wakko and Dot, the Warner brothers and sister—jumped to the big screen in 1994 with their first theatrical cartoon, "I'm Mad," which opened nationwide with Don Bluth's full-length animated feature, *Thumbelina*, based on the classic Hans Christian Andersen fairy tale. The success of their weekday television series—which premiered on the FOX Network in 1993—sparked a desire on the part of executive producer Steven Spielberg, senior producer Tom Ruegger and executive in charge of production Jean MacCurdy to bring the characters to a wider audience by featuring them in a series of theatrical cartoon shorts that never went beyond its initial entry. *Directed by Rich Arons, Audu Paden and Dave Marshall. Technicolor. An Amblin Entertainment/Warner Brothers Animation Production released by Warner Bros.*

*Voices*
**Yakko Warner:** Rob Paulsen; **Wakko Warner:** Jess Harnell; **Dot Warner:** Tress MacNeille

**1994:** "I'm Mad" (Mar. 30).

## ANIMATED ANTICS

This series evolved from Max Fleischer's *Gulliver's Travels* (1939). testing various supporting characters from the classic animated feature in a new animated series. Films spotlighted character favorites, such as Twinkletoes and Sneak, Snoop and Snith, in animated adventures. *Produced by Max Fleischer and directed by Dave Fleischer. Black-and-white. A Fleischer Studios Production released through Paramount Pictures.*

**1940:** "The Dandy Lion" (with Sneak, Snoop, Snitch, Twinkletoes/Sept. 20); Sneak, Snoop and Snitch" (Oct. 25); "Mommy Loves Puppy" (with Sneak, Snoop and Snitch);

*Yakko, Wakko and Dot Warner, also known as the Animaniacs, make their motion picture debut in their first and only theatrical cartoon short, "I'm Mad," also shown as an episode of television's* Steven Spielberg Presents Animaniacs. © *Warner Brothers. All rights reserved.*

and "Bring Himself Back Alive" (with Sneak, Snoop, Snitch, Twinkletoes, Hyde Skinner).

**1941:** "Zero the Hound" (with Sneak, Snoop, Snitch, Twinkletoes/© Feb. 14); "Twinkletoes Gets the Bird" (with Sneak, Snoop, Snitch, Twinkletoes/Mar. 14); "Sneak, Snoop and Snitch in Triple Trouble" (with Sneak, Snoop, Snitch, Twinkletoes/May 9); "Twinkletoes— Where He Goes, Nobody Knows" (with Sneak, Snoop, Snitch, Twinkletoes, King Bombo/June 27); "Copy Cat" (with Sneak, Snoop, Snitch, Twinkletoes/July 18); "The Wizard of Arts" (with Sneak, Snoop, Snitch, Twinkletoes/Aug. 8); and "Twinkletoes in Hat Stuff" (with Sneak, Snoop, Snitch, Twinkletoes/Aug. 29).

## THE ANT AND THE AARDVARK

The misadventures of a purple, vacuumed-nosed aardvark in pursuit of his meal: a tiny red ant. In his ill-fated attempts to sniff out the ant, the aardvark instead picks up gunpowder, tacks, dynamite and virtually every object imaginable during its prowl. Episodes were later featured as part of the television series, *The New Pink Panther Show. Directors were Gerry Chiniquy, Art Davis, Friz Freleng, George Gordon and Hawley Pratt. Technicolor. A Mirisch-DePatie-Freleng Enterprises Production released through United Artists.*

*Voices*
**The Ant/The Aardvark:** John Byner.

***Additional Voices***
Athena Lorde and Marvin Miller.

**1969:** "The Ant and the Aardvark" (Freleng/Mar. 5); "Hasty But Tasty" (Chiniquy/Mar. 6); "The Ant from Uncle" (Gordon/Apr. 2); "I've Got Ants in My Plans" (Chiniquy/May 14); "Technology, Phooey" (Chiniquy/June 25); "Never Bug an Ant" (Davis/Sept. 12); "Dune Bug" (Davis/Oct. 27); and "Isle of Caprice" (Chiniquy/ Dec. 18).

**1970:** "Scratch a Tiger" (Pratt/Jan. 28); "Odd Ant Out" (Chiniquy/Apr. 20); "Ants in the Pantry" (Pratt/June 10); "Science Friction" (Chiniquy/June 28); "Mumbo Jumbo" (Davis/Sept. 27); "The Froze Nose Knows" (Chiniquy/Nov. 18); and "Don't Hustle an Ant with Muscle" (Davis/Dec. 27).

**1971:** "Rough Brunch" (Davis/Jan. 3); and "From Bed to Worse" (Davis/May 16).

## ASTRONUT

This friendly, outer-space gremlin first appeared in a *Deputy Dawg* episode before starring in a theatrical series of his own. Each adventure followed Astronut's frolics across Earth with his friend and companion, Oscar Mild. *Directors were Connie Rasinski, Dave Tendlar, Arthur Bartsch and Cosmo Anzilotti. Technicolor. A Terrytoons and CBS Films, Inc., Production released through 20th Century Fox.*

*Voices*
**Astronut:** Dayton Allen, Lionel Wilson, Bob McFadden; **Oscar:** Bob McFadden

**1964:** "Brother from Outer Space" (Rasinski/Mar.); "Kisser Plant" (Rasinski/June); "Outer Galaxy Gazette" (Rasinski/Sept.); and "Molecular Mixup" (Tendlar/Dec.).

**1965:** "The Sky's the Limit" (Tendlar/Feb. 1); "Weather Magic" (Anzilotti/May 1); "Robots in Toyland" (Rasinski/Aug. 1); and "Twinkle, Twinkle Little Telestar" (Bartsch/Nov. 1).

**1966:** "Gems from Gemini" (Tendlar/Jan.); and "Haunted Housecleaning" (Rasinski/May 1).

**1969:** "Space Pet" (Mar.); "Scientific Sideshow" (June 12); and "Balloon Snatcher" (Sept.).

**1970:** "Going Ape" (Jan.); and "Martian Moochers" (May).

**1971:** "Oscar's Birthday Present" (Jan.); "Oscar's Thinking Cap" (May); and "No Space Like Home" (Oct.).

## ◎ BABBIT AND CATSTELLO

Bob Clampett created this pair of loquacious cats based on the antics of the movie comedy greats Abbott and Costello. Originally designed as one-shot characters. The funny felines first appeared in 1942's "A Tale of Two Kitties," which marked the debut of Tweety Bird (who was unofficially called Orson in the cartoon). They later returned in two more cartoons before the studio retired them. *Directed by Bob Clampett, Frank Tashlin and Robert McKimson. Technicolor. A Leon Schlesinger Studios/Warner Bros. Cartoons, Inc. Production released by Warner Bros.*

### Voices
**Babbit:** Ted Pierce; **Catstello:** Mel Blanc

### Merrie Melodies

**1942:** "A Tale of Two Kitties" (with Tweety/Clampett/Nov. 21).

**1946:** "The Mouse-Merized Cat" (McKimson/Oct. 19).

### Looney Tunes

**1945:** "A Tale of Two Mice" (Tashlin/June 30).

## ◎ BABY-FACE MOUSE

In the late 1930s, Walter Lantz introduced a flurry of new characters to the screen in one-shot cartoons and potential series. Baby-Face Mouse was among the lot, featured in a short-lived series of his own, who bore some resemblance to Warner Bros.' Sniffles the Mouse and was introduced to moviegoers that same year (1938). *Directed by Alex Lovy and Les Kline. Black-and-white. A Walter Lantz Production released through Universal Pictures.*

**1938:** "Cheese-Nappers" (with Butch Face Rat/Lovy/July 14); "The Big Cat and the Little Mouse" (Kline/Aug. 15); "The Cat and the Bell" (Lovy/Oct. 3); "Sailor Mouse" (Lovy/Nov. 7); and "The Disobedient Mouse" (Kline/Nov. 28).

## ◎ BABY HUEY

Baby Huey was the inspiration of Paramount/Famous Studios, which also brought the likes of Casper the Friendly Ghost, Little Audrey and Herman and Katnip to the screen. The studio was formed in 1942, following Paramount's removal of Max and Dave Fleischer from control of its animation studio; thereafter it was renamed and staffed with new personnel.

Like those of his cohorts, Baby Huey's cartoons can be best described as "formula" with little room for imagination. The premise: a husky, strong baby duck whose complete naivete makes him a prime target for one hungry fox that is repeatedly thwarted by Huey's immense strength, rendering him virtually indestructible in a clumsy sort of way. Comedian Syd Raymond, who created the voice of Katnip, also provided the voice characterization for Huey.

In the fall of 1995, the five-foot-tall, 250-pound baby duck with a heart of gold returned, this time to the small screen in a new syndicated animated television series, *The Baby Huey Show. Directed by Isadore Sparber, Seymour Kneitel and Dave Tendlar. Technicolor. A Famous Studios Production released through Paramount Pictures.*

### Voices
**Baby Huey:** Syd Raymond

**1950:** (Each listed title was from the *Noveltoons* series): "Quack-a-Doodle-Doo" (with Fox, Mrs. Duck/Sparber/May 3).

**1951:** "One Quack Mind" (with Fox/Sparber/Jan. 12); "Party Smarty" (with Fox, Oscar/Kneitel/Aug. 3); and "Scout Fellow" (Kneitel/Dec. 21).

**1952:** "Clown on the Farm" (with Fox/Kneitel/Aug. 22).

**1953:** "Starting from Hatch" (with Mommy, Fox/Kneitel/Mar. 6); and "Huey's Ducky Daddy" (with Hubert Duck/Sparber/Nov. 20).

**1955:** "Git Along Li'l Duckie" (with Fox/Tendlar/Mar. 25).

**1956:** "Swab the Duck" (Tendlar/May 11).

**1957:** "Pest Pupil" (with Mom, Dad, German Tutor, Shark/Tendlar/Jan. 25); and "Jumping with Toy" (with Fox, Santa Claus/Tendlar/Oct. 4).

**1959:** "Huey's Father's Day" (with Father, Mr. Quack/Kneitel/May 8).

## ◎ BARNEY BEAR

MGM developed several promising animated film stars, one of which was the lumbering but lovable Barney Bear, whose slow-burn reactions, sympathetic nature and vocal patterns were reminiscent of actor Wallace Beery, who, incidentally, was an MGM star in the 1930s.

The character was redesigned in the late 1940s by animators Preston Blair and Michael Lah, the latter an understudy of director Tex Avery. Lah also directed the series following Rudolf Ising's departure in 1943. The fourth cartoon in the series, 1941's "Rookie Bear," was nominated for an Academy Award for best short subject but lost that year to Walt Disney's Pluto cartoon, "Lend a Paw." *Directed by Preston Blair, George Gordon, Rudolf Ising, Dick Lundy and Michael Lah. Technicolor. A Metro-Goldwyn-Mayer Cartoon Production released by Metro-Goldwyn-Mayer.*

### Voices
**Barney Bear:** Billy Bletcher, Rudolf Ising, Paul Frees

**1939:** "The Bear That Couldn't Sleep" (Ising/June 10).

**1940:** "The Fishing Bear" (Ising/Jan. 20).

**1941:** "The Prospecting Bear" (Ising/Mar. 8); "Rookie Bear" (Ising/May 17/A.A. nominee); and "The Flying Bear" (Ising/Nov. 1).

**1942:** "The Bear and the Beavers" (Ising/Mar. 28); "Wild Honey" (Ising/Nov. 7/working title: "How to Get Along Without a Ration Book"); and "Barney Bear's Victory Garden" (Ising/Dec. 26).

**1943:** "Bah Wilderness" (Ising/Feb. 13); and "The Uninvited Pest" (Ising/July 17/re: Apr. 29, 1950).

**1944:** "Bear Raid Warden" (Gordon/Sept. 9); and "Barney Bear's Polar Pest" (Gordon/Dec. 30/working title: "Bedtime for Barney").

**1945:** "The Unwelcome Guest" (Gordon/Feb. 17/working title: "Skunk Story").

**1948:** "The Bear and the Bean" (Lah, Blair/Jan. 31); and "The Bear and the Hare" (Lah, Blair/June 26/working title: "Snowshoe Baby").

**1949:** "Goggle Fishing Bear" (Blair, Lah/Jan. 15/working title: "Goggle Fishing").

*Barney Bear looks disgusted over his "big" catch in a scene from MGM's "The Fishing Bear" (1949). © Turner Entertainment*

**1952:** "Little Wise Quacker" (Lundy/Nov. 8); and "Busybody Bear" (Lundy/Dec. 20).

**1953:** "Barney's Hungry Cousin" (Lundy/Jan. 31); "Cobs and Robbers" (Lundy/Mar. 14); "Heir Bear" (Lundy/May 30); "Wee Willie Wildcat" (Lundy/June 20); and "Half-Pint Palomino" (Lundy/Sept. 26).

**1954:** "Impossible Possum" (Lundy/Mar. 28); "Sleepy-Time Squirrel" (Lundy/June 19); and "Bird-Brain Bird Dog" (Lundy/July 30).

## BARNEY GOOGLE

Producer Charles Mintz, who wanted another established star in Columbia Pictures' cartoon stable, brought this popular comic-strip character to the screen by special arrangement with its creator, Billy DeBeck. The character appeared in only four films before the series was abandoned. *Directed by Art Davis. Technicolor. A Columbia Pictures Corporation Production released by Columbia Pictures.*

**1935:** "Tetched in the Head" (Oct. 24); and "Patch Mah Britches" (Dec. 19).

**1936:** "Spark Plug" (Apr. 12); and "Major Google" (May 24).

## BEAKY BUZZARD

Bob Clampett dreamed up this misfit buzzard who was as stupid as he looked. Beaky, a shy, Mortimer Snerd type (who was also known as the Snerd Bird), first appeared in 1942's "Bugs Bunny Gets the Boid," which Clampett directed. He reappeared three years later in 1945's "The Bashful Buzzard." The character was voiced in these earlier adventures by an actor named Kent Rogers. After Clampett left Warner Bros. in 1946, Beaky was resurrected four years later in "The Lion's Busy." By then Mel Blanc replaced Rogers as the voice as the voice of Beaky. *Directed by Bob Clampett, Friz Freleng and Robert McKimson. Technicolor. A Warner Bros. Cartoons, Inc. Production released by Warner Bros.*

### Voice
**Beaky Buzzard:** Kent Rogers, Mel Blanc

### Looney Tunes

**1945:** "The Bashful Buzzard" (Clampett/Sept. 5).

**1950:** "The Lion's Busy" (Freleng/Feb. 18); and "Strife with Father" (McKimson/Apr. 1).

### Merrie Melodies

**1942:** "Bugs Bunny Gets the Boid" (Clampett/July 11).

## BEANS

One of Warner Bros. earliest cartoon stars, this mischievous black cat was used primarily as a supporting character in *Looney Tunes* cartoons produced in the mid-1930s. Created by Bob Clampett, Beans's first appearance was in the 1935 *Merrie Melodies* cartoon, "I Haven't Got a Hat," which also marked the debut of Porky Pig. *Directed by Jack King, Tex Avery and Friz Freleng. Black-and-white. A Vitaphone and Warner Bros. Production released by Warner Bros.*

### Looney Tunes

**1935:** "A Cartoonist's Nightmare" (King/Sept. 21); and "Hollywood Capers" (King/Oct. 19).

**1936:** "Gold Diggers of '49" (with Porky/Avery/Jan. 6); "The Phantom Ship" (with Ham and Ex/King/Feb. 1); "Boom Boom" (with Porky/King/Feb. 29); "Alpine Antics" (King/Mar. 9); "The Fire Alarm" (with Ham and Ex/King/Mar. 9); and "Westward Whoa" (with Porky/King/Apr. 25).

### Merrie Melodies

**1935:** "I Haven't Got a Hat" (with Porky/Freleng/Mar. 9).

## THE BEARY FAMILY

Modern cave-life situations run amuck when father Charlie, children Junior and Suzy and wife Bessie battle everyday problems of a bear's life. The series was inspired by TV's *Life of Riley* starring William Bendix, and lasted nine years. *Former Disney director Jack Hannah and veteran Lantz animator Paul J. Smith directed the series. Technicolor. A Walter Lantz Production released through Universal Pictures.*

### Voices
**Charlie Beary:** Paul Frees; **Bessie Beary:** Grace Stafford; **Junior:** Paul Frees; **Suzy:** Grace Stafford

**1962:** "Fowled-Up Birthday" (Hannah/Apr. 1); and "Mother's Little Helper" (Hannah/June 1).

**1963:** "Charlie's Mother-in-Law" (Smith/Apr. 1); "Goose in the Rough" (Smith/Aug. 1); and "Goose Is Wild" (Smith/Oct. 1).

**1964:** "Rah Rah Ruckus" (Smith/June 1); and "Rooftop Razzle-Dazzle" (Smith/Oct. 1).

**1965:** "Guest Who?" (Smith/Mar. 1); and "Davy Cricket" (Smith/May 1).

**1966:** "Foot Brawl" (Smith/Jan. 1).

**1967:** "Window Pains" (Smith/Jan. 1); and "Mouse in the House" (Smith/Apr. 1).

**1968:** "Jerky Turkey" (Smith); "Paste Makes Waste" (Smith); and "Bugged by a Rug" (Smith).

**1969:** "Gopher Broke" (Smith); "Charlie's Campout" (Smith); and "Cool It Charlie" (Smith).

**1970:** "Charlie in Hot Water" (Smith); "Charlie's Golf Classic" (Smith); and "The Unhandy Man" (Smith).

**1971:** "Charlie the Rainmaker" (Smith); "The Bungling Builder" (Smith); and "Moochin Pooch" (Smith).

**1972:** "Let Charlie Do It" (Smith); "A Fish Story" (Smith); "Rain Rain, Go Away" (Smith) and "Unlucky Potluck" (Smith).

## ◎ BETTY BOOP

In "Dizzy Dishes," the sixth cartoon of Max Fleischer's *Talkartoon* series, this bubbling beauty of the cartoon world was first introduced. Initially she was nothing like the femme fatale who later seduced a nation of filmgoers with her cute button nose, wide-sparkling eyes, flapper-style dress and saucy "Boop-Boop-a-Doop" tag line.

Grim Natwick, who later animated for Ub Iwerks and Walt Disney, fashioned Betty after singer/actress Helen Kane, who happened to be a Paramount star. (The Betty Boop cartoons were released by the same studio.) Natwick based Betty's looks on Kane, after seeing the singer's face on a song sheet cover. He took Kane's own physical features and blended them with a French poodle. Thus, in her screen debut, Betty looks more like a hybrid of a dog, sporting long floppy ears and other characteristics that were more doglike in manner.

By 1932 Betty's character was completely modified and she returned with her new look in a number of cartoons under the *Talkartoon* banner. She was actually without a name until her appearance in "Stopping the Show," billed as the first official *Betty Boop* cartoon, that same year.

Dave Fleischer, Max Fleischer's brother, was responsible for standardizing Betty's appearance, making her feminine. She exhibited the true Betty Boop personality for the first time in "Minnie the Moocher," featuring Cab Calloway and his orchestra. (Calloway was Rotoscoped as a ghost walrus who dances to the sounds of the orchestra.)

The films' sexual themes ultimately became the series' downfall. By the mid-1930s, with stricter censorship laws enforced against cartoons, Betty underwent substantial changes again. Her garter, short skirt and decolletage were soon gone, undermining her appeal. Cast members Bimbo and Koko the Clown, who had come out of retirement, were given pink slips as well.

National Television Associates (NTA) bought the package of *Betty Boop* one-reelers in the late 1950s to distribute the series to television. *Directed by Dave Fleischer. Black-and-white. A Fleischer Studios Production released through Paramount Pictures.*

*Voices*
**Betty Boop:** Mae Questel, Ann Rothschild, Margie Heinz, Kate Wright, Bonnie Poe

**1930:** "Dizzy Dishes" (Aug. 9/*Talkartoon*).

**1931:** "Silly Scandals" (May 23/*Talkartoon*); "Bimbo's Initiation" (July 24/*Talkartoon*); "Bimbo's Express" (Aug. 22/*Talkartoon*); "Minding the Baby" (Sept. 26/*Talkartoon*); "Mask-a-Raid" (Nov. 7/*Talkartoon*); "Jack and the Beanstalk" (Nov. 21/*Talkartoon*); and "Dizzy Red Riding Hood" (Dec. 12).

**1932:** "Any Rags" (Jan. 2/*Talkartoon*); "Boop-Oop-a-Doop" (Jan. 16/*Talkartoon*); "Minnie the Moocher" (with Cab Calloway/Mar. 1); "Swim or Sink" (Mar. 11/*Talkartoon*); "Crazy Town" (Mar. 25/*Talkartoon*); "The Dancing Fool" (Apr. 18/*Talkartoon*); "A Hunting We Will Go" (Apr. 28); "Admission Free" (June 10/*Talkartoon*); "The Betty Boop Limited" (July 1/*Talkartoon*); "Rudy Vallee Melodies" (Aug. 5/*Screen Song*); "Stopping the Show" (Aug. 12); "Betty Boop Bizzy Bee" (Aug. 19); "Betty Boop, M.D." (Sept. 2); "Betty Boop's Bamboo Isle" (with Royal Samoans with Miri/Sept. 23); "Betty Boop's Ups and Downs" (Oct. 14); "Betty Boop for President" (Nov. 4); "I'll Be Glad When You're Dead You Rascal You" (with Louis Armstrong/Nov. 25); and "Betty Boop's Museum" (Dec. 16).

**1933:** "Betty Boop's Ker-Choo" (Jan. 6); "Betty Boop's Crazy Inventions" (Jan. 27); "Is My Palm Read" (Feb. 17); "Betty Boop's Penthouse" (Mar. 10); "Snow-White" (Mar. 31); "Betty Boop's Birthday Party" (Apr. 21); "Betty Boop's May Party" (May 12); "Betty Boop's Big Boss" (June 2); "Mother Goose Land" (June 23); "Popeye the Sailor" (Popeye's debut/July 14); "The Old Man of the Mountain" (with Cab Calloway/Aug. 4); "I Heard" (with Don Redman/Sept. 1); "Morning, Noon and Night" (with Rubinoff/Oct. 6); "Betty Boop's Hallowe'en Party" (Nov. 3); and "Parade of the Wooden Soldiers" (with Rubinoff/Dec. 1).

**1934:** "She Wrong Him Right" (Jan. 5); "Red Hot Mama" (Feb. 2); "Ha! Ha! Ha!" (Mar. 2); "Betty in Blunderland" (Apr. 6); "Betty Boop's Rise to Fame" (May 18); "Betty Boop's Trial" (June 15); "Betty Boop's Life Guard" (July 13); "There's Something About a Soldier" (Aug. 17); "Betty Boop's Little Pal" (Sept. 21); "Betty Boop's Prize Show" (Oct. 19); "Keep in Style" (Nov. 16); and "When My Ship Comes In" (Dec. 21).

*Beloved "boop-boop-a-doop" girl, Betty Boop, and sidekick Bimbo in a promotional still for the popular Max Fleischer cartoon series.*

**1935:** "Baby Be Good" (Jan. 18); "Taking the Blame" (Feb. 15); "Stop That Noise" (Mar. 15); "Swat the Fly" (Apr. 19); "No! No! A Thousand Times No!" (May 24); "A Little Soap and Water" (June 21); "A Language All My Own" (July 19); "Betty Boop and Grampy" (Aug. 16); "Judge for a Day" (Sept. 20); "Making Stars" (Oct. 18); "Betty Boop, with Henry the Funniest Living American" (Nov. 22); and "Little Nobody" (Dec. 27).

**1936:** "Betty Boop and the Little King" (Jan. 31); "Not Now" (Feb. 28); "Betty Boop and Little Jimmy" (Mar. 27); "We Did It" (Apr. 24); "A Song a Day" (May 22); "More Pep" (June 19); "You're Not Built That Way" (July 17); "Happy You and Merry Me" (Aug. 21); "Training Pigeons" (Sept. 18); "Grampy's Indoor Outing" (Oct. 16); "Be Human" (Nov. 20); and "Making Friends" (Dec. 18).

**1937:** "House Cleaning Blues" (Jan. 15); "Whoops! I'm a Cowboy" (Feb. 12); "The Hot Air Salesman" (Mar. 12); "Pudgy Takes a Bow-Wow" (Apr. 19); "Pudgy Picks a Fight" (May 14); "The Impractical Joker" (June 18); "Ding Dong Doggie" (July 23); "The Candid Candidate" (Aug. 27); "Service with a Smile" (Sept. 23); "The New Deal Show" (Oct. 22); "The Foxy Hunter" (Nov. 26); and "Zula Hula" (Dec. 24).

**1938:** "Riding the Rails" (Jan. 28); "Be Up to Date" (Feb. 25); "Honest Love and True" (Mar. 25); "Out of the Inkwell" (Apr. 22); "Swing School" (May 27); "Pudgy and the Lost Kitten" (June 24); "Buzzy Boop" (July 29); "Pudgy the Watchman" (Aug. 12); "Buzzy Boop at the Concert" (Sept. 16); "Sally Swing" (Oct. 14); "On with the New" (Dec. 2); and "Pudgy in Thrills and Chills" (Dec. 23).

**1939:** "My Friend the Monkey" (Jan. 27); "So Does an Automobile" (Mar. 31); "Musical Mountaineers" (May 12); "The Scared Crows" (June 9); "Rhythm on the Reservation" (July 7); and "Yip Yip Yippy" (Aug. 11/officially released as a *Betty Boop* cartoon even though she does not appear).

**◉ BLACKIE THE LAMB**

Innocent-looking Blackie the Lamb was always the target of a lamb-hungry Wolf, whose level of frustration mounted every time his attempt to capture the wool-skinned creature failed in this series of cartoon shorts released under the *Noveltoons* banner. The director of the first cartoon in the series is unknown. *Directed by Isadore Sparber. Technicolor. A Famous Studios Production released by Paramount Pictures.*

**1943:** "No Mutton for Nuttin'" (Nov. 26).

**1945:** "A Lamb in a Jam" (Sparber/May 4).

**1946:** "Sheep Shape" (Sparber/June 28).

**1947:** "Much Ado About Mutton" (Sparber/July 18).

**◉ THE BLUE RACER**

In the tradition of the Road Runner and Coyote cartoons, this series followed a similar "chase" premise in each episode, with the fast-moving sissy blue snake (self-billed as "the fastest little ol' snake west of the pecos") pursuing the ever-elusive Japanese beetle, a self-proclaimed black belt karate champion who is always one step ahead in outwitting the sly reptile. *Directed by Gerry Chiniquy, Bob Balser, Art Davis, David Deneen, Cullen Houghtaling, Robert McKimson and Sid Marcos. Technicolor. A DePatie-Freleng/Mirisch Cinema Company Production released through United Artists.*

**Voices**
**The Blue Racer:** Larry D. Mann; **Japanese Beetle:** Tom Holland

*A blue rattler is known as "the fastest little snake west of the Pecos" in the DePatie-Freleng theatrical cartoon series* The Blue Racer. *© DePatie-Freleng Enterprises*

**1972:** "Nippon Tuck" (Chiniquy/July); "Hiss and Hers" (Chiniquy/July 3); "Support Your Local Serpent" (Davis/July 9); "Punch and Judo" (Davis/July 23); "Love and Hisses" (Chiniquy/Aug. 3); "Camera Bug" (Davis/Aug. 6); "Yokahama Mamma" (Chiniquy/Dec. 24); and "Blue Racer Blues" (Davis/Dec. 31).

**1973:** "The Boa Friend" (Chiniquy/Feb. 11); "Wham and Eggs" (Davis/Feb. 18); "Blue Aces Wild" (Chiniquy/May 16); "Killarney Blarney" (Chiniquy/May 16); "Fowl Play" (McKimson/June 1); "Freeze a Jolly Good Fellow" (Marcus/June 1); "Aches and Snakes" (Deneen/Aug. 10); and "Snake Preview" (Houghtaling/Aug. 10).

**1974:** "Little Boa Peep" (Balser/Jan. 16).

**◉ BOBO**

Bobo, a sorrowful-looking, usually nontalking baby pink elephant, finds success in the big city in this short-lived *Looney Tunes* series. *Directed by Robert McKimson. Technicolor. A Warner Bros. Cartoons, Inc. Production released by Warner Bros.*

**Voices**
Mel Blanc

*Looney Tunes*

**1947:** "Hobo Bobo" (May 17).

**1954:** "Gone Batty" (Sept. 4).

**◉ BOOBIE BABOON**

This klutzy baboon was one of several incidental starring cartoon characters brought to the screen in Paramount's *Modern Madcaps* of the 1960s. Boobie starred in only two cartoons, his first being "Solitary Refinement," produced in 1965. The series was written by newspaper cartoonist Jack Mendelsohn, who also directed another short-lived series for Paramount, *Jacky's Whacky World. Directed by Howard Post. Technicolor. A Famous Studios Production released through Paramount Pictures.*

**1965:** "Solitary Refinement" (Sept./*Modern Madcap*); and "The Outside Dope" (Nov./*Modern Madcap*).

## ◎ BOSKO

In 1929 former Disney animators Hugh Harman and Rudolf Ising, who turned to animating independent productions, completed a three-minute pilot starring a black minstrel character they hoped to develop into a series. Called "Bosko the Talkink Kid," the film's lead character resembled a humanized Mickey Mouse who favored a derby and spoke in a Southern Negro dialect.

Animator Friz Freleng cartooned the pilot one-reeler, with animator Hugh Harman making the first drawing of Bosko, who he had "behave like a little boy." The film was previewed for several distributors but no offers were made to distribute it.

Leon Schlesinger, president of Pacific Arts and Titles, had a different opinion. He later viewed the film and used his connections at Warner Bros. to have the series contracted by the studio, with the three men coproducing it. The first *Bosko* cartoon for Warners was also the first *Looney Tunes* cartoon, called "Sinkin' in the Bathtub." (The title was a play on the popular song title introduced in a Warner feature, *The Show of Shows.*)

The film was so well received that Bosko became a mainstay at Warner Bros. for several years. His costars were Honey, Bosko's girlfriend (a thinly disguised Minnie Mouse); Pluto, their dog (Harman and Ising's version of Pluto); and Bruno. The films were populated by visual puns and other exaggerations set to popular tunes of the day, recorded by the studio's orchestra. (Abe Lyman Brunswick Record Orchestra played on several of the first releases before relinquishing his duties.)

In 1932 Ising, the idea man of the two, left the series to work on the studio's fledgling *Merrie Melodies* cartoons. The *Bosko* series was never the same. A year later he and Harman departed Warner for good, taking *Bosko* with them to MGM, where they revived the series two years later but with little success.

Besides Freleng, the series' animators included Rollin Hamilton, Paul J. Smith and Carmen Maxwell, who also supplied the voice of Bosko. *Directed by Hugh Harman, Rudolf Ising and Friz Freleng. Black-and-white and Technicolor. A Hugh Harman-Rudolf Ising and Vitaphone Production released through Warner Bros. A Metro-Goldwyn-Mayer Production released by Metro-Goldwyn-Mayer.*

### Voices

**Bosko:** Carmen Maxwell; **Honey, his girlfriend:** Rochelle Hudson

**1930:** "Sinkin' in the Bathtub" (with Honey/Harman, Ising/Apr. 19); "Congo Jazz" (Harman, Ising/Sept.); "Hold Anything" (Harman, Ising/Oct.); "The Booze Hangs High" (Harman, Ising/Nov.); and "Box Car Blues" (Harman, Ising/Dec.).

**1931:** "Big Man from the North" (with Honey/Harman, Ising); "Ain't Nature Grand!" (Harman, Ising/Feb); "Ups 'N Downs" (Harman, Ising/Mar.); "Dumb Patrol" (with Honey/Harman, Ising/Apr.); "Yodeling Yokels" (with Honey/Harman, Ising/May); "Bosko's Holiday" (with Honey/Harman, Ising/June); "The Tree's Knees" (Harman, Ising/July); "Bosko Shipwrecked!" (Harman, Ising/Sept. 19); "Bosko the Doughboy" (Harman/Oct. 17); "Bosko's Soda Fountain" (with Honey/Nov. 14); and "Bosko's Fox Hunt" (Harman/Dec. 12).

**1932:** "Bosko and Honey" (with Honey/Harman); "Battling Bosko" (with Honey/Feb. 6); "Big-Hearted Bosko" (with Bruno/

Harman, Ising/Mar. 5/originally "Bosko's Orphans"); "Bosko's Party" (with Honey/Harman/Apr. 2); "Bosko and Bruno" (with Bruno/Harman/Apr. 30); "Bosko's Dog Race" (with Honey, Bruno/Harman/June 25); "Bosko at the Beach" (with Honey, Bruno/Harman/July 23); "Bosko's Store" (with Honey, Bruno/Harman/Aug. 13); "Bosko the Lumberjack" (with Honey/Harman/Sept. 3); "Ride Him, Bosko!" (with Honey/Harman/Sept. 17); "Bosko the Drawback" (Harman/Oct. 22); "Bosko's Dizzy Date" (with Honey, Bruno/Harman/Nov. 19); and "Bosko's Woodland Daze" (with Bruno/Harman/Dec. 17).

**1933:** "Bosko in Dutch" (with Honey, Bruno, Wilber, Goopy Geer/Harman, Freleng (uncredited)/Jan.14); "Bosko in Person" (with Honey/Harman/Feb. 11); "Bosko the Speed King" (with Honey/Harman/Mar. 22); "Bosko's Knight-Mare" (with Honey, Bruno/Harman/Apr. 29); "Bosko the Sheep-Herder" (Harman/June 3); "Beau Bosko" (with Honey/Harman, Freleng (uncredited)/July); "Bosko's Mechanical Man" (with Honey, Bruno/Harman/July 29); "Bosko the Musketeer" (with Honey, Bruno/Harman/Aug. 12); and "Bosko's Picture Show" (with Honey, Bruno/Harman, Freleng (uncredited)/Aug. 26).

### MGM Bosko cartoons released as Happy Harmonies

**1934:** (in Technicolor) "Bosko's Parlor Pranks" (with Honey/Harman/Nov. 24).

**1935:** "Hey-Hey Fever" (with Honey, Bruno/Harman/Jan. 9); and "Run, Sheep, Run" (with Honey/Dec. 14).

**1936:** "The Old House" (with Honey, Bruno/Harman/May 2).

**1937:** "Circus Daze" (with Honey/Harman/Jan. 16); "Bosko's Easter Eggs" (with Honey, Bruno/Harman/Mar. 17); "Little Ol' Bosko and the Pirates" (with Honey/Harman/May 1); and "Little Ol' Bosko and the Cannibals" (with Honey/Harman/Aug. 28).

**1938:** "Little Ol' Bosko in Bagdad" (with Honey/Harman/Jan. 1).

## ◎ BUDDY

As a replacement for Bosko, producer Leon Schlesinger unveiled Buddy, a nondescript, wide-eyed boy, as the new lead in the *Looney Tunes* series. A pale imitation at best, Buddy was "Bosko in white-face" and had little impact on moviegoers, proving to be "a nothing," recalled Bob Clampett, a series animator.

The Disney influence was apparent again in this series, the third for Warner Bros.' young animation studio. Like Bosko, Buddy had Disneyish costars: a flapper girlfriend, Cookie (Minnie Mouse in costume) and, later, a dog named Towser (yet another Pluto-like clone).

Chuck Jones, a young in-betweener at the time, graduated to animator on the series and as he recalled, "Nothing in the way of bad animation could make Buddy worse than he was anyway."

Surprisingly, with such internal unrest over the character, Buddy lasted two years in 23 cartoon adventures released from 1933 to 1935. *Series direction was handled by Earl Duvall, Ben Hardaway, Friz Freleng, Tom Palmer and Jack King. Black-and-white. A Vitaphone Production released through Warner Bros.*

### Voices

**Buddy:** Jack Carr

**1933:** "Buddy's Day Out" (with Cookie, Elmer, Happy/Palmer/Sept. 9); "Buddy's Beer Garden" (with Cookie/Duvall/Nov. 18); and "Buddy's Show Boat" (with Cookie/Duvall/Dec. 9).

**1934:** "Buddy the Gob" (Freleng/Jan. 13); "Buddy and Towser" (with Towser/Freleng/Feb. 24); "Buddy's Garage" (with Cookie/Duvall/Apr. 14); "Buddy's Trolley Troubles" (with Cookie/Freleng/May 5); "Buddy of the Apes" (Hardaway/May 26); "Buddy's Bearcats" (with Cookie/King/June 23); "Buddy's Circus" (King/Aug. 25); "Buddy the Detective" (with Cookie/King/Sept. 15); "Viva Buddy" (King/Sept. 29); "Buddy the Woodsman" (with Cookie/King/Oct. 20); "Buddy's Adventures" (with Cookie/Hardaway/Nov. 17); and "Buddy the Dentist" (with Cookie, Buddy's Dog/Hardaway/Dec. 15).

**1935:** "Buddy of the Legion" (Hardaway/Jan. 12); "Buddy's Theatre" (with Cookie/Hardaway/Feb. 16); "Buddy's Pony Express" (with Cookie/Hardaway/Mar. 9); "Buddy in Africa" (Hardaway/Apr. 20); "Buddy's Lost World" (King/May 18); "Buddy's Bug Hunt" (with Cookie/King/June 22); "Buddy Steps Out" (with Cookie/King/July 20); and "Buddy the Gee Man" (King/Aug. 24).

## ◎ BUGS BUNNY

Long a staple of the Warner Bros. cartoon roster, Bugs Bunny still remains one of the most popular cartoon characters in animation history. The long-eared, screwy rabbit who chomped on carrots and uttered in Brooklynese the famous words of "Eh, What's up, Doc?" starred in 150 cartoons during his 25 years on screen, the most of any character in Warner Bros. cartoon history.

First appearing in cartoons in a formative stage between 1938-39, Bugs's characterization became the basis for ridiculous situations that were offbeat and outrageously funny. Often the humor was more pointed and self-serving, with the brunt of the situational gags taken by a handful of supporting characters, including Elmer Fudd, Daffy Duck, Yosemite Sam and others.

The story behind Bugs's origin has gone through several versions over the years, mostly due to several animators' attempts to claim credit for his creation. For a long time the most accepted version was that Ben "Bugs" Hardaway, who was directing a second rabbit picture, enlisted a fellow by the name of Charlie Thorson to make a drawing of a crazy rabbit like Woody Woodpecker. When Thorson sent the drawing back to Hardaway, he labeled the corner of the page "Bugs' bunny"—and that's how Bugs supposedly got his name.

New research has revealed otherwise. Bugs did not receive his name until two years after the first model sheet was drawn. He first appeared as an "unnamed rabbit" in three cartoons "Porky's Hare Hunt" (1938), "Prest-O Change-O" (1939) and "Hare-Um Scare-Um" (1939).

Bob Clampett wrote the story for the first cartoon, "Porky's Hare Hunt," using some leftover gags from "Porky's Duck Hunt" and reshaping them for the rabbit. In this first appearance, several key aspects of Bugs's character emerged: chomping on a carrot; the fake dying act ("You got me!"); and the Groucho Marx line of "Of course, you know this means war!" When Clampett's story timed short, Hardaway added a few other touches, like having Bugs bounce across the scene à la studio contemporary Daffy Duck. (By the second cartoon, Bugs was portrayed as more high strung in the fashion of Woody Woodpecker in both voice and actions.)

Bugs's creation initially stirred some controversy, however. Some people at Walt Disney Studios cried foul as he resembled Disney's own rabbit character, Max Hare, who made his cartoon debut in "The Tortoise and the Hare" (1935), which won an Academy Award.

Ah, yes—the name. In 1940 animator Tex Avery took over the series. He directed the first official Bugs Bunny cartoon and also

helped the studio, which was getting nervous since the rascally rabbit was fast becoming a rising star, decide on what to call him. It was before producing "A Wild Hare" that the studio opened discussions on naming the character.

Tex wanted to call the character Jack Rabbit, but the idea didn't stick. Finally it was suggested that he be named Bugsy after the famed West Coast mobster Bugsy Siegel, but producer Leon Schlesinger nixed that idea. Another round of discussions ensued before the issue was settled. The name that won out over all the others was Bugs Bunny.

During production of this first Bugs Bunny cartoon, Avery created the character's trademark phrase, "What's up, Doc?" partly inspired by an idea given to him by Bob Clampett, Tex's key gag man from the Termite Terrace days, who suggested the line of "What's up, Duke?" (used in the screwball comedy *My Man Godfrey*) and from Avery's own recollection of expressions used in his native Texas—"Hey, Doc? Whaddya know?" and "How ya been today, Doc?"

Introduced during the cartoon's first confrontation between Bugs and Elmer Fudd, the befuddled hunter ("I'm hunting wabbit! Heh-heh-heh-heh-heh!"), Avery believes the phrase was the key to Bugs's success while giving audiences something they never expected.

"We decided he [Bugs] was going to be a smart-aleck rabbit, but casual about it. That opening line of 'Eh, What's up, Doc?' in the very first picture floored them [the audience]," Avery told biographer Joe Adamson. "They expected the rabbit to scream, or anything but make a casual remark. For here's a guy pointing a gun in his face! It got such a laugh that we said, 'Boy, we'll do that every chance we get.'"

Besides his long-running feud with Elmer Fudd, Bugs developed several other rivalries with his costars Yosemite Sam, a pint-size Westerner (his classic line, "I'm the roughest, toughest, meanest hombre ever to terrorize the West") and Daffy Duck, the ever-malevolent wise quacker who was always jealous of Bugs stealing the spotlight from him. (The most popular gag between both characters was "Duck Season! Rabbit Season!" instrumented by Chuck Jones in several cartoons.)

Bugs's final cartoon appearance was in 1964, a year after Warner Bros. closed its animation department and made special arrangements with Friz Freleng's new company, DePatie-Freleng Enterprises, to produce a series of new *Looney Tunes* and *Merrie Melodies*. (Warner reopened its department in 1967, hiring a new staff to head its productions.)

*Hollywood trade paper advertisement for Warner Bros.' "new" Bugs Bunny cartoon series. © Warner Brothers, Inc.*

In 1991 Bugs returned to the screen in an all-new *Looney Tunes* theatrical short, "Box-Office Bunny," the studio's first Bugs Bunny cartoon in 27 years. The film opened nationwide with the Warner Bros. feature "The Neverending Story II: The Next Chapter." Jeff Bergman took over as the voice of Bugs Bunny and his costars Elmer Fudd and Daffy Duck, succeeding Mel Blanc, who died that year. Produced by Kathleen Helppie-Shipley and directed by Darrell Van Citters, the short was created to mark the 50th anniversary of Bugs's cartoon debut. The studio starred Bugs in a follow-up *Looney Tunes* cartoon, "Invasion of the Bunny Snatchers" (a spoof of the 1950s' sci-fi classic *Invasion of the Body Snatchers*, in which Bugs's pals are replaced by alien look-alikes), directed by Greg Ford and Terry Lennon, released to theaters along with a new *Merrie Melodies* starring Bugs, Daffy Duck, Elmer Fudd and Yosemite Sam entitled "(blooper) Bunny!"

Bugs marked another milestone in 1992 with the debut of the much-talked-about "Hare Jordan" television commercial for Nike, broadcast during the Super Bowl. In the $1 million spot, Bugs outsmarted basketball superstar Michael Jordan, along with a host of other Warner Bros. characters, marking the beginning of a surge of television commercials that mixed live action with animated cartoon characters. Four years later Bugs and company would team up with Jordan to star in the blockbuster live-action/animated feature *Space Jam*.

In 1995 two new Bugs Bunny cartoons were produced. Bugs starred in "Carrotblanca," a cartoon parody of the classic 1942 Warner Bros. feature *Casablanca*, produced by Warner Bros. Classic Animation division. Douglas McCarthy served as director. Legendary animator Chuck Jones produced and directed a handful of new cartoon shorts for Warner Bros. beginning in 1994 (under the auspices of Chuck Jones Film Productions, a new animation unit located on the Warner Bros. lot), including the 1995 Bugs Bunny–Yosemite Sam pairing, "From Hare to Eternity," dedicated to fellow animator Friz Freleng, who died in May of that year. Unfortunately, the cartoon was never released to theaters. (It was later released on home video.) Greg Burson provided the voice of Bugs Bunny; veteran comedian Frank Gorshin (who played The Riddler in the *Batman* television series starring Adam West) voiced Yosemite Sam.

Jones formed the new animation unit to supply theatrical cartoons for Warner Bros. and to re-create the spirit of Termite Terrace, the nickname of the old Warner Bros. animation headquarters during the studio's heyday when his colleagues included Tex Avery, Bob Clampett, Friz Freleng, Frank Tashlin, Robert McKimson and others. In April of 1997, after producing only six new cartoon shorts for the studio, Jones's animation unit closed its doors, leaving Warner Bros. Classic Animation Division as the studio's sole producer of theatrical cartoon shorts.

In 2003, Bugs headed an all-star cast of characters in his second full-length feature, the live-action/animated film, *Looney Tunes: Back in Action*. A year later, Warner Bros. planned and storyboarded five new *Looney Tunes* in which he was to star—that were cancelled and never finished—including "Badda Bugs," "Beach Bunny," "Deep Sea Bugs," "Guess Who's Coming to Meet the Parents," and "What's Hip, Doc?" to be directed by Rich Moore, Dan Povenmire, Peter Shin, and Bill Kopp. In 2005, Bugs did star in a new direct-to-video *Looney Tunes* directed by them as well, called, "Hare and Loathing in Las Vegas." *Series directors included Friz Freleng, Ben Hardaway, Robert McKimson, Bob Clampett, Frank Tashlin, Charles "Chuck" M. Jones, Abe Levitow, Dave Detiege, Tex Avery, Gerry Chiniquy, Cal Dalton, Art Davis, Ken Harris, Maurice Noble, Hawley Pratt, Darrel Van Citters, Greg Ford, Terry Lennon and Douglas McCarthy, Rich Moore, Dan Povenmire,* *Peter Shin and Bill Kopp. Black-and-white. Technicolor. A Vitaphone/ Leon Schlesinger Studios/Warner Bros. Cartoons, Inc./Warner Bros./ Warner Bros. Pictures, Inc./Vitagraph/Warner Bros./Chuck Jones Film/Warner Bros. Animation/Warner Bros. Production released by Warner Bros., Warner Bros. Seven Arts, and Warner Bros. Family Entertainment.*

*Voices*
**Bugs Bunny:** Mel Blanc, Jeff Bergman, Greg Burson

*Looney Tunes*

### Vitaphone Productions releases

**1938:** "Porky's Hare Hunt" (with Porky Pig/Hardaway/Apr. 30/ features Bugs Bunny prototype).

### Leon Schlesinger Studios releases

**1940:** "Patient Porky" (with Porky Pig/Clampett/Aug. 24/Porky Pig cartoon/Note: Bugs Bunny prototype makes a cameo appearance).

**1943:** "Porky Pig's Feat" (with Porky Pig, Daffy Duck/Tashlin/ July 17/Porky Pig cartoon).

**1944:** "Buckaroo Bugs" (Clampett/Aug. 26).

### Warner Bros. Cartoons, Inc. releases

**1945:** "Hare Conditioned" (Jones/Aug. 11); and "Hare Tonic" (with Elmer Fudd/Jones/Nov. 10).

**1946:** "Baseball Bugs" (Freleng/Feb. 2); "Hair-Raising Hare" (Jones/May 25); "Acrobatty Bunny" (McKimson/June 29); "Racketeer Rabbit" (with Edward G. Robinson, Peter Lorre characters Nero and Hugo/Freleng/Sept. 14); and "The Big Snooze" (with Elmer Fudd/Clampett/Oct. 5).

**1947:** "Easter Yeggs" (with Elmer Fudd/McKimson/June 28).

**1948:** "Gorilla My Dreams" (with Gruesome Gorilla, Mrs. Gruesome Gorilla/McKimson/Jan. 3); "A Feather in His Hare" (Jones/Feb. 7); "Buccaneer Bunny" (with Yosemite Sam/Freleng/ May 8); "Haredevil Hare" (with Commander X-2 Marvin Martian, K-9/Jones/July 24); and "A-Lad-in His Lamp" (with Genie McKimson/Oct. 23).

**1949:** "Mississippi Hare" (Jones/Feb. 26); "High Diving Hare" (with Yosemite Sam/Freleng/Apr. 30); "Long-Haired Hare" (Jones/ June 25); "The Grey Hounded Hare" (McKimson/Aug. 6); and "The Windblown Hare" (McKimson/Aug. 27).

**1950:** "Mutiny on the Bunny" (with Yosemite Sam/Freleng/Feb. 11); "Big House Bunny" (with Yosemite Sam/Freleng/Apr. 22); "What's Up Doc?" (with Elmer Fudd/McKimson/June 17); "8 Ball Bunny" (with Penguin, Bogart/Jones/July 8); "Bushy Hare" (McKimson/Nov. 11); and "Rabbit of Seville" (with Elmer Fudd/ Jones/Dec. 16).

**1951:** "Rabbit Every Monday" (with Yosemite Sam/Freleng/Feb. 10); "The Fair Haired Hare" (with Yosemite Sam/Freleng/Apr. 14); "Rabbit Fire" (with Daffy Duck, Elmer Fudd/Jones/May 19); and "His Hare Raising Tale" (with Clyde Bunny, Bugs's nephew, Elmer Fudd cameo/Freleng/Aug. 11).

**1952:** "Operation: Rabbit" (with Wile E. Coyote/Jones/Jan. 19); "14 Carrot Rabbit" (with Yosemite Sam/Freleng/Feb. 16); "Water, Water Every Hare" (Jones/Apr. 19); "The Hasty Hare" (with Commander X-2 Marvin Martian, K-9/Jones/June 7); and "Hare Lift" (with Yosemite Sam/Freleng/Dec. 20).

**1953:** "Forward March Hare" (Jones/Feb. 4); "Southern Fried Rabbit" (with Yosemite Sam/Freleng/May 2); "Bully for Bugs" (Jones/Aug. 8); and "Robot Rabbit" (with Elmer Fudd/Freleng/Dec. 12).

**1954:** "Bugs and Thugs" (with Rocky, Mugsy/McKimson/Mar. 2); "No Parking Hare" (McKimson/May 1); "Dr. Jekyll's Hide" (with Spike [Alfie] and Chester/Freleng/May 8); "Devil May Hare" (with Tasmanian Devil/McKimson/June 19); "Bewitched Bunny" (with Witch Hazel/Jones/July 24); "Yankee Doodle Bugs" (with Clyde Bunny/Freleng/Aug. 28); and "Lumber-Jack Rabbit" (with Paul Bunyan, Smidgen/Jones/Nov. 13/released in 3-D; Warner Bros.' only cartoon produced in 3-D).

**1955:** "Sahara Hare" (with Yosemite Sam, Daffy Duck cameo/Freleng/Mar. 26); "Rabbit Rampage" (Jones/June 11); "Hyde and Hare" (Freleng/Aug. 27); and "Roman-Legion Hare" (with Yosemite Sam/Freleng/Nov. 12).

**1956:** "Broom-Stick Bunny" (with Witch Hazel, Genie/Jones/Feb. 25); "Rabbitson Crusoe" (with Yosemite Sam/Freleng/Apr. 28); "Barbary Coast Bunny" (with Nasty Canasta/Jones/July 21); and "A Star Is Bored" (with Daffy Duck, Elmer Fudd, and Yosemite Sam/Freleng/Sept. 15).

**1957:** "Piker's Peak" (with Yosemite Sam/Freleng/May 25); "Bugsy and Mugsy" (with Rocky and Mugsy/Freleng/Aug. 31); and "Show Biz Bugs" (with Daffy Duck/Freleng/Nov. 2).

**1958:** "Hare-Way to the Stars" (with Commander X-2 Marvin Martian, K-9/Jones/Mar. 29); "Now, Hare This" (McKimson/May 31); "Knighty Knight Bugs" (with Yosemite Sam/Freleng/Aug. 23/A.A. winner); and "Pre-Hysterical Hare" (with Elmer Fudd/McKimson/Nov. 1).

**1959:** "Baton Bunny" (Jones, Levitow/Jan. 10); "Wild And Woolly Hare" (with Yosemite Sam/Freleng/Aug. 1); and "A Witch's Tangled Hare" (with Witch Hazel/Levitow/Oct. 31).

**1960:** "Horse Hare" (with Yosemite Sam/Freleng/Feb. 13); and "Rabbit's Feat" (with Wile E. Coyote/Jones/June 4).

### Warner Bros. Pictures, Inc./Vitagraph releases

**1961:** "The Abominable Snow Rabbit" (with Daffy Duck, Hugo/Jones, Noble/May 20); and "Prince Violent" (with Yosemite Sam/Freleng, Pratt/Sept. 2).

**1962:** "Wet Hare" (McKimson/Jan. 20); and "Skiska Bugs" (with Yosemite Sam/Freleng/Dec. 8).

**1963:** "The Million Hare" (McKimson/Apr. 6); and "Hare-Breadth Hurry" (with Wile E. Coyote/Jones, Noble/June 8).

**1964:** "The Iceman Ducketh" (with Daffy Duck/Monroe, Noble/May 16); and "False Hare" (with Foghorn Leghorn cameo/McKimson/July 16).

### Warner Bros. releases

**1991:** "Box-Office Bunny" (with Daffy Duck, Elmer Fudd/Van Citters/Feb. 11.); and "Invasion of the Bunny Snatchers" (with Daffy Duck, Elmer Fudd, Yosemite Sam, and Porky Pig cameo/Ford, Lennon).

### Warner Bros. Animation releases

**1995:** "Carrotblanca" (with Daffy Duck, Yosemite Sam, Sylvester, Tweety, Pepe Le Pew, Foghorn Leghorn, Penelope/McCarthy/Aug. 25).

### Warner Bros./Chuck Jones Film Productions releases

**1997:** "From Hare to Eternity" (with Yosemite Sam/Jones/dedicated to the memory of Friz Freleng).

### Merrie Melodies

### Warner Bros./Vitaphone Productions releases

**1939:** "Prest-O Change-O" (with Two curious puppies, formative Bugs Bunny/Jones/Mar. 25); and "Hare-Um Scare-Um" (with formative Bugs Bunny/Hardaway, Dalton/Aug. 12).

### Leon Schlesinger Studios releases

**1940:** "Elmer's Candid Camera" (with Elmer Fudd/Jones/Mar. 2/first Elmer Fudd cartoon); and "A Wild Hare" (with Elmer Fudd/Avery/July 27/A.A. nominee/first official Bugs Bunny cartoon).

**1941:** "Elmer's Pet Rabbit" (with Elmer Fudd/Jones/Jan. 4); "Tortoise Beats Hare" (with Cecil Turtle, Chester Turtle/Avery/Mar. 15); "Hiawatha's Rabbit Hunt" (Freleng/June 7/A.A. nominee); "The Heckling Hare" (Avery/July 5); "All This and Rabbit Stew" (Avery/Sept. 13); and "Wabbit Twouble" (with Elmer Fudd/Clampett/Dec. 20/Note: Bob Clampett is credited as director under the name of "Wobert Clampett").

**1942:** "Crazy Cruise" (with Bugs Bunny cameo/Avery/Mar. 14); "The Wabbit Who Came to Supper" (with Elmer Fudd/Freleng/Mar. 28); "The Wacky Wabbit" (with Elmer Fudd/Clampett/May 2); "Hold the Lion, Please!" (Jones/June 13); "Bugs Bunny Gets the Boid" (with Beaky Buzzard/Clampett/June 11); "Fresh Hare" (with Elmer Fudd/Freleng/Aug. 22); "The Hare-Brained Hypnotist" (with Elmer Fudd/Freleng/Oct. 31); and "Case of the Missing Hare" (Jones/Dec. 22).

**1943:** "Tortoise Wins by a Hare" (Clampett/Feb. 20); "Super Rabbit" (Jones/Apr. 3); "Jack-Wabbit and the Beanstalk" (Freleng/June 12); "Wackiki Wabbit" (Jones/July 3); "A Corny Concerto" (with Elmer Fudd, Porky Pig/Clampett/Sept. 18); and "Falling Hare" (with Gremlin/Clampett/Oct. 30).

**1944:** "Little Red Riding Rabbit" (Freleng/Jan. 4); "What's Cookin' Doc?" (Clampett/Jan. 8); "Bugs Bunny and the Three Bears" (with The Three Bears/Jones/Feb. 26); "Bugs Bunny Nips the Nips" (Freleng/Apr. 22); "Hare Ribbin'" (Clampett/June 24); "Hare Force" (Freleng/July 22).

### Warner Bros. Cartoons, Inc. releases

**1944:** "The Old Grey Hare" (with Elmer Fudd/Clampett/Oct. 28); and "Stage Door Cartoon" (with Elmer/Freleng/Dec. 30).

**1945:** "Herr Meets Hare" (with Herman Goering, Adolph Hitler/Freleng/Jan. 13); "The Unruly Hare" (with Elmer Fudd/Tashlin/Feb. 10); and "Hare Trigger" (with Yosemite Sam/Freleng/May 5).

**1946:** "Hare Remover" (with Elmer Fudd/Tashlin/Mar. 23); "Hair-Raising Hare" (Jones/May 25); and "Rhapsody Rabbit" (Freleng/Nov. 9).

**1947:** "Rabbit Transit" (Freleng/May 10); "A Hare Grows in Manhattan" (with Lola Beverly/Freleng/May 22); and "Slick Hare" (with Elmer Fudd/Freleng/Nov. 1).

**1948:** "Rabbit Punch" (Jones/Apr. 10); "Bugs Bunny Rides Again" (with Yosemite Sam/Freleng/June 12); "Hot Cross Bunny" (McKimson/Aug. 21); "Hare Splitter" (Freleng/Sept. 25); and "My Bunny Lies Over the Sea" (Jones/Dec. 14).

**1949:** "Hare Do" (with Elmer/Freleng/Jan. 15); "Rebel Rabbit" (McKimson/Apr. 9); "Bowery Bugs" (Davis/June 4); "Knights Must Fall" (Freleng/July 16); "Frigid Hare" (Jones/Oct. 7); and "Rabbit Hood" (Jones/Dec. 24).

**1950:** "Hurdy-Gurdy Hare" (McKimson/Jan. 21); "Homeless Hare" (Jones/Mar. 11); "Hillbilly Hare" (McKimson/Aug. 12); and "Bunker Hill Bunny" (with Yosemite Sam/Freleng/Sept. 23).

**1951:** "Hare We Go" (McKimson/Jan. 6); "Bunny Hugged" (Jones/Mar. 10); "French Rarebit" (McKimson/June 30); "Ballot Box Bunny" (with Yosemite Sam/Freleng/Oct. 6); and "Big Top Bunny" (McKimson/Dec. 12).

**1952:** "Foxy by Proxy" (Freleng/Feb. 23); "Oily Hare" (McKimson/July 26); "Rabbit Seasoning" (with Daffy Duck, Elmer Fudd/Jones/Sept. 20); and "Rabbit's Kin" (McKimson/Nov. 15).

**1953:** "Duck Amuck" (with Daffy Duck/Jones/Feb. 28); "Upswept Hare" (with Elmer Fudd/McKimson/Mar. 14); "Hare Trimmed" (with Yosemite Sam/Freleng/June 20); and "Duck! Rabbit, Duck!" (with Daffy Duck, Elmer Fudd/Jones/Oct. 3).

**1954:** "Captain Hareblower" (with Yosemite Sam/Freleng/Feb. 16); and "Baby Buggy Bunny" (Jones/Dec. 18).

**1955:** "Beanstalk Bunny" (with Daffy Duck, Elmer Fudd/Jones/Feb. 12); "Hair Brush" (with Elmer Fudd/Freleng/May 7); "This Is a Life?" (with Daffy Duck, Elmer Fudd, Yosemite Sam/Freleng/July 9); and "Knight-Mare Hare" (Jones/Oct. 1).

**1956:** "Bugs Bonnets" (with Elmer Fudd/Jones/Jan. 14); "Napoleon Bunny-Part" (Freleng/June 16); "Half-Fare Hare" (McKimson/Aug. 18); "Wideo Wabbit" (with Elmer Fudd/McKimson/Oct. 27); and "To Hare Is Human" (with Wile E. Coyote/Jones/Dec. 15).

**1957:** "Ali Baba Bunny" (with Daffy Duck, Hassan/Jones/Feb. 9); "Bedevilled Rabbit" (with Tasmanian Devil/Jones/Apr. 13); "What's Opera, Doc?" (with Elmer Fudd/Jones/July 6); and "Rabbit Romeo" (with Elmer Fudd/McKimson/Dec. 14).

**1958:** "Hare-Less Wolf" (Freleng/Feb. 1).

**1959:** "Hare-abian Nights" (with Yosemite Sam/Harris/Feb. 28); "Apes of Wrath" (Freleng/Apr. 18); "Backwoods Bunny" (McKimson/June 13); and "Bonanza Bunny" (McKimson/Sept. 5).

*Warner Bros. releases*

**1959:** "People Are Bunny" (with Daffy Duck, Art Lamplighter/McKimson/Dec. 19).

*Warner Bros. Pictures, Inc./Vitagraph releases*

**1960:** "Person to Bunny" (with Daffy Duck, Elmer Fudd/Freleng/Apr. 1); "From Hare to Heir" (with Yosemite Sam/Freleng/Sept. 3); and "Lighter than Hare" (with Yosemite Sam/Freleng/Dec. 17).

**1961:** "COMpressed Hare" (with Wile E. Coyote/Jones/July 29).

**1962:** "Bill of Hare" (with Tasmanian Devil/McKimson/June 9).

**1963:** "Devil's Feud Cake" (with Yosemite Sam/Freleng/Feb. 9); "The Unmentionables" (with Rocky, Mugsy/Freleng/Sept. 7); "Mad as a Mars Hare" (with Commander X-2 Marvin Martian/Jones, Noble/Oct. 19); and "Transylvania 6-500" (Jones, Noble/Nov. 30).

**1964:** "Dumb Patrol" (with Josemite Sam, Porky Pig/Chiniquy/Jan. 18); and "Dr. Devil and Mr. Hare" (with Tasmanian Devil/McKimson/Mar. 28).

*Warner Bros. releases*

**1991:** "(blooper) Bunny!" (with Daffy Duck, Elmer Fudd, Yosemite Sam/Moore, Povenmire, Shin, Kopp).

## ◉ BUNNY AND CLAUDE

One of Warner Bros.' last cartoon series, this one featured two outlaw rabbits, Bunny and Claude, who steal carrots for a living, hotly pursued by a mean redneck sheriff in comical misadventures inspired by the hit Warner feature *Bonnie and Clyde*. *Directed by Robert McKimson. Technicolor. A Warner Bros. Production released by Warner Bros. Seven Arts.*

*Voices*
**Bunny:** Pat Wodell; **Claude:** Mel Blanc; **Sheriff:** Mel Blanc

**1968:** "Bunny and Claude (We Rob Carrot Patches)" (Nov. 9/Merrie Melodies).

**1969:** "The Great Carrot Train Robbery" (Jan. 25/Merrie Melodies).

## ◉ BURT GILLETT'S TODDLE TALES

This series was Burt Gillett's first following his defection from Walt Disney Studios to direct new cartoons for Van Beuren. Only three films were made in the series, which blended live-action sequences of two children with animated animal characters in each adventure. The filmed openings led into each story, which might involve why dogs wag their tails or how ducks evolved, based on discussions with these animals. *Directors were Burt Gillett, Steve Muffati, Jim Tyer and Tom Palmer. Black-and-white. Cinecolor. A Van Beuren Studios Production released by RKO Radio Pictures.*

**1934:** "Grandfather's Clock" (Gillett, Tyler/June 29); "Along Came a Duck" (Gillett, Muffati/Aug. 10); and "A Little Bird Told Me" (Gillett, Tyer/Sept. 7).

## ◉ BUTCH

William Hanna and Joseph Barbera created this sharp and shrewd alley cat as a supporting player in their seven-time Oscar-winning *Tom and Jerry* cartoon series for Metro-Goldwyn-Mayer. First introduced to moviegoers in 1943's "Baby Puss," he appeared in three cartoons without a name before he was officially called Butch in the 1947 cartoon short, "A Mouse in the House." Thereafter, Butch appeared in nine more *Tom and Jerry* cartoons, including one of his funniest performances in 1951's "Casanova Cat," in which he undermines Tom's romantic play for beautiful felines, namely the lovely Toodles. *Directed by William Hanna and Joseph Barbera. Technicolor. CinemaScope. A Metro-Goldwyn-Mayer Cartoon Production released by Metro-Goldwyn-Mayer.*

**1943:** "Baby Puss" (with Tom and Jerry/Dec. 25).

**1946:** "Springtime for Thomas" (with Tom and Jerry, Toodles/Mar. 30); and "Trap Happy" (with Tom and Jerry/June 29).

**1947:** "A Mouse in the House" (with Tom and Jerry/Aug. 30/first cartoon as Butch).

**1949:** "Heavenly Puss" (with Tom and Jerry/July 9); and "Tennis Chumps" (with Tom and Jerry/Dec. 10).

**1951:** "Casanova Cat" (with Tom and Jerry, Toodles/Jan. 6); and "Jerry's Cousin" (with Tom and Jerry/Apr. 7/A.A. nominee).

**1954:** "Baby Butch" (with Tom and Jerry/Aug. 14).

**1955:** "Smarty Cat" (with Tom and Jerry/Oct. 14).

**1956:** "Muscle Beach Tom" (with Tom and Jerry/Sept. 7/ CinemaScope); and "Blue Cat Blues" (with Tom and Jerry/Nov. 6/CinemaScope).

**1957:** "Mucho Mouse" (with Tom and Jerry/Sept. 6/ CinemaScope).

## ⊚ BUZZ BUZZARD

In 1948, Walter Lantz introduced this con man buzzard as a comic foil opposite his studio's wacky film star, Woody Woodpecker, in the Dick Lundy–directed cartoon short, "Wet Blanket Policy." Besides unveiling Woody's newest co-star, the film also was the first to feature smash hit song, "The Woody Woodpecker Song," sung by Gloria Wood and Harry Babbit, becoming the only animated cartoon short to ever be nominated for an Oscar for best song.

Following his screen debut, Buzz appeared in two more Woody Woodpecker cartoons through 1949, among them, "Drooler's Delight," not only the last cartoon Lundy directed for Walter Lantz's studio, but also the last short distributed to theaters by United Artists. In addition, the cartoon marked the final time Ben Hardaway voiced the character of Woody; thereafter, he was replaced by Lantz's real-life wife, Grace Stafford, who actually auditioned for the part unbeknownst to her famous animator husband. Lantz's original film distributor, Universal Pictures, released subsequent films in the series, with the unscrupulous buzzard co-starring in 23 Woody Woodpecker films altogether through 1972, the same year Lantz closed his studio, including the studio's only cartoon to be released in 3-D, "Hypnotic Hick" (1953). *Directed by Dick Lundy, Walter Lantz, Don Patterson and Paul J. Smith. Technicolor. A Walter Lantz Production released by United Artists and Universal Pictures.*

### Voices

**Buzz Buzzard:** Dallas McKennon.

### United Artists releases

**1948:** "Wet Blanket Policy" (with Woody Woodpecker/Lundy/ Aug. 27) and "Wild and Woody!" (with Woody Woodpecker/ Lundy/Dec. 31).

**1949:** "Drooler's Delight" (with Woody Woodpecker/Lundy/ Mar. 25).

### Universal Pictures releases

**1951:** "Puny Express" (with Woody Woodpecker/Lantz/Jan. 22); "Slingshot 6 7/8" (with Woody Woodpecker/Lantz/July 23); and "Destination Meatball" (with Woody Woodpecker/Lantz/Dec. 24/spoofs George Pal's live-action sci-fi feature, "Destination Moon").

**1952:** "Stage Hoax" (with Woody Woodpecker, Wally Walrus/ Lantz/Apr. 21); "Scalp Treatment" (with Woody Woodpecker/ Lantz/Sept. 18/Lantz's final film as a director); and "The Great Who Dood It" (with Woody Woodpecker/Patterson/Oct. 20).

**1953:** "Buccaneer Woodpecker" (with Woody Woodpecker/ Patterson/Apr. 20); "Operation Sawdust" (with Woody Woodpecker, Wally Walrus/Patterson/June 15); "Belle Boys" (with Woody Woodpecker/Patterson/Sept. 14); "The Hypnotic Hick" (with Woody Woodpecker/Patterson/Sept. 26/the only Lantz cartoon released in 3-D); and "Hot Noon or 12 O'Clock for Sure" (with Woody Woodpecker/Smith/Oct. 12).

**1954:** "Socko in Morocco" (with Woody Woodpecker/Patterson/ Jan. 18); "Alley to Bali" (with Woody Woodpecker/Patterson/Mar. 15); "Hot Road Huckster" (with Woody Woodpecker/Patterson/ July 5); and "Real Gone Woody" (with Woody Woodpecker, Winnie Woodpecker/Smith/Sept. 20).

**1955:** "Bunco Busters" (with Woody Woodpecker/Smith/ Nov. 21).

**1969:** "Tumble Weed Greed" (with Woody Woodpecker/ Smith).

**1972:** "Indian Corn" (with Woody Woodpecker/Smith); "Show Biz Beagle" (with Woody Woodpecker/Smith); and "The Genie with the Light Touch" (with Woody Woodpecker/Smith).

## ⊚ BUZZY THE CROW

Buzzy the Crow was the star of several *Noveltoons* cartoons in which his wise-cracking, fast-talking ways enabled him to successfully outsmart his feline enemy, Katnip, in a series of comic misadventures. *Directed by Seymour Kneitel and Isadore Sparber. Technicolor. A Famous Studios Production released by Paramount Pictures.*

**1947:** "The Stupidstitious Cat" (Kneitel/Apr. 25).

**1950:** "Sock a Bye Kitty" (with Katnip/Kneitel/Dec. 2).

**1951:** "As the Crow Lies" (Kneitel/June 1/re: Sept. 28, 1956); and "Cat-Choo" (with Katnip/Kneitel/Oct. 12).

**1952:** "The Awful Tooth" (with Katnip/Kneitel/May 2).

**1953:** "Better Bait Than Never" (with Katnip/Kneitel/June 5).

**1954:** "Hair Today, Gone Tomorrow" (with Katnip/Kneitel/Apr. 16); and "No If's, Ands or Butts" (with Katnip/Sparber/Dec. 17).

## ⊚ CAPTAIN AND THE KIDS

United Features Syndicate and MGM reached an agreement in the late 1930s to coproduce a sound cartoon series of Rudolf Dirks's famous *Katzenjammer Kids* comic strip, retitling the series and featuring most of the same cast of characters as the silent version.

Fred Quimby, MGM's cartoon studio head, produced the series, while former Warner Bros. director Friz Freleng joined forces with the studio to help direct. Freleng, who broke his contract with Warner (it ran out in October of that year), accepted Quimby's offer based on the understanding that "I could could hire anyone I wanted, that money was no object, and I could use any character I saw fit."

Once he arrived at MGM, Freleng found out differently. Quimby and the studio's board of directors had already struck a deal to produce the *Captain and the Kids* series, eliminating his opportunity to invent something original. (This was what attracted Freleng to MGM in the first place.)

"I went over to MGM because they offered me a lot more money than I was making at Warners," remembered Freleng. "But I knew the Katzenjammer Kids wouldn't sell. They were humanoid characters. Humanoids were not selling, only animal pairs like Tom and Jerry were."

As Freleng feared, the series failed. The budgets were much larger than the Warner Bros. cartoons', but "it didn't help much since the audience didn't recognize that."

Freleng returned to Warner Bros. the same year of the series demise, while codirectors William Hanna, of Hanna and Barbera fame, and Robert Allen remained. Most cartoons in the series were filmed in black and white and released in "sepiatone," and only one cartoon was shot in full Technicolor: 1938's "The Captain's Christmas." *Black-and-white/Sepiatone and Technicolor. A Metro-Goldwyn-Mayer and United Feature Syndicate Production released through Metro-Goldwyn-Mayer.*

**Voices**
**Captain:** Billy Bletcher

**1938:** "Cleaning House" (Allen/Feb. 19/Sepiatone); "Blue Monday" (Hanna/Apr. 2/Sepiatone); "Poultry Pirates" (Freleng/Apr. 16/Sepiatone); "Captain's Pup" (Allen/Apr. 30/Sepiatone); "A Day at the Beach" (Freleng/June 25/Sepiatone); "What a Lion!" (Hanna/July 16/Sepiatone); "The Pygmy Hunt" (Freleng/Aug. 6/Sepiatone); "Old Smokey" (Hanna/Sept. 3/Sepiatone); "Buried Treasure" (Allen/Sept. 17/Sepiatone/formerly "Treasure Hunt"); "The Winning Ticket" (Oct. 1/Sepiatone); "Honduras Hurricane" (Oct. 15/Sepiatone/formerly "He Couldn't Say No"); and "The Captain's Christmas" (Dec. 17/formerly "The Short Cut"/Technicolor).

**1939:** "Petunia National Park" (Jan. 14); "Seal Skinners" (Jan. 28/Sepiatone); and "Mamma's New Hat" (Feb. 11/Sepiatone).

## ⊚ CASPER, THE FRIENDLY GHOST

His appearance frequently met by shrieks of "It's a g-g-ghost!" Casper, the Friendly Ghost, became a huge moneymaker for Paramount Pictures' Famous Studio, the same studio responsible for cartoon stalwarts like Baby Huey and others. Producer/animator Joseph Oriolo, who later revived Felix the Cat on television, created the friendly ghost, who in each adventure wished he had "someone to play with me." (Oriolo collaborated with Sy Reit on the character's conception.)

Oriolo lost out on millions of dollars in revenue the studio earned in merchandise and other licensed products, including a long-running comic-book series based on the character. He was paid by Paramount Pictures the paltry sum of $175 for the initial pilot in 1945, never making another dime.

"It's a shame that I never held onto the Casper series," explained Oriolo, "for Paramount and the Harvey people have made literally millions of dollars from the series from which I made mere pennies."

Since then several animators have claimed credit for masterminding Casper, but the first story, "The Friendly Ghost," was actually drafted by Seymour Wright. The character did not appear again on screen until 1948, and after the 1949 cartoon, "A-Haunting We Will Go," he was finally given his name.

In 1954, Casper starred in Famous Studios' second 3-D color cartoon, "Boo Moon," the first being the 1953 Popeye cartoon,

"Popeye the Ace of Space." Paramount released the Casper 3-D cartoon on Friday the 13th, in February of that year.

Made into a regular series in 1950, Casper scored a bigger hit on television in the 1960s, when a new series of films were commissioned, aimed strictly at children. Like the theatrical series, the new cartoons were built around the same premise: Casper's eternal search for a friend.

In 1995 Casper returned to the screen after a 36-year absence in an all-new live action/animated feature, *Casper*, for Universal Pictures. The movie was a smash hit with adults and children and spawned a made-for-video sequel. *Series directors were Isadore Sparber, Bill Tytla and Seymour Kneitel. A Famous Studios Production released through Paramount Pictures.*

**Voices**
**Casper:** Mae Questel, Norma McMillan, Gwen Davies, Cecil Roy

**1945:** "The Friendly Ghost" (Sparber/Nov. 16/*Noveltoon*).

**1948:** "Flip Flap" (with Flip Flap the Seal/Sparber/Feb. 13/*Noveltoon*); "There's Good Boos Tonight" (Sparber/Apr. 23/*Noveltoon*).

**1949:** "A Haunting We Will Go" (Kneitel/May 13/*Noveltoon*/narrator: Frank Gallop).

**1950:** "Casper's Spree under the Sea" (Tytla/Oct. 13); and "Once upon a Rhyme" (Sparber/Dec. 20).

**1951:** "Boo Hoo Baby" (Kneitel/Mar. 30); "To Boo or Not to Boo" (Kneitel/June 8); "Boo Scout" (Sparber/July 27); "Casper Comes to Clown" (Sparber/Aug. 10); and "Casper Takes a Bow-Wow" (Sparber/Dec. 7).

**1952:** "The Deep Boo Sea" (Kneitel/Feb. 15); "Ghost of the Town" (Sparber/Apr. 11); "Spunky Skunky" (Sparber/May 30); "Cage Fright" (Kneitel/Aug. 8); "Pig-a-Boo" (Sparber/Sept. 12); and "True Boo" (Sparber/Oct. 24).

**1953:** "Fright Day the 13th" (Sparber/Feb. 13/released on Friday, February 13, 1953); "Spook No Evil" (Kneitel/Mar. 13); "North Pal" (Sparber/May 29); "By the Old Mill Scream" (Kneitel/July 3); "Little Boo Peep" (Kneitel/Aug. 28); "Do or Diet" (Sparber/Oct. 16); and "Boos and Saddles" (Sparber/Dec. 25).

**1954:** "Boo Moon" (Kneitel, Sparber/Jan. 1/first released in 3-D; re-released in flat prints on Mar. 5); "Zero the Hero" (Kneitel/Mar. 26); "Casper Genie" (Kneitel/May 28); "Puss 'n' Boos" (Kneitel/July 16); "Boos and Arrows" (Kneitel/Oct. 15); and "Boo Ribbon Winner" (Sparber/Dec. 3).

**1955:** "Hide and Shriek" (Kneitel/Jan. 28); "Keep Your Grin Up" (Sparber/Mar. 4); "Spooking with a Brogue" (Kneitel/May 27); "Bull Fright" (Kneitel/July 15); "Red, White and Boo" (Sparber/Oct. 21); and "Boo Kind to Animals" (Sparber/Dec. 23).

**1956:** "Ground Hog Play" (Kneitel/Feb. 10); "Dutch Treat" (Sparber/Apr. 20); "Penguin for Your Thoughts" (Kneitel/June 15); "Line of Screammage" (Kneitel/Aug. 17); and "Fright from Wrong" (Kneitel/Nov. 2).

**1957:** "Spooking About Africa" (Kneitel/Jan. 4); "Hooky Spooky" (Kneitel/Mar. 1); "Peekaboo" (Kneitel/May 24); "Ghost of Honor" (Sparber/July 19); "Ice Scream" (Kneitel/Aug. 30); and "Boo Bop" (Kneitel/Nov. 11).

**1958:** "Heir Restorer" (Sparber/Jan. 24); "Spook and Span" (Kneitel/Feb. 28); "Ghost Writers" (Kneitel/Apr. 25); "Which Is Witch" (Kneitel/May 2); and "Good Scream Fun" (Kneitel/Sept. 12).

EYES IN CENTER OF HEAD — FAIRLY LARGE WITH PUPIL TAKING UP ABOUT ⅔ OF EYE

SHOW SLIGHT CHEEK (ONLY ON ONE SIDE AT A TIME)

KEEP NOSE AND MOUTH VERY SMALL

LITTLE CASPER IS SHORT, CHUBBY, SQUAT AND COMPACT

*Original concept drawing for the popular friendly ghost, Casper, co-created by producer Joseph Oriolo. © Harvey Cartoons*

**1959:** "Doing What's Fright" (Kneitel/Jan. 16); "Down to Mirth" (Kneitel/Mar. 20); "Not Ghoulty" (Kneitel/June 5); and "Casper's Birthday Party" (Kneitel/July 31).

## ◎ THE CAT

This series features a feline British supersleuth whose voice is patterned after Cary Grant's. Each time the cat escapes trouble he happily sings, "When you're wearing a new kind of hat." *Directed by Seymour Kneitel. Technicolor. A Famous Studios Production released through Paramount Pictures.*

**Voices**
**The Cat:** Dayton Allen

**1960:** "Top Cat" (July); and "Shootin' Stars" (Aug. 19/*Modern Madcap*).

**1961:** "Cool Cat Blues" (Jan. 19); "Bopin' Hood" (Aug. 15/ *Modern Madcap*); and "Cane and Able" (Oct. 19).

## ◎ CHARLIE DOG

Chuck Jones invented this wise-guy, orphan dog in stories shaped around his relentless search for a new master. Charlie was introduced to moviegoers in 1947's "Little Orphan Airedale," starring Porky Pig. The character appeared opposite Porky Pig in three cartoons before he was cast in a short-lived cartoon series of his own, beginning with 1950's "Dog Gone South." *Directed by Chuck Jones. Technicolor. A Warner Bros. Cartoons, Inc. Production released by Warner Bros.*

**Voices**
**Charlie Dog:** Mel Blanc

*Looney Tunes*

**1947:** "Little Orphan Airedale" (with Porky Pig/Oct. 4).

**1949:** "Often an Orphan" (with Porky Pig/Aug. 13).

**1951:** "A Hound for Trouble" (Apr. 28).

*Merrie Melodies*

**1949:** "Awful Orphan" (with Porky Pig/Jan. 29).

**1950:** "Dog Gone South" (Aug. 26/first Charlie Dog cartoon).

## ◎ CHILLY WILLY

Chilly Willy, a mute penguin, was one of Walter Lantz's most productive film characters next to Woody Woodpecker. The character was Chaplinesque in nature, scooting around corners using Chaplin's famed one-legged stand, to elude his enemies in sticky situations. The series was initiated in 1953 in a film bearing the character's own name.

Unfortunately, Chilly was not well received, and Lantz brought in Tex Avery, of Warner Bros. and MGM fame, to redesign the character, which he was determined to make into a star. As Avery told biographer Joe Adamson: "The penguin wasn't funny. There was nothing to it, no personality, no nothing."

In 1954 Avery's direction of Chilly Willy in "I'm Cold" made a splash with critics and theatergoers alike. The film even earned an Academy Award nomination for best short subject of that year.

Avery remained on the series only for a short time, however. He left over a salary dispute in 1955, at which time Alex Lovy took over as the series' director. The series was terminated in 1960, having amassed 35 cartoons during its lifetime. *Directed by Paul J. Smith, Alex Lovy, Jack Hannah, Tex Avery and Sid Marcus. Technicolor. A Walter Lantz Production released through Universal Pictures.*

*Mute penguin Chilly Willy, who displayed Charlie Chaplin's famous stiff-legged walk, outwitted his adversaries in a host of Walter Lantz cartoons. © Walter Lantz Productions*

**Voices**
**Chilly Willy:** Daws Butler

**1953:** "Chilly Willy" (Smith/Dec. 21).

**1954:** "I'm Cold" (with Smedley the Dog/Avery/Nov. 29/A.A. nominee/a.k.a. "Some Like It Not").

**1955:** "The Legend of Rockabye Point" (Avery/Apr. 11/A.A. nominee/a.k.a. "Rockabye Legend"); and "Hot and Cold Penguin" (Lovy/Oct. 24/originally storyboarded by Tex Avery).

**1956:** "Room and Wrath" (Lovy/June 4); and "Hold That Rock" (Lovy/July 30).

**1957:** "Operation Cold Feet" (Lovy/May 6); "The Big Snooze" (Lovy/Aug. 30); and "Swiss Miss-Fit" (Lovy/Dec. 2).

**1958:** "Polar Pests" (Lovy/May 19); "A Chilly Reception" (Lovy/ June 16); and "Little Tellevillain" (Lovy/Dec. 8).

**1959:** "Robinson Gruesome" (Smith/Feb. 2); and "Yukon Have It" (Lovy/Mar. 30).

**1960:** "Fish Hooked" (Smith/Aug. 10).

**1961:** "Clash and Carry" (Hannah/Apr. 25); "St. Moritz Blitz" (Smith/May 16); and "Tricky Trout" (Smith/Sept. 5).

**1962:** "Mackerel Moocher" (Hannah/Apr. 10).

**1963:** "Fish and Chips" (Hannah/Jan. 8); "Salmon Loafer" (Marcus/May 28); and "Pesky Pelican" (Marcus/Sept. 24).

**1964:** "Deep-Freeze Squeeze" (Marcus/Mar.); "Lighthouse Keeping Blues" (Marcus/Aug.); and "Ski-Napper" (Marcus/Nov.).

**1965:** "Fractured Friendship" (Marcus/Mar.); "Half Baked Alaska" (Marcus/Apr.); and "Pesty Guest" (Marcus/June 1).

**1966:** "Snow Place Like Home" (Smith/Feb. 1); "South Pole Pals" (Smith/Mar. 1); "Polar Fright" (Smith/Apr. 1); and "Teeny Weeny Meany" (Marcus/May 1).

**1967:** "Operation Shanghai" (Smith/Jan.); "Vicious Viking" (Smith/Feb.); "Hot Time on Ice" (Smith/Mar.); "Chilly and the Woodchopper" (Smith/May); and "Chilly Chums" (Smith/June).

**1968:** "Under Sea Dogs" (Smith); "Highway Hecklers" (Smith/Sept. 1); and "Chiller Dillers" (Smith).

**1969:** "Project Reject" (Smith/May); "Chilly and Looney Gooney" (Smith/July); and "Sleepy Time Bear" (Smith/Dec.).

**1970:** "Gooney's Goofy Landing" (Smith/Mar.); "Chilly's Ice Folly" (Smith/June); and "Chilly's Cold War" (Smith/Nov.).

**1971:** "A Gooney Is Born" (Smith/Jan.); "Airlift a la Carte" (Smith); and "Chilly's Hide-a-Way" (Smith).

**1972:** "The Rude Intruder" (Smith).

## ◉ CHIP 'N' DALE

These two pesty, buck-toothed chipmunks were mainly supporting characters in cartoons for Walt Disney, usually a source of irritation to the irascible Donald Duck. Formative versions of the characters first appeared in 1943's "Private Pluto" and "Squatter's Rights," also with Pluto, which was nominated for an Academy Award. The squeaky-voiced duo were given their rightful names in the Donald Duck cartoon, "Chip 'n' Dale," in 1947. They appeared in several more Donald Duck one-reelers before the studio featured the characters in their own series. The first series entry was 1951's "Chicken in the Rough." *Directed by Jack Hannah and Jack Kinney. Technicolor. A Walt Disney Studios Production released by RKO Radio Pictures.*

### Voices
**Chip/Dale:** Dessie Miller; Helen Silbert

(*Cartoons listed are from the* Chip 'n' Dale *series only.*)

**1951:** "Chicken in the Rough" (Hannah/Jan. 19).

**1952:** "Two Chips and a Miss" (Hannah/Mar. 21).

**1954:** "The Lone Chipmunks" (Kinney/Apr. 7).

## ◉ CHUCK JONES MGM CARTOONS

Director Chuck Jones's prolific career was footnoted at Warner Bros. for his direction of cartoon stars Bugs Bunny, Pepe Lew Pew and the Road Runner. In the 1960s he coproduced MGM's *Tom and Jerry* cartoons, besides directing several miscellaneous one-reelers for the studio, one of which won an Academy Award. *Technicolor. A Metro-Goldwyn-Mayer Production released by Metro-Goldwyn-Mayer.*

**1965:** "The Dot and the Line" (Dec. 31/A.A. winner).

**1967:** "The Bear that Wasn't" (Dec. 31).

## ◉ CLAUDE CAT

Created by Chuck Jones, this paranoid yellow cat was usually menaced by wise-guy mice, Hubie and Bertie, with shock of red hair in a series of Warner Bros. cartoons. Claude first appeared in 1949's "Mouse Wreckers," which was nominated for an Academy Award. A year later Jones cast Claude opposite a new adversary: a floppy-eared, hyperactive pup named Frisky Puppy. The pair wreaked havoc on the screen in three cartoons, beginning with 1950's "Two's a Crowd." *Directed by Chuck Jones and Robert McKimson. Technicolor. A Warner Bros. Cartoons, Inc. Production released by Warner Bros.*

### Voices
**Claude Cat:** Mel Blanc

### Looney Tunes

**1949:** "Mouse Wreckers" (with Hubie and Bertie/Jones/Apr. 23/A.A. nominee).

**1950:** "Two's a Crowd" (with Frisky Puppy/Jones/Dec. 30).

**1952:** "Mouse Warming" (with Hubie and Bertie/Jones/Sept. 8).

**1954:** "Feline Frame-Up" (with Marc Antony, Pussyfoot/Jones/Feb. 13).

### Merrie Melodies

**1950:** "The Hypo-Condri-Cat" (with Hubie and Bertie/Jones/Apr. 15).

**1951:** "Cheese Chasers" (with Hubie and Bertie/McKimson/Aug. 28).

**1952:** "Terrier Stricken" (with Frisky Puppy/Jones/Nov. 29).

**1954:** "No Barking" (with Frisky Puppy, Tweety/Jones/Feb. 27).

## ◉ CLINT CLOBBER

Fully named DeWitt Clinton Clobber, this bombastic superintendent and sanitary engineer of the Flamboyant Arms Apartments was reminiscent of comedian Jackie Gleason, especially the famed comedian's gruff demeanor. The series was one of several new *Terrytoons* creations made during the reign of the studio's creative director Gene Deitch from 1956 to 1958.

Initially, *Terrytoons* cameraman Doug Moye, previously the voice of the father Terry Bears character, was the voice of Clint Clobber. Moye did not last long in the role, however. "Doug was not quite up to the acting ability we needed for Clobber, who was a more complex character," recalled Gene Deitch. "So we went with another actor."

Longtime voice actor Allen Swift replaced Moye as the voice of Clint Clobber for the remainder of the series. *Directed by Connie Rasinski and Dave Tendlar. Technicolor and CinemaScope. A Terrytoons and CBS Films, Inc., Production released through 20th Century Fox.*

### Voices
**Clint Clobber:** Allen Swift, Doug Moye

**1957:** "Clint Clobber's Cat" (Rasinski/July).

**1958:** "Springtime for Clobber" (Rasinski/Jan.); "Camp Clobber" (Tendlar/July); "Old Mother Clobber" (Rasinski/Sept.); and "Signed, Sealed, and Clobbered" (Rasinski/Nov.).

**1959:** "Clobber's Ballet Ache" (Rasinski/Jan.); and "The Flamboyant Arms" (Rasinski/Apr.).

## ◉ COLOR CLASSICS

Max Fleischer followed Walt Disney into the color cartoon arena with this series of charming fables produced in Cinecolor and two-strip and then three-strip Technicolor. The series was initially filmed in Cinecolor and two-strip Technicolor because Walt Disney had exclusive rights to three-strip Technicolor. Fleischer began filming the series in full-blown Technicolor in 1936, beginning with "Somewhere in Dreamland." Betty Boop was featured in the series opener, a fairy-tale spoof called "Poor Cinderella," released in 1934. *Directed by Dave Fleischer. Cinecolor and Technicolor. A Fleischer Studios Production released through Paramount Pictures.*

**1934:** "Poor Cinderella" (with Betty Boop/Aug. 3/Cinecolor); "Little Dutch Mill" (Oct. 26/Cinecolor); and "An Elephant Never Forgets" (Dec. 28).

1935: "The Song of the Birds" (Mar. 1 /two-color Technicolor); "The Kids in the Shoe" (May 19/two-color Technicolor); "Dancing on the Moon" (July 12/two-color Technicolor); "Time for Love" (Sept. 6/two-color Technicolor); and "Musical Memories" (Nov. 8/two-color Technicolor).

All cartoons listed below were filmed in three-color Technicolor.

1936: "Somewhere in Dreamland" (Jan. 17); "The Little Stranger" (Mar. 13); "The Cobweb Hotel" (May 15); "Greedy Humpty Dumpty" (July 10); "Hawaiian Birds" (Aug. 28); "Play Safe" (Oct. 16); and "Christmas Comes But Once a Year" (Dec. 4).

1937: "Bunny Mooning" (Feb. 12); "Chicken a La King" (Apr. 16); "A Car-Tune Portrait" (June 26); "Peeping Penguins" (Aug. 26); "Educated Fish" (Oct. 29); and "Little Lamby" (Dec. 31).

1938: "The Tears of an Onion" (Feb. 26); "Hold It!" (Apr. 29); "Hunky and Spunky" (June 24); "All's Fair at the Fair" (Aug. 26); and "The Playful Polar Bears" (Oct. 28).

1939: "Always Kickin'" (Jan. 26); "Small Fry" (Apr. 21); "Barnyard Brat" (June 30); and "The Fresh Vegetable Mystery" (Sept. 29).

1940: (Copyright dates are marked by a ©.) "Little Lambkins" (© Feb. 2); "Ants in the Plants" (Mar. 15); "A Kick in Time" (May 17/Note: Animator Shamus Culhane credits himself as director, even though Dave Fleischer is given credit); "Snubbed by a Snob" (July 19); and "You Can't Shoe a Horsefly" (Aug. 23).

## ⊚ COLOR RHAPSODIES

In an effort to emulate Walt Disney's *Silly Symphonies*, Columbia Pictures cartoon division created a similar fairy-tale series using the same commercial format of storyboarding music, children's tales and various cartoon calamities. The cartoons were initially produced using a two-strip color process over the three-strip Technicolor, for which Disney had exclusive rights at the time. (Later, full Technicolor films were produced after Disney lost his exclusivity.)

The series remained popular until Columbia's animation department closed in 1948. *Produced by Charles Mintz, Dave Fleischer and Ray Katz. Directed by Ub Iwerks, Ben Harrison, Manny Gould, Art Davis, Sid Marcus, Paul Fennell, Frank Tashlin, Alec Geiss, Bob Wickersham, Paul Sommer, John Hubley, Dun Roman, Howard Swift and Alex Lovy. Black-and-white and Technicolor. A Columbia Pictures Corporation Production released by Columbia Pictures.*

1934: "Holiday Land" (with Scrappy/Nov. 9/A.A. nominee); and "Babes at Sea" (Nov. 30).

1935: "The Shoemaker and the Elves" (Jan. 20); "The Make Believe Revue" (Mar. 22); "A Cat, a Mouse, and a Bell" (May 10); "Little Rover" (June 28); "Neighbors" (Aug. 15); "Monkey Love" (Sept. 12); and "Bon Bon Parade" (Oct. 10).

1936: "Doctor Bluebird" (with Scrappy, Margie, Yippy/Feb. 5); "Football Bugs" (Apr. 29); "Glee Worms" (June 24); "Playing Politics" (with Scrappy, Margie, Yippy/July 8); "Untrained Seal" (July 26); "The Novelty Shop" (Aug. 15); "In My Gondola" (with Scrappy, Margie/Sept. 3); "Merry Mutineers" (Oct. 2); "Birds in Love" (Oct. 28); "Two Lazy Crows" (Iwerks/Nov. 26); and "A Boy and His Dog" (with Scrappy, Yippy/Dec. 23).

1937: "Hollywood Picnic"; "Gifts from the Air" (Jan. 1); "Skeleton Frolics" (Iwerks/Jan. 29); "Merry Mannequins" (Iwerks/Mar. 19); "Let's Go" (Apr. 10); "Mother Hen's Holiday" (May 7); "The Foxy Pup" (Iwerks/May 21); "The Stork Takes a Holiday" (June 11); "Indian Serenade" (July 16); "Spring Festival" (Aug. 6); "Scary Crows" (Aug. 20); "Swing Monkey Swing" (Sept. 10); "The Air Hostess" (Oct. 22); "The Little Match Girl" (Nov. 5); and "Hollywood Panic" (Dec. 18).

1938: "Bluebirds' Baby" (Jan. 21); "The Horse on the Merry-Go-Round" (Iwerks/Feb. 17); "The Foolish Bunny" (Davis/Mar. 26); "Snowtime" (Iwerks/Apr. 14); "The Big Birdcast" (May 13); "Window Shopping" (Marcus/June 3); "Poor Little Butterfly" (Harrison/July 4); "Poor Elmer" (Marcus/July 22); "The Frog Pond" (Iwerks/Aug. 12); "Hollywood Graduation" (Davis/Aug. 26); "Animal Cracker Circus" (Harrison/Sept. 23); "Happy Birthday" (with Scrappy, Margie, Yippy/Oct. 7); "Little Moth's Big Flame" (Marcus/Nov. 3); "Midnight Frolics" (Iwerks/Nov. 24); and "The Kangaroo Kid" (Harrison/Dec. 23).

1939: "Peaceful Neighbors" (Marcus/Jan. 26); "The Gorilla Hunt" (Iwerks/Feb. 24); "Happy Tots" (Harrison/Mar. 31); "The House that Jack Built" (Marcus/Apr. 14); "Lucky Pigs" (Harrison/May 26); "Nell's Yells" (Iwerks/June 30); "Hollywood Sweepstakes" (Harrison/July 28); "Jitterbug Knights" (Marcus/Aug. 11); "Crop Chasers" (Iwerks/Sept. 22); "Dreams on Ice" (Marcus/Oct. 20); "Mountain Ears" (Gould/Nov. 3); and "Mother Goose in Swingtime" (Gould/Dec. 18).

1940: "A Boy, a Gun and Birds" (Harrison/Jan. 12); "Happy Tots' Expedition" (with Happy Tots/Harrison/Feb. 9); "Blackboard Revue" (Iwerks/Mar. 15); "The Greyhound and the Rabbit" (Marcus/Apr. 19); "The Egg Hunt" (Iwerks/May 31); "Ye Old Swap Shoppe" (Iwerks/June 28); "The Timid Pup" (Harrison/Aug. 1); "Tangled Television" (Marcus/Aug. 30); "Mr. Elephant Goes to Town" (Davis/Oct. 4); "The Mad Hatter" (Marcus/Nov. 3); and "Wise Owl" (Iwerks/Dec. 6).

1941: "A Helping Paw" (Marcus/Jan. 7); "Way of All Pests" (Davis/Feb. 28); "The Carpenters" (Fennell/Mar. 14); "The Land of Fun" (Marcus/Apr. 18); "Tom Thumb's Brother" (Marcus/June 12); "The Cuckoo I.Q." (Marcus/July 24); "Who's Zoo in Hollywood" (Davis/Nov. 15); "The Fox and the Grapes" (with Fox and the Crow/Tashlin/Dec. 5); and "Red Riding Hood Rides Again" (Marcus/Dec. 5).

1942: "A Hollywood Detour" (Tashlin/Jan. 23); "Wacky Wigwams" (Geiss/Feb. 22); "Concerto in B-Flat Minor" (Tashlin/Mar. 20); "Cinderella Goes to a Party" (Tashlin/May 3); "Woodman Spare That Tree" (Wickersham/June 19); "Song of Victory" (Wickersham/Sept. 4); "Tito's Guitar" (with Tito/Wickersham/Oct. 30); "Toll Bridge Troubles" (with Fox and the Crow/Wickersham/Nov. 27); and "King Midas, Junior" (Sommer, Hubley/Dec. 18).

1943: "Slay It with Flowers" (with Fox and the Crow/Wickersham/Jan. 8); "There's Something About a Soldier" (Geiss/Feb. 26); "Professor Small and Mister Tall" (Sommer, Hubley/Mar. 26); "Plenty Below Zero" (with Fox and the Crow/Wickersham/May 14); "Tree for Two" (with Fox and the Crow/Wickersham/June 21); "He Can't Make It Stick" (Sommer, Hubley/June 11); "A Hunting We Won't Go" (with Fox and the Crow/Wickersham/Aug. 23); "The Rocky Road to Ruin" (Sommer/Sept. 16); "Imagination" (Wickersham/Oct. 29/A.A. nominee); and "The Herring Murder Mystery" (Roman/Dec. 30).

1944: "Disillusioned Bluebird" (Swift/May 26).

1945: "Dog, Cat and Canary" (with Flippy/Swift/Jan. 5); "Fiesta Time" (with Tito/Wickersham/Apr. 4); "Rippling Romance"

(Wickersham/June 21); "Hot Foot Lights" (Swift/Aug. 2); "Carnival Courage" (with Willoughby Wren/Swift/Sept. 6); and "River Ribber" (with Professor Small and Mr. Tall/Sommer/Oct. 4).

**1946:** "Polar Playmates" (Swift/Apr. 25); "Picnic Panic" (Wickersham/June 20); and "Cagey Bird" (with Flippy/Swift/July 18).

**1947:** "Loco Lobo" (Swift/Jan. 9); "Cockatoos for Two" (Wickersham/Feb. 13); "Big House" (with Flippy/Swift/Mar. 6); "Mother Hubba-Hubba Hubbard" (Wickersham/May 29); "Up 'n' Atom" (Marcus/July 10); "Swiss Tease" (Marcus/Sept. 1); and "Boston Beany" (Marcus/Dec. 4).

**1948:** "Flora" (Lovy/Mar. 18); "Pickled Puss" (Swift/Sept. 2); and "Lo, the Poor Buffalo" (Lovy/Nov. 14).

**1949:** "Grape Nutty" (with Fox and the Crow/Lovy/Apr. 14); and "Cat-Tastrophy" (Marcus/June 30).

## ◎ COMIC KINGS

The series starred the kings of Sunday comic strips, from Beetle Bailey to Krazy Kat, in madcap animated adventures simultaneously released to theaters and television. (Entries from the theatrical cartoon series, with the exception of *Little Lulu*, became part of the *King Features Trilogy*, featuring 50 episodic films of each character, broadcast in syndication.) The first entry in the theatrical series was a new *Little Lulu* cartoon, "Frog's Legs," coproduced by Lulu's creator, Marjorie H. Buell. Al Brodax, who produced a series of *Popeye* cartoons for television as well as the syndicated *King Features Trilogy*, was the executive producer of the theatrical series (except for the *Little Lulu* cartoon). *Directed by Seymour Kneitel and Gene Deitch. Technicolor. A Famous Studios Production released through Paramount Pictures.*

### Voices

**Private Beetle Bailey:** Howard Morris; **Sgt. Orville Snorkel, General Halftrack:** Allan Melvin; **Cookie, Beetle Bailey's girlfriend:** June Foray; **Snuffy Smith:** Howard Morris; **Barney Google:** Allan Melvin; **Krazy Kat:** Penny Phillips; **Ignatz Mouse:** Paul Frees

**1962:** "Frog's Legs" (with Little Lulu/Kneitel/Apr.); "Home Sweet Swampy" (with Beetle Bailey/Kneitel/May 19); "Hero's Reward" (with Beetle Bailey/Kneitel/May 19); "Snuffy's Song" (with Snuffy Smith, Barney Google/Kneitel/June); "Et Tu Otto" (with Beetle Bailey/Kneitel/June 19); "The Hat" (with Snuffy Smith, Barney Google/Kneitel/July); "Keeping up with Krazy" (with Krazy Kat, Ignatz Mouse, Officer Pupp/Deitch/Oct. 1); "A Tree Is a Tree Is a Tree" (with Beetle Bailey/Kneitel/Oct. 19); "The Method and the Maw" (with Snuffy Smith, Barney Google/Kneitel/Oct. 19); "Take Me to Your Gen'rul" (with Snuffy Smith/Kneitel/Oct. 19); and "Mouse Blanche" (with Krazy Kat, Ignatz Mouse, Officer Pupp/Kneitel/Nov. 1).

## ◎ COMICOLOR CARTOONS

Veteran animator Ub Iwerks, a former Disney protégé, directed these cartoon fables from 1933 to 1936. They were formula-type adventures using music and fanciful story lines in the Disney mold. The films were produced in Cinecolor, a two-color process combining red and blue hues, which was the forerunner to three-strip Technicolor.

The series' first entry, "Jack and the Beanstalk," premiered in 1933. In 1934 Iwerks broadened the scope of these films by adding his most prestigious invention: multiplane animation, a technique Max Fleischer later used in Paramount's two-reel Popeye cartoons.

Iwerks unveiled the process in "The Headless Horseman," based on Washington Irving's "The Legend of Sleepy Hollow." The technique added a three-dimensional foreground and background to cartoons by using a multiplane camera, capable of shooting through layers of animated background, moving either forward or backward, to project on film elaborate backgrounds and a greater feeling of depth. Not all *ComiColor* cartoons were produced using the multiplane camera, but all had the highest quality animation and stories.

The last cartoon of the series, "Happy Days" (1936), was also the pilot for a new series Iwerks wanted to animate based on Gene Byrnes's widely syndicated strip, *Reg'lar Fellers*. Plans for the series, scheduled for the 1936–37 season, never materialized.

Musical director Carl Stalling, long at Warner Bros., scored the *ComiColor* series. *Produced by Ub Iwerks. Directed by Ub Iwerks. Cinecolor. P.A. Powers Production released by Celebrity Productions Inc.*

**1933:** "Jack and the Beanstalk" (Nov. 30).

**1934:** "The Little Red Hen" (Feb. 16); "The Brave Tin Soldier" (Apr. 7); "Puss in Boots" (May 17); "The Queen of Hearts" (June 25); "Aladdin and the Wonderful Lamp" (Aug. 10); "The Headless Horseman" (Oct. 1); "The Valiant Tailor" (Oct. 29); "Don Quixote" (Nov. 26); and "Jack Frost" (Dec. 24).

**1935:** "Little Black Sambo" (Feb. 6); "The Brementown Musicians" (Mar. 6); "Old Mother Hubbard" (Apr. 3); "Mary's Little Lamb" (May 1); "Summertime" (June 15/originally "In the Good Ol' Summertime"); "Sinbad the Sailor" (July 30); "The Three Bears" (Aug. 30); "Balloonland" (Sept. 30/a.k.a. "The Pincushion Man"); "Simple Simon" (Nov. 15); and "Humpty Dumpty" (Dec. 30).

**1936:** "Ali Baba" (Jan. 30); "Tom Thumb" (Mar. 30); "Dick Whittington's Cat" (May 30); "Little Boy Blue" (July 30); and "Happy Days" (Sept. 30).

## ◎ CONRAD CAT

Dimwitted Conrad Cat was created for the screen by Warner Brothers veteran Chuck Jones and was loosely based on rubber-limbed comedian Ben Blue, who coincidentally starred in several comedy short subjects at Warner Brothers. The character first starred as an errand boy for the Arctic Palm Company in "The Bird Came C.O.D.," a *Merrie Melodies* cartoon. Pinto Colvig, of Walt Disney voice fame (best known as the voice of Goofy), provided the voice of Conrad. *Directed by Chuck Jones. Technicolor. A Warner Bros. Cartoons Inc. Production released by Warner Bros.*

### Voices

**Conrad Cat:** Pinto Colvig

### Merrie Melodies

**1942:** "The Bird Came C.O.D." (Jan. 17); and "Conrad the Sailor" (with Daffy Duck/Feb. 28).

## ◎ COOL CAT

This series, one of the last at Warner Bros. starred a hip kind of tiger created by Alex Lovy, who was hired in 1967 to direct a new series of Speedy Gonzales and Daffy Duck cartoons for the studio's newly formed animation department. Actor Larry Storch of TV's *F Troop* provided the character's "co-o-ol" voice. *Directed by Alex Lovy and Robert McKimson. Technicolor. A Warner Bros. Production released by Warner Bros. Seven Arts.*

*Voices*
**Cool Cat:** Larry Storch

**1967:** "Cool Cat" (Lovy/Oct. 14/*Looney Tunes*/song: "He's Just a Cool Cat," sung by The Clingers).

**1968:** "Big Game Haunt" (Lovy/Feb. 10/*Merrie Melodies*); "Hippydrome Tiger" (Lovy/Mar. 30/*Looney Tunes*); and "3 Ring Wing Ding" (Lovy/July 13/*Looney Tunes*).

**1969:** "Bugged by a Bee" (McKimson/July 26/*Looney Tunes*).

### ◎ CRACKPOT CRUISE
In the spring of 1939, Walter Lantz produced an animated comedy cruise cartoon directed by veteran animator Alex Lovy, entitled "Crackpot Cruise," for his *Cartune Classics* series. The cartoon inspired its own, albeit brief, full Technicolor series of spin-offs that same year. Lovy directed the entire series. *Directed by Alex Lovy. Technicolor. A Walter Lantz Production released by Universal Pictures.*

**1939:** "Crackpot Cruise" (Apr. 10/*Cartoon Classics*); "Bolo-Mola Land" (May 28); and "Slaphappy Valley" (Aug. 21).

### ◎ CUBBY THE BEAR
In 1933 George Stallings was appointed director of Van Beuren's animation department. Studio chief Amadee J. Van Beuren's first request was for Stallings to develop a lead character that brought life to the studio's sagging cartoon productions.

Animator Mannie Davis suggested a portly bear with round ears and an impish grin, animated in the same style as Mickey Mouse. Davis submitted a sketch to Stallings for consideration. Named Cubby, the character won immediate approval and Davis directed the series opener, "Opening Night," released in February of that year.

Unfortunately, the series never caught on, so in 1934 Van Beuren laid off personnel and to save costs subcontracted the production company of animators Rudolf Ising and Hugh Harman to animate and direct three cartoons for the series: "Cubby's World Flight," "Gay Gaucho" and "Mischievous Mice." "Mischievous Mice" was never released because Van Beuren broke off relations with the famed animators after its completion. *Produced by Amadee J. Van Beuren and George Stallings. Directed by Harry Bailey, Eddie Donnelly, Steve Muffati, George Stallings, Mannie Davis, Rudolf Ising and Hugh Harman. Black-and-white. A Van Beuren Studios Production released through RKO Radio Pictures.*

**1933:** "Opening Night" (Davis/Feb. 10); "The Last Mail" (Davis/Mar. 24); "Runaway Blackie" (Bailey/Apr. 7); "Bubbles and Troubles" (Davis/Apr. 28); "The Nut Factory" (Stallings/Aug. 11); "Cubby's World Flight" (Stallings/Aug. 26); "Cubby's Picnic" (Muffati, Donnelly/Oct. 6/a.k.a. "Picnic Problems"); "The Gay Gaucho" (Harman, Ising/Nov. 3); "Galloping Fanny" (Muffati, Donnelly/Dec. 1); and "Croon Crazy" (Muffati/Dec. 29).

**1934:** "Robin Hood Rides Again" (Jan. 1); "Sinister Stuff" (Muffati/Jan. 26/a.k.a. "Villain Pursues Her"); "Goode Knight" (Stallings/Feb. 23); "How's Crops?" (Stallings/Mar. 23/a.k.a. "Brownie's Victory Garden"); "Cubby's Stratosphere Flight" (Stallings/Apr. 20); "Mild Cargo" (Stallings/May 18/a.k.a. "Brownie Bucks the Jungle"); "Fiddlin' Fun" (Stallings/June 15); and "Mischievous Mice" (Harman, Ising/never released).

### ◎ DAFFY DITTIES
John Sutherland Productions, the same company that produced industrial cartoons for MGM, produced this series. Most were regular animated cartoons, with a few done in stop-motion animation using plastic-and-clay figures à la George Pal's *Puppetoons*. *Directors and voice credits are unknown. Technicolor. A John Sutherland Production released through United Artists.*

**1945:** "The Cross-Eyed Bull."

**1946:** "The Lady Said No" (Apr. 26); "Pepito's Serenade" (July 5); "Choo Choo Amigo" (Aug. 16); and "The Flying Jeep" (Aug. 20).

**1947:** "The Fatal Kiss" (Nov. 7).

### ◎ DAFFY DUCK
Daffy was a wisecracking duck whose screen antics originated at Warner Bros. in the late 1930s. The web-footed looney, who first appeared as a costar in Tex Avery's 1937 cartoon "Porky's Duck Hunt," was not officially christened until his second cartoon appearance, "Daffy Duck and Egghead," the following year.

At first, Daffy was nothing like the character audiences grew to love. He was more screwball than the later witty sophisticate who spouted verbal gems in his adversarial sparrings with Bugs Bunny, Porky Pig and Elmer Fudd. Instead, cross-eyed with a squat and round physique, he made the quick, jerky movements of a lunatic on the loose, performing handstands, somersaults and other acrobatics that underscored his manic "Woo-hoo! Woo-hoo!" laugh (reportedly inspired by comedian Hugh Herbert's famous "Hoo-hoo! Hoo-hoo!" tag line).

Daffy's unique personality proved infectious, winning support to cast him in additional cartoons of his own. As director Bob Clampett, who animated Daffy's first screen appearance, recalled in an interview: "At the time, audiences weren't accustomed to seeing a cartoon character do these things. And so, when it hit the theaters it was like an explosion. People would leave the theaters talking about this 'daffy duck.'"

Through the 1940s Daffy's character remained "out of control" in the films that followed under the effective direction of Clampett, who streamlined Daffy's design, making him taller, skinnier and thin-limbed. Daffy showed signs of screwballness in his first star-billed effort, "Daffy and the Dinosaur" (1939), directed by

*Porky Pig orders Daffy Duck to sit on and hatch a mysterious egg in a scene from Bob Clampett's 1946 cartoon, "Baby Bottleneck." © Warner Brothers* (COURTESY: BOB CLAMPETT ANIMATION ART)

Chuck Jones, but Clampett took the character to greater extremes in such notable efforts as "Draftee Daffy" (1945), "The Great Piggy Bank Robbery" (1946), "Book Revue" (1946), and "Baby Bottleneck" (1946).

By the 1950s Daffy became more malevolent in nature and was transformed into a hilarious cartoon foil for Warner cartoon stars Bugs Bunny and Porky Pig in a host of cartoons. It was during this period that Daffy's speech impediment evolved—he was unable to pronounce words having an "s" sound (thus "despicable" became "desthpicable"). In the 1960s, with DePatie-Freleng as his producer, Daffy's character became even more hard-edged when he was cast as a villain of sorts opposite Speedy Gonzales in a series of cartoons.

According to Chuck Jones, the successful formula for Daffy was having him victimized by his own ego: "Daffy was insane. He never settled down. His personality was very self-serving, as if to say 'I may be mean, but at least I'm alive.'"

Perhaps the most memorable cartoons in the series include the Bugs Bunny/Daffy Duck pairings about rabbit/duck season—"Rabbit Fire" (1951), "Rabbit Seasoning" (1952) and "Duck! Rabbit, Duck!" (1953)—as well as the science-fiction favorite, "Duck Dodgers in the 24½th Century" (1953), each directed by Jones. (In 1977 Jones directed a sequel, "The Return of Duck Dodgers in the 24½th Century," intended for theatrical release but instead broadcast as the centerpiece of a TV special, *Daffy Duck's Thank-for-Giving Special* in 1981.)

After a 19-year absence from the silver screen, Daffy starred in an all-new *Looney Tunes* cartoon in 1987, "The Duxorcist," a spoof of the chilling horror flick *The Exorcist,* followed by a new *Merrie Melodies* cartoon a year later: "Night of the Living Duck," this time parodying the cult horror classic *Night of the Living Dead.* Both were directed by Greg Ford and Terry Lennon and were the last Daffy Duck theatrical cartoons to feature the voice of Mel Blanc as Daffy. Blanc died in 1989 at the age of 81.

In the 1990s Daffy appeared in four new cartoon shorts, three of them as costar opposite Bugs Bunny: 1990's "Box-Office Bunny," followed by "Invasion of the Bunny Snatchers," which was never released theatrically, and "Carrotblanca" (1995), a cartoon parody of the Warner Bros. classic, *Casablanca* (voiced by Joe Alaskey), directed by Douglas McCarthy. In 1996 Daffy returned to star in the Michael Jordan–Bugs Bunny smash hit feature *Space Jam* and in the first new Daffy Duck cartoon in nine years: "Superior Duck" (voiced by Frank Gorshin), in which Daffy tries to be a superhero. Warner Bros. cartoon legend Chuck Jones produced and directed the film, one of six new *Looney Tunes* he produced and/or directed (under the Chuck Jones Film Productions banner) for the studio after forming a new animation unit on the studio grounds. The cartoon was released jointly to theaters nationwide by Warner Bros. Family Entertainment with the live-action comedy feature *Carpool,* starring Tom Arnold. The cartoon was the last to be directed by the Jones animation unit, which ceased operation in April of 1997.

A year after costarring with Warner Bros. cartoons counterparts Bugs Bunny, Porky Pig and others in his second live-action/animated feature, *Looney Tunes: Back in Action,* in 2004, the studio either produced, planned or storyboarded several new theatrical *Looney Tunes* cartoon shorts starring Daffy that were never released. Among them were "A Very Daffy Christmas"; "Badda Bugs," co-starring Bugs Bunny; "Daffy Contractor," with Porky Pig; "Duck Suped"; and "Slacker Quacker," also with Porky Pig. In February of 2005, Daffy costarred in a brand-new *Looney Tunes* cartoon, "Attack of the Drones," with Daffy reprising his role as the far-out space avenger, Duck Dodgers. *Directed by Tex Avery, Bob Clampett, Norm McCabe, Charles M. Jones, Frank Tashlin, Friz Freleng, Robert McKimson, Phil Monroe, Art Davis, Rudy Larriva, Alex Lovy, Maurice Noble, Ted Bonnicksen, Greg Ford, Terry Lennon, Darrel Van Citters, Douglas McCarthy, Bill Kopp, Rich Moore, Dan Povenmire and Peter Shin. Black-and-white. Technicolor. A Vitaphone/Leon Schlesinger Studios/Warner Bros. Cartoons, Inc./Warner Bros. Pictures, Inc./DePatie-Freleng Enterprises/Format Films/Warner Bros. Animation/Chuck Jones Film/Warner Bros. Production released by Warner Bros., Warner Bros. Seven Arts and Warner Bros. Family Entertainment.*

**Voices**
**Daffy Duck:** Mel Blanc, Jeff Bergman, Greg Burson, Frank Gorshin

### Looney Tunes

#### Vitaphone Production releases

**1937:** "Porky's Duck Hunt" (with Porky Pig/Avery/Apr. 17).

**1938:** "What Price Porky" (with Porky/Clampett/Feb. 26); "Porky & Daffy" (with Porky/Clampett/Aug. 6); and "The Daffy Doc" (with Porky Pig/Clampett/Nov. 26).

**1939:** "Scalp Trouble" (with Porky Pig/Clampett/June 24); and "Wise Quacks" (with Porky Pig/Clampett/Aug. 5).

#### Leon Schlesinger Studios releases

**1940:** "Porky's Last Stand" (with Porky Pig/Clampett/Jan. 6); and "You Ought to Be in Pictures" (with Porky Pig/Freleng/May 18).

**1941:** "A Coy Decoy" (with Porky Pig/McCabe/June 7); and "The Henpecked Duck" (with Porky Pig, Mrs. Daffy Duck/Clampett/Aug. 30).

**1942:** "Daffy's Southern Exposure" (McCabe/May 2); "The Impatient Patient" (McCabe/Sept. 5); "The Daffy Duckaroo" (McCabe/Oct. 24); and "My Favorite Duck" (with Porky Pig/Jones/Dec. 5).

**1943:** "To Duck or Not to Duck" (with Elmer Fudd/Jones/Mar. 6); "The Wise Quacking Duck" (Clampett/May 1); "Yankee Doodle Daffy" (with Porky Pig/Freleng/July 3); "Porky Pig's Feat" (with Porky Pig, Bugs Bunny/Tashlin/July 17); "Scrap Happy Daffy" (Tashlin/Aug. 21); and "Daffy—The Commando" (Freleng/Nov. 20).

**1944:** "Tom Turk and Daffy" (with Porky Pig/Jones/Feb. 12); "Tick Tock Tuckered" (with Porky Pig/Clampett/Apr. 8/remake of "Porky's Badtime Story"); and "Duck Soup to Nuts" (with Porky Pig/Freleng/May 27).

#### Warner Bros. Cartoons, Inc. releases

**1944:** "Plane Daffy" (Tashlin/Sept. 16); and "The Stupid Cupid" (with Elmer Fudd/Tashlin/Nov. 25).

**1945:** "Draftee Daffy" (Clampett/Jan. 27); and "Ain't That Ducky" (Freleng/May 19).

**1946:** "Book Revue" (Clampett/Jan. 5); "Baby Bottleneck" (with Porky Pig/Clampett/Mar. 16); "Daffy Doodles" (with Porky Pig/McKimson/Apr. 6); and "The Great Piggy Bank Robbery" (Clampett/July 20).

**1947:** "Birth of a Notion" (with Peter Lorre, Joe Besser–like goose/McKimson/Apr. 12); "Along Came Daffy" (with Yosemite Sam/Freleng/June 4); and "Mexican Joy Ride" (Davis/Nov. 29).

**1948:** "What Makes Daffy Duck?" (with Elmer Fudd/Davis/Feb. 14/Cinecolor); "The Up-Standing Sitter" (McKimson/July 13);

"Riff Raffy Daffy" (with Porky Pig/Davis/Nov. 7/Cinecolor); and "The Stupor Salesman" (Davis/Nov. 20).

**1949:** "Wise Quackers" (with Elmer Fudd/Freleng/Jan. 1); and "Daffy Duck Hunt" (with Porky Pig/McKimson/Mar. 26).

**1950:** "Boobs in Woods" (with Porky Pig/McKimson/Jan. 28); "The Scarlet Pumpernickel" (with Porky Pig, Sylvester the Cat, Elmer Fudd, Momma Bear/Jones/Mar. 4); "The Ducksters" (with Porky Pig/Jones/Sept. 2); and "The Prize Pest" (with Porky Pig/McKimson/Dec. 22).

**1951:** "Rabbit Fire" (with Bugs Bunny, Elmer Fudd/Jones/May 19).

**1952:** "Thumb Fun" (with Porky Pig/McKimson/Mar. 1); "The Super Snooper" (McKimson/Nov. 1); and "Fool Coverage" (with Porky Pig/McKimson/Dec. 13).

**1954:** "Design for Leaving" (with Elmer Fudd/McKimson/Mar. 27).

**1955:** "Dime to Retire" (with Porky Pig/McKimson/Sept. 3).

**1956:** "The High and the Flighty" (with Foghorn Leghorn/McKimson/Feb. 18); "Stupor Duck" (McKimson/July 17); "A Star Is Bored" (with Elmer Fudd, Bugs Bunny/Freleng/Sept. 15); and "Deduce, You Say" (with Porky Pig/Jones/Sept. 29).

**1957:** "Boston Quackie" (with Porky Pig/McKimson/June 22); and "Show Biz Bugs" (with Bugs Bunny/Freleng/Nov. 2).

**1959:** "China Jones" (with Porky/McKimson/Feb. 14).

### Warner Bros. Pictures, Inc. releases

**1961:** "The Abominable Snow Rabbit" (with Bugs Bunny/Jones, Noble/May 20); and "Daffy's Inn Trouble" (with Porky Pig/McKimson/Sept. 23).

**1962:** "Good Noose" (McKimson/Nov. 10).

**1964:** "The Iceman Ducketh" (with Bugs Bunny/Monroe, Noble/May 16).

### DePatie-Freleng Enterprises releases

**1965:** "It's Nice to Have Mouse Around the House" (with Speedy Gonzales, Sylvester, Granny/Freleng, Pratt/Jan. 16); "Moby Duck" (with Speedy Gonzales/McKimson/Mar. 27); "Well Worn Daffy" (with Speedy Gonzales/McKimson/May 22); "Tease for Two" (with Goofy Gophers/McKimson/Aug. 28); and "Chili Corn Corny" (with Speedy Gonzales/McKimson/Oct. 23).

**1966:** "The Astroduck" (with Speedy Gonzales/McKimson/Jan. 1); "Daffy Rents" (with Speedy Gonzales/McKimson/Apr. 29); "A-Haunting We Will Go" (with Speedy Gonzales, Witch Hazel/McKimson/Apr. 16); "A Squeak in the Deep" (with Speedy Gonzales/McKimson/July 19); and "Swing Ding Amigo" (with Speedy Gonzales/McKimson/Sept. 17).

### Format Films releases

**1967:** "Quacker Tracker" (with Speedy Gonzales/Larriva/Apr. 29).

### Warner Bros. releases

"Rodent to Stardom" (with Speedy Gonzales/Lovy/Sept. 23); and "Fiesta Fiasco" (Lovy/Dec. 9/originally "The Rain Maker").

**1968:** "See Ya Later Gladiator" (with Speedy Gonzales/Lovy/June 29).

**1987:** "The Duxorcist" (Ford, Lennon/Nov. 20).

**1991:** "Invasion of the Bunny Snatchers" (with Bugs Bunny, Elmer Fudd, Yosemite Sam, Porky Pig/Ford, Lennon); and "Box-Office Bunny" (with Bugs Bunny, Elmer Fudd/Van Citters/Feb. 11).

### Warner Bros. Animation releases

**1995:** "Carrotblanca" (with Bugs Bunny, Yosemite Sam, Sylvester, Tweety, Foghorn Leghorn, Pepe Le Pew, Penelope/McCarthy/Aug. 25).

### Warner Bros./Chuck Jones Film Productions releases

**1996:** "Marvin the Martian in the Third Dimension" (with Marvin Martian, K-9/McCarthy/June); and "Superior Duck" (with Superman/Jones/Aug. 23).

### Warner Bros. releases

**2005:** "Attack of the Drones" (with Daffy as Duck Dodgers/Moore, Povenmire, Shin, Kopp/Feb. 8).

## Merrie Melodies

### Vitaphone Production releases

**1938:** "Daffy Duck and Egghead" (with Egghead/Avery/Jan. 1); and "Daffy Duck in Hollywood" (Avery/Dec. 3).

**1939:** "Daffy Duck and the Dinosaur" (Jones/Apr. 22).

### Leon Schlesinger Studios releases

**1942:** "Conrad the Sailor" (with Conrad Cat/Jones/Feb. 28).

**1944:** "Slightly Daffy" (with Porky Pig/Freleng/June 17).

### Warner Bros. Cartoons, Inc. releases

**1945:** "Nasty Quacks" (Tashlin/Dec. 1).

**1946:** "Hollywood Daffy" (with Bette Davis, Johnny Weissmuller, Charlie Chaplin, Jimmy Durante, Jack Benny, Bing Crosby, Joe Besser caricatures/Freleng/June 22).

**1947:** "A Pest in the House" (with Elmer Fudd/Jones/Aug. 3).

**1948:** "Daffy Duck Slept Here" (with Porky Pig/McKimson/Mar. 6); "You Were Never Duckier" (with Henery Hawk/Jones/Aug. 7); and "Daffy Dilly" (Jones/Oct. 30/Cinecolor).

**1949:** "Holiday for Drumsticks" (with Tom Turk/Davis/Jan. 22/Cinecolor).

**1950:** "His Bitter Half" (Freleng/May 20); and "Golden Yeggs" (with Porky Pig, Rocky, Nick/Freleng/Aug. 5).

**1951:** "Dripalong Daffy" (with Porky Pig/Jones/Nov. 17); and "The Prize Pest" (with Porky Pig/McKimson/Dec. 22).

**1952:** "Cracked Quack" (with Porky Pig/Freleng/July 5); and "Rabbit Seasoning" (with Bugs Bunny, Elmer Fudd/Jones/Sept. 20).

**1953:** "Duck Amuck" (with Bugs Bunny/Jones/Feb. 28/working title: "Daffy Pull"); "Muscle Tussle" (McKimson/Apr. 18); "Duck Dodgers in the 24½th Century" (with Porky Pig, Marvin Martian/Jones/July 25); and "Duck! Rabbit, Duck!" (with Bugs Bunny, Elmer Fudd/Jones/Oct. 3).

**1954:** "Quack Shot" (with Elmer Fudd/McKimson/Oct. 30); and "My Little Duckaroo" (with Porky Pig, Nasty Canasta/Jones/Nov. 27).

**1955:** "Beanstalk Bunny" (with Bugs Bunny, Elmer Fudd/Jones/Feb. 12); "Stork Naked" (with Daffne Duck/Freleng/Feb. 26); and "This Is a Life?" (with Elmer Fudd, Bugs Bunny, Yosemite Sam/Freleng/July 9).

**1956:** "Rocket Squad" (with Porky Pig/Jones/Mar. 10).

**1957:** "Ali Baba Bunny" (with Bugs Bunny, Hassan/Jones/Feb. 9); and "Ducking the Devil" (with Tasmanian Devil/McKimson/Aug. 17).

**1958:** "Don't Axe Me" (with Elmer Fudd/McKimson/Jan. 4); and "Robin Hood Daffy" (with Porky Pig/Jones/Mar. 8).

*Warner Bros. releases*

**1959:** "People Are Bunny" (with Bugs Bunny, Art Lamplighter/McKimson/Dec. 19).

**1960:** "Person to Bunny" (with Bugs Bunny, Elmer Fudd/Freleng/Apr. 2).

*Warner Bros. Pictures, Inc./Vitaphone releases*

**1962:** "Quackodile Tears" (with Mrs. Daffy Duck/Davis/Mar. 31).

**1963:** "Fast Buck Duck" (McKimson, Bonnicksen/Mar. 9); and "Aqua Duck" (McKimson/Sept. 28).

*DePatie-Freleng Enterprises releases*

**1965:** "Assault and Peppered" (with Speedy Gonzales/McKimson/Apr. 24); "Suppressed Duck" (McKimson/June 26); and "Go Go Amigo" (with Speedy Gonzales/McKimson/Nov. 20).

**1966:** "Muchos Locos" (with Speedy Gonzales/McKimson/Feb. 5); "Mexican Mousepiece" (with Speedy Gonzales/McKimson/Feb. 26); "Snow Excuse" (with Speedy Gonzales/McKimson/May 21); "Feather Finger" (with Speedy Gonzales/McKimson/Aug. 20); and "A Taste of Catnip" (with Speedy Gonzales/McKimson/Dec. 3).

*Warner Bros. releases*

**1967:** "Daffy's Diner" (with Speedy Gonzales/McKimson/Jan. 21).

*Format Films releases*

**1967:** "The Music Mice-Tro" (with Speedy Gonzales/Larriva/May 27); and "The Spy Swatter" (with Speedy Gonzales/Larriva/June 24).

*Warner Bros. releases*

**1967:** "Speedy Ghost to Town" (with Speedy Gonzales/July 29); and "Go Away Stowaway" (with Speedy Gonzales/Lovy/Sept. 30).

*Warner Bros./Seven Arts releases*

**1968:** "Skyscraper Caper" (with Speedy Gonzales/Lovy/Mar. 9).

*Warner Bros. releases*

**1980:** "Duck Dodgers and the Return of the 24½th Century" (with Porky Pig, Marvin Martian, Gossamer/Jones).

**1988:** "Night of the Living Duck" (Ford, Lennon/Sept. 23).

**1991:** "(blooper) Bunny!" (with Bugs Bunny, Elmer Fudd/Ford).

## ◎ DEPUTY DAWG

Spurred by the success of *The Deputy Dawg Show*, which premiered on television in 1960, 20th Century Fox released a number of these made-for-TV cartoons, featuring a not-so-bright lawman trying to maintain law and order in Mississippi, to theaters nationwide two years later. The series was one of Terrytoons' most successful in the 1960s. During this period, the Terrytoons name was not hyphenated in its films. *Produced by Bill Weiss and directed by George Gordon, Bob Kuwahara, Dave Tendlar and Bill Tytla.*

*Technicolor. A Terrytoons and CBS Films Inc., production released through 20th Century Fox.*

*Voices*

**Deputy Dawg:** Dayton Allen

**1962:** "Shotgun Shambles" (Sept. 8); "Space Varmit" (Sept. 8); "The Yoke's on You" (Sept. 8); "Li'l Whooper" (Sept. 15); "Seize You Later, Alligator" (Sept. 15); "Welcome Mischa Mouse" (Sept. 15); "Cotton Pickin' Picnic" (Sept. 22); "Henhouse Hassle" (Sept. 22); "Law and Disorder" (Sept. 22); "Deputy Dawg's Nephew" (Sept. 29); "Friend Fox" (Sept. 29); "Rabid Rebel" (Sept. 29); "Aig Plant" (Oct. 6); "Dog-Gone Catfish" (Oct. 6); "National Spoof Day" (Oct. 6); "Kin Folk" (Oct. 13); "Penguin Panic" (Oct. 13); "People's Choice" (Oct. 13); "Lynx th' Jinx" (Oct. 20); "The Bird Burglar" (Oct. 20); "Watermelon Watcher" (Oct. 20); "Dragon My Foot" (Oct. 27); "Star for a Day" (Oct. 27); "The Two Inch Inchworm" (Oct. 27); "Honey Tree" (Nov. 3); "Where There's Smoke" (Kuwahara/Nov. 3); "Nobody's Ghoul" (Tendlar/Nov. 3); "Oil Tycoons" (Nov. 10); "Rebel Trouble" (Tendlar/Nov. 10); "Big Chief, No Treaty" (Kuwahara/Nov. 10); "Beaver Battle" (Nov. 17); "Ship Aha Ha" (Nov. 17); "The Fragrant Vagrant" (Nov. 17); "Noise Annoys" (Nov. 24); "Peanut Pilferer" (Nov. 24); "Tennessee Walkin' Horse" (Nov. 24); "Little Red Fool House" (Dec. 1); "Mr. Moose" (Dec. 1); and "National Lazy Day" (Dec. 1).

**1963:** "Echo Park" (Jan. 5); "Physical Fatness" (Jan. 5); "Astronut" (Rasinski/Jan. 5); "Corn Cribber" (Jan. 12); "Heat Wave" (Jan. 12); "Herman the Hermit" (Jan. 12); "Dagnabit, Rabbit" (Jan. 19); "Long Island Duckling" (Jan. 19); "Tents Moments" (Jan. 19); "Dry Spell" (Jan. 26); "Orbit a Little Bit" (Jan. 26); "Tourist Tirade" (Jan. 26); "Low Man Lawman" (Feb. 2); "Safe 'an Insane 4th" (Feb. 2); "Terrific Traffic" (Feb. 2); "Open Wide" (Feb. 9); "Th' Catfish Poachin' Pelican" (Feb. 9); "The Milkweed From Space" (Feb. 9); "Bad Luck Day" (Feb. 16); "Royal Southern Dismounted Police" (Feb. 16); "Stuck Duck" (Feb. 16); "Champion Whooper Teller" (Feb. 23); "Go Go Gor-rilla" (Feb. 23); "Grandpa Law" (Feb. 23); "Daddy Frog Legs" (Mar. 2); "On the Lam with Ham" (Mar. 2); "Science Friction" (Mar. 2); "Just Ghost to Show You" (Mar. 9); "Lawman to the Rescue" (Mar. 9); "Mama Magnolia's Pecan Pies" (Mar. 9); "Feud for Thought" (Mar. 16); "Peach Pluckin' Kangaroo" (Mar. 16); "The Never Glades" (Mar. 16); "Diamonds in the Rough" (Mar. 23); "Double-Barreled Boom Boom" (Mar. 23); "The Poster Caper" (Mar. 23); "Chicken Bull" (Mar. 30); "Spare That Tree" (Mar. 30); "The Pig Rustler" (Mar. 30); "Catfish Crisis" (Apr. 6); "Hex Marks the Spot" (Apr. 6); "Something to Crow About" (Apr. 6); "How Biz Whiz" (Apr. 13); "Pinch Hittin' for a Pigeon" (Apr. 13); "Save Ol' Piney" (Apr. 13); "Mountain Melvin Meets Hairy Harry" (Apr. 20); "Mule-Itary Maneuvers" (Apr. 20); "Prostein' Pilot" (Apr. 20); "All Tuckered Out" (Apr. 27); "Millionaire Deputy" (Apr. 27); "The Hungry Astronaut" (Apr. 27); "Museum of th' South" (May 4); "Scare Cure" (May 4); "The Great Train Robbery" (May 4); "Corn Pone Limited" (May 11); "Space Invitation" (May 11); "You're Fired an' I'm Fired" (May 11); "Imperfect Crime" (May 18); "Obnoxious Obie" (May 18); "The Pink Flamingo" (May 18); "Elusive Louie" (May 25); "The Governor's Guide" (May 25); and "Home Cookin'" (June 2).

## ◎ DIMWIT

As the character's name implies, Dimwit was anything but smart in this early 1950s series of *Terry-Toon* cartoon adventures. *Directed by Connie Rasinski. Technicolor. A Terry-Toon Cartoons Production released through 20th Century Fox.*

**1953:** "How to Keep Cool" (with Spike-the Bulldog/Oct.).

**1954:** "How to Relax" (Feb.).

**1957:** "Daddy's Little Darling" (Apr.).

## ⊚ DINGBAT

This nutty cuckoo bird with a wacky laugh and a penchant for causing trouble starred in this short-lived *Terry-Toons* cartoon series, following his appearance in the 1949 Gandy Goose cartoon "Dingbat Land" (a sort of *Terry-Toons* version of the Warner Bros. classic, "Porky in Wackyland"). *Directed by Connie Rasinski and Mannie Davis. Technicolor. A Terry-Toon Cartoons Production released through 20th Century Fox.*

**1949:** "Dingbat Land" (with Gandy Goose, Sourpuss/Rasinski/ Feb. 1)

**1950:** "All This and Rabbit Stew" (with the Fox/Rasinski/July 1); and "Sour Grapes" (with the Fox/Davis/Dec.)

## ⊚ DINKY DUCK

A number of studios had a duck star. Walt Disney had Donald Duck and Warner Bros. had Daffy Duck. *Terry-Toons* producer Paul Terry developed his own duck character to compete with his cartoon rivals: Dinky Duck. Dinky splashed onto the silver screen to the delight of millions of moviegoers in "The Orphan Duck" (1939). The character managed to endure despite the competition, continuing to entertain audiences in new adventures until 1957. *Directed by Eddie Donnelly, Connie Rasinski, Mannie Davis and Win Hoskins. Black-and-white. Technicolor. A Terry-Toons Cartoons and Terrytoons/CBS Films, Inc. production released through 20th Century Fox.*

**1939:** "The Orphan Duck" (Rasinski/Oct. 6).

**1940:** "Much Ado About Nothing" (Rasinski/Mar. 22); and "The Lucky Ducky" (Rasinski/Sept. 6/Technicolor).

**1941:** "Welcome Little Stranger" (Rasinski/Oct. 3).

**1942:** "Life with Fido" (Rasinski/Aug. 21).

(All cartoons in Technicolor.)

**1946:** "Dinky Finds a Home" (Donnelly/June 7).

**1950:** "The Beauty Shop" (Donnelly/Apr. 28).

**1952:** "Flat Foot Fledgling" (Davis/Jan. 25); "Foolish Duckling" (Davis/May 16); and "Sink or Swim" (Rasinski/Aug. 29).

**1953:** "Wise Quacks" (Davis/Feb.); "Featherweight Champ" (Donnelly/Feb. 6); "The Orphan Egg" (Donnelly/Apr. 24); and "The Timid Scarecrow" (Donnelly/Aug. 28).

**1957:** "It's a Living" (Hoskins/Nov. 15).

## ⊚ DR. SEUSS

Based on the Dr. Seuss children's stories and written by Irving A. Jacoby. Musical score by Phillip Sheib. *Black-and-white. A Warner Bros. Production released by Warner Bros.*

**1931:** "'Neath the Bababa Tree" (June 1); and "Put on the Spout" (June 1).

## ⊚ DOGFACE

This talking mutt premiered on the silver screen in the 1945 *Noveltoon* cartoon, "A Self Made Mongrel," in which he appeared as a companion to a rich man. The character was reprised in a second cartoon four years later, this time becoming jealous of a black kit-

ten in a second *Noveltoon* "A Mutt in a Rutt." *Directed by Dave Tendlar and Isadore Sparber. Technicolor. A Famous Studios Production released through Paramount Pictures.*

**1945:** "A Self Made Mongrel" (Tendlar/June 29)

**1949:** "A Mutt in a Rutt" (Sparber/May 27).

## ⊚ THE DOGFATHER

Spoofing Marlon Brando's role in *The Godfather,* Dogfather and canine subordinates, Louie and Pugg, carry out heists and other jobs that run amuck. *Directed by Hawley Pratt, Gerry Chiniquy and Art Leonardi. A DePatie-Freleng Enterprises/Mirisch Cinema Company Production released through United Artists. Technicolor. A DePatie-Freleng/Mirisch Cinema Company Production released through United Artists.*

### Voices
**Dogfather:** Bob Holt; **Louie/Pugg:** Daws Butler

### Additional Voices
Frank Welker

**1974:** "The Dogfather" (Pratt/June 27); "The Goose that Laid a Golden Egg" (Pratt/Oct. 4); "Heist and Seek" (Chiniquy/Oct. 4); "The Big House Ain't a Home" (Chiniquy/Oct. 31); "Mother Dogfather" (Leonardi/Oct. 31); "Bows and Errors" (Chiniquy/Dec. 29); and "Deviled Yeggs" (Chiniquy/Dec. 29).

**1975:** "Watch the Birdie" (Chiniquy/Mar. 20); "Saltwater Tuffy" (Leonardi/Mar. 20); "M-O-N-E-Y Spells Love" (Leonardi/Apr. 23); "Roc-A-Bye Maybe" (Chiniquy/Apr. 23); "Haunting Dog" (Chiniquy/May 2); "Eagles Beagles" (Chiniquy/May 5); "From Nags to Riches" (Chiniquy/May 5); "Goldilox & the Three Hoods" (Chiniquy/Aug. 28); and "Rockhounds" (Leonardi/Nov. 20).

**1976:** "Medicur" (Chiniquy/Apr. 30).

## ⊚ DONALD DUCK

The ill-tempered Donald Duck made his debut in 1934 in Walt Disney's *Silly Symphony* cartoon, "The Wise Little Hen." Like

*The Dogfather gives directions to his henchmen in the cartoon series spoof of Marlon Brando's* The Godfather, *called* The Dogfather. *© DePatie-Freleng Enterprises*

Warner's Daffy Duck, Donald's features were greatly exaggerated in the beginning: He featured a longer bill, a skinnier neck, a fatter body and overly webbed feet highlighted by a tailor-made navy-blue jacket. (Donald's initial design was by studio animator Dick Lundy.) By the 1940s Donald's physique was modified into the figure known and recognized worldwide today.

Though Donald's first appearance won the unanimous acceptance of moviegoers, it wasn't until his second appearance in "Orphan's Benefit" that his true personality was revealed—that of "a cocky showoff with a boastful attitude that turns into anger as soon as he is crossed," according to animator Fred Spencer, who later animated MGM's *Tom and Jerry* cartoons.

Donald's success onscreen was largely due to his distinctive voice, which broke into nondescriptive jibberish when he became angry. Actor Clarence Nash was the talented individual who created Donald's voice. An Oklahoma native, Nash started at age 13 imitating animal sounds for friends down on the farm, never dreaming that one day he would voice cartoons professionally.

Walt Disney discovered Nash one evening while listening to a Los Angeles radio show. Nash was a local milk company spokesman. "I was talking duck talk on the radio one night when Disney just happened to tune in," Nash once explained. Disney immediately had the studio's personnel director set up a voice audition for Nash and from there everything fell into place.

"When I was 13, I used to recite 'Mary Had a Little Lamb' to my friends, and they'd just cut up," remembered Nash, prior to his death in 1985. "When I got there [the studio], I stuck my tongue into the left side of my mouth and recited the same old 'Mary Had a Little Lamb.' I didn't know it, but the engineer had flipped the switch and my voice was being piped over an intercom into Walt's office."

Midway through Nash's recital, Walt ran out of his office declaring "That's our duck! You're Donald Duck!"

Nash's most difficult voice challenge was presented in dubbing Donald Duck cartoons in foreign languages for theatrical release abroad. "Words were written out for me phonetically," he once recalled. "I learned to quack in French, Spanish, Portuguese, Japanese, Chinese, and German."

Among Nash's favorite cartoons were "The Band Concert," in which Mickey Mouse's attempt to play the "William Tell Overture" is marred by Donald's spiteful insistence at playing "Turkey in the Straw" on a piccolo, and the TV show, *A Day in the Life of Donald Duck*, made in the 1950s, in which he appears with his alter ego.

As the series blossomed, so did Donald's supporting cast. In 1937's "Don Donald," Donald was paired with a young, attractive senorita named Donna, who later became Daisy Duck, Donald's girlfriend. A year later Huey, Dewey and Louie, Donald's hellion nephews, were cast as regulars in the series.

Donald's meteoric rise led to roles in more than 150 cartoon shorts as well as appearances in several memorable feature films, among them: *The Reluctant Dragon* and *The Three Caballeros*. In 1983 he appeared in a featurette cartoon with pals Mickey Mouse and Goofy entitled *Mickey's Christmas Carol*.

Jack King, formerly of Warner Bros., directed the series from 1937 to 1947. King was joined by Jack Hannah and Jack Kinney, who shared assignments with King until his retirement. Kinney is best remembered for directing the 1943 Academy Award–winning Donald Duck wartime short, "Der Fuehrer's Face," winner in the best short film (cartoon) of the year category. The series reaped an additional nine Academy Award nominations during its run. Other Oscar-nominated cartoons included "Good Scouts" (1938), directed by Jack Kinney; "Truant Officer Donald" (1941) and "Donald's Crime" (1945), both directed by Jack King; "Chip an' Dale"

*Donald Duck gets a shovelful of problems in the form of these pesky chipmunks, Chip 'n' Dale, in a scene from "Corn Chips."* © *Walt Disney Productions. All rights reserved.*

(1947), "Tea for Two Hundred" (1948), "Toy Tinkers" (1949), "Rugged Bear" (1953) and "No Hunting" (1955), all directed by Jack Hannah; and, finally, "Donald in Mathmagic Land" (1959), directed by Hamilton Luske and nominated for best documentary. In 1947, Hannah won the series' second Oscar for the Donald Duck cartoon, "Chip an' Dale." *Additional series directors included Clyde Geronimi, Ben Sharpsteen, Dick Lundy, Riley Thomson, Wilfred Jackson, Bob Carlson, Charles Nichols, Hamilton Luske and Bill Roberts. Technicolor. A Walt Disney Production released through United Artists, RKO Radio Pictures and Buena Vista Pictures.*

**Voices**
**Donald Duck:** Clarence Nash

***United Artists releases***

**1934:** "The Wise Little Hen" (Jackson/June 9/*Silly Symphony*).

**1936:** "Donald and Pluto" (with Mickey Mouse, Pluto Sharpsteen/ Sept. 12/Mickey Mouse cartoon).

**1937:** "Don Donald" (with Mickey Mouse, Donna Duck Sharpsteen/Jan. 9/Mickey Mouse cartoon); "Modern Inventions" (King/May 29/released as a Mickey Mouse cartoon without Mickey).

***RKO-Radio Pictures releases***

**1937:** "Donald's Ostrich" (King/Dec. 10).

**1938:** "Self Control" (King/Feb. 11); "Donald's Better Self" (King/Mar. 11); "Donald's Nephews" (with Huey, Dewey, and Louie/King/Apr. 15); "Polar Trappers" (with Goofy/Sharpsteen/ June 17); "Good Scouts" (with Huey, Dewey, and Louie/King/July 8/A.A. nominee); "The Fox Hunt" (with Mickey Mouse, Goofy/ Sharpsteen/July 29); and "Donald's Golf Game" (with Huey, Dewey, and Louie/King/Nov. 4).

**1939:** "Donald's Lucky Day" (King/Jan. 13); "The Hockey Champ" (with Huey, Dewey, and Louie/King/Apr. 28); "Donald's Cousin Gus" (King/May 19); "Beach Picnic" (with Pluto/Geronimi/ June 9); "Sea Scouts" (with Huey, Dewey, and Louie/Lundy/June 30); "Donald's Penguin" (King/Aug. 11); "The Autograph Hound" (King/Sept. 1); and "Officer Duck" (Geronimi/Oct. 10).

**1940:** "The Riveter" (Lundy/Mar. 15); "Donald's Dog Laundry" (with Pluto/King/Apr. 5); "Billposters" (with Goofy/Geronimi/May 17); "Mr. Duck Steps Out" (with Daisy Duck, Huey, Dewey, and Louie/King/June 7); "Put-Put Troubles" (with Pluto/Thomson/July 19); "Donald's Vacation" (King/Aug. 9); "Window Cleaners" (with Pluto/King/Sept. 20); and "Fire Chief" (with Huey, Dewey, and Louie/King/Dec. 3).

**1941:** "Timber" (King/Jan. 10); "Golden Eggs" (Jackson/Mar. 7); "A Good Time for a Dime" (with Daisy Duck/Lundy/May 9); "Early to Bed" (King/July 11); "Truant Officer Donald" (with Huey, Dewey, and Louie/King/Aug. 1/A.A. nominee); "Old MacDonald Duck" (King/Sept. 12); "Donald's Camera" (Lundy/Oct. 24); and "Chef Donald" (King/Dec. 5).

**1942:** "The Village Smithy" (Lundy/Jan. 16); "The New Spirit" (Jackson, Sharpsteen/Jan. 23); "Donald's Snow Fight" (with Huey, Dewey, and Louie/King/Apr. 10); "Donald Gets Drafted" (King/May 1); "Donald's Garden" (Lundy/June 12); "Donald's Gold Mine" (Lundy/July 24); "The Vanishing Private" (King/Sept. 25); "Sky Trooper" (King/Nov. 6); and "Bell Boy Donald" (King/Dec. 18).

**1943:** "Der Fuehrer's Face" (Kinney/Jan. 1/A.A. winner); "The Spirit of '43" (King/Jan. 7); "Donald's Tire Trouble" (Lundy/Jan. 29); "Flying Jalopy" (Lundy/Mar. 12); "Fall Out, Fall In" (King/Apr. 23); "The Old Army Game" (King/Nov. 5); and "Home Defense" (with Huey, Dewey, and Louie/King/Nov. 26).

**1944:** "Trombone Trouble" (King/Feb. 18); "Donald Duck and the Gorilla" (King/Mar. 31); "Contrary Condor" (King/Apr. 21); "Commando Duck" (King/June 2); "The Plastics Inventor" (King/Sept. 1); and "Donald's Off Day" (with Huey, Dewey, and Louie/Hannah/Dec. 8).

**1945:** "The Clock Watcher" (King/Jan. 26); "The Eyes Have It" (with Pluto/Hannah/Mar. 30); "Donald's Crime" (with Daisy Duck, Huey, Dewey, and Louie/King/June 29/A.A. nominee); "Duck Pimples" (Kinney/Aug. 10); "No Sail" (with Goofy/Hannah/Sept. 7); "Cured Duck" (with Daisy Duck/King/Oct. 26); and "Old Sequoia" (King/Dec. 21).

**1946:** "Donald's Double Trouble" (with Daisy Duck/King/June 28); "Wet Paint" (King/Aug. 9); "Dumbbell of the Yukon" (with Daisy Duck/King/Aug. 30); "Lighthouse Keeping" (Hannah/Sept. 20); and "Frank Duck Brings 'Em Back Alive" (with Goofy/Hannah/Nov. 1).

**1947:** "Straight Shooters" (with Huey, Dewey, and Louie/Hannah/Apr. 18); "Sleepy Time Donald" (with Daisy Duck/King/May 9); "Clown of the Jungle" (Hannah/June 20); "Donald's Dilemma" (with Daisy Duck/King/July 11); "Crazy with the Heat" (with Goofy/Carlson/Aug. 1); "Bootle Beetle" (Hannah/Aug. 22); "Wide Open Spaces" (King/Sept. 12); and "Chip an' Dale" (with Chip 'n' Dale/Hannah/Nov. 28/A.A. winner).

**1948:** "Drip Dippy Donald" (King/Mar. 5); "Daddy Duck" (Hannah/Apr. 16); "Donald's Dream Voice" (with Daisy Duck/King/May 21); "The Trial of Donald Duck" (King/July 30); "Inferior Decorator" (Hannah/Aug. 27); "Soup's On" (with Huey, Dewey, and Louie/Hannah/Oct. 15); "Three for Breakfast" (with Chip 'n' Dale/Hannah/Nov. 5); and "Tea for Two Hundred" (Hannah/Dec. 24/A.A nominee).

**1949:** "Donald's Happy Birthday" (Hannah/Feb. 11); "Sea Salts" (Hannah/Apr. 8); "Winter Storage" (with Chip 'n' Dale/Hannah/June 3); "Honey Harvester" (Hannah/Aug. 5); "All in a Nutshell" (with Chip 'n' Dale/Hannah/Sept. 2); "The Greener Yard" (Hannah/Oct. 14); "Slide, Donald, Slide" (Hannah/Nov. 25); and "Toy Tinkers" (with Chip 'n' Dale/Hannah/Dec. 16/A.A. nominee).

**1950:** "Lion Around" (with Huey, Dewey, and Louie/Hannah/Jan. 20); "Crazy Over Daisy" (with Daisy Duck, Chip 'n' Dale/Mickey Mouse, Minnie Mouse, and Goofy/Hannah/Mar. 24); "Trailer Horn" (with Chip 'n' Dale/Hannah/Apr. 28); "Hook, Lion and Sinker" (Hannah/Sept. 1); "Bee at the Beach" (Hannah/Oct. 13); and "Out on a Limb" (with Chip 'n' Dale/Hannah/ Dec. 15).

**1951:** "Dude Duck" (Hannah/Mar. 2); "Corn Chips" (with Chip 'n' Dale/Hannah/Mar. 23); "Test Pilot Donald" (with Huey, Dewey, and Louie/with Chip 'n' Dale/Hannah/June 8); "Lucky Number" (Hannah/July 20); "Out of Scale" (with Chip 'n' Dale/Hannah/Nov. 2); and "Bee on Guard" (Hannah/Dec. 14).

**1952:** "Donald Applecore" (with Chip 'n' Dale/Hannah/Jan. 18); "Let's Stick Together" (Hannah/Apr. 25); "Uncle Donald's Ants" (Hannah/July 18); and "Trick or Treat" (with Huey, Dewey, and Louie/Hannah/Oct. 10).

**1953:** "Don's Fountain of Youth" (Hannah/May 30); "The New Neighbor" (Hannah/Aug. 1); "Rugged Bear" (with Humphrey Bear/Hannah/Oct. 23/A.A. nominee); "Working for Peanuts" (with Chip 'n' Dale/Hannah/Nov. 11/3-D); and "Canvas Back Duck" (Hannah/Dec. 25).

**1954:** "Spare the Rod" (with Huey, Dewey, and Louie/Hannah/Jan. 15); "Donald's Diary" (with Daisy Duck, Huey, Dewey, and Louie/Kinney/Mar. 5); "Dragon Around" (with Chip 'n' Dale/Hannah/July 16); "Grin and Bear It" (with Humphrey Bear, Ranger J. Aubudon Woodlore/Hannah/Aug. 13); "The Flying Squirrel" (Hannah/Nov. 12); and "Grand Canyonscope" (Ranger J. Audubon Woodlore, Louie the Mountain Lion/Nichols/Dec. 23/CinemaScope; Buena Vista release).

*RKO Radio releases*

**1955:** "No Hunting" (Hannah/Jan. 14/A.A. nominee/CinemaScope); "Lake Titicaca" (Roberts/Feb. 18/segment from *Saludos Amigos* feature); "Blame It on the Samba" (with José Carioca/Geronimi/Apr. 1/from *Melody Time* feature); "Bearly Asleep" (with Humphrey Bear/Hannah/Aug. 19/CinemaScope); "Beezy Bear" (with Humphrey Bear, Ranger J. Audubon Woodlore/Hannah/Sept. 2/CinemaScope); and "Up a Tree" (with Chip 'n' Dale/Hannah/Sept. 23).

**1956:** "Chips Ahoy" (with Chip 'n' Dale/Kinney/Feb. 24/CinemaScope); and "How to Have an Accident in the Home" (Nichols/July 8/CinemaScope/Buena Vista release).

*Buena Vista releases*

**1959:** "Donald in Mathmagic Land" (Luske/June 26/A.A. nominee, best documentary); and "How to Have an Accident at Work" (Nichols/Sept. 2).

**1961:** "Donald and the Wheel" (with Junior, Spirit of Progress/Luske/June 21); and "The Litterbug" (with Huey, Dewey, and Louie/Luske/June 21).

## ◎ DROOPY

Dwarfed, sad-eyed, unflappable bloodhound Droopy had a Buster Keaton physique and comedy style. His creator, Tex Avery, who directed the series until he left MGM in 1954, based the character on Wallace Wimple, a supporting character in radio's *The Fibber McGee and Molly Show*, played by Bill Thompson, who also voiced Droopy. (Thompson was later replaced by veteran voice artists Daws Butler and Don Messick in succession.)

Most adventures followed Avery's trademark survival-of-the-fittest theme, pitting the tiny basset hound against a scene-stealing Wolf, featured between 1949 and 1952, and pesky bulldog, Spike, in situational duels with meek, low-key Droopy always emerging victorious. Situations often were earmarked by imaginative sight gags and hyperboles, complementing Droopy's notorious deadpan, which, like Keaton, convulsed audiences into laughter often without ever uttering a line of dialogue.

Michael Lah was named Avery's successor, directing five cartoons in all, including "One Droopy Knight" (1957), which was nominated for an Academy Award. (Lah actually codirected several of Avery's last films before he was given full reign.) Dick Lundy, an MGM cartoon veteran, also directed occasional episodes. *Technicolor. CinemaScope. A Metro-Goldwyn-Mayer Cartoon Production released by Metro-Goldwyn-Mayer.*

### Voices
**Droopy:** Bill Thompson, Daws Butler, Don Messick

**1943:** "Dumb-Hounded" (Avery/Mar. 20).

**1945:** "The Shooting of Dan McGoo" (Avery/Mar. 3/re: Apr. 14, 1951/originally "The Shooting of Dan McScrew," a take-off of MGM's feature *Dan McGrew*); and "Wild and Woolfy" (Avery/Nov. 3/re: Oct. 4, 1952/working title: "Robinson's Screwball").

**1946:** "Northwest Hounded Police" (Avery/Aug. 13/re: Sept. 19, 1953/working title: "The Man Hunt").

**1949:** "Señor Droopy" (Avery/Apr. 9/re: Dec. 7, 1956); "Wags to Riches" (with Spike/Avery/Aug. 13/working title: "From Wags to Riches"); and "Out-Foxed" (Avery/Oct. 12).

**1950:** "The Chump Champ" (with Spike/Avery/Nov. 4).

**1951:** "Daredevil Droopy" (with Spike/Avery/Mar. 31); "Droopy's Good Deed" (Avery/May 5); and "Droopy's 'Double Trouble'" (with Droopy, Spikel/Avery/Nov. 17).

**1952:** "Caballero Droopy" (with Slick the Wolf/Lundy/Sept. 27).

**1953:** "Three Little Pups" (Avery/Dec. 26).

*The Wolf has the curvaceous sexpot Red right where he wants her in Tex Avery's hilarious cartoon romp "Wild and Woolfy." © Metro-Goldwyn-Mayer*

**1954:** "Drag-A-Long Droopy" (with the Wolf/Avery/Feb. 20); "Home-steader Droopy" (with the Wolf, Mrs. Droopy, Baby Droopy/Avery/July 10); and "Dixieland Droopy" (Avery/Dec. 4/first in CinemaScope).

**1955:** "Deputy Droopy" (Avery, Lah/Oct. 28).

**1956:** (All in CinemaScope); "Millionaire Droopy" (Avery/Sept. 21).

**1957:** "Grin and Share It" (Lah/May 17/produced by William Hanna and Joseph Barbera); "Blackboard Jumble" (Lah/Oct. 4/produced by William Hanna and Joseph Barbera); and "One Droopy Knight" (Lah/Dec. 6/produced by William Hanna and Joseph Barbera).

**1958:** "Sheep Wrecked" (Lah/Feb. 7/produced by William Hanna and Joseph Barbera); "Mutts about Racing" (Lah/Apr. 4/produced by William Hanna and Joseph Barbera); and "Droopy Leprechaun" (Lah/July 4/produced by William Hanna and Joseph Barbera).

## ⊚ DUCKWOOD
This ordinary-looking duck, who got into all sorts of fixes, was a minor star in this early 1960s Terry-Toons cartoon series, starring in only three cartoons for the studio. *Directed by Dave Tendlar. Technicolor. A Terrytoons/CBS Films, Inc., Production released through 20th Century Fox.*

**1964:** "The Red Tractor" (Feb.); "Short Term Sheriff" (with Dokey Otie); and "Oil Thru the Day."

## ⊚ EGGHEAD, JR.
Often pawned off on the southern-accented Foghorn Leghorn by his husband-seeking mother, Miss Prissy, thinking he would make a good stepfather (and husband) by teaching the boy some things she knew, this poker-faced chicken sporting an egg-shaped head, big glasses and a high I.Q. costarred in a handful of Warner Bros. cartoons. Naturally, the brainy bird proved to be heads-and-tails smarter than the older rooster, resulting in all-out laughs. The character was first introduced in the 1954 *Looney Tunes* cartoon, "Little Boy Boo." Egghead, Jr. was no relation to the bulbous-nosed human, Egghead, who later morphed into the now-famous rabbit hunter, Elmer Fudd. Veteran Warner Bros. animator Robert McKimson directed the entire series. *Directed by Robert McKimson. Technicolor. A Warner Bros. Cartoons, Inc., and Warner Bros. Production released by Warner Bros.*

### Voices
**Egghead, Jr.:** Mel Blanc

*Looney Tunes*

**1954:** "Little Boy Boo" (with Foghorn Leghorn, Miss Prissy/June 5).

*Merrie Melodies*

**1955:** "Feather Dusted" (with Foghorn Leghorn, Miss Prissy/Jan. 15).

**1960:** "Crockett-Doodle-Doo" (with Foghorn Leghorn, Miss Prissy/June 25).

## ⊚ ELMER FUDD
A "wabbit hunter" by trade, Elmer J. Fudd's comic adventures onscreen often involved his relentless pursuit of his adversarial costar, Bugs Bunny, who successfully outwitted Fudd ("Be vew-wy quiet, I'm hunting wabbits!") in numerous animated film triumphs.

The plump, chipmunk-cheeked hunter originally debuted in a different body and face as Egghead, a comic-relief character in early Warner Bros. cartoons, replete with brown derby and a nose the color of wine. Patterned after famed radio/film comedian Joe Penner, whose trademark phrase was "Wanna buy a duck?" Cliff Nazzaro has been credited with supplying the character's voice. It is now believed that Dave Weber, who provided the voices of various minor characters in several Warner Bros. cartoons as early as 1938, actually did the voice of Egghead. Among his other voice characterizations were impersonations of Rochester, Jack Benny's sidekick, Fred Allen and Walter Winchell.

After 11 cartoons, Warner Bros. animators decided to change the character to Elmer Fudd, appearing as such for the first time in "Dangerous Dan McFoo" (1939), supervised by Tex Avery. (Avery also directed Bugs Bunny's first official screen appearance, "A Wild Hare" [1940], in which Fudd also starred.) For this cartoon, Warner Bros. hired a new man to do the voice of Elmer: Arthur Q. Bryan, best known as Doc Gamble on the *Fibber McGee and Molly* radio program and an actor who did bit parts in movies, including Bela Lugosi's cult classic *The Devil Bat* (1941).

Even with a new name and face, Elmer went through several additional design changes, beginning with Bob Clampett's "Wabbit Twouble" (1941) and three subsequent cartoons in which he appeared exceedingly portly. According to Clampett, Elmer was redesigned because "we artists were never satisfied with the way he looked—he didn't look funny."

By now Elmer resembled his alter ego, Arthur Q. Bryan. By Friz Freleng's "The Hare-Brained Hypnotist" (1942), Elmer appeared in the style and form filmgoers would remember, including his most memorable trait—his inability to pronounce the letter *r*.

In the 1990s Elmer popped up on the screen in three new Bugs Bunny cartoons, "Box Office Bunny" (1991), "Invasion of the Bunny Snatchers" (1991) and "(blooper) Bunny!" (1991), and in the Michael Jordan-Bugs Bunny megahit movie, *Space Jam* (1996). In 2003, he costarred in a second live-action/animated feature for Warner Bros. opposite Steve Martin, Bugs, Daffy and many others, *Looney Tunes: Back in Action. Directed by Tex Avery, Frank Tashlin, Ben Hardaway, Cal Dalton, Bob Clampett, Charles M. Jones, Friz Freleng, Darrel Van Citters, and Greg Ford. Black-and-white. Technicolor. A Vitaphone/Leon Schlesinger Studios/Warner Bros. Cartoons Inc./Warner Bros. Production released by Warner Bros.*

### Voices
**Egghead:** Dave Weber, Cliff Nazzaro; **Elmer J. Fudd:** Arthur Q. Bryan, Mel Blanc, Jeff Bergman

### Merrie Melodies

#### Vitaphone Production releases

**1937:** "Egghead Rides Again" (Avery/July 17); and "Little Red Walking Hood" (Avery/Nov. 6).

**1938:** "Daffy Duck and Egghead" (with Daffy Duck/Avery/Jan. 1); "The Isle of Pingo Pongo" (Avery/May 28); "Cinderella Meets Fella" (Avery/July 23); "A Feud There Was" (Avery/Sept. 24); "Johnny Smith and Poker-Huntas" (Avery/Oct. 22); and "Count Me Out" (Hardaway, Dalton/Dec. 17).

**1939:** "Hamateur Night" (Avery/Jan. 28); A Day at the Zoo" (Avery/Mar. 11); "Believe It or Else" (Avery/June 25); and "Dangerous Dan McFoo" (character's named changed to Elmer Fudd/Avery/July 15).

#### Leon Schlesinger Studios releases

**1940:** "Elmer's Candid Camera" (with Bugs Bunny/Jones/Mar. 2); "Confederate Honey" (Freleng/May 30); "A Wild Hare" (with Bugs Bunny/Avery/July 27/A.A. nominee); and "Good Night Elmer" (Jones/Oct. 26).

**1941:** "Elmer's Pet Rabbit" (with Bugs Bunny/Jones/Jan. 4); "All This and Rabbit Stew" (with Bugs Bunny/Avery/Sept. 13); and "Wabbit Twouble" (with Bugs Bunny/Clampett/Dec. 20).

**1942:** "The Wabbit Who Came to Supper" (with Bugs Bunny/ Freleng/Mar. 28); "The Wacky Wabbit" (with Bugs Bunny/Clampett/ May 2); "Fresh Hare" (with Bugs Bunny/Freleng/Aug. 22); and "The Hare-Brained Hypnotist" (with Bugs Bunny/Freleng/Oct. 31).

**1943:** "A Corny Concerto" (with Bugs Bunny, Porky Pig/ Clampett/Sept. 18); and "An Itch in Time" (Clampett/Dec. 4).

#### Warner Bros. Cartoons, Inc. releases

**1944:** "The Old Grey Hare" (with Bugs Bunny/Clampett/Oct. 28); and "Stage Door Cartoon" (with Bugs Bunny/Freleng/Dec. 30).

**1945:** "The Unruly Hare" (with Bugs Bunny/Tashlin/Feb. 10).

**1946:** "Hare Remover" (with Bugs Bunny/Tashlin/Mar. 23); and "Bacall to Arms" (with Bugs Bunny/Clampett/Aug. 3).

**1947:** "A Pest in the House" (with Daffy Duck/Jones/Aug. 3).

**1948:** "Back Alley Oproar" (with Sylvester/Freleng/Mar. 27).

**1949:** "Hare Do" (with Bugs Bunny/Freleng/Jan. 15); and "Each Dawn I Crow" (Freleng/Sept. 23).

**1952:** "Rabbit Seasoning" (with Bugs Bunny, Daffy Duck/Jones/ Sept. 20).

**1953:** "Duck! Rabbit, Duck!" (with Bugs Bunny, Daffy Duck/ Jones/Oct. 3).

**1954:** "Quack Shot" (with Daffy Duck/McKimson/Oct. 30).

**1955:** "Pest for Guests" (with Goofy Gophers/Freleng/Jan. 29); and "Beanstalk Bunny" (with Bugs Bunny, Daffy Duck/Jones/Feb. 12).

**1956:** "Bugs Bonnets" (with Bugs Bunny/Jones/Jan. 14); "Yankee Dood It" (with Sylvester/Freleng/Oct. 13); and "Wideo Wabbit" (with Bugs Bunny/McKimson/Oct. 27).

**1957:** "What's Opera, Doc?" (with Bugs Bunny/Jones/July 6); and "Rabbit Romeo" (with Bugs Bunny/McKimson/Dec. 14).

**1958:** "Don't Axe Me" (with Daffy Duck/McKimson/Jan. 4).

#### Warner Bros. releases

**1960:** "Person to Bunny" (with Bugs Bunny, Daffy Duck/Freleng/ Apr. 1); and "Dog Gone People" (McKimson/Nov. 12).

**1991:** "(blooper) Bunny!" (with Bugs Bunny, Daffy Duck, Yosemite Sam/Ford).

### Looney Tunes

#### Vitaphone Productions releases

**1938:** "The Daffy Doc" (with Daffy Duck, Porky Pig/Clampett/ Nov. 26).

#### Warner Bros. Cartoons, Inc. releases

**1944:** "The Stupid Cupid" (with Daffy Duck/Tashlin/Nov. 25).

**1945:** "Hare Tonic" (with Bugs Bunny/Jones/Nov. 10).

**1946:** "The Big Snooze" (with Bugs Bunny/Clampett/Oct. 5).

**1947:** "Easter Yeggs" (with Bugs Bunny/McKimson/June 28).

**1948:** "Kit for Cat" (with Sylvester/Freleng/Nov. 6).

*Elmer Fudd, Bugs Bunny and Daffy Duck comically sort out duck and rabbit season in a scene from Chuck Jones's 1951 Warner Bros. cartoon short "Rabbit Fire."* © *Warner Bros. All rights reserved.*

**1949:** "Wise Quackers" (with Daffy Duck/Freleng/Jan. 1).

**1950:** "The Scarlet Pumpernickel" (with Daffy Duck, Porky Pig, Sylvester, Momma Bear/Jones/Mar. 4); "What's Up Doc?" (with Bugs Bunny/McKimson/June 17); and "The Rabbit of Seville" (with Bugs Bunny/Jones/Dec. 16).

**1951:** "Rabbit Fire" (with Bugs Bunny, Daffy Duck/Jones/May 19).

**1953:** "Ant Pasted" (Freleng/May 9); and "Robot Rabbit" (with Bugs Bunny/Freleng/Dec. 12).

**1954:** "Design for Living" (with Daffy Duck/McKimson/Mar. 27).

**1955:** "Hare Brush" (with Bugs Bunny/Freleng/May 7).

**1956:** "Heir-Conditioned" (with Sylvester/Freleng/Nov. 26).

**1958:** "Pre-Hysterical Hare" (with Bugs Bunny/McKimson/Nov. 1).

**1959:** "A Mutt in a Rut" (McKimson/May 23).

*Warner Bros. Pictures, Inc. releases*

**1961:** "What's My Lion?" (McKimson/Oct. 21).

*Warner Bros. releases*

**1991:** "Box-Office Bunny" (with Bugs Bunny, Daffy Duck/Van Citters/Feb. 25) and "Invasion of the Bunny Snatchers" with Daffy Duck, Yosemite Sam, and Porky Pig cameo/Ford, Lennon).

### ◉ FABLES

In addition to *Color Rhapsodies,* producer Charles Mintz, who began his career producing silent cartoons, produced another series based on popular children's tales called *Fables. Directors included Sid Marcus, John Hubley, Lou Lilly, Frank Tashlin, Alec Geiss, Bob Wickersham and Art Davis. Technicolor. A Columbia Pictures Corporation Production released by Columbia Pictures.*

**1939:** "Park Your Baby" (with Scrappy, Yippy/Dec. 22).

**1940:** "Practice Makes Perfect" (with Scrappy, Yippy/Apr. 5); "Barnyard Babies" (Davis/June 14); "Pooch Parade" (with Scrappy, Yippy/July 19); "A Peep in the Deep" (with Scrappy, Yippy/Aug.

23); "Farmer Tom Thumb" (with Scrappy, Yippy/Sept. 27); "Mouse Meets Lion" (Oct. 25) and "Paunch 'n' Judy" (Dec. 13).

**1941:** "The Streamlined Donkey" (Marcus/Jan. 17); "It Happened to Robinson Crusoe" (Mar. 14); "Kitty Gets the Bird" (June 13); "Dumb Like a Fox" (July 18); "Playing the Pied Piper" (Lilly/Aug. 18); "The Great Cheeze Mystery" (Davis/Oct. 27); and "The Tangled Angler" (Tashlin/Dec. 26).

**1942:** "Under the Shedding Chestnut Tree" (Wickersham/Feb. 22); "Wolf Chases Pigs" (Tashlin, Hubley/Apr. 20); and "The Bulldog and the Baby" (Geiss/July 3).

### ◉ FANNY ZILCH

Paul Terry produced this *Terry-Toons* cartoon series parody of old movie serial melodramas, starting with 1933's "The Banker's Daughter." The serials followed the exploits of beautiful heroine Fanny Zilch and her love interest, Strongheart, who was more concerned about his good looks while the villainous Oil Can Harry snatched Fanny right from under his nose. The series inspired the later *Mighty Mouse* operetta format that became common in that series, and, in 1937, Oil Can Harry was spun off into a short-lived series of his own. *Directed by Paul Terry and Frank Moser. Black and white. A Terry-Toons Cartoon Production released through Educational Pictures and Fox Film Corporation.*

**1933:** "The Banker's Daughter" (with Oil Can Harry/June 25); "The Oil Can Mystery" (with Oil Can Harry, Strongheart/July 9); "Fanny in the Lion's Den" (with Oil Can Harry, Strongheart/Aug. 1); "Hypnotic Eyes" (with Oil Can Harry, Strongheart/Aug. 11); and "Fanny's Wedding Day" (with O./Can Harry, Strongheart/Oct. 6).

### ◉ FARMER AL FALFA

The white-bearded hayseed who first appeared in the silent days returned to star in new sound cartoon adventures under the *Terry-Toons* banner for creator Paul Terry. Later adventures costarred two other *Terry-Toons* stars, Kiko the Kangaroo and Puddy the Pup. *Directed by Paul Terry, Frank Moser, Mannie Davis, John Foster, George Gordon and Jack Zander. Black-and-white. A Terry-Toon Cartoon Production released through Educational Pictures, Fox Film Corporation and 20th Century Fox.*

**1931:** "Club Sandwich" (Terry, Moser/Jan. 25/known on studio records as "Dancing Mice"); "Razzberries" (Terry, Moser/Feb. 8); "The Explorer" (Terry, Moser/Mar. 22); "The Sultan's Cat" (Terry, Moser/May 17); "Canadian Capers" (Terry, Moser/Aug. 23); and "The Champ" (Terry, Moser/Sept. 20).

**1932:** "Noah's Outing" (Terry, Moser/Jan. 24); "Ye Olde Songs" (Terry, Moser/Mar. 20); "Woodland" (Terry, Moser/May 1); "Farmer Al Falfa's Bedtime Story" (Terry, Moser/June 12); "Spring Is Here" (Terry, Moser/July 24); "Farmer Al Falfa's Ape Girl" (Terry, Moser/Aug. 7); and "Farmer Al Falfa's Birthday Party" (Terry, Moser/Oct. 2).

**1933:** "Tropical Fish" (Terry, Moser/May 14); "Pick-Necking" (Terry, Moser/Sept. 22); "The Village Blacksmith" (Terry, Moser/Nov. 3); and "Robinson Crusoe" (Terry, Moser/Nov. 17/copyrighted as "Shipwrecked Brothers").

**1934:** "The Owl and the Pussycat" (Terry, Moser/Mar. 9); and "Why Mules Leave Home" (Terry, Moser/Sept. 7).

**1935:** "What a Night" (Terry, Moser/Jan. 25); "Old Dog Tray" (Terry, Moser/Mar. 21); "Flying Oil" (Terry, Moser/Apr. 5); "Moans and Groans" (Terry, Moser/June 28); and "A June Bride" (Terry, Moser/Nov. 1).

**1936:** "The 19th Hole Club" (Terry, Moser/Jan. 24); "Home Town Olympics" (Terry Moser/Feb. 7); "The Alpine Yodeler" (Terry, Moser/Feb. 21); "Barnyard Amateurs" (Terry, Moser/Mar. 6); "The Western Trail" (Terry, Moser/Apr. 3); "Rolling Stones" (Terry, Moser/May 1); "The Runt" (Terry, Moser/May 15); "The Hot Spell" (with Puddy the Pup/Davis, Gordon/July 10); "Puddy the Pup and the Gypsies" (with Puddy the Pup/Davis, Gordon/July 24); "Farmer Al Falfa's Prize Package" (with Kiko the Kangaroo/July 31); "The Health Farm" (Davis, Gordon/Sept. 4); and "Farmer Al Falfa's Twentieth Anniversary" (Davis, Gordon/Nov. 27).

**1937:** "The Tin Can Tourist" (Davis, Gordon/Jan. 22); "The Big Game Hunt" (Davis, Gordon/Feb. 19); "Flying South" (Davis, Gordon/Mar. 19); "The Mechanical Cow" (Zander/June 25); "Pink Elephants" (Gordon/July 9); "Trailer Life" (with Puddy the Pup/Aug. 20); "A Close Shave" (with Ozzie/Davis/Oct. 1); "The Dancing Bear" (Oct. 15); and "The Billy Goat Whiskers" (with Puddy the Pup/Foster/Dec. 10).

## ◎ FELIX THE CAT

The silent era's first major merchandising phenomena and one of the biggest stars of its time, this crafty, pointy-eared black cat was created by pioneer animator Otto Messmer but produced and directed by Pat Sullivan, who owned all rights to the character and credited himself as its creator, even on film, though Messmer invented the wily feline, who reportedly starred in an estimated 150 to 175 cartoon shorts through 1930.

Like Walt Disney's Mickey Mouse, Felix transitioned to sound, unfortunately with poor results. Up until Walt Disney made cinematic history with the release of his first talking cartoon with a synchronized soundtrack, "Steamboat Willie" (1928), Sullivan seemed disinterested in producing "talking" cartoon, in part because of his unwillingness to bear the cost of adding sound to his films—but he embraced the idea following Disney's success in the medium.

That year, Sullivan inked a deal with First National Pictures to distribute cartoons, including some older ones with sound added, but the deal never lasted. It ended in 1929. A year later, Sullivan went to California to establish a new studio with plans to release new *Felix the Cat* cartoons in sound and in color, with former Bray Studios manager-turned producer Jacques Kopfstein distributing the films with post-synchronized music effects and soundtracks (with an ad in *Film Daily* magazine proclaiming in Jolson-esque manner, "You ain't heard nothin' yet!").

Unfortunately, the brace of films that Copley Pictures Corporation released, including such titles as "Felix the Cat in False Vases," "Felix the Cat Woos Whoopee," "Felix the Cat in April Maze," and "Felix the Cat in Oceantics," did little to raise Felix to the status of Disney's acclaimed mouse or Sullivan's prized franchise with movie audiences. As a result of poor health and a host of medical problems, Sullivan never fully completed his quest to open a new studio and produce *Felix the Cat* sound cartoons in color. His wife, Marjorie, died in March 1932, and his health really tail-spinned following an alcoholic depression; Sullivan died nearly a year after his wife, in 1933.

Two years after Sullivan's death, Van Beuren Studios president Amadee J. Van Beuren contacted Messmer about returning Felix to the screen in a series of new cartoon shorts. Messmer passed but suggested to Van Beuren that former Pat Sullivan studios animator Burt Gillett, then heading Van Beuren's animation unit, animate the series. Van Beuren subsequently licensed the rights to the character from Sullivan's brother and starred Felix in a handful of new shorts in color and sound, produced as part of Burt Gillett's *Rainbow Parades*. Gillett, who helmed the series with Van Beuren animator/director Tom Palmer, altered the clever feline's established personality in the films, accompanied by a musical soundtrack, in which he acted in pantomime in stories that were throwbacks to the silent days of filmmaking. *Directed by Pat Sullivan, Burt Gillett and Tom Palmer. Black-and-white. Technicolor. A Pat Sullivan Production released through First National Pictures and Copley Pictures Corporation/A Van Beuren Studios Production released through RKO Radio Pictures.*

### First National Pictures releases

**1928–29:** (Some previously released cartoons with sound added were re-released to theaters; the exact dates and releases remain unknown.)

### Copley Pictures Corporation releases

**1929:** "False Vases" (Sullivan); "One Good Turn" (Sullivan); and "Roameo" (Sullivan).

**1930:** "April Maze" (Sullivan); "Felix Woos Whoopee" (Sullivan); "Forty Winks" (Sullivan); "Hootchy Kootchy Parlais Vous" (Sullivan); "Oceantics" (Sullivan); "Skulls and Sculls" (Sullivan); and "Tee Time" (Sullivan).

### Van Beuren/RKO Radio Pictures releases

**1936:** "Felix the Cat and the Goose that Laid the Golden Eggs" (Gillett, Palmer/Feb. 7); "Neptune Nonsense" (Gillett, Palmer/Mar. 20); and "Bold King Cole" (Gillett, Palmer/May 29).

## ◎ FIGARO

This series starred the mischief-making cat Figaro, formerly of Walt Disney's *Pinocchio* (1940), in his eternal quest to catch the ever-elusive Cleo the goldfish who likewise debuted in the feature-film classic. Figaro also appeared separately as a supporting player in Pluto cartoons. *Directed by Jack Kinney and Charles Nichols. Technicolor. A Walt Disney Production released through RKO Radio Pictures.*

### Voices
**Figaro:** Clarence Nash, Kate-Ellen Murtagh

**1943:** "Figaro and Cleo" (Kinney/Oct. 15).

**1946:** "Bath Day" (Nichols/Oct. 11).

**1947:** "Figaro and Frankie" (Nichols/May 30).

## ◎ FINNEGAN AND CHARLIE

In the late 1950s, Famous Studios produced this short-lived pairing for Paramount Pictures casting them in two Technicolor *Noveltoons* cartoons, first in 1958's "Finnegan's Flea," directed by Isadore Sparber, in which the recently paroled con man, Finnegan, who served time in Alcatraz, happens upon a singing flea that repeatedly sings one song, "It's a Hap Hap Happy!," landing a $1,000-a-week movie contract. The cartoon's plotline was similar to Chuck Jones's Warner Bros. classic, "One Froggy Evening," in which a construction worker sees dollar signs after discovering the now-famous dancing-singing frog, Michigan J. Frog. A year later, director Seymour Kneitel starred the duo in the flying saucer send-up, "Out of This Whirl." *Directed by Isadore Sparber and Seymour Kneitel. Technicolor. A Famous Studios Production released through Paramount Pictures.*

**1958:** "Finnegan's Flea" (with Charlie the Singing Flea/Sparber/Apr. 4).

**1959:** "Out of This Whirl" (with Charlie/Kneitel/Nov. 13).

## ◎ FINX FOX

Wearing a crumpled top hat, white collar and faint green dress tie, this smooth-talking fox was the second of two foxes (the first was Wolfie Wolf) given the difficult job of catching one wily woodpecker, Walter Lantz's Woody Woodpecker, in two Woody Woodpecker Technicolor shorts: "Dumb Like a Fox" (1964), in an unbilled role, and "Sioux Me" (1965), in which he was introduced in the opening credits. Veteran animator Sid Marcus directed both cartoons. *Directed by Sid Marcus. Technicolor. A Walter Lantz Production released by Universal Pictures.*

**1964:** "Dumb Like a Fox" (with Woody Woodpecker/Marcus/ first appearance of Finx Fox).

**1965:** "Sioux Me" (with Woody Woodpecker/Marcus/June).

## ◎ FLIPPY

The "chase" formula, so popular in *Terry-Toons* and MGM's *Tom and Jerry*, was the basis of this series that revolved around the adventures of a thin yellow canary, Flippy, who is chased by an adversarial cat, Flop. That's until Sam the Dog, the neighborhood watchdog, intervenes. Flippy in some ways resembles Warner Bros.' Tweety bird. The series later inspired its own comic book series. *Directed by Howard Swift and Bob Wickersham. Technicolor. A Columbia Pictures Corporation Production released by Columbia Pictures.*

**1945:** "Dog, Cat and Canary" (Swift/Jan. 5/*Color Rhapsody*).

**1946:** "Catnipped" (Wickersham/Feb. 14); "Cagey Bird" (Swift/ July 18); and "Silent Treatment" (Wickersham/Sept. 19).

**1947:** "Big House Blues" (Swift/Mar. 6/*Color Rhapsody*).

## ◎ FLIP THE FROG

The star of Ub Iwerks's first Celebrity Pictures animated series, this web-footed amphibian was featured in 38 cartoon adventures released by Metro-Goldwyn-Mayer. Each film had a ragtime musical soundtrack and other vocal effects, as none of the characters in the films ever talked.

Originally to be called Tony the Frog, Flip's debut was in the 1930 cartoon "Fiddlesticks," made in two-strip Cinecolor two years before Walt Disney produced the first Technicolor short,

*Flip the Frog gets "reeled in" in a scene from Ub Iwerks's "Nurse Maid" (1932). (COURTESY: BLACKHAWK FILMS)*

"Flowers and Trees." With the aid of a small staff, Iwerks animated most of the cartoons himself.

After two cartoons, Flip's character was modified at the request of Iwerks's producer Pat Powers, making him "less froglike" with more human qualities. (Taller, he was dressed in plaid pants, white shoes and hand mittens.) The changes to his character were apparent in the 1930 release "The Village Barber," which enabled Powers to sell the series to MGM for distribution.

Most cartoons in the series, except for those filmed in two-strip Cinecolor, cost an average of $7,000 to produce and proved extremely profitable. "The Village Barber," for example, grossed $30,000 in ticket receipts in the United States alone, and the series overall grossed $304,666.61, of which Pat Powers made $110,000 in profit.

The *Flip the Frog* series was MGM's first animated venture and lasted four years. Carl Stalling, who first scored Walt Disney's *Silly Symphony* series and later Warner Bros.' *Merrie Melodies* and *Looney Tunes*, served as the series' musical director. Most cartoons were produced in black-and-white with a few filmed in the then-experimental Cinecolor. *Directed by Ub Iwerks. A Celebrity Pictures Production released through Metro-Goldwyn-Mayer.* (Copyright dates are marked by ©.)

**1930:** "Fiddlesticks" (Aug. 16/Cinecolor); "Flying Fists" (Sept. 6); "The Village Barber" (Sept. 27); "Little Orphan Willie" (Oct. 18); "Cuckoo Murder Case" (Oct. 18); and "Puddle Pranks" (Dec.).

**1931:** "The Village Smitty" (Jan. 31); "The Soup Song" (Jan. 31); "Laughing Gas" (Mar. 14); "Ragtime Romeo" (May 2); "The New Car" (July 25); "Movie Mad" (Aug. 29); "The Village Specialist" (Sept. 12); "Jail Birds" (Sept. 26); "Africa Squeaks" (Oct. 17); and "Spooks" (Dec. 21).

**1932:** "The Milkman" (Feb. 20); "Fire! FIRE!" (Mar. 5); "What a Life" (Mar. 26); "Puppy Love" (Apr. 30); "School Days" (May 14); "Bully" (June 18); "The Office Boy" (July 16); "Room Runners" (Aug. 13); "Stormy Seas" (Aug. 22); "Circus" (Aug. 27); "The Goal Rush" (© Oct. 3); "Phoney Express" (© Oct. 27); "The Music Lesson" (Oct. 29); "Nurse Maid" (Nov. 26), and "Funny Face" (Dec. 24).

**1933:** "Cuckoo the Magician" (Jan. 21); "Flip's Lunch Room" (Apr. 3); "Techno-Cracked" (May 8/Cinecolor); "Bulloney" (May 30); "Chinaman's Chance" (June 24); "Pale-Face" (Aug. 12); and "Soda Squirt" (Oct. 12).

## ◎ FOGHORN LEGHORN

A loudmouthed Southern rooster known for his boisterous babblings on ("Pay attention, boy . . . now listen here!"), Foghorn Leghorn was another popular character in Warner Bros.' stable of cartoon stars. The braggart was first featured in Warner's 1946 release "Walky Talky Hawky," appearing opposite a precocious chicken hawk named Henery Hawk, whose single greatest ambition is to "catch chickens."

Surprisingly, the cartoon won an Academy Award nomination for best short subject that year. It also won Foghorn a permanent spot on the Warner's cartoon roster; he was cast in his own starring cartoon series for the next 16 years.

Warner's animator Robert McKimson actually modeled Foghorn, originally considered a parody of the Senator Claghorn character from Fred Allen's radio show, after a sheriff character from an earlier radio program, *Blue Monday Jamboree*. It was from this broadcast that McKimson adapted many of Foghorn's distinctive traits, among them his overstated repartee and other standard lines for which he became famous.

Mel Blanc, the man of 1,000 cartoon voices, was the voice of Foghorn Leghorn. Blanc derived the idea for the character's voice from a 1928 vaudeville show he attended as a teenager. "When I was just a youngster, I had seen a vaudeville act with this hard-of-hearing sheriff. And the fellow would say, 'Say! P-pay attenshun. I'm talkin' to ya, boy. Don't ya know what I'm ah talkin' about.' I thought, 'Gee, this might make a good character if I made a big Southern rooster out of him.' And that's how I happened to get the voice of Foghorn Leghorn," Blanc recalled prior to his death in 1989.

Since pairing Henery Hawk with Foghorn was so successful the first time around, McKimson made the character a regular in the series, alternating him in a supporting role with Br'er Dog, a grumpy backyard dog, as Foghorn's chief nemesis. For romantic interest, Miss Prissy, the husband-seeking hen, was later featured in several films, along with her son, Egghead Jr. (also known as "Junior" in earlier adventures), a bookwormish child prodigy whose intelligence was vastly superior to that of Foghorn's.

In the 1990s Foghorn returned to the screen, first in a minor role in a new Bugs Bunny cartoon: "Carrotblanca" (1995), which pokes fun at the 1942 Warner Bros.' classic *Casablanca* (with Greg Burson as the voice of Foghorn). Then in 1997 Foghorn returned starred in his first new cartoon short in 34 years, entitled "Pullet Surprise," produced by legendary animator Chuck Jones and directed by Darrel Van Citters. Foghorn's nemesis was the slightly impaired Pete Puma (as voiced by Stan Freberg); Frank Gorshin did the voice of Foghorn. The cartoon was the fifth new cartoon short produced by Jones, who had formed a new animation unit on the Warner Bros. lot three years earlier. The short opened with the full-length animated feature *Cats Don't Dance*. Foghorn made his feature-film debut a year earlier in the Michael Jordan–Bugs Bunny hit, *Space Jam*.

Eight years later, in 2005, Foghorn Leghorn starred in a new direct-to-video Looney Tunes cartoon, "Cock-A-Doodle Duel," directed by Rich Moore, Dan Povenmire, Peter Shin and Bill Kopp. *Directed by Robert McKimson, Art Davis, Douglas McCarthy and Darrel Van Citters. Technicolor. A Warner Bros. Cartoons Inc./Warner Bros. Pictures, Inc./Vitagraph/Warner Bros. Production released by Warner Bros. and Warner Bros. Family Entertainment.*

**Voices**
**Foghorn Leghorn:** Mel Blanc, Greg Burson, Frank Gorshin; **Henery Hawk:** Mel Blanc; **Miss Prissy:** Mel Blanc, Bea Benadaret, June Foray, Julie Bennett

*Merrie Melodies*

*Warner Bros. Cartoons, Inc. releases*

**1946:** "Walky Talky Hawky" (with Henery Hawk/McKimson/Aug. 31/A.A. nominee).

**1948:** "The Foghorn Leghorn" (with Henery Hawk/McKimson/Oct. 9).

**1950:** "A Fractured Leghorn" (McKimson/Sept. 16).

**1951:** "Leghorn Swoggled" (with Henery Hawk/McKimson/July 28).

**1952:** "The EGGcited Rooster" (with Henery Hawk/McKimson/Oct. 4).

**1955:** "Feather Dusted" (with Prissy, Junior/McKimson/Jan. 15).

**1957:** "Fox Terror" (McKimson/May 11).

**1958:** "Feather Bluster" (McKimson/May 10); and "Weasel While You Work" (McKimson/Aug. 6).

**1960:** "Crockett-Doodle-Doo" (with Egghead Jr./McKimson/June 25); and "The Dixie Fryer" (McKimson/Sept. 24).

*Warner Bros. Pictures, Inc./Vitagraph releases*

**1961:** "Strangled Eggs" (with Henery Hawk/McKimson/Mar. 18).

**1962:** "Mother Was a Rooster" (McKimson/Oct. 20).

**1963:** "Banty Raids" (McKimson/June 29).

*Looney Tunes*

*Warner Bros. Cartoons, Inc. releases*

**1947:** "Crowing Pains" (with Sylvester, Henery Hawk/McKimson/July 12).

**1948:** "The Rattled Rooster" (Davis/June 26).

**1950:** "The Leghorn Blows at Midnight" (with Henery Hawk/McKimson/May 6).

**1951:** "Lovelorn Leghorn" (with Miss Prissy/McKimson/Sept. 8).

**1952:** "Sock-a-Doodle Doo" (McKimson/May 10).

**1954:** "Little Boy Boo" (with Widow Hen, Junior/McKimson/June 5).

**1955:** "All Fowled Up" (with Henery Hawk/McKimson/Feb. 19).

**1956:** "The High and the Flighty" (with Daffy Duck/McKimson/Feb. 18).

**1959:** "A Broken Leghorn" (McKimson/Sept. 26).

*Warner Bros. Pictures, Inc./Vitagraph releases*

**1962:** "The Slick Chick" (with Widow Hen, Junior/McKimson/July 21).

**1995:** "Carrotblanca" (with Bugs Bunny, Daffy Duck, Yosemite Sam, Sylvester, Tweety, Pepe Le Pew, Penelope/McCarthy/Aug. 25).

*Warner Bros./Chuck Jones Film Productions releases*

**1997:** "Pullet Surprise" (with Pete Puma/Van Citters/Mar. 26/produced by Chuck Jones).

## ◎ FOOFLE

Gene Deitch, the creative director for *Terrytoons* (whose name ceased to be hyphenated) in the late 1950s, created this hapless, voiceless character who pantomimed his way through one failure after another. Deitch derived the concept for Foofle from another one of his sad-sack creations, Nudnik, who appeared in 13 cartoons for Paramount. *Directed by Dave Tendlar. Technicolor and Cinema-Scope. A Terrytoons/CBS Films, Inc., Production released through 20th Century Fox.*

**1959:** "Foofle's Train Ride" (May).

**1960:** "Foofle's Picnic" (Mar./CinemaScope); and "The Wayward Hat" (July/CinemaScope).

## ◎ FOOLISH FABLES

Various spoofs of popular children's fables had been done before. That same formula inspired this short-lived series by Walter Lantz Production, which faltered after only two cartoons. *Directed by Paul J. Smith. Technicolor. A Walter Lantz Production released through Universal Pictures.*

**1953:** "The Mouse and the Lion" (May 11); and "The Flying Turtle" (June 29).

### ◎ THE FOX AND THE CROW

The slick-talking black crow and gluttonous bow-tied fox were the most flamboyant Columbia Pictures cartoon characters to appear on movie screens. The brainchild of director Frank Tashlin, who wrote and directed the first cartoon, "Fox and Grapes" (1941), the characters' wild pursuits of each other served as inspiration for Chuck Jones's blackout-style humor (a series of gags joined together by one common theme) in his Road Runner and Coyote series for Warner Bros. From 1941 through most of 1943, they initially starred in seven *Color Rhapsodies* before they were featured in their own series, beginning with 1943's "Room and Bored."

Charles Mintz initially produced the series, with Dave Fleischer and Ray Katz succeeding him as the series producer.

When Columbia Pictures closed its cartoon department, United Productions of America (UPA) picked up the series and continued its production, with Steve Bosustow serving as producer. The characters received two Academy Award nominations: 1948's "Robin Hoodlum," the first *Fox and the Crow* cartoon for UPA, and 1949's "The Magic Fluke." *Series directors were Bob Wickersham, Frank Tashlin, Howard Swift and John Hubley. Technicolor. A Columbia Pictures Corporation UPA Productions released by Columbia Pictures Corporation.*

*Voices*
**Fox:** Frank Graham; **Crow:** Paul Frees

**Columbia Pictures releases**

**1941:** "Fox and Grapes" (Tashlin/Dec. 5/*Color Rhapsody*).

**1942:** "Woodman Spare That Tree" (Wickersham/July 2/*Color Rhapsody*); and "Toll Bridge Troubles" (Wickersham/Nov. 27/*Color Rhapsody*).

**1943:** "Slay It with Flowers" (Wickersham/Jan. 8/*Color Rhapsody*); "Plenty Below Zero" (Wickersham/May 14/Color Rhapsody); "Tree for Two" (Wickersham/June 21); "A Hunting We Won't Go" (Wickersham/Aug. 23/*Color Rhapsody*); "Room and Bored" (Wickersham/Sept. 30/first *Fox and the Crow* cartoon); and "Way Down Yonder in the Corn" (Wickersham/Nov. 25).

**1944:** "The Dream Kids" (Wickersham/Jan. 5/last cartoon produced by Fleischer); "Mr. Moocher" (Wickersham/Sept. 8); "Be Patient, Patient" (Wickersham/Oct. 27); and "The Egg-Yegg" (Wickersham/Dec. 8).

**1945:** "Kuku-Nuts" (Wickersham/Mar. 30); "Treasure Jest" (Wickersham/Aug. 30); and "Phoney Baloney" (Wickersham/Sept. 13).

**1946:** "Foxey Flatfoots" (Wickersham/Apr. 11); "Unsure Runts" (Swift/May 16); and "Mysto Fox" (Wickersham/Aug. 29).

**1947:** "Tooth or Consequences" (Swift/June 5/Phantasy cartoon).

**UPA Productions releases**

**1948:** "Robin Hoodlum" (Hubley/Dec. 23/produced by Steve Bosustow/A.A. nominee).

**1949:** "The Magic Fluke" (Hubley/Mar. 27/produced by Steve Bosustow/A.A. nominee).

**1950:** "Punchy De Leon" (Hubley/Jan. 12/Jolly Frolics).

### ◎ FOXY

Foxy, who resembled Mickey Mouse with pointy ears and a bushy tail, was an early *Merrie Melodies* star who headlined three series entries in 1931. The character was featured in episodes shaped around popular songs of the day. Hugh Harman and Rudolf Ising produced the series, with Ising directing. Frank Marsales served as musical director for animation. *Black-and-white. Voice credits unknown. A Hugh Harman-Rudolf Ising/Vitaphone Pictures Production released by Warner Bros.*

**1931:** "Lady, Play Your Mandolin!" (with Roxy/Ising/Sept.); "Smile, Darn Ya, Smile!" (with Roxy/Ising/Sept. 5); and "One More Time" (with Roxy/Ising/Oct. 3).

### ◎ FRACTURED FABLES

A series of outlandish tall tales directed by Ralph Bakshi, of *Lord of the Rings* and *Fritz the Cat* fame, and James "Shamus" Culhane. Bakshi also served as executive producer of the series, beginning with 1967's "The Fuz." *Technicolor. A Famous Studios Production released through Paramount Pictures.*

**1967:** "My Daddy the Astronaut" (Culhane/Apr./released in conjunction with *2001: A Space Odyssey*); "The Stuck-Up Wolf" (Culhane/Sept.); "The Stubborn Cowboy" (Culhane/Oct.); "The Fuz" (Bakshi/Dec.); "The Mini-Squirts" (Bakshi/Dec.); and "Mouse Trek" (Bakshi/Dec. 31).

### ◎ GABBY

Gabby first appeared as a town crier in the animated feature *Gulliver's Travels* (1939), produced by Max Fleischer. After his film debut, he starred in his own cartoon series. Stories were shaped around Gabby's inability to do anything right. He tried everything,

*Gabby, a character in the Max Fleischer feature* Gulliver's Travels *(1939), starred in his own cartoon series, shaped around his inability to do anything right.* (COURTESY: REPUBLIC PICTURES)

from diapering a baby to cleaning a castle, with predictably disastrous results.

Pinto Colvig, the original voice of Walt Disney's Goofy, provided the voice of Gabby. *Directed by Dave Fleischer. Technicolor. A Fleischer Studios Production released through Paramount Pictures.*

### Voices
**Gabby:** Pinto Colvig

**1940:** "King for a Day" (Oct. 18); and "The Constable" (Nov. 15).

**1941:** "All's Well" (Jan. 17); "Two for the Zoo" (Feb. 21); "Swing Cleaning" (Apr. 11); "Fire Cheese" (June 20); "Gabby Goes Fishing" (July 18); and "It's a Hap-Hap-Happy Day" (Aug. 15).

## ◎ GABBY GATOR
Over the years, legendary Walter Lantz incorporated several recurring co-stars in his studio's comical *Woody Woodpecker* cartoons. One of them was this profoundly talkative gator, featured in 10 *Woody Woodpecker* one-reel shorts in the late 1950s and 1960s, first as the prototype Ali Gator in "Everglade Raid" (1958) and "Romp in the Swamp" (1959). Gabby made his first "official" appearance in Woody Woodpecker's "Southern <u>Fried</u> Hospitality" (1960). Daws Butler voiced the character up to his final Woody Woodpecker film, 1963's "Greedy Gabby Gator." *Directed by Jack Hannah, Sid Marcus and Paul J. Smith. Technicolor. A Walter Lantz Production released by Universal Pictures.*

### Voices
**Gabby Gator:** Daws Butler

**1958:** "Everglade Raid" (with Woody Woodpecker/Smith/Aug. 11/first appearance of prototype character, Ali Gator).

**1959:** "Romp in the Swamp" (with Woody Woodpecker/Smith/Aug. 7/second and last appearance of prototype character, Ali Gator).

**1960:** "Southern Fried Hospitality" (with Woody Woodpecker/Hannah/Nov. 28/first official appearance of Gabby Gator).

**1961:** "Gabby's Diner" (with Woody Woodpecker/Hannah/Apr.) and "Woody's Kook-Out" (with Woody Woodpecker/Hannah/Nov.).

**1962:** "Rock-a-Bye Gator" (with Woody Woodpecker/Jan.); "Rocket Racket" (with Woody Woodpecker/Hannah/Apr.); "Voo-Doo Boo-Hoo" (with Woody Woodpecker/Hannah/Aug.); and "Little Woody Riding Hood" (with Woody Woodpecker/Smith/Oct.).

**1963:** "Greedy Gabby Gator" (with Woody Woodpecker/Marcus/Jan.).

## ◎ GABBY GOAT
Cast as a sidekick in Warner Bros. enormously popular Porky Pig cartoons, this highly irritable, hot-tempered goat made his screen debut in the 1937 *Looney Tunes* cartoon, "Porky and Gabby." That same year, he returned to the screen two more times in "Porky's Badtime Story" and "Get Rich Porky," but was unceremoniously dropped from the series when his character was not well received. Warner Bros. animator/director Cal Howard provided the character's voice. *Directed by Ub Iwerks and Bob Clampett. Black-and-white. A Vitaphone Production released by Warner Bros.*

### Voices
**Gabby Goat:** Cal Howard

### *Looney Tunes*
**1937:** "Porky and Gabby" (with Porky Pig/June 5); "Porky's Badtime Story" (with Porky Pig/Clampett/July 24); and "Get Rich Porky" (with Porky Pig/Clampett/Aug. 28).

## ◎ GANDY GOOSE
Inspired by comedian Ed Wynn's fluttery voice and mannerisms, sweet-natured Gandy was another *Terry-Toons* attempt at copying the success of a noted personality in animated form. Unlike other attempts, this character proved to be a major disappointment after it was first introduced to filmgoers in 1938's "Gandy the Goose." There was no real chemistry or magic to the early films.

Rather than scrap Gandy altogether, the studio resurrected a one-shot cat character, Sourpuss, from an earlier cartoon, "The Owl and the Pussycat," to pair with Gandy in future escapades. The teaming saved the series, with the cat's offbeat personality, which was reminiscent of comedian Jimmy Durante, sparking more interest from theater audiences. The series became so successful that studio animators repeated the Gandy-Sourpuss formula for 10 years until the series ended in 1955.

Several *Terry-Toons* veterans were responsible for directing the series. They included John Foster, Eddie Donnelly, Connie Rasinski, Volney White and Mannie Davis. *Black-and-white. Technicolor. A Terry-Toons Cartoons Production released through 20th Century Fox.*

### Voices
**Gandy/Sourpuss:** Arthur Kay

(The following cartoons were all produced (in black-and-white unless noted otherwise.)

**1938:** "Gandy the Goose" (Foster/Mar. 4); "Goose Flies High" (Foster/Sept. 9); "Doomsday" (Rasinski/Dec. 16); and "The Frame-Up" (Rasinski/Dec. 30).

**1939:** "G-Man Jitters" (Donnelly/Mar. 10); "A Bully Romance" (Donnelly/June 16); Barnyard Baseball" (Davis/July 14); "Hook, Line and Sinker" (Donnelly/Sept. 8/first Technicolor); and "The Hitchhiker" (Donnelly/Dec. 1).

**1940:** "It Must Be Love" (Rasinski/Apr. 5); and "The Magic Pencil" (White/Nov. 15).

**1941:** "Fishing Made Easy" (Donnelly/Feb. 21); "The Home Guard" (Davis/Mar. 7/Technicolor); "The One Man Navy" (Davis/Sept. 5/Technicolor); "Slap Happy Hunters" (Donnelly/Oct. 31/Technicolor); and "Flying Fever" (Davis/Dec. 26).

**1942:** "Sham Battle Shenanigans" (Rasinski/Mar. 20/Technicolor); "Lights Out" (Donnelly/Apr. 17/Technicolor); "Tricky Business" (Donnelly/May 1); "The Outpost" (Davis/July 10); "Tire Trouble" (Donnelly/July 24); "Night Life in the Army" (Davis/Oct. 12/Technicolor); and "Ickle Meets Pickle" (Rasinski/Nov. 13/*Terry-Toons* cartoon).

(The following cartoons were all produced in Technicolor.)

**1943:** "Scrap for Victory" (Rasinski/Jan. 22/*Terry-Toons* cartoon); "Barnyard Blackout" (Davis/Mar. 5/*Terry-Toons* cartoon); "The Last Round Up" (Davis/May 14/*Terry-Toons* cartoon); "Camouflage" (Donnelly/Aug. 27); "Somewhere in Egypt" (Davis/Sept. 17); and "Aladdin's Lamp" (Donnelly/Oct. 22).

**1944:** "The Frog and the Princess" (Donnelly/Apr. 7); "Gandy Goose in the Ghost Town" (Davis/Sept. 22); and "Gandy's Dream Girl" (Davis/Dec. 8).

**1945:** "Post War Inventions" (Rasinski/Mar. 23); "Fisherman's Luck" (Donnelly/Mar. 23); "Mother Goose Nightmare" (Rasinski/May 4); "Aesop's Fables: The Mosquito" (Davis/June 29); "Who's Who in the Jungle" (Donnelly/Oct. 19); and "The Exterminator" (Donnelly/Nov. 23).

**1946:** "Fortune Hunters" (Rasinski/Feb. 8); "It's All in the Stars" (Rasinski/Apr. 12); "The Golden Hen" (Davis/May 24); and "Peace-Time Football" (Davis/July 19).

**1947:** "Mexican Baseball" (Davis/Mar. 14).

**1948:** "Gandy Goose and the Chipper Chipmunk" (Davis/Mar. 9).

**1949:** "Dingbat Land" (Rasinski/Feb. 1); "The Covered Pushcart" (with Sourpuss/Davis/Aug. 26); and "Comic Book Land" (Davis/Dec. 23).

**1950:** "Dream Walking" (Rasinski/June 9); and "Wide Open Space" (Donnelly/Nov. 1).

**1951:** "Songs of Erin" (Rasinski/Feb. 25); and "Spring Fever" (Davis/Mar. 18).

**1955:** "Barnyard Actor" (Rasinski/Jan. 25).

## GASTON LE CRAYON

Appearing in several new *Terrytoons* series launched in the late 1950s, this talented French artist made his drawings come to life in assorted misadventures. Screen debut: "Gaston Is Here," released in CinemaScope in 1957. *Directed by Connie Rasinksi and Dave Tendlar. Technicolor. CinemaScope. A Terrytoons and CBS Films, Inc., Production released through 20th Century Fox.*

**1957:** "Gaston Is Here" (Rasinski/May 1).

**1958:** "Gaston's Baby" (Rasinski/Mar.); "Gaston, Go Home" (Rasinski/May); and "Gaston's Easel Life" (Tendlar/Oct.).

**1959:** "Gaston's Mama Lisa" (Rasinski/June).

## GEORGE AND JUNIOR

Parodying characters George and Lenny from John Steinbeck's novel *Of Mice and Men*, this short-lived series featured stupid, overweight George and his clever straight man bear Junior. They were an uproarious and destructive pair, fashioned by Tex Avery, who also directed the series. *Technicolor. A Metro-Goldwyn-Mayer Cartoon Production released by Metro-Goldwyn-Mayer.*

*Voices*
**George:** Frank Graham; **Junior:** Tex Avery

**1946:** "Henpecked Hoboes" (Avery/Oct. 26).

**1947:** "Hound Hunters" (Avery/Apr. 12); and "Red Hot Rangers" (Avery/May 31).

**1948:** "Half-Pint Pygmy" (Avery/Aug. 7).

*George and Junior, the Abbott and Costello of cartoons, starred in riotous misadventures directed by Tex Avery for MGM. © Turner Entertainment*
(COURTESY: MARK KAUSLER)

## ◎ GEORGE PAL PUPPETOONS

Director George Pal, noted for producing such science-fiction classics as *War of the Worlds* and *When Worlds Collide*, created this widely acclaimed stop-action animation series starring the wide-eyed little black boy Jasper and his constant companions, Professor Scarecrow and Black Crow, in Huckleberry Finn–like tales shaped around black folklore.

The characters, which were actually wooden puppets, had flexible limbs that enabled them to move realistically. Pal and his 45 staff members, whom he credits for the series' success, diligently prepared background sets and other movable miniatures before filming each eight-minute one-reel short. A typical production cost $25,000 to create.

According to Pal, "We had all these creative people bouncing ideas around. We were our own masters. We didn't have to get this approval and that approval, the way you do in feature motion pictures. All I had to do was pick up the phone to Paramount and tell them we had an idea, and they said, 'Go ahead.'"

The series won six Academy Award nominations in the best short subject category and critical acclaim from film industry officials, who were amazed by the dexterity of Pal's creations. *Directed by George Pal. Narration by Rex Ingram and Victor Jory. Technicolor. A Paramount Pictures Production released by Paramount Pictures.*

**1941:** "Western Daze" (Jan. 7/*Madcap Model* cartoon); "Dipsy Gypsy" (Apr. 4); "Hoola Boola" (June 27); "The Gay Knighties" (Aug. 22); and "Rhythm in the Ranks" (Dec. 26/A.A. nominee).

**1942:** "Jasper and the Watermelons" (Feb. 26/*Madcap Model* cartoon); "Sky Princess" (Mar. 27); and "Jasper and the Haunted House" (Oct. 23).

**1943:** "Jasper and the Choo-Choo" (Jan. 1/*Madcap Model* cartoon); "Tulips Shall Grow" (Jan. 26/A.A. nominee); "Bravo Mr. Strauss" (Feb. 26); "The 500 Hats of Bartholomew Cubbins" (Apr. 30/A.A. nominee); "Mr. Strauss Takes a Walk" (May 8); "Jasper's Music Lesson" (May 21); "The Truck Goes Fishing" (Oct. 8); and "Good Night Rusty" (Dec. 3).

**1944:** "Package for Jasper" (Jan. 28); "Say, Ah Jasper" (Mar. 10); "And to Think I Saw It on Mulberry Street" (July 28/with original story by Dr. Seuss); "Jasper Goes Hunting" (July 28); "Jasper's Paradise" (Oct. 13); and "Two-Gun Rusty" (Dec. 1).

**1945:** "Hot Lips Jasper" (Jan. 5); "Jasper Tell" (Mar. 23); "Jasper's Minstrels" (May 25); "A Hatful of Dreams" (July 6); "Jasper's Close Shave" (Sept. 28); "Jasper and the Beanstalk" (Oct. 9/A.A. nominee); and "My Man Jasper" (Dec. 14).

**1946:** "Olio for Jasper" (Jan. 25); "Together in the Weather" (Mar. 22); "John Henry and the Inky Poo" (Sept. 6/A.A. nominee); "Jasper's Derby" (Sept. 20); and "Jasper in a Jam" (Oct. 18).

**1947:** "Shoe Shine Jasper" (Feb. 28); "Wilbur the Lion" (Apr. 18); "Tubby the Tuba" (July 11); "Date with Duke" (Oct. 31); and "Rhapsody in Wood" (Dec. 29).

## ◎ GERALD MCBOING BOING

Based on a Dr. Seuss children's record, Gerald McBoing Boing, a curly-topped, mute boy, uttered only the sound of "Boing Boing" when communicating with his parents and friends. Introduced in 1951, the first cartoon, titled after the character, was released to theaters under the *Jolly Frolics* series produced by United Productions of America (UPA). The film garnered an Academy Award for best short subject of the year.

Three years later the series was distributed under the *Gerald McBoing Boing* name, with the final series release, "Gerald McBoing! Boing! on the Planet Moo" (1956), winning the series' second Oscar in five years. *Directed by Bob Cannon. Narrated by Hal Peary. Technicolor. A UPA Productions released through Columbia Pictures.*

**1951:** "Gerald McBoing Boing" (Cannon/Jan. 25/A.A. winner/*Jolly Frolics*).

**1953:** "Gerald McBoing Boing's Symphony" (Cannon/July 15/*Jolly Frolics*).

**1954:** "How Now Boing Boing" (Cannon/Sept. 9).

**1956:** "Gerald McBoing! Boing! on the Planet Moo" (Cannon/Feb. 9/A.A. winner).

## ◎ GO-GO TOONS

One of Famous Studios' last cartoon series, *Go-Go Toons* features a wide assortment of outlandish cartoon tales, each starring various characters. *Directed by Ralph Bakshi, James "Shamus" Culhane and Chuck Harriton. Technicolor. A Famous Studios Production released through Paramount Pictures.*

**1967:** "The Space Squid" (Culhane/Jan.); "The Squaw-Path" (Culhane/May); "The Plumber" (Culhane/May); "A Bridge Grows in Brooklyn" (Harriton/Oct.); "The Opera Caper" (Culhane. Bakshi/Nov. 1/Culhane also served as executive producer); "Keep the Cool, Baby" (Harriton/Nov.); and "Marvin Digs" (Bakshi/Dec. 1/Bakshi also served as executive producer).

## ◎ GOOD DEED DAILY

The name of this character, whose lifeblood was performing "good deeds," defined the plot line of this short-lived *Terry-Toons* series. *Directed by Connie Rasinski. Technicolor and CinemaScope. A Terrytoons and CBS Films, Inc. Production released through 20th Century Fox.*

**1955:** "Good Deed Daily" (Apr. 1).

**1956:** "Scouts to the Rescue" (Apr.); and "Cloak and Stagger" (Aug./CinemaScope).

## ◎ GOODIE THE GREMLIN

Famous Studios introduced this lovable gremlin, who tries fitting into Earthly situations, in a series of *Noveltoons*. The character's career was short-lived, however; he appeared in only five cartoons. *Directed by Seymour Kneitel. Technicolor. A Famous Studios Production released through Paramount Pictures.*

**1961:** "Goodie the Gremlin" (Apr./*Noveltoon*).

**1962:** "Good and Guilty" (Feb./*Noveltoon*); and "Yule Laff" (Kneitel/Oct./*Noveltoon*).

**1963:** "Goodie's Good Deed" (Nov./*Modern Madcap*); and "Hiccup Hound" (Nov./*Noveltoon*).

## ◎ GOOFY

A cross between Mortimer Snerd and Snuffy Smith, Walt Disney's hayseed Goofy lit up the screen with his apologetic laugh, "Uh-hyulk, uh-hyulk . . . yep . . . uh-hyulk," in a series of misadventures that played up his silly but harmless nature.

Affectionately nicknamed the "Goof" by studio animators, Goofy first appeared in the early 1930s as a stringbean character, Dippy Dawg, in a Disney cartoon adventure. Later renamed, his actual personality never came into focus until studio animator Art Babbitt molded Goofy into "a composite of an everlasting optimist, a gullible Good Samaritan, a halfwit and a hick with a philosophy of the barber shop variety," who seldom completes his objectives or what he has started.

Babbitt, who first worked for Paul Terry in New York in 1932, became the studio expert at animating Goofy, with director Jack Kinney, who directed the most memorable cartoons in the series, using the character to good measure. Kinney's "How to Play Football" (1944), one in a series of classic Goofy sports "how-tos," received the series' first Academy Award nomination. Seventeen years later in 1961, director Wolfgang Reitherman earned the series' second Oscar nomination for the hilarious cartoon short, "Aquamania."

In 1992 Goofy celebrated his 60th birthday by starring in his own daily cartoon series, *Goof Troop*, which premiered in September of that year as part of the Disney Afternoon, a two-hour weekday syndicated cartoon block. The series was the first Disney cartoon series to feature a member of the "Classic 5" characters as its star; Mickey Mouse, Minnie Mouse, Donald Duck and Pluto are the others. The program centered on the slapstick adventures of Goofy and his son, Max. Three years later Goofy starred opposite Max in his first full-length animated feature, *A Goofy Movie*. *Series directors were Dick Huemer, Jack Kinney, Jack Hannah, Bob Carlson, Clyde Geronimi, Les Clark and Woolie Reitherman. Technicolor. A Walt Disney Production released through RKO Radio Pictures and Buena Vista Pictures.*

**Voices**
**Goofy:** Pinto Colvig (1931–39, 1944–67); George Johnson (1933–44); Bob Jackman (1950–51)

**RKO Radio Pictures releases**

**1939:** "Goofy and Wilbur" (Huemer/Mar. 17).

**1940:** "Goofy's Glider" (Kinney/Nov. 22).

**1941:** "Baggage Buster" (Kinney/Apr. 18); "The Art of Skiing" (Kinney/Nov. 14); and "The Art of Self Defense" (Kinney/Dec. 26).

**1942:** "How to Play Baseball" (Kinney/Sept. 4); "The Olympic Champ" (Kinney/Oct. 9); "How to Swim" (Kinney/Oct. 23); and "How to Fish" (Kinney/Dec. 4).

**1943:** "Victory Vehicles" (with Pluto/Kinney/July 30).

**1944:** "How to be a Sailor" (Kinney/Jan. 28); "How to Play Golf" (Kinney/Mar. 10); and "How to Play Football" (Kinney/Sept. 15/A.A. nominee).

**1945:** "Tiger Trouble" (with Dolores the Elephant/Kinney/Jan. 5/first appearance by Dolores the Elephant); "African Diary" (Kinney/Apr. 20); "Californy er Bust" (Kinney/July 15); and "Hockey Homicide" (Kinney/Sept. 21).

**1946:** "A Knight for a Day" (Hannah/Mar. 8); and "Double Dribble" (Hannah/Dec. 20).

**1947:** "Crazy with the Heat" (with Donald Duck/Carlson/Aug. 1); and "Foul Hunting" (with Clementine Duck/Hannah/Oct. 31)

**1948:** "They're Off" (Hannah/Jan. 23); and "The Big Wash" (with Dolores the Elephant/Geronimi/Feb. 6).

**1949:** "Tennis Racquet" (Kinney/Aug. 26); and "Goofy Gymnastics" (Kinney/Sept. 23).

**1950:** "How to Ride a Horse" (Kinney/Feb. 24/part of *The Reluctant Dragon* feature); "Motor Mania" (Kinney/June 30); and "Hold That Pose" (Kinney/Nov. 3).

**1951:** "Lion Down" (with Louie the Mountain Lion/Kinney/Jan. 5); "Home Made Home" (Kinney/Mar. 23); "Cold War" (Kinney/Apr. 27); "Tomorrow We Diet" (Kinney/June 29); "Get Rich Quick" (Kinney/Aug. 31); "Fathers Are People" (with Goofy Junior, Mrs. Goofy/Kinney/Oct. 21); and "No Smoking" (Kinney/Nov. 23).

**1952:** "Father's Lion" (with Goofy Junior, Louie, the Mountain Lion/Kinney/Jan. 4); "Hello, Aloha" (Kinney/Feb. 29); "Man's Best Friend" (Kinney/Apr. 4); "Two-Gun Goofy" (Kinney/May 16); "Teachers Are People" (Kinney/June 27); "Two Weeks Vacation" (Kinney/Oct. 31); and "How to Be a Detective" (Kinney/Dec. 12).

**1953:** "Father's Day Off" (with Goofy Junior, Mrs. Goofy/Kinney/Mar. 28); "For Whom the Bulls Toil" (Kinney/May 9); "Father's Week-End" (with Goofy Junior/Kinney/June 20); "How to Dance" (Kinney/July 11); and "How to Sleep" (Kinney/Dec. 25).

**1955:** "El Gaucho Goofy" (Kinney/June 10/part of *Saludos Amigos*).

**Buena Vista Pictures releases**

**1961:** "Aquamania" (with Goofy Junior/Reitherman/Dec. 20/ A.A. nominee).

**1965:** "Freeway Phobia No. 1" (Clark/Feb. 13); and "Goofy's Freeway Trouble" (Clark/Sept. 22).

## ⊚ GOOFY GOPHERS

This pair of polite, swift-talking gophers vaguely resembled Walt Disney's popular Chip 'n' Dale characters, not only in voice but in facial and body features.

Introduced in a 1947 cartoon of the same name, Warner's director Bob Clampett designed the gophers, whose demeanor was modeled after two mild-mannered character actors of the time, Edward Everett Horton and Franklin Pangborn. (The gophers appeared earlier in a 1941 Warner's cartoon, "Gopher Goofy," but were not similar to Clampett's version.) Clampett wrote the story for the first cartoon, which was directed by Art Davis, Clampett's successor. Clampett left Warner's after completing the story to join Columbia Pictures' animation department.

The gophers' inquisitive ways landed them in a half-dozen cartoons. They were often cast in situations that enabled them to display exaggerated politeness towards one another to resolve their differences. The characters acquired the nicknames of "Mac and Tosh" when they later appeared on television's *The Bugs Bunny Show. Directors included Robert McKimson, Friz Freleng and Arthur Davis. Cinecolor. Technicolor. A Warner Bros. Cartoons Inc. Production released by Warner Bros.*

**Voices**
**Mac:** Mel Blanc; **Tosh:** Stan Freberg

**Looney Tunes**

**1947:** "Goofy Gophers" (with Bugs Bunny/Davis/Jan. 25).

**1949:** "A Ham in a Role" (McKimson/Dec. 31).

**1951:** "A Bone for a Bone" (Freleng/Apr. 7).

**1955:** "Lumber Jerks" (Freleng/June 25).

**1958:** "Gopher Broke" (McKimson/Nov. 15).

**Merrie Melodies**

**1948:** "Two Gophers from Texas" (Davis/Dec. 27/Cinecolor).

**1954:** "I Gopher You" (Freleng/Jan. 30).

**1955:** "Pests for Guests" (with Elmer Fudd/Freleng/Jan. 29).

## ◎ GOOPY GEER

Considered the first *Merrie Melodies* star, Goopy is a consummate performing dog—he sings, dances and plays the piano—who appeared in a number of music-and-dance shorts for Warner Bros. Unfortunately, Goopy's stardom was short-lived; he appeared in only three *Merrie Melodies* cartoons. *Produced by Hugh Harman and Rudolf Ising and directed by Rudolf Ising. Black-and-white. A Hugh Harman-Rudolf Ising and Vitaphone Pictures Production released by Warner Bros.*

**1932:** "Goopy Geer" (Apr. 16); "Moonlight for Two" (June 11); and "The Queen Was in the Parlor" (July 9).

## ◎ GRAN' POP MONKEY

This was one of animator Ub Iwerks's last cartoon series, a British-financed production produced by Cartoons Limited, an animation studio headed by Walt Disney veteran Paul Fennell. The short-lived series featured Gran' Pop, an artful and ancient ape created by noted British painter/illustrator Lawson Wood. Wood actually drew many of the key drawings for the series starring this cheerful old chimp in a handful of full-color cartoon shorts. *Produced and directed by Ub Iwerks. Technicolor. A Cartoons Limited Production released through Monogram Pictures.*

**1940:** "A Busy Day"; "Beauty Shoppe"; and "Baby Checkers."

## ◎ HALF PINT

This incidental *Terry-Toons* star—a tiny Dumboesque elephant who everyone frowned on and yet managed to get into trouble—was unleashed onto the screen in two cartoon shorts, both produced in 1951. Walt Disney later did a similar version of the character in the 1960 Wolfgang Reitherman–directed short, "Goliath II." *Directed by Mannie Davis. Technicolor. A Terry-Toons Cartoons Production released through 20th Century Fox.*

**1951:** "Stage Struck" (Feb.); and "The Elephant Mouse" (May).

## ◎ HAM AND EX

This pair of troublesome pups was first featured as part of an ensemble cast in 1935's "I Haven't Got a Hat," in which Porky Pig made his first official appearance. The characters were later paired with Beans, a mischievous cat, in several *Looney Tunes* cartoons. *Directed by Friz Freleng and Jack King. Black-and-white. A Vitaphone Production released by Warner Bros.*

### Merrie Melodies

**1935:** "I Haven't Got a Hat" (with Porky Pig, Beans/Freleng/Mar. 2).

### Looney Tunes

**1936:** "The Phantom Ship" (with Beans/King/Feb. 1); and "The Fire Alarm" (with Beans/King/Mar. 9).

## ◎ HAM AND HATTIE

In the last theatrical series of United Productions of America (UPA), Ham and Hattie made their screen debut in the 1948 release, "Trees and Jamaica Daddy," which received the studio's final Academy Award nomination. Each episode paired two three-and-a-half-minute cartoons, the first featuring the adventures of a little girl named Hattie, with the second shaped around the music of Hamilton Ham. *Directed by Lew Keller. Technicolor. A UPA Production released through Columbia Pictures.*

© 1958 UPA PICTURES, INC.

# "HAM and HATTIE"

*UPA's last theatrical cartoon series,* Ham and Hattie, *paired two separate cartoons shaped around the adventures of Ham Hamilton (left) and a girl named Hattie (right). © UPA Productions*

**1958:** "Trees and Jamaica Daddy" (Jan. 30/A.A. nominee); "Sailing and Village Band" (Feb. 27); and "Spring and Saganaki" (Oct. 16).

**1959:** "Picnics Are Fun and Dino's Serenade" (Jan. 16).

## ◎ HAPPY HARMONIES

Another attempt by former Disney animators Hugh Harman and Rudolf Ising to rival Walt Disney's "personality animation," this series of musical cartoons is similar to Disney's celebrated *Silly Symphony* series. This type of cartoon had been mastered before by both animators, who had directed Warner Bros.' *Merrie Melodies* series.

*Happy Harmonies* resulted after the pair left Warner Bros. in 1933. They formed their own production company in conjunction with MGM to produce cartoons for theatrical release by the studio. Metro developed its own cartoon studio four years later, spurred by Harman's and Ising's inability to keep their films under budget. Animated by MGM's new animation department, the series continued through 1938. The series produced two Academy Award–nominated cartoons, 1935's "The Calico Dragon," directed by Rudolf Ising, and 1937's "The Old Mill Pond," directed by Hugh Harman. *Produced by Hugh Harman and Rudolf Ising. Directed by Rudolf Ising, Hugh Harman and William Hanna. Technicolor and Cinecolor. A Hugh Harman and Rudolf Ising and Metro-Goldwyn-Mayer Cartoon Production released by Metro-Goldwyn-Mayer.*

**1934:** "The Discontented Canary" (Ising/Sept. 1); "The Old Pioneer" (Ising/Sept. 29/Cinecolor); "A Tale of the Vienna

Woods" (Harman/Oct. 27); "Bosko Parlor Pranks" (with Bosko, Honey/Harman/Nov. 24); and "Toyland Broadcast" (Ising/Dec. 22).

**1935:** "Hey-Hey Fever" (Harman/Jan. 9); "When the Cat's Away" (Ising/Feb. 16); "The Lost Chick" (Harman/Mar. 9); "The Calico Dragon" (Ising/Mar. 30/A.A. nominee); "Good Little Monkeys" (Harman/Apr. 13); "The Chinese Nightingale" (Ising/Apr. 27); "Poor Little Me" (Harman/May 11); "Barnyard Babies" (Ising/May 25); "The Old Plantation" (Ising/Sept. 21); "Honeyland" (Ising/Oct. 19); "Alias St. Nick" (with Little Cheeser/Ising/Nov. 16/first appearance of Little Cheeser); and "Run, Sheep, Run" (with Bosko, Honey/Harman/Dec. 14).

**1936:** "Bottles" (Harman/Jan. 11); "The Early Bird and the Worm" (Ising/Feb. 8); "The Old Mill Pond" (Harman/Mar. 7/with Two Puppies); "Two Little Pups" (Ising/Apr. 4/A.A. nominee); "The Old House" (with Bosko, Honey, Bruno/Harman/May 2); "Pups' Picnic" (Ising/May 30); "To Spring" (Hanna/June 4); "Little Cheeser" (Ising/July 11); and "The Pups' Christmas" (with Two Pups/Ising/Dec. 12).

**1937:** "Circus Daze" (with Bosko, Honey/Harman/Jan. 16); "Swing Wedding" (Harman/Feb. 13); "Little Ol' Bosko and the Pirates" (with Honey/Harman/May 1); "The Hound and the Rabbit" (Ising/May 29); "The Wayward Pups" (with Two Pups/Ising/July 10); "Little Ol' Bosko and the Cannibals" (with Bosko, Honey/Harman/Aug. 28).

**1938:** "Little Ol' Bosko in Bagdad" (with Bosko, Honey/Harman); "Pipe Dreams" (Harman/Feb. 5); and "The Little Bantamweight" (Ising/Mar. 12).

## ◎ HAPPY TOTS

This group of tiny elves, who made their screen debut in 1939, starred in a pair of *Color Rhapsody* cartoon shorts for Columbia Pictures. *Directed by Ben Harrison. Technicolor. A Columbia Pictures Production released by Columbia Pictures Corporation.*

**1939:** "Happy Tots" (Mar. 31).

**1940:** "Happy Tots' Expedition" (Feb. 9).

## ◎ HASHIMOTO

Created by Terrytoons animator Bob Kuwahara, Japanese house mouse Hashimoto, a judo expert, was launched in the 1959 *Terrytoons* "Hashimoto San." The series pilot and subsequent adventures dealt with Hashimoto's reminiscences about the legends of his country, its romantic tradition and numerous other aspects of Japanese lore for American newspaper correspondent G.I. Joe. The cartoon shorts costarred his wife, Hanako, and his children, Yuriko and Saburo. A series of new cartoons were produced as part of NBC's *The Hector Heathcote Show* in the 1960s. *Directors were Bob Kuwahara, Dave Tendlar, Connie Rasinski, Mannie Davis and Art Bartsch. A Terrytoons and CBS Films, Inc., Production released through 20th Century Fox.*

### Voices
**Hashimoto/Hanako/Yuriko/Saburo:** John Myhers

**1959:** "Hashimoto-San" (Kuwahara, Tendlar/Sept. 6).

**1960:** "House of Hashimoto" (Rasinski/Nov. 30).

**1961:** "Night Life in Tokyo" (Davis/Feb.); "So Sorry, Pussycat" (Bartsch/Mar.); "Son of Hashimoto" (Rasinski/Apr. 12); "Strange Companion" (Davis/May 12); and "Honorable Cat Story" (Rasinski/Nov.).

**1962:** "Honorable Family Problem" (Kuwahara/Mar. 30); "Loyal Royalty" (Kuwahara/May 18); and "Honorable Pain in the Neck" (Kuwahara/Aug. 22).

**1963:** "Tea House Mouse" (Kuwahara/Jan.); "Pearl Crazy" (Kuwahara/May); "Cherry Blossom Festival" (Kuwahara/June 17); and "Spooky-Yaki" (Kuwahara/Nov. 13).

## ◎ HECKLE AND JECKLE

Conniving, talking magpies Heckle and Jeckle were popular cartoon stars through the mid-1960s. Paul Terry, head of *Terry-Toons*, inspired the characters' creation after dreaming of starting a series featuring cartoon twins or look-alikes. Terry's idea came to fruition in "The Talking Magpies," the first Heckle and Jeckle cartoon, released in 1946.

The comical pair were identical in appearance yet featured contrasting accents—Brooklyn and British respectively. The characters became Terry's answer to the bombastic stars of rival Warner Bros. and MGM, becoming his most popular characters next to Mighty Mouse. The cartoons revitalized the "chase" formula characteristic of the Terry-Toons cartoons.

Heckle and Jeckle experienced a brief revival when their films were syndicated to television in the 1960s. *Directors were Mannie Davis, Connie Rasinski, Eddie Donnelly, Martin B. Taras, Dave Tendlar, George Bakes and Al Chiarito. Technicolor. A Terry-Toons Cartoons and Terrytoons/CBS Films, Inc., Production released through 20th Century Fox.*

### Voices
**Heckle/Jeckle:** Dayton Allen, Ned Sparks, Roy Halee

### *Terry-Toon Cartoons Productions releases*

**1946:** "The Talking Magpies" (Davis/Jan. 4); and "The Uninvited Pests" (Rasinski/Nov. 29).

**1947:** "McDougal's Rest Farm" (Davis/Jan. 31); "Happy Go Lucky" (Rasinski/Feb. 28); "Cat Trouble" (Rasinski/Apr. 11); "The Intruders" (Donnelly/May 9); "Flying South" (Davis/Aug. 15); "Fishing by the Sea" (Rasinski/Sept. 19); "The Super Salesman" (Donnelly/Oct. 24); and "The Hitch Hikers" (Rasinski/Dec. 12).

*Paul Terry's talking magpies Heckle and Jeckle lasted 20 years on screen as mischief makers for Terry-Toons.* © *Viacom International*

**1948:** "Taming the Cat" (Rasinski/Jan.); "A Sleepless Night" (Rasinski/June 24); "Magpie Madness" (Donnelly/July); "Out Again In Again" (Rasinski/Nov. 1); "Free Enterprise" (Davis/Nov. 23); "Goony Golfers" (Rasinski/Dec. 1); and "Power of Thought" (Donnelly/Dec. 31).

**1949:** "The Lion Hunt" (Donnelly/Mar.); "The Stowaways" (Rasinski/Apr.); "Happy Landing" (June); "Hula Lula Land" (Davis/June 22); and "Dancing Shoes" (Davis/Dec.).

**1950:** "The Fox Hunt" (Rasinski/Feb. 17); "A Merry Chase" (Davis/May); and "King Tut's Tomb" (Davis/Aug.).

**1951:** "Rival Romeos" (Donnelly/Jan.); "Bulldozing the Bull" (Donnelly/Mar. 11); "The Rainmakers" (Rasinski/June); "Steeple Jacks" (Rasinski/Sept.); and "Sno' Fun" (Donnelly/Nov.).

**1952:** "Movie Madness" (Rasinski/Jan.); "Seaside Adventure" (Davis/Feb.); "Off to the Opera" (Rasinski/May); "House Busters" (Rasinski/Aug.); and "Moose on the Loose" (Davis/Nov.).

**1953:** "Hair Cut-Ups" (Donnelly/Feb.); "Pill Peddlers" (Rasinski/Apr.); "Ten Pin Terrors" (Rasinski/June); "Bargain Daze" (Davis/Aug.); and "Log Rollers" (Davis/Nov.).

**1954:** "Blind Date" (Donnelly/Feb.); "Satisfied Customers" (Rasinski/May); and "Blue Plate Symphony" (Rasinski/Oct. 29.).

*Terrytoons/CBS Films, Inc., Productions releases*

**1956:** "Miami Maniacs" (Rasinski/Feb.).

**1957:** "Pirate's Gold" (Donnelly/Jan.).

**1959:** "Wild Life" (Taras/Sept.).

**1960:** "Thousand Smile Checkup" (Taras/Jan.); "Mint Men" (Tendlar/June 23); "Trapeze Please" (Rasinski/June 12); "Deep Sea Doddle" (Tendlar/Sept. 16); and "Stunt Men" (Taras/Nov. 23).

**1961:** "Sappy New Year" (Nov. 10).

**1966:** "Messed Up Movie Makers" (Bakes, Chiarito/Mar.).

## ◉ HECTOR HEATHCOTE

As with Deputy Dawg, this series was originally produced for television. It focused on the adventures of this good-natured, Revolutionary War-era boy who plays an integral part in the events of this country's history. (George Washington would have never crossed the Delaware River if Hector hadn't built the rowboat.)

Ed Bower, a Terrytoons designer, is credited with creating the character. Cartoons produced for television in the early 1960s also received theatrical distribution. *Produced by Bill Weiss and Gene Deitch. Directed by Arthur Bartsch, Dave Tendlar, Connie Rasinski, Bill Tytla and Bob Kuwahara. Technicolor. CinemaScope. A Terrytoons Cartoons and CBS Films, Inc., Production released through 20th Century Fox.*

*Voices*

Hector Heathcote: John Myhers

**1959:** "The Minute and 1/2 Man" (Tendlar/July/CinemaScope).

**1960:** "The Famous Ride" (Rasinski/Apr./CinemaScope); and "Daniel Boone, Jr." (Tendlar/Dec./CinemaScope).

**1961:** 'High Flyer" (Tendlar/Apr.); "Railroaded to Fame" (Tendlar/May); "Barrel of Fun" (Tendlar/May); "Drum Roll" (Tendlar/May); "Expert Explorer" (Tendlar/May); "Foxed by a Fox" (Tendlar/May); "Hats Off to Hector" (Tendlar/May); "Hold the Fort!" (Tendlar/May); "Ice Cream for Help" (Tendlar/May); "Peace Pipe" (Tendlar/May); "Pig in a Poke" (Tendlar/May);

"Search for a Symbol" (Tendlar/May); "The First Telephone" (Tendlar/May); "Valley Forge Hero" (Tendlar/May); "Wind Bag" (Tendlar/May); "The First Fast Mail" (Tendlar/May); "Crossing the Delaware" (June); and "Unsung Hero" (July).

**1962:** "Klondike Strike Out" (Tendlar/Jan.); "He-Man Seaman" (Bartsch/Mar.); "River Boat Mission" (Tendlar/May); "First Flight Up" (Tytla/Oct.); and "A Flight to the Finish" (Tendlar/Dec.).

**1963:** "Tea Party" (Tendlar/Apr.); "A Bell for Philadelphia" (Kuwahara/July); and "The Big Clean-Up" (Tendlar/Sept.).

**1970:** "Land Grab" (Feb.), "Lost and Foundation" (June); and "Belabour Thy Neighbor" (Oct.).

**1971:** "Train Terrain" (Feb.).

## ◉ HENERY HAWK

This temperamental diminutive chicken hawk with a fiery attitude was intended to be a "star" in his own right. Known for his supporting roles in mostly Foghorn Leghorn cartoons, Henery was introduced to the screen in 1942 with the intention of featuring him in his own series. Created by legendary Warner Bros. animator Chuck Jones, Henery first splashed onto the screen in "The Squawkin' Hawk," a *Merrie Melodies* cartoon. Four years later he was meant to star in what would be the follow-up cartoon to his first screen appearance, "Walky Talky Hawky," directed by Robert McKimson (which was nominated for an Academy Award). Instead, McKimson turned the cartoon into a starring vehicle for a new character he planned to introduce: a loudmouthed, cantankerous rooster named Foghorn Leghorn. Henery also appeared opposite Daffy Duck in one cartoon, "You Were Never Duckier," a 1948 *Merrie Melodies* directed by Chuck Jones.

The voice of Henery was provided by none other than venerable Warner Bros. voice artist Mel Blanc. *Directed by Chuck Jones and Robert McKimson. A Leon Schlesinger Studios, Warner Bros. Cartoons Inc., Warner Bros. Pictures, Inc./Vitaphone Production released by Warner Bros.*

*Voices*

Henery Hawk: Mel Blanc

*Merrie Melodies*

*Warner Bros. Cartoons, Inc. releases*

**1942:** "The Squawkin' Hawk" (Jones/Aug. 8).

**1946:** Walky Tawky Hawky" (with Foghorn Leghorn/McKimson/Aug. 31/A.A. nominee).

**1948:** "You Were Never Duckier" (with Daffy Duck/Jones/Aug. 7).

**1951:** "Leghorn Swoggled" (with Foghorn Leghorn/McKimson/July 18).

**1952:** "The Egg-Cited Rooster" (with Foghorn Leghorn/McKimson/Oct. 4).

*Warner Bros. Pictures, Inc./Vitagraph releases*

**1961:** "Strangled Eggs" (with Foghorn Leghorn/McKimson/Mar. 18).

*Looney Tunes*

*Warner Bros. Cartoons, Inc. releases*

**1947:** "Crowing Pains" (with Foghorn Leghorn, Sylvester/McKimson/July 12).

**1950:** "The Leghorn Blows at Midnight" (with Foghorn Leghorn/McKimson/May 6).

**1955:** "All Fowled Up" (with Foghorn Leghorn/McKimson/Feb. 19)

## ◉ HERMAN AND KATNIP

The idea of a cat-and-mouse team already proved successful for MGM with *Tom and Jerry*. What worked for one studio seemed liked it could work again, so Famous Studios unveiled their own feuding tandem in 1950: Herman, a slick city mouse, and Katnip, a country-bumpkin cat. Herman had made his screen debut in 1944 and starred in a handful of *Noveltoons* before pairing with Katnip. For the next 10 years, the pair starred in a series of misadventures with Herman being the target of Katnip's desires to nab him as his personal prize. They made their first joint appearance that year in the *Noveltoon* cartoon, "Mice Meeting You." Like MGM's Jerry, Herman emerged unscathed through his sheer inventiveness and ability to outwit the cat. Initially, the madcap duo starred in cartoons produced under the *Noveltoons* banner before they were given their own series in 1952, the first entry of which was "Mice-Capades." The pair also appeared independently of each other in individual *Noveltoons*. *Directors were Isadore Sparber, Seymour Kneitel, Bill Tytla and Dave Tendlar. Technicolor. A Famous Studios Production released through Paramount Pictures Corporation.*

*Country bumpkin cat Katnip and slick city mouse Herman often feuded on screen with, naturally, the cat always on the losing end. © Harvey Cartoons*

**Voices**

**Herman:** Arnold Stang; **Katnip:** Syd Raymond

**1950:** "Mice Meeting You" (Kneitel/Nov. 10/*Noveltoon*).

**1951:** "Mice Paradise" (Sparber/Mar. 9/*Noveltoon*); and "Cat Tamale" (Kneitel/Nov. 9/*Noveltoon*).

**1952:** "Cat Carson Rides Again" (Kneitel/Apr. 4/*Noveltoon*); and "Mice-Capades" (Kneitel/Oct. 3/first cartoon in the *Herman and Katnip* series).

**1953:** "Of Mice and Magic" (Sparber/Feb. 20); "Herman the Cartoonist" (Sparber/May 15); "Drinks on the Mouse" (Tendlar/Aug. 28); and "Northwest Mousie" (Kneitel/Dec. 28).

**1954:** "Surf and Sound" (Tendlar/Mar. 5); "Of Mice and Menace" (Kneitel/June 25); "Ship A-Hooey" (Sparber/Aug. 20); and "Rail-Rodents" (Tendlar/Nov. 26).

**1955:** "Robin Rodenthood" (Tendlar/Feb. 25); "A Bicep Built for Two" (Kneitel/Apr. 8); "Mouse Trapeze" (Sparber/Aug. 5); and "Mousieur Herman" (Tendlar/Nov. 25).

**1956:** "Mouseum" (Kneitel/Feb. 24); "Will Do Mouse-work" (Kneitel/June 29); "Mousetro Herman" (Sparber/Aug. 10); and "Hide and Peak" (Tendlar/Dec. 7).

**1957:** "Cat in the Act" (Tendlar/Feb. 22); "Sky Scrappers" (Tendlar/June 14); "From Mad to Worse" (Kneitel/Aug. 16); and "One Funny Knight" (Tendlar/Nov. 22).

**1958:** "Frighty Cat" (Sparber/Mar. 14); and "You Said a Mouseful" (Kneitel/Aug. 29).

**1959:** "Owly to Bed" (Kneitel/Jan. 2); "Felineous Assault" (Kneitel/Feb. 20); "Fun on the Furlough" (Kneitel/Apr. 3); and "Katnip's Big Day" (Kneitel/Oct. 30).

**1960:** "Miceniks" (Kneitel/Dec.).

### Herman by Himself

**1944:** "Henpecked Rooster" (with Henry the Rooster/Kneitel/Feb. 18/*Noveltoon*).

**1945:** "Scrappily Married" (with Henry the Rooster/Kneitel/Mar. 30/*Noveltoon*).

**1946:** "Cheese Burglar" (Sparber/Feb. 22/*Noveltoon*); and "Sudden Fried Chicken" (with Henry the Rooster/Tytla/Oct. 18/*Noveltoon*); "Naughty but Mice" (Kneitel/Oct. 10/*Novelton*).

**1949:** "Campus Capers" (Tytla/July 1/*Noveltoon*).

### Katnip by Himself

**1952:** "City Kitty" (Sparber/July 18/*Noveltoon*); and "Feast and Furious" (with Finny the Goldfish/Sparber/Dec. 26/*Noveltoon*).

## ◉ HICKORY, DICKORY AND DOC

Walter Lantz first introduced this highly sophisticated cat, replete with bow tie, top hat and spindly cane, opposite two troublesome mice, Hickory and Dickory, in 1959's "Space Mouse," directed by Alex Lovy. The character starred in seven additional cartoons through 1962.

Director Alex Lovy left the series in 1960, with Jack Hannah, a former Disney veteran, succeeding him in that role. *Directed by Alex Lovy and Jack Hannah. Technicolor. A Walter Lantz Production released through Universal Pictures.*

**Voices**

**Doc:** Paul Frees; **Hickory/Dickory:** Dal McKennon

## ⊚ HIPPETY HOPPER

The high-jumping kangaroo was originally created by Robert McKimson as a running gag in a cartoon with lisping Sylvester. Resembling an overgrown mouse, Hippety became more than a one-shot joke. He lasted for 16 years as a nontalking costar in a dozen cartoons with Sylvester, with his actions speaking louder than words.

In 1950 McKimson added another character to play off Hippety: Sylvester's son, Sylvester Jr., who encounters the kangaroo in situations where he questions his father's knowledge of animals. (Sylvester often mistakes Hippety for a "mouse.") *Directed by Robert McKimson. Technicolor. A Warner Bros. Cartoons, Inc./ Warner Bros. Pictures, Inc./Vitagraph Production released by Warner Bros.*

### Looney Tunes

#### Warner Bros. Cartoons, Inc. releases

**1948:** "Hop Look and Listen" (with Sylvester/McKimson/Apr. 17).

**1950:** "Pop 'Im Pop!" (with Sylvester, Sylvester Jr./McKimson/ Oct. 28).

**1952:** "Hoppy-Go-Lucky" (with Sylvester/McKimson/Aug. 9).

**1956:** "Too Hop to Handle" (with Sylvester, Sylvester Jr./ McKimson/Jan. 28).

#### Warner Bros. Pictures Inc./Vitagraph releases

**1961:** "Hoppy Daze" (with Sylvester/McKimson/Feb. 11).

**1964:** "Freudy Cat" (McKimson/Mar. 14).

### Merrie Melodies

#### Warner Bros. Cartoons, Inc. releases

**1949:** "Hippety Hopper" (with Sylvester/McKimson/Nov. 19).

**1953:** "Cat's Aweigh" (with Sylvester, Sylvester Jr./McKimson/ Nov. 28).

**1954:** "Bell Hoppy" (with Sylvester/McKimson/Apr. 17).

**1955:** "Lighthouse Mouse" (with Sylvester/McKimson/Mar. 12).

**1956:** "The Slap-Hoppy Mouse" (with Sylvester/McKimson/ Sept. 1).

**1957:** "Mouse-Taken Identity" (with Sylvester, Sylvester Jr./ McKimson/Nov. 16).

## ⊚ HOMER PIGEON

A 1940s' addition to Walter Lantz's cartoon gallery, this rubelike country bird was based on comedian Red Skelton's famed radio character, Clem Kadiddlehopper. The straw-hatted bird, who was originally cast as comic relief in a number of films, first appeared in the Walter Lantz Cartune Special, "Pigeon Patrol," in 1942. His only other starring appearance came 14 years later before retiring from the screen. *Directed by Alex Lovy. Technicolor. A Walter Lantz Production released through Universal Pictures.*

### Voices
**Homer Pigeon:** Dal McKennon

**1942:** "Pigeon Patrol" (Aug. 3).

**1956:** "Pigeon Holed" (Jan. 16).

## ⊚ HONEY HALFWITCH

In an attempt to come up with something different, Famous Studios, producers of *Casper* and *Herman and Katnip*, launched this series featuring Honey Halfwitch, a sweet-natured apprentice who manages to escape trouble through the power of witchcraft. The series' theme song was composed by Winston Sharples, the studio's musical director. *Directors were Howard Post, James "Shamus" Culhane and Chuck Harriton. Technicolor. A Famous Studios Production released through Paramount Pictures Corporation.*

**1965:** "Shoeflies" (Post/Oct.).

**1966:** "Baggin' the Dragon" (Post/Feb.); "From Nags to Witches" (Post/Feb.); "Trick or Cheat" (Post/Mar.); "The Rocket Racket" (Post/Mar.); "The Defiant Giant" (Culhane/June); "Throne for a Loss" (Culhane/July); and "Potions and Notions" (Culhane/Aug.).

**1967:** "Alter Egotist" (Harriton/Apr.); "Clean Sweep" (Harriton/ June); "High but Not Dry" (Culhane/Aug.); and "Brother Bat" (Harriton/Aug.).

## ⊚ THE HONEY-MOUSERS

What began as a one-shot parody of television's classic comedy series *The Honeymooners* turned into a brief series of hilarious spoofs featuring Ralph (Ralph Crumden), Alice (Alice Crumden), Norton (Ned Morton) and Trixie (Trixie Morton) as mice. Warner Bros. veteran Robert McKimson brought the characters to the screen for the first time in 1956's "The Honey-Mousers." Comedian Jackie Gleason allegedly was unhappy with the idea of a cartoon spoof and threatened to block its release by the studio. McKimson sent Gleason a print of the cartoon and after watching it, Gleason was pleased and dropped his objections. *Directed by Robert McKimson. Technicolor. A Warner Bros. Cartoons, Inc. Production released by Warner Bros.*

### Voices
**Ralph Crumden/Ned Morton:** Daws Butler; **Alice Crumden:** June Foray, Julie Bennett; **Trixie Morton:** June Foray

### Looney Tunes

**1956:** "The Honey-Mousers" (Dec. 8).

**1957:** "Cheese It, The Cat" (May 4).

**1960:** "Mice Follies" (Aug. 20).

## ⊚ HOOT KLOOT

A redneck, fat-bellied sheriff saddles up to maintain law and order with the help of his silly but faithful horse, Confederate, in cartoon adventures lampooning the Wild West. *Directors were Bob Balser, Durward Bonaye, Gerry Chiniquy, Arthur Leonardi, Sid Marcus, Roy Morita and Hawley Pratt. Technicolor. A DePatie-Freleng Enterprises/Mirisch Cinema Company Production released through United Artists.*

### Voices
**Hoot Kloot:** Bob Holt; **Confederate:** Larry D. Mann

### Additional Voices
Joan Gerber, Allan Melvin, Hazel Shermet

**1973:** "Kloot's Kounty" (Pratt/Jan. 19); "Apache on the County Seat" (Pratt/June 16); "The Shoe Must Go On" (Chiniquy/June 16); "A Self-Winding Sidewinder" (Morita/Oct. 9); "Pay Your Buffalo Bill" (Chiniquy/Oct. 9); "Stirrups and Hiccups" (Chiniquy/ Oct. 15); and "Ten Miles to the Gallop" (Leonardi/Oct. 15).

**1974:** "Phony Express" (Chiniquy/Jan. 4); "Giddy-Up Woe" (Marcus/Jan. 9); "Gold Struck" (Morita/Jan. 16); "As the Tumbleweed Turns" (Chiniquy/Apr. 8); "The Badge and the

*Fat-bellied sheriff Hoot Kloot prepares for trouble in a scene from DePatie-Freleng's cartoon series spoofing the Old West. © DePatie-Freleng Enterprises*

Beautiful" (Balser/Apr. 17); "Big Beef at the O.K. Corral" (Balser/Apr. 17); "By Hoot or by Crook" (Balser/Apr. 17); "Strange on the Range" (Bonaye/Apr. 17); "Mesa Trouble" (Marcus/May 16); and "Saddle Soap Opera" (Chiniquy/May 16).

## ◎ HUBIE AND BERTIE

Chuck Jones created these two troublesome mice, Hubie and Bertie, who were added to the Warner Bros. cartoon roster in 1943. In subsequent adventures they were paired with a mouse-hungry cat, Claude Cat. The short-lived series produced one Academy Award nomination for the 1949 release "Mouse Wreckers," the pair's second cartoon. *Directed by Chuck Jones. Technicolor. A Leon Schlesinger Studios and Warner Bros. Cartoons, Inc. Production released by Warner Bros.*

**Voices**
Hubie: Mel Blanc; *Bertie:* Mel Blanc, Stan Freberg

*Merrie Melodies*

*Leon Schlesinger Studios releases*

**1943:** "The Aristo Cat" (June 12).

*Warner Bros. Cartoons, Inc. releases*

**1948:** "House-Hunting Mice" (Oct. 7).

**1949:** "Mouse Wreckers" (with Claude Cat/Apr. 23/A.A. nominee).

**1950:** "The Hypo-Condri-Cat" (with Claude Cat/Apr. 15).

**1951:** "Cheese Chasers" (with Claude Cat/Aug. 28).

*Looney Tunes*

*Warner Bros. Cartoons, Inc. releases*

**1946:** "Roughly Squeaking" (Nov. 23).

**1952:** "Mouse Warming" (with Claude Cat/Sept. 8).

## ◎ HUBLEY CARTOONS

Seven-time Oscar-nominated series, including three winners, of quirky, unusual and innovative independently produced theatrical cartoon shorts comprised of flatly drawn characters and streamlined backgrounds and largely shown at film festivals and art houses; produced and directed by former animator Disney and United Productions of America (UPA) founder John Hubley and his wife and partner, Faith Hubley.

Relocating to New York after he was blacklisted in Hollywood for refusing to testify before the House Committee on Un-American Activities during the McCarthy era, the Hubleys established their own animation studio, Storyboard Inc. (later renamed the Hubley Studio, Inc.), first producing animated commercials (in which John's work went uncredited), before co-producing 22 films together. Their first theatrical cartoon short collaboration was *The Adventures of an \** (1956), the first of many groundbreaking and oddly distinctive cartoon short subjects with extemporized dialogue and musical scores by such famous jazz musicians and composers as Benny Carter, Dizzy Gillespie, Quincy Jones, William Russo and others.

The Hubleys' subsequent widely praised film shorts, which they produced and directed, played at film festivals around the world and won a bevy of international awards and honors. Three of them included such Oscar winners as *Moonbird* (1959), which John Hubley directed with Faith (under the name of Faith Elliot) coproducing; the alarming nuclear holocaust short, *The Hole* (1962), about a nuclear holocaust; and *Herb Alpert and the Tijuana Brass Double Feature* (1966), both codirected by husband John. Four additional shorts they produced received Oscar nominations: *Windy Day* (1968), *Of Men and Demons* (1969), *Voyage to Next* (1974), and *The Doonesbury Special* (1977), an adaptation of Garry Trudeau's hugely successful comic strip, which was also broadcast in November of 1977 as a special on NBC. Faith completed the project following her husband's death after a heart attack that same year after he'd finished work on the 1976 CBS television special, *Everybody Rides the Carousel*, which also played at numerous film festivals.

Going solo, Faith Hubley made 25 additional film that she designed, produced and directed, usually visual explorations that confronted social issues, different aspects of mythology or the origins of the universe, including the highly acclaimed *Whither Weather* (1977), *Step by Step* (1978), *The Big Bang and Other Creation Myths* (1979), *Enter Life* (1982), *Time of the Angels* (1987), *Who Am I?* (1989), featuring animation by her daughter Emily, *Rainbows of Hawaii* (1995) and her final solo film, *Northern Ice, Golden Sun* (2001).

After years of suffering from various illnesses, Hubley died of cancer in 2001 at her home in New Haven, Connecticut, at the age of 77, four days before her last film premiered at UCLA in Los Angeles; it later aired on the Sundance Channel.

Besides their praiseworthy short-subject work, the Hubleys also produced two independent features beloved by critics: 1961's *Of Stars and Men*, which Hubley directed and Faith coproduced, and 1986's *The Cosmic Eye*, which Faith produced and directed nine years after his death. *Produced and directed by John Hubley, Faith Hubley, and Garry Trudeau. Color. A Storyboard Films, Inc. and Hubley Studio, Inc. Production released by Paramount Pictures, the National Film Board of Canada, and Paramount Pictures.*

**Voices:**
Mark Hubley, Ray Hubley, Emily Hubley, Georgia Hubley, Dizzy Gillespie, George Mathews, Dudley Moore, Anita Ellis, David Burns, Grady Tate, Maureen Stapleton, Jack Warden, Morris Carnovsky, Phil Leeds, Dee Dee Bridgewater, Barbara Harris,

Richard Cox, James Smith Jackson, Michael Ontkean, Sam Hubley.

### John and Faith Hubley releases

**1957:** "The Adventures of An *" (J. Hubley/music by Benny Carter).

**1958:** "Harlem Wednesday" (J. Hubley/music by Benny Carter); "The Tender Game" (J. Hubley/music by Ella Fitzgerald and the Oscar Peterson Trio); and "Old Whiff" (J. Hubley).

**1959:** "Moonbird" (J. Hubley/A.A. winner).

**1961:** "Children of the Sun" (Hubleys/coproduced by UNICEF).

**1962:** "The Hole" (Hubleys/A.A. winner).

**1963:** "The Hat" (Hubleys/working title: "The Hat: Is the War Necessary?").

**1966:** "Herb Alpert and the Tijuana Brass Double Feature" (J. Hubley/A.A. winner/with music by Herb Alpert and the Tijuana Brass); and "Urbanissimo" (J. Hubley/music by Benny Carter).

**1967:** "The Cruise" (J. Hubley/music by Benny Carter); and "A Windy Day" (Hubleys/A.A. nominee).

**1969:** "Zuckerhandl" (J. Hubley); and "Of Men and Demons" (J. Hubley/A.A. nominee/music by Quincy Jones).

**1970:** "Eggs" (J. Hubley/music by Quincy Jones).

**1972:** "Dig" (Hubleys).

**1973:** "Cockaboody" (Hubleys).

**1974:** "Upkeep" (Hubleys); and "Voyage to Next" (Hubleys/music by Dizzy Gillespie/A.A. nominee).

**1975:** "People, People, People" (Hubleys/music by Benny Carter); "Everybody Rides the Carousel" (J. Hubley/CBS network special also released to film festivals/music by William Russo); and "A Doonesbury Special" (Hubleys, Trudeau/also an NBC special/ A.A. nominee).

### Faith Hubley releases

**1976:** "Second Chance: Sea" (F. Hubley/music by William Russo).

**1977:** "Wow (Women of the World)" (F. Hubley/music by William Russo/Cannes Film Festival, Golden Palm best short film nominee).

**1978:** "Whither Weather" (F. Hubley/music by William Russo).

**1979:** "Step by Step" (F. Hubley/music by Elizabeth Swados).

**1980:** "Sky Dance" (F. Hubley/music by Elizabeth Swados).

**1981:** "The Big Bang and Other Creation Myths" (F. Hubley/music by Elizabeth Swados).

**1982:** "Enter Life" (F. Hubley/music by Elizabeth Swados).

**1983:** "Starlore" (F. Hubley/music by Conrad Cummings).

**1984:** "Hello" (F. Hubley/music by William Russo).

**1987:** "Time of the Angels" (F. Hubley/music by William Russo).

**1988:** "Yes We Can" (F. Hubley/music by Don Christensen).

**1989:** "Who Am I?" (F. Hubley/music by Don Christensen).

**1990:** "Amazonia" (F. Hubley/music by Don Christensen).

**1991:** "Upside Down" (F. Hubley).

**1992:** "Tall Time Tales" (F. Hubley).

**1994:** "Seers and Clowns" (F. Hubley)

**1995:** "Rainbows of Hawaii" (F. Hubley).

**1996:** "My Universe Inside Out" (F. Hubley/May 1).

**1997:** "Beyond the Shadow Place" (F. Hubley).

**1998:** "Africa" (F. Hubley).

**1999:** "Witch Madness" (F. Hubley).

**2000:** Our Spirited Earth" (F. Hubley).

**2001:** "Northern Ice, Golden Sun" (F. Hubley/Dec. 11).

## ◎ HUGH HARMAN CARTOONS

In the early 1930s Hugh Harman and partner Rudolf Ising moved from Warner Bros. to MGM to produce cartoons independently for their new studio. In 1939, after a brief departure, Harman returned to Metro following overtures from Fred Quimby, head of the studio's new cartoon department. Quimby hired Harman to develop a fresh, new cartoon series that would help establish the studio as a leader in the field of cartoon animation.

Using a familiar formula, Harman produced and directed a series of musical cartoons similar to his former *Merrie Melodies* for Warner Bros., featuring various animated characters as the stars. His finest effort came in 1939 during his first year back at the studio, when his "Peace on Earth," a timely war-themed cartoon released that year, won an Academy Award nomination for best short subject and a *Parents Magazine* medal of distinction.

Veteran animator Friz Freleng, who briefly defected to MGM from Warner Bros., directed one cartoon under the series. *Directed by Hugh Harman and Friz Freleng. Technicolor. A Metro-Goldwyn-Mayer Cartoon Production released by Metro-Goldwyn-Mayer.*

**1939:** "Art Gallery" (Harman/May 13); "Goldilocks and the 3 Bears" (Harman/July 15/re: Nov. 22, 1947); "Bear Family" (Abandoned); "The Bookworm" (Freleng/Aug. 26); "The Blue Danube" (Harman/Oct. 28); "Peace on Earth" (Harman/Dec. 9/ A.A. nominee); and "The Mad Maestro" (Harman/Dec. 30).

**1940:** "A Rainy Day" (Harman/Apr. 20); "Tom Turkey and His Harmonica Humdingers" (Harman/June 8); "The Bookworm

*Two determined cherubs of the forest pick blueberries so they can color the nearby waters of the land in Hugh Harman's MGM cartoon short "The Blue Danube" (1939). © Turner Entertainment*

Turns" (Harman/July 20); "Papa Gets the Bird" (Harman/Sept. 7); and "The Lonesome Stranger" (Harman/Nov. 23).

**1941:** "Abdul the Bulbul-Ameer" (Harman/Feb. 22); "The Little Mole" (Harman/Apr. 5); "The Alley Cat" (Harman/July 5); and "The Field Mouse" (Harman/Dec. 27).

**1942:** "The Hungry Wolf" (Harman/Feb. 21).

## ◎ INKI

Paired with a pesty minah bird, Inki, who was a little black jungle boy with a bone in his hair, was used occasionally in a number of Warner Bros. cartoons directed by creator Chuck Jones. Inki first appeared in 1939's "The Little Lion Hunter." *Directed by Chuck Jones. Technicolor. A Leon Schlesinger Studios and Warner Bros. Cartoons, Inc. Production released by Warner Bros.*

### Voices
Mel Blanc

### Leon Schlesinger Studios releases

### Merrie Melodies

**1939:** "The Little Lion Hunter" (Oct. 7).

**1941:** "Inki and the Lion" (July 19).

**1943:** "Inki and the Minah Bird" (Nov. 6).

### Warner Bros. Cartoons, Inc. releases

**1947:** "Inki at the Circus" (June 21).

### Looney Tunes

**1950:** "Caveman Inki" (Nov. 25).

## ◎ THE INSPECTOR

The blundering French sleuth of *Pink Panther* fame, Inspector Clouseau starred in a series of cartoon shorts based on Blake Edwards's film character, played by actor-comedian Peter Sellers in several feature films in the 1960s and 1970s.

In 1965 the animated character, who bears more than a fleeting resemblance to Sellers, made his debut along with his equally lamebrained aide, Sergeant Deudeux, when United Artists simultaneously released the James Bond thriller *Thunderball* and the cartoon "The Great DeGaulle Stone" nationwide.

As in the successful feature film series, the animated adventures dealt with Clouseau's inherent ability to solve important cases despite his obvious ineptitude. Blake Edwards actually suggested the idea for the series. *Directors were Gerry Chiniquy, Friz Freleng, Robert McKimson and George Singer. Technicolor. A Mirisch-Geoffrey-DePatie-Freleng Enterprises Production released through United Artists.*

### Voices
**The Inspector/Sergeant Deudeux:** Pat Harrington Jr.; **The Chief:** Paul Frees, Marvin Miller

### Additional Voices
June Foray, Helen Gerald, Joan Gerber, Diana Maddox, Mark Skor, Hal Smith, Larry Storch, Lennie Weinrib

**1965:** "The Great DeGaulle Stone Operation" (Freleng, Chiniquy/Dec. 21).

**1966:** "Reaux, Reaux, Reaux Your Boat" (Chiniquy/Feb. 1); "Napoleon Blown-Aparte" (Chiniquy/Feb. 2); "Cirrhosis of the Louvre" (Chiniquy/Mar. 9); "Plastered in Paris" (Chiniquy/Apr. 5); "Cock-a-Doodle Deux Deux" (McKimson/June 15); "Ape Suzette" (Chiniquy/June 24); "The Pique Poquette of Paris" (Singer/Aug. 24); "Sicque! Sicque! Sicque!" (Singer/Sept. 23); "That's No Lady—That's Notre Dame" (Singer/Oct. 26); "Unsafe and Seine" (Singer/Nov. 9); and "Toulouse La Trick" (McKimson/Dec. 30).

**1967:** "Sacre Bleu Cross" (Chiniquy/Feb. 1); "Le Quiet Squad" (McKimson/May 17); "Bomb Voyage" (McKimson/May 22); "Le Pig-Al Patrol" (Chiniquy/May 24); "Le Bowser Bagger" (Chiniquy/May 30); "Le Escape Goat" (Chiniquy/June 29); "Le Cop on Le Rocks" (Singer/July 3); "Crow De Guerre" (Chiniquy/Aug. 16); "Canadian Can-Can" (Chiniquy/Sept. 20); "Tour De Farce" (Chiniquy/Oct. 25); and "The Shooting of Caribou Lou" (Chiniquy/Dec. 20).

**1968:** "London Derriere" (Chiniquy/Feb. 7); "Les Mise-robots" (Chiniquy/Mar. 21); "Transylvania Mania" (Chiniquy/Mar. 26); "Bear De Guerre" (Chiniquy/Apr. 26); "Cherche Le Phantom" (Chiniquy/June 13); "Le Great Dane Robbery" (Chiniquy/July 7); "La Feet's De Feat" (Chiniquy/July 24); and "Le Ball and Chain Gang" (Chiniquy/July 24).

**1969:** "French Freud" (Chiniquy/Jan. 22); "Pierre and Cottage Cheese" (Chiniquy/Feb. 26); and "Carte Blanched" (Chiniquy/May 14).

## ◎ INSPECTOR WILLOUGHBY

Believing the time was ripe for a new cartoon character to grace the screen, Walter Lantz enlisted former Disney director Jack Hannah to develop story ideas for a new series. Hannah responded with a revised version of a character from his Disney days named Ranger Willoughby, who was renamed Inspector Willoughby. Making a few minor alterations, he gave the character a new identity and new profession as a burly mustachioed secret agent, 6 7/8. Willoughby's low-key demeanor and speaking voice were humanized versions of Tex Avery's popular basset hound, Droopy.

Hannah directed the premiere episode of the series, "Hunger Strife," in 1960, plus a subsequent cartoon, "Eggnapper," the following year. The rest of the series was directed by Lantz veteran Paul J. Smith until 1965. *Directed by Jack Hannah and Paul J. Smith. Technicolor. A Walter Lantz Production released through Universal Pictures.*

### Voices
**Inspector Willoughby:** Dal McKennon

**1960:** "Hunger Strife" (with Fatso the Bear/Hannah/Oct. 5).

**1961:** "Rough and Tumbleweed" (Smith/Jan. 31); "Eggnapper" (Hannah/Feb. 14); "Mississippi Slow Boat" (Smith/July); and "Case of the Red-Eyed Ruby" (Smith/Nov. 28).

**1962:** "Phoney Express" (Smith/May 15); and "Hyde and Sneak" (with Woody Woodpecker cameo/Smith/July 24).

**1963:** "Coming-Out Party" (Smith/Feb. 1); "Case of the Cold-Storage Yegg" (Smith/Mar. 1); and "Hi-Seas Hi-Jacker" (Smith/May 1).

**1964:** "The Case of the Maltese Chicken" (Smith/Feb. 4).

**1965:** "The Case of the Elephant's Trunk" (Smith/Jan. 1).

## ◎ JACKY'S WHACKY WORLD

Based on the comic strip *Jacky's Diary* by cartoonist Jack Mendelsohn that relates a young boy's fractured views of history and fairy tales, Mendelsohn wrote and directed this brief Paramount cartoon series, produced as *Noveltoons* cartoons. *Technicolor. Voice credits unknown. A Famous Studios Production released through Paramount Pictures Corporation.*

**1965:** "The Story of George Washington" (Feb./*Noveltoon*); and "A Leak in the Dike" (Mar./*Modern Madcap*).

## ⊚ JAMES HOUND

Inspired by Ian Fleming's fictional James Bond character, Terry-Toons introduced this canine counterpart of the famed super-sleuth in animated escapades featuring international spies and farfetched gadgets on a smaller scale. Ralph Bakshi, who made his *Terrytoons* directorial debut in 1964, directed the series. *Directed by Ralph Bakshi. Technicolor. A Terrytoons Production released through 20th Century Fox.*

### Voices

**James Hound:** Dayton Allen

**1966:** "Dr. Ha Ha Ha" (Feb. 1/working title: "Doctor Ha-Ha"); "Dr. Rhinestone's Theory" (Mar. 12); "The Monster Maker" (July 1); "Rain Drain" (Sept. 1); "Dream-Napping" (Nov. 1); and "The Phantom Skyscraper" (Dec. 1).

**1967:** "Voodoo Spell" (Jan.); "Mr. Win Lucky" (Feb. 1); "It's for the Birds" (Mar. 1); "The Heat's Off" (Apr. 1); "Traffic Trouble" (May 1); "Bugged by a Bug" (June 1); "Fancy Plants" (July 1); "Give Me Liberty" (Aug. 1); "Which Is Witch?" (Sept. 1); "Frozen Sparklers" (Nov. 1); and "Baron Von Go-Go" (Dec. 1).

## ⊚ JEEPERS AND CREEPERS

This brief series starred a comic pair of dogs, Jeepers and Creepers, who were the original version of another Paramount cartoon team, Swifty and Shorty, who debuted two years later. *Directed by Seymour Kneitel. Technicolor. A Famous Studios Production released through Paramount Pictures Corporation.*

### Voices

**Jeepers:** Jack Mercer; **Creepers:** Syd Raymond, Allen Swift, Jack Mercer

**1960:** "The Boss Is Always Right" (Jan. 15); "Trouble Date" (Mar. 11/*Modern Madcap*); "Busy Buddies" (June); and "Scouting for Trouble" (Sept. 19).

## ⊚ THE JERKY JOURNEYS

Two years after Republic Pictures released animator Bob Clampett's experimental TruColor cartoon, "It's a Grand Old Nag," starring Charlie Horse and Hay-dy LaMare, the studio produced this series of animated travelogue spoofs without the guidance of Clampett, who left the studio after producing his single effort. Studio president Herbert Yates proposed making the series to further exploit its new color process in the same manner Disney made Technicolor into a success with his *Silly Symphony* cartoons.

The series became Republic's first and only cartoon series. Produced by Leonard Lewis Levinson and Art Heineman, these low-budget cartoons starred Professor Cassius Mugglesby and his wife, Mrs. Mugglesby, and their daughter, Penelope, and such supporting characters as Dr. Livingston I Presume, Rembrandt Schultz and Cecil Bravado. *TruColor. An Impossible Pictures Production released by Republic Pictures.*

**1949:** "Beyond Civilization to Texas" (Mar. 15); "The 3 Minnies: Sota, Tonka & Ha Ha!" (Apr. 15); "Bungle in the Jungle" (May 15); and "Romantic Rumbolia" (June 15).

## ⊚ JOCK AND JILL

A boy (Jock) and girl (Jill) monkey duo, billed as "the Simple Simeons" even though the correct spelling is "Simians," that first debuted on the screen in Walter Lantz's 1938 cartoon, "Ghost Town Frolics," directed by Lester Kline. Jock would appear by himself in a second Walter Lantz cartoon that same year, "The Rabbit Hunt," for Lantz's *Cartune Comedy* series, also known as *Walter Lantz Cartune Classics. Directed by Lester Kline. Black-and-white. A Walter Lantz Production released by Universal Pictures Company, Inc.*

**1938:** "Ghost Town Frolics" (with Jock and Jill, the Simple Simeons/Kline/Sept. 5/working title: "Ghost Town"/first appearances of Jock and Jill, the Simple Simeons); and "The Rabbit Hunt" (with Jock/Kline/Oct. 10/*Cartune Comedy* cartoon).

## ⊚ JOHN DOORMAT

The ups-and-downs of suburban life in the 1950s are comically portrayed in this *Terrytoons* series featuring John Doormat, a poor soul whose encounters deal with a variety of everyday issues created by Terrytoons creative director Gene Deitch, who served as a supervising director and producer of the series. Writer Jules Feiffer later joined the series, changing the direction of the cartoons to a more Thurberish outlook on life. Lionel Wilson, who supplied all the voice characterizations for TV's *Tom Terrific* series, did the voice of John Doormat. *Directed by Connie Rasinski and Al Kouzel. Technicolor. CinemaScope. A Terrytoons and CBS Film, Inc., Production released through 20th Century Fox.*

### Voices

**John Doormat:** Lionel Wilson

**1957:** "Topsy TV" (Rasinski/Jan.); and "Shove Thy Neighbor" (Rasinski/June).

**1958:** "Dustcap Doormat" (Kouzel/June).

**1959:** "Another Day, Another Doormat" (Kouzel/Mar.)

## ⊚ JOLLY FROLICS

When Columbia Pictures' animation department closed down, United Productions of America (UPA) independently produced new cartoons for distribution through the studio to replace the *Phantasy* color classics series. The first cartoon to launch the series was 1949's "The Ragtime Bear," starring the myopic Mr. Magoo.

Magoo, Gerald McBoing Boing and other stalwarts from UPA's cartoon gallery appeared in several episodes of this new series. *Directors were John Hubley, Art Babbitt, Steve Bosustow, Bob Cannon, Pete Burness and Ted Parmelee. Technicolor. A UPA Production released through Columbia Pictures.*

**1949:** "The Ragtime Bear" (with Mr. Magoo, Waldo/Hubley/Sept. 8).

**1950:** "Punchy DeLeon" (Hubley/Jan. 16); "The Miner's Daughter" (Cannon/May 25); "Giddyap" (Babbitt/July 27); and "The Popcorn Story" (Babbitt/Nov. 30).

**1951:** "Gerald McBoing Boing" (Cannon/Jan. 25); "The Family Circus" (Babbit/Jan. 25); "Georgie the Dragon" (Cannon/Sept. 27); and "Wonder Gloves" (Cannon/Nov. 29).

**1952:** "The Oompahs" (Cannon/Jan. 24); "Rooty Tooty Toot" (Hubley/Mar. 27/A.A. winner); "Pete Hothead" (Parmelee/Sept. 25); and "Madeline" (Cannon/Nov. 27/A.A. nominee).

**1953:** "The Fifty First Dragon"; "Little Boy with a Big Horn" (Cannon/Mar. 26); "The Emperor's New Clothes" (Parmelee/Apr. 30); "Christopher Crumpet" (Cannon/June 25/A.A. nominee); and "Gerald McBoing Boing's Symphony" (Cannon/July 5).

**1954:** "How Now McBoing Boing" (Cannon/Sept. 9).

## ◎ KARTUNES

In the early 1950s Paramount's Famous Studios resurrected a familiar formula—sing-a-long musical cartoons with no named stars—when it introduced *Kartunes*, animated in the same style and manner as its former success, *Noveltoons*.

*Kartunes* never equaled the success of *Noveltoons* in terms of popularity and longevity. The series only lasted three years. *Directed by Isadore Sparber and Seymour Kneitel. A Famous Studios Production released through Paramount Pictures Corporation.*

**1951:** "Vegetable Vaudeville" (Sparber/Nov. 9); and "Snooze Reel" (Kneitel/Dec. 28).

**1952:** "Off We Glow" (Sparber/Feb. 29); "Fun at the Fair" (Sparber/May 9/song: "Wait Till the Sun Shines, Nellie"); "Dizzy Dinosaurs" (Kneitel/July 4); "Gag and Baggage" (Sparber/Aug. 8); and "Forest Fantasy" (Kneitel/Nov. 14).

**1953:** "Hysterical History" (Sparber/Jan. 23/song: "Yankee Doodle Boy"); "Philharmaniacs" (Kneitel/Apr. 3); "Aero-Nutics" (Kneitel/May 8); "Invention Convention" (Sparber/June 10); and "No Place Like Rome" (Sparber/July 31).

## ◎ KIKO THE KANGAROO

First appearing in *Farmer Al Falfa* cartoons, Kiko was a playful kangaroo cast in numerous misadventures. The character was created by Paul Terry, who featured the character in his own series of animated shorts beginning in 1936 in "Kiko and the Honey Bears," written by Joe Barbera, who briefly worked as a storyman for the studio. *Directed by Mannie Davis and George Gordon. Black-and-white. A Terry-Toon Cartoons Production released through 20th Century Fox.*

**1936:** "Kiko and the Honey Bears" (Davis, Gordon/Aug. 21); "Kiko Foils a Fox" (Davis, Gordon/Oct. 2); "A Battle Royal" (Davis, Gordon/Oct. 31); and "Skunked Again" (Davis, Gordon/ Dec. 25).

**1937:** "Red Hot Music" (Davis, Gordon/Mar. 5); "The Hay Ride" (Davis, Gordon/Apr. 12); "Ozzie Ostrich Comes to Town" (Davis, Gordon/May 28); "Play Ball" (Davis/June 11); and "Kiko's Cleaning Day" (Gordon/Sept. 17).

## ◎ KRAZY KAT

The advent of sound revived many silent-film favorites, including George Herriman's popular animated feline, Krazy Kat. Krazy had gained fame by starring in more than 80 silent cartoons. He was brought back to life when Columbia Pictures, wanting to become a major force in the cartoon industry, agreed to distribute this proven property in a series of new cartoons produced by Charles Mintz.

The sound cartoons had the same basic stories as the silent adventures, with some dialogue and musical soundtrack accompaniment. Krazy's soft-speaking voice was like Mickey Mouse, who inspired several other sound-alike characters, among them, Warner Bros.' Bosko and Buddy.

As had happened in the silent series, the series suffered several setbacks because of creative differences in bringing Krazy's innate style of humor to the screen. No attempt was made to stay true to creator George Herriman's style or story lines. Consequently, Offisa Pup was rarely used, and the romance between Ignatz and Krazy, ever popular in the comic strip series, was virtually ignored.

At the same time Mintz produced the series for Columbia, Walt Disney supplied cartoons for the studio for release. In 1932, after Disney parted company with Columbia, Mintz became the studio's sole supplier of cartoons, with Krazy leading the pack. (Coincidentally, Mintz was the same producer responsible for taking the *Oswald the Rabbit* series from Disney years earlier.)

Manny Gould and Ben Harrison, who wrote most of the cartoon stories, jointly directed and supervised the animation of each cartoon. Music was supplied by Joe De Nat, a former New York pianist, whose peppy musical scores enlivened each film. *Directed by Manny Gould and Ben Harrison. Black-and-white. Technicolor. A Columbia Pictures Corporation Production released by Columbia Pictures. Voice credits unknown.*

**1929:** "Ratskin" (Aug. 15); "Canned Music" (Sept. 12); "Port Whines" (Oct. 10); "Sole Mates" (Nov. 7); and "Farm Relief" (Dec. 30).

**1930:** "The Cat's Meow" (Jan. 2); "Spook Easy" (Jan. 30); "Slow Beau" (Feb. 27); "Desert Sunk" (Mar. 27); "An Old Flame" (Apr. 24); "Alaskan Knights" (May 23); "Jazz Rhythm" (June 19); "Honolulu Wiles" (July 17); "Cinderella" (Aug. 14); "The Band Master" (Sept. 8); "The Apache Kid" (Oct. 9); "Lambs Will Gamble" (Nov. 1); and "The Little Trail" (Dec. 3).

**1931:** "Take for a Ride" (Jan.); "Rodeo Dough" (Feb. 13); "Swiss Movements" (Apr. 4); "Disarmament Conference" (Apr. 27); "Soda Poppa" (May 29); "Stork Market" (July 11); "Svengarlic" (Aug. 3); "Weenie Roast" (Sept. 14); "Bars and Stripes" (Oct. 15); "Hash House Blues" (Nov. 2); and "The Restless Sax" (Dec. 1).

**1932:** "Piano Mover" (Jan. 4); "Love Krazy" (Jan. 25); "Hollywood Goes Krazy" (Feb. 13); "What a Knight" (Mar. 14); "Soldier Old Man" (Apr. 2); "Birth of Jazz" (Apr. 13); "Ritzy Hotel" (May 9); "Hic-Cups the Champ" (May 28); "The Paper Hanger" (June 21); "Lighthouse Keeping" (Aug. 15); "Seeing Stars" (Sept. 12); "Prosperity Blues" (Oct. 8); "The Crystal Gazebo" (Nov. 7); "The Minstrel Show" (Nov. 21); and "Show Time" (Nov. 30).

**1933:** "Wedding Bells" (Jan. 10); "The Medicine Show" (Feb. 7); "Wooden Shoes" (Feb. 25); "Bunnies and Bonnets" (Mar. 29); "The Broadway Malady" (Apr. 18); "Russian Dressing" (May 1); "House Cleaning" (June 1); "Antique Antics" (June 14); "Out of the Ether" (Sept. 5); "Whacks Museum" (Sept. 29); "Krazy Spooks" (Oct. 13); "Stage Krazy" (Nov. 13); "The Bill Poster" (Nov. 24); and "The Curio Shop" (Dec. 15).

**1934:** "The Autograph Hunter" (Jan. 5); "Southern Exposure" (Feb. 5); "Tom Thumb" (Feb. 16); "Cinder Alley" (Mar. 9); "Bowery Daze" (Mar. 30); "Busy Bus" (Apr. 20); "Masquerade Party" (May 11); "The Trapeze Artist" (Sept. 1); "Katnips of 1940" (Oct. 12); "Krazy's Waterloo" (Nov. 16); and "Goofy Gondolas" (Dec. 21).

**1935:** (All the following cartoons were produced in Technicolor.) "The Bird Man" (Feb. 1); "Hotcha Melody" (Mar. 15); "The Peace Conference" (Apr. 26); "The King's Jester" (May 20); "Garden Gaieties" (Aug. 1); "A Happy Family" (Sept. 27); and "Kannibal Kapers" (Dec. 27).

**1936:** "The Bird Stuffer" (Feb. 1); "Lil' Ainjil" (Mar. 19); "Highway Snobbery" (Aug. 9); "Krazy's Newsreel" (Oct. 24); and "Merry Cafe" (Dec. 26).

**1937:** "The Lyin' Hunter" (Feb. 12); "Krazy's Race of Time" (May 6); "The Masque Raid" (June 25); and "Railroad Rhythm" (Nov. 20).

**1938:** "Sad Little Guinea Pigs" (Feb. 22); "The Auto Clinic" (Mar. 4); "Little Buckaroo" (Apr. 11); "Krazy Magic" (May 20); "Krazy's Travel Squawks" (July 4); "Gym Jams" (Sept. 9); "Hot Dogs on Ice" (Oct. 21); and "The Lone Mountie" (Dec. 10).

**1939:** "Krazy's Bear Tale" (Jan. 27); "Golf Chumps" (Apr. 6); "Krazy's Shoe Shop" (May 12); and "Little Lost Sheep" (Oct. 6).

**1940:** "The Mouse Exterminator" (Jan. 26/*Phantasy* cartoon); and "News Oddities" (July 19).

## ◎ LADDY AND HIS LAMP

This brief Paramount cartoon series—following the adventures of a young boy and the genie of the lamp—was brought to the screen in 1964, when studio animators introduced a variety of one-shot characters (including Buck and Wingy, Homer Ranger and King Artie) in the studio's popular *Noveltoons* series. *Directed by Seymour Kneitel. Technicolor. A Famous Studios Production released through Paramount Pictures Corporation.*

**1964:** "Laddy and His Lamp" (Sept./*Noveltoon*); and "A Tiger's Tail" (Dec./*Noveltoon*).

## ◎ LAND OF THE LOST

The popular children's radio show *The Insgrigs* inspired this series of fantasy cartoons produced as part of Famous Studios' *Noveltoons* series. *Directed by Isadore Sparber and Seymour Kneitel. Technicolor. A Famous Studios Production released through Paramount Pictures Corporation.*

**1948:** "Land of the Lost" (Sparber/June 7).

**1950:** "Land of the Lost Jewels" (Sparber/Jan. 6).

**1951:** "Land of Lost Watches" (Kneitel/May 4).

## ◎ LIL' ABNER

Few comic-strip characters were successful in an animated cartoon environment. Columbia Pictures had learned this before with Krazy Kat and Barney Google, the latter an earlier comic strip-to-film adaptation that failed. Yet the studio tried again, this time with a short-lived series of cartoon shorts based on Al Capp's hillbilly character. Produced by Dave Fleischer, the series was dropped after only five films, which pleased creator Capp, who repeatedly expressed his disdain with the studio's simplifications of the characters and situations from his nationally syndicated strip. *Directors were Sid Marcus, Bob Wickersham and Howard Swift. Technicolor. A Columbia Pictures Corporation Production released by Columbia Pictures.*

**1944:** "Amoozin but Confoozin" (Marcus/Mar. 3); "Sadie Hawkins Day" (Wickersham/May 4); "A Peekoolyar Sitcheeyshun" (Marcus/Aug. 11); "Porkulia Piggy" (Wickersham/Oct. 13); and "Kickapoo Juice" (Swift/Dec. 1).

## ◎ LIL' EIGHTBALL

Former Disney protégé Burt Gillett was responsible for creating this stereotyped black youngster who, after a brief opportunity at movie stardom, resurfaced in Walter Lantz's comic books of the 1940s. *Directed by Burt Gillett. Black-and-white. Technicolor. A Walter Lantz Production released through Universal Pictures.*

**1939:** "The Stubborn Mule" (July 3); "Silly Superstition" (Aug. 28/last black-and-white Lantz cartoon); and "A Haunting We Will Go" (Sept. 4/first Lantz cartoon made in three-strip Technicolor).

## ◎ LITTLE AUDREY

When Paramount lost the rights to Little Lulu in late 1947, the studio produced a series of Little Audrey cartoons as her replacement. This series revolved around the life and loves of a sweet little girl who earlier claimed fame as a Harvey comic-book character. Stories depict her matching wits with a prank-loving boy, Melvin, tracking down hoodlums and lending a helping hand to anyone needing assistance.

Mae Questel, who did most of the female and children's voices for the studio, was Audrey in the series. The first little Audrey comic book was published four months before the series' first cartoon. *Directed by Isadore Sparber, Seymour Kneitel and Bill Tytla. Technicolor. A Famous Studios Production released through Paramount Pictures Corporation.*

### Voices

**Little Audrey:** Mae Questel

(All series cartoons were released under the *Noveltoons* banner.)

**1948:** "Butterscotch and Soda" (Kneitel/July 6).

**1949:** "The Lost Dream" (Tytla/Mar. 18); and "Song of the Birds" (Tytla/Nov. 18).

**1950:** "Tarts and Flowers" (Tytla/May 26); and "Goofy Goofy Gander" (Tytla/Aug. 18).

**1951:** "Hold the Lion Please" (Sparber/Apr. 27); and "Audrey the Rainmaker" (Sparber/Oct. 26).

**1952:** "Law and Audrey" (Sparber/May 23); and "The Case of the Cockeyed Canary" (Kneitel/Dec. 19).

**1953:** "Surf Bored" (Sparber/July 17).

**1954:** "The Seapreme Court" (Kneitel/Jan. 29).

**1955:** "Dizzy Dishes" (Sparber/Feb. 4); and "Little Audrey Riding Hood" (Kneitel/Oct. 14).

**1957:** "Fishing Tackler" (Sparber/Mar. 29).

**1958:** "Dawg Gawn" (Kneitel/Dec. 12).

## ◎ LITTLE CHEESER

Rudolph Ising created this cute, cuddly mouse who briefly appeared on the screen in two cartoons of his own. Little Cheeser's first appearance was in a *Happy Harmonies* cartoon bearing his name. *Produced by Hugh Harman and Rudolf Ising. Ising also directed the series. Technicolor. A Metro-Goldwyn-Mayer Cartoon Production released by Metro-Goldwyn-Mayer.*

### Voice

**Little Cheeser:** Bernice Hansen

**1936:** "Little Cheeser" (July 11/*Happy Harmonies*).

**1937:** "Little Buck Cheeser" (Dec. 15).

## ◎ LITTLE KING

Based on the popular comic-strip character penned by cartoonist Oscar E. Soglow, this animated version marked yet another attempt by Van Beuren Studios to find a successful screen character to upgrade its image in the already crowded cartoon marketplace.

Unfortunately, the series never quite lived up to the studio's expectations as a "cartoon savior." The king never talked but acted out his response in pantomime, which may have been part of the reason for the series failure. (Strangely, the king later appeared in several Paramount Betty Boop cartoons and was given a speaking voice for those appearances.) *Directed by Jim Tyer and George Stallings. Black-and-white. A Van Beuren Studios Production released through RKO Radio Pictures.*

**1933:** "The Fatal Note" (Tyer/Sept. 29); "Marching Along" (Tyer/Mar. 27); "On the Pan" (Nov. 24); and "Pals" (Tyer/Dec. 22).

**1934:** "Jest of Honor" (Stallings/Jan. 19); "Jolly Good Felons" (Stallings/Feb. 16); "Sultan Pepper" (Stallings/Mar. 16); "A Royal Good Time" (Stallings/Apr. 13); "Art for Art's Sake" (Stallings/May 11); and "Cactus King" (Stallings/June 8).

## ⊚ LITTLE LULU

Animator Max Fleischer adapted the Marjorie H. Bell comic-strip character, Little Lulu, to stories that relate the activities and frustrations of a mischievous little girl trying to show her parents how grown up she can be. Already a favorite in *Saturday Evening Post* cartoon panels, Fleischer added the series to the Paramount/Famous Studios 1943–44 roster.

As he had hoped, Lulu's childish mischief spelled success for his studio, with adventures pitting her against next-door neighbor Tubby, who always harasses her but is vanquished by Lulu's childlike wit.

The series' theme song was written by Fred Wise, Sidney Lippman and Buddy Kaye, becoming as successful a hit as the cartoon series itself.

Paramount dropped the series in 1948 when it was unable to renegotiate the rights to continue with the character. (Thirteen years later Lulu returned to the screen in "Alvin's Solo Flight," a *Noveltoon* coproduced by Lulu's creator Majorie H. Buell.) Lulu ultimately was replaced by a new little girl character, Little Audrey, whose inspiration was clear by her Lulu-like voice and manner.

In 1995 the character experienced a resurgence of interest, starring in an all-new animated television series produced for HBO. *Directors were Isadore Sparber, Seymour Kneitel and Bill Tytla.*

*Marjorie H. Buell's popular comic-strip character Little Lulu was turned into a theatrical cartoon series by Max Fleischer in 1944.* (COURTESY: NATIONAL TELEFILM ASSOCIATES)

Technicolor. *A Famous Studios Production released through Paramount Pictures Corporation.*

**Voices**
**Little Lulu:** Mae Questel, Cecil Roy

**1943:** "Eggs Don't Bounce" (Sparber/Dec. 24).

**1944:** "Hullaba-Lulu" (Kneitel/Feb. 25); "Lulu Gets the Birdie" (Sparber/Mar. 31); "Lulu in Hollywood" (Sparber/May 19); "Lucky Lulu" (Kneitel/June 30); "It's Nifty to Be Thrifty" (Kneitel/Aug. 18); "I'm Just Curious" (Kneitel/Sept. 8); "Indoor Outing" (Sparber/Sept. 29); "Lulu at the Zoo" (Sparber/Nov. 17); and "Lulu's Birthday Party" (Sparber/Dec. 29).

**1945:** "Magica-Lulu" (Kneitel/Mar. 2); "Beau Ties" (Kneitel/Apr. 20); "Daffydilly Daddy" (Kneitel/May 25); "Snap Happy" (Tytla/June 22); and "Man's Pest Friend" (Kneitel/Nov. 30).

**1946:** "Bargain Counter Attack" (Sparber/Jan. 11); "Bored of Education" (Tytla/Mar. 1); and "Chick and Double Chick" (Kneitel/Aug. 16).

**1947:** "Musica-Lulu" (Sparber/Jan. 24); "A Scout with the Gout" (Tytla/Mar. 24); "Loose in a Caboose" (Kneitel/May 23); "Cad and Caddy" (Sparber/July 18); "A Bout with a Trout" (Sparber/Oct. 30); "Super Lulu" (Tytla/Nov. 21); and "The Baby Sitter" (Kneitel/Nov. 28).

**1948:** "The Dog Show-Off" (Kneitel/Jan. 30).

**1961:** "Alvin's Solo Flight" (Kneitel/Apr./*Noveltoon*/coproduced by Marjorie H. Buell and William C. Erskine).

**1962:** "Frog's Legs" (Kneitel/Apr./*Comic King*/coproduced by Marjorie H. Buell and William C. Erskine).

## ⊚ LITTLE QUACKER

This lovable, charming duck who grew into a malicious troublemaker became a popular mainstay in Metro-Goldwyn-Mayer's *Tom and Jerry* cartoon series, featured in eight cartoon shorts beginning with 1950's "Little Quacker." Two years lapsed between appearances before the duckling returned to the screen in the 1952 cartoon short, "The Duck Doctor," recast as a comical sidekick for Jerry, a successful formula that was duplicated in 1953's "Just Ducky." The latter was followed by four additional film appearances in the *Tom and Jerry* series: "Downhearted Duckling" (1954); "Southbound Duckling" (1955), the first released in CinemaScope; "That's My Mommy" (1955), the first *Tom and Jerry* film short produced by directors William Hanna and Joseph Barbera; "Happy Go Lucky Duck" (1958); and "The Vanishing Duck" (1958). *Produced and directed by William Hanna and Joseph Barbera. Technicolor. CinemaScope. A Metro-Goldwyn-Mayer Cartoon Production released by Metro-Goldwyn-Mayer.*

**Voices**
**Little Quacker:** Red Coffee

**1950:** "Little Quacker" (with Tom and Jerry, Mama Duck/Jan. 7).

**1952:** "The Duck Doctor" (with Tom and Jerry/Feb. 16).

**1953:** "Just Ducky" (with Tom and Jerry, Mother Duck/Sept. 5).

**1954:** "Downhearted Duckling" (with Tom and Jerry/Nov. 13).

**1955:** "Southbound Duckling" (with Tom and Jerry/Mar. 12/CinemaScope) and "That's My Mommy" (with Tom and Jerry/Nov. 19/CinemaScope/first Tom and Jerry cartoon produced by directors William Hanna and Joseph Barbera).

**1958:** "Happy Go Lucky Duck" (with Tom and Jerry/Jan. 3/working title: "One Quack Mind"/CinemaScope) and "The Vanishing Duck" (with Tom and Jerry, George/May 2/CinemaScope).

## ⊚ LITTLE ROQUEFORT

MGM's Tom and Jerry and Famous Studios' Herman and Katnip preceded this cat-and-mouse tandem—a pesky, pint-size mouse, Little Roquefort, and nemesis cat, Percy—who starred in assorted *Terry-Toons* cartoon "chases" reminiscent of the style and humor first popularized in the *Tom and Jerry* series. Unfortunately, most comparisons of the two series end here. The *Terry-Toons* version ran five years, while MGM's cat-and-mouse stars remained popular for 26 years, winning seven Academy Awards in the process. *Directed by Connie Rasinski, Mannie Davis and Ed Donnelly. Technicolor. A Terry-Toon Cartoons Production released through 20th Century Fox.*

### Voices
**Little Roquefort/Percy the Cat:** Tom Morrison

**1950:** "Cat Happy" (Rasinski/Sept.); and "Mouse and Garden" (Davis/Oct.).

**1951:** "Three Is a Crowd" (Rasinski/Feb.); "Musical Madness" (Donnelly/May); "Seasick Sailors" (Davis/July); "Pastry Panic" (Davis/Oct.); and "The Haunted Cat" (Donnelly/Dec.).

**1952:** "City Slicker" (Davis/Feb.); "Hypnotized" (Davis/June); "Good Mousekeeping" (Davis/Oct.); and "Flop Secret" (Donnelly/Dec.).

**1953:** "Mouse Meets Bird" (Rasinski/Mar.); "Playful Puss" (Davis/May); "Friday the 13th" (Davis/July); and "Mouse Menace" (Donnelly/Sept.).

*Cartoon stars Little Roquefort (pictured) and his nemesis cat, Percy, starred for Terry-Toons in cartoon "chases" reminiscent of MGM's Tom and Jerry. © Viacom International*

**1954:** "Runaway Mouse" (Davis/Jan.); "Prescription for Percy" (Davis/Apr.); and "Cat's Revenge" (Davis/Sept.).

**1955:** "No Sleep for Percy" (Rasinski/Mar. 1).

## ⊚ LOONEY TUNES

*Looney Tunes* were cartoon specials originally produced and animated in the style of Walt Disney's *Silly Symphony* cartoons, featuring popular music and assorted characters to tell a story. By the late 1930s, following structural changes, the series became a stamping ground for many of Warner Bros.' most renowned characters, including Bugs Bunny, Daffy Duck and Porky Pig.

From 1930 to 1933 the series was directed by Rudolf Ising and Hugh Harman, two ex-Disney animators who later joined MGM to head up its new cartoon department. After Harman and Ising's departure, producer Leon Schlesinger named Friz Freleng head director of the series. Freleng had worked alongside both directors since the inception of Warner's cartoon department. He served as chief animator on Harman and Ising's *Bosko* series. Incidentally, Bosko was the *Looney Tunes* series first regular cartoon star.

Beside Bosko, cartoons featured such studio favorites as Babbit and Catstello, Beaky Buzzard, Beans, Bobo, Buddy, Bugs Bunny, Claude Cat, Conrad Cat, Daffy Duck, Elmer Fudd, Foghorn Leghorn, Goofy Gophers, Hippety Hopper, The Honey-Mousers, Hubie and Bertie, Marc Antony, Pepe Le Pew, Ralph Wolf and Sam Sheepdog, Road Runner, Speedy Gonzales, Sylvester and Tweety and the Three Bears. (See individual entries for series episode titles.) *Other series directors included Jack King, Bob Clampett, Norm McCabe, Frank Tashlin, Chuck Jones, Art Davis, Abe Levitow, Maurice Noble, Hawley Pratt, Alex Lovy and Robert McKimson. Black-and-white. Technicolor. A Leon Schlesinger Studios/Warner Bros. Cartoons, Inc./Warner Bros. Pictures, Inc./Warner Bros. Production released by Warner Bros. and Warner Bros. Seven Arts.*

### Voices
Mel Blanc, June Foray, Stan Freberg, Dick Beals, Daws Butler

(The following filmography is made up of *Looney Tunes* that do not feature a major star.)

### *Leon Schlesinger Studios releases*

**1941:** "The Haunted Mouse" (Avery/Feb. 15); and "Joe Glow, the Firefly" (Jones/Mar. 8).

**1942:** "Saps in Chaps" (Freleng/Apr. 11); "Nutty News" (Clampett/May 23); "Hobby Horse-Laffs" (McCabe/June 6); "Gopher Goofy" (McCabe/June 27); "Wacky Blackout" (Clampett/July 11); "The Ducktators" (McCabe/Aug. 1); "Eatin' on the Cuff" (or, The Moth Who Came to Dinner) (Clampett/Aug. 22); "Fox Pop" (Jones/Sept. 5/film title was a spoof of a popular radio program); and "The Hep Cat" (Clampett/Oct. 3/first Technicolor *Looney Tunes*).

**1943:** "Hop and Go" (McCabe/Mar. 27); "Tokio Jokio" (McCabe/May 15); and "Puss N' Booty" (Tashlin/Dec. 11/last black-and-white *Looney Tunes*).

(All the following cartoons were in Technicolor.)

**1944:** "I Got Plenty of Mutton" (Tashlin/Mar. 11); "Angel Puss" (Jones/June 3); and "From Hand to Mouse" (Jones/Aug. 5).

### *Warner Bros. Cartoons, Inc. releases*

**1945:** "Behind the Meat Ball" (Tashlin/Apr. 7).

**1946:** "Of Thee I Sting" (Freleng/Aug. 17).

**1948:** "The Rattled Rooster" (Davis/June 26); "The Shell Shocked Egg" (McKimson/July 10); and "A Horse Fly Fleas" (McKimson/Dec. 13).

**1949:** "Swallow the Leader" (McKimson/Oct. 14).

**1950:** "It's Hummer Time" (McKimson/July 22).

**1951:** "Chow Hound" (Jones/June 16).

**1953:** "A Peck o' Trouble" (McKimson/Mar. 28); "There Auto Be a Law" (McKimson/Jones/June 6); "Easy Peckins" (McKimson/Oct. 17); and "Punch Trunk" (Jones/Dec. 19).

**1954:** "From A to Z-Z-Z-Z" (Jones/Oct. 16/A.A. nominee/voice by Dick Beals).

**1955:** "The Hole Idea" (McKimson/Apr. 16).

**1956:** "Mixed Master" (McKimson/Apr. 14).

**1957:** "Three Little Bops" (Freleng/Jan. 5/narrator: Stan Freberg); and "Go Fly a Kit" (Jones/Feb. 23).

**1958:** "A Waggily Tale" (Freleng/Apr. 26); and "Dog Tales" (McKimson/July 26).

**1959:** "Mouse-Placed Kitten" (McKimson/Jan. 24).

***Warner Bros. Pictures, Inc./Vitagraph releases***

**1960:** "High Note" (Jones/Dec. 3/A.A. nominee).

**1962:** "Martian Through Georgia" (Jones, Levitow/co-director: Noble/Dec. 29).

**1963:** "Now Hear This" (Jones/codirector: Noble/Apr. 27/A.A. nominee).

**1964:** "Señorella and the Glass Huarache" (Pratt/Aug. 1).

***Warner Bros. releases***

**1968:** "Flying Circus" (Lovy/Sept. 14).

## ◎ LOOPY DE LOOP

The indomitable French wolf's broken English caused unending communications gaffes that usually resulted in chaos. Loopy was the first theatrical cartoon series produced by William Hanna and Joseph Barbera for their studio, Hanna-Barbera Productions, which they cofounded after leaving MGM in 1957. Loopy later found new life through syndication of the old shorts to television in the 1960s. *Directed by William Hanna and Joseph Barbera. Technicolor. A Hanna-Barbera Production released through Columbia Pictures.*

*Voices*

**Loopy De Loop:** Daws Butler

**1959:** "Wolf Hounded" (Nov. 5); and "Little Bo Bopped" (Dec. 3).

**1960:** "Tale of a Wolf" (Mar. 3); "Life with Loopy" (Apr. 7); "Creepy Time Pal" (May 19); "Snoopy Loopy" (June 16); "The Do Good Wolf" (July 14); "Here, Kiddie, Kiddie" (Sept. 1); and "No Biz Like Shoe Biz" (Sept. 8).

**1961:** "Count Down Clown" (Jan. 5); "Happy Go Lucky" (Mar. 2); "Two Faced Wolf" (Apr. 6); "This My Ducky Day" (May 4); "Fee Fie Foes" (June 9); "Zoo Is Company" (July 6); "Child Sock-Cology" (Aug. 10); "Catch Meow" (Sept. 14); "Kooky Loopy" (Nov. 16); and "Loopy's Hare-Do" (Dec. 14).

**1962:** "Bungle Uncle" (Jan. 18); "Beef For and After" (Mar. 1); "Swash Buckled" (Apr. 5); "Common Scents" (May 10);

"Bearly Able" (June 28); "Slippery Slippers" (Sept. 7); "Chicken Fraca-See" (Oct. 11); "Rancid Ransom" (Nov. 15); and "Bunnies Abundant" (Dec. 13).

**1963:** "Just a Wolf at Heart" (Feb. 14); "Chicken Hearted Wolf" (Mar. 14); "Whatcha Watchin" (Apr. 18); "A Fallible Fable" (May 16); "Sheep Stealers Anonymous" (June 13); "Wolf in Sheep Dog's Clothing" (July 11); "Not in Nottingham" (Sept. 5); "Drum-Sticked" (Oct. 3); "Bear Up!" (Nov. 7); "Crook Who Cried Wolf" (Dec. 12); and "Habit Rabbit" (Dec. 31).

**1964:** "Raggedy Rug" (Jan. 2); "Elephantastic" (Feb. 6); "Bear Hug" (Mar. 5); "Trouble Bruin" (Sept. 17); "Bear Knuckles" (Oct. 15); and "Habit Troubles" (Nov. 19).

**1965:** "Horse Shoo" (Jan. 7); "Pork Chop Phooey" (Mar. 18); "Crow's Fete" (Apr. 14); and "Big Mouse Take" (June 17).

## ◎ LUNO

The flying horse Luno and his young master Tim relive history and fairy tales through transcendental powers of the great white stallion. *Directed by Connie Rasinski and Arthur Bartsch. Technicolor. A Terrytoons Production released through 20th Century Fox.*

*Voices*

**Luno, the white stallion/Tim, his companion:** Bob McFadden

**1963:** "The Missing Genie" (Rasinski/Apr. 1); and "Trouble in Baghdad" (Rasinski/Sept. 13).

**1964:** "Roc-a-Bye Sinbad" (Bartsch/Jan.); "King Rounder" (Rasinski); "Adventure by the Sea" (Bartsch/July 15); and "The Gold Dust Bandit" (Bartsch/Sept.).

## ◎ MAGGIE AND SAM

Domestic trouble was the basis for comedy misadventures of this husband-and-wife pair who starred briefly in this Walter Lantz series. *Directed by Alex Lovy. Technicolor. A Walter Lantz Production released through Universal Pictures.*

*Voices*

**Maggie:** Grace Stafford; **Sam:** Daws Butler

**1956:** "The Ostrich and I" (Apr. 9) and "The Talking Dog" (Aug. 27).

**1957:** "Fowled Up Party" (Jan. 14).

## ◎ MAMMY-TWO-SHOES

Deliberately hidden from view in earlier films except for her rotund form and ordinary white apron and housedress, this black stereotyped maid costarred as Tom's owner in Metro-Goldwyn-Mayer's Academy Award–winning *Tom and Jerry* cartoon series.

Her name was actually derived from old Disney model sheets, though never actually referred to on film. *Mammy-Two-Shoes* was primarily voiced by actress Lillian Randolph, best remembered for her role as Birdie the maid in *The Great Gildersleeve* radio program in the 1940s. She voiced many other MGM and Walt Disney cartoons, appeared in 18 *Tom and Jerry* shorts in the 1940s and 1950, and made her screen debut in 1940 in their first cartoon and first Oscar nominee, "Puss Gets the Boot," starring Tom as Jasper and Jerry as Jinks.

During her more than two decades on film, Mammy-Two-Shoes became a valued supporting cast member with moviegoers getting occasional glimpses of her physical attributes other than the lower half of her body. Her chin was seen on camera and her entire form is in the distance in the final shot of "Part Time Pal"

(1947). Her entire body was shown in the shadows, and the back of her head got a smack with a frying pan and shovel by Tom and Butch in "Mouse Cleaning" (1948). Two years later, moviegoers finally saw her full figure and face in "Saturday Evening Puss" (1950).

Fans of the *Tom and Jerry* series apparently couldn't stand the suspense of not knowing what Mammy-Two-Shoes looked like. In a 1951 article in the *Hollywood Reporter*, MGM producer Fred Quimby explained: "A young lady, after seeing a *Tom and Jerry* cartoon, inquired about the maid's face, which is never shown. To quote her (and we have it in writing lest there be any doubters among you): 'It gave me the impression that the operators in the booth must be having some sort of party, since every time the maid came on the screen, the only thing I could see was her feet. My curiosity is killing me. Before I go stark, raving mad, please tell me what she looks like.' In this instance, we had an artist draw a special head of the maid to accompany the reply. We also explained that since Tom and Jerry were the stars of the pictures, we did not wish to do anything that might distract attention from them."

Nonetheless, Mammy-Two-Shoes continued to dole out laughs until her last appearance in the 1952 Tom and Jerry short, "Push-Button Kitty." *Directed by William Hanna and Joseph Barbera. Technicolor. A Metro-Goldwyn-Mayer Cartoon Production released by Metro-Goldwyn-Mayer.*

### Voices
**Mammy-Two-Shoes:** Lillian Randolph

**1940:** "Puss Gets the Boot" (with Tom as "Jasper" and Jerry as "Jinks"/Feb. 10/first appearance of Mammy-Two-Shoes/A.A. nominee).

**1941:** "The Midnight Snack" (with Tom and Jerry/July 19).

**1942:** "Fraidy Cat" (with Tom and Jerry/Jan. 17); "Dog Trouble" (with Tom and Jerry/Apr. 1942); and "Puss 'n' Toots" (with Tom and Jerry/May 30).

**1943:** "The Lonesome Mouse" (with Tom and Jerry/May 22).

**1945:** "The Mouse Comes to Dinner" (with Tom and Jerry/May 5/working title: "Mouse to Dinner").

**1947:** "Part Time Pal" (with Tom and Jerry/Mar. 1947); and "A Mouse in the House" (with Tom and Jerry, Butch/Aug. 30).

**1948:** "Old Rockin' Chair Tom" (with Tom and Jerry, Lightnin'/Sept. 18); and "Mouse Cleaning" (with Tom and Jerry/Dec. 11).

**1949:** "Polka-Dot Puss" (with Tom and Jerry/Feb. 26).

**1950:** "Saturday Evening Puss" (with Tom and Jerry/Jan. 14) and "The Framed Cat" (with Tom and Jerry, Butch [Spike]/Oct. 21).

**1951:** "Sleepy-Time Tom" (with Tom and Jerry/May 26) and "Nit-Witty Kitty" (with Tom and Jerry/Oct. 6).

**1952:** "Triplet Trouble" (with Tom and Jerry/Apr. 19); and "Push-Button Kitty" (with Tom and Jerry/Sept. 6).

### ◎ MARC ANTONY
A ferocious, bellowing bulldog is reduced to a softie by an adorable tiny pussycat, Pussyfoot, in this Warner Bros. cartoon series. The characters were created by Chuck Jones. *Directed by Chuck Jones. Technicolor. A Warner Bros. Cartoons, Inc. Production released by Warner Bros.*

### Voices
**Marc Antony/Pussyfoot:** Mel Blanc

### *Additional Voices*
Bea Benadaret

### *Merrie Melodies*

**1952:** "Feed the Kitty" (Feb. 2).

### *Looney Tunes*

**1953:** "Kiss Me Cat" (Feb. 21).

**1958:** "Cat Feud" (Dec 20).

### ◎ MARTIAN MOOCHERS
Created under the reign of legendary animator Ralph Bakshi, supervising director of *Terrytoons* in 1966, these weird little outer space mice wreaked havoc before making their escape in their spaceship in this short-lived series of adventures. *Directed by Bob Kuwahara. Technicolor. A Terrytoons and CBS Films, Inc., Production released through 20th Century Fox.*

**1966:** "Champion Chump" (Apr.); and "The Cowardly Watchdog" (Aug.).

### ◎ MARVIN MARTIAN
This dwarf, super-intelligent being, whose face was kept hidden under an oversize space helmet, zapped his way into the hearts of filmgoers in the 1948 Bugs Bunny cartoon "Haredevil Hare." Warner's animator Chuck Jones created Marvin for the screen, along with his Commander Flyer Saucer X-2 spacecraft, featuring the character in several command performances. Marvin's most memorable appearance was opposite Daffy Duck and Porky Pig in the 1953 classic, "Duck Dodgers in the 24½th Century."

In 1980, following a 17-year absence, Marvin returned to the screen, at least the small screen, in two cartoons: "Spaced-Out Bunny," produced as part of the *Bugs Bunny's Bustin' Out All Over* TV special for CBS, and "Duck Dodgers and the Return of the 24½th Century," the long-awaited sequel to "Duck Dodgers in the 24½th Century." The latter was originally produced for theaters but never released; it made its television debut on *Daffy Duck's Thank-for-Giving Special* on NBC.

In the 1990s, Marvin reappeared in two new *Looney Tunes* cartoon shorts, one produced and directed by Chuck Jones, "Another Froggy Evening" (1995), the sequel to the cult favorite, "One Froggy Evening" (1955), starring Michigan J. Frog, and another directed by Douglas McCarthy, "Marvin Martian in the Third Dimension" (1996), produced in 3-D.

In 2003, also for Warner Bros., Marvin and his Looney Tunes costar K-9 costarred in their first feature-length production, the live-action/animated feature, *Looney Tunes: Back in Action. Directed by Chuck Jones, Maurice Noble, and Douglas McCarthy. Technicolor. A Warner Bros. Cartoons, Inc./Warner Bros. Pictures Inc./Vitagraph/Chuck Jones Film Productions/Warner Bros. Production released by Warner Bros.*

### Voices
**Marvin Martian:** Mel Blanc

### *Looney Tunes*

### *Warner Bros. Cartoons, Inc. releases*

**1948:** "Haredevil Hare" (with Bugs Bunny/Jones/July 24).

**1952:** "The Hasty Hare" (with Bugs Bunny/Jones/June 7).

**1958:** "Hare-Way to the Stars" (with Bugs Bunny/Jones/Mar. 29).

*Chuck Jones Film Productions releases*

**1995:** "Another Froggy Evening" (with Michigan J. Frog/Jones/Sept.).

*Warner Bros. releases*

**1996:** "Marvin Martian in the Third Dimension" (with Daffy Duck, K-9/McCarthy/June/released in 3-D).

*Merrie Melodies*

*Warner Bros. Cartoons, Inc., releases*

**1953:** "Duck Dodgers in the 24½th Century" (with Daffy Duck, Porky Pig/Jones/July 25).

*Warner Bros. Pictures, Inc./Vitagraph releases*

**1963:** "Mad as a Mars Hare" (with Bugs Bunny/Jones, Noble/Oct. 19).

*Warner Bros. releases*

**1980:** "Duck Dodgers and the Return of the 24½th Century" (with Daffy Duck, Porky/Jones).

### ◎ MAW AND PAW

The pug-nosed hillbilly Maw was half the size of her lean, bald husband, Paw. The two characters bore striking resemblances to Marjorie Main and Percy Kilbride, stars of Universal's long-running *Ma and Pa Kettle* film series, on which the cartoon series was based.

Grace Stafford, Walter Lantz's wife and voice of Woody Woodpecker, supplied the voice of Maw. *Directed by Paul J. Smith. Technicolor. A Walter Lantz Production released through Universal Pictures.*

**Voices**
Maw: Grace Stafford; Paw: Dal McKennon

**1953:** "Maw and Paw" (with the Kids and Milfred the Pig/Smith/Aug. 10); and "Plywood Panic" (Smith/Sept. 28).

© 1977 Walter Lantz

*Universal's successful* Ma and Pa Kettle *feature film series inspired this cartoon spinoff,* Maw and Paw, *created by Walter Lantz.* © *Walter Lantz Productions*

**1954:** "Pig in a Pickle" (Smith/Aug. 30).

**1955:** "Paw's Night Out" (Smith/Aug. 16).

### ◎ MEANY, MINY AND MOE

Walter Lantz first introduced these three circus-dressed monkeys as supporting players in an Oswald the Lucky Rabbit cartoon, "Monkey Wretches," in 1935. The characters were so well received that Lantz starred the trio in their own series, his fourth for Universal. Each episode incorporated the broad comedy gags that had made the Three Stooges popular, here with the monkeys acting out stories in pantomime.

Thirteen cartoons were produced between 1936 and 1937, with the first official Meany, Miny and Moe cartoon being "Turkey Dinner," released in November 1936. Lantz cut the number of Oswald cartoons he usually produced in half so he could start production of this new series, costing roughly $8,250 for each episode. Lantz discontinued the series in late 1937. "There just wasn't much else we could do with the characters," he said. *Directed by Walter Lantz. Black-and-white. A Walter Lantz Production released through Universal Pictures.*

**1935:** "Monkey Wretches" (with Oswald the Lucky Rabbit/Nov. 11/*Oswald the Lucky Rabbit* cartoon).

**1936:** "Farming Fools" (with Oswald the Lucky Rabbit/Mar. 25/*Oswald the Lucky Rabbit* cartoon); "Beauty Shoppe" (with Oswald the Lucky Rabbit/Mar. 30/*Oswald the Lucky Rabbit* cartoon); "Turkey Dinner" (Nov. 30); and "Knights for a Day" (Dec. 25).

**1937:** "The Gofers" (Jan. 11); "House of Magic" (Feb. 8); "The Big Race" (Mar. 8); "The Lumber Camp" (Mar. 15); "The Steel Workers" (Apr. 26); "The Stevedores" (May 24); "The Country Store" (July 5); "Fireman's Picnic" (Aug. 16); "The Rest Resort" (Aug. 23); "Ostrich Feathers" (Sept. 6); and "The Air Express" (Sept. 20).

### ◎ MELLO-DRAMAS

First produced by Walter Lantz in 1938 for his studio's *Walter Lantz Cartune Classics* series, these animated 1890s melodrama spoofs evolved into their own short-lived series in 1938. *Directed by Alex Lovy. Black-and-white. A Walter Lantz Production released by Universal Pictures.*

**1938:** "Nellie the Sewing Machine Girl or Honest Hearts and Willing Hands" (Apr. 11/*Cartune Classics* cartoon); and "Nellie the Indian's Chief's Daughter" (June 6/*Cartune Classics* cartoon).

**1939:** "Nellie of the Circus" (June 19/working title: "Under the Big Top"); and "The Bird on Nellie's Hat" (June 19/working title: "The Bird on Nellie's Cap").

### ◎ MERLIN THE MAGIC MOUSE

Reminiscent of W.C. Fields—even sounding like the great bulbous-nosed comedian—Merlin the Magic Mouse was the second new cartoon creation by Alex Lovy for Warner Bros.' animation department after its reopening in 1967. Stories were based on the globe-trotting adventures of the mouse, who never made a lasting impression on filmgoers and was quickly retired after only five film appearances. Larry Storch (of TV's *F Troop* fame) provided the voice of Merlin in all but one cartoon, that being the first: 1967's "Merlin the Magic Mouse" (voiced by Daws Butler). *Directed by Alex Lovy and Robert McKimson. Technicolor. A Warner Bros. Production released by Warner Bros. Seven Arts.*

**Voices**
Merlin the Magic Mouse: Larry Storch, Daws Butler

*Merrie Melodies*

**1967:** "Merlin the Magic Mouse" (Lovy/Nov. 18).

**1968:** "Feud with a Dude" (Lovy/May 25).

**1969:** "Shamrock and Roll" (McKimson/June 28).

*Looney Tunes*

**1968:** "Hocus Pocus Pow Wow" (Lovy/Jan. 13).

**1969:** "Fistic Mystic" (McKimson/Mar. 29).

## ⊚ MERRIE MELODIES

Directors Rudolf Ising and Hugh Harman, two former Disney animators, produced independently through Warner Bros. a series based on popular melodies of that era. Leon Schlesinger later served as producer when Harman and Ising left Warner in 1933 to lend their talent to studio rival MGM, which was entering the cartoon field for the first time.

The earliest picture in the series made use of Abe Lyman's Recording Orchestra on soundtracks, playing "whoopee tunes" of the day, like "Smile, Darn Ya Smile" and "Freddie the Freshman." Other initial series entries revolved around "period" subjects—the vaudeville stage, the college football craze, and so on—and spot references to popular culture and current trends.

In the beginning, the series' closest thing to a star was Goopy Geer, a wisecracking entertainer—"part comedian, part musician and part dancer"—inspired by vaudeville showmen of that period. Throughout its history, the series featured a vast array of major and less notable cartoon stars and miscellaneous one-shot characters.

The series' stars were Babbit and Catstello, Beaky Buzzard, Bobo, Bunny and Claude, Bugs Bunny, Bunny and Claude, Charlie Dog, Claude Cat, Conrad Cat, Cool Cat, Daffy Duck, Elmer Fudd, Foxy, Goofy Gophers, Goopy Geer, Hippety Hopper, Hubie and Bertie, Inki, Marc Antony, Merlin the Magic Mouse, Pepe Le Pew, Piggy, Ralph Phillips, Rapid Rabbit, Ralph Wolf and Sam Sheepdog, the Road Runner and Coyote, Speedy Gonzales, Sylvester, The Three Bears, Tweety and Two Curious Dogs. (See individual entries for aforementioned characters for episodic listings.) *Besides Harman and Ising, series directors included Tex Avery, Bernard Brown, Bob Clampett, Cal Dalton, Art Davis, Earl Duvall, Friz Freleng, Ben Hardaway, Chuck Jones, Abe Levitow, Alex Lovy, Frank Marsales, Robert McKimson, Ken Mundie, Tom Palmer, Frank Tashlin, Rich Moore, Dan Povenmire, Peter Shin and Bill Kopp. Black-and-white. Technicolor. A Hugh Harman-Rudolf Ising/Vitaphone Pictures/Leon Schlesinger Studios/Warner Bros. Cartoons, Inc./Warner Bros. Pictures Inc./Vitagraph/Warner Bros. Production released by Warner Bros.*

*Voices*

Mel Blanc, Pinto Colvig, Bea Benadaret, June Foray, Daws Butler

**Additional Voices**

Vivian Dandrige, Tex Avery, Leslie Barrings

(The following filmography is comprised of "Merrie Melodies" that do not feature major Warner cartoon stars.)

**Hugh Harmon-Rudolf Ising releases**

**1931:** "Red-Headed Baby" (Ising/Dec. 26).

**1932:** "Pagan Moon" (Ising/Jan. 23); "Freddy the Freshman" (Ising/Feb. 20); "Crosby! Columbo and Vallee" (Ising/Mar. 19); "It's Got Me Again" (Ising/May 14/A.A. nominee); "I Love a Parade" (Ising/Aug. 6); "You're Too Careless with Your Kisses"

(Ising/Sept. 10); "I Wish I Had Wings" (Ising/Oct. 15); "A Great Big Bunch of You" (Ising/Nov. 12); and "Three's a Crowd" (Ising/Dec. 10).

**1933:** "The Shanty Where Santa Lives" (Ising/Jan. 7); "One Step Ahead of My Shadow" (Ising/Feb. 4); "Young and Healthy" (Ising/Mar. 4); "The Organ Grinder" (Ising/Apr. 8); "Wake Up the Gypsy in Me" (Ising/May 13); "I Like Mountain Music" (Ising/June 13); "Shuffle Off to Buffalo" (Freleng/July 8); "The Dish Ran Away with the Spoon" (Ising/Aug. 5); "We're in the Money" (Ising/Aug. 26); "I've Got to Sing a Torch Song" (Palmer/Sept. 23); and "Sittin' on a Backyard Fence" (Duvall/Sept. 16).

*Vitaphone Pictures releases*

**1934:** "Pettin' in the Park" (Brown/Jan. 27); "Honeymoon Hotel" (Duvall/Feb. 17/Cinecolor); "Beauty and the Beast" (Freleng/Apr. 14/Cinecolor); "Those Were Wonderful Days" (Brown/Apr. 26); "Goin' to Heaven on a Mule" (Freleng/May 19); "How Do I Know It's Sunday" (Freleng/June 9); "Why Do I Dream Those Dreams?" (Freleng/June 30); "The Girl at the Ironing Board" (Freleng/Aug. 23); "The Miller's Daughter" (Freleng/Oct. 13); "Shake Your Powder Puff" (Freleng/Oct. 17); "Those Beautiful Dames" (Freleng/Nov. 10/two-strip Technicolor); and "Pop Goes Your Heart" (Freleng/Dec. 18/two-strip Technicolor).

**1935:** "Mr. and Mrs. Is the Name" (Freleng/Jan. 19/two-strip Technicolor); "Rhythm in Bow" (Hardaway/Feb. 1/last *Merrie Melodies* in black-and-white; following were all produced in two-strip Technicolor); "Country Boy" (with Peter Rabbit/Freleng/Feb. 9/); "Along Flirtation Walk" (Freleng/Apr. 6); "My Green Fedora" (with Peter Rabbit/Freleng/May 4); "Into Your Dance" (Freleng/June 8); "Country Mouse" (Freleng/July 13); "The Merry Old Soul" (Freleng/Aug. 17); "The Lady in Red" (Freleng/Sept. 7); "Little Dutch Plate" (Freleng/Oct. 19); "Billboard Frolics" (Freleng/Nov. 9); and "Flowers for Madame" (Freleng/Nov. 20).

(All in Technicolor.)

**1936:** "I Wanna Play House" (Freleng/Jan. 11); "The Cat Came Back" (Freleng/Feb. 8); "Miss Glory" (Avery/Mar. 7); "I'm a Big Shot Now" (Freleng/Apr. 11); "Let It Be Me" (Freleng/May 2); "I Love to Take Orders from You" (Avery/May 18); "Bingo Crosbyana" (Freleng/May 30); "When I Yoo Hoo" (Freleng/June 27); "I Love to Singa" (Avery/July 18); "Sunday Go to Meetin' Time" (Freleng/Aug. 8); "At Your Service Madame" (Freleng/Aug. 29); "Toytown Hall" (Freleng/Sept. 19); "Boulevardier from the Bronx" (Freleng/Oct. 10); "Don't Look Now" (Avery/Nov. 7); and "The Coo Coo Nut Grove" (Freleng/Nov. 28).

**1937:** "He Was Her Man" (Freleng/Jan. 2); "Pigs Is Pigs" (Freleng/Jan. 30); "I Only Have Eyes for You" (Avery/Mar. 6); "The Fella with the Fiddle" (Freleng/Mar. 27); "She Was an Acrobat's Daughter" (Freleng/Apr. 10); "Ain't We Got Fun" (Avery/Apr. 17); "Clean Pastures" (Freleng/May 22); "Uncle Tom's Bungalow" (Avery/June 5); "Streamlined Greta Green" (Freleng/June 19); "Sweet Sioux" (Freleng/June 26); "Plenty of Money and You" (Freleng/July 31); "A Sunbonnet Blue" (Avery/Aug. 21); "Speaking of the Weather" (Tashlin/Sept. 4); "Dog Daze" (Freleng/Sept. 18); "I Wanna Be a Sailor" (Avery/Sept. 25); "The Lyin' Mouse" (Freleng/Oct. 16); "The Woods Are Full of Cuckoos" (Tashlin/Dec. 4); and "September in the Rain" (Freleng/Dec. 18).

**1938:** "My Little Buckaroo" (Freleng/Jan. 29); "Jungle Jitters" (Freleng/Feb. 19); "The Sneezing Weasel" (Avery/Mar. 12); "A Star Is Hatched" (Freleng/Apr. 2); "The Penguin Parade" (Avery/

Apr. 16); "Now That Summer Is Gone" (Tashlin/May 14); "The Isle of Pingo Pongo" (Avery/May 28); "Katnip Kollege" (Hardaway, Dalton/June 11); "Have You Got Any Castles" (Tashlin/June 25); "Love and Curses" (Hardaway, Dalton/July 9); "The Major Lied 'Till Dawn" (Tashlin/Aug. 13); "Cracked Ice" (Tashlin/Sept. 10); "Little Pancho Vanilla" (Tashlin/Oct. 8); "You're an Education" (Tashlin/Nov. 5); "The Night Watchman" (Jones/Nov. 19); and "The Mice Will Play" (Avery/Dec. 31).

**1939:** "Robinhood Makes Good" (Jones/Feb. 11); "Gold Rush Daze" (Hardaway, Dalton/Feb. 25); "Bars and Stripes Forever" (Hardaway, Dalton/Apr. 8); "Thugs with Dirty Mugs" (Avery/May 6); "Hobo Gadget Band" (Hardaway, Dalton/June 17); "Believe It or Else" (Avery/June 25); "Dangerous Dan McFoo" (Avery/July 15); "Snowman's Land" (Jones/July 29); and "Detouring America" (Avery/Aug. 26/A.A. nominee).

### Leon Schlesinger Studios releases

**1939:** "Sioux Me" (Hardaway, Dalton/Sept. 9); "Land of the Midnight Fun" (Avery/Sept. 23); "The Good Egg" (Jones/Oct. 21); "Fresh Fish" (Avery/Nov. 4); "Fagin's Freshman" (Hardaway, Dalton/Nov. 18); and "Screwball Football" (Avery/Dec. 16).

**1940:** "The Early Worm Gets the Bird" (Avery/Jan. 13); "Mighty Hunters" (Jones/Jan. 27); "Busy Bakers" (Hardaway, Dalton/Feb. 10); "Cross Country Detours" (Avery/Mar. 16); "The Bear's Tale" (Avery/Apr. 13); "A Gander at Mother Goose" (Avery/May 25); "Tom Thumb in Trouble" (Jones/June 8); "Circus Today" (Avery/June 22); "Little Blabbermouse" (Freleng/July 6); "Ghost Wanted" (Jones/Aug. 10); "Ceiling Hero" (Avery/Aug. 24); "Malibu Beach Party" (Freleng/Sept. 14); "Stage Fright" (Jones/Sept. 28); "Holiday Highlights" (Avery/Oct. 12); "Wacky Wildlife" (Avery/Nov. 9); "Of Fox and Hounds" (Avery/Dec. 7); and "Shop, Look and Listen" (Freleng/Dec. 21).

**1941:** "The Fighting 69½th" (Freleng/Jan. 18); "The Crackpot Quail" (Avery/Feb. 15); "The Cat's Tale" (Freleng/Mar. 1); "Goofy Groceries" (Clampett/Mar. 29); "The Trial of Mister Wolf" (Freleng/Apr. 26); "Farm Frolics" (Clampett/May 10); "Hollywood Steps Out" (with The Three Stooges, Clark Gable, Bing Crosby, Jimmy Stewart, William Powell, Peter Lorre, Groucho Marx, Harpo Marx and Buster Keaton caricatures/Avery/May 24); "The Wacky Worm" (Freleng/June 21); "Aviation Vacation" (Avery/Aug. 2); "Sport Chumpions" (Freleng/Aug. 16); "Snowtime for Comedy" (Jones/Aug. 30); "Bug Parade" (Avery/Oct. 11); "Rookie Revue" (Freleng/Oct. 25); "Saddle Silly" (Jones/Nov. 8); "The Cagey Canary" (Avery, Clampett/Nov. 22); and "Rhapsody in Rivets" (Freleng/Dec. 6/A.A. nominee).

**1942:** "Hop, Skip, and a Chump" (with Laurel and Hardy–like crows/Freleng/Jan. 3); "Aloha Hooey" (Avery/Jan. 30); "Crazy Cruise" (Avery, Clampett/Mar. 14/with Bugs Bunny cameo); "Horton Hatches the Egg" (Clampett/Apr. 11/based on the story by Dr. Seuss); "Dog Tired" (Jones/Apr. 25); "The Draft Horse" (Jones/May 9); "Lights Fantastic" (Freleng/May 23); "Double Chaser" (Freleng/June 27); "Foney Fables" (Freleng/Aug. 1); "The Dover Boys" at Pimento University or the Rivals of Roquefort Hall (Jones/Sept. 10); "The Sheepish Wolf" (Freleng/Oct. 17); and "Ding Dog Daddy" (Freleng/Dec. 5).

**1943:** "Coal Black and de Sebben Dwarfs" (Clampett/Jan. 16/So White voiced by Vivian Dandrige); "Pigs in a Polka" (Freleng/Feb. 2/A.A. nominee); "The Fifth-Column Mouse" (Freleng/Mar. 6); "Flop Goes the Weasel" (Jones/Mar. 20); "Greetings Bait" (Freleng/May 15/A.A. nominee); "Tin Pan Alley Cats" (Clampett/July 17); "Hiss and Make Up" (Freleng/Sept. 11); and "Fin'n Catty" (Jones/Oct. 23).

**1944:** "Meatless Flyday" (Freleng/Jan. 29/spider voiced by Tex Avery); "The Weakly Reporter" (Jones/Mar. 25); and "Russian Rhapsody" (Clampett/May 20).

### Warner Bros. Cartoons, Inc. releases

**1944:** "Goldilocks and the Jivin' Bears" (Freleng/Sept. 2).

**1945:** "Fresh Airedale" (Jones/Aug. 25).

**1946:** "Holiday for Shoestrings" (with Laurel and Hardy elves/Freleng/Feb. 23); "Quentin Quail" (Jones/Mar. 2); "Hollywood Canine Canteen" (with Edward G. Robinson, Jimmy Durante, Laurel and Hardy, Bing Crosby, Bob Hope, Jerry Colonna, Abbott and Costello, Blondie and Dagwood, Joe Besser and Harry James caricatures in the images of dogs/McKimson/Apr. 20); "The Eager Beaver" (Jones/July 13); and "Fair and Worm-er" (Jones/Sept. 28).

**1947:** "The Gay Anties" (Freleng/Feb. 15); and "The Foxy Duckling" (Davis/Aug. 23).

**1948:** "A Hide, a Slick, and a Chick" (with Elmo, Daisy Lou, Blackie, Hernan/Davis/Mar. 13); "Bone Sweet Bone" (with Shep Professor, Bulldog/Davis/May 22/Cinecolor); "Dough Ray Me-Ow" (with Heathcliff, Louie/Davis/Aug. 14); "A Horse Fly Fleas" (McKimson/Dec. 13/Cinecolor).

**1951:** "A Fox in a Fix" (McKimson/Jan. 20); "Corn Plastered" (McKimson/Mar. 3); "Early to Bet" (McKimson/May 12); and "Sleepy Time Possum" (McKimson/Nov. 3).

**1952:** "Kiddin' the Kitten" (with Dodsworth/McKimson/Apr. 5); and "The Turn-Tale Wolf" (McKimson/June 28).

**1953:** "Much Ado about Nutting" (Jones/May 23).

**1954:** "Wild Wife" (McKimson/Feb. 20); "The Oily American" (with Moe Hican/McKimson/July 10); and "Goo Goo Goliath" (Freleng/Sept. 18).

**1955:** "Pizzicato Pussycat" (Freleng/Jan. 1); and "One Froggy Evening" (with Michigan J. Frog/Jones/Dec. 31).

**1956:** "Rocket-Bye Baby" (Jones/Aug. 4); and "Two Crows from Tacos" (Freleng/Nov. 24).

**1958:** "To Itch His Own" (with Mighty Angelo/Jones/June 28).

**1959:** "Mouse-Placed Kitten" (with Kitten, Matilda, Clyde/McKimson/Jan. 24); "The Mouse that Jack Built" (with Jack Benny, Rochester, Mary Livingston and Don Wilson as mice/McKimson/Apr. 4/voices performed by Jack Benny, Mary Livingston, Rochester, Don Wilson and Mel Blanc); and "Unnatural History" (Levitow/Nov. 14).

### Warner Bros. releases

**1960:** "Wild Wild World" (McKimson/Feb. 27).

### Warner Bros. Pictures, Inc./Vitagraph releases

**1961:** "The Mouse on 57th Street" (Jones/Feb. 25); and "Nelly's Folly" (with Nelly the Giraffe/Jones, Noble, Levitow/Dec. 30/A.A. nominee).

**1963:** "I Was a Teenage Thumb" (with George Ebeneezer Thumb, Ralph K. Merlin Jr., King Arthur/Jones, Noble/Jan. 19).

**1964:** "Bartholomew Versus the Wheel" (McKimson/Feb. 29).

*Warner Bros. releases*

**1968:** "Chimp & Zee" (with Chimp Zee/Lovy/Oct. 12).

**1969:** "Rabbit Stews and Rabbits Too" (with Rapid Rabbit/McKimson/June 7).

**2005:** "Meet Me in Chicago" (with Cow/Moore, Povenmire, Shin, Kopp).

## ◉ MERRY MAKERS

This was the last cartoon series launched by Paramount's Famous Studios. James "Shamus" Culhane produced and directed each cartoon short, shaped around everyday situations and starring various animated characters. Paramount shut down its cartoon department after the 1967 season, the same year *Merry Makers* was created.

*Directed by James "Shamus" Culhane. Technicolor. A Famous Studios Production released through Paramount Picture Corporation.*

**1967:** "Think or Sink" (Mar.); "Halt, Who Grows There?" (May); "From Orbit to Obit" (June); and "Forget-Me-Nuts" (Aug.).

## ◉ MGM CARTOONS

The Metro-Goldwyn-Mayer lot was known for more than just producing its share of big-budget musicals and epic films. The studio also produced a number of quality, theatrical sound cartoons. In the early 1930s Hugh Harman and Rudolf Ising produced and directed MGM cartoons, and in the 1940s the studio produced a series of cartoons featuring major stars like Tom and Jerry, Droopy and Barney Bear. During the cartoon division's halcyon days it also produced an assortment of cartoons featuring some recurring and lesser-known characters that, for the most part, were equally entertaining. The following is a listing of the studio's miscellaneous cartoons that were released under the studio's trademark MGM lion logo. (For MGM series entries, see *Barney Bear, Captain and the Kids, Droopy, George and Junior, Happy Harmonies, Screwy Squirrel, Spike and Tyke, Tom and Jerry* and Tex Avery, Hugh Harman and Rudolf Ising listings.) *Produced by Hugh Harman, Rudolf Ising, Fred Quimby, John Sutherland, William Hanna, Joseph Barbera, Chuck Jones, Les Goldman and Frank Tashlin. A Metro-Goldwyn-Mayer Cartoon Production released by Metro-Goldwyn-Mayer.*

**1937:** "Little Buck Cheeser" (with Little Cheeser/Ising/Dec. 15).

**1939:** (Sepia-tone) "Jitterbug Follies" (with J.R. the Wonder Dog, Count Screwloose/Gross/Feb. 25); "Wanted: No Master" (with J.R. the Wonder Dog, Count Screwloose/Gross/Mar. 18); (All the following cartoons were produced in Technicolor) "The Little Goldfish" (Ising/Apr. 15); "Art Gallery" (Harman/May 13); "Goldilocks and the Three Bears" (with Pappa Bear, Momma Bear and Junior Bear/Harman/July 15); "The Bookworm" (Freleng/Aug. 26); "One Mother's Family" (Ising/Sept. 30); "The Blue Danube" (Harman/Oct. 28); "Peace on Earth" (Harman/Dec. 9/A.A. nominee; Nobel Peace Prize nominee; *Parents Magazine* medal winner); and "The Mad Maestro" (Harman/Dec. 30).

**1940:** "Home on the Range" (Ising/Mar. 23); "A Rainy Day" (with Pappa Bear, Momma Bear and Junior Bear/Harman/Apr. 20); "Swing Social" (Hanna, Barbera/May 18); "Tom Turkey and His Harmonica Humdingers" (Harman/June 8); "The Milky Way" (with Three Little Kittens/Ising/June 22/A.A. winner); "The Bookworm Turns" (Harman/July 20); "Romeo in Rhythm" (Ising/Aug. 10); "Papa Gets the Bird" (with Pappa Bear, Momma Bear and Junior Bear/Harman/Sept. 7); "The Homeless Flea" (Ising/Oct. 12); "Gallopin' Gals" (Hanna, Barbera/Oct. 26); "The Lonesome Stranger" (with the Lonesome Stranger, Sliver/Harman/Nov. 23); and "Mrs. Ladybug" (Ising/Dec. 21).

**1941:** "Abdul the Bulbul-Ameer" (Harman/Feb. 22); "The Little Mole" (Harman/Apr. 5); "The Goose Goes South" (Hanna, Barbera/Apr. 26); "Dance of the Weed" (Ising/June 7); "The Alley Cat" (Harman/July 5); "Little Cesario" (Allen/Aug. 30); "Officer Pooch" (Hanna, Barbera/Sept. 6); and "The Field Mouse" (Harman/Dec. 27).

**1942:** "The Hungry Wolf" (Harman/Feb. 21); "The First Swallow" (Brewer/Mar. 14); "Little Gravel Voice" (Ising/May 16); "Bats in the Belfry" (Brewer/July 4); "Blitz Wolf" (with the Wolf/Avery/Aug. 22/A.A. nominee); "The Early Bird Dood It" (Avery/Aug. 29); and "Chips off the Old Block" (Allen/Sept. 12).

**1943:** "The Boy and the Wolf" (Ising/Apr. 24); "Red Hot Riding Hood" (with the Wolf, Red/Avery/May 8); "Who Killed Who?" (Avery/June 19); "One Ham's Family" (with the Wolf, Junior Pig/Avery/Aug. 14); "War Dogs" (with Private Smiley/Hanna, Barbera/Oct. 9); "Stork's Holiday" (Gordon/Oct. 23); and "What Buzzin' Buzzard?" (Avery/Nov. 27).

**1944:** "Innertube Antics" (Gordon/Jan. 22/working titles: "Strange Innertube" and "Innertube Interlude"); "Batty Baseball" (Avery/Apr. 22); and "The Tree Surgeon" (Gordon/June 3).

**1945:** "Jerky Turkey" (Avery/Apr. 7); and "Swing Swift Cinderella" (with the Wolf, Cinderella, Fairy Godmother/Avery/Aug. 25).

**1946:** "The Hick Chick" (Avery/June 15).

**1947:** "Uncle Tom's Cabana" (Avery/June 19); and "King-Size Canary" (Avery/Dec. 6).

**1948:** "Make Mine Freedom" (Hanna, Barbera/Feb. 25); "What Price Fleadom" (Avery/Mar. 20); "Little 'Tinker" (Avery/June 15); and "The Cat that Hated People" (Avery/Nov. 12).

**1949:** "Bad Luck Blackie" (Avery/Jan. 22); "The House of Tomorrow" (Avery/June 11); "Doggone Tired" (Avery/July 30); and "Little Rural Riding Hood" (Avery/Sept. 17).

**1950:** "Why Play Leapfrog?" (produced by John Sutherland for Harding College); "The Cuckoo Clock" (Avery/June 10); and "The Peachy Cobbler" (Avery/Dec. 9).

**1951:** "Symphony in Slang" (Avery/June 6); "Meet Joe King" (produced by John Sutherland for Harding College/Sept. 13); "Car of Tomorrow" (Avery/Sept. 22); "Inside Cackle Corners" (produced by John Sutherland for Harding College/Nov. 13); and "Fresh Laid Plans" (produced by John Sutherland for Harding College/Dec. 11).

**1952:** "Magical Maestro" (Avery/Feb. 9); and "One Cab's Family" (Avery/May 15).

**1953:** "Little Johnny Jet" (Avery/Apr. 18/A.A. nominee); and "T.V. of Tomorrow" (Avery/June 6).

**1954:** "Billy Boy" (Avery/May 8); "The Farm of Tomorrow" (Avery/Sept. 18); and "Flea Circus" (Avery/Nov. 6).

**1955:** "Field and Scream" (Avery/Apr. 30); "The First Bad Man" (Avery/Sept. 30); "Cellbound" (with Spike/Avery, Lah/Nov. 25); "Good Will to Men" (Hanna, Barbera/Dec. 23/A.A. nominee).

**1957:** "Cat's Meow" (Avery/Jan. 25).

**1965:** "The Dot and the Line" (Jones, Noble/Dec. 31/A.A. winner).

**1967:** "The Bear That Wasn't" (Jones, Noble/Dec. 31).

## ⊚ MICHIGAN J. FROG

This high-stepping song-and-dance amphibian, known today to television audiences as the corporate mascot of the WB Television Network, was the brainchild of legendary animator Chuck Jones. Jones introduced him as a nameless frog in the 1956 *Merrie Melodies* cartoon "One Froggy Evening," considered a cult classic in which the top-hatted frog is exploited for his dancing talent and singing of "Hello, My Ragtime Gal."

In 1995, after forming a new animation studio to produce theatrical cartoon shorts for his former studio, Jones directed a sequel to the original masterpiece, entitled, what else, "Another Froggy Evening." The short continues the story of the mysterious amphibian with a beautiful voice who refuses to sing in public. Jeff McCarthy supplied the crooning in the sequel (following this gig he starred on Broadway as the Beast in the stage rendition of Disney's *Beauty and the Beast*). The film was originally scheduled to be released nationwide with the Batman sequel, *Batman Forever*, but Warner Bros. decided not to release it. The cartoon instead made its premiere at the Telluride Film Festival in September 1995. *Directed by Chuck Jones. Technicolor. A Warner Bros. Cartoons, Inc./Chuck Jones Film Productions/Warner Bros. Production released by Warner Bros.*

### Voices
**Michigan J. Frog:** Jeff McCarthy

**1956:** "One Froggy Evening (Dec. 31/*Merrie Melodies*).

**1995:** "Another Froggy Evening" (with Marvin Martian/Sept.).

## ⊚ MICKEY MOUSE

Button-eyed, mischievous Mickey Mouse has been a lovable world-renowned character for more than 60 years. New generations of television viewers continue to rediscover the superstar rodent through reruns of *The Mickey Mouse Club* and Mickey Mouse cartoons.

In the early cartoons, Mickey displayed some of the same physical features as Walt Disney's Oswald the Rabbit character: He wore short, button-down pants and pure-white, four-finger gloves. Disney and veteran animator Ub Iwerks first drew the soft-talking Mickey, and Disney himself supplied the voice through the late 1940s.

In 1928, inspired by the enormous success of *The Jazz Singer*, the first talking picture, which had been released the previous year, Disney cashed in on the opportunity by providing something unique—the first synchronized sound cartoon, "Steamboat Willie," starring Mickey as the captain of his own steamboat.

The cartoon came about following initial tests by Disney and his staff. He first screened a scene using synchronized sound—a process renovated by animator Ub Iwerks—when the film was half finished. The effect of the screening was "nothing less than electric," Disney once said. The reaction was duplicated months later when audiences witnessed this latest innovation for the first time on theater screens across the country.

This landmark film changed the course of cartoon animation, and Disney immediately added soundtracks to two previously produced silent Mickey Mouse cartoons, "Plane Crazy" and "Gallopin' Gaucho," releasing both films with music arranged and composed by Carl Stalling, who later became Warner Bros.' musical director.

Mickey experienced unprecedented worldwide fame in the years ahead, spawning hundreds of thousands of licensed merchandise items, such as games and toys. (The first Mickey Mouse stuffed doll was designed by animator Bob Clampett, then a high school student, and his enterprising aunt, Charlotte Clark.) In fact, in 1932 Disney even received a special Academy Award in recognition of Mickey's creation and resulting impact on the cartoon industry.

Supporting characters in the series were Minnie Mouse, Peg Leg Pete, Horace Horsecollar and Clarabelle Cow, each appearing in several episodes during the life of the series.

In 1990 Mickey Mouse starred along with pals Goofy, Donald Duck and Pluto in an all-new 35-minute featurette, *The Prince and the Pauper*, based on the original Mark Twain tale. The film was simultaneously released with the full-length Disney feature *The Rescuers Down Under*. Animator George Scribner, who had worked with legendary animators Chuck Jones and Ralph Bakshi (on the features *American Pop* and *Lord of the Rings* and at Hanna-Barbera (on the feature *Heidi's Song*) and Disney (on the features *The Black Cauldron* and *The Great Mouse Detective*), directed the film.

Following a five-year absence, Mickey returned to the screen in an all-new cartoon adventure, "Runaway Brain," in which he encounters a Frankenstein-like mad scientist who switches his brain with that of his monster creation. It was Mickey's 119th cartoon short and his first in 42 years. The seven-minute cartoon opened with the live-action feature, *A Kid in King Arthur's Court.* Mickey was redesigned for the occasion by supervising animator Andreas Deja and his fellow animators (so was costar Minnie Mouse, who had a retro makeover; the film also featured Pluto). They reviewed Mickey's other short films and archival "model sheets," 67 years' worth of drawings, before settling on the personality and look Mickey had around 1941 in films such as "The Nifty Nineties." Wayne Allwine, who took over as the voice of Mickey in 1983, provided Mickey's voice characterization, with wife Russi Taylor as Minnie and Kelsey Grammer as the mad scientist. The short was produced by Ron Tippe and directed by Chris Bailey. *Directors were Walt Disney, Wilfred Jackson, Bert Gillett, David Hand, Ben Sharpsteen, Hamilton Luske, Pinto Colvig, Walt Pfeiffer, Ed Penner, Jack King, Dick Huemer, Bill Roberts, Clyde Geronimi, Riley Thomson, Charles Nichols, Jack Hannah, Milt Schaffer, Burny Mattinson, George Scribner and Chris Bailey. Black-and-white. Technicolor. A Walt Disney Production released through Celebrity Pictures, Columbia Pictures, United Artists, RKO Radio Pictures and Buena Vista Pictures.*

### Voices
**Mickey Mouse:** Walt Disney (to 1947), Jim MacDonald (1947–83), Wayne Allwine (1983– ); **Minnie Mouse:** Marcellite Garner (to 1940), Thelma Boardman (1940), Ruth Clifford (after 1942), Russi Taylor

### *Celebrity Pictures releases*

**1928:** "Plane Crazy" (with Minnie Mouse/Disney/May as a silent cartoon/released in 1929 in sound); "Gallopin' Gaucho" (Disney/August as a silent cartoon/released in 1929 in sound); and "Steamboat Willie" (with Minnie Mouse, Pegleg Pete/Disney/Nov. 18/first sound cartoon).

**1929:** "The Barn Dance" (with Minnie Mouse, Pegleg Pete/Disney/Mar. 14); "The Opry House" (with Kat Nipp/Disney/Mar. 28); "When the Cat's Away" (with Minnie Mouse, Kat Nipp/Disney/Apr. 11); "The Barnyard Battle" (with Pegleg Pete/Disney/Apr. 25); "The Plow Boy" (with Minnie Mouse, Horace Horsecollar, Clarabelle Cow/Disney/May 9); "The Karnival Kid" (with Minnie Mouse, Kat Nipp, Horace Horsecollar, Clarabelle Cow/Disney/May 23); "Mickey's Choo-Choo" (with Minnie Mouse, Clarabelle Cow/Disney/June 20); "Mickey's Follies" (with Minnie Mouse, Patricia Pig/Jackson/June 26); "The Jazz Fool" (with Horace Horsecollar/Disney/July 5); "The Haunted House" (Disney/Aug. 1); "Wild Waves" (with Minnie Mouse/Gillett/Aug. 15); and "Jungle Rhythm" (Disney/Nov. 15).

*Columbia Pictures releases*
(The studio took over distributorship of all previous films as well as new releases.)

**1930:** "The Barnyard Concert" (with Horace Horsecollar, Clarabelle Cow/Disney/Mar. 3); "Just Mickey" (Disney/Mar. 14/ formerly "Fiddlin' Around"); "The Cactus Kid" (with Minnie Mouse, Pegleg Pete, Horace Horsecollar/Disney/Apr. 11); "The Shindig" (with Minnie Mouse, Horace Horsecollar, Clarabelle Cow and Patricia Pig/Gillett/July 11); "The Fire Fighters" (with Minnie Mouse, Horace Horsecollar/Gillett/Aug. 6); "The Chain Gang" (with Pluto, Pegleg Pete/Gillett/Aug. 18); "The Gorilla Mystery" (with Minnie Mouse, Beppo the Gorilla/Gillett/Oct. 1); "The Picnic" (with Minnie Mouse, Pluto as "Rover"/Gillett/Nov. 14); and "Pioneer Days" (with Minnie Mouse, Horace Horsecollar/ Gillett/Dec. 10).

**1931:** "The Birthday Party" (with Minnie Mouse, Horace Horsecollar, Clarabelle Cow and Clara Cluck/Gillett/Jan. 6); "Traffic Troubles" (with Minnie Mouse, Percy Pig and Pegleg Pig/Gillett/Mar. 20); "The Castaway" (Jackson/Apr. 6); "The Moose Hunt" (with Pluto/Gillett/May 8); "The Delivery Boy" (with Minnie Mouse/Gillett/June 15); "Mickey Steps Out" (with Minnie Mouse, Pluto/Gillett/June 22); "Blue Rhythm" (with Minnie Mouse, Clarabelle Cow, Horace Horsecollar and Pluto/ Gillett/Aug. 8); "Fishin' Around" (with Pluto/Gillett/Sept. 14); "The Barnyard Broadcast" (with Minnie Mouse, Clarabelle Cow and Horace Horsecollar/Gillett/Oct. 19); "The Beach Party" (with Minnie Mouse, Clarabelle Cow, Horace Horsecollar and Pluto/ Gillett/Nov. 4); "Mickey Cuts Up" (with Minnie Mouse, Pluto/ Gillett/Dec. 2); and "Mickey's Orphans" (with Minnie Mouse, Pluto/Gillett/Dec. 14/A.A. nominee).

**1932:** "The Duck Hunt" (with Pluto/Gillett/Jan. 28); "The Grocery Boy" (with Minnie Mouse, Pluto/Jackson/Feb. 3); "The Mad Dog" (with Pluto, Pegleg Pete/Gillett/Mar. 5); "Barnyard Olympics" (with Minnie Mouse, Pluto, Clarabelle Cow, and Horace Horsecollar/Jackson/Apr. 18); "Mickey's Revue" (with Minnie Mouse, Pluto, Clarabelle Cow, Horace Horsecollar and Dippy Dawg [Goofy]); "Musical Farmer" (with Minnie Mouse/ Jackson/July 11); and "Mickey in Arabia" (with Minnie Mouse, Pegleg Pete/Jackson/July 20).

*United Artists releases*

**1932:** "Mickey's Nightmare" (with Minnie Mouse, Pluto/Gillett/ Aug. 13); "Trader Mickey" (with Pluto/Hand/Aug. 10); "The Whoopee Party" (with Minnie Mouse, Dippy Dawg (Goofy), Clarabelle Cow and Horace Horsecollar/Jackson/Sept. 17); "Touchdown Mickey" (with Minnie Mouse, Goofy, Clarabelle Cow and Horace Horsecollar/Jackson/Oct. 5); "The Wayward Canary" (with Minnie Mouse, Pluto/Gillett/Nov. 12); "The Klondike Kid" (with Minnie Mouse, Pluto, Dippy Dawg (Goofy) and Pegleg Pete/Jackson/Nov. 12); and "Mickey's Good Deed" (with Pluto/Gillett/Dec. 17).

**1933:** "Building a Building" (with Minnie Mouse, Pluto, Pegleg Pete/Hand/Jan. 7/A.A. nominee); "The Mad Doctor" (with Pluto/Hand/Jan. 21); "Mickey's Pal Pluto" (with Minnie Mouse, Pluto/ Gillett/Feb. 18); "Mickey's Mellerdrammer" (with Minnie Mouse, Clarabelle Cow and Dippy Dawg (Goofy); "Ye Olden Days" (with Minnie Mouse, Clarabelle Cow, Dippy Dawg (Goofy)); "The Mail Pilot" (with Minnie Mouse, Pegleg Pete/Hand/May 13); "Mickey's Mechanical Man" (with Minnie Mouse, Beppo/Jackson/June 17); "Mickey's Gala Premiere" (with Minnie Mouse, Clarabelle Cow, Horace Horsecollar and Pluto/Gillett/July 1); "Puppy Love" (with

Minnie Mouse, Pluto, Fifi/Jackson/Sept. 2); "The Steeplechase" (with Minnie Mouse/Gillett/Sept. 30); "The Pet Store" (with Minnie Mouse, Beppo/Jackson/Oct. 28); and "Giantland" (with Minnie Mouse/Gillett/Nov. 25).

**1934:** "Shanghaied" (with Minnie Mouse, Pegleg Pete/Gillett/ Jan. 13); "Camping Out" (with Minnie Mouse, Clarabelle Cow, Horace Horsecollar/Hand/Feb. 17); "Playful Pluto" (with Pluto/ Gillett/Mar. 3); "Gulliver Mickey" (Gillett/May 19); "Mickey's Steam Roller" (with Minnie Mouse/Hand/June 16); "Orphan's Benefit" (with Donald Duck, Goofy, Clarabelle Cow, Clara Cluck, Horace Horsecollar/Gillett/Sept. 29); "The Dognapper" (with Donald Duck, Fifi, Pluto, Pegleg Pete/Hand/Nov. 17); and "Two-Gun Mickey" (with Minnie Mouse, "Pistol" Pete/ Sharpsteen/Dec. 15).

**1935:** "Mickey's Man Friday" (Hand/Jan. 9); "The Band Concert" (with Donald Duck, Goofy, Clarabelle Cow, Horace Horsecollar, Pegleg Pete, Paddy Pig/Jackson/Feb. 23/first color); "Mickey's Service Station" (with Donald Duck, Goofy, Pegleg Pete/ Sharpsteen/Mar. 16); "Mickey's Kangaroo" (with Pluto, Hoppy/ Hand/Apr. 13/last black-and-white Mickey Mouse cartoon); "Mickey's Fire Brigade" (with Donald Duck, Goofy, Clarabelle Cow/Sharpsteen/Aug. 3); "Pluto's Judgement Day" (with Pluto/ Hand/Aug. 31); and "On Ice" (with Minnie Mouse, Donald Duck, Goofy, Clarabelle Cow, Horace Horsecollar/Sharpsteen/Sept. 28).

**1936:** "Mickey's Polo Team" (with Donald Duck, Clarabelle Cow, Goofy/Hand/Jan. 4); "Orphans' Picnic" (with Donald Duck/ Sharpsteen/Feb. 15) "Mickey's Grand Opera" (with Donald Duck, Pluto, Goofy, Clara Cluck, Clarabelle Cow, Horace Horsecollar/ Jackson/Mar. 7); "Thru the Mirror" (Hand/May 30); "Moving Day" (with Donald Duck, Goofy, Pegleg Pete/Sharpsteen/June 20); "Mickey's Rival" (with Minnie Mouse, Mortimer Mouse/ Jackson/June 20); "Alpine Climbers" (with Donald Duck, Pluto/ Hand/July 25); "Mickey's Circus" (with Minnie Mouse, Donald Duck/Sharpsteen/Aug. 1); and "Mickey's Elephant" (with Pluto, Bobo/Luske/Oct. 10).

**1937:** "The Worm Turns" (with Pluto, Pegleg Pete/Sharpsteen/Jan. 2); "Don Donald" (with Donald Duck, Donna Duck/Sharpsteen/Jan. 9); "Moose Hunters" (with Donald Duck, Goofy/Sharpsteen/Feb. 20); "Mickey's Amateurs" (with Donald Duck, Goofy, Clarabelle Cow, Clara Cluck, Horace Horsecollar/Colvig, Pfeiffer, Penner/Apr. 17); and "Modern Inventions" (with Donald Duck).

*RKO Radio Pictures releases*

**1937:** "Hawaiian Holiday" (with Donald Duck, Goofy, Pluto/ Sharpsteen/Sept. 24); "Clock Cleaners" (with Donald Duck, Goofy/Sharpsteen/Oct. 15); and "Lonesome Ghosts" (with Donald Duck, Goofy/Gillett/Dec. 24).

**1938:** "Boat Builders" (with Minnie Mouse, Donald Duck, Goofy/Sharpsteen/Feb. 25); "Mickey's Trailer" (with Donald Duck, Goofy/Sharpsteen/May 6); "The Whalers" (with Donald Duck, Goofy/Huemer/Aug. 19); "Mickey's Parrot" (with Pluto/ Roberts/Sept. 9); and "Brave Little Tailor" (with Minnie Mouse, the King, Willie the Giant/Gillett/Sept. 23/A.A. nominee).

**1939:** "Society Dog Show" (with Pluto, Fifi/Roberts/Feb. 3); and "The Pointer" (with Pluto/Geronimi/July 21/A.A. nominee).

**1940:** "Tugboat Mickey" (with Donald Duck, Goofy/Geronimi/ Apr. 26); "Pluto's Dream House" (with Pluto/Geronimi/Aug. 30); and "Mr. Mouse Takes a Trip" (with Pluto, Pegleg Pete/Geronimi/ Oct. 1).

**1941:** "The Little Whirlwind" (Minnie Mouse/Thomson/Feb. 14); "The Nifty Nineties" (with Donald Duck, Goofy, Daisy Duck, Huey/Dewey and Louie/Thomson/June 20); and "Orphan's Benefit" (with Donald Duck, Goofy, Clarabelle Cow, Horace Horsecollar, Clara Cluck/Thomson/Aug. 12).

**1942:** "Mickey's Birthday Party" (with Minnie Mouse, Donald Duck, Clarabelle Cow, Horace Horsecollar, Clara Cluck, Goofy/Thomson/Feb. 7); and "Symphony Hour" (with Donald Duck, Pegleg Pete, Clarabelle Cow, Clara Cluck, Horace Horsecollar, Goofy/Thomson/Mar. 20).

**1947:** "Mickey's Delayed Date" (with Minnie Mouse, Pluto/Nichols/Oct. 3).

**1948:** "Mickey Down Under" (with Pluto/Nichols/Mar. 19); and "Mickey and the Seal" (Nichols/Dec. 3/A.A. nominee).

**1951:** "Plutopia" (with Pluto/Nichols/May 18); and "R'coon Dawg" (with Pluto/Nichols/Aug. 10).

**1952:** "Pluto's Party" (with Pluto/Schaffer/Sept. 19); and "Pluto's Christmas Tree" (with Chip 'n' Dale, Donald Duck, Goofy, Minnie Mouse, Clarabelle Cow, Horace Horsecellar/Hannah/Nov. 21).

**1953:** "The Simple Things" (with Pluto/Nichols/Apr. 18).

*Buena Vista Pictures releases*

**1983:** "Mickey's Christmas Carol" (Mattinson/Dec. 16/A.A. nominee).

**1990:** "The Prince and the Pauper" (with Goofy, Donald Duck, Pluto/Scribner/Nov. 16).

**1994:** "Runaway Brain" (with Minnie Mouse, Pluto/Bailey/Aug. 11).

## ◎ THE MIGHTY HEROES

Under the supervision of animator Ralph Bakshi, this series emerged in response to the growing craze for superhero cartoons, only this one poked fun at the idea. Episodes featured five defenders of justice—Diaper Man, Tornado Man, Rope Man, Strong Man and Cuckoo Man—a group of half witted superheros who battle the evil doings of such notorious villains as the Stretcher, the Shrinker and, of course, the Enlarger.

Originally, 26 episodes were made for television, with a scant few actually released to theaters nationwide in the late 1960s and early 1970s. Bakshi was named supervising director of Terrytoons in 1966, the same year the series was first broadcast on television. *Directed by Ralph Bakshi and Bob Taylor. Technicolor. A Terrytoons Production released through 20th Century Fox.*

*Voices:*
**The Mighty Heroes:** Herschel Benardi, Lionel Wilson

**1969:** "The Stretcher" (Apr.); "The Frog" (Oct.); and "The Toy Man" (Dec.).

**1970:** "The Ghost Monster" (Apr.); "The Drifter" (Aug.); "The Proton Pulsator" (Sept.); and "The Shocker" (Dec.).

**1971:** "The Enlarger" (Apr.); "The Dusters" (Aug.); and "The Big Freeze" (Dec.).

## ◎ MIGHTY MOUSE

Combining the power of Superman and the body of Mickey Mouse, Mighty Mouse was animator Paul Terry's most popular cartoon star. For more than 15 years, the character defended the rights of mice in need of his superstrength to stave off trouble and restore order.

*Original character design of Paul Terry's Mighty Mouse (originally called Super Mouse).*

I. Klein, a Terry-Toons storyman, originated the Mighty Mouse character several years after joining the studio in the spring of 1940. Since most animated characters at that time were humanized animals and insects, Klein initially sketched a "super fly," replete with a red Superman-like cape. The sketches quickly attracted Terry's attention.

"We were putting up ideas for a cartoon at the start of a new cartoon story. It crossed my mind that a 'takeoff' of the new comic-strip sensation, *Superman*, could be a subject for a *Terry-Toons* cartoon," Klein once recalled.

Terry changed Klein's superfly to a mouse, dubbing him "Super Mouse," as the character was billed in four cartoons beginning in 1942 with "The Mouse of Tomorrow." (He was actually more like a superrat than supermouse in this film.) The cartoon series ultimately saved Terry-Toons from losing its distribution contract with 20th Century Fox, which had considered dropping the studio's cartoons from its roster. With the success of the *Mighty Mouse* series, 20th Century Fox immediately changed its mind and signed a new deal with Terry-Toons to continue releasing its cartoons to theaters.

A year after the cartoon's debut, Terry changed the name of the character, but not because of possible legal action from D.C. Comics, the license holder of Superman, for copyright infringement, as reported elsewhere. A former Terry-Toons employee had contributed his own version of the character to a new comic book called *Coo Coo Comics*, with the first issue appearing the same month that "The Mouse of Tomorrow" was officially released. Terry decided he didn't want to compete with a character that was so similar in nature, so he renamed his superrodent "Mighty Mouse."

As a result of the name change, the early Super Mouse cartoons were retitled before the films were syndicated to television. The films reappeared on television as part of CBS's *Mighty Mouse Playhouse* in 1955. *Directors were Mannie Davis, Connie Rasinski, Eddie Donnelly, Bill Tytla, and Dave Tendlar. Technicolor. A Terry-Toon Cartoons and Terrytoons/CBS Films, Inc., Production released through 20th Century Fox.*

*Voices*
**Mighty Mouse:** Tom Morrison

**1942:** "The Mouse of Tomorrow" (Donnelly/Oct. 16); and "Frankenstein's Cat" (Davis/Nov. 27).

**1943:** "He Dood It Again" (Donnelly/Feb. 5); "Pandora's Box" (Rasinski/June 11); "Super Mouse Rides Again" (Davis/Aug. 6/ a.k.a. "Mighty Mouse Rides Again"); "Down with Cats" (Rasinski/ Oct. 7); and "Lion and the Mouse" (Davis/Nov. 12).

**1944:** "The Wreck of Hesperus" (Davis/Feb. 11/first cartoon billed as Mighty Mouse); "The Champion of Justice" (Davis/ Mar. 17); "Mighty Mouse Meets Jekyll and Hyde Cat" (Davis/ Apr. 28); "Eliza on Ice" (Rasinski/June 16); "Wolf! Wolf!" (Davis/June 22); "The Green Line" (Donnelly/July 7); "Mighty Mouse and the Two Barbers" (Donnelly/Sept. 1); "Sultan's Birthday" (Tytla/Oct. 13); and "Mighty Mouse at the Circus" (Donnelly/Nov. 17).

**1945:** "Mighty Mouse and the Pirates" (Rasinski/Jan. 12); "Port of Missing Mice" (Donnelly/Feb. 2); "Raiding the Raiders" (Rasinski/Mar. 9); "The Kilkenny Cats" (Davis/Apr. 13); "The Silver Streak" (Donnelly/June 8); "Mighty Mouse and the Wolf" (Donnelly/July 20); "Gypsy Life" (Rasinksi/Aug. 3/A.A. nominee); "Mighty Mouse Meets Bad Bill Bunion" (Davis/Nov. 9); and "Mighty Mouse in Krakatoa" (Rasinski/Dec. 14).

**1946:** "Svengali's Cat" (Donnelly/Jan. 18); "The Wicked Wolf" (Davis/Mar. 8); "My Old Kentucky Home" (Donnelly/Mar. 29); "Throwing the Bull" (Rasinski/May 3); "The Johnstown Flood" (Rasinksi/June 28); "The Trojan Horse" (Davis/July 26); "Winning the West" (Donnelly/Aug. 16); "The Electronic Mouse Trap" (Davis/Sept. 6); "The Jail Break" (Davis/Sept. 20); "The Crackpot King" (Donnelly/Nov. 15); and "Mighty Mouse and the Hep Cat" (Davis/Dec. 6).

**1947:** "Crying Wolf" (Rasinski/Jan. 10); "Deadend Cats" (Donnelly/Feb. 14); "Aladdin's Lamp" (Donnelly/Mar. 28); "The Sky Is Falling" (Davis/Apr. 25); "Mighty Mouse Meets Deadeye Dick" (Rasinski/May 30); "A Date for Dinner" (Donnelly/Aug. 29); "The First Snow" (Davis/Oct. 10); "Fight to the Finish" (Rasinski/Nov. 14); "Swiss Cheese Family Robinson" (Davis/Dec. 19); and "Lazy Little Beaver" (Donnelly/Dec. 26).

**1948:** "Mighty Mouse and the Magician" (Donnelly/Mar.); "The Feudin' Hillbillies" (Rasinski/June 23); "The Witch's Cat" (Davis/ July 15); "Love's Labor Won" (Davis/Sept. 15); "Triple Trouble" (Davis/Sept. 30); "The Mysterious Stranger" (Davis/Oct.); and "Magic Slipper" (Davis/Dec.).

**1949:** "Racket Buster" (Davis/Feb.); "Cold Romance" (Davis/ Apr. 10); "The Catnip Gang" (Donnelly/July 22); "Perils of Pearl Pureheart" (Donnelly/Oct. 11); and "Stop, Look and Listen" (Donnelly/Dec.).

**1950:** "Anti-Cats" (Davis/Mar.); "Law and Order" (Donnelly/ June 23); "Beauty on the Beach" (Rasinski/Nov.); and "Mother Goose's Birthday Party" (Rasinski/Dec.).

**1951:** "Sunny Italy" (Rasinski/Mar.); "Goons from the Moon" (Rasinski/Apr. 1); "Injun Trouble" (Donnelly/June); "A Swiss Miss" (Davis/Aug.); and "A Cat's Tale" (Davis/Nov.).

**1952:** "Prehistoric Perils" (Rasinski/Mar.); "Hansel and Gretel" (Rasinski/June); and "Happy Holland" (Donnelly/Nov.).

**1953:** "A Soapy Opera" (Rasinski/Jan.); "Hero for a Day" (Davis/ Apr.); "Hot Rods" (Donnelly/June); and "When Mousehood Was in Flower" (Rasinski/July).

**1954:** "Spare the Rod" (Rasinski/Jan.); "Helpless Hippo" (Rasinski/Mar.); and "Reformed Wolf" (Rasinski/Oct.).

**1959:** "Outer Space Visitor" (Tendlar/Nov.).

**1961:** "The Mysterious Package" (Davis/Dec. 15); and "Cat Alarm" (Rasinski/Dec. 31).

## ◎ MISTER MAGOO

For a long time United Productions of America (UPA) cartoon producer John Hubley wanted to get away from "funny" cartoon animals and try something different—a human character with a distinct personality of his own. Columbia Pictures, UPA's distributor, reluctantly approved Hubley's new concept: a nearsighted, crotchety old man named Mr. Magoo.

The studio bought the idea when Hubley added an animal character—a bear—to the first cartoon, "The Ragtime Bear," released in 1949. Success was immediate, and soon after the studio requisitioned more Magoo cartoon shorts, which became UPA's top moneymaking short-subject series during its long, award-winning run.

Millard Kaufman, who wrote "The Ragtime Bear," was the person most responsible for Magoo's creation. Hubley handled the series from the beginning, producing and directing two more cartoons until he assigned Pete Burness to direct the series. Under Burness, the *Magoo* series received four Academy Award nominations, winning twice for "When Magoo Flew" (1954) and "Magoo's Puddle Jumper" (1956) as best short subjects of the year.

Magoo's character was actually derived from several real-life figures—a bullheaded uncle of Hubley's and bulbous-nosed comedian W. C. Fields, among others. Jim Backus, the voice of Magoo, also drew from remembrances of his businessman father for the character's crinkly voice.

Backus was hired to voice Magoo at the recommendation of Jerry Hausner, who played Magoo's nephew, Waldo, in the series. According to Hausner, Backus "invented a lot of things and brought to the cartoons a fresh, wonderful approach."

By the 1950s Magoo's personality was softened, and he was made into a more sentimental character. Director Pete Burness contends that the character "would have been stronger if he had continued crotchety, even somewhat nasty." Nonetheless, Magoo continued to charm moviegoers with his slapdash humor until 1959, when the series ended. The character later experienced a rebirth in popularity when UPA produced a brand-new series of cartoons for television in the early 1960s.

In 1997 Leslie Nielsen, of *Naked Gun* film fame, reprised the role of Mr. Magoo in a live-action feature film, based on the popular cartoon character. The film fared poorly at the box office and was panned by critics. *Series directors were John Hubley, Pete Burness, Robert Cannon, Rudy Larriva, Tom McDonald, Gil Turner, Chris Ishii and Bill Hurtz. Technicolor. CinemaScope. A UPA Production released through Columbia Pictures.*

***Voices***

**Mr. Magoo:** Jim Backus; **Waldo:** Jerry Hausner, Daws Butler

**1949:** "The Ragtime Bear" (Hubley/Sept. 8/Jolly Frolics cartoon).

**1950:** "Spellbound Hound" (Hubley/Mar. 16/first official Mr. Magoo cartoon in the series); "Trouble Indemnity" (Burness/Sept. 4/A.A. nominee); and "Bungled Bungalow" (Burness/Dec. 28).

**1951:** "Barefaced Flatfoot" (Business/Apr. 26); "Fuddy Duddy Buddy" (Hubley/Oct. 18); and "Grizzly Golfer" (Burness/Dec. 20).

**1952:** "Sloppy Jalopy" (Burness/Feb. 21); "The Dog Snatcher" (Burness/May 29); "Pink and Blue Blues" (Burness/Aug. 28/A.A.

nominee/working title "Pink Blue Plums"); "Hotsy Footsy" (Hurtz/Oct. 23); and "Captains Outrageous" (Burness/Dec. 25).

**1953:** "Safety Spin" (Burness/May 21); "Magoo's Masterpiece" (Burness/July 30); and "Magoo Slept Here" (Burness/Nov. 19).

**1954:** "Magoo Goes Skiing" (Burness/Mar. 11); "Kangaroo Courting" (Burness/July 1); and "Destination Magoo" (Burness/Dec. 16).

**1955:** "When Magoo Flew" (Burness/Jan. 6/A.A. winner); "Magoo's Check-Up" (Burness/Feb. 24); "Magoo Express" (Burness/May 19); "Madcap Magoo" (Burness/June 23); "Stage Door Magoo" (Burness/Oct. 6); and "Magoo Makes News" (Burness/Dec. 15/CinemaScope).

**1956:** "Magoo's Caine Mutiny" (Burness/Mar. 8/originally "Canine Mutiny"); "Magoo Goes West" (Burness/Apr. 19/CinemaScope); "Calling Dr. Magoo" (Burness/May 24/CinemaScope); "Magoo Beats the Heat" (Burness/June 21/CinemaScope); "Magoo's Puddle Jumper" (Burness/July 26/A.A. winner/CinemaScope); "Trailblazer Magoo" (Burness/Sept. 13/CinemaScope); "Magoo's Problem Child" (Burness/Oct. 18/CinemaScope); and "Meet Mother Magoo" (Burness/Dec. 27/CinemaScope).

**1957:** "Magoo Goes Overboard" (Burness/Feb. 21/CinemaScope); "Matador Magoo" (Burness/May 30/CinemaScope); "Magoo Breaks Par" (Burness/June 27/CinemaScope); "Magoo's Glorious Fourth" (Burness/July 25/CinemaScope); "Magoo's Masquerade" (Larriva/Aug. 15/CinemaScope); "Magoo Saves the Bank" (Burness/Sept. 26/CinemaScope); "Rock Hound Magoo" (Burness/Oct. 24); "Magoo's House Hunt" (Cannon/Nov. 28); and "Magoo's Private War" (Larriva/Dec. 19).

**1958:** "Magoo's Young Manhood" (Burness/Mar. 13/working title: "The Young Manhood of Mr. Magoo"); "Scoutmaster Magoo" (Cannon/Apr. 10); "The Explosive Mr. Magoo" (Burness/May 8); "Magoo's Three-Point Landing" (Burness/June 5); "Magoo's Cruise" (Larriva/Sept. 11); "Love Comes to Magoo" (McDonald/Oct. 2); and "Gumshoe Magoo" (Turner/Nov.).

**1959:** "Bwana Magoo" (McDonald/Jan. 9); "Magoo's Homecoming" (Turner/Mar. 5); "Merry Minstrel Magoo" (Larriva/Apr. 9); "Magoo's Lodge Brother" (Larriva/May 7); and "Terror Faces Magoo" (Ishii/July 9).

### ◎ MODERN MADCAPS

This series was a lame attempt by Paramount's cartoon department to provide a launch for other potential cartoon series. A few notable characters to appear in this series during its nine-year run were Boobie Baboon, The Cat, Goodie the Gremlin, Honey Halfwitch, Professor Herman Schwaltz and Sir Blur. (See individual series entries of aforementioned characters for filmographies and more information.) *Directed by Seymour Kneitel, James "Shamus" Culhane, Howard Post and Gene Deitch. Gene Deitch and Allen Swift were series producers. Technicolor. A Famous Studios Production released through Paramount Pictures Corporation.*

**1958:** "Right Off the Bat" (Kneitel/Nov. 7).

**1959:** "Fit to Be Toyed" (Kneitel/Feb. 6); "La Petite Parade" (Kneitel/Mar. 6); "Spooking of Ghosts" (Kneitel/June 12); "Talking Horse Sense" (Kneitel/Sept. 11); and "T.V. Fuddlehead" (Kneitel/Oct. 16).

**1960:** "Mike the Masquerader" (Kneitel/Jan. 1); "Fiddle Faddle" (with Professor Schmaltz/Kneitel/Feb. 26); "Trouble Date" (with Jeepers and Creepers/Kneitel/Mar. 11); "From Dime to Dime" (Kneitel/Mar. 25); "Trigger Treat" (Kneitel/Apr. 19); "The Shoe Must Go On" (Kneitel/June); "Electronica" (Kneitel/July); "Shootin' Stars" (with the Cat/Kneitel/Aug. 19); "Disguise the Limit" (Kneitel/Sept. 19); "Galaxia" (Kneitel/Oct. 19); "Bouncing Benny" (Kneitel/Nov. 19); and "Terry the Terror" (with Professor Schmaltz/Kneitel/Dec. 19).

**1961:** "Phantom Moustacher" (with Mike the Moustacher/Kneitel/Jan. 19); "The Kid from Mars" (Kneitel/Feb. 19); "The Mighty Termite" (with Professor Schmaltz/Kneitel/Apr.); "In the Nicotine" (Kneitel/June); "The Inquisit Visit" (Kneitel/July); "Bopin' Hood" (with The Cat/Kneitel/Aug.); and "The Plot Sickens" (Kneitel/Dec. 19).

**1962:** "Perry Popgun" (with Perry Popgun/Kneitel); "Crumley Cogwheel" (with Crumley Cogwheel/Kneitel/Jan. 19); "Popcorn and Politics" (Kneitel/Feb. 19); "Samson Scap" (Deitch/Mar.); "Giddy Gadgets" (with Professor Schmaltz, Lena/Kneitel/Mar. 19); "Funderful Suburbia" (Kneitel/Mar. 19); "Penny Pals" (Kneitel/Oct. 19); "The Robot Ringer" (Kneitel/Nov. 19); and "One of the Family" (Kneitel/Dec. 19).

**1963:** "Ringading Kid" (Kneitel/Jan.); "Drump Up a Tenant" (Kneitel/Feb.); "One Weak Vacation" (Kneitel/Mar.); "Trash Program" (Kneitel/Apr.); "Harry Happy" (Kneitel/Sept.); "Tell Me a Badtime Story" (with Goodie the Gremlin/Kneitel/Oct.); "The Pigs' Feat" (Kneitel/Oct.); "Sour Gripes" (Kneitel/Oct.); "Goodie's Good Deed" (with Goodie the Gremlin/Kneitel/Nov.); and "Muggy-Doo Boycat" (with Myron Walman, Boy Animator and Beverly Arnold, Girl Creator/Kneitel/Dec./produced by Hal Seeger of TV's *Batfink* and *Milton the Monster* fame).

**1964:** "Robot Rival" (with Zippy Zephyr/Kneitel/Sept.); "And So Tibet" (Kneitel/Oct.); "Reading, Writhing and 'Rithmetic" (with Buck and Wingy/Kneitel/Nov.); and "Near Sighted and Far Out" (Kneitel/Nov.).

**1965:** "Cagey Business" (Post/Feb.); "The Itch" (Post/May); "Solitary Refinement" (with Boobie Baboon/Post/Sept.); and "The Outside Dope" (with Boobie Baboon/Post/Nov.).

**1966:** "Two by Two" (Post/Jan.); and "I Want My Mummy" (with José Jimenez/Post/Mar./voiced by Bill Dana).

### ◎ MOTHER GOOSE PRESENTS

Legendary stop-motion animation special effects artist Ray Harryhausen, who had served as an animator on George Pal's Academy Award-winning *Puppetoons* series for Paramount Pictures, produced, directed and animated this independently produced series of stop-motion animated fairy tales. During his service in the navy, he managed to acquire thousands of feet of old Kodachrome film stock; in 1946, after his discharge he used it to produce the first film—which lasted about two minutes—in the series, "Little Miss Muffet." The film was combined with three other Mother Goose rhymes and stories—"Old Mother Hubbard," "The Queen of Hearts" and "Humpty Dumpty"—co-animated by Fred Blasauf and released to theaters as a 10-minute short, entitled "Mother Goose Stories," by Bailey Films.

Harryhausen went on to produce four other 10-minute shorts photographed in three-dimensional animation that were subsequently released to theaters, taking as long as four months to finish them: "The Story of Little Red Riding Hood" (1949), "The Story of Hansel and Gretel" (1951) and "The Story of King Midas" (1953). In 1952, he began production of his fifth and final short in the series, "The Story of the Tortoise and the Hare," but quit the project when he found working in feature films was far more lucrative.

Fifty years later, in 2002, with the help of filmmakers Mark Caballero and Seamus Walsh, Harryhausen came out of retirement to help animate some scenes and complete the short, which was released that same year. *Directed by Ray Harryhausen. Technicolor. A Ray Harryhausen Production released by Bailey Films and Screen Novelties International.*

**Bailey Films releases**

**1946:** "Mother Goose Stories."

**1949:** "The Story of Little Red Riding Hood."

**1951:** "The Story of Hansel and Gretel" and "The Story of Rapunzel."

**1953:** "The Story of King Midas."

**Screen Novelties International releases**

**2002:** "The Story of the Tortoise and the Hare" (Sept. 27).

## ◎ MUSICAL MINIATURES

Putting music to animation took new direction with this animated series by Walter Lantz, which used classical music as a backdrop for story elements and character development on screen. Music was performed by a 50-piece orchestra that Universal Pictures, the series' distributor, loaned out to Lantz. Woody Woodpecker's "The Poet and Peasant" inaugurated the series in 1946 and was held over by some theaters for four to six weeks. The films cost more than $30,000 to produce—the most expensive pictures Lantz ever made. *Directed by Dick Lundy. Technicolor. A Walter Lantz Production released through Universal Pictures.*

**1946:** "The Poet & Peasant" (with Woody Woodpecker, Andy Panda/Lundy/Mar. 18/A.A. nominee).

**1947:** "Musical Moments from Chopin" (with Andy Panda, Woody Woodpecker/Lundy/Feb. 24/A.A. nominee); and "The Overture to William Tell" (with Wally Walrus/Lundy/June 16).

**1948:** "Kiddie Concert" (Lundy/Apr. 23); and "Pixie Picnic" (Lundy/May).

## ◎ NANCY AND SLUGGO

Breaking tradition, Paul Terry purchased the rights to an established comic-strip character, in this case Ernie Bushmiller's *Nancy*, which he turned into a short-lived cartoon series. *Technicolor. A Terry-Toon Cartoons Production released through 20th Century Fox.*

**1942:** "School Daze" (Sept. 18); and "Doing Their Bit" (Oct. 30).

## ◎ NERTSERY RHYMES

Legendary animator Walter Lantz produced this brief series of three-strip Technicolor animated re-tellings of popular children's nursery rhymes for movie theaters in the late 1930s. *Directed by Lester Kline and Burt Gillett. Technicolor. A Walter Lantz Production released by Universal Pictures.*

**1939:** "The Magic Beans" (Kline/Feb. 13); and "The Sleeping Princess" (Gillett/Dec. 4).

## ◎ NEW UNIVERSAL CARTOONS

In 1934, pioneer animator Walter Lantz began producing a series of musical novelties called "specials," comprised of one-shots or individual cartoons featuring incidental characters, released to theaters as *Walter Lantz Cartune Classics.* Four years later, with the release of "The Rabbit Hunt," that series was alternately billed as "Cartune Comedy" and later "Cartunes." Emerging that same year was this entertaining collection of black-and-white cartoons under the banner of "A New Universal Cartoon." Alex Lovy helmed the series' first cartoon, an 1890s melodrama spoof entitled "Nellie the Sewing Machine Girl (or Honest Hearts & Willing Hands)." The comedy one-reeler spawned a second effort that same year, "Nellie the Indian Chief's Daughter," and was then spun-off into its own *Mello-Drama* cartoons the following year. Additional series entries starred Lantz newcomers Baby-Face Mouse and a pair of boy and girl monkeys, Jock and Jill, the Simple Simeons, and longtime star, Oswald the Lucky Rabbit, in the final stages of his career. Besides Lovy, the series marked the directing debuts of Lantz studio animators Lester Kline, Rudy Zamora and Fred Kopietz. *Directed by Alex Lovy, Lester Kline, Rudy Zamora and Fred Kopietz. Black-and-white. Voice credits unknown. A Walter Lantz Production released by Universal Pictures Company, Inc.*

**1938:** "Nellie the Sewing Machine Girl (or Honest Hearts & Willing Hands)" (Lovy/Apr. 11/first New Universal Cartoon release); "Tail End" (Kline/Apr. 25/Lester Kline's directorial debut); "Problem Child" (Zamora/May 16/working title: "Wildcat Willie"/Rudy Zamora's directorial debut); "Movie Phoney News" (Lovy/May 30); "Nellie the Indian Chief's Daughter" (Lovy/June 6); "Happy Scouts" (with Oswald the Rabbit/Kopietz/June 20/Fred Kopietz's directorial debut); "Cheese-Nappers" (with Baby-Face Mouse/Lovy/July 4/first appearance of Baby-Face Mouse); "Voodoo in Harlem" (Zamora/July 18/working title: "Black Magic"); "Silly Seals" (Kline/July 25/copyrighted as "The Silly Seals"); "Barnyard Romeo" (Lovy/Aug. 1/working title: "Fine Feathers"); "Queen's Kittens" (Kline/Aug. 8); "The Big Cat and the Little Mouse" (with Baby-Face Mouse/Lovy/Aug. 15); "Ghost Town Frolics" (with Jock and Jill, the Simple Simeons/Kline/Sept. 5/working title: "Ghost Town"/first appearance of Jock and Jill, the Simple Simeons); "Pixie Land" (Perkins/Sept. 12/working title: "The Busy Body"); "The Cat and the Bell" (with Baby-Face Mouse/Lovy/Oct. 3); "Hollywood Bowl" (Perkins/Oct. 5/final "A New Universal Cartoon" release).

## ◎ NIBBLES AND TUFFY

This sweet, inquisitive gray mouse with a large appetite first appeared as the ward of Jerry the Mouse in William Hanna and Joseph Barbera's Oscar–winning *Tom and Jerry* series. As Nibbles, the character made his screen debut in the 1946 cartoon, "The Milky Waif," and appeared in five more films thereafter, including two Academy Award winners: "The Little Orphan" (1949) and "The Two Mouseketeers" (1952).

In 1954, Nibbles was renamed Tuffy, costarring in six more cartoon shorts, among them "Touché, Pussy Cat!" (1954), the last *Tom and Jerry* cartoon nominated for an Oscar. Tuffy spoke in French only twice, "C'est la guerre!" and singing, "Frère Jacques." He sang this again in his swan song—his final *Tom and Jerry* cartoon—the outrageous Robin Hood send-up, "Robin Hoodwinked" (1958). *Directed by William Hanna and Joseph Barbera. Technicolor. CinemaScope. A Metro-Goldwyn-Mayer Cartoon Production released by Metro-Goldwyn-Mayer.*

**As Nibbles**

**1946:** "The Milky Waif" (with Tom and Jerry/May 18).

**1949:** "The Little Orphan" (with Tom and Jerry, Mammy-Two-Shoes/May 30/A.A. winner).

**1950:** "Safety Second" (with Tom and Jerry/July 1).

**1952:** "The Two Mouseketeers" (with Tom and Jerry/Mar. 15/A.A. winner).

**1953:** "Two Little Indians" (with Tom and Jerry, Spike/Oct. 17) and "Life With Tom" (with Tom and Jerry, Spike/Nov. 21).

### As Tuffy

**1954:** "Little School Mouse" (with Tom and Jerry/May 29); "Mice Follies" (with Tom and Jerry/Sept. 14), and "Touché, Pussy Cat!"(with Tom and Jerry/Dec. 18/A.A. nominee/last Tom and Jerry cartoon nominated for an Oscar).

**1955:** "Tom and Cherie" (with Tom and Jerry/Sept. 9).

**1957:** "Feedin' the Kiddie" (with Tom and Jerry/June 7/ CinemaScope).

**1958:** "Royal Cat Nap" (with Tom and Jerry/Mar. 7/CinemaScope) and "Robin Hoodwinked" (with Tom and Jerry/June 6/Tuffy's last appearance/CinemaScope).

## ◎ NOVELTOONS

A stalwart array of familiar and lesser-known cartoon stars appeared in these full-color productions, created by Paramount's Famous Studios. The series' featured players were Baby Huey, Blackie the Lamb, Buzzy the Crow, Casper the Friendly Ghost, Dog Face, Finnegan and Charlie, Goodie the Gremlin, Herman and Katnip, Little Audrey, Little Lulu, Tommy Tortoise and Moe Hare, Spunky and Swifty and Shorty, and a few short-lived characters who starred in cartoons of their own: *Jacky's Whacky World, Laddy and His Lamp* and *Raggedy Ann and Raggedy Andy*. (See series entries for aforementioned characters for filmographies and series information.) The studio had used this formula successfully before and found it worth repeating, especially for characters who did not warrant series of their own. *Directors were Seymour Kneitel, Isadore Sparber, Bill Tytla, Dave Tendlar, Howard Post, James "Shamus" Culhane, Jack Mendelsohn and Gene Deitch. Cinecolor. Technicolor. A Famous Studios Production released through Paramount Pictures Corporation.*

### Voices

Jackson Beck, Syd Raymond, Arnold Stang

**1944:** "Henpecked Rooster" (with Herman and Henry/Kneitel/ Feb. 18); "Cilly Goose" (with Goose that laid golden eggs/Kneitel/ Mar. 24); and "Gabriel Church-kitten (from the book by Margot Austin/Kneitel/Dec. 15).

**1945:** "When G.I. Johnny Comes Homes" (Feb. 2/Kneitel); "A Self Made Mongrel" (with Dog Face/Tendlar/June 29); and "Old MacDonald Had a Farm" (Kneitel/Dec. 28/first to revive "Bouncing Ball" format of Fleischer *Song Car-Tunes*).

**1946:** "The Goal Rush" (Sparber/Sept. 27); and "Spree for All" (with Snuffy Smith/Kneitel/Oct. 18/Cinecolor).

**1947:** "Madhattan Island" (Kneitel/June 27/narrated by Kenneth Roberts); "The Wee Men" (Tytla/Aug. 8); "The Mild West" (Kneitel/Aug. 22); and "Santa's Surprise" (Kneitel/Dec. 5).

**1948:** "Cat o' Nine Ails" (with Little Audrey/Kneitel/Jan. 9); "Flip Flap" (with Casper, Flip Flap the Seal/Sparber/Feb. 13); "We're in the Honey" (Kneitel/Mar. 19); "The Bored Cuckoo" (Tytla/Apr. 19); "The Mite Makes Right" (with Tom Thumb/ Tytla/Sept. 3); and "Hector's Hectic Life" (with Hector the Dog at Christmas/Tytla/Nov. 19).

**1949:** "The Little Cutup" (Sparber/Jan. 21); "Hep Cat Symphony" (Kneitel/Feb. 4); "Little Red School Mouse" (Apr. 15); "A Mutt in a Rut" (with Martin Kanine/Sparber/May 27); and "Leprechaun's Gold" (Tytla/Oct 14).

**1950:** "Quack-a-Doodle-Doo" (Sparber/Mar. 3); "Teacher's Pest" (with Junior/Sparber/Mar. 31); "Ups and Downs Derby" (with Lightning/Kneitel/June 9); "Pleased to Eat You" (with The Hungry Lion/Sparber/July 21); "Saved by the Bell" (Kneitel/Sept. 15); and "The Voice of the Turkey" (with turkey voiced by Arnold Stang/Tytla/Oct. 13).

**1951:** "Slip Us Some Redskin" (with Hep Indians/Kneitel/July 6); and "By Leaps and Hounds" (with Herbert the Dog/Sparber/ Dec. 14).

**1952:** "Feast and Furious" (with Finny the Goldfish, Katnip/ Sparber/Dec. 26).

**1954:** "Crazytown" (a gag anthology/Sparber/Feb. 26); "Candy Cabaret" (Tendlar/June 11); "The Oily Bird" (with Inchy the Worm/Sparber/July 30); and "Fido Beta Kappa" (with Martin Kanine, Fido/Sparber/Oct. 29).

**1955:** "News Hound" (with Snapper the Dog/Sparber/June 10); "Poop Goes the Weasel" (with Wishbone Duck and Waxy Weasel/ Tendlar/July 8); and "Kitty Cornered" (with Kitty Cuddles/ Tendlar/Dec. 30).

**1956:** "Pedro and Lorenzo" (Tendlar/July 13); "Sir Irving and Jeames" (Kneitel/Oct. 19); and "Lion in the Roar" (with Louie the Lion/Kneitel/Dec. 21).

**1957:** "L'Amour the Merrier" (Kneitel/July 5); "Possum Pearl" (with Possum Pearl/Kneitel/Sept. 20); "Jolly the Clown" (Kneitel/ Oct. 25); and "Cock-a-Doodle Dino" (with Danny Dinosaur, Mother Hen/Sparber/Dec. 6).

**1958:** "Dante Dreamer" (with Little Boy, Dragon/Sparber/Jan. 3); "Sportickles" (compilation of scenes from earlier cartoons/ Kneitel/Feb. 14); "Grateful Gus" (with Grateful Gus/Tendlar/Mar. 7); "Chew Chew Baby" (Sparber/Aug. 15); "Travelaffs" (compilation of scenes from earlier cartoons/Sparber/Aug. 22); and "Stork Raving Mad" (Kneitel/Oct. 3).

**1959:** "The Animal Fair" (Kneitel/Jan. 16); and "Hound-about" (Kneitel/Apr. 10).

**1960:** "Be Mice to Cats" (with Skit and Skat/Kneitel/Feb. 5); "Monkey Doodles" (Kneitel/Apr.); "Silly Science" (Kneitel/May); "Peck Your Own Home" (Kneitel/May); "The Shoe Must Go On" (Kneitel/June); "Counter Attack" (with Scat Cat/Kneitel/ July); "Fine Feathered Fiend" (Kneitel/Sept.); "Munro" (with Munro/Deitch/Sept./A.A. winner/produced by William Snyder and Rembrandt Films); "The Planet Mouseola" (Kneitel/Oct.); and "Northern Mites" (Kneitel/Nov.).

**1961:** "The Lion's Busy" (Kneitel/Feb.); "Hound About That" (Kneitel/Apr.); "Trick or Tree" (Kneitel/July); "Cape Kidnaveral" (Kneitel/Aug.); "Abner the Baseball" (Kneitel/Nov./two reel documentary cartoon about the life of a baseball); and "Kozmo Goes to School" (Kneitel/Nov.).

**1962:** "Anatole" (Deitch/Sept.); "It's for the Birdies" (Kneitel/ Nov.); and "Fiddlin' Around" (Kneitel/Dec.).

**1963:** "Ollie the Owl" (Kneitel/Jan.); "Good Snooze Tonight" (Kneitel/Feb.); "A Sight for Squaw Eyes" (Kneitel/Mar.); "Gramps to the Rescue" (Kneitel/Sept.); "Hobo's Holiday" (Kneitel/Oct.); "Hound for Pound" (Kneitel/Oct.); and "The Sheepish Wolf" (Kneitel/Nov.).

**1964:** "Whiz Quiz Kid" (Kneitel/Feb.); and "Homer on the Range" (with Homer Ranger/Post/Dec.).

**1965:** "Horning In" (with King Artie/Post/Jan.); "A Hair Raising Tale" (Post/Jan.); "Horning In" (Post/Jan.); "Tally-Hokum" (with Hangdog and Moxie Foxie/Post/Oct.); and "Geronimo and Son" (Culhane/Dec.).

**1966:** "Sick Transit" (with Roadhog and Rapid Rabbit/Post/ Jan.); "Op Pop Wham and Bop" (Post/Jan.); and "Space Kid" (Kneitel/Feb./this cartoon was released a year and a half after Kneitel's death).

**1967:** "The Trip" (Culhane/Apr.); and "Robin Hood-winked" (with Sir Blur/Culhane/June).

## ◎ NUDNIK

By the early 1960s Paramount began distributing cartoon properties produced overseas, including this Czechoslovakian-made series featuring a galactic alien named Nudnik, animated in the fashion of Terry-Toons' *Astronut*.

Nudnik was based on a character named Foofle, who won critical acclaim in a *Terry-Toons* cartoon short. Its creator was William Snyder, who produced the Academy Award–winning cartoon "Munro," also released by Paramount. Nudnik was introduced in the 1964 Academy Award-winning short, "Nudnik #2," produced by Snyder's Rembrandt Films. Rembrandt Films produced subsequent cartoons for Famous Studios.

Story lines centered on Nudnik's problems communicating with Earthlings. Narration and sound effects were used in place of dialogue as the character did not speak. *Directed by Gene Deitch. Technicolor. A Rembrandt Films/Famous Studios Production released through Paramount Pictures.*

**1964:** "Nudnik #2" (Nov. 1/A.A. winner).

**1965:** "Here's Nudnik" (Aug.); and "Drive On, Nudnik" (Dec.).

**1966:** "Home Sweet Nudnik" (Mar.); "Nudnik on a Shoestring" (Mar. 12); "Welcome Nudnik" (May); "Nudnik on the Roof" (July); and "From Nudnik with Love" (Sept.).

**1967:** "Nudnik on a Showcase"; "Nowhere with Nudnik" (Mar.); "Goodnight Sweet Nudnik" (Apr.); "Who Needs Nudnik?" (May); "Nudnik on the Beach" (May); "Good Neighbor Nudnik" (June); "Nudnik's Nudnickel" (Aug.); and "I Remember Nudnik" (Sept.)

## ◎ OIL CAN HARRY

Villainous Oil Can Harry, costar of the Terry-Toons *Fanny Zilch* cartoon melodrama series of the early 1930s, was cast in his own series of "cartoon serials" four years after his screen debut. The series was short-lived, lasting only two cartoons. *Series directors included Connie Rasinski. Black-and-white. A Terry-Toon Cartoons Production released through Educational Pictures.*

**1937:** "The Villain Still Pursued Her" (Sept. 3); and "The Saw Mill Mystery" (Rasinki/Oct. 29).

## ◎ OSWALD THE LUCKY RABBIT

Originally a silent cartoon star, Oswald the Lucky Rabbit made the transition to sound, unlike many other characters from that era. Walt Disney originated the series but lost the rights to the character in 1927 after holding out for more money. His partnership with series producer Charles Mintz came to an abrupt end as a result.

Mintz contracted his brother-in-law, George Winkler, to set up a cartoon studio to animate new Oswalds. Universal Pictures, which owned the rights to Oswald, intervened and awarded the series to animator Walter Lantz. Mintz and Winkler were thus put out of business, and Lantz was put in charge of the studio's first cartoon department.

Lantz's first job was to staff his animation department. He hired several former Disney animators, such as Hugh Harman, Rudolf Ising and Friz Freleng. He then added sound to six unreleased Oswald cartoons Winkler had completed, the first called "Ozzie of the Circus."

"It was funny how we did it," Lantz once said, remembering how he stuck sound to the cartoons. "We had a bench with all the props on it—the bells, and so. And we'd project the cartoon on the screen and all of us would stand there in front of the cartoon. As the action progressed, we'd make the sound effects, dialogue, and all. We never prescored these films. We did everything as we watched the picture. It was the only way we knew how to add sound."

Lantz also changed Oswald's character, giving him a cuter look. He shortened the ears and humanized Oswald to resemble a Mickey Mouse–type character. "The Disney stories were great, mind you . . . very funny," he said, "but I didn't like the rabbit. He was just black and white. He wouldn't have any appeal for commercial items like comic books, or that sort of thing. So I redesigned him."

Mickey Rooney, who was nine years old at the time, was the first person to voice Oswald. Lantz hired him because "he had the right squealing voice for Oswald." Rooney had previously starred in a series of Mickey McGuire comedy two-reel shorts. Bernice Hansen, also the voice of Warner Bros.' Sniffles, replaced Rooney when he left the series.

Over the years, Oswald was redesigned and his name was also shortened from Oswald the Lucky Rabbit to Oswald Rabbit. In 1938, he was featured in the final cartoon in the Oswald Rabbit series, "Feed The Kitty," directed by Alex Lovy. Afterward, he would appear in only two more cartoons, the *Cartune Classic*, "Happy Scouts" (1938), and the *Swing Symphony*, "The Egg-Cracker Suite" (1943), his only Technicolor cartoon and the only Lantz cartoon directed by Ben Hardaway and Emery Hawkins.

In 1933, Lantz directed the series' only Academy Award-nominated short, "The Merry Old Soul." Aside from regular cartoon shorts, Lantz animated the first two-strip Technicolor sequence for Universal's all-talking extravaganza, *The King of Jazz*, a revue featuring an animated Oswald and famed bandleader Paul Whiteman.

Lantz directed most cartoons in the series. William C. Nolan codirected with Lantz from 1931 to 1934, with additional films supervised by Friz Freleng, Ben Hardaway, Emery Hawkins, Alex Lovy, Fred Kopietz, Lester Kline, Rudy Zamora and Elmer Perkins directed during the series' last years of production. While many cartoons originally listed Lantz and Nolan as co-directors in the opening credits, in many cases the films were directed by only one of them. Directors listed in the filmography in this case are based on who actually directed these shorts and are not based on those directors listed in the credits. *Black-and-white. Technicolor. A Walter Lantz Production released through Universal Pictures.*

**Voices**
**Oswald the Rabbit:** Bernice Hansen, Mickey Rooney

**1929:** "Race Riot" (Lantz/Sept. 2); "Oil's Well" (Lantz/Sept. 16); "Permanent Wave" (Lantz/Sept. 29); "Cold Turkey" (Lantz/Oct. 15); "Pussy Willie" (Lantz/Oct. 28); "Amature Nite" (Lantz/Nov. 11); "Hurdy Gurdy" (Lantz/Nov. 24); "Snow Use" (Lantz/Nov. 25); "Nutty Notes" (Dec. 9); and "Ozzie of the Circus" (Lantz/Dec. 23).

**1930:** "Kounty Fair" (Lantz/Jan. 6); "Chile Con Carmen" (Lantz/ Jan. 15); "Kisses and Kurses" (Lantz/Feb. 17); "Broadway Folly" (Lantz/Mar. 3); "Bowery Bimbos" (Lantz/Mar. 18/working title:

"Bowling Bimboes"); "The Hash Shop" (Lantz/Apr. 12/working title: "The Hash House"); "The Prison Panic" (Lantz/Apr. 30); "Tramping Tramps" (Lantz/May 6); "Hot for Hollywood" (Lantz/May 19/working title: "Hollywood"); "Hells Heels" (Lantz/June 2); "My Pal Paul" (Lantz/June 20); "Not So Quiet" (Lantz/June 30); "Spooks" (Lantz/July 14); "Sons of the Saddle" (Lantz/July 20); "Cold Feet" (Lantz/Aug. 13); "Snappy Salesman" (Lantz/Aug. 18); "The Singing Sap" (Lantz/Sept. 8); "Fanny the Mule" (Lantz/Sept. 15); "The Detective" (Lantz/Sept. 22); "The Fowl Ball" (Lantz/Oct. 13); "Strange as It Seems" (Lantz/Oct. 27); "The Navy" (Lantz/Nov. 3); "Mexico" (Lantz/Nov. 17); "Africa" (Lantz/Dec. 1); "Alaska" (Lantz/Dec. 15); and "Mars" (Lantz/Dec. 29).

**1931:** "China" (Lantz, Nolan/Jan. 12); "College" (Lantz, Nolan/Jan. 27); "Shipwreck" (Lantz, Nolan/Feb. 9); "The Farmer" (Lantz, Nolan/Mar. 23); "The Fireman" (Lantz, Nolan/Apr. 6); "Sunny South" (Lantz, Nolan/Apr. 20); "Country School" (Lantz, Nolan/May 5); "The Bandmaster" (Lantz, Nolan/May 18); "Northwoods" (Lantz, Nolan/June 1); "Stone Age" (Lantz, Nolan/July 15); "Radio Rhythm" (Lantz, Nolan/July 27); "Kentucky Belles" (Lantz, Nolan/Sept. 2/working title: "The Horse Race"); "Hot Feet" (Lantz, Nolan/Sept. 14); "The Hunter" (Lantz, Nolan/Oct. 12); "Wonderland" (Lantz, Nolan/Oct. 26); "Trolley Troubles" (Lantz, Nolan/Nov. 23); "The Hare Mail" (Lantz, Nolan/Nov. 30); "The Fisherman" (Lantz, Nolan/Dec. 7); and "The Clown" (Lantz, Nolan/Dec. 21).

**1932:** "Grandma's Pet" (Lantz, Nolan/Jan. 18); "Mechanical Man" (Lantz, Nolan/Feb. 15); "Wins Out" (Lantz, Nolan/Mar. 14); "Beau and Arrows" (Lantz, Nolan/Mar. 28); "Making Good" (Lantz, Nolan/Apr. 11); "Let's Eat" (Lantz, Nolan/Apr. 21/working title: "Foiled!"); "The Winged Horse" (Lantz, Nolan/May 9); "To the Rescue" (Lantz, Nolan/May 23); "Cat Nipped" (Lantz, Nolan/May 23); "A Wet Knight" (Lantz, Nolan/June 20); "A Jungle Jumble" (Lantz, Nolan/July 4); "Day Nurse" (Nolan/Aug. 1); "The Busy Barber" (Lantz, Nolan/Sept. 12); "Carnival Capers" (Nolan/Oct. 10); "Wild and Woolly" (Nolan/Nov. 21); and "Teacher's Pest" (Nolan/Dec. 19).

**1933:** "The Plumber" (Nolan/Jan. 16); "The Shriek" (Nolan/Feb. 27); "Going to Blazes" (Nolan/Apr. 10); "Beau Best" (Nolan/May 22); "Ham and Eggs" (Nolan/June 19); "Confidence" (Nolan/July 31/working title: "A New Deal"); "Five and Dime" (Nolan/Sept. 18); "The Zoo" (Nolan/Nov. 6); "The Merry Old Soul" (Lantz/Nov. 27/A.A. nominee); and "Parking Space" (Nolan/Dec. 18).

**1934:** "Chicken Reel" (Lantz/Jan. 1); "The Candy House" (Lantz/Jan. 15); "The County Fair" (Nolan/Feb. 5); "The Toy Shoppe" (Lantz/Feb. 19); "Kings Up" (Nolan/Mar. 12); "Wolf! Wolf!" (Lantz/Apr. 12); "The Gingerbread Boy" (Apr. 16); "Goldilocks and the Three Bears" (Lantz/May 14); "Annie Moved Away" (Nolan/May 28); "The Wax Works" (Lantz/June 25); "William Tell" (Lantz/July 9); "Chris Columbus, Jr." (Lantz/July 23); "The Dizzy Dwarf" (Nolan/Aug. 6); "Ye Happy Pilgrims" (Lantz/Sept. 3); "Sky Larks" (Lantz/Oct. 22); and "Spring in the Park" (Nolan/Nov. 12).

**1935:** "Robinson Crusoe Isle" (Lantz/Jan. 7); "The Hillbillys" (Lantz/Feb. 1); "Two Little Lambs" (Lantz/Mar. 11); "Do a Good Deed" (Lantz/Mar. 25); "Elmer the Great Dane" (Lantz/Apr. 29); "Towne Hall Follies" (Lantz/June 3); "At Your Service" (Lantz/July 8); "Bronco Buster" (Lantz/Aug. 5); "Amateur Broadcast" (Lantz/Aug. 26); "The Quail Hunt" (Lantz/Sept. 23); "Monkey Wretches" (with Meany, Miny, and Moe/Lantz/Nov. 11); "Case of the Lost Sheep" (Lantz/Dec. 9); and "Doctor Oswald" (Lantz/Dec. 30).

**1936:** "Soft Ball Game" (Lantz/Jan. 27); "Alaska Sweepstakes" (Lantz/Feb. 7); "Slumberland Express" (Lantz/Mar. 9); "Beauty Shoppe" (with Meany, Miny, and Moe/Lantz/Mar. 30); "The Barnyard Five" (Lantz/Apr. 20); "Fun House" (Lantz/May 4); "Farming Fools" (with Meany, Miny, and Moe/Lantz/May 25); "Battle Royal" (Lantz/June 22); "Music Hath Charms" (Lantz/Sept. 7); "Kiddie Revue" (Lantz/Sept. 21); "Beach Combers" (Lantz/Oct. 5); "Night Life of the Bugs" (Lantz/Oct. 19); "Puppet Show" (Lantz/Nov. 2); "The Unpopular Mechanic" (Lantz/Nov. 6); and "Gopher Trouble" (Lantz/Nov. 30).

**1937:** "Everybody Sing" (Lantz/Feb. 22); "Duck Hunt" (Lantz/Mar. 8); "The Birthday Party" (Lantz/Mar. 29); "Trailer Thrills" (Lantz/May 3); "The Wily Weasel" (June 7); "The Playful Pup" (July 12); "Lovesick" (Oct. 4); "Keeper of the Lions" (Lantz/Oct. 18); "The Mechanical Handyman" (Lantz/Nov. 8); "Football Fever" (Lantz/Nov. 15); "The Mysterious Jug" (Lantz/Nov. 29); and "The Dumb Cluck" (Lantz/Dec. 20).

**1938:** "The Lamp Lighter" (Jan. 10); "Man Hunt" (Lantz/Feb. 7); "Yokel Boy Makes Good" (with Snuffy Skunk/Lantz/Feb. 21); "Trade Mice" (Lantz/Feb. 28); "Feed the Kitty" (Lovy/Mar. 14/final Oswald the Rabbit series cartoon); and "Happy Scouts" (Kopietz/June 20/Cartune Classic).

**1943:** "The Egg-Cracker Suite" (Hardaway, Hawkins/Mar. 22/ *Swing Symphony*).

## ⊚ PARAMOUNT CARTOON SPECIALS

In the 1960s Paramount Pictures distributed a handful of new cartoon shorts labeled as "cartoon specials." Most were produced and directed by outside producers and animators, with one exception: 1961's "Abner the Baseball," which tells the story of Abner Doubleday, the founder of major league baseball. The cartoon was produced by the studio's Famous Studios cartoon division and directed by veteran animator Seymour Kneitel. "Abner" was an animated two-reeler—it was twice as long as the usual seven-minute cartoon normally produced by the studio. Eddie Lawrence, who supplied the voice of Paramount cartoon stars Swifty and Shorty, wrote and narrated the film.

The bulk of the studio's "cartoon specials" were produced by William Snyder and directed by Gene Deitch, a Czechoslovakian director and former artistic director of Terry-Toons. (Deitch created the critically acclaimed *Tom Terrific* cartoon series for TV's *Captain Kangaroo* and in the 1960s directed a new series of *Tom and Jerry* cartoons for MGM.) In 1960 the pair produced and directed the studio's Academy Award–winning cartoon, "Munro." Subsequently they teamed up to produce three more cartoons for Paramount—a *Modern Madcap*, entitled "Samson Scrap," followed by the *Noveltoon*, "Anatole" and a Krazy Kat cartoon, "Keeping Up with Krazy," part of the *Comic Kings* series featuring famous King Features comic-strip characters in animated form. Al Brodax, who produced the *Popeye* cartoon series for television in the 1960s, was executive producer of the series. In 1963 Hal Seeger, who produced the 1960s' TV cartoon series *Out of the Inkwell*, *The Milton the Monster Show* and *Batfink*, independently produced under his Hal Seeger Productions (and employing primarily former and moonlighting Paramount animators) the *Modern Madcap* "Muggy Doo Boy Cat: Boy Pest with Osh," featuring Myron Waldman, Boy Animator and Beverly Arnold, Girl Creator. It was the only outside cartoon Seeger produced for the studio.

Three years later Oscar-winning producer/director John Hubley, formerly of United Productions of America (UPA), produced and directed another independent release, *Herb Alpert and the*

*Tijuana Brass Double Feature*. The cartoon was nominated for an Academy Award.

It would be 26 years before Paramount released another "cartoon special." In 1992 the studio distributed, *The Itsy Bitsy Spider*, a cartoon featurette that inspired the television series of the same name for USA Network. The film, produced by Hyperion Studios and directed by Matthew O'Callaghan, was released to theaters with the Paramount animated feature *BeBe's Kids. Directed by Gene Deitch, Hal Seeger, John Hubley and Matthew O'Callaghan. Technicolor. A Famous Studios/Rembrandt Films/Hal Seeger/Storyboard Films/Hyperion Pictures Production released through Paramount Pictures Corporation.*

**1960:** "Munro" (with Munro/Deitch/Sept./*Noveltoon*/A.A. winner).

**1961:** "Abner the Baseball" (Kneitel/Nov./two reels/narrated by Eddie Lawrence/*Noveltoon*).

**1962:** "Keeping Up with Krazy" (with Krazy Kat, Ignatz Mouse, Officer Pupp/Deitch/Oct. 1/*Comic Kings* cartoon).

**1963:** "Muggy Doo Boy Cat" (Seeger/Dec./*Noveltoon*).

**1966:** *Herb Alpert and the Tijuana Brass Double Feature* (Hubley/ A.A. winner).

**1992:** *The Itsy Bitsy Spider* (O'Callaghan/Jan. 14).

## ◎ PEPÉ LE PEW

Warner Bros.' storyman Michael Maltese created and refined Pepé Le Pew, the suave French skunk who charmed moviegoers for more than a decade with his aromatic adventures.

Pepé's unctuous accent and irresistible personality were based on French actor Charles Boyer and others. (His name was derived from Boyer's Pepé Le Moko character in the 1938 film classic *Algiers*.) The character first appeared in Chuck Jones's 1945 *Looney Tunes* cartoon, "Odor-Able Kitty," but not as Pepé Lew Pew. (On model sheets he was called "Stinky.") Two years later the character was so named and starred in the first "official" Pepé Le Pew film, "Scent-Imental Over You."

In 1949, after just three cartoons, Pepé won an Academy Award for his starring role in "For Scent-Imental Reasons," which Jones also directed. The award marked the second such honor for Jones, who won three Academy Awards during his career.

In an interview, Jones once remarked that he had no problem identifying with Pepé's romantic foibles: "Pepé was everything I wanted to be romantically. Not only was he quite sure of himself but it never occurred to him that anything was wrong with him. I always felt there must be great areas of me that were repugnant to girls, and Pepé was quite the opposite of that."

The series remained a popular Warner Bros. entry through 1962, when "Louvre Come Back to Me," the final Pepé Le Pew cartoon, was released to theaters.

Pepé returned to the screen in the 1990s, first in a new Bugs Bunny cartoon, "Carrotblanca" (1995), a parody of the 1942 Warner Bros. classic, *Casablanca* (with Greg Burson as the voice of Pepé), then in the 1996 hit feature *Space Jam. In addition to Jones, series directors were Abe Levitow, Art Davis and Douglas McCarthy. Technicolor. Cartoons, Inc./Warner Bros. Pictures, Inc./Vitagraph/Warner Bros./Warner Bros. Animation Production released by Warner Bros.*

### Voices
**Pepé Le Pew:** Mel Blanc, Greg Burson

### Merrie Melodies

### Warner Bros. Cartoons, Inc. releases

**1951:** "Scentimental Romeo" (Jones/Mar. 24).

**1952:** "Little Beau Pepé" (Jones/Mar. 29).

**1955:** "Past Perfumance" (Jones/May 21); and "Two Scent's Worth" (Jones/Oct. 15).

**1956:** "Heaven Scent" (Jones/Mar. 31).

**1957:** "Touché and Go" (Jones/Oct. 12).

**1959:** "Really Scent" (Levitow/July 27).

### Looney Tunes

### Warner Bros. Cartoons, Inc. releases

**1945:** "Odor-Able Kitty" (Jones/Jan. 6).

**1947:** "Scent-Imental Over You" (Jones/Mar. 8).

**1949:** "For Scent-Imental Reasons" (Jones/Nov. 12/A.A. winner).

**1953:** "Wild Over You" (Jones/July 11).

**1954:** "The Cat's Bah" (Jones/Mar. 20).

### Warner Bros. releases

**1960:** "Who Scent You?" (Jones/Apr. 23).

### Warner Bros. Pictures, Inc./Vitagraph releases

**1961:** "A Scent of the Matterhorn" (Jones/June 24).

**1962:** "Louvre Come Back to Me!" (Jones/Aug. 18).

### Warner Bros. Animation releases

**1995:** "Carrotblanca" (with Bugs Bunny, Daffy Duck, Yosemite Sam, Tweety, Sylvester, Foghorn Leghorn, Penelope/McCarthy/ Aug. 25).

## ◎ PETE HOTHEAD

Longtime United Productions of America (UPA) animator Ted Parmelee created this quick-tempered character—supposedly modeled after UPA's hot-tempered director Pete Burness—who managed to make a mess of everything in his life as a result of his temper. Parmelee made his directing debut in 1952, helming the first of two *Jolly Frolics* cartoons, one of which was *Pete Hothead*. Three years after the character's debut, Parmelee directed a second cartoon, this time a *UPA Cartoon Special*, featuring the character and his wife. *Directed by Ted Parmelee. Technicolor. A United Productions of America (UPA) Production released by Columbia Pictures.*

**1952:** "Pete Hothead" (with Mrs. Hothead/Sept. 25/*Jolly Frolics* cartoon).

**1955:** "Four Wheels, No Brake" (with Mrs. Hothead/Mar. 24/ *UPA Cartoon Special*).

## ◎ PHANTASY CARTOONS

In addition to Krazy Kat and Scrappy, its two major cartoon stars, Columbia Pictures' cartoon department produced several catchall series featuring no-name animated characters. The *Phantasy* cartoons were the last of these series, comprised of black-and-white and Technicolor oddities. The series was discontinued in 1948 when Columbia's animation department closed down. United Productions of America (UPA) later replaced the series with *Jolly Frolics. Producers were Charles Mintz, Dave Fleischer, Raymond Katz, and Henry Binder. Directors were Art Davis, Frank Tashlin, Alec Geiss, Paul Sommer, Howard Swift, Allen Rose, John Hubley, Sid Marcus, Bob Wickersham and Alex Lovy. Black-and-white. Technicolor. A Columbia Pictures release.*

**1939:** "The Charm Bracelet" (with Scrappy, Margie, Yippie, Oopie, Vonsey/Sept. 1); and "Millionaire Hobo" (with Scrappy, Margie, Yippie, Oopie, Vonsey/Nov. 24).

**1940:** "The Mouse Exterminator" (with Krazy Kat/Jan. 26); "Man of Tin" (with Scrappy, Margie, Yippie, Oopie, Vonsey/Feb. 23); "Fish Follies" (May 10); "News Oddities" (with Krazy Kat/July 19); "Schoolboy Dreams" (with Scrappy, Margie, Yippie, Oopie, Vonsey/Sept. 24); and "Happy Holidays" (with Scrappy, Margie, Yippie, Oopie, Vonsey/Oct. 25).

**1941:** "The Little Theatre" (with Scrappy, Margie, Yippie, Oopie, Vonsey/Feb. 7); "There's Music in Your Hair" (Davis/Mar. 28); "The Cute Recruit" (Davis/May 2); "The Wall Flower" (July 3); "The Merry Mouse Cafe" (Aug. 15); and "The Crystal Gazer" (Davis/Sept. 26).

**1942:** "Dog Meets Dog" (with Butch, Puppy/Tashlin/Mar. 6); "The Wild and Woozy West" (Rose/Apr. 30); "A Battle for a Bottle" (Geiss/May 29); "Old Blackout Joe" (Sommer, Hubley/ Aug. 27); "The Gullible Canary" (Geiss/Sept. 18); "The Dumb Conscious Mind" (with Butch, Puppy/Sommer, Hubley/Oct. 23); "Malice in Slumberland" (Geiss/Nov. 20); and "Cholly Polly" (Geiss/Dec. 18).

**1943:** "The Vitamin G Man" (Sommer, Hubley/Jan. 22); "Kindly Scram" (Geiss/Mar. 5); "Willoughby's Magic Hat" (with Willoughby Wren/Wickersham/Apr. 30); "Duty and the Beast" (Geiss/May 28); "Mass Mouse Meeting" (Geiss/June 25); "The Fly in the Ointment" (Sommer/July 23); "Dizzy Newsreel" (Geiss/Aug. 27); "Nursery Crimes" (Geiss/Oct. 8); "The Cocky Bantam" (Sommer/ Nov. 12); and "The Playful Pest" (Sommer/Dec. 3).

**1944:** "Polly Wants a Doctor" (Swift/Jan. 6); "Magic Strength" (Wickersham/Feb. 4); "Lionel Lion" (Sommer/Mar. 3); "Giddy Yapping" (Swift/Apr. 7); "Tangled Travels" (Geiss/June 9); "Mr. Fore by Fore" (Swift/July 7); "Case of the Screaming Bishop" (Swift/Aug. 4); "Mutt 'n' Bones" (Sommer/Aug. 25); and "As the Fly Flies" (Swift/Nov. 17).

**1945:** "Goofy News Views" (Marcus/Apr. 27); "Booby Socks" (Swift, Wickersham/July 12); and "Simple Siren" (Sommer/ Sept. 20).

**1946:** "Kongo-Roo" (Swift/Apr. 18); "Snap Happy Traps" (Wickersham/June 6); and "The Schooner the Better" (Swift/July 14).

**1947:** "Fowl Brawl" (Swift/Jan. 9); "Uncultured Vulture" (Wickersham/Feb. 6); "Wacky Quacky" (Lovy/Mar. 20); "Leave Us Chase It" (Swift/May 15); "Tooth or Consequences" (with Fox and the Crow/Swift/June 5); and "Kitty Caddy" (Marcus/Nov. 6).

**1948:** "Topsy Turkey" (Marcus/Feb. 5); and "Short Snort on Sports" (Lovy/June 3).

**1949:** "Coo Coo Bird Dog" (Marcus/Feb. 3).

## ◎ PHONEY BALONEY

Phoney Baloney, a teller of tall tales who stretched the truth a bit, was a lesser-known character cast in a brief series of one-reel shorts under the *Terry-Toons* banner. *Directed by Connie Rasinski. Technicolor. A Terry-Toon Cartoons and Terrytoons CBS Films, Inc., Production released through 20th Century Fox.*

**1954:** "Tall Tale Teller" (Mar).

**1957:** "African Jungle Hunt" (Mar.).

## ◎ PIGGY

Warner Bros. introduced this happy-go-lucky musical pig, called "Patty Pig" on studio model sheets, in a series of musical *Merrie Melodies* cartoon shorts. *Directed by Rudolf Ising. Voice credits are unknown. Black-and-white. A Hugh Harman and Rudolf Ising and Vitaphone Pictures Production released by Warner Bros.*

### Merrie Melodies

**1931:** "You Don't Know What You're Doin'!'" (Oct. 21); and "Hittin' the Trail to Hallelujah Land" (Nov. 28).

## ◎ THE PINK PANTHER

The egocentric panther was first introduced during the credits of Blake Edwards's popular spy spoof *The Pink Panther,* named after the jewel in the movie. Edwards contracted DePatie-Freleng Enterprises, headed by David H. DePatie and Friz Freleng, to animate titles for the movie using a sly panther being hotly pursued by a cartoon version of Inspector Clouseau.

The film's clever title sequence set the stage for a series of Pink Panther cartoons that followed, produced by DePatie-Freleng for United Artists. The studio unanimously approved the idea after witnessing the widespread attention the character received for its brief appearance in the Blake Edwards feature.

The first "official" Pink Panther cartoon, "The Pink Phink," premiered in 1964 with Billy Wilder's feature *Kiss Me, Stupid* at Grauman's Chinese Theatre in Hollywood. The cartoon was a huge success in more ways than one. It garnered the coveted Oscar statuette for best short subject (it was the only time a cartoon studio won an Oscar with its first cartoon release; only one other Pink Panther cartoon was ever nominated for an Oscar: 1966's "The Pink Blueprint"), and DePatie-Freleng was commissioned to produce one new cartoon per month following the success of their first effort in order to satisfy the public's thirst for more.

The nonspeaking panther did break his silence in two cartoons. In 1965's "Sink Pink," Paul Frees, in a Rex Harrison–type voice, spoke the first lines of dialogue in the character's history ("Why can't man be more like animals?") at the end of film in which he outsmarts a big-game hunter who tries capturing animals of every species by building an ark. He spoke again, this time with more extensive dialogue, in 1965's "Pink Ice" (voiced by Rich Little).

Silent film comedies of the 1920s served as a source of inspiration for creating the series' brand of humor. Many films reenact visual bits first made famous by Charlie Chaplin and Buster Keaton, two of filmdom's greatest slapstick comedians. Even a lively ragtime musical score accompanied the cartoons, similar to the music organists played in theaters to back silent film comedies as they were screened for audiences.

Friz Freleng, who found his niche at Warner Bros., first directed the series before turning it over to his longtime assistant Hawley Pratt. Storyman John Dunn is credited with writing the wildly innovative and clever stories for the series.

In 1993 the Pink Panther returned, this time in a new syndicated television cartoon series, in which he talked (voiced by Matt Frewer of TV's *Max Headroom* fame). The series was produced by MGM/United Artists (UA) in association with Claster Corporation. Creator Friz Freleng and longtime partner David DePatie served as creative consultants on the series, which was produced and directed by Charles Grosvenor and Byron Vaughns. Two years later the Pink Panther was back on the silver screen when MGM/ UA released an episode from the television series as a new theatrical cartoon short, "Driving Mr Pink," featuring a new sidekick: Voodoo Man. The short, produced and directed by Grosvenor and Vaughns, opened with Don Bluth's full-length animated feature

*The Pebble and the Penguin.* Directed by Friz Freleng, Brad Case, Gerry Chiniquy, Art Davis, Dave Detiege, Cullen Houghtaling, Art Leonardi, Sid Marcus, Robert McKimson, Hawley Pratt, Bob Richardson, Charles Grosvenor and Byron Vaughns. Technicolor. A Mirisch-Geoffrey-DePatie-Freleng Enterprises Production released through United Artists and MGM/United Artists.

*Voices*
**Pink Panther:** Paul Frees, Rich Little, Matt Frewer

*Additional voices*
Rich Little, Mel Blanc, Paul Frees, Dave Barry, Ralph James

*United Artists releases*

**1964:** "The Pink Phink" (Freleng, Pratt/Dec. 18/A.A. winner); and "Pink Pajamas" (Freleng, Pratt/Dec. 25).

**1965:** "We Give Pink Stamps" (Freleng, Pratt/Feb. 12); "Dial 'P' for Pink" (Freleng, Pratt/Mar. 17); "Sink Pink" (Freleng, Pratt/Apr. 12/Note: Friz Freleng is uncredited as codirector); "Pickled Pink" (Freleng, Pratt/May 12); "Shocking Pink" (Freleng, Pratt/May 13); "Pinkfinger" (Freleng, Pratt/May 13); "Pink Ice" (Freleng, Pratt/June 10); "The Pink Tail Fly" (Freleng, Pratt/Aug. 25); "Pink Panzer" (Pratt/Sept. 15/incorporates live-action footage of tanks in action); "An Ounce of Pink" (Pratt/Oct. 20); "Reel Pink" (Pratt/Nov. 16); and "Bully for Pink" (Pratt/Dec. 14).

**1966:** "Pink Punch" (Pratt/Feb. 21); "Pink Pistons" (Pratt/Mar. 16); "Vitamin Pink" (Pratt/Apr. 6); "The Pink Blue Print" (Pratt/May 25/A.A. nominee); "Pink, Plunk, Plink" (Pratt/May 25/Note: Contains cameo appearance by Pink Panther theme composer Henry Mancini); "Smile Pretty, Say Pink" (Pratt/May 29); "Pink-a-Boo" (Pratt/June 26); "Genie with the Light Pink Fur" (Pratt/Sept. 14); "Super Pink" (Pratt/Oct. 12); and "Rock A Bye Pinky" (Pratt/Dec. 23).

**1967:** "Pinknic" (Pratt/Jan. 6); "Pink Panic" (Pratt/Jan. 11); "Pink Posies" (Pratt/Apr. 26); "Pink of the Litter" (Pratt/May 17); "In the Pink" (Pratt/May 18); "Jet Pink" (Chiniquy/June 13); "Pink Paradise" (Chiniquy/June 24); "Pinto Pink" (Pratt/July 19); "Congratulations It's Pink" (Pratt/Oct. 27); "Prefabricated Pink" (Pratt/Nov. 22); "Hand Is Pinker Than the Eye" (Pratt/Dec. 20); and "Pink Outs" (Chiniquy/Dec. 27).

**1968:** "Sky Blue Pink" (Pratt/Jan. 3); "Pinkadilly Circus" (Pratt/Feb. 21); "Psychedelic Pink" (Pratt/Mar. 13); "Come on In! The Water's Pink" (Pratt/Apr. 10); "Put-Put, Pink" (Chiniquy/Apr. 14); "G.I. Pink" (Pratt/May 1); "Lucky Pink" (Pratt/May 7); "The Pink Quarterback" (Pratt/May 22); "Twinkle, Twinkle Little Pink" (Pratt/June 30); "Pink Valiant" (Pratt/July 10); "The Pink Pill" (Chiniquy/July 31); "Prehistoric Pink" (Pratt/Aug. 7); "Pink in the Clink" (Chiniquy/Sept. 18); "Little Beaux Pink" (Pratt/Oct. 2); "Tickled Pink" (Chiniquy/Oct. 6); "Pink Sphinx" (Pratt/Oct. 23); "Pink Is a Many Splintered Thing" (Chiniquy/Nov. 20); "The Pink Package Plot" (Davis/Dec. 11); and "Pinkcome Tax" (Davis/Dec. 20).

**1969:** "Pink-a-Rella" (Pratt/Jan. 8); "Pink Pest Control" (Chiniquy/Feb. 12); "Think Before You Pink" (Chiniquy/Mar. 19); "Slink Pink" (Pratt/Apr. 2); "In the Pink of the Night" (Davis/May 18); "Pink on the Cob" (Pratt/May 29); and "Extinct Pink" (Pratt/June 20).

**1971:** "A Fly in the Pink" (Pratt/June 23); "Pink Blue Plate" (Chiniquy/July 18); "Pink Tuba-Dore" (Davis/Aug. 4); "Pink Pranks" (Chiniquy/Aug. 28); "The Pink Flea" (Pratt/Sept. 15);

"Psst Pink" (Davis/Sept. 5); "Gong with the Pink" (Pratt/Oct. 20); and "Pink-in" (Davis/Oct. 20).

**1972:** "Pink 8 Ball" (Pratt/Feb. 6).

**1974:** "Pink Aye" (Chiniquy/May 16); and "Trail of the Lonesome Pink" (Chiniquy/June 27).

**1975:** "Pink DaVinci" (McKimson/June 23); "Pink Streaker" (Chiniquy/June 27); "Salmon Pink" (Chiniquy/July 25); "Forty Pink Winks" (Chiniquy/Aug. 8); "Pink Plasma" (Leonardi/Aug. 8); "Pink Elephant" (Chiniquy/Oct. 20); "Keep Our Forests Pink" (Chiniquy/Nov. 20); "Bobolink Pink" (Chiniquy/Dec. 30); "It's Pink But Is It Mink?" (McKimson/Dec. 30); "Pink Campaign" (Leonardi/Dec. 30); and "The Scarlet Pinkernel" (Chiniquy/Dec. 30).

**1976:** "Mystic Pink" (McKimson/Jan. 6); "The Pink Arabee" (Chiniquy/Mar. 13); "The Pink Pro" (McKimson/Apr. 12); "Pink Piper" (Houghtaling/Apr. 30); "Pinky Doodle" (Marcus/May 28); "Sherlock Pink" (McKimson/June 29); and "Rocky Pink" (Leonardi/July 9).

**1977:** "Therapeutic Pink" (Chiniquy/Apr. 1).
(The following 32 Pink Panther cartoons were originally produced for television's *All New Pink Panther Show*, which aired on ABC from 1978 to 1979, and were released theatrically.)

**1978:** "Pink Pictures" (Chiniquy/Oct. 21); "Pink Arcade" (Marcus/Oct. 25); "Pink Lemonade" (Chiniquy/Nov. 4); "Pink Trumpet" (Davis/Nov. 4); "Sprinkle Me Pink" (Richardson/Nov. 11); "Dietetic Pink" (Marcus/Nov. 11); "Pink Lightning" (Case/Nov. 17); "Pink U.F.O." (Detiege/Nov. 16); "Pink Daddy" (Chiniquy/Nov. 18); "Cat and the Pinkstalk" (Detiege/Nov. 18); "Pink S.W.A.T." (Marcus/Nov. 22); "Pink and Shovel" (Chiniquy/Nov. 25); "Pinkologist" (Chiniquy/Dec. 2); "Yankee Doodle Pink" (Marcus/Dec. 2/reissue of "Pinky Doodle"); "Pink Press" (Davis/Dec. 9); "Pet Pink Pebbles" (Chiniquy/Dec. 9/reissue of "Rocky Pink"/Note: Art Leonardi is uncredited as codirector); "The Pink of Bagdad" (Davis/Dec. 9/reissue of "The Pink of Arabee"/Note: Gerry Chiniquy is uncredited as codirector); "Pink in the Drink" (Marcus/Dec. 20); "Pink Bananas" (Davis/Dec. 22); "PinkTails for Two" (Davis/Dec. 22); "Pink Z-Z-Z" (Marcus/Dec. 23); and "Star Pink" (Davis/Dec. 23).

**1979:** "Pink Breakfast" (Case/Feb. 1); "Pink Quackers" (Case/Apr. 4); "Toro Pink" (Marcus/Apr. 4); "String Along in Pink" (Chiniquy/Apr. 12); "Pink in the Woods" (Case/Apr. 27); "Pink Pull" (Marcus/June 15); "Spark Plug Pink" (Case/June 28); "Doctor Pink" (Marcus/Nov. 16); "Pink Suds" (Davis/Dec. 19).

**1980:** "Supermarket Pink" (Case/Feb. 1).

*MGM/United Artists release*

**1995:** "Driving Mr. Pink" (with Voodoo Man/Grosvenor, Vaughns/Apr.).

## ◎ PIXAR CARTOONS
Predating the studio's later blockbuster features, including *Toy Story* (1995), *A Bug's Life* (1998), *Finding Nemo* (2003) and others, was this series of highly original and highly entertaining Academy Award-winning computer short-subjects, begun in 1984 by former Disney animator John Lasseter and still in production today. Lasseter became interested in the immense possibilities of computer animation while working on the studio's partially computer-animated feature, *TRON* (1982). Thereafter, he produced a 30-second film utilizing traditional and computer-rendered animation

based on Maurice Sendak's classic children's book, *Where the Wild Things Are*, with fellow Disney animator Glean Keane.

Desiring to do more in the medium, in 1984 Lasseter left Disney to join Lucasfilm's Industrial Light and Magic Computer Division, where he directed his first 3-D animated short, *Andre and Willy B.* (1984), which premiered at SIGGRAPH, the largest computer graphics conference in the world. Two years later, after Macintosh founder Steve Jobs bought Lucasfilm's computer graphics division for $10 million and changed its name to Pixar, Lasseter stayed on to write, produce and direct television commercials and computer-animated film shorts, many of them winners of numerous film festival awards. His first under the Pixar banner was the two-minute father-kid lamp adventure *Luxo Jr.* (1986), the first widely seen short using computer animation and the studio's first Academy Award-nominated short in the best short film (animated) category.

Over the next three years, Lasseter directed three more award-winning shorts: *Red's Dream* (1987), about a bicycle store unicycle dreaming of a better future; *Tin Toy* (1988), a film containing 55 shots about the escapades of a destructive tot that debuted that October at the Ottawa '88 International Animation Festival and became the first computer-animated film to win an Oscar for best short film (animated); and, finally, *knick knack* (1989), a comical 3-D stereoscopic film about an overly eager snowman hoping to crack open his snow globe to join a beautiful bathing suit-clad woman at a party.

While assuming greater responsibility for the day-to-day operations of the studio, Lasseter has since served as executive producer on computer-animated shorts directed by Pixar animators Jan Pinkava, Ralph Eggleston, Bud Luckey, Peter Docter, Roger Gould, Mark Andrews and Andrew Jimenez. Among them were two more Academy Award shorts, *Geri's Game* (1997), about an elderly man's attempt to play a game of chess, and *For the Birds* (2000), in which a dopey bird drops in on some snooty birds on a telephone pole wire, plus three other Oscar nominees: *Mike's New Car* (2003), featuring the characters James P. "Sulley" Sullivan and Mike Wzowski from the Pixar hit feature *Monsters, Inc.*; *Boundin* (2004), starring a banjo-playing, high-stepping woolly lamb; and *One Man Band*, in which two street performers compete for a kid's last piece of change. *Directed by John Lasseter, Jan Pinkava, Ralph Eggleston, Bud Luckey, Peter Docter, Roger Gould, Mark Andrews and Andrew Jimenez. Color. A Pixar Animation Studios Production released by Lucasfilms Ltd., 20th Century Fox Film Corp. and Buena Vista Pictures.*

### Lucafilms Ltd. releases

**1984:** *The Adventures of Andre and Wally B.* (Lasseter).

### Buena Vista Pictures releases

**1986:** *Luxo Jr.* (Lasseter/A.A. nominee)

**1987:** *Red's Dream* (Lasseter/July 6).

**1988:** *Tin Toy* (Lasseter/A.A. winner)

### 20th Century Fox Film Corp. releases

**1989:** *knick knack* (Lasseter)

### Buena Vista Pictures releases

**1997:** *Geri's Game* (Pinkava/Nov. 27/A.A. winner)

**2000:** *For the Birds* (Eggleston/June 5/A.A. winner)

**2002:** *Mike's New Car* (Docter, Gould/May 24/A.A. nominee)

**2003:** *Boundin'* (Luckey/Dec./A.A. nominee).

**2005:** *One Man Band* (Andrews, Jimenez/June 8/A.A. nominee)

## ◉ PLUTO

His lovable, mischievous nature spelled instant stardom for Mickey Mouse's playful pet Pluto in a number of memorable Walt Disney cartoons. By contrast to other cartoon stars of this era, his popularity was somewhat surprising since he displayed few human characteristics and didn't even talk. Nonetheless, film audiences fell in love with this canine creation following his first screen appearance in the 1930 Mickey Mouse cartoon "The Chain Gang."

Norman Ferguson, who animated Pluto in his first cartoon, was mostly responsible for establishing him as a major star. He embellished the dog's personality, adding exaggerated facial expressions and pantomime to his repertoire. Audiences were so taken by Pluto's screen presence that by the 1940s he actually outranked his mentor Mickey Mouse in popularity.

In 1937 Pluto starred in his own series, lasting 15 consecutive years before it was discontinued. *Directors were Ben Sharpsteen, Jack Kinney, Norman Ferguson, Clyde Geronimi, Charles Nichols, Jack Hannah and Milt Schaffer. Technicolor. A Walt Disney Production released through RKO Radio Pictures.*

**1937:** "Pluto's Quin-Puplets" (Sharpsteen/Nov. 26).

**1940:** "Bone Trouble" (Kinney/June 28); and "Pantry Pirate" (Geronimi/Dec. 27).

**1941:** "Pluto's Playmate" (Ferguson/Jan. 24); "A Gentleman's Gentleman" (with Mickey Mouse/Geronimi/Mar. 28); "Canine Caddy" (with Mickey Mouse/Geronimi/May 30); and "Lend a Paw" (with Mickey Mouse/Geronimi/Oct. 3/A.A. winner).

**1942:** "Pluto Junior" (with Pluto Junior/Geronimi/Feb. 28); "The Army Mascot" (Geronimi/May 22); "The Sleepwalker" (with Dinah/Geronimi/July 3); "T-Bone for Two" (with Dinah, Butch/Geronimi/Aug. 14); and "Pluto at the Zoo" (Geronimi/Nov. 20).

**1943:** "Pluto and the Armadillo" (with Mickey Mouse/Geronimi/Feb. 19); and "Private Pluto" (with formative Chip 'n' Dale/Geronimi/Apr. 2).

**1944:** "Springtime for Pluto" (Nichols/June 23); and "First Aiders" (with Minnie Mouse, Figaro, Fifi/Nichols/Sept. 22).

**1945:** "Dog Watch" (Nichols/Mar. 16); "Canine Casanova" (with Dinah, Butch/Nichols/July 27); "The Legend of Coyote Rock" (Nichols/Aug. 24); and "Canine Patrol" (Nichols/Dec. 7).

**1946:** "Pluto's Kid Brother" (with Pluto's Kid Brother, Butch, Lucifer/Nichols/Apr. 12); "In Dutch" (with Dinah/Nichols/May 10); "Squatter's Rights" (with Chip 'n' Dale, Mickey Mouse/Hannah/June 7/A.A. nominee); and "The Purloined Pup" (with Butch/Nichols/July 19).

**1947:** "Pluto's Housewarming" (with Butch/Nichols/Feb. 21); "Rescue Dog" (Nichols/Mar. 21); "Mail Dog" (Nichols/Nov. 14); and "Pluto's Blue Note" (Nichols/Dec. 26/A.A. nominee).

**1948:** "Bone Bandit" (Nichols/Apr. 30); "Pluto's Purchase" (with Mickey Mouse, Butch/Nichols/July 9); "Cat Nap Pluto" (Nichols/Aug. 13); and "Pluto's Fledgling" (Nichols/Sept. 10).

**1949:** "Pueblo Pluto" (with Mickey Mouse/Nichols/Jan. 14); "Pluto's Surprise Package" (Nichols/Mar. 4); "Pluto's Sweater" (with Minnie Mouse, Figaro, Butch/Nichols/Apr. 29); "Bubble Bee" (Nichols/June 24); and "Sheep Dog" (Nichols/Nov. 4).

**1950:** "Pluto's Heart Throb" (with Dinah, Butch/Nichols/Jan. 6); "Pluto and the Gopher" (with Minnie Mouse/Nichols/Feb. 10); "Wonder Dog" (with Dinah, Butch/Nichols/Apr. 7); "Primitive

Pluto" (Nichols/May 19); "Puss-Cafe" (Nichols/June 9); "Pests of the West" (Nichols/July 21); "Food for Feudin'" (with Chip 'n' Dale/Nichols/Aug. 11); and "Camp Dog" (Nichols/Sept. 22).

**1951:** "Cold Storage" (Kinney/Feb. 9); "Plutopia" (with Mickey Mouse/Nichols/May 18); and "Cold Turkey" (Nichols/Sept. 21).

## ◉ PLYMPTOONS

Award-winning series of offbeat, ridiculous and strangely original cartoons animated, written, directed and produced by one of the industry's most successful independent American animators and former illustrator and political cartoonist, Bill Plympton, exhibited at hundreds of film festivals, movie theaters and art houses throughout the world.

While working as a free-lance artist in 1977, Plympton, who lives and works in New York, animated and directed his first cartoon short starring a young corncob who learns to grow up, *Lucas the Ear of Corn*. He returned to the screen six years later, directing and animating *Boomtown* (1985), his first film that Valeria Wasilewski (of the Android Sisters) and Connie D'Antuono adapted from the popular Jules Feiffer song of the same name. The Cold War musical parable played at numerous film festivals and, from the $2,000 he won in award money, he financed and started a third short, combining live-action and animation, *Drawing Lesson #2* (1988). Before its completion, he produced the acclaimed short scored by Maureen McElheron, *Your Face* (1987), the adventures of a group of sleazy crooners that garnered dozens of awards, including his first Academy Award nomination for best animated short.

Since then, Plympton has produced an onslaught of memorable animated one-reelers, among them, *Love in the Fast Lane* (1987), *One of Those Days* (1988), *How to Kiss* (1989), *25 Ways to Quit Smoking* (1989), *Plymptoons* (1990), *Tango Schmango* (1990) and *Dig My Do* (1990), not to mention his first cartoon feature, *The Tune* (1992). To continue to finance the film, Plympton finished and released parts of the feature as individual cartoon shorts, *The Wiseman* (1990) and *Push Comes to Shove* (1991), which won the 1991 Prix du Jury at the Cannes Film Festival. Following its theatrical release, *The Tune* premiered at many major film festivals, winning many awards, including the Houston WorldFest GoldJury Special Award and a Spirit Award nomination for best film score.

Between making two live-action features, *J. Lyle* (1994) and *Guns on the Clackamas: A Documentary* (1995), Plympton continued to produce, direct and animate many more distinctive cartoon shorts, including *Draw* (1993), *Faded Roads* (1994), *Nosehair* (1994), *How to Make Love to a Woman* (1995), *Smell the Flowers* (1995), *Boney D* (1996) and *Plympmania* (1996). In addition to producing two more full-length films, the cartoon compilation, *Mondo Plympton* (1997) and *I Married a Strange Person* (1998), he likewise animated a host of other acclaimed films, including: *Sex and Violence* (1997), *The Exciting Life of a Tree* (1998), *General Chaos: Uncensored Animation* (1998), *More Sex and Violence* (1998), *Surprise Cinema* (1999), *Can't Drag Race with Jesus* (2000), *Mutant Aliens, Eat* (2001) and *Parking* (2002), plus his third live-action feature, *Walt Curtis: The Peckerneck Poet* (1997), and first prime-time animated special for the Cartoon Network, *12 Tiny Christmas Tales* (2001).

In 2004, Plympton's clever cartoon, *Guard Dog*, nabbed him his second Academy Award nomination, after which he animated the widely received short, *Fan and the Flower* (2005), written and produced by Dan O'Shannon and starring the voice of Paul Giamatti, and his fourth animated feature, *Hair High* (2006). *Produced, directed, and animated by Bill Plympton. Color. A Bill Plympton, Big Man Pictures Corporation, Acme Filmworks, Plymptoons and Atomic Television Production released by E.D. Distribution.*

**1977:** *Lucas the Ear of the Corn*

### E.D. Distribution

**1985:** *Boomtown.*

**1987:** *Your Face* (A.A. nominee) and *Love in the Fast Lane.*

**1988:** *Drawing Lesson #2* and *One of Those Days.*

**1989:** *25 Ways to Quit Smoking* and *How to Kiss.*

**1990:** *Plymptoons; Tango Schmango; Dig My Do;* and *The Wiseman.*

**1991:** *Push Comes to Shove* (first cartoon produced by Big Man Pictures Corp.).

**1993:** *Draw.*

**1994:** *Faded Roads* and *Nose Hair.*

**1995:** *How to Make Love to a Woman.*

**1996:** *Smell the Flowers; Boney D;* and *Plympmania.*

**1997:** *Sex and Violence.*

**1998:** *The Exciting Life of a Tree* and *More Sex and Violence.*

**1999:** *Surprise Cinema.*

**2000:** *Can't Drag Race with Jesus* and *Eat.*

**2002:** *Parking.*

**2004:** *Guard Dog* (May/A.A. nominee).

**2005:** *The Fan and the Flower.*

## ◉ POOCH THE PUP

A cuddly canine, whose happy disposition was typical of other 1930s' cartoon stars, was the central figure in this series launched by creator Walter Lantz. The series was short-lived despite its strong characterizations and story lines based on familiar children's fairy tales and everyday themes with strong morals. *Directed and animated by Walter Lantz and William Nolan. No voice credits. Black-and-white. A Walter Lantz Production released through Universal Pictures.*

**1932:** "The Athlete" (Aug. 29/spoof of the 1932 Summer Olympics in Los Angeles); "The Butcher Boy" (Sept. 26); "The Crowd Snores" (Oct. 24/satire of the Warner Bros. feature, *The Crowd Roars*); "The Under Dog" (Nov. 7); and "Cats and Dogs" (Dec. 5).

**1933:** "Merry Dog" (Jan. 2); "The Terrible Troubadour" (Jan. 30); "The Lumber Champ" (Mar. 13); "Nature's Workshop" (June 5); "Pin Feathers" (July 3); "Hot and Cold" (Aug. 14/working title: "S.O.S. Icicle"); "King Klunk" (Sept. 4/spoof of RKO Radio feature, *King Kong*); and "She Done Him Right" (Oct. 9).

## ◉ POPEYE THE SAILOR

The most loved sailor of all time, Popeye came into the cartoon world in 1919 when Elzie Segar, a world-famous comic-strip artist, first conceived the musclebound sailor, originally known as Ham Gravy, for the classic strip *Thimble Theatre*. Gravy was featured in the strip along with his sticklike girlfriend, Olive Oyl. The strip became enormously popular, and Segar experimented with the Gravy character, changing his name to Popeye on January 17, 1929.

Even then, Popeye displayed many of the same traits that moviegoers became accustomed to in later cartoons: a gruff, straight-talking, hard-hitting sailor whose main source of energy was his can of spinach. The sailor's initial appearance was so well received that Segar made him a regular in the strip. Then, in 1932, Max Fleischer bought the film rights to the character from King Features, which syndicated the strip nationally, to produce a series of Popeye cartoons.

Popeye's first film appearance was in a Betty Boop cartoon, "Popeye the Sailor" (1933). Fleischer chose to feature him opposite a known star like Betty to measure public reaction before starring him in his own series, which began in earnest that same year. Early titles were derived from many of Popeye's popular catch lines, such as "Blow Me Down," "I Eats My Spinach" and others.

Through the years Popeye's voice changed—from gruff to even solemn—due to the switchover in voice artists who played him. William Costello was the first man to do Popeye (he won the job after Fleischer heard a recording of songs from his nightclub act as Red Pepper Sam) but was let go after "success went to his head." Costello was succeeded by another man, whom Dave Fleischer, Max's younger brother, overheard talking while buying a newspaper at a street corner. Fleischer hired the gentleman on the spot. His name was Jack Mercer, who, ironically, was an in-betweener at the Fleischer Studios.

Mercer remained the voice of Popeye for more than 45 years altogether, counting cartoons later produced for television. He gave the character greater dimension through memorable mutterings and other under-his-breath throwaway lines during recording sessions that added to the infectious humor of the series. A singer named Gus Wickie was the original voice of Bluto, who never appeared in the *Thimble Theatre* strip. (He was adapted from a one-shot villain in the strip, Bluto the Terrible.) As for Olive Oyl, Mae Questel, also the voice of Betty Boop, lent her voice for Popeye's lovestruck girlfriend. Questel demonstrated her versatility throughout the series, even doing the voice of Popeye for a handful of cartoons when Mercer was sent overseas during World War II.

Many early cartoons were built around songs by lyricist Sammy Lerner and musician Sammy Timberg, who wrote the original "Popeye the Sailor Man" song for the first Paramount cartoon. In time, various costars were added to the series, among them the hamburger-mooching Wimpy, Swee'Pea and other Segar creations, such as the Jeep, Poopdeck Pappy and the Goon. In the 1940s the series introduced Popeye's nephews: Peep-eye, Pip-eye, Pup-eye and Poop-eye, obviously inspired by Donald Duck's own nephews, Hewey, Dewey and Louie.

Besides starring in hundreds of one-reel shorts, Popeye and his cast of regulars appeared in a series of two-reel Technicolor "featurettes" before Walt Disney's breakthrough *Snow White and the Seven Dwarfs*. Adventures included *Popeye the Sailor Meets Sindbad the Sailor* (1936), *Popeye the Sailor Meets Ali Baba's Forty Thieves* (1937); and *Aladdin and His Wonderful Lamp* (1939).

In all, the Popeye series lasted 24 consecutive years, becoming the longest-running cartoon series in motion picture history. *Produced by Max Fleischer. Directors were Dave Fleischer, Isadore Sparber, Dan Gordon, Seymour Kneitel, Bill Tytla and Dave Tendlar. Black-and-white. Technicolor. A Fleischer Studios and Famous Studios release through Paramount Pictures Corporation.*

### Voices

**Popeye:** William Costello (to 1933), Jack Mercer, Mae Questel; **Olive Oyl:** Mae Questel; **Bluto:** Gus Wickie, Pinto Colvig, William Pennell, Jackson Beck; **Swee'pea:** Mae Questel; **Poopdeck Pappy/Peep-eye/Pip-eye/Pup-eye/Poop-eye/Wimpy:** Jack Mercer; **Shorty:** Arnold Stang

### Fleischer Studios releases

(The following cartoons are black-and-white unless indicated otherwise.)

**1933:** "Popeye the Sailor" (Fleischer/July 14); "I Yam What I Yam" (Fleischer/Sept. 29); "Blow Me Down!" (Fleischer/Oct. 27); "I Eats My Spinach" (Fleischer/Nov. 17); "Seasin's Greetniks!" (Fleischer/Dec. 17); and "Wild Elephinks" (Fleischer/Dec. 29).

**1934:** "Sock-A-Bye Baby" (Fleischer/Jan. 19); "Let's You and Him Fight" (Fleischer/Feb. 16); "The Man on the Flying Trapeze" (Fleischer/Mar. 16); "Can You Take It" (Fleischer/Apr. 27); "Shoein' Hosses" (Fleischer/June 1); "Strong to the Finish" (Fleischer/June 29); "Shiver Me Timbers!" (Fleischer/July 27); "Axe Me Another" (Fleischer/Aug. 30); "A Dream Walking" (Fleischer/© Sept. 26); "The Two-Alarm Fire" (Fleischer/Oct. 26); "The Dance Contest" (Fleischer/Nov. 23); and "We Aim to Please" (Fleischer/Dec. 28).

**1935:** "Beware of Barnacle Bill" (Fleischer/Jan. 25); "Be Kind to 'Animals'" (Fleischer/Feb. 22); "Pleased to Meet Cha!" (Fleischer/Mar. 22); "The 'Hyp-Nut-Tist'" (Fleischer/Apr. 26); "Choose Your 'Weppins'" (Fleischer/May 31); "For Better or Worser" (Fleischer/June 28); "Dizzy Divers" (Fleischer/July 26); "You Gotta Be a Football Hero" (Fleischer/Aug. 30); "King of the Mardi Gras" (Fleischer/Sept. 27); "Adventures of Popeye" (Fleischer/Oct. 25); and "The Spinach Overture" (Fleischer/Dec. 7).

**1936:** "Vim, Vigor and Vitaliky" (Fleischer/Jan. 3); "A Clean Shaven Man" (Fleischer/Feb. 7); "Brotherly Love" (Fleischer/Mar 6); "I-Ski Love-Ski You-Ski" (Fleischer/Apr. 3); "Bridge Ahoy!" (Fleischer/May 1); "What—No Spinach?" (Fleischer/May 7); "I Wanna Be a Lifeguard" (Fleischer/June 26); "Let's Get Movin'" (Fleischer/July 24); "Never Kick a Woman" (Fleischer/Aug. 28); "Little Swee' Pea" (Fleischer/Sept. 25); "Hold the Wire" (Fleischer/Oct. 23); "The Spinach Roadster" (Fleischer/Nov. 26); and "I'm in the Army Now" (Fleischer/Dec. 25).

**1937:** "The Paneless Window Washer" (Fleischer/Jan. 22); "Organ Grinder's Swing" (Fleischer/Feb. 19); "My Artistical Temperature" (Fleischer/Mar. 19); "Hospitaliky" (Fleischer/Apr. 16); "The Twisker Pitcher" (Fleischer/May 21); "Morning, Noon and Night Club" (Fleischer/June 18); "Lost and Foundry" (Fleischer/July 16); "I Never Changes My Altitude" (Fleischer/Aug. 20); "I Like Babies and Infinks" (Fleischer/Sept. 18); "The Football Toucher Downer" (Fleischer/Oct. 15); "Proteck the Weakerist" (Fleischer/Nov. 19); and "Fowl Play" (Fleischer/Dec. 17).

**1938:** "Let's Celebrake" (Fleischer/Jan. 21); "Learn Polikeness" (Fleischer/Feb. 18); "The House Builder Upper" (Fleischer/Mar. 18); "Big Chief Ugh-Amugh-Ugh" (Fleischer/Apr. 25); "I Yam Love Sick" (Fleischer/May 29); "Plumbin' Is a Pipe" (Fleischer/June 17); "The Jeep" (Fleischer/July 15); "Bulldozing the Bull" (Fleischer/Aug. 19); "Mutiny Ain't Nice" (Fleischer/Sept. 23); "Goonland" (Fleischer/Oct. 21); "A Date to Skate" (Fleischer/Nov. 18); and "Cops Is Always Right" (Fleischer/Dec. 29).

**1939:** "Customers Wanted" (Fleischer/Jan. 27); "Leave Well Enough Alone" (Fleischer/Apr. 28); "Wotta Nitemare" (Fleischer/May 19); "Ghosks Is the Bunk" (Fleischer/June 14); "Hello, How Am I?" (Fleischer/July 14); "It's the Natural Thing to Do" (Fleischer/July 30); and "Never Sock a Baby" (Fleischer/Nov. 3).

**1940:** "Shakespearian Spinach" (Fleischer/Jan. 19); "Females Is Fickle" (Fleischer/Mar. 8); "Stealin' Aint Honest" (Fleischer/Mar. 22); "Me Feelins Is Hurt" (Fleischer/Apr. 12); "Onion Pacific" (Fleischer/May 24); "Wimmen Is a Myskery" (Fleischer/June 7);

"Nurse-Mates" (Fleischer/June 21); "Fightin Pals" (Fleischer/July 12); "Doing Impossikible Stunts" (Fleischer/Aug. 2); "Wimmin Hadn't Oughta Drive" (Fleischer/Aug. 16); "Puttin' On the Act" (Fleischer/Aug. 30); "Popeye Meets William Tell" (Fleischer/Sept. 20/Note: Shamus Culhane credits himself as director, even though Fleischer is listed); "My Pop, My Pop" (Fleischer/© Oct. 18); "With Poopdeck Pappy" (Fleischer/Nov. 15); and "Popeye Presents Eugene, the Jeep" (Fleischer/Dec. 13).

**1941:** "Problem Pappy" (Fleischer/Jan. 10); "Quiet! Pleeze" (Fleischer/Feb. 7/uses footage from "Sock-a-Bye Baby"); "Olive's $weep$take Ticket" (Fleischer/Mar. 7); "Flies Ain't Human" (Fleischer/Apr. 4); "Popeye Meets Rip Van Wrinkle" (Fleischer/May 9); "Olive's Boithday Presink" (Fleischer/June 13); "Child Psykolojiky" (Fleischer/July 11); "Pest Pilot" (Fleischer/Aug. 8); "I'll Never Crow Again" (Fleischer/Sept. 19); "The Mighty Navy" (Fleischer/Nov. 14); and "Nix on Hypnotricks" (Fleischer/Dec. 19).

**1942:** "Kickin' the Conga 'Round" (Fleischer/Jan. 16); "Blunder Below" (Fleischer/Feb. 13); "Fleets of Stren'th" (Fleischer/Mar. 13); "Pip-Eye, Pup-Eye, Poop-Eye an' Peep-Eye" (Fleischer/Apr. 10); "Olive Oyl and Water Don't Mix" (Fleischer/May 8); "Many Tanks" (Fleischer/May 15); and "Baby Wants a Bottleship" (Fleischer/July 3/last cartoon directed by Fleischer).

### Famous Studios releases

**1942:** "You're a Sap, Mr. Jap" (Gordon/Aug. 7); "Alona on the Sarong Seas" (Sparber/Sept. 4); "A Hull of a Mess" (Sparber/Oct. 16); "Scrap the Japs" (Kneitel/Nov. 20); and "Me Musical Nephews" (Kneitel/Dec. 25).

**1943:** "Spinach fer Britain" (Sparber/Jan. 22); "Seein' Red, White 'N' Blue" (Gordon/Feb. 19); "Too Weak to Work" (Sparber/Mar. 19); "A Jolly Good Furlough" (Gordon/Apr. 23); "Ration fer the Duration" (Kneitel/May 28); "The Hungry Goat" (Gordon/June 25); "Happy Birthdaze" (Gordon/July 16); "Wood-Peckin'" (Sparber/Aug. 6); "Cartoons Ain't Human" (Kneitel/Aug. 27/last Paramount black-and-white cartoon); "Her Honor the Mare" (Sparber/Nov. 26/re: Oct 6, 1950/first Technicolor); and "The Marry-Go-Round" (Kneitel/Dec. 31).

(The following cartoons are in Technicolor unless indicated otherwise.)

**1944:** "W'ere on Our Way to Rio" (Sparber/Apr. 21/re: Oct. 20, 1950); "The Anvil Chorus Girl" (Sparber/May 26/re: Oct. 5, 1951/remake of "Shoein' Hosses"); "Spinach Packin' Popeye" (Sparber/July 21/re: Oct. 5, 1951/footage used from *Popeye the Sailor Meets Ali Baba's Forty Thieves* and *Popeye the Sailor Meets Sindbad the Sailor*); "Puppet Love" (Kneitel/Aug. 11/re: Oct. 3, 1952); "Pitching Woo at the Zoo" (Sparber/Sept. 1/re: Oct. 3, 1953); "Moving Aweigh" (Sept. 22); and "She-Sick Sailors" (Kneitel/Dec. 8/re: Oct. 5, 1951).

**1945:** "Pop-Pie a la Mode" (Sparber/Jan. 26/re: Nov. 3, 1950); "Tops in the Big Top" (Sparber/Mar. 16); "Shape Ahoy" (Sparber/Apr. 27/re: Nov. 17, 1950); "For Better or Nurse" (Sparber/June 8/re: Oct. 5, 1951/remake of "Hospitaliky"); and "Mess Production" (Kneitel/Aug. 24/re: Oct. 3, 1952).

**1946:** "House Tricks?" (Kneitel/Mar. 15/re: Oct. 5, 1952/remake of "House Builder Uppers"); "Service with a Guile" (Tytla/Apr. 19); "Klondike Casanova" (Sparber/May 31); "Peep in the Deep" (Kneitel/June 7/remake of "Dizzy Divers"); "Rocket to Mars" (Tytla/Aug. 9/Cinecolor); "Rodeo Romeo" (Sparber/Aug. 16);

"The Fistic Mystic" (Kneitel/Nov. 29); and "The Island Fling" (Tytla/Nov. 29).

**1947:** "Abusement Park" (Sparber/Apr. 25); "I'll Be Skiing Ya" (Sparber/June 13); "Popeye and the Pirates" (Kneitel/Sept. 12); "The Royal Four-Flusher" (Kneitel/Sept. 12); "Wotta Knight" (Sparber/Oct. 24); "Safari So Good" (Sparber/Nov. 7); and "All's Fair at the Fair" (Sparber/Dec. 19/Cinecolor).

**1948:** "Olive Oyl for President" (Sparber/Jan. 30); "Wigwam Whoopee" (Sparber/Feb. 27); "Pre-Hysterical Man" (Kneitel/Mar. 26); "Popeye Meets Hercules" (Tytla/June 18/Polacolor); "A Wolf in Sheik's Clothing" (Sparber/July 30); "Spinach vs. Hamburgers" (Kneitel/Aug. 27/footage used from "Anvil Chorus Girl," "She-Sick Sailors" and "Pop-Pie a la Mode"); "Snow Place Like Home" (Kneitel/Sept. 3); "Robin Hoodwinked" (Kneitel/Nov. 12/Polacolor); and "Symphony in Spinach" (Kneitel/Dec. 31/Polacolor).

**1949:** "Popeye's Premiere" (Mar. 25/footage used from *Aladdin and His Wonderful Lamp*); "Lumberjack and Jill" (Kneitel/May 27); "Hot Air Aces" (Sparber/June 24); "A Balmy Swami" (Sparber/July 22); "Tar with a Star" (Tytla/Aug. 12); "Silly Hillbilly" (Sparber/Sept. 9); "Barking Dogs Don't Fite" (Sparber/Oct. 28/remake of "Proteck the Weakerist"); and "The Fly's Last Flight" (Kneitel/Dec. 23).

**1950:** "How Green Is My Spinach" (Kneitel/Jan. 27); "Gym Jam" (Sparber/Mar. 17/remake of "Vim, Vigor and Vitaliky"); "Beach Peach" (Kneitel/May 12); "Jitterbug Jive" (Tytla/June 23); "Popeye Makes a Movie" (Kneitel/Aug. 11/footage used from *Popeye the Sailor Meets Ali Baba's Forty Thieves*); "Baby Wants Spinach" (Kneitel/Sept. 29); "Quick on the Vigor" (Kneitel/Oct. 6); "Riot in Rhythm" (Kneitel/Nov. 10/remake of "Me Musical Nephews"); and "The Farmer and the Belle" (Kneitel/Dec. 1).

**1951:** "Vacation with Play" (Sparber/Jan. 19); "Thrill of Fair" (Kneitel/Apr. 20/remake of "Li'l Swee Pea"); "Alpine for You" (Sparber/May 18/remake of "I-Ski Love-Ski You-Ski"); "Double-Cross-Country Race" (Kneitel/June 15); "Pilgrim Popeye" (Sparber/July 13); "Let's Stalk Spinach" (Kneitel/Oct. 19/remake of "Popeye and the Beanstalk"); and "Punch and Judo" (Sparber/Nov. 16).

**1952:** "Popeye's Pappy" (Kneitel/Jan. 25); "Lunch with a Punch" (Sparber/Mar. 14); "Swimmer Take All" (Kneitel/May 16); "Friend or Phony" (Sparber/June 30/footage used from "Tar with a Star" and "I'll Be Skiing Ya"); "Tots of Fun" (Kneitel/Aug. 15); "Popalong Popeye" (Kneitel/Aug. 29); "Shuteye Popeye" (Sparber/Oct. 3); and "Big Bad Sinbad" (Kneitel/Dec. 12/footage used from *Popeye the Sailor Meets Sindbad the Sailor*).

**1953:** "Ancient History" (Kneitel/Jan. 30); "Child Sockology" (Sparber/Mar. 27); "Popeye's Mirthday" (Kneitel/May 22); "Toreadorable" (Kneitel/June 12); "Baby Wants a Battle" (Kneitel/July 24); "Firemen's Brawl" (Sparber/Aug. 21); "Popeye, the Ace of Space" (Kneitel/Oct. 2/released in 3-D); and "Shaving Muggs" (Kneitel/Oct. 9/remake of "A Clean Shaven Man").

**1954:** "Floor Flusher" (Sparber/Jan. 1/remake of "Plumbing Is a Pipe"); "Popeye's 20th Anniversary" (Sparber/Apr. 2); "Taxi-Turvy" (Kneitel/June 4); "Bride and Gloom" (Sparber/July 2); "Greek Mirthology" (Kneitel/Aug. 13); "Fright to the Finish" (Kneitel/Aug. 27); "Private Eye Popeye" (Kneitel/Nov. 12); and "Gopher Spinach" (Kneitel/Dec. 10).

**1955:** "Cooking with Gags" (Sparber/Jan. 14); "Nurse to Meet Ya" (Sparber/Feb. 11/remake of "Hospitaliky," "Nurse-Mates" and

"For Better or Nurse"); "Penny Antics" (Kneitel/Mar. 11/remake of "Customers Wanted"); "Beaus Will Be Beaus" (Sparber/May 20); "Gift of Gag" (Kneitel/May 27); "Car-azy Drivers" (Kneitel/July 22); "Mister and Mistletoe" (Sparber/Sept. 30); "Cops Is Tops" (Sparber/Nov. 4); and "A Job for a Gob" (Kneitel/Dec. 9).

**1956:** "Hill-billing and Cooing" (Kneitel/Jan. 13); "Popeye for President" (Kneitel/Mar. 30); "Out to Punch" (Kneitel/June 8); "Assault and Flattery" (Sparber/July 6/footage used from "The Farmer and the Belle," "Friend or Phony" and "A Balmy Swami"); "Insect to Injury" (Tendlar/Aug. 10); "Parlez Vous Woo" (Sparber/Sept. 12); "I Don't Scare" (Sparber/Nov. 16); and "A Haul in One" (Sparber/Dec. 14/remake of "Let's Get Movin'").

**1957:** "Nearlyweds" (Kneitel/Feb. 8); "The Crystal Brawl" (Kneitel/Apr. 5/footage used from "Alpine for You" and "Quick on the Vigor"); "Patriotic Popeye" (Sparber/May 10); "Spree Lunch" (Kneitel/June 21); and "Spooky Swabs" (Sparber/Aug. 9).

### Popeye Two-Reel Featurettes

**1936:** *Popeye the Sailor Meets Sindbad the Sailor* (Fleischer/Nov. 27/A.A nominee).

**1937:** *Popeye the Sailor Meets Ali Baba's Forty Thieves* (Fleischer/Nov. 26/Technicolor).

**1939:** *Aladdin and His Wonderful Lamp* (Fleischer/Apr. 7/Technicolor).

### ◎ PORKY PIG

When Warner Bros. began testing several characters as replacements for Hugh Harman's *Buddy* series, director Friz Freleng introduced this timid, simpleminded pig who spoke with a stutter in 1935's "I Haven't Got a Hat," an animal version of Hal Roach's *Our Gang* series. (The idea for the film was suggested by producer Leon Schlesinger, who liked the classic short-subject series.) Created as part of a team called "Pork and Beans" (named after a can of Campbell's Pork & Beans) by animator Bob Clampett, Freleng renamed the pig Porky after a childhood playmate he recalled as being "very fat."

While the other characters had their moments, Porky's recital of "Mary Had a Little Lamb" was the most memorable. Warner Bros. agreed. Afterward they gave the stammering pig his own starring series and, as they say, the rest is history.

Actor Joe Dougherty, a Warner Bros. bit player whose credits included *The Jazz Singer* and *Ziegfeld Girl*, was first hired to do the voice of Porky. Dougherty got the job because he actually stammered when he spoke, which turned out to be a problem as the series progressed since it was difficult for him to record his lines of dialogue. Dougherty lasted in the role for only two years; according to Freleng, "When he delivered his lines, he used up excessive amounts of soundtrack film since he couldn't control his stammerings. It just became too expensive to keep him so we finally let him go."

At the advice of Warner story editor Treg Brown, actor Mel Blanc was auditioned as Dougherty's replacement. He was so convincing that Freleng hired him on the spot and Blanc not only became the voice of Porky but practically every Warner Bros. cartoon character until the demise of the animation department in 1963. Blanc created Porky's famous sign-off line of "Th-th-th-th-that's all, folks!" used at the end of most Warner Bros. cartoons.

Porky remained a headliner in his series throughout the 1930s and 1940s. During the 1930s Clampett almost exclusively directed Porky in such early classics as "Porky's Hero Agency" (1937), "Porky in Wackyland" (1938), and "The Lone Stranger and

*Promotional lobby card from the Porky Pig cartoon "Porky's Hotel," directed by Bob Clampett. © Warner Brothers. All rights reserved.*

Porky" (1939), a Grand Shorts Award winner, plus two key 1940s films, "Baby Bottleneck" (1946) and "Kitty Kornered" (1946). In the late 1930s Porky was given a sidekick: a short-tempered, irritable goat named Gabby Goat, who appeared in only three cartoons: "Porky's Badtime Story," "Porky and Gabby" and "Get Rich Porky," all produced in 1937. (Gabby was voiced by Warner Bros. animator/director Cal Howard.) Gabby was dropped from the series after movie audiences found his characterization offensive.

Although Porky was a major star, the studio often used him in supporting roles to play off other characters on the studio roster. He was a supporting character for the first appearances of Daffy Duck in "Porky's Duck Hunt" (1937) and of Bugs Bunny in "Porky's Hare Hunt" (1938). At various times he played other comic relief roles. His most notable performances in this realm were under director Chuck Jones, who made Porky more adult-looking and cast him opposite Daffy Duck in a series of misadventures. Their most memorable appearance together is the space-age encounter "Duck Dodgers in the 24½th Century" (1953), which Jones directed. By the 1950s Porky seemed so well suited as a "second banana" that the studio utilized him more often in this capacity for the remainder of his career.

Porky did not remain completely indifferent to members of the opposite sex. In the late 1930s he was given a girlfriend who appeared in a handful of cartoon shorts. Her name: Petunia Pig. Petunia was introduced to moviegoers in 1937's "Porky's Romance."

Porky was reunited with his Bugs Bunny and his *Looney Tunes* pals in two films: "Invasion of the Bunny Snatchers," a 1990s Bugs Bunny cartoon that was never released to theaters, and *Space Jam*, the 1996 feature starring Michael Jordan and Bugs Bunny. Bob Bergen provided the voice of Porky for the latter. After costarring in his second live-action/animated feature, 2003's *Looney Tunes: Back in Action*, in 2004 Porky was to star in several new *Looney Tunes* theatrical cartoon shorts that were planned and storyboarded but never produced and released, including "The Pig Stays in the Picture" and "Daffy Contractor," with Daffy Duck, to be directed by Rich Moore, Dan Povenmire, Peter Shin and Bill Kopp. *Series directors were Friz Freleng, Tex Avery, Jack King, Frank Tashlin, Ub Iwerks, Bob Clampett, Cal Dalton, Cal Howard, Ben Hardaway, Norm McCabe, Chuck Jones, Art Davis, Robert McKimson and Irv Spector. Black-and-white. Technicolor. A Vitaphone/Leon Schlesinger/Warner Bros. Cartoons, Inc/Warner Bros./Warner Bros. Pictures, Inc./Vitagraph/DePatie-*

*Freleng Enterprises/Warner Bros. Animation/Warner Bros. Production released by Warner Bros.*

**Voices**
**Porky Pig:** Joe Dougherty (to 1937), Mel Blanc, Jeff Bergman; **Gabby Goat:** Cal Howard

*Looney Tunes*

*Vitaphone Productions releases*

**1935:** "Gold Diggers of '49" (with Beans/Avery/Nov. 2).

**1936:** "Plane Dippy" (with Oliver Owl, Little Kitty/Avery/Jan. 4); "Alpine Antics" (with Beans, Kitty/King/Jan. 18); "Boom Boom" (with Beans/King/Feb. 29); "The Blow Out" (Avery/Apr. 4); "Westward Whoa" (with Beans, Ham, Ex, Kitty/King/Apr. 25); "Fish Tales" (King/May 23); "Shanghaiied Shipmates" (King/June 26); "Porky's Pet" (King/July 11); "Porky the Rain-Maker" (Avery/Aug. 1); "Porky's Poultry Plant" (Tashlin/Aug. 22); "Milk and Money" (Avery/Oct. 3); "Porky's Moving Day" (King/Oct. 7); "Little Beau Porky" (Tashlin/Nov. 14); "The Village Smithy" (Avery/Dec. 5); and "Porky of the North Woods" (Tashlin/Dec. 19).

**1937:** "Porky the Wrestler" (Avery/Jan. 9); "Porky's Road Race" (Tashlin/Feb. 6); "Picador Porky" (Avery/Feb. 27); "Porky's Romance" (with Petunia Pig/Tashlin/Apr. 3); "Porky's Duck Hunt" (with Daffy Duck; his first appearance/Avery/Apr. 17); "Porky and Gabby" (with Gabby Goat/Iwerks/May 15); "Porky's Building" (Tashlin/June 19); "Porky's Super Service" (Iwerks/July 3); "Porky's Badtime Story" (with Gabby Goat/Clampett/July 24); "Porky's Railroad" (Tashlin/Aug. 7); "Get Rich Quick Porky" (Clampett/Aug. 28); "Porky's Garden" (Avery/Sept. 11); "Rover's Rival" (Clampett/Oct. 9); "The Case of the Stuttering Pig" (with Petunia Pig/Tashlin/Oct. 30); "Porky's Double Trouble" (with Petunia Pig/Tashlin/Nov. 13); and "Porky's Hero Agency" (Clampett/Dec. 4).

**1938:** "Porky's Poppa" (Clampett/Jan. 15); "Porky at the Crocadero" (Tashlin/Feb. 5); "What Price Porky" (Clampett/Feb. 26); "Porky's Phoney Express" (Howard, Dalton/Mar. 19); "Porky's Five & Ten" (Clampett/Apr. 6); "Porky's Hare Hunt" (with formative Bugs Bunny/Hardaway/Apr. 30); "Injun Trouble" (Clampett/May 21); "Porky the Fireman" (Tashlin/June 4); "Porky's Party" (Clampett/June 25); "Porky's Spring Planting" (Tashlin/July 25); "Porky & Daffy" (with Daffy Duck/Clampett/Aug. 6); "Wholly Smoke" (Tashlin/Aug. 27); "Porky in Wackyland" (Clampett/Sept. 24); "Porky's Naughty Nephew" (Clampett/Oct. 15); "Porky in Egypt" (Clampett/Nov. 5); "The Daffy Doc" (with Daffy Duck/Clampett/Nov. 26); and "Porky the Gob" (Hardaway, Dalton/Dec. 17).

**1939:** "The Lone Stranger and Porky" (with Daffy Duck/Clampett/Jan. 7); "It's an Ill Wind" (Hardaway, Dalton/Jan. 28); "Porky's Tire Trouble" (Clampett/Feb. 18); "Porky's Movie Mystery" (Clampett/Mar. 11); "Chicken Jitters" (Clampett/Apr. 1); "Porky and Teabiscuit" (Hardaway, Dalton/Apr. 22); "Kristopher Kolumbus, Jr." (Clampett/May 13); "Polar Pals" (Clampett/June 3); "Scalp Trouble" (with Daffy Duck/Clampett/June 24); "Porky's Picnic" (with Petunia Pig/Clampett/July 15); "Wise Quacks" (with Daffy Duck, Mrs. Daffy Duck/Clampett/Aug. 5); and "Porky's Hotel" (Clampett/Sept. 2).

*Leon Schlesinger Studios releases*

**1939:** "Jeepers Creepers" (Clampett/(Sept. 23); "Naughty Neighbors" (Clampett/Oct. 7); "Pied Piper Porky" (Clampett/Nov. 4); "Porky the Giant Killer" (Hardaway, Dalton/Nov. 18); and "The Film Fan" (Clampett/Dec. 16).

**1940:** "Porky's Last Stand" (with Daffy Duck/Clampett/Jan. 6); "Africa Squeaks" (Clampett/Jan. 27); "Ali-Baba Bound" (Clampett/Feb. 17); "Pilgrim Porky" (Clampett/Mar. 16); "Slap Happy Porky" (Clampett/Apr. 13); "Porky's Poor Fish" (Clampett/Apr. 27); "You Ought to Be in Pictures" (with Daffy Duck/Freleng/May 18); "The Chewin' Bruin" (Clampett/June 8); "Porky's Baseball Broadcast" (Freleng/July 6); "Patient Porky" (with Bugs Bunny/Clampett/Aug. 24); "Calling Dr. Porky" (Freleng/Sept. 21); "Prehistoric Porky" (Clampett/Oct. 12); "The Sour Puss" (Clampett/Nov. 2); "Porky's Hired Hand" (Freleng/Nov. 30); and "The Timid Toreador" (Clampett, McCabe/Dec. 21).

**1941:** "Porky's Snooze Reel" (Clampett, McCabe/Jan. 11); "Porky's Bear Facts" (Freleng/Mar. 29); "Porky's Preview" (Avery/Apr. 19); "Porky's Ant" (Jones/Apr. 10); "A Coy Decoy" (with Daffy Duck/Clampett/June 7); "Porky's Prize Pony" (Jones/June 21); "Meet John Doughboy" (Clampett/July 5); "We, the Animals-Squeak!" (Clampett/Aug. 9); "The Henpecked Duck" (with Daffy Duck/Clampett/Aug. 30); "Notes to You" (Freleng/Sept. 20); "Robinson Crusoe, Jr." (McCabe/Oct. 25); "Porky's Midnight Matinee" (Jones/Nov. 22); and "Porky's Pooch" (Clampett/Dec. 27).

**1942:** "Who's Who in the Zoo" (McCabe/Feb. 14); "Porky's Cafe" (with Conrad Cat/Jones/Feb. 21); and "My Favorite Duck" (with Daffy Duck/Jones/Dec. 5).

**1943:** "Confusions of a Nutzy Spy" (McCabe/Jan. 23); "Yankee Doodle Daffy" (with Daffy Duck/Freleng/July 3); and "Porky Pig's Feat" (with Daffy Duck/Tashlin/July 17).

**1944:** "Tom Turk and Daffy" (with Daffy Duck/Jones/Feb. 12); "Tick Tock Tuckered" (with Daffy Duck/Clampett/Apr. 8); "Swooner Crooner" (Tashlin/May 6/A.A. nominee), "Duck Soup to Nuts" (with Daffy Duck/Freleng/May 27); and "Brother Brat" (Tashlin/July 15).

*Warner Bros. Cartoons, Inc. releases*

**1945:** "Trap Happy Porky" (with Hubie and Bertie Jones/Feb. 24).

**1946:** "Baby Bottleneck" (with Daffy Duck, Tweety cameo/Clampett/Mar. 16); "Daffy Doodles" (with Daffy Duck/McKimson/Apr. 16); "Kitty Kornered" (with Sylester/Clampett/June 8); and "Mouse Menace" (Davis/Nov. 2).

**1947:** "Little Orphan Airedale" (with Charlie Dog/Jones/Oct. 4).

**1948:** "The Pest That Came to Dinner" (Davis/Sept. 11); and "Riff Raffy Daffy" (with Daffy Duck/Davis/Nov. 7/Cinecolor).

**1949:** "Porky Chops" (Davis/Feb. 12); "Paying the Piper" (McKimson/Mar. 12); "Daffy Duck Hunt" (with Daffy Duck/McKimson/Mar. 26); "Curtain Razor" (with Tweety cameo/Freleng/May 21); and "Often an Orphan" (with Charlie Dog/Jones/Aug. 13).

**1950:** "Boobs in the Woods" (with Daffy Duck/McKimson/Jan. 28); "The Scarlet Pumpernickel" (with Daffy Duck, Sylester the Cat, Elmer Fudd, Momma Bear/Jones/Mar. 4); and "The Ducksters" (with Daffy Duck/Jones/Sept. 2).

**1951:** "The Wearing of the Grin" (Jones/July 14); and "The Prize Pest" (with Daffy Duck/McKimson/Dec. 22).

**1952:** "Thumb Fun" (with Daffy Duck/McKimson/Mar. 1); and "Fool Coverage" (with Daffy Duck/McKimson/Dec. 13).

**1955:** "Dime to Retire" (with Daffy Duck/McKimson/Sept. 3).

**1956:** "Deduce, You Say" (with Daffy Duck/Jones/Sept. 29).

**1957:** "Boston Quackie" (with Daffy Duck/McKimson/June 22).

**1959:** "China Jones" (with Daffy Duck/McKimson/Feb. 14).

*Warner Bros. Pictures, Inc./Vitagraph releases*

**1961:** "Daffy's Inn Trouble" (with Daffy Duck/McKimson/Sept. 23).

**1964:** "Dumb Patrol" (with Bugs Bunny, Daffy Duck, Yosemite Sam/Chiniquy/Jan. 18/Porky Pig cameo/Bugs Bunny cartoon).

*Warner Bros. releases*

**1991:** "Invasion of the Bunny Snatchers" (with Bugs Bunny, Daffy Duck, Elmer Fudd, Yosemite Sam/Ford, Lennon/Porky Pig cameo/Bugs Bunny cartoon).

*Merrie Melodies*

*Vitaphone Productions releases*

**1935:** "I Haven't Got a Hat" (first Porky Pig cartoon/Freleng/Mar. 9); and "Into Your Dance" (Freleng/June 8).

(The following cartoons are in Technicolor unless indicated otherwise.)

**1939:** "Old Glory" (Jones/July 1).

**1942:** "Porky's Pastry Pirates" (Freleng/Jan. 17).

*Leon Schlesinger Studios releases*

**1943:** "A Corny Concerto" (with Bugs Bunny, Elmer Fudd/Clampett/Sept. 18).

**1944:** "Slightly Daffy" (with Daffy Duck/Freleng/June 17).

*Warner Bros. Cartoons, Inc. releases*

**1945:** "Wagon Heels" (Clampett/July 28).

**1947:** "One Meat Brawl" (McKimson/Jan. 18).

**1948:** "Daffy Duck Slept Here" (with Daffy Duck/McKimson/Mar. 6); "Nothing but the Tooth" (Davis/May 1); and "Scaredy Cat" (with Sylvester/Jones/Dec. 18).

**1949:** "Awful Orphan" (with Charlie Dog/Jones/Jan. 29); "Dough for the Do-Do" (Freleng/Sept. 3/remake of "Porky in Wackyland"); and "Bye, Bye Bluebeard" (Davis/Oct. 21).

**1950:** "An Egg Scramble" (with Miss Prissy/McKimson/May 27); and "Golden Yeggs" (with Daffy Duck/Freleng/Aug. 5).

**1951:** "Drip-Along Daffy" (with Daffy Duck/Jones/Nov. 17); and "Dog Collared" (McKimson/Dec. 2).

**1952:** "Cracked Quack" (with Daffy Duck/Freleng/July 5).

**1953:** "Duck Dodgers in the 24½th Century" (with Daffy Duck, Commander X-2 Marvin Martian/Jones/July 25).

**1954:** "Claws for Alarm" (with Sylvester/Jones/May 22); and "My Little Duckaroo" (with Daffy Duck/Jones/Nov. 27).

**1955:** "Jumpin' Jupiter" (with Sylvester/Jones/Aug. 6).

**1956:** "Rocket Squad" (with Daffy Duck/Jones/Mar. 10).

**1958:** "Robin Hood Daffy" (with Daffy Duck/Jones/Mar. 8).

*DePatie-Freleng Enterprises releases*

**1965:** "Corn on the Cop" (with Daffy Duck/Spector/July 24).

*Warner Bros. releases*
"Duck Dodgers and the Return of the 24½th Century" (with Daffy Duck, Marvin Martian, Gossamer/Jones).

## ◎ POSSIBLE POSSUM

Set in the tiny town of Happy Hollow, this series spin-off from Terrytoons' *Deputy Dawg* was composed of more Southern-flavored tales, this time featuring the carefree, guitar-playing Possible Possum and his loyal swamp friends, Billy the Bear, Owlawishus Owl and Macon Mouse. *The cartoons were animated and directed by Terry-Toons veterans Connie Rasinski, Art Bartsch, Bob Kuwahara, Cosmo Anzilotti and Dave Tendlar. Technicolor. A Terrytoons and CBS Films, Inc., Production released through 20th Century Fox.*

*Voices*
**Possible Possum/Billy Bear/Owlawishus Owl/Macon Mouse:** Lionel Wilson

**1965:** "Freight Fright" (Rasinski/Mar.); "Darn Barn" (Rasinski/June); "Get That Guitar" (Bartsch/Sept.); and "The Toothless Beaver" (Rasinski/Dec.).

**1966:** "Watch the Butterfly" (Tendlar/Oct.).

**1968:** "Big Bad Bobcat" (Anzilotti/Apr.); "Surprisin' Exercisin'" (Anzilotti/July); "The Rock Hounds" (Tendlar/Oct.); "Mount Piney" (Bartsch/Dec.); "The Pickle Pirate" (Dec.); "Kooky Cucumbers" (Dec.); "Black and Blue Jay" (Dec.); "Hobo Hassle" (Dec.); "Southern Super Market" (Dec.); "Don't Burro Trouble" (Dec.); "Happy Hollow Hay Ride" (Dec.); "Findin' the Phantom" (Dec.); "The Bold Eagle" (Dec.); "Surface Surf Aces" (Dec.); "Trestle Hassle" (Dec.); "Happy Hollow Turkey Trot" (Dec.); "Swamp Water Taffy" (Dec.); "Rootin' Tootin' Pumpkin Lootin'" (Dec.); "The Red Swamp Fox" (Dec.); "Popcorn Poachers" (Dec.); "Showboat Showoff" (Dec.); "Slinky Mink" (Dec.); "Berry Funny" (Dec.); "Friendship" (Dec.); "Big Mo" (Dec.); "The Chestnut Nut" (Dec.); "Sleep Slip Up" (Dec.); "The General's Little Helpers" (Dec.); "Pirate Plunder Blunder" (Dec.); "Swamp Snapper" (Dec.); "Harm Sweet Home" (Dec.); and "The Steel Stealer" (Dec.).

## ◎ PROFESSOR SCHMALTZ

This eccentric professor who did everything from illustrating how music calmed the savage beast to inventing new household gadgets to make life easier for his wife, Lena, starred in four *Modern Madcap* cartoons directed by Seymour Kneitel for Famous Studios. *Directed by Seymour Kneitel. Technicolor. A Famous Studios Production released through Paramount Pictures.*

**1960:** "Fiddle Faddle" (Feb. 26); and "Terry the Terror" (Dec. 19).

**1961:** "The Mighty Termite" (Apr. 19).

**1962:** "Giddy Gadgets" (with Lena, his wife/Mar. 19)

## ◎ PROFESSOR SMALL AND MR. TALL

This capricious pair, who were the complete opposites of their names—the "tall" Professor Small and "small" Mr. Tall—appeared in a short-lived cartoon series for Columbia Pictures. Situations revolved around the twosome's clumsy attempts to refute various superstitions of life. *Directed by John Hubley and Paul Sommer. Technicolor. A Columbia Pictures Corporation Production released by Columbia Pictures.*

**1943:** "Professor Small and Mister Tall" (Sommer, Hubley/Mar. 26/*Color Rhapsody*).

**1945:** "River Ribber" (Sommer/Oct. 4/*Color Rhapsody*).

## ◎ PUDDY THE PUP

Paul Terry created this frisky little pup who first appeared opposite Farmer Al Falfa before starring in a theatrical sound series of his own.

*Directed by Paul Terry, Frank Moser, Mannie Davis, George Gordon and Connie Rasinski. Black-and-white. A Terry-Toon Cartoons Production released through 20th Century Fox.*

**1935:** "The Bullfight" (Terry, Moser/Feb. 8).

**1936:** "Sunken Treasure" (Davis, Gordon/Oct. 16); "Cats in the Bag" (Davis, Gordon/Dec. 11); "Puddy the Pup and the Gypsies" (with Farmer Al Falfa/Davis, Gordon/Dec. 12); and "The Hot Spell" (with Farmer Al Falfa/Davis, Gordon/Dec. 12).

**1937:** "The Dog and the Bone" (Gordon/Nov. 12).

**1938:** "His Off Day" (Rasinski/Feb. 4); "Happy and Lucky" (Rasinksi/Mar. 18); "The Big Top" (Davis/May 12); and "The Big Build-Up" (Davis/Sept. 4).

## ◎ RAGGEDY ANN AND RAGGEDY ANDY

Three years after Max Fleischer's two-reel special *Raggedy Ann and Raggedy Andy*, based on the characters and stories created by Johnny Gruelle, Famous Studios produced this short-lived series of one-reel shorts starring Raggedy Ann, which premiered with 1944's "Suddenly It's Spring." The cartoons were released as part of the studio's *Noveltoons* series. *Directed by Dave Fleischer and Seymour Kneitel. Cinecolor. Technicolor. A Fleischer Studios/Famous Studios Production released through Paramount Pictures Corporation.*

**1941:** "Raggedy Ann and Raggedy Andy" (Fleischer/April 11).

**1944:** "Suddenly It's Spring" (Apr. 28).

**1947:** "The Enchanted Square" (May 9).

## ◎ RAINBOW PARADES

Former Disney director Burt Gillett, who won Academy Awards for his Walt Disney classics "Flowers and Trees" (1932) and "The Three Little Pigs" (1933), created and directed this series of musical children's fables for Van Beuren Studios, whose stars were generally lesser known. Gillett, who had joined the studio in 1933, launched the idea following completion of his first series there, *Toddle Tales*, which combined live-action sequences with animated characters and plot lines.

*Rainbow Parades* became the first color series for Van Beuren, initially filmed in a two-color process and then in three-strip Technicolor. The cartoons alternated between one-shot stories and episodes with continuing characters, becoming popular installments for the studio.

The series was released to television in the 1950s after Official Films purchased Van Beuren's entire cartoon library to distribute to this thriving medium. *Other series directors were Ted Eshbaugh, Steve Muffati, Tom Palmer, James "Shamus" Culhane and Dan Gordon. Technicolor. A Van Beuren Studio Production released by RKO Radio Pictures.*

**1934:** "Pastry Town Wedding" (Gillett, Eshbaugh/July 27); and "The Parrotville Fire Department" (Gillett, Eshbaugh/Sept. 14).

**1935:** "The Sunshine Makers" (Gillett, Eshbaugh/Jan. 11); "Parrotville Old Folks" (Gillett, Palmer/Jan. 25); "Japanese Lanterns" (Gillett, Eshbaugh/Mar. 8); "Spinning Mice" (Gillett, Palmer/Apr. 5); "Picnic Panic" (Gillett, Palmer/May 3); "The Merry Kittens" (Gillett, Culhane/May 15); "The Foxy Terrier" (Gillett/May 31); "Parrotville Post Office" (Gillett, Palmer/June 28); "Rag Dog" (Gillett/July 19); "Putting on the Dog" (Gillett/July 19); "The Hunting Season" (Gillett/Aug. 9); "Scotty Finds a Home" (Gillett/Aug. 23); "Bird Scouts" (Gillett, Palmer/Sept. 20); "Molly Moo-Cow and the Butterflies" (Gillett, Palmer/Nov. 15); "Molly Moo-Cow and the Indians" (Gillett, Palmer/Nov. 15); and "Molly Moo-Cow and Rip Van Wrinkle" (Gillett, Palmer/Nov. 17).

**1936:** "Toonerville Trolley" (Gillett, Palmer/Jan. 17); "Felix the Cat and the Goose That Laid the Golden Egg" (Gillett, Palmer/Feb. 7); "Molly Moo-Cow and Robinson Crusoe" (Gillett, Palmer/Feb. 28); "Neptune Nonsense" (Gillett, Palmer/Mar. 20); "Bold King Cole" (with Felix the Cat/Gillett/May 29); "A Waif's Welcome" (Palmer/June 19); "Trolley Ahoy" (Gillett/July 3/ Toonerville Trolley cartoon); "Cupid Gets His Man" (Palmer/July 24); "It's a Greek Life" (Gordon/Aug. 2); and "Toonerville Picnic" (Gillett/Oct. 2/*Toonerville Trolley* cartoon).

## ◎ RALPH PHILLIPS

Chuck Jones brought this young boy with an overactive imagination, who daydreams of heroic deeds inspired by everyday events in the fashion of Walter Mitty, to the screen in 1954's "From A to Z-Z-Z-Z," which was nominated for an Academy Award. Ralph appeared in only two cartoons altogether, his second being "Boyhood Daze" (1957), a *Merrie Melodies* cartoon. *Directed by Chuck Jones. Technicolor. A Warner Bros. Cartoons, Inc. Production released by Warner Bros.*

**Voices**
**Ralph Phillips:** Dick Beals

*Looney Tunes*

**1954:** "From A to Z-Z-Z-Z" (Oct. 16/A.A. nominee/voice of teacher by Bea Benadaret).

*Merrie Melodies*

**1957:** "Boyhood Daze" (Apr. 20).

## ◎ RALPH WOLF AND SAM SHEEPDOG

Ralph, a scheming wolf who resembles Wile E. Coyote, tries everything possible to steal sheep under the nose of one clever sheepdog, Sam—only during working hours—in this rib-tickling cartoon series created by Chuck Jones for Warner Bros. The battling pair first starred in 1953's "Don't Give Up the Sheep." *Directed by Chuck Jones, Phil Monroe and Richard Thompson. Technicolor. A Warner Bros. Cartoons, Inc. and Warner Bros. Pictures Production released by Warner Bros.*

**Voices**
Mel Blanc

*Looney Tunes*

**1953:** "Don't Give Up the Sheep" (Jan. 3).

**1955:** "Double or Mutton" (July 13).

**1957:** "Steal Wool" (June 8).

*Merrie Melodies*

**1954:** "Sheep Ahoy" (Dec. 11).

**1960:** "Ready, Woolen and Able" (July 30).

**1962:** "A Sheep in the Deep" (Feb. 10).

**1963:** "Woolen Under Where" (Monroe, Thompson/May 11).

## ◎ RECORD TOONS

Legendary animator James "Shamus" Culhane produced and directed this short-lived, ultra-limited animated series of seven-minute theatrical cartoons on a shoestring budget in 1957 based on popular novelty tunes of the day. Besides serving as a creative supervisor on the series, UPA animator Ed Nofziger, best known for his work on UPA's *Mister Magoo* cartoons, designed and animated the films along with fellow animators Cecil Beard, Joe Messerli (of TV's *Captain Fathom* fame) and Milt Feldman, and films were drawn by animators Fred Crippen, Jack Heiter, Ed Levitt and Shirley Silvey. A few 16-mm prints that exist today are in black and white, though it is possible the series was made in color. Listed below are known titles. *Produced and directed by James "Shamus" Culhane. Black and white. A Shamus Culhane Production.*

**1957:** "Dinky Pinky"; "Pepe the Possum"; and "D-O-G Spells Dog."

## ⊙ ROAD RUNNER AND COYOTE

Director Chuck Jones and storyman Michael Maltese created the incredibly speedy ostrich-necked Road Runner ("Beep! Beep!") and his relentless pursuer Wile E. Coyote in what became known as the "longest chase" in cartoon history.

Jones had always aspired to animate a series using "blackouts" and sound effects in classic fashion. He admits to having been influenced by a series of a similar nature, Columbia Pictures' *Fox and the Crow* cartoons, which was based on the same chase formula but to a different extreme.

As for Road Runner's voice, Jones recalls he and Maltese got the idea from, of all places, the hallways of Warner Bros.' cartoon studio. "Curiously enough, Mel Blanc didn't come up with the 'Beep! Beep!' That was done by a fellow named Paul Julian. He was walking down the hall carrying a load of backgrounds and couldn't see where he was going," Jones recalled. "He had about 60 drawings in front of him and he kept going 'Beep! Beep!' as he went by to keep people out of his way. Mike and I were laying out the first picture when Paul went by our door making that sound. We looked at each other and thought that must have been the sound Road Runner makes. Mike looked up and said, 'Okay, God, we'll take it from here.'"

The characters were first introduced in the 1948 Technicolor release, "Fast and Furry-Ous," featuring the type of lunacy that became a staple of the series. Jones imposed certain disciplines when animating the series: Road Runner always stayed on the road. He was never injured; Coyote injured himself instead. The same Arizona desert was used in each picture. Sympathy was always on

*Coyote's never-ending pursuit of Road Runner is about to end in disaster in the long-running Warner Brothers cartoon series created by Chuck Jones. © Warner Brothers*

the side of Coyote. No dialogue was furnished for either character, with the exception of Road Runner's traditional "Beep! Beep!" sound, which sound-effects man Treg Brown invented while using an electronic horn called a claxon. (Mel Blanc mimed the sound vocally for the second cartoon, "Beep Beep!" [1952], when the instrument got lost. Blanc's sound was used for each and every cartoon thereafter.) The splash technique of Coyote falling off the cliff was incorporated into almost every film. And, last, Coyote never catches Road Runner.

Jones directed the most cartoons in the series, one of which was nominated for an Academy Award for best short subject: 1961's "Beep Prepared." After Warner Bros. shut down its animation department, the series resumed under DePatie-Freleng Enterprises, which produced a new series of Warner cartoons before the studio reopened its animation division in 1967.

In 1980, Chuck Jones produced and directed a brand-new Road Runner and Coyote cartoon, entitled "Soup or Sonic." The cartoon premiered on the CBS special *Bugs Bunny's Busting Out All Over.*

In 1994 Road Runner and Coyote returned to the screen in their first all-new theatrical cartoon in 28 years, "Chariots of Fur," which opened with the live-action feature *Richie Rich,* starring Macaulay Culkin. Series creator Chuck Jones opened a 1990s' version of Termite Terrace, the name of the animation unit in Warner Bros. heyday, to produce new animated cartoon shorts for theaters. The Road Runner cartoon was to be animated by the new unit.

The first new Road Runner and Coyote cartoons since Chuck Jones's 1994 cartoon short "Chariots of Fur" was produced in the 2000s, "Little Go Beep" (2000), directed by Spike Brandt and "Whizzard of Ow" (2003), directed by Bret Haaland. *Other series directors were Maurice Noble, Rudy Larriva, Abe Levitow, Robert McKimson, Spike Brandt and Bret Haaland. Technicolor. A Warner Bros. Cartoons, Inc./Warner Bros. Pictures, Inc/Vitagraph/Warner Bros./DePatie-Freleng Enterprises/Format Films/Warner Bros./Chuck Jones Film Production released by Warner Bros. and Warner Bros. Family Entertainment.*

### Voices
**Road Runner:** Mel Blanc

### *Merrie Melodies*

### *Warner Bros. Cartoons, Inc. releases*

**1952:** "Beep, Beep" (Jones/May 24); and "Going! Going! Gosh!" (Jones/Aug. 23).

**1953:** "Zipping Along" (Jones/Sept. 10).

**1954:** "Stop! Look! and Hasten" (Jones/Aug. 14).

**1958:** "Whoa, Be-Gone!" (Jones/Apr. 12); and "Hip Hip—Hurry" (Jones/Dec. 6).

**1959:** "Wild About Hurry" (Jones/Oct. 10).

**1960:** "Hopalong Casualty" (Jones/Oct. 8)

**1961:** "Zip 'n' Snort" (Jones/Jan. 21); and "Beep Prepared" (Jones/Nov. 11/A.A. nominee).

**1962:** "Zoom at the Top" (Jones, Noble/June 30).

**1963:** "To Beep or Not to Beep" (Jones, Noble/Dec. 28).

**1965:** "Zip Zip Hooray!"

### *DePatie-Freleng Enterprises/Format Films releases*

**1965:** "Rushing Roulette" (McKimson/July 31); "Run, Run, Sweet Road Runner" (Larriva/Aug. 21); "Tired and Feathered" (Larriva/Sept. 18); "Boulder Wham!" (Larriva/Oct. 9); "Just Plane

Beep" (Larriva/Oct. 30); "Harried and Hurried" (Larriva/Nov. 13); and "Chaser on the Rocks" (Larriva/Dec. 25).

**1966:** "Out and Out Rout" (Larriva/Jan. 29).

*Looney Tunes*

*Warner Bros. Cartoons, Inc. releases*

**1949:** "Fast and Furry-Ous" (Jones/Sept. 16/first Road Runner cartoon).

**1955:** "Ready . . . Set . . . Zoom!" (Jones/Apr. 30); and "Guided Muscle" (Jones/Dec. 10).

**1956:** "Gee Whiz-z-z" (Jones/May 5); and "There They Go-Go-Go!" (Jones/Nov. 10).

**1957:** "Scramble Aches" (Jones/Jan. 26); and "Zoom and Bored" (Jones/Sept. 14).

**1958:** "Hook, Line and Stinker" (Jones/Oct. 11).

*Warner Bros. releases*

**1959:** "Hot-Rod and Reel!" (Jones/May 9).

**1960:** "Fastest with the Mostest" (Jones/Jan. 19).

*Warner Bros. Pictures, Inc./Vitagraph releases*

**1961:** "Lickety-Splat" (Jones, Levitow/June 3).

**1964:** "War and Pieces" (Jones, Noble/June 6).

*DePatie-Freleng Enterprises/Format Films releases*

**1965:** "Highway Runnery" (Larriva/Dec. 11).

**1966:** "Shot and Bothered" (Larriva/Jan. 8); "The Solid Tin Coyote" (Larriva/Feb. 29); "Clippety Clobbered" (Larriva/Mar. 12); and "Sugar and Spies" (McKimson/Nov. 5).

*Warner Bros./Chuck Jones Film Productions releases*

**1994:** "Chariots of Fur" (Jones/Dec.).

## ◉ ROCKY AND MUGSY

Longtime supporting players in Warner Bros. cartoons directed by Friz Freleng, this hilarious gangster team—featuring Rocky, the diminutive tough guy with the tall hat and ever-present cigar, and Mugsy, his gullible, dumb sidekick—were used mostly as comic relief in cartoons starring Bugs Bunny. Rocky actually was introduced first on screen in 1950's "Golden Yeggs" starring Daffy Duck and Porky Pig. He appeared next in the 1953 Tweety and Sylvester cartoon, "Catty Cornered," in which he was joined by a sidekick named Nick. In 1954 Rocky and Mugsy made their first joint appearance in "Bugs and Thugs" starring Bugs Bunny, followed by their second appearance three years later in "Bugsy and Mugsy," also a Bugs Bunny cartoon. In 1960 Freleng cast the gangster duo in their only starring vehicle, "The Unmentionables," a clever spoof of TV's *Untouchables*. It was also their final appearance on the screen. *A Warner Bros. Cartoons, Inc. and Warner Bros. Pictures, Inc. Production released by Warner Bros.*

*Voices*
**Rocky/Mugsy/Nick:** Mel Blanc

*Merrie Melodies*

*Warner Bros. Cartoons, Inc. releases*

**1950:** "Golden Yeggs" (with Daffy Duck/Porky Pig/Freleng/Aug. 5/introduced the character Rocky by himself).

**1953:** "Catty Cornered" (with Tweety and Sylvester/Freleng/Oct. 31).

*Warner Bros. Pictures, Inc.*

**1963:** "The Unmentionables" (with Bugs Bunny/Freleng/Sept. 7/narrator: Ralph James).

*Looney Tunes*

*Warner Bros. Cartoons, Inc. releases*

**1954:** "Bugs and Thugs" (with Bugs Bunny, Freleng/Mar. 2).

**1957:** "Bugsy and Mugsy" (with Bugs Bunny/Freleng/Aug. 31).

## ◉ ROGER RABBIT

Following up on the success of *Who Framed Roger Rabbit*, Walt Disney Studios launched this series of fast-paced, funny tributes to Hollywood cartoons of the 1940s reuniting the film's principal cartoon stars, the zany Roger Rabbit, his voluptuous wife, Jessica Rabbit and the temper-tantrum-throwing Baby Herman.

Under the Maroon Cartoons banner—the fictional studio that employed Roger in the box-office smash cartoon feature—Disney released its first theatrical animated short in 25 years, the 1989 madcap adventure "Tummy Trouble," double-billed with the studio's feature-length *Honey, I Shrunk the Kids*, which grossed more than $87 million at the box office in the first five weeks.

Like the movie, it again paired Roger Rabbit and Baby Herman, who has been left in Roger's less-than-adroit care. When Baby swallows a rattle, Roger rushes the tyke to the hospital—St. Nowhere—and bedlam ensues. Roger's sexy, curvaceous wife, Jessica, plays a nurse in the film (again voiced by Kathleen Turner), and MGM's sorrowful bloodhound Droopy makes a cameo appearance as an elevator operator.

In June 1990 Disney again tied the release of the series' second short, "Rollercoaster Rabbit," with the nationwide premiere of Warren Beatty's long-awaited feature-length comic-strip adaptation *Dick Tracy*. A year later the crazy cottontail character was to return to the screen in another cartoon short, entitled "Hare in My Soup," but the film was never produced.

After a three-year absence from the screen, Roger starred again with Jessica Rabbit in an all-new cartoon, "Trail Mix Up." Directed by Barry Cook, the nine-minute short, produced at Disney-MGM Studios in Florida, opened in theaters with the live-action feature *A Far Off Place*. *Directed by Rob Minkoff, Barry Cook and Frank Marshall (live action). Technicolor. A Walt Disney/Amblin Entertainment Production released through Touchstone Pictures.*

*Voices*
**Roger Rabbit:** Charles Fleischer; **Jessica Rabbit:** Kathleen Turner; **Young Baby Herman:** April Winchell; **Adult Baby Herman:** Lou Hirsch; **Droopy:** Richard Williams

**1989:** "Tummy Trouble" (Minkoff, Marshall/July 23).

**1990:** "Rollercoaster Rabbit" (Minkoff, Marshall/June 15).

**1993:** "Trail Mix-Up" (Cook/March 12).

## ◉ ROLAND AND RATTFINK

DePatie-Freleng Enterprises seemingly took over where Warner Bros.' animation department left off, producing new cartoon series mirroring the style and humor of the classic Warner cartoons, only with new stars in the leading roles. Produced in the late 1960s, Roland and Rattfink was based on the idea of good versus evil. The series paired Roland, a blond, good-looking upholder of justice, against Rattfink, that all-around sleazy, dastardly, good-for-nothing

*Good-looking champion of justice Roland makes peace with all-around sleaze Rattfink in the DePatie-Freleng Enterprises theatrical cartoon series, Roland and Rattfink. © DePatie-Freleng Enterprises*

bad guy who always seems to be on the wrong side of the law. *Series directors were Gerry Chiniquy, Art Davis, Hawley Pratt and Grant Simmons. Technicolor. A DePatie-Freleng Enterprises/Mirisch Films Production released through United Artists.*

**Voices**
**Roland:** Leonard Weinrib, Dave Barry; **Rattfink:** Leonard Weinrib, John Byner

***Additional Voices***
June Foray, Peter Halton, Athena Lorde

**1968:** "Hawks and Doves" (Pratt/Dec. 18).

**1969:** "Hurts and Flowers" (Pratt/Feb. 11); "Flying Feet" (Chiniquy/Apr. 10); "The Deadwood Thunderball" (Pratt/June 6); "Sweet and Sourdough" (Davis/June 25); and "A Pair of Sneakers" (Davis/Sept. 17).

**1970:** "Say Cheese, Please" (Davis/June 7); "A Taste of Money" (Davis/June 24/Note: Only Rattfink appears in this cartoon); "The Foul Kin" (Simmons/Aug. 5); "Bridgework" (Davis/Aug. 26); "Robin Goodhood" (Chiniquy/Sept. 9); "War and Pieces" (Davis/Sept. 20); and "Gem Dandy" (Chiniquy/Oct. 25).

**1971:** "Trick or Retreat" (Davis/Mar. 3); "The Great Continental Overland Cross Country Race" (Davis/May 23); "A Fink in the Rink" (Davis/July 4); and "Cattle Battle" (Davis/Aug. 4).

## ◎ RUDOLF ISING CARTOONS

Producer/animator Rudolf Ising, a former Disney animator, produced and directed this series of musical cartoons, starring miscellaneous characters, on his return visit to MGM in the late 1930s. Ising felt right at home, having worked for the studio previously in 1933 after a brief stint at Warner Bros. Following his arrival, he was responsible for directing MGM's *Barney Bear* series and the studio's first Academy Award-winning cartoon, "Milky Way" (1940).

For additional Rudolf Ising cartoons, see *Barney Bear* series entry. *Directed by Rudolf Ising. Voice credits unknown. Technicolor. A Metro-Goldwyn-Mayer Cartoon Production released by Metro-Goldwyn-Mayer.*

**1939:** "The Little Goldfish" (Ising/Apr. 15/re: Nov. 10, 1948); and "One Mother's Family" (Ising/Sept. 30).

**1940:** "Home on the Range" (Ising/Mar. 23); "The Milky Way" (Ising/June 22/re: Feb. 14, 1948/A.A. winner); "Romeo Rhythm"

(Ising/Aug. 10); "The Homeless Flea" (Ising/Oct. 12); and "Mrs. Lady Bug" (Ising/Dec. 21/re: Jan. 17, 1958).

**1941:** "Dance of the Weed" (Ising/June 7).

**1942:** "Little Gravel Voice" (Ising/May 16).

**1943:** "The Bear and the Beavers" (Ising/Mar. 28); and "The Boy and the Wolf" (Ising/Apr. 24).

## ◎ SAD CAT

Ralph Bakshi, after being elevated to the role of director at Terry-Toons, created and directed this series about a scraggly-haired, droopy-eyed cat and his friends, Gadmouse, Impressario, Letimore and Fenimore, in numerous backwoods adventures. Following two seasons, Bakshi turned over the directorial reins to Arthur Bartsch, another Terrytoons veteran. *Directed by Ralph Bakshi and Arthur Bartsch. Technicolor. A Terrytoons and CBS Films, Inc., Production released through 20th Century Fox.*

**Voices**
**Sad Cat/Impressario/Letimore/Fenimore:** Bob McFadden

**1965:** "Gadmouse the Apprentice Good Fairy" (Bakshi/Jan.); "Don't Spill the Beans" (Bakshi/Apr.); "Dress Reversal" (Bakshi/July); and "The Third Musketeer" (Bakshi/Oct.).

**1966:** "Scuba Duba Do" (Bakshi/June).

**1968:** "Dribble Drabble" (Bartsch/Jan.); "Big Game Fishing" (Bartsch/Feb.); "Grand Prix Winner" (Bartsch/Mar.); "Commander Great Guy" (Bartsch/May); "All Teed Off" (Bartsch/June); "Judo Kudos" (Bartsch/Aug.); "The Abominable Mountaineers" (Bartsch/Sept.); and "Loops and Swoops" (Bartsch/Nov.).

## ◎ SAM SMALL

This British-made cartoon series was the only foreign—animated series to be distributed theatrically in the United States, outside of Gene Deitch's Czechoslovakian—produced cartoons for MGM and Paramount in the 1960s. It starred a defiant soldier of the king's army who was also a teller of tall tales. Sam was created by famed British comedian Stanley Holloway and English cartoonist Anson Dyer. Astor Pictures distributed the series in America. *Narrated by Stanley Holloway. Technicolor. An Astor Pictures Corporation release.*

**1937:** "Halt, Who Goes There" (Apr. 15); "Carmen" (May); "Sam and His Musket" (June); "Sam's Medal" (July); "Beat the Retreat" (Aug.); and "Drummed Out" (Sept.).

## ◎ SCRAPPY

Produced as a companion to Columbia's *Krazy Kat*, Dick Huemer devised this curly-topped, button-eyed boy and his faithful dog, Yippy, in plots associated with childhood themes and encounters with juvenile nemeses, Vonsey and Oopie. When Huemer left the series in 1933 to join Walt Disney Studios, Art Davis and Sid Marcus, who contributed most of the series' stories, continued with its production. *Directed by Dick Huemer, Ub Iwerks, Sid Marcus, Art Davis, Ben Harrison, Manny Gould and Howard C. Brown. Produced by Charles Mintz. Black-and-white. Technicolor. A Columbia Pictures Corporation Production released by Columbia Pictures.*

**1931:** "The Little Pest" (Huemer/Aug. 15); "Sunday Clothes" (Huemer/Sept. 15); "The Dog Snatcher" (Huemer/Oct. 15); "Showing Off" (Huemer/Nov. 11); and "Minding the Baby" (Huemer/Nov. 16).

**1932:** "Chinatown Mystery" (Huemer/Jan. 4); "Treasure Runt" (Huemer/Feb. 25); "Railroad Wrecth" (Huemer/Mar. 23); "The

Pet Shop" (Huemer/Apr. 28); "Stepping Stones" (Huemer/May 17); "Battle of the Barn" (Huemer/May 31); "Fare-Play" (Huemer/July 2); "Camping Out" (Huemer/Aug. 10); "The Black Sheep" (Huemer/Sept. 17); "The Great Bird Mystery" (Huemer/Oct. 20/working title: "The Famous Bird Case"); "Flop House" (Huemer/Nov. 9); "The Bad Genius" (Huemer/Dec. 1); and "The Wolf at the Door" (Huemer/Dec. 29).

**1933:** "Sassy Cats" (Huemer/Jan. 25); "Scrappy's Party" (Huemer/Feb. 13); "The Beer Parade" (Huemer/Mar. 4); "The False Alarm" (Huemer/Apr. 22); "The Match Kid" (Huemer/May 9); "Technocracket" (Huemer/May 20); "The World's Affair" (Huemer/June 5); "Movie Struck" (Huemer/Sept. 8); "Sandman Tales" (Huemer/Oct. 6); "Hollywood Babies" (Huemer/Nov. 10); and "Auto Show" (Huemer/Dec. 8).

**1934:** "Scrappy's Art Gallery" (Jan. 12); "Scrappy's Television" (Jan. 29); "Aw, Nurse" (Mar. 9); "Scrappy's Toy Shop" (Apr. 13); "Scrappy's Dog Show" (May 18); "Scrappy's Theme Song" (June 15); "Scrappy's Relay Race" (July 7); "The Great Experiment" (July 27); "Scrappy's Expedition" (Aug. 27); "Concert Kid" (Gould, Harrison/Nov. 2); "Holiday Land" (Nov. 9/Color Rhapsody/A.A. nominee); and "Happy Butterfly" (Dec. 20).

**1935:** "The Gloom Chasers" (Jan. 18); "The Gold Getters" (Mar. 1); "Graduation Exercises" (Apr. 12); "Scrappy's Ghost Story" (May 24); "The Puppet Murder Case" (Davis/June 21); "Scrappy's Big Moment" (July 28); "Scrappy's Trailer" (Aug. 29); and "Let's Ring Doorbells" (Davis/Nov. 7).

**1936:** "Scrappy's Boy Scouts" (Davis/Jan. 2); "Scrappy's Pony" (Mar. 16); "Scrappy's Camera Troubles" (June 5); "Playing Politics" (July 8/Color Rhapsody); "The Novelty Shop" (Davis/Aug. 15/Color Rhapsody); "In My Gondola" (Sept. 3/Color Rhapsody); "Looney Balloonists" (Sept. 24); "Merry Mutineers" (Davis/Oct. 2/Color Rhapsody); "Birds in Love" (Oct. 28/Color Rhapsody); and "A Boy and His Dog" (Davis/Dec. 23/Color Rhapsody).

*Scrappy shares a moment with faithful companion, Yippy, in a scene from the popular Columbia Pictures cartoon series. © Columbia Pictures*

**1937:** "Skeleton Frolic" (Iwerks/Jan. 29/Color Rhapsody); "Merry Mannequins" (Iwerks/Mar. 19/Color Rhapsody); "Puttin' Out the Kitten" (Davis/Mar. 26); "Scrappy's Band Concert" (Apr. 29); "Scrappy's Music Lesson" (Davis/June 4); "I Want to Be an Actress" (July 18); "Scary Crows" (Davis/Aug. 20/Color Rhapsody); "Swing Monkey Swing" (Sept. 10/Color Rhapsody); "Canine Capers" (Brown/Sept. 16); "The Fire Plug" (Oct. 16); "The Clock Goes Round and Round" (Nov. 6); "Dizzy Ducks" (Nov. 18); and "Scrappy's News Flashes" (Dec. 8).

**1938:** "Scrappy's Trip to Mars" (Feb. 4); "Scrappy's Playmates" (Mar. 27); "The Early Bird" (Sept. 16); and "Happy Birthday" (Oct. 7/Color Rhapsody).

**1939:** "Scrappy's Added Attraction" (Jan. 13); "Scrappy's Side Show" (Mar. 3); "A Worm's Eye View" (Apr. 28); "Scrappy's Rodeo" (June 2); "The Charm Bracelet" (Sept. 1 /Phantasy cartoon); "Millionaire Hobo" (Davis/Nov. 24/Phantasy cartoon); and "Park Your Baby" (Dec. 22/Fable cartoon).

**1940:** "Man of Tin" (Feb. 23/Phantasy cartoon); "Practice Makes Perfect" (Apr. 5/Fable cartoon); "Pooch Parade" (July 19/Fable cartoon); "A Peep in the Deep" (Aug. 23/Fable cartoon); "Schoolboy Dreams" (Sept. 24/Phantasy cartoon); "Farmer Tom Thumb" (Sept. 27/Fable cartoon); and "Happy Holidays" (Oct. 25/Phantasy cartoon).

**1941:** "The Little Theatre" (Feb. 7/Phantasy cartoon).

### ◎ SCREEN SONGS

Animator Seymour Kneitel created the *Follow the Bouncing Ball* series, which was first produced in the late 1920s and was revived in the late 1940s by Famous Studios. The cartoons worked on the concept popularized in movie theaters of song slides showing lyrics of well-known tunes to invite audiences to sing along with live singers or musicians. Max and Dave Fleischer adapted the idea, committing it to animated drawings with live-action footage featuring the talents of famous musical personalities within the context of the films. The early series installments were actually filmed without sound; the dialogue and sound were synchronized later. In the late 1940s series revival, the animated stars led the sing-a-longs, this time in Technicolor. As before, the bouncing ball was incorporated into the onscreen lyrics. *Directed by Dave Fleischer, Isadore Sparber and Seymour Kneitel. Black-and-white. Technicolor. A Flesicher Studios and Famous Studios release through Paramount Pictures Corporation.*

#### Voices
Jack Mercer and Mae Questel

#### *Fleischer Studios releases*

**1929:** "The Sidewalks of New York" (Fleischer/Feb. 5); "Yankee Doodle Boy Fleischer/Mar. 1); "Old Black Joe" (Fleischer/Apr. 5); "Ye Olde Melodies" (Fleischer/© May 3); "Daisy Bell" (Fleischer/May 31); "Mother Pin a Rose on Me" (Fleischer/© July 6); "Dixie" (Fleischer/Aug. 17); "Chinatown My Chinatown" (Fleischer/Aug. 29); "Goodbye My Lady Love" (Fleischer/© Aug. 3); "My Pony Boy" (Fleischer/© Sept. 13); "Smiles" (Fleischer/Sept. 27); "Oh You Beautiful Doll" (Fleischer/Oct. 14); "After the Ball" (Fleischer/Nov. 8); "Put On Your Old Gray Bonnet" (Fleischer/Nov. 22); and "I've Got Rings on My Fingers" (Dec. 17)

**1930:** "Bedilla" (Fleischer/Jan. 3); "In the Shade of the Old Apple Tree" (Fleischer/Jan. 16); "I'm Afraid to Come Home in the Dark" (Fleischer/Jan. 30); "Prisoner's Song" (Fleischer/Mar. 1); "La Paloma" (Fleischer/Mar. 20); "I'm Forever Blowing Bubbles"

(Fleischer/Mar. 30); "Yes! We Have No Bananas" (Fleischer/Apr. 25); "Come Take a Trip in My Airship" (Fleischer/May 23); "In the Good Old Summer Time" (Fleischer/June 6); "A Hot Time in the Old Town Tonight" (Fleischer/Aug. 1); "The Glow Worms" (Fleischer/Aug. 18); "The Stein Song" (with Rudy Vallee/Fleischer/Sept. 5); "Strike Up the Band" (Fleischer/Sept. 26); "My Gal Sal" (Fleischer/Oct. 18); "Marituch" (Fleischer/Nov. 15); "One Sunday Afternoon" (Fleischer/Nov. 25); and "Row, Row, Row" (Fleischer/Dec. 19).

**1931:** "Please Go 'Way and Let Me Sleep" (Fleischer/June 9); "By the Beautiful Sea" (Fleischer/Jan. 23); "I Wonder Who's Kissing Her Now" (Fleischer/Feb. 13); "I'd Climb the Highest Mountain" (Fleischer/Mar. 6); "Somebody Stole My Gal" (Fleischer/© Mar. 20); "Any Little Girl That's a Nice Little Girl" (Fleischer/Apr. 16); "Alexander's Ragtime Band" (Fleischer/May 9); "And the Green Grass Grew All Around" (Fleischer/June 1); "My Wife's Gone to the Country" (Fleischer/© June 12); "That Old Gang of Mine" (Fleischer/© July 9); "Betty Co-Ed" (with Rudy Vallee/Fleischer/Aug. 1); "Mr. Gallagher and Mr. Shean" (Fleischer/Aug. 29); "You're Driving Me Crazy" (Fleischer/Sept. 19); "Little Annie Rooney" (Fleischer/Oct. 10); "Kitty from Kansas City" (with Rudy Vallee/Fleischer/Nov. 1); "By the Light of the Silvery Moon" (Fleischer/Nov. 14); "My Baby Cares for Me" (Fleischer/Dec. 5); and "Russian Lullabye" (with Arthur Tracy/Fleischer/Dec. 26).

**1932:** "Sweet Jenny Lee" (Fleischer/Jan. 9); "Show Me the Way to Go Home" (Fleischer/Jan. 30); "When the Red Red Robin Comes Bob Bob Bobbin' Along" (Fleischer/Feb. 19); "Wait Till the Sun Shines, Nellie" (Fleischer/Mar. 4); "Just One More Chance" (Fleischer/Apr. 1); "Oh! How I Hate to Get Up in the Morning" (Fleischer/Apr. 22); "Shine On Harvest Moon" (with Alice Joy/Fleischer/May 6); "Let Me Call You Sweetheart" (with Ethel Merman/Fleischer/May 20); "I Ain't Got Nobody" (with the Mills Brothers/Fleischer/June 17); "You Try Somebody Else" (with Ethel Merman/Fleischer/July 29); "Rudy Vallee Melodies" (with Betty Boop/Fleischer/Aug. 5); "Down Along the Sugar Cane" (with Lillian Roth/Fleischer/Aug. 26); "Just a Gigolo" (with Irene Bordoni/Fleischer/Sept. 9); "School Days" (with Gus Edwards/Fleischer/Sept. 30); "Romantic Melodies" (with Arthur Tracy/Fleischer/Oct. 21); "When It's Sleepy Time Down South" (with the Boswell Sisters/Fleischer/Nov. 11); "Sing a Song" (with James Melton/Fleischer/Dec. 2); and "Time on My Hands" (with Ethel Merman/Fleischer/Dec. 23).

**1933:** "Dinah" (with the Mills Brothers/Fleischer/Jan. 13); "Ain't She Sweet?" (with Lillian Roth/Fleischer/Feb. 3); "Reaching for the Moon" (with Arthur Tracy/Fleischer/Feb. 24); "Aloha Oe" (with the Royal Samoans/Fleischer/Mar. 17); "Popular Melodies" (with Arthur Jarrett/Fleischer/Apr. 7); "The Peanut Vendor" (with Armida/Fleischer/Apr. 28); "Song Shopping" (with Ethel Merman, Johnny Green/Fleischer/May 19); "Boilesk" (with the Watson Sisters/Fleischer/June 9); "Sing, Sisters, Sing!" (with the Three X Sisters/Fleischer/June 30); "Down By the Old Mill Stream" (with the Funny Boners/Fleischer/July 21); "Stoopnocracy" (with Stoopnagle and Budd/Fleischer/Aug. 18); "When Yuba Plays the Rumba on the Tuba" (with the Mills Brothers/Fleischer/Sept. 15); "Boo, Boo, Theme Song" (with the Funny Boners/Fleischer/Oct. 3); "I Like Mountain Music" (with the Eton Boys/Fleischer/Nov. 10); "Sing, Babies, Sing" (with Baby Rose Marie/Fleischer/Dec. 15).

**1934:** "Let's Sing with Popeye" (with Popeye the Sailor/Fleischer); "Keeps Rainin' All the Time" (with Gertrude Niesen/

Fleischer/Jan. 12); "Let's All Sing Like the Birdies Sing" (with Reis and Dunn/Fleischer/Feb. 9); "Tune Up and Sing" (with Lanny Ross/Mar. 9); "Lazy Bones" (with Borrah Minnevitch and His Harmonica Rascals/Fleischer/Apr. 13); "This Little Piggie Went to the Market" (with Singin' Sam/Fleischer/May 25); "She Reminds Me of You" (with The Eton Boys/Fleischer/June 22); and "Love Thy Neighbor" (with Mary Small/July 20).

**1935:** "I Wished on the Moon" (with Abe Lyman and His Orchestra/Fleischer/Jan. 24); and "It's Easy to Remember" (with Richard Humber and His Orchestra/Fleischer/Nov. 29).

**1936:** "No Other One" (with Hal Kemp and His Orchestra/ Fleischer/Jan. 24); "I Feel Like a Feather in the Breeze" (with Jack Denny and His Orchestra/Fleischer/Mar. 27); "I Don't Want to Make History" (with Vincent Lopez and His Orchestra/Fleischer/ May 22); "The Hills of Wyomin" (with the Westerners/Fleischer/ July 31); "I Can't Escape from You" (with Joe Reitchman and His Orchestra/Fleischer/Sept. 25); and "Talking Through My Heart' (with Dick Stable and His Orchestra/Fleischer/Nov. 27).

**1937:** "Never Should Have Told You" (with Nat Brandywine and His Orchestra/Fleischer/Jan. 29); "Twilight on the Trail" (with the Westerners/Fleischer/Mar. 26); "Please Keep Me in Your Dreams" (with Henry King and His Orchestra/Fleischer/ May 28); "You Came to My Rescue" (with Shep Fields and His Orchestra/Fleischer/July 30); "Whispers in the Dark" (with Gus Arnheim and His Orchestra/Fleischer/Sept. 24); and "Magic on Broadway (with Jay Freeman and His Orchestra/Fleischer/Nov. 26).

**1938:** "You Took the Words Right Out of My Heart" (with Jerry Blaine and His Orchestra/Fleischer/Jan. 28); "Thanks for the Memory" (with Bert Block and His Orchestra/Fleischer/Mar. 25); "You Leave Me Breathless" (with Jimmy Dorsey and His Orchestra/Fleischer/May 27); and "Beside a Moonlit Stream" (with Frank Dailey and His Orchestra/Fleischer/July 29).

### *Famous Studios releases*

**1947:** "The Circus Comes to Town" (Sparber/Dec. 26).

**1948:** "Base Brawl" (Kneitel/Jan. 23); "Little Brown Jug" (Kneitel/Feb. 20); "The Golden State" (Kneitel/Mar. 12); "Winter Draws On" (Kneitel/Mar. 19); "Sing or Swim" (Kneitel/June 16); "Camp Town Races" (Kneitel/July 30); "The Lone Star State" (Sparber/Aug. 20); and "Readin', Writin', and Rhythmetic" (Kneitel/Oct. 22).

**1949:** "The Funshine State" (Kneitel/Jan. 7/Polacolor/narrator: Charles Irving); "The Emerald Isle" (Kneitel/Feb. 25/song: "McNamara's Band"); "Comin' Round the Mountain" (Sparber/ Mar. 11); "The Stork Market" (Kneitel/Apr. 8); "Spring Song" (Sparber/June 3); "The Ski's the Limit" (Sparber/June 24); "Toys Will Be Toys" (Kneitel/July 15); "Farm Foolery" (Kneitel/Aug. 5); "Our Funny Finny Friends" (Kneitel/Aug. 26); "Marriage Wows" (Sparber/Sept. 16); "The Big Flame-Up" (Sparber/Sept. 30); "Strolling Thru the Park" (Kneitel/Nov. 4); "The Big Drip" (Sparber/Nov. 25/song: "Ain't Gonna Rain No More"); and "Snow Foolin'" (Sparber/Dec. 16/song: "Jingle Bells").

**1950:** "Blue Hawaii" (Kneitel/Jan. 13); "Detouring Thru Maine" (Kneitel/Feb. 17/song: "Maine Stein Song"); "Short'nin Bread" (Sparber/Mar. 24); "Win, Place and Showboat" (Sparber/Apr. 28/song: "Waitin' for the Robert E. Lee"); "Jingle Jangle Jungle" (Kneitel/May 19/song: "Civilization—Bongo Bongo Bongo"); "Heap Hep Injuns" (Sparber/June 30/song: "My Pony Boy"); "Gobs of Fun" (Sparber/July 28/song: "Strike Up the Band");

"Helter Swelter" (Kneitel/Aug. 25/song: "In the Good Old Summertime"); "Boos in the Night" (Sparber/Sept. 22/song: "Pack Up Your Troubles"); "Fiesta Time" (Kneitel/Nov. 17/song: "El Rancho Grande"); and "Fresh Yeggs" (Kneitel/Nov. 17/song: "Give My Regards to Broadway").

**1951:** "Tweet Music" (Sparber/Feb. 9/song: "Let's All Sing Like the Birdies Sing"); "Drippy Mississippi" (Kneitel/Apr. 13/song: "M-i-s-s-i-s-s-i-p-p-i"); "Miners Forty Niners" (Sparber/May 18/song: "Clementine"); and "Sing Again of Michigan" (Sparber/June 29/song: "I Wanted to Go Back to Michigan Down on the Farm").

### ◎ SCREWY SQUIRREL

The bushy-tailed squirrel was a short-lived MGM character who manifested on screen animator/creator Tex Avery's wild and brash humor. During the planning stages of the first cartoon, MGM animators simply dubbed the character "the squirrel" before he was named. Nonetheless, MGM made quite an effort to sell the new character, releasing three cartoons in the first year. Unfortunately, Screwy was a bit too wild for filmgoers' tastes. Exhibiting the same brashness as Bugs Bunny and Woody Woodpecker, in the eyes of

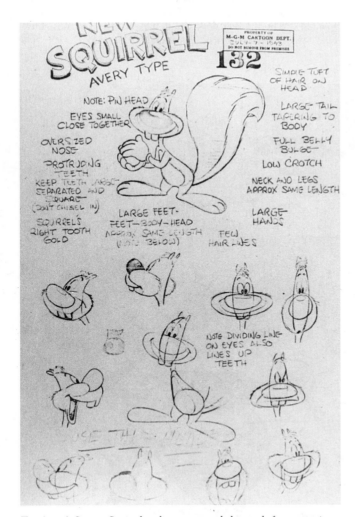

*Tex Avery's Screwy Squirrel underwent several changes before appearing in his first cartoon, "Screwball Squirrel." This was the second model sheet for the character who, up to this point, was nameless. © Turner Entertainment*

the public, he lacked the endearing qualities that were necessary to make him a "likable" star. *Directed by Tex Avery. Technicolor. Voice credits unknown. A Metro-Goldwyn-Mayer Cartoon Production released by Metro-Goldwyn-Mayer.*

**1944:** "Screwball Squirrel" (Apr. 1); "Happy-Go-Nutty" (June 24); and "Big Heel-Watha" (Oct. 21/working title: "Buck of the North").

**1945:** "The Screwy Truant" (Jan. 13).

**1946:** "Lonesome Lenny" (Mar. 9).

### ◎ SIDNEY THE ELEPHANT

The final creation of Gene Deitch's regime as creative director for Terrytoons, this series helped restore the studio's image as a major cartoon producer. Deitch, who joined the studio in 1956, developed a number of starring characters after revamping the animation department. Sidney was by far his most likable character, a neurotic, frustrated elephant who sucks on his trunk for security and feels ill-suited for life in the jungle. Pals Stanley the Lion and Cleo the Giraffe were always on hand to protect him from serious danger.

The series' second cartoon, "Sidney's Family Tree," marked another breakthrough for the studio: It won the first Academy Award nomination for Terrytoons. Thirteen episodes were later broadcast on television as part of *The Hector Heathcote Show*. *Directors were Arthur Bartsch, Martin B. Taras, Gene Deitch, Dave Tendlar and Connie Rasinski. Technicolor. CinemaScope. A Terrytoons and CBS Films, Inc., Production released through 20th Century Fox.*

**Voices**
**Sidney the Elephant:** Lionel Wilson, Dayton Allen; **Stanley the Lion/Cleo the Giraffe:** Dayton Allen

**1958:** "Sick, Sick Sidney" (Bartsch/Aug.) and "Sidney's Family Tree" (Bartsch/Dec. 1/A.A. nominee).

**1960:** "Hide and Go Sidney" (Bartsch/Jan./CinemaScope); "Tusk Tusk" (Taras/Apr. 3); "The Littlest Bully" (Taras/Aug. 9/CinemaScope); and "Two Ton Baby Sitter" (Tendlar/Sept. 4/CinemaScope).

**1961:** "Banana Binge" (Deitch/CinemaScope); "Clown Jewels" (Deitch/CinemaScope); "Meet Drink and Be Merry" (Tendlar/CinemaScope); "Really Big Act" (Deitch/CinemaScope); "The Fleet's Out" (Bartsch/CinemaScope); and "Tree Spree" (Deitch/CinemaScope).

**1962:** "Peanut Battle" (Rasinski/Apr. 25/CinemaScope); "Send Your Elephant to Camp" (Bartsch/July 4/CinemaScope); and "Home Life" (Rasinski/CinemaScope).

**1963:** "To Be or Not to Be" (Rasinski/CinemaScope); "Sidney's White Elephant" (Bartsch/May 1); and "Driven to Extraction" (Bartsch/June 28).

### ◎ SILLY SYMPHONIES

Long wanting a series in the form of *Aesop's Fables*, Walt Disney fulfilled his dream by producing this series of nonstandard character cartoons that evoked settings, seasons and events. The series was actually proposed by musical director Carl Stalling, who had composed and arranged music for Mickey Mouse's historic "Steamboat Willie" (1928).

The first cartoon officially to launch the series was entitled "The Skeleton Dance," animated by Disney's longtime associate Ub Iwerks. The series went on to introduce the first three-strip Technicolor cartoon, "Flowers and Trees," perhaps the most imaginatively drawn cartoon from this era. (The film appropriately won an Academy Award for best short film [cartoon].)

The addition of color ensured the success of the *Silly Symphony* series, which lasted six more years and produced more classic cartoons like "Three Little Pigs." *Directors were Walt Disney, Ub Iwerks, Burt Gillett, Wilfred Jackson, David Hand, Ben Sharpsteen, Dick Lundy, Hugh Harman, Rudolf Ising, Jack Cutting, Dick Rickard and Graham Heid. Black-and-white. Technicolor. A Walt Disney Studios Production released through Celebrity Pictures, Columbia Pictures, United Artists and RKO Radio Pictures.*

### Celebrity Pictures releases

**1929:** "The Skeleton Dance" (Disney/Aug. 22); "El Terrible Toreador" (Disney/Sept. 7); "Springtime" (Iwerks/Oct. 24); "Hell's Bell's (Iwerks/Oct. 30); and "The Merry Dwarfs" (Disney/Dec. 16).

### Columbia Pictures releases

**1930:** "Summer" (Iwerks/Jan. 6); "Autumn" (Iwerks/Feb. 13); "Cannibal Capers" (Gillett/Mar. 13); "Frolicking Fish" (Gillett/May 8); "Arctic Antics" (Iwerks/June 5); "In a Toy Shop" (Gillett/July 3/copyrighted as "Midnight in a Toy Shop"); "Night" (Disney/July 31); "Monkey Melodies" (Gillett/Aug. 10); "Winter" (Gillett/Nov. 5); and "Playful Pan" (Gillett/Dec. 28).

**1931:** "Birds of a Feather" (Gillett/Feb. 10); "Mother Goose Melodies" (Apr. 17); "The China Plate" (Jackson/May 25); "The Busy Beavers" (Jackson/June 22); "The Cat's Out" (Jackson/July 28/originally "The Cat's Nightmare"); "Egyptian Melodies" (Jackson/Aug. 21); "The Clock Store" (Jackson/Sept. 30/originally "In a Clock Store"); "The Spider and the Fly" (Jackson/Oct. 16); "The Fox Hunt" (Jackson/Nov. 18); and "The Ugly Duckling" (Jackson/Dec. 16).

**1932:** "The Bird Store" (Jackson/Jan. 16).

### United Artists releases

**1932:** "The Bears and the Bees" (Jackson/July 9); "Just Dogs" (Gillett/July 30); "Flowers and Trees" (Gillett/Sept. 30/first color *Silly Symphony* cartoon); "King Neptune" (Gillett/Sept. 10); "Bugs in Love" (Gillett/Oct. 1); "Babes in the Woods" (Gillett/Nov. 19/all *Silly Symphony* cartoons in color from this point on); and "Santa's Workshop" (Jackson/Dec. 10).

**1933:** "Birds in the Spring" (Hand/Mar. 11); "Father Noah's Ark" (Jackson/Apr. 8); "Three Little Pigs" (Gillett/May 27/A.A. winner); "Old King Cole" (Hand/July 29); "Lullaby Land" (Jackson/Aug. 19); "The Pied Piper" (Jackson/Sept. 16); and "The Night Before Christmas" (Jackson/Dec. 9).

**1934:** "The China Shop" (Jackson/Jan. 13); "Grasshopper and the Ants" (Jackson/Feb. 10); "Funny Little Bunnies" (Jackson/Mar. 24); "The Big Bad Wolf" (Gillett/Apr. 14); "The Wise Little Hen" (Jackson/June 9/first appearance of Donald Duck); "The

*The Three Little Pigs enjoy themselves, unaware of what lurks outside, the Big Bad Wolf, in a scene from Walt Disney's Silly Symphony cartoon "Three Little Pigs," which won an Oscar for Best Short Subject. © Walt Disney Productions. All rights reserved.*

Flying Mouse" (Hand/July 14); "Peculiar Penguins" (Jackson/Sept. 1); and "The Goddess of Spring" (Jackson/Nov. 3).

**1935:** "The Tortoise and the Hare" (Jackson/Jan. 5/A.A. winner); "The Golden Touch" (Disney/Mar. 22); "The Robber Kitten" (Hand/Apr. 20); "Water Babies" (Jackson/May 11); "The Cookie Carnival" (Sharpsteen/May 25); "Who Killed Cock Robin?" (Hand/June 29/A.A. nominee); "Music Land" (Jackson/Oct. 5); "Three Orphan Kittens" (Hand/Oct. 26/A.A. winner); "Cock o' the Walk" (Sharpsteen/Nov. 30); and "Broken Toys" (Sharpsteen/Dec. 14).

**1936:** "Elmer Elephant" (Jackson/Mar. 28); "Three Little Wolves" (Hand/Apr. 18); "Toby Tortoise Returns" (Jackson/Aug. 22); "Three Blind Mouseketeers" (Hand/Sept. 26); "The Country Cousin" (Jackson/Oct. 31/A.A. winner); "Mother Pluto" (Nov. 14); and "More Kittens" (Hand/Dec. 19).

**1937:** "Woodland Cafe" (Jackson/Mar. 13); and "Little Hiawatha" (Hand/May 15).

### RKO Radio Pictures releases

**1937:** "The Old Mill" (Jackson/Nov. 5/A.A. winner).

**1938:** "Moth and the Flame" (Gillett/Apr. 1); "Wynken, Blynken and Nod" (Heid/May 27); "Farmyard Symphony" (Cutting/Oct. 14); "Merbabies" (supervised by Disney, Sharpsteen, Hand, Englander; directed by Rudolf Ising for Harman-Ising Studios/Dec. 9); and "Mother Goose Goes Hollywood" (Jackson/Dec. 23/A.A. nominee).

**1939:** "The Practical Pig" (Rickard/Feb. 24); and "The Ugly Duckling" (Cutting/Apr. 7/A.A. winner).

## ◎ SIR BLUR

A nearsighted knight in King Arthur's time who always has trouble with his glasses, Sir Blur was one of several late 1960s' cartoon creations featured in Paramount/Famous Studios' *Modern Madcap* theatrical cartoon series. The myopic knight made his screen debut in 1966's "A Balmy Knight," directed by James "Shamus" Culhane. *Culhane directed the entire series. Technicolor. Voice credits unknown. A Famous Studios Production released by Paramount Picture Corporation.*

**1966:** "A Balmy Knight" (June/*Modern Madcap*); and "A Wedding Knight" (Aug./*Modern Madcap*).

**1967:** "Black Sheep Blacksmith" (Jan./*Modern Madcap*).

## ◎ SNIFFLES

Director Chuck Jones created this naive, bewhiskered mouse who spoke with a squealing dialect and constantly found himself in precarious situations. Sniffles personified the "cute" personalities that launched the careers of animators Hugh Harman and Rudolf Ising at Warner Bros. In fact, in some respects, Jones's character bore a striking resemblance to Harman's Little Buck Cheeser.

Introduced in 1939's "Naughty But Mice," even Jones admitted the Sniffles cartoons were "often too long. When I had extra time, I'd tend to make the pans too long and the movement too slow."

Sniffles's squeaky voice was provided by Bernice Hansen, a veteran voice artist best known for her animal characters. Jones derived Sniffles's name from the fact he always had "a code in da nose." In 1940, his efforts to bring the character to the big screen paid off by earning him his first Academy Award nomination for "The Egg Collector." *Directed by Chuck Jones. Technicolor. A Warner Bros, Vitaphone/Leon Schlesinger Studios/Warner Bros. Cartoons, Inc. Production released by Warner Bros.*

### Voices

**Sniffles:** Bernice Hansen

### Merrie Melodies

### Vitaphone Productions releases

**1939:** "Naughty But Mice" (Jones/May 20); "Little Brother Rat" (Jones/Sept. 2); and "Sniffles and the Bookworm" (Jones/Dec. 2).

### Leon Schlesinger Studios releases

**1940:** "Sniffles Takes a Trip" (Jones/May 11); "The Egg Collector" (Jones/July 20/A.A. nominee); and "Bedtime for Sniffles" (Jones/Nov. 23).

**1941:** "Sniffles Bells the Cat" (Jones/Feb. 1); "Toy Trouble" (Jones/Apr. 12); and "The Brave Little Bat" (Jones/Sept. 27).

**1943:** "The Unbearable Bear" (Jones/Apr. 17).

**1944:** "Lost and Foundling" (Jones/Aug. 30).

### Looney Tunes

### Warner Bros. Cartoons, Inc. releases

**1946:** "Hush My Mouse" (Jones/May 4).

## ◎ SNUFFY SKUNK

After making his screen debut in Walter Lantz's 1938 Oswald the Rabbit cartoon, "Yokel Boy Makes Good," this likable skunk headlined a year later in his own starring cartoon short, "Snuffy's Party," directed by Elmer Perkins. Snuffy would appear in two more cartoons (both in Technicolor) "Life Begins for Andy Pandy" (1939) and in a cameo role in the 1941 *Swing Symphony* cartoon, "$21 a Day Once a Month," featuring Andy Panda and Woody Woodpecker. *Directed by Walter Lantz, Elmer Perkins and Alex Lovy. Black-and-white. Technicolor. A Walter Lantz Production released by Universal Pictures.*

**1938:** "Yokel Boy Makes Good" (with Oswald the Rabbit/Lantz/Feb. 21).

**1939:** "Snuffy's Party" (Perkins/Aug. 7/working title: "Snuffy Skunk's Party"); and "Life Begins for Andy Panda" (with Andy Panda/Lovy/Aug. 9).

**1941:** "$21 a Day Once a Month" (with Andy Panda and Woody Woodpecker/Lantz/Dec. 1).

## ◎ SPEEDY GONZALES

Possessing the speed of the Road Runner and the quickwittedness of Tweety bird Speedy Gonzales was the mischievous Mexican mouse, jaunty in his chic sombrero, who boasted a spitfire running speed of 100 miles per hour. He was often paired with Sylvester and Daffy Duck in adventures reminiscent of MGM's *Tom and Jerry* cartoons.

The idea for Speedy's character originated in a Robert McKimson cartoon of 1953 called "Cat-Tails for Two." The story was about an idiotic cat-and-dog team who sneak into a Mexican strip in search of mice but discover that the rodents are too fast to be caught. The head mouse is unnamed in the film and bears little resemblance to the Speedy movie audiences grew up with.

Friz Freleng remembered McKimson's mouse character two years later and redesigned him with animator Hawley Pratt into "the fastest mouse in all of Mexico." Speedy's first cartoon was the 1955 entry "Speedy Gonzales." The film was accorded the film industry's highest honor, an Academy Award, for best cartoon of the year. Three other Speedy cartoons were also nominated for

Oscars: "Tabasco Road" (1957), "Mexicali Shmoes" (1959); and "The Pied Piper of Guadalupe" (1961).

In later adventures, Speedy was given a comic sidekick, Slowpoke Rodriguez, whose lethargic personality never caught on. He was limited to occasional guest appearances. *Directors were Robert McKimson, Friz Freleng, Hawley Pratt, Rudy Larriva and Alex Lovy. Technicolor. A Warner Bros. Cartoons, Inc./Warner Bros. Pictures, Inc./DePatie-Freleng Enterprises/Format Films/Warner Brothers Production released by Warner Bros. and Warner Bros. Seven Arts.*

*Voices*
**Speedy Gonzales:** Mel Blanc

*Merrie Melodies*

*Warner Bros. Cartoons, Inc. releases*

**1953:** "Cat-Tails for Two" (McKimson/Aug. 29).

**1955:** "Speedy Gonzales" (with Sylvester/Freleng/Sept. 17/A.A. winner).

**1957:** "Tabasco Road" (with Sylvester/McKimson/July 20/A.A. nominee); and "Gonzales' Tamales" (with Sylvester/Freleng/Nov. 30).

**1960:** "West of the Pesos" (with Sylvester/McKimson/Jan. 23).

**1963:** "Mexican Cat Dance" (Freleng/Apr. 20); and "Chili Weather" (with Sylvester/Freleng/Aug. 17).

*DePatie-Freleng Enterprises/Format Films releases*

**1964:** "Road to Andalay" (with Sylvester/Freleng, Pratt/Dec. 26).

**1965:** "Cats and Bruises" (with Sylvester/Freleng, Pratt/Jan. 30); "The Wild Chase" (Freleng, Pratt/Feb. 27); and "Go Go Amigo" (with Daffy Duck/McKimson/Nov. 20).

**1966:** "Muchos Locos" (with Daffy Duck/McKimson/Feb. 5); "Mexican Mousepiece" (with Daffy Duck/McKimson/Feb. 26); "Snow Excuse" (with Daffy Duck/McKimson/May 21); "Feather Finger" (with Daffy Duck/McKimson/Aug. 20); and "A Taste of Catnip" (with Daffy Duck/McKimson/Dec. 3).

**1967:** "Daffy's Diner" (with Daffy Duck/McKimson/Jan. 21); "The Music Mice-Tro" (with Daffy Duck/Larriva/May 27); "Speedy Ghost to Town" (with Daffy Duck/Miguel/Lovy/July 29); and "Go Away Stowaway" (with Daffy Duck/Lovy/Sept. 30).

**1968:** "Skyscraper Caper" (with Daffy Duck/Lovy/Mar. 9).

*Looney Tunes*

*Warner Bros. Cartoons, Inc. releases*

**1958:** "Tortilla Flaps" (McKimson/Jan. 18).

**1959:** "Mexicali Shmoes" (with Slowpoke Rodriguez/Freleng/July 4/A.A. nominee); and "Here Today, Gone Tamale" (with Sylvester/Freleng/Aug. 29).

**1961:** "Cannery Woe" (with Sylvester/McKimson/Jan. 7); and "The Pied Piper of Guadalupe" (with Sylvester, Slowpoke Rodriguez/Freleng, Pratt/Aug. 19/A.A. nominee).

**1962:** "Mexican Boarders" (with Sylvester, Slowpoke Rodriguez/Freleng, Pratt/May 12).

**1964:** "A Message to Gracias" (with Sylvester/McKimson/Feb. 8); and "Nuts and Volts" (with Sylvester/Freleng/Apr. 25).

*DePatie-Freleng Enterprises/Format Films releases*

**1964:** "Pancho's Hideaway" (Freleng, Pratt/Oct. 24).

**1965:** "It's Nice to Have Mouse Around the House" (with Daffy Duck, Sylvester/Freleng, Pratt/Jan. 16); "Well Worn Daffy" (with Daffy Duck/McKimson/May 22); "Tease for Two" (with Daffy Duck, Goofy Gophers/McKimson/Aug. 28); and "Chili Corn Corny" (with Daffy Duck/McKimson/Oct. 23).

**1966:** "The Astroduck" (with Daffy Duck/McKimson/Jan. 1); "Daffy Rents" (with Daffy Duck/McKimson/Mar. 26); "A-Haunting We Will Go" (with Daffy Duck, Witch Hazel/McKimson/Apr. 16); "A Squeak in the Deep" (with Daffy Duck/McKimson/July 19); and "Swing Ding Amigo" (with Daffy Duck/McKimson/Sept. 17).

*Format Films/Warner Bros. releases*

**1967:** "Quacker Tracker" (with Daffy Duck/Larriva/Apr. 29).

**1968:** "See Ya Later Gladiator" (with Daffy Duck/Lovy/June 29).

## ◎ SPIKE

Originally developed as a supporting nemesis character in MGM's *Droopy* series, Tex Avery featured this gentle bulldog pushed to his limits in traditional chaotic cartoon situations in a starring series of his own. Bill Thompson, also the voice of Droopy, played Spike in the series. *Directed by Tex Avery. Technicolor. A Metro-Goldwyn-Mayer Cartoon Production released by Metro-Goldwyn-Mayer.*

*Voices*
**Spike:** Bill Thompson

**1949:** "The Counterfeit Cat" (Dec. 24).

**1950:** "Ventriloquist Cat" (May 27); and "Garden Gopher" (Sept. 30/working title: "Sting Time in the Rockies").

**1951:** "Cock-a-Doodle Dog" (Feb. 10).

**1952:** "Rock-a-Bye Bear" (July 12).

## ◎ SPIKE AND CHESTER

Spike, a tough streetwise dog, and his admiring pal, Chester, were short-lived screen stars, paired with Sylvester (of *Tweety and Sylvester* fame) in two Warner Bros. cartoons. The tandem began their screen careers in 1952's "Tree for Two." *Directed by Friz Freleng. Technicolor. A Warner Bros. Cartoons, Inc. Production released by Warner Bros.*

*Voices*
**Spike:** Mel Blanc; **Chester:** Stan Freberg

*Merrie Melodies*

**1952:** "Tree for Two" (with Sylvester/Oct. 4).

*Looney Tunes*

**1954:** "Dr. Jerkyl's Hide" (with Sylvester/May 8).

## ◎ SPIKE AND TYKE

This popular father-and-son dog pairing—Spike, the gruff father, and Tyke, the impish son—sprang on to the screen in the late 1940s as costars in Metro-Goldwyn-Mayer's Academy Award–winning *Tom and Jerry* cartoon series directed by creators William Hanna and Joseph Barbera. Spike originated as a sleeping "Bull Dog" in the 1942 *Tom and Jerry* cartoon, "Dog Trouble," evolving into a character that particularly loathed cats but, despite his stern exterior, was a softie when it came to mice. He was named Spike in subsequent cartoons (and voiced by Daws Butler), beginning with the 1944 *Tom and Jerry* cartoon, "The Bodyguard." Early in his career at Metro, he costarred in the Academy Award-winning *Tom and Jerry* cartoon, "Quiet Please" (1945).

Beginning with 1947's "A Mouse in the House," Spike went under the name of "Butch" in the series until 1952 in cartoons that included "The Truce Hurts" (1948), "Heavenly Puss" (1949), "The Framed Cat" (1950), "Cat Napping" (1951) and "Fit to Be Tied" (1952).

Tyke made his debut as "Pup" opposite Spike (as Butch) in the 1949 *Tom and Jerry* cartoon, "Love That Pup," and appeared again, two years later, in "Slicked-up Pup" (1951). In 1952, Spike was so-named in the hilarious *Tom and Jerry* cartoon, "The Dog House." A year later, Pup officially became known as Tyke, and was paired with Spike in "That's My Pup" (1953). Sticking with those names, the lovable father-and-dog team costarred in four more *Tom and Jerry* cartoons, including "Hic-Cup Pup" (1954), "Pup on a Picnic" (1955), the first in CinemaScope, "Barbecue Brawl" (1956) and "Tom's Photo Finish" (1957), which by now Hanna and Barbera also produced as well as directed. In the late 1950s, Hanna and Barbera modified and cast the pair in their own series, beginning with "Give and Tyke" (1957) and ending with "Scat Cats" (1957), produced that same year. Unfortunately, the series lasted a short time.

Spike and Tyke later served as the basis for Hanna and Barbera's popular television characters, Augie Doggy and Doggy Daddy. *Directed by William Hanna and Joseph Barbera. Technicolor. CinemaScope. A Metro-Goldwyn-Mayer Cartoon Production released by Metro-Goldwyn-Mayer.*

**Voices**
**Spike:** Daws Butler

**1942:** "Dog Trouble" (with Tom and Jerry, Bulldog/Apr. 18/ introduces Spike as "Bulldog").

**1944:** "The Bodyguard" (with Tom and Jerry/Apr. 18); and "Puttin' On the Dog" (with Tom and Jerry/Oct. 28).

**1945:** "Quiet Please" (with Tom and Jerry/Dec. 22/A.A. winner).

**1946:** "Cat Fishin'" (with Tom and Jerry/Feb. 22); and "Solid Serenade" (with Tom and Jerry/Aug. 31).

**1947:** "The Invisible Mouse" (with Tom and Jerry/Sept. 27).

**1948:** "The Truce Hurts" (with Tom and Jerry/July 17).

**1949:** "Heavenly Puss" (with Tom and Jerry/July 9); and "Love That Pup" (with Tom and Jerry/Oct. 1/with Spike as "Butch"; introduces Tyke as "Pup").

**1951:** "Slicked-up Pup" (with Tom and Jerry/Sept. 8).

**1952:** "Fit to Be Tied" (with Tom and Jerry, Spike as "Butch"/ July 26); and "The Dog House" (with Tom and Jerry/Nov. 29).

**1953:** "That's My Pup" (with Tom and Jerry/July 26/first official Spike and Tyke appearance); "Two Little Indians" (with Tom and Jerry, Spike/Oct. 17); and "Life With Tom" (with Tom and Jerry, Spike and Tyke/Nov. 21).

**1954:** "Hic-Cup Pup" (with Tom and Jerry, Spike and Tyke/ Apr. 1); and "Pet Peeve" (with Tom and Jerry, Spike/Nov. 20/ CinemaScope).

**1955:** "Pup on a Picnic" (with Tom and Jerry, Spike and Tyke/ Apr. 30/CinemaScope); and "Smarty Cat" (with Tom and Jerry, Spike/Oct. 14/CinemaScope).

**1956:** "Barbecue Brawl" (with Tom and Jerry/Dec. 14/ CinemaScope).

**1957:** "Tops with Pops" (with Tom and Jerry, Spike and Tyke/ CinemaScope); "Give and Tyke" (Mar. 29/first Spike and Tyke series cartoon/CinemaScope); "Scat Cats" (July 26/last Spike and Tyke series cartoon/CinemaScope); and "Tom's Photo Finish" (with Tom and Jerry, Spike/Nov. 1/CinemaScope).

## ⊚ SPLINTER AND KNOTHEAD
Rambunctious niece and nephew opposite their great uncle Woody Woodpecker in three cartoon shorts produced by Walter Lantz and directed by Paul J. Smith, beginning with 1956's "Get Lost." Veteran voice actor June Foray provided the voice of both characters. *Directed by Paul J. Smith. Technicolor. A Walter Lantz Production released by Universal Pictures.*

**Voices**
**Splinter/Knothead:** June Foray

**1956:** "Get Lost" (with Woody Woodpecker/Smith/Mar. 12).

**1957:** "The Unbearable Salesman" (with Woody Woodpecker/ Smith/June 3).

**1962:** "Careless Caretaker" (with Woody Woodpecker/May 29).

## ⊚ SPUNKY
Spunky, one of several minor *Noveltoons* characters, appeared on the screen for the first time in 1944's "Yankee Doodle Donkey." The character did not star again in another cartoon until 14 years after his screen debut. *Directed by Isadore Sparber. Technicolor. A Famous Studios Production released through Paramount Pictures Corporation.*

**1944:** "Yankee Doodle Donkey" (Nov. 27).

**1958:** "Okey Dokey Donkey" (May 16).

## ⊚ STONE AGE CARTOONS
Following the success of *Gulliver's Travels* (1939), Max Fleischer unveiled two cartoon series, the first featuring the comic exploits of Stone Age life. The series predated TV's *The Flintstones* by 20 years but, unlike the television classic, this novel series died a quick death. No central characters starred in the films, which may have been one reason for the series' failure. *Directed by Dave Fleischer. Technicolor. A Fleischer Studios Production released through Paramount Pictures Corporation.*

**1940:** "Way Back When a Triangle Had Its Points" (Jan. 26); "Way Back When a Nag Was Only a Horse" (Mar. 8); "Way Back When a Nightclub Was a Stick" (Mar. 15); "Granite Hotel" (Apr. 26); "The Fool Ball Player" (May 24); "The Ugly Dino" (June 14); "Wedding Belts" (July 5); "Way Back When a Razzberry Was a Fruit" (July 26/working title: "Bear Facts"); "The Fulla Bluff Man" (Aug. 9); "Springtime in the Rock Age" (Aug. 30); "Pedagogical Institution (College to You)" (Sept. 13); and "Way Back When Women Had Their Weigh" (Sept. 26).

## ⊚ SUGARFOOT
In 1954, Walter Lantz attempted to cast the lame horse Sugarfoot, later a supporting character in Woody Woodpecker cartoons in the late 1960s, in a cartoon series of his own. The series did not produce much interest, however, as only two films were produced. *Directed by Paul J. Smith. Technicolor. A Walter Lantz Production released through Universal Pictures.*

**1954:** "A Horse's Tale" (Feb. 15); and "Hay Rube" (June 7).

**1968:** "Lotsa Luck" (with Woody Woodpecker).

**1969:** "Phoney Pony" (with Woody Woodpecker/Nov. 1).

## ⊚ SUPERMAN
First conceived by Jerry Siegel and Joe Schuster as a newspaper strip and finally published in *Action Comics*, this legendary man of steel was adapted to the screen in 1941.

As in the comics, the city of Metropolis was the newspaper beat for mild-mannered reporter Clark Kent of the *Daily Planet*. Beneath his meek exterior was a Herculean superhero able to leap tall buildings in a single bound, more powerful than a locomotive and faster than a speeding bullet.

The supporting cast of characters was also intact: pretty newspaper gal Lois Lane, cub reporter Jimmy Olsen and blustering editor-in-chief Perry White.

Both Fleischer Studios and Famous Studios produced the series. "The Japoteurs" was the first Famous cartoon. The original Fleischer cartoons used Rotoscoping to give animation a semirealistic look and attention to detail never to be matched in later television versions of the series. Action and special effects were key elements of the series, which was backed by a tremendous promotional campaign when it was introduced.

Director Dave Fleischer contracted two actors from the radio version, Bud Collyer and Joan Alexander, to voice Clark Kent/Superman and Lois Lane. *Directors were Dave Fleischer, Seymour Kneitel, Isadore Sparber and Dan Gordon. Technicolor. A Fleischer Studios and Famous Studios Production released through Paramount Pictures Corporation.*

*Voices*
**Clark Kent/Superman:** Clayton "Bud" Collyer; **Lois Lane:** Joan Alexander

*Fleischer Studios releases*

**1941:** "Superman" (Fleischer/Sept. 26/working title: "The Mad Scientist"/A.A. nominee); and "The Mechanical Monsters" (Kneitel/Nov. 21).

**1942:** "Billion Dollar Limited" (Fleischer/Jan. 9); "The Arctic Giant" (Fleischer/Feb. 27); "The Bulleteers" (Fleischer/Mar. 26); "The Magnetic Telescope" (Fleischer/Apr. 24); "Electric Earthquake" (Fleischer/May 15); "Volcano" (Fleischer/July 10); and "Terror on the Midway" (Fleischer/Aug. 28).

*Famous Studios releases*

**1942:** "Japoteurs" (Kneitel/Sept. 18); "Showdown" (Sparber/Oct. 16); "Eleventh Hour" (Gordon/Nov. 20); and "Destruction, Inc." (Sparber/Dec. 25).

**1943:** "The Mummy Strikes" (Sparber/Feb. 19); "Jungle Drums" (Gordon/Mar. 26); "Underground World" (Kneitel/June 18); and "Secret Agent" (Kneitel/July 30).

## ◎ SWIFTY AND SHORTY

A fast-talking con man, Swifty, and his pudgy friend, Shorty, appeared in this series of misadventures patterned after comedy greats Abbott and Costello. Formerly "Jeepers and Creepers," the characters under their new identities were recast in several cartoon shorts—*Noveltoon* and *Modern Madcap* releases—before being given their own star-billed series in 1964. (In the three cartoons released in 1962, they were known as Ralph and Percy.) Comedian Eddie Lawrence supplied the voices for this series. *Directed by Seymour Kneitel and Howard Post. Technicolor. A Famous Studios Production released through Paramount Pictures Corporation.*

*Voices*
**Swifty/Shorty:** Eddie Lawrence

**1962:** "Without Time or Reason" (Kneitel/Jan./Noveltoon); "Hi-Fi Jinx" (Kneitel/Mar./Modern Madcap); and "T.V. or No T.V." (Kneitel/Mar./Noveltoon).

**1964:** "Panhandling on Madison Avenue" (Kneitel/Apr.); "Fizzicle Fizzle" (Kneitel/Apr.); "Sailing Zero" (Kneitel/Apr.); "Fix That Clock" (Kneitel/May); "A Friend in Tweed" (Kneitel/May); "The Once-Over" (Kneitel/June); "Service with a Smile" (Kneitel/June); "Call Me a Taxi" (Kneitel/July); "Highway Slobbery" (Kneitel/July); "Hip Hip Ole" (Kneitel/Sept.); "Accidents Will Happen" (Kneitel/Sept.); and "The Bus Way to Travel" (Kneitel/Oct.).

**1965:** "Inferior Decorator" (Post/June); "Ocean Bruise" (Post/Sept.); "Getting Ahead" (Post/Dec.); and "Les Boys" (Post/Dec.).

## ◎ SWING SYMPHONIES

Popular jazz tunes of the 1940s were the basis of this series produced and created by Walter Lantz. Episodes featured no running characters, and early versions concentrated on boogie-woogie type music evidenced by such series titles as "Yankee Doodle Swing Shift" and "Cow-Cow Boogie."

Lantz paid a hefty price to produce these ambitious musical oddities, from $9,500 to $12,000 per one-reeler. As he told biographer Joe Adamson: "I loved to make musicals, but you can't cheat on musicals. You've got to animate to the beat."

By 1944 the series had run its course. Two years later Lantz replaced it with another musical series entitled *Musical Miniatures*. *Directed by Walter Lantz, Alex Lovy, Ben Hardaway, Emery Hawkins, James "Shamus" Culhane and Dick Lundy. Black-and-white. Technicolor. A Walter Lantz Production released through Universal Pictures.*

**1941:** "$21 a Day Once a Month" (with Woody Woodpecker, Andy Panda, Snuffy Skunk Lantz/Dec. 1).

**1942:** "The Hams That Couldn't Be Cured" (Lantz/Mar. 4); "Juke Box Jamboree" (Lovy/July 27); "Yankee Doodle Swing Shift" (Lovy/Sept. 21); and "Boogie Woogie Sioux" (Lovy/Nov. 30).

**1943:** "Cow-Cow Boogie" (Lovy/Jan. 5); "The Egg Cracker Suite" (with Oswald the Rabbit/Hardaway, Hawkins/Mar. 22/first appearance of Oswald the Rabbit); "Swing Your Partner" (with Homer Pigeon/Lovy); "Pass the Biscuits Mirandy!" (Culhane/Aug. 23); and "Boogie Woogie Man" (Will Get You If You Don't Watch Out) (Culhane/Sept. 27).

**1944:** "The Greatest Man in Siam" (Culhane/Mar. 27); "Jungle Jive" (Culhane/May 15); and "Abou Ben Boogie" (Culhane/Sept. 18).

**1945:** "The Pied Piper of Basin Street" (Culhane/Jan. 15); and "The Sliphorn King of Polaroo" (Lundy/Mar. 19/narrated by Hans Conried).

## ◎ SYLVESTER

Sylvester enjoyed an accomplished solo career before teaming up with the slippery yellow canary Tweety. The lisping cat, whose voice was similar to Daffy Duck's, was first used in Friz Freleng's 1945 "Life with Feathers," ironically appearing with a lovelorn lovebird. In this film debut he uttered his now-famous line of "Sufferin' succotash."

Sylvester next appeared in Freleng's "Peck Up Your Troubles" (1945), this time opposite a woodpecker, and as a ringleader of a quartet of cats in Bob Clampett's "Kitty Kornered" (1946), before Freleng paired the exasperated cat with Tweety the bird in 1947's "Tweety Pie." (Clampett did the preliminary story for the film, but Freleng assumed the property after Clampett left the studio that same year.)

While the cartoon became the first starring role for Sylvester (in the film, he is referred to as Thomas, not Sylvester), it also became the first Warner cartoon to win an Oscar for best short subject of the year. It was Sylvester's second of three Oscar-nominated cartoons. His first was 1945's "Life with Feathers"; his third and final nominated cartoon was 1961's "The Pied Piper of Guadalupe" starring Speedy Gonzales.

Sylvester was given a series of his own in 1953, appearing in 11 cartoons opposite his ever-energetic son, Sylvester Jr. (simply known as "Junior"), and seven with Hippety Hopper, the hopping kangaroo, whom Sylvester constantly mistakes for an oversize mouse. The sly pussycat made intermittent appearances with Elmer J. Fudd and Porky Pig and was paired with Speedy Gonzales in other cartoon misadventures.

In the 1990s Sylvester resurfaced in minor film roles, first in the new Bugs Bunny cartoon "Carrotblanca" (1995), followed by an appearance in the hit feature *Space Jam* (1996), starring Michael Jordan and the *Looney Tunes* characters. In 1997 Sylvester starred in an all-new cartoon short—his first in 35 years—"Father of the Bird," which opened in theaters with the live-action comedy *The Man Who Knew Too Little*, starring Bill Murray. Produced by legendary animator Chuck Jones (who four years earlier had formed a new animation unit at Warner Bros. to produce new theatrical cartoon shorts for the studio) and directed by Jones's protégé Steve Fossati, the cartoon introduced a new nemesis: Cornbread, a fiesty little bird, voiced by veteran voice artist June Foray. Joe Alaskey provided the voice of Sylvester. (See *Tweety and Sylvester* for Tweety and Sylvester cartoons.) *Directed by Friz Freleng, Charles M. Jones, Bob Clampett, Robert McKimson, Hawley Pratt, Gerry Chiniquy, Douglas McCarthy and Steve Fossati. Technicolor. A Warner Bros. Cartoons, Inc./Warner Bros. Pictures, Inc./Vitagraph/DePatie-Freleng Enterprises/Warner Bros. Animation/Warner Bros./Chuck Jones Film Production released by Warner Bros. and Warner Bros. Family Entertainment.*

**Voices**
Sylvester: Mel Blanc, Joe Alaskey; **Sylvester Jr./Tweety:** Mel Blanc; **Cornbread:** June Foray

*Merrie Melodies*

**Warner Bros. Cartoons, Inc. releases**

**1945:** "Life with Feathers" (Freleng/Mar. 24/A.A. nominee); and "Peck Up Your Troubles" (Freleng/Oct. 20).

**1947:** "Dog Gone Cats" (Davis/Oct. 25).

**1948:** "Back Alley Oproar" (with Elmer Fudd/Freleng/Mar. 27); and "Scaredy Cat" (with Porky Pig/Jones/Dec. 18).

**1949:** "Mouse Mazurka" (Freleng/June 11); and "Hippety Hopper" (with Hippety Hopper/McKimson/Nov. 19).

**1952:** "Little Red Rodent Hood" (with Granny/Freleng/May 3); and "Tree for Two" (with Spike, Chester/Freleng/Oct. 4).

**1953:** "A Mouse Divided" (with Mrs. Sylvester/Freleng/Jan. 31); "A Peck o' Trouble" (McKimson/Mar. 28); and "Cats A-Weigh!" (with Sylvester Jr., Hippety Hopper/McKimson/Nov. 28).

**1954:** "Bell Hoppy" (with Hippety Hopper/McKimson/Apr. 17); and "Claws for Alarm" (with Porky Pig/Jones/May 22).

**1955:** "Lighthouse Mouse" (with Hippety Hopper/McKimson/Mar. 12); "Jumpin' Jupiter" (with Porky Pig/Jones/Aug. 6); "A Kiddie's Kitty" (Freleng/Aug. 20); "Speedy Gonzales" (with Speedy Gonzales/Freleng/Sept. 17/A.A. winner); and "Pappy's Puppy" (with Butch J. Bulldog/Freleng/Dec. 17).

**1956:** "The Unexpected Guest" (McKimson/June 2); "The Slap-Hoppy Mouse" (with Hippety Hopper, Sylvester Jr./McKimson/Sept. 1); and "Yankee Dood It" (with Elmer Fudd/Freleng/Oct. 13).

**1957:** "Tabasco Road" (with Speedy Gonzales/McKimson/July 20/A.A. nominee); "Mouse-Taken Identity" (with Hippety Hopper, Sylvester Jr./McKimson/Nov. 10); and "Gonzales' Tamales" (with Speedy Gonzales/Freleng/Nov. 30).

**1960:** "West of Pesos" (with Speedy Gonzales/McKimson/Jan. 23).

*Warner Bros. Pictures, Inc./Vitagraph releases*

**1961:** "D'Fightin' Ones" (Freleng/Apr. 22).

**1963:** "Chili Weather" (with Speedy Gonzales/Freleng/Aug. 17); and "Claws in the Lease" (with Junior/McKimson/Nov. 9).

*DePatie-Freleng Enterprises Releases*

**1964:** "Road to Andalay" (with Speedy Gonzales/Freleng, Pratt/Dec. 26).

**1965:** "Cats and Bruises" (with Speedy/Freleng, Pratt/Jan. 30).

*Looney Tunes*

**Warner Bros. Cartoons, Inc. releases**

**1946:** "Kitty Kornered" (with Porky Pig/Clampett/June 8).

**1948:** "Hop Look and Listen" (with Hippety Hopper/McKimson/Apr. 17); and "Kit for Cat" (with Elmer/Freleng/Nov. 6).

**1949:** "Swallow the Leader" (McKimson/Oct. 14).

**1950:** "The Scarlet Pumpernickel" (with Daffy Duck, Porky Pig, Elmer Fudd and Momma Bear/Jones/Mar. 4); and "Pop 'Im Pop!" (with Hippety, Sylvester Jr./McKimson/Nov. 6).

**1951:** "Canned Feud" (Freleng/Feb. 3).

**1952:** "Who's Kitten Who" (with Hippety Hopper, Sylvester Jr./McKimson/Jan. 5); and "Hoppy-Go-Lucky" (with Hippety Hopper/McKimson/Aug. 9).

**1954:** "Dr. Jerkyl's Hide" (with Spike and Chester/Freleng/May 8); and "By Word of Mouse" (Freleng/Oct. 2).

**1955:** "Heir-Conditioned" (with Elmer Fudd/Freleng/Nov. 26).

**1956:** "Too Hop to Handle" (with Hippety Hopper, Sylvester Jr./McKimson/Jan. 28).

**1959:** "Cat's Paw" (with Sylvester Jr./McKimson/Aug. 15); and "Here Today, Gone Tamale" (with Speedy Gonzales/Freleng/Aug. 29).

**1960:** "Goldimouse and the Three Cats" (with Junior/Freleng/Mar. 19); and "Mouse Garden" (with Junior, Sam/Freleng/July 16/A.A. nominee).

*Warner Bros. Pictures/Vitagraph releases*

**1961:** "Cannery Woe" (with Speedy Gonzales/McKimson/Jan. 7); "Hoppy Daze" (with Hippety Hopper/McKimson/Feb. 11); "Birds of a Father" (with Junior/McKimson/Apr. 1); and "The Pied Piper of Guadalupe" (with Speedy Gonzales, Slowpoke Rodriguez/Freleng, Pratt/Aug. 19/A.A. nominee).

**1962:** "Fish and Slips" (with Junior/McKimson/Mar. 10); and "Mexican Boarders" (with Speedy Gonzales, Slowpoke Rodriguez/Freleng, Pratt/May 12).

**1964:** "A Message to Gracias" (with Speedy Gonzales/McKimson/Feb. 8); "Freudy Cat" (with Hippety Hopper, Sylvester Jr./McKimson/Mar. 14); and "Nuts and Volts" (with Speedy Gonzales/Freleng/Apr. 25).

*DePatie-Freleng Enterprises releases*

**1965:** "It's Nice to Have Mouse Around the House" (with Speedy Gonzales, Daffy Duck/Freleng, Pratt/Jan. 16).

*Warner Bros. Animation releases*

**1995:** "Carrotblanca" (with Bugs Bunny, Daffy Duck, Yosemite Sam, Tweety, Pepe Le Pew, Foghorn Leghorn, Penelope/McCarthy/Aug. 25).

*Warner Bros./Chuck Jones Film Productions releases*

**1997:** "Father of the Bird" (with Cornbread/Fossati/Nov. 14).

### ◎ SYLVESTER JR.

Small-fry version of his cartoon father (whom he affectionately referred to as "Dear Old Father"), right down to his dad's famous lisp, costarred in a series of Warner Bros. cartoons often cast in comical situations where he was ashamed of his dad's antics, all directed, except for two of them, by longtime Warner Bros. animator Robert McKimson. Simply referred to as Junior, the pint-sized clone was first paired with his famous father in the 1950 *Looney Tunes*, "Pop 'Im Pop!," opposite the high-hopping kangaroo, Hippety Hopper, with whom they starred in six more *Looney Tunes* and *Merrie Melodies* releases until 1964's "Freudy Cat." The latter, coincidentally, marked Hippety and Sylvester Jr.'s final screen appearance.

Sylvester Jr. likewise starred in a similar role in a single Tweety and Sylvester cartoon, 1959's "Tweet Dreams," directed by Friz Freleng, and other cartoons of his own, including "Goldimouse and the Three Cats" (1960), also directed by Freleng. Unlike most cartoons in the series, this one featured the flip side of his character as a spoiled brat besides introducing a Mrs. Sylvester to the world. *Directed by Robert McKimson and Friz Freleng. Technicolor. A Warner Bros. Cartoons, Inc., Warner Bros. Pictures, Inc., Vitaphone Production released by Warner Bros.*

*Voices*
**Sylvester Jr:** Mel Blanc

*Looney Tunes*

*Warner Bros. Cartoons, Inc., releases*

**1950:** "Pop 'Im Pop!" (with Sylvester, Hippety Hopper/McKimson/Oct. 28/first appearance of Sylvester Jr.).

**1952:** "Who's Kitten Who?" (with Sylvester, Hippety Hopper/McKimson/Jan. 5).

**1956:** "Too Hop Too Handle" (with Sylvester, Hippety Hopper/McKimson/Jan. 28).

**1959:** "Cat's Paw" (with Sylvester/McKimson/Aug. 15) and "Tweet Dreams" (with Tweety, Granny/Freleng/Dec. 5).

**1960:** "Goldimouse and the Three Cats" (with Sylvester/Freleng/Mar. 19).

*Warner Bros. Pictures, Inc./Vitaphone releases*

**1961:** "Birds of a Father" (with Sylvester/McKimson/Apr. 1).

**1962:** "Fish and Slips" (with Sylvester/McKimson/Mar. 10).

**1964:** "Freudy Cat" (with Sylvester, Hippety Hopper/McKimson/Mar. 14/last appearance of Sylvester Jr. and Hippety Hopper).

*Merrie Melodies*

*Warner Bros. Cartoons, Inc. releases*

**1953:** "Cat's-a-Weigh!"(with Sylvester, Hippety Hopper/McKimson/Nov. 28).

**1956:** "The Slap-Hoppy Mouse" (with Sylvester, Hippety Hopper/McKimson/Sept. 1).

**1957:** "Mouse-Taken Identity" (with Sylvester, Hippety Hopper/McKimson/Nov. 10).

*Warner Bros. Pictures, Inc./Vitaphone release*

**1963:** "Claws in the Lease" (with Sylvester/McKimson/Nov. 9).

### ◎ TALKARTOONS

Billed as "actual talking pictures" in theater ads, this series represented the Fleischer Studios' initial entrance into the sound cartoon arena. Films starred a host of subsequently famous characters, including Betty Boop, Bimbo and Koko the Clown.

Early entries featured postsynched dialogue and music added after the productions were complete with dialogue being kept to a minimum and peppy musical scores carrying the films. In the beginning, having no accomplished musical director to create songs, the Fleischers purchased the rights of popular songs to use as soundtracks. The series' first star was Bimbo, resurrected by the Fleischers from the *Out of the Inkwell* series.

While the series celebrated Bimbo's return to the screen, the series' sixth cartoon release of 1930, "Dizzy Dishes," introduced another character in her formative stages—Betty Boop, invented and drawn by animator Grim Natwick. In 1931 Koko the Clown was brought back as a supporting player in the series, after a brief retirement from the screen. *Directed by Dave Fleischer. Black-and-white. A Fleischer Studios Production released through Paramount Picture Corporation.*

(Copyright dates are marked by a ©.)

**1929:** "Noah's Lark" (© Oct. 25); and "Accordion Joe" (© with Bimbo/Dec. 12).

**1930:** "Marriage Wows" (© Jan. 8); "Radio Riot" (Feb. 13); "Hot Dog" (with Bimbo/Mar. 29); "Fire Bugs" (May 9); "Wise Flies" (July 18); "Dizzy Dishes" (with Betty Boop, Bimbo/Aug. 9); "Barnacle Bill" (with Betty Boop, Bimbo/Aug. 31); "Swing, You Sinner!" (with Bimbo/Sept. 24); "The Grand Uproar" (with Bimbo/Oct. 3); "Sky Scraping" (with Bimbo/Nov. 1); "Up to Mars" (Nov. 20); and "Mysterious Mose" (with Betty Boop, Bimbo/Dec. 26).

**1931:** "The Ace of Spades" (with Bimbo, Koko the Clown/Jan. 16); "Tree Saps" (with Bimbo/Feb. 3); "Teacher's Pest" (with Bimbo, Koko the Clown); "The Cow's Husband" (with Bimbo, Koko the Clown); "The Bum Bandit" (with Betty Boop, Bimbo/Apr. 3); "The Male Man" (with Bimbo, Koko the Clown/Apr. 24); "Twenty Legs Under the Sea" (with Bimbo/May 5); "Silly Scandals" (with Betty Boop, Bimbo/May 23); "The Herring Murder Case" (with Bimbo, Koko the Clown/June 26); "Bimbo's Initiation" (with Betty Boop, Bimbo/July 24); "Minding the Baby" (with Betty Boop, Bimbo/Sept. 26); "In the Shade of the Old Apple Sauce" (with Bimbo, Koko the Clown/Oct. 16); "Mask-a-Raid" (with Betty Boop, Bimbo/Nov. 7); "Jack and the Beanstalk" (with Betty Boop, Bimbo/Nov. 21); and "Dizzy Red Riding-Hood" (with Betty Boop, Bimbo/Dec. 12).

**1932:** "Any Rags" (with Betty Boop, Bimbo, Koko the Clown/Jan. 2); "Boop-Oop-A-Doop" (with Betty Boop, Bimbo, Koko the Clown/Jan. 16); "The Robot" (with Betty Boop, Bimbo, Koko the Clown/Feb. 5); "Minnie the Moocher" (with Betty Boop, Bimbo, Cab Calloway and His Orchestra/Feb. 26); "Swim or Sink" (with Betty Boop, Bimbo, Koko the Clown/Mar. 11); "Crazy Town" (with Betty Boop, Bimbo, Koko the Clown/Mar. 25); "The Dancing Fool" (with Betty Boop, Bimbo, Koko the

Clown/Apr. 8); "A Hunting We Will Go" (with Betty Boop, Bimbo, Koko the Clown/Apr. 29); "Chess-Nuts" (with Betty Boop, Bimbo, Koko the Clown/May 13); "Hide and Seek" (with Betty Boop, Bimbo, Koko the Clown/May 26); "Admission Free" (with Betty Boop, Bimbo, Koko the Clown/June 10); and "Betty Boop Limited" (with Betty Boop, Bimbo, Koko the Clown/July 1).

## ◎ TASMANIAN DEVIL

One Warner Bros. star who was very popular on screen in a handful of cartoon misadventures was that whirling dervish, the Tasmanian Devil, who buzzsawed his way through everything in his path. Robert McKimson originated the character and Mel Blanc supplied the voice. Blanc, who described his characterization as "growl slobbering, indecipherable gibberish," supposedly told McKimson while voicing the first cartoon, "I defy you or anybody else to tell me he doesn't sound like a Tasmanian Devil."

In all, the Tasmanian Devil appeared in five cartoons, most of them opposite Bugs Bunny.

The character resurfaced again, in a different form, in 1990 on the hit Warner Bros. TV series, *Tiny Toon Adventures*. Known as Dizzy Devil, he made occasional appearances on the show. In 1991 Warner Bros. renamed him "Taz" and awarded him his own series, *Taz-Mania*, which premiered on the Fox Network in 1991. The character later appeared in a supporting role in the critically acclaimed feature *Space Jam* (1996), starring basketball superstar Michael Jordan. *Directed by Robert McKimson. Technicolor. A Warner Bros. Cartoons, Inc. and Warner Bros. Pictures, Inc. Production released by Warner Bros.*

### Voices
**Tasmanian Devil:** Mel Blanc

### *Looney Tunes*

**Warner Bros. Cartoons, Inc. release**

**1954:** "Devil May Hare" (with Bugs Bunny/McKimson/June 19).

### *Merrie Melodies*
**Warner Bros. Cartoons, Inc. releases**

**1957:** "Bedevilled Rabbit" (with Bugs Bunny/McKimson/Apr. 13); and "Ducking the Devil" (with Daffy Duck/McKimson/Aug. 17).

**1962:** "Bill of Hare" (with Bugs Bunny/McKimson/June 9).

**1964:** "Dr. Devil and Mr. Hare" (with Bugs Bunny/McKimson/Mar. 28).

## ◎ TERRY BEARS

Originally Terry-Toons' mascots, these rascally twin bears starred in their own cartoon series for the studio. *Directors were Connie Rasinski, Ed Donnelly and Mannie Davis. Technicolor. A Terry-Toon Cartoons and Terrytoons/CBS Films, Inc., Production released through 20th Century Fox.*

### Voices
**Terry Bears:** Roy Halee, Phillip A. Scheib, Doug Moye

**1951:** "Tall Timber Tale" (Rasinski/July); and "Little Problems" (Donnelly/Sept.).

**1952:** "Thrifty Cubs" (Davis/Jan.); "Snappy Snap Shots" (Donnelly/Mar.); "Papa's Little Helpers" (Davis/Jan.); "Papa's Day of Rest" (Davis/Mar.); "Little Anglers" (Rasinski/July); "Nice Doggy" (Donnelly/Oct.); and "Picnic with Papa" (Davis/Dec.).

**1953:** "Plumber's Helpers" (Rasinski/May); "Open House" (Donnelly/Aug.); "The Reluctant Pup" (Davis/ Oct.); and "Growing Pains" (Donnelly/Dec.).

**1954:** "Pet Problems" (Donnelly/Apr.); and "Howling Success" (Rasinski/July).

**1955:** "Duck Fever" (Rasinski/Feb.).

**1956:** "Baffling Business" (Rasinski/Apr.).

## ◎ TERRY-TOONS

Featuring assembly-line animation and repetitive story formulas, *Terry-Toons* was, surprisingly, one of the longest-running continuous series in cartoon history. The series never achieved the critical success or cult status of Disney, Warner and MGM cartoons, yet it endured despite the fact most films starred incidental characters.

Paul Terry created the series after forming his own studio in 1929, with partner Frank Moser. Audio-Cinema Studios agreed to finance the cartoons and provided working space for the animators at the old Edison studio in the Bronx. Under the agreement, Terry and Moser worked without pay until Audio Cinema recouped its costs for these animated adventures.

Educational Pictures distributed the first cartoons, released with a synchronized soundtrack based on popular music of the day. In 1934 Terry broke ground and built his Terry-Toons studio in New Rochelle, New York, where the vast majority of these films were produced until the studio closed down in 1968.

Despite the addition of sound, Terry relied mostly on ragtime musical soundtracks and loads of action, featuring little dialogue between characters in these episodes. Except for some films produced in the 1950s, most cartoons had no main character.

Terry was one of the last to change over to color, filming the series in black-and-white. In 1938 he finally gave in to industry pressures and produced his first color *Terry-Toons*, "String Bean Jack." However, Terry remained unconvinced about producing more color cartoons because of the great expense; black-and-white animation was considerably less costly. He therefore used color sparingly until 1943, when he completely converted over to the process since black-and-white had faded in popularity altogether.

The late 1950s and 1960s marked a new period of *Terry-Toons* under the guidance of veteran animator Gene Deitch, who was named creative director in 1956, and later Ralph Bakshi, who was elevated to supervising director 10 years later. In these later films, the hyphen was dropped from the Terrytoons name and a new more modern contemporary logo was spelled out in lowercase script in the opening credits of some films, including John Doormat's "Topsy TV."

(For additional *Terrytoons* entries, see *Aesop's Fables, Astronut, Clint Clobber, Deputy Dawg, Dinky Duck, Dimwit, Dingbat, Duckwood, Fanny Zilch, Farmer Al Falfa, Foofle, Gandy Goose, Gaston Le Crayon, Good Deal Daily, Half Pint, Hashimoto, Heckle and Jeckle, Hector Heathcote, James Hound, John Doormat, Kiko the Kangaroo, Little Roquefort, Luno, Martian Moochers, Mighty Mouse, Oil Can Harry, Phoney Baloney, Possible Possum, Puddy the Pup, Sad Cat, Sidney the Elephant, the Terry Bears and Willie the Walrus.) Directors were Paul Terry, Frank Moser, Mannie Davis, George Gordon, Jack Zander, Dan Gordon, John Foster, Connie Rasinski, Volney White, Ed Donnelly, Bob Kuwahara, Dave Tendlar, Al Kouzel and Martin B. Taras. Black-and-white. Technicolor. CinemaScope. A Terry-Toon Cartoons and Terrytoons/CBS Films, Inc., Production released through Educational Pictures and 20th Century Fox.*

### *Educational Pictures releases*

**1930:** "Caviar" (Terry, Moser/Feb. 23); "Pretzels" (Terry, Moser/Mar. 9); "Spanish Onions" (Terry, Moser/Mar. 23); "Indian

Pudding" (Terry, Moser/Apr. 6); "Roman Punch" (Terry, Moser/Apr. 20); "Hot Turkey" (Terry, Moser/May 4); "Hawaiian Pineapple" (Terry, Moser/May 4); "Swiss Cheese" (Terry, Moser/May 18); "Codfish Balls" (Terry, Moser/June 1); "Hungarian Goulash" (Terry, Moser/June 15); "Bully Beef" (Terry, Moser/July 13); "Kangaroo Steak" (Terry, Moser/July 27); "Monkey Meat" (Terry, Moser/Aug. 10); "Chop Suey" (Terry, Moser/Aug. 24); "French Fried" (Terry, Moser/Sept. 7); "Dutch Treat" (Terry, Moser/Sept. 21); "Irish Stew" (Terry, Moser/Oct. 5); "Fried Chicken" (Terry, Moser/Oct. 19); "Jumping Beans" (Terry, Moser/Nov. 2); "Scotch Highball" (Terry, Moser/Nov. 16); "Salt Water Taffy" (Terry, Moser/Nov. 30); "Golf Nuts" (Terry, Moser/Dec. 14); and "Pigskin Capers" (Terry, Moser/Dec. 28).

**1931:** "Popcorn" (Terry, Moser/Jan. 11); "Go West, Big Boy" (Terry, Moser/Feb. 22); "Quack Quack" (Terry, Moser/Mar. 8); "Clowning" (Terry, Moser/Apr. 5); "Sing Sing Prison" (Terry, Moser/Apr. 19); "The Fireman's Bride" (Terry, Moser/May 3); "A Day to Live" (Terry, Moser/May 31); "2000 B.C." (Terry, Moser/June 14); "Blues" (Terry, Moser/June 28); "By the Sea" (Terry, Moser/July 12); "Her First Egg" (Terry, Moser/July 26); "Jazz Mad" (Terry, Moser/Aug. 9); "Jesse and James" (Terry, Moser/Sept. 6); "Around the World" (Terry, Moser/Oct. 4); "Jingle Bells" (Terry, Moser/Oct. 18); "The Black Spider" (Terry, Moser/Nov. 1); "China" (Terry, Moser/Nov. 15); "The Lorelei" (Terry, Moser/Nov. 29); "Summertime" (Terry, Moser/Dec. 13); and "Aladdin's Lamp" (Terry, Moser/Dec. 27).

**1932:** "The Villain's Curse" (Terry, Moser/Jan. 10); "The Spider Talks" (Terry, Moser/Feb. 7); "Peg Leg Pete" (Terry, Moser/Feb. 21); "Play Ball" (Terry, Moser/Mar. 6); "Bull-Ero" (Terry, Moser/Apr. 3); "Radio Girl" (Terry, Moser/Apr. 17); "Romance" (Terry, Moser/May 15); "Bluebeard's Brother" (Terry, Moser/May 29); "The Mad King" (Terry, Moser/June 26); "Cocky Cockroach" (Terry, Moser/July 10); "Sherman Was Right" (Terry, Moser/Aug. 21); "Burlesque" (Terry, Moser/Sept. 4); "Southern Rhythm" (Terry, Moser/Sept. 18); "College Spirit" (Terry, Moser/Oct. 16); "Hook and Ladder Number One" (Terry, Moser/Oct. 30); "The Forty Thieves" (Terry, Moser/Nov. 13); "Toyland" (Terry, Moser/Nov. 27); "Hollywood Diet" (Terry, Moser/Dec. 11); and "Ireland or Bust" (Terry, Moser/Dec. 25)

**1933:** "Jealous Lover" (Terry, Moser/Jan. 8); "Robin Hood" (Terry, Moser/Jan. 22); "Hansel and Gretel" (Terry, Moser/Feb. 5); "Tale of a Shirt" (Terry, Moser/Feb. 19); "Down on the Levee" (Terry, Moser/Mar. 5); "Who Killed Cock Robin?" (Terry, Moser/Mar. 19); "Oh Susanna" (Terry, Moser/Apr. 2); "Romeo and Juliet" (Terry, Moser/Apr. 16); "Pirate Ship" (Terry, Moser/Apr. 30); "Cinderella" (Terry, Moser/May 28); "King Zilch" (Terry, Moser/June 11); "Grand Uproar" (Terry, Moser/Aug. 25); "A Gypsy Fiddler" (Terry, Moser/Oct. 6); "Beanstalk Jack" (Terry, Moser/Oct. 20); "Little Boy Blue" (Terry, Moser/Nov. 30); "In Venice" (Terry, Moser/Dec. 15); and "The Sunny South" (Terry, Moser/Dec. 29).

**1934:** "Holland Days" (Terry, Moser/Jan. 12); "The Three Bears" (Davis/Jan. 26); "Rip Van Winkle" (Terry, Moser/Feb. 9); "The Last Straw" (Terry, Moser/Feb. 23); "A Mad House" (Terry, Moser/Mar. 23); "Joe's Lunch Wagon" (Terry, Moser/Apr. 6); "Just a Clown" (Terry, Moser/Apr. 20); "The King's Daughter" (Terry, Moser/May 4); "The Lion's Friend" (Terry, Moser/May 18); "Pandora" (Terry, Moser/June 1); "Slow But Sure" (Terry, Moser/June 15); "See the World" (Terry, Moser/June 29); "My Lady's Garden" (Terry, Moser/July 13); "Irish Sweepstakes" (Terry, Moser/July 27); "Busted Blossoms" (Terry, Moser/Aug. 10); "Mice in Council" (Terry, Moser/Aug. 24); "Jail Birds" (Terry, Moser/Sept.

21); "The Black Sheep" (Terry, Moser/Oct. 5); "The Magic Fish" (Terry, Moser/Oct. 17); "Hot Sands" (Terry, Moser/Nov. 2); "Tom, Tom the Piper's Son" (Terry, Moser/Nov. 16); "Jack's Snack" (Terry, Moser/Nov. 30); "South Pole or Bust" (Terry, Moser/Dec. 14); and "The Dog Show" (Terry, Moser/Dec. 28).

**1935:** "The First Show" (Terry, Moser/Jan. 11); "Fireman Save My Child" (Terry, Moser/Feb. 22); "The Moth and the Spider" (Terry, Moser/Mar. 8); "Peg Leg Pete, The Pirate" (Terry, Moser/Apr. 19); "A Modern Red Riding Hood" (Terry, Moser/May 3); "Five Puplets" (Terry, Moser/May 17); "Opera" (Terry, Moser/May 31); "King Looney XIV" (Terry, Moser/June 14); "Amateur Night" (Terry, Moser/July 12); "The Foxy-Fox" (Terry, Moser/July 26); "Chain Letters" (Terry, Moser/Aug. 9); "Birdland" (Terry, Moser/Aug. 23); "Circus Days" (Terry, Moser/Sept. 6); "Hey Diddle Diddle" (Terry, Moser/Sept. 20); "Football" (Terry, Moser/Oct. 18); "Aladdin's Lamp" (Terry, Moser/Nov. 15); "Southern Horse-Pitality" (Terry, Moser/Nov. 29); "Ye Olde Toy Shop" (Terry, Moser/Dec. 13); and "The Mayflower" (Terry, Moser/Dec. 27).

**1936:** "The Feud" (Terry, Moser/Jan. 10); "Off to China" (Terry, Moser/Mar. 20); "A Wolf in Cheap Clothing" (Terry, Moser/Apr. 17); "The Busy Bee" (May 29); "The Sailor's Home" (June 12); "A Tough Egg" (Terry, Moser/June 26); "A Bully Frog" (Terry, Davis, Gordon/Sept. 18); and "Robin Hood in an Arrow Escape" (Davis, Gordon/Nov. 13).

**1937:** "Salty McGuire" (Davis, Gordon/Jan. 8); "Bug Carnival" (Davis, Gordon/Apr. 16); "Schoolbirds" (Davis, Gordon/Apr. 30); "The Paper Hangers" (Davis/July 30); "The Timid Rabbit" (Davis/Nov. 26); "The Billy Goat Whiskers" (Foster/Dec. 10); and "The Barnyard Boss" (Rasinski/Dec. 24).

**1938:** "The Lion Hunt" (Davis/Jan. 7); "Bugs Beetle and His Orchestra" (Foster/Jan. 21); "Just Ask Jupiter" (Davis/Feb. 18); "A Mountain Romance" (Davis/Apr. 1); "Robinson Crusoe's Broadcast" (Foster/Apr. 15); "Maid in China" (Rasinski/Apr. 29); "Devil of the Deep" (Foster/May 27); "Here's to Good Old Jail" (Donnelly/June 10); "The Last Indian" (Rasinski/June 24); "Milk for Baby" (Davis/July 8); "Mrs. O'Leary's Cow" (Donnelly/July 22); and "Eliza Runs Again" (Rasinski/July 29/last Educational Pictures release).

### 20th Century Fox releases

**1938:** "Chris Columbo" (Donnelly/Aug. 12); "String Bean Jack" (Foster/Aug. 26/first in Technicolor); "The Wolf's Side of the Story" (Rasinski/Sept. 23); "The Glass Slipper" (Davis/Oct. 7); "The Newcomer" (with Panda Bear/Davis/Oct. 21); "The Stranger Ride Again" (Davis/Nov. 4); "Housewife Herman" (Donnelly/Nov. 18); and "Village Blacksmith" (Davis/Dec. 2).

**1939:** "The Owl and the Pussycat" (Donnelly/Jan. 13/Technicolor); "One Gun Gary in the Nick of Time" (with One Gun Gary/Donnelly/Jan. 27); "The Three Bears" (Davis/Feb. 10/Technicolor); "Frozen Feet" (Rasinski/Feb. 24); "The Nutty Network" (Davis/Mar. 24/Technicolor); "The Cuckoo Bird" (Davis/Apr. 7); "Their Last Bean" (Donnelly/Apr. 21); "Barnyard Eggcitement" (Davis/May 5); "Nick's Coffee Pot" (Rasinski/May 19); "The Prize Guest" (Davis/June 2); "Africa Squawks" (Rasinski/June 30); "Old Fire Horse" (Donnelly/July 28); "Two Headed Giant" (Rasinski/Aug. 11); "The Golden West" (Davis/Aug. 25); "Sheep in the Meadow" (Davis/Sept. 22); "The Watchdog" (Donnelly/Oct. 20); "One Mouse in a Million" (Rasinski/Nov. 3); "A Wicky Wacky Romance" (Davis/Nov. 17); "The Ice Pond" (Davis/Dec. 15); and "The First Robin" (Rasinski/Dec. 29/Technicolor).

**1940:** "A Dog in a Mansion" (Donnelly/Jan. 12); "Edgar Runs Again" (Davis/Jan. 26); "Harvest Time" (Rasinski/Feb. 9/Technicolor); "The Hare and the Hounds" (Donnelly/Feb. 23); "All's Well That Ends Well" (Davis/Mar. 8); "Just a Little Bull" (Donnelly/Apr. 19/Technicolor); "Wot's All th' Shootin' Fer" (White/May 3); "Swiss Ski Yodelers" (Donnelly/May 17); "Catnip Capers" (Davis/May 31); "Professor Offkeyski" (Rasinski/June 14); "Rover's Rescue" (White/June 28); "Rupert the Runt" (Davis/July 12); "Love in a Cottage" (White/July 28); "Billy Mouse's Akwakade" (Donnelly/Aug. 9/Technicolor); "Club Life in Stone Age" (Davis/Aug. 23); "Touchdown Demons" (White/Sept. 20); "How Wet Was My Ocean" (Donnelly/Oct. 4/Technicolor); "Happy Haunting Grounds" (Davis/Oct. 18); "Landing of the Pilgrims" (Rasinski/Nov. 1/Technicolor); "Plane Goofy" (Donnelly/Nov. 29); "Snowman" (Davis/Dec. 13); and "Temperamental Lion" (Rasinski/Dec. 27/Technicolor).

**1941:** "What a Little Sneeze Will Do" (Donnelly/Jan. 10); "Hairless Hector" (White/Jan. 24); "Mississippi Swing" (Rasinski/Feb. 7/Technicolor); "When Knights Were Bold" (White/Mar. 21); "The Baby Seal" (Rasinski/Apr. 10); "Uncle Joey" (Davis/Apr. 18/Technicolor); "A Dog's Dream" (Donnelly/May 2); "The Magic Shell" (Davis/May 16); "What Happens at Night" (Rasinski/May 30); "Horse Fly Opera" (Donnelly/June 13); "Good Old Irish Tunes" (Rasinski/June 27); "Twelve O'Clock and All Ain't Well" (Donnelly/July 25); "The Old Oaken Bucket" (Rasinski/Aug. 8); "The Ice Carnival" (Donnelly/Aug. 22); "Uncle Joey Comes to Town" (Davis/Sept. 19); "The Frozen North" (Rasinski/Oct. 17); "Back to the Soil" (Donnelly/Nov. 14); "The Bird Tower" (Davis/Nov. 28/Technicolor); and "A Yarn About Yarn" (Rasinski/Dec. 12).

**1942:** "The Torrid Toreador" (Donnelly/Jan. 9/Technicolor); "Happy Circus Days" (Rasinski/Jan. 23/Technicolor); "Funny Bunny Business" (Donnelly/Feb. 6); "Cat Meets Mouse" (Davis/Feb. 20/Technicolor); "Eat Me Kitty, Eight to a Bar" (Davis/Mar. 6); "Oh Gentle Spring" (Rasinski/Apr. 3); "Neck and Neck" (Davis/May 15/Technicolor); "The Stork's Mistake" (Donnelly/May 29); "All About Dogs" (Rasinski/June 12/Technicolor); "Wilful Willie" (Rasinski/June 26); "All Out for 'V'" (Davis/Aug. 7/Technicolor/A.A. nominee); "School Daze" (with Nancy/Sept. 18/Technicolor); "Doing Their Bit" (with Nancy/Oct. 30/a.k.a. "Nancy's Little Theatre"); "Barnyard WAAC" (Donnelly/Dec. 11); and "Somewhere in the Pacific" (Davis/Dec. 25/Technicolor).

(All cartooons below in Technicolor.)

**1943:** "Shipyard Symphony" (Donnelly/Mar. 19); "Patriotic Pooches" (Rasinski/Apr. 9); "Mopping Up" (Donnelly/June 25); "Keep 'Em Growing" (Davis/July 28); "Yokel Duck Makes Good" (Donnelly/Nov. 26); and "The Hopeful Donkey" (Davis/Dec. 17).

**1944:** "The Butcher of Seville" (Donnelly/Jan. 7); "The Helicopter" (Donnelly/Jan. 21); "A Day in June" (Donnelly/Mar. 3); "My Boy Johnny" (May 12/A.A. nominee); "Carmen Veranda" (Davis/July 28); "The Cat Came Back" (Rasinski/Aug. 18); "A Wolf's Tale" (Rasinski/Oct. 27); and "Dear Old Switzerland" (Donnelly/Dec. 22).

**1945:** "Ants in Your Pantry" (Davis/Feb. 16); "Smoky Joe" (Rasinski/May 25); "The Fox and the Duck" (Davis/Aug. 24); "Swooning the Swooners" (Rasinski/Sept. 14); and "The Watch Dog" (Donnelly/Sept. 28).

**1946:** "The Tortoise Wins Again" (Rasinski/Aug. 9); "The Snow Man" (Rasinski/Oct. 11); "The Housing Problem" (Davis/Oct. 25); and "Beanstalk Jack" (Donnelly/Dec. 20).

**1947:** "One Note Tony" (Rasinski/© Oct. 22); and "The Wolf's Pardon" (Donnelly/Dec. 5).

**1948:** "Felix the Fox" (Davis/Jan.); "Hounding the Hares" (Donnelly/June); "Mystery in the Moonlight" (Donnelly/July); "Seeing Ghosts" (Davis/Aug.); and "The Hard Boiled Egg" (Rasinski/Sept.).

**1949:** "The Wooden Indian" (Rasinski/Jan.); "The Lyin' Lion" (Rasinski/May); "The Kitten Sitter" (Donnelly/Aug. 12); "Mrs. Jones Rest Farm" (Donnelly/Oct. 12); "A Truckload of Trouble" (Rasinski/Oct. 25); "Flying Cops and Saucers" (Rasinski/Nov.); and "Paint Pot Symphony" (Rasinski/Dec.).

**1950:** "Better Late Than Never" (with Victor the Volunteer/Donnelly/Mar. 1); "The Red Headed Monkey" (Davis/July 1); "The Dog Show" (Donnelly/Aug.); and "If Cats Could Sing" (Donnelly/Oct.).

**1951:** "Squirrel Crazy" (with Nutsy/Davis/Jan.); "Woodman Spare That Tree" (Donnelly/Feb.); "Aesop's Fable: Golden Egg Goosie" (Donnelly/Aug.); "The Helpful Genie" (Rasinski/Oct.); and "Beaver Trouble" (Rasinski/Dec.).

**1952:** "Mechanical Bird" (Donnelly/Feb.); "Time Gallops On" (Davis/Apr.); "The Happy Cobblers" (Davis/May); "Flipper Frolics" (Rasinski/July); and "The Mysterious Cowboy" (Davis/Sept.).

**1954:** "Nonsense Newsreel" (Davis/Mar.); and "Pride of the Yard" (with Percival Sleuthound/Donnelly/Aug.).

**1955:** "A Yokohama Yankee" (Rasinski/Jan.); "Bird Symphony" (Rasinski/Apr./CinemaScope); "Phoney News Flashes" (Rasinski/May); "Foxed by a Fox" (Rasinski/May); "Last Mouse of Hamlin" (Rasinski/June); and "Little Red Hen" (Rasinski/July/CinemaScope).

**1956:** "Clockmakers Dog" (Rasinski); and "Park Avenue Pussycat" (Rasinski/CinemaScope).

*20th Century Fox Terrytoons/CBS Films, Inc., Productions releases*

**1956:** "Uranium Blues" (Rasinski/Mar./CinemaScope); "Hep Mother Hubbard" (Rasinski/Mar.); "Oceans of Love" (Rasinski/May/CinemaScope); "Lucky Dog" (Rasinski/June/CinemaScope); "Police Dogged" (with Clancy the Bull/Rasinski/July/CinemaScope); and "The Brave Little Brave" (Davis/July).

**1957:** "Gag Buster" (with Spoofy/Rasinski/Feb./CinemaScope); "A Hare Breadth Finish" (Rasinski/Feb.); "A Bum Steer" (with Beefy/Davis/Mar./CinemaScope); "The Bone Ranger" (with Sniffer/Rasinski/Apr./CinemaScope); "Love Is Blind" (Davis/May); and "Flebus" (Pintoff/Aug./CinemaScope).

(All cartoons in CinemaScope.)

**1958:** "The Juggler of Our Lady" (Kouzel/Apr.).

**1959:** "A Tale of a Dog" (Tendlar/Feb.); "The Fabulous Firework Family" (Kouzel/Aug.); and "The Leaky Faucet" (Taras/Dec.).

**1960:** "The Misunderstood Giant" (Rasinski/Feb.); "Hearts and Glowers" (Taras/June); and "Tin Pan Alley Cat" (Tendlar/Oct.).

**1964:** "Search for Misery" (with Pitiful Penelope/Kuwahara).

## ⊚ **TEX AVERY CARTOONS**

Tex Avery, the former Warner Bros. director who joined MGM in 1942, supervised various spoofs and comedy-musical cartoons with the basic Avery humor of hyperbole and character gyrations intact. His cartoons featured fast-paced, violent, zany moments, punctuated with outrageous takes by his cartoon stars. When a character does a take in an Avery cartoon, his eyes literally pop out, his jaw drops to the floor like porch steps and his tongue gyrates vigorously as he screams. Avery's cartoons were based on the survival-of-the-fittest theme, obviously to some extremes.

Avery produced practically every other major non-Hanna and Barbera MGM cartoon from 1942 to 1955, starting with "Blitz Wolf," which won an Academy Award for best short subject. Like his other MGM series—*Droopy, George and Junior,* and *Screwy Squirrel*—these cartoon specialties delved into the unusual only as Tex Avery could, from lampooning detective mysteries in "Who Killed Who?" (1943) to discovering the formula to create a giant-size canary in "King-Size Canary" (1947).

Avery also took a subject that was taboo—sex—to another level of lunacy, directing his own "updated" versions of nursery tales: "Red Hot Riding Hood" (1943); "Swing Shift Cinderella" (1945) and "Uncle Tom's Cabana" (1947), all starring a lustful Wolf who at the sight of a curvacious female costar turns into a human pretzel of delirious sexual desire.

In 1954 Avery left MGM to join Walter Lantz Studios, where he directed the *Chilly Willy* series. See *Droopy, George and Junior, Screwy Squirrel* and *Spike* for additional entries. *Directed by Tex Avery. Technicolor. A Metro-Goldwyn-Mayer Cartoon Production released by Metro-Goldwyn-Mayer.*

**Voices**
June Foray

**1942:** "The Blitz Wolf" (Aug. 22/A.A. winner); and "The Early Bird Dood It" (Aug. 29).

**1943:** "Red Hot Riding Hood" (May 8); "Who Killed Who?" (June 5); "One Ham's Family" (Aug. 14); and "What's Buzzin' Buzzard" (Nov. 27).

**1944:** "Batty Baseball" (Apr. 22).

**1945:** "Jerky Turkey" (Apr. 7); and "Swing Shift Cinderella" (Aug. 25/working titles: "Wolf," "Swingshift Cindy," "Red Hot Cinderella," and "The Glass Slipper").

**1946:** "The Hick Chick" (June 15).

**1947:** "Uncle Tom's Cabana" (July 19); "Slap Happy Lion" (Sept. 20/re: May 28, 1955); and "King-Size Canary" (Dec. 6/re: Oct. 21, 1955).

**1948:** "What Price Fleadom" (Mar. 20/re: Dec. 2, 1955); "Little Tinker" (May 15/re: May 14, 1955); and "The Cat That Hated People" (Nov. 12/re: Jan. 20, 1956).

**1949:** "Bad Luck Blackie" (Jan. 22/re: Nov. 9, 1956/working title: "Two Black Cats"); "House of Tomorrow" (June 11/re: Mar. 16, 1956); "Doggone Tired" (July 30/re: Apr. 6, 1956); and "Little Rural Red Riding Hood" (Sept. 17/re: Dec. 28, 1956).

**1950:** "The Cuckoo Clock" (June 10/re: Jan. 19, 1957); and "The Peachy Cobbler" (Dec. 9/re: May 24, 1957).

**1951:** "Symphony in Slang" (June 6/re: June 13, 1958); and "Car of Tomorrow" (Sept. 22).

**1952:** "Magical Maestro" (Feb. 9); "One Cab's Family" (May 15); and "Rock-a-Bye Bear" (July 12).

**1953:** "Little Johnny Jet" (Apr. 18/A.A. nominee); and "T.V. of Tomorrow" (June 6).

**1954:** "Billy Boy" (May 8); "Farm of Tomorrow" (Sept. 18); and "The Flea Circus" (Nov. 6).

**1955:** "Field and Scream" (Apr. 30); "The First Bad Man" (Sept. 30); and "Cellbound" (Nov. 25).

**1957:** "The Cat's Meow" (Jan. 25/remake of "Ventriloquist Cat").

## ◉ THE THREE BEARS

Warner animator Chuck Jones originated this series depicting domestic life of an American family, with bears playing the roles of Papa, Mamma and Junyer. The trio first appeared in 1944, in "Bugs Bunny and the Three Bears," reenacting the Goldilocks fable with a comical twist. Jones brought the characters back to the screen in four more cartoon adventures, each one offering a humorous view of the trials and tribulations of this abnormal family. *Directed by Chuck Jones. Technicolor. A Leon Schlesinger Studios/ Warner Bros. Cartoons, Inc. Production released by Warner Bros.*

**Voices**
**Papa Bear:** Mel Blanc, Billy Bletcher; **Mamma Bear:** Bea Benadaret; **Junyer Bear:** Stan Freberg

**Merrie Melodies**

**1944:** "Bugs Bunny and the Three Bears" (with Bugs Bunny/ Feb. 26).

**1949:** "The Bee-Deviled Bruin" (May 14).

**1951:** "A Bear for Punishment" (Oct. 20).

**Looney Tunes**

**1948:** "What's Brewin', Bruin?" (Feb. 28).

**1949:** "Bear Feat" (Dec. 10).

## ◉ TIJUANA TOADS

This late-1960s series followed the humorous exploits of a bossy Spanish-accented toad, Poncho, who demonstrates for his inexperienced, skinny apprentice, Toro, how to catch flies and cope with basic necessities of life as a toad in inventively funny situations. The toads were later renamed "The Texas Toads" (the characters also changed their names to Fatso and Banjo) when segmented on TV's *The Pink Panther Laff and a Half Hour and a Half Show. Directors were Hawley Pratt, Gerry Chiniquy, Art Davis and Grant Simmons. Technicolor. A DePatie-Freleng Enterprises/Mirisch Films Production released through United Artists.*

**1969:** "Tijuana Toads" (Pratt/Aug. 6); "A Pair of Greenbacks" (Davis/Dec. 16); and "Go for Croak" (Pratt/Dec. 25).

**1970:** "The Froggy Froggy Duo" (Pratt/Mar. 15); "Hop and Chop" (Simmons/June 17); "Never on Thirsty" (Pratt/Aug. 5); and "A Dopey Hacienda" (Pratt/Dec. 6).

**1971:** "Snake in the Gracias" (Pratt/Jan. 24); "Two Jumps and a Chump" (Chiniquy/Mar. 28); "Mud Squad" (Davis/Apr. 28); "The Egg of Ay-Yi-Yi!" (Chiniquy/June 6); "The Fastest Tongue in the West" (Chiniquy/June 20); "A Leap in the Deep" (Chiniquy/ June 20); "Croakus Pocus" (Davis/Dec. 26); and "Serape Happy" (Chiniquy/Dec. 26).

**1972:** "Frog Jog" (Chiniquy/Apr. 23); and "Flight to the Finish" (Davis/Apr. 30).

## ◉ TIMON AND PUMBAA

Timon, the wisecracking meerkat, and Pumbaa, his warthog sidekick, from the Disney animated classic *The Lion King* returned to the silver screen in 1995, this time as stars of their first theatrical cartoon short, "Stand by Me." The cartoon, based on the popular song of the same name, opened in theaters nationwide with the live-action feature-length adventure *Tom and Huck,* starring Jonathan Taylor (of TV's *Home Improvement*). Three months before the release of the three-minute cartoon short, the characters starred in their own television series, *The Lion King's Timon and Pumbaa,* which premiered in syndication and on CBS that fall. Nathan Lane, who provided the voice of Timon in *The Lion King,* did not return to reprise the character. The character, in the short and on the television series, was voiced by Kevin Schoen. *Directed by Steve Moore. A Walt Disney Studios Production released by Buena Vista Pictures.*

*Voices*
**Timon:** Kevin Schoen; *Pumbaa:* Ernie Sabella

**1995:** "Stand by Me" (Dec. 22).

## ◎ TITO

The adventures of a small, portly Mexican boy named Tito and his burro companion, Burrito, comprised this short-lived series for Columbia Pictures. The characters, who were created by Dave Fleischer, later found new life in *Real Screen* and *Fox and the Crow* comics. *Directed by Bob Wickersham and Howard Swift. Produced by Dave Fleischer and later Ray Katz. Technicolor. A Columbia Pictures Corporation Production released by Columbia Pictures.*

**1942:** "Tito's Guitar" (Wickersham/Oct. 30/Color Rhapsody).

**1945:** "Fiesta Time" (Wickersham/Apr. 4/Color Rhapsody).

**1947:** "Loco Lobo" (Swift/Jan. 9/Color Rhapsody).

## ◎ TOBY THE PUP

Columbia producer Charles Mintz, who produced several major cartoon series for the studio, hired two of Max Fleischer's best animators, Dick Huemer and Sid Marcus, to head a new animation unit in California to expand his cartoon operations and sell a separate series to RKO Radio Pictures. It was Marcus who devised the character for that series, Toby the Pup, a malicious, frisky pup who headlined in only 11 films. *Directed by Dick Huemer and Sid Marcus. Black-and-white. A Van Beuren Studios Production released by RKO Radio Pictures.*

**1930:** "Toby the Fiddler" (Sept. 1); "Toby the Miner" (Oct. 1); "Toby the Showman" (Nov. 22); and "The Bug House" (Dec. 7).

**1931:** "Circus Time" (Jan. 25); "Toby the Milkman" (Feb. 25); "Brown Derby" (Mar. 22); "Down South" (Apr. 15); "Halloween" (May 1); "Toby the Bull Thrower" (June 7); and "Aces Up."

## ◎ TOM AND JERRY (VAN BEUREN)

This was not MGM's famous cat-and-mouse team but rather an earlier duo of rawboned leader Tom and his dumpy cohort Jerry in primitively animated stories combining action and ragtime music with little onscreen dialogue. The series, produced by Van Beuren, was developed by John Foster and studio newcomers George Stallings and George Rufle, both veteran animators of the New York animation circuit. Following the series' first entry, "Wot a Night" (1931), the studio produced 26 cartoons over the next three years before the characters were retired. *Directors were John Foster, George Stallings, Frank Tashlin, George Rufle, Frank Sherman and Harry Bailey. Black-and-white. A Van Beuren Studios Production released by RKO Radio Pictures.*

**1931:** "Wot a Night" (Foster, Stallings/Aug. 1); "Polar Pals" (Foster, Rufle/Sept. 5); "Trouble" (Foster, Stallings/Oct. 10); "Jungle Jam" (Foster, Rufle/Nov. 14); and "A Swiss Trick" (Foster, Stallings/Dec. 19).

**1932:** "Rocketeers" (Foster, Rufle/Jan. 30); "Rabid Hunters" (Foster, Stallings/Feb. 27); "In the Bag" (Foster, Rufle/Mar. 26); "Joint Wipers" (Foster, Stallings/Apr. 23); "Pet and Pans" (Foster, Rufle/May 14); "The Tuba Tooter" (Foster, Stallings/June 4); "Plane Dumb" (Foster, Rufle/June 25); "Redskin Blues" (Foster, Stallings/July 23); "Jolly Fish" (Foster, Stallings/Aug. 19); "Barnyard Bunk" (Foster, Rufle/Sept. 6); "A Spanish Twist" (Foster, Stallings/Oct. 7); "Piano Tooners" (Foster, Rufle/Nov. 11); and "Pencil Mania" (Foster, Stallings/Dec. 9).

**1933:** "Tight Rope Tricks" (Foster, Rufle/Jan. 6); "The Magic Mummy" (Foster, Stallings/Feb. 7); "Panicky Pup" (Foster, Bailey/Feb. 24/*Aesop's Fable*); "Puzzled Pals" (Stallings, Sherman/© Mar. 31); "Happy Hoboes" (Stallings, Rufle/Mar. 31); "Hook and Ladder Hokum" (Stallings, Tashlin/Apr. 28); "In the Park" (Sherman, Rufle/©May 26); "Doughnuts" (Sherman, Rufle/July 10); and "The Phantom Rocket" (Sherman, Rufle/July 31).

## ◎ TOM AND JERRY (MGM)

MGM's madcap adventures of the feuding alley cat, Tom, and his mischief-making nemesis, Jerry the mouse, won seven Academy Awards during their heyday.

The idea for this pairing came from veteran animators William Hanna and Joseph Barbera, who later created the likes of Yogi Bear, Ruffy and Reddy and countless other characters after opening their own studio in the late 1950s. "We asked ourselves what would be a normal conflict between characters provoking comedy while retaining a basic situation from which we could continue to generate plots and stories," Hanna once recalled. "We almost decided on a dog and a fox before we hit on the idea of using a cat and a mouse."

Hanna and Barbera named the characters based on hundreds of suggestions submitted by studio employees in a contest staged at the MGM lot. (In their screen debut Tom was actually called "Jasper" and Jerry "Jinks.") The first Tom and Jerry cartoon, "Puss Gets the Boot," was produced and released in 1940, despite producer Fred Quimby's reservations about the characters. ("What can you do with a cat and a mouse that would be different?")

The first cartoon quickly established the entire tone of the series: Tom, the mischievous house cat, trying to outfox the equally clever mouse, Jerry. The formula remained the same throughout the history of the series, though the characters underwent gradual changes in their appearance.

*Tom and Jerry in their first screen appearance, "Puss Gets the Boot" (1940). The characters were created by William Hanna and Joseph Barbera. © Turner Entertainment*

In addition to earning a second Academy Award for their fourth cartoon, "The Night before Christmas" (1941), Hanna and Barbera's Tom and Jerry series dominated the annual Oscar derby, earning 13 nominations and winning seven times, more than any other theatrical cartoon series starring the same characters. Besides being nominated for "Dr. Jekyll and Mr. Mouse" (1947), "Hatch Up Your Troubles" (1949), "Jerry's Cousin" (1951) and "Touché, Pussy Cat!" (1954), they won the coveted gold statuette for such classic cartoons as "The Yankee Doodle Mouse" (1943), "Mouse Trouble" (1944), "Quiet Please" (1945), "The Cat Concerto" (1946), "The Little Orphan" (1948), "The Two Mouseketeers" (1952) and "Johann Mouse" (1953).

Besides starring in cartoon shorts, Tom and Jerry also appeared as animated characters in live-action sequences of two classic MGM musicals: Gene Kelly's *Anchors Aweigh* (1944) (Jerry only) and Esther Williams's *Dangerous When Wet* (1953), featuring both characters swimming with Williams in complete synchronization.

The Tom and Jerry series produced a stable of popular supporting characters. One recurring cult favorite who appeared as Tom's owner in 18 cartoons in the 1940s and the 1950s, was Mammy-Two-Shoes (but never referred to by name). Known usually to moviegoers only by the lower half of her portly body and by the broom she used to wallop Tom when he misbehaved, she was the stereotyped black maid attired in a simple house dress and white apron. Actress Lillian Randolph, best known as Birdie the maid on *The Great Gildersleeve* radio program in the 1940s and for her roles in Walt Disney cartoons, originally voiced the character. In a few cases, moviegoers got a better glimpse of Mammy, including her chin in "Part Time Pal" (1947); a shadow of her entire body as she walks down the street in "Mouse Cleaning" (1948); and her whole body and face in "Saturday Evening Puss" (1950). In 1952, this popular series fixture made her final screen appearance in the Tom and Jerry cartoon, "Push-Button Kitty."

Another popular fixture and supporting cast member in 13 films, created as comical counterpart for Tom, was the street-smart alley cat, Butch. Nameless in his first three cartoons, beginning with the 1943 cartoon short, "Baby Puss," in which he appeared as one of three alley cat pals of Tom who become a thorn in Jerry's side, he officially became Butch in the 1947 one-reeler, "A Mouse in the House." In subsequent films, Butch often spoiled Tom's romantic overtures with attractive felines that were in town, such as Tom's luscious love interest, Toodles, in 1951's "Casanova Cat," before making his final appearance in the 1957 CinemaScope cartoon, "Mucho Mouse." Toodles, the attractive white feline co-star, first appeared sunbathing while reading the latest issue of *Har-Puss Bazaar* in 1946's "Springtime for Thomas."

Jerry frequently shared center stage with another costar, a curious, perpetually hungry, little gray mouse and ward named Nibbles, who frequently became a source of exasperation for not only him but also his mouse-chasing cat costar, Tom. Debuting in the 1946 one-reeler, "The Milky Waif," this sweet, innocent mouse, who by 1954 had become known as Tuffy, starred in 13 films, including three Academy Award–winning shorts: "The Little Orphan" (1949), "The Two Mouseketeers" (1952), winners of an Oscar for best short subject, and the Oscar-nominated "Touché, Pussy Cat!" (1954), the last Tom and Jerry cartoon nominated for an Academy Award. In the latter, Tuffy not only said, "C'est la guerre!" but also sang "Frère Jacques." He spoke again in his last screen appearance—and his final Tom and Jerry cartoon—the hilarious Robin Hood–inspired spoof, "Robin Hoodwinked" (1958).

When Nibbles wasn't giving Tom fits (to the delight of Jerry), it was an adorable, innocent-looking yellow duck, Little Quacker, who later evolved into a mischievous troublemaker, that wreaked havoc in eight cartoons. The cute duckling debuted in the self-titled 1950 comedy cartoon short, "Little Quacker," in which Tom steals an egg for dinner from a mother duck and out pops Little Quacker; Tom comes up short when the duckling and mother are reunited. After the character was redesigned and retooled, the duckling was cast in a second cartoon, 1952's "The Duck Doctor," becoming a comical sidekick for Jerry, a pattern that was repeated in 1953's "Just Ducky," in which Jerry tries to teach Little Quacker how to swim, with Tom envisioning him as his latest meal. The character starred in four more cartoons with the dueling cat-and-mouse tandem, including "Downhearted Duckling" (1954); "Southbound Duckling" (1955), the first in wide screen CinemaScope; "That's My Mommy" (1955), the first Tom and Jerry cartoon produced by directors William Hanna and Joseph Barbera; the Easter-themed "Happy Go Lucky Duck" (1958); and, finally, "The Vanishing Duck" (1958).

Quimby produced the series until his retirement in 1955; from then through 1958 Hanna and Barbera performed dual roles as the series' producers and directors.

The popular screen tandem lost some of their comedy flair after Hanna and Barbera left MGM to launch their own production company, Hanna-Barbera Productions. From 1961 to 1962 Gene Deitch, a former artistic director of Terry-Toons and a Czechoslovakian cartoon director (whose claim to fame was creating TV's critically acclaimed *Tom Terrific*), tried animating new Tom and Jerry adventures that were unmemorable at best.

In 1963 former Warner Bros. animator/director Chuck Jones and producer Les Golden, who formed Sib-Tower 12 Productions (later renamed MGM Animation/Visual Arts), convinced MGM to allow them to produce a third series of films. But even under the watchful eye of Jones the films failed to generate much excitement. As one anonymous MGM executive remarked after a board of directors screening: "Those are god awful!"

Even Jones has admitted making the cartoons was a mistake: "They were not my characters and I didn't really understand them as well as, let's say, the Road Runner and Coyote. The Tom and Jerrys I did look like the Road Runner and Coyote in cat and mouse drag!"

Other series directors included Maurice Noble, Ben Washam, Abe Levitow, Tom Ray and Jim Pabian. Veteran voice artist June Foray provided occasional supporting character voices in a number of cartoons for the series. *Technicolor. CinemaScope. A Metro-Goldwyn-Mayer Cartoon/Rembrandt Films/Sib-Tower 12 Production released by Metro-Goldwyn-Mayer.*

### Metro-Goldwyn-Mayer releases

**1940:** "Puss Gets the Boot" (as Jasper and Jinks with Mammy-Two-Shoes/Hanna, Barbera/Feb. 10).

**1941:** "The Midnight Snack" (with Mammy-Two-Shoes/Hanna, Barbera/July 19/re: Feb. 27, 1948); and "The Night Before Christmas" (Hanna, Barbera/Dec. 6/A.A. nominee).

**1942:** "Fraidy Cat" (with Mammy-Two-Shoes/Hanna, Barbera/Jan. 17); "Dog Trouble" (with Spike and Mammy/Hanna, Barbera/Apr. 18); "Puss 'n' Toots" (with Mammy-Two-Shoes/Hanna, Barbera/May 30); "The Bowling Alley-Cat" (Hanna, Barbera/July 18); and "Fine Feathered Friend" (Hanna, Barbera/Oct. 10/re: Jan. 1, 1949).

**1943:** "Sufferin' Cats" (with Meathead/Hanna, Barbera/Jan. 16/re: June 4, 1949); "Lonesome Mouse" (with Mammy-Two-Shoes/Hanna, Barbera/May 22/re: Nov. 26, 1949); "The Yankee Doodle Mouse" (Hanna, Barbera/June 26/A.A. winner); and "Baby Puss" (with Meathead/Hanna, Barbera/Dec. 25).

**1944:** "Zoot Cat" (Hanna, Barbera/Feb. 26); "The Million Dollar Cat" (Hanna, Barbera/May 6/re: May 6, 1954); "The Bodyguard" (with Spike/Hanna, Barbera/July 22); "Puttin' on the Dog" (with Spike/Hanna, Barbera/Oct. 28/re: Oct. 20, 1951); and "Mouse Trouble" (Hanna, Barbera/Nov. 23/re: Dec. 12, 1951/A.A. winner/working titles: "Cat Nipped" and "Kitty Foiled").

**1945:** "The Mouse That Comes to Dinner" (with Toots, Mammy-Two-Shoes/Hanna, Barbera/May 5/re: Jan. 19, 1952/working title: "Mouse to Dinner"); "Mouse in Manhattan" (Hanna, Barbera/July 7/working title: "Manhattan Serenade"); "Tee for Two" (Hanna, Barbera/July 21); "Flirty Birdy" (Hanna, Barbera/Sept. 22/re: July 4, 1953/working title: "Love Boids"); and "Quiet Please" (with Spike/Hanna, Barbera/Dec. 22/A.A. winner).

**1946:** "Springtime for Thomas" (with Toots/Hanna, Barbera/Mar. 30); "The Milky Waif" (with Nibbles/Hanna, Barbera/May 18); "Trap Happy" (with Meathead/Hanna, Barbera/June 29/re: Mar. 6, 1954); and "Solid Serenade" (with Spike, Meathead/Hanna, Barbera/Aug. 31).

**1947:** "Cat Fishin'" (with Spike/Hanna, Barbera/Feb. 22/re: Oct. 30, 1954); "Part Time Pal" (with Mammy-Two-Shoes/Hanna, Barbera/Mar. 15/working title: "Fair Weathered Friend"); "The Cat Concerto" (Hanna, Barbera/Apr. 26/A.A. winner); "Dr. Jekyll and Mr. Mouse" (Hanna, Barbera/June 14/A.A. nominee); "Salt Water Tabby" (July 12); "A Mouse in the House" (with Mammy-Two-Shoes/Spike/Hanna, Barbera/Aug. 30); and "The Invisible Mouse" (with Spike/Hanna, Barbera/Sept. 27).

**1948:** "Kitty Foiled" (Hanna, Barbera/June 1); "The Truce Hurts" (with Butch (Spike)/Hanna, Barbera/July 17); "Old Rockin' Chair Tom" (with Mammy-Two-Shoes, Lightnin'/Hanna, Barbera/Sept. 18); "Professor Tom" (Hanna, Barbera/Oct. 30); and "Mouse Cleaning" (with Mammy-Two-Shoes/Hanna, Barbera/Dec. 11/A.A. winner).

**1949:** "Polka-Dot Puss" (with Mammy-Two-Shoes/Hanna, Barbera/Feb. 26/re: Sept. 28, 1956); "The Little Orphan" (with Mammy-Two-Shoes/Nibbles/Hanna, Barbera/Apr. 30/A.A. winner); "Hatch Up Your Troubles" (Hanna, Barbera/May 14/A.A. nominee/remade as "The Egg and Jerry"); "Heavenly Puss" (with Butch/Hanna, Barbera/July 9/re: Oct. 26, 1956); "The Cat and Mermouse" (Hanna, Barbera/Sept. 13); "Love That Pup" (with Butch (Spike), Pup (Tyke)/Hanna, Barbera/Oct. 1); "Jerry's Diary" (Hanna, Barbera/Oct. 22); and "Tennis Chumps" (Hanna, Barbera/Dec. 10).

**1950:** "Little Quacker" (Hanna, Barbera/Jan. 7); "Saturday Evening Puss" (with Mammy-Two-Shoes/Hanna, Barbera/Jan. 19/working title: "Party Cat"); "Texas Tom" (Hanna, Barbera/Mar. 11); "Jerry and the Lion" (Hanna, Barbera/Apr. 8/working title: "Hold That Lion"); "Safety Second" (with Nibbles/Hanna, Barbera/July 1/working title: "F'r Safety Sake"); "Tom and Jerry in the Hollywood Bowl" (Hanna, Barbera/Sept. 16); "The Framed Cat" (with Mammy-Two-Shoes, Butch (Spike), Hanna, Barbera/Oct. 21); and "Cueball Cat" (Hanna, Barbera/Nov. 25).

**1951:** "Casanova Cat" (with Toodles/Hanna, Barbera/Jan. 6); "Jerry and the Goldfish" (Hanna, Barbera/Mar. 3); "Jerry's Cousin" (Hanna, Barbera/Apr. 7/working title: "City Cousin" and "Muscles Mouse"/A.A. nominee); "Sleepy-Time Tom" (with Mammy-Two-Shoes/Hanna, Barbera/May 26); "His Mouse Friday" (Hanna, Barbera/July 7); "Slicked Up Pup" (with Butch (Spike)/Pup (Tyke)/Hanna, Barbera/Sept. 8); "Nit-Witty Kitty" (with Mammy-Two-Shoes/Hanna, Barbera/Oct. 6); and "Cat Napping" (with Butch (Spike)/Hanna, Barbera/Dec. 8).

**1952:** "The Flying Cat" (Hanna, Barbera/Jan. 12); "The Duck Doctor" (with Little Quacker/Hanna, Barbera/Feb. 16); "Two Mouseketeers" (with Nibbles Hanna, Barbera/Mar. 15/A.A. winner with Mammy-Two-Shoes); "Smitten Kitten" (Hanna, Barbera/Apr. 12); "Triplet Trouble" (with Mammy-Two-Shoes/Hanna, Barbera/Apr. 19); "Little Runaway" (Hanna, Barbera/June 14); "Fit to Be Tied" (with Butch (Spike)/Hanna, Barbera/July 26); "Push-Button Kitty" (Hanna, Barbera/Sept. 6); "Cruise Cat" (Hanna, Barbera/Oct. 18); and "The Dog House" (with Spike/Hanna, Barbera/Nov. 29).

**1953:** "The Missing Mouse" (Hanna, Barbera/Jan. 10); "Jerry and Jumbo" (Hanna, Barbera/Feb. 21); "Johann Mouse" (Hanna, Barbera/Mar. 21/A.A. winner/narration by Hans Conried); "That's My Pup" (with Spike and Tyke/Hanna, Barbera/May 28); "Just Ducky" (with Little Quacker/Hanna, Barbera/Sept. 5); "Two Little Indians" (Hanna, Barbera/Oct. 17); and "Life with Tom" (with Spike, Tyke, Nibbles/Hanna, Barbera/Nov. 21).

**1954:** "Puppy Tale" (Hanna, Barbera/Jan. 23); "Posse Cat" (Hanna, Barbera/Jan. 30); "Hic-Cup Pup" (with Spike and Tyke/Hanna, Barbera/Apr. 17/working title: "Tyke Takes a Nap"); "Little School Mouse" (with Tuffy/Hanna, Barbera/May 29); "Baby Butch" (Hanna, Barbera/Aug. 14); "Mice Follies" (with Tuffy/Hanna, Barbera/Sept. 4); "Neopolitan Mouse" (Hanna, Barbera/Oct. 21); "Downhearted Duckling" (Hanna, Barbera/Nov. 13); "Pet Peeve" (with Spike/Hanna, Barbera/Nov. 20/CinemaScope); and "Touché Pussy Cat" (with Tuffy/Hanna, Barbera/Dec. 18/re: May 21, 1955/CinemaScope).

**1955:** "Southbound Duckling" (Hanna, Barbera/Mar. 12/re: June 25, 1955/CinemaScope); "Pup on a Picnic" (with Spike and Tyke/Hanna, Barbera/Apr. 30/CinemaScope); "Mouse for Sale" (Hanna, Barbera/May 21/CinemaScope); "Designs on Jerry" (Hanna, Barbera/Sept. 2/CinemaScope); "Tom and Cherie" (with Tuffy/Hanna, Barbera/Sept. 9/CinemaScope); "Smarty Cat" (Hanna, Barbera/Oct. 14/CinemaScope); "Pecos Pest" (Hanna, Barbera/Nov. 11); and "That's My Mommy" (Hanna, Barbera/Nov. 19/CinemaScope).

(The following were all in CinemaScope.)

**1956:** "The Flying Sorceress" (Hanna, Barbera/Jan. 27); "The Egg and Jerry" (Hanna, Barbera/Mar. 23/remake of "Hatch Up Your Troubles"); "Busy Buddies" (Hanna, Barbera/May 4); "Muscle Beach Tom" (with Butch/Hanna, Barbera/Sept. 7); "Down Beat Bear" (Hanna, Barbera/Oct. 21); "Blue Cat Blues" (with Butch/Hanna, Barbera/Nov. 6); and "Barbecue Brawl" (with Spike and Tyke/Hanna, Barbera/Dec. 14).

**1957:** "Tops with Pops" (Hanna, Barbera/Feb. 22/remake of "Love That Pup"); "Timid Tabby" (Hanna, Barbera/Apr. 19); "Feedin' the Kiddie" (with Tuffy/Hanna, Barbera/June 7/remake of "The Little Orphan"); "Mucho Mouse" (with Butch/Hanna, Barbera/Sept. 6); and "Tom's Photo Finish" (with Spike/Hanna, Barbera/Nov. 1).

**1958:** "Happy Go Ducky" (with Little Quacker/Hanna, Barbera/Jan. 3/working title: "One Quack Mind"); "Royal Cat Nap" (Hanna, Barbera/Mar. 7); "The Vanishing Duck" (with Little Quacker/Hanna, Barbera/May 2); "Robin Hoodwinked" (with Tuffy/Hanna, Barbera/June 6); and "Tot Watchers" (with Spike/Hanna, Barbera/Aug. 1).

*Rembrandt Films releases*

**1961:** "Switchin' Kitten" (Deitch/Sept. 7); "Down and Outing" (Deitch/Oct. 26); and "It's Greek to Me-Ow" (Deitch/Dec. 7).

**1962:** "High Steaks" (Deitch/Jan.); "Mouse Into Space" (Deitch/Feb. 1); "Landing Stripling" (Deitch/Apr. 1); "Calypso Cat" (Deitch/June 1); "Dicky Moe" (Deitch/July 1); "The Tom and Jerry Cartoon Kit" (Deitch/Aug. 1); "Tall in the Trap" (Deitch/Sept. 1); "Sorry Safari" (Deitch/Oct. 1); "Buddies Thicker Than Water" (Deitch/Nov. 1); and "Carmen Get It!" (Deitch/Dec. 1).

### Sib-Tower 12 Productions releases

**1963:** "Pent House Mouse" (Jones).

**1964:** "Much Ado about Nothing" (Jones, Noble); "Somebody Loves Me" (Jones, Noble); "The Cat Above and The Mouse Below" (Jones); "Is There a Doctor in the Mouse?" (Jones, Noble); and "The Unshrinkable Jerry Mouse" (Jones, Noble).

**1965:** "Tom-ic Energy" (Jones, Noble); "Ah, Sweet Mouse-Story of Life" (Jones, Noble); "Haunted Mouse" (Jones, Noble); "I'm Just Wild about Jerry" (Jones, Noble); "Of Feline Bondage" (Jones, Noble); "The Year of the Mouse" (Noble, Jones); "Jerry-Go-Round" (Levitow); "Bad Day at Cat Rock" (Jones, Noble); "Jerry-Go-Round" (Levitow); "The Cat's Me-Ouch" (Jones, Noble); and "The Brothers Carry-Mouse-Off" (Pabian, Jones).

**1966:** "Guide Mouse-Ille" (Levitow); "O-Solar-Meow" (Levitow); "Puss 'n' Boats" (Levitow); "Love Me, Love My Mouse" (with Toots/Jones); "Cat and Dupli-Cat" (Jones, Noble); "Catty-Cornered" (Levitow); "Filet Meow" (Levitow); "Duel Personality" (Jones, Noble); "The A-Tominable Snowman" (Levitow); "Matinee Mouse" (with Spike/Ray); and "Jerry, Jerry, Quite Contrary" (Jones).

**1967:** "Rock 'n' Rodent" (Levitow); "Cannery Rodent" (Jones, Noble); "Advance and Be Mechanized" (Washam); "Surf-Bored Cat" (Levitow); "The Mouse from H.U.N.G.E.R." (Levitow); "Shutter Bugged Cat" (Ray, Hanna, Barbera/with scenes from Hanna and Barbera's "The Yankee Doodle Mouse" [1943]); "Heavenly Puss" (1949); "Designs on Jerry" (1955); and "Purr-Chance to Dream" (Washam).

## ◎ TOMMY TORTOISE AND MOE HARE

Loosely based on the concept of the timeless children's fable "Tortoise and the Hare," this series concerned the humorous exploits of a smart rabbit, Moe, and a dumb tortoise, Tommy, who somehow manages to outsmart the superintelligent hare in outlandish situations. The films were produced for Paramount's *Noveltoons* series. *Directed by Isadore Sparber and Dave Tendlar. Technicolor. A Famous Studios Production released through Paramount Picture Corporation.*

**1953:** "Winner by a Hare" (Sparber/Apr. 17).

**1955:** "Rabbit Punch" (Tendlar/Sept. 30).

**1956:** "Sleuth But Sure" (Tendlar/Mar. 23).

**1957:** "Mr. Money Gags" (Sparber/June 7).

**1960:** "Turning The Fables" (Kneitel/Aug.).

**1961:** "Turtle Scoop" (Kneitel/Oct.).

## ◎ TOODLES

In the early 1940s, Tom and Jerry cocreators William Hanna and Joseph Barbera developed this attractive white feline costar and love interest for Tom, instantly becoming known to filmgoers for her appearance in 1946's "Springtime for Thomas," sunbathing while perusing the most recent issue of *Har-Puss Bazaar*. In 1951, she reprised her role, instead playing a rich kitten who inherits a million dollars that Tom tries to impress in "Casanova Cat." *Directed by William Hanna and Joseph Barbera. Technicolor. A Metro-Goldwyn-Mayer Cartoon Production released by Metro-Goldwyn-Mayer.*

**1946:** "Springtime for Thomas" (with Tom and Jerry/Mar. 30).

**1951:** "Casanova Cat" (with Tom and Jerry, Butch/Jan. 6).

## ◎ TOONERVILLE TROLLEY

Fontaine Fox's popular comic strip inspired this abbreviated three-strip Technicolor sound cartoon series, featuring the Skipper, the Powerful Katrinka and the Terrible-tempered Mr. Bang, which was released under the RKO Radio Pictures-Van Beuren *Rainbow Parade* series. Director Burt Gillett purchased the rights to make the films in hopes of insuring greater box-office success for the fledgling Van Beuren cartoon studio. *Directed by Burt Gillett and Tom Palmer. Black-and-white. A Van Beuren Studios Production released by RKO Radio Pictures.*

**1936:** "Toonerville Trolley" (Gillett, Palmer/Jan. 17); "Trolley Ahoy" (Gillett/July 3); and "Toonerville Picnic" (Gillett/Oct. 2).

## ◎ TWEETY AND SYLVESTER

The bird-hungry cat Sylvester plotted fruitlessly against the clever canary Tweety, whose immortal battle cry for 15 years upon Sylvester's entrance was "I tawt I taw a puddy tat. I did, I did see a puddy tat!"

Both characters made separate film debuts before becoming a team. They shared top billing in 39 cartoons between 1947 and 1964, garnering two Academy Awards—for "Tweetie Pie" (1947) and "Birds Anonymous" (1957)—and three Oscar nominations. The films alternately featured another series regular, sweet, bespectacled Granny, Tweety's owner, who was far from sweet when Sylvester was around, pounding on him whenever he attempted to lay his lands on her baby-faced, baby-voiced pet bird.

Mel Blanc voiced both characters. His voice for Sylvester was similar to Daffy Duck's, featuring the same sputtering delivery and slurred voice. The only difference was his recorded dialogue was sped

*Tweety unknowingly walks into the mouth of a cat who plans on making him his next meal in Bob Clampett's 1944 cartoon "Birdy and the Beast." It was the second Tweety cartoon.* © *Warner Brothers* (COURTESY: BOB CLAMPETT ANIMATION ART)

up in the sound studio. As for the voice of Tweety, Bob Clampett developed the idea of what the small bird should sound like. Top layout artist Michael Sasanoff and animator/director Robert McKimson both recalled that Clampett used to talk in the "baby-talk voice" later used for Tweety while just kidding around at the studio.

Clampett created Tweety, basing the baby bird's wide-eyed stare on a childhood picture of himself. Tweety's famous catch phrase, "I tawt I taw a putty tat," was actually derived from a phrase Clampett had used years earlier in letters to a friend next to a drawing of a little bird. (The catch phrase became so popular that in 1950 Warner Bros. story man Warren Foster composed a song using the phrase as its title. The record sold more than 2 million copies and became a novelty in England.)

Clampett directed the first three cartoons in the series, beginning with 1942's "A Tale of Two Kitties," which costarred Babbit and Catstello, a pair of cats resembling famed comedians Abbot and Costello. Friz Freleng took over the series after Clampett left the studio in 1946. Freleng directed the bulk of the series, with additional titles produced under the direction of Hawley Pratt and Gerry Chiniquy. (See *Sylvester* entry for other Sylvester cartoon appearances.)

Tweety and Sylvester returned to the screen in supporting roles in the 1995 Bugs Bunny cartoon short "Carrotblanca," lampooning the Humphrey Bogart-Lauren Bacall classic *Casablanca* and in the 1996 live-action/animated feature *Space Jam* starring Michael Jordan. Tweety was voiced by Bob Bergen; Sylvester by Joe Alaskey. In 2003, the rollicking pair starred in a brand-new *Looney Tunes* cartoon short, "Museum Scream," directed by Rich Moore, Peter Shin and Bill Kopp. *Technicolor. Directed by Bob Ciampetti, Friz Freleng, Gerry Chiniquy, Greg Ford, Terry Lennon, Douglas McCarthy, Rich Moore, Dan Povenmire, Peter Shin and Bill Kopp. A Leon Schlesinger Studios/Warner Bros. Cartoons, Inc./Warner Bros. Pictures, Inc./Vitagraph/Warner Bros. Animation/Warner Bros. Production released by Warner Bros.*

### Voices
**Tweety:** Mel Blanc, Bob Bergen; **Sylvester the Cat:** Mel Blanc, Joe Alaskey; **Granny:** Bea Benaderet, June Foray

*Merrie Melodies*

*Leon Schlesinger Studios releases*

**1942:** "A Tale of Two Kitties" (with Babbit and Catstello/Clampett/Nov. 21/first Tweety cartoon).

**1944:** "Birdy and the Beast" (Clampett/Aug. 19).

*Warner Bros. Cartoons, Inc. releases*

**1945:** "A Grusome Twosome" (Clampett/June 9).

**1947:** "Tweetie Pie" (Freleng/May 3/A.A. winner).

**1948:** "I Taw a Putty Tat" (Freleng/Apr. 2).

**1949:** "Bad Ol' Putty Tat" (Freleng/July 23).

**1950:** "Home Tweet Home" (Freleng/Jan. 14).

**1951:** "Room and Bird" (Freleng/June 2); and "Tweety's S.O.S." (with Granny/Freleng/Sept. 22).

**1953:** "Fowl Weather" (Freleng/Apr. 4); "Tom Tom Tomcat" (Freleng/June 27); and "Catty Cornered" (Freleng/Oct. 31).

**1954:** "Muzzle Tough" (Freleng/June 26).

**1955:** "Tweety's Circus" (Freleng/June 4).

**1956:** "Tree Cornered Tweety" (Freleng/May 19); and "Tugboat Granny" (with Granny/Freleng/June 23).

**1957:** "Tweet Zoo" (Freleng/Jan. 12); "Tweety and the Beanstalk" (Freleng/May 16); and "Birds Anonymous" (Freleng/Aug. 10/A.A. winner).

**1958:** "A Bird in a Bonnet" (Freleng/Sept. 27).

**1959:** "Trick or Tweet" (Freleng/Mar. 21); and "Tweet and Lovely" (Freleng/July 18).

*Warner Bros. releases*

**1960:** "Hyde and Tweet" (Freleng/May 14); and "Trip for Tat" (Freleng/Oct. 29).

*Warner Bros. Pictures. Inc./Vitagraph releases*

**1961:** "The Last Hungry Cat" (Freleng, Pratt/Dec. 2).

**1964:** "Hawaiian Aye Aye" (Chinquy/June 27).

*Looney Tunes*

*Warner Bros. Cartoons, Inc. releases*

**1950:** "All A-Bir-r-r-d" (Freleng/June 24); and "Canary Row" (Freleng/Oct. 7).

**1951:** "Puddy Tat Trouble" (Freleng/Feb. 24); and "Tweet Tweet Tweety" (Freleng/Dec. 15).

**1952:** "Gift Wrapped" (Freleng/Feb. 16); "Ain't She Tweet" (Freleng/June 21); and "Bird in a Guilty Cage" (Freleng/Aug. 30).

**1953:** "Snow Business" (Freleng/Jan. 17); and "A Streetcar Named Sylvester" (Freleng/Sept. 5).

**1954:** "Dog Pounded" (Freleng/Jan. 2).

**1955:** "Sandy Claws" (Freleng/Apr. 2/A.A. nominee); and "Red Riding Hoodwinked" (Freleng/Oct. 29).

**1956:** "Tweet and Sour" (Freleng/Mar. 24).

**1957:** "Greedy for Tweety" (Freleng/Sept. 28).

**1958:** "A Pizza Tweety Pie" (Freleng/Feb. 22).

*Warner Bros. Pictures, Inc./Vitagraph releases*

**1959:** "Tweet Dreams" (Freleng/Dec. 5).

**1961:** "The Rebel Without Claws" (Freleng/July 15).

**1962:** "The Jet Cage" (Freleng/Sept. 22).

*Warner Bros. releases*

**1991:** "Invasion of the Bunny Snatchers" (with Bugs Bunny/Ford, Lennon).

*Warner Bros. Animation releases*

**1995:** "Carrotblanca" (with Bugs Bunny, Daffy Duck, Yosemite Sam, Pepe Le Pew, Foghorn Leghorn, Penelope/McCarthy/Aug. 25).

*Warner Bros. releases*

**2003:** "Museum Scream" (Moore, Povenmire, Shin, Kopp/Nov. 14).

## ☺ TWO CURIOUS PUPPIES

This nontalking, comical pair—a large brown boxer and a spotted puppy—were introduced by Chuck Jones to moviegoers in 1939, usually cast in everyday situations in which things ran afoul. The entertaining duo starred in two *Merrie Melodies* that first year, "Dog Gone Modern," marking their screen debut, followed by "Curious Puppy." It would be two years before moviegoers were again treated to their unusual antics with the debut of "Snowtime for Comedy," their third and final appearance on the big screen. *The series was directed by Chuck Jones. Technicolor. A Warner Bros. release.*

### Merrie Melodies

**1939:** "Dog Gone Modern" (Jan. 14); and "Curious Puppy" (Dec. 30).

**1941:** "Snowtime for Comedy" (Aug. 30).

## ◎ UPA CARTOON SPECIALS

This series featured previous characters such as Gerald McBoing Boing and other cartoon stars in cartoon specials produced by United Productions of America (UPA), which later produced television strips based on Dick Tracy and Mr. Magoo.

One cartoon in the series, "The Tell-Tale Heart" (1953), was adapted from a story by Edgar Allen Poe. Only one film was nominated for an Academy Award, the series' last entry, "The Jaywalker" (1956). *Directors were Bill Hurtz, Art Babbitt, Theodore Tee Hee, Ted Parmelee, Bob Cannon, Abe Liss, Paul Julian and Osmond Evans. Technicolor. A UPA Production released through Columbia Pictures.*

**1953:** "A Unicorn in the Garden" (Hurtz/Sept. 24); and "The Tell-Tale Heart" (Parmelee/Dec. 27/narrated by actor James Mason).

**1954:** "Bringing Up Father" (Hurtz/Jan. 14); "Ballet-Oop" (Cannon/Feb. 11); "The Man on the Flying Trapeze" (Parmelee/Apr. 8); "Fudget's Budget" (Cannon/June 17); "Kangaroo Courting" (Burness/July 22); and "How Now Boing Boing" (with Gerald McBoing Boing/Cannon/Sept. 9).

**1955:** "Spare the Child" (Liss/Jan. 27); "Four Wheels' No Brake" (with Pete Hothead/Parmelee/Mar. 24); "Baby Boogie" (Julian/May 19); "Christopher Crumpet's Playmate" (Cannon/Sept. 8); and "Rise of Duton Lang" (Evans/Dec. 1).

**1956:** "The Jaywalker" (Cannon/May 31/A.A. nominee).

## ◎ WALLY WALRUS

Making his screen debut in the 1944 cartoon, "Beach Nut," this slow-witted walrus with a Swedish accent—originally voiced by actor Hans Conried—costarred as comic relief for nine years in numerous Woody Woodpecker cartoons, plus two cartoons from Lantz's two-time Academy Award *Musical Miniature* series, "The Overture to William Tell" (1947) and "Kiddie Koncert" (1948). Likewise, he starred as a dogcatcher in the Andy Panda cartoon, "Dog Tax Dodgers" (1948).

Following a seven-year hiatus after his last cartoon, 1953's "Operation Sawdust," Wally took his final bows in 1961 in two Chilly Willy cartoons, "Clash and Carry" and "Tricky Trout." The character was tremendously popular in comic books, storybooks, records, and other merchandise licensed by the studio. In 1999, Wally was re-introduced to a new generation of viewers in brand-new episodes on FOX Network's Saturday-morning series *The All New Woody Woodpecker Show. Directed by James "Shamus" Culhane, Dick Lundy, Walter Lantz, Don Patterson, and Jack Hannah. Technicolor. A Walter Lantz Production released by Universal Pictures.*

### Voices:
**Wally Walrus:** Hans Conried (1944–48), Paul Frees (1961).

**1944:** "The Beach Nut" (with Woody Woodpecker/Culhane/Oct. 16); and "Ski for Two" (with Woody Woodpecker/Culhane/Nov. 13).

**1945:** "Chew-Chew Baby" (with Woody Woodpecker/Culhane/Feb. 5); and "The Dippy Diplomat" (with Woody Woodpecker/Culhane/Aug. 27).

**1946:** "Bathing Buddies" (with Woody Woodpecker/Lundy/Aug. 1); and "The Reckless Driver" (with Woody Woodpecker/Culhane/Aug. 26).

**1947:** "Smoked Hams" (with Woody Woodpecker/Lundy/Apr. 28); "The Overture to William Tell" (Lundy/June 16/*Musical Miniature*); and "Well Oiled" (with Woody Woodpecker/Lundy/June 30).

**1948:** "The Mad Hatter" (with Woody Woodpecker/Lundy/Feb. 16); "Banquet Busters" (with Woody Woodpecker/Lundy/Mar. 3); "Kiddie Koncert" (Lundy/Apr. 21/*Musical Miniature*); "Wacky-Bye Baby" (with Woody Woodpecker/Lundy/May 2); and "Dog Tax Dodgers" (with Andy Panda/Lundy/Nov. 26).

**1951:** "Sleep Happy" (with Woody Woodpecker/Lantz/Mar. 26); "Slingshot 6 7/8" (with Woody Woodpecker/Lantz/July 23); and "The Woody Woodpecker Polka" (with Woody Woodpecker/Lantz/Oct. 29).

**1952:** "Stage Hoax" (with Woody Woodpecker/Lantz/Apr. 21).

**1953:** "What's Sweepin'" (with Woody Woodpecker/Patterson/Jan. 5/working title: "The Big Clean-Up"); "Buccaneer Woodpecker" (with Woody Woodpecker/Patterson/Apr. 20); and "Operation Sawdust" (with Woody Woodpecker/Patterson/June 15).

**1961:** "Clash and Carry" (with Chilly Willy/Hannah/May); and "Tricky Trout" (Hannah/Sept.).

## ◎ WALT DISNEY SPECIALS

When *Silly Symphonies* faded into screen history, Walt Disney produced new cartoon specials to replace the old animated favorites. This long-running series proved equally successful for the studio, reaping eight Academy Award nominations and three Oscar statuettes for best short subject of the year.

Over the years several well-known Disney characters appeared in the series, including Scrooge McDuck, Winnie the Pooh and Roger Rabbit. *Directors were Dick Rickard, Norm Ferguson, Eric Larson, Bob Cormack, Gerry Geronimi, Bill Roberts, Hamilton Luske, Jack Kinney, Charles Nichols, Jack Hannah, Wilfred Jackson, Ward Kimball, Bill Justice, Woolie Reitherman, Les Clark, John Lounsbery, Don Bluth, Tim Burton, Darrell Van Citters, Rick Reinert, Michael Cedeno, Rob Minkoff, Frank Marshall, David Block, Steve Moore, Barry Cook, Mark Henn, Dominique Monfery, John Hench and Mike Gabriel. Technicolor. A Walt Disney Studios/Walt Disney Pictures Production released through RKO Radio Pictures and later Buena Vista Pictures.*

### RKO Radio Pictures releases

**1938:** "Ferdinand the Bull" (Rickard/Nov. 25/A.A. winner).

**1939:** "The Practical Pig" (Rickard/Feb. 24).

**1943:** "Education for Death" (Geronimi/Jan. 15); "Reason and Emotion" (Roberts/Aug. 27/A.A. nominee); and "Chicken Little" (Geronimi/Dec. 17).

**1944:** "The Pelican and the Snipe" (Luske/Jan. 7).

**1950:** "The Brave Engineer" (Kinney/Mar. 3); and "Morris the Midget Moose" (Hannah/Nov. 24).

**1952:** "Lambert the Sheepish Lion" (Hannah/Feb. 8/A.A. nominee); "Susie the Little Blue Coupe" (Geronimi/June 6); and "The Little House" (Jackson/Aug. 8).

**1953:** "Melody" (Nichols, Kimball/May 28/a.k.a.: "Adventures in Music"/Disney's first 3-D cartoon); "Football Now and Then" (Kinney/Oct. 2); "Toot, Whistle, Plunk and Boom" (Nichols, Kimball/Nov. 10/A.A. winner/Disney's first CinemaScope cartoon/a Buena Vista release); and "Ben and Me" (Luske/Nov. 10/A.A. nominee/a Buena Vista release).

**1954:** "Two for the Record" (Kinney/Apr. 23/from "Make Mine Music"); "Pigs Is Pigs" (Kinney/May 21/A.A. nominee); "Johnny Fedora and Alice Bluebonnet" (Kinney/May 21/from *Make Mine Music*); "Casey Bats Again" (Kinney/June 18); "The Martins and the Coys" (Kinney/June 18/from *Make Mine Music*); "Casey at the Bat" (Geronimi/July 16/from *Make Mine Music*); "Little Toot" (Geronimi/Aug. 13/from *Melody Time*); "Willie the Operatic Whale" (Geronimi, Luske, Cormack/Aug. 17/from *Make Mine Music*/a Buena Vista release); "Once Upon a Wintertime" (Luske/Sept. 17/from *Melody Time*); and "Social Lion" (Kinney/Oct. 15).

**1955:** "Man and the Moon" (Kimball/Jan. 28/originally broadcast on ABC's *Disneyland* television show); "Contrasts in Rhythm" (Kinney, Luske/Mar. 11/from *Melody Time*); "Pedro" (Luske/May 13/from *Saludos Amigos*); "Aquarela Do Brasil" (Jackson/June 24/from *Saludos Amigos*); "The Flying Gauchito" (Ferguson, Larson/July 15/from *The Three Caballeros*); "Peter and the Wolf" (Geronimi/Sept. 14/from *Make Mine Music*/a Buena Vista release); and "Johnny Appleseed" (Jackson/Dec. 25/from *Melody Time*/a Buena Vista release).

### Buena Vista releases

**1956:** "Hooked Bear" (Hannah/Apr. 27/CinemaScope); "Jack and Old Mac" (Justice/July 18); "Man in Space" (Kimball/July 18/originally broadcast on ABC's *Disneyland* television show/A.A. nominee, "Best Documentary"); "In the Bag" (Hannah/July 27/CinemaScope); and "A Cowboy Needs a Horse" (Justice/Nov. 6).

**1957:** "The Story of Anyburg U.S.A." (Geronimi/June 19); "The Truth About Mother Goose" (Reitherman, Justice/Aug. 28/A.A. nominee); and "Mars and Beyond" (Kimball/Dec. 26/originally broadcast on ABC's *Disneyland* television show).

**1958:** "Paul Bunyan" (Clark/Aug. 1); "Our Friend the Atom" (Luske/Aug.); and "The Legend of Sleepy Hollow" (Kinney, Geronimi/Nov. 26/from "The Adventures of Ichabod and Mr. Toad").

**1959:** "Noah's Ark" (Justice/Nov. 10/A.A. nominee).

**1960:** "Goliath II" (Reitherman/Jan. 21/A.A. nominee).

**1961:** "The Saga of Windwagon Smith" (Nichols/Mar. 16).

**1962:** "A Symposium on Popular Songs" (Justice/Dec. 19/A.A. nominee).

**1966:** "Winnie the Pooh and the Honey Tree" (Reitherman/Feb. 4).

**1967:** "Scrooge McDuck and Money" (Luske/Mar. 23).

**1968:** "Winnie the Pooh and the Blustery Day" (Reitherman/Dec. 20/A.A. winner).

**1969:** "It's Tough to Be a Bird" (Kimball/Dec. 10/A.A. winner).

**1970:** "Dad, Can I Borrow the Car" (Kimball/Sept. 30).

**1971:** "Bongo" (Kinney/Jan. 20/from *Fun and Fancy Free*).

**1974:** "Winnie the Pooh and Tigger Too" (Lounsbery/Dec. 20/A.A. nominee).

**1975:** "The Madcap Adventures of Mr. Toad" (Kinney/Dec. 25/from *The Adventures of Ichabod and Mr. Toad*).

**1978:** "The Small One" (Bluth/Dec. 16).

**1980:** "Mickey Mouse Disco" (June 25/compilation cartoon).

**1981:** "Once Upon a Mouse" (July 10/compilation cartoon).

**1982:** "Vincent" (Burton/Oct. 1); and "Fun with Mr. Future" (Van Citters/Oct. 27).

**1983:** "Winnie the Pooh and a Day for Eeyore" (Reinert/Mar. 11).

**1987:** "Oilspot and Lipstick" (Cedeno/July 28).

**1989:** "Tummy Trouble" (with Roger Rabbit, Jessica Rabbit, Baby Herman, Droopy/animation directed by Rob Minkoff; live action by Frank Marshall/July 23).

**1990:** "Rollercoaster Rabbit" (with Roger Rabbit, Jessica Rabbit, Baby Herman/Minkoff, Marshall/June 15).

**1992:** "Petal to the Metal" (with Bonkers D. Bobcat/Block/Aug. 7).

**1993:** "Trail Mix-Up" (with Roger Rabbit, Jessica Rabbit, Baby Herman, Droopy/Cook/Mar. 12).

**1995:** "Stand by Me" (with Timon, Pumbaa/Moore/Dec. 22).

**2000:** "John Henry" (Henn/Oct. 30).

**2003:** "Destino" (Monféry, Hench (uncredited)/June 2/A.A. nominee).

**2004:** "Lorenzo" (Gabriel/Mar/A.A. nominee).

## ⊚ WALTER LANTZ CARTUNE CLASSICS

Walter Lantz, creator of Woody Woodpecker, Andy Panda and others, lived out his love for music by initiating this series of musical cartoon novelties in 1934, produced in the same form as Disney's *Silly Symphonies* and Warner's early *Merrie Melodies*. No main characters were prominent in these animated efforts, which were based on hit songs of the day. Early titles were filmed in two-strip Cinecolor and then later three-strip Technicolor. In 1938, cartoons began to be released under the banner of "A New Universal Cartoon," with subsequent cartoons, beginning with "The Rabbit Hunt," directed by Lester Kline, called a "Cartune Comedy" and later "Cartune." *Directors were Walter Lantz, Lester Kline, Alex Lovy, Burt Gillett, Ben Hardaway, Emery Hawkins, James "Shamus" Culhane, Dick Lundy, Elmer Perkins, Paul J. Smith, Tex Avery, Pat Lenihan, Grant Simmons, Don Patterson and Jack Hannah. Cinecolor. Technicolor. A Walter Lantz Production released through Universal Pictures.*

### Universal Pictures releases

**1934:** "Jolly Little Elves" (Lantz/Oct. 1/A.A. nominee); and "Toyland Premiere" (Lantz/Dec. 10).

**1935:** "Candyland" (Lantz/Apr. 22); "Springtime Serenade" (May 27); "Three Lazy Mice" (Lantz/July 15); and "Fox and the Rabbit" (Lantz/Sept. 30).

**1938:** "Nellie the Sewing Machine Girl or Honest Hearts and Willing Hands" (Lovy/Apr. 11); "Tail End" (Kline/Apr. 25/Lester Kline's directorial debut); "Problem Child" (Zamora/May 16/working title: "Wildcat Willie"/Rudy Zamora's directorial debut); "Movie Phoney News" (Lovy/May 30); "Nellie, the Indian Chief's Daughter" (Lovy/June 6); "Happy Scouts" (with Oswald Rabbit/Kopietz/June 20/Fred Kopietz's directorial debut); "Cheese-Nappers" (with Baby-Face Mouse/Lovy/July 4); "Voodoo in Harlem" (Zamora/July 18/working title: "Black Magic"); "Silly Seals" (Kline/July 25); "Barnyard Romeo" (Lovy/Aug. 1/working title: "Fine Feathers"); "Queen's Kittens" (Kline/Aug. 8); "Pixie Land" (Perkins/Aug. 12/working title: "The Busy Body"/Elmer Perkins directorial debut); "The Big Cat and the Little Mousie" (with Baby-Face Mouse/Lovy/Aug. 15); "Ghost Town Frolics" (with Jock and Jill, the Simple Simeons/Kline/Sept. 3/working title: "Ghost Town"); "The Cat and the Bell" (with Baby-Face Mouse/Lovy/Oct. 3); "The Rabbit Hunt" (Kline/Oct. 10); "Sailor Mouse" (with BabyFace Mouse/Lovy/Nov. 7); "The Disobedient Mouse" (with Baby-Face Mouse/Kline/Nov. 28); "Baby Kittens" (Lovy/Dec. 19); and "Little Blue Blackbird" (Lenihan/Dec. 26).

**1939:** "Soup to Mutts" (Kline/Jan. 9); "I'm Just a Jitterbug" (Lovy/Jan. 23); "The Birth of a Toothpick" (Gillett/Feb. 27); "Little Tough Mice" (with Baby-Face Mouse/Lovy/Mar. 13); "The One-Armed Bandit" (Lovy/Mar. 27); "Crackpot Cruise" (Lovy/Apr. 10); "Charlie Cuckoo" (Perkins/Apr. 24); "Nellie of the Circus" (Lovy/May 8); "Bolo-Mola Land" (Lovy/May 28); "The Bird on Nellie's Hat" (Lovy/June 19); "The Arabs with Dirty Fezzes" (Lovy/July 31); "Snuffy Party" (with Snuffy Skunk/Perkins/Aug. 7); "Slaphappy Valley" (Lovy/Aug. 31/*Crackpot Cruise* cartoon); and "A Haunting We Will Go" (with Lil's Eightball Gillett/Sept. 4/first cartoon in three-strip Technicolor; previous cartoons filmed in two-strip Cinecolor).

**1940:** "Kittens' Mittens" (Lovy/Feb. 12); "Adventures of Tom Thumb Jr." (Gillett/Mar. 4); "Recruiting Daze" (Lantz/Oct. 28/ working title: "Be Prepared"); and "Syncopated Sioux" (Lantz/ Dec. 30).

**1941:** "Fair Today" (Lantz/Feb. 24); "Scrub Me Mama with a Boogie Beat" (Lantz/Mar. 28); "Hysterical Highspots in American History" (Lantz/Mar. 31); "Salt Water Daffy" (Lantz/June 9); "Boogie Woogie Bugle Boy of Company 'B'" (Lantz/Sept. 1/A.A. nominee); and "Man's Best Friend" (Lantz/Oct. 20).

**1942:** "Mother Goose on the Loose" (Lantz/Apr. 13).

**1943:** "Canine Commandos" (Lovy/June 28).

*Universal Pictures releases*

**1953:** "The Dog That Cried Wolf" (Smith/Mar. 23).

**1954:** "Dig That Dog" (Simmons, Patterson/Apr. 12); and "Broadway Bow Wow's" (Patterson/Aug. 2).

**1955:** "Crazy Mixed-Up Pup" (Avery/Feb. 14/A.A. nominee); and "Flea for Two" (Patterson/July 20).

**1957:** "Plumber of Seville" (with Hercules/Lovy/Mar. 11); "The Goofy Gardener" (Lovy/Aug. 26); and "The Bongo Punch" (with Pepito Chickeeto/Lovy/Dec. 30).

**1960:** "Hunger Strife" (with Fatso the Bear/Hannah/Oct. 5).

**1961:** "Eggnapper" (Hannah/Feb.); "Papoose on the Loose" (Smith/Apr. 11); "Bears and the Bees" (Hannah/May); and "Tin Can Concert" (with Hickory, Dickory, Doc/Hannah/Oct. 31).

## ◎ WARNER BROS. CARTOON SPECIALS

In 1968, a year after studio head Jack Warner reorganized Warner Bros.' animation department and put William L. Hendricks in place as the studio's newest cartoon producer, Hendricks produced the studio's first and only "Cartoon Special," a non-*Looney Tunes* and *Merrie Melodies* cartoon, entitled "Norman Normal." A contemporary satire on business methods and social behavior as experienced by a young man with a conscience (Norman), the cartoon

features the vocal and singing talents of singer/songwriter Noel (Paul) Stookey (Paul of Peter, Paul and Mary fame), who provides all of the character voices but Norman's, and Dave Dixon, the voice of Norman (who is incorrectly identified as Paul Dixon in the opening credits). Stookey and Dixon wrote the story on which the cartoon was based. The theme song, "Norman Normal," sung in the cartoon, was released on Peter, Paul and Mary's 1967 Warner Bros. album *Album*. *Directed by Alex Lovy. Technicolor. A Warner Bros.–Seven Arts Production released by Warner Bros.*

**1968:** "Norman Normal" (Feb. 3).

## ◎ WILLIE THE WALRUS

As an experiment, Terry-Toons cast a walrus in Arctic misadventures in an effort to develop new cartoon star material. This series, like several other attempts, was short-lived. *Directed by Mannie Davis and Connie Rasinski. Technicolor. A Terry-Toon Cartoons Production released through 20th Century Fox.*

**1954:** "Arctic Rivals" (Davis/June).

**1955:** "An Igloo for Two" (Rasinski/Mar.).

## ◎ WILLIE WHOPPER

When animator Ub Iwerks ceased production of his *Flip the Frog* series, he created this screen replacement, an imaginative liar named Willie Whopper whose tall tales were the foundation for unusual stories and situations. Adventures opened with Willie standing in front of a *Looney Tunes*-type oval, bragging to viewers "Say, did I ever tell you this one?" The roly-poly, freckle-faced boy never matched the popularity of Iwerks's Flip the Frog, however, and was soon abandoned. The character was first featured in a pilot film, "The Air Race," which was never released but later shown on local television kids' shows in the 1950s. Actress Jane Withers, best known as Josephine the Plumber in TV's Comet Cleanser commercials, supplied the voice of Willie when she was seven years old. It was one of her first paying jobs. *Produced and directed by Ub Iwerks. Black-and-white. Cinecolor. A Celebrity Pictures Production released through Metro-Goldwyn-Mayer.*

*Voice*
**Willie Whopper:** Jane Withers

**1933:** "Play Ball" (Sept. 6); "Spite Flight" (Oct. 14); "Stratos Fear" (Nov. 11); and "Davy Jones" (Dec. 9/Cinecolor).

**1934:** "Hell's Fire" (Jan. 6/Cinecolor); "Robin Hood, Jr." (Feb. 3); "Insultin' the Sultan" (Apr. 14); "Reducing Creme" (May 19); "Rasslin' Round" (© June 1); "The Cave Man" (July 6); "Jungle Jitters" (July 24); "Good Scout" (© Sept. 1); and "Viva Willie" (© Sept. 20).

## ◎ WILLOUGHBY WREN

This abbreviated Columbia Pictures cartoon series starred a canarylike bird who acquires tremendous strength each time he dons a magical cap containing particles of hair from Samson, the legendary strongman. Without the hat, he loses his power and becomes meek and helpless. The cartoons were released under the *Phantasy* and *Color Rhapsody* cartoon banners. Directors were Bob Wickersham and Howard Swift. *Technicolor. Voices credits unknown. A Columbia Pictures Corporation Production released by Columbia Pictures.*

**1943:** "Willoughby's Magic Hat" (Wickersham/Apr. 30/Phantasy cartoon).

**1944:** "Magic Strength" (Wickersham/Feb. 4/Phantasy cartoon).

**1945:** "Carnival Courage" (Swift/Sept. 6/Color Rhapsody).

## ☺ WINDY

Featured in various misadventures, this dumbfounded country bear starred briefly in his own series for creator Walter Lantz. Costarring in these comical cartoon adventures was the diminutive Breezy, whose character later became known as Inspector Willoughby and starred in his own cartoon series for Lantz studios. Veteran voice artist Daws Butler provided vocal characterization for both characters. *Directed by Paul J. Smith. Technicolor. A Walter Lantz Production released through Universal Pictures.*

*Voice*
**Windy:** Daws Butler

**1958:** "Salmon Yeggs" (with Breezy/Smith/Mar. 24/first appearance of character later known as Inspector Willoughby); and "Three Ring Fling" (Lovy/Oct. 6).

**1959:** "Truant Student" (with Breezy/Smith/Jan. 5); "Bee Bopped" (with Breezy/Smith/June 15).

## ☺ WINNIE THE POOH

Honey-loving Winnie the Pooh, created by children's author A.A. Milne, was adapted for the screen in a series of delightfully animated cartoon shorts produced by Walt Disney under the studio's *Walt Disney Specials* banner. Joined by Eeyore, Piglet, Rabbit, Tigger and Christopher Robin, Pooh first appeared on movie screens in 1966's "Winnie the Pooh and the Honey Tree," directed by Woolie Reitherman. The series received two Academy Award nominations, winning an Oscar for 1968's "Winnie the Pooh and the Blustery Day." All short subjects in the series were later rebroadcast as prime-time network specials. In 1977 Pooh starred in his first full-length feature. *The Many Adventures of Winnie the Pooh.* He also appeared in his own animated series for ABC, *The New Adventures of Winnie the Pooh*, premiering in the fall of 1988. *Directed by Woolie Reitherman, John Lounsbery and Rick Reinert. Technicolor. A Walt Disney Production released through Buena Vista Pictures.*

*Voices*
**Winnie the Pooh:** Sterling Holloway, Hal Smith; **Eeyore:** Ralph Wright; **Owl:** Hal Smith; **Piglet:** John Fiedler; **Christopher Robin:** Bruce Reitherman, John Walmsley, Kim Christianson; **Kanga:** Barbara Luddy, Julie McWhirter Dees; **Roo:** Clint Howard, Dori Whitaker, Dick Billingsley; **Rabbit:** Junius Matthews, Will Ryan; **Tigger:** Paul Winchell; **Gopher:** Howard Morris

**1966:** "Winnie the Pooh and the Honey Tree" (Reitherman/Feb. 4).

**1968:** "Winnie the Pooh and the Blustery Day" (Reitherman/Dec. 20/A.A. winner).

**1974:** "Winnie the Pooh and Tigger Too" (Lounsbery/Dec. 20/A.A. nominee).

**1981:** "Winnie the Pooh Discover the Seasons" (Sept.).

**1983:** "Winnie the Pooh and a Day for Eeyore" (Reinert/Mar. 11).

## ☺ WOLFIE WOLF

Director James "Shamus" Culhane unveiled this latest nemesis for Walter Lantz's *Woody Woodpecker* series in the 1946 cartoon, "Who's Cookin' Who." The character was so well received he returned in a second cartoon later that year, "Fair Weathered Fiends," becoming the last cartoon on which Culhane received screen credit. Eleven years lapsed before the wily wolf costarred again, this time in the 1957 Woody Woodpecker cartoon, "Red Riding Hoodlum," directed by veteran Lantz director Paul J. Smith. *Directed by James Culhane and Paul J. Smith. Technicolor. A Walter Lantz Production released by Universal Pictures.*

**1946:** "Who's Cookin' Who? (with Woody Woodpecker/Culhane/June 24) and "Fair Weathered Fiends" (with Woody Woodpecker/Culhane/Nov. 18).

**1957:** "Red Riding Hoodlum" (with Woody Woodpecker/Smith/Feb. 11).

## ☺ WOODY WOODPECKER

This hammering woodpecker with the "Ha-hah-ha-hah" laugh was Walter Lantz's prized creation. Screwball by nature, the redheaded menace was first introduced as the perfect foil in Andy Panda's 1940 cartoon, "Knock Knock," bearing a strong resemblance to the nutty characterizations of Warner's early Daffy Duck and Bugs Bunny. Legend long had it that Lantz invented Woody after honeymooning with his wife, former Broadway/screen actress Grace Stafford. A pesky woodpecker that pounded the roof of their honeymoon cottage provided inspiration. Unfortunately, the story was a Hollywood press agent's fabrication since Lantz's honeymoon actually occurred one year after Woody's first cartoon appearance.

"My wife suggested that since I had animated animals like mice, rabbits and so forth that maybe I should invent some kind of woodpecker character. I thought it was a good idea so I created Woody," Lantz later recalled.

1941　1945
WOODY WOODPECKER®
1950　© Walter Lantz　1960

*Walter Lantz's Woody Woodpecker experienced many physical changes during his years as a screen star. © Walter Lantz Productions*

In 1941 Lantz officially launched Woody in his own series, casting the malicious woodpecker in an eponymous cartoon. Veteran actor Mel Blanc supplied the voice of Woody in the first four or five cartoons. Ben "Bugs" Hardaway, who left Warner to become a story man for Lantz, lent his vocal talents to the character after Blanc's departure and continued to develop new stories for the series.

Hardaway did not handle the dual responsibility for long. In 1948 Lantz decided a change was needed and auditioned 50 actors for the "new" voice of Woody. Lantz was not present at the auditions, but he was responsible for making the final choice. Of those who auditioned on tape, he picked the talent who sounded the best. His selection: Grace, his wife, who had "tried out" without informing her husband.

Stafford was first employed in the 1948 Woody Woodpecker release "Banquet Busters" and remained the voice of Woody until the series ended 24 years later in 1972. By her request, she did not receive voice credit until 1952; she was afraid children would be "disillusioned if they knew a woman" had voiced the famed woodpecker.

Adding to the series fresh comical adventures and longevity were a cast of supporting characters featured during the series' long and successful run. Among them were the slow-witted walrus with a Swedish accent, Wally Walrus, who made his screen debut in the 1944 Woody Woodpecker cartoon, "Beach Nut." Originally voiced by actor Hans Conreid and later by Paul Frees, this comic-relief character costarred for nine years in 23 films, including two from Lantz's two-time Academy Award *Musical Miniature* series, "The Overture to William Tell" (1947) and "Kiddie Koncert" (1948). Likewise, he starred as a dogcatcher in the Andy Panda cartoon, "Dog Tax Dodgers" (1948). Following a seven-year hiatus after 1953's "Operation Sawdust," Wally took his final bows in 1961 in two Chilly Willy cartoons, "Clash and Carry" and "Tricky Trout." The character was tremendously popular in comic books, storybooks, records, and other merchandise licensed by the studio. In 1999, the Wally was introduced to a new generation of viewers in brand-new episodes on Fox Network's Saturday-morning series, *The All New Woody Woodpecker Show*.

In 1948, Lantz added the popular mainstay and comical nemesis, the con-man Buzz Buzzard (featured in 23 films), who was first featured opposite the wacky woodpecker in "Wet Blanket Policy" directed by Dick Lundy. The film not only introduced Woody's newest costar but also was the first cartoon to include the sensational hit song "The Woody Woodpecker Song," sung by Gloria Wood and Harry Babbitt. (Coincidentally, the cartoon earned the distinction of becoming the only animated cartoon short to ever be nominated for an Academy Award for best song.) Buzz went on to star in two more cartoons through 1949, including "Drooler's Delight," which was the final cartoon Lundy directed for the studio and also the last cartoon short released by United Artists. Likewise, the cartoon marked the final time Ben Hardaway provided the voice of Woody (Lantz's real-life wife, Grace Stafford, assumed the role thereafter). Lantz's former distribution partner, Universal Pictures, released subsequent films featuring the shyster buzzard and Lantz's famous woodpecker through 1972, the same year Lantz closed his studio, including the studio's only cartoon to be released in 3-D, "Hypnotic Hick" (1953).

Another mainstay and comical costar of Woody's was the talkative gator, Gabby Gator, who starred in 10 animated one-reelers, first as the prototype character called Ali Gator in two cartoons produced in the late 1950s, "Everglade Raid" (1958) and "Romp in the Swamp" (1959). The talkative gator then made his first "official" appearance in the 1960 Woody Woodpecker cartoon, "Southern Fried Hospitality." As in the previous cartoons, Daws Butler provided the character's voice until his last screen appearance, 1963's "Greedy Gabby Gator," also starring Woody Woodpecker.

Woody had his share of other comical foils over the years, both foxes, Wolfie Wolf and later Finx Fox. Wolfie Wolf was introduced in the 1946 short, "Who's Cookin' Who," directed by James "Shamus" Culhane." He reprised the character in a second cartoon that same year, "Fair Weathered Fiends," the last studio cartoon on which Culhane received screen credit. Eleven years after he was shelved, the wolf returned to the screen to costar in the 1957 Woody Woodpecker cartoon, "Red Riding Hoodlum." The fast-talking Finx Fox, outfitted in a crushed top hat, white collar and pale green dress tie, with the unenviable task of trying to catch Woody, first appeared, unbilled, in the 1964 cartoon short, "Dumb Like a Fox." A year later, he was officially introduced in a second Technicolor one-reeler, "Sioux Me," in which he was billed in the opening credits ("Introducing Finx Fox").

Like Walt Disney's Donald Duck before him, Woody also romped on the screen with a rambunctious niece and nephew and chips off the ol' block, Splinter and Knothead. The characters were featured in three cartoons produced by Lantz and directed by longtime helmsman, Paul J. Smith, beginning with 1956's "Get Lost," followed by "The Unbearable Salesman" (1957) and "Careless Caretaker" (1962). June Foray provided the voices of both characters.

Lantz later packaged the early Woody cartoons in a half-hour television series, *The Woody Woodpecker Show*, which was first broadcast in 1957 on ABC and was sponsored by Kellogg for nine consecutive seasons. The films are still syndicated today throughout most U.S. television markets and abroad. *Directors were Walter Lantz, Don Patterson, Paul J. Smith, Alex Lovy, Jack Hannah, Sid Marcus, Emery Hawkins, Milt Schaffer, James "Shamus" Culhane, Dick Lundy, Ben Hardaway and Cal Dalton. Technicolor. A Walter Lantz Production released through Universal Pictures and United Artists.*

### Voices

**Woody Woodpecker:** Mel Blanc, Ben Hardaway, Grace Stafford; Buzz Buzzard; Dallas McKennon; Gabby Gator: Daws Butler; Wally Walrus; Hans Conreid (1944–48), Paul Frees (1961); Splinter/Knothead, June Foray

### Universal Pictures releases

**1940:** "Knock Knock" (with Andy Panda/Lantz/Nov. 25).

**1941:** "Woody Woodpecker" (Lantz/July 7/working title: "The Cracked Nut"); "The Screwdriver" (Lantz/Aug. 11); and "Pantry Panic" (Lantz/Nov. 24/working title: "What's Cookin'?").

**1942:** "The Hollywood Matador" (Lantz/Feb. 9); "Ace in the Hole" (Lovy/June 22); and "The Loan Stranger" (Lovy/Oct. 19).

**1943:** "The Screwball" (Lovy/Feb. 15); "The Dizzy Acrobat" (Lovy/May 31/A.A. nominee); and "Ration Bored" (Hawkins, Schaffer/June 22).

**1944:** "The Barber of Seville" (Culhane/Apr. 10); "The Beach Nut" (Culhane/Oct. 16); and "Ski for Two" (Culhane/Nov. 13).

**1945:** "Chew-Chew Baby" (Culhane/Feb. 5); "Woody Dines Out" (Culhane/May 14); "The Dippy Diplomat" (Culhane/Aug. 27); and "The Loose Nut" (Culhane/Dec. 17).

**1946:** "Who's Cookin' Who?" (Culhane/June 24); "Bathing Buddies" (Lundy/July 1); "The Reckless Driver" (Culhane/Aug. 26); and "Fair Weather Friends" (Culhane/Nov. 18).

*United Artists releases*

**1947:** "Musical Moments from Chopin" (with Andy Panda/Lundy/Feb. 24/A.A. nominee/Musical Miniature); "Smoked Hams" (Lundy/Apr. 28); "The Coo Coo Bird" (Lundy/June 9); "Well Oiled" (Lundy/June 30); "Solid Ivory" (Lundy/Aug. 25); and "Woody the Giant Killer" (Lundy/Dec. 15).

**1948:** "The Mad Hatter" (Lundy/Feb. 16); "Banquet Busters" (with Andy Panda/Lundy/Mar. 3); "Wacky-Bye Baby" (Lundy/May 2); "Wet Blanket Policy" (Lundy/Aug. 27/first appearance of Buzz Buzzard); and "Wild and Woody!" (Lundy/Dec. 31).

**1949:** "Drooler's Delight" (Lundy/Mar. 25).

*Universal Pictures releases*

**1951:** "Puny Express" (Lantz/Jan. 22); "Sleep Happy" (Lantz/Mar. 26); "Wicket Wacky" (Lantz/ May 28); "Slingshot 6 7/8" (Lantz/July 23); "The Redwood Sap" (Lantz/Oct. 1); "The Woody Woodpecker Polka" (Lantz/Oct. 29); and "Destination Meatball" (Lantz/Dec. 24).

**1952:** "Born to Peck" (Lantz/Feb. 25); "Stage Hoax" (Lantz/Apr. 21); "Woodpecker in the Rough" (Lantz/June 16); "Scalp Treatment" (Lantz/Sept. 18); "The Great Who-Dood-It" (Lantz/Oct. 20); and "Termites from Mars" (Patterson/Dec. 8).

**1953:** "What's Sweepin'" (Patterson/Jan. 5); "Bucaneer Woodpecker" (Patterson/Apr. 20); "Operation Sawdust" (Patterson/June 15); "Wrestling Wrecks" (Patterson/July 20); "Hypnotic Hick" (Patterson/Sept. 26/the only Lantz cartoon made in 3-D); "Belle Boys" (Patterson/Sept. 14); and "Hot Noon" (or/2'O'Clock For Sure) (Smith/Oct. 12).

**1954:** "Socko in Morocco" (Patterson/Jan. 18); "Alley to Bali" (Patterson/Mar. 15); "Under the Counter Spy" (Patterson/May 10); "Hot Rod Huckster" (Patterson/July 5); "Real Gone Woody" (Smith/Sept. 20); "A Fine Feathered Frenzy" (Patterson/Oct. 25); and "Convict Concerto" (Patterson/Nov. 20).

**1955:** "Helter Shelter" (Smith/Jan. 17); "Witch Crafty" (Smith/Mar. 14); "Private Eye Pooch" (Smith/May 9); "Bedtime Bedlam" (Smith/July 4); "Square Shootin' Square' (Smith/Sept. 1); "Bunco Busters" (Smith/Nov. 21); and "The Tree Medic" (Lovy/Dec. 9).

**1956:** "After the Ball" (Smith/Feb. 13); "Get Lost" (Smith/Mar. 12); "Chief Charlie Horse" (Smith/May 7); "Woodpecker from Mars" (Smith/July 2); "Calling All Cuckoos" (Smith/Sept. 24); "Niagra Fools" (Smith/Oct. 22); "Arts and Flowers" (Smith/Nov.19); and "Woody Meets Davy Crewcut" (Lovy/Dec. 17).

**1957:** "Red Riding Hoodlum" (Smith/Feb. 11); "Box Car Bandit" (Smith/Apr. 8); "The Unbearable Salesman" (Smith/June 3); "International Woodpecker" (Smith/July 1); "To Catch a Woodpecker" (Lovy/July 29); "Round Trip to Mars" (Smith/Sept. 23); "Fodder and Son" (Smith/Nov. 4); and "Dopey Dick and the Pink Whale" (Smith/Nov. 15).

**1958:** "Misguided Missile" (Smith/Jan. 27); "Watch the Birdie" (Lovy/Feb. 24); "Half Empty Saddles" (Smith/Apr. 21); "His Better Elf" (Smith/July 14); "Everglade Raid" (Smith/Aug. 11); "Tree's a Crowd" (Smith/Sept. 8); and "Jittery Jester" (Smith/Nov. 3).

**1959:** "Tom Cat Combat" (Smith/Mar. 2); "Log Jammed" (Smith/Apr. 20); "Panhandle Scandal" (Lovy/May 18); "Woodpecker in the Moon" (Lovy/July 1); "The Tee Bird" (Smith/July 13); "Romp in a Swamp" (Smith/Aug. 7); and "Kiddie League" (Smith/Nov. 3).

**1960:** "Billion Dollar Boner" (Lovy/Jan. 5); "Pistol-Packin' Woodpecker" (Smith/Mar. 2); "Heap Big Hepcat" (Smith/Mar. 30); "Ballyhooey" (Lovy/Apr. 20); "How to Stuff a Woodpecker" (Smith/May 18); "Bats in the Belfry" (Smith/June 16); "Ozark Lark" (Smith/July 13); "Southern <u>Fried</u> Hospitality" (with Gabby Gator/Hannah/Nov. 28); and "Fowled Up Falcon" (Smith/Dec. 20).

**1961:** "Poop Deck Pirate" (Hannah/Jan. 10); "The Bird Who Came to Dinner" (Smith/Mar. 7); "Gabby's Diner" (with Gabby Gator/Hannah/Apr.); "Sufferin' Cats" (Smith/June); "Franken-stymied" (Hannah/July 4); "Busman's Holiday" (Smith/Aug.); "Phantom of the Horse Opera" (Smith/Oct.); and "Woody's Kook-Out" (Hannah/Nov.).

**1962:** "Rock-a-Bye Gator" (with Gabby Gator/Hannah/Jan. 9); "Home Sweet Homewrecker" (Smith/Jan. 30); "Room and Bored" (Smith/Mar. 6); "Rocket Racket" (with Gabby Gator/Hannah/Apr. 24); "Careless Caretaker" (Smith/May 29); "Tragic Magic" (Smith/July 3); "Voo-Doo Boo-Hoo" (Hannah/Aug. 14); "Growin' Pains" (Smith/Sept.); and "Little Woody Riding Hood" (with Gabby Gator/Smith/Oct.).

**1963:** "Greedy Gabby Gator" (with Gabby Gator/Marcus/Jan.); "Robin Hood Woody" (Smith/Mar.); "Stowaway Woody" (Marcus/May); "Shutter Bug" (Smith/June); "Coy Decoy" (Marcus/July 9); "The Tenant's Racket" (Marcus/Aug. 30); "Short in the Saddle" (Smith/Sept. 30); "Teepee for Two" (Marcus/Oct. 29); "Science Friction" (Marcus/Nov.); and "Calling Dr. Woodpecker" (Smith/Dec. 24).

**1964:** "The Case of the Maltese Chicken" (Smith); "Dumb Like a Fox" (with Finx Fox/Marcus/Jan. 7); "Saddle-Sore Woody" (Smith/Apr. 7); "Woody's Clip Joint" (Marcus/May); "Skinfolks" (Marcus/July 7); "Get Lost! Little Doggy" (Marcus/Sept.); "Freeway Fracus" (Smith/Sept.); and "Roamin' Roman" (Smith/Dec.).

**1965:** "Three Little Woodpeckers" (Marcus/Jan. 1); "Woodpecker Wanted" (Smith/Feb. 1); "Birds of a Feather" (Marcus/Mar. 1); "Canned Dog Feud" (Smith/Apr. 1); "Janie Get Your Gun" (with Finx Fox/Smith/May 1); "Sioux Me" (Marcus/June); and "What's Peckin'" (Smith/July 1).

**1966:** "Rough Riding Hood" (Marcus/Jan. 1); "Lonesome Ranger" (Smith/Feb. 1); "Woody and the Beanstalk" (Smith/Mar. 1); "Hassle in a Castle" (Smith/Apr.); "The Big Bite" (Smith/Apr. 1); "Astronut Woody" (Smith/May); "Monster of Ceremonies" (Smith/May); and "Practical Yolk" (Smith/May 1).

**1967:** "Sissy Sheriff" (Smith/Jan. 1); "Have Gun' Can't Travel" (Smith/Feb. 1); "The Nautical Nut" (Smith/Mar. 1); "Hot Diggity Dog" (Smith/Mar. 1); "Horse Play" (Smith/Apr. 1); and "Secret Agent Woody Woodpecker" (Smith/May 1).

**1968:** "Lotsa Luck" (Smith); "Fat in the Saddle" (Smith/June 1); "Feudin' Fightin-n-Fussin'" (Smith/June 1); "A Peck of Trouble" (Smith/July 1); "A Lad in Bagdad" (Smith/Aug. 1); "One Horse Town" (Smith/Oct. 1); and "Woody the Freeloader" (Smith).

**1969:** "Hook Line and Stinker" (Smith); "Little Skeeter" (Smith); "Woody's Knight Mare" (Smith/May 1); "Tumble Weed Greed" (Smith/June 1); "Ship Ahoy, Woody" (Smith/Aug. 1); "Prehistoric Super Salesman" (Smith/Sept. 1); and "Phoney Pony" (Smith/Nov. 1).

**1970:** "Film Flam Fountain" (Smith/Jan. 5); "Seal on the Loose" (Smith/May 1); "Wild Bill Hiccup" (Smith/June 1); "Coo Coo Nuts" (Smith/July 1); "Hi-Rise Wise Guys" (Smith/Aug. 1); "Buster's Last Stand" (Smith/Oct. 1); and "All Hams on Deck" (Smith/Nov. 9).

**1971:** "Sleepy Time Chimes" (Smith/Feb. 1); "The Reluctant Recruit" (Smith); "How to Trap a Woodpecker" (Smith); "Woody's Magic Touch" (Smith); "Kitty from the City" (Smith); "The Snoozin' Bruin Woody" (Smith); and "Shanghai Woody" (Smith).

**1972:** "Indian Corn" (Smith); "Gold Diggin' Woodpecker" (Smith); "Pecking Holes in Poles" (Smith); "Chili Con Corny" (Smith); "Show Biz Eagle" (Smith); "For the Love of Pizza" (Smith); "The Genie with the Light Touch" (Smith); and "Bye, Bye Blackboard" (Smith).

## ◎ YOSEMITE SAM

A primary cartoon foil for Bugs Bunny, this pint-size, short-tempered cowboy who called himself "the roughest, toughest hombre" in the West came out guns ablazing in his screen debut opposite the carrot-eating rabbit in 1945's "Hare Trigger."

Friz Freleng, who directed the film, was responsible for creating Yosemite. "I was looking for a character strong enough to work against Bugs Bunny. . . . So I thought to use the smallest guy I could think of along with the biggest voice I could get," Freleng told Warner Bros. historian Steven Schneider.

In his 1944 "Stage Door Cartoon," Freleng used a similar character who looked and sounded like Yosemite and had only a walk-on part. According to writer Michael Maltese, Freleng drew from several personas—himself included—in developing the loud-mouthed Yosemite. His primary influences were Red Skelton's Sheriff Deadeye, a boneheaded cowboy short on smarts, Bob Clampett's gunslinger character based on Deadeye and comic-strip star Red Ryder in his 1944 "Buckaroo Bugs."

Yosemite's appearances were limited to supporting roles throughout his career; he never starred in his own series. Today the character is still seen daily in television reruns of the studio's *Merrie Melodies* and *Looney Tunes* package and in frequent prime-time animated specials.

In 1995 Yosemite returned to movie screens as costar in a brand-new Bugs Bunny cartoon, "Carrotblanca," a spoof of the Humphrey Bogart-Lauren Bacall classic, *Casablanca*, directed by Douglas McCarthy. Voice impressario Maurice LaMarche took over as the voice of Yosemite Sam. Two years later, after returning to Warner Bros. to produce and direct new cartoon shorts, legendary animator Chuck Jones directed Yosemite in a second cartoon opposite Bugs Bunny, "From Hare to Eternity," (1997) intended as Jones's tribute to fellow animator, the late Friz Freleng. Comedian/impressionist Frank Gorshin, best known as the Riddler on the *Batman* TV series, lent his voice as Yosemite. In 2003, Yosemite joined his fellow Warner Bros. cartoon stars, including Bugs Bunny, Daffy Duck and others, to costar in the live-action animated feature—and second full-length film since 1993's *Space Jam*—*Looney Tunes: Back in Action*. A year later, the studio cast him in a brand-new *Looney Tunes* cartoon that was planned and storyboarded but cancelled and never released, entitled "Deep Sea Bugs" with Bugs Bunny. *Directors were Friz Freleng, Ken Harris, Hawley Pratt, Gerry Chiniquy, Douglas McCarthy. Rich Moore, Dan Povenmire, Peter Shin and Bill Kopp. Technicolor. A Warner Bros. Cartoons, Inc./Warner Bros. Pictures, Inc./Vitagraph/Warner Bros. Animation/Chuck Jones Film Production released by Warner Bros. and Warner Bros. Family Entertainment.*

**Voices**
**Yosemite Sam:** Mel Blanc, Maurice LaMarche, Frank Gorshin

**Additional Voices**
June Foray, Billy Booth

### Looney Tunes

*Warner Bros. Cartoons, Inc. releases*

**1948:** "Bucaneer Bunny" (with Bugs Bunny/Freleng/May 8).

**1950:** "Mutiny on the Bunny" (with Bugs Bunny/Freleng/Feb. 11); and "Big House Bunny" (with Bugs Bunny/Freleng/Apr. 22).

**1951:** "Rabbit Every Monday" (with Bugs Bunny/Freleng/Feb. 10); and "The Fair Haired Hare" (with Bugs Bunny/Freleng/Apr. 14).

**1952:** "14 Carrot Rabbit" (with Bugs Bunny/Freleng/Feb. 16); and "Hare Lift" (with Bugs Bunny/Freleng/Dec. 20).

**1955:** "Sahara Hare" (with Bugs Bunny/Freleng/Mar. 26); and "Roman Legion-Hare" (with Bugs Bunny, Nero/Freleng/Nov. 12).

**1956:** "Rabbitson Crusoe" (with Bugs Bunny/Freleng/Apr. 28).

**1957:** "Piker's Peak" (with Bugs Bunny/Freleng/May 25).

**1958:** "Knighty Knight Bugs" (with Bugs Bunny/Freleng/Aug. 23/A.A. winner).

**1959:** "Wind and Woolly Hare" (with Bugs Bunny/Freleng/Aug. 1).

**1960:** "Horse Hare" (with Bugs Bunny/Freleng/Feb. 13).

*Warner Bros. Pictures, Inc./Vitagraph releases*

**1961:** "Prince Violent" (with Bugs Bunny/Freleng, Pratt/Sept. 2).

**1962:** "Shishkabugs" (with Bugs Bunny/Freleng/Dec. 8).

*Warner Bros. Animation releases*

**1995:** "Carrotblanca" (with Bugs Bunny, Daffy Duck, Yosemite Sam, Tweety and Sylvester, Foghorn Leghorn, Pepe Le Pew, Penelope/McCarthy).

*Warner Bros./Chuck Jones Film Productions releases*

**1997:** "From Hare to Eternity" (with Bugs Bunny/Jones)

### Merrie Melodies

*Warner Bros. Cartoons, Inc. releases*

**1945:** "Hare Trigger" (with Bugs Bunny/Freleng/May 5)

**1948:** "Bugs Bunny Rides Again" (with Bugs Bunny/Freleng/June 12).

**1950:** "Bunker Hill Bunny" (with Bugs Bunny/Freleng/Sept. 23).

**1951:** "Ballot Box Bunny" (with Bugs Bunny/Freleng/Oct. 6).

**1953:** "Southern Fried Rabbit" (with Bugs Bunny/Freleng/May 2); and "Hare Trimmed" (with Bugs Bunny/Freleng/June 20).

**1954:** "Captain Hareblower" (with Bugs Bunny/Freleng/Feb. 16).

**1959:** "Hare-abian Nights" (with Bugs Bunny/Harris/Feb. 28).

**1960:** "From Hare/d'Heir" (with Bugs Bunny/Freleng/ Sept. 3); and "Lighter than Hare" (with Bugs Bunny/Freleng/Dec. 17).

*Warner Bros. Pictures, Inc./Vitagraph releases*

**1962:** "Honey's Money" (Freleng/Sept. 1).

**1963:** "Devil's Feud Cake" (with Bugs Bunny/Freleng/Feb. 9).

**1964:** "Dumb Patrol" (with Bugs Bunny, Porky Pig/Chiniquy/ Jan. 18).

*Warner Bros. releases*

**1991:** "(blooper) Bunny!" (with Daffy Duck, Elmer Fudd/Moore, Povenmire, Shin, Kopp).

# FULL-LENGTH ANIMATED FEATURES

The following section is a complete listing of full-length animated features that received limited and wide theatrical distribution in the United States only. This section excludes feature-length cartoon documentaries, outright compilations, direct-to-video features (unless they were also released theatrically) and mostly live-action films that combine animation.

Films that have minor animated sequences that are not mentioned in this section include: *King of Jazz* (1930), which features a four-minute animated opening by Walter Lantz (the first animation to be done in two-color Technicolor); *Hollywood Party* (MGM, 1934), in which an animated Mickey Mouse appears; *She Married a Cop* (1939), featuring Paddy the Pig in a cartoon segment, also seen in the film's remake *Sioux City Sue* (1947), starring Gene Autry; *Anchors Aweigh* (MGM, 1944), featuring Gene Kelly and Jerry Mouse in a popular dance sequence; *So Dear to My Heart* (Disney, 1945); *My Dream Is Yours* (Warner, 1949), the Doris Day-Jack Carson film highlighted by animated appearances of Bugs Bunny and Tweety bird (Bugs appeared one year earlier in another Jack Carson film, *Two Guys from Texas*); *Destination Moon* (1950), featuring Woody Woodpecker in a brief bit of animated business; *Dangerous When Wet* (MGM, 1953), which teams Tom and Jerry with Esther Williams in an underwater sequence; *Mary Poppins* (1965), in which Julie Andrews and Dick Van Dyke dance in perfect synchronization with several animated penguins; and *Bedknobs and Broomsticks* (1971).

Additional, essentially live-action films featuring animated or computer-generated characters, such as *Casper* (1995), *Stuart Little* (1999), *Stuart Little 2* (2002), *Scooby Doo* (2002) and *Scooby Doo 2: Monster Unleashed* (2004), *Garfield: The Movie* (2004) and others, are not covered.

When animated characters play a major part in the story structure of live action/animated films (e.g. *The Incredible Mr. Limpet*, *Pete's Dragon* and *Who Framed Roger Rabbit*), those productions have been included.

Technical credits appear with each listing, limited to the production staff (producer, director, writer, musical director and supervising animators) and voice artists. Production sidelights and

other tidbits of interest have been entered under notes about the production (abbreviated as "PN") whenever appropriate.

The following key can be used to translate abbreviations for technical staff listed under each film:

**3-D anim supervisor:** three-dimensional animation supervisor
**anim dir:** animation director
**anim leads:** animation leads
**anim prod:** animation producer
**anim prod dir:** animation production director
**anim superv:** animation supervisor
**anim tech dir:** animation technical director
**anim:** animator
**assoc prod:** associate producer
**asst anim dir:** assistant animation director
**asst anim superv:** assistant animation supervisor
**asst dir:** assistant director
**CG superv:** computer generation supervisor
**CGI lead anim:** computer generated imagery lead animator
**char anim:** character animator
**char anim superv:** character animation supervisor
**char design:** character design
**char dev superv:** character development supervisor
**char superv:** character supervisor
**chief anim:** chief animator
**chief key aim superv:** chief key animation supervisor
**co-exec prod:** co-executive producer
**cpd:** coproducer
**dir anim:** directing animator
**dir of anim:** director of animation
**dir:** director
**exec prod:** executive producer
**f/x anim superv:** effects animation supervisor
**f/x anim:** effects animator
**head anim:** head animator
**head char anim:** head character animator
**host seq dir:** host sequence director
**key anim:** key animator

key anim superv: key animation supervisor
key seq anim: key sequence animator
l/a dir: live-action director
l: lyrics
lead anim superv: lead animation supervisor
lead anim: lead animator
m/a: music associate
m/l: music and lyrics
m/s: music and songs
m: music
md: musical direction
ms: musical supervision
orig p: original play
orig s: original story
p: producer
prod dir: production director
prod superv: production supervisor
s: songs by
scr: screenplay
scr/st: screenplay and story
scr st: screen story
senior anim: senior animator
senior superv anim: senior supervising animator
seq dir: sequence director
seq superv: sequence supervisor
st: story
st dev: story development
superv anim: supervising animators
superv anim dir: supervising animation director
superv d: supervising directors
superv seq dir: supervising sequence director
superv tech dir: supervising technical director
U.S. dub dir: United States dub director
unit anim dir: unit animation director
w: writer

## ◎ AARON'S MAGIC VILLAGE (1997)

An Avalanche Releasing and Columbia Tri-Star Home Video Production released by Avalanche Releasing. **p:** Dora Benousilio, Jacqueline Galia Benousilio, Albert Hanan Kaminski, Peter Völkle; **d:** Albert Hanan Kaminski, Jacqueline Galia Benousilio; Buzz Potamkin; **scr:** Albert Hanan Kaminski, Jacqueline Galia Benousilio (based on *Stories for Children* by Isaac Bashevis Singer); **m:** Michel Legrand. **Running time:** 80 minutes. **Released:** September 19, 1997.

### Voices

**Aaron:** Tommy J. Michaels; **Uncle Shlemiel:** Ronn Carroll; **Aunt Sarah/Zlateh the Goat/Matchmaker:** Tovah Feldshuh; **The Sorcerer:** Steve Newman; **The Lantuch:** Ivy Austin; **Gronam Ox:** Harry Goz; **Narrator:** Fyvush Finkel

### Additional Voices

Lewis J. Stadlen, Lee Wilkof, Chip Zien

An orphan boy (Aaron) who lives in the small village of Chelm with his aunt and uncle foils an evil sorcerer who stole the Book of Marvels and intends to use it to destroy the town in this adaptation of four fables from Isaac Bashevis Singer's book *Stories for Children*.

## ◎ THE ADVENTURES OF ICHABOD AND MR. TOAD (1949)

A Walt Disney Production released by RKO Radio Pictures. **p:** Walt Disney; **prod superv:** Ben Sharpsteen; **d:** Jack Kinney, Clyde Geronimi, James Algar; **dir anim:** Frank Thomas, Ollie Johnston, Wolfgang Reitherman, Milt Kahl, John Lounsbery, Ward Kimball; **st:** Erdman Penner, Winston Hibler, Joe Rinaldi, Ted Sears, Homer Brightman, Harry Reeves; **md:** Oliver Wallace. **Songs:** "Ichabod," "Katrina," "The Headless Horseman" and "Merrily on Our Way." **Running time:** 68 minutes. **Released:** October 5, 1949.

### Voices

**Mr. Toad:** Eric Blore; **Cyril:** J. Pat O'Malley; **Rat:** Claude Allister; **John Ployard:** John McLeish; **Mole:** Colin Campbell; **Angus MacBadger:** Campbell Grant; **Winky:** Alec Harford. "Ichabod" narrated by Bing Crosby. "Willows" narrated by Basil Rathbone.

This somewhat forgotten Disney feature combines two half-hour adaptations: Washington Irving's *Legend of Sleepy Hollow*, the story of schoolmaster Ichabod Crane's encounter with the famed horseman and his Jack-o'-lantern head, and Kenneth Grahame's *Wind in the Willows*, featuring the misadventures of Mr. Toad Hall, a whimsical toad who is wrongly accused of car thievery and tries proving his innocence. Bing Crosby ("Ichabod") and Basil Rathbone ("Willows") provided narration for the films.

**PN:** The film's original title was *Two Fabulous Characters* but was changed prior to its release.

## ◎ THE ADVENTURES OF MARK TWAIN (1986)

A Will Vinton Associates/Harbour Tower Production released by Atlantic Releasing. **p & d:** Will Vinton; **exec prod:** Frank Moynihan; **scr:** Susan Shandburne; **m:** Billy Scream; **char anim:** Barry Bruce, William L. Fiesterman, Tom Gasek, Mark Gustafson, Craig Burdett, Bruce McKean; **anim:** Don Merkt, Will Vinton, Mat Wuerker. **Running time:** 90 minutes. **Released:** January 17, 1986.

### Voices

**Mark Twain:** James Whitmore; **Becky Thatcher:** Michelle Mariana; **Huck Finn:** Gary Krug; **Tom Sawyer:** Chris Ritchie; **Eve:** Carol Edelman; **Adam:** John Morrison

Aboard his interplanetary balloon, Mark Twain recalls for his stowaways (Huck Finn, Tom Sawyer and Becky Thatcher) his many tall-tale adventures on a trip to Halley's Comet to achieve his "destiny" in this feature-length Claymation fantasy.

**PN:** Claymation creator Will Vinton of California Raisins fame produced and directed this animated feature of the Twain legend.

## ◎ THE ADVENTURES OF MR. WONDERBIRD (1957)

A Les Gemeaux/Clarge Distributors Production released by Fine Arts Films Production. **p:** André Sarrut; **d:** Paul Grimault, Pierre Grimault; **scr:** Paul Grimault, Jacques Prévert (based on Hans Christian Andersen's "The Sheperdess and the Chimney Sweep"); **m/l:** Joseph Losmma; **anim:** Pierre Watrin, Jacques Vausseur; **U.S. dub dir:** Pierre Rouvre. **Running time:** 63 minutes. **Released:** February 1, 1957.

### Voices

(English version): **Mr. Wonderbird:** Peter Ustinov; **The Shepherdess:** Claire Bloom; **The Chimney Sweep:** Denholm Elliott; **The King:** Max Adrian; **The Blind Man:** Alex Clunes; **The Statue:** Cecil Trouncer; **Chief of Police:** Phillip Stainton; **The Old Beggar:** Harcourt Williams; **The Killer:** Joan Heal; **Commentator:** Frank Muir

A magical mockingbird helps a lowly chimney sweep and his beloved shepherdess escape from the kingdom of Upandownia, but not before obliterating the palace of a ruthless king who tries to come between them, in this French animated feature based on

Han Christian Andersen's *The Shepherdess and the Chimney-Sweep.*

**PN:** Producer Andre Sarraut and writer/director Paul Grimault, who catapulted to fame producing animated shorts and commercials in France through their studio, Les Gemeaux, started production of this feature-length project in 1946. After years of toiling on the film and after receiving pressure from their distributor, they released the film in France in 1953. Four years later, in 1957, the film was dubbed in English and made a limited run in theaters across the United States. Also known as *Wonderbird, Mr. Wonderbird, The Curious Mr. Wonderbird* and *The King and Mr. Bird,* the film's French title is *La Bergere et Le Ramoneur.*

## THE ADVENTURES OF PRINCE ACHMED (1926)

A UFA Production. **d:** Lotte Reiniger; **scr:** Lotte Reiniger (based on stories from *The Arabian Nights*); **m:** Wolfgang Zeller; **anim:** Walter Ruttmann, Berthold Bartosch, Walter Turck, Alexander Kardan, Lotte Reiniger. **Running time:** 65 minutes. **Released:** September 23, 1926.

A heroic prince, who is tricked by a wicked sorcerer into riding a wild magical flying horse that he learns to control, embarks on a series of adventures that include defeating an army of demons and winning the love of a beautiful princess.

**PN:** Based on stories from *The Arabian Nights,* female writer/director Lotte Reiniger of Germany, who produced experimental films for a studio she joined in 1918, launched production of this animated feature in 1923, 14 years before Walt Disney's first full-length feature, *Snow White and the Seven Dwarfs* (1937). The stop-motion animated film employed an early version of multiplane animation, giving the black-and-white production a three-dimensional look by using movable cardboard and mental cutouts positioned in front of illuminated sheets of glass, also creating a silhouette effect. After completing the film three years later, Reiniger was initially unable to find a German distributor interested in distributing a film advanced for that time. That year, the film's musical composer, Wolfgang Zeller, after receiving permission from Reiniger, premiered the film at a concert hall to rave reviews. It subsequently played at a theater in Paris for a full year and was distributed around the world, including the United States, where the film premiered in 1931 at Town Hall in New York.

## THE ADVENTURES OF ROCKY AND BULLWINKLE (2000)

A Capella International/KC Medien AG/Tribeca Productions Production released by Universal Pictures. **p:** Jane Rosenthal, Robert DeNiro; **d:** Des McAnuff; **scr:** Kenneth Lonergan (based on characters by Jay Ward); **anim prod:** Leslie Arvio, Allison P. Brown; **exec prod:** Tiffany Ward, David Nikkay; **m:** Mark Mothersbaugh; **anim superv:** David Andrews; **anim leads:** Jean Emberly, Julie Lenrie, Julie Nelson, Steve Nichols, Steve Rawlins, Scott Wirtz. **Songs:** "Be Ya Self," "Cryptik Souls Crew," "Side by Side," "Secret Agent Man," "America," "Blue Danube," "America the Beautiful," "Hooray for Hollywood," "Dreamer," "Bad Boys," "Rocky Show Theme," "Duelin' Banjoes," "Rocky the Flying Squirrel," "Hail, Hail, Pottsylvania" and "Through the Eyes of a Child." **Running time:** 88 minutes. **Released:** June 30, 2000.

### Live-Action Cast
**Nastasha Fatale:** Rene Russo; **Boris Badenov:** Jason Alexander; **Fearless Leader:** Robert De Niro; **FBI Director Cappy von Trapment:** Randy Quaid; **FBI Agent Karen Sympathy:** Piper Perabo; **Others:** Janeane Garofalo, John Goodman, Kenan Thompson,

Kel Mitchell, David Alan Grier, Carl Reiner, Jonathan Winters, Whoopi Goldberg, Billy Crystal.

### Voices
**Rocket J. "Rocky" Squirrel/Narrator's Mother/Animated Natasha Fatale:** June Foray; **Bullwinkle J. Moose/Narrator/Animated Boris Badenov/Animated Fearless Leader/Pottsylvanian TV Announcer:** Keith Scott; **Weasel:** Susan Berman

Television cartoon stars Rocky and Bullwinkle are lured out of retirement to help the FBI stop their notorious arch-rivals Boris and Natasha who have crossed over from the cartoon world to the real world, and their boss, Fearless Leader, who now heads a major media empire of his own, from successfully taking over the United States in this live-action/computer-animated feature, based on animate Jay Ward's famed characters.

## THE ADVENTURES OF THE AMERICAN RABBIT (1986)

A Toei Animation Production released by Clubhouse Pictures. **p:** Masaharu Etoh, Masahisa Saeki, John G. Marshall; **d:** Fred Wolf, Nobutaka Nishizawa; **w:** Norm Lenzer (based on the characters created by Stewart Moskowitz); **m/l:** Mark Volman, Howard Kayland, John Hoier. **Running time:** 85 minutes. **Released:** February 14, 1986.

### Voices
**Theo:** Bob Arbogast; **Tini Meeny:** Pat Fraley; **Rob/American Rabbit:** Barry Gordon; **Rodney:** Bob Holt; **Dip/Various Characters:** Lew Horn; **Bruno:** Norm Lenzer; **Vultor/Buzzard:** Ken Mars; **Toos Loose:** John Mayer; **Lady Pig:** Maitzi Morgan; **Ping Pong:** Lorenzo Music; **Bunny O'Hare:** Laurie O'Brien; **Mentor:** Hal Smith; **Mother:** Russi Taylor; **Fred Red:** Fred Wolf

Loosely based on Superman, mild-mannered, bespectacled Rob Rabbit obtains supernatural powers following a bizarre encounter with a mystical rabbit wizard, enabling him to restore peace and order as a superrabbit.

## AKIRA (1988)

An Akira Committee Production released by Streamline Pictures. **p:** Akira Committee; **d:** Mamoru Oshii, Katsuhiro Otomo; **scr:** Isao Hashimoto (based on the comic created by Katsuhiro Otomo); **m:** Shoji Yamashiro. **Songs:** "Kaneda," "Battle Against Clown," "Winds over the Neo-Tokyo," "Tetsuo," "Dolls' Polyphony," "Shohmyoh," "Mutation," "Exodus from the Underground Fortress," "Illusion" and "Requiem." **Running time:** 124 minutes. **Released:** December 25, 1989.

### Voices
**Kaneda:** Mitsuo Iwata; **Tetsuo:** Nozomu Sasaki; **Kei:** Mami Koyama; **Kai:** Takeshi Kusao; **The Colonel:** Tara Ishida

### Additional Voices
Jimmy Flanders, Barbara Larsen, Lewis Lemay, Drew Thomas

A secret military project endangers Neo-Tokyo when it turns a biker gang member into a rampaging psychopath with telekinetic powers that only a group of teenagers (from the motorcycle gang from which he came) can stop, in this apocalyptic story based on the popular Japanese comic book novel.

## ALADDIN (1992)

A Walt Disney Picture released by Buena Vista. **p & d:** John Musker, Ron Clements; **scr:** Ron Clements, John Musker, Ted Elliott, Terry Rossio; **m:** Alan Menken (with songs by Howard Ashman, Alan Menken, Tim Rice); **superv anim:** Randy Cartwright, Andreas Deja, Will Finn, Eric Goldberg, Mark Henn, Glen Keane,

Duncan Marjoribanks. **Songs:** "Arabian Nights," "Legend of the Lamp," "One Jump Ahead," "Street Urchins," "Friend Like Me," "To Be Free," "Prince Ali," "A Whole New World," "Jafar's Hour," "The Ends of the Earth," "The Kiss," "On a Dark Night," "Jasmine Runs Away," "Marketplace," "Cave of Wonders," "Aladdin's Word," "The Battle" and "Happy End in Agrabah." **Running time:** 90 minutes. **Released:** November 11, 1992.

*Voices*

**Aladdin:** Scott Weinger; **Genie:** Robin Williams; **Jasmine:** Linda Larkin; **Jafar:** Jonathan Freeman; **Abu:** Frank Welker; **Iago:** Gilbert Gottfried; **Sultan:** Douglas Seale; **Rajah:** Aaron Blaise; **Merchant (singing):** Bruce Adler; **Aladdin (singing):** Brad Kane; **Jasmine (singing):** Lea Salonga; **Gazem/Achmed:** T. Daniel Hofstedt; **Guard:** Chris Wahl; **Beggar/Snake Jafar:** Kathy Zielinski

*Additional Voices*

Jack Angel, Corey Burton, Philip L. Clarke, Jim Cummings, Jennifer Darling, Debi Derryberry, Bruce Gooch, Jerry Houser, Vera Lockwood, Sherry Lyn, Mickie McGowan, Patrick Pinney, Philip Proctor

Accompanied by his faithful monkey friend Abu, street-urchin Aladdin, with the aid of a mysterious magic lamp with a powerful Genie inside (played for laughs by Robin Williams) who will grant him three wishes, goes up against the evil Jafar, who plots to rule the city of Agrabah. Aladdin falls in love with Princess Jasmine in the process and saves the city from Jafar's ruthless attempt to rule.

**PN:** *Aladdin* marked a departure from tradition for Disney animated features. Unlike past efforts, this film was an irreverent, high-stakes gamble featuring outrageous one-liners, sight gags and pop references. Comedian Robin Williams, known for his free-form shtick, improvised freely during the recording of dialogue for the film. This was a challenge for the directors: The first scene he recorded for the film he did 25 times, in 25 different ways, to the point that scenes originally meant to last 30 seconds suddenly ended up 10 minutes long.) Williams reportedly mimicked 55 different personalities for the film, with many more ending up on the cutting room floor, including imitations of President Bush and well-known sex therapist Dr. Ruth Westheimer. The work paid off as the film earned a record $217 million in revenue, at one time making it the highest-grossing animated feature film ever. The film was nominated for five Academy Awards, winning the award for best original score and best song (for the song: "A Whole New World"). Robin Williams was honored with a special Golden Globe award for his vocal work on the film. Two made-for-video sequels were produced following the success of the animated feature: *The Return of Jafar* (1993) and *Aladdin and the King of Thieves* (1996). Robin Williams reprised his role of the Genie only for the latter.

## ⊚ ALADDIN AND HIS MAGIC LAMP (1975)

A Les Films Jean Image Production released by Paramount Pictures. **p:** Les Films Jean Image; **d:** Jean Image; **scr:** Jean Image; **anim:** Denis Boutin, Guy Lehideux, Marcel Breuil, Ch. El J. Clairfeuille, J.P. Nantis, Alberto Ruiz, J.F. Sornin, Sante Vilani, Jose Xavier; **m:** Fred Freed; **songs:** Christian Sarrel. **Running time:** 70 minutes. **Released:** July 1, 1975.

*Voices*

(French version) George Atlas, Lucie Dolene, Richard Francoeur, Michel Gudin, Paul Guez, Claire Guibert, Rene Hieronimus, Jean-Pierre Leroux, Lita Recio

A dastardly magician successfully steals a magic lamp from a young boy (Aladdin) who has used its wish-making powers to help his mother and to woo a beautiful princess, whom the magician also kidnaps, but not before he is outsmarted and banished for good by the lamp's original owner.

**PN:** Produced over a grueling seven months beginning in April 1969 by French animator Jean Image, this animated feature was released in France in 1970 and five years later by Paramount Pictures as a Saturday matinee feature film attraction in theaters in the United States.

## ⊚ ALAKAZAM THE GREAT (1961)

A Toei Animation Production released by American International Pictures. **p:** Lou Rusoff (U.S.), Hiroshi Okawa (Japan); **d:** Lee Kresel (U.S.), Teiji Yabushita, Osamu Tezuka, Daisaku Shirakawa (Japan); **scr:** Lou Rusoff, Lee Kresel (U.S.), Keinosuke Uekusa (Japan); **m:** Les Baxter. **Songs:** "Ali the Great," "Bluebird in the Cherry Tree," "Under the Waterfall" and "Aliki-Aliko-Alakazam." **Running time:** 84 minutes. **Released:** July 26, 1961.

*Voices*

**Alakazam:** Frankie Avalon; **De De:** Dodie Stevens; **Sir Quigley Broken-Bottom:** Jonathan Winters; **Lulipop:** Arnold Stang; **Narrator:** Sterling Holloway

Alakazam, a shy and modest monkey, is chosen by his peers to be the monarch of all animals on earth. When the power goes to his head, King Amo, ruler of Majutsoland, the celestial island where all retired magicians reside, imprisons Alakazam in a cave to teach him a lesson. He is later released from confinement with the stipulation that he go about the countryside performing good deeds.

**PN:** Released in Japan in 1960 in ToeiScope as *Saiyu-ki*, the film was reedited and retitled for American release, running four minutes shorter than the original production. Also known as *The Enchanted Monkey*.

## ⊚ ALIBABA (2002)

A Pentamedia Graphics/Ivory Pictures release. **p:** NS Riyaz Babu, M. Alagarsamy, M. Venkata Krishnan; **d:** Usha Ganesarajan; **m:** Pravin Mani. **Running time:** 85 minutes. **Released:** November 22, 2002.

*Voices*

Robert Andrew, Ravi Khajuria, Sadie LeBlanc, Chris Nolan, Manny Rush

After uncovering a cave of stolen gold with the Forty Thieves, Ali Baba constructs a castle while distributing the newfound wealth to others and warding off a team of ruthless thieves who plot to steal the gold.

**PN:** Also known as *Ali Baba and the Forty Thieves*, India's Pentamedia Graphics, the company behind *Sinbad: Beyond the Veil of Mists*, the world's first 100 percent motion-capture CGI feature film, and Pentamedia Graphics, which also worked on Warner Bros.' animated version of *The King and I*, produced this full-length feature using computer-generated imagery. The film premiered in Los Angeles for Academy Award consideration in 2002.

## ⊚ ALICE IN WONDERLAND (1951)

A Walt Disney Production released by RKO Radio Pictures. **p:** Walt Disney; **prod superv:** Ben Sharpsteen; **d:** Clyde Geronimi, Hamilton Luske, Wilfred Jackson; **anim dir:** Milt Kahl, Ward Kimball, Frank Thomas, Eric Larson, John Lounsbery, Ollie Johnston, Wolfgang Reitherman, Marc Davis, Les Clark, Norman Ferguson; **st:** Winston Hibler, Bill Peet, Joe Rinaldi, Bill Cottrell, Joe Grant, Del Connell, Ted Sears, Erdman Penner, Milt Banta, Dick Kelsey, Dick Huemer, Tom Oreb, John Walbridge; **m/sc:** Oliver

Wallace. **Songs:** "Very Good Advice," "In a World of My Own," "All in a Golden Afternoon," "Alice in Wonderland," "The Walrus and the Carpenter," "The Caucus Race," "I'm Late," "Painting the Roses Red," "March of the Cards," "Twas Brillig," "The Unbirthday Song," "We'll Smoke the Blighter Out," "Old Father William" and "A E I O U." **Running time:** 75 minutes. **Released:** July 28, 1951.

*Voices*

**Alice:** Kathryn Beaumont; **Mad Hatter:** Ed Wynn; **Caterpillar:** Richard Haydn; **Cheshire Cat:** Sterling Holloway; **March Hare:** Jerry Colonna; **Queen of Hearts:** Verna Felton; **Walrus/Carpenter/Tweedledee and Tweedledum:** J. Pat O'Malley; **White Rabbit/Dodo:** Bill Thompson; **Alice's Sister:** Heather Angel; **Door Knob:** Joseph Kearns; **Bill Card Painter:** Larry Grey; **Nesting Mother Bird:** Queenie Leonard; **King of Hearts:** Dink Trout; **The Rose:** Doris Lloyd; **Dormouse:** James Macdonald; **Card Painters:** The Mello Men; **Flamingoes:** Pinto Colvig; **Card Painter:** Ken Beaumont

Based on Lewis Carroll's two books, *Alice in Wonderland* and *Through the Looking Glass*, this classic Disney feature traces young Alice's dream of falling through space and time into a magical land of make-believe where she meets everything from the disappearing Cheshire Cat to the White Rabbit ("I'm late, I'm late for a very important date!").

### ⊚ ALICE OF WONDERLAND IN PARIS (1966)

A Rembrandt Films Production released by Childhood Productions. **p:** William L. Snyder; **d:** Gene Deitch; **m/l:** Victor Little, Paul Alter. **Running time:** 52 minutes. **Released:** February 5, 1966.

*Voices*

**Alice:** Norma McMillan; **Francios/The King:** Allen Swift; **Anatole:** Carl Reiner; **Frowning Prince:** Howard Morris; **Minstrel/Royal Mathematician:** Lionel Wilson; **Princess Lenore:** Trinka Snyder; **Queen:** Luce Ennis

After eating some magic cheese to reduce her to the size of a mouse, young Alice gets her wish to go to Paris and bicycles there with François the mouse and takes a journey through Storybook-land, reliving many classic children's tales—"Anatole," "The Frowning Prince," "Many Moons" and "Madeline and the Bad Hat"—in this full-length animated adaptation of Lewis Carroll's *Through the Looking Glass* and other well-known children's stories.

**PN:** Producer William Snyder and three-time Academy Award-nominated director/animator Gene Deitch (who produced a slate of cartoons in the 1960s, including Paramount's "Nudnik," later MGM Tom and Jerry theatrical cartoon shorts, and King Features' Krazy Kat and Popeye cartoons for television, for their company Rembrandt Films in Prague, Czechoslovakia) produced and directed this full-length feature, also known as *Alice in a New Wonderland*.

### ⊚ ALL DOGS GO TO HEAVEN (1989)

A Sullivan Bluth Studios Ireland, Ltd. Production in association with Goldcrest Films released by United Artists. **p:** Don Bluth, Gary Goldman, John Pomeroy; **d:** Don Bluth; **scr:** Davis Weiss; **st:** Don Bluth, Ken Cromar, Gary Goldman, Larry Leker, Linda Miller, Monica Parker, John Pomeroy, Guy Schulman, David Steinberg, David N. Weiss; **m:** Ralph Burns; **anim dir:** John Pomeroy, Linda Miller, Ralph Zondag, Dick Zondag, Lorna Pomeroy-Cook, Jeff Etter, Ken Duncan. **Songs:** "You Can't Keep a Good

*Charlie (voiced by Burt Reynolds) leads an all-canine conga line in* All Dogs Go to Heaven *(1989)*, a tale of rascals, puppies and true love. © Goldcrest & Sullivan Bluth, Ltd.

Dog Down," "Let Me Be Surprised," "What's Mine Is Yours," "Let's Make Music Together," "Soon You'll Come Home" and "Hallelujah." **Running time:** 85 minutes. **Released:** November 17, 1989.

*Voices*

**Charlie B. Barkin:** Burt Reynolds; **Itchy:** Dom DeLuise; **Dog Caster:** Daryl Gilley; **Vera:** Candy Devine; **Killer:** Charles Nelson Reilly; **Carface:** Vic Tayback; **Whippet Angel:** Melba Moore; **Anne-Marie:** Judith Barsi; **Harold:** Rob Fuller; **Kate:** Earleen Carey; **Stella Dallas:** Anna Manahan; **Sir Reginald:** Nigel Pegram; **Flo:** Loni Anderson; **King Gator:** Ken Page; **Terrier:** Godfrey Quigley; **Mastiff:** Jay Stevens; **Puppy:** Cyndi Cozzo; **Gambler Dog:** Thomas Durkin; **Puppy:** Kelly Briley; **Fat Pup:** Dana Rifkin; **The Don Bluth Players:** John Carr, John Eddings, Jeff Etter, Dan Hofstedt, Dan Kuenster, Dan Molina, Mark Swan, Taylor Swanson, David Weiss, Dick Zondag.

Set in the canine world of New Orleans, c. 1939, this fun-filled, heartwarming story traces the exploit of Charlie B. Barkin, a German shepherd with a con man's charm, who gets a reprieve (he is sent back from heaven to perform some acts of goodness before he will be allowed in) and befriends a little orphan girl, Anne-Marie, kidnapped by his scurvy old gang.

**PN:** More than 1.5 million individual drawings were needed to produce this animated adventure. The film features a musical score by Academy Award-winning composer Ralph Burns (*Cabaret, All That Jazz*) and original songs by Charles Strouse (*Annie*). The film marked the first production for the Sullivan Bluth Studios, relocated from Hollywood to Dublin, Ireland.

### ⊚ ALL DOGS GO TO HEAVEN 2 (1996)

A Metro-Goldwyn-Mayer Production released by Metro-Goldwyn-Mayer/United Artists. **p:** Jonathan Dern, Paul Sabella; **d:** Larry Leker, Paul Sabella; **scr:** Arnie Olsen, Kelly Ward; **m:** Mark Watters. **Songs:** "It's Too Heavenly Here," "Count Me Out," "My Afghan Hairless," "It Feels So Good to Be Bad," "On Easy Street" and "I Will Always Be with You." **Running time:** 82 minutes. **Released:** March 29, 1996.

*Voices*

**Charlie B. Barkin:** Charlie Sheen; **Sasha:** Sheena Easton; **Carface:** Ernest Borgnine; **Itchy:** Dom DeLuise; **Red:** George Hearn; **Anabelle:** Bebe Neuwirth; **David:** Adam Wylie; **Labrador:** Wallace Shawn

Mischievous mutt Charlie B. Barkin is asked to retrieve Gabriel's horn when it is stolen from heaven and returns to earth, joined by sidekick Itchy, only to get sidetracked into trouble in this sequel to 1989's *All Dogs Go to Heaven.*

**PN:** Don Bluth, who produced and directed the original, was not involved in producing the sequel, which fared poorly at the box office, grossing $8.62 million in ticket sales. Actor Charlie Sheen took over the role of Charlie B. Barkin, which was played by Burt Reynolds in the original movie.

## ALLEGRO NON TROPPO (1977)

A Bruno Bozetto Film Production released by Specialty Films. **p & d:** Bruno Bozetto; **scr:** Guido Manuli, Maurizo Nichetti, Bruno Bozetto; **m:** Debussy, Dvorak, Ravel, Sibelius, Vivaldi, Stravinsky. **Running time:** 75 minutes. **Released:** July 27, 1977.

### Cast (live action)

Maurizo Nichetti, Nestor Garay, Maurizio Micheli, Maria Luisa Giovannini

A parody of Walt Disney's famed *Fantasia* featuring six different animated stories fitted to classical music conducted by such noted artists as Herbert von Karajan, Hans Stadlmair and Lorin Maazel. The film intersperses live action between each of the symphonic pieces, which feature English subtitles and animation. Musical selections are: "Prelude of a Faun" by Debussy, "Slavonic Dance No. 7" by Dvorak, "Bolero" by Ravel, "Valse Triste" by Sibelius, "Concerto in C Minor" by Vivaldi and "The Firebird" by Stravinsky.

## AMERICAN POP (1981)

A Ralph Bakshi Film released by Columbia Pictures. **p:** Martin Ransohoff; **d:** Ralph Bakshi; **scr:** Ronnie Kern; **m:** Lee Holdridge. **Songs:** "A Hard Rain's a Gonna Fall" (by Bob Dylan), "American Pop Overture" (arranged by Lee Holdridge), "Anything Goes," "As Time Goes By," "Bill," "Blue Suede Shoes," "Body & Soul," "California Dreamin'," "Cantaloupe Island," "Charleston," "Crazy on You," "Devil with the Blue Dress On," "Don't Think Twice It's Allright," "Free Bird" (performed by Lynrd Skynrd), "Give My Regards to Broadway," "Hell Is for Children," "I Don't Care," "I Got Rhythm," "I'm Waiting for the Man," "Look for the Silver Lining," "Maple Leaf Rag," "Moanin'" (performed by Al Blakey), "Mona Lisa," "Nancy (with the Laughing Face)," "Night Moves," "Onward Christian Soldiers," "Over There," "Palm Leaf Rag," "People Are Strange," "Pretty Vacant," "Purple Haze," "Say Si Si," "Sing, Sing, Sing," "Slaughter on Tenth Avenue," "Smiles," "Somebody Loves Me," "Somebody to Love," "Summertime," "Sweet Georgia Brown," "Take Give" (performed by Dave Brubeck Quartet), "This Train," "Turn Me Loose" (performed by Fabian), "Up, Up and Away," "When the Saints Go Marching In" and "You Send Me." **Running time:** 97 minutes. **Released:** February 13, 1981.

### Voices

**Izzy:** Gene Borkan; **Prostitute:** Beatrice Colen; **Crisco:** Frank DeKova; **Nicky Palumbo:** Ben Frommer; **Louie:** Jerry Holland; **Eva Tanguay:** Roz Kelly; **Nancy:** Amy Levitt; **Zalmie:** Jeffrey Lippu; **Poet:** Richard Moll; **Bella:** Lisa Jane Perksy; **Hannele:** Elsa Raven; **Theatre Owner:** Vincent Schiarelli; **Benny:** Richard Singer; **Frankie:** Marya Small; **Leo:** Leonard Stone; **Little Pete:** Eric Taslitz; **Tony:** Ron Thompson; **The Blonde:** Lynda Wiesmeier; **Other:** Hilary Beane

Beginning in 19th-century Russia, this animated musical odyssey follows the adventures of a troubled but talented family and chronicles popular American music from the turn of the century—from the pre-jazz age through soul, '50s rock, drug-laden psychadelia, punk and finally new wave of the early 1980s.

## AN AMERICAN TAIL (1986)

An Amblin Entertainment Production released by Universal Pictures. **p:** Don Bluth, John Pomeroy, Gary Goldman; **d:** Don Bluth; **w:** Judy Freudberg, Tony Geiss (based on the story by David Kirschner, Judy Freudberg, Tony Geiss); **m:** James Horner; **anim dir:** John Pomeroy, Dan Kuenster, Linda Miller. **Songs:** "There Are No Cats in America," "Never Say Never," "Somewhere Out There," "A Duo" and "Stars and Stripes Forever." **Running time:** 74 minutes. **Released:** November 21, 1986.

### Voices

**Mama Mousekewitz:** Eric Yohn; **Papa Mousekewitz:** Nehemiah Persoff; **Tanya Mousekewitz:** Amy Green; **Fievel Mousekewitz:** Phillip Glasser; **Henri:** Christopher Plummer; **Warren T. Rat:** John Finnegan; **Digit:** Will Ryan; **Moe:** Hal Smith; **Tony Toponi:** Pat Musick; **Bridget:** Cathianne Blore; **Honest John:** Neil Ross; **Gussie Mausheimer:** Madeline Kahn; **Tiger:** Dom DeLuise

When a clan of Jewish mice are forced to emigrate, little Fievel Mousekewitz is separated from his family, who is en route to New York. The cherubic mouse makes it to the New Land via a glass bottle and encounters many adventures—including his share of cats—until he is successfully reunited with his family.

**PN:** This was Steven Spielberg's first animated motion picture. It grossed $47 million and earned the honor of being the highest-grossing animated feature of that time. The song "Somewhere Out There" received a 1986 Oscar nomination for best song. A year later the home video edition was released and sold a whopping 1.3 million units.

## AN AMERICAN TAIL: FIEVEL GOES WEST (1991)

A Steven Spielberg and Amblin Entertainment Production released by Universal Pictures. **d:** Phil Nebblink, Simon Wells; **p:** Steven Spielberg, Robert Watts; **exec prod:** Franik Marshall, Kathleen Kennedy, David Kirschner; **st:** Charles Swenson; **scr:** Flint Dille; **m:** James Horner, Will Jennings; **superv anim:** Nancy Beiman, Bibo Begeron, Ulrich W. Meyer, Christoph Serrand, Robert Stevenhagen. **Songs:** "Dreams to Dream," "American Tail Overture," "Cat Rumble," "Headin' Out West," "Way Out West," "Green River/Trek Through the Desert," "Building a New Town," "Sacred Mountain," "Reminiscing," "Girl You Left Behind," "In Training," "Shoot-Out" and "New Land." **Running time:** 75 minutes. **Released:** November 22, 1991.

### Voices

**Fievel Mousekewitz:** Phillip Glasser; **Mama:** Erica Yohn, **Papa:** Nehemiah Persoff; **Tanya:** Cath Cavadini; **Cat R. Waul:** John Cleese; **Tiger, Fievel's vegetarian cat friend:** Dom DeLuise; **Wylie Burp, over-the-hill marshall:** James Stewart; **Miss Kitty:** Amy Irving; **T.R. Chula:** Jon Lovitz

Two years after arriving in New York City from Russia, Fievel and his family discover the streets in America are "not paved with cheese" and decide to head West to seek a new promised land in this sequel to the 1986 original.

**PN:** A follow-up to the 1986 smash hit *An American Tail*, the Universal/Steven Spielberg animated movie premiered on Thanksgiving weekend opposite Disney's *Beauty and the Beast.* Don Bluth, who directed the highly successful *An American Tail*, was replaced by Phil Nibbelink and Simon Wells to direct the sequel, and animation was done by a new group of artists. The song "Dreams to Dream" received a Golden Globe nomination for best original song.

## ⊚ ANASTASIA (1997)

A Fox Family/20th Century Fox/Fox Animation Studios Production released by 20th Century Fox. **p & d:** Don Bluth, Gary Goldman; **exec prod:** Maureen Donley; **scr:** Susan Gauthier, Bruce Graham, Bob Tzudiker, Noni White; **m:** David Newman (with songs by Stephen Flaherty); **dir anim:** Sandro Cleuzo, John Hill, Fernando Moro, Paul Newberry, Troy Saliba, Len Simon. **Songs:** "Once Upon a December," "A Rumor in St. Petersburg," "Journey to the Past," "In the Dark of the Night," "Learn to Do It," "Paris Holds the Key (to Your Heart)" and "At the Beginning." **Running time:** 94 minutes. **Released:** November 21, 1997.

### Voices

**Anastasia:** Meg Ryan; **Dimitri:** John Cusack; **Vladimir:** Kelsey Grammer; **Rasputin:** Christopher Lloyd; **Bartok:** Hank Azaria; **Sophie:** Bernadette Peters; **Young Anastasia:** Kirsten Dunst; **Dowager Empress Marie:** Angela Lansbury; **Anastasia (singing):** Liz Calloway; **Young Anastasia (singing):** Lacey Chabert; **Rasputin (singing):** Jim Cummings; **Dimitri (singing):** Jonathan Dokuchitz; **Czar Nicholas/Servant/Revolutionary Soldier/Ticket Agent:** Rick Jones; **Phlegmenkoff/Old Woman:** Andrea Martin; **Young Dimitri:** Glenn Walker Harris Jr.; **Actress:** Debra Mooney; **Travelling Man/Major Domo:** Arthur Malet; **Anastasia Impostor:** Charity James

An orphaned peasant girl who was a Russian princess finds true love in this modern-day romantic fairy tale. This classically animated musical explores what might have happened to the little girl long rumored to have survived the massacre of Russia's royal Romanovs.

**PN:** The first full-length animated feature ever produced by 20th Century Fox—and first by the studio's Fox Animation Studios, based in Phoenix, Arizona—*Anastasia* was produced and directed by legendary animator Don Bluth and partner Gary Goldman. (Bluth is Fox Animation's studio head.) Costing an estimated $53 million to produce, the animated musical opened on 2,478 movie screens nationwide, grossing $14.242 million its first weekend and more than $48.36 million (through December 1997).

## ⊚ ANIMAL FARM (1955)

A Halas and Batchelor Films Production released by DCA (Distributors Corporation of America). **p & d:** John Halas and Joy Batchelor; **scr:** John Halas, Joy Batchelor, Joseph Bryan III, Borden mace, Philip Stapp, Lothar Wolff (based on the novel, *Animal Farm*, by George Orwell"); **m:** Matyas Seiber; **anim dir:** John F. Reed; **anim:** Ralph Ayres, Arthur Humberstone, Frank Moysey, Edric Radage, Harold Whitaker. **Running time:** 75 minutes. **Released:** January 5, 1955.

### Voices

**Napoleon Snowball/Old Major/Squealer/Sheep/Jones/All Animal Sounds:** Maurice Denham; **Narrator:** Gordon Heath

When the animals of Farmer Jones's Manor Farm are treated unfairly, they launch a revolutionary coup to take over the farm but find things are far worse after the pigs establish a dictatorship in this animated political satire of George Orwell's classic novel.

**PN:** Produced, directed and written by Britain's award-winning husband-and-wife team John Halas and Joy Batchelor, this Disney-esque film became Britain's first commercially produced full-length animated feature.

## ⊚ THE ANT BULLY (2006)

A Playtone Productions/DNA Productions Production released by Warner Bros. **p:** Tom Hanks, Gary Goetzman, John A. Davis; **exec prod:** Keith Alcorn, William Fay, Scott Mednick, Thomas Tull; **d:** John A. Davis; **scr:** John A. Davis (based on a book by John Nickle, *The Ant Bully*); **m:** John Debney; **anim superv:** Rena Archer. **Songs:** "The Ants Go Marching," "Sugar Sugar," "I Got Ants in My Pants, Part 1, " "I Got Stung," "Take a Giant Step," "Wooly Bully," "Antmusic," "Cruel to Be Kind," "Go Where You Wanna Go," "Mr. Big Stuff," "Let's Work Together" and "Grazing in the Grass." **Running time:** 82 minutes. **Released:** July 28, 2006.

### Voices

**Hova:** Julia Roberts; **Zoc:** Nicolas Cage; **Queen Ant:** Meryl Streep; **Stan Beals:** Paul Giamatti; **Lucas Nickle:** Zach Tyler; **Kreela:** Regina King; **Fugax:** Bruce Campbell; **Mommo:** Lily Tomlin; **Fred Nickle:** Larry Miller; **Doreen Nickle:** Cheri Oteri; **Tiffany Nickle:** Allison Mack; **Blue Teammate:** Austin Majors; **Head of Council:** Ricardo Mountalban; **Steve:** Myles Jeffrey; **Nicky:** Jake T. Austin; **Beetle:** Rob Paulsen; **Glow Worm/Wasp Survivor:** S. Scott Bullock; **Fly:** Mark DeCarlo; **Spindle/Frog/Caterpillar:** Frank Welker; **Sleeping Ant #1/Head Lice #1/Brett:** Paul Greenberg; **Sleeper Ant:** David Kaye; **Slacker Ant:** Alfred Jackson; **Albert:** Denzel Whitaker; **Shigeko:** Casey Masamitsu; **Fernando:** Bryan Fernando Fabian; **Mullet Boy:** Creagen Dow; **Ant #18/Pupa/Soldier Ant #3:** Keith Alcorn; **Ant #19:** John A. Davis; **Drone Ant/Ant #2/Ant #5:** Tom Kenny; **Mother Ant:** Sarah Mensinga; **Ant #1/Ant #7:** Nika Futterman; **Ant #3:** Scott Holst; **Ant #4:** Susan Silo; **Ant #5:** Paul Rugg; **Ant #8:** Larry Cedar; **Ant #9:** Nicole Sullivan; **Nurse Ant #3:** Candi Milo; **Billo:** Nissa Alcorn; **Ant Council #1:** Pat Fraley; **Blue Teammate #1:** Tyler James Williams; **Blue Teammate #4:** Jaishon Fisher; **Blue Teammate #5:** Aaron Michael Drozin; **Blue Teammate #6:** Max Burkholder; **Red Teammate #3:** Sam Green; **Red Teammate #4:** Colin Ford; **Red Teammate #5:** Kendall Saunders; **Red Teammate #6:** Shane Baumel; **Wasp #1/#5:** Neil Ross; **Wasp #2:** Bob Joles; **Wasp #3:** Wally Wingert; **Wasp #4:** Leon Morenzie; **Wasp #6:** Jonathan Teague Cook; **Guard Ant:** Ken Mitchroney; **Soldier Ant #1:** Sean Donnellan; **Old Council Ant:** Tress MacNeille; **Wasp Leader:** Richard Green; **Soldier Ant:** Don Frye; **Hova's Wasp:** Clive Robertson; **Head Nurse:** Vernee Watson-Johnson; **Kid:** Benjamin Bryan; **Ant:** Jordan Orr; **Football Kid:** Paul Price; **Blonde Boy:** Zack Shada; **Additional Voices:** Jessie Flower

After moving to a new town, and without friends, a 10-year-old boy (Lucas), who is repeatedly tormented by a neighborhood bully, takes out his frustration on a nearby anthill by flooding an ant colony with his water gun. The ants retaliate, using a magic potion that shrinks the boy down to their size and sentence him to live like them in their underground world, where he learns many valuable lessons about friendship while discovering the courage to stand up for himself.

**PN:** Featuring an all-star voice cast of Nicolas Cage, Julia Roberts, Meryl Streep and Lily Tomlin, Academy Award–winning actor Tom Hanks coproduced this CGI-animated feature through his company, Playtone Productions, with John Davis's (creator of *Jimmy Neutron: Boy Genius*) DNA Productions. Costing around $50 million to produce, the film opened in traditional movie houses throughout the United States, besides playing in 3-D in IMAX theaters in 50 cities in the United States and Canada. Despite its all-star cast, stylized visuals and surreal setting, the film made more than $28 million in revenue in the United States and $26 million abroad.

## ⊚ ANTZ (1998)

A DreamWorks SKG and Pacific Data Images (PDI) Production released by DreamWorks SKG. **p:** Brad Lewis, Aron Warner, Patty

Wooton; **d:** Eric Darnell, Tim Johnson; **dir anim:** Sean Curran; **scr:** Todd Alcott, Chris Weitz, Paul Weitz; **m:** Harry Gregson-Williams, John Powell, Gavin Greenaway, Steve Jablonsky, Geoff Zanelli; **superv anim:** Rex Gridnon, Raman Huii; **dir anim:** Denis Couchon, Sean Curran, Donnachada Daly. **Songs:** "I Can See Clearly Now," "High Hopes," "Almost Being in Love," "Give Peace a Chance" and "Guantanamera." **Running time:** 83 minutes. **Released:** October 2, 1998.

*Voices*

**Z:** Woody Allen; **Chip:** Dan Aykroyd; **Queen:** Anne Bancroft; **Muffy:** Jane Curtin; **Barbatus:** Danny Glover; **General Mandible:** Gene Hackman; **Azteca:** Jennifer Lopez; **Grebs/Drunk Scout/ Other Voices:** John Mahoney; **Psychologist:** Paul Mazursky; **Foreman:** Grant Shaud; **Weaver:** Sylvester Stallone; **Princess Bala:** Sharon Stone; **Colonel Cutter:** Christopher Walken; **Bartender/Other Voices:** Jerry Sroka

*Additional Voices*

Jim Cummings, April Winchell

A neurotic, lowly worker-ant, Z (voiced by Woody Allen), becomes a hero after he discovers his individuality and saves the colony from the totalitarian actions of the evil General Mandible, who plans to destroy the colony's entire worker population, while falling in love with the ant, Princess Bala (voiced by Sharon Stone), in the process.

**PN:** This first animated feature from DreamWorks SKG in association with Pacific Data Images, featuring the voice of comedian Woody Allen as Z, grossed more than $91 million in the United States after its theatrical release in 1998. It remains Allen's most successful film to date.

## ◉ APPLESEED (2005)

A Digital Frontier/Geneon Entertainment (USA) Inc./Mainichi Broadcasting/Micott & Basara/TBS/Toho/TYO/Yamato Production released by Geneon Entertainment Inc. **p:** Hidenori Ueki, Naoko Watanabe, SORI; **d:** Shinji Aramaki; **scr:** Haruka Hana, Tsutomu Kamishiro (based on the comic by Shirow Masamune); **m:** Paul Oakenfold, T. Raumschmiere, Ryuichi Sakamoto. **Running time:** 103 minutes. **Released:** January 14, 2005.

*Voices*

(English version) Jack Aubree; William Bassett; Michael Forest; William Knight; Steve Kramer; Michael McConnohie; Mary Elizabeth McGlynn; Liam O'Brien; Kristy Pape; Bob Papenbrook; Jamieson Price; Mike Reynolds; Cindy Robinson; Lee Rush; Deborah Sale Butler; Michael Sorich; Doug Stone; Kim Strauss; Amanda Winn Lee; Dave Wittenberg.

The future of humanity rests on the shoulders of a female survivor (Deunan Knute) of a global war who lives in what appears to be the perfect city of Utopia, where artificial humans called Bioroids war to overtake mankind and her past holds the key to resolving the war.

## ◉ ARABIAN KNIGHT (1995)

An Allied Filmmakers/Majestic Film Production released by Miramax Films. **p:** Imogene Sutton, Richard Williams; **d:** Richard Williams; **st:** Margaret French; **scr:** Richard Williams, Margaret French; **m/sc:** Robert Folk. **Songs:** "Am I Feeling Love?" "Tack and Thief," "Polo Game," "She Is More," "The Courtroom," "The Brigands," "Pole Vault," "Club Sahara," "So Incredible," "Bom, Bom, Bom Beem, Bom," "Thief Gets the Ball," "One Eyes Advance," "Witch Riddle" and "Thief After the Balls." **Running time:** 72 minutes. **Released:** August 25, 1995.

*Voices*

**Tack, the Cobbler:** Matthew Broderick; **Princess Yum Yum:** Jennifer Beals; **The Thief:** Jonathan Winters; **King Nod:** Clive Revill; **Zigzag:** Vincent Price; **Phido:** Eric Bogosian; **Nurse/Good Witch:** Toni Collette; **One-Eye:** Kevin Dorsey; **Princess Yum Yum (singing):** Bobbi Page

*Additional Voices*

Donald Pleasance

A timid shoemaker (Tack) recovers the three enchanted Golden Balls that protect the ancient city of Baghdad after they were stolen by a wicked wizard, saving the beloved city from destruction.

**PN:** Originally titled *The Thief and the Cobbler.* Oscar-winning animator Richard Williams, of *Who Framed Roger Rabbit* fame, ran into financial trouble trying to get this film finished and released. In May of 1992 the film was over budget, prompting a Los Angeles completion bond firm to take control of the project. That company fired Williams and his London-based crew and hired TV producer Fred Calvert to finish the production. Because of his firing, Williams ceased operation of his London-based Richard Williams Animation and laid off about 30 animators plus other personnel. Warner Bros. originally intended to release the movie at Christmas. (The finished film was released instead by Miramax.) Williams had begun production in 1965. When he lost control of the project, only 70 minutes of the full-length feature had been completed, with 17 minutes of footage left to be animated. Some of the finest American animators came out of retirement to work on the film, including Grim Natwick, the creator of Betty Boop; Art Babbit, who animated the dancing mushroom and thistles in *Fantasia,* and two of the top animators of Warner Bros. cartoons: Ken Harris (who animated many of the Road Runner cartoons) and Emery Hawkins. It was the last animation done by all four, each of whom died before the film was completed. The finished film included animation, dialogue and music added after Williams departed the project. In 1995 Miramax Films released Williams's long-awaited masterpiece to mixed reviews and an even less enthusiastic moviegoing public. Final ticket sales totaled $500,000. The home video release was issued under the film's original title.

## ◉ THE ARISTOCATS (1970)

A Walt Disney Production released by Buena Vista Pictures. **p:** Wolfgang Reitherman, Winston Hibler; **d:** Wolfgang Reitherman; **st:** Larry Clemmons, Vance Gerry, Frank Thomas, Julius Svendsen, Ken Anderson, Eric Cleworth, Ralph Wright (based on a story by Tom McGowan and Tom Rowe); **m:** George Bruns; **s:** Richard M. Sherman, Robert B. Sherman; **dir anim:** Milt Kahl, Frank Thomas, Ollie Johnston, John Lounsbery. **Songs:** "The Aristocats," "Scales and Arpeggios," "She Never Felt Alone" and "Thomas O'Malley Cat." **Running time:** 78 minutes. **Released:** December 24, 1970.

*Voices*

**Thomas O'Malley:** Phil Harris; **Duchess:** Eva Gabor; **Roquefort:** Sterling Holloway; **Scat Cat:** Scatman Crothers; **Chinese Cat:** Paul Winchell; **English Cat:** Lord Tim Hudson; **Italian Cat:** Vito Scotti; **Russian Cat:** Thurl Ravenscroft; **Berlioz:** Dean Clark; **Marie:** Liz English; **Toulouse:** Gary Dubin; **Frou-Frou:** Nancy Kulp; **Georges Hautecourt:** Charles Lane; **Madame Adelaide Bonafamille:** Hermione Baddeley; **Edgar:** Roddy Maude-Roxby; **Uncle Waldo:** Bill Thompson; **Lafayette:** George Lindsey; **Napoleon:** Pat Buttram; **Abigail Gabble:** Monica Evans; **Amelia Gabble:** Carole Shelley; **French Milkman:** Pete Renoudet

Duchess, a cat, and her three well-bred kittens, Berlioz, Toulouse and Marie, try to find their way back to Paris after a jealous butler (Edgar) angrily abandons them in the countryside.

## ⊚ ATLANTIS: THE LOST EMPIRE (2001)

A Walt Disney Pictures Production released by Buena Vista Pictures. **p:** Don Hahn; **d:** Kirk Wise and Gary Trousdale; **st:** Kirk Wise, Gary Trousdale, Tab Murphy, Bryce Zabel, Jackie Zaebl (based on *Atlantis Story* by Plato); **scr:** Tab Murphy; **m:** James Newton Howard; **superv anim:** John Pomeroy, Mike Surrey, Randy Haycock, Russ Emonds, Ron Husband, Yoshimichi Tamura, Anne Marie Bardwell, Dave Pruiksma, Shawn Keller, Anthony DeRosa, Michael Cedeno, Mike "Moe" Merrell. **Songs:** "Where the Dream Takes You" and "Atlantis 2002." **Running time:** 95 minutes. **Released:** June 3, 2001.

### Voices
**Milo James Thatch:** Michael J. Fox; **Gaetan "The Mole" Molierre:** Corey Burton; **Helga Katrina Sinclair:** Claudia Christian; **Captain Lyle Tiberius Rourke:** James Garner; **Preston B. Whitmore:** John Mahoney; **Dr. Joshua Strongbear Sweet:** Phil Morris; **King Kashekim Nedakh:** Leonard Nimoy; **Vincenzo "Vinny" Santorini:** Don Novello; **Audrey Rocio Ramirez:** Jacqueline Obradors; **Wilhelmina Bertha Packard:** Florence Stanley; **Fenton Q. Harcourt:** David Ogden Stiers; **Princess Kida Kidagakash:** Cree Summer; **Young Kida:** Natalie Storm; **Jebediah Allardyce "Cookie" Farnsworth:** Jim Varney

### Additional Voices
Jim Cummings, Patrick Pinney, Steve Barr

Milo Thatch, the grandson of the great adventurer Thaddeus Thatch, embarks on an intrepid and privately financed undersea journey with a team of five explorers to uncover the mysterious lost city of Atlantis, encountering danger and corruption along the way.

**PN:** Billed as Walt Disney Pictures' first animated science fiction adventure and produced at a cost of nearly $100 million, this high-budget production, codirected by Kirk Wise and Gary Trousdale of Disney's *Beauty and the Beast* fame, turned out to be a box-office bust for the studio, grossing only $84 million domestically.

## ⊚ BABAR: THE MOVIE (1989)

A Nelvana Production released by New Line Cinema. **p:** Patrick Loubert, Michael Hirsh, Clive A. Smith; **d:** Alan Bunce; **scr:** Peter Sauder, J.D. Smith, John De Klein, Raymond Jaffelice, Alan Bunce (adapted from a story by Sauder, Loubert and Hirsh based on characters created by Jean and Laurent de Brunhoff); **m/s:** Milan Kymlicka; **anim dir:** John Laurence Collins. **Songs:** "Elephantland March," "The Best We Both Can Be," "Monkey Business," "Committee Song" and "Rataxes Song." **Running time:** 70 minutes. **Released:** July 28, 1989.

### Voices
**King Babar/the Elder:** Gordon Pinsent; **Queen Celeste/Old Lady:** Elizabeth Hanna; **Isabelle:** Lisa Yamanaka; **Flora:** Marsha Moreau; **Pom:** Bobby Becken; **Alexander:** Amos Crawley: **Boy Babar:** Gavin Magrath; **Young Celeste:** Sarah Polley; **Pompadour:** Stephen Ouimette; **Cornelius:** Chris Wiggins; **Zephir:** John Stocker; **Rataxes:** Charles Kerr; **Old Tusk:** Stuart Stone; **Celeste's Mom:** Angela Fusco

In the form of a bedtime story, King Babar recalls for his children his first day as boy-king of Elephantland and his ensuing battle to save the nearby village—the home of his sweetheart, Celeste—from decimation by a tyrannical cult of elephant-enslavening rhinos.

## ⊚ BALTO (1995)

A Universal Pictures/Amblin Entertainment Production released by Universal Pictures. **p:** Steve Hickner; **d:** Simon Wells; **exec prod:** Steven Spielberg, Kathleen Kennedy, Bonnie Radford; **st:** Clif Ruby, Elana Lesser (based on a true story); **scr:** Cliff Ruby, Elana Lesser, David Steven Cohen, Roger S.H. Schulman; **m:** James Horner (with song "Reach for the Light" written by Barry Mann and James Horner); **superv anim:** David Bowers, Shahin Ersoz, Rodolphe Guenoden, Nicolas Marlet, Patrick Mate, William Salazar, Christoph Serrand, Robert Stevenhagen, Jeffrey James Varab, Dick Zondag. **Songs:** "Reach for the Light." **Running time:** 74 minutes. **Released:** December 22, 1995.

### Cast (live action)
**Grandma:** Miriam Margolyes; **Granddaughter:** Lola Bates-Campbell

### Voices
**Balto:** Kevin Bacon; **Boris:** Bob Hoskins; **Jenna:** Bridget Fonda; **Steele:** Jim Cummings; **Muk/Luk:** Phil Collins; **Nikki:** Jack Angel; **Kaltag:** Danny Mann; **Star:** Robbie Rist; **Rosy:** Juliette Brewer; **Sylvie/Dixie/Rosy's Mother:** Sandra Searles Dickinson; **Doc:** Donald Sinden; **Rosy's Father:** William Roberts; **Telegraph Operator:** Garrick Hagon; **Butcher:** Bill Bailey; **Town Dog:** Big Al; **Grandma Rosy:** Miriam Margolyes; **Granddaughter:** Lola Bates-Campbell

### Additional Voices
Michael McShane, Austin Tichenor, Reed Martin, Adam Long, Jennifer Blanc, Jim Carter, Christine Cavanaugh, Brendan Fraser, Michael Shannon

In 1925 a courageous dog named Balto, who is half wolf, half husky, leads a team of sled dogs on a 600-mile trip across the Alaskan wilderness, braving blizzard conditions for five days, to deliver antitoxin to the diphtheria-stricken residents of Nome, Alaska. Based on a true story.

**PN:** This Steven Spielberg film, with its largely British production team, was headed by Simon Wells and Steve Hickner, who previously supervised animation for Disney's milestone animated feature *Who Framed Roger Rabbit*. The film grossed a disappointing $11.268 million in the United States.

## ⊚ BAMBI (1942)

A Walt Disney Production released by RKO Radio Pictures. **p:** Walt Disney; **superv dir:** David D. Hand; **st (adaptation):** Larry Morey; **st dev:** George Stallings, Melvin Shaw, Carl Fallberg, Chuck Couch, Ralph Wright (based on the book by Felix Salten); **m:** Frank Churchill, Edward H. Plumb; **seq dir:** James Algar, Bill Roberts, Norman Wright, Sam Armstrong, Paul Satterfield, Graham Heid; **superv anim:** Franklin Thomas, Milt Kahl, Eric Larson, Oliver M. Johnston Jr. **Songs:** "Love Is a Song," "Let's sing a Gay Little Spring Song," "Little April Shower" and "Looking for Romance (I Bring You a Song)." **Running time:** 69 minutes. **Released:** August 13, 1942.

### Voices
**Bambi:** Bobby Stewart; **Bambi:** Donnie Dunagan; **Bambi:** Hardy Albright; **Bambi:** John Sutherland; **Bambi's mother:** Paula Winslowe; **Faline:** Cammie King, Ann Gillis; **Aunt Ena/Mrs. Possum:** Mary Lansing; **Prince of the Forest:** Fred Shields; **Friend Owl:** Bill Wright; **Flower:** Stanley Alexander; **Flower:** Sterling Holloway; **Thumper:** Peter Behn; **Thumper/Flower:** Tim Davis; **Mrs. Quail:** Thelma Boardman; **Mrs. Rabbit:** Marjorie Lee

*Additional Voices*

Bobette Audrey, Janet Chapman, Jeanne Christy, Dolyn Bramston Cook, Marion Darlington, Otis Harlan, Jack Horner, Thelma Hubbard, Babs Nelson, Sandra Lee Richards, Francesca Santoro, Elouise Woodward

A newborn prince of the forest (Bambi) learns about love, friendship and survival—with the help of fellow forest dwellers including Flower the skunk and Thumper the rabbit—as he conquers both man and nature to take his rightful place as king of the forest.

## ◎ BAREFOOT GEN (1992)

A Gen Productions released by Tara Releasing. **p:** Masao Murayama, Carl Macek; **d:** Mori Masaki; **scr:** Kenji Nakazawa; **char design/anim dir:** Kazuo Tomizawa; **m:** Kentaro Haneda; **assist anim dir:** Nobuko Yuasa. **Running time:** 85 minutes. **Released:** July 3, 1992.

*Voices*

**Gen Nakaoka:** Catherine Battistone; **Kimie Nakaoka:** Barbara Goodson; **Shinji Nakaoka/Eiko Nakaoka:** Wendee Lee

A six-year-old boy witnesses the aftermath of the atomic bombing of Hiroshima in this animated feature based on the autobiographical comics by Kenji Nakazawa.

## ◎ BARNYARD: THE ORIGINAL PARTY ANIMALS (2006)

An Omation Studios/Nickelodeon Movies Production released by Paramount Pictures. **p:** Steve Oedekerk, Paul Marshal; **exec prod:** Julia Pistor, Albie Hecht; **d & w:** Steve Oedekerk; **m:** John Debney; **lead anim superv:** David Andrews; **anim superv:** Steve Baker. **Songs:** "Mud," "Hittin' the Hay," "Down on the Farm (They All Ask for You)," "Won't Back Down," "2StepN," "Hillbilly Holla," "Kick It," "Father, Son," "Freedom Is a Voice," "Popsickle," "Wild and Free" and "Boombastic." **Running time:** 83 minutes. **Released:** July 28, 2006.

*Voices*

**Otis the Cow:** Kevin James; **Daisy the Cow:** Courteney Cox Arquette; **Miles the Mule:** Danny Glover; **Ben the Cow:** Sam Elliott; **Bessy the Cow:** Wanda Sykes; **Mrs. Beady: Etta the Hen:** Andie MacDowell; **Hanna the Hen:** Megan Cavanagh; **Dag the Coyote:** David Koechner; **Pip the Mouse:** Jeffrey Garcia; **Freddy the Ferret:** Cam Clarke; **Peck the Rooster/Skunk:** Rob Paulsen; **Pig the Pig:** Tino Insana; **Duke the Dog:** Dom Irrera; **Eddy the Jersey Cow:** S. Scott Bullock; **Budd the Jersey Cow/Officer O'Hanlon:** John DiMaggio; **Igg the Jersey Cow:** Maurice LaMarche; **Maddy the Chick:** Madeline Lovejoy; **Root the Rooster:** Earthquake; **Mr. Beady/Snotty Boy/Snotty Boy's Father:** Steve Oedekerk; **Snotty Boy's Mother:** Jilly Talley; **Mrs. Beady:** Maria Bamford; **Farmer:** Fred Tatasciore; **Snotty's Boy Friend #1:** Laraine Newman; **Snotty Boy's Friend #2:** Katie Leigh; **Little Girl:** Zoe Raye; **Chick:** Paul Butcher

A carefree cow (Otis) (voiced by TV's *King of Queens* star Kevin James) and his misfit animal pals have fun playing tricks on humans, along with singing, dancing and partying, until someone takes charge and the responsibility then falls on Otis, who finds the courage and confidence to lead.

**PN:** Budgeted at $51 million, this CGI-animated Omation Studios and Nickleodeon Movies coproduction, originally entitled *Barnyard* in preproduction, grossed more than $101 million, with 71.5 percent of its revenue from theaters throughout the United States and the rest from foreign markets.

## ◎ BATMAN: MASK OF THE PHANTASM (1993)

A Warner Bros. Production released by Warner Bros. **p:** Benjamin Melniker, Michael Uslan; **cpd:** Alan Burnett, Erich Radomski, Bruce W. Timm; **exec prod:** Tom Ruegger; **d:** Eric Radomski, Bruce W. Timm; **scr:** Alan Burnett, Paul Dini, Martin Pasko, Michael Reaves (based on the DC Comics character created by Bob Kane); **m:** Shirley Walker; **anim dir:** Se-Won Kim, Young-Hwan Sang, Chung Ho Kim, Sun Hee Lee, Yukio Suzuki, Yutaka Oka, Noburo Takahashi; **superv anim:** Ric Machin. **Songs:** "I Never Even Told You" (performed by Tia Carrere). **Running time:** 76 minutes. **Released:** December 25, 1993.

*Voices*

**Batman/Bruce Wayne:** Kevin Conroy; **Andrea Beaumont:** Dana Delany; **Councilman Arthur Reeves:** Hart Bochner; **Phantasm/Carl Beaumont:** Stacy Keach Jr.; **Salvatore Valestra:** Abe Vigoda; **Chuckie Sol:** Dick Miller; **Buzz Bronski:** John P. Ryan; **Alfred the Butler:** Efrem Zimbalist Jr.; **Commissioner Gordon:** Bob Hastings; **Detective Bullock:** Robert Coztanzo; **The Joker:** Mark Hamill

*Additional Voices*

Jeff Bennett, Jane Downs, Ed Gilbert, Mark Hamill, Marilu Henner, Charles Howarton, Vernee Watson-Johnson, Pat Musick, Thom Pinto, Peter Renaday, Neil Ross

Batman tries to save face after being accused of a series of murders he did not commit and attempts to uncover the real killer, known as The Phantasm, in this absorbing, first-ever full-length animated feature based on the popular DC Comics character. A sequel, *Batman: Sub-Zero*, was released direct-to-video in 1998.

*Batman faces two adversaries, the Phantasm (left), and his old enemy, the Joker (right), in Warner Bros.' big-screen animated adventure* Batman: Mask of the Phantasm. © *Warner Brothers/DC Comics. All rights reserved.*

**PN:** Warner Bros. originally planned to produce this animated feature spun off from the popular animated TV series directly to video but, after the project was substantially completed, deemed it strong enough for theatrical release. The feature tallied $5.6 million in ticket sales and was a big hit on home video as well. The film's original working title was *Batman: The Animated Movie*.

## ◎ BEAUTY AND THE BEAST (1991)

A Walt Disney Picture released by Buena Vista Pictures. **p:** Don Hahn; **d:** Gary Trousdale, Kirk Wise; **exec prod:** Don Hahn; **scr:** Linda Woolverton; **m:** Alan Menken; **superv anim:** Ruben A. Aquino, James Barter, Andreas Deja, Will Winn, Mark Henn, David Pruiksma, Nik Ranieri, Chris Wahl. **Songs:** "Beauty and the Beast," "Be Our Guest," "Belle," "How Long Must This Go On," "If I Can't Love Her," "Something There," "The Mob Song" and "Maison des Lumes." **Running time:** 85 minutes. **Released:** November 15, 1991.

*Voices*

**Belle:** Paige O'Hara; **Beast:** Robby Benson; **Gaston:** Richard White; **Lumiere:** Jerry Orbach; **Cogsworth/Narrator:** David Ogden Stiers; **Mrs. Potts:** Angele Lansbury; **Chip:** Bradley Michael Pierce; **Maurice:** Rex Everhart; **LeFou:** Jesse Corti; **Philippe:** Hal Smith; **Wardrobe:** Jo Anne Worley; **Bimbette:** Mary Kay Bergman; **Stove:** Brian Cummings; **Bookseller:** Alvin Epstein; **Monsieur D'Arque:** Tony Jay; **Baker:** Alec Murphy; **Featherduster:** Kimmy Robertson; **Footstool:** Frank Welker; **Mimbette:** Kath Soucie

A cruel prince who is turned into a hideous beast must win the love of a beautiful young enchantress to break the spell cast upon him in this animated musical version of the classic children's fairy tale.

**PN:** In the first eight weeks, *Beauty and the Beast* earned $82.5 million in box-office revenue and broke the previous record set by *The Little Mermaid* (which had earned $84.3 million during its release), becoming the first animated feature to surpass the $100-million mark (final gross: $144.8 million). Originally a dark, straightforward, nonmusical retelling of this classic fairy tale was planned, but it was scuttled after Disney executives saw the first reel. Nominated for six Academy Awards (including an unprecedented three nominations for the film's musical score and songs), it became the first animated feature ever nominated for best picture. Joe Grant, who developed the characters and stories for Walt Disney's *Snow White and the Seven Dwarfs*, *Pinocchio*, *Dumbo*, *Fantasia*, among others and had left the studio in 1949, returned for a second stint to work on this film, after a 40-year absence from the film business. He also worked on subsequent Disney animated features, including *Aladdin*, *The Lion King* and *Pocahontas* (the latter at 86 years of age).

## ◎ BEAVIS AND BUTT-HEAD DO AMERICA (1996)

A Geffen Pictures/MTV/Paramount Production released by Paramount Pictures. **p:** Abby Terkuhle; **d:** Mike Judge, Yvette Kaplan; **cpd:** John Andrews; **exec prod:** David Gale, Van Toffler; **scr:** Mike Judge, Joe Stillman (based on the television series, *Beavis and Butt-Head*); **m:** John C. Frizzell. **Songs:** "Two Cool Guys," "Love Rollercoaster," "Ain't Nobody," "Ratfinks, Suicide Tanks and Cannibal Girls," "I Wanna Riot," "Walk on Water," "Snakes," "Pimp'n Aint Ez," "Lord Is a Monkey," "White Trash," "Gone Shootin'" and "Lesbian Seagull." **Running time:** 80 minutes. **Released:** December 20, 1996.

*Voices*

**Beavis/Butt-Head/Tom Anderson/Mr. Van:** Mike Judge; **FBI Agent Flemming:** Robert Stack; **Martha:** Cloris Leachman; **Agent Hurly:** Jacqueline Barba; **Flight Attendant/White House Tour Guide:** Pamela Blair; **Ranger:** Eric Bogosian; **Man on Plane/Second Man in Confession Booth/Old Guy/Jim:** Kristofor Brown; **Motley Crue Roadie #2/Tourist Man:** Tony Darling; **Airplane Captain/White House Representative:** John Donman; **Petrified Forest Recording:** Jim Flaherty; **Hoover Guide/ATF Agent:** Tim Guinee; **Motley Crue Roadie #1:** David Letterman; **TV Chief #2/Concierge/Bellboy/Male TV Reporter:** Toby Huss; **Limo Driver/TV Chief #1/Man in Confession Booth #1/Petrified Forest Ranger:** Sam Johnson; **Tour Bus Driver:** Richard Linklater; **Flight Attendant #2:** Rosemary McNamara; **Indian Dignitary:** Harsh Nayyar; **Announcer in Capitol:** Karen Phillips; **President Clinton:** Dale Reeves; **Hoover Technician/General at Strategic Air Command:** Michael Ruschak; **Flight Attendant #3/Female TV Reporter:** Gail Thomas; **FBI Agent Bork:** Greg Kinnear; **Dallas Grimes:** Demi Moore; **Muddy Grimes:** Bruce Willis

*Additional Voices*

David Spade

MTV junkies Beavis and Butt-Head wake up to find their television stolen. They embark on an epic journey across America to recover it, only to become wanted by the FBI (they're mistaken for two of America's most dangerous men alive) in their first full-length animated feature, based on the popular television series.

**PN:** Produced at a cost of $12 million, this crudely animated feature opened on 2,190 movie screens and grossed a stunning $20.114 million the weekend it opened. The film's total domestic gross was $63.071 million.

## ◎ BEBE'S KIDS (1992)

A Hudlin Bros./Hyperion Studio Production released by Paramount Pictures. **p:** William Carroll, Thomas L. Wilhite, David Robert Cobb; **d:** Bruce Smith; **exec prod:** Reginald Hudlin, Warrington Hudlin; **scr:** Reginald Hudlin (based on the album *Bebe's Kids* by Robin Harris); **m:** John Barnes; **superv anim:** Lennie K. Graves. **Songs:** "On Our Worst Behavior," "Standing on the Rock of Love," "Can't Say Goodbye," "I Got the 411," "Your Love Keep Working on Me," "All My Love," "Straight Jackin'," "Freedom Song" and "Oh No." **Running time:** 73 minutes. **Released:** July 31, 1992.

*Voices*

**Robin Harris:** Faizon Love; **Jamika:** Vanessa Bell Calloway; **Leon:** Wayne Collins Jr.; **LaShawn:** Jonell Green; **Kahill:** Marques Houston; **Pee Wee:** Tone Loc; **Dorothea:** Myra J.; **Vivian:** Nell Carter; **Card Player #1:** John Witherspoon; **Card Player #2:** Chino "Fats" Williams; **Card Player #3:** Rodney Winfield; **Card Player #4:** George D. Wallace; **Bartender:** Brad Sanders; **Lush:** Reynaldo Rey; **Barfly:** Bebe Drake-Massey; **Richie:** Jack Lynch; **Opie:** Phillip Glasser; **Security Guard #1:** Louie Anderson; **Security Guard #2:** Tom Everett; **Security Guard #2/Fun World Patrolman:** Kerrigan Mahan; **Ticket/Lady/Saleswoman/Nuclear Mother/Rodney Rodent:** Susan Silo; **Announcer/President Lincoln/Impericon/Tommy Toad:** Pete Renaday; **President Nixon:** Rich Little; **Titanic Captain:** David Robert Cobb; **Nuclear Father/Motorcycle Cop:** Barry Diamond

*Additional Voices*

Stanley B. Clay, Michelle Davison, Judi M. Durand, Greg Finley, Maui France, Jaquita Green, Jamie Gunderson, J.D. Hall, Doris Hess, Barbara Iley, Daamen J. Krall, John Lafayette, Tina Lifford,

*Robin Harris (in cartoon form) has his own troubles in this scene from the animated musical based on the late comedian's life,* Bebe's Kids. © *Paramount Pictures*

Josh Lindsay, Arvie Lowe Jr., DeVaughn Nixon, David Randolph, Noreen Reardon, Gary Schwartz, Cheryl Tyre Smith

In this amusing animated musical comedy, based on characters created by the late comedian Robin Harris, Robin's first date with a beautiful woman is foiled when she insists that her well-mannered son and her friend Bebe's three irrepressible kids accompany them, turning their trip to an amusement park into a nightmare.

**PN:** The first animated featured produced by Hyperion Studios as part of a multifilm deal with Paramount Pictures, *Bebe's Kids* was also the first animated theatrical feature to star all–African American characters. The film was promoted as "Animation with an attitude."

## ◎ THE BLACK CAULDRON (1985)

A Walt Disney Production in association with Silver Screen Partners II released through Buena Vista Pictures. **p:** Joe Hale; **d:** Ted Berman, Richard Rich; **st:** David Jonas, Vance Gerry, Al Wilson, Roy Morita, Ted Berman, Peter Young, Richard Rich, Art Stevens, Joe Hale (based on Lloyd Alexander's five *Chronicles of Prydain* books); **m:** Elmer Bernstein. **Running time:** 80 minutes. **Released:** July 24, 1985.

*Voices*

**Taran:** Grant Bardsley; **Eilonwy:** Susan Sheridan; **Dallben:** Freddie Jones; **Fflewddur Fflam:** Nigel Hawthorne; **King Eidilleg:** Arthur Malet; **Gurgi/Doli:** John Byner; **Orddu:** Eda Reiss Merin; **Orwen:** Adele Malia-Morey; **Orgoch:** Billie Hayes; **The Horned King:** John Hurt; **Creeper/Henchman:** Phil Fondacaro; **Narrator:** John Huston; **Fairfolk:** Lindsday Ric, Brandon Call, Gregory Levinson; **Henchmen:** Peter Renaday, James Almanzar, Wayne Allwine, Steve Hale, Phil Nibbelink, Jack Laing

Taran, a young man who dreams of becoming a warrior, is put to the test as he battles the evil Horned King, who is determined to gain possession of the "black cauldron," a source of supernatural power, to use to further his misdeeds. Taran is joined by a cast of characters in his quest, including Princess Eilonwy, Hen Wen, a psychic pig and Gurgi, a sycophantic creature.

**PN:** More than 2.5 million drawings were used to create this $25-million feature, which took 10 years to complete. The film was shot in 70 millimeter, only the second to ever be done in that wide-screen format. (The first was *Sleeping Beauty* in 1959.) The movie was also the first Disney cartoon feature to merit a PG rating.

## ◎ BLOOD: THE LAST VAMPIRE (2001)

A I.G. Studio production released by Manga Entertainment/Palm Pictures. **p:** Mitsuhisa Ishikawa, Yukio Nagasaki, Mamorou Oshii; **d:** Hiroyuki Kitakubo; **scr:** Kenji Kamiyama, Katsuya Terad; **exec prod:** Akira Sato, Ryuzo Shirakawa; **anim dir:** Kazuchika Kise, Hiroyuki Kitabuko. **Running time:** 48 minutes. **Released:** August 17, 2001.

*Voices*

**Saya:** Youki Kudoh; **Nurse Mahiko Caroline Amano:** Saemi Nakamura; **Dave:** Joe Romersa; **Louis:** Stuart Robinson; **Sharon:** Rebecca Forstadt; **Teacher:** Tom Charles; **S.P. #1:** Fitz Houston; **S.P. #2:** Steven Blum; **School Headmaster:** Paul Carr

Around Halloween in 1966, three agents in Japan, including a young girl (Saya) with vampire-like tendencies, are sent undercover by the U.S. military to track down and destroy supernatural vampires who act like humans and have attacked the Yokota Air Base in Fussa-shi, Tokyo, in this Japanese-made horror-action adventure.

## ◎ BON VOYAGE, CHARLIE BROWN (*AND DON'T COME BACK!*) (1980)

A Lee Mendelson–Bill Melendez Production released through Paramount Pictures. **p & d:** Lee Mendelson, Bill Melendez; **w:** Charles M. Schulz (based on the *Peanuts* characters); **m:** Ed Bogas, Judy Munsen. **Running time:** 75 minutes. **Released:** May 30, 1980.

*Voices*

**Charlie Brown:** Arrin Skelley; **Peppermint Patty:** Laura Planting; **Marcie:** Casey Carlson; **Linus:** Daniel Anderson; **Sally Brown:** Annalisa Bartolin; **Snoopy:** Bill Melendez; **Waiter/Baron/Driver/Tennis Announcer/English Voice/American Male:** Scott Beach

As exchange students, Charlie Brown and the gang visit both England, where Snoopy competes at Wimbeldon, and France, where they find themselves the guests of a mysterious benefactor in a historic chateau.

## ◎ A BOY NAMED CHARLIE BROWN (1969)

A Lee Mendelson Films and Cinema Center 100 Production released by New General Pictures. **p:** Lee Mendelson, Bill Melendez; **d:** Bill Melendez; **w:** Charles M. Schulz; **m:** Vince Guaraldi; **m/s:** Rod McKuen. **Songs:** "Piano Sonata Opus 13 (Pathetique)," "Failure Face," "Champion Charlie Brown," "Cloud Dreams," "Charlie Brown and His All Stars," "We Lost Again," "Blue Charlie Brown," "Time to Go to School," "I Only Dread One Day at a Time," "By Golly I'll Show 'Em," "Class Champion," "School Spelling Bee," "Start Boning Up on Your Spelling, Charlie Brown," "You'll Either Be a Hero . . . or a Goat," "Bus Station," "Do Piano Players Make a Lot of Money?" "I've Got to Get My Blanket Back," "Big City," "Found Blanket," "National Spelling Bee," "B-E-A-G-L-E," "Homecoming," "I'm Never Going to School Again," "Welcome Home, Charlie Brown" and "I Before E." **Running time:** 85 minutes. **Released:** December 4, 1969.

*Voices*

**Charlie Brown:** Peter Robbins; **Lucy:** Pamelyn Ferdin; **Linus:** Glenn Gilger; **Sally:** Erin Sullivan; **Patty:** Sally Dryer Barker; **Violet:** Ann Altieri, **Pigpen:** Christopher Defaria; **Schroeder:** Andy Pforsich; **Frieda:** Linda Mendelson; **Singers:** Betty Allan; Loulie Norman, Gloria Wood; **Boys:** David Carey, Guy Pforsich; **Snoopy:** Bill Melendez

Charlie Brown, who never seems able to do anything right, surprises himself and his friends by being chosen for the national spelling bee in New York. True to form, he loses, on national television no less, but is nevertheless given a hero's welcome when he returns home.

## ◎ THE BRAVE LITTLE TOASTER (1987)
A Kushner-Locke/Hyperion Pictures Production released by Walt Disney Pictures. **p:** Donald Kushner, Thomas L. Wilhite; **d:** Jerry Rees; **coprod:** Cleve Reinhard; **exec prod:** Willard Carroll, Peter Locke; **st:** Joe Ranft, Jerry Reese, Brian McEntee (based on the novella by Thomas M. Disch); **scr:** Joe Ranft, Jerry Rees; **m:** David Newman (with songs by Van Dyke Parks); **anim dir:** Randy Cartwright, Joe Ranft, Rebecca Rees. **Songs:** "City of Light," "It's a B-Movie," "Cutting Edge," "Worthless," "Hidden Meadow," "Tutti Frutti," "My Mammy" and "April Showers." **Running time:** 80 minutes. **Released:** July 10, 1987.

### Voices
**Radio:** Jon Lovitz; **Lampy/Zeke:** Tim Stack; **Blanky/Young Master/Kirby:** Thurl Ravenscroft; **Toaster:** Deanna Oliver; **Air Conditioner/Hanging Lamp:** Phil Hartman; **Elmo St. Peters:** Joe Ranft; **Mish-Mash/Two-Face Sewing Machine:** Judy Toll; **Rob:** Wayne Katz; **Chris:** Colette Savage; **Mother/Two-Face Sewing Machine:** Mindy Stern; **Plugsy:** Jim Jackman; **Entertainment Center:** Randy Cook; **Computer:** Randy Bennett; **Black and White TV:** Jonathan Benair; **Spanish Announcer:** Louis Conti

Based on Thomas M. Disch's charming 1986 novella, five household appliances—Toaster (also known as "Slots" to his pals), Blankey, the electric blanket, Kirby, the grumpy vacuum cleaner, Lampy, the desk lamp, and Radio, the wise-guy chatterbox—abandoned in a rustic family cabin, set out to find their 13-year-old Master, who gave their secret lives meaning.

**PN:** Following completion of this $1.8-million animated feature, the producers had trouble securing a distributor for the film. In 1988 the film was broadcast on the Disney Channel; in 1989 and 1990 it played in theaters in selected cities.

## ◎ BRAVESTARR: THE LEGEND (1988)
A Filmation Production released by Taurus Entertainment. **p:** Lou Scheimer; **d:** Tom Tataranowicz; **scr:** Bob Forward, Steve Hayes; **m:** Frank W. Becker; **superv anim:** Brett Hisey. **Running time:** 91 minutes. **Released:** September 17, 1988.

### Voices
Charlie Adler, Susan Blu, Pat Fraley, Ed Gilbert, Alan Oppenheimer, Eric Gunden, Erika Scheimer

Bravestarr, who comes from a place steeped in Indian culture to futuristic New Texas, meets his nemesis, Tex-Hex, for the first time.

**PN:** In movie theater ads, this film was billed as *Bravestarr, The Movie*, even though initially prints of the film reflected the original title, *Bravestarr, The Legend*.

## ◎ BROTHER BEAR (2003)
A Walt Disney Pictures Production release by Buena Vista Pictures. **p:** Chuck Williams; **d:** Aaron Blaise, Robert Walker; **scr:** Steve Bencich, Lorne Cameron, Ron J. Friedman, David Hoselton, Tab Murphy; **m/sc:** Phil Collins, Mark Mancina; **l:** Howard Ashman; **superv anim:** Ruben A. Aquinio, Byron Howard, James V. Jackson, Broose Johnson, Alex Kuperschmidt, Anthony Wayne Michaels, Tony Stanley. **Songs:** "Great Spirits," "Transformation," "Welcome," "On My Way," "No Way Out" (theme from *Brother Bear*) and "Look Through My Eyes." **Running time:** 85 minutes. **Released:** November 7, 2003.

### Voices
**Kenai:** Joaquin Phoenix; **Koda:** Jeremy Suarez; **Denahi:** Jason Raiz; **Old Denahi:** Harold Gould; **Sitka:** D.B. Sweeney; **Rurt:** Rick Moranis; **Tewk:** Dave Thomas; **Tanana:** Joan Copeland; **Tug:** Michael Clarke Duncan; **Ram #1:** Paul Christie; **Ram #2:** Daniel Mastrogiorgio; **Old Lady Bear:** Estelle Harris; **Boy Lover Bear:** Greg Proops; **Girl Lover Bear:** Pauley Perette; **Croatian Bear:** Darko Cesar; **Chipmunks:** Bumper Robinson

A young Inuit hunter (Kenai) vengefully kills a bear involved in the accidental death of his older brother, disturbing the Great Spirits, who teach him a valuable lesson by transforming him into a cub bear while his other brother, Denahi, pursues him, unaware of his sudden transformation.

**PN:** Produced by Walt Disney Productions, this beautifully rendered film—dubbed by some as *Beauty and Bear*—grossed $85.2 million in the United States and was nominated for an Academy Award for best animated feature in 2003. Grammy award-winning singer/songwriter Phil Collins wrote the film's "transformation song," and the script reportedly went through 12 drafts before completion.

## ◎ BUGS BUNNY, SUPERSTAR (1975)
A Hair Raising Films Inc. release through Warner Bros. **p & d:** Larry Jackson; **anim dir:** Chuck Jones, Bob Clampett, Tex Avery, Friz Freleng, Robert McKimson. **Running time:** 91 minutes. **Released:** January 11, 1975.

### Voices
**Bugs Bunny/Elmer Fudd/Daffy Duck/Porky Pig/Sylvester/Tweety/Henery Hawk/Foghorn Leghorn/Barnyard Dog/Rudolph (Gossamer)/Mad Scientist:** Mel Blanc; **Narrator:** Orson Welles

Famed Warner Warner Bros. animators Friz Freleng, Tex Avery and Bob Clampett appear in this documentary film on Warner Bros. cartoons of the 1940s. Interspersed between interview segments are complete cartoon versions of "A Wild Hare" (1940), "My Favorite Duck" (1942), "A Corny Concerto" (1943), "What's Cookin' Doc?" (1944), "The Old Grey Hare" (1944), "Rhapsody Rabbit" (1946), "Walky Talky Hawky" (1946), "Hair-Raising Hare" (1946) and "I Taw a Putty Tat" (1948).

## ◎ THE BUGS BUNNY/ROAD RUNNER MOVIE (1979)
A Warner Bros. release. **p & d:** Chuck Jones; **w:** Michael Maltese, Chuck Jones; **m:** Carl Stalling, Milt Franklyn. **Running time:** 92 minutes. **Released:** September 30, 1979.

### Voices
**Bugs Bunny/Daffy Duck:** Mel Blanc

Bugs Bunny looks back on his past triumphs in this entertaining compilation that ties in 20 minutes of new animation with old Warner cartoons, in full or part. (New footage has Bugs giving audiences a tour of his Beverly Hills estate as he fondly recalls the highlights of his 40-year career.) The five complete cartoons featured are "Hareway to Stars," "What's Opera, Doc?" "Duck Amuck," "Bully for Bugs" and "Rabbit Fire," plus excerpts from eight others, along with an 11-minute Road Runner tribute consisting of 31 gags culled from 16 cartoons.

**PN:** Warner Bros. had a difficult time deciding what to call this feature. The original titles that were bantered about included *The Great Bugs Bunny/Road Runner Chase* and *The Great American Bugs Bunny/Road Runner Chase*.

## BUGS BUNNY'S THIRD MOVIE: 1001 RABBIT TALES (1982)

A Warner Bros. release. **p:** Friz Freleng; **seq dir:** Dave Detiege, Friz Freleng; **m:** Rob Walsh, Bill Lava, Milt Franklyn, Carl Stalling. **Running time:** 76 minutes. **Released:** November 19, 1982.

*Voices*

**Bugs Bunny/Daffy Duck/Sultan Yosemite Sam:** Mel Blanc; **Prince Abadaba:** Lennie Weinrib; **Old Servant:** Shep Menken

As rival book salesmen for "Rambling House Publishers," Bugs Bunny and Daffy Duck travel the world to find new areas to market their wares, including the Arabian desert. Other characters featured include Yosemite Sam, Tweety and Sylvester. New animated wraparounds introduce several complete cartoons, previously released to theaters: "Ali Baba Bunny," (1957)," "Apes of Wrath" (1959), "Bewitched Bunny" (1954), "Cracked Quack" (1952), "Goldimouse and the Three Cats" (1960), "Mexican Boarders" (1962), "One Froggy Evening" (1955), "The Pied Piper of Guadalupe" (1961) and others.

**PN:** The sequel to this third Bugs Bunny compilation is 1983's *Daffy Duck's Movie: Fantastic Island.*

## A BUG'S LIFE (1998)

A Pixar Animation Studios and Walt Disney Studios Production released by Buena Vista Pictures. **p:** Darla K. Anderson, Kevin Reher; **d:** John Lasseter, Andrew Stanton; **st:** John Lasseter, Andrew Stanton, Joe Ranft; **scr:** Andrew Stanton, Donald McEnery, Bob Shaw; **m:** Randy Newman; **superv anim:** Glenn McQueen, Rich Quade. **Song:** "The Time of Your Life." **Running time:** 96 minutes. **Released:** November 20, 1998.

*Voices*

**Flik:** Dave Foley; **Hopper:** Kevin Spacey; **Atta:** Julia Louis-Dreyfus; **Dot:** Hayden Panettiere; **Queen:** Phyllis Diller; **Molt:** Richard Kind; **Slim:** David Hyde Pierce; **Heimlich:** Joe Ranft; **Francis:** Denis Leary; **Manny:** Jonathan Harris; **Gypsy:** Madeline Kahn; **Rosie:** Bonnie Hunt; **P.T. Flea:** John Ratzenberger; **Dim:** Brad Garrett; **Mr. Soil:** Roddy McDowell

A misfit ant, Flik, and a group of flea circus performers he mistakenly recruits set out to find "bigger bugs" to save the colony from evil encroaching grasshoppers who are endangering the colony's existence.

## THE CARE BEARS ADVENTURE IN WONDERLAND (1987)

A Nelvana Production released by Cineplex Odeon Films. **p:** Michael Hirsh, Patrick Loubert, Clive A. Smith; **d:** Raymond Jafelice; **w:** Susan Snooks, John De Klein (based on a story by Peter Sauder); **m:** Trish Cullen; **m/l:** John Sebastian, Maribeth Solomon; **superv anim:** John Laurence Collins. **Running time:** 75 minutes. **Released:** August 7, 1987.

*Voices*

**Grumpy Bear:** Bob Dermer; **Swift Heart Rabbit:** Eva Almos; **Brave Heart Lion/Dum:** Dan Hennessey; **Tenderheart Bear:** Jim Henshaw; **Good Luck Bear:** Marla Lukofsky; **Lots-a-Heart Elephant:** Louba Goy; **White Rabbit:** Keith Knight; **Alice:** Tracey Moore; **Wizard:** Colin Fox; **Dim/Cheshire Cat:** John Stocker; **Caterpillar:** Don McManus; **Queen of Wonderland:** Elizabeth Hanna; **Flamingo:** Alan Fawcett; **Mad Hatter/Jabberwocky:** Keith Hampshire; **Princess:** Alyson Court

Combining the flavor of Lewis Carroll's *Alice in Wonderland* and Frank Baum's *Wizard of Oz*, this third Care Bears feature casts the cuddly characters in Wonderland where they search for Alice, who has been abducted by an evil-doing wizard who has designs on ruling the great land. Along the way they meet up with all sorts of interesting characters—The Mad Hatter, Tweedledee and Tweedledum, Cheshire Cat and others—who appeared in the Disney classic *Alice in Wonderland.*

**PN:** Nelvana produced this third and final Care Bears feature, which earned a disappointing $3 million. The first movie in the series made almost three times as much at the box office.

## THE CARE BEARS MOVIE (1985)

A Nelvana Production released by Samuel Goldwyn. **p:** Michael Hirsch, Patrick Loubert, Clive Smith; **d:** Arna Selznick; **w:** Peter Sauder; **m:** John Sebastian, Walt Woodward, Trish Cullen; **m/l:** John Sebastian, title song. **Running time:** 75 minutes. **Released:** March 29, 1985.

*Voices*

**Mr. Cherrywood:** Mickey Rooney; **Love-a-Lot Bear:** Georgia Engel; **Brave Heart Lion:** Harry Dean Stanton

In the land of Care-A-Lot two orphaned siblings, Kim and Jason, develop friendships with the Care Bears and experience the warm, good feelings of these cuddly creatures. Such feelings are temporarily dashed by the Evil Spirit, who casts a third child, Nicholas, under his power. Nicholas is to help the Evil Spirit by creating spells that remove all the care and feeling from the world.

## CARE BEARS MOVIE II: A NEW GENERATION (1986)

A Nelvana Production released by Columbia Pictures. **p:** Michael Hirsh, Patrick Loubert, Clive A. Smith; **d:** Dale Schott; **scr:** Peter Sauder; **m:** Patricia Cullen; **anim dir:** Charles Bonifacio. **Songs:** "Our Beginning," "Flying My Colors," "I Care for You," "Growing Up," "Care Bears Cheer Song" and "Forever Young." **Running time:** 77 minutes. **Released:** March 21, 1986.

*Voices*

**True Heart Bear:** Maxine Miller; **Noble Heart Horse:** Pam Hyatt; **Dark Heart/The Boy:** Hadley Kay; **Christy:** Cree Summer Francks; **Dawn:** Alyson Court; **John:** Michael Fantini

*Noble Heart Horse (left) and True Heart Bear (second from left), the cofounders of the Care Bears Family, and Care Bears Cubs, Secret Cub (second from right) and Tenderheart (right) look on as Care Bears Cousin Bright Heart Racoon slides down a rainbow in* Care Bears Movie II: A New Generation *(1986).* (COURTESY: NELVANA LIMITED)

True Heart Bear and Noble Heart Horse venture from their home base at the Great Wishing Star on a mission to a summer camp to teach a couple of self-centered youngsters the virtues of sharing and caring.

**PN:** This Nelvana theatrical cartoon feature release grabbed $8 million in ticket sales.

## ◎ CARS (2006)

A Walt Disney Pictures/Pixar Animation Studios Production released by Buena Vista Pictures. **p:** Darla K. Anderson; **d:** John Lasseter; **scr:** Dan Fogelman, Dan Gerson; **st:** Jorgen Klubien, John Lasseter, Philip Loren, Kiel Murray, Joe Ranft; **m:** Randy Newman; **superv anim:** Scott Clark, Doug Sweetland. **Songs:** "Life Is a Highway," "The Star Spangled Banner," "Reveille," "Westbound Sign," "Real Gone," "Our Town," "Behind the Clouds" and "Find Yourself." **Running time:** 96 minutes. **Released:** June 9, 2006.

*Voices*

**Lightning McQueen:** Owen Wilson; **Doc Hudson:** Paul Newman; **Sally Carrera:** Bonnie Hunt; **Mater:** Larry the Cable Guy; **Ramone:** Cheech Marin; **Luigi:** Tony Shalhoub; **Guido:** Guido Quaroni; **Flo:** Jennifer Lewis; **Sarge:** Paul Dooley; **Sheriff:** Michael Wallis; **Fillmore:** George Carlin; **Lizzie:** Katherine Helmond; **Mack/Hamm Truck/Abominable Snow Plow/P.T. Flea Car:** John Ratzenberger; **Red/Peterbuilt:** Joe Ranft; **Chick Hicks:** Michael Keaton; **"The King" Strip Weathers:** Richard Petty; **Harv:** Jeremy Piven; **Bob Cutlass:** Bob Costas; **Darrell Cartrip:** Darrell Waltrip; **Van:** Richard Kind; **Minny:** Edie McClurg; **Tex:** H.A. "Humpy" Wheeler; **Rusty Rust-eze:** Tom Magliozzi; **Dusty Rust-eze:** Ray Magliozzi; **Mrs. The King:** Lynda Petty; **Fred:** Andrew Stanton; **Junior:** Dale Earnhardt Jr.; **Michael Schumacher Ferrari:** Michael Schumacher; **Jay Lino:** Jay Leno; **Mario Andretti:** Mario Andretti; **Kori Turbowitz:** Sarah Clark; **Not Chuck:** Mike Nelson; **Boost:** Jonas Rivera; **Snotrod:** Lou Romano; **Wingo:** Adrian Ochoa; **DJ:** E.J. Holowicki; **Tia:** Elissa Knight; **Mia:** Lindsey Collins; **Motorhome Race Fan #1:** Larry Benton; **Motorhome Race Fan #3:** Douglas Keever; **Woody Car:** Tom Hanks; **Buzz Lightyear Car:** Tim Allen; **Mike Car:** Billy Crystal; **Sullivan Truck:** John Goodman; **Flik Car:** Dave Foley; **Various Others:** Sherry Lynn

En route cross-country to complete in the big Piston Cup Championship in California, hot-shot, rookie stock-car racer Lightning McQueen (voiced by Owen Wilson) takes an unexpected detour off Route 66 to the sleepy town of Radiator Springs, where he bonds with its offbeat cast of characters—Sally, a snazzy 2002 Porsche; Doc Hudson, a 1951 Hudson Hornet; and Mater, a rusty tow truck—who help him discover there are more important things than racing, such as family and friendship.

**PN:** This 2006 Disney-Pixar offering from John Lasseter, director of *Toy Story*, *A Bug's Life* and *Toy Story 2*, featured the voices of Owen Wilson as upstart Lightning McQueen, Paul Newman as Doc Hudson (who laid down his voice at a New York sound studio and donated his salary to his Newman's Hole in the Wall Camp for kids), Larry the Cable Guy as Mater, as well as famed NASCAR champions Richard Petty as The King, a 1970 Plymouth Superbird, and Darrell Waltrip as Darrell Cartrip and Lowe's Motor Speedway owner H.A. "Humpy" Wheeler as Tex, a 1975 Cadillac Coupe de Ville. On May 26, 2006, the racing-theme film fittingly premiered at Lowe's Motor Speedway in Charlotte, North Carolina, in front of 30,000 race car fans, with proceeds benefiting Speedway Children's Charities. Billed as "the first multiple-screen digital cinema premiere ever," the fully computer-animated movie was shown on four 50-foot-high by 115-foot-wide outdoor screens. Two weeks later, on June 9, 2006, the high-octane adventure comedy debuted number-one at the box office, opening on close to 7,000 screens at 3,985 theaters nationwide and hauling in $62.8 million, about $8 million short of some analysts' predictions. Becoming Pixar Animation Studios' seventh straight number-one grossing film, the $120-million computer-animated feature marked the third highest-grossing opening for a June release and sixth best among animated features overall, besides becoming 2006's top-grossing film of the year with more than $461 million in revenue worldwide.

## ◎ THE CASTLE OF CAGLIOSTRO (1991)

A Tokyo Movie Sinsha (TMS) Co. Ltd. Production released by Streamline Pictures. **p:** Yutaka Fujoka; **d:** Hayao Miyazaki; **scr:** Hayao Miyazaki, Haruya Yamazaki; **st:** Monkey Punch; **anim:** Yasunao Aoki, Nobumasa Arakawa, Hideo Kawauchi, Joji Manabe, Shoji Maruyama, Masami Ozaki, Yoko Sakurai, Junko Shimozaki, Masako Shinohara, Atsuko Tanaka, Tsukasa Tannai, Nobuo Tomizawa, Kazahide Tomonaga, Mikako Osato. **Running time:** 100 minutes. **Released:** April 3, 1991.

*Voices*

(English version) **Arsene Lupino III:** Bob Bergen; **Cagliostro:** Michael McConnohie

A good thief, Arsene Lupin III, and his gang attempt to free Princess Clarisse from her marriage to the evil Count Cagliostro and uncover the secret of a hidden treasure to which she possesses the key.

## ◎ CATS DON'T DANCE (1997)

A Turner Pictures/Turner Feature Animation/David Kirschner Production released by Warner Bros. **p:** Bill Bloom, Paul Gertz, David Kirschner; **d:** Mark Dindal; **cpd:** Jim Katz, Barry Weiss; **exec prod:** David Steinberg, Charles L. Richardson, Sandy Russell Gartin; **st:** Mark Dindal, Robert Lence, Brian McEntee, Rick Schneider, David Womersley, Kelvin Yasuda; "**scr:** Robert Gannaway, Cliff Ruby, Elana Lesser, Theresa Pettengell; **m:** Steve Goldstein (with songs by Randy Newman); **dir anim:** Jill Culton, Lennie K. Graves, Jay Jackson, Kevin Johnson, Bob Scott, Frans Vischer; **superv anim:** Chad Stewart, Steven Wahl. **Songs:** "Our Time Has Come," "I Do Believe," "Danny's Arrival Song," "Little Boat on the Sea," "Animal Jam," "Big and Loud," "Tell Me Lies," "Nothing's Gonna Stop Us Now," "Once Upon a Time . . ." and "Tea Time for Danny." **Running time:** 77 minutes. **Released:** March 26, 1997.

*Voices*

**Danny:** Scott Bakula; **Sawyer (speaking):** Jasmine Guy; **Sawyer (singing):** Natalie Cole; **Darla Dimple (speaking):** Ashley Peldon; **Darla Dimple (singing):** Lindsay Rideway; **Tillie Hippo:** Kathy Najimy; **Woolie Mammoth:** John Rhys-Davies; **L.B. Mammoth:** George Kennedy; **Flanigan:** Rene Auberjonois; **Francis:** Betty Lou Gerson; **Cranston:** Hal Holbrook; **T.W. Turtle:** Don Knotts; *Pudge the Penguin:* Matthew Harried, **Francis Betty:** Lou Gerson; **Farley Wink:** Frank Welker; **Bus Driver:** David Johansen; **Max:** Mark Dindal

A young, optimistic cat named Danny heads to Hollywood, with a song in his heart and dance moves in his feet, to become a film star, only to learn that Hollywood is a cruel and unforgiving town.

**PN:** Songs for *Cats Don't Dance* were written by Randy Newman, of "I Love L.A." fame, who also penned the Oscar-nominated songs for Disney's *Toy Story*. The songs were sung by Natalie

Cole. The movie's song-and-dance numbers were choreographed by famed MGM song-and-dance man Gene Kelly, who died that year. A high-speed digital ink and paint system, created by USAnimation, was used to create the film's digitally composited 2-D cel animation look, replacing traditional painting and camera methods. Even though the film was beautifully animated, *Cats Don't Dance* lasted only one week in movie theaters, grossing a mere $3.562 million at the box office.

### ◎ CHARLOTTE'S WEB (1973)

A Hanna-Barbera Production released by Paramount Pictures. **p:** William Hanna, Joseph Barbera; **d:** Charles A. Nichols, Iwao Takamoto; **w:** Earl Hamner Jr. (based on the book by E.B. White); **m:** Richard M. Sherman, Robert B. Sherman. **Songs:** "Charlotte's Web," "A Veritable Smorgasbord," "There Must Be Something More," "I Can Talk," "Mother Earth and Father Time," "We've Got Lots in Common," "Deep in the Dark" and "Zukerman's Famous Pig." **Running time:** 94 minutes. **Released:** March 1, 1973.

*Voices*

**Charlotte:** Debbie Reynolds; **Templeton:** Paul Lynde; **Wilbur:** Henry Gibson; **Narrator:** Rex Allen; **Mrs. Arable:** Martha Scott; **Old Sheep:** Dave Madden; **Avery:** Danny Bonaduce; **Geoffrey:** Don Messick; **Lurvy:** Herb Vigran; **The Goose:** Agnes Moorehead; **Fern Arable:** Pam Ferdin; **Mrs. Zuckerman/Mrs. Fussy:** Joan Gerber; **Homer Zuckerman:** Robert Holt; **Arable:** John Stephenson; **Henry Fussy:** William B. White

Wilbur, a runt pig who has been a pet of a New England farmer, is sold to a neighbor where he is told by a sheep that he is ticketed for the slaughterhouse. His life changes upon meeting a spider named Charlotte, who devotes all her energies to saving Wilbur from a pig's fate.

### ◎ CHICKEN LITTLE (2005)

A Walt Disney Studios Production released by Buena Vista Pictures. **p:** Randy Fullmer; **d:** Mark Dindal; **scr:** Steve Bencich, Ron J. Friedman, Ron Anderson; **st:** Mark Dindal, Mark Kennedy; **m:** John Debney. **Songs:** "Stir It Up," "One Little Slip," "Ain't No Mountain High Enough," "Don't Go Breaking My Heart," "It's the End of the World as We Know It," "We Are Champions," "All I Know," "Shake a Tail Feather," "Nants' Ingonyama," "Raiders of the Lost Ark Theme," "Gonna Make You Sweat," "I Will Survive," "Stayin' Alive," "Wannabe," "It's Too Late" and "Lollipop." **Running time:** 81 minutes. **Released:** November 4, 2005.

*Voices*

**Chicken Little:** Zach Braff; **Buck Cluck:** Garry Marshall; **Abby Mallard:** Joan Cusack; **Runt of the Litter:** Steve Zahn; **Foxy Loxy:** Amy Sedaris; **Mayor Turkey Lurkey:** Don Knotts; **Dog Announcer:** Harry Shearer; **Mr. Woolensworth:** Patrick Stewart; **Principal Fetchit:** Wallace Shawn: **Melvin, Alien Dad:** Fred Willard; **Tina, Alien Mom:** Catherine O'Hara; **Ace, Hollywood Chicken Little:** Adam West; **Alien Cop:** Patrick Warburton; **Morkubine Porcupine/Coach:** Mark Didal; **Fish out of Water:** Dan Molina; **Rodriguez/Acorn Mascot/Umpire:** Joe Whyte; **Kirby, Alien Kid:** Sean Elmore, Evan Dunn, Matthew Michael Josten; **Mama Runt:** Kelly Hoover; **Hollywood Fish:** Will Finn; **Hollywood Abby:** Dara McGarry; **Hollywood Runt:** Mark Kennedy

*Additional Voices*

Brad Abrell, Tom Amundsen, Steve Bencich, Greg Berg, Julianne Buescher, David Cowgill, Terri Douglas, Chris Edgerly,

Amanda Fein, Caitlin Fein, Patrick Fraley, Eddie Frierson, Jackie Gonneau, Archie Hahn, Jason Harris, Brittney Lee Harvey, Brian Hershkowitz, Amanda Kaplan, Nathan Kress, Anne Lockhart, Connor Matheus, Mona Marshall, Scott Menville, Rene Mujica, Jonathan Nichols, Paul Pape, Aaron Spann, Pepper Sweeney

In this offbeat retelling of the classic children's story, a young chicken causes chaos when he mistakes a falling acorn for part of the sky falling, ruining his reputation forever, until he saves his fellow citizens from an alien invasion of their town.

**PN:** Joining Pixar and DreamWorks as a producer of computer-animated features, this was Disney's first in-house all-CG animated feature. Opening in theatres nationwide on November 4, 2005, and at a few venues in 3-D, the 76-minute comedy claimed the number-one spot for two straight weeks, grossing more than $80.8 million in that time and more than $133 million overall in the United States. To create the title character of Chicken Little, animators computer animated more than 76,000 individual feathers—55,000 alone on his head and roughly 9,000 on each arm—to cover his body.

### ◎ CHICKEN RUN (2000)

An Aardman Animations Production released by DreamWorks Pictures SKG in association with Pathé. **p:** Peter Lord, David Sproxton, Nick Park; **exec prod:** Jake Eberts, Jeffrey Katzenberg, Michael Rose; **d:** Peter Lord, Nick Park; **st:** Peter Lord, Nick Park; **scr:** Karey Kirkpatrick; **superv anim:** Loyd Price; **key anim:** Merline Crossingham, Sergio Delfino, Suzy Fagan, Guionne Leroy, Dave Osmand, Darren Robbie, Jason Spencer-Galsworthy. **Songs:** "Ave Maria," "Barwick Green," "Flip Flop and Fly," "Over the Waves" and "The Wanderer." **Running time:** 85 minutes. **Released:** June 21, 2000.

*Voices*

**Rocky:** Mel Gibson; **Ginger:** Julia Sawalha; **Mrs. Tweety:** Miranda Richardson; **Fowler:** Benjamin Whirrow; **Mr. Tweedy:** Tony Haygarth; **Fetcher:** Phil Daniels; **Mac:** Lynn Ferguson; **Babs:** Jane Horrocks; **Nick:** Timothy Spall; **Bunty:** Imelda Staunton; **Circus Man:** John Sharian

Held captive at Tweedy's Egg Farm where they ultimately face extinction, heroic "flying hen" Rocky the rooster (voiced by Mel

*Rocky the rooster (voiced by Mel Gibson, front center) is the center of attention in the henhouse with (front, left to right) Bunty, Babs, and Ginger in Aardman Animations' smash-hit clay animation comedy adventure* Chicken Run. © *Aardman Animations. All rights reserved.*

Gibson) leads his fellow "inmates" and love interest, Ginger, to freedom in 1950s England in this claymation comedy reminiscent of the 1963 live-action drama *The Great Escape*.

**PN:** *Chicken Run* was Britain's Aardman Animations' first feature-length film following its success producing stop-motion clay-animated and cel-animated cartoon shorts and featurettes, including the Oscar-nominated *Wallace & Gromit* cartoons. Met by widespread critical raves and nominated for 22 awards, winning 19 times including a Golden Globe for best motion picture–comedy/musical, the film grossed an astounding $105.5 million in the United States.

### ◎ THE CHIPMUNK ADVENTURE (1987)

A Bagdasarian Production released by Samuel Goldwyn. **p:** Ross Bagdasarian Jr.; **d:** Janice Karman; **w:** Janice Karman, Ross Bagdasarian Jr.; **m:** Randy Edelman. **Songs:** "Witch Doctor," "Come on-a My House," "Diamond Dolls," "The Girls of Rock and Roll," "Wooly Bully," "I, Yi, Yi, Yi, Yi/Cuanto Le Gusta," "My Mother" and "Getting Lucky." **Running time:** 90 minutes. **Released:** May 22, 1987.

*Voices*

**Alvin/Simon/Dave Seville:** Ross Bagdasarian Jr.; **Theodore/Brittany/Jeanette/Eleanor:** Janice Karman; **Miss Miller:** Dodie Goodman; **Claudia Furschtien:** Susan Tyrell; **Klaus Furschtien:** Anthony DeLongis; **Sophie:** Frank Welker

*Additional Voices*

Charles Adler, Nancy Cartwright, Phillip Clark, Pat Pinney, George Poulos, Ken Samson

Dave Seville goes off to Europe, leaving the unhappy Chipmunks home with their babysitter, Miss Miller. Alvin dreams of world travel and convinces Simon and Theodore to enter a hot-air balloon race around the world against the Chipettes, Brittany, Jeanette and Eleanor. During their globe-trotting the Chipmunks and Chipettes unwittingly assist a pair of international diamond smugglers, hiding illegal gems in toy dolls at shops in Greece, Africa, Egypt, Rio and several other faraway places.

*Alvin, Theodore and Simon travel the world to several faraway places in their first full-length feature, The Chipmunk Adventure (1987).* (COURTESY: BAGDASARIAN PRODUCTIONS)

*The glass slipper appears to be a perfect fit for poor orphaned Cinderella in a scene from Walt Disney's full-length cartoon release,* Cinderella *(1950). © Walt Disney Productions* (COURTESY: MUSEUM OF MODERN ART/FILM STILLS ARCHIVE)

### ◎ CINDERELLA (1950)

A Walt Disney Production released by RKO Radio Pictures. **p:** Walt Disney; **prod superv:** Ben Sharpsteen; **d:** Wilfred Jackson, Hamilton Luske, Clyde Geronimi; **dir anim:** Eric Larson, Ward Kimball, Norman Ferguson, Marc Davis, John Lounsbery, Milt Kahl, Wolfgang Reitherman, Les Clark, Ollie Johnston, Frank Thomas; **st:** Kenneth Anderson, Ted Sears, Homer Brightman, Joe Rinaldi, William Peet, Harry Reeves, Winston Hibler, Erdman Penner (based on the traditional story as told by Charles Perrault); **md:** Oliver Wallace, Paul J. Smith. **Songs:** "Bibbidi-Bobbidi-Boo," "So This Is Love," "A Dream Is a Wish Your Heart Makes," "Cinderella," "The Work Song" and "Oh Sing, Sweet Nightingale." **Running time:** 74 minutes. **Released:** February 15, 1950.

*Voices*

**Cinderella:** Ilene Woods; **Prince Charming:** William Phipps; **Stepmother:** Eleanor Audley; **Stepsisters:** Rhoda Williams, Lucille Bliss; **Fairy Godmother:** Verna Felton; **King/Grand Duke:** Luis Van Rooten; **Jaq/Gus/Bruno:** James Macdonald

Poor orphaned Cinderella is a slave to her stepmother and two stepsisters in an environment she can endure only through her friendship with animals. Her fairy godmother transforms her rags into a beautiful gown, and she is given only until midnight to attend the king's ball where his son (Prince Charming) yearns to find the girl of his dreams.

### ◎ CLEOPATRA, QUEEN OF SEX (1972)

A Mushi Pro Productions released by Xanadu. **p:** Yoneyama Abiko; **d:** Eiichi Yamamoto, Osamu Tezuka; **scr:** Shigemi Satoyoshi; **m:** Isao Tomita; **anim:** Kazuko Nakamura, Gisaburo Sugii. **Running time:** 100 minutes. **Released:** April 24, 1972.

*Voices*

**Cleopatra:** Nakayama Chinatsu; **Ceasar:** Hana Takamura; **Antonius:** Nabe Osami; **Libya:** Yoshimura Miko; **Apollodrius:** Hatsui Kotoe; **Lupa:** Yanagiya Tsubame; **Ionius:** Tsukamoto Nobuo; **Carpania:** Imai Kazuko; **Cabagonis:** Abe Susumu; **Chief Tarabach:** Kato Yoshio; **Octavian:** Nozawa Nachi

Was Cleopatra a great lover? Three friends argue this point and time-travel to the past to Egypt to see if the legend is true in this erotic animated fantasy parody.

**PN:** Originally produced in 1970 by Japanese animator Osamu Tezuka (best known as the father of television's *Astro Boy*), this X-rated film was redubbed in English and released in the United States on April 24, 1972, about two weeks after the release of Ralph Bakshi's milestone feature *Fritz the Cat* (1972), the first X-rated animated feature in film history.

## ◎ CLIFFORD'S REALLY BIG MOVIE (2004)

A Scholastic Entertainment Inc./Big Red Dog Production released by Warner Bros. Pictures. **p:** Deborah Forte; **d:** Robert Ramirez; **scr:** Robert C. Ramirez, Rhett Reese; **m:** Jody Gray; **songs:** Jody Gray, David Steven Cohen; **anim dir:** Murray Debus. **Running time:** 73 minutes. **Released:** February 20, 2004.

### Voices

**Clifford the Big Red Dog:** John Ritter; **Shackelford:** Wayne Brady; **Emily Elizabeth:** Grey DeLisle; **Dorothy:** Jenna Elfman; **George Wolfsbottom:** John Goodman; **Dirk:** Jess Harnell; **T-Bone:** Kel Mitchell; **Larry:** Judge Reinhold; **Jetta/Madison:** Kath Soucie; **Cleo:** Cree Summer; **Rodrigo:** Wilmer Valderrama; **Mr. Bleakman:** Earl Boen; **P.T.:** Ernie Hudson

Under the assumption that his owner can't afford to feed him, Clifford runs away from home and embarks on the adventure of a lifetime where he joins a carnival and, in the process, wins a dog food talent contest with the prize of a lifetime supply of Tummy Yummies.

**PN:** Based on the best-selling children's book series by author/illustrator Norman Bridwell, this feature-length project followed the successful PBS animated series, also based on the books, produced in 2000. Unfortunately, the film had limited distribution and did poorly at the box office, grossing $2.8 million from box-office ticket sales. (Conversely, the film was a big seller on DVD.) The late actor John Ritter voiced the character Clifford in the film and in the television series.

## ◎ COOL WORLD (1992)

A Frank Mancuso Production released by Paramount Pictures. **p:** Frank Mancuso Jr.; **d:** Ralph Bakshi; **scr:** Michael Grais, Mark Victor, Larry Gross (uncredited); **m:** Mark Isham, John Dickson. **Songs:** "Play with Me," "My Ideal," "Under," "N.W.O.," "Ah-Ah," "The Devil Does Drugs," "The Witch," "Holli's Groove," "Sex on Wheelz," "Do That Thing," "Papua New Guinea," "Next Is the E," "Her Sassy Kiss," "Industry and Seduction," "Mindless," "Sedusa," "Let's Make Love," "Disappointed," "Real Cool World" and "That Old Black Magic." **Running time:** 102 minutes. **Released:** July 9, 1992.

### Cast/Voices

**Holli Would:** Kim Basinger; **Jack Deebs:** Gabriel Byrne; **Jennifer Malley:** Michele Abrams; **Isabelle Malley:** Deidre O'Connell; **Mom Harris:** Janni Brenn-Lowen; **Frank Harris:** Brad Pitt; **Cop:** William Frankfather; **Cop:** Greg Collins; **Sparks:** Michael David Lally; **Comic Bookstore Cashier:** Michele Abrams; **Comic Store Patron:** Stephen Worth; **Lonette (performance model):** Jenine Jennings; **Interrogator:** Joey Camen; **Mash:** Maurice LaMarche; **Bash:** Gregory Snegoff; **Bob:** Candi Milo; **Nails:** Charles Adler; **Bouncer:** Patrick Pinney; **Isabelle Malley:** Deidre O'Connell; **Himself:** Frank Sinatra; **Lucky's Bouncer:** Lamont Jackson; **Valet:** Paul Ben-Victor, **Mash (performance model):** Gary Friedkin, **Lonette (performance model):** Clare Hoak; **Dock Whiskers (performance model):** Antonio Hoyos; **Nails (performance model):** Leroy Thompson, **Bob (performance model):** Robert N. Bell

None-too-stable cartoonist Jack Deebs (Gabriel Byrne), who has just finished a jail term for murdering his wife's lover (a return-ing World War II soldier played by Brad Pitt), is willed into a cartoon world by a character of his own devising: sexy cartoon seductress Holli Would (voiced by Kim Basinger). Trying to return to the real world, Deebs encounters a universe of strange animated "doodles" (cartoon characters) through adventures in Las Vegas, in this live-action/animated fantasy directed by legendary animator Ralph Bakshi of *Fritz the Cat*, *Heavy Traffic* and *Coonskin* fame and often compared to *Who Framed Roger Rabbit* but taken to extremes.

**PN:** Animator Ralph Bakshi toned down his trademark outrageousness for this film, which received a PG-13 rating. Screenwriter Larry Gross, of *48 Hours* fame, wrote most of the other screenplay for the film but his work was uncredited. The film cost an estimated $28 million to produce. As with most Bakshi productions, the film was not without controversy; following its release, Jenine Jennings, a 21-year-old actress listed as the film's choreographer and music consultant, went public, claiming that it was she who played the animated Holli Would in the film. Jennings reported that she did the dancing, acting and even the "very hot" love scene with Gabriel Byrne (in the movie Byrne and the animated Holli Would do more than kiss), and dressed in skimpier and skimpier outfits for the animators to get the idea of what the Basinger cartoon character should act like. Frank Sinatra Jr. appeared in the film as himself and also sang the duet, "Let's Make Love," with the film's costar Kim Basinger, who had the dubious distinction of being nominated for a 1993 Razzie Award for Worst Actress for her performance. Rocker David Bowie also sang a song for the film, entitled "Real Cool World."

## ◎ COONSKIN (1975)

An Albert S. Ruddy Production released by Paramount and Bryanston Pictures. **p:** Albert S. Ruddy; **d & w:** Ralph Bakshi; **m:** Chico Hamilton; **seq anim:** Irven Spence, Charlie Downs, Ambrozi Palinoda, John E. Walker Sr. **Running time:** 82 minutes. **Released:** August 1, 1975.

### Voices

**Samson/Brother Bear:** Barry White; **Preacher/Brother Fox:** Charles Gordone; **Pappy/Old Man Bone:** Scatman Crothers; **Randy/Brother Rabbit:** Phillip Thomas

Three rural black men seek new direction in their lives to escape the ghetto life of crime and other vices.

**PN:** Paramount Pictures was originally supposed to release this film, which combined live action and animation, but passed due its strong racial content. Upon its release, the film provoked objections to its depictions of blacks from the Congress of Racial Equality (CORE). In 1975, after a brief run, the film was shelved. To calm racial tension, the film was later released on video under a new title: *Streetfight*. The film's working titles were *Bustin' Out*, *Coon Skin* and *Coonskin No More*.

## ◎ THE COSMIC EYE (1986)

A Hubley Studios Production released by Upfront Releasing. **p & d:** Faith Hubley; **w:** John Hubley, Faith Hubley; **anim:** Fred Burns, William Littlejohn, Emily Hubley, Robert Cannon, Ed Smith, Georia Hubley, Tissa David, Phil Duncan, Katherine Woddell. **Running time:** 72 minutes. **Released:** June 6, 1986.

### Voices

**Father Time/Musician:** Dizzy Gillespie; **Musician:** Sam Hubley; **Musician:** Linda Atkinson; **Mother Earth:** Maureen Stapleton; **Rocko:** Jack Warden

Homeward bound to a distant planet that orbits Sirius, the Dog Star, a trio of space musicians who suffer from acute nostalgia, take a whirling out-of-the-body spin in a rose-tinted sky, only to return to their bodies and observe life on Earth through a series of animated shorts before joyously returning to their home planet.

**PN:** Faith Hubley, the wife of animator/producer/director John Hubley, produced, designed and directed this innovative feature-length project, originally produced in 1985 and screened at film festivals around the world before being released theatrically in 1986 by Upfront Releasing. The film won numerous awards, including a Grand Jury Prize nomination at the 1986 Sundance Film Festival.

### ◎ COWBOY BEBOP: THE MOVIE (2003)

A Sunrise Inc./Bandai Visual Production released by Sony Pictures and Destination Films/Samuel Goldwyn Films. **p:** Kazuhiko Ikeguchi, Haruyo Kanesaku, Yutaka Maseba, Masahiko Minami; **d:** Shinichiro Watanabe; **scr:** Marc Handler (English version), Akihiko Inari, Sadayuki Murai, Keiko Nobumoto, Dai Sato, Shinichiro Watanabe, Ryota Yamaguchi, Michiko Yokote; **m:** Yoko Kanno. **Running time:** 114 minutes. **Released:** April 4, 2003.

*Voices*

(English version) **Jet Black:** Beau Billingslea; **Spike Spiegel:** Steven Blum

A team of space cowboys on Mars, headed by the bounty-hunting Bebop, tries to catch a cold-blooded terrorist who plans to unleash an army of microscopic robots to destroy all life on the planet.

**PN:** Also known as *Cowboy Bebop: The Movie: Knockin' on Heaven's Door*, this film, redubbed in English, was shown in limited release and took in slightly more than $1 million in box-office receipts in the United States. The motion picture followed the successful, adult action, 26-episode cartoon series of the same name produced in 1998.

### ◎ CURIOUS GEORGE (2006)

A Universal Pictures/Imagine Entertainment Production in association with David Kirschner/Jon Shapiro Productions released by Universal Pictures. **p:** Ron Howard, David Kirschner, Jon Shapiro; **exec prod:** Bonne Radford, Ken Tsumura, James Whitaker, David Bernardi; **d:** Matthew O'Callaghan; **scr:** Ken Kaufman; **st:** Ken Kaufman, Mike Werb (based on the books by Margret and H.A. Rey); **m:** Heitor Pereira; **songs:** Jack Johnson; **lead anim:** D. Brewster, Anthony DeRosa, Jeffrey P. Johnson, John Pomeroy, Stevan Wahl, Frans Vischer. **Songs:** "Broken," "People Watching," "Talk of the Town" and "Upside Down" (written and performed by Jack Johnson). **Running time:** 86 minutes. **Released:** February 10, 2006.

*Voices*

**Ted, the Man with the Yellow Hat:** Will Ferrell; **Maggie:** Drew Barrymore; **Bloomsberry Jr.:** David Cross; **Clovis:** Eugene Levy; **Bloomsberry:** Dick Van Dyke; **George:** Frank Welker

A timid museum employee travels to the jungles of Africa to locate a rare artifact for an exhibit and encounters a wide-eyed, curious and playful monkey who follows him back to civilization.

**PN:** Nearly 65 years after the first book by the late author/illustrator tandem of H.A. Rey and his wife, Margret, was published, Universal Pictures and Imagine Entertainment produced this full-length, ink-and-paint animated adaptation. In producing this cartoon version of the Reys' immortal troublemaking monkey from their popular 1940s children's stories, producers made a few modern revisions to the story and characterizations. For starters, Curious George's human pal, simply known as "the man in the yellow hat," was given the name Ted (voiced by Will Ferrell) and

a much bigger role in the movie than in the children's books. In the books, the Man actually captures George and brings him back with him, whereas, in the movie George stows away on the Man's ship bound for America. Licensing deals for *Curious George* reportedly topped $500 million, with Universal licensing consumer promotions for everything from postage stamps to cold medicines and other products, to more than 100 vendors worldwide. In the fall of 2006, PBS debuted a new 30-episode half-hour animated Curious George series aimed at preschoolers.

### ◎ DAFFY DUCK'S MOVIE: FANTASTIC ISLAND (1983)

A Warner Bros. release. **p & d:** Friz Freleng; **scr:** John Dunn, David Detiege, Friz Freleng; **seq dir:** David Detiege, Friz Freleng, Phil Monroe, **Running time:** 78 minutes. **Released:** August 5, 1983.

*Voices*

**Daffy Duck/Speedy Gonzales/Yosemite Sam/Bugs Bunny/Tasmanian Devil/Porky Pig/Foghorn Leghorn:** Mel Blanc; **Granny/Miss Prissy:** June Foray; **Spirit of the Well:** Les Tremayne

In this spoof of TV's *Fantasy Island*, Daffy Duck and Speedy Gonzales become shipwrecked on a desert island. After finding a treasure map belonging to Yosemite Sam, they begin digging for buried treasure and instead discover a wishing well that—after making a wish—magically changes the island into a fantasy paradise. This new footage introduces several complete cartoons: "Bucaneer Bunny" (1948), "Greedy for Tweety" (1957), "Tree for Two" (1952), "Curtain Razor" (1949), "A Mouse Divided (1953), "From Hare to Heir" (1960), "Stupor Duck" (1956), "Banty Raids" (1963) and "Louvre Come Back to Me" (1962).

### ◎ DAFFY DUCK'S QUACKBUSTERS (1989)

A Warner Bros. Production released by Warner Bros. **p:** Steven S. Greene, Kathleen Helppie-Shipley; **d & w:** Greg Ford, Terry Lennon; **m:** Carl Stalling, Milt Franklyn, Bill Lava. **Running time:** 72 minutes. **Released:** September 24, 1989.

*Voices*

**Daffy Duck/Bugs Bunny/Sylvester the Cat/Tweety/J.P. Cubish/Monsters** Mel Blanc; **Singing Voice of Daffy Duck:** Mel Torme;

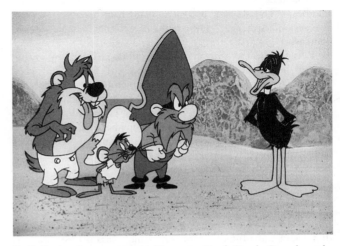

*Daffy Duck calls a meeting with Tasmanian Devil, Speedy Gonzales and Yosemite Sam in Daffy Duck's Movie: Fantastic Island, produced and directed by Friz Freleng. © Warner Brothers. All rights reserved.*

**Zed Koppell/Lawyer:** Roy Firestone; **Thelma/Operator:** B.J. Ward; **Count Bloodcount:** Ben Frommer; **Emily/Agatha:** Julie Bennett

After inheriting $1 million, Daffy starts a ghost-busting business with Bugs Bunny and Porky Pig for the sole purpose of destroying the ghost of J.B. Cubish, his benefactor. Cartoons featured: "Daffy Dilly" (1948), "Water Water Every Hare" (1952), "Claws for Alarm" (1954), "The Abdominable Snow Rabbit" (1961), "Transylvania 6-5000" (1963), "Punch Trunk" (1953), "Jumpin' Jupiter" (1955), "Hyde and Go Tweet" (1960) and "The Prize Pest" (1951). The film also contained the first new cartoon short produced by the studio in several decades: "The Duxorcist" (1987).

**PN:** This compilation featured grossed a dismal $300,000 following its opening.

### ◎ THE DAYDREAMER (1966)

A Joseph E. Levine/Arthur Rankin Jr. and Jules Bass/Videocraft International Production released by Embassy Pictures. **p:** Arthur Rankin Jr.; **d:** Jules Bass; **exec prod:** Joseph E. Levine, **scr:** Arthur Rankin Jr. (based on the stories and characters created by Hans Christian Andersen; with additional dialogue by Romeo Muller); **m/l:** Jules Bass, Maury Laws (with the theme "The Daydreamer" sung by Robert Goulet). **Songs:** "The Daydreamer," "Wishes and Teardrops," "Luck to Sell," "Happy Guy," "Who Can Tell," "Simply Wonderful," "Isn't It Cozy Here," "Tivoli Bells," "Voyage of the Walnut Shell" and "Waltz for a Mermaid." Filmed in Animagic. **Running time:** 98 minutes. **Released:** July 29, 1966.

*Cast/Voices*

**The Sandman:** Cyril Ritchard; **Chris Andersen:** Paul O'Keefe; **Papa Andersen:** Jack Gilford; **The Pieman:** Ray Bolger; **Mrs. Klopplebobbler:** Margaret Hamilton; **The Little Mermaid:** Hayley Mills; **Father Neptune:** Burl Ives; **The Sea Witch:** Tallulah Bankhead; **The First Tailor:** Terry-Thomas; **The Second Tailor:** Victor Borge; **The Emperor:** Ed Wynn; **Thumbelina:** Patty Duke; **The Rat:** Boris Karloff; **The Mole:** Sessue Hayakawa

*Additional Voices*

Robert Harter, Larry Mann, Billie Richards, James Daugherty, William Marine

Famous storyteller Hans Christian Andersen, as a young boy, daydreams about his best-loved fairytale adventures—incorporating the tales of "The Little Mermaid," "The Emperor's New Clothes," "Thumbelina" and "The Garden of Paradise"—in this live-action/"Animagic," full-length feature that includes an all-star cast.

**PN:** *Daydreamer* was one of three films produced by Arthur Rankin Jr. and Jules Bass in association with famed Hollywood producer Joseph E. Levine. The motion picture was the combined efforts of five countries, the United States, Canada, England, France and Japan. The movie's title song, "The Daydreamer," was sung by Robert Goulet. Other musical numbers were sung by the film's costars, among them: "Wishes and Teardrops" (by Hayley Mills), "Happy Guy" (by Patty Duke), "Who Can Tell" (by Ray Bolger), "Simply Wonderful" (by Ed Wynn).

### ◎ DIGIMON: THE MOVIE (2000)

A Toei Company Ltd./Saban Entertainment, Inc. Production released by 20th Century Fox. **p:** Seki Hiromi, Terri-Lei O'Malley; **d:** Takaaki Yamashita, Hisashi Nayayama, Masahiro Aizawa; **scr:** (English version) Jeff Nimoy, Bob Bucholz; **m:** Udi Harpaz, Amorz Plessner. **Running time:** 85 minutes. **Released:** October 6, 2000.

*Voices*

**Kari:** Jill Miller; **Tai:** Joshua Seth; **Red Greymon:** Bob Papenbrook; **T.K:** Doug Erholtz; **Parrotman:** David Lodge; **Mrs. Kamiya:** Dorothy Melendrez: **Big Agumon/Gargomon/Miko:** Michael Sorich; **Botamon:** Peggy O'Neal; **Sora:** Colleen O'Shaughnessey; **Koromon:** Brianne Siddall

*Additional Voices*

Mona Marshall, Michael Lindsay, Michael Reisz, Wendee Lee, Mike Reynolds, Kirk Thornton; Laura Summer: Edie Mirman; Dave Mallow, Robert Axelrod

While attending summer camp, three youngsters cross over into the computer world where they encounter digital monsters (Digimon) who look like dinosaurs that help them battle bad Digimon infected by a computer virus that threatens mankind, in this compilation animated feature featuring three cartoon shorts from the *Digimon* television series.

### ◎ DINOSAUR (2000)

A Walt Disney Studios Production released by Buena Vista Pictures. **p:** Pam Marsden; **d:** Ralph Zondag, Eric Leighton; **scr:** John Harrison, Robert Nelson Jacobs, Walon Green; **st:** Thom Erinquez, John Harrison, Robert Nelson Jacobs, Ralph Zondag; **m:** John Newton Howard; **superv anim:** Mark Anthony Austin, Trey Thomas, Tom Roth, Bill Fletcher, Larry White, Eamonn Butler, Joel Fletcher, Dick Zondag, Michael Belzer, Gregory William Griffith, Atsushi Sato. **Running time:** 82 minutes. **Released:** May 19, 2000.

*Voices*

**Aladar:** D.B. Sweeney; **Plio:** Alfre Woodard; **Suri:** Hayden Panettiere; **Yar:** Ossie Davis; **Zini:** Max Cassella; **Neera:** Julianna Margulies; **Kron:** Samuel E. Wright; **Bruton:** Peter Siragusa; **Baylene:** Joan Plowright

Raised by a family of lemurs who adopt him as their own, an orphaned iguanodon (Aladar) takes a remarkable journey across desert terrain after a meteor shower annihilates the island on which they live to find a new sanctuary to call home in this partially live-action and CGI-animated fantasy adventure.

**PN:** Grossing more than $136.5 million in the United States alone but never turning a profit due to the high costs of production, this prehistoric fantasy was Walt Disney Studios' first computer-animated feature combining CGI-animated characters and live-action backgrounds.

### ◎ DIRTY DUCK (1977)

A Murakami-Wolf Production released by New World Pictures. **p:** Jerry Good; **d, w & anim:** Charles Swenson; **m:** Mark Volman, Howard Kaylan-Flo and Eddie. **Running time:** 75 minutes. **Released:** July 13, 1977.

*Voices*

**Willard:** Mark Volman

*Additional Voices*

Robery Ridgeley, Walker Emiston, Cynthia Adler, Janet Lee, Lurene Tuttle, Jerry Good, Howard Kaylan

Willard Eisenbaum, a shy, lonely, inept, sexually frustrated insurance company employee, is thrown by fate into the company of a large, sailor-suited duck who is convinced that some good sex will straighten Willard out.

**PN:** Like Ralph Bakshi's *Fritz the Cat*, this film was X-rated.

### ◎ DOOGAL (2006)

A Weinstein Company Production in association with Pathé Image/U.K. Film Council/Pathé Renn Productions/France 2 Cinema/Canal+/Films Action/SPZ Entertainment/Bolexbrothers Ltd. Productions released by the Weinstein Company. **p:** Laurent Rodon, Pascal Rodon, Claude Gorsky; **exec prod:** Francois Ivernel, Cameron McCracken, Jill Sinclair; **d:** Jean Duval, Frank Passingham, Dave Borthwick; **scr:** Paul Bassett, Serge Danot, Tad Safran, Raolf Sanoussi, Stephanie Sanoussi (based on characters created by Serge Danot and Martine Danot); **m:** Mark Thomas; **anim:** Benoit Gagne, David Hubert. **Running time:** 85 minutes. **Released:** February 24, 2006.

### Voices

**Doogal:** Daniel Tay; **Dylan:** Jimmy Fallon; **Zeebad:** Jon Stewart; **Ermintrude:** Whoopi Goldberg; **Brian:** William H. Macy; **Train:** Chevy Chase; **Narrator:** Judi Dench; **Florence:** Kylie Minogue; **Zebedee:** Ian McKellen; **Moose:** Kevin Smith; **Soldier Sam:** Bill Hader; **Coral:** Heidi Brook Myers

### Additional Voices

Cory Edwards, John Krasinski

A group of animal friends embarks on a dangerous journey in an effort to imprison their oppressor, the evil wizard Zebedee.

**PN:** Created by the late Serge Danot, the character Doogal actually began as a series of five-minute, black-and-white, stop-motion cartoons animated by English toonster Ivor Wood on French television in 1964 as *Le Manège Enchanté*. The BBC later bought it as a children's television series that was broadcast in the United Kingdom with narration and all voices supplied by actor Eric Thompson, and it became a cult favorite with more than 500 episodes that was extremely popular with adults and children. Thompson later voiced a feature-length version of the show, entitled *Dougal and the Blue Cat* (1970). This newest computer-animated feature was a British/French coproduction that first opened at a charity event on January 30, 2005, with the French version being released in that country on February 2, 2005, as *Pollux! Le Manège Enchanté* (Pollux being dougal), featuring a heavyweight French-voice cast that included Vanessa Paradis, Michel Galabru, Gerard Jugnot, Valerie Lemercier and Eddy Mitchell. The British version then opened in the United Kingdom nine days later.

Coproduced by Harvey Weinstein's Weinstein Company, the American version of this $20-million feature was redubbed with the voices of popular American stars, including Jimmy Fallon, Whoopi Goldberg, William H. Macy and Chevy Chase. Hoping to replicate the success of Pixar and DreamWorks Animation, it opened in the United States a year later, on February 24, 2006, becoming a commercial and critical flop, grossing a dismal $3.6 million the weekend it opened and only $7,578,946 overall.

### ◎ DOUG'S 1ST MOVIE (1999)

A Jumbo Pictures/Plus One Animation, Inc. Production released by Walt Disney Pictures. **p:** Jim Jinkins, David Campbell, Melanie Grisanti, Jack Spillum; **d:** Maurice Joyce; **scr:** Ken Scarborough (based on characters created by Jim Jinkins); **m:** Mark Watters; **songs:** Dan Sawyer, Fred Newman, Krysten Osborne, Linda Garvey, William Squier, Jeffrey Lodin; **superv dir (Japan):** Choon-Man Lee; **anim dir (Japan):** Hon-Gil Oh, Hyeon-Deok Ma, Soeng-Chean Shin, Joon-Bok Kim; **anim (New York):** Mike Foran, Ray daSilva. **Songs:** "Deep Deep Water," "Someone Like Me," "Mona Mo" and "Disney's Doug: Original Theme." **Running time:** 81 minutes. **Released:** March 26, 1999.

### Voices

**Doug Funnie/Lincoln:** Thomas McHugh; **Skeeter/Mr. Dink/ Porkchop/Ned/Vocal Effects:** Fred Newman; **Roger Klotz/**
**Boomer/Larry/Mr. Chiminy:** Chris Phillips; **Patti Mayonaisse:** Constance Schulman; **Herman Melville:** Frank Welker; **Mr. Funnie/Mr. Bluff/Willie/Chalky/Bluff Agent #1:** Doug Preis; **Guy Graham:** Guy Hadley; **Beebe Bluff/Elmo:** Alice Playten; **Al and Moo Sleech/Robocrusher:** Eddie Korbich; **Stentorian Announcer:** David O'Brien

Having heard tales about a mythological monster that supposedly lives in polluted Lucky Duck Lake, 12-year-old Doug Funnie and his best friend, Skeeter, decide to find out once and for all, if the endangered lake creature really exists. When they find that he does, they also discover a major cover-up by one of Bluffington's leading residents.

**PN:** Based on the writer/director/animator Jim Jinkins's character Doug Funnie, star of the cartoon series *Doug*, originally broadcast on Nickelodeon and later on ABC (after Disney acquired Jinkins's company, Jumbo Pictures), this film received mixed reviews from critics and grossed a modest $19.4 million at theaters in the United States.

### ◎ DUCKTALES THE MOVIE: THE TREASURE OF THE LOST LAMP (1990)

A Walt Disney Animation (France) S.A. Production released by Buena Vista. **p & d:** Bob Hathcock; **scr:** Alan Burnett; **m:** David Newman; **seq dir:** Paul Brizzi, Gaetan Brizzi, Clive Pallant, Mattias Marcos Rodric, Vincent Woodcock; **anim:** Gary Andrews, James Baker, Javier Gutierrez Blas, Eric Bouillette, Moran Caouissin, Caron Creed, Caroline Cruikshank, Roberto Curilli, Sylvain DeBoissy, Joe Ekers, Mark Eoche-Duval, Pierre Fassal, Al Gaivoto, Manolo Galiana, Bruno Gaumetou, Dina Gellert-Nielsen, Arnold Gransac, Teddy Hall, Peter Hausner, Francisco Alaminos Hodar, Daniel Jeannette, Nicholas Marlet, Bob McKnight, Ramon Modiano, Sean Newton, Brent Odell, Catherine Poulain, Jean-Christopher Roger, Pascal Ropars, Stephane Sainte-Foi, Alberto Conejo Sanz, Anna Saunders, Ventura R. Vallejo, Jan Van Buyten, Duncan Varley, Simon Ward-Horner and Johnny Zeuten. **Songs:** "Duck Tales Theme." **Running time:** 73 minutes. **Released:** August 3, 1990.

### Voices

**Scrooge McDuck:** Alan Young; **Launchpad:** Terence McGovern; **Huey/Duey/Louie/Webby:** Russi Taylor; **Dijon:** Richard Libertini; **Merlock:** Christopher Lloyd; **Mrs. Featherby:** June Foray; **Duckworth:** Chuck McCann; **Mrs. Beakley:** Joan Gerber; **Genie:** Rip Taylor

### Additional Voices

Charlie Adler, Jack Angel, Steve Bulen, Sherry Lynn, Mickie T. McGowan, Patrick Pinney, Frank Welker

Scrooge McDuck travels to the far ends of the earth in search of the elusive buried treasure of legendary thief Collie Baba. With his companions Huey, Dewey and Louie, Webby and Launchpad McQuack, Scrooge discovers not only the treasure but also that there's a mysterious madman named Merlock who's out to stop him.

**PN:** The success of the *DuckTales* syndicated TV series inspired this feature-length release. Box-office receipts totaled $18 million.

### ◎ DUMBO (1941)

A Walt Disney Production released by RKO Radio Pictures. **p:** Walt Disney; **super dir:** Ben Sharpsteen; **scr st:** Joe Grant, Dick Huemer (based on a story by Helen Aberson and Harold Pearl); **st dev:** Bill Peet, Aurie Battaglia, Joe Rinaldi, George Stallings, Webb Smith; **m:** Oliver Wallace, Frank Churchill, Ned Washington; **seq**

*Baby elephant Dumbo takes his first flight in a scene from the classic Walt Disney feature* Dumbo *(1941). © Walt Disney Productions* (COURTESY: MUSEUM OF MODERN ART/FILM STILLS ARCHIVE)

**dir:** Norman Ferguson, Wilfred Jackson; Bill Roberts, Jack Kinney, Sam Armstrong; **anim dir:** Vladimir Tytla, Fred Moore, Ward Kimball, John Lounsbery, Arthur Babbitt, Wolfgang Reitherman. **Songs:** "Look Out for Mr. Stork," "Baby Mine," "Pink Elephants on Parade," "Casey Junior," "Song of the Roustabouts," "When I See an Elephant Fly." **Running time:** 64 minutes. **Released:** October 23, 1941.

*Voices*
**Narrator:** John McLeish; **Timothy Mouse:** Ed Brophy; **Ringmaster:** Herman Bing; **Casey Jr.:** Margaret Wright; **Messenger Stork:** Sterling Holloway; **Elephant:** Verna Felton; **Elephant:** Sarah Selby; **Elephant:** Dorothy Scott; **Elephant:** Noreen Gamill; **Joe/Clown:** Billy Sheets; **Clown:** Billy Bletcher; **Skinny:** Malcolm Hutton; **Crows:** Cliff Edwards; **Crows:** Jim Carmichael; **Crows:** Hall Johnson Choir; **Clown:** Eddie Holden; **Roustabouts:** The King's Men; **Boy:** Harold Manley; **Boy:** Tony Neil; **Boy:** Charles Stubbs

Mrs. Jumbo, a circus elephant, patiently awaits the stork's delivery of her own baby elephant. The young elephant is like no other—with ears as large as sails, he is affectionately dubbed "Dumbo." Dumbo's imperfection becomes an asset when he discovers he can use his ears to fly. He is billed as a top circus attraction, experiencing triumphs and failures of circus life.

## ◎ EDEN (2002)
A Poland, Europa Ltd. Production released by Europa. **p:** Thomasz Filipczak; **d & w:** Andrzej Czeczot; **m:** Michał Urbaniak. **Running time:** 85 minutes. **Released:** December 13, 2002.

*Voices*
Urszula Dudziak, Eugene Lazarotti

Produced in Poland *Eden* features a Czeczot "everyman," Youzeck, as a flute-playing shepherd who travels through hell and heaven until finally ending up in New York aboard Noah's Ark. He meets many well-known characters from the Bible, Greek mythology, pop culture and history, including Prometheus, Janosik, Salvador Dali, Elvis Presley, President Bill Clinton with Monica Lewinsky, plus an assortment of bizarre animals and monsters, a witch, angels, and, for good measure, God himself in this animated fable for adults.

**PN:** Famed illustrator Andrzej Czeczot, who immigrated to the United States, wrote, directed and animated this feature-length odyssey that was entirely hand-painted on to celluloid film. Production lasted six years, commencing in 1996 and wrapping in 2002. In 2003, the film previewed in Los Angeles and earned an Academy Award nomination for best animated feature.

## ◎ EIGHT CRAZY NIGHTS (2002)
A Happy Madison/Meatball Animation Production released by Columbia TriStar and Sony Pictures. **p:** Adam Sandler, Jack Giarrupto, Allen Covert; **d:** Seth Kearsley; **scr:** Brooks Arthur, Allen Covert, Brad Isaacs, Adam Sandler; **m:** Ray Ellis, Marc Ellis, Teddy Castelluci; **char anim superv:** Stephan Franck; **superv anim:** Steve Cunningham, Ralph Fernan, Holger Leige, Melina Sydney Padua. **Songs:** "Davey's Song," "Patch Song," "Long Ago," "Technical Foul," "Mr. Roboto," "Intervention Song," "Bum Biddy," "Grand Finale/It's Your Moment, Whitey!" and "The Chanukah Song Part 3." **Running time:** 86 minutes. **Released:** November 27, 2002.

*Voices*
**Davey Stone/Whitey Duvall/Eleanore Duvall/Deer:** Adam Sandler; **Jennifer:** Jackie Tinone; **Benjamin:** Austin Stout; **Mayor Stewey Dewey:** Kevin Nealon; **Chinese Waiter/Narrator:** Rob Schneider; **Judge:** Norm Crosby; **Tom Baltezor:** Jon Lovitz

*Additional Voices*
Tyra Banks, Blake Clark, Peter Dante, Ellen Albertini Dow, Kevin Farley, Lari Friedman, Tom Kenny, Cole Sprouse, Dylan Sprouse, Carl Weathers, Jamie Alcroft, Brooks Arthur, James Barbour, Allen Covert, J.D. Donaruma, Archie Hahn, Todd Holland, Lainie Kazan

Determined to make sure nobody enjoys the holidays in the small town of Dukesberry where he lives, a holiday-loathing, former local basketball champ, Davey Stone (voiced by Adam Sandler), goes on a destructive rampage during Hanukah and is sentenced to 10 years in prison, only to have his sentence commuted when a kindly old basketball referee, Whitey, agrees to take full responsibility for him, after which Darey Stone redeems himself and changes his Scrooge-like behavior during the holidays.

## ◎ THE EMPEROR'S NEW GROOVE (2000)
A Walt Disney Pictures Production released by Buena Vista Pictures. **p:** Randy Fullmer; **d:** Mark Dindal; **scr:** David Reynolds; **orig st:** Roger Allers; **st:** Chris Williams, Mark Dindal; Matthew Jacobs; **m/sc:** John Debney; **superv anim:** Nik Ranieri, Bruce W. Smith, Dale Baer, Tony Bancroft; **superv anim (Paris unit):** Dominque Monferey. **Songs:** "Perfect World" and "My Funny Friend and Me." **Running time:** 79 minutes. **Released:** December 15, 2000.

*Voices*
**Kuzco:** David Spade; **Pacha:** John Goodman; **Yzma:** Eartha Kitt; **Kronk:** Patrick Warburton; **ChiCha:** Wendie Malick; **Chaca:** Kellyann Kelso; **Tipo:** Eli Russell Linnerty; **Bucky:** Bob Bergen; **Theme Song Guy:** Tom Jones; **Waitress:** Patti Deutsch; **Old Man:** John Fiedler

Aided by Pacha, a peasant llama herder, Kuzco, a miserable, egomanical Incan emperor-turned llama attempts to regain the power of his throne and return to his original form.

**PN:** Film and television stars John Goodman, David Spade and Wendie Malick (the latter co-stars of the NBC comedy series, *Just Shoot Me*) lent their voices to this outrageous comical, whose title is derived from the popular Danish children's story. *The Emperor's New Clothes*, produced by Walt Disney Pictures and directed by Mark Dindal. Originally it was made as a musical drama—first called *Kingdom in the Sun,* then *Kingdom of the Sun*—and Inca version of Mark Twain's story, *The Prince and the Pauper.* Built around six songs by Grammy Award-winning rock star Sting, the film was transformed into a comedy after the finished film test-screened badly. Afterward, the film was deconstructed and retooled and the film's original codirector Roger Allers (credited with writing the film's original story) was dropped, an expensive undertaking that cost $100 million. Receiving mostly good reviews, the film grossed $89,296,573 in the United States and $169,296,573 abroad. Sting and composer David Hartley wrote the film's songs, including the Academy Award-nominated "My Funny Friend and Me." Sting singlehandedly penned "Perfect World," which was sung by Tom Jones. Six other songs were ditched when the film turned from a musical into a comedy feature. In September 2002, a feature-length documentary describing the making of this animated feature opened in theaters.

## ◎ THE EMPEROR'S NIGHTINGALE (1951)

A Trick Brothers (Studio)/Rembrandt Films Production released by New Trends Associates. **p:** Jiri Trnka, William L. Snyder; **d:** Jiri Trnka; **scr:** Jiri Brdecka, Jiri Trnka; **m:** Vaclav Trojan. **Running time:** 75 minutes. **Released:** May 25, 1951.

*Voices*

**Narrator:** Boris Karloff; **The Girl:** Helena Patockova; **The Boy:** Jaromir Sobotoa

When a young boy (seen in live-action) imagines in his dreams that his toys are real, his dream comes to life (as stop-motion animated puppets) with a Chinese emperor befriending a nightingale whose song he loves to hear. This live-action/puppet animated feature was based on the classic Hans Christian Andersen fairy tale, narrated by Boris Karloff.

**PN:** Czechoslovakian animator Jiri Trnka, one of Europe's premier stop-motion animators, first produced this film in 1948 at his Trick Brothers studio in Prague, which he and Jiri Brdecka adapted for the screen. Before distributing the film to the United States in 1951, Rembrandt Films, which acquired the English-speaking rights, hired legendary horror film star Boris Karloff to provide new narration for the film. It marked the actor's first voice credit on an animated production.

## ◎ ESCAFLOWNE (2002)

A Bandai Entertainment release. **p:** Masahiko Minami, Minoru Takanashi, Masuo Ueda, Toyoyuki Yokohama; (English adaptation) Charles McCarter; **d:** Kazuki Akane; **scr:** Kazuki Sekine, Ryota Yamaguchi; **anim dir:** Nobuteru Yuki; **m:** Yoko Kanno, Hajime Mizoguchi, Inon Zur. **Running time:** 96 minutes. **Released:** January 25, 2002.

*Voices*

**Shesta:** Trevor Devall; **Nukushi:** Brian Dobson; **Dryden:** Michael Dobson; **Folken:** Paul Dobson; **Allen:** Brian Drummond; **Dilandau:** Andrew Francis; **Sora:** Mayumi Iizuka; **Yukari:** Willow Johnson; **Mole Man:** Terry Klassen; **Old Woman:** Hisako Kyoda

After overcoming her depression on Earth, a young Japanese high school female student named Hitomi, travels to the alternate world of Gaea, where she teams up with the enigmatic young king Van. Empowered by a mystical dragon armor they wear, they defeat the country's enemies to save its future.

**PN:** Dubbed in English, this feature-length project was based on the popular 26-episode cartoon series produced in Japan in 1996 and released four years later as a film entitled, *Escaflowne: A Girl in Gaea* before being released in the United States two years later.

## ◎ EVERYONE'S HERO (2006)

An IDT Entertainment Production released by 20th Century Fox. **p:** Ron Tippe, Igor Khait; **exec prod:** Christopher Reeve, Dana Reeve, Janet Healy, Jerry Davis, Stephen R. Brown, Morris Berger; **d:** Christopher Reeve, Dan St. Pierre, Colin Brady; **scr:** Robert Kurtz, Jeff Hand (based on a story by Howard Jonas); **m:** John Debney; **CG superv:** Jeff Bell. **Songs:** "The Best," "Keep on Swinging," "Dream Like New York," "Chicago (That Toddling Town)," "The Best Day of My Life," "Keep Your Eye on the Ball," "What You Do," "Swing It," "Take Me Out to the Ballgame," "The Bug," "The Tigers" and "At Bat." **Running time:** 86 minutes. **Release date:** September 15, 2006.

*Voices*

**Yankee Irving:** Jake T. Austin; **Babe Ruth:** Brian Dennehy; **Darlin:** Whoopi Goldberg; **Bully:** Gideon Jacobs; **Lefty Maginnis:** William H. Macy; **Stanley Irving:** Mandy Pankin; **Emily Irving:** Dana Reeve; **Marti:** Raven; **Screwie:** Rob Reiner; **Yankees' Manager:** Joe Torrre; **Mr. Robinson:** Robert Wagner; **Lonnie Brewster:** Forest Whitaker; **Hobo Andy/Maitre:** Richard Kind; **Arnold:** Conor J. White; **Tommy:** Tyler James Williams; **Officer Bryant/Other Voices:** Ritchie Allen; **Rosetta Brewster:** Cherise Boothe; **Sandlot Kid #2:** Ralph Coppola; **Announcer:** Jason Harris; **Hobo Louie:** Ed Helms; **Conductors/Umpire:** Ray Iannicelli; **Bully Kid Tubby:** Gideon Jacobs; **Bully Kid Arnold:** Conor J. White; **Willie:** Marcus Maurice

*Additional Voices*

Rochelle Hogue; Sondra James; Matthew Laborteaux; Greta Martin; Christie Moreau; Sean Oliver; Charles Parnell; Dennis Pressey; Tyler James Williams; Cornell Womack

A young boy who recovers Babe Ruth's stolen bat takes a memorable thousand-mile journey with his dad to New York to return it to the famed homerun slugger and help the New York Yankees win the World Series in this heartwarming, G-rated Depression-era comedy-adventure.

**PN:** Originally to be called *Yankee Irving,* the film's originating director and executive producer, Christopher Reeve, inspired the project's theme of perseverance against all odds. The basis of the film was born out of a bedtime yarn that writer Howard Jonas told his kids. After Christopher and Dana Reeve, who served as a coproducer and was the voice of Emily, died, cowriter Robert Kurtz said there were no plans to shelve the movie. "They would have never forgiven us," Kurtz said. Released to theaters in September 2006 and despite mixed critical reviews, the movie took third place in the weekend box-office results, opening on 2,896 screens and grossing slightly more than $6 million. Overall, the computer-animated feature pulled in a paltry $15.2 million, worldwide.

## ◎ FANTASIA (1940)

A Walt Disney Production released by RKO Radio Pictures. **p:** Walt Disney; **prod superv:** Ben Sharpsteen; "Toccata and Fugue in D Minor" by Johann Sebastian Bach: **d:** Samuel Armstrong; **st:** Lee Blair, Elmer Plummer, Phil Dike; "The Nutcracker Suite" by Peter Ilich Tchaikovsky: **d:** Samuel Armstrong; **st:** Sylvia Moberly-Holland, Norman Wright, Albert Heath, Bianca Majolie, Graham Heid; "The Sorcerer's Apprentice" by Paul Dukas: **d:** James Algar; **st:** Perce Pearce, Carl Fallberg; **superv anim:** Fred Moore, Vladimir Tytla; "The Rite of Spring" by Igor Stravinsky: **d:** Bill Roberts, Paul Satterfield; **st:** William Martin, Leo Thiele, Robert Sterner, John Fraser McLeish; **superv anim:** Wolfgang Reitherman, Joshua

*Mickey Mouse hypnotizes the brooms to do his chores in "The Sorcerer's Apprentice" segment of Walt Disney's* Fantasia *(1940). © Walt Disney Productions* (COURTESY: MUSEUM OF MODERN ART/FILM STILLS ARCHIVE)

Meador; "Pastoral Symphony" by Ludwig van Beethoven: **d:** Hamilton Luske, Jim Handley, Ford Beebe; **st:** Otto Englander, Webb Smith, Erdman Penner, Joseph Sabo, Bill Peet, George Stallings: **superv anim:** Fred Moore, Ward Kimball, Eric Larson, Arthur Babbitt, Oliver M. Johnston Jr., Don Towsley; "Dance of the Hours" by Amilcare Ponchielli: **d:** T. Hee, Norman Ferguson; **superv anim:** Norman Ferguson; "Night on Bald Mountain" by Modest Mussorgsky and "Ave Maria" by Franz Schubert: **d:** Wilfred Jackson; **st:** Campbell Grant, Arthur Heinemann, Phil Dike; **superv anim:** Vladimir Tytla. **Running time:** 120 minutes. **Released:** November 13, 1940.

### Cast

**Himself:** Deems Taylor; **Themselves:** Leopold Stokowski and the Philadelphia Symphony Orchestra; **Sorcerer's Apprentice:** Mickey Mouse

Walt Disney set new standards for animation with this film, featuring eight different pieces of classical music—Tchaikovsky's "The Nutcracker Suite," Bach's "Toccata and Fugue in D Minor" and others—visually interpreted by the Disney artists. The most memorable moment of the film is Mickey Mouse's performance in "The Sorcerer's Apprentice," where he tries to cast his master's spells.

**PN:** Among Walt Disney's plans for this animated, symphony-laden classic was to shoot the film in wide screen and stereophonic sound, film some scenes in 3-D and perfume theaters with floral scent during the "Nutcracker Suite" flower ballet. Although tight money stymied Disney's plans, he did embellish the film with an innovative, fully directional sound system he called "Fantasound."

### ⊚ FANTASIA/2000 (1999)

A Walt Disney Studios Production released by Buena Vista Pictures. **p:** Donald W. Ernst; **exec prod:** Roy Edward Disney; **d:** Pixote Hunt ("Symphony No. 5"); Hendel Butoy ("Pines of Rome," "Piano Concerto No. 2, Allegro, Opus 102"); Eric Goldberg ("Rhapsody in Blue," "Carnival of the Animals" [Le Carnival des Animaux] Finale); James Algar ("The Sorcerer's Apprentice"); Francis Glebas ("Pomp and Circumstance"—Marches 1, 2, 3 and 4); Gaetan Brizzi and Paul Brizzi ("Firebird Suite—1919 Version") **superv anim dir:** Hendel Butoy; **host seq dir:** Don Hahn; **m:** James Levine, with the Chicago Symphony Orchestra; **Running time:** 75 minutes. **Released:** December 31, 1999.

### Voices

**Mickey Mouse:** Tony Anselmo; **Daisy Duck:** Russi Taylor; **"Pomp and Circumstance" Soprano:** Kathleen Battle; **"Pomp and Circumstance" Choral:** Chicago Symphony Chorus

### Live-action Cast

Leopold Stokowski, Bette Midler, Steve Martin, Penn and Teller, Itzhak Perlman, Quincy Jones, James Earl Jones, Angela Lansbury

Seven new animated sequences set to classical music—Beethoven's "Symphony No. 5"; Gershwin's "Rhapsody in Blue"; Stravinsky's "Firebird Suite" and "Pomp and Circumstance," featuring Donald Duck as Noah's helper; "Pines of Rome"; Dmitri Shostakovich's "Steadfast Tin Soldier" (Piano Concerto No. 2); and "Carnival of the Animals"—plus "The Sorcerer's Apprentice" with Mickey Mouse from the original film are featured in this animated musical sequel to Disney's 1940 masterpiece *Fantasia*.

**PN:** Produced 59 years after Walt Disney's imaginative mixture of animation and music revered by critics the world over, this continuation—and the first film released to theaters in the United States with the millennium as part of its title—was originally presented in the big-screen IMAX format and was released exclusively to 75 IMAX theaters worldwide from January 1 through April 30, 2000. The release marked a significant breakthrough for IMAX, becoming the first feature film to be screened in the large-format IMAX process. Previously, IMAX presentations, due to film size and projector capacity, had been limited to films no more than 45 minutes long. On June 16, Disney released a digitally projected, 35 millimeter version to 1,300 screens nationwide. The 2-D animated film made a short of list of Academy Award–nominated films in 2000.

### ⊚ FANTASTIC PLANET (1973)

A Les Films Armorial/Service De Recherche Ortif Production released by New World Pictures. **p:** Simon Damiani, Andre Valio-Cavaglione; **d:** Rene Laloux; **w:** Rene Laloux, Roland Topor (based on the novel *Ems en Serie* by Stefen Wul); **m:** Alain Gorogeur. **Running time:** 71 minutes. **Released:** December 1, 1973.

### Voices

**Terr:** Barry Bostwick; **Chief of the Oms/Master Kon:** Marvin Miller; **Master Taj:** Olan Soule; **Master Sihn/Om Sorcerer:** Hal Smith; **Hollow Log/Chief/Traag Child:** June Foray

### Additional Voices

Cynthia Adler, Nora Heflin, Mark Gruner, Monika Ramirez

This avant-garde-styled film is a tale of social injustice, relating the story of the Draggs, 39-foot-tall inhabitants of the planet Yagam, who keep the Oms—who have evolved from humans—as pets. Terr, one of the Oms, is accidentally educated by the Draggs and, after uniting with his people, helps them achieve equality with the Draggs once and for all.

**PN:** This French Czech full-length animated fantasy was winner of a Grand Prix award at the 1973 Cannes Film Festival.

### ⊚ FERNGULLY . . . THE LAST RAINFOREST (1992)

An FAI Films Production in association with Youngheart Productions released by 20th Century Fox. **p:** Peter Faiman, Wayne Young, Jim Cox, Brian Rosen, Richard Harper; **d:** Bill Kroyer; **exec prod:** Ted Field, Robert W. Cort, Jeff Dowd, William F. Willett; **scr:** Jim Cox (based on the stories of *Ferngully* by Diana Young); **m:** Alan Silvestri: **m/sc:** Tim Sexton, Becky Mancuso; **anim dir:** Tony Fucile. **Songs:** "Life Is a Magic Thing," "Batty Rap," "If I'm Gonna Eat (It Might as Well Be You)," "Toxic Love," "Raining

Like Magic," "Land of a Thousand Dances," "A Dream Worth Keeping," "Lithuanian Lullaby," "Spis, Li Milke Le," "Bamnqo-bile," "Tri Jetrve," "Some Other World." **Running time:** 74 minutes. **Released:** April 10, 1992.

*Voices*

**Hexxus:** Tim Curry; **Crysta, a fairy wise-woman-in-training:** Samantha Mathis; **Pips, Crysta's boyfriend:** Christian Slater; **Zak, a young human logger:** Jonathan Ward; **Batty Koda:** Robin Williams; **Magi Lune, the wise forest mother:** Grace Zabriski; **Ralph:** Geoffrey Blake; **Tony:** Robert Pastorelli; **Stump:** Cheech Marin; **Root:** Tommy Chong; **The Goanna, a ravenous blue goanna lizard:** Tone Loc; **Knotty:** Townsend Coleman; **Ock:** Brian Cummings; **Elder #1:** Kathleen Freeman; **Fairy #1:** Janet Gilmore: **Elder #2:** Naomi Lewis; **Ash/Voice Dispatch:** Danny Mann; **Elder #3:** Neil Ross; **Fairy #2:** Pamela Segall; **Rock:** Anderson Wong

*Additional Voices*

Lauri Hendler, Rosanna Huffman, Harvey Jason, Dave Mallow, Paige Nan Pollack, Holly Ryan, Gary Schwartz

In this animated ecological fantasy, the lives of rain forest inhabitants nestled in a secret world known as FernGully, home to an unusual girl named Crysta and her friend Pips, the rowdy Beetle Boys, a singing lizard and a bat named Batty, are threatened by the forces of destruction. The only human who has ever been there fights to save them and their magical place.

**PN:** Adapted from stories by Australian author Diana Young and written for the screen by Jim Cox, who penned Disney's *The Rescuers Down Under*, the film marked the feature-film directorial debut of Bill Kroyer and was the first feature for Kroyer's Kroyer Films. Released in the spring of 1992, the film grossed $25 million. Music for the film was performed by Sheena Easton, Elton John, Johnny Clegg, Tone Loc, and Raffi among others.

## ◎ FINAL FANTASY: THE SPIRITS WITHIN (2001)

A Columbia Pictures/Square Pictures Production released by Sony Pictures Entertainment. **p:** Jun Aida, Chris Lee; **d:** Hinrobu Saka-guchi; **scr:** Al Reinert, Jeff Vinnar; **anim dir:** Andy Jones; **seq**

**superv:** Eiji Fujii, Hiroyuki Hayashida, Kenichi Isaka, Takumi Kimura, Claudea Precourt, Steve Preeg, Teru "Yosh" Yoshida. **Running time:** 106 minutes. **Released:** July 11, 2001.

*Voices*

**Dr. Aki Ross:** Ming-Na; **Captain Gray Edwards:** Alec Baldwin; **Ryan:** Ving Rhames; **Neil:** Steve Buscemi; **Jane:** Peri Gilpin; **Dr. Sid:** Donald Sutherland; **General Hein:** James Woods; **Council Member #1:** Keith David; **Council Member #2:** Jean Simmons; **Major Elliott:** Matt McKenzie; **BFW Soldier #1:** John DiMaggio

When a meteor crashes and unleashes millions of alien creatures with plans to extinguish all life on the planet, a group of surviving scientists, led by the beautiful and brilliant Dr. Aki Ross, tries to save the planet from extinction in this animated science fiction action-adventure.

**PN:** *Final Fantasy: The Spirits Within* was the first major film release to feature an entire cast of human characters using computer-generated imagery and motion-capture technology. Based on the popular video game, first produced in 1987 and created by Hironobu Sakaguchi, the film topped $32 million in box-office revenue in the United States.

## ◎ FINDING NEMO (2003)

A Pixar Animation Studios/Walt Disney Studios Production released by Buena Vista Pictures. **p:** Graham Walters; **exec prod:** John Lasseter; **d:** Andrew Stanton; **co-dir:** Lee Unkrich; **scr:** Andrew Stanton, Bob Peterson, David Reynolds; **st:** Andrew Stanton; **m:** Thomas Newman; **superv tech dir:** Oren Jacob; **superv anim:** Dylan Brown; **CG superv:** Brian Green, Lisa Forssell, Danielle Feinberg, David Eisenmann, Jesse Hollander, Steve May, Michael Fong, Anthony A. Apodaca, Michael Lorenzen. **Songs:** "The Girl from Ipanema," "Fandango," "Psycho (The Murder)" and "Beyond the Sea." **Running time:** 100 minutes. **Released:** May 30, 2003.

*Voices*

**Marlin:** Albert Brooks; **Dory:** Ellen DeGeneres; **Nemo:** Alexander Gould; **Gill:** Willem Dafoe; **Bloat:** Brad Garrett; **Peach:** Allison Janney; **Gurgle:** Austin Pendleton; **Bubbles:** Stephen Root; **Deb and Flo:** Vicki Lewis; **Jacques:** Joe Ranft; **Nigel:** Geoffrey Rush; **Crush:** Andrew Stanton; **Coral:** Elizabeth Perkins; **Bruce:** Barry Humphries; **Anchor:** Eric Bana; **Fish School:** John Ratzenberger

Nemo, a tiny clown fish, finds that danger lurks along the Great Barrier Reef when he swims off alone and becomes lost and his single-parent father, Marlin, searches for him. Thanks to a friendly but absentminded fish, Dory, he meets along the way, he eventually finds his way back home, but not before experiencing an undersea adventure of a lifetime in this computer-animated fantasy.

**PN:** The fourth feature of a five-picture deal for Pixar Animation Studios with Walt Disney Studios, *Finding Nemo* was not only the summer sensation of 2003—grossing an amazing $339 million in the United States alone—but also won an Academy Award that year for Best Animated Feature.

## ◎ FIRE AND ICE (1983)

A Ralph Bakshi/Frank Frazetta Production released by 20th Century Fox/Producers Sales Organization. **p:** Ralph Bakshi, Frank Frazetta; **d:** Ralph Bakshi; **w:** Roy Thomas, Gerry Conway (based on a story and characters by Ralph Bakshi); **m:** William Kraft. **Running time:** 81 minutes. **Released:** August 27, 1983.

*Voices*

**Larn:** Randy Norton; **Teegra:** Cynthia Leake; **Darkwolf:** Steve Sandor; **Nekron:** Sean Hannon; **Jarol:** Leo Gordon; **Taro:** William Ostrander; **Juliana:** Eileen O'Neill; **Roleil:** Elizabeth Lloyd Shaw; **Otwa:** Micky Morton; **Tutor:** Tamara Park; **Monga:** Big Yank; **Pako:** Greg Elam; **Subhuman Priestess:** Holly Frazetta; **Envoy:** Alan Koss; **Defender Captain:** Hans Howes; **Subhumans:** James Bridges, Shane Callan, Archie Hamilton, Michael Kellogg, Dale Park, Douglas Payton

Teegra, the beautiful young daughter of the evil Ice Lord, is taken hostage by the Subhumans, which were considered extinct after the glacial destruction of the city Fire Keep. The Subhumans prove to be no match for the Ice Lord and his powerful Dragonhawks, but a mysterious hero, Darkwolf, prevails in destroying the sorcerer once and for all.

**PN:** Working title: *Sword and the Sorcery.*

## ◎ FIST OF THE NORTH STAR (1991)

A Toei Animation Company Ltd. Production released by Streamline Pictures. **p:** Shoji Kishimoto; (English dub) Carl Macek; **d:** Toyoo Ashida; **scr:** Susumu Takahisa; **m:** Katsuhisa Hattori, Tsuyoshi Ujiki; **anim dir:** Msami Suda. **Running time:** 100 minutes. **Released:** September 27, 1991.

*Voices*

**Ken:** John Vickery; **Ryuken:** Jeff Corey; **Alei:** Barbara Goodson; **Old Woman:** Catherine Battistone; **Shin:** Michael McConnohie; **Wise Man:** Steve Bulen; **Jackel:** Michael Forest; **Pillage Victim:** Wendee Lee; **Hart:** Dave Mallow; **Bat:** Tony Oliver; **Lynn:** Holly Sidell; **Ray/Uygle:** Gregory Snegoff; **Julia:** Melodee Spevack; **Torture Victim:** Doug Stone; **Head Banger:** Kirk Thorton; **Thugmeister:** Tom Wyner

Ken, a martial arts master and leader of the North Star once thought to be dead, rises from the ashes of a post-apocalyptic world to protect the weak while seeking revenge against a group of sadistic mutant giants who have abducted his fiancée in this feature-length adaptation of the popular Japanese cartoon series.

**PN:** Produced by Toei Animation in 1986, *Fist Of The North Star* was based on the 1984 cartoon series, *Hokuto no Ken,* which was adapted from the Japanese graphic novels, translated and published stateside in 1989 by Viz Comics, which also spawned a popular Nintendo video game.

## ◎ FLUSHED AWAY (2006)

An Aardman Animations Studio/DreamWorks Animation Production released by DreamWorks SKG. **p:** Cecil Kramer, David Sproxton; **exec prod:** Peter Lord; **d:** Sam Fell, Henry F Anderson III, David Bowers; **scr:** Dick Clement, Ian La Frenias; **m:** Harry Gregson-Williams; **superv anim:** Lionel Gallat, Jakob Hjort Jensen, Fabrice Joubert, Fabio Lignini, Simon Otto. **Songs:** "Dancing with Myself," "Are You Gonna Be My Girl," "She's a Lady," "Don't Worry, Be Happy 2," "Bohemian Like You," "Proud Mary," "What's New Pussycat?" and "Wonderful Night." **Running time:** 86 minutes. **Release date:** November 3, 2006.

*Voices*

**Roderick "Roddy" St. James:** Hugh Jackson; **Rita:** Kate Winslet; **The Toad:** Ian McKellen; **Le Frog:** Jean Reno; **Whitey:** Bill Nighy; **Spike:** Andy Serkis; **Syd:** Shane Richie; **Rita's Mum:** Kathy Burke; **Rita's Dad:** David Suchet; **Rita's Grandma:** Miriam; **Tabitha:** Rachel Rawlinson; **Mother:** Susan Duerden; **Father:** Miles Richardson; **Football Commentator:** John Motson; **Newspaper Seller:** Douglas Weston; **Policeman/Balloon Seller:** Roger Blake; **Thimblenose Ted/Cockroach Passerby:** Christopher Fair-

bank; **Pegleg:** Paul Shardlow; **Take Out:** Conrad Vernon; **Barnacle:** Jonathan Kydd; **Tex:** Newell Alexander; **Edna:** Susan Fitzer; **Fergus:** Joshua Silk; **Rita's Little Sister:** Meredith Wells; **Rita's Sister #2:** Ashleigh-Louis Elliot; **Rita's Sister #3:** Ashleigh Ludwig; **Fat Barry/Market Trader:** Christopher Knights; **Fly-Lady/Passerby #2:** Emma Tate; **Action Figure/Artist:** Tom McGrath; **Liam Prophet/Ladykiller/Fanseller:** Sam Fell; **Goldfish/Fly/Shocky/Henchfrog #1/Tadpole:** David Bowers; **Slugs #2:** Karey Kirkpatrick; **Slugs #1:** Nick Park

A snooty, pampered, upscale-living pet rat, Roddy, who tries to get rid of a pesky sewer rat, must fend for himself when he flushes himself down the toilet of his luxurious penthouse apartment into the sewers of London, where he encounters a mobster toad and his henchman and discovers a whole new world and way of life.

**PN:** This latest coproduction by British animation studio, Aardman Animations, producers of such stop-motion hit films as *Wallace & Gromit: The Curse of the Were-Rabbit* (2005) and *Chicken Run* (2000), and DreamWorks employed the high-tech tools of computer animation rather than Aardman's traditional clay animation to bring this comedy to life. The film did not look as polished and perfect as most CGI-animated films do and codirector Sam Fell told *USA Today*, "We scruffed up the film and added wonky imperfections," and the characters were fully "Aardman-ized." They have wide smiles, round edges, and spherical eyes close together." Budgeted at $148 million, the computer-animated comedy opened in third place with $18.8 million from 4,800 screens at 3,707 theaters nationwide and right behind the Disney/Tim Allen holiday comedy *Santa Claus 3.* The film opened stronger than the previous Aardman Animations/DreamWorks picture, *Wallace & Gromit: The Curse of the Were-Rabbit*, which debuted with $16 million and $56.1 million in total box-office revenue, with $57 million in 24 days of release and more than $64 million worldwide.

## ◎ THE FOX AND THE HOUND (1981)

A Walt Disney Production released through Buena Vista Pictures. **p:** Wolfgang Reitherman, Art Stevens; **d:** Art Stevens, Ted Berman, Richard Rich; **st:** Larry Clemmons, Ted Berman, Peter Young, Steve Hulett, David Michener, Burny Mattinson, Earl Kress, Vance Gerry (based on the book by Daniel P. Mannix); **superv anim:** Randy Cartwright, Cliff Nordberg, Frank Thomas, Glen Keane, Ron Clements, Ollie Johnston. **Running time:** 83 minutes. **Released:** July 10, 1981.

*Voices*

**Tod:** Mickey Rooney; **Cooper:** Kurl Russell; **Big Mama:** Pearl Bailey; **Amos Slade:** Jack Albertson; **Vixey:** Sandy Duncan; **Widow Tweed:** Jeanette Nolan; **Chief:** Pat Buttram; **Porcupine:** John Fiedler; **Badger:** John McIntire; **Dinky:** Dick Bakalyan; **Boomer:** Paul Winchell; **Young Tod:** Keith Mitchell; **Young Cooper:** Corey Feldman

A young fox and a puppy become the best of friends one summer but are separated when the dog's owner, a hunter, takes the dog away for the winter. Returning the following spring, the dog (now a fully trained hunting dog) and the fox learn what it is like to be enemies.

**PN:** The first Disney feature to display the talents of a new crop of artists developed during a 10-year program at the studio under the supervision of veteran Disney animators Wolfgang Reitherman, Eric Larson and Art Stevens. Working title: *The Fox and the Hounds.*

## ◎ FREDDIE AS F.R.O.7 (1992)

A Shapiro Glickenhaus/Hollywood Motion Pictures (of London) Ltd. Production released by Miramax Films. **p:** Norman Priggen,

Jon Acevski; **d:** Jon Acevski; **scr:** Jon Acevski, David Ashton; **m:** David Dundas, Rick Wentworth; **anim dir:** Ton Guy. **Songs:** "The Narrator," "I'll Keep Your Dreams Alive," "Evilmainya," "Shy Girl," "Lay Down Your Arms," "Fear Not the Sword My Son," "F. R.O.7," and "Suite from Freddie." **Running time:** 90 minutes. **Released:** August 28, 1992.

*Voices*
**Freddie:** Ben Kingsley; **El Supremo:** Brian Blessed; **Trilby:** Jonathan Pryce; **Nessie:** Phyllis Logan: **Brigadier G:** Nigel Hawthorne; **King:** Michael Hordern; **Queen/Various Voices:** Prunella Scales; **Daffers:** Jenny Agutter; **Messina:** Billie Whitelaw; **Scott/Various Voices:** John Sessions

An extraordinary young frog prince–turned–secret agent with superpowers and a leaping green fighting machine battles the forces of evil to stop the wicked Aunt Messina from conquering the earth in this animated fantasy adventure.

**PN:** Of the non-Disney features released in 1992, this one fared the worst, grossing only $1 million in revenue. Songs featured in the production were sung by such well-known recording artists as George Benson, Grace Jones and Boy George. The film is also known as *Freddie the Frog*.

## ◉ FRITZ THE CAT (1972)
A Steve Krantz Production released by Cinemation Industries. **p:** Steve Krantz; **d & w:** Ralph Bakshi (based on characters created by Robert Crumb); **m:** Ed Bogas, Ray Shanklin; **superv anim:** Virgil Ross, Manuel Perez, John Sparey. **Running time:** 78 minutes. **Released:** April 12, 1972.

*Voices*
**Fritz:** Skip Hinnant; **Big Bertha:** Rosetta LeNoire; **Pig Cop #1 "Ralph":** Phil Seuling; **Pig Cop #2:** Ralph Bakshi

*Additional Voices*
John McCurry, Judy Engles

Re-creating the pop culture and social agonies of the 1960s, this political, racial and sexual satire traces the sexual and political exploits of Fritz the Cat, a college-age cat who dabbles in drugs, radical politics and hedonism. By film's end, following his many encounters, he rejects violence and cruelty but still embraces sex.

**PN:** The first animated film ever to receive an X rating. The feature was to become the first of three projects planned by producer Steve Krantz. The others: *Arrivederci, Rudy!* based on the life of Valentino, and *Dick Tracy, Frozen, Fried and Buried Alive,* tracing the career of Chester Gould's detective through the 1930s and 1940s. These two films were never produced.

## ◉ FRIZ FRELENG'S LOONEY LOONEY BUGS BUNNY MOVIE (1981)
A Warner Bros. release. **p & d:** Friz Freleng; **scr:** John Dunn, David Detiege, Friz Freleng, Phil Monroe, Gerry Chinquy; **m:** Rob Walsh, Don McGinnis, Milt Franklyn, Bill Lava, Shorty Rogers, Carl Stalling. **Running time:** 80 minutes. **Released:** November 20, 1981.

*Voices*
Mel Blanc, June Foray, Frank Nelson, Frank Welker, Stan Freberg, Ralph James

Veteran Warner Bros. director Friz Freleng was given a shot at producing and directing this compilation feature following the success of Chuck Jones's *The Bugs Bunny/Road Runner Movie.* Freleng combined new animation with previously presented cartoons, broken into three acts: Yosemite Sam, playing the devil (shaped around 1963's "Devil's Feud Cake"); Bugs outsmarting a dopey gangster duo, Rocky and Mugsy, who are holding Tweety hostage; and Bugs serving as master of ceremonies for a humorous spoof of Hollywood awards programs. Cartoons featured during the film are: "Knighty Knight Bugs," "Sahara Hare," "Roman Legion Hare," "High Diving Hare," "Hare Trimmed," "Wild and Wooly Hare," "Catty Cornered," "Golden Yeggs," "The Unmentionables," "Three Little Bops" and "Show Biz Bugs," the latter an Academy Award winner.

## ◉ FUN AND FANCY FREE (1947)
A Walt Disney Production released by RKO Radio Pictures. **p:** Walt Disney; **prod superv:** Ben Sharpsteen; **l/a dir:** William Morgan; **anim dir:** Jack Kinney, Bill Roberts, Hamilton Luske; **st:** Homer Brightman, Harry Reeves, Ted Sears, Lance Nolley, Eldon Dedini, Tom Oreb, with "Bongo" based on an original story by Sinclair Lewis; **md:** Charles Wolcott; **m/sc:** Paul J. Smith, Oliver Wallace, Eliot Daniel; **anim dir:** Ward Kimball, Les Clark, John Lounsbery, Fred Moore, Wolfgang Reitherman. **Songs:** "Fun and Fancy Free, "Lazy Countryside," "Too Good to Be True," "Say It with a Slap," "Fee Fi Fo Fum," "My Favorite Dream," "I'm a Happy Go-Lucky Fellow," "Beanero" and "My, What a Happy Day." **Running time:** 73 minutes. **Released:** September 27, 1947.

*Cast*
Edgar Bergen, Luana Patten, Charlie McCarthy, Mortimer Snerd

*Voices*
**Narrator/Bongo:** Dinah Shore; **The Singing Harp:** Anita Gordon; **Jiminy Cricket:** Cliff Edwards; **Willie the Giant:** Billy Gilbert; **Donald Duck:** Clarence Nash; The King's Men, The Dinning Sisters, and The Starlighters

Radio stars Edgar Bergen and Charlie McCarthy and cartoon star Jiminy Cricket appear in this Walt Disney feature composed of two animated stories threaded together by live action and animated wraparounds. Cartoon sequences include: "Bongo, the Wonder Bear," about a circus bear who escapes from the circus and finds the companionship of Lulubelle, a cute female bear, and "Mickey and the Beanstalk," a clever retelling of the famed "Jack and the Beanstalk" tale featuring Mickey, Donald, Goofy and, of course, the Giant (Willie).

## ◉ GALAXY EXPRESS (1981)
A Toei Animation Company Ltd. Production released by New World Pictures. **p:** Roger Corman; **d:** Rintaro; **scr:** Kon Ichikawa, Shiro Ishimori, Leiji Matsumoto; **m:** Nozomu Aoki, Yukihide Takekawa; **anim:** Tomeko Horikawa, Yoshinobu Ineno, Yoshinori Kanada, Reiko Kuwahara, Joji Manabe, Shigeo Matoba, Hiroshi Oikawa, Rintaro, Kazuhide Tomonaga, Emiko Tsukima, Koichi Tsunoda. **Running time:** 91 minutes. **Released:** August 8, 1981.

*Voices*
**Tetsuro Hoshino:** Masako Nozawa; **Queen Emeralda:** Reiko Tajima; **Captain Harlock:** Makio Inoue; **Narrator:** Tatsuya Jo; **Conductor:** Kaneta Kimotsuki; **Maettel:** Masako Ikeda; **Claire:** Yoko Asagama; **Tochiro's Mother:** Miyoko Aso; **Shadow:** Toshiko Fujita; **Captain of the Guard:** Banjo Ginga; **Antares:** Yasuo Hisamatsu; **Queen Promethium:** Kimiya; **Tochiro Oyama:** Kei Tomiyama

A brave young orphan (Joey) travels to Andromedia on the Galaxy Express train to outer space to avenge the death of his mother and the Cyborgs who killed her in this animated scientific fiction adventure based on the Japanese cartoon series *Galaxy Express 999.*

*Mewsette, a naive country girl cat (voiced by Judy Garland), is the object of boyfriend Jaune-Tom's love in* Gay Purr-ee *(1962). © Warner Brothers*

### ◎ GAY PURR-EE (1962)

A UPA (United Pictures of America) Production released by Warner Bros. **p:** Henry G. Saperstein; **d:** Abe Levitow; **w:** Dorothy and Chuck Jones, Ralph Wright. **Songs:** "Mewsette," "Roses Red-Violets Blue," "Take My Hand, Paree," "The Money Cat," "Little Drops of Rain," "Rubbles," "Paris Is a Lonely Town" and "The Horses Won't Talk." **Running time:** 86 minutes. **Released:** October 24, 1962.

#### Voices

**Mewsette:** Judy Garland, **Jaune-Tom:** Robert Goulet; **Robespierre:** Red Buttons; **Mme. Rubens-Chatte:** Hermione Gingold; **Meowrice:** Paul Frees

#### Additional Voices

Morey Amsterdam: Mel Blanc; Julie Bennett; and Joan Gardiner

Mewsette, a naive country girl cat, becomes tired of peasant-type cats and leaves the farm on the next train to Paris to explore new adventures. She is followed on foot by her boyfriend, Jaune Tom, and his tiny companion, Robespierre, who set out to rescue her from Meowrice, a suave city cat who plans to marry her.

### ◎ GHOST IN THE SHELL (1996)

A Production I.G./Bandai Visual Production released by Manga Entertainment and Palm Pictures. **p:** Shigeru Watanabe, Laurence Guinness, Yoshimasa Mizuo, Ken Iyadomi, Mitsuhisa Ishikawa; **d:** Mamoru Oshii; **scr:** Kazunori Ito; **m:** Brian Eno, Kenji Kawai; **key anim superv:** Kazuchika Kise, Hiroyuki Okiura; **anim dir:** Toshihiko Nishikubo. **Running time:** 81 minutes. **Released:** March 29, 1996.

#### Voices

**Puppet Master:** Abe Lasser; **Aramaki:** William Frederick; **Nakamura:** Simon Prescott; **Bateau:** Richard Epcair; **Togusa:** Christopher Joyce; **Minister:** Henry Douglas; **Ishikawa:** Michael Sorich; **Dr. Willis:** Phil Williams; **Section 9 Cyberneticist/Coroner:** Steve Bulen

In the year 2029, a sophisticated computer terrorist, the Puppet Master, seeks a physical life form to obtain the remarkable strengths and abilities of humans to penetrate any network on the planet Earth.

### ◎ GHOST IN THE SHELL 2: INNOCENCE (2004)

A Production I.G./Bandai Visual/Studio Ghibli Production released by Go Fish Pictures. **p:** Mitsuhisa Ishikawa, Toshio Suzuki; **d:** Mamoru Oshii; **scr:** Mamoru Oshii; **m:** Kenji Kawai; **anim dir:** Toshihiko Hishikubo; **superv anim:** Kazuchika Kise, Tetsuya Nishio. **Running time:** 99 minutes. **Released:** September 17, 2004.

#### Voices

**Batô:** Akio Otsuka; **Motoko Kusanagi:** Atsuko Tanaka; **Togusa:** Loichi Yamadera; **Kim:** Naoto Takenaka; **Ararmaki:** Tamio Oki; **Ishikawa:** Yutaki Nakano; **Haraway:** Yoshiko Sakaibara; **Mysterious Young Girl:** Sumi Mutoh

In the year 2032 Batô, a cyborg detective, investigates the case of a woman sex robot killed by her owner in this sequel to 1996's *Ghost in the Shell*.

### ◎ GOBOTS: BATTLE OF THE ROCKLORDS (1986)

A Hanna-Barbera/Tonka Toys Production released by Clubhouse Pictures/Atlantic Releasing. **p:** Kay Wright; **d:** Ray Patterson; **w:** Jay Segal; **md:** Hoyt Curtin; **anim dir:** Paul Seballa; **superv anim:** Janine Dawson. **Running time:** 73 minutes. **Released:** March 21, 1986.

#### Voices

**Solitaire:** Margot Kidder; **Nuggit:** Roddy McDowall; **Boulder:** Michael Nouri; **Magmar:** Telly Savalas; **Turbo/Cop-Tur/Talc:** Arthur Burghardt; **Nick:** Ike Eisenmann; **Cy-Kill:** Bernard Erhard; **Crasher:** Marilyn Lightstone; **Matt:** Morgan Paull; **Leader-1** Lou Richards; **A.J.:** Leslie Speights; **Scooter/Zeemon/Rest-Q/Pulver Eye/Sticks/Narliphant:** Frank Welker; **Slime/Stone/Granite/Narligator:** Michael Bell; **Stone Heart/Fossil Lord:** Foster Brooks; **Vanguard:** Ken Campbell; **Herr Friend/Crack-Pot/Tork:** Philip Lewis Clarke; **Pincher/Tombstone/Stone:** Peter Cullen; **Brimstone/Klaws/Rock Narlie:** Dick Gautier; **Marbles/Hornet:** Darryl Hickman; **Small Foot:** B.J. Ward; **Fitor:** Kelly Ward; **Heat Seeker:** Kirby Ward

The evil Rock Lord Magmar is bent on seizing control of the entire planet of Quartex, which is peopled by various species of living rock. This spurs the noble Guardian Go-Bots into action, using a variety of devices to thwart the enemy Renegade GoBots to prevent the Rock Lords from taking control.

### ◎ THE GOLDEN LAWS (2003)

A Toei Animation Company Ltd./Colorado FX Production released by the IRH Press Company. **p:** Seikyo Oda, Kujyou Ogawa, Naifumi Sato; **exec prod:** Ryuho Okawa; **d:** Takaaki Ishiyama; **anim:** Masami Suda, Keizo Shimizu, Yukiyoshi Hane, Marisuke Eguchi. **Running time:** 110 minutes. **Released:** December 5, 2004.

Voice credits unkown.

In the 25th Century New Atlantis, a 15-year-old boy and girl travel beyond time and space and over thousands of years in a time machine to ancient Egypt, Greece, India, China, and Israel, and encounter many famous spiritual leaders in history in this spiritual adventure.

**PN:** This anime film by Japanese director Ryuho Okawa premiered in Los Angeles on December 5, 2003, at the Laemmle Fairfax theater, and was based on Okawa's best-selling book of the same name. Many top Japanese animators worked on this innovative feature, including Takeaki Ishiyama (*Sakura Taisen*), Isamu Imakake (*Lupin the Third: Dead or Alive*), Masami Suda (*Gatcha-*

man, *Hokuto No Ken* [*Fist of North Star*]), Keizo Shimizu (*Ginga Eiyuu Densetsu* [*Legend of the Galactic Heroes*]), Yukiyoshi Hane (*Kiki's Delivery Service, Nausicaa of the Valley of the Wind*) and Marisuke Eguchi (*Street Fighter, Ginga Tetsudou no Yoru* [*Night on the Galactic Railroad*]).

## A GOOFY MOVIE (1995)
A Walt Disney Pictures Production released by Buena Vista Pictures. **p:** Dan Rounds; **d:** Kevin Lima; **st:** Jymm Magon; **scr:** Jymn Magon, Chris Matheson, Brian Pimenthal; **m/sc:** Carter Burwell (with songs by Tom Snow, Jack Feldman, Patrick DeRener and Roy Freeland); **anim superv:** Nancy Beiman, Matias Marcos, Dominique Monfery, Stephane Sainte-Foi. **Songs:** "After Today," "Stand Out," "Leslie's Possum Pork," "On the Open Road," "121" and "Nobody Else But You." **Running time:** 78 minutes. **Released:** April 7, 1995.

*Voices*
**Goofy:** Bill Farmer; **Max:** Jason Marsden; **Pete:** Jim Cummings; **Roxanne:** Kellie Martin, **PJ:** Rob Paulsen; **Principal Mazur:** Wallace Shawn; **Stacey:** Jenna von Oy; **Bigfoot:** Frank Welker; **Lester:** Kevin Lima; **Waitress:** Florence Stanley; **Miss Maples:** Jo Anne Worley; **Photo Studio Girl:** Brittany Alyse Smith; **Lester's Grinning Girl:** Robyn Richards; **Lisa:** Julie Brown; **Tourist Kid:** Klee Bragger; **Chad:** Joey Lawrence; **Possum Park Emcee:** Pat Buttram (listed as Butrum in credits); **Mickey Mouse:** Wayne Allwine; **Security Guard:** Herschel Sparber; **Powerline:** Tevin Campbell; **Max (singing):** Aaron Lohr; **Robert Zimmeruski (Bobby):** Pauly Shore

*Additional Voices*
Dante Basco, Sheryl Bernstein, Corey Burton, Pat Carroll, Elizabeth Daily, Carol Holiday, Steve Moore, Brian Pimental, Jason Willinger

Lovable canine klutz Goofy is a suburban dad who tries to bond and regain the closeness he once had with his teenage son, Max, during a cross-country trip.

**PN:** A spinoff of the Disney animated series *Goof Troop*, Disney struck gold with this new animated feature (and the first full-length animated feature to star the 63-year-old canine), grossing $35 million at the box office. Principal animation was produced overseas at studio facilities in France and Sydney, Australia, as well as at the Burbank studios.

## GREAT CONQUEST: THE ROMANCE OF THREE KINGDOMS (1994)
A Toei Animation Company Ltd. Production released by Streamline Pictures. **p:** Yusuke Okada, Takamasa Yoshinari; **d:** Mashahara Okuwaki; **scr:** Kazuo Kasahara; **st:** Takamasa Yoshinari, Shoji Yazawa; **m:** Seiji Yokoyama; **anim dir:** Koichi Tsunoda. **Running time:** 118 minutes. **Released:** April 21, 1994.

*Voices*
**Narrator:** Pat Morita

Epic tale of three rival kingdoms and leaders in ancient China—Sun Jian, the tiger of Jiang Dong and ruler of Wu, Lui Pei, ruler of Shu, and Cao, magnificent ruler of Wei—who fight to unite China under one dynasty in this animated adaptation of the popular Chinese literary classic *The Romance of Three Kingdoms*.

## THE GREAT MOUSE DETECTIVE (1986)
A Walt Disney/Silver Screen Partners II Production released by Buena Vista Pictures. **p:** Burny Mattinson; **d:** John Musker, Ron Clements, Dave Michener, Burny Mattinson; **st dev:** Pete Young, Vance Gerry, Steve Hulett, Ron Clements, John Musker, Bruce M.

Morris, Matthew O'Callaghan, Burny Mattinson, Dave Michener, Melvin Shaw (based on the book *Basil of Baker Street* by Eve Titus); **m:** Henry Mancini; **superv anim:** Mark Henn, Glen Keane, Robert Minkoff, Hendel Butoy. **Songs:** "The World's Greatest Criminal Mind," "Goodbye, So Soon" and "Let Me Be Good to You." **Running time:** 74 minutes. **Released:** July 2, 1986.

*Voices*
**Professor Ratigan:** Vincent Price; **Basil/Bartholomew:** Barrie Ingham; **Dawson:** Val Bettin; **Olivia:** Susanne Pollatschek; **Fidget:** Candy Candido; **Mrs. Judson:** Diana Chesney; **The Mouse Queen:** Eve Brenner; **Flaversham:** Alan Young; **Sherlock Holmes:** Basil Rathbone; **Watson:** Laurie Main; **Lady Mouse:** Shani Wallis; **Bar Maid:** Ellen Fitzhugh; **Citizen/Thug Guard:** Walker Edmiston; **Thug Guards:** Wayne Allwine, Val Bettin, Tony Anselmo

Ratigan, an evil rat, wants to control the mouse world and kidnaps a brilliant mouse toymaker to build a mechanical rodent robot to begin his quest. His initial plans are to dethrone the mouse queen, but he never counted on two factors getting in his way: Basil and Dr. Dawson, two Holmesian mice hired by the toymaker's daughter to track down her father. The pair not only find the toymaker but successfully thwart Ratigan's plans.

**PN:** This Disney mouse-tale/adventure grossed $25 million at the box office and used digital animation for the first time in an animated movie.

## GRENDEL, GRENDEL, GRENDEL (1982)
An Al et al. Studios/Animation Australia Property Ltd. Production released by Satori Productions. **p:** Phillip Adams; **d:** Alexander Stitt; **scr:** Alexander Stitt; **anim dir:** Frank Hellard; **anim:** Frank Hellard, David Atkinson, Ralph Peverill, Gus McClaren, Anne Jolliffe, Alexander Stitt. **Running time:** 90 minutes. **Released:** April 1, 1982.

*Voices*
**Grendel:** Peter Ustinov; **Beowulf:** Keith Mitchell; **King Hrothgar:** Arthur Dignam; **King's Mistress:** Julie McKenna

*Additional Voices*
Ed Rosser, Ric Stone, Bobby Bright, Ernie Bourne, Alison Bird, Barry Hill

Peter Ustinov narrates this entertaining tale, told from his viewpoint as the towering monster Grendel, who challenges the hero, the legendary Beowulf, in order to survive in this animated feature produced in Australia.

**PN:** Australian director Alexander Stiff produced this adaptation of John Gardner's acclaimed novel 10 years after its publication. Made in 1981, the film cost between $560,000 and $680,000 to complete and was released in the United States the following spring.

## GULLIVER'S TRAVELS (1939)
A Fleischer Studios Production released by Paramount Pictures. **p:** Max Fleischer; **d:** Dave Fleischer; **w:** Dan Gordon, Ted Pierce, Izzy Sparber, Edmond Seward (based on a story by Seward from the novel by Jonathan Swift); **m:** Victor Young; **anim dir:** Seymour Kneitel, Willard Bowsky, Tom Palmer, Grim Natwick, William Hanning, Rolland Crandall, Tom Johnson, Robert Leffingwell, Frank Kelling, Winfield Hoskins, Orestes Calpini: **Songs:** "It's a Hap-Hap-Happy Day," "Bluebirds in the Moonlight," "All's Well," "We're All Together Again," "Forever," "Faithful" and "Faithful Forever." **Running time:** 74 minutes. **Released:** December 22, 1939.

*In an effort to rival Disney's feature-length cartoons, Max Fleischer countered with his own full-length film, Gulliver's Travels (1939).*
(COURTESY: REPUBLIC PICTURES)

### Voices

**Singing voice of the Prince:** Lanny Ross; **Singing voice of the Princess:** Jessica Dragonette.

With the success of Walt Disney's *Snow White and the Seven Dwarfs*, animators Max and Dave Fleischer tried their own hand at a full-length animated feature shaped around the popular romance of Jonathan Swift. The film centers on the adventures of shipwrecked Lemuel Gulliver on an island inhabited by tiny people in the kingdom of Lilliput and his attempts to escape the island and return to his homeland.

### ◎ GULLIVER'S TRAVELS BEYOND THE MOON (1966)

A Toei Animation Co. Ltd. Production released through Continental Distributing. **p:** Hiroshi Okawa; **d:** Yoshio Kuroda; **w:** Shinichi Sekizawa (based on the character in the novel by Jonathan Swift); **m/s:** Milton and Anne Delugg; **anim dir:** Hideo Furusawa. **Songs:** "The Earth Songs," "I Wanna Be Like Gulliver," "That's the Way It Goes" and "Keep Your Hopes High." **Running time:** 78 minutes. **Released:** July 23, 1966.

### Voices

**(English version) Professor Gulliver:** Robert Harter; **Pug:** Herb Duncan; **Princess:** Darla Hood

Hit by a car and knocked unconscious, a young boy dreams he is with Dr. Gulliver, a toy-soldier colonel, a crow and a dog on a trip to the planet Hope. There they discover a princess who tells them the planet is being run by robots who have gone out of control. The boy and Dr. Gulliver destroy the robots—who melt when hit by water—and free the planet.

**PN:** Produced in Japan by Toei Animation Co. Ltd., Japan's largest producer of animation, this full-length animated feature was retitled for American release. It was formerly titled *Gulliver No Uchu Ryoko*.

### ◎ GUMBY: THE MOVIE (1995)

An Arrow/Premavision Production released by Arrow Releasing. **p:** Art Clokey, Gloria Clokey; **d:** Art Clokey; **scr:** Art Clokey, Gloria Clokey; **m/sc:** Jerry Gerber (with songs by David Ozzie Ahlers). **Songs:** "Take Me Away," "Rockin' Arc Park," "This Way 'n That" and "He Was Once." **Running time:** 88 minutes. **Released:** December 8, 1995.

### Voices

**Gumby/Claybery/Fatbuckle/Kapp:** Charles Farrington; **Pokey/Prickle/Gumbo:** Art Clokey; **Goo:** Gloria Clokey; **Thinbuckle:** Manny LaCarruba; **Ginger:** Alice Young; **Gumba:** Janet MacDuff; **Lowbelly/Farm Lady:** Bonnie Rudolph; **Tara:** Patti Morse; **Radio Announcer:** Ozzie Ahlers

In this spinoff of the 1950's "claymation" cartoon series, the spunky green clay hero and his orange sidekick Pokey experience thrills and spills as they travel to Camelot, Toyland and beyond in their first feature-length adventure.

### ◎ HAIR HIGH (2004)

A Plymptoons Production released by E.D. Distribution. **p, d, w & anim:** Bill Plympton; **co-prod:** Martha Plimpton; **m:** Hank Bones, Maureen McElheron. **Running time:** 75 minutes. **Released:** February 14, 2005.

### Voices

**Rev. Sidney Cheddar:** Ed Begley, Jr.; **Sarge:** Craig Beirko; **Mr. Snerd:** David Carradine; **JoJo:** Keith Carradine; **Darlene:** Beverly D'Angelo; **Buttercup:** Hayley Dumond; **Spud:** Eric Gilliland; **Dill:** Matt Groening; **Hill:** Don Hertzfeldt; **Coach:** Peter Jason; **Dwayne:** Justin Long; **Rod:** Dermot Mulroney; **Principal:** Tom Noonan; **Zip:** Zak Orth; **Miss Crumbles:** Martha Plimpton; **Football Announcer:** Jay O. Sanders; **Wally:** Michael Showalter; **Cherri:** Sarah Silverman

Bizarre adult send-up of the late '50s and early '60s high school told by a soda jerk, JoJo (voiced by Keith Carradine), who chronicles the tragic love triangle of class nerd, Spud, head cheerleader, Cherri, and star quarterback, Ro, who retaliates when Spud takes his girl to the prom by murdering them—with their car-crashed corpses returning to the dance to avenge their deaths.

**PN:** Independent filmmaker/animator Bill Plympton wrote, produced, directed and animated this limited-animated feature—and his first cartoon featuring a "name" voice cast—that was shown at film festivals during 2004 and 2005. It made its West Coast premiere on February 14, 2005, at the San Francisco Film Festival, and premiered on the East Coast on March 5, 2005, at the Florida Film Festival in Maitland, Florida, besides receiving limited distribution to theaters.

### ◎ HANSEL AND GRETEL (1954)

An RKO Pictures Inc. Production released by RKO Radio Pictures Inc. **p:** Michael Myerberg; **d:** John Paul; **orig p:** Adelheid Wette; **st (adaptation):** Padraic Colum; **m:** Engelbert Humperdinck; **anim:** Joseph Horstmann, Inez Anderson, Daniel Diamond, Ralph Emory, Hobart Rosen, Don Sahlin, Teddy Shapard, Nathalie Schulz. **Running time:** 72 minutes. **Released:** October 10, 1954.

### Voices

**Hansel/Gretel:** Constance Brigham; **Rosina Rubylips the Witch:** Anna Russell; **Mother:** Mildred Dunson; **Father:** Frank Rogier; **Sandman:** Delbert Anderson; **Dew Fairy:** Helen Boatright; **Angels/Children and Chorus:** Apollo Boys' Choir

Stop-motion puppet animated version of the classic Grimm fairy tale in which the evil witch lures two innocent children, Hansel and Gretel, into her fabled candy house with plans to eat them but they manage to escape.

**PN:** Produced in 1954 by Broadway producer Michael Myerberg using hand-sculpted dolls and stop-motion technology, this film's musical score of the 1893 Humperdinck opera was sung by none other than pop music sensation Engelbert Humperdinck. That year, Humperdinck's song was nominated for a Grammy Award.

## ◉ HAPPILY EVER AFTER (1993)

A Filmation/First National Production released by Kel-Air Entertainment and later First National. **p:** Lou Scheimer; **d:** John Howley; **scr:** Robby London, Martha Moran; **m:** Frank W. Becker; **seq dir:** Gian Celestri, Ka Moon Song, Lawrence White. **Running time:** 74 minutes. **Released:** May 28, 1993.

*Voices*

**Snow White:** Irene Cara; **Scowl:** Edward Asner; **Muddy:** Carol Channing; **Looking Glass:** Dom DeLuise; **Mother Nature:** Phyllis Diller; **Blossom:** Zsa Zsa Gabor; **Critterina/Marina:** Linda Gary; **Sunflower:** Jonathan Harris; "**Prince:** Michael Horton; **Sunburn:** Sally Kellerman; **Lord Maliss:** Malcolm McDowell; **Moonbeam/Thunderella:** Tracey Ullman; **Batso:** Frank Welker

The evil queen's brother, Lord Maliss, seeks to avenge his sister's death by evening the score with Snow White, who is rescued by the Prince.

**PN:** This unauthorized sequel to the Walt Disney classic *Snow White and the Seven Dwarfs* began production in 1986 simultaneously with another unauthorized sequel to a Disney masterpiece, *Pinocchio and the Emperor of the Night*, which was released in 1987. Originally the film was slated to be released in 1990 by First National Film Corporation, but a dispute between them and its producer, Filmation, ensued, delaying the film's theatrical release until 1993. Unlike the Disney original, the film produced a small return, grossing only $3.2 million at the box office.

## ◉ HAPPILY N'EVER AFTER (2007)

A BAF Berlin Animation Film/Greenlight Media/Vanguard Films/BFC Berliner Film Companie/Odyssey Entertainment Production released by Lions Gate. **p:** John H. Williams; **co-prod:** Chad Hammes, Volker Bass, Silke Zakarneh, Wilhelm Auer, Peter Widmann; **exec prod:** Ralph Kamp, Louise Goodsill, Carl Woebcken; **d:** Paul J. Bolger, Yvette Kaplan; **scr:** Douglas Langdale, Robert Moreland; **m:** Paul Buckley. **Running time:** 75 minutes. **Released:** January 5, 2007.

*Voices*

**Frieda:** Sigourney Weaver; **Ella:** Sarah Michelle Gellar; **Rick:** Freddie Prinze Jr.; **Mr. Prince Humperdink:** Patrick Warburton; **Mambo:** Andy Dick; **Munk:** Wallace Shawn; **Wizard:** George Carlin; **Rumpelstiltskin:** Michael McShane; **Dwarf 1/Dwarf 2/Giant:** John DiMaggio; **Fairy Godmother:** Lisa Kaplan

Comical variation of the classic children's tale of the beautiful Cinderella (voiced by Sarah Michelle Gellar) under the rule of the evil stepmother, who takes control of Fairy Tale Land, and what Cinderella's life would be like if she did not end up with the handsome prince in this CGI-animated U.S.–German coproduction.

## ◉ HAPPY FEET (2006)

A Warner Bros. Pictures, Inc./Village Roadshow Pictures Entertainment/Kennedy/Miller Productions Production released by Warner Bros. Pictures, Inc. **p:** Bill Miller, George Miller, Doug Mitchell; **d:** George Miller; **scr:** Warren Coleman, John Collee, George Miller, Judy Morris; **m:** John Powell; **anim dir:** Daniel Jeannette. **Songs:** "Song of the Heart," "Hit Me Up," "Tell Me Something Good," "Somebody to Love," "I Wish," "Jump N' Move," "Do It Again," "The Joker," "My Way," "Kiss," "Boogie Wonderland," "Golden Slumbers/The End" and "The Story of Mumble Happyfeet." **Running time:** 98 minutes. **Released:** November 17, 2006.

*Voices*

**Mumble:** Elijah Wood; **Noah/Ramone/Adelie/Lovelace:** Robin Williams; **Gloria:** Brittany Murphy; **Memphis:** Hugh Jackman; **Norma Jean:** Nicole Kidman; **Young Mumble:** Elizabeth Daily; **Baby Mumble:** Khamani Griffin; **Nestor:** Carlos Alazraqui; **Actress:** Denise Blasor; **Young Penguin:** Kwesi Boakye; **Squaw Bird:** Michael Cornacchia; **Female Penguin:** Sonje Fortag; **Lil Girl:** Zoe Raye; **Gloria Hatchling:** Alyssa Shafer; **Miss Viola:** Magda Szubanski

*Additional Voices*

Mark Klastorin, Alyssa Smith

In the land of emperor penguins in Antarctica, a young and enthusiastic penguin, Mumble, needs to sing a special song to win over a soul mate. Unfortunately, he can't sing very well but he can sure tap dance.

**PN:** George Miller, the man who made pigs talk in the delightfully entertaining *Babe* movies, coproduced, cowrote and directed this cartoon adventure. He conceived the idea for the combined computer- and stop-motion animated feature after seeing the BBC documentary *Life in the Freezer*. As he told an interviewer, "I had no idea what extraordinary creatures they [penguins] were. It was a chance to look at how individuals in a community can't survive without depending on one another." Opening in 3,804 regular theaters nationwide the weekend before Thanksgiving, the animated penguin romp grabbed first place with $42.3 million in box-office receipts, edging out the James Bond 007 feature, *Casino Royale*, which opened with $40.6 million. After its first 10 days of release, the feature remained the number-one grossing film in America, with $99,256,766 in ticket sales. Produced in stunning 2-D animation, the film was likewise released in eye-popping IMAX 3-D to theaters across the United States.

## ◉ HEATHCLIFF: THE MOVIE (1986)

A DIC-Audiovisual-LBS Communications-McNaught Syndicate Production released by Atlantic Releasing and Clubhouse Pictures. **p:** Jean Chalopin; **d:** Bruno Bianchi; **w:** Alan Swayze (based on the comic strip *Heathcliff* by George Gately). **Running time:** 73 minutes. **Released:** January 17 1986.

*Voices*

**Heathcliff:** Mel Blanc

*Additional Voices*

Donna Christie, Peter Cullen, Jeannie Elias, Stan Jones, Marilyn Lightstone, Danny Mann, Derek McGrath, Marilyn Schreffler, Danny Wells, Ted Zeigler

Featuring new introductory footage, the film incorporates numerous adventures from the television series with the famed comic-strip feline becoming involved in all kinds of escapades.

## ◉ HEAVY METAL (1981)

An Ivan Reitman/Leonard Mogel Production released by Columbia Pictures. **p:** Ivan Reitman; **d:** Gerald Potterton; **w:** Dan Goldberg and Len Blum (based on work and stories by Richard Corben, Angus McKie, Dan O'Bannon, Thomas Warkentin, Berni Wrightson); **m:** Elmer Bernstein. **Running time:** 90 minutes. **Released:** August 7, 1981.

*Voices*

**Grimaldi:** Don Francks; **Grimaldi's Student:** Caroline Semple; **Harry Canyon:** Richard Romanus; **Girl/Satellite:** Susan Roman; **Rudnick:** Al Waxman; **Alien:** Harvey Atkin; **Dan/Den/Desk Sergeant/Robot:** John Candy; **Queen/Whore:** Marilyn Lightstone;

**Prosecutor:** John Vernon; **Captain Lincoln F. Sternn/Edsel/Mal Reporter:** Eugene Levy; **Lawyer Charlie/General:** Joe Flaherty; **Hanover First/Dr. Anrak:** Rodger Bumpass; **Regolian:** Douglas Kenney, **Zeke:** Harold Ramis

Seven segments backed by original rock music comprise this adult cartoon fantasy based on stories from *Heavy Metal* magazine.

## ◉ HEAVY TRAFFIC (1973)

A Steve Krantz Production released by American International Pictures. **p:** Steve Krantz; **d & scr:** Ralph Bakshi, **m:** Ray Shanklin, Ed Bogas. **Running time:** 76 minutes. **Released:** August 15, 1973.

*Voices*

**Michael:** Joseph Kaufman; **Carole:** Beverly Hope; **Angie:** Frank De Kova, **Ida:** Terri Haven; **Molly:** Mary Dean Lauria; **Rosalyn:** Jacqueline Mills; **Rosa:** Lilian Adams

*Additional Voices*

Jim Bates, Michael Brandon, Jaime Farr, Robert Easton, Charles Gordon, Candy Candido, Jay Lawrence, Morton Lewis, Bill Striglos, Lee Weaver, Helene Winston

Young cartoonist Michael, the virginal offspring of a Mafia member, leaves home after quarreling violently with his Jewish mother and takes a black girl, Rosa, as his mistress.

**PN:** Like *Fritz the Cat*, the film received an X rating, even though the content was not as visually and aurally explicit as Bakshi's first effort. It was originally to be based on Hubert Selby's *Last Exit to Brooklyn*, but a deal between Selby and Bakshi fell through. In 1974 a scattering of scenes from the film were reanimated for an R rating so the film could be reissued on a double bill with *The Nine Lives of Fritz the Cat*.

## ◉ HEIDI'S SONG (1982)

A Hanna-Barbera Production released by Paramount Pictures. **p:** Joseph Barbera, William Hanna; **d:** Robert Taylor; **st:** Joseph Barbera, Jameson Brewer (based on the novel *Heidi* by Johanna Spyri); **scr:** Joseph Barbera, Robert Taylor, Jameson Brewer; **m:** Hoyet S. Curtin; **m/l:** Sammy Cahn, Burton Lane. **Songs:** "Friends," "It's a Christmas Day," "She's a Nothing!," "Can You Imagine," "An Unkind Word" and "You're Not Rat Enough to Be a Rat!" **Running time:** 94 minutes. **Released:** November 19, 1982.

*Voices*

**Grandfather:** Lorne Greene; **Head Ratte:** Sammy Davis Jr.; **Heidi:** Margery Gray; **Gruffle:** Peter Cullen; **Peter:** Roger DeWitt; **Herr Sessman:** Richard Erdman; **Sebastian:** Fritz Feld; **Klara:** Pamela Ferdin; **Fraulein Rottenmeier:** Joan Gerber; **Willie:** Michael Bell; **Aunt Dete:** Virginia Gregg; **Tinette:** Janet Waldo; **Schnoddle/Hootie:** Frank Welker; **Mountain:** Michael Winslow

Based on Johanna Spyri's enduring, tear-jerking novel *Heidi*, this animated musical version tells the story of Heidi, who is separated from her beloved grandfather and forced to live with a wealthy crippled girl and a mean-spirited governess who detests her, only to be reunited with her grandfather and her friends in the end.

**PN:** After years of intensive preparation, *Heidi's Song* was the next major animated feature produced by William Hanna and Joseph Barbera (who also cowrote the story and screenplay), following their last effort, 1973's *Charlotte's Web*.

## ◉ HERCULES (1997)

A Walt Disney Production released by Buena Vista Pictures. **p:** Ron Clements, Alice Dewey, John Musker; **d:** Ron Clements, John Musker; **st:** Barry Johnson; **scr:** Ron Clements, Don McEnery, Irene Mecchi, John Musker, Bob Shaw; **m:** Alan Menken; **superv anim:** Chris Bailey, Nancy Beiman, Andreas Deja, Ken Duncan, Eric Goldberg. **Songs:** "Long Ago . . . ," "Gospel Truth," "Go the Distance," "Oh Mighty Zeus," "One Last Hope," "Zero to Hero," "I Won't Say (I'm in Love)," "Star Is Born," "Big Olive," "Prophecy," "Destruction of the Agora," "Phil's Island," "Rodeo," "Speak of the Devil," "Hydra Battle," "Meg's Garden," "Hercules' Villa," "All Time Chump," "Cutting the Thread" and "True Hero." **Running time:** 93 minutes. **Released:** June 27, 1997.

*Voices*

**Hercules:** Tate Donovan; **Young Hercules (speaking):** Josh Keaton; **Young Hercules (singing):** Roger Bart; **Phi:** Danny DeVito; **Hades:** James Woods; **Meg (Megara):** Susan Egan; **Pain:** Bob Goldthwait; **Panic:** Matt Frewer; **Zeus:** Rip Torn; **Hera:** Samantha Eggar; **Alcmene:** Barbara Barrie; **Hermes:** Paul Shaffer; **The Fates:** Amanda Plummer, Carole Shelley, Paddi Edwards; **Narrator:** Charlton Heston; **Cyclops:** Patrick Pinney; **Calliope:** Lillias White; **Clio:** Vanesse Thomas; **Melpomene:** Cheryl Freeman; **Terpsichore:** La Chanze; **Thalia:** Roz Ryan; **Burnt Man:** Corey Burton; **Nessus:** Jim Cummings; **Apollo:** Keith David; **The Earthquake Lady:** Mary Kay Bergman; **Heavyset Woman:** Kathleen Freeman; **Little Boy:** Bug Hall; **Little Boy:** Kellen Hathaway; **Demetrius:** Wayne Knight; **Ithicles:** Aaron Michael Metchik

*Additional Voices*

Tawatha Agee, Jack Angel, Shelton Becton, Bob Bergen, Rodger Bumpass, Jennifer Darling, Debi Derryberry, Bill Farmer, Milt Grayson, Sherry Lynn, Mickie McGowan, Denise Pickering, Philip Protor, Jan Rabson, Riley Steiner, Fronzi Thornton, Erik von Detten, Ken Williams

Pumped-up Greek muscleman Hercules conquers the villainous Hades' hostile takeover of Mount Olympus in this souped-up, fiendishly funny animated musical-comedy from the producers of *The Little Mermaid* and *Aladdin*.

**PN:** Much like *The Hunchback of Notre Dame*, *Hercules* was a high-stakes risk for Walt Disney Productions, though the film fared better than expected. Opening the same week as the hit suspense/thriller *Face Off* starring John Travolta, *Hercules* came in a close second, raking in $21.454 million the weekend it premiered and going on to gross more than $99.0446 million nationwide.

## ◉ HERE COME THE LITTLES (1985)

A DIC Enterprises Production released by Atlantic Releasing. **p:** Jean Chalopin, Andy Heyward, Tetsuo Katayama; **d:** Bernard Deyries; **w:** Woody Kling; **m:** Haim Saban, Shuky Levy; **anim dir:** Tsukasa Tannai, Yoshinobu Michihata. **Running time:** 77 minutes. **Released:** May 24, 1985.

*Voices*

**Henry Bigg:** Jimmy E. Keegan; **Lucy Little:** Bettina Bush; **Tom Little:** Donovan Freberg; **Uncle Augustus:** Hal Smith; **William Little:** Gregg Berger; **Helen Little:** Patricia Parris; **Grandpa Little:** Alvy Moore; **Dinky Little:** Robert David Hall; **Mrs. Evans:** Mona Marshall

When Henry Bigg's parents are lost in Africa, the boy is sent to live with his mean Uncle Augustus, who wants to be Henry's guardian so he can tear down Henry's house and build a shopping center. The Littles, Tom and Lucy, who accidentally wind up in Henry's suitcase, reveal themselves to Henry, who is astonished to learn of their existence but pledges to help them escape.

## ⊚ HEY ARNOLD! THE MOVIE (2002)

A Paramount Pictures/Nickelodeon Movies/Snee-Oosh Production in association with Nickelodeon Animation Studios released by Paramount Pictures. **p:**Craig Bartlett, Albie Hecht; **exec prod:** Marjorie Cohn, Julia Pistor; **d:** Tuck Tucker; **scr:** Craig Bartlett, Steve Viksten; **m:** Jim Lang; **anim dir:** Christine Kolosov, Frank Weiss. **Songs:** "2 Way," "Coconut" and "Life Is Just a Bowl of Cherries." **Running time:** 75 minutes. **Released:** June 28, 2002.

*Voices*

**Arnold:** Spencer Klein; **Helga Geraldine Pataki/Deep Voice:** Francesca Marie Smith; **Gerald Martin Johanssen/Rasta Guy:** Jamil Walker Smith; **Grandpa "Steely" Phil/Nick Vermicelli:** Dan Castellaneta; **Grandma Gertie "Pookie"/Mayor Dixie/Red:** Tress MacNeille; **Scheck:** Paul Sorvino; **Bridget:** Jennifer Jason Leigh; **Coroner:** Christopher Lloyd; **Mr. Bailey:** Vincent Schiavelli; **Big Bob Pataki/Head of Security:** Maurice LaMarche; **Miriam Pataki/Reporter:** Kath Soucie; **Stinky Peterson:** Christopher Walberg; **Mrs. Vitello:** Elizabeth Ashley; **Brainy/Murray/Grubby/Monkeyman:** Craig Bartlett

Arnold and his friends try to track down a document declaring his town a historical landmark in an effort to stop a greedy corporation from razing his neighborhood.

**PN:** Marking yet another attempt by Nickelodeon and Paramount Pictures to turn a popular television cartoon series into a feature film franchise, this feature-length adaptation of Nickelodeon's beloved series *Hey, Arnold!* proved to be a tough sell, grossing a paltry $13.6 million in the United States.

## ⊚ HEY GOOD LOOKIN' (1982)

A Ralph Bakshi Production released through Warner Bros. **p, d & w:** Ralph Bakshi; **m:** John Madara, Ric Sandler. **Running time:** 76 minutes. **Released:** October 1, 1982.

*Voices*

**Vinnie:** Richard Romanus; **Crazy Shapiro:** David Proval; **Roz:** Tina Bowman; **Eva:** Jesse Welles; **Solly:** Angelo Grisanti; **Stompers:** Danny Wells, Bennie Massa, Gelsa Palao, Paul Roman, Larry Bishop, Tabi Cooper; **Waitress:** Juno Dawson, **Chaplain:** Shirley Jo Finney; **Yonkel:** Martin Garner; **Alice:** Terry Haven; **Max:** Allen Joseph; **Chaplain:** Philip M. Thomas; **Old Vinnie:** Frank DeKova; **Sal:** Candy Candido; **Italian Man:** Ed Peck; **Italian Women:** Lillian Adams, Mary Dean Lauria; **Gelsa:** Donna Ponterotto; **The Lockers Staging and Choreography:** Toni Basil

Vinnie, a slicked-hair, 1950's type (drawn to look like John Travolta), is the head of a white youth street gang, The Stompers, whose rivals are a black group known as the Chaplains in this 1950's genre spoof.

**PN:** Ralph Bakshi completed principal work on this animated feature in 1975, but it was shelved by Warner Bros. for seven years before it was released.

## ⊚ HEY THERE, IT'S YOGI BEAR! (1964)

A Hanna-Barbera Production released by Columbia Pictures. **p & d:** William Hanna, Joseph Barbera; **w:** William Hanna, Joseph Barbera, Warren Foster; **m:** Marty Paich; **anim dir:** Charles A. Nichols. **Songs:** "Hey There, It's Yogi Bear," "Ven-E, Ven-O, Ven-A," "Like I Like You," "Wet Whistle," "St. Louie" and "Ash Can Parade." **Running time:** 89 minutes. **Released:** June 3, 1964.

*Voices*

**Yogi Bear:** Daws Butler; **Boo Boo/Ranger Smith:** Don Messick; **Cindy Bear:** Julie Bennett; **Grifter:** Mel Blanc; **Corn Pone:** Hal Smith; **Snively:** J. Pat O'Malley

*Additional Voices*

James Darren; Jean Vander Pyl

Yogi Bear, the self-proclaimed king of Jellystone Park, and pal Boo Boo travel cross-country in search of Yogi's girlfriend, Cindy, who has been captured by a circus. The adventure winds up in New York, where Ranger Smith comes to the rescue of all three.

**PN:** The film was Yogi's first full-length animated feature and the first cartoon feature ever for Hanna-Barbera Productions.

## ⊚ HOME ON THE RANGE (2004)

A Walt Disney Pictures Production released by Buena Vista Pictures. **p:** Alice Dewey Goldstone; **d:** Will Finn, John Sanford; **scr:** Will Finn, John Sanford; **st:** Will Finn, John Sanford, Michael LaBash, Sam Levine, Mark Kennedy, Robert Lence; **m:** Alan Menken; **songs:** Alan Menken, Glenn Slater; **f/x anim:** Mauro Maressa; **anim:** Tim Allen, Dale Baer, James Baker, Tony Bancroft, Dan Boulos, Chris Buck, Andreas Deja, Frank Dietz, Russ Edmonds, Will Finn, Steven E. Gordon, Mark Henn, Jay Jackson, Shawn Keller, James Lopez, Duncan Marjoribanks, Mark Pudleiner, Chris Sauve, Bruce W. Smith, Marc Smith, Michael Stocker, Michael Surrey, Barry Temple, Andreas Wesel-Therborn; Dougg Williams, Ellen Woodbury, Phillip Young. **Songs:** "(You Ain't) Home on the Range," "Home on the Range (Echo Mine Reprise)," "Little Patch of Heaven," "Yodle-Adle-Eedle-Idle-Oo," "Will the Sun Ever Shine Again," "Wherever the Trail May Lead," "Anytime You Need a Friend" and "Little Patch of Heaven" (Finale). **Running time:** 75 minutes. **Released:** April 2, 2004.

*Voices*

**Maggie:** Roseanne Barr; **Mrs. Caloway:** Judi Dench; **Grace:** Jennifer Tilly; **Almeda Slim:** Randy Quaid; **Buck:** Cuba Gooding Jr.; **Lucky Jack:** Charles Haid; **Annie:** Anne Richards; **Sheriff Sam Brown:** Richard Riehle; **The Willie Brothers:** Sam J. Levine; **Jeb:** Joe Flaherty; **Ollie:** Charlie Dell; **Mr. Wesley:** Steve Buscemi; **Rico:** Charles Dennis; **Junior:** Lance LeGault; **Audrey:** Estelle Harris; **Barry/Bob:** Marshall Efron, **Piggy:** Bobby Block; **Little Pigs:** Keaton Savage, Ross Simanteris; **Patrick:** Patrick Warburton; **Pearl Gesner:** Carole Cook; **Rusty:** G.W. Bailey

After the ranch owner of the Patch of Heaven dairy farm is suddenly served with a notice that her farm will be auctioned unless she pays the $750 mortgage payment, a herd of cows, led by the plump, prize-winning show cow, Maggie, a fussy British cow, Mrs. Calloway, and a spacey, New-Age cow, Grace, nab a cattle rustler to collect a ransom to pay off the debt.

**PN:** Costing an extraordinary $110 million to make and returning less than half of that in box-office revenue in the United States after its release—some $50 million—*Home on the Range* officially marked the end of Walt Disney Studios' reign as a producer of 2-D animated movies. In fact, the studio shut down its traditional animation department and turned its attention to computer-animated features instead.

## ⊚ HOODWINKED (2005)

A Kanbar Entertainment Production in association with Kanbar Animation and Blue Younder Films released by the Weinstein Company LLC. **p:** Maurice Kanbar, David Lovegren, Sue Bea Montgomery, Preston Stutzman; **d:** Cory Edwards, Todd Edwards, Tony Leech; **scr:** Cory Edwards, Todd Edwards, Tony Leech; **m/sc:** John Mark Painter; **songs:** Todd Edwards. **Songs:** "Great Big World." **Running time:** 80 minutes. **Released:** January 13, 2006.

*Voices*

**Red:** Anne Hathaway; **The Wolf:** Patrick Warburton; **Granny:** Glenn Close; **The Woodsman:** James Belushi; **Detective Bill**

**Stork:** Anthony Anderson; **Nicky Flippers:** David Ogden Stiers; **Chief Grizzly:** Xzbit; **Woolworth the Sheep:** Chazz Palimenteri; **Boingo:** Andy Dick; **Twitchy:** Cory Edwards; **Sandwich Man:** Todd Edwards; **Dolph:** Tye Edwards; **Japeth the Goat:** Benjy Gaither; **Jimmy Lizard:** Joshua J. Greene; **Raccoon Jerry:** Ken Marino; **P-Biggie:** Kevin Michael Richardson; **Zorra:** Tara Strong

Updated version of the classic children's fable described as the "real story" of Little Red Riding Hood and the Wolf, with a few adult-humored twists.

**PN:** The first animated feature acquisition released by the Weinstein Company, this film opened in Los Angeles for a one-week Oscar-qualifying run on December 15, 2005, before going citywide on January 13, 2006. Despite receiving mixed reviews, the CGI-animated feature narrowly came in second in box-office sales the week it opened following Jerry Bruckheimer's basketball drama, *Glory Road*, which took in $16.9 million to *Hoodwinked*'s $16.8 million. Overall, the film grossed more than $51.1 million in revenue during its release.

## ◎ HOWL'S MOVING CASTLE (2005)

A Studio Ghibli Production in association with Tokuma Stoten/Dentsu Inc./Nippon Television Network/Buena Vista Home Entertainment/Touhoku Sinsha/Walt Disney Pictures released by Walt Disney Pictures. **p:** Toshio Suzuki, Rick Dempsey, Ned Lott; **d:** Hayao Miyazaki; **scr:** Reiko Yoshida, Hayao Miyazaki (based on the novel, *Howl's Moving Castle*, by Diana Wynne Jones); **m:** Joe Hisaishi; **superv anim:** Akihiro Yamashita, Takeshi Inamura, Kitaro Kosaka. **Running time:** 119 minutes. **Released:** June 10, 2005.

*Voices*

**Howl:** Christian Bale; **Young Sophie:** Emily Mortimer; **Old Sophie:** Jean Simmons; **Witch of the Waste:** Lauren Bacall; **Calcifer:** Billy Crystal; **Markl:** Josh Hutcherson; **Madam Suliman:** Blythe Danner; **Honey:** Jane Alan; **Prince Turnip:** Crispin Freeman; **Lettie:** Jena Malone; **Madge:** Liliana Mumy; **King:** Mark Silverman

*Additional Voices*

Carlos Alazraqui, Newell Alexander, Rosemary Alexander, Julia Barnett, Susan Blakeslee, Leslie Carrara, Mitch Carter, David Cowgill, Holly Dorff, Moosie Drier, Ike Eisenmann, Will Friedle, Bridget Hoffman, Richard Steven Horvitz, Sherry Hursey, Hope Levy, Christina MacGregor, Joel McCrary, Edie Mirman, Daran Norris, Pete Renaday, Kristen Rutherford, Warren Sroka

After the wicked Witch of the Waste turns her into a 90-year-old woman, the formerly shy teenager, Sophie, befriends the Witch Howl and his companions to help her break the spell.

**PN:** Japanese animator Hayao Miyazaki, the Oscar-winning director of *Spirited Away*, wrote and directed this clever and often enchanting story inspired by popular British children's author Diana Wynne Jones's novel. Toho first released the film in Japan on November 20, 2005. As part of a deal with Japan's Studio Ghibli, the film's original producer, Walt Disney Pictures, acquired the rights to distribute the film through its Buena Vista Pictures in the United States, dubbing the film in English. Disney's release grossed $4.7 million in revenue.

## ◎ HUGO THE HIPPO (1976)

A Brut/Hungarofilm Pannonia Filmstudio Production released by 20th Century-Fox. **p:** Robert Halmi; **d:** Bill Feigenbaum; **scr:** Thomas Baum; **m:** Bert Keyes; **anim dir:** Joszef Gemes. **Songs:** "It's Really True," "I Always Wanted to Make a Garden," "Somewhere

*A forlorn baby hippo struggles to survive against hippo-haters of the world in the Hungarian-produced feature* Hugo the Hippo *(1976). © 20th Century Fox*

You Can Call Home," "H-I-P-P-O-P-O-T-A-M-U-S," "You Said a Mouthful," "Best Day Ever Made," "Mr. M'Bow-Wow," "Wherever You Go, Hugo," "Harbor Chant" and "Zing Zang." **Running time:** 90 minutes. **Released:** July 14, 1976.

*Voices*

**Narrator:** Burl Ives; **The Sultan:** Robert Morley; **Aban Khan:** Paul Lynde; **Jorma:** Ronnie Cox; **Jorma's Father:** Percy Rodriguez; **Royal Magician:** Jesse Emmette; **Judge:** Len Maxwell; **Grown Ups and Children:** Tom Scott; Don Marshall, H.B. Barnum III, Marc Copage, Charles Walken, Lee Weaver, Richard Williams, Frank Welker, Ron Pinkard, Michael Rye, Marc Wright. Ellsworth Wright, Vincent Esposito, Court Benson, Peter Benson, Mona Tera, Bobby Eilbacher, Len Maxwell, Peter Fernandez, Allen Swift, Derek Power, Frederick O'Neal, Al Fann, Thomas Anderson, Jerome Ward, Shawn Campbell, Lisa Huggins, John McCoy, Alicia Fleer, Lisa Kohane, Bobby Dorn, Pat Bright, Robert Lawrence; **Special Voice Effects:** Frank Welker, Nancy Wible, Jerry Hausner; **Vocalists:** Marie Osmond, Jimmy Osmond

A forlorn baby hippo struggles to survive against hippo-haters of the world, led by Aban Khan (voiced by Paul Lynde), and seeks the companionship of others to feel needed and loved.

## ◎ THE HUNCHBACK OF NOTRE DAME (1996)

A Walt Disney Production released by Buena Vista Pictures. **p:** Roy Conli, Don Hahn; **d:** Gary Trousdale, Kirl Wise; **st:** Tab Murphy (based on the novel *Notre-Dame de Paris*); **scr:** Irene Mecchi, Tab Murphy, Jonathan Roberts, Bob Tzudiker, Noni White; **m:** Alan Menken, Stephen Schwartz; **superv anim:** James Baxter, Dave Burgess, Russ Edmonds, Will Finn, Tony Fucile, Ron Husband, David Pruiksma, Mike Surrey, Kathy Zielinski. **Songs:** "The Bells of Notre Dame," "Out There," "Topsy Turvy," "Humiliation," "God Help the Outcasts," "The Bell Tower," "Heaven's Light/Hellfire," "A Guy Like You," "Paris Burning," "The Court of Miracles," "Sanctuary," "And He Shall Smite the Wicked" and "Someday." **Running time:** 86 minutes. **Released:** July 21, 1996.

*Voices*

**Quasimodo:** Tom Hulce; **Esmeralda:** Demi Moore; **Frollo:** Tony Jay; **Phoebus:** Kevin Kline; **Clopin:** Paul Kandel; **Hugo:** Jason

Alexander; **Victor:** Charles Kimbrough; **Laverne:** Mary Wickes; **The Archdeacon:** David Odgen Stiers; **Esmeralda (singing):** Heidi Mollenhauer; **Quasimodo's Mother:** Mary Kay Bergman; **Brutish Guard:** Corey Burton; **Miscellaneous Guards/Gypsies:** Jim Cummings; **Oafish Guard:** Bill Fagerbakke; **Miscellaneous Guards/Gypsies:** Patrick Pinney; **The Old Heretic:** Gary Trousdale; **Baby Bird:** Frank Welker; **Laverne (additional dialogue:** Jane Withers

Quasimodo, the 15th-century misshapen, gentle-souled bell ringer who lives in the belltower of the Notre Dame cathedral, defends the beautiful gypsy girl Esmeralda and the very cathedral he calls home from the evil Minister of Justice in this animated retelling of the classic Victor Hugo story.

**PN:** Costing $70 million to produce, *The Hunchback of Notre Dame* was not as successsful as some of Disney's other animated features in the 1990s. The film grossed $100.117 million in this country and $184.7 million worldwide. Talented songwriter/lyricist Alan Menken, who penned the award-winning musical scores for *Beauty and the Beast*, *Aladdin* and others, wrote the original music for the film along with Stephen Schwartz. Menken and Schwartz were honored with an Academy Award nomination for best original score for their work.

### ◎ ICE AGE (2002)

A Blue Sky Studios/20th Century Fox Animation Production released by 20th Century Fox. **p:** Lori Forte; **exec prod:** Chris Meledandri; **d:**Chris Wedge, Carlos Saldanha; **scr:** Michael Berg, Michael J. Wilson, Peter Ackerman; **st:** Michael J. Wilson; **m:** David Newman; **seq dir:** Mark Baldo, Jan Carle; **lead anim:** James Bresnahan, Michael Thurmeier; **anim:** Nina Bafaro, Floyd Bishop, Jr., Thomas Bisogno, James Campbell, Jaime Andres Castaneda, Galen T. Chu, Nick Craven, Marcelo Fernandes DeMoura, Everett Downing Jr., Aaron J. Hardine, James Hundertmark, Jeffrey K. Joe, Kompin Kerngunird, Dean Kalman Lennert, Rodrigo Blass, Simi Nallasetg, Dana O'Connor, Davis S. Peng, Andreas Procopiou, Mika Ripatti, Scott Robideau, David J. Smith, David B. Vallone, Joshua West. **Songs:** "Sound Off (Duckworth Chant)," "Send Me on My Way" and "The Comedians." **Running time:** 80 minutes. **Released:** March 15, 2002.

*Voices*

**Manfred:** Ray Romano; **Sid:** John Leguizamo, **Diego:** Denis Leary; **Soto:** Goran Visnjic; **Zeke:** Jack Black; **Roshan:** Tara Strong, **Rhino:** Cedric the Entertainer; **Rhino/Start:** Stephen Root; **Sabertooth Tiger:** Diedrich Bader; **Scrat/Dodo:** Chris Wedge; **Oscar/Dab the Dodo:** Alan Tudyk; **Female Sloths:** Lorri Bagley, Jane Krakowski; **Dodo/Macrauchenia:** Peter Ackerman; **Dodo:** P. J. Benjamin; **Dodo/Aardvark:** Josh Hamilton

Back when dinosaurs roamed the Earth, an unlikely foursome of prehistoric animals—a dumb sloth, Sid; a woolly mammoth, Manny; a saber-toothed tiger, Diego; and an hilarious acorn-loving squirrel, Scrat—band together to journey across harsh elements and frozen tundra to take a child back to his rightful tribe.

**PN:** This CGI-animated feature was the first produced by Blue Sky Studios of New York, which previously had produced several award-winning computer-animated shorts, including the Oscar-winning cartoon, "Bunny," directed by *Ice Age* codirector Chris Wedge. This first entry into feature-film producing became a smash hit and brought critical success to the studio—it grossed an astounding $175 million in the United States—that spawned a successful cartoon short starring Scrat, "Gone Nutty" (2002), which was nominated for an Academy

Award for best short subject (animated), and a sequel, *Ice Age 2: The Meltdown* (2006).

### ◎ ICE AGE 2: THE MELTDOWN (2006)

A Blue Sky Studios/20th Century Fox Animation Production released by 20th Century Fox. **p:** Lori Forte; **exec prod:** Christopher Meledandri, Chris Wedge; **d:** Carlos Saldahna; **scr:** Peter Gaulke, Gerry Swallow, Jim Hecht; **st:** Peter Gaulke, Gerry Swallow; **m:** John Powell. **Running time:** 91 minutes. **Released:** March 31, 2006.

*Voices*

**Manny:** Ray Romano; **Sid:** John Leguizamo; **Diego:** Denis Leary; **Crash:** Seann William Scott; **Eddie:** Josh Peck; **Ellie:** Queen Latifah; **Lone Gunslinger Vulture:** Will Arnett; **Fast Tony:** Jay Leno; **Scrat:** Chris Wedge; **Dung Beetle Dad:** Peter Ackerman; **Glypto Boy Billy/Beaver Girl:** Caitlin Rose Anderson; **Rhino Boy/Beaver Boy:** Connor Anderson; **Elk Boy:** Jack Crocicchia; **Condor Chick:** Peter DeSeve

It's no picnic this time around for Manny, the woolly mammoth, Sid, the sloth, Diego, the saber-toothed tiger, or Scat, the hapless squirrel when a global thaw threatens a massive meltdown and they must warn their fellow creatures to move to safer ground.

**PN:** Not often in Hollywood does a sequel outdo the first film, but this sequel to 2002's *Ice Age* did just that by out-grossing the original film with more than $187.5 million in ticket sales. A trio of comic newcomer was introduced in this computer-animated hit: Ellie, a womanly woolly mammoth and a potential mate for Manny voiced by Queen Latifah; Crash and Eddie, a pair of playful possum brothers featuring the voices of Seann William Scott of *The Dukes of Hazard* movie and Josh Peck of TV's *Drake and Josh*; and Fast Tony, a shady armadillo whose voice was supplied by comedian Jay Leno. Carlos Saldahna, who codirected the original film, soloed as director this time around.

### ◎ I GO POGO (1980)

A Stowar Enterprises/Possum Production released by 21st Century Distribution. **p, d & w:** Marc Paul Chinoy; **m:** Gary Baker, Thoma Flora; **anim dir:** Stephen Chiodo; **senior anim:** Diedre A. Knowlton, Stephen Oakes. **Running time:** 82 minutes. **Released:** August 1, 1980.

*Voices*

**Pogo:** Skip Hinnant; **Porky Pine/Mole/Wiley Katt:** Jonathan Winters; **The Deacon Mushrat:** Vincent Price; **Mam'zelle Hepsibah/Miz Beaver:** Ruth Buzzi; **Albert Alligator:** Stan Freberg; **P.T. Bridgeport:** Jimmy Breslin; **Churchy La Femme:** Arnold Stang; **Howland Owl/Bothered Bat:** Bob McFadden; **Bewitched Bat/Seminole Sam/Narrator:** Len Maxwell; **Bewildered Bat:** Bob Kaliban; **Miz Beetle:** Marcia Savella; **Freemount Bug:** Mike Schultz

Election year fever sweeps the Okenfenokee Swamp as everyone's favorite possum suddenly finds himself recruited for the nation's highest office by all of his friends, including Albert, Howland and Porky Pine.

**PN:**Produced in stop-motion animation and based on Walt Kelly's unforgettable Pogo comic strip, this film is also known as *Pogo for President*.

### ◎ I MARRIED A STRANGE PERSON (1998)

A PlympCorp Production in association with Italtoons released by Lions Gate Entertainment. **p, d, w & anim:** Bill Plympton; **m:** Maureen McElheron. **Running time:** 72 minutes. **Released:** October 28, 1998.

*Voices*

**Grant Boyer:** Tom Larson; **Keri Boyer:** Charis Michelsen (as Charis Michaelson); **Larson P. Giles:** Richard Spore; **Col. Ferguson:** Chris Cooke; **Keri's Mom:** Ruth Ray; **Keri's Dad:** J.B. Adams, **Bud Sweeny:** John Russo; **Smiley:** Jennifer Senko; **Jackie Jason:** John Holderried; **Sex Video Model:** Etta Valeska; **Announcer:** Bill Martone; **Solly Jim:** Tony Rossi

After a strange growth on his neck bestows him with supernatural abilities to change people or objects, a corporate CEO aims to achieve world domination of man.

## ◎ THE INCREDIBLE MR. LIMPET (1964)

A Warner Bros. Pictures Production released by Warner Bros. **p:** John C. Rose; **l/a dir:** Arthur Lubin; **scr:** James Brewer and John C. Rose; **m:** Frank Perkins; **anim dir:** Vladimir Tytla, Gerry Chiniquy, Hawley Pratt; **seq dir:** Robert McKimson. **Running time:** 102 minutes. **Released:** March 28, 1964.

*Cast*

**Henry Limpet:** Don Knotts; **Bessie Limpet:** Carole Cook; **George Stickle:** Jack Weston; **Commander Harlock:** Andrew Duggan; **Admiral Spewter:** Larry Keating; **Admiral Fivestar:** Charles Meredith; **Admiral Doemitz:** Oscar Beregi

*Voices*

**Limpet:** Don Knotts; **Ladyfish:** Elizabeth MacRae; **Crusty:** Paul Frees

In this live-action/animated feature, Don Knotts plays a retiring Walter Mitty–type bookkeeper who, depressed by his inability to join the navy (he's classified as 4-F because of his eyesight), accidentally falls into the ocean and is suddenly transformed into a fish. In his new role, he makes friends, finds a sweetheart and aides the U.S. war effort by helping convoys cross the ocean to knock off enemy U-boats.

**PN:** Working titles were *Henry Limpet*, *Mister Limpet* and *Be Careful How You Wish.*

## ◎ THE INCREDIBLES (2004)

A Pixar Animation Studios/Walt Disney Pictures Production released by Buena Vista Pictures. **p:** John Walker; **exec prod:** John Lasseter; **d:** Brad Bird; **scr:** Brad Bird; **m:** Michael Giacchino; **superv anim:** Tony Fucile, Steven Clay Hunter, Alan Barillaro. **Running time:** 115 minutes. **Released:** November 5, 2004.

*Voices*

**Bob Parr/Mr. Incredible:** Craig T. Nelson; **Helen Parr/Elastgirl:** Holly Hunter; **Lucius Best/Frozone:** Samuel L. Jackson; **Buddy Pine/Syndrome:** Jason Lee; **Violet Parr:** Sarah Vowell; **Dash Parr:** Spencer Fox; **Edna "E" Mode:** Brad Bird; **Mirage:** Elizabeth Pena; **Gilbert Huph:** Wallace Shawn; **The Underminer:** John Ratzenberger; **Jack Jack:** Maeve Andrews, Eli Fucile; **Mrs. Hogenson:** Jean Sincere; **Rick Dicker:** Bud Luckey; **Kari:** Bret Parker; **Newsreel Narrator:** Teddy Newton; **Tony Rydinger:** Michael Bird; **Honey:** Kimberly Adair Clark; **Bomb Voyage:** Dominique Louis; **Principal:** Wayne Canney

After attempting to live a normal suburban life, a family of superheroes, who has gone undercover to protect their identities, comes out of retirement to save the world while bonding as a family.

**PN:** Unlike his first animated feature for Warner Bros., *The Iron Giant,* which was largely a critical success but a major disappointment at the box office mostly due to poor studio marketing of the film, Brad Bird's second foray into feature-film directing and second animated feature overall, this time for computer-animation giant Pixar, *The Incredibles,* was a monstrous hit. It grossed more than $261 million in the United States and was nominated for 28 awards, including four Academy Awards, winning twice for best achievement in sound editing, and, more importantly, for best animated feature. Paired with the film during its release was the Oscar-winning cartoon short, "Boundin'," directed by Pixar animator Bud Luckey. Making cameo appearances in the film were legendary Disney animators Frank Thomas and Ollie Johnson, who also had cameos in Bird's *The Iron Giant.* In 2005, *The Incredibles* DVD edition became the number-one best-selling DVD of the year with more than 17.38 million units sold. On May 31, 2006, Disney's DVD edition of *The Incredibles* won "Best of Show" at the second annual DVD Critics Awards in Los Angeles and also was named "Best Children's DVD of 2005" by a panel of 10 critics.

## ◎ IRON GIANT (1999)

A Warner Bros. Feature Animation Production released by Warner Bros. **p:** Allison Abbate, Des McAnuff; **d:** Brad Bird; **scr:** Tim McCanlies; **st:** Brad Bird (based on the book, *The Iron Man,* by Ted Hughes); **m:** Michael Kamen; **head anim:** Tony Fucile; **superv anim:** Richard Bazley, General Rogard, Bob Davies, Stephan Franck, Tony Fucile, Gregory S.E. Manwaring, Steven Markowski, Mike Nguyen, Wendy Perdue, Christopher Sauve, Dean Wellings. **Songs:** "Honeycomb," "I Got a Rocket in My Pocket," "Comin' Home Baby," "Duck and Cover," "Blue Rumba," "Genius after Hours," "Capitolizing," "Cha-Hua-Hua," "Blues Walk," "Let's Do the Cha Cha" and "Searchin'." **Running time:** 86 minutes. **Released:** August 6, 1999.

*Voices*

**Hogarth Hughes:** Eli Marienthal; **The Iron Giant:** Vin Diesel; **Kent Mansley:** Christopher McDonald; **Dean McCoppen:** Harry Connick Jr.; **Annie Hughes:** Jennifer Aniston; **General Rogard:** John Mahoney; **Earl Stutz:** M. Emmet Walsh; **Foreman Marv Loach/Floyd Turbeaux:** James Gammon; **Mrs. Tensedge:** Cloris Leachman; **B-Movie Scientist:** Bill Farmer; **Train Engineer:** Ollie Johnston; **Frank the Train Brakeman:** Frank Thomas

A giant alien robot that a paranoid government wants to destroy after it crash-lands on Earth and frightens the residents of a small town in Maine befriends a young boy fighting fear and prejudice in this Cold War fable.

**PN:** Brad Bird, who years earlier toiled as an animator and director on such television series as *The Simpsons* and *Family Dog,* made his feature film directing debut with this film, based on British poet laureate Ted Hughes's children's book, *The Iron Man,* first published in 1968. While the film fared poorly at the box office during its theatrical release, but garnered widespread praise from critics for its quality craftsmanship and wonderful story, the movie became a major success on home video. Likewise, it won several major awards, including the BAFTA Children's Award for best feature film, a Los Angeles Film Critics Association Award for best animation–feature length, and was also nominated for 13 awards, including science fiction's Hugo Award for best dramatic presentation. Coincidentally, Warner Bros. did a major push with the home video release of the movie by distributing 535 copies to every member of the U.S. Senate and Congress, hoping that praise from key legislators of the G-rated, morality-friendly movie would boost sales. Actor Vin Diesel, still struggling to establish himself as filmdom's next action hero, provided the voice of the Cold War era metal giant.

## ◎ JACK AND THE BEANSTALK (1976)

A Group TAC Production released by Columbia Pictures. **p:** Katsumi Furukawa; **exec prod:** Mikio Nakada; **d:** Gisaburo Sugii, Peter J. Solmo (U.S. director); **scr:** Shuji Hirami; **anim:** Shigeru,

Yamaoto, Yasuo Maeda, Teruhito Kamiguchi, Takateru Miwa, Kazuko Nakamura, Toshio Hirata, Kanji Akabori, Sadao Ysukioka. **Running time:** 82 minutes. **Released:** February 13, 1976.

### Voices

(English version) **Jack/Madame Hecuba:** Billie Lou Watt; **Princess Margaret:** Corinne Orr

Fantasy adventure based on the popular English folktale in which Jack and his faithful dog companion, Crosby, climb to the top of the magical beanstalk Jack planted and where they encounter an evil witch and rescue a princess who is under a spell that makes her believe she is in love with the witch's dumb giant.

## ◎ JAMES AND THE GIANT PEACH (1996)

A Walt Disney/Skellington Production released by Buena Vista Pictures. **p:** Tim Burton; **d:** Henry Selick; **cpd:** John Engel, Henry Selick; **exec prod:** Jake Eberts; **scr:** Steven Bloom, Karey Kirkpatrick, Jonathan Roberts (based on the novel by Roald Dahl); **m:** Randy Newman; **anim superv:** Paul Berry. **Songs:** "My Name Is James," "That's Life," "Eating the Peach," "Family," "Heroes Return" and "Sail Away." **Running time:** 80 minutes. **Released:** April 12, 1996.

### Cast/Voices

**Grasshopper:** Simon Callow; **Centipede:** Richard Dreyfuss, **Ladybug:** Jane Leeves; **Aunt Spiker:** Joanna Lumley; **The Glowworm/Aunt Sponge:** Miriam Margolyes; **Old Man:** Pete Postlethwaite; **Spider:** Susan Sarandon; **James:** Paul Terry; **Earthworm:** David Thewlis; **Reporter #2:** J. Stephen Coyle; **James's Father:** Steven Culp; **Girl with Telescope:** Cirocco Dunlap; **Reporter #1:** Michael Girardin; **Reporter #3:** Tony Haney; **Woman in Bathrobe:** Katherine Howell; **Newsboy:** Chae Kirby; **Hard Hat Man:** Jeff Mosely; **Cabby:** Al Nalbandian; **Beat Cop:** Mike Starr; **James's Mother:** Susan Turner-Cray; **Street Kid:** Mario Yedidia

### Additional Voices

Emily Rosen

After saving the life of a spider, a wildly imaginative young boy (James) embarks on a fantastic adventure after boarding a magical giant peach, only to become friends with a ladybug and a centipede who help him with his plan to get to New York, in this live-action/stop-motion animated featured based on Roald Dahl's popular children's story.

**PN:** Randy Newman, who scored the music for the Disney blockbuster feature *Toy Story*, wrote the music for this feature and received an Oscar nomination for best original score.

## ◎ JESTER TILL (2003)

A Munich Animation Film GmbH. Production release. **p:** Eberhard Junkersdorf, Dieter Meyer, Roland Pellegrino, Linda Van Tulden; **d:** Eberhard Junkersdorf; **scr:** Peter Carpentier, Eberhard Junkersdorf, Christopher Vogler; **m:** Soren Hyldgaard, George Keller; **anim dir:** Jon McClenahan. **Running time:** 84 minutes. **Released:** December 12, 2003.

### Voices

(English version) Lee Evans, Sharon Alexander, Doug Parker, Ellen Kennedy, David Kaye, Ian James Corlett, Richard Newman

A wise-cracking kid, Jester Till, who usually does anything to draw attention to himself, becomes sidetracked when he rescues his Uncle Marcus, a great wizard who is in trouble, helps a young king assume control of his kingdom from his evil advisers and fancies the mayor's clever daughter, Nele, in this animated fantasy

adventure based on the legendary medieval trickster of European folklore.

**PN:** Originally titled *Till Eulenspiegel*, this German-made 2-D and 3-D animated family musical premiered in Los Angeles on December 5, 2003, making a preliminary short list of 11 nominated films for the Academy Awards' best animated feature.

## ◎ JETSONS: THE MOVIE (1990)

A Hanna-Barbera Production released by Universal Pictures. **p & d:** William Hanna and Joseph Barbera; **w:** Dennis Marks; **m:** John Debney (with original songs by Tiffany); **anim dir:** David Michener; **anim:** Frank Adriana, Oliver "Lefty" Callahan, David Feiss, Don MacKinnon, and Irv Spence. **Songs:** "Jetsons Main Title," "Gotcha," "Maybe Love, Maybe Not," "Staying Together," "I Always Thought I'd See You Again," "First Time in Love," "You and Me," "Home," "We're the Jetsons" (Jetsons' RAP) and "With You All the Way." **Running time:** 81 minutes. **Released:** July 6, 1990.

### Voices

**George Jetson:** George O'Hanlon; **Cosmo C. Spacely:** Mel Blanc; **Jane Jetson:** Penny Singleton; **Judy Jetson:** Tiffany; **Elroy Jetson:** Patric Zimmerman; **Astro:** Don Messick; **Rosie the Robot:** Jean Vander Pyl; **Rudy 2:** Ronnie Schell; **Lucy 2:** Patti Deutsch; **Teddy 2:** Dana Hill; **Fergie Furbelow:** Russi Taylor; **Apollo Blue:** Paul Kreppel; **Rocket Rick:** Rick Dees

### Additional Voices

Michael Bell, Jeff Bergman, Brian Cummings, Brad Garrett, Rob Paulsen, Susan Silo, Janet Waldo, B.J. Ward, Jim Ward, Frank Welker

This film version of the classic cartoon show finds the fun-loving foursome, accompanied by their faithful companion/dog, Astro, moving to outer space when George receives a promotion. While their family adjusts to their new home in the Intergalactical Garden estates, George heads for his new job as vice president of the Spacely Sprocket factory. Trouble looms, however, with the discovery that someone is sabotaging the factory and its machinery.

**PN:** Based on the popular 1960s' TV show, this full-length feature grossed $5 million during the first weekend of its release and $20 million overall. One unpopular move was the ousting of actress Janet Waldo, the original voice of Judy Jetson, who recorded all her dialogue and was then dumped for the youthful pop singer Tiffany. The film's settings and vehicles were designed using advanced computer-animated techniques created by deGraf/Wahrman and Kroyer Films.

## ◎ JIMMY NEUTRON, BOY GENIUS (2001)

A DNA Productions/Nickelodeon Movies/O Entertainment Production released by Paramount Pictures. **p:** Steve Oedekerk, John A. Davis, Albie Hecht; **exec prod:** Julia Pistor, Keith Alcorn; **d:** John A. Davis; **scr:** John A. Davis, David N. Weiss, J. David Stern, Steve Oedekerk; **st:** John A. Davis, Steve Oedekerk; **m:** John Debney; **seq dir:** Russell Calabrese, John Eng, Raul Garcia, Robert LaDuca; **anim dir:** Keith Alcorn, John A. Davis; **anim superv:** Paul C. Allen, Renata Dos Anjos, Mike Gasaway, Bryan Hillestad, Troy Saliba. **Songs:** "Go Jimmy, Jimmy," "Leave It up to Me," "AC's Alien Nation" and "Pop." **Running time:** 83 minutes. **Released:** December 21, 2001.

### Voices

**James "Jimmy" Isaac Neurton:** Debi Derryberry; **Cindy Vortex:** Carolyn Lawrence; **Carl Wheezer/Carl's Mom and Dad/Kid in the Classroom/Kid:** Rob Paulsen; **Judy Neutron, VOX:** Megan Cavanagh; **Hugh Neutron/Pilot/Arena Guard:** Mark De Carlo; Sheen Estevez: Jeffrey Garcia; **Mrs. Fowl:** Andrea Martin; **Nick**

**Dean/Brittany/PJ:** Candi Milo; **Libby:** Crystal Scales; **Ooblar:** Martin Short; **King Goobot:** Patrick Stewart; **Ultra Lord/Mission Control:** Jim Cummings; **Yokian Guard/Gus:** David L. Lander; **Newscasters:** Bob Goen, Mary Hart

When an experiment goes haywire causing the parents in his neighborhood to be abducted by aliens, brainy Retroville resident inventor, Jimmy Neutron, his mechanical dog, Goddard, and his classmates travel into space to rescue them.

**PN:** *Jimmy Neutron* creator John A. Davis, of his Dallas-based DNA Productions, directed, coproduced and cowrote with Steve Odekerk and others this full-length animated family adventure that preceded the award-winning Nickelodeon cartoon series. The sixth joint venture by Paramount Pictures and Nickelodeon Movies, this big-screen production was originally going to be made as the pilot for an animated cartoon television series, but after Paramount executives saw some early footage and preliminary plans, they decided to finance it as a feature instead. Davis originally created the character in a 40-second video short he produced in 1995 called "Runaway Rocket Boy," which he eventually lengthened into "The Adventures of Johnny Quasar." Leading up to this feature film release, Jimmy Neutron appeared in various forms on Nickelodeon throughout the year, along with new Internet and videogames, in preparation for the network's September 2002 launch of the weekly series, *The Adventures of Jimmy Neutron: Boy Genius.* Actor Martin Sheen, whose real name is Ramon Estevez, inspired the name of the character, Sheen Estevez, in the film and subsequent television series. Costing approximately $25 million to make, the G-rated movie was not only loved by critics—and was nominated for an Academy Award for best animated feature—but also became a major hit with families and kids, earning more than $80,920,948 in U.S. box-office revenue and $102,970,948 worldwide. Pop stars Aaron Carter and 'N Sync performed songs in the film.

## ◎ JIN-ROH: THE WOLF BRIGADE (2001)

A Production I.G. Production released by Bandai Entertainment. **p:** (Japan) Tsutomu Sugita, Hidekazu Terakawa, (U.S.) Satoshi Kanuma, Toshifumi Yoshida; **d:** Hiroyuki Okiura; **scr/st:** Mamoru Oshii, (U.S. version) Kevin Mckeown; **anim dir:** Kenji Kamiyama. **Running time:** 98 minutes. **Released:** August 3, 2001.

*Voices*
**Kazuki Fuse:** Michael Dobson; **Kei Amamiya:** Moneca Stori; **Atsushi Henmi:** Colin Murdoch; **Bunmei Hiroto:** Dale Wilson; **Hachiro Tobe/Narrator:** Doug Abrahams

Kazuki Fuse, a Special Force Unit paramilitary rookie of Tokyo's Capital Police who fails to shoot a suicidal female terrorist, becomes smitten with the terrorist's surviving sister, Kei, who turns out to be a terrorist as well.

## ◎ JOHNNY THE GIANT KILLER (1953)

A Films Jean Image/Lippert Pictures Production released by Cine Selection. **p & d:** Jean Image, Charles Frank; **scr:** Paul Colline, Charles Frank, Nesta MacDonald (English version); **chief anim:** Albert Chapeaux; **anim:** Denis Boutin, Marcel Breuil, Albert Champeaux, O'Klein. **Running time:** 62 minutes. **Released:** June 5, 1953.

Voice credits unknown.

After going on an expedition with his friends to a castle, Johnny and his friends are captured by an evil giant who reduces them all to the size of a bee using a high-tech machine. After becoming a hero to the Queen Bee, Johnny forms an alliance with the bees and they attack the giant while restoring themselves to the rightful human size with the giant's machine.

**PN:** Winner of a Grand Prix award for children's films at the 1951 Venice Film festival, this feature, while produced in France, was first released in Hollywood and in the United States by Hollywood's Lippert Pictures. No voice actors were credited in the film.

## ◎ JONAH: A VEGGIE TALES MOVIE 2002)

A Big Idea Productions Inc. released by FHE Pictures. **p:** Ameake Owens; **exec prod:** Terry Botwick, Dan Philips, Phil Vischer; **d:** Phil Vischer, Mike Nawrocki; **scr:** Phil Vischer, Mike Nawrocki; **st:** Tim Hodge; **m/s:** Kurt Heinecke, David Mullen, Mike Nawrocki, Phil Vischer; **anim dir:** Marc Vulcano; **anim:** Andy Arnett, Justin Barett, Tom Danen, Thom Falter, Joe Gorski, Christopher Hickman, Amber Rudolph, Nathan Tungseth, Danny Wawrzaszek. **Running time:** 82 minutes. **Released:** October 4, 2002.

*Voices*
**Archibald Asparagus/Jonah/Twippo/Bob the Tomato/Mr. Lunt/Pirate Lunt/Percy Pea/Phillipe Pea/Pa Pea #2:** Phil Vischer; **Larry the Cucumber/Pirate Larry/Jean Claude Pea/Cockney Pea #1/Self-Help Tape Voice/Jerry Gourd/Whooping BBQ Pea:** Mike Nawrocki; **Khalil:** Tim Hodge; **Junior Asparagus:** Lisa Vischer; **Dad Asparagus:** Dan Anderson; **Laura Carrot:** Kristin Blegen; **Annie:** Shelby Vischer; **Scooter/Townsperson:** Jim Poole; **City Official/Crazy Jopponian:** Ron Smith; **Message from the Lord Choir:** Sarah Catherine Brooks

As a messenger of God, Jonah treks across arid deserts and stormy seas to take his message of hope and mercy to the sinful people of Nineveh, aided in his journey by the Pirates Who Don't Do Anything, a trio of root beer guzzling buccaneers and a new cast addition, a cheery half-worm, half-caterpillar carpet salesman, in this G-rated family adventure.

**PN:** Replete with biblical themes and moral lessons, this CGI-animated feature was inspired by a hugely successful direct-to-video series starring the parable-spinning veggies, created in 1992 by Phil Vischer and Mike Nawrocki of Big Idea Productions, raising more than $25.5 million in box-office revenue following its theatrical release. Vischer and Nawrocki not only provided most of the character voices for the film, but also cowrote and codirected the feature.

## ◎ JOURNEY BACK TO OZ (1974)

A Seymour Bordel Filmation Associates Production released by EBA. **p:** Norm Prescott, Lou Scheimer; **w:** Fred Ladd, Norm Prescott **d:** Hal Sutherland; **m/l:** Sammy Cahn, James Van Heusen; **anim superv:** Amby Paliwoda. **Running time:** 102 minutes. **Released:** June 19, 1974.

*Voices*
**Dorothy:** Liza Minelli; **Scarecrow:** Mickey Rooney; **Tin-Man:** Danny Thomas; **Cowardly Lion:** Milton Berle; **Aunt Em:** Margaret Hamilton; **Mombi, the Bad Witch;** Ethel Merman; **Glinda, the Good Witch:** Rose Stevens; **Pumpkinhead:** Paul Lynde; **Woodenhead:** Herschel Bernardi; **The Signpost:** Jack E. Leonard

*Additional Voices*
Mel Blanc, Paul Ford, Dallas McKennon, Larry Storch

Ever since the classic 1939 MGM/Judy Garland film filmakers have wanted to return to the land of Oz, which is the focal point of this animated sequel featuring the same well-known characters—Dorothy, Tin Man, Scarecrow and the Cowardly Lion—in all-new adventures in the "land over the rainbow."

**PN:** This animated feature was originally produced in 1964 but was not released until nearly 10 years later.

*Dorothy, Tin Man, Scarecrow and the Cowardly Lion return to Oz in the full-length animated feature,* Journey Back to Oz. © *Filmation*

### ◉ THE JUNGLE BOOK (1967)

A Walt Disney Production released by Buena Vista Pictures. **p:** Walt Disney; **d:** Wolfgang Reitherman; **dir anim:** Milt Kahl, Frank Thomas, Ollie Johnston Jr., John Lounsbery; **st:** Larry Clemmons, Ralph Wright, Ken Anderson, Vance Gerry (based on Rudyard Kipling's *The Jungle Book* stories); **m:** George Bruns; **s:** Richard M. Sherman, Robert B. Sherman; **Songs:** "I Wanna Be Like You," "Trust in Me," "My Own Home," "That's What Friends Are For," "Colonel Hathi's March" and "The Bare Necessities." **Running time:** 78 minutes. **Released:** October 18, 1967.

*Voices*

**Baloo the Bear:** Phil Harris; **Bagheera the Panther:** Sebastian Cabot; **King Louise of the Apes:** Louis Prima; **Shere Kahn, the tiger:** George Sanders; **Kaa, the snake:** Sterling Holloway; **Colonel Hathi, the elephant:** J. Pat O'Malley; **Mowgli, the man-cub:** Bruce Reitherman; **Elephants:** Verna Felton, Clint Howard; **Vultures:** Chad Stuart, Lord Tim Hudson, J. Pat O'Malley, Digby Wolfe **Wolves:** John Abbott, Ben Wright; **Girl:** Darleen Carr

This animated adaptation of Rudyard Kipling's classic stories deals with Mowgli, an Indian boy abandoned at birth who is raised as a wolf cub and 10 years later is returned to his people by Bagheera, the panther who protected him as a child. In his jungle setting, Mowgli makes friends with Baloo, a happy-go-lucky bear, and lives life anew in the jungle, but not without a few close encounters with King Louie, Colonel Hathi and Shere Khan.

**PN:** The last animated film to bear the creative stamp of Walt Disney, who died in 1966.

### ◉ THE JUNGLE BOOK 2 (2003)

A Walt Disney Pictures/DisneyToon Studios Production released by Buena Vista Pictures. **p:** Mary Thorne, Christopher Chase; **d:** Steve Trenbirth; **scr:** Karl Geurs; **superv anim:** Kevin Peaty, Kelly Baigent, Simon Ashton; **anim superv:** Bob Paster; **senior anim:** Davide Benvenuti, Andrew Brooks, Bernard Derriman, Adam Murphu, Myke Sutherland, Jozef Szekeres, Marc Wasik, Robert Fox, Ian Harrowell, Andries Maritz, Manny Banados, Lianne Hughes, Alexis Staderman. **Songs:** "Jungle Rhythm," "W - I - L - D," "Right Where I Belong," "Bare Necessities," "I Wan'na Be Like You" and "Colonel Hathi's March." **Running time:** 72 minutes. **Released:** April 9, 2003.

*Voices*

**Mowgli:** Haley Joel Osmont; **Baloo:** John Goodman; **Shanti:** Mae Whitman; **Bagheera:** Bob Joles; **Shere Khan:** Tony Jay; **Ranjan:** Connor Funk; **Kaa/Col. Hathi:** Jim Cummings; **Ranjan's father:** John Rhys-Davies; **Lucky the Vulture:** Phil Collins

*Additional Voices*
Bobby Edner, J. Grant Albrecht

After his old friend, Baloo the Bear, pays a visit to the civilized village where he lives, Mowgli becomes nostalgic and runs off with Baloo to return to the bare necessities of the jungle and his old friends, unaware of the danger that awaits him in the wild.

**PN:** Originally intended to be produced as a direct-to-video animated production, this big-screen sequel, produced 36 years after the 1967 classic original, amassed $47.8 million in box-office revenue, even though critics' reviews were mixed. While a lightweight by comparison, this film was among 11 films that made the Academy Awards' short list of nominees for best animated feature.

## ◎ KAENA: THE PROPHECY (2004)

A Motion Pictures International/Sony Pictures Entertainment/ StudioCanal/TVA International/Xilam Production released by IDP Distribution. **p:** Denis Friedman, **exec prod:** Manuel Chiche, Marc Du Pontavice, Andre Belanger; **d:** Chris Delaporte; **co-dir:** Pascal Pinon; **scr:** Chris Delaporte, Tarik Hamdine (based on an original idea by Patrick Daher and Chris Delaporte); **m:** Farid Russlan; **anim dir:** Patrick Bonneau, Patrick Daher, Phillip Giles. **Running time:** 91 minutes. **Released:** June 25, 2004.

*Voices*
**Commander:** Keith David; **Kaena:** Kirsten Dunst; **Opaz:** Richard Harris; **The Queen:** Angelica Huston

*Additional Voices*
Michael McShane, Greg Proops

A rebellious teenage girl, Kaena, whose village on the distant planet, Axis, is in danger of extinction, battles to save her planet and people.

**PN:** Budgeted at $26 million, this French PG-13-rated film, based on an idea for a video II game by Patrick Daher and Chris Delaporte, was produced in 3-D CGI animation. Commencing production in January 1999, Le StudioCanal Plus provided the majority of the financing while Motion Pictures International and Xilam provided the remainder. Xilam purchased rights from Chaman Productions when Chaman went bankrupt in March 2002. Receiving limited theatrical distribution, the film, released in New York and Los Angeles, took in only $8,593 in box-office revenue.

## ◎ THE KING AND I (1999)

A Morgan Creek Productions/Rankin/Bass/Nest Entertainment Production released by Warner Bros. **p:** James G. Robinson, Arthur Rankin, Peter Bakalian; **d:** Richard Rich; **scr:** Peter Bakalian, Jacqueline Feather, David Seidler; **st (adaptation):** Arthur Rankin; **superv anim:** Patrick Gleeson, Colm Duggan. **Songs:** "Getting to Know You," "Hello Young Lovers," "I Whistle a Happy Tune," "A Puzzlement" and "Shall We Dance." **Running time:** 90 minutes. **Released:** March 19, 1999.

*Voices*
**Anna Leanowens, speaking:** Miranda Richardson; **Anna, singing:** Christiane Nell; **The King of Siam:** Martin Vidnovic; **The Kralahome:** Ian Richardson; **Master Little:** Darrell Hammond; **Prince Chulalangkorn:** Allen D. Hong; **Prince Chulalangkorn, singing:** David Burnham; **Tuptim:** Armi Arrabee; **Tuptim, singing:** Tracy Venner Warren; **Louis Leanowens:** Adam Wylie

Full-length animated adaptation of the famed Richard Rodgers and Oscar Hammerstein II Broadway and film musical in which a young British school teacher, Anna, moves to Siam to instruct the king's children and, in doing so, must deal with his highness the king.

**PN:** This animated movie was a coproduction involving several interests, including Morgan Creek Productions and long-time film and television producers Rankin/Bass Productions, now run by original cofounder Arthur Rankin and Peter Bakalian (who cowrote the screenplay based on a story adapted by Rankin), with animation produced by Richard Rich's Nest Entertainment, makers of *The Swan Princess* (1994) and its sequel, *Swan Princess II: Escape from Castle Mountain* (1997).

## ◎ KING DICK (1982)

An Aquarius Releasing release. **p:** Claudio Monti; **d:** Gioacchino Libratti. **Running time:** 65 minutes. **Released:** July 3, 1982.
Voice credits unknown.

To break a wicked spell on the prince and princess he serves, a midget falls in love with the ugly witch, Nymphomania, in this animated sex comedy from Italy.

**PN:** This X-rated animated feature is also known as *Little Dick, The Mighty Midget*.

## ◎ KIRIKOU AND THE SORCERESS (2000)

An Artmattan Productions released by Gebeka. **p:** Didier Brunner, Jacques Vercruvssen, Paul Thiltges; **d & w:** Michael Ocelot; **m:** Youssou N'Dour. **Running time:** 70 minutes. **Released:** February 28, 2000.

*Voices*
**Karaba:** Antoinette Kellerman; **Uncle: Fezele Mpeka; The Mother:** Kombisile Sangweni; **The Wise Man/Viellard:** Mabutho "Kid" Sithole

Kirikou, an African-born villager whose village is under a horrendous spell placed on it by Karaba the sorceress, frees the village of the curse by keeping the Wise Man in the Forbidden to find out the secret of why Karaba is so wicked and challenge the evil sorceress in this animated blend of African folk tales produced in France.

## ◎ LADY AND THE TRAMP (1955)

A Walt Disney Production released by Buena Vista. **p:** Walt Disney; **d:** Hamilton Luske, Clyde Geronimi, Wilfred Jackson; **dir anim:** Milt Kahl, Frank Thomas, Ollie Johnston, John Lounsbery, Wolfgang Reitherman, Eric Larson, Hal King, Les Clark; **st:** Erdman Penner, Joe Rinaldi, Ralph Wright, Donald Da Gradi (based on an original story by Ward Greene); **m/sc:** Oliver Wallace. **Songs:** "He's a Tramp," "La La Lu," "Siamese Cat Song," "Peace on Earth" and "Bella Notte." **Running time:** 75 minutes. **Released:** June 22, 1955.

*Voices*
**Darling/Si/Am/Peg:** Peggy Lee; **Lady:** Barbara Luddy; **Tramp:** Larry Roberts; **Trusty:** Bill Baucom; **Aunt Sarah:** Verna Felton; **Tony:** George Givot; **Jim Dear/Dog Catcher:** Lee Millar; **Bull/ Dachsie/Jock/Joe:** Bill Thompson: **Beaver/Pet-Store Clerk:** Stan Freberg; **Boris:** Alan Reed; **Toughby/Professor/Pedro:** Dallas McKennon; **Dogs in Pound:** The Mello Men

Lady, a pretty female cocker spaniel, falls in love with Tramp, a stray who values his liberty above all else. The heart of the story deals with the unusual bonding of the two characters—the more refined Lady and the outcast Tramp, who battles with two neighborhood mutts, Jock and Caesar, who yearn for Lady's love.

## ◎ THE LAND BEFORE TIME (1988)

A Sullivan Bluth Studios Production released by MGM/United Artists. **p:** Don Bluth, Gary Goldman, John Pomeroy; **d:** Don Bluth; **scr:** Stu Krieger; **st:** Judy Freudberg; Tony Geiss; **m:** James Horner; **anim dir:** John Pomeroy, Linda Miller, Ralph Zondag,

Dan Kuenster, Lorna Pomeroy, Dick Zondag. **Running time:** 66 minutes. **Released:** November 18, 1988.

*Voices*

**Narrator/Rooter:** Pat Hingle; **Littlefoot's Mother:** Helen Shaver; **Littlefoot:** Gabriel Damon; **Grandfather:** Bill Erwin; **Cera:** Candy Hutson; **Daddy Topps:** Burke Barnes; **Ducky:** Judith Barsi; **Petrie:** Will Ryan

A young brontosaurus named Littlefoot is orphaned when a tyrannosaurus attacks and separates his herd. He sets off in search of the Great Valley, a legendary land of lush vegetation where dinosaurs can live and thrive in peace. Along the way he meets four other youngsters, each a member of a different dinosaur family. Together they encounter incredible obstacles while learning unforgettable lessons about life.

**PN:** Thirteen direct-to-video sequels were produced following the original feature through 2007: *The Land Before Time II: The Great Valley Adventure* (1994); *The Land Before Time III: The Time of the Great Giving* (1995); *The Land Before Time IV: Journey Through the Mists* (1996), the last sequel to feature the original voice cast from the original full-length feature; *The Land Before Time V: The Mysterious Island* (1997); *The Land Before Time VI: The Secret of Saurus Rock* (1998); *The Land Before Time VII: The Stone of Cold Fire* (2000); *The Land Before Time VIII: The Big Freeze* (2001); *The Land Before Time IX: Journey to Big Water* (2002); *The Land Before Time X: The Great Longneck Migration* (2003); *The Land Before Time XI: Invasion of the Tinysauruses* (2004); *The Land Before Time XII: The Great Day of the Flyers* (2006); and *The Land Before Time XIII: The Wisdom of Friends* (2007).

## ◎ LAPUTA: CASTLE IN THE SKY (1989)

A studio Ghibli Production released by streamline Pictures. **p:** Isao Takahata; **exec prod:** Yasuyoshi Tokuma; **d:** Hayao Miyazaki; **st/scr:** Hayao Miyazaki **m:** Joe Hisaishi; **anim:** Toyosaki Emura, Masaaki Endo, Tadashi Fukuda, Makiko Futaki, Megumi Kagawa, Yoshinori Kanada, Toshio Kawaguchi, Kazuhiro Kinoshita, Kazuyuki Kobayashi, Katusya Kondo, Kitaro Kosaka, Mahiro Maeda, Noriko Moritomo, Osamu Nabeshima, Yasuhiro Nakura, Shinji Otsuka, Michiyo Sakuraim, Masako Shinohara, Tsukasa Tannai, Kazuhide Tomonaga, Atsuko Otani. **Running time:** 124 minutes. **Released:** March 24, 1989.

*Voices*

(U.S. version) **Pazu:** James Van Der Beek; **Sheeta:** Anna Paquin; **Dola:** Cloris Leachman; **Col. Muska:** Mark Hamill

After being seized by government agents, escaping and surviving an attack on her family by sky pirates, a young orphaned girl, Sheeta, seeks to find the secret of the legendary floating city in the sky and the lost civilization of Laputa in this mythical 19th-century fantasy/adventure.

**PN:** Japanese animation maestro Hayao Miyazaki wrote, designed and directed this science fiction fantasy adventure, becoming his third full-length feature. In 1996, Walt Disney Studios, after licensing the rights to all of his films from Japan's Studio Ghibli, re-issued the film, dubbed in English and retitled *Castle in the Sky*.

## ◎ THE LAST UNICORN (1982)

A Rankin-Bass/Jensen-Farley Production released by ITC. **p & d:** Arthur Rankin Jr., Jules Bass; **w:** Peter S. Beagle (based on the novel by Peter S. Beagle); **m:** Jimmy Webb. **Running time:** 85 minutes. **Released:** November 19, 1982.

*Voices*

**Schmendrick the Magician:** Alan Arkin; **Prince Lir:** Jeff Bridges; **The Last Unicorn/Lady Amalthea:** Mia Farrow; **Molly Grue:** Tammy Grimes; **The Butterfly:** Robert Klein; **Mommy Fortuna:** Angela Lansbury; **King Haggard:** Christopher Lee; **Capt. Cully:** Keenan Wynn; **The Talking Cat:** Paul Frees; **The Speaking Skull:** Rene Auberjonois

A young unicorn accompanied by a magician journeys to release the rest of her species from the tyranny of an evil king.

## ◎ THE LEGEND OF BUDDHA (2004)

A Pentamedia Graphics Ltd./Blazeway Production in association with Economic Development Board of Singapore. **d:** Shamboo Phalke. **Running time:** 88 minutes. **Released:** October 22, 2004.

Voice credits unknown.

Remarkable true story of Prince Siddartha Gautama who abandons the trappings of his kingdom and wealth to become the historic, inspirational leader, Buddha, the Enlightened One, in this animated family adventure.

**PN:** Pentamedia Graphics Ltd., which produced the 3-D animated films *Sinbad: Beyond the Veil of Mist* (2000), *Alibaba* (2002) and *Son of Aladdin* (2003), and which helped animate Warner Bros.' *The King and I* (1999), coproduced this $6.3 million, 2-D animated film in association with the Economic Development Board of Singapore at studios in India, Singapore and the Philippines. Expected to make $10 to $12 million worldwide during the year and half following its release, the film used some 200,000 drawings made by 400 artists at Pentamedia's Manila subsidiary, Kingdom Animasia, supported by 1,000 3-D animated backgrounds created by artists in Chennai, to bring this story of Prince Siddhartha to the screen. The movie made a short list of 11 animated films that contended for an Academy Award for best animated feature in 2005, becoming the studio's second Oscar contender since 2002's *Alibaba*.

## ◎ LEGEND OF THE OVERFIEND (1993)

A West Cape Corporation Production released by Anime 21. **p:** Yoshinobu Nishzaki; **d:** Hideki Takayama; **scr:** Sho Aikawa, Michael Lawrence, Toshio Maeda; **m:** Masamichi Amano; **anim dir:** Shiro Kasami, Dan Kongoji, Mari Mizuta. **Running time:** 108 minutes. **Released:** March 11, 1993.

*Voices*

**Ozaki:** Bick Balse; **Tatsuo Nagumo:** Danny Bush; **Amano Jyaku:** Christopher Courage; **Akemi Ito:** Rebel Joy: **Megumi Amano:** Lucy Morales; **Kuroko:** Rose Palmer; **Niki:** Bill Timoney; **Suikakujyu:** Jurgen Offen

When a young man metamorphisizes into the super-powerful being, Overfiend, he bridges the human world with dimensions inhabited by demons and man-beasts who recruit women to his cause through rape and torture.

## ◎ LENSMAN (1990)

An E. E. "Doc" Smith/MK Company/Toho Production released by Streamline Pictures. **p:** Carl Macek (U.S. version); **d:** Yoshiaki Kawajiri, Kazuyuki Hirokawa; **scr:** Soji Yoshikawa; **m:** Akira Inoue; **anim:** Hiroyuki Kitakubo, Koji Morimoto. **Running time:** 107 minutes. **Released:** August 31, 1990.

*Voices*

**Kimball Kinnison:** Kerrigan Mahan; **Worsel:** Steve Kramer; **Lens:** Alexandra Kenworthy; **Van Buskirk:** Michael McConnohie; **Clarisse:** Edie Mirman; **Sol:** Robert Axelrod; **Admiral Haines:** Michael Forest; **Zuiik:** Milton James; **Thorndyke:** Dave Mallow; **Gary Kinnison:** Mike Reynolds; **Admiral Haynes:** Gregory Snegoff; **Lekesly:** Doug Stone; **Lord Helmuth:** Tom Wyner

Entrusted with supernatural power in the form of a legendary crystal lens embedded in his hand by a dying Galactic Patrol agent, young Kimball Kinnison, and his friend, Buskirk, ward off intergalactic enemies in this futuristic, 25th-century science fiction adventured based on the popular Lensman novels by Edward E. Smith published in the 1930s and 1940s.

## ◎ LIGHT YEARS (1988)

A Col. Ima. Son/Films A2/Revcom Television/Centre National de la Cinematographie/Ministre de la Culture et de la Communication Production released by Miramax Films. **p:** Bob Weinstein, Henry Rollin, Jean-Claude Delynre; **d:** Rene Laloux, Harvey Weinstein; **scr (French):** Raphael Cluzel; **st (adaptation):** Rene Laloux (based on the novel, *Metal Men against Gandahar,* by Jean-Pierre Andrevan); **m:** Gabriel Yared, Bob Jewett, Jack Maeby; **anim:** Phillippe Caza. **Running time:** 83 minutes. **Released:** January 28, 1988.

*Voices*
**Queen Ambisextra:** Glenn Close; **Altelle:** Jennifer Grey; **Metamorphosis:** Christopher Plummer; **Sylvain:** John Shea; **Chief of the Deformed:** Penn Jillette; **Shaol:** David Johansen; **The Collective Voice:** Terrence Mann; **Gemmen:** Charles Busch; **Historian/Head #2:** Bridget Fonda; **Council Spokeswoman/Head #3:** Sheila McCarthy; **Opeflow:** Paul Shaffer; **Octum:** Teller; **Maxum, Chief of the Deformed:** Earl Hyman; **Blaminhoe:** Earl Hammond; **Apod/Metal Man:** Alexander Marshall; **Head #3/Metal Men:** Dennis Predovic; **Head #1/Metal Men:** Chip Bolcik; **The Metal Men:** Kevin O'Rourke, Ray Owens; **Announcer:** Jill Haworth

Sent by the queen to investigate the deaths of the mirror birds, guardians of the utopian world of Gandahar, heroic warrior Sylvain joins forces with mutant warriors, whom he first mistakes as his enemies, to battle the menacing surface-dwelling Metal Men who threaten their existence in this futuristic science fiction action-adventure.

**PN:** Famed French animation filmmaker Rene Laloux wrote and directed this adaptation of Jean-Pierre Andrevan's novel, which premiered at the Cannes Film Festival in 1987 and was distributed in the United States by Harvey Weinstein's Miramax Films. Costing $5.5 million to produce, the film, despite its comic book story, generated little interest in America, grossing a meager $370,698 in limited release. The film's original working title was *Gandahar.*

## ◎ LILO AND STITCH (2002)

A Walt Disney Pictures Production released by Buena Vista Pictures. **p:** Clark Spender; **exec prod:** Don Hahn; **d & w:** Chris Saunders, Dean Debois; **scr:** Chris Sanders, Dean DeBois; **st:** Ed Gombert, Chris Williams, John Sanford, Roger Allers; **m:** Alan Silvestri; **superv anim:** Alex Kuperschmidt, Andreas Deja, Stephanie Sainte Foi, Byron Howard, Bolhem Bouchiba, Ruben A. Aquino; **lead anim:** James Young Jackson, Theodore Anthony Lee Ty, Dominic M. Carola; Mark Henn. **Songs:** "You're the Devil in Disguise," "Hawaiian Roller Coaster Ride," "Hound Dog" and "Suspicious Minds." **Running time:** 85 minutes. **Released:** June 16, 2002.

*Voices*
**Lilo:** Daveigh Chase; **Stitch:** Chris Sanders; **Nani:** Tia Carrere; **Dr. Jumba Jookiba:** David Ogden Stiers; **Agent Pleakley:** Kevin McDonald; **Cobra Bubbles:** Ving Rhames; **Grand Councilwoman of the United Galactic Federation:** Zoe Caldwell; **David Kawena:** Jason Scott Lee; **Captain Gantu:** Kevin Michael Richardson; **Animal Rescue Lady:** Susan Hegarty; **Mrs. Hasagawa:** Amy Hill

A five-year-old Hawaiian girl, who enjoys taking care of animals, befriends an alien that crash lands on the island and teaches her the real meaning of family and friendship.

**PN:** Making its world premiere at Hollywood's renovated El Capitan Theater before going nationwide a week later, Chris Sanders, who had actually created the character Stitch in 1986, wrote and directed this movie, which originally was set in Kansas instead of the tropical islands of Hawaii. Seven Elvis Presley songs add to the flavor of the film's upbeat musical score by composer Alan Silvestri. Budgeted at $80 million, the film returned nearly double that amount with a box-office gross of $146 million. Likewise, this Disney feature was nominated for an Academy Award for best animated feature.

## ◎ THE LION KING (1994)

A Walt Disney Production released by Walt Disney Pictures. **p:** Don Hahn; **d:** Roger Allers, Rob Minkoff; **exec prod:** Sarah McArthur, Thomas Schumacher; **scr:** Irene Mecchi, Jonathan Roberts, Linda Woolverton; **m:** Elton John, Hans Zimmer; **superv anim:** Tony Fucile, Mark Henn, Ellen Woodbury, Anthony de Rosa. **Songs:** "Circle of Life," "I Just Can't Wait to Be King," "Be Prepared," "Hakuna Matata," "Can You Feel the Love Tonight," "The Lion Sleeps Tonight," "I've Got a Lovely Bunch of Coconuts," "It's a Small World," "Hawaiian War Chant" and "Rhythm of the Pride Lands." **Running time:** 88 minutes. **Released:** June 15, 1994.

*Voices*
**Adult Simba:** Matthew Broderick; **Young Simba:** Jonathan Taylor Thomas; **Mafasa:** James Earl Jones; **Adult Nala:** Moira Kelly; **Young Nala:** Niketa Calame; **Shenzi:** Whoopi Goldberg; **Banzai:** Cheech Marin; **Timon:** Nathan Lane; **Pumbaa:** Ernie Sabella; **Scar:** Jeremy Irons; **Rafiki:** Robert Guillaume; **Sarabi:** Madge Sinclair; **Sarafina:** Zoe Leader; **Zazu:** Rowan Atkinson; **Ed, the Laughing Hyena:** Jim Cummings; **Adult Simba (singing):** Joseph Williams; **Young Simba (singing):** Jason Weaver; **Adult Nala (singing):** Sally Dworsky; **Young Nala (singing):** Laura Williams

*Additional Voices*
Cathy Cavadini, Judi M. Durand, Daamen J. Krall, David McCharen, Linda Phillips, Philip Proctor, David J. Randolph, Frank Welker

Set amid the majestic beauty of the Serengeti, this coming-of-age saga tells of the love between a proud lion ruler, Mufasa, and his son, Simba, and follows Simba's heroic journey when he is forced into exile by his evil uncle after the death of his father, the King.

**PN:** This Disney animated feature was the most successful in the studio's history, earning $312.8 million in ticket sales and winning two Oscars for best original score and best song. The home video release did even better than the movie, grossing more in its first two weeks than its entire theatrical run. A mild controversy followed the release of the film. Cult "Japanimation" fans raised questions over similarities between the hit Disney film and the 1960s' Japanese-created TV cartoon series *Kimba the White Lion*, which was based on a comic-book series from the 1950s called *The Jungle Emperor* by animator Osamu Tezuka, crowned "the Walt Disney of Japan." Disney cited *Hamlet* as one of the film's main influences. Disney pulled the movie from theaters in late September 1994, after grossing more than $270 million through the summer and falling out of the Top 10 for the first time since opening. The studio re-released the film at Thanksgiving, breeding new life at the box office and sending it on its way to the biggest-grossing animated feature in motion picture history. On Christmas Day, 2002, the film was re-released in the IMAX format to IMAX theaters.

### ◎ THE LITTLE MERMAID (1989)

A Walt Disney Pictures presentation in association with Silver Screen Partners IV released by Buena Vista. **p:** Howard Ashman, John Musker; **d:** Ron Clements, John Musker; **scr:** Ron Clements, John Musker; **m:** Alan Menken; **anim dir:** Mark Henn, Glen Keane, Duncan Marjoribanks, Ruben Aquino, Andreas Deja, Matthew O'Callaghan. **Songs:** "Under the Sea," "Part of Your World," "Poor Souls," "Les Poissons," "Fathoms Below" and "Daughters of Triton." **Running time:** 82 minutes. **Released:** November 17, 1989.

*Voices*

**Louis:** Rene Auberjonois; **Eric:** Christopher Daniel Barnes; **Ariel:** Jodi Benson: **Ursula:** Pat Carroll; **Scuttle:** Buddy Hackett; **Flounder:** Jason Marin; **Triton:** Kenneth Mars; **Grimsby:** Ben Wright; **Sebastian:** Samuel E. Wright

Against her father's wishes, young mermaid princess Ariel travels beyond her world to the one above the sea, where she falls in love with a human prince in this cartoon adaptation of the Hans Christian Andersen tale.

**PN:** *Little Mermaid* set a box-office record for a modern-day fully animated feature, grossing $84.4 million. The record was soon surpassed by *Beauty and the Beast,* which grossed more than $141 million. Prior to *Little Mermaid's* record-setting performance, Disney's *Oliver & Company* (1988) was the studio's top animated performer with $53.1 million.

### ◎ LITTLE NEMO: ADVENTURES IN SLUMBERLAND (1992)

A Tokyo Movie Sinsha Company Production released by Hemdale Pictures Corporation. **p:** Yutaka Fujioka; **d:** Masami Hata, William T. Hurtz; **scr:** Chris Columbus, Richard Outten (based on the comic strip by Winsor McCay and on a concept for the screen by Ray Bradbury); **st:** Jean Mobius Giraud, Yutaka Fujioka; **m:** Thomas Chase, Steve Rucker; **s:** Richard M. Sherman and Robert B. Sherman; **superv anim:** Kazuhide Tomonaga, Nobuo Tomizawa. **Running time:** 85 minutes. **Released:** July 24, 1992.

*Ariel is fascinated by her discussion with crustacean guardian Sebastian and her friend Flounder in a scene from Walt Disney Pictures' 28th full-length animated feature,* The Little Mermaid. © *Walt Disney Company. All rights reserved.*

*Voices*

**Little Nemo:** Gabriel Damon; **Flip:** Mickey Rooney; **Professor Genius:** Rene Auberjonois; **Icarus:** Danny Mann; **Princess Camille:** Laura Mooney; **King Morpheus:** Bernard Erhard; **Nightmare King:** William E. Martin; **Oomp:** Alan Oppenheimer; **Oompy:** Michael Bell; **Oompe:** Sidney Miller; **Oompa:** Neil Ross; **Oompo:** John Stephenson; **Nemo's Mother:** Jennifer Darling; **Nemo's Father/Flap:** Greg Burson; **Bon Bon:** Sherry Lynn; **Dirigible Captain:** John Stephenson; **Courtier/Cop:** Guy Christopher; **Page:** Nancy Cartwright; **Page:** Ellen Gerstell; **Elevator Creature:** Tress MacNeille; **Etiquette Master:** Michael McConnohie; **Teacher #1/Cop:** Beau Weaver; **Teacher #2:** Michael Gough; **Dance Teacher:** Kathleen Freeman; **Fencing Teacher:** Michael Sheehan; **Librarian:** June Foray; **Equestrian Master:** Gregg Barger; **Goblin General:** Ben Kramer; **Woman:** Bever-Leigh Banfield

A young boy (Little Nemo) falls asleep and is carried off by a blimp to Slumberland, where he helps Princess Camille and her father, King Morpheus, defeat the armies of the evil Nightmare King in this feature-length adaptation of Winsor McCay's stylistic newspaper strip and animated cartoon of the same name.

**PN:** This feature was in production for 15 years before it was finally released. The film was a big flop, grossing only $1.1 million in ticket sales. Famed fantasy novelist Ray Bradbury conceived the story of this feature-length treatment, and *Home Alone* director Chris Columbus was one of the film's screenwriters. Former Disney and UPA animator William T. Hurtz codirected the movie, and veteran Disney animators Frank Thomas and Oliver Johnston served as story consultants. Original songs for the movie were written by Richard M. Sherman and Robert B. Sherman, the famed songwriting brothers who wrote the music for the Disney classic *Mary Poppins.* The title songs for the movie were sung by famed singer/songwriter Melissa Manchester.

## ◎ THE LITTLE PRINCE AND THE EIGHT-HEADED DRAGON (1964)

A Toei Animation Company Ltd. Production released by Columbia Pictures. **d:** Yugo Serikawa; **co-dir:** Isao Takahata, Kimio Yabuki; **scr:** Ichiro Ikeda, Kei Lijima; **m:** Akira Ifukube; **anim:** Sanae Yamamoto, Yasuji Mori, Hideo Furusawa. **Running time:** 85 mninutes. **Released:** January 1, 1964.

Voice credits unknown

After his mother dies, a young prince, Susano, searches with his pet rabbit to uncover the spirit of his deceased mother but encounters plenty of trouble along the way, including an eight-headed dragon.

**PN:** Titled *Wanpaku ôji no orochi taiji* in Japan, this film was produced by Toei Animation Co. and first released in Japan in March 1963 and then redubbed in English and distributed to theaters in the United States by Hollywood's Columbia Pictures, which touted the movie in its advertising as being presented "in Magicolor and Wonderscope."

## ◎ THE LITTLEST WARRIOR (1962)

A Toei Animation Company Ltd. Production released by Signal International. **p:** Isamu Takahashi; **d:** Taiji Yabushita; **scr:** Sumi Tanaka; **m:** Tadashi Kishimo; **anim dir:** Sanae Yamamoto; **anim:** Akira Daikuhara, Hideo Furusawa, Masao Kumagawa, Daikichiro Kusube, Ysuji Mori, Yasuo Otsuka. **Running time:** 70 minutes. **Released:** March 1, 1962.

*Voices*

**Anjue:** Yoshiko Sakuma; **Zooshio:** Kinya Kitaoji

A young boy grows up to become a fantastic samurai warrior and seek revenge after he is separated from his family by a no-good emperor.

**PN:** Japan's Toei Animation Co. produced and animated this historical fantasy, also known as *The Orphan Brother (Anju To Zushio-Maru)*, based on the Japanese book *Sansho Dayu* by Ogai Mori. After being released in its own country in July 1961, an English-speaking version was released in the United States the following year.

## ◎ THE LIVING FOREST (2002)

A DYGRA Films release. **p:** Angel de la Cruz; **d:** Angel de la Cruz, Manolo Gomez; **scr:** Angel de la Cruz (based on the novel by Wenceslao Fernandez Florez); **m:** Arturo B. Kress; **songs:** Luz Casal; **anim dir:** Julio Diez. **Running time:** 80 minutes. **Released:** November 8, 2002.

*Voices*

(Spanish version) **Furi:** Nacho Aldeguer; **Linda:** Mar Bordallo; **Carballo:** Claudio Rodriguez; **Pino:** Juan Miguel Cuesta; **Poste:** Hector Cantolla; **Eucalipto:** Javier Franquelo; **Encina:** Marla Romero; **Castano/Rosendo/Cuscus:** Rafael Azcarraga; **Abedul:** Francisco Javier Martinez; **Sabela:** M. Teresa Neila; **Senora D'Abondo:** Roberto Cuenca; **Morrina/Raton:** Pilar Martin; **Piorno:** Jose Padilla; **Luci:** Beatriz Berciano

When a mole finds the love of his life and his entire colony has suddenly vanished, other animals in the forest join him to help save them.

**PN:** The first fully computer-generated full-length feature made in Spain (and in Europe), this cartoon feature, originally called *El Bosque Animado*, premiered on October 27, 2002, at the Chicago International Children's Film Festival and then made a qualifying run in Los Angeles for Academy Award consideration. The film subsequently made a preliminary list of eligible films that were nominated for an Academy Award for best animated feature.

## ◎ LOONEY TUNES: BACK IN ACTION (2003)

A Warner Bros. Feature Animation Production released by Warner Bros. **p:** Paula Weinstein, Bernie Goldmann; **exec prod:** Chris DeFaria, Larry Doyle; **l/a dir:** Joe Dante; **dir anim:** Eric Goldberg; **anim prod:** Allison Abbate; **scr:** Larry Doyle; **m:** Jerry Goldsmith, John Debney; **lead anim:** David Brewster, Anthony DeRosa, Bert Klein, Frank Molieri, Jeff Siergey. **Songs:** "The Gremlin Rag," "Pictures at an Exhibition," "Orphée aux Enfers," "Powerhouse," "What's Up, Doc?" and "Primavera." **Running time:** 92 minutes. **Released:** November 14, 2003.

*Live-Action Cast*

**DJ Drake/Himself:** Brendan Fraser; **Kate Houghton:** Jenna Elfman; **Damien Drake:** Timothy Dalton; **Mother:** Joan Cusack; **Dusty Tails:** Heather Locklear; **Mr. Chairman:** Steve Martin

*Voices*

**Bugs Bunny/Daffy Duck/Beaky Buzzard/Sylvester/Ma Bear:** Joe Alaskey; **Yosemite Sam/Foghorn Leghorn/Nasty Canasta:** Jeff Glen Bennett; **Elmer Fudd/Peter Lorre:** Billy West; **Tweety Bird/Marvin the Martian/Speedy Gonzales:** Eric Goldberg; **Pepe Le Pew:** Bruce Lanoil; **Granny:** June Foray; **Porky Pig:** Bob Bergen; **Tazmanian Devil/Tazmanian She-Devil:** Brendan Fraser; **Shaggy:** Casey Kasem; **Scooby Doo:** Frank Welker; **Cottontail Smith:** Danny Chambers; **Baby Bear:** Stan Freberg; **Papa Bear:** Will Ryan; **Robo Dog/Spy Car:** Danny Mann; **Gremlin Car (archival**

recordings of "The Maxwell" from *The Jack Benny Program*)**:** Mel Blanc

Bugs Bunny teams up with Daffy Duck to help a Warner Bros. studio executive who's been fired, but Daffy goes off with a studio guard, who also has been given the pink slip, to locate the guard's well-known father who was recently abducted by the now-evil ACME corporation.

**PN:** The first Warner Bros. cartoon feature to star its legendary Looney Tunes characters since 1996's *Space Jam* starring Michael Jordan, this follow-up film came seven years later and was largely dismissed by critics as a huge Technicolor and Panavision flop at the box office. It pulled in slightly more than $20.9 million in domestic revenue and $54.5 million worldwide and was a live-action/2-D cel-animated movie that cost $80 million, four times its U.S. box-office receipts. Nonetheless, the move made a short list of films that competed for Academy Award consideration for best animated feature and premiered a week before its nationwide release to qualify.

Although the film mixed live-action and animation, it met the Academy's criteria that at least 75 percent of the film be animated.

### ◉ LORD OF THE RINGS (1978)

A Fantasy Films/Saul Zaentz Production released by United Artists. **p:** Saul Zaentz; **d:** Ralph Bakshi; **w:** Chris Conkling, Peter S. Beagle (based on the stories by J.R.R. Tolkien); **m:** Leonard Roseman. **Running time:** 133 minutes. **Released:** November 21, 1978.

*Voices*

**Frodo:** Christopher Guard; **Gandalf:** William Squire; **Sam:** Michael Scholes; **Aragorn:** John Hurt; **Merry:** Simon Chandler; **Pippin:** Dominic Guard; **Bilbo:** Norman Bird; **Boromir:** Michael Graham-Fox; **Legolas:** Anthony Daniels; **Gimli:** David Buck; **Gollum:** Wood Thorpe; **Saruman:** Fraser Kerr; **Theoden:** Phillip Stone; **Wormtongue:** Michael Deacon; **Elrond:** Andre Murell; **Innkeeper:** Alan Tilvern; **Galadriel:** Annette Crosbie; **Treebeard:** John Westbrook

The Dark Lord Sauron possesses rings of great evil with which he can control Middle Earth, but that all changes when one of the rings falls into the hands of Hobbit Bilbo Baggins, who passes the ring and its inherent power on to his nephew, Frodo, to take up the battle.

**PN:** The film employs Bakshi's Rotoscope technique of animating live-action characters to create a lifelike effect.

### ◉ MACROSS II: LOVERS AGAIN (1993)

A Bandai/Big West/Hero/MBS/Shogakukan/AIC/Oniro/Macross Project Production released by Tara Releasing. **p:** Shinichi Iguchi, Hiroaki Inoue, Hiroshi Kakoi, Hirotake Kanda, Keiji Kusano; **exec prod:** Katushi Murakami, Hirohiko Suckichi, Minoru Takanashi, Eiji Taki, Yoshiaki Onishi; **d:** Kenichi Yatagai, Quint Lancaster; **scr:** Raymon Garcia; **m:** Shiro Sagisu. **Running time:** 134 minutes. **Released:** June 4, 1993.

*Voices*

(U.S. version) **Hibiki:** Jonathan Charles; **Marduk:** Raymond Garcia; **Marduk Commander:** Tom Fahn; **Ishtar:** Debra Jean Rogers; **Lord Feff/Major Nexx:** Steven Blum; **Exxegran:** Hal Cleaveland; **Lord Emperor Ingues:** Bill Kestin; **Wendy Ryder:** Trish Ledoux

With the help of ace Valkyrie pilot Silvie Gena, Scramble News Network (SNN) investigative reporter Hibiki Kanzaki becomes embroiled in a battle to rescue the enigmatic princess,

Zentraedi, from imminent "reprogramming" by the renegade alien invaders, the Zentraedi, and reactivate the Macross to defend Earth again in this high-flying, high-spirited film sequel to the popular Japanese anime television series, *Super-Dimension Fortress Macross* (1982–83).

### ◉ MADAGASCAR (2005)

A DreamWorks Animation SKG/Pacific Data Images Production released by DreamWorks SKG. **p:** Mirelle Soria; **co-prod:** Teresa Cheng; **d:** Eric Darnell, Tom McGrath; **scr:** Mark Burton, Billy Frolick, Eric Darnell, Tom McGrath; **m:** Hans Zimmer; **char superv:** Milana Huang, Robert Vogt; **superv anim:** Denis Couchon; **head char anim:** Rex Grignon. **Songs:** "Born Free," "I Like to Move It" and "American Beauty." **Running time:** 86 minutes. **Released:** May 27, 2005.

*Voices*

**Alex:** Ben Stiller; **Marty the Zebra:** Chris Rock; **Melman the Giraffe:** David Schwimmer; **Gloria:** Jada Pinkett; **Julien:** Sacha Baren Cohen; **Maurice:** Cedric the Entertainer; **Mort:** Andy Richter; **Skipper/Fossa/Panicky Man on Subway:** Tom McGrath; **Private:** Christopher Knights; **Kowalski:** Chris Miller; **Mason:** Conrad Vernon; **Zoo Announcer/Lemur #1/Fossa/Subway Car Announcer:** Eric Darnell; **Police Horse:** David Cowgill; **Police Officer:** Steve Apostolina; **Old Lady:** Elisa Gabrielli; **News Reporter:** Devika Parikh; **Spider/Lemur #2:** David P. Smith; **Willie:** Cody Cameron; **Zoo Animal:** Bob Saget

*Additional Voices*

Jason Alexander, Julia Louis-Dreyfus, Ricky Martin, Mel Gibson

When four motley animals—a zebra Marty, a hippo Gloria, a hypochondriac giraffe Melman, and lion Alex—from Central Park Zoo are transferred back to the wild by an animal rights organization that believes they are better off there, they find themselves unprepared for life in the jungle after their ship capsizes and leaves them stranded in Madagascar.

**PN:** DreamWorks Animation, the studio responsible for such monster hits as *Shark Tale* and *Shrek 2*, produced this CGI-animated feature, which was codirected by Eric Darnell (*Antz*) and Tom McGrath (*Ren and Stimpy Show*). Like many of the studio's features, this movie was a big hit with adults and children, generating more than $193 million in box-office revenue in the United States alone. The DreamWorks DVD version was equally successful, tying for third with the studio's other hit animated film, *Shark Tales*, and was among 2005's top 10-selling DVDs with 10 million units sold.

### ◉ MAD MONSTER PARTY? (1969)

A Rankin Bass Videocraft International Production released by Embassy Pictures. **p:** Arthur Rankin Jr.; **d:** Jules Bass; **exec prod:** Joseph E. Levine; **scr:** Len Korobkin, Harvey Kurtzman, Forrest J. Ackerman (based on a story by Rankin); **m/l:** Maury Laws, Jules Bass. **Songs:** "Mad Monster Party," "Waltz for a Witch," "Never Was a Love," "Cocktails," "The Mummy," "Drac," "The Baron," "You're Different," "Our Time to Shine" and "One Step Ahead." Filmed in Animagic. **Running time:** 94 minutes. **Released:** March 8, 1969.

*Voices*

**Baron Boris von Frankenstein:** Boris Karloff; **Monster's Mate:** Phyllis Diller; **Francesca:** Gale Garnett; **Felix Flankin/Dracula/Yetch/Invisible Man/Dr. Jekyll & Mr. Hyde/Mr. Cronkite/Chef Machiavelli/Hunchback of Notre Dame/Werewolf Howis:** Allen Swift; **Vocalist:** Ethel Ennis

*Additional Voices*
Ethel Ennis, Gale Garnett, Allen Swift

Using 3-D figures in a process called Animagic, this stop-action animated film lampoons the horror-film genre. This musical comedy features all the monsters—The Werewolf, Dracula, the Creature from the Black Lagoon, King Kong, Dr. Jekyll and Mr. Hyde, The Mummy and others—as attendees at a convention for the Worldwide Organization of Monsters. Their purpose: to select a new leader for the soon-to-be-retired Baron Boris von Frankenstein.

**PN:** Produced between 1966 and 1967, this was the third and final full-length theatrical release produced by Arthur Rankin and Jules Bass in association with Joseph E. Levine for Embassy Pictures and was the most popular of the three. Veteran character designer Jack Davis did the character designs for the film. He was later responsible for the character designs for such popular Rankin/Bass television series as *The King Kong Show* and *The Jackson 5*. The character Yetch was modeled after well-known horror film star Peter Lorre, who died in 1964. Newspaper advertisements used to promote the film featured the headline, "At long last a Motion Picture with absolutely no cultural value!!"

## ◉ MAGIC BOY (1961)

A Toei Animation Company Production released by Metro-Goldwyn-Mayer (MGM). **p:** Sanae Yamamoto; **d:** Taiji Yabushita, Akira Okuwara; **scr:** Toppei Marsumura; **st:** Kazuo Dan, Dohei Muramatsu; **dir anim:** Sanae Yamamoto; **m:** Satoshi Funemura; **anim:** Taku Sugiyama, Gisaburo Sugli, Notio Hikone, Masatake Kita, Shuji Konno, Daikichiro Kusube, Kazuko Nakamura, Reiko Okuyama, Chikao Tera. **Running time:** 82 minutes. **Released:** June 22, 1961.

*Voices*

**Sarutobi Sasuke:** Teruo Miyazaki; **Yukimura Sanada:** Katsuo Nakamura; **Oyu:** Hiroko Sakuramachi; **Okei-chan:** Tomoko Matsushima; **Master Tozawa Hakuun:** Kenji Usuda; **Omon Yayamata:** Harue Akagi; **Gonkuro the Mountain Storm:** Yoshio Yoshida

A young boy who is fascinated with magic employs his craft to overcome an evil sorceress.

**PN:** Also known as *The Adventures of the Little Samurai* (*Shonen Sarutobi Sasuke,* 1959), this second full-length feature by Japan's Toei Animation Co. was redubbed in English and released in the United States by Metro-Goldwyn-Mayer (MGM).

## ◉ THE MAGIC HORSE (1949)

A Soyuzmultfilm Studios Production released by Artkino. **p:** C.B. Wismar; **d:** Ivan Ivanov-Vano; **scr:** George Malko (based on the Russian folktale adapted by Peter Yershow); **m:** Tom Ed Williams; **anim:** Lev Milchin, V. Rodzhero, I. Troyanova, A. Bewlyakov. **Songs:** "Ride a Magic Pony," "Lonely Child," "A Whale of a Day" and "On This Beautiful Day." **Running time:** 60 minutes. **Released:** April 18, 1949.

*Voices*

(1977 U.S. video version) **King:** Jim Backus; **Red-Haired Groom:** Hans Conried; **Zip the Pony:** Erin Moran; **Ivan:** Johnny Whitaker

*Additional Voices*

Diane Alton, Robb Cigne, John Craig, Wayne Heffley, Jason Wingreen, Sandra Wirth

A young boy, Ivan, with the aide of his magical flying horse goes on a fascinating adventure in which he thwarts the king, saves the princess and, in the end, assumes the duties of prime minister in this animated version of the classic Russian folktale.

**PN:** Produced by Moscow's Soyuzmultfilm Studios, this first animated feature made in the then Soviet Union took two years to complete, using more than 150,000 drawings and color renderings. Premiering in Russia in 1947, two years later it became only the second foreign animated feature since 1926's *The Adventures of Prince Achmed* to be commercially distributed in the United States, with a dubbed version released to theaters in 1949. In 1977, the film was redubbed and released on home video as *The Magic Pony.* Also known as *Over the Rainbow.*

## ◉ MAKE MINE MUSIC (1946)

A Walt Disney Production released by RKO Radio Pictures. **p:** Walt Disney; **prod superv:** Joe Grant; **d:** Jack Kinney, Clyde Geronimi, Hamilton Luske, Robert Cormack, Joshua Meador; **st:** Homer Brightman, Dick Huemer, Dick Kinney, John Walbridge, Tom Oreb, Dick Shaw, Eric Gurney, Sylvia Holland, T. Hee, Dick Kelsey, Jesse Marsh, Roy Williams, Ed Penner, James Bodero, Cap Palmer, Erwin Graham; **md:** Charles Wolcott; **m/a:** Ken Darby, Oliver Wallace, Edward H. Plumb. **Songs:** "Johnny Fedora and Alice Bluebonnet," "All the Cats Join In," "Without You," "Two Silhouettes," "Casey, the Pride of Them All," "The Martins and the Coys," "Blue Bayou," "After You've Gone" and "Make Mine Music." **Running time:** 74 minutes. **Released:** August 15, 1946.

*Voices*

Nelson Eddy, Dinah Shore, Benny Goodman and Orchestra, The Andrew Sisters, Jerry Colonna, Andy Russell, Sterling Holloway, The Pied Pipers, The King's Men, The Ken Darby Chorus, and featuring Tania Riabouchinska and David Lichine

Like *Fantasia,* this Disney production adapted popular music to the screen, featuring a collection of melodies in animated sequences, including "The Martins and the Coys," a cartoon version of an age-old hillbilly feud; "A Tone Poem," a mood piece based on Ken Darby's chorus of "Blue Bayou"; "A Jazz Interlude," with Benny Goodman and his orchestra leading a vignette drawn version of "All the Cats Join In."

## ◉ THE MAN CALLED FLINTSTONE (1966)

A Hanna-Barbera Production released by Columbia Pictures. **p & d:** William Hanna, Joseph Barbera; **w:** Harvey Bullock, R.S. Allen (based on a story by Harvy Bullock and R.S. Allen and story material by Joseph Barbera, William Hanna, Warren Foster, Alex Lovy); **m:** Marty Paich, Ted Nichols; **anim dir:** Charles A. Nichols. **Songs:** "Pensate Amore," "Team Mates," "Spy Type Guy," "The Happy Sounds of Paree," "The Man Called Flintstone," "When I'm Grown Up" and "Tickle Toddle." **Running time:** 87 minutes. **Released:** August 3, 1966.

*Voices*

**Fred Flintstone:** Alan Reed Sr.; **Barney Rubble:** Mel Blanc; **Wilma Flintstone:** Jean Vander Pyl; **Betty Rubble:** Gerry Johnson

*Additional Voices*

Paul Frees, June Foray, Harvey Korman, Don Messick, John Stephenson, Janet Waldo

Resembling American spy Rock Slag, who was wounded while chasing international spy Green Goose and his girlfriend, Tanya, Fred Flintstone is asked to take Rock's place and fly to Rome (with his family, of course) to help corral Green Goose once and for all. The whole thing turns out to be a trap and the real Slag, now fully recovered, comes to Fred's rescue.

**PN:** The film's working title was *That Man Flintstone.*

## ◉ THE MAN FROM BUTTON WILLOW (1965)

An Eagle Film Production released by United Screen Artists. **p:** Phyllis Bounds Detiege; **d & w:** Dave Detiege; **m:** George Stoll,

Robert Van Eps. **Running time:** 81 minutes. **Released:** February 1, 1965.

*Voices*
**Justin Eagle:** Dale Robertson; **Sorry:** Edgar Buchanan; **Stormy:** Barbara Jean Wong

*Additional Voices*
Herschel Bernardi, Buck Buchanan, Pinto Colvig, Cliff Edwards, Verna Felton, John Hiestand, Howard Keel, Ross Martin, Shep Menken, Clarence Nash, Edward Platt, Thurl Ravenscroft

Intrigue and espionage are key elements of this action-packed adventure about the first U.S. government undercover agent, Justin Eagle, who recovers a kidnapped government official and thwarts plans to sabotage a state railroad.

## ◎ THE MANY ADVENTURES OF WINNIE THE POOH (1977)

A Walt Disney Production released through Buena Vista Pictures. **p:** Wolfgang Reitherman; **d:** Wolfgang Reitherman, John Lounsbery; **st:** Larry Clemmons, Vance Gerry, Ken Anderson, Ted Berman, Ralph Wright, Xavier Atencio, Julius Svendsen, Eric Cleworth; **m/l:** Richard Sherman, Robert B. Sherman. **Running time:** 74 minutes. **Released:** March 11, 1977.

*Voices*
**Narrator:** Sebastian Cabot; **Winnie the Pooh:** Sterling Holloway; **Tigger:** Paul Winchell; **Roo:** Clint Howard; **Roo:** Dori Whitaker; **Christopher Robin:** Timothy Turner; **Christopher Robin:** Bruce Reitherman; **Christopher Robin:** Jon Walmsley; **Kanga:** Barbara Luddy; **Eeyore:** Ralph Wright; **Rabbit:** Junius Matthews; **Gopher:** Howard Morris; **Piglet:** John Fiedler; **Owl:** Hal Smith

A.A. Milne's beloved children's stories come alive in this collection of Winnie the Pooh cartoon shorts ("Winnie the Pooh and the Honey Tree," "Winnie the Pooh and the Blustery Day" and "Winnie the Pooh and Tigger Too") combined with new animation and released as a full-length feature.

## ◎ MARCO POLO JR. (1973)

A Premore/Animation International/Porter Animations Production released by Premore. **p & d:** Eric Porter; **scr:** Sheldon Moldoff; **m:** Joel Herron; **anim:** Jerry Grabner; Gairden Cooke, Stan Walker, Richard Jones, Paul McAdam, Ray Nowland, Dick Dunn, Wallace Logue, Yvonne Pearsall, Cynthia Leech, Vivienne Ray, Peter Luschwitz, George Youssef. **Running time:** 85 minutes. **Released:** April 12, 1973.

*Voices*
Bobby Rydell, Arnold Stang, Corie Sims, Kevin Golsby, Larry Best, Gordon Hammer, Lionel Wilson, Arthur Andersen, Merril Joels, Sam Gray

Marco Polo Jr. embarks on a high-seas adventure to find the other half to the magical medallion he possesses when his plans are disrupted by the evil Red Dragon who imprisons the Princess Ming-Yu and Marco Polo must rescue her.

**PN:** Australian animator Eric Porter, who originally made his mark producing television commercials, film titles and local animation at his studios in Sydney, produced and directed this epic film—also known as *Marco Polo, Marco Polo and the Red Dragon* and *The Red, Red Dragon*—the first animated feature produced in Australia and widely released in that country. Reportedly, the film played on 25 movie screens in Sydney alone and in other countries, including the United States. American pop singer Bobby Rydell provided the voice of Marco in the movie, which was remade 28 years later as *Marco Polo: Return to Xanadu* (2001).

## ◎ MARCO POLO: RETURN TO XANADU (2001)

A Tooniversal Company Production released by Koan, Inc. **p:** Ron Merk, Chris Holter, Igor Meglic; **d:** Ron Merk; **scr:** Ron Merk, Chris Holter, Sheldon Moldoff; **m:** Chris Many. **Running time:** 86 minutes. **Released:** December 28, 2001.

*Voices*
**Marco:** Nicholas Gonzalez; **Wong Wei:** Paul Ainsley; **Pangu:** Alan Altshuld; **Mingu:** Elea Bartling; **Malgo the Vulture:** John C. Hyke; **Kubla Khan:** Michael Kostroff; **Helmsman:** Robert Kramer; **The Delicate Dinosaur:** John Matthew; **Space Station Captain:** Tim Owen; **Babu:** Tony Pope

Following the same plotline as its 1973 predecessor, Marco Polo's descendant takes to the high seas to unite the two halves of a magical medallion but plans change when he must rescue Princess Ming-Yu from the evil ruler Foo-Ling.

**PN:** Ron Merk of Universal's animation division, Tooniversal, produced and directed this updated cel-animated feature that combined new animation with sequences from Eric Porter's 1973 original feature, *Marco Polo Jr.* Premiering in Los Angeles, the film was among nine animated features that made a short list of nominees for an Academy Award for best animated feature, the first such Oscar to be presented that year under a new category at the 74th Academy Awards. Other contenders included DreamWorks' *Shrek*; Disney/Pixar's *Monsters, Inc.*; Sony's *Final Fantasy: The Spirits Within*; Paramount/Nickelodeon's CG holiday feature, *Jimmy Neutron, Boy Genius*; Richard Linklater's *Waking Life*; Warner Bros.' live-action/animated *Osmosis Jones*; Yugo Sako's Indian Ramayana epic, *The Prince of Light* (featuring the voice of "Malcolm in the Middle's" Bryan Cranston); and Terry L. Noss and Richard Rich's adaptation of E.B. White's literary classic, *The Trumpet of the Swan*.

## ◎ MEET THE ROBINSONS (2007)

A Walt Disney Pictures/Walt Disney Feature Animation Production released by Buena Vista Pictures. **p:** Dorothy McKim; **exec prod:** Clark Spencer; **d:** Steven J. Anderson; **scr:** Michelle Bochner (based on the book, *A Day with Wilbur Robinson*, by William Joyce); **m:** Danny Elfman. **Running time:** 92 minutes. **Release date:** March 30, 2007.

*Voices*
**Mildred:** Angela Bassett; **Wilbur:** Spencer Fox; **Lewis:** Jordan Fry; **Mr. Willerstein:** Tom Kenny; **Stanley:** Paul Butcher; **Young Franny:** Jessie Flower

*Additional Voices*
Kelly Ripa, Ethan Sandler, Wesley Singerman, Adam West, Harland Williams

A boy genius creates a fantastic machine that allows him to recover the lost memories of the past. What he unlocks instead is the future, with a family and a world whose survival is up to him.

**PN:** Originally titled *A Day with Wilbur Robinson*, Walt Disney Feature Animation produced this computer-animated feature. Originally scheduled for release on December 15, 2006, as a holiday feature, the film's release was postponed to March 30, 2007. Released to 3,435 theaters in 2-D and also shown in digital 3-D in select theaters nationwide, the cartoon comedy grossed an impressive $25,123,781 its first weekend and more than $97 million in its first two and a half weeks of release worldwide.

## ◎ MEGAZONE 23, PART ONE (1994)

An Artland/Artmic Production released by Streamline Pictures. **p:** Toru Moiru; **d:** Noboru Ishiguro; **scr:** Hiroyuki Hoshiyama;

**anim dir:** Toshihiro Hirano; **anim:** Kiyotoshi Aoi, Yoshiharu Fukushima, Yoko Kadokami, Narumi Kakinouchi, Hiroyuki Kitazume, Toru Miyoshi, Sadami Morikawa, Hiroaki Okami, Haruhiko Sato, Hideaki Shimada, Yasuomi Umetsu, Masahito Yamashita, Nobuteru Yuuki. **Running time:** 80 minutes. **Released:** February 2, 1994.

*Voices*

**Shogo Yahagi:** Masato Kubota; **Tomomi Murashita:** Mina Tominaga; **Mai Yumekano:** Mayumi Sho; **B.D.:** Kanero Shiosawa; **Coco:** Hitoshi Takagi; **Eigen Yumekano:** Kiyoshi Kobayashi; **Morii:** Yuji Mitsuya; **Chonbo:** Katsumi Toriumi.

Shogo Yahagi, a young, fun-loving teenager who likes to bike with his friends, discovers a prototype military motorcycle that makes him a marked man by government agents as he unravels a conspiracy involving a giant computer beneath Tokyo that is actually a world-destroying satellite.

## ◎ MEGAZONE 23, PART TWO (TELL ME THE SECRET) (1994)

An Artland/Artmic Production released by Streamline Pictures. **p:** Toru Miura; **d:** Toshihiro Hirano; **scr:** Hiroyuki Hoshiyama; **anim:** Kiyotoshi Aoi, Yoshiharu Fukushima, Yoko Kadokami, Narumi Kakinouchi, Hiroyuki Kitazume, Toru Miyoshi, Sadami Morikawa, Hiroaki Okami, Haruhiko Sato, Hideaki Shimada, Yasuomi Umetsu, Masahito Yamashita, Nobuteru Yuuki. **Running time:** 60 minutes. **Released:** February 2, 1994.

*Voices*

**Shougo Yahagi:** Vic Mignogna; **Yui Takanaka:** Alison Shipp; **Admiral:** Phil Ross; **Morley:** Kurt Stoll; **Coco:** John Swasey; **Eigen:** John Tyson; **Nakao:** Mike Vance

Anime science fiction-fantasy adventure continuing the saga of 1985's *Megazone 23, Part One,* in which a teenage biker and his friends war against the government while trying to save humanity from automated weapons left over from another war.

## ◎ MELODY TIME (1948)

A Walt Disney Production released by RKO Radio Pictures. **p:** Walt Disney; **prod superv:** Ben Sharpsteen; **anim dir:** Clyde Geronimi, Wilfred Jackson, Hamilton Luske, Jack Kinney; **st:** Winston Hibler, Harry Reeves, Ken Anderson, Erdman Penner, Homer Brightman, Ted Sears, Joe Rinaldi, Art Scott, Bob Moore, Bill Cottrell, Jesse Marsh, John Walbridge. "Little Toot" by Hardie Gramatky; **md:** Eliot Daniel, Ken Darby; **dir anim:** Eric Larson, Ward Kimball, Milt Kahl, Oliver M. Johnston Jr., John Lounsbery, Les Clark. **Songs:** "Melody Time," "Little Toot," "The Lord Is Good to Me," "The Pioneer Song," "Once Upon a Wintertime," "Blame It on the Samba," "Blue Shadows on the Trail," "Pecos Bill," "Trees" and "The Flight of the Bumblebee." **Running time:** 75 minutes. **Released:** May 27, 1948.

*Cast*

Roy Rogers, Luana Patten, Bobby Driscoll, Ethel Smith, Bob Nolan, the Sons of the Pioneers

*Voices/Musicians*

**Master of Ceremonies:** Buddy Clark; The Andrews Sisters; Fred Waring and his Pennsylvanians: Frances Langford; Dennis Day; **Aracaun Bird:** Pinto Colvig; with Freddy Martin and His Orchestra featuring Jack Fina

The last of Disney's musical fantasies, this musical melange features live action and animated episodes based on popular songs of the day. Several key animated sequences make up the film, among them: "Blame It on the Samba," with Donald Duck and

*Saludos Amigos* costar Jose Carioca in this animated samba backed by Ethel Smith and the Dinning Sisters; "Johnny Appleseed," featuring the voice of actor/singer Dennis Day as narrator; and "Little Toot," the story of a young tugboat's determination to be successful, sung by the Andrews Sisters.

## ◎ METAMORPHOSES (1978)

A Sanrio Films release. **p:** Terry Ogisu, Hiro Tsugawa, Takashi; **d & w:** Takashi (based on Ovid's *Metamorphoses*); **seq dir:** Jerry Eisenberg, Richard Huebner, Sadao Miyamoto, Amby Paliwoda, Ray Patterson, Manny Perez, George Singer, Stan Walsh. **Running time:** 89 minutes. **Released:** May 3, 1978.

Six of the most familiar Greek and Roman myths—creation; the hunter Actaeon turned into a stag by the goddess Diana; Orpheus and Eurydice; Mercy and the House of Envy; Perseus and Medusa; and Phaeton and the sun chariot—are integrated into this cartoon adaptation of five tales of classic mythology by Ovid.

**PN:** Three years in the making, *Metamorphoses* was first screened in the fall of 1977 but pulled back from general release for some additional postproduction work.

## ◎ METROPOLIS (2002)

A Madhouse Production released by TriStar Pictures. **p:** Yutaka Maseba, Tasao Maruyama, Iwao Yamaki; **d:** Rin Taro; **scr:** Katsuhiro Otomo (based on the manga by Osamu Tezuka); **chief key anim superv:** Yasuhiro Nakura; **anim superv:** Shigeo Akahori, Kunihiko Sakurai, Shigeru Fujita; **asst anim superv:** Shigeto Tsuji, Toshio Hirata. **Running time:** 107 minutes. **Released:** January 25, 2002.

*Voices*

**Tima:** Rebecca Forstadt; **Kenichi/Fifi:** Brianne Siddall; **Rock:** Michael Reisz; **Duke Red:** Jamieson K. Price; **Shunsaku Ban:** Tony Pope; **Pero:** Dave Mallow; **Dr. Laughton:** Simon Prescott; **Dr. Ponkotsu:** Doug Stone; **President Boon:** Steve McGowan; **Notarlin:** William Knight; **Skunk:** Dan Woren; **Lamp:** Steve Blum; **Ham and Egg:** Robert Axelrod; **Mayor Lyon:** Peter Spellos; **Atlas:** Scott Weinger; **Enmy:** Barbara Goodson

Set in the futuristic Metropolis, a detective named Shunsaku Ban and his nephew, Kenichi, join forces with a powerful robot girl, Tima, to thwart plans by the military to take control of the city in this animated science fiction drama based on Japanese manga writer/animator Osamu Tezuka's 1949 cartoon novel of the same name.

## ◎ A MIDSUMMER NIGHT'S DREAM (1961)

A Ceskoslovenský Státní Film Production released by Showcorporation. **p:** Erna Kminkovc, Jaroslav Morris; **d:** Jiri Trnka; **st:** Jiri Trnka, Jiri Brdecka, Josef Kainar, Howard Sackler (based on the play by William Shakespeare); **m:** Vaclav Trojan; **anim:** Jan Adams, Vlasta Jurajdovc, Jan Karpas, Stanislav Lctal, Bretislav Pojar, Bohuslav Srcmek. **Running time:** 74 minutes. **Released:** December 28, 1961.

*Voices*

**Narrator:** Richard Burton; **Oberon:** Jack Gwillim, **Titania:** Barbara Jefford; **Puck:** Roger Shepherd; **Demetrius:** Michael Meacham; **Lysander:** Tom Criddle; **Hermia:** Anne Bell; **Helena:** Barbara Leigh-Hunt; **Bottom:** Alec McCowen; **Theseus:** Hugh Manning; **Quince:** Joss Ackland; **Hippolyta:** Laura Graham; **Flute:** Stephen Moore; **Egeus:** John Warner

Puppet-animated reenactment of William Shakespeare's play about four young lovers and a band of amateur actors and their romantic adventures under a moonlit sky and interactions with the faeries who live there.

**PN:** Master Czechoslovakian animator/sculptor/illustrator Jiri Trnka wrote and directed this colorful, puppet-animated, silent (with no dialogue) adaptation of William Shakespeare's romantic comedy, written in the mid-1590s, and one of Shakespeare's most popular and most performed plays. The film was first released in Czechoslovakia in 1959 and won the Grand Prix award at that year's Cannes Film Festival. A much shorter version of Trnka's original film—edited to 74 minutes—was produced with an added soundtrack and dialogue voiced by an English cast that included actor Richard Burton as the narrator. This version was released in the United States two years later.

## ◉ THE MIGHTY KONG (1998)

A Lana Film Production released by Legacy Releasing Corporation. **p:** Lyn Henderson, Denis deVallance; **d:** Art Scott; **exec prod:** George W. Drysdale, Koichi Motohashi; **scr:** William J. Kennan (based on material by Merian C. Cooper, Delos Lovelace and Edgar Wallace); **m/sc:** David Siebels; **m/s:** Richard M. Sherman, Robert B. Sherman; **anim superv:** Franco Cristofani, Karl Fischer, Junzo Nakajima, Lynn Singer. **Running time:** 78 minutes. **Released:** May 29, 1998.

*Voices*
**Carl Denham/King Kong:** Dudley Moore; **Ann Darrow:** Jodi Benson; **Jack Driscoll:** Randy Hamilton; **Roscoe/Other Voices:** William Sage, **Ricky:** Jason Gray-Stanford; **Captain:** Richard Newman

*Additional Voices*
Don Brown, Michael Richard Dobson, Paul Dobson, Ian James Corlett

An animated musical remake of the famed beast of the jungle held in captivity for the entire world to see.

**PN:** Shown in limited release, this latest attempt to revive the King Kong story featured the voices of Dudley Moore as the manic filmmaker Carl Denham, and Jodi Benson as the budding film actress Ann Darrow, with songs by famed Disney composers Richard and Robert Sherman.

## ◉ MIGHTY MOUSE IN THE GREAT SPACE CHASE (1982)

A Filmation Associates/Viacom Productions, Inc. Production released by Filmation Associates. **p:** Don Christensen, Norm Prescott, Lou Scheimer. **d:** Ed Friedman, Lou Kachivas, Marsh Lamore, Gwen Wetzler, Kay Wright, Lou Zukor. **Running time:** 88 minutes. **Released:** December 10, 1982.

*Voices*
**Mighty Mouse:** Alan Oppenheimer; **Pearl Pureheart:** Diane Pershing

Mighty Mouse encounters many perilous adventures as he tries to save the space queen, Pearl Pureheart, from the villainous Harry the Heartless and his Doomsday Machine.

**PN:** Trying to cash-in on the *Star Wars* craze in the early 1980s, Filmation Associates produced this compilation feature stringing together various episodes of its Saturday-morning cartoon series, "The New Adventures of Mighty Mouse." The film opened as a Saturday matinee attraction at theaters in the United States but did not fare well at the box office.

## ◉ MILLENNIUM ACTRESS (2003)

A Madhouse Production released by Go Fish Pictures (DreamWorks). **p:** Taro Maki; **d:** Satoshi Kon; **scr:** Satoshi Kon, Sadayuki Murai; **m:** Susumu Hirasawa. **Running time:** 87 minutes. **Released:** September 12, 2003.

*Voices*
**Chiyoko Fujiwara, 70s:** Miyoko Shoji; **Chiyoko Fujiwara, 20-40s:** Mami Koyama; **Chiyoko Fujiwara, 10-20s:** Furniko Orikasa; **Genya Tachibana:** Shozo Izuka; **Eiko Shimao:** Shouko Tsuda; **Junichi Ootaki:** Hirotaka Suzuoki; **Mother:** Hisako Kyoda; **Senior Manager of Ginei:** Kan Tokumaru; **Mino:** Tomie Katoaka; **Genya:** Masamichi Sato; **Kyoji Ida:** Masaya Onosaka

Documentary director Genya Tachibana interviews one of her country's most reclusive actresses, celebrated film star Chiyoko Fujiwara, who talks about her life and loves by revisiting her most famous film performances.

**PN:** The first American release for Go Fish Pictures, a distribution division of DreamWorks that specializes in art films, the feature grossed $37,285 in the United States.

## ◉ MR. BUG GOES TO TOWN (1941)

A Fleischer Studios Production released by Paramount Pictures. **p:** Max Fleischer; **d:** Dave Fleischer; **w:** Dave Fleischer, Dan Gordon, Ted Pierce, Isadore Sparber, William Turner, Mike Meyer, Graham Place, Bob Wickersham, Cal Howard; **md:** Leigh Harline; **m/l:** Hoagy Carmichael, Frank Loesser, Herman Timberg, Four Marshals and Royal Guards. **Songs:** "We're the Couple in the Castle," "Boy, Oh Boy," "Katy-Did, Katy-Didn't," "Bee My Little Baby Bumble Bee" and "I'll Dance at Your Wedding." **Running time:** 77 minutes. **Released:** December 4, 1941.

*Voices*
Kenny Gardner, Gwen Williams, Jack Mercer, Ted Pierce, Mike Meyer, Stan Freed, Pauline Loth

Bug life on Broadway sets the stage for this second feature by animators Max and Dave Fleischer chronicling an insect colony's never-ending battle against the human race. The film's central characters are Honey Bee and grasshopper Hoppity, the love interests of the story, and the nasty C. Bagley Beetle and his hoodlum henchmen, Swat the Fly and Smack the Mosquito, who make life miserable in bug town.

**PN:** Also known as *Hoppity Goes to Town.*

## ◉ MONSTER HOUSE (2006)

A Sony Pictures Animation/Imagemovers Production released by Columbia Pictures. **p:** Jack Rapke, Steve Starkey; **exec prod:** Jason Clark, Steven Spielberg, Robert Zemeckis; **d:** Gil Kenan; **scr:** Gil Kenan, Dan Harmon, Rob Schrab, Pamela Pettler; **m:** Douglas Pipes; **st:** Gil Kenan; **anim superv:** Troy Saliba, T. Daniel Hofstedt. **Songs:** "Eliza's Song." **Running time:** 91 minutes. **Released:** July 21, 2006.

*Voices*
**D.J.:** Michael Tate Musso; **Chowder:** Sam Lerner; **Jenny:** Spencer Locke-Bonney; **Nebbercracker:** Steve Buscemi; **Zee:** Maggie Gyllenhaal; **Bones:** Jason Lee; **Officer Landers:** Kevin James; **Officer Lister:** Nick Cannon; **D.J.'s Mom:** Catherine O'Hara; **D.J.'s Dad:** Fred Willard; **Eliza:** Ryan Newman; **Paramedic #1:** Woody Schulz; **Paramedic #2:** Ian McConnel; **Reginald "Skull" Skulinski:** Jon Heder; **Constance:** Kathleen Turner; **Cameron:** Erik Walker; **Ryan:** Matthew Fahey; **Jenny:** Brittany Curran (uncredited); **Additional Voices:** Marc Musso

After three teenagers find a neighbor's house is not a house at all but actually a real monster, even though their parents find the discovery hard to believe, they intervene to save the neighborhood in this motion capture/computer-animated fantasy.

**PN:** Marking Gil Kenan's directorial debut, this animated horror film, using the same performance-capture animation as *The Polar Express*, was a monstrous hit with moviegoers. Opening in

3,553 theaters, the film, produced at a cost of $75 million and also shown in 3-D in some theaters throughout the United States, scared up $22,217,226 in revenue its opening weekend and topped more than $135 million worldwide.

## ◉ MONSTERS INC. (2001)

A Pixar Animation Studios/Walt Disney Studios Production released by Buena Vista Pictures. **p:** Darla K. Anderson; **exec prod:** John Lasseter, Andrew Stanton; **d:** Peter Docter; **co-dir:** Lee Unkrich, David Silverman; **scr:** Andrew Stanton, Daniel Gerson; **st:** Pete Docter, Jill Culton, Jeff Pidgeon, Ralph Eggleston; **m:** Randy Newman; **superv anim:** Glenn McQueen, Rich Quade; **dir anim:** Doug Sweetland, Scott Clark. **Songs:** "If I Didn't Have You." **Running time:** 92 minutes. **Released:** November 2, 2001.

*Voices*

**James P. "Sulley" Sullivan:** John Goodman; **Mike Mazowski:** Billy Crystal; **Boo:** Mary Gibbs; **Randall Boggs:** Steve Buscemi; **Henry J. Watermoose:** James Coburn; **Celia:** Jennifer Tilly; **Roz:** Bob Peterson; **Yeti:** John Ratzenberger; **Fungus:** Frank Oz; **Needleman/Smitty:** Daniel Gerson; **Floor Manager:** Steve Susskind; **Flint:** Bonnie Hunt; **Bile:** Jeff Pidgeon; **George:** Sam Black

Two employees of the largest scare factory in Monsteropolis, the intimidating furry blue monster, James "Sully" Sullivan, and his one-eyeballed best friend and scare assistant, Mike Wazowski, deal with a major catastrophe when a tiny girl turns their world upside-down.

**PN:** With Pixar Animation's fourth CG-animated feature in association with Walt Disney Studios, Pixar once again maintained its box-office domination as this latest cartoon fantasy enjoyed the largest opening day debut for an animated film, earning $65,577,067. Overall, this delightfully entertaining comedy-adventure amassed more than $255 million in ticket sales and was nominated for an Academy Award for best animated feature, losing to DreamWorks' *Shrek*, the first year this category was established by the Academy. However, the film went on to win three Oscars for best music, best original score and original song for Randy Newman's "If I Didn't Have You" and best sound effects editing.

## ◉ THE MOUSE AND HIS CHILD (1978)

A DeFaria-Lockhart-Murakami-Wolf/Sanrio Films Production released by Sanrio. **p:** Walt DeFaria; **d:** Fred Wolf, Chuck Swenson; **w:** Carol Mon Pere (based on the novel by Russell Hoban); **m:** Roger Kellaway. **Running time:** 83 minutes. **Released:** May 24, 1978.

*Voices*

**Manny:** Peter Ustinov; **Eutrepe:** Cloris Leachman; **Seal:** Sally Kellerman; **Frog:** Andy Devine; **Mouse:** Alan Barzman; **Mouse Child:** Marcy Swenson; **Iggy:** Neville Brand; **Clock/Hawk:** Regis Cordic; **Elephant:** Joan Gerber; **Muskrat:** Bob Holt; **Startling/Teller:** Maitzi Morgan; **Crow:** Frank Nelson; **Crow:** Cliff Norton; **Serpentina:** Cliff Osmond; **The Paper People:** Iris Rainer; **Jack in the Box:** Bob Ridgely; **Blue Jay/The Paper People:** Charles Woolf; and Mel Leven

Based on Russell Hoban's novel, the film centers around the story of a mechanical mouse and his son who have one wish: to be self-winding.

## ◉ MUHAMMAD: THE LAST PROPHET (2004)

A RichCrest Animation Studios/Badr International Corporation Production released by Fine Media Group. **p:** Mowafak El-Harthy; **d:** Richard Rich; **scr:** Brian Nissen; **m:** William Kidd. **Running time:** 90 minutes. **Released:** November 14, 2004.

*Voices*

**Abu Talib:** Eli Allem; **Abu Jahl/Tribal Leader/Counselor:** Richard Epcar; **Abu Lahab/Tribal Leader:** David Llewellyn; **Soothsayer/Poor Man/Tribal Leader:** Donal O'Sullivan; **Al Walid:** Lawrence Ross; **Abu Ben Alas/The Spy:** Bob Johnson; **Khaleed:** Robert Cottrell; **Hamzah/Tribal Leader:** C.S. Berkeley; **Malek:** Brian Nissen; **Slave Merchant:** Andrew Craig; **Salman:** Anthony Mozdy; **Tribal Leader/Guard:** Ed Trotta; **Old Woman:** Alena Sheley; **Bread Maker:** Don Oscar Smith; **Archer:** Bernie Van De Yacht

*Additional Voices*

Nick Kadi, Catherine Lavin, Tiffany Johnson, Mark Hunt, Lauren Schaffel, Anthony Michael Jr., Jerome Dinon, D. Hunter White, Leon Morenzie, Spencer Beglarian, Mary Louise Gemmill, Jacob Livingston, F. Blossom DeWitt

An animated retelling of the events surrounding the birth of Islam and the humble origins of the man who would become its most celebrated spiritual leader, based on the classic children's fable.

**PN:** Originally released in Islamic countries in 2002 and set to premiere that same year in the United States, the film was shelved after the 9/11 terrorist attacks on the World Trade Center and Pentagon for fear of anti-Muslim sentiment at the time. The film was directed by Richard Rich who also helmed such animated features as Disney's *The Fox and the Hound* and Warner Bros.' *The King and I*, under the banner of his RichCrest Animation Studios (so-named after Rich Animation Studios was acquired by Crest, a company in India). Pared down from its original 4½-hour length to 90 minutes, the hand-drawn and partly computer-animated feature premiered two years later, opening the week of November 14 in 100 theaters and some 40 cities in the United States and Canada. Its release coincided with Eid al-Fitr, a Muslim holiday marking the end of Ramadan. The film was among a short list of contenders from lesser-known studios nominated for an Academy Award for best animated feature in 2004.

## ◉ MULAN (1998)

A Walt Disney Pictures Production released by Buena Vista Pictures. **p:** Pam Coats; **d:** Barry Cook, Tony Bancroft; **scr:** Rita Hsiao, Christopher Sanders, Philip La Zebnik, Raymond Singer, Eugenia Bostwick Singer (based on a story by Robert D. San Souci); **m:** Jerry Goldsmith; **songs:** Matthew Wilder, David Zippel; **superv anim:** Mark Henn, Ruben A. Aquino, Tom Bancroft, Aaron Blaise, Broose Johnson, Pres Antonio Romanillos, Alex Kuperschmidt, Jeffrey J. Varab, Barry Temple. T. Daniel Hoffstedt, Rob Bekuhrs. **Songs:** "Honor to Us All," "Reflection," "I'll Make a Man Out of You," "A Girl Worth Fighting For," "True to Your Heart," "The Emperor's New Clothes" and "Reflejo." **Running time:** 88 minutes. **Released:** June 19, 1998.

*Voices*

**Mulan:** Ming Na Wen; **Mulan singing:** Lea Salonga; **Fa Zhou:** Soon Teck; **Fa Li:** Freda Foh Shen; **Mushu:** Eddie Murphy; **Shang:** B.D. Wong; **Shang singing:** Donny Osmond; **Ling:** Gedde Watanabe; **Chein-Po:** Jerry S. Tondo; **Yao:** Harvey Fierstein; **Shan-Yu:** Miguel Ferrer; **Chi Fu:** James Hong; **The Emperor:** Pat Morita; **First Ancestor:** George Takei; **Grandmother Fa:** June Foray

In ancient China a tradition-bucking young girl, Mulan, who disguises herself as a man, joins the army to replace her ill father in this story of female-empowerment based on a Chinese folk tale.

**PN:** First-time directors Barry Cook, then a 17-year veteran at Walt Disney Studios, and Tony Bancroft, a Disney character animator on several films, codirected this film based on Chinese legend. Comedian Eddie Murphy provided comic relief as the voice of Mushu. Budgeted for $90 million, this animated fairy tale, released in June of 1998, was a summer hit and did big business at the box office, making $120 million in the United States and more than $303.5 million worldwide. In December of that year, the film passed the $100 million mark in box-office revenue overseas with Disney's distribution division, Buena Vista Pictures, as well. Likewise, *Mulan* was the studio's seventh consecutive full-length animated feature to do well at the box office in foreign markets, including the United Kingdom ($14.6 million), France ($10.2 million), Germany ($8.6 million) and Japan ($6.4 million).

## ⊚ MUTANT ALIENS (2002)

A Plymptoons Production released by E.D. Distribution and Apollo Cinema. **p, d, w & anim:** Bill Plympton; **assoc prod:** John Holderried; **m:** Hank Bones. **Running time:** 83 minutes. **Released:** April 19, 2002.

*Voices*

**Earl Jensen:** Dan McComas; **Josie Jensen/Squeeze Rod Voice:** Francine Lobis; **Darby/Tomkins:** Matthew Brown; **Dr. Frubar/President:** George Casden; **Boris/NASA Technician/Alien Voices:** Jay Cavanaugh; **Secretary:** Amy Allison; **Preacher:** Kevin Kolack; **Signe Bullwinkel:** Vera Beren; **Guard:** Bill Plympton; **Young Josie:** Thea Burton; **Alien Voices:** Silkie O'Ishi; **Computer Access Voice:** Samantha Ridgway

Earl Jensen, an astronaut stranded in outer space, returns to Earth 20 years later with an army of aliens seeking revenge against the space-industry tycoon Dr. Frubar.

**PN:** Released in 2001, this film by independent animator Bill Plympton, which screened in New York and Los Angeles, was an entry at that year's Sundance Film Festival and winner of the Grand Prize at the Annecy Animation Festival.

## ⊚ MY LITTLE PONY: THE MOVIE (1986)

A Sunbow/Marvel Production in association with Hasbro, Inc. released by DeLaurentis Films. **p:** Joe Bacal, Tom Griffin, Michael Joens; (no director listed); **w:** George Arthur Bloom; **m:** Rob Walsh (theme song "My Little Pony" by Spencer Michilin and Ford Kinder); **superv anim:** Pierre DeCelles, Michael Fallows, Ray Lee. **Running time:** 89 minutes. **Released:** June 20, 1986.

*Voices*

**Grundle King:** Danny DeVito; **Droggle:** Madeline Kahn; **Hydia:** Cloris Leachman; **Reeka:** Rhea Perlman; **The Moonchick:** Tony Randall; **Megan:** Tammy Amerson; **The Snooze:** Jon Bauman; **Baby Lickety Split/Bushwoolie #1:** Alice Playten; **Spike/Woodland Creature:** Charlie Adler; **Grundle:** Michael Bell; **Buttons/Woodland Creature/Bushwoolie:** Sheryl Bernstein; **Lofty/Grundle/Bushwoolie:** Susan Blu; **North Star:** Cathy Cavadini; **Gutsy/Bushwoolie #4:** Nancy Cartwright; **Grundle/Ahgg:** Peter Cullen; **Sundance/Bushwoolie #2:** Laura Dean; **Magic Star:** Ellen Gerstell; **Molly:** Keri Houlihan; **Fizzy/Baby Sunshine:** Katie Leigh; **Danny:** Scott Menville; **Sweet Stuff:** Laurel Page; **Wind Whistler:** Sarah Partridge; **Morning Glory/Rosedust/Bushwoolie/Shunk:** Russi Taylor; **Shady/Baby Lofty:** Jill Wayne; **Grundle/Bushwoolie #3:** Frank Welker

In Ponyland, the Little Ponies' annual Spring Festival is about to begin. While they are enjoying their festive spring party, the evil witch Hydia is plotting to turn Ponyland into a wasteland. When her attempt fails, she decides to cover Ponyland with a purple ooze called the "Smooze."

## ⊚ MY NEIGHBOR TOTORO (1993)

A Studio Ghibli Production released by 50th Street Films/Troma, Inc. **p:** Toru Hara (American producer: Carl Macek); **d:** Hayao Miyazaki (American director: Greg Snegoff); **exec prod:** Yasuyoshi Tokuma; **scr:** Hayao Miyazaki; **m:** Jo Hisaishi; **dir anim:** Yoshiharu Sato. **Songs:** "Sanpo" and "Tonarino Totoro." **Running time:** 89 minutes. **Released:** May 7, 1993.

*Voices*

Lisa Michaelson, Cheryl Chase, Greg Snegoff, Kenneth Hartman, Alexandra Kenworthy, Natalie Core, Steve Kramer, Lara Cody, Melanie McQueen

After moving to the country with their professor-father, two young children befriend a giant, lovable supernatural spirit known as Totoro who becomes their magical guardian in a series of high-flying adventures.

**PN:** Released originally in 1988 in Japan, this English-dubbed version enjoyed modest success in the United States and was directed by accomplished Japanese director Hayao Miyazaki. The movie was a Film Advisory Board award winner.

## ⊚ NEO-TOKYO/SILENT MOBIUS (1992)

A Kadokawa Films Production released by Streamline Pictures. **p:** Haruki Kadokawa; **d:** (*Neo-Tokyo*) Rin Taro, Yoshiaki Kawajiri, Katsuhiro Otomo; (*Silent Mobius*) Michitaka Kikuchi; **scr:** (*Neo-Tokyo*) Yoshiaki Kawajiri ("The Running Man"), Katsuhiro Otomo ("The Order to Cease Construction"), Rintaro ("Labyrinth-Labyrintos"); **anim:** Nobumasa Arakawa, Atsuko Fukushima, Kengo Inagaki, Toshio Kawaguchi, Reiko Kurihara, Koji Morimoto, Takashi Nakamura, Shinji Otsuka, Kunihiko Sakurai, Manabu Ohashi; (*Silent Mobius*) **scr:** Kei Shigema, Michitaka Kikuchi; **st:** Kia Asamiya; **m:** Kaora Wada. **Running time:** 50 minutes. **Released:** November 20, 1992.

*Voices*

(*Neo-Tokyo*) **Tsutomu Sugioka:** Robert Axelrod; **Sachi:** Cheryl Chase; **Mother:** Barbara Goodson; **Chief Technician/Boat Pilot:** Steve Kramer; **Reporter:** Michael McConnohie; **Robot 444-1:** Jeff Winkless; **Tech/Boss:** Tom Wyner; (*Silent Mobius*) **Katsumi:** Iona Morris; **Miyuka:** Alexandra Kensworthy; **Kiddy:** Joyce Kurtz; **Lucifer Hawke:** Jeff Winkless; **Nami:** Wendee Lee; **Rally:** Melora Harre; **Lebia:** Barbara Goodson; **Yuki:** Julie Donald

This double-feature combined two short Japanese films on the same bill: *Neo-Tokyo*, a trilogy of futuristic stories—animator Rin Taro's *Labyrinth*; Yoshiaki Kawajiri's *Running Man* and Katsuhiro Otomo's *Order to Cease Construction*—and *Silent Mobius*, about a special police unit comprised of six women, each with special abilities, who battle demons on the loose in Tokyo.

## ⊚ NINE LIVES OF FRITZ THE CAT (1974)

A Steve Krantz Production released by American International Pictures, Inc. **p:** Steve Krantz; **exec prod:** Samuel Z. Arkoff; **d:** Robert Taylor; **scr:** Fred Halliday, Eric Monte, Robert Taylor (based on the comic books by Robert Crumb); **m:** Tom Scott and the LA Express; **anim:** Robert Taylor, Jim Davis, Don Williams, Herb Johnson, Paul Sommer, Jack Foster, Manny Perez, Volus Jones, Manny Gould, Bob Maxfield, Bob Bachman, Cosmo Anzilotti, Art Vitello, John Gentilella, Milt Gray, Marty Taras, Fred Hellmich, Frank Andrina, Bob Bransford, Bob Bemiller, John Bruno. **Running time:** 76 minutes. **Released:** June 26, 1974.

*Voices*

**Fritz the Cat:** Skip Hinnant; **Fritz's Old Lady:** Reva Rose; **Numerous Voices:** Bob Holt; **"Bowery Buddies"/"Black New Jersey":** Robert Ridgeley; **"Bowery Buddies":** Fred Smoot; **"Sweet" (various):** Dick Whittington; **Various Voices:** Luke Walker; **Juan/Various Voices:** Peter Leeds; **Fritz's Sister:** Louise Mortiz; **The Roach:** Sarina C. Grant

After losing one of his lives, pot-smoking Fritz the Cat is a henpecked husband who is married—and hates it—to the point that he lights up a reefer and fantasizes about his eight other lives, from being on breadlines during the Great Depression to taking a rocket-ship trip to Mars, in this 1974 sequel.

**PN:** Former Bakshi Studios animator Robert Taylor, one of Ralph Bakshi's main collaborators during his days at New York's Terry-Toons studio, wrote, directed, and co-animated this sequel to Bakshi's 1972 X-rated original, *Fritz the Cat*, which Bakshi rejected after producer Steve Krantz approached Bakshi about re-upping to do a second feature based on the character created by R. Crumb. This film was selected as an entry at the 27th annual Cannes Film Festival, marking the first time in the festival's history that an animated film competed.

### ◎ NUTCRACKER FANTASY (1979)

A Sanrio Films Production released by Sanrio. **p:** Walt DeFaria, Mark L. Rosen, Arthur Tomioka; **d:** Takeo Nakamura; **w:** Thomas Joachim, Eugene Fornier (based on *The Nutcracker and the Mouse King* by E.T.A. Hoffman, adaptation by Shintaro Tsuji; **m:** Peter Illych Tchaikovsky (adapted and arranged by Akihito Wakatsuki,

Kentaro Haneda). **Running time:** 82 minutes. **Released:** July 7, 1979.

*Voices*

**Narrator:** Michele Lee; **Clara:** Melissa Gilbert; **Aunt Gerda:** Lurene Tuttle; **Uncle Drosselmeyer/Street Singer/Puppeteer/Watchmaker:** Christopher Lee; **Queen Morphia:** Jo Anne Worley; **Chamberlain/Poet/Wiseman:** Ken Sansom; **King Goodwin:** Dick Van Patten; **Franz Fritz:** Roddy McDowall; **Indian Wiseman/Viking Wiseman:** Mitchel Gardner; **Chinese Wiseman/Executioner:** Jack Angel; **Otto Von Atra/French Wiseman/Clovis:** Gene Moss; **Queen of Time:** Eva Gabor; **Mice Voices:** Joan Gerber, Maxine Fisher; **Princess Mary:** Robin Haffner

A young girl dreams of romance and adventure in a world inhabited by a king whose daughter has been turned into a sleeping mouse and can only be transformed and reawakened by a heroic prince.

**PN:** This Japanese production, filmed and dubbed in English for American release, featured puppet animation.

### ◎ THE NUTCRACKER PRINCE (1990)

A Lacewood Production released by Warner Bros. **p:** Kevin Gillis; **d:** Paul Schibli; **scr:** Patricia Watson (based on *The Nutcracker and the Mouseking* by E.T.A. Hoffman); **m:** Peter Ilyich Tchaikovsky (arranged by Victor Davies and performed by the London Symphony Orchestra under the direction of Boris Brott). **Running time:** 75 minutes. **Released:** November 23, 1990.

*The Nutcracker Prince (voiced by Kiefer Sutherland) battles the evil Mouseking in the animated fantasy* The Nutcracker Prince.

*Voices*
**Nutcracker Prince:** Kiefer Sutherland; **Clara:** Megan Follows; **Mouseking:** Mike MacDonald; **Uncle Drosselmeier:** Peter Boretski; **Mousequeen:** Phyllis Diller; **Pantaloon:** Peter O'Toole

Young Clara Stahlbaum discovers a wooden nutcracker in the shape of a toy soldier under her Christmas tree. Her eccentric Uncle Drosselmeier tells her the story of the nutcracker, a young man named Hans, who was put under a spell by a wicked, vengeful Mousequeen. Clara dismisses the story, but that night everything her uncle told her unfolds before her eyes.

## ◎ OF STARS AND MEN (1964)

A story based Films Production released by Brandon Films Inc. **p:** John and Faith Hubley; **d:** John Hubley; **w:** John and Faith Hubley, Harlow Shapley (based on the book *Of Stars and Men* by Shapley); **anim dir:** William Littlejohn, Gary Mooney. **Running time:** 53 minutes. **Released:** May 13, 1964.

*Voices*
Dr. Harlow Shapley, Mark Hubley, Hamp Hubley

Man's scientific world is interpreted in this film by animation husband-and-wife team John and Faith Hubley. The film's central character, Man, recalls his place in the universe—in space, time, matter and energy—and the meaning of life.

## ◎ OLIVER & COMPANY (1988)

A Walt Disney/Silver Screen Partners III Production released by Buena Vista Pictures. **d:** George Scribner; **st:** Vance Gerry, Mike Gabriel, Joe Ranft, Jim Mitchell, Chris Bailey, Kirk Wise, Dave Michener, Roger Allers, Gary Trousdale, Kevin Lima, Michael Cedeno, Pete Young, Leon Joosen (based on Charles Dickens's *Oliver Twist*); **scr:** Jim Cox, Timothy J. Disney, James Mangold; **m:** Carole Childs (original score by J.A.C. Redford); **superv anim:** Mike Gabriel, Glen Keane, Ruben A. Aquino, Hendel Butoy, Mark Hehn, Doug Krohn. **Running time:** 72 minutes. **Released:** November 18, 1988.

*Voices*
**Oliver:** Joey Lawrence; **Dodger:** Billy Joel; **Tito:** Cheech Marin; **Einstein:** Richard Mulligan; **Francis:** Roscoe Lee Browne; **Rita:** Sheryl Lee Ralph; **Fagan:** Dom DeLuise; **Roscoe:** Taurean Blacque; **Desoto:** Carl Weintraub; **Sykes:** Robert Loggia; **Jenny:** Natalie Gregory; **Winston:** William Glover; **Georgette:** Bette Midler

A rollicking take-off of Dickens's masterpiece with little orphan Oliver, a homeless kitten, taken in and cared for and taught "street smarts" by a pack of lovable hip dogs led by a human Fagin.

**PN:** *Oliver & Company* proved to be Disney's most successful fully animated feature in the 1980s, grossing a record $53.1 million.

## ◎ OLIVER TWIST (1974)

A Filmation Associates Production released by Warner Bros. **p:** Lou Scheimer, Norman Prescott; **exec prod:** Jacqueline Smith; **d:** Hal Sutherland; **m:** George Blais. **Running time:** 75 minutes. **Released:** May 1, 1974.

*Voices*
**Oliver Twist:** Josh Albee; **Fagin:** Les Tremayne.

*Additional Voices*
Phil Clark, Cathleen Cordell, Michael Evans, Lola Fischer, Robert Holt, Davy Jones, Larry D. Mann, Dallas McKennon, Billy Simpson, Larry Storch, Jane Webb, Helen Winston

In mid-19th-century London, an orphan boy finds that he is really the heir to a large fortune in this musical version of Charles Dickens's timeless novel.

**PN:** Originally released as a full-length feature, the film was reedited and broadcast as a prime-time special on NBC in 1981.

## ◎ ONCE UPON A FOREST (1993)

A Hanna-Barbera Production released by 20th Century Fox. **p:** David Kirschner, Jerry Mills; **d:** Charles Grosnevor, David Michener; **scr:** Mark Young, Kelly Ward; **st:** Rae Lambert; **m:** James Horner. **Songs:** "Once Upon a Time With Me," "Forest," "Cornelius's Nature Lesson," "Accident," "Bedside Vigil," "Please Wake Up," "Journey Begins," "He's Back," "Flying," "Escaping from the Yellow Dragons/The Meadow," "Flying Home to Michelle" and "Children/Maybe One Day . . . Maybe One Day." **Running time:** 80 minutes. **Released:** June 18, 1993.

*Voices*
**Cornelius:** Michael Crawford; **Phineas:** Ben Vereen; **Abigail:** Ellen Blain; **Edgar:** Ben Gregory; **Russell:** Paige Gosney; **Michelle:** Elizabeth Moss; **Abigail's Father:** Paul Eiding; **Edgar's Mother:** Janet Waldo; **Russell's Mother:** Susan Silo; **Willy:** Will Estes; **Waggs:** Charles Adler; **Bosworth:** Rickey Collins; **Bosworth's Mother:** Angel Harper; **Marshbird:** Don Reed; **Truck Driver:** Robert David Hall; **Russell's Brother:** Benjamin Smith; **Russell's Sister:** Haven Hartman

Exploring humans' cavalier encroachment on nature, this politically correct storybook fantasy details the adventures of four young forest animals—a wood mouse named Abigail, a mole named Edgar, a hedgehog named Russell and their little badger friend Michelle—and a wise old badger, Cornelius, who try to stop the deforestation of the forest by man and retrieve an herbal antidote that grows there to save the life of Michelle, who becomes seriously ill after a tanker crashes and releases poison gas in the air.

**PN:** Box-office gross for this Hanna-Barbera feature only totaled $6.2 million.

## ◎ ONCE UPON A GIRL (1976)

A Producers Releasing Organization release. **p:** Joel Siebel; **exec prod:** William B. Silberkleit, David Winters; **d & w:** Don Jurwich; **m:** Martin Slavin. **Running time:** 77 minutes. **Released:** June 20, 1976.

*Live-Action Cast*
**Mother Goose:** Hal Smith

*Voices*
Richmond Johnson, Frank Welker

Norwegian-produced animated sex comedy with live-action segments of actor Hal Smith, best known for his role as Otis the town drunk on TV's *The Andy Griffith Show*, in drag as the famous children's fairy tale character, Mother Goose, defending her fairy tales against charges of depravity and corruption that segue into a series of X-rated versions of classic fairy tales, including Cinderella, Jack and the Beanstalk and Little Red Riding Hood.

## ◎ ONCE UPON A TIME (1976)

A N.W. Russo Production released by G.G. Communications, Inc. **p:** Rolf Kauka; **d:** Rolf Kauka, Roberto Gavioli; **scr:** Rolf Kauka; **m:** Peter Thomas. **Running time:** 83 minutes. **Released:** October 1, 1976.

*Voices*
Dolphy, Chuckie Dreyfuss, Richard Gomez, Tessie Tomas

A beautiful young girl from an underprivileged family, Maria D'Oro, raised by her wicked stepsister and whose only friend is her little dog, Bello, seeks a happier life away from her stepmother and stepsister when she encounters a handsome prince, disguised as a woodsman, in the forest in this feature-length fantasy.

**PN:** Also known as *Maria D'Oro and Bello Blue*, this Italian/West German co-production was originally produced in 1975, with an English-language version released in the United States in 1976 by G.G. Communications, the same distributor that brought *Pippi Longstocking* to the big screen. Taking approximately three years to complete, internationally renowned cartoonist Rolf Kauka wrote, produced and directed this full-length animated feature with a team of animators that mirrored the expressionism and classic look of Disney animation and is reputedly the only animated feature to tell the tale of Frau Holle, Queen of the Wonderworld, a classic German fairy tale that previously had been adapted into several live-action films.

## ⊚ ONE HUNDRED AND ONE DALMATIANS (1961)

A Walt Disney Production released by Buena Vista. **p:** Walt Disney; **d:** Wolfgang Reitherman, Hamilton Luske, Clyde Geronimi; **st:** Bill Peet (based on *The Hundred and One Dalmatians* by Dodie Smith); **m:** George Bruns; **dir anim:** Milt Kahl, Frank Thomas, Marc Davis, John Lounsbery, Ollie Johnston, Eric Larson. **Songs:** "Cruelle De Vil," "Dalmatian Plantation" and "Kanine Krunchie Commercial." **Running time:** 79 minutes. **Released:** December 25, 1961.

*Voices*

**Pongo:** Rod Taylor; **Perdita:** Lisa Daniels; **Perdita:** Cate Bauer; **Roger Radcliff:** Ben Wright; **Anita Radcliff:** Lisa Davis; **Nanny/Queenie/Lucy:** Martha Wentworth; **The Colonel/Jaspar Badun/etc.:** J. Pat O'Malley, Horace Badun; **Inspector Craven:** Fred Worlock; **Cruella De Vil/Miss Birdwell:** Betty Lou Gerson; **Towser:** Tudor Owen; **Quizmaster/Collie:** Tom Conway; **Danny:** George Pelling; **The Captain:** Thurl Ravenscroft; **Sergeant Tibs:** Dave Frankham; **Television Announcer/Labrador:** Ramsay Hill; **Princess:** Queenie Leonard; **Duchess:** Marjorie Bennett; **Rolly:** Barbara Beaird; **Patch:** Mickey Maga; **Penny:** Sandra Abbott; **Lucky:** Mimi Gibson; **Rover:** Barbara Luddy; **Dirty Dawson:** Paul Frees; **Singer of TV Commercial:** Lucille Bliss

*Additional Voices*

Sylvia Marriott, Dallas McKennon, Basil Ruysdael, Max Smith, Rickie Sorensen, Bob Stevens

The spotted dogs owned by British couple Roger and Anita grow to multitudes when their prized pets Pongo and Perdita produce 15 beautiful Dalmatian puppies. The newborns fall prey to a rich and cunning woman, Cruella De Vil, a self-professed fur lover. Aided by henchmen Jasper and Horace, she steals the poor pups and makes plans to turn them into fur coats!

**PN:** Costing approximately $4 million to produce, this Disney classic featured the use of Xerography, whereby Disney animators made multiple copies of drawings, thus eliminating the necessity to draw 101 separate dogs for the mass character scenes.

## ⊚ 1001 ARABIAN NIGHTS (1959)

A UPA (United Productions of America) Production released by Columbia Pictures. **p:** Steve Bosustow; **d:** Jack Kinney; **scr:** Czeni Ormonde; **st:** Dick Kinney, Leo Salakin, Pete Burness, Lew Keller, Ed Notziger, Ted Allan, Margaret Schneider, and Paul Schneider; **m:** George Duning; **dir anim:** Abe Levitow. **Songs:** "You Are My Dream," "Three Little Maids from Damascus" and "Magoo's Blues." **Running time:** 76 minutes. **Released:** December 1, 1959.

*Voices*

**Uncle Abdul Azzia Magoo:** Jim Backus; **Princess Yasminda:** Kathryn Grant; **Aladdin/Magoo's nephew:** Dwayne Hickman;

*Nearsighted Mister Magoo takes a flying carpet ride he'll never forget in* Columbia Pictures' 1001 Arabian Nights. *© Screen Gems*

**The Wicked Wazir:** Hans Conried; **The Jinni of the Lamp:** Herschel Bernardi; **Sultan:** Alan Reed; **Omar the Rug Maker:** Daws Butler; **Three Little Maids from Damascus:** The Clark Sisters

Nearsighted, bumbling Baghdad lamp dealer Azziz Magoo wants his carefree nephew Aladdin to wed and settle down. Aladdin likes his own way of life until he falls in love with the beautiful Princess Yasminda. Yasminda is to wed the Wicked Wazir, who craves absolute power but can't have it until he also gets possession of a magic lamp that lies buried in a treasure cave. Magoo is fooled into giving up the magic lamp to the Wicked Wazir, although Wazir's victory is short-lived as Magoo triumphs in the end by defeating him entirely.

**PN:** The Technicolor film marked the first full-length feature for UPA and the first animated feature starring the myopic Mr. Magoo.

## ⊚ OPEN SEASON (2006)

A Sony Pictures Animation Production released by Sony Pictures. **p:** Christopher Jenkins, Michelle Murdocca; **exec prod:** John B. Carls, Steve Moore; **d:** Roger Allers, Jill Culton, Anthony Stacchi; **scr:** Steve Bencich, Ron. J. Friedman; **m:** Ramin Djawadi; **superv anim:** Renato Dos Anjos, Chris Hurtt, Sean P. Mullen, Todd Wilderman. **Songs:** "Meet Me in the Meadow," "Love You in the Fall," "I Belong," "I Wanna Lose Control," "Better Than This," "Wild Wild Life," "Right to Arm Bears," "Good Day," "All About Me," "Wild as I Wanna Be," "Whisper Me Luck" and "I Belong." **Running time:** 110 minutes. **Released:** September 29, 2006.

*Voices*

**Boog the Grizzly Bear:** Martin Lawrence; **Elliot the Mule Deer:** Ashton Kutcher; **Reilly the Beaver:** Jon Favreau; **Shaw:** Gary Sinise; **Giselle:** Jane Krakowski; **Forest Ranger Beth:** Debra Messing; **McSquizzy:** Billy Connolly; **Porcupine/Others:** Matthew W. Taylor; **Bobbie:** Georgia Engel; **Serge/Deni:** Danny Mann; **Gordy:** Gordon Tootoosis; **Ian:** Patrick Warburton; **Mr. Weenie:** Cody Cameron; **Rosie:** Nika Futterman; **Hunter:** Jack McGee; **Maria:** Michelle Murdocca; **O'Toole:** Fergal Reilly

*Additional Voices*

Kirk Baily, Jack Blessing, Ranjani Brow, David Cowgill, Caitlin Cutt, Elisa Gabrielli, Jackie Gonneau, Wendy Hoffman, Scott Menville, Renee Robert, André Sogliuzzo, Hans Tester, Paul Westerberg

A female forest ranger embarks on a desperate search to locate her 900-pound domesticated grizzly bear who gets lost during hunting season but is saved by a fast-talking, one-antlered mule deer who teaches him about life in the woods.

**PN:** Former Disney animator Roger Allers codirected this CGI-animated buddy comedy based on the edgy humor of cartoonist Steve Moore (*In the Bleachers*) for Sony Pictures Animation—its first feature-length animated venture—featuring comedian Martin Lawrence as the voice of the annoyed grizzly bear, Boog, and actor Ashton Kutcher as his one-horned mule deer pal, Elliot. Released to more than 3,800 theaters domestically, the cartoon comedy rustled up more than $23 million in ticket sales its first weekend from more than 5,000 screens at 3,833 theaters, including nearly $1.5 million from 66 IMAX screens in the United States that simultaneously screened a remastered version in IMAX 3-D, and more than $160 million worldwide. Coincidentally, the Martin Lawrence-Ashton Kutcher feature topped all features that weekend, including Kutcher's live-action Disney drama, *The Guardian*, costarring Kevin Costner, which finished in second place.

## ◉ OSMOSIS JONES (2001)

A Conundrum Entertainment Production released by Warner Bros. **p:** Peter Farrelly, Bobby Farrelly, Bradley Thomas, Zak Penn, Dennis Edwards; **l/a dir:** Peter Farrelly, Bobby Farrelly; **anim dir:** Piet Kroon, Tom Sito; **scr:** Marc Hyman; **m:** Randy Edelman; **superv anim:** Richard Bazley, Dave Brewster, Ricardo Curtis, Tony Fucile, Wendy Perdue, Deean Williams; **lead anim:** Stephan Franck, Lennie K. Graves, Duncan Marjoribanks, Mike Nguyen. **Running time:** 98 minutes. **Released:** August 10, 2001.

### Live-Action Cast

**Frank:** Bill Murray; **Mrs. Boyd:** Molly Shannon; **Bob:** Chris Elliott; **Shane:** Elena Franklin; **Zookeeper Superintendent:** Danny Murphy; **Zookeeper:** Jack McCullough; **Volcano Lady:** Kathy Wege; **Oyster Boy:** Will Dunn; **School Janitor:** Jackie Flynn

### Voices

**Osmosis Jones:** Chris Rock; **Thrax:** Laurence Fishburne; **Drix:** David Hyde Pierce; **Leah:** Brandy Norwood; **The Mayor:** William Shatner; **Tom Colonic:** Ron Howard; **Kidney Rock:** Kenny Olson; **The Chief:** Joel Silver

A cocky renegade white blood cell cop, Osmosis Jones, teams up with a 12-hour cold tablet, Drix, to zap the deadly virus Thrax, which threatens the life of a recently widowed, mundane zookeeper, Frank Detorri, who catches it after consuming a germ-infested hard-boiled egg that a chimp throws away in this live-action/animated comedy.

**PN:** Produced and directed by the famed live-action comedy brother team of Peter and Bobby Farrelly of *There's Something About Mary* and *Dumb and Dumber* fame, with animation sequences directed by Piet Kroon and Tom Sito, the film's gross-out humor and subject matter didn't translate well at the box office where it earned only $13,483,306 for a film but cost $75 million to produce. Actor Bill Murray played the widower zookeeper, Frank Detorri, in live-action sequences, while comedian Chris Rock provided the voice of germ-fighter Osmosis Jones, with David Hyde Pierce of TV's *Fraser* fame as the cold pill Drix. The combination live-action/animated feature reportedly had the most interplay of live-action and animation since Walt Disney Studios' acclaimed live-action/animated film *Who Framed Roger Rabbit*.

## ◉ OVER THE HEDGE (2006)

A DreamWorks SKG/DreamWorks Animation Production released by Paramount Pictures and United International Pic-tures. **p:** Bonnie Arnold; **exec prod:** Bill Damaschke, Jim Cox; **d:** Tim Johnson, Karey Kirkpatrick; **scr:** Karey Kirkpatrick, Lorne Cameron, David Hoselton, Len Blum; **st:** Chris Poche (based on the comic strip, "Over the Hedge," by Michael Fry and T. Lewis); **m:** Rupert Gregson-Williams. Songs: "Family of Me," "Heist" and "Still." **Running time:** 87 minutes. **Released:** May 19, 2006.

### Voices

**RJ:** Bruce Willis; **Verne:** Garry Shandling; **Hammy:** Steve Carell; **Stella:** Wanda Sykes; **Ozzie:** William Shatner; **Vincent:** Nick Nolte; **Dwayne:** Thomas Haden Church; **Gladys:** Allison Janney; **Lou:** Eugene Levy; **Penny:** Catherine O'Hara; **Heather:** Avril Lavigne; **Tiger:** Omid Djalili; **Bucky:** Sami Kirkpatrick; **Spike:** Shane Baumel; **Quillo:** Madison Davenport; **Mackenzie:** Zoe Randol; **Shelby:** Jessica Di Cicco; **Debbie:** Debra Wilson; **Police Officer:** Sean Bishop; **Janis:** Jeannie Elias; **Timmy:** Kejon Kesse; **Skeeter:** Paul Butcher; **BBQ Barry:** Sean Yazbeck; **Ranger:** Geoffrey Pomeroy; **Dr. Dennis:** Joel McCrary; **Lunch Table Larry:** Lee Beinstock; **Nugent the Dog:** Brian Stepanek

### Additional Voices

Steve Alterman, Kirk Baily, Jessie Flower, Nicholas Guest, David Hiller, Bridget Hoffman, Sandy Holt, Talula Holt, Erin Lander, Jordan Orr, Michelle Ruff, Greyson Spann, April Struebing, Marcelo Tubert, Ariel Winter

A fast-talking conniving raccoon RJ and his cautious turtle pal, Verne, along with their forest denizens—a hibernating bear, Vincent; a father-daughter pair of opossums, Ozzie and Heather; a manic squirrel, Hammy; a sarcastic skunk, Stella and a pair of porcupines, Lou and Penny—form an unbreakable bond when an housing development encroaches upon their habitat and they exploit their new world.

**PN:** Featuring an all-star voice cast of Bruce Willis, Nick Nolte, Steve Carell, Allison Janney, William Shatner, Wanda Sykes and Avril Lavigne, this PG-rated, digitally animated Dream-Works Animation feature, based on Michael Fry and T. Lewis's popular comic strip, received rave reviews from critics across the board and pulled in an amazing $38,457,003 during its first three days of release, coming in second to Sony Pictures' and Ron Howard's live-action drama *The Da Vinci Code*, based on author Dan Brown's best-selling book of the same name.

## ◉ THE PAGEMASTER (1994)

A 20th Century Fox/Turner Pictures/David Kirschner Production released by 20th Century Fox. **p:** David Kirschner, Paul Gertz (animation producers: David J. Steinberg, Barry Weiss; live-action scenes produced by Michael R. Joyce); **d:** Maurice Hunt (animation), Joe Johnston (live action); **st:** David Kirschner, David Casci; **scr:** David Casci, David Kirschner, Ernie Contreras; **m:** James Horner. Songs: "Dream Away" and "Whatever You Imagine." **Running time:** 75 minutes. **Released:** December 23, 1994.

### Cast/Voices

**Richard Tyler:** Macaulay Culkin; **Mr. Dewey and the Pagemaster:** Christopher Lloyd; **Alan Tyler:** Ed Begley Jr.; **Claire Tyler:** Mel Harris; **Adventure:** Patrick Stewart; **Fantasy:** Whoopi Goldberg; **Horror and Dragon:** Frank Welker; **Dr. Jekyll & Mr. Hyde:** Leonard Nimoy; **Captain Ahab:** George Hearn; **Jamaican Pirates:** Dorian Harewood; **George Merry:** Ed Gilbert; **Pirates:** Richard Erdmann, Fernando Escandon, Robert Picardo; **Tom Morgan:** Phil Hartman; **Long John Silver:** Jim Cummings; **Queen of Hearts:** B.J. Ward; **Neighborhood kids:** Canan J. Howell, Alexis Kirschner, Jessica Kirschner, Guy Mansker, Brandon McKay, Stephen Sheehan

Richard Tyler, a bookwormish young boy, is transported to an animated world in which fictional characters from his favorite books come to life—Captain Ahab, Long John Silver, Dr. Jekyll (and Mr. Hyde)—and knowledge is the only key to get him home in this live-action/animated adventure.

## PANDA AND THE MAGIC SERPENT (1961)

A Toei Animation Co. Ltd. Production released by Globe Releasing Company. **p:** Hiroshi Okawa, Hideyuki Takahashi, Sanae Yamamoto; **d:** Taiji Yabushita, Kazuhiko Okabe; **scr:** Taiji Yabushita, Yasuji Mori (based on the book, *The White Snake Enchantress*); **m:** Chuji Kinoshira, Msayoshi Ikeda; **anim:** Yasuo Otsuka, Kazuko Nakamura, Reiko Okukyama, Yusaku Sakamoto, Taku Sugiyama, Gisaburo Sugii. **Running time:** 80 minutes. **Released:** July 8, 1961.

*Voices*

**Isao Ota:** Richard Epcar; **Boat Captain:** Steve Kramer; **Hitomi Misaki:** Julie Maddalena; **Police Captain:** Dan Martin; **Kiichi Goto:** Daran Norris; **Baseball Player:** Tony Oliver; **Toshiro Kurisuo:** Simon Prescott; **Shizuo Miyaomori:** Steven Chester Prince; **Noa Izumi:** Michelle Ruff; **Kieko Misaki:** Helen Storm; **Takeshi Kusumi:** Alfred Thor; **Col. Goro Ishihara:** Kirk Thorton; **Saeko Misaki:** Kari Wahlgren; **Shinichiro Hata:** Dave Wittenberg.

Fantasy adventure based on an ancient Chinese folk tale in which a young boy befriends a snake he rescues and turns it into his pet who, later in his life, is reincarnated as a beautiful maiden whom he marries but that a wicked magician believes is possessed with an evil spirit and tries to kill.

**PN:** Originally produced and released in Japan in October 1958 under the title of *Hakuja Den*, this redubbed English version, released in the United States in 1961, was part of a wave of animated features imported into this country in the 1960s by Toei, which wanted to become known as "the Disney of the East."

## THE PEBBLE AND THE PENGUIN (1995)

A Don Bluth Limited Production released by Metro-Goldwyn-Mayer/United Artists. **p:** Russell Boland; **d:** Don Bluth, Gary Goldman; **exec prod:** James Butterworth; **scr:** Rachel Koretsky, Steve Whitestone; **m/sc:** Mark Watters (with original songs by Barry Manilow and Bruce Sussman); **dir anim:** John Pomeroy, Len Simon, Richard Brazley, Silvia Hoefnagels, Ralf Palmer, John Hill, John Power. **Songs:** "Now and Forever," "Sometimes I Wonder," "The Good Ship Misery," "Don't Make Me Laugh" and "Looks I Got a Friend." **Running time:** 74 minutes. **Released:** April 12, 1995.

*Voices*

**Narrator:** Shani Wallis; **Chubby/Gentoo:** S. Scott Bullock; **Hubie:** Martin Short; **Marina:** Annie Golden; **Priscilla/Chinstrap:** Louise Vallance; **Pola/Chinstrap:** Pat Music; **Gwynne/Chinstrap:** Angeline Ball; **Timmy:** Kendall Cunningham; **Petra:** Alissa King; **Beany:** Michael Nunes; **Drake:** Tim Curry; **Scrawny:** Neil Ross; **King:** Philip L. Clarke; **Megellenic #1:** B.J. Ward; **Mellegenic #2:** Hamilton Camp; **McCallister:** Stanley Jones; **Royal/Tika:** Will Ryan; **Rocko:** James Belushi

Escaping to Antarctica with his streetwise friend Rocko, Hubie, a lovable but introverted penguin, plans to present his betrothal pebble to the bird of his dreams in this Don Bluth–animated feature, with original songs by award-winning singer/songwriter Barry Manilow.

**PN:** American filmgoers never warmed up to this film, which was the last feature to originate from Don Bluth's Irish studio. It opened the same weekend as Disney's *A Goofy Movie* and took in only $3.9 million. The original story for the film was based on mating habits observed among Antarctica's Adelie penguins,

which engage in an elaborate ritual involving brightly colored stones. A special added attraction, featured with the full-length animated feature, was an all-new Pink Panther cartoon, "Driving Mr. Pink," featuring a new character: Voodoo Man. Five months after its theatrical release, Warner Bros. released the film on home video. During its first two weeks, it ranked number one in sales, according to VideoScan, Inc.

## PERFECT BLUE (1999)

A Madhouse Production released by Manga Entertainment. **p:** Haruyo Kanesaku, Hiroaki Inoue, Masao Murayama, Yutaka Maseba; **exec prod:** Marvin Gleicher, Laurence Guinness, Koshiro Kanda, Yuichi Tsurumi; **d:** Satoshi Kon; **scr:** Sadayuki Murai (based on a novel by Yoshihazu Takeuchi); **m:** Masahiro Ikumi; **anim:** Koichi Arai, Nobumasa Arakawa, Shigero Fujita, Hiroshi Haga, Shinji Hashimoto, Takeshi Honda, Mitsuo Iso, Kumiko Kawana, Yoshihiro Kitano, Makota Koga, Masahiro Morita, Morifumi Naka, Katsuichi Nakayama, Toshiya Nidome, Hideki Nimura, Takuo Noda, Michiyo Suzuki, Masaharu Tada, Shin'ya Takahashi, Kunio Takahide, Hikaru Takanashi, Makoto Yamada, Takaaki Yamashita. **Running time:** 80 minutes. **Released:** October 8, 1999.

*Voices*

**Mima Kirigoe:** Ruby Marlowe; **Tadakoro:** Barry Stigler; **Rumi:** Wendee Lee; **Me-Mania:** Bob Marx; **Director:** Richard Plantagenet; **Mureno:** Jamieson Price; **Yamashiro:** Kirk Thorton; **Cham Manager:** Dylan Tully.

A young female pop star-turned-actress, who is being stalked by a killer, thinks she is losing her mind when her nightmares become reality in this Japanese animated feature.

## PETER PAN (1953)

A Walt Disney Production released by RKO Radio Pictures. **p:** Walt Disney; **d:** Hamilton Luske, Clyde Geronimi, Wilfred Jackson; **dir anim:** Milt Kahl, Frank Thomas, Wolfgang Reitherman, Ward Kimball, Eric Larson, Ollie Johnston, Marc Davis, John Lounsbery, Les Clark, Norman Ferguson; **st:** Ted Sears, Bill Peet, Joe Rinaldi, Erdman Penner, Winston Hibler, Milt Banta, Ralph Wright, Bill Cottreoll (adapted from the play and books by Sir James M. Barrie); **m/sc:** Oliver Wallace. **Songs:** "The Elegant Captain Hook," "The Second Star to the Right," "What Makes the Red Man Red?" "You Can Fly, You Can Fly, You Can Fly," "Your Mother and Mine," "A Pirate's Life," "March of the Lost Boys (Tee Dum Tee Dee)" and "Never Smile at a Crocodile." **Running time:** 77 minutes. **Released:** February 5, 1953.

*Voices*

**Peter Pan:** Bobby Driscoll; **Wendy:** Kathryn Beaumont; **Captain Hook/Mr. Darling:** Hans Conried; **Mr. Smee and other pirates:** Bill Thompson; **Mrs. Darling:** Heather Angel; **John Darling:** Paul Collins; **Michael:** Tommy Luske; **Indian Chief:** Candy Candido; **Narrator:** Tom Conway

Left in the care of a nursemaid, Wendy, Michael and John, the children of Mr. and Mrs. Darling of Bloomsbury, London, are swept away to fascinating adventures with fairy-tale hero Peter Pan, who, along the way, saves the children from his longtime nemesis, Captain Hook.

## PETE'S DRAGON (1977)

A Walt Disney Production released by Buena Vista. **p:** Ron Miller, Jerome Courtland; **d:** Don Chaffey; **anim dir:** Don Bluth; **w:** Malcolm Marmorstein (based on a story by Seton I. Miller and S.S. Field); **m:** Irwin Kostal. **Songs:** "Candle on the Water," "I Saw a

Dragon," "It's Not Easy," "Every Little Piece," "The Happiest Home in These Hills," "Brazzle Dazzle Day," "Boo Boo Bopbopbop (I Love You Too)," "There's Room for Everyone," "Passamashloddy" and "Bill of Sale." **Running time:** 134 minutes. **Released:** November 3, 1977.

*Cast*
**Nora:** Helen Reddy; **Dr. Terminus:** Jim Dale; **Lampie:** Mickey Rooney; **Hoagy:** Red Buttons; **Lena Gogan:** Shelley Winters; **Pete:** Sean Marshall; **Miss Taylor:** Jean Kean; **The Mayor:** Jim Backus; **Merle:** Charles Tyner; **Grover:** Gary Morgan; **Willie:** Jeff Conway; **Paul:** Cal Bartlett; **Captain:** Walter Barnes; **Store Proprietor:** Robert Easton; **Man with Visor:** Roger Price; **Old Sea Captain:** Robert Foulk; **Egg Man:** Ben Wrigley; **Cement Man:** Joe Ross; **Fishermen:** Al Checco, Henry Slate, Jack Collins

*Voices*
**Elliott the Dragon:** Charlie Callas

Pete, an orphaned little boy, runs away from his foster family and makes friends with an animated dragon named Elliott, who becomes the child's new companion.

**PN:** Elliott was the film's only animated star, appearing in live-action scenes with characters throughout the film. The film was cut by 30 minutes for its 1984 rerelease.

## ◎ THE PHANTOM TOLLBOOTH (1970)

A Chuck Jones Production released by Metro-Goldwyn-Mayer. **p:** Chuck Jones, Abe Levitow, Les Goldman; **d:** Chuck Jones, Abe Levitow, David Monahan; **w:** Chuck Jones, Sam Rosen (based on the book by Norton Juster); **m:** Dean Elliott; **anim dir:** Ben Washam, Hal Ambro, George Nicholas. **Songs:** "Milo's Song," "Time Is a Gift," "Word Market," "Numbers Are the Only Things That Count," "Rhyme and Reason Reign," "Don't Say There's Nothing to Do in the Doldrums" and "Noise, Noise, Beautiful Noise." **Running time:** 90 minutes. **Released:** November 7, 1970.

*Cast*
**Milo:** Butch Patrick

*Voices*
**Tock:** Shep Menken; **King Azaz, The Mathemagician:** Hans Conried; **Officer Short Shrift/Dodecahedron/Word Man/Demon of Insincerity/Lethargians/Minsters:** Mel Blanc; **Humbug/Poet:** Les Tremayne; **Faintly Macabre/Princess of Pure Reason:** June Foray; **Whether Man/Senses Taker/Terrible Trivium/Gelatinous Giant:** Daws Butler; **Spelling Bee/Chroma the Great/Ministers:** Cliff Norton; **Dr. Kakofanus A. Dischord/ Tollbooth Speaker Voice/Lethargians:** Larry Thor; **Awful DYNN/Lethargians:** Candy Candido; **Princess of Sweet Rhyme/Teacher Voice:** Patti Gilbert; **Lethargians:** Thurl Ravenscroft; **Overbearing Know-It-All:** Herb Vigran

Milo, a young lad bored with life, is taken to the Kingdom of Wisdom where he embarks on a magical journey with new friends, Tock and Humburg, to rescue the Princesses of Rhyme and Reason. He returns home through the tollbooth in his room from which he came. The film opens and closes with live-action sequences of Milo, played by *Munsters* star Butch Patrick, who is transformed into an animated character once he is transported into this land of make-believe.

**PN:** Chuck Jones directed this film, the first full-length feature of his career and the first for MGM.

## ◎ PIGLET'S BIG MOVIE (2003)

A Walt Disney Pictures/DisneyToons Studios Production released by Buena Vista Pictures. **d:** Francis Glebas; **p:** Michelle Papalardo-Robinson; **scr:** Brian Hohlfeld (with additional screenplay material by Ted Henning adapted from and inspired by the works of A.A. Milne); **m:** Carl Johnson; **m/l:** Carly Simon, Richard M. Sherman, Robert B. Sherman; **anim dir:** Takeshi Atomurra; **assist dir:** Furno Maczono, Yumiko Suzuki. **Songs:** "Winnie the Pooh," "The Wonderful Thing about Tiggers," "If I Wasn't So Small (The Piglet Song)," "Mother's Intuition," "Sing Ho for the Life of a Bear," "The More It Snows," "With a Few Good Friends," "With a Few Good Friends," "The More I Look Inside" and "Comforting to Know." **Running time:** 75 minutes. **Released:** March 21, 2003.

*Voices*
**Piglet:** John Fiedler; **Winnie the Pooh/Tigger:** Jim Cummings; **Owl:** Andre Stojka; **Kanga:** Kath Soucie; **Roo:** Nikita Hopkins; **Eeyore:** Peter Cullen; **Rabbit:** Samson; **Christopher Robin:** Tom Wheatley

After big-hearted Piglet, who's feeling down in the dumps, goes missing, Winnie the Pooh and his Hundred Acre Wood pals use Piglet's Book of Memories to locate him while realizing his importance in their lives.

**PN:** During a protracted legal battle between the studio and the estate of "Winnie the Pooh" creator, A.A. Milne, over the rights to the characters, Walt Disney Studios continued to mine the "Winnie the Pooh" franchise as it had done since the 1960s by producing a series of award-winning cartoon shorts and later television cartoon series and specials and produced this full-length animated feature adapted from the popular tales by Milne. Unlike previous film and television versions of the "Pooh" characters, this 2-D animated feature was hardly a huge financial success, grossing a mere $23,073,611 in ticket sales in the United States following its release.

## ◎ PINOCCHIO (1940)

A Walt Disney Production released by RKO Radio Pictures. **p:** Walt Disney; **superv dir:** Ben Sharpsteen, Hamilton Luske; **seq dir:** Bill Roberts, Norman Ferguson, Jack Kinney, Wilfred Jackson, T. Hee; **anim dir:** Fred Moore, Franklin Thomas, Milton Kahl, Vladimir Tytla, Ward Kimball, Arthur Babbitt, Eric Larson, Wolfgang Reitherman; **st (adaptation):** Ted Sears, Otto Englander, Webb Smith, William Cottrell, Joseph Sabo, Erdman Penner, Aurelius Battaglia (based on the story by Collodi a.k.a. Carlo Lorenzini); **m/l:** Leigh Harline, Ned Washington, Paul J. Smith. **Songs:** "When You Wish upon a Star," "Little Woodenhead," "Hi Diddle Dee Dee (An Actor's Life for Me)," "I've Got No Strings" and "Give a Little Whistle." **Running time:** 88 minutes. **Released:** February 7, 1940.

*Voices*
**Pinocchio:** Dickie Jones; **Geppetto:** Christian Rub; **Jiminy Crickett:** Cliff Edwards; **The Blue Fairy:** Evelyn Venable; **J. Worthington Foulfellow:** Walter Catlett; **Gideon:** Mel Blanc; **Lampwick:** Frankie Darro; **Stromboli and the Coachman:** Charles Judels; **Barker:** Don Brodie

The story of toymaker Geppetto and his wooden puppet creation, Pinocchio, became Walt Disney's second feature-length attempt in three years. Given life by the Blue Fairy, Pinocchio is joined by Jiminy Cricket, appointed as "his conscience," to lead him through real-life adventures of boyhood.

## ◎ PINOCCHIO AND THE EMPEROR OF THE NIGHT (1987)

A Filmation Associates Production released by New World Pictures. **p:** Lou Scheimer; **d:** Hal Sutherland; **w:** Robby London, Barry O'Brien, Dennis O'Flaherty (based on a story by Dennis

O'Flaherty from *The Adventures of Pinocchio* by Collodi a.k.a. Carlo Lorenzini); **m:** Anthony Marinelli, Brian Banks; **m/l:** Will Jennings, Barry Mann, Steve Tyrell, Anthony Marinelli; **superv anim:** John Celestri, Chuck Harvey, Kamoon Song. **Songs:** "Love Is the Light Inside Your Heart," "You're a Star," "Do What Makes You Happy" and "Neon Cabaret." **Running time:** 91 minutes. **Released:** December 25, 1987.

*Voices*
**Scalawag:** Edward Asner; **Geppetto:** Tom Bosley; **Twinkle:** Lana Beeson; **Emperor of the Night:** James Earl Jones; **Fairy Godmother:** Rickie Lee Jones; **Gee Willikers:** Don Knotts; **Pinocchio:** Scott Grimes; **Bee-Atrice:** Linda Gary; **Lt. Grumblebee:** Jonathan Harris; **Puppetino:** William Windom; **Igor:** Frank Welker

Woodcarver mentor Geppetto assigns former puppet creation Pinocchio to deliver a jewel box to the mayor. Despite a friendly warning from Gee Willikers, a toy glowbug brought to life by the Blue Fairy, Pinocchio becomes sidetracked along the way. He encounters a shifty raccoon and monkey assistant who con him out of the jewel box. Ashamed, he joins the traveling circus and continues search for the missing jewel box.

**PN:** Despite a concerted effort to market the film to fans of the original Disney *Pinocchio*, this Filmation-produced full-length animated feature grossed only $3 million in ticket revenue.

## ◉ PINOCCHIO IN OUTER SPACE (1965)

A Swallow/Belvision Production released by Universal Pictures. **p:** Norm Prescott, Fred Ladd; **d:** Ray Goossens; **w:** Fred Laderman (based on an idea by Prescott from the story by Carlo Collodi); **m:** F. Leonard, H. Dobelaere, E. Schurmann; **m/l:** Robert Sharp, Arthur Korb. **Running Time:** 90 minutes. **Released:** December 22, 1965.

*Voices*
**Nurtle the Turtle:** Arnold Stang; **Pinocchio:** Peter Lazer; **Gepetto:** Jess Cain; **Blue Fairy:** Mavis Mims; **G. Codline Sharp:** Conrad Jameson; **Blue Fairy's Mother:** Minerva Pious; **Groovy:** Cliff Owens

*Additional Voices*
Norman Rose, Kevin Kennedy

Turned back into a puppet by Gepetto, Pinocchio becomes friends with an outer-space creature, Nurtle the Turtle, whose spaceship has accidentally landed on Earth. Pinocchio helps Nurtle get back on course and joins him on a trip to Mars where they encounter the menacing Astro the Flying Whale, who plans to invade Earth.

**PN:** Film was titled *Pinocchio dans le space* for its Belgian release. Working title: *Pinocchio's Adventure in Outer Space*.

## ◉ PIPPI LONGSTOCKING (1997)

An AB Svensk Filmindustri/Iduna Film/TFC Trickcompany and Nelvana Limited Production released by Legacy Releasing Corp. **p:** Waldemar Bergendahl, Hasmi Giakoumis, Merle-Anne Ridley, Michael Shaack; **d:** Clive Smith; **exec prod:** Michael Hirsh, Patrick Loubert, Clive Smith, Lennart Wilkund (co-exec prod: David Ferguson); **scr:** Catharina Stackelberg (with additional dialogue written by Frank Nissen and Ken Sobol, based on the books by Astrid Lindgren); **m:** Anders Bergund; **anim dir:** Ute V. Minchon-Pohl, Edson Basarin, Robin Budd, Bill Giggle. **Songs:** "What Shall I Do Today," "Hey-Ho I'm Pippi," "Recipe for Life," "A Bowler and a New Gold Tooth," "Pluttifikation" and "The Schottish." **Running time:** 75 minutes. **Released:** August 22, 1997.

*Voices*
**Pippi Longstocking:** Melissa Altro; **Mrs. Prysselius:** Catherine O'Hara; **Teacher:** Carole Pope; **Thunder-Karlsson:** Dave Thomas; **Captain Longstocking:** Gordon Pinset; **Dunder-Karlsson:** Peter Karlsson; **Constable Kling:** Jan Sigurd; **Constable Klang:** Phillip Williams; **Mrs. Settergren:** Karen Bernstein; **Mr. Settergren:** Martin Zavut; **Mrs. Prysselius:** Wallis Grahn; **Tommy:** Noah Reid; **Blom:** Wayne Robson; **Annika (vocals):** Judy Tate; **Mr. Nillson/Dog:** Richard Binsley; **O'Malley/King:** Rick Jones; **Fridolf:** Chris Wiggins; **Mrs. Klang:** Mari Trainer; **Mrs. Kling:** Elva Mai Hoover; **Ringmaster:** Phillip Williams; **Snake Lady:** Melleny Melody; **Adolp:** Howard Jerome; **Kids:** Kyle Farley; **Zachary Spider:** Brown Smith; **Group Singers:** Brent Barkman, Emily Barlow, Marleve Herington

A nine-year-old girl lives the way all children wish they could—in charge of their own destiny—in this animated musical adaptation of Astrid Lindgren's popular children's books.

**PN:** This Canadian-Swedish–produced animated feature was shown in limited release in the United States, opening at only 73 theaters. Consequently, the film did not muster up much in ticket sales, producing a total box-office gross of $478,113.

## ◉ THE PLAGUE DOGS (1983)

A Nepenthe Productions released by United International Pictures. **p, d & w:** Martin Rosen; **m:** Patrick Gleason; **anim dir:** Tony Guy, Colin White. **Running time:** 103 minutes. **Released:** December 17, 1983.

*Voices*
**Snitter:** John Hurt; **Rowf:** Christopher Benjamin; **The Tod:** James Bolam; **Dr. Boycott:** Nigel Hawthorne; **Tyson/Wag:** Warren Mitchell; **Stephen Powell:** Bernard Bepton; **Laboratory Assistant:** Brian Stirner; **Lynn Driver:** Penelope Lee; **Farmer:** Geoffrey Matthews; **Farmer's Wife:** Barbara Leigh-Hunt; **Don:** John Bennett; **Williamson:** John Franklyn-Robbins; **Editor:** Bill Maynard; **Robert Lindsay:** Malcolm Terris; **Pekinese:** Judy Geeson; **Civil Servant #1:** Phillip Locke; **Civil Servant #2:** Brian Spink; **Civil Servant #3:** Tony Church; **Civil Servant #4:** Anthony Valentine; **Civil Servant #5:** William Lucas; **Phyllis Dawson:** Dandy Nichols; **Vera Dawson:** Rosemary Leach; **Major:** Patrick Stewart; **Animal Vocalizations:** Percy Edwards

Two dogs, one of whom already was the victim of experimental brain surgery, escape from a government research establishment in England's Lake District. Their mission is to find a kind master and an island where they may be safe from pursuit and their own dread.

**PN:** Filmmaker Martin Rosen, of *Watership Down* fame, produced this film, which was originally previewed in London two years before its American release. On December 17, 1983, the film had a test engagement in Seattle, Washington, before premiering in New York in January 1985.

## ◉ POCAHONTAS (1995)

A Walt Disney Production released by Walt Disney Pictures. **p:** James Pentecost; **d:** Mike Gabriel, Eric Goldberg; **scr:** Carl Binder, Susannah Grant, Philip LaZebnik; **m:** Alan Menken, Stephen Schwartz; **superv anim:** Renee Holt-Bird, Glen Keane, Duncan Marjoribanks, David Pruiksma. **Songs:** "Virginia Company," "Ship at Sea," "Steady as the Beating Drum," "Just Around the Riverbend," "Grand-mother Willow," "Listen with Your Heart," "Mine, Mine, Mine," "Colors of the Wind," "Savages, Part 1," "Savages, Part 2," "I'll Never See Him Again," "Pocahontas," "Council Meeting," "Percy's Bath," "River's Edge," "Skirmish," "Getting Acquainted," "Ratcliffe's Plan," "Picking Corn,"

"Warriors Arrive," "John Smith Sneaks Out," "Execution," "Farewell" and "If I Never Knew You." **Running time:** 81 minutes. **Released:** June 23, 1995.

### Voices

**John Smith:** Mel Gibson; **Pocahontas:** Irene Bedard; **Lon:** Joe Baker; **Thomas:** Christian Bale; **Ben:** Billy Connolly; **Kocoum:** James Apaumut Fall; **Grandmother Willow:** Linda Hunt; **Meeko:** Jon Kassir; **Pocahontas (singing):** Judy Kuhn; **Percy:** Danny Mann; **Powhatan:** Russell Means; **Governor Ratcliffe/Wiggins:** David Odgen Stiers; **Nakoma:** Michelle St. John; **Kekata:** Gordon Tootoosis; **Flit:** Frank Welker

A courageous and free-spirited Indian woman defies her father by falling in love with Captain John Smith, leader of a rag-tag band of English sailors and soldiers to the New World who plunder its riches, even though she has already been pledged to marry a great Indian warrior.

**PN:** Disney premiered this feature in New York's Central Park, attracting more than 100,000 filmgoers. Overall, the film drummed up less business at the box office than Disney's previous blockbusters *Beauty and the Beast* and *The Lion King*, as it faced stronger-than-usual competition from *Casper*, *Batman Forever* and *Mighty Morphin Power Rangers: The Movie*, released during the summer. Budgeted at $55 million, the film grossed $141.6 million nationally and $342.6 million worldwide.

### ◎ POKÉMON 4-EVER (2002)

A Pokémon USA Inc. and 4Kids Entertainment Production released by Miramax Films. **p:** Yukako Matsusako, Takemoto Mori, Choji Yoshikawa; **d:** Kunihiko Yuyama, Jim Malone (English version); **scr:** Hideki Sonoda (based on characters created by Satoshi Tajiri). **Running time:** 79 minutes. **Released:** October 11, 2002.

### Voices

**Ash Ketchum:** Veronica Taylor; **Misty/Jesse:** Rachael Lillis; **Brock/James:** Eric Stuart; **Meowth:** Madeleine Blaustein; **Pikachu:** Ikue Ootani; **The Iron Masked Marauder/Other Voices:** Dan Green; **Professor Samuel Oak:** Stan Hart; **Samuel "Sammy" Oak:** Tara Jayne; **Narrator:** Phillip Bartlett

### Additional Voices

Roxanne Beck, Amy Birnbaum, Ken Gates, Roger Kay, Ed Paul, Kayzie Rogers, Marc Thompson, Kerry Williams

Ash and his trainer friends, Misty and Brock, aid a young boy and new Pokémon creature, Celebi, also known as "The Voice of the Forest," flee an evil bounty hunter who plans to create a destructive forest monster.

**PN:** The first film released by its new distributor, Miramax Films, this fourth installment in the Pokémon film series hardly produced a blip on the radar screen at the box office, where it took in only $1,669,596 in U.S. ticket sales.

### ◎ POKÉMON HEROES (2003)

A Pokémon USA and 4Kids Entertainment Presentation of a Pikachu Project 2002 Production released by Miramax Films. **p:** Yukako Matsusako, Takemoto Mori, Choji Yoshikawa, Kathryn A. Borland; **d:** Kunihiko Yuyama, Jim Malone (English version); **scr:** Hideki Sonoda (based on characters created by Satoshi Tajiri). **Running time:** 79 minutes. **Released:** May 16, 2003.

### Voices

**Ash Ketchum:** Veronica Taylor; **Misty/Jessie:** Rachael Lillis; **Brock/James/Lorenzo:** Eric Stuart; **Meowth:** Madeleine Blaustein; **Pikachu:** Ikue Ootani; **Latios:** Masashi Ebara; **Annie:** Megan Hollingshead; **Natalie:** Ashley Fox Linton; **Bianca/Oakley:** Lisa Ortiz

### Additional Voices

Ken Gates, Wayne Grayson, Tara Jayne, Ed Paul, Kayzie Rogers, Michael Sinterniklaas, Kerry Williams

Lead trainer Ash, his loyal Pokémon, Pikachu, and fellow trainers Misty and Brock square off with a pair of nefarious teenaged Pokémon, Annie and Oakley, who plan to steal a precious and powerful jewel guarded by the winged brother-and-sister pair of Latios and Latias on the island city of Alto Mare for the villainous mastermind, Giovanni, in this fifth feature-length adventure.

**PN:** Further proof that the Pokémon craze was over in America, at least as a major film franchise, this fifth and final feature was a huge disappointment, amassing a meager $746,381 in box-office revenue in the United States, but managed to make the Academy Awards' short list of nominees in 2003 for best animated feature. Subsequently, a sixth and seventh movie were produced as direct-to-video releases in the United States.

### ◎ POKÉMON THE FIRST MOVIE: MEWTWO STRIKES BACK (1999)

A Kids WB!/Pikachu Project '98-Shogakukan Inc. Production in association with 4Kids Entertainment released by Warner Bros. Family Entertainment. **p:** Tomoyuki Igarashi, Takemoto Mori, Norman J. Grossfeld (English version); **d:** Kunihiko Yuyama, Michael Haigney; **scr:** Takeshi Shudo (based on characters created by Satoshi Tajiri). **Running time:** 75 minutes. **Released:** November 12, 1999.

### Voices

**Ash Ketchum:** Veronica Taylor; **Misty/Jessie/Jigglypuff:** Rachael Lillis; **Brock/James/Squirtle/Pikachu/Raichu/Other Voices:** Ikue Ootani; **Narrator/Mewtwo:** Phillip Bartlett; **Meowth/Other Voices:** Madeleine Blaustein; **Meowth:** Tommy Karlsen; **Giovanni/Cubone/Weezing:** Ted Lewis; **Officer Jenny/Nurse Joy:** Amy Birnbaum; **Mewtwo's Servant:** Megan Hollingshead; **Vulpix/Ninetales/Bulbasaur/Venusaur/Other Voices:** Tara Jayne; **Neesha:** Lisa Ortiz; **Giovanni/Corey:** Ed Paul; **Arbok/Hitmonlee/Onix/Victreebel/Farfetch'd:** Kayzie Rogers; **Mew:** Koichi Yamadera; **Fergus:** Jimmy Zoppi

A mysterious mistress invites eager Pokémon trainers to a remote island competition to help conquer the world.

**PN:** This Japanese production in association with Kids WB! and 4Kids Entertainment was the first full-length feature, based on the huge commercial franchise and Japanese television series starring the characters created by Satoshi Tajiri, that also became a popular import broadcast in the United States on the WB! network. A huge financial success at the box office that grossed $85,744,662 in the United States and $163,644,662 worldwide, the film inspired four less successful sequels, *Pokémon the Movie 2000* (2000), *Pokémon 3: The Movie* (2001), *Pokémon 4-Ever* (2002) and *Pokémon Heroes* (2003), which made a short list of animated features contending for an Academy Award nomination for best animated feature.

### ◎ POKÉMON THE MOVIE 2000 (2000)

A Kids WB!/Pikachu Project '99-Shogakukan Inc. Production in association with 4Kids Entertainment released by Warner Bros. Family Entertainment. **p:** Yukako Matsusako, Takemoto Mori, Choji Yoshikawa; **d:** Kunihiko Yuyama, Michael Haigney (English version); **scr:** Takeshi Shudo (based on characters created by Satoshi Tajiri). **Running time:** 100 minutes. **Released:** July 21, 2000.

### Voices

**Ash Ketchum/Mrs. Delia Ketchum:** Veronica Taylor; **Misty/Jesse:** Rachael Lillis; **Tracey Sketchit:** Ted Lewis; **James/Chariz-**

ard: Eric Stuart; **Meowth:** Madeleine Blaustein; **Pikachu:** Ikue Ootani; **Professor Samuel Oak:** Stan Hart; **Professor Felinda Ivy/Mr. Mime:** Kayzie Rogers; **Melody:** Amy Birnbaum; **Lugia:** Dan Green; **Computer:** Megan Hollingshead; **Erin:** Tara Jayne; **Maren:** Julie Lund; **The Collector (a.k.a Lawrence III):** Neil Stewart

*Additional Voices*

Norman Altman, John Corallo, Ken Gates, Michaelle Goguen, Cassidy Kahn, Roger Kay, Emily Niebo, Robert O'Gorman, Ed Paul, Nathan Price, Eric Rath, Jack Taylor

Ash once again encounters British bad-guy rival, Lawrence III, who flies around in a massive flying machine and whose goal is to capture three rare Poke-birds, representing fire (Moltres), lightning (Zapdos) and ice (Articuno), to lure the powerful amphibious sea-air beast, Lugia, who is capable of destroying the world.

**PN:** Paired with the short, "Pikachu's Rescue Adventure," this sequel to 1999's smash-hit, *Pokémon the First Movie: Mewtwo Strikes Back,* opened in Japan in the summer of 1999 under the longwinded title of *Pocket Monsters the Movie: The Phantom Pokémon: Lugia's Explosive Birth* before premiering in theaters in the United States, where box-office receipts declined dramatically compared to its predecessor, taking a less than resounding $43.7 million, an indicator that the widespread mania over the franchise was on the downslope.

## ◎ POKÉMON 3: THE MOVIE (2001)

A Kids WB!/Pikachu Project 2000-Shogakukan Inc. Production in association with 4Kids Entertainment released by Warner Bros. Family Entertainment. **p:** Yukako Matsusako, Takemoto Mori, Choji Yoshikawa; **d:** Kunihiko Yuyama, Michael Haigney (English version); **scr:** Norman J. Grossfeld, Michael Haigney (based on characters created by Satoshi Tajiri). **Running time:** 90 minutes. **Released:** April 6, 2001.

*Voices*

**Ash Ketchum/Mrs. Delia Ketchum:** Veronica Taylor; **Misty/Jesse:** Rachael Lillis; **Brock/James:** Eric Stuart; **Meowth:** Madeleine Blaustein; **Pikachu:** Ikue Ootani; **Molly Hale:** Amy Birnbaum; **Spencer Hale/Entei:** Dan Green; **Professor Samuel Oak:** Stan Hart; **Skyler:** Ed Paul

*Additional Voices*

Lisa Ortiz, Kathy Pilon, Peter R. Bird, Kayzie Rogers, Ken Gates, Tara Jayne

Ash, Brock and Misty along with Team Rocket thwart the efforts of the legendary Unown, freeing a daughter whose parents have been cloned for evil purposes.

**PN:** Opening in theaters in May 2001 with the short, "Pikachu and Pichu," this third full-length feature in the Pokémon franchise had the poorest showing of the three films to date, bringing in a mere $17,052,128. Following the series' continuing decline at the box office since its first feature, Warner Bros. ceased as the series' distributor and was replaced by Miramax Films.

## ◎ THE POLAR EXPRESS (2004)

A Warner Bros./Castle Rock Entertainment Production in association Shangri-La Entertainment/Playtone/ImageMovers/Golden Mean Productions released by Warner Bros. **p:** Steve Starkey, Robert Zemeckis, Gary Goetzman, William Teitler, Steve Boyd; **exec prod:** Tom Hanks, Jack Rapke, Chris Van Allsburg; **d:** Robert Zemeckis; **scr:** Robert Zemeckis (based on the book, *The Polar Express,* by Chris Van Allsburg); **m:** Alan Silvestri; **anim prod dir:** Robin A. Linn; **char anim:** Tom Bruno Jr. **Songs:** "Here Comes Santa Claus," White Christmas," "Winter Wonderland," "Santa Claus Is Coming to Town," "Silver Bells," "I'll Be Home for Christmas," "Frosty the Snowman" and "It's Beginning to Look a Lot Like Christmas." **Running time:** 132 minutes. **Released:** November 10, 2004.

*Voices*

**Conductor/Santa Claus/Hobo/Father:** Tom Hanks; **Hero Boy:** Daryl Sabara; **Hero Girl:** Nona Gaye; **Lonely Boy:** Jimmy Bennet; **Know-It-All:** Eddie Deezen; **El General:** Charles Fleischer; **Smokey/Steamer:** Andre Sogliuzzo; **Sister Sarah:** Isabella Peregrina; **Elf Singer:** Steven Tyler

Classic tale of a young boy who is afraid Santa Claus doesn't exist, then embarks on a magical train ride to the North Pole where he discovers his suspicions are false.

**PN:** Coproduced by Warner Bros. and Castle Rock Entertainment in association with several production partners, including Tom Hanks' company, Playtone. Hanks loved this classic storybook by author Chris Van Allsburg so much that he teamed with the author to develop the book into a feature-length film with director Robert Zemeckis of *Who Framed Roger Rabbit* fame at the helm. With the promising, groundbreaking "performance capture" (also called motion capture) animation technique of using CGI technology to replicate humans in photoreal digital form, this costly $165 million, G-rated epic opened on November 10, 2004, five days before Disney/Pixar's smash-hit *The Incredibles.* The film had the added value of an IMAX 3-D version, which was released simultaneously to IMAX theaters (becoming the first mainstream film to achieve this feat) with the standard print issued to conventional theaters. Despite mixed reviews, the film did very respectable business in the United States, topping $170 million in ticket sales, with an additional $45 million at IMAX theaters and more than $296 million worldwide. It also received three Academy Award nominations, for best original song (for the song "Believe" by Glen Ballard and Alan Silvestri), best sound by William B. Kaplan, Randy Thom, Tom Johnson and Dennis S. Sands, and best sound editing by Randy Thom and Dennis Leonard. The film's 2005 DVD release was the fifth best-selling DVD of the year's top-10-selling DVDs with more than 8.13 million units sold.

## ◎ POOH'S HEFFALUMP MOVIE (2005)

A Walt Disney Pictures/DisneyToons Studios Production released by Buena Vista Pictures. **p:** Jessica Koplos-Miller; **d:** Frank Nissen; **scr:** Brian Hohlfeld, Evan Spiliotopoulos (based on characters created by A.A. Milne); **m:** Joel McNeely; **m/l** Carly Simon, Brian Hohfeld, Richard M. Sherman, Robert B. Sherman; **anim dir:** Don MacKinnon. **Songs:** "Winnie the Pooh," "The Horribly Hazardous Heffalumps!" "Little Mr. Roo," "The Name Game," "Shoulder to Shoulder" and "In the Name of the Hundred Acre Wood / What Do You Do?" **Running time:** 67 minutes. **Released:** February 11, 2006.

*Voices*

**Winnie the Pooh/Tigger:** Jim Cummings; **Piglet:** John Fiedler; **Roo:** Nikita Hopkins; **Kanga:** Kath Soucie; **Rabbit:** Ken Sansom; **Eeyore:** Peter Cullen; **Mama Heffalump:** Brenda Blethyn; **Lumpy:** Kyle Stanger

Distressed by evidence of the dreaded elephant, Heffalump, roaming around near the Hundred Acre Wood, Winnie the Pooh, Tigger, Piglet, Rabbit and Eeyore try to capture the creature, while their spunky little friend, Roo, befriends a younger Heffalump named Lumpy.

**PN:** Originally intended as a direct-to-video release, this 67-minute feature, replete with rather unremarkable animation, backgrounds and landscapes lacking detail, and original songs by songwriter Carly Simon, probably would have done better had it been exclusively released on home video. As it was, the film opened to lukewarm reviews and topped $18,098,433 in ticket sales in the United States. Reportedly more than 900 children auditioned in the United States for the part of Lumpy, with five-year-old Kyle Stanger cast as the voice of the character. Singer/songwriter Carly Simon, who wrote and sung original songs in the film, is credited with coming up with the character's full name, Heffridge Trumpler Brompet Heffalump, for the movie.

## ◎ POUND PUPPIES AND THE LEGEND OF BIG PAW (1988)

A Family Home Entertainment and Tonka Corp. presentation of an Atlantic/Kushner-Locke Production in association with the Maltese Companies released by Tri-Star. **p:** Donald Kushner, Peter Locke; **d:** Pierre DeCelles; **scr:** Jim Carlson, Terrence McDonnell; **m:** Steve Tyrell. **Running time:** 76 minutes. **Released:** March 18, 1988.

### Voices

**McNasty:** George Rose; **Whopper:** B. J. Ward; **Nose Marie:** Ruth Buzzi; **Cooler:** Brennan Howard; **Collette:** Cathy Cadavini; **Bright Eyes:** Nancy Cartwright

The Pound Puppies foil the efforts a nasty old man with an evil laugh (McNasty) whose goal is to take over the world by recovering the Bone of Scone, a mystical relic possessing great magical powers.

## ◎ THE POWERPUFF GIRLS (2002)

A Cartoon Network Production released by Warner Bros. **p:** Donna Castricone; **exec prod:** Craig McCracken, Brian A. Miller; **co-exec prod:** Mike Lazzo, Linda Simensky, Mark Norman; **d:** Craig McCracken; **scr:** Charlie Bean, Lauren Faust, Craig McCracken, Paul Rudish, Don Shank; **st:** Amy Keating Rogers; **m:** James L. Venable; **anim dir:** Genndy Tartakovsky. **Running time:** 74 minutes. **Released:** July 3, 2002.

### Voices

**Blossom:** Catherine Cavadini; **Bubbles:** Tara Strong; **Buttercup:** E.G. Daily; **Mojo Jojo:** Roger L. Jackson; **Professor Utonium:** Tom Kane; **Ms. Keane:** Jennifer Hale; **Narrator/Mayor/Mitch/Punk:** Tom Kenny; **Sara Bellum:** Jennifer Martin; **Ace/Big Billy/Grubber/Hotcha Chatcha:** Jeff Glen Bennett; **Linda/Woman at Zoo:** Grey DeLisle; **I.P. Host/Local Anchor:** Phil LaMarr; **Hota Wata/Killa Drilla/Cukor the Pickle Man:** Rob Paulsen; **Rocko Socko/Ojo Tango:** Kevin M. Richardson; **Whole Lotta Monkeys:** Frank Welker

Sweet, square-jawed scientist Professor Utonium invents three perfect super-powered girls representing sugar, spice and everything nice, who end up preventing the professor's pet—accidentally transformed into the evil Mojo Jojo when an experiment went wrong—from taking control of Townsville.

**PN:** Advertised on promotional posters and in coming attraction trailers as *The Powerpuff Girls Movie*, this feature-length version of the popular Cartoon Network series, created by Craig McCracken, faced some tough competition, becoming the third cartoon feature to open (with the *Dexter's Laboratory* short, "Chicken Scratch") the same weekend opposite Disney's *Lilo and Stitch* and Nickelodeon's *Hey Arnold! The Movie*. Of these, Disney's *Lilo and Stitch* prevailed, becoming the top box-office draw with $146 million, while *The Powerpuff Girls* mustered up a measly $9,589,131 (less than its $10 million budget) in ticket sales in the United States.

## ◎ THE PRINCE OF EGYPT (1998)

A DreamWorks Pictures SKG Production released by Dream-Works SKG. **p:** Penney Finkelman Cox, Sandra Rabins; **exec prod:** Jeffery Katzenberg; **d:** Brenda Chapman, Steven Hickner, Simon Wells; **scr:** Philip LaZebnik (based on the biblical book of Exodus); **m:** Hans Zimmer; **m/l:** Stephen Schwartz; **superv anim:** Kristof Serrand, William Salazar, David Brewster, Sergei Kouchnerov, Rodolphe Guenoden, Gary Perkovac, Patrick Mate, Bob Scott, Fabio Lignini, Rick Farmiloe, Jurgen Gross. **Songs:** "The Prince of Egypt (When You Believe)," "Deliver Us," "All I Ever Wanted (with Queen's Reprise)," "Goodbye Brother," "Through Heaven's Eyes," "Playing with the Big Boys," "Cry," "The Plagues," "When You Believe," "River Lullaby" and "Humanity." **Running time:** 97 minutes. **Released:** December 18, 1998.

### Voices

**Moses/God:** Val Kilmer; **Rameses:** Ralph Fiennes; **Tzipporah:** Michelle Pfeiffer; **Miriam:** Sandra Bullock; **Aaron:** Jeff Goldblum; **Jethro:** Danny Glover; **Pharaoh Seti:** Patrick Stewart; **The Queen:** Helen Mirren; **Hotep:** Steve Martin; **Huy:** Martin Short; **Rameses' son:** Bobby Motown; **Young Miriam:** Eden Riegel; **Yocheved:** Ofra Haza; **Moses, singing:** Amick Byram; **Jethro, singing:** Brian Stokes Mitchell; **Miriam, singing:** Sally Dworsky; **The Queen, singing:** Linda Dee Shayne

### Additional Voices

Mel Brooks (uncredited)

Richly animated adaptation of the much-loved story of the biblical character Moses who is empowered by God and goes on to part the Red Sea in remarkable fashion.

**PN:** A labor of love for DreamWorks cofounder Jeffrey Katzenberg, who had been responsible, at Walt Disney Studios, for helping to develop such box-office smashes as *Beauty and the Beast* and *The Lion King,* this traditional and CGI animated, loose adaptation of the famed biblical story featured nine songs interwoven into the plot, including the opening theme, "Deliver Us," performed by Ofra Haza and Eden Riegel, "The Plagues," sung by Ralph Fiennes and Moses' singing voice Amick Byram, and the inspirational "I Will Get There" by Boyz II Men. It took four years to make, at a cost of more than $75 million. Taking greats pains to make the film as accurate a representation of the story as possible, Katzenberg consulted more than 500 archaeologists, historians and religious leaders, and employed some 400 animators. While the film did not become the huge blockbuster he had anticipated, it did open on 3,118 screens its first week with $14 million in ticket sales, and also at an unprecedented 8,000 to 10,000 theaters in 40 countries and in two dozen languages in the weeks leading up to Christmas. Considering its cost and years in production, the final U.S. gross was perhaps disappointing, tallying $101 million in revenue.

## ◎ THE PRINCE OF LIGHT: THE LEGEND OF RAMAYANA (2001)

A Nippon Ramayana/MRI Inc. Production released by Showcase Entertainment Inc. **p:** Yugo Sako, Krishna Shah; **exec prod:** Atsushi Matsuo; **d:** Yugo Sako; **scr:** Yugo Sako, Krishna Shah (based on *The Ramayana* by Valmiki); **m:** Vanraj Bhatia, Alan Howarth; **anim dir:** WRS Motion Picture and Video Lab color, Kazuyuki Koyabayashi. **Running time:** 96 minutes. **Released:** November 9, 2001.

### Voices

**Ram:** Bryan Cranston; **Sita:** Edie Mirman; **Ravan:** Tom Wyner; **Lakshman:** Richard Cansino; **Hanuman:** Michael Sorich; **Dasharatha:** Mike L. Reynolds; **Vishwarmitra:** Tony Pope; **Kumshaharn:** Barbera Prescott; **Shoorpanakha:** Barbara Goodson

Entails the legendary heroic exploits of two brothers, Ram and Lakshman, who, along with the Monkey King, save a young princess held captive by the evil King Ravan.

**PN:** In 2001, this Japanese-Indian coproduction of the widely known Indian legend, in the fashion of such ancient-world animated masterpieces as Disney's *Aladdin* (1992) and *Hercules* (1997), premiered in Los Angeles and made a list of eligible films nominated for an Academy Award for best animated feature.

## ◎ THE PRINCESS AND THE GOBLIN (1994)

A Siriol/Pannonia Filmstudio/S4C Wales/NHK Enterprises International Production released by Hemdale Pictures Corporation. **p:** Robin Lyons; **d:** Jozsef Grimes; **exec prod:** Steve Walsh, Marietta Dardai; **scr:** Robin Lyons (adapted from the novel by George MacDonald); **m:** Istvah Lerch; **anim dir:** Les Orton. Song: "A Spark Inside Us." **Running time:** 82 minutes. **Released:** June 3, 1994.

### Voices
**Princess Irene:** Sally Ann Marsh; **The King:** Joss Ackland; **Mump:** Roy Kinnear; **Froglip:** Rik Mayall; **Curdi:** Peter Murray; **Fairy Godmother:** Claire Bloom; **Goblin Queen:** Peggy Mount; **Glump:** Victor Spinetti; **Nanny Lootie:** Mollie Sugden; **Goblin King:** Robin Lyons

### Additional Voices
Frank Rozelaar Green, Steve Lyons, William Hootkins

When a peaceful kingdom is menaced by an army of monstrous goblins, a brave and beautiful princess teams up with a resourceful peasant boy to rescue the noble king and his people in this thrilling adventure based on the timeless fairy tale from master storyteller George MacDonald.

**PN:** This 1993 British-Hungarian coproduction, known as *A Hercengno es a kobold*, was released in the United States on Memorial Day, 1994. The G-rated feature was winner of the Film Advisory Board's Award of Excellence, The Dove Seal of Approval from the Dove Foundation Review Board and the Best Children's Film Award from the Fort Lauderdale International Film Festival.

## ◎ THE PRINCESS AND THE PEA (2002)

A Feature Films for Families/Swan Animation Production released by Feature Films for Families. **p:** Forest S. Baker III, Don Judd; **d:** Mark Swan; **m/sc:** Alan Williams; **songs:** Alan Williams, David Pomeranz; **anim:** Pannoniafilm (Budapest), Exist Studios, Kecskemet Studios (Hungary). **Running time:** 75 minutes. **Released:** October 25, 2002.

### Voices
**Heath:** Lincoln Hambert; **Sebastian, The Court Historian:** Nigel Lambert; **Laird, The Evil Prince:** Ronan Vibert; **Button/King Windham:** Richard Ridings; **Daria, The Princess:** Amanda Waring; **Prince Rollo:** Steven Webb; **Other Voices:** Alex Gerrish, Frank Gerrish

Hoping to find a bride to marry, Prince Rollo travels to the kingdom of Corazion where he meets and falls in love with a beautiful peasant girl who happens to be a princess.

**PN:** Mark Swan of the Utah-based Swan Animation directed this classically animated adaptation screened at a few festivals and played in Los Angeles, making a list of 17 eligible animated features that initially competed for an Academy Award for best animated feature. Other preliminary nominees included Adam Sandler's *Eight Crazy Nights, Alibaba & the Forty Thieves, Eden, El Bosque Animado (The Living Forest), Hey Arnold! The Movie, Ice Age, Jonah–A VeggieTales Movie, Lilo & Stitch, Mutant Aliens, The Powerpuff Girls, Return To Never Land, Spirit: Stallion of the Cimarron, Spirited Away, Stuart Little 2* and *Treasure Planet.*

## ◎ PRINCESS MONONOKE (1999)

A Studio Ghibli/Tokuma Shoten Publishing Company/Nippon Television Network Corporation Production released by Miramax Films. **p:** Toshio Suzuki; **d:** Hayao Miyazaki; **scr:** Hayao Miyazaki, Neil Gaiman (English version); **m:** Joe Hisaishi; **anim dir:** Masashindo, Yoshifumi Kondo, Katsuya Kondo, Kitaro Kosaka. **Running time:** 133 minutes. **Released:** October 29, 1999.

### Voices
**Moro:** Gillian Anderson; **Prince Ashitaka:** Billy Crudup; **San/The Princess Mononoke:** Claire Davis; **Okkoto:** Keith David; **Kohroku:** John DeMita; **Lady Eboshi:** Minnie Driver; **Toki:** Jada Pinkett Smith; **Kaya:** Tara Strong; **Jigo:** Billy Bob Thornton

Infected with an incurable disease, a young prince will die unless he finds a cure. He travels to the Far East to seek help from a deer god and gets caught in a war between the forest gods, led by a beautiful princess raised by wolves, and an iron-mining town.

**PN:** Considered a "jewel" of Japanese animation, this historical fantasy-adventure first opened in Japan on July 12, 1997, and in addition to posting record box-office sales along with U.S. films, helped set a new attendance mark that year at Japanese movie theaters, posting a 17.7% gain over the previous year.

## ◎ THE PROFESSIONAL: GOLGO 13 (1992)

A Tokyo Movie Shinsha (TMS) Production released by Streamline Pictures. **d:** Osamu Dezaki, Shichiro Kobayashi, Hirotaka Takahashi; **m:** Toshiyuki Omori; **anim dir:** Akio Sugino; **key anim:** Atsuko Fukushima, Shinji Otsuka; **anim:** Koji Morimoto. **Running time:** 95 minutes. **Released:** October 23, 1992.

### Voices
**General T. Jefferson:** Kiyoshi Kobayashi; **Golgo 13:** Tetsuro Sagawa; **Leonard Dawson:** Goro Naya; **Bishop Moretti:** John Dantona; **Thomas Waltham:** Carlos Ferro; **E. Young:** Michael Forest; **Gold:** Eddie Frierson; **Albert:** Milt Jamin; **Paco:** Steve Kramer; **Cindy:** Joyce Kurtz; **Pablo/Silver:** Kerrigan Mahan; **General Jefferson:** Edward Mannix; **Leonard Dawson:** Michael McConnohie; **Rita:** Diana Michelle; **Emily:** Karlyn Michelson; **Laura:** Edie Mirman; **Robert Dawson:** Tony Oliver; **F. Garvin:** David Povall; **Lt. Bob Bragen:** Mike Reynolds; **Duke "Golgo 13" Togo/Snake:** Gregory Snegoff; **Informant:** Jeff Winkless

An assassin called Golgo 13 murders the son of a wealthy business tycoon, Leonard Dawson, and becomes the target of the CIA and the U.S. Army after Dawson hires them to avenge the death of his son.

**PN:** Based on Takao Saito's popular and longest running adult action adventure manga published since 1970.

## ◎ THE PUPPETOON MOVIE (1987)

An Expanded Entertainment release. **p, d & w:** Arnold Leibovit; **m:** Brady Baker; **anim dir:** Gene Warren, Jr. **Running time:** 80 minutes. **Released:** June 12, 1987.

### Voices
**Arnie the Dinosaur/Pillsbury Doughboy:** Paul Frees; **Gumby/Gremlin:** Dallas McKennon; **Pokey:** Art Clokey; **Speedy Alka-Seltzer:** Dick Beals

Gumby and Pokey star with Arnie the Dinosaur in this long-overdue tribute to the animated film work of *Puppetoons* creator George Pal who influenced the creators of Gumby and other stop-motion animated characters, including television commercial stars Pillsbury Doughboy and Speedy Alka-Seltzer. The feature contains nine film shorts from 1937 and 1947: "Phillip's Broadcast of 1938," "Phillips Cavalcade," "John Henry and the Inky Poo,"

"Together in the Weather," "Jasper in a Jam," "The Sleeping Beauty," "Southseas Sweetheart," "Tulips Shall Grow" and "Tubby the Tuba.

## ⊚ QUEST FOR CAMELOT (1998)

A Warner Bros. Production released by Warner Bros. **p:** Dalisa Cooper Cohen; **d:** Frederik Du Chau; **scr:** Kirk DiMicco, William Schifrin, Jacqueline Feather, Dave Seidler (based on the novel *The King's Damosel* by Vera Chapman); **m:** Patrick Doyle; **m/l:** David Foster, Carole Bayer-Sager, Steven Schwartz; **superv anim:** (U.K.) Russell Hall; **lead anim:** Nassos Vakalis, Chrystal S. Klabunde, Alexander Williams, Dan Wagner, Cynthia L. Overman, Stephen A. Franck, Mike Nguyen, Lennie K. Graves, Alyson Hamilton. **Songs:** "Looking Through Your Eyes (LeAnn Rimes)," "Ruber," "I Stand Alone," "United We Stand," "The Prayer (Celine Dion)," "On My Father's Wings" "The Prayer (Andrea Bocelli)" and "If I Didn't Have You." **Running time:** 85 minutes. **Released:** May 15, 1998.

*Voices*
**Kayley:** Jessalyn Gilsig; **Garrett:** Cary Elwes; **Baron Ruber:** Gary Goldman; **Devon:** Eric Idle; **Cornwall:** Don Rickles; **Lady Juliana:** Jane Seymour; **King Arthur:** Pierce Brosnan; **Merlin:** Sir John Gielgud; **The Griffin:** Bronson Pinchot; **Bladebeak:** Jaleel White; **Sir Lionel:** Gabriel Byrne; **Lynnit:** Jessica Hathaway; **Ayden:** Frank Welker; **Knight:** Al Roker; **Minion:** Jess Harnell; **Young Kayley:** Sarah Freeman; **Kayley, singing:** Andrea Corr; **Garrett, singing:** Bryan White; **Lady Juliana, singing:** Celine Dion; **King Arthur, singing:** Steve Perry

Joined by blind warrior Garrett and a funny two-headed dragon, Kayley, a plucky girl who dreams of following her late father as a Knight of the Round Table, sets out to find the legendary sword Excalibur, before an ousted knight can steal it, in order to save King Arthur and Camelot in this Arthurian fantasy/adventure.

**PN:** Attempting to compete with Walt Disney's dominance in feature-length animation, Warner Bros. produced this cartoon fantasy about Arthurian legend; originally set to premiere in November 1997, its release changed to May 1998 to open a full-month before Disney's animated feature *Mulan*. Regardless of when this film was released it did poorly, grossing a mere $6 million over the weekend of May 15–17, and a meager $22.7 million overall in the United States. (In Europe, the film was released as *The Magic Sword*.)

## ⊚ RACE FOR YOUR LIFE CHARLIE BROWN (1977)

A Bill Melendez Production released by Paramount Pictures. **p:** Lee Mendelson, Bill Melendez; **d:** Bill Melendez, Phil Roman; **w:** Charles M. Schulz (based on the *Peanuts* characters by Schulz); **m:** Ed Bogas. **Songs:** "Race for Your Life, Charlie Brown," "The Greatest Leader," "Charmine" and "She'll Be Comin' Round the Mountain." **Running time:** 76 minutes. **Released:** August 24, 1977.

*Voices*
**Charlie Brown:** Duncan Watson; **Schroeder:** Gregory Felton; **Peppermint Patty:** Stuart Brotman; **Sally:** Gail Davis; **Linus:** Liam Martin; **Lucy:** Melanie Kohn; **Marcie:** Jimmie Ahrens; **Bully:** Kirk Jue; **Another Bully:** Jordan Warren; **Another Bully:** Tom Muller; **Singers:** Ed Bogas, Larry Finlayson, Judith Munsen, David Riordan, Roberta Vandervort

*Additional Voices*
Fred Van Amburg, Bill Melendez

The Peanuts gang is off to camp for a summer of misadventures, including building a raft for the "big race," only to be outdone by the competing team, which "buys" its raft. Aside from the race, Snoopy has an altercation with a nasty feline and Lucy leads the other girls in an antiboy campaign.

## ⊚ RAGGEDY ANN AND ANDY (1977)

A Lester Osterman Production released by 20th Century-Fox. **p:** Richard Horner; **d:** Richard Williams; **scr:** Patricia Thackray and Max Wilk (based on the stories and characters created by Johnny Gruelle); **m:** Joe Raposo; **seq dir:** Gerald Potterton. **Songs:** "I Look and What Do I See!" "No Girl's Toy," "Rag Dolly," "Poor Babette," "A Miracle," "Ho-Yo," "Candy Hearts," "Blue," "The Mirage," "I Never Get Enough," "I Love You," "Loony Anthem," "It's Not Easy Being King," "Hooray for Me," "You're My Friend" and "Home." **Running time:** 84 minutes. **Released:** April 1, 1977.

*Cast*
**Marcella:** Claire Williams

*Voices*
**Raggedy Ann:** Didi Conn; **Raggedy Andy:** Mark Baker; **The Camel with the Wrinkled Knees:** Fred Struthman; **Babette:** Niki Flacks; **Captain Contagious:** George S. Irving; **Queasy:** Arnold Stang; **The Greedy:** Joe Silver; **The Loony Knight:** Alan Sues; **King Koo-Koo:** Marty Brill; **Gazooks:** Paul Dooley; **Grandpa:** Mason Adams; **Maxi-Fixit:** Allen Swift; **Susie Pincushion:** Hetty Galen; **Barney Beanbag/Socko:** Sheldon Harnick; **Topsy:** Ardyth Kaiser; **The Twin Pennies:** Margery Gray, Lynne Stuart

A search ensues for Babette, a French doll, who is kidnapped by another doll, Captain Contagious, in the toy-filled playroom of a young girl named Marcella, seen in live action in this animated feature. Doll makes Raggedy Ann and Andy embark on a magical journey to rescue Babette, successfully managing through a forbidding forest, a tossing sea, a looney kingdom and other dangers.

**PN:** Film was originally designed as a Hallmark Hall of Fame television special; Liza Minnelli and Goldie Hawn were considered for Raggedy Ann's role. Also known as *Raggedy Ann and Andy: A Musical Adventure*.

## ⊚ RAINBOW BRITE AND THE STAR STEALER (1985)

A DIC Enterprises Production released by Warner Bros. **p:** Jean Chalopin, Andy Heyward, Tetsuo Katayama; **d:** Bernard Deyries, Kimio Yabuki; **w:** Howard R. Cohen (based on a story by Chalopin, Howard R. Cohen, and characters developed by Hallmark Properties); **m:** Haim Saban, Shuki Levy. **Songs:** "Brand New Day" and "Rainbow Brite and Me." **Running time:** 97 minutes. **Released:** November 15, 1985.

*Voices*
**Rainbow Brite:** Bettina; **Lurky/On-X/Buddy Blue/Dog Guard/Spectran/Slurthie/Glitterbot:** Patrick Fraley; **Murky/Castle Monster/Glitterbot/Guard/Skydancer/Slurthie:** Peter Cullen; **Twin/Shy Violet/Indigo/La La Orange/Spectran/Sprites:** Robbie Lee; **Starlite/Wizard/Spectran:** Andre Stojka; **Krys:** David Mendenhall; **The Princess/The Creature:** Rhonda Aldrich; **Orin/Bombo/TV Announcer:** Les Tremayne; **Red Butler/Witch/Castle Creature/Spectran/Patty O'Green/Canary Yellow:** Mona Marshall; **Count Blogg:** Jonathan Harris; **Stormy:** Marissa Mendenhall; **Brian:** Scott Menville; **Popo:** Charles Adler; **Sergeant Zombo:** David Workman

A spoiled princess steals the planet Spectra for her "jewel collection." Little Rainbow, riding her flying horse Starlites, saves the planet, accompanied by a young boy, Krys, on his mechanical horse, On-X.

## ◎ RECESS: SCHOOL'S OUT (2001)

A Walt Disney Pictures/Walt Disney Television Animation Production released by Buena Vista Pictures. **p:** Paul Germain, Joe Ansolabehere, Stephen Swofford; **d:** Chuck Sheetz; **scr:** Jonathan Greenberg; **st:** Joe Ansolabehere, Paul Germain, Jonathan Greenberg; **m:** Denis M. Hannigan. **Running time:** 84 minutes. Released: January 16, 2004.

*Voices*

**Vince:** Rickey D'Shon Collins; **Mikey:** Jason Davis; **Gretchen:** Ashley Johnson; **T.J.:** Andy Lawrence; **Gus:** Courtland Mead; **Spinelli:** Pam Segall; **Principal Prickly:** Dabney Coleman; **Mikey's Singing Voice:** Robert Goulet; **Becky:** Melissa Joan Hart; **Fenwick:** Peter MacNicol; **Ms. Finster/Mrs. Detweiler:** April Winchell; **Benedict:** James Woods

When a rotten ex-principal plans to build a powerful ray gun that will alter the moon, create permanent frigid weather and banish summer forever, T.J. and the gang and the school's new principal band against him.

**PN:** This big-screen spin-off of the highly rated ABC Saturday-morning series *Disney's Recess* was the studio's next television cartoon series-to-feature transfer after 1999's *Doug's 1st Movie*, which generated $22.8 million in ticket sales worldwide. Budgeted at $10 million, the G-rated movie exceeded its cost, bringing in $36,696,761 at the box office at theaters in the United States.

## ◎ THE RELUCTANT DRAGON (1941)

A Walt Disney Production released by RKO Radio Pictures. **p:** Walt Disney; **l/a dir:** Alfred L. Werker; **anim dir:** Hamilton Luske, Jim Handley, Ford Beebe, Erwin Verity, Jasper Blystone; **scr:** Ted Sears, Al Perkins, Larry Clemmons, Bill Cottrell, Harry Clark. **Songs:** "Oh Fleecy Cloud," "To an Upside Down Cake," "Radish So Red," "'Tis Evening" and "The Reluctant Dragon." **Running time:** 72 minutes. **Released:** June 30, 1941.

*Cast*

**Robert Benchley:** Himself; **Studio artist:** Frances Gifford; **Mrs. Benchley:** Nana Bryant; **Studio guide:** Buddy Pepper; **Florence Gill and Clarence Nash:** Themselves; Alan Ladd, John Dehner, Truman Woodworth, Hamilton McFadden, Maurice Murphy, Jeff Corey; **Studio cop:** Henry Hall; **Orchestra leader:** Frank Faylen; **Slim:** Lester Dorr; **Guard:** Gerald Mohr; and members of the staff, including Walt Disney, Ward Kimball and Norman Ferguson

*Voices*

**The Dragon:** Barnett Parker; **Sir Giles:** Claud Allister; **The Boy:** Billy Lee; **Themselves:** The Rhythmaires; **Donald Duck:** Clarence Nash; **Goofy:** Pinto Colvig; **Baby Weems's narrator:** Gerald Mohr; **Baby Weems:** Leone LeDoux, Raymond Severn; **John Weems:** Ernie Alexander; **Mrs. John Weems:** Linda Marwood; **FDR:** Art Gilmore; **Walter Winchell:** Edward Marr; **How to Ride a Horse narrator:** John McLeish; **Reluctant Dragon narrator:** J. Donald Wilson

Part live action and part animation, this film delves into the behind-the-scenes making of cartoons, with comedian Robert Benchley, in live action, being persuaded by his onscreen wife (Nana Bryant) to approach Walt Disney about producing a cartoon based on *The Reluctant Dragon*, a delightful children's book by Kenneth Grahame. The film traces Benchley's visit to the Disney studio and the ultimate production of this tale about a dragon who loathes terrorizing people. Goofy appears in the film showing animator Ward Kimball making his latest cartoon, "How to Ride a Horse."

## ◎ RESCUE HEROES: THE MOVIE (2003)

A Nelvana Production released by Artisan/Family Home Entertainment. **p:** Pamela Lehn; **d:** Ron Pitts; **scr:** Brent Piaskoski; **m:** Amin Bhatia; **char anim:** Mark Stanger; **anim:** Dana Boadway, Kelly Brennan, Bill Giggie, Brian Harris, Marion Kulyk, Luc Marier, Virginia Mielke, Sara Newman, Robert Padovan, Dave Simmons. **Running time:** 78 minutes. **Released:** October 24, 2003.

*Voices*

**Billy Blazes:** Norm Spencer; **Rocky Canyon:** Joe Motiki; **Wendy Waters:** Lenore Zann; **Ariel Flyer:** Deb Odell; **Jack Hamer:** Rod Wilson; **Jake Justice:** Martin Roach; **Rip Rockefeller:** Cal Dodd; **Matt Medic:** Andrew Pifko; **Warren Waters:** John Bourgeois; **Roger Houston:** Chris Earle; **Pat Pending:** Donald Burda; **Bob Sled:** Andrew Sabiston; **Hal E. Copter:** Tony Daniels; **Sam Sparks:** Dwayne Hill; **Tony:** Colin Glazer

After a volcano erupts, spouting a strange agent into the atmosphere and causing a series of ravaging storms and worldwide panic, this brawny, globe-saving team scampers to the scene to avert a cataclysmic storm heading toward Greenland from merging with the atmosphere before it is too late.

**PN:** Based on the popular television series, this CGI-animated feature opened in Chicago. Lionsgate Home Entertainment subsequently released the film on DVD.

## ◎ THE RESCUERS (1977)

A Walt Disney Production released by Buena Vista. **p:** Wolfgang Reitherman; **d:** Wolfgang Reitherman, John Lounsbery, Art Stevens; **st:** Larry Clemmons, Ken Anderson, Vance Gerry, David Michener, Burny Mattinson, Frank Thomas, Fred Lucky, Ted Berman, Dick Sebast (from *The Rescuers* and *Miss Bianca* by Margery Sharp); **m:** Artie Butler (songs by Carol Connors, Ayn Robbins, Sammy Fain, and Robert Crawford); **anim dir:** Ollie Johnston, Frank Thomas, Milt Kahl, Don Bluth. **Songs:** "The Journey," "Rescue Aid Society," "Tomorrow Is Another Day," "Someone's Waiting for You" and "The U.S. Air Force Song." **Running time:** 77 minutes. **Released:** June 22, 1977.

*Voices*

**Bernard:** Bob Newhart; **Miss Bianca:** Eva Gabor; **Mme. Medusa:** Geraldine Page; **Mr. Snoops:** Joe Flynn; **Ellie Mae:** Jeanette Nolan; **Luke:** Pat Buttram; **Orville:** Jim Jordan; **Rufus:** John McIntire; **Penny:** Michelle Stacy; **Chairman:** Bernard Fox; **Gramps:** Larry Clemmons; **Evinrude:** James Macdonald; **Deadeye:** George Lindsey; **TV Announcer:** Bill McMillan; **Digger:** Dub Taylor; **Deacon:** John Fiedler

Two mice, Bernard and Miss Bianca, set out to rescue a girl, Penny, held captive in a swamp by the evil Mme. Medusa.

**PN:** This beautifully animated feature took four years to make at a cost of nearly $8 million.

## ◎ THE RESCUERS DOWN UNDER (1990)

A Walt Disney Pictures Production in association with Silver Screen Partners IV released by Buena Vista. **p:** Thomas Schumacher; **d:** Hendel Butoy and Mike Gabriel; **scr:** Jim Cox, Karey Kirkpatrick, Byron Simpson, Joe Ranft; **m:** Bruce Broughton; **superv anim:** Glen Keane, Mark Henn, Russ Edmonds, David Cutler, Ruben A. Aquino, Nik Ranieri, Ed Gombert, Anthony De Rosa, Kathy Zielinski, Duncan Marjoribanks; **anim:** James Baxter, Ron Husband, Will Finn, David Burgess, Alexander S. Kupershmidt, Chris Bailey, Mike Cedeno, Rick Farmiloe, Jacques Muller, Dave Pruiksma, Rejean Bourdages, Roger Chiasson, Ken Duncan, Joe Haidar, Ellen Woodbury, Jorgen Klubien, Gee Fwee Border,

Barry Temple, David P. Stephan, Chris Wahl, Larry White, Brigitte Hartley, Doug Krohn, Phil Young, Tom Roth, Leon Joosen. **Songs:** "Black Slacks" and "Waltzing Matilda." **Running time:** 74 minutes. **Released:** November 16, 1990.

### Voices

**Bernard:** Bob Newhart; **Miss Bianca:** Eva Gabor; **Wilbur:** John Candy; **Jake:** Tristan Rogers; **Cody:** Adam Ryen; **McLeach:** George C. Scott; **Frank:** Wayne Robson; **Krebs:** Douglas Seale; **Joanna/Special Vocal Effects:** Frank Welker; **Chairmouse/Doctor:** Bernard Fox; **Red:** Peter Firth; **Baitmouse:** Billy Barty; **François:** Ed Gilbert; **Faloo/Mother:** Carla Meyer; **Nurse Mouse:** Russi Taylor

In Australia, young Cody discovers that evil McLeach has captured the magnificent eagle Marahute. He manages to set her free only to be kidnapped himself and later to see her recaptured.

**PN:** This sequel to Disney's *The Rescuers* was released simultaneously with a brand-new Mickey Mouse short, *The Prince and the Pauper*, costarring pals Goofy, Donald Duck and Pluto.

## ◉ RETURN TO NEVERLAND (2002)

A Walt Disney Pictures/Walt Disney Television Animation Production released by Buena Vista Pictures. **p:** Christopher Chase, Michelle Robinson, Dan Rounds; **scr:** Temple Matthews; **d:** Robin Budd; **m:** Joel McNeely; **m/l:** Jonatha Brooke, John Flansburg, John Linnell; **anim dir:** Charlie Bonifaco, Keith Ingham, Ryan O'Loughlin, Larry Whitaker; **superv anim:** Lianne Hughes, Andrew Collins, Pierre Lommerse, Bob Baxter, Ryan O'Loughlin. **Songs:** "I'll Try," "They Might Be Giants" and "Do You Believe in Magic." **Running time:** 72 minutes. **Released:** February 15, 2002.

### Voices

**Jane/Young Wendy:** Harriet Owen; **Peter Pan:** Blayne Weaver; **Captain Hook:** Corey Burton; **Smee/Pirates:** Jeff Bennett; **Wendy:** Kath Soucie; **Danny:** Andrew McDonough; **Edward:** Roger Rees; **Cubby:** Spencer Breslin; **Nibs:** Bradley Pierce; **Slightly:** Quinn Beswick

When Wendy's daughter, Jane, is abducted by the rapscallion, Captain Hook, Peter Pan and his companions, the Lost Boys, rescue her and Tinkerbell so they can fly home in this World War II-era story set in London.

**PN:** Produced nearly 50 years after the Disney animated classic *Peter Pan* (1953), this G-rated sequel, which cost $20 million to make, did modest business in the United States taking in $48,423,368, and $107,423,368 in revenue worldwide. The film did well enough, apparently, to become eligible for an Academy Award nomination for best animated feature, along with 16 others that made a preliminary list of nominees.

## THE ROAD TO EL DORADO (2000)

A DreamWorks SKG Production released by DreamWorks SKG. **p:** Bonnie Radford, Brooke Breton; **d:** Eric "Bibo" Bergeron, Don Paul; **scr:** Ted Elliott, Terry Rosio; **m:** Hans Zimmer, John Powell; **m/l:** Elton John, Tim Rice; **seq dir:** Will Finn, David Silverman; **seq superv (Stardust Pictures):** Rob Stevenhagen; **senior superv anim:** James Baxter, David Brewster; **superv anim:** William Salazar, Sergei Kouchnerov, Bob Scott, Rodolphe Guenoden, Kathy Zielinski, Frans Vischer, Kristof Serrand, Sylvain Deboissy, Nicolas Marlet, Patrick Mate, Erik Schmidt. **Songs:** "El Dorado," "Someday out of the Blue," "Without Question," "Friends Never Say Goodbye," "The Trail We Blaze," "16th Century Man," "The Panic in Me," "It's Tough to Be a God," "Trust Me," "My Heart Dances," "Queen of Cities," "Cheldorado," "The Brig" and "Won-

ders of the New World." **Running time:** 88 minutes. **Released:** March 31, 2000.

### Voices

**Tulio:** Kevin Kline; **Miguel:** Kenneth Branagh; **Chel:** Rosie Perez; **Tzekel-Kan:** Armand Assante; **Chief:** Edward James Olmos; **Cortes:** Jim Cummings; **Altivo:** Frank Welker; **Zaragosa:** Tobin Bell; **Acolyte:** Duncan Majoribanks; **Kid #1:** Elijah Chang; **Kid #2:** Cyrus Shaki-Khan; **Narrator:** Elton John

Two Spanish swindlers—the dark-haired Tulio (voiced by Kevin Kline) and blond-maned Miguel (voiced by Kenneth Branagh)—become stowaways on one of Cortes', ships headed across the Atlantic to the New World in 1519 to find a map that will lead them to the fabled city of gold, El Dorado.

**PN:** After going through two sets of directors, various concepts and five years of production at a cost of $95 million, DreamWorks produced this high-budget, cel-animated 16th-century epic with songs by Elton John and composer Tim Rice, combining the successful formula of Paramount's Bob Hope and Bing Crosby's "Road" pictures and John Huston's live-action adventure, *The Man Who Would Be King* (1975). Unlike the studio's previous box-office successes, *Antz* (1998) and *The Prince of Egypt* (1998), this historical adventure film failed to make a profit in the United States, returning $50,802,661 in domestic revenue and $65,700,000 worldwide.

## ◉ ROBIN HOOD (1973)

A Walt Disney Pictures Production released by Buena Vista. **p:** Wolfgang Reitherman; **d:** Wolfgang Reitherman; **st:** Larry Clemmons (based on character and story conceptions by Ken Anderson); **m:** (songs by) Roger Miller, Floyd Huddleston, George Bruns, Johnny Mercer; **dir anim:** Milt Kahl, Frank Thomas, Ollie Johnston, John Lounsbery. **Songs:** "Not in Nottingham," "Whistle Stop," "Love" and "The Phoney King of England." **Running time:** 83 minutes. **Released:** November 8, 1973.

### Voices

**Allan-a-Dale:** Roger Miller; **Prince John/King Richard:** Peter Ustinov; **Sir Hiss:** Terry-Thomas; **Robin Hood:** Brian Bedford; **Maid Marian:** Monica Evans; **Little John:** Phil Harris; **Friar Tuck:** Andy Devine; **Lady Kluck:** Carole Shelley; **Sheriff of Nottingham:** Pat Buttram; **Trigger:** George Lindsay; **Nutsy:** Ken Curtis; **Skippy:** Billy Whitaker; **Sis:** Dana Laurita; **Tagalong:** Dora Whitaker; **Toby Turtle:** Richie Sanders; **Otto:** J. Pat O'Malley; **Crocodile:** Candy Candido; **Mother Rabbit:** Barbara Luddy; **Church Mouse:** John Fiedler

All the familiar characters appear in this animated version of the classic story, featuring cartoon animals in the title roles—Robin Hood and Maid Marian are foxes, Little John is a bear and the ever-villainous Prince John is a mangy lion—in this return to Sherwood Forest and Robin's battles with the Sheriff of Nottingham.

## ◉ ROBOT CARNIVAL (1991)

An A.P.P.P. Production released by Streamline Pictures. **p:** Kazufumi Nomura; **d:** Katsuhiro Otomo, Atsuko Fukushima, Kouji Morimoto, Kiroyuki Kitazume, Mao Lamdo, Hidetoshi Ohmori, Yasuomi Umetsu, Hiroyuki Kitakubo, Takashi Nakamura; **scr:** Katsuhiro Otomo, Atsuko Fukushima, Kouji Morimoto, Hiroyuki Kitazume, Mao Lamdo, Hidetoshi Ohmori; **m:** Joe Hisaishi, Isaku Fujita, Yasunori Honda. **Running time:** 91 minutes. **Released:** January 25, 1991.

### Voices

**The Man:** Michael McConnohie; **His Robot, Yayoi:** Lisa Michelson; **His Wife:** Barbara Goodson; **The Gent/Daimaru:** Tom

Wyner; **Sankichi:** Bob Bergen; **Kukusuke:** Eddie Frierson; **Denjiro:** Kerrigan Mahan; **Volkeson:** Steve Kramer

Japanese science fiction anthology of nine cartoon shorts, each mixing comedy and drama and with storylines involving futuristic robots; directed by Japan's most famous anime directors, it played at art theaters and film festivals worldwide.

## ◎ ROBOTECH: THE MOVIE (1986)

A Harmony Gold Production released by Cannon Films. **p:** Ahmed Agrama, Miurra Toru; **d:** Carl Macek, Ishiguro Noburo; **scr:** Ardwright Chamberlain (based on a story by Carl Macek); **m:** Three Dog Night, Joanne Harris, Michael Bradley, Gigi Agrama. **Running time:** 80 minutes. **Released:** July 25, 1986.

*Voices*

**Mark Landry:** Ryan O'Flannigan, Kerrigan Mahan; **Colonel B.D. Andrews:** Greg Snow, Gregory Snegoff; **Becky Michaels:** Brittany Harlow; **Eve:** Muriel Fargo; **General Leonard:** Guy Garrett; **Rolf Emerson:** Jeffrey Platt; **Kelly:** Penny Sweet, Edie Merman; **Stacey:** Wendee Swan, Wendee Lee; **Professor Embrey:** Merle Pearson; **Robotech Master:** A. Gregory; **Robotech Master:** Guy Garrett; **Todd Harris:** Don Warner; **Nick:** Anthony Wayne

*Additional Voices*

Dave Mallow, Colin Philips, Tom Wyner, Drew Thomas, Mike Reynolds, Ray Michaels

Set in the year 2027 when an armada of alien Robotech Masters invades Earth to seize control of lost technology so they can destroy the planet, Mark Landry holds the key that unlocks the power to save the planet from destruction.

**PN:** Budgeted at $8 million, this re-edited Japanese feature-length production mined material from the serialized Japanese cartoon series *Super Dimensional Calvary Southern Cross* and the made-for-video release *Megazone 23, Part One*.

## ◎ ROBOTS (2005)

A Blue Sky Studios Production released by 20th Century Fox. **p:** Jerry Davis, William Joyce, John Dorkin; **d:** Chris Wedge, Carlos Saldanha; **scr:** Lowell Ganz, Babaloo Mandel; **st:** Jim McClain, Ron Mita; **m/l:** Ian Ball, John Powell, Adam Schlesinger; **superv anim:** James Bresnahan, Michael Thurmeier; **CG superv:** Michael J. Travers; **seq dir:** Jimmy Hayward. **Songs:** "Tell Me What You Already Did," "Get Up Offa That Thing," "Right Thurr," "From Zero to Hero," "Pomp and Circumstance," "Il barbiere di Siviglia," "Thritsch-Tratsch Polka" and "Underground." **Running time:** 89 minutes. **Released:** March 11, 2005.

*Voices*

**Rodney Copperbottom:** Ewan McGregor; **Fender:** Robin Williams; **Cappy:** Halle Berry; **Ratchet:** Greg Kinnear; **Big Weld:** Mel Brooks; **Crank:** Drew Carey; **Piper:** Amanda Byrnes; **Madame Gasket:** Jim Broadbent; **Aunt Fanny:** Jennifer Coolidge; **Tim the Gate Guard:** Paul Giamatti; **Watch:** Paula Abdul; **Pigeon Lady:** Lucille Bliss; **Broken Arm Bot:** Terry Bradshaw; **Youngest Rodney:** Dylan Denton; **Young Rodney:** Will Denton; **Lamppost/Toilet Bot/Bass Drum/Microphone:** Marshall Efron; **Stage Announcer:** Damien Fahey; **Mr. Gasket:** Lowell Ganz

A callow young inventor 'bot, Rodney Copperbottom, journeys from the boondocks of Rivet Town to the vast metropolis of Robot City where he befriends a group of outmoded male robots to take on a corporate shark who wants to stop manufacturing replacement parts and buy upgraded robots, making them all obsolete.

**PN:** Follow-up film from the producers of the 2002 smash-hit *Ice Age,* this second 20th Century Fox-Blue Sky Studios coproduction more impressively utilized the vivid and realistically rendered three-dimensional CGI animation than its previous feature. Unlike *Ice Age,* which grossed $176 million domestically, this $80 million, futuristic robotic fantasy, featuring the voices of Halle Berry as Cappy, Ewan McGregor (of *Star Wars* prequel fame) as Rodney, Robin Williams as the comical Fender, and Greg Kinnear as the scumbag corporate executive Ratchet, made an impressive $128,200,012 in ticket revenue in the United States and $260,700,012 worldwide.

## ◎ ROCK*A*DOODLE (1992)

A Goldcrest Films/Sullivan Bluth Studios Ireland Ltd. Production released by Samuel Goldwyn Company. **p:** Don Bluth, Gary Goldman, John Pomeroy; **d:** Don Bluth; **cd:** Gary Goldman, Dan Kuenster; **exec prod:** John Quested, Morris F. Sullivan; **st:** Don Bluth, John Pomeroy, David Steinberg, David N. Weiss, T.J. Kuenster, Gary Goldman; **scr:** David N. Weiss; **m/sc:** Robert Folk (with original songs by T.J. Kuenster). **Songs:** "Sun Do Shine," "We Hate the Sun," "Come Back to You," "Bouncers' Theme Song," "Tweedle Te Dee," "Treasure Hunting Fever," "Sink or Swim," "Kiss 'n Cod," "Back to the Country," "The Owl's Picnic" and "Tyin' Your Shoes." **Running time:** 77 minutes. **Released:** April 3, 1992.

*Cast (live action)*

**Edmond:** Toby Scott Ganger; **Mother:** Kathryn Holcomb; **Dad:** Stan Ivar; **Scott:** Christian Hoff; **Mark:** Jason Marin

*Voices*

**Narrator/Patou:** Phil Harris; **Chanticleer:** Glen Campbell; **Snipes, the magpie:** Eddie Deezen; **The Grand Duke:** Christopher Plummer; **Peepers, the mouse:** Sandy Duncan; **Stuey:** Will Ryan; **Hunch, Grand Duke's inept nephew:** Charles Nelson Reilly; **Goldie:** Ellen Greene; **Pinky:** Sorrell Booke

When a young farmboy (Edmond) is turned into an animated kitten by an evil owl, he and his barnyard friends go in search of the singing Elvis-like rooster Chanticleer (who has been banished to a cartoon-world Las Vegas, known as Big City, after he fails to crow one morning), to enlist his help in getting back home in this live-action/animated musical from the creator of *The Secret of NIMH* and *Land Before Time*.

## ◎ ROCK AND RULE (1985)

A Nelvana Limited Production released by Metro-Goldwyn-Mayer/United Artists. **p:** Patrick Loubert, Michael Hirsh; **d:** Clive A. Smith; **scr:** Peter Sauder, John Halfpenny; **st:** Patrick Loubert, Peter Sauder; **m:** Patrick Cullen. **Songs:** "Angel's Song," "Invocation Song," "Send Love Through," "Pain and Suffering," "My Name Is Mok," "Born to Raise Hell," "I'm the Man," "Ohm Sweet Ohm," "Dance, Dance, Dance" and "Hot Dogs and Sushi." **Running time:** 83 minutes. **Released:** August 5, 1985.

*Voices*

**Mok:** Don Francks; **Omar:** Paul Le Mat; **Angel:** Susan Roman; **Mok's Computer:** Sam Langevin; **Dizzy:** Dan Hennessey; **Stretch/Zip:** Greg Duffell; **Toad:** Chris Wiggins; **Sleazy:** Brent Titcomb; **Quadhole/1st Radio Announcer:** Donny Burns; **Mylar/2nd Radio Announcer:** Martin Lavut; **Cindy:** Catherine Gallant; **Other Computers:** Keith Hampshire; **Carnegie Hall Groupie:** Melleny Brown; **Edna:** Anna Bourque; **Borderguard:** Nick Nichols; **Uncle Mikey:** John Halfpenny; **Sailor:** Maurice LaMarche; **Aunt Edith:** Catherine O'Hara

The war is over. The only survivors are street animals—dogs, cats and rats. From them a new race of mutants evolve. In this new world Mok, an aging superstar, tries to find the last element in a diabolical plan to raise a demon that will give him immense power. The missing element is a voice, and he finds that voice in Angel,

*When the only survivors of a war are street animals, a new race of mutants evolves in the fantasy-adventure* Rock and Rule *(1984). The film was the first feature-length production by Nelvana Limited in Canada.* (COURTESY: NELVANA LIMITED)

a female singer who plays with a local band in the small town of Ohmtown. He steals her away to post-apocalypse Nuke York to launch his plan into action.

**PN:** The first full-length feature film for Nelvana Limited, a Canadian-based animation company (producers of *The Care Bears*). The film features an original soundtrack by rock artists Cheap Trick, Debbie Harry, Lou Reed, Iggy Pop and a special performance by Earth, Wind and Fire.

## ◎ ROUJIN Z (OLD MAN Z) (1996)

An A.P.P.P./Kit Parker Films Production released by Rapid Eye Movies and Wardour Films Ltd. **p:** Yasuku Kazama, Yoshiaki Motoya, Kazufumi Nomura, Yasuhito Nomura; **d:** Hiroyuki Kitabuko; **scr:** Katsuhiro Otomo; **m:** Bun Itakura; **anim:** Kouji Morimoto. **Running time:** 80 minutes. **Released:** January 5, 1996.

### Voices

**Haruko:** Toni Barry; **Haru:** Nicolette McKenzie; **Nobuko:** Barbara Barnes; **Terada:** Allan Wenger; **Norie:** Jana Carpenter; **Hasegawa:** Jay Fitzgerald; **Maeda:** Adam Henderson; **Reporter:** Peter Marinker; **Ian:** Ian Thompson

Chaos reigns when a revolutionary hospital bed equipped with a sixth-generation computer—from the Department of Health's so-called "Project Z"—escapes with an elderly man strapped to it.

## ◎ ROVER DANGERFIELD (1991)

A Rodney Dangerfield/Hyperion Pictures Production released by Warner Bros. **p:** Willard Carroll, Thomas L. Wilhite; **d:** Jim George, Bob Seeley; **exec prod:** Rodney Dangerfield; **st:** Roger Dangerfield, Harold Ramis (based on an idea by Rodney Dangerfield) **scr:** Rodney Dangerfield; **m:** David Newman (with songs by Rodney Dangerfield and Billy Tragesser); **seq dir:** Steve Moore, Matthew O'Callaghan, Bruce Smith, Dick Sebast, Frans Vischer, Skip Jones. **Songs:** "It's a Dog's Life," "Somewhere There's a Party," "I'd Give Up a Bone for You," "I'm in Love with the Dog Next Door," "I'll Never Do It on a Christmas Tree," "I Found a Four-Leaf Clover When I Met Rover," "Respect," "Happy Birthday to You," "Merrily We Roll Along," "I'm Just a Country Boy at Heart," "It's a Big Wide Wonderful World" and "Winter Wonderland." **Running time:** 74 minutes. **Released:** August 6, 1991.

### Voices

**Rover Dangerfield:** Rodney Dangerfield; **Daisy:** Susan Boyd; **Eddie:** Ronnie Schell; **Raffles:** Ned Luke; **Connie:** Shawn Southworth; **Danny:** Dana Hill; **Rocky:** Sal Landi; **Coyote/Rooster:** Tom Williams; **Big Boss/Coyote/Sparky/Wolf/Horse:** Chris Collin; **Gangster/Farm Voice:** Robert Bergen; **Count:** Paxton Whitehead; **Mugsy/Bruno:** Ron Taylor; **Max:** Bert Kramer; **Champ:** Eddie Barth; **Truck Driver:** Ralph Monaco; **Queenie/Chorus Girls/Hen/Chickens/Turkey:** Tress MacNeille; **José/Sheep:** Michael Sheehan; **Gigi/Chorus Girl/Sheep:** Lara Cody; **Fisherman #1:** Owen Bush; **Fisherman #2:** Ken White; **Cal:** Gregg Berger; **Katie:** Heidi Banks; **Lem:** Dennis Blair; **Clem:** Don Stuart; **Duke:** Robert Pine; **Wolvies:** Danny Mann, Bernard Erhard

In this canine adventure, Rover Dangerfield, a street-smart dog owned by a Las Vegas showgirl, becomes separated from his owner and winds up living on an idyllic farm where he finds true love and respect.

**PN:** Comedian Rodney Dangerfield came up with the idea for this animated feature and served as the film's executive producer, writer and lyricist. The movie had its Los Angeles premiere at the Fourth Los Angeles International Animation Celebration.

## ◎ RUDOLPH AND FROSTY'S CHRISTMAS IN JULY (1979)

A Rankin-Bass Production released by Avco-Embassy. **p & d:** Arthur Rankin Jr., Jules Bass; **scr:** Romeo Muller; **m:** Maury Laws; **m/l:** Steve Nelson, Jack Rollins ("Frosty the Snowman"); **anim superv:** Akikazu Kono; **anim:** Seiichi Araki, Shigeru Ohmachi, Hiroshi Tabata. **Running time:** 97 minutes. **Released:** July 1, 1979.

### Voices

**Rudolph:** Billie Mae Richards; **Frosty:** Jackie Vernon; **Milton:** Red Buttons; **Lilly Loraine:** Ethel Merman; **Santa Claus:** Mickey Rooney; **Mrs. Santa Claus:** Darlene Conley; **Crystal:** Shelley Winters; **Winterbolt/Jack Frost/Policeman:** Paul Frees; **Scratcher, the jealous reindeer:** Alan Sues; **Big Ben:** Harold Peary

### Additional Voices

Don Messick, Nellie Bellflower, Steffi Calli, Howard Shapiro, Eric Hines, Cynthia Adler, Bob McFadden

Beloved Christmas legends Rudolph the Reindeer and Frosty the Snowman aid an ailing circus owner and get back to the North Pole in time to confront the evil King Winterbolt who is on the loose.

**PN:** Produced by Rankin/Bass, the producers of such timeless television cartoon specials as *Rudolph, the Red-Nosed Reindeer* and *Frosty the Snowman*, this updated, stop-motion puppet-animated production starring Frosty and Rudolph received limited theatrical distribution and also aired as a prime-time network special on ABC.

## ◎ RUDOLPH THE RED-NOSED REINDEER (1998)

A Tundra Productions Inc./Goodtimes Entertainment/Cyrus Brothers Productions Production released by Legacy Releasing Corporation. **p:** William R. Kowalchuk, Jonathon Flom; **exec prod:** Eric Ellenbogen, Andrew Greenberg, Seth M. Willenson; **d:** Bill Kowalchuk; **scr:** Michael Aschner; **st:** Robert May; **m:** Al Kasha, Michael Lloyd. **Running time:** 83 minutes. **Released:** October 19, 1998.

### Voices

**Younger Rudolph:** Eric Pospisil; **Older Rudolph/Twinkle the Sprite:** Kathleen Barr; **Santa Claus:** John Goodman, **Mrs.**

Prancer/School Teacher/Mitzi, Rudolph's Mother: Debbie Reynolds; Stormella, the Evil Ice Queen: Whoopi Goldberg, Leonard the Polar Bear: Bob Newhart; Blitzen, Rudolph's Father: Garry Chalk; Dasher/Elf Referee at Games: Paul Dobson; Boone: Richard Simmons; Slyly the Fox: Eric Idle; Doggie: Alec Willows; Ridley: Lee Tockar; Blitzen: Gary Chalk; Arrow/Donner: Christopher Gray; Young Zoey: Vanessa Morley; Glitter the Sprite/Older Zoey/Schoolroom Doe #1: Miriam Sirois; Elf Crowd Member #2: Jim Byrnes; Cupid: David Kaye; Dancer: Terry Klassen; Comet: Colin Murdock; Aurora the Sprite/Zoey's Mother/Elf Crowd Member #3: Elizabeth Carol Savankoff; Schoolroom Buck #1: Tyler Thompson; Ridley, Stormella's Butler/Milo the Elf/Vixen: Lee Tocklar; Sparkle the Sprite/Elf Crowd Member #1: Cathy Weseluck; Dogle/Prancer: Alec Willows

In this holiday themed musical Rudolph, who survived a childhood accident that makes his nose glow red, overcomes his trepidation about being different and saves Christmas, despite the evil Stormella's effort to unleash bad weather to ruin it.

PN: Featuring John Goodman, Debbie Reynolds, Whoopi Goldberg and Bob Newhart as character voices, this $10-million feature-length version of the classic Christmas tale opened in theatres in limited release on October 19, 1998, two months before Christmas; the home video version was released a month later.

### ◎ RUGRATS GO WILD (2003)

A Klasky Csupo/Nickelodeon Movies Production released by Paramount Pictures. p: Gabor Csupo, Arlene Klasky; exec prod: Albie Hecht, Julia Pistor, Eryk Casemiro, Hal Waite; co-prod: Tracy Kramer, Terry Thoren, Patrick Stapleton; d: Norton Virgien, John Eng and Kate Boutilier; scr: Kate Boutilier (based on Rugrats characters created by Arlene Klasky, Gabor Csupo, Paul Germain, and The Wild Thornberrys characters created by Klasky, Csupo, Steve Pepoon, David Silverman, Stephen Sustarsic; st: Edmund Fong; m: George Acogny; m/l: Elizabeth Daily, Greg De Belles, Curtis Hudson, Jeff Lynne, Mark Mothersbaugh, Joe Perry, Lisa Stevens, Steven Tyler; seq dir: Raymie Reynolds. Songs: "Changing Faces," "Holiday," "Lizard Love," "It's a Jungle Out There," "Lust for Life," "The Morning After," "Should I Stay or Should I Go," "Message in a Bottle" and "She's on Fire." Running time: 80 minutes. Released: June 13, 2003.

*Voices*

Tommy Pickles: E. G. Daily; Chuckie Finster: Nancy Cartwright; Eliza Thornberry: Lacey Chabert; Nigel Thornberry: Tim Curry; Donnie: Flea; Debbie Thornberry: Danielle Harris; Spike: Bruce Willis; Angelica Pickles: Cheryl Chase; Phil/Lil/Betty DeVille: Kath Soucie; Darwin: Tom Kane; Marianne Thornberry: Jodi Carlisle; Susie Carmichael: Cree Summer; Kimi Finster: Dionne Quan; Grandpa Lou: Joe Alaskey; Charlotte Pickles: Tress MacNeille; Drew Pickles/Chas Finster: Michael Bell; Didi Pickles: Melanie Chartoff; Kira Finster: Julia Kato; Howard DeVille: Philip Proctor; Stu Pickles: Jack Riley; Dil Pickles: Tara Strong; Siri: Chrissie Hynde; Dr. Lipschitz: Tony Jay; Toa: Ethan Phillips

The creature-comfort-craving Rugrats become shipwrecked on a tropical island and encounter the globetrotting Thornberrys, producers of a television nature documentary series, who are after an elusive white leopard as the subject of their latest documentary.

PN: This third feature-length production from producers Arlene Klasky and Gabor Csupo and Nickelodeon's Rugrats television series franchise followed the pair's 1998 hit, The Rugrats Movie, which hit $100 million domestically and $55 million overseas, and the surprise hit sequel two years later, Rugrats in Paris (2000), which generated $77 million in the United States but only $28 million abroad. Despite these successes, Klasky and Csupo did not fare as well with the big-screen version of their popular TV series, The Wild Thornberrys, which produced $40 million in ticket sales and half that worldwide. In order to boost box office revenue for this latest feature combining two of their most successful franchises, Paramount Pictures, the film's distributor, released it midway between the Disney-Pixar collaboration Finding Nemo and DreamWorks' Sinbad: Legend of the Seven Seas. While proving to be no competition for the behemoth Finding Nemo, Rugrats Go Wild came in second, raking in $39.4 million overall compared to DreamWorks' effort, which grossed $26 million in the United States. Even with its marginal victory, this third film in the franchise has been its last to date.

### ◎ RUGRATS IN PARIS: THE MOVIE (2000)

A Klasky Csupo/Nickelodeon Movies Production released by Paramount Pictures. p: Arlene Klasky, Gabor Csupo; exec prod: Albie Hecht, Julia Pistor, Eryk Casemiro, Hal Waite; co-prod: Tracy Kramer, Terry Thoren, Norton Virgienl; d: Stig Bergqvist, Paul Demeyer, scr: J. David Stem, David N. Weiss, Jill Gorey, Barbara Herndon, Kate Boutilier (based on characters created by Arlene Klasky, Gabor Csupo, Paul Germain); m: Mark Mothersbaugh; m/l: Laurent Boutonnat, Lee Hazelwood, Cyndi Lauder, Mark Mothersbaugh, Tionne "T-Boz" Watkins; seq dir: John Eng, Raul Garcia, John Holmquist, Andrei Svislotski, Greg Tiernan; f/x anim superv: Brice Mallier; CGI lead anim: Barbara Wright. Songs: "L'histoire d'une fée. . .C'est," "These Boots Are Made for Walkin'," "I Want a Mom That Will Last Forever," "My Get Away" and "Bad Girls." Running time: 78 minutes. Released: November 17, 2000.

*Voices*

Tommy Pickles: E.G. Daily; Dil Pickles: Tara Charendoff; Angelica Pickles: Cheryl Chase; Chuckie Finster: Christine Cavanaugh; Susie Carmichael: Cree Summer; Phil/Lil/Betty DeVille: Kath Soucie; Drew Pickles/Chas Finster: Michael Bell; Charlotte Pickles: Tress MacNeille; Wedding DJ: Casey Kasem; Grandpa Lou Pickles: Joe Alaskey; Lulu Pickles: Debbie Reynolds; Stu Pickles: Jack Riley; Coco LaBouche: Susan Sarandon; Jean-Claude: John Lithgow; Kita Watanabe: Julie Kato; Kimi Watanabe: Dionne Quan; Didi Pickles: Melanie Chartoff; Howard DeVille: Phil Proctor; Sumo Singers: Tim Curry, Billy West

Tommy, Chuckie, Angelica, Phil, Lil, Dil, Didi and the entire Rugrats troupe follow Stu to Paris where they enlist the services of a giant theme park robot to stop Chuckie's dad, who started dating again, from getting married to the park's female executive.

PN: Released two weeks before Thanksgiving and two years after The Rugrats Movie (1998) joined the elite group of cartoon features to reach the $100 million plateau in box-office gross, Paramount Pictures commissioned this sequel from producers Arlene Klasky and Gabor Csupo, co-creators with producer Paul Germain of the popular Nickelodeon cartoon series on which the film was based. For comic effect, reflecting its association with Paramount Pictures, the G-rated, $30-million feature's opening title, Rugrats II, morphs into a Godfather-style graphic (Paramount produced the Godfather series) featuring the Rugrats-type Pickles play-acting. Songs include "When You Love," beautifully warbled by Sinead O'Connor. More widely praised by critics than its previous effort, Rugrats in Paris: The Movie came in a close second to its predecessor, grossing $76,501,438 domestically and $103,284,813 in foreign markets.

## THE RUGRATS MOVIE (1998)

A Klasky Csupo/Nickelodeon Movies Production released by Paramount Pictures. **p:** Arlene Klasky, Gabor Csupo; **exec prod:** Alby Hecht, Debby Beece; **d:** Norton Virgien, Igor Kovalyov; **scr:** David N. Weiss, J. David Stern (based on characters created by Arlene Klasky, Gabor Csupo, Paul Germain); **m:** Mark Mothersbaugh; **m/l:** Elvis Costello, Nigel Harrison, Busta Rhymes, Gwen Stefani; **seq dir:** Zhenia Delioissine, Paul Demeyr, Raymie Muzquiz, Peter Chin, Andrei Svislotsky. **Songs:** "I Throw My Toys Around" and "One Way or Another." **Running time:** 79 minutes. **Released:** November 25, 1998.

*Voices*

**Tommy Pickles:** E.G. Daily; **Chuckie Finster:** Christine Cavanaugh; **Phil/Lil/Betty DeVille:** Kath Soucie; **Didi Pickles/Minka:** Melanie Chartoff; **Howard DeVille/Igor:** Phil Proctor; **Susie Carmichael:** Cree Summer; **Aunt Miriam:** Andrea Martin; **Chas Finster/Grandpa Boris/Drew Pickles:** Michael Bell; **Charlotte Pickles:** Tress MacNeille; **Stu Pickles:** Jack Riley; **Reptar Wagon:** Busta Rhymes; **Grandpa Lou Pickles:** Joe Alaskey; **Angelica Pickles:** Cheryl Chase; **Dr. Lipschitz:** Tony Jay; **Newborn Babies:** Laurie Anderson, Beck, B. Real, Jakob Dylan, Phife, Gordon Gano, Iggy Pop, Lenny Kravitz, Lisa Loeb, Lou Rawls, Patti Smith, Dawn Robinson, Fred Schneider, Kate Pierson, Cindy Wilson; **Lieutenant Klavin:** Margaret Cho; **Rex Pester:** Tim Curry; **Ranger Margaret:** Whoopi Goldberg; **Ranger Frank:** David Spade

While vacationing, precocious toddlers Tommy, Angelica, Chuckie, Lil and Phil become lost after riding their Reptar Wagon into the woods then try to find their way back home in this animated comedy adventure.

**PN:** Based on the Emmy award–winning Nickelodeon cartoon series, co-created by producers Arlene Klasky, Gabor Csupo and Paul Germain, this big-screen adaptation was the first of three feature-length productions starring the famed moppets, becoming a monster hit with pee-wee audiences and families and topping the $100-million mark in ticket sales in the United States. The film spawned two sequels: *Rugrats in Paris: The Movie* (2000) and *Rugrats Go Wild* (2003).

## SAKURA WARS THE MOVIE (2003)

A Production I.G. Production released by Pioneer Entertainment. **p:** Toshimichi Orsuki; **d:** Mitsuro Hongo; **scr:** Mitsuro Hongo, Hiroyuki Nishimura, Nobutoshi Terdo, Ohji Hiroi; **st:** Ohji Hiroi; **m:** Kohei Tanaka; **char anim superv:** Takuya Saito; **key anim superv:** Mitsuru Ishihara. **Running time:** 85 minutes. **Released:** July 18, 2003.

*Voices*

(English version) **Lachette Altair:** Julie Anne Taylor; **Sakuta Shinguji:** Wendee Lee; **Li Kohran:** Annie Pastrano; **Iris Chateaubriand:** Carrie Savage; **Captain Ichiro Oogami:** Dave Lelyveld; **Maria Tachibana:** Jane Alan; **Sumire Kanzaki:** Michelle Ruff; **Yuichi Kayama:** David Lucas; **Ikki Yoneda:** David Orozco; **Kaeda Fujieda:** Lia Sargent

Acclaimed fantasy-adventure featuring a female troupe of special agents who are put on alert to thwart an attack on Tokyo by demons. Based on the popular videogame, original video animation and the Japanese cartoon series created in 1996 by Ohji Hiroi.

## SALUDOS AMIGOS (1943)

A Walt Disney Production released by RKO Radio Pictures. **p:** Walt Disney; **st:** Homer Brightman, Ralph Wright, Roy Williams, Harry Reeves, Dick Huemer, Joe Grant; **md:** Charles Wolcott; **m:** Ed Plumb, Paul Smith; **seq dir:** Bill Roberts, Jack Kinney, Hamilton Luske, Wilfred Jackson. **Songs:** "Saludos Amigos," "Brazil" and "Tico Tico." **Running time:** 43 minutes. **Released:** February 6, 1943.

*Voices*

**Donald Duck:** Charles Nash; **Joe Carioca:** José Oliveira; **Goofy:** Pinto Colvig

This animated production, though far short of feature-film length, was released by Disney as an animated feature. Travelogue footage—filmed on location in South America—is incorporated into the film, which features four cartoon shorts strung together to portray the Latin American influence on the United States.

Sequences include Donald Duck as a naive tourist who runs into trouble while sightseeing; the adventures of Pedro the airplane, who grows up to be an airmail plane just like his dad; "El Gaucho Goofy," the misadventures of Goofy playing out the life of a gaucho—with little success; and, finally, tropical bird José (or Joe) Carioca, who takes Donald on a tour of South America, teaching him the samba along the way.

## SANTA AND THE THREE BEARS (1970)

A R and S Film Enterprises Production released by Ellman Enterprises. **p, w & d:** Tony Benedict; **m:** Doug Goodwin, Tony Benedict, Joe Leahy. **Running time:** 63 minutes. **Released:** November 7, 1970.

*Cast*

**Grandfather:** Hal Smith; **Beth:** Beth Goldfarb; **Brian:** Brian Hobbs

*Voices*

**Ranger/Santa Claus:** Hal Smith; **Nana:** Jean Vander Pyl; **Nikomi:** Annette Ferra; **Chinook:** Bobby Riaj

*Additional Voices*

Joyce Taylor; Ken Engels; Leonard Kerth; Kathy Lemon; Roxanne Poole; Michael Rodriguez

Two cute wide-eyed bear cubs (Nikomi and Chinook) put off hibernating in Yellowstone National Park to wait for the arrival of Santa Claus. So the cubs are not disappointed, the park's cheery, grandfatherly forest ranger agrees to impersonate Santa Claus at the request of their mother. The film opens, in live action, with a kindly old grandfather (played by Hal Smith) relating the tale to his grandchildren.

## A SCANNER DARKLY (2006)

A Warner Independent Pictures/3 Arts Entertainment/Detour Filmproduction/Thousand Words/Section Eight Production released by Warner Independent Pictures. **p:** Tommy Palotta, Jonah Smith, Erwin Stoff, Anne Walker-McBay, Palmer West, Erin Ferguson; **exec prod:** George Clooney, John Sloss, Steven Soderbergh; **d:** Richard Linklater, Bob Sabiston; **scr:** Richard Linklater (based on the novel by Philip K. Dick); **m:** Graham Reynolds. **Running time:** 100 minutes. **Released:** July 7, 2006.

*Voices*

**Fred/Bob Arctor:** Keanu Reeves; **Brown Bear Lodge Host:** Mitch Baker; **Barris:** Robert Downey Jr.; **Donna:** Winona Ryder; **Luckman:** Woody Harrelson; **Freck:** Rory Cochrane; **Girl at Scanning Station:** Casey Chapman; **Arctor's Wife:** Melody Chase; **Mike:** Dameon Clarke; **Police Officer:** Jack Cruz; **New Path Farm Manager:** Jason Douglas; **New Path Staff Member #1:** Hugo Perez; **New Path Attendant:** Jaki Davis; **New Path Girl:** Heather Kafka; **New Path Resident:** Christopher Ryan; **New Path Resident:** Rommel Sulit; **New Path Resident #2:** Leila Plummer; **Medical Technician #1:** Chamblee Ferguson; **Donald:** Marco Perella;

**Future Cop:** Steven Chester Prince; **Medical Deputy:** Angela Rawna; **P.A. Announcer:** Andrew Sparkes; **Daughter:** Eliza Stevens; **Scanner (uncredited):** Lisa Del Dotto

*Additional Voices*
Alex Jones, Mona Lee Fultz

A reluctant government-recruited undercover cop, addicted to a popular drug used by many other agents that causes split personalities, is ordered to spy on his friends in this computer-enhanced Rotoscope animated science fiction adventure set in futuristic, suburban Orange County, California.

### ◉ THE SECRET OF NIMH (1982)

A United Artists/Aurora Productions released through MGM/UA. **p:** Don Bluth, Gary Goldman, John Pomeroy; **d:** Don Bluth; **anim dir:** John Pomeroy, Gary Goldman; **st:** Don Bluth, John Pomeroy, Gary Goldman, Will Finn (based on the novel *Mrs. Frisby and the Rats of NIMH* by Robert C. O'Brien); **m:** Jerry Goldsmith. **Running time:** 82 minutes. **Released:** July 2, 1982.

*Voices*
Elizabeth Hartman, Dom DeLuise, Hermione Baddeley, Arthur Malet, Peter Strauss, Paul Shenar, Derek Jacobi, John Carradine, Shannen Doherty, Will Wheaton, Jodi Hicks, Ian Fried, Tom Hatten, Lucille Bliss, Aldo Ray

A recently widowed mother mouse (Mrs. Bisby) desperately tries finding a new home for her brood before the old one is destroyed by spring plowing. Her task gets complicated by the severe illness of her son, who is too sick to move.

**PN:** Co-creators of the film were Don Bluth, Gary Goldman, and John Pomeroy, all three former Disney animators who left the studio in a dispute over standards and struck out on their own. Working title: *Mrs. Frisby and the Rats of NIMH*.

### ◉ THE SECRET OF THE SWORD (1985)

A Filmation Associates Production released by Atlantic Releasing. **p:** Arthur Nadel; **d:** Ed Friedman, Lou Kachivas, Marsh Lamore, Bill Reed, Gwen Wetzler; **scr:** Larry Ditillo, Robert Forward. **Running time:** 88 minutes. **Released:** March 29, 1985.

*Voices*
**He-Man:** John Erwin; **She-Ra:** Melendy Britt; **Hordak:** George DiCenzo

*Justin (center) tries to fend off dastardly Jenner, while Mrs. Brisby looks on in a scene from* The Secret of NIMH *(1982). © United Artists*

*Additional Voices*
Linda Gary, Eric Gunden, Erika Scheimer, Alan Oppenheimer

He-Man discovers he has a twin sister, She-Ra, who was kidnapped shortly after birth by the evil Hordak. She has been raised by Hordak to combat He-Man. He-Man sets about to reunite her with their family.

**PN:** Prior to its release the film was called *Princess of Power*.

### ◉ SHAME OF THE JUNGLE (1979)

An International Harmony Production released by 20th Century Fox. **p:** Boris Szulinger, Michael Gast; **d:** Picha; **co-dir:** Boris Szulinger; **scr:** Pierre Bartier, Picha, Anne Beatts, Michael O'Donoghue; **m:** Teddy Lasry; **anim dir:** Vivian Miessen, Claude Monfort, Kjeld Simonsen, Alan Ball; **anim:** Malcolm Draper, Jack Stokes, Arthur Button, Richard Cox, Tom Barker, Michael Stuart, Denis Rich. **Running time:** 73 minutes. **Released:** September 14, 1979.

*Voices*
**Shame:** Johnny Weissmuller Jr.; **Perfect Master:** John Belushi; **Chief M'Bulu:** Christopher Guest; **Queen Bazonga:** Pat Bright; **June:** Emily Prager; **Speaker:** Bill Murray; **Brutish:** Adolph Caesar; **Siamese Twin 1:** Brian Doyle-Murray; **Siamese Twin 2:** Andrew Duncan; **Steffanie Starlet:** Judy Graubert; **Professor Cedric Addlepate:** Guy Sorel; **Narrator:** Bob Perry

Vine-swinging Shame, ape man of the jungle, tangles with hunters, a lion and the Molar Men before rescuing his woman, Jane, who is held captive by the balding Queen Bazonga, in this R-rated animated sex-comedy spoof of the Tarzan legend from Belgium, featuring the voices of Johnny Weissmuller Jr., the son of Tarzan film star, Johnny Weissmuller, as Shame, and then *Saturday Night Live* stars, comedians John Belushi and Bill Murray.

### ◉ SHARK TALE (2004)

A DreamWorks Animation SKG Production released by DreamWorks SKG. **p:** Bill Damaschke, Janet Healy, Allison Lyon Segan; **exec prod:** Jeffrey Katzenberg; **d:** Bibo Bergeron, Vicky Jenson, Rob Letterman; **scr:** Michael J. Wilson, Rob Letterman; **m:** Hans Zimmer; **m/l:** Missy "Misdemeanor" Elliott, Cheryl Lynn; **superv anim:** Ken Stuart Duncan, Lionel Gallat, Fabrice Joubert, Fabio Lignini, William Salazar, Bill Diaz. **Songs:** "Car Wash" and "Sweet Kind of Life." **Running time:** 89 minutes. **Released:** October 1, 2004.

*Voices*
**Oscar:** Will Smith; **Don Lino:** Robert De Niro; **Angie:** Renee Zellweger; **Lenny:** Jack Black; **Lola:** Angelina Jolie; **Sykes:** Martin Scorsese; **Ira Feinberg:** Peter Falk; **Frankie:** Michael Imperioli; **Luca:** Vincent Pastore; **Bernie:** Doug E. Doug; **Ernie:** Ziggy Marley; **Katie Current:** Katie Couric; **Shrimp/Worm/Starfish #1/Killer Whale #2:** David Soren; **Crazy Joe:** David P. Smith

Oscar, a fast-talking, bottom-feeding, big-dreaming little yellow fish (voiced by Will Smith), takes credit for killing the son of a shark mob boss, Don Lino (voiced by Robert DeNiro), and discovers that making such a claim has "serious consequences" in this animated underwater comedy.

**PN:** DreamWorks' fourth fully computer-animated feature, this fish-out-of-water tale not only was the surprise hit of the season, topping $160 million in ticket sales, but also was nominated for an Academy Award for best animated feature. In 2005, the movie's DVD edition tied for third with DreamWorks' *Madagascar* among the top-10-selling DVDs of the year with 10 million units sold.

## ⊚ SHINBONE ALLEY (1971)

A Fine Arts Film released by Allied Artists. **p:** Preston M. Fleet; **d:** John David Wilson; **w:** Joe Darion (based on the book for the musical play by Darion and Mel Brooks, from the "archy and mehitabel" stories by Don Marquis); **m:** George Kleinsinger. **Songs:** "I Am Only a Poor Humble Cockroach," "Blow Wind Out of the North," "Cheerio My Deario (Toujours Gai)," "Ah, the Theater, the Theater," "What Do We Care If We're Down and Out?" "The Moth Song," "Lullaby for Mehitabel's Kittens," "The Shinbone Alley Song," "The Lightning Bug Song," "Here Pretty Pretty Pussy," "Ladybugs of the Evening," "Archy's Philosophies," "They Don't Have It Here," "Romeo and Juliet" and "Come to Meeoww." **Running time:** 83 minutes. **Released:** June 18, 1971.

*Voices*

**Mehitabel:** Carol Channing; **Archy:** Eddie Bracken; **Big Bill Sr.:** Alan Reed; **Tyrone T. Tattersall:** John Carradine; **Newspaperman:** Byron Kane; **Freddie the Rat/Prissy Cat/Mabel/Pool Player:** Hal Smith; **Penelope the Fat Cat/Ladybugs of the Evening:** Joan Gerber; **Rosie the Cat:** Ken Sansom; **Beatnik Spider:** Sal Delano; **Singing Alley Cats/Kittens:** The Jackie Ward Singers

A poet is transmigrated into the body of a cockroach named archy, whose back-alley adventures and love for a sexy street cat (mehitabel) make up the plot line of this surrealistic tale.

**PN:** Based on the long-running musical of the same name (which was based on Don Marquis's comic strip of the 1920s and 1930s), Carol Channing and Eddie Bracken re-created roles originally played by Eartha Kitt and Bracken on Broadway.

## ⊚ SHREK (2001)

A DreamWorks SKG/Pacific Data Images Production released by DreamWorks Pictures SKG. **p:** Aron Warner, John H. Williams, Jeffrey Katzenberg; **exec prod:** Penney Finkelman Cox, Sandra Rabins, Steven Spielberg (uncredited); **co-prod:** Ted Elliott, Terry Rossio; **co-exec prod:** David Lipman; **d:** Andrew Adamson, Victoria Jensen; **scr:** Ted Elliott, Terry Rossio, Joe Stillman, Roger S.H. Schulman (based on the book by William Steig); **m:** Harry Gregson-Williams, John Powell; **superv anim:** Raman Hui; **dir anim:** Tim Cheung, Paul Chung, Denis Couchon, Donnachada Daly, James Satoru Straus. **Songs:** "All Star," "On the Road Again," "Friends," "Whipped Cream," "Escape (The Piña Colada Song)," "My Beloved Monster," "You Belong to Me," "Hallelujah," "Try a Little," "I'm a Believer," "Meditation," "Welcome to Duloc," "Bad Reputation," "I'm on My Way," "Merry Men," "Stay Home," "Best Years of Our Lives," "Like Wow!" and "It Is You (I Have Loved)." **Running time:** 89 minutes. **Released:** May 16, 2001.

*Voices*

**Shrek:** Mike Myers; **Donkey:** Eddie Murphy; **Princess Fiona:** Cameron Diaz; **Lord Faraquaad:** John Lithgow; **Monsieur Hood:** Vincent Cassel; **Ogre Hunter:** Peter Dennis; **Ogre Hunter:** Clive Pearse; **Captain of Guards:** Jim Cummings; **Baby Bear:** Bobby Block; **Geppetto/Magic Mirror:** Chris Miller; **Pinocchio/Three Pigs:** Cody Cameron; **Old Woman:** Kathleen Freeman; **Peter Pan:** Michael Galasso; **Blind Mouse/Thelonious:** Christopher Knight; **Blind Mouse:** Simon J. Smith; **Gingerbread Man:** Conrad Vernon; **Wrestling Fan:** Jacquie Barnbrook; **Merry Man:** Guillaume Aretos; **Merry Man:** John Bisom; **Merry Man:** Matthew Gonder; **Merry Man:** Calvin Remsberg; **Merry Man:** Jean-Paul Vignon; **Bishop:** Val Bettin

Joined by his faithful chatterbox, Donkey, a reclusive, giant green ogre takes a fanciful journey to Duloc to rescue the imprisoned Princess Fiona, held by the tyrannical midget, Lord Faraquaad, who plans to marry her so he can become king.

**PN:** Based on the popular children's book by William Steig, DreamWorks produced this CG-animated feature in collaboration with Pacific Data Images after optioning the story in November 1995, originally casting comedian Chris Farley of *Saturday Night Live* fame as Shrek until he died of a drug overdose in December 1997. By then, the studio had already spent $34 million to develop the feature, including storyboarding and recorded voiceovers. Thereafter, *Saturday Night Live* star Mike Myers was signed on for the role. The weekend it opened, the film enjoyed the second largest opening of any feature in film history, making a record $42.3 million and also becoming the largest opening of any movie produced by DreamWorks. The enjoyable fairy-tale romp tallied more than $277.8 million in ticket sales worldwide and was a major hit on DVD, selling more than 43 million units worldwide. Academy Award voters did not overlook the success of the film that year, with the film being nominated for best animated feature. The monster hit inspired a sequel, *Shrek 2* released three years later.

## ⊚ SHREK 2 (2004)

A DreamWorks SKG and Pacific Data Images Production released by DreamWorks Pictures SKG. **p:** Aron Warner, David Lipman, John H. Williams; **exec prod:** Jeffrey Katzenberg; **d:** Andrew Adamson, Kelly Asbury, Conrad Vernon; **scr:** Andrew Adamson, Joe Stillman, J. David Stern, David N. Weiss; **st:** Andrew Adamson (based on the book by William Steig); **m:** Harry Gregson-Williams, Ryeland Allison; **songs:** Adam Duritz, Mark Everett; **superv anim:** James Baxter, Rex Grignon, Raman Hui. **Songs:** "Holding Out for a Hero" "Livin' la Vida Loca," "Fairy Godmother Song," "Changes," "Accidentally in Love," "Funkytown," "Little Drop of Poison," "As Lovers Go," "People Ain't No Good," "Ever Fallen in Love," "One," "Le Freak," "Hawaii Five-O," "Theme from 'Rawhide," "I Need Some Sleep," "Ain't No Stoppin' Us Now," "Tomorrow," "Mission Impossible," "I Love Bosco," "All by Myself" and "You're So True." **Running time:** 88 minutes. **Released:** May 19, 2004.

*Voices*

**Shrek:** Mike Myers; **Donkey:** Eddie Murphy; **Princess Fiona:** Cameron Diaz; **Queen Lillian:** Julie Andrews; **Puss in Boots:** Antonio Banderas; **King Harold:** John Cleese; **Prince Charming:** Rupert Everett; **Fairy Godmother:** Jennifer Saunders; **Wolf:** Aron Warner; **Page/Elf/Nobleman/Nobleman's Son:** Kelly Asbury; **Pinocchio/Three Pigs:** Cody Cameron; **Gingerbread Man/Cedric/Announcer/Muffin Man/Mongo:** Conrad Vernon; **Blind Mouse:** Christopher Knight; **Mirror/Dresser:** Mark Moseley; **Ugly Stepsister:** Larry King; **Joan Rivers:** Joan Rivers

Lovable oaf Shrek and his bride-to-be, Princess Fiona, are invited to dine with Fiona's parents to celebrate their pending nuptials, but not if evil Fairy Godmother and her no-good son, Prince Charming, can help it as they plot against them in this animated sequel.

**PN:** Comedians Mike Myers and Eddie Murphy and actress Cameron Diaz, the original costars of 2001's *Shrek*, all signed to star in this sequel, along with actor Antonio Banderas as the voice of Puss in Boots. Celebrated CNN talk-show host Larry King as the Ugly Stepsister was added to the cast. Amazingly, this $70-million sequel greatly surpassed the 2001 box-office sensation. It actually outsold its predecessor, grossing $44.8 million in one day, and $108 million in its opening weekend, greatly surpassing the previous record holder, Disney-Pixar's *Finding Nemo*, which set an opening weekeend high of $70.3 million. Six months following its release, *Shrek 2* became the highest-grossing animated movie, earning a jaw-dropping $436,471,036 domestically. Of course, its overall box-office success may have been helped by the fact that the film enjoyed the widest release of any film in DreamWorks history—shown on 4,163 screens nationwide. *Shrek 2* was also nominated for an Academy Award—in the same category as the original—for best animated feature.

### ◎ SINBAD: BEYOND THE VEIL OF MISTS (2000)

A Pentafour Production released by Trimark Pictures. **p:** Sririam Rajan, G.V. Babu; **exec prod:** Usha Ganesh; **d:** Evan Ricks, Allan Jacobs; **scr:** Jeff Wolverton; **m:** Chris Desmond; **anim tech dir:** Vinnakota Gupta. **Running time:** 85 minutes. **Released:** January 28, 2000.

*Voices*

**Sinbad:** Brendan Fraser; **Princess Serena:** Jennifer Hale; **Captain of the Guard:** Mark Hamill; **Akron/Baraka/King Chandra:** Leonard Nimoy; **Babu:** K.W. Miller; **King Akron/Baraka:** John Rhys-Davies; **King's Guard/Executioner:** Robert Allen Mukes; **Other Voices:** Jeff Wolverton

After the evil sorcerer Baraka switches bodies with King Chandra and tosses the king's old body into the dungeon, the king's adventure-seeking daughter, Princess Serena, enlists the services of the roguish Captain Sinbad and his crew to rescue her father and to reverse the spell before the wizard beheads the real king in this computer-animated, motion-capture fantasy adventure.

**PN:** Indian software giant, Pentafour, known mostly as a computer games manufacturer, produced this film, which it promoted as "the first full-length use of motion-capture technology," a process that was extensively used in computer games and was a modern-day version of Rotoscoping, which involved filming live actors whose actions were then digitally recorded and animated to replicate more life-like movement.

### ◎ SINBAD: LEGEND OF THE SEVEN SEAS (2003)

A DreamWorks Animation SKG Production released by DreamWorks Pictures. **p:** Jeffrey Katzenberg, Mireille Soria; **d:** Tim Johnson, Patrick Gilmore; **scr:** John Logan; **m:** Harry Gregson-Williams; **anim superv:** Kristoff Serrand; **lead anim superv:** Jacob Hjott Jensen; **superv anim:** James Baxter, Simon Otto, William Salazar, Dan Wagner, Rodolphe Guenoden, Bruce Ferriz, Fabio Lignini, Sergei Kouchnerov, Steve Horrocks, Pres Romanillos, Fabrice Joubert, Michael Spokas, Michelle Cowart. **Running time:** 86 minutes. **Released:** July 2, 2003.

*Voices*

**Sinbad:** Brad Pitt; **Marina:** Catherine Zeta-Jones; **Eris:** Michelle Pfeiffer; **Proteus:** Joseph Fiennes; **Kale:** Dennis Haysbert; **Dymas:** Timothy West; **Rat:** Adriano Giannini; **Jin:** Raman Haui; **Li:** Chung Chan; **Luca/Council Judge/Dignitary/Guard/Others:** Jim Cummings; **Jed:** Conrad Vernon; **Grum/Chum:** Andrew Birch; **Tower Guard:** Chris Miller; **Sirens:** Lisbeth Scott

After the evil goddess Eris steals the hallowed Book of Peace and then frames Sinbad for the crime, Sinbad and his seafaring crew set sail with a beautiful shipboard stowaway, Marina (voiced by Catherine Zeta-Jones), to recover the book; otherwise, his childhood friend, Princess Proteus, will die by execution in his place.

**PN:** Codirected by Tim Johnson, codirector of DreamWorks' *Antz* (1998) and interactive-game veteran Patrick Gilmore, writer John Logan, who penned the live-action feature, *Gladiator* (2000),

scripted this King Arthur-Guinevere-Lancelot story and final 2-D animated feature from DreamWorks (which mixed 3-D animation for Sinbad's ship and the film's nifty creatures); it grossed a meager $26,466,286 domestically.

### ◎ SINBAD THE SAILOR (1962)

A Toei Animation Company Production released by Signal International. **exec prod:** Okawa Hiroshi; **d:** Masao Kuroda, Taiji Yabushita; **scr:** Morio Kita, Osamu Tezuka; **m:** Isao Tomita; **anim:** Akira Daikuhara, Hideo Furusawa, Yasuo Otsuka. **Running time:** 81 minutes. **Release date:** July 21, 1962.

Voice credits unknown.

Pirate ship stowaways Sinbad and his sidekick, Ali, convince the ship's captain to change course to rescue the sultan's daughter, Princess Samir, imprisoned by the grand vizier, and encounter many perilous adventures while finding secret treasure.

**PN:** Japanese animation giant Toei Animation Co. produced this 1962 adaptation of the well-known Arabian Nights tale that was among a series of Japanese animated features that it produced—*Panda and the Magic Serpent* (*Hakujaden*, 1958), *Alakazam The Great* (*Saiyu-Ki*, 1960) and *The Littlest Warrior* (*Anjo To Zushiomaru*, 1961)—redubbed in English, shortened, and released in the United States.

### ◎ SKY BLUE (2004)

A Tin House production released by Maxmedia/Endgame Entertainment. **p:** Kay Hwang, J. Ethan Park (English version), Park Sunmin; **d:** Moon Sang Kim, Park Sunmin (English version); **scr:** Michael Keyes, Moon-saeng Kim; **m:** Jaell Sim, Il Won; **3-D anim superv:** Young-Min Park; **anim dir:** Yeong-ki Yoon. **Running time:** 86 minutes. **Released:** December 31, 2004.

*Voices*

**Shua:** Marc Worden; **Jay:** Cathy Cavadini

*Additional Voices*

David Naughton, Joon-ho Chung, Hye-jin Yu, Ji-tae Yu

Futuristic, apocalyptic tale of the survivors of the last human city of Ecoban who, unless a young man can stop them, plan to destroy the outside city of Marr and its inhabitants to acquire a much-needed energy source that is also a deadly pollutant.

### ◎ SLEEPING BEAUTY (1959)

A Walt Disney Production released through Buena Vista. **p:** Walt Disney; **dir superv:** Clyde Geronimi; **st:** Erdmann Penner, Joe Rinaldi, Ralph Wright, Donald Da Gradi (based on an original story by Ward Greene); **m:** Oliver Wallace; **dir anim:** Milt Kahl, Frank Thomas, Marc Davis, Ollie Johnston Jr., John Lounsbery; **seq dir:** Eric Larson, Wolfgang Reitherman, Les Clark. **Songs:** "Once Upon a Dream," "Hail the Princess Aurora," "I Wonder," "The Skumps" and "Sleeping Beauty Song." **Running time:** 75 minutes. **Released:** January 29, 1959.

*Voices*

**Princess Aurora/Briar Rose:** Mary Costa; **Maleficent:** Eleanor Audley; **Merryweather:** Barbara Luddy; **King Stefan:** Taylor Holmes; **Prince Phillip:** Bill Shirley; **Flora:** Verna Felton; **Fauna:** Barbara Jo Allen; **King Hubert:** Bill Thompson; **Maleficent's Goons:** Candy Candido, Pinto Colvig, Bob Amsberry; **Owl:** Dallas McKennon; **Narrator:** Marvin Miller

Aurora, the daughter of good king Stephen and his wife, is given beauty, goodness and charm by three good fairies only to become victimized by a bad fairy, who casts a spell on her that she will prick her finger on a spindle when she is 16 and die. Fortunately, one of the good fairies intervenes and changes the spell so that Aurora's fate is deep sleep rather than death. She will awaken only with a loving kiss.

## THE SMURFS AND THE MAGIC FLUTE (1983)

A First Performance Pictures/Studios Belvision coproduction in association with Stuart R. Ross released by Atlantic Releasing Corporation. **p:** José Dutillieu; **d & w:** John Rust; **m:** Michel Legrand; **superv anim:** Eddie Lateste. **Running time:** 74 minutes. **Released:** November 25, 1983.

*Voices*
Cam Clarke, Grant Gottschall, Patty Foley, Mike Reynolds, Ted Lehman, Bill Capizzi, Ron Gans, X. Phifer, Dudly Knight, John Rust, Richard Miller, David Page, Durga McBroom, Michael Sorich, Robert Axelrod

Somehow a magic flute—which has the power to make people dance uncontrollably when it is played—has gotten out of Smurfland and into the hands of young practical joker Peewit and good knight Johan. But when Peewit loses the flute to the sinister bandit Oilycreep, the Smurfs make plans to retrieve the magical instrument.

**PN:** Film was called *V'la Les Schtroumpfs* for its Belgian release.

## SNOOPY COME HOME (1972)

A Cinema Center 100 and Sopwith Productions production released by National General Pictures. **p:** Lee Mendelson, Bill Melendez; **d:** Bill Melendez; **scr:** Charles Schultz; **m:** Donald Ralke; **m/l:** Richard M. Sherman, Robert B. Sherman. **Songs:** "Snoopy, Come Home," "Lila's Tune," "Fun on the Beach," "Best of Buddies," "Changes," "Partners," "Getting It Together" and "No Dogs Allowed." **Running time:** 80 minutes. **Released:** August 9, 1972.

*Voices*
**Charlie Brown:** Chad Webber; **Lucy Van Pelt:** Robin Kohn; **Linus Van Pelt:** Stephen Shea; **Schroeder:** David Carey; **Lila:** Johanna Baer; **Sally:** Hilary Momberger; **Peppermint Patty:** Chris DeFaria; **Clara:** Linda Ecroli; **Freida:** Linda Mendelson; **Snoopy:** Bill Melendez

Snoopy learns that his previous owner, Lila, is sick in the hospital and goes to see her. He vows to return to Lila for good, so he drafts a "Last Will and Testament" for the gang, which throws him a farewell party.

## THE SNOW QUEEN (1959)

A Soyuzmultfilm Production released by Universal-International. **p:** (American) Robert Faber; **d:** Lev Atamanov (American directors: Bob Fisher, Phil Patton, Alan Lipscott); **scr:** Soyuzmultfilm Productions (based on a story of Hans Christian Andersen; live-action prologue and adaptation written by Alan Lipscott, Bob Fisher); **m:** Frank Skinner. **Songs:** "The Snow Queen," "Do It While You're Young" and "The Jolly Robbers." **Running time:** 70 minutes. **Released:** November 20, 1959.

*Cast (live action)*
Art Linkletter, Tammy Marihugh, Jennie Lynn, Billy Booth, Rickey Busch

*Voices*
**Gerda:** Sandra Dee; **Kay:** Tommy Kirk; **Angel:** Patty McCormack; **Snow Queen:** Louise Arthur; **Ol' Dreamy/The Raven:** Paul Frees; **Henrietta Eskimo Woman:** June Foray; **The Princess:** Joyce Terry; **The Prince:** Richard Beals; **Granny:** Lillian Buyeff; **Ole Lukoje:** Vladimir Gribkov; **Karraks:** Sergie Martinson

Two inseparable companions—a boy, Kay, and a girl, Gerda—search for the girl's brother, held captive in the palace of the evil Snow Queen, in this Russian animated color feature, based on the classic Hans Christian Andersen fairy tale, which was rescored and redubbed in English for its American release.

**PN:** A six-minute live-action prologue, featuring well-known television personality Art Linkletter (host of *House Party* and *Kids Say the Darndest Things*) and a cast of child actors, was produced and added to the film. Dialogue for the animated story was redubbed by American actors, including 1950s' and 1960s' teen stars Sandra Dee and Tommy Kirk (best known for his roles in Disney films, including *The Shaggy Dog, The Absent-Minded Professor* and *Old Yeller*).

## SNOW WHITE AND THE SEVEN DWARFS (1937)

A Walt Disney Production released by RKO Radio Pictures. **p:** Walt Disney; **superv d:** David Hand; **seq dir:** Perce Pearce, Larry Morey, William Cottrell, Wilfred Jackson, Ben Sharpsteen; **w:** Ted Sears, Otto Englander, Earl Hurd, Dorothy Ann Blank, Richard Creedon, Dick Richard, Merrill De Maris, Webb Smith (based on the fairy tale "Sneewittchen" in collection of *Kinder-und Hausmarchen* by Jacob Grimm, Wilhelm Grimm); **m:** Frank Churchill, Leigh Harline, Paul Smith, Morey; **superv anim:** Hamilton Luske, Vladimir Tytla, Fred Moore, Norman Ferguson. **Songs:** "I'm Wishing," "One Song," "With a Smile and a Song," "Whistle While You Work," "Heigh Ho," "Bluddle-Uddle-Um-Dum," "The Dwarfs' Yodel Song" and "Some Day My Prince Will Come." **Running time:** 83 minutes. **Released:** December 21, 1937.

*Voices*
**Snow White:** Adriana Caselotti; **The Prince:** Harry Stockwell; **The Queen:** Lucille LaVerne; **Bashful:** Scotty Mattraw; **Doc:** Roy Atwell; **Grumpy:** Pinto Colvig; **Happy:** Otis Harlan; **Sleepy:** Pinto Colvig; **Sneezy:** Billy Gilbert; **The Magic Mirror:** Moroni Olsen; **Humbert, the Queen's Huntsman:** Stuart Buchanan

Classic good versus evil tale of ever-sweet orphan princess Snow White, who although she is forced to work as a household servant to the Queen, a vain woman who will have no rival, becomes the most beautiful in the land. In retaliation, the Queen casts a spell on Snow White—brought on by a bite of a poisonous

*Walt Disney's* Snow White and the Seven Dwarfs *(1937) was the first full-length animated feature in cartoon history. The film remains one of the top-grossing cartoon features of all time. © Walt Disney Productions* (COURTESY: MUSEUM OF MODERN ART/FILM STILLS ARCHIVE)

apple—which can be broken only by a kiss from the Prince to bring her back to life.

**PN:** The first full-length animated feature of any kind, this film is still considered a milestone in animated cartoon history. The picture took four years to complete and went over budget. (Originally set at $250,000, the film cost $1,488,000 to produce.) It grossed $8.5 million during its first release (then the highest-grossing first release film of all time). Subsequent reissues in 1944, 1952, 1967, 1975, 1983 and 1987 have proven even more worthwhile. The 1987 release alone grossed over $50 million.

One sequence involving Snow White's mother dying in childbirth was cut from the story during production, even though stills from the scene were published in *Look* magazine's preview of the film as well as in authorized book versions, comic strips and comic books based on the film.

## ◎ SONG OF THE SOUTH (1946)

A Walt Disney Production released by RKO Radio Pictures. **p:** Walt Disney; **anim dir:** Wilfred Jackson; **scr:** Dalton Reymond, Morton Grant, Maurice Rapf; **st:** Dalton Reymond (based on the *Tales of Uncle Remus* by Joel Chandler Harris); **cart st:** William Peet, Ralph Wright, George Stallings; **md:** Charles Wolcott; **cart sc:** Paul J. Smith; **dir anim:** Milt Kahl, Eric Larson, Oliver M. Johnston Jr., Les Clark, Marc Davis, John Lounsbery. **Songs:** "How Do You Do?" "Song of the South," "That's What Uncle Remus Said," "Sooner or Later," "Everybody's Got a Laughing Place," "Zip-a-Dee-Doo-Dah," "Let the Rain Pour Down" and "Who Wants to Live Like That?" **Running time:** 94 minutes. **Released:** November 2, 1946.

### Cast

**Sally:** Ruth Warrick; **Uncle Remus:** James Baskett; **Johnny:** Bobby Driscoll; **Ginny:** Luana Patten; **Grandmother:** Lucile Watson; **Aunt Tempy:** Hattie McDaniel; **Toby:** Glenn Leedy; **The Faver Boys:** George Nokes, Gene Holland; **John:** Erik Rolf; **Mrs. Favers:** Mary Field; **Maid:** Anita Brown

### Voices

**Brer Fox:** James Baskett; **Brer Bear:** Nicodemus Stewart; **Brer Rabbit:** Johnny Lee

In Tom Sawyer–like fashion, Uncle Remus recalls the simple truths of the Old South instilling good morals in the mind of Johnny, a youngster who comes to rely on Remus as his main companion. The two are joined by a friendly little girl, Ginny, and along the way many of Remus's old tales come to life via animated sequences featuring the likes of Brer Rabbit, Brer Fox and Brer Bear.

## ◎ SON OF ALADDIN (2003)

A Pentamedia Graphics Production release. **d:** Rao Singeetam; **scr:** Mark Zaslove. **Running time:** 90 minutes. **Released:** August 29, 2003.

Voice credits unknown.

Prince Aladdin's son, Mustapha, grows into a swashbuckling sailor who woos a haughty priness and defeats the wicked wizard Zee Zee Ba, who tries hunting him down after discovering that the young prince's destiny is to kill him in this animated high-seas fantasy-adventure.

**PN:** This $3.6-million fantasy adventure was produced in nine months by India's Pentamedia Graphics using motion-capture technology and some 1,100 shots and a total of 125 characters, 32 sets and 2,000 rendered images. Released in the United States in late August, the film opened on the East Coast, where theaters were only 24 percent full during its first weekend. Distri-

bution of the film later expanded to multiplexes in major-market cities.

## ◎ SOUTH PARK: BIGGER, LONGER AND UNCUT (1999)

A Scott Rudin/Trey Park/Matt Stone Production in association with Comedy Central released by Paramount Pictures/Warner Bros. **p:** Trey Parker, Matt Stone; **exec prod:** Scott Rudin, Adam Schroeder; **cpd:** Anne Garefino, Deborah Liebling; **d:** Trey Parker; **scr:** Trey Parker, Matt Stone, Pam Brady; **m:** James Herfield; **songs:** Trey Parker, Bobby Guy, Ernie Lake, Marc Shairman; **dir anim:** Eric Stough; **superv anim:** Martin Cendrada, Toni Nugnes. **Songs:** "Mountain Town," "Uncle Fucka," "Wendy's Song," "It's Easy, Mmmkay," "Hell Isn't Good," "Blame Canada," "Kyle's Mom's a Bitch," "What Would Brian Boitano Do?" "Up There," "La Resistance (Medley)," "I Can Change," "I'm Super," "The Mole's Reprise," "Mountain Town (Reprise)," "What Would Brian Boitano Do? Pt. II" and "Eyes of a Child." **Running time:** 80 minutes. **Released:** June 30, 1999.

### Voices

**Stan Marsh/Eric Cartman/Mr. Garrison/Mr. Hat/Officer Barbrady:** Trey Parker; **Kyle Broflovski/Kenny McCormick/Pip/Jesus/Jimbo:** Matt Stone; **Mrs. Cartman/Sheila Broflovski/Sharon Manson/Mrs. McCormick/Wendy Testaburger/Principal Victoria/Mole Child/Female Bodypart:** Mary Kay Bergman; **Chef:** Isaac Hayes; **Dr. Gouache:** George Clooney; **Conan O'Brien:** Brent Spiner; **Brooke Shields:** Minnie Driver; **Baldwin Brothers:** Dave Foley; **Dr. Vosknocker:** Eric Idle; **American Soldier #1:** Stewart Copeland; **Kenny's Goodbye:** Mike Judge

After potty-mouthed third-graders Stan, Kyle, Cartman and Kenny attend an R-rated movie, *Asses of Fire,* starring their Canadian television favorites, Terrence and Philip, the film's graphic vocabulary causes a major uproar with the parents of South Park, led by Kyle's mom, who launches an anti-Canadian campaign that soon lands the film's stars in a U.S. prison.

**PN:** *South Park* cocreators Trey Parker and Matt Stone coproduced, with Parker directing, this feature-length version of the hit Comedy Central series known for its crude paper cutout animated characters and gross humor. Costing $21 million to produce, this R-rated feature made $52 million domestically, with the film's title song, "Blame Canada," being nominated for an Academy Award for best song.

## ◎ SPACE ADVENTURE COBRA (1995)

A Tokyo Movie Shinsha (TMS) Production released by Tara Releasing Corporation. **p:** Yutaka Fujioka, Tetsuo Katayama; **d:** Osamu Dezaki; **scr:** Buichi Terasawa, Hauya Yamazaki; (English version) Michael Charles Hill; **m:** Osamu Shoji; **anim dir:** Akio Sugino; **anim:** Yukari Kobayashi, Hayao Miyazaki, Koji Morimoto, Setusko Shibuichi. **Running time:** 109 minutes. **Released:** August 20, 1995.

### Voices

**Cobra:** Dan Woren; **Crystal Boy:** Jeff Winkless; **Professor Topolov:** Kirk Thornton; **Catherine:** Jane Alan; **Sandra:** Catherine Battistone; **Jane:** Barbara Goodson; **Dominique:** Wendee Lee

Teamed with the beauteous android bounty hunter, Jane Flower, the handsome, charismatic space pirate, Cobra, defeats the Galactic Guild and his sinister archrival, Crystal Boy, in this cult-classic, 24th-century science fiction adventure.

**PN:** Based on the Japanese manga adventure of the same name by Buichi Terasawa first published in 1978, this animated feature debuted in Japan on July 3, 1982, followed by a 31-episode cartoon series that aired on Japanese television from October 1982 through May 1983. In 1995, the film was released in the United States.

## ◎ SPACE JAM (1996)

A Uli Meyer Features/Warner Brothers/Character Builders/Charles Gammage Animation/Courtside Seats/Northern Lights Entertainment/Rees-Leiva/Spaff Animation/Stardust Pictures Production released by Warner Bros. **p:** Daniel Goldberg, Steven Paul Leiva, Joe Medjuck, Ivan Reitman; **d:** Joe Pytka (live action), Tony Cervone (animation), Bruce W. Smith (animation); **exec prod:** David Falk, Ken Ross; **scr:** Leonardo Benvenuti, Timothy Harris, Steve Rudnick, Herschel Weingrod; **m:** James Newton Howard. **Songs:** "Fly Like an Eagle," "Winner," "Space Jam," "I Believe I Can Fly," "Hit 'em High," "I Found My Smile Again," "For You I Will," "Upside Down ('Round-n-Round)," "Givin' U All That I've Got," "Basketball Jones," "I Turn to You," "All of My Days," "That's the Way (I Like It)" and "Buggin." **Running time:** 87 minutes. **Released:** November 15, 1996.

### Cast (live action)

**Himself:** Michael Jordan; **Stan Podolak:** Wayne Knight; **Juanita Jordan:** Theresa Randle; **Jeffery Jordan:** Manner Washington; **Marcus Jordan:** Eric Gordon; **Jasmine Jordan:** Penny Bae Bridges; **Michael Jordan, age 10:** Brandon Hammon; **Himself:** Larry Bird; **James Jordan:** Thom Barry; **Themselves:** Charles Barkley, Patrick Ewing, Tyrone Bogues, Larry Johnson, Shawn Bradley, Ahmad Rashad, Del Harris, Vlade Divac, Cedric Ceballos, Jim Rome, Paul Westphal, Danny Ainge; **Jordan Housekeeper:** Bebe Drake; **Woman Fan:** Patricia Heaton; **Male Fan:** Dan Castellaneta; **Female Seer:** Linda Lutz; **Basketball Girl:** Nicky McCrimmon; **Little League Girl:** Kelly Vint; **Golfer:** Willam G. Schilling; **Psychiatrist:** Albert Hague; **Doctor:** Michael Alaimo; **NBA Referee:** James O'Donnell; **Charlotte Coach:** David Ursin; **Commissioner:** Douglas Robert Jackson; **Themselves:** Alonzo Mourning, A.C. Green, Charles Oakley, Derek Harper, Jeff Malone, Anthony Miller, Sharone Wright; **Umpire (as Rosey Brown):** Andre Rosey Brown; **Stars Catcher:** Brad Henke; **Owner's Girlfriend:** Connie Ray; **Baron's Manager:** John Roselius; **Baron's Catcher:** Charles Hoyes; **Players:** Luke Torres, Steven Shenbaum, Bean Miller; **Barons Coach:** Joy Bays; **Himself:** Bill Murray (uncredited)

### Voices

**Bugs Bunny/Elmer Fudd:** Billy West; **Daffy Duck/Tazmanian Devil/Bull:** Dee Bradley Baker; **Swackhammer:** Danny DeVito; **Porky Pig:** Bob Bergen; **Sylvester/Yosemite Sam/Foghorn Leghorn:** Bill Farmer; **Granny:** June Foray; **Pepe Le Pew:** Maurice LaMarche; **Lola Bunny:** Kath Soucie; **Nerdluck Pound:** Jocelyn Blue; **Nerdluck Blanko:** Charity James; **Nerdluck Bang:** June Melby; **Nerdluck Bupkus:** Catherine Reitman; **Nerdluck Nawt/Sniffles:** Colleen Wainwright; **Monstar Bupkus:** Dorian Harewood; **Monstar Ban:** Joey Camen; **Monstar Nawt:** T.K. Carter; **Monstar Pound:** Darnell Suttles; **Monster Blanko/Announcer:** Steve Kehela

Basketball superstar Michael Jordan is recruited by Bugs Bunny and the Looney Tunes characters to compete in a high-stakes basketball game (their opponent is the Monstars, a team of pumped-up aliens who've stolen the skills of some NBA stars) to win their freedom from an evil amusement park owner who plans to enslave them as his top attractions.

**PN:** Opening on 2,650 movie screens nationwide, *Space Jam* was an instant hit, grossing $27.528 million during its first weekend and more than $90 million in the United States alone.

## ◎ SPIRITED AWAY (2002)

A Studio Ghibli Production in association with Tokuma Shoten Co., Nippon TV Network Co., Dentsu, Buena Vista Home Entertainment (Japan), Tohokushinsha Film and Mitsubishi released by Walt Disney Studios. **p:** Toshio Suzuki; **exec prod:** Yasuyoshi Tokuma, Takeyoshi Matsushita, Seiichiro Ujiie, Yutaka Narita, Koji Hoshino, Banjiro Uemura, Hironori Aihara, (U.S. version) John Lasseter; **d:** Hayao Miyazaki; **scr:** Hayao Miyazaki; **m:** Joe Hisaishi; **songs:** Wakako Kaku, Youmi Kimura; **anim dir:** Masashi Ando. **Running time:** 125 minutes. **Released:** September 20, 2002.

### Voices

**Chihiro:** Daveigh Chase; **Yubaba/Zeniba:** Suzanne Pleshette; **Haku:** Jason Marsden; **Lin:** Susan Egan; **Kamaji:** David Ogden Stiers; **Chihiro's Mother:** Lauren Holly; **Chihiro's Father:** Michael Chiklis; **Assistant Manager:** John Ratzenberger; **Boh–Baby:** Tara Strong; **Bath House Woman:** Mickie McGowan; **Radish Spirit:** Jack Angel; **No-Face/The Frog:** Bob Bergen; **Bouncing Heads:** Rodger Bumpass; **Frog-Like Chef:** Phil Proctor

While moving to their new family home, a bratty, 10-year-old girl, Chihiro, and her parents, Akio and Yugo, get lost in a forest and end up in an abandoned theme park where, after her parents are turned into pigs, Chihiro wanders off into a world inhabited by ghosts, animals and demons whom she must thwart before restoring her parents to their human form and returning to the real world.

**PN:** Following the success of his acclaimed eco-parable, *Princess Mononoke* (1997), legendary Japanese animator and Studio Ghibli cofounder Hayao Miyazaki wrote, designed and directed this Nipponese *Alice in Wonderland* story. Originally opening in movie theaters in Japan on July 27, 2001, the $19 million, 19th-century fantasy became Japan's top-grossing movie of all time, earning more than $230 million in revenue—six times more than the science fiction sequel, *Jurassic Park III* (2001), and more than four times that of director Michael Bay's Academy Award-winning *Pearl Harbor* (2001). Redubbed in English more than a year later, Walt Disney Studios released this PG-rated film to theaters in the United States on September 20, 2002, where it won widespread acclaim and grossed slightly more than $10 million. Despite its poor box-office showing, the film won an Academy Award that year for best animated feature.

## ◎ SPIRIT: STALLION OF THE CIMARRON (2002)

A DreamWorks Animation SKG Production released by DreamWorks Pictures SKG. **p:** Jeffery Katzenberg, Mireille Soria; **d:** Kelly Asbury, Lorna Cook; **scr:** John Fusco; **m:** Hans Zimmer, Steve Jablonsky; **songs:** Bryan Adams; **anim superv:** Kristoff Serrand; **senior superv anim:** James Baxter; **superv anim:** Steve Horrocks, Jakob Hjort Jensen, Dan Wagner, Bruce Ferriz, Pres Antonio Romanillos, William Salazar, Fabio Lignini, Sylvain Deboissy, Lionel Gallat, Erik C. Schmidt, Alex Williams, Phillipe LeBrun, Mary Ann Malcomb, Simon Otto, Patrick Mate. **Running time:** 83 minutes. **Released:** May 24, 2002.

### Voices

**Spirit:** Matt Damon; **Little Creek:** Daniel Studi; **The Colonel:** James Cromwell; **Sgt. Adams:** Chopper Bernet; **Murphy/Railroad Foreman:** Jeff LeBeau; **Soldier:** John Rubano; **Bill:** Richard McConagle; **Joe:** Matthew Levin; **Pete:** Adam Paul; **Jake:** Robert Cait; **Roy:** Charles Napier; **Little Indian Girl:** Meredith Wells; **Little Creek's Friends:** Zahn McClarnon, Michael Horse; **Train Pull Foreman:** Don Fullilove

Spirit, a fast, headstrong mustang that matures into an untamed stallion roped and captured by a harsh army colonel who is determined to break him, falls in love with a pretty pinto, Rain, after her owner, an Indian native, sets him free, only to escape with Rain on a suspenseful adventure through forests, rivers and open country while trying to return to his homeland.

**PN:** Actor Matt Dillon narrated this noble Old West story told from the horse's point of view of "my spirit will never be broken" as its central theme, marking the codirecting debut of directors Kelly Asbury and Lorna Cook, formerly story supervisors of DreamWorks' *The Prince of Egypt* (1998), which combined elements of traditional hand-drawn animation and 3-D computer work, grossed $73,215,310 domestically and was nominated for an Academy Award for best animated feature.

### ◎ THE SPONGEBOB SQUAREPANTS MOVIE (2004)

A Nickelodeon Movies Production in association with United Plankton Pictures released by Paramount Pictures. **p:** Stephen Hillenburg, Julia Pistor; **exec prod:** Albie Hecht, Gina Shay, Derek Drymon; **d:** Stephen Hillenburg; **scr:** Derek Drymon, Tim Hill, Stephen Hillenburg, Kent Osborne, Aaron Springer, Paul Tibbitt (based on a story and the series created by Stephen Hillenburg); **m:** Gregor Nabholz; **seq dir:** Derek Drymon, Kent Osborne; **superv anim dir:** Alan Smart. **Running time:** 99 minutes. **Released:** November 19, 2004.

*Voices*
**SpongeBob:** Tom Kenny; **Patrick Star:** Bill Fagerbakke; **Mr. Krabs:** Clancy Brown; **Squidward:** Rodger Bumpass; **Plankton:** Mr. Lawrence; **Dennis:** Alec Baldwin; **David Hasselhoff:** Himself; **Mindy:** Scarlett Johansson; **King Neptune:** Jeffrey Tambor; **Karen (The Computer Wife):** Jill Talley; **Sandy:** Carolyn Lawrence; **Mrs. Puff:** Mary Jo Catlett

After scheming restaurateur Plankton, owner of the unsuccessful Chum Bucket, successfully campaigns to take customers from the Krusty Krab and steals the crown of the king of Neptune at the same time (while convincing the good king that Mr. Krabs is the guilty party who took it), SpongeBob and Patrick battle sea monsters, a scary biker hit man named Dennis (voiced by Alec Baldwin) and live-action *Baywatch* television star David Hasselhoff to recover the stolen crown and save SpongeBob's greedy, encrusted boss before it's too late.

**PN:** Based on Nickelodeon's biggest cartoon series hit since its debut in 1999, *SpongeBob SquarePants* creator Stephen Hillenburg cowrote, directed and produced this feature-length version. Hillenburg, a CalArts graduate (after Oscar-winning animators John Lasseter and Brad Bird) created the cult favorite underwater characters after working in marine biology. The movie, which was made on a shoestring budge of $30 million, featured the crudely hand-drawn animated adventures and was a major box-office hit, earning $85,416,609 domestically and $140,416,609 worldwide.

### ◎ SPRIGGAN (2001)

A Studio 4°C Production released by A.D.V. Films. **p:** Ayao Ueda, Kazuhiko Ikeguchi, Kazuya Hamana, Haruo Sai, Eiko Tanaka, (English adaptation) Matt Greenfield; **d:** Hirotsugu Kawasaki; **scr:** Yasutaka Ito, Hirotsugu Kawasaki (based on the manga by Hiroshi Takashige and Ryoji Minagawa); **m:** Kuniaki Haishima **Running time:** 90 minutes. **Released:** October 12, 2001.

Voice credits unknown.

A top superhuman agent (Yu) employed by the secret organization, ARCAM, dedicated to protecting ancient artifacts, must stop a foreign military unit from gaining control of one of the most prized artifacts of all, Noah's Ark, which turns out to be an alien spaceship possessing great power in this Japanese science fiction animated adventure.

### ◎ STARCHASER: THE LEGEND OF ORIN (1985)

A Steven Hahn Production released by Atlantic Releasing. **p:** Steven Hahn; **d:** Steven Hahn, John Sparey; **w:** Jeffrey Scott; **m:** Andrew Belling; **anim dir:** Mitch Rochon, Jang-Gil Kim. **Running time:** 98 minutes. **Released:** November 22, 1985.

*Voices*
**Orin:** Joe Colligan; **Dagg:** Carmen Argenziano; **Elan Aviana:** Noelle North; **Zygon:** Anthony Delongis; **Arthur:** Les Tremayne; **Silica:** Tyke Caravelli; **Magreb:** Ken Samson; **Auctioneer/Z. Gork:** John Moschita Jr.; **Minemaster:** Mickey Morton; **Pung/Hopps:** Herb Vigran; **Shooter:** Dennis Alwood; **Kallie:** Mona Marshall; **Aunt Bella:** Tina Romanus

*Additional Voices*
Daryl T. Bartley, Phillip Clarke, Joseph Dellasorte, John Garwood, Barbera Harris and Company, Ryan MacDonald, Thomas H. Watkins, Mike Winslow

A young robot/human retrieves a magic sword and overtakes a piratical captain of a spaceship to free other humans in the underground world.

**PN:** Film was released in 3-D.

### ◎ STEAMBOY (2005)

A Studio 4°C/Steamboy Committee/Sunrise VAP Production released by Triumph Films. **p:** Shinji Komori, Hideyuki Tomioka; **d:** Katsuhiro Otomo; **scr:** Sadayuki Murai, Katsuhiro Otomo; **m:** Steve Jablonsky; **anim dir:** Shinji Takagi; **anim superv:** Tatsuya Tomaru. **Running time:** 140 minutes. **Released:** March 18, 2005.

*Voices*
(English version) **James Ray Steam:** Anna Paquin; **Dr. Eddie Steam:** Alfred Molina; **Dr. Lloyd Steam:** Patrick Stewart; **Scarlett O'Hara:** Kari Wahlgren; **David:** Robin Atkin Downes; **Jason:** David S. Lee; **Emma:** Paula J. Newman; **Cliff/Tommy/Other Voices:** Moira Quirk; **Alfred:** Mark Bramhall; **Mrs. Steam:** Kim Thomson

*Additional Voices*
Julian Stone

Set in mid-19th-century England, a child inventor is suddenly transformed into a superhero after he obtains a mysterious invention coveted by governments and businesses. Known as the Steam Ball, the device emits a powerful stream of energy source that he uses to fight evil forces who want to use its menacing power for mass destruction.

**PN:** Acclaimed Japanese filmmaker Katsuhiro Otomo wrote and directed this Neo-Toyko science fiction fantasy, his first full-length cartoon feature since his watershed film, *Akira* (1988). The 128-minute production was redubbed in English and opened in the United States in limited release.

### ◎ THE SWAN PRINCESS (1994)

A Nest Entertainment/Rich Animation Studios Production released by Columbia Pictures. **p&d:** Richard Rich; **exec prod:** Jared F. Brown, Seldon Young; **st:** Brian Nissen, Richard Rich; **st:** Richard Rich, Brian Nissen; **scr:** Brian Nissen; **m:** Lex de Azevedo (with songs by David Zippel and Lex de Azevedo). **Songs:** "Far Longer Than Forever," "Eternity," "This Is My Idea," "Practice,

Practice, Practice," "No Fear," "No More Mr. Nice Guy" and "Princess on Parade." **Running time:** 90 minutes. **Released:** November 18, 1994.

*Voices*
**Rothbart:** Jack Palance; **Prince Derek:** Howard McGillin; **Princess Odette:** Michelle Nicastro; **Jean-Bob:** John Cleese; **Speed:** Steven Wright; **Puffin:** Steve Vinovich; **Lord Rogers:** Mark Harelik; **Chamberlain:** James Arrington; **Bromley:** Joel McKinnon Miller; **King William:** Dakin Matthews; **Queen Uberta:** Sandy Duncan; **Narrator:** Brian Nissen; **Young Derek:** Adam Wylie; **Young Odette:** Adrian Zahiri; **Musician:** Tom Alan Robbins; **Hag:** Bess Hopper; **Dancers:** Cate Coplin, Tom Slater, Jim Pearce; **Odette (singing voice):** Liz Callaway; **Rothbart (singing voice):** Lex De Azevedo; **Chamberlain (singing voice):** Davis Gaines

A beautiful young princess (Odette) is transformed into a swan by an evil sorcerer's spell, which can be broken only by a vow of everlasting love in this magical musical adventure based on the classic fairy tale *Swan Lake*.

**PN:** Turner's New Line Cinema lost the battle at the box office with this beautifully animated feature that went head-to-head against 20th Century Fox's release of Turner's *The Pagemaster*, Disney's *The Lion King* and live-action *The Santa Clause* starring Tim Allen of TV's *Home Improvement*. Final ticket sales totaled only $3 million. At the 1994 Cannes Film Festival in France, 300 guests were given their first peek of the $35-million full-length animated feature at a party held in a medieval castle overlooking the Mediterranean. The film's fairy-tale story was based on the German folk tale, *Swan Lake* (which was also the film's original working title). Eight original songs were written for the movie by Broadway veterans Lex de Azevedo and David Zippel, the same composers who wrote Broadway's *The Goodbye Girl* and *City of Angels*, a Tony Award winner. The song "Far Longer than Forever" was nominated for a Golden Globe award for best original song. Richard Rich and Matt Mazur, two former Disney employees (Rich is best known for directing the animated feature *Fox and the Hound*) produced the feature as well as the 1997 sequel, *Swan Princess: Escape from Castle Mountain*, which Rich also directed.

## ◎ THE SWAN PRINCESS II: ESCAPE FROM CASTLE MOUNTAIN (1997)

A Nest Entertainment/Seldon O. Young/Jared F. Brown/K. Douglas Martin presentation of a Rich Animation Studios Production released by Legacy Releasing Corporation. **p:** Jared F. Brown, Richard Rich; **exec prod:** Jared F. Brown, K. Douglas Martin, Seldon O. Young; **d:** Richard Rich; **scr:** Brian Nissen; **st:** Brian Nissen, Richard Rich; **m:** Lex de Azevedo; **songs:** Lex de Azevedo, Clive Romney; **anim dir:** Sang Man Hong, Han Won Lee. **Running time:** 71 minutes. **Released:** July 18, 1997.

*Voices*
**Princess Odette:** Michaelle Nicastro; **Derek:** Douglas Sills; **Clavius:** Jake Williamson; **Uberta:** Christy Landers; **Jean-Bob:** Donald Sage MacKay; **Speed:** Doug Stone; **Puffin:** Steve Vinovich; **Knuckles:** Joey Camen; **Chamberlain:** James Arrington; **Bridget:** Rosie Mann; **Lord Rogers:** Joseph Medrano; **Bromley:** Owen Miller

After morphing into a swan when her husband is seized, the lovely Princess Odette embarks on a dangerous mission on the day of their first wedding anniversary to rescue her handsome Prince Derek from the clutches of the evil Clavius, who aspires to conquer the world using a globe-sized orb he has obtained that contains the powers of the Forbidden Arts.

**PN:** Follow-up to the 1994 original, this was released by New Line Cinema but grossed only $9.8 million domestically despite major product tie-ins and a widespread marketing campaign. Coproduced, cowritten and directed by the film's original producer-director, animator Richard Rich, this sequel opened the weekend of July 19, 1997, in only 97 theaters nationwide, grossing a meager $50,208.

## ◎ THE SWORD IN THE STONE (1963)

A Walt Disney Production released by Buena Vista. **p:** Walt Disney; **d:** Wolfgang Reitherman; **dir anim:** Frank Thomas, Milt Kahl, Ollie Johnston, John Lounsbery; **st:** Bill Peet (based on the book by T.H. White); **m:** George Bruns. **Songs:** "A Most Befuddling Thing," "Blue Oak Tree," "Mad Madame Mim," "That's What Makes the World Go Round," "Higitus Figitus" and "The Legend of the Sword in the Stone." **Running time:** 75 minutes. **Released:** December 25, 1963.

*Voices*
**Wart:** Ricky Sorenson; **Sir Ector/Narrator:** Sebastian Cabot; **Merlin:** Karl Swenson; **Archimedes:** Junius Matthews; **Sir Pelinore:** Alan Napier; **Sir Kay:** Norman Alden; **Madame Mim/Granny Squirrel:** Martha Wentworth; **Girl Squirrel:** Ginny Tyler; **Scullery Maid:** Barbara Jo Allen; **Wart:** Richard and Robert Reitherman

As the title implies, the sword embedded in stone is central to this story featuring Wart, a foster son of Sir Ector, who undertakes lessons in life from Merlin the Magician. Setting off for a jousting tournament in London with Ector and his son Sir Kay, Wart returns to retrieve Kay's forgotten sword. To save time, he pulls a sword from the legendary stone, unaware that the man who does so becomes the rightful king of all of England.

## ◎ TAMALA 2010 (2003)

A Kinetique Production released by Vitagraph Films. **p:** Seiichi Tsukada, Kazuko Mio, t.o.L.; **d, scr, & anim::** trees of Life (t.o.L.). **Running time:** 92 minutes. **Released:** December 19, 2003.

*Voices*
**Tamala:** Hisayo Mochizuki; **Michelangelo:** Shinji Takeda; **Tatla the Machine God:** Beatrice Dalle; **Zombie Cat:** Takeshi Kato

Futuristic space-age adventures of a carefree, one-year-old feline advertising icon, Tamala, controlled by an influential corporate empire, Catty & Co., who embarks on a spaceship journey to discover the planet of her origin.

**PN:** Written, animated and scored by a group of producers collectively known as "t.o.L.," this international film festival favorite was first released in Japan on October 19, 2002. Debuting in the United States more than a year after its original release, the surreal black-and-white and color film, which combined Flash and full 2-D animation, was promoted as the first of a feature film trilogy and planned television series, which has yet to materialize.

## ◎ TARZAN (1999)

A Walt Disney Pictures Production released by Buena Vista Pictures. **p:** Bonnie Arnold; **d:** Kevin Lima, Chris Buck; **scr:** Tab Murphy, Bob Tzudiker, Noni White (based on the story *Tarzan of the Apes* by Edgar Rice Burroughs, with additional screenplay material by David Reynolds and Jeffrey Stepakoff); **m/l:** Phil Collins, Mark Mancina; **superv anim:** Glen Keane, Ken Stuart Duncan, Russ Edmonds, John Ripa, Michael Surry, Randy Haycock, David Burgess, Bruce W. Smith, Sergio Fabios, Dominique Monfery, Jay Jackson, T. Daniel Hofstedt, Chris Wahl. **Songs:** "Two

Worlds," "You'll Be in My Heart," "Son of Man," "Trashin' the Camp," "Strangers Like Me" and "True Colors." **Running time:** 88 minutes. **Released:** June 18, 1999.

### Voices

**Tarzan:** Tony Goldwyn; **Young Tarzan:** Alex D. Linz; **Jane Porter:** Minnie Driver; **Kerchak:** Lance Henriksen; **Kala:** Glenn Close; **Professor Porter:** Nigel Hawthorne; **Clayton:** Brian Blessed; **Terk:** Rosie O'Donnell; **Tantor:** Wayne Knight; **Young Tantor:** Taylor Dempsey; **Baby Apes:** Aria Noelle Curzon

A man raised by gorillas in the wilds of the African jungles comes to the realization that he is human after he falls in love with a female expeditioner in this animated musical adventure based on Edgar Rice Burroughs's classic novel.

**PN:** Walt Disney Studios produced this feature-length version of the improbable feats of the vine-swinging ape man of the jungle created by author Edgar Rice Burroughs, bringing this first-ever animated version of Burroughs's legendary African tale to the screen after 47 previous Tarzan features by other studios, all of them live action. Considered a viable project for animation dating back to 1936, after seeing the studio's first full-length animated feature, *Snow White and the Seven Dwarfs* (1937), Burroughs reportedly wrote Walt Disney about adapting his famed novel into a cartoon feature. Burroughs said that although the story seemed well suited for animation, any "cartoon must be good. It must approximate Disney excellence." Disney's G-rated 1999 release lived up to those expectations with exceptional 2-D animation meshed with vivid 3-D special effects and backgrounds codirected by Chris Buck and Kevin Lima and produced by Disney's Burbank and Paris studios. Lead animator Glen Keane, who led a team of animators in Paris, noted that Tarzan's remarkably fluid swinging through the jungle was inspired by watching his skateboarding son. With songs, including the title song, "You'll Be in My Heart" (which won an Oscar for best music, original song), produced and arranged by Grammy award-winning pop-singer Phil Collins with composer Mark Mancina and sung by Collins, the musical epic did blockbuster business at the box office, where it grossed $172 million domestically and inspired the direct-to-video sequel released five years later, *Tarzan and Jane* (2004).

### ◎ TEACHER'S PET (2004)

A Walt Disney Pictures/Walt Disney Television Animation Production released by Buena Vista Pictures. **p:** Stephen Swofford; **exec prod:** Gary Baseman, Bill and Cheri Steinkellner; **d:** Timothy Bjorklund; **scr:** Bill and Cheri Steinkellner; **m:** Stephen James Taylor; **songs:** Randy Peterson, Kevin Quinn, Cheri Steinkeller, Brian Woodbury, Peter Lurye; **unit anim dir:** Dante Clemente; **assist anim superv:** Nowell Villano. **Running time:** 73 minutes. **Released:** January 16, 2004.

### Voices

**Spot/Scott:** Nathan Lane; **Dr. Krank:** Kelsey Grammer; **Leonard:** Shaun Fleming; **Mrs. Helperman:** Debra Jo Rupp; **Jolly:** David Ogden Stiers; **Pretty Boy:** Jerry Stiller; **Dennis:** Paul Reubens; **Adele:** Megan Mullally; **Ian:** Rob Paulsen; **Principal Strickler:** Wallace Shawn; **Mrs. Boogin:** Estelle Harris; **Barry Anger:** Jay Thomas; **Ian Wazelewski:** Rob Paulsen; **Marcia/Marcia:** Genie Francis; **John/Juan:** Anthony Geary; **Beefeater:** David Maples; **Trevor/Taylor/Tyler:** Pamela Segall; **Daddy:** Timothy Stack; **Little Girl:** Emma Steinkeller; **Officer White:** Ken Swafford; **Younghee:** Lauren Tom; **Conductor:** Kevin Michael Richardson

Disguised as a bright fourth-grader named Scott Leadready II, Spot, a turquoise talking dog who dreams of becoming a "boy," heads to Florida with his owner and best friend, eight-year-old Leonard Helperman, and his mother. In Florida spot meets up with a mad scientist who fulfills his wish by turning him into a man who then falls in love with Leonard's mother.

**PN:** Based on the three-time Emmy Award-winning *Disney's Teacher's Pet* Saturday-morning cartoon series that aired as part of ABC's "One Saturday Morning" lineup, this fast-paced, low-budget, big-screen version finally came to the screen after numerous delays reunited the creative team behind the hit cartoon series: Nathan Lane as the voice of Spot; illustrator Gary Baseman; writers Bill and Cheri Steinkellner; and director Timothy Bjorklund. Also lending her voice to this project was Debra Jo Rupp of Fox television's *That 70's Show* as Leonard Helperman's mother. Among a list of 11 features that made a short list of nominees for an Academy Award for best animated feature in 2004, this enjoyable 73-minute romp was a tremendous critical success, but largely ignored by the public, grossing only $6,426,692 in the United States—less than half of its original budget.

### ◎ TEENAGE MUTANT NINJA TURTLES (2007)

An Imagi International Holdings Ltd. Production released by Warner Bros. **p:** Galen Walker, Paul Wang, Felix Ip; **exec prod:** Peter A. Laird, Francis Kao, Gary Richardson, Frederick Fierst; **d:** Kevin Munroe; **scr:** Kevin Munroe, **m:** Klaus Badelt; **superv anim:** Kim Ooi. **Running time:** 90 minutes. **Release date:** March 23, 2007.

### Voices

**Raphael/Nightwatcher:** Nolan North; **Donatello:** Mitchell Whitfield; **Michaelangelo:** Mikey Kelley; **Leonardo:** James Arnold Taylor; **Maximillian J. Winters:** Patrick Steweart; **April O'Neil:** Sarah Michelle Gellar; **Karai:** Zivi Zhang; **Casey Jones:** Chris Evans; **Splinter:** Mako; **Diner Cook:** Kevin Smith

Having grown apart after successfully defeating their famed arch rival, the Shredder, Splinter restores a sense of urgency into the shelled superheroes Raphael, Michaelangelo, Leonardo and Donatello in time to battle a tycoon industrialist who has unleashed four ancient stone warriors on New York City.

**PN:** Opening in theaters the week before Walt Disney's computer-animated comedy, *Meet the Robinsons*, this computer-animated update of the famed animated cartoon and live-action movie characters, debuted at number one with $25.45 million in ticket sales its first weekend.

### ◎ TENCHI MUYO IN LOVE (1996)

An Anime International Company (A.I.C.) Production released by Pioneer Entertainment. **p:** Take W. Abe, Naoju Nakamura, Hidemi Satani; **d:** Hiroshi Negishi; **scr:** Hiroshi Negishi, Ryoe Tsukimura; **m:** Christopher Franke; **anim prod:** Toru Miura; **anim dir:** Kazuya Kuroda, Michiyo Suzuki, Takahiro Kishida. **Running time:** 95 minutes. **Released:** August 16, 1996.

### Voices

**Tenchi Masaki:** Masami Kikuchi; **Ryoko:** Ai Orikasa; **Achika:** Megumi Hayashibara; **Ayeka:** Yumi Takada; **Sasami:** Chisa Yokoyama; **Ryo-Ohki:** Etsuko Kozakura; **Kain:** Ryuzaburo Otomo; **Young Nobuyuki Masaki:** Toshiyuki Morikawa; **Washu:** Yuko Kobayashi; **Mihoshi:** Yuko Mizutani; **Kiyone:** Yuri Amano

Tenchi Masaki and his adolescent friends time-travel back to the 1970s to stop a demonic space villain, who has escaped from prison and destroyed Galaxy Police headquarters, from killing Tenchi's mother before his birth. This science fiction adventure was based on the popular Japanese direct-to-video series, OAV specials and a 26-episode cartoon series produced between September 1992 and September 1995.

## THE THREE CABALLEROS (1945)

A Walt Disney Production released by RKO Radio Pictures. **p:** Walt Disney; **prod superv/dir:** Norman Ferguson; **seq d:** Clyde Geronimi, Jack Kinney, Bill Roberts; **d:** Harold Young (Patzcuaro, Veracruz, Acapulco); **st:** Homer Brightman, Ernest Terrazzas, Ted Sears, Bill Peet, Ralph Wright, Elmer Plummer, Roy Williams, William Cottrell, Del Connell, James Bodrero; **md:** Charles Wolcott, Paul J. Smith, Edward H. Plumb. **Songs:** "The Three Caballeros," "Os Quindins De Yaya," "You Belong to My Heart," "Mexico," "Have You Ever Been to Bahia?" "Pandeiro & Flute," "Pregoes Carioca" and "Lilongo." **Running time:** 70 minutes. **Released:** February 3, 1945.

### Cast

Aurora Miranda, Carmen Molina, Dora Luz, Nestor Amaral, Almirante, Trio Calaveras, Ascencio del Rio Trio and Padua Hill Players

### Voices

**Donald Duck:** Clarence Nash; **José Carioca:** José Oliveira; **Panchito:** Joaquin Garay; **Narrator:** Fred Shields; **Narrator:** Frank Graham; **Narrator:** Sterling Holloway. "Mexico" sung by Carlos Ramirez

The Latin American setting of Brazil serves as a background for this musical combining live-action personalities and cartoon figures on the same screen. Donald Duck is the central cartoon character in the animated story line of his journey to the native lands of Bahia, where he falls in love with a beautiful saleslady and sees the city aboard a magic flying serape. Donald is paired in the film with old pal José Carioca, a tropical bird friend who appeared with Donald in 1943's *Saludos Amigos*, and new addition Panchito, a Mexican charro rooster.

## THUMBELINA (1994)

A Don Bluth Film released by Warner Brothers. **p:** Don Bluth, Gary Goldman, John Pomeroy; **d:** Don Bluth, Gary Goldman; **scr:** Don Bluth; **m:** William Ross, Barry Manilow (with original songs by Barry Manilow, Jack Feldman, Bruce Sussman); **superv anim:** John Pomeroy; **dir anim:** John Hill, Richard Bazley, Jean Morel, Len Simon, Piet Derycker, Dave Kupcyk. **Songs:** "Follow Your Heart," "Thumbelina's Theme," "Soon," "Let Me Be Your Wings," "On the Road," "Follow Your Heart," "You're Beautiful Baby," "Marry the Mole." **Running time:** 94 minutes. **Released:** March 30, 1994.

### Voices

**Jacquimo:** Gino Conforti; **Mother:** Barbara Cook; **Thumbelina:** Jodi Benson; **Hero:** Will Ryan; **Queen Tabitha:** June Foray; **King Colbert:** Kenneth Mars; **Prince Cornelius:** Gary Imhoff; **Grundel:** Joe Lynch; **Mrs. (Ma) Toad:** Charo; **Mozo:** Danny Mann; **Gringo:** Loren Michaels; **Baby Bug:** Kendall Cunningham; **Gnatty:** Tawny Sunshine Glover; **Li'l Bee:** Michael Nunes; **Mr. Beetle:** Gilbert Gottfried; **Mrs. Rabbit:** Pat Muisick; **Mr. Fox/Mr. Bear:** Neil Ross; **Ms. Fieldmouse:** Carol Channing; **Mr. Mole:** John Hurt; **Reverend Rat:** Will Ryan

This animated adaptation of the timeless Hans Christian Andersen fairy tale tells the enchanting story of a tiny, out-of-place girl ("no bigger than a thumb") who tries to find her place in a giant world, thus setting the stage for a series of romantic adventures that begin with the arrival of a fairy prince and lead to romance by an ugly, wise-cracking beetle who wants to steal her from the handsome prince.

**PN:** This film marked Don Bluth's last production for his Ireland-based animation studio, producing a disappointing $11 million in ticket sales. Two months following the release of the film,

*Thumbelina and Prince Cornelius find true happiness together at last in Don Bluth's animated fantasy* Thumbelina. *© Don Bluth Limited*

Bluth was hired to head up 20th Century Fox's theatrical animation studio in Phoenix, Arizona. Opening with the film nationwide was the Steven Spielberg produced short subject, "I'm Mad," the first theatrical short starring TV's Animaniacs.

## THE TIGGER MOVIE (2000)

A Walt Disney Pictures/DisneyToons Studio Production released by Buena Vista Pictures. **p:** Cheryl Abood; **d:** Jun Falkenstein; **scr:** Jun Falkenstein; **st:** Eddie Guzelian (based on characters created by A.A. Milne); **m:** Harry Gregson-Williams; **m/l:** Kenny Loggins, Richard M. Sherman, Robert B. Sherman. **Songs:** "Your Heart Will Lead You Home," "The Wonderful Thing about Tiggers," "Someone Like Me Lullabee," "The Whoop-de-Dooper-Bounce," "Pooh's Lullabee," "Round My Family Tree" and "How to Be a Tigger." **Running time:** 77 minutes. **Released:** February 11, 2000.

### Voices

**Tigger/Winnie the Pooh:** Jim Cummings; **Roo:** Nikita Hopkins; **Rabbit:** Ken Samson; **Piglet:** John Fiedler; **Eeyore:** Peter Cullen; **Owl:** Andre Stojka; **Kanga:** Kath Soucie; **Christopher Robin:** Tom Attenborough; **Narrator:** John Hurt

### Additional Voices

Frank Welker

After discovering there are no other creatures like him in the Hundred Acre Wood, the usually happy-go-lucky, bouncy tiger, Tigger, decides to investigate his family tree to see if there are other members still around, only to realize, in the end, who his real friends are.

**PN:** With 60 percent of the film's animation produced at Walt Disney's Japan studio and the rest completed at its Burbank studios, this $20-million big-screen variation of A.A. Milne's prized characters starred Winnie-the-Pooh's gregarious and enthusiastic, bouncing tiger friend, voiced by actor Jim Cummings, who replaced Paul Winchell as the voice of Tigger, a character Winchell previously voiced on Disney's *The New Adventures of Winnie-the-Pooh* series in the late 1980s. The film also marked first Disney film since 1971's *Bedknobs and Broomsticks* to feature songs by former studio mainstays, the award-winning composer brothers, Richard M. and Robert B. Sherman; having previously scored several "Pooh" featurettes, they served up six new songs including the spirited "Round My Family Tree."

## TIM BURTON'S CORPSE BRIDE (2005)

A Tim Burton Animation Company/Laika Entertainment Production feature released by Warner Bros. **p:** Tim Burton, Allison Abbate; **exec prod:** Jeffrey Auerbach, Joe Ranft; **d:** Mike Johnson, Tim Burton; **scr:** John August, Caroline Thompson, Pamela Pettler (based on original characters created by Tim Burton and Carlos Grangel); **m:** Danny Elfman; **anim superv:** Anthony Scott. **Running time:** 78 minutes. **Released:** September 16, 2005.

### Voices

**Victor Van Dort:** Johnny Depp; **Corpse Bride:** Helena Bonham Carter; **Victoria Everglot:** Emily Watson; **Nell Van Dort/Hildegarde:** Tracey Ullman; **William Van Dort/Mayhew/Paul the Head Waiter:** Paul Whitehouse; **Maudeline Everglot:** Joanna Lumley; **Finis Everglot:** Albert Finney; **Barkis Bittern:** Richard E. Grant; **Pastor Galswells:** Christopher Lee; **Elder Gutknecht:** Michael Gough; **Black Widow Spider/Mrs. Plum:** Jane Horrocks; **Maggot/Town Crier:** Enn Reitel; **General Bonesapart:** Deep Roy; **Bonejangles:** Danny Elfman; **Emil:** Stephen Ballantyne; **Solemn Village Boy:** Lisa Kay

Nineteenth-century tale of a shy, remarkably gifted pianist, Victor, the offspring of snooty old-money parents, who mistakenly weds a mysterious Corpse Bride, while his actual, equally timid bride, Victoria, waits for him among the living in this macabre stop-motion animated musical.

**PN:** Originally debuting at film festivals in Venice, Toronto and Deauville, Tim Burton and Mike Johnson co-helmed this ghoulishly wicked production featuring stop-motion animated models designed by Alex McDowell and songs penned by award-winning composer-lyricist Danny Elfman, including the snazzy title song, "According to Plan," cowritten with Burton. After opening at three film festivals, the film opened in theaters in the United States on September 16, 2005, earning $53,359,111 in ticket sales.

## TIM BURTON'S THE NIGHTMARE BEFORE CHRISTMAS (1993)

A Skellington Production released by Touchstone Pictures. **p:** Tim Burton, Denise Di Novi, Kathleen Gavin; **d:** Henry Selick; **scr:** Caroline Thompson (with adaptation by Michael McDowell based on a poem by Tim Burton); **m:** Danny Elfman. **Songs:** "Overture," "Opening," "This Is Halloween," "Jack's Lament," "Doctor Finklestein/In the Forest," "What's This?" "Town Meeting Song," "Jack & Sally Montage," "Jack's Obsession," "Kidnap the Sandy Claws," "Making Christmas," "Nabbed," "Oogie Boogie's Song," "Sally's Song," "Christmas Eve," "Poor Jack," "To the Rescue," "Finale," "Closing" and "End Titles." **Running time:** 75 minutes. **Released:** October 29, 1993.

### Voices

**Jack Skellington (singing)/Barrel/Clown with the Tear-Away Face:** Danny Elfman; **Jack Skellington (speaking):** Chris Sarandon; **Sally/Shock:** Catherine O'Hara; **Dr. Finkelstein:** William Hickey; **Mayor:** Glenn Shadix; **Lock:** Paul Reubens; **Oogie Boogie:** Ken Page; **Santa:** Ed Ivory; **Big Witch:** Susan McBride; **Corpse Kid/Corpse Mom/Small Witch:** Debi Durst; **Harlequin Demon/Devil/Sax Player:** Greg Proops; **Man Under Stairs/Vampire/Corpse Dad:** Kerry Katz; **Mr. Hyde/Behemoth/Vampire:** Randy Crenshaw; **Mummy/Vampire:** Sherwood Ball; **Undersea Gal/Man Under the Stairs:** Carmen Twillie; **Wolfman:** Glenn Walters; **Narrator:** Patrick Stewart

### Additional Voices

Mia Brown, L. Peter Callender, Ann Fraser, Jess McClurg, Robert Olague, Jennifer Levey, Elena Praskin, Judi M. Durand, John Morris, Daamen J. Krall, David McCharen, Bobbi Page, David J. Randolph, Trampas Warman, Doris Hess, Christina MacGregor, Gary Raff, Gary Schwartz

Jack Skellington, the Pumpkin King of Halloween Town, discovers the joys of Christmas Town and attempts to fill Santa's shoes in this ghoulish yet wickedly funny dark, stop-motion animated holiday tale, based on a story by Tim Burton.

**PN:** Unlike the Disney blockbuster animated features, *The Nightmare Before Christmas* was filmed in a laborious process called "stop-motion animation," for which animators move puppets around miniature sets, filming them frame by frame with computerized cameras. Grossing $50 million in box-office revenue, this feature-length treatment was responsible for revitalizing the stop-motion animation industry. Twelve years before making this film, Burton worked as an animator at Disney. Stop-motion expert Henry Selick, the genius behind Pillsbury Doughboy commercials and MTV spots, directed the film. Thirteen years after its original release, Burton's spooky stop-motion animated cult classic was re-released in the United States, this time in 3-D. Opening in 168 theaters on Friday, October 20, 2006, the PG-rated feature scared up $3,277,004 in ticket sales its first week and $8,481,774 in domestic box-office receipts overall. Burton told *USA Today* that seeing the film in three-dimension made it "weirdly better; you just see it the way it was meant to be—completely dimensional." Unlike other filmmakers who have re-issued their films to new audiences, Burton avoided the temptation of tampering or altering the film prior to re-issuing it.

## TITAN A.E. (2000)

A 20th Century Fox Animation/Gary Goldman Production in association with David Kirschner Productions, released by 20th Century Fox. **p:** David Kirschner, Don Bluth, Gary Goldman; **exec prod:** Paul Gertz; **d:** Don Bluth, Gary Goldman; **scr:** Ben Edlund, John August, Joss Whedon; **st:** Hans Bauer, Randall McCormick; **m:** Graeme Revell; **dir of anim:** Len Simon; **anim dir:** Troy Saliba, John Hill, Robert Fox, Renato Dos Anjos, Edison Goncalves, Paul Newberry. **Running time:** 95 minutes. **Released:** June 16, 2000.

### Voices

**Cale:** Matt Damon; **Akima:** Drew Barrymore; **Korso:** Bill Pullman; **Gune:** John Leguizamo; **Preed:** Nathan Lane; **Stith:** Janeane Garofalo; **Prof. Sam Tucker:** Ron Perlman; **Young Cale:** Alex D. Linz; **Tek:** Tone-Loc; **The Cook:** Jim Breuer; **Queen Drei:** Christopher Scarabosio; **Chowquin:** Jim Cummings; **Firrikash/Slave Trader Guard:** Charles Rocket; **Po:** Ken Campbell; **Old Woman:** Tsai Chin; **Drifter Girl:** Crystal Scales; **The Mayor:** David L. Lander; **Male Announcer:** Thomas A. Chantler; **Citizen:** Elaine A. Clark; **Second Human:** Roy Conrad; **First Human/Other Voices:** Leslie Hedger; **First Alien:** Roger L. Jackson; **Female Announcer:** Shannon Orrock; **Soldier:** Alex Pels; **Alien:** Erin Schniewind; **Colonist:** Stephen W. Stanton

Fifteen years into the future, after fleeing Earth on a Titan spaceship before the planet was destroyed, a now-20-year-old, jaded blue-collar worker, Cale, teams up with other survivors to find the hidden spacecraft before an alien species finds it, while hopefully restoring the human race.

**PN:** Codirected by longtime partners Don Bluth and Gary Goldman, this futuristic science fiction adventure, following the pair's big-screen rags-to-riches fantasy, *Anastasia* (1997), produced by Fox Animation Studios in Phoenix, Arizona, had been in development by 20th Century Fox studios since 1994, first as *Treasure Planet* (not to be confused with the much later Disney version directed by John Musker and Ron Clements) starring Mel Gibson as the voice of Long John Silver, and then as *Planet Ice*, to be produced as a combined traditional-animated/CG-animated feature by Blue Sky Studios in New York, which Fox had bought. Fox's studio president, Bill Mechanic, later offered the property to Bluth, giving him 19 months to finish it. The $75 million production, retitled *Titan A.E.*, was originally to be released in 1999 but was bumped to the summer of 2000. Unfortunately, even though it opened on 2,734 screens nationwide, the film, featuring the voice talents of Matt Damon and Drew Barrymore, sputtered at the box office. It grossed $9.4 million its opening weekend, and a disappointing $22.8 million overall. After laying off 255 of Fox Animation Studios' 320 employees four months before the film's release, two weeks after *Titan A.E.*'s sluggish box-office results, Fox permanently closed the facility.

## ⊚ TOKYO GODFATHERS (2003)

A Tokyo Godfathers Committee Production in association with Mad House (Tokyo) and Sony Pictures (Japan) released by Samuel Goldwyn/Destination Films. **p:** Masao Maruyama; **exec prod:** Shinichi Kobayashi, Taro Maki, Masao Takiyama; **d:** Satoshi Kon; **scr:** Satoshi Kon, Keiko Nobumoto; **st:** Satoshi Kon; **m:** Moonriders, Keiichi Suzuki; **anim dir:** Ken'ichi Konishi. **Running time:** 92 minutes. **Released:** December 5, 2003.

### Voices

**Gin:** Toru Emori; **Miyuki:** Aya Okamoto; **Hana:** Yoshiaki Umegaki; **Oota:** Shozo Izuka; **Mother:** Seizo Kato

While rummaging through trash on Christmas Day in Tokyo, a homeless young girl, a transvestite and a middle-aged bum find an abandoned newborn baby and try tracking down its parents, encountering numerous adventures along the way.

**PN:** Acclaimed Japanese animator Satoshi Kon, who began his career as a Manga artist, wrote and directed this acclaimed anime feature following his two previous successful artful films, *Perfect Blue* (1999), one of the top-selling anime DVDs of all time, and *Millennium Actress* (2000). In August 2003, the film made its world premiere at the Big Apple Anime Fest in New York and thereafter played at other international film festivals, before being released to Japanese and American art theaters on December 5, 2003, including a brief Oscar-qualifying run in New York and Los Angeles as one of 11 films considered for an Academy Award for best animated feature. The film then opened in additional theaters nationwide on January 16.

## ⊚ TOM AND JERRY: THE MOVIE (1993)

A Turner Entertainment/WMG Film/Film Roman Production released by Miramax Films. **p&d:** Phil Roman; **cpd:** Bill Schultz; **exec prod:** Roger Mayer, Jack Petrik, Hans Brockman, Justin Ackerman; **scr:** Dennis Marks; **m/sc:** Henry Mancini (with songs by Henry Mancini and lyrics by Leslie Bricusse); **seq dir:** John Sparey, Monte Young, Bob Nesler, Adam Kuhlman. **Songs:** "Tom and Jerry Theme," "Friends to the End," "What Do We Care? (The Alley Cat Song)," "(Money Is Such) A Beautiful Word," "God's Little Creatures," "I Miss You—Robyn's Song," "I've Done It" and "All in How Much We Give." **Running time:** 80 minutes. **Released:** May 28, 1993.

### Voices

**Tom:** Richard Kind; **Jerry:** Dana Hill; **Robyn Starling:** Anndi McAfee; **Lickboot:** Tony Jay; **Captain Kiddie/carnival sea captain:** Rip Taylor; **Doctor Applecheeks, an evil pet snatcher:** Henry Gibson; **Ferdinand/Straycatcher #1:** Michael Bell; **Puggsy/Daddy Starling:** Ed Gilbert; **Frankie Da Flea:** David L. Lander; **Squawk:** Howard Morris; **Straycatcher #2:** Sydney Lassick; **Alleycat/Bulldog:** Raymond McLeod; **Alleycat:** Mitchell D.

Moore; **Alleycat:** Scott Wojahn; **Patrolman:** Tino Insana; **Droopy:** Don Messick; **Woman's Voice:** B.J. Ward; **Man:** Greg Burson; **Aunt Pristine Figg, Robyn's aunt:** Charlotte Rae

In their first full-length feature, squabbling cat-and-mouse duo Tom and Jerry are left homeless after Tom's owners accidentally move without him. The lovable duo help a runaway rich girl named Robyn find her missing father.

**PN:** Tom and Jerry spoke and sang in this movie, which was a joint effort between Turner Entertainment and Film Roman Productions, but not for the first time as the film's promoters made the public believe. Tom spoke many times before in the duo's MGM cartoon shorts, including "Solid Serenade" (1946), in which he used four different voices. Jerry's most notable talking film appearance was in the MGM feature *Anchors Aweigh*, in which he sang and danced with costar Gene Kelly. Despite the prospects of an all-talking Tom and Jerry feature, the movie proved to be a major disappointment, however, taking in just $3.5 million. Joseph Barbera, who co-created Tom and Jerry with partner Bill Hanna, served as a creative consultant on the film.

## ⊚ TOY STORY (1995)

A Walt Disney/Pixar Animation Studios Production released by Walt Disney Pictures. **p:** Bonnie Arnold, Ralph Guggenheim; **d:** John Lasseter; **st:** John Lasseter, Andrew Stanton, Peter Docter, John Ranft; **scr:** Joss Whedon, Andrew Stanton, Joel Cohen, Alec Sokolow; **m:** Randy Newman; **dir anim:** Ash Brannon. **Songs:** "You've Got a Friend in Me," "Strange Things," "I Will Go Sailing No More," "Andy's Birthday," "Soldier's Mission," "Presents," "Buzz," "Sid," "Woody And Buzz," "Mutants," "Woody's Gone," "Big One," "Hang Together," "Big One," "On the Move" and "Infinity and Beyond." **Running time:** 81 minutes. **Released:** November 22, 1995.

### Voices

**Woody:** Tom Hanks; **Buzz Lightyear:** Tim Allen; **Mr. Potato Head:** Don Rickles; **Slinky Dog:** Jim Varney; **Rex:** Wallace Shawn; **Hamm:** John Ratzenberger; **Bo Peep:** Annie Potts; **Andy:** John Morris; **Sid:** Erik von Detten; **Mrs. Davis:** Laurie Metcalf; **Sergeant:** R. Lee Ermey; **Hannah:** Sarah Freeman; **TV Announcer:** Penn Jillette

### Additional Voices

Jack Angel, Spencer Aste, Gregg Berger, Lisa Bradley, Kendall Cunningham, Debie Derryberry, Cody Dorkin, Bill Farmer, Craig Good, Gregory Grudt, Danielle Judovits, Sam Lasseter, Brittany Levenbrown, Sherry Lynn, Scott McAfee, Mickie McGowan, Ryan O'Donohue, Jeff Pidgeon, Patrick Pinney, Philip Proctor, Jan Rabson, Joe Ranft, Andrews Stanton, Shane Sweet

A pull-string cowboy toy named Woody ("Reach for the sky") falls out of favor with his six-year-old owner when the young boy receives a flashy space ranger (Buzz Lightyear), sporting laser action and pop-out wings, as a birthday present. The two rival toys become friends in order to defeat the toy-torturing boy next door in this heartwarming, entertaining computer-animated adventure.

**PN:** A joint venture between Disney and Pixar, this feature was seven years in the making and the first fully computer animated feature made in America. Produced at a cost of $30 million, the film grossed an astounding $191 million in the United States and $354 million worldwide, and was nominated for three Academy Awards: best writing (screenplay written directly for the screen), best original score and best song (for "You've Got a Friend in Me," written and performed as a solo by Randy Newman and as a duet with Lyle Lovett in the film). Director John Lasseter previously directed five groundbreaking computer-animated shorts for Pixar prior to doing *Toy Story*, including two Oscar-nominated films for Best Short Films: 1988's *Tin Toy* and 1989's *Knicknack*.

## ◎ TOY STORY 2 (1999)

A Walt Disney Pictures/Pixar Animation Studios Production released by Buena Vista Pictures. **p:** Helene Plotkin, Karen Robert Jackson; **exec prod:** Sarah McArthur; **d:** John Lasseter, Ash Brannon, Lee Unkrich; **scr:** Andrew Stanton, Rita Hsiao, Doug Chamberlin, Chris Webb; **st:** John Lasseter, Pete Docter, Ash Brannon, Andrew Stanton; **m:** Randy Newman; **superv anim:** Glenn McQueen; **dir anim:** Kyle Balda, Dylan Brown. **Songs:** "When She Loved Me," "You've Got a Friend in Me," "You've Got a Friend in Me" (Wheezy's version)," "You've Got a Friend in Me" (Instrumental version), "Woody's Roundup" theme and "Also Sprach Zarathrustra." **Running time:** 92 minutes. **Released:** November 24, 1999.

*Voices*

**Woody:** Tom Hanks; **Buzz Lightyear:** Tim Allen; **Jessie:** Joan Cusack; **Stinky Pete the Prospector:** Kelsey Grammer; **Mr. Potato Head:** Don Rickles; **Slinky Dog:** Jim Varney; **Rex the Green Dinosaur:** Wallace Shawn; **Hamm the Piggy Bank:** John Ratzenberger; **Bo Peep:** Annie Potts; **Al McWhiggin:** Wayne Knight; **Andy Davis:** John Morris; **Andy's Mom:** Laurie Metcalf; **Mrs. Potato Head:** Estelle Harris; **Sarge:** R. Lee Ermey; **Barbie:** Jodi Benson; **The Cleaner:** Jonathan Harris; **Wheezy the Penguin:** Joe Ranft; **Evil Emperor Zurg:** Andrew Stanton; **Aliens:** Jeff Pidgeon

After Woody, whose arm was broken after playing with kid owner, Andy, inadvertently winds up in a yard sale bin for 25 cents and is stolen by a greedy toy collector, Al McWhiggin, owner of the local Al's Toy Barn, Buzz Lightyear and his pals come to the rescue in this sequel to 1995's monster hit, *Toy Story*.

**PN:** Pixar Animation's John Lasseter codirected and cowrote this long-awaited sequel to the studio's original film, which grossed $362 million worldwide. Unlike that film, this sequel was much costlier—budgeted at $90 million—and the first completely digitally created, mastered and screened film in movie history. In addition to achieving this milestone, the film outpaced the original at the box office, earning $245,024,222 domestically and easily surpassed that film's worldwide gross totals, earning an astounding $485,800,000 in ticket revenue. Oscar-winning composer Randy Newman, who scored the sequel, penned the film's title song, "When She Loved Me," sung by Sarah McLachlan, which was nominated for an Academy Award for best original song.

## ◎ THE TRANSFORMERS: THE MOVIE (1986)

A Sunbow-Marvel Entertainment Production released by DEG. **p:** Joe Bacal, Tom Griffin; **d:** Nelson Shin, Kozo Morishita; **w:** Ron Friedman, Flint Dille (based on the Hasbro toy, "The Transformers"); **m:** Vince DiCola. **Running time:** 86 minutes. **Released:** August 8, 1986.

*Voices*

**Planet Unicron:** Orson Welles; **Ultra Magnus:** Robert Stack; **Galvatron:** Leonard Nimoy; **Wreck Gar:** Eric Idle; **Hot Rod/ Rodimus Prime:** Judd Nelson; **Kup:** Lionel Stander; **Blurr:** John Moschitta; **Kranix:** Norm Alden; **Astrotrain:** Jack Angel; **Prowl/ Scrapper/Swoop/Junkion:** Michael Bell; **Grimlock:** Gregg Berger; **Arcee:** Susan Blu; **Devastator:** Arthur Burghardt; **Spike/Brown/ Shockwave:** Cory Burton; **Cyclonus/Quintession Leader:** Roger C. Carmel; **Quintession Judge:** Rege Cordic; **Prime/Ironhide:** Peter Cullen; **Jazz:** Scatman Crothers; **Dirge:** Bud Davis; **Inferno:** Walker Edmiston; **Perceptor:** Paul Eiding; **Blitzwing:** Ed Gilbert; **Bumblebee:** Dan Gilvean; **Blaster:** Buster Jones; **Scourge:** Stan Jones; **Cliffjumper:** Casey Kasem; **Starscream:** Chris Latta; **Daniel:** David Mendenhall; **Gears:** Don Messick; **Shrapnel:** Hal Rayle; **Kickback:** Clive Revill; **Bonecrusher/Hook/Springer/ Slag:** Neil Ross; **Soundwave/Megatron/Rumble/Frenzy/Wheelie/ Junkion:** Frank Welker

Set in the year 2005, the Transformers and their archenemies, the Decepticons, are at war with each other when an Earthly group, the Autobots, enters the picture and helps send the Decepticons into outer space. The Decepticons return rejuvenated after Unicron, a powerful planetary force, intercedes and refits the group's leader with a new body and new name (he's now called Galvatron) so they can renew the war with Autobots.

**PN:** *Citizen Kane* director Orson Welles was the voice of Unicron.

## ◎ TREASURE ISLAND (1972)

A Filmation Associates Production released by Warner Bros. **p:** Lou Scheimer, Norman Prescott; **d:** Hal Sutherland; **m:** George Blais. **Songs:** "Fifteen Men on a Dead Man's Chest," "Find the Boy/Find the Mouse and We Find the Map" and "Proper Punishment." **Running time:** 75 minutes. **Released:** November 1972.

*Voices*

**Long John Silver:** Richard Dawson; **Captain Flint:** Larry Storch; **Jim Hawkins:** Davy Jones; **Squire Trelawney:** Larry D. Mann; **Mother:** Jane Webb; **Parrot:** Dallas McKennon

Young Jim Hawkins and his newfound friend Hiccup the Mouse take to the high seas in search of buried treasure in this musical version of Robert Louis Stevenson's classic children's tale.

**PN:** In 1980 NBC aired this feature-length movie as a primetime special, edited for broadcast.

## ◎ TREASURE PLANET (2002)

A Walt Disney Pictures Production released by Buena Vista Pictures. **p:** Roy Conli, John Musker, Ron Clements; **d:** Ron Clements, John Musker; **scr:** Ron Clements, John Musker, Rob Edwards (adapted from the novel *Treasure Island* by Robert Louis Stevenson); **st:** Ron Clements, John Musker, Ted Elliott, Terry Rossio; **m:** James Newton Howard; **m/l:** John Rzeznik; **superv anim:** John Ripa, Glen Keane, Ken Duncan, Sergio Pablos, Oskar Urretabizkaia, Michael Show, Jared Beckstrand, T. Daniel Hofstedt, Nancy Beiman, Adam Dykstra, Ellen Woodbury, Brian Ferguson, Mac Smith, John Pomeroy. **Songs:** "I'm Still Here (Jim's Theme)," "Always Know Where You Are" and "Alasdair Fraser's Compliments to Lorna Mitchell." **Running time:** 95 minutes. **Released:** November 27, 2002.

*Voices*

**Jim Hawkins:** Joseph Gordon-Levitt; **John Silver:** Brian Murray; **Doctor Doppler:** David Hyde Pierce; **Captain Amelia:** Emma Thompson; **Scroop:** Michael Wincott; **B.E.N.:** Martin Short; **Sarah:** Laurie Metcalf; **Billy Bones:** Patrick McGoohan; **Morph:** Dane A. Davis; **Mr. Arrow:** Roscoe Lee Browne; **Onus:** Corey Burton; **Hands:** Michael McShane; **Young Jim:** Austin Majors; **Narrator:** Tony Jay

During their journey across the universe aboard a majestic spaceship to a distant planet in search of treasure, antsy shipmate Jim Hawkins, the owner of an intergalactic treasure map, discovers that his charismatic cyborg cook, John Silver, is no friend at all when he tries to steal the treasure for himself.

**PN:** Disney golden boys Ron Clements and John Musker, creators of such major box-office hits as *The Little Mermaid* and *Hercules,* cohelmed this futuristic, mostly 2-D animated (with some computer-generated effects) retelling of Robert Louis Stevenson's classic 1883 novel, *Treasure Island* (an idea they originally pitched to the studio in 1985), which cost between $140 million and $180 million to make. Unfortunately, things didn't pan out as well as they or the studio had hoped. Released to theaters during a time when computer-animated features were dominating the box-office, luring adults and kids to theaters in droves, this pitiful film became the studio's largest financial flop in its history—netting a mere $38,120,554—resulting in the closure of its 2-D animation studio. Despite this fact, the film was nominated for an Academy Award for best animated feature.

### ◎ THE TRIPLETTES OF BELLEVILLE (2003)

A Les Armateurs/Production Champion/Vivi Film, France 3 Cinema/RGP France Production with the support of Canal Plus, Telefilm Canada, CNC, Fonds Film in Vlaanderen and National Loterij in association with BBC Bristol and BBC Worldwide, with support of Cartoon, the Media Programme of the European Community and Procirep, released by Sony Pictures Classics. **p:** Didier Brunner, Paul Cadieux; **d & w:** Sylvain Chomet; **m:** Benoit Charest; **anim superv:** Jean-Christophe Lie, Benoit Feroumont. **Running time:** 82 minutes. **Released:** November 26, 2003.

*Voices*
Jean-Claude Donda, Charles Prevost Linton; Michel Robin, Monica Viegas, Charles Prevost Linton; **Triplets singing voices:** Beatric Bonifassi

A retired 1930s singing trio, the Belleville Sisters, helps a friend rescue her kidnapped grandson and champion bicyclist, who goes missing during the famed Tour de France, from his abductors.

**PN:** Award-winning animator/director Sylvain Chomet, whose 1997 cartoon short, *La Vielle Dame et les Pigeons* (*The Old Lady and the Pigeons*), earned him an Academy Award nomination for best animated short film, wrote and directed this traditional and 3-D animated independent feature, which received scores of critical accolades and film festival awards, in addition to two Academy Award nominations for best animated feature film and best music and original song for the delightful tune, "Belleville Rendezvous."

### ◎ A TROLL IN CENTRAL PARK (1994)

A Don Bluth Ireland Ltd. Production released by Warner Bros. Family Entertainment. **p:** Don Bluth, Gary Goldman; **d:** Don Bluth, Gary Goldman; **st:** Don Bluth, Gary Goldman, John Pomeroy, T.J. Kuenster, Stu Krieger; **scr:** Stu Krieger; **m:** Robert Folk (with original songs by Barry Mann, Cynthia Well, Norman Gimbel and Robert Folk); **superv anim:** John Pomeroy. **Songs:** "Queen of Mean," "Welcome to My World," "Absolutely Green" and "Friends Like Us." **Running time:** 76 minutes. **Released:** October 7, 1994.

*Voices*
**Stanley:** Dom DeLuise; **Queen Gnorga:** Cloris Leachman; **King Llort:** Charles Nelson Reilly; **Alan:** Jonathon Pryce; **Hilary:** Hayley Mills; **Gus:** Philip Glasser; **Rosie:** Tawny "Sunshine" Glover; **Boss:** Will Ryan; **Snuffy:** Pat Musik

Stanley, a kindly troll with a sweet disposition and a penchant for growing beautiful plants, is exiled by the wicked queen to New York City for growing one too many flowers and to learn how to act like the other trolls (who are mean and like to scare humans) in this classically animated fantasy/adventure from legendary animator Don Bluth.

### ◎ THE TRUMPET OF THE SWAN (2001)

A Nelvana Ltd./TriStar Pictures Production released by Sony Pictures. **p:** Lin Oliver, Richard Rich, Thomas L. Tobin, Terry L. Noss; **exec prod:** Seldon O. Young; **d:** Richard Rich, Terry L. Noss; **scr:** Rothman Rofe (based on the book, *The Trumpet of the Swan,* by E.B. White); **m:** Marcus Miller. **Running time:** 75 minutes. **Released:** May 11, 2001.

*Voices*
**Father:** Jason Alexander; **Mother:** Mary Steenburgen; **Serena:** Reese Witherspoon; **Boyd:** Seth Green; **Mrs. Hammerbotham:** Carol Burnett; **Monty:** Joe Mantegna; **Sam Beever:** Sam Gifaldi; **Louie:** Dee Baker; **Billie:** Melissa Disney

A mute swan (voiced by *Seinfeld*'s Jason Alexander), who is ridiculed by others and communicates only by playing a brass horn, discovers how to read and write and enjoys success with his music in this adaptation of E.B. White's acclaimed novel.

**PN:** Former Disney veteran Richard Rich, whose claim to fame included *The Swan Princess* (1994), produced and directed this G-rated adaptation of E.B. White's children's novel. The film, including an all-star voice cast led by Alexander, Mary Steenburgen, Reese Witherspoon and Carol Burnett, was so poorly received that it opened in only 125 theaters nationwide, totaling $102,202 in domestic box-office gross, and was soon thereafter released on home video and DVD.

### ◎ TUBBY THE TUBA (1975)

A New York Institute of Technology (NYIT) Production released by Avco-Embassy; **p:** Barry B. Yellin, Steven R. Carlin, Alexander Schure; **d:** Alexander Schure **st:** Paul Tripp; **m:** George Kleinsinger; **superv anim:** John Gentilella. **Running time:** 81 minutes. **Released:** April 1, 1975.

*Voices*
**Tubby the Tuba:** Dick Van Dyke; **Pee-Wee the Piccolo:** David Wayne; **Narrator:** Paul Tripp; **Mrs. Elephant:** Pearl Bailey; **The Herald:** Jack Gilford; **The Great Pepperino:** Ray Middleton; **Celeste:** Jane Powell; **The Frog:** Cyril Ritchard; **The Haughty Violin:** Ruth Enders; **Miss Squeek:** Hermione Gingold

Longing to find a melody he can play on the tuba and call his own, a shy tuba embarks on a whirlwind adventure in which he learns to use his talent at a circus and in the pit of an orchestra in Singing City.

**PN:** Adapted from the 1945 musical story created by actor/kid-show host/songwriter/musician Paul Tripp (who died in 2002) that became a popular Decca children's record, recorded by Danny Kaye, and the subject of an Academy Award-nominated George Pal *Puppetoon* in 1947, this full-length feature, featuring the voice of actor/comedian Dick Van Dyke as Tubby, was directed and coproduced by Alexander Schure and New York Institute of Technology's (NYIT) Animation Department, Visual Arts Center and Tech Sound Lab in Woodbury, Long Island. Schure founded NYIT in 1974.

### ◎ THE TUNE (1992)

A Bill Plympton Production released by October Films. **p & d:** Bill Plympton; **scr:** Maureen McElheron, Bill Plympton, P.C. Vey; **m:** Maureen McElheron; **anim:** Bill Plympton. **Running time:** 69 minutes. **Released:** December 4, 1992.

*Voices*
**Del:** Daniel Nieden; **Didi:** Maureen McElheron; **Mayor/Mr. Mega/Mrs. Mega:** Marty Nelson; **Dot:** Emily Bindiger; **Wiseone/Surfer/Tango Dancer/Note:** Chris Hoffman; **Cabbie:** Jimmy Ceribello; **Houndog:** Ned Reynolds; **Bellhop:** Jeff Knight; **Surfer/Note:** Jennifer Senko

This entertaining series of musical shorts follows the adventures of a songwriter's (Del) quest to write a hit song, leading him to the wacky world of Flooby Nooby, where he learns to write songs from the heart.

**PN:** This was the first feature film produced almost entirely by an independent animator in a one-room New York loft. Producer-director Bill Plympton worked three years to bring the movie to the big screen. Unlike big-budget animated features which often employ hundreds of people, *The Tune* was made by scarcely a handful of artists. Plympton animated the entire film (using approximately 30,000 drawings) himself while two assistants inked and painted. Financed entirely by Plympton, sections of the feature were released as short films to generate funds to finance the film, including "The Wiseman" and "Push Comes to Shove," which won the 1991 Prix du Jury at the Cannes Film Festival.

## ◎ TWICE UPON A TIME (1983)

A Korty Films and Lucasfilm Ltd. Production released by the Ladd Company through Warner Bros. **p:** Bill Couturie; **d:** John Korty, Charles Swenson; **scr:** John Korty, Charles Swenson, Suella Kennedy, Bill Couturie; **m:** Dawn Atkinson, Ken Melville; **seq dir:** Brian Narelle, Carl Willat, Henry Selick. **Songs:** "Twice upon a Time," "Life Is But a Dream," "Out on My Own," "Heartbreak Town" and "Champagne Time." **Running time:** 75 minutes. **Released:** August 5, 1983.

*Voices*
**Ralph, the All-Purpose Animal:** Lorenzo Musi; **The Fairy Godmother:** Judith Kahan Kampmann; **Synonamess Botch:** Marshall Efron; **Rod Rescueman/Scuzzbopper:** James Crana; **Flora Fauna:** Julie Payne; **Greensleeves:** Hamilton Camp; **Narrator/Chief of State/Judges and Bailliff:** Paul Frees

Action-adventure-fantasy-comedy about two oddballs, Ralph, the All-Purpose Animal, and Mum, his prankster sidekick, who are so eager to be heroes that they do something very wrong in trying to do something very right.

**PN:** This film was the first to utilize a revolutionary new animation process, Lumage animation, developed by Korty Films. The technique enables depth, translucent color and textural effects usually impossible to achieve in standard cel animation.

## ◎ TWILIGHT OF THE COCKROACHES (1989)

A TYO Productions/Kitty Entertainment Group Production released by Streamline Pictures. **p:** Hiroaki Yoshida, Hidenori Taga; **exec prod:** Tatsumi Eatanabe, Mayumi Izumi; **d:** Hiroaki Yoshida; **scr:** Hiroaki Yoshida; **m:** Morgan Fisher; **anim dir:** Toshio Hirata, Yoshinori Kamemori, Kinichirou Suzuki. **Running time:** 105 minutes. **Released:** May 5, 1989.

*Voices*
Michael Forest, Gregory Snegoff

A colony of cockroaches living in Mr. Saito's messy bachelor's apartment struggles to survive when the owner's girlfriend suddenly moves in and things change in this live-action/animated fantasy.

## ◎ VALIANT (2005)

A Touchstone Pictures/Vanguard Animation (U.S.)/Ealing Studios/U.K. Film Council Production in association with Odyssey Entertainment, Take Film Partnerships, Baker Street Finance (U.K.) released by Buena Vista Pictures. **p:** John H. Williams, Shuzo John Shiota, Eric M. Bennett, Curtis Auspurger, Buckley Collum; **exec prod:** Barnaby Thompson, Ralph Kamp, Neil Braun, Robert Jones, Keith Evans; **d:** Gary Chapman; **scr:** Jordan Katz, George Webster, George Melrod (based on a story by George Webster); **m:** George Fenton; **anim dir:** Richard Purdum; **char dev superv:** Rodney J. McFall; **CG superv:** Grey Horsfield, Ron Brinkmann. **Songs:** "(There'll Be Bluebirds over) the White Cliffs of Dover," "Non Je Ne Regrette Rien," "Shoo Shoo Baby," "Pathe News Fanfare," "Horse & Hound," "Presenting Sport," "Busy Life" and "Da Jodel-Rudel." **Running time:** 76 minutes. **Released:** August 19, 2005.

*Voices*
**Valiant:** Ewan McGregor; **Bugsy:** Ricky Gervais; **General Von Talon:** Tim Curry; **Sergeant:** Jim Broadbent; **Gutsy:** Hugh Laurie; **Toughwood:** Brian Lonsdale; **Tailfeather:** Dan Roberts; **Mercury:** John Cleese; **Felix:** John Hurt; **Lofty:** Pip Torrens

Inspired by the work of his squadron leader, Valiant, a patriotic wooden pigeon, joins the Royal Homing Pigeon Service during World War II in this computer-animated spoof of World War II fly-boys loosely based on the role that real-life carrier pigeons played during the war.

**PN:** This British animated production from *Shrek* producer John H. Williams, featuring all-avian characters and named British vocal cast—including Ewan McGregor as Valiant, John Cleese as fellow squadron leader, Mercury, and Tim Curry as the Nazi falcon, General Von Talon—did soaring business when it opened Easter weekend 2005 in the United Kingdom. Released in the United States that August by Disney's Buena Vista Pictures, the CGI-animated toon laid an egg with critics and, more importantly, moviegoers, grossing only $19,229,436 domestically.

## ◎ VAMPIRE HUNTER D (1993)

An Ashi Production Co. Production released by Streamline Pictures. **p:** Hiroshi Kato, Mitsushisa Koeda, Yukio Nagasaki; **d:** Toyoo Ashida; **scr:** Yasushi Hirano, Tom Wyner (based on the novel by Hideyuki Kikuchi); **m:** Tetsuya Komuro. **Running time:** 80 minutes. **Released:** March 26, 1993.

*Voices*
**D:** Michael McConnohie; **Lamika:** Lara Cody; **Doris Rudman:** Barbara Goodson; **Meier:** John Rafter Lee; **Reiganse:** Kerrigan Mahan; **Benge:** Dwight Schultz; **Leila Markus:** Pamela Segall; **Dan Rumm:** Karen Prell

D, a half-human, half-vampire warrior who kills other vampires wherever they roam, rescues the beautiful Doris from the demonic vampire lord, Count Lee, who claims her as his bride, in this futuristic horror fantasy based on the popular selling manga novel series; originally made for the home video market, inspiring the 2001 sequel, *Vampire Hunter D: Bloodlust.*

## ◎ VAMPIRE HUNTER D: BLOODLUST (2001)

A Madhouse Studios/Urban Vision Entertainment Production released by Urban Vision Entertainment. **p:** Mata Yamamoto, Masao Muruyama, Taka Nagasawa, Mataichiro Yamamoto, Meileen Choo; **d:** Yoshiaki Kawajiri; **scr:** Yoshiaki Kawajiri (based on the novel by Kideyuki Kikuchi); **m:** Maro D'Ambrosio; **anim dir:**

Yutaka Minowa. **Running time:** 103 minutes. **Released:** October 5, 2001.

*Voices*
D: Andrew Philpot; **Meier Link:** John Rafter; **Leila:** Pamela Segall; **Charlotte:** Wendee Lee; **Left Hand:** Michael McShane; **Carmila:** Julia Fletcher; **Borgoff:** Matt McKenzie; **John Elbourne/ Nolt/Mashira:** John Di Maggio; **Kyle:** Alex Fernandez; **Grove:** Jack Fletcher

The half-breed son of a human mother and vampire father races to save a rich heiress, abducted by a vampire count, from falling in love with him in this sequel to the 1993 anime feature, *Vampire Hunter D.*

## ⊚ VICTORY THROUGH AIR POWER (1943)
A Walt Disney Studios Production released by United Artists. **p:** Walt Disney; **l/a dir:** H.C. Potter; **superv anim dir:** David Hand; **st:** Perce Peerce (adapted from the book by Alexander P. de Seversky); **m:** Edward Plumb, Paul J. Smith, Oliver Wallace; **seq dir:** Clyde Geronimi, Jack Kinney, James Algar; **anim:** Ward Kimball, Josh Meador, John Lounsbery, Carleton Boyd, Hugh Fraser, Bill Justice, George Rowley, Ed Aardal, John Sibley, John McManus, Norm Tate, Oliver M. Johnston Jr., Vladimir Tytla, Marvin Woodward, Harvey Toombs. **Running time:** 65 minutes. **Released:** July 17, 1943.

*Voices*
**Himself:** Alexander de Seversky; **Narrator:** Art Baker

Topical World War II live-action/animated propaganda documentary recounting the development of air warfare but, more importantly, promoting Major Alexander de Seversky's theories of using strategic air power to quickly end the war (based on his book of the same name); features the animated segment, "The History of Aviation."

## ⊚ THE WACKY WORLD OF MOTHER GOOSE (1966)
A Joseph E. Levine/Arthur Rankin Jr. and Jules Bass/Videocraft International Production released by Embassy Pictures. **p:** Arthur Rankin Jr.; **d:** Jules Bass; **exec prod:** Joseph E. Levine; **st:** Arthur Rankin Jr.; **scr:** Romeo Muller (based on characters created by Charles Perrault in the book *Mother Goose Tales*); **m/l:** George Wilkins, Jules Bass. **Songs:** "I Still Believe," "It's Never Too Late," "Half a Chance," "S.S. BBC," "You're Predictable" and "Great Big Wacky World." **Running time:** 77 minutes. **Released:** December 2, 1967.

*Voices*
**Mother Goose:** Margaret Rutherford

*Additional Voices*
Robert McFadden, Bradley Bolke, Laura Leslie, James Daugherty, Craig Sechler, Susan Melvin, Kevin Gavin, Bryma Kaeburn, Robert Harter, William Marine

Fabled storybook character Mother Goose gets mixed up with secret agents and well-known storybook characters Sleeping Beauty, Tom Thumb and others in this full-color fantasy adventure.

**PN:** *The Wacky World of Mother Goose* was the first cel-animated theatrical feature produced by Arthur Rankin Jr. and Jules Bass, who achieved fame with their "Animagic"-produced television specials using stop-motion puppets.

## ⊚ WAKING LIFE (2001)
An Independent Film Channel/Thousand Words/Line Research/ Detour Filmproduction Production released by Fox Searchlight. **p:** Anne Walker-McBay, Tommy Pallotta, Palmer West, Jonah Smith; **exec prod:** Jonathan Sehring, Caroline Kaplan, John Sloss; **d:** Richard Linklater, Bob Sabiston; **scr:** Richard Linklater (with additional dialogue by various cast members); **m:** Glover Gill. **Running time:** 99 minutes. **Released:** October 19, 2001.

*Voices*
**Hit-and-Run Driver:** Peter Atherton; **Main Character:** Wiley Wiggins; **Kierkegaard Disciple:** Louis Black; **Bartender:** Ken Webster; **Young Boy Playing Paper Game:** Trevor Jack Brooks; **Celine:** Julie Delpy; **Jesse:** Ethan Hawke; **Angry Man in Jail:** Charles Gunning; **Man in Car with P.A.:** Alex Jones; **Quiet Woman:** Mona Lee; **Young Girl:** Lorelei Linklater; **Artist:** Edith Mannix; **Himself:** Caveh Zahedi; **Himself:** Timothy "Speed" Levitch; **Himself:** Steven Soderbergh; **Himself:** Louis Mackey; **Himself:** Robert Solomon

*Additional Voices*
Richard Linklater, Bill Wise, Steven Prince, Steve Brudniak, John Cristensen, Nicky Katt, Kim Krizan

In his dreams a young man encounters a menagerie of people who share their various theories and philosophies of life in this computer-enhanced animated fantasy.

**PN:** Austin-based writer/director Richard Linklater wrote and directed this innovative independent feature that was filmed on digital video, cut, then "animated" using a computer technique called interpolated Rotoscoping, producing a more pointed, impressionistic, artistic effect. Computer animator Bob Sabiston was in charge in the post-production process and worked with 31 animators to draw over Linklater's live-action footage, with each artist assigned to animate separately, allowing for a variety of styles and interpretations. After premiering at the 2001 Sundance Film Festival, the critically acclaimed film received limited distribution, playing at international film festivals, art houses and campus theaters and grossing a mere $2.8 million domestically.

## ⊚ WALLACE & GROMIT: THE CURSE OF THE WERE-RABBIT (2005)
An Aardman Animations/DreamWorks Animation SKG Production released by DreamWorks SKG. **p:** Claire Jennings, Carla Shelley, Peter Lord, David Sproxton, Nick Park; **exec prod:** Michael Rose, Cecil Kramer; **d:** Nick Park, Steve Box; **scr:** Steve Box, Nick Park, Bob Baker, Mark Burton (based on characters created by Nick Park); **m:** Julian Nott, Hans Zimmer; **anim superv:** Lloyd Price. **Songs:** "The Planets, Op.32: Venus, the Bringer of Peace," "We Plow the Fields and Scatter," "The Stripper," "Bright Eyes," "Symphony No.1 in A Flat Major, Op. 55: 1st Movement" and "The Planet's Opus 32:2. Venus, the Bringer of Peace." **Running time:** 85 minutes. **Released:** October 7, 2005.

*Voices*
**Wallace/Hutch:** Peter Sallis; **Victor Quartermaine:** Ralph Fiennes; **Lady Campanula Tottington:** Helena Bonham Carter; **PC Mackintosh:** Peter Kay; **Reverend Clement Hedges:** Nicholas Smith; **Mrs. Mulch:** Liz Smith; **Mr. Mulch:** Dicken Ashworth; **Mr. Windfall:** John Thompson; **Miss Blight:** Mark Gatiss; **Mr. Caliche:** Vincent Ebrahim; **Miss Thripp:** Geraldine McEwan; **Mr. Growbag:** Edward Kelsey; **Mr. Dibber:** Robert Horwath; **Mr. Crock:** Pete Atkin; **Mrs. Girdling:** Noni Lewis

After a monstrous bunny ravages the town's sacred gardens right before its annual Giant Vegetable Competition, pest control business operators Wallace and his dog pal try to find the culprit and humanely eradicate it.

**PN:** Academy Award-winning animator Nick Park, who joined British animation giant Aardman Animations in 1985, codirected, coproduced and cowrote this full-length animated feature, produced in association with DreamWorks Animation. Originally entitled *Wallace & Gromit: The Great Vegetable Plot*, it was based on Park's popular stop-motion, clay-animated short-subject stars—the cheese-addicted inventor and his faithful dog companion (who Park first created as a cat, but then settled for "man's best friend" and changed him to a dog that was supposed to talk before he became Chaplinesque)—previously featured in three award-winning cartoon shorts, beginning with 1989's "A Grand Day Out." The hilarious cartoon one-reeler earned the distinction of being nominated for both an Academy Award and a British Academy of Film and Television Arts (BAFTA) Academy Award that same year, winning the latter. Park then won two consecutive Academy Awards for two follow-up shorts, "Wrong Trousers" (1987) and "Close Shave" (1995). The pair's first feature again combined the painstaking process of animating clay figures one frame at a time, along with subtlely using CGI animation in some cases. On September 16, 2005, the claymation comedy made its North American premiere at the Toronto Film Festival before opening nationwide on October 7. Well-received by critics and film lovers alike, the $30 million, G-rated feature was the top-grossing film the weekend it opened, taking in more than $16.1 million. The film, which won an Academy Award for best animated feature and a BAFTA Alexander Korda Award for best British film, went on to gross $56,201,000 domestically and $184,601,000 worldwide. Coinciding with the film's opening was DreamWorks Home Entertainment's release of *Wallace & Gromit in Three Amazing Adventures*, a DVD edition featuring the celebrated claymation man-and-dog duo's three Oscar-lauded shorts, along with *Cracking Contraptions*, a collection of 10 mini-shorts never before seen in the United States. As in the previous cartoon comedies, 84-year-old British actor Peter Sallis provided the voice of Wallace.

## ◎ WARRIORS OF THE WIND (1986)

A Hakuhodo Incorporated/Studio Ghibli/Tokuma Shoten Production released by New World Pictures. **p:** Isao Takahata; **exec prod:** Tohru Hara, Michio Kondo, Yasuyoshi Tokuma; **d:** Hayao Miyazaki; **scr:** Hayao Miyazaki; **m:** Joe Hisaishi; **anim dir:** Kazuo Komatsubara. **Running time:** 95 minutes. **Released:** April 15, 1986.

*Voices*
**Princess Lastelle:** Emily Bauer; **Prince Milo:** Cam Clarke; **Mayor of Pejite:** Mark Hamill; **Asbel:** Shia LeBeouf; **Nausicaä:** Alison Lohman; **Kurotawa:** Chris Sarandon; **Lord Yupa:** Patrick Stewart; **Kushana:** Uma Thurman

Zandra, a young warrior princess ("Nausicaä" in the original), averts the evil queen Selena from unleashing another cataclysmic war in the Valley of the Wind that results in the total annihilation of her people and the planet in this post-apocalyptic science fiction fantasy.

**PN:** Internationally revered Japanese animator Hayao Miyazaki wrote and directed this 118-minute epic, originally produced through Studio Ghibli—under the title of *Nausicaä (Kaze no Tani no Nausicaä)*—and released in Japan in 1984. Two years later, New World Pictures distributed a radically altered version, cutting 23 minutes from the film and changing the name of its main character to Zandra from Nausicaä, to theaters in the United States. Angered by New World Pictures' treatment of his film, Miyazaki swore he would never again license his films for distribution in the United States unless he had contractual control that prohibited altering their content. In 1996, Walt Disney Studios agreed to Miyazaki's terms to license and release his films. In February 2005 Disney issued a redubbed version of this film on home video.

## ◎ THE WATER BABIES (1979)

A Productions Associates and Adridne Films Production released by Pethurst International. **p:** Peter Shaw; **d:** Lionel Jeffries; **scr:** Michael Robson (based on Charles Kingsley's novel); **st:** Phil Coulter, Bill Martin; **superv anim:** Mirsolaw Kijowiez (Film Polski), J. Stokes (Cuthbert Cartoons). **Running time:** 93 minutes.

*Cast*
**Grimes:** James Mason, **Mrs. Doasyouwouldbedoneby:** Billie Whitelaw; **Masterman:** Bernard Cribbins; **Lady Harriet:** Joan Greenwood; **Sir John:** David Tomlinson; **Sladd:** Paul Luty; **Tom:** Tommy Pender; **Ellie:** Samantha Gates

A young chimney sweep's apprentice and his dog accidentally fall into a pond and are transformed into "water babies" who inhabit an eternal underwater playground.

**PN:** Based on Charles Kingsley's children's novel, the film combines live action and animation. Budget: $2 million.

## ◎ WATERSHIP DOWN (1978)

A Nepenthe Production released by Avco Embassy Pictures. **p, d & w:** Martin Rosen (based on the novel by Richard Adams); **m:** Angela Morley, Malcolm Williamson; **superv anim:** Philip Duncan; **anim dir:** Tony Guy; **superv anim:** Philip Duncan. **Running time:** 92 minutes. **Released:** November 1, 1978.

*Voices*
**Hazel:** John Hurt; **Fiver:** Richard Briers; **Bigwig:** Michael Graham-Cox; **Capt. Holly:** John Bennett; **Blackberry:** Simon Cadell; **Pipkin:** Roy Kinnear; **Dandelion:** Richard O'Callaghan; **Silver:** Terence Rigby; **Chief Rabbit:** Sir Ralph Richardson; **Cowslip:** Denholm Elliott; **Kehaar:** Zero Mostel; **Clover:** Mary Maddox; **Hyzenthlay:** Hannah Gordon; **Cat:** Lyn Farleigh; **Gen. Woundwort:** Harry Andrews; **Campion:** Nigel Hawthorne; **Blackavar:** Clifton Jones; **Black Rabbit:** Joss Ackland; **Narrator:** Michael Hordern

A colony of rabbits, threatened by the destruction of their warren, run off to find a new home safe from the menace of human rule.

**PN:** First U.S. showing was at the World Science Fiction and Fantasy Convention in Phoenix, Arizona. World premiere: London. Singer/songwriter Art Garfunkel sings two songs in the film.

*A scene from* Watership Down *(1978), based on Richard Adams's celebrated best seller about a colony of rabbits who flock to escape the menace of human rule.* © *Avco Embassy Pictures*

## ☺ WE'RE BACK! A DINOSAUR'S STORY (1993)

An Amblin Entertainment Production released by Universal Pictures. **p:** Steve Hickner; **d:** Dick Zondag, Ralph Zondag, Phil Nibbelink, Simon Wells; **cpd:** Thad Weinlein; **exec prod:** Kathleen Kennedy, Frank Marshall, Steven Spielberg; **scr:** John Patrick Stanley (based on the book by Hudson Talbott); **m:** James Horner (with original songs by James Horner and Thomas Dolby); **superv anim:** Jeffrey J. Varab, Bibo Bergeron, Kristof Serrand, Rob Stevenhagen, Thierry Schiel, Sahin Ersoz, Borge Ring. **Songs:** "Roll Back the Rock (to the Dawn of Time)." **Running time:** 72 minutes. **Released:** November 24. 1993.

### Voices

**Rex:** John Goodman; **Buster:** Blaze Berdahl; **Mother Bird:** Rhea Perlman; **Vorb:** Jay Leno; **Woog:** Rene Le-Vant; **Elsa:** Felicity Kendal; **Dweeb:** Charles Fleischer; **Captain NewEyes:** Walter Cronkite; **Louie:** Joe Shea; **Dr. Bleeb:** Julia Child; **Professor ScrewEyes, Captain NewEyes' evil brother:** Kenneth Mars; **Cecilia:** Yeardley Smith; **Stubbs the Clown:** Martin Short

### Additional Voices

Eddie Deezen, Larry King, John Malkovich

Four dinosaurs, Elsa, Woog, Rex and Dweeb, are plucked from prehistory by an eccentric captain who raises their IQs with a high-tech breakfast cereal and offers them a chance to grant the wishes of modern-day children.

**PN:** Based on the popular 32-page children's book by Hudson Talbott, this was the fourth Spielberg-produced animated feature and the second from his London-based Amblimation studio (after *An American Tail: Fievel Goes West*). This film was the least successful of Spielberg's animated films. Adding to its difficulties at the box office was the fact it opened the same weekend as Robin Williams's smash-hit comedy, *Mrs. Doubtfire*. Former CBS newscaster Walter Cronkite lent his voice to the character of Captain NewEyes, making his animated film debut, and Charles Fleischer, the voice of Roger Rabbit, also worked on the film.

## ☺ WHEN THE WIND BLOWS (1988)

A National Film Finance Corp./Film Four International/TVC London Production released by Kings Road Entertainment. **p:** John Coates; **exec prod:** Iain Harvey; **d:** Jimmy T. Murakami; **scr:** Raymond Briggs (based on a novel by Briggs); **m:** Roger Waters; **m/l:** David Bowie; **key seq anim:** Tony Guy, Bill Speers, Dave Varwin, Malcolm Draper, Joe Ekers, John McGuire, Hilary Audus, Joanna Harrison, Gary McCarver, Roger Mainwood. **Running time:** 85 minutes. **Released:** March 11, 1988.

### Voices

**Hilda:** Peggy Ashcroft; **Jim:** John Mills; **Announcer:** Robin Houston

### Additional Voices

James Russell, David Dundas, Matt Irving

Jim and Hilda, an older British couple, build a shelter in preparation for an oncoming nuclear attack and survive, but are unaware they have contracted radiation poisoning following the blast and are slowly dying; based on Raymond Briggs's best-selling book of the same name.

**PN:** John Coates of TVC London, producer of the Oscar-nominated short and television special, *The Snowman* (1982), produced this grim, $3-million adaptation, which was directed by former UPA animator and original founder of Murakami Wolf (and later Murakami Wolf Swenson), Jimmy Murakami.

## ☺ WHO FRAMED ROGER RABBIT (1988)

An Amblin Entertainment/Touchstone Pictures Production released by Buena Vista. **d:** Richard Zemeckis; **scr:** Jeffrey Price, Peter Seaman (based on novel *Who Censored Roger Rabbit?* by Gary K. Wolf); **m:** Alan Silvestri; **anim dir:** Richard Williams; **superv anim:** Andreas Beja; Russell Hall, Phil Nibbelink, Simon Wells. **Running time:** 103 minutes. **Released:** June 22, 1988.

### Cast

**Eddie Valiant:** Bob Hoskins; **Judge Doom:** Christopher Lloyd; **Dolores:** Joanna Cassidy; **Marvin Acme:** Stubby Kaye; **R.K. Maroon:** Alan Tilvern; **Lt. Santino:** Richard Le Parmentier

### Voices

**Roger Rabbit/Benny the Cab:** Charles Fleischer; **Jessica Rabbit:** Kathleen Turner; **Baby Herman:** Lou Hirsch; **Betty Boop:** Mae Questel; **Daffy Duck/Porky Pig/Tweety/Sylvester the Cat/Bugs Bunny:** Mel Blanc; **Hippo:** Mary T. Radford; **Yosemite Sam:** Joe Alaskey; **Droopy:** Richard Williams; **Lena Hyena:** June Foray; **Mickey Mouse:** Wayne Allwine; **Bullet #1:** Pat Buttram; **Bullet #2:** Jim Cummings; **Bullet #3:** Jim Gallant; **Singing Sword:** Frank Sinatra; **Minnie Mouse:** Russi Taylor; **Goofy/Wolf:** Tony Pope; **Woody Woodpecker:** Cherry Davis

Famed cartoon star Roger Rabbit is sabotaging his screen career by worrying over his wife's carrying on with another "toon." The studio assigns a detective to follow the wife and spy on her in this live-action/animated romp.

**PN:** This classic live-action/animated feature was rumored to have cost $45 million to produce. It became the most popular film of 1988, grossing an astronomical $154 million in the United States and the same number overseas. In November 1991 the film premiered on CBS, featuring four never-before seen animated minutes cut from the original film. In the added footage, detective Eddie Valiant snoops around Jessica Rabbit's dressing room and gets caught by Judge Doom, who has the Weasels take him to Toontown and give him a "Toonaroo"—they paint a cartoon head on him. The four-minute scene cost $500,000 to produce. Paul Reubens, of "Pee Wee Herman" fame, was originally chosen to do the voice of Roger Rabbit when the film was first in development in 1981. At the time Darrell Van Citters was to be the film's animation director. Mike Giaimo developed the original character design for Roger when Van Citters was handling the project. Some years later, when Robert Zemeckis took over the project, he considered Giaimo's character design "too clownlike" and asked Giaimo to redesign, suggesting that he make Roger "a little more like Michael J. Fox." Fox was then star of TV's *Family Ties* and had recently wrapped up production of the comedy feature *Back to the Future*, which Zemeckis directed.

## ☺ WICKED CITY (1993)

A Japan Home Video/Madhouse Studios Production released by Streamline Pictures. **p:** Yoshio Masumizu, Koohei Kuri; **d:** Yoshiaki Kawajiri; **scr:** Kisei Choo (based on the novel by Hideyuki Kikuchi); **m:** Osamu Shooji. **Running time:** 90 minutes. **Released:** August 20, 1995.

### Voices

**Taki Renzaburo:** Greg Snegoff; **Spider Woman:** Edie Mirman; **Black Guard's Japan Section Chief:** Robert V. Barron; **Makie:** Gaye Kruger; **Giuseppe Mayart:** Mike Reynolds; **Teito Hotel Manager:** David Povall; **Jin:** Kerrigan Mahan; **Mr. Shadow/Head Black World Terrorist:** Jeff Winkless

Supernatural demons from a parallel universe known as "Black World" cross over into the human world to feast on humans and to undermine the signing of a new peace treaty negotiated by a human diplomat who is protected by a police detective in this Japanese animated fantasy based on Hideyuki Kikuchi's horror novel *Yogu Toshi*.

## ◎ THE WILD (2006)

A Walt Disney Pictures/Sir Zip Studios/Hoytyboy Pictures/Complete Pandemonium/Core Technologies/Contrafilm Production released by Buena Vista Pictures. **p:** Clint Goldman, Beau Flynn, Ed Decter, John J. Strauss, Jane Park; **exec prod:** Kevin Lima, Will Vinton, Stefano Simchowitz; **d:** Steve Williams; **scr:** Ed Decter, John J. Strauss, Mark Gibson, Philip Halprin (based on a story by Mark Gibson and Philip Halprin); **m:** Alan Silvestri; **superv lead anim:** Warren Leathem; **char superv:** Ken Ouellette; **seq superv:** Terry Bradley, Todd Jahnke. Songs: "Good Enough," "Big Time Boppin' (Go Man Go)," "Really Nice Day," "Clocks" and "Lovin' You." **Running time:** 82 minutes. **Released:** April 14, 2006.

*Voices*

**Samson:** Kiefer Sutherland; **Benny:** Jim Belushi; **Nigel:** Eddie Izzard; **Bridget:** Janeane Garofalo; **Kazar:** William Shatner; **Larry:** Richard Kind; **Ryan:** Greg Cipes; **Fergus Flamingo:** Colin Hay; **Duke:** Miles Marsico; **Eze:** Jack De Sena; **Penguin MC:** Don Cherry; **Hamir:** Christian Argueta; **Hamir:** David Cowgill; **Carmine:** Lenny Venito; **Hyrax:** Joseph Siravo; **Rock Hyrax:** Colin Cunningham; **Blag:** Patrick Warburton; **Scab:** Jonathan Kimmel; **Scraw:** Eddie Gossling; **Mama Hippo:** Clinton Leupp; **Samson's Father:** Kevin Michael Richardson; **Young Samson:** Dominic Scott Kay; **Dung Beetle #1:** Nika Futterman; **Dung Beetle #2:** Julianne Bueschler; **Cloak:** Chris Edgerly; **Camo/Ringleader:** Bob Joles

*Additional Voices*

Keith Anthony, Greg Berg, Bob Bergen, Jason Connery, Debi Derryberry, Terri Douglas, Jeannie Elias, Pat Fraley, Eddie Frierson, Nicholas Guest, Jess Harnell, Jason Harris, Bridget Hoffman, Emily Johnson, John Kassir, Daniel Kaz, Josh Keaton, Carolyn Lawrence, Danny Mann, Mona Marshall, Laraine Newman, Nolan North, Paul Pape, Peter Pamela Rose, Fred Tatasciore, Audrey Wasilewski, Hannah Williams, Steve "Spaz" Williams

Zoo pals Samson the Lion, Benny the Squirrel, Nigel the Koala, Bridget the Giraffe and Larry the Anaconda journey to Africa to find their young lion friend, Ryan, who was mistakenly transported from their home in the New York Zoo to Africa, and to bring him back home with them in this computer-animated comedy/adventure.

**PN:** More than 400 animators worked on this Canadian G-rated, fully digitally animated-comedy feature in association with Walt Disney Pictures, becoming the largest production ever produced in that country and one of the costliest, a whopping $80 million. Featuring the voices of Kiefer Sutherland (of TV's *24*), Jim Belushi, Eddie Izzard, Janeane Garofalo and William Shatner among others, this cross between Pixar's *Finding Nemo* and DreamWorks's *Madagascar* opened to mixed reviews in the United States, where it grossed $35,297,670 domestically (and $70,797,670 worldwide). Sutherland, who played the character of Samson the lion, reportedly practiced the lion's roar while driving on the freeway rather than at home with his two daughters around, much to the delight of a woman driver in the adjoining lane who watched him.

## ◎ THE WILD THORNBERRYS MOVIE (2002)

A Paramount Pictures/Nickelodeon Movies/Klasky Csupo Production released by Paramount Pictures. **p:** Arlene Klasky, Gabor Csupo, Tracy Kramer, Terry Thoren, Norton Virgien, Sean Lurie; **exec prod:** Albie Hecht, Julia Pistor, Eryk Casemiro, Hal Waite; **d:** Jeff McGrath, Cathy Malkasian; **scr:** Kate Boutilier (based on characters created by Arlene Klasky, Gabor Csupo, Steve Pepoon, David Silverman, Stephen Sustarsic); **m:** Drew Neumann, Randy Kerber, Brandy Norwood, J. Peter Robinson; **m/l:** Paul Simon; **seq dir:** Paul Demeyer, Raul Garcia, John Holmquist, Sylvia Keulen, Frank Marino, Mark Risley, Greg Tiernan. Songs: "The Wild Thornberrys Theme," "Iwoya," "Accident," "Father and Daughter," "I Am the Very Model of a Modern Major-General," "She's a Lady," "Monkey Man," "This Dream," "Get Out of London," "Animal Nation," "Don't Walk Away," "Shaking the Tree (02 Remix)," "End of Forever," "Oombe," "Motla Le Pula (The Rainmaker)," "Africa (Ila Re Waisco)," "Awa Awa," "Dance with Us," "Bridge to the Stars (theme from the Wild Thornberrys)" and "Happy." **Running time:** 94 minutes. **Released:** December 20, 2002.

*Voices*

**Eliza Thornberry:** Lacey Chabert; **Darwin:** Tom Kane; **Nigel Thornberry/Colonel Thornberry:** Tim Curry; **Cordelia Thornberry:** Lynn Redgrave; **Marianne Thornberry:** Jodi Carlisle; **Debbie Thornberry:** Danielle Harris; **Donnie Thornberry:** Flea; **Sloan Blackburn:** Rupert Everett; **Bree Blackburn:** Marisa Tomei; **Sarah Wellington:** Melissa Greenspan; **Shaman Mnyambo:** Kevin Michael Richardson; **Boko:** Obba Babatunde; **Akela:** Alfre Woodard; **Jomo:** Brock Peters; **Mrs. Fairgood:** Brenda Blethyn; **Rhino:** Billy Brown; **Tim, the Park Ranger:** Jeff Coopwood; **Ranger/BaAka Villager:** Didier M. Ngole; **Ranger:** Anthony Okungbowa; **Zebu:** James Brown Orleans; **Cart Owner:** Michael Chinyamurindi; **Gorilla:** Earl Boen; **Boko:** Obba Babatunde; **BaAka Leader:** Malonga Casquelourd; **BaAka Villagers:** Alu Amina, Nsaka Kaninda, B. Dido Tshimanga, Camille Ntoto, Lunbeka Tezo, Jeanne Klimi, Inousca Kayombo, Mata Mokwala; **Poacher:** Keith Szarabajka; **Loris:** Victoria Hoffman

*Additional Voices*

Victoria Hoffman, Laraine Newman, Joanna Rubiner, Lauren Tom

During an African safari, Eliza and her clan try to save a chimpanzee and pack of elephants from becoming prey to a group of no-good poachers.

**PN:** *Wild Thornberrys* co-creators Arlene Klasky and Gabor Csupo produced this PG-rated, $35-million spin-off of their Emmy-nominated cartoon series originally broadcast from 1998 to 2001 on cable television giant, Nicklodeon. Garnering lukewarm reviews from critics, the film did only modest business at theaters in the United States after it opened, taking in $39,835,592. Among a list of animated features eligible to be nominated for a 2003 Academy Award for best animated feature, the film's song, "Father and Daughter" by Paul Simon, was nominated for an Oscar for best song, original music.

## ◎ WILLY MCBEAN AND HIS MAGIC MACHINE (1965)

An Arthur Rankin Jr./Videocraft International/Dentsu Motion Picture Production released by Magna Pictures Distribution Corporation. **p, d & scr:** Arthur Rankin Jr.; **assoc prod:** Jules Bass, Larry Roemer; **m/l:** Edward Thomas, Gene Forrell, James Polack; **anim superv:** Tad Mochinaga. Filmed in Animagic. **Running time:** 94 minutes. **Released:** June 23, 1965.

*Voices*

**Willie McBean:** Billie Richards; **Professor Von Rotten:** Larry Mann

*Additional Voices*

Alfie Scopp, Paul Kligman, Claude Ray, Corrine Connely, James Doohan, Pegi Loder, Paul Soles

A young boy (Willie McBean) and his sidekick monkey (Pablo) follow a mad professor (Professor Von Rotten) take a mad romp through time on a magic time machine to the days of Christopher Columbus, King Tut, King Arthur, Buffalo Bill and the cavemen—in this "Animagic" color musical comedy-fantasy.

**PN:** Produced in "Animagic," a lifelike stop-motion process using three-dimensional objects and puppets that move on the screen without strings or hands, this was the first full-length stop-motion animated theatrical feature by the team of Arthur Rankin and Jules Bass, known for such popular television specials as *Rudolph, The Red-Nosed Reindeer, Frosty the Snowman* and others. The movie was produced simultaneously with the *Rudolph, The Red-Nosed Reindeer* special, which premiered first on NBC on December 6, 1964. Actor James Doohan, who later became known as Scotty on TV's *Star Trek*, was one of the voice artists on the film.

The movie had its world premiere in San Francisco on June 23, 1965, in a multiple engagement of 47 theaters.

## ◎ THE WINGS OF HONNEAMISE: ROYAL SPACE FORCE (1995)

A Bandai Visual Co. Ltd./Gainax Ltd. Production released by Tara Releasing Corporation. **p:** Hiroaki Inoue, Hirohiko Suekichi; **d:** Hiroyuki Yamaga; **scr:** Mason Hiroshi Onogi, Hiroyuki Yamaga; **m:** Ryuichi Sakamoto. **Running time:** 125 minutes. **Released:** March 10, 1995.

*Voices*

**Shiro Lhadatt:** Leo Morimoto; **Leiquinni Nondelaiko:** Mitsuki Yayoi; **Majaho:** Masahiro Anzai; **Dr. Gnomm:** Chikao Otsuka; **Yanatan:** Bin Shimada; **Marty:** Kazuyuki Sogabe; **Domorhot:** Hirotaka Suzuoki; **Tchallichammi:** Koji Totani; **Nekkerout:** Yoshito Yasuhara

The first manned space flight from the distant planet of Kingdom, featuring Shilo, the planet's first astronaut, results in political problems and war in this fictional adventure.

**PN:** Originally entitled *Oneamisu no Tsubasa: Ouritsu Uchuugun*, this Japanese-produced 1986 animated science fiction adventure—to be based on the story of the U.S.-Soviet space race until its producer changed course—was the first feature-length anime film produced by a new studio, Gainax Limited. Helmed by Hiroyuki Yamaga, it was one of the costliest anime films ever produced, costing $800 million yen (or U.S.$7,164,606). A retitled American version, called *Star Quest*, premiered in February 1986 at Hollywood's famed Chinese Theater, but after its coproducer, Bandai, filed for breach of contract against the film's U.S. producer for its failure to produce "an accurate translation," the film was pulled from distribution and not released again theatrically in the United States until March 1995.

## ◎ WIZARDS (1977)

A Bakshi Production released by 20th Century Fox. **w, p & d:** Ralph Bakshi; **m:** Andrew Belling; **seq anim:** Irv Spence. **Running time:** 81 minutes. **Released:** March 2, 1977.

*Original hand-painted animation production cel from Ralph Bakshi's 1977 fantasy film* Wizards.

*Voices*

**Avatar:** Bob Holt; **Elinore:** Jesse Wells; **Weehawk:** Richard Romanus; **Peace:** David Proval; **President:** James Connell; **Blackwolf:** Steve Gravers; **Fairy:** Barbara Sloane; **Frog:** Angelo Grisant; **Priest:** Hyman Wien; **Deewhittle:** Christopher Tayback; **Sean:** Mark Hamill; **General:** Peter Hobbs; **Prostitute:** Tina Bowman

An evil twin brother/wizard named Blackwolf seeks to extend the evil sphere of his domain in the land of Scortch. He battles for supremacy against his brother Avatar, wizard of Montagar, who is totally the opposite of Blackwolf in personality and beliefs.

## ◎ THE WORLD OF HANS CHRISTIAN ANDERSEN (1971)

A Toei Animation Company Production released by United Artists. **p & d:** Chuck McCann, Al Kilgore (U.S.); **exec prod:** Herbert Gelbspan, Bill Yellin; **d:** Kimio Yabuki (Japan); **m:** Ronald Frangiapane, Seiichiro Uno. **Running time:** 80 minutes. **Released:** March 1, 1971.

*Voices*

**Uncle Oley:** Chuck McCann; **Hans:** Hetty Galen; **Elisa:** Corinne Orr; **Kaspar Kat:** Jim MacGeorge; **Hannibal Mouse:** Lionel G. Wilson; **Lullaby vocal:** Linda November

*Additional Voices*

Ruth Bailew, Sidney Filson, Earl Hammond

A series of classic tales, including *Thumbelina, The Ugly Duckling, The Little Match Girl, The Red Shoes* and others, unfold in this fantasy adventure—inspired by the works of famous storyteller Hans Christian Andersen—told from his perspective as a 10-year-old boy and son of an early-19th-century Danish cobbler.

**PN:** Japanese animation giant Toei Animation Company produced this animated fantasy-musical based on the life of noted storyteller Hans Christian Andersen, which was first released to theaters in its native country on March 19, 1968, then re-dubbed in English and distributed in the United States three years later by United Artists. Legendary comedy film producer Hal Roach, of Laurel and Hardy and Our Gang comedies fame, presented this dubbed American version on behalf U.S.–based Sean Productions, becoming the last film he presented.

## ◎ WXIII: PATLABOR THE MOVIE 3 (2003)

A Production I.G. Production released by Pioneer Entertainment. **p:** Takuji Endo; **exec prod:** Kazumi Kawashiro, Fumihiko Takayama; **d:** Takuji Endo, Fumihiko Takayama; **scr:** Tori Miki; **st:** Masami Yuki; **m:** Kenji Kawai. **Running time:** 105 minutes. **Released:** January 10, 2003.

*Voices*

(English version) **Asuma Shinohara/Kishida/Lab Researcher/Officer Mimura:** Richard Cansino; **Isao Ota/Director/Other-Voices:** Richard Epcar; **Takeshi Kusumi:** Michael Forest; **Hitomi Misaki:** Julie Maddalena; **Saeko Misaki:** Kari Wahlgren; **Shinchiro Hata:** Dave Wittenberg (as Dave Lelyveld); **Boat Captain/Detective/Labor Technician/Security Guard/Police Officer/Yoshitake Misaki/Engineer/Other Voices:** Steve Kramer; **Police Captain:** Jake Martin; **Kiichi Goto:** Daran Norris (as Bob Thomas); **Baseball Player/Rude Boyfriend/Other Voices:** Tony Oliver; **Toshiro Kurisu/Fisherman:** Simon Prescott; **Shizuo Miyanomor/Police Officer:** Derek Stephen Prince; **Noa Izumi/ Student/Computer System/Reporter/Translator/Other Voices:** Michelle Ruff; **Sign Language Interpreter/Stage Actress/Disbatch Operator/Kieko Misaki:** Ellyn Stern; **Col. Goro Ishihara/Labor Technician/Other Voices:** Kirk Thornton

When a strange sea beast rampages Tokyo Bay, two police detectives, Kusumi and Hata, are assigned to investigate in this science fiction adventure of a giant robot police force unit.

**PN:** Also known as *WXIII Patlabor: Wasted Thirteen*, this Japanese production was the third theatrical feature film in the *Patlabor, the Mobile Police* series, which generated two direct-to-video productions, an animated series and two other full-length animated features produced from 1988 to 1994—the work of famed anime director Mamoru Oshii.

## ◎ X (2000)

An X Committee Clamp/Manga Entertainment Production in association with Kadokawa Shoten Publishing Co., Bandai Visual Co., Marubeni Corp., Shelty Co., Sega Enterprises, Victor Entertainment, Animation Studio Mad House Co., Movie Co. Ltd. released by Manga Entertainment. **p:** Kazuhiko Ikeguchi, Kazuo Kokoyama, Masanori Maruyama; **exec prod:** Tsuguhiko Kadokawa; **d:** Rintaro; **scr:** Nanase Okawa, Asami Watanabe; **st:** Mokona Apapa, Satsuki Igarashi, Mick Nekoi; **m:** Yasuaki Shimizu, X-Japan; **anim dir:** Nobuteru Yuuki; **anim:** Yoshinori Kanada. **Running time:** 98 minutes. **Released:** March 24, 2000.

*Voices*

**Karen Kasumi:** Toni Barry; **Seiichirou Aoki:** David Lucas; **Shuogo Asagi:** Rupert Degas; **Kanoe:** Denica Fairman; **Sorata Arisugawa:** Mike Fitzpatrick; **Arashi Kishu:** Teresa Gallagher; **Kusangi:** Jeff Harding; **Fuma Summit:** Adam Henderson; **Hinoto:** Stacey Jefferson; **Yuzuriha Nekoi:** Annemarie Lawless; **Kamui Shirou:** Alan Marriott; **Kotari Summit:** Larissa Murray; **Toshiu:** Liza Ross

In 1999, the Year of Destiny, the young teen Kaumi Shiro will determine the future of humanity when he battles and must destroy one of two clashing forces—the Seven Dragons of Heaven or the Seven Dragons of Earth—in this literal adaptation of the apocalypse from the *Book of Revelation*, first released in Japan in 1996.

## ◎ YELLOW SUBMARINE (1968)

An Apple Films/King Features Production released by United Artists. **p:** Al Brodax; **d:** George Dunning; **st:** Lee Minoff (based on a song by John Lennon and Paul McCartney); **scr:** Lee Minoff, Al Brodax, Jack Mendelsohn, Erich Segal; **md:** George Martin; **anim**

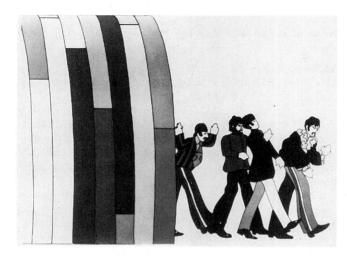

*The Beatles, in animated form, fight to save the undersea kingdom of Pepperland from a horde of antimusic monsters in* Yellow Submarine *(1968).* (COURTESY: KING FEATURES PRODUCTIONS)

**dir:** Jack Stokes, Bob Balser. **Running time:** 85 minutes. **Released:** November 13, 1963.

*Voices*

**John:** John Clive; **Paul:** Geoff Hughes; **Ringo/Chief Blue Meanie:** Paul Angelis; **George:** Paul Batten; **Old Fred:** Lance Percival; **Jeremy Hilary Boob, Ph.D. (Nowhere Man)/Lord Mayor/Max:** Dick Emery; **The Beatles Singing Voices:** Paul McCartney, Ringo Starr, John Lennon, George Harrison

Inspired by its title song, this musical fantasy (billed as a "modyssey") finds the legendary lads from Liverpool fighting to save the undersea kingdom of Pepperland from a horde of antimusic monsters, the Blue Meanies. The fearless four meet a multitude of strange and original characters throughout their voyage: the U.S. Cavalry, King Kong, Paul's Clean Old Grandad and Lucy in the Sky with Diamonds.

**PN:** First previewed at the Pavillion in London in July 1968. The film began its exclusive Los Angeles engagement November 13 at the Village Theatre, Westwood. Lance Percival, one of the film's vocal talents, earlier voiced the characters of Paul and Ringo in the 1960's animated television series, which, coincidentally, was produced by Al Brodax, also producer of the Fab Four's animated feature.

## ◎ YU-GI-OH! THE MOVIE: PYRAMID OF LIGHT (2004)

A Kids WB!/4Kids Entertainment Production released by Warner Bros. **p:** Noriko Kobayashi, Naoki Sasada, Lloyd Goldfine, Katia Milani, Michael Pecoriello; **exec prod:** Hideyuki Nagai, Tamizo Suzuki, Hideki Yamashita, Alfred R. Kahn, Norman J. Grossfeld; **d:** Hatsuki Tsuji; **scr:** Matthew Drdek, Lloyd Goldfine, Norman J. Grossfeld, Michael Pecoriello (based on characters created by Kazuki Takahashi, Studio Dice); **st:** Junki Takegami, Masahiro Hikokubo; **m:** Elik Alvarez, John Angier, Joel Douek, Ralph Schuckett, Wayne Sharpe, Freddy Sheinfeld, Gil Talmi; **anim dir:** Nak Soo Choi, Hee Nam Cho, Koung Tae Kim. **Running time:** 88 minutes. **Released:** August 13, 2004.

*Voices*

(English version) **Yugi Moto/Yami Yugi:** Dan Green; **Seto Kaiba:** Eric Stuart; **Anubis:** Scottie Ray; **Joey Wheeler:** Wayne Grayson;

**Tristan Taylor:** Frank Frankson; **Mokuba Kaiba:** Tara Jayne; **Solomon Moto:** Madeleine Blaustein; **Max-a-Million Pegasus:** Darren Dunstan; **Newscaster:** Mike Pollock

### Additional Voices
Andrew Paull, Ed Paul, Lisa Oritz, Marc Thompson, Sebastian Arcelus

Awakened from his centuries-old sleep, the ancient, evil Egyptian spirit Anubis plans to rid the world of Yugi and claim it as his own.

**PN:** Produced entirely for American film audiences with no Japanese-language version ever made (even though the film was produced in Japan), this feature-length knock-off of the phenomenal manga-turned-video game franchise based on Kazuki Takahashi's 1996 comic book serial, *Yu-Gi-Oh! (King of Games)*, and later hit animated television series, *Yu-Gi-Oh! Duel Monsters*, was broadcast in the United States on the Kids' WB Television Network in 2001. This first-time feature did so-so business in the United States, earning $19,742,947 in ticket sales.

## ANIMATED TELEVISION SPECIALS

### ⊚ ABEL'S ISLAND

Abel, an articulate and sophisticated mouse, is stranded on an island for a full year, separated from his new wife, Amanda, and worried about her, in this award-winning film and Emmy-nominated half-hour special from animator Michael Sporn. Based on a book by William Steig, this intelligent retelling debuted on the long-running PBS anthology series, *Long Ago & Far Away. A Michael Sporn Animation Production in association with Italtoons Corporation. Half-hour. Premiered on PBS: February 11, 1989. Rebroadcast on PBS: November 30, 1990; November 1, 1992.*

#### Voices
**Abel:** Tim Curry; **Gower the Frog:** Lionel Jeffries; **Amanda:** Heidi Stallings

### ⊚ ACCELERACERS: BREAKING POINT

Inventor Dr. Tezla's human race car drivers, the AcceleRacers, take their confrontation into two new realms, the Neon Pipeline Realm and Junk Realm, first encountering the mysterious Silencerz team in the new outer-dimension and then the evil Gelorum and deadly Racing Drones, who capture Kurt's brother, Markie, in this third of four exciting, fast-paced CGI-animated specials for the Cartoon Network, based on Mattel's toy car line of the same name. Three months after its premiere, the fourth and final special in the series aired on Cartoon Network: *AcceleRacers: The Ultimate Race.* In March 2006, nearly a year after its television debut, the special was released on DVD by Warner Bros. Home Video. *A Mainframe Entertainment/Mattel Inc. Production. Color. One hour. Premiered on CAR: June 25, 2005.*

#### Voices

**ACCELERACERS: Shirako Takamoto:** Kirby Morrow; **Deezel "Porkchop" Riggs:** David Kaye; **Tork Maddox:** Adrian Holmes; **Nolo Pasaro:** Dexter Bell; **Karma Eiss:** Lisa Ann Beley; **RD-L3/RD-L4:** Mark Oliver; **Mitch "Monkey" McClurg:** Andrew Duncan

**OTHERS: Dr. Peter Tezla:** Michael Donovan; **Lani Tam:** Venus Terzo; **Vert Wheeler:** Andrew Francis; **Kurt Wylde:**

Brian Drummond; **Markie Wylde:** Will Sanderson, **GIG:** Kasper Michaels, **Gelorum:** Kathleen Barr; **Taro Kitano:** Kevin Ohtsji

### ⊚ ACCELERACERS: IGNITION

After discovering the technology that allows superfast cars to enter other-dimensional environments to race on tracks underwater, in a strange city or elsewhere, Dr. Peter Tezla recruits two human race teams, the Teku and Metal Maniacs, featuring World Race holdovers Vert Wheeler, Kurt Wylde, Taro Kitano and Mark Wylde, to compete in the high-speed, action-packed battleground of the Racing Realms and retrieve the all-powerful AcceleChargers from the deadly robotic racers, the Deadly Drones, in this first of four CGI-animated quarterly specials, based on Mattel's futuristic *Hot Wheels AcceleRacers* toy franchise. Joining the teams in their mission were former World Race drivers Lani Tam and Kadeem and Dr. Tezla, along with his sidekick, Gig, who worked behind the scenes.

Airing on Cartoon Network, this exciting series of specials took place at the conclusion of the *Hot Wheels Highway 35: World Race* series, where the ultimate prize was discovered: the Wheel of Power. During production, professional racecar drivers were consulted for real-life racing skills that were incorporated into the program's racing sequences. Also entitled *HotWheels AcceleRacers: Ignition,* the hour-long special was the first sequel to 2003's five-part *Hot Wheels Highway 35* half-hour cartoon series (also known as *Hot Wheels World Race*), which also ran on Cartoon Network. Three months later in March 2005, the second special in the series, *The Speed of Silence,* premiered on Cartoon Network around the same time that a DVD of the first special was released. Other specials to air included *AcceleRacers: Breaking Point* and *AcceleRacers: The Ultimate Race.* Vancouver, British Columbia, Canada-based Mainframe Entertainment, which also produced *ReBoot,* produced the entire series in association with Mattel. *A Mainframe Entertainment/Mattel Inc. Production. Color. One hour. Premiered on CAR: January 8, 2005.*

#### Voices

**ACCELERACERS: Shirako Takamoto:** Kirby Morrow; **Deezel "Porkchop" Riggs:** David Kaye; **Tork Maddox:** Adrian Holmes; **Nolo Pasaro:** Dexter Bell; **Karma Eiss:** Lisa Ann Beley; **RD-**

**L3/RD-L4:** Mark Oliver; **Mitch "Monkey" McClurg:** Andrew Duncan

**OTHERS: Dr. Peter Tezla:** Michael Donovan; **Lani Tam:** Venus Terzo; **Vert Wheeler:** Andrew Francis; **Kurt Wylde:** Brian Drummond; **Markie Wylde:** Will Sanderson, **GIG:** Kasper Michaels, **Gelorum:** Kathleen Barr; **Taro Kitano:** Kevin Ohtsji

## ⊚ ACCELERACERS: THE SPEED OF SILENCE

Once again, the techno-charged human race car teams, the Teky and Metal Maniacs, compete against each other, this time in new outer-dimensional environments, the Water Realm and the Metro Realm, to hold off the wicked Gelorum and his scary Racing Drones from claiming the AcceleCharger that provides unique powers to vehicles that the AcceleRacers' inventor Dr. Peter Tezla seeks to claim first in this second of four CGI-animated specials, based on Mattel's Hot Wheels *AcceleRacers* toy car line, for Cartoon Network. This follow-up special to the first, *AcceleRacers: Ignition*, was also released on DVD. Two additional specials were telecast on Cartoon Network: *AcceleRacers: Breaking Point* and *AcceleRacers: The Ultimate Race*. A *Mainframe Entertainment/Mattel Inc. Production. Color. One hour and six minutes. Premiered on CAR: March 19, 2005.*

*Voices*

**ACCELERACERS: Shirako Takamoto:** Kirby Morrow; **Deezel "Porkchop" Riggs:** David Kaye; **Tork Maddox:** Adrian Holmes; **Nolo Pasaro:** Dexter Bell; **Karma Eiss:** Lisa Ann Beley; **RD-L3/RD-L4:** Mark Oliver; **Mitch "Monkey" McClurg:** Andrew Duncan

**OTHERS: Dr. Peter Tezla:** Michael Donovan; **Lani Tam:** Venus Terzo; **Vert Wheeler:** Andrew Francis; **Kurt Wylde:** Brian Drummond; **Markie Wylde:** Will Sanderson, **GIG:** Kasper Michaels, **Gelorum:** Kathleen Barr; **Taro Kitano:** Kevin Ohtsji

## ⊚ ACCELERACERS: THE ULTIMATE RACE

Dr. Peter Tezla's futuristic race car teams, the Teku and Metal Maniacs, defy gravity as they enter the surreal Cosmic Realm to infiltrate the deadly Racing Drones' headquarters and rescue Kurt's captured brother, Wylde, only to encounter a new problem when Gelorum steals the all-powerful AcceleCharger to speed toward the finish line and become the one and only AccleRacer until Vert can stop her first in this fourth and final CGI-animated special, based on Mattel's Hot Wheels AcceleRacers franchise, for Cartoon Network. A *Mainframe Entertainment/Mattel Inc. Production. Color. One hour. Premiered on CAR: October 1, 2005.*

*Voices*

**ACCELERACERS: Shirako Takamoto:** Kirby Morrow; **Deezel "Porkchop" Riggs:** David Kaye; **Tork Maddox:** Adrian Holmes; **Nolo Pasaro:** Dexter Bell; **Karma Eiss:** Lisa Ann Beley; **RD-L3/RD-L4:** Mark Oliver; **Mitch "Monkey" McClurg:** Andrew Duncan

**OTHERS: Dr. Peter Tezla:** Michael Donovan; **Lani Tam:** Venus Terzo; **Vert Wheeler:** Andrew Francis; **Kurt Wylde:** Brian Drummond; **Markie Wylde:** Will Sanderson, **GIG:** Kasper Michaels, **Gelorum:** Kathleen Barr; **Taro Kitano:** Kevin Ohtsji

## ⊚ ACE VENTURA CHRISTMAS SPECIAL

Famous pet detective Ace Ventura (in cartoon form) and his monkey sidekick Spike go after a bunch of reindeer-nappers who've made off with Santa's prized reindeer in this prime-time animated special, based on the popular CBS Saturday morning series. A *Nelvana Enterprises/Morgan Creek Production. Color. Half-hour. Premiered on CBS: December 13, 1995.*

*Voices*

**Ace:** Michael Hall; **Spike:** Richard Binsley; **Shickadance:** Vince Corraza; **Aguado:** Al Waxman; **Emilio:** Bruce Tubbe; **Woodstock:** David Beatty

## ⊚ ACTION MAN: "DÉJÀ VU" (1986)

One of the world's greatest athletes is transformed into a superhuman fighting machine with supernatural abilities after a life-changing accident as he battles, along with his "Team Extreme" members Jacques, Knuck and Natalie, the maniacal Dr. X in this halfhour animated special, syndicated in the United States and based on Hasbro Toys' famed toy action figure. Animation giant, DIC Entertainment, produced the action-packed animated adaptation that Hasbro originally commissioned to produce as a half-hour pilot for a potential weekly series. A *DIC Entertainment Production in association with Hasbro Toys. Color. Halfhour. Premiered: October 13, 1986. Syndicated.*

## ⊚ ACTION MAN: "THE CALL TO ACTION" (2000)

After surviving a deadly accident in the Acceleration Games, an international extreme sports competition, Alex Mann, one of the top competitors in his field, emerges with a newfound ability to plan and perform death-defying stunts as he battles the mysterious Dr. X, who plans to exploit his powers for evil purposes in this CGI-animated special that launched a weekly half-hour, 26-episode action/adventure series in August 2006 on FOX, produced by Canada's Mainframe Entertainment A *Mainframe Entertainment Production. Color. One hour. Premiered on FOX: May 20, 2000.*

*Voices*
**Alex Mann:** Mark Hildreth; **Desmond "Grindre" Sinclair:** Michael Dobson; **Templeton Storm/Tempest:** Andrew Francis; **Nick Masters:** Mackenzie Gray; **Fidget Wilson:** Tabitha St. Germain; **Simon Grey:** Christopher Judge; **Rikkie Syngh-Baines:** Peter Kelamis; **Brandon Caine:** Tyler Labine; **Dr. X:** Campbell Lane.

## ⊚ THE ADVENTURE MACHINE

Buttons, the cub bear, and Rusty, the fox, stars of this fifth in a series of syndicated Chucklewood Critters specials, become stranded in a forest where they meet some unusual characters in this entertaining holiday half-hour program. An *Encore Enterprises Production. Color. Half-hour. Premiered: 1990. Premiered in USA: April 11, 1993. Syndicated.*

*Voices*
**Buttons:** Barbara Goodson; **Rusty:** Mona Marshall

## ⊚ ADVENTURES FROM THE BOOK OF VIRTUES: "COMPASSION"

When an immigrant family loses its home in a terrible fire, Plato and Aurora counter Zach's excuses not to get involved with several inspiring stories about the need for compassion in this installment of the popular PBS inspirational series, first broadcast as part of an hour-long block of specials. A *PorchLight Entertainment Production in association with KCET/Hollywoood and FOX Animation Studios. Color. Half-hour. Premiered on PBS: September 3, 1996. Rebroadcast on PBS: September 21, 1996.*

*Voices*

**Plato:** Kevin Richardson; **Ari:** Jim Cummings; **Aurora/Annie:** Kath Soucie; **Zach:** Pam Segall; **Socrates:** Frank Welker

## ◎ ADVENTURES FROM THE BOOK OF VIRTUES: "COURAGE"

When Annie Redfeather hits a hurdle and falls flat on her face during a track meet, her friends at Plato's Peak offer several stories to bolster her courage so she can face the next big race in this half-hour episode of the critically acclaimed PBS series, which debuted on PBS as part of an hour-long block of specials. *A PorchLight Entertainment Production in association with KCET/Hollywood and FOX Animation Studios. Color. Half-hour. Premiered on PBS: September 4, 1996. Rebroadcast on PBS: September 21, 1996.*

*Voices*

**Plato:** Kevin Richardson; **Ari:** Jim Cummings; **Aurora/Annie:** Kath Soucie; **Zach:** Pam Segall; **Socrates:** Frank Welker

*Wraparound*

**Starter:** Jim Cummings; **Bobbi:** Pam Segall

**THE MINOTAUR: Theseus:** Mark Hamill; **Minotaur/Aegeus:** Frank Welker; **King Minos:** Tim Curry; **Guard #1:** Ed Begley Jr.; **Ariadne:** B.J. Ward; **Father:** Jim Cummings

**THE BRAVE MICE: Skinny Male Mouse:** Mark Hamill; **Young Lady Mouse:** Kath Soucie; **Old Lady Mouse:** B.J. Ward; **Chubby Mouse:** Kevin Richardson

**WILLIAM TELL: William Tell:** Ed Begley Jr.; **Gessler:** Tim Curry; **Soldier #1:** Mark Hamill; **Willie:** B.J. Ward; **Soldier #2:** Kevin Richardson

## ◎ ADVENTURES FROM THE BOOK OF VIRTUES: "FAITH"

When Annie's elderly friend and neighbor dies suddenly, she questions the use of faith in the telling of three related stories in this half-hour edition of the award-winning PBS cartoon series—and part of a second batch of half-hour specials—aired in an hour-long block. *A PorchLight Entertainment Production in association with KCET/Hollywood and FOX Animation Studios. Color. Half-hour. Premiered on PBS: February 16, 1997.*

*Voices*

**Plato:** Kevin Richardson; **Ari:** Jim Cummings; **Aurora/Annie:** Kath Soucie; **Zach:** Pam Segall; **Socrates:** Frank Welker

## ◎ ADVENTURES FROM THE BOOK OF VIRTUES: "FRIENDSHIP"

When Annie's "new best friend" breaks her promise and chooses someone else to be her partner on a canoe trip, Annie's feelings are hurt, provoking a discussion about the meaning of true friendship in this animated half-hour—and second grouping of six specials from the critically acclaimed PBS series—which premiered as part of an hour-long block. *A PorchLight Entertainment Production in association with KCET/Hollywood and FOX Animation Studios. Color. Half-hour. Premiered on PBS: February 9, 1997.*

*Voices*

**Plato:** Kevin Richardson; **Ari:** Jim Cummings; **Aurora/Annie:** Kath Soucie; **Zach:** Pam Segall; **Socrates:** Frank Welker

**"FOR EVERYTHING THERE IS A SEASON" (POEM):** Sarah West: Catherine Cavadini; **Betty RedFeather:** Christine Avila

**WAUKEWA'S EAGLE: Waukewa:** Alex Dent; **Father:** Michael Horse; **Eagle:** Frank Welker

**WHY FROG AND SNAKE DON'T PLAY TOGETHER: Frog Child:** Christine Cavanaugh; **Snake Child:** Kath Soucie; **Frog Father:** Frank Welker; **Snake Mother:** Catherine Cavanaugh

**DAMON & PYTHIAS: Damon:** George Newbern; **Pythias/-Soldier #1:** Jim Cummings; **King Dionysius:** Peter Strauss

## ◎ ADVENTURES FROM THE BOOK OF VIRTUES: "GENEROSITY"

After collecting canned goods for a local shelter, Plato realizes that Zach and Annie are more concerned about getting recognition for their generosity than actually helping people in this animated half-hour–part of a second collection of specials from the popular PBS inspirational series–aired in an hour-long block. *A PorchLight Entertainment Production in association with KCET/Hollywood and FOX Animation Studios. Color. Half-hour. Premiered on PBS: February 23, 1997.*

*Voices*

**Plato:** Kevin Richardson; **Ari:** Jim Cummings; **Aurora/Annie:** Kath Soucie; **Zach:** Pam Segall; **Socrates:** Frank Welker

**ROCKING HORSE LAND: Fredolin:** Mike Hughes; **Rocking Horse (Rollande):** Jim Cummings; **Attendant:** Chris Sarandon

**OLD MR. RABBIT'S THANKSGIVING DINNER: Old Mr. Rabbit:** Lewis Arquette; **Billy Chipmunk:** Frank Welker; **Molly Mouse:** Tippi Hedren; **Tommy Chickadee:** Jim Cummings

**THE GIFT OF THE MAGI: Salesman:** Lewis Arquette; **Della:** Joanna Gleason; **Madame Sofroni:** Tippi Hedren; **Jim:** Chris Sarandon

## ◎ ADVENTURES FROM THE BOOK OF VIRTUES: "HONESTY"

When Zach Nichols breaks one of his father's cameras, he concocts a story to escape blame in this half-hour edition of the award-winning PBS series, which debuted as part of an hour-long block of specials. *A PorchLight Entertainment Production in association with KCET/Hollywood and FOX Animation Studios. Color. Half-hour. Premiered on PBS: September 2, 1996. Rebroadcast on PBS: September 21, 1996.*

*Voices*

**Plato:** Kevin Richardson; **Ari:** Jim Cummings; **Aurora/Annie:** Kath Soucie; **Zach:** Pam Segall; **Socrates:** Frank Welker

*Wraparound*

**Mr. Nichols:** Jim Cummings

**THE FROG PRINCE: Frog/Frog Prince:** Jeff Bennett; **Princess** Page O'Hara; **King:** Frank Welker

**GEORGE WASHINGTON AND THE CHERRY TREE: George Washington:** Kath Soucie; **Mr. Washington:** Frank Welker; **Washington's Siblings:** Page O'Hara, Jeff Bennett

**THE INDIAN CINDERELLA: Strong Wind/Chief:** Michael Horse; **Sharp Eyes/Morning Light:** Irene Bedard; **Quiet Fire:** Candi Milo; **Mountain Cloud/Maiden:** Jennifer Hale

## ◎ ADVENTURES FROM THE BOOK OF VIRTUES: "HUMILITY"

When Annie wins the class presidency, the power goes to her head, prompting several stories about the virtue of humility in this animated half-hour, part of second group of six specials aired in hour-long blocks. *A PorchLight Entertainment Production in associa-*

tion with KCET/Hollywood and FOX Animation Studios. Color. Half-hour. Premiered on PBS: February 23, 1997.

### Voices

**Plato:** Kevin Richardson; **Ari:** Jim Cummings; **Aurora/Annie:** Kath Soucie; **Zach:** Pam Segall; **Socrates:** Frank Welker; **Russ:** Adam Wylie; **Kara:** Pat Musick; **Mrs. Mathers:** Mary Gregory

**THE EMPEROR'S NEW CLOTHES: Emperor:** Jim Cummings; **Prime Minister:** Frank Welker; **Royal Treasurer** Pat Musick; **Wills/Servant:** Hamilton Camp; **Nils/Child in Crowd:** Charlie Adler; **Herald:** Neilson Ross

**KING CANUTE AT THE SEASHORE: King Canute:** Neilson Ross; **Courtier #1:** Adam Wylie; **Courtier #2:** Pat Musick; **Courtier #3:** Jim Cummings

**PHAETON: Phaeton:** John Christian Graas; **Croseus:** Adam Wylie; **Clymene:** Pat Musick; **Phoebus Apollo:** Michael Dorn

## ◎ ADVENTURES FROM THE BOOK OF VIRTUES: "LOYALTY"

When Zach accidentally breaks a memorial plaque in an "overgrown park, his elderly friend is angered and Zach doesn't understand why until Plato helps by telling several stories about loyalty in this half-hour special from the popular PBS inspirational cartoon series, part of a second batch of specials aired in hour-long blocks. A PorchLight Entertainment Production in association with KCET/Hollywood and FOX Animation Studios. Color. Half-hour. Premiered on PBS: February 9, 1997.

### Voices

**Plato:** Kevin Richardson; **Ari/Mr. Cleveland:** Jim Cummings; **Aurora/Annie:** Kath Soucie; **Zach:** Pam Segall; **Socrates:** Frank Welker

**YUDISTHIRA AT HEAVEN'S GATE: King Yudisthira:** Richard Libertini; **Mongrel Dog:** Frank Welker; **God Indra:** Malcolm McDowell; **God Dharma:** Frank Welker

**THE CAP THAT MOTHER MADE: Anders/Anders's Sister/ Princess:** E.G. Daily; **Lars:** Kath Soucie; **King:** Peter Renaday

**QUEEN ESTHER: King Ahasuerus:** Brock Peters; **Guest #1:** Peter Renaday; **Queen Vashti:** Kath Soucie; **Haman:** Michael Des Barres; **Queen Esther:** Joan Van Ark; **Mordecai:** Jim Cummings; **Assassin #1:** Kevin Richardson; **Assassin #2:** Frank Welker; **Royal Guards:** Michael Des Barres, Kevin Richardson; **Merchant #1:** Richard Libertini; **Merchant #2:** Brock Peters

## ◎ ADVENTURES FROM THE BOOK OF VIRTUES: "RESPECT"

When Zach and Annie are rude to a friendly junkyard man who is helping them build a go cart for an upcoming race, Plato decides to tell several stories about the virtue of respect in this uplifting half-hour, part of a second offering of six specials from the PBS animated series. A PorchLight Entertainment Production in association with KCET/Hollywood and FOX Animation Studios. Color. Half-hour. Premiered on PBS: February 16, 1997.

### Voices

**Plato:** Kevin Richardson; **Ari:** Jim Cummings; **Aurora/Annie:** Kath Soucie; **Zach:** Pam Segall; **Socrates:** Frank Welker

**PLEASE: Dick:** Kath Soucie; **John:** B.J. Ward; **Dick's Please:** Henry Gibson; **John's Please:** Arte Johnson; **Father:** Frank Welker; **Mother:** Joan Gerber

## ◎ ADVENTURES FROM THE BOOK OF VIRTUES: "RESPONSIBILITY"

Annie vows to safely deliver her mother's cakes on her new bike, but she is tempted by Zach's challenge to a bike race, resulting in an accident that wrecks her new bike and the cakes in this episode about the nature of responsibility from the PBS series, first introduced as part of an hour-long block of specials. A PorchLight Entertainment Production in association with KCET/Hollywood and FOX Animation Studios. Color. Half-hour. Premiered on PBS: September 3, 1996. Rebroadcast on PBS: September 21, 1996.

### Voices

**Plato:** Kevin Richardson; **Ari:** Jim Cummings; **Aurora/Annie:** Kath Soucie; **Zach:** Pam Segall; **Socrates:** Frank Welker

### Wraparound

**Betty Redfeather:** Christine Avila

**ICARUS AND DAEDALUS: Daedalus:** John Forsythe; **Icarus:** Elijah Wood; **King Minos:** Tim Curry; **The Minotaur:** Frank Welker

**KING ALFRED AND THE CAKES: King Alfred:** Jim Cummings; **Woodcutter's Wife:** Carolyn Seymour; **Woodcuttter:** Tim Curry

**THE CHEST OF BROKEN GLASS: Old Woman:** Judy Geeson; **Charles:** Charles Shaughnessy; **Emma:** Carolyn Seymour; **Henry:** Julian Sands

## ◎ ADVENTURES FROM THE BOOK OF VIRTUES: "SELF-DISCIPLINE"

Zach gets into a heated argument with his mother when she refuses to advance him his allowance, prompting several stories from Plato and Aurora about the pitfalls of impatience and losing one's temper. The program premiered on PBS as part of an hour-long block of specials. A PorchLight Entertainment Production in association with KCET/Hollywood and FOX Animation Studios. Color. Half-hour. Premiered on PBS: September 3, 1996. Rebroadcast on PBS: September 21, 1996.

### Voices

**Plato:** Kevin Richardson; **Ari:** Jim Cummings; **Aurora/Annie:** Kath Soucie; **Zach:** Pam Segall; **Socrates:** Frank Welker

**KING MIDAS: King Midas:** Clive Revill; **Marygold:** Sherry Lynn; **Stranger:** Frank Welker

**GENGHIS KAHN AND HIS HAWK: Khan:** Jim Cummings

**THE MAGIC THREAD: Liese:** Pam Dawber; **Peter's Mother/ Teacher:** Tress MacNeille; **Old Woman:** Kathy Najimy; **Peter:** Rob Paulsen; **Foreman:** Kevin Richardson; **Priest:** Clive Revill

## ◎ ADVENTURES FROM THE BOOK OF VIRTUES: "WORK"

When a violent thunderstorm wrecks Plato's Peak, everyone works together to clean up the debris except Sock (short for Socrates), who finds no virtue in "work," in this half-hour episode of the popular PBS animated series. The program premiered as part of an hour-long block of specials. A PorchLight Entertainment Production in association with KCET/Hollywood and FOX Animation Studios. Color. Half-hour. Premiered on PBS: September 2, 1996. Rebroadcast on PBS: September 21, 1996.

### Voices

**Plato:** Kevin Richardson; **Ari:** Jim Cummings; **Aurora/Annie:** Kath Soucie; **Zach:** Pam Segall; **Socrates:** Frank Welker

**HOW THE CAMEL GOT HIS HUMP: Camel:** Jim Cummings; **Horse:** Daniel Davis; **Dog/The Man:** Bronson Pinchot; **Genie:** Paula Poundstone

**TOM SAWYER GIVES UP THE BRUSH: Tom Sawyer:** Matthew Lawrence; **Joe:** Dana Hill; **School Master:** Daniel Davis; **Aunt Polly:** Kath Soucie; **Ben:** Andrew Lawrence; **Jim:** Pam Segall

## ◎ THE ADVENTURES OF ENERGY

One in a series of syndicated specials under the title of *LBS Children's Theatre*, this half-hour show chronicled the ways in which man harnessed energy throughout the ages. *A DIC Audiovisual Production. Color. Half-hour. Premiered: 1983—84. Syndicated.*

## ◎ THE ADVENTURES OF HUCKLEBERRY FINN

Mark Twain's classic adventure is faithfully retold, from rafting down the Mississippi to Huck's friendship with runaway slave Jim, in this animated special sponsored by Kenner Toys. A "Kenner Family Classics" special. *A John Erichsen Production in association with Triple Seven Concepts. Color. Half-hour. Premiered on CBS: November 23, 1984.*

## ◎ THE ADVENTURES OF JIMMY NEUTRON, BOY GENIUS: "ATTACK OF THE TWONKIES"

Jimmy soon finds that this cute and cuddly pet that stows away on his ship is more dangerous than he thought after it mutates and threatens to take over Retroville in this hour-long animated special, featuring two half-hour episodes, for Nickelodeon based on the popular cartoon series. *A DNA Productions Inc. Production. Color. One hour. Premiered on NICK: November 11, 2004. Rebroadcast on NICK: November 13, 2004; November 14, 2004; November 16, 2004; November 26, 2004; December 12, 2004; January 1, 2005; April 22, 2005; September 11, 2005; December 31, 2005; February 1, 2006; March 31, 2006; May 3, 2006; May 29, 2006; June 30, 2006; July 18, 2006; August 7, 2006; August 24, 2006; October 22, 2006; April 18, 2007.*

*Voices*

**James Isaac "Jimmy" Neutron:** Debi Derryberry; **Goddard:** Frank Welker; **Carl Wheezer:** Rob Paulsen; **Cindy Vortex/Tina Sue:** Carolyn Lawrence; **Nick:** Candi Milo; **Sheen:** Jeffrey Garcia; **Libby Folfax:** Crystal Scales; **Hugh Beaumont Neutron, his father:** Mark DeCarlo; **Judy Neutron, his mother/VOX 2000:** Megan Cavanagh; **Ms. Winifred Fowl:** Andrea Martin; **Nick's singing voice:** Jeff Gunn; **Graystar:** Themselves

## ◎ THE ADVENTURES OF JIMMY NEUTRON, BOY GENIUS: "HOLLY JOLLY JIMMY"

Convinced that Santa isn't real, boy genius Jimmy Neutron and his best friends, Carl and Sheen, head to the North Pole to prove his theory true. Instead, they find that Santa does, in fact, exist, including Santa's workshop, but are unconvinced until a homing device Jimmy sets off accidentally emits a blast of energy and puts Santa temporarily out of commission. It is then up to Jimmy to save Christmas for the people of Retroville before they replace it with a different holiday altogether in this original Nickelodeon Christmas special. *A DNA Productions Inc. Production. Color. Half-hour. Premiered on NICK: December 8, 2003. Rebroadcast on NICK: December 13, 2003; December 16, 2003; December 21, 2003; December 25, 2003; December 15, 2004; December 18, 2004; December 24, 2004; December 25, 2004; December 8, 2005; December 13, 2005; December 17, 2005; December 20, 2005; December 21, 2005; December 22,* 2005; December 24, 2005; December 25, 2005; December 8, 2006; December 11, 2006; December 16, 2006; December 24, 2006; December 25, 2006. Rebroadcast on NICKT: December 24, 2003; December 25, 2003; December 21, 2004; December 23, 2004; December 18, 2005; December 22, 2005; December 13, 2006; December 29, 2006.

*Voices*

**James Isaac "Jimmy" Neutron:** Debi Derryberry; **Hugh Beaumont Neutron, his father/Octopus Man:** Mark DeCarlo; **Judy Neutron, his mother:** Megan Cavanagh; **Cynthia Aurora "Cindy" Vortex:** Carolyn Lawrence; **Miss Winifred Fowl:** Andrea Martin; **Goddard/Wendell/Officer Tubbs/Father:** Frank Welker; **Liberty Danielle "Libby" Folfax:** Crystal Scales; **Carlton Ulysses Wheezer/Butch/Elf:** Rob Paulsen; **Juarerra Estevez/Nathan:** Jeffrey Garcia; **Nick Dean:** Candi Milo; **Sam/Lou/Reporter:** Billy West; **Santa Claus:** Mel Brooks

## ◎ THE ADVENTURES OF JIMMY NEUTRON, BOY GENIUS: "LEAGUE OF THE VILLAINS"

King Goobot's notorious League of Villains, comprised of Jimmy Neutron's primary adversaries—Professor Finbar Calamitous, Beautiful Gorgeous, his evil genius baby cousin, Eddie, the Junkman, Eustace Strytch, Grandma Taters and the Space Bandits (Zix, Travoltron and Tee)—have one mission: to go after Jimmy and get him once and for all in this half-hour special from the creators of the popular Nickelodeon cartoon series. *A DNA Productions Inc. Production. Color. Half-hour. Premiered on NICK: June 18, 2005. Rebroadcast on NICK: June 19, 2005; June 24, 2005; July 4, 2005; July 9, 2005; July 25, 2005; August 8, 2005; September 5, 2005; September 30, 2005; October 16, 2005; November 25, 2005; February 11, 2006; July 24, 2006; August 21, 2006; April 17, 2007.*

*Voices*

**James Isaac "Jimmy" Neutron:** Debi Derryberry; **Goddard:** Frank Welker; **Carl Wheezer/Eustace Strytch:** Rob Paulsen; **Cindy Vortex/Tina Sue:** Carolyn Lawrence; **Nick Dean:** Candi Milo; **Sheen:** Jeffrey Garcia; **Libby Folfax:** Crystal Scales; **Hugh Beaumont Neutron, his father:** Mark DeCarlo; **Judy Neutron, his mother/VOX 2000:** Megan Cavanagh; **Ms. Winifred Fowl:** Andrea Martin; **Sam:** Billy West; **Professor Calamitous:** Tim Curry; **Tee:** Kevin Michael Richardson; **Brobot:** Paul Greenberg; **Barbarino:** Jeff Bennett; **Zia:** Maurice LaMarche; **King Goobot:** S. Scott Bullock; **Grandma Taters:** Edie McClurg; **Baby Eddie:** Mark DeCarlo; **Beautiful Gorgeous:** Wendie Malick; **Junkman:** Charlie Adler

## ◎ THE ADVENTURES OF JIMMY NEUTRON, BOY GENIUS: "LOVE POTION #976/J"

When Jimmy mistakenly shows Carl and Sheen his latest invention—a love pheromone—that makes anyone who comes in contact with the magic potion fall in love with the first person they meet. Carl becomes the first victim after accidentally opening it and exposing them all, including Jimmy, who hopelessly falls for the first girl he sees, the dreaded aggressive arch-rival, Cindy Vortex, in this Valentine's Day special for Nickelodeon. *A DNA Productions Inc. Production. Color. Half-hour. Premiered on NICK: February 13, 2004. Rebroadcast on NICK: February 14, 2004; May 9, 2005; July 14, 2005; August 5, 2005; August 17, 2005; October 13, 2005; November 18, 2005; December 17, 2005; December 24, 2005; February 14, 2006; June 2, 2006; February 14, 2007; March 30, 2007. Rebroadcast on NICKT: February 13, 2005; February 14, 2005; May 29, 2006; February 12, 2006; February 14, 2006; February 14, 2007.*

*Voices*

**James Isaac "Jimmy" Neutron/Emily:** Debi Derryberry; **Hugh Beaumont Neutron, his father:** Mark DeCarlo; **Judy Neutron, his mother:** Megan Cavanagh; **Cynthia Aurora "Cindy" Vortex:** Carolyn Lawrence; **Miss Winifred Fowl:** Andrea Martin; **Goddard:** Frank Welker; **Liberty Danielle "Libby" Folfax:** Crystal Scales; **Carlton Ulysses Wheezer/Oleander:** Rob Paulsen; **Juarerra Estevez:** Jeffrey Garcia; **Nick Dean/Britney:** Candi Milo; **Goddard:** Frank Welker; **Sam:** Billy West

### ◉ THE ADVENTURES OF JIMMY NEUTRON, BOY GENIUS: "MAKE ROOM FOR DADDY-O"

When Jimmy learns he has to perform with his dorky dad, Hugh, in the Father's Day Talent Show in front of the entire school, he invents a device that transforms his father into the coolest dad in Retroville to prevent him from embarrassing Jimmy in this Father's Day cartoon special—also known as *The Father's Day Special* and *Ring-A-Ding Dad*—based on the hit Nickelodeon cartoon series. Famed rock star Peter Frampton appeared as a guest voice of the character "Cool" High. *A DNA Productions Inc. Production. Color. Half-hour. Premiered on NICK: June 6, 2003. Rebroadcast on NICK: June 15, 2003; June 19, 2004; June 20, 2004; June 19, 2005; June 18, 2006; July 9, 2006; July 15, 2006; July 28, 2006; August 22, 2006; September 6, 2006; September 20, 2006; October 6, 2006; October 23, 2006; November 7, 2006; November 23, 2006; February 26, 2007; March 14, 2007; April 2, 2007; April 20, 2007. Rebroadcast on NICKT: June 15, 2003; June 19, 2005.*

*Voices*

**James Isaac "Jimmy" Neutron:** Debi Derryberry; **Goddard/Wendell:** Frank Welker; **Carl Wheezer/Principal Willoughby/Butch:** Rob Paulsen; **Cindy Vortex/Tina Sue:** Carolyn Lawrence; **Nick Dean:** Candi Milo; **Sheen:** Jeffrey Garcia; **Libby Folfax/Libby's Little Brother:** Crystal Scales; **Hugh Beaumont Neutron, his father/Mr. Vortex:** Mark DeCarlo; **Judy Neutron, his mother/VOX 2000:** Megan Cavanagh; **Ms. Winifred Fowl:** Andrea Martin; **Sam/Corky Shimazu:** Billy West; **"Cool" High:** Peter Frampton

### ◉ THE ADVENTURES OF JIMMY NEUTRON, BOY GENIUS: "MY BIG FAT SPY WEDDING"

When Jimmy is assigned to a new mission from the BTSO to follow Beautiful Gorgeous (voiced by Wendie Malick), he uncovers something he didn't expect: that she and Jet Fusion are getting married in this prime-time, half-hour animated special spun-off from the popular Nickelodeon cartoon series. *A DNA Productions Inc. Production. Color. Half-hour. Premiered on NICK: July 22, 2005. Rebroadcast on NICK: July 23, 2005; July 24, 2005; August 1, 2005; September 1, 2005; September 5, 2005; September 19, 2005; October 18, 2005; November 16, 2005; November 19, 2005; December 7, 2005; December 22, 2005; January 7, 2006; February 4, 2006; February 25, 2006; March 14, 2006; March 30, 2006; April 16, 2006; May 3, 2006; May 16, 2006; June 9, 2006; June 22, 2006; July 5, 2006; July 21, 2006; July 30, 2006; August 2, 2006; August 11, 2006; August 15, 2006; August 28, 2006; September 11, 2006; September 26, 2006; October 4, 2006; October 12, 2006; November 6, 2006; November 21, 2006; December 10, 2006; December 15, 2006; December 24, 2006; January 11, 2007; January 28, 2007; March 20, 2007; April 6, 2007; April 24, 2007.*

*Voices*

**James Isaac "Jimmy" Neutron:** Debi Derryberry; **Hugh Beaumont Neutron, his father:** Mark DeCarlo; **Judy Neutron, his mother:** Megan Cavanagh; **Cynthia Aurora "Cindy" Vortex:** Carolyn Lawrence; **Miss Winifred Fowl:** Andrea Martin; **Goddard:** Frank Welker; **Liberty Danielle "Libby" Folfax:** Crystal Scales; **Carlton Ulysses Wheezer:** Rob Paulsen; **Juarerra Estevez:** Jeffrey Garcia; **Goddard:** Frank Welker; **Professor Calamitous:** Tim Curry; **Monkey/Colonel McSwain:** Mike Gasaway; **Monkey:** Joe E. Elwood; **Monkey:** Rena Archer; **Commander Baker:** Michael Clarke Duncan; **Jet Fusion:** Christian Slater; **Beautiful Gorgeous:** Wendie Malick

### ◉ THE ADVENTURES OF JIMMY NEUTRON, BOY GENIUS: "NIGHTMARE IN RETROVILLE"

Jimmy's Neutronic Monster-Maker machine works all too well after transforming Sheen (Werewolf), Carl (Vampire) and his dad, Hugh (Frankenstein), into real monsters and Carl and Sheen bite Cindy and Libby, turning them into monsters, too, who want him next in this half-hour Halloween special based on the Emmy Award-winning Nickelodeon cartoon series. Jeff Garcia, the voice of Sheen Estevez, won a 2004 Annie Award for voice acting in an animated television production in the special. *A DNA Productions Inc. Production. Color. Half-hour. Premiered on NICK: October 29, 2003. Rebroadcast on NICK: October 31, 2003; November 1, 2003; November 8, 2003; October 29, 2004; October 30, 2004; October 31, 2004; October 28, 2005; October 29, 2005; October 30, 2005; October 31, 2005; June 5, 2006; June 17, 2006; October 17, 2006; October 27, 2006; October 28, 2006; October 30, 2006; October 31, 2006; November 3, 2006. Rebroadcast on NICKT: October 31, 2003; November 24, 2003; December 29, 2003; October 30, 2004; October 31, 2004; October 29, 2005; October 30, 2005; October 28, 2006.*

*Voices*

**James Isaac "Jimmy" Neutron:** Debi Derryberry; **Goddard/Wendell:** Frank Welker; **Carl Wheezer/Principal Willoughby:** Rob Paulsen; **Cindy Vortex/Tina Sue:** Carolyn Lawrence; **Nick Dean:** Candi Milo; **Sheen Estevez:** Jeffrey Garcia; **Libby Folfax:** Crystal Scales; **Hugh Beaumont Neutron, his father/Octopus Man:** Mark DeCarlo; **Judy Neutron, his mother:** Megan Cavanagh; **Ms. Winifred Fowl:** Andrea Martin; **Sam/Man:** Billy West

### ◉ THE ADVENTURES OF JIMMY NEUTRON, BOY GENIUS: "OPERATION: RESCUE JET FUSION"

Recruited by a top-secret agency to act as a spy and armed with super high-tech gadgets, whiz kid Jimmy Neutron teams up with his action-hero movie idol, Jet Fusion, to save the world from the mad scientist Professor Calamitous in this hour-long animated special based on the television series. A video-game version of the show was simultaneously released to stores on the day the special debuted on Nickelodeon. *A DNA Productions Inc. Production. Color. One hour. Premiered on NICK: October 13, 2003. Rebroadcast on NICK: October 15, 2003; October 17, 2003; October 18, 2003; October 19, 2003; October 25, 2003; November 16, 2003; November 22, 2003; November 27, 2003; November 28, 2003; December 26, 2003; December 31, 2003; January 2, 2004; January 16, 2004; March 13, 2004; April 11, 2004; April 24, 2004; May 30, 2004; July 25, 2004; September 12, 2004; October 24, 2004; November 21, 2004; December 12, 2004; January 23, 2005; January 24, 2005; August 1, 2005; September 5, 2005; November 4, 2005; November 23, 2005; January 14, 2006; February 22, 2006; March 29, 2006; July 3, 2006; August 18, 2006; September 9, 2006; November 24, 2006; April 18, 2007.*

*Voices*

**James Isaac "Jimmy" Neutron:** Debi Derryberry; **Goddard:** Frank Welker; **Carl Wheezer:** Rob Paulsen; **Cindy Vortex:** Carolyn Lawrence; **Nick Dean:** Candi Milo; **Sheen Estevez:** Jeffrey Garcia; **Hugh Beaumont Neutron, Jimmy's father:** Mark DeCarlo; **Judy Neutron, Jimmy's mother:** Megan Cavanagh; **Ms. Fowl:** Andrea Martin; **Professor Crank:** Dan Castellaneta; **Professor Finbarr Calamitous:** Tim Curry; **Commander Baker:** Michael Clarke Duncan; **Beautiful Gorgeous:** Wendie Malick; **Chief:** Ving Rhames; **Jet Fusion:** Christian Slater; **Betty:** Kath Soucie

### ◎ THE ADVENTURES OF JIMMY NEUTRON: BOY GENIUS: "WIN, LOSE AND KABOOM"

After a suspicious meteor crash lands in Retroville, Jimmy deciphers a mysterious alien message engraved on it and he and his friends, Cindy, Libby, Sheen, Carl, Bobli and Goddard, are subsequently "sucked" into deep space where they become contestants on an intergalactic reality-game show, with the losers—as their consolation prize—having their home planets destroyed by aliens in this 90-minute special, originally titled "You Bet Your Life Form." The special was one of seven expanded versions of the award-winning Nickelodeon cartoon series produced in the summer of 2004 for the network's *Nicktoons Movie Summer* festival. *A DNA Productions Inc. Production. Color. Ninety minutes. Premiered on NICK: July 9, 2004. Rebroadcast on NICK: July 10, 2004; July 11, 2004; July 19, 2004; August 13, 2004; August 14, 2004; August 15, 2004; September 3, 2004; September 6, 2004; November 26, 2004; December 27, 2004; January 9, 2005; February 27, 2005; April 8, 2005; August 20, 2005; October 9, 2005; November 23, 2005; November 25, 2005; February 4, 2006; March 4, 2006; May 13, 2006; June 30, 2006; August 9, 2006; September 4, 2006; November 24, 2006; December 25, 2006; March 18, 2007; April 18, 2007. Rebroadcast on NICKT: July 9, 2005; July 10, 2005; September 3, 2005; September 4, 2005; September 5, 2005; August 20, 2006.*

*Voices*

**James Isaac "Jimmy" Neutron/Alien Actress/Alien Woman:** Debi Derryberry; **Goddard/Wendell:** Frank Welker; **Carl Wheezer/Principal Willoughby/Test Pilot/Announcer/Mr. Wheezer/Mrs. Wheezer:** Rob Paulsen; **Cindy Vortex/Tina Sue:** Carolyn Lawrence; **Nick Dean:** Candi Milo; **Sheen Estevez/Army Guard:** Jeffrey Garcia; **Libby Folfax/Mrs. Scales:** Crystal Scales; **Hugh Beaumont Neutron, his father/Octopus Man/Ambercrombie/Emergency System/Alien Man/Eleason Like Creature:** Mark DeCarlo; **Judy Neutron, his mother/Mrs. Vortex:** Megan Cavanagh; **Ms. Winifred Fowl:** Andrea Martin; **Sam/Corky:** Billy West; **Gorlock #1/Mayor/Dad Gorlock/Other Gorlocks/Brain #2:** Jim Cummings; **Gorlock #2/Brain #1:** Jeff Bennett; **Bolbi Stroganovsky/British Tourist:** Phil LaMarr; **Vandanna:** Grey DeLisle; **Meldar:** Tim Allen; **April:** Alyssa Milano; **Mr. Estevez:** Joe Lala; **Other Voices:** Jess Harnell

### ◎ THE ADVENTURES OF MOLE

Mole and his civilized compatriots, Rat, Badger and Toad, discover the joys of fellowship in this hour-long special, based on characters from Kenneth Grahame's *The Wind in the Willows*. The program, preceded by 1995's half-hour holiday special *Mole's Christmas*, debuted on the Disney Channel. *An All Time Entertainment Production. Color. One hour. Premiered on DIS: May 7, 1996.*

*Voices*

**Rat:** Richard Briers; **Badger:** Paul Eddington; **Toad:** Hugh Laurie; **Mole:** Peter Davison; **Otter/Various Others:** Gary Martin; **Additional Voices:** Imelda Staunton, Richard Tate

### ◎ THE ADVENTURES OF SINBAD

Sinbad volunteers to recover Baghdad's magic lantern and its genie from the wicked Old Man of the Sea but is met by danger at every turn in this half-hour special produced by Australia's Air Programs International under the series banner *Famous Classic Tales*. *An Air Programs International Production. Color. Half-hour. Premiered on CBS: November 27, 1980.*

*Voices*

Peter Corbett, Barbara Frawley, Ron Haddrick, Phillip Hinton, Bevan Wilson

### ◎ THE ADVENTURES OF THE GET ALONG GANG

Six friendly animals—Montgomery, Dotty, Bingo, Zipper, Portia and Woolma—find their values of honesty and friendship tested as they participate in a big scavenger hunt, which is undermined by slimeballs Catchum Crocodile and Leland Lizard. Produced as a TV pilot for the weekly Saturday-morning series, the special aired on CBS the same year the weekly series debuted. *A Scholastic Production in association with Those Characters From Cleveland and Nelvana Limited. Color. Half-hour. Premiered on CBS: 1984.*

*Voices*

**Montgomery Moose:** Charles Haid; **Dotty Dog:** Mara Hobel; **Zipper Cat:** Jim Henshaw; **Bingo Beaver:** Maria Lufofsky; **Portia Porcupine:** Gloria Figura; **Woolma Lamb:** Julie Cohen; **Catchum Crocodile:** Dan Hennessey; **Leland Lizard:** Dave Thomas; **Officer Growler:** Mark Gordon; **Mr. Hoofnagel:** Wayne Robson; **The Announcer:** Bruce Pirrie

### ◎ THE ADVENTURES OF THE SCRABBLE PEOPLE IN "A PUMPKIN NONSENSE"

At the site of a magical pumpkin patch, a small boy (Tad) and a girl (Terry), accompanied by Mr. Scrabble, are transported to a town called Nonsense, where they learn of the unhappiness of the Scrabble People and try to help spread goodness among them. *An Arce Production with James Diaz Studios. Color. Half-hour. Premiered: October 31, 1985. Syndicated.*

*Voices*

**Tad/Terry:** Brianne Sidall; **Sir Scrabble:** Kevin Slattery; **Rot:** Bob Singer; **Muddler:** George Atkins; **Lexa:** Melissa Freeman; **Rotunda:** Kathy Hart Freeman

### ◎ THE ADVENTURES OF TOAD

Motor-crazy Mr. Toad ends up on the wrong side of the local constabulary, only to discover upon his return that his mansion has been overrun by rowdies in this second of two one-hour specials to air on The Disney Channel, based on Kenneth Grahame's bestselling novel, *The Wind in the Willows*. *An All Time Entertainment Production. Color. One hour. Premiered on DIS: June 25, 1996.*

### ◎ AESOP'S FABLES

Comedian Bill Cosby, appearing in live-action wraparounds, hosts two animated *Aesop's Fables* about the tortoise and the hare and the tale of two children (Joey and Marta), in live-action/animation, who are lost in an enchanted forest—in this half-hour special. Cosby's appeal with children was the principal reason for his hosting this special, as his Filmation-produced *Fat Albert and the Cosby Kids* was a popular Saturday-morning installment on CBS, which also aired the special. *A Filmation Associates Production in association with Lorimar Productions. Color. Half-hour. Premiered on CBS: October 31, 1971. Rebroadcast on CBS: December 23, 1974. Rebroadcast on DIS: February 21, 1993.*

*Cast*
**Aesop:** Bill Cosby; **Joey:** Keith Hamilton; **Marta:** Jerelyn Fields

*Voices*
**Tortoise:** John Byner; **Hare:** Larry Storch; **Eagle:** Roger C. Carmel; **Lady Eagle:** Jane Webb; **Donkey:** John Erwin; **Owl:** Dal McKennon

## ◉ THE ALAN BRADY SHOW

When his show's staff offers to develop a 50th anniversary retrospective special in his honor, their cantankerous boss, Alan Brady (voiced by Carl Reiner), counters instead with an altogether different concept, a *Who Wants to Marry Alan Brady?* special, in this CGI-animated and first original special in TV Land's seven-year history, written by Carl Reiner and adapted from CBS's classic live-action television sitcom, *The Dick Van Dyke Show* (which Reiner also created), produced by George Shapiro, Howard West and Sal Maniaci. *A Shapiro/West Production. Color. Half-hour. Premiered on TVLND: August 17, 2003. Rebroadcast on TVLND: August 17, 2003; August 18, 2003; August 20, 2003; August 22, 2003; August 23, 2003; October 5, 2003; May 18, 2004.*

*Voices*
**Alan Brady:** Carl Reiner; **Mal:** S. Scott Bullock; **The Secretary:** Rose Marie; **Webb:** Dick Van Dyke; **The Announcer:** Gary Owens; **Other Voices:** Carol Leifer, Rob Paulsen, Katy Selverstone

## ◉ ALICE IN WONDERLAND (1966)

This musical spoof of the Lewis Carroll classic, follows the adventures of Alice and her dog Fluff in Wonderland where they meet an amusing assortment of characters including several new creations: Hedda Hatter, a female counterpart of the Mad Hatter; Humphrey Dumpty, whose voice was patterned after that of Humphrey Bogart; and the White Knight, voiced by Bill Dana in his José Jimenez character. The full title of the program was *Alice in Wonderland (or "What's a Nice Kid Like You Doing in a Place Like This?").* *A Hanna-Barbera Production. Color. Half-hour. Premiered on ABC: March 30, 1966. Rebroadcast on ABC: November 19, 1967.*

*Voices*
**Alice:** Janet Waldo, Doris Drew (singing); **Cheshire Cat:** Sammy Davis Jr.; **White Knight:** Bill Dana; **Queen of Hearts:** Zsa Zsa Gabor; **White Rabbit:** Howard Morris; **Hedda Hatter:** Hedda Hopper; **Mad Hatter:** Harvey Korman; **Alice's Father/Humphrey Dumpty:** Allan Melvin; **King of Hearts/March Hare:** Daws Butler; **Dormouse/Fluff, Alice's dog:** Don Messick; **Caterpillar:** Alan Reed, Mel Blanc

## ◉ ALICE IN WONDERLAND (1973)

Arthur Rankin Jr. and Jules Bass, who created such classic specials as *Rudolph, the Red-Nosed Reindeer* and *Frosty the Snowman,* produced this second animated version of the children's fairy tale, with Alice making that familiar visit to Wonderland. This wonderfully entertaining syndicated special was broadcast under the umbrella title of *Festival of Family Classics. A Rankin-Bass Production in association with Mushi Studios. Color. Half-hour. Premiered: February 11, 1973. Syndicated.*

*Voices*
Carl Banas, Len Birman, Bernard Cowan, Peg Dixon, Keith Hampshire, Peggi Loder, Donna Miller, Frank Perry, Henry Ramer, Billie Mae Richards, Alfie Scopp, Paul Soles

## ◉ ALICE'S ADVENTURES IN WONDERLAND

Slipping into dreamland, Alice becomes caught up in the whimsical world of Wonderland. Met by the frenetic March Hare, who is late for a very important date, they end up at a tea party with the Mad Hatter, where the rest of her madcap adventure unfolds. *A Greatest Tales Production. Color. Half-hour. Premiered: 1983–84. Syndicated.*

*Voices*
Peter Fernandez, Gilbert Mack, Ray Owens, Billie Lou Watt

## ◉ ALIENS FIRST CHRISTMAS

Christmas comes to the Cosmos when Roger and Fran Peoples and their son Benny try to celebrate the holidays in their new home on the planet Zolognia, marred by unexpected problems in this second in a series of half-hour animated *Aliens* specials. *A Perennial Pictures Film Corporation Production in association with Paragon International. Color. Half-hour. Premiered on DIS: November 12, 1991. Rebroadcast on DIS: December 21, 1991. Rebroadcast on FOX FAM: December 4, 1998/December 22, 1998.*

*Voices*
**Roger Peoples:** Jerry Reynolds; **Fran Peoples:** Brett Sears; **Mavo Zox:** Rachel Rutledge; **Charlick Zox:** Will Gould

## ◉ ALIENS NEXT DOOR

Transferred to a new job and feeling insecure, the Peoples family arrives on the planet Zolognia and are as frightened of their new neighbors (Charlick and Mavo Zox) as their neighbors are of them in this first of two charming *Aliens* cartoon specials. *A Perennial Pictures Film Corporation Production in association with Paragon International. Color. Half-hour. Premiered on DIS: November 3, 1990. Rebroadcast on DIS: February 8, 1992; February 17, 1992.*

*Voices*
**Roger Peoples:** Jerry Reynolds; **Fran Peoples:** Peggy Powis; **Mavo Zox:** Rachel Rutledge; **Charlick Zox:** Will Gould; **Boonka Frinx:** Miki Mathioudakis

## ◉ ALL ABOUT ME

A young boy falls asleep in class and dreams of taking a tour of his own body in this musical fantasy that explores the functions of various organs and other biological wonders. *An Animated Cartoon Production. Color. Half-hour. Premiered on NBC: January 13, 1973 (NBC's Children's Theater).*

## ◉ ALL-AMERICAN SPORTS NUTS

Disney sports cartoons comprise this salute to athletes and Olympic gold medalists, produced for the Disney Channel. *A New Wave Production for The Disney Channel. Color. One hour. Premiered on DIS: October 16, 1988.*

## ◉ ALL GROWN UP!: "DUDE, WHERE'S MY HORSE?"

After having dreamed as kids about being cowboys someday, Tommy and his grown-up Rugrats pals get to do it for real by spending an entire week on a dude ranch and participating in a horse drive in this second hour-long special—the title parodied the live-action comedy feature, *Dude, Where's My Car?*—based on the Nickelodeon cartoon series. Other hour-long special spin-offs included *Interview with a Campfire* (2004) and *R.V. Having Fun Yet?* (2005). *A Klasky Csupo/Viacom Production. Color. One hour. Premiered on NICK: July 16, 2005.*

*Voices*
**Tommy Pickles:** Elizabeth Daily; **Charles "Chuckie" Finster Jr.:** Christine Cavanaugh; **Angelica C. Pickles:** Cheryl Chase; **Phil/Lil/Betty DeVille:** Kath Soucie; **Dil Pickles:** Tara Strong; **Charlotte C. Pickles:** Tress MacNeille; **Didi Pickles:** Melanie Chartoff; **Stu Pickles:** Jack Riley; **Kimi Watanabe-Finster:** Dionne Quan; **Susie Carmichael:** Cree Summer; **Grandpa Lou Pickles/Rustler #2:** Joe Alaskey; **Enrique/Doctor:** Joe Lala; **Reject/Truck Driver/Ostriches:** Dee Bradley Baker; **Big Red/Crazy Australian:** Jeffrey R Nordling; **Tiny:** Stefan Marks; **Little Red:** Nikka Futterman; **Red/Rustler #1:** Grant Albrecht

## ◎ ALL GROWN UP: "INTERVIEW WITH A CAMPFIRE"

Creepy things happen when pre-teens Tommy, Chuckie, Angelica and the rest of the Rugrats travel with their parents to Camp Everwood, where Tommy unravels the truth behind a supposed curse and mysterious disappearance of early settlers in this, the first of two one-hour specials based on the top-rated Nickelodeon cartoon series, *All Grown Up!*, produced in the summer of 2004 for Nickelodeon's *Nicktoons Movie Summer* festival. *A Klasky Csupo Production in association with Viacom International. Color. One hour. Premiered on NICK: June 25, 2004. Rebroadcast on NICK: June 26, 2004; June 27, 2004; July 4, 2004; August 9, 2004; August 27, 2004; August 29, 2004; September 6, 2004; November 26, 2004; January 1, 2005; January 30, 2005; May 29, 2005; September 5, 2005; November 25, 2005; August 3, 2006.*

*Voices*
**Tommy Pickles:** Elizabeth Daily; **Charles "Chuckie" Finster Jr.:** Nancy Cartwright; **Angelica C. Pickles:** Cheryl Chase; **Phil/Lil/Betty DeVille:** Kath Soucie; **Dylan "Dil" Pickles/Eliza Lockheart's Real Voice:** Tara Strong; **Charlotte Pickles:** Tress MacNeille; **Didi Pickles:** Melanie Chartoff; **Stu Pickles:** Jack Riley; **Drew Pickles/"Chazz" Finster Sr.:** Michael Bell; **Susie Carmichael:** Cree Summer; **Kimi Watanabe-Finster:** Dionne Quinn; **Lucy Carmichael:** Hattie Winston; **Kira Finster:** Julia Kato; **Howard DeVille:** Phil Proctor; **Mac and Cher:** Amy Guzenhauser; **Bean:** Lauren Tom; **Randy Carmichael:** Ron Glass

## ◎ ALL GROWN UP!: "R.V. HAVING FUN YET?"

When their friend Susie is picked to perform in the Gracy's Day Parade, her fellow tween-age Rugrats crisscross America en route to New York with Phil and Chuckie trying to find a girl who will kiss Chuckie while Lil tries breaking a world record for playing with a soccer ball in this third and final hour-long special adapted from Nickelodeon's famed animated television series. The fun-filled special followed two others: *Interview with a Campfire* (2004) and *Dude, Where's My Horse?* (2005). *A Klasky Csupo/Viacom Production. Color. One hour. Premiered on NICK: October 10, 2005.*

*Voices*
**Tommy Pickles:** Elizabeth Daily; **Charles "Chuckie" Finster Jr.:** Christine Cavanaugh; **Angelica C. Pickles:** Cheryl Chase; **Phil/Lil/Betty DeVille:** Kath Soucie; **Dil Pickles:** Tara Strong; **Charlotte C. Pickles:** Tress MacNeille; **Didi Pickles:** Melanie Chartoff; **Stu Pickles:** Jack Riley; **Kimi Watanabe-Finster:** Dionne Quan; **Susie Carmichael:** Cree Summer; **Grandpa Lou Pickles:** Joe Alaskey; **Adenoidal Girl/Parade Representative:** Denise Pickering; **Amish Boy/The Rogers Clones:** Scott Menville; **Amish Father:** Ed Begley Jr.; **Rachel:** Meagan Smith; **Mariachi Singer:** David Michie

## ◎ AN ALL NEW ADVENTURE OF DISNEY'S SPORT GOOFY

Popular Disney canine Goofy is the star of this prime-time special, which included scenes from various cartoon shorts (narrated by Stan Freberg) previously released to theaters (including "Hold That Pose [1950]," "Goofy's Glider" [1940], "Lion Down" [1951], "Mickey's Birthday Party" and "Goofy Gymnastics" [1949]) and combined new footage, narrated by Los Angeles Lakers sports announcer Chick Hearn, who calls the "play by play," leading up to a new 20-minute short, "Sport Goofy in Soccermania." *A Happy Feets Production for Walt Disney Television. Color. One hour. Premiered on NBC: May 27, 1987.*

*Voices*
**Goofy (old):** Pinto Colvig; **Goofy (new):** Jack Angel, Tony Pope; **Scrooge McDuck:** Will Ryan; **Beagle Boys/Gyro Gearloose:** Will Ryan; **Huey/Dewey/Louie:** Russi Taylor; **Museum Curator:** Phil Proctor; **Narrator:** Stan Freberg; **Sportscaster:** Chick Hearn

## ◎ ALLOSAURUS: A WALKING WITH DINOSAURS SPECIAL

The incredible life and death struggle and peculiar traits and characteristics of the ferocious Jurassic period predator dinosaur Allosaurus, nicknamed "Big Al," are vividly told in this moving, state-of-the-art computer-animated special, produced by the BBC and Discovery Channel. Narrated by Avery Brooks, this prime-time Emmy-winning sequel to the highly successful digitally-animated specials, *Walking with Dinosaurs* and *Walking with Prehistoric Beasts*, became the basis of the popular NBC and Discovery Kids children's series *Prehistoric Planet*. The latest special was seen by an estimated 80 million households during its April 8, 2001, premiere on Discovery Channel. *A Stone House Productions/BBC/Discovery Channel Production. Color. One hour. Premiered on DSC: April 8, 2001.*

*Voices*
**Narrator:** Avery Brooks

## ◎ ALOHA SCOOBY-DOO!

Scooby-Doo, Shaggy and the rest of the Mystery, Inc., gang venture to the island of Hawaii for a big surfing contest and wind up instead solving the mysterious appearance of the Wiki-Tiki before a nearby volcano erupts in this eighth direct-to-video production. *A Warner Bros. Animation Production for Warner Home Video. Color. Seventy minutes. Premiered on CAR: May 13, 2005.*

*Voices*
**Scooby-Doo/Fred Jones/Wiki-Tiki:** Frank Welker; **Shaggy Rogers:** Casey Kasem; **Daphne Blake/Auntie Mahina/Local Woman #2:** Grey DeLisle; **Velma Dinkley:** Mindy Cohn; **Manu Tuiana:** Mario Lopez; **Little Jim:** Ray Bumatai; **Mayor Molly Quinn:** Teri Garr; **Jared Moon:** Adam West; **Ruben Laluna:** Tom Kenny; **Snookie:** Tia Carrere; **Tiny Tiki/Surfer on Bike/California Surfer Dude/Local Guy #1/Wild Pig/Gecko/Flame Thrower:** Dee Bradley Baker

## ◎ ALVIN AND THE CHIPMUNKS TRICK OR TREASON: THE STORY OF PUMPKINHEAD

Alvin tries to pass an initiation to become a member of the exclusive Monster Club in this half-hour, made-for-cable animated special. The Halloween-themed program includes the Chipmunks' rendition of the hit song "Monster Mash." *A Bagdasarian Production in association with The Krislin Company. Color. Half-hour. Premiered on USA: October 28, 1994.*

*Voices*
**Alvin/Simon:** Ross Bagdasarian Jr.; **Theodore:** Janice Karman

## ◎ THE AMAZING BUNJEE VENTURE
Accidentally sent back to the year 100 million B.C., Karen and Andy Winsborrow encounter prehistoric animals; become friends with an elephantlike creature who can fly (Bunjee); and experience modern-day adventures together in this two-part, one-hour ABC Weekend Special. A Hanna-Barbera Production. Color. One hour. Premiered on ABC: March 24 and March 31, 1984. Rebroadcast on ABC: September 15, 1984 and September 22, 1984; January 18, 1986 and January 25, 1986; September 12, 1987 and September 19, 1987; December 10, 1988 and December 17, 1988.

*Voices*
**Bunjee:** Frank Welker; **Karen Winsborrow:** Nancy Cartwright; **Andy Winsborrow:** Robbie Lee; **Mr. Winsborrow:** Michael Rye; **Mrs. Winsborrow/Baby #1:** Linda Gary; **Baby #2:** Nancy Cartwright; **Waxer/Drasto:** John Stephenson; **Willy/Pterodactyl/Tyrannosaur:** Frank Welker

## ◎ THE AMAZING ZORRO
The famed masked, swashbuckling avenger, alias Don Diego Vega, fights for the rights of the common people and other families and ranchers in 1820s southern California who are under attack by a corrupt government in this $2 million, made-for-TV movie created by DIC Entertainment and directed by Scott Herning, that debuted three days before Christmas Day 2002 as part of DIC's Incredible Movie Toons on Nickelodeon. A DIC Entertainment Production in association with Zorro Productions. Color. Seventy-two minutes. Premiered on NICK: December 22, 2002.

*Voices*
**Zorro/Don Diego Vega:** Cusse Mankuma; **Don Carlos Pulido:** Mark Acheson; **Dona Catalina:** Carmen Aguirre; **Nico Pulido:** Kathleen Barr; **Sergeant Garcia:** Eli Gabay; **Caballero #3:** Santo Lombardo; **His Excellency, the Governor:** John Novak; **Luisa:** Sylvia Maldonado; **Captain Ramon:** Dale Wilson

## ◎ THE ANGEL AND THE SOLDIER BOY
A toy soldier and a toy angel try to rescue the contents of their owner's piggy bank from ruthless pirates, who've popped up from a book somebody forgot to put away, in this half-hour special originally produced for Showtime. A BMG Video Production. Color. Half-hour. Premiered on SHO: May 14, 1991.

*Voices*
Marie Brennan (vocals)

## ◎ ANIMALYMPICS: WINTER GAMES
Olympic-style sports competition takes on a new meaning as animals compete in events of the first Animalia Winter Games in this cartoon spoof built around songs and vignettes. A Lisberger Production. Color. Half-hour. Premiered on NBC: February 1, 1980. Rebroadcast on NBC: July 4, 1982. Rebroadcast on DIS: August 20, 1993.

*Voices*
**Henry Hummel:** Michael Fremer; **Rugs Turkel:** Billy Crystal; **Keen Hacksaw:** Harry Shearer; **Barbara Warbles/Brenda Springer:** Gilda Radner

## ◎ ANIMATED EPICS: BEOWULF
The great sixth-century Scandinavian warrior faces three mortal enemies—the monster Grendel, Grendel's vengeful mother and a fire-breathing dragon—in this epic story, part of HBO's Emmy Award–winning series of half-hour specials, Animated Epics. Narrated by Derek Jacobi and featuring the voice of actor Joseph Fiennes as the beastly Viking hero Beowulf, this program was the second installment of a continuing series of half-hour specials—and one of the more ambitious attempts to bring classic literature to television in animated form, coproduced in 1998 by Welsh studio 24C, HBO and BBC Wales. Creating the program as well as this series of specials involved using a medley of different media, styles, collaborators and techniques of animation, including stop-motion, with Russia's Christmas Films, Cardiff's Beryl Productions and London's Pizazz each contributing their unique styles of animation to each special. Other adaptations included the two-part The Canterbury Tales (1999), Don Quixote (2000) and Moby Dick (2000). Premiering on HBO in 1998, the program was subsequently rebroadcast on HBO's sister network, HBO Family. A S4C/HBO/BBC Wales Production in association with a.k.a. Pizazz/Beryl Productions/Christmas Films/Picasso Pictures/Right Angle in association with Home Box Office. Color. Half-hour. Premiered on HBO: 1998. Rebroadcast on HBO FAM: December 14, 2001; December 18, 2001; December 22, 2001.

*Voices*
**Narrator:** Derek Jacobi; **Beowulf:** Joseph Fiennes; **Hrothgar:** Timothy West; **Queen Wealtheow:** Anna Calder-Marshall; **Wiglaf:** Michael Sheen; **Hygelac:** John Castle; **Peasant:** James Greene; **Unferth:** Michael Feast; **Aschere:** Nicholas Woodeson; **Wulfgar:** Robert Blythe; **Slave:** Wayne Forester

## ◎ ANIMATED EPICS: CANTERBURY TALES
Animated adaptations of Chaucer's legendary tales, including "The Nun's Priest Tale," "The Knight's Tale" and "The Wife of Bath's Tale"—with character voices provided by members of the Royal Shakespeare Company. Nominated in 1998 for an Oscar for best short film animated and winner of four prime time Emmy Awards for outstanding individual achievement (for "Leaving London—The Wife of Bath's Tale"), this stunningly animated program, incorporating traditional animation along with model work, oil painting and sketch art, premiered on HBO in two parts, at 6:30 P.M., May 26, 1999, and 2:30 P.M., May 27, 1999. A S4C/HBO/BBC Wales Production in association with a.k.a. Pizazz/Beryl Productions/Christmas Films/Picasso Pictures/Right Angle in association with Home Box Office. Color. Ninety minutes. Premiered on HBO: May 26, 1999 (Part 1); May 27, 1999 (Part II).

*Voices*
**Chaucer:** Bob Peck; **Canon:** Ken Dodd; **the Pardoner:** Tim McInnerny; **Friar:** David Troughton; **Squire:** Ronan Vibert; **Nun's Priest:** Sean Bean; **the Prioress:** Imelda Stanton; **Harry Bailey:** Robert Lindsay; **the Knight:** John Wood; **the Wife of Bath:** Billie Whitelaw; **the Merchant:** Bill Nighy; **Saturn/the Franklin:** Richard Griffiths; **the Miller:** Neil Dudgeon; **Chanticleer:** Mark Williams; **Pertelote/Dorigen:** Geraldine Somerville; **the Summoner:** Michael Feast; **the Hag:** Liz Smith; **the Cook:** Jonathan Cullen; **Venus:** Haydn Gwynne

## ◎ ANIMATED EPICS: DON QUIXOTE
Joined by his faithful squire, Sancho Panzo, self-annointed 18th-century Spanish knight, Don Quixote de la Mancha, seeks to right the wrongs of the world, including fighting for the honor of the beautiful peasant, Dulcinella, in this cartoon adaptation of Miguel de Cervantes's classic literary tale. Part of HBO's series of half-hour recreations of characters and stories from classic literature, Animated Epics, the special bowed on HBO in October 2000. A S4C/HBO/BBC Wales Production in association with a.k.a. Pizazz/

*Beryl Productions/Christmas Films/Picasso Pictures/Right Angle in association with Home Box Office. Color. Half-hour. Premiered on HBO: October 9, 2000.*

**Voices**

**Don Quixote:** Simon Callow; **Sancho Panza:** Paul Bradley; **Antonia/Landlady/Peasant Girl Dulcinella:** Ruth Jones; **Jeronimo Perez:** Christian Rodska; **Housekeeper/Duchess:** Julie Higginson; **Page/Nicholas:** Richard Pearce; **Samson Carasco/Barber:** Simon Harris; **Steward/Merlin/Merchant:** Michael Tudor Barnes; **Landlord/Master Peter/Merchant 2:** Brian Smith

### ⊚ ANIMATED EPICS: MOBY DICK

Captain Ahab's relentless journey to capture the gigantic white whale that devoured his leg comes to life in this half-hour animated version of author Herman Melville's epic story, produced in 2000 for HBO's *Animated Epics* anthology series. Academy Award- winner Rod Steiger provided the voice of Captain Ahab. *A S4C/HBO/BBC Wales Production in association with a.k.a. Pizazz/Beryl Productions/Christmas Films/Picasso Pictures/Right Angle in association with Home Box Office. Color. Half-hour. Premiered on HBO: 2000.*

**Voices**

**Captain Ahab:** Rod Steiger; **Ishmael:** Tim Guinee; **Starbuck:** William Hootkins; **Peter Coffin/Flask:** William Hope; **Fedallah:** Burt Kwuk; **Tashtego/Stubb:** Kerry Shale

### ⊚ THE ANIMATRIX

More than three years of collaboration between writers-producers-directors Larry and Andy Wachowski, creators of *The Matrix* film series, and animators from studios in Japan, Korea and the United States went into producing this anthology of feature-film quality shorts based on *The Matrix* and its sequels, created by world-renowned anime directors Peter Chung ("Matriculated"), Andy Jones ("Final Flight of the Osiris"), Yoshiaki Kawajiri ("Program"), Takeshi Koike ("World Record"), Mahiro Maeda ("The Second Renaissance Part I & II"), Kôji Morimoto ("Beyond") and Shin-ichirô Watanabe ("Kid's Story" and "A Detective Story"). The English-language version, re-dubbed with American actors, was released on DVD and premiered on Cartoon Network. *A Square USA Inc./ Studio 4°C/Madhouse/Sayao/H-Studio/ Production. Color. Eighty-nine minutes. Premiered on CAR: April 17, 2004.*

**Voices**

**FINAL FLIGHT OF THE OSTRIS: Jue:** Pamela Adlon; **Thaddeus:** Kevin Michael Richardson; **Pilot:** Rick Gomez; **Crewman:** John DiMaggio; **Crew Woman:** Tara Strong; **Operator:** Tom Kenny; **Old Woman:** Bette Ford

**THE SECOND RENAISSANCE, PARTS I & II: Kid: The Instructor:** Julia Fletcher; Debi Derryberry; **Mother:** Jill Talley; **01 Versatran Spokesman:** Dane Davis; **Other Voices:** Dwight Schulz, James Arnold Taylor

**KID'S STORY: Michael Karl Popper/The Kid:** Clayton Watson; **Teacher:** John DeMita; **Neo:** Keanu Reeves; **Trinity:** Carrie-Ann Moss; **Cop:** Kevin Michael Richardson; **Other Voices:** James Arnold Taylor

**PROGRAM: Cis:** Hedy Burress; **Duo:** Phil LaMarr; **Kaiser:** John DiMaggio

**WORLD RECORD: Dan:** Victor Williams; **Tom:** Alex Fernandez; **Reporter:** Allison Smith; **Nurse:** Tara Strong; **Dan's dad:** John Wesley; **Agent #1:** Matt McKenzie; **Agent #2:** Kevin Michael Richardson; **Narrator:** Julia Fletcher

**BEYOND: Manabu:** Pamela Adlon; **Yoko:** Hedy Burress; **Agent/Housewife/Kenny:** Tress MacNeile; **Agent/Ash:** Matt McKenzie; **Masa/Pudgy/Sara:** Kath Soucie; **Misha:** Tara Strong; **Other Voices:** Jack Fletcher, Tom Kenny, Dwight Schultz, Jill Talley

**A DETECTIVE STORY: Ash:** James Arnold Taylor; **Trinity:** Carrie-Ann Moss; **Agent:** Matt McKenzie

**MATRICULATED: Alexa:** Melinda Clarke; **Sandro:** Jack Fletcher; **Chyron:** Rodney Saulsberry; **Nonaka:** Dwight Schulz; **Raul:** James Arnold Taylor; **Rox:** Olivia d'Abo

### ⊚ ANNABELLE'S WISH

A lovable calf named Annabelle, born on Christmas Eve, makes friends with a young boy (Billy) who cannot talk and a friendly bunch of barnyard animals, and has one very special wish—to fly like one of Santa's reindeer—in this tender holiday tale, narrated by and starring country music superstar Randy Travis. *A Ralph Edwards Films/Baer Animation Production. Color. One hour. Premiered on FOX: November 30, 1997.*

**Voices**

**Adult Billy/Narrator:** Randy Travis; **Aunt Agnes:** Cloris Leachman; **Grandpa:** Jerry Van Dyke; **Scarlett the Horse:** Rue McClanahan; **Mr. Holder:** Jim Varney; **Annabelle:** Kath Soucie; **Ears:**

*A little calf's special Christmas wish becomes legendary in the Fox special* Annabelle's Wish. © *Ralph Edwards Productions*

Jay Johnson; **Emily:** Aria Noelle Curzon; **Young Billy:** Hari Oziol; **Santa:** Kay E. Kuter; **Star the Cow:** Jennifer Darling; **Lawyer/Sheriff:** Clancy Brown; **Buste/Bucky Holder:** James Lafferty, Charlie Cronin; **The Doctor:** Stu Rosen; **Slim the Pig:** Jerry Houser; **Brewster the Rooster:** Brian Cummings; **The Hens:** Mary Kaye Bergman, Tress MacNeille; **Owliver the Owl:** Steven Mackall; **Speaking Animals:** Frank Welker

## ◉ THE ARABIAN KNIGHTS

A courageous young teenager Pindar tries to win the hand of his love, Fatha, from her uncle Omar, the Thief of Baghdad, by capturing the treasure guarded by the great and powerful Genie of the lamp and the magic slippers of the Cruel Caliph in this half-hour syndicated *Festival of Family Classics* special. *A Rankin-Bass Production in association with Mushi Studios. Color. Half-hour. Premiered: February 4, 1973. Syndicated.*

### Voices

Carl Banas, Len Birman, Bernard Cowan, Peg Dixon, Keith Hampshire, Peggi Loder, Donna Miller, Frank Perry, Henry Ramer, Billie Mae Richards, Alfie Scopp, Paul Soles

## ◉ ARABIAN NIGHTS

Yogi Bear, Boo Boo, Magilla Gorilla, Scooby-Doo and Shaggy star in this politically correct version of the classic children's tale, broken into three separate acts. The 90-minute special, adapted from *The Book of One Thousand and One Nights* and reissued on VHS and DVD as *Scooby-Doo in Arabian Nights* and *Scooby-Doo! Arabian Nights*, made its debut on Superstation WTBS. *A Hanna-Barbera Production. Color. Ninety minutes. Premiered on TBS: September 3, 1994. Rebroadcast on CAR: December 25, 1997.*

### Voices

**ACT 1:** Alliyah-Din and the Magic Lamp: **Yogi Bear:** Greg Burson; **Boo Boo:** Don Messick; **Haman:** John Kassir; **Lord of the Amulet:** Tony Jay; **Sultan:** Brian Cummings; **Prince:** Rob Paulsen; **Scribe:** Paul Eiding; **Alliyah-Din:** Jennifer Hale; **Princess:** Kath Soucie

**ACT II:** Sinbad: **Captain:** Charlie Adler; **Magilla Gorilla:** Allan Melvin; **Cyclops:** Maurice LaMarche; **Mrs. Rukh/Baby Rukh:** Frank Welker

**ACT III:** Scheherazade: **Scooby-Doo:** Don Messick; **Shaggy:** Casey Kasem; **Chef:** Greg Burson; **Kitchen Worker/Dress Maker:** Nick Jameson; **Caliph:** Eddie Deezen; **Driver/Guard:** Brian Cummings

## ◉ ARCHIE AND HIS NEW FRIENDS

Familiar comic-book characters Archie, Jughead, Betty and Veronica are joined by a new character, Sabrina the Teenage Witch, in this prime-time special that tells the story of Sabrina's attempt to fit in with the rest of the Riverdale High School crowd. Sabrina was formally introduced to television audiences one day earlier with the debut of CBS's *The Archie Comedy Hour. A Filmation Associates Production. Color. Half-hour. Premiered on CBS: September 14, 1969.*

### Voices

**Archie Andrews:** Dal McKennon; **Jughead Jones:** Howard Morris; **Veronica Lodge/Betty Cooper/Sabrina:** Jane Webb; **Reggie Mantle/Moose:** John Erwin

## ◉ THE ARCHIES IN JUG MAN

A new geothermal heating system that is installed deep below the surface of Riverdale High manages to thaw out Jughead's hairy Neanderthal ancestor, Jug Man, who becomes the "toast of Riverdale," with Archie and the gang intervening to stop Reggie from unleashing one of his classic money-making schemes in the fifth feature-length installment of Nickelodeon's *DIC's Incredible Movie*

*Toons* series. *A DIC Entertainment Production. Color. Ninety minutes. Premiered on NICK: November 3, 2002.*

### Voices

**Archie:** Andy Rannells; **Jughead/Jugman:** Chris Lundquist; **Midge:** Jill Anderson; **Dilton:** Ben Beck; **Mrs. Weatherbee:** Kim Carlson; **Furnace Repairman/Coach Cleats:** Matt Geiler; **Bits:** Nils Haaland; **Lana Manana:** Anadella Lamas; **Mr. Lodge:** John Lee; **Moose:** Jerry Longe; **Veronica:** Camille Schmidt; **Pop Tate:** Ryle Smith; **Reggie:** Paul Sosso; **Mr. Weatherbee:** Tony Wike; **Betty:** Danielle Young

## ◉ THE ARCHIE, SUGAR SUGAR, JINGLE JANGLE SHOW

Selected scenes from the Saturday-morning series *The Archies* were featured in this half-hour special, which presented four popular songs (performed by the rock group The Archies) from the earlier series with comic vignettes. Songs included the Archies' number-one hit record in 1969, "Sugar Sugar." *A Filmation Associates Production. Color. Half-hour. Premiered on CBS: March 22, 1970.*

### Voices

**Archie Andrews:** Dal McKennon; **Jughead Jones:** Howard Morris; **Betty Cooper/Veronica Lodge/Sabrina:** Jane Webb; **Reggie Mantle/Moose:** John Erwin

## ◉ AROUND THE WORLD IN 80 DAYS

The familiar Jules Verne voyage of Phileas Fogg, who tries to win a wager by making a trip around the globe in 80 days, is the premise of this two-part *Festival of Family Classics* special. *A Rankin-Bass Production in association with Mushi Studios. Color. Half-hour. Premiered: November 12 and 19, 1972. Syndicated. Rebroadcast on NICK: March 28, 1992; July 16, 1993.*

### Voices

Carl Banas, Len Birman, Bernard Cowan, Peg Dixon, Keith Hampshire, Peggi Loder, Donna Miller, Frank Perry, Henry Ramer, Billie Mae Richards, Alfie Scopp, Paul Soles

## ◉ ARTHUR AND BUSTER'S THANKSGIVING SPECTACULAR

Two-hour holiday block of classic stories about food, friendship and family starring the famed animated aardvark, Arthur, and his pal, Buster Bunny, with episodes from the PBS Emmy Award–winning series, *Arthur*, and *Arthur* spin-off, *Postcards from Buster*, and live-action video footage of kids sharing their thoughts about Thanksgiving, hosted by Kyle and Taylor of the kids' variety show *Zoom.* (See *Arthur* and *Postcards from Buster* for complete voice credits.) The special aired only once on PBS on November 24, 2005. *A CINAR Animation/Cookie Jar Entertainment Inc./WGBH Boston/Mark Brown Studios/AKOM Productions Production. Color. Two hours. Premiered on PBS Kids: November 24, 2005.*

## ◉ ARTHUR: "IT'S ONLY ROCK 'N' ROLL"

Arthur the popular aardvark from PBS's longest-running, Emmy Award-winning daytime children's series, stars in this hour-long special—and second prime-time special—spoofing the Beatles' cult-classic film, *A Hard Day's Night* (1964), and featuring a guest appearance by the Backstreet Boys as cartoon rabbits and bears, broadcast during the series' seventh season on PBS. *A CINAR Animation/Cookie Jar Entertainment Inc./WGBH Boston/Mark Brown Studios/AKOM Productions Production. Color. One hour. Premiered on PBS: September 1, 2002.*

### Voices

**Arthur Timothy Read:** Mark Rendall; **Dora Winifred "D.W." Read:** Oliver Grainger; **Binky/David "Dad" Read:** Bruce Dinsmore; **Jane "Mom" Read:** Sonja Ball; **Buster Baxty:** Danny Brochu; **Francine Alice Frensky:** Jodi Resther; **Mary Alice "Muffy" Crosswire:** Melissa Altro; **Alan "The Brain" Powers:** Alex Hood; **Mr. Ratburn:** Arthur Holden; **Prunella:** Tammy Kaslov; **Sue Ellen Armstrong:** Patricia Rodriguez; **Principal Herbert Haney:** Walter Massey; **Grandma Thora Read:** Joanne Noyes; **Grandpa Dave/Ed Crosswire:** A.J. Henderson; **Mrs. Sarah MacGrady:** Bronwen Mantel; **Fern Walters:** Holly G. Frankel; **Paige Turner:** Kate Hutchinson; **Nadine:** Hayley Reynolds; **George Nordgren:** Mitchell David; **Baby Kate Read:** Tracy Braunstein; **Marie-Helen:** Jessica Kardos; **Emily:** Vanessa Lengies; **Nemo the Cat:** Greg Kramer; **Pal the Dog:** Simon Peacock; **Rabbits:** Brian Littrell, Howie Dorough; **Bears:** Kevin Scott Richardson, Nick Carter, A.J. McLean; **Perky Newswoman:** Eleanor Noble; **Molly McDonald:** Maggie Castle

## ◎ ARTHUR'S MISSING PAL

Arthur searches with the help of Buster the bunny and his friends for his dog Pal, who suddenly ends up missing, and learns a valuable lesson along the way, in this computer-animated feature—and first cartoon feature—based on PBS's award-winning educational series. Originally made as a direct-to-DVD release, this feature-length adaptation, with some of the voices of the original actors from the series, was released to theaters in select cities in July 2006 and was released on DVD that August, the same month it premiered on PBS. A *Mainframe Entertainment/Lionsgate Production. Color. Sixty-eight minutes. Premiered on PBS: August 18, 2006.*

### Voices

**Arthur Timothy Read:** Carr Thompson; **Buster Baxter:** Daniel Brochu; **Jodie Resther:** Francine Frensky; **Steven Crowder:** Alan "The Brain" Powers II; **Father Dave Read/Binky Barnes:** Bruce Dinsmore; **Mother Jane Read:** Sonja Ball; **Grandpa Dave Read/ Ed Crosswire:** A.J. Henderson; **Timmy Tibble/Tommy Tibble:** Jonathan Koensgen; **Prunella:** Wendee Lee; **Emily:** Vanessa Lengies; **Sarah MacGrady:** Bronwen Mantel; **Mary Alice "Muffy" Crosswire:** Melissa Altro; **TV Announcer:** Dave Mallow; **Dora Winifred "D.W." Read:** Luciano Rauso

## ◎ ARTHUR'S PERFECT CHRISTMAS

Arthur, D.W. and their family and friends, including Buster, Muffy, Alan, Francine and Binky, do everything possible to make the holiday season "perfect" in every way, from buying perfect gifts, to planning perfect parties, to even having perfect family traditions for Christmas, Hanukah and Kwanzaa. Unfortunately, in the end, Arthur discovers that the real joy of the season is the imperfect world in which he lives in this first prime-time special based on the Emmy Award–winning series for PBS. A companion CD, featuring many songs from the television special, such as "Boogie Woogie Christmas" and "Baxter Day," was also released. New tunes produced for the hour-long special included a rock version of "Silent Night" performed by Fern and "Here We Come A' Wassailing." A *CINAR Animation/WGBH/Mark Brown Studios Production. Color. One hour. Premiered on PBS: November 23, 2000; Rebroadcast on PBS: November 24, 2000; December 20, 2000; December 24, 2000; December 25, 2000; December 26, 2000; November 19, 2001; December 24, 2001; December 25, 2001; December 21, 2002; December 25, 2002; December 24, 2003; December 25, 2003; December 26, 2003; November 29, 2004; December 8, 2004; December 9, 2004; December 11, 2004; December 12, 2004; December 13, 2004; December 25, 2004; December 26, 2004; November 21, 2005; December 15, 2005; December 24, 2005; December 25, 2005; December 25, 2006.*

### Voices

**Arthur:** Michael Yarmush; **D.W.:** Oliver Grainger; **Binky/Dad:** Bruce Dinsmore; **Brain:** Steven Crowder; **Buster:** Danny Brochu;

**Francine:** Jodie Resther; **Muffy:** Melissa Altro; **Mr. Rathburn:** Arthur Holden; **Mom/Quackers:** Sonja Ball; **Grandma Thora:** Joanna Noyes; **Tommy Tibble:** Jonathan Koensgen; **Timmy Tibble:** Ricky Mabe; **Oliver Frensky/Security Guard:** Mark Camacho; **George:** Mitchel David Rothman; **Bitzi/Old Woman:** Ellen David

## ◎ AS TOLD BY GINGER: "EVEN STEVEN HOLIDAY SPECIAL"

After discovering she is one-quarter Jewish, Ginger becomes so involved in her newfound faith that Dodie thinks she has given up on Christmas altogether, while Carl still believes Santa exists and a special visitor Mr. Foutley arrives on Christmas Eve. This is the second holiday special based on creator Emily Kapnek's acclaimed Nickelodeon cartoon series, *As Told by Ginger. A Klasky Csupo/ Anivision Korea/Sunwoo Digital International Production. Color. Half-hour. Premiered on NICK: December 10, 2001.*

### Voices

**Ginger Foutley:** Melissa Disney; **Dodie Bishop:** Aspen Miller; **Macie Lightfoot:** Jackie Harris; **Carl Foutley:** Jeannie Elias; **Hoodsey Bishop:** Tress MacNeille; **Courtney Gripling:** Liz Georges; **Miranda Killgallen:** Cree Summer; **Darren Patterson:** Kenny Blank; **Blake Gripling:** Kath Soucie; **Lois Foutley:** Laraine Newman; **Winston:** John Kassir; **Mitchey Mekelburg:** Richard Horvitz; **Santa Claus #2:** Arthur Burghardt

## ◎ AS TOLD BY GINGER: "FAR FROM HOME"

Bright, thoughtful tween Ginger Foutley wins a scholarship to the Avalanche Arts Academy and suffers a severe case of separation anxiety when she spends a semester away from her family and classmates until she makes new friends, including a potential love interest, while her younger brother, Carl, falls for a telekinetic girl—and a new character—Noelle (voiced by the show's creator, Emily Kapnek), in this second TV-movie adapted from the hit Nickelodeon series following the Emmy-nominated (and third consecutive nominated) episode, "And She Was Gone." Originally titled *Foutleys on Ice,* the title was changed in the United States to *Far from Home* while the program aired in the United Kingdom under its original title. In July 2001, Ginger and company starred in their first 90-minute movie special on Nick, *Summer of Camp Caprice. A Klasky Csupo/Anivision Korea/Sunwood Digital International Production. Color. Ninety minutes. Premiered on NICK: August 9, 2003. Rebroadcast on NICK: August 10, 2003; August 11, 2003; August 30, 2003; September 1, 2003; October 12, 2003; October 26, 2003; November 28, 2003; December 30, 2003; January 10, 2004*

### Voices

**Ginger Foutley:** Melissa Disney; **Dodie Bishop:** Aspen Miller; **Macie Lightfoot:** Jackie Harris; **Carl Foutley/Hysterical Citizen:** Jeannie Elias; **Hoodsey Bishop/Space Cannibal:** Tress MacNeille; **Courtney Gripling:** Liz Georges; **Miranda Killgallen:** Cree Summer; **Darren Patterson/Punk Kid:** Kenny Blank; **Blake Gripling:** Kath Soucie; **Lois Foutley/Silver-Haired Woman:** Laraine Newman; **Winston/Turtle Eater:** John Kassir; **Noelle Sussman:** Emily Kapnek; **Thea:** Joey Lauren Adams; **Fred:** Toran Caudell; **Cheese Attendant:** Eryk Casemiro; **Bus Driver:** Wes Parnell; **Radio Voice/ Train Conductor:** Chris Parnell; **Hip Art Student:** Lauren Tom

## ◎ AS TOLD BY GINGER: "I SPY A WITCH"

Accused of defacing a statue at school as part of a Halloween prank, Ginger loses out on playing the lead in the school musical until the ghost of Maude reveals who really did the crime in this half-hour Halloween special, based on Nickelodeon's Emmy-nominated animated series. The first-ever prime-time special bowed on Nickelodeon on Friday, October 26, 2001, at 8:30 P.M. (ET). A *Klasky Csupo/Anivision Korea/Sunwoo Digital International Production. Color. Half-hour. Premiered on NICK: October 26, 2001. Rebroadcast on NICK: October 31, 2001; February 2, 2002; October 27, 2002; October 31, 2002; March 28, 2004; October 31, 2004; October 30, 2005.*

### Voices

**Ginger Foutley:** Melissa Disney; **Dodie Bishop:** Aspen Miller; **Macie Lightfoot:** Jackie Harris; **Carl Foutley:** Jeannie Elias; **Hoodsey Bishop:** Tress MacNeille; **Courtney Gripling:** Liz Georges; **Miranda Killgallen:** Cree Summer; **Darren Patterson:** Kenny Blank; **Blake Gripling:** Kath Soucie; **Lois Foutley:** Laraine Newman; **Winston:** John Kassir; **Lizzie Laypoff:** R. Samantha Lee; **Girls:** Hope Levy, Tia Texada; **Piano Player:** Matt Farnsworth

## ◉ AS TOLD BY GINGER: "NO TURNING BACK"

Ginger overcomes her paranoia that she and her friends will grow apart once they graduate and attend different classes at high school, while her mother wraps up final preparations for her wedding and Carl and Hoodsey make plans to go to Lucky Jr. High in this third and final TV-movie special and last episode of the three-time Emmy-nominated series for Nickelodeon. A *Klasky Csupo/Anivision Korea/Sunwoo Digital International Production. Color. One hour. Premiered on NICK: June 11, 2004. Rebroadcast on NICK: June 12, 2004; June 13, 2004; August 23, 2004; September 6, 2004; November 7, 2004.*

### Voices

**Ginger Foutley:** Melissa Disney; **Dodie Bishop:** Aspen Miller; **Macie Lightfoot:** Jackie Harris; **Carl Foutley:** Jeannie Elias; **Hoodsey Bishop:** Tress MacNeille; **Courtney Gripling:** Liz Georges; **Miranda Killgallen:** Cree Summer; **Darren Patterson:** Kenny Blank; **Blake Gripling:** Kath Soucie; **Lois Foutley:** Laraine Newman; **Winston:** John Kassir

## ◉ AS TOLD BY GINGER: "SUMMER OF CAMP CAPRICE"

Spoiled rich girl Courtney heads to summer camp with Ginger and friends Dodie and Macie and nearly ruins Ginger's chances with a boy she meets named Sasha. Darren and Miranda make the best of military camp where Miranda's father works and Carl and Hoodsey go after dognappers in this first 90-minute TV-movie special, combining three half-hour episodes, based on the successful Nickelodeon cartoon series. Neil Patrick Harris of TV's *Doogie Howser* fame does a guest voice as the swimming counselor, Jed. Two years later, the characters returned to star in a second 90-minute feature-length special, *Far from Home*. A *Klasky Csupo/Anivision Korea/Sunwoo Digital International Production. Color. Ninety minutes. Premiered on NICK: July 7, 2001. Rebroadcast on NICK: July 8, 2001; July 15, 2001; July 28, 2001; July 29, 2001; July 30, 2001; August 25, 2001; August 26, 2001; September 2, 2001; September 29, 2001; September 30, 2001; November 17, 2001; November 18, 2001; November 23, 2001; January 1, 2002; January 5, 2002; March 3, 2002; April 14, 2002; June 29, 2002; June 30, 2002; August 3, 2002; August 4, 2002; November 29, 2002; January 1, 2003; March 16, 2003; June 13, 2003; October 10, 2004; June 5, 2005.*

### Voices

**Ginger Foutley:** Melissa Disney; **Dodie Bishop:** Aspen Miller; **Macie Lightfoot:** Jackie Harris; **Carl Foutley/Girl in Movie:** Jeannie Elias; **Hoodsey Bishop/Georgia, Principal Milty's Date:** Tress MacNeille; **Courtney Gripling:** Liz Georges; **Miranda Killgallen:** Cree Summer; **Darren Patterson/Policeman:** Kenny Blank; **Blake Gripling/Cinnamon Ann:** Kath Soucie; **Lois Foutley/Courtney's**

Seamstress/Boy in Movie: Laraine Newman; **Winston/Jarhead:** John Kassir; **Sarah, Ginger's Friend:** Candi Milo; **Sasha:** Evan Bonifant; **Melanie, Sasha's Sister:** Hope Levy; **Margie, Head Counselor:** Carol Rosenthal; **Policeman:** Jeff D. Beuhl; **Field Hockey Player:** Jackie Harris; **Jed, Swimming Counselor:** Neil Patrick Harris; **Farmhand:** Jerry Houser; **Giselle:** Kate Movius; **Doctor in Soap Opera:** Tony Plana; **Sergeant:** Andre Ware

## ◉ AS TOLD BY GINGER: "TEN CHAIRS"

Ginger springs a surprise guest, Jonas, on the Foutley family for Thanksgiving, which makes her younger brother, Carl, unhappy. Meanwhile, he and his fellow vegan friend, Hoodsey, buy a turkey and set it free in this final episode and third half-hour special—following *I Spy a Witch* (2001) and *The Even Steven Holiday Special* (2001) Halloween and Christmas specials, respectively, based on the Nickelodeon series. A *Klasky Csupo/Anivision Korea/Sunwoo Digital International Production. Color. Half-hour. Premiered on NICK: November 24, 2004.*

### Voices

**Ginger Foutley:** Melissa Disney; **Dodie Bishop:** Aspen Miller; **Macie Lightfoot:** Jackie Harris; **Carl Foutley:** Jeannie Elias; **Hoodsey Bishop:** Tress MacNeille; **Courtney Gripling:** Liz Georges; **Miranda Killgallen:** Cree Summer; **Darren Patterson:** Kenny Blank; **Blake Gripling:** Kath Soucie; **Lois Foutley:** Laraine Newman; **Winston:** John Kassir; **Dr. Dave's Mother:** Patti Deutsch; **Dodie/Mr. Talbit, Hoodsey's Father (Turkey Farm Owner):** Dan Castellaneta; **Jonas Foutley:** Tom Virtue

## ◉ ATOMIC BETTY: "THE NO-L-9"

After Supreme Overlord Maximus I.Q. shrinks some planets down to size to keep for himself, Admiral DeGill calls on Betty, joined by Sparky's mom, Robot X-5 and his Uncle B-1, to save a long-forgotten mythical constellation of singing planets, No-L-9, where she meets an old man who turns out to be her Grandpa, returning to Earth with him for a memorable family reunion in this hour-long Christmas special based on the popular Cartoon Network series. An *Atomic Cartoons/Breakthrough Films/TeleImages Kids Production. Color. One hour. Premiered on CAR: December 4, 2005. Rebroadcast on CAR: December 18, 2005; December 24, 2005; December 25, 2005.*

### Voices

**Betty:** Taija Isen; **Minumus P.U.:** Len Carlson; **Noah:** Laurie Elliot; **Supreme Overlord Maximus I.Q.:** Colin Fox; **Robot X-5:** Bruce Hunter; **Mom:** Kristina Nicoll; **Dad:** Patrick McKenna; **Admiral DeGill:** Adrian Truss; **Penelope Lang/Sarah:** Catherine Disher; **Sparky:** Rick Miller; **Betty's Grandma:** Jayne Eastwood; **Betty's Grandpa:** William Shatner; **Max Sr.:** Don Francks

## ◉ AU CLAIR DE LA LUNE

The Prince of Darkness puts the person responsible for changing night into day, into a deep slumber, part of his evil plan to have eternal darkness in this half-hour animated special from CINAR Films' cartoon anthology series, *The Real Story of . . . (a.k.a. Favorite Songs)*, first produced for Canadian television in 1992, then premiering on HBO. A *CINAR Films/France Animation Production. Color. Half-hour. Premiered on HBO: January 15, 1994.*

### Voices
**Prince of Darkness:** Milton Berle

## ◉ AVATAR: THE LAST AIRBENDER: "THE BOY IN THE ICEBERG"

When Aang and his pet flying bison, Appa, become trapped in an iceberg, teenage siblings Sokka and Katara come to the rescue, with

Aang learning that he is the planet's only surviving Airbender in this two-part, one-hour series premiere special for Nickelodeon's top-rated action fantasy series. A *Nickelodeon Studios Production. Color. One hour. Premiered on NICK: February 21, 2005.*

*Voices*
**Avatar Roku:** James Garrett; **Katara:** Mae Whitman; **Uncle Iroh:** Makato Iwamasto; **Prince Zuko:** Dante Basco; **Sokka:** Jack DeSena; **Appa/Momo/Others:** Dee Bradley Baker; **Aang:** Zack Tyler Eisen; **Gran Gran:** Melendy Britt

## ◎ AVATAR: THE LAST AIRBENDER: "THE FURY OF AANG"

When the gang visits the Spirit Library, Sokka discovers secrets to use against the Fire Nation while Aang becomes upset over Appa's capture in this hour-long prime-time special combining two episodes, "The Library" and "The Desert." Executive produced by series' creators Michael DiMartino and Bryan Knoietzko, the special marked the program's 60th episode produced by Burbank, California's Nickelodeon Studios. A *Nickelodeon Studios Production. Color. One hour. Premiered on NICK: July 14, 2005.*

*Voices*
**Avatar Roku:** James Garrett; **Katara:** Mae Whitman; **Uncle Iroh:** Makato Iwamasto; **Prince Zuko:** Dante Basco; **Sokka:** Jack DeSena; **Appa/Momo/Others:** Dee Bradley Baker; **Aang:** Zack Tyler Eisen; **Gran Gran:** Melendy Britt; **Princess Yue:** Johanna Braddy; **Master Pakku:** Victor Brandt; **Chief Arnook:** Jon Polto; **Hahn:** Ben Diskin; **Koh:** Erik Dellums; **Toph:** Jessie Flower; **Wan Shi Tong:** Hector Elizondo; **Professor Zei:** Raphael Sharge; **Master Yu:** Sab Shimono; **Colonel Mongke:** Malachi Throne; **Xin Fu:** Marc Graue; **Sha-Mo:** Bill Bolender; **Fung:** Peter Jessop; **Ghashiun:** Paul McKinney

## ◎ AVATAR: THE LAST AIRBENDER: "THE GURU"/"THE CROSSROADS TO DESTINY"

Toph learns the art of "metalbending" while Xin Fu and Master Yu send Toph to visit her parents, and Aang dreams that Katara faces serious danger as he, Sooka and Toph hurry back from the city of Ba Sing Se to save her in this fifth hour special—and second season finale—comprised of two episodes from Nickelodeon's weekly cartoon series. A *Nickelodeon Studios Production. Color. One hour. Premiered on NICK: December 1, 2006.*

*Voices*
**Avatar Roku:** James Garrett; **Katara:** Mae Whitman; **Uncle Iroh:** Makato Iwamasto; **Prince Zuko:** Dante Basco; **Sokka:** Jack DeSena; **Appa/Momo/Others:** Dee Bradley Baker; **Aang:** Zack Tyler Eisen; **Gran Gran:** Melendy Britt; **Princess Yue:** Johanna Braddy; **Master Pakku:** Victor Brandt; **Chief Arnook:** Jon Polto; **Hahn:** Ben Diskin; **Koh:** Erik Dellums; **Toph:** Jessie Flower; **Ty Lee:** Olivia Hack; **General H. Cricket:** Jim Meskimen; **Hakoda:** Andre Sogliuzzo; **Long Feng:** Clancy Brown; **Master:** Sab Shimono; **Guru Pathik:** Brian George; **Bato:** Richard McGonagle; **Earth King:** Phil LaMarr; **Xin Fu:** Marc Graue

## ◎ AVATAR: THE LAST AIRBENDER: "SECRET OF THE FIRE NATION"

After crossing the dangerous Serpent's Pass by ferry with Iroh to the city of Ba Sing Se, Zuko decides whether to join the Freedom Fighters with his new friend, Jet, while Ang discovers a weapon aimed at destroying the great wall that protects the city. Combining two episodes, "The Serpent's Pass" and "The Drill," the movie was the fourth one-hour special overall and first during the series'

second season on Nickelodeon. A *Nickelodeon Studios Production. Color. One hour. Premiered on NICK: September 15, 2006.*

*Voices*
**Avatar Roku:** James Garrett; **Katara:** Mae Whitman; **Uncle Iroh:** Makato Iwamasto; **Prince Zuko:** Dante Basco; **Sokka:** Jack DeSena; **Appa/Momo/Others:** Dee Bradley Baker; **Aang:** Zack Tyler Eisen; **Toph:** Jessie Flower; **Wan Shi Tong:** Hector Elizondo; **Professor Zei:** Raphael Sharge; **War Minister:** Kristoffer Tabori; **General Sung:** Barry Dennen; **Bureaucrat:** Karen Maruyama; **Than:** Brian Tochi; **Ying:** Kim Mai Guest; **Smellerbee:** Nika Futterman; **Jet:** Crawford Wilson

## ◎ AVATAR: THE LAST AIRBENDER: "SIEGE OF THE NORTH"

After Admiral Zhao launches a fierce battle with the Fire Nation, Avatar turns to one of the oldest spirits in the Spirit World for help in this action-packed, two-part hour-long movie special—and first season finale—featuring the voice of *Stars Wars'* Luke Skywalker, Mark Hamill, as Fire Lord Ozai, aired on Nickelodeon. A *Nickelodeon Studios Production. Color. One hour. Premiered on NICK: December 2, 2005.*

*Voices*
**Avatar Roku:** James Garrett; **Katara:** Mae Whitman; **Uncle Iroh:** Makato Iwamasto; **Prince Zuko:** Dante Basco; **Sokka:** Jack DeSena; **Appa/Momo/Others:** Dee Bradley Baker; **Aang:** Zack Tyler Eisen; **Princess Yue:** Johanna Braddy; **Master Pakku:** Victor Brandt; **Chief Anook:** Jon Polito; **Hahn:** Ben Diskin; **Fire Lord Ozai:** Mark Hamill; **Koh:** Erik Dellums

## ◎ BAA BAA BLACK SHEEP

The toughest sheep in Muttonville Prison break out to set up a wool racket that leaves the whole town fleeced in this cartoon special, featuring the voices of Shelley Long and Robert Stack. The show aired on HBO as part of the Saturday-morning anthology series *The Real Story of . . . (a.k.a. Favorite Stories).* A *CINAR Films/France Animation Production. Color. Half-hour. Premiered on HBO: January 1, 1994.*

*Voices*
**Lieutenant Littleboy:** Robert Stack; **The Dame:** Shelley Long

## ◎ BABAR, THE LITTLE ELEPHANT

The story of the elephant who would be king is told in this first primetime special based on the first three books from the popular French children's book series. The program was originally entitled *The Story of Babar, the Little Elephant.* A *Lee Mendelson–Bill Melendez Production in association with Laurent de Brunhoff and the cooperation of Random House. Color. Half-hour. Premiered on NBC: October 21, 1968. Rebroadcast on NBC: April 21, 1969; Rebroadcast on DIS: June 6, 1993.*

*Voices*
**Narrator:** Peter Ustinov

## ◎ BABAR AND FATHER CHRISTMAS

King Babar successfully spoils the plans of Retaxes the Rhinoceros, who stops at nothing to foil Father Christmas's goodwill gesture to visit the people of Celesteville in Elephant Land. An *Atkinson Film-Arts/MTR Ottawa Production in association with the CBC. Color. Half-hour. Premiered on HBO: December 5, 1986. Rebroadcast on HBO: December 9–24, 1986; December 22, 1991; December 24, 1991.*

*Voices*
**Babar:** Jim Bradford; **Celeste:** Louise Villeneuve; **Arthur:** Kemp Edwards; **Zephir/Lazarro/Podular/Mice:** Rick Jones; **Retaxes/ Father Christmas:** Les Lye; **Pom:** Amie Charlebois; **Flora:** Courtney Caroll; **Alexander:** Kai Engstead; **Professor:** Noel Council; **Secretary/Elf #1:** Bridgitte Robinson; **Elderberry/Elf #2/Boatman;** Derek Diorio; **Gendarme:** Roch Lafortune

## ◎ BABAR COMES TO AMERICA

King Babar and his wife, Queen Celeste, receive a telegram inviting them to America to make a movie in Hollywood in this second animated special based on two of the Babar books—*Travels of Babar* by Jean de Brunhoff and *Babar in America* by his son, Laurent de Brunhoff, who also penned the script. *A Lee Mendelson–Bill Melendez Production in association with Laurent de Brunhoff and with the cooperation of Random House. Color. Half-hour. Premiered on NBC: September 7, 1971. Rebroadcast on NBC: February 27, 1972.*

*Voices*
**Babar, King of Elephant Land/Celeste, his queen/Arthur, Babar's cousin/Cornelius, the elder elephant/Narrator:** Peter Ustinov

## ◎ BACK TO SCHOOL WITH FRANKLIN

It's back to school for Franklin the Turtle, his sister, Harriet, and his many other animal friends in this new direct-to-video feature. Based on the popular children's books by Paulette Bourgeois, this 75-minute cartoon adventure follows the highly successful Nick Jr. series and two previous made-for-video movies, *Franklin's Magic Christmas* (2001) and *Franklin and the Green Knight* (1999), each debuting on Canada's Family Channel before subsequently airing in the United States on Nick Jr. and Noggin.

Broadcast in a 90-minute time slot, the cartoon feature made its U.S. television premiere on Nick Jr. in August 2003 and was first rebroadcast on Noggin on August 30, 2004 at 11:00 A.M. (EST), followed by an encore performance rebroadcast that afternoon. Noggin has repeated the "back-to-school" special multiple times on its fall schedule each year since its debut. Three new voice actors were featured in the movie that launched the program's sixth season: Cole Caplan, replacing Noah Reid as the voice of Franklin the Turtle; Bryn McAuley as his sister Harriet; and Carolyn Scott as Franklin's new teacher, Miss Koala. *A Nelvana Ltd. Production. Color. Ninety minutes. Premiered on NICK JR.: August 19, 2003. Premiered on NOG: August 30, 2004. Rebroadcast on Noggin: August 30, 2004; August 31, 2004; September 1, 2004; September 2, 2004; September 3, 2004; September 4, 2004; September 5, 2004; August 29, 2005; August 30, 2005; August 31, 2005; September 1, 2005; September 2, 2005; September 3, 2005; September 4, 2005; September 4, 2006; September 6, 2006; September 8, 2006; September 9, 2006; September 10, 2006.*

*Voices*
**Franklin:** Cole Caplan; **Harriett, His Sister:** Bryn McAuley; **Miss Koala:** Carolyn Scott; **Additional Voices:** Amanda Soha, Carolyn Scott, James Rankin, Scott Beaudin, Kristen Bone, Valerie Boyle, Elizabeth Brown, Leah Cudmore, Kyle Fairlie, Luca Perlman, Richard Newman, Ruby Smith-Merowitz

## ◎ THE BACKYARDIGANS: "MISSION TO MARS"

After hearing a strange "boinga, boinga!" sound coming from outer space, backyard pals-turned Mission Control specialists Tyrone and Tasha send their friends, now astronauts, Uniqua, Pablo and Austin on an important mission to find life on Mars in this half-hour epic

musical adventure and second special, based on the popular Nick Jr. cartoon series, *The Backyardigans*. Nine-time Grammy Award-winning recording artist Alicia Keys guest starred as the voice of Mommy Martian, along with her niece, Shakyra Lipscomb, as the baby Martian, Boinga. Keys also sang an original song for the special, entitled "Almost Everything Is Boinga Here."

Premiering at 10:30 A.M. (ET) on Columbus Day in 2005, the half-hour special preceded the second season debut on October 16 of the top-rated, CGI-animated weekday series with a special week of new episodes through October 19 on Nick Jr. The day after the special aired, Nickelodeon Home Entertainment and Paramount Home Entertainment released the program on DVD and VHS, featuring the title episode with three other adventures.

Of her experience working on the special, Keys said, "After speaking with kids who said they loved 'The Backyardigans,' I knew this would be a great project for me to get involved in. Working alongside my niece was so much fun and the people at Nick Jr. helped to make it a great experience. I can't wait to see it all put together to make one great episode." *A Nelvana Limited/ Nickelodeon Production. Color. Half-hour. Premiered on NICK JR.: October 9, 2005. Rebroadcast on NICK JR.: October 11, 2006; October 13, 2006; November 2, 2006; November 13, 2006; November 22, 2006; December 13, 2006; January 23, 2007; January 31, 2007; March 23, 2007; April 10, 2007; May 3, 2007.*

*Voices*
**Tyrone:** Reginald Davis Jr.; **Tasha:** Naelee Rae; **Uniqua:** LeShawn Jeffries; **Pablo:** Sean Curley; **Austin:** Jonah Bobo; **Tyrone Singing:** Corwin C. Tuggles; **Tasha Singing:** Kristen Danielle Klabunde; **Uniqua Singing:** Jamia Simone Nash; **Pablo Singing:** Zach Tyler; **Austin Singing:** Thomas Sharkey; **Mommy Martian:** Alicia Keys; **Little Martian/Boinga:** Shakyra Lipscomb

## ◎ THE BACKYARDIGANS: "RACE TO THE TOWER OF POWER"

The high-spirited backyard friends embark on a salsa-themed, super-imaginative musical adventure from the frozen North to the high seas as Pablo and Tyrone play supervillains who try ruling the world, but meet their match in the form of Unique and Austin who turn into superheroes to stop them. Featuring four original songs and actual dance steps—choreographed by former Alvin Ailey Dance School director Beth Bogush and recreated in CGI and 3-D animation, this half-hour special—and first based on the popular Nick Jr. series—debuted Monday, July 18, 2005, at 11:00 A.M. during Nick Jr.'s weekday morning pre-school block. A week before the special's premiere, Nick Records and Sony BMG Music Entertainment released the first-ever collection of songs from the series, featuring many different musical genres, including reggae, jazz and opera. *A Nelvana Limited/Nickelodeon Production. Color. Half-hour. Premiered on NICK JR.: July 18, 2005. Rebroadcast on NICK JR.: July 18, 2005; July 22, 2005; July 26, 2005; August 23, 2005; September 14, 2005; October 12, 2005; November 4, 2005; December 1, 2005; December 28, 2005; March 10, 2006; April 25, 2006; May 24, 2006; June 20, 2006; July 21, 2006; August 25, 2006; September 25, 2006; October 24, 2006; November 14, 2006; December 5, 2006; December 26, 2006; January 12, 2007; February 1, 2007; March 21, 2007; April 9, 2007.*

*Voices*
**Tyrone:** Reginald Davis Jr.; **Tasha:** Naelee Rae; **Uniqua:** LeShawn Jeffries; **Pablo:** Sean Curley; **Austin:** Jonah Bobo; **Tyrone Singing:** Corwin C. Tuggles; **Tasha Singing:** Kristen Danielle Klabunde; **Uniqua Singing:** Jamia Simone Nash; **Pablo Singing:** Zach Tyler; **Austin Singing:** Thomas Sharkey

## ◉ THE BACKYARDIGANS: THE SECRET OF SNOW

Uniqua journeys to the frigid North to uncover the secret of snow from Ice Lady Tasha and is joined in her quest by Cowboy Pablo, Tarzan Tyrone and Ice Lady Tasha's assistant, Austin, whom she befriends along the way in this Christmas special based on the beloved Nick Jr. preschool series. In December 2006, the 30-minute special premiered on Nick Jr.'s "Frosty Fridays" on the same day as the half-hour Christmas special, *Lazy-Town Snow Monster*, from *The LazyTown* television series, and also aired on the commercial-free pre-school network, Noggin. *A Nelvana Limited/Nickelodeon Production. Color. Half-hour. Premiered on NICK JR.: December 15, 2006. Premiered on NOG: December 15, 2006. Rebroadcast on NICK JR.: December 21, 2006; December 25, 2006; December 29, 2006. Rebroadcast on NOG: December 17, 2006.*

### Voices
**Tyrone:** Reginald Davis Jr.; **Tasha:** Naelee Rae; **Uniqua:** LeShawn Jeffries; **Pablo:** Sean Curley; **Austin:** Jonah Bobo; **Tyrone Singing:** Corwin C. Tuggles; **Tasha Singing:** Kristen Danielle Klabunde; **Uniqua Singing:** Jamia Simone Nash; **Pablo Singing:** Zach Tyler; **Austin Singing:** Thomas Sharkey

## ◉ BAD CAT

Based on two children's books about one cat's struggle for acceptance, this half-hour adaptation tells the story of Bad Cat, the undisputed "King Cat" of Fulton Street, who, despite his reputation for being a troublemaker, is really a good cat. First, he must overcome the animosity of a new group of cats, led by bully cat Riff, who challenges him to a mouse-catching contest to prove one's superiority over the other. *An ABC Weekend Special. A Ruby-Spears Enterprises Production. Color. Half-hour. Premiered on ABC: April 14, 1984. Rebroadcast on ABC: September 29, 1984; October 28, 1985; November 12, 1988; July 8, 1995; May 18, 1996.*

### Voices
**Bad Cat:** Bart Braverman; **Gordon:** Hal Smith; **Neddy:** Tress MacNeille; **Vernon Turner:** Bobby Ellerbee; **Jim Harrison:** Alan Young; **Steve Harrison:** Steve Spears; **Pam Harrison:** Amy Tunik; **Champ:** Frank Welker; **Diedra:** Judy Strangis; **Dimples:** Didi Conn; **Riff:** Jon Bauman; **Mouser:** Marvin Kaplan

## ◉ BAH, HUMDUCK! A LOONEY TUNES CHRISTMAS

Daffy Duck, as a modern-day Scrooge and heartless owner of the incredibly successful "Lucky Duck" department store chain, learns the importance of giving and the true meaning of Christmas through the example of Porky Pig's daughter, Priscilla, and visits from the ghosts of Christmas past, present and future (played by *Looney Tunes* stars Granny, Tweety, Yosemite Sam and Tasmanian Devil), as well as Bug Bunny's relentless prodding, in this 44-minute first-ever made-for-video *Looney Tunes* feature directed by Charles Visser—and latest spoof on the classic Charles Dickens tale—that was released on DVD on November 14, 2006, before premiering in an hour time slot on Cartoon Network that December. *A Warner Bros. Television Animated Production. Color. One hour. Premiered on CAR: December 1, 2006. Rebroadcast on CAR: December 17, 2006. December 22, 2006; December 24, 2006.*

### Voices
**Daffy Duck/Sylvester/Marvin the Martian:** Joe Alaskey; **Yosemite Sam (The Ghost of Christmas Present):** Jeff Bennett; **Porky**

**Pig/Speedy Gonzales/Tweety:** Bob Bergen; **Taz/Ghost of Christmas Future/Gossamer:** Jim Cummings; **Granny/Ghost of Christmas Past:** June Foray; **Pepé Le Pew:** Maurice LaMarche; **Priscilla Pig:** Tara Strong; **Bugs Bunny/Elmer Fudd:** Billy West

## ◉ THE BALLAD OF PAUL BUNYAN

Known for his legendary feats of skill and strength as a respected axeman, a giant lumberjack who wields a magic axe, maintains his title by beating the hated Panhandle Pete, a ruthless lumber boss, in log-rolling, arm-wrestling and hole-digging competitions in this *Festival of Family Classics* special. *A Rankin-Bass Production in association with Mushi Studios. Color. Half-hour. Premiered: January 7, 1973. Syndicated.*

### Voices
Carl Banas, Len Birman, Bernard Cowan, Peg Dixon, Keith Hampshire, Peggi Loder, Donna Miller, Frank Perry, Henry Ramer, Billie Mae Richards, Alfie Scopp, Paul Soles

## ◉ THE BALLAD OF SMOKEY THE BEAR

Movie tough guy Jimmy Cagney, as Smokey the Bear's big brother Big Bear, narrates this charming, half-hour special that recalls the trials and tribulations of the U.S. Forest Service fire-prevention campaign spokesperson, from his early challenges as a tiny cub to his courageous acts on behalf of those in trouble as a wise adult. The special was filmed using the spectacularly lifelike stop-motion animation process called Animagic. *A Rankin-Bass Production in association with Videocraft International. Color. Half-hour. Premiered on NBC: November 24, 1966. Rebroadcast on NBC: May 5, 1968; May 4, 1969.*

### Voices
**Big Bear:** James Cagney; **Smokey:** Barry Pearl

*Smokey's friends:*
**Turtle:** William Marine; **Beaver:** Herbert Duncan; **Mrs. Beaver:** Rose Marie Jun; **Fox:** George Petrie; **Mama:** Bryna Raeburn

## ◉ THE BALLOONATIKS®: "CHRISTMAS WITHOUT A CLAUS"

The Balloontiks® (Flator, Squeeker, Airhead, Bouncer and Stretch), five balloon creatures from the planet Balloona whose mission on Earth is to battle dastardly deeds, search for the kidnapped Santa in this animated special, based on the comic-book characters created by Anthony Diloia. The half-hour Saturday-morning special was produced by Jay Poynor, winner of three Emmy Awards for his television work as executive producer of the Film Roman animated *Garfield* prime-time specials for CBS. The Balloonatiks is a registered trademark of Animagic Entertainment Group. *An Animagic Entertainment Group Production. Color. Half-hour. Premiered on FOX: December 14, 1996.*

### Voices
**Flator/Al Pinhead:** James Andrew Pearsons; **Airhead/Boy:** Alexandra Rhodie; **Squeeker/Girl/Mom:** Ashley Albert; **Bouncer:** Brian Mitchell; **L.A. Tee/Santa:** Doug Preis; **Dr. "Pop" Swellhead:** Don Peoples; **Keedler/Tacky Pinhead/Squirt:** Chris Phillips; **Penny Nails/Baloonimal:** Giovanna Godard; **Stinky Pinhead:** Marcia Savella; **Dad/Ned Carpool/Dan Blather:** George Flowers

## ◉ BALTO II: WOLF'S QUEST

This beautifully rendered direct-to-video sequel to Universal Studios' 1995 full-length feature finds half-wolf Balto embarking on a treacherous journey to follow his daughter, Aleu, as she discovers the truth about her mixed heritage with her father on her trail. Winner of a 2002 Humanitas Prize Award for children's animation, the movie premiered on Cartoon Network. *A Universal Cartoon Studios Production. Color. One hour and 16 minutes. Premiered on CAR: November 21, 2001.*

### Voices
**Balto:** Maurice LaMarche; **Jenna:** Jodi Benson; **Aleu:** Lacey Chabert; **Nava the Wolf Shaman:** David Carradine; **Niju the Evil Wolf:** Mark Hamill; **Boris:** Charles Fleischer; **Muru:** Peter MacNicol; **Terrier/Suman/Wolverine 2:** Rob Paulsen; **Dingo:** Nicolette Little; **Saba:** Melanie Spore; **Muc/Luc/Wolverine 1:** Kevin Schon; **Hunter/Nuk:** Joe Alaskey; **Aniu:** Monnae Michaell; **Fox/Wolverine 3:** Mary Kay Bergman; **Yak:** Jeff Bennett

### ◎ BANANA SPLITS IN HOCUS POCUS PARK

Costumed live-action animals Fleegle (the dog), Drooper (the lion), Bingo (the gorilla) and Snorky (the elephant) stars of TV's *The Banana Splits Adventure Hour*, appear in this live-action/animated fantasy in which they meet a magician with special powers. *A Hanna-Barbera Production. Color. One hour. Premiered on ABC: November 25, 1972 (on The ABC Saturday Superstar Movie). Rebroadcast on CAR: October 28, 1994; October 30, 1994; October 31, 1994; October 29, 1995 (Mr. Spim's Cartoon Theatre).*

### Voices
**Snorky:** (no voice); **Drooper:** Allan Melvin; **Bingo/Frog/Octopus:** Daws Butler; **Fleegle/Tree:** Paul Winchell; **Witch:** Joan Gerber; **Hocus/Pocus:** Howard Morris

### ◎ BANJO, THE WOODPILE CAT

Banjo, an adventurous young cat, runs away to the big city where he becomes lost. Together with his newfound friend, Crazy Legs, he searches for a truck, from which he came, to take him back home. Program preceded the network premiere of *Stanley, the Ugly Duckling. A Banjo Production in association with Don Bluth Productions. Color. Half-hour. Premiered on ABC: May 1, 1982. Rebroadcast on ABC: August 7, 1983.*

### Voices
**Banjo, the Woodpile Cat:** Sparky Marcus; **Crazy Legs:** Scatman Crothers; **Zazu:** Beah Richards; **Papa Cat/Freeman:** Jerry Harper; **Mama Cat/Cleo:** Georgette Rampone; **Jean:** Ann E. Beesley; **Emily:** Robin Muir; **Farmer/Warehouseman:** Ken Samson; **Announcer:** Mark Elliott; **Vocalists:** Jackie Ward, Sally Stevens, Sue Allen

### ◎ BARBIE AND THE ROCKERS: OUT OF THIS WORLD

After a successful worldwide concert tour ends, Barbie reveals to the group her greatest tour ever—a concert in outer space. The one-hour, two-part syndicated special was based on the popular Mattel Toys doll. *A DIC Enterprises Production in association with Mattel. Color. One hour. Premiered: Fall 1987. Syndicated.*

### Voices
**Barbie:** Sharon Lewis

### ◎ BATMAN: THE ANIMATED SERIES: "ON LEATHER WINGS"

Terrorized by the strange, swift-moving, bat-like creature with super powers known as the Dark Knight, Gotham City's police department investigates the matter while the mysterious superhero attempts to clear his name in this prime time series preview special that aired on FOX during the network's "Batman Premiere Week"

in September 1992. *A Warner Bros. Television Production. Color. Half-hour. Premiered on FOX: September 6, 1992.*

### Voices
**Batman/Bruce Wayne:** Kevin Conroy; **Alfred Pennyworth:** Clive Revill; **Robin/Dick Grayson:** Loren Lester; **Mayor Hamilton Hill:** Lloyd Bochner; **Commissioner Jim Gordon:** Bob Hastings; **Harvey Dent:** Richard Moll; **Detective Harvey Bullock:** Robert Costanzo; **Dr. Kirk Langstrom/Man-Bat:** Marc Singer; **Dr. March:** Rene Auberjonois; **Female Lab Technician:** Pat Musick; **Francine:** Meredith MacRae

### ◎ BATTLETOADS

Three Oxnard, California, junior high school students (Morgan, Dave and George) who become powerful humanoid toads with magical superpowers known as Zitz, Rash and Pimple—the mighty BattleToads—battle General Slaughter and the Beast Police to rescue Princess Angelica who's been kidnapped by the evil Black Queen who wants the magical amulet that controls the universe. The BattleToads then travel back from the planet Murania to defend Oxnard from the evil Black Queen in this half-hour fantasy adventure special that premiered on FOX. *A DIC Entertainment Production. Color. Half-hour. Premiered on FOX: December 25, 1991.*

### Voices
**Zitz:** Ian James Corlett; **Rash:** Jason Michas; **Pimple:** Andrew Kavadas; **Princess:** Lalaina Lindiberg; **Professor T-Bird/Principal Block:** Mike Donovan; **General Slaughter:** Scott McNeil; **Dark Queen:** Kathleen Barr; **Mr. Thorpe:** Alvin Sanders

### ◎ B.C.: A SPECIAL CHRISTMAS

Inspired by Johnny Hart's daily comic strip, Peter and Wiley make plans to cash in on the Christmas season by selling trees and gift rocks that are supposedly from a mythical gift giver they have created named Santa Claus in this half-hour yuletide special. *A Cinera Production in association with Hardlake Animated Pictures and Field Enterprises. Color. Half-hour. Premiered: 1971. Syndicated.*

### Voices
**Peter:** Bob Elliott; **Wiley:** Ray Goulding; **Fat Broad:** Barbara Hamilton; **Cute Chick:** Melleny Brown; **Thor:** Henry Ramer; **Clumsy:** Keith Hampshire; **Curls:** John Stocker

### ◎ B.C.: THE FIRST THANKSGIVING

Since "there's only one way to flavor rock soup and that's with a dead turkey," Fat Broad sends the cavemen (Peter, Wiley, Thor and Curls) all out on a cross-country chase for the bird, complicated by the fact that nobody knows what a turkey is, in this special based on Johnny Hart's popular strip of the same name. *A Levitow-Hanson Films Production in association with Field Enterprises. Color. Half-hour. Premiered on NBC: November 19, 1972.*

### Voices
**Peter/Thor/Turkey:** Don Messick; **Wiley/Grog:** Bob Holt; **Clumsy:** Daws Butler; **Fat Broad/Cute Chick:** Joanie Sommers

### ◎ THE BEAR WHO SLEPT THROUGH CHRISTMAS

Ted E. Bear, who has never seen Christmas because he's always snoozing through winter, decides to fight hibernation to witness the glorious event for the first time in his life. *A Sed-bar Production in association with DePatie-Freleng Enterprises. Color. Half-hour. Premiered on NBC: December 17, 1973. Rebroadcast on NBC: December 16, 1974; December 25, 1977; December 19, 1978; December 23, 1980; CBS: December 15, 1979.*

*Voices*
**Ted E. Bear:** Tom Smothers; **Patti Bear:** Barbara Feldon; **Professor Werner Von Bear:** Arte Johnson; **Santa Claus:** Robert Holt; **Weather Bear:** Kelly Lange; **Honey Bear:** Michael Bell

### ◎ BEAUTY AND THE BEAST (1983)

Of five children who live in a plush mansion, only one is kind and good and full of love. Her name is Beauty. While the others are selfish and greedy, especially sisters Jacqueline and Erwina, Beauty makes the best of everything in life, even when her father falls on hard times and they are forced to move from their mansion to a tiny cottage and lead a meager lifestyle. Based on the Madame Leprince de Beaumont children's story. A Kenner Family Classics daytime special. *A Ruby-Spears Enterprises Production in association with TCG Products. Color. Half-hour. Premiered on CBS: November 25, 1983. Rebroadcast on CBS: November 22, 1984.*

*Voices*
**Beauty/Jacqueline/Queen/Old Crone:** Janet Waldo; **Beast/Prince:** Robert Ridgely; **Erwina/Stately Lady/Messenger Boy:** Linda Gary; **Merchant/Sailor/Male Voice:** Stacy Keach Jr.; **Rene/Cockatoo:** Alan Young; **Gerard:** Paul Kirby

### ◎ BEAUTY AND THE BEAST (1989)

A merchant's daughter volunteers to live in the enchanted palace of the Beast to save her father's life in this half-hour animated film, originally produced by Joshua Greene for Lightyear Entertainment as part of his "Stories to Remember" series, a collection of international children's stories told in picture books, recordings and animated films. Narrated by actress Mia Farrow (who also portrays the voice of every character), the award-winning production debuted as an installment of the long-running PBS live-action/animated anthology series, *Long Ago & Far Away*. *A Lightyear Entertainment Production. Color. Half-hour. Premiered on PBS: September 8, 1990. Rebroadcast on PBS: December 20, 1992.*

*Voices*
**Narrator/All Others:** Mia Farrow

### ◎ BEAVIS AND BUTT-HEAD CHRISTMAS SPECIAL (1993)

The moronic twosome starred in what was billed as their "first" Christmas special for music cable network, MTV, featuring back-to-back cartoon episodes. *An MTV Production. Color. Half-hour. Premiered on MTV: December 1993.*

*Voices*
**Beavis/Butt-Head:** Mike Judge

### ◎ BEAVIS AND BUTT-HEAD CHRISTMAS SPECIAL (1995)

In comic twists, Beavis and Butt-Head star in a pair of holiday parodies—"It's a Miserable Life," in which the boys receive a visit from their guardian angel Charlie, and "Huh Huh Humbug," wherein Beavis nods off at Burger World and dreams he's the Scrooge-like manager—in this second prime-time Christmas special for MTV. *An MTV Production. Color. Half-hour. Premiered on MTV: December 19, 1995.*

*Voices*
**Beavis/Butt-Head:** Mike Judge

### ◎ BEAVIS AND BUTT-HEAD HALLOWEEN SPECIAL

The B&B boys get into the Halloween spirit in this half-hour spooky spectacular featuring the animated episode "Buttonween," in which an evening of trick-or-treating takes a strange turn when Beavis becomes the Great Cornholio (Beavis's alter ego, who first appeared in four episodes a year earlier). *An MTV Production. Color. Half-hour. Premiered on MTV: October 31, 1995.*

*Voices*
**Beavis/Butt-Head:** Mike Judge

### ◎ BEFORE THE DINOSAURS

Avery Brooks narrates this three-part, digitally-animated special examing Earth when giant scorpions and lumbering reptiles dominated the planet, in this primetime Emmy Award–winning, 3-D, CGI-animated prequel to Discovery Channel's *Walking with Dinosaurs*, coproduced by the BBC and Discovery Channel. *A BBC/Discovery Channel Production. Two hours. Premiered on DSC: November 5, 2005.*

*Voices*
**Narrator:** Avery Brooks

### ◎ BE MY VALENTINE, CHARLIE BROWN

It's Valentine's Day and Cupid is already busy at work, especially at Birchwood School, where Linus displays his affection for his homeroom teacher by buying her a huge box of candy and Sally thinks the candy is for her. Meanwhile, Lucy continues her quest to win Schroeder's affection, while poor hopeless heart Charlie Brown continues to wait for his cards to arrive in the mail. Beginning in February 1998 Nickelodeon, which began re-airing CBS's *The Charlie Brown & Snoopy Show* and dozens of original *Peanuts* specials made for the network, rebroadcast this Valentine's special the Friday night before Valentine's Day. *A Lee Mendelson–Bill Melendez Production in cooperation with United Feature Syndicate. Color. Half-hour. Premiered on CBS: January 28, 1975. Rebroadcast on CBS: February 10, 1976; February 14, 1977; February 9, 1979; February 11, 1983; February 11, 1984; February 14, 1987. Rebroadcast on NICK: February 13, 1998; February 14, 1998; February 12, 1999; February 14, 1999; February 12, 2000; February 13, 2000.*

*Voices*
**Charlie Brown:** Duncan Watson; **Linus Van Pelt:** Stephen Shea; **Lucy Van Pelt:** Melanie Kohn; **Sally Brown:** Lynn Mortensen; **Schroeder:** Greg Felton; **Violet/Frieda:** Linda Ercoli

### ◎ BEN 10: "MERRY CHRISTMAS"

Ben, Grandpa Max and Gen uncover a mysterious curse that has left a village frozen in time at Christmas in the 1930s and run by a strange man who mistakes Grandpa Max for Santa Claus. Spun-off from the popular weekly cartoon series, the holiday special premiered during the series' third season on Cartoon Network. *A Cartoon Network Studios Production. Color. Half-hour. Premiered on CAR: December 11, 2006*

*Voices*
**Ben Tennyson/Upgrade:** Tara Strong; **Grandpa Max Tennyson:** Paul Eiding; **Gwen Tennyson:** Meagan Smith; **Grey Matter:** Richard Horvitz; **Stinkfly/Wildmutt/Grandpa Elsgood:** Dee Bradley Baker; **Diamond Head/XLR8/Wildvine:** Jim Ward; **Mr. Jingles:** Richard Doyle; **Elsgood/Grandkid/Kid #1:** Kim Mai Guest

### ◎ BEN 10: "WASHINGTON B.C."

Ben springs into action to ward off the evil scientist Dr. Animo who plans to build a highly advanced device called a Transmodulator to bring the dead to life in this second episode following the series' pilot that premiered as a special on Cartoon Network. *A Cartoon Network Studios Production. Color. Half-hour. Premiered on CAR: January 13, 2006.*

*Voices*

**Ben Tennyson/Young Boy:** Tara Strong; **Grandpa Max Tennyson:** Paul Eiding; **Gwen Tennyson:** Meagan Smith; **Grey Matter/Robber #1/VIP#1:** Richard Horvitz; **Heatblast:** Steven Jay Blum; **Fourarms:** Richard McGonagle; **Stinkfly:** Dee Bradley Baker; **Dr. Animo/Police Officer/VIP #2:** Dwight Schultz

### ◎ THE BERENSTAIN BEARS' CHRISTMAS TREE

Papa Bear goes against the advice of Mama Bear not to get a Christmas tree by deciding to find the perfect tree himself in the woods of Bear Valley. During his journey, he encounters the animals of the forest and realizes that by taking a tree he could jeopardize the homes of other creatures less fortunate. *A Cates Brothers Company Production in association with Perpetual Motion Pictures. Color. Half-hour. Premiered on NBC: December 3, 1979. Rebroadcast on NBC: December 15, 1980.*

*Voices*

**Papa Bear:** Ron McLarty; **Mama Bear:** Pat Lysinger; **Brother Bear:** Jonathan Lewis; **Sister Bear:** Gabriela Glatzer; **Narrator:** Ron McLarty

### ◎ THE BERENSTAIN BEARS' EASTER SURPRISE

With no sign of spring in sight, Papa Bear takes it upon himself to find the Easter Hare, Boss Bunny, and see why Easter hasn't arrived on time. *A Joseph Cates Production in association with Perpetual Motion Pictures. Color. Half-hour. Premiered on NBC: April 14, 1981. Rebroadcast on NBC: April 6, 1982; April 20, 1984.*

*Voices*

**Papa Bear:** Ron McLarty; **Mama Bear:** Pat Lysinger; **Brother Bear:** Knowl Johnson; **Sister Bear:** Gabriela Glatzer; **Boss Bunny:** Bob McFadden; **Narrator:** Ron McLarty

### ◎ THE BERENSTAIN BEARS' LITTLEST LEAGUER

The moral of this children's special is that parents should never heap their expectations upon their children. Papa Bear finds that out for himself, in a big way, when he tries making his son—and later his daughter—into successful Little League ballplayers with the dream of them someday turning pro. *A Joseph Cates Production in association with Buzzco Productions. Color. Half-hour. Premiered on NBC: May 6, 1983. Rebroadcast on NBC: May 20, 1984 (as The Berenstain Bears Play Ball).*

*Voices*

**Papa Bear:** Ron McLarty; **Mama Bear:** Pat Lysinger; **Brother Bear:** Knowl Johnson; **Sister Bear:** Gabriela Glatzer; **Narrator:** Ron McLarty

### ◎ THE BERENSTAIN BEARS MEET BIG PAW

The legend of Big Paw—a monster who eats bears at Thanksgiving to punish them because they're "insufficiently grateful" for nature's bounty—is the premise of this holiday prime-time special. *A Joseph Cates Production in association with Perpetual Motion Pictures. Color. Half-hour. Premiered on NBC: November 20, 1980. Rebroadcast on NBC: November 24, 1981.*

*Voices*

**Papa Bear:** Ron McLarty; **Mama Bear:** Pat Lysinger; **Brother Bear:** Jonathan Lewis; **Sister Bear:** Gabriela Glatzer; **Big Paw/Announcer:** Bob Kaliban; **Narrator:** Ron McLarty

### ◎ THE BERENSTAIN BEARS' VALENTINE SPECIAL

Cupid's arrows get the best of Brother Bear and Sister Bear as both critters become preoccupied with the idea of loving someone. *A Joseph Cates Production in association with Perpetual Motion Pictures. Color. Half-hour. Premiered on NBC: February 13, 1982. Rebroadcast on NBC: February 12, 1983.*

*Voices*

**Papa Bear:** Ron McLarty; **Mama Bear:** Pat Lysinger; **Brother Bear:** Knowl Johnson; **Sister Bear:** Gabriela Glatzer; **Bearcaster/Others:** Jerry Sroka; **Narrator:** Ron McLarty

### ◎ BILL AND BUNNY

Tells the story of a young boy (Bill) who can't wait for his baby sister (Bunny) to grow up and become a true playmate, based on the book by Gunilla Bergstroms. The Swedish-produced program premiered on the PBS anthology series *Long Ago & Far Away*. *A Svenska Filminstitutet, Sweden Production. Color. Half-hour. Premiered on PBS: April 29, 1989. Rebroadcast on PBS: December 14, 1990.*

### ◎ BILL THE MINDER

A clever inventor (Bill) who solves problems for his family and friends by constructing absurd and elaborate machines. Based on a classic picture-book series by W. Heath Robinson, the award-winning film was televised as a special on the PBS anthology series *Long Ago & Far Away*. *A Bevanfield Film, Britain Production in association with Link Licensing Ltd. Color. Half-hour. Premiered on PBS: November 3, 1990. Rebroadcast on PBS: January 17, 1993.*

*Voices*
**Narrator:** Peter Chelsom

### ◎ THE BIRTHDAY DRAGON

Young Emily invites her age-old dragon friend to her birthday party, while taking time to stop two dragon hunters and make the world safe for dragons once again, in this sequel to 1991's *The Railway Dragon*. *A Lacewood Production. Color. Half-hour. Premiered on DIS: September 15, 1992.*

*Young Emily helps celebrate her dragon friend's birthday in Lacewood Production's half-hour animated special* The Birthday Dragon. *© Lacewood Productions. All rights reserved.*

## ⊚ THE BLACK ARROW

Adapted from the Robert Louis Stevenson story, this half-hour special re-creates the adventures of a young heir, orphaned at birth, who joins the band of forest outlaws known as the Brotherhood of the Black Arrow. A *Famous Classic Tales* special. *An Air Programs International Production. Color. Half-hour. Premiered on CBS: December 2, 1973. Rebroadcast on CBS: September 22, 1974.*

*Voices*

Alistair Duncan, Jeannie Drynan, Tim Elliott, Barbara Frawley, Ron Haddrick, John Llewellyn, Owen Weingott

## ⊚ BLACK BEAUTY

Born and raised in the lush English countryside, a sweet-tempered horse named Black Beauty is taught by his mother to be a friend to man. In true testimony to his mother, Beauty's faith in the goodness of man is put to the test again and again in this touching and heartwarming story based on Anna Sewell's children's novel, first published in 1877. A *Famous Classic Tales* special. *A Hanna-Barbera Production. Color. Half-hour. Premiered on CBS: October 28, 1978. Rebroadcast on CBS: November 11, 1979; November 6, 1983 (as Kenner Family Classics).*

*Voices*

Alan Young (Narrator), Robert Comfort, Cathleen Cordell, Alan Dinehart, Mike Evans, David Gregory, Colin Hamilton, Laurie Main, Patricia Sigris, Barbara Stevens, Cam Young

## ⊚ THE BLINKINS

Blink, Sparkle, Flicker, Flashy and Shady are selected to perform in the annual Flower of Spring Ceremony to bring the first ray of spring sunshine to Blinkin Land but Slime, a swamp monster, has different plans. *An MCA Television Production in association with TMS Entertainment. Color. Half-hour. Premiered: Spring 1986. Syndicated.*

*Voices*

**Mr. Benjamin the Owl:** Burgess Meredith; **Grog the Frog:** Paul Williams; **Blink:** Missy Gold; **Shady:** Tracey Gold; **Baby Twinkle:** Brandy Gold; **Flashy:** Sagan Lewis; **Sparkle:** Carrie Swenson; **Flicker/Pettiford:** Louise Chamis; **Slime:** Chris Latta; **Announcer:** Henry Gibson

## ⊚ THE BLINKINS AND THE BEAR

New challenges await the spunky Blinkins as they follow Mr. Benjamin Owl's advice by gathering food for the winter—but their precious supply is endangered by bad guys, Grog the Frog and Sneed the Bear, who disrupt the proceedings. *An MCA Television Production in association with TMS Entertainment. Color. Half-hour. Premiered: September, 1986. Syndicated.*

*Voices*

**Blink:** Noelle North; **Flash:** Daryl Wood; **Sparkle:** Carrie Swenson; **Flicker/Baby Twinkle:** Louise Chamis; **Shady:** Jennifer Darling; **Mr. Benjamin the Owl:** Burgess Meredith; **Sneed the Bear:** Chris Latta; **Grog the Frog:** Hamilton Camp; **Announcer:** Alan Young

## ⊚ THE BLINKINS AND THE BLIZZARD

The Blinkins come to the aid of a poor little girl who is lost in the woods after she loses her precious doll. Villainous Grog the Frog and Sneed the Bear make life miserable for them until the Blinkins lead the girl home safely. *An MCA Television Production in association with TMS. Color. Half-hour. Premiered: December, 1986. Syndicated.*

*Voices*

**Blink:** Noelle North; **Flashy:** Daryl Wood; **Sparkle:** Carrie Swenson; **Flicker/Baby Twinkle:** Louis Chamis; **Shady:** Jennifer Darling; **Mr. Benjamin, the Owl:** Burgess Meredith; **Sneed the Bear:** Chris Latta; **Grog the Frog:** Hamilton Camp; **Announcer:** Alan Young

## ⊚ BLONDIE AND DAGWOOD

The world's favorite comic-strip couple trade places when Blondie gets a job after Dagwood Bumstead gets fired. Loni Anderson provides the voice of Blondie. Based on the comic strip *Blondie* by Dean Young and Stan Drake. *A Marvel Animation Production with King Features Entertainment in association with Toei Animation. Color. Half-hour. Premiered on CBS: May 15, 1987. Rebroadcast on CBS: October 12, 1988.*

*Voices*

**Blondie Bumstead:** Loni Anderson; **Dagwood Bumstead:** Frank Welker; **Alexander Bumstead:** Ike Eisenmann; **Cookie Bumstead:** Ellen Gerstell; **Daisy, the Bumsteads' dog:** Pat Fraley; **Julius Dithers:** Alan Oppenheimer; **Cora Dithers/Mrs. Hannon:** Russi Taylor; **Tootsie Woodley:** Laurel Page; **Mr. Beasley/Herb Woodley:** Jack Angel

## ⊚ BLONDIE AND DAGWOOD: "SECOND WEDDING WORKOUT"

In their second prime-time special, the Bumsteads' 20th wedding anniversary falls on the same day as the deadline for a building project Dagwood must complete in order to receive a bonus to pay for Blondie's new ring—which he loses. *A King Features Entertainment Production in association with King Services Inc. Color. Half-hour. Premiered on CBS: November 1, 1989.*

*Voices*

**Blondie Bumstead:** Loni Anderson; **Dagwood Bumstead:** Frank Welker; **Alexander Bumstead:** Ike Eisenmann; **Cookie Bumstead:** Ellen Gerstell; **Daisy, the Bumsteads' dog:** Pat Fraley; **Julius Dithers:** Alan Oppenheimer; **Cora Dithers:** Russi Taylor

## ⊚ BLUETOES, THE CHRISTMAS ELF

One pint-size, clumsy elf, appropriately named Small One can't seem to do anything right, until his misadventures land him on Santa's toy-filled sleigh to deliver toys to all the children of the world (earning him the name, Bluetoes) in this adorable half-hour animated special, originally produced in 1988 for Canadian television by Lacewood Productions. *A Lacewood Production. Color. Half-hour. Premiered on DIS: December 8, 1991. Rebroadcast on DIS: December 20, 1992; December 7, 1993.*

*Voices*

**Small One (Bluetoes):** Polly Jones; **Santa Claus:** Dave Broadfoot; **Woody:** James Bradford; **The Girl:** Jennifer Finestone; **Lonesome/Whitey:** Rick Jones; **Hattie/Elf:** Anna MacCormack; **Elf/Gummy:** Michael O'Reilly; **Boy/Elf:** Ben Mulroney

## ⊚ BOB THE BUILDER: PROJECT BUILD IT: "BOB'S BIG PLAN"

After learning that Sunflower Valley, where he and his brother once camped, is about to be bulldozed and developed into a garish resort with nightclubs, skyscrapers and restaurant by Bobsville architect Mr. Adams, Bob and his handy crew save the day when their design to build a more environmentally friendly town wins out in this first of two specials based on the stop-motion animated preschool series for PBS. *A HOT Animation/HIT Entertainment Limited/Keith Chapman Production. Color. Half-hour. Premiered on PBS Kids: September 3, 2005.*

**Voices**

**Bob the Builder:** Greg Proops; **Robert, Bob's Dad:** Richard Briers; **Dot, Bob's Mum:** June Whitfield; **Spud:** Rob Rackstraw; **Scrambler:** Rupert Dugas; **Wendy/Dizzy:** Kate Harbour

## ◎ BOB THE BUILDER: PROJECT BUILD IT: "SNOWED UNDER: THE BOBBLESBERG GAMES"

Facing cancelation when they are unable to build courses necessary for the famed Bobblesberg Winter Games, popular build-it guy Bob and his construction gang come through by building what is needed to the delight of the town's mayor and invited dignitaries in this hour-long special spun-off from the award-winning PBS children's series. The stop-motion animated program followed the series' first half-hour special, *Bob's Big Plans*, which premiered in February. *A HOT Animation/HIT Entertainment Limited/Keith Chapman Production. Color. One hour. Premiered on PBS Kids: December 1, 2005.*

**Voices**

**Bob the Builder:** Greg Proops; **Robert, Bob's Dad:** Richard Briers; **Dot, Bob's Mum:** June Whitfield; **Spud:** Rob Rackstraw; **Scrambler:** Rupert Dugas; **Wendy/Dizzy:** Kate Harbour

## ◎ THE BOLLO CAPER

On the verge of extinction, two leopards—Bollo and Nefertiti—try to save their species from a band of trappers who are capturing and killing the animals to sell the skins to their boss, a famed New York furrier. An *ABC Weekend Special*. *A Rick Reinert Pictures Production. Color. Half-hour. Premiered on ABC: February 2, 1985. Rebroadcast on ABC: November 16, 1985; August 16, 1986; November 29, 1986; July 11, 1987; October 5, 1991; January 9, 1993; April 26, 1997.*

**Voices**

**Bollo:** Michael Bell; **Nefertiti/Lulu La Looche:** Ilene Latter; **Clamper Carstair:** Hal Smith; **Snag Carstair:** Will Ryan; **Lion/Iceberg/Emperor:** Hal Smith; **Chestnut/Monkey #1:** Will Ryan; **Felix the Furrier:** Pete Renaday; **President/Monkey #2:** Pete Renaday

## ◎ BOO! CHRISTMAS SPECIAL

Boo, Growling Tiger, Laughing Duck and Sleeping spend time together decorating their Christmas tree while waiting patiently for Santa to deliver their Christmas presents in this half-hour holiday special featuring the stars of the popular British-produced 2002 animated children's series that aired among a slate of holiday specials on ION Network (formerly PAX-TV). *A Tell-Tale Productions Ltd. Production. Color. Half-hour. Premiered on ION: December 15, 2006.*

## ◎ BOO! TO YOU TOO, WINNIE THE POOH

Winnie the Pooh and friends, Tigger and Piglet, prepare to celebrate the Bestest Halloween ever and find themselves caught up in an adventure on Halloween night, during which Piglet finds his courage and learns the benefits of sticking together. A winner of two 1996 Emmy Awards for outstanding achievement in animation and outstanding music and lyrics for the song, "I Wanna Scare Myself," on Halloween Eve 2001, the Disney cartoon classic was rebroadcast on ABC following the perennial pumpkin favorite, *It's the Great Pumpkin, Charlie Brown*, ABC's highest-rated show of the night, and they averaged 11.9 million viewers, combined. The two specials also generated the network's strongest kids' ratings in the hour in two-and-a-half years. *A Walt Disney Television Animation Production. Color. Half-hour. Pre-*

*miered on CBS: October 25, 1996. Rebroadcast on ABC: October 31, 1998; October 30, 2001.*

**Voices**

**Winnie the Pooh/Tigger:** Jim Cummings; **Piglet:** John Fiedler; **Eeyore:** Peter Cullen; **Rabbit:** Ken Samson; **Gopher:** Michael Gough; **Owl:** Andre Stojka; **Narrator:** John Rhys-Davies

## ◎ THE BOY WHO DREAMED CHRISTMAS

A greedy boy learns about giving when Nilus the Snowman transports him to the North Pole on Christmas Eve in this holiday special, first aired on Disney Channel. *A Cambium Film & Video/Delaney and Friends Production. Color. Half-hour. Premiered on DIS: December 10, 1991. Rebroadcast on DIS: December 22, 1991.*

## ◎ THE BRADY KIDS ON MYSTERIOUS ISLAND

Teenagers Greg, Peter, Bobby, Marcia, Janice and Cindy of television's *The Brady Bunch* perform as rock musicians and encounter a few spooks on a strange island in this one-hour animated adventure, which officially launched the first season for *The ABC Saturday Superstar Movie*. *A Filmation Associates Redwood Productions Production for Paramount Television. Color. One hour. Premiered on ABC: September 9, 1972.*

**Voices**

**Greg Brady:** Barry Williams; **Peter Brady:** Christopher Knight; **Bobby Brady:** Michael Lookinland; **Marcia Brady:** Maureen McCormick; **Janice Brady:** Eve Plumb; **Cindy Brady:** Susan Olsen; **Marlon:** Larry Storch

## ◎ THE BRAK SHOW: "LEAVE IT TO BRAK: MR. BAWK BA GAWK"

Brak is convinced by his friend Zorak that he will become really popular at school if he steals Jerkwater High School's mascot in this animated pilot that aired as a cartoon special on Cartoon Network. The program launched the successful weekly 15-minute series that debuted in September 2001 on Cartoon Network's late-night *Adult Swim* programming block. *A Williams Street/Turner Production. Color. Fifteen minutes. Premiered on CAR: December 21, 2000.*

**Voices**

**Brak:** Andy Merrill; **Zorak Jones:** C. Martin Croker; **Brak's Mom:** Marsha Crenshaw; **Brak's Dad:** George Lowe; **Thunderclease:** Carey Means

## ◎ THE BRAK SHOW: "NEW YEAR'S EVE PARTY AT BRAK'S HOUSE"

Brak throws a New Year's Eve bash joined by his best friend Zorak and other *Adult Swim* cartoon series stars in this end-of-the-year holiday special, featuring premiere episodes from *Adult Swim* late-night programming block favorites, including *Aqua Teen Hunger Force*, *Harvey Birdman, Attorney at Law* and *Sealab 2021*, as well as all-time favorite episodes of *Family Guy* and *Futurama*. *A Williams Street/Wild Hare Studios/Turner Production. Color. Three hours. Premiered on CAR: December 31, 2003.*

**Voices**

**Voldemar H. "Brak" Guerta/Clarence:** Andy Merill; **Zorak/Moltar:** C. Martin Croker; **Brak's Mom:** Joanna Daniel; **Brak's Dad/Space Ghost/Himself:** George Lowe; **Thundercleese/Frylock:** Carey Means; **Marlon:** Don Kennedy; **Phil Ken Sebben:** Stephen Colbert; **Debbie:** Kate Miller; **Hesh:** Chris Ward; **Meatwad, Carl:** Dave Willis; **Master Shake:** Dana Snyder

## ◎ "BUBSY WHAT COULD POSSIBLY GO WRONG?"

In his first celluloid adventure, Bubsy, an unpredictable bobcat with an attitude and a heart of gold, and his reluctant sidekick Arnold, the Armadillo, set out to test mad scientist Virgil Reality's new invention, the Virtual Reality helmet. The villainous Allycassandra and her henchmen scheme to steal in this half-hour syndicated special, broadcast Thanksgiving weekend 1993 as part of Bohbot Entertainment's "Kid's Day Off" block. *A Calico Entertainment/Imagination Factory Inc. Production in association with Accolade Inc. Color. Half-hour. Premiered: November 27–28, 1993. Syndicated.*

**Voices**
**Bubsy:** Rob Paulsen; **Arnold, the Armadillo/Virgil Reality:** Pat Fraley; **Sid, the Vicious Shrew:** Jim Cummings; **Oblivia/Bubsy Twin:** Tress MacNeille; **Bozwell, the Gourmet Buzzard/Bubsy Twin:** Neil Ross; **Allycassandra:** B.J. Ward

## ◎ BUGS BUNNY: ALL-AMERICAN HERO

The carrot-eating rabbit recalls past events in America's glorious history in this half-hour special, which combines full versions and clips from several old Warner's cartoons reedited to tell a complete story. The program was primarily shaped around the 1954 Bugs Bunny cartoon "Yankee Doodle Bugs." Other cartoons, in whole or in part, included: "Bunker Hill Bunny," "Dumb Patrol," "Rebel Without Claws" and "Ballot Box Bunny." *A Warner Bros. Television Production. Color. Half-hour. Premiered on CBS: May 4, 1981.*

*Bubsy, a bobcat who is a loose cannon with a heart of gold, stars in his first cartoon adventure, "Bubsy What Could Possibly Go Wrong?" produced by Calico Creations. © Accolade. All rights reserved. Property of Calico Entertainment/Imagination Factory, Inc.*

*Rebroadcast on CBS: March 10, 1982; April 16, 1983; May 26, 1984; May 10, 1985; January 7, 1986; June 18, 1987; September 20, 1988; September 5, 1990; July 1, 1993.*

**Voices**
Mel Blanc, June Foray

## ◎ THE BUGS BUNNY EASTER SPECIAL

When the Easter Bunny becomes ill, Granny turns to Bugs to help her find the right recruit who can deliver baskets of eggs to children throughout the world. Offered the job himself, Bugs demurs but stages an audition for others to apply for the position. (One persistent applicant is Daffy Duck, who doesn't understand why he isn't taken seriously for the job.) Program includes complete versions of theatrical cartoon favorites, such as "For Scenti-mental Reasons," "Knighty Knight Bugs," "Robin Hood Daffy," "Sahara Hare" and "Birds Anonymous," plus clips from five other cartoons. *A DePatie-Freleng Production for Warner Bros. Television. Color. Half-hour. Premiered on CBS: April 7, 1987. Rebroadcast on CBS: March 18, 1978; April 13, 1979; April 2, 1980; April 14, 1984; March 30, 1985; March 25, 1989.*

**Voices**
Mel Blanc, June Foray

## ◎ BUGS BUNNY IN SPACE

Following the box-office sensation of *Star Wars*, CBS aired this half-hour collection of the best moments from science-fiction–oriented Warner Bros. cartoons put together to represent a common theme. The special contained several cartoons featuring Bugs Bunny as well as the classic "Duck Dodgers in the 24½th Century." *A Warner Bros. Television Production. Color. Half-hour. Premiered on CBS: September 6, 1977. Rebroadcast on CBS: April 18, 1978.*

**Voices**
Mel Blanc

## ◎ THE BUGS BUNNY MOTHER'S DAY SPECIAL

When Bugs and Granny encounter a blundering stork, their discussion turns to Mother's Day, which acts as a bridge to various sequences culled from Warner Bros. cartoons, including "Stork Naked," "Apes of Wrath" and "Goo Goo Goliath." *A Warner Bros. Television Production. Color. Half-hour. Premiered on CBS: May 12, 1979. Rebroadcast on CBS: May 12, 1984; May 10, 1985; May 8, 1987; May 8, 1991.*

**Voices**
Mel Blanc, June Foray

## ◎ THE BUGS BUNNY MYSTERY SPECIAL

In the role of Alfred Hitchcock, Porky Pig hosts this compilation of crime cartoons, both complete cartoons and excerpts, which entail a string of "whodunit" plots starring a melange of Warner characters. *A Warner Bros. Television Production. Color. Half-hour. Premiered on CBS: October 15, 1980. Rebroadcast on CBS: December 5, 1981; March 8, 1983; March 10, 1984; September 14, 1984; June 5, 1987.*

**Voices**
Mel Blanc

## ◎ BUGS BUNNY'S BUSTIN' OUT ALL OVER

Three new cartoons created by Chuck Jones are presented in this half-hour special: Bugs recalling his childhood and first encounter with an infant Elmer Fudd; his capture by Marvin Martian; and

Wile E. Coyote's near completion of a 30-year chase to catch the Road Runner. *A Chuck Jones Enterprises Production in association with Warner Bros. Television. Color. Half-hour. Premiered on CBS: May 21, 1980. Rebroadcast on CBS: March 20, 1981; May 5, 1984; April 6, 1985; June 5, 1987; April 19, 1988; April 19, 1989; April 22, 1993.*

**Voices**
Mel Blanc

### ◉ BUGS BUNNY'S CREATURE FEATURES
Animated science fiction parodies starring Bugs Bunny and Daffy Duck, with new introductions by that carrot-chomping rabbit, make up this animated trilogy, including a new 1991 cartoon short, "Invasion of the Bunny Snatchers," and two theatrical cartoon shorts, "The Duxorcist" (1987) and "Night of the Living Duck (1988)." *A Warner Bros. Television Animation Production. Color. Half-hour. Premiered on CBS: February 1, 1992. Rebroadcast on CAR: October 31, 1997.*

**Voices**
Jeff Bergman

### ◉ BUGS BUNNY'S HOWL-OWEEN SPECIAL
Monstrous events occur in this compendium of old Warner Bros. cartoons as Tweety, Daffy Duck, Porky Pig, Sylvester the Cat and, of course, Bugs Bunny experience strange encounters of the Halloween kind. Cartoons featured are "Bedeviled Rabbit," "Rabbit Every Monday" and clips from eight additional one-reelers, including "Beep Beep," "Canned Feud" and "Trip for Tat." *A Warner Bros. Television Production. Color. Half-hour. Premiered on CBS: October 26, 1977. Rebroadcast on CBS: October 25, 1978; October 31, 1979; October 29, 1980; October 27, 1981; October 25, 1989; Rebroadcast on CAR: October 31, 1997.*

**Voices**
Mel Blanc, June Foray

### ◉ BUGS BUNNY'S LOONEY CHRISTMAS TALES
Warner cartoon directors Friz Freleng and Chuck Jones animated three all-new cartoons, each with a Christmas theme, for this half-hour special that spotlights the traditional values of the yuletide season in using an assortment of Warner characters. Included are "Bugs Bunny's Christmas Carol" (directed by Freleng), a spoof of Charles Dickens's classic with Porky Pig as Bob Cratchit, Yosemite Sam as Scrooge and Tweety as Tiny Tim; "Freeze Frame" (directed by Jones), starring Wile E. Coyote and the Road Runner chasing each other through the ice and snow; and "Fright Before Christmas" (by Freleng), featuring the Tasmanian Devil, who visits Bugs's house dressed as Santa. *A DePatie-Freleng Enterprises Production with Chuck Jones Enterprises and Warner Bros. Television. Color. Half-hour. Premiered on CBS: November 27, 1979. Rebroadcast on CBS: December 13, 1980; November 27, 1981; December 6, 1982; December 4, 1984; December 24, 1987; December 17, 1988; December 8, 1990; December 4, 1991; Rebroadcast on FAM: December 11, 1996; December 25, 1996.*

**Voices**
Mel Blanc, June Foray

### ◉ BUGS BUNNY'S MAD WORLD OF TELEVISION
In new footage, Bugs Bunny is the new head of entertainment for the QTTV Network. His first task is to bolster the station's sagging ratings with new, original programming. He explores a number of options, most of which are represented in footage from previously exhibited cartoons made for theaters. *A Warner Bros. Television Production. Color. Half-hour. Premiered on CBS: January 11, 1982. Rebroadcast on CBS: April 2, 1983; September 14, 1983; July 28, 1984; September 6, 1985.*

**Voices**
Mel Blanc

### ◉ BUGS BUNNY'S OVERTURES TO DISASTER
Bugs Bunny stars in this half-hour animated tribute to classical music, featuring the rabbit's own classic cartoon shorts, "What's Opera, Doc?" (1957), "Rabbit of Seville" (1950) and "Baton Bunny" (1959), and including new sequences of Daffy and Porky (in a cartoon version of "The William Tell Overture" directed by Daniel Haskett), with appearances by Mr. Meek, The Three Bears, Yosemite Sam and Granny. Debuting in 1991, the prime-time special kicked off CBS's "Toon Night," a weekly Wednesday-night attraction featuring animated specials and animated series. *A Warner Bros. Television Production. Color. Half-hour. Premiered on CBS: April 17, 1991.*

**Voices**
Jeff Bergman, Mel Blanc, June Foray, Stan Freberg, Ronnie Scheib

### ◉ BUGS BUNNY'S THANKSGIVING DIET
Bugs Bunny, playing a diet doctor, counsels his patients—Porky Pig, Sylvester the Cat and others—against holiday overeating, presenting his favorite cure: a series of cartoons to reduce the urge. Features full versions of "Bedeviled Rabbit" and "Rabbit Every Monday" and clips from eight others. *A Warner Bros. Television Production. Color. Half-hour. Premiered on CBS: November 15, 1979. Rebroadcast on CBS: November 10, 1981; November 12, 1983; November 20, 1984; November 26, 1985; November 26, 1987; November 23, 1988; November 22, 1989.*

**Voices**
Mel Blanc, June Foray

### ◉ BUGS BUNNY'S VALENTINE
In the unusual role of "Cupid," Elmer Fudd strikes love into the heart of Bugs Bunny, who experiences the fresh bloom of romance through a series of classic Warner cartoons, complete and edited, strung together in one common theme. *A Warner Bros. Television Production. Color. Half-hour. Premiered on CBS: February 14, 1979. Rebroadcast on CBS: February 13, 1980; February 4, 1981; February 2, 1982; February 11, 1984; February 11, 1986; February 4, 1988.*

**Voices**
Mel Blanc

### ◉ BUGS BUNNY'S WILD WORLD OF SPORTS
The "Sportsman of the Year Award" is announced in ceremonies at the Arthur Q. Bryan Pavillion, utilizing many clips of sporting activities from previous Warner Bros. cartoons, including "Raw Raw Rooster," "Sports Chumpions," "To Duck or Not to Duck" and others. Oh, yes, the winner is Foghorn Leghorn, of all characters. *A Warner Bros. Television Production. Color. Half-hour. Premiered on CBS: February 15, 1989.*

**Voices**
Mel Blanc, Roy Firestone, Paul Kuhn

## ◉ BUGS VS. DAFFY: BATTLE OF THE MUSIC VIDEO STARS

As cross-town rival disc jockeys, Bugs Bunny, of music channel W.A.B.B.I.T., and Daffy Duck, of radio station K.P.U.T., try topping each other as they introduce various song sequences from old Warner cartoons. Naturally, Bugs gets the higher ratings. *A Warner Bros. Television Production. Color. Half-hour. Premiered on CBS: October 21, 1988.*

**Voices**
Mel Blanc

## ◉ A BUNCH OF MUNSCH: "BLACKBERRY SUBWAY JAM" AND "MOIRA'S BIRTHDAY"

Robert Munsch's beloved stories come to life in this half-hour edition of Showtime's *A Bunch of Munsch* series, featuring two episodes: "Blackberry Subway Jam," about a little boy who accepts a man's help to stop a train showing up in his house in exchange for blackberry jam, and "Moira's Birthday," about a young girl whose parents insist she can only invite six of her friends to her birthday party but 200 show up instead. *A CINAR/TMP IX Limited Partnership Production in association with CTV Television Network/ Showtime Networks Inc./The Maclean Hunter Television Fund/Telefilm Canada. Color. Half-hour. Premiered on SHO: December 2, 1992.*

**Voices**
Andrew Bauer-Gabor, Holly Frankel-Gauthier, A.J. Henderson, Gary Jewell, Rick Jones, Tamar Kozlov, Shayne Olszynko-Gryn, Patricia Rodriguez, Terence Scammell, Jory Steinberg, Jacob D. Tierney, Jane Woods

## ◉ A BUNCH OF MUNSCH: "FIRE STATION" AND "ANGELA'S AIRPLANE"

Part of Showtime's original *A Bunch of Munsch* children's series, this sixth half-hour special spotlights two adventures: "The Fire Station," about a boy (Michael) and a girl (Sheila) who get into "fun" kind of trouble after exploring a real fire station; and "Angela's Airplane," which follows the adventures of a young girl (Angela) and her stuffed rabbit (Ralph). *A CINAR/TMP IX Limited Partnership Production in association with CTV Television Network/Showtime Networks Inc./The Maclean Hunter Television Fund/Telefilm Canada. Color. Half-hour. Premiered on SHO: November 11, 1992. Rebroadcast on SHO: December 23, 1992.*

*Bugs Bunny tops his crosstown rival deejay Daffy Duck in the half-hour CBS cartoon special* Bugs vs. Daffy: Battle of the Music Video Stars.

**Voices**
Sonja Ball, Tia Caroleo, Richard Dumont, Norman Groulx, Arthur Holden, Liz MacRae, Carlyle Miller, George Morris, Haley Reynolds, Jacob D. Tierney, June Wallack

## ◉ A BUNCH OF MUNSCH: "MURMEL, MURMEL, MURMEL" AND "THE BOY IN THE DRAWER"

Combined in this half-hour adaptation of the work of famous children's author Robert Munsch are two separate animated stories presented in one broadcast: "Murmel, Murmel, Murmel," about a young girl's (Robin) quest to find a home for a very small baby she uncovers in a sandbox; and "The Boy in the Drawer," which follows the exploits of an impish gnome messing up the life a schoolgirl (Shelley). *A CINAR/TMP IX Limited Partnership Production in association with CTV Television Networks/Showtime Networks Inc./The Maclean Hunter Television Fund/Telefilm Canada. Color. Half-hour. Premiered on SHO: November 4, 1992. Rebroadcast on SHO: December 16, 1992.*

**Voices**
Amy Fulco, Eramelinda Boquer, Harry Standjofsky, Tamar Kozlov, Sonja Ball, Liz MacRae, Kathleen Fee, Michael Rudder, Rick Jones

## ◉ A BUNCH OF MUNSCH: "THE PAPER BAG PRINCESS"

Princess Elizabeth, an itty-bitty tyke, has a vivid picture of the man she likes and that man is Ronald, the "perfect prince next door," in this faithful half-hour rendition of a book by Robert Munsch (also narrated by him), broadcast as part of this Showtime anthology series. The episode was the only installment of the series to feature one complete 30-minute story. Subsequent episodes combined two stories per half-hour. *A CINAR/TMP IX Limited Partnership in association with CTV Television Network/Showtime Networks Inc./The Maclean Hunter Television Fund/Telefilm Canada. Color. Half-hour. Premiered on SHO: October 14, 1992.*

**Voices**
Robert Munsch (Narrator), Mark Hellman, Rick Jones, Jory Steinberg, Christian Tessier

## ◉ A BUNCH OF MUNSCH: "PIGS" AND "DAVID'S FATHER"

Another entertaining half-hour from this 1992 Showtime series, produced by Canada's CINAR Films, highlighting two animated adaptations of author Robert Munsch's children's stories: "Pigs," in which a young girl named Megan thinks pigs are "stupid" until she finds out otherwise; and "David's Father," about a boy who claims his father is really a "giant," much to the disbelief of his next-door neighbor (Julie). *A CINAR/TMP IX Limited Partnership Production in association with CTV Television Networks/Showtime Networks Inc./The Maclean Hunter Television Fund/Telefilm Canada. Color. Half-hour. Premiered on SHO: October 21, 1992. Rebroadcast on SHO: November 25, 1992.*

**Voices**
Sonja Ball, Rick Jones, Gordon Masten, Michael O'Reilly, Mark Hellman, Lianne Picard-Poiriero, Matthew Barrot, Tia Caroleo, Jess Gryn, Lisa Hull, Kaya Scott, Vlasta Vrana, Carlysle Miller

## ◉ A BUNCH OF MUNSCH: "SOMETHING GOOD" AND "MORTIMER"

Robert Munsch's best selling children's books, "Something Good," about a grocery store expedition with three kids (Julie, Andrew and Tyya) run amok and an exasperated father who is forced to buy something good for his daughter (Julie); and "Mortimer," about a rambunctious child who creates pandemonium in his quiet suburban town by making "tumultous noise," comprise this half-hour special and third installment of the critically acclaimed Showtime series *A Bunch of Munsch*. *A CINAR/TMP IX Limited Partnership Production in association with CTV Television Network/Showtime Networks Inc./The Maclean Hunter Television Fund/Telefilm Canada. Color. Half-hour. Premiered on SHO: October 28, 1992. Rebroadcast on SHO: December 9, 1992.*

*Voices*
Sonja Ball, Liz MacRae, Haley Reynolds, Gabriel Taraboulsy, Michael Rudder, Lisa Hull, Mark Hellman, Bronwen Mantel, Carlyle Miller, Rick Jones, Terrence Scammel, Kathleen Fee, Harry Standjofsky, Thor Bishopric, Patricia Rodriguez, Norman Groulx

### ◎ A BUNCH OF MUNSCH: "THOMAS'S SNOWSUIT" AND "FIFTY BELOW ZERO"

Two cartoon adaptations of stories by world-renowned author Robert Munsch appear in this half-hour special (part of the *A Bunch of Munsch* series), which aired on Showtime in 1992. Included are: "Thomas's Snowsuit," about a young boy whose mother forces him to wear his new ugly brown snowsuit; and "Fifty Below Zero," the companion episode about the freezing cold and a boy named Jason who deals with his father's sleepwalking problem. *A CINAR/TMP IX Limited Partnership Production in association with CTV Television Network/Showtime, Inc./The Maclean Hunter Television Fund/Telefilm Canada. Color. Half-hour. Premiered on SHO: November 18, 1992.*

*Voices*
Julian Bailey, Sonja Ball, Rick Jones, Gordon Masten, Michael O'Reilly, Anik Matern, Liz MacRae

### ◎ BUNNICULA, THE VAMPIRE RABBIT

This spooky but comical tale tells the story of a supernatural rabbit and his loving friendship with a small-town family and its pets as told by the family's dog, Harold, an easygoing, intelligent mutt, in this adaptation of Deborah and James Howe's popular children's book, *Bunnicula, A Rabbit-Tale of Mystery*. *An ABC Weekend Special. A Ruby-Spears Enterprises Production. Color. Half-hour. Premiered on ABC: January 9, 1982. Rebroadcast on ABC: April 17, 1982; October 9, 1982; October 29, 1983.*

*Voices*
**Harold/Roy:** Jack Carter; **Chester/Stockboy/Hank:** Howard Morris; **Toby Monroe:** Pat Peterson; **Mr. Monroe/Storekeeper:** Alan Young; **Mrs. Monroe/Gertie/Alice:** Janet Waldo; **Boss/Andy:** Alan Dinehart

### ◎ BUTT-BOWL (1994)

MTV offered this alternative to traditional Super Bowl halftime fare with the network's first "Butt-Bowl" special, featuring two brand-new Beavis and Butt-Head cartoons. *An MTV Production. Color. Half-hour. Premiered on MTV: January 1994.*

*Voices*
**Beavis/Butt-Head:** Mike Judge

### ◎ BUTT-BOWL (1995)

Two cartoon adventures highlight this second annual "Butt-Bowl" special broadcast during 1995's Super Bowl halftime on MTV: "The Party," in which the world's biggest losers get thrown out of their "own" party; and "Wet Behind the Rears," in which the boys

are forced to take a shower during gym class. *An MTV Production. Color. Half-hour. Premiered on MTV: January 29, 1995.*

*Voices*
**Beavis/Butt-Head:** Mike Judge

### ◎ BUTT-BOWL (1996)

Beavis and Butt-Head return for more halftime Super Bowl antics in this MTV special, highlighted by two cartoon shorts: "Prank Call," in which the boys engage in prank calls with disastrous results with a person they pick out of the phone book; and "No Service," wherein Beavis gets a call to work at Burger World and Butt-Head shows up to harass him. *An MTV Production. Color. Half-hour. Premiered on MTV: January 26, 1996.*

*Voices*
**Beavis/Butt-Head:** Mike Judge

### ◎ BUTT-BOWL (1997)

MTV continued the Super Bowl halftime tradition with the airing of this half-hour special, starring Beavis and Butt-Head, which included the animated episode "Vaya Con Cornholio," in which Beavis is mistaken for an illegal alien when federal agents conduct a spot check at Burger World. *An MTV Production. Color. Half-hour. Premiered on MTV: January 26, 1997.*

*Voices*
**Beavis/Butt-Head:** Mike Judge

### ◎ THE CABBAGE PATCH KIDS' FIRST CHRISTMAS

When the Cabbage Patch Kids help a disabled girl and one of their own get adopted, they discover the true meaning of Christmas spirit in this Ruby-Spears animated holiday special. *A Ruby-Spears Enterprises Production in association with Heywood Kling Productions. Color. Half-hour. Premiered on ABC: December 7, 1984. Rebroadcast on ABC: December 13, 1985. Rebroadcast on TBS: December 19, 1993.*

*Voices*
**Otis Lee:** Scott Menville; **Dawson Glenn:** Josh Rodine; **Cannon Lee:** David Mendenhall; **Sybil Sadie:** Phenina Segal; **Rachel "Ramie" Marie:** Ebony Smith; **Tyler Bo:** Vaughn Jelks; **Paula Louise:** Ann Marie McEvoy; **Jenny:** Gini Holtzman; **Colonel Casey:** Hal Smith; **Xavier Roberts:** Sparky Marcus; **Lavender Bertha:** Tress MacNeille; **Cabbage Jack/Gus:** Arthur Burghardt; **Beau Weasel/Fingers:** Neil Ross

### ◎ CABBAGE PATCH KIDS: THE NEW KID

The Cabbage Patch Kids learn an important lesson about accepting others when they meet a new kid in town who saves the school's talent show. This stop-motion, animated, direct-to-video musical adventure aired Saturday morning on FOX Kids Network The program was the second special featuring the famed toy dolls following Ruby-Spears Productions' 1984 cel-animated effort, *The Cabbage Patch Kids' First Christmas*. *A Goldhill Entertainment Production in association with BMG Home Video. Color. Half-hour. Premiered on FOX: August 26, 1995.*

### ◎ THE CANTERVILLE GHOST

When the Otis family moves into their new house in Canterville, they get more than they bargained for when a 300-year-old ghost attempts to scare them from the house in this delightful adaptation of the Oscar Wilde story. *A CBS Television Production in association with Orkin-Flaum Productions and Calabash Productions. Color. Half-hour. Premiered: Fall 1988. Syndicated. Rebroadcast on DIS: October 26, 1991. Rebroadcast on USA: October 28, 1994.*

*Voices*
**The Ghost:** Dick Orkin; **General:** Brian Cummings; **Father:** Louis Arquette; **Mother:** Janet Waldo; **Virginia Otis, their daughter:** Susan Blu; **Washington:** Michael Sheehan; **Ned and Ted, the twins:** Nancy Cartwright, Mona Marshall; **Mrs. Umney, the maid:** Kathleen Freeman

## ◉ CAP'N O.G. READMORE MEETS CHICKEN LITTLE

A true child of the TV age, Chicken Little now believes the sky is falling when his hero, Rocket Rooster, experiences danger in an episode, and it's up to the traveling librarian Cap'n O.G. to save him from a broadcast-manipulating Foxy Loxy. *An ABC Entertainment Production in association with Rick Reinert Pictures. Color. Half-hour. Premiered on ABC: April 18, 1992. Rebroadcast on ABC: October 24, 1992; June 10, 1995; April 27, 1996.*

*Voices*
**Cap'n O.G. Readmore/Rocket Rooster:** Neil Ross; **Foxy Loxy/ Ol' Tome:** Stanley Jones; **Goosey Loosy/Kitty Literature:** Ilene Latter; **Turkey Lurkey/Ducky Lucky:** Hal Smith; **Chicken Little:** Susan Blu; **Kitty Literature:** Lucille Bliss

## ◉ CAP'N O.G. READMORE MEETS DR. JEKYLL AND MR. HYDE

While holding their Friday Night Book Club meeting, Cap'n O.G. and his friends, Kitty Literature, Ol' Tome Cat, Wordsy and Lickety Page, turn to reading the Robert Louis Stevenson classic, *The Strange Case of Dr. Jekyll and Mr. Hyde.* The story becomes so enthralling that Wordsy is sucked into it—literally—and Cap'n O.G. follows to save him in this *ABC Weekend Special. An ABC Entertainment Production in association with Rick Reinert Pictures. Color. Half-hour. Premiered on ABC: September 13, 1986. Rebroadcast on ABC: August 8, 1987; May 3, 1989; November 4, 1989; January 18, 1992; January 23, 1993; October 28, 1995.*

*Voices*
**Cap'n O.G. Readmore:** Neil Ross; **Wordsy/Ol' Tome Cat/Poole:** Stanley Jones; **Vendor/Master of Ceremonies:** Neil Ross; **Robert Louis Stevenson:** Stanley Jones; **Kitty Literature/Olivia/Heathpote:** Ilene Latter; **Lickety Page/Calypso LaRose:** Lucille Bliss; **Edward Hyde/Newcommon:** Hal Smith

## ◉ CAP'N O.G. READMORE MEETS LITTLE RED RIDING HOOD

To teach him a lesson for hating villains, Cap'n O.G. is turned into the Big Bad Wolf from the classic children's tale "Little Red Riding Hood," so he can understand what being a villain is really like. *An ABC Entertainment Production in association with Rick Reinert Pictures. Color. One hour. Premiered on ABC: October 1, 1988. Rebroadcast on ABC: January 13, 1990; April 14, 1990; November 13, 1993; April 15, 1995; February 17, 1996; August 17, 1996; April 19, 1997.*

*Voices*
**Cap'n O.G. Readmore:** Neil Ross; **Lickety Page:** Lucille Bliss; **Ol' Tome:** Stanley Ross; **Wordsy:** Will Ryan; **Kitty Literature:** Ilene Latter

## ◉ CAP'N O.G. READMORE'S JACK AND THE BEANSTALK

In an effort to promote reading, this Saturday-afternoon special takes a unique approach, featuring a bright, articulate cat, Cap'n O.G. Readmore and his friends, Kitty Literature, Ol' Tome Cat, Wordsy, Lickety Page and Dog-Eared, as vehicles to encourage a love of literature among young people. As members of the Friday Night Book Club, they meet to discuss classic literature. Their discussion of the favorite fairy tale, *Jack and the Beanstalk* transports them to this land of make-believe. *An ABC Weekend Special. An ABC Entertainment Production in association with Rick Reinert Pictures. Color. Half-hour. Premiered on ABC: October 12, 1985. Rebroadcast on ABC: October 4, 1986; January 7, 1989; July 15, 1995; June 8, 1996.*

*Voices*
**Cap'n O.G. Readmore:** Neil Ross; **Kitty Literature:** Ilene Latter; **Ol' Tome Cat:** Stanley Jones; **Wordsy:** Will Ryan; **Lickety Page:** Lucille Bliss; **Jack:** Stanley Jones; **Jack's Mother:** Lucille Bliss; **Giant:** Hal Smith; **Giant's Wife:** Ilene Latter; **Harp:** Ilene Latter; **Humpty Dumpty:** Will Ryan; **Little Old Man:** Hal Smith; **Hen:** Lucille Bliss

## ◉ CAP'N O.G. READMORE'S PUSS IN BOOTS

It turns out the original "Puss in Boots" is an ancestor of literate feline, Cap'n O.G., who stars, along with his friends Lickety Page, Ol' Tome and Kitty Literature, in this faithful retelling of the well-known fairy tale, broadcast as an *ABC Weekend Special. An ABC Entertainment Production in association with Rick Reinert Pictures. Color. One hour. Premiered on ABC: September 10, 1988. Rebroadcast on ABC: January 13, 1990; May 22, 1993.*

*Voices*
**Cap'n O.G. Readmore/Puss:** Neil Ross; **Lickety Page:** Lucille Bliss; **Ol' Tome/King:** Stanley Jones; **Kitty Literature/Princess:** Ilene Latter; **Wordsy/Francois:** Will Ryan; **The Giant:** Hal Smith

## ◉ THE CARE BEARS BATTLE THE FREEZE MACHINE

Diabolical Professor Coldheart plans to use his Freeze Machine to no good by freezing all the children in town. The Care Bears (with new characters, Hugs and Tugs) prevent this fiendish plot from being carried out. *A MAD Production in association with Those Characters from Cleveland and Atkinson Film-Arts. Color. Half-hour. Premiered: April, 1984. Syndicated.*

*Voices*
Dominic Bradford, Bob Dermer, Abby Hagyard, Rick Jones, Les Lye, Anna MacCormack, Brodie Osome, Noreen Young

## ◉ THE CARE BEARS IN THE LAND WITHOUT FEELINGS

The Care Bears, popular greeting card characters, bring friendship, love and caring to a young boy named Kevin, a runaway, who becomes ensared by the evil Professor Coldheart. The program was the first special based on this wholesome gang. *A MAD Production in association with Those Characters from Cleveland and Atkinson Film-Arts. Color. Half-hour. Premiered: April, 1983.*

*Voices*
Andrea Blake, Justin Cammy, Abby Hagyard, Rick Jones, Les Lye, Anna MacCormack, Kathy MacLennan

## ◉ THE CARE BEARS NUTCRACKER SUITE

A tyrant takes over Toyland in this feature-length story produced in 1986 by Canadian animation giant Nelvana around the same time as the studio's popular ABC Saturday-morning series *The Care Bears Family.* The animated production, which ultimately was released on home video, received airplay in the United States on the Disney Channel. *A Nelvana Limited Production in association with Global Television Network/Telefilm Canada. Color. Sixty-five minutes. Premiered on DIS: December 1988.*

**Voices**
**Grumpy Bear:** Bob Dermie; **Braveheart Lion/Loyal Heart Dog/ Good Luck Bear:** Dan Hennessey; **Mr. Beastley:** John Stocker; **Birthday Bear:** Melleny Brown; **Lotsa Heart Elephant/Gentle Heart Lamb:** Luba Goy; **Tenderheart Bear:** Billie Mae Richards

## ◎ CARLTON YOUR DOORMAN

This misfit of society who was heard but not seen on the television sitcom *Rhoda*, was transformed into a full-figure character whose adventures were unusual at best in this prime-time special based on the character created by James L. Brooks, Allan Burns, David Davis and Lorenzo Music (the voice of the Carlton in the sitcom and the special). *An MTM Production in association with Murakami-Wolf-Swenson. Color. Half-hour. Premiered on CBS: May 21, 1980.*

**Voices**
**Carlton:** Lorenzo Music; **Charles Shaftman:** Jack Somack; **Mrs. Shaftman:** Lucille Meredith; **Carlton's Mother:** Lurene Tuttle; **Darlene:** Kay Cole; **Mr. Gleanson/Fat Man:** Paul Lichtman; **Dog Catcher:** Alan Barzman; **Parrot:** Bob Arbogast; **Pop:** Charles Woolf; **D.J.:** Roy West

## ◎ CARNIVAL OF ANIMALS

Chuck Jones wrote, produced and animated this half-hour special based on the music of Camille Saint-Saens and the poetry of Ogden Nash, starring a variety of animals—lions, roosters, elephants and others—and Warner cartoon stars Bugs Bunny, Daffy Duck and Porky Pig. One major highlight: Bugs and Daffy, resplendent in black tie and tails, playing twin concert pianos along with a live orchestra conducted by Michael Tilson Thomas. *A Chuck Jones Enterprises Production in association with Warner Bros. Television. Color. Half-hour. Premiered on CBS: November 22, 1976. Rebroadcast on CBS: July 12, 1979.*

**Voices**
**Bugs Bunny/Daffy Duck/Porky Pig:** Mel Blanc

## ◎ CARTOON ALL-STARS TO THE RESCUE

More than 20 animated characters from Saturday-morning cartoon shows band together to help a 14-year-old (Michael) lick his addiction to drugs in this half-hour special shown on all three networks, some 200 independent stations and numerous cable services. The antidrug program produced a record-high 22.0 rating (more than 30 million viewers), the highest rating ever for a Saturday-morning children's program. The program's theme song: "Wonderful Ways to Say 'No.'" *An Academy of Television Arts and Sciences Foundation Production in cooperation with Alien Productions, Bagdasarian Productions, Columbia Pictures Television, DIC Enterprises, Film Roman, Hanna-Barbera Productions, Henson Associates, Marvel Productions, Murakami-Wolf-Swenson Films, Southern Star Productions, The Walt Disney Company and Warner Brothers. Color. Half-hour. Premiered: April 21, 1990. Syndicated.*

**Voices**
**Michael:** Jason Marsden; **Corey:** Lindsey Parker; **Mom:** Laurie O'Brien; **Dad:** Townsend Coleman; **Alf:** Paul Fusco; **Bugs Bunny/ Daffy Duck:** Jeff Bergman; **The Chipmunks: Alvin/Simon:** Ross Bagdasarian; **Theodore:** Janice Karman; **Papa Smurf:** Don Messick; **Brainy Smurf:** Danny Goldman; **Smurfette:** Julie Dees; **Garfield:** Lorenzo Music; **Huey/Duey/Louie:** Russi Taylor; **Winnie the Pooh/Tigger:** Jim Cummings; **Slimer/Baby Kermit:** Frank Welker; **Michaelangelo:** Townsend Coleman; **Baby Piggy:** Laurie O'Brien; **Baby Gonzo:** Russi Taylor; **Smoke:** George C. Scott

## ◎ CARTOON NETWORK BLOOPERS AND OTHER EMBARRASSING MOMENTS

First-ever hour-long special delivering the best outtakes from the world of animation, including the wackiest technical gaffes, blown lines and comical mishaps from world-famous cartoon stars, such as Ed, Edd and Eddy, the Flintstones, Johnny Bravo, Foghorn Leghorn and the Jetsons. Hosted by veteran cartoon voice artist Tom Kenny, best known as the voice of Nickelodeon's *SpongeBob SquarePants* and characters from many other Cartoon Network shows (*The Powerpuff Girls, Dexter's Laboratory* and *Johnny Bravo*), the world premiere special also included two Warner Bros. theatrical cartoon shorts showing what happens when things go amuck on the set: *Duck Amuck* (1953) and *(blooper) Bunny!* (1991). *A Cartoon Network Studios Production. Color. One hour. Premiered on CAR: June 6, 2003.*

## ◎ CARTOON NETWORK'S GREATEST MUSICAL MOMENTS

Thirty of animation's most memorable musical performances culled from Cartoon Network's library of more than 8,000 titles, including four classic cartoons shown complete and uncut, were showcased in this hour-long prime-time special. Among the titles included in this melodic retrospective were Bugs Bunny in "What's Opera, Doc?" (1957) and "Rabbit of Seville" (1950); Tom and Jerry in their Oscar-winning short, "The Cat Concerto" (1947); and Popeye's "Me Musical Nephews" (1942). Some of animation's most beloved songs were also featured, among them, Fred Flintstone's hit, "The Twitch" and Pebbles and Bamm-Bamm's "Let Sunshine In," as well as performances by Droopy, the Hillbilly Bears, Magilla Gorilla, the Powerpuff Girls and many others. *A Cartoon Network Studios Production. Color. One hour. Premiered on CAR: March 7, 2003. Rebroadcast on CAR: March 9, 2003; May 8, 2003.*

## ◎ CASPER'S FIRST CHRISTMAS

A joyful group of characters—Yogi Bear, Boo Boo, Snagglepuss and others—get lost and decide to make Christmas Eve merry by visiting Casper. Hairy Scary tries to scare their Christmas spirits away until a touching gesture changes his heart. *A Hanna-Barbera Production. Color. Half-hour. Premiered on NBC: December 18, 1979. Rebroadcast on NBC: December 5, 1980; December 14, 1981. Rebroadcast on DIS: December 12, 1990; December 13, 1991; December 15, 1992; December 7, 1993; December 20, 1994. Rebroadcast on CAR: November 25, 1995.*

**Voices**
**Casper:** Julie McWhirter; **Hairy Scary:** John Stephenson; **Augie Doggie/Doggie Daddy:** John Stephenson; **Huckleberry Hound:** John Stephenson; **Quick Draw McGraw:** John Stephenson; **Snagglepuss/Quick Draw McGraw:** John Stephenson; **Yogi Bear:** John Stephenson; **Boo Boo:** Don Messick; **Santa Claus:** Hal Smith

## ◎ CASPER'S HALLOWEEN SPECIAL

It's Halloween night and Casper, the friendly ghost, decides to dress up and go out trick or treating like the rest of the children. Hairy Scary tries to spoil the fun by playing a few pranks and goes beyond the limits of good fun when he disappoints a group of orphan children. The special's story title was "He Ain't Scary, He's Our Brother." *A Hanna-Barbera Production. Color. Half-hour. Premiered on NBC: October 30, 1979. Rebroadcast on NBC: November 1, 1981. Rebroadcast on DIS: October 16, 1991; October 25, 1992; October 18, 1993; October 30, 1994.*

*Voices*

**Casper:** Julie McWhirter; **Hairy Scary:** John Stephenson; **Mr. Duncan/Skull:** Hal Smith; **J.R.:** Diane McCannon; **Winifred the Witch:** Marilyn Schreffler; **Black Cat:** Frank Welker; **Butler/Rural Man:** John Stephenson; **Nice Man/Dog:** Frank Welker; **Lovella:** Ginny Tyler; **Bejewelled Dowager/Rural Lady:** Ginny Tyler; **Gervais/Carmelita/Nice Lady:** Lucille Bliss; **Screech:** Michael Sheehan; **Dirk:** Greg Alter

## ⊚ CASPER'S HAUNTED CHRISTMAS

Casper is ordered by the supreme ruler of ghosts, Kibosh, to scare at least *one* person before Christmas Day: the Jollimore family in Massachusetts. When his kindhearted manner prevents him from doing so, the Ghostly Trio secretly hires Spooky to pose as the goody-two-shoes Casper and finish the job instead in this 90-minute special originally produced in October 2000 directly for home video by MCA/Universal. The program made its television debut five years later on Cartoon Network. A *Mainframe Entertainment/Harvey Entertainment Production. Color. Ninety minutes. Premiered on CAR: December 1, 2005. Rebroadcast on CAR: December 13, 2005; December 20, 2005; December 24, 2005; December 1, 2006; December 17, 2006; December 21, 2006; December 22, 2006; December 24, 2006.*

*Voices*

**Casper:** Brendon Ryan Barrett; **Carol Jollimore:** Kathleen Barr; **Little Kid:** Ian James Corlett; **Fatso:** Graeme Kingston; **Skinkie:** Terry Klassen; **Stretch:** Scott McNeil; **Holly Jollimore:** Tegan Moss; **Kibosh:** Colin Murdock; **Poil:** Tabitha St. Germain; **Snivel:** Lee Tockar; **Spooky:** Samuel Vincent; **Narrator:** David Kaye

## ⊚ CASPER'S SCARE SCHOOL

Casper is sent back to school to learn how to scare people or else, but retreats to his old good-natured ways upon learning of an evil plan to take over the world and tries to stop it in this direct-to-video full-length computer-animated movie released in September 2006. Featuring the vocal talents of Jim Belushi, Bob Saget, Phyllis Diller and Dan Castellaneta, the ghost-and-goblin cartoon feature, with Devon Werkheiser taking over as the voice of the harmless goblin, premiered on Cartoon Network as part of the channel's lineup of Halloween programming. A *MoonScoop/Classic Media/DQ Entertainment Production. Color. Ninety minutes. Premiered on CAR: October 20, 2006.*

*Voices*

**Casper/Casper's Shadow:** Devon Werkheiser; **Stinkie/Frankengymteacher:** John Di Maggio; **Fatso/Figurehead:** Billy West; **Banana Lady/History Teacher:** Debi Derryberry; **Punk Kid/Scare Center Host #2/Pumpkinhead/Braniac/Pool Guy:** Scot Menville; **Jimmy:** Brett DelBuono; **Scare Center Host #1/Wolfie/Narrator/Werewolf:** Pat Fraley; **Kibosh:** Kevin Michael Richardson; **Gargoyle/Flyboy/Skinny Ghost/Coach:** Jason Harris; **Monaco:** Nika Futterman; **Ra:** Kendre Berry; **Pirate/Thurdigree Burns:** Maurice LaMarche; **Parrot:** Kevin McDonald; **Fish Boy/Drip:** Terri Douglas

## ⊚ CASTLE

This public television special, based on the book by David Macaulay (also one of the principal voice artists), follows the construction of a 13th-century Welsh castle while examining life in medieval England, combining live action and animation. A *Unicorn Projects Production. Color. One hour. Premiered on PBS: October 5, 1983.*

*Voices*

Sarah Bullen, David Macaulay

## ⊚ CATDOG: "CATDOG AND THE GREAT PARENT MYSTERY"

With Nearburg holdings its Parents' Day festival CatDog feel left out and decide to go find their parents and to learn where they came from in this half-hour special based on the popular Nickelodeon comedy series. A *Peter Hannan Productions/Studio B/Viacom International Production. Color. Half-hour. Premiered on NICK: November 25, 2000.*

*Voices*

**Cat:** Jim Cummings; **Dog/Cliff:** Tom Kenny; **Winslow T. Oddfellow/Lube:** Carlos Alzraqui; **Shriek Dubois:** Maria Bamford; **Lola Caricola:** Nika Frost; **Dunglap/Mervis:** John Kassir; **Eddie the Squirrel:** Dwight Schultz; **Rancid Rabbit:** Pete Zarustica

## ⊚ CATHY

Comic-strip heroine Cathy Andrews searches for happiness in this half-hour animated special based on creator Cathy Guisewite's nationally syndicated strip. The story comically plays the upswing in Cathy's career (a nomination for her company's "Employee of the Year") against the downswing in her personal life (her long-time boyfriend is seeing another woman). Seeing red, Cathy reluctantly renews her quest for Mr. Right, prodded by her chum Andrea. In 1987, the special won an Emmy Award for outstanding animated program. A *Lee Mendelson–Bill Melendez Production in association with Universal Press Syndicate and Bill Melendez Productions. Color. Half-hour. Premiered on CBS: May 15, 1987. Rebroadcast on CBS: January 5, 1988.*

*Voices*

**Cathy:** Kathleen Wilhoite; **Irving:** Robert F. Paulsen; **Andrea:** Allison Argo; **Anne, Cathy's mother:** Shirley Mitchell; **Bill, Cathy's father:** William L. Guisewite; **Charlene:** Emily Levine; **Mr. Pinkley:** Gregg Berger; **Brenda:** Desiree Goyette; **M.C.:** Robert Towers

## ⊚ CATHY'S LAST RESORT

While on a romantic island vacation with Charlene, the receptionist, career woman Cathy manages to meet a nice single guy and must contend with the sudden appearance of her ever-undependable, workaholic boyfriend, Irving, who, at the last minute, had backed out on the trip. Program was written and illustrated by *Cathy* creator/cartoonist Cathy Guisewite. A *Lee Mendelson–Bill Melendez Production in association with Universal Press Syndicate. Color. Half-hour. Premiered on CBS: November 11, 1988.*

*Voices*

**Cathy:** Kathleen Wilhoite; **Irving, her boyfriend:** Robert F. Paulsen; **Anne, Cathy's mother:** Shirley Mitchell; **Bill, Cathy's father:** William L. Guisewite; **Andrea:** Allison Argo; **Mr. Pinkley:** Gregg Berger; **Charlene:** Emily Levine

*Additional Voices*

Heather Kerr, Jamie Neal, Frank Welker

## ⊚ CATHY'S VALENTINE

Cathy and boyfriend, Irving, try rekindling their romance before Valentine's Day, with Cathy going all out to impress her beau by getting a makeover and buying a new dress even though her mother believes "romance has nothing to do with what you wear, it's what you have in your cupboard." A *Lee Mendelson–Bill Melendez Production in association with Universal Press Syndicate. Color. Half-hour. Premiered on CBS: February 10, 1989.*

*Voices*

**Cathy:** Kathleen Wilhoite; **Irving:** Robert F. Paulsen; **Anne, Cathy's mother:** Shirley Mitchell; **Bill, Cathy's father:** William

L. Guisewite; **Andrea:** Allison Argo; **Mr. Pinkley:** Gregg Berger; **Charlene:** Emily Levine

### ☉ CELEBRITY DEATHMATCH DEATHBOWL '98

Clay rendering of today's hottest celebrities from the worlds of music and television appeared as commentators and competitors in three no-holds-barred fights (Howard Stern vs. Kathie Lee Gifford, Pamela Anderson vs. RuPaul and Hanson vs. The Spice Girls) in this MTV Super Bowl half-time special that premiered in 1998. Sports commentator Marv Albert made a special "clay animated" guest appearance. *An MTV Animation Production. Color. Half-hour. Premiered on MTV: January 25, 1998.*

### ☉ CHALKZONE

Everything about Rudy Tabootie is normal except for one of his favorite possessions: a magical piece of chalk that transports him into a special world beyond the chalkboard, the ChalkZone, in which anything that he draws or erases comes to life in this four-minute cartoon short pilot, entitled "Rudy's First Adventure," which premiered on Nickelodeon's half-hour anthology series, *Oh Yeah! Cartoons,* and later inspired the half-hour weekly series on Nickelodeon in 2002. *A Frederator Incorporated Production. Color. Half-hour. Premiered on NICK: October 17, 1998 (Oh Yeah! Cartoons).*

*Voices*
**Rudy Tabootie:** Elizabeth Daily; **Snap:** Candi Milo; **Penny Sanchez:** Hynden Walch; **Joe Tabootie:** Jess Harnell; **Mildred "Millie" Tabootie:** Miriam Flynn; **Mr. Wilter/Blocky:** Robert Cait; **Biclops:** Rodger Bumpass; **Queen Rapsheeba:** Rosslynn Taylor; **Penny Sanchez (singing voice):** Robbyn Kirmsse; **Mrs. Sanchez:** Nika Futterman; **Additional Voices:** Daran Norris, Robin Atkin Downes

### ☉ CHALKZONE: "THE BIG BLOW UP"

Assisted by Penny and Snap, Rudy develops a cure for a fast-spreading disease called Baloonemia, which causes its victims to blow up like parade-size balloons in this Nickelodeon movie special based on the popular weekly series. The feature-length special was one of seven animated movies—each based on a Nickelodeon cartoon series—that premiered on the network's *Nicktoons Movie Summer* festival in 2004. *A Frederator Incorporated Production. Color. Two hours. Premiered on NICK: August 6, 2004. Rebroadcast on NICK: August 7, 2004; August 8, 2004; August 16, 2004; September 6, 2004; November 26, 2004; January 1, 2005; August 29, 2005.*

*Voices*
**Mildred "Millie" Tabootie:** Miriam Flynn; **Penny Sanchez:** Hynden Walch; **Rudy Tabootie:** Elizabeth Daily; **Snap/Reggie Bullnerd:** Candi Milo; **Mr. Wilter:** Robert Cait; **Joe Tabootie:** Jess Harnell; **Barney the Encyclocentopedia:** Malcolm McDowell; **Biclops:** Rodger Bumpass

### ☉ CHARLES DICKENS' DAVID COPPERFIELD

Young quixotic feline David Copperfield is forced into the employ of his villainous stepfather at a moldy London cheese factory in this two-hour musical spectacular, loosely based on Charles Dickens's classic 1849 novel. *A Cinemotion Inc/PMMP National Production. Color. Two hours. Premiered on CBS: December 10, 1993.*

*Voices*
**David Copperfield:** Julian Lennon; **Agnes:** Sheena Easton; **Murdstone:** Michael York; **Mealy:** Howie Mandel; **Micawber:** Joseph Marcell; **Clara:** Kelly LeBrock

### ☉ CHARLIE AND LOLA: "HOW MANY MORE MINUTES UNTIL CHRISTMAS?"

With Christmas only a few days away, Charlie and Lola find their holidays nearly ruined when the flap for Christmas on their advent calendar mysteriously vanishes and they investigate what happened in this cut-out and collage-animated special and the first half-hour special that premiered the popular preschool series' second season on the Disney Channel. The program was double the length of the show's usual 11-minute cartoon episodes. *A Tiger Aspect Production. Color. Half-hour. Premiered on DIS: December 16, 2006. Rebroadcast on DIS: December 24, 2006; December 25, 2006.*

*Voices*
**Charlie Summer:** Daniel Mayers; **Lola Summer:** Clementine Cowell; **Marv Lowe:** Ryan Harris; **Lotta:** Morgan Gayle; **Soren Lorenson:** Stanley Street; **Morten Lowe, Marv's little brother:** Macauley Keeper; **Elves:** Battina Berg, Nicolai Berg, Thale Krohn-Patterson; **Evie:** Lara Mayers; **Mini Reader:** Katie Hedges; **Arnold Wolf:** E'oin O'Sullivan

### ☉ A CHARLIE BROWN CELEBRATION

This one-hour animated special consists of several different stories of various lengths derived from the best comic strips ever done by *Peanuts* creator/cartoonist Charles Schulz. Segments include Charlie Brown's ill-fated attempt at kite flying, Peppermint Patty going to Dog Obedience School and Lucy and Schroeder at the piano discussing marriage. Schulz hosts the program, which was originally to be called *The Best of Charlie Brown.* In March 1998, the fun-filled special re-aired for the first time—in two parts over two consecutive days—on cable network giant Nickelodeon. *A Lee Mendelson–Bill Melendez Production in association with Charles M. Schulz Creative Associates and United Feature Syndicate. Color. Half-hour. Premiered on CBS: May 24, 1982. Rebroadcast on CBS: February 18, 1984. Rebroadcast on NICK: March 12, 1998 (Part I); March 13, 1998 (Part II); April 23, 1998 (Part I); April 14, 1998 (Part II); May 26, 1998 (Part I); May 27, 1998 (Part II); June 29, 1998 (Part I); June 30, 1998 (Part II); July 28, 1998 (Part I); July 29, 1998 (Part II); August 17, 1998 (Part I); August 18, 1998 (Part II); October 13, 1998 (Part I); October 14, 1998 (Part II); November 12, 1998 (Part I); November 13, 1998 (Part II); December 17, 1998 (Part I); December 18, 1998 (Part II); April 7, 1999 (Part I); April 8, 1999 (Part II); June 1, 1999 (Part I); June 2, 1999 (Part II); July 29, 1999 (Part I); July 30, 1999 (Part II).*

*Voices*
**Charlie Brown:** Michael Mandy; **Lucy Van Pelt:** Kristen Fullerton; **Linus Van Pelt:** Earl "Rocky" Reilly; **Sally Brown:** Cindi Reilly; **Schroeder:** Christopher Donohoe; **Peppermint Patty:** Brent Hauer; **Polly/Truffles:** Casey Carlson; **Marcie:** Shannon Cohn; **Snoopy:** Bill Melendez; **Announcer:** John Hiestand

### ☉ A CHARLIE BROWN CHRISTMAS

It may be Christmas but Charlie Brown is depressed. Acting as his psychiatrist, Lucy suggests that he get involved with the holiday festivities by directing their Christmas play. To set the proper mood, he is sent out to find the "perfect" Christmas tree to decorate the stage. The first *Peanuts* special ever produced (prompted by some Coca-Cola advertising executives who asked producer Lee Mendelson and creator Charles Schulz if they had ever considered doing a Christmas special for TV), the program was the first half-hour prime-time cartoon without a laugh track and the first to have kids—not adults—do the voices. The special won Emmy and Peabody awards for program excellence. For its 1997 encore showing, CBS restored the 1965 special to its original format, including a 45-second scene, since cut from network reairings, focusing on Linus's use of his blanket in a snowball fight.

The perennial favorite switched to a new network, ABC, in 2001. That year the program was rebroadcast on two nights back-to-back, along with a new half-hour documentary special, *The Making of a Charlie Brown Christmas*, hosted by Whoopi Goldberg.

In 2003, ABC aired a digitally remastered version of this beloved Christmas special for the first time. The repeat telecast drew its biggest viewing audience ever on the network with 11.5 million viewers.

Two years later, in December 2005, *TV Guide* named the perennial yuletide classic "Best Christmas Special." It also ranked number one in ratings across all key adult demographics (adults 18–34, 18–49, 25–54), teens 12–14 and kids 2–11, drawing 13.8 million viewers—the special's best numbers ever on ABC.

In 2006, the 40th annual airing of the holiday classic included a retelecast of the short 2002 special, *Charlie Brown's Christmas Tales*, and averaged 15.3 million viewers, its largest total audience since ABC claimed the *Peanuts* franchise from CBS in 2001. *A Lee Mendelson–Bill Melendez Production in association with Charles M. Schulz Creative Associates and United Feature Syndicate. Color. Half-hour. Premiered on CBS: December 9, 1965. Rebroadcast on CBS: December 11, 1966; December 10, 1967; December 8, 1968; December 7, 1969; December 5, 1970; December 7, 1971; December 12, 1972; December 6, 1973; December 17, 1974; December 15, 1975; December 18, 1976; December 12, 1977; December 18, 1978; December 10, 1979; December 9, 1980; December 10, 1981; Decem-*

*ber 16, 1982; December 12, 1983; December 5, 1984; December 4, 1985; December 12, 1986; December 11, 1987; December 14, 1988; December 22, 1989; December 19, 1990; December 20, 1991; December 2, 1992; December 22, 1993; December 7, 1994; December 9, 1995; December 19, 1996; December 3, 1997; December 2, 1998; December 3, 1999; December 11, 2000; Rebroadcast on ABC: December 6, 2001; December 16, 2001; December 8, 2002; December 13, 2002; December 2, 2003 (digitally remastered version); December 7, 2004; December 16, 2004; December 16, 2005; November 28, 2006.*

**Voices**
**Charlie Brown:** Peter Robbins; **Lucy Van Pelt:** Tracy Stratford; **Linus Van Pelt:** Christopher Shea; **Schroeder:** Chris Doran; **Peppermint Patty:** Karen Mendelson; **Sally Brown:** Cathy Steinberg; **Freida:** Ann Altieri; **Pigpen/Shermy:** Chris Doran; **Violet:** Sally Dryer-Barker

## ◎ CHARLIE BROWN'S ALL STARS

His team having just lost their 99th game in row, Charlie Brown reaches new depths of depression until his team is sponsored—to be in a real league with real uniforms. Unfortunately, he later learns that his sandlot crew can't play in the real league because his players include a dog and several girls. On Friday, March 6, 1998, the baseball-themed special was rebroadcast at 3 P.M. (ET) on Nickelodeon, which had begun re-airing many original CBS *Peanuts* specials and the Saturday-morning cartoon series, *The Charlie Brown & Snoopy Show*. *A Lee Mendelson–Bill Melendez Production in association with Charles M. Schulz Creative Associates*

*Baseball isn't Charlie Brown's thing, as he finds out in the half-hour animated special* Charlie Brown's All-Stars. © *United Feature Syndicate*
(COURTESY: BILL MELENDEZ PRODUCTIONS)

*and United Feature Syndicate. Color. Half-hour. Premiered on CBS: June 6, 1966. Rebroadcast on CBS: April 10, 1967; April 6, 1968; April 13, 1969; April 12, 1970; April 3, 1982. Rebroadcast on NICK: January 25, 1998; March 6, 1998; May 3, 1998; June 3, 1998; July 29, 1998; August 21, 1998; September 22, 1998; October 21, 1998; November 19, 1998; December 10, 1998; December 21, 1998; December 28, 1998; January 14, 1999; February 4, 1999; July 1, 1999; July 8, 1999; September 2, 1999; April 15, 2000.*

*Voices*

**Charlie Brown:** Peter Robbins; **Linus Van Pelt:** Christopher Shea; **Lucy Van Pelt:** Sally Dryer-Barker; **Schroeder:** Glenn Mendelson; Sally Brown: Cathy Steinberg; **Peppermint Patty:** Lynn Vanderlip; **Frieda:** Ann Altieri; **Pigpen:** Jeff Ornstein; **Violet:** Karen Mendelson; **Shermy/Umpire:** Kip DeFaria

### ◎ CHARLIE BROWN'S CHRISTMAS TALES

A year after winning the broadcast rights to the *Peanuts* specials over CBS, which had aired the programs for 35 years, ABC commissioned this new mini-special starring each of the beloved *Peanuts* characters, Charlie Brown, Snoopy, Linus, Lucy and Sally, in a series of five Christmastime vignettes—"Happy Holidays from Snoopy," "Yuletide Greetings from Linus," "Season's Greetings from Sally," "Peace On Earth from Lucy," and "Merry Christmas from Charlie Brown"—adapted from the work of the famed comic strip's creator Charles Schulz, who died in February 2000.

ABC decided to pair this new, shorter special with a rebroadcast of the classic 1965 Christmas specials *A Charlie Brown Christmas*, unedited and uncut, in a full-hour block. (Over the years, CBS had edited the special, including the closing credits and final song, "Hark! The Herald Angels Sing," angering viewers, to trim the program to a half-hour.) In doing so, ABC had an extra 18 minutes of air time to fill, thus the network created this new holiday-themed special to fill the hour. Previously in 2001, its first year of ownership of broadcast of broadcast rights, ABC produced a new original 17-minute documentary, *The Making of a Charlie Brown Christmas*, which aired immediately after its first rebroadcast of *A Charlie Brown Christmas*. *A Lee Mendelson-Bill Melendez Production in association with United Features Syndicate. Color. Half-hour. Premiered on ABC: December 8, 2002.*

*Voices*

**Charlie Brown:** Wesley Singerman; **Lucy Van Pelt:** Serena Berman; **Linus Van Pelt:** Coney Padhos; **Renun Van Pelt:** Tim Deter **Schroeder:** Christopher Ryan Johnson; **Sally Brown:** Hannah Leigh Dworkin; **Lydia:** Lauren Schaffel; **Snoopy/Woodstock:** Bill Melendez

### ◎ A CHARLIE BROWN THANKSGIVING

Charlie Brown celebrates America's oldest holiday in a rather unorthodox fashion. With his little stand-by, Linus, and the slightly questionable help of Snoopy and Woodstock, Charlie devises the most unusual Thanksgiving menu (potato chips, popcorn, jelly beans, buttered toast and ice cream) since 1621, served, traditionally enough, around a Ping Pong table in Charlie's backyard. After airing for the last time on CBS in 1989, 12 years later the former perennial favorite returned to network television on ABC (which picked up the rights to the classic *Peanuts* special). ABC has rebroadcast it ever since. *A Lee Mendelson–Bill Melendez Production in association with Charles M. Schulz Creative Associates and United Feature Syndicate. Color. Half-hour. Premiered on CBS: November 20, 1973. Rebroadcast on CBS: November 21, 1974; November 22,*

*1975; November 22, 1976; November 21, 1977; November 15, 1978; November 19, 1979; November 25, 1980; November 23, 1981; November 20, 1984; November 26, 1985; November 25, 1986; November 24, 1987; November 23, 1989. Rebroadcast on ABC: November 16, 2001; November 22, 2001; November 21, 2002; November 23, 2003; November 25, 2004; November 24, 2005; November 21, 2006.*

*Voices*

**Charlie Brown:** Todd Barbee; **Linus Van Pelt:** Stephen Shea; **Lucy Van Pelt:** Robin Kohn; **Peppermint Patty:** Kip DeFaria; **Sally Brown:** Hilary Momberger; **Marcie:** Jimmy Ahrens; **Franklin:** Robin Reed; **Snoopy:** Bill Melendez

### ◎ THE CHARMKINS

The Charmkins find themselves in the throes of danger when their friend Lady Slipper, a talented dancer, is abducted by Dragonweed and his band of henchmen. His scheme to keep her is foiled by the Charmkins, who rescue Lady Slipper and return her to Charm World unharmed. *A Sunbow Production in association with Marvel Productions. Color. Half-hour. Premiered: June 1983. Syndicated.*

*Voices*

**Dragonweed:** Ben Vereen; **Brown-Eyed Susan:** Aileen Quinn; **Poison Ivy:** Sally Struthers; **Skunkweed:** Ivy Austin; **Willie Winkle:** Martin Biersbach; **Lady Slipper:** Lynne Lambert; **Bramble Brother #1:** Chris Murney; **Bramble Brother #2:** Bob Kaliban; **Briarpatch/Crocus:** Chris Murney; **Thorny:** Gary Yudman; **Popcorn:** Peter Waldren; **Blossom:** Freddi Webber; **Announcer:** Patience Jarvis, Tina Capland; **Vocalists:** Helen Leonhart; Jamie Murphy; Helen Miles

### ◎ A CHILD'S GARDEN OF VERSES

Nursed by his parents, a young Robert Louis Stevenson fights a childhood illness and is allowed to let his imagination run wild in this half-hour animated special featuring songs and poems from the book by Robert Louis Stevenson. The program was part of the popular cartoon anthology series *HBO Storybook Musicals*. *A Michael Sporn Animation Production in association with Italtoons Corporation. Color. Half-hour. Premiered on HBO: April 13, 1992. Rebroadcast on HBO: August 8, 1993.*

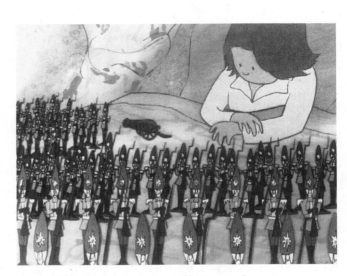

*A sick child lets her imagination run wild in a scene from animator Michael Sporn's A Child's Garden of Verses for HBO. © Michael Sporn Animation*

*Voices*
**Narrator (grown Robert Louis Stevenson):** Jonathan Pryce; **The Mother:** Heidi Stallings

## ◎ A CHIPMUNK CHRISTMAS

The Chipmunks (Alvin, Theodore and Simon) show their Christmas spirit when helping a gravely ill boy (Tommy Waterford) by giving him Alvin's prized harmonica to perform at Carnegie Hall on Christmas Eve. *A Bagdasarian Production. Color. Half-hour. Premiered on NBC: December 14, 1981. Rebroadcast on NBC: December 13, 1982; December 9, 1983; December 5, 1986; December 16, 1988. Rebroadcast on USA: December 11, 1991; December 17, 1992; December 8, 1993; December 1, 1994; December 16, 1995.*

*Voices*
**Alvin/Simon/David Seville:** Ross Bagdasarian Jr.; **Theodore:** Janice Karman

## ◎ A CHIPMUNK REUNION

Alvin, Theodore and Simon embark on a personal journey to uncover their real mother, while David Seville and the Chipettes—Brittany, Jeanette and Elenore—form a search party to find them. *A Bagdasarian Production in association with Ruby-Spears Productions. Color. Half-hour. Premiered on NBC: April 13, 1985. Rebroadcast on NBC: December 22, 1985.*

*Voices*
**Alvin/Simon/David:** Ross Bagdasarian Jr.; **Theodore/Brittany/Jeanette/Elenore:** Janice Karman; **Vinnie:** June Foray

## ◎ THE CHIPMUNKS ROCKIN' THROUGH THE DECADES

Alvin, Theodore and Simon headline this pop-music retrospective, hosted by Will Smith (star of TV's *Fresh Prince*) and featuring guest appearances by Little Richard, Kenny Loggins, Ben Vereen, Shelly Duvall, Raven Symone, Richard Moll and Markie Post. Also included is a special music video by Michael Jackson. *A Bagdasarian Production. Color. Half-hour. Premiered on NBC: December 9, 1990. Rebroadcast on USA: December 17, 1992; December 19, 1992; December 8, 1993; December 19, 1993.*

*Voices*
**Alvin/Simon:** Ross Bagdasarian Jr.; **Theodore:** Janice Karman

## ◎ CHIP 'N DALE RESCUE RANGERS TO THE RESCUE

Chip and Dale try solving a big ruby heist when they help Detective Don Drake and Plato, a police dog, who suspect the notorious Clawdane is somehow behind the crime in this two-hour special based on the hit syndicated series. *A Walt Disney Television Animation Production. Color. Two hours. Premiered: September 30, 1989. Syndicated.*

*Voices*
**Chip/Gadget:** Tress MacNeille; **Dale/Zipper/Snout/Mole:** Corey Burton; **Kirby/Muldoon:** Peter Cullen; **Monterey Jack/Fat Cat/Professor Nimnul:** Jim Cummings

## ◎ A CHRISTMAS CAROL (1970)

In this hour-long adaptation of Charles Dickens's classic tale money-grubbing businessman Ebenezer Scrooge is visited by several ghostly beings that make him understand the importance of giving. *A Famous Classic Tales special. An Air Programs International Production. Color. One hour. Premiered on CBS: December 13, 1970. Rebroadcast on CBS: December 12, 1971; December 10, 1972; December 8, 1973; December 14, 1974; December 13, 1975; December 18, 1976; December 10, 1977; November 26, 1978; November 25, 1979; November 28, 1980; December 6, 1981; November 28, 1982; December 4, 1983.*

*Voices*
C. Duncan, Ron Haddrick, John Llewellyn, T. Mangan, Bruce Montague, Brenda Senders, T. Kaff (vocalist), C. Bowden (vocalist)

## ◎ A CHRISTMAS CAROL (1971)

Actor Alistair Sim, who portrayed the character of Scrooge in a 1951 live-action feature, re-creates the role in this half-hour special that tells the story of one man's greed versus the true meaning of Christmas. *A Richard Williams Production. Color. Half-hour. Premiered on ABC: December 21, 1971. Rebroadcast on ABC: December 15, 1972; December 14, 1973; December 7, 1974.*

*Voices*
**Ebenezer Scrooge:** Alistair Sim; **Bob Cratchit:** Melvin Hayes; **Mrs. Cratchit:** Joan Sims; **Tiny Tim:** Alexander Williams; **Marley's Ghost:** Sir Michael Hordern; **Ragpicker/Fezziwig:** Paul Whitsun-Jones; **Scrooge's nephew/Charity Man:** David Tate; **Ghost of Christmas Past:** Diana Quick; **Ghost of Christmas Present:** Felix Felton; **Ghost of Christmas Yet to Come:** Annie West; **Mrs. Dilber:** Mary Ellen Ray; **Narrator:** Sir Michael Redgrave

## ◎ A CHRISTMAS CAROL (1984)

Unlike previous versions, this syndicated special based on the Charles Dickens story was 90 minutes in length, faithfully re-creating the famed children's classic for another generation of television viewers. *A Burbank Films Production. Color. Ninety minutes. Premiered: November 1984. Syndicated.*

*Voices*
Bill Conn, Barbara Frawley, Ron Haddrick, Philip Hinton, Anne Hardy, Sean Hinton, Liz Horne, Derani Scarr, Robin Stewart

## ◎ A CHRISTMAS CAROL (1997)

Feature-length animated musical version of Charles Dickens's legendary tale of the notorious skinflint, Ebenezer Scrooge, who, after being visited one night by three spirits—the ghosts of Christmas past, present and future—realizes the importance of giving at Christmas. Produced by DIC Entertainment in 1997 with voices by Ed Asner, Jodi Benson, Tim Curry, Whoopi Goldberg and Michael York, this 72-minute direct-to-video production was released on home video that October. Two weeks after its release, this latest adaptation, also known as *Charles Dickens' A Christmas Carol*, made its world television premiere on the premium pay channel Starz! Thereafter, the yuletide special was replayed multiple times annually, including in the month of July, on Starz!, Encore WAM! and Starz! Kids & Family through December 2002. That December, the film was rebroadcast on Nickelodeon in a 90-minute time slot as part of its *DIC's Incredible Movie Toons* series. Then, in 2004, DIC repackaged the special along with other DIC cartoon series and programs for its syndicated DIC Kids' Network three-hour programming block. *A DIC Entertainment/20th Century Fox Entertainment Production. Color. Ninety minutes. Premiered on STRZ: October 27, 1997. Rebroadcast on STRZ: December 20, 1997; December 21, 1997; December 24, 1997; December 25, 1997; July 25, 1998; July 26, 1998; December 2, 1998; December 5, 1998; December 10, 1998; December 14, 1998; December 16, 1998; December 20, 1998; December 21, 1998; December 25, 1998; December 2, 2000; December 7, 2000; December 12, 2000; December 15, 2000; December 20, 2000; December 24, 2000. Rebroadcast on EWAM: December 20, 1998; December 25, 1998. Rebroadcast on STRZK&F: June 1, 1999; June 5, 1999; June 11, 1999; July 2, 2001; July 15, 2001;*

*July 24, 2001; July 30, 2001; December 17, 2001; December 20, 2001; December 24, 2001; December 25, 2001; July 4, 2002; July 5, 2002; July 12, 2002; July 15, 2002; July 23, 2002; July 24, 2002; December 2, 2002; December 10, 2002; December 14, 2002; December 22, 2002; December 25, 2002. Rebroadcast on NICK: December 8, 2002 (DIC's Incredible Movie Toons). Syndicated: 2004.*

**Voices**
**Ebenezer Scrooge:** Tim Curry; **Bob Cratchit:** Michael York; **Mrs. Cratchit:** Kath Soucie; **Marley:** Edward Asner; **Debit:** Frank Welker; **Belle:** Jodi Benson; **Spirit of Christmas Present:** Whoopi Goldberg; **Other Voices:** Bettina Bush, Amick Byram, John Garry, Jerry Houser, Jarrad Kritzstein, Joe Lala, Kelly Lester, Anna Mathias, Sidney Miller, Judy Ovitz, Cathy Riso, Sam Saletta, Alan Shearman, David Wagner, Ian Whitcomb

## ◎ CHRISTMAS CARTOON CLASSICS
A selection of public-domain, holiday-themed cartoons from the 1930s and 1940s, including Ub Iwerks's "Jack Frost," the Max Fleischer Color Classic "Christmas Comes But Once a Year" and several Paramount theatrical cartoons, such as "Santa's Surprise" and "Hector's Hectic Life," highlight this one-hour syndicated extravaganza. *A Starcross Entertainment/Cable Films/Originamics Production. Color. One hour. Premiered: December 21, 1991. Syndicated.*

## ◎ CHRISTMAS COMES TO PAC-LAND
When Santa Claus develops sleigh trouble and crash lands in Pac-Land, the Pac family, along with policemen Morris and O'Pac, pool their resources to repair the sleigh and get Santa and his reindeer back on course. *A Hanna-Barbera Production. Color. Half-hour. Premiered on ABC: December 16, 1982. Rebroadcast on ABC: December 8, 1983. Rebroadcast on CAR: December 24, 1992; November 28, 1993; December 17, 1993; December 24, 1993. Rebroadcast on TNT: November 29, 1993 (as Pac-Man's Christmas). Rebroadcast on CAR: November 26, 1994.*

**Voices**
**Pac-Man:** Marty Ingels; **Mrs. Pac:** Barbara Minkus; **Pac-Baby:** Russi Taylor; **Chomp Chomp/Morris/Reindeer:** Frank Welker; **Sour Puss/Santa:** Peter Cullen; **O'Pac/Blinky/Pinky Monsters:** Chuck McCann; **Sue Monster:** Susan Silo; **Clyde Monster:** Neilson Ross; **Inky Monster:** Barry Gordon

## ◎ THE CHRISTMAS DINOSAUR
A young boy is hopelessly downcast at Christmas after receiving a petrified dinosaur egg, instead of the robotic dinosaur toy he wished for, until the egg hatches a real flying pterosaur that he tries hiding from his parents until he can reunite the young dino with his true parents. Produced by Los Angeles's PorchLight Entertainment and India's Escotoonz studios, this original hour-long animated Christmas special, featuring songs and music by Craig Dobbin and Brian Mann, debuted on Cartoon Network five days before Christmas 2004. *A PorchLight Entertainment/Escotoonz India/Slightly Offbeat Production. Color. One hour. Premiered on CAR: December 20, 2004.*

**Voices**
Jules De Jongh, Tom Eastwood, Anjella Mackintosh, Jo Ruiz Rodriguez, Ben Small

## ◎ CHRISTMAS EVERY DAY
Based on a short story by William Dean Howells, this first-run special tells the story of a young girl (Lucy) who wishes that

Christmas lasted forever. Her father relates a story, told in flashback, of another girl who made the same wish but lived to regret it. *A CBS Television Production in association with Orkin-Flaum Productions and Calabash Productions. Color. Half-hour. Premiered: December 20, 1986. Syndicated. Rebroadcast on USA: December 15, 1993; December 7, 1994; December 16, 1995.*

**Voices**
**Tilly/Cissy:** Stacy Q. Michaels; **Ned/Butcher/Policemen:** Brian Cummings; **Helen/Franny/Will:** Miriam Flynn; **Christmas Fairy:** Edie McClurg; **Grace/Lucy:** Marla Frumkin; **George/Pete:** Dick Orkin

## ◎ CHRISTMAS IS
The religious meaning of Christmas is witnessed through the eyes of a young boy (Benji) and his shaggy dog (Waldo) who are sent back to the scene of the Nativity, where Christ is born. The characters appeared in three additional specials, each underwritten by the International Lutheran Layman's League. *A Screen Images Production for Lutheran Television. Color. Half-hour. Premiered: November 7, 1970. Syndicated.*

**Voices**
**Benji:** Richard Susceno; **Innkeeper:** Hans Conried; **Waldo/Joseph:** Don Messick; **Mary:** Colleen Collins

## ◎ THE CHRISTMAS LAMB
Jodi Benson (*The Little Mermaid*), Mark Hamill (*Star Wars*) and Robby Benson (*Beauty and the Beast*) head an all-star cast in this retelling of Christ's birth in a manger and the animals who witnessed it, a story of self-worth and acceptance based on author Max Lucado's award-winning children's book, *The Crippled Lamb*. Written and directed by Rob Loos and George Taweel, this half-hour, direct-to-video production, retitled *The Christmas Lamb*, featured two original songs sung by Jodi Benson, including a new arrangement of "Away in a Manger." The inspirational holiday program made its television debut on the PAX-TV cable network, along with a second Tommy Nelson made-for-video, live-action production entitled "Jacob's Gift." *A Startoons/TLC Entertainment Production. Color. Half-hour. Premiered on PAX: December 9, 2000.*

**Voices**
**Joshua:** Jodi Benson; **Other Voices:** Robby Benson, Jessi Corti, Jeannie Elias, Mark Hamill

## ◎ CHRISTMAS LOST AND FOUND
Young Davey Hansen, star of the stop-motion animation series *Davey and Goliath*, conveys the Christian meaning of the yuletide season in this holiday special—one of six specials sponsored by the Lutheran Church of America—as he helps a discouraged young boy find happiness by letting him play the part of a king in an upcoming Christmas pageant, a role originally intended for Davey. Gumby creator Art Clokey produced the special. *A Clokey Production for the Lutheran Church of America. Color. Half-hour. Premiered: 1965. Syndicated.*

**Voices**
**Davey Hansen/Sally Hansen/Mary Hansen:** Norma McMillan, Nancy Wible; **Goliath/John Hansen:** Hal Smith

## ◎ THE CHRISTMAS MESSENGER
Encouraged by a friendly stranger whose real identity is later revealed, a young boy joins a group of Christmas carolers, which enhances his appreciation of the holiday season. Richard Cham-

berlain narrated the special. *A Shostak and Schwartz/Gerald Potterton Production in association with Narrator's Digest. Color. Half-hour. Premiered: 1975. Syndicated.*

**Voices**

**Narrator:** Richard Chamberlain

### ◎ THE CHRISTMAS ORANGE

When six-year-old Anton Stingley discovers on Christmas morning that Santa ignored his 16-page gift list and gave him an orange instead, he sues the legendary St. Nick for "breach of contract" with Santa deciding to retire and never deliver another Christmas present again in this animated special adapted from the award-winning 1998 children's book of the same name, written by Don Gillmor and illustrated by Marie-Louise Gay. Originally produced by Vancouver-based Bardel Entertainment for Canada's first and only 24-hour-a-day cartoon network, Teletoon, the half-hour yuletide special debuted in United States in December 2002 as part of ABC Family's annual "25 Days of Christmas." *A Bardel Entertainment Inc./The Christmas Orange Productions Inc. Production. Color. Half-hour. Premiered on ABC FAM: December 9, 2002. Rebroadcast on ABC FAM: December 14, 2002; December 15; 2002; December 22, 2002; December 17, 2003; December 24, 2004.*

**Voices**

**Anton Stingley:** Danny McKinnon; **Wiley Studpustle:** Don Brown; **Santa:** French Tickner; **Lenny the Elf Foreman:** Scott McNeil; **Judge Marion Oldengray:** Ellen Kennedy

### ◎ THE CHRISTMAS RACCOONS

Cyril Sneer, in his desire to harvest all the trees in the Evergreen Forest, cuts down the "Raccoondominium" of Ralph, Melissa and Bert. The Raccoons set out to thwart Cryil's plans and save the forest. Based on the characters of the Canadian-produced series *The Raccoons. A Gillis-Wiseman Production in association with Atkinson Film-Arts. Color. Half-hour. Premiered: December 1980. Syndicated.*

**Voices**

**Dan:** Rupert Holmes; **Julie:** Tammy Bourne; Tommy: Hadley Kay; **Schaeffer:** Carl Banas; **Ralph:** Bobby Dermer; **Melissa:** Rita Coolidge; **Bert:** Len Carlson; **Cyril Sneer:** Michael Magee; **Cedric Sneer:** Fred Little; **Narrator:** Rich Little; **Vocalists:** Rita Coolidge, Rupert Holmes

### ◎ A CHRISTMAS STORY

With Christmas not too far away, Timmy, a bright little boy, makes a special request of Santa in the form of a letter he believes has been mailed but instead has been misplaced. Pals Goober the dog and Gumdrop the mouse discover the letter and set out to deliver it to Santa so Timmy's wish comes true at Christmas. *A Hanna-Barbera Production. Color. Half-hour. Premiered: December, 1972. Syndicated. Rebroadcast on CAR: November 28, 1992. Rebroadcast on TNT: December 20, 1992. Rebroadcast on CAR: December 15, 1993; November 26, 1994; December 14, 1994; November 25, 1995.*

**Voices**

**Mother/Girl:** Janet Waldo; **Timmy/Boy:** Walter Tetley; **Dad/Squirrel:** Don Messick; **Goober/Sleezer/Runto:** Paul Winchell; **Gumdrop/Second Dog:** Daws Butler; **Santa/Fatcat:** Hal Smith; **Polecat/Postman/First Dog:** John Stephenson; **Vocalists:** Paul DeKorte, Randy Kemner, Stephen McAndrew, Susie McCune, Judi Richards

### ◎ A CHRISTMAS TREE

Charles Dickens himself, in animated form, takes two children, Peter and Mary, on the adventure of their lives as they relive tales of the Christmases of his youth, including the story of a magical Christmas tree that grows as high as the sky, in this *Festival of Family Classics* special. *A Rankin-Bass Production in association with Mushi Studios. Color. Half-hour. Premiered: December 17, 1972. Syndicated. Rebroadcast on USA: December 17, 1991; December 17, 1992; December 5, 1993.*

**Voices**

Carl Banas, Len Birman, Bernard Cowan, Peg Dixon, Keith Hampshire, Peggi Loder, Donna Miller, Frank Perry, Henry Ramer, Billie Mae Richards, Alfie Scopp, Paul Soles

### ◎ THE CHRISTMAS TREE TRAIN

Buttons, a young bear, and Rusty, a young fox, are accidentally transported, along with evergreens cut by lumberjacks, to the big city on a train known as "The Christmas Tree Train." Rusty's and Buttons's parents, Rosey and George Fox and Bridget and Abner Bear, seek help in finding them from Jonesy, the Ranger of the forest. The first in a series of Chucklewood Critters specials. *An Encore Enterprises Production. Color. Half-hour. Premiered: December, 1983. Syndicated. Rebroadcast on USA: December 11, 1991; December 12, 1992; December 4, 1993.*

**Voices**

**Rusty/Rosie:** Kathy Ritter; **Buttons:** Barbara Goodson; **Ranger Jones:** Bill Boyett; **Abner/Santa Claus:** Alvy Moore; **George:** Bill Ratner; **Bridgett:** Morgan Lofting

### ◎ THE CHRISTMAS WITCH

Angela Lansbury tells the story of a neophyte witch named Gloria who doesn't cut it at the wicked-witch academy and decides to become a good witch instead in this special holiday edition of *Shelley Duvall's Bedtime Stories*, airing on Showtime. *A Think Entertainment/MCA Family Entertainment/Universal Cartoon Studios Production. Color. Half-hour. Premiered on SHO: December 11, 1994.*

**Voices**

**Narrator:** Angela Lansbury

### ◎ CHRISTOPHER THE CHRISTMAS TREE

A pint-size pine tree gets his heartfelt wish of being cut down so he can be displayed with all the trimmings in the home of a loving family in this half-hour musical cartoon special, which showed on FOX Network's Saturday-morning schedule. This direct-to-video special, featuring such delightful holiday tunes as "The Ballad of Christopher the Christmas Tree," "Hoot Hoot Hootey," "Christopher We Love You" and "I'm the Whole World's Christmas Tree," aired one month after its DVD release Saturday morning on FOX Kids. *A Chuck Glaser/Delaney and Friends Production in association with 20th Century Fox Home Video. Color. Half-hour. Premiered on FOX: December 24, 1994.*

**Voices**

Bill Reiter, Lelani Marrell, Kyle Lebine, Tony Dakota, Chuck Glaser, George Bowers, Babs Shula, Kathleen Barr, Kevin Hayes, Hugh Delaney, Jim Glaser, Scott McNeil, Paul Dobson, John Payne, Mikal Grant

### ◎ A CHUCKLEWOOD EASTER

Rusty and Buttons are put on trial for stealing eggs after invading the secret home of the Easter Bunny in this entertaining half-hour

*Buttons and Rusty learn a valuable lesson when they are put on trial for stealing eggs from the Easter Bunny in the fourth in a series of Chucklewood Critters specials, entitled A Chucklewood Easter © Encore Enterprises. All rights reserved.*

and fourth in a series of Chucklewood Critters specials. *An Encore Enterprise Production. Color. Half-hour. Premiered: April, 1987. Syndicated. Rebroadcast on USA: April 11, 1993.*

**Voices**
**Rusty/Bluebell:** Mona Marshall; **Buttons:** Barbara Goodson; **Abner:** Alvy Moore; **George/Easter Bunny:** Robert Axelrod; **Bridgett:** Oceana Mars; **Skipper:** Dan Roth; **Ranger Jones:** Bill Boyett

## ◎ CINDERELLA
Clever spoof of the classic children's tale in which the misfit Cinderella is transformed into a radiant beauty by her fairy godmother. The other characters are not as perfect as they seem, however; Cinderella's fairy godmother is absentminded; Prince Charming is a bumbling fool. Yet somehow everything comes out right as Cinderella and Prince Charming get married in this first-run special for television. *A Festival of Family Classics special. A Rankin-Bass Production. Color. Half-hour. Premiered: September 17, 1972. Syndicated.*

**Voices**
Carl Banas, Len Birman, Bernard Cowan, Peg Dixon, Keith Hampshire, Peggi Loder, Donna Miller, Frank Perry, Henry Ramer, Billie Mae Richards, Alfie Scopp, Paul Soles

## ◎ CIRCUS DREAMS
Enchanced by sophisticated animation, this program takes viewers inside the magical world of a traveling circus in this imaginative program (and sequel to the French clay-animated "The Happy Circus") which premiered on the PBS series *Long Ago & Far Away*. *A La Maison du Cinema de Grenoble/Antenne 2/Folimage-Valence Production. Color. Half-hour. Premiered on PBS: September 29, 1990. Rebroadcast on PBS: February 7, 1993.*

**Voices**
**Narrator:** Tammy Grimes

## ◎ A CITY THAT FORGOT ABOUT CHRISTMAS
When Benji is impatient with the long wait for Christmas, his grandfather relates to him, his friend Martin and Benji's dog,

Waldo, the story of a visitor (Matthew) who changed the lives of the townspeople in preparation for the coming of Jesus on Christmas Eve. *A Screen Images Production for Lutheran Television. Color. Half-hour. Premiered: December, 1974. Syndicated.*

**Voices**
**Benji's grandfather:** Sebastian Cabot; **Benji:** David Kelly; **Matthew, the wood carver:** Sebastian Cabot; **Wicked Mayor:** Charles Nelson Reilly; **Henchman:** Louis Nye; **Waldo, Benji's dog:** Don Messick

## ◎ CLASSICAL BABY
A diaper-clad maestro leads an all-animal symphonic orchestra to the classical music of Johann Sebastian Bach, Irving Berlin, Johann Strauss II, Pyotr Ilyich Tchaikovsky and other legendary composers, introducing youngsters to music, art and dance, in this prime-time special from the Emmy and Peabody Award-winning producer and director Amy Schatz of *Goodnight Moon & Other Sleepytime Tales*; culled from the three-part *Classical Baby* video series featuring two- to three-minute musical pieces with animation inspired by famed artists Claude Monet, Joan Miro and Fernand Leger, for HBO. Promoted by HBO before its May 2005 debut as its "first evening special for infants, babies and parents," the half-hour program won two Emmy Awards for outstanding children's program and outstanding individual achievement in animation and also a 2006 Peabody Award. *A Home Box Office Production. Color. Half-hour. Premiered on HBO: May 14, 2005.*

## ◎ A CLAYMATION CHRISTMAS CELEBRATION
The California Raisins join a host of other animated clay figures in song-and-dance renditions of traditional Christmas carols. In 1992 the special was rebroadcast on The Disney Channel under the title of *Will Vinton's Claymation Christmas Special*. In 1988, the special ended up winning a prime time Emmy Award for outstanding animated program (for programming one hour or less). *A Will Vinton Production. Color. Half-hour. Premiered on CBS: December 21, 1987. Rebroadcast on CBS: December 23, 1988; December 21, 1989; December 7, 1990; December 6, 1991. Rebroadcast on DIS: December 11, 1992 (as* Will Vinton's Claymation Christmas*); December 4, 1993; December 22, 1994; December 17, 1995; December 21, 1996.*

**Voices**
**Herb:** Tim Conner; **Red:** Johnny Counterfit; **Singers:** Greg Black, Ron Tinsley

## ◎ CLAYMATION COMEDY OF HORRORS SHOW
The ever-scheming Wilshire Pig talks Sheldon Snail into visiting the castle of Dr. Frankenswine to seek scientific secrets that could be worth a fortune in this prime-time comedy/adventure Halloween special, produced by claymation-master Will Vinton (of *California Raisins* fame). In 1991, the half-hour special received two Emmy Award nominations for outstanding animated program (for programming one hour or less) and outstanding individual achievement in animation, winning the latter. *A Will Vinton Associates Production. Color. Half-hour. Premiered on CBS: May 29, 1991.*

**Voices**
Tim Conner, Brian Cummings, Krischa Fairchild, Todd Tolces

## ◎ CLAYMATION EASTER
Porkster Wilshire Pig kidnaps the Easter Bunny, then dresses up as a cottontail to enter a competition to become the rabbit's successor in this third in a series of prime-time "claymation" specials.

The special won two 1992 prime time Emmy Awards for outstanding animated program (for programming one hour or less) and outstanding individual achievement in animation. A *Will Vinton Associates Production. Color. Half-hour. Premiered on CBS: April 19, 1992.*

*Voices*
Tim Conner, Brian Cummings, Krischa Fairchild, Todd Tolces

## ◉ CLEROW WILSON AND THE MIRACLE OF P.S. 14

Re-creating characters introduced on his NBC series, *The Flip Wilson Show*, comedian Flip Wilson, as the voice of his nine-year-old self Clerow Wilson (his rightful name), recalls the struggle of his early childhood at the New Jersey school he attended in this prime-time network special, one of two based on Wilson's childhood adventures. A *DePatie-Freleng Enterprises Production in association with Clerow Productions and NBC. Color. Half-hour. Premiered on NBC: November 12, 1972. Rebroadcast on NBC: November 19, 1973.*

*Voices*
**Clerow/Geraldine Jones/Herbie/Reverend LeRoy/The Devil:** Flip Wilson; **Freddie:** Richard Wyatt Jr.; **Miss Davis:** Vivian Bonnett; **Li'l David:** Kenney Ball; **Robert Jackson:** Phillip Brown; **Dicke Porter:** Larry Oliver

## ◉ CLEROW WILSON'S GREAT ESCAPE

Comedian Flip Wilson plays many of his favorite characters—Geraldine Jones, Freddie the playboy, Ralph the invisible dog, Li'l David, Reverend Leroy and others—in this animated story as a small boy who is adopted into a mean family and attempts to escape. A *DePatie-Freleng Enterprises Production in association with Clerow Productions and NBC. Color. Half-hour. Premiered on NBC: April 3, 1974. Rebroadcast on NBC: December 16, 1974.*

*Voices*
**Clerow Wilson/Geraldine Jones/Ralph/Reverend LeRoy/Herbie/The Devil:** Flip Wilson

## ◉ CLIFFORD'S PUPPY DAYS: "CLIFFORD THE SCARY PUPPY/THINGS THAT GO BUMP"

The adorable red puppy with the giant-sized heart learns an important lesson that spooky sights and sounds are scary only in his imagination in two back-to-back episodes: "Clifford the Scary Puppy," in which Evan plays some tricks on Emily Elizabeth and her friends Nina and Shun dressed like animals for trick-or-treating, but finds a surprise of his own; and "Things That Go Bump," in which Clifford starts hearing funny noises that sound like those Mr. Solomon described while reading his latest Flo and Zo adventure, "Scaredy Cats," to Emily Elizabeth and her friends during a sleep-out on another Halloween night, in this half-hour Halloween special from the popular animated preschool series on PBS. A *Scholastic Entertainment Inc. Production. Color. Half-hour. Premiered on PBS Kids: October 26, 2005. Rebroadcast on PBS Kids: October 28, 2005; October 30, 2005; October 31, 2005; December 7, 2005; December 11, 2005.*

*Voices*
**Puppy Clifford:** Lara Jill Miller; **Emily Elizabeth Howard:** Grey DeLisle; **Zo:** Ogie Banks; **Brown:** Evan Thomas; **Mark Howard:** Cam Clarke; **Nina:** Masiela Lusha (Stacey Haglund); **Jorge:** Jess Harnell; **Daffodil:** Kath Soucie; **Shun:** Lauren Tom; **Norville:** Henry Winkler

## ◉ CODENAME: KIDS NEXT DOOR: "OPERATION N.A.U.G.H.T.Y."

After a group posing as the Kids Next Door steals Santa's invaluable gift-giving device, the R.E.I.N.D.E.E.R. 4000, the real covert kids group (Numbuh One, Numbuh Two, Numbuh Three, Numbuh Four and Numbuh Five) uncovers the real culprits while battling an elite squad of superpowered elves and finding the missing device before every present around the world suddenly turns to coal in this half-hour holiday special—and first special—based on the popular Cartoon Network series. A *Curious Pictures/Cartoon Network/Rough Draft Studios Inc. Production. Color. Half-hour. Premiered on CAR: December 6, 2005. Rebroadcast on CAR: December 8, 2005; December 12, 2005; December 16, 2005; December 21, 2005; December 23, 2005; December 24, 2005; December 25, 2005; December 12, 2006; December 17, 2006; December 20, 2006; December 21, 2006; December 22, 2006; December 24, 2006; December 25, 2006.*

*Voices*
**Numbuh One/Numbuh Two:** Benjamin Diskin; **Numbuh Three:** Lauren Tom; **Numbuh Four/Thesaurus Rex/Wintergreen:** Dee Bradley Baker; **Numbuh Five:** Cree Summer; **French Kid/Narrator:** Tom Kenny; **Edna Jucation:** Candi Milo; **Mr. Physically Fitastic:** Daran Norris; **Other Voices:** Dave Wittenberg

## ◉ CODENAME: KIDS NEXT DOOR: "OPERATION Z.E.R.O."

The Kids Next Door battle an evil power who suddenly turns kids and adults into tapioca-loving, grotesquely wrinkled Senior Citizombies in their first made-for-TV movie special, based on the top-rated Cartoon Network series created by Tom Warburton, which also was released on DVD in widescreen format. The acronym in the title stood for "Zero Explanation Reveals Origin." A *Cartoon Network Studios Production. Color. Ninety minutes. Premiered on CAR: August 11, 2006.*

*Voices*
**Nigel "Numbuh 1" Uno/Hoagie Pennywhistle "Numbuh 2" Gilligan Jr/Numbuh 101:** Ben Diskin; **Kuki "Numbuh 3" Sanban:** Lauren Tom; **Wally "Numbuh 4" Beatles/Mr. Fibb/Toilenator/Joaquin/Tommy Gilligan:** Dee Bradley Baker; **Abigail "Numbuh 5" Lincoln/Former Numbuh 11:** Cree Summer; **Mr. Boss/Mr. Fizz/Benedict Wigglestein:** Jeff Bennett; **Numbuh 94:** Steven Jay Blum; **Crazy Old Cat Lady/Gramma Stuffum:** Grey DeLisle; **Numbuh 26:** Michael Clarke Duncan; **Numbuh 86:** Jennifer Hale; **Stickybeard:** Mark Hamill; **Chad Dickson:** Jason Harris; **Sonya, Numbuh 83/Lee, Numbuh 84:** Janice Kawaye; **Numbuh 130/Knightbrace/Chester/Mr. Wink/Other Voices:** Tom Kenny; **Father:** Maurice LaMarche; **Numbuh 60:** Matt Levin; **Numbuh 362:** Rachael MacFarlane; **Count Spankulot/Janitor:** Daran Norris; **Grandfather:** Neil Ross; **Numbuh 18:** James Arnold Taylor; **Monty Uno:** Frank Welker; **Numbuh Zero:** Dave Wittenberg; **Other Voices:** Cam Clarke

## ◉ COMPUTERS ARE PEOPLE, TOO!

The technology of computer animation is demonstrated through a variety of film clips showing the marvels of computer-generated images. The tale is told by talking computers and hosted by Elaine Joyce, who takes viewers through this world of visual entertainment. A *Walt Disney Production. Color. One-hour. Premiered: May 22, 1982. Syndicated.*

*Voices*
Billy Bowles, Joe Campanella, Nancy Kulp

## COMPUTER WARRIORS

In this half-hour fantasy adventure, based on the popular Mattel toy line, four computer warriors (Rod, Grid, Micron and Scanner) are developed to neutralize malfunctioning A1 programs, which have transformed into dangerous computer viruses (named Megahert, Indexx, Hull and Minus) and have the potential to cause irreparable damage to a computer network they've entered unless they are stopped. The program was produced by Carl Macek and directed by Bill Kroyer, who also cowrote the script. *A Kroyer Films Production in association with Mattel Toys/Island Animation and American Film Technologies. Color. Half-hour. Premiered: September 23, 1990. Syndicated.*

## THE CONEHEADS

That unusual alien family from the planet Remulak, first seen in a series of comedy sketches on NBC's *Saturday Night Live,* continue their mission to rebuild their space fleet, using humans as their slaves. Based on characters created by Dan Aykroyd, Tom Davis and Lorne Michaels. *A Rankin-Bass Production in association with Broadway Video Color. Half-hour. Premiered on NBC: October 14, 1983.*

### Voices
**Beldar:** Dan Aykroyd; **Prymaat:** Jane Curtin; **Connie:** Laraine Newman

## A CONNECTICUT RABBIT IN KING ARTHUR'S COURT

Bugs Bunny plays a wise-guy Connecticut "rabbit" as Daffy Duck (King Arthur), Porky Pig (a varlat), Elmer Fudd (Sir Elmer Fudd) and Yosemite Sam join the fun in this loosely based adaptation of the Mark Twain classic "plagiarized" by Chuck Jones, who produced this all-new special for CBS. The program was later retitled *Bugs Bunny in King Arthur's Court. A Chuck Jones Enterprises Production for Warner Brothers Television. Color. Half-hour. Premiered on CBS: February 23, 1978. Rebroadcast on CBS: November 22, 1978; (as Bugs Bunny in King Arthur's Court) November 17, 1979; August 19, 1981; March 10, 1982.*

### Voices
Mel Blanc

## A CONNECTICUT YANKEE IN KING ARTHUR'S COURT

Through clever thinking and the use of modern inventions, the inventive Connecticut Yankee encounters the likes of Merlin the Magician and King Arthur's knights in a series of medieval battles in this made-for-television daytime special under the *Famous Classic Tales* banner. *An Air Programs International Production. Color. Half-hour. Premiered on CBS: November 26, 1970. Rebroadcast on CBS: November 25, 1971; November 23, 1972 (in New York on WPIX).*

### Voices
**Connecticut Yankee:** Orson Bean

## COOL LIKE THAT: THE CHRISTMAS SPECIAL

Urban depiction of holidays in the 'hood following the exploits of a 15-year-old inner-city teen named Orlando (voiced by Tommy Davison of *In Living Color* fame) and his band of homeboys who experience Christmas in an underprivileged neighborhood. *A Warner Bros. Television Animation/Quincy Jones Production. Color. Half-hour. Premiered on FOX: December 23, 1993.*

### Voices
**Orlando:** Tommy Davison; **Orlando's Mom/Drug Dealer:** Whoopi Goldberg

## A COSMIC CHRISTMAS

Three creatures from outer space and their pet mascot journey to Earth on their mission to discover the bright star, the Star of Bethlehem, and find the true meaning of Christmas. *A Nelvana Limited Production in association with the CBC. Color. Half-hour. Premiered: December 6, 1977. Syndicated.*

### Voices
**Peter:** Joey Davidson; **Dad/Plutox/Santa Joe:** Martin Lavut; **Lexicon:** Richard Davidson; **Amalthor:** Duncan Regehr; **Mom:** Patricia Moffat; **Grandma:** Jane Mallett; **Police Chief Snerk:** Marvin Goldhar; **Marvin:** Greg Rogers; **The Mayor:** Chris Wiggins; **Townies:** Nick Nichols, Marion Waldman

## THE COUNT OF MONTE CRISTO

Escaping from prison 15 years after his imprisonment Edmond Dantes, a young sailor, assumes the identify of his dead companion and sets sail to the Isle of Monte Cristo, where he uncovers fabulous treasure and acquires a new persona, the Count of Monte Cristo, with which to wage war on his enemies. *A Hanna-Barbera Production. Color. One hour. Premiered on CBS: September 23, 1973. Rebroadcast on CBS: December 7, 1974. Rebroadcast on CAR: October 22, 1995 (Mr. Spim's Cartoon Theatre).*

### Voices
Elizabeth Crosby, Tim Elliott, Barbara Frawley, Ron Haddrick, Richard Meike

## THE COUNTRY MOUSE AND THE CITY MOUSE: A CHRISTMAS TALE

Emily, a humble mouse living underneath the floor of a quaint country home, is invited by her cousin Alexander to spend Christmas with him in New York. They encounter trouble when the owner of the restaurant where Alexander lives purchases a "Christmas Cat" to help get rid of pests, and the two barely escape with their lives in this half-hour animated special, produced as part of the *HBO Storybook Musicals* series. *A Michael Sporn Animation Production in association with Italtoons Corporation. Color. Half-hour. Premiered on HBO: December 8, 1993. Rebroadcast on HBO: December 11, 1993.*

### Voices
**Emily, the Country Mouse:** Crystal Gayle; **Alexander, the City Mouse:** John Lithgow

## THE CRICKET IN TIMES SQUARE

Adapted from the 1960 book by George Selden, a liverwurst-loving cricket named Chester C. Cricket is transported in a picnic basket from a field in Connecticut to the Times Square subway. There the genteel Chester is befriended by Tucker Mouse, Harry the Cat and Mario the Newsboy, whose parents' newsstand is suffering from a severe lack of sales. When Tucker and Harry discover that Chester has the uncanny gift of being able to reproduce any music he hears, they convince him to perform during rush hour to attract business to the newsstand. The special was the recipient of the Parents' Choice Award for excellence in television programming. *A Chuck Jones Enterprises Production. Color. Half-hour. Premiered on ABC: April 24, 1973. Rebroadcast on ABC: January 30, 1974; November 9, 1974. Rebroadcast on NICK: March 14, 1992.*

*Voices*
**Chester C. Cricket/Harry the Cat:** Les Tremayne; **Tucker the Mouse:** Mel Blanc; **Mario Bellini:** Kerry MacLane; **Mario's Father:** Les Tremayne; **Mario's Mother:** June Foray; **Music Teacher:** Les Tremayne

## ◉ THE CRICKET ON THE HEARTH

Cricket Crockett is no ordinary cricket. He has a heart and soul and becomes the saving grace of poor toymaker Caleb Plummer and his troubled daughter, Bertha, who make him a permanent member of their family at Christmas, in this musical adaptation of the Charles Dickens fantasy. The one-hour special starred Danny Thomas and was broadcast during his weekly network series, *The Danny Thomas Hour*. Daughter Marlo Thomas costarred and joined Thomas in several musical numbers, their first such feat on film together. *A Rankin-Bass Production in association with Videocraft International. Color. One hour. Premiered on NBC: December 18, 1967 (on The Danny Thomas Hour). Rebroadcast on NBC: November 25, 1971.*

*Voices*
**Cricket Crockett:** Roddy McDowell; **Caleb Plummer:** Danny Thomas; **Bertha:** Marlo Thomas; **Edward:** Ed Ames; **Tackleton:** Hans Conried; **Moll:** Abbe Lane; **Uriah/Sea Captain:** Paul Frees

## ◉ CURIOUS GEORGE

Named for his natural inquisitiveness, this little monkey and his big-city friend, the Man in the Yellow Hat, encounter numerous misadventures in this half-hour special comprised of several four-minute cartoons from the *Curious George* cartoon series broadcast on Canadian television. *A Lafferty, Harwood and Partners Production in association with Milktrain Productions. Color. Half-hour. Premiered: 1983. Syndicated.*

*Voices*
**Narrator:** Jack Duffy

## ◉ CYRANO

French folk hero Cyrano de Bergerac conquers injustice in his quest to help his beautiful friend, Roxanne, in this adaptation of Edmond de Rostand's romantic play. The special was first broadcast as an ABC Afterschool Special. *A Hanna-Barbera Production. Color. Half-hour. Premiered on ABC: March 6, 1974. Rebroadcast on ABC: April 9, 1975. Rebroadcast on DIS: April 22, 1992. Rebroadcast on CAR: October 22, 1995 (Mr. Spim's Cartoon Theatre).*

*Voices*
**Cyrano de Bergerac:** José Ferrer; **Roxanne:** Joan Van Ark; **Ragueneau:** Kurt Kasznar; **Comte de Guiche:** Martyn Green; **Christian de Neuvillette:** Victor Garber; **Duenna:** Jane Connell; **First Cadet/de Brigny:** Alan Oppenheimer; **Richelieu:** John Stephenson

## ◉ DAFFY DUCK AND PORKY PIG MEET THE GROOVIE GOOLIES

Warner Bros.' cartoon stars Daffy Duck and Porky Pig join forces with Horrible Hall's the Groovie Goolies in this comic tale of Phantom's efforts to sabotage the movie studio. The made-for-television cartoon premiered on *The ABC Saturday Superstar Movie*. *A Filmation Associates Production in cooperation with Warner Bros. Color. One hour. Premiered on ABC: December 16, 1972 (on ABC Saturday Superstar Movie). Rebroadcast on ABC: December 29, 1973.*

*Voices*
**Daffy Duck/Porky Pig:** Mel Blanc; **The Groovie Goolies: Count Dracula/Hagatha/Frankie/Bella La Ghostly/Sabrina/Wolfie/Bonapart/Mummy/Dr. Jekyll-Hyde/Ghouliland/Hauntleroy/Ratso and Batso:** Jane Webb, Howard Morris, Larry Storch, Larry D. Mann

## ◉ DAFFY DUCK'S EASTER SHOW

The malevolent mallard stars in three new cartoon adventures related to the Easter season—"Yolks on You," "The Chocolate Chase" and "Daffy Goes North"—in his first-ever prime-time special, which preceded NBC's Saturday-morning series *The Daffy and Speedy Show*, introduced in the fall of 1981. In 1992 CBS rebroadcast the show under a new title: "Daffy Duck's Easter Egg-citement." *A DePatie-Freleng Enterprises Production for Warner Bros. Television. Color. Half-hour. Premiered on NBC: April 1, 1980. Rebroadcast on NBC: April 14, 1981; April 6, 1982. Rebroadcast on CBS: April 16, 1984; April 6, 1985; April 18, 1992 (as Daffy Duck's Easter Egg-citement).*

*Voices*
Mel Blanc

## ◉ DAFFY DUCK'S THANK-FOR-GIVING SPECIAL

In trying to convince the studio to buy his idea for a sequel to his classic film, "Duck Dodgers in the 24½th Century," Daffy Duck shows the producer all of his great films of the past, interspersed with clips from his earlier theatrical film accomplishments. After the producer finally relents, the show concludes with a screening of "The Return of Duck Dodgers in the 24½th Century," a 1977 cartoon Chuck Jones produced as a companion piece for the science-fiction thriller, *Star Wars*. In 1991, the special was rebroadcast on CBS and retitled, *Daffy Duck Goes Hollywood*, ranking second in the ratings behind ABC's powerhouse sitcom, *Growing Pains*. *A Chuck Jones Enterprises Production for Warner Bros. Television. Color. Half-hour. Premiered on NBC: November 20, 1980. Rebroadcast on NBC: November 24, 1981. CBS: November 12, 1983; November 26, 1987; May 1, 1991 (as Daffy Duck Goes Hollywood).*

*Voices*
Mel Blanc

## ◉ DAISY-HEAD MAYZIE

A little girl (Mayzie) becomes an instant celebrity—and the target of exploitation—when a daisy grows out of her head one morning in this Emmy-nominated half-hour animated special, based on a 20-year-old unpublished manuscript written by the late Dr. Seuss (alias Ted Geisel). *A Hanna-Barbera/Tony Collingwood Production. Color. Half-hour. Premiered on TNT: February 5, 1995. Rebroadcast on TNT: February 11, 1995.*

*Voices*
**Mayzie:** Fran Smith; **Cat in the Hat:** Henry Gibson; **Finagle:** Tim Curry; **Mayor:** George Hearn; **Principal:** Lewis Arquette; **Dr. Eisenbart:** Jonathan Winters; **Miss Sneetcher:** Susan Silo; **Mrs. McGrew:** B.J. Ward; **Mr. McGrew:** Paul Eiding; **Finch:** Robert Ridgely

## ◉ DANIEL BOONE

Daniel Boone tells his true life story, separating fact from fable, as he reflects upon his life and accomplishments for the benefit of a writer eager to portray the real story in this daytime children's special produced for CBS's *Famous Classic Tales* series. *A Hanna-*

Legendary pioneer Daniel Boone appears surrounded and with no visible way out in Hanna-Barbera's half-hour animated special Daniel Boone.

Barbera Production. Color. Half-hour. Premiered on CBS: November 27, 1981. Rebroadcast on CBS: November 25, 1982.

**Voices**
**Daniel Boone:** Richard Crenna; **Rebecca:** Janet Waldo; **Daniel Boone, age 14:** Bill Callaway; **Henry Miller:** Mike Bell; **Running Fox:** Bill Callaway; **First Settler/Mr. Harding:** Mike Bell; **Stearns/Assemblyman/Squire Boone:** John Stephenson; **Sarah/James/Quiet Dove:** Joan Gerber; **Washington/Col. Morgan/Second Settler:** Joe Baker; **White Top/Painter/Floor Leader:** Vic Perrin; **Blackfish/Business Man/Indian Dragging Canoe:** Barney Phillips; **Girty/Oconostata/Finley:** Michael Rye

### ◎ DANNY PHANTOM: "FRIGHT BEFORE CHRISTMAS"

Danny is cast as the star of a ghostly Christmas story by its author, Ghost Writer, after the young teen accidentally destroys the writer's only copy of the story and he then tries pinning the blame on Danny for a series of unexplainable catastrophes that almost ruin Christmas for the residents of Amity Park. The half-hour prime time holiday special was first telecast in December 2005 on Nickelodeon as part of its *Ha Ha Holidays* schedule of specials and holiday-theme cartoon series episodes. A *Nicktoons Productions/Billinfold Production. Color. Half-hour. Premiered on NICK: December 6, 2005. Rebroadcast on NICK: December 17, 2005; December*

19, 2005; December 25, 2005; December 16, 2006; December 18, 2006; December 24, 2006; December 25, 2006. Premiered on NICKT: December 9, 2006.

**Voices**
**Danny Fenton/Danny Phantom/Kids Walla:** David Kaufman; **Jack Fenton/The Box Ghost/Kid Walla:** Rob Paulsen; **Maddie Fenton/Lunch Lady Ghost:** Kath Soucie; **Jazz Fenton:** Colleen O'Shaughnessey; **Tucker Foley:** Rickey D'Shon Collins; **Samantha "Sam" Manson:** Grey DeLisle; **Vice-Principal Lancer:** Ron Perlman; **Dash Baxter:** Scott Bullock; **Paulina:** Maria Canals; **Qwan:** Dat Phan; **Ember/Penelope Spectra/Tiffany Snow/Baby Danny:** Tara Strong; **Skulker:** Kevin Michael Richardson; **Lance Thunder/News Reporter/Mikey:** Dee Bradley Baker; **Ghost Writer:** Will Arnett; **Walker:** James Arnold Taylor; **Bertrand:** Jim Ward; **Young Blood:** Taylor Lautner

### ◎ DANNY PHANTOM: "REALITY TRIP"

The ghost-hunting teen superhero goes up against the evil ringmaster Freakshow and his ghostly minions who have escaped from jail and kidnapped Danny, Sam and Tucker's families to seek revenge in this hour-long special, which also previewed new fall episodes. This second one-hour special from the famed Nickelodeon cartoon series was originally entitled *School Spirit*. A *Nicktoons Productions/Billinfold Production. Color. One hour. Premiered* on NICK: June 9, 2006. Rebroadcast on NICK: June 10, 2006; June 11, 2006; June 16, 2006; June 17, 2006; June 19, 2006; July 14, 2006; August 7, 2006; August 22, 2006; September 1, 2006; September 2, 2006; September 4, 2006; December 27, 2006.

**Voices**

**Danny Fenton/Danny Phantom/Walla:** David Kaufman; **Jack Fenton/The Box Ghost/Auto Jack/Stuffed Animal #1/Geek Danny/Nicolai Technus:** Rob Paulsen; **Maddie Fenton/Empress She-Wolf/Walla:** Kath Soucie; **Jazz Fenton/Nerd Girl/Walla:** Colleen O'Shaughnessey; **Tucker Foley:** Rickey D'Shon Collins; **Samantha "Sam" Manson/Police Dispatcher:** Grey DeLisle; **Vice-Principal Lancer:** Ron Perlman; **Dash Baxter/Jeremy/Operative O:** S. Scott Bullock; **Paulina/Stuffed Animal #2:** Maria Canals; **Qwan:** Dat Phan; **Operative K/Generic TV Reporter/Scarlet Samarai/Lance Thunder/Nerds:** Dee Bradley Baker; **Lydia/Walla:** Tara Strong; **Maurice Foley/Old Man/Nerd:** Phil LaMarr; **Freakshow:** Jon Cryer; **Qwan:** James Sie

### ◎ DANNY PHANTOM: "REIGN STORM"

In a race against time, after the town of Amity Park is sucked into the Ghost Zone, half-human and half-ghost teenage Danny Fenton, alias Danny Phantom, battles the sinister Ghost King to save his family and friends before it's too late in this first hour-long animated special based on the highly-rated Nickelodeon cartoon series. A *Nicktoons Productions/Billinfold Production. Color. One hour. Premiered on NICK: July 29, 2005. Rebroadcast on NICK: July 30, 2005; July 31, 2005; August 1, 2005; August 3, 2005; August 4, 2005; August 5, 2005; August 6, 2005; August 7, 2005; August 15, 2005; August 27, 2005; August 29, 2005; September 5, 2005; October 2, 2005; October 7, 2005; November 18, 2005; November 23, 2005; November 25, 2005; December 26, 2005; December 31, 2005; January 28, 2006; March 1, 2006; April 22, 2006; May 17, 2006; June 5, 2006; July 27, 2006; September 4, 2006; October 28, 2006; November 24, 2006; January 13, 2007.*

**Voices**

**Danny Fenton/Phantom:** David Kaufman; **Maddie Fenton, Danny's mom/Lunch Lady Ghost:** Kath Soucie; **Jack Fenton, Danny's dad/The Box Ghost:** Rob Paulsen; **Paulina:** Maria Canals; **Mr. Lancer:** Ron Perlman; **Tucker Foley:** Rickey D'Shon Collins; **Jazz Fenton:** Colleen O'Shaughnessey; **Skulker:** Kevin Michael Richardson; **Mikey/Nathan/Lance:** Dee Bradley Baker; **Kwan:** James Sie; **Ember/Tiffany Snow:** Tara Strong; **Klemper/Box Store Owner/Dash Baxter:** S. Scott Bullock; **Pam:** Laraine Newman; **Samantha "Sam" Manson:** Grey DeLisle; **Vlad Plasmius:** Martin Mull; **Valerie:** Cree Summer; **Damon:** Phil Morris; **Poindexter:** Peter MacNicol; **Pariah Dark:** Brian Cox; **Fright Knight:** Michael Dorn

### ◎ DANNY PHANTOM: "THE ULTIMATE ENEMY"

Time-traveling 10 years into the future, Danny comes to grips with the death of his family and friends and becomes the most powerful and evil ghost the world has ever known in this second hour-long special following 2005's first, "Reign Storm," to air in prime time on Nickelodeon, based on creator Butch Hartman's popular science-fiction fantasy cartoon series. A *Nicktoon Productions/Billinfold Production. Color. One hour. Premiered on NICK: September 16, 2005. Rebroadcast on NICK: September 17, 2005; September 18, 2005; September 20, 2005; September 23, 2005; October 2, 2005; November 11, 2005; November 26, 2005; December 30, 2005; January 22, 2006; February 8, 2006; March 22, 2006; May 6, 2006; May 29, 2006; June 3, 2006; July 15, 2006; August 2, 2006;*

August 29, 2006; October 22, 2006; December 3, 2006; March 24, 2007.

**Voices**

**Danny Fenton/Danny Phantom:** David Kaufman; **Jack Fenton/The Box Ghost:** Rob Paulsen; **Maddie Fenton:** Kath Soucie; **Jazz Fenton:** Colleen O'Shaughnessey; **Tucker Foley:** Rickey D'Shon Collins; **Samantha "Sam" Manson:** Grey DeLisle; **Vice-Principal Lancer:** Ron Perlman; **Dash Baxter:** Scott Bullock; **Paulina:** Maria Canals; **Qwan:** Dat Phan; **Irving/Observant #1/Guy:** Dee Bradley Baker; **Clockwork:** David Carradine; **Fright Knight:** Michael Dorn; **Daman/Observant #2:** Phil Morris; **Vlad Masters:** Martin Mull; **Skulker:** Kevin Michael Richardson; **Dark Danny:** Eric Roberts; **Ember–Nasty Burger Employee:** Tara Strong; **Valerie Grey:** Cree Summer

### ◎ DANNY PHANTOM: "URBAN JUNGLE"

When an evil plant eco-ghost Undergrowth tries turning Amity Park into a literal urban jungle, half-phantom boy Danny masters and unleashes his newfound freezing power to chill the town and save it from a villainous takeover by his latest nemesis in this half-hour special—also released as new Game Boy Advance and Nintendo DS video games—from *Danny Phantom* series creator Butch Hartman for Nickelodeon. A *Nicktoons Productions/Billinfold Production. Color. Half-hour. Premiered on NICK: October 9, 2006. Rebroadcast on NICK: October 11, 2006; October 20, 2006; November 18, 2006; December 10, 2006; January 2, 2007; January 23, 2007; February 12, 2007; March 7, 2007.*

**Voices**

**Danny Fenton/Danny Phantom:** David Kaufman; **Jack Fenton/The Box Ghost:** Rob Paulsen; **Maddie Fenton:** Kath Soucie; **Jazz Fenton:** Colleen O'Shaughnessey; **Tucker Foley:** Rickey D'Shon Collins; **Samantha "Sam" Manson:** Grey DeLisle; **Vice-Principal Lancer:** Ron Perlman; **Dash Baxter.** Scott Bullock; **Paulina:** Maria Canals; **Qwan:** Dat Phan

### ◎ DARIA IN IS IT COLLEGE YET?

Pressure mounts and frustrations flare as Daria, Tom, Jane and their fellow Lawndale High seniors face the prospect of graduating and applying for college in this 90-minute special television movie finale of MTV's *Daria* cartoon series, also titled *Is It College Yet?* An *MTV Animation/Plus One Animation Production in association with Music Television and Sony Pictures Entertainment. Color. Ninety minutes. Premiered on MTV: January 21, 2002.*

**Voices**

**Daria Morgendorffer:** Tracy Grandstaff; **Janet Brach/Tiffany:** Ashley Albert; **Charles "Upchuck" Ruttheimer III:** Geoffrey Arend; **Stacy Rowe:** Sarah Drew; **Trent Lane:** Alvaro J. Gonzalez; **Thomas "Tom" Sloane, Daria's Boyfriend:** Russell Hankin; **Lindy:** Jessica Hardin; **Jane Lane/Helen Barksdale Morgendorffer/ Quinn Morgendorffer:** Wendy Hoopes; **Joey:** Steven Huppert; **Jodie Abigail Landon:** Jessica Cyndee Jackson; **Angela Li:** Nora Laudani; **Andrea/Sandi Griffin/Brittany Taylor:** Janie Mertz; **Jeffy:** Tim Novikoff; **Jake:** Julian Rebolledo; **Jesse:** Willy Schwenz; **Mr. Anthony DeMartino/Mr. Timothy O'Neill/Kevin Thompson/Jamie White:** Marc Thompson; **Mack:** Amir Williams; **Professor Bill Woods:** H.R. Bridges; **Lisa Goldwyn:** Becca Lish; **Lisa:** Stefanie Layne; **Shauna:** Jennifer Visalli

### ◎ DARK WATER: "BETRAYAL"

After Bloth captures Ren and Niddler, Ren comes face-to-face with one of his father's captains in this half-hour fantasy/adventure special, part of the five-part miniseries that debuted on FOX.

*A Hanna-Barbera Production in association with Fils-Cartoons, Inc. and Tama Production Co. Color. Half-hour. Premiered on FOX: February 28, 1991.*

**Voices**
**Konk:** Tim Curry; **Mantus:** Peter Cullen; **Tula:** Jodi Benson; **Nidder:** Roddy McDowall; **Ren:** George Newbern; **Bloth:** Brock Peters; **Lugg Brother #1:** Earl Boen; **Lugg Brother #2:** Frank Welker

### ◉ DARK WATER: "BREAKUP"

Tracking down Konk on the island of Pandwa, Ren and his gang find out firsthand about Niddler's troubled past. This third half-hour special was one of a five-part miniseries to premiere on FOX. *A Hanna-Barbera Production in association with Fils-Cartoons, Inc. and Tama Production Co. Color. Half-hour. Premiered on FOX: February 27, 1991.*

**Voices**
**Konk:** Tim Curry; **Mantus:** Peter Cullen; **Tula:** Jodi Benson; **Nidder:** Roddy McDowall; **Ren:** George Newbern; **Bloth:** Brock Peters; **Queen:** Jessica Walter; **Lugg Brother #1:** Earl Boen; **Lugg Brother #2:** Frank Welker

### ◉ DARK WATER: "DISHONOR"

After eluding Bloth, Ren and his able crew are abducted by the Atari warriors in his second half-hour special in the five-part miniseries, originally produced for FOX. *A Hanna-Barbera Production in association with Fils-Cartoons, Inc. and Tama Production Co. Color. Half-hour. Premiered on FOX: February 26, 1991.*

**Voices**
**Konk:** Tim Curry; **Mantus:** Peter Cullen; **Tula:** Jodi Benson; **Nidder:** Roddy McDowall; **Ren:** George Newbern; **Bloth:** Brock Peters; **Lugg Brother #1:** Earl Boen; **Lugg Brother #2:** Frank Welker

### ◉ DARK WATER: "THE QUEST"

After rescuing his father at sea, Ren embarks on a noble journey to uncover the Thirteen Treasures of the Rule in this first installment of a five-part sword-and-sorcery miniseries produced by Hanna-Barbera Productions, which bowed Saturday mornings on FOX in 1991. That September, ABC picked up the series for a full season, renaming it *Pirates of Dark Water*. Actor Roddy McDowall provided the voice of Niddler in the original miniseries. *A Hanna-Barbera Production in association with Fils-Cartoons, Inc. and Tama Production Co. Color. Half-hour. Premiered on FOX: February 25, 1991.*

**Voices**
**Konk:** Tim Curry; **Mantus:** Peter Cullen; **Tula:** Jodi Benson; **Nidder:** Roddy McDowall; **Ren:** George Newbern; **Bloth:** Brock Peters

### ◉ DARK WATER: "VICTORY"

Ren and his crew obtain the coveted First Treasure from Bloth while trying to escape in this fifth and final installment of the Saturday-morning high adventure cartoon miniseries that debuted on FOX. *A Hanna-Barbera Production in association with Fils-Cartoons, Inc. and Tama Production Co. Color. Half-hour. Premiered on FOX: March 1, 1991.*

**Voices**
**Konk:** Tim Curry; **Mantus:** Peter Cullen; **Tula:** Jodi Benson; **Nidder:** Roddy McDowall; **Ren:** George Newbern; **Bloth:** Brock Peters

### ◉ DARKWING DUCK: IT'S A WONDERFUL LEAF

Bushroot plots to ruin Christmas by making Christmas trees in order to steal the presents in this half-hour holiday special, based on the popular *Disney Afternoon* syndicated series. *A Walt Disney Television Animation Production. Color. Half-hour. Premiered: December 23, 1991. Syndicated.*

**Voices**
**Darkwing Duck:** Jim Cummings; **Gosalyn Mallard:** Christine Cavanaugh; **Launchpad McQuack:** Terry McGovern; **Bushroot:** Tino Insana

### ◉ THE DARKWING DUCK PREMIERE/BACK TO SCHOOL WITH THE MICKEY MOUSE CLUB

The debut of Disney's newest cartoon series, *Darkwing Duck*, and the return of the Disney Channel's *The Mickey Mouse Club* are celebrated in this two-hour, first-run syndicated special featuring the episode "Darkly Dawns the Duck," which tells the origin of Darkwing Duck, and several segments from a new season of *The Mickey Mouse Club*. *A Walt Disney Television Animation Production. Color. Two hours. Premiered: September 8, 1991. Syndicated.*

**Cast (live action)**
Fred Newman, Terri Misner, Josh Ackerman, Lindsey Alley, Rhona Bennett, Nita Booth, Mylin Brooks, Blaine Carson, JC Chasez, Tasha Danner, Dale Godboldo, Tony Lucca, Ricky Lunda, Jennifer McGill, Terra McNair, Ilana Miller, Jason Minor, Matt Morris, Kevin Osgood, Keri Russell, Marc Worden. **The Party:** Albert Fields, Tiffini Hale, Chase Hampton, Deedee Magno, Damon Pampolina

**Voices**
**Darkwing Duck:** Jim Cummings; **Gosalyn Mallard:** Christine Cavanaugh; **Launchpad McQuack:** Terry McGovern; **Taurus Bulba:** Tim Curry; **Hammerhead Hannigan:** Laurie Faso; **Huge Jerk:** Hal Rayle; **Clovis/Mrs. Cavanaugh:** Marcia Wallace

### ◉ DAVEY AND GOLIATH'S SNOWBOARD CHRISTMAS

Davey and Goliath embark on an exciting new adventure by honing their snowboarding skills on the slippery slopes and learning some dazzling maneuvers, plus some valuable lessons about the true meaning of Christmas and respecting others who are different, in this case two new friends of different faiths. The hour-long special, which premiered on the Hallmark Channel, was the first new *Davey and Goliath* production in 30 years. The modern-day stop-motion animated program cost an estimated $1 million to produce. *A Premavision Production. Color. One hour. Premiered on HLMRK: December 19, 2004. Rebroadcast on HLMRK: December 26, 2004; December 18, 2005; December 17, 2006.*

**Voices**
**Davey:** Kerry O'Malley; **Sally/Yasmeen:** Tara Sands; **Other Voices:** Brad Abelle, Deb Rabbai, Lloyd Floyd, Gary Littman, Chris Phillips

### ◉ DAVID COPPERFIELD

The story of David Copperfield, one of Charles Dickens's most beloved creations, is revealed in this 90-minute cable-television special that takes viewers through every stage of his life and the many struggles he encounters along the way. *A Burbank Films Production. Color. Ninety minutes. Premiered on HBO: October 2, 1984.*

*Voices*

Ross Higgins, Phillip Hinton, Robyn Moore, Judy Nunn, Moya O'Sullivan, Robin Steward, John Stone

## DAVY CROCKETT ON THE MISSISSIPPI

American frontiersman Davy Crockett and his talking pet bear, Honeysuckle, are joined by an orphaned boy, Matt Henry, as they journey to meet the Indians on behalf of the U.S. president as part of a peacekeeping mission. *A Hanna-Barbera Production. Color. One hour. Premiered on CBS: November 20, 1976. Rebroadcast on CBS: October 22, 1977; November 2, 1980; November 26, 1982. Rebroadcast on CAR: October 8, 1995 (Mr. Spim's Cartoon Theatre).*

*Voices*

**Davy Crockett:** Ned Wilson; **Matt Henry:** Randy Gray; **Honeysuckle/Pete/The Settler:** Mike Bell; **Mike Fink/Flatboat Sailor:** Ron Feinberg; **Running Wolf/Jake:** Kip Niven; **Settler's Wife/Amanda/Susie:** Pat Parris; **Sloan/Andrew Jackson/Blacksmith:** John Stephenson

## DECK THE HALLS

It is nearly Christmas when two recently orphaned children have to choose with which of their relatives they will live—eccentric, stingy Aunt Edwina or kindly Uncle Robert—only to have surprises in store for them when they make their choices in this half-hour holiday special, produced for first-run syndication. *A Perennial Pictures Film Corporation Production. Color. Half-hour. Premiered: November 24, 1994. Syndicated.*

*Voices*

**Aunt Edwina:** Rachel Rutledge; **Uncle Robert/Baxter:** Jerry Reynolds; **Wadsworth:** Chris Cawthorne; **Andrew:** Peter Schmutte; **Allison:** Kimberly Ann Harris

*Edwina Benson puts the crowning touch on her Christmas tree as her nephew, niece and butler look on in Deck the Halls, a half-hour animated special from Perennial Pictures. © Perennial Pictures*

## DECK THE HALLS WITH WACKY WALLS

Six Wallwalkers (Wacky, Big Blue, Springette, Stickum, Crazylegs and Bouncing Baby Boo) are sent to Earth from their distant planet to find what Christmas is all about in this half-hour animated special based on the Wacky Wallwalker toys. *An NBC Entertainment Production in association with Buzzco Productions. Color. Half-hour. Premiered on NBC: December 11, 1983.*

*Voices*

**Wacky:** Daws Butler; **Big Blue:** Peter Cullen; **Springette:** Tress MacNeille; **Stickum:** Marvin Kaplan; **Crazylegs:** Howard Morris; **Bouncing Baby Boo:** Frank Welker; **Darryl:** Scott Menville

## DEFENDERS OF DYNATRON CITY

The master of evil, Dr. Mayhem, unleashes an army of Robot Drone Soldiers to claim Dynatron City as his own, but not before Monkey Kid uses his atomic-powered Proto-Cola syrup to mutate a bunch of youngsters—Jet Headstrong, Buzzsaw Girl, Ms. Megawatt—and their dog, Radium, to defend the city against Mayhem and his evil drones and save the day in this cartoon special produced by DIC Entertainment in association with Lucasfilms. The half-hour fantasy adventure bowed on the FOX Kids Network in February 1992, followed by a repeat performance that May and also via syndication in some markets throughout the year. *A DIC Entertainment/Lucasfilms Ltd. Production. Color. Half-hour. Premiered on FOX: February 22, 1992. Rebroadcast on FOX: May 16, 1992. Syndicated.*

*Voices*

**Mary Middlefield/Ms. Megwatt:** Whoopi Goldberg; **Brett Headlong:** Pat Fraley; **Dr. Mayhem:** Charlie Adler; **Atom Ed:** Tim Curry; **Kid Monkey:** David Coburn; **Buzzsaw Girl:** Candi Milo

## DENNIS THE MENACE: CRUISE CONTROL

Mr. Wilson's plan to get far away from his menacing neighbor, Dennis, by going on a long-planned cruise goes amuck when Dennis and his friends and family tag along and Dennis befriends a seven-year-old princess whom he and his friends have to save, ruining Mr. Wilson's vacation in the process, in this fourth of 13 animated made-for-TV movies aired on Nickelodeon's *DIC Incredible Movie Toons* series. *A DIC Entertainment Production. Color. Ninety minutes. Premiered on NICK: October 27, 2002.*

*Voices*

**Mr. Wilson:** Tom Arnold; **Dennis:** Peter Cronkite; **Kraigor:** Jim Byrnes; **Hector:** Gary Chalk; **Margaret/Joey:** Jeannie Elias; **Henry Mitchell, Dennis's father:** Maurice LaMarche; **Martha Wilson/Alice Mitchell, Dennis's mother:** Marilyn Lightstone; **Jinks:** Richard Newman; **Liana:** Tabitha St. Germain; **Ruff:** Lee Tockar

## DENNIS THE MENACE: MAYDAY FOR MOTHER

In his first prime-time special, neighborhood terror Dennis the Menace encounters a variety of problems in attempting to create a special Mother's Day gift for his mother, Alice Mitchell. The special was based on an original story by creator Hank Ketcham. *A DePatie-Freleng Enterprises Production in association with Mirisch Films. Color. Half-hour. Premiered on NBC: May 8, 1981. Rebroadcast on NBC: May 6, 1983.*

*Voices*

**Dennis Mitchell:** Joey Nagy; **Alice Mitchell:** Kathy Garver; **Henry Mitchell:** Bob Holt; **George Wilson:** Larry D. Mann; **Martha Wilson:** Elizabeth Kerr; **Margaret:** Nicole Eggert

## ◎ THE DEVIL AND DANIEL MOUSE

Jan and Daniel Mouse, recently unemployed folk singers, try making a fresh start with their careers, only for Jan to sign a contract with B.L. Zebub, the devil in disguise, to sell her soul to become a rock star legend. *A Nelvana Limited Production in association with the CBC. Color. Half-hour. Premiered: October 22, 1978. Syndicated.*

*Voices*

**Daniel Mouse:** Jim Henshaw, John Sebastian (singing); **Jan:** Annabelle Kershaw, Laurel Runn (singing); **B.L. Zebub, the devil:** Chris Wiggins; **Weez Weasel/Pawnbroker:** Martin Lavut; **Rock Emcee:** John Sebastian; **Interviewer:** Dianne Lawrence

## ◎ DEXTER'S LABORATORY: "EGO TRIP"

When Dexter is attacked by a group of superevil robots who want to destroy him for saving the future, he travels back in time in his famous time machine to see how he changed the outcome in this half-hour animated special based on the four-time Emmy Award–nominated Cartoon Network series. In 2000, Christine Cavanaugh, the voice of Dexter, won an Annie Award for outstanding individual achievement for voice acting by a female performer in an animated television production. *A Hanna-Barbera Productions/Rough Draft Studios Production. Color. One hour. Premiered on CAR: December 10, 1999.*

*Voices*

**Dexter:** Christine Cavanaugh; **Dee Dee:** Kathryn Cressida; **Dexter's Mom/The Computer:** Kath Soucie; **Mandark:** Eddie Deezen; **Dad:** Jeff Bennett

## ◎ DIG

Explaining the wonders of Earth, Adam and his dog, Bones, explore the geological structure of the planet during a fascinating journey in which they meet strange characters and encounter various phenomena. The special aired in place of CBS's *The Monkees*, which was in reruns on Saturday mornings. *A Hubley Studios Production. Color. Half-hour. Premiered on CBS April 8, 1972. Rebroadcast on CBS: May 5, 1973.*

*Voices*

**Adam:** Ray Hubley; **Mother:** Maureen Stapleton; **Rocco:** Jack Warden; **Fossil Pillar:** Morris Carnovsky; **First Rock:** Phil Leeds; **Vocalists:** Harry "Sweets" Edison, Don Elliott, Ruth Price

## ◎ DINOSAUR ISLAND

Four teens picked to star in a *Survivor*-type television series pilot find that the island on which they end up has dinosaurs and cavemen roaming a South American jungle and the teens must work together to make it out alive. This 90-minute animated made-for-TV movie was the sixth installment of Nickelodeon's *DIC Incredible Movie Toons* series. *A DIC Entertainment Production. Color. Ninety minutes. Premiered on NICK: November 10, 2002.*

*Voices*

**Alex:** Phillip Chen; **Jackie Rodriguez:** Anadella Lamas; **Stu Ellison:** Paul Sosso; **Leo Bryant:** Ronelle Tipler; **Margaret Tim:** Hillary Williams; **Professor:** John Lee; **Copter Pilot:** Nils Haaland; **Pilot:** Jerry Longe; **Cameraman:** D. Kevin Williams; **Alex's Father:** Don Nyugen; **Alex's Mother:** Loreen Pickle; **Leo's Mom:** Lynette Moore; **Proud Mother:** Kim Carlson; **Narrator:** Cork Ramer

## ◎ A DISNEY CHANNEL CHRISTMAS

Jiminy Cricket hosts (and also sings a special version of "When You Wish Upon a Star") this holiday look at the Christmas season featuring a medley of clips from numerous Christmas-themed car-

*Hot-tempered high-tech genius Dexter gets a closer view during an experiment in his enormous home laboratory. © Hanna-Barbera Cartoons. All rights reserved.*

toons, including "A Night Before Christmas," "Santa's Workshop" and "Pluto's Christmas Tree," plus a look at "Mickey's Christmas Carol" in this Disney Channel original production. *A Film Landa Inc. Production for The Disney Channel. Color. Ninety minutes. Premiered on DIS: December 3, 1983.*

## ◎ A DISNEY CHRISTMAS GIFT

Favorite scenes from Walt Disney Studios' classic animated features, including *Bambi*, *Peter Pan*, *The Three Caballeros* and *Cinderella* and a few memorable cartoon shorts, namely "The Clock Watcher" starring Donald Duck, are tied together in this prime-time holiday special celebrating Christmases past. *A Walt Disney Television Production. Color. One hour. Premiered on CBS: December 20, 1983.*

*Voices*

**Peter Pan:** Bobby Driscoll; **Fairy Godmother:** Verna Felton; **Cinderella:** Ilene Woods

## ◎ A DISNEY HALLOWEEN

Disney's treatment of witches, ghosts and goblins from the studio's classic films and cartoons make up this Disney Channel original production. It includes Mickey, Donald and Goofy as ghost hunters, the frenzied dance demons from the classic animated feature *Fantasia* (1940) and Donald Duck in the 1952 cartoon short, "Trick Or Treat." *A Film Landa Inc. Production for The Disney Channel. Color. Ninety minutes. Premiered on DIS: October 1, 1983.*

## ◎ DISNEY'S ALL-STAR MOTHER'S DAY ALBUM

The subject of motherhood is celebrated in this compilation special featuring clips from assorted Disney cartoons including the memorable feature film *Peter Pan* (1953), and many classic cartoon shorts, among them "Mickey and the Seal" (1948), "Pluto's Fledgling" (1948) and "Donald's Nephews" (1938). The special closes with a segment featuring the fairy godmother from *Cinderella* (1950) transforming a depressed girl into a fairy princess. *A Walt Disney Television Production. Color. One hour. Premiered on CBS: May 11, 1984.*

## ◎ DISNEY'S ALL-STAR VALENTINE PARTY

Popular Los Angeles radio disc jockey Rick Dees narrates this collection of scenes from classic Disney cartoons that depict love and friendship. Scenes were culled from "Mickey's Rival" (1936), "The Brave Tin Soldier" (1938), "Pluto's Heart Throb" (1949)

and others. *A Walt Disney Television Production. Color. One hour. Premiered on CBS: February 14, 1984.*

**Voices**
**Narrator:** Rick Dees

## ◎ DISNEY'S DTV DOGGONE HITS
(See DISNEY'S DTV DOGGONE VALENTINE.)

## ◎ DISNEY'S DTV DOGGONE VALENTINE
Hosted by Mickey Mouse, Minnie Mouse, Professor Ludwig von Drake and others, this one-hour special salutes man's best friend with a series of entertaining clips of favorite dog scenes and characters, culled from Disney full-length features and cartoon shorts, set to a rock beat and featuring the music of Kenny Rogers, Huey Lewis and Deniece Williams. *An Andrew Solt Production in association Walt Disney Television. Color. One hour. Premiered on NBC: February 13, 1987. Rebroadcast on NBC: February 19, 1988 (as Disney's DTV Doggone Hits). Rebroadcast on DIS: February 4, 1992; February 2, 1994.*

**Voices**
**Mickey Mouse:** Wayne Allwine; **Minnie Mouse/Dalamation Puppy:** Russi Taylor; **Professor Ludwig von Drake:** Albert Ash; **Jiminy Cricket:** Eddie Carroll; **Goofy:** Bill Farmer; **Pongo:** Will Ryan; **Dalamation Puppies:** Lisa St. James; **Radio Announcer:** Maurice LaMarche; **Announ-cer:** J.J. Jackson

## ◎ DISNEY'S DTV MONSTER HITS
In the style of past "DTV" specials, Disney salutes Halloween in this slightly scary collection of cartoon clips featuring scenes from classic Disney cartoons set to music. Includes "Lonesome Ghosts" (1937), starring Mickey Mouse, Donald Duck and Goofy, with Ray Parker's "Ghostbusters" theme, "Bad Moon Rising" by Creedence Clearwater Revival and Bobby "Boris" Pickett's classic Halloween romp, "Monster Mash." Also included is a special montage salute to Disney's villains set to the Eurythmics' hit song "Sweet Dreams." *A Walt Disney Television Production. Color. Half-hour. Premiered on NBC: October 30, 1987. Rebroadcast on DIS.*

## ◎ DISNEY'S DTV ROMANCIN'
(See DISNEY'S DTV VALENTINE.)

## ◎ DISNEY'S DTV VALENTINE
Clips from Disney cartoons timed to rock-and-roll music highlight this Valentine's Day special hosted by Mickey Mouse, Donald Duck, Jiminy Cricket and Professor Ludwig von Drake. *An Andrew Solt Production in association with Walt Disney Television. Color. One hour. Premiered on NBC: February 14, 1986. Rebroadcast on NBC: September 7, 1986 (as Disney's DTV Romancin').*

**Voices**
**Mickey Mouse:** Les Perkins; **Donald Duck:** Tony Anselmo; **Jiminy Cricket:** Eddie Carroll; **Professor Ludwig von Drake:** Paul Frees; **Gruffi Gummi:** Corey Burton; **Goofy/Pongo:** Will Ryan; **Chip/Dale/Female Voice:** Judith Searle; **Dalmatian Puppies:** Lisa St. James; **Sleeping Beauty:** Mary Costa; **Princess Aura:** Mary Costa; **Prince Phillip:** Bill Shirley; **Announcer:** Paul Frees

## ◎ DISNEY'S FLUPPY DOGS
Off course from their real destination, several out-of-this-universe dogs (Stanley, Ozzie, Tippi, Bink and Dink), who possess magical powers, arrive on Earth, where they are forced to act like normal dogs when their real presence sends panic into local citizens. Their teenage friends, Jaimie and Claire, aid their escape in order for them to return home through the interdimensional doorway from

which they came. *A Walt Disney Television Production in association with TMS Entertainment. Color. One hour. Premiered on ABC: November 27, 1986. Rebroadcast on ABC: August 30, 1987 (as The Sunday Disney Movie).*

**Voices**
**Jaimie Bingham:** Carl Stevens; **Bink/Tippi:** Susan Blu; **Stanley:** Marshall Efron; **Mrs. Bingham:** Cloyce Morrow; **Ozzie:** Lorenzo Music; **Claire:** Jessica Pennington; **Wagstaff:** Michael Rye; **Haimish/Attendant/Dink:** Hal Smith

## ◎ DISNEY'S GOOF TROOP
Disney's syndicated series *Goof Troop* premiered as this two-hour special season opener in which Goofy returns to his hometown of Spoonerville with his teenage son Max to experience a whole new series of adventures as a 1990s-style dad. Also featured: a new music video, "Gotta Be Gettin' Goofy" by rap artist The CEO and "The Goofy Success Story," a cartoon short chronicling Goofy's remarkable career. *A Walt Disney Television Animation Production. Color. Two hours. Premiered: September 5, 1992.*

## ◎ DISNEY'S HALLOWEEN TREAT
Halloween is the theme of this Disney prime-time special, featuring witches, goblins and ghouls and classic Disney characters in a collection of excerpts from favorite screen moments of the past. *A Walt Disney Television Production. Color. One hour. Premiered on CBS: October 30, 1982. Rebroadcast on NBC: October 29, 1983. Rebroadcast on DIS: October 18, 1992.*

**Voices**
**Peter Pan:** Bobby Driscoll; **Si/Am (Lady and the Tramp):** Peggy Lee

## ◎ DISNEY'S KIM POSSIBLE: A SITCH IN TIME
Kim faces perhaps her fiercest challenge as arch-enemies Dr. Drakken, Monkey Fist and Duff Killigan deploy an ancient time-travel device to not only rule the world but also to influence Kim's past, present and future, including her partnership with Ron as they begin a new school year and find that Ron's family is relocating to Norway, in this first animated made-for-TV movie, based on the popular Disney Channel cartoon series. Premiering in prime time at 8:00 P.M. (ET) three days after Thanksgiving in November 2003, the hour-long adventure, which enjoyed two encore performances on the same night as its debut, has re-aired numerous times on the Disney Channel. In April 2005, a second hour-long special, *Disney's Kim Possible: So the Drama*, also bowed on the Disney Channel. *A Disney Television Animation/Starburst Animation Co. Ltd. Production. Color. One hour. Premiered on DIS: November 28, 2003. Rebroadcast on DIS: November 28, 2003; November 30, 2003; December 11, 2003; June 21, 2004; July 25, 2004; August 19, 2004; September 24, 2004; April 1, 2005; May 3, 2005; June 24, 2005; August 21, 2005; August 26, 2005; November 24, 2005; December 8, 2005; January 15, 2006; April 19, 2006; June 17, 2006; August 14, 2006; November 17, 2006; January 22, 2007; February 11, 2007.*

**Voices**
**Kimberly Ann "Kim" Possible:** Christy Carlson Romano; **Ron Stoppable:** Will Friedle; **Rufus:** Nancy Cartwright; **Wade:** Tahj Mowry; **Dr. Possible, Kim's dad:** Gary Cole; **Dr. Possible, Kim's mom:** Jean Smart; **Dr. Drakken:** John DiMaggio; **Rufus 3000:** Michael Dorn; **Future Wade:** Michael Clarke Duncan; **Pre-school Ron Stoppable:** Harrison Fahn; **Pre-school Kim Possible:** Dakota Fanning; **Jim and Tim Possible:** Shaun Fleming; **Future Jim and Tim Possible:** Freddie Prinze Jr.; **Future Monique:** Vivica A. Fox;

**Duff Killagan:** Brian George; **McHenry:** Richard Gilliland; **Mr. Stoppable:** Elliott Gould; **Mrs. Stoppable:** Andrea Martin; **Monkey Fist/Real Estate Agent:** Tom Kane; **Monique:** Raven; **Future Bonnie:** Kelly Ripa; **Pre-school Teacher/Mrs. Mahoney:** Kath Soucie; **Bonnie Rockwaller:** Kirsten Storms; **Shego:** Nicole Sullivan

## ◎ DISNEY'S KIM POSSIBLE: SO THE DRAMA

Evil Dr. Drakken's plan to uncover Kim Possible's weakness—a handsome new Middleton High School student named Eric, who spurs Ron to demonstrate his feelings for Kim, which turn into something more than friendship—runs amuck in this second animated movie based on Disney's *Kim Possible* series. The first was 2003's ratings hit, *A Sitch in Time.* Mixing traditional animation and computer-generated imagery, posting a 3.6 Nielsen rating with approximately 3.1 million viewers tuning in for its premiere, the 60-minute adventure, mixing traditional animation and computer-generated imagery, was cable television's top-rated program the week it debuted on the Disney Channel. The production also featured Christy Carlson Romano's hit single, "Could It Be." *A Disney Television/Rough Draft Studios Co. Ltd. Production. Color. One hour. Premiered on DIS: April 8, 2005. Rebroadcast on DIS: April 9, 2005; April 10, 2005; July 8, 2005; August 18, 2005; August 20, 2005; September 28, 2005; November 3, 2005; November 21, 2005; November 24, 2005; December 18, 2005; March 13, 2006; April 29, 2006; July 30, 2006; September 5, 2006; September 17, 2006; November 23, 2006; February 9, 2007; February 10, 2007.*

### Voices
**Kimberly Ann "Kim" Possible:** Christy Carlson Romano; **Ron Stoppable:** Will Friedle; **Rufus:** Nancy Cartwright; **Wade:** Tahj Mowry; **Dr. Possible, Kim's dad:** Gary Cole; **Dr. Possible, Kim's mom:** Jean Smart; **Tim Possible/Jim Possible:** Shaun Fleming; **Lars:** Diedrich Bader; **Ned:** Eddie Deezen; **Dr. Drakken:** John DiMaggio; **Nakasumi:** Clyde Kusatu; **"Big Daddy" Brotherson:** Maurice LaMarche; **Monique:** Raven; **Sumo Ninja/Dr. Gooberman:** Kevin Michael Richardson; **Cowboy Gambler:** Stephen Root; **Bonnie Rockwaller:** Kirsten Storms; **Brick Flagg:** Rider Strong; **Shego:** Nicole Sullivan; **Yoshiko:** Lauren Tom; **Eric:** Ricky Ullman; **Reporter:** April Winchell; **Other Voices:** Phil LaMarr

## ◎ DISNEY'S ROOTIN' TOOTIN' ROUNDUP

Animated host Saddlesore Sam introduces this showcase of classic Disney cartoons about the Wild West including "The Legend of Coyote Rock," "Donald's Gold Mine," "Little Hiawatha" and "The Lone Chipmunks," which are presented in this Disney Channel original production. *A Robert Heath Inc. Production for The Disney Channel. Color. Ninety minutes. Premiered on DIS: 1990.*

## ◎ DISNEY'S SALUTE TO MOM

Memorable clips from Disney full-length features and cartoon shorts—including *Bambi, Lady and the Tramp, Dumbo* and *One Hundred and One Dalmatians*—are featured in this hour-long clip fest, originally shown on the Disney Channel in 1994 under the title *A Tribute to Mom* (a 90-minute version), which celebrated mothers of all ages. *A Film Landa Inc. Production for The Disney Channel. Color. One hour. Premiered on DIS: May 14, 1955.*

## ◎ DISNEY'S TALE SPIN PLUNDER & LIGHTNING

Cargo pilot Baloo is aided by a young thief named Kit Cloudkicker (who hides in Baloo's plane) in foiling the evil Don Karnage, who plots to steal a precious jewel in this two-hour pilot for the Disney weekday syndicated series *Tale Spin. A Walt Disney Television Animation Production. Color. Two hours. Premiered: September 7, 1990. Syndicated.*

### Voices
**Baloo:** Ed Gilbert; **Don Karnage/Louie:** Jim Cummings; **Kit Cloudkicker:** R.J. Williams; **Rebecca Cunningham:** Sally Struthers; **Molly Cunningham:** Janna Michaels; **Shere Khan:** Tony Jay; **Dumptruck:** Chuck McCann; **Mad Dog:** Charlie Adler; **Wildcat:** Pat Fraley

## ◎ DISNEY'S THE LITTLE MERMAID: "A WHALE OF A TALE"

Beautiful young mermaid Ariel tries to prevent King Triton from finding about her pet killer whale, whom he feels would be better off in the wild, in this half-hour "preview" special to the Saturday-morning series that aired on CBS. *A Walt Disney Television Animation Production. Color. Half-hour. Premiered on CBS: September 11, 1992. Rebroadcast on CBS: September 10, 1993.*

### Voices
**Ariel:** Jodi Benson; **Sebastian:** Samuel E. Wright; **Flounder:** Edan Gross; **King Triton:** Kenneth Mars

## ◎ DR. SEUSS' HALLOWEEN IS GRINCH NIGHT

The people of Whoville are plagued by a "sour-sweet wind," suggesting only one thing—the nasty Grinch, who dwells atop dreadful Mt. Crumpit, cannot be far away. A young lad, Ukariah, bravely faces the evil Grinch in order to save his people. Joining the Grinch in his acts of evildoing: his dog, Max. Hans Conried, effective in earlier specials, returns as the program's narrator. *A Dr. Seuss and A.S. Giesel Production in association with DePatie-Freleng Enterprises. Color. Premiered on ABC: October 29, 1977. Rebroadcast on ABC: October 26, 1978; October 28, 1979; October 30, 1980. Rebroadcast on DIS: October 13, 1991; October 17, 1992. Rebroadcast on CAR: November 1, 1997.*

### Voices
**Grinch:** Hans Conried; **Grandpa Joseph:** Hal Smith; **Grandma Mariah:** Irene Tedrow; **Ukariah:** Gary Shapiro

## ◎ DR. SEUSS' HORTON GEARS A WHO!

Hearing a small voice—"as if some tiny person were calling for help"—Horton the Elephant discovers microscopic creatures floating aboard a speck of dust, headed by the minuscule Dr. Whoovy, who is trying to convince his followers there is another world outside theirs. For "pretending" to talk to his unseen dust friends, Horton is finally seized by his jungle companions, but all comes to a happy ending as Whoovy in turn hears a voice from an even smaller fleck of dust. Based on the Dr. Seuss children's fable of the same name, the program played up the theme: "A person's a person no matter how small." *A Chuck Jones Enterprises Production in association with The Cat in the Hat Productions and MGM-TV. Color. Half-hour. Premiered on CBS: March 19, 1970. Rebroadcast on CBS: September 19, 1971; July 31, 1972; April 20, 1973; February 4, 1974; March 24, 1975; March 19, 1976; May 13, 1977; August 4, 1978. Rebroadcast on CAR: June 3, 1994 (Turner Family Showcase); August 14, 1995; November 29, 1998.*

### Voices
**Narrator:** Hans Conried

## ◎ DR. SEUSS' HOW THE GRINCH STOLE CHRISTMAS

Perennial favorite based on the popular Dr. Seuss fable about old meanie Grinch almost ruining Christmas for the townspeople of the little village of Whoville because either "his heart was two sizes small or he wore tight shoes." CBS reportedly spent $350,000 for this animated special, originally sponsored by the Foundation for Commercial Banks. The program preempted the network's *Lassie* series, airing in its time slot. After airing on CBS through December 1987, the holiday classic was replayed on Cartoon Network, TBS and TNT. In 2004, the special aired for the first time on the WB Television Network, and, two years later, on ABC. *A Chuck Jones Enterprises Production in association with The Cat in the Hat Productions and MGM-TV. Color. Half-hour. Premiered on CBS: December 18, 1966. Rebroadcast on CBS: December 17, 1967; December 22, 1968; December 21, 1969; December 2, 1970; December 7, 1971; December 4, 1972; December 10, 1973; December 13, 1974; December 12, 1975; December 18, 1976; December 10, 1977; December 16, 1978; December 19, 1979; November 28, 1980; December 16, 1981; December 18, 1982; December 12, 1983; December 5, 1984; December 7, 1985; December 17, 1986; December 11, 1987. Rebroadcast on TNT: December 6, 1990; December 5, 1991 (opposite Dr. Seuss' The Butter Battle Book); December 1, 1992. Rebroadcast on TBS: December 13, 1992; November 28, 1993. Rebroadcast on TNT: November 29, 1993. Rebroadcast on TBS: December 5, 1993. Rebroadcast on CAR: November 25, 1995; December 4, 1996. Rebroadcast on TNT: December 14, 1996. Rebroadcast on TBS: December 17, 1995; December 6, 1996. Rebroadcast on CAR: December 24, 1997; December 22, 1998; December 21, 1999; December 25, 2000; December 23, 2001; December 24, 2002; December 6, 2003; December 15, 2003; December 21, 2003; December 24, 2004; December 25, 2003; December 3, 2004; December 13, 2004; December 18, 2004; December 23, 2004; December 24, 2004; December 25, 2004; December 12, 2005; December 16, 2005; December 19, 2005; December 21, 2005; December 22, 2005; December 24, 2005; December 25, 2005; December 6, 2006; December 15, 2006; December 21, 2006; December 24, 2006; December 25, 2006. Rebroadcast on WB: December 10, 2004. Rebroadcast on ABC: December 11, 2006.*

**Voices**
**Grinch:** Thurl Ravenscroft (singing); **Cindy Lou:** June Foray; **Narrator:** Boris Karloff

### ◎ DR. SEUSS ON THE LOOSE

Dr. Seuss returns in this animated trilogy based on three of his classic fables—*The Sneetches*, featuring ostrichlike creatures who learn to treat each other as equals; *Green Eggs and Ham*, showing the silliness of prejudging; and *The Zax*, dealing with the subject of stubborness—which Seuss (Ted Geisel) coproduced. *A DePatie-Freleng Enterprises Production in association with CBS. Color. Half-hour. Premiered on CBS: October 15, 1973. Rebroadcast on CBS: October 28, 1974; November 21, 1975; March 9, 1976; July 12, 1979. Rebroadcast on ABC FAM: December 21, 2006.*

**Voices**
**The Cat in the Hat (host):** Allan Sherman; **Zax (narrator):** Hans Conried; **Joey/Sam-I-Am:** Paul Winchell; **Zax/Sylvester McMonkey McBeam:** Bob Holt

### ◎ DR. SEUSS' PONTOFFEL POCK, WHERE ARE YOU?

Misfit Pontoffel Pock has blown his opportunity at the pickle factory and gets a second chance when some good fairies provide him with a push-button piano that has the power to transport him anywhere. *A Dr. Seuss and A.S. Gelsel Production in association with DePatie-Freleng Enterprises. Color. Half-hour. Premiered on ABC: May 2, 1980. Rebroadcast on ABC: July 31, 1981. Rebroadcast on DIS: February 23, 1992. Rebroadcast on CAR: August 17, 1995.*

**Voices**
**Pontoffel Pock:** Wayne Morton; **Neepha Pheepha:** Sue Allen; **McGillicuddy:** Hal Smith

### ◎ DR. SEUSS' THE BUTTER BATTLE BOOK

In the first new Dr. Seuss special in seven years, a musical adaptation of Dr. Seuss's parable about the arms race, the Yooks square off against the Zooks, separated by a Great Wall and by a philosophical disagreement over which side to butter their bread on. *A Bakshi Production in association with Ted S. Geisel. Color. Half-hour. Premiered on TNT: November 13, 1989. Rebroadcast on TNT: September 29, 1991. Rebroadcast on CAR: June 3, 1994: (Turner Family Showcase); March 5, 1995 (Mr. Spim's Cartoon Theatre); May 26, 1996 (Mr. Spim's Cartoon Theatre).*

**Voices**
**Narrator:** Charles Durning

### ◎ DR. SEUSS' THE CAT IN THE HAT

Two children who are bored by the prospects of staying home all day because of the rain are greeted by a surprise visitor, the Cat in the Hat, who turns the house upside down looking for his moss-covered three-handled gradunza. He virtually destroys the home in the process, but magically restores the structure to its former state before the kids' mother returns. *A DePatie-Freleng Enterprises Production. Color. Half-hour. Premiered on CBS: March 10, 1971. Rebroadcast on CBS: April 11, 1972; February 20, 1973; January 4, 1974; January 31, 1975; March 30, 1976; August 20, 1979; September 20, 1980; May 15, 1987; January 5, 1988. Rebroadcast on CAR: August 15, 1995; November 29, 1998. Rebroadcast on ABC FAM: December 21, 2006.*

**Voices**
**Cat in the Hat:** Allan Sherman; **Karlos K. Krinklebein:** Daws Butler; **Boy:** Tony Frazier; **Girl:** Pamelyn Ferdin; **Mother:** Gloria Camacho; **Thing 1:** Thurl Ravenscroft; **Thing 2:** Lewis Morford

### ◎ DR. SEUSS' THE GRINCH GRINCHES THE CAT IN THE HAT

Grouchy Grinch employs a variety of self-made contraptions to get even with the Cat in the Hat but instead is taught manners by the amiable cat. *A Dr. Seuss and A.S. Geisel Production in association with Marvel Productions. Color. Half-hour. Premiered on ABC:*

*Which side of the bread to butter becomes a source of disagreement for the Yooks and the Zooks in the animated parable* Dr. Seuss' The Butter Battle Book. *© Bakshi Productions*

*May 20, 1982. Rebroadcast on ABC: August 7, 1983. Rebroadcast on DIS: November 2, 1991; May 5, 1992.*

**Voices**
Mason Adams, Joe Eich, Bob Holt, Marilyn Jackson, Melissa Mackay, Frank Welker, Richard B. Williams

### ◎ DR. SEUSS' THE HOOBER-BLOOB HIGHWAY

Young humans are sent down an imaginary ribbon of light—known as the Hoober-Bloob Highway—to Earth by the chief dispatcher, Hoober-Bloob, who briefs them on the pros and cons of Earth-bound living. Dr. Seuss (Ted Geisel) wrote the special. *A De-Patie Freleng Enterprises Production. Color. Half-hour. Premiered on CBS: February 19, 1975. Rebroadcast on CBS: March 23, 1976; November 15, 1977; September 9, 1981. Rebroadcast on DIS: October 31, 1993. Rebroadcast on CAR: May 26, 1996 (Mr. Spim's Cartoon Theatre); November 29, 1998.*

**Voices**
Bob Holt, Hal Smith

### ◎ DR. SEUSS' THE LORAX

The Lorax, a spokesman for saving trees from the woodsman's axe, sets out to stop the evil Once-ler from destroying all the trees in the forest to help local industrialists prosper. Program originally aired in the time slot usually reserved for CBS's *Gunsmoke*. *A DePatie-Freleng Enterprises Production. Color. Half-hour. Premiered on CBS: February 14, 1972. Rebroadcast on CBS: March 28, 1973; March 25, 1974; July 19, 1977; August 4, 1978. Rebroadcast on DIS: October 26, 1993. Rebroadcast on CAR: August 16, 1995; May 26, 1996 (Mr. Spim's Cartoon Theatre); November 29, 1998.*

**Voices**
**Lorax/Once-ler:** Bob Holt; **Boy:** Harlen Carraher; **Other Voices:** Athena Lorde; **Narrator:** Eddie Albert

### ◎ DONALD'S 50TH BIRTHDAY

Donald Duck's illustrious career is recounted through clips from many of his cartoon and film appearances in this 90-minute special for the Disney Channel. *A Film Landa Inc. Production for the Disney Channel. Color. Ninety minutes. Premiered on DIS: 1984.*

### ◎ DONNER

Donner, one of Santa's other reindeer, helps save Christmas in this CGI-animated holiday special, written and directed by Kevin Munroe, and the first commissioned under Sunbow Entertainment's TV-Loonland banner. The 30-minute holiday special made its television debut in December 2001 on the newly renamed ABC Family, formerly known as the Family Channel. *A Sunbow Entertainment/Rainbow Studios/ABC Family/TV-Loonland AG Production. Color. Half-hour. Premiered on ABC FAM: December 1, 2001.*

**Voices**
**Skeezer:** Jimmy Kimmel

### ◎ A DOONESBURY SPECIAL

Zonker Harris, the lead character in Garry Trudeau's popular *Doonesbury* strip, reflects on social and political issues of the past—flower children, college campus bombings and other cynical observations—in this nostalgic half-hour special, which was released to theaters as well as television and received an Academy Award nomination for best animated film. *A Hubley Studios Production in association with Universal Press Syndicate. Color. Half-hour. Premiered on NBC: November 27, 1977.*

**Voices**
**Zonker Harris:** Richard Cox; **Joanie Caucus:** Barbara Harris; **Mike:** David Grant; **Mark Slackmeyer/Ralphie:** Charles Levin; **B.D.:** Richard Bruno; **Boopsie:** Rebecca Nelson; **Rev. Scott Sloan:** Rev. William Sloane Coffin Jr.; **Referee:** Jack Gilford; **Kirby:** Mark Baker; **Frank:** Eric Elice; **Calvin:** Ben Haley, Jr.; **Sportscaster:** Will Jordan; **Ellie:** Linda Baer; **Howie:** Eric Jaffe; **Jeannie:** Michelle Browne; **Rufus:** Thomas Baxton; **Magus:** Lenny Jackson; **Virgin Mary:** Patrice Leftwich; **Jimmy Thudpacker:** Jimmy Thudpacker

### ◎ DORA THE EXPLORER CHRISTMAS SPECIAL

Adorable little Dora and her red-boot-wearing monkey, Boots, commence an exciting adventure with her talking Backpack and singing Map to the North Pole to deliver special treats to Santa in this half-hour holiday special—also known as "A Present for Santa—for Nick Jr. Howie Dorough of the famed pop group the Backstreet Boys provides the voice of Santa Claus. *A Nickelodeon Production. Color. Half-hour. Premiered on NICK JR.: December 11, 2002. Rebroadcast on NICK JR.: December 16, 2006. Rebroadcast on NOG: January 5, 2004.*

**Voices**
**Dora Jones:** Kathleen Herles; **Boots:** Harrison Chad; **The Map/Swiper:** Marc Weiner; **Tico:** Jose Zelaya; **Backpack:** Sasha Tora; **Benny:** Jake Burbage; **Isa:** Ashley Fleming; **Grumpy Old Troll:** Chris Guifford; **Santa Claus:** Howie Dorough; **Additional Voices:** Elaine del Valle, Adam Seitz

### ◎ DORA THE EXPLORER: "DORA'S DANCE TO THE RESCUE"

Accompanied by her faithful companion, Boots, Dora dances, spins, shakes and wiggles her way to rescue Swiper the Fox, who is trapped inside a magic bottle. Premiering on Nick Jr. on November 11, 2005, at 11:00 A.M., this delightful, tune-filled hour-long educational special was the second-highest-rated cable, program attracting 1.4 million preschoolers and 1.4 million viewers grades 2 through 5 (2.8 million viewers overall), beating out all competition on basic cable that week. Only one program ranked higher, the January 2005 special *Dora's Private Adventure*, which was also the number-four-ranked program on television in 2005 with grades 2 through 5 behind the Super Bowl, the Super Bowl kick-off and Dora's "The Pirate Adventure." The special was repeated on Nick Jr. on Thanksgiving Day and in December 2005, and sporadically in March and December 2006 and January 2007. *A Nicktoon Production. Color. One-hour. Premiered on NICK JR.: November 11, 2005. Rebroadcast on NICK JR.: November 25, 2005; December 5, 2005; December 27, 2005; March 3, 2006; December 6, 2006; January 25, 2007.*

**Voices**
**Dora:** Kathleen Herles; **Boots:** Harrison Chad; **Benny:** Jake Burbage; **The Map/Swiper:** Marc Weiner; **Backpack:** Sasha Tora; **Tico:** Muhammed Cunningham; **Isa:** Ashley Flemming; **Grumpy Old Troll:** Chris Guifford

### ◎ DORA THE EXPLORER: "DORA'S SUPER SILLY FIESTA"

Seven-year-old heroine Dora is invited to the Super Silly Fiesta hosted by the Big Red Chicken and helps out by bringing a cake to the party, where she plays games and solves riddles and sings silly songs with her friends Boots, Swiper, the Silly Mail Bird and her cousin, Diego, who starred in his own spin-off series, *Go, Diego, Go!*, in the fall. Based on the number-one rated preschool show on commercial television, *Dora the Explorer*, that aired at 10 A.M. and 11 A.M. weekdays on Nick Jr. and weekends on CBS, the all-new special premiered during the show's third season in prime time at 8 P.M. in April 2004. In conjunction with the special's debut, Nickjr.com launched a Super Silly Costume Maker game for preschool children to play and dress up like Dora and her cousin, Diego, for the event. Actor/comedian John Leguizamo provided the voice of Silly Mail Bird. *A Nicktoon Production. Color. Half-hour. Premiered on NICK JR.: April 12, 2004. Rebroadcast on NOG: April 13, 2004.*

*Voices*

**Dora:** Kathleen Herles; **Boots:** Harrison Chad; **Benny:** Jake Burbage; **The Map/Swiper:** Marc Weiner; **Backpack:** Sasha Tora; **Tico:** Muhammed Cunningham; **Isa:** Ashley Flemming; **Silly Mail Bird:** John Leguizamo; **Diego:** Jake T. Austin

### ◎ DORA THE EXPLORER: "DORA'S WORLD ADVENTURE"

Dora and her friends undertake a remarkable global journey to France, Tanzania, Russia and China, with she and Swiper saving Friendship Day while learning about each country's native language, culture and customs in this hour-long prime-time special that premiered on November 19, 2006, at 8:00 P.M. on Nickelodeon. The special was subsequently rebroadcast weekday mornings and afternoons on Nick Jr. in November-December 2006 and January 2007. *A Nickelodeon Production. Color. One hour. Premiered on NICK: November 19, 2006. Rebroadcast on NICK JR.: November 20, 2006; November 22, 2006; November 24, 2006; December 4, 2006; December 8, 2006; January 23, 2007; January 26, 2007.*

*Voices*

**Dora Jones:** Kathleen Herles; **Boots:** Harrison Chad; **The Map/Swiper:** Marc Weiner; **Tico:** Jose Zelaya; **Backpack:** Sasha Tora

### ◎ DORA THE EXPLORER: FAIRYTALE ADVENTURE

After entering Fairytale Land, Dora and Boots meet all kinds of classic fairytale characters, including a mean old witch who (voiced by Chita Rivera). Boots falls under the witch's spell after eating one of a banana that she's cursed and he can awaken only when hugged by a true princess. The hour-long, song-filled special bowed on Nick Jr. on October 11, 2004, at 10 A.M. (ET), followed by repeat airings annually. *A Nicktoon Production. Color. One-hour. Premiered on NICK JR.: September 24, 2004. Rebroadcast on NICK JR.: October 11, 2004; November 26, 2004; December 29, 2004; March 21, 2005; April 8, 2005; July 25, 2005; July 29, 2005; October 10, 2005; November 11, 2005; December 19, 2005; March 31, 2006; November 22, 2006; December 5, 2006; December 17, 2006; January 24, 2007.*

*Voices*

**Dora:** Kathleen Herles; **Boots:** Harrison Chad; **Benny:** Jake Burbage; **The Map/Swiper:** Marc Weiner; **Backpack:** Sasha Tora; **Tico:** Muhammed Cunningham; **Isa:** Ashley Flemming; **Witch:** Chita Rivera

### ◎ DORA THE EXPLORER: "MOTHER'S DAY SPECIAL"

It's Mother's Day and with Boots's help Dora finds three ingredients she needs—bananas, nuts and chocolate—to bake a special cake for Mama on this most special day of the year in this half-hour special (also known as "Dia de las Madres"), adapted from the enormously successful Nick Jr. weekday preschool series created by Chris Gifford, Valerie Walsh and Eric Weiner. Famed stage and screen star Gregory Hines did a guest stint as the character Michael Jones. *A Nickelodeon Production. Color. Half-hour. Premiered on NICK JR.: May 8, 2002. Rebroadcast on NICK JR.: May 10, 2002. Rebroadcast on NOG: May 14, 2006.*

*Voices*

**Dora Jones:** Kathleen Herles; **Boots:** Harrison Chad; **The Map/Swiper:** Marc Weiner; **Tico:** Jose Zelaya; **Backpack:** Sasha Tora; **Michael Jones:** Gregory Hines

### ◎ DORA THE EXPLORER: THE PIRATE ADVENTURE

Planning to perform a musical pirate play for their closest friends and relatives, Dora, Boots, Diego and company discover one major problem: The Pirate Pigs have stolen the treasure chest containing their costumes. Dora leads the way to recover the costumes by crossing the Seven Seas with her friends to Treasure Island to which the pigs have headed in this hour-long preschool special that debuted on Nickelodeon's Nick Jr. in the 9 A.M. time slot. *A Nicktoon Production. Color. One hour. Premiered on NICK JR.: January 17, 2005. Rebroadcast on NICK JR.: January 18, 2005; January 21, 2005; February 18, 2005; June 13, 2005; June 17, 2005; August 5, 2005; September 5, 2005; October 28, 2005; November 11, 2005; December 12, 2005; January 16, 2006; January 20, 2006; May 29, 2006; December 7, 2006; January 22, 2007.*

*Voices*

**Dora:** Kathleen Herles; **Boots:** Harrison Chad; **Benny:** Jake Burbage; **The Map/Swiper:** Marc Weiner; **Backpack:** Sasha Tora; **Tico:** Muhammed Cunningham; **Isa:** Ashley Flemming

### ◎ DOUG AND RUGRATS CHRISTMAS

Two half-hour holiday episodes from Nickelodeon's popular animated series, *Doug* and *Rugrats*, were repackaged in this hour-long syndicated special. *A Jumbo Pictures/Klasky Csupo Production. Color. One hour. Premiered: December 1, 1996. Syndicated.*

### ◎ DOUG'S HALLOWEEN ADVENTURE

Bristle-haired Doug and his best friend Skeeter go to an amusement park for the grand opening of "the scariest ride ever made" in his first prime-time cable network special, spun off from the popular Nickelodeon cartoon series. *A Jumbo Pictures Production. Color. Half-hour. Premiered on NICK: October 30, 1993.*

*Voices*

**Doug Funnie:** Billy West; **Skeeter Valentine:** Fred Newman

### ◎ DOUG'S SECRET CHRISTMAS

Doug experiences a major crisis (at least major to him) in his life: He doesn't understand why his family fails to celebrate Christmas in the traditional way in this prime-time holiday special, based on the ABC animated series *Brand Spanking New Doug*. The program premiered opposite *Edith Ann's Christmas* on ABC. *A Jumbo Pictures Production in association with Walt Disney Television. Color. Half-hour. Premiered on ABC: December 14, 1996.*

*Voices*

**Doug Funnie:** Billy West; **Judy Funnie:** Becca Lish; **Skeeter Valentine:** Fred Newman; **Patti Mayonnaise:** Constance Shulman

## ◎ DOWN AND OUT WITH DONALD DUCK

The up-and-down life of Donald Duck is chronicled in this *60 Minutes*–style "duckumentary" that combines clips from more than 30 hours of previously exhibited Donald Duck cartoons. *A Garen-Albrecht Production in association with Walt Disney Television. Color. One hour. Premiered on NBC: March 25, 1987. Rebroadcast on NBC: April 29, 1988.*

*Voices*

**Donald Duck/Daisy Duck:** Tony Anselmo; **Huey/Dewey/Louie:** Tony Anselmo; **Professor Ludwig von Drake:** Albert Ash; **Mickey Mouse:** Les Perkins; **Goofy/Peg-Leg Pete:** Will Ryan; **Narrator:** Stan Freberg; **Announcer:** Harry Shearer

## ◎ DRAGONS: FIRE & ICE

Two unlikely rivals teenage dragon warrior—Prince Dev and Princess Kyra—come together to fight and end a 1,000-year-old war between their two kingdoms in this first of two CG-animated direct-to-video specials based on the top-selling Mega Blocks toy line. It first aired on Canada's YTV network and premiered in the United States on the Disney Channel in September 2005. The Bardel Entertainment-produced movie debuted the week of September 12 through September 15, highlighted by the premiere of its sequel, *Dragons: Metal Ages*, along with *Digimon: The Movie* and *Silverwing: A Glimpse of the Son. A Bardel Entertainment, Inc./Fury Productions Production in association with Lionsgate Family Entertainment/Alliance Atlantis Communication/Bardel Distribution/YTV. Color. Seventy-two minutes. Premiered on DIS: September 2005.*

*Voices*

**Dev:** Michael Adamthwaite, Mark Hildreth; **Kyra:** Chiara Zanni

## ◎ DRAGONS: THE METAL AGES

After the well-armed Odaku warriors handily defeat a team of Ferroch commandos, Prince Dev and Princess Kyra encounter a greater evil, witch queen Scylla, who has built an immense army and teamed with the dragon-traitor Stendhal and two Shadow-Dragons to conquer both the Human World and the Dragon World, unless Dev and Kyra stop them. This sequel to the computer-animated direct-to-video release, *Dragons: Fire & Ice*, first aired on Canada's YTV network and in the United States on Disney Channel. *A Bardel Entertainment, Inc./Fury Productions Production in association with Lionsgate Family Entertainment/Alliance Atlantis Communication/Bardel Distribution/YTV. Color. Seventy-two minutes. Premiered on DIS: September 2005.*

*Voices*

**Dev:** Michael Adamthwaite, Mark Hildreth; **Kyra:** Chiara Zanni

## ◎ DTV²: THE SPECIAL

Classic Disney animation, set to the music of Huey Lewis, Elton John and other performers and featuring such hit songs as "1, 2, 3," "Come On, Let's Go" and "Heart and Soul," fill out this music video-styled (dubbed "DTV") live-action/animated special hosted by Nina Peoples for Disney Channel. *A Brighton Group Production for Disney Channel. Color. Half-hour. Premiered on DIS: 1989.*

## ◎ DUCKTALES: "TIME IS MONEY"

When Scrooge McDuck buys an island that ends up being full of diamonds, his heartless rival, the notorious Flintheart Glomgold, blows the island in two so he'll have all the diamonds while McDuck has only the other worthless half in this two-hour special based on the syndicated series. The special was later rebroadcast in five parts. *A Walt Disney Television Animation Production. Color. Two hours. Premiered: November 25, 1988.*

*Voices*

**Uncle Scrooge McDuck:** Alan Young; **Launchpad McQuack:** Terence McGovern; **Huey/Dewey/Louie/Webbigail Vanderduck:** Russi Taylor; **Duckworth:** Don Hills, Chuck McCann; **Gyro Gearloose/Flintheart Glomgold:** Hal Smith; **Mrs. Beakley/Webra Walters:** Joan Gerber; **Sen-Sen:** Haunani Minn; **Bubba Duck/Big Time Beagle:** Frank Welker; **Myng-Ho:** Keone Young

## ◎ DUCKTALES: "TREASURE OF THE GOLDEN SUNS"

Donald Duck's cantankerous canard uncle, Scrooge McDuck, the world's richest tightwad, is joined by Donald's nephews, Huey, Dewey and Louie, in daring exploits and risky undertakings in this two-hour preview special of the popular syndicated series, which debuted three days later. The special was then shown in five parts during the series' regular syndicated run. *A Walt Disney Television Animation Production. Color. Two hours. Premiered: September 18, 1987.*

*Voices*

**Uncle Scrooge McDuck:** Alan Young; **Donald Duck:** Tony Anselmo; **Huey/Dewey/Louie:** Russi Taylor; **Duckworth:** Joan Gerber, Chuck McCann; **El Capitan:** Peter Cullen, Jim Cummings; **Skittles:** Terence McGovern, Patty Parris

## ◎ DUEL MASTERS: "PLAYING WITH A FULL DECK"

Becoming one of a few elite players in the world of the special trading game "Duel Masters" Shobu Kirifuda magically brings to life the card game's creatures by employing the powerful martial art "Kaijudo" while seeking to become a champion in the art much like his father in this 90-minute special that introduced the weekly Saturday night series on Cartoon Network. *A Shogakukan Productions Co. Ltd./Plastic Cow/Elastic Media Corp./Howling Cat Productions. Color. Ninety minutes. Premiered on CAR: February 27, 2004.*

*Voices*

**Shobu Kirifuda:** Joshua Seth; **Rekuta:** Alex Gold; **Knight/Shori Kirifuda:** Brahan Lee; **Boy George:** Tim Diamond; **Jimera:** David Jeremiah; **Mai Kirifuda:** Cindy Alexander; **Mimi:** Janice Lee; **Aiken:** Brian Beacock; **Kokujoh:** Terrence Stone; **Dr. Root/Multi-Card Monty:** Derek Stephen Prince; **Hakuoh:** Doug Erholtz; **Knight:** Kirk Thorton; **Your Mama:** Michelle Ruff; **Sho/Extreme Bucket Man:** Steven Jay Blum; **Prince Eugene the Mean:** Bob Papenbrook. **Rikuda's Father/Tohru:** Cam Clarke; **Saiyuki:** Dee Dee Green; **Prince Irving the Terrible:** Jamieson Price; **Kintaro:** Jay Max; **Rekuta's father:** Joe Ochman; **Benny Haha:** Kerrigan Mahan; **Mikuni:** Udel R. Deet; **Johnny Coolburns:** Paul St. Peter; **Fritz:** Richard Steven Horvitz; **Robbie Rotten:** Yuri Lowenthal

## ◎ THE EASTER BUNNY IS COMIN' TO TOWN

Through the wonders of Animagic, Fred Astaire, as old friend/mailman S.D. Kluger from *Santa Claus Is Comin' to Town*, relates how the traditions of Easter and the excitement brought by the holiday—the Easter bunny, decorating eggs and chocolate bunnies—first came about in the town of Kidville, a city reserved for children. Astaire sings the title song and "Can Do," one of six original songs written for the program. *A Rankin-Bass Production. Color. One hour. Premiered on ABC: April 6, 1977. Rebroadcast on*

ABC: *March 20, 1978; April 14, 1978; April 5, 1980. Rebroadcast on DIS: March 23, 1994; March 29, 1997. Rebroadcast on FOX FAM: April 22, 2000; April 23, 2000. Rebroadcast on ABC FAM: April 14, 2004: March 27, 2005.*

**Voices**
**S.D. Kluger (narrator):** Fred Astaire; **Sunny, the Easter Bunny:** Skip Hinnant; **Chugs:** Robert McFadden; **Hallelujah Jones:** Ron Marshall; **King Bruce:** James Spies; **Lilly Longtooth:** Meg Sargent

### ◉ THE EASTER EGG ADVENTURE

When the thieving Take-Its steal Egg Town's Easter eggs, a group of residents from the idyllic village brave the dangers of crossing the swamp to the "Take-Its" lair to recover the eggs and bring joy back to Easter in this feature-length animated children's film, originally produced in 2004 by Vancouver-based Waterfront Pictures. Becoming the first animated and first children's film to be accepted into the prestigious Boston Film Festival in September 2004, the cartoon feature, written and directed by renowned children's author John Michael Williams (*Rules of the Road Toads* and *Wondering William and the Sandman*), played at other festivals, including the Jackson Hole Film Festival, where it won that year's Cowboy Award.

Starring the voices of James Woods, Brooke Shields, Joe Pantoliano, Sandra Bernhard, Eli Wallach and two-time Olympic medalist Nancy Kerrigan, the PG-rated movie debuted to U.S. television audiences as an Easter special on Starz! Kids (subsequently changed to Starz! Kids & Family) on Easter Sunday morning in 2005. John Michael Williams also recorded the production's theme song, "Crazy About You," with Grammy award-winning recording artist Natalie Cole. *A Waterfront Pictures/MarVista Entertainment Production. Color. Ninety minutes. Premiered on STZK: March 27, 2005. Rebroadcast on STZK&F: July 6, 2005; July 12, 2005; July 17, 2005; July 22, 2005; July 28, 2005; July 29, 2005; November 2, 2005; November 6, 2005; November 25, 2005; January 16, 2006; February 2, 2006; February 8, 2006; February 18, 2006; February 24, 2006.*

**Voices**
**Horrible Harriet Hare:** Brooke Shields; **Grab Takit:** James Woods; **Terrible Timmy Takit:** Joe Pantoliano; **Claralyne Cluck:** Sandra Bernhard; **Bernadette Baker/Helen Hen:** Nancy Kerrigan; **Big Boring Benedict:** John Michael Williams; **Narrator:** Eli Wallach; **Good Gracious Grasshopper:** Gary Littman; **Boss Baker:** Rob Bartlett; **Tiny Tessie:** Becca Lish; **Additional Voices:** Tara Sands

### ◉ EASTER EGG MORNIN'

The voice and songs of pop music superstar Bobby Goldsboro highlight this animated Easter tale following the adventures of Picasso "Speedy" Cottontail. Known to boast of his fame as the "egg-painting Easter bunny," Cottontail finds himself in a fix when, with Easter fast approaching, the chickens go on strike and won't lay eggs. This half-hour holiday special was produced by Goldsboro. *A Bobby Goldsboro Production in association with Peeler-Rose Productions. Color. Half-hour. Premiered on DIS: 1990.*

**Voices**
**Picasso "Speedy" Cottontail:** Bobby Goldsboro; **Henrietta/Snake:** Pat Childs; **Owlbert:** Tim Tappan

### ◉ EASTER FEVER

The Easter Bunny, alias Jack the Rabbit, is the subject of a celebrity-type roast in honor of his retirement from the Easter egg business. Don Rattles and Steed Martin (animal characterizations of comedians Don Rickles and Steve Martin) head the all-star salute.

Just when he thinks his career is over, however, Jack is convinced by a pleading aardvark to change his mind. *A Nelvana Limited Production in association with the CBC. Color. Half-hour. Premiered: March 30, 1980. Syndicated.*

**Voices**
**Jack, the Easter Bunny:** Garrett Morris; **Don Rattles/Steed Martin:** Maurice LaMarche; **Santa Claus/Baker:** Chris Wiggins; **Madame Malegg:** Jeri Craden; **Aardvark:** Jim Henshaw; **Scarlett O'Hare:** Catherine O'Hara; **Scrawny Chicken:** Melleny Brown; **Ratso Rat:** Larry Mollin; **Announcer:** Don Ferguson

### ◉ EASTER IS

Benji is confronted with the prospect of losing his pet dog, Waldo, if he doesn't pay the dog's captor ransom: $5. Waldo manages to escape, making his return home even more dramatic by coming back to his master on Easter morning. *A Screen Images Production for Lutheran Television. Color. Half-hour. Premiered: March, 1974. Syndicated.*

**Voices**
**Benji:** David Kelly; **Schoolteacher:** Leslie Uggams; **Martin:** Phillip Morris

### ◉ ED, EDD N EDDY'S BOO-HAW-HAW HALLOWEEN SPECIAL

On Halloween night, Ed, Edd and Eddy dress up to find the legendary trick-or-treat filled neighborhood of "Spooke-E-Ville," with Ed, after preparing for a night out by spending all day watching horror movies, believing he is being stalked by monsters. Debuting five days before Halloween in 2005, the special was the third featuring the oddball stars of Cartoon Network's long-running weekly series. *An a.k.a. Cartoon Production. Color. Half-hour. Premiered on October 26, 2005. Rebroadcast on CAR: October 27, 2006.*

**Voices**
**Ed:** Matt Hill; **Edd "Double D:** Samuel Vincent; **Eddy:** Tony Sampson; **Jimmy:** Keenan Christenson; **Sarah/Lee Kanker:** Janyse Jaud; **Kevin/Marie Kanker:** Kathleen Barr; **May Kanker/Nazz:** Erin Fitzgerald, **Rolf:** Peter Kelamis

### ◉ ED, EDD N EDDY'S HANKY PANKY HULLABALOO

Valentine's Day at Peach Creek High almost proves disastrous when one of the famous Kanker sisters, May, falls for Edd instead of Ed, making Ed and Eddy unhappy until harmony is restored after May's other two sisters, Lee and Marie, fix everything so everyone has someone special in their lives in this new 30-minute special based on the popular Cartoon Network series. *An a.k.a. Cartoon Production. Color. Half-hour. Premiered on CAR: February 11, 2005. Rebroadcast on CAR: February 14, 2005.*

**Voices**
**Ed:** Matt Hill; **Edd "Double D":** Samuel Vincent; **Eddy:** Tony Sampson; **May Kanker/Nazz:** Erin Fitzgerald; **Sarah/Lee Kanker:** Janyse Jaud; **Kevin/Marie Kanker:** Kathleen Barr; **Jimmy:** Keenan Christenson; **Jonny:** David Paul Grove

### ◉ ED, EDD N EDDY'S JINGLE JINGLE JANGLE

After discovering his yet-to-be unwrapped Christmas gifts are the usual socks, underwear and other unwanted presents, Eddie takes matters into his own hands by trying to get adopted by his friends, families to replace his gifts with theirs but learns instead the importance of spreading good cheer with his best friends, Ed and Edd. The all-new 30-minute holiday special was the first of three based on the runaway hit Cartoon Network series that aired during the program's fourth season. *An a.k.a. Cartoon Production. Color. Half-hour. Premiered on CAR: December 3, 2004. Rebroadcast on CAR: December 15, 2004; December 22, 2004; December 24, 2004; December 25, 2004; December 16, 2005; December 17, 2005; December 18, 2005; December 20, 2005; December 21, 2005; December 23, 2005; December 24, 2005; December 4, 2006; December 15, 2006; December 16, 2006; December 19, 2006; December 22, 2006; December 24, 2006.*

**Voices**
**Ed:** Matt Hill; **Edd "Double D":** Samuel Vincent; **Eddy:** Tony Sampson; **Jimmy:** Keenan Christenson; **Sarah/Lee Kanker:** Janyse Jaud; **Jonny:** David Paul Grove; **Kevin/Marie Kanker:** Kathleen Barr; **May Kanker/Nazz:** Erin Fitzgerald; **Rolf:** Peter Kelamis

## ◉ EDGAR & ELLEN: "ACCEPT NO SUBSTITUTES"

With others dreading the first day of school, mischievous twins, Edgar and Ellen, unleash their unusual brand of twisted mayhem on their fellow classmates in this first of six planned half-hour specials, preceding their half-hour weekly television series debut in October 2007 on Nicktoons. The special premiered in primetime on Saturday, September 2 at 8:30 P.M. (EST). *A StarFarm Productions LLC/Bardel Entertainment Inc. Production in association with Nickelodeon and YTV. Color. Half-hour. Premiered on NICKT: September 2, 2006.*

## ◉ EDGAR & ELLEN: "COLD MEDALISTS"

After originally trying to sabotage their own town, against their better wishes Edgar and Ellen team up with their arch-nemesis, Stephanie Knightleigh, to defeat the rotten Smelterburg team in the Nod's O-Limb-pics Winter Games to win the grand-prize trophy and save the town's beloved sewers in this third half-hour special adaptation in 2006 of the acclaimed Simon & Schuster children's book series. Premiering in prime time on Christmas Eve of 2006, on cable's Nicktoons, the outlandish holiday special was rebroadcast four more times through the holiday season. *A StarFarm Productions LLC/Bardel Entertainment Inc. Production in association with Nickelodeon and YTV. Color. Half-hour. Premiered on NICKT: December 23, 2006. Rebroadcast on NICKT: December 24, 2006; December 25, 2006; December 27, 2006; December 29, 2006.*

## ◉ EDGAR & ELLEN: "TRICK OR TWINS"

Dressed as aliens and robots, the twisted twins of Nod's Limb turn their 13-story mansion into a spooky house of horrors to scare the neighbors but to no avail, while one of Edgar's weird experiments does monstrous things to Ellen's carnivorous plant, Berenice, in this half-hour prime time Halloween special—and second of six specials—costarring the popular Simon & Schuster children's book characters. Following their first special that coincided with the back-to-school season in September, this half-hour comedy scare-fest premiered in prime time on the Nicktoons Network at 8:30 P.M. in late October 2006. *A StarFarm Productions LLC/Bardel Entertainment Inc. Production in association with Nickelodeon and YTV. Color. Half-hour. Premiered on NICKT: October 28, 2006.*

## ◉ EDITH ANN: A FEW PIECES OF THE PUZZLE

Upset that nobody in her family remembered her birthday, Edith Ann plays hooky and lands in the school counselor's office. Her meeting with the counselor and subsequent situations provide a waif's-eye view of her imperfect life in the first of three half-hour

animated adaptations of Lily Tomlin's classic comedy character, written by Tomlin's longtime collaborator Jane Wagner. Two more specials followed this effort: *Edith Ann: Homeless Go Home* (1994) and *Edith Ann Christmas* (1996), also on ABC. *A Klasky Csupo/Anivision/Tomlin/Wagner Production. Color. Half-hour. Premiered on ABC: January 18, 1994.*

**Voices**
**Edith Ann:** Lily Tomlin

## ◉ EDITH ANN: HOMELESS GO HOME

Edith Ann opposes a petition that would ban a proposed shelter for the homeless, which one petitioner claims would leave Edgetown jammed with "bums and bag ladies bumper to bumper," in this second in a series of Edith Ann specials. *A Klasky Csupo/Tomlin/Wagner Production. Color. Half-hour. Premiered on ABC: May 27, 1994.*

**Voices**
**Edith Ann:** Lily Tomlin

## ◉ EDITH ANN'S CHRISTMAS

When Edith's older sister Irene gets her bottom tattooed, Edith tattles to her parents, causing Irene to run away and leaving Edith trying to patch things up in time for Christmas in this third half-hour outing based on Lily Tomlin's popular character. *A Kurtz & Friends/Tomlin and Wagner Theatricalz Production. Color. Half-hour. Premiered on ABC: December 14, 1996.*

**Voices**
**Edith Ann:** Lily Tomlin

## ◉ EEK! THE CAT CHRISTMAS

Eek! gets into the holiday spirit by helping his mortal enemy Sharkey the Sharkdog search for his missing relatives and aiding Santa in settling a dispute with his reindeer in this prime-time animated special based on the popular Saturday-morning cartoon series. *A Nelvana/Savage Studios Production in association with Fox Children's Network. Color. Half-hour. Premiered on FOX: December 5, 1993.*

**Voices**
**Eek! the Cat:** Bill Kopp

## ◉ THE ELECTRIC PIPER

Set in the late 1960s, a Jimi Hendrix–like guitarist annihilates the rats from the suburban community of Hamlin and takes revenge on the mayor for not awarding him his prize—a Harley Davidson motorcycle—in this rock opera version of the Pied Piper tale, the first feature-length musical by Nickelodeon Studios, featuring the voices of celebrities Rodney Dangerfield, Rob Schneider, George Segal and others. The 78-minute movie premiered as a 90-minute special on the Nickelodeon network. *A Nickelodeon Studios Production. Color. Ninety minutes. Premiered on NICK: February 2, 2003.*

**Voices**
**Sly, The Electric Piper:** Wayne Brady; **Rat-A-Tat-Tat:** Rodney Dangerfield; **Pat Dixon:** Christine Ebersole; **Janet Dixon:** Lesli Margherita; **Mick Dixon:** Robbie Rist; **Mrs. Robinson:** Laura San Giacomo; **Mrs. Jones:** Rodney Saulsberry; **Abby Jones:** Crystal Scales; **Rinky-Dink-Dink:** Rob Schneider; **Mayor Nick Dixon:** George Segal

## ◉ THE ELEPHANT'S CHILD

Rudyard Kipling's most beloved "Just So" story about how the elephant got his trunk is told in this half-hour animated special, produced as part of Rabbit Ears Video's *Storybook Classics* series. A *Rabbit Ears Video Production. Color. Half-hour. Premiered on SHO: 1989.*

*Voices*
**Narrator:** Jack Nicholson

### ◎ THE ELF AND THE MAGIC KEY
Santa Claus is kidnapped on Christmas Eve and it's up to Toby the elf to free him in time for Christmas in this holiday half-hour. *A RIM/World Production. Color. Half-hour. Premiered on USA: December 4, 1993. Rebroadcast on USA: December 5, 1993; December 14, 1994; December 24, 1995.*

*Voices*
**Toby:** Wendy J. Cooke; **Santa Claus:** Harry Frazier; **Hoot:** Barry Livingston; **Trixie:** Lee Wilson; **Smitty:** F. Thom Spadaro; **Head Elf:** Roger Perry; **Mrs. Buzzard:** Jo Anne Worley; **Buzzard Brother #1:** Dink O'Neal; **Buzzard Brother #2:** Lara Teeter

### ◎ THE ELF WHO SAVED CHRISTMAS
Disappointed Santa tries to retire when no children's letters arrive, so a determined elf (Toby) sets out in this half-hour holiday special to find the messages in order to change Santa's mind. *A RIM/World Production. Color. Half-hour. Premiered on USA: December 12, 1992. Rebroadcast on USA: December 4, 1993; December 24, 1995.*

*Voices*
**Toby, the Elf:** Wendy Cooke; **Santa Claus:** Harry Frazier; **Hoot:** Barry Livingston; **Trixie:** Lee Wilson; **Smitty:** F. Thom Spadaro; **Head Elf:** Roger Perry; **Mrs. Buzzard:** Jo Anne Worley; **Robin:** Linda Denise Martin

### ◎ ELOISE: LITTLE MISS CHRISTMAS
With Christmas right around the corner, the most famous six-year-old resident of New York City's Plaza Hotel, Eloise, and her friends plan a holiday extravaganza to end all holiday shows in this two-part one-hour animated special based on Kay Thompson and Hillary Knight's best-selling children's book series. On New Year's Day 2007, the special was rebroadcast as part of an "Eloise" marathon on Starz! Kids & Family, beginning at 6:00 A.M. (ET). *A Film Roman/Handmade Films Production. Color. One hour. Premiered on STZK&F: December 2, 2006. Rebroadcast on STZK&F: December 8, 2006; December 12, 2006; December 17, 2006; December 21, 2006; December 25, 2006; January 1, 2007.*

*Voices*
**Eloise:** Mary Matilyn Mouser; **Nanny:** Lynn Redgrave; **Mr. Salamone:** Tim Curry; **Mrs. Thorton:** Kathleen Gati; **Other Voices:** Curtis Armstrong, Matthew Lillard

### ◎ THE EMPEROR AND THE NIGHTINGALE
Actress Glenn Close tells this story of the Emperor and his court in ancient China who discover a little gray bird with an enchanting song, part of Rabbit Ears Video's award-winning *Storybook Classics* series. *A Rabbit Ears Video Production. Color. Half-hour. Premiered on SHO: 1989.*

*Voices*
**Narrator:** Glenn Close

### ◎ THE EMPEROR'S NEW CLOTHES (1972)
Danny Kaye lends his voice to this animated version of the Hans Christian Andersen classic about the vain Emperor Klockenlocher, who is duped into paying $1 million for a suit made from "invisible cloth" in this live-action/animation special featuring the stop-motion process of Animagic, which utilizes the lifelike qualities of three-dimensional figures and the magical fantasy of animation. Portions of the special were shot on location in Andersen's native Denmark. Kaye was most familiar with the famed storyteller, as he played the title role in a 1952 movie about Andersen's life. *A Rankin-Bass Production. Color. One hour. Premiered on ABC: February 21, 1972 (as The Enchanted World of Danny Kaye: The Emperor's New Clothes).*

*Voices*
**Marmaduke (narrator):** Danny Kaye; **Emperor Klockenlocher:** Cyril Ritchard; **Princess Klockenlocher:** Imogene Coca; **Mufti:** Allen Swift; **Jasper:** Robert McFadden

### ◎ THE EMPEROR'S NEW CLOTHES (1989)
Two clever swindlers claiming to be the creators of the richest and most beautiful cloth in the world take advantage of the emperor's passion for new clothes in this animated retelling of the popular Hans Christian Andersen tale, part of Rabbit Ears Video's *Storybook Classics* series. *A Rabbit Ears Video Production. Color. Half-hour. Premiered on SHO: 1989.*

*Voices*
**Narrator:** Sir John Gielgud

### ◎ THE EMPEROR'S NEW CLOTHES (1991)
The tale of a little weaver who convinces a vain emperor that he is wearing the finest garments in the land—until a young child dares to point out that he is wearing nothing at all—in this PBS animated special based on Hans Christian Andersen's timeless tale. Produced by Emmy-award winning animator Michael Sporn (whose affinity for the stories of Hans Christian Andersen is seen in his animated versions of "The Little Match Girl" and "The Red Shoes") and narrated by Regis Philbin, the half-hour adventure aired as part of PBS's award-winning series, *Long Ago & Far Away*. *A Michael Sporn Animation/WGBH Boston Production in association with Italtoons Corporation. Color. Half-hour. Premiered on PBS: October 19, 1991. Rebroadcast on PBS: September 20, 1992.*

*Voices*
**Emperor/Narrator:** Regis Philbin; **Scribe:** Courtney Vance; **Mancy:** Peggy Cass; **Treasurer:** Barnard Hughes; **Dresser:** Heidi Stallings; **Weaver:** Phillip Schopper

*A vain emperor comes to the realization that he is wearing nothing at all in Emmy award–winning animator Michael Sporn's half-hour adaptation of Hans Christian Andersen's classic tale The Emperor's New Clothes.*

*Scene from John and Faith Hubley's cartoon special about the eight stages of life, Everybody Rides the Carousel. © Hubley Studios*

## ⊚ EVERYBODY RIDES THE CAROUSEL

Based on the works of psychiatrist Erik H. Erikson, this unusual 90-minute prime-time special deals with the eight stages of human life—from infancy to old age—presented in fablelike form and skillfully animated by John and Faith Hubley. Cicely Tyson hosted the special and actress Meryl Streep contributed her voice to the production. *A Hubley Studios Production. Color. Ninety minutes. Premiered on CBS: September 10, 1976.*

### Voices
**Mother:** Judith Coburn; **Baby #1/Maura #2/Adolescent:** Georgia Hubley; **Baby #2:** Ray Hubley; **Baby (cries)/Emily/Adolescent #5:** Emily Hubley; **Babies' Relative #1/Cafeteria Woman:** Jane Hoffman; **Babies' Relative #2:** Lou Jacobi; **Babies' Relative #3:** Lane Smith; **Babies' Relative #4:** Eleanor Wilson; **Maura #1:** Maura Washburn; **Maura's Mother:** Linda Washburn; **Maura's Father:** Mike Washburn; **Bruce/Student #2:** Bruce E. Smith; **Bruce's Mother:** Jane E. Smith; **Bruce's Father:** Mortimer Shapiro; **Student #1:** John Infantanza; **Boy:** Leeds Atkinson; **Girl:** Jenny Lumet; **Oracle:** Jo Carrol Stoneham; **Adolescent #1:** Alvin Mack; **Adolescent #2:** Michael Hirst; **Adolescent #3:** Barbara Gittleman; **Lovers:** Charles Levin, Meryl Streep; **Dinah:** Dinah Manoff; **Dinah's Father:** John Randolph; **Dinah's Mother:** Sarah Cunningham; **Tulane:** Tulane Bridgewater; **Tulane's Mother:** DeeDee Bridgewater; **Librarian:** William Watts; **Couple in Bed:** Lawrence (David) Pressman, Lanna Saunders; **Cafeteria Man:** Jack Gilford; **Halloween Woman:** Juanita Moore; **Halloween Man:** Harry Edison

## ⊚ THE FABULOUS SHORTS

Lee Mendelson, coproducer of television's *Peanuts* specials, produced this collection of Academy Award–winning cartoons, which included domestic and foreign winners. Clips were featured from nearly 20 films, including Mickey Mouse's "Steamboat Willie" (1928), Bugs Bunny's "Knighty Knight Bugs" (1958) and two Mister Magoo shorts, "When Magoo Flew" (1955) and "Magoo's Puddle Jumper" (1956). The special was hosted by actor Jim Backus, also the voice of Mr. Magoo. *A Lee Mendelson Production. Color. Half-hour. Premiered on NBC: October 17, 1968.*

## ⊚ FAERIES

Oisin, a middle-age hunter who is magically transformed into a 15-year-old, offers his help to the Trows to save the faerie world from the evil shadow of the Faerie King, who is threatening their very existence. *An MHV and Friends Production in association with Tomorrow Entertainment. Color. Half-hour. Premiered on CBS: February 25, 1981. Rebroadcast on CBS: July 31, 1982; August 13, 1983.*

### Voices
**Faerie King/Shadow:** Hans Conried; **Oisin:** Craig Schaefer; **Princess Niamh:** Morgan Brittany; **Puck/Fir Darrig:** Frank Welker; **Kobold:** Bob Arbogast; **Hags:** June Foray, Linda Gary; **Trows/Hunters:** Mel Wells, Frank Welker, Bob Arbogast

## ⊚ THE FAIRLY ODDPARENTS: ABRA-CATASTROPHE THE MOVIE

Cosmo and Wanda's plans to throw a party for Timmy to celebrate his one-year anniversary of having godparents goes awry when Mr. Crocker introduces them to a magic muffin that grants the person who eats it one wish, in this made-for-TV movie written and directed by Butch Hartman, creator of Nickelodeon's smash-hit series, *The Fairly OddParents. A NickToon Productions in association with Viacom International. Color. Ninety minutes. Premiered on NICK: July 11, 2003. Rebroadcast on NICK: July 13, 2003; July 14, 2003; August 16, 2003; August 17, 2003; August 18, 2003; September 1, 2003; September 20, 2003; September 28, 2003; October 10, 2003; October 11, 2003; November 15, 2003; November 28, 2003; December 20, 2003; December 29, 2003; January 17, 2004; February 7, 2004; February 29, 2004; March 14, 2004; March 28, 2004; April 25, 2004; May 23, 2004; July 10, 2004; September 5, 2004; October 17, 2004; December 5, 2004; January 1, 2005; February 6, 2005; March 27, 2005; May 1, 2005; July 11, 2005; August 1, 2005; August 21, 2005; September 5, 2005; October 2, 2005; November 25, 2005; January 29, 2006; April 16, 2006; August 8, 2006; August 30, 2006; September 9, 2006; October 15, 2006; November 24, 2006; January 7, 2007; April 21, 2007.*

### Voices
**Timmy Turner/Kid/Fairy #1/Kid #1:** Tara Strong; **Cosmo/Mr. Turner/Jorgen Von Strangle:** Darran Norris; **Wanda/Mrs. Turner:** Susan Blakeslee; **Vicky/Principal Waxelplax:** Grey DeLisle; **Bad Guy/Business Man:** Kevin Richardson; **Chester McBadbat:** Jason Marsden; **A.J.:** Gary LeRoi Gray; **Mr. Crocker/Ape #2:** Carlos Alazraqui; **Sanjay/Binky/Bippy/Fairy Private/Kid #2:** Dee Bradley Baker; **Cupid/Muffin Man/Another Kid//Fairy Sergeant/Others:** Tom Kenny; **Easter Bunny/Construction Worker Ape/Ape Truck Driver:** Bobby Constanzo; **Francis/Ape #1:** Faith Abrahams; **Flashback Boy/Web-Eared Guy/Third Kid/Orderly:** Butch Harman; **Flashback Girl/Female Ape #1/Gorilla Business Woman:** Carla Newman Ruyle; **Bowling Pin/Warthog:** Steve Marmel

## ⊚ THE FAIRLY ODDPARENTS: "CHANNEL CHASERS"

Timmy's wish to use a magic remote control that transports him inside television is thwarted when Vicky ruins the Turner home after babysitting and blames it all on Timmy, who gives the remote control to her, unaware of her evil plot to conquer the world. The two-hour movie was broadcast along with six other films adapted from Nickelodeon cartoon series as part of the network's 2004 *Nicktoons Movie Summer* festival. *A NickToon Production. Color. Two hours. Premiered on NICK: July 23, 2004. Rebroadcast on NICK: July 25, 2004; August 2, 2004; August 20, 2004; August 21, 2004; August 22, 2004; September 6, 2004; September 10, 2004; September 12, 2004; October 3, 2004; November 26, 2004; December 31, 2004; January 1, 2005; January 22, 2005; February 21,*

2005; April 29, 2005; May 22, 2005; July 25, 2005; August 19, 2005; September 5, 2005; November 6, 2005; November 26, 2005; December 18, 2005; January 8, 2006; January 25, 2006; February 25, 2006; April 5, 2006; July 17, 2006; August 14, 2006; August 23, 2006; September 4, 2006; October 1, 2006; October 22, 2006; November 5, 2006; March 25, 2007; April 21, 2007. Rebroadcast on NICKT: June 4, 2005; June 5, 2005; July 23, 2005; July 24, 2005; July 30, 2006.

*Voices*

**Young Timmy Turner/Paula Poundcake/Vicky and Tootie's Mom/Others:** Tara Strong; **Mr. Turner/Cosmo/Others:** Daran Norris; **Mrs. Turner/Wanda/Others:** Susan Blakeslee; **Vicky/Tootie/Others:** Grey DeLisle; **Denzel Crocker/Sheldon Dinkleburg/Dinkledog/Tony Futurelli/Man #1/Additional Voices:** Carlos Alazraqui; **Chester McBadbatt/Jeff/Adult Chester/Johnny Hunt/Additional Voices:** Dee Bradley Baker; **Adult AJ/Dad's Boss/Snoop/Donnie Donut/Additional Voices:** Kevin Michael Richardson; **Chet Ubetcha/Mr. Joel/Doug Dimmadome/Blackbird/Additional Voices:** Jim Ward; **T.V. Host//Wrestler #1/Bird/Man#2/Various:** S. Scott Bullock; **Race Official/Man on Puppet Show (from deleted alternate scene)/Additional Voices:** Butch Hartman; **Adam West:** himself; **Adult Timmy Turner:** Alec Baldwin; **Other Voices:** Cara Newman Ruyle

## ⊚ THE FAIRLY ODDPARENTS: "CRASH NEBULA"

Before becoming a big-time space hero, Sprig Speevak, star of Timmy Turner's favorite television show, Crash Nebula, has one major obstacle he must first overcome: attending space high school at the Celestial Academy in this parody of Disney/Pixar's Buzz Lightyear character from the blockbuster computer-animated features, *Toy Story* and *Toy Story 2*.

*The Fairly OddParents* creator Butch Hartman originally produced this program as an 11-minute pilot intended to be spun-off into a regular weekly series, chronicling the adventures of his fictional space star. Hartman extended the program to 30 minutes by incorporating wraparound segments of his *Fairly OddParents'* star Timmy Turner, with Nickelodeon subsequently airing it as a special in the summer of 2004. A *NickToon/Frederator Inc. Production. Color. Half-hour. Premiered on NICK: July 2, 2004. Rebroadcast on NICK: July 3, 2004; July 4, 2004; July 9, 2004; September 6, 2004; October 9, 2004; November 24, 2004; December 28, 2004; January 1, 2005; March 13, 2005; October 3, 2005; October 8, 2005; October 24, 2005; November 14, 2005; December 3, 2005; December 20, 2005; January 12, 2006; January 27, 2006; February 7, 2006.*

*Voices*

**Timmy Turner/Sprout:** Tara Strong; **Cosmo/Mr. Turner/Jorgen von Strangle:** Daran Norris; **Wanda/Mrs. Turner/Galaxandra:** Susan Blakeslee; **Vicky/Veronica/Tootie:** Grey DeLisle; **Denzel Crocker/Felos:** Carlos Alazraqui; **Gil/Pa Speevak:** Jim Ward; **A.J.:** Gary LeRoi Gray; **Francis:** Faith Abrahams; **Chester:** Jason Marsden; **Lance Thraster:** Pat Fraley; **Ani:** Nika Frost; **Ving:** Justin Berfield; **Rockwall:** Michael Clarke Duncance; **Pam Dromeda:** Queen Latifah; **Chuck:** Richard Steven Horwitz; **Sprig Speevak/Crash Nebula:** James Arnold Taylor

## ⊚ THE FAIRLY ODDPARENTS: "FAIRY IDOL"

After Norm the Genie unleashes his evil plan to become a Fairy Godparent by making Cosmo and Wanda disappear, plucky 10-year-old Timmy Turner travels to Fairy World to locate them while a wide-scale talent search is underway for every wish-granting creature in the universe to audition to become new fairy godparents in The Fairly OddParents cartoon parody of FOX television's runaway hit reality series, *American Idol*. Premiering on Nickelodeon in May 2006, the prime-time special attracted 3 million viewers who tuned in for its debut. A *NickToon Productions/Frederator Inc. Production. Color. One hour. Premiered on NICK: May 19, 2006.*

*Voices*

**Timmy Turner:** Tara Strong; **Vicky/Veronica/Tootie:** Grey DeLisle; **Chester McBadbat:** Jason Marsden; **Francis:** Faith Abrahams; **Wanda/Mrs. Turner:** Susan Blakeslee; **Mr. Denzel Crocker/Wandisimo:** Carlos Alazraqui; **Cosmo/Mr. Turner/Jorgen von Strangle/Grandpa Pappy:** Daran Norris; **Chip Skylark [Archive Recording]:** Chris Kirkpatrick; **Cupid/Anchorman:** Tom Kenny; **Santa/Penguin/Scientists:** Butch Hartman; **Cosmo's Singing Voice:** Diana DeGarmo; **Sanderson's Rapping Voice:** Method Man; **The Pixies:** Ben Stein; **Norm the Genie:** Robert Gait

## ⊚ THE FAIRLY ODDPARENTS: "SCHOOL'S OUT! THE MUSICAL"

After misbehaving badly during their summer break, Timmy Turner and his friends are sent to Flappy Bob's Peppy Happy Learn-A-Torium to correct their behavior, unaware of an evil plot by the Pixies (voiced by Ben Stein) to take over the world unless Timmy and his fairy godparents, Cosmo and Wanda, can sing their way out of it in this one-hour animated musical and third movie special, featuring 11 musical numbers, that premiered during the sixth season of creator Butch Hartman's top-rated Nickelodeon cartoon series. A *NickToon/Frederator Inc. Production. Color. One hour. Premiered on NICK: June 10, 2004.*

*Voices*

**Timmy Turner:** Tara Strong; **Vicky/Veronica/Tootie:** Grey DeLisle; **Chester McBadbat:** Jason Marsden; **Francis:** Faith Abrahams; **Wanda/Mrs. Turner:** Susan Blakeslee; **Mr. Denzel Crocker/Wandisimo:** Carlos Alazraqui; **Cosmo/Mr. Turner/Jorgen von Strangle/Grandpa Pappy:** Daran Norris; **Chip Skylark [Archive Recording]:** Chris Kirkpatrick; **Cupid/Anchorman:** Tom Kenny; **Santa/Penguin/Scientists:** Butch Hartman; **Cosmo's Singing Voice:** Diana DeGarmo; **Sanderson's Rapping Voice:** Method Man; **The Pixies:** Ben Stein; **Norm the Genie:** Robert Gait

## ⊚ A FAMILY CIRCUS CHRISTMAS

Daddy, Mommy, Billy, P.J., Dolly and Jeffy are preparing for Christmas when Jeffy gives Santa a near-impossible request: bring his deceased grandfather back to visit the family for the holidays. A *Cullen-Kasden Production in association with the Register and Tribune Syndicate. Color. Half-hour. Premiered on NBC: December 18, 1979. Rebroadcast on NBC: December 5, 1980; December 20, 1981. Rebroadcast on DIS: December 21, 1992; December 21, 1993; December 13, 1994.*

*Voices*

**Mommy:** Anne Costello; **Daddy:** Bob Kaliban; **Billy:** Mark McDermott; **Dolly:** Missy Hope; **Jeffy/P.J.:** Nathan Berg; **Santa Claus:** Allen Swift; **Vocalist:** Sarah Vaughan

## ⊚ A FAMILY CIRCUS EASTER

Billy, Dolly and Jeffy succeed in trapping the Easter Bunny to find out why it hides the eggs in this prime-time holiday special that premiered on NBC. A *Cullen-Kasden Productions in association with the Register and Tribune Syndicate. Color. Half-hour. Premiered on NBC: April 8, 1982. Rebroadcast on NBC: April 1, 1983. Rebroadcast on DIS: March 20, 1992; April 16, 1995; April 7, 1996.*

### Voices

**Mommy:** Anne Costello; **Daddy:** Bob Kaliban; **Billy:** Mark McDermott; **Dolly:** Missy Hope; **Jeffy/D.J.:** Nathan Berg; **Easter Bunny:** Dizzy Gillespie

### ◎ THE FAMILY DOG

The story of a suburban middle-class family and their pet pooch is told from the dog's perspective in three related stories that showcase the animal's true feelings about its owners in humorous fashion. The program was billed as "A Special Animated Adventure" of Steven Spielberg's short-lived NBC series, *Amazing Stories. A Hyperion-Kushner-Locke Production in association with Amblin Entertainment and Universal Television. Color. Half-hour. Premiered on NBC: February 16, 1987 (on Amazing Stories). Rebroadcast on NBC: September 11, 1987.*

### Voices

**Father:** Stan Freberg; **Mother:** Mercedes McCambridge; **Billy:** Scott Menville; **Baby Sister:** Annie Potts

### ◎ FAMILY GUY: "DEATH HAS A SHADOW"

Premiering as a half-hour special on Super Bowl Sunday in 1999 in this episode entitled "Death Has a Shadow," Peter loses his job at the factory and, too embarrassed to tell Lois, finds he can make a fortune through benefits instead. The program officially launched the weekly prime time series that began airing on FOX that April. *A Film Roman Productions Production. Color. Half-hour. Premiered on FOX: January 31, 1999.*

### Voices

**Peter Griffin/Brian Griffin/Stewie Griffin:** Seth MacFarlane; **Lois Griffin:** Alex Borstein; **Chris Griffin:** Seth Green; **Meg Griffin:** Lacy Chabert; **Himself:** Pat Summerall; **Freddy (on Scooby Doo):** Frank Welker; **Other Voices:** Joey Slotnick

### ◎ THE FAT ALBERT CHRISTMAS SPECIAL

The true meaning of Christmas—to love one another—is portrayed in this third Fat Albert special. Tyrone, the owner of the junkyard where Fat Albert's clubhouse sits, threatens to demolish the shack as an act of nastiness while the Cosby Kids, busily working up a Christmas pageant, help a little boy (voiced by Marshall Franklin) whose father and pregnant mother are stranded outside in their car. *A Filmation Associates Production in association with Bill Cosby Productions. Color. Half-hour. Premiered on CBS: December 18, 1977. Rebroadcast on CBS: November 27, 1978; November 27, 1979; December 24, 1980.*

### Voices

**Fat Albert/Mushmouth/Bill:** Bill Cosby; **Russell:** Jan Crawford; **Weird Harold:** Gerald Edwards; **Rudy:** Eric Suter; **Little Boy:** Marshall Franklin

### ◎ THE FAT ALBERT EASTER SPECIAL

The spirit of Easter is conveyed as Fat Albert and the gang observe the joy of the holiday season by spreading good cheer to others. *A Filmation Associates Production in association with Bill Cosby Productions. Color. Half-hour. Premiered on CBS: April 3, 1982. Rebroadcast on CBS: March 10, 1983.*

### Voices

**Fat Albert/Mushmouth/Mudfoot/Bill:** Bill Cosby; **Russell:** Jan Crawford; **Weird Harold:** Gerald Edwards; **Rudy:** Eric Suter

### ◎ THE FAT ALBERT HALLOWEEN SPECIAL

Fat Albert and the Cosby Kids are treated to an old-fashioned Halloween, with a trip to the cemetery where a witch jumps out, a visit to that ol' bum Mudfoot who teaches them how to get tricked out of their treats and an encounter with a frightening widow who lives in a house on the hill. *A Filmation Associates Production in association with Bill Cosby Productions. Color. Half-hour. Premiered on CBS: October 24, 1977. Rebroadcast on CBS: October 24, 1978; October 22, 1979; October 22, 1980; October 27, 1981.*

### Voices

**Fat Albert/Mushmouth/Bill:** Bill Cosby; **Russell:** Jan Crawford; **Weird Harold:** Gerald Edwards; **Rudy:** Eric Suter; **Other Voices:** Erika Carroll

### ◎ FATHER CHRISTMAS

After delivering presents one Christmas season, a weary Santa Claus decides to spend "the other 364 days" tending his garden, doing housework and basking in the sunny climes on a holiday adventure. He returns home in time to prepare Christmas stockings for another yuletide season in this British-produced hour-long animated special that aired on PBS. *An Iain Harvey/Blooming Production in association with Channel 4 International. Color. One hour. Premiered on PBS: December 21, 1994.*

### Voices

**Santa Claus:** Mel Smith

### ◎ THE FIRST CHRISTMAS: "THE STORY OF FIRST CHRISTMAS SNOW"

In this heartwarming holiday special set in a small abbey in the south of France, a nun cares for a young boy (Lukas) who is blinded by a lightning bolt. *A Rankin-Bass Production. Color. Half-hour. Premiered on NBC: December 19, 1975. Rebroadcast on NBC: December 18, 1976; December 15, 1979. Rebroadcast on FAM: December 3, 1992; November 28, 1993; December 4, 1997. Rebroadcast on FOX FAM: December 3, 1998; December 24, 1998; July 13, 1999; December 2, 1999; December 24, 1999; December 25, 1999; December 4, 2000; December 18, 2000; December 24, 2000. Rebroadcast on ABC FAM: December 1, 2001; December 4, 2001; December 6, 2001; December 24, 2001; December 2, 2002; December 16, 2002; December 20, 2002; December 3, 2003; December 6, 2003; December 18, 2003; December 4, 2004; December 13, 2004; December 22, 2004; December 2, 2005; December 5, 2006; December 9, 2006; December 24, 2006.*

### Voices

**Sister Theresa (narrator):** Angela Lansbury; **Father Thomas:** Cyril Ritchard; **Lukas:** David Kelly; **Sister Catherine:** Iris Rainer; **Sister Jean:** Joan Gardner; **Louisa:** Diana Lynn

### ◎ THE FIRST EASTER RABBIT

Folksy Burl Ives sings and tells the story of the first Easter rabbit, whose special assignment from the good fairy is to deliver painted Easter eggs to children. His mission is not without its obstacles, however, as three comedic con bunnies try to stop him. Adapted from the bestselling book *The Velveteen Rabbit.* Ives sings four songs, including Irving Berlin's famous melody, "Easter Parade." *A Rankin-Bass Production. Color. Half-hour. Premiered on NBC: April 9, 1976. Rebroadcast on NBC: March 19, 1978; April 7, 1979; April 9, 1981. Rebroadcast on DIS: March 24, 1993; March 19, 1994. Rebroadcast on FOX FAM: April 23, 2000. Rebroadcast on ABC FAM: April 11, 2004; March 27, 2005.*

### Voices

**Great Easter Bunny (narrator):** Burl Ives; **Stuffy:** Robert Morse; **Flops:** Stan Freberg; **Zero/Spats:** Paul Frees; **Mother:** Joan Gardner; **Whiskers:** Don Messick; **Glinda:** Dina Lynn; **Vocalists:** Burl Ives, Robert Morse, Christine Winter

## ⊚ THE FISHERMAN AND HIS WIFE

Academy Award–winning actress Jodie Foster narrates this animated half-hour adaptation of the Brothers Grimm tale about a poor fisherman who catches and then frees an enchanted flounder who is able to grant him any wish. Produced for Rabbit Ears Video's *Storybook Classics* series. *A Rabbit Ears Video Production. Color. Half-hour. Premiered on SHO: 1989.*

*Voices*
**Narrator:** Jodie Foster

## ⊚ FIVE WEEKS IN A BALLOON

Inspired by the Jules Verne story, three adventurers travel across the wilds of Africa via a hot-air balloon, led by famed explorer Dr. Samuel Ferguson, to reclaim for Queen Victoria a priceless diamond thought to be located on Devil's Peak. *A Hanna-Barbera Production. Color. One hour. Premiered on CBS: November 24, 1977. Rebroadcast on CBS: September 30, 1978; November 23, 1981.*

*Voices*
**Narrator:** John Stephenson; **Dr. Samuel Ferguson/Duke of Salisbury:** Laurie Main; **Oliver:** Loren Lester; **Queen Victoria:** Cathleen Cordell; **Irumu/King Umtali:** Brooker Bradshaw; **Le Griffe/1st & 2nd Poacher:** Johnny Hayner; **Native:** Gene Whittington

## ⊚ THE FLAGSTONES SPECIAL

Part of a two-month celebration of all things stone age, the Cartoon Network aired this two-hour special featuring the never-before seen, full-color pilot of *The Flintstones* cartoon series. Known as "The Flagstones," the existence of this 1-minute 45-second clip was rumored for over 30 years before it was finally discovered in a warehouse. Featured during the broadcast were original black-and-white prints of the first three episodes of *The Flintstones* with vintage commercials. *A Hanna-Barbera Production. Black-and-white. Color. Two hours. Premiered on CAR: May 7, 1994. Rebroadcast on CAR: May 14, 1994.*

*Voices*
**Fred Flintstone:** Daws Butler; **Barney Rubble:** Mel Blanc; **Betty Rubble:** June Foray

## ⊚ FLASH GORDON: THE GREATEST ADVENTURE OF ALL

This full-length, made-for-television fantasy tells the complete story of space-age hero, Flash Gordon, who, as a State Department employee in Warsaw, takes it upon himself to prevent the powerful Ming the Merciless from bringing his wave of destruction to the planet Earth. *A Filmation Associates Production in association with King Features. Color. Two hours. Premiered on NBC: August 21, 1982. Rebroadcast on NBC: September 5, 1982; September 26, 1982.*

*Voices*
**Flash Gordon:** Robert Ridgely; **Dale Arden:** Diane Pershing; **Dr. Zarkov:** David Opatoshu; **Ming the Merciless:** Bob Holt; **Vultan:** Vic Perrin; **Princess Aura:** Melendy Britt; **Prince Barin:** Robert Douglas; **Thun:** Ted Cassidy

## ⊚ THE FLIGHT OF DRAGONS

The good wizards select a young Boston writer, Peter Dickenson, to stop the menacing Red Wizards and reclaim a magic crown belonging to their race in this two-hour stop-motion (Animagic) special, produced by Arthur Rankin Jr. and Jules Bass of *Rudolph, The Red-Nosed Reindeer* and *Frosty the Snowman* television fame. A Rankin-Bass Production. *Color. Two hours. Premiered on ABC: August 3, 1986. Rebroadcast on DIS: December 1, 1992. Rebroadcast on CAR: July 30, 1995 (Mr. Spim's Cartoon Theatre).*

*Voices*
**Peter Dickenson:** John Ritter; **Carolinus:** Harry Morgan; **Ommadon:** James Earl Jones; **Smrgol:** James Gregory; **Gorbash:** Cosie Costa; **Arak:** Victor Buono; **Danielle:** Nellie Bellflower; **Princess Melisande:** Alexandra Stoddart; **Pawnbroker:** Larry Storch; **Vocalist:** Don McLean

## ⊚ A FLINTSTONE CHRISTMAS

Fred's holiday job as a part-time Santa at a Bedrock department store lands him in the real Santa's shoes on Christmas Eve in this half-hour holiday special, which was subtitled "How the Flintstones Saved Christmas." The week of December 15, 2003, the yuletide favorite was rebroadcast in three time slots on the fifth day of an amazing 240-hour Flintstones holiday marathon on Boomerang. *A Hanna-Barbera Production. Color. Half-hour. Premiered on NBC: December 7, 1977. Rebroadcast on NBC: December 11, 1978. Rebroadcast on CAR: December 13, 1992, November 28, 1993. Rebroadcast on TNT: November 29, 1993. Rebroadcast on CAR: December 18, 1993, November 26, 1994. Rebroadcast on TBS: December 17, 1995. Rebroadcast on TNT: December 13, 1995; December 12, 1996; December 7, 1997. Rebroadcast on BOOM: December 19, 2003.*

*Voices*
**Fred Flintstone:** Henry Corden; **Barney Rubble:** Mel Blanc; **Betty Rubble:** Gay Hartwig; **Wilma Flintstone:** Jean VanderPyl; **Pebbles Flintstone:** Gay Hartwig; **Bamm-Bamm Rubble:** Lucille Bliss; **Mrs. Santa:** Virginia Gregg; **Real Santa:** Hal Smith; **Ed the Foreman/Otis:** Don Messick; **George Slate, Fred's boss:** John Stephenson

## ⊚ A FLINTSTONE FAMILY CHRISTMAS

In the spirit of the holiday season, Fred and Wilma invite a caveless street urchin named Stony from "the wrong side of the tarpits" into their home and face a world of trouble while trying to teach the boy the difference between naughty and nice. *A Hanna-Barbera Production. Color. Half-hour. Premiered on ABC: December 18, 1993.*

*Voices*
**Fred Flintstone:** Henry Corden; **Wilma Flintstone:** Jean VanderPyl; **Barney Rubble:** Frank Welker; **Betty Rubble/Dino:** B.J. Ward

## ⊚ THE FLINTSTONE KIDS' "JUST SAY NO" SPECIAL

While Freddy, Betty, Barney and Philo are vacationing in exotic locales, Wilma's stuck in Bedrock. Lonely, she makes some new friends, one of whom (Stoney) tries turning Wilma on to drugs. This half-hour prime-time special tied in with former First Lady Nancy Reagan's national campaign to fight drug addiction. A cartoon take-off of rock singer Michael Jackson (called "Michael Jackstone") appears on the program. Featured songs: LaToya Jackson's "Just Say No" and Michael Jackson's "Beat It," with new lyrics added. The program was first broadcast in primetime and then rebroadcast as an ABC Weekend Special. *A Hanna-Barbera Production. Color. Half-hour. Premiered on ABC: September 15, 1988. Rebroadcast on ABC: September 24, 1988 (on ABC Weekend Special).*

*Voices*
**Wilma:** Elizabeth Lyn Fraser; **Freddy:** Scott Menville; **Barney:** Hamilton Camp; **Betty:** B.J. Ward; **Philo:** Bumper Robinson;

**Stoney:** Dana Hill; **Dottie:** Shuko Akune; **Joey:** David Markus; **Clyde:** Scott Menville; **Mr. Slaghoople:** Michael Rye; **Mrs. Slaghoople/Fluffy Woman:** Jean VanderPyl; **Dino/Fang/Crusher:** Frank Welker; **Officer Quartz:** Rene Levant; **Edna Flintstone:** Henry Corden; **Irate Man:** Michael Rye; **Angry Adult:** Jean VanderPyl; **Mrs. Gravelson/Female Announcer:** B.J. Ward; **Michael Jackstone:** Kip Lennon

## ◎ A FLINTSTONES CHRISTMAS CAROL

Christmas is nearly ruined when Fred, who plays Ebenezer Scrooge in the Bedrock Community Players Christmas production, becomes a scrooge himself in this 1994 Christmas special produced for first-run syndication. In December 2003, the beloved 1994 tele-film was rebroadcast multiple times on two different days of Boomerang's festive, 240-hour Flintstones holiday marathon of classic movies and specials. *A Hanna-Barbera Production. Color. Half-hour. Premiered: December 1994. Syndicated. Rebroadcast on TBS: December 15, 1995; December 6, 1996. Rebroadcast on TNT: December 7, 1997. Rebroadcast on BOOM: December 19, 2003; December 21, 2003.*

### Voices
**Fred Flintstone:** Henry Corden; **Wilma Flintstone:** Jean VanderPyl; **Barney Rubble/Spirit of Christmas Past/Belle:** Frank Welker; **Betty Rubble/Dino/Bronto/Cragit/Fezzing:** B.J. Ward; **Urchin #1 /Kid/Joe Rockhead:** Don Messick; **Bamm-Bamm/Pin Bird/Slate:** John Stephenson; **Marbly/Banner Hanger #1/Whistle Bird/Santa Claus:** Brian Cummings; **Pebbles/Spirit of Christmas Present/Passerby/Wrapper/Constable:** Russi Taylor; **Martha/Garnet Shale/Saleswoman/Ned:** Will Ryan; **Miss Feldspar:** Marsha Clark; **Fanny/Maggie/Urchin #2/Chip:** Maurice LaMarche; **Mother Pterodactyl/Banner Hanger #1/Philo Quartz/Customer #1:** Rene Levant

## ◎ THE FLINTSTONES: FRED'S FINAL FLING

With just 24 hours to live (or so he believes), Fred takes a final fling until his eyes close . . . with exhaustion. He awakens to discover the predictions of his demise were premature, but the lesson he learned will last a lifetime. In December 2003, the half-hour special aired three times on a single day to help kick off a remarkable week-long, 240-hour Flintstones holiday marathon on Boomerang. *A Hanna-Barbera Production. Color. Half-hour. Premiered on NBC: October 18, 1981. Rebroadcast on NBC: August 1, 1982. Rebroadcast on DIS: February 30, 1992. Rebroadcast on CAR: November 5, 1995 (Mr. Spim's Cartoon Theatre). Rebroadcast on BOOM: December 15, 2003.*

### Voices
**Fred Flintstone:** Henry Corden; **Barney Rubble:** Mel Blanc; **Betty Rubble:** Gay Autterson; **Wilma Flintstone/Pebbles Flintstone:** Jean VanderPyl; **Dino:** Mel Blanc; **Frank Frankenstone:** John Stephenson; **Monkey #2/Turtle #2:** Henry Corden; **Elephant:** Jean VanderPyl; **Monkey #3:** Mel Blanc; **Nurse/Turtle #1:** Gay Autterson; **Dinosaur/Monkey #1:** John Stephenson; **Doctor/Fish #1 & 2/Parrot/Pigasaurus:** Don Messick

## ◎ THE FLINTSTONES: JOGGING FEVER

Fred gets it from all sides about his bulging waistline. Even his boss, Mr. Slate, tells him to shape up. Fred decides to take up jogging and finds out how badly out of shape he is. In December 2003, Boomerang re-aired the special during the week of December 15 as part of a first-ever 240-hour Flintstones holiday marathon. *A Hanna-Barbera Production. Color. Half-hour. Premiered on NBC:*

*October 11, 1981. Rebroadcast on NBC: July 25, 1982. Rebroadcast on DIS: December 31, 1991; January 26, 1992; June 6, 1993. Rebroadcast on BOOM: December 17, 2003.*

### Voices
**Fred Flintstone:** Henry Corden; **Barney Rubble:** Mel Blanc; **Wilma Flintstone:** Jean VanderPyl; **Betty Rubble:** Gay Autterson; **Pebbles Flintstone:** Jean VanderPyl; **Dino:** Mel Blanc; **Frank Frankenstone/George Slate, Fred's boss:** John Stephenson; **Nurse #1:** Jean VanderPyl; **Nurse #2:** Gay Autterson; **Workman #2:** Henry Corden; **Turtle:** Mel Blanc; **Dinosaur/Pterodactyl/Bird/Snake:** John Stephenson; **Creeply/Announcer:** Frank Welker; **Control Tower Operator/Workman #1/Hipposaurus:** Wayne Norton

## ◎ THE FLINTSTONES: LITTLE BIG LEAGUE

Fred and Barney go to bat as coaches of opposing Little League teams and find their friendship crumbles as the big playoff game approaches in this hour-long, primetime special. Twenty-two years after its making, this 1981 television special was rebroadcast in December 2003 during a week-long, 240-hour Flintstones holiday marathon on the Cartoon Network's sister channel, Boomerang. *A Hanna-Barbera Production. Color. One hour. Premiered on NBC: April 6, 1976. Rebroadcast on NBC: October 10, 1980. Rebroadcast on CAR: June 4, 1994; November 5, 1995 (Mr. Spim's Cartoon Theatre). Rebroadcast on BOOM: December 16, 2003.*

### Voices
**Fred Flintstone:** Henry Corden; **Barney Rubble:** Mel Blanc; **Wilma Flintstone:** Jean VanderPyl; **Betty Rubble:** Gay Hartwig; **Pebbles Flintstone:** Pamela Anderson; **Bamm-Bamm Rubble:** Frank Welker; **Dino:** Mel Blanc; **Officer:** Ted Cassidy; **Judge:** Herb Vigran; **Dusty:** Lucille Bliss; **Lefty:** Randy Gray

## ◎ THE FLINTSTONES MEET ROCKULA AND FRANKENSTONE

The Flintstones and the Rubbles don crazy costumes to compete on the "Make a Deal or Don't" game show and to win a romantic trip to Count Rockula's castle in Rocksylvania. *A Hanna-Barbera*

*Pebbles shows Bamm-Bamm her "stuff" as Fred and Barney look on in a scene from the Hanna-Barbera special* The Flintstones: Little Big League. *© Hanna-Barbera Productions*

Production. Color. One hour. Premiered: on NBC: October 3, 1980. Rebroadcast on CAR: June 4, 1994: October 29, 1995 (Mr. Spim's Cartoon Theatre).

*Voices*
**Fred Flintstone:** Henry Corden; **Barney Rubble:** Mel Blanc; **Wilma Flintstone:** Jean VanderPyl; **Betty Rubble:** Gay Autterson; **Count Rockula:** John Stephenson; **Frankenstone:** Ted Cassidy; **Frau G.:** Jean VanderPly; **Monty Marble:** Casey Kasem; **Igor/Wolf:** Don Messick; **Silica/Bat:** Lennie Weinrib

## ◎ THE FLINTSTONES' NEW NEIGHBORS

Fred and Wilma are reluctant to greet their new neighbors, the Frankenstones, whose house is furnished with the weirdest creature comforts. A *Hanna-Barbera Productions. Color. Half-hour. Premiered on NBC: September 26, 1980. Rebroadcast on DIS: September 26, 1991. Rebroadcast on CAR: November 5, 1995 (Mr. Spim's Cartoon Theatre).*

*Voices*
**Fred Flintstone:** Henry Corden; **Barney Rubble:** Mel Blanc; **Wilma Flintstone:** Jean VanderPyl; **Betty Rubble:** Gay Autterson; **Pebbles Flintstone:** Jean VanderPyl; **Bamm-Bamm Rubble:** Don Messick; **Dino:** Mel Blanc; **Frank Frankenstone:** John Stephenson; **Oblivia Frankenstone:** Pat Parris; **Stubby Frankenstone:** Jim MacGeorge; **Hidea Frankenstone:** Julie McWhirter; **Creeply/Mother Pterodactyl:** Frank Welker; **Scorpion:** Henry Corden; **Vulture:** Don Messick; **Pterodactyl Chicks:** Don Messick, Mel Blanc, Frank Welker

## ◎ THE FLINTSTONES ON THE ROCKS

With their marriage in trouble, Fred and Wilma meet with a marriage counselor before going on an exotic vacation, an anniversary gift to them from the Rubbles. Fred's obnoxious behavior and tendency to take her for granted deeply disturb Wilma until she thinks he has bought her an expensive diamond pendant when her handbag is replaced by a jewel thief who steals the wrong one, in this made-for-television movie special that premiered on Cartoon Network. Winner of a 2003 Annie Award for outstanding achievement in an animated television production. *A Hanna-Barbera/Cartoon Network Production. Color. Ninety minutes. Premiered on CAR: November 3, 2001.*

*Voices*
**Fred Flintstone/Parking Guard/Vendor:** Jeff Bergman; **Wilma Flintstone:** Tress MacNeille; **Barney Rubble/Hector/Jewel Guard:** Kevin Michael Richard; **Betty Rubble/Mystery Woman:** Grey DeLisle; **Dino/Monkey/Elevator Guy:** Frank Welker; **Bellboy/Mammoth Vendor/Bed Monkey/Bowling Announcer:** Tom Kenny; **Stoney Altruda:** Joey Altruda; **Concierge/Bartender/Border Guard/Florist:** John Kassir; **Mr. Slate/Old Man:** John Stephenson; **Baritone Singer:** Oren Waters; **Soprano Singer:** Maxi Anderson; **Tenor Singer:** Carmen Twillie; **Bass Singer:** Willie Wheaton; **Xavier, the villain/Club Announcer/Pool Waiter:** Jeff Bennett; **Dino:** Mark Mangini; **Psychiatrist:** Zelda Rubenstein

## ◎ THE FLINTSTONES' 25TH ANNIVERSARY CELEBRATION

Using clips from past *Flintstones* episodes, along with all-new animation created especially for this program, Tim Conway, Harvey Korman and Vanna White, seen in live-action segments, host this nostalgic special tracing the unique history of television's first prime-time animated program. *A Hanna-Barbera Production. Color. One hour. Premiered on CBS: May 20, 1986.*

*Voices*
**Fred Flintstone:** Alan Reed, Henry Corden; **Wilma Flintstone:** Jean VanderPyl; **Barney Rubble:** Mel Blanc; **Betty Rubble:** Bea Benadaret; **Yogi Bear/Huckleberry Hound/Quick Draw McGraw:** Daws Butler; **Scooby-Doo/Scrappy-Doo:** Don Messick

## ◎ THE FLINTSTONES: WIND-UP WILMA

Wilma's mean wind-up in the supermarket, where she throws a melon and knocks two thieves unconscious for trying to steal her grocery money, turns her into an instant local celebrity. She is offered a baseball contract to pitch for the local Bedrock Dodger team, who since their attendance is lagging, could use her talent to boost interest in the team. On December 18, 2003, the 1981 Hanna-Barbera special was rebroadcast multiple times on Boomerang as part of a 240-hour Flintstones holiday marathon, including classic specials and movies. *A Hanna-Barbera Production. Color. Half-hour. Premiered on NBC: October 4, 1981. Rebroadcast on NBC: March 7, 1982. Rebroadcast on DIS: September 3, 1991. Rebroadcast on BOOM: December 18, 2003.*

*Voices*
**Fred Flintstone:** Henry Corden; **Barney Rubble:** Mel Blanc; **Wilma Flintstone:** Jean VanderPyl; **Betty Rubble:** Gay Autterson; **Pebbles Flintstone:** Jean VanderPyl; **Dino:** Mel Blanc; **Frank Frankenstone:** Julie McWhirter; **Turtle #2/Elephant:** Henry Corden; **Clothespin Bird:** Jean VanderPyl; **Female Cop/Cuckoo Bird:** Gay Autterson; **Animal/La Shale/Rocky:** Julie McWhirter; **Announcer/Bird #1/Turtle #1:** Don Messick; **Mean/Checker/Chick #1:** Joe Baker; **Stub/Cop:** Jim MacGeorge; **Sheep/Rooster/Umpire/Reporter #1/Thief/1st Man/Voice:** Paul Winchell; **Creeply/Bird #2/Finrock:** Frank Welker

## ◎ THE FOOL OF THE WORLD AND THE FLYING SHIP

Nearly two years went into producing this endearing two-part, stop motion puppet animated production derived from a classic Russian folktale (presented in two half-hour installments on PBS's *Long Ago and Far Away* anthology series) which tells the story a kind-hearted peasant boy (Pyotr) who tries to win an evil czar's daughter's hand in marriage by bringing him a "flying ship." David Suchet, best known as Agatha Christie's Poirot on the PBS series *Mystery!* narrates both segments. *A Cosgrove Hall/WGBH Boston Production. Color. Half-hour. Premiered on PBS: October 5, 1991 (Part 1) and October 12, 1991 (Part 2). Rebroadcast on PBS September 6, 1992 (Part 1) and September 13, 1992 (Part 2).*

*Voices*
**Narrator:** David Suchet

## ◎ FOR BETTER OR FOR WORSE: "A STORM IN APRIL"

Elly is discouraged when the whole Patterson family seems to be constantly self-absorbed: Michael is playing video games nonstop, Elizabeth is working madly on a school project on the electric typewriter, John is busy puttering about his electric train set and April is glued to the television set. So when Elly is asked to work more hours at the library, she jumps at the chance, only to find life isn't so easy when their regular babysitter is unavailable and she tries to take baby April to work with her in this sixth and final half-hour special in the *For Better or for Worse* series, which premiered on Disney Channel. *A Lacewood Production. Color. Half-hour. Premiered on DIS: October, 1992.*

## FOR BETTER OR FOR WORSE: "THE BABE MAGNET"

Michael complains that though he now has a driver's license, he never gets to use the Patterson family car. He and a friend decide to buy their own car—the perfect "Babe Magnet"—and hope that it will attract girls in this half-hour *For Better or for Worse* special. The program was the fifth of six specials, originally produced for Canadian television, to air on the Disney Channel. *A Lacewood Production. Color. Half-hour. Premiered on DIS: September, 1992.*

## FOR BETTER OR FOR WORSE: "THE BESTEST PRESENT"

Originally made for Canadian television audiences, this special—the first based on cartoonist Lynn Johnston's syndicated comic strip, *For Better or for Worse*—deals with the nightmarish adventures of the Patterson family during Christmas when daughter Lizzie loses her precious stuffed bunny while Christmas shopping. *An Atkinson Film-Arts Production in association with Telefilm, Canada. Color. Half-hour. Premiere (U.S.) on HBO: December 1986. Rebroadcast on DIS: December 11, 1991; December 12, 1993; December 6, 1994; December 2, 1996.*

*Voices*
**Michael Patterson:** Aaron Johnston; **Elizabeth "Lizzy" Patterson:** Katherine Johnston; **Elly Patterson:** Abby Hagyard; **John Patterson:** William H. Stevens, Jr.; **Walter Lederhaus:** Billy Van; **Connie:** Anna MacCormick; **Lawrence:** Dominic Bradford; **Vocalist:** Scott Binkley

## FOR BETTER OR FOR WORSE: "THE CHRISTMAS ANGEL"

"Too little to be big and too big to be little," Lizzie is suffering from the middle-child syndrome. When the rest of the Patterson family seems to have no time for her or for decorating their Christmas tree, Lizzie undertakes the task herself, aided and abetted by the family dog, Farley, which leads to disaster in this half-hour holiday special, part of the *For Better or for Worse* series specials. *A Lacewood Production. Color. Half-hour. Premiered on DIS: September, 1992. Rebroadcast on DIS: December 7, 1992; December 19, 1993; December 6, 1994; December 2, 1996.*

## FOR BETTER OR FOR WORSE: "THE GOOD FOR NOTHING"

The Patterson family is busily preparing for the fall fair—Elizabeth is grooming Farley for the dog show and Elly is planning to enter the squash from her garden—only for things to go from bad to worse when Farley makes a mess of Elly's garden and his performance in the dog show is a fiasco. The half-hour special, originally produced for Canadian television, premiered in the United States as part of a series of *For Better or for Worse* cartoon specials on the Disney Channel. *A Lacewood Production. Color. Half-hour. Premiered on DIS: September, 1992. Rebroadcast on DIS: December 20, 1992; November 1, 1994.*

## FOR BETTER OR FOR WORSE: "THE LAST CAMPING TRIP"

In this half-hour animated special based on cartoonist Lynn Johnston's popular comic strip, Michael is looking forward to the last day of school and to going up to his friend's cottage but is horrified to discover that his parents have planned a camping trip to the East Coast and insist that he go with them. The Canadian-produced special was the first of six *For Better or for Worse* specials to air on The Disney Channel. *A Lacewood Production. Color. Half-hour. Premiered on DIS: August 28, 1992.*

## FOR BETTER OR FOR WORSE: "VALENTINE FROM THE HEART"

Difficulties abound when Michael cons his parents into letting him throw a Valentine's Day party, only to have bully Brad Luggsworth crash the event and wreak unintentional havoc when the rest of the kids turn against him. Michael and his friends later try to make amends when Brad decides to leave town in this half-hour *For Better or for Worse* special, one of six animated specials broadcast on the Disney Channel. *A Lacewood Production. Color. Half-hour. Premiered on DIS: September, 1992. Rebroadcast on DIS: February 6, 1993.*

## FOSTER'S HOME FOR IMAGINARY FRIENDS: "A LOST CLAUS"

After questioning whether Santa Claus is real or not, Mac and Bloo try proving his existence scientifically, only to have their experiments backfire and restore their faith in Santa in this half-hour special based on the Flash-animated original series created by Craig McCracken, creator of *The Powerpuff Girls*, for the Cartoon Network. *A Cartoon Network Studios Production. Color. Half-hour. Premiered on CAR: December 1, 2005. Rebroadcast on CAR: December 6, 2005; December 16, 2005; December 21, 2005; December 23, 2005; December 24, 2005; December 25, 2005; December 6, 2006; December 16, 2006; December 18, 2006; December 21, 2006; December 22, 2006; December 24, 2006; December 25, 2006.*

*Voices*
**Frances "Frankie" Foster/Duchess/Mac's Mom:** Grey DeLisle; **Blooregard "Bloo" Q. Kazoo/Fireman:** Keith Ferguson; **Coco/Madame Foster:** Candi Milo; **Eduardo/Mail Santa Manager:** Tom Kenny; **Mr. Herriman/Imaginary Santa #2:** Tom Kane; **Terrence:** Tara Strong; **Mac:** Sean Marquette; **Wilt:** Phil LaMarr

## FOSTER'S HOME FOR IMAGINARY FRIENDS: "GOOD WILT HUNTING"

Having no success attracting a visitor to the Foster's Creator Reunion Picnic again, a despondent Wilt treks cross-country in hopes of reuniting with his long-lost creator. Meanwhile, Bloo and the Foster gang take to the road to find him, encountering many unexpected twists and turns while discovering more about Wilt's mysterious past in the first-ever original movie based on creator Craig McCracken's (of TV's *The Powerpuff Girls* fame) series, *Foster's Home for Imaginary Friends*. Preceded by a 12-hour marathon of mostly thankful episodes from the hit series beginning at 7 A.M., the hour-long special bowed in prime time at 7 P.M. on Thanksgiving Day eve. *A Cartoon Network Studios/Boulder Media, Ltd. Production. Color. One hour. Premiered on CAR: November 24, 2006.*

*Voices*
**Frankie/Duchess/Mom:** Grey DeLisle; **Bloo/Host/Friend #4:** Keith Ferguson; **Mr. Herriman/Nature Show Host/Funky/Friend #5:** Tom Kane; **Eduardo/Australian Host/Scissors/Friend #2/Friend #6/Unicorn #2:** Tom Kenny; **Wilt/Announcer/Friend #3/Snooty Dad:** Phil LaMarr; **Mac:** Sean Marquette; **Coco/Friend #1/Unicorn #1:** Candi Milo; **Terrence/Sultry Woman/Boy/Snooty Girl/Snooty Mom:** Tara Strong

## FOSTER'S HOME FOR IMAGINARY FRIENDS: "HOUSE OF BLOO'S"

After being forced to give up his imaginary friend Bloo, Mac, a shy eight-year-old boy, finds the ideal place for him to live: Foster's Home for Imaginary Friends, where, besides becoming friends with many of the other kid residents, Eduardo, Wilt,

Coco and others, they adopt Bloo, but not before standing up against an evil 13-year-old friend who puts Bloo in danger in this 90-minute pilot for the series, *Foster's Home for Imaginary Friends*, that aired as a special from *Powerpuff Girls* creator Craig McCracken on Cartoon Network. *A Cartoon Network Studios/ Boulder Media, Ltd. Production. Color. Ninety minutes. Premiered on CAR: July 16, 2004.*

**Voices**
**Frankie/Duchess/Mom:** Grey DeLisle; **Bloo/Host/Friend #4:** Keith Ferguson; **Mr. Herriman/Nature Show Host/Funky/Friend #5:** Tom Kane; **Eduardo/Australian Host/Scissors/Friend #2/ Friend #6/Unicorn #2:** Tom Kenny; **Wilt/Announcer/Friend #3/Snooty Dad:** Phil LaMarr; **Mac:** Sean Marquette; **Coco/Friend #1/Unicorn #1:** Candi Milo; **Terrence/Sultry Woman/Boy/ Snooty Girl/Snooty Mom:** Tara Strong

## ◎ THE FOURTH KING

Spotting a "strange new light in the sky"—the star of Bethlehem—the animals of the land decide to send emissaries of their own—a lion, sparrow, rabbit, beaver and turtle—so they also will be represented along with the three traveling kings at the manger where the Christ child is to be born. *A RAI Television Production in association with NBC. Color. Half-hour. Premiered on NBC: December 23, 1977.*

**Voices**
**Lion:** Ted Ross; **Sparrow:** Laurie Beechman; **Turtle:** Arnold Stang; **Beaver:** Bob McFadden; **Rabbit:** Ed Klein

## ◎ FRANKLIN AND THE GREEN KNIGHT

With winter nearly over, Franklin looks forward to spring and the birth of a new baby sister, after which he embarks on a long quest as a knight with his friend Snail as his squire, based on a mythical story his mother told him called *The Quest of the Green Knight*, in this first made-for-video feature-length movie. Produced in 1999, the 75-minute adventure, which preceded the popular weekly Nick Jr. cartoon series, subsequently aired on Canada's Family Channel and the United States' Nick Jr. and Noggin cable networks. Two additional straight-to-video movies followed, each of which were eventually broadcast on the same networks in Canada and the United States: *Franklin's Magic Christmas* (2001) and *Back to School with Franklin* (2003). *A Nelvana LimitedHong Guang Animation Production. Color. Half-hour. Premiered on NICK JR.: August 19, 2003. Rebroadcast on Noggin: March 15, 2004; March 16, 2004; March 17, 2004; March 18, 2004; March 19, 2004; March 20, 2004; March 21, 2004; March 21, 2005; March 22, 2005; March 23, 2005; March 24, 2005; March 26, 2005; March 27, 2005; March 20, 2006; March 22, 2006; March 24, 2006; March 25, 2006; March 26, 2006.*

**Voices**
**Franklin Turtle:** Noah Reid; **Mr. Turtle/Great Grandfather Turtle:** Richard Newman; **Mrs. Turtle:** Elizabeth Brown; **Rabbit:** Kyle Fairlie; **Beaver:** Leah Cudmore; **Goose:** Olivia Garratt; **Bear:** Luca Perlman; **Snail:** Kristen Boone; **Badger:** Ruby Smith-Merovitz; **Mr. Owl:** James Rankin; **Granny Turtle:** Corinne Conley; **Mrs. Goose:** Catherine Disher; **Mr. Fox:** Paul Haddad; **Green Knight:** Juan Chioran; **Squire:** Paul Essiembre; **Goblin:** Jonathan Wilson; **Lynx:** Gary Krawford; **Mrs. Beaver:** Valerie Boyle; **Mr. Beaver:** Adrian Truss; **Mrs. Fox/Eagle:** Elizabeth Hanna; **Gopher:** Jim Jones; **Warbler:** Debra McGrath; **Armadillo:** Annick Obonsawin; **Additional Voices:** Shirley Douglas, Ali Mukaddam, Luca Perlman

## ◎ FRANKLIN'S MAGIC CHRISTMAS

After becoming annoyed with his sister Harriet for causing him to leave his favorite stuffed toy behind while visiting their grandparents at Faraway Farm, thanks to some holiday magic Franklin patches things up with his sibling in the true spirit of Christmas in this second direct-to-video and DVD movie, following the first, *Franklin and the Green Knight* (1999).

In 1997, Franklin was featured in a weekly series, produced by Canada's Nelvana Limited, which premiered in the United States on Nick Jr. Besides debuting on Canada's Family Channel, the feature-length production likewise premiered in November 2001 in the United States on Nick Jr. Noggin has rebroadcast the animated adventure multiple times on its morning and afternoon schedules every holiday season since its first telecast in December 2004. In 2003 a third made-for-video movie was produced, *Back to School with Franklin*, which subsequently aired on Noggin and other networks as well. *A Nelvana Limited Production. Color. Half-hour. Premiered on NICK JR.: November 6, 2001. Rebroadcast on Noggin: December 13, 2004; December 14, 2004; December 15, 2004; December 16, 2004; December 17, 2004; December 18, 2004; December 19, 2004; December 24, 2004; December 25, 2004; November 26, 2005; November 27, 2005; November 28, 2005; November 29, 2005; November 30, 2005; December 1, 2005; December 2, 2005; December 3, 2005; December 4, 2005; December 24, 2005; December 25, 2005; December 11, 2006; December 16, 2006; December 23, 2006; December 24, 2006; December 25, 2006.*

**Voices**
**Franklin Turtle:** Noah Reid; **Mr. Turtle/Great Grandfather Turtle:** Richard Newman; **Mrs. Turtle:** Elizabeth Brown; **Narrator:** Janet-Laine Green; **Bear:** Luca Perlman; **Beaver:** Leah Cudmore; **Goose:** Olivia Garratt; **Beatrice/Young Grandmother Jenny Turtle:** Kristen Bone; **Mr. Bear:** Donald Burda; **Mr. Collie:** Chris Wiggins; **Dr. Bear:** Mari Trainor; **Grandmother Jenny Turtle:** Joyce Gordon; **Grandfather Turtle:** Eric Peterson; **Mrs. Collie:** Araby Lockhart

## ◎ FREEDOM IS

In his dreams, Benji and his pet dog, Waldo, are transported back in time to the Revolutionary War, where they learn all about freedom with the help of new friend, Jeremiah Goodheart. *A Screen Images Production for Lutheran Television. Color. Half-hour. Premiered: Summer 1976. Syndicated.*

**Voices**
**Benji:** David Kelly; **Jeremiah Goodheart:** Jonathan Winters; **Samuel:** Richard Roundtree; **Ben Franklin:** Joseph Cotton; **John Adams:** Edward Asner; **Thomas Jefferson:** Dan Dailey; **Jason:** Philip Morris

## ◎ A FREEZERBURNT CHRISTMAS

When an evil toy magnate grounds Santa's reindeer, shy Freezerburnt and his best friends, Anna, and the penguin, Chill, save Christmas by helping Santa Claus deliver Christmas gifts in a magical flying ice cream truck in this stop-motion, clay-animated special voiced by comedian Darrell Hammond, Horatio Sanz and other cast members from NBC's late-night comedy series, *Saturday Night Live*. The special was written and directed by Michael Bannon, co-founder of Wreckless Abandon Studios, a New England–based production company that produces award-winning clay animation, stop-motion and 3-D-computer-animated commercials, including the groundbreaking Davey and Goliath Mountain Dew ad, and other productions. *A Freezerburnt Christmas* was in development for four years before premiering on NBC in December 2002. *A Wreckless Abandon Studios Production. Color. Half-hour. Premiered on NBC: December 21, 2002.*

**Voices**
Darrell Hammond, Horatio Sanz.

## ◎ FRÈRE JACQUES

Frere Jacques is in trouble until, with the help of his friend, the Wizard Owl, he breaks an evil spell of eternal sleep cast upon the king in this half-hour animated interpretation of the classic children's song, which aired as part of HBO's Storybook Musicals *"The Real Story of . . . "* series. Best-selling recording star Stevie Nicks (of Fleetwood Mac fame) provides the voice of the owl. *A CINAR Films/France Animation Production. Color. Half-hour. Premiered on HBO: January 3, 1994.*

**Voices**
**The Wizard Owl:** Stevie Nicks

## ◎ FROG AND TOAD

Nine of Arthur Lobel's best-loved "Frog and Toad" stories—from *Frog and Toad Together* and *Frog and Toad Are Friends*—come to life in this two-part stop-motion puppet-animated special, following the adventures of the blustery Toad and patient Frog, produced for PBS's award-winning series *Long Ago & Far Away. A Churchill Films Production. Color. Half-hour. Premiered on PBS: May 6, 1989 (Part 1) and May 13, 1989 (Part 2). Rebroadcast on PBS: November 24, 1990 (Part 1) and December 1, 1990 (Part 2); February 21, 1992 (Part 1) and February 28, 1992 (Part 2).*

## ◎ FROM DISNEY, WITH LOVE

This 90-minute animated salute to Disney's female characters, produced by The Disney Channel to tie in with Valentine's Day, features clips from many of the studio's classic films, including *Lady and the Tramp, Bambi, Snow White, Cinderella* and *Sleeping Beauty*, among others. *A Film Landa Inc. Production for The Disney Channel. Color. Ninety minutes. Premiered on DIS: 1984.*

## ◎ FROM THE EARTH TO THE MOON

The early triumphs of an adventurous group, the Gun Club, that attempts to reach the moon by launching a manned vessel is related in this half-hour syndicated special produced overseas. *An Air Programs International Production. Color. Half-hour. Premiered: 1976. Syndicated.*

**Voices**
Alistair Duncan, Ron Haddrick, Phillip Hinton, Shane Porteous

## ◎ FROSTY RETURNS

The lovable snowman with the "corncob pipe and a button nose and two eyes made out of coal" (voiced by John Goodman) battles a nasty old inventor, Mr. Twitchell, who wows the town of Beansborough with his Summer Wheeze de-icing spray. The spray threatens to alter weather cycles dramatically and put an end to Frosty's existence, when the jolly old snowman comes up with a plan that saves the day (thanks to his new pal, a little girl named Holly), in this second sequel to the 1969 holiday classic *Frosty the Snowman. A Bill Melendez Production in association with Broadway Video and CBS Entertainment Productions. Color. Half-hour. Premiered on CBS: December 1, 1995. Rebroadcast on CBS: December 6, 1996; December 12, 1997.*

**Voices**
**Frosty the Snowman:** John Goodman; **Narrator:** Jonathan Winters

## ◎ FROSTY'S WINTER WONDERLAND

In this first sequel to 1969's *Frosty the Snowman*, Frosty's moppet friends create a wife for the usually joyful snowman whom they find is really lonely. Jack Frost, jealous of the snowman's newfound happiness, makes every effort to make life miserable for him once again. Andy Griffith narrates and sings in this imaginatively wrought special. Songs featured include "Frosty" and "Winter Wonderland." *A Rankin-Bass Production. Color. Half-hour. Premiered on ABC: December 2, 1976. Rebroadcast on ABC: December 3, 1977; December 13, 1978; November 25, 1979; December 23, 1981; December 1, 1982: Rebroadcast on DIS: December 4, 1993. Rebroadcast on FAM: December 10, 1995. Rebroadcast on DIS: December 25, 1996. Rebroadcast on FOX FAM: December 7, 1998; December 17, 1998; December 20, 1998; July 13, 1999; December 6, 1999; December 10, 1999; December 18, 1999; December 23, 1999; December 24, 1999; December 13, 2000; December 18, 2000; December 21, 2000; December 24, 2000. Rebroadcast on ABC FAM: December 1, 2001; December 4, 2001; December 12, 2001; December 15, 2002; December 22, 2002; December 24, 2002; December 6, 2003; December 17, 2003; December 22, 2003; December 1, 2004; December 4, 2004; December 19, 2004; December 24, 2004; December 1, 2005; December 3, 2005; December 6, 2005; December 24, 2005; December 1, 2006; December 9, 2006; December 19, 2006; December 24, 2006.*

**Voices**
**Frosty the Snowman:** Jackie Vernon; **Crystal the Snowgirl:** Shelley Winters; **Parson:** Dennis Day; **Jack Frost:** Paul Frees; **Children:** Shelley Hines, Eric Stern; **Others:** Manfred Olea, Barbara Jo Ewing; **Narrator:** Andy Griffith; **Vocalists:** The Wee Winter Singers

## ◎ FROSTY THE SNOWMAN (1953)

In 1953, America's favorite snowman, Frosty, was brought to life in this three-minute stop-motion animated short produced by Hollywood's United Productions of America (UPA) backed by a jazzy rendition of the popular song—written by Steve "Jack" Rollins and Steve Nelson and made famous by recording artist Gene Autry—that made its television debut that December on WGN-TV's *Garfield Goose and Friends*, hosted by Frazier Thomas. Such other classic yuletide shorts as *Suzy Snowflake* and *Hardrock, Coco and Joe: The Three Little Dwarfs* became perennial favorites on the network. Over the years WGN replayed all three classic cartoons on its popular children's variety programs, including *Bozo's Circus, Garfield Goose and Friends* and *The Ray Rayner Show*. In December 2005, this vintage holiday short was rebroadcast nationally as part of WGN-TV's children's programming retrospective, *Bozo, Gar, & Ray. A UPA Studios Production. Black and white. Three minutes. Premiered on WGN: 1955. December 1953.*

## ◎ FROSTY THE SNOWMAN (1969)

Based on a song of the same name by Jack Rollins and Steve Nelson, this perennial favorite traces the origin of America's best-known snowman—brought to life by a magic hat on Christmas Eve—and his struggle to get to the North Pole before spring arrives. *A Rankin-Bass Production. Color. Half-hour. Premiered on CBS: December 7, 1969. Rebroadcast on CBS: December 5, 1970; December 5, 1971; December 4, 1972; December 10, 1973; December 8, 1974; December 12, 1975; December 17, 1976; December 10, 1977; November 30, 1978; December 8, 1979; November 28, 1980; November 27, 1981; December 21, 1982 December 14, 1983; December 11, 1984; December 7, 1985; December 12, 1986; December 9, 1987; November 28, 1988; December 22, 1989; December 19, 1990;*

*December 18, 1991; December 16, 1992; December 6, 1993; November 30, 1994; December 1, 1995; December 6, 1996; December 12, 1997; December 1998; December 1999; December 2000; December 2001; December 2002; December 2003; December 2004; December 17, 2005; December 8, 2006. Rebroadcast on CAR: December 24, 2003.*

**Voices**
**Frosty the Snowman:** Jackie Vernon; **Professor Hinkle:** Billy DeWolfe; **Karen, Frosty's friend:** June Foray; **Santa Claus:** Paul Frees; **Narrator:** Jimmy Durante

### ◎ A GARFIELD CHRISTMAS SPECIAL

Jon goes home to the farm for the holidays. While Odie works on a mystery gift, Garfield plans to surprise Grandma. An Emmy Award nominee. *A Film Roman Production in association with United Media and Paws. Color. Half-hour. Premiered on CBS: December 21, 1987. Rebroadcast on CBS: December 23, 1988; December 21, 1989; December 7, 1990: December 6, 1991; December 2, 1992; December 19, 1996.*

**Voices**
**Garfield:** Lorenzo Music; **Jon Arbuckle:** Thom Huge; **Odie:** Gregg Berger; **Mom:** Julie Payne; **Dad:** Pat Harrington; **Doc Boy:** David Lander; **Grandma:** Pat Carroll

### ◎ GARFIELD GETS A LIFE

Follows the hapless social antics of Garfield's dweeb owner, Jon, as Garfield tries to help him "get a life" and a girlfriend. This prime-time half-hour special features music by Lou Rawls, B.B. King and The Temptations. *A Film Roman Production in association with United Media/Mendelson and Paws Inc. Color. Half-hour. Premiered on CBS: May 8, 1991.*

**Voices**
**Garfield:** Lorenzo Music; **Jon:** Thom Huge; **Odie:** Gregg Berger; **Lorenzo:** Frank Welker; **Mona:** June Foray

**Additional Voices**
Julie Payne

### ◎ GARFIELD GOES HOLLYWOOD

When the TV show *Pet Search* announces a pet talent, contest Jon devises an act for himself, Garfield and Odie: Jonny Bop and the Two Steps. They win the local event and head to Hollywood for the finals, where Garfield and Odie cut Jon out of the act and become The Dancing Armandos. An Emmy Award nominee. *A Film Roman Production in association with United Media and Paws. Color. Half-hour. Premiered on CBS: May 8, 1987. Rebroadcast on CBS: March 16, 1988.*

**Voices**
**Garfield:** Lorenzo Music; **Jon Arbuckle:** Thom Huge; **Odie/Bob/Grandma Fogerty/Announcer:** Gregg Berger; **Herbie:** Nino Tempo; **National TV Host:** Frank Welker

### ◎ GARFIELD: HIS NINE LIVES

Garfield hosts a look at his nine lives. At the end, he is luckily given an additional nine. Ten segments actually make up the special: "In the Beginning," with the "creator" deciding to design a cat; "Cave Cat," showing the prehistoric origins of cats; "King Cat," revealing Garfield's royal heritage; "In the Garden," the story of Garfield's sharing joy in a whimsical world of fantasy with a young girl (Cloey); "Court Musician," with Garfield as the inventor of jazz; "Stunt Rat," featuring Garfield working in silent films; "Diana's Piano," a touching tale about the cycle of life and death;

"Lab Animal," offering a strange tale of an experiment that goes awry; "Garfield," the origin of the famed comic-strip character; and "Space Cat," his travels in the distant future and a distant galaxy. *A Film Roman Productions in association with United Media and Paws. Color. One hour. Premiered on CBS: November 22, 1988.*

**Voices**
**Garfield:** Lorenzo Music; **Odie:** Gregg Berger; **The Creator:** Lindsay Workman; **Narrator ("Cave Cat"):** Gregg Berger; **Junior:** Thom Huge; **Black Bart:** Nino Tempo; **Announcer ("In the Garden"):** Desiree Goyette; **Jester ("Court Musician"):** Gregg Berger; **Director ("Stunt Kat"):** Jim Davis; **Sara ("Diana's Piano"):** Desiree Goyette; **Jon Arbuckle ("Garfield"):** Thom Huge; **Garfield's Mom ("Garfield"):** Desiree Goyette; **Captain Mendelson ("Space Cat"):** Frank Welker

### ◎ GARFIELD IN PARADISE

Garfield, Odie and Jon vacation in the tropics at a cheap resort. When they go exploring, they meet a lost tribe that worships 1950's automobiles and is preparing a human and cat sacrifice for the volcano god. An Emmy Award nominee. *A Film Roman Production in association with United Media and Paws. Color. Half-hour. Premiered on CBS: May 27, 1986. Rebroadcast on CBS: January 16, 1987; November 23, 1988; April 24, 1989.*

**Voices**
**Garfield:** Lorenzo Music; **Jon Arbuckle:** Thom Huge; **High Rama Lama:** Wolfman Jack; **Hotel Clerk/Salesman:** Frank Nelson; **Odie Pigeon:** Gregg Berger; **Owooda:** Desiree Goyette; **Mai Tai/Stewardess:** Julie Payne; **Monkey:** Nino Tempo; **Woman/Cat:** Carolyn Davis; **B.G. Voices:** Hal Smith; **Vocalists:** Desiree Goyette, Thom Huge, Lorenzo Music, Lou Rawls

### ◎ GARFIELD IN THE ROUGH

Garfield's enthusiasm for a vacation wanes when he discovers Jon plans a camping trip. Life in the wild gets dangerous when an escaped panther enters the campgrounds. An Emmy Award winner. *A Film Roman Production in association with United Media and Paws. Color. Half-hour. Premiered on CBS: October 26, 1984. Rebroadcast on CBS: March 23, 1985; August 21, 1987.*

*Garfield's enthusiastic arrival at a flea-bitten resort is further punctuated by the discovery of Odie, who has stowed away in a suitcase, in the prime-time special* Garfield in Paradise. *© United Feature Syndicate*
(COURTESY: CBS)

*Voices*
**Garfield:** Lorenzo Music; **Jon Arbuckle:** Thom Huge; **Odie/ Ranger #1/Announcer:** Gregg Berger; **Ranger #2:** George Wendt; **Dicky Beaver:** Hal Smith; **Billy Rabbit:** Orson Bean; **Girl Cats/ Arlene:** Desiree Goyette; **Vocalists:** Desiree Goyette, Thom Huge, Lou Rawls

## GARFIELD ON THE TOWN
On the way to the vet's, Garfield slips out of the car and attempts to make it as a street cat. While in the inner city, he discovers his birthplace and family. An Emmy Award winner. *A Lee Mendelson–Bill Melendez Production in association with United Media Productions. Color. Half-hour. Premiered on CBS: October 28, 1983. Rebroadcast on CBS: March 10, 1984; December 28, 1985; September 5, 1990.*

*Voices*
**Garfield:** Lorenzo Music; **Jon Arbuckle:** Thom Huge; **Raoul:** George Wendt; **Ali Cat:** Gregg Berger; **Mom, Garfield's mother:** Sandi Huge; **Liz:** Julie Payne; **Grandfather:** Lindsay Workman; **Girl Cat #2 & #3:** Allyce Beasley; **Girl Cat #1:** Desiree Goyette; **Vocalists:** Desiree Goyette, Lou Rawls

## GARFIELD'S BABES AND BULLETS
In this satire of detective films of the 1940s, Garfield fantasizes (in black-and-white) on a rainy day about being Sam Spayed, a private investigator handling a case involving a mysterious woman. An Emmy Award winner. *A Film Roman Production in association with United Media and Paws. Color. Half-hour. Premiered on CBS: May 23, 1989.*

*Voices*
**Garfield:** Lorenzo Music; **Jon Arbuckle:** Thom Huge; **Odie/Burt Fleebish:** Gregg Berger; **Thug:** Thom Huge; **Kitty:** Julie Payne; **Tanya:** Desiree Goyette; **Professor O'Felix:** Lindsay Workman; **Lt. Washington:** Nino Tempo

## GARFIELD'S FELINE FANTASIES
Garfield and Odie fantasize that they are on a Middle East mission to retrieve the Banana of Bombay, the symbol of humor to nations around the world. The prime-time half-hour special, which debuted on Friday, May 18, 1990, in the 8:30–9:00 P.M. time period, was nominated for an Emmy Award the following year. *A Film Roman Production in association with United Media and Paws. Color. Half-hour. Premiered on CBS: May 18, 1990.*

*Voices*
**Garfield/Lance Sterling:** Lorenzo Music; **Jon Arbuckle:** Thom Huge; **Odie/Slobber Job:** Gregg Berger

## GARFIELD'S HALLOWEEN ADVENTURE
Garfield and Odie get dressed up as pirates to go trick or treating. They accidentally end up at a haunted house where ghostly pirates are expected any minute. An Emmy Award winner. *A Film Roman Production in association with United Media Productions. Color. Half-hour. Premiered on CBS: October 30, 1985. Rebroadcast on CBS: October 24, 1986; October 23, 1987; October 28, 1988; October 30, 1989.*

*Voices*
**Garfield:** Lorenzo Music; **Jon Arbuckle:** Thom Huge; **Odie:** Gregg Berger; **Old Man:** Lindsay Workman; **TV Announcer:** Gregg Berger; **Woman:** Desiree Goyette; **Vocalists:** Lorenzo Music, Lou Rawls

## GARFIELD'S THANKSGIVING SPECIAL
The day before Thanksgiving, Garfield is put on a diet and Liz, the veterinarian, agrees to have Thanksgiving dinner with Jon. However, when Jon's manages to destroy the meal, Grandma arrives in time to save the day and Garfield is given a reprieve from fasting. An Emmy Award winner. *A Film Roman Production in association with United Media and Paws. Color. Half-hour. Premiered on CBS: November 22, 1989.*

*Voices*
**Garfield:** Lorenzo Music; **Jon Arbuckle:** Thom Huge; **Odie:** Gregg Berger; **Liz/Scale:** Julie Payne; **Grandma:** Pat Carroll; **Vocalists:** Lou Rawls, Desiree Goyette

## GARY LARSON'S TALES FROM THE FAR SIDE
Syndicated cartoonist Gary Larson's sadistic comic strip *The Far Side* comes to life in this humorous Halloween-themed special showcasing his trademark bugs, monsters, redneck hunters and zombies as they meet their comical fates in parodies of familiar spooky tales. *An International Rocketship Production for FarWorks Inc. Color. Half-hour. Premiered on CBS: October 26, 1994.*

*Voices*
Kathleen Barr, Doug Parker, Lee Tokar, Dale Wilson

## GIDGET MAKES THE WRONG CONNECTION
In this animated spinoff of the *Gidget* television series, Frances "Gidget" Lawrence and her surfer friends expose a ring of gold smugglers in this one-hour movie originally broadcast on the *The ABC Saturday Superstar Movie* series. *A Hanna-Barbera Production. Color. One hour. Premiered on ABC: November 18, 1972 (on The ABC Saturday Superstar Movie). Rebroadcast on ABC: October 6, 1973; March 16, 1974. Syndicated.*

*Voices*
**Gidget:** Kathy Gori; **Rink/Steve:** Denny Evans; **Killer/Gorgeous Cat/Capt. Parker:** Don Messick; **Ralph Hightower/R.C. Man:** Mike Road; **Radio (Voice):** Don Messick; **Bull/Capt. Shad:** Bob Hastings; **Barbara Hightower:** Virginia Gregg; **Jud:** David Lander

## G.I. JOE: GREATEST EVIL
The G.I. Joe team and COBRA organization unite in the war against drugs, forming the Drug Elimination Force (DEF), and make the Head Man's local drug factory their primary target in this hour-long special, which premiered in daytime syndication in 1991. The program was rebroadcast in syndication in 1992 as a two-part special in most markets. *A DIC Enterprises Production. Color. One hour. Premiered: December 1, 1991. Rebroadcast: October 24, 1992–November 7, 1992. Syndicated.*

## G.I. JOE: SPY TROOPS THE MOVIE
The Spy Troops, an elite G.I. Joe force, battle the Cobra forces, who disguise themselves as the G.I. Joe team to steal new technology and capture Scarlett, whom the Spy Troops go undercover to rescue while infiltrating the Cobra forces to save the world in this 44-minute, direct-to-video, CGI-animated movie, based on the Hasbro Spy Troops toy line, that premiered on Cartoon Network in September 2003. The movie followed an eight-week trial run of episodes of Sunbow/Marvel Productions' syndicated 1980s *G.I. Joe: A Real American Hero* series, that began with a 30-episode midnight marathon that aired on the Cartoon Network on July 1, 2002. *A Reel FX Production. Color. One hour. Premiered on CAR: September 27, 2003.*

**Voices**
**Duke:** John Payne; **Beachheead:** Matt Hill, **Scarlett:** Lisa Ann Beley; **Shipwreck:** Lee Tockar; **Wild Bill:** Don Davis; **Hightech:** Mark Hildreth; **Cobra Commander:** Michael Dobson; **Destro:** Scott McNeil; **Baroness:** Teryl Rothery; **Dr. Mindbender:** Jim Foronda; **Tunnel Rat:** Doron Bell; **Flint:** Brian Dobson; **Barrel Roll:** Paul Dobson; **Torpedo:** Phil Hayes; **Dusty:** Alessandro Juliani: **Polly:** Peter Kelamis; **Heavy Duty:** Blu Mankuma; **Zartan:** Colin Murdock; **Storm Shadow:** Ty Olsson; **SnakeEyes:** Jake Parker; **Agent Faces:** Ward Perry

## THE GINGHAM DOG AND THE CALICO CAT

Popular singer Amy Grant tells this story of two bickering stuffed animals—a dog and a cat—who fall out of Santa's sleigh, and work together to find their way to their new home in this half-hour animated special. First broadcast on Showtime, it featured a music soundtrack by country music guitar legend Chet Atkins. Part of Rabbit Ears *Holiday Classics* video series. *A Rabbit Ears Video Production. Color. Premiered on SHO: December 3, 1991. Rebroadcast on SHO: December 23, 1991.*

**Voices**
**Narrator:** Amy Grant

## GLOBE HUNTERS: AN AROUND THE WORLD IN 80 DAYS ADVENTURE

Three animals who escape from a genetics lab—a sassy lady Cheetah; a nervous bespectacled parrot; and a rebellious gorilla—embark on a musical 'round-the-world adventure to satisfy a bet while eluding a hunter sent to find them in this animated movie loosely based on Jules Verne's classic novel, *Around the World in Eighty Days.* Featuring an all-star voice cast including Sid Caesar, Willem Dafoe, Chaka Kahn and Carl Reiner, this 11th of 13 television features was part of *DIC's Incredible Movie Toons* anthology series that aired on Nicklelodeon. *A DIC Entertainment Production. Color. Ninety minutes. Premiered on NICK: December 15, 2002.*

**Voices**
**Jacob:** Sid Caesar; **Hunter:** Willem Dafoe; **Marla:** Chaka Khan; **Max:** Carl Reiner; **Eddie:** Lee Cherry; **Sasha:** Kenna Ramsey; **Trevor:** Brian Beacock; **Raj Kangaroo/Circus Baboon:** Wally Wingert; **Dr. Burke:** Dwight Schultz; **Dr. Wilkins/Spume/British Gentleman:** Quinton Flynn; **Leopard/French Newswoman:** Pat Musick; **Old Lion/Tiger:** Greg Eagles; **Security Guard:** Frank Welker

## THE GLO FRIENDS SAVE CHRISTMAS

When the Wicked Witch of the North Pole unveils her fiendish plans to prevent Santa Claus from delivering toys to the creatures of Gloland, the Glo Friends unleash their own counterattack on the mean witch so Santa can spread his good cheer to everyone. *A Sunbow Production in association with Marvel Productions. Color. Half-hour. Premiered: November 1985. Syndicated.*

**Voices**
**Santa Claus:** Carroll O'Connor; **Blanche, Wicked Witch of the North Pole:** Sally Struthers

## GNOMES

Revenge is the order of the day when Tor, a young gnome, is set to marry Lisa from the city, but the archrival trolls, angry because the gnomes keep releasing their prey before they can eat it, decide to grab the unsuspecting gnomes when they're assembled for the nuptial ceremony. *A Zander's Animation Parlour Production in association with Tomorrow Entertainment. Color. One hour. Premiered on CBS: November 11, 1980. Rebroadcast on CBS: August 28, 1982; August 27, 1983.*

**Voices**
Arthur Anderson, Rex Everhart, Anne Francine, Hetty Galen, Gordon Halliday, Bob McFadden, Corrinne Orr, Joe Silver

## GO, DIEGO, GO!: "DIEGO SAVES CHRISTMAS"

Dora the Explorer's animal rescuer cousin, Diego, makes Christmas bright when he rescues Santa and his reindeer after their sleigh gets stuck under a snow hill in this first half-hour special and first preschool holiday special based on the popular Nick Jr. series that also aired on Noggin. On Friday, December 8, 2006, the program debuted at noon, followed at 12:30 P.M. by a second special, *The Wonder Pets Save the Reindeer,* with the special rebroadcast on Nickelodeon's commercial-free children's programming network, Noggin. *A Nicklelodeon Studios Production. Color. Half-hour. Premiered on NICK JR.: December 8, 2006. Rebroadcast on NICK JR.: December 12, 2006. Rebroadcast on NOG: December 16, 2006.*

**Voices**
**Diego:** Jake T. Austin; **Alicia:** Constanza Sperakis; **Click:** Rosie Perez

## GOING BONKERS

A group of once-famous cartoon characters are replaced by muscle-bound movie stars in this one-hour preview special to the syndicated series *Disney's Bonkers. A Walt Disney Production. Color. One hour. Premiered: September 4, 1993. Syndicated.*

**Voices**
**Bonkers D. Bobcat/Lucky Piquel:** Jesse Corti, Jim Cummings; **W.W. Wacky:** David Doyle; **Grumbles Grizzly:** Rodger Bumpass; **Jitters D. Dog:** Jeff Bennett; **Police Chief Leonard Kanifky:** Earl Boen; **Donald Duck:** Tony Anselmo; **Fawn Deer:** Nancy Cartwright; **Marilyn Piquel:** Sherry Lynn; **Dylandra "Dyl" Piquel:** April Winchell; **Fall Apart Rabbit/Toots/Toon Radio:** Frank Welker; **Toon Siren:** Charlie Adler

## GOLDILOCKS

The familiar children's tale of "Goldilocks and the Three Bears" is re-created in this live-action/animation version, which features the voices of the Crosby family (Bing, Kathryn, Mary Frances and Nathaniel). *A DePatie-Freleng Enterprises Production in association with NBC. Color. Half-hour. Premiered on NBC: March 31, 1970. Rebroadcast on NBC: October 24, 1970.*

**Voices**
**Goldilocks:** Mary Frances Crosby; **Papa Bear:** Bing Crosby; **Mama Bear:** Kathryn Crosby; **Baby Bear:** Nathaniel Crosby; **Bobcat:** Paul Winchell

**Other Voices**
Avery Schreiber

## GOOD NIGHT MOON AND OTHER SLEEPYTIME TALES

Billy Crystal, Natalie Cole and Susan Sarandon narrate this original cartoon adaptation of one of the most beloved children's books, produced and animated by Emmy award–winning New York animator Michael Sporn for HBO. In 2000, the special walked away with two Emmy Awards for outstanding children's program (tied with *The Color of Friendship*) and outstanding individual achievement in animation for two segments: "Brahm's Lullaby" and "Twinkle, Twinkle Little Star." The special has since been repeatedly rebroadcast on HBO's offspring channels HBO Family and HBO Kids. A *Michael Sporn Animation Production. Color. Half-hour. Premiered on HBO: December 6, 1999. Rebroadcast on HBO: December 11, 1999; December 15, 1999; December 21, 1999; December 21, 1999; December 30, 1999; August 5, 2000; August 9, 2000; August 13, 2000; August 24, 2000; August 28, 2000; December 3, 2000; December 7, 2000; December 23, 2000; December 28, 2000. Rebroadcast on HBO FAM: March 4, 2006; March 17, 2006; March 27, 2006; March 29, 2006; March 31, 2006; May 1, 2006. Rebroadcast on HBO KIDS: March 20, 2006.*

*Voices*

**Narrators:** Billy Crystal, Natalie Cole, Susan Sarandon; **Other Voices:** Tony Bennett, Lauryn Hill, Patti LaBelle, Aaron Neville

### ◎ THE GOOD, THE BAD AND HUCKLEBERRY HOUND

Huckleberry Hound cleans up the Old West town of Two Bit, after the notorious Dalton gang (Dinky, Pinky and Frinky) steal his gold nugget, so he becomes the new sheriff. First in a series of feature-length cartoons made for first-run syndication for "Hanna-Barbera's Superstars 10" package. A *Hanna-Barbera Production. Color. Two hours. Premiered: 1988, Syndicated. Rebroadcast on CAR: March 19, 1995 (Mr. Spim's Cartoon Theatre). Rebroadcast on DIS: December 5, 1996.*

*Voices*

**Huckleberry Hound:** Daws Butler; **Baba Looey/Peter Potamus/ Yogi Bear/Hokey Wolf/Snagglepuss/Quick Draw McGraw:** Daws Butler; **Boo Boo/Narrator:** Don Messick; **Finky/Fat Boy Kid/Rooster/Baby/Little Boy:** Pat Fraley; **Magilla Gorilla/Dinky/ Announcer:** Alan Melvin; **Pinky/News Anchorman/Pig:** Charlie Adler; **Stinky/Steer/Station Announcer/Bailiff/Laughing Donkey:** Michael Bell; **Dentist/Governor/Mr. Peebles/Photographer/ Chuckling Chipmunk:** Howie Morris; **Judge Flopner/Horse/ Chef/Race Track Announcer/Mission Control:** Frank Welker; **Rusty/Desert Flower/Wife/Little Old Lady/Fat Girl:** B.J. Ward; **Red Eye:** Pat Buttram

### ◎ A GOOF TROOP CHRISTMAS

Pete and his family take off on a ski vacation to Aspirin, Colorado, only to have Goofy and son Max follow (in the episode entitled "Have Yourself a Goofy Little Christmas") in this half-hour holiday special spun off from the popular series *Goof Troop.* The special, which first aired in syndication in 1992, was comprised of two holiday-themed episodes, including "Have Yourself a Goofy Little Christmas, "Up a Tree, The Art of Skiing" and a behind-the-scenes look at some of Disney's animated classics. The program returned in 1993, still featuring the "Have Yourself a Goofy Little Christmas" episode, plus two new animated additions: "On Ice, the Hockey Champ" and "Toy Tinkers." A *Walt Disney Television Animation Production. Color. Half hour. Premiered: December 5, 1992; December 11, 1993. Syndicated.*

*Voices*

**Goofy:** Bill Farmer; **Max:** Dana Hill; **Pete:** Jim Cummings; **Pistol:** Nancy Cartwright; **P.J.:** Rob Paulsen; **Peg:** April Winchell; **Grizz/ Waffles/Chainsaw:** Frank Welker

### ◎ GOOFY'S GUIDE TO SUCCESS

Featuring clips from classic cartoons, this Disney Channel original production takes a look at Goofy's success in the workforce, with the help of the show's animated host, Paddy O'Riley. A *Robert*

*Heath Production for Disney Channel. Color. Ninety minutes. Premiered on DIS: November 18, 1990.*

### ◎ GOOFY'S SALUTE TO FATHER

Goofy's life from his devil-may-care bachelor days to the joys and frustration of parenthood is chronicled in this collection of snippets from past Goofy cartoons. A *Walt Disney Production. Color. Half-hour. Premiered on DIS: June 19, 1994.*

### ◎ GRANDMA GOT RUN OVER BY A REINDEER

After discovering, much to the disbelief of his parents, sister and grandpa, his beloved grandma is missing on Christmas Eve, grandson Jake Spankenheimer sets out to find her while saving the family store from being taken over by their conniving cousin, Mel. Jake finds his grandmother and proves that Santa Claus really exists in this hilarious half-hour holiday romp, loosely based on the popular 1979 Christmas song with music and lyrics by Randy Brooks.

Directed by six-time Emmy Award–winning animator Phil Roman, this goofy and heartwarming yuletide comedy, scripted by Jim Fisher and Jim Staahl (TV's *Bobby's World*) from a story by Fred A. Rappoport, was originally produced and released as a direct-to-video production in October 2000 and then subsequently premiered in prime time on WB Television Network in December 2001, followed by repeat performances in 2002 in prime time and on Saturday morning's Kids' WB! and WB Television Network through 2005. In December 2002, the outrageous escapade was also rebroadcast for the first time on Turner Broadcasting's 24-hour Cartoon Network. Five songs, including the title song, were featured in the program, including "Grandma's Killer Fruitcake," "Grandma's Spending Christmas with the Superstars," "Grandpa's Gonna Sue the Pants Off Santa" and "Feels Like Christmas." A *Fred Rappoport Company/Phil Roman Productions/Atomic Cartoons/KOKO Enterprises Production in association with Warner Home Video and SFM Entertainment LLC. Color. One hour. Premiered on WB: December 21, 2001. Rebroadcast on WB: December 12, 2002; December 23, 2002 (Kids WB!); December 9, 2004; December 25, 2004; December 11, 2005; December 16, 2005. Rebroadcast on CAR: December 16, 2002; December 21, 2004, December 22, 2004, December 24, 2004, December 25, 2004; December 9, 2005; December 16, 2005; December 18, 2005; December 19, 2005; December 23, 2005; December 24, 2005; December 8, 2006; December 13, 2006; December 18, 2006; December 21, 2006; December 22, 2006; December 23, 2006; December 24, 2006; December 25, 2006. Rebroadcast on CW (formerly the WB): December 3, 2006; December 17, 2006.*

*Voices*

**Jake Spankenheimer:** Alex Doduk; **Grandma Spankenheimer:** Susan Blu; **Grandpa Spankenheimer/Narrator:** Elmo Shropshire; **Daphne Spankenheimer:** Maggie Blue O'Hara; **Cousin Mel:** Michele Lee; **Austin Bucks:** Cam Clarke; **Santa Claus:** Jim Staahl; **Other Voices:** Kathleen Barr, Jim Fisher, Jim Flinders, Christopher Gaze, Phil Hayes, Scott McNeil, Pauline Newstone, Maggie Blue O'Hara, Drew Rechett, Venus Terzo

### ◎ GRANDPA

A kindly old grandfather (voiced by Peter Ustinov) lovingly introduces his granddaughter Emily to the worlds of books and imagination in this half-hour animated adaptation of John Burningham's book of the same name, first aired on Showtime. A *TVC Grandpa Ltd. Production for TVS Television and Channel 4. Premiered on SHO: November 5, 1991. Rebroadcast on SHO: November 20, 1991; November 29, 1991.*

*Voices*
**Grandpa:** Peter Ustinov; **Emily:** Emily Osborne

## ◎ THE GREAT BEAR SCARE

In the small forest community of Bearbank, the resident bear population is menaced by a group of monsters. Ted E. Bear (voiced by Tommy Smothers) is selected to quell the dastardly bunch and becomes hero to the populace and to his special friend, Patti Bear, anchorbear for the local TV station's "Bear Witness News." A *DimenMark Films Production. Color. Half-hour. Premiered: October 1982. Syndicated.*

*Voices*
**Ted E. Bear:** Tom Smothers; **Patti Bear:** Sue Raney; **Professor Werner Von Bear:** Hans Conried; **Dracula:** Louis Nye; **C. Emory Bear:** Hal Smith; **Miss Witch:** Lucille Bliss

## ◎ THE GREAT CHRISTMAS RACE

The Lollipop Dragon and his friends must defeat Baron Bad Blood to save the children from having to eat liver lollipops on Christmas morning. *A Blair Entertainment Production in association with Pannonia Film. Color. Half-hour. Premiered: November 1986. Syndicated.*

*Voices*
**Lollipop Dragon:** Gary Wilmot; **Princess Gwendolyn:** Jill Lidstone; **Prince Hubert:** Pat Starr; **Blue Eyes:** Karen Fernald; **Glider/Queen:** Eva Hadden; **Baron Bad Blood:** Stephen Thorne; **Cosmo the Cunning/King:** Dennis Greashan

## ◎ THE GREAT EXPECTATIONS

Overcoming early misfortunes as a child, Phillip Pirrip—called "Pip"—inherits a sizable fortune and learns many valuable lessons in a series of adventures that follow. *A Burbank Films Production. Color. Half-hour. Premiered: Fall, 1984. Syndicated.*

*Voices*
Barbara Frawley, Marcus Hale, Philip Hinton, Simon Hinton, Liz Horne, Bill Kerr, Moya O'Sullivan, Robin Stewart

## ◎ THE GREAT HEEP

In this hour-long fantasy/adventure, *Star Wars* droids R2-D2 and C-3PO arrive on the planet Biitu to meet their new master. They are shocked to find that a gigantic evil droid, the Great Heep, has turned the planet into a wasteland and captured their master, Mungo Baobab, a merchant/explorer. *A Nelvana Limited Production in association with Hanho Heung-Up and Mi-Hahn Productions for Lucasfilm. Color. One hour. Premiered on ABC: June 7, 1986.*

*Voices*
**C3-PO:** Anthony Daniels; **R2-D2:** (electronic); **Mungo Baobab:** Winston Rekert; **Admiral Screed:** Graeme Campbell; **Fridge:** Noam Zylberman; **Captain Cag/Announcer/Gulper:** Dan Hennessey; **KT-10/Darva:** Melleny Brown; **The Great Heep:** Long John Baldry

## ◎ THE GRIM ADVENTURES OF BILLY & MANDY

It's Manny's birthday and the life of his pet hamster, Mr. Snuggles, who's advanced in years, depends on who wins the bet after Manny and Billy play a game with Grim Reaper in this 10-minute *Cartoon Cartoon* pilot that premiered in August 2000 on Cartoon Network's successful late-night programming block, *Adult Swim.* Also known as *Meet the Reaper,* the 2-D animated pilot also spawned a half-hour special that aired a year later, *Grim & Evil. A*

*Rough Draft Studios, Inc. Production. Color. Ten minutes. Premiered on CAR: August 24, 2000 (Adult Swim).*

*Voices*
**Mandy:** Grey DeLisle; **Grim Reaper:** Greg Eagles; **Billy:** Richard Horvitz

## ◎ THE GRIM ADVENTURES OF BILLY & MANDY: "BILLY & MANDY SAVE CHRISTMAS"

Grim travels to the North Pole with Billy and Mandy to prove to them, once and for all, that Santa Claus (voiced by Gilbert Gottfried) really does exist, arriving after Santa has suffered a horrible accident that turned him into a vampire. It is up to Billy, Mandy and Grim Reaper to help Mrs. Claus (voiced by Carol Kane) find the antidote and save Christmas before an army of vampires take control in this second half-hour holiday special produced in 2005 during the fifth season of Cartoon Network's popular weekly series. *A Rough Draft Studios Production. Color. Half-hour. Premiered on CAR: December 2, 2005. Rebroadcast on CAR: December 5, 2005; December 11, 2005; December 16, 2005; December 18, 2005; December 20, 2005; December 23, 2005; December 24, 2005; December 25, 2005. Rebroadcast on CAR: December 15, 2006; December 17, 2006; December 21, 2006; December 22, 2006; December 24, 2006; December 25, 2006.*

*Voices*
**Billy:** Richard Steven Horvitz; **Mandy/Doll:** Grey DeLisle; **Grim/Sperg:** Greg Eagles; **Baron Von Ghoulish:** Malcolm McDowell; **Female Parent/Mother Earth/Kid #2:** B.J. Ward; **Dad/Man in Cave/Snow Creature/Bat/Kid:** Dee Bradley Baker; **Male Parent/Man/Father Time:** Richard McGonagle; **Cassie/Elf:** Amber Hood; **Mrs. Claus:** Carol Kane; **Santa Claus:** Gilbert Gottfried; **General Skarr:** Armin Shimerman

## ◎ THE GRIM ADVENTURES OF BILLY & MANDY: "BILLY & MANDY'S BIG BOOGEY ADVENTURE"

After Grim is stripped of his incredible powers, Billy and Mandy and their sidekick Irwin race across the high seas to claim the powerful Hand of Horror, capable of turning anyone into the scariest creature, before Grim's longtime arch-rival, the Boogey Man, does. The wacky 90-minute swashbuckling action-adventure debuted Friday, March 30, 2007, at 7 P.M. on Cartoon Network, preceded by a three-hour *The Grim Adventures of Billy & Mandy* marathon. Noted screen star George Segal signed on as the voice of Horror, along with series regulars Grey DeLisle (Mandy), Richard Horvitz (Billy), Greg Eagles (Grim) and Fred Willard (the Boogey Man) reprising their roles. On April 3, four days after the premiere, Warner Home Video released the movie on DVD. *A Cartoon Network Studios/Castle Creek Production. Color. Ninety minutes. Premiered on CAR: March 30, 2007.*

*Voices*
**Billy:** Richard Steven Horvitz; **Mandy:** Grey DeLisle; **Grim Reaper:** Greg Eagles; **Boogey Man:** Fred Willard; **Horror:** George Segal

## ◎ THE GRIM ADVENTURES OF BILLY & MANDY: "BILLY AND MANDY'S JACKED UP HALLOWEEN"

When Billy and Mandy go trick-or-treating, Grim Reaper recounts the story of the legendary Halloween figure Jack O'Lantern, only to have the famed character steal Grim's scythe on Halloween night after Billy accidentally ends up on his doorstep; he hopes to use its hidden powers for revenge, until Mandy comes up with a plan to save the day in this half-hour animated special based on the popular Cartoon Network series, *The Grim Adventures of Billy & Mandy*. First shown in prime time on Wednesday, October 1, 2003, at 8:00 P.M., the ghostly animated fare has spooked viewers during multiple repeat broadcasts annually. *A Rough Draft Studios, Inc. Production. Color. Half-hour. Premiered on CAR: October 1, 2003. Rebroadcast on CAR: October 8, 2003; October 30, 2003; October 31, 2003; January 30, 2004; September 18, 2004; October 8, 2004; October 12, 2004; October 22, 2004; October 29, 2004; October 30, 2004; October 31, 2004; July 24, 2005; August 3, 2005; September 3, 2005; October 7, 2005; October 9, 2005; October 10, 2005; October 17, 2005; October 20, 2005; October 28, 2005; October 29, 2005; October 31, 2005; October 8, 2006; October 22, 2006; October 27, 2006; October 31, 2006.*

*Voices*
**Billy/Guy:** Richard Horvitz; **Mandy/Granny/Cowgirl:** Grey DeLisle; **The Grim Reaper/Spirit/Knight:** Greg Eagles; **Irwin/Toilet Paper Woman:** Vanessa Marshall; **Jack O'Lantern:** Wayne Knight; **Giant Pumpkin/Lumber Jack:** Billy West

## ⊚ GRIM & EVIL: "GRIM & EVIL/EVIL CON CARNE"

After losing a bet, Grim Reaper is forced to play with two kids, the dimwitted boy, Billy, and devious girl, Mandy ("Grim & Evil"), while the dismembered brain of a man, Hector Con Carne, plots to take over the world ("Evil Con Carne") in this two-episode half-hour special starring characters featured in Cartoon Network's 2000 pilot and 2001 weekly series, *The Grim Adventures of Billy & Mandy*. The special premiered in August 2001 on the network's late-night "Adult Swim" cartoon block. *A Rough Draft Studios Inc. Production. Color. Half-hour. Premiered on CAR: August 24, 2001.*

*Voices*
**Mandy/Major Dr. Ghastly:** Grey DeLisle; **Grim:** Greg Eagles; **Billy:** Richard Horvitz; **Hector Con Carne:** Phil LaMarr; **General Skarr:** Armin Shimerman; **Boskov the Bear:** Frank Welker

## ⊚ THE GROOVENIANS

Two oddballs (the Groovenians) create art while having fun at the same time after escaping to the Bohemian planet of Groovenia in this original CGI-animated half-hour special and first all-3-D animated half-hour program for the Cartoon Network written, produced, and directed by Jordan Reichek and animated by S4 Studios in Sherman Oaks, California. Created and designed by famed pop artist Kenny Scharf, the milestone special premiered on Cartoon Network's *Adult Swim* programming block. Nominated for an Annie Award for outstanding achievement in an animated short subject, the program's theme song was written and performed by the B52s. *A S4 Studios Production. Color. Half-hour. Premiered on CAR: November 10, 2002 (Adult Swim).*

*Voices*
**Suavo:** Jeff Bennett; **Glindy:** Drena De Niro; **Nixon:** Vincent Gallo; **Dad/King Normans:** Dennis Hopper; **Lalasha/Mom/Zazzy:** Ann Magnuson; **Cuckoo Bird/Swirly/Yalda:** Debi Mazar; **Funbus Captain:** Floyd Peterson; **Jet/The Bubble:** Paul Reubens; **Champagne Courvoisier:** RuPaul

## ⊚ GROOVE SQUAD

Featuring the voice of actress Jennifer Love Hewitt (TV's *Ghost Whisperer*), three high school cheerleaders (Chrissy, Ping and McKenzie), endowed with special powers, including X-ray vision and the ability to fly, and their male mascot friend battle the evil and powerful Dr. Nightingale, along with his hippie-looking accomplices and his evil cheerleader daughter, while attempting to win the school's annual cheerleading competition in this feature-length animated movie and ninth installment of *DIC's Incredible Movie Toons* series broadcast on Nickelodeon. *A DIC Entertainment Production. Color. Ninety minutes. Premiered on NICK: November 17, 2002.*

*Voices*
**Chrissy:** Jennifer Love Hewitt; **Roxanne:** Kathleen Barr; **Star:** Meghan Black; **Mackenzie "Mac":** Tina Bush; **Zeke:** Andrew Francis; **Dr. Nightingale:** Mackenzie Gray; **Fernando:** Santo Lombardo; **Coach:** Blu Mankuma; **Stacy:** Vanessa Morley; **Ping:** Valerie Sing Turner; **Larry:** Alec Willows; **Heifer Cheerleaders:** Stefanie Abramson, J.C. Cheng, Cat Sides; **Other Voices:** Andrea Libman

## ⊚ GROWING AND CHANGING

Produced for UNICEF in conjunction with the International Day of the Child in 1995. First Lady Hillary Clinton introduces this half-hour animated special, narrated by Dr. T. Berry Brazelton and produced by Emmy Award–winning animator Michael Sporn for Disney Channel. *A Michael Sporn Animation Production in association with Italtoons Corporation. Color. Half-hour. Premiered on DIS: December 8, 1995.*

## ⊚ GRUNT AND PUNT

An animated pig and boar illustrate for children the rough-and-tumble sport of professional football while also critiquing live-action footage of NFL plays of the week in this traditional cel-animated four-episode series—also known as *The Grunt and Punt Show* created by well-known children's television creative director Howard Hoffman and designed by Oscar-nominated animator and *Courage the Cowardly Dog* creator John R. Dilworth—that aired Saturday mornings on FOX. Hoffman developed the pilot for Jumbo Pictures with the series of specials being produced for Indigo Entertainment. The premiere episode debuted in late October 1994, preempting the popular weekly cartoon series *Where on Earth Is Carmen Sandiego?* Three additional episodes aired in November and December and in January 1995. The program was also offered in syndication. *A Jumbo Pictures/Indigo Entertainment/NFL Films Production. Color. Half-hour. Premiered on FOX: October 29, 1994; November 26, 1994; December 17, 1994; January 28, 1995. Syndicated.*

## ⊚ GULLIVER'S TRAVELS

The adventure-seeking Gulliver learns the true meaning of friendship as he assists the Lilliputians in this colorful adaptation of the Jonathan Swift classic. *A CBS Famous Classic Tales special. A Hanna-Barbera Production. Color. One hour. Premiered on CBS: November 18, 1979. Rebroadcast on CBS: November 9, 1980.*

*Voices*
**Gulliver:** Ross Martin; **Filmnap/Jester Pirate:** Hal Smith; **Bolgolam/Lilliputian King/Brobdingnag King:** John Stephenson; **Lilliputian/Mob Member #1:** Ross Martin; **Reldresal/Old Fisherman/Blefuscu King:** Don Messick; **Farmer/Brobdingnag Minister/Mob Member #2:** Regis Cordic; **Lilliputian Queen/Brogdingnag Queen:** Julie Bennett; **Farmer's Wife/Glumdalclitch:** Janet Waldo

## ⊚ HAGAR THE HORRIBLE: "HAGAR KNOWS BEST"

Hagar the Horrible, the most famous Viking of all, is on his way home from a two-year business trip ravaging foreign lands. As his

*The most famous Viking of all heads home from a two-year business trip, but home doesn't quite meet his expectations in the CBS prime-time special* Hagar the Horrible: Hagar Knows Best. © *King Features Entertainment*

ship nears the port, visions of a *Father Knows Best* family life dance in his helmeted head. But once he is home, reality doesn't match up. *A Hanna-Barbera Production in association with King Entertainment. Color. Half-hour. Premiered on CBS: November 1, 1989.*

**Voices**
**Hagar:** Peter Cullen; **Honi:** Lydia Cornell; **Helga:** Lainie Kazan; **Hamlet:** Josh Rodine; **Lucky Eddie:** Jeff Doucett; **Olaf:** Hank Saroyan; **Lute/Instructor:** Donny Most; **Doorman:** Hank Saroyan; **Kid:** Josh Rodine; **Principal:** Frank Welker; **Joe:** Jeff Doucette; **Al/Snert/Kvaak:** Frank Welker; **Teacher:** Jack Tice; **Narrator:** Frank Welker

### ◎ THE HALLOWEEN TREE

Well-known novelist Ray Bradbury is author and narrator of this 90-minute animated tale about five young children who take a frightful journey 4,000 years into the past to rescue the spirit of their friend Pip from the malevolent Mr. Moundshroud (voiced by Leonard Nimoy, alias Mr. Spock from TV's original *Star Trek*), who introduces them to the holiday's customs in various ages and countries. *A Hanna-Barbera Production. Color. Ninety minutes. Premiered on TBS. Syndicated: October 30, 1993.*

**Voices**
**Narrator:** Ray Bradbury; **Mr. Moundshroud:** Leonard Nimoy; **Pip:** Alex Greenwald; **Jenny:** Annie Barker

### ◎ HALLOWEEN WHO-DUN-IT?

Davey Hansen and his dog, Goliath, stars of the popular religious stop-motion animation series *Davey and Goliath*, return in this first-run special providing a new lesson on Christian living tied in with Halloween. *A Clokey Production for the Lutheran Church of America. Color. Half-hour. Premiered: 1977. Syndicated.*

**Voices**
**Davey Hansen/Sally Hansen/Mary Hansen:** Norma McMillan, Nancy Wible; **Goliath/John Hansen:** Hal Smith

### ◎ HAMTARO: "HAM-HAM BIRTHDAY SPECIAL"

After meeting a new hamster, Heidi, at summer camp, the ever-curious Ham-Hams help her find a special treasure to boost the spirits of her sick grandmother ("Ham-Hams Ahoy"), while the Ham-Hams stage a gigantic birthday party for Hamtaro and Cappy ("Happy Ham-Ham Birthday") in this two-part hour-long special based on the popular Japanese anime series that aired on Cartoon Network. *A Shogakukan Music & Digital Entertainment/R Kawai/SMDE/TV Tokyo/Ocean Group/ShoPro Entertainment Production. Color. One hour. Premiered on CAR: August 31, 2003.*

**Voices**
**Hamtaro:** Chiara Zanni; **Laura:** Carly McKillip; **Boss:** Ted Cole; **Bijou:** Chantal Strand; **Maxwell:** Brad Swaile; **Dexter/Forrest Haruna, Laura's father:** Sam Vincent; **Mr. Yoshi:** Scott McNeil; **Elder Ham:** Dave "Squatch" Ward; **Elder Ham:** Donald Brown; **Kana Iwata:** Daniella Evangelista; **Kaitlin Endo:** Pauline Newstone; **Stan:** Noel Fisher; **Sabu:** Richard Ian Cox; **Sandy:** Brittney Wilson; **Cappy:** Tabitha St. Germain; **Howdy:** Paul Dobson; **Jingle:** Terry Klassen; **Travis:** Matthew Smith; **Dylan:** Michael Donovan; **Oxnard:** Saffron Henderson; **Panda:** Jillian Michaels; **Pashmina:** Jocelyne Loewen; **Laura Haruna:** Moneca Stori; **Pepper/Penelope/Marion Haruna, Laura's mother:** Cathy Weseluck; **Laura's grandfather:** Richard Newman; **Cindy Iwata, Kana's mother:** Ellen Kennedy; **Conrad Iwata, Kana's father:** Trevor Devall; **Grandma Willow:** Kathy Morse; **Other Voices:** Anna Cummer, Michael Coleman, Marcy Goldberg, Pam Hyatt

### ◎ HAMTARO: "HAM-HAM GAMES"

Fun-loving and inquisitive Hamtaro pays tribute to the Athens Summer Olympic Games in this Olympic Games–like adventure in which he and his fellow Ham-Hams travel to attend the legendary games, played only every 8,656 years, where they confront the mischievous Rainbow Girls while helping the wild Djungarian hamsters with their allies, the rowdy Ham-Pirates, in this exciting fun-filled adventure. Based on the top-rated anime series redubbed in English, this original hour special debuted Saturday, August 21, 2004, at 3 P. M. on Cartoon Network. *A Shogakukan Music & Digital Entertainment/R Kawai/SMDE/TV Tokyo/Ocean Group/ShoPro Entertainment Production. Color. One hour. Premiered on CAR: August 21, 2004.*

**Voices**
**Hamtaro:** Chiara Zanni; **Laura:** Carly McKillip; **Boss:** Ted Cole; **Bijou:** Chantal Strand; **Maxwell:** Brad Swaile; **Dexter/Forrest Haruna, Laura's father:** Sam Vincent; **Mr. Yoshi:** Scott McNeil; **Elder Ham:** Dave "Squatch" Ward; **Elder Ham:** Donald Brown; **Kana Iwata:** Daniella Evangelista; **Kaitlin Endo:** Pauline Newstone; **Stan:** Noel Fisher; **Sabu:** Richard Ian Cox; **Sandy:** Brittney Wilson; **Cappy:** Tabitha St. Germain; **Howdy:** Paul Dobson; **Jingle:** Terry Klassen; **Travis:** Matthew Smith; **Dylan:** Michael Donovan; **Oxnard:** Saffron Henderson; **Panda:** Jillian Michaels; **Pashmina:** Jocelyne Loewen; **Laura Haruna:** Moneca Stori; **Pepper/Penelope/Marion Haruna, Laura's mother:** Cathy Weseluck; **Laura's grandfather:** Richard Newman; **Cindy Iwata, Kana's mother:** Ellen Kennedy; **Conrad Iwata, Kana's father:** Trevor Devall; **Grandma Willow:** Kathy Morse; **Rosie:** Alexandra Carter; **Mrs. Charlotte Yoshi:** Venus Terzo; **Other Voices:** Sharon Alexander, Michael Coleman, Annette Ducharine, Brian Drummond, Matt Hill, Kelly Sheridan, Ellen Kennedy

### ◎ HAMTARO: "HAM-HAM HALLOWEEN"

Thinking that Laura and Kana are going to a "Hamoween" party, Hamtaro excitedly gets into the spirit by making costumes to attend the event after he is mysteriously invited, only for Hamtaro and the Ham-Hams to be scared out of their minds when heading off to the event in this half-hour special adapted from the famed anime series for Cartoon Network. *A Shogakukan Music & Digital Entertainment/R Kawai/SMDE/TV Tokyo/Ocean Group/ShoPro Entertainment Production. Color. Half-hour. Premiered on CAR: October 21, 2003.*

*Voices*
**Hamtaro:** Chiara Zanni; **Laura:** Carly McKillip; **Boss:** Ted Cole; **Bijou:** Chantal Strand; **Maxwell:** Brad Swaile; **Dexter/Forrest Haruna, Laura's father:** Sam Vincent; **Mr. Yoshi:** Scott McNeil; **Elder Ham:** Dave "Squatch" Ward; **Elder Ham:** Donald Brown; **Kana Iwata:** Daniella Evangelista; **Kaitlin Endo:** Pauline Newstone; **Stan:** Noel Fisher; **Sabu:** Richard Ian Cox; **Sandy:** Brittney Wilson; **Cappy:** Tabitha St. Germain; **Howdy:** Paul Dobson; **Jingle:** Terry Klassen; **Travis:** Matthew Smith; **Dylan:** Michael Donovan; **Oxnard:** Saffron Henderson; **Panda:** Jillian Michaels; **Pashmina:** Jocelyne Loewen; **Laura Haruna:** Moneca Stori; **Pepper/Penelope/Marion Haruna, Laura's mother:** Cathy Weseluck; **Laura's grandfather:** Richard Newman; **Cindy Iwata, Kana's mother:** Ellen Kennedy; **Conrad Iwata, Kana's father:** Trevor Devall; **Grandma Willow:** Kathy Morse; **Rosie:** Alexandra Carter; **Mrs. Charlotte Yoshi:** Venus Terzo; **Other Voices:** Sharon Alexander, Michael Coleman, Annette Ducharine, Brian Drummond, Matt Hill, Kelly Sheridan, Ellen Kennedy

## ☺ HAPPILY EVER AFTER

Troubled by the news of her parents' divorce, Molly Conway, who like most children dreams of living happily ever after, forms a group with her offbeat friends ("The Skywalkers") to try to prevent her parents from breaking up. *A JZM–Bill Melendez Production in association with Wonderworks and Bill Melendez Productions, London, England. Color. One hour. Premiered on PBS: October 21, 1985 (on PBS's Wonderworks anthology series).*

*Voices*
**Narrator:** Carol Burnett; **Molly Conway:** Cassandra Coblentz; **Alice Conway:** Carrie Fisher; **Carl Conway:** Henry Winkler; **Tommy Johnson:** Danny Colby; **George Johnson:** Danny DeVito; **Rose Johnson:** Rhea Perlman; **Joey Fabrizio:** Jeremy Schoenberg; **Dom Fabrizio:** Dana Ferguson; **Mary O'Connell:** Gini Holtzman; **Darlene Kashitani:** Karrie Ullman; **Woody Coleman:** Carl Stevens; **Molly's Daughter:** Keri Houlihan; **What's His Name:** Brett Johnson

## ☺ HAPPY BIRTHDAY BUNNYKINS

Mr. and Mrs. Bunnykin overlook making plans for a birthday for their son William, who hopes to get his very own marching drum, like the one used in his father's band. This half-hour animated special, originally produced for Canada's CTV network in 1995, was based on the Bunnykins China by Royal Doulton. The program debuted in the United States on The Disney Channel. *A Rabbits Unlimited/Lacewood Production in association with CTV Television Network/Cat's Pyjamas/MTR Entertainment. Color. Half-hour. Premiered on DIS: April 7, 1996.*

*Voices*
**Mr. Bunnykins:** James Bradford; **Mrs. Bunnykins:** Denis Killock; **Susan:** Rebecca Overall; **William:** Tia Carello; **Harry:** Amy Fulco; **Lady Rattley:** Leonie Gardner; **Stoatworth:** Terrence Scammel; **Reginald:** Dylan Shaw Lane; **Queen Sophie:** Natalie Stern; **Mr. Shortbread:** Dean Hagopian; **Adrian:** Catherine Lewis

*Other Voices*
Rick Jones

## ☺ HAPPY BIRTHDAY, DONALD DUCK

Expanding on the story of the 1949 cartoon "Donald's Happy Birthday," Huey, Dewey and Louie, Donald's mischievous nephews, make plans for a special birthday party for their famed but temperamental uncle. Donald surprises his nephews with his own plans for his birthday—watching footage of his old cartoons. The special was retitled and rebroadcast in two other versions on NBC after its initial premiere on rival network ABC. *A Walt Disney Television Production. Color. One hour. Premiered on ABC: November 21, 1956 (as "At Home with Donald Duck" on the program Disneyland.) Rebroadcast on ABC: May 8, 1957. Rebroadcast on NBC: November 7, 1976 (on The Wonderful World of Disney); April 4, 1979 (as Happy Birthday, Donald Duck).*

*Voices*
**Donald Duck:** Clarence Nash

## ☺ HAPPY BIRTHDAY MICKEY

Mickey Mouse's illustrious career is highlighted in this birthday special loaded with clips from his first screen appearances and his roles in *Fantasia* and *The Mickey Mouse Club*, originally produced for The Disney Channel. *A Film Landa Inc. Production for The Disney Channel. Color. Ninety minutes. Premiered on DIS: 1983.*

## ☺ HAPPY BIRTHDAY TO YOU

It's Olivia Orderly's birthday and her only friend at Orderly Mansion is Charley the Horse . . . until Barnaby the stable hand shows up. This story of one girl's search for the perfect birthday song was part of Canadian television's *The Real Story of . . .* series (a.k.a. *Favorite Songs*) produced in 1991 by CINAR Films. It premiered in the U.S. a year later on HBO's popular anthology series *HBO Storybook Musicals*. *A CINAR/France Animation Production in association with Western Publishing Company Inc/The Family Channel/Telefilm Canada/Cofimage 3. Color. Half-hour. Premiered on HBO: January 4, 1992.*

*Voices*
**Barnaby:** Roger Daltrey; **Charley the Horse:** Ed Asner

## ☺ THE HAPPY CIRCUS

Three magical episodes from the French claymation series *Le Cirque Bonheur*, which takes viewers into a world of dreams, fantasy and childhood with unusual stories, all set in a traveling circus, are featured in this half-hour special based on original stories by Jacques-Remy Girerd, Renaud Terrier and Toni Bauza. It was first introduced to American television audiences on the award-winning PBS series *Long Ago & Far Away*. *A La Maison du Cinema de Grenoble/Antenne 2/Folimage-Valence, France Production. Color. Half-hour. Premiered on PBS: February 18, 1989.*

## ☺ HAPPY EASTER

The lesson of Easter is delivered as Davey attends the Easter pageant and is overtaken by emotion after watching a rehearsal of the Passion Play.

   A restored version of the original 1967 Easter special, "Davey and Goliath's Happy Easter," aired on cable's Hallmark Channel in 2004 and 2005. *A Clokey Production for the Lutheran Church of America. Color. Half-hour. Premiered: 1967. Syndicated. Rebroadcast on HLMRK: March 27, 2004; March 27, 2005.*

*Voices*
**Davey Hansen/Sally Hansen/Mary Hansen:** Norma McMillan, Nancy Wible; **Goliath/John Hansen:** Hal Smith

## ◎ THE HAPPY ELF

Velvety-voiced singer Harry Connick Jr. narrates this story of Santa's helper, Eubie the Elf, whose overly enthusiastic, rose-colored view of the holiday season is put to the test when he tries bringing good cheer to the dreary town of Bluesville in this 3-D, computer-animated network holiday special featuring the voices of Lewis Black, Carol Kane, Rob Paulsen, and songs by Connick himself. The hour-long special, which premiered on NBC in December 2005, came in third with 5.7 million viewers to CBS's annual holiday favorite, *Rudolph the Red-Nosed Reindeer*, which pulled in an amazing 15.8 million viewers. In December 2006, the popular yuletide program was rebroadcast on the commercial-free Starz! Kids and Family premium channel. *An IDT Entertainment/HC Production. Color. One hour. Premiered on NBC: December 2, 2005. Rebroadcast on STZK&F: December 2, 2006; December 7, 2006; December 17, 2006; December 22, 2006; December 25, 2006.*

### Voices

**The Happy Elf/Narrator:** Harry Connick Jr.; **Eubie the Elf:** Rob Paulsen; **Gilda:** Carol Kane; **Santa Claus:** Mickey Rooney; **Derek/Tucker/Mayor/Toady:** Kevin Michael Richardson; **Molly:** Mae Whitman; **Norbert:** Lewis Black; **Curtis:** Candi Milo; **Brother:** Rory Thost; **Sister:** Lilianna Mumy; **Other Voices:** Charlie Adler

## ◎ HAPPY NEW YEAR, CHARLIE BROWN

The *Peanuts* gang rings in 1986 with Marcie and Peppermint Patty throwing a big New Year's Eve bash that Charlie Brown at first decides not to attend. The New Year's special was one of 58 Peanuts programs Nickelodeon began rebroadcasting in 1998, along with the popular CBS Saturday morning series, *The Charlie Brown & Snoopy Snow*. *A Lee Mendelson–Bill Melendez Production in association with Charles M. Schulz Creative Associates and United Feature Syndicate. Color. Half-hour. Premiered on CBS: January 1, 1986. Rebroadcast on CBS: January 1, 1987; December 28, 1988. Rebroadcast on NICK: December 31, 1998; January 1, 1999.*

### Voices

**Charlie Brown:** Chad Allen; **Charlie Brown (singing):** Sean Collins; **Peppermint Patty:** Kristi Baker; **Lucy Van Pelt:** Melissa Guzzi; **Lucy Van Pelt (singing):** Tiffany Billings; **Linus Van Pelt:** Jeremy Miller; **Sally Brown:** Elizabeth Lyn Fraser; **Schroeder:** Aron Mandelbaum; **Marcie:** Jason Muller; **Off-Camera Singer:** Desiree Goyette

## ◎ THE HAPPY PRINCE

The story of a royal statue that makes friends with a small swallow is told in this bittersweet tale based on the Oscar Wilde story. *A Gerald Potterton Production in association with Narrator's Digest. Color. Half-hour. Premiered: 1975. Syndicated.*

### Voices

**Statue:** Christopher Plummer; **Swallow:** Glynis Johns

## ◎ HAPPY TO BE NAPPY AND OTHER STORIES OF ME

Award-winning New York animator Michael Sporn animated and directed this original live-action/animated feature for HBO Family, featuring a star-studded voice cast, about the importance of accepting not only all people but also one's self. Premiering on February 29, 2004, at 6:30 P.M., the program won a prime time Emmy Award that year for outstanding children's program. Since its debut, the enlightening production has replayed multiple times mornings, afternoons and evenings on HBO Family. *A Michael Sporn Animation, Inc. Production. Color. Half-hour. Premiered on HBO FAM: February 29, 2004. Rebroadcast on HBO FAM: March 1, 2004; March 5, 2004; March 9, 2004; March 13, 2004; March 17, 2004; March 23, 2004; March 24, 2004; March 28, 2004; April 11, 2004; April 19, 2004; April 28, 2004; June 9, 2004; June 14, 2004; June 15, 2004; June 20, 2004; June 24, 2004; September 10, 2004; September 19, 2004; September 30, 2004; December 4, 2004; December 23, 2004; December 24, 2004; February 1, 2005; February 10, 2005; February 15, 2005; February 24, 2005; February 24, 2005; May 2, 2005; May 10, 2005; May 12, 2005; August 5, 2005; August 7, 2005; August 13, 2005; August 16, 2005; August 29, 2005; January 2, 2007; January 6, 2007; January 8, 2007; January 17, 2007; January 18, 2007; January 21, 2007; January 23, 2007; January 31, 2007.*

### Voices

Mikhail Baryshnikov, Mary J. Blige, Harvey Fierstein, Melanie Griffith, Isaac Mizrahi, Rita Moreno, Vanessa Williams

## ◎ HARDROCK, COCO AND JOE: THE THREE LITTLE DWARFS

First introduced on WGN-TV in the mid-1950s and produced by Centaur Productions in 1951, this nearly three-minute, primitively made, stop-motion animated film was based on the popular song written by Stuart Hamblen for Hill and Range Music and recorded by the Les Tucker Singers. This delightful ditty went on to become an annual Christmas tradition on WGN, which first aired it on the station's *Garfield Goose and Friends* and shown annually with other yuletide animated favorites, *Frosty the Snowman* and *Suzy Snowflake*. Since their original premiere, WGN annually rebroadcast all three cartoons on the station's popular kid shows, including *Bozo's Circus*, *Garfield Goose and Friends*, and *The Ray Rayner Show*. Years later, the cartoon was re-introduced to a new generation of television viewers on the Comedy Central series, *TV Funhouse*, and in 2005 was rebroadcast on WGN-TV's retrospective special, *Bozo, Gar & Ray*. *A Centaur Productions/Hill and Range Music Production. Black and white. Two minutes. Premiered on WGN: December 18, 1956.*

## ◎ THE HARLEM GLOBETROTTERS MEET SNOW WHITE

The wizards of the basketball court play gargoyles working for a wicked witch—really a vain queen—who has cast a spell on Snow White. *A Hanna-Barbera Production. Color. Ninety minutes. Premiered on NBC: September 27, October 4, October 11 and October 18, 1980 (as a four-part serial on* Fred and Barney Meet the Shmoo*). Syndicated.*

### Voices

**Curly Neal:** Stu Gilliam; **Geese:** John Williams; **Marques:** Robert DoQui; **Li'l John:** Buster Jones; **Dunbar:** Adam Wade; **Nate:** Scatman Crothers; **Baby Face Paige:** Mork Davitt; **Snow White:** Russi Taylor; **Prince:** Michael Bell; **Marva:** Diane McCannon; **Queen of Grimmania:** Gay Autterson; **Count Revolta:** John Stephenson

## ◎ HARVEY BIRDMAN, ATTORNEY AT LAW: "BANNON CUSTODY BATTLE"

Now working for a prestigious law firm, ex-superhero-turned-attorney Harvey Birdman represents Dr. Benton Quest in a messy custody battle in which his long-time partner Roger "Race" Bannon attempts to gain custody of Benton's son, Jonny Quest, and his friend, Hadji, in this 11-minute pilot that debuted on Cartoon Network's programming block for mature audiences, *Adult Swim*. Produced by J.J. Sedelmaier and Williams Street Productions, the well-received special spawned a second one in September 2001, *Harvey Birdman, Attorney At Law: Very Personal Injury*, before becoming a regular series on *Adult Swim* in 2002, which, unlike the original pilot, was produced by a new studio, Allied Arts and Science. *A J.J. Sedelmaier Productions/Williams Street Production. Color. Eleven minutes. Premiered on CAR: December 30, 2000.*

**Voices**

**Harvey Birdman/Judge Mightor:** Gary Cole; **Myron Reductor Esq.:** Stephen Colbert; **Race Bannon:** Thom Pinto; **Jonny Quest:** Dee Bradley Baker; **Hadji:** Wally Wingert; **Dr. Benton Quest:** Neil Ross; **Dr. Zin:** Billy West

### ◎ HARVEY BIRDMAN, ATTORNEY AT LAW: "VERY PERSONAL INJURY"

Famed superheroes' attorney Harvey Birdman sues the Javalux company for damages after his client, Native American Super Friends member Apache Chief, accidentally spills hot coffee on himself, burning his groin, in this second of two specials to air on Cartoon Network's *Adult Swim* cartoon block. The special was followed by a weekly series that began airing on *Adult Swim* in 2002. *An Allied Arts and Science Production. Color. Eleven minutes. Premiered on CAR: September 23, 2001.*

**Voices**

**Harvey Birdman/Judge Mightor:** Gary Cole; **Myron Reductor Esq.:** Stephen Colbert; **Apache Chief:** Maurice LaMarche; **Zan:** Michael Bell; **Supervolt:** Michael Bell; **Sybil Schussler:** Laraine Newman; **Vulturo:** Neil Ross

### ◎ THE HAUNTED PUMPKIN OF SLEEPY HOLLOW

In this direct-to-video special, originally produced in 2002 by PorchLight Entertainment and inspired by Washington Irving's classic tale, two friends Nick and Kate vow to stop the legendary Headless Horseman in the small town of Sleepy Hollow after discovering the pumpkin they found is haunted. The holiday production made its U.S. television premiere three years later on Cartoon Network. *A PorchLight Entertainment Production in association with VIDEAL. Color. One hour. Premiered on CAR: October 21, 2005. Rebroadcast on CAR: October 27, 2006.*

**Voices**

**Nick:** Joanna Ruiz; **Kate/Mrs. Wentworth:** Jules De Jongh; **Nathaniel/Mr. Van Tassel:** Eric Meyers; **Leo/Grunk:** Tom Clarke-Hill; **Mrs. Van Tassel:** Regine Candler; **Ichabod Crane:** Benjamin Small

### ◎ HE-MAN AND SHE-RA—A CHRISTMAS SPECIAL

The villainous Skeletor, archrival of He-Man and She-Ra, tries to stop the spread of Christmas joy on Earth, but his diabolical plan is squelched when Prince Adam (He-Man) and Princess Adora (She-Ra) launch their own counterattack. *A Filmation Associates Production. Color. One hour. Premiered: November 1985. Syndicated.*

**Voices**

**Adam/He-Man:** John Erwin; **Adora/She-Ra:** Melendy Britt; **Skeletor:** Alan Oppenheimer; **Madam Razz/Shadow Weaver:** Linda Gary; **Hordak/Bow:** George DiCenzo; **Orko:** Eric Gunden

### ◎ HEMO THE MAGNIFICENT

Professor Frank Baxter and some animated friends tell the story of blood and the human circulatory system, including its function to support the heart, lung and nervous system, in this hour-long live-action/animated special directed by Oscar-winning filmmaker Frank Capra. The special made its television debut on the syndicated *Bell Telephone Science Hour* series in 1957, and won an Emmy the following year for best cinematography for television. Noted animator James "Shamus" Culhane created the animation for the program. *A Bell Science/Frank Capra Productions/Shamus Culhane Productions Production. Color. One hour. Premiered: March 20, 1957. Syndicated.*

**Cast (live action)/Voices**

**Dr. Frank Baxter:** Himself; **Richard Carlson:** Himself; **Lab Assistant:** Sterling Holloway

### ◎ HENRY'S CAT: "THE MYSTERY OF THE MISSING SANTA" AND "WHEN TIME WENT WRONG"

The bedraggled orange feline, star of the British imported animated series *Henry's Cat*, appears in two madcap holiday adventures, which were combined into this half-hour special that premiered on Showtime. (It also aired the *Henry's Cat* cartoon series.) In the opener, Henry plays the "world-famous master detective" when Santa is found missing; then, in the second adventure, he finds himself in a time-tripping predicament. *A Bob Godfrey Films Ltd. Production. Color. Half-hour. Premiered on SHO: December 24, 1991. Rebroadcast on SHO: December 4, 1994; December 20, 1994; December 23, 1994.*

**Voices**

Bob Godfrey

### ◎ HERCULES AND XENA—THE ANIMATED MOVIE: THE BATTLE FOR MOUNT OLYMPUS

Suspecting his mother, Alemene, has been kidnapped by Zeus, Hercules (voiced by Kevin Sorbo) embarks on a dangerous mission to rescue her while Zeus's jealous wife, Hera, unleashes four imprisoned Titans to attack Mount Olympus. Hercules then teams up with Xena and their trusty sidekicks Iolaus and Gabrielle to save the city from destruction in this 80-minute direct-to-DVD movie that premiered Saturday morning on FOX. *A Renaissance Pictures Production. Color. Eighty minutes. Premiered on FOX: September 4, 1999.*

**Voices**

**Hercules:** Kevin Sorbo; **Xena:** Lucy Lawless; **Iolaus:** Michael Hurst; **Gabrielle:** Renee O'Connor; **Crius:** Ted Raimi; **Aclmene/Artemis:** Josephine Davison; **Zeus:** Peter Rowley; **Tethys/Mnemosyne:** Alison Wall; **Aphrodite:** Alexandra Tydings; **Hera:** Joy Watson; **Prophyrion:** David Mackie

### ◎ HERE COMES GARFIELD

In his first prime-time animated special, Garfield the cat lives up to his reputation as being "both thorny and funny" when he and his pint-size playmate, Odie the mutt, play havoc with a nasty neighbor. Unfortunately, their friskiness lands Odie in the city pound and it is up to rueful Garfield to get him out. An Emmy Award nominee. *A Lee Mendelson–Bill Melendez Production in association with United Feature Syndicate. Color. Half-hour. Premiered on CBS: October 25, 1982. Rebroadcast on CBS: November 26, 1983; May 17, 1985; October 12, 1988.*

*Voices*
**Garfield:** Lorenzo Music; **Jon Arbuckle:** Sandy Kenyon; **Odie:** Gregg Berger; **Hubert:** Henry Corden; **Reba/Skinny:** Hal Smith; **Fast Eddie/Fluffy:** Hank Garrett; **Salesman:** Gregg Berger; **Little Girl:** Angela Lee; **Vocalists:** Lou Rawls, Desiree Goyette

### ◉ HERE COMES PETER COTTONTAIL
Danny Kaye hosts and narrates this whimsical hour-long Animagic special—using stop-motion puppet animation—recounting the delightful tale of Peter Cottontail and his efforts to deliver more eggs than Irontail, an evil rabbit, who is interested in dethroning him as "the Easter Rabbit." Based on the popular children's book *The Easter That Overslept*, the program was conceived by the same team that produced earlier seasonal favorites, including *Rudolph, The Red-Nosed Reindeer* and *Little Drummer Boy*. A *Rankin-Bass Production in association with Videocraft International. Color. One hour. Premiered on ABC: April 4, 1971. Rebroadcast on ABC: March 30, 1972. Rebroadcast on CBS: April 13, 1976; April 8, 1977; March 24, 1978; April 10, 1979; March 28, 1980; April 10, 1981.*

*Voices*
**Seymour S. Sassafrass:** Danny Kaye; **Peter Cottontail:** Casey Kasem; **Irontail:** Vincent Price; **Donna:** Iris Rainer; **Antoine/Wellington B. Bunny:** Danny Kaye; **Bonnie:** Joan Gardner

### ◉ HERE COMES THE BRIDE
Actress/comedienne Carol Kane lends her voice to this imaginative adaptation of the well-known song in which klutzy Maximillian Mole meets acrobat Margaret Mouse when the circus comes to town and it's love at first sight. From CINAR Films *The Real Story of . . .* series. *A CINAR Films/France Animation Production. Color. Half-hour. Premiered on HBO: January 24, 1994.*

*Voices*
**Margaret Mouse:** Carol Kane

### ◉ HE'S A BULLY, CHARLIE BROWN
While attending summer camp with their friends and learning to play a game of marbles, camp bully Joe Agate cheats, taking every kid's marbles, including Rerun's. Never having played the game before, Charlie Brown uses his own marbles to play and recover the marbles that have been stolen. Produced by Lee Mendelson and Bill Melendez, the all-new special—originally titled, *It's Only Marbles, Charlie Brown*—was based on an original *Peanuts* strip published in April 1995 and on an idea *Peanuts* creator Charles Schulz had pitched and worked on before his death in February 2000. The special debuted on Monday, November 20, 2006, on ABC after the annual rebroadcast of the classic *Peanuts* special, *A Charlie Brown Thanksgiving*. *A Lee Mendelson-Bill Melendez Production in association with United Feature Syndicate. Color. Half-hour. Premiered on ABC: November 20, 2006.*

*Voices*
**Charlie Brown:** Spencer Robert Scott; **Lucy Van Pelt:** Stephanie Patton; **Linus Van Pelt:** Benjamin Bryan; **Peppermint Patty:** Rory Thost; **Marcie:** Jessica Gordon; **Sally Brown:** Sierra Marcoux; **Rerun Van Pelt:** Jimmy Bennett; **Joe Agate:** Taylor Lautner; **Snoopy:** Bill Melendez; **Girl:** Katie Fischer; **Violet Gray:** Jolean Bejbe; **Boy:** Paul Butcher

### ◉ HE'S YOUR DOG, CHARLIE BROWN
Snoopy's sudden attack of bad manners makes him so unpopular with the *Peanuts* clan that Charlie Brown decides to send him back to the Daisy Hill Puppy Farm for a refresher course in obedi-

ence training. The program marked Snoopy's first starring role in primetime. In March 1998, Nickelodeon re-aired the special for the first time, followed by additional rebroadcasts after picking up the broadcasting rights to nearly five dozen *Peanuts* programs that had originally aired on CBS. *A Lee Mendelson–Bill Melendez Production in association with Charles M. Schulz Creative Associates and United Feature Syndicate. Color. Half-hour. Premiered on CBS: February 14, 1968. Rebroadcast on CBS: February 20, 1969; February 15, 1970; February 13, 1971; February 14, 1972; June 5, 1973. Rebroadcast on NICK: March 9, 1998; April 10, 1998; May 12, 1998; June 21, 1998; July 27, 1998; August 28, 1998; September 29, 1998; November 8, 1998; December 14, 1998; March 6, 1999; April 27, 1999; June 15, 1999; August 13, 1999; December 4, 1999.*

*Voices*
**Charlie Brown:** Peter Robbins; **Linus Van Pelt:** Chris Shea; **Lucy Van Pelt:** Sally Dryer-Barker; **Peppermint Patty:** Gail DeFaria; **Frieda/Patty:** Anne Altieri; **Violet:** Linda Mendelson

### ◉ HEY ARNOLD!: "ARNOLD'S THANKSGIVING"
After comparing how others celebrate Thanksgiving, including Mr. Simmons and his family's "perfect" celebrations Arnold's family realizes that how they mark the holiday isn't so bad after all in this second half-hour holiday special since 1996's *Hey Arnold! The Christmas Show* from the third season of Nickelodeon's popular cartoon series, *Hey Arnold! A Games Animation Production. Color. Half-hour. Premiered on NICK: November 18, 1998.*

*Voices*
**Arnold:** Phillip Van Dyke; **Helga:** Francesca Marie Smith; **Mr. Simmons:** Dan Butler; **Gerald:** Jamil Smith; **Phoebe/Joy:** Anndi L. McAfee; **Harold:** Justin Shenkarow; **Eugene:** Ben Diskin; **Rhonda:** Olivia Hack; **Stinky:** Christopher Walberg; **Brainy (uncredited):** Craig Bartlett; **Grandpa/Peter:** Dan Castellaneta; **Grandma:** Tress MacNeille; **Ernie:** Dom Irrera; **Oskar:** Stephen Viksten; **Suzie:** Mary Scheer; **Mr. Hyunh:** Baoan Coleman; **Big Bob Pataki/Chuck:** Maurice LaMarche; **Miriam Pataki:** Kath Soucie; **Olga Pataki:** Nika Futterman; **Pearl, Mr. Simmons' mother:** Mitzi McCall; **Mayor Dixie:** Maria Bamford

### ◉ HEY ARNOLD! THE CHRISTMAS SHOW
Entitled "Arnold's Christmas," this half-hour holiday special follows the adventures of street-smart fourth-grader Arnold as he arranges an elaborate gift for lonely Mr. Hyunh by reuniting him with his long-lost daughter. *A Games Animation Production in association with Snee-Osh, Inc. Color. Half-hour. Premiered on NICK: December 14, 1996. Rebroadcast on NICK: December 20, 1996; December 25, 1996.*

*Voices*
**Arnold:** Toran Caudell (Lane T. Caudell); **Gerald:** Jamil W. Smith; **Helga:** Francesca Marie Smith; **Grandma:** Tress MacNeille; **Grandpa:** Dan Castellaneta; **Oskar:** Steve Viksten; **Harold:** Justin Shenkarow; **Phoebe:** Anndi McAfee; **Stinky:** Christopher P. Walberg; **Brainy:** Craig M. Bartlett; **Rhonda:** Olivia Hack; **Mr. Hyunh:** Baoan Coleman; **Big Bob Pataki/Shoe Salesman:** Maurice LaMarche; **Mrs. Pataki:** Kath Soucie; **Ernie:** Dom Irrera; **Mai Hyunh:** Hiep Thi Le; **Mr. Bailey #2:** Vincent Schiavelli

### ◉ HEY, HEY, HEY, IT'S FAT ALBERT
The first cartoon adaptation of comedian Bill Cosby's fictional childhood characters, this half-hour special combined sketchy-

style animated drawings superimposed over live-action footage to tell the story of Cosby's boyhood chums from North Philadelphia who are preparing for a big football match against rival street-gang members the Green Street Terrors. *A Filmation Associates Production in association with Bill Cosby Productions. Color. Half-hour. Premiered on NBC: November 12, 1969. Rebroadcast on NBC: April 17, 1970; September 12, 1971.*

**Voices**
**Fat Albert/Mushmouth/Mudfoot/Dumb Donald:** Bill Cosby; **Russell:** Stephen Cheatham; **Weird Harold:** Gerald Edwards; **Bucky:** Jan Crawford; **Rudy:** Eric Suter

### ◎ HIAWATHA

Legendary brave Hiawatha encounters his greatest test of courage when his tribe is put under the spell of Pearl Feather, an evil medicine man, who seeks revenge by starving the tribe. Based on the Henry Wadsworth Longfellow poem, this program was broadcast in syndication as part of the *Festival of Family Classics*. *A Rankin-Bass Production in association with Mushi Studios. Color. Half-hour. Premiered: September 24, 1972. Syndicated.*

**Voices**
Carl Banas, Len Birman, Bernard Cowan, Peg Dixon, Keith Hampshire, Peggi Loder, Donna Miller, Frank Perry, Henry Ramer, Billie Mae Richards, Alfie Scopp, Paul Soles

### ◎ THE HOBBIT

Self-doubting hobbit Bilbo Baggins leads a quest through Middle Earth to recover stolen treasure from the terrifying dragon, Smaug, and finds a magical ring in this 90-minute special based on the J.R.R. Tolkien literary classic. Glen Yarborough sings the special's theme song, "The Greatest Adventure." *A Rankin-Bass Production. Color. Ninety minutes. Premiered on NBC: November 27, 1977.* Rebroadcast on CBS: May 19, 1979. *Rebroadcast on DIS: December 4, 1992. Rebroadcast on CAR: June 18, 1995 (Mr. Spim's Cartoon Theatre).*

**Voices**
**Bilbo Baggins:** Orson Bean; **Gandalf the wizard:** John Huston; **Thorin Oakenshield, king dwarf:** Hans Conried; **Dragon Smaug:** Richard Boone; **Gollum:** Theodore; **Elvenking:** Otto Preminger; **Elrond:** Cyril Ritchard

### ◎ HOLIDAZE: THE CHRISTMAS THAT ALMOST DIDN'T HAPPEN

Frustrated by playing a much smaller role in helping Santa prepare for Christmas, despondent Rusty the Reindeer heads from the North Pole to the Big City where he finds support and encouragement from holiday icons who have also lost their way—Albert, the Thanksgiving Day Turkey; Candie, the southern Eastern Bunny; Mr. C., the grouchy Cupid; and the moody teenaged twin Halloween Ghosts, Trick and Treat—and the true meaning of Christmas along the way. Produced by Los Angeles–based production studio Madison Road Entertainment in association with PorchLight Entertainment and designed in the style of Rankin-Bass's classic '60s and '70s stop-motion animated specials, this hour-long direct-to-video production, featuring the voice talents of Harland Williams, Gladys Knight, Paul Rodriguez, Emily Osment, Brenda Song, Fred Willard, John O'Hurley and others, aired in first-run syndication and on the ION network (previously PAX-TV) in December 2006. PorchLight Entertainment handled worldwide distribution, excluding the United States, for television, DVD, licensing and merchandising. Prince, Jak Severson and Kelli Baxter coexecutive-produced the holiday special. *A Madison Road Entertainment Production. Color. One hour. Premiered: December 9, 2006. Syndicated. Premiered on ION: December 15, 2006.*

**Voices**
**Rusty the Reindeer:** Fred Savage; **Albert, the Thanksgiving Day Turkey:** Harland Williams; **Candie, the Easter Bunny:** Gladys Knight; **Grouchy Cupid:** Paul Rodriguez; **Trick and Treat, Halloween Ghosts:** Emily Osment, Brenda Song; **Santa Claus:** Fred Willard; **Mrs. Claus:** Edie McClurg; **Kringle:** John O'Hurley; **Photographer Elf/Tech Elf/Dad/Italian Chef:** Andrew Block; **Kids:** Dylan Sprouse, Cole Sprouse

### ◎ HOLLY HOBBIE & FRIENDS: "CHRISTMAS WISHES"

Christmas has arrived in Clover and Holly, who is in the town pageant with the Hey Girls Club, finds out that not everyone has reason to be joyous when she tries helping a recently widowed mother, Kelly Deegan, and her twin sons, Joey and Paul, in this second of two heartwarming cartoon specials, following the first, *Holly Hobbie & Friends: Surprise Party*, to premiere on Nickelodeon's Nick Jr. block; based on American Greetings' classic *Holly Hobbie* brand by Academy Award-winning producer Julia Pistor and writers of *Jimmy Neutron* and *The Wild Thornberrys* and the popular children's book, *Little Simon*, written by Bonnie Pinehurst and illustrated by Kellee Riley. The program included traditional Christmas carols, including "O Holy Night," and music from Grammy Award-winning recording artist LeAnn Rhimes, also the voice of the young widow. Real-life father and former child star Bill Mumy, best known as Will Robinson in TV's *Lost in Space*, played the father of Amy, voiced by his daughter, Lilana. Three days after its premiere, the cartoon special was released on DVD by Sony Wonder. *A Sony Wonder/AG Properties/American Greetings Production. Color. One hour. Premiered on NICK JR.: November 13, 2006. Rebroadcast on NICK JR.: December 14, 2006.*

**Voices**
**Holly Hobbie:** Alyson Stoner; **Robby Hobbie:** Jansen Panettiere; **Joan Hobbie/Minnie:** Jane Lynch; **Gary Hobbie/Ted:** Rob Paulsen; **Uncle Dave:** Diedrich Bader; **Aunt Jesse:** Rusty Schwimmer; **Carrie Baker:** Tinasha Kachungwe; **Amy Morris:** Lilana Mumy: **Kyle Morris:** Paul Butcher; **Bud, Amy's Father:** Bill Mumy; **Kelly Deegan:** LeAnn Rhimes; **Joey Deegan:** Spencer Ganus; **Paul Deegan:** Harrison Fahn; **Carolyn:** Dawnn Lewis; **Jim Bidderman:** Michael McShane; **Mrs. Palmer:** Sirena Irwin

### ◎ HOLLY HOBBIE & FRIENDS: SURPRISE PARTY

To celebrate Aunt Jessie's birthday, Holly works in tandem with Amy and Carrie, becoming overbearing at times, to send out invitations, bake a cake and practice her special song that she plans to sing as they learn the importance of teamwork and honesty in the first direct-to-DVD animated movie based on the popular American Greetings character. Airing at 10 A.M. on Nickelodeon's Nick Jr., the hour-long special preceded a second direct-to-DVD special that aired on Nick that November, *Holly Hobbie & Friends: Christmas Wishes. An AG Properties/American Greetings Production. Color. Half-hour. Premiered on NICK JR.: February 10, 2006.*

**Voices**
**Holly Hobbie:** Alyson Stoner; **Aunt Jessie:** Rusty Schwimmer; **Amy:** Liliana Mumy; **Carrie:** Tinashe Kachungwe; **Joan Hobbie/Minnie:** Jane Lynch; **Robby Hobbie:** Jansen Panettiere; **Uncle Dave:** Diedrich Bader; **Bud, Amy's father:** Bill Mumy

## ⊚ HOLLYROCK-A-BYE BABY

When Pebbles and Bamm-Bamm, now married, move to Hollyrock, the first thing they produce is a "double" feature: twins. Meanwhile, Fred tangles with jewel thieves and a glamorous starlet while helping his son-in-law sell a screenplay in this two-hour made-for-TV animated special. In December 2003, the made-for-TV holiday movie was rebroadcast on the Cartoon Network's sister channel, Boomerang, as part of the first-ever 240-hour, week-long Flintstones holiday movies and specials marathon. A *Hanna-Barbera Production. Color. Two hours. Premiered on ABC: December 5, 1993. Rebroadcast on BOOM: December 18, 2003; December 21, 2003.*

### Voices
**Fred Flintstone:** Henry Corden; **Wilma Flintstone:** Jean Vander-Pyl; **Barney Rubble/Dino/J. Rocko:** Frank Welker; **Betty Rubble:** B.J Ward; **Pebbles Flintstone Rubble:** Kath Soucie; **Bamm-Bamm Rubble:** Jerry House; **Mr. Slate:** John Stephenson; **Mrs. Slaghoople:** June Foray; **Rocky:** Charlie Adler; **Mr. Pyrite:** Michael Bell; **Big Rock:** Brad Garrett; **Slick:** Mark Hamill; **Mary Hartstone:** Mary Hart; **John Teshadactyl:** John Tesh; **Shelly Millstone:** Raquel Welch

## ⊚ A HOLLYWOOD HOUNDS CHRISTMAS

A Caucasian country guitar-playing dog learns cultural tolerance and understanding when he teams up with an African American sax-playing canine and a timbale-playing Latina cat to form the first multiethnic pet singing group and discover the true meaning of Christmas. A *DIC Enterprises Production in association with Bohbot Entertainment. Color. Half-hour. Premiered: November 25, 1994. Syndicated.*

### Voices
**Rosie:** Candi Milo; **Dude:** Jeff Bennett; **Cuz:** Chris Broughton; **Michael:** Theodore Borders; **Holly:** Jania Foxworth

## ⊚ HOORAY FOR THE THREE WISEMEN

In the year 2000, three wise men are sent to Earth in a spacecraft to deliver gifts to the newborn Christ child in this Italian-produced special made in six episodes. A *Cineteam Realizzazioni Production in association with Radiotelevisione Italiana. Color. One hour. Premiered: 1987. Syndicated.*

### Voices
**Gaspar:** Albert Eddy; **Balthasar:** Leroy Villanueva; **Melchor:** Tony McShear; **Kid:** Dennis Khalili-Borna; **Joseph:** Michael Connor; **Mary:** Eric Rose; **Herod:** Ken Dana, Michael McComohle; (singing); **Shepherd:** Simon Prescott

## ⊚ THE HORSE THAT PLAYED CENTERFIELD

The New York Goats, a professional baseball team, are perennial losers. Their luck turns when a baseball-playing horse, Oscar, joins the team. The *ABC Weekend Special* was aired in two parts. A *Ruby-Spears Enterprises Production for ABC. Color. Half-hour. Premiered on ABC: February 24, 1979 and March 3, 1979. Rebroadcast on ABC: September 29, 1969 and October 6, 1969; July 5, 1980 and July 12, 1980; June 13, 1981 and 20, 1981; June 5, 1982 and June 12, 1982; May 28, 1983 and June 4, 1983; June 15, 1985 and June 22, 1985; March 4, 1989 and March 11, 1989; September 16, 1989 and September 23, 1989.*

### Voices
John Erwin, Joan Gardner, Allan Melvin, Don Messick, Howard Morris, Alan Oppenheimer, Brad Sanders

## ⊚ HOT WHEELS HIGHWAY 35: "WORLD RACE: DESERT HEAT"

Kadeem, leader of race car team Dune Ratz, almost achieves the impossible when he claims the Wheel of Power first to win the World Race and grand prize that would help his family back home in this third of five half-hour specials, based on Mattel's *Hot Wheels* toy car line. A *Mainframe Entertainment/Mattel Inc. Production. Color. Half-hour. Premiered on CAR: July 26, 2003.*

### Voices
**Dr. Peter Tezla:** Michael Donovan; **Vert Wheeler:** Andrew Francis; **Kurt Wylde:** Brian Drummond; **Markie Wylde:** Will Sanderson; **Taro Kitano:** Kevin Ohtsji; **Lani Tam:** Venus Terzo; **Gig:** Kasper Michaels; **Gelorum:** Kathleen Barr; **Other Voices:** Scott McNeil, Cusse Mankuma, John Payne II

## ⊚ HOT WHEELS HIGHWAY 35: "WORLD RACE: FROZEN FIRE"

Older brother Kurt Wylde competes for the crown against his rival younger brother, Mark, racing through deadly ice-covered mountains on Highway 35, while hoping to collect the Wheel of Power and win the race in this fourth of five half-hour specials, based on Mattel's *Hot Wheels* toy car line. A *Mainframe Entertainment/Mattel Inc. Production. Color. Half-hour. Premiered on CAR: August 2, 2003.*

### Voices
**Dr. Peter Tezla:** Michael Donovan; **Vert Wheeler:** Andrew Francis; **Kurt Wylde:** Brian Drummond; **Markie Wylde:** Will Sanderson; **Taro Kitano:** Kevin Ohtsji; **Lani Tam:** Venus Terzo; **Gig:** Kasper Michaels; **Gelorum:** Kathleen Barr; **Other Voices:** Scott McNeil, Cusse Mankuma, John Payne II

## ⊚ HOT WHEELS HIGHWAY 35: "WORLD RACE: GREATEST CHALLENGE"

The notorious Wave Rippers, Scorchers, Street Breed, Dune Ratz and Road Beats encounter perhaps their greatest challenge in the World Race competition—a monstrous and deadly road-blocking device—while continuing on their fast-track journey to pick up the all-powerful Wheel of Power. Meanwhile, Kurt Wylde's younger brother Mark joins the adventure and Vert, who is impressed by his driving skills, asks him to join his brother's rival team in this second of five half-hour specials, based on Mattel's *Hot Wheels* toy car line. The specials were produced in celebration of the toys' 35th anniversary. In December 2003, Family Home Entertainment released a 110-minute feature-length compilation of all five episodes on DVD. In 2005, a series of hour-long sequels, called *AcceleRacers*, were produced for Cartoon Network. A *Mainframe Entertainment/Mattel Inc. Production. Color. Half-hour. Premiered on CAR: July 19, 2003.*

### Voices
**Dr. Peter Tezla:** Michael Donovan; **Vert Wheeler:** Andrew Francis; **Kurt Wylde:** Brian Drummond; **Markie Wylde:** Will Sanderson; **Taro Kitano:** Kevin Ohtsji; **Lani Tam:** Venus Terzo; **Gig:** Kasper Michaels; **Gelorum:** Kathleen Barr; **Other Voices:** Scott McNeil, Cusse Mankuma, John Payne II

## ⊚ HOT WHEELS HIGHWAY 35: "WORLD RACE: RING OF FIRE"

Five World Race teams, Wave Rippers, Scorchers, Street Breed, Dune Ratz and Road Beasts, featuring world-famous racers and others recruited by Dr. Peter Tezla, embark on a daring high-speed competition on Highway 35, including their first challenge, a lava-filled Volcana Track, in their quest to pick up the coveted

Wheel of Power, in this first of the five-part series of half-hour specials based on Mattel's *Hot Wheels* franchise. Marking the 35th anniversary of these popular toy collectibles, the special premiered on Cartoon Network in July 2003. That December, Family Home Entertainment released a 110-minute feature-length compilation of all five episodes on DVD. In 2005, the series spawned four successful hour-long sequels, called *AcceleRacers*. *A Mainframe Entertainment/Mattel Inc. Production. Color. Half-hour. Premiered on CAR: July 12, 2003.*

**Voices**
**Dr. Peter Tezla:** Michael Donovan; **Vert Wheeler:** Andrew Francis; **Kurt Wylde:** Brian Drummond; **Markie Wylde:** Will Sanderson; **Taro Kitano:** Kevin Ohtsji; **Lani Tam:** Venus Terzo; **Gig:** Kasper Michaels; **Gelorum:** Kathleen Barr; **Other Voices:** Scott McNeil, Cusse Mankuma, John Payne II

### ◎ HOT WHEELS HIGHWAY 35: "WORLD RACE: WHEEL OF POWER"

Dr. Tezla wins the World Race and the highly sought after Wheel of Power, but not before evil forces try taking it from him, forcing the World Race team leaders to team up and make sure it doesn't fall into the wrong hands in this fifth and final installment of the five-part series of Cartoon Network half-hour specials, based on Mattel's *Hot Wheels* toy car line. *A Mainframe Entertainment/Mattel Inc. Production. Color. Half-hour. Premiered on CAR: August 2, 2003.*

**Voices**
**Dr. Peter Tezla:** Michael Donovan; **Vert Wheeler:** Andrew Francis; **Kurt Wylde:** Brian Drummond; **Markie Wylde:** Will Sanderson; **Taro Kitano:** Kevin Ohtsji; **Lani Tam:** Venus Terzo; **Gig:** Kasper Michaels; **Gelorum:** Kathleen Barr; **Other Voices:** Scott McNeil, Cusse Mankuma, John Payne II

### ◎ HOW BUGS BUNNY WON THE WEST

Actor Denver Pyle, well-known for various roles in movie westerns, tells how Bugs Bunny and Daffy Duck were true pioneers of the West in this half-hour special featuring excerpts from previously released Warner cartoons. *A Warner Bros. Television Production. Color. Half-hour. Premiered on CBS: November 15, 1978. Rebroadcast on CBS: September 10, 1979; September 18, 1980; March 8, 1983; January 13, 1984; May 30, 1984; January 18, 1985; September 20, 1985; August 21, 1987.*

**Voices**
Mel Blanc

### ◎ HOW DO YOU SPELL GOD?

Children from diverse religious and cultural backgrounds answer candid and touching questions emphasizing the importance of unity and understanding among people of all faiths in this HBO special, featuring cartoon renditions of the Hindu parable "The Blind Men and the Elephant" as well as works by Maya Angelou, Isaac Bashevis Singer and A.A. Milne. Opening the half-hour program is a live-action introduction by the Dalai Lama. *A Debra Solomon/Michael Sporn Animation/HBO Production. Color. Half-hour. Premiered on HBO: December 22, 1996. Rebroadcast on HBO: December 25, 1996; December 27, 1996; December 31, 1996; January 6, 1997; January 9, 1997; January 11, 1997; April 6, 1997; June 15, 1997; July 1, 1997; July 13, 1997; July 24, 1997; July 28, 1997; December 1, 1997; December 5, 1997; December 11, 1997; December 14, 1997; December 25, 1997; June 5, 1998; June 10, 1998; June 18, 1998; June 27, 1998; June 30, 1998; October 2, 1998; October 10, 1998; October 13, 1998; October 26, 1998; July 3, 1999; July 9, 1999; July 11, 1999; July 12, 1999; December 1,*

*1999; December 4, 1999; December 14, 1999; December 20, 1999; December 25, 1999; December 30, 1999; September 13, 2000; September 18, 2000; September 24, 2000. Rebroadcast on HBO FAM: April 1, 1997; April 3, 1997; April 10, 1997; April 18, 1997; April 21, 1997; April 25, 1997; April 28, 1997; July 5, 1997; July 8, 1997; July 14, 1997; July 17, 1997; July 25, 1997; September 8, 1997; September 12, 1997; September 16, 1997; September 27, 1997; December 2, 1997; December 13, 1997; December 15, 1997; December 21, 1997; December 24, 1997; December 29, 1997; June 3, 1998; June 8, 1998; June 13, 1998; June 16, 1998; June 21, 1998; June 26, 1998; October 4, 1998; October 16, 1998; October 21, 1998; October 14, 1998; October 27, 1998; February 10, 1999; February 18, 1999; February 22, 1999; February 25, 1999; March 2, 1999; March 5, 1999; May 5, 1999; May 14, 1999; May 22, 1999; May 28, 1999; May 31, 1999; June 1, 1999; September 8, 1999; September 9, 1999; September 14, 1999; September 18, 1999; September 28, 1999; December 4, 1999; December 7, 1999; December 19, 1999; December 23, 1999; May 8, 2000; May 18, 2000; May 23, 2000; September 4, 2000; September 15, 2000; September 19, 2000; September 22, 2000; December 3, 2000; December 25, 2000; December 28, 2000; January 1, 2001; March 3, 2001; March 8, 2001; March 9, 2001; March 26, 2001; July 1, 2001; July 4, 2001; July 14, 2001; July 19, 2001.*

**Voices**
**Narrator:** Fred Savage; **Other Voices:** Hayden Panettiere

### ◎ HOW THE LEOPARD GOT HIS SPOTS

Actor Danny Glover narrates this beloved children's tale of a light-coated African leopard whose only chance of survival is to acquire spots for himself in this inspired half-hour animated adaptation of the Rudyard Kipling classic, produced as part of Rabbit Ears Video's *Storybook Classics* series. *A Rabbit Ears Video Production. Color. Half-hour. Premiered on SHO: 1989.*

**Voices**
**Narrator:** Danny Glover

### ◎ HOW THE RHINOCEROS GOT HIS SKIN/ HOW THE CAMEL GOT HIS HUMP

Two of Rudyard Kipling's best-known "Just So" stories—the first about a man who seeks revenge on a nasty piggish rhino, the second about how arrogance becomes the downfall of a lazy camel— are presented in this half-hour animated adaptation, told by award-winning actor Jack Nicholson. Produced for Rabbit Ears Video's *Storybook Classics* series, it made its debut on Showtime. *A Rabbit Ears Video Production. Color. Half-hour. Premiered on SHO: 1989.*

**Voices**
**Narrator:** Jack Nicholson

### ◎ HULK HOGAN: ALL-TIME CHAMP

World Wrestling Federation (WWF) champion wrestler Hulk Hogan faces a series of new challenges with some help from his friends in this original hour-long *DIC Holiday Theater* cartoon special for first-run syndication. *A DIC Entertainment Production. Color. One hour. Premiered: October 27, 1992. Syndicated.*

**Voices**
**Hulk Hogan:** Himself

### ◎ HUNGARIAN FOLK TALES

Produced by MTV Enterprises in Hungary, these three delightful animated folktales—"John Raven," about a young man's journey to find his fortune, and two others, "The Hedgehog" and "Pinko," classic stories of unlikely heroes rewarded for their kindness and remarkable feats—debuted in the United States on PBS's long-running *Long Ago & Far Away* series. *A MTV Enterprises, Hungary Production. Color. Half-hour. Premiered on PBS: February 25, 1989. Rebroadcast on PBS: November 23, 1990.*

## ◉ THE ICE QUEEN'S MITTENS

With no kitten fur for mittens to warm her hands during the upcoming winter, Freezelda, the evil Ice Queen bribes her henchman, Hoodwink the Rat, to fetch three little kittens to make fur, only to have Old Man Winter summon a blizzard and thwart her in this half-hour animated musical, originally produced for Canadian television as part of CINAR Films' *The Real Story of . . .* series (retitled from *Three Little Kittens*). The special aired on HBO under the pay-cable network's *HBO Storybook Musicals* series. *A CINAR Films/Crayon Animation Production in association with Western Publishing Company/CTV Television Network/Telefilm Canada. Color. Half-hour. Premiered on HBO: October 2, 1991. Rebroadcast on HBO: October 7, 1991; October 18, 1991; October 31, 1991.*

*Voices*
**Freezelda, the Ice Queen:** Lauren Bacall; **Hoodwink:** Bryan Adams

## ◉ I LOVE CHIPMUNKS, VALENTINE SPECIAL

Valentine's Day to the Chipmunks marks the long-awaited social event of the year—the Valentine's Day dance and a chance to win the prestigious Valentine's couple award. Alvin and Chipette Brittany learn a lesson in honesty and love as they become the model Valentine's couple. *A Ruby-Spears Enterprises Production in association with Ross Bagdasarian Productions. Color. Half-hour. Premiered on NBC: February 12, 1984. Rebroadcast on NBC: February 13, 1985.*

*Voices*
**Alvin/Simon/David Seville:** Ross Bagdasarian Jr.; **Theodore:** Janice Karman; **The Chipettes: Brittany/Jeanette/Elenore:** Janice Karman

## ◉ THE INCREDIBLE BOOK ESCAPE

Actress Quinn Cummings, as a young boy named P.J. (in live action), accidentally gets locked in the children's reading room of the local public library and becomes acquainted with the characters from several picture books who come to life in a blend of live action and animation. *A CBS Library Special. A Bosustow Entertainment Production. Color. One hour. Premiered on CBS: June 3, 1980. Rebroadcast on CBS: November 28, 1980.*

*Voices*
**Mrs. Page:** Ruth Buzzi; **Myra:** Penelope Sundrow; **Ghost-in-the-Shed:** George Gobel; **Princess:** Tammy Grimes; **Lord Garp/Prince:** Arte Johnson; **Professor Mickimecki:** Hans Conried; **Melvin Spitznagle:** Sparky Marcus; **Mrs. Spitznagle:** June Foray; **Mr. Spitznagle:** Jack Angel

## ◉ THE INCREDIBLE CRASH DUMMIES

After crash dummy Ted severs his head during a crash test, Dr. Zub replaces it with that of the evil Junkman who, thanks to Zub's powerful new "uncrashable" Torso 9000 prototype armor, then escapes from the Crash Test facility in Dummyland with plans to destroy the crash dummies until Steve and Slick save the day in this computer-animated half-hour special—and one of the first computer-animated movies ever made—inspired by the popular safe-driving public service announcements ("Don't You Be a Dummy. Buckle Your Safety Belt") produced for television in the early 1990s. Executive produced and co-written by *Eek! The Cat* creators Savage Steve Holland and Bill Kopp, the program premiered on Saturday, May 1, 1993, on FOX Kids Network, with an encore performance that September, and was later resold on home video in conjunction with Tyco's popular Crash Dummy action figure toy line. Twelve years later, the characters were recast in their own series of animated interstitials airing Saturday mornings on FOX. *A Lamb & Company, Inc./ Nelvana Limited Production. Color. Half-hour. Premiered on FOX: May 1, 1993. Rebroadcast on FOX: September 11, 1993.*

*Voices*
**Slick/Jackhammer:** James Rankin; **Spin:** Michael Caruana; **Doctor Zub/Horst:** John Stocker; **Junkman:** Dan Hennessey; **Ted:** Lee MacDougall; **Spare Tire/Pistonhead:** Richard Bineley; **Bull/Daryl:** Paul Haddad; **Computer Voice:** Susan Roman

## ◉ THE INCREDIBLE DETECTIVES

On a visit to a local museum, Davey Morrison is kidnapped by two guards with few clues left behind for the police to track his whereabouts. Davey's three talented pets—Madame Cheng, a slightly vain Siamese cat; Hennesy, a gabby black crow; and Reggie, a sophisticated but stuffy bulldog—investigate Davey's whereabouts. *A Ruby-Spears Enterprises Production. Color. Half-hour. Premiered on ABC: November 17, 1979. Rebroadcast on ABC: March 20, 1980; September 27, 1980.*

*Voices*
**Madame Chen:** Mariene Aragon; **Reggie:** Laurie Main; **Hennesey:** Frank Welker; **Davey Morrison:** Albert Eisenmann

## ◉ THE INCREDIBLE, INDELIBLE, MAGICAL, PHYSICAL MYSTERY TRIP

This educational and entertaining fantasy entails the journey of two young children, Joey and Missy, through the mistreated body of their Uncle Carl, who has done little in his life to maintain his health. The kids make their trip after being miniaturized by their cartoon companion, Timer, in this *ABC Afterschool Special* that combines live action and animation. *A DePatie-Freleng Enterprises Production in association with ABC. Color. Half-hour. Premiered on ABC: February 7, 1973. Rebroadcast on ABC: October 24, 1973; March 4, 1978 (on ABC Weekend Specials).*

*Reggie the bulldog, Madame Cheng the cat and Hennesy the crow become detectives to right the wrong and save the day in the Ruby-Spears cartoon special* The Incredible Detectives. *© Ruby-Spears Enterprises*

*Voices*
**Timer:** Len Maxwell; **Joey:** Peter Broderick; **Missy:** Kathy Buch

## ◎ INSPECTOR GADGET SAVES CHRISTMAS

There's trouble at the North Pole: Dr. Claw has changed the elves into drones and jailed the real Santa. His plot to ruin Christmas is thwarted by Inspector Gadget's tag-along friends Brain and Penny, as well as some fast bumbling on the part of the great inspector himself in this Emmy-nominated holiday special. In the fall of 2004, the hilarious yuletide adventure was re-offered in syndication as part of DIC Entertainment's three-hour DIC Kids Network programming block. *A DIC Enterprises Production. Color. Half-hour. Premiered on NBC: December 4, 1992. Rebroadcast on ABC: December 14, 1996.*

*Voices*
**Inspector Gadget:** Don Adams

## ◎ INSPECTOR GADGET'S LAST CASE

After bidding farewell to his antiquated Gadgetmobile and being assigned a more advanced replacement vehicle, the super bionic Inspector Gadget battles to save his job after his famous archenemy Dr. Claw employs a competing crime-fighter to discredit him. This second premiere episode was part of *DIC's Incredible Movie Toons* anthology series, consisting of 13 animated movies that were telecast on the Nickelodeon network. *A DIC Entertainment Production. Color. Ninety minutes. Premiered on NICK: October 13, 2002.*

*Voices*
**Lieutenant Gadget:** Maurice LaMarche; **Female Superhero:** Tina Bush; **Chief Quimby:** Jim Byrnes; **R2K:** Michael Richard Dobson; **Dr. Claw:** Brian Drummond; **Velvetmobile:** Blu Mankuma; **Penny:** Tegan Moss; **Professor Gorgonzola:** Colin Murdock; **Otto:** Richard Newman; **Devon Debonair:** Dale Wilson; **Anchorwoman:** Kim Hawthorne

## ◎ INTERGALACTIC THANKSGIVING

Two families who are dissimilar in nature (one is hardworking and dedicated, the other is self-centered) travel in space to parts unknown in search of a new planet where they can settle in this Canadian produced holiday special. *A Nelvana Limited Production in association with the CBC. Color. Half-hour. Premiered: October 1979. Syndicated.*

*Voices*
**King Goochie:** Sid Caesar; **Ma Spademinder:** Catherine O'Hara; **Pa Spademinder:** Chris Wiggins; **Victoria Spademinder:** Jean Walker; **Magic Mirror:** Martin Lavut; **Notfunnyenuf:** Derek McGrath; **The Bug:** Al Waxman; **Bug Kid:** Toby Waxman

## ◎ INUYASHA: AFFECTIONS TOUCHING ACROSS TIME

Along with Kagome, Shippo, Sango and Miroku, InuYasha comes face-to-face with the evil Menomaru in his relentless quest to recover the powerful Shikon Jewel shards in this first of four movies—based on the popular anime series—that debuted at midnight on Cartoon Network's *Adult Swim* block. *A Yomimuri TV/Bandai Visual/Sunrise Inc. Production. Color. One hour. Premiered on CAR: May 15, 2005.*

*Voices*
**Kagome Higurashi:** Moneca Stori; **InuYasha:** Richard Cox; **Kohaku:** Alex Doduk; **Rin:** Brenna O'Briend; **Sessho-maru:** David Kaye; **Jaken:** Don Brown; **Shippo:** Jillian Michaels; **Sango:** Kelly Sheridan; **Miroku:** Kirby Morrow; **Myonga/Naraku:** Paul Dobson; **Kiga:** Scott McNeil; **Kikyo:** Willow Johnson; **Gatenmaru:** Adam Henderson; **InuYasha's Mom:** Alaina Burnett; **Mushin:** Alec Willows; **Momiji:** Alexandra Carter; **Toran:** Alison Matthew; **Hakkaku:** Alistair Abell; **Manten:** Alvin Sanders; **Hiten/Tsuyu's Lord:** Andrew Francis; **Serina:** Anna Cummer; **Nobunaga:** Brad Swaile; **Muso/Shouga:** Brian Dobson; **Juromaru/Kageromaru/Renkotsu:** Brian Drummond; **Suzuna:** Brittany Wilson; **Ayumi/Bunza/Fake Princess/Flesh-Eating Mask/Hakudoushi/Kagome's Mom/Urasue:** Cathy Weseluck; **Asuka/Mayu:** Chantal Strand; **Hakudoshi/The Infant/Yura of the Hair:** Chiara Zanni; **Orochidayu/Royakan/Sango's Father/Water God:** Colin Murdock

## ◎ INUYASHA: CASTLE BEYOND THE LOOKING GLASS

After successfully defeating Naraku, InuYasha and his friends enjoy a brief break back home until they must confront a new enemy, the ruler of eternal light, Kaguya, in this second of four made-for-TV movies adapted from the Japanese cartoon series, first shown in August 2005 at midnight and rerun at 3:00 A.M. on Cartoon Network. *A Yomimuri TV/Bandai Visual/Sunrise Inc. Production. Color. One hour. Premiered on CAR: August 27, 2005.*

*Voices*
**Kagome Higurashi:** Moneca Stori; **InuYasha:** Richard Cox; **Kohaku:** Alex Doduk; **Rin:** Brenna O'Briend; **Sessho-maru:** David Kaye; **Jaken:** Don Brown; **Shippo:** Jillian Michaels; **Sango:** Kelly Sheridan; **Miroku:** Kirby Morrow; **Myonga/Naraku:** Paul Dobson; **Kiga:** Scott McNeil; **Kikyo:** Willow Johnson; **Gatenmaru:** Adam Henderson; **InuYasha's Mom:** Alaina Burnett; **Mushin:** Alec Willows; **Momiji:** Alexandra Carter; **Toran:** Alison Matthew; **Hakkaku:** Alistair Abell; **Manten:** Alvin Sanders; **Hiten/Tsuyu's Lord:** Andrew Francis; **Serina:** Anna Cummer; **Nobunaga:** Brad Swaile; **Muso/Shouga:** Brian Dobson; **Juromaru/Kageromaru/Renkotsu:** Brian Drummond; **Suzuna:** Brittany Wilson; **Ayumi/Bunza/Fake Princess/Flesh-Eating Mask/Hakudoushi/Kagome's Mom/Urasue:** Cathy Weseluck; **Asuka/Mayu:** Chantal Strand; **Hakudoshi/The Infant/Yura of the Hair:** Chiara Zanni; **Orochidayu/Royakan/Sango's Father/Water God:** Colin Murdock

## ◎ INUYASHA: FIRE ON THE MYSTIC ISLAND

InuYasha and his friends face their greatest foes yet when four evil gods, the Shitoushin, seek to attain the immense supernatural powers to maintain life on the island of Houraijima that mysteriously reappears 50 years after its disappearance in this fourth and final movie featuring characters from Cartoon Network's top-rated *Toonami* action block series. *A Yomimuri TV/Bandai Visual/Sunrise Inc. Production. Color. One hour. Premiered on CAR: December 23, 2006.*

*Voices*
**Kagome Higurashi:** Moneca Stori; **InuYasha:** Richard Cox; **Kohaku:** Alex Doduk; **Rin:** Brenna O'Briend; **Sessho-maru:** David Kaye; **Jaken:** Don Brown; **Shippo:** Jillian Michaels; **Sango:** Kelly Sheridan; **Miroku:** Kirby Morrow; **Myonga/Naraku:** Paul Dobson; **Kiga:** Scott McNeil; **Kikyo:** Willow Johnson; **Gatenmaru:** Adam Henderson; **InuYasha's Mom:** Alaina Burnett; **Mushin:** Alec Willows; **Momiji:** Alexandra Carter; **Toran:** Alison Matthew; **Hakkaku:** Alistair Abell; **Manten:** Alvin Sanders; **Hiten/Tsuyu's Lord:** Andrew Francis; **Serina:** Anna Cummer; **Nobunaga:** Brad Swaile; **Muso/Shouga:** Brian Dobson; **Juromaru/Kageromaru/Renkotsu:** Brian Drummond; **Suzuna:** Brittany Wilson; **Ayumi/Bunza/Fake Princess/Flesh-Eating Mask/Hakudoushi/Kagome's Mom/Urasue:**

Cathy Weseluck; **Asuka/Mayu:** Chantal Strand; **Hakudoshi/The Infant/Yura of the Hair:** Chiara Zanni; **Orochidayu/Royakan/ Sango's Father/Water God:** Colin Murdock

## ◉ INUYASHA: SWORDS OF AN HONORABLE RULER

InuYasha and his brother, Sessho-maru, must stop the legendary sword, So'unga, which their father once fought for, from destroying Earth and all mankind in this third of four movie specials spun-off from the English-dubbed Japanese anime series, debuting in August 2006 at 11 A.M. on Cartoon Network. *A Yomimuri TV/ Bandai Visual/Sunrise Inc. Production. Color. One hour. Premiered on CAR: August 12, 2006.*

*Voices*
**Kagome Higurashi:** Moneca Stori; **InuYasha:** Richard Cox; **Kohaku:** Alex Doduk; **Rin:** Brenna O'Briend; **Sessho-maru:** David Kaye; **Jaken:** Don Brown; **Shippo:** Jillian Michaels; **Sango:** Kelly Sheridan; **Miroku:** Kirby Morrow; **Myonga/Naraku:** Paul Dobson; **Kiga:** Scott McNeil; **Kikyo:** Willow Johnson; **Gatenmaru:** Adam Henderson; **InuYasha's Mom:** Alaina Burnett; **Mushin:** Alec Willows; **Momiji:** Alexandra Carter; **Toran:** Alison Matthew; **Hakkaku:** Alistair Abell; **Manten:** Alvin Sanders; **Hiten/Tsuyu's Lord:** Andrew Francis; **Serina:** Anna Cummer; **Nobunaga:** Brad Swaile; **Muso/Shouga:** Brian Dobson; **Juromaru/ Kageromaru/Renkotsu:** Brian Drummond; **Suzuna:** Brittany Wilson; **Ayumi/Bunza/Fake Princess/Flesh-Eating Mask/Hakudoushi/Kagome's Mom/Urasue:** Cathy Weseluck; **Asuka/Mayu:** Chantal Strand; **Hakudoshi/The Infant/Yura of the Hair:** Chiara Zanni; **Orochidayu/Royakan/Sango's Father/Water God:** Colin Murdock

## ◉ IRA SLEEPS OVER

Based on the book by Bernard Waber, a young boy (Ira) spends his first night away from home at his playmate Reggie's house. Even though he's afraid that his friend will tease him, he brings along his beloved teddy bear in this half-hour animated musical special, part of the *HBO Storybook Musicals* series. *A Michael Sporn Animation Production in association with Italtoons Corporation. Color. Half-hour. Premiered on HBO: November 6, 1991. Rebroadcast on HBO: November 15, 1991.*

*Voices*
**Ira:** Danny Gerard; **Sister:** Grace Johnston

*Ira is excited at the invitation to sleep over at his best friend Reggie's house in Ira Sleeps Over. © Michael Sporn Animation*

## ◉ IS IT FALL YET?

Daria and her Lawndale High classmates, Kevin, Brittany, Quinn, Mack, Jodie, Jane and others go their separate ways during summer vacation enjoying different challenges with Daria helping a troubled 12-year-old who reminds her of herself in this animated made-for-TV movie, based on MTV's hit *Daria* cartoon series. Also entitled *Daria in Is It Fall Yet?* and *Daria: Is It Fall Yet?* the movie debuted after the conclusion of the series' fourth season on MTV. *An MTV Animation/Plus One Animation Production in association with Music Television and Sony Pictures Entertainment. Color. Ninety minutes. Premiered on MTV: August 27, 2000.*

*Voices*
**Daria Morgendorffer:** Tracy Grandstaff; **Stacy Rowe:** Sarah Drew; **Jane Lane/Helen Barksdale Morgendorffer/Quinn Morgendorffer:** Wendy Hoopes; **Joey:** Steven Huppert; **Andrew Landon:** Bart Fastbender; **Trent Lane:** Alvaro J. Gonzalez; **Jodie Abigail Landon:** Jessica Cyndee Jackson; **Angela Li:** Nora Laudani; **Mr. Anthony DeMartino/Mr. Timothy O'Neill/Kevin Thompson/ Jamie White:** Marc Thompson; **Thomas "Tom" Sloane, Daria's boyfriend:** Russell Hankin; **Sandi/Brittany:** Janie Mertz; **Jeffy:** Tim Novikoff; **Tiffany:** Ashley Albert; **Jake:** Julian Rebolledo; **Jesse:** Willy Schwenz; **Mack:** Amir Williams; **David:** Carson Daly; **Daniel:** David Grohl; **Alison:** Bif Naked; **Other Voices:** Rachel Anton, Brett Barsky, Amanda Fox, Maggie Frederic, Amy Goldman, James Woods, Amy Palmer, David Moritt, Rhodri J. Murphy, Lemon Krasny, Corey Block, Cindy E. Brolsma, Joseph Buoye

## ◉ IS THIS GOODBYE, CHARLIE BROWN?

In this funny yet poignant treatment of the trauma friends suffer when they must separate, Lucy and Linus's father is transferred to a new job in another city and the children must move away from their pint-size community. Charlie Brown finds the situation so appalling that he's left speechless . . . well, almost. This original CBS special was among a slate of specials as well as the Saturday-morning series, *The Charlie Brown & Snoopy Show*, rebroadcast on cable's Nickelodeon network, beginning in 1998. *A Lee Mendelson–Bill Melendez Production in association with Charles M. Schulz Creative Associates and United Media Syndicate. Color. Half-hour. Premiered on CBS: February 21, 1983. Rebroadcast on CBS: February 13, 1984. Rebroadcast on NICK: January 3, 1998; March 4, 1998; April 7, 1998; May 7, 1998; June 10, 1998; July 12, 1998; August 17, 1998; September 17, 1998; October 18, 1998; November 17, 1998; December 25, 1998; March 20, 1999; May 12, 1999; June 28, 1999; August 29, 1999; February 26, 2000.*

*Voices*
**Charlie Brown:** Brad Kesten; **Linus Van Pelt:** Jeremy Schoenberg; **Lucy Van Pelt:** Angela Lee; **Marcie:** Michael Dockery; **Sally Brown:** Stacy Heather Tolkin; **Peppermint Patty:** Victoria Vargas; **Schroeder/Franklin:** Kevin Brando; **Snoopy:** José C. Melendez

## ◉ IT'S A BRAND NEW WORLD

Four children experience the wonders of the Bible in stories about Noah and Samson told in music and song. The program was one of six specials that aired on NBC under the heading "NBC Special Treat." *An Elias Production in association with D & R Productions. Color. One hour. Premiered on NBC: March 8, 1977. Rebroadcast on NBC: April 9, 1977; December 5, 1977.*

*Voices*
**Teacher/Noah:** Joe Silver; **Elijah/Samson:** Malcolm Dodd; **Aaron:** Dennis Cooley; **Jezebel:** Boni Enten; **Barnabas:** George Hirsch;

**Samson's Brother:** Charmaine Harma; **Vocalists:** Sylvester Fields, Hilda Harris, Maeretha Stewart

### ◎ IT'S A MYSTERY, CHARLIE BROWN

Sally needs something to bring to show and tell at school and takes Woodstock's nest as an example of a prehistoric bird nest. Meanwhile, Snoopy, thinking he's Sherlock Holmes, tries to find the thief of his little friend's nest. In 1998, cable giant Nickelodeon began re-airing the special almost monthly on weekdays and weekends, along with several other *Peanuts* specials and Saturday morning's *The Charlie Brown & Snoopy Show*, originally broadcast on CBS, to which it had bought the broadcasting rights. *A Lee Mendelson–Bill Melendez Production in association with Charles M. Schulz Creative Associates and United Feature Syndicate. Color. Half-hour. Premiered on CBS: February 1, 1974. Rebroadcast on CBS: February 17, 1975. Rebroadcast on NICK: January 28, 1998; March 3, 1998; April 6, 1998; May 6, 1998; June 14, 1998; July 14, 1998; August 18, 1998; September 18, 1998; December 9, 1998; February 21, 1999; April 22, 1999; June 11, 1999; August 9, 1999; December 5, 1999.*

*Voices*

**Charlie Brown:** Todd Barbee; **Lucy Van Pelt:** Melanie Kohn; **Linus Van Pelt:** Stephen Shea; **Peppermint Patty:** Donna Forman; **Marcie:** Jimmie Ahrens; **Sally Brown:** Lynn Mortensen; **Pigpen:** Thomas A. Muller

### ◎ IT'S AN ADVENTURE, CHARLIE BROWN

This one-hour animated special was one of a series of programs featuring different stories based on the best comic strips by *Peanuts* cartoonist Charles M. Schulz. Segments include Lucy's plot to get rid of Linus's security blanket and Peppermint Patty's and Marcie's stint as "caddies" at a golf course. Host: Charles M. Schulz. Nickelodeon later rebroadcast the special beginning in 1998 in two parts on back-to-back days, along with an entire package of Peanuts specials and Saturday morning's *The Charlie Brown & Snoopy Show*, originally aired on CBS. *A Lee Mendelson–Bill Melendez Production in association with Charles M. Schulz Creative Associates and United Feature Syndicate. Color. Half-hour. Premiered on CBS: May 16, 1983. Rebroadcast on CBS: November 5, 1983; September 19, 1987. Rebroadcast on NICK: March 16, 1998 (Part I); March 17, 1998 (Part II); April 27, 1998 (Part I); April 28, 1998 (Part II); June 3, 1998 (Part I); June 4, 1998 (Part II); July 6, 1998 (Part I); July 7, 1998 (Part II); September 7, 1998 (Part I); September 8, 1998 (Part II); October 1, 1998 (Part I); October 2, 1998 (Part II); October 26, 1998 (Part I); October 27, 1998 (Part II); December 2, 1998 (Part I); December 3, 1998 (Part II); April 1, 1999 (Part I); April 2, 1999 (Part II); May 24, 1999 (Part I); May 25, 1999 (Part II); July 21, 1999 (Part I); July 22, 1999 (Part II).*

*Voices*

**Charlie Brown:** Michael Catalano; **Lucy Van Pelt:** Angela Lee; **Linus Van Pelt:** Earl "Rocky" Reilly; **Sally Brown:** Cindi Reilly; **Peppermint Patty:** Brent Hauer; **Schroeder:** Brad Schachter; **Marcie:** Michael Dockery; **Ruby:** Jenny Lewis; **Austin:** Johnny Graves; **Leland:** Joel Graves; **Milo:** Jason Muller; **Caddymaster:** Gerard Goyette Jr.; **Camp Kids:** Brandon Crane, Brian Jackson, Kevin Brando; **Snoopy:** José Melendez; **Announcer:** John Hiestand

### ◎ IT'S ARBOR DAY, CHARLIE BROWN

Sally's lack of knowledge of the significance of Arbor Day inspires some members of the *Peanuts* gang to set things right by embarking on a seed-planting spree using the baseball field as their garden plot. Meanwhile, unsuspecting Charlie Brown is busy preparing strategy for the opening game of the baseball season, unaware that the baseball diamond has been turned into a jungle without his consent. The final *Peanuts* special featuring original music by composer Vince Guaraldi, who died of a heart attack several hours after finishing the soundtrack for the special. Nickelodeon began reshowing it in April 1998, followed by additional airings. The program was part of a package of *Peanuts* programs first seen on CBS that the network had acquired and re-aired. *A Lee Mendelson–Bill Melendez Production in association with Charles M. Schulz Creative Associates and United Feature Syndicate. Color. Half-hour. Premiered on CBS: March 16, 1976. Rebroadcast on CBS: March 14, 1977; April 10, 1978; March 24, 1980. Rebroadcast on NICK: April 24, 1998; June 1, 1998; July 3, 1998; August 1, 1998; September 2, 1998; October 12, 1998; October 15, 1998; October 17, 1998; November 16, 1998; December 22, 1998; April 30, 1998; June 17, 1999; August 16, 1999; January 18, 2000.*

*Voices*

**Charlie Brown:** Dylan Beach; **Lucy Van Pelt:** Sarah Beach; **Linus Van Pelt:** Liam Martin; **Schroeder:** Greg Felton; **Frieda:** Michelle Muller; **Sally Brown:** Gail Davis; **Peppermint Patty:** Stuart Brotman; **Rerun/Pigpen:** Vinny Dow

### ◎ IT'S A WONDERFUL TINY TOONS CHRISTMAS

In this parody of the Jimmy Stewart classic *It's a Wonderful Life*, Buster Bunny is fired as director of the Christmas pageant and wishes he had never been on Tiny Toons. He gets his wish and an angel shows him what life would have been like in Acme Acres without him in the first prime-time animated special starring the characters of the popular animated series. *A Warner Bros./Amblin Entertainment Production. Color. Half-hour. Premiered on FOX: December 6, 1992. Rebroadcast on FOX: December 5, 1993; December 25, 1994. Rebroadcast on NICK: December 25, 1996.*

*Voices*

**Buster Bunny:** Charlie Adler; **Babs Bunny:** Tress MacNeille; **Hamton J. Pig:** Don Messick; **Plucky Duck:** Joe Alaskey; **Elmyra Duff:** Cree Summer; **Dizzy Devil:** Maurice LaMarche; **Shirley Loon:** Gail Matthius

### ◎ IT'S CHRISTMAS TIME AGAIN, CHARLIE BROWN

After airing the first *Peanuts* holiday special, *A Charlie Brown Christmas*, for 26 consecutive seasons, CBS ordered this new holiday-themed half-hour—a series of vignettes that focus on the normal *Peanuts* characters and themes. Features music by the late Vince Guaraldi (as performed by jazz pianist David Benoit), who wrote and performed the classic music from the Christmas and Halloween Charlie Brown specials. The 1992 special was the first for creator Charles M. Schulz since the 40th anniversary Charlie Brown retrospective airing in 1990. *A Lee Mendelson–Bill Melendez Production in association with Charles M. Schulz Creative Associates and United Media. Color. Half-hour. Premiered on CBS: November 27, 1992.*

*Voices*

Lindsay Bennish, John Graas, Philip Lucier, Minday Martin, Sean Mendelson, Marne Patterson, Matthew Slowik, Jamie Smith, Denna Tello, Brittany Thornton

### ◎ IT'S FLASHBEAGLE, CHARLIE BROWN

Snoopy plays a John Travolta-type character in this animated musical parody of such films as *Flashdance* and *Staying Alive*, featuring various musical vignettes that center around a hoedown, aerobic exercise, a game of "Lucy Says" and, of course, Snoopy on the disco dance floor. In the late 1990s, the special was rebroadcast, along with many other original CBS specials and the Saturday-morning cartoon series, *The Charlie Brown & Snoopy Show*, on Nickelodeon. *A Lee Mendelson–Bill Melendez Production in association with Charles M. Schulz Creative Associates and United Feature Syndicate. Color. Half-hour. Premiered on CBS: April 16, 1984. Rebroadcast on CBS: January 1, 1985; May 27, 1986; April 19, 1988. Rebroadcast on NICK: February 2, 1998; February 19, 1998; March 23, 1998; May 1, 1998; May 29, 1998; July 2, 1998; July 30, 1998; August 26, 1998; November 6, 1998; December 7, 1998; January 6, 1999; January 27, 1999; February 9, 1999; March 10, 1999; May 1, 1999; September 11, 1999.*

*Voices*

**Charlie Brown:** Brett Johnson, Brad Kesten; **Charlie Brown (singing):** Kevin Brando; **Sally Brown:** Stacy Ferguson; **Peppermint Patty:** Gini Holtzman; **Marcie:** Keri Houlihan; **Schroeder/ Tommy, the kid:** Gary Goren, Kevin Brando; **Linus Van Pelt:** Jeremy Schoenberg; **Linus (singing):** David Wagner; **Lucy Van Pelt:** Heather Stoneman; **Lucy (singing):** Jessie Lee Smith; **Snoopy:** José Melendez; **Vocalists:** Joseph Chemay, Joey Harrison Scarbury, Desiree Goyette

## ◎ IT'S MAGIC, CHARLIE BROWN

While practicing magic tricks, Snoopy succeeds at making Charlie Brown invisible, but he encounters trouble in making him reappear. In 1998, the special resurfaced in reruns on Nickelodeon. *A Lee Mendelson–Bill Melendez Production in association with Charles M. Schulz Creative Associates and United Feature Syndicate. Color. Half-hour. Premiered on CBS: April 28, 1981. Rebroadcast on CBS: March 22, 1982; March 23, 1985; May 24, 1988. Rebroadcast on January 29, 1998; February 17, 1998; March 19, 1998; April 23, 1998; May 22, 1998; June 25, 1998; July 30, 1998; August 27, 1998; September 29, 1998; November 9, 1998; December 3, 1998; December 31, 1998; January 25, 1999; February 5, 1999; March 8, 1999; April 29, 1999; October 2, 1999; February 19, 2000.*

*Voices*

**Charlie Brown:** Michael Mandy; **Snoopy:** José Melendez; **Linus:** Earl "Rocky" Reilly; **Sally:** Cindi Reilly; **Marcie:** Shannon Cohn; **Peppermint Patty:** Brent Hauer; **Lucy:** Sydney Penny; **Schroeder/ Kid/Franklin:** Christopher Donohoe

## ◎ IT'S SPRING TRAINING, CHARLIE BROWN

After new kid-on-the-block Leland joins his baseball team, Charlie Brown and his teammates earn new uniforms when they win their first game of the season. They lose their next contest only to realize that how they play on the field is more important than how they look in this half-hour special originally made in 1992 but never broadcast. In January 1996, the program was officially released for public consumption on VHS by Paramount Home Video, and officially debuted on television on Nickelodeon in February 1998. That year, Nick had acquired the broadcasting rights to a package of CBS *Peanuts* specials as well as the network's popular Saturday-morning cartoon program, *The Charlie Brown & Snoopy Show*, which it began re-airing. *A Lee-Mendelson-Bill Melendez Production in association with Charles M. Schulz Creative Associates and United Feature Syndicate. Color. Half-hour. Premiered on NICK: February 23, 1998. Rebroadcast on NICK: March 25, 1998; April 26, 1998; May 27, 1998; July 26, 1998; September 1, 1998; October 16, 1998; March 1, 1999; April 25, 1999; June 14,* 1999; August 12, 1999; December 18, 1999; June 5, 2000; June 19, 2000.

*Voices*

**Charlie Brown:** Justin Shenkarov; **Linus Van Pelt:** John Christian Graas; **Lucy Van Pelt:** Marnette Patterson; **Leland:** Gregory Grudt; **Schroeder:** Travis Boles; **Kid on Opposing Team:** Michael Sander; **Franklin:** Jessica Nwafor; **Snoopy:** Bill Melendez

## ◎ IT'S THE EASTER BEAGLE, CHARLIE BROWN

Linus insists that an Easter beagle will magically appear to hand out candy on Easter morning. But, with fresh memories of their futile vigil for the Great Pumpkin, the *Peanuts* gang make their own novel preparations, including boiling eggs without the shells. In 1998 cable giant Nickelodeon, which had begun re-airing *The Charlie Brown and Snoopy Show* and assorted *Peanuts* specials, (except *It's the Great Pumpkin, Charlie Brown, A Charlie Brown Thanksgiving* and *A Charlie Brown Christmas*), televised the springtime special over Easter weekend and rebroadcast it again in 1999 and 2000. In 2005, two years after airing on Canada's YTV cable network, ABC bought the broadcast rights to the 1974 holiday special and televised it for the first time that March. *A Lee Mendelson–Bill Melendez Production in association with Charles M. Schulz and United Feature Syndicate. Color. Half-hour. Premiered on CBS: April 9, 1974. Rebroadcast on CBS: March 26, 1975; April 12, 1976; April 4, 1977; March 19, 1978; April 9, 1979; March 26, 1986. Rebroadcast on DIS: April 7, 1996. Rebroadcast on NICK: April 10, 1998; April 11, 1998; April 12, 1998; April 2, 1999; April 3, 1999; April 4, 1999; April 22, 2000. Rebroadcast on ABC: March 25, 2005; April 11, 2006.*

*Voices*

**Charlie Brown/Schroeder:** Todd Barbee; **Lucy Van Pelt:** Melanie Kohn; **Linus Van Pelt:** Stephen Shea; **Peppermint Patty:** Linda Ercoli; **Sally Brown/Violet/Frieda:** Lynn Mortensen; **Marcie:** James Ahrens

## ◎ IT'S THE GIRL IN THE RED TRUCK, CHARLIE BROWN

Live action and animation combine in this tale of puppy love in the desert as Snoopy's brother Spike relates in a letter to Charlie Brown and Snoopy that he has found a special someone who brings new meaning to his quiet, carefree days of cooking flapjacks and listening to French-language tapes. She is Jenny (played by Jill Schulz, the daughter of *Peanuts* creator Charles M. Schulz), a perky aerobics instructor who drives a clunky red pickup truck. But Spike's happiness does not last: Jenny has a boyfriend, Jeff, who lures her from the idyllic desert life she has come to love. *A Lee Mendelson–Bill Melendez Production in association with Charles M. Schulz Creative Associates and United Feature Syndicate. Color. One hour. Premiered on CBS: September 27, 1988.*

*Voices*

**Charlie Brown:** Jason Riffle; **The French Instructor:** Steve Stoliar

*Cast (live action)*

**Jenny:** Jill Schulz; **Jeff:** Greg Deason; **Mollie:** Mollie Boice

## ◎ IT'S THE GREAT PUMPKIN, CHARLIE BROWN

The Halloween season is here and Linus convinces Charlie and his pals from the Charles Schulz *Peanuts* comic strip that the arrival of the Great Pumpkin "with his bag of toys for all the good children" is near. The show featured the first appearance of

Snoopy's Red Baron character. Because of Charlie Brown's complaint that all he got for Halloween was a "rock," gifts poured in to CBS and Charles Schulz's office after the special first aired. The special began airing on ABC in October 1996. In 2003, sixteen years after its first rebroadcast on CBS and seven years after its first rebroadcast its new network, the Halloween-themed special attracted its largest audience since 1991, leading its time slot with 13.2 million viewers, including 5 million adults ages 18–49, and became the highest-rated program among kids ages 2–11 on television since May of that year. The October 2006 airing marked the 40th anniversary of the Halloween favorite. *A Lee Mendelson–Bill Melendez Production in association with Charles M. Schulz Creative Associates and United Feature Syndicate. Color. Half-hour. Premiered on CBS: October 27, 1966. Rebroadcast on CBS: October 26, 1967; October 24, 1968; October 26, 1969; October 24, 1970; October 23, 1971; October 28, 1974; October 23, 1976; October 30, 1978; October 22, 1979; October 24, 1980; October 30, 1981; October 25, 1982; October 28, 1983; October 26, 1984; October 30, 1985; October 24, 1986; October 23, 1987; October 25, 1989; October 30, 1991. Rebroadcast on ABC: October 25, 1996; October 31, 1997; October 30, 1998; October 29, 1999; October 30, 2001; October 25, 2002; October 28, 2003; October 26, 2004; October 25, 2002; October 26, 2004; October 25, 2005; October 27, 2006.*

**Voices**
**Charlie Brown:** Peter Robbins; **Linus Van Pelt:** Chris Shea; **Lucy Van Pelt:** Sally Dryer-Barker; **Sally Brown:** Cathy Steinberg; **Frieda/Violet:** Anne Altieri; **Peppermint Patty:** Kip DeFaria; **Pigpen:** Gail DeFaria; **Patty:** Lisa DeFaria; **Schroeder** (*off camera*)/ **Shermy:** Glenn Mendelson

## ◎ IT'S VALENTINE'S DAY, JOHNNY BRAVO

On this special day of the year, Valentine's and his birthday, the self-involved pompadoured Elvis ladies man sound-a-like Johnny Bravo is sent on a blind date by his Mama with a smart, attractive woman named Heather (who visually resembles Jennifer Garner from TV's *Alias*) and passes out after kissing her. He requires the help of pop singer Donny Osmond to teach him how to treat a lady and save face with the stiletto heel-wearing beauty in this half-hour special—and second in the series—for Cartoon Network. Featuring the voices of guest stars Maureen McCormick, Molly Shannon, Joe McIntyre and Donny Osmond, Cartoon Network premiered the special following an hour block of Johnny Bravo's most memorable dates from six episodes: "Date with an Antelope," "The Unsinkable Johnny Bravo," "Buffoon Lagoon," "Luke Perry's Guide to Love," "Red Faced in the White House" and "Jailbird Johnny." *A Cartoon Network Studios Production. Color. Half-hour. Premiered on CAR: February 14, 2003.*

**Voices**
**Johnny Bravo:** Dwayne Johnson; **Bunny Bravo, His Mother:** Brenda Vaccaro; **Little Suzy:** Mae Whitman; **Donny Osmond:** Himself; **Other Voices:** Maureen McCormick, Molly Shannon, Joe McIntyre

## ◎ IT'S YOUR FIRST KISS, CHARLIE BROWN

Unlikely hero Charlie Brown is faced with two horrendous challenges in this half-hour animated special: He is the kicker for the local football team at the annual homecoming football game and he has been chosen to escort Heather, the homecoming queen, to the celebration dance and give her the "traditional kiss." Reruns of the special were shown on Nickelodeon beginning in 1998. *A Lee Mendelson–Bill Melendez Production in association with Charles M. Schulz Creative Associates and United Feature Syndicate. Color.*

*Half-hour. Premiered on CBS: October 24, 1977. Rebroadcast on CBS: January 8, 1979; January 14, 1980; January 30, 1981; November 24, 1987. Rebroadcast on NICK: March 2, 1998; March 31, 1998; May 31, 1998; July 1, 1998; August 25, 1998; September 26, 1998; November 5, 1998; December 1, 1998; December 29, 1998; January 21, 1999; January 31, 1999; February 23, 1999; March 4, 1999; July 4, 1999; September 18, 1999; February 12, 2000.*

**Voices**
**Charlie Brown/Roy/Kid:** Arrin Skelley; **Peppermint Patty:** Laura Planting; **Linus/Schroeder:** Daniel Anderson; **Lucy/Heather:** Michelle Muller; **Franklin/Shermy/Pigpen:** Ronald Hendrix

## ◎ IT WAS A SHORT SUMMER, CHARLIE BROWN

Assigned to write a 500-word theme on his summer vacation, Charlie Brown agonizes over the remembrance of things past, including summer camp and his tent-mates' competing against the girls in baseball, swimming and canoeing, all ending in defeat and disaster. His last hope of beating the girls is the Masked Marvel (Snoopy), who enters a wrist-wrestling match against Lucy. Directed by Bill Melendez (also the voice of Snoopy), this original CBS special was part of a package of network specials, along with the popular Saturday-morning series spin-off *The Charlie Brown & Snoopy Show*, reshown on Nickelodeon after the cable giant acquired the broadcasting rights in 1998. *A Lee Mendelson–Bill Melendez Production in association with Charles M. Shulz Creative Associates and United Feature Syndicate. Color. Half-hour. Premiered on CBS: September 27, 1969. Rebroadcast on CBS: September 16, 1970; September 29, 1971; September 7, 1972; June 27, 1983. Rebroadcast on NICK: January 25, 1998; February 6, 1998; March 10, 1998; April 13, 1998; May 13, 1998; June 15, 1998; July 31, 1998; September 1, 1998; October 12, 1998; November 11, 1998; December 28, 1998; January 30, 1999; February 26, 1999; March 24, 1999; May 16, 1999; October 10, 1999.*

**Voices**
**Charlie Brown:** Peter Robbins; **Lucy Van Pelt:** Pamelyn Ferdin; **Linus Van Pelt:** Glenn Gilger; **Sally Brown:** Hilary Momberger; **Peppermint Patty:** Kip DeFaria; **Frieda:** Ann Altieri; **Sophie/Shirley/Clara:** Sally Dryer-Barker; **Shermy:** David Carey; **Pigpen:** Gail DeFaria; **Violet:** Linda Mendelson; **Schroeder:** John Daschback; **Roy/Kid/Boy:** Matthew Liftin; **Snoopy:** Bill Melendez

## ◎ IT ZWIBBLE: EARTHDAY BIRTHDAY

Two star-touched baby dinosaurs join forces and recruit other creatures to save the planet. Led by the magical dinosaur fairy, It Zwibble, and the Zwibble Dibbles, a group of adorable, socially responsible baby dinosaurs who pledge to care for the Earth and give it a birthday party, this half-hour tied in with the international celebration of Earth Day, April 22, 1990. Featuring a voice cast that included actors Christopher Reeve (as It Zwibble), Fred Gwynne (of TV's *The Munsters* fame) and acclaimed songstress/actress Lainie Kazan, the program was produced and directed by Emmy-nominated animator Michael Sporn (*Lyle, Lyle Crocodile*). *A Michael Sporn Animation Production. Color. Half-hour. Premiered on HBO: April 22, 1990. Rebroadcast on HBO: April 22, 1991; April 22, 1992; April 22, 1993; April 22, 1994; April 22, 1995; April 22, 1996; April 22, 1997.*

**Voices**
Christopher Reeve, Lainie Kazan, Fred Gwynne, Gregory Perler, Jonathan Goch, Jonathan Gold, Meghan Andrews, Gina Marle Huaman, Larry White, John Cannemaker

## ⊚ IVANHOE
Twelfth-century knight Ivanhoe, aided by Robin Hood and his Merry Men, rescues Lady Rebecca, held captive by Prince John in this loosely based adaptation of Sir Walter Scott's romantic fantasy adventure. *An Air Programs International Production. Color. Half-hour. Premiered on CBS: November 27, 1975. Syndicated.*

*Voices*
Alistair Duncan, Barbara Frawley, Chris Haywood, Mark Kelly, John Llewellyn, Helen Morse, Bevan Wilson

## ⊚ I WANT A DOG FOR CHRISTMAS, CHARLIE BROWN
Linus and Lucy's younger brother, ReRun, wants a dog for Christmas, so Snoopy invites his canine brother, Spike, to visit. After being given the responsibility of taking care of Spike, ReRun has trouble handling this newfound responsibility in this all-new, hour-long *Peanuts* Christmas special. Produced and animated by Lee Mendelson and Bill Melendez (the same team responsible for many earlier classic *Peanuts* cartoon specials), ABC debuted the program in prime time on December 9, 2003, at 8:00 P.M. *A Lee Mendelson-Bill Melendez Production. Color. One hour. Premiered on ABC: December 9, 2003. Rebroadcast on ABC: December 14, 2004; December 9, 2005; December 19, 2006.*

*Voices*
**Charlie Brown:** Adam Taylor Gordon; **Lucy Van Pelt:** Ashley Rose Orr; **Linus Van Pelt:** Corey Padnos; **Schroeder:** Nick Price; **Pig Pen/Franklin:** Jake Miner; **Sally Brown:** Hannah Leigh Dworkin; **ReRun Van Pelt:** Jimmy Bennett; **Snoopy:** Bill Melendez; **Little Girl:** Kaitlyn Maggio.

## ⊚ I YABBA-DABBA DO!
Longtime sweethearts Pebbles Flintstone and Bamm-Bamm Rubble tie the knot (get married, in other words), making Fred and Barney proud parents in this two-hour made-for-TV movie extravaganza directed by cartoon legend William Hanna (who also coproduced with longtime partner Joseph Barbera). The ABC special was the first of two new animated specials by the Oscar-winning cartoon team, followed by the sequel, *Hollyrock-a-Bye Baby* (1993), also for ABC. Ten years after its network premiere, the made-for-TV movie was rebroadcast on Boomerang as part of its week-long, 240-hour Flintstones holiday marathon in December 2003. *A Hanna-Barbera Production. Color. Two hours. Premiered on ABC: February 7, 1993. Rebroadcast on ABC: December 31, 1994. Rebroadcast on BOOM: December 17, 2003; December 21, 2003.*

*Voices*
**Fred Flintstone:** Henry Corden; **Wilma Flintstone:** Jean Vander-Pyl; **Barney Rubble/Dino:** Frank Welker; **Betty Rubble:** B.J. Ward; **Pebbles Flinstone:** Megan Mullaly; **Bamm-Bamm Rubble:** Jerry Houser

## ⊚ IZZY'S QUEST FOR GOLD
Young Izzy asks the Tribunal Elders if he can compete in the Olympic Games and they agree if he first obtains the Five Olympic Rings given for perseverance, integrity, sportsmanship, excellence and brotherhood before taking his giant leap into Olympic-hood. This half-hour animated special featured the mascot of the 1996 Summer Olympics Games, produced less than a year before the games were held in Atlanta. The special was the first of a planned two-part series of cartoon specials to be produced by Emmy Award–winning animation giant Film Roman (producers of such hits as *The Simpsons* and *Garfield and Friends*) for Turner Network Television, but only the first special was ever produced. *A Film Roman Production in association with Atlanta Centennial Olympic Properties. Color. Half-hour. Premiered on TNT: August 12, 1995. Rebroadcast on CAR: August 3, 1996; August 4, 1996.*

*Voices*
**Izzy:** Justin Shenkarow; **Coriba:** Alice Ghostly; **Fortius:** Victoria Carroll; **Citius:** Kay E. Kuter; **Altius:** Jeff Bennett; **Mom:** Tress MacNeille; **Dad:** Rob Paulsen; **Martin:** Scott Menville; **Spartin:** Mike Simmrin; **Narrator:** Jim Cummings

## ⊚ JACK AND THE BEANSTALK
Gene Kelly heads the cast of live actors and animated characters who appear in this live-action/animation musical based on the popular children's fable. The original story remains intact as Jack (played by Bobby Riha) is conned by street peddler Jeremy Keen (Gene Kelly) into exchanging the family cow for a handful of magic beans that will sprout a giant beanstalk and take him to the giant's skyward castle, where treasures of every kind abound. The special reunited Kelly with producers Joe Barbera and William Hanna, who animated Kelly's spectacular dance sequence with Jerry Mouse (of *Tom and Jerry* fame) in the 1945 MGM musical *Anchors Aweigh*. *A Hanna-Barbera Production. Color. One hour. Premiered on NBC: February 26, 1967. Rebroadcast on NBC: January 16, 1968. Rebroadcast on CBS: January 15, 1971. Syndicated.*

*Cast*
**Jeremy Keen:** Gene Kelly; **Jack:** Bobby Riha; **Mother:** Marian McKnight

*Voices*
**Around the Mouse:** Chris Allen; **Monster Cat:** Dick Beals; **Princess Serena:** Janet Waldo, Marni Nixon (singing); **Giant:** Ted Cassidy; **Woggle Bird:** Cliff Norton; **Announcer:** Art Gilmore

*Other Voices*
Jack DeLeon

## ⊚ JACK FROST
After falling in love with beautiful blond Elisa of January Junction—a village terrorized by Kubla Kraus, an ogre who lives in a castle—Jack Frost is granted his wish to become human but is foiled in his pursuit of the girl when she falls for a handsome knight instead. *A Rankin-Bass Production. Color. One hour. Premiered on NBC: December 13, 1979. Rebroadcast on NBC: December 5, 1980. Rebroadcast on DIS: December 15, 1992; December 4, 1993. Rebroadcast on FOX FAM: December 3, 1998; December 13, 1998; December 22, 1998; July 11, 1999; July 14, 1999; December 2, 1999; December 5, 1999; December 10, 1999; December 24, 1999; December 3, 2000; December 6, 2000; December 8, 2000; December 14, 2000; December 20, 2000; December 21, 2000. Rebroadcast on ABC FAM: December 1, 2001; December 2, 2001; December 7, 2001; December 18, 2001; December 21, 2001; December 22, 2001; December 24, 2001; December 1, 2002; December 4, 2002; December 12, 2002; December 15, 2002; December 18, 2002; December 21, 2002; December 24, 2002; December 6, 2003; December 8, 2003; December 21, 2003; December 4, 2004; December 14, 2004; December 23, 2004; December 3, 2005; December 5, 2005; December 21, 2005; December 24, 2005; December 8, 2006; December 24, 2006. Syndicated.*

*Voices*
**Pardon-Me-Pete, the groundhog:** Buddy Hackett; **Jack Frost:** Robert Morse; **Elisa:** Debra Clinger; **Elisa's Father/Danny, the ventriloquist's dummy:** Larry Storch; **Elisa's Mother:** Dee Stratton; **Kubla Kraus/Father Winter:** Paul Frees; **Snip, the Snow-**

flake Maker: Don Messick; **Holly:** Diana Lynn; **TV Announcer:** Dave Garroway

*Other Voices*
Sonny Melendrez

### ◎ THE JACKIE BISON SHOW
Animation and live action were blended in this unsold comedy pilot that aired as a prime-time special about a buffalo (billed as "America's beast of buffoonery") who is the host of his own TV show. The program was inspired by *The Jack Benny Show*. A Stein *& Illes Production in association with Brillstein/Grey Productions, Akom Productions and Broadcast TV Arts. Color. Half-hour. Premiered on NBC: July 2, 1990.*

*Voices*
**Jackie Bison:** Stan Freberg; **Larry J. Lizard, his announcer:** Richard Karron; **Jill St. Fawn, his girlfriend:** Jane Singer; **Mrs. St. Fawn, Jill's mother:** Jayne Meadows

### ◎ JACK O'LANTERN
In an unusual plot line, Jack O'Lantern, a staple of Halloween, encounters trouble in the form of an evil witch, Zelda, who is fervent in her attempt to snatch Jack's magic pot of gold, and her doting warlock husband, Sir Archibald. The tale is recalled by the grandfather of two children, Michael and Colleen, whose interest in the story serves as a subplot. *A Festival of Family Classics special. A Rankin-Bass Production in association with Mushi Studios. Color. Half-hour. Premiered: October 29, 1972. Syndicated.*

*Voices*
Carl Banas, Len Birman, Bernard Cowan, Peg Dixon, Keith Hampshire, Peggi Loder, Donna Miller, Frank Perry, Henry Ramer, Billie Mae Richards, Alfie Scopp, Paul Soles

### ◎ JAZZTIME TALE
In New York City circa 1919 a young city girl (Lucinda) befriends a lonely girl (Rose) from the other side of town, who feels left out

*The spooky spirit of Halloween is captured in the Rankin-Bass animated fantasy* Jack O'Lantern. *© Rankin-Bass Productions*

of her father's busy schedule. They experience Jazztime history while forming a lifelong friendship in this half-hour animated special from animator Michael Sporn, broadcast in 1991 on PBS's award-winning anthology series *Long Ago & Far Away*. *A Michael Sporn Animation/WGBH Boston Production in association with Ital-toons Corporation. Color. Half-hour. Premiered on PBS: November 2, 1991. Rebroadcast on PBS: October 4, 1992.*

*Voices*
**Old Lucinda/Narrator:** Ruby Dee

### ◎ THE JEAN MARSH CARTOON SPECIAL
Jean Marsh and Grover Monster, one of the original Muppets, host this collection of animated cartoons for children, including films by animators Chuck Jones, John Hubley and others. Program is also known as *The Grover Monster Cartoon Special*. *A KQED-TV Production for PBS. Color. One hour. Premiered on PBS: March 10, 1975.*

### ◎ THE JETSONS MEET THE FLINTSTONES
A time machine catapults the Jetsons (George, Jane, Judy and Elroy) back in time to come face to face with Stone Age citizens Fred and Wilma Flintstone and their best friends, Betty and Barney Rubble, in this two-hour special, the third in a series of original animated movies for first-run syndication distributed as part of *Hanna-Barbera's Superstars 10* package. Sixteen years after its making, the made-for-TV movie was rebroadcast on Cartoon Network's sister channel, Boomerang, as part of its week-long, 240-hour Flintstones holiday marathon of classic movies and specials in December 2003. *A Hanna-Barbera Production. Color. Two hours. Premiered: 1987. Syndicated. Rebroadcast on TBS: September 5, 1993. Rebroadcast on CAR: May 28–30, 1994. Rebroadcast on BOOM: December 16, 2003; December 21, 2003.*

*Voices*
**Fred Flintstone/Knight:** Henry Corden; **Wilma Flintstone/Rosie/Mrs. Spacely:** Jean VanderPyl; **Barney Rubble/Cosmo C. Spacely/Dino:** Mel Blanc; **Betty Rubble/Jet Rivers/Investor/Panelist/Harem Girl:** Julie Dees; **George Jetson:** George O'Hanlon; **Jane Jetson:** Penny Singleton; **Judy Jetson/Female computer:** Janet Waldo; **Elroy Jetson/Cogswell/Henry:** Daws Butler; **Astro/Rudi/Mac/Announcer/Store Manager/Robot:** Don Messick; **Didi:** Brenda Vaccaro; **George Slate/Moderator/Investor/Poker Player:** John Stephenson; **Turk Tarpit:** Hamilton Camp; **Iggy:** Jon Bauman; **Dan Rathmoon/Johnny/Mr. Goldbrick:** Frank Welker

### ◎ JIM HENSON'S MUPPET BABIES
Stars of their own successful Saturday-morning cartoon show, the Muppet Babies made their first appearance in cartoon form in this prime-time special for CBS. The premise has the characters acting like show-biz stars in situations taped before a video camera, including a movie take-off (*Star Wars*) and a rock music video. The story title for the program was "Gonzo's Video Show." *A Henson Associates Production in association with Marvel Productions. Color. Half-hour. Premiered on CBS: December 18, 1984.*

*Voices*
**Kermit/Beaker:** Frank Welker; **Piggie:** Laurie O'Brien; **Fozzie/Scooter:** Greg Berg; **Rowlf:** Katie Lee; **Skeeter/Animal:** Howie Mandel; **Gonzo:** Russi Taylor; **Nanny:** Barbara Billingsley

### ◎ JIMINY CRICKET: STORYTELLER
Famous fables and fairy tales make up this 90-minute special, hosted by Jiminy Cricket, and later released overseas on home video as *Jiminy Cricket's Fabulous Fables, Fairy Tales and Other*

*Wonderful Stuff.* The program premiered on the Disney Channel. *A Disney Channel Production. Color. Ninety minutes. Premiered on DIS: 1986.*

**Voices**
**Jiminy Cricket:** Eddie Carroll

### ⊚ THE JIMMY TIMMY POWER HOUR

Science and magic collides as Timmy Turner, who appears bound to fail science class, desires to have "the greatest lab in the universe," which happens to belong to Jimmy Neutron. Together, they are teleported to Retroville where they work on retooling Jimmy's mechanical dog, Goddard, while Timmy unexpectedly downloads a violent video game and falls in love with Jimmy's arch-rival, Cindy Vortex. Meanwhile, a fairy-consumed teacher (Denzel Crocker) uses Jimmy's scientific know-how to take control of Fairy World in this hour-long movie special and fourth in a series of Nickelodeon crossover specials. *An O Entertainment/DNA Productions/Frederator Incorporated Production. Color. One hour. Premiered on NICK: May 7, 2004. Rebroadcast on NICK: May 8, 2004; May 9, 2004; May 14, 2004; May 15, 2004; May 16, 2004; May 21, 2004; May 30, 2004; May 31, 2004; June 4, 2004; June 20, 2004; September 12, 2004; November 11, 2004; January 2, 2005; February 5, 2005; March 13, 2005; May 6, 2005; June 12, 2005; August 22, 2005; August 28, 2005; September 5, 2005; October 14, 2005; November 27, 2005; February 18, 2006; May 29, 2006; July 9, 2006; August 18, 2006; August 19, 2006; October 14, 2006; November 24, 2006; December 28, 2006; January 26, 2007; April 19, 2007.*

**Voices**
**James Isaac "Jimmy" Neutron:** Debi Derryberry; **Timmy Turner:** Tara Strong; **Hugh Beaumont Neutron, Jimmy's father:** Mark DeCarlo; **Judy Neutron, Jimmy's mother:** Megan Cavanagh; **Carl Wheezer/Announcer:** Rob Paulsen; **Sheen Estevez:** Jeffrey Garcia; **Cindy Vortex:** Carolyn Lawrence; **Libby Folfax:** Crystal Scales; **Goddard:** Frank Welker; **Wanda:** Susan Blakeslee; **Cosmo/Mr. Turner/Jorgen von Strangle:** Daran Norris; **Vicky/Principal Waxelplex:** Grey DeLisle; **Denzel Crocker:** Carlos Alazaqui; **Sanjay/Elmer/Fairy Agent #1:** Dee Bradley Baker; **A.J.:** Gary LeRoi Gray II

### ⊚ THE JIMMY TIMMY POWER HOUR 2: WHEN NERDS COLLIDE

When Timmy can't find a date to his school's Friday the 13th dance, he leaves for Retroville with the intention of asking the last person on the planet, Cindy Vortex. It turns out that Jimmy also plans to ask her to accompany him to his school's dance. Meanwhile, after the boys engage in a duel of magic vs. science, Jimmy's archenemy, Professor Calamitous, launches yet another attempt to destroy Jimmy. This time, he engages the villainous Anti-Cosmo, who betrays Calamitous to help him free the Anti-Faeries from prison and spread bad luck everywhere on Friday the 13th in this second installment of the crossover trilogy, between Nickelodeon's *The Fairly OddParents* and *The Adventures of Jimmy Neutron: Boy Genius.* The special was the third-highest-rated cable program on basic cable networks the week it premiered, attracting 5.48 million viewers and was beamed into 4.09 million homes. *An O Entertainment/DNA Productions/Frederator Incorporated Production. Color. One hour. Premiered on NICK: January 16, 2006. Rebroadcast on NICK: January 18, 2006; January 19, 2006; January 20, 2006; January 21, 2006; February 20, 2006; April 2, 2006; May 29, 2006; July 16, 2006; July 31, 2006; August 18, 2006; August 19, 2006; August 20, 2006; October 14, 2006; November 24, 2006; December 28, 2006; January 26, 2007; April 19, 2007.*

**Voices**
**James Isaac "Jimmy" Neutron:** Debi Derryberry; **Timmy Turner:** Tara Strong; **Hugh Beaumont Neutron, Jimmy's father:** Mark DeCarlo; **Judy Neutron, Jimmy's mother:** Megan Cavanaugh; **Carl Wheezer:** Rob Paulsen; **Sheen Estevez:** Jeffrey Garcia; **Cindy Vortex:** Carolyn Lawrence; **Libby Folfax:** Crystal Scales; **Goddard:** Frank Welker; **Wanda/Mrs. Turner/Anti-Wanda:** Susan Blakeslee; **Cosmo/Mr. Turner/Jorgen Von Strangle/Anti-Cosmo:** Daran Norris; **Vicky/Principal Waxelplex:** Grey DeLisle; **Denzel Crocker:** Carlos Alazaqui; **A.J.:** Gary LeRoi Gray II; **Francais:** Faith S. Abrahams; **Professor Calamitous:** Tim Curry; **Chester:** Jason Marsden; **Other Voices:** Dee Bradley Baker

### ⊚ THE JIMMY TIMMY POWER HOUR 3: THE JERKINATORS

In this third and final part of the crossover trilogy of Nickelodeon's *The Fairly OddParents* and *The Adventures of Jimmy Neutron: Boy Genius,* Timmy Turner befriends the brainy Jimmy Neutron and accidentally creates a new villain who changes their worlds in this hour-long prime-time movie event broadcast on Nickelodeon. *An O Entertainment/DNA Productions/Frederator Incorporated Production. Color. One hour. Premiered on NICK: July 21, 2006. Rebroadcast on NICK: July 22, 2006; July 23, 2006; July 26, 2006; July 30, 2006; August 18, 2006; August 19, 2006; August 20, 2006; September 4, 2006; October 14, 2006; November 24, 2006; December 22, 2006; December 28, 2006; January 26, 2007; April 19, 2007.*

**Voices**
**Jimmy Neutron:** Debi Derryberry; **Timmy Turner:** Tara Strong; **Wanda/Mrs. Turner:** Susan Blakeslee; **Judy Neutron, Jimmy's mother:** Megan Cavanagh; **Hugh Beaumont Neutron, Jimmy's father:** Mark DeCarlo; **Sheen Estevez:** Jeffrey Garcia; **Villain:** Jeff Garlin; **Cindy Vortex:** Carolyn Lawrence; **Nega-Chin:** Jay Leno; **Cosmo/Mr. Turner:** Daran Norris; **Carl Wheezer:** Rob Paulsen; **Libby Folfax:** Crystal Scales; **Sam:** Billy West

### ⊚ JINGLE BELL RAP

The K9-4 (Fetch, Licks, Rollover and Bones) is a merry group of musical dogs that rap and rock their way back to their hometown for a special Christmas concert and a very special reunion for Rollover in this colorful half-hour Christmas special, first broadcast in first-run syndication in 1991. *A Perennial Pictures Film Corporation Production. Color. Half-hour. Premiered: November 1991. Syndicated.*

**Voices**
**Rollover:** Scott Tyring; **Fetch/Licks:** Jerry Reynolds; **Roxie:** Rachel Rutledge; **Dad:** Russ Harris; **Collie Flower:** Lisa Roe Ward

### ⊚ JINGLE BELL ROCK

Santa is forced to lay off some of his elves as a result of "budget cuts." And three of them decide to hoof it to Hollywood to raise money by competing for the big cash prize on a *Star Search*–type variety show (hosted and voiced by an animated Milton Berle). But the show's host has rigged the contest so his niece will win in this prime-time holiday special for ABC. Burbank, California, producer DIC Entertainment later resyndicated the program in the fall of 2004 as part of its DIC Kids Network three-hour programming block to television stations nationwide. *A DIC Enterprises Production. Color. Half-hour. Premiered on ABC: December 22, 1995. Syndicated.*

**Voices**
Milton Berle, Jay Brazeau, Terry King

## JIRIMPIMBIRA: AN AFRICAN FOLKTALE

Temba, a lionhearted young boy whose kindness is as great as "the generosity of his heart," sets off with a trio of ill-intentioned peers to search for food and water to save his starving North African village. He gets off track after meeting a mysterious old man who gives him some magic bones that will grant him his every wish (after saying the magic word: "jirimpimbira") in this half-hour *ABC Weekend Special*, produced in celebration of Black History Month, based on the classic African folktale of the same name. *A Ruby-Spears/Huff-Douglas Production in association with Greengrass Productions. Premiered on ABC: February 25, 1995. Rebroadcast on ABC: March 15, 1997.*

**Voices**
**Temba:** Jamil Smith; **Old Man:** Paul Winfield; **Featherbrain:** Dave Fennoy; **Greedy:** Rembrandt Sabel; **Rat:** Meshach Taylor; **Mother:** Bianca Fergusso; **Storyteller:** Diahann Carroll; **Sly:** Greg Eagles; **Headman:** James Avery; **She Hawk:** Gwen Shepard; **Sister:** Dawn Lewis; **Villager:** Kelly Huff

## JOHANN'S GIFT TO CHRISTMAS

In a small mountain village in the early 19th century, a mouse named Johann takes shelter in a church on Christmas Eve and, with the help of a guiding angel, writes a song (with an elderly church mouse, Viktor). In this live-action/clay-animated holiday special produced in 1991, the song provides the inspiration for the church's pastor and his organist to create the classic yuletide carol "Silent Night." The U.S. premiere date is unknown, but the program aired on Nickelodeon in 1993. Clay-animation sequences were directed by Anthony LaMolinera and Jeff Mulcaster (of California Raisins commercials fame). *An O'B & D Films Production. Color. Half-hour. Broadcast on NICK: December 9, 1993.*

**Cast (live action)**
**Father Mohr:** Heath Lamberts; **Angel:** Sarah Polley; **Others:** Zacri Crane, Michael Polley, Gerry Quigley

**Voices**
**Viktor:** John Neville; **Johann:** Illya Woloshyn

## JOHNNY APPLESEED

Folk hero Johnny Appleseed goes up against a quack doctor who claims his bottled medicine cures more ills than Johnny's own bottle of apple medicine. *A Family Festival of Classics special. A Rankin-Bass Production in association with Mushi Studios. Color. Half-hour. Premiered: November 5, 1972. Syndicated.*

**Voices**
Carl Banas, Len Birman, Bernard Cowan, Peg Dixon, Keith Hampshire, Peggi Loder, Donna Miller, Frank Perry, Henry Ramer, Billie Mae Richards, Alfie, Scopp, Paul Soles

## A JOHNNY BRAVO CHRISTMAS

Teaming up on a wild sleigh ride adventure with pop star Donny Osmond, Johnny Bravo personally delivers his Christmas "wish" list to Santa in this half-hour special based on the long-running weekly cartoon series for the Cartoon Network. *A Cartoon Network Studios Production. Color. Half-hour. Premiered on CAR: December 21, 2001. Rebroadcast on CAR: December 2, 2002; December 14, 2002; December 24, 2002; December 25, 2002; July 25, 2003; December 1, 2003; December 12, 2003; December 23, 2003; December 24, 2003; December 25, 2003; December 13, 2004; December 21, 2004; December 22, 2004; December 24, 2004; December 25, 2004; December 7, 2005; December 23, 2005; December 24, 2005; December 25, 2005; December 12, 2006; December 16, 2006; December 24, 2006.*

**Voices**
**Johnny Bravo:** Jeff Bennett; **Little Suzi:** Mae Whitman; **Mama:** Brenda Vaccaro

## JOHNNY BRAVO GOES HOLLYWOOD

After a Big Time Studios producer picks Johnny to star in his new movie, *Lunchlady S'Uprise!*, bulked-up film star wannabe Johnny makes the long trek by bus to Hollywood to work with his costars—his leading lady, Jessica Biel; his arch nemesis in the film, Alec Baldwin; and his mentor in showbiz culture Don Knotts, playing a hair-footed Hobbit and dinosaur (all of whom provided their voices)—only to be replaced before even filming his first scene by a CGI-animated Mark Hamill. This prime-time animated special was the third and final special based on the series, that aired on Cartoon Network. Of his experience working on the special, Academy Award and Golden Globe nominated actor Alec Baldwin said, "In my career, I've had the opportunity to work with some really great actors—Al Pacino, Anthony Hopkins, Jack Lemmon. They each brought a certain amount of class and professionalism to the set. Working with Johnny Bravo was not like that at all." *A Cartoon Network Studios Production. Color. Half-hour. Premiered on CAR: February 20, 2004.*

**Voices**
**Johnny Bravo:** Dwayne Johnson; **Bunny Bravo, his mother:** Brenda Vaccaro; **Little Suzy:** Mae Whitman; **Jessica Biel:** Herself; **Alec Baldwin:** Himself; **Don Knotts/Hairy Hobbit/Dinosaur:** Don Knotts; **CG Mark Hamill:** Mark Hamill

## JOLLY OLD ST. NICHOLAS

Scuddle Mutt and Clawdia dress up as elves and sing "Jolly Old St. Nicholas" to win the $50 first prize at a talent show. During the Christmas Eve performance, two of Santa's elves are mistaken for the impostors and are pushed on stage to sing while the real Scuddle Mutt and Clawdia go on an unexpected sleigh ride with Santa they'll never forget in this heartwarming, half-hour syndicated special. *A Perennial Pictures Film Corporation Production. Color. Half-hour. Premiered: November 24, 1994. Syndicated.*

**Voices**
**Scuddle Mutt/O'Toole the Mule:** Jerry Reynolds; **Clawdia/Miss Posey:** Rachel Rutledge; **Santa Claus:** Andy Kuhn; **Poinsetta Pig:** Lisa Buetow

## JONNY QUEST VS. THE CYBER INSECTS

The Quest Team again matches wits with the evil Dr. Zin (he's baaaack!) and his army of genetically engineered insects as Zin wreaks havoc on Earth's climate through the use of high-tech satellites in this second feature-length adventure starring the characters from the popular 1960s cartoon series, animated in their original form. Originally titled *Jonny's Global Impact*, the two-hour cartoon spectacular marked the last appearance of Jonny Quest and the gang in their original animated form before the arrival of a new animated series, *The Real Adventures of Jonny Quest*, in the fall of 1996, featuring 1990s' makeovers. *A Hanna-Barbera Production. Color. Two hours. Premiered on TNT: November 19, 1995.*

**Voices**
**Jonny Quest:** Kevin Michaels; **Dr. Benton Quest:** Don Messick; **Race Bannon:** Granville Van Dusen; **Hadji:** Rob Paulsen; **Jessie:** Anndi McAfee; **Dr. Zin:** Jeffrey Tambor; **Dr. Belage:** Teresa Saldana; **4-DAC:** Tim Matheson; **Atacama:** Hector Elizondo

## JONNY'S GOLDEN QUEST

Jonny, Dr. Quest, Race Bannon, Hadji and company battle the evil Dr. Zin and his ecosystem-threatening genetic mutants in a global chase that takes them to such international locales as Peru, Tokyo, Rome and Australia in this full-length and first-ever animated feature produced exclusively for USA Network. Produced 28 years after the original 1964–65 television series, *The Adventures of Jonny Quest*, the film introduced two new female characters: Mrs. Quest, the wife of Dr. Quest (said to have been "lost" all this time), and Jessie Bannon, daughter of Race Bannon (also now married). *A Hanna-Barbera Production in association with USA Network and Fil-Cartoons Inc., Philippines. Color. Two hours. Premiered on USA: April 4, 1993. Rebroadcast on USA: August 20, 1995.*

*Voices*

**Jonny Quest:** Will Nipper; **Race Bannon/Stilt Walker/Cook:** Granville Van Dusen; **Dr. Benton Quest/Bandit/Man:** Don Messick; **Hadji/Announcer:** Rob Paulsen; **Rachel Quest:** Meredith MacRae; **Jade Kenyon:** JoBeth Williams; **Dr. Zin/Guard:** Jeffrey Tambor; **3-Dac/Ms. Moo Moo:** B.J. Ward; **Jessie:** Anndi McAfee; **Dr. Devlon/Scientist #1/Stilt Walker:** Peter Renaday; **Commander/College President/Robot:** Ed Gilbert; **Chief/Policeman/Local Boy:** Marcelo Tubert; **Snipe/Replicant/Dolphins:** Frank Welker; **President/Scientist #2/Chikara:** George Hearn; **Agent Melendez/Local Boy/Stilt Walker:** Pepe Serna; **Young Jonny Quest:** Whitby Hertford

## JOURNEY BACK TO OZ

Dorothy and her friends, the Scarecrow, the Tin-Man and the Cowardly Lion, return to save Oz from Mombi, the Bad Witch, in this sequel to the 1939 MGM classic that was released originally to theaters and later repackaged as a holiday special with additional live-action sequences of Bill Cosby as the program's Host Wizard. Margaret Hamilton, an original *Wizard of Oz* cast member, played the role of Aunt Em. *A Filmation Associates Production. Color. Two hours. Premiered on ABC: December 5, 1976. Syndicated. Rebroadcast: December 1978 (SFM Holiday Network).*

*Voices*

**Dorothy:** Liza Minelli; **Scarecrow:** Mickey Rooney; **Tin-Man:** Danny Thomas; **Cowardly Lion:** Milton Berle; **Aunt Em:** Margaret Hamilton; **Mombi, the Bad Witch:** Ethel Merman; **Glinda, the Good Witch:** Rise Stevens; **Pumpkinhead:** Paul Lynde; **Woodenhead:** Herschel Bernardi; **The Signpost:** Jack E. Leonard

## JOURNEY TO THE CENTER OF THE EARTH

Professor Linderbrook, his friend Alex and their guide Hans take the journey of their lifetimes as they head out on a mission to explore Earth's core in this animated adaptation of the Jules Verne science-fiction novel. *A Famous Classic Tales special. An Air Programs International Production. Color. One hour. Premiered on CBS: November 13, 1977. Rebroadcast on CBS: November 23, 1978. Syndicated.*

*Voices*

Lynette Curran, Alistair Duncan, Barbara Frawley, Ron Haddrick, Bevan Wilson

## JUNE'S EGG-CELLENT ADVENTURE: JUNIPER LEE MEETS THE EASTER BUNNY

To stop a feud that has erupted between the bunnies and the chickens started by Monroe, two Easter bunnies call upon Juniper, Ray Ray and Monroe to step in and put an end to it in this half-hour Easter special based on the popular Cartoon Network series. *A Cartoon Network Studios Production. Color. Half-hour. Premiered on CAR: April 24, 2006.*

*Voices*

**Juniper Lee:** Lara Jill Miller; **Jasmine Lee:** Amy Hill; **Monroe Connery Boyd Carlyle McGregor Scott Lee V:** Carlos Alazaqui; **Ray Ray Lee:** Kath Soucie; **Marcus Conner:** Phil LaMarr; **Heather:** Kath Soucie; **Beatrice:** Tara Strong; **Mitch the Enchanted Rhino/Derek:** Dee Bradley Baker; **William/King Teddy:** Martin Jarvis

## JUSTICE LEAGUE: "A LEAGUE OF THEIR OWN"

The evil Brainiac becomes a free man after Watchtower suffers a sudden power drain, releasing him from confinement, and neither Static—whom the Justice League bring into the fold to re-energize the station so it doesn't redeploy into the atmosphere—or Gear are aware of his sudden escape, in this two-part, hour-long special from the popular *Justice League* cartoon series produced by Warner Bros. Television Animation and broadcast on consecutive Saturdays in March 2003 on Cartoon Network. *A Warner Bros. Television Animation Production. Color. One hour. Premiered on CAR: March 1, 2003 (Part 1); March 8, 2003 (Part II).*

*Voices*

**Batman/Bruce Wayne:** Kevin Conroy; **Superman/Clark Kent/Kal-El:** George Newbern; **Green Lantern/John Stewart:** John LaMarr; **Wonder Woman/Diana Prince:** Susan Eisenberg; **Hawkgirl/Shayera Hol:** Maria Canals; **Martian Manhunter/J'onn J'onnz:** Carl Lumbly; **The Flash/Wally West:** Michael Rosenbaum; **Brainiac:** Corey Burton; **Richie "Gear" Foley:** Jason Marsden; **Hotstreak:** Danny Cooksey; **Puff:** Kimberly Brooks; **Carmen Dillo:** Jason Marsden; **Virgil "Static" Hawkins:** Phil LaMarr

## JUSTICE LEAGUE: "COMFORT & JOY"

The world's greatest superheroes of the famed Justice League—Batman, Flash, Green Lantern, Hawkman, Superman and Wonder Woman—complete one final mission to save two planets that are about to collide, before breaking for a week's vacation for the Christmas holidays. The brand-new holiday special, based on Cartoon Network's top-rated original animated series and the popular DC Comics series, premiered Saturday, December 13, 2003, at 10 P.M. (ET). Real-life Hollywood couple Mike Farrell and Shelley Fabares provided the voices of Superman's parents. *A Warner Bros. Television Animation Production. Color. Half-hour. Premiered on CAR: December 13, 2003.*

*Voices*

**Batman/Bruce Wayne:** Kevin Conroy; **Superman/Clark Kent/Kal-El:** George Newbern; **Green Lantern/John Stewart:** John LaMarr; **Wonder Woman/Diana Prince:** Susan Eisenberg; **Hawkgirl/Shayera Hol:** Maria Canals; **Martian Manhunter/J'onn J'onnz:** Carl Lumbly; **The Flash/Wally West:** Michael Rosenbaum; **UltraHumanite:** Ian Buchanan; **Pa Kent:** Mike Farrell; **Ma Kent:** Shelley Fabares; **Mrs. Saunders:** Kimberly Saunders; **Mr. Hana:** Robert Ito; **Little Boy:** Little Stevie; **Little Girl:** Amber Hood

## KABLAM! PRESENTS THE HENRY & JUNE SHOW

Famous cartoon hosts—the energetic, disaster-prone Henry, and sarcastic and more practical partner, June—of the Nickelodeon's popular, long-running children's anthology series *KaBlam!* star in their first and only spin-off special. Premiering on Friday, June 25,

1999, at 8:00 P.M. (ET) on Nicklelodeon, the half-hour special was the third in the *KaBlam!* series, following 1998's *Life with Loopy Birthday Gala-bration* and 1999's *The Off-Beats Valentine's Special*. A Nicklelodeon Production. Color. Half-hour. Premiered on NICK: June 25 1999.

**Voices**
**Henry:** Noah Segan; **June:** Julia McIlvane

### ⊚ KAPPA MIKEY: "A CHRISTMAS MIKEY"

Ready to return to America after Czu shuns him, Mikey receives a surprise visit from his guardian angel that shows him what his friends' lives would be like without him, while ghosts of Japanese Christmas visit Czu to correct his mistake in this half-hour special inspired by Charles Dickens's classic story, *A Christmas Carol*. The holiday special—spun-off from the popular anime-styled series—premiered on Nicktoons in December 2006, followed by an encore performance that night. An *Animation Collective Production*. Color. Half-hour. Premiered on NICKT: December 7, 2006. Rebroadcast on NICKT: December 9, 2006; December 10, 2006; December 16, 2006; December 24, 2006.

**Voices**
**Mikey Simon:** Michael Sinterniklaas; **Czu:** Stephen Moverley; **Gonard:** Sean Schemmel; **Lily:** Annice Moriarty; **Mitsuki:** Evelyn Lanton; **Guano:** Gary Mack; **The Yes Man:** Jesse Adams; **Japanese Ghost of Christmas Present:** Lex Woutas; **Japanese Ghost of Christmas Future:** Dan Green

### ⊚ KIDNAPPED

David Balfour, the rightful heir of the Master of the House of Shaws, gets kidnapped so that his uncle can control his inheritance and remove him from the picture altogether. Program was adapted from the Robert Louis Stevenson novel. A *Famous Classic Tales* special. An *Air Programs International Production*. Color. One hour. Premiered on CBS: October 22, 1973. Syndicated.

### ⊚ THE KINGDOM CHUMS: LITTLE DAVID'S ADVENTURE

Based on the biblical story of David and Goliath, this holiday special, which opens with live-action footage, details the adventures of Little David, Christopher and Magical Mose who welcome three children—transformed into cartoon form—to the world of the Kingdom Chums where the world's greatest stories unfold, all leading up to David's man-to-man challenge of Goliath. An *ABC Production in association with DIC Enterprises and Diana Kerew Productions*. Color. One hour. Premiered on ABC: November 28, 1986. Rebroadcast on ABC: August 15, 1992 (Part 1) and August 22, 1992 (Part 2).

**Cast**
**Mary Ann:** Jenna Van Oy; **Peter:** Christopher Fitzgerald; **Sauli:** Andrew Cassese

**Voices**
**Little David:** Scott Menville, Sandi Patti (singing); **Magical Mose:** John Franklin; **Christopher/Cat Soldier:** Billy Bowles; **Goliath/Fox Soldier #3:** Jim Cummings; **Eliab/Fox Soldier #2:** Townsend Coleman; **King Saul:** Paul Winchell; **Frog Servant/Fox Soldier #1/Rat Soldier #1:** Phil Proctor; **Vocalists:** John Franklin, Sandi Patti, Mitchell Winfield

### ⊚ THE KINGDOM CHUMS: ORIGINAL TOP TEN

Debby Boone, Tony Orlando, Marilyn McCoo, Billy Preston and Frankie Valli lend their voices to this tuneful, inspirational tale of

*The biblical story of David and Goliath is transformed into cartoon form in the ABC Weekend Special* The Kingdom Chums: Little David's Adventure. *© American Broadcasting Companies. All rights reserved.*
(COURTESY: DIC ENTERPRISES)

three kids who discover the original Top 10 Songs were the Ten Commandments in this two-part, hour-long animated special for Saturday-morning's *ABC Weekend Specials* series. Originally produced in 1989, the program was shelved when ABC's children's programming head left the network. Briefly offered on home video via point-of-purchase television commercials with an 800-number (the idea was dropped when sales were less than expected), it premiered three years after its making. A *Rick Reinert Pictures Production*. Color. One hour. Premiered on ABC: August 15, 1992 and August 22, 1992. Rebroadcast on ABC: April 10, 1993 and April 17, 1993.

**Voices**
**Essie:** Debby Boone; **Miriam:** Marilyn McCoo; **Christopher:** Tony Orlando; **Mose:** Billy Preston; **Little David:** Frankie Valli; **Petey:** Mayim Bialik; **Osborn:** Scott Menville; **Annie:** Marine Patterson

### ⊚ THE KING KONG SHOW

The great ape, whose colossal strength and great size enable him to conquer others, was featured in two episodes shown back to back in this one-hour preview of the Saturday-morning series that premiered on ABC. A *Rankin-Bass Production*. Color. One-hour. Premiered on ABC: September 6, 1966

### ⊚ KING OF THE BEASTS

The animal cast from TV's *Noah's Ark* returns in this half-hour sequel about a lion who assumes the role of "king of the beasts," only to drive one of his rivals, Croc the crocodile, into setting up his own solitary kingdom atop a mount. Songs and story were written by executive producer Charles G. Mortimer Jr., director Shamus Culhane and John Culhane. A *Shamus Culhane Production in association with Westfall Productions*. Color. Half-hour. Premiered on NBC: April 9, 1977. Rebroadcast on NBC: April 19, 1978: Rebroadcast on DIS: July 29, 1993; August 6, 1993. Syndicated.

**Voices**
**Noah:** Henry Ramer; **Crocodile:** Paul Soles; **Lion:** Carl Banas; **Male Elephant:** Murray Westgale; **Female Elephant:** Bonnie Brooks; **Male Giraffe/Camel:** Jay Nelson; **Polar Bear:** Don Mason; **Ostrich/Female Penguin:** Ruth Springford; **Walrus:** Jack Mather; **Female Baby Croc:** Judy Sinclair; **Male Baby Croc/Mouse:** Cardie Mortimer

## ⊚ KISSYFUR: BEAR ROOTS

Gus and Kissyfur, a father-and-son team of performing circus bears, escape from the big top to join the community of Paddlecab County, but are not welcomed by the other resident animals until they rescue the community from the jaws of two hungry alligators, Jolene and Floyd. The program was based on characters created by Phil Melendez and also inspired their own Saturday-morning series. *An NBC Production in association with DIC Enterprises. Color. Half-hour. Premiered on NBC: December 22, 1985.*

### Voices
**Kissyfur:** R.J. Williams; **Gus:** Edmund Gilbert; **Jolene:** Terence McGovern; **Floyd/Stuckey:** Stu Rosen; **Duane:** Neil Ross; **Beehonie/Miss Emmy/Toot:** Russi Taylor; **Lennie:** Lennie Weinrib; **Uncle Shelby:** Frank Welker

## ⊚ KISSYFUR: THE BIRDS AND THE BEARS

In their attempt to impress Miss Emmy Lou's smarter-than-average niece, Donna, Kissyfur and his swamp friends build a raft and recklessly travel upstream, only to get caught in a strong undertow and become the target of swamp 'gators, Jolene and Floyd, returning characters from the first Kissyfur special, *Bear Roots. An NBC Production in association with DIC Enterprises. Color. Half-hour. Premiered on NBC: March 30, 1986.*

### Voices
**Kissyfur:** R.J. Williams; **Gus:** Edmund Gilbert; **Jolene:** Terence McGovern; **Floyd/Stuckey:** Stu Rosen; **Duane:** Neil Ross; **Beehonie/Miss Emmy/Toot:** Russi Taylor; **Lennie:** Lennie Weinrib; **Uncle Shelby:** Frank Welker

## ⊚ KISSYFUR: THE LADY IS A CHUMP

When the search begins for a new babysitter for Kissyfur, Gus hires a sweet nanny who turns out to be Floyd the alligator—bent on a good meal—in disguise. *An NBC Production in association with DIC Enterprises. Color. Half-hour. Premiered on NBC: June 1, 1986.*

### Voices
**Kissyfur:** R.J. Williams; **Gus:** Edmund Gilbert; **Jolene:** Terence McGovern; **Floyd/Stuckey:** Stu Rosen; **Duane:** Neil Ross; **Beehonie/Miss Emmy/Toot:** Russi Taylor; **Lennie:** Lennie Weinrib; **Uncle Shelby:** Frank Welker

## ⊚ KISSYFUR: WE ARE THE SWAMP

Old buzzard Floyd and his snake Reggie lure Kissyfur and his swamp buddies up to a magical place high in a tree where anything is possible—even swimming in a water-filled hole—as part of a plan to make the critters their main dish for dinner. *An NBC Production in association with DIC Enterprises. Color. Half-hour. Premiered on NBC: July 6, 1986.*

### Voices
**Kissyfur:** R.J. Williams; **Gus:** Edmund Gilbert; **Jolene:** Terence McGovern; **Floyd/Stuckey:** Stu Rosen; **Duane:** Neil Ross; **Beehonie/Miss Emmy/Toot:** Russi Taylor; **Lennie:** Lennie Weinrib; **Uncle Shelby:** Frank Welker; **Flo:** Marilyn Lightstone

## ⊚ THE KOALA BROTHERS OUTBACK CHRISTMAS

After inviting some friends and looking forward to spending a festive Christmas Day together down under in the Australian Outback, brother koalas Frank and Buster, whose mission in life is to help others, hastily embark on a trip to Antarctica to find their stranded friend, Penny the Penguin, to celebrate Christmas together back home. Originally titled *Frank and Buster's Christmas in the Outback,* this half-hour puppet-animated special, using plasticine, clay-like figures and traditional stop-motion techniques, premiered in December 2005 in the United Kingdom on BBC2 and in the United States on the Disney Channel. Since 2003, the characters have starred in their own 57-episode weekly cartoon series called *The Koala Brothers* airing on the BBC and the Disney Channel's *Playhouse Disney* weekday-morning programming block. *A Famous Flying Films/Spellbound Entertainment Production in association with the British Broadcasting Corporation and Momentum Pictures. Color. Half-hour. Premiered on DIS: December 21, 2005. Rebroadcast on DIS: December 24, 2005; December 25, 2005; December 16, 2006; December 24, 2006.*

### Voices
**Narrator:** Jonathan Coleman; **Frank/Archie/Sammy:** Keith Wickham; **Other Voices:** Lucinda Cowden, Rob Rackstraw, Janet James

## ⊚ KONG: KING OF ATLANTIS

Created from DNA of the original beast of the jungle, a stronger, more agile, and more primal Kong is born as an ancient prophecy comes true with the sunken city of Atlantis rising from the ocean. It is up to Kong's human "brother" Jason to save him and the island and its inhabitants from the evil Queen Reptilla who enslaves the amazing beast to unite the warring clans of Atlantis for her own evil purpose. Based on the animated television series *Kong: The Animated Series* that also aired on Toon Disney, this 78-minute feature-length fantasy adventure premiered on Toon Disney in December 2005 in a 90-minute time slot. *A BKN Studios Production. Color. Ninety minutes. Premiered on TDIS: December 14, 2005.*

### Voices
**Jason Jenkins/Frazetti:** Kirby Morrow; **Eric "Tan" Tannenbaum IV:** Scott McNeil; **Professor Ramon De La Porta:** David Kaye; **Lua:** Saffron Henderson; **Harpy:** Pauline Newstone; **Dr. Lorna Jenkins:** Daphne Goldrick

## ⊚ KORGOTH OF BARBARIA

Possessing massive bulging biceps and physically endowed with brute strength, a merciless barbarian named Korgoth (voiced by Diedrich Bader, best known as Oswald on TV's *The Drew Carey Show*) survives in a dark post-apocalyptic wasteland inhabited by scantily clad maidens, overweight innkeepers and (naturally) a fair amount of medieval deviants and henchmen, including Baron Gog-Ma-Gogg and the evil wizard Specules, in this animated sword-and-sorcery parody from veteran storyboard writer/director Aaron Springer (*Dexter's Laboratory, The Grim Adventures of Billy & Mandy* and *SpongeBob SquarePants*) that debuted with a half-hour pilot special on Cartoon Network in June 2006. Picked up as a series by Cartoon Network, the action-comedy was to officially debut as a regular weekly component of *Adult Swim* in late spring 2007 but has yet to air. *A Cartoon Network Studios Production. Color. Half-hour. Premiered on CAR: June 3, 2006.*

### Voices
**Korgoth:** Diedrich Bader; **Gog-Ma-Gogg:** Craig T. Raisner, **Hargon:** Tom Kenny, **Narrator/Specules:** Corey Burton; **Stink/Scrotus:** John DiMaggio; **Orala:** Susan Spano

## ⊚ KRYPTO THE SUPERDOG: "STORYBOOK HOLIDAY"

Kevin learns about the importance of family when he and Krypto magically end up in Storybook Land, where the characters he meets resemble his relatives in this two-part half-hour holiday special based on the popular Cartoon Network and CW Network Kids'

WB! series, *Krypto the Superdog*, produced by Warner Bros. Television Animation. *A Warner Bros. Television Animation Production. Color. Half-hour. Premiered on CAR: December 5, 2005. Rebroadcast on CAR: December 16, 2005; December 17, 2005; December 19, 2005; December 23, 2005; December 24, 2005; December 25, 2005. Rebroadcast on CW (Kids' WB!): December 9, 2006.*

**Voices**
**Krypto:** Samuel Vincent; **Kevin Whitney:** Alberto Chisi; **Superman:** Michael Daingerfield; **Hot Dog:** Trevor Devall; **Lex Luthor:** Brian Dobson; **Streaky the Cat:** Brian Drummond; **Tail Terrier:** Peter Kelamis; **Brainy Barker:** Ellen Kennedy; **Ignatius/Ace the Bathound:** Scott McNeil; **Kevin's Mom:** Nicole Oliver; **Andrea/Melanie:** Tabitha St. Germain; **Mammoth Mutt:** Kelly Sheridan; **Paw Pooch:** Dale Wilson

### ◉ LASSIE AND THE SPIRIT OF THUNDER MOUNTAIN

Television's most famous collie appeared in cartoon form for the first time in this one-hour feature-length story, later rebroadcast as two episodes on Saturday-morning's *Lassie Rescue Rangers* series. *A Filmation Associates Production with Lassie Television. Color. One hour. Premiered on ABC: November 11, 1972 (on The ABC Saturday Superstar Movie).*

**Voices**
**Ben Turner:** Ted Knight; **Laura Turner, his wife:** Jane Webb; **Susan Turner:** Lane Scheimer; **Jackie Turner:** Keith Sutherland; **Ben Turner/Gene Fox:** Hal Harvey; **Lassie:** Lassie; **Narrator:** Ted Knight

### ◉ THE LAST HALLOWEEN

Blending live action and computer-generated animation, four bumbling Martians—Gleep, Romtu, Scoota and Bing—crash-land on Earth in search of candy (called "koobie" on their planet) to replenish their planet's supply. They hook up with two small-town kids who help the aliens with their mission and take them trick-or-treating, only to discover an evil scientist (played by Rhea Perlman) who has been stealing the lake water for her experiments in this half-hour Halloween special originally broadcast on CBS. The special's animated stars, Gleep, Romtu, Scoota and Bing, were originally created at Industrial Light & Magic for a series of television commercials. *A Hanna-Barbera/Pacific Data Images Production. Color. Half-hour. Premiered on CBS: October 28, 1991.*

**Cast (live action)**
**Michael:** Will Nipper; **Jeanie:** Sarah Martineck; **Mrs. Gizborne, evil scientist:** Rhea Perlman; **Hans, her sinister henchman:** Richard Moll; **Grandpa:** Eugene Roche; **Hubble:** Stan Ivar; **Accountant:** Michael D. Roberts; **Others:** Grant Gelt, Tim Anderson, Sean Roche, Darwyn Carson, Bill Hanna

**Voices**
**Gleep:** Paul Williams; **Romtu:** Don Messick; **Scoota/Bing:** Frank Welker

### ◉ THE LAST OF THE CURLEWS

Native to the arctic shoreland, the curlews, tall striped birds, are on the verge of extinction. As the two survivors search for mates to keep their species alive, they encounter hunters who are unconcerned with their survival. This *ABC Afterschool Special* was an Emmy Award winner. *A Hanna-Barbera Production. Color. One hour Premiered on ABC: October 4, 1972. Rebroadcast on ABC: March 7, 1973. Rebroadcast on CAR: September 10–12, 1993, April 1, 1994 (Turner Family Showcase).*

**Voices**
**Stan:** Ross Martin; **Mark:** Vinnie Van Patten; **Bird Calls:** Ginny Tyler; **Narrator:** Lee Vines

### ◉ THE LAST OF THE MOHICANS

During the French and Indian War, Cora, the daughter of French Commander Allan Munro, is abducted by the traitorous Magua Indians. Scout Hawkeye and the last two Mohicans, Chingachook and his son, Unca, work to free the girl from her captors and aid the French in the capture of the Magua tribe. Based on a novel by James Fenimore Cooper. *A Famous Classic Tales special. A Hanna-Barbera Production. Color. One hour. Premiered on CBS: November 27, 1975. Rebroadcast on CBS: November 25, 1981. Syndicated.*

**Voices**
**Hawkeye:** Mike Road; **Uncas:** Casey Kasem; **Chingachook:** John Doucette; **Cora Munro:** Joan Van Ark; **Alice Munro:** Kristina Holland; **Duncan Heyward:** Paul Hecht; **Magua/Soldier:** Frank Welker; **Colonel Allen Munro/Delaware Chief:** John Stephenson

### ◉ THE LAST OF THE RED-HOT DRAGONS

A once-powerful old flying dragon who has lost his fire-breathing ability regains it in time to save Noah's ark-bound animals, who are left stranded at the North Pole by melting a block of ice that traps them in a dark cave. *A Shamus Culhane Production in association with Erredia Productions and Westfall Productions. Color. Ninety minutes. Premiered on NBC: April 1, 1980. Syndicated. Rebroadcast on DIS: August 14, 1993.*

**Voices**
**Dragon:** John Culhane; **King Lion:** Carl Banas; **Crocodile:** Paul Soles; **Elephant:** Murray Westgate; **Penguin:** Ruth Springford; **Polar Bear:** Don Mason; **Baby Girl Crocodile:** Judy Sinclair; **Baby Boy Crocodile:** Cardie Mortimer

### ◉ LATE NIGHT WITH CONAN O'BRIEN

Smart aleck NBC late-night television host/funnyman Conan O'Brien starred in this 90-minute special redone from a live-action episode first broadcast in October 2000, with the red-headed comedian and his entire cast appearing as clay animated figures. O'Brien and his show's staff thought doing a show in clay would put a "fresh spin on old material," so many months were spent on crafting clay models and laboriously animating them in stop-motion, including the program's original title opening. O'Brien's monologue, and guests Johnny Knoxville, Richard Lewis, rock legend David Bowie and Mr. T, featured in the show's "Year 2000" sketches. As O'Brien joked in an interview, "This may be the best show we've ever done—in clay." *A Broadway Video Production. Color. Ninety minutes. Premiered on NBC: May 15, 2003.*

**Voices**
**Host:** Conan O'Brien; **Announcer:** Joel Godard; **Music Director:** Max Weinberg; **Johnny Knoxville:** Himself; **Richard Lewis:** Himself; **David Bowie:** Himself; **Mr. T:** Himself

### ◉ LEGEND OF THE DRAGON: "TRIAL BY FIRE"

Two-part one-hour pilot that premiered as a special Jetix Blockbuster presentation on ABC Family following the martial arts adventures of one fraternal twin Ang chosen over the other, Ling, to become guardian of the secret Temple of the Dragons and their 15-year-old sister deciding to fight for the forces of evil as the

Shadow Dragon that launched the daily hit animated series on Toon Disney. *A BKN Production. Color. Half-hour. Premiered on ABC FAM: August 14, 2006.*

**Voices**
**Ling/Shadow Dragon/Cobra:** Larissa Murray; **Ang/Golden Dragon:** Alan Marriot; **Xuan Chi:** Mark Silk; **Master Chin/Chow/Dog Guardian Wang Lee:** Dan Russell; **Beingal/Ming/Rat Guardian:** Lucy Porter

### ◎ THE LEGEND OF FROSTY THE SNOWMAN

Burt Reynolds lends his voice as the narrator of this updated version of the story of the famed snowman who teaches the perfect, tiny town of Evergreen the joys of snowballs, sleigh rides and other winter wonderland fun until the evil Principal Pankley dethrones the good-natured Mayor Tinkerton and wants to make things more orderly and less fun. Fortunately, the mayor's son, Tommy, and his new best friend, Frosty, make sure that doesn't happen. Originally produced as a direct-to-video release in October 2003 by Sony Music Distribution and Classic Media, the special debuted two years later on Cartoon Network. *A Sony Music Distribution/Classic Media Production in association with Greg Sullivan and Studio B. Color. Half-hour. Premiered on CAR: December 15, 2005. Rebroadcast on CAR: December 22, 2005; December 23, 2005; December 5, 2006; December 16, 2006; December 20, 2006; December 21, 2006; December 22, 2006.*

**Voices**
**Frosty the Snowman:** Bill Fagerbakke; **Mayor Tinkerton:** Tom Kenny; **Tommy Tinkerton:** Kath Soucie; **Sara Simple:** Tara Strong; **Principal Hank Pankley:** Larry Miller; **Narrator:** Burt Reynolds

### ◎ THE LEGEND OF HAWAIIAN SLAMMERS

On the tropical island paradise of Oahu, Ronnie, a local cap-playing champion, unleashes a team of good slammer-powered superheroes, called "Sun Slammers," including Rain Slammer, Earth Slammer, Gold Slammer and Ice Slammer, to overtake the evil archaeologist Dr. Karl Von Fragman's team of "evil" slammers and their sinister spirits whom he's released—Lava Slammer, Storm Slammer, Lead Slammer, Fire Slammer and Shadow Slammer—to conquer the world in a classic battle of good vs. evil in this half-hour syndicated special by Emmy award-winning writer Jeffrey Scott (son of Three Stooges producer Norman Maurer). *A DIC Entertainment Production. Color. Half-hour. Premiered: 1991. Syndicated.*

**Voices**
**Shadow:** Long John Baldry; **Von Fragman:** Jim Byrnes; **Fire:** Babz Chula; **Michael:** Chad Dormer; **Ice:** Edward Glen; **Gold:** Marcy Goldberg; **Rain:** Saffron Henderson; **Heavy Hitter:** Andrew Kavadas; **Sun:** David Kaye; **Storm:** Shirley Milliner; **Ronnie:** Jesse Moss; **Earth:** John Novak; **Lava:** Dale Wilson

### ◎ THE LEGEND OF HIAWATHA

Great Indian legend Hiawatha, who is half man and half god, teaches his people how to meet the challenges of everyday life in this adaptation of the famed Henry Wadsworth Longfellow poem. *A Kenner Family Classics special. An Atkinson Film-Arts Production in association with Triple Seven Concepts. Color. One hour. Premiered on CBS: November 24, 1983. Rebroadcast on NBC: December 4, 1984 (as NBC Special Treat). Syndicated.*

**Voices**
Tim Atkinson, Barry Edward Blake, Gary Chalk, Arline Van Dine, Les Lye, Anna MacCormick, Michael Voss

### ◎ THE LEGEND OF LOCHNAGAR

A reclusive Scotsman's quest for peace and quiet and a warm bath bring him to a cave carved into Lochnagar Mountain, where, boasting an "encyclopedic knowledge of indoor plumbing," he outfits his new home with all the modern conveniences. The plumbing ultimately causes ecological problems that threaten elfin creatures who live beneath Earth's surface in this *ABC Weekend Special*, written and narrated by England's Prince Charles (who appears in a live-action introduction). The prince wrote the story when he was 21 and first told it to his younger brothers, Andrew and Edward. *A Mike Young Production in association with Dave Edwards Ltd. Color. Half-hour. Premiered on ABC: April 24, 1993. Rebroadcast on ABC: April 1, 1995; November 4, 1995.*

**Voices**
**Scotsman:** Robbie Coltrane; **Narrator:** Prince Charles

### ◎ THE LEGEND OF ROBIN HOOD

The classic tale of Robin Hood and his Merry Men, who rob from the rich to give to the poor, is colorfully retold in this hour-long adaptation that traces Robin's crusade to rid England of the underhanded Prince John. *A Famous Classic Tales special. An Air Programs International Production. Color. One hour. Premiered on CBS: November 14, 1971. Rebroadcast on CBS: November 11, 1972; September 30, 1973. Syndicated.*

**Voices**
Tim Elliott, Peter Guest, Ron Haddrick, John Kingley, John Llewellyn, Helen Morse, Brenda Senders

### ◎ THE LEGEND OF SLEEPY HOLLOW

Washington Irving's eerie tale of romantic rivalry along the Hudson River, pitting the new schoolmaster, Ichabod Crane, against the local hero and bully, Brom Bones, is told by Oscar-winning actress Glenn Close in this spirited 1988-produced, half-hour adaptation, part of Rabbit Ears Video's *Holiday Classics* video series, which aired on Showtime. *A Rabbit Ears Video Production. Color. Half-hour. Premiered on SHO: 1989. Rebroadcast on DIS: December 20, 1991.*

**Voices**
**Narrator:** Glenn Close

### ◎ THE LEPRECHAUN'S CHRISTMAS GOLD

Art Carney, as the oldest of the Killakilarney clan, narrates and sings this story of a young cabin boy lost on an uncharted island who unwittingly frees a caterwauling Banshee who tries to steal the leprechauns' pot of gold. *A Rankin-Bass Production. Color. Half-hour. Premiered on ABC: December 23, 1981. Syndicated. Rebroadcast on ABC: December 20, 1983. Rebroadcast on DIS: December 22, 1992. Rebroadcast on FOX FAM: July 14, 1999; December 2, 1999; December 10, 1999; December 15, 1999; December 23, 1999; December 25, 1999; December 4, 2000; December 13, 2000; December 18, 2000; December 24, 2000. Rebroadcast on ABC FAM: December 1, 2001; December 15, 2001; December 18, 2001; December 23, 2001; December 4, 2002; December 12, 2002; December 24, 2002; December 6, 2003; December 4, 2004; December 20, 2004; December 13, 2005; December 24, 2006.*

Voices

**Barney Killakilarney (narrator):** Art Carney; **Faye Killakilarney:** Peggy Cass; **Dinty Doyle:** Ken Jennings; **Old Mag:** Christine Mitchell; **Child/Others:** Glynnis Bieg; Michael Moronosk

## ◎ LIBERTY AND THE LITTLES

On their way to New York City for the Fourth of July, a storm forces the Littles (Dinky, Grandpa, William, Helen, Tom and Lucy) to crash near the Statue of Liberty. There they make friends with two children, Michelle and Pierre, and help them escape from a tiny 19th-century community contained inside the statue. Michelle and Pierre learn the meaning of liberty in a free land. Based on John Peterson's popular children's book series, the special aired in three parts as an *ABC Weekend Special*. The characters appeared in their own successful Saturday-morning series, *The Littles*, also broadcast on ABC. *An ABC Entertainment Production in association with DIC Enterprises. Color. Half-hour. Premiered on ABC: October 18, October 25 and November 1, 1986. Rebroadcast on ABC: August 18, August 25 and September 1, 1989; June 20, June 27 and July 4, 1992.*

Voices

**Tom Little:** David Wagner; **Lucy Little:** Bettina Rush; **Grandpa Little:** Alvy Moore; **Dinky Little:** Robert David Hall; **Helen Little:** Patti Parris; **William Little:** Gregg Berger; **Michelle/Pierre:** Katie Lee; **Pere Egalitaire:** Jim Morgan; **General/Massey:** Earl Boen

## ◎ THE LIFE AND ADVENTURES OF SANTA CLAUS

The origin of jolly old St. Nick, alias Santa Claus, is recounted in this Animagic stop-motion animation special that traces the life of this merry old soul, from his early childhood to his rise as the world's foremost agent of goodwill in this hour-long holiday special adaptation of the 1902 story by *Wizard of Oz* author L. Frank Baum. *A Rankin-Bass Production. Color. One hour. Premiered on CBS: December 17, 1985. Rebroadcast on CBS: December 2, 1986; December 3, 1987; December 24, 1988. Rebroadcast on DIS: December 11, 1992; December 14, 1993; December 12, 1995.*

Voices

**Great Ak:** Alfred Drake; **Old Santa:** Earl Hammond; **Young Santa:** J.D. Roth; **Tingler:** Robert McFadden; **Necile:** Lesley Miller; **King Awgwa:** Earle Hyman; **Wind Demon:** Larry Kenney; **Weekum:** Joey Grasso; **Children:** Amy Anzelowitz, Josh Blake, Ari Gold, Jamie Lisa Murphy; **Others:** Lynne Liptor, Peter Newman; **Vocalists:** Al Dana, Margaret Dorn, Arlene Mitchell, Marty Nelson, David Ragaini, Robert Ragaini; Annette Sanders

## ◎ LIFE IS A CIRCUS, CHARLIE BROWN

Snoopy leaves home, becomes a big-top star ("Hugo the Great") in a traveling circus and falls in love with a fancily preened French poodle named Fifi, a circus performer. Charlie Brown is understandably distraught over his lost pet, receiving little comfort from Linus, who philosophizes, "It's difficult not to be enticed by romance and excitement, Charlie Brown. There's more to life than a plastic supper dish." The special was rebroadcast at various dates and times on Nickelodeon beginning in February 1998. *A Lee Mendelson–Bill Melendez Production in association with Charles M. Schulz Creative Associates and United Feature Syndicate. Color. Half-hour. Premiered on CBS: October 24, 1980. Rebroadcast on CBS: January 11, 1982; January 17, 1983. Rebroadcast on NICK: February 25, 1998; March 26, 1998; May 31, 1998; July 2, 1998; July 31, 1998; August 28, 1998; September 30, 1998; October 23, 1998; November 20, 1998; December 2, 1998; December 30, 1998; January 22, 1999; February 4, 1999; March 5, 1999; April 26, 1999; July 7, 1999; September 26, 1999.*

Voices

**Charlie Brown:** Michael Mandy; **Snoopy:** Bill Melendez; **Schroeder/Kids:** Christopher Donohoe; **Linus Van Pelt:** Earl "Rocky" Reilly; **Lucy Van Pelt:** Kristen Fullerton; **Peppermint Patty:** Brent Hauer; **Marcie:** Shannon Cohn; **Polly:** Casey Carlson

## ◎ LIFE WITH LOOPY BIRTHDAY GALABRATION

Steven Holman of his San Francisco–based production company (W)Holesome Products Inc. created and produced this mixture of stop-motion animation, puppetry and live-action spun-off from the popular mixed-media skit *Life with Loopy* on Nickelodeon's popular alternative animated variety show *KaBlam!* featuring an imaginative, adventurous young girl, Loopy (short for Lupicia) Cooper, in strange, surreal adventures narrated by her dweeby older brother, Larry. On Friday, September 25, 1998, the half-hour special premiered in prime time at 8:00 P.M. (ET) on Nickelodeon. *A (W)Holesome Products Inc. Production. Color. Half-hour. Premiered on NICK: September 25, 1998.*

## ◎ LIFE WITH LOUIE: A CHRISTMAS SURPRISE FOR MRS. STILLMAN

Stand-up comedian Louie Anderson, as his eight-year-old alter ego, helps his father decorate his lonely neighbor's house in this half-hour holiday misadventure that preceded the popular Fox Saturday-morning series. *A Hyperion Animation Production. Color. Half-hour. Premiered on FOX: December 18, 1994. Rebroadcast on FOX: December 24, 1994.*

Voices

**Little Louie/Dad (Andy Anderson)/Narrator:** Louie Anderson; **Mom (Ora Anderson):** Edie McClurg; **Tommy:** Miko Hughes; **Mike Grunewald/Glen Glenn:** Justin Shenkarow; **Jeannie Harper:** Debi Derryberry; **Mrs. Stillman:** Liz Sheridan

## ◎ LIFE WITH LOUIE: "DAD GETS CANNED"

Louie and his family come up with various ways to save money after his dad, Andy, loses his job in this second of two prime time specials to air on FOX based on the popular Saturday-morning cartoon series featuring the voice—and narrated by—comedian Louie Anderson. *A Hyperion Animation Production. Color. Premiered on FOX: June 18, 1995.*

Voices

**Little Louie/Andy Anderson, his father/Narrator:** Louie Anderson; **Ora Anderson, Louie's mother:** Edie McClurg; **Tommy Anderson:** Miko Hughes; **Mike Grunewald/Glenn Glenn:** Justin Shenkarow; **Jeannie Harper:** Debi Derryberry; **Grandma:** Mary Wickes; **Other Voices:** Joe Alaskey

## ◎ THE LION, THE WITCH AND THE WARDROBE

Based on the children's book of the same name, four children are magically transported, via a giant wardrobe, into the wonderful land of Narnia, where they help a kingly lion vanquish a wicked queen who holds the land in the grip of winter. The Emmy Award-winning program was broadcast in two parts. *A Children's Television Workshop Production in association with Bill Melendez Productions, the Episcopal Radio-TV Foundation, T.V. Cartoons and Pegbar Productions. Color. Two hours. Premiered on CBS: April 1 and April 2,*

*1979. Rebroadcast on CBS: April 22 and April 23, 1980. Rebroadcast on DIS: May 9, 1992; September 4, 1993; October 6, 1995.*

**Voices**
Lucy: Rachel Warren; **Susan:** Susan Sokol; **Peter:** Reg Williams; **Edmund:** Simon Adams; **Mr. Tumnus:** Victor Spinetti; **Professor:** Dick Vosburgh; **Mr. Beaver:** Don Parker; **Mrs. Beaver:** Liz Proud; **Asian:** Stephen Thorne; **White Witch:** Beth Porter

### ◎ THE LITTLE BROWN BURRO

A dejected little burro, who finds he has no place in society, is reassured when he is bought by Joseph and travels to Bethlehem, carrying Mary to the site of baby Jesus' birth. *A Titlecraft/Atkinson Film-Arts Production in association with D.W. Reid Films. Color. Half-hour. Premiered (U.S.): December, 1978. Syndicated.*

**Voices:**
**Little Brown Burro:** Bonnie Brooks; **Omar:** Paul Soles; **Narrator:** Lorne Greene

### ◎ THE LITTLE CROOKED CHRISTMAS TREE

Christopher Plummer narrates this timeless story of a Christmas tree that is spared from being chopped down to protect a nest of dove's eggs. The 1993 special originally produced for Canadian television, aired in the United States on The Disney Channel. *A Lacewood Production. Color. Half-hour. Premiered on DIS: 1993.*

**Voices**
**Narrator:** Christopher Plummer

### ◎ LITTLE DRUMMER BOY

An exceptional tale set in ancient times about Aaron, a six-year-old orphaned drummer boy, who, along with his drum and three animal friends—a lamb, a camel and a donkey—learns the lesson of love and the true meaning of the holy season by journeying with the Three Wise Men to Bethlehem to witness the birth of the Christ child. The Teachers Guide to Television listed the special as "a specially selected program of educational value" prior to its network premiere. Animation for the program was by Animagic, a stop-motion process using puppets and making their movements appear life-like. The program was backed by the Vienna Boys Choir. *A Videocraft International Production in association with NBC. Color. Half-hour. Premiered on NBC: December 19, 1968. Rebroadcast on NBC: December 18, 1969; December 16, 1970; December 14, 1971; December 10, 1972; December 9, 1973; December 14, 1974; December 14, 1975; December 23, 1977; December 23, 1980. Rebroadcast on FAM: December 11, 1996. Rebroadcast on FOX FAM: December 2, 1998; December 18, 1998; December 24, 1998; July 10, 1999; July 14, 1999; December 2, 1999; December 16, 1999; December 24, 1999; December 4, 2000; December 16, 2000; December 24, 2000. Rebroadcast on ABC FAM: December 1, 2002; December 3, 2002; December 24, 2002; December 6, 2003; December 10, 2003; December 4, 2004; December 9, 2004; December 22, 2004; December 3, 2005; December 14, 2006; December 24, 2006.*

**Voices**
**Aaron:** Teddy Eccles; **Haramed:** José Ferrer; **Ali/Other voices:** Paul Frees; **Narrator:** Greer Garson

### ◎ LITTLE DRUMMER BOY, BOOK II

In this sequel to 1968's *The Little Drummer Boy*, Aaron returns to undertake an incredible journey with one of the wise men, Melchoir—to find a man named Simeon who has constructed a

*Aaron, a six-year-old orphan, conveys his happiness by beating his drum in a scene from the perennial Christmas favorite* Little Drummer Boy. *© Rankin-Bass Productions.* (COURTESY: FAMILY HOME ENTERTAINMENT)

set of Silver Bells to be rung to herald the birth of Christ. This Animagic special was produced by Arthur Rankin Jr., and Jules Bass, who created such perennial holiday special favorites as *Santa Claus Is Comin' to Town* and *Frosty the Snowman*. Greer Garson, who narrated the first special, served as the program's story teller. *A Rankin-Bass Production. Color. Half-hour. Premiered on NBC: December 13, 1976. Rebroadcast on NBC: December 23, 1977; December 21, 1978; December 23, 1980. Rebroadcast on FAM: December 9, 1995; December 13, 1996. Rebroadcast on FOX FAM: December 9, 1998; December 18, 1998; July 10, 1999; December 7, 1999; December 24, 1999; December 12, 2000; December 24, 2000. Rebroadcast on ABC FAM: December 1, 2001; December 18, 2001; December 24, 2001; December 1, 2002; December 3, 2002; December 24, 2002; December 6, 2003; December 10, 2003; December 4, 2004; December 9, 2004; December 3, 2005; December 9, 2005; December 14, 2006; December 24, 2006.*

**Voices**
**Aaron:** David Jay; **Melchoir:** Allen Swift; **Brutus:** Zero Mostel; **Simeon:** Ray Owens; **Plato:** Robert McFadden; **Narrator:** Greer Garson

### ◎ LITTLE EINSTEINS: "CHRISTMAS WISH"

The junior explorers blast off to the Himalayas to recover a missing Christmas present from atop snowy Mt. Everest in this second half-hour holiday special featuring Ludwig van Beethoven's "Für Elise," based on the popular cartoon series *Little Einsteins* for Disney Channel. *A Curious Pictures Production. Color. Half-hour. Premiered on DIS: December 12, 2005. Rebroadcast on DIS: December 14, 2005; December 17, 2005; December 22, 2005; December 23, 2005; December 24, 2005; December 25, 2005; December 4,*

*2006; December 16, 2006; December 20, 2006; December 24, 2006; December 25, 2006.*

**Voices**
**Leo:** Jesse Schwartz; **June:** Erica Huang; **Quincy:** Aiden Pompey; **Annie:** Natalia Wojcik

### ⊚ LITTLE EINSTEINS: "LITTLE EINSTEINS' HALLOWEEN"

While celebrating Halloween in Europe, Leo, June, Quincy and Annie plan to go trick-or-treating, with their first stop a medieval castle supposedly haunted by ghosts in this first half-hour special, based on the popular Disney Channel series. *A Curious Pictures/ Baby Einstein Company Production. Color. Half-hour. Premiered on DIS: October 29, 2005. Rebroadcast on DIS: October 30, 2005; October 31, 2005; October 28, 2006; October 29, 2006; October 30, 2006; October 31, 2006.*

**Voices**
**Leo:** Jesse Schwartz; **June:** Erica Huang; **Quincy:** Aiden Pompey; **Annie:** Natalia Wojcik

### ⊚ THE LITTLE ENGINE THAT COULD

The plucky little locomotive of children's storybook fame who pulls a trainload of toys over a treacherous, snow-packed mountain, chugging "I think I can" learns the power of positive thinking to overcome difficult odds in this half-hour, made-for-video adaptation of the age-old children's classic by Watty Piper. First released on home video, the program also aired as an Easter special for two weeks—the end of March through early April of 1993—on 56 independent stations around the country. *A Dave Edwards Studio Production in association with MCA/Universal. Color. Half-hour. Premiered: March–April 1993. Syndicated.*

**Voices**
Bever-Leigh Banfield, Peter Cullen, Scott Menville, Billy O'Sullivan

### ⊚ LITTLE GOLDEN BOOKLAND

Little Golden Bookland is in danger. Storms have created a hole in the breakwater, and Harbortown and Beamer, the venerable old lighthouse, could be washed away. Scuffy the Tugboat saves the day, along with his friends Tootle the Train, Katy Caboose, Pokey Little Puppy and Shy Little Kitten in this animated version of the well-known children's book characters. *A DIC Enterprises Production in association with Western Publishing Company. Color. Half-hour. Premiered: 1989.*

**Voices**
**Tootle the Train:** Dillan Bouey; **Pokey Little Puppy:** Chiara Zanni; **Shy Little Kitten:** Tony Balshaw; **Katy Caboose:** Emily Perkins; **Scuffy the Tugboat:** Tony Ail; **Tawny Scrawny Lion:** Graham Andrews; **Saggy Raggy Elephant:** Lelani Marrell; **Baby Brown Bear:** Tony Dakota; **Beamer:** Imbert Orchard

### ⊚ THE LITTLE MATCH GIRL

Young Angela is selling matches on the streets of New York on New Year's Eve 1999. In order to survive the freezing weather, she lights three of her matches and has visions of warmth, great feats, loved ones and powerful people who can help her and the homeless in this modern-day adaptation of the Hans Christian Andersen fairy tale. Produced by New York animator Michael Sporn, the special aired on *HBO's Storybook Musicals* series. *A Michael Sporn Animation Production in association with Italtoons Corporation. Color. Half-hour. Premiered on HBO: December 10, 1990.*

**Voices**
**Narrator:** F. Murray Abraham; **Angela, the Match Girl:** Theresa Smythe

### ⊚ THE LITTLE MERMAID

Once comfortable with her lifestyle under the sea, a beautiful mermaid princess experiences a change of heart when she is saved by a young prince in this philosophical adaptation of the popular Han Christian Andersen tale. The program preceded a rebroadcast of *Dr. Seuss's Horton Hears a Who* in its original broadcast on CBS. *A Gerald Potterton Production in association with Narrator's Digest. Color. Half-hour. Premiered on CBS: February 4, 1974. Rebroadcast on CBS: January 31, 1975. Syndicated.*

**Voices**
**Narrator:** Richard Chamberlain

### ⊚ THE LITTLE RASCALS CHRISTMAS SPECIAL

Filmdom's *The Little Rascals*, who cavorted in more than 100 live-action comedy shorts for Hal Roach in the 1920s and 1930s, return in a prime-time animated special revolving around Spanky and his younger brother, Porky, who mistakenly think they're getting an electric train for Christmas. Former "Rascals" Darla Hood Granson (playing Spanky's mother) and Matthew "Stymie" Beard (the town butcher), both since deceased, lend their voices to the program. *A King World Presentation in association with Muller-Rosen Productions and Murakami-Wolf-Swenson Films. Color. Half-hour. Premiered on NBC: December 3, 1979. Rebroadcast on NBC: December 15, 1980; December 20, 1981.*

**Voices**
**Alfalfa:** Jimmy Gatherum; **Spanky:** Phillip Tanzini; **Darla:** Randi Kiger; **Stymie:** Al Jocko Fann; **Porky:** Robby Kiger; **Mom:** Darla Hood Granson; **Sidewalk Santa:** Jack Somack; **Butcher:** Matthew "Stymie" Beard; **Man:** Cliff Norton; **Sales Clerk:** Frank Nelson; **Delivery Man:** Melville A. Levin; **Uncle Hominy:** Hal Smith; **Sales Lady:** Naomi Lewis; **Tough Kid:** Ike Eisenmann

### ⊚ LITTLE SPARROW: A PRECIOUS MOMENTS THANKSGIVING SPECIAL

A settler boy and a young Indian brave overcome their differences to work together to find the special berry that will cure the sickness affecting both their families in this half-hour Thanksgiving special, aired in first-run syndication on the Bohbot Kids Network. The program was one of five Precious Moments specials. Only two ever aired on U.S. television, the first being 1991's *Timmy's Gift*—produced by Westlake Village, California–based Rick Reinert Pictures, producers of the popular *Cap'n O.G. Readmore/ABC Weekend Specials. A Rick Reinert Pictures Production. Color. Half-hour. Premiered: November 24, 1995. Syndicated.*

**Voices**
**Little Sparrow:** Alex McKenna; **Jon:** E.G. Daily; **Timmy:** Justin Garms; **Angie:** Debi Derryberry; **Indian Father/Settler Father:** Neil Ross

### ⊚ THE LITTLEST LIGHT ON THE CHRISTMAS TREE

Heartwarming half-hour, post–World War II animated story about an abandoned Christmas tree light and an eight-year-old who loves it and helps others find their way in the world, featuring the voices of actors Jane Seymour and James Naughton, as well as six original songs. Sponsored by Model Fitness, the animated musical, which won a 2004 Accolade Award for best show and an Award of

Excellence from the Film Advisory Board, made its television debut on the home-shopping channel, QVC, in November 2004 and was rebroadcast a year later on the WB Television Network. *A KeyFrame Digital Production in association with Abrams Gentile Entertainment. Color. Half-hour. Premiered on QVC: November 2, 2004. Rebroadcast on WB: December 24, 2005.*

**Voices**
**Maggie Wiggins:** Jane Seymour; **Timothy Wiggins:** Jordan Duffy; **Melissa Wiggins:** Brianna Steinhilber; **Emanuel Girthmore:** Kenneth Kantor; **Mr. Jeepers:** Bruce Linser; **Mr. Goodly:** Scott Robertson; **Colonel:** Jacob (Jay) Harran; **Watley/Little Light:** Eddie Korbich; **Woman Greeter:** Donna Daley; **Narrator:** James Naughton

## ⊚ THE LITTLE TROLL PRINCE

Set among the rustic fjords and snow-covered villages of scenic Norway, this delightful parable tells the story of Bu, the crown prince of the trolls, who learns the true meaning of Christmas. This first-run syndicated special was produced in conjunction with the International Lutheran Laymen's League. *A Hanna-Barbera Production in association with Wang Film Productions, Inc. and Cuckoo Nest Studios. Color. Half-hour. Premiered: 1987. Syndicated.*

**Voices**
**Bu:** Danny Cooksey; **Borch, his two-headed brother:** Rob Paulsen; Laurie Faso; **Prag, his two-headed brother:** Neilson Ross; Frank Welker; **King Ulvik Head #1:** Vincent Price; **King Ulvik Head #2:** Jonathan Price; **Queen Sirena:** Cloris Leachman; **Professor Nidaros:** Don Knotts; **Stav:** Charlie Adler; **Ribo/Krill/ Father:** Michael Bell; **Kristi:** Ami Foster; **Sonja:** Christina Lange; **Bjorn:** William Christopher; **Witch/Mrs. Bjorn:** B.J. Ward; **Spectator #1:** Rob Paulsen; **Spectator #2:** Laurie Faso; **Spectator #3:** Neilson Ross; **Troll:** Frank Welker

## ⊚ LOST IN SPACE

Hopping aboard their space shuttle *Jupiter II*, Craig Robinson and his crew embark on a peace-saving mission to help the peaceful Throgs ward off the Tyranos, metallic creatures who have declared war on the Throg planet, in this animated version of television's popular science-fiction series, *Lost in Space.* The hour-long movie, which featured several new characters, premiered on *The ABC Saturday Superstar Movie* series. *A Hanna-Barbera Production. Color. One hour. Premiered on ABC: September 8, 1973 (on The ABC Saturday Superstar Movie). Rebroadcast on ABC: January 5, 1974. Syndicated.*

**Voices**
**Craig Robinson:** Mike Bell; **Deana Carmichael:** Sherry Alberoni; **Linc Robinson:** Vince Van Patten; **Dr. Smith:** Jonathan Harris; **Robot:** Don Messick

*Throgs:*
**Lar/Tyrano Twin One:** Sidney Miller; **Kal/Tyrano Twin Two:** Ralph James; **Brack (child)/Announcer/Narrator:** Don Messick; **Tyrano Guard:** Mike Bell

## ⊚ LOVE AMERICAN STYLE: "LOVE AND THE OLD-FASHIONED FATHER"

Tom Bosley, of TV's *Happy Days* fame, plays the father of teenage daughter (Alice), who creates consternation in her middle-class American home when she asks her parents' permission to go away on a water-skiing weekend with her hippie boyfriend in this *All in the Family*–style cartoon scripted by R.S. Allen and Harvey Bullock, executive producers of the live-action *Love American Style*

series. The all-animated show was one of two half-hour pilots produced and directed by William Hanna and Joseph Barbera. (Its predecessor was entitled, *Love and the Private Eye.*) *A Hanna-Barbera Production for Paramount Television. Color. Half-hour. Premiered on ABC: February 11, 1972.*

**Voices**
**Father:** Tom Bosley; **Mother:** Joan Gerber; **Alice:** Tina Holland

## ⊚ LOVE AMERICAN STYLE: "LOVE AND THE PRIVATE EYE"

Private eye Melvin Danger, a master of disguises who believes he is irresistible to women, delivers a large payroll to an industrial tycoon but loses both payroll and tycoon in the process in this half-hour pilot produced and directed by William Hanna and Joseph Barbera. Originally entitled *Melvin Danger Plus Two*, the story was written by R.S. Allen and Harvey Bullock. Voice artist Lennie Weinrib is credited with having done six character voices for the show. *A Hanna-Barbera Production for Paramount Television. Color. Half-hour. Premiered on ABC: January 28, 1972.*

**Voices**
**Melvin Danger:** Richard Dawson; **Others:** Lennie Weinrib

## ⊚ LUCKY LUKE

This made-for-television movie returns viewers to the wild and woolly days of the Old West, with all the ingredients of a classic sagebrush saga: the strong, silent hero (Lucky Luke), his gallant horse (Jolly), the loyal dog (Bushwhack) and the gang of hardened desperadoes (the Dalton Boys) in an affectionate spoof of the western. *A Hanna-Barbera Production in association with Gaumont Productions and Dargaud Editeur. Color. Two hours. Premiered: 1985. Syndicated.*

**Voices**
**Lucky Luke:** Bill Callaway; **Jolly Jumper:** Bob Ridgely; **Averell:** Bob Holt; **Ma Dalton:** Mitzi McCall; **Jack:** Rick Dees; **Bushwhack:** Paul Reubens; **William:** Fred Travalena; **Joe:** Frank Welker

## ⊚ LUCY, DAUGHTER OF THE DEVIL

A rebellious 21-year-old college student in the role of the anti-Christ battles three Special Fathers who are dispatched to the Vatican to stop her and the devil and DJ Jesus (also known as "C2") and the second coming of Christ in this 15-minute, CGI-animated, satanic horror-comedy cartoon pilot episode that premiered on Cartoon Network's late-hour cartoon block, *Adult Swim.* Lauren Bouchard, who served as an editor, storywriter, producer and director of the award-winning Comedy Central cartoon series *Dr. Katz, Professional Therapist*, created the cartoon. In 2006, Cartoon Network announced plans to produce a ten-episode series based on the pilot that premiered in September 2007. *A Fluid Production. Color. Fifteen minutes. Premiered on CAR: October 30, 2005 (Adult Swim).*

**Voices**
**Lucy:** Jessi Klein; **Ethan:** Todd Barry; **Becky, the Devil's Advocate:** Melissa Bardin Galsky; **Satan/Special Father #1:** H. Jon Benjamin; **The Senator/Special Father #2:** Sam Seder; **DJ Jesus:** Jon Glaser.

## ⊚ LUCY MUST BE TRADED, CHARLIE BROWN

Charlie Brown trades Lucy to Peppermint Patty's baseball team, hopefully to obtain a better player in return and win some more baseball games as a result in this half-hour, prime-time special for ABC. The program was the first of two new specials produced for ABC in 2003, along with *Charlie Brown's Christmas Tales,* which premiered that December. Following the special's premiere that summer, a complete storyboard reproduction from the program was displayed at the Charles M. Schulz Museum in Santa Rosa, California, in conjunction with a baseball-themed exhibit, including baseball-related cartoon cels from previous shows. A *Lee Mendelson-Bill Melendez Production. Color. Half-hour. Premiered on ABC: August 29, 2003. Rebroadcast on ABC: June 12, 2004.*

*Voices*
**Charlie Brown:** Wesley Singerman; **Lucy Van Pelt:** Serena Berman; **Peppermint Patty:** Daniel Hansen; **Schroeder:** Christopher Johnson; **Linus:** Corey Padnos; **Marcie Johnson:** Melissa Montoya; **Snoopy:** Bill Melendez

### ⊚ LYLE, LYLE CROCODILE: THE MUSICAL: "THE HOUSE ON EAST 88TH ST."

This music-filled family special tells the enchanting tale about a family who moves into a new home to find it's already inhabited by a talented reptile named Lyle the Crocodile. The charming green character wins their hearts, until Lyle's rightful owner returns to claim him in this animated version of Bernard Waber's popular tale, "The House on East 88th St." Animator Michael Sporn produced and directed this program, which was first released as a theatrical cartoon short in 1985, then given its world television premiere on the *HBO Storybook Musicals* series showcase. A *Michael Sporn Animation Production in association with Italtoons Corporation. Color. Half-hour. Premiered on HBO: November 18, 1987. Rebroadcast on HBO: November 23, 1987.*

*Voices*
**Hector P. Valenti/Narrator:** Tony Randall; **Mrs. Primm:** Liz Callaway; **Joshua:** Devon Michaels

### ⊚ MADELINE

Twelve little girls live in an old vine-covered house in Paris. The smallest and bravest of them all is Madeline. She experiences many adventures with her housemates and their loving guardian, Miss Clavel, in this musical tale based on the classic 1930s' children's book. The Emmy-nominated special premiered as part of the *HBO Storybook Musicals* series. A *DIC Enterprises Production. Color. Ninety minutes. Premiered on HBO: November 7, 1988. Rebroadcast on FAM: October 7, 1990.*

*Voices*
**Madeline:** Marsha Moreau; **Miss Clavel:** Judith Orban; **Vendor:** John Stocker; **Madeline's friends:** Loretta Jafelice, Linda Kash, Wendy Lands, Daccia Bloomfield, Tara Charendoff; **Narrator:** Christopher Plummer

### ⊚ MADELINE AND THE BAD HAT

Madeline and crew try to tame Pepito, the son of a Spanish ambassador ("The Bad Hat," as Madeline calls him with-with a capital "B"), who pulls all sorts of dastardly deeds on them. One day the young boy goes too far and must learn his lesson in the second of four half-hour specials produced for The Family Channel. A *DIC Enterprises Production. Color. Half-hour. Premiered on FAM: March 3, 1991. Rebroadcast on FAM: October 18, 1991; February 7, 1992.*

*Voices*
**Madeline:** Marsha Moreau; **Narrator:** Christopher Plummer

### ⊚ MADELINE AND THE GYPSIES

Pepito invites Madeline and the girls to a Gypsy carnival and, after getting separated, Pepito and Madeline meet the Gypsy mama who dresses them in a lion's costume. They roam the countryside, inadvertently frightening people and animals alike and discovering, like many children before them, that there's "no place like home," in this half-hour special produced for The Family Channel. A *DIC Enterprises Production. Color. Half-hour. Premiered on FAM: October 14, 1991. Rebroadcast on FAM: August 21, 1992.*

*Voices*
**Madeline:** Marsha Moreau; **Narrator:** Christopher Plummer

### ⊚ MADELINE IN LONDON

Pixieish Parisian Madeline, Miss Clavel and her friends surprise Pepito, who's moved to London with his father, the Spanish ambassador, by giving him a horse. Madcap mishaps ensue and Madeline ends up with a medal from the queen in this Family Channel special whose debut coincided with the repeat performance of 1990's *Madeline's Christmas.* A *DIC Enterprises Production. Color. Half-hour. Premiered on FAM: November 28, 1991. Rebroadcast on FAM: December 20, 1991; April 12, 1992.*

*Voices*
**Madeline:** Marsha Moreau; **Narrator:** Christopher Plummer

### ⊚ MADELINE: MY FAIR MADELINE

While visiting the world-famous Louvre museum in Paris with her friends, Madeline successfully prevents the heist of the famed Mona Lisa painting but is scolded afterward for misbehaving and subsequently deported to a London finishing school to learn better manners. This time, she foils the same thieves again when they try to steal the highly coveted British Crown Jewels in this feature-length special animated in the style of Ludwig Bemelman's original children's books on which this special was based. In 2003, the 90-minute special—part of Nickelodeon's *DIC's Incredible Movie Toons* series—was nominated for a Daytime Emmy Award for outstanding special class animated program. A *DIC Entertainment Production. Color. Ninety minutes. Premiered on NICK: November 11, 2002. Rebroadcast on NICK: November 13, 2002.*

*Voices*
**Miss Clavel:** Whoopi Goldberg; **Madeline:** Chantal Strand; **Mayor of Paris:** Jim Brynes; **Chloe:** Shannon Chan-Kent; **Narrator:** Christopher Gaze (as Chris Gaze); **Mr. Henry:** Mackenzie Gray; **Danielle:** Brittney Irvin; **Miss Higginsbottom:** Marilyn Lightstone; **Emma:** Annick Obonsawin; **Lord Cucuface:** French Tickner; **Nicole:** Jessie Young; **Lady Bovine Ribsby:** Jane Mortifee

### ⊚ MADELINE'S CHRISTMAS

One year at Christmastime, Madeline, her friends and Miss Clavel get ready by making presents for family and friends, but the holiday is nearly ruined when the whole group (except for Madeline) come down with bad colds in this original half-hour special produced for The Family Channel. A *DIC Enterprises Production. Color. Half-hour. Premiered on FAM: November 11, 1990. Rebroadcast on FAM: December 20, 1991; December 3, 1992.*

*Voices*
**Madeline:** Marsha Moreau; **Narrator:** Christopher Plummer

### ⊚ MADELINE'S RESCUE

Madeline's teacher Miss Clavel almost dies, after nearly being scared to death during Madeline's clowning around. She survives thanks to the intercession of a charming dog who becomes the "hero of the day" in this Family Channel original production. *A DIC Enterprises Production. Color. Half-hour. Premiered on FAM: June 6, 1991. Rebroadcast on FAM: June 9, 1991; March 12, 1992; February 5, 1993.*

**Voices**
**Madeline:** Marsha Moreau; **Narrator:** Christopher Plummer

### ◉ THE MAD, MAD, MAD COMEDIANS

The comedy routines of several well-known comedians, culled from excerpts of radio programs and television sketches, are brought to life in this simplistic animated special. *A Bruce Stark Production in association with ABC. Color. Half-hour. Premiered on ABC: April 7, 1970.*

**Voices**
**Jack Benny:** himself; **George Burns:** himself; **The Marx Brothers:** Groucho Marx, Chico Marx, Harpo Marx; **Smothers Brothers:** Tom Smothers, Dick Smothers; **Christopher Columbus:** Flip Wilson; **George Jessel:** himself; **Phyllis Diller:** herself; **Jack E. Leonard:** himself; **Henny Youngman:** himself; **W.C. Fields:** Paul Frees

### ◉ MAD, MAD, MAD MONSTERS

Baron von Frankenstein invites his old friends—Count Dracula, the Wolfman, the Mummy, the Invisible Man and his wife, and his own assistant, Igor—to the ballroom of the Transylvania-Astoria to witness his monster's wedding to the "perfect bride" he has created for him in this hour-long program that was first broadcast as part of the *ABC Saturday Superstar Movie* series. The production was later broadcast on its own as a children's special in reruns on the network and then in syndication. *A Rankin-Bass Production. Color. One hour. Premiered on ABC: September 23, 1972 (on ABC Saturday Superstar Movie). Syndicated.*

**Voices**
Bradley Bolke, Rhoda Mann, Bob McFadden, Allen Swift

### ◉ THE MAGICAL MYSTERY TRIP THROUGH LITTLE RED'S HEAD

Live action and animation are combined in this story of Little Red, a young girl, who is used in an experiment by two youngsters (Carol and Larry) who, reduced in size, explore the girl's mind and learn how people express and deal with their feelings from the inside. An *ABC Afterschool Special. A DePatie-Freleng Enterprises Production. Color. One hour. Premiered on ABC: May 15, 1974. Rebroadcast on ABC: December 11, 1974; April 29, 1978 (as ABC Weekend Specials).*

**Voices**
**Timer:** Lennie Weinrib; **Carol:** Diane Murphy; **Larry:** Ike Eisenmann; **Little Red:** Sarah Kennedy; **Mother/Adeline/Diane:** Joan Gerber

### ◉ THE MAGIC FLUTE

Prince Tamino (voiced by Mark Hamill) embarks on an adventurous quest and, with help from the magic flute, subdues dragons, mercenaries and a duplicitious queen in order to rescue a kidnapped princess in this two-part, hour-long animated adaptation of the famous Mozart opera, broadcast as an *ABC Weekend Special. A Ruby-Spears Production in association with Greengrass Productions. Color. One hour. Premiered on ABC: April 30, 1994 (Part 1) and May 7, 1994 (Part 2). Rebroadcast on ABC: March 18, 1995 (Part 1) and March 25, 1995 (Part 2); February 3, 1996 (Part 1) and* February 10, 1996 (Part 2); June 29, 1996 (Part 1) and July 6, 1996 (Part 2); March 1, 1997 (Part 1) and March 8, 1997 (Part 2).

**Voices**
**Prince Tamino:** Mark Hamill; **Sarastro:** Michael York

### ◉ THE MAGIC LOLLIPOP ADVENTURE

In his animated debut, Lollipop Dragon, named for his love of lollipops, appears doomed when Baron Bad Blood, bent on undermining the success of the lollipop industry in the land of Tumtum, steals the magic wand that gives the lollipops their flavor. *A Blair Entertainment Production in association with Pannonia Film. Color. Half-hour. Premiere: 1986. Syndicated.*

**Voices**
**Lollipop Dragon/Hairy Troll:** Gary Wilmot; **Cosmo the Cunning/King/Herald:** Dennis Greashan; **Baron Bad Blood:** Stephen Thorne; **Blue Eyes:** Karen Fernald; **Magic Mirror/Prince Hubert:** Pat Starr; **Princess Gwendolyn:** Jill Lidstone; **Glider/Queen/Lady of the Forest:** Eva Hadden

### ◉ THE MAGIC OF DR. SNUGGLES

Kindly Dr. Snuggles enters the great balloon race in hopes of winning prize money to help Granny Toots build a new cat hospital. However, a couple of treacherous hoodlums have their own plan to win the race—at any cost. This hour-long special was based on the popular television series *Dr. Snuggles. An American Way Production in association with DePatie-Freleng Enterprises. Color. One hour. Premiered: 1985. Syndicated.*

**Voices**
Cindy Kozacik, Lacoya Newsome, Danielle Romeo, Tony Rosscia, David Scott, Pearl Terry

### ◉ THE MAGIC PAINTBRUSH

Nib, a young boy, acquires a magic paintbrush with which he grants life to objects he chooses to illustrate. The mystical gift brings him more heartache than fulfillment in this prime-time animated special, based on Robin Muller's book of the same name. Sponsored by McDonald's (dubbed *McDonald's Family Theater*), the half-hour program premiered in prime time on CBS. In 1995 ABC reaired the special on its Saturday-evening schedule. *A Marvel Films Production in association with American Film Technologies. Color. Half-hour. Premiered on CBS: April 22, 1993. Rebroadcast on ABC (ABC Weekend Special): June 25, 1995; July 1, 1995.*

**Voices**
**Greedy King:** Michael York; **Nib:** Aaron Metchik; **Sara:** Christa Larson

### ◉ THE MAGIC PEARL

Follows the story of a Chinese American brother and sister, Peter and Jamie Leung, and their grandfather, Popo, who are magically transported to mythical ancient China where they encounter an evil sorceress protected by a white pearl that possesses extraordinary powers in this 90-minute animated special first aired as part of ABC's *Kids Movie Matinee* series. *A Film Roman Production in association with Greengrass Productions. Color. One hour and a half. Premiered on ABC: August 4, 1996. Rebroadcast on ABC: (as an ABC Weekend Special) February 8, 1997 (Part 1) and February 15, 1997 (Part II).*

**Voices**
**Jamie:** Lana McKissack; **Ha Ping:** George Takei; **Other Voices:** Tsai Chin, Amy Hill, France Nuyen

## ⊚ THE MAGIC SCHOOL BUS FAMILY HOLIDAY SPECIAL

Award-winning country singer Dolly Parton provides the voice of Ms. Frizzle's cousin, teaching her students all about "the gift that keeps on giving-recycling," in this hour-long, song-filled yuletide animated special, based on the long-running PBS animated series. A *Nelvana/Scholastic Production. Color. One hour. Premiered on PBS: December 25, 1996.*

### Voices

**Ms. Valerie Frizzle:** Lily Tomlin; **Katrina Eloise "Murph" Murphy, Frizzle's cousin:** Dolly Parton; **Producer:** Malcolm-Jamal Warner; **Ralphael "Ralphie" Tennelli:** Stuart Stone; **Arnold Perlstein:** Danny Tamberelli; **Dorothy Ann:** Tara Meyer; **Wanda Li:** Lisa Yamanaka; **Carlos Ramon:** Daniel DeSanto; **Keesha Franklin:** Erica Luttrell; **Timothy:** Andre Ottley-Lorant

## ⊚ THE MAGIC SCHOOL BUS HALLOWEEN

Ms. Frizzle (voiced by Lily Tomlin) and her gang visit a museum where three classmates get separated from the pack and overcome their fears of unusual creatures in this hour-long live-action/animated adventure based on the popular PBS cartoon series. A *Nelvana/Scholastic Production. Color. One hour. Premiered on PBS: (week of) October 28, 1995.*

### Voices

**Ms. Valerie Frizzle/Institute Inhabitant:** Lily Tomlin; **Producer:** Malcolm-Jamal Warner; **Ralphael "Ralphie" Tennelli:** Stuart Stone; **Arnold Perlstein:** Danny Tamberelli; **Dorothy Ann:** Tara Meyer; **Wanda Li:** Lisa Yamanaka; **Carlos Ramon:** Daniel DeSanto; **Keesha Franklin:** Erica Luttrell; **Timothy:** Andre Ottley-Lorant

## ⊚ THE MAGIC SCHOOL BUS: "INSIDE RALPHIE"

Despite coming down with a high fever and sore throat, Ralphie hosts the planned broadcast on the inner workings of the human bloodstream on the Frizzle News Network from his bed while learning from the story itself the cause of his illness in this half-hour preview special that aired Saturday morning on FOX before the regular weekday series premiere on PBS. Actress Tyne Daly of CBS's *Cagney & Lacey* fame provided the voice of Ralphie's mother. A *Nelvana/Scholastic Production. Color. Half-hour. Premiered on FOX: September 10, 1994.*

### Voices

**Ms. Valerie Frizzle:** Lily Tomlin; **Producer:** Malcolm-Jamal Warner; **Ralphael "Ralphie" Tennelli:** Stuart Stone; **Arnold Perlstein:** Danny Tamberelli; **Dorothy Ann:** Tara Meyer; **Wanda Li:** Lisa Yamanaka; **Carlos Ramon:** Daniel DeSanto; **Keesha Franklin:** Erica Luttrell; **Timothy:** Andre Ottley-Lorant; **Dr. Tennelli, Ralphie's mom:** Tyne Daly

## ⊚ THE MAN WHO PLANTED TREES

Winner of 1988 Oscar for Best Animated Short Subject, this inspiring story of how one man, shepherd Elzear Bouffler, selflessly dedicates his life to growing a forest in a barren, desolate region of the French Alps premiered as a half-hour special on the PBS anthology series *Long Ago & Far Away.* Based on an original story by Jean Giono, Christopher Plummer narrates the film, originally produced by animator Frederic Back in 1987. A *Societe Radio-Canada Production. Color. Half-hour. Premiered on PBS: April 15, 1989. Rebroadcast on PBS: December 7, 1990; November 8, 1992.*

### Voices

**Narrator:** Christopher Plummer

## ⊚ MARCO POLO

Famed adventurer Marco Polo is thrust in the middle of a war between the forces of Kublai Khan and the city of Siang-yan Fu in China in the year A.D. 1260. Aided by his servant Ton-Ton, Polo wins the respect of the Khan as he saves the province of Yunnan from destruction and returns the Khan's captured daughter to safety. An *Air Programs International Production. Color. One hour. Premiered: 1972. Syndicated.*

### Voices

Alistair Duncan, Tim Elliott, Ron Haddrick, Mark Kelly, John Llewellyn, Helen Morse

## ⊚ MARVIN: BABY OF THE YEAR

Tom Armstrong's witty, precocious, diapered comic-strip character is entered into a "baby of the year" contest by his grandparents in the first prime-time special based on Armstrong's beloved creation. A *Southern Star Production. Color. Half-hour. Premiered on CBS: March 10, 1989. Rebroadcast on DIS: August 1, 1992; September 11, 1993.*

### Voices

**Marvin:** Dana Hill; **Chrissy's Mother:** Ruth Buzzi; **Grandma:** Erin Donica; **Meagan:** Patti Dworkin; **Mom:** Kathy Garver; **Dad:** Dave Madden; **Vince:** Jerry Sroka; **Grandpa:** John Stephenson; **Announcer:** Frank Welker

## ⊚ MARVIN—FIRST FLIGHT

Marvin, a man of average looks who builds robots in his underground laboratory, creates a robot (Maxwell) that can change shape, from robot to rocket to automobile, to accommodate Marvin with whatever form of transportation he requires. This program aired on *Special Delivery* on Nickelodeon several years after its United Kingdom television debut. All character voices were performed by voice artist Chris Harris. A *Link Licensing Limited Production. Color. Half-hour. Premiered on NICK: August 1, 1987.*

### Voices

Chris Harris

## ⊚ MARVIN—LONDON CALLING

Sid and Stan are a couple of naughty but likable villains who have invented a "Blitzer"—a gun that stuns people briefly, enabling the bad guys to steal lots of money from shops and banks. With help from his robots Buffer, Maxwell and Micron, Marvin puts the culprits behind bars where they belong. A *Link Licensing Limited Production. Color. Half-hour. Premiered on NICK: 1989.*

### Voices

Chris Harris

## ⊚ THE MARZIPAN PIG

The tale of the marzipan pig, whose sweetness would enchant a lonely mouse, a lovesick owl, a curious bee and a weary hibiscus flower, inspires a dance of love under the light of the moon in this half-hour animated special produced by Emmy Award–winning animator Michael Sporn for HBO, based on Russell Hoban's acclaimed children's book. A *Michael Sporn Animation Production in association with Italtoons Corporation. Color. Half-hour. Premiered on HBO: November 5, 1990.*

### Voices

**Narrator:** Tim Curry

## ⊚ THE MASTERMIND OF MIRAGE POKÉMON

While watching a demonstration of a new Mirage system created by Pokémon scientist Dr. Yung, the high-tech machine runs amok with a Mirage Aerodactyl kidnapping the enigmatic scientist as Ash, Misty and Professor Oak everything possible to thwart the madman's plan in this 10th anniversary one-hour special that debuted on Cartoon Network. *A TV Tokyo/Shogakukan Production Co./Oriental Light and Magic/Goldenball Animation/Hanil Animation//Nintendo/Pokémon USA/TAJ Production in association with Viz Media. Color. One hour. Premiered on CAR: April 29, 2006.*

**Voices**
**Ash Ketchum/Max:** Jamie Peacock; **Misty/May:** Michele Knotz; **Brock:** Bill Rogers; **James/Meowth:** Billy Beach; **Meowth:** Jimmy Zoppi; **Mew:** Katsuyuki Konishi; **Jessie:** Michele Knotz; **Officer Jenny/Nurse Joy:** Diane Stillwell; **Officer Jenny:** Erica Schroeder; **Professor Oak:** Billy Beach; **Mirage Master/Dr. Yung:** Billy Regan; **Narrators:** Ken Gates, Rodger Parsons

## ◎ MASTER OF THE WORLD

Captain Robur, the mad inventor of a fantastic flying machine who bills himself as "Master of the World," sets out to destroy Washington, D.C., with Inspector Strock of the Federal Police fresh on his heels. *A Famous Classic Tales special. An Air Programs International Production. Color. One hour. Premiered on CBS: October 23, 1976. Syndicated.*

**Voices**
Tim Elliott, John Ewart, Ron Haddrick, Judy Morris, Matthew O'Sullivan

## ◎ MEET JULIE

David McAlister, owner of a small security company, takes his nine-year-old daughter along on a trip to Paris, where he has been assigned to guard a jeweled collar to be worn by a rare snow leopard at an exhibit. As an added surprise, he gives his daughter a special computerized doll, Julie, to take with her on the trip. *A DIC Enterprises Production. Color. Half-hour. Premiered: Fall 1987. Syndicated.*

**Voices**
**Julie:** Nicole Lyn; **Carol:** Karen Burthwright

## ◎ MEET THE RAISINS: THE STORY OF THE CALIFORNIA RAISINS

The California Raisins return in their second prime-time special, this time given recognizable personalities and names (A.C., Red, Stretch, and Beebop), in a clever rock documentary parody, tracing the Raisins' rise to stardom from their early days in a band called the Vine-yls. *A Will Vinton Production. Color. Half-hour. Premiered on CBS: November 4, 1988. Rebroadcast on CBS: August 22, 1990. Rebroadcast on DIS: November 7, 1992.*

## ◎ MERLIN AND THE DRAGONS

Kevin Kline narrates this animated chronicle highlighted by dark magic, flying serpents, valorious knights, and wicked and bold adventure. In the days of the wise magical warlord Merlin, young King Arthur doubts his ability to rule. Arthur's prophetic dream leads to Merlin's downfall and reveals to Arthur that he is the true heir to the throne in this animated half-hour based on the characters from the King Arthur legends. Originally produced by Lightyear Entertainment for its *Stories to Remember* series (a series of videos and audio recordings), the program debuted on the PBS anthology series *Long Ago & Far Away. A Lightyear Entertainment Production. Color. Half-hour. Premiered on PBS: November 9, 1991. Rebroadcast on PBS: October 11, 1992.*

**Voices**
**Narrator:** Kevin Kline

## ◎ A MERRY MIRTHWORM CHRISTMAS

Bert Worm, a new resident of Wormingham, is banned from the town's annual holiday pageant after he bungles preparations for the event. The clumsy worm is given a second chance when he proves he can sing in this half-hour holiday special originally produced for Showtime. The special was the first of three Mirthworm specials, followed by 1987's *A Mirthworm Masquerade* and 1988's *Mirthworms on Stage*, each produced for first-run syndication. *A Perennial Pictures Film Corporation Production. Color. Half-hour. Premiered on SHO: December 14, 1984. Syndicated.*

**Voices**
**Bert Worm/Teddy Toddlers/Wilbur Diggs/Baggs:** Jerry Reynolds; **Crystal Crawler:** Rachel Rutledge; **Wormaline Wiggler:** Miki Mathioudakis; **Eulalia Inch/Agnes/Dribble:** Peggy Nicholson; **Mayor Filmore Q. Pettiworm/Eudora Vanderworm:** Russ Harris

## ◎ MICKEY'S CHRISTMAS CAROL

Walt Disney's beloved cartoon creations—Mickey Mouse, Donald Duck, Goofy and others—are cast in this updated version of Charles Dickens's Christmas classic, which features new animation and three previously exhibited adventures—"The Art of Skiing" (1941), "Donald's Snow Fight" (1942) and "Pluto's Christmas Tree" (1952)—in this one-hour holiday special first released as a brand-new theatrical short in 1983. *A Walt Disney Television Production. Color. One hour. Premiered on NBC: December 10, 1984. Rebroadcast on NBC: December 22, 1985; December 15, 1986; December 4, 1987: December 17, 1990. Rebroadcast on CBS: December 13, 1991; December 1, 1993. Rebroadcast on DIS: December 12, 1991; December 23, 1993. Rebroadcast on CBS: December 22, 1994; December 21, 1995; December 19, 1996. Rebroadcast on DIS: December 23, 1995; December 21, 1996. Rebroadcast on CBS: December 19, 1997.*

**Voices**
**Mickey Mouse (Bob Cratchit):** Wayne Allwine; **Uncle Scrooge McDuck (Ebenezer Scrooge):** Alan Young; **Donald Duck (Fred):** Clarence Nash; **Goofy (Ghost of Jacob Marley):** Hal Smith; **Jiminy Cricket (Ghost of Christmas Past):** Eddie Carroll; **Willie the Giant (Ghost of Christmas Present)/Black Pete (Ghost of Christmas Future):** Will Ryan; **Morty (Tiny Tim):** Susan Sheridan; **Daisy Duck (Isabel):** Pat Parris

## ◎ MICKEY'S HAPPY VALENTINE

Mickey, Minnie, Donald Duck and Daisy Duck wrestle with romance in a series of animated sequences accompanied by rock music in this hour-long prime-time special. Included is the 1938 cartoon "Brave Little Tailor," in which Mickey saves mouse-in-distress Minnie from a giant. *A Walt Disney Television Production. Color. One hour. Premiered on NBC: February 12, 1989 (on The Magical World of Disney).*

**Voices**
**Mickey Mouse:** Walt Disney; **Minnie Mouse:** Marcellite Garner; **Donald Duck:** Clarence Nash .

## ◎ MICKEY'S ONCE UPON A CHRISTMAS

Direct-to-video production originally produced in 1999 featuring three all-new Christmas stories starring Mickey and friends: "Stuck on Christmas," with Huey, Dewey and Louie finding that wishing everyday was like Christmas isn't what they'd hoped for; "A Very Goofy Christmas," with Goofy trying to convince his son, Max, to believe in Santa again after his neighbor, Pete, tells him that Santa doesn't exist; and "The Gift of the Magi," with Mickey and Minnie discovering their most cherished gift at Christmas is their love for each other. In December 2000, the 71-minute holiday-themed production, narrated by Kelsey Grammer of TV's *Cheers* and *Frasier* fame, debuted in prime time on the Disney Channel. *A Walt Disney Studios/Walt Disney Animation Canada, Inc./Animation Studio Basara Co., Ltd. Production for Buena Vista Home Video. Color. Seventy-one minutes. Premiered on DIS: December 11, 2000. Rebroadcast on DIS: December 25, 2000; December 17, 2001; December 25, 2001; October 31, 2002; November 29, 2004; December 12, 2004; December 23, 2004; December 25, 2004; December 19, 2005; December 25, 2005; December 1, 2006; December 2, 2006; December 24, 2006.*

**Voices**
**Narrator:** Kelsey Grammer; **Mickey Mouse:** Wayne Allwine; **Minnie/Huey/Dewey/Louie:** Russi Taylor; **Donald Duck:** Tony Anselmo; **Daisy/Chip/Aunt Gertie:** Tress MacNeille; **Uncle Scrooge:** Alan Young; **Goofy:** Bill Farmer; **Dale:** Corey Burton; **Max:** Shaun Flemming; **Pete/Santa/Mailman/Fire Chief:** Jim Cummings; **Mr. Mortimer/Dad:** Jeff Bennett; **Mr. Anderson:** Gregg Berger; **Figaro/The Turkey:** Frank Welker

### ⊚ MIKE MULLIGAN AND HIS STEAM SHOVEL

Mike Mulligan is sure that his steam shovel, Mary Anne, can dig more in one day than 100 men could dig in a week. One terrible day he and Mary Anne lose their job. In desperation, he offers to dig the cellar for Popperville's new town hall for free in this half-hour animated special from the *HBO Storybook Musicals* series. *A Michael Sporn Animation Production in association with Italtoons Corporation. Color. Half-hour. Premiered on HBO: September 10, 1990. Rebroadcast on HBO: September 22, 1991.*

**Voices**
**Narrator:** Robert Klein

### ⊚ THE MINI-MUNSTERS

Herman, Grandpa and the rest of TV's *The Munsters* clan, in animated form, discover that their hearse-dragster runs on music instead of gas in this made-for-television feature that aired on *The ABC Saturday Superstar Movie. A Universal Television Production. Color. One hour. Premiered on ABC: October 27, 1973. Rebroadcast on ABC: January 12, 1974.*

**Voices**
**Herman Munster:** Richard Long; **Lily Munster:** Cynthia Adler; **Grandpa Munster:** Al Lewis; **Mr. Grundy:** Henry Gibson; **Other Voices:** Bobby Diamond, Ron Feinberg

### ⊚ MINORITEAM: "OPERATION BLACKOUT"

A unique band of superheroes possessing their own stereotype-inspired superhuman strengths (El Jefe, Nonstop, Fasto, Jewcano, and Dr. Wang) that fight discrimination wherever it lurks set out to rescue a man (Sebastian Jefferson) who has been kidnapped, waging battle with such evil doers as the White Shadow, the Corporate Ladder and Standardized Testing, in this 15-minute pilot episode, entitled, "Operation Blackout," that premiered as an animated special on Cartoon Network's *Adult Swim*. The program was so successful that the network subsequently commissioned a 20-episode weekly series. *A Cartoon Network Studios Production. Color. Fifteen minutes. Premiered on CAR: November 6, 2005 (on "Adult Swim").*

**Voices**
**Jewcano:** Enn Reitel; **El Jefe:** Nick Puga; **Dr. Wang/Corporate Ladder:** Dana Snyder; **Fasto:** Rodney Saulsberry; **Nonstop:** Keith Lal; **Racist Frankenstein:** Adam De La Pena

### ⊚ THE MIRACLE MAKER

Predominantly stop-motion, clay-animated retelling of the life of Jesus, mixing surreal 2-D animated sequences for Jesus's visions and focusing on his later public life as the world's greatest inspirational figure and miracle worker to those around him and his inevitable crucifixion, featuring a mostly British voice cast, including actors Ralph Fiennes (as Jesus), Julie Christie and Miranda Richardson. Jointly produced in 1999 in Britain and Russia by Emmy winners Christopher Grace and Elizabeth Babakhina of PBS's *Shakespeare: The Animated Tales*, this two-hour epic, originally released to theaters in the United Kingdom in January 2000, debuted in the United States that April on ABC as a prime-time Easter Sunday event. *A Cartwn Cymru/Christmas Films Production. Color. Two hours. Premiered on ABC: April 23, 2000.*

**Voices**
**Jesus:** Ralph Fiennes; **Voice of God/The Doctor:** Michael Byrant; **Rachel, Rebecca:** Julie Christie; **Tamar:** Callard; **Thomas:** James Frain; **Pontius Pilate:** Ian Holm; **Jairus:** William Hurt; **Herod:** Anton Lesser; **Cleopas:** Daniel Massey; **Barabbas:** Tim McInnerny; **Simon the Pharisee:** Alfred Molina; **Joseph of Arimathea:** Bob Peck; **Mary Magdalene:** Miranda Richardson; **Ben Azra:** Anthony Sher; **Andrew:** Ewan Stewart; **Simon Peter:** Ken Stott; **Judas:** David Thewlis

### ⊚ A MIRTHWORM MASQUERADE

In this half-hour springtime special, the evil Miss Wormaline Wiggler spoils the fun for the Mirthworms annual Masquerade Ball when she tries to have herself crowned Queen of the Masquerade Ball. The second in a series of *Mirthworms* specials. *A Perennial Pictures Film Corporation Production. Color. Half-hour. Premiered: April 11, 1987. Syndicated. Rebroadcast on DIS: October 17, 1991.*

**Voices**
**Bert Worm/Teddy Toddlers/Wilbur Diggs/Prince Pringle/Homer/Armbruster:** Jerry Reynolds; **Crystal Crawler:** Rachel Rutledge; **Wormaline Wiggler:** Miki Mathioudakis; **Eulalia Inch/Agnes/Dribble:** Peggy Nicholson; **Eudora Vanderworm/Mayor Filmore Q. Pettiworm:** Russ Harris; **Brooks:** Michael N. Ruggiero; **Chester/Arnold:** Adam Dykstra

*Crystal Crawler and Bert Worm get all dressed up for the Wormingham Masquerade Ball in a scene from* A Mirthworm Masquerade.
© *Perennial Pictures*

## ⊙ MIRTHWORMS ON STAGE

It's curtains for the Wormingham Bowl if the Mirthworms don't put on a successful play in this third *Mirthworms* animated special. A *Perennial Pictures Film Corporation Production. Color. Half-hour. Premiered: December 18, 1998. Syndicated.*

### Voices

**Crystal Crawler:** Rachel Rutledge; **Bert Worm/Teddy Toddlers/Wilbur Diggs:** Jerry Reynolds; **Wormaline Wiggler:** Miki Mathioudakis; **Eulalia Inch/Agnes/Dribble:** Peggy Rowis; **Mayor Filmore Q. Pettiworm:** Russ Harris

## ⊙ MISS SPIDER'S SUNNY PATCH KIDS

Actress Brooke Shields, nearly seven months pregnant at the time, lent her voice as the sweet-natured Miss Spider who marries a noble, bespectacled bug named Holley; they become parents to a family of curious siblings, including their smallest son, Squirt, who wanders in the forest and becomes trapped in the web of the menacing arachnid, Spiderus, but everything turns out well in the end in this hour-long, 3-D computer-animated special based on best-selling author David Kirk's *Miss Spider* children's book series. In September 2004, the film spawned a weekly half-hour series, with actress Kristen Davis of TV's *Sex and the City* replacing Shields as the voice of Miss Spider, broadcast on Nickelodeon's Nick Jr. morning preschool program block. *A Nickelodeon/Nelvana Limited/Callaway & Kirk Production. Color. One hour. Premiered on NICK: March 31, 2003.*

### Voices

**Miss Spider:** Brooke Shields; **Holley:** Rick Moranis; **Spiderus:** Tony Jay; **Squirt:** Scott Beaudin; **Shimmer:** Rebecca Brenner; **Roxie:** Stacey DePass; **Spinner:** Austin Di Iulio; **Wiggle:** Marc Donato; **Pansy:** Aaryn Doyle; **Dragon:** Mitchell Eisner; **Betty Beetle:** Patricia Gage; **Beatrice:** Catherine Gallant; **Snowdrop:** Alexandra Lai; **Bounce:** Julie Lemieux; **Stinky:** Scott McCord; **Gus:** Peter Oldring; **Eunice:** Cara Pifko; **Mr. Mantis:** Wayne Robson; **Mama Snake:** Alison Sealy-Smith; **Grub:** Robert Tinkler; **Ant 1:** Jonathan Wilson; **Ant 2:** Philip Williams

## ⊙ MISS SPIDER'S SUNNY PATCH KIDS: "FROGGY DAY IN SUNNY PATCH"

After hearing scary sounds while playing with Taddy Puddle, thinking the story of a legendary monster is true, Squirt, Shimmer and Spinner are relieved to discover it's only a frog named Felix, whom they befriend and keep secret while the frog-hating Spiderus creates a squad to get rid of them in this all-new half-hour special (also known as *Secret Frog*)—the first of three—based on Nelvana's popular weekday afternoon series on Nickelodeon's Nick Jr. *A Nelvana Limited/Absolute Digital/Callaway Arts & Entertainment Production. Color. Half-hour. Premiered on NICK JR.: June 20, 2005. Rebroadcast on NICK JR.: June 22, 2005.*

### Voices

**Miss Spider:** Kristen Davis; **Holley Spider:** Robert Smith; **Spiderus:** Tony Jay; **Squirt:** Scott Beaudin; **Bounce:** Julie Lemieux; **Shimmer:** Rebecca Brenner; **Dragon:** Mitchell Eisner; **Snowdrop:** Alexandra Lai; **Pansy:** Aaryn Doyle; **Spinner:** Austin Di Iulio; **Wiggle:** Marc Donato; **Stinky:** Scott McCord; **Gus:** Peter Oldring; **Frank:** Keith Knight; **Felix:** Richard Binsley

## ⊙ MISS SPIDER'S SUNNY PATCH KIDS: "THE PRINCE, THE PRINCESS AND THE BEE"

After Shimmer realizes she may be a princess, Miss Spider takes her on an exciting high-flying adventure to see what it is like to come from royalty in this first hour-long movie adventure based on the popular Nick Jr. preschool series. *A Nelvana Limited/Absolute Digital/Callaway Arts & Entertainment Production. Color. One hour. Premiered on NICK JR.: July 24, 2006. Rebroadcast on NICK JR.: July 28, 2006.*

### Voices

**Miss Spider:** Kristen Davis; **Holley Spider:** Robert Smith; **Spiderus:** Tony Jay; **Squirt:** Scott Beaudin; **Bounce:** Julie Lemieux; **Shimmer:** Rebecca Brenner; **Dragon:** Mitchell Eisner; **Snowdrop:** Alexandra Lai; **Pansy:** Aaryn Doyle; **Spinner:** Austin Di Iulio; **Wiggle:** Marc McMulkin; **Betty Beetle:** Patricia Gage; **Mr. Mantis:** Wayne Robson; **Stinky:** Scott McCord; **Eunice Earwig:** Carar Pifko; **Gus:** Peter Oldring; **Beetrice:** Catherine Gallant; **Ned:** Jonathan Wilson; **Ted:** Philip Williams; **Felix:** Richard Binsley; **Lil Sis:** Tajja Isen; **Ruby:** Alessandra Cannito; **Jasper, Ruby's Dad:** Adrian Truss; **Druey, Ruby's Mom:** Catherine Disher; **Feather:** Miranda Jones; **Queen Sapphire:** Laura De Carteret; **King Rigel:** Donald Burda; **Auntie Figwort:** Ellen Ray Hennessy; **Honey:** Isabel de Carteret

## ⊙ MISS SWITCH TO THE RESCUE

In this two-part, hour-long special based on the characters created by Barbara Brooks Wallace, Miss Switch, a good witch in the form of a substitute teacher, comes to the aid of young Rupert when a bad warlock he unwittingly lets out of the bottle kidnaps the boy's friend, Amelia, in this ABC Weekend Special. *A Ruby-Spears Enterprises Production. Color. One hour. Premiered on ABC: January 16, 1982 and January 23, 1982. Rebroadcast on ABC: April 24, 1982 and May 1, 1982; June 18, 1983 and June 25, 1983; February 9, 1985 and February 16, 1985; July 5, 1986 and July 12, 1986; April 4, 1987 and April 11, 1987; February 11, 1989 and February 18, 1989.*

### Voices

**Miss Switch/Guinevere:** Janet Waldo; **Rupert P. Brown III/Peatmouse:** Eric Taslitz; **Amelia Matilda Daley:** Nancy McKeon; **Mordo:** Hans Conried; **Smirch:** Hal Smith; **Banana/Conrad:** Phillip Tanzini; **Bathsheba/Saturna (Crone):** June Foray; **Witch's Book/Old Salt/Mayor:** Walker Edmiston; **Teacher/Barmaid:** Anne Lockhart; **Hector:** Alan Dinehart

## ⊙ MISTER MAGOO'S CHRISTMAS CAROL

Lovable bumbler Mister Magoo is cast as the skinflint Ebenezer Scrooge in this first made-for-TV animated special presented as a play within a play with Magoo headlining a Broadway production based on the Charles Dickens classic. *A UPA Productions of America Production.* In 2003, the perennial holiday favorite was rebroadcast in prime time for the first time in the 8:00 P.M. (ET) time slot on Cartoon Network, followed by annual re-airings through 2005. *Color. One hour. Premiered on NBC: December 18, 1962. Rebroadcast on NBC: December 13, 1963; December 18, 1964; December 17, 1965: December 17, 1966; December 17, 1967. Rebroadcast on DIS: December 3, 1991; December 12, 1992. Rebroadcast on CAR: December 10, 2003; December 23, 2003; December 25, 2003; December 16, 2004; December 24, 2004; December 25, 2004; December 24, 2005; December 25, 2005. Syndicated.*

### Voices

**Ebenezer Scrooge (Mister Magoo):** Jim Backus; **Bob Cratchit:** Jack Cassidy; **Mrs. Cratchit/Children:** Laura Olsher; **Tiny Tim/Christmas Past:** Joan Gardner; **Belle Fezzlwig, Scrooge's first love:** Jane Kean; **Marley's Ghost:** Royal Dano; **Brady/James:** Morey Amsterdam; **Christmas Present:** Les Tremayne; **Old Fezzlwig/Undertaker/Men:** Paul Frees; **Young Scrooge:** Marie Matthews; **Stage Manager/Billings/Milkman:** John Hart

## MISTER MAGOO'S STORYBOOK SNOW WHITE

The fairy-tale version of "Snow White and the Seven Dwarfs" is updated in this prime-time special, featuring Mister Magoo (George) as the elder member of the dwarfs (each the spitting image of him), who protect Snow White from danger. Unlike Walt Disney's feature-length treatment, the dwarfs have names dissimilar to those of the original characters: Axlerod (the leader); Bartholomew (a wizard); Cornelius (a magician); Dexter (a legal expert); George (a daydreamer); Eustes and Ferdinand, who possess no special abilities whatsoever.

Originally broadcast as a two-part episode on NBC's weekly series *The Famous Adventures of Mister Magoo*, the program was rebroadcast in syndication as *Mister Magoo's Storybook*, an hour-long format encompassing three fanciful fables starring Mister Magoo (the others: "Don Quixote" and "A Midsummer Night's Dream" and "Mister Magoo's Storybook Snow White"). *A UPA Productions of America Production. Color. Half-hour. Premiered on NBC: 1964 (as part of* The Famous Adventures of Mister Magoo). *Syndicated.*

### Voices
**George (Mister Magoo)/Axlerod/Bartholomew/Cornelius/Dexter/Eustes/Ferdinand:** Jim Backus; **Snow White:** Julie Bennett; **Queen/Bertha the Peddler/Zelda the Gypsy/Old Crone:** Joan Gardner; **Prince Valor:** Howard Morris; **Demon/Hunter:** Marvin Miller

## MISTER MAGOO'S TREASURE ISLAND

A pack of cutthroat pirates (Blind Pew, Black Dog and others) discover that the proprietor of a seaside inn has a map leading to buried treasure. Led by the seafaring Long John Silver (played by Mister Magoo) and his crew, they set out to find the treasure. The program was originally produced as an episode of NBC's *The Famous Adventures of Mister Magoo* and later rebroadcast as a syndicated special. *A UPA Productions of America Production. Color. Half-hour. Premiered on NBC: 1964–65 (as part of* The Famous Adventures of Mister Magoo). *Syndicated.*

### Voices
**Long John Silver (Mister Magoo):** Jim Backus; **Jim Hawkins:** Dennis King; **Jarvis:** Marvin Miller

## MISUNDERSTOOD MONSTERS

Three terrific monster tales—"Beauty and the Beast," "Creole," and "The Reluctant Dragon"—are featured in this live-action/animation afternoon children's special that combines filmed scenes of host Meeno Peluce, star of TV's *The Voyagers* and *The Bad News Bears. A Bosustow Entertainment Production. Color. One hour. Premiered on CBS: April 7, 1981. Rebroadcast on CBS: January 1, 1982. Syndicated.*

### Voices
**Mouth:** Avery Schreiber; **Creole:** Mickey Rooney; **Bird:** Georgia Engel; **Alligator:** Arte Johnson; **Reluctant Dragon:** Alan Sues; **St. George:** Louis Nye; **Boy:** Sparky Marcus; **Beauty:** Claire Bloom; **Beast:** Michael York; **Narrators:** John Carradine, James Earl Jones, Mickey Rooney

## MOBY DICK

Herman Melville's tragic story of the great white whale, Moby Dick, relentlessly pursued by Captain Ahab and his crew, is retold in this first-run hour-long animated special. *An Air Programs International Production. Color. One hour. Premiered: 1975. Syndicated.*

### Voices
Alistair Duncan, Tim Elliott, Ron Haddrick, Mark Kelly, John Llewellyn

*Mister Magoo and the other six dwarves gather around Snow White in the half-hour primetime network special,* Mister Magoo's Storybook Snow White.

## MOLE'S CHRISTMAS

Christmas Eve finds Mole and Rat unwittingly evading highway thieves as they search for Mole End, Mole's old home, in this holiday half-hour special adapted from Kenneth Grahame's *The Wind in the Willows. An All Time Entertainment Production. Color. Half-hour. Premiered on DIS: December 12, 1995. Rebroadcast on DIS: December 19, 1996.*

### Voices
**Mole:** Peter Davison; **Rat:** Richard Briers; **Young Girl:** Ellie Beaven; **Field Mouse Carol Singers:** Alexander Britten, Benjo Fraser, Oliver Howard, Amanda Lake, Tanya Lake, Sophie Mullen; **Additional Voices:** Arthur Boni, Kees Coolen, Stephen Donald, Jonathan Gabb, Olivia Hallinan, Imelda Staunton, Richard Tate, Paul van Gorcum

## MON COLLE KNIGHTS: "JUST ANOTHER MON-DAY"

Mondo and his girlfriend, Rockna, the daughter of famed scientist Professor Hiragi, embark on their first adventure to stop the evil Prince Eccentro and his mighty minions from unleashing monsters of the dimensional world, called Mon World, in this hour-long special that preceded the weekly Saturday morning series on FOX. *A Studio Deen/Saban Entertainment Production. Color. One hour. Premiered on FOX: July 26, 2001.*

### Voices
**Mondo Ooya:** Derek Stephen Prince; **Rockna:** Brianne Siddall; **Professor Hiragi:** Jamieson Price; **Prince Eccentro:** Joe Ochman; **Tenaka:** Michael Sorich; **Gluko:** Dina Sherman

## MONSTER BED

Trapped in a world of monsters, a young boy tries to go home in this *ABC Weekend Special. A Marvel Production. Color. One hour. Premiered on ABC: September 9, 1989 (on ABC Weekend Special). Rebroadcast on ABC: October 26, 1991.*

### Voices
Charlie Adler, Brandon Crane, Peter Cullen, Katie Leigh, Laurie O'Brien, Hank Saroyan

## MONSTER MASH

Three monsters—Frank (Frankenstein), Drac (Dracula) and Wolf (The Werewolf)—have 24 hours to prove they can scare the Tinklemeister family or they will be sentenced to forever performing at children's parties in this animated musical spin-off of the popular 1960s recording produced in the United States and Italy. On October 22, 1999, the musical special aired in first-run syndication, premiering on Los Angeles's the WB Television Network affiliate KTLA and 10 days later on Halloween on the WB Television Network station WUTV in New York. A year later, the production was released on home video and in 2004 was included among series and specials syndicated to stations across the United States as part of DIC Entertainment's DIC Kids' Network three-hour programming block. *A Guido Manuli/DIC Entertainment/RAI Production. Color. One hour. Premiered: October 22, 1999. Syndicated.*

**Voices**
**Frank:** David Sobolov; **The Wolfman:** Scott McNeil; **Spike/Mom:** Janyse Jaud; **Yorick (singing):** Phil Trainer; **Other Voices:** Ian James Corlett, Robert O. Smith, Jim Byrnes, Patricia Drake, French Tickner, Phil Hayes, Tabitha St. Germain, Dave Ward; **Monster Mash:** David Pavlovitch, W. Harlan May, Jason Michas

### ◎ THE MOO FAMILY® HOLIDAY HOE-DOWN
During the performance of their Christmas special, live from the island of Cowaii, the "moosical" Moo Family (Daddy Moo, Momma Moo, Patty Moo and Baby Moo) hooks up via "saddle-lite" to the North Pole, only to discover that Santa Cow's new Turbo Sleigh and his ace sled jockey, Chuck Steaker, have vanished. First in a series of Moo Family syndicated specials produced by Calico Entertainment. The Moo Family® is a registered trademark of Calico Creations, Ltd. *A Calico Entertainment Production. Color. Half-hour. Premiered: November 1992. Syndicated. Rebroadcast: November 26–27, 1993 (as part of Bohbot Entertainment's Kid's Day Off block).*

**Voices**
**Professor Albert Holstein/Santa Cow:** Jim Cummings; **Chuck Steaker:** Pat Fraley; **Momma Moo:** Tress MacNeille; **Chick Bantam/T. Bone:** Rob Paulsen; **Daddy Moo:** Brian Cummings; **Patty Moo/Baby Moo:** B.J. Ward

### ◎ THE MOO FAMILY® STALL OF FAME
While the Moo Family is preparing for a reunion and concert, Bad Moos! Professor Holstein's Time Tracker goes haywire, sending the

*Santa takes his new Turbo Sleigh for a ride in the first in a series of Moo Family syndicated specials produced by Calico Entertainment, The Moo Family® Holiday Hoe-Down. © Calico Creations Ltd. All rights reserved.*

beloved bovines into the past on one radical hayride, where there they meet a herd of their bulldacious ancestors. The Moo Family® is a registered trademark of Calico Creations, Ltd. *A Calico Entertainment Production. Color. Half-hour. Premiered: November 27–28, 1993. Syndicated.*

**Voices**
**Professor Albert Holstein:** Jim Cummings; **Chuck Steaker/Robin Hoof:** Pat Fraley; **Momma Moo:** Tress MacNeille; **Chick Bantam/Two-Ton-Cow-Man:** Rob Paulsen; **Daddy Moo:** Brian Cummings; **Patty Moo/Baby Moo/Cowapatra:** B.J. Ward

### ◎ MORAL OREL: THE BEST CHRISTMAS EVER
Trying his best to be a good Christian but often misinterpreting theology, which causes problems in the end, Orel believes that his younger brother Shapey, lying in a manger scene at a local church, is "the second coming" of Christ in this offbeat, 15-minute cartoon—described as a cross between *Davey and Goliath* and *South Park*—created by Dino Stamatopoulos of *Late Night with Conan O'Brien*, *Mr. Show* and *TV Funhouse* fame. The pilot premiered as a special on Cartoon Network's *Adult Swim* late night cartoon block for mature audiences. Its success spawned a series of 10 episodes ordered by the network. *A Moral Oral/Shadow Machine Films/Williams Street Production. Color. Fifteen minutes. Premiered on CAR: December 13, 2005 (Adult Swim). Rebroadcast on CAR: December 24, 2006.*

**Voices**
**Orel:** Carolyn Lawrence; **Shapey, his younger brother:** Tigger Stamatopoulos; **Clay/Doughy:** Scott Adsit; **Coach Stopframe/Officer Papermouth/Principal Fakey:** Jay Johnston; **Reverend Putty:** William Salyers; **Bloberta/Stephanie/Miss Sculptham/Nurse Blinkless/Tommy:** Britta Phillips

### ◎ MORE HUNGARIAN FOLKTALES
Hungary's MTV Enterprises produced this sequel to the popular *Hungarian Folktales*, an animated collection of short films broadcast on PBS's live-action/animated series *Long Ago & Far Away*. This second animated half-hour offered four short animated films, each based on traditional folktales from Hungary. *An MTV Enterprises, Hungary Production. Color. Half-hour. Premiered on PBS: October 6, 1990.*

**Voices**
**Narrator:** Tammy Grimes

### ◎ MOTHER GOOSE: A RAPPIN' AND RHYMIN' SPECIAL
Having had enough of "all of this rhymin' stuff," Mother Gooseberg decides to retire. Her fairy-tale friends Old King Cole, Humpty Dumpty, Jack and Jill and a host of others try to persuade her to change her mind in this prime-time half-hour special, part of HBO's *Happily Ever After: Fairy Tales for Every Child* series. *A Hyperion Animation Production. Color. Ninety minutes. Premiered on HBO October 12, 1997.*

**Voices**
**Mother Gooseberg:** Whoopi Goldberg; **Humpty Dumpty/Crooked Man:** Denzel Washington; **Old King Cole:** Jimmy Smits; **Jack and Jill:** Regis Philbin, Kathie Lee Gifford; **The Three Little Kittens:** Salt-N-Peppa; **Little Bo Beep:** Jackee Harry; **Mary/Little Lamb:** Nell Carter; **Little Miss Muffet:** Lauren Tom; **Spider:** Dave Chappelle; **Sgt. Louie:** Robert Pastorelli; **Mother Hubbard:** Marla Gibbs; **Farmer:** George Wallace; **Pigs #1–#5:** Rockapella;

**Tommy Tucker:** Franklin Wright; **Boogie Man:** Steve Wright; **Child:** Camille Winbush

## MOUSE ON THE *MAYFLOWER*

In this animated retelling of the first Thanksgiving, Willum Mouse (voiced by Tennessee Ernie Ford) accompanies the Pilgrims to America and aids the valiant pioneers in their struggle for freedom in a new world. *A Rankin-Bass Production. Color. Half-hour. Premiered on NBC: November 23, 1968. Rebroadcast on NBC: November 25, 1971; Rebroadcast on DIS: November 11, 1995. Syndicated.*

*Voices*

**Willum Mouse (narrator):** Tennessee Ernie Ford; **Pricilla Mullens:** Joanie Sommers; **John Alden:** John Gary; **Miles Standish:** Eddie Albert; **William Bradford/Quizzler/Others:** Paul Frees; **Indian Mouse/Scurv/Others:** June Foray

## MOUSE SOUP

A small but clever mouse (voiced by comedian Buddy Hackett) evades a hungry weasel by telling him stories in this delightful program based on the book by award-winning children's author/illustrator Arnold Lobel. The show debuted on PBS's award-winning series *Long Ago & Far Away*. *A Churchill Films Production. Color. Half-hour. Premiered on PBS: November 29, 1992.*

*Voices*

**Pete:** Buddy Hackett; **Other Voices:** Pat Musick, Hal J. Rayle, Will Ryan

## MOWGLI'S BROTHERS

Roddy McDowall narrates the story of a small boy raised by wolves and taught about love, justice and the jungle code of loyalty in this final installment based on Rudyard Kipling's *The Jungle Book* and adapted for television by Chuck Jones. *A Chuck Jones Enterprises Production. Color. Half-hour. Premiered on CBS: February 11, 1976. Rebroadcast on CBS: May 6, 1977; April 4, 1978; June 16, 1979; August 19, 1981. Rebroadcast on NICK: October 12, 1991. Syndicated.*

*Voices*

**Mowgli/Shere Khan/Akela/Tabaqui/Babheera/Baloo:** Roddy McDowall; **Mother Wolf:** June Foray

## ¡MUCHA LUCHA!'S "THE MATCH BEFORE CHRISTMAS" (A.K.A. "A MUCHO MUCHA CHRISTMAS")

Led by Buena Girl, the Luchadores (The Flea, Rikochet and Snow Pea) save Christmas by stopping Santa Claus's evil twin brother, Rudo Claus, and rescuing the real Santa who has been infected with pink eye in this half-hour special from the popular weekly series, *¡Mucha Lucha!*, originally entitled *A Mucho Mucha Christmas* and broadcast on the WB Television Network's Kids' WB! in December 2004. A year later the program was retitled *¡Mucha Lucha!'s The Match before Christmas* and rebroadcast on Cartoon Network. *A Warner Bros. Animation Production. Color. Half-hour. Premiered on Kids' WB!: December 11, 2004. Rebroadcast on CAR: December 9, 2005.*

*Voices*

**Buena Girl/Snow Pea:** Kimberly Brooks; **The Flea:** Candi Milo; **Rikochet:** Carlos Alazraqui; **Timmy of a Thousand Masks:** Matt Hill

## MUMFIE'S WHITE CHRISTMAS

The lovable little elephant with the great big heart fulfills a promise to his friends, Scarecrow and Pinkey, that their Christmas will

*Scene from Britt Alcroft's* Magic Adventures of Mumfie *series. © Britt Alcroft Limited*

be "white" in this special half-hour edition of the Saturday-morning series, *Adventures of Mumfie*, which premiered on the Fox Network. *A Britt Allcroft Production. Color. Half-hour. Premiered on FOX: December 23, 1995.*

*Voices*

**Mumfie/Narrator:** Patrick Breen

## MY FRIEND LIBERTY

The story of the Statue of Liberty is told by the green goddess herself in this half-hour "claymation" special, featuring cameo celebrity caricatures. The program, produced by Mimi Mervis, debuted on The Disney Channel. *A Illustrious Entertainment, Ltd. Production. Color. Half-hour. Premiered on DIS: June 9, 1992. Rebroadcast on DIS: June 15, 1993.*

## MY GYM PARTNER'S A MONKEY: "THE BIG FIELD TRIP"

Adam joins the school's band in order to participate in the annual field trip, but his much-anticipated trip becomes a much bigger adventure when the tour bus crashes, stranding Adam, his friends and faculty members in the woods in this hour-long original movie that premiered in prime time on Sunday, January 14, 2006, on Cartoon Network. The special was preceded by an all-day *My Gym Partner's a Monkey* marathon, starting at 9 A.M. *A Cartoon Network Studios Production. Color. One hour. Premiered on CAR: January 14, 2006. Rebroadcast on CAR: March 5, 2007; March 31, 2007.*

*Voices*

**Adam Lyon:** Nikka Futterman; **Jake Spidermonkey:** Tom Kenny; **Lupe Toucan:** Grey DeLisle; **Mrs. Tusk:** Cree Summer

## MY LIFE AS A TEENAGE ROBOT: "ESCAPE FROM CLUSTER PRIME"

After accidentally ending up on the planet Cluster Prime, ruled by Queen Vexus and her army of robots, Jenny rescues enslaved robots while being deceived by a new robot friend. Meanwhile, back on Earth, Mrs. Wakeman and the boys band together to prevent Vexus from launching a full-scale invasion of Earth in this 60-minute movie special, based on the critically-acclaimed Nickelodeon cartoon series created by Rob Renzetti that debuted on Nickelodeon in August 2005. The special was nominated for a 2006 Emmy

Award for animated program (for programming one hour or more). *A Frederator Incorporated Production. Color. One hour. Premiered on NICK: August 12, 2005. Rebroadcast on NICK: August 13, 2005; August 14, 2005; August 15, 2005; September 5, 2005; September 9, 2005; November 20, 2005; December 31, 2005.*

**Voices**
**Jenny:** Janice Kawaye; **Brad:** Chad Doreck; **Tuck:** Audrey Wasilewski; **Mrs. Wakeman:** Candi Milo; **Sheldon Lee:** Quinton Flynn; **Brit Krust:** Moira Quirk; **Tiff Krust:** Cree Summer; **Krackus:** Jim Ward; **Vega:** Thora Birch; **Queen Vexus:** Eartha Kitt; **Smytus:** Steven Jay Blum

### ◎ MY LITTLE PONY

Thirteen-year-old Megan and her pony friends, who live in magical Dream Valley, find their perfect life ruined when the villainous half-horse Tirac arranges for the Stratadons to kidnap several of the ponies and whisk them away to his dingy Midnight Castle in this fantasy adventure. *A Sunbow Production in association with Marvel Productions. Color. Half-hour. Premiered: April 1984. Syndicated.*

**Voices**
**Firefly:** Sandy Duncan; **Moochick:** Tony Randall

### ◎ MY LITTLE PONY: ESCAPE FROM CATRINA

Following a costume ball in her honor, Megan must save the baby ponies of Dream Valley from the evil catlike creature, Catrina, in this second first-run special based on the popular greeting card characters. *A Sunbow Production in association with Marvel Productions and Toei Animation. Color. Half-hour. Premiered: April 1985. Syndicated.*

**Voices**
**Rep:** Paul Williams; **Catrina:** Tammy Grimes

### ◎ MY SMURFY VALENTINE

Smurfette learns an important lesson about love as the Smurfs save the world from the spell of the evil sorceress, Chlorhydris, who plans to cause a total eclipse of the sun in this Valentine's Day special. *A Hanna-Barbera Production in association with SEPP International. Color. Half-hour. Premiered on NBC: February 13, 1983.*

**Voices**
**Papa Smurf/Azrael/Vulture:** Don Messick; **Harmony/Greedy/Ogre:** Hamilton Camp; **Handy/Lazy/Grouchy:** Michael Bell; **Vanity:** Alan Oppenheimer; **Brainy/Serpent/Ogre:** Danny Goldman; **Clumsy/Bear/Serpent #1:** Bill Callaway; **Smurfette:** Lucille Bliss; **Gargamel:** Paul Winchell; **Jokey/Smurfberry Bird:** June Foray; **Poet/Hefty/Cat:** Frank Welker; **Cupid:** Joe Besser; **Chlorhydris:** Amanda McBroom

### ◎ THE MYSTERIOUS ISLAND

Five Confederate prisoners (Gideon, Herbert, Neb, Captain Harding and Captain Jack) escape during the Civil War in a hot-air balloon, only to crash-land on a remote island in the Pacific, where they encounter danger and destruction in this adaptation of the Jules Verne novel. *A Famous Classic Tales special. An Air International Production. Color. One hour. Premiered on CBS: November 15, 1975. Rebroadcast on CBS: November 25, 1976; April 14, 1990. Syndicated.*

**Voices**
Alistair Duncan, Tim Elliott, Ron Haddrick, Mark Kelly, John Llewellyn

### ◎ NANNY AND THE PROFESSOR

The story of Phoebe Figalilly, the enchanting housekeeper of Professor Harold Everett, who possesses the ability to spread love and joy, is caricatured in this hour-long animated story based on the popular 1970s' television show of the same name. *A Fred Calvert Production. Color. One hour. Premiered on ABC: September 30, 1972. Rebroadcast on ABC: December 8, 1973. Syndicated.*

**Voices**
**Nanny (Phoebe Figalilly):** Juliet Mills; **Professor Everett:** Richard Long; **Hal Everett:** David Doremus; **Prudence Everett:** Kim Richards; **Butch Everett:** Trent Lehman; **Aunt Henrietta:** Joan Gerber

### ◎ NANNY AND THE PROFESSOR AND THE PHANTOM OF THE CIRCUS

When Aunt Henrietta reports the mysterious disappearance of several performers from her traveling circus, Nanny, Professor Everett and company try locating the source of the problem in this sequel to 1972's animated version of television's *Nanny and the Professor* series. The special was originally broadcast on *The ABC Saturday Superstar Movie* series. *A Fred Calvert Production. Color. One hour. Premiered on ABC: November 17, 1973 (on The ABC Saturday Superstar Movie). Syndicated.*

**Voices**
**Nanny (Phoebe Figalilly):** Juliet Mills; **Professor Everett:** Richard Long; **Hal Everett:** David Doremus; **Prudence Everett:** Kim Richards; **Butch Everett:** Trent Lehman; **Aunt Henrietta:** Joan Gerber; **Waldo:** Thurl Ravenscroft; **Zambini:** Walker Edmiston; **Lazlo:** Paul Shively; **Arturo:** Dave Ketchum

### ◎ THE NANNY CHRISTMAS SPECIAL: "OY TO THE WORLD"

Fran Fine (played by Fran Drescher) takes Brighton and the gang on a *Wizard of Oz*–like journey to the North Pole, where she flirts with a sexy Santa Claus, sings with elves and battles an evil princess in this prime-time animated holiday special based on the popular CBS sitcom. Regulars from the live-action series (who first appear in a live-action opening) provide voices for this animated holiday outing. *A Sternin-Frasier Ink Production. Color. Half-hour. Premiered on CBS: December 18, 1995.*

**Cast/Voices**
**Fran Fine:** Fran Drescher; **Maxwell Sheffield:** Charles Shaughnessy; **Niles, the butler:** Daniel Davis; **C.C. Babcock:** Lauren Lane; **Margaret "Maggie" Sheffield:** Nicholle Tom; **Brighton Sheffield:** Benjamin Salisbury; **Grace Sheffield:** Madeline Zima

### ◎ NASCAR RACERS: THE MOVIE

Consisting of three half-hour episodes strung together—"The Real Thing," "The Stakes," and "Heroes,"—Team Fastex outraces the evil Team Rexcor in this futuristic, animated NASCAR movie. Originally called *NASCAR Racers: The Movie, Part I* and *NASCAR Racers: The Movie, Part II*, respectively, the film spawned a weekly Saturday-morning series on FOX and its sister cable network, FOX Family Channel. *A Saban Entertainment Production. Color. Two hours. Premiered on FOX: November 20, 1999.*

**Voices**
**Mark "Charger" McCutchen:** Ian James Corlett; **Megan "Spitfire" Fassler:** Kathleen Barr; **Carlos "Stunts" Rey:** Rino Romano;

Steve "Flyer" Sharp: Roger R. Cross; **Miles McCutchen:** Andrew Francis; **Garner Rexton:** Ron Halder; **Redline:** Kirby Morrow; **Specks:** Richard Newman; **Mike Hauger:** Dale Wilson

## ◎ NESTOR, THE LONG-EARED CHRISTMAS DONKEY

Nestor, a young, ridiculous-looking donkey, is chosen above all others to guide Mary and Joseph to Bethlehem in this animated variation of "The Ugly Duckling" based on a song by Gene Autry. Singer/songwriter Roger Miller narrates the Animagic production, featuring additional music and lyrics by Maury Laws and Jules Bass. Writer Romeo Muller, the man behind such holiday classics as *Rudolph, The Red-Nosed Reindeer, Frosty the Snowman* and *The Little Drummer Boy*, originally wrote the story for his mother, who died December 23, 1947. *A Rankin-Bass Production. Color. Half-hour. Premiered on ABC: December 3, 1977. Rebroadcast on ABC: December 13, 1978; December 7, 1979; Rebroadcast on FAM: December 15, 1995; December 13, 1996. Rebroadcast on FOX FAM: December 3, 1998; December 22, 1998; December 2 1999; December 24, 1999; December 14, 2000; December 18, 2000; December 24, 2000. Rebroadcast on ABC FAM: December 1, 2001; December 5, 2001; December 21, 2001; December 24, 2001; December 2, 2002; December 24, 2002; December 4, 2003; December 6, 2003; December 4, 2004; December 20, 2004; December 2, 2005; December 3, 2005; December 13, 2005; December 9, 2006; December 19, 2006; December 24, 2006. Syndicated.*

### Voices

**Nestor, the long-eared donkey:** Eric Stern; **Nestor's Mother:** Linda Gray; **Tillie, the cherub:** Brenda Vaccaro; **Olaf:** Paul Frees; **Girl Donkey #1:** Iris Rainer; **Girl Donkey #2:** Shirley Hines; **Roman Soldier:** Don Messick; **Narrator:** Roger Miller

## ◎ THE NEW ADVENTURES OF MOTHER GOOSE

A young publisher (played by Emmanuel Lewis of *Webster* fame) enjoins Mother Goose (Sally Struthers from TV's *All in the Family*) to "communicate with kids today and write gentle rhymes for happy times" in this hour-long live-action/animated special featuring retooled versions of popular nursery rhymes, including "Three Blind Mice" (as "Three Kind Mice"). *A Martindale-Hiller Entertainment Production. Color. One hour. Premiered: April 15, 1995. Syndicated.*

### Cast/Voices

**Publisher:** Emmanuel Lewis; **Mother Goose:** Sally Struthers

## ◎ NEW KIDS ON THE BLOCK CHRISTMAS SPECIAL

Donnie Wahlberg (in cartoon form) and the rest of the group help to make Christmas brighter for an eight-year-old Puerto Rican boy named Albert, his mother, Rosa, and less fortunate children, only to learn later that Albert was an angel in disguise. This prime-time, live-action/animated special was first broadcast on ABC. Featuring music from several of the pop-music group's albums as background and live-action segments of the "real" New Kids recalling Yuletides past and performing "This One's for the Children" (closing the show), the half-hour special was spun off from the Saturday-morning series, also broadcast on ABC. *A DIC Animation City/Big Step Production. Color. Half-hour. Premiered on ABC: December 14, 1990.*

### Voices

**Donnie Wahlberg:** David Coburn; **Jordan Knight:** Loren Lester; **Joe McIntyre:** Scott Menville; **Danny Wood:** Brian Mitchell; **Jonathan Knight:** Matt E. Mixer; **Dick Scott:** Dave Fennoy; **Biz-** cut: J.D. Hall; **Rosa:** Theresa Saldana; **Hubbie:** Pat Fraley; **Albert:** Joshua Weiner

## ◎ THE NEW MISADVENTURES OF ICHABOD CRANE

Based on the Washington Irving novel, cowardly schoolteacher Ichabod Crane rescues the tiny village of Sleepy Hollow from the supernatural forces of the Headless Horseman and the evil witch, Velma Van Dam, who has cast a spell upon the quiet little town. This syndicated special was originally produced for Canadian television. *A Titlecraft-Lou Reda Production in association with Atkinson Film-Arts Productions. Color. Half-hour. Premiered (U.S.): October 1979. Syndicated.*

### Voices

**Ichabod Crane:** The Amazing Kreskin; **Washington:** Pat Buttram; **Wolf:** George Lindsay; **Velma Van Dam:** Hazel Shermet; **Rip Van Winkle:** Larry D. Mann; **Mayor:** Monty Morgan; **Vocalist:** Bobby Van

## ◎ NEW YEAR PROMISE

Young Davey Hansen resolves that he won't yell at his little sister, Sally, any more. He decides the only way he can keep his promise is not to talk to her at all, causing her to run away in this religious special produced in conjunction with the Lutheran Church of America. Art Clokey, creator of Gumby, produced the special featuring puppets brought to life by stop-motion animation. *A Clokey Production for the Lutheran Church of America. Color. Half-hour. Premiered: January 1967. Syndicated.*

### Voices

**Davey Hansen/Sally Hansen/Mary Hansen:** Norma McMillan, Nancy Wible; **Goliath/John Hansen:** Hal Smith

## ◎ NICHOLAS NICKLEBY

Nicholas Nickleby, a young energetic lad, learns some valuable lessons about life through a series of misadventures including the kidnapping of his sister and death of his longtime friend Smike, in this colorfully produced adaptation of Charles Dickens's classic novel. *A Burbank Films Production. Color. Half-hour. Premiered: Fall 1984. Syndicated.*

## ◎ NICK AND NOEL

Beautiful house cat Noel enlists the help of her neighbor, the more worldly dog Nick, in search of the one thing that will make a wish come true for Noel's dreamy-eyed little girl owner, Sarah. They embark on a series of heart-pounding adventures in this half-hour animated special narrated by Grammy Award–winning singer/composer Paul Williams (as the lovable old mouse Barnaby) and backed by original songs. *A Film Roman Production in association with Toys 'R' Us and Bohbot Entertainment. Color. Half-hour. Premiered: 1994. Syndicated.*

### Voices

**Noel:** Kath Soucie; **Nick:** Jerry Houser; **Barnaby:** Paul Williams; **Sarah:** Anndi McAfee; **Leslie:** Lorna Patterson; **Howard:** Mark Taylor; **Doberman Duck:** Frank Welker

## ◎ THE NIGHT BEFORE CHRISTMAS (1968)

Television star Art Linkletter hosts this yuletide special about Clement Clark Moore, a professor who writes a special story, "A Visit from St. Nicholas," for his ailing daughter, Charity, who was seriously ill with pneumonia. The special was backed by the music of the Norman Luboff Choir. *An ELBA Production in association* with *Playhouse Pictures. Color. Half-hour. Premiered: December 1968. Syndicated.*

**Voices**
Douglas Crowther, Barbara Eiler, Virginia Gregg, Hal Smith, Olan Soule, Laura Turnbull, Shari Turnbull

### ◎ THE NIGHT BEFORE CHRISTMAS (1991)
Clement C. Moore's beloved poem and stirring illustrated renditions of popular Christmas carols are read by actress Meryl Streep in this half-hour adaptation which premiered on Showtime. The program was part of Rabbit Ear Video's *Holiday Classics* video series. *A Rabbit Ears Video Production. Color. Half-hour. Premiered on SHO: 1991. Rebroadcast on SHO: December 20, 1992. Rebroadcast on FAM: December 11, 1997. Rebroadcast on FOX FAM: December 19, 1998; December 25, 1998; July 10, 1999; December 3, 1999; December 24, 1999; December 8, 2000; December 15, 2000. Rebroadcast on ABC FAM: December 8, 2001.*

**Voices**
**Narrator:** Meryl Streep

### ◎ THE NIGHT BEFORE CHRISTMAS: A MOUSE TALE
Left cold and homeless on Christmas Eve after their underground home is tragically bulldozed over, the Mouse family takes up residence in the Atwell family home where they learn the true meaning of Christmas in this delightful animated special based on the beloved poem by Clement C. Moore. Produced in 2002 by Los Angeles's PorchLight Entertainment, the hour-long direct-to-video holiday production premiered three years later on Cartoon Network. *A PorchLight Entertainment Production in association with VIDEAL. Color. One hour. Premiered on CAR: December 17, 2005. Rebroadcast on CAR: December 19, 2005; December 21, 2005.*

**Voices**
Jane Alan, Ron Allen, Donald Bradford, Kathy Franks, Bruce D. Johnson, Wendee Lee, Julie Maddalena, Bob Marx, B.G. Mills, Brian Richard Peck

### ◎ THE NIGHT B4 CHRISTMAS
Original 2003 holiday tale about one of Santa's elves Elvin who leaves the North Pole to embark on an improbable journey, joined by a gnome, a dog (Pup Daddy) and a girl (Jel-O) he meets along the way, to fulfill his lifelong dream of becoming a pop music star in this hip-hop-infused animated special featuring the vocal talents of Aries Spears (of FOX's *MADTV*), recording artist Chali 2NA of Jurassic 5 and comedian Earthquake from Paramount's live-action comedy feature, *Kings of Comedy 2*. Directed by Tom Tataranowicz and produced by Korea's Sunwoo Entertainment and Nite B4 Productions, the 70-minute direct-to-video production debuted on Cartoon Network in December 2003. *A Sunwoo Entertainment/Nite B4Production in association with Urban Works Entertainment. Color. One hour and 10 minutes. Premiered on CAR: December 2, 2003. Rebroadcast on CAR: December 9, 2003; December 22, 2003; December 23, 2003; December 3, 2004; December 24, 2004; December 7, 2005; December 21, 2005; December 22, 2005; December 23, 2005; December 24, 2005; December 25, 2005; December 21, 2006; December 24, 2006; December 25, 2006.*

**Voices**
**Elvin:** Aries Spears; **Pup Daddy:** Chali 2NA; **Santa:** Earthquake

### ◎ THE NIGHTINGALE
Based on the classic Hans Christian Andersen fairy tale, this faithful retelling is the story of a lonely emperor and the captivating songbird that comes to live in his beautiful palace. The emperor is entranced by the sweetness of the bird's song until a dazzling mechanical bird with a wind-up song comes between them. This half-hour animated film, created especially for PBS's long-running series *Long Ago & Far Away*, was produced by award-winning animator Michael Sporn for PBS. *A Michael Sporn Animation in association with Italtoons Corporation Production. Color. Half-hour. Premiered on PBS: November 22, 1992.*

**Voices**
**The Emperor:** Mako

### ◎ NIGHT OF THE HEADLESS HORSEMAN
Timid 18th-century schoolmaster Ichabod Crane encounters the ghostly night rider, the Headless Horseman, summoned by the evil Brom Bones who stops at nothing to teach Crane a lesson for trying to romance the same woman he's in love with, the beautiful Katrina Van Tassel, in this motion-captured, computer-animated version of the classic Washington Irving story directed by Shane Williams and written by John Shirley for the FOX network. *A Fox Television Studios/Cinematek/Computed Animated Technology/Locomotion Studios Production. Color. One hour. Premiered on FOX: October 29, 1999.*

**Voices**
**Ichabod Crane:** William H. Macy; **Brom Bones:** Luke Perry; **Van Ripper:** Mark Hamill; **Katrina Van Tassel:** Tia Carrere; **Hessian Trooper:** Clancy Brown

### ◎ THE NIGHT THE ANIMALS TALKED
Animals reenact the scene of the Nativity where the Christ child is born, with a new wrinkle—the animals accept the "visitor" and spread the message of love to all mankind. *A Gamma Films Production. Color. Half-hour. Premiered on ABC: December 9, 1970. Rebroadcast on ABC: December 17, 1971; December 15, 1972; December 15, 1973; December 24, 1977. Syndicated.*

**Voices**
**Donkey:** Frank Porella; **Ox:** Joe Silver; **Cow:** Pat Bright; **Goat:** Bob Kaliban

### ◎ NINE DOG CHRISTMAS
When Santa's famous reindeer suddenly come down with the flu with only a few days left until Christmas, nine amazing dogs step in to replace them after a near-sighted elf mistakes them for reindeer, and help the old St. Nick bring joy and presents to children all over the world in this holiday special, narrated by James Earl Jones and produced by California-based Earthworks Entertainment and JRS Properties. The one-hour special, which also was released to the DVD/home video market, premiered on Sunday, December 19, 2004, at 3:00 P.M. (ET) on Cartoon Network. *An Earthworks Entertainment/JRS Properties Production. Color. Half-hour. Premiered on CAR: December 19, 2004. Rebroadcast on CAR: December 23, 2004; December 24, 2004; December 25, 2004; December 24, 2005; December 24, 2006.*

**Voices**
**Narrator:** James Earl Jones; **Buzz:** Scott Hamilton; **Agnes Ann:** Christy Lynn

### ◎ NOAH'S ANIMALS
The biblical story of Noah's Ark is retold in animated form. The animals are led to safety by a raven whom Noah has trusted to

bring them aboard for the 40-day voyage. *A Shamus Culhane Production in association with Westfall Productions. Color. Half-hour. Premiered on ABC: April 5, 1976. Rebroadcast on ABC: December 25, 1977. Syndicated. Rebroadcast on DIS: May 14, 1993.*

**Voices**
**Noah:** Henry Ramer; **Crocodile:** John Soles; **Female Elephant:** Bonnie Brooks; **Male Giraffe/Camel:** Jay Nelson; **Ostrich:** Ruth Springford; **Polar Bear:** Don Mason; **Lion:** Carl Banas; **Walrus:** Jack Mather; **Male Elephant:** Murray Westgate; **Female Baby Crocodile:** Judy Sinclair; **Male Baby Crocodile:** Cardie Mortimer; **Others:** Wendy Thatcher

## ⊚ NOAH'S ARK

In preparation for his cleansing the world by flood, God instructs Noah and his family to build a huge ark and take aboard it one pair of every creature on Earth in this animated retelling of one of the Bible's most beloved stories, based on Peter Spier's Caldecott Award–winning book. Originally produced for Lightyear Entertainment's *Stories to Remember* video and audio recording series, the half-hour program made its television premiere on PBS's *Long Ago & Far Away* series. *A Lightyear Entertainment/Shangai Animation Studio Production. Color. Half-hour. Premiered on PBS: September 15, 1990. Rebroadcast on PBS: December 27, 1992.*

**Voices**
**Narrator:** James Earl Jones

## ⊚ NODDY: "ANYTHING CAN HAPPEN AT CHRISTMAS"

Mrs. Claus (played by Betty White) teaches a small wooden boy named Noddy and his friends the importance of sharing in the true spirit of the holiday season in this half-hour live-action/animated holiday special based on British animators Brian Cosgrove and Mark Hall's Emmy Award-winning weekday stop-motion animated children's series that debuted weekday mornings and at night on selected PBS station affiliates in December 1998. *A BBC Children's International/BBC Worldwide America/TV Ontario/CBC/Cosgrove-Hall/Catalyst/Enid Boyton Production. Color. Half-hour. Premiered on PBS: December 18, 1998. Rebroadcast on PBS: December 24, 1999; December 25, 1999.*

**Cast (live-action)**
**Noah:** Sean McCann; **Kate:** Katie Boland; **Truman:** Max Morrow; **Mrs. Claus:** Betty White

**Voices**
**Noddy:** Denise Bryer; **Gertie Gator:** Taborah Johnson

## ⊚ NOEL

Actor Charlton Heston, in his first animated project, narrates this story about a red Christmas tree ornament that comes to life. The half-hour special was written by acclaimed screenwriter Romeo Muller, creator of such perennial holiday classics as *Rudolph the Red-Nosed Reindeer* and *Frosty the Snowman. A Burt Strattford Production. Color. Half-hour. Premiered on NBC: December 4, 1992.*

**Voices**
**Narrator:** Charlton Heston; **Noel:** Blaze Berdahl

## ⊚ NOËL NOËL

Leslie Nielsen of filmdom's *Naked Gun* fame narrates this traditional Christmas tale of a misguided billionaire who, thanks to a young girl named Zoey, her faithful dog Snooze and a blue-eyed reindeer, finds that money doesn't ensure happiness and discovers the importance of listening to his heart instead. Written by

*A small group of animals celebrates the victory of a band of condors against a local construction company in the CBS network special* No Man's Valley. *© Lee Melendez-Phil Howard Productions* (COURTESY: BILL MELENDEZ PRODUCTIONS)

Martin Barry, directed by Nicola Lemay and produced by Marc Bertrand, Jean-Jacques Leduc and Marcy Page, the half-hour yuletide special was originally produced by the National Film Board of Canada as a 22-minute two-reel short and simultaneously released to theaters in English and French in December 2003. Nominated for the prestigious Gemini Award for best animated program or series in 2004, the colorful cartoon production premiered in the United States on VOOM's Animania HD channel and on Cartoon Network in December 2004. *A National Film Board of Canada Production. Color. Half-hour. Premiered on ANI: December 5, 2004. Premiered on CAR: December 25, 2004.*

**Voices**
**Narrator:** Leslie Nielsen (English), Benoit Briere (French); **Other Voices:** Joanne Leveille, Benoit Rousseau, Rick Jones, Helene Lasnier

## ⊚ NO MAN'S VALLEY

In this Thanksgiving special, a construction company threatens the sanctuary of a band of condors which sends out a scout, Elliot, in search of a fabled animal refuge for endangered species known as No Man's Valley. One of its inhabitants, Pat the Passenger Pigeon, returns with Elliot to guide the other condors back so they will be safe from extinction. *A Lee Mendelson–Phil Howort Production in association with Frank Fehmers Productions and Bill Melendez Productions. Color. Half-hour. Premiered on CBS: November 23, 1981. Rebroadcast on CBS: September 12, 1982. Syndicated. Rebroadcast on DIS: April 13, 1993.*

**Voices**
**Chief:** Henry Corden; **Elliot:** Frank Buxton; **Abe:** Art Metrano; **George:** Hal Smith; **Nipponia:** Chanin Hale; **Fred Firmwing:** Arnold Stang; **Pere David:** Barney Phillips; **Daniel:** Joe E. Ross; **Pat:** Desiree Goyette; **Nobody Panda:** Richard Deacon; **Herman:** John Stephenson

## ⊚ NONESENSE AND LULLABYES: NURSERY RHYMES

Well-known stage and screen personalities Karen Allen, Eli Wallach, Linda Hunt, Grace Johnston, Heidi Stallings and Courtney Vance narrate this likable half-hour collection of 18 nursery rhymes assembled in animated one-minute segments that aired on USA Network and Nickelodeon in 1993. The entire package was rebroadcast as one-minute program bridges on Disney Channel. *A Michael Sporn Animation Production. Color. Half-hour. Premiered on USA Network: 1993. Rebroadcast on DIS.*

**Voices**
**Narrators:** Karen Allen, Eli Wallach, Linda Hunt, Grace Johnston, Heidi Stallings, Courtney Vance, Phillip Schopper

### ◎ NONESENSE AND LULLABYES: POEMS FOR CHILDREN

Award-winning New York animator Michael Sporn produced this second half-hour assemblage of delightful children's poems including animated renditions of Edward Lear's "The Owl and the Pussy-cat," Jack Prelutsky's "The Creature in the Classroom" and two poems by Robert Louis Stevenson. *A Michael Sporn Animation Production. Color. Half-hour. Premiered on USA Network: 1993. Rebroadcast on DIS.*

**Voices**
**Narrators:** Karen Allen, Eli Wallach, Linda Hunt, Grace Johnston, Heidi Stallings, Courtney Vance, Phillip Schopper

### ◎ THE NOTORIOUS JUMPING FROG OF CALAVERAS COUNTY

Dan'l Webster and Reverend Leonidas W. "Jim" Smiley, two members of a small mining community, wager $40 with a stranger in a bet over which frog can jump the farthest in this humorous half-hour special based on Mark Twain's famous short story. *A Severo Perez Production. Color. Half-hour. Premiere: 1983–84. Syndicated.*

### ◎ THE NUTCRACKER

A housemaid of a rich European family discovers one wooden soldier—known as a nutcracker—left under the Christmas tree and dreams what it would be like to have the brave soldier go into battle. *A Soyuzmultifilm Studios Production. Color. Half-hour. Premiered on CBS: November 25, 1978. Rebroadcast on CBS: November 27, 1980. Syndicated.*

### ◎ THE NUTCRACKER SCOOB

This regular two-part episode was from the popular ABC Saturday-morning series *The New Scooby-Doo Mysteries*, originally produced in 1984–85, in which Scooby-Doo and the gang search for a hidden emerald that's also sought by the evil Mr. Nickelby and a ghost. USA Network, which aired *Scooby-Doo, Where Are You?* (in reruns) and subsequent off-network Scooby-Doo mystery series from Hanna-Barbera as part of its cartoon program block, *Cartoon Express*, rebroadcast the episode—melded into a half-hour—as a holiday special in 1991. It was later replayed on the Cartoon Network. *A Hanna-Barbera Production. Color. Half-hour. Premiered on USA: December 5, 1991. Rebroadcast on USA: December 8, 1991: Rebroadcast on CAR: November 25, 1995.*

**Voices**
**Scooby-Doo/Scrappy-Doo:** Don Messick; **Freddy Jones:** Frank Welker; **Shaggy Rogers:** Casey Kasem; **Daphne Blake:** Heather North; **Velma Dace Dinkley:** Maria Frumkin

### ◎ O CHRISTMAS TREE (1991)

Adapted from the popular yuletide nursery rhyme, a brave evergreen (called Tannenbaum) stands up to King Winter, leaving it up to his new friend (Anneka) to save him in this half-hour holiday special, originally produced as part of CINAR Films' *The Real Story of . . .* series. *A CINAR Films/France Animation Production in association with Western Publishing Company/CTV Television Network/Telefilm Canada. Color. Half-hour. Premiered on HBO: January 17, 1994.*

**Voices**
**Anneka:** Deborah Harry; **Piney:** John Ritter; **Other Voices:** Jason Ritter

### ◎ O CHRISTMAS TREE (1996)

Santa's neighbors, two feuding bears named Iggy Lou Bear and Edgar Allan Snow, each wants a Christmas tree for his own igloo. The only trouble is, there is only one tree in the whole frozen North Pole. This colorful half-hour Christmas special was produced for The Family Channel. *A Perennial Pictures Film Corporation Production. Color. Half-hour. Premiered on FAM: December 5, 1996.*

**Voices**
**Edgar Allan Snow:** Russ Harris; **Iggy Lou Bear:** Jerry Reynolds

### ◎ AN OFF-BEATS VALENTINE'S SPECIAL

Tommy engages in an illicit romance with one of the off-limit The Populars in this half-hour Valentine's special, written, produced and directed by Mo Willems, creator of the popular Nickelodeon cartoon characters, *The Off-Beats*, produced from 1995 to 1998 first as a series of shorts for Nick's "Creative Lab" and then as segments for the network's popular animated variety show *KaBlam! A Curious Pictures Production. Color. Half-hour. Premiered on NICK: February 12, 1999.*

**Voices**
**Tommy:** Mark Wagner; **Beth:** Tara Ketterer; **Betty Anne Bongo:** Mischa Barton; **Repunzil:** Trisha Hedgecock; **Tina:** Kathleen Fasolino; **September/Grubby Groo:** Mo Willems; **Billy:** Jimmy McQuaid; **P Boy:** Tim Duffy; **Hat Boy:** Keith Franklin; **Back Boy:** John Morgan; **Cool's Leader:** Todd Honig; **Brad:** Bradley Glenn; **February:** Kris Greengrove; **All Yelling/Heartometer 4000:** Kevin Seal

### ◎ OFF ON A COMET

Led by French Captain Hector Servadac, a band of people of all races and ethnic origins becomes stranded on a comet racing through space only to find their existence threatened when they realize the comet is headed on a crash course with Earth in this hour-long special based on the Jules Verne novel *Hector Servadac: Travels and Adventures Through the Solar System. An Air Programs International Production. Color. One hour. Premiered: 1976. Syndicated.*

**Voices**
Barbara Frawley, Ron Haddrick, Philip Hinton, Shane Porteous, Bevan Wilson

### ◎ OH, MR. TOAD

The beloved characters of Cosgrove Hall Productions' award-winning *The Wind in the Willows* return in this two-part, hour-long stop-motion puppet-animated story of friendship (also inspired by Kenneth Grahame's best-selling novel), told in two half-hour broadcasts, in which the underhanded Weasels kidnap the lovable aristocrat Mr. Toad and hire an impersonator to take his place. *A Cosgrove Hall Production. Color. Half-hour. Premiered on PBS: October 20, 1990 (Part 1) and October 27, 1990 (Part 2). Rebroadcast on PBS: January 3, 1993 (Part 1) and January 10, 1993 (Part 2).*

**Voices**
Sir Michael Hordern, David Jason, Richard Pearson, Peter Sullis

## THE OLD CURIOSITY SHOP

The tragic tale of one granddaughter's love for her poor grandfather is the basis of this 90-minute special in which the young girl (Little Nell) takes to the road to raise money to lift her grandfather out of debt. The program was based on the Charles Dickens novel of the same name. *A Burbank Films Production. Color. Ninety minutes. Premiered: 1984. Syndicated.*

*Voices*

John Benton, Jason Blackwell, Wallas Eaton, Penne Hackforth-Jones, Brian Harrison, Doreen Harrop, Ross Higgins, Sophie Horton, Jennifer Mellett

## OLIVER AND THE ARTFUL DODGER

When it is revealed that Oliver is named as heir to the estate of the wealthy Mr. Brownlow, his wicked nephew, Snipe, sets out to find the will and destroy it. He is unsuccessful in preventing Oliver's inheritance, thanks to some help from Oliver's special friend, the Artful Dodger, in this animated re-creation (first broadcast as a two-part episode of *The ABC Saturday Superstar Movie* series) of Charles Dickens's popular novel *Oliver Twist*. *A Hanna-Barbera Production. Color. One hour. Premiered on ABC: October 21, 1972 and October 28, 1972 (on The ABC Saturday Superstar Movie). Rebroadcast on ABC: December 15, 1973 and December 22, 1973. Rebroadcast on CAR: March 4, 1994 (Turner Family Showcase). Syndicated.*

*Voices*

**Oliver:** Gary Marsh; **The Dodger/Fishmonger:** Mike Bell; **Flip/Boy:** John Walmsley; **Deacon/Happy Harry/Twig:** Darryl Pollack; **Louisa/Lilibit:** Pamelyn Ferdin; **Snipe/Furniture Man:** Dick Dawson; **Mrs. Puddy/Rose/Tess/Old Hag:** Joan Gerber; **Mr. Bumble/Coachman:** Ronald Long; Mrs. Grunch/Mistress Dreadly/Farmer's Wife/The Old Crone: Anna Lee; **Mr. Grunch/Goodfriend/Butcher/Mr. Brownlow/Mr. Highbottle:** John Stephenson; **The Doctor/Farmer/Constable/Master Dreadly:** Bernard Fox; **Pastry Cook/House Agent/Midget/Workman/Hero (Dog):** Don Messick; **Narrator:** Michael Evans

## OLIVER TWIST (1981)

Charles Dickens's classic novel inspired this hour-long program, which was first released as a full-length feature and then reedited for television. This time Oliver is paired with a new friend, Squeaker the Cricket, who helps search for Oliver's inheritance while matching wits with several colorful villains (Fagin, Mr. Bumble, the Artful Dodger and Bill Sikes). *A Filmation Associates Production in association with Warner Bros. Television. Color. One hour. Premiered on NBC: April 14, 1981 (as NBC Special Treat). Rebroadcast on CAR: July 2, 1995 (Mr. Spim's Cartoon Theatre), August 27, 1995 (Mr. Spim's Cartoon Theatre).*

*Voices*

**Oliver Twist:** Josh Albee; **Fagin:** Les Tremayne

## OLIVER TWIST (1984)

The story of impoverished orphan Oliver Twist, who struggles to find his inheritance, is captured in this 90-minute special created for first-run syndication. *A Burbank Films Production. Color. Ninety minutes. Premiered: 1984. Syndicated.*

*Voices*

Faye Anderson, Bill Conn, Wallas Eaton, Barbara Frawley, Ross Higgins, Sean Hinton, Robin Ramsey, Derani Scarr, Robin Stewart

## OLIVE, THE OTHER REINDEER

After misunderstanding a radio broadcast that Santa is canceling Christmas because one of his reindeers is injured, Olive the dog quickly heads to the North Pole to volunteer his services and meets some interesting characters along the way, including an evil postman who's sick and tired of delivering Christmas mail and a penguin who helps him fulfill his dream in this hour-long special, based on the popular children's book by J. Otto Seibold and Vivian Walsh and created by Matt Groening of *The Simpsons*.

Directed by Steve Moore, who is credited as Oscar Moore, the Emmy-nominated holiday special premiered in prime time on FOX in December 1999. In 2002, the dog-who-thinks-she's-a-reindeer favorite was rebroadcast for the first time on Cartoon Network. *A DNA Productions, Inc./Curiosity Company/Flower Films/Fox Television Studios Production. Color. One hour and nine minutes. Premiered on FOX: December 17, 1999. Rebroadcast on FOX: December 14, 2000. Rebroadcast on CAR: December 14, 2002; December 22, 2003; December 10, 2004; December 18, 2004; December 22, 2004; December 24, 2004; December 25, 2004; December 23, 2005; December 24, 2005; December 17, 2006; December 21, 2006; December 22, 2006.*

*Voices*

**Olive:** Drew Barrymore; **The Postman:** Dan Castellaneta; **Martini, the penguin:** Joe Pantoliano; **Santa Claus:** Edward Asner; **Mrs. Claus/Mrs. Eskimo:** Tress MacNeille; **Mr. Eskimo:** Billy West; **Fido:** Peter MacNicol; **Richard Stands:** Tim Meadows; **Tim:** Jay Mohr; **Schnitzel:** Michael Stipe; **Zoo Director:** Diedrich Bader; **Guard Shack Elf:** David Herman; **Round John Virgin/Comet:** Mitch Rouse; **Arturo:** Matt Groening; **Other Voices:** Kath Soucie

## THE ONLINE ADVENTURES OF OZZIE THE ELF

Spun off from a cyber-site character created by America Online and one of the last projects spearheaded by programming executive Brandon Tartikoff, this half-hour computer and stop-motion animated special follows the adventures of the blue-tinted, techno-savvy elf as he upgrades Santa's workshop from its old-fashioned system to an automated assembly line, leaving veteran elves unhappy and some reindeer out of a job—not a good thing at Christmas. *An Will Vinton Production. Color. Half-hour. Premiered on ABC: December 13, 1997.*

*Voices*

**Ozzie:** Cam Clarke; **Santa:** Jim Cummings; **Comet/Blitzen:** Dan Castellaneta; **Clover:** Tom Kenny; **Other Voices:** Rob Paulsen, Kath Soucie

## ON VACATION WITH MICKEY MOUSE AND FRIENDS

Jiminy Cricket hosts this wacky look at the most memorable vacations of several of Walt Disney's most beloved characters in this collection of previously released theatrical cartoons—"Hawaiian Holiday" (1937), "Goofy and Wilbur" (1939), "Canine Caddy" (1941), "Bubble Bee" (1949), "Dude Duck" (1951) and "Mickey's Trailer" (1951)—which was first broadcast as an episode of ABC's prime-time series, *Disneyland*, in 1956. The program was later retitled and rebroadcast on both NBC and ABC as an hour-long special. *A Walt Disney Television Production. Color. One hour. Premiered on ABC: March 7, 1956 (on Disneyland). Rebroadcast on NBC: April 11, 1979 (as On Vacation with Mickey Mouse and Friends). Rebroadcast on ABC: June 29, 1986 (on The Disney Sunday Movie).*

*Voices*

**Jiminy Cricket (host):** Cliff Edwards; **Mickey Mouse:** Wayne Allwine; **Donald Duck:** Clarence Nash

## ◎ OUR FRIEND, MARTIN

During a class field trip to a museum a group of students, led by a young black teenager, Miles, and his friends—Randy, Kyle, and Maria—are sent back in time to meet Dr. Martin Luther King and learn firsthand what he did for the ages, from denouncing segregation to his famous "I Have a Dream" speech, in this live-action/animated time-travel adventure special inspired by the life of the famed civil rights leader. Nominated for a 1999 Emmy Award for outstanding animated program (for programming more than one hour) the hour-long tribute, featuring the voices of such well-known film and television stars as LeVar Burton, Oprah Winfrey, Danny Glover, Whoopi Goldberg, Samuel L. Jackson, Ashley Judd, John Travolta and many others, premiered on the premium cable channel Starz!, and was subsequently rebroadcast multiple times on Starz Entertainment LLC's offspring networks, including Starz! WAM!, Starz! In Black, Starz! Kids, Starz! Family and Starz! Family & Kids, until March 2005. A DIC Entertainment/Hang Yang Productions Production. Color. One Hour. Premiered on STZ: January 10, 1999. Rebroadcast on STZ: April 3, 1999; April 6, 1999; April 20, 1999; April 21, 1999; April 25, 1999; November 8, 1999; November 11, 1999; November 21, 1999; November 25, 1999; May 11, 2000; May 19, 2000; May 27, 2000; May 30, 2000; November 19, 2004; November 23, 2004; January 1, 2005; January 12, 2005; January 17, 2005; January 18, 2005; January 23, 2005. Rebroadcast on STZ WAM!: August 28, 1999; January 17, 1999 (twice); May 5, 2005; May 9, 2005; May 17, 2005. Rebroadcast on STZB: February 13, 1999; March 6, 1999; June 5, 1999; June 17, 1999; June 21, 1999; June 27, 1999; October 4, 1999; October 14, 1999; October 22, 1999; October 31, 1999; February 12, 2000; February 23, 2000; February 27, 2000; March 5, 2000; July 1, 2000; July 2, 2000; July 7, 2000; July 10, 2000; July 11, 2000; July 19, 2000; August 4, 2000; August 10, 2004; August 12, 2004; August 15, 2004; August 24, 2004; August 27, 2004; December 9, 2004; December 19, 2004; December 22, 2004; April 4 2005; June 7, 2005. Rebroadcast on STZK: July 25, 2004; July 26, 2004; July 27, 2004; July 28, 2004; July 29, 2004; July 30, 2004; July 31, 2004; August 1, 2004; March 1, 2005; March 6, 2005; March 9, 2005; March 19, 2005. Rebroadcast on STZF: May 12, 1999; May 19, 1999; May 25, 1999; May 30, 1999; September 1, 1999; September 9, 1999; September 20, 1999; September 25, 1999; April 4, 2000; April 16, 2000; April 20, 2000; April 21 2000; April 24, 2000; August 4, 2000; August 10, 2000; August 11, 2000; June 25, 2004; June 29, 2004; June 30, 2004; October 1, 2004; October 5, 2004; October 6, 2004; October 16, 2004; October 21, 2004; October 25, 2004; October 31, 2004; March 1, 2005; March 6, 2005; March 9, 2005; March 19, 2005; March 31, 2005. Rebroadcast on STZK&F: March 31, 2005.

### Voices
**Miles:** Robert Richard; **Randy:** Lucas Black; **Kyle:** Zachary Leigh; **Maria:** Jessica Garcia; **Mr. Harris:** Ed Asner; **Miles's Mom:** Angela Bassett; **Martin Luther King, age 12:** Theodore Borders; **Martin Luther King, age 15:** Jaleel White; **Martin Luther King, age 26:** LeVar Burton; **Martin Luther King, age 34:** Dexter Scott King; **Corretta Scott King:** Oprah Winfrey; **Train Conductor:** Danny Glover; **Mrs. Peck:** Whoopi Goldberg; **Turner:** Samuel L. Jackson; **Daddy King:** James Earl Jones; **Mrs. Dale:** Ashley Judd; **Mr. Willis:** Richard Kind; **Christine King:** Yolanda King; **Mrs. Clark:** Susan Sarandon; **Kyle's Dad:** John Travolta; **Adam Wylie:** Sam Dale; **Bull Connor/Chihuahua:** Frank Welker; **Reporter/Demonstrator:** Jess Harnell; **Reporter/Demonstrator:** Joe Lala; **Man/Demonstrator:** John Wesley; **Old Woman/Demonstrator:** Elizabeth Primm; **Other Voices:** Jodi Carlisle

## ◎ OUR MR. SUN

Live action-animated educational special—the first for the Bell Telephone Science Hour series (1956–64)—written and produced by Academy Award-winning movie director Frank Capra and codirected by Capra (live action) and animator William T. Hurtz (animation), featuring animation by Hollywood's United Productions of America (UPA). In this hour-long installment, Mr. Sun and Father demonstrate the importance of the Sun as well as solar energy and thermonuclear reactors. Nominated for an Emmy Award in 1957 for best editing of a film for television, the special and entire series was hosted by Dr. Frank Baxter and featured the voice of actor Sterling Holloway. Shamus Culhane Productions and Disney later produced animation for the series. A Bell Science/Frank Capra Productions/UPA Studios Production. Color. One hour. Premiered on CBS: November 19, 1956.

### Cast (live-action)/Voices
**Dr. Research:** Frank Baxter; **The Fiction Writer:** Eddie Albert; **Chloro Phyll:** Sterling Holloway; **Mr. Sun:** Marvin Miller

## ◎ PAC-MAN HALLOWEEN SPECIAL

Pac-Baby experiences Halloween for the first time, but Mezmaron and his chomping Ghost Monsters threaten to disrupt the seasonal fun in this half-hour prime-time special based on the popular Atari video game characters. Entitled "Trick or Chomp," the program was originally broadcast on the characters' popular Saturday-morning series. A Hanna-Barbera Production. Color. Half-hour. Premiered on ABC: October 30, 1982.

### Voices
**Pac-Man:** Marty Ingels; **Ms. Pac:** Barbara Minkus; **Baby Pac:** Russi Taylor; **Chomp Chomp:** Frank Welker; **Sour Puss:** Peter Cullen; **Mezmaron:** Alan Lurie; **Sue Monster:** Susan Silo; **Inky Monster:** Barry Gordon; **Blinky Monster/Pinky Monster:** Chuck McCann; **Clyde Monster:** Neilson Ross

## ◎ PADDINGTON GOES TO SCHOOL

Disaster strikes the Brown household when Paddington is told he must attend school in this 1986 special—the third in a series of puppet-animated specials from producer George Clutterback of FilmFair Animation-directed by Martin Pullen. The program, along with the other two, made its American television debut on the Disney Channel. A FilmFair Animation/Paddington & Company, Ltd. Production. Color. Half-hour. Premiered on DIS. Rebroadcast on DIS: September 17, 1990; September 11, 1991.

### Voices
**Narrator:** Sir Michael Hordern

## ◎ PADDINGTON GOES TO THE MOVIES

The incorrigible Paddington, inspired by the magic of the "silver screen" and a sudden rainstorm, follows the famous footsteps of Gene Kelly and in his own way "dances in the rain" with hilarious consequences in this half-hour special produced by FilmFair Animation (producers of the 1981 PBS stop-motion animated series Paddington Bear. A FilmFair Animation/Paddington & Company, Ltd. Production. Color. Half-hour. Premiered on DIS. Rebroadcast on DIS: June 2, 1992.

### Voices
**Narrator:** Sir Michael Hordern

## ◎ PADDINGTON'S BIRTHDAY BONANZA

Mr. Brown's birthday is drawing near and Paddington is worried because he can't afford to buy him a present in this half-hour puppet-animated special—the first in a series produced by London's

FilmFair Animation in 1986. *A FilmFair Animation/Paddington & Company, Ltd. Production. Color. Half-hour. Premiered on DIS. Rebroadcast on DIS: August 11, 1991; February 21, 1993.*

*Voices*
**Narrator:** Sir Michael Hordern

## ⊚ PARTY WAGON

Teenager Randolph P. McDuff (voiced by Sean Astin) embarks on a wagon trip west along the Oregon Trail to find his fortune while staying ahead of his ex-fiancé's family, hot on his trail in this clever animated western send-up, written and co-directed by Craig Bartlett, the creator of TV's *Hey Arnold! A Cartoon Network Production. Color. Ninety minutes. Premiered on CAR: February 27, 2004.*

*Voices*
**Randall P. McDuff/Josiah:** Sean Astin; **Sublimity Jill/Daughter #2:** Pamela Hayden; **Lewis Clark Jefferson/Cowpoke #3:** Scott Lawrence; **Bumpy Snits/Ferryman #1/Cowpoke #2:** Maurice LaMarche; **Ornery Sue/Wagonmaster's Wife/Daughter #3:** Carolyn Lawrence; **Romeo Jones/Ferryman #2/Cheyenne #1:** Craig Bartlett; **Billie Bartley/Manifest Destiny:** Andrea Bowen; **Toad E. Bartley:** Josh Hutcherson; **Wagonmaster/Pioneer #1/Cowpoke #1:** Dan Conroy; **Three-Eyed Jack/Wall-Eyed Tom:** Danny Mann; **Daughter #1:** Christie Insley; **Wild Bill Hickok/Clerk/Cheyenne #2:** Dan Castellaneta

## ⊚ PEGASUS

Narrated by Mia Farrow, this contemporary animated half-hour captures the glorious adventures of the mythic winged horse who helps slay a three-headed monster and survives a falling out with Zeus, only to be made immortal. The program aired on PBS's long-running *Long Ago & Far Away* series. *A Lightyear Entertainment Production. Color. Half-hour. Premiered on PBS: November 16, 1991. Rebroadcast on PBS: October 18, 1992.*

*Voices*
**Narrator:** Mia Farrow

## ⊚ PENGUINS BEHIND BARS

Framed by her boyfriend Charlie and imprisoned for 10 years for a pearl robbery she didn't commit, penguin Doris Fairfeather learns from her cellmate Mad'm Millie how to clear her name in this 22-minute animated short directed by Oscar-winning animator Janet Perlman, who cowrote the story with her former husband, the late Derek Lamb. The film premiered on Cartoon Network's *Adult Swim* animation block. *A Hulascope/National Film Board of Canada Production. Color. Half-hour. Premiered on CAR: July 20, 2003 (Adult Swim).*

*Voices*
**Doris Fairfeather:** Lili Taylor; **Charlie Abaloney:** Richard Clarkin; **Mad'm Millie:** Patricia Collins; **Oily Doily Valdeez:** Sonja Ball; **Flotsam:** Catherine Fitch; **Mike the Lawyer:** Craig Francis; **Matron Hruffwater:** Patricia Gage; **District Attorney/Judge:** Dan Lett; **The Warden:** Maria Vacratsis; **Babs:** Alberta Watson

## ⊚ PERFECT HAIR FOREVER

Following the same absurd humor and style of Cartoon Network's *Space Ghost Coast to Coast, Aqua Teen Hunger Force* and *Sealab 2021*, this CGI-animated pilot followed the adventures of a bald young boy named Gerald who attempts to remedy his premature baldness by embarking on a quest for perfection. The 15-minute episode premiered on Cartoon Network's *Adult Swim* in a time slot originally scheduled for the world television premiere of the pilot for *Squidbillies*, but was shelved when it wasn't ready for broadcast. In the fall of 2005, Cartoon Network offered a six-episode series, based on the pilot, as part of its *Adult Swim* program block that included the debuts of two other new series: *Squidbillies* and *12 Oz. Mouse. A Williams Street Production. Color. Fifteen minutes. Premiered on CAR: November 7, 2004. Rebroadcast on CAR: November 20, 2005.*

*Voices*
**Gerald:** Kim Manning; **Coffo/Uncle Grandfather/Catman:** Dave Willis; **Comedy Tree:** Nick Ingkatanuwat

## ⊚ PETER AND THE MAGIC EGG

Peter Paas the rabbit helps Mama and Papa Doppler, who raised him, save their farm from greedy Tobias Tinwhiskers in this Easter tale told by Uncle Amos Egg, an egg farmer, whose mortgage is about to be foreclosed on by the same evil Tinwhiskers. *An RLR Associates in association with Murakami-Wolf-Swenson Films. Color. Half-hour. Premiered: March, 1983. Syndicated. Rebroadcast on DIS: March 20, 1992; March 7, 1993; March 22, 1994.*

*Voices*
**Uncle Amos Egg:** Ray Bolger; **Tobias Tinwhiskers/Cotton:** Bob Ridgely; **Peter Paas:** Al Eisenmann; **Terrence:** Charles Woolf; **Feathers:** Joan Gerber; **Lollychops:** Russi Taylor; **Papa Doppler/Kookybird:** Bob Holt

## ⊚ PETER AND THE WOLF

Kirstie Alley narrates this warm-hearted story of a family reunion, based on Sergei Prokofiev's classic musical tale, told in live action and animation (the latter by cartoon legend Chuck Jones). The hour-long spectacular premiered in prime time on ABC, with versions of the program also offered on home video, audiocassette and CD-ROM. *An IF/X Production/Chuck Jones Enterprises Production for BMG Entertainment International. Color. One hour. Premiered on ABC: December 8, 1995.*

*Cast/Voices*
**Annie, Peter's Mother:** Kirstie Alley; **Peter:** Ross Malinger; **Grandfather:** Lloyd Bridges

## ⊚ PETROUSHKA

After founding his independent animation studio, Fine Arts Film, Wimbledon-born animator John Wilson adapted Igor Stravinsky's famous ballet score, "Petroushka," into what would become American television's first fully-animated prime-time special. Stravinsky scored the 15-minute black-and-white film that Wilson animated and directed, with Stravinsky conducting the music with the Los Angeles Philharmonic Orchestra. The film premiered as a segment on NBC's *Sol Hurok Music Hour* in 1956. Wilson went on to produce films for children, including film shorts for NBC's *Exploring* series, which won the prestigious Peabody Award. *A Fine Arts Films Production. Black-and-white. Fifteen minutes. Premiered on NBC: 1956 (Sol Hurok Music Hour).*

## ⊚ THE PICKWICK PAPERS

The humorous escapades of Samuel Pickwick and the members of his literary group, the Pickwick Club, are the premise for this 90-minute adaptation of the Charles Dickens novel. *A Burbank Films Production. Color. Ninety minutes. Premiered: 1985.*

## ⊚ THE PIED PIPER OF HAMELIN

A mysterious stranger saves the town of Hamelin from a plague of rats by luring them away with his magic pipe in this half-hour stop-motion puppet-animated special produced by England's Cosgrove Hall Productions for the award-winning PBS anthology series *Long Ago & Far Away*. *A Cosgrove Hall Production. Color. Half-hour. Premiered on PBS: January 28, 1989. Rebroadcast on PBS: November 10, 1990; February 28, 1992.*

**Voices**
Narrator: Robert Hardy

### ◎ PINK PANTHER IN "A PINK CHRISTMAS"

In this heartwarming animated holiday special, the Pink Panther, appearing in his first prime-time animated special, is alone, cold and hungry in New York's Central Park in the 1890s, trying desperately to get himself a Christmas dinner even if it entails getting arrested. The holiday special earned two prime-time Emmy Award nominations for outstanding individual achievement–animation program for the main title song by John Bradford and Doug Goodwin, and music and lyrics for the other songs by Doug Goodwin. *A DePatie-Freleng Enterprises Production in association with Mirisch-Geoffrey Productions. Color. Half-hour. Premiered on ABC: December 7, 1978. Rebroadcast on ABC: December 16, 1979. Syndicated.*

### ◎ PINK PANTHER IN "OLYMPINKS"

Timed to coincide with the 1980 Winter Olympics, the Pink Panther finds the odds stacked against him in this cartoon version of the Olympics—called "Olympinks"—in which he tries to win at any cost but often pays the price for his effort. The special aired during the Lake Placid Winter Olympics and was also broadcast on ABC. The sports spoof special was nominated for two Emmy Awards for outstanding animated program and outstanding individual achievement–animation program for direction (Friz Freleng). *A DePatie-Freleng Enterprises Production in association with Mirisch-Geoffrey Productions. Color. Half-hour. Premiered on ABC: February 22, 1980. Syndicated.*

### ◎ PINK PANTHER IN "PINK AT FIRST SIGHT"

In this Valentine's Day special, the Pink Panther longs for a lady panther and fantasizes about every female he meets. He is ready to give up until a pretty panther comes along and wins not only his attention but his love. *A Marvel Production in association with Mirisch-Geoffrey Productions and DePatie-Freleng Enterprises. Color. Half-hour. Premiered on ABC: May 10, 1981. Rebroadcast on ABC: May 29, 1982. Syndicated.*

**Voices**
Weaver Copeland, Brian Cummings, Marilyn Schreffler, Hal Smith, Frank Welker

### ◎ A PINKY AND THE BRAIN CHRISTMAS

Traveling to the North Pole, Brain sets up in Santa's workshop to mass produce a "fantastically powerful doll" that he will use to broadcast hypnotic suggestions to unsuspecting viewers in this Emmy Award–winning half-hour special based on the popular WB Television Network series. *A Warner Bros. Television Animation/Amblin Entertainment Production. Color. Half-hour. Premiered on WB: December 17, 1995. Rebroadcast on WB: December 22, 1996.*

**Voices**
Pinky: Rob Paulsen; **The Brain:** Maurice LaMarche; **Santa Claus:** Earl Boen; **Other Voices:** Tress MacNeille, Frank Welker

### ◎ PINOCCHIO'S CHRISTMAS

Back in an all-new Christmas adventure, Pinocchio falls in love with a little girl marionette, Julietta. Along the way he meets up with a sly old fox and money-hungry cat and, of course, Papa Geppetto in this Animagic adventure. *A Rankin-Bass Production. Color. One hour. Premiered on ABC: December 3, 1980. Rebroadcast on ABC: December 24, 1982. Syndicated. Rebroadcast on FAM: December 10, 1996; December 11, 1997. Rebroadcast on FOX FAM: December 5, 1998; December 21, 1998; July 11, 1999; July 15, 1999; December 4, 1999; December 24, 1999; December 8, 2000; December 14, 2000; December 24, 2000. Rebroadcast on ABC FAM: December 1, 2001; December 10, 2001; December 20, 2001; December 24, 2001; December 1, 2002; December 4, 2002; December 24, 2002; December 6, 2003; December 4, 2004; December 10, 2004; December 3, 2005; December 12, 2005; December 6, 2006; December 9, 2006; December 24, 2006.*

**Voices**
Pinocchio: Todd Porter; **Geppetto:** George S. Irving; **Maestro Fire-Eater:** Alan King; **The Cat:** Pat Bright; **Julietta/Lady Azura:** Diane Leslie; **Dr. Cricket:** Robert McFadden; **Children:** Tiffany Blake, Carl Tramon, Alice Gayle

### ◎ P.J. FUNNYBUNNY: A VERY COOL EASTER

Floppy-eared P.J. tries desperately to instill some Easter spirit into his otherwise-occupied family in this third in a series of ABC Weekend Specials, produced by animator Marija Miletic-Dail's Animation Cottage. *An Animation Cottage Production in association with ABC. Color. Half-hour. Premiered on ABC: March 30, 1996.*

**Voices**
P.J. Funnybunny: Jason Barnhill; **Honey Bunny:** Christine Cavanaugh

### ◎ P.J. FUNNYBUNNY: THE LIFESTYLES OF THE FUNNY AND FAMOUS

Determined to escape another boring family reunion, young P.J. embarks on a "hare-larious" quest for fame and fortune, only to discover that being famous has far-out consequences in this ABC Weekend Special. The program introduced Christine Cavanaugh (the melodious voice of the pig in the movie *Babe*) as the voice of P.J.'s sister, Honey Bunny. (It was her first cartoon voiceover job.) *An Animation Cottage Production in association with ABC. Color. Half-hour. Premiered on ABC: February 4, 1989. Rebroadcast on ABC: July 13, 1996.*

*Model sheet drawings of P.J. Funnybunny from the ABC Weekend Special P.J. Funnybunny: A Very Cool Easter. © Capital Cities/ABC Entertainment* (COURTESY: ANIMATION COTTAGE)

*Voices*

**P.J. Funnybunny:** Jason Barnhill; **Honey Bunny:** Christine Cavanaugh

## ⊚ THE PJ'S CHRISTMAS SPECIAL: "HOW THE SUPER STOLED CHRISTMAS"

Unable to get his wife Muriel a computer for Christmas, Thurgood (voiced by Eddie Murphy) steals Christmas presents from the other tenants in his building and pawns them so he can buy the computer anyway in this half-hour holiday special based on the prime-time stop-motion animated series for FOX. The program repeated on Christmas Day 1999, with holiday episodes of FOX's *Futurama* and *The Simpsons* and was rebroadcast in 2000 when the series moved to the WB Television Network. *An Eddie Murphy/ Imagine Television/Will Vinton Studios/Touchstone Television Production. Color. Half-hour. Premiered on FOX: December 17, 1999. Rebroadcast on FOX: December 25, 1999. Rebroadcast on WB: December 24, 2000.*

*Voices*

**Thurgood Stubbs:** Eddie Murphy; **Muriel Stubbs:** Loretta Devine; **Mrs. Avery:** Ja'net DuBois; **Calvin Banks:** Crystal Scales; **Juicy Hudson:** Michele Morgan; **Jimmy Ho:** Michael Paul Chan; **Walter:** Marc Wilmore; **Tarnell:** James Black; **Smokey:** Shawn Michael Howard; **Ms. Mambo Garcelle (Haiti Lady):** Cheryl Francis Harrington; **Mr. Sanchez:** Pepe Serna; **Sharique:** Wanda Christine; **Papa Hudson/Rasta Man:** Kevin Michael Richardson; **Bebe Ho:** Jenifer Lewis; **Smokey:** Shawn Michael Howard; **Tarnell:** James Black; **HUD Woman:** Cassi Davis

## ⊚ P.J.'S UNFUNNYBUNNY CHRISTMAS

P.J. Funnybunny and his friends Pots, Ricky and Buzz save the day when they provide some lonely children at a local orphanage with toys at Christmas in this second in a series of *ABC Weekend Special. An Animation Cottage Production in association with ABC. Color. Half-hour. Premiered on ABC: December 11, 1993. Rebroadcast on ABC: December 24, 1994; December 16, 1995; December 24, 1996.*

*Voices*

**P.J. Funnybunny:** Jason Barnhill; **Honey Bunny:** Christine Cavanaugh

## ⊚ PLAY IT AGAIN, CHARLIE BROWN

For years Lucy has tried to get Schroeder's attention. She makes yet another attempt after Peppermint Patty tells her that she has an opening in the PTA program at school for Schroeder to play the piano. Lucy thus offers Schroeder his first "big break," for which he is most appreciative, but her only reward is a "thank you" in return. Cable giant Nickelodeon re-aired the special for two seasons beginning in 1998. *A Lee Mendelson–Bill Melendez Production in association with Charles M. Schulz Creative Associates and United Feature Syndicate. Color. Half-hour. Premiered on CBS: March 28, 1971. Rebroadcast on CBS: April 11, 1972; February 11, 1973. Rebroadcast on NICK: January 26, 1998; February 27, 1998; March 30, 1998; May 5, 1998; June 7, 1998; July 3, 1998; August 3, 1998; September 2, 1998; September 27, 1998; October 13, 1998; November 12, 1998; December 23, 1998; December 30, 1998; January 18, 1999; February 5, 1999; February 25, 1999; July 3, 1999; September 4, 1999; March 25, 2000.*

*Voices*

**Charlie Brown:** Chris Inglis; **Lucy Van Pelt:** Pamelyn Ferdin; **Linus Van Pelt:** Stephen Shea; **Sally Brown:** Hilary Momberger; **Schroeder:** Danny Hjeim; **Frieda:** Linda Mendelson; **Peppermint Patty:** Kip DeFaria

## ⊚ THE POGO SPECIAL BIRTHDAY SPECIAL

Walt Kelly's charming comic-strip character, known for his wit and pointed satire, comes to life in this television special based on classic Pogo stories. Kelly, who coproduced the special with animator Chuck Jones, is credited with writing the program and providing voices for three of the characters. *A Chuck Jones Enterprises Production in association with MGM-TV. Color. Half-hour. Premiered on NBC: May 18, 1969. Rebroadcast on NBC: February 22, 1970; February 20, 1971.*

*Voices*

**Pogo Possum/Mam'selle Hepzibah:** June Foray; **Porky Pine/ Bunny Rabbit/Basil the Butterfly:** Chuck Jones; **P.T. Bridgeport the Bear/Albert the Alligator/Dr. Howland Owl:** Walt Kelly; **Churchy-la-Femme/Beauregard Bugleboy:** Les Tremayne

## ⊚ THE POINT

Oblio, a young lad, searches for acceptance after he is banished from his homeland to the Pointless Forest because his head is not pointed like the rest of the locals and because not having a "point" is against the law. Academy Award–winning actor Dustin Hoffman originally narrated this 90-minute special produced for ABC's *Movie of the Week.* (In rebroadcasts of the program, Hoffman was replaced by Alan Barzman [1974] as the father/narrator; Ringo Starr [1976] performed the same task for the videocassette version.) Harry Nilsson, who wrote the original story, also composed seven songs for the program. In August of 1993, the Dustin Hoffman version was rebroadcast in nationwide syndication and on PBS stations. *A Nilsson House Music Production in association with Murakami-Wolf-Swenson Films. Color. Ninety minutes. Premiered on ABC: February 2, 1971. Rebroadcast on ABC: December 7, 1974. Rebroadcast on PBS: December 25, 1993. Syndicated: (week of) August 14, 1993.*

*Voices*

**Father (narrator):** Dustin Hoffman, Alan Barzman, Ringo Starr; **Son/Oblio:** Michael Lookinland; **Oblio's Father:** Alan Thicke; **The King/Leaf Man:** Paul Frees; **The Count:** Lennie Weinrib; **Rockman:** Bill Martin; **Oblio's Mother:** Joan Gerber; **Count's Son:** Buddy Foster

*Oblio, a young lad, searches for acceptance in* The Point. © *Nilsson House Music/Murakami-Wolf Productions* (COURTESY: MURAKAMI-WOLF-SWENSON)

## POKÉMON: CELEBI: VOICE OF FOREST

Ash, Misty and Brock help a young boy and the newest Pokémon creature, Celebi (better known as the Voice of the Forest), escape from a sinister bounty hunter who is developing a powerful forest monster in this fourth theatrical feature film in the illustrious Pokémon franchise, which also premiered as a Saturday-morning movie special on the WB Television Network's Kids' WB! A *Pokémon USA/4Kids Entertainment Production in association with Summit Media Group. Color. Ninety minutes. Premiered on the WB (Kids' WB!): October 11, 2002.*

*Voices*

**Ash Ketchum:** Veronica Taylor; **Misty/Jesse:** Rachael Lillis; **Brock/James:** Eric Stuart; **Meowth:** Madeleine Blaustein; **Pikachu:** Ikue Ootani; **The Iron Masked Marauder/Other Voices:** Dan Green; **Professor Samuel Oak:** Stan Hart; **Samuel "Sammy" Oak:** Tara Jayne; **Narrator:** Phillip Bartlett; **Other Voices:** Roxanne Beck, Amy Birnbaum, Ken Gates, Roger Kay, Ed Paul, Kayzie Rogers, Marc Thompson, Kerry Williams

## POKÉMON CHRONICLES: PIKACHU'S WINTER VACATION: "CHRISTMAS NIGHT"/"KANGA GAME"

Leaving Pikachu at home with his friends isn't a good idea as they get into all sorts of mischief while also showing baby Kangaskhan the wonder of playing in the snow in this two-episode, half-hour holiday special based on Cartoon Network's popular anime series aired during its high-rated Saturday night *Toonami* action block. (See listing under "Animated Television Series" section for voice credits.) A *TV Tokyo/Shogakukan Production Co./4Kids Entertainment Production. Color. Half-hour. Premiered on CAR: December 11, 2006. Rebroadcast on CAR: December 21, 2006; December 22, 2006; December 24, 2006.*

## POKÉMON: DESTINY DEOXYS

Ash and Pikachu face perhaps their toughest challenge yet: stopping a major battle that is raging between the powerful Deoxys and Rayquaza in this latest movie special to air on Kids' WB!'s Saturday-morning schedule. A *TV Tokyo/Softix/Shogakukan Production Co. (ShoPro)/J P Kikaku/Nintendo/CREATURES/GameFreak/4Kids Entertainment Production in association with Summit Media Group. Color. Ninety minutes. Premiered on the WB (Kids' WB!): January 22, 2005.*

*Voices*

**Ash Ketchum/May:** Veronica Taylor; **Jessie:** Rachael Lillis; **Brock/James:** Eric Stuart; **Meowth:** Madeleine Blaustein; **Pikachu:** Ikue Ootani; **Max:** Amy Birnbaum; **Professor Lund:** Ed Paul; **Yuko:** Kayzie Rogers; **Rebecca:** Lisa Ortiz; **Rafe:** Sebastian Arcelus; **Tory:** Tara Jayne; **Computer:** Darren Dunstan; **Rayquaza:** Katsuyuki Konishi; **Sid:** Matthew Charles; **Office Jenny:** Megan Hollingshead; **Narrator:** Mike Pollock; **Andrea/Catherine:** Rebecca Honig

## POKÉMON HEROES: LATIOS AND LATIAS

Head trainer Ash Ketchum, his fellow trainers, Misty and Brock, and trusty *Pokémon*, Pikachu battle the evil teenage *Pokémons*, Annie and Oakley, who swipe a powerful gem guarded by the winged brother-and-sister duo, Latios and Latias, in this fifth animated feature released to theaters—as *Pokémon Heroes* (2003)—and shown as a Saturday-morning special on Kids' WB! A *Pokémon USA/Pikachu Project 2002 Production/4Kids Entertainment Production. Color. Ninety minutes. Premiered on the WB (Kids' WB!): May 16, 2003.*

*Voices*

**Ash Ketchum:** Veronica Taylor; **Misty/Jessie:** Rachael Lillis; **Brock/James/Lorenzo:** Eric Stuart; **Meowth:** Madeleine Blaustein; **Pikachu:** Ikue Ootani; **Latios:** Masashi Ebara; **Annie:** Megan Hollingshead; **Natalie:** Ashley Fox Linton; **Bianca/Oakley:** Lisa Ortiz; **Other Voices:** Ken Gates, Wayne Grayson, Tara Jayne, Ed Paul, Kayzie Rogers, Michael Sinterniklaas, Kerry Williams

## POKÉMON: JIRACHI WISH MAKER

Ash, Pikachu, Max and company rescue the all-powerful Jirachi from an evil scientist who wants to mine Jirachi's remarkable energy source to become the most powerful *Pokémon* in the world in this 90-minute movie special for Kids' WB! That also aired the latest rendition of the *Pokémon* franchise, *Pokémon: Advanced Challenge.* A *TV Tokyo/Softix/Shogakukan Production Co. (ShoPro)/J P Kikaku/Nintendo/CREATURES/GameFreak/4Kids Entertainment Production in association with Summit Media Group. Color. Ninety minutes. Premiered on the WB (Kids' WB!): June 1, 2004.*

*Voices*

**Ash Ketchum/May:** Veronica Taylor; **Misty/Jessie:** Rachael Lillis; **Brock/James/Ludicolo:** Eric Stuart; **Meowth:** Madeleine Blaustein; **Pikachu:** Ikue Ootani; **Max:** Amy Birnbaum; **Jirachi:** Kerry Williams; **Butler:** Wayne Grayson; **Diane:** Megan Hollingshead

## POKÉMON: LUCARIO AND THE MYSTERY OF MEW

While traveling with Ash, Brock, Max and May to compete in a tournament honoring Prince Aaron, the mischievous Mew kidnaps Pikachu and Ash goes to great danger to save him in this eighth movie to air, this time on Cartoon Network, which began airing (in June 2006) the latest incarnation in the *Pokémon* franchise, *Pokémon Chronicles,* after the WB and UPN networks merged to become the CW Network. A *TV Tokyo/Softix/Shogakukan Production Co. (ShoPro)/J P Kikaku/Nintendo/CREATURES/GameFreak/4Kids Entertainment Production in association with Viz Media.Color. Ninety minutes. Premiered on CAR: September 19, 2006.*

*Voices*

**Ash Ketchum/May:** Veronica Taylor; **Jessie:** Rachael Lillis; **Brock/James:** Eric Stuart; **Meowth:** Madeleine Blaustein; **Pikachu:** Ikue Ootani; **Max:** Amy Birnbaum; **Satoshi:** Rika Matsumoto; **Aaron:** Jason Griffith; **Lucario:** Sean Schemmel; **Kidd Summers:** Lisa Ortiz; **Narrator:** Mike Pollock

## POKÉMON: MEWTWO RETURNS

After Ash, Misty and Brock manage to rescue Pikachu after Jessie James of Team Rocket abducts him, the sinister Giovanni plots to capture Mewtwo himself to relaunch his plan to unleash an army of bio-engineered Pokémon on the world. Debuting Saturday morning on Kids' WB!, this hour-long animated special was a sequel to the feature-length *Pokémon: The First Movie.* A *TV Tokyo/Softix/Shogakukan Production Co. (ShoPro)/J P Kikaku/Nintendo/CREATURES/GameFreak/4Kids Entertainment Production in association with Summit Media Group. Color. One hour. Premiered on the WB (Kids' WB!): December 4, 2001.*

*Voices*

**Ash Ketchum/Delia:** Veronica Taylor; **Mewtwo:** Dan Green; **Brock:** Eric Stuart; **Pikachu:** Ikue Ohtani; **Misty/Jesse:** Rachael Lillis; **Giovanni:** Ted Lewis; **James:** Eric Stuart; **Domino:** Kerry Williams; **Duplicate Meowth:** Mayumi Shintani; **Pikatwo:** Megumi Hayashibara; **Chikorita:** Mika Kanai; **Narrator:** Phillip

Bartlett; **Persian:** Rica Matsumoto; **Topegi:** Satomi Koorogi; **Golbat/Staryu:** Shinichiro Miki; **Onix:** Unshou Ishizuka

## POKÉMON: MEWTWO STRIKES BACK

Ash, Misty and Brock spoil Mewtwo's devilish plan to defeat all the great Pokémasters and rule the world in the world television premiere of this first action-packed movie—also known as *Pokémon the First Movie*—broadcast on Saturday morning on Kids' WB! two days before the release of the 90-minute feature to movie theaters. *A Kids' WB!/Pikachu Project '98–Shogakukan Inc. Production/4Kids Entertainment Production in association with Warner Bros. Family Entertainment. Color. Ninety minutes. Premiered on the WB (Kids' WB!): November 10, 1999.*

### Voices

**Ash Ketchum:** Veronica Taylor; **Misty/Jessie/Jigglypuff:** Rachael Lillis; **Brock/James/Squirtle/Pikachu/Raichu/Other Voices:** Ikue Ootani; **Narrator/Mewtwo:** Phillip Bartlett; **Meowth/Other Voices:** Madeleine Blaustein; **Meowth:** Tommy Karlsen; **Giovanni/Cubone/Weezing:** Ted Lewis; **Officer Jenny/Nurse Joy:** Amy Birnbaum; **Mewtwo's Servant:** Megan Hollingshead; **Vulpix/Ninetales/Bulbasaur/Venusaur/Other Voices:** Tara Jayne; **Neesha:** Lisa Ortiz; **Giovanni/Corey:** Ed Paul; **Arbok/Hitmonlee/Onix/Victreebel/Farfetch'd:** Kayzie Rogers; **Mew:** Koichi Yamadera; **Fergus:** Jimmy Zoppi

## POKÉMON MYSTERY DUNGEON: TEAM GO-GETTERS OUT OF THE GATE!

Joined by Chikorita and Charmander, Squirtle leads the Go-Getters team to find Pichu's older brother competing against the evil rival Team Meanie team, featuring Medicham and Gengar, in this half-hour special based on the new video game of the same name, broadcast on Cartoon Network. The special marked the premiere of the all-new series, *Pokémon: Battle Frontier. A TV Tokyo/Softix/Shogakukan Production Co. (ShoPro)/J P Kikaku/Nintendo/CREATURES/GameFreak/4Kids Entertainment Production in association with Viz Media. Color. Half-hour. Premiered on CAR: September 30, 2006.*

### Voices

**Squirtle:** Kayzie Rogers; **Whiscash:** Ken Gates; **Chikorita:** Michelle Knotz; **Gengar:** Jimmy Zoppi; **Medicham/Baby Kangaskhan:** Sarah Natochenny

## POKÉMON RANGER AND THE TEMPLE OF THE SEA

Ash and his friends encounter a greedy pirate, Phantom, who plans to use the powerful egg of Manaphy for evil purposes in this 90-minute movie special that bowed on Cartoon Network. *A TV Tokyo/Shogakukan Production Co./Oriental Light and Magic/Goldenball Animation/Hanil Animation//Nintendo/4Kids Entertainment Production in association with Viz Media. Color. One hour. Premiered on CAR: March 23, 2007.*

### Voices

**Ash Ketchum/Max:** Sarah Natochenny; **Misty/May:** Michele Knotz; **Brock:** Bill Rogers; **James/Meowth:** Billy Beach; **Meowth:** Jimmy Zoppi; **Mew:** Katsuyuki Konishi; **Pikachu:** Ikue Ohtani; **Jessie/Manaply:** Michele Knotz; **Officer Jenny/Nurse Joy:** Diane Stillwell; **Officer Jenny:** Erica Schroeder; **Professor Oak:** Billy Beach; **Chef:** Armen Mazlumian; **Merideth:** Annie Silver; **Lizabeth:** Emily Williams II; **Phantom:** Eric Schussler; **Phantom's Assistant/Ship Caregiver:** Craig Blair; **Jack Walker/Pirate/Kyle/Ship Caregiver:** Bill Rogers; **Narrator/Intercom Pilot:** Ken Gates

## POKÉMON: SPELL OF THE UNOWN

Grief stricken over her father's sudden disappearance, Molly accidentally empowers the Unown to invent her own dream world with Entei kidnapping Ash's mom, with Misty and Brock coming to her rescue in this third 90-minute movie released to theaters under the title of *Pokémon 3 the Movie: Spell of the Unown* (2001), adapted from the world-renowned Japanese anime series broadcast on the Kids' WB! *A Kids' WB!/Pikachu Project 98-Shogakukan Inc. Production/4Kids Entertainment Production in association with Warner Bros. Color. Ninety minutes. Premiered on Kids' WB!: March 29, 2001.*

### Voices

**Ash Ketchum/Delia:** Veronica Taylor; **Misty/Jesse:** Rachael Lillis; **Togepi:** Satomi Koorogi; **Pikachu:** Ikue Ohtani; **Tracy:** Ted Lewis; **Brock/James:** Eric Stuart; **Professor Ivy:** Kayzie Rogers; **Professor Oak:** Stan Hart; **Spencer/Entei:** Dan Green; **Skyler:** Eddie Paulson; **Molly:** Amy Birnbaum

## POKÉMON: THE POWER OF ONE

After the greedy Pokémon collector Lawrence III disrupts the balance of nature in the universe, Ash faces the ultimate challenge as he saves the world in this second feature-length theatrical movie—also known as *Pokémon the Movie 2000*—first shown on Kids' WB! in January 2000. *A Kids' WB!/Pikachu Project '99-Shogakukan Inc. Production/4Kids Entertainment Production in association with Warner Bros. Family Entertainment. Color. Ninety minutes. Premiered on the WB (Kids' WB!): January 21, 2000.*

### Voices

**Ash Ketchum/Mrs. Delia Ketchum:** Veronica Taylor; **Misty/Jesse:** Rachael Lillis; **Tracey Sketchit:** Ted Lewis; **James/Charizard:** Eric Stuart; **Meowth:** Madeleine Blaustein; **Pikachu:** Ikue Ootani; **Professor Samuel Oak:** Stan Hart; **Professor Felinda Ivy/Mr. Mime:** Kayzie Rogers; **Melody:** Amy Birnbaum; **Lugia:** Dan Green; **Computer:** Megan Hollingshead; **Erin:** Tara Jayne; **Maren:** Julie Lund; **The Collector Lawrence III:** Neil Stewart; **Additional Voices:** Norman Altman, John Corallo, Ken Gates, Michaelle Goguen, Cassidy Kahn, Roger Kay, Emily Niebo, Robert O'Gorman, Ed Paul, Nathan Price, Eric Rath, Jack Taylor

## THE POKY LITTLE PUPPY'S FIRST CHRISTMAS

A playful little puppy wanders off while the family searches for the perfect Christmas tree, only to fall into a deep hole through the fresh snow. He's rescued later, but that's not the last of the family's misfortunes in this half-hour animated special based on the popular children's storybooks. *A Michael Sporn Animation Production for Italtoons Corporation and Western Publishing Co. Inc. Color. Half-hour. Premiered on SHO: December 13, 1992. Rebroadcast on SHO: December 10, 1993.*

### Voices

**Narrator:** Donald Sutherland; **Mother:** Heidi Stallings; **Herman:** Andrew Harrison Leeds; **Girl:** Grace Johnston

## POOCHIE

Poochie, a lovable pink pup, goes on an exciting journey to Egypt with her computer robot, Hermes, to help a young boy, Danny Evans, find his father, who has disappeared inside a pyramid. *A DIC Enterprises Production in association with Mattel. Color. Half-hour. Premiered: June 1984. Syndicated.*

*Voices*
**Poochie:** Ellen Gerstell; **Hermes:** Neil Ross; **Zipcode:** Fred Travalena; **Koom:** Jennifer Darling; **Danny Evans:** Katie Leigh

## ◎ POPEYE MEETS THE MAN WHO HATED LAUGHTER

Seafaring sailor Popeye and a bumper crop of comic-strip favorites (Blondie and Dagwood, the Katzenjammer Kids, the Little King, Steve Canyon, Flash Gordon, the Phantom, Tim Tyler, Beetle Bailey, and Jiggs and Maggie) who appear in animation for the first time meet their match when an evil man tries to prevent the spread of laughter in the world in this *ABC Saturday Superstar Movie*. The made-for-television feature was directed by cartoon veterans Jack Zander and Hal Seeger and written by Lou Silverton. Original music was scored by Elliott Schiprut. *A King Features Production. Color. One hour. Premiered on ABC: October 7, 1972 (on The ABC Saturday Superstar Movie). Rebroadcast on ABC: February 9, 1974. Syndicated.*

*Voices*
**Popeye/Wimpy:** Jack Mercer; **Other Voices:** Bob McFadden

## ◎ THE POPEYE SHOW

Aired in prime time, this half-hour special was comprised of four excerpts from the Saturday-morning series *The All-New Popeye Hour*, in which the spinach-gulping sailor; stringbean girlfriend, Olive, and world-class bully, Bluto, are subjected to a series of misadventures. *A Hanna-Barbera Production in association with King Features Entertainment. Color. Half-hour. Premiered on CBS: September 13, 1978.*

*Voices*
**Popeye:** Jack Mercer; **Olive Oyl:** Marilyn Schreffler; **Bluto:** Allan Melvin; **Wimpy:** Daws Butler

## ◎ POPEYE'S VOYAGE: THE QUEST FOR PAPPY

After dreaming that his long-lost Pappy has encountered sea monsters, the world's favorite spinach-gulping sailor takes to the high seas to rescue him with the help of Olive Oyl, Swee'pea, Wimpy (who becomes a stowaway) and Bluto, who serves as his first-mate and joins forces to battle Popeye's famed arch-enemy, the Sea Hag (voiced by Oscar-winning actress Kathy Bates). Available in 22- and 44-minute versions, the all-new 3-D computer-animated prime-time television and home entertainment special—Popeye's first appearance in CGI animation and produced to commemorate the character's 75th anniversary—premiered in December 2004 on FOX, preceded by an hour-long DVD/VHS version released on Artisan Home Entertainment featuring new and classic bonus material. On July 15th of that year, producers of the special showcased it before national television critics and reporters at the Television Critics Association Press Tour, including a Popeye-themed luncheon that featured spinach salad topped with an "Olive Oyl" red wine vinaigrette. A month before its FOX debut, the Museum of Television and Radio premiered the holiday special along with classic Popeye cartoons. Actor/comedian Paul Reiser (of TV's *Mad About You*), a life-long Popeye fan, cowrote the special with Jim Hardison (*Gary and Mike*). *A Mainframe Entertainment Production. Color. Half-hour. Premiered on FOX: December 17, 2004. Rebroadcast on FOX: December 30, 2005.*

*Voices*
**Popeye/Pappy:** Billy West; **Olive Oyl/Swee'pea:** Tabitha St. Germain; **Bluto:** Gary Chalk; **Wimpy:** Sanders Whiting; **The Sea Hag:** Kathy Bates

## ◎ THE POPEYE VALENTINE SPECIAL

Olive Oyl sets sail on a Valentine's Day Sweetheart Cruise, captained by hamburger-eating Wimpy, in search of "Mr. Right." She discovers in the end that the best man for her is Popeye. The story title of the program was "Sweethearts at Sea." *A Hanna-Barbera Production in association with King Features Entertainment. Color. Half-hour. Premiered on CBS: February 14, 1979. Rebroadcast on CBS: February 13, 1980; January 30, 1981; February 2, 1982.*

*Voices*
**Popeye:** Jack Mercer; **Olive Oyl/Sea Hag/Bathing Beauty #1:** Marilyn Schreffler; **Bluto:** Allan Melvin; **Wimpy:** Daws Butler; **King Neptune/Man-In-The-Moon:** Barney Phillips; **Jeep/Princess/Bathing Beauty #2:** Ginny McSwain

## ◎ POUND PUPPIES

The Pound Puppies operate the Pound Puppy Mission Control Center. Their mission is to find homes for hapless puppies that get caught in the net of Dabney Nabbit, the diligent if sloppy dogcatcher in this first-run movie inspired by the Saturday-morning series *Pound Puppies*, which was broadcast on ABC. *A Hanna-Barbera Production. Color. One hour. Premiered: October 1985. Syndicated.*

*Voices*
**Cooler:** Dan Gilvezan; **Violet/TV Newscaster:** Gail Matthius; **Scounger:** Ron Palillo; **Bright Eyes/Mom:** Adrienne Alexander; **Howler/Fat Cat:** Frank Welker; **Barkerville/Dad:** Alan Oppenheimer; **Mayor Fisk:** Sorrell Brooke; **Chief Williams:** Garrett Morris; **Bigelow:** Jonathan Winters; **Tubbs/Pound Puppy #4:** Avery Schreiber; **Nabbit/Pound Puppy #3:** Henry Gibson; **The Nose:** Jo Anne Worley; **Flack/Nathan/Pound Puppy #1:** Charles Adler; **Itchy/Snitchy/Louie:** Don Messick; **Fist/Pound Puppy #2:** Ed Begley Jr.; **Mother Superior/Old Lady:** June Foray; **Doc West/Chelsea:** Victoria Carroll; **Sarah:** Laura Duff

## ◎ THE POWERPUFF GIRLS: "'TWAS THE FRIGHT BEFORE CHRISTMAS"

When Townville's greedy Princess Morbucks tries stealing Christmas by switching every child's "wish" list to make it look like the Powerpuff Girls and other children have been naughty and not nice, Bubbles, Blossom and Buttercup stir up a nasty blizzard to prevent the Princess from making Christmas disappear altogether. Originally broadcast on Friday, December 12, 2003, at 9:00 P.M., followed by two encore performances that weekend on Cartoon Network, the hour-long direct-to-video holiday special was nominated in 2004 for an Emmy Award for outstanding animated program (for programming one hour or more). The program has appeared in reruns on Cartoon Network since its original broadcast. *A Hanna-Barbera Studios Production. Color. One hour. Premiered on CAR: December 12, 2003. Rebroadcast on CAR: December 13, 2003; December 14, 2003; December 22, 2003; December 23, 2003; December 24, 2003; December 25, 2003; December 17, 2004; December 24, 2004; December 25, 2004; December 9, 2005; December 16, 2005; December 17, 2005; December 23, 2005; December 25, 2005; November 16, 2006; November 25, 2006; December 3, 2006; December 14, 2006; December 15, 2006; December 16, 2006; December 21, 2006; December 22, 2006; December 24, 2006; December 25, 2006.*

*Voices*
**Bubbles:** Tara Strong; **Blossom:** Cathy Cavadini; **Buttercup:** Elizabeth Daily; **Princess Morbucks/Ms. Keane:** Jennifer Hale; **Professor Utonium:** Tom Kane; **Narrator/Mitch Mitchellson:** Tom Kenny; **Santa Claus:** Michael Bell

### ◎ THE PRINCE AND THE PAUPER

This 1990, 35-minute theatrical featurette starring Mickey Mouse, Pluto, Donald Duck and Goofy, first premiered by itself on Disney Channel in 1992 and a year later was broadcast on ABC as an hour-long prime-time "world premiere event"—in which Mickey, in a comic variation of the Mark Twain classic, plays a royal heir-head and a look-alike urchin who trade places. The ABC presentation included the broadcast of "Mickey and the Beanstalk" (narrated by Corey Burton as Ludwig Von Drake), an animated sequence from the 1947 Disney full-length classic *Fun and Fancy Free*. *A Walt Disney Production. Color. Thirty-five minutes. One hour. Premiered on DIS: January 12, 1992. Rebroadcast on ABC: March 26, 1993.*

*Voices*
**Mickey Mouse/The Prince:** Wayne Allwine; **Pluto/GoofyHorace/Weasel #1:** Bill Farmer; **Donald Duck:** Tony Anselmo; **Clarabelle:** Elvia Allman; **Pete:** Arthur Burghardt; **Archbishop/Dying King:** Frank Welker; **Weasels #2 and #3/Pig:** Charles Adler; **Kid #1:** Tim Eyster; **Kid #2:** Rocky Krakoff; **Narrator (The Prince and the Pauper):** Roy Dotrice; **Ludwig Von Drake:** Corey Burton

### ◎ THE PRINCE'S RAIN

Inspired by the popular children's nursery rhyme "Rain, Rain, Go Away," this half-hour adaptation tells the tale of cool Prince Vince who angers Mother Nature by asking the palace magician to stop the skies from raining on his tanning season in this animated musical special, broadcast as part of the *HBO Musical Storybook* series in 1991. Canadian animation giant CINAR Films produced the special, which was part of the 13-part *The Real Story of . . .* anthology series. *A CINAR Films/Crayon Animation in association with Western Publishing Company/Global Television Network/Telefilm Canada. Color. Half-hour. Premiered on HBO: November 13, 1991. Rebroadcast on HBO: November 21, 1991, November 26, 1991, November 29, 1991.*

*Voices*
**Prince Vince:** Joe Piscopo; **Narrator:** Robin Leach

### ◎ PRINCE VALIANT: KNIGHT OF THE ROUND TABLE

In this intriguing saga, Prince Valiant struggles with his own sense of pride and must choose his path—to remain true to his father's throne or to continue his journey to become a knight of the Round Table in this feature-length compilation of episodes of the Family Channel's original series *The Legend of Prince Valiant*. *A Hearst/IDDH Groupe Bruno Rene Huchez/Polyphonfilm und Fernsehen GmbH/Sei Young Studios/King Features/Family Channel Production. Premiered on FAM: September 4, 1992.*

*Voices*
**Prince Valiant:** Robby Benson; **Arn:** Michael Horton; **King Arthur:** Efrem Zimbalist, Jr; **Guinevere:** Samantha Eggar; **Sir Gawain:** Tim Curry

### ◎ PRINCE VALIANT: THE VOYAGE OF CAMELOT

This feature-length companion-the first of two reedited from The Family Channel's *The Legend of Prince Valiant* series—tells the story of how the young Valiant comes to serve King Arthur. It features the voices of Robby Benson (Prince Valiant) and Efrem Zimbalist Jr. (King Arthur). *A Hearst/IDDH Groupe Bruno Rene Huchez/Polyphonfilm und Fernsehen GmbH/Sei Young Studios/King Features/Family Channel Production. Premiered on FAM: January 3, 1992. Rebroadcast on FAM: July 24, 1992.*

*Voices*
**Prince Valiant:** Robby Benson; **King Arthur:** Efrem Zimbalist Jr.

### ◎ PRIVATE EYE PRINCESS

A half-hour special—created by award-winning animator Debra Solomon, creator of the acclaimed cartoon short *Mrs. Matisse* and an animator of Disney's *Lizzie McGuire*—about the kooky misadventures of an idiotic female sleuth who vanquishes the forces of the evilest man on earth, Mr. Meenie. Debuting on Cartoon Network, the program's musical score was composed by Jody Gray and Andy Ezrin. In November 2002, Solomon held a premiere screening and reception of her special at ASIFA-East in New York. *A Pharoh Films/Sunwoo Entertainment Production. Color. Half-hour. Premiered on CAR: November 29, 2002.*

*Voices*
**Private Eye Princess:** Candi Milo

### ◎ THE PROUD FAMILY MOVIE

Plans for Penny's 16th birthday party are cancelled when Oscar catches her kissing a young rap star. Meanwhile, the mad scientist offers to send the entire Proud family on a tropical island vacation in exchange for Oscar's snack formula, promising to make them multimillionaires. One problem: Oscar won't budge, so Dr. Carver holds them hostage while sending peanut-sized clones back home in their places in this feature-length movie special, based on the popular Disney Channel cartoon series. *A Walt Disney Television Animation/Jambalaya Studios/Hyperion Studios Production. Color. Ninety minutes. Premiered on DIS: August 19, 2005. Rebroadcast on DIS: August 19, 2005; August 20, 2005; August 21, 2005; August 24, 2005; September 1, 2005; September 11, 2005; September 21, 2005; January 18, 2006; January 31, 2006; February 24, 2006; April 2, 2006; April 27, 2006; May 11, 2006; June 14, 2006; November 23, 2006; February 16, 2007.*

*Voices*
**Penny Proud:** Kyla Pratt; **Oscar Proud:** Tommy Davidson; **Trudy Parker-Proud:** Paula Jai Parker; **Bobby Proud:** Cedric the Entertainer; **Bebe Proud/Cece Proud/Cashew:** Tara Strong; **Suga Mama:** Jo Marie Payton-Noble; **Sticky Webb:** Orlando Brown; **Zoey:** Soleil Moon Frye; **Papi Boulevardez:** Alvaro Gutierrez; **LaCienega Boulevardez:** Alisa Reyes; **Felix Boulevardez:** Carlos Mencia; **Sunset Boulavardez:** Maria Canals; **Wizard Kelly:** Aries Spears; **The Gross Sisters:** Racquel Lee; **Dijonay Jones:** Karen Malina White; **Dr. Carver:** Arsenio Hall; **Peanut Head:** Marcy Perlson; **Wally:** Jeremy Suarez; **Puff/Board Member:** Carlos Alazraqui; **Board Member 2:** Matthew Charles; **Fifteen Cent:** Omarion Grandberry; **Dr. Carver in Disguise/Board Member:** Phil LaMarr; **Big Boy:** Himself; **Nubia Gross:** Raquel Lee; **Attorney/Hot Dog Ventor:** Christian Mills; **Japanese Kid/Announcer:** Masi Oka; **Wizard Kelly/Board Member:** Aries Spear; **Board Member/Cab Driver:** Billy West; **Sea Beast/The Mangler/Narrator:** Kevin Michael Richardson

### ◎ PUFF AND THE INCREDIBLE MR. NOBODY

An insecure young boy (Terry) creates his own imaginary friend, Mr. Nobody. He soon believes his ability to make up songs, jokes and games and to paint pictures originates from the mythical character. Puff the Magic Dragon teaches the young lad that his creativity comes from within and not from his friend. *A Yarrow-Muller/Murakami-Wolf-Swenson Films Production for the My Company. Color. Half-hour. Premiered on CBS: May 17, 1982.*

*Rebroadcast on CBS: August 30, 1985. Syndicated. Rebroadcast on DIS: May 19, 1992; May 30, 1992.*

**Voices**
**Puff:** Burgess Meredith; **Terry:** David Mendenhall; **Mr. Nobody:** Robert Ridgely; **Girl:** Diana Dumpis; **Boy:** Billy Jacoby; **Mom:** Joan Gerber; **Dad:** Bob Holt; **Professor K:** Hal Smith

## ◎ PUFF THE MAGIC DRAGON

Puff comes to the aid of a small boy who is afraid to face life and helps solve the boy's problems by taking him on a trip to his homeland, teaching him to be brave and to see things as they really are. Based on the Peter, Paul and Mary song of the same name, writer Peter Yarrow added new lyrics to go with the story. *A Yarrow-Muller/Murakami-Wolf-Swenson Films Production for the My Company. Color. Half-hour. Premiered on CBS: October 30, 1978. Rebroadcast on CBS: September 10, 1979; April 28, 1981. Syndicated. Rebroadcast on DIS: April 25, 1992.*

**Voices**
**Puff:** Burgess Meredith; **Jackie Draper:** Phillip Tanzini; **Pirate/Pieman/Sneeze:** Bob Ridgely; **Mother/Star:** Maitzi Morgan; **Father:** Peter Yarrow; **Bald Doctor:** Regis Cordic; **Tall Doctor:** Frank Nelson; **Short Doctor:** Charles Woolf

## ◎ PUFF THE MAGIC DRAGON IN THE LAND OF THE LIVING LIES

The irresistible Puff deals with a young girl who lies to make herself feel better after her parents' divorce by taking her to the Land of Living Lies so she can recognize that her lying fools nobody and only hurts herself. *A Yarrow-Muller/Murakami-Wolf-Swenson Films Production for the My Company. Color. Half-hour. Premiered on CBS: November 17, 1979. Rebroadcast on CBS: October 22, 1980. Syndicated.*

**Voices**
**Puff:** Burgess Meredith; **Sandy:** Mischa Lenore Bond; **Talking Tree:** Alan Barzman; **Kid Umpire/Boy Who Cried Wolf/Boy with Huge Ears:** Ike Eisenmann; **Mother/Talking Pumpkin/Little Girl:** Joan Gerber; **Judge/Bailiff/Zealot:** Gene Moss; **Baron Munchausen/Snake/Attorney/Basketball Player:** Robert Ridgely; **Father:** Peter Yarrow

## ◎ THE PUPPY'S AMAZING RESCUE

While celebrating Tommy's birthday in his parents' mountaintop cabin, Petey the puppy and Dolly, Tommy's sister, get separated from Tommy and his father during a massive snowslide. Petey and Dolly head up a search party to find them. *An ABC Weekend Special. A Ruby-Spears Enterprises Production. Color. Half-hour. Premiered on ABC: January 26, 1980. Rebroadcast on ABC: May 3, 1980; September 6, 1980; March 26, 1983.*

**Voices**
**Petey:** Bryan Scott; **Tommy:** John Joseph Thomas; **Dolly:** Nancy McKeon

## ◎ THE PUPPY SAVES THE CIRCUS

In his fourth afternoon children's special, Petey, the frisky pup, suffers a serious bout of amnesia after he is accidentally struck by a car and, with no memory of his past, he winds up performing in the circus (as Rags II, the Funny Wonder Puppy), where his life is put in great danger. The program marked the fifth-season debut of the ABC Weekend Specials. *A Ruby-Spears Enterprises Production. Color. Half-hour. Premiered on ABC: September 12, 1981. Rebroadcast on ABC: March 6, 1982; October 23, 1982; March 3, 1984.*

**Voices**
**Petey:** Sparky Marcus; **Dolly:** Nancy McKeon; **Tommy:** Tony O'Dell; **George Goodbee/Sligh:** Alan Young; **Gloria Goodbee:** Janet Waldo; **Emily:** Linda Gary; **Dad/Abdullah:** John Stephenson; **Kiki/Vet:** Alan Dinehart; **Tiger/Lead Pony/Clown:** Frank Welker

## ◎ THE PUPPY'S GREAT ADVENTURE

Petey the puppy's happiness turns to bitter sorrow when his master, Tommy, is adopted out of the Public Home for Boys by a wealthy jeweler and his wife who refuse to take Petey in this sequel to *The Puppy Who Wanted a Boy*. *An ABC Weekend Special. A Ruby-Spears Enterprises Production. Color. Half-hour. Premiered on ABC: February 3, 1979. Rebroadcast on ABC: May 12, 1979; September 2, 1979.*

**Voices**
**Petey:** Bryan Scott; **Tommy:** John Joseph Thomas; **Dolly:** Nancy McKeon

## ◎ THE PUPPY WHO WANTED A BOY

The natural bond between a dog and a boy is the core of this half-hour special, adapted from Catherine Woolley's sentimental children's story in which Sonny, a lonely puppy, seeks the companionship of a 12-year-old orphan (Tommy) to fulfill his search for an owner to call his own. *An ABC Weekend Special. A Ruby-Spears Enterprises Production. Color. Half-hour. Premiered on ABC: May 6, 1978. Rebroadcast on ABC: September 23, 1978; January 21, 1979; October 27, 1979.*

**Voices**
**Sonny/Petey:** Todd Turquand; **Tommy:** John Joseph Thomas

## ◎ PUSS-IN-BOOTS

Wearing boots that possess magical powers, Orlando the cat is given the ability to speak and uses his newfound talent to elevate his master (Jacques) in the community, thus enabling him to pursue his first and only love—the king's daughter. *A Rankin-Bass Production in association with Mushi Studios. Color. Half-hour. Premiered: December 9, 1972. Syndicated. Rebroadcast on NICK: May 6, 1993.*

**Voices**
Carl Banas, Len Birman, Bernard Cowan, Peg Dixon, Keith Hampshire, Peggi Loder, Donna Miller, Frank Perry, Henry Ramer, Billie Mae Richards, Alfie Scopp, Paul Soles

## ◎ THE RACCOONS AND THE LOST STAR

Bert Raccoon and his friends foil the evil Cyril Sneer's plan to recover a special "gold star," and to conquer Earth in this third special based on the popular Canadian cartoon series *Raccoons*. *A Gillis-Wiseman Production in association with Atkinson Film-Arts Productions. Color. Half-hour. Premiered (U.S.): December, 1983. Syndicated.*

**Voices**
**Bert Raccoon/Pig General:** Len Carlson; **Ralph Raccoon:** Bobby Dermer; **Melissa Raccoon:** Dottie West; **Julie:** Tammy Bourne; **Tommy:** Hadley Kay; **Dan the Ranger:** John Schneider; **Schaeffer, Julie and Tommy's dog:** Carl Banas; **Cyril Sneer/Snag:** Michael Magee; **Cedric Sneer/Pig General:** Fred Little; **Sophia Tu Tu/Broo:** Sharon Lewis; **Narrator:** Rich Little

## ◎ RACCOONS ON ICE

The Raccoons and their friends wage a courageous effort to save Evergreen Lake, climaxing with an exciting game of ice hockey against sinister Cyril Sneer's ferocious team of "Bears" in this half-hour syndicated cartoon that coincided with the beginning of the 1982 National Hockey League Stanley Cup playoffs. *A Gillis-Wiseman Production in association with Atkinson Film-Arts Productions. Color. Half-hour. Premiered: December 20, 1981. Syndicated.*

**Voices**
**Bert Raccoon:** Len Carlson; **Ralph Raccoon:** Bobby Dermer; **Melissa Raccoon:** Rita Coolidge; **Schaeffer:** Carl Banas; **Cyril Sneer/Snag:** Michael Magee; **Cedric Sneer:** Fred Little; **Sophia Tu Tu:** Sharon Lewis; **Julie:** Tammy Bourne; **Tommy:** Hadley Kay; **Ferlin:** Danny Gallivan; **Narrator:** Rich Little; **Vocalist:** Leo Sayer

## ◉ RAGGEDY ANN AND ANDY IN THE GREAT SANTA CLAUS CAPER

Alexander Graham Wolf, the inventor of "Gloopstick," plans to use the breakable plastic cube to sabotage Christmas, but not before Raggedy Ann and Raggedy Andy ruin his sinister scheme. *A Chuck Jones Enterprises Production in association with Bobbs-Merrill Company. Color. Half-hour. Premiered on CBS: November 30, 1978. Rebroadcast on CBS: December 10, 1979; December 9, 1980. Syndicated. Rebroadcast on DIS: December 23, 1991; December 25, 1993.*

**Voices**
**Raggedy Ann/Comet:** June Foray; **Raggedy Andy:** Daws Butler; **Alexander Graham Wolf/Santa:** Les Tremayne

## ◉ RAGGEDY ANN AND ANDY IN THE PUMPKIN WHO COULDN'T SMILE

Raggedy Ann and Raggedy Andy bring together a lonely boy and lonely pumpkin—to make Halloween special in this touching tale based on the famous ragdoll characters created by Johnny Gruelle. *A Chuck Jones Enterprises Production in association with Bobbs-Merrill Company. Color. Half-hour. Premiered on CBS: October 31, 1979. Rebroadcast on CBS: October 29, 1980. Syndicated. Rebroadcast on DIS: October 27, 1991; October 18, 1992; October 26, 1993; October 30, 1994; October 21, 1995.*

**Voices**
**Raggedy Ann/Aunt Agatha:** June Foray; **Raggedy Andy:** Daws Butler; **The Pumpkin:** Les Tremayne; **Ralph:** Steven Rosenberg

## ◉ THE RAILWAY DRAGON

Keenly aware of the magic that lurks beneath the old railway tunnel, young Emily's ultimate wish comes true in the form of a centuries-old dragon who takes her on an exciting, fun-filled adventure. This Canadian-animated half-hour special was the first of two *Railway Dragon* produced by Canada's Lacewood Productions. *A Lacewood Production. Color. Half-hour. Premiered on DIS: 1991.*

**Voices**
**Narrator:** Leslie Nielsen; **The Dragon:** Barry Morse; **Emily:** Tracey Moore; **Father/Conductor:** Noel Counsil; **Mother:** Beverly Wolfe; **A Dragon/Hunter:** Chuck Collins; **Hunter's Son/Chef:** Rick Jones

## ◉ RAINBOW BRITE: PERIL IN THE PITS

Archenemy Murky Dismal and his henchman, Lurky, try to drain Earth of its color and remove all the happiness from the world but are foiled by Rainbow Brite and her special friends of Rainbowland in this animated special based on the popular greeting card characters. *A Hallmark Properties Production in association with DIC Enterprises Productions. Color. Half-hour. Premiered: June 1984. Syndicated.*

*Emily and a dragon share an adventure learning more about themselves and their world in the half-hour animated special* The Railway Dragon. © *Lacewood Productions (now Paragon Entertainment)*

**Voices**
**Rainbow Brite:** Bettina Rush; **Starlite/Spectran:** Andre Stojka; **Brian:** Scott Menville; **Murky Dismal:** Peter Cullen; **Lurky/Buddy Blue/Puppy Brite:** Patrick Fraley; **Twink/Shy Violet/Indigo/La La Orange:** Robbie Lee; **Krys:** David Mendenhall; **Count Blogg:** Jonathan Harris; **Stormy:** Marissa Mendenhall; **Princess/Moonglow/Tickled Pink:** Ronda Aldrich; **Patty O'Green/Red Butler/Canary Yellow/Castle Creature:** Mona Marshall

## ◉ RAINBOW BRITE: THE BEGINNING OF RAINBOWLAND

In this two-part special based on the Hallmark greeting card characters, Rainbow Brite relates the history of Rainbowland, including the beginning of her own magical power. Broadcast in half-hour time slots over two consecutive days. *A Hallmark Properties Production in association with DIC Enterprises Productions. Color. One hour. Premiered: April 1985. Syndicated.*

**Voices**
**Rainbow Brite:** Bettina Rush; **Starlite/Spectran:** Andre Stojka; **Brian:** Scott Menville; **Murky Dismal:** Peter Cullen; **Lurky/Buddy Blue/Puppy Brite:** Patrick Fraley; **Twink/Shy Violet/Indigo/La La Orange:** Robbie Lee; **Krys:** David Mendenhall; **Count Blogg:** Jonathan Harris; **Stormy:** Marissa Mendenhall; **Princess/Moonglow/Tickled Pink:** Ronda Aldrich; **Patty O'Green/Red Butler/Canary Yellow/Castle Creature:** Mona Marshall

## ◉ RAINBOW BRITE: THE MIGHTY MONSTROMURK MENACE

Terror strikes Rainbowland when Monstromurk, a powerful monster held captive in a bottle for 700 years, is let loose by that good-for-nothing aardvark Murky Dismal, who wants to make the people of this happy-go-lucky world as miserable as he is. *A Hallmark Properties Production in association with DIC Enterprises Productions. Color. One hour. Premiered: December 1984. Syndicated.*

**Voices**
**Rainbow Brite:** Bettina Rush; **Starlite/Spectran:** Andre Stojka; **Brian:** Scott Menville; **Murky Dismal:** Peter Cullen; **Lurky/Buddy Blue/Puppy Brite:** Patrick Fraley; **Twink/Shy Violet/Indigo/La La Orange:** Robbie Lee; **Krys:** David Mendenhall; **Count Blogg:** Jonathan Harris; **Stormy:** Marissa Mendenhall;

**Princess/Moonglow/Tickled Pink:** Ronda Aldrich; **Patty O'Green/ Red Butler/Canary Yellow/Castle Creature:** Mona Marshall

## ◎ THE RAISINS SOLD OUT!

In this fanciful claymation rockumentary, slick manager Leonard Limabean pressures the California Raisins to accept a new member into the group, hotshot performer Lick Broccoli, in this stop-motion animated special. A Will Vinton Associates Production. Color. Half-hour. Premiered on CBS: May 2, 1990. Rebroadcast on DIS: February 18, 1993; November 26, 1994.

### Voices

Brian Cummings, Jim Cummings, Dorian Harewood, Brian Mitchell, David Scully, Todd Tolces

## ◎ RARG

British animator Tony Collingwood created this award-winning animated film, based on his original short story (written in 1982) about a place called Rarg in which the sun never rises and things are blissful until the citizens discover that they exist in the dream of a man who is about to wake up. Premiered on PBS anthology series Long Ago & Far Away. A Hit Communications Production. Color. Half-hour. Premiered on PBS: September 22, 1990. Rebroadcast on PBS: December 13, 1992.

### Voices

Nigel Hawthorne, Michael Gough, Ronnie Stevens

## ◎ THE REAL GHOSTBUSTERS CHRISTMAS

Those ghostbusting fools—Peter, Egon, Ray and Winston—unwittingly aid Ebenezer Scrooge when they trap the ghosts of Christmas Past, Present and Future in this regular episode from the popular Saturday-morning series, rebroadcast as a holiday special on USA Network in 1993. (For voice credits, see series entry in Animated Television Series section.) A DIC Enterprises Production in association with Columbia Pictures Television. Color. Half-hour. Premiered on USA: December 19, 1993.

## ◎ REALLY ROSIE

Singer-composer Carole King takes on the role of Rosie, who, dressed up like a film star, persuades her friends, the Nutshell Kids, into making musical screen tests for a picture she wants to make. Based on characters from Maurice Sendak's Nutshell Library. A Sherriss Production in association with D & R Productions. Color. Half-hour. Premiered on CBS: February 19, 1975. Rebroadcast on CBS: June 8, 1976 (as Maurice Sendak's Really Rosie). Rebroadcast on DIS: September 2, 1993.

### Voices

**Rosie:** Carole King

## ◎ RECESS CHRISTMAS: "MIRACLE ON THIRD STREET"

The Recess kids try convincing the Third Elementary Street School teachers that miracles come true in this direct-to-video compilation of four episodes from the popular Saturday-morning cartoon series, Disney's Recess), including the 1998 Christmas special, Yes Mikey, Santa Does Shave. The 65-minute movie guest stars the voices of Dick Clark, Robert Goulet and James Earl Jones. Produced in 2003, the production was followed by two more direct-to-video films that same year: Recess: Taking the Fifth Grade and Recess: All Growed Down. A Walt Disney Television Animation Production. Color. One hour and five minutes. Premiered on TDIS: December 11, 2004. Rebroadcast on TDIS: December 17, 2004; December 24, 2004; December 9, 2005; December 19, 2005; Decem-

ber 23, 2005; December 24, 2005; December 25, 2005; December 19, 2006; December 20, 2006; December 24, 2006; December 25, 2006. Syndicated: December 3, 2006 (Tribune Broadcasting).

### Voices

**Theodore J. "T.J." Detweiler:** Andrew Lawrence; **Vincent Pierre "Vince" LaSalle:** Rickey D'Shon Collins; **Michael "Mikey" Blumberg:** Jason Davis; **Gretchen Grundler:** Ashley Johnson; **Gustav Patten "Gus" Griswald:** Courtland Mead; **Ashley Spinelli:** Pamela Segall; **Miss Alordayne Grotkey:** Allyce Beasley; **Miss Muriel P. Finster:** April Winchell; **Principal Peter Prickly:** Dabney Coleman; **Erwin Lawson:** Erik von Detten; **Dick Clark:** Himself; **Santa Claus:** James Earl Jones; **Michael "Mikey" Blumberg (singing):** Robert Goulet; **Theodore J. "T.J." Detweiler (scenes "The Great Can Drive"):** Ross Malinger; **Mr. Bream (scenes from "Yes, Mikey, Santa Does Shave"):** Michael McKean

## ◎ THE RED BARON

When the princess of Pretzelheim is kidnapped by the evil cat, Putzi, legendary flying ace the Red Baron (played by a schnauzer) leads a new squadron of flyers to reclaim the princess and defeat Catahari, the mastermind behind the sinister plan. Program originally aired as an episode of The ABC Saturday Superstar Movie. A Rankin-Bass Production. Color. Half-hour. Premiered on ABC: December 9, 1972 (on The ABC Saturday Superstar Movie). Rebroadcast on ABC: January 26, 1974. Syndicated.

### Voices

Bradley Bolke, Rhoda Mann, Robert McFadden, Allen Swift

## ◎ RED RIDING HOOD AND GOLDILOCKS

Actress Meg Ryan narrates this half-hour animated retelling of two of the most cherished stories in children's literature. Part of Rabbit Ear Video's Storybook Classics series. A Rabbit Ears Video Production. Color. Half-hour. Premiered on SHO: 1989.

### Voices

**Narrator:** Meg Ryan

## ◎ THE RED SHOES

Based on a story by Hans Christian Andersen, this animated rendition weaves a timeless tale about the importance of friendship. Two girls, Lisa and Jennie, are best friends until Lisa's parents win the lottery. Thereafter Lisa ignores Jennie, until a pair of magic dancing shoes appears and teaches her that money cannot buy happiness. Part of the award-winning anthology series HBO Storybook Musicals. A Michael Sporn Animation Production in association with Italtoons Corporation. Color. Half-hour. Premiered on HBO: February 7, 1990.

### Voices

**The Shoemaker/Narrator:** Ossie Davis

## ◎ THE RELUCTANT DRAGON

In this stop-motion, puppet-animated half-hour special based on the book by Kenneth Grahame, a simple shepherd's son discovers lurking in a cave a dragon who is more inclined to compose poetry than attack frightened villagers. Produced by England's Cosgrove Hall Productions, the special, winner of the British Academy of Film and Television Arts' best animation award, premiered on PBS's critically acclaimed anthology series Long Ago & Far Away. A Cosgrove Hall Production. Color. Half-hour. Premiered on PBS: February 4, 1989. Rebroadcast on PBS: November 17, 1990; November 15, 1992.

### Voices

**Boy/Narrator:** Martin Jarvis; **Dragon:** Simon Callow

## ⊚ THE REMARKABLE ROCKET

An incredible fireworks rocket (Remarkable Rocket) that displays the attitudes and emotions of humans is the subject of this charming adaptation of the Oscar Wilde story about the experiences of a group of fireworks that prepare to be set off during a royal wedding celebration. *A Potterton Production in association with Narrator's Digest. Color. Half-hour. Premiered: 1974. Syndicated.*

**Voices**
**Narrator:** David Niven; **Other Voices:** Graham Stark

## ⊚ REN & STIMPY ADULT CARTOON PARTY: "MAN'S BEST FRIEND"

George Liquor attempts to teach Ren and Stimpy the true meaning of obedience and make them "champions" in this half-hour special that bowed on cable's Spike TV and preceded the debut of *Ren & Stimpy* creator John Kricfalusi's all-new *Ren & Stimpy Adult Cartoon Party* as part of the network's new adult program block, *The Strip*, in June 2003. The special was actually originally produced during the fifth season of the widely popular Nickelodeon series, but the network banned it from the airwaves, deeming it too violent and sadistic for young viewers. *A Spumco Production. Color. Half-hour. Premiered on TNN/SPIKE: June 23, 2003.*

**Voices**
**Ren Hoek:** John Kricfalusi; **Stimpson J. "Stimpy" Cat:** Eric Bauza; **George Liquor:** Michael Pataki; **Other Voices:** Cheryl Chase, Harris Peet, Tom Hay, Mike Kricfalusi

## ⊚ THE RETURN OF THE BUNJEE

Bunjee, the elephantlike prehistoric creature, and his two young friends, Karen and Andy, wind up in the Middle Ages when the children's father's time-traveling machine is accidentally switched on in this sequel to *The Amazing Bunjee Venture*, adapted from the popular children's book *The Bunjee Venture* by Stan McMurty. *A Hanna-Barbera Production. Color. Half-hour. Premiered on ABC: April 6 and 12, 1985. Rebroadcast on ABC: September 21 and 28, 1985; April 21 and 28, 1990.*

**Voices**
**Bunjee:** Frank Welker; **Karen Winsborrow:** Nancy Cartwright; **Andy Winsborrow:** Robbie Lee; **Mr. Winsborrow:** Michael Rye; **Mrs. Winsborrow:** Linda Gary; **Others:** Peter Cullen, Pat Musick; **Narrator:** Michael Rye

## ⊚ THE RETURN OF THE KING

Continuing J.R.R. Tolkein's saga of the Hobbits, Frodo—kin to the aged Bilbo—sets off to destroy the now-evil Ring in the fires of Mount Doom, thereby making it possible for the noble Aragon to return to his kingdom victorious over the hideous realm of Sauron. *A Rankin-Bass Production in association with Toei Animation. Color. Two hours. Premiered on ABC: May 11, 1980. Rebroadcast on ABC: July 21, 1983. Syndicated. Rebroadcast on CAR: June 25, 1995 (Mr. Spim's Cartoon Theatre).*

**Voices**
**Frodo:** Orson Bean; **Samwise:** Roddy McDowall; **Gandalf:** John Huston; **Aragorn:** Theodore Bikel; **Denethor:** William Conrad; **Gollum:** Theodore; **Minstrel:** Glenn Yarborough

## ⊚ RETURN TO OZ

In this *General Electric Fantasy Hour* production, Dorothy returns to the Land of Oz to help her former cronies—Socrates (Strawman), Rusty (Tinman) and Dandy Lion (Cowardly Lion)—who have lost their brain, heart and courage, respectively. The program

marked the first special produced by filmmakers Arthur Rankin Jr. and Jules Bass. *A Rankin-Bass Production in association with Videocraft International and Crawley Films. Color. One hour. Premiered on NBC: February 9, 1964. Rebroadcast on NBC: February 21, 1965. Syndicated. Rebroadcast on DIS: November 25, 1995.*

**Voices**
**Dorothy:** Susan Conway; **Dandy Lion/Wizard:** Carl Banas; **Socrates (Strawman):** Alfie Scopp; **Rusty (Tinman):** Larry D. Mann; **Munchkins:** Susan Morse; **Glinda/Wicked Witch:** Peggi Loder

## ⊚ RIKKI-TIKKI-TAVI

Adopted by a British family in India, Rikki-Tikki-Tavi, a brave mongoose, fights to protect the people who've been so kind to him, saving them from two dreaded cobras in this wonderful cartoon adaptation of Rudyard Kipling's *The Jungle Book. A Chuck Jones Enterprises Production. Color. Half-hour. Premiered on CBS: January 9, 1975. Rebroadcast on CBS: April 12, 1976; April 4, 1977; January 23, 1978; February 9, 1979. Syndicated. Rebroadcast on NICK: October 12, 1991; February 29, 1992.*

**Voices**
**Rikki-Tikki-Tavi:** Orson Welles; **Nag/Chuchundra:** Shepard Menken; **Teddy:** Michael LeClaire; **Nagaina/Dazee's Wife/ Mother:** June Foray; **Father:** Les Tremayne; **Darzee:** Lennie Weinrib; **Narrator:** Orson Welles

## ⊚ RING RAIDERS

A group of heroic aviators from all eras of flight, led by Ring Commander Victor Vector defend the world from the evil pilots of the Skull Squadron and Skull Commander Scorch in this two-hour special (entitled "Ring Fire"), partially inspired by the box-office success of the Tom Cruise movie *Top Gun.* The special preceded a five-part daily animated series that aired in syndication. *A DIC Enterprises Production in association with Those Characters from Cleveland and Bohbot Entertainment. Color. Half-hour. Premiered: 1989. Syndicated.*

**Voices**
**Victor Vector:** Dan Gilvezan; **Joe Thundercloud:** Efrain Figueroa; **Hubbub:** Stuart Goetz; **Cub Jones:** Ike Eisenmann; **Kirchov:** Gregory Martin; **Mako:** Jack Angel; **Jenny Gail:** Chris Anthony; **Max Miles:** Roscoe Lee Browne; **Scorch:** Rodger Bumpass; **Yasu Yakamura:** Townsend Coleman; **Baron Von Clawdeitz:** Chuck McCann; **Siren:** Susan Silo

## ⊚ THE RISE AND FALL OF HUMPTY DUMPTY

The walking, talking egg of children's nursery rhyme fame saves a beautiful princess from the curses of an evil witch in this half-hour animated special originally produced in 1991 for CINAR Films' *The Real Story of . . .* (retitled from its former name, simply *Humpty Dumpty*). HBO premiered the special as part of its musical cartoon anthology series *HBO Storybook Musicals. A CINAR Production in association with Crayon Animation. Color. Half-hour. Premiered on HBO: December 18, 1991. Rebroadcast on HBO: December 20, 1991.*

**Voices**
**Glitch the Witch:** Glenda Jackson; **Scratch the Cat:** Huey Lewis

## ⊚ ROBBIE THE REINDEER IN HOOVES OF FIRE

Rudolph the Reindeer's son, Robbie, enters the famous Reindeer Games, running the race of his life as he tries beating his pal,

Blitzen, who cheats in this stop-motion animated special. Featuring an all-star cast of British actors, the special, which originally premiered in Great Britain on BBC1 on Christmas Day 1999 and debuted one year later in the United States on FOX network and cable sister channel FOX Family Channel (and reran on its successor ABC Family), went on to win 19 international awards, including the highly coveted Annecy for best TV special and BAFTA Television Award for best entertainment (programme or series).

In 2002, the 30-minute special was revoiced by an American cast, including such well-known stars as Ben Stiller, Britney Spears, James Belushi and James Woods. Hugh Grant was the lone British actor added to voice the character of Blitzen. In addition, CBS Sports personalities Dan Dierdorf and Dick Enberg lent their voices to the project as announcers for the Reindeer Races. CBS purchased the broadcast rights to both this special and its 2001 sequel, *Robbie the Reindeer in Legend of the Lost Tribe*, also first shown on British television, from BBC Worldwide. Both programs were produced by the BBC's animation unit, Bristol Animation, in association with BBC Worldwide and Comic Relief U.K., with 100 percent of the net profits from the specials benefiting the Comic Relief charity.

After re-airing on CBS for three consecutive years, the special moved to Nickelodeon's sister channel, Nicktoons, along with *Robbie the Reindeer in Legend of the Lost Tribe*, where it was rerun multiple times in December 2006. A *BBC Bristol Animation Production in association with BBC Worldwide and Comic Relief U.K. Color. Half-hour. Premiered on FOX: December 19, 2000. Premiered on FOX FAM: December 30, 2000 (British version). Rebroadcast on FOX FAM: December 12, 2000; December 13, 2000; December 18, 2000; December 20, 2000. Rebroadcast on ABC FAM: December 3, 2001; December 12, 2001; December 20, 2001; December 22, 2001; December 25, 2001. Premiered on CBS (American version): December 13, 2002. Rebroadcast on CBS: December 20, 2003; December 11, 2004, December 17, 2005. Rebroadcast on NICKT: December 2, 2006; December 3, 2006; December 8, 2006.*

### Voices

(U.S. version) **Narrator:** James Woods; **Robbie the Reindeer:** Ben Stiller; **Prancer:** Brad Garrett; **Donner:** Britney Spears; **Blitzen:** Hugh Grant; **Vixen:** Leah Remini; **Old Jingle:** Jerry Stiller; **Des Yeti:** Dick Enberg; **Alan Snowman:** Dan Dierdorf; **Tapir:** James Belushi; (British version) **Narrator:** Robbie Williams; **Robbie the Reindeer:** Ardal O'Hanlon; **Prancer:** Paul Whitehouse; **Donner:** Jane Horrocks; **Blitzen:** Steve Coogan; **Vixen:** Caroline Quentin; **Mrs. Claus:** Jean Alexander; **Santa Claus:** Ricky Tomlinson; **Head Elf:** Rhys Ifans; **Old Jingle:** Harry Enfield; **Elf #3:** Tony Anscombe; **Des Yeti/Alan Snowman:** Alistair McGowan

## ◉ ROBBIE THE REINDEER IN LEGEND OF THE LOST TRIBE

Robbie and his group of reindeer run into trouble when their tour guide business starts losing money and the evil Blitzen, who's recently been released from prison, promises to help turn their business around only to double-cross them in this sequel to 1999's *Robbie the Reindeer in Hooves of Fire*. Produced in Britain and re-voiced by an American voice cast including Ben Stiller, Hugh Grant, Britney Spears, Brad Garrett and Jim Belushi, CBS imported this stop-motion animated half-hour holiday special as part of a package deal with BBC Worldwide, airing it back-to-back in prime time on December 13, 2002, with the first special. The sequel originally premiered a year earlier on BBC1. *A BBC Bristol Animation Production in association with BBC Worldwide and Comic Relief U.K. Color. Half-hour. Premiered on CBS: December 13, 2002. Rebroadcast on CBS: December 20, 2003; December 11,*

2004; December 17, 2005. Rebroadcast on NICKT: December 30, 2006; December 31, 2006.

### Voices

**Robbie the Reindeer:** Ardal O'Hanlon; **Donner/Arctic Fox:** Jane Horrocks; **Blitzen:** Steve Coogan; **Prancer:** Paul Whitehouse; **Old Jingle:** Harry Enfield; **White Rabbit:** Jeff Goldblum; **David Attenborough:** Himself; **Penguin:** Ricky Gervais; **Prison Guard:** Rob Brydon; **Tapir:** Sean Hughes; **Koala:** Natalie Imbruglia; *Vikings:* Jeremy Dyson, Mark Gatiss, Steven Pemberton, Reece Shearsmith

## ◉ ROBIN HOOD

The Sheriff of Nottingham finally captures Robin Hood and his Merry Men with a plan involving a woodcutter, his son and the boy's sheepdog in this new version of the popular tale. A *Festival of Family Classics* special. *A Rankin-Bass Production. Color. Half-hour. Premiered: November 26, 1973. Syndicated.*

### Voices

Carl Banas, Len Birman, Bernard Cowan, Peg Dixon, Keith Hampshire, Peggi Locker, Donna Miller, Frank Perry, Henry Ramer, Billie Mae Richards, Alfie Scopp, Paul Soles

## ◉ ROBIN HOODNIK

Animals are cast in human roles in this colorful rendition of the classic fantasy tale. This time, Robin and his pack of happy critters are prime targets of the Sheriff of Nottingham (aided by his faithful deputy, Oxx) who tries to stop Robin from marrying the lovely Maid Marian by using a secret potion. The hour-long program first aired on *The ABC Saturday Superstar Movie* series (the working title of the production was *Cartoon Adventures of Robin Hound*). A *Hanna-Barbera Production. Color. One hour. Premiered on ABC: November 4, 1972 (on The ABC Saturday Superstar Movie). Syndicated.*

### Voices

**Robin Hood/Alan Airedale/Whirlin' Merlin/Lord Scurvy/Friar Pork/Little John:** Lennie Weinrib; **Sheriff of Nottingham/Carbuncle:** John Stephenson; **Oxx:** Joe E. Ross; **Donkey/Town Crier/Buzzard:** Hal Smith; **Scrounger/Richard the Iron-Hearted:** Daws Butler; **Maid Marian/Widow Weed:** Cynthia Adler

## ◉ ROBINSON CRUSOE (1972)

The resourceful Robinson Crusoe is shipwrecked on a tropical island and must find new means of survival until the day he will be rescued in this animated retelling of Daniel Defoe's beloved adventure novel. A *Famous Classic Tales* special. *An Air Programs International. Color. One hour. Premiered on CBS: November 23, 1972. Rebroadcast on CBS: October 8, 1973. Syndicated.*

### Voices

Alistair Duncan, Ron Haddrick, Mark Kelly, John Llewellyn, Owen Weingott

## ◉ ROBINSON CRUSOE (1973)

Robinson Crusoe and his talking parrot, Poll, save the captain of a ship from his mutinous crew and find their ticket to freedom from the island on which they have been stranded in this *Festival of Family Classics* special for first-run syndication. *A Rankin-Bass Production in association with Mushi Studios. Color. Half-hour. Premiered: February 18, 1973. Syndicated.*

### Voices

Carl Banas, Len Birman, Bernard Cowan, Peg Dixon, Keith Hampshire, Peggi Loder, Donna Miller, Frank Perry, Henry Ramer, Billie Mae Richards, Alfie Scopp, Paul Soles

## ROBOTMAN AND FRIENDS

An evil robot (Roberon) tries to convert three friendly robots (Robotman, Stellar and Oops) into hating people instead of loving them, but fails on all counts thanks to the robot's Earthbound friends. Based on the Kenner toy product, which was also turned into a daily comic strip for United Features Syndicate in 1985. *A DIC Enterprises Production in association with United Media. Color. Ninety minutes. Premiered: October, 1985. Syndicated.*

### Voices

**Robotman:** Greg Berg; **Roberon/Sound-Off:** Frank Welker; **Stellar:** Katie Leigh; **Uncle Thomas Cooper:** Phil Proctor; **Michael/Oops:** Adam Carl

## ROCKET POWER: "A ROCKET X-MAS"

When Ray is unable to buy the 10-foot longboard he wants for Christmas, Reggie and Otto pool their money together and surprise him by buying it for him in this half-hour holiday special—and the series' first 30-minute episode—based on the popular Nickelodeon cartoon series. *A Klasky Csupo/Viacom International Production. Color. Half-hour. Premiered on NICK: December 15, 2003.*

### Voices

**Ray "Raymundo" Rocket:** John Kassir; **Regina "Reggie" Rocket/Dani Rocket:** Shayna Fox; **Oswald "Otto" Rocket:** Joseph Anton; **Tito Makami Jr.:** Ray Bumatai; **Noelani:** Kim Mai Guest; **Lars "Twister" Rodriguez:** Lombardo Boyar; **Trish/Sherry:** Lauren Tom; **Maurice "Twister" Rodriguez:** Gilbert Leal Jr.; **Sammy "The Squid" Dullard:** Gary Leroi Gray; **Eddie "Prince of the Netherworld" Valentine:** Jordan Warkol; **Lifeguard/Tony/Eggs/Lame-o the Clown/PA Announcer/Rocker #2/Various Others:** Gregory Jbara; **Paula Dullard:** Jennifer Hale; **Sputz Piston:** Dominic Armato; **Maori:** Stan Harrington; **Trent:** Gregory Coolidge; **Keoni Makami:** Mathew Stephen Liu

## ROCKET POWER: "ISLAND OF THE MENEHUNE"

While on summer vacation in Hawaii, Ray rekindles his relationship with Tito's cousin, Noelani, canceling his extreme sports plans with Reggie and Otto who surf the perilous Banzai Pipeline, even though Noelani tells them it's too dangerous. They find out she was right in this third cartoon special based on the weekly Nickelodeon series. Aired in a 90-minute time slot, the 75-minute film was among seven feature-length cartoons produced for Nick's *Nicktoons Movie Summer* festival in 2004. Steve Guttenberg of *Police Academy* fame guest starred as the character Billy Joe. *A Klasky Csupo Production. Color. Ninety minutes. Premiered on NICK: July 16, 2004. Rebroadcast on NICK: July 17, 2004; July 18, 2004; July 26, 2004; August 22, 2004; September 6, 2004; November 26, 2004; December 29, 2004. Rebroadcast on NICKT: August 6, 2005; August 7, 2005.*

### Voices

**Ray "Raymundo" Rocket:** John Kassir; **Regina "Reggie" Rocket/Dani Rocket:** Shayna Fox; **Oswald "Otto" Rocket:** Joseph Anton; **Tito Makami Jr.:** Ray Bumatai; **Noelani:** Kim Mai Guest; **Trish/Sherry:** Lauren Tom; **Lars "Twister" Rodriguez:** Lombardo Boyar; **Lifeguard/Tony Eggs/Lame-o the Clown/P.A. Announcer/Rocker #2/Various Voices:** Gregory Jbara; **Sammy "The Squid" Dullard:** Sean Marquette; **Paula Dullard:** Jennifer Hale; **Sputz Piston:** Dominic Armato; **Maori:** Stan Harrington; **Eddie "Prince of the Netherworld" Valentine:** Jordan Warkol; **Trent:** Gregory Coolidge; **Keoni Makami:** Matthew Stephen Liu; **Mommi, Tito's mom:** Brooks Almy; **Billie Joe:** Steve Guttenberg; **Cousin Leilani:** Tinashe Kachingwe

## ROCKET POWER: RACE ACROSS THE ISLAND

In their first-ever movie special for Nickelodeon, the Rocket Power gang head to New Zealand to compete in the "The Junior Waikikamukau Games," with Otto Rocket going up against the son of an athlete who beat Ray's father—and cheated in the process—at a similar race, while his sister Reggie tries to gain the attention of Otto during the competition. *A Klasky Csupo Production. Color. Ninety minutes. Premiered on NICK: February 16, 2002. Rebroadcast on NICK: February 17, 2002; February 18, 2002; March 10, 2002; April 28, 2002; July 20, 2002; July 21, 2002; August 24, 2002; November 30, 2002; January 1, 2003; February 9, 2003; March 9, 2003; August 4, 2003; August 8, 2003; October 18, 2003; November 28, 2003; February 21, 2004. Rebroadcast on NICKT: June 11, 2005; June 12, 2005; July 30, 2005; July 31, 2005.*

### Voices

**Ray "Raymundo" Rocket:** John Kassir; **Regina "Reggie" Rocket/Dani Rocket:** Shayna Fox; **Oswald "Otto" Rocket:** Joseph Anton; **Tito Makami Jr.:** Ray Bumatai; **Noelani, Tito's cousin:** Kim Mai Guest; **Trish/Sherry:** Lauren Tom; **Lars "Twister" Rodriguez:** Lombardo Boyar; **Sammy "The Squid" Dullard:** Sean Marquette; **Mommi, Tito's mom:** Brooks Almy; **Cousin Leilani:** Tinashe Kachingwe; **Cousin Makami:** Matty Liu

## ROCKET POWER: "REGGIE'S BIG (BEACH) BREAK"

The Rocket Power gang enjoys spring break-type sports and a music beach festival in this second 90-minute movie special based on the series that debuted on Nickelodeon in July of 2003. *A Klasky Csupo Production. Color. Ninety minutes. Premiered on NICK: July 19, 2003. Rebroadcast on NICK: July 20, 2003; July 21, 2003; July 25, 2003; August 23, 2003; August 24, 2003; August 25, 2003; September 1, 2003; September 27, 2003; October 18, 2003; November 2, 2003; November 28, 2003; December 31, 2003; January 18, 2004; February 25, 2004; January 16, 2005.*

### Voices

**Ray "Raymundo" Rocket:** John Kassir; **Regina "Reggie" Rocket/Dani Rocket:** Shayna Fox; **Oswald "Otto" Rocket:** Joseph Anton; **Tito Makami Jr.:** Ray Bumatai; **Noelani:** Kim Mai Guest; **Lars "Twister" Rodriguez:** Lombardo Boyar; **Sammy "The Squid" Dullard:** Sean Marquette; **Mommi, Tito's mom:** Brooks Almy; **Billie Joe:** Steve Guttenberg; **Cousin Leilani:** Tinashe Kachingwe

## ROCKET POWER: "THE BIG DAY"

Ray Rocket of the Rocket Power gang plans to wed Tito's cousin, Noelani, in Hawaii, while Otto tries postponing the ceremony to compete in the Zero Gravity Zone skating competition to play with the pros in this hour-long special—and last new episode—that debuted as part of Nickelodeon's *Nicktoons Movie Summer* festival in July 2004. *A Klasky Csupo Production. Color. One hour. Premiered on NICK: July 30, 2004. Rebroadcast on NICK: August 1, 2004; August 30, 2004; November 26, 2004.*

### Voices

**Ray "Raymundo" Rocket:** John Kassir; **Regina "Reggie" Rocket/Dani Rocket:** Shayna Fox; **Oswald "Otto" Rocket:** Joseph Anton; **Tito Makami Jr.:** Ray Bumatai; **Noelani:** Kim Mai Guest; **Trish/Sherry:** Lauren Tom; **Lars "Twister" Rodriguez:** Lombardo

Boyar; **Lifeguard/Tony Eggs/Lame-o the Clown/P.A. Announcer/ Rocker #2/Various Voices:** Gregory Jbara; **Sammy "The Squid" Dullard:** Sean Marquette; **Paula Dullard:** Jennifer Hale; **Sputz Piston:** Dominic Armato; **Maori:** Stan Harrington; **Eddie "Prince of the Netherworld" Valentine:** Jordan Warkol; **Trent:** Gregory Coolidge; **Keoni Makami:** Matthew Stephen Liu; **Mommi, Tito's mom:** Brooks Almy; **Billie Joe:** Steve Guttenberg; **Cousin Leilani:** Tinashe Kachingwe

## ◎ ROCKIN' WITH JUDY JETSON

News of intergalactic rock star Sky Rocker's surprise concert sends George and Jane Jetson's teenage daughter, Judy, into orbit, inspiring her to write a song for her music idol in this two-hour movie based on the *Jetsons* cartoon series. *A Hanna-Barbera Production. Color. Two hours. Premiered: 1988. Syndicated. Rebroadcast on CAR: March 5, 1995 (Mr. Spim's Cartoon Theatre).*

### Voices

**Judy Jetson:** Janet Waldo; **Jane Jetson, her mother:** Penny Singleton; **George Jetson, her father:** George O'Hanlon; **Elroy Jetson, her brother:** Daws Butler; **Rosie, the Jetson's maid:** Jean VanderPyl; **Astro, the Jetson's dog:** Don Messick; **Mr. Microchips/Manny:** Hamilton Camp; **Nicky:** Eric Suter; **Ramm/Dee-Jay:** Beau Weaver; **Iona:** Cindy McGee; **Starr/Fan Club President/Zowie:** Pat Musick; **Felonia:** Ruth Buzzi; **Quark/Zappy:** Charlie Adler; **Gruff/Commander Comsat/Bouncer:** Peter Cullen; **Sky Rocker/Zany:** Rob Paulsen; **Rhoda Starlet:** Selette Cole; **High Loopy Zoomy:** P.L. Brown; **Zippy:** B.J. Ward; **Zilchy:** Pat Fraley; **Cosmo C. Spacely:** Mel Blanc

## ◎ ROCKO'S MODERN LIFE CHRISTMAS AND TATTERTOWN

This hour-long syndicated special features two half-hour Christmas episodes from Nickelodeon's *Rocko's Modern Life*, in which Rocko's Christmas party guestlist includes his new neighbors-the elves-and Ralph Bashki's 1988 Nickelodeon special, *Tattertown*, about a stranger who visits a world populated by unwanted objects. *A Games Animation/Bakshi Animation Production. Color. One hour. Premiered: December 10, 1995. Syndicated.*

## ◎ THE ROMANCE OF BETTY BOOP

It's 1939 and Betty's working two jobs to keep body and soul together: selling shoes by day and headlining at her Uncle Mischa's club at night. While dreaming of millionaire Waldo, she is pursued by humble iceman Freddie and gangster Johnny Throat, Uncle Mischa's ruthless creditor. Desiree Goyette, who displayed her singing prowess in several Charlie Brown television specials, is the voice of Betty. *A King Features Entertainment Production in association with Lee Mendelson–Bill Melendez Productions. Color. Half-hour. Premiered on CBS: March 20, 1985. Rebroadcast on CBS: December 31, 1987.*

### Voices

**Betty Boop:** Desiree Goyette; **Freddie:** Sean Allen; **Waldo Van Lavish:** Derek McGrath; **Johnny Throat/Punchie:** George R. Wendt; **Mischa Bubbles:** Sandy Kenyon; **Parrot:** Frank W. Buxton; **Chuckles:** Robert Towers; **Ethnic Voices:** Ron Friedman; **Announcer:** John Stephenson; **Vocalists:** Desiree Goyette, Sean Allen

## ◎ ROMAN CITY

This hour-long live-action/animated special, winner of a nighttime Emmy Award for outstanding animated program, tells the story of life in a fictional but historically accurate Roman city, Verbonia. Based on the book by acclaimed author-illustrator David Macaulay, the PBS special examines the social significance of Roman cities and the age-old conflict between the generations. *A Unicorn Films Production. Color. One hour. Premiered on PBS: May 7, 1994.*

## ◎ ROMIE-O AND JULIE-8

Two robots fall in love with each other and are kept apart by the two companies that manufactured them in this innovative rendition of the classic love story. *A Nelvana Limited Production in association with CBC. Color. Half-hour. Premiered (U.S.): April 1979. Syndicated.*

### Voices

**Romie-O:** Greg Swanson; **Julie-8:** Donann Cavin; **Mr. Thunderbottom:** Max Ferguson; **Ms. Passbinder:** Marie Aloma; **Gizmo:** Nick Nichols; **Junk Monster:** Bill Osler; **Vocalists:** John Sebastian, Rory Block, Richard Manuel

## ◎ A ROOM NEARBY

Intimate interviews with five culturally dissimilar people from Harlem-born writer Lynn Blue to Hollywood film director Milos Forman reflecting on the problems they faced with loneliness and what they learned from their experiences, blended with distinctive CGI-animation in this educational film that premiered at the Margaret Meade Festival in New York City in November 2003. Produced and directed by acclaimed animator Paul Fierlinger, the film went on to become a Grand Prize winner at the 2004 Ottawa International Animation Festival. Less than 18 months after its making, the 2006 Peabody Award-winning production debuted in prime time in the 10:30 to 11:00 P.M. time slot on PBS stations in March 2005. *An AR&T Animation Production. Color. Half-hour. Premiered on PBS: March 23, 2005. Rebroadcast on PBS: March 23, 2005; March 28, 2005; June 7, 2005; June 10, 2005; June 13, 2005; February 11, 2007.*

### Voices

**Paul Fierlinger:** Himself; **Sandra Fierlinger:** Herself; **Lynn Blue:** Herself; **Domingo D'Achille:** Himself; **Milos Forman:** Himself; **Tom McMan:** Himself; **Pamela Tang:** Herself

## ◎ ROSE-PETAL PLACE

A magical flower's beauty and kindness triumphs over evil in an enchanting garden world known as Rose-Petal Place in this live-

*Two robots, kept apart by the companies who manufactured them, fall hopelessly in love in the* Romeo and Juliet–*inspired* Romie-O and Julie-8. © *Nelvana Limited*

action/animation special. *A Ruby-Spears Enterprises Production. Color. Half-hour. Premiered: May, 1984. Syndicated.*

**Cast**
**Little Girl in the Garden:** Nicole Eggert

**Voices**
**Rose-Petal:** Marie Osmond; **Nastina:** Marilyn Schreffler; **Sunny Sunflower/Daffodil:** Susan Blu; **Orchid/Little Girl/Lily Fair:** Renae Jacobs; **Iris:** Candy Ann Brown; **P.D. Centipede/Seymour J. Snailsworth/Tumbles/Elmer/Horace Fly:** Frank Welker

## ROSE-PETAL PLACE II: REAL FRIENDS

In this sequel to *Rose-Petal Place*, Rose Petal returns to help her garden friends learn an important lesson about friendship and trust. *A Ruby-Spears Enterprises Production in association with David Kirschner Productions and Hallmark Properties. Color. Half-hour. Premiered: April, 1985. Syndicated.*

**Cast**
**Little Girl in the Garden:** Nicole Eggert

**Voices**
**Rose-Petal:** Marie Osmond; **Sunny Sunflower/Canterbury Belle/Fuschia:** Susan Blu; **Elmer/Horace Fly/Seymour J. Snailsworth/P.D. Centipede/Tumbles:** Frank Welker; **Nastina/Lily Fair/Marigold:** Marilyn Schreffler; **Sweet Violet/Cherry Blossom:** Renae Jacobs; **Ladybug:** Stacy McLaughlin

## THE ROSEY AND BUDDY SHOW

Pulling their motorhome into Cartoonland, Rosey and Buddy (played by then real husband and wife Roseanne and Tom Arnold) star in their own television show and find out that the network Powers (as in "the powers that be") care only about profits. *A Little Rosey Production in association with Wapello County Productions/Nelvana Limited. Color. Half-hour. Premiered on ABC: May 15, 1992.*

**Voices**
**Rosey:** Roseanne Arnold; **Buddy:** Tom Arnold

## ROSIE O'DONNELL'S KIDS ARE PUNNY

Inspired by O'Donnell's book of the same name published by Warner Books, this half-hour special, from the creators of the acclaimed 1997 HBO special *How Do You Spell God?* combined live-action footage of kids swapping jokes and stories with animated shorts from award-winning animators based on classic humorous stories featuring an all-star cast of celebrity voices. Animation included Debra Solomon's "The Parable of the Clown," voiced by Jackie Mason and Mary Tyler Moore; Maciek Albrecht of Ink Tank's "Tito the Frog," featuring multiple voices by John Leguizamo; Santiago Cohen of Ink Tank's "How Nehemiah Got Free"; Michael Sporn of Michael Sporn Animation's "The Camel Dances," narrated by Madonna, and "Lila's Last Smile." O'Donnell also served as executive producer. *An Amy Schatz/Home Box Office Production. Color. Half-hour. Premiered on HBO: December 6, 1998. Rebroadcast on HBO: December 13, 1998; December 19, 1998; December 25, 1998; December 28, 1998.*

**Cast (live-action)/Voices**
Rosie O'Donnell, Hazelle Goodman, Geoffrey Holder, John Leguizamo, Madonna, Jackie Mason, Mary Tyler Moore, Chris Rock, Marlo Thomas

## ROTTEN RALPH: "NOT SO ROTTEN RALPH"

Inspired by many weeks of being grounded, Rotten Ralph tries his best to be good and behave himself, but his good deeds have unpredicted results. Second in a series of *Rotten Ralph* specials for Disney Channel. *An Italtoons Corporation/Matthews Production. Color. Half-hour. Premiered on DIS: August 26, 1996.*

**Voices**
**Rotten Ralph:** Hal Rayle; **Mae Whitman/Maggie Roswell:** Corey Burton

## ROTTEN RALPH: "THE TAMING OF THE RALPH"

The Disney Channel originally commissioned four episodes for this stop-motion animated series of specials, but stopped production after only two programs. In this first installment, Ralph watches silly TV shows all day and annoys everyone in the family. As punishment for his rotten deeds, Ralph has to stay home while the rest of the family goes to the circus. The specials were based on the popular children's books written by Jack Gantos and illustrated by Nicole Rubel, published by Houghton-Mifflin. *An Italtoons Corporation/Matthews Production. Color. Half-hour. Premiered on DIS: May 18, 1996.*

**Voices**
**Rotten Ralph:** Hal Rayle; **Mae Whitman/Maggie Roswell:** Corey Burton

## RUDOLPH AND FROSTY'S CHRISTMAS IN JULY

Frosty the Snowman and Rudolph the Red-Nosed Reindeer leave the cozy confines of the North Pole to help an ailing circus but find trouble in the form of the villainous Winterbolt. *A Rankin-Bass Production. Color. Half-hour. Premiered on ABC: November 25, 1979. Rebroadcast on ABC: December 20, 1981. Rebroadcast on CBS: December 22, 1991. Rebroadcast on DIS: December 18, 1996. Rebroadcast on FOX FAM: December 4, 1998; December 13, 1998; December 25, 1998. Rebroadcast on ABC FAM: December 10, 2001; December 14, 2001; December 21, 2001; December 23, 2001; December 2, 2002; December 11, 2002; December 19, 2002; December 24, 2002; December 4, 2003; December 21, 2003; December 5, 2004; December 3, 2005; December 18, 2005; December 27, 2005; December 9, 2006; December 24, 2006.*

**Voices**
**Santa Claus (narrator):** Mickey Rooney; **Rudolph:** Billie Richards; **Frosty:** Jackie Vernon; **Crystal, Frosty's wife:** Shelley Winters; **Mrs. Santa Claus:** Darlene Conley; **Winterbolt:** Paul Frees; **Milton, the ice cream salesman:** Red Buttons; **Scratcher, the jealous reindeer:** Alan Sues; **Lilly, the circus owner:** Ethel Merman; **Lanie, Lilly's daughter:** Shelby Flint; **Big Ben:** Harold Peary

## RUDOLPH'S SHINY NEW YEAR

Happy, the Baby New Year, has run away from Father Time and unless he's found there will be no new year and the calendar will remain locked on December 31st forever. Rudolph the Red-Nosed Reindeer saves the day with Santa's help. Program features an original score by Johnny Marks, including his original hit song, "Rudolph the Red-Nosed Reindeer." *A Rankin-Bass Production. Color. One hour. Premiered on ABC: December 10, 1976. Rebroadcast on ABC: December 11, 1977; December 9, 1978; December 16, 1979; December 14, 1980; December 10, 1981; December 6, 1982. Rebroadcast on DIS: December 22, 1992; December 1, 1993; December 6, 1993; December 18, 1993; December 23, 1993; December 20, 1995; December 25, 1996. Rebroadcast on FOX FAM: December 2, 1998; December 14, 1998; December 20, 1998; December 25, 1999; July 11, 1999; July 15, 1999; July 16, 1999; December 3, 1999; December 8, 1999; December 12, 1999; December 18, 1999; December 24, 1999; December 25, 1999; December 5, 2000; December 11,*

2000; December 13, 2000; December 20, 2000; December 21, 2000; December 24, 2000; December 25, 2000. Rebroadcast on ABC FAM: December 1, 2001; December 3, 2001; December 14, 2001; December 20, 2001; December 23, 2001; December 24, 2001; December 1, 2002; December 3, 2002; December 12, 2002; December 14, 2002; December 22, 2002; December 24, 2002; December 6, 2003; December 11, 2003; December 21, 2003; December 24, 2003; December 3, 2004; December 4, 2004; December 15, 2004; December 19, 2004; December 24, 2004; December 1, 2005; December 3, 2005; December 14, 2005; December 22, 2005; December 24, 2005; December 30, 2005; December 4, 2006; December 9, 2006; December 13, 2006; December 22, 2006; December 24, 2006. Syndicated.

**Voices**
**Father Time (narrator):** Red Skelton; **Rudolph:** Billie Richards; **Sir Tentworthree/Camel:** Frank Gorshin; **One Million B.C.:** Morey Amsterdam; **Santa Claus/Aeon:** Paul Frees; **Big Ben:** Hal Peary

### ◎ RUDOLPH THE RED-NOSED REINDEER

Inspired by Johnny Marks's bestselling song (recorded in 1949 and selling more than 8 million copies), this gaily colored Animagic special tells the story of Rudolph, the reindeer with the illuminating red nose, who saves Christmas by safely guiding Santa through a terrible storm on Christmas Eve. Burl Ives, appearing as Sam the Snowman, narrates the program, which was first broadcast on NBC in 1964 under the title of General Electric's Fantasy Hour.

In a break from tradition, CBS aired a remastered version of this classic holiday favorite in late November 1998. The following year, Rudolph shined bright for CBS, propelling it, along with a Hallmark Hall of Fame special "The Runaway," to first place in the weekly Nielsen ratings. In 2001, the annual Christmas special was the highest rated show of the night in the age 18–49 demographic and in total households, improving its viewership in its second half-hour by 14 percent.

In 2005, the perennial holiday favorite became the highest rated special among kids, ages 2–11, attracting more than 3.6 million viewers and 15.8 viewers overall, its largest audience in six years, easily edging out ABC's rerun of the animated Santa Claus Is Comin' to Town (8.7 million) and NBC's computer-animated The Happy Elf (5.7 million). A Videocraft International Production. Color. Half-hour. Premiered on NBC: December 6, 1964 (on General Electric Fantasy Hour). Rebroadcast on NBC: December 5, 1975; December 4, 1966; December 8, 1967; December 6, 1968; December 5, 1969; December 4, 1970; December 6, 1971. Rebroadcast on CBS: December 8, 1972; December 7, 1973; December 13, 1974; December 3, 1975; December 1, 1976; November 30, 1977; December 6, 1978; December 6, 1979; December 3, 1980; December 14, 1981; December 1, 1982; December 3, 1983; December 1, 1984; December 3, 1985; December 9, 1986; December 15, 1987; December 5, 1988; December 15, 1989; December 14, 1990; November 29, 1991; December 11, 1992; December 2, 1993; November 29, 1994; November 28, 1995; November 29, 1996; December 1, 1997. Rebroadcast on CBS: November 30, 1998; December 8, 1999; December 4, 2000; November 24, 2001; December 13, 2002; December 10, 2003; December 1, 2004; November 30, 2005; December 7, 2006.

**Voices**
**Sam the Snowman (narrator):** Burl Ives; **Rudolph:** Billie Richards; Hermy the Elf: Paul Soles; **Yukon Cornelius:** Larry D. Mann; **Santa Claus:** Stan Francis; **Clarice:** Janet Orenstein

### ◎ RUGRATS: "ALL GROWED UP!"

The Rugrats ditch their diapers and see how they turn out when they travel 10 years into the "footure" in an imaginary time

machine in this hour-long adventure, based on the long-running, Emmy Award-winning Nickelodeon cartoon series. A Klasky Csupo Production. Color. One hour. Premiered on NICK: July 21, 2001. Rebroadcast on NICK: July 22, 2001; July 23, 2001; July 25, 2001; July 27, 2001; July 28, 2001; October 13, 2001; October 14, 2001; November 10, 2001; November 25, 2001; January 1, 2002; January 13, 2002; March 31, 2002; May 19, 2002; July 6, 2002; July 7, 2002; August 31, 2002; November 29, 2002; January 1, 2003; February 26, 2003; March 30, 2003; April 20, 2003; August 10, 2003; November 30, 2003; December 7, 2003; January 1, 2004; January 3, 2004; January 23, 2004; May 31, 2004.

**Voices**
**Tommy Pickles:** E. G. Daily; **Chuckie Finster Jr.:** Christine Cavanaugh; **Angelica C. Pickles:** Cheryl Chase; **Phil/Lil/Betty DeVille:** Kath Soucie; **Dil Pickles:** Tara Strong; **Suzie Pickles:** Cree Summer; **Charlotte C. Pickles:** Tress MacNeille; **Didi Pickles:** Melanie Chartoff; **Stu Pickles:** Jack Riley; **Grandpa Pickles:** Joe Alaskey; **Drew Pickles/Chazz Finster Sr.:** Michael Bell; **B-Movie Mad Scientist:** Charlie Adler; **Kira Watanabe-Finster:** Julia Kato; **Samantha Shane:** Laraine Newman; **Kimi Watanabe-Finster:** Dione Quan

### ◎ RUGRATS: "A RUGRATS VACATION"

Taking their RV on the road, the Pickles family travels to the entertainment capital of the world—Las Vegas—with the trouble-making toddlers setting free "kitties from prison" that turn out to be a prized pair of Siberian tigers owned by the famed Vegas performers, Heimlich and Bob, in this direct-to-video movie that preceded Paramount Pictures' full-length theatrical release The Rugrats Movie (1998) on Nickelodeon, which aired as a half-hour springtime special. Originally scheduled to air in March 1998, the hour-long program premiered on Nickelodeon that May instead and was nominated that year for an Annie Award for best home video production. A Klasky Csupo Production. Color. One hour. Premiered on NICK: May 29, 1998. Rebroadcast on NICK: May 31, 1998; June 9, 1998; July 16, 1998; March 14, 1999; June 21, 1999; June 26, 1999; November 27, 1999; December 10, 1999; April 22, 2000; June 4, 2000; June 5, 2000; January 15, 2001; January 31, 2001; February 24, 2001; April 21, 2001; July 28, 2001; October 13, 2001; November 23, 2001; December 29, 2001; March 23, 2002; June 29, 2002; July 22, 2002; February 24, 2003; July 28, 2003.

**Voices**
**Tommy Pickles:** E. G. Daily; **Chuckie Finster Jr.:** Christine Cavanaugh; **Phil/Lil/Betty Deville:** Kath Soucie; **Stu Pickles:** Jack Riley; **Angelica C. Pickles:** Chery Chase; **Chazz Finster Sr./Drew Pickles:** Michael Bell; **Charlotte Pickles:** Tress MacNeille; **Howard Deville:** Phil Proctor; **Grandpa Lou Pickles:** Joe Alaskey; **Didi Pickles:** Melanie Chartoff; **Head Clown/Bellhop/Oarsman:** Hadley Kay

### ◎ RUGRATS: "BABIES IN TOYLAND"

After greedy little Angelica drives Santa (voiced by Jim Belushi) to quit, Tommy and the rest of the Rugrats bring Santa back to make Christmas a joyous occasion for Dil, who believes Angelica that they don't receive any presents and won't be able to celebrate Christmas again. Debuting in December 2002 on Nickelodeon, the hour-long program was the Rugrats' second Christmas special and fourth holiday special on Nick. A Klasky Csupo Production. Color. One hour. Premiered on NICK: December 9, 2002. Rebroadcast on NICK: December 18, 2002; December 24, 2002; December 11, 2003; December 13, 2003; December 21, 2003; December 24, 2003; December 25, 2003; December 16, 2004; December 24, 2004;

December 25, 2004; December 15, 2005; December 24, 2005; December 20, 2006; December 24, 2006; December 25, 2006.

*Voices*

**Tommy Pickles:** E. G. Daily; **Chuckie Finster Jr.:** Nancy Cartwright; **Angelica C. Pickles:** Cheryl Chase; **Phil/Lil/Betty DeVille:** Kath Soucie; **Dil Pickles/Timmy McNulty:** Tara Strong; **Susie Carmichael:** Cree Summer; **Charlotte C. Pickles:** Tress MacNeille; **Didi Pickles:** Melanie Chartoff; **Stuart "Stu" Pickles:** Jack Riley; **Grandpa Pickles:** Joe Alaskey; **Drew Pickles/Chazz Finster Sr.:** Michael Bell; **Randy Carmichael:** Ron Glass; **Lulu Pickles:** Debbie Reynolds; **Howard DeVille:** Phil Proctor; **Fake Santa:** Jim Belushi; **Hermie the Elf:** Paul Reubens

## ◉ RUGRATS CHANUKAH

It's Chanukah and everyone's off to the synagogue to watch Grandpa Boris perform at the holiday fair, while the Rugrats track down a mysterious "villain" of their own in this 1997 holiday special based on the popular Nickelodeon cartoon series. (For voice credits, see series entry in Television Cartoon Series section.) *A Klasky Csupo Production. Color. Half-hour. Premiered on NICK: December 20, 1997.*

## ◉ RUGRATS: "CURSE OF THE WEREWUFF"

Before their parents take them trick-or-treating for the first time at a local amusement park, Chuckie, dressed like a werewolf, has nightmares after Angelica tells the Rugrats that they will permanently turn into the costumed characters they play in this Halloween-themed episode of TV's *Rugrats* that has morphed into a traditional Halloween special on Nickelodeon and its offshoot network, Nicktoons. *A Klasky Csupo Production. Color. Half-hour. Premiered on NICK: October 28, 2003. NICKT: October 31, 2003; October 31, 2004; February 14, 2005; October 29, 2005; October 30, 2005; October 27, 2006; October 31, 2006.*

*Voices*

**Tommy Pickles:** E. G. Daily; **Charles "Chuckie" Finster Jr.:** Nancy Cartwright; **Angelica C. Pickles:** Cheryl Chase; **Phil/Lil/Betty DeVille:** Kath Soucie; **Dylan Prescott "Dil" Pickles/Timmy McNulty:** Tara Strong; **Suzie Pickles:** Cree Summer; **Charlotte C. Pickles:** Tress MacNeille; **Didi Pickles:** Melanie Chartoff; **Stuart "Stu" Pickles:** Jack Riley; **Louis "Grandpa" Pickles:** Joe Alaskey; **Drew Pickles/Charles "Chazz" Finster Sr.:** Michael Bell; **Randy Carmichael:** Ron Glass; **Susie Carmichael:** Cree Summer; **Lulu Pickles:** Debbie Reynolds; **Howard DeVille:** Phil Proctor

## ◉ RUGRATS: "HOLLYWEEN"

Tommy Pickles and the rest of his preschool age friends get a lesson in trick-or-treating and suspect there's a monster in the garage in their first prime-time animated special based on the popular Nickelodeon cartoon series. (For voice credits, see series entry in "Television Cartoon Series" section.) *A Klasky Csupo Production. Color. Half-hour. Premiered on NICK: October 30, 1993.*

## ◉ A RUGRATS KWANZAA

The Rugrats learn that everyone is important in their own way when their Great Aunt T pays them a visit to celebrate the joyous holiday of Kwanzaa in this half-hour special based on the Emmy award-winning Nickleodeon cartoon series. Eight months before making its U.S. premiere on Nick in December 2001, the half-hour holiday special debuted in Britain. The special was also known as *Carmichael's Special* on Nick Australia. *A Klasky Csupo Production. Color. Half-hour. Premiered on NICK: December 11, 2001. Rebroadcast: December 15, 2001; December 16, 2001; December 19, 2001;*

December 25, 2001; December 26, 2001; December 5, 2002; December 23, 2002; December 26, 2002; December 26, 2003; December 26, 2004; December 26, 2005. Rebroadcast on NICKT: December 26, 2003; December 27, 2003; December 28, 2003; December 29, 2003; December 30, 2003; December 31, 2003; January 1, 2004.

*Voices*

**Tommy Pickles:** E.G. Daily; **Chuckie Finster Jr.:** Christine Cavanaugh; **Angelica C. Pickles:** Cheryl Chase; **Phil/Lil/Betty DeVille:** Kath Soucie; **Chazz Finster Sr./Drew/Boris:** Michael Bell; **Didi Pickles/Minka:** Melanie Chartoff; **Howard DeVille:** Phil Proctor; **Stu Pickles:** Jack Riley; **Dr. Lucy Carmichael:** Cheryl Carter; **Charlotte:** Tress MacNeille; **Susie Carmichael:** Cree Summer; **Dylan Prescott "Dil" Pickles:** Tara Strong; **Great Aunt T:** Irma P. Hall

## ◉ RUGRATS MOTHER'S DAY SPECIAL

While the precocious kids scurry around to find the right Mother's Day gifts for their moms, first they lend a hand to Chuckie, who doesn't have a mother, to find an appropriate surrogate in this half-hour special featuring the cast of characters from the Nickelodeon cartoon series. (For voice credits, see series entry in Television Cartoon Series section.) *A Klasky Csupo Production. Color. Half-hour. Premiered on NICK: May 6, 1997.*

## ◉ A RUGRATS PASSOVER

On Seder night, after locking the kids in the attic, Grandpa Boris entertains them with the story of Passover ("the greatest holiday of the year") in this prime-time animated special. (For voice credits, see entry in Television Cartoon Series section.) *A Klasky Csupo Production. Color. Half-hour. Premiered on NICK: April 13, 1995. Rebroadcast on NICK: March 30, 1996.*

## ◉ "RUGRATS: RUNAWAY REPTAR"

When Grandpa takes the Rugrats to the drive-in movie theater to see the latest horror thriller *Runaway Reptar*, the gang becomes unhappy when they discover the giant monster is aiding his evil twin in destroying the city, so they imagine themselves helping Reptar save the city instead. The direct-to-video production aired as a three-part hour-long special Saturday, November 27, 1999, at 8:00 P.M. on Nickelodeon. *A Klasky Csupo Production. Color. One hour. Premiered on NICK: November 27, 1999. Rebroadcast on NICK: January 14, 2000; March 12, 2000; April 15, 2000; August 5, 2000; August 6, 2000; August 25, 2000; September 9, 2000; September 10, 2000; February 19, 2001; June 30, 2001; July 28, 2001; January 1, 2002; March 17, 2002; July 6, 2002; July 7, 2002; August 31, 2002; December 1, 2002; January 1, 2003; February 16, 2003; March 30, 2003; August 1, 2003; December 30, 2003; February 28, 2004; March 21, 2004; April 18, 2004; June 6, 2004; August 15, 2006.*

*Voices*

**Tommy Pickles:** E.G. Daily; **Chuckie Finster Jr.:** Christine Cavanaugh; **Angelica C. Pickles:** Cheryl Chase; **Phil/Lil/Betty DeVille:** Kath Soucie; **Chazz Finster Sr./Drew/Boris:** Michael Bell; **Didi Pickles/Minka:** Melanie Chartoff; **Howard DeVille:** Phil Proctor; **Stu Pickles:** Jack Riley; **Dr. Lucy Carmichael:** Cheryl Carter; **Charlotte:** Tress MacNeille; **Susie Carmichael:** Cree Summer; **Dylan Prescott "Dil" Pickles:** Tara Strong; **Grandpa Pickles:** Joe Alaskey

## ◉ RUGRATS: "STILL BABIES AFTER ALL THESE YEARS"

Narrated by Nickelodeon teen star Amanda Bynes (also the voice of Taffy in *Rugrats*), this half-hour live-action/animated documentary offers an inside look into the world of America's favorite television toddlers, featuring clips, fan testimonials and interviews with the cast and producers of the Emmy-winning series. The program aired the same night, one hour after the debut of the *Rugrats* 10th anniversary cartoon special, *Rugrats: All Growed Up!* at 9 P.M. (ET). *A Klasky Csupo Production. Color. Half-hour. Premiered on NICK: July 21, 2001.*

## ◎ RUGRATS: TALES FROM THE CRIB: "SNOW WHITE"

Taffy recounts the Rugrats' own version of the timeless fable of Snow White (Susie) and her Seven Dwarfs—Baldy (Tommy), Spazzy (Kimi), Scardey (Chuckie), Icky (Phil), Sticky (Lil), Furball (Spike) and Drooly (Dil)—and the devious Wicked Queen's (Angelica) plan to rid the world of the pretty princess and her seven sweet babies and become the land's "fairest of them all" with love conquering all. Featuring the voices of Kenan Thompson, Amanda Bynes and Jeffrey Licon, this first of two direct-to-DVD *Rugrats Tales from the Crib* specials aired on Nickelodeon. *A Klasky Csupo Production. Color. One hour. Premiered on NICK: September 9, 2005. Rebroadcast on NICK: November 13, 2005; November 23, 2005.*

### Voices
**Taffy:** Amanda Bynes; **Snow White/Susie Pickles:** Cree Summer; **Baldy/Tommy Pickles:** Elizabeth Daily; **Spazzy/Kimi Watanabe-Finster:** Dione Quan; **Chuckie Finster Jr./Scaredy:** Christine Cavanaugh; **Icky/Phil/Sticky/Lil:** Kath Soucie; **Wicked Queen/Angelica C. Pickles:** Cheryl Chase; **Drooly/Dil Pickles:** Tara Strong; **Other Voices:** Kenan Thompson, Jeffrey Licon

## ◎ RUGRATS: TALES FROM THE CRIB: "3 JACKS & A BEANSTALK"

Clever retelling of the classic children's fairy tale, *Jack and the Beanstalk*, with Angelica as the evil giant trying to get the best of the stalk-climbing Rugrats gang in this second of two direct-to-video specials that aired only once, at noon on Sunday, November 5, 2006, more than one year after the first production, *Rugrats: Tales from the Crib: Snow White*, debuted on Nickelodeon. Starring the guest voice talents of Amanda Bynes, Mo'Nique and Kathy Najimy, the special was based on the long-running, Emmy-winning Nickelodeon cartoon series. *A Klasky Csupo Production. Color. One hour. Premiered on NICK: November 5, 2006.*

### Voices
**Tommy Pickles:** E. G. Daily; **Chuckie Finster Jr.:** Christine Cavanaugh; **Angelica C. Pickles:** Cheryl Chase; **Phil/Lil/ DeVille:** Kath Soucie; **Dil Pickles:** Tara Strong; **Susie Carmichael:** Cree Summer; **Kimi Watanabe-Finster:** Dione Quan; **Tammy:** Amanda Bynes; **Other Voices:** Mo'Nique, Kathy Najimy

## ◎ RUGRATS THE SANTA EXPERIENCE

The families spend Christmas together in the mountains where Tommy and Chuckie set traps for Santa Claus in this fun-filled, prime-time holiday special. (For voice credits, see entry in Television Cartoon Series section.) *A Klasky Csupo Production. Color. Half-hour. Premiered on NICK: December 21, 1996. Rebroadcast on NICK: December 25, 1996.*

## ◎ RUGRATS VACATION

Taking their RV on the road, the Pickles family travels to the entertainment capital of the world—Las Vegas—in this springtime half-hour special. (For voice credits, see series entry in Tele-

vision Cartoon Series section.) *A Klasky Csupo Production. Color. Half-hour. Premiered on NICK: March 3, 1998.*

## ◎ RUMPELSTILTSKIN

A maiden is forced to spin straw into gold to save her father or face death in this animated rendition of the Grimm Brothers' fairy tale which debuted on Canadian television and was syndicated in the United States. *An Atkinson Film-Arts Production in association with Telefilm Canada and CTV. Color. Half-hour. Premiered (U.S.): December 1985. Syndicated. Rebroadcast on NICK: February 8, 1992; April 4, 1992.*

### Voices
**Rumplestiltskin:** Robert Bockstael; **Miller:** Les Lye; **Miller's Daughter/Queen:** Charity Brown; **King:** Al Baldwin; **Narrator:** Christopher Plummer

## ◎ THE RUNAWAY TEAPOT

Toby the Teapot and Jenny the Milk Jug escape from the clutches of the Mad Hatter and find true love in New York City in this half-hour animated musical, part of the *HBO Storybook Musicals* series, inspired by Lewis Carroll's children's classic *Alice in Wonderland*. Originally called *I'm a Little Teapot*, the special was originally produced as part of CINAR Films' 13-part *The Real Story of . . .* series. *A CINAR Films/Crayon Animation Production in association with Western Publishing Company Inc./Global Television Network. Color. Half-hour. Premiered on HBO: December 4, 1991. Rebroadcast on HBO: December 11, 1991.*

### Voices
Julian Lennon

## ◎ RUPERT AND THE FROG SONG

Music legend Paul McCartney, in live-action wraparounds, hosts (he also produced) this half-hour program featuring two animated stories of popular British cartoon characters Seaside Woman and Oriental Nightfish (for which McCartney and wife, Linda, provided some of the voices), which premiered in the United States on Disney Channel. *An MPL Communications Production. Color. Half-hour. Premiered on DIS: September 20, 1986.*

### Voices
**Rupert/Edward/Bill/Boy Frog:** Paul McCartney; **Rupert's Father/Father Frog:** Windsor Davies; **Rupert's Mother:** June Whitfield; **Other Voices:** Linda McCartney

## ◎ SABRINA: FRIENDS FOREVER

After deciding to enter the Witch Academy, Sabrina is afraid she won't be accepted so she keeps a secret from everyone, including her teachers and classmates—she's only half-mortal. After meeting another girl who's just like her, they support each other in becoming full witches and proving they belong in this 90-minute cartoon special—also known as *Sabrina the Teenage Witch in Friends Forever* and *Sabrina's Secret Life: Friends Forever*—for DIC's *Incredible Movie Toons* on Nickelodeon. *A DIC Entertainment Production. Color. Ninety minutes. Premiered on NICK: October 6, 2002.*

### Voices
**Sabrina Spellman:** Britt McKillip; **Uncle Eustace:** Jay Brazeau; **Aunt Zelda:** Tina Bush; **Nicole:** Alexandra Carter; **Warlock:** Gary Chalk; **Miss Hag:** Marilyn Gann; **Salem Saberhagen:** Louis Chirillo; **Flat Ears:** Andrew Kavadas; **Portia:** Carly McKillip; **Bree:** Vanessa Morle; **Enchantra:** Jane Mortifee; **Miss Fetid:** Teryl

Rothery; **Aunt Hilda:** Moneca Stori; **Craven:** Samuel Vincent; **Mr. Rancid:** Dale Wilson; **Hockey Players:** Colin Murdock, Alistair Abell, Brent Miller

## ◎ SADDLE RASH

Somewhere in a small Old West town, armless gunslinger Slim seeks revenge against the ruthless Tommy Morgan, who has posted a $1,000 bounty on his head, while also falling in love with Hanna Headstrong, daughter of a well-known local rancher, in this Flash-animated cartoon special, narrated by old prospector Gummy, that also served as the pilot for a proposed comedy cartoon series created by Loren Bouchard, co-creator of *Home Movies*, which aired on Cartoon Network's *Adult Swim*. A *Flickerlab/Ka-Plunk Productions/Loren Bouchard Production. Color. Half-hour. Premiered on CAR: March 1, 2002.*

*Voices*
**Gummy/Tommy Morgan:** H. Jon Benjamin; **Slim:** Sam Seder; **Hanna Headstrong:** Sarah Silverman; **Kitty the Kid:** Todd Barry; **Additional Voices:** David Frizzell, Mitch Hedberg, Waylon Jennings, Doug Stone

## ◎ SAILOR MOON: THE RETURN OF SAILOR MOON

Endowed with amazing powers, five average-looking teenagers, dubbed Sailor Moon, Sailor Mares, Sailor Mercury, Sailor Jupiter and Sailor Venus, fight the nefarious Queen Beryl in this half-hour series preview special that aired Saturday morning on FOX one week before the DIC Entertainment-produced series debuted in first-run syndication. (See entry, *Sailor Moon*, in "Animated Television Series" section for details.) A *DIC Entertainment Production. Color. Half-hour. Premiered on FOX: September 2, 1995.*

## ◎ SAILOR MOON S, THE MOVIE: HEARTS ON ICE

When an evil snow queen (Kaguya) decides to freeze Earth, the Inner Sailor Scouts with the help of the Outers try to stop her from unleashing her diabolical plan in this English-dubbed version of the second of three Sailor Moon theatrical movies based on the popular Japanese-imported cartoon series *Sailor Moon*. Originally produced in 1994, the movie premiered six years later in November 2001 in the United States on Cartoon Network, which previously aired the half-hour series. A *Toei Animation/Kodansha/Cloverway/Pioneer Entertainment L.P. Production. Color. One hour. Premiered on CAR: November 9, 2001.*

*Voices*
**Sailor Moon/Serena:** Linda Ballantyne; **Sailor Mercury/Amy:** Liza Balkan; **Sailor Mars/Raye:** Katie Griffin; **Sailor Jupiter/Lita:** Susan Roman; **Sailor Venus/Mina:** Emilie Barlow; **Sailor Uranus/Amara Tenoh:** Sarah LeFleur; **Sailor Neptune/Michelle Kaiou:** Barbara Radecki; **Sailor Saturn/Hotaru Tomoe:** Jennifer Gould; **Sailor Mini-Moon/Rini:** Stephanie Beard; **Sailor Pluto/Trista Meioh:** Susan Aceron; **Tuxedo Mask/Darien:** Vince Corazza; **Luna:** Jill Frappier; **Artemis:** Ron Rubin; **Mimet:** Catherine Disher; **Grandpa Hino:** David Fraser; **Dr. Souichi Tomoe:** Jeff Lumby; **Andrew:** Joel Feeney; **Kaori Knight:** Kirsten Bishop; **Eugeal:** Loretta Jafelice; **Molly:** Mary Long; **Melvin:** Roland Parliament; **Chad:** Steven Bednarski; **Mistress 9:** Susan Aceron

## ◎ SAILOR MOON SUPER S, THE MOVIE: BLACK DREAM HOLE

After the evil Madame Vadiane kidnaps the children of the Earth to put them all into a permanently dream-filled sleep, Sailor Moon rescues Chibi-Usa while transforming Usagi before it is too late in this third Sailor Moon movie. Based on the popular Japanese *Tales of Suspense* comic book series (editions 63 and 64), the feature-length movie made its U.S. television premiere on Cartoon Network in November 2001, one week after the network debut of the 1995 English-dubbed *Sailor Moon* theatrical feature, *Sailor Moon S, The Movie: Hearts on Ice*. A *Toei Animation/Kodansha/Cloverway/Pioneer Entertainment L.P. Production. Color. One hour. Premiered on CAR: November 16, 2001.*

*Voices*
**Sailor Moon/Serena:** Linda Ballantyne; **Sailor Mercury/Amy:** Liza Balkan; **Sailor Mars/Raye:** Katie Griffin; **Sailor Jupiter/Lita:** Susan Roman; **Sailor Venus/Mina:** Emilie Barlow; **Sailor Mini-Moon/Rini:** Stephanie Beard; **Tuxedo Mask/Darien:** Vince Corazza; **Luna:** Jill Frappier; **Artemis:** Ron Rubin; **Diana/Eugeal:** Loretta Jafelice, Naomi Emmerson; **Ikuko Tsukino, Serena's mom:** Barbara Radecki; **Grandpa Hino:** David Fraser; **Hawk's-eye:** Benji Plener; **Fisheye:** Deborah Drakeford; **Tiger's-eye:** Jason Barr; **Sammy Tsukino:** Julie Lemieux; **Queen Nehellenia:** Lisa Dalbello; **Junjun/Miharu/Molly:** Mary Long; **Pegasus/Helios:** Robert Bockstael; **Melvin:** Roland Parliament; **Chad:** Steve Bednarski; **Elizabeth:** Susan Aceron; **Melanie:** Tanya Donato; **Dentist:** Tony Daniels

## ◎ SANTA AND THE THREE BEARS

Two bear cubs, Nikomi and Chinook, experience the joy and magic of Christmas for the very first time in this hour-long musical originally released theatrically in 1970 and rebroadcast via syndication as a holiday special. Live-action sequences of a kindly old grandfather relating the tale to his grandchildren introduce the animated story. A *Tony Benedict Production in association with Key Industries. Color. One hour. Premiered: 1970. Syndicated. Rebroadcast on USA Network: December 5, 1991; December 12, 1992; December 1, 1993; December 25, 1994; December 24, 1995. Rebroadcast on FAM: December 24, 1995; December 6, 1996; December 10, 1997.*

*Cast*
**Grandfather:** Hal Smith; **Beth:** Beth Goldfarb; **Brian:** Brian Hobbs

*Voices*
**Ranger:** Hal Smith; **Nana:** Jean VanderPyl; **Nikomi:** Annette Ferra; **Chinook:** Bobby Riha

## ◎ SANTA BABY!

Noel, a struggling songwriter who desperately wants to write a hit song, takes his frustrations out on his family while his daughter, Dakota, outdoes her father by penning her own song and wishes that he will be granted the same opportunity in this colorful, hour-long holiday special produced by Rankin/Bass Productions and sponsored by Coca-Cola that premiered on FOX. Directed by Lee Dannacher and executive produced by Arthur Rankin Jr. in the tradition of classic Rankin/Bass Christmas specials like *Rudolph the Red-Nosed Reindeer* and *Frosty the Snowman*, the prime-time special featured the voices of Gregory Hines, Eartha Kitt, Patti LaBelle and Vanessa Williams, plus original music composed by Glen Roven as well as many timeless holiday classics. A *Rankin-Bass Production. Color. Half-hour. Premiered on FOX: December 17, 2001. Rebroadcast on FOX: December 24, 2002.*

*Voices*
**Noel:** Gregory Hines; **Dakota:** Kianna Underwood; **Alicia:** Vanessa Williams; **Emerald:** Eartha Kitt; **Melody Songbird:** Patti LaBelle; **Mr. Sweet:** Tom Joyner

## ◎ SANTABEAR'S FIRST CHRISTMAS

Santa Claus recognizes a young bear's giving nature and appoints him as his helper to deliver toys to the animals of the forest. Thus he becomes known as Santabear. *A Rabbit Ears Video Production. Color. Half-hour. Premiered on ABC: November 22, 1986. Rebroadcast on SHO: December 17, 1991; December 22, 1991.*

**Voices**
**Narrator:** Kelly McGillis; **Santabear/Bullybear:** Bobby McFerrin; **Santa Claus:** John Malkovich

## ◎ SANTABEAR'S HIGH-FLYING ADVENTURE

Santa Claus asks Santabear to deliver his toys to the South Pole, but when the naughty Bullybear steals Santabear's bag of toys and his identity, all chances for a merry Christmas seem lost. Second in a series of Santabear Christmas specials. *A Michael Sporn Animation Production. Color. Half-hour. Premiered on CBS: December 24, 1987.*

**Voices**
**Santabear/Bullybear:** Bobby McFerrin; **Missy Bear:** Kelly McGillis; **Santa Claus:** John Malkovich

## ◎ THE SANTA CLAUS BROTHERS

Santa Claus's bumbling sons desperately try proving to their famous father that they are capable of stepping into his jet-black shoes when he retires in this Canadian-produced, CGI-animated holiday special featuring a star-studded voice cast and inspired by the artwork of Canadian pop artist Michael Beard. The hour-long prime-time adventure debuted on Canada's YTV and in the United States on Disney Channel. *A Nelvana Limited/Film Roman/Sitting Ducks Production. Color. One hour. Premiered on DIS: December 13, 2001. Rebroadcast on DIS: December 14, 2001; December 19, 2001; December 23, 2001; December 24, 2001; December 25, 2001; October 31, 2002; December 7, 2002; December 10, 2002; December 22, 2002; December 25, 2002; December 14, 2003; December 25, 2003; December 24, 2005; December 25, 2005.*

**Voices**
**Santa Claus:** Bryan Cranston; **Mrs. Claus:** Caroline Rhea; **Daryl:** Harland Williams; **Roy:** Richard Kind; **Mel:** Kevin McDonald; **Snorkel:** Joe Flaherty; **Other Voices:** Stephanie Beard

## ◎ SANTA CLAUS IS COMING TO TOWN

The life and times of Santa Claus—his abandonment as a child, his christening as Kris Kringle, and his eventual marriage to Jessica, the schoolmarm—are the essence of this holiday favorite produced in Animagic and narrated by actor/singer Fred Astaire, who likewise appears, in puppet form, as the town's mailman, S.D. Kluger. *A Rankin-Bass Production. Color. Half-hour. Premiered on ABC: December 14, 1970. Rebroadcast on ABC: December 3, 1971; December 1, 1972; November 30, 1973; December 5, 1974; December 9, 1975; December 12, 1976; December 1, 1977; December 10, 1978; December 2, 1979; December 8, 1980; December 19, 1981. Syndicated. Rebroadcast on FAM: December 4, 1996. Rebroadcast on FOX FAM: December 3, 1998; December 12, 1998; December 16, 1998; July 13, 1999; December 2, 1999; December 5, 1999; December 11, 1999; December 15, 1999; December 20, 1999; December 24, 1999; December 7, 2000; December 9, 2000; December 11, 2000; December 12, 2000; December 15, 2000; December 20, 2000; December 24, 2000. Rebroadcast on ABC FAM: December 1, 2001; December 2, 2001; December 7, 2001; December 12, 2001; December 18, 2001; December 21, 2001; December 24, 2001.* December 1, 2002; December 5, 2002; December 11, 2002; December 16, 2002; December 20, 2002; December 24, 2002; December 1, 2003; December 6, 2003; December 7, 2003; December 15, 2003; December 21, 2003; December 24, 2003; December 25, 2003; December 2, 2004; December 4, 2004; December 6, 2004; December 15, 2004; December 19, 2004; December 24, 2004; December 3, 2005; December 7, 2005; December 13, 2005; December 19, 2005; December 24, 2005; December 30, 2005; December 7, 2006; December 9, 2006; December 15, 2006; December 18, 2006; December 24, 2006.

**Voices**
**S.D. Kluger (narrator):** Fred Astaire; **Kris Kringle:** Mickey Rooney; **Jessica:** Robie Lester; **Winter Warlock:** Keenan Wynn; **Tanta Kringle:** Joan Gardner; **Burgermeister:** Paul Frees; **Children:** Diana Lyn, Greg Thomas

## ◎ SANTA MOUSE AND THE RATDEER

Featuring the voice of Melissa Joan Hart of TV's *Sabrina the Teenage Witch* sitcom fame as Molly Mouse, this charming animated special, based on Thatcher Hurd's illustrated children's book, follows the adventures of a well-meaning mouse (Rosie) who is more excited about Christmas than her friends and family and convinces Santa Mouse's exasperated ratdeer to help Santa deliver presents this year even though circumstances are less than ideal, or the holiday will be lost forever. *A KickStart Production. Color. Half-hour. Premiered on FOX FAM: December 22, 2000. Rebroadcast on FOX FAM: December 25, 2000. Rebroadcast on ABC FAM: December 1, 2001; December 14, 2001; December 19, 2001; December 23, 2001.*

**Voices**
**Santa Mouse:** Ewan "Sudsy" Clark; **Rosie:** Emily Hart; **Molly:** Melissa Joan Hart; **Basher:** Phil Hayes; **Blunder:** Saffron Henderson; **Bugsy/Easter Squirrel:** Peter Kelamis; **Loopy:** Scott McNeil; **Lousy:** Alistair Abell; **Twizzebum:** Colin Murdock; **Mom:** Ellen Kennedy; **Honest Wease:** John Payne

## ◎ SANTA'S FIRST CHRISTMAS

Santa recalls the fascinating tale of his evolution, from his childhood as a six-year-old boy, to recruiting his original elves, to training his famous reindeer and even bumbling his first delivery of toys to children around the world in this British-produced cartoon special. Produced by Robin Lyons and Juergen Egenolf and directed by Les Orton, *Santa's First Christmas* premiered on Christmas Day 1992 on BBC1 in the United Kingdom. Six years later, in December 1998, the special was first telecast in the United States on the FOX Family Channel. In October 2000, BMG Home Video released the special in the United States on DVD under the title of *Santa Stories* with a second half-hour yuletide cartoon special entitled *Santa and the Tooth Fairies. A Siriol Production with Cologne Cartoon for Eva Animation Production in association with S4C/Filmstiftung NRW/Rhewes Film. Color. Half-hour. Premiered on FOX FAM: December 9, 1998. Rebroadcast on FOX FAM: December 3, 1999; December 16, 1999.*

**Voices**
**Old Santa:** David Ellison; **Romauld:** Nigel Planer; **Grandpa Ivy:** Kenneth Waller; **Holly:** Emma Wray; **Mistletoe:** Will Brenton; **Santa's Mother:** Julie Higginson; **Young Santa:** Susan Sheridan

## ◎ SANTA VS. THE SNOWMAN

A lonely snowman (in a nonspeaking role) grows jealous of all the attention Santa Claus always receives and creates an army of snow-minions out of ice cubes, waging an all-out battle against Santa and his elves in this computer-generated holiday special. Created by Steve Oedekerk (of *Ace Ventura: When Nature Calls*

*Santa and the Snowman square off in a scene from the ABC holiday special* Santa vs. the Snowman. © O Entertainment

fame) and writer-animator John Davis. *An O Entertainment Production. Color. Half-hour. Premiered on ABC: December 13, 1997.*

**Voices**
**Santa Claus:** Jonathan Winters; **Security Elf:** Mark Decarlo; **Tour Guide Elf:** Ben Stein; **Communications Elf:** Victoria Jackson; **Narrator:** Don LeFontaine

## ◉ THE SAVIOR IS BORN

Morgan Freeman reads this poignant retelling of Mary and Joseph's journey to Bethlehem culminating in the birth of Jesus. Part of Rabbit Ears Video's *Holiday Classics* video series, the program debuted on The Family Channel. *A Rabbit Ears Video Production. Color. Half-hour. Premiered on FAM: December 24, 1992.*

**Voices**
**Narrator:** Morgan Freeman

## ◉ SCARY GODMOTHER: HALLOWEEN SPOOKTAKULAR

The first of two 3-D CGI-animated hour-long specials—adapted from artist Jill Thompson's well-known children's book and comic-books—follows the first trick-or-treating adventure of a young Hannah Marie, who ditches her older, mean cousin/babysitter, Jimmy, in the basement of a haunted house, only to enjoy an unforgettable Halloween party with Scary Godmother and her famous monster friends, Skully Pettibone, Harry the Werewolf, Orson, Bug-A-Boo and others, while Jimmy's scheme to frighten her backfires.

Produced by Canada's Mainframe Entertainment in 2003, the entertaining spookfest made its U.S. television debut in October 2004 on Cartoon Network. In October 2005, the special was broadcast on Halloween as part of a spooky double-feature that included a rebroadcast of the second special, *Scary Godmother 2: The Revenge of Jimmy*, which premiered earlier in the month. *A Mainframe Entertainment Production. Color. One hour. Premiered on CAR: October 1, 2004. Rebroadcast on CAR: October 31, 2005; October 6, 2006; October 31, 2006.*

**Voices**
**Scary Godmother/Ruby:** Tabitha St. Germain; **Hannah:** Britt McKillip; **Skully Pettibone/Count Max:** Scott McNeil; **Orson, Count Max's Son:** Adam Pospisil; **Harry the Werewolf/Bug-A-Boo:** Gary Chalk

## ◉ SCARY GODMOTHER 2: THE REVENGE OF JIMMY

The second of two hour-long computer-animated specials, based on author Jill Thompson's acclaimed children's book and comic book series, with Scary Godmother planning to host another spectacular spooky Halloween party, which Hannah's cousin, Jimmy, hopes to spoil this time with his dastardly plan. Premiering on Cartoon Network in early October 2005, the spooky special was rebroadcast numerous times by itself, and also as a part of a double feature on Halloween with the first special produced two years earlier, *Scary Godmother: Halloween Spooktakular. A Mainframe Entertainment Production. Color. One hour. Premiered on CAR: October 7, 2005. Rebroadcast on CAR: October 10, 2005; October 18, 2005; October 30, 2005; October 31, 2005.*

**Voices**
**Harry the Werewolf/Bug-A-Boo:** Gary Chalk; **Skully Pettibone/ Count Max:** Scott McNeil; **Orson, Count Max's son:** Adam Pospisil; **Scary Godmother:** Tabitha St. Germain

## ◉ SCOOBY AND THE GHOUL SCHOOL

Scooby-Doo, Shaggy and Scrappy-Doo get mixed up with monsters when they accept jobs as gym teachers at a girls' finishing school in this two-hour made-for-television movie. Part of *Hanna-Barbera's Superstars 10* movie package for first-run syndication. *A Hanna-Barbera Production. Color. Two hours. Premiered: 1988. Syndicated.*

**Voices**
**Scooby-Doo/Scrappy-Doo:** Don Messick; **Shaggy:** Casey Kasem; **Miss Grimwood:** Glynis Johns; **Elsa Frankensteen:** Pat Musick; **Winnie Werewolf:** Marilyn Schreffler; **Sibella Dracula:** Susan Blu; **Tannis the Mummy:** Patty Maloney; **Phantasma the Phantom:** Russi Taylor; **Matches/Papa Werewolf:** Frank Welker; **Colonel Calloway:** Ronnie Schell; **Daddy Dracula/Frankenstein Senior:** Zale Kessler; **Phantom Father:** Hamilton Camp; **Mummy Daddy/The Grim Creeper:** Andre Stojka; **Revolta:** Ruta Lee; **Baxter:** Rene Auberjonois; **Tug:** Scott Menville; **Miguel:** Aaron Lohr; **Jamaal:** Bumper Robinson; **Grunt:** Jeff B. Cohen

## ◉ SCOOBY-DOO AND THE ALIEN INVADERS

Scooby-Doo and company are stranded in a remote desert town and find themselves searching for clues about the mystery of alien invaders in this third in a series of direct-to-video cartoon features based on Hanna-Barbera's popular Saturday-morning franchise. The 80-minute film debuted on Cartoon Network. *A Hanna-Barbera Cartoons Production for Warner Home Video. Color. Eighty minutes. Premiered on CAR: October 2000.*

**Voices**
**Scooby-Doo/Shaggy Rogers:** Scott Innes; **Fred Jones:** Frank Welker; **Daphne Blake:** Mary Kay Bergman; **Velma Dinkley:** B. J. Ward; **Lester:** Jeff Bennett; **Crystal:** Candi Milo; **Steve:** Mark Hamill; **Laura:** Audrey Wasilewski; **Max:** Kevin Michael Richardson; **Dottie:** Jennifer Hale; **Sergio:** Neil Ross

## ◉ SCOOBY-DOO AND THE CYBERCHASE

The Mystery, Inc., gang—Scooby-Doo, Shaggy, Fred, Daphne and Velma—embark on one of their most electrifying adventures (literally) after being zapped into a computer game in pursuit of the game's virtual villain, Phantom Virus, in this fourth direct-to-video feature and last "official" production by Hanna-Barbera Studios, which was folded into Warner Bros. Animation after the death of cofounder William Hanna in 2001. *A Hanna-Barbera Cartoons Production for Warner Home Video. Color. Seventy-five minutes. Premiered on CAR: October 2001.*

*Voices*

**Scooby-Doo/Cyber Scooby-Doo/Shaggy Rogers/Cyber Shaggy Rogers:** Scott Innes; **Fred Jones/Cyber Fred Jones:** Frank Welker; **Daphne Blake/Cyber Daphne Blake:** Grey DeLisle; **Velma Dinkley/Cyber Velma Dinkley:** B. J. Ward; **Officer Wembley:** Joe Alaskey; **Eric Staufer:** Bob Bergen; **Professor Robert Kaufman:** Tom Kane; **Bill McLemore:** Mikey Kelley; **Phantom Virus:** Gary Sturgis

### ◎ SCOOBY-DOO AND THE LEGEND OF THE VAMPIRE

Masquerading as a heavy metal band, Those Meddling Kids, Scooby-Doo and the gang travel to a music festival in Australia where a legendary vampire, Yowie Yahoo, is kidnapping musical acts in this fifth direct-to-video Scooby-Doo animated feature released in February 2003 and produced by Cartoon Network Studios and Hanna-Barbera cofounder Joseph Barbera that premiered that March on Cartoon Network. *A Cartoon Network Studios Production for Warner Home Video. Color. Seventy-two minutes. Premiered on CAR: March 4, 2003.*

*Voices*

**Scooby-Doo/Fred Jones:** Frank Welker; **Shaggy Rogers:** Casey Kasem; **Daphne Blake:** Heather North; **Velma Dinkley:** Nicole Jaffe; **Daniel Illiwara:** Phil LaMarr; **Jasper Ridgeway:** Jeff Bennett; **Malcolm Illiwara/Yowie Yahoo:** Kevin Michael Richardson; **Thorn:** Jennifer Hale; **Dusk:** Jane Wiedlin; **Luna:** Kimberly Brooks; **Russell/Dark Skull:** Michael Neill; **Harry/Stormy Weathers and Barry/Lightning Strikes:** Tom Kenny

### ◎ SCOOBY-DOO AND THE LOCH NESS MONSTER

On vacation in Scotland, the Mystery, Inc., gang (Scooby-Doo, Shaggy, Fred, Daphne and Velma) encounter the famed Loch Ness Monster, or so they think, while trying to unravel one of history's greatest unsolved mysteries in this seventh in a series of direct-to-video cartoon features that premiered on Cartoon Network two days before its video release in June 2004. *A Warner Bros. Animation Production for Warner Home Video. Color. Seventy-four minutes. Premiered on CAR: June 22, 2004.*

*Voices*

**Scooby-Doo/Fred Jones:** Frank Welker; **Shaggy Rogers:** Casey Kasem; **Daphne Blake:** Grey DeLisle; **Velma Dinkley:** Mindy Cohn; **Professor Fiona Pembrooke:** Sheena Easton; **Del Chillman/Sir Ian Locksley:** Jeff Bennett; **Angus Haggart:** Phil LaMarr; **Colin Haggart:** John DiMaggio; **Duncan MacGubbin/Mcintyre:** Michael Bell

### ◎ SCOOBY-DOO AND THE MONSTER OF MEXICO

Scooby-Doo, Shaggy, Fred, Daphne and Velma take on Mexico's towering legendary Chupacabra monster that is terrifying locals and tourists with their clues leading them into danger in this sixth direct-to-video feature that also debuted on Cartoon Network. *A Warner Bros. Animation Production for Warner Home Video. Color. Seventy-five minutes. Premiered on CAR: September 30, 2003.*

*Voices*

**Scooby-Doo/Fred Jones:** Frank Welker; **Shaggy Rogers:** Casey Kasem; **Daphne Blake:** Heather North; **Velma Dinkley:** Nicole Jaffe; **Jorge Otero:** Brandon Gonzalez; **Luis Otero:** Jesse Borrego; **Charlene Otero/Museum Guide:** Candi Milo; **Doña Dolores:** Rita Moreno; **Sofia Otero:** Maria Canals; **Mr. Smiley/Ghost of** **Señor Otero:** Rip Taylor; **Señor Fuente:** Castulo Guerra; **El Curandero:** Benito Martinez; **Alejo Otero:** Eddie Santiago

### ◎ SCOOBY AND THE RELUCTANT WEREWOLF

Scooby-Doo and Shaggy are funny-car drivers, who get into monstrous trouble involving a new werewolf. Produced for *Hanna-Barbera's Superstar 10* movie package for first-run syndication. *A Hanna-Barbera Production. Color. Two hours. Premiered: 1988. Syndicated. Rebroadcast on TBS: December 13, 1992. Rebroadcast on CAR: March 12, 1995 (Mr. Spim's Cartoon Theatre). Rebroadcast on DIS: October 31, 1996; October 31, 1997.*

*Voices*

**Scooby-Doo/Scrappy-Doo:** Don Messick; **Shaggy:** Casey Kasem; **Googie:** B.J. Ward; **Vana Pira:** Pat Musick; **Dracula:** Hamilton Camp; **Dreadonia:** Joan Gerber; **Repulsa:** B.J. Ward; **Bonejangles:** Brian Mitchell; **Frankenstein/Skull Head:** Jim Cummings; **Mummy:** Alan Oppenheimer; **Brunch:** Rob Paulsen; **Crunch:** Frank Welker; **Screamer:** Mimi Seton; **Dr. Jeckyll/Mr. Hyde:** Ed Gilbert

### ◎ SCOOBY-DOO AND THE WITCH'S GHOST

Scooby-Doo, Shaggy, Fred, Daphne and Velma are invited by a famous horror writer, Ben Ravencroft, to investigate the frightfully strange goings-on of a witch's ghost that is haunting the quaint New England village where he lives in this second direct-to-video animated feature released on home video on October 5, 1999 and also broadcast that Halloween on Cartoon Network. *A Hanna-Barbera Cartoons/Warner Bros. Television Animation Production for Warner Home Video. Color. Seventy minutes. Premiered on CAR: October 31, 1999.*

*Voices*

**Scooby-Doo/Shaggy Rogers:** Scott Innes; **Fred Jones:** Frank Welker; **Daphne Blake:** Mary Kay Bergman; **Velma Dinkley:** B. J. Ward; **Ben Ravencroft:** Tim Curry; **Dusk:** Jane Wiedlin; **Thorn:** Jennifer Hale; **Sarah Ravencroft:** Tress MacNeille; **Jack:** Bob Joles; **Mr. McKnight:** Peter Renaday; **Mayor Corey:** Neil Ross

### ◎ A SCOOBY-DOO CHRISTMAS

After staying at Daphne's uncle's condo in the quaint town of Winter Hollow, Scooby-Doo and the gang quickly find that a ghostly headless snowman is terrorizing the locals, destroying their homes and ruining their holiday spirit. The brand-new half-hour holiday special, featuring the guest voices of Jim Belushi, Mark Hamill, Peter Scolari and Kathy Kinney, debuted in 2002 on Kids' WB! *A Warner Bros. Animation Production. Color. Half-hour. Premiered on Kids' WB!: December 13, 2002. Rebroadcast on the WB! (Kids' WB!): December 18, 2003; December 25, 2004; December 16, 2005.*

*Voices*

**Scooby-Doo/Freddy Jones:** Frank Welker; **Norville "Shaggy" Rodgers:** Casey Kasem; **Velma Dinkley:** Mindy Cohn; **Daphne Blake:** Grey DeLisle; **Tommy:** Daryl Sabara; **Mortimer, Tommy's father:** Mark Hamill; **Professor William Fagan Higginson:** Peter Scolari; **Sheriff Ellen Perkins:** Kathy Kinney; **Asa Buchwald:** Jim Belushi; **Jeb:** M. Emmet Walsh; **Headless Snowman of Winter Hollow:** Frank Welker

### ◎ SCOOBY-DOO IN WHERE'S MY MUMMY?

When archaeologist and supersleuth Velma goes to Egypt to restore an ancient Sphinx statue, she finds more than she bargained for when she uncovers a lost ruby ankh necklace originally owned by Cleopatra (voiced by Oscar-winning actress Virginia Madsen)—with the help of Scooby, Shaggy, Fred and Daphne who make a surprise appearance—that unlocks a secret tomb protected by a curse and one thousand mummified warriors. Produced by Warner Bros. Television Animation, this ninth direct-to-video animated movie featuring the popular Great Dane and friends debuted three weeks before its release on DVD by Warner Bros. Home Video, on Thanksgiving, November 24, 2005, on Cartoon Network. *A Warner Bros. Television Animation Production. Color. Seventy-five minutes. Premiered on CAR: November 24, 2005.*

*Voices*

**Scooby-Doo/Fred Jones:** Frank Welker; **Shaggy Rogers:** Casey Kasem; **Daphne Blake/Natasha:** Grey DeLisle; **Velma Dinkley:** Mindy Cohn; **Amelia von Butch:** Christine Baranski; **Prince Omar:** Ajay Naidu; **Cleopatra:** Virginia Madsen; **Rock Rivers:** Jeremy Piven; **Hotep/Ancient One #2:** Ron Perlman; **Campbell:** Wynton Marsalis

## ◎ SCOOBY-DOO MEETS THE BOO BROTHERS

A search for lost treasure turn the visit of Scooby-Doo, Scrappy-Doo and Shaggy to a Southern plantation into spine-tingling adventure. Part of *Hanna-Barbera's Superstar 10* syndicated movie package. *A Hanna-Barbera Production. Color. Two hours. Premiered: 1987. Syndicated.*

*Voices*

**Scooby-Doo/Scrappy-Doo/Hound:** Don Messick; **Shaggy:** Casey Kasem; **Sheriff:** Sorrell Booke; **Farquard/Skull Ghost/Skeleton:** Arte Johnson; **Freako/Demonstrator Ghost:** Ronnie Schell; **Shreako:** Rob Paulsen; **Meako:** Jerry Houser; **Sadie Mae:** Victoria Carroll; **Billy Bob/Confederate Ghost/Uncle Beauregard/Ape:** Bill Callaway; **Mayor:** Michael Rye

## ◎ SCOOBY-DOO ON ZOMBIE ISLAND

First in a series of largely successful direct-to-video features in which the lovable cartoon mutt Scooby-Doo and the gang—Shaggy, Fred, Daphne and Velma—investigate the ghost of Moonscar the Pirate whose swashbuckling spirit is haunting an island in the bayou. Warner Bros. rolled out what they called "the biggest promotional and merchandising campaign" for a direct-to-video title in the studio's history to tie in with the video's release and premiere on Cartoon Network on Halloween in 1998. *A Hanna-Barbera Cartoon/Warner Bros. Television Animation Production in association with Warner Home Video. Color. Seventy-seven minutes. Premiered on CAR: October 31, 1998.*

*Voices*

**Scooby-Doo:** Scott Innes; **Shaggy:** Billy West; **Fred Jones:** Frank Welker; **Daphne Blake:** Mary Kay Bergman; **Velma Dinkley:** B. J. Ward; **Simone:** Adrienne Barbeau; **Lena:** Stara Strong; **Beau Neville:** Cam Clarke; **Jacques:** Jim Cummings; **Snakebite Scruggs:** Mark Hamill

## ◎ SCOOBY-DOO: PIRATES AHOY!

Scooby-Doo and the gang go on a creepy cruise to the famed Bermuda Triangle where, after encountering ghost pirates, they may walk the plank and become the Triangle's latest victims unless, of course, they can solve the greatest of all unsolved maritime mysteries in this direct-to-video, high-seas adventure that debuted on Cartoon Network. *A Warner Bros. Television Animation Production. Color. One hour and 20 minutes. Premiered on CAR: October 6, 2006.*

*Voices*

**Scooby-Doo/Fred:** Frank Welker; **Shaggy:** Casey Kasem; **Daphne:** Grey DeLisle; **Velma:** Mindy Cohn; **Mr. Mysterio/Woodenleg:**

Dan Castellaneta; **Skip Jones:** Tim Conway; **Captain Crothers:** Arsenio Hall; **Peggy Jones/Sea Salt Sally:** Edie McClurg; **Sunny St. Cloud:** Kathy Najimy; **Captain Skunkbeard/Biff Wellington:** Ron Perlman; **Rupert Garcia:** Freddy Rodriguez

## ◎ SCOOBY GOES HOLLYWOOD

Scooby-Doo, the clumsy but lovable canine, romps through delightful capers in order to hit the big time in Hollywood by landing his own prime-time television show. *A Hanna-Barbera Production. Color. One hour. Premiered on ABC: December 23, 1979. Rebroadcast on ABC: January 25, 1981.*

*Voices*

**Scooby-Doo/Bulldog/Second Man:** Don Messick; **Shaggy/First Man/Pilot's Voice:** Casey Kasem; **Fred/Afghan/The Groove:** Frank Welker; **Velma/First Woman/Lucy Lane:** Pat Stevens; **Daphne/Treena/Mail girl:** Heather North Kenney; **Baby Scooby-Doo:** Frank Welker; **C.J.:** Rip Taylor; **Director/First V.P./Terrier:** Stan Jones; **Jesse Rotten/V.P./Jackie Carlson:** Michael Bell; **Cherie/Sis/Receptionist:** Marilyn Schreffler; **Lavonne/Second Woman/Waitress:** Joan Gerber; **Kerry/Girl Fan/Executive Secretary:** Ginny McSwain; **Brother/Guard/Announcer's Voice:** Patrick Fraley

## ◎ SCHOOL . . . WHO NEEDS IT?

Davey (of TV's *Davey and Goliath*) and his friends protest going back to school but come around when their teacher extends an understanding hand and initiates the beginning of a special friendship. *A Clokey Production for the Lutheran Church of America. Color. Half-hour. Premiered: August-September 1971. Syndicated.*

*Voices*

**Davey Hansen/Sally Hansen/Teacher:** Norma McMillan, Nancy Wible; **Goliath:** Hal Smith

## ◎ SCRUFFY

In this three-part adventure, Scruffy, an orphaned puppy, searches for a new home and seeks to find true love in her life for the first time, becoming friends with a Shakespearean street actor, Joe Tibbles, and another stray dog, Butch, in this *ABC Weekend Special. A Ruby-Spears Enterprises Production. Color. Half-hour. Premiered on ABC: October 4, October 11 and October 18, 1980. Rebroadcast on ABC: February 7, February 14 and February 21, 1981; February 13, February 20 and February 27, 1982; February 26, March 5 and March 12, 1983.*

*Voices*

**Scruffy:** Nancy McKeon; **Tibbles:** Hans Conried; **Butch:** Michael Bell; **Dutchess:** June Foray; **Narrator:** Alan Young

## ◎ SEALAB 2021: "HAPPY CAKE"

The second of three 11-minute pilots following the exploits of insane captain Hazel "Hank" Murphy who probes his oddball crew of scientists about the sudden disappearance of a Happy Cake Oven in this update of Hanna-Barbera's classic 1970s cartoon series, *Sealab 2020*, first shown on Cartoon Network in late December 2000. The other two pilots included the first, "Radio Free Sealab," and the last, "I, Robot." *A 70-30 Productions/Williams Street Production. Color. Eleven minutes. Premiered on CAR: December 30, 2000.*

*Voices*

**Captain Hazel "Hank" Murphy:** Harry Goz; **Derek "Stormy" Waters:** Ellis Henican; **Jodene Sparks:** Bill Lobley; **Debbie DuPree:** Kate Miller; **Doctor Quentin Q. Quinn:** Brett Butler;

Marco Rodrigo Diaz de Vivar Gabriel Garcia Marquez: Erik Estrada; **Other Voices:** Molly Charette, John J. Miller, Adam Reed, Matt Thompson

### ◎ SEALAB 2021: "I, ROBOT"

With the Sealab about to implode after being severely damaged by a hurricane, Captain Murphy and his crew try repairing it to save their undersea facility while discussing implanting their brains in the bodies of robots in this third of three pilots to Cartoon Network's *Adult Swim* animation block, *Sealab 2021*. A *70-30 Productions/Williams Street Production. Color. Eleven minutes. Premiered on CAR: December 30, 2000.*

#### Voices

**Captain Hazel "Hank" Murphy:** Harry Goz; **Derek "Stormy" Waters:** Ellis Henican; **Jodene Sparks:** Bill Lobley; **Debbie DuPree:** Kate Miller; **Doctor Quentin Q. Quinn:** Brett Butler; **Marco Rodrigo Diaz de Vivar Gabriel Garcia Marquez:** Erik Estrada; **Other Voices:** Molly Charette, John J. Miller, Adam Reed, Matt Thompson

### ◎ SEALAB 2021: "RADIO FREE SEALAB"

After none of his crewmembers will play with him, madman captain Hank Murphy siphons all of Sealab's power to launch a pirate radio station and host his own call-in radio show, insulting all of his listeners, in this first of three pilots, followed by "Happy Cake" and "I, Robot," for the off-the-wall undersea remake of Hanna-Barbera's memorable 1970s Saturday-morning series, *Sealab 2020*, broadcast on Cartoon Network. A *70-30 Productions/Williams Street Production. Color. Eleven minutes. Premiered on CAR: December 30, 2000.*

#### Voices

**Captain Hazel "Hank" Murphy:** Harry Goz; **Derek "Stormy" Waters:** Ellis Henican; **Jodene Sparks:** Bill Lobley; **Debbie DuPree:** Kate Miller; **Doctor Quentin Q. Quinn:** Brett Butler; **Marco Rodrigo Diaz de Vivar Gabriel Garcia Marquez:** Erik Estrada; **Orphan:** Molly Charette; **Ted from Accounting [uncredited]:** Dave Willis; **Other Voices:** John J. Miller, Adam Reed, Matt Thompson

### ◎ THE SECRET GARDEN

Sent to live in Yorkshire, England, at the manor house of her aloof, hunchbacked uncle, 11-year-old orphan Mary Lennox finds refuge in her magical hideaway in this animated musical adaptation—and first offering of ABC's quarterly *Kids Movie Matinees* series—of Frances Hodgson Burnett's book. A *Mike Young Production in association with Greengrass Productions. Color. Ninety minutes. Premiered on ABC: November 5, 1994.*

#### Voices

**Mary Lennox:** Anndi McAfee; **Mrs. Medlock:** Honor Blackman

### ◎ THE SECRET WORLD OF OG

Five brothers and sisters—Penny, Pamela, Patsy, Peter and their baby brother, Pollywog—are taken to a world of games and make-believe in a strange underground world called OG, inhabited by small green creatures who live in mushroom-shape buildings and play games. A *Hanna-Barbera Production. Color. Ninety minutes (three parts). Premiered on ABC: April 30, 1983, May 7, 1983 and May 14, 1983. Rebroadcast on ABC: December 3, 1983, December 10, 1983 and December 17, 1983; October 27, 1984, November 10, 1984 and November 17, 1984: March 15, 1986, March 22, 1986 and March 29, 1986; February 21, 1987, February 28, 1987 and March 7, 1987; March 7, 1992, March 14, 1992 and March 21, 1992.*

#### Voices

**OG:** Fred Travalena; **Penny:** Noelle North; **Pamela:** Marissa Mendenhall; **Patsy:** Brittany Wilson; **Peter:** Josh Rodine; **Pollywog/Green Lady/Woman's Voice:** Julie McWhirter Dees; **Mother/Old Lady:** Janet Waldo; **Old Man/Glub Villager:** Fred Travalena; **Yukon "Yukie" Pete, family dog/Earless, Pollywog's cat/Long John Silver:** Peter Cullen; **Flub/Blib/Little Green Man #2/; Sheriff/Little Green Man #1; Butcher/Villager/Mushroom Harvester:** Hamilton Camp; **Teacher:** Beth Clopton; **Pirate #1/Mayor/Man's Voice:** Dick Erdman; **Worker/Cowboy #1/Green Deputy/Narrator:** Michael Rye; **Victim #2/Green Man:** Joe Medalis; **Victim #1/Elder OG/OG Father:** Andre Stojka

### ◎ THE SELFISH GIANT

A giant, who sees his selfish ways, makes an effort to reform himself, opening up his heart to a stray child in this faithful retelling of Oscar Wilde's short story of the same name. Originally produced for theaters, the film was nominated for an Academy Award as best animated short subject in 1972. The program had first been broadcast in Canada. David Niven narrated the original version of the production and was later replaced by Paul Hecht. A *Gerald Potterton Production in association with Narrator's Digest. Color. Half-hour. Premiered on CBS: March 28, 1973. Rebroadcast on CBS: March 25, 1974; April 6, 1976. Syndicated. Rebroadcast on DIS: September 12, 1991.*

#### Voices

**Narrator:** David Niven, Paul Hecht

### ◎ SHEEP IN THE BIG CITY: "IN THE BAA-INNING"

After living on a small country farm and being chosen to power a new sheep-powered ray gun, a runaway sheep escapes to the Big City to hide from General Specific and his Top Secret Military Organization, finding romance, adventures, problems and all sorts of unwelcome characters (including his love interest, Swanky the Poodle, and Swanky's sheep-loathing owner, Lady Richington) in this animated comedy series originally broadcast on the Cartoon Network.

Created by Mo Willems, who also served as executive producer, this half-hour program originated as a 15-minute pilot special called *In the Baa-inning* that aired in early November 2000 on Cartoon Network's *Adult Swim* cartoon block. Then, in mid-November, the 27-episode program, featuring two episodes per 30-minute broadcast, joined the *Adult Swim* lineup, becoming Cartoon Network's ninth original animated series. A *Curious Pictures/Cartoon Network Production. Color. Half-hour. Premiered CAR: November 4, 2000.*

#### Voices

**Sheep/General Specific/Ranting Swede:** Kevin Seal; **Farmer John/Private Public:** James Godwin; **Narrator/Ben Plotz:** Ken Schatz; **Angry Scientist:** Mo Willems; **Lady Richington:** Stephanie D'Abruzzo; **Wonderful Boy:** Christine Walters; **Other Voices:** Ruth Buzzi, Bradley Glenn

### ◎ SHE'S A GOOD SKATE, CHARLIE BROWN

Peppermint Patty enters her first major ice skating competition. With her coach, Snoopy, and faithful companion Marcie at her side, she runs into the usual Charlie Brown–like problems en route to the competition, where a real disaster strikes. Woodstock saves the day. Beginning in January 1998, the special was rerun for two seasons on Nickelodeon. A *Lee Mendelson–Bill Melendez Production in association with Charles M. Schulz Creative Associates and United Feature Syndicate. Color. Half-hour. Premiered on CBS: February 25, 1980. Rebroadcast on CBS: February 25, 1981; February 10, 1982;*

*Charlie Brown and the gang help Peppermint Patty prepare for her first ice-skating competition in the original CBS animated special* She's a Good Skate, Charlie Brown. © *United Features Syndicate* (COURTESY: BILL MELENDEZ PRODUCTIONS)

*February 23, 1988. Rebroadcast on NICK: January 29, 1998; February 15, 1998; March 18, 1998; April 21, 1998; May 21, 1998; June 24, 1998; July 22, 1998; August 25, 1998; September 25, 1998; November 4, 1998; December 11, 1998; February 6, 1999; April 19, 1999; June 8, 1999; August 5, 1999; November 28, 1999.*

**Voices**

**Charlie Brown:** Arrin Skelley; **Marcie:** Casey Carlson; **Peppermint Patty:** Patricia Patts; **Coach/Announcer:** Scott Beach; **Teacher:** Debbie Muller; **Bully:** Tim Hall; **Snoopy:** José Melendez; **Woodstock (singing):** Jason Serinus; **Singer:** Rebecca Reardon

## ◎ SILENT NIGHT

The heartwarming tale of Austrian pastor Joseph Mohr, who wrote the famed Christmas carol, is the premise of this animated production, which tells the origin of the popular yuletide song and its author, including the first time it was performed on Christmas Eve in 1818. *A National Telefilm Associates Presentation. Color. Half-hour. Premiered: December 1977. Syndicated.*

## ◎ SILVERHAWKS

In the year 2839 a volunteer android team—part metal and part human—is sent by Earth to keep law and order in the galaxy in this hour-long special marking the debut of the first-run syndicated series. *A Rankin-Bass Production in association with Pacific Animation. Color. One hour. Premiered: January 1986. Syndicated.*

**Voices**

**Quicksilver:** Peter Newman; **Melodia/Steelheart:** Maggie Jackson; **Windhammer:** Doug Preis; **Mon*Star/Stargazer:** Earl Hammond; **Poker-Face/BlueGrass/Time-Stopper:** Larry Kenney; **HardWare/Steelwill/Yes-Man/Mo-Lec-U-Lar:** Robert McFadden; **Hotwing:** Adolph Caesar, Doug Preis

## ◎ SILVERWING: A GLIMPSE OF THE SUN

A rebellious undersized teenage bat named Shade Silverwing breaks the law forbidding him and legions of bats before him from ever seeing the sun in order to find his father in this first of three made-for-TV movies adapted from the popular fantasy novel series. Produced by Vancouver's Bardel Entertainment, the 72-minute movie and both sequels, *Towers of Fire* and *Redemption*, as well as the half-hour animated series, premiered on Toon Disney.

*A Bardel Entertainment Production. Color. Seventy-two minutes. Premiered on TDIS: August 22, 2006.*

**Voices**

**Shade Silverwing:** Bill Switzer; **Breeze:** Louise Vallance; **Goth:** Michael Dobson; **Chinook:** Matt Hill; **Ursa:** Candus Churchill; **Frieda:** Pam Hyatt; **Throbb/Brutus/Zephyr:** Richard Newman; **Luger/Romulus:** Lee Tockar; **Mercury/Scirocco:** Ian James Corlett; **Marina:** Sharon Alexander

## ◎ SILVERWING: REDEMPTION

Conclusion to the three-part science fiction-fantasy adventure of a runt bat seeking revenge after trying to reconnect with his father and freeing his fellow nocturnal beasts from an unjust punishment, based on Kenneth Oppel's original fantasy novel that aired on Toon Disney. *A Bardel Entertainment Production. Color. Seventy-two minutes. Premiered on TDIS: August 24, 2006.*

**Voices**

**Shade Silverwing:** Bill Switzer; **Breeze:** Louise Vallance; **Goth:** Michael Dobson; **Chinook:** Matt Hill; **Ursa:** Candus Churchill; **Frieda:** Pam Hyatt; **Throbb/Brutus/Zephyr:** Richard Newman; **Luger/Romulus:** Lee Tockar; **Mercury/Scirocco:** Ian James Corlett; **Marina:** Sharon Alexander

## ◎ SILVERWING: TOWERS OF FIRE

The second of three feature-length fantasy adventures following the exploits of undaunted Shade Silverwing that made its world premiere on Toon Disney, following the first installment in the series, *Silverwing: A Glimpse of the Sun. A Bardel Entertainment Production. Color. Seventy-two minutes. Premiered on TDIS: August 23, 2006.*

**Voices**

**Shade Silverwing:** Bill Switzer; **Breeze:** Louise Vallance; **Goth:** Michael Dobson; **Chinook:** Matt Hill; **Ursa:** Candus Churchill; **Frieda:** Pam Hyatt; **Throbb/Brutus/Zephyr:** Richard Newman; **Luger/Romulus:** Lee Tockar; **Mercury/Scirocco:** Ian James Corlett; **Marina:** Sharon Alexander

## ◎ SIMPLE GIFTS

The spirit of holiday gift-giving in its simplest form is the running theme of this one-hour collection of cartoon segments—each adapted from well-known stories and produced by some of America's most noted animators and artists hosted by Colleen Dewhurst. *An R.O. Blechman Production for PBS. Color. One hour. Premiered on PBS: December 16, 1978.*

**Voices**

**Narrators:** José Ferrer ("A Memory of Christmas"); Hermione Gingold ("The Great Frost")

## ◎ SIMPLY MAD ABOUT THE MOUSE

Songs performed by contemporary artists, including Billy Joel, Harry Connick Jr., LL Cool J, Ric Ocasek and Michael Bolton, accompany clips from classic Disney cartoons in this half-hour compilation first released on home video, then broadcast on The Disney Channel. *A Walt Disney Production. Color. Half-hour. Premiered on DIS: 1992.*

## ◎ THE SIMPSONS CHRISTMAS SPECIAL

It's rough sledding for husband and father Homer, who is forced to resort to desperate measures when his Christmas bonus is canceled and Marge's family money goes to erase the tattoo son Bart thought would be the perfect gift. Entitled "Simpsons Roasting Over an Open Fire," the show was originally produced as part of the first season of *The Simpsons* television show. *A Gracie Films/Klasky Csupo Production in association with 20th Century Fox Television. Color. Half-hour. Premiered on FOX: December 17, 1989. Rebroadcast on FOX: December 23, 1989; July 1, 1990; December 19, 1991.*

**Voices**

**Homer J. Simpson/Krusty:** Dan Castellaneta; **Marge Simpson:** Julie Kavner; **Bart Simpson:** Nancy Cartwright; **Lisa Simpson:** Yeardley Smith; **Maggie Simpson:** (no voice); **Other Voices:** Harry Shearer

### ◎ THE SIMPSONS HALLOWEEN MARATHON: "TREEHOUSE OF HORROR V"

This two-hour spooky spectacular sandwiches a brand-new half-hour trilogy featuring tributes to more favorite horror and sci-fi movies between reruns of past Halloween specials from 1991 to 1993. In "The Shinning," Mr. Burns cuts off beer and cable TV to caretaker Homer who then becomes an axe-wielding maniac. "Time and Punishment" casts Homer as a time traveler who returns to the present under the totalitarian rule of Ned Flanders. "Nightmare Cafeteria" tells the tale of students at Springfield Elementary who go to detention only to return as "lunch." *A Gracie Films/Film Roman Production in association with 20th Century Fox Television. Color. Two hours. Premiered on FOX: October 30, 1994.*

**Voices**

**Homer J. Simpson:** Dan Castellaneta; **Marge Simpson:** Julie Kavner; **Bart Simpson:** Nancy Cartwright; **Lisa Simpson:** Yeardley Smith; **Maggie Simpson:** (no voice); **Charles Montgomery Burns/Ned Flanders:** Harry Shearer

### ◎ THE SIMPSONS HALLOWEEN SPECIAL: "TREEHOUSE OF HORROR"

Bart and Lisa swap scary stories about moving into a haunted house ("Bad Dream House"), their family's abduction by one-eyed extraterrestials ("Hungry Are the Damned") and their own rendition of Edgar Allan Poe's "The Raven" in their first prime-time Halloween special. *A Gracie Films/Klasky Csupo Production in association with 20th Century Fox Television. Color. Half-hour. Premiered on FOX: October 25, 1990. Rebroadcast on FOX: December 27, 1990; October 31, 1993; October 30, 1994.*

**Voices**

**Homer J. Simpson/Kodos:** Dan Castellaneta; **Marge Simpson:** Julie Kavner; **Bart Simpson/Raven:** Nancy Cartwright; **Lisa Simpson:** Yeardley Smith; **Maggie Simpson:** (no voice); **Moving Man/Serak The Preparer/Narrator:** James Earl Jones; **House:** Harry Shearer

### ◎ THE SIMPSONS HALLOWEEN SPECIAL: "TREEHOUSE OF HORROR VIII"

More bizarre Halloween tales are told in this eighth annual prime-time trilogy. Homer is the last man left in Springfield after a neutron missile explodes; Bart mixes up his DNA with that of a fly; and Marge and her sisters go trick-or-treating during witch-hunting season. (For voice credits, see entry in Television Cartoon Series section.) *A Gracie Films/Film Roman Production in association with 20th Century Fox Television. Color. Half-hour. Premiered on FOX: October 26, 1997. Rebroadcast on FOX: October 25, 1998; October 29, 1998.*

### ◎ THE SIMPSONS HALLOWEEN: "TREEHOUSE OF HORROR III"

Homer Simpson is stalked by a murderous Krusty the Clown doll who threatens to kill him; Mr. Burns and Smithers put Homer's giant, shackled form on stage as a monstrous ape; and son Bart unleashes brain-eating zombies into the world in this third annual

half-hour Halloween cartoon trilogy. *A Gracie Films/Film Roman Production in association with 20th Century Fox Television. Color. Half-hour. Premiered on FOX: October 29, 1992. Rebroadcast on FOX: October 30, 1994.*

**Voices**

**Homer J. Simpson/Krusty:** Dan Castellaneta; **Marge Simpson:** Julie Kavner; **Bart Simpson:** Nancy Cartwright; **Lisa Simpson:** Yeardley Smith; **Maggie Simpson:** (no voice); **House of Evil Owner:** James Hong

### ◎ THE SIMPSONS NEW HALLOWEEN SPECIAL: "TREEHOUSE OF HORROR II"

Following the success of their first Halloween special produced in 1990, the Simpsons starred in this hilarious trilogy of terrifying tales in which Lisa buys a magic monkey's paw that grants four wishes; Mr. Burns fires Homer then cuts out his brain; and everyone in Springfield fears Bart for his mind-reading abilities. *A Gracie Films/Klasky Csupo Production in association with 20th Century Fox Television. Color. Half-hour. Premiered on FOX: October 31, 1991. Rebroadcast on FOX: October 31, 1993; October 30, 1994.*

**Voices**

**Homer Simpson:** Dan Castellaneta; **Marge Simpson:** Julie Kavner; **Bart Simpson:** Nancy Cartwright; **Lisa Simpson:** Yeardley Smith

### ◎ THE SIMPSONS THANKSGIVING SPECIAL: "BART VS. THANKSGIVING"

It's Thanksgiving Day and Bart leaves rather than apologize to Lisa after accidentally destroying her historical centerpiece in this prime-time Thanksgiving special. *A Gracie Films/Klasky Csupo Production in association with 20th Century Fox Television. Color. Half-hour. Premiered on FOX: October 25, 1990. Rebroadcast on FOX: March 21, 1991; November 28, 1991.*

**Voices**

**Homer Simpson:** Dan Castellaneta; **Marge Simpson:** Julie Kavner; **Bart Simpson:** Nancy Cartwright; **Lisa Simpson:** Yeardley Smith; **Rory:** Gregg Berger

### ◎ THE SIMPSONS: "TREEHOUSE OF HORROR IV"

In this spook-tacular Halloween trilogy Homer and the gang parody "The Twilight Zone" episode "Nightmare at 20,000 Feet" called "Nightmare at 5 1/2 Feet"; Homer sells his soul to Ned Flanders as the devil; Mr. Burns is suspected of being a vampire. *A Gracie Films/Film Roman Production in association with 20th Century Fox Television. Color. Half-hour. Premiered on FOX: October 30, 1993.*

**Voices**

**Homer Simpson:** Dan Castellaneta; **Marge Simpson:** Julie Kavner; **Lisa Simpson:** Nancy Cartwright; **Bart Simpson:** Yeardley Smith

### ◎ THE SIMPSONS: "TREEHOUSE OF HORROR VI"

In the sixth annual Simpsons Halloween trilogy, a two-dimensional Homer Simpson gets trapped in a weird 3-D universe; an animated Paul Anka croons to help Springfield combat giant advertising characters; and Groundskeeper Willie menaces children (á la Freddy Krueger). *A Gracie Films/Film Roman Production in association with 20th Century Fox Television. Color. Half-hour. Premiered on FOX: October 29, 1995.*

**Voices**

**Homer J. Simpson/Groundskeeper Willie:** Dan Castellaneta; **Marge Simpson:** Julie Kavner; **Bart Simpson:** Nancy Cartwright; **Lisa Simpson:** Yeardley Smith; **Paul Anka:** Himself

## THE SIMPSONS: "TREEHOUSE OF HORROR VII"

Three unrelated stories make up this seventh annual "Treehouse of Horror" trilogy special. Aliens Kang and Kudos interrogate Homer about the identity of Earth's leaders; the Simpsons search for a missing Siamese twin; and Lisa's lost baby tooth is turned into a miniature city. (For voice credits, see entry in Television Cartoon Series section.) *A Gracie Films/Film Roman Production in association with 20th Century Fox Television. Color. Half-hour. Premiered on FOX: October 27, 1996.*

## THE SIMPSONS: "TREEHOUSE OF HORROR IX"

The ninth annual Halloween trilogy featuring America's favorite TV cartoon family in three laugh-filled episodes: "Hell Toupée," with Homer's newfound hair, received from an electrocuted death row convict, Snake, seeking revenge on his behalf; "The Terror of Tiny Toon," with Marge and Lisa ending up in an episode of *Itchy & Scratchy* after Lisa substitutes plutonium for batteries in the TV remote; and "Starship Poopers," in which Maggie grows fangs and tentacles for legs after confessing Kang is her father and goes on *The Jerry Springer Show* with Homer to settle the dispute. *A Gracie Films/Film Roman/20th Century Fox Television Production. Color. Half-hour. Premiered on FOX: October 25, 1998.*

### Voices

**Homer Simpson/Abraham Simpson/Krusty the Klown/Barney/ Willy/Sideshow Mel/Mayor Quimby/Hans Moleman/Gil/Itchy/ Scott Chr:** Dan Castellaneta; **Marjorie "Marge" Bouvier Simpson/Patty Bouvier/Selma Bouvier/Jacqueline Ingrid Bouvier/ Others:** Julie Kavner; **Bart Simpson/Nelson Muntz/Ralph Wiggum/Todd Flanders/Kearney:** Nancy Cartwright; **Lisa Simpson:** Yeardley Smith; **Apu/Moe/Police Chief Wiggum/Carl/Comic Book Guy/Dr. Nick Riviera/Professor Frink, Cletus/Sea Captain/Kirk Van Houten/Superintendent:** Hank Azaria; **Mr. Burns/ Smithers/Dr. Marvin Monroe/Ned Flanders/Principal Skinner/ Otto/Kent Brockman/Dr. Hibert/Lenny/Reverend Lovejoy/ Raine:** Harry Shearer; **Freddy Krueger:** Robert Englund; **Herself:** Kathie Lee Gifford; **Himself:** Ed McMahon; **Himself:** Regis Philbin; **Himself:** Jerry Springer

## THE SIMPSONS: "TREEHOUSE OF HORROR X"

The Simpsons return in this 10th collection of three spellbinding, hilarious stories featured in this half-hour special that premiered on Halloween night in 1999 on FOX. Included are "I Know What You Diddlily-Iddly-Did," in which Marge thinks she's killed Ned Flanders and then tries to cover it up; "Desperately Xeeking Xena," with Lisa and Bart, transformed into the superhuman Stretch Dude and Clobber Girl, battling the Comic Booky Guy who has kidnapped Xena (voiced by Lucy Lawless) to add to his priceless collection; and "Life's a Glitch, Then You Die," about a Y2K bug striking the networks at Homer's nuclear plant, resulting in mass destruction. *A Gracie Films/Film Roman/20th Century Fox Television Production. Color. Half-hour. Premiered on FOX: October 31, 1999.*

### Voices

Homer Simpson/Abraham Simpson/Krusty the Klown/Barney/ Willy: Dan Castellaneta; **Marjorie "Marge" Bouvier Simpson/ Patty Bouvier/Selma Bouvier:** Julie Kavner; **Bart Simpson/Nelson Muntz/Todd Flanders:** Nancy Cartwright; **Lisa Simpson:** Yeardley Smith; **Apu/Moe/Police Chief Wiggum/Dr. Nick Riviera:** Hank Azaria; **Mr. Burns/Smithers/Dr. Marvin Monroe/Ned Flanders/ Principal Skinner/Otto/Kent Brockman:** Harry Shearer; **Himself:** Tom Arnold; **Himself:** Dick Clark; **Herself:** Lucy Lawless

## THE SIMPSONS: "TREEHOUSE OF HORROR XI"

Homer's horoscope turns real when he dies after eating broccoli but isn't allowed into Heaven until he performs one good deed in "G-G-Ghost D-D-Dad"; Bart and Lisa wind up in the woods where they meet an evil witch who lives in a gingerbread house while Homer and Marge search for them in the fairy-tale send-up, "Scary Tales Can Come True"; and Lisa saves a dolphin who seeks revenge against the humans in "Night of the Dolphin" in this 11th annual half-hour Halloween scare-fest for FOX, based on the long-running animated sitcom. *A Gracie Films/Film Roman/20th Century Fox Television Production. Color. Half-hour. Premiered on FOX: November 1, 2000.*

### Voices

**Homer Simpson/Abraham Simpson/Krusty the Klown/Barney/ Willy:** Dan Castellaneta; **Marjorie "Marge" Bouvier Simpson/ Patty Bouvier/Selma Bouvier:** Julie Kavner; **Bart Simpson/Nelson Muntz/Todd Flanders:** Nancy Cartwright; **Lisa Simpson:** Yeardley Smith; **Apu/Moe/Police Chief Wiggum/Dr. Nick Riviera:** Hank Azaria; **Mr. Burns/Smithers/Dr. Marvin Monroe/Ned Flanders/Principal Skinner/Otto/Kent Brockman/McBain:** Harry Shearer; **Other Voices:** Tress MacNeille

## THE SIMPSONS: "TREEHOUSE OF HORROR XII"

Halloween takes on a whole new meaning—and dimension—in this outlandish half-hour special comprised of three new episodes: "hex and the city," with Homer falling under a gypsy's curse and nabbing a leprechaun to have it lifted; "House of Whacks," about Simpson's upgraded computer, the Ultrahouse 3000 (voiced by Pierce Brosnan), falling hopelessly in love with Marge while trying to kill Homer; and "Wiz Kids," following an evil lord who captures Lisa while she and Bart attend wizard school. Actor Matthew Perry, costar of long-running hit NBC comedy series *Friends*, appears as himself. *A Gracie Films/Film Roman/20th Century Fox Television Production. Color. Half-hour. Premiered on FOX: November 6, 2001.*

### Voices

**Homer Simpson/Abraham Simpson/Krusty the Klown/Barney/ Willy:** Dan Castellaneta; **Marjorie "Marge" Bouvier Simpson/ Patty Bouvier/Selma Bouvier:** Julie Kavner; **Bart Simpson/Nelson Muntz/Todd Flanders:** Nancy Cartwright; **Lisa Simpson:** Yeardley Smith; **Apu/Moe/Police Chief Wiggum/Dr. Nick Riviera:** Hank Azaria; **Mr. Burns/Smithers/Dr. Marvin Monroe/Ned Flanders/Principal Skinner/Otto/Kent Brockman:** Harry Shearer; **Edna Krabappel:** Marcia Wallace; **Ultrahouse 3000:** Pierce Brosnan; **Himself:** Matthew Perry

## THE SIMPSONS: "TREEHOUSE OF HORROR XIII"

When the Simpsons hold a séance with Ned Flanders, the ghost of Maude Flanders returns and opens a book that introduces three ghostly tales—"Send in the Clones," "The Right to Keep and Scare Harms," and "The Island of Dr. Hibbert"—in this 13th prime-time Halloween special for FOX network. *A Grace Films/ Film Roman/20th Century Fox Television Production. Color. Half-hour. Premiered on FOX: November 3, 2002.*

### Voices

**Homer Simpson/Abraham Simpson/Krusty the Klown/Barney/ Willy:** Dan Castellaneta; **Marjorie "Marge" Bouvier Simpson/ Patty Bouvier/Selma Bouvier:** Julie Kavner; **Bart Simpson/Nelson Muntz/Todd Flanders:** Nancy Cartwright; **Lisa Simpson:** Yeardley Smith; **Apu/Moe/Police Chief Wiggum/Dr. Nick Riviera:** Hank

Azaria; **Mr. Burns/Smithers/Dr. Marvin Monroe/Ned Flanders/ Principal Skinner/Otto/Kent Brockman/McBain:** Harry Shearer; **Maude Flanders:** Maggie Roswell; **Milhouse Van Houten:** Pamela Hayden; **Other Voices:** Tress MacNeille, Kal Wiedergott

## ◉ THE SIMPSONS: "TREEHOUSE OF HORROR XIV"

Homer becomes the Grim Reaper after killing the real one and deciding to kill Marge next in "Reaper Madness"; Homer helps a soon-to-be Nobel Prize-winning professor (voiced by Jerry Lewis) bring his father back to life to attend the awards ceremony in "Frinkenstein"; and Bart and Milhouse hold the power to stop time in "Stop the World, I Want to Goof Off," a spoof of the feature film *Clockstoppers* (2002) in this 14th annual prime-time Halloween special. Also making guest voice appearances are actress Jennifer Garner and boxing champion Oscar De La Hoya. *A Gracie Films/Film Roman/20th Century Fox Television Production. Color. Half-hour. Premiered on FOX: November 2, 2003.*

*Voices*

**Homer Simpson/Abraham Simpson/Krusty the Klown/Barney/ Willy:** Dan Castellaneta; **Marjorie "Marge" Bouvier Simpson/ Patty Bouvier/Selma Bouvier:** Julie Kavner; **Bart Simpson/Nelson Muntz/Todd Flanders:** Nancy Cartwright; **Lisa Simpson:** Yeardley Smith; **Apu/Moe/Police Chief Wiggum/Dr. Nick Riviera:** Hank Azaria; **Mr. Burns/Smithers/Dr. Marvin Monroe/Ned Flanders/Principal Skinner/Otto/Kent Brockman/McBain:** Harry Shearer; **Martin Prince:** Russi Taylor; **Milhouse Van Houten:** Pamela Hayden; **Miss Hoover:** Maggie Roswell; **Professor John Frink Sr.:** Jerry Lewis; **Herself:** Jennifer Garner; **Himself:** Dudley Herschbach; **Himself:** Oscar De La Hoya; **Other Voices:** Tress MacNeille, Pamela Hayden, Karl Wiedergott

## ◉ THE SIMPSONS: "TREEHOUSE OF HORROR XV"

The Simpsons trot out more Halloween surprises in this annual prime-time trilogy special produced in 2004. After suffering a serious head injury when Homer knocks himself unconscious with his bowling ball (duh!), Ned Flanders awakens to foresee the future and predicts Homer's death in "The Ned Zone." Meanwhile, the Simpsons try saving Maggie after a science experiment goes wrong that shrinks her in size and she is accidentally swallowed by Mr. Burns in "In the Belly of the Boss," a send-up of the science-fiction film *Fantastic Voyage* (1966). Finally, Lisa and Bart try catching the famous Muttonchop Murder serial killer in "Four Beheadings and a Funeral." *A Gracie Films/Film Roman/20th Century Fox Television Production. Color. Half-hour. Premiered on FOX: November 7, 2004.*

*Voices*

**Homer Simpson/Abraham Simpson/Krusty the Klown/Barney/ Willy:** Dan Castellaneta; **Marjorie "Marge" Bouvier Simpson/ Patty Bouvier/Selma Bouvier:** Julie Kavner; **Bart Simpson/Nelson Muntz/Todd Flanders:** Nancy Cartwright; **Lisa Simpson:** Yeardley Smith; **Apu/Moe/Police Chief Wiggum/Dr. Nick Riviera:** Hank Azaria; **Mr. Burns/Smithers/Dr. Marvin Monroe/Ned Flanders/ Principal Skinner/Otto/Kent Brockman/McBain:** Harry Shearer; **Other Voices:** Marie Cain, Tress MacNeille, Karl Wiedergott

## ◉ THE SIMPSONS: "TREEHOUSE OF HORROR XVI"

After a diving accident lands Bart on his head and in a coma, the Simpsons find what they believe to be the ideal substitute, a robot Bart, in "Bartificial Intelligence," the first of three Halloween-themed romps, including "Survival of the Fattest" and "I've Grown

a Costume on Your Face," in this 16th annual prime-time special. Featured as guest voices on the special as themselves were football Hall of Famer Terry Bradshaw and basketball great Dennis Rodman. *A Gracie Films/Film Roman/20th Century Fox Television Production. Color. Half-hour. Premiered on FOX: November 6, 2005.*

*Voices*

**Homer Simpson/Abraham Simpson/Krusty the Klown/Barney/ Willy/Sideshow Mel/Mayor Quimby/Hans Moleman/Gil/Itchy:** Dan Castellaneta; **Marjorie "Marge" Bouvier Simpson/Patty Bouvier/Selma Bouvier:** Julie Kavner; **Bart Simpson/Nelson Muntz/ Ralph Wiggum/Todd Flanders/Kearney:** Nancy Cartwright; **Lisa Simpson:** Yeardley Smith; **Apu/Moe/Police Chief Wiggum/Dr. Nick Riviera/Comic Book Guy/Carl/Professor Frink/Cletus/Sea Captain/Kirk Van Houten/Superintendent:** Hank Azaria; **Mr. Burns/Smithers/Dr. Marvin Monroe/Ned Flanders/Principal Skinner/Otto/Kent Brockman/Dr. Hibert/Lenny/Ray/Lovejoy/ Raine:** Harry Shearer; **Milhouse Van Houten:** Pamela Hayden; **Martin Prince:** Russi Taylor; **Himself:** Terry Bradshaw; **Himself:** Dennis Rodman; **Other Voices:** Tress MacNeille, Terry W. Greene

## ◉ THE SIMPSONS: "TREEHOUSE OF HORROR XVII"

Three new scary tales are offered in this 17th *Treehouse of Horror* special, featuring the voices of Dr. Phil McGraw, Fran Drescher and Richard Lewis. Among them are "Married to the Blob," in which Homer changes and eats everything in sight after consuming a strange green substance that came from a meteorite; "You Gotta Know When to Golem," with Bart forcing the ancient statue of Jewish folklore to do what he wishes; and "The Day the Earth Looked Stupid," a parody of Orson Welles's famous *War of the Worlds* radio broadcast set in 1938 Springfield. *A Gracie Films/ Film Roman/20th Century Fox Television Production. Color. Half-hour. Premiered on FOX: November 5, 2006.*

*Voices*

**Homer Simpson/Abraham Simpson/Krusty the Klown/Barney/ Willy/Sideshow Mel/Mayor Quimby/Hans Moleman/Gil/Itchy:** Dan Castellaneta; **Marjorie "Marge" Bouvier Simpson/Patty Bouvier/Selma Bouvier:** Julie Kavner; **Bart Simpson/Nelson Muntz/Ralph Wiggum/Todd Flanders/Kearney:** Nancy Cartwright; **Lisa Simpson:** Yeardley Smith; **Apu/Moe/Police Chief Wiggum/Dr. Nick Riviera/Comic Book Guy/Carl/Professor Frink/Cletus/Sea Captain/Kirk Van Houten/Superintendent:** Hank Azaria; **Mr. Burns/Smithers/Dr. Marvin Monroe/Ned Flanders/Principal Skinner/Otto/Kent Brockman/Dr. Hibert/ Lenny/Ray/Lovejoy/Raine:** Harry Shearer; **Edna Krabappel:** Marcia Wallace; **Milhouse Van Houten:** Pamela Hayden; **Golem:** Richard Lewis; **Orson Welles:** Maurice LaMarche; **Female Golem:** Fran Drescher; **Himself:** Phil McGraw; **Other Voices:** Tress MacNeille, Six Mix-A-Lot, Karl Wiedergott

## ◉ SLEEPING BEAUTY

This show retells the story of the beautiful young princess who is cast under a spell by the wicked old witch, but with a new twist. During her curse, the princess and all the subjects in the kingdom remain in perpetual sleep. None of them, including the princess, can be awakened until the handsome, bravehearted Prince Daring puckers up and kisses the sleeping beauty. *A Festival of Family Classics* special. *A Rankin-Bass Production in association with Mushi Studios. Color. Half-hour. Premiered: January 21, 1973. Syndicated.*

*Voices*

Carl Banas, Len Birman, Bernard Cowan, Peg Dixon, Keith Hampshire, Peggi Loder, Donna Miller, Frank Perry, Henry Ramer, Billie Mae Richards, Alfie Scopp, Paul Soles

## SLIMER! AND THE REAL GHOSTBUSTERS: "THE HALLOWEEN DOOR"

In their first prime-time special, the Ghostbusters are hired by the chairman of the Citizens United Against Halloween assist him in his crusade to abolish the holiday and its traditions. Originally produced as an episode of the popular Saturday-morning series on ABC. *A DIC Enterprises Production in association with Columbia Pictures Television. Color. Half-hour. Premiered on ABC: October 29, 1989.*

### Voices

**Slimer/Ray Stantz:** Frank Welker; **Peter Venkman:** Dave Coulier; **Winston Zeddmore:** Edward L. Jones; **Egon Spengler:** Maurice LaMarche; **Janine Melintz:** Kath Soucie

## THE SMURFIC GAMES

The Smurfs discover the spirit of friendly competition when they hold their first Olympic-style "Smurfic Games," and Gargamel tries to activate a special medallion with deadly powers to use against them. Nominated for an Emmy. *A Hanna-Barbera Production in association with SEPP International. Color. Half-hour. Premiered on NBC: May 20, 1984. Rebroadcast on NBC: May 11, 1985.*

### Voices

**Papa Smurf/Azrael:** Don Messick; **Baby Smurf:** Julie McWhirter Dees; **Smurfette:** Lucille Bliss; **Clumsy/Painter/Dragon:** Bill Callaway; **Grouchy/Handy/Lazy/Argus:** Michael Bell; **Greedy/Harmony:** Hamilton Camp; **Jokey:** June Foray; **Hefty/Frog/Bird/Poet:** Frank Welker; **Tailor:** Kip King; **Gargamel:** Paul Winchell; **Bigmouth:** Lennie Weinrib; **Vanity:** Alan Oppenheimer

## SMURFILY EVER AFTER

As the Smurfs celebrate the wedding of their beloved Laconia, the mute wood elf, Smurfette hopes to find her own "Mr. Right." The special was closed-captioned for the hearing impaired. *A Hanna-Barbera Production in association with SEPP International. Color. Half-hour. Premiered on NBC: February 13, 1985. Rebroadcast on NBC: March 30, 1986.*

### Voices

**Papa Smurf/Azrael:** Don Messick; **Smurfette:** Lucille Bliss; **Hefty/Monster:** Frank Welker; **Handy/Lazy/Grouchy:** Michael Bell; **Jokey:** June Foray; **Gargamel:** Paul Winchell; **Clumsy:** Bill Callaway; **Vanity:** Alan Oppenheimer; **Brainy:** Danny Goldman; **Greedy/Woody:** Hamilton Camp; **Tailor:** Kip King; **Farmer:** Alan Young; **Elderberry:** Peggy Webber; **Bramble:** Robbie Lee; **Pansy:** Susan Blu; **Lilac:** Janet Waldo; **Holly:** Alexandria Stoddart; **Acorn:** Patti Parris

## THE SMURFS

Two months after its successful debut on Saturday morning, this colony of little blue people was featured in their first prime-time special, featuring three episodes from their weekly series: "Supersmurf," "The Smurfette" and "The Baby Smurf." *A Hanna-Barbera Production in association with SEPP International. Color. One hour. Premiered on NBC: November 29, 1981.*

### Voices

**Papa Smurf/Azrael:** Don Messick; **Gargamel:** Paul Winchell; **Brainy:** Danny Goldman; **Clumsy:** Bill Callaway; **Hefty:** Frank Welker; **Jokey:** June Foray; **Smurfette:** Lucille Bliss; **Vanity:** Alan Oppenheimer; **Greedy/Harmony:** Hamilton Camp; **Lazy/Handy/Grouchy:** Michael Bell

## THE SMURFS' CHRISTMAS SPECIAL

The Smurfs must use every little ounce of goodness they can muster to battle an even greater evil than Gargamel in this half-hour holiday special. *A Hanna-Barbera Production in association with SEPP International. Color. Half-hour. Premiered on NBC: December 13, 1982. Rebroadcast on NBC: December 9, 1983; December 22, 1984; December 5, 1986. Rebroadcast on CAR: December 24, 1992; November 28, 1992. Rebroadcast on TNT: November 29, 1993. Rebroadcast on CAR: December 13, 1993; December 12, 1994; November 25, 1995.*

### Voices

**Papa Smurf/Azrael/Horse:** Don Messick; **Harmony/Greedy/Bailiff:** Hamilton Camp; **Jokey/Squirrel:** June Foray; **Gargamel:** Paul Winchell; **Smurfette:** Lucille Bliss; **Grouchy/Lazy/Handy:** Michael Bell; **Grandfather/Vanity/Servant:** Alan Oppenheimer; **Stranger:** Rene Auberjonois; **William:** David Mendenhall; **Gwenevere:** Alexandra Stoddart; **Brainy:** Danny Goldman; **Clumsy/Painter/Wolf #1:** Henry Polic; **Hefty:** Frank Welker

## THE SMURFS SPRINGTIME SPECIAL

The Smurfs prepare for their big Easter festival, while Gargamel, the Smurfs' archenemy, conspires with his wizardly godfather, Balthazar, to ruin the festivities. An Emmy Award winner. *A Hanna-Barbera Production in association with SEPP International. Color. Half-hour. Premiered on NBC: April 8, 1982. Rebroadcast on NBC: April 1, 1983; April 20, 1984.*

### Voices

**Gargamel:** Paul Winchell; **Papa Smurf/Azrael:** Don Messick; **Smurfette:** Lucille Bliss; **Mother Nature/Jokey:** June Foray; **Handy/Grouchy/Lazy:** Michael Bell; **Clumsy:** Bill Callaway; **Harmony:** Hamilton Camp; **Balthazar:** Keene Curtis; **Brainy/Tailor:** Danny Goldman; **Vanity:** Alan Oppenheimer; **Hefty/Poet/Duckling:** Frank Welker

## SNOOPY'S GETTING MARRIED, CHARLIE BROWN

Snoopy's plans to marry a worldly French poodle who runs off with a golden retriever. *A Lee Mendelson–Bill Melendez Production in association with Charles M. Schulz Creative Associates and United Feature Syndicate. Color. Half-hour. Premiered on CBS: March 20, 1985. Rebroadcast on CBS: January 16, 1987; March 16, 1988. Rebroadcast on NICK: February 3, 1998; February 20, 1998; March 24, 1998; May 4, 1998; May 24, 1998; June 25, 1998; July 26, 1998; August 27, 1998; September 28, 1998; November 7, 1998; December 8, 1998; January 7, 1999; January 28, 1999; February 10, 1999; March 11, 1999; May 2, 1999; October 3, 1999.*

### Voices

**Charlie Brown:** Bett Johnson; **Lucy Van Pelt:** Heather Stoneman; **Linus Van Pelt:** Jeremy Schoenberg; **Schroeder:** Danny Colby; **Peppermint Patty:** Gini Holtzman; **Sally Brown:** Stacy Ferguson; **Sally (singing):** Dawnn S. Leary; **Marcie:** Keri Houlihan; **Pigpen/Franklin:** Carl Steven; **Snoopy:** José Melendez

## SNOOPY'S REUNION

Glancing into the *Peanuts* past, the story of Snoopy's life is told in this nostalgic and entertaining prime-time animated special, written by *Peanuts* creator Charles M. Schulz. The half-hour program was highlighted by a vignette involving Snoopy's first owner, an apparent reference to the 1972 animated feature *Snoopy Come Home*. The CBS special was later rebroadcast on Nickelodeon along with several dozen specials acquired by Nickelodeon in 1998. *A Bill Melendez Production in association with Charles M. Schulz Creative Association and United Media. Color. Half-hour.*

*Premiered on CBS: May 1, 1991. Rebroadcast on NICK: February 3, 1998; March 5, 1998; April 9, 1998; May 11, 1998; June 14, 1998; July 13, 1998; August 15, 1998; September 16, 1998; October 20, 1998; November 19, 1998; December 9, 1998; January 8, 1999; February 15, 1999; March 12, 1999; May 3, 1999; June 18, 1999; August 17, 1998; January 9, 2000.*

**Voices**
**Charlie Brown:** Philip Shafran; **Sally:** Kaitlyn Walker; **Farmer/Bus Driver:** Steve Stoliar; **Linus:** Josh Weiner; **Mother:** Laurel Page; **Little Girl:** Megan Parlen; **Other Voices:** Bill Melendez

## ◉ SNOOPY: THE MUSICAL

Based on the popular 1974 play, this one-hour animated special is comprised of a series of tuneful vignettes, with Snoopy headlining. Musical interludes include "Edgar Allen Poe," a clever melody about the jitters experienced when being called on in school; "Poor Sweet Baby," a lighthearted ballad pairing hapless Charlie Brown and lovelorn Peppermint Patty; and "The Vigil," a song about Linus's woeful watch for the Great Pumpkin. Music and lyrics were written by Larry Grossman and Hal Hackady. Beginning in March 1998, Nickelodeon re-aired the specials in two parts over two seasons. *A Lee Mendelson–Bill Melendez Production in association with Charles M. Schulz Creative Associates and United Feature Syndicate. Color. One hour. Premiered on CBS: January 29, 1988. Rebroadcast on NICK: March 23, 1998 (Part I); March 24, 1998 (Part II); April 29, 1998 (Part I); April 30, 1998 (Part II); June 1, 1998 (Part I); June 2, 1998 (Part II); July 6, 1998 (Part I); July 7, 1998 (Part II); August 4, 1998 (Part I); August 5, 1998 (Part II); September 7, 1998 (Part I); September 8, 1998 (Part II); October 1, 1998 (Part I); October 2, 1998 (Part II); October 22, 1998 (Part I); October 23, 1998 (Part II); November 23, 1998 (Part I); November 24, 1998 (Part II); March 29, 1998 (Part I); March 30, 1998 (Part II); May 20, 1999 (Part I); May 21, 1999 (Part II); July 19, 1999 (Part I); July 20, 1999 (Part II).*

**Voices**
**Snoopy:** Cameron Clarke; **Charlie Brown:** Sean Collins; **Lucy:** Tiffany Billings; **Peppermint Patty:** Kristi Baker; **Linus:** Jeremy Miller; **Sally:** Ami Foster

## ◉ SNOWDEN'S CHRISTMAS

After movers pack young Adam's favorite toys—Snowden, the snowman; Drummer, a pessimistic drum-playing teddy bear; Footloose, a bunny with extra large feet; and Tiny, a claustrophobic elephant—the box containing the four mismatched toys falls out of the truck and the toys are stranded outside of New York City, miles from the boy who loves them. They trek cross-country to be reunited with him by Christmas in this delightful half-hour, stop-motion and cel-animated special that debuted on CBS. Toronto, Canada-based Cuppa Coffee Animation produced this $700,000 special, with CBS hiring producer Adam Shaheen, following the success of the studio's first series *Crashbox! Crashbox!* for HBO Family, to produce the program. *A Cuppa Coffee Animation/CBS Worldwide Inc./Dayton Hudson Brands Inc. Production. Color. Half-hour. Premiered on CBS: December 3, 1999. Rebroadcast on CBS: December 14, 2000.*

**Voices**
**Snowden:** Peter MacNicol **Adam:** Jeffrey Schoeny

## ◉ THE SNOWMAN

Tells the story of a young boy who builds a snowman that comes to life during a dream on Christmas Eve in this Oscar-winning animated film based on the book by Raymond Briggs (who also wrote the screenplay). Film premiered as a half-hour special on HBO in 1983 and was subsequently rebroadcast on PBS with rocker David Bowie serving as host. *A Snowman Enterprises Production for Channel 4 in association with TVC London. Color. Half-hour. Premiered on HBO: December 26, 1983. Rebroadcast on PBS: December 2, 1985; December 25, 1986. Rebroadcast on SHO: October 22, 1991; Rebroadcast on DIS: December 20, 1991; November 21, 1992; December 22, 1993.*

## ◉ THE SNOW QUEEN

Two small children, Gerta and Kay, embark on a dangerous journey to rescue Gerta's brother, who has been kidnapped by the evil Snow Queen in this charming adaptation of the Hans Christian Andersen classic. Originally produced overseas, the program was reedited and redubbed for American broadcast. *A Greatest Tales Production. Color. Half-hour. Premiered: 1977. Syndicated.*

**Voices**
**Gerta:** Donna Ellio; **Kay:** Peter Nissen

## ◉ SNOW WHITE

Ruled by her cruel stepmother, the Queen, the enslaved Snow White escapes to the forest where she receives shelter and protection from the Seven Dwarfs, only to be hunted down by the Queen disguised as a wicked old witch, who sells her a poisoned apple. *A Festival of Family Classics special. A Rankin-Bass Production in association with Mushi Studios. Color. Half-hour. Premiered: March 4, 1973. Syndicated. Rebroadcast on NICK: February 22, 1992.*

**Voices**
Carl Banas, Len Birman, Bernard Cowan, Peg Dixon, Keith Hampshire, Peggi Loder, Donna Miller, Frank Perry, Henry Ramer, Alfie Scopp, Paul Soles

## ◉ A SNOW WHITE CHRISTMAS

Adapted from the Grimm Brothers' fairy tale, the story of Snow White is given a new twist and new characters as she teams up with seven giants (not dwarfs)—Thinker, Finicky, Corney, Brawny, Tiny, Hicker and Weeper—to stop the evil Queen from ruining Christmas. *A Filmation Studios Production. Color. One hour. Premiered on CBS: November 19, 1980. Rebroadcast on CBS: December 7, 1983.*

**Voices**
**Snow White:** Erika Scheimer; **Finnicky/Corney/Tiny/Brawny/Hicker/Weeper/Villager:** Arte Johnson; **Wicked Queen/Hag:** Melendy Britt; **Queen:** Diane Pershing; **Grunyon:** Charlie Bell; **Mirror:** Larry D. Mann; **Thinker:** Clinton Sundberg

## ◉ SOLARMAN

Endowed with superhuman strength, supersonic flight and the abilities to survive in deep space and harness light energies, teenager-turned-superhero Solarman (alias Benjamin Tucker) foils the evil warlord Kraal's plan to destroy the sun in this animated adventure based on the popular Marvel Comic. Created by Marvel Comics icon Stan Lee and the comic-book's creator David Oliphant and produced in 1989, this half-hour pilot debuted on FOX Kids in place of the highly anticipated comic book superhero adaptation, *X-Men*, which was slated to air but was delayed due to production problems and was pulled from the lineup at the last minute. *A Marvel Production. Color. Half-hour. Premiered on FOX: October 24, 1992.*

## ◉ THE SOLDIER'S TALE

In this post–World War I story, a young soldier sells his soul—represented by his violin—to the Devil, only to have second thoughts

A trio of human-sized food products solves crimes between trying "get-rich-quick" schemes in Cartoon Network's popular animated comedy Aqua Teen Hunger Force. © Cartoon Network. All rights reserved.

Tiny humanlike creatures are discovered by a normal-sized young boy in DIC Enterprises' original ABC Saturday morning series The Littles. © DIC Enterprises. All rights reserved.

Dashing leader Saber Rider leads his team of special frontier fighters into battle in a scene from the futuristic space western series Saber Rider and the Star Sheriffs. © World Events Productions Ltd. All rights reserved.

The lovable bears of Care-a-Lot come down to earth in their cloud-mobiles to help children with their problems in the first-run, syndicated series The Care Bears. The program was based on the popular children's book of the same name. © 1985 American Greetings Corp. All program material © 1985 Kenner Parker Toys.

Eight castoffs of the cartoon, comic book and video game world try living together on Comedy Central's animated reality spoof of MTV's Real World, Drawn Together. © Comedy Central. All rights reserved.

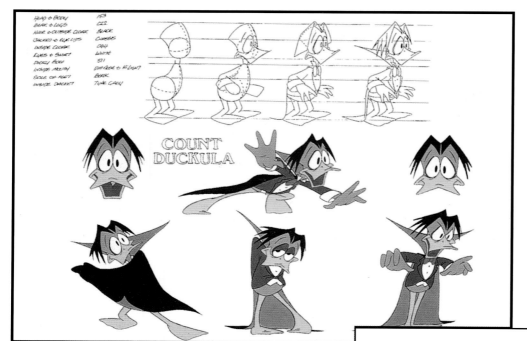

Model sheet for Count Duckula, *a reluctant vampire with an aversion to blood who tries to find fame and fortune in show business. The British-produced series was a hit in the United States on Nickelodeon. © 1988 Cosgrove Hall Productions.* (COURTESY: COSGROVE HALL PRODUCTIONS)

Charlie Brown *decides to send Snoopy back to obedience school after Snoopy suffers from a sudden attack of bad manners in the prime-time CBS television special* He's Your Dog, Charlie Brown. © United Features Syndicate. (COURTESY: BILL MELENDEZ PRODUCTIONS)

*Robbie the Reindeer has his bags packed and ready to go in a scene from the popular BBC original animated special Robbie the Reindeer in Hooves of Fire. © BBC. All rights reserved.*

*Hermey the Elf sings joyfully as friend Rudolph looks on in the perennial prime-time Christmas special* Rudolph the Red-Nosed Reindeer. *© Rankin-Bass Productions.* (COURTESY: FAMILY HOME ENTERTAINMENT)

Miyagi (center) demonstrates the fine art of self-defense for Taki and Daniel in the animated adaptation of the famed motion picture The Karate Kid. © 1989 Columbia Pictures Television. All rights reserved. (COURTESY: DIC ENTERPRISES)

Morry the moose, Dotty the pooch, Woolma the lamb and Zipper the cat lend a helping hand in the half-hour Saturday morning series adapted from a series of popular children's books called The Get Along Gang. © DIC Enterprises. All rights reserved.

Madeline, the smallest and bravest of 12 girls, experiences many new adventures shaped around the importance of love, sharing and friendship in the HBO special Madeline. © 1988 DIC Enterprises. (COURTESY: DIC ENTERPRISES)

Opening title sequence from the popular HBO animated series The Little Lulu Show. © 1997 CINAR Productions. Little Lulu is a trademark of Western Publishing Company. (COURTESY: CINAR PRODUCTIONS)

Television tough guy Mr. T fights crime with a team of teenage gymnasts in Saturday morning's Mister T. © 1983 Ruby-Spears Enterprises. (COURTESY: RUBY-SPEARS ENTERPRISES)

Actors Adam West and Burt Ward reprised the roles of their famed caped-crusading characters in The New Adventures of Batman, *originally produced for CBS. Joining the cast: Batmite (far left). © Filmation Associates–DC Comics.* (COURTESY: FILMATION)

Noted playboy film producer Robert Evans was cast in unusual
adventures parodying his rise in Hollywood in the short-lived
Comedy Central cartoon series Kid Notorious. © Comedy
Central. All rights reserved.

A young girl is forced to sell matches on the streets of New York
on New Year's Eve in order to survive in the Michael Sporn
animated special The Little Match Girl, produced for HBO.
© Michael Sporn Animation. (COURTESY: MICHAEL SPORN
ANIMATION)

A courageous young girl endowed with a powerful rainbow-making belt travels the world spreading joy to others in DIC Enterprises' half-hour animated series Rainbow Brite. © Hallmark Cards. (COURTESY: DIC ENTERTAINMENT)

Europe's leading animated film studio, Halas and Batchelor, produced this television series adaptation of Alexander Dumas's classic novel The Count of Monte Cristo. © Halas and Batchelor Productions.

*Television tough guy Mr. T fights crime with a team of teenage gymnasts in Saturday morning's* Mister T. *© 1983 Ruby-Spears Enterprises.* (COURTESY: RUBY-SPEARS ENTERPRISES)

*Actors Adam West and Burt Ward reprised the roles of their famed caped-crusading characters in* The New Adventures of Batman, *originally produced for CBS. Joining the cast: Batmite (far left). © Filmation Associates–DC Comics.* (COURTESY: FILMATION)

*Uncle Martin and his magazine reporter friend Tim O'Hara, of TV's* My Favorite Martian, *joined by two new cast members, Andromeda, Martin's nephew (far left), and Katy O'Hara, Tim's niece (second from left), experienced all-new animated adventures in the Saturday morning spin-off* My Favorite Martians. © Filmation. (COURTESY: FILMATION)

*Felix the Cat with his magic bag of tricks has the last laugh in this original cel from Joe Oriolo's* Felix the Cat *series. © Joe Oriolo Productions.* (COURTESY: JOE ORIOLO PRODUCTIONS)

A fearless cadet member of an international rescue team defends
the world from disasters in the British-animated cartoon series
Thunderbirds 2086. © ITC Entertainment. All rights reserved.

The universe-zapping exploits of Flash Gordon, originally
brought to the screen by Buster Crabbe as a favorite movie
matinee serial in the 1930s, were revived by Filmation Studios
in the form of the Saturday morning cartoon series The New
Adventures of Flash Gordon. © Filmation/King Features
Syndicate. (COURTESY: KING FEATURES SYNDICATE)

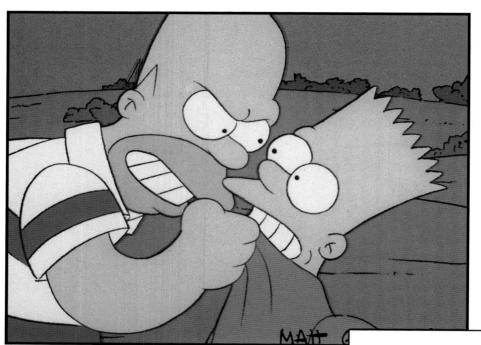

Homer Simpson shows his smart-mouthed son Bart that he means business in a scene from the critically acclaimed, long-running FOX animated series The Simpsons. © 1990 20th Century Fox Film Corp. (COURTESY: KLASKY/CSUPO PRODUCTIONS)

A team of newly trained cadets, members of Robotech Defense Force, defend Earth from being destroyed by a fleet of giant alien spaceships in the Japanese television series cult favorite Robotech. © 1984 Tasunoko Productions Co., Ltd. Robotech is a trademark owned and licensed by Revell, Inc. (COURTESY: HARMONY GOLD)

*Captain Harlock (pointing), head of an interstellar space galleon, protects and defends his home planet in the Japanese-imported series* Captain Harlock and the Queen of a Thousand Years. © 1981 ZIV International. All rights reserved. (COURTESY: HARMONY GOLD)

*The robotic droids R2-D2 and C-3PO from the* Star Wars *film series returned in animated form in the ABC Saturday morning series* Droids: The Adventures of R2-D2 and C-3PO. *The series was produced in association with Star Wars creator George Lucas's company, Lucasfilm.* © *and* ™ *1985 Lucasfilm Ltd. All rights reserved.* (COURTESY: LUCASFILM LTD.)

A bright spotlight freezes Foo Foo in his tracks in Britain's Halas and Batchelor studio's imported animated series Foo Foo. © Halas Batchelor Ltd. All rights reserved.

Handyman Bob the Builder teaches kids the importance of working together in the successful PBS educational cartoon series Bob the Builder. © HIT Entertainment PLC and Keith Chapman. All rights reserved.

A strong and intimidating ogre finds love and
adventure with a beautiful, down-to-earth and
feisty princess and a talkative donkey in the
blockbuster computer-animated feature Shrek,
the first computer-animated feature to win an
Academy Award for best animated feature.
© DreamWorks SKG. All rights reserved.

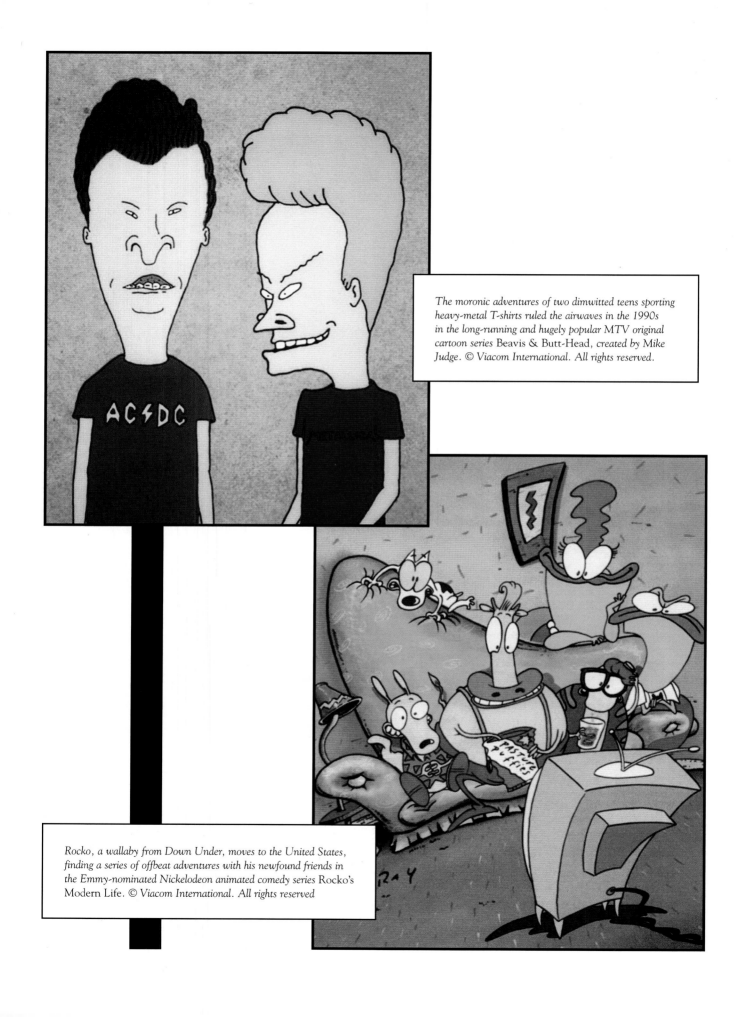

The moronic adventures of two dimwitted teens sporting heavy-metal T-shirts ruled the airwaves in the 1990s in the long-running and hugely popular MTV original cartoon series Beavis & Butt-Head, created by Mike Judge. © Viacom International. All rights reserved.

Rocko, a wallaby from Down Under, moves to the United States, finding a series of offbeat adventures with his newfound friends in the Emmy-nominated Nickelodeon animated comedy series Rocko's Modern Life. © Viacom International. All rights reserved

*Arthur the aardvark confronts and solves problems in the half-hour PBS cartoon series Arthur. © 1997 WGBH Educational Foundation and CINAR Productions. All rights reserved.*

*Popular recording stars Alvin and the Chipmunks in a scene from their 1960s animated series The Alvin Show. © 1961 Bagdasarian Productions.*

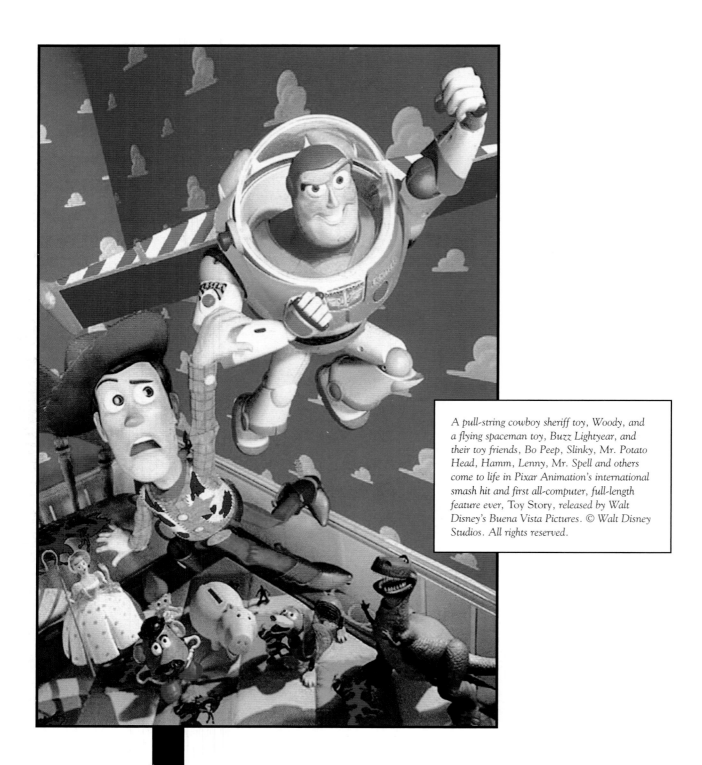

A pull-string cowboy sheriff toy, Woody, and a flying spaceman toy, Buzz Lightyear, and their toy friends, Bo Peep, Slinky, Mr. Potato Head, Hamm, Lenny, Mr. Spell and others come to life in Pixar Animation's international smash hit and first all-computer, full-length feature ever, Toy Story, released by Walt Disney's Buena Vista Pictures. © Walt Disney Studios. All rights reserved.

about the idea in this animated version of the classic Russian children's fable written by Igor Stravinsky. *An R.O. Blechman Production for PBS. Color. One hour. Premiered on PBS: March 19, 1981. Rebroadcast on PBS: October 30, 1981.*

**Voices**
**Devil:** Max Von Sydow; **Princess:** Galina Panova; **Narrator:** André Gregory

## ◎ SOMEDAY YOU'LL FIND HER, CHARLIE BROWN

Charlie Brown falls in love with a little girl (Mary Jo) he sees on television during the telecast of a local football game and sets out to find her with the help of codetective Linus. By 1998, the special re-emerged in reruns, along with an entire package of former CBS *Peanuts* specials and the Saturday-morning cartoon series, *The Charlie Brown & Snoopy Show,* on Nickelodeon. *A Lee Mendelson–Bill Melendez Production in association with Charles M. Schulz Creative Associates and United Features Syndicate. Color. Half-hour. Premiered on CBS: October 30, 1981. Rebroadcast on CBS: March 21, 1983. Rebroadcast on NICK: January 30, 1998; February 18, 1998; March 20, 1998; April 27, 1998; May 28, 1998; July 1, 1998; July 29, 1998; August 24, 1998; September 25, 1998; November 4, 1998; December 4, 1998; January 5, 1999; January 26, 1999; February 8, 1999; March 9, 1999; April 4, 1999; July 6, 1999; September 25, 1999.*

**Voices**
**Charlie Brown:** Grant Wehr; **Linus Van Pelt:** Earl Reilly; **Little Girl (Mary Jo):** Jennifer Gaffin; **Snoopy:** José Melendez; **Loretta:** Nicole Eggert; **Teenager:** Melissa Strawmeyer; **Singer:** Rebecca Reardon

## ◎ SONIC CHRISTMAS BLAST

While shopping for a present for Princess Sally, Sonic and Tails discover that the evil Dr. Robotnik, disguised as Santa Claus, has stolen every gift in the world while locking up the real Santa. Meanwhile, a special ring Sally gives Sonic will help him teach super-speed if he passes a few tests in this half-hour holiday adventure originally created as part of the *Adventures of Sonic the Hedgehog* series. The 30-minute program aired two years after the final original series episode as a Christmas special in 1996. In 1998 Toon Disney began annually rebroadcasting the special mostly during the holiday season until December 2001. In the fall of 2004, the popular yuletide program was re-offered in syndication as part of DIC Entertainment's DIC Kids' Network three-hour programming block carried by 450 stations throughout the United States. *A DIC Entertainment/SEGA America Production. Color. Half-hour. Premiered: November 24, 1996. Syndicated. Rebroadcast on TDIS: December 13, 1998; December 19, 1998; December 25, 1998; December 24, 1999; December 25, 1999; November 24, 2000; December 1, 2000; December 24, 2000; December 25, 2000; July 21, 2001; December 1, 2001.*

**Voices**
**Sonic the Hedgehog:** Jaleel White; **Miles "Tails" Prower:** Christopher Evan Welch; **Gounder:** Gary Chalk; **Coconuts:** Ian James Corlett; **Scratch:** Phil Hayes; **Dr. Ivo Robotnik:** Long John Baldry

## ◎ THE SORCERER'S APPRENTICE

A poor young boy (Hans) accepts a job as the Sorcerer's apprentice, only to learn that the Sorcerer uses his magical powers for the purposes of evil in this adaptation of the Jacob Grimm fairytale classic. *A Gary Moscowitz Production in association with Astral Bellevue Pathé. Color. Half-hour. Premiered: October, 1984. Syndicated.*

**Voices**
**Narrator:** Vincent Price

## ◎ SPACE GHOST COAST TO COAST HOLIDAY SPECIAL

Interplanetary superhero Space Ghost and his less-than-merry archenemies Moltar and Zorak are featured in three encore presentations of the Cartoon Network's critically acclaimed talk show *Space Ghost Coast to Coast,* plus a brand-new 15-minute Christmas episode in this holiday-filled hour special. Originally premiering in December 1994 on Cartoon Network, the special, later retitled *Space Ghost Coast to Coast Christmas,* has become an annual favorite in reruns on the Cartoon Network. *A Hanna-Barbera/Cartoon Network Production. Color. One hour. Premiered on CAR: December 21, 1994. Syndicated: December 1995. Rebroadcast on CAR: December 17, 2000; December 24, 2004; December 24, 2005.*

**Voices**
**Space Ghost:** George Lowe; **Moltar/Zorak:** C. Martin Croker

## ◎ THE SPECIAL MAGIC OF HERSELF THE ELF

Nasty King Thorn and his daughter, Creeping Ivy, steal Herself the Elf's magical wand in order to take nature into their own evil hands in this half-hour syndicated special featuring music composed and performed by Judy Collins. *A Scholastic Production in association with Those Characters From Cleveland and Nelvana Limited. Color. Half-hour. Premiered: April 1983. Syndicated.*

**Voices**
**Herself the Elf:** Priscilla Lopez; **Creeping Ivy:** Ellen Greene; **King Thorn:** Jerry Orbach; **Willow Song:** Georgia Engel; **Meadow Morn:** Denny Dillon; **Snow Drop:** Terri Hawkes; **Wilfie:** Jim Henshaw; **Wood Pink:** Susan Roman; **Vocalist:** Judy Collins

## ◎ A SPECIAL VALENTINE WITH THE FAMILY CIRCUS

In this television debut of Bill Keane's *Family Circus* characters, P.J., Dolly, Billy and Jeffy do everything possible to outdo each other in impressing their parents with "love" for Valentine's Day. *A Cullen-Kasden Production in association with the Register and Tribune Syndicate. Color. Half-hour. Premiered on NBC: February 10, 1978. Rebroadcast on NBC: February 8, 1980; February 13, 1983; Rebroadcast on DIS: February 6, 1993; February 1, 1994; February 12, 1994.*

**Voices**
**Mommy:** Anne Costello; **Daddy:** Bob Kaliban; **Billy:** Mark McDermott; **Dolly:** Missy Hope; **Jeffy:** Nathan Berg; **P.J./Teacher:** Suzanne Airey; **Bus Driver:** Sammy Fain

## ◎ SPIDER JUNIOR HIGH

Itsby Bitsy ("I.B." for short) Spider yearns to play in the Three Bad Bugs. He tags along with an ultra-cool school rock band from Spider Junior High, having to rescue them after they get sealed in a jar in this update of the popular children's nursery rhyme. Premiering in 1991 on HBO's popular anthology series *HBO Storybook Musicals,* the half-hour special was originally produced under the title *Itsy Bitsy Spider* for CINAR Films' *The Real Story of . . .* series. *A CINAR Films/Crayon Animation Production in association with Western Publishing Company/CTV Television Network/Telefilm Canada. Color. Half-hour. Premiered on HBO: October 16, 1991. Rebroadcast on HBO: October 21, 1991.*

*Voices*
**Miss Widow:** Patti LaBelle; **Spinner:** Malcolm-Jamal Warner

## ◎ SPIDER-MAN: "NIGHT OF THE LIZARD"

The web-slinging comic-book superhero springs into action in this half-hour Saturday-morning special that premiered before the popular Fox Network animated series. *A Marvel Films/New World Entertainment/Saban Entertainment/Graz Entertainment Production. Color. Half-hour. Premiered on FOX: November 19, 1994.*

*Voices*
**Peter Parker/Spider-Man:** Christopher Daniel Barres

## ◎ THE SPIRIT OF '76

Historical events relating to the birth of the United States are presented through live action, animation and song in this overture of five-minute stories. *An MG Films Productions. Color. Half-hour. Premiered: July, 1984. Syndicated.*

*Voices*
**Narrator:** Oscar Brand

## ◎ SPONGEBOB SQUAREPANTS: "BEST DAY EVER"

SpongeBob can't help but think he is going to have his best day ever since he gets to work at the Krusty Krab, meet Sandy, then jellyfish with Pat and attend Squidward's clarinet rectical. Of course, nothing goes as he planned with his friends all sharing their problems and, in the end, having to cheer him up. *A Nick-Toons Production in association with Viacom International. Color. Half-hour. Premiered on NICK: November 10, 2006.*

*Voices*
**SpongeBob SquarePants/Gary/Mr. SquarePants/Narrator:** Tom Kenny; **Mr. Eugene H. Krabs:** Clancy Brown; **Patrick Star:** Bill Fagerbakke; **Sandy Cheeks:** Carolyn Lawrence; **Squidward Tentacles:** Rodger Bumpass; **Plankton/Larry the Lobster/Other Voices:** Mr. Lawrence; **Mrs. Puff/Mrs. SquarePants:** Mary Jo Catlett

## ◎ SPONGEBOB SQUAREPANTS: "CHRISTMAS WHO?"

Super square-shaped SpongeBob brings Christmas to the residents of Bikini Bottom with his fan club president, Patchy the Pirate, showing the results of his endeavor in this half-hour holiday special, also known as the *Patchy Pirate Presents the SpongeBob SquarePants Christmas Special* and *The SpongeBob SquarePants Christmas Special*, from the second season of Nickelodeon's most-watched cartoon series, *SpongeBob SquarePants*. *A NickToon Production in association with Viacom International. Color. Half-hour. Premiered on NICK: December 6, 2000. Rebroadcast on NICK: December 18, 2000; December 23, 2000; December 24, 2000; December 25, 2000; December 3, 2001; December 15, 2001; December 25, 2001; December 3, 2002; December 11, 2002; December 13, 2002; December 17, 2002; December 23, 2002; December 25, 2002; December 2, 2003; December 19, 2003; December 21, 2003; December 25, 2003; December 14, 2004; December 18, 2004; December 24, 2004; December 25, 2004; October 17, 2005; December 7, 2005; December 9, 2005; December 12, 2005; December 15, 2005; December 16, 2005; December 17, 2005; December 20, 2005; December 22, 2005; December 24, 2005; December 25, 2005; December 4, 2006; December 8, 2006; December 16, 2006; December 19, 2006; December 24, 2006; December 25, 2006. Rebroadcast on NICK: June 12, 2002; June 29, 2002; December 21, 2002; December 22, 2002; December 25, 2002; December 19, 2003; December 20, 2003; December 21, 2003; December 23, 2003; December 24, 2003; December 25, 2003; December 24, 2004; Decem-*

*ber 19, 2005; December 21, 2005; December 25, 2005; December 7, 2006; December 20, 2006; December 26, 2006.*

*Voices*
**SpongeBob SquarePants/Gary/Mr. SquarePants/Narrator/Patchy the Pirate/Old Fish/Singer #1/Jellyfish:** Tom Kenny; **Mr. Eugene H. Krabs:** Clancy Brown; **Patrick Star/Singer #2:** Bill Fagerbakke; **Squidward Tentacles/Singer #3:** Rodger Bumpass; **Sandy Cheeks:** Carolyn Lawrence; **Plankton/Larry the Lobster/Fish #2/Announcer:** Mr. Lawrence; **Santa Claus:** Michael Bell; **Potty the Parrot/Director:** Stephen Hillenburg; **Little Boy:** Austin Stout; **Painting:** Patrick Pinney; **Puppeteer:** Jonathan Silsby; **Woman Fish:** Sirena Irwin; **Little Girl:** Sara Paxton; **Singer #4:** Clancy Brown; **Fish #1-4/Singer #5/Mr. Krabs Solo:** Dee Bradley Baker

## ◎ SPONGEBOB SQUAREPANTS: "DUNCES AND DRAGONS" ("LOST IN TIME")

SpongeBob and Patrick are transported back in time, after a bizarre jousting accident at a Medieval Times restaurant, to a medieval version of Bikini Bottom where, mistaken as knights, King Krabs entrusts *them* with the job of saving his daughter, Princess Pearl, from an evil lord who has abducted her and slaying a menacing dragon for good measure before returning to the present. Aired in prime time, the half-hour animated time-travel special sopped up more than 8.6 million viewers, making it Nickelodeon's top telecast since 2001 and most-watched episode among kids to date. *A NickToon Production in association with Viacom International. Color. Half-hour. Premiered on NICK: February 20, 2006.*

*Voices*
**SpongeBob SquarePants/Gary/Mr. SquarePants/Narrator:** Tom Kenny; **Mr. Eugene H. Krabs:** Clancy Brown; **Patrick Star:** Bill Fagerbakke; **Sandy Cheeks:** Carolyn Lawrence; **Squidward Tentacles:** Rodger Bumpass; **Plankton/Larry the Lobster/Other Voices:** Mr. Lawrence; **Pearl Krabs:** Lori Alan; **Other Voices:** Dee Bradley Baker, Sirena Irwin

## ◎ SPONGEBOB SQUAREPANTS: "FOOLS IN APRIL"/"NEPTUNE'S SPATULA"

It's April Fool's Day and SpongeBob gets into the act by playing practical jokes on everyone, including Squidward who decides to play a trick of his own ("Fools in April"), and then manages to ruin a cook-off he attends at the Fry Cook Hall of Fame ("Neptune's Spatula") in this third half-hour prime-time special adapted from the top-rated Nickelodeon animated series. *Seinfeld* alumnus John O'Hurley provided the voice of Neptune. *A NickToons Production in association with Viacom International. Color. Half-hour. Premiered on NICK: April 1, 2000.*

*Voices*
**SpongeBob SquarePants/Gary/Mr. SquarePants/Narrator:** Tom Kenny; **Mr. Eugene H. Krabs:** Clancy Brown; **Patrick Star:** Bill Fagerbakke; **Squidward Tentacles:** Rodger Bumpass; **Sandy Cheeks:** Carolyn Lawrence; **Plankton/Larry the Lobster:** Mr. Lawrence; **Lou:** Dee Bradley Baker; **Neptune:** John O'Hurley; **Other Voices:** Camryn Walling

## ◎ SPONGEBOB SQUAREPANTS: "HAVE YOU SEEN THIS SNAIL?"

Television's most popular little squirt finds his world turned upside down when his beloved pet snail, Gary, runs away, and he and his pal Patrick desperately search the streets of Bikini Bottom to bring him home in this half-hour special and the series' final new episode of the 2005 season. The absurd underwater adventure (also known as "Where's Gary?"), shown in prime time, was the highest-rated program on all television with kids ages two to 11 for the year, behind the Super Bowl and the Super Bowl kick-off, and the highest-rated play on all of cable with kids two to 11 and six to 11 in 2005. In addition, at the time it aired, the half-hour comedy special was the highest-rated episode ever of *SpongeBob SquarePants* with six to 11 year olds. *A NickToons Production. Color. Half-hour. Premiered on NICK: November 11, 2005. Rebroadcast on NICK: November 12, 2005; November 13, 2005; November 16, 2005; November 23, 2005; November 25, 2005; December 20, 2005; January 20, 2006; January 21, 2006; February 21, 2006; March 7, 2006; March 10, 2006; March 11, 2006; March 20, 2006; March 31, 2006; April 13, 2006; April 16, 2006; May 9, 2006; May 19, 2006; May 27, 2006; June 12, 2006; June 18, 2006; July 1, 2006; July 5, 2006; July 7, 2006; July 21, 2006; July 24, 2006; July 28, 2006; August 6, 2006; August 15, 2006; August 21, 2006; September 5, 2006; September 18, 2006; September 29, 2006; October 12, 2006; October 20, 2006; October 27, 2006; November 10, 2006; November 12, 2006; November 22, 2006; November 25, 2006; November 27, 2006; December 9, 2006; December 11, 2006; December 29, 2006; January 5, 2007; January 12, 2007; January 30, 2007; February 24, 2007; March 21, 2007; March 31, 2007; April 15, 2007; April 28, 2007.*

**Voices**
SpongeBob SquarePants/Gary/Mr. SquarePants/Narrator/Patchy the Pirate/Various Others: Tom Kenny; **Mr. Eugene H. Krabs:** Clancy Brown; **Patrick Star:** Bill Fagerbakke; **Grandma:** Amy Poehler

### ⊚ SPONGEBOB SQUAREPANTS: "SCAREDY PANTS"/"I WAS A TEENAGE GARY"

Nothing is more frightening for SpongeBob than Halloween in the two episodes—"Scaredy Pants," with SpongeBob dressing up like the legendary Flying Dutchman until the real one shows up; and "I Was a Teenage Gary," with SpongeBob finding what it is like to be a snail after accidentally taking Gary's medicine—of this first half-hour prime-time special based on the popular Nickelodeon cartoon series. *A NickToons Production in association with Viacom International. Color. Half-hour. Premiered on NICK: October 28, 1999.*

**Voices**
SpongeBob SquarePants/Gary/Mr. SquarePants/Narrator: Tom Kenny; **Mr. Eugene H. Krabs:** Clancy Brown; **Patrick Star:** Bill Fagerbakke; **Squidward Tentacles:** Rodger Bumpass; **Sandy Cheeks:** Carolyn Lawrence; **Plankton/Larry the Lobster:** Mr. Lawrence; **Mrs. Puff/Mrs. SquarePants:** Mary Jo Catlett; **Pearl Krabs:** Lori Alan; **Karen:** Jill Talley; **Flying Dutchman:** Brian Doyle-Murray; **Doctor Fish/Guy at Party #2:** Carlos Alazraqui; **Witch/Mummy:** Sara Paxton; **Other Voices:** Camryn Walling, Dee Bradley Baker, Sirena Irwin

### ⊚ SPONGEBOB SQUAREPANTS: "SHANGHAIED" ("YOU WISH SPECIAL")

Prime-time half-hour animated special, also known as *You Wish Special*, featuring two back-to-back *SpongeBob SquarePants* episodes: "Shanghaiied," with SpongeBob, Patrick and Squidward stumbling upon the remains of the Flying Dutchman's ship and being granted three wishes; and "Gary Takes a Bath," with SpongeBob resorting to all kinds of tactics to encourage Gary to take a bath, only to take one himself. *A NickToons Production in association with Viacom International. Color. Half-hour. Premiered on NICK: March 7, 2001. Rebroadcast on NICK: July 26, 2003; July 27, 2003; August 11, 2003; September 2, 2003; October 4, 2003;*

*October 14, 2003; October 21, 2003; November 6, 2003; December 10, 2003; December 24, 2003; January 6, 2004; January 31, 2004; February 13, 2004; February 27, 2004; March 9, 2004; March 22, 2004; April 2, 2004; April 3, 2004; April 16, 2004; April 27, 2004; May 13, 2004; May 18, 2004; May 28, 2004; June 19, 2004; June 26, 2004; July 12, 2004; July 26, 2004; August 9, 2004; August 23, 2004; September 7, 2004; September 22, 2004; October 7, 2004; November 9, 2004; November 23, 2004; December 13, 2004; December 31, 2004; January 5, 2005; January 21, 2005; February 8, 2005; March 21, 2005; April 12, 2005; May 3, 2005; May 24, 2005; June 7, 2005; June 21, 2005; July 5, 2005; July 19, 2005; July 27, 2005; August 3, 2005; August 10, 2005; August 16, 2005; August 24, 2005; September 5, 2005; October 3, 2005; October 18, 2005; November 10, 2005; November 11, 2005; November 13, 2005; November 14, 2005; November 30, 2005; December 4, 2005; December 11, 2005; December 17, 2005; January 2, 2006; January 18, 2006; February 3, 2006; February 7, 2006; February 18, 2006; February 24, 2006; March 10, 2006; March 22, 2006; April 4, 2006; April 22, 2006; May 6, 2006; May 22, 2006; June 10, 2006; June 16, 2006; June 28, 2006; July 17, 2006; July 24, 2006; August 7, 2006; August 12, 2006; August 21, 2006; September 3, 2006; September 17, 2006; September 30, 2006; October 13, 2006; November 2, 2006; November 17, 2006; December 1, 2006; December 13, 2006; December 20, 2006; December 31, 2006; January 4, 2007; January 19, 2007; February 15, 2007; February 28, 2007; March 12, 2007; April 5, 2007; April 18, 2007.*

**Voices**
SpongeBob SquarePants/Gary/Mr. SquarePants: Tom Kenny; **Mr. Eugene H. Krabs:** Clancy Brown; **Patrick Star:** Bill Fagerbakke; **Sandy Cheeks:** Carolyn Lawrence; **Squidward Tentacles:** Rodger Bumpass; **Pearl Krabs:** Lori Alan; **Mrs. Puffs/Mrs. SquarePants:** Mary Jo Catlett; **Mermaid Man/Plankton/Larry the Lobster:** Mr. Lawrence; **Karen:** Jill Talley; **The Flying Dutchman:** Brian Doyle-Murray; **Kid Fish:** Sara Paxton; **Additional Voices:** Dee Bradley Baker, Sirena Irwin, Camryn Walling

### ⊚ SPONGEBOB SQUAREPANTS: "SPONGEBOB BC" (BEFORE COMEDY)

SpongeBob, Patrick and Squidward's ancestors SpongeGar, Patar and Squog discover fire in this half-hour animated special—also known as *SpongeBob BC (The Prehistoric Special)* and UGH!—from the 2003–04 season of Nickelodeon's immensely popular *SpongeBob SquarePants* cartoon series. Premiering on March 5, 2004, Paramount Home Video released the nighttime special as part of a retitled 110-minute DVD extravaganza, *SpongeBob Goes Prehistoric*, including five fun-filled episodes from the broadcast, including "Nature Pants" (1999), "Fools in April" (2000), "I'm with Stupid" (2001) and 2003's half-hour special, *SpongeBob BC*. *A NickToons Production. Color. Half-hour. Premiered on NICK: March 5, 2004. Rebroadcast on NICK: March 6, 2004; March 7, 2004; March 9, 2004; April 2, 2004; April 12, 2004; May 7, 2004; May 22, 2004; May 24, 2004; May 31, 2004; June 7, 2004; June 21, 2004; November 18, 2004; November 27, 2004; December 30, 2004; January 18, 2005; February 5, 2005; February 25, 2005; March 18, 2005; April 9, 2005; April 30, 2005; May 20, 2005; June 6, 2005; June 19, 2005; July 3, 2005; July 16, 2005; July 31, 2005; August 30, 2005; September 16, 2005; October 8, 2005; November 1, 2005; November 17, 2005; December 4, 2005; December 21, 2005; January 4, 2006; January 29, 2006; February 20, 2006; February 28, 2006; March 13, 2006; March 27, 2006; April 22, 2006; May 5, 2006; May 19, 2006; August 28, 2006; September 11, 2006; September 24, 2006; October 6, 2006; November 4, 2006; November 10, 2006; November 21, 2006; December 6, 2006; January 1,*

2007; January 7, 2007; January 16, 2007; January 31, 2007; February 3, 2007; February 7, 2007; February 13, 2007; February 26, 2007; March 10, 2007; March 23, 2007; April 4, 2007; April 17, 2007; April 30, 2007. *Rebroadcast on NICKT: May 27, 2006; May 28, 2006; June 20, 2006; July 14, 2006; August 9, 2006; September 3, 2006; September 28, 2006; October 24, 2006; November 14, 2006; December 11, 2006; January 7, 2007; February 4, 2007; March 5, 2007; March 23, 2007; April 19, 2007.*

*Voices*

**SpongeBob SquarePants/Gary/Mr. SquarePants/Patchy the Pirate/Announcer/Tom/Grandpa SquarePants/Old Man Jenkins/ Robot/Various Others:** Tom Kenny; **Mr. Eugene H. Krabs:** Clancy Brown; **Patrick Star/Cavey the Caveman:** Bill Fagerbakke; **Mrs. Puff/Mrs. SquarePants:** Mary Jo Catlett; **Sandy Cheeks:** Carolyn Lawrence; **Squidward Tentacles:** Rodger Bumpass; **Plankton/Larry the Lobster/Other Voices:** Mr. Lawrence; **Pearl Krabs:** Lori Alan; **Stagehand:** Dennis Hoerter; **Potty:** Stephen Hillenburg; **Stunt Dancer:** Mark "Biz" Burke; **Puppeteer:** Jonathan Silsby; **Stunt Robot:** Kent Osbourne; **Other Voices:** Dee Bradley Baker, Sirena Irwin, Camryn Walling

## ◎ SPONGEBOB SQUAREPANTS: "SPONGEBOB'S HOUSE PARTY"

After buying a "Throw the Best Party Ever" kit, SpongeBob throws a big house party for 177 of his closest friends and is mistaken for a burglar trying to break in when he accidentally locks himself out and spends the entire night in jail after being arrested in this half-hour animated special, originally titled *Party Pooper Pants,* based on the hit Nickelodeon cartoon series and hosted by Patchy the Pirate. *A NickToons Production in association with Viacom International. Color. Half-hour. Premiered on NICK: May 17, 2002. Rebroadcast on NICK: May 18, 2002; May 19, 2002; May 22, 2002; November 30, 2002; December 31, 2002; February 24, 2003; March 23, 2003; April 12, 2003; May 17, 2003; June 1, 2003; June 16, 2003; July 2, 2003; July 15, 2003; December 31, 2003; April 3, 2004; November 18, 2004; November 27, 2004; December 18, 2004; November 23, 2005; December 8, 2005.*

*Voices*

**SpongeBob SquarePants/Gary/Mr. SquarePants/Narrator/ Patchy the Pirate/Other Voices:** Tom Kenny; **Mr. Eugene H. Krabs:** Clancy Brown; **Patrick Star:** Bill Fagerbakke; **Squidward Tentacles:** Rodger Bumpass; **Sandy Cheeks:** Carolyn Lawrence; **Pearl Krabs:** Lori Alan; **Mermaid Man:** Mr. Lawrence; **Mrs. Puffs/Mrs. SquarePants:** Mary Jo Catlett; **Plankton/Larry the Lobster/Other Voices:** Mr. Lawrence; **Karen:** Jill Talley; **Scooter/ Lou/Other Voices:** Dee Bradley Baker; **Minnie Mermaid/Wife Fish/Officer O'Malley/Other Voices:** Sirena Irwin; **Potty:** Stephen Hillenburg; **King Neptune:** Kevin Michael Richardson; **Fisherman:** Paul Tibbit; **Additional Voices:** Camryn Walling

## ◎ SPONGEBOB SQUAREPANTS: "THE SPONGE WHO COULD FLY" ("THE LOST EPISODE SPECIAL")

After jellyfishing, SpongeBob decides he wants to fly like a jelly-fish, too, so he tries inventing different ways to fly with little success, until he puts a hair dryer in his pants that fills them with hot air, in this half-hour special based on the famed Nickelodeon cartoon series, also known as *The Lost Episode Special. A NickToons Production in association with Viacom International. Color. Half-hour. Premiered on NICK: March 21, 2003. Rebroadcast on NICK: March 22, 2003; March 23, 2003; March 24, 2003; March 29, 2003; April 11, 2003; May 17, 2003; July 1, 2003; December 31, 2003; January*

19, 2004; January 31, 2004; April 4, 2004; May 1, 2004; May 18, 2004; May 18, 2004; November 13, 2004; November 27, 2004; December 16, 2004; February 3, 2006; February 20, 2006; March 6, 2006; March 10, 2006; March 19, 2006; March 31, 2006; April 12, 2006; April 24, 2006; May 8, 2006; May 22, 2006; June 16, 2006; July 13, 2006; July 22, 2006; August 4, 2006; September 14, 2006; September 28, 2006; October 11, 2006; October 26, 2006; November 8, 2006; December 7, 2006; December 27, 2006; January 11, 2007; January 26, 2007; January 30, 2007; February 8, 2007; February 13, 2007; February 21, 2007; March 5, 2007; March 17, 2007; March 30, 2007; April 11, 2007; April 24, 2007. *Rebroadcast on NICKT: August 19, 2006; September 14, 2006; October 10, 2006; November 4, 2006; November 21, 2006; December 18, 2006; January 14, 2007; February 11, 2007; March 8, 2007; April 22, 2007.*

*Voices*

**SpongeBob SquarePants/Gary/Mr. SquarePants:** Tom Kenny; **Mr. Eugene H. Krabs:** Clancy Brown; **Patrick Star:** Bill Fagerbakke; **Squidward Tentacles:** Rodger Bumpass; **Sandy Cheeks:** Carolyn Lawrence; **Pearl Krabs:** Lori Alan; **Mermaid Man:** Mr. Lawrence; **Mrs. Puffs/Mrs. SquarePants:** Mary Jo Catlett; **Plankton/Larry the Lobster/Other Voices:** Mr. Lawrence; **Farmer Jenkins/Various Voices:** Dee Bradley Baker; **Potty:** Stephen Hillenburg; **Other Voices:** Sirena Irwin, Camryn Walling

## ◎ SPONGEBOB SQUAREPANTS: "VALENTINE'S DAY"/"THE PAPER"

Everything SpongeBob tries goes awry—as it usually does—when he plans a Valentine's Day surprise for Patrick that backfires ("Valentine's Day") and whom he creates a fabulous toy using a gum wrapper, much to Squidward's displeasure, in this second half-hour prime-time special for Nickelodeon. *A NickToons Production in association with Viacom International. Color. Half-hour. Premiered on NICK: February 14, 2000.*

*Voices*

**SpongeBob SquarePants/Gary/Mr. SquarePants/Narrator:** Tom Kenny; **Mr. Eugene H. Krabs:** Clancy Brown; **Patrick Star:** Bill Fagerbakke; **Squidward Tentacles:** Rodger Bumpass; **Sandy Cheeks:** Carolyn Lawrence; **Plankton/Larry the Lobster:** Mr. Lawrence; **Mrs. Puff/Mrs. SquarePants:** Mary Jo Catlett; **Pearl Krabs:** Lori Alan; **Little Fish/Fran:** Sirena Irwin; **Frank/Fish #4:** Dee Bradley Baker; **Other Voices:** Camryn Walling; **Kid:** Sara Paxton

## ◎ SPORT GOOFY IN SOCCERMANIA

Uncle Scrooge donates an old beat-up trophy for Huey, Dewey and Louie's soccer tournament. But when he finds out that it is actually worth a million dollars, he has to put together a ragtag team, led by Goofy, to win it back. This short began production before Michael Eisner became head of Disney and was completed after his ascension to power. Originally intended for theatrical release (presumably with a new Disney feature film), the production instead debuted on NBC in late May 1987 as a prime-time half-hour special. *A Walt Disney Production. Color. Half-hour. Premiered on NBC: May 27, 1987.*

*Voices*

**Goofy:** Tony Pope; **Scrooge McDuck/The Beagle Boys/Gyro Gearlose:** Will Ryan; **Huey/Dewey/Louie:** Russi Taylor

## ◎ SPOT'S MAGICAL CHRISTMAS

Based on Eric Hill's lift-the-flap books, Spot and his friends come to the aid of Santa's reindeer to help them find his lost sleigh. This direct-to-video special premiered on The Disney Channel. *A King Rollo Films Ltd./Walt Disney Home Video Production. Color. Half-*

*hour. Premiered on DIS: December 25, 1995. Rebroadcast on DIS: December 4, 1997.*

## ◎ SQUIRREL BOY: "LINE IN THE SANDWICH"/"TREE FOR TWO"

Andy's brainy, mischievous, know-it-all squirrel, Rodney, disagrees with Andy over who makes the best sandwich and why customers prefer one over the other, while Rodney tries recovering Andy's rocket that's stuck in a tall tree with disastrous results in this two-episode, half-hour Summer Preview Special that preceded the 13-episode wacky Cartoon Network comedy series created by *Duckman* creator Everett Peck. *A Cartoon Network Studios Production. Color. Half-hour. Premiered on CAR: May 29, 2006.*

### Voices
**Rodney J. Squirrel/Boy Wood Gnome/Customer #3:** Richard Steven Horvitz; **Andy Johnson/Customer #2/Girl Wood Gnome:** Pamela Segall; **Bob Johnson:** Kurtwood Smith; **Lucy Johnson:** Nancy Sullivan; **Darlene:** Monica Lee Gradischek; **Leon:** Tom Kenny; **Salty Mike/Pigeon/Motorist #2/Child:** Carlos Alazraqui; **Kyle Finkster:** Billy West; **Announcer/Motorist #1/Customer #1:** Brad Abrell; **Oscar:** Jason Spisak; **Park Ranger Stu:** Corey Burton

## ◎ STANLEY, THE UGLY DUCKLING

A klutzy young duck tries to be anything but a duck and becomes friends with a loner fox who tries to help him become somebody. *An ABC Weekend Special. A Fine Arts Production in association with I Like Myself Productions. Color. Half-hour. Premiered on ABC: May 1, 1982. Rebroadcast on ABC: February 4, 1984. Rebroadcast on NICK: July 20, 1986.*

### Voices
**Stanley:** Susan Blu; **Nathan the Fox:** Jack DeLeon; **Eagle One:** Wolfman Jack

## ◎ STAR FAIRIES

A tiny band of star creatures (Spice, Nightsong, Jazz, True Love and Whisper) embarks on a very special mission—to grant the wishes of every child in the world—in this half-hour special broadcast as part of a two-hour package that included *Pound Puppies* and *The Harlem Globetrotters Meet Snow White*. *A Hanna-Barbera Production. Color. Two hours. Premiered: October, 1985. Syndicated.*

### Voices
**Spice:** Didi Conn; **True Love:** Jean Kasem; **Jazz:** Susan Blu; **Nightsong:** Ta Tanisha; **Whisper:** Marianne Chinn; **Sparkle/Michelle/Mother:** B.J. Ward; **Troll:** Billy Barty; **Giant:** Michael Nouri; **Dragon Head #1:** Howard Morris; **Dragon Head #2:** Arte Johnson; **Harvey:** Shavar Ross; **Benjamin:** Matthew Gotlieb; **Jennifer:** Holly Berger; **Puppy/Lavandar/Vanity:** Frank Welker; **Freddie/Frump/Spectre:** Michael Bell; **Giggleby:** Jerry Houser; **Blunderpuff/Elf:** Don Messick; **Wishing Well:** Herschel Bernardi; **Winthrop the Wizard:** Jonathan Winters; **Hillary:** Drew Barrymore

## ◎ A STAR FOR JEREMY

On Christmas Eve, young Jeremy learns in a dream the meaning of the Christmas star that transports him to the place where God assigns stars to their place in the universe. *A TPC Communications Production. Color. Half-hour. Premiered: December 1984. Syndicated.*

### Voices
Leif Ancker, James Gleason, Charlotte Jarvis, Larry Kenny, Stacy Melodia, Christopher Potter, Tia Relbling

## ◎ THE STEADFAST TIN SOLDIER

Actor Jeremy Irons tells this story of the tin soldier and the hardships he endures for the love of a beautiful ballerina in a delightful half-hour animated adaptation of Hans Christian Andersen's classic tale. Part of Rabbit Ears Video's *Storybook Classics* series. *A Rabbit Ears Video Production. Color. Half-hour. Premiered on SHO: 1989.*

### Voices
**Narrator:** Jeremy Irons

## ◎ STILL LIFE WITH ANIMATED DOGS

Award-winning animator Paul Fierlinger produced this hand-drawn educational film dealing with dogs and the divine power of nature that premiered on PBS in 2001. The critically acclaimed production also won a prestigious 2002 Peabody Award and a Special Jury Award at the Zagreb World Festival of Animated Films. *An AR&T Animation Production. Color. Half-hour. Premiered on PBS: March 2001.*

## ◎ THE STINGIEST MAN IN TOWN

Charles Dickens's classic *A Christmas Carol* is revisited, set in 1840s London with the phantoms, known as Christmas Past and Christmas Present, paying the penny-pinching Scrooge a visit to change his self-centered ways. *A Rankin-Bass Production. Color. One hour. Premiered on NBC: December 23, 1978. Rebroadcast on NBC: December 22, 1979. Syndicated. Rebroadcast on DIS: December 14, 1992; December 7, 1993; December 19, 1995; December 17, 1996.*

### Voices
**B.A.H. Humbug (narrator):** Tom Bosley; **Ebenezer Scrooge:** Walter Matthau; **Young Scrooge:** Robert Morse; **Ghost of Marley:** Theodore Bikel; **Fred:** Dennis Day; **Tiny Tim:** Robert Rolofson; **Mrs. Cratchit:** Darlene Conley; **Ghost of Christmas Past:** Paul Frees; **Martha:** Debra Clinger; **Belinda:** Steffanie Calli; **Peter:** Eric Hines; **Boy:** Charles Matthau; **Scrooge's fiancee:** Diana Lee

## ◎ THE STORY OF SANTA CLAUS

A kindly old toymaker named Nicholas Claus starts the tradition of delivering a toy on Christmas to every child around the world in this prime-time one-hour animated musical. *An Arnold Shapiro/Film Roman Production in association with CBS Productions. Color. One hour. Premiered on CBS: December 4, 1996. Rebroadcast on CBS: December 12, 1997.*

### Voices
**Nicholas Claus:** Ed Asner; **Gretchen Claus:** Betty White; **Nostros:** Tim Curry; **Clement:** Miko Hughes; **Aurora:** Kathryn Zaremba

## ◎ THE STORY OF THE DANCING FROG

George is a multifaceted frog whose leaps and bounds in this parody of a Hollywood musical bring him fame and fortune as he and his devoted friend, Gertrude, set out on a dance adventure around the world. *An HBO Storybook Musicals series special. A Michael Sporn Animation Production in association with Italtoons Corporation. Color. Half-hour. Premiered on HBO: October 3, 1989.*

### Voices
**Narrator:** Amanda Plummer; **Gertrude:** Heidi Stallings

## ◎ STRAWBERRY SHORTCAKE AND THE BABY WITHOUT A NAME

Strawberry Shortcake and her friends, Plum Puddin' and Peach Blush, set out to rescue Baby Without a Name, only to be kidnapped themselves by the evil Peculiar Purple Pieman and Sour Grapes. The special was one of six programs based on the American Greetings card characters. *A MAD Production in association with Those Characters From Cleveland and Nelvana Limited. Color. Half-hour. Premiered: March 1984. Syndicated.*

**Voices**

**Sun (narrator):** Chris Wiggins; **Strawberry Shortcake:** Russi Taylor; **Peculiar Purple Pieman:** Bob Ridgely; **Sour Grapes/Fig-Boot:** Jeri Craden; **Plum Puddin':** Laurie Waller; **Lemon Meringue/Lime Chiffon:** Melleny Brown; **Peach Blush/Orange Blossom:** Susan Roman; **Lullaberry Pie:** Monica Parker; **Orange Blossom:** Cree Summer Francks

### ◎ STRAWBERRY SHORTCAKE: "BERRY, MERRY CHRISTMAS"

Strawberry Shortcake and Honey Pie Pony travel to the magical Holidayland looking for the perfect Christmas presents for their friends—including a trip to the North Pole to see Santa—but her carefully selected presents are almost ruined when snowballs melt all over them in this direct-to-video special—and third in the series—to air on HBO. *A DIC Entertainment Production. Color. One hour. Premiered on HBO: November 7, 2003.*

**Voices**

**Strawberry Shortcake:** Sarah Heinke; **Orange Blossom:** Dejare Barfield; **Huckleberry:** Daniel Canfield; **Pupcake:** Nils Haaland; **Honey Pie Pony:** Hannah Koslosky; **Custard the Cat:** Sarah Koslosky; **Apple Dumplin':** Katie Labosky; **Ginger Snap:** Samantha Triba; **Angel Cake:** Rachel Ware

### ◎ STRAWBERRY SHORTCAKE: "GET WELL ADVENTURE"

Honey Pie Pony is upset after she hurts her leg and is unable to go on a grand adventure with Strawberry Shortcake, but her friends tell her stories and sing songs to cheer her up and get well faster. This fourth direct-to-video special debuted on HBO and was rebroadcast on PAX. *A DIC Entertainment Production. Color. One hour. Premiered on HBO: November 10, 2003. Rebroadcast on PAX: December 20, 2004.*

**Voices**

**Strawberry Shortcake:** Sarah Heinke; **Orange Blossom:** Dejare Barfield; **Huckleberry:** Daniel Canfield; **Pupcake:** Nils Haaland; **Honey Pie Pony:** Hannah Koslosky; **Custard the Cat:** Sarah Koslosky; **Apple Dumplin':** Katie Labosky; **Ginger Snap:** Samantha Triba; **Angel Cake:** Rachel Ware

### ◎ STRAWBERRY SHORTCAKE IN BIG APPLE CITY

Strawberry Shortcake ventures to Big Apple City to compete in a bake-off against the nasty Peculiar Purple Pieman, who does everything possible to prevent her from winning. *An RLR Associates Production in association with Those Characters From Cleveland and Perpetual Motion Pictures. Color. Half-hour. Premiered: April 1981. Syndicated. Rebroadcast on DIS: September 25, 1993.*

**Voices**

**Sun (narrator):** Romeo Muller; **Strawberry Shortcake:** Russi Taylor; **Peculiar Purple Pieman:** Bob Ridgely; **Coco Nutwork:** Bob Holt; **Orange Blossom:** Diane McCannon; **Blueberry Muffin/Apple Dumplin'/Apricot:** Joan Gerber; **Vocalists:** Flo and Eddie

### ◎ STRAWBERRY SHORTCAKE: "MEET STRAWBERRY SHORTCAKE"

With her sister Apple Dumplin' about to celebrate her first birthday, Strawberry Shortcake goes all out to plan a special birthday partner

*Strawberry Shortcake displays her homemade strawberry shortcake in a scene from the half-hour syndicated special* Strawberry Shortcake in Big Apple City. *© RLR Associates/Those Characters From Cleveland*

in her honor, heading off to pick up the perfect party supplies while meeting five new friends in the process (Orange Blossom, Angel Cake, Ginger Snap, Honey Pie Pony and Huckleberry). This first of four direct-to-video specials aired in first-run syndication in March 2003 and was rebroadcast that August followed by two more specials that November. *A DIC Entertainment Production. Color. One hour. Syndicated: March 29, 2003. Rebroadcast on HBO: August 1, 2003.*

**Voices**

**Strawberry Shortcake:** Sarah Heinke; **Orange Blossom:** Dejare Barfield; **Huckleberry:** Daniel Canfield; **Pupcake:** Nils Haaland; **Honey Pie Pony:** Hannah Koslosky; **Custard the Cat:** Sarah Koslosky; **Apple Dumplin':** Katie Labosky; **Ginger Snap:** Samantha Triba; **Angel Cake:** Rachel Ware

### ◎ STRAWBERRY SHORTCAKE MEETS THE BERRYKINS

Thanks to Strawberry Shortcake and her friends, the Peculiar Purple Pieman and Sour Grapes are foiled in their plan to make exotic perfume out of the little Berrykins, tiny fairies who give scent and flavor to fruit. *A MAD Production in association with Those Characters From Cleveland and Nelvana Limited. Color. Half-hour. Premiered: Spring 1985. Syndicated.*

**Voices**

**Sun (narrator):** Chris Wiggins; **Strawberry Shortcake:** Russi Taylor; **Peculiar Purple Pieman:** Bob Ridgely; **Sour Grapes:** Jeri Craden; **Banana Twirl/Banana Berrykin:** Melleny Brown; **Berry Princess/Peach Blush/Peach Berrykin:** Susan Roman; **Plum Puddin'/Plum Berrykin/Orange Blossom:** Laurie Waller; **Raspberry Tart/Blueberry Muffin:** Susan Snooks; **VO:** Patrick Black; **Vocalists:** Nadia Medusa, Ben Sebastian, John Sebastian, Russi Taylor, Nicole Wills

### ◎ STRAWBERRY SHORTCAKE: PETS ON PARADE

Strawberry Shortcake is entrusted with guarding a new tricycle that will be given to the winner of the annual pet show and parade from the villainous Peculiar Purple Pieman and his cohort Sour Grapes who try to ruin all of the fun. *A Muller-Rosen Production in association with Those Characters From Cleveland and Murakami-Wolf-Swenson Films and Toei Doga Productions. Color. Half-hour. Premiered: April 1982. Syndicated.*

*Voices*

**Sun (narrator):** Romeo Muller; **Strawberry Shortcake:** Russi Taylor; **Pecular Purple Pieman:** Bob Ridgely; **Blueberry Muffin/ Apple Dumplin':** Joan Gerber; **Huckleberry Pie:** Julie McWhirter; **Vocalists:** Flo and Eddie

## ◎ STRAWBERRY SHORTCAKE'S HOUSEWARMING SURPRISE

After Strawberry Shortcake moves into a big new house, her friends give her a surprise housewarming party, but two uninvited guests— Peculiar Purple Pieman and Sour Grapes—try to eat everything in sight and steal Strawberry Shortcake's famous recipes. *A MAD Production in association with Those Characters From Cleveland and Nelvana Limited. Color. Half-hour. Premiered: April 1983. Syndicated.*

*Voices*

**Sun (narrator):** Chris Wiggins; **Strawberry Shortcake:** Russi Taylor; **Pecular Purple Pieman:** Bob Ridgely; **Sour Grapes:** Jeri Craden; **Captain Cackle/VO:** Jack Blum; **Lime Chiffon:** Melleny Brown; **Huckleberry/Parfait/Lem:** Jeanine Elias; **Blueberry/Crepe Suzette/Ada:** Susan Roman; **Vocalists:** Phil Glaston, Bill Keith, Sharon McQueen, Ben Sebastian, John Sebastian

## ◎ STRAWBERRY SHORTCAKE: "SPRING FOR STRAWBERRY SHORTCAKE"

When Spring in Strawberryland is delayed on its first official day by cold weather and frost on the ground, Strawberry Shortcake and her friends, Orange Blossom and Ginger Snap, locate Spring herself to convince her to make Spring happen for everyone in this second of four direct-to-video specials produced by DIC Entertainment for HBO. *A DIC Entertainment Production. Color. One hour. Premiered on HBO: August 1, 2003.*

*Voices*

**Strawberry Shortcake:** Sarah Heinke; **Orange Blossom:** Dejare Barfield; **Huckleberry:** Daniel Canfield; **Pupcake:** Nils Haaland; **Honey Pie Pony:** Hannah Koslosky; **Custard the Cat:** Sarah Koslosky; **Apple Dumplin':** Katie Labosky; **Ginger Snap:** Samantha Triba; **Angel Cake:** Rachel Ware

## ◎ SUPER DUCKTALES

Scrooge McDuck, Huey, Dewey and Louie fight the Beagle Boys' attempts to steal the McDuck fortune in this prime-time special based on the popular weekday series *DuckTales. A Walt Disney Television Production. Color. One hour. Premiered on NBC: March 26, 1989 (on The Magical World of Disney).*

*Voices*

**Scrooge McDuck:** Alan Young; **Huey/Dewey/Louie:** Russi Taylor

## ◎ SUPERMAN

The infant Kal-El is sent to Earth before his home planet, Krypton, explodes. Raised by adoptive parents, he develops great powers, which he uses to combat crime in Metropolis in this 90-minute prime-time movie detailing the origins of the "Man of Steel." Also the series opener for 1996's *Superman* animated series, based on the popular DC Comics character. *A Warner Bros. Television Animation Production in association with DC Comics. Color. Ninety minutes. Premiered on the WB: September 8, 1996.*

*Voices*

**Clark Kent/Superman:** Tim Daly; **Lois Lane:** Dana Delany; **Perry White:** George Dzundza; **Martha Kent:** Shelley Fabares; **Jonathan Kent:** Mike Farrell; **Jor-El:** Christopher McDonald; **Lara-El:** Finola Hughes; **Lex Luthor:** Clancy Brown

## ◎ SUPERMAN: BRANIAC ATTACKS

Tim Daley and Dana Delany reprise their roles from "Superman: The Animated Series" in this straight-to-DVD movie in which the Man of Steel faces a combined threat from two of his biggest foes, Lex Luthor and Braniac, while struggling with the need to disclose his true identity to Lois because he loves her. In June 2006, Cartoon Network previewed the 75-minute feature with a special one-day showing one day before its release to retail stores. *A Warner Bros. Animation Production. Color. Seventy-five minutes. Premiered on CAR: June 17, 2006.*

*Voices*

**Clark Kent/Superman:** Timothy Daly; **Lois Lane:** Dana Delany; **Jonathan Kent:** Mike Farrell; **Martha Kent:** Shelley Fabares; **Perry White:** George Dzundza; **Jimmy Olsen:** David Kaufman; **Braniac:** Lance Henriksen; **Lex Luthor:** Powers Boothe; **Mercy Graves:** Tara Strong

## ◎ SUPER ROBOT MONKEY TEAM HYPER FORCE GO! SPECIAL

Creator and executive producer Ciro Nieli presented his favorite episodes from this popular series' third season in this two-part special with widescreen versions of "Wormhole" and "Belly of the Beast" that premiered one week apart on Toon Disney's *Jetix* action/adventure block. *A Walt Disney Studios Production. Color. Half-hour. Premiered on TDIS: February 13, 2006 ("Wormhole"); February 20, 2006 ("Belly of the Beast")*

*Voices*

**Antauri:** Kevin Michael Richardson; **Chiro:** Greg Cipes; **Gibson:** Tom Kenny; **Nova:** Kari Wahlgren; **Otto:** Clancy Brown; **Sprx-77:** Corey Feldman; **The Skeleton King:** Mark Hamill; **The Being:** Jim Cummings ("Wormhole")

## ◎ THE SUPER TROLLS

After escaping from the underground kingdom of Trolland to San Francisco, the evil troll wizard, Dredmor, hatches his evil plan to use "human magic" combined with troll magic by inventing a giant half-mechanical, half-magical creature, the Trollminator, to conquer both the troll and human worlds on his behalf. That is, until King Astar transforms three average-looking trolls into Super Trolls to thwart him and his killing machine in an action-packed climax on the Golden Gate Bridge in this half-hour cartoon special written by Jeffrey Scott. Produced by Burbank's DIC Entertainment, the special aired in first-run syndication. *A DIC Entertainment Production. Color. Half-hour. Premiered: 1992. Syndicated.*

*Voices*

**Narrator/Greeb/Trollminator:** Dale Wilson; **Dredmor:** Don Brown; **Saliva/Mayor Funstein:** Babs Chula; **Tastar:** Ian James Corlett; **Warpy/Mother/Baby:** Cathy Weseluck; **Hulkules/Dispatcher:** Scott McNeil; **Bendar:** Jason Michas; **Chief of Police:** Don Brown

## ◎ SUR LE PONT D'AVIGNON

A ghost appears before a clock shop's owner (Amedee Carillon) and his grandson (Jerome), who have been threatened with eviction from their clock shop. They embark on an exciting adventure to find gold, save the ghost's reputation and keep their shop in this half-hour animated musical that premiered on HBO's cartoon anthology series *The Real Story of. . . . A CINAR Films/France Animation Production in association with Western Publishing Company/The Family Channel/Telefilm Canada/Cofimage 3. Color. Half-hour. Premiered on HBO: January 10, 1994.*

*Voices*
**Amedee Carillon:** Robert Guillaume

## ◎ SUZY SNOWFLAKE

A spindly but fragile fairy spreads good cheer amidst the dark and blizzardy winter landscape in this rudimentary stop-motion animated short adapted from Hill and Range Music's popular song of the same name. In December 1956, the two-minute film premiered on then-local, now-Chicago superstation WGN on the legendary *Garfield Goose and Friends*, becoming a traditional favorite, along with *Frosty the Snowman* and *Hardrock, Coco and Joe: The Three Little Dwarfs*. The short holiday film was then replayed annually with the others as part of WGN's holiday programming on kid-vid variety shows, including *Bozo's Circus* and *The Ray Rayner Show*. In 2005, the iconic cartoon and the two others were rebroadcast nationally on WGN's retrospective special, *Bozo, Gar & Ray*. *A Little World Films/Hill and Range Music Production. Black and white. Two minutes. Premiered on WGN: December 18, 1956.*

## ◎ SVATOHOR (SAINT MOUNTAIN)

A young Russian hunter must complete a seemingly impossible task to save the czar from his enemies and win the hand of the czar's daughter in this stop-motion puppet-animated film based on a popular Russian folktale. From PBS's award-winning series *Long Ago & Far Away*. *A Czechoslovak Television Production. Color. Half-hour. Premiered on PBS: March 25, 1989.*

## ◎ SWAMP THING: EXPERIMENT IN TERROR

Swamp Thing is abducted by scientists for use in a top-secret government experiment in New Orleans, when Delbert, J.T. (who witnessed his capture) and Bayou Jack come to the rescue, while Dr. Arcane views this as his best opportunity yet to recapture the Swamp Thing for his own evil purposes in this final installment of the five-part miniseries that aired as half-hour specials Saturday mornings on CBS. Episodes in the entire series were rebroadcast in 1991 on FOX and later on Disney Channel. *A DIC Entertainment/Batfilm Production. Color. Half-hour. Premiered on CBS: September 1990. Rebroadcast on FOX: May 11, 1991; July 27, 1991.*

*Voices*
**Dr. Alex Holland/Swamp Thing:** Len Carlson; **Dr. Anton Arcane:** Don Francks; **Abby, Dr. Arcane's Niece:** Paulina Gillis; **Bayou Jack:** Phillip Atkin; **Tomahawk:** Harvey Atkin; **J.T.:** Richard Yearwood; **Delbert:** Jonathan Potts; **Dr. Deemo:** Errol Slue; **Weed Killer:** Joe Matteson; **Skin Man:** Gordon Masten

## ◎ SWAMP THING: FALLING RED STAR

Joined by his friends Bayou Jack and Tomahawk, Swamp Thing recovers a nuclear-powered NASA satellite that crash lands in the swamp, while the evil Dr. Arcane sets his sights on retrieving it to power his UN-Men and forces of evil in this third installment of a five-part series adapted from the DC Comics character that debuted on CBS in September 1990 and re-aired on FOX Kids Network and Disney Channel. *A DIC Entertainment/Batfilm Production. Color. Half-hour. Premiered on CBS: September 1990. Rebroadcast on FOX: April 27, 1991; July 13, 1991.*

*Voices*
**Dr. Alex Holland/Swamp Thing:** Len Carlson; **Dr. Anton Arcane:** Don Francks; **Abby, Dr. Arcane's Niece:** Paulina Gillis; **Bayou Jack:** Phillip Atkin; **Tomahawk:** Harvey Atkin; **J.T.:** Richard Yearwood; **Delbert:** Jonathan Potts; **Dr. Deemo:** Errol Slue; **Weed Killer:** Joe Matteson; **Skin Man:** Gordon Masten

## ◎ SWAMP THING: LEGEND OF THE LOST CAVERN

Determined to fulfill his goal of attaining immortality, Dr. Arcane goes in search of the fabled Fountain of Youth housed in the Lost Caverns, dishonoring the Indian burial grounds of Tomahawk's ancestors in the process. First airing Saturday mornings on CBS, this half-hour special was the fourth installment of the DC Comics miniseries adaptation that was originally developed as a weekly series that CBS decided not to pick up. In 1991, the special was rebroadcast on the FOX Kids Network and later Disney Channel. *A DIC Entertainment/Batfilm Production. Color. Half-hour. Premiered on CBS: September 1990. Rebroadcast on FOX: May 4, 1991; July 20, 1991.*

*Voices*
**Dr. Alex Holland/Swamp Thing:** Len Carlson; **Dr. Anton Arcane:** Don Francks; **Abby, Dr. Arcane's Niece:** Paulina Gillis; **Bayou Jack:** Phillip Atkin; **Tomahawk:** Harvey Atkin; **J.T.:** Richard Yearwood; **Delbert:** Jonathan Potts; **Dr. Deemo:** Errol Slue; **Weed Killer:** Joe Matteson; **Skin Man:** Gordon Masten

## ◎ SWAMP THING: THE UN-MEN UNLEASHED

The evil Dr. Anton Arcane transforms two kids, J.T. and Delbert, into mutants, known as the UN-Men, to attack the slimy Louisiana swampland creature, Swamp Thing, only for them to be rescued by Arcane's niece, Abby, in this first of a five-part miniseries that aired on CBS and was later rebroadcast on the FOX Kids Network and Disney Channel. *A DIC Entertainment/Batfilm Production. Color. Half-hour. Premiered on CBS: September 1990. Rebroadcast on FOX: October 31, 1990.*

*Voices*
**Dr. Alex Holland/Swamp Thing:** Len Carlson; **Dr. Anton Arcane:** Don Francks; **Abby, Dr. Arcane's Niece:** Paulina Gillis; **Bayou Jack:** Phillip Atkin; **Tomahawk:** Harvey Atkin; **J.T.:** Richard Yearwood; **Delbert:** Jonathan Potts; **Dr. Deemo:** Errol Slue; **Weed Killer:** Joe Matteson; **Skin Man:** Gordon Masten

## ◎ SWAMP THING: TO LIVE FOREVER

Notorious Dr. Arcane and his mutant UN-Men head to the Amazon rainforest where they enlist the help of a local Indian tribe to mine the sap of "the trees that never die," but Swamp Thing arrives in time to put an end to Arcane's evil plan. This half-hour special was the second installment in the five-part miniseries that aired on CBS in the fall of 1990. In April 1991, FOX rebroadcast the complete series, which was later rerun on Disney Channel. *A DIC Entertainment/Batfilm Production. Color. Half-hour. Premiered on CBS: September 1990. Rebroadcast on FOX: April 20, 1991; July 6, 1991.*

*Voices*
**Dr. Alex Holland/Swamp Thing:** Len Carlson; **Dr. Anton Arcane:** Don Francks; **Abby, Dr. Arcane's Niece:** Paulina Gillis; **Bayou Jack:** Phillip Atkin; **Tomahawk:** Harvey Atkin; **J.T.:** Richard Yearwood; **Delbert:** Jonathan Potts; **Dr. Deemo:** Errol Slue; **Weed Killer:** Joe Matteson; **Skin Man:** Gordon Masten

## ◎ THE SWISS FAMILY ROBINSON (1973)

Fritz and Franz, the shipwrecked sons of the Robinson family, return to civilization with a young girl they discover on the island. *A Family of Festival Classics special. A Rankin-Bass Production in association with Mushi Studios. Color. Half-hour. Premiered: January 13, 1973. Syndicated.*

**Voices**

Carl Banas, Len Birman, Bernard Cowan, Peg Dixon, Keith Hampshire, Peggi Loder, Donna Miller, Frank Perry, Henry Ramer, Billie Mae Richards, Alfie Scopp, Paul Soles

## ◎ THE SWISS FAMILY ROBINSON (1973)

Survival is the name of the game for a family of travelers who become shipwrecked on a deserted island in this one-hour special based on Johann Wyss's popular adventure story. *An Air Programs International Production. Color. One hour. Premiered on CBS: October 28, 1973. Rebroadcast on CBS: November 28, 1974. Syndicated.*

**Voices**

Jeannie Drynan, Alistair Duncan, Barbara Frawley, Ron Haddrick, Brender Senders

## ◎ TABITHA AND ADAM AND THE CLOWN FAMILY

Tabitha and Adam Stephens, the offspring from television's *Bewitched*, are a teenage witch and warlock in a circus setting in this hour-long animated spinoff of the popular weekly sitcom. *A Hanna-Barbera Production. Color. One hour. Premiered on ABC: December 2, 1972 (on The ABC Saturday Superstar Movie). Syndicated.*

**Voices**

**Tabitha Stephens:** Cindy Eilbacher; **Adam Stephens/Scooter:** Michael Morgan; **Max/Glenn/Yancy:** John Stephenson; **Julie:** Shawn Shepps; **Ernie:** Gene Andrusco; **Mike:** Frank Welker; **Ronk/Mr. McGurk/Haji/Ducks/Railroad Conductor:** Paul Winchell; **Muscles/Boris/Third Cyclone:** Hal Smith; **Big Louie/Count Krumley/Mr. McGuffin:** Lennie Weinrib; **Second Cyclone/Trumpet/Voice:** Don Messick; **Marybell/Georgia:** Janet Waldo; **Hi-Rise/First Cyclone:** Pat Harrington

## ◎ THE TAILOR OF GLOUCESTER

Sensitive retelling of Beatrix Potter's wry tale of a tailor who, thanks to his naughty cat Simpkin, has no more silk thread to finish the coat he has promised the mayor for his wedding on Christmas day. Part of Rabbit Ears Video's *Holiday Classics* video series, produced in 1988. *A Rabbit Ears Video Production. Color. Half-hour. Premiered on SHO: 1989.*

**Voices**

**Narrator:** Meryl Streep

## ◎ TAKE ME UP TO THE BALLGAME

A sandlot baseball team consisting of animals is pitted against the Outer-Space All-Stars, a team that has never lost a game, in an intergalactic playoff to determine the best team in the universe. The half-hour fantasy special aired in Canada and in the United States. *A Nelvana Limited Production in association with CBC. Color. Half-hour. Premiered (U.S.): September 1980. Syndicated.*

**Voices**

**Irwin:** Phil Silvers; **Beaver:** Bobby Dermer; **Eagle:** Derek McGrath; **Commissioner:** Don Ferguson; **Announcer:** Paul Soles; **Edna:** Anna Bourque; **Jake:** Maurice LaMarche; **Mole:** Melleny Brown; **Vocalist:** Rick Danko

## ◎ THE TALE OF PETER RABBIT

Mrs. Rabbit tells her children—Flopsy, Mopsy, Cottontail and Peter—to stay out of Mr. McGregor's garden, but naughty Peter disobeys. This leads to a high-speed chase with an angry Mr. McGregor in pursuit. An *HBO Storybook Musicals* series special. A Hare Bear Production. *Color. Half-hour. Premiered on HBO: June 11, 1991. Rebroadcast on HBO: June 17, 1991; April 5, 1993.*

**Voices**

**Narrator/Mrs. Rabbit/Mr. McGregor's cat:** Carol Burnett

## ◎ THE TALE OF PETER RABBIT AND THE TALE OF MR. JEREMY FISHER

Two enchanting stories by Beatrix Potter—the first about a curious and disobedient rabbit, the second about a gentleman frog's minnow-fishing trip that turns into a surprising adventure—are featured in this delightful half-hour adaptation, narrated by actress Meryl Streep. Part of Rabbit Ears Video's *Storybook Classics* series. *A Rabbit Ears Video Production. Color. Half-hour. Premiered: 1989. Syndicated.*

**Voices**

**Narrator:** Meryl Streep

## ◎ A TALE OF TWO CITIES

During the French Revolution, Sidney Carton, a dispirited English barrister, saves French aristocrat Charles Darnay from execution at the guillotine in this vivid adaptation of Charles Dickens's well-known story. *A Burbank Films Production. Color. Ninety minutes. Premiered: 1984. Syndicated.*

**Voices**

John Benton, John Everson, Phillip Hinton, Liz Horne, Moya O'Sullivan, Robin Stewart, John Stone, Henri Szeps, Ken Wayne

## ◎ A TALE OF TWO WISHES

In this live-action/animated special about wish-making, Jane, a girl whose wishes never seem to come true, becomes friends with Skeeter (voiced by rock-'n'-roll legend Rick Nelson), a wise but gentle storyteller. As hosts they introduce a series of animated tales that help Jane understand how to turn her dreams into reality. *A Bosustow Entertainment Production. Color. One hour. Premiered on CBS: November 8, 1981. Rebroadcast on CBS: July 6, 1982. Syndicated.*

**Cast**

**Jane:** Tracey Gold; **Skeeter:** Rick Nelson; **Grandmother:** Bibi Osterwald; **Mother:** Judy Farrell; **Father:** Bob Ross; **Margaret:** Seeley Ann Thumann; **Daniel:** Chad Krentzman

## ◎ TALES OF WASHINGTON IRVING

Author Washington Irving's two most popular folktales, "The Legend of Sleepy Hollow" and "Rip Van Winkle," are featured in this one-hour special produced as part of CBS's *Famous Classic Tales* package of animated children's specials. *An Air Programs International Production. Color. One hour. Premiered on CBS: November 1, 1970. Rebroadcast on CBS: October 24, 1971. Syndicated.*

**Voices**

Mel Blanc, George Firth, Joan Gerber, Byron Kane, Julie McWhirter, Don Messick, Ken Samson, Lennie Weinrib, Brian Zax, Larraine Zax

## ◎ THE TALKING EGGS

When a young girl named Selina befriends a mystical elderly woman, magical things happen. This half-hour animated production—one of three new half-hours produced for the fourth season of the PBS series *Long Ago & Far Away*. *A Michael Sporn Animation Production. Color. Half-hour. Premiered on PBS: December 6, 1992.*

**Voices**

**Narrator:** Danny Glover

## ◉ THE TALKING PARCEL

A 12-year-old girl and talking parrot set out on a remarkable journey to return the land of Mythologia to its rightful leader in this two-part special, based on the book by Gerald Durrell (and adapted by Rosemary Anne Sisson). Originally debuting in syndication in 1983, the special was rebroadcast in 1989 on the award-winning PBS anthology series *Long Ago & Far Away*. A *Cosgrove-Hall Production. Color. Half-hour. Premiered: 1983–84. Syndicated. Rebroadcast on PBS: March 4, 1989 (Part 1) and March 11, 1989 (Part II).*

### Voices

**Penelope:** Lisa Norris; **Parrot:** Freddie Jones; **Hortense, the Flying Train:** Mollie Sugden; **Ethelred:** Roy Kinnear; **H.H. Junketbury:** Edward Kelsey; **Chief Cockatrice:** Windsor Davies; **Oswald, the Sea Serpent:** Sir Michael Hordern; **Werewolf:** Peter Woodthorpe; **Duke Wensleydale:** Harvey Ashby; **Others:** Raymond Mason, Daphne Oxenford

## ◉ THE TANGERINE BEAR

An all-star cast, including Tom Bosley, Jenna Elfman, David Hyde Pierce, Jonathan Taylor Thomas, Marlon Wayans and Howie Mandel, lent their voices to this heartwarming 90-minute holiday tale of a stuffed teddy bear with an upside-down smile who struggles to find a home and a family amongst a rag-tag group of thrift store toys. Originally released on home video in November 2000, the program first debuted on German television in December 2001 before making its U.S. television premiere on Cartoon Network on Saturday, December 18, 2004 at 3:00 P.M., followed by three encore performances, including two on Christmas Eve. *A Family Home Entertainment Production. Color. Ninety minutes. Premiered on CAR: December 18, 2004. Rebroadcast on CAR: December 20, 2004; December 24, 2004; December 20, 2005.*

### Voices

**Narrator:** Trisha Yearwood; **Tangie:** Jonathan Taylor Thomas; **Louie Blue:** Marlon Wayans; **Lorelei:** Jenna Elfman; **Jack:** Howie Mandel; **Bird:** David Hyde Pierce

## ◉ TATTERTOWN

In a mystical town where everything comes to life—misfit toys, broken machines and discarded musical instruments—Debbie, a young girl, tries to prevent her stuffed doll, Muffett, from joining forces with the evil Sidney Spider to take over the town. The half-hour Christmas special was the pilot for what was announced as the first prime-time animated series for the all-kids network, Nickelodeon. Ralph Bakshi based the idea on a concept he originated 30 years earlier called "Junk Town." *A Bakshi Animation Production. Color. Half-hour. Premiered on NICK: December 1988. Rebroadcast: December 10, 1995 (as Rocko's Modern Life Christmas and Tattertown); December 1, 1996 (syndication).*

### Voices

**Sidney the Spider:** Charles Adler; **Saxaphone/Others:** Keith David; **Other Voices:** Jennifer Darling, Adrian Arnold, Arthur Burghardt, Sherry Lynn, Patrick Pinney

## ◉ TAZ-MANIA: "LIKE FATHER LIKE SON"/ "FRIGHTS OF PASSAGE"

After getting to know each other better, Taz finds he has more in common with his dad, Hugh, than he realized in this half-hour prime-time series preview special, comprised of two episodes, that aired on FOX six days before the premiere of the new weekly Warner Bros. Television Animation series based on the classic *Looney Tunes* character. *A Warner Bros. Television Animation Production. Color. Half-hour. Premiered on FOX: September 1, 1991.*

### Voices

**Taz/Bushwhacker Bob/Buddy Boar/Wendel T. Wolf:** Jim Cummings; **Jean:** Miriam Flynn; **Mr. Thickley:** Dan Castellaneta; **Molly Tasmanian Devil:** Kellie Martin; **Bull Gator:** John Astin; **Willie Wombat:** Phil Proctor; **Hugh:** Maurice LaMarche; **Constance:** Rosalyn Landor; **Didgeri Dingo III/Axle Dog the Turtle:** Rob Paulsen; **Jake:** Debi Derryberry; **Didgeri Dingo:** Kevin Thudeau; **Other Voices:** Edward Paulsen

## ◉ THE TEDDY BEARS' CHRISTMAS

Ben, an adorable teddy bear, wants to buy his boy owner's little sister, Sally, a teddy bear for Christmas in this sequel to 1989's *The Teddy Bears' Picnic*. *A Lacewood Production. Color. Half-hour. Premiered on DIS: December 19, 1992. Rebroadcast on DIS: December 24, 1995; December 19, 1996.*

### Voices

**Benjamin Bear:** Jonathan Crombie; **Simon:** Ryan Lindsay; **Sally:** Kylie Schibli

## ◉ THE TEDDY BEARS' PICNIC

Two warmhearted teddys, Wally and Benjamin Bear, come to the aid of a sad and lost little girl named Amanda in this first of two Teddy Bears specials, produced by Canada's Lacewood Productions. Originally produced for Canadian television, the half-hour special debuted in the United States on Disney Channel. *A Lacewood Productions/Hinton Animation Studios Production in association with C.T.V. and Telefilm Canada. Color. Half-hour. Premiered on DIS: 1989.*

### Voices

**Benjamin Bear:** Jonathan Crombie; **Amanda:** Marsha Moreau; **Wally:** Stuart Stone; **Doc:** Tracey Moore; **Sally:** Elissa Marcus

## ◉ TEENAGE MUTANT NINJA TURTLES: "PLANET OF THE TURTLETOIDS"

The animated reptiles go out of this world to save a peaceful planet from a monster in their second half-hour prime-time special. *A Murakami-Wolf-Swenson Production in association with Mirage Studios. Color. Half-hour. Premiered on CBS: August 31, 1991.*

### Voices

**Michaelangelo:** Townsend Coleman; **Leonardo:** Cam Clarke; **Donatello:** Barry Gordon; **Raphael:** Rob Paulsen

## ◉ TEENAGE MUTANT NINJA TURTLES: "THE CUFFLINK CAPER"

Following its decision to pick up the hit syndicated series based on the early 1980s' comic books about the Turtles, CBS premiered this episode as a prime-time special the night before the show's Saturday morning bow. In the special the Turtles join the mob of a notorious gangster (Big Louie) to find out why the big-time crook is robbing all the best places and taking only cuff links. *A Murakami-Wolf-Swenson Production in association with Mirage Studios. Color. Half-hour. Premiered on CBS: September 14, 1990.*

### Voices

**Michaelangelo:** Townsend Coleman; **Leonardo:** Cam Clarke; **Donatello:** Barry Gordon; **Raphael:** Rob Paulsen

## ◉ TEEN TITANS: TROUBLE IN TOKYO

The first made-for-TV movie based on the DC Comics-inspired series *Teen Titans*, this time with teen superheroes Robin,

Starfire, Cyborg, Raven and Beast Boy spurred into action when the mysterious and menacing Japanese criminal Brushogen sends a high-tech ninja to attack Titans Tower. The film premiered on Cartoon Network in September 2006. In February 2007, Warner Home Video released the 75-minute full-length feature on DVD. A *Warner Bros. Television Animation Production. Color. Seventy-five minutes. Premiered CAR: September 15, 2006. Rebroadcast on CAR: September 16, 2006; November 24, 2006; November 26, 2006.*

**Voices**
**Robin/Japanese Boy:** Scott Menville; **Starfire/Mecha-Boi:** Hynden Walch; **Cyborg:** Khary Payton; **Raven/Computer Voice:** Tara Strong; **Beast Boy:** Greg Cipes; **Aqualad:** Wil Wheaton; **Brushogen:** Cary-Hiroyuki Tagawa; **Scarface/Japanese Biker:** Yuri Lowenthal; **Mayor/Bookstore Owner:** Robert Ito; **Commander Uehara Daizo/Saico-Tek/Sushi Shop Owner:** Keone Young; **Nya-Nya/Timoko:** Janice Kawaye

### ◎ THANKSGIVING IN THE LAND OF OZ

Dorothy returns to Oz and joins forces with her friends Jack Pumpkinhead (the Scarecrow), the Hungry Tiger (the Cowardly Lion) and Tic-Toc (the Tin Man) to stop Tyrone the Terrible Toy Maker, from gaining control of Winkle Country. Later retitled and rebroadcast as *Dorothy in the Land of Oz*. A *Muller-Rosen Production in association with Murakami-Wolf-Swenson Films. Color. Half-hour. Premiered on CBS: November 25, 1980. Rebroadcast on CBS: December 10, 1981 (as Dorothy in the Land of Oz). Rebroadcast on SHO: November 1985; November 1986. Syndicated.*

**Voices**
**Wizard of Oz (narrator):** Sid Caesar; **Dorothy:** Mischa Bond; **Jack Pumpkinhead/Tyrone, the Terrible/Toy Tinker:** Robert Ridgely; **Tic Toc/Ozma, Queen of Oz:** Joan Gerber; **Hungry Tiger:** Frank Nelson; **Aunt Em:** Lurene Tuttle; **Uncle Henry:** Charles Woolf

### ◎ THE THANKSGIVING THAT ALMOST WASN'T

Johnny Cooke, a young Pilgrim boy, and Little Bear, an Indian boy, are discovered to be missing. Jeremy Squirrel hears of his friends' plight and goes to find them in the woods, putting himself at risk. The story ends happily as the Pilgrims and Indians invite Jeremy to be their guest of honor for Thanksgiving. A *Hanna-Barbera Production. Color. Half-hour. Premiered: November, 1972. Syndicated. Rebroadcast on CAR: November 21, 1993; November 23, 1994; November 19, 1995.*

**Voices**
**Johnny Cooke:** Bobby Riha; **Little Bear:** Kevin Cooper; **Janie/Mom/Mary Cooke:** Marilyn Mayne; **Jimmy/Son Squirrel/Mom Squirrel:** June Foray; **Jeremy Squirrel/Dad:** Hal Smith; **Dad Squirrel/Francis Cooke/Indian (Massa-soit):** Vic Perrin; **Wolf/Rabbit/Sparrow #1:** Don Messick; **Sparrow #2:** John Stephenson

### ◎ THAT GIRL IN WONDERLAND

Marlo Thomas, in the role of Ann Marie from her popular primetime series *That Girl*, portrays a children's book editor who daydreams and imagines herself as the heroine of various fairy tales. Originally broadcast as part of *The ABC Saturday Superstar Movie*. A *Rankin-Bass Production. Color. One hour. Premiered on ABC: January 13, 1973 (on The ABC Saturday Superstar Movie). Rebroadcast on ABC: March 2, 1974. Syndicated.*

**Voices**
**Ann Marie:** Marlo Thomas; **Other Voices:** Patricia Bright, Dick Heymeyer, Rhoda Mann, Ted Schwartz

### ◎ THERE'S NO TIME FOR LOVE, CHARLIE BROWN

Charlie Brown and his gang go on a school field trip to the local supermarket (they mistake it for a museum) and do their report on that instead. Discovering their mistake, they all fear that they'll get failing grades. Reruns of the special played on Nickelodeon, beginning in January 1998. A *Lee Mendelson–Bill Melendez Production in association with Charles M. Schulz Creative Associates and United Feature Syndicate. Color. Half-hour. Premiered on CBS: March 11, 1973. Rebroadcast on CBS: March 17, 1974. Rebroadcast on NICK: January 28, 1998; February 10, 1998; March 12, 1998; April 15, 1998; May 15, 1998; June 16, 1998; August 19, 1998; September 19, 1998; November 2, 1998; December 25, 1998; January 20, 1999; February 2, 1999; March 3, 1999; March 26, 1999; May 17, 1999; October 16, 1999.*

**Voices**
**Charlie Brown:** Chad Webber; **Linus Van Pelt:** Stephen Shea; **Lucy Van Pelt:** Robin Kohn; **Sally Brown:** Hillary Momberger; **Peppermint Patty:** Kip DeFaria; **Schroeder:** Jeffrey Bailly; **Franklin:** Todd Barbee; **Marcie:** Jimmie Ahrens

### ◎ THIS IS YOUR LIFE, DONALD DUCK

Spoofing Ralph Edwards's *This Is Your Life* television series, host Jiminy Cricket recounts the life of honored guest Donald Duck, in a series of cartoon flashbacks derived from several classic Disney cartoons—"Donald's Better Self" (1938), "Donald's Lucky Day" (1938), "Donald Gets Drafted" (1942), "Sky Trooper" (1942), "Working for Peanuts" (1953), "Mickey's Amateurs" (1937), "Bee at the Beach" (1950) and "Donald's Diary" (1954)—in this hourlong special that first aired on ABC in 1960. The program was later rebroadcast in primetime on NBC as an episode of *The Wonderful World of Disney* and then in 1980 as an NBC special. A *Walt Disney Television Production. Color. One hour. Premiered on ABC: March 11, 1960 (as Walt Disney Presents). Rebroadcast on NBC: February 13, 1977 (on The Wonderful World of Disney); February 22, 1980 (as NBC Special).*

**Voices**
**Jiminy Cricket:** Cliff Edwards; **Donald Duck:** Clarence Nash

### ◎ THE THREE BILLY GOATS GRUFF AND THE THREE LITTLE PIGS

Two popular nursery rhymes—the first about a greedy troll who is no match for the biggest of the Billy Goats Gruff, the second based on one of the most beloved children's classics, about a wolf who threatens to blow the three little pigs' house down—are featured in this colorful half-hour special, part of Rabbit Ears Video's *Storybook Classics* series. A *Rabbit Ears Video Production. Color. Half-hour. Premiered on SHO: 1989.*

**Voices**
**Narrator:** Holly Hunter

### ◎ THE THREE FISHKETEERS

A trio of adventuresome fish—(Toby, Finner and Gillis) comically help a "damsel" (Tika) recover a large pearl, then learn what heroism really is in this half-hour animated special produced for first-run syndication. A *Perennial Pictures Film Corporation Production. Color. Half-hour. Premiered: November 21, 1987. Syndicated.*

*Voices*
**Finner:** Jerry Reynolds; **Gillis:** Russ Harris; **Toby:** Adam Dykstra; **Tika:** Rachel Rutledge

## ◎ THE THREE MUSKETEERS

Swashbuckling heroes Athos, Porthos and Aramis foil the plan of the ruthless Cardinal de Richelieu who conspires against the honorable King Louis XIII in this colorful rendition of Alexandre Dumas's famed historical novel. *A Hanna-Barbera Production. Color. One hour. Premiered on CBS: November 23, 1973. Rebroadcast on CBS: November 28, 1974; November 22, 1979. Syndicated. Rebroadcast on CAR: October 8, 1995 (Mr. Spim's Cartoon Theatre).*

*Voices*
James Condon, Neil Fitzpatrick, Barbara Frawley, Ron Haddrick, Jane Harders, John Martin, Richard Meikle

## ◎ THUGABOO: A MIRACLE ON D-ROC'S STREET

D-Roc, Dee-Dee, Chad, Slime and the entire Thugaboo gang brighten up the lives of a less fortunate kid named Gavin and his family by bringing the real meaning of Christmas to their humble home in this hour-long holiday special—and second of three cartoon specials focused on the experiences of inner-city kids—that premiered on Nicktoons and Nickelodeon. Nicktoons first aired the Christmas special at 7:00 P.M. on Saturday, December 16, 2006, followed by an encore performance that same night at 10:00. *A Nickelodeon Production. Color. One hour. Premiered on NICKT: December 16, 2006. Rebroadcast on NICKT: December 16, 2006; December 17, 2006; December 22, 2006. Premiered on NICK: December 21, 2006.*

*Voices*
Shawn Wayans, Marlon Wayans, Keenen Ivory Wayans, Kim Wayans, Michael Rapaport, George Gore II, Aries Spears, David Alan Grier and Charlie Murphy

## ◎ THUGABOO: SNEAKER MADNESS

Comedic brothers Shawn, Marlon and Keenen Ivory Wayans of *I'm Gonna Git You Sucka!*, *Little Man*, *Scary Movie* and *White Chicks* movie fame created, coproduced and cowrote and supplied some of the voices for this series of three specials, which they described as ". . . a throwback to the old Fat Albert and Charlie Brown days, but packaged in something cooler and hipper . . . and very funny but also very educational," focused on the trials and tribulations in the lives of nine inner city kids in "Boo" York City, based on their experiences growing up. Joining the Wayans for the first special was an impressive all-star cast, including sister Kim Wayans (*In Living Color*), Michael Rapaport (*Dr. Doolittle 2*), George Gore II (*My Wife & Kids*), Aries Spears (*MADTV*), David Alan Grier (*Life with Bonnie*) and Charlie Murphy (*Chappelle's Show*).

Entitled *Sneaker Madness*, the hour-long special premiered in August 2006 on Nickelodeon with a back-to-school parody of the popular sneakers, Air Jordans, with D-Roc seeking Soo-Young's help to make Air Jareds for him out of Air Johnsons, with a DVD of the special released within weeks of its debut. The program was followed by two more half-hour specials on Nicktoons, a Christmas special, *A Miracle on D-Roc's Street* that debuted in December 2006, and *Don't Judge a Boo by Its Cover* that addressed how a person's appearance oftentimes is misleading that has yet to air. *A Nickelodeon Production. Color. One hour. Premiered on NICK: August 11, 2006. Premiered on NICKT: August 12, 2006. Rebroadcast on NICK: August 13, 2006.*

*Voices*
Shawn Wayans, Marlon Wayans, Keenen Ivory Wayans, Kim Wayans, Michael Rapaport, George Gore II, Aries Spears, David Alan Grier and Charlie Murphy

## ◎ THUMBELINA

A beautiful baby girl, no bigger than a thumb, is snatched from her family by an ugly toad who wants to marry her in this colorful half-hour animated adaptation of the classic Hans Christian Andersen story. From Rabbit Ears Video's *Storybook Classics* series. *A Rabbit Ears Video Production. Color. Half-hour. Premiered on SHO: 1989.*

*Voices*
**Narrator:** Kelly McGillis

## ◎ THUNDERCATS

Years into the future a group of noble, moralistic humanoids from a distant planet thwart the evil efforts of an ageless devil-priest. Based on characters created by Ted Wolf, this one-hour special preceded the popular syndicated series. *A Rankin-Bass Production in association with Pacific Animation. Color. One hour. Premiered: January–February 1985. Syndicated.*

*Voices*
**Lion-O/Jackalman:** Larry Kenney; **Snarft/S-S-Slithe:** Robert McFadden; **Cheetara/Wilykit:** Lynne Lipton; **Panthro:** Earle Hyman; **Wilykat/Monkian/Tygra:** Peter Newman; **Mumm-Ra/Vultureman/Jaga:** Earl Hammond

## ◎ THUNDERCATS HO!

The Thundercats square off again with their archenemy Mumm-Ra, who assigns the evil Ma-Mut to search out and destroy the heroic gladiators of outer space. The feature-length special was later edited into five half-hour segments to be broadcast as a mini-series. *A Rankin-Bass Production in association with Pacific Animation. Color. Two hours. Premiered: October 1986. Syndicated.*

*Voices*
**Lion-O/Jackalman:** Larry Kenney; **Lynx-O/Snarf/S-S-Slithe:** Robert McFadden; **Cheetara/Wilykit:** Lynne Lipton; **Panthro:** Earle Hyman; **Wilykat/Monkian/Ben-Gali/Tygra:** Peter Newman; **Mumm-Ra/Vultureman/Jaga:** Earl Hammond; **Pumyra:** Gerrianne Raphael

## ◎ THE TICK: "THE TICK LOVES SANTA!"

Jolted by an electric billboard he smashes into while being chased following a bank robbery disguised as Santa Claus, a small-time crook is suddenly endowed with the power to clone himself, becoming known as Multiple Santa, with Tick, Arthur and their superhero friends having to rid the city of this new menace. Originally aired on Saturday, Thanksgiving Day, 1996, FOX re-aired this episode as a half-hour holiday special—and only special based on Saturday-morning cartoon series—in prime time that December. *An Akom/Graz Entertainment/Sunbow Production. Color. Half-hour. Premiered on FOX: December 15, 1996.*

*Voices*
**The Tick:** Townsend Coleman; **Arthur:** Rob Paulsen; **Sewer Urchin:** Jess Harnell; **Die Fledermaus:** Cam Clarke; **Multiple Santa:** Jim Cummings; **Santa Claus:** Ron Feinberg; **American Maid:** Kay Lenz; **Four-Legged Man:** Roger Rose; **Feral Boy:** Kevin Schon

## ◎ TIME KID

Following the death of his wife, Tom's father invents a time-traveling machine to go back in time to find a cure so his wife might live. His teenage son, Tom Spender, follows to rescue his famed scientist father and bring him home to 1902 America. This third feature-length adventure, adapted from H.G. Wells's *Time Machine*, debuted as part of *DIC's Incredible Movie Toon* series on Nickelodeon. *A DIC Entertainment Production. Color. Ninety minutes. Premiered on NICK: October 20, 2002.*

**Voices**
**Tom Spender:** Michael Monroe Heyward; **Lira:** Danielle Young; **Rose:** Kim Carlson; **Asian Man:** Philip Chen; **Luman:** John Dittrick; **Brall:** Nils Haaland; **Potts:** Travis Howe; **Umpire:** Matt Kamprath; **Zorog:** Jon Kodera; **Second Street Kid:** Ian Lee; **Mr. Spender:** John Lee; **Henry Spender:** Jerry Longe; **Outfielder:** Chris Lundquist; **Skinhead:** Ryle Smith; **First Brahmin:** Paul Sosso; **Bottomley:** Aaron Wilhoft; **Policeman:** Tony Wike; **Brittany:** Hillary Williams; **Foreman:** D. Kevin Williams; **Harney:** Spencer Williams

## ◉ TIMMY'S GIFT: A PRECIOUS MOMENTS CHRISTMAS SPECIAL

One of heaven's smallest and most inexperienced angels helps deliver a priceless crown to a special giant, in the first of two Precious Moments holiday specials. The special was one of five Precious Moments specials that were produced but only two ever aired on U.S. television. *A Rick Reinert Pictures Production. Color. Half-hour. Premiered on NBC: December 25, 1991.*

**Voices**
**Timmy:** Zachary Bostrom; **Baruch:** Billy O'sullivan; **Simon:** Jaclyn Bernstein; **Simon:** Ziad LeFlore; **Harold:** Giant Gelt; **Nicodemus:** Dom DeLuise; **Titus:** Don Knotts; **Snowflake:** Julie DiMattia

## ◉ TIMOTHY TWEEDLE THE FIRST CHRISTMAS ELF

Timothy (voiced by Jonathan Taylor Thomas) becomes the first Christmas elf when he comes to Santa's aid after all the toys disappear from the workshop in this delightfully entertaining, hour-long special first aired on Christmas Day morning in 2000 on the Disney Channel. *An Evening Sky/Wang Film Production. Color. One hour. Premiered on DIS: December 25, 2000. Rebroadcast on DIS: December 25, 2001; December 25, 2002; December 14, 2003; December 25, 2003; December 25, 2004.*

**Voices**
**Timothy Tweedle:** Jonathan Taylor Thomas

## ◉ THE TIN SOLDIER

The one-legged Tin Soldier of the famed Hans Christian Andersen tale comes to life in this colorful adaptation, featuring two new characters, a pair of mice named Fred and Sam, who befriend the Tin Soldier. *An Atkinson Film-Arts Production in association with Telefilm Canada and CTV. Half-hour. Premiered (U.S.): December 1986. Syndicated. Rebroadcast on NICK: August 10, 1991.*

**Voices**
**Fred:** Terrence Scammell; **Sam:** Pier Kohl; **Boy:** Adam Hodgins; **Lefty/Rat #1/Rat #3:** Rick Jones; **King Rat/Rat #2/Rat #4:** Robert Bockstael; **Narrator:** Christopher Plummer

## ◉ TINY TOON ADVENTURES: HOW I SPENT MY VACATION

Plucky Duck joins Hamton on a nightmarish car trip to the ultimate amusement park—Happy World Land. Elmyra terrorizes Wild Safari Zoo; Fifi sets her sights on movie star Johnny Pew; and Buster harasses Babs, only to have her retaliate in this hour-long, prime-time "summer vacation" special featuring the characters from the popular series *Tiny Toon Adventures*. *A Warner Bros./ Amblin Entertainment Production. Color. One hour. Premiered on FOX: September 5, 1993.*

**Voices**
**Buster Bunny:** Charlie Adler; **Babs Bunny:** Tress MacNeille; **Plucky Ducky:** Joe Alaskey; **Hamton J. Pig:** Don Messick; **Elmyra Duff:** Cree Summer; **Dizzy Devil:** Maurice LaMarche; **Shirley Loon:** Gail Matthius; **Wade Pig:** Jonathan Winters; **Winnie Pig:** Edie McClurg; **Uncle Stinky:** Frank Welker; **Big Daddy Boo:** Sorrell Booke; **Foulmouth:** Rob Paulsen; **Fifi:** Kath Soucie; **Sweetie:** Candi Milo

## ◉ TINY TOON ADVENTURES SPRING BREAK SPECIAL

It's Spring Break at the ACME Looniversity and the gang heads to sunny Fort Lauderdale, where Plucky Duck finally meets his "dream girl" and Elmyra mistakes Buster for the Easter Bunny. *A Warner Bros./Amblin Entertainment Production. Color. Half-hour. Premiered on FOX: March 27, 1994.*

**Voices**
**Buster Bunny:** Charles Adler; **Babs Bunny:** Tress MacNeille; **Plucky Duck:** Joe Alaskey; **Hamton J. Pig:** Don Messick; **Montana Max:** Danny Cooksey; **Dizzy Devil:** Maurice LaMarche; **Elmyra Duff:** Cree Summer

## ◉ TINY TOON ADVENTURES: THE LOONEY BEGINNING

Warner Bros.' adolescent versions of the studio's popular Looney Tunes characters—Buster and Babs Bunny (as in Bugs), Plucky Duck (as in Daffy), Hamton Pig (as in Porky) and others—were introduced to television audiences in this "sneak preview" prime-time special prior to the premiere of their hit syndicated series *Tiny Toon Adventures*. The Friday night half-hour special premiered on CBS opposite the Teenage Mutant Ninja Turtles special, "The Cufflink Caper," in 1990. *A Warner Bros./Amblin Entertainment Production. Color. Half-hour. Premiered on CBS: September 14, 1990.*

**Voices**
**Buster Bunny:** Charles Adler; **Babs Bunny:** Tress MacNeille; **Plucky Duck:** Joe Alaskey; **Hamton J. Pig:** Don Messick; **Montana Max:** Danny Cooksey; **Dizzy Devil:** Maurice LaMarche

## ◉ TINY TOONS' NIGHT GHOULERY

Emmy-nominated prime-time scarefest in which the Tiny Toons Gang poke fun at popular TV horror anthology series such as *Night Gallery* and *The Twilight Zone* and cult creature features from *Frankenstein* to *Night of the Living Dead* (even executive producer Steven Spielberg's TV-suspenser *Duel*, is played for laughs). Hosted by Babs Bunny. *A Warner Bros./Amblin Entertainment Production. Premiered on FOX: May 28, 1995. Rebroadcast on CAR: October 31, 1997.*

**Voices**
**Plucky Duck:** Joe Alaskey; **Babs Bunny:** Tress MacNeille; **Buster Bunny:** John Kassir; **Hamton J. Pig:** Don Messick; **Elmyra Duff:** Cree Summer; **Dizzy Devil:** Maurice LaMarche; **Shirley Loon:** Gail Matthius; **Sneezer (the Sneezin' Ghost):** Kath Soucie; **Montana Max:** Danny Cooksey; **Furrball:** Frank Welker; **Mr. Scratch:** Ron Perlman; **Paddy:** Jim Cummings; **Shamus:** Jeff Bennett; **Witch Hazel:** June Foray

## ◉ THE TINY TREE

A lonely young crippled girl and several small meadow animals transform a tiny whispering tree into a glowing Christmas tree. Johnny Marks provides music and lyrics for the songs, with narrator

Buddy Ebsen singing one of the melodies in this half-hour Christmas special produced under the *Bell System Family Theatre* banner. *A DePatie-Freleng Enterprises Production. Color. Half-hour. Premiered on NBC: December 14, 1975 (on Bell System Family Theatre). Rebroadcast on NBC: December 12, 1976. Rebroadcast on ABC: December 18, 1977. Rebroadcast on CBS: December 16, 1978; December 19, 1979. Syndicated.*

**Voices**
**Squire Badger (narrator):** Buddy Ebsen; **Hawk:** Allan Melvin; **Turtle:** Paul Winchell; **Lady Bird/Little Girl:** Janet Waldo; **Boy Bunny/Girl Raccoon:** Stephen Manley; **Groundhog/Father/Beaver/Mole:** Frank Welker; **Vocalist:** Roberta Flack

### ⊚ 'TIS THE SEASON TO BE SMURFY
The other Smurfs learn a lesson about the true meaning of Christmas when they help bring some holiday cheer to the lives of an old toy seller and his gravely ill wife. *A Hanna-Barbera Production in association with SEPP International. Color. Half-hour. Premiered on NBC: December 13, 1987. Rebroadcast on CAR: December 14, 1993;December 13, 1994; November 25, 1995.*

**Voices**
**Papa Smurf/Azrael/Chitter:** Don Messick; **Smurfette:** Lucille Bliss; **Hefty/Monster/Poet/Puppy:** Frank Welker; **Handy/Lazy/Grouchy:** Michael Bell; **Jokey:** June Foray; **Gargamel:** Paul Winchell; **Clumsy/Rich Man:** Bill Callaway; **Vanity/Doctor:** Alan Oppenheimer; **Brainy:** Danny Goldman; **Greedy/Woody:** Hamilton Camp; **Tailor:** Kip King; **Farmer:** Alan Young; **Timber:** Bernard Erhard; **Snappy/Anna:** Pat Musick; **Slouchy:** Noelle North; **Nat/Thief:** Charlie Adler; **Baby Smurf/Sassette:** Julie Dees; **Grandpa:** Jonathan Winters; **Gustav:** Les Tremayne; **Hans:** Justin Gocke; **Willem:** William Schallert; **Elise:** Peggy Weber; **Sheriff:** Jess Douchette

### ⊚ TOM & JERRY: SHIVER ME WHISKERS
After finding a treasure map, Tom ships off to discover buried treasure with stowaway Jerry in tow, encountering coconut-throwing monkeys, a gigantic octopus and pirates, in this direct-to-video, swashbuckling adventure produced in 2006 that premiered on Cartoon Network. Tom and Jerry cocreator Joseph Barbera served as an executive producer on the production. *A Warner Bros. Television Animation Production. Color. One hour and 14 minutes. Premiered on CAR: August 18, 2006.*

**Voices**
**Blue Parrot Betty:** Kathy Najimy; **Red Parrot Stan:** Charles Nelson Reilly; **Red Pirate Ron/Blue Pirate Bob/Purple Parrot:** Kevin Michael Richardson; **Purple Pirate/Narrator:** Wallace Shawn

### ⊚ TOM SAWYER
An animated Mark Twain narrates this popular story that follows the adventures of Tom Sawyer and Becky Sharpe who get lost during a cave exploration and are thought to be dead by the townspeople. *A Festival of Family Classics special. A Rankin-Bass Production in association with Mushi Studios. Color. Half-hour. Premiered: February 25, 1973. Syndicated. Rebroadcast on NICK: April 13, 1993.*

**Voices**
Carl Banas, Len Birman, Bernard Cowan, Peg Dixon, Keith Hampshire, Peggi Loder, Donna Miller, Frank Perry, Henry Ramer, Billie Mae Richards, Alfie Scopp, Paul Soles

### ⊚ TOONS FROM PLANET ORANGE
Half-hour collection of eight animated shorts commissioned by Nickelodeon and directed by animators from various countries including Australia, Germany, Latin America, the United Kingdom, and the United States. The purpose of the special—the first animated project by Nickelodeon's Worldwide Development Group—was "to discover fresh talent from around the globe and provide [them] the opportunity to develop and produce their innovative, irreverent ideas," said Albie Hecht, president of Nickelodeon Film and Television Entertainment, "[as well as] a chance to develop their characters into future Nickelodeon toon stars."

Films showcased included "Agent Green and Ego from Mars" by Kapow Productions, "Snout" by Fudge Puppy Productions, "Helmut and the Killer Nose" by Anton Reidel, "La Hora de Hombre Cacto" by Darío Adanti and Bárbara Perdiguera, "Vida De Sapos" by Metrovisión Post Producción, "Spider and Fly" by Elm Road on the Box and "Hector the Get Over Cat" by John R. Dilworth. The special was simultaneously broadcast on Nickelodeon channels in several different languages around the world. *A NickToons Production. Color. Half-hour. Premiered on NICK: August 22, 1998. Rebroadcast on NICK: August 25, 1998; December 13, 1998.*

### ⊚ TOOT & PUDDLE: "I'LL BE HOME FOR CHRISTMAS"
World traveler Toot visits his Great Aunt Peg in Scotland to celebrate her 100th birthday, while Puddle stays home in Woodcock Pocket to prepare for his return in time to enjoy Christmas with her cousin, Opal, barring a snowstorm preventing him from making it back. Based on the acclaimed children's author and illustrator Holly Hobbie's best-selling book series, this hour-long direct-to-video special bowed on the commercial-free preschool channel, Noggin, and was also released on DVD through Warner Home Video. *A Grand Slamm Children's Films/National Geographic Kids Entertainment Production in association with Warner Home Video and Nelvana. Color. One hour. Premiered on NOG: December 15, 2006.*

### ⊚ TOP CAT AND THE BEVERLY HILLS CATS
The fortunes for Top Cat and his pals (Benny the Ball, Brain, Spook, Fancy and Choo Choo) suddenly change when Benny inherits the Beverly Hills estate of an eccentric old lady. Part of *Hanna-Barbera's Superstars 10* movie package. *A Hanna-Barbera Production. Color. Two hours. Premiered: 1988. Syndicated.*

**Voices**
**Top Cat:** Arnold Stang; **Benny the Ball:** Avery Schreiber; **Choo Choo:** Marvin Kaplan; **Spook/Brain:** Leo de Lyon; **Fancy-Fancy/Officer Dibble:** John Stephenson; **Mrs. Vandergelt:** Linda Gary; **Snerdly:** Henry Polic II; **Rasputin:** Frank Welker; **Kitty Glitter:** Teresa Ganzel; **Sid Buckman/Manager:** Dick Erdman; **Lester Pester:** Rob Paulson; **Warden:** Kenneth Mars

### ⊚ TO THE RESCUE
During summer camp, Davey, his dog Goliath and a group of youngsters form an emergency rescue squad to help a man and his daughter trapped in the wreckage of their light airplane. *A Clokey Production for the Lutheran Church of America. Color. Half-hour. Premiered: 1975. Syndicated.*

**Voices**
**Davey Hansen/Sally Hansen/Mary Hansen:** Norma McMillan, Nancy Wible; **Goliath/John Hansen:** Hal Smith

### ⊚ THE TOWN THAT SANTA FORGOT
In this Emmy-nominated, prime-time holiday special, Dick Van Dyke is the voice of a kindly grandfather who tells his grandchil-

dren the story of Jeremy Creek, a spoiled brat of a boy who learns that it is better to give than receive. *A Hanna-Barbera Production. Color. Half-hour. Premiered on NBC: December 3, 1993.*

**Voices**
**Narrator/Old Jeremy Creek:** Dick Van Dyke; **Young Jeremy Creek:** Miko Hughes; **Granddaughter:** Ashley Johnson; **Santa Claus:** Hal Smith

## ☺ TRANSFORMERS: ARMADA

Hoping to form a powerful alliance with a newly discovered race of Transformers robots, the Autobot and Decepticons fight to the finish to partner up with the Mini-Cons and tilt the future of Earth and the universe in their favor in this 90-minute made-for-television special featuring three half-hour episodes ("First Encounter," "Metamorphosis" and "Base"). Based on Hasbro's best-selling toy franchise, the special, which was redubbed in English, premiered in the United States one week before the regular series' debut on Cartoon Network. *An Aeon Inc./Dangun Pictures/Hangzhou Feilong Donghua/MSJ/Sabella-Dern Entertainment/Hasbro/Cartoon Network Production. Color. Half-hour. Premiered on CAR: August 23, 2002.*

**Voices**
**Rad:** Kirby Morrow; **Carlos:** Matt Hill; **Alexis:** Tabitha St. Germain; **Billy:** Andrew Francis; **Fred:** Tony Sampson; **Optimus Prime:** Gary Chalk; **Hotshot:** Brent Miller; **Red Alert:** Brian Dobson; **Demolisher:** Alvin Sanders; **Cyclonus:** Donald Brown; **Thrust:** Scott McNeil; **Smokescreen:** Dale Wilson; **Narrator:** Jim Conrad

## ☺ TREASURE ISLAND (1971)

In this high-seas journey, young Jim Hawkins joins Long John Silver and his crew of buccaneers in search of the buried treasure. This hour-long special is based on Robert Louis Stevenson's illustrious pirate story. *A Famous Classic Tales special. An Air Programs International Production. Color. One hour. Premiered: November 28, 1971. Syndicated.*

**Voices**
Ron Haddrick, John Kingley, John Llewellyn, Bruce Montague, Brenda Senders, Colin Tilley

## ☺ TREASURE ISLAND (1980)

Young Jim Hawkins's quest to uncover buried treasure and save his life at the same time is recounted in this musical version based on Robert Louis Stevenson's popular adventure story. This time several new faces are added to the standard cast of characters, among them Hiccup the Mouse, Jim's special friend, who keeps him safe although trouble lurks around every corner. The program was originally released in 1972 as a full-length feature and reedited for television broadcast. Melissa Sue Anderson hosted the program. *A Filmation Studios Production in association with Warner Bros. Television. Color. One hour. Premiered on NBC: April 29, 1980. Rebroadcast on NBC: January 31, 1981. Syndicated. Rebroadcast on CAR: August 8, 1995 (Mr. Spim's Cartoon Theatre).*

**Voices**
**Long John Silver:** Richard Dawson; **Captain Flint:** Larry Storch; **Jim Hawkins:** Davy Jones; **Squire Trelawney:** Larry D. Mann; **Mother:** Jane Webb; **Parrot:** Dal McKennon

## ☺ TREASURE ISLAND REVISITED

Long John Silver, Jim Hawkins and the rest of the cast are depicted as animals in this rendition of the familiar children's tale. Made for Japanese television, the program was later dubbed into English and released in the United States. *An American International Television Production in association with Toei Animation and Titan Productions. Color. One hour. Premiered: February 1972. Syndicated.*

## ☺ A TRIBUTE TO MOM

The Disney Channel's look at the importance of mothers through an assemblage of clips culled from memorable Disney cartoons and featuring such popular songs as "Your Mother and Mine," by Sammy Fain and Sammy Cahn, and "The Bare Necessities," sung by Phil Harris. The original 90-minute special (1984) was shortened to an hour and rebroadcast in 1995 with the title *Disney's Salute to Mom. A Film Landa Inc. Production for Disney Channel. Color. Ninety minutes. Premiered on DIS: May 13, 1984.*

**Voices**
**Narrator:** Charles Aidman

## ☺ TROLLIES CHRISTMAS SING-ALONG

When the evil Trouble Trollies steal a Christmas tree to ruin the holidays, the impish Trollies save the day in this half-hour musical sing-along special, featuring the famed Peter Pan Records characters, which premiered on FOX Kids Network. *A PPI/Peter Pan, Inc. Production. Color. Half-hour. Premiered on FOX: December 24, 1993.*

## ☺ THE TROLLS AND THE CHRISTMAS EXPRESS

Christmas is almost ruined when six dastardly trolls dress up as elves to prevent the delivery of toys on Christmas Eve. *A Titlecraft Production in association with Atkinson Film-Arts. Color. Half-hour. Premiered on HBO: December 9, 1981.*

**Voices**
**Trogio:** Hans Conried; **Narrator:** Roger Miller

## ☺ THE TROUBLE WITH MISS SWITCH

A good witch disguised as a schoolteacher enlists two students to help her carry out a special plan to foil the bad witch Saturna and become a witch of good standing again in this two-part fantasy/adventure. *An ABC Weekend Special. A Ruby-Spears Enterprises Production. Color. Half-hour. Premiered on ABC: February 16 and 23, 1980. Rebroadcast on ABC: May 31 and June 7, 1980; September 13 and 20, 1980; April 18 and 25, 1981; July 3 and 10, 1982; January 22 and 29, 1983; May 25 and June 1, 1985; October 14 and 21, 1989.*

**Voices**
**Miss Switch:** Janet Waldo; **Rupert P. Brown III ("Rupe"):** Eric Taslitz; **Amelia Matilda Daley:** Nancy McKeon; **Bathsheba/Saturna:** June Foray

## ☺ TUKIKI AND HIS SEARCH FOR A MERRY CHRISTMAS

A young Eskimo boy travels around the world and experiences the meaning of Christmas through a variety of celebrations. *A Titlecraft Production in association with Atkinson Film-Arts. Color. Half-hour. Premiered (U.S.): December 1979. Syndicated.*

**Voices**
**Tukiki:** Adam Rich; **The North Wind:** Sterling Holloway; **Vocalist:** Stephanie Taylor

## ☺ THE TURKEY CAPER

In this third Chucklewood Critters special, bear cub Buttons and his young fox friend Rusty encounter two young turkeys, who ask for their help in rescuing the wild turkeys of the forest that have been captured. *An Encore Enterprises Production. Color. Half-hour. Premiered: November 1985. Syndicated. Rebroadcast on USA: November 23, 1991; November 21, 1992; November 21, 1993.*

### Voices
**Rusty/Rosie:** Kathy Ritter; **Buttons:** Barbara Goodson; **Ranger Jones:** Bill Boyett; **Abner:** Alvy Moore; **George:** Bill Ratner; **Bridgett:** Morgan Lofting

## ◎ 'TWAS THE NIGHT: A HOLIDAY CELEBRATION
Acclaimed live-action and animated special from producer/director Amy Schatz (HBO's *Through a Child's Eyes: September 11, 2001*) and the makers of the Emmy Award-winning *Goodnight Moon & Other Sleepytime Tales,* blended beloved children's stories and traditional holiday songs with footage of actual children ages four to eight discussing their holiday wishes, hopes and dreams.

Inspired by Grandma Moses's 1948 illustration *The Night before Christmas,* the multicultural half-hour special featured recordings of popular Christmas songs sung by Nat King Cole, Frank Sinatra, Judy Garland, Louis Armstrong and Bette Midler including "Have Yourself a Merry Little Christmas," "Jingle Bells," "Winter Wonderland," "The Christmas Song" and "Hannukah Oh Hannukah," each brought to life by a group of animators, including the final segment "A Visit from St. Nicholas" (a.k.a. "The Night before Christmas"), read by Louis Armstrong in his final recording. The program won a 2002 Emmy Award for outstanding individual achievement in animation for the segments "The Christmas Song," "Feliz Navidad," and "Have Yourself a Merry Little Christmas." *An Amy Schatz/Home Box Office/Michael Sporn Animation Production. Color. Half-hour. Premiered on HBO: December 17, 2001. Rebroadcast on HBO: December 24, 2001; December 25, 2001; December 17, 2002; December 20, 2002; December 24, 2002; December 28, 2002; December 22, 2003; December 24, 2003; December 15, 2004; December 21, 2004; December 24, 2004; December 27, 2004; December 22, 2005; December 24, 2005. Rebroadcast on HBO FAM: December 19, 2001; December 22, 2001; December 23, 2001; December 24, 2001; December 25, 2001; December 26, 2001; December 28, 2001; December 29, 2001; December 30, 2001; December 31, 2001; March 6, 2002; March 9, 2002; March 13, 2002; March 24, 2002; June 4, 2002; June 15, 2002; June 19, 2002; June 28, 2002; September 8, 2002; September 14, 2002; September 17, 2002; September 24, 2002; December 4, 2002; December 15, 2002; December 20, 2002; December 21, 2002; December 24, 2002; December 25, 2002; December 30, 2002; March 11, 2003; March 28, 2003; June 6, 2003; June 11, 2003; June 20, 2003; June 21, 2003; June 25, 2003; June 29, 2003; September 2, 2003; September 9, 2003; September 17, 2003; September 18, 2003; December 5, 2003; December 8, 2003; December 24, 2003; December 25, 2003; December 28, 2003; December 29, 2003; December 31, 2003; March 4, 2004; March 9, 2004; March 30, 2004; July 4, 2004; July 8, 2004; July 19, 2004; July 24, 2004; November 22, 2004; November 23, 2004; November 25, 2004; November 26, 2004; November 30, 2004; December 9, 2004; December 10, 2004; December 20, 2004; December 24, 2004; December 25, 2004; April 1, 2005; April 12, 2005; April 17, 2005; April 19, 2005; April 22, 2005; April 26, 2005; July 4, 2005; July 5, 2005; July 8, 2005; July 24, 2005; July 27, 2005; October 5, 2005; October 8, 2005; October 19, 2005; October 24, 2005; December 4, 2005; December 10, 2005; December 13, 2005; December 17, 2005; December 20, 2005; December 24, 2005; December 25, 2005; December 26, 2005; March 3, 2006; March 10, 2006; March 11, 2006; March 17, 2006; March 20, 2006; March 25, 2006; July 2, 2006; July 7, 2006; July 12, 2006; July 17, 2006; July 22, 2006; July 27, 2006; July 30,* *2006; October 5, 2006; October 11, 2006; December 2, 2006; December 10, 2006; December 20, 2006; December 24, 2006; December 25, 2006; December 27, 2006.*

## ◎ 'TWAS THE NIGHT BEFORE BUMPY
Mr. Bumpy and his pal Squishington take a trip to the North Pole to snag some of Santa's presents. En route, they become sidetracked and held captive in the jungles of Peru by an earthworm soldier (voiced by Cheech Marin), in this 90-minute Saturday-morning special spunoff from the popular television series, *Bump in the Night. A Danger/Greengrass Production. Color. Ninety minutes. Premiered on ABC: December 19, 1995. Rebroadcast on ABC: December 14, 1996.*

## ◎ 'TWAS THE NIGHT BEFORE CHRISTMAS
The hearts of every child in Junctionville are broken when their letters to Santa Claus are returned marked "Not Accepted by Addressee!" Father Mouse sets out to find the culprit responsible so his children and others are not disappointed in this holiday special loosely based on Clement Moore's Christmas poem. *A Rankin-Bass Production. Color. Half-hour. Premiered on CBS: December 8, 1974. Rebroadcast on CBS: December 9, 1975; December 17, 1976; December 12, 1977; December 18, 1978; December 8, 1979; December 13, 1980; December 16, 1981; December 18, 1982; December 14, 1983; December 11, 1984; December 4, 1985; December 17, 1986; December 9, 1987; December 8, 1990; December 11, 1991; December 24, 1992; December 23, 1993. Rebroadcast on FAM: December 9, 1995; December 11, 1996. Rebroadcast on FOX FAM: December 2, 1998; December 6, 1998; December 24, 1998; December 3, 2000; December 9, 2000; December 12, 2000; December 13, 2000; December 20, 2000; December 24, 2000; December 25, 2000. Rebroadcast on ABC FAM: December 1, 2001; December 3, 2001; December 12, 2001; December 20, 2001; December 24, 2001; December 5, 2002; December 11, 2002; December 16, 2002; December 24, 2002; December 2, 2003; December 6, 2003; December 18, 2003; December 22, 2003; December 1, 2004; December 4, 2004; December 13, 2004; December 19, 2004; December 24, 2004; December 1, 2005; December 3, 2005; December 6, 2005; December 24, 2005; December 5, 2006; December 9, 2006; December 24, 2006.*

### Voices
**Joshua Trundel, the Clockmaker (narrator):** Joel Grey; **Albert Mouse:** Tammy Grimes; **Mayor of Junctionville:** John McGiver; **Father Mouse:** George Gobel; **Vocalists:** The Wee Winter Singers

## ◎ TWEETY'S HIGH FLYING ADVENTURE
To raise enough cash to save a local children's park, Granny wagers that Tweety can fly around the world in 80 days with Sylvester in tow hoping to finally catch the yellow canary himself in this 72-minute feature-length direct-to-DVD adventure that premiered on Cartoon Network. *A Warner Bros. Television Animation Production. Color. Seventy-two minutes. Premiered on CAR: April 13, 2002.*

### Voices
**Tweety/Sylvester:** Joe Alaskey; **Granny:** June Foray; **Other Voices:** Julie Bernstein, Steve Bernstein, Jim Cummings, Stan Freberg, Elizabeth Lamers, Tress MacNeille, Pat Musick, Rob Paulsen, Frank Welker

## ◎ TWELVE DAYS OF CHRISTMAS
Based on that age-old Christmas carol ("12 lords-a-leaping, 11 ladies dancing, 10 pipers piping" . . . not to mention "a partridge

in a pear tree") a blowhard boss, Sir Carolbloomer, wants to use the abovementioned gifts to woo the gloomy Princess Silverbelle. The program was premiered on NBC opposite another new Hanna-Barbera Christmas special, *The Town That Santa Forgot*. *A Hanna-Barbera Production. Color. Half-hour. Premiered on NBC: December 3, 1993.*

**Voices**
Carter Cathcart, John Crenshaw, Donna Divino, Merwin Goldsmith, Earl Hammond, Phil Hartman, Larry Kenny, Frank Sims, Marcia Savella

## ◎ 12 TINY CHRISTMAS TALES

First prime-time animated special by award-winning independent animator Bill Plympton featuring a series of Christmas tales based on cards he created over the years. Plympton told an interviewer that working with the Cartoon Network's then-head of programming, Linda Simensky, was a "dream" and the "only restriction was [to] make it funny." *A Plympton Production. Color. Half-hour. Premiered on CAR: December 21, 2001.*

## ◎ 20,000 LEAGUES UNDER THE SEA (1972)

Scientific journalist Pierre Aronnax, his 16-year-old assistant Conrad, and famed harpooner Ned Land join Captain Nemo for a fantastic undersea journey to the fabled lost continent of Atlantis in this two-part special based on Jules Verne's famous novel. *A Festival of Family Classics special. A Rankin-Bass Production in association with Mushi Studios. Color. One hour. Premiered: October 1972. Syndicated.*

**Voices**
Carl Banas, Len Birman, Bernard Cowan, Peg Dixon, Keith Hampshire, Peggi Loder, Donna Miller, Frank Perry, Henry Ramer, Billie Mae Richards, Alfie Scopp, Paul Soles

## ◎ 20,000 LEAGUES UNDER THE SEA (1973)

Captain Nemo dispels the rumor about a giant sea monster by bringing his ship *Nautilus* to the surface and making believers out of marine research scientist Pierre Aronnax and famed harpooner Ned Land. *A Famous Classic Tales special. A Hanna-Barbera Production. Color. Half-hour. Premiered on CBS: November 22, 1973. Rebroadcast on CBS: November 16, 1974. Syndicated.*

**Voices**
Tim Elliott, Ron Haddrick, Don Pascoe, John Stephenson

## ◎ 20,000 LEAGUES UNDER THE SEA (2002)

Jules Verne's classic novel inspired this feature-length animated adaptation following the famed reclusive genius Captain Nemo as he takes a group of captive adventurers on a perilous undersea voyage on his magnificent, highly advanced submarine, *The Nautilus*, in this last original made-for-TV movie aired as part of Nickelodeon DIC's *Incredible Movie Toons* series. *A DIC Entertainment Production. Color. Ninety minutes. Premiered on NICK: December 29, 2002.*

**Voices**
**Captain Nemo:** John Lee; **Bernadette:** Jennifer Andrews Anderson; **Dr. Aronnax:** Anthony Clark-Kaczmarek; **Delivery Boy:** Nils Haaland; **Darren:** Michael Hartig; **Farragut:** Matt Kamprath; **Grace:** Hannah Koslosky; **Conseil:** Jerry Longe; **Jason:** Andy Monbouquette; **Diver:** Ryle Smith: **Reporter:** Paul Sosso; **Bernadette's Father:** Tony Wike; **Ned:** D. Kevin Williams

## ◎ TWINKLE TWINKLE LITTLE STAR

A young girl (Lea), who should be practicing her violin, fiddles with her dad's super telescope and, with her dog Paggy and a very young rematerialized Mozart, float through space and come upon a tap-dancing star named Twinkle. From CINAR Films' *The Real Story of . . .* series. *A CINAR Films/France Animation Production in association with Western Publishing Company/The Family Channel/Telefilm Canada/Cofimage 3. Color. Half-hour. Premiered on HBO: January 22, 1994.*

**Voices**
**Twinkle:** Vanna White; **Mozart:** Martin Short

## ◎ THE 2000 YEAR OLD MAN

Carl Reiner and Mel Brooks wrote and created this half-hour animated special, geared more toward adults than children, featuring an interviewer (Reiner) talking about life with a 2,000-year-old man who has lived a full life. ("When I say 'the old days' I don't mean the George M. Cohan days!") Dialogue for the special was recorded before a live studio audience. *A Crossbow/Acre Enterprises Production in association with Leo Salkin Films. Color. Half-hour. Premiered on CBS: January 11, 1975. Rebroadcast on CBS: April 11, 1975. Syndicated.*

**Voices**
**Interviewer:** Carl Reiner; **Old Man:** Mel Brooks

## ◎ THE UGLY DUCKLING

Award-winning singer/actress Cher narrates this adaptation of the beloved Hans Christian Andersen fairy tale about a lonely outcast duckling who is transformed into a beautiful swan. Produced in 1987, it was shown two years later on Showtime as part of Rabbit Ears Video's *Storybook Classics* series. *A Rabbit Ears Video Production. Color. Half-hour. Premiered on SHO: 1989.*

## ◎ UNCLE ELEPHANT

Based on the award-winning book by author-illustrator Arnold Lobel, this animated musical relates a sensitive story about the special bond between a wistful young elephant who mourns the disappearance of his parents at sea and his older Uncle Elephant, who introduces his nephew to a world full of hope and wonder. This beautifully animated half-hour premiered on PBS's *Long Ago & Far Away* series. *A Churchill Films/WGBH Boston Production. Color. Half-hour. Premiered on PBS: October 26, 1991. Rebroadcast on PBS: September 27, 1992.*

**Voices**
Pat Musick, Will Ryan

## ◎ UNCLE SAM MAGOO

Myopic Mr. Magoo wanders through the full spectrum of American history and encounters the likes of George Washington, Ben Franklin, Davy Crockett, Mark Twain and Paul Bunyan in this well-written animated special with a lively musical score by award-winning composer Walter Scharf. *A UPA Production. Color. One hour. Premiered on NBC: February 15, 1970. Syndicated. Rebroadcast on DIS: June 23, 1992; June 29, 1992; June 15, 1993; July 9, 1993.*

**Voices**
**Mr. Magoo:** Jim Backus; **Uncle Sam/John Alden/Miles/Standish/Paul Revere/Davy Crockett/James Marshall/Johnny Appleseed/Captain John Parker/Robert E. Lee/Daniel Webster/John F. Kennedy:** Lennie Weinrib; **Mark Twain/John Sutter/President/Daniel Boone/Patrick Henry/U.S. Grant/Martin Luther

*Mr. Magoo retraces moments in American history in a scene from the NBC network special* Uncle Sam Magoo. *© UPA Productions*

King/Abraham Lincoln: Barney Phillips; **Indian Chief (American)/Indian Chief (Tropical)/John Smith/Powhattan/Massasoit/Francis Scott Key/Kit Carson/Paul Bunyan/Franklin D. Roosevelt/Harry Truman/Wendell Willkie:** Bob Holt; **Leif Ericson/Columbus/Elder Brewster/Tom Paine/Thomas Jefferson/Woodrow Wilson:** Dave Shelley; **Priscilla/Betsy Ross/Tom Sawyer/Amelia Earhart/Eleanor Roosevelt/Susan B. Anthony:** Patti Gilbert; **George Washington/Walt Whitman/Oliver Wendell Holmes:** John Himes; **Dwight D. Eisenhower/Herbert Hoover/Carl Sandburg:** Bill Clayton; **Benjamin Franklin/Thomas Wolfe/George Washington Carver:** Sid Grossfield; **Others:** Sam Rosen

## ⊚ UP ON THE HOUSETOP

In this half-hour syndicated Christmas special Curtis Calhoun just isn't in the mood for Christmas and wishes it would all go away. It appears he has gotten his wish, at least until he finds a strange little man in a red suit stuck in his chimney on Christmas Eve. *A Perennial Pictures Film Corporation Production. Color. Half-hour. Premiered: November 1993. Syndicated.*

### Voices
**Curtis Calhoun/Dad/David/Santa:** Jerry Reynolds; **Gash:** Russ Harris; **Mrs. Wimbley:** Rachel Rutledge; **Reporter:** Natalie Bridgegroom Harris; **Mr. Peterson:** Michael N. Ruggiero

## ⊚ VEGGIETALES CHRISTMAS SPECTACULAR

Bob the Tomato, Larry the Cucumber, Annie, Wally P. Nezzer, the Pea Family, including Percy Pea and Li'l Pea, the Carrot Family and the rest of the VeggieTales gang star in this inspirational and educational computer-animated half-hour children's special teaching children that Christmas is about the greatest gift of all: the birth of baby Jesus. Featuring the original VeggieTales episode, "The Toy That Saved Christmas" (1996), plus more than 10 minutes of new animation, this CGI-animated half-hour special premiered in December 1998 on PAX. *A Big Idea Production. Color. Half-hour. Premiered on PAX: December 1998. Rebroadcast on PAX: November 27, 1999; December 16, 2000.*

### Voices
**Bob the Tomato/Grandpa George/Mr. Nezzer/Mr. Lunt/Pa Grape/Scallion/Dad Carrot/Dad Pea/Percy Pea:** Phil Vischer; **Larry the Cucumber:** Mike Nawrocki; *Buzzsaw Louie:* Mike Sage; **Junior Asparagus/Mom Asparagus:** Lisa Vischer; **Annie:** Phoebe Vischer

## ⊚ THE VELVETEEN RABBIT (1985)

Academy Award winning actress Meryl Streep narrates the story of a velveteen toy rabbit given to a small boy at Christmas. The rabbit is made real by the child's love in this award-winning half-hour, part of Rabbit Ear Video's *Storybook Classics* series. *A Rabbit Ears Production in association with Random House Home Video. Color. Half-hour. Premiered on PBS: March 9–24, 1985. Rebroadcast on SHO: December 10, 1991. Rebroadcast on ABC (ABC Weekend Special): April 11, 1992. Rebroadcast on SHO: April 29, 1992; May 7, 1992; May 18, 1992. Rebroadcast on ABC (ABC Weekend Special): March 13, 1993; December 23, 1995.*

### Voices
**Narrator:** Meryl Streep; **Velveteen Rabbit/Little Princess:** Marie Osmond; **The Little Boy:** Joshua Tenney; **Rabbit #1:** Craig Call; **Rabbit #3:** Jason Ayon; **Other Voices:** Chub Bailey, Josh Rodine

## ⊚ THE VELVETEEN RABBIT (1985)

Margery Williams's classic tale of a stuffed toy rabbit who comes to life in this special narrated by actor Christopher Plummer. *An Atkinson Film-Arts Production in association with Telefilm Canada and CTV. Color. Half-hour. Premiered (U.S.): April, 1985. Syndicated.*

### Voices
**Jones:** Don Westwood; **Tin Soldier:** Jim Bradford; **Rabbit #1/Rabbit #2:** Rick Jones; **Skin Horse:** Bernard McManus; **Doctor:** Eddie Nunn; **Fairy Queen:** Charity Brown; **Narrator:** Christopher Plummer

## ⊚ THE VELVETEEN RABBIT (1985)

Young Robert's favorite Christmas gift is a velveteen toy rabbit named Velvee. The special friendship they share is threatened when Robert turns seriously ill and Velvee is on the verge of being destroyed. *A Hanna-Barbera Production. Color. Half-hour. Premiered on ABC: April 20, 1985. Rebroadcast on ABC: October 19, 1985; December 20, 1986.*

### Voices
**Velvee:** Chub Bailey; **Robert:** Josh Rodine; **Skin Horse/Nana:** Marilyn Lightstone; **Father:** Peter Cullen; **Tug:** Bill Scott; **Scungilli:** Barry Dennen; **Spinner:** Hal Smith; **Mouse:** Frank Welker; **Brenda:** Jodi Carlisle; **Harry:** Brian Cummings; **Mother/Nursery Fairy:** Beth Clopton

## ⊚ THE VENTURE BROS.: "A VERY VENTURE CHRISTMAS"

Dr. Venture finds he still has shopping left to do for his annual Christmas Eve bash; Brock demonstrates his own yuletide traditions; Dean and Hank, who still think Santa is real, unlock a magical demon who plans to kill all of the guests at Dr. Venture's party; and the Monarch reveals plans to destroy the Ventures' campground as a gift for Dr. Girlfriend in this half-hour Christmas special, based on the popular *Adult Swim* series for Cartoon Network. *A Noodlesoup/Astro Base Go! Production. Color. Half-hour. Premiered on CAR: December 19, 2004.*

### Voices
**Dr. Thaddius S. "Rusty" Venture/The Phantom Limb:** James Urbaniak; **Hank Venture/the Monarch/Peter White:** Christopher McCulloch; **Dean Venture:** Michael Sinterniklaas; **Brock Samson:** Patrick Warburton; **Dr. Girlfriend/Master Billy Boy:** Doc Hammer; **Triana Orpheus:** Lisa Hammer; **Dr. Byron Orpheus:** Steven Ratazzi; **H.E.L.P.eR.:** Soul Bot

## ⊚ THE VENTURE BROS.: "THE TERRIBLE SECRET OF TURTLE BAY"

Acting like castoffs from the 1960s with a penchant for using outdated vocabulary, thrill-seeking identical twins Hank and Dean Venture head out on a wild adventure with their famous scientist father, Dr. Venture, and their loyal bodyguard, Brock Samson, encountering everything from ninjas to strange-looking zombies in this half-hour animated pilot special that debuted on Cartoon Network's *Adult Swim* programming block. The program launched the short-lived action adventure series of the same name that debuted in August 2004. *A Noodlesoup Production. Color. Half-hour. Premiered on CAR: February 16, 2003.*

*Voices*

**Dr. Thaddeus Venture/Other Voices:** James Urbaniak; **Hank Venture/the Monarch/Other Voices:** Christopher McCullough; **Dean Venture/Other Voices:** Michael Sinterniklaas; **Brock Samson:** Patrick Warburton; **Dr. Girlfriend/Master Billy Quizboy/Other Voices:** Doc Hammer

## ⊚ A VERY BARRY CHRISTMAS

A luckless Australian entrepreneur and unlikely hero, Barry Buckley, who provides shelter to animals in need, accidentally trades lives with Santa Claus following a chance meeting between them, resulting in a mix-up of epic proportions and whirlwind magical Christmas adventure from the snow-capped North Pole to the sun-drenched Australian Outback, in this stop-motion animated special produced in 2004 by Toronto's Cuppa Coffee Animation for CBC network. A year later, the prime-time program debuted in the United States on ABC Family. The special's voice cast includes Canadian comedian Colin Mochrie (of TV's *Who's Line Is It Anyway?*) as Santa Claus and Australian icon Roy Billing as Barry Buckley. *A Cuppa Coffee Animation Production. Color. Half-hour. Premiered on ABC FAM: December 3, 2005. Rebroadcast on ABC FAM: December 20, 2005.*

*Voices*

**Santa Claus:** Colin Mochrie; **Barry Buckley:** Roy Billing; **Nutmeg Reindeer:** Jacqueline Pillon; **Mrs. Claus:** Shannon Lawson; **Lily:** Gail Knight; **Walter:** Michael Lamport; **Nigel:** Lily Jim Pike; **Dasher:** Phil Williams; **Warrun:** Aaron Pederson; **Polar Bear:** Stewart Horsley; **Ms. Hollyjolly:** Deanna Aubert

## ⊚ THE VERY FIRST NOEL

Created by award-winning animation team Carrie and Yarrow Cheney as a seven-year labor of love, this stunning 3-D computer-animated half-hour holiday program, made in the tradition of other classic animated Christmas specials from the '60s and '70s, retells one of the world's most beloved biblical stories: the tale of Melchior, one of the Three Wise Men—in musical rhyme and narrated by Andy Griffith as the voice of Melchior—who traveled from the east to see the newborn King of Kings. The new animated Christmas special premiered on DirecTV on Thanksgiving Day Eve and aired daily through December 2006. The program's captivating soundtrack of Christmas carols was performed by the Brothers Cazimero from Hawaii. *An Exclaim Entertainment Production. Color. Half-hour. Premiered on DirecTV: November 24, 2006. Rebroadcast on DirecTV: November 25, 2006-December 31, 2006.*

*Voices*

**Melchior:** Andy Griffith; **Mary:** Catherine Gilbert; **Joseph/Tall Shepherd:** Ernie Gilbert; **Gabriel Herod:** Steve Twitchell; **Caspar/Scribe:** Rod Goldfarb; **Balthasar:** Ben Chambers; **Inn Keeper:** Jonna Wiseman; **Short Shepherd/Caesar/Tax Man/Townsperson:** Matthew W. Taylor

## ⊚ A VERY MERRY CRICKET

Chester C. Cricket returns in this sequel to 1973's *The Cricket in Times Square*, this time with pals Tucker R. Mouse and Harry the Cat. Tired of the cacophony and commercialism of Manhattan yuletide, they set off from Connecticut to return Chester to the Big Apple and use his musical attributes to bring the real meaning back to Christmas. *A Chuck Jones Enterprises Production. Color. Half-hour. Premiered on ABC: December 14, 1973. Rebroadcast on ABC: November 28, 1974; December 5, 1978. Syndicated. Rebroadcast on NICK: December 22, 1991; December 9, 1993.*

*Voices*

**Chester C. Cricket/Harry the Cat:** Les Tremayne; **Tucker the Mouse/Alley Cat:** Mel Blanc

## ⊚ A VERY SPECIAL ACTION LEAGUE NOW! SPECIAL

Four hapless crimefighting action-figure heroes, known as the Action League (from Nickelodeon's *Kablam!* series), take on two missions—first, to save the pop star Blandi (voiced by Swedish singer Robyn) from a marauding robot, then to rescue Stinky Diver from the clutches of the dreaded canine Spotzilla, in their first prime-time special. *A Nickelodeon Production. Color. Half-hour. Premiered on NICK: March 28, 1998.*

*Voices*

**The Chief:** Victor Hart; **Meltman/Announcer:** Scott Paulsen; **ThunderGirl:** Chris Winters; **The Flesh/Stinky Diver/The Mayor/Bill the Lab Guy/Johnny Cool:** Jim Krenn; **Justice:** Alyssa Grahm; **Generic Boy:** Stephen Gaich

## ⊚ VIRTUAL BILL

When President Bill Clinton made his State of the Union Address to the nation in January of 1998, MTV countered with this computer-animated special featuring America's first artificially intelligent bio-digital President who engaged in his own one-hour "fireside chat." The special was written and voiced by Scott Dikkers. *An MTV Animation Production. Color. One hour. Premiered on MTV: January 27, 1998.*

*Voice*

**Virtual Bill:** Scott Dikkers

## ⊚ VOLTRON: DEFENDER OF THE UNIVERSE

In the 25th century, Voltron, a giant flying samurai robot, battles the evil reptile alien King Zorkon of Planet Doom and his army in this 90-minute feature-length cartoon, first syndicated in 1983. The special, shown in 76 markets, was the "pilot" for the weekly half-hour series of the same name, which premiered a year later. *A World Events Production. Color. Ninety minutes. Premiered: 1983. Syndicated.*

*Voices*

Jack Angel, Michael Bell, Peter Cullen, Tress MacNeille, Neil Ross, B.J. Ward, Lennie Weinrib

## ⊚ WALKING WITH DINOSAURS

Prime-time Emmy Award-winning special for outstanding animated program (for programming more than one hour) examining the Triassic, Jurassic and Cretaceous eras when prehistoric beasts dominated Earth. The special preceded the popular weekly, half-hour, state-of-the-art CGI-animated series narrated by Ben Stiller and produced by the BBC for Discovery Kids and NBC. The special was narrated by actor Avery Brooks (with actor Kenneth Branagh doing the honors in the BBC original), and the three-hour extravaganza showed in prime-time on the Discovery Channel with segments from the special rebroadcast in the spin-off series. *A Stone House Productions/BBC/Discovery Channel Production. Color. Three hours. Premiered on DSC: April 16, 2000.*

**Voices**
**Narrator:** Avery Brooks

### ⊚ WALKING WITH PREHISTORIC BEASTS

The rise of forgotten prehistoric mammals over the last 49 million years, including the immense Indricothere, is revealed in this three-hour digitally animated special, combining digital technology and animatronics, which debuted on cable's Discovery Channel. Winner of a 2002 Emmy Award for outstanding animated program (for programming one hour or more), footage from this and the previous special, *Walking with Dinosaurs* (2001), was incorporated into the popular weekly Discovery Kids and NBC series *Walking with Dinosaurs. A Stone House Productions/BBC/Discovery Channel Production. Color. Three hours. Premiered on DSC: December 9, 2001.*

**Voices**
**Narrator:** Avery Brooks

### ⊚ WALLACE & GROMIT'S A GRAND DAY OUT

The absent-minded, cheese-addicted inventor, Wallace, and his mute dog companion, Gromit, go to great lengths when they realize they have run out of cheese and travel to the moon since "everybody knows the moon is made of cheese" in this Oscar-nominated short subject, directed and animated by creator/animator Nick Park for British animation giant Aardman Animations. Produced in 1989, the 24-minute film premiered as a half-hour Saturday-morning special on FOX in 1995. *An Aardman Animations Production. Color. Half-hour. Premiered on FOX: September 30, 1995.*

**Voices**
**Wallace:** Peter Sallis

### ⊚ WALT DISNEY PRESENTS SPORT GOOFY'S OLYMPIC GAMES SPECIAL

Like the previously syndicated "Sports Goofy" specials, this version features a selection of memorable Goofy sports cartoons, among them, "Olympic Champ" (1942), "Goofy Gymnastics" (1949), "How to Swim" (1942) and "The Art of Self-Defense" (1941). *A Walt Disney Television Production. Color. Half-hour. Premiered: June 8, 1984. Syndicated.*

**Voices**
**Goofy:** Pinto Colvig, George Johnson

### ⊚ WALT DISNEY'S MICKEY AND DONALD PRESENTS SPORT GOOFY

Athletic competition and sporting events comprise this half-hour compilation special starring lovable dope Goofy in a collection of theatrical shorts from the 1940s, including "How to Play Baseball" (1942), "How to Swim" (1942) and "Tennis Racquet" (1949). *A Walt Disney Television Production. Color. Half-hour. Premiered: May 21–June 12, 1983. Syndicated.*

**Voices**
**Goofy:** Pinto Colvig, George Johnson

### ⊚ WALT DISNEY'S MICKEY AND DONALD PRESENTS SPORT GOOFY #2

Goofy returns in this second in a series of half-hour compilation specials of sports-oriented cartoons: "How to Play Football" (1944), "Goofy's Glider" (1940) and "Get Rich Quick" (1951). *A Walt Disney Television Production. Color. Half-hour. Premiered: August 21, 1983–September 24, 1983. Syndicated.*

**Voices**
**Goofy:** Pinto Colvig, George Johnson

### ⊚ WALT DISNEY'S MICKEY AND DONALD PRESENTS SPORT GOOFY #3

In his third sports spoof special, Goofy is featured in four memorable cartoons originally released to theaters: "Hockey Homicide" (1945), "Double Dribble" (1946), "The Art of Skiing" (1941) and "Aquamania" (1961). *A Walt Disney Television Production. Color. Half-hour. Premiered: November 6–December 19, 1983. Syndicated.*

**Voices**
**Goofy:** Pinto Colvig, George Johnson

### ⊚ WALT DISNEY'S MICKEY, DONALD AND SPORT GOOFY: GETTING WET

Goofy, Mickey Mouse, Pluto, Donald Duck and Chip and Dale are all featured in this half-hour special—part of a continuing series of Goofy sports specials—originally produced for syndication. Among the cartoons featured are: "The Simple Things" (1953), starring Mickey Mouse and Pluto; "Chips Ahoy" (1956), featuring that pesky pair Chip and Dale; and "Aquamania" (1961), with Goofy. *A Walt Disney Production. Half-hour. Color. Premiered: September 14, 1984. Syndicated.*

**Voices**
**Goofy:** Pinto Colvig; **Mickey Mouse:** Jim MacDonald; **Donald Duck:** Clarence Nash

### ⊚ WALT DISNEY'S MICKEY, DONALD AND SPORT GOOFY: HAPPY HOLIDAYS

Mickey Mouse, Donald Duck and Goofy star in a collection of old cartoon shorts in this holiday season compilation entitled *Happy Holidays.* The show features "Pluto's Christmas Tree" (1952), "The Clock Watcher" (1945) and "How to Ride a Horse" from *The Reluctant Dragon* (1941) full-length feature. *A Walt Disney Television Production. Color. Half-hour. Premiered: December 14, 1984. Syndicated.*

**Voices**
**Mickey Mouse:** Jim MacDonald; **Donald Duck:** Clarence Nash; **Goofy:** Pinto Colvig

### ⊚ WALT DISNEY'S MICKEY, DONALD AND SPORT GOOFY SHOW: SNOWTIME

Subtitled *Snowtime,* various Disney characters appear in this first-run special presenting a collection of previously released cartoons, including "Lend a Paw" (1941), "Chip 'n' Dale" (1947) and "How to Fish" (1942). *A Walt Disney Television Production. Color. Half-hour. Premiered: November 30, 1984.*

**Voices**
**Mickey Mouse:** Jim MacDonald; **Donald Duck:** Clarence Nash; **Goofy:** Pinto Colvig

### ⊚ WALTER MELON: "THE FAR FLOWER RANGERS"/"THE MARK OF ZORRO"

Notoriously rotund and clumsy "Hero for Hire" Walter Melon saves the world by filling in for literary and comic book superheroes and pop culture characters from film and television in this half-hour Saturday-morning preview special, comprised of two episodes that aired Saturday morning on FOX and preceded the debut of the weekly, English-dubbed and French-animated series on FOX Family Channel. *A Saban France Production. Color. Half-hour. Premiered on FOX: August 8, 1998.*

**Voices**
David Kaye, Michael McConnohie, Mary Kay Bergman, Dave Mallow

## ◎ WEEP NO MORE, MY LADY

In the Mississippi backwoods, Skeeter, a 13-year-old boy, adopts a stray dog, (he names My Lady) and accepts a challenge from Alligator Ike to see whose dog is the best. *An ABC Weekend Special. A Ruby-Spears Enterprises Production. Color. Half-hour. Premiered on ABC: February 10, 1979. Rebroadcast on ABC: May 19, 1979; September 8, 1979; July 19, 1980; May 30, 1981; September 5, 1981; April 9, 1983; June 2, 1984; May 30, 1981; September 5, 1981; April 9, 1983; June 2, 1984.*

**Voices**
**Skeeter:** Jeremy Lawrence; **Uncle Jess:** Alan Oppenheimer; **Alligator Ike:** Larry D. Mann; **Mr. Rackman:** Michael Rye

## ◎ WEIRD HAROLD

Fat Albert relies on Weird Harold to participate with the group in the Great Go-Cart Race. Unfortunately, the race turns into disaster when Weird Harold and Young Bill crash their soap-box derbies and are arrested. This program was the second Fat Albert special following 1969's *Hey, Hey, Hey, It's Fat Albert. A Filmation Associates Production in association with Bill Cosby Productions. Color. Half-hour. Premiered on NBC: May 4, 1973. Rebroadcast on NBC: September 7, 1973.*

**Voices**
**Fat Albert/Mushmouth/Young Bill/Father:** Bill Cosby; **Weird Harold:** Gerald Edwards; **Judge:** Henry Silva

## ◎ WELCOME TO ELTINGVILLE: "BRING ME THE HEAD OF BOBA FETT"

Animated comedy series pilot based on Evan Dorkin's comic book, *Dork*, about the comical exploits of four nerdy teenagers—Jason Harris, Troy Metcalf, Corey Brill, and Larc Spies—and their outlandish dorky adventures, from sneaking into science fiction and horror movies to tracking down rare action-figure collectibles, as members of the Eltingville Club, a science fiction, horror, comic book and fantasy gaming club they organized and operate. The premiere episode, titled "Bring Me the Head of Boba Fett," debuted on Cartoon Network's *Adult Swim* on March 3, 2002, but never went beyond the pilot stage to become a weekly series. Besides re-airing the special, on November 7, 2005, Cartoon Network featured it on AdultSwim.com.'s *Friday Night Fix.*

Dorkin formerly created the acerbic *Milk & Cheese: Dairy Products Gone Bad* comics and was a writer on Cartoon Network's popular live-action/animated talk show, *Space Ghost Coast to Coast* and the WB's *Superman* animated series. The program's opening and closing themes were written and performed by the Aquabats. *A Cartoon Network Studios Production. Color. Half-hour. Premiered on CAR: March 3, 2002 (Adult Swim).*

**Voices**
**Jason Harris:** Bill Dickey; **Troy Metcalf:** Josh levy; **Corey Brill:** Jerry Stokes; **Larc Spies:** Pete DiNunzio; **Chris Ward:** Ward Willoughby; **Tara Sands:** Jane Dickey; **Evan Dorkin:** Ironjaw.

## ◎ WE WISH YOU A MERRY CHRISTMAS (1996)

A shellless turtle named Harold, who uses an army helmet as a substitute, suddenly becomes popular (under the name of Bob)—that is, until he is called upon to save the life of a drowning baby turtle. *A Perennial Pictures Film Corporation Production. Color. Half-hour. Premiered on FAM: December 5, 1996.*

**Voices**
**Harold (Bob):** Scott Tyring; **Monsieur Volture:** Jerry Reynolds; **Celeste:** Rachel Rutledge; **Mother Turtle:** Lisa Buetow; **Butch:** Russ Harris

## ◎ WE WISH YOU A MERRY CHRISTMAS (1998)

The amazing story of how Christmas carols evolved and how the tiny town of Harmony, including three down-on-their-luck orphans (Ollie, Ted and Cindy), rediscovered the true spirit of Christmas in this 1998-produced, magical, music-filled holiday special, featuring the vocal talents of Nell Carter, Lacey Chabert, John Forsythe, Travis Tritt and others. In August 2002, Lionsgate Home Entertainment released the hour-long production on DVD. Three years later, the program was broadcast on Cartoon Network. *A Lionsgate Home Entertainment Production. Color. One hour. Premiered on CAR: December 20, 2005.*

**Voices**
**Ollie:** Tahj Mowry; **Ted:** Elizabeth Daily; **Cindy:** Lacey Chabert; **Mr. Ryan:** John Forsythe; **Mrs. Claus:** Nell Carter; **Little Reindeer:** Travis Tritt; **Little Girl/Old Woman/Little Boy/Boy/Mom/Young Woman:** Jeannie Elias; **Santa/Man#1/Angry Man/Elves:** Jess Harnell; **Singers:** Randall Crissman, Scott Haskell, Laura Lively, Kellie Coffey, Scott Finch, Geoff Koch, James W. Lively

## ◎ WHAT A NIGHTMARE, CHARLIE BROWN

After devouring too much pizza, Snoopy has a nightmare that he is at the North Pole as part of a husky dog sled team and, in the adventures that follow, attempts to adapt to being a "real dog." After premiering on CBS, the special was rebroadcast on the network and cable giant Nickelodeon. *A Lee Mendelson–Bill Melendez Production in association with Charles M. Schulz Creative Associates and United Feature Syndicate. Color. Half-hour. Premiered on CBS: February 23, 1978. Rebroadcast on CBS: April 13, 1987. Rebroadcast on NICK: January 25, 1998; February 11, 1998; March 13, 1998; April 16, 1998; May 18, 1998; June 19, 1998; July 20, 1998; August 21, 1998; September 22, 1998; November 6, 1998; December 10, 1998; February 27, 1998; April 23, 1999; June 12, 1999; August 10, 1999; December 11, 1999.*

**Voices**
**Charlie Brown:** Liam Martin; **Snoopy:** Bill Melendez

## ◎ WHAT HAVE WE LEARNED, CHARLIE BROWN?

In this mostly serious and reflective Memorial Day salute, Charlie Brown reminisces about the *Peanuts* group's adventures while taking part in a student-exchange program in France. Their visit to Omaha Beach triggers a retelling of the D-day attack in animation and newsreel footage. A later visit to the World War I battlefield of Ypres in Belgium sparks historical views on the "war to end all wars," with Linus movingly reciting John McCrae's famous poem, "In Flanders Field." *Peanuts* creator Charles Schulz hosted the program. Bowing in prime time on CBS, the network subsequently rebroadcast the special before moving to Nickelodeon as part of a package of *Peanuts* programs in 1998. *A Lee Mendelson–Bill*

*Melendez Production in association with Charles M. Schulz Creative Associates and United Feature Syndicate. Color. Half-hour. Premiered on CBS: May 30, 1983. Rebroadcast on CBS: May 26, 1984; May 29, 1989. Rebroadcast on NICK: May 4, 1998; May 18, 1998.*

**Voices**
**Charlie Brown:** Brad Kesten; **Sally Brown:** Stacey Heather Tolkin; **Linus Van Pelt:** Jeremy Schoenberg; **Marcie/Shermy:** Michael Dockery; **Peppermint Patty:** Victoria Vargas; **French Madam:** Monica Parker; **Snoopy:** Bill Melendez

### ◎ WHEN DINOSAURS ROAMED AMERICA

Actor/comedian John Goodman narrates this entertaining animated documentary depicting the life of dinosaurs that lived in North America 220 million years ago during what was known as the Mesozoic period, combining nature, photography and computer graphics similar to its 1999 predecessor *Walking with Dinosaurs*. Produced by the BBC and Discovery Channel, the two-hour 3-D CGI-animated special—directed by Pierre de Lespinois—first aired on Discovery Channel in 2001 and was nominated for a prime-time Emmy Award for outstanding animated program (for programming more than one hour), losing to the competing Discovery Channel animated documentary *Walking with Prehistoric Beasts*. The special was the seventh highest watched cable program of the week. *A Stone House Productions/BBC/Discovery Channel Production. Color. Two hours. Premiered on DSC: July 15, 2001.*

**Voices**
**Narrator:** John Goodman

### ◎ WHICH WITCH IS WITCH?

Buttons and Rusty, stars of the Chucklewood Critters specials, experience their first Halloween together, dressed up in costumes, and overcome trouble at a Halloween party thrown by Ranger Jones. *An Encore Enterprises Production. Color. Half-hour. Premiered: October 1984. Syndicated. Rebroadcast on USA: October 26, 1991; October 27, 1991; October 31, 1992.*

**Voices**
**Rusty/Rosie:** Kathy Ritter; **Buttons/Christie:** Barbara Goodson; **Abner:** Alvy Moore; **George:** Bill Ratner; **Bridgett:** Morgan Lofting; **Ranger Jones:** Bill Boyett

*Ranger Jones shows Buttons the bear and Rusty the fox the right way to carve a pumpkin in the Halloween special* Which Witch Is Witch? © *Encore Enterprises*

### ◎ WHITE BEAR'S SECRET

Bumbling bachelor Brown Bear (in this sequel to the United Kingdom television hit *Brown Bear's Wedding*) finds that adapting to married life isn't easy in this half-hour special from London's FilmFair Animation that premiered on Disney Channel. *A FilmFair Animation Production. Color. Half-hour. Premiered on DIS: August 1, 1992. Rebroadcast on DIS: August 4, 1992.*

**Voices**
**Brown Bear:** Joss Ackland; **White Bear:** Helena Bonham-Carter; **Owl:** Hugh Laurie

### ◎ THE WHITE SEAL

In the second of two *Jungle Book* animated specials ordered for the 1974–75 season by CBS, Roddy McDowall narrates the story of Kotick the white seal, who grows up from playful sprout to become leader of his group, taking them to a spectacular island safe from the savage seal hunters. *A Chuck Jones Enterprises Production. Color. Half-hour. Premiered on CBS: March 24, 1975. Rebroadcast on CBS: October 17, 1975; May 13, 1977; September 9, 1981. Syndicated.*

**Voices**
**Kotick/Sea Catch/Sea Cow/Killer Whale/Walrus:** Roddy McDowall; **Matkah:** June Foray; **Narrator:** Roddy McDowall

### ◎ WHITEWASH

Attacked and sprayed white by a gang of young white men, a young black girl comes to terms with what has happened and goes on with her life thanks to her loving grandmother, in this half-hour animated special, written by Ntozake Shange and produced by award-winning animator Michael Sporn for HBO. *A Michael Sporn Animation Production. Color. Half-hour. Premiered on HBO: August 16, 1994.*

**Voices**
**Grandmother:** Ruby Dee; **Teacher:** Linda Lavin; **Helene Angel:** Serena Henry; **Mauricio:** Ndehru Roberts; **Shades:** Michael McGruther; **Detective:** Joel Briel; **Reporter:** Heidi Stallings

### ◎ WHY, CHARLIE BROWN, WHY?

Janice, a new *Peanuts* character, is a school friend of Linus and Charlie Brown's who develops leukemia. The story traces her treatment—and eventual recovery—and how the gang deals with it. *A Lee Mendelson–Bill Melendez Production in association with Charles M. Schulz Creative Associates and United Feature Syndicate. Color. Half-hour. Premiered on CBS: March 16, 1990.*

**Voices**
**Charlie Brown:** Kaleb Henley; **Janice Emmons:** Olivia Burnette; **Linus Van Pelt:** Brandon Stewart; **Sally Brown:** Andrienne Stiefel; **Little Sister:** Brittany Thorton; **Big Sister:** Lindsay Sloane; **The Bully:** Dion Zamora

### ◎ THE WILD THORNBERRYS: "ORIGIN OF DONNIE"

While planning Donnie's birthday party in Borneo, Indonesia, the Thornberrys encounter a series of problems, including Grandma Sophie's (voiced by television comedy legend Betty White) decision to visit on the day that Nigel and Marianne need to capture a wild orangutan or lose their film funding in this 90-minute made-for-TV movie—and first prime-time special—that aired on Saturday, August 18, 2001, from 8 to 9 P.M. on Nickelodeon based on the popular network cartoon series. *A Klasky Csupo Production. Color. Ninety minutes. Premiered on NICK: August 18, 2001.*

## Voices
**Eliza Thornberry:** Lacey Chabert; **Debbie Thornberry:** Danielle Harris; **Donnie Thornberry:** Flea; **Nigel Thornberry:** Tim Curry; **Marianne Thornberry:** Jodi Carlisle; **Darwin the Chimp:** Tom Kane; **Grandma Sophie:** Betty White

## ⊚ THE WILD THORNBERRYS: "SIR NIGEL"
While visiting Nigel's parents in Scotland, Nigel (voiced by Tim Curry) receive the highest honor when he is knighted by the Queen of England and is then pressured by his mother to accept a professorship at Oxford in this hour-long special entitled *Sir Nigel*, featuring the characters from the popular Nickelodeon cartoon series, *The Wild Thornberrys*. The actual knighthood ceremony was originally to be included in the full-length *The Wild Thornberrys Movie* (2002), but was edited from the film's final version to improve the pacing of the story. Produced by Hollywood's Emmy Award-winning Klasky Csupo, creators of *The Rugrats*, the program aired in prime time on Sunday, March 30, 2003, from 8 to 9 P.M. on Nickelodeon. *A Klasky Csupo Production. Color. One hour. Premiered on NICK: March 30, 2003. Rebroadcast on NICK: April 6, 2003; July 28, 2003.*

## Voices
**Eliza Thornberry:** Lacey Chabert; **Debbie Thornberry:** Danielle Harris; **Donnie Thornberry:** Flea; **Nigel Thornberry/Colonel Thornberry:** Tim Curry; **Marianne Thornberry:** Jodi Carlisle; **Darwin the Chimp:** Tom Kane; **Kip O'Donnell:** Keith Szarabajka; **Neil Beidermann:** Jerry Sroka

## ⊚ WILLIE MAYS AND THE SAY-HEY KID
Baseball great Willie Mays, playing himself, recounts the tale of the near-impossible catch he made to clinch the National League pennant, thanks to a special wish he is granted by an eccentric angel, and a poor orphan girl (Veronica) who turns out to be his godchild in this one-hour special, which originally aired as part of *The ABC Saturday Superstar Movie series. A Rankin-Bass Production. Color. One hour. Premiered on ABC: October 14, 1972 (on The ABC Saturday Superstar Movie). Rebroadcast on ABC: September 22, 1973; February 16, 1974. Syndicated.*

## Voices
**Willie Mays:** himself; **Veronica:** Tina Andrews; **Iguana:** Paul Frees; **Veronica's aunt:** Ernestine Wade

## ⊚ THE WILLOWS IN WINTER
Michael Palin and Vanessa Redgrave lent their voices to this 90-minute sequel to a British animated production of Kenneth Grahame's *The Wind in the Willows*, one of two feature-length coproductions produced by Carlton UK Television, HIT Entertainment and Animation House, TVC London. The Emmy-nominated sequel premiered in the United States on The Family Channel. *A TVC London/HIT Entertainment/Carlton UK Television Production. Color. Ninety minutes. Premiered on FAM: September 8, 1996.*

## Voices
**Rat:** Michael Palin; **Badger:** Michael Gambon; **Toad:** Rik Mayall; **Mole:** Alan Bennett; **Otter:** Enn Reitel; **Mole's Nephew:** Adrian Scarborough; **Portly:** Zoot Lynam; **Prendergast:** Peter Cellier; **Chief Weasel:** Mark Lockyer; **Chief Judge:** Ronald Fraser; **Commissioner of Police:** Windsor Davis; **Magistrate:** James Villiers; **Gaoler/Clerk:** David Sinclair; **Pilot:** Mike Grady; **Sweep:** Bill Oddie

## ⊚ WILL VINTON'S CLAYMATION COMEDY OF HORRORS SHOW
The ever-scheming Wilshire Pig talks Sheldon Snail into visiting the castle of Dr. Frankenswine to seek scientific secrets that could be worth a fortune in this prime-time comedy/adventure Halloween special, produced by claymation-master Will Vinton (of *California Raisins* fame). In 1991, the half-hour special received two Emmy Award nominations for outstanding animated program (for programming one hour or less) and outstanding individual achievement in animation, winning the latter. *A Will Vinton Associates Production. Color. Half-hour. Premiered on CBS: May 29, 1991.*

## Voices
Tim Conner, Brian Cummings, Krischa Fairchild, Todd Tolces

## ⊚ THE WIND IN THE WILLOWS (1987)
Ratty, Badger and Mole struggle to keep boastful Mr. Toad from danger and try to save Toad Hall from destruction by evil weasels in this two-hour made-for-television movie based on Kenneth Grahame's popular children's classic. *A Rankin-Bass Production in association with Cuckoos Nest Animation. Color. Two hours. Premiered on ABC: July 5, 1987. Rebroadcast on ABC: September 12, 1987. Rebroadcast on NICK: March 28, 1992.*

## Voices
**Mr. Toad:** Charles Nelson Reilly; **Ratty:** Roddy McDowall; **Badger:** José Ferrer; **Moley:** Eddie Bracken; **Wayfarer:** Paul Frees; **Magistrate:** Robert McFadden; **Vocalist:** Judy Collins

## ⊚ THE WIND IN THE WILLOWS (1989)
England's Cosgrove Hall Productions produced this two-hour, stop-motion, puppet-animated film following an unusual group of friends (wise old Badger, kind and innocent Mole, brave and generous Rat and reckless and impetuous Toad)—and their misadventures in 1908 Edwardian England, based on the book by Kenneth Grahame. Part of the award-winning series *Long Ago & Far Away* on PBS, it was the only film from the series longer than a half hour. *A Cosgrove Hall Production. Color. Two hours. Premiered on PBS: March 18, 1989. Rebroadcast on PBS: December 25, 1992 (as a 90-minute special).*

## Voices
**Badger:** Sir Michael Hordern; **Rat:** Ian Carmichael; **Toad:** David Jason; **Mole:** Richard Pearson

## ⊚ THE WIND IN THE WILLOWS (1996)
Kenneth Grahame's prized literary classic—featuring the prudent Rat, the impulsive Mole, the cantankerous Badger and the audacious but likeable Toad who learn important lessons about life, responsibility, justice and friendship—comes to life in this enchanting, beautifully animated feature, the second of two coproductions by TVC London, Carlton UK Television and HIT Entertainment after *The Willows in Winter*, narrated by Oscar-winning actress Vanessa Redgrave as the Grandmother. The 90-minute film, which won the "Best of Fest" and "Children's Jury Award" at the 1996 Chicago International Children's Film Festival, debuted in the United States on the Family Channel in December 1996. *A TVC London/HIT Entertainment/Carlton UK Television Production. Color. Ninety minutes. Premiered on FAM: December 16, 1996.*

## Voices
**Mole:** Alan Bennett; **Rat:** Michael Palin; **Badger:** Michael Gambon; **Toad:** Rik Mayall; **Magistrate:** James Villiers; **Gaoler's Daughter:** Emma Chambers; **Barge Woman:** Judy Cornwell; **Grandmother:** Vanessa Redgrave; **Alexandra:** Jemima Ffyne; **Emma:** Jordan Hollywood; **Edward:** Tom Stourton; **Boatman:** Barry Foster; **Additional Voices:** Erin Reitel, David Sinclair, Mark Lockyer

## ◎ WINNIE THE POOH AND A DAY FOR EEYORE

Winnie the Pooh and his friends—Rabbit, Piglet and Roo—happen to forget Eeyore's birthday and with Christopher Robin's help, they throw a surprise party for the sorrowful-looking donkey. The special was the first production starring the characters since *Winnie the Pooh and Tigger Too* produced 12 years earlier. *A Walt Disney Television Production. Color. Half-hour. Premiered on DIS: May 6, 1986.*

*Voices*
**Winnie the Pooh:** Hal Smith; **Eeyore:** Ralph Wright; **Piglet:** John Fiedler; **Rabbit:** Will Ryan; **Christopher Robin:** Kim Christianson; **Roo:** Dick Billingsley; **Kanga:** Julie McWhirter Dees; **Tigger:** Paul Winchell

## ◎ WINNIE THE POOH AND CHRISTMAS, TOO

Winnie the Pooh and the gang write a letter to Santa Claus and take it upon themselves to make sure all their friends in the woods get they want in this prime-time half-hour special that marked the return of TV legend Paul Winchell as the voice of Tigger. *A Walt Disney Television Animation Production. Color. Half-hour. Premiered on ABC: December 14, 1991. Rebroadcast on ABC: December 11, 1992; December 8, 1993. Rebroadcast on DIS: December 10, 1994; December 20, 1994; December 23, 1994; December 25, 1994. Rebroadcast on CBS: December 21, 1995; December 5, 1996; December 5, 1997.*

*Voices*
**Winnie the Pooh:** Jim Cummings; **Tigger:** Paul Winchell; **Piglet:** John Fiedler; **Eeyore:** Peter Cullen; **Christopher Robin:** Edan Gross, Tim Hoskins; **Rabbit:** Ken Sansom; **Gopher:** Michael Gough; **Narrator:** Laurie Mann

## ◎ WINNIE THE POOH AND THE BLUSTERY DAY

Broadcast as a prime-time special, this Academy Award–winning short subject relates Pooh and Piglet's frightening encounter with a giant windstorm that blows them skyward, crashing into and destroying the Owl's treehouse. *A Walt Disney Television Production. Color. Half-hour. Premiered on NBC: November 30, 1970. Rebroadcast on NBC: December 1, 1971; November 29, 1972; November 28, 1973; November 26, 1974; December 1, 1978.*

*Voices*
**Winnie the Pooh:** Sterling Holloway; **Eeyore:** Ralph Wright; **Owl:** Hal Smith; **Christopher Robbin:** Jon Walmsley; **Kanga:** Barbara Luddy; **Roo:** Clint Howard; **Rabbit:** Junius Matthews; **Gopher:** Howard Morris; **Tigger:** Paul Winchell; **Piglet:** John Fiedler; **Narrator:** Sebastian Cabot

## ◎ WINNIE THE POOH AND THE HONEY TREE

Winnie the Pooh's love for honey gets the better of him as he becomes overweight from overconsumption of the sweet stuff in this theatrical short subject broadcast as a prime-time special. *A Walt Disney Television Production. Color. Half-hour. Premiered on NBC: March 10, 1970. Rebroadcast on NBC: March 22, 1971; March 14, 1972; April 4, 1973: March 26, 1974; November 25, 1977; January 21, 1990 (on Magical World of Disney).*

*Voices*
**Winnie the Pooh:** Sterling Holloway; **Eeyore:** Ralph Wright; **Owl:** Hal Smith; **Christopher Robin:** Bruce Reitherman; **Kanga:** Barbara Luddy; **Roo:** Clint Howard; **Rabbit:** Junius Matthews; **Gopher:** Howard Morris; **Narrator:** Sebastian Cabot

## ◎ WINNIE THE POOH AND TIGGER TOO

Tigger is so joyfully bouncy that his friends Pooh, Rabbit and Piglet look for ways to "unbounce" him in this animated special originally produced as a theatrical cartoon short. *A Walt Disney Television Production. Color. Half-hour. Premiered on NBC: November 28, 1975 (as NBC Holiday Special). Rebroadcast on ABC: November 25, 1976; CBS: December 11, 1982; August 30, 1983.*

*Voices*
**Winnie the Pooh:** Sterling Holloway; **Tigger:** Paul Winchell; **Rabbit:** Junius Matthews; **Piglet:** John Fiedler; **Kanga:** Barbara Luddy; **Roo:** Dori Whitaker; **Christopher Robin:** Timothy Turner; **Narrator:** Sebastian Cabot

## ◎ WINNIE THE POOH A VALENTINE FOR YOU

It's that most special day of the year and time to show affection for each other, but Rabbit wants to cancel Valentine's Day because of how many cards littered the Hundred Acre Wood from the previous year. Everyone goes along with Rabbit's wish, until Pooh wins him over with a pot of honey in this originally titled, *Winnie the Pooh's Un-Valentine's Day*, direct-to-video production, produced in 1995 and broadcast four years later on ABC as *Winnie the Pooh A Valentine for You*. Featuring three original songs, the half-hour special received two prime-time Emmy Awards nominations for outstanding music composition for a miniseries or a movie (dramatic underscore) by composer Carl Johnson and outstanding music and lyrics by composer Michael Silversher and lyricist Patty Silversher for the song "Place in the Heart." *A Walt Disney Television Animation Production. Color. Half-hour. Premiered on ABC: February 13, 1999. Rebroadcast on ABC: February 14, 2002; February 12, 2005.*

*Voices*
**Winnie the Pooh/Eeyore:** Jim Cummings; **Christopher Robin:** Brady Bluhm; **Tigger:** Paul Winchell; **Piglet:** John Fiedler; **Eeyore:** Peter Cullen; **Roo:** Jerome Beidler; **Gopher:** Michael Gough; **Rabbit:** Ken Sansom; **Owl:** Andre Stojka; **Narrator:** David Warner

## ◎ A WINNIE THE POOH THANKSGIVING

When Thanksgiving dinner is served in the Hundred Acre Wood, Rabbit complains that the meal is unacceptable because it doesn't include turkey, cranberry sauce and pumpkin pie, which Winnie the Pooh and his friends end up finding to make the holiday festivities complete. First telecast in prime time on ABC in 1998, this original half-hour holiday special was nominated for an Emmy Award for outstanding children's program. *A Walt Disney Television Animation Production. Color. Half-hour. Premiered on ABC: November 26, 1998. Rebroadcast on ABC: November 16, 2001; November 21, 2002; November 23, 2003.*

*Voices*
**Winnie the Pooh/Tigger (singing):** Jim Cummings; **Tigger:** Paul Winchell; **Piglet:** John Fiedler; **Eeyore:** Peter Cullen; **Rabbit:** Ken Sansom; **Owl:** Tim Hoskins; **Gopher:** Michael Gough

## ◎ A WISH FOR WINGS THAT WORK: OPUS & BILL'S FIRST CHRISTMAS SPECIAL

Characters from Berkeley Breathed's *Bloom County* and *Outland* comic strips star in this half-hour Christmas special in which Opus the Penguin writes to Santa to ask for wings that work—since he can't handle being a bird that can't fly. Missing from holiday television schedules since its network premiere, on Friday, December 15, 2006, the Bloom County comic-inspired special returned to the small screen on the ION network (formerly PAX), along with a brace of other animated and live-action Christmas programs including *Boo! Christmas Special* and *Holidaze: The Christmas That*

*Almost Didn't Happen. A Universal Cartoon Studios/Amblin Entertainment Production. Color. Half-hour. Premiered on CBS: December 18, 1991. Rebroadcast on CBS: December 24, 1992. Rebroadcast on ION: December 15, 2006. Syndicated.*

### Voices
**Opus the Penguin:** Michael Bell; **Bill the Cat:** John Byner; **Cockroach:** Sudy Nun; **Truffles/The Ducks:** Joe Alaskey; **The Chicken:** Tress MacNeille; **The Kiwi:** Robin Williams (as Sudy Nim); **Ronald-Ann:** Alexandria Simmons; **Santa:** Andrew Hill Newman; **Santa Claus:** Frank Welker

### ◎ THE WISH THAT CHANGED CHRISTMAS
A lonely orphan, a lonely Christmas doll and a lonely childless couple each wish to change their lives at Christmas in this animated adaptation of Rumer Godden's heart-warming story "The Story of Holly and Ivy." *A Children's Television Workshop Production. Color. Half-hour. Premiered on CBS: December 20, 1991. Rebroadcast on CBS: December 16, 1992. Rebroadcast on ABC: December 23, 1994.*

### Voices
**The Owl:** Jonathan Winters; **Mr. Smith:** Paul Winfield; **Ivy:** Brittany Thornton; **Holly:** Lea Floden; **Officer Jones:** Bill Boyett; **Mrs. Jones:** Tress MacNeille; **Mrs. Sheperd:** Beverly Garland; **Mr. Blossom:** Lindsey Workman; **Peter:** Marc Robinson

### ◎ WITCH'S NIGHT OUT
Gilda Radner provides the voice of a washed-up witch who turns two small children into the monsters of their choice only to fulfill the fantasies of the town's entire adult population as well in this prime-time Halloween special. *A Leach-Rankin Production in association with Rankin-Bass Productions. Color. Half-hour. Premiered on NBC: October 27, 1978. Rebroadcast on NBC: October 30, 1979. Syndicated. Rebroadcast on DIS: October 25, 1992; October 31, 1992; October 30, 1993.*

### Voices
**Witch ("The Godmother"):** Gilda Radner; **Rotten:** Bob Church; **Goody:** John Leach; **Tender:** Naomi Leach; **Small:** Tony Molesworth; **Malicious:** Catherine O'Hara; **Mincely:** Fiona Reid; **Bazooey:** Gerry Salsberg

### ◎ WOLVES, WITCHES AND GIANTS
British comic Spike Milligan narrates and provides character voices for three classic children's fairy tales—"Red Riding Hood," "The Witch and the Comb" and "The Little Tailor"—featured in this half-hour special, which premiered on Disney Channel. The program was culled from a series of 10-minute episodes originally produced for United Kingdom's ITV Network. *A Honeycomb Animation Production. Color. Half-hour. Premiered on DIS: January 29, 1997.*

### Voices
**Narrator/Other Voices:** Spike Milligan

### ◎ THE WOMAN WHO RAISED A BEAR AS HER SON
Set in the high Arctic, an old Inuit woman, who lives alone becomes an unlikely mother when an orphaned polar cub tumbles into her life—in this heartwarming adventure adapted from Arctic legend. *A Lacewood Production. Color. Half-hour. Premiered on DIS: 1990.*

### ◎ THE WONDER PETS SAVE THE REINDEER
The Wonder Pets head to the North Pole on Christmas Eve to rescue Santa's Baby Reindeer. The 30-minute cartoon special, based on the popular preschool series, bowed on Nick Jr. *A Little Airplane Productions, Inc. Production. Color. Half-hour. Premiered on NICK JR.: December 8, 2006. Rebroadcast on NICK: December 14, 2006. Rebroadcast on NOG: December 14, 2006.*

### Voices
**Linny the Guinea Pig:** Sofie Zamchick; **Ming-Ming Duckling:** Ming-Ming Duckling; **Tuck the Turtle:** Teala Dunn; **Jazz Mouse:** Matthew Black; **Mamma Cow:** Emyln Elisabeth Morinelli

### ◎ THE WORLD OF PETER RABBIT AND FRIENDS
Originally airing on The Family Channel, CBS broadcast this hour-long re-creation of books by Beatrix Potter, culled from two previously broadcast half-hours: "The Tale of Peter Rabbit and Benjamin Bunny" and "The Tale of Flopsy Bunnies and Mrs. Tittlemouse." (For full voice credit information, see the series entry in the Television Cartoon Series section.) *A TVC London Production for Frederick Warne and Co./BBC in association with Pony Canyon, Inc. Color. One hour. Premiered on CBS: March 27, 1997.*

### Cast (live action)
**Beatrix Potter:** Niamh Cusack

### ◎ THE WORLD OF PETER RABBIT AND FRIENDS: "THE TAILOR OF GLOUCESTER"
This timeless yuletide tale, featuring an ailing tailor and an altruistic group of mice, weaves a story about the joy of giving in this fourth animated installment of the Emmy-nominated Family Channel series, adapted from work of well-known children's author Beatrix Potter. (For full voice credit information, see the series entry in the Television Cartoon Series section.) *A TVC London Production for Frederick Warne and Co./BBC in association with Pony Canyon, Inc. Color. Half-hour. Premiered on FAM: November 26, 1993. Rebroadcast on FAM: November 29, 1993; December 5, 1993; December 12, 1993; December 4, 1994; December 23, 1994; December 25, 1994; January 8, 1995; May 7, 1995; December 2, 1995; December 17, 1995; December 22, 1995; December 7, 1996; December 8, 1997; December 19, 1997.*

### Cast (live action)
**Beatrix Potter:** Niamh Cusack

### ◎ THE WORLD OF PETER RABBIT AND FRIENDS: "THE TALE OF FLOPSY BUNNIES AND MRS. TITTLEMOUSE"
Two more timeless tales—the first dealing with a group of bunnies who naughtily get into Mr. McGregor's lettuce patch, the second following the exploits of a tidy little wood mouse who lives under a hedge—by renowned children's author Beatrix Potter are featured in this colorfully animated installment of the popular Family Channel series. (For full voice credit information, see the series entry in the Television Cartoon Series section.) *A TVC London Production for Frederick Warne and Co./BBC in association with Pony Canyon, Inc. Color. Half-hour. Premiered on FAM: November 13, 1995. Rebroadcast on FAM: November 16, 1995; November 24, 1995.*

### Cast (live action)
**Beatrix Potter:** Niamh Cusack

### ◎ THE WORLD OF PETER RABBIT AND FRIENDS: "THE TALE OF MRS. TIGGY-WINKLE AND MR. JEREMY FISHER"
The sixth of the Family Channel's Emmy-nominated live-action/animated series, this half-hour special combines two of Beatrix

Potter's favorite stories in this seven-part series of specials, following the adventures of a young farm girl, Lucie Carr, a talkative pet hedgehog, Mrs. Tiggy-Winkle and a gentleman frog, Mr. Jeremy Fisher, who have a frightful story of their own. (For full voice credit information, see the series entry in the Television Cartoon Series section.) *A TVC London Production for Frederick Warne and Co./BBC in association with Pony Canyon, Inc. Color. Half-hour. Premiered on FAM: April 3, 1994. Rebroadcast on FAM: April 4, 1994; April 11, 1994; April 17, 1994; October 9, 1994; November 18, 1994; March 27, 1995.*

**Cast** *(live action)*
**Beatrix Potter:** Niamh Cusack

### ☉ THE WORLD OF PETER RABBIT AND FRIENDS: "THE TALE OF PETER RABBIT AND BENJAMIN BUNNY"

Cousins Peter and Benjamin experience some hair-raising escapades in Mr. McGregor's vegetable patch in this first installment in a series of half-hour live-action/animated specials, based on two of Beatrix Potter's popular children's stories. The series of specials were produced for The Family Channel. (For full voice credit information, see the series entry in the Television Cartoon Series section.) *A TVC London Production for Frederick Warne and Co./BBC in association with Pony Canyon, Inc. Color. Half-hour. Premiered on FAM: March 29, 1993. Rebroadcast on FAM: April 4, 1993; April 11, 1993; May 10, 1993; May 16, 1993; September 13, 1993; November 16, 1993; March 13, 1994; March 21, 1994; March 27, 1994; April 3, 1994; April 29, 1994; October 3, 1994; November 11, 1994; April 3, 1995; April 9, 1995; November 16, 1995.*

**Cast** *(live action)*
**Beatrix Potter:** Niamh Cusack

### ☉ THE WORLD OF PETER RABBIT AND FRIENDS: "THE TALE OF PIGLING BLAND"

In this fifth of six animated specials based on Beatrix Potter's lovable and laughable creations, Pigling and his addle-brained brother Alexander head to the market, ignoring the sage advice of Aunt Pettitoes, and find themselves in a stew. (For full voice credit information, see the series entry in the Television Cartoon Series section.) *A TVC London Production for Frederick Warne and Co./BBC in association with Pony Canyon, Inc. Color. Half-hour. Premiered on FAM: March 13, 1994. Rebroadcast on FAM: March 21, 1994; March 27, 1994; October 3, 1994; March 27, 1995; May 8, 1995.*

**Cast** *(live action)*
**Beatrix Potter:** Niamh Cusack

### ☉ THE WORLD OF PETER RABBIT AND FRIENDS: "THE TALE OF SAMUEL WHISKERS AND THE ROLY-POLY PUDDING"

When Mrs. Kitten misplaces her rebellious son Tom, Kitten Dumpling Roly-Poly Pudding becomes the dinner item of choice for a rotund cat named Samuel Whiskers, in this delightful animated half-hour, part of *The World of Peter Rabbit and Friends* series, produced by Oscar-winning British producer John Coates for The Family Channel. (For full voice credit information, see the series entry in the Television Cartoon Series section.) *A TVC London Production for Frederick Warne and Co./BBC in association with Pony Canyon, Inc. Color. Half-hour. Premiered on FAM: May 10, 1993. Rebroadcast on FAM: May 16, 1993; May 23, 1993; September 19, 1993; November 17, 1993; December 5, 1993; November 17, 1994; May 8, 1995.*

**Cast** *(live action)*
**Beatrix Potter:** Niamh Cusack

### ☉ THE WORLD OF PETER RABBIT AND FRIENDS: "THE TALE OF TOM KITTEN AND JEMIMA PUDDLE-DUCK"

This richly animated half-hour special combines two fine adaptations of Beatrix Potter's classic children's stories. The opener follows the adventures of three little mischievous kittens named Tom Kitten, Mittens and Moppet. Next is a farmyard tale of a duck who becomes annoyed when the farmer's wife won't let her hatch her own eggs. Both premiered on this Emmy-nominated series, produced for The Family Channel. (For full voice credit information, see the series entry in the Television Cartoon Series section.) *A TVC London Production for Frederick Warne and Co./BBC in association with Pony Canyon, Inc. Color. Half-hour. Premiered on FAM: September 13, 1993. Rebroadcast on FAM: September 19, 1993; September 26, 1993; November 19, 1993; November 29, 1993; April 3, 1994; April 4, 1994; April 11, 1994; October 9, 1994; November 15, 1994; January 8, 1995; May 7, 1995; November 13, 1995.*

**Cast** *(live action):*
**Beatrix Potter:** Niamh Cusack

### ☉ THE WORLD OF SECRET SQUIRREL AND ATOM ANT

The first cartoon preview aired in prime time, this hour-long special gave viewers a glimpse of the characters from the Saturday-morning series, *The Atom Ant/Secret Squirrel Show* in two back-to-back episodes. The series officially debuted on October 2, 1965. *A Hanna-Barbera Production. Color. One hour. Premiered on NBC: September 12, 1965.*

**Voices**
**Secret Squirrel:** Mel Blanc; **Morocco Mole:** Paul Frees; **Atom Ant:** Howard Morris; **Mr. Moto/Others:** Don Messick

### ☉ THE WORLD OF STRAWBERRY SHORTCAKE

In this Easter special based on the popular greeting card characters, the happiness of Strawberry Shortcake and her friends of the fantasy world, Strawberry Land, is intruded upon by the diabolical Peculiar Purple Pieman, who is always out to spoil their fun. The first of six Strawberry Shortcake specials produced for first-run syndication. *An RLR Associates Production in association with Those Characters From Cleveland and Murakami-Wolf-Swenson Films. Color. Half-hour. Premiered: March–April, 1980. Syndicated. Rebroadcast on DIS: August 11, 1992.*

**Voices**
**Sun (narrator):** Romeo Muller; **Strawberry Shortcake:** Russi Taylor; **Peculiar Purple Pieman:** Bob Ridgely; **Huckleberry Pie:** Julie McWhirter; **Blueberry Muffin/Apple Dumplin:** Joan Gerber; **Raspberry Tart:** Pamela Anderson; **Ben Bean/Escargot:** Bob Holt; **Vocalists:** Flo and Eddy

### ☉ WOW! WOW! WUBBZY!: "THE SNOW SHOO SHOO"

Worried that they haven't spotted Snow Shoo-Shoo in quite some time, Walden, Wubbzy and Widget head off to Mt. Zubba to locate the friendly creature in this half-hour holiday special based on the Nick Jr. preschool series. *A Bolder Media for Boys and Girls Production in association with IDT Entertainment/Film Roman. Premiered on NICK JR.: December 1, 2006. Rebroadcast on NICK JR.: December 21, 2006. Rebroadcast on NOG: December 19, 2006.*

*Voices*
**Wubbzy:** Grey DeLisle; **Walden:** Carlos Alazaqui; **Widget:** Lara Jill Miller

### ◎ X-MEN: "NIGHT OF THE SENTINELS"

The X-Men (Cyclops, Wolverine, Storm, Rogue, Gambit, the Beast and Jean Grey) uncover a mutant registration program associated with the government and a group of mutant-thriving robots called the Sentinels while rescuing a mutant teenage girl named Jubilee. The two-part Saturday-morning series preview special, comprised of two half-hour episodes that preceded the program's official debut in January 1993, aired one week apart on FOX's FOX Kids. A *Marvel Films/Saban Entertainment Production. Color. Half-hour. Premiered on FOX: October 31, 1992 (Part I); November 7, 1992 (Part II).*

*Voices*
**Scott Summers/Cyclops:** Norm Spencer; **Logan/Wolverine:** Cal Dodd; **Ororo Monroe/Storm:** Iona Morris; **Gambit:** Chris Potter; **Jean Grey/Phoenix:** Catherine Disher; **Dr. Hank McCoy/The Beast:** George Buza; **Rogue:** Lenore Zann; **Jubilation Lee/Jubilee:** Alyson Court; **Professor Charles Xavier:** Cedric Smith; **Henry Peter Gyrich/Guardian Vindicator/James MacDonald Hudson:** Barry Flatman; **Sabertooth/Victor Creed/Puck Eugene Milton Judd/Shaman/Dr. Michael Twoyoungmen:** Don Francks; **Sentinels Mastermold:** David Fox; **Senator Robert Kelly:** Len Carlson; **Morph:** Ron Ruben

### ◎ X-MEN: "OUT OF THE PAST"

A band of vicious cyborg mercenaries and a mysterious woman from Wolverine's past use him to uncover the secrets of a buried alien spaceship while the X-Men battle the villainous alien, Spirit Drinker, who sucks the life out of Jubilee and Reavers in this two-part special aired Sunday night in prime time from the popular FOX Kids Saturday-morning cartoon series. The special was the first of two to air in prime time during the 1994–95 season, followed by *Weapon X, Lies and Videotape.* A *Marvel Films/Saban Entertainment Production. Color. Half-hour. Premiered on FOX: July 29, 1994 (Part I); August 5, 1994 (Part II).*

*Voices*
**Scott Summers/Cyclops:** Norm Spencer; **Logan/Wolverine:** Cal Dodd; **Ororo Monroe/Storm:** Iona Morris; **Gambit:** Chris Potter; **Jean Grey/Phoenix:** Catherine Disher; **Dr. Hank McCoy/The Beast:** George Buza; **Rogue:** Lenore Zann; **Jubilation Lee/Jubilee:** Alyson Court; **Professor Charles Xavier:** Cedric Smith

### ◎ X-MEN: "WEAPON X, LIES AND VIDEO TAPE"

Haunted by his past, Wolverine learns little about himself that is good while visiting a Canadian government facility with Beast in this second half-hour special that bowed Sunday night in prime time, based on FOX's weekly Saturday-morning cartoon series. A *Marvel Films/Saban Entertainment Production. Color. Half-hour. Premiered on FOX: June 11, 1995.*

*Voices*
**Scott Summers/Cyclops:** Norm Spencer; **Logan/Wolverine:** Cal Dodd; **Ororo Monroe/Storm:** Iona Morris; **Gambit:** Chris Potter; **Jean Grey/Phoenix:** Catherine Disher; **Dr. Hank McCoy/The Beast:** George Buza; **Rogue:** Lenore Zann; **Jubilation Lee/Jubilee:** Alyson Court; **Professor Charles Xavier:** Cedric Smith

### ◎ THE X'S: TRUMAN X: SUPER VILLAIN

After being punished by the X's for destroying their advanced super-jet and selling all of his high-tech spy gadgets at a garage sale, rebellious tween Truman goes over to the "dark" side in retaliation after the nefarious Glowface convinces him to join S.N.A.F.U. with his first assignment being to destroy his entire family in this feature-length movie for Nickelodeon based on the hit fantasy adventure series. First telecast during the summer of 2006, the cartoon feature was among a slate of all-new animated telefilms to premiere based on several hit Nickelodeon series, including *Avatar: The Last Airbender, Danny Phantom* and *The Fairly OddParents.* A *Nickelodeon Studios Production. Color. Ninety minutes. Premiered on NICK: June 16, 2006.*

*Voices*
**Mr. X (Aaron Truman Extreme Sr.):** Patrick Warburton; **Mrs. X (Andrea Martha Cohen Extreme):** Wendie Malick; **Tuesday X (Tabbatha Tuesday Extreme):** Lynsey Bartilson; **Truman X (Aaron Truman Extreme Jr.):** Jansen Panettiere; **Homebase:** Stephen Root; **Glowface (Arthur Emmons):** Chris Hardwick; **Minions:** Carlos Ramos

### ◎ XYBER 9: NEW DAWN: "NEW ACQUAINTAINCES"/"ENTER IKIRA"

A troublesome young orphan, Jack, who dreams of becoming a hero gets his opportunity after finding an all-powerful super computer, Xyber 9, while coming to the aide of the legendary swordsman, Lord Ikira, in this two-part, CGI-animated hour-long special that launched the weekly Saturday-morning cartoon series on FOX. A *Saban Entertainment/Bokabi Productions Production. Color. One hour. Premiered on FOX: September 5, 1999.*

*Voices*
**Xyber 9:** Rene Auberjonois; **Jack:** Jason Marsden; **King Renard:** Tim Curry; **Mick:** Quinton Flynn; **Anakonda:** Nika Frost; **Lord Machestro:** Tony Jay; **Princess Rozalyn/Ana:** Jolie Jenkins; **Willy:** Rodney Saulsberry; **Ikira:** Christopher Marquette; **Other Voices:** Obba Babatundé, Phil Buckman, Victor Brandt, David Jeremiah, Tom Kane, Neil Ross, Tom Strauss, Keith Szarabajka, Jim Ward, Frank Welker

### ◎ YABBA DABBA 2

Host Bill Bixby salutes the prolific careers of animators William Hanna and Joseph Barbera in this compilation special of clips from their cartoon successes, from their MGM days and their days as the head of their own studio, Hanna-Barbera Productions. The show featured clips of Tom and Jerry, Scooby-Doo, Ruff and Reddy, the Flintstones, and others. A *Hanna-Barbera Production in association with Robert Guenette Productions. Color. One hour. Premiered on CBS: October 12, 1979. Rebroadcast on CBS: June 1, 1982. Rebroadcast on CAR: June 4, 1994.*

### ◎ YANKEE DOODLE

The spirit of the Revolutionary War, including Paul Revere's historic midnight ride to warn the colonials, is witnessed by Danny, a 12-year-old boy, and his Midnight Militia friends, Freddy and Timmy, in this special about freedom and independence. A *Festival of Family Classics special.* A *Rankin-Bass Production in association with Mushi Studios. Color. Half-hour. Premiered: 1972–1973. Syndicated.*

*Voices*
Carl Banas, Len Birman, Bernard Cowan, Peg Dixon, Keith Hampshire, Peggi Loder, Donna Miller, Frank Perry, Henry Ramer, Billie Mae Richards, Alfie Scopp, Paul Soles

### ◎ YANKEE DOODLE CRICKET

Chester C. Cricket, star of *The Cricket in Times Square* and *A Very Merry Cricket,* stars in this fanciful view of American history re-created by the ancestors of Chester, Harry the Cat and Tucker R. Mouse. *A Chuck Jones Enterprises Production. Color. Half-hour. Premiered on ABC: January 16, 1975. Rebroadcast on ABC: June 28, 1976. Syndicated.*

*Voices*

**Chester C. Cricket/Harry the Cat:** Les Tremayne; **Tucker R. Mouse:** Mel Blanc; **Other Voices:** June Foray

### ◎ THE YEAR WITHOUT A SANTA CLAUS

This stop-motion "Animagic" special features the voice of Mickey Rooney, again picking up Santa's reins—as he did in the 1970 *Santa Claus Is Coming to Town*—only this time feeling the world has lost the Christmas spirit. Santa recovers from his disenchantment in time to make his traditional sleigh ride on Christmas Eve to distribute toys to the children of the world. Features the hit songs "Blue Christmas" and "Here Comes Santa Claus." *A Rankin-Bass Production. Color. One hour. Premiered on ABC: December 10, 1974. Rebroadcast on ABC: December 10, 1975; December 14, 1976; December 9, 1977; December 10, 1978; December 9, 1979; December 21, 1980; Rebroadcast on DIS: December 18, 1992; December 14, 1993; December 13, 1995; December 14, 1996; December 10, 1997. Rebroadcast on DIS: December 13, 1995; December 15, 1995; December 24, 1995; December 25, 1995; July 14, 1996; December 9, 1996; December 14, 1996; December 16, 1996; December 20, 1996; December 24, 1996; December 10, 1997; December 13, 2006; December 24, 1997. Rebroadcast on FOX FAM: December 2, 1998; December 6, 1998; December 15, 1998; December 25, 1998; December 4, 2000; December 9, 2000; December 11, 2000; December 12, 2000; December 15, 2000; December 18, 2000; December 24, 2000. Rebroadcast on ABC FAM: December 1, 2001; December 7, 2001; December 11, 2001; December 18, 2001; December 22, 2001; December 24, 2001; December 1, 2002; December 6, 2002; December 7, 2002; December 15, 2002; December 18, 2002; December 24, 2002; December 2, 2003; December 6, 2003; December 7, 2003; December 16, 2003; December 21, 2003; December 23, 2003; December 24, 2003; December 25, 2003; December 2, 2004; December 4, 2004; December 8, 2004; December 15, 2004; December 19, 2004; December 24, 2004; December 1, 2005; December 3, 2005; December 7, 2005; December 13, 2005; December 14, 2005; December 24; 2005; December 4, 2006; December 9, 2006; December 15, 2006; December 20, 2006; December 24, 2006. Syndicated.*

*Voices*

**Mrs. Santa Claus (narrator):** Shirley Booth; **Santa Claus:** Mickey Rooney; **Snowmiser:** Dick Shawn; **Heatmiser:** George S. Irving; **Jingle Bells:** Robert McFadden; **Jangle Bells:** Bradley Bolke; **Mother Nature:** Rhoda Mann; **Mr. Thistlewhite:** Ron Marshall; **Ignatius Thistlewhite:** Colin Duffy; **Blue Christmas Girl/Vocalists:** Christine Winter

### ◎ YES, VIRGINIA, THERE IS A SANTA CLAUS

Animated retelling of eight-year-old Virginia O'Hanlon's letter to a *New York Sun* editor in 1897 asking if Santa Claus really exists. Program was coproduced by Bill Melendez, who was also associated with Charles M. Schulz's *Peanuts* specials—cornerstones of prime-time animation. *A Burt Rosen Company Production in association with Wolper Productions and Bill Melendez Production. Color. Half-hour. Premiered on ABC: December 6, 1974. Rebroadcast on ABC: December 5, 1975. Syndicated. Rebroadcast on CBS: December 22, 1991. Rebroadcast on USA: December 17, 1993; December 7, 1994; December 24, 1995. Rebroadcast on FAM: December 11, 1996; December 4, 1997.*

*Voices*

**Virginia O'Hanlon:** Courtney Lemmon; **Miss Taylor:** Susan Silo; **Billie:** Billie Green; **Specs:** Sean Manning; **Mary Lou:** Tracy Bel-

land; **Arthur:** Christopher Wong; **Amy:** Vickey Ricketts; **Peewee:** Jennifer Green; **Officer Riley:** Herb Armstrong; **Sergeant Muldoon:** Arnold Ross; **Vocalist:** Jimmy Osmond; **Narrator:** Jim Backus

### ◎ YOGI AND THE INVASION OF THE SPACE BEARS

Yogi Bear is on a rampage—and no picnic basket is safe in Jellystone Park. He swears to turn over a new leaf but before he does so, he and Boo Boo are kidnapped by aliens who plan to clone them. Part of *Hanna-Barbera's Superstar 10* movie package. *A Hanna-Barbera Production. Color. Two hours. Premiered: 1988. Syndicated.*

*Voices*

**Yogi Bear:** Daws Butler; **Boo Boo/Ranger Smith:** Don Messick; **Cindy Bear:** Julie Bennett; **Ranger Jones/Guy:** Michael Rye; **Ranger Brown/Ranger Two:** Patric Zimmerman; **Ranger Roubidoux/Owner:** Peter Cullen; **Boy/Zor Two/Wife:** Rob Paulson; **Little Girl:** Maggie Roswell; **Man/Zor One/Boy:** Townsend Coleman; **Dax Nova/Worker Kid:** Frank Welker; **Mountain Bear/Ranger One:** Sorrell Booke; **Girl:** Victoria Carroll

### ◎ YOGI AND THE MAGICAL FLIGHT OF THE SPRUCE GOOSE

Everyone's favorite bear leads a gang of his friends on a tour of the Spruce Goose, the largest cargo plane ever built. To their amazement, the plane suddenly takes off, taking them on the voyage of a lifetime. Syndicated as part of *Hanna-Barbera's Superstar 10* movie package. *A Hanna-Barbera Production. Color. Two hours. Premiered: 1988. Syndicated. Rebroadcast on DIS: December 3, 1996.*

*Voices*

**Yogi Bear/Quick Draw McGraw/Snagglepuss/Huckleberry Hound/Augie Doggie:** Daws Butler; **Boo Boo/Mumbley:** Don Messick; **Doggie Daddy/Pelican:** John Stephenson; **Dread Baron:** Paul Winchell; **Merkin:** Frank Welker; **Firkin:** Dave Coulier; **Bernice:** Marilyn Schreffler

### ◎ YOGI BEAR'S ALL-STAR COMEDY CHRISTMAS CAPER

Yogi Bear and Boo Boo sneak off into the city and make Christmas merry for a lonely little rich girl, Judy Jones, with some help from their old friends in this all-star Hanna--Barbera holiday special. *A Hanna-Barbera Production. Color. Half-hour. Premiered on CBS: December 21, 1982. Rebroadcast on CBS: December 18, 1984. Rebroadcast on DIS: December 12, 1990; December 13, 1991; December 19, 1992; December 7, 1993.*

*Voices*

**Yogi Bear/Quick Draw McGraw/Huckleberry Hound/Snagglepuss/Hokey Wolf/Snooper/Blabber/Augie Doggie/Mr. Jinks/Dixie/Wally Gator:** Daws Butler; **Boo Boo/Ranger Smith/Pixie:** Don Messick; **Judy Jones:** Georgi Irene; **Doggie Daddy/Butler/Announcer:** John Stephenson; **Mr. Jones/Zookeeper #1/Sergeant:** Hal Smith; **Mrs. Jones/P.A. Voice/Lady in the Street:** Janet Waldo; **Yakky Doodle/Zookeeper #2:** Jimmy Weldon; **Magilla Gorilla/Chief Blake/Murray:** Allan Melvin; **Fred Flintstone/Policeman/Security Guard #1:** Henry Corden; **Barney Rubble/Bulldog/Security Guard #2:** Mel Blanc

### ◎ YOGI'S ARK LARK

The biblical tale of Noah's Ark is given a different twist in this animated rendering featuring Yogi Bear, Boo Boo and a host of Hanna-Barbera cartoon favorites. The feature-length story, which originally aired on *The ABC Saturday Superstar Movie*, served as the successful pilot for the Saturday-morning series *Yogi's Gang*, in which the program was rebroadcast in two parts. *A Hanna-Barbera Production. Color. One hour. Premiered on ABC: September 16, 1972 (on The ABC Saturday Superstar Movie). Syndicated.*

*Voices*
**Yogi Bear/Baba Looey/Wally Gator/Huckleberry Hound/Lambsy/Quick Draw McGraw/Snagglepuss/Top Cat:** Daws Butler; **Boo Boo/Atom Ant/So So/Moby Dick/Touche' Turtle:** Don Messick; **Paw Rugg/1st Truck Driver/Paw Rugg:** Henry Corden; **Magilla Gorilla/2nd Truck Driver:** Allan Melvin; **Maw Rugg/Floral Rugg/Woman:** Jean VanderPyl; **Squiddly/Hokey Wolf/Yakky Doodle:** Walker Edmiston; **Cap'n Noah:** Lennie Weinrib; **Benny/Doggie Daddy/Hardy:** John Stephenson

### ◎ YOGI'S FIRST CHRISTMAS

Huckleberry Hound, Snagglepuss, Augie Doggie and Doggie Daddy all arrive at Jellystone Lodge for their annual Christmas celebration with cartoon pals Yogi Bear and Boo Boo. Their festivities gain added meaning when they discover that the owner, Mrs. Throckmorton, plans to sell the lodge to make way for a freeway in this two-hour made-for-television movie. *A Hanna-Barbera Production. Color. Half-hour. Premiered: November 22, 1980. Syndicated. Rebroadcast: December 22, 1991 (syndication). Rebroadcast on DIS: December 12, 1992; December 7, 1993. Rebroadcast on CAR: November 26, 1994; July 23, 1995 (Mr. Spim's Cartoon Theatre). Rebroadcast on TNT: December 17, 1995; December 1, 1996.*

*Voices*
**Yogi Bear/Huckleberry Hound/Augie Doggie/Snagglepuss:** Daws Butler; **Boo Boo/Ranger Smith/Herman the Hermit:** Don Messick; **Doggie Daddy/Mr. Dingwell:** John Stephenson; **Cindy Bear/Mrs. Throckmorton:** Janet Waldo; **Otto the Chef/Santa Claus:** Hal Smith; **Snively:** Marilyn Schreffler

### ◎ YOGI'S GREAT ESCAPE

Because of a financial crisis, Jellystone Park will be closed and Yogi Bear and all the other bears must move to a zoo. To avoid incar-

*Yogi Bear heads a cast of characters in some yuletide fun in the two-hour, made-for-television movie Yogi's First Christmas. © Hanna-Barbera Productions*

ceration, Yogi and his diminutive sidekick, Boo Boo, lead Ranger Smith on a cross-country chase in this two-hour made-for-television movie, broadcast as part of *Hanna-Barbera's Superstar 10* series of first-run animated films for television. *A Hanna-Barbera Production. Color. Two hours. Premiered: 1987. Syndicated.*

*Voices*
**Yogi Bear/Quick Draw McGraw/Wally Gator/Snagglepuss:** Daws Butler; **Boo Boo/Ranger Smith:** Don Messick; **Buzzy/Little Cowgirl/Swamp Fox Girl/Girl/Swamp Fox Kid #2:** Susan Blu; **Bopper/Yapper/Real Ghost:** Frank Welker; **Bitsy:** Edan Gross; **Skinny Kid:** Josh Rodine; **Chubby Kid:** Dustin Diamond; **Leader Kid:** Scott Menville; **Trapper/Dad:** Bill Callaway; **Bandit Bear:** Allan Melvin; **Li'l Brother Bear:** Hamilton Camp; **Reporter/Cowboy Kid #1/Swamp Fox Kid:** Patrick Fraley; **Swamp Fox Boy/Cowboy Kid #2/Mom/Boy:** Tress MacNeille

### ◎ YOGI THE EASTER BEAR

In this first-run syndicated special, after swiping the sweets marked for the Jellystone Easter Jamboree, Yogi hatches a plan to pacify the enraged Ranger Smith and find the Easter Bunny in time for the big event. *A Hanna-Barbera Production. Color. Half-hour. Premiered: April 3, 1994. Syndicated. Rebroadcast on CAR: April 16, 1995 (Mr. Spim's Cartoon Theatre).*

*Voices*
**Yogi Bear:** Greg Burson; **Boo Boo/Ranger Smith:** Don Messick; **Paulie:** Charlie Adler; **Clarence:** Gregg Berger; **Easter Chicken:** Marsha Clark; **Ernest:** Jeff Doucette; **Commissioner:** Ed Gilbert; **Easter Bunny:** Rob Paulsen; **Mortimer/Grand Grizzly:** Jonathan Winters

### ◎ YOU'RE A GOOD MAN, CHARLIE BROWN

This hour-long cartoon adaptation of the 1967 off-Broadway musical featuring the *Peanuts* characters charts the ups and downs of hapless Charlie Brown, for whom life is a constant source of frustration. The program marked Snoopy's speaking debut, with his voice supplied by Robert Tower, a member of the 1967 Los Angeles stage cast. Reshown in two parts over two consecutive dates on Nickelodeon beginning in March 1998. *A Lee Mendelson–Bill Melendez Production in association with Charles M. Schulz Creative Associates and United Feature Syndicate. Color. Half-hour. Premiered on CBS: November 6, 1985. Rebroadcast on NICK: March 18, 1998 (Part I); March 19, 1998 (Part II); June 8, 1998 (Part I); June 9, 1998 (Part II); July 14, 1998 (Part I); July 15, 1998 (Part II); August 3, 1998 (Part I); August 4, 1998 (Part II); September 3, 1998 (Part I); September 4, 1998 (Part II); October 5, 1998 (Part I); October 6, 1998 (Part II); October 28, 1998 (Part I); October 29, 1998 (Part II); December 7, 1998 (Part I); December 8, 1999 (Part II); April 5, 1999 (Part I); April 6, 1999 (Part II); May 26, 1999 (Part I); May 27, 1999 (Part II); July 26, 1999 (Part I); July 27, 1999 (Part II); November 13, 1999 (Part I); November 14, 1999 (Part II); February 12, 2000 (Part I); February 13, 2000 (Part II).*

*Voices*
**Charlie Brown:** Brad Keston; **Charlie Brown (singing):** Kevin Brando; **Linus Van Pelt:** David Wagner; **Lucy Van Pelt:** Jessie Lee Smith; **Schroeder:** Jeremy Reinbolt; **Marcie:** Michael Dockery; **Sally Brown:** Tiffany Reinbolt; **Snoopy:** Robert Tower

### ◎ YOU'RE A GOOD SPORT, CHARLIE BROWN

Charlie Brown enters a motocross race, but not until Lucy pulls the ol' place-kick trick on him. To win the race, Charlie finds himself up against some pretty stiff competition: Peppermint Patty and the Masked Marvel (Snoopy). In a separate subplot, Snoopy gets a "tennis lesson" from his pal Woodstock. *A Lee Mendelson–Bill Melendez Production in association with Charles M. Schulz Creative Associates and United Feature Syndicate. Color. Half-hour. Premiered on CBS: October 28, 1975. Rebroadcast on CBS: January 23, 1978. Rebroadcast on NICK: January 25, 1998; February 26, 1998; March 27, 1998; May 17, 1998; June 18, 1998; July 17, 1998; August 20, 1998; September 21, 1998; October 19, 1998; November 20, 1998; December 31, 1998; April 18, 1999; June 6, 1999; August 3, 1999; November 21, 1999.*

**Voices**

**Charlie Brown:** Duncan Watson; **Linus Van Pelt:** Liam Martin; **Lucy Van Pelt:** Melanie Kohn; **Peppermint Patty:** Stuart Brotman; **Marcie:** Jimmie Ahrens; **Sally Brown:** Gail M. Davis; **Schroeder:** Liam Martin; **Loretta:** Melanie Kohn; **Franklin/Kid:** Duncan Winston

### ◎ YOU'RE IN LOVE, CHARLIE BROWN

For the first time, Charlie Brown is in love! The object of his affection is a little girl in his class. Gravel-voiced, tomboy Peppermint Patty makes her debut in the program, first trying to solve "Chuck's" baseball problems and what she thinks is "an affair d'amour" between Charlie and Lucy. Rebroadcasts of the special were shown from 1998 to 2000 on Nickelodeon. *A Lee Mendelson–Bill Melendez Production in association with Charles M. Schulz Creative Associates and United Feature Syndicate. Color. Half-hour. Premiered on CBS: June 12, 1967. Rebroadcast on CBS: June 10, 1968; June 11, 1969; June 10, 1970; June 7, 1971; June 3, 1972. Rebroadcast on NICK: January 25, 1998; February 13, 1998; March 17, 1998; May 10, 1998; June 10, 1998; July 31, 1998; August 31, 1998; October 4, 1998; October 22, 1998; November 21, 1998; December 22, 1998; December 29, 1998; January 15, 1999; February 11, 1999; February 13, 1999; July 2, 1999; September 3, 1999; March 18, 2000.*

**Voices**

**Charlie Brown:** Peter Robbins; **Linus Van Pelt:** Christopher Shea; **Sally Brown:** Cathy Steinberg; **Lucy Van Pelt:** Sally Dryer-Barker; **Peppermint Patty:** Gail DeFaria; **Violet:** Anne Altieri

### ◎ YOU'RE IN THE SUPER BOWL, CHARLIE BROWN

Coached by that ever-feisty Snoopy ("the Bear Bryant of the beagle and birdie world") who uses all the motivation he can muster to overcome their brawnier opponents, Woodstock and his fine-feathered team of Grid Iron birds take on the Bison in a football free-for-all in this 1993 prime-time special, which bowed on NBC (the station that also carried the year's Super Bowl in Atlanta). *A Lee Mendelson–Bill Melendez Production in association with Charles Schulz Creative Associates and United Media. Color. Half-hour. Premiered on NBC: January 18, 1993.*

**Voices**

**Charlie Brown:** Jimmy Guardino; **Linus:** John Graas; **Lucy:** Molly Dunham; **Peppermint Patty:** Haley Peel; **Marcie:** Nicole Fisher; **Melody:** Crystal Kuns; **Announcer:** Steve Stoliar; **Snoopy/Woodstock:** Bill Melendez

### ◎ YOU'RE NOT ELECTED, CHARLIE BROWN

After taking a private poll, Lucy determines that Charlie Brown is not suited to run for student body president at school but finds that her insecure brother, Linus, is the perfect candidate. Linus has the election in the bag, but throws it all away during a debate with his opponent by mentioning "the Great Pumpkin," whereupon he is laughed out of the election. From 1998 to 2000, Nickelodeon re-aired the special along with a package of original CBS *Peanuts* specials and Saturday morning's *The Charlie Brown & Snoopy Show*. *A Lee Mendelson–Bill Melendez Production in association with Charles M. Schulz Creative Associates and United Feature Syndicate. Color. Half-hour. Premiered on CBS: October 29, 1972. Rebroadcast on CBS: October 15, 1973; September 23, 1976. Rebroadcast on NICK: January 27, 1998; February 9, 1998; March 11, 1998; April 14, 1998; May 14, 1998; June 28, 1998; July 23, 1998; August 26, 1998; November 3, 1998; December 24, 1998; January 19, 1999; February 1, 1999; March 2, 1999; March 25, 1999; July 5, 1999; September 19, 1999; April 29, 2000.*

**Voices**

**Charlie Brown:** Chad Webber; **Lucy Van Pelt:** Robin Kohn; **Linus Van Pelt:** Stephen Shea; **Sally Brown:** Hilary Momberger; **Russell:** Todd Barbee; **Violet:** Linda Ercoli; **Schroeder:** Brian Kazanjian; **Loud Child in Audience:** Brent McKay

*Additional Voices*

Danny Lettner, Joshua McGowan, Jay Robertson, David Zuckerman

### ◎ YOU'RE THE GREATEST, CHARLIE BROWN

With his school hosting the local Junior Olympics, Charlie Brown enters the decathalon event in hopes of helping his school win. Everyone has faith in him except the Peanuts gang. *A Lee Mendelson–Bill Melendez Production in association with Charles M. Schulz Creative Associates and United Feature Syndicate. Color. Half-hour. Premiered on CBS: March 19, 1979. Rebroadcast on CBS: March 5, 1980; March 20, 1981. Rebroadcast on NICK: February 12, 1998; March 16, 1998; April 20, 1998; May 20, 1998; June 23, 1998; July 28, 1998; August 20, 1998; September 21, 1998; November 5, 1998; December 12, 1998; February 7, 1999; April 20, 1999; June 9, 1999; August 6, 1999; December 12, 1999; May 8, 2000.*

**Voices**

**Charlie Brown:** Arrin Skelley; **Lucy Van Pelt/Girl:** Michelle Muller; **Marcie/Crowd:** Casey Carlson; **Linus Van Pelt/Crowd:** Daniel Anderson; **Fred Fabulous:** Tim Hall; **Peppermint Patty:** Patricia Patts; **Announcer:** Scott Beach; **Snoopy:** Bill Melendez

### ◎ ZIGGY'S GIFT

Accident-prone Ziggy gets scammed by a bogus street-corner Santa and afterward dedicates himself to doing nothing but good deeds for Christmas, unknowingly cracking the case for the police who want to break the "Santa ring." Based on Tom Wilson's popular comic strip, this prime-time Emmy Award-winning half-hour special premiered on ABC. *A Welcome Enterprises Production in association with Universal Press Syndicate. Color. Half-hour. Premiered on ABC: December 1, 1982.*

**Voices**

**Ziggy:** (non-speaking); **Crooked Santa:** Richard Williams; **Officer O'Connor:** Tom McGreevey; **Butcher:** Tony Giorgio; **Announcer:** John Gibbons

# TELEVISION CARTOON SERIES

## ● AAAHH!!! REAL MONSTERS

From the producers of *The Simpsons* and *Rugrats* comes this half-hour series (whose working title was simply *Real Monsters*) about three funny-looking teenage monsters—Ickis, Krumm and Oblina—who learn to scare people at the subterranean Monster Academy (where their teacher is the charming, high-pitched voiced Gromble). Produced in 11-minute half episodes per half-hour, with occasional full half-hour episodes, the series began airing Saturday nights on Nickelodeon in 1994. *A Klasky Csupo Production. Color. Half-hour. Premiered on NICK: October 29, 1994–December 6, 1997.*

**Voices**
**Ickis:** Charlie Adler; **Krumm:** David Eccles; **Oblina:** Christine Cavanaugh; **The Gromble:** Gregg Berger; **Bradley:** Brett Alexander; **The Library Monster:** Beverly Archer; **Simon the Monster Hunter:** James Belushi; **Zimbo:** Tim Curry; **Dizzle:** Cynthia Mann; **Exposia:** Lisa Raggio; **Hairyette:** Marcia Strassman; **Slickis:** Billy Vera; **Dr. Buzz Kutt:** Edward Winter

## ● ABBOTT AND COSTELLO

The antics of one of Hollywood's most memorable comedy teams, Bud Abbott and Lou Costello, inspired this series of 156 five-minute animated misadventures. Bud Abbott, the fast-talking straightman in dire financial straits at the time of the filming, actually voiced his own character. Abbott passed away in 1974. His gullible partner, roly-poly Lou Costello, who succumbed to a heart attack in 1959, was played by actor Stan Irwin. *A Hanna-Barbera Production for RKO-Jomar Productions. Color. Half-hour. Premiered: Fall 1967. Syndicated.*

**Voices**
**Bud Abbott:** Himself; **Lou Costello:** Stan Irwin

## ● THE ABC SATURDAY SUPERSTAR MOVIE

This popular Saturday-morning series marked the birth of feature-length cartoons for television. Famous television and cartoon figures were adapted into hour-long stories, along with new concepts especially made for television. In all, 16 films were made during the first season, each costing approximately $300,000 to produce.

A number of popular television sitcoms of the 1960s and 1970s were spun off into feature-length cartoons during the series' first season. *The Brady Bunch*, which enjoyed a five-season run on ABC (1970–74), starred in *The Brady Kids on Mysterious Island* (Filmation), with cast members supplying their own voices. The movie, originally titled *Jungle Bungle*, was the "pilot" for the Saturday-morning cartoon series *The Brady Kids*, broadcast on ABC from 1972 to 1974. Other animated adaptations included: *Nanny and the Professor* (Fred Calvert Productions), based on the television comedy series starring Juliet Mills and Richard Long; *That Girl in Wonderland* (Rankin-Bass), featuring Marlo Thomas as the character Ann Marie (from the ABC sitcom *That Girl*) in this loosely based version of the classic children's story *Alice in Wonderland*; *Gidget Makes a Wrong Connection* (Hanna-Barbera Productions), an animated spin-off of the mid-1960s' teen comedy sensation starring Sally Field (with voice artist Kathy Gori assuming the role); and *Tabitha and Adam and the Clown Family* (Hanna-Barbera), featuring the teenage offspring from television's *Bewitched*.

Other live-action characters turned animated that first season were: *Lassie and the Spirit of Thunder Mountain* (Fred Calvert Productions), featuring television's most famous collie in her first animated adventure (Lassie later starred in the ABC Saturday-morning animated series *Lassie's Rescue Rangers*, from 1973 to 1975); *Mad, Mad, Mad Monsters* (Rankin-Bass), reuniting Count Dracula, the Wolfman, the Mummy and the Invisible Man in stop-motion animated form; and even baseball great Willie Mays in an animated retelling of the 1951 feature film *Angels in the Outfield*, entitled *Willie Mays and the Say-Hey Kid* (Rankin-Bass), in which Mays did his own voice.

Popular animated film and television stars were also cast in feature-length cartoons. Hanna-Barbera produced *Yogi's Ark Lark*, starring "everyone's favorite bear" Yogi Bear, in an animated rendition of the biblical tale of Noah's Ark. King Features brought back the spinach-eating Popeye the Sailor in *Popeye Meets the Man Who Hated Laughter*, while Warner Bros. and Filmation merged some of their most popular characters in *Daffy Duck and Porky Pig Meet the*

*Groovie Goolies.* (The latter were introduced on 1970's *Sabrina and the Groovie Goolies* series on CBS.)

Other original made-for-television feature-length stories were presented during that first season: the two-part *Oliver Twist; and the Artful Dodger,* an animated re-creation of the classic Charles Dickens novel *Oliver Twist; Robin Hoodnik* (originally to be called *Cartoon Adventures of Robin Hood*), a colorful rendition of the classic character Robin Hood in animal form; *The Banana Splits in Hocus Pocus Park,* featuring the popular costumed live-action animals from TV's *The Banana Splits Adventure Hour.* (The last three shows were all produced by Hanna-Barbera.) Two other feature-length stories were *The Red Baron* (Rankin-Bass), the story of the legendary flying ace; and *Luvcast U.S.A.*

In 1973–74 the series returned for a second season (retitled *The New Saturday Superstar Movie*), featuring mostly reruns of shows from the first season and only three new cartoons: *Lost in Space,* based on the space-traveling Robinson family ("Danger! Danger!") from the 1960s' cult classic television show; *Nanny and the Professor and the Phantom Circus* and *The Mini-Munsters,* spotlighting Herman and the gang (from the cult television comedy classic *The Munsters*) in their first and only animated adventure.

Most series entries were produced by Hanna-Barbera Productions, then considered the leading producer of animated cartoons for television. Additional series entries were produced by Rankin-Bass Productions, Fred Calvert Productions and King Features Productions. (Details for each production, except for *Luvcast U.S.A.*, are available in the Animated Television Specials section.) A *Hanna-Barbera/Rankin-Bass/Fred Calvert/Filmation/Warner Brothers/King Features Production. Color. One hour. Premiered on ABC: September 9, 1972–August 31, 1974.*

## ◎ ABC WEEKEND SPECIALS

Mostly a weekly offering of live-action dramas, this Saturday anthology series occasionally featured hour-long animated specials produced by several major studios. Some stories were one-shot productions, while others were told over the course of two or more broadcasts.

Series installments included the critically acclaimed *The Trouble with Miss Switch* (1980) and *Miss Switch to the Rescue* (1982), about a witch who tries to do good with her witchcraft, each two-part specials, and *Scruffy* (1980), the adventures of an orphaned puppy; all were produced by Ruby-Spears Productions.

Other popular specials included the three-part *Liberty and the Littles* (1986), in which the tiny, near-human Littles learn about liberty, based on John Peterson's popular children's book series and spun off from the ABC animated series *The Littles,* produced by DIC Enterprises. The *Cap'n O.G. Readmore* (Rick Reinert Pictures) series of specials about a literature-loving, articulate cat who discusses classic literature with members of his "Friday Night Book Club" also was popular and included *Cap'n O.G. Readmore's Jack and the Beanstalk* (1985), *Cap'n O.G. Readmore Meets Dr. Jekyll and Mr. Hyde* (1986), *Cap'n O.G. Readmore Meets Little Riding Hood* (1988) and *Cap'n O.G. Readmore's Puss in Boots* (1988). Additional half-hours were comprised of Marvel Productions' *The Monster Bed* (1989), about a young boy trapped in a world of monsters, and *P.J. Funnybunny: Lifestyles of the Funny and Famous* (1989), the first of three such specials produced by independent animator Marija Diletic Dail's Animation Cottage.

More half-hour specials followed between 1992 and 1997, including *The Kingdom Chums: Original Top Ten* (1992), an inspirational tale of three young kids who discover the original top 10 were the 10 Commandments; *The Legend of Lochnagar* (1993), a Scottish story written and narrated by Prince Charles of Wales; *The Magic Flute* (1994), adapted from the famous Mozart opera; *The Magic Paintbrush* (1993), a prime-time animated special originally broadcast on CBS, based on Robin Muller's book; *Jirimpimbira: An African Folktale* (1995), produced in celebration of Black History Month; and *The Magic Pearl* (1996), the story of a Chinese American brother and sister that originally premiered on ABC's quarterly *Kids Movie Matinee* series. (For each title, see the entries in Animated Television Specials section for further details.) A *Hanna-Barbera/Ruby-Spears/Dave Edwards Ltd./DIC Entertainment/Film Roman/Greengrass/Huff-Douglas/Marvel Films/Rick Reinert Pictures/Mike Young Production. Color. One hour. Premiered on ABC: September 10, 1977.*

## ◎ ACE VENTURA: THE ANIMATED SERIES

Wacky pet detective Ace Ventura and his sidekick, Spike the monkey, tackle new capers in this half-hour cartoon series spinoff based on the box-office comedy hit movie starring comedian Jim Carrey. Carrey did not supply his voice for this Saturday-morning cartoon version, which began as a midseason replacement on CBS. A *Nelvana Entertainment Production in association with Morgan Creek Productions. Color. Half-hour. Premiered on CBS: January 20, 1996–August 30, 1997. Rebroadcast on NICK: September 13, 1999–March 3, 2000.*

**Voices**
**Ace Ventura:** Michael Hall; **Spike:** Richard Binsley; **Shickadance:** Vince Corraza; **Aguado:** Al Waxman; **Emilio:** Bruce Tubbe; **Woodstock:** David Beatty

## ◎ ACTION LEAGUE NOW!

Loving danger at every corner and one of the biggest group of bumblers ever assembled, an unusual team of crime-fighting toy action figures, toys and dolls—The Chief, Meltman, ThunderGirl, The Flesh and Stinky Diver—come to life thanks to a child's imagination and find adventure and, of course, danger in the form of the Sinkhole of Doom (better known as a household garbage disposal) and a ferocious German shepherd named Spotzilla in this hilarious series of combined stop-motion animated/live-action shorts created by Tim Hill using the so-called method of "Chuckimation," which begun as a component of Nickelodeon's popular children's anthology series, *KaBlam!* On Friday, October 25, 1996, this oddball league of superheroes was introduced in a two-part adventure that aired on consecutive Friday nights. Two years later, Nickelodeon starred the four hapless heroes in their first prime-time special, *A Very Special Action League Now! Special.* The characters were voiced by Pittsburgh's WDVE radio station personalities. Episodes of *Action League Now!* were subsequently rerun on Nickelodeon as part of *KaBlam!* until late June 2006.

As a result of the amazing popularity of their Friday night adventures on *KaBlam!*, in September 2003 Nick spun them off into their own half-hour series, beginning with the premiere episode, "Thunder and Lightning." Airing Sunday afternoons, 38 additional half-hours (excluding one unaired episode) were produced through November 2004. Broadcast on Nickelodeon until June 2006, Nick's sister network, Nicktoons, began re-airing the original *KaBlam!* shorts in May 2002 and later the half-hour series as well. A *Nickelodeon Production. Two minutes. Half-hour. Premiered on NICK: October 25, 1996 (KaBlam!). Premiered on NICK (series): September 14, 2003–November 11, 2004. Rebroadcast on NICKT: May 5, 2002–June 30, 2006.*

**Voices**
**The Chief:** Victor Hart; **Meltman/Announcer:** Scott Paulsen; **ThunderGirl:** Chris Winters; **The Flesh/Stinky Diver/The Mayor/Bill the Lab Guy/Johnny Cool:** Jim Krenn; **Justice:** Alyssa Grahm; **Generic Boy:** Stephen Gaich

## ⊚ ACTION MAN (1995)

Billed as "The Ultimate Extreme Action Hero," Alex Mann (a.k.a. Action Man) and his elite multinational task force, including computer expert Jacques, ex-Green Beret Knuck and beauteous blond Natalie, race to save the world from the evil Dr. X and his minions, while trying to uncover the secret to his past identity in this computer-animated half-hour action-adventure series, featuring live-action wraparounds of series' stars Mark Griffin (Action Man) and Rolf Leenders (Dr. X), based on Hasbro Toys' popular action figure toyline. Produced in the style of the *James Bond 007* and *Indiana Jones* movies by Burbank, California's DIC Entertainment, the thrilling 26-episode series began airing in first-run syndication in the United States in September 1995. The series remained on the air for three years until 1998. Previously, Hasbro had commissioned DIC to produce a half-hour pilot starring the famed action hero that was instead syndicated as an animated special in October 1986. In 2000, the top-selling action figure returned to star in a brand-new half-hour series for the FOX network. *A Hasbro/DIC Enterprises Production. Color. Half-hour. Premiered: September 23, 1995. Syndicated.*

### Voices

**Action:** Mark Griffin; **Dr. X:** Rolf Leenders; **Knuck:** Dale Wilson; **Natalie:** Joely Collins; **Jacques:** Richard Cox; **Norris:** Gary Chalk; **Gangrene:** David Hay; **Vira:** Iris Quinn

### Additional Voices

Patti Allen, Gillian Gaber, Nigel Bennett, Lisa Bunting, Babs Chula, Brian Drummond, Christopher Gaze, Paulina Gillis, L. Harvey Gold, Mark Hildreth, Chris Humphreys, Art Irizawa, Scott McNeil, David Morse, Colin Murdock, Simon Pidgeon, Rick Poltaruk, Ken Roberts, William Samples, Devon Sawa, Kelly Sheridan, Tasha Simms, Tracey Lee Smythe, Raimund Stramm, Ingrid Tesch, French Tickner, Louise Vallance, Dave "Squatch" Ward, Richard Yee

## ⊚ ACTION MAN (2000)

While traveling the world to compete in heart-pounding sports competitions with his team, incredible, thrill-seeking athlete Alex Mann (a.k.a. Action Man) possesses the unique ability known as AMP (Alternative Motor & Physical) Factor, which gives him a split-second advantage to anticipate and react to danger. He returns again to fight the nefarious Dr. X, who is hell-bent on duplicating the famed action hero's AMP Factor for evil purposes and global domination. Produced by Canada's Mainframe Entertainment, this weekly 2-D cel and CGI-animated half-hour action-adventure was introduced to television viewers on FOX in May 2000 as a half-hour "preview" special of the series pilot entitled *The Call to Action*, with the Saturday-morning series debuting that August. In this second television cartoon series adaptation following DIC Entertainment's 1995 syndicated series, Mann was to learn of his hidden connection to Dr. X, but FOX never aired the finale or episodes offering this important revelation. The series was cancelled only four months after its debut. *A Mainframe Entertainment Production. Color. One-hour. Premiered on FOX: May 20, 2000 (special); Premiered on FOX: August 5, 2000–December 28, 2000 (series).*

### Voices

**Alex Mann/Action Man:** Mark Hildreth; **Desmond "Grinder" Sinclair:** Michael Dobson; **Templeton Storm/Tempest:** Andrew Francis; **Nick Masters:** Mackenzie Gray; **Fidget Wilson:** Tabitha St. Germain; **Simon Grey:** Christopher Judge; **Rikkie Syngh-Baines:** Peter Kelamis; **Brandon Caine:** Tyler Labine; **Dr. X:** Campbell Lane; **Asazi:** Janyse Jaud

## ⊚ THE ADDAMS FAMILY (1973)

Popular TV ghouls Gomez Addams, wife Morticia, bald Uncle Fester and zombie butler Lurch travel across the country with the rest of the family, telling hair-raising stories in a haunted wagon, complete with moat. The 16-episode series enjoyed a two-season run on NBC. *A Hanna-Barbera Production. Characters' copyrights owned by Charles Addams. Color. Half-hour. Premiered on NBC: September 8, 1973–August 30, 1975. Rebroadcast on CAR: June 1, 1996– (Saturdays).*

### Voices

**Gomez Addams:** Lennie Weinrib; **Morticia Addams/Granny:** Janet Waldo; **Uncle Fester:** Jackie Coogan; **Lurch:** Ted Cassidy; **Pugsley:** Jodie Foster; **Wednesday:** Cindy Henderson; **Other Voices:** Josh Albee, John Carver, Pat Harrington Jr., Bob Holt, John Stephenson, Don Messick, Herb Vigran, Howard Caine

## ⊚ THE ADDAMS FAMILY (1992)

Cartoonist Charles Addams's macabre characters live in the suburb of Happydale Heights, where their normal neighbors seem weird, in brand-new half-hour animated adventures inspired by the success of the 1991 live-action feature. John Astin, who portrayed Gomez in the original hit television series, reprised the character for the new series. *A Hanna-Barbera/Fils-Cartoons Production. Color. Half-hour. Premiered on ABC: September 12, 1992–January 7, 1995.*

### Voices

**Gomez:** John Astin; **Morticia:** Nancy Linari; **Wednesday:** Debi Derryberry; **Pugsley:** Jeannie Elias; **Uncle Fester:** Rip Taylor; **Granny:** Carol Channing; **Lurch:** Jim Cummings; **Cousin Itt:** Pat Fraley; **Mrs. Normanmeyer:** Rob Paulsen; **N.J. Normanmeyer:** Dick Beals

## ⊚ ADVENTURES FROM THE BOOK OF VIRTUES

Positive topics using classic American stories, European fairy tales, African fables, biblical adventures, Greek mythology, Asian folktales and Native American legends were brought to life in this first-ever, half-hour prime-time animated series for PBS, based on

*Time-honored stories from Greek mythology, European fairy tales, African folklore and other sources illustrate different virtues for young Zach and Annie in the award-winning PBS cartoon series* Adventures from the Book of Virtues. © *PorchLight Entertainment*

William J. Bennett's bestseller, *The Book of Virtues*. The series was originally presented as a series of 10 prime-time specials and aired in hour-long blocks, first in September of 1996, then in February of 1997 (two half-hour episodes, back to back). (See Animated Television Specials section for details.) This was before the series entered its regular weekly run. *A PorchLight Entertainment/Fox Animation Studios Production in association with KCET/Hollywood. Color. Half-hour. Premiered on PBS: September 2, 1996 (as a series of specials).*

**Voices (main cast)**
**Plato:** Kevin Richardson; **Ari:** Jim Cummings; **Aurora/Annie:** Kath Soucie; **Zach:** Pam Segall; **Socrates:** Frank Welker

## ◎ THE ADVENTURES OF BATMAN
In Gotham City, millionaire playboy Bruce Wayne and his youthful ward, Dick Grayson, battle the nefarious schemes of the Joker, the Penguin, the Riddler, the Catwoman, Mr. Freeze, Mad Hatter and Simon the Pieman in this half-hour action series spun off from 1968's *The Batman/Superman Hour* (see entry for information), which was broadcast on CBS. *A Filmation Associates Production in association with Ducovny Productions and National Periodicals. Color. Half-hour. Premiered on CBS: September 13, 1969–September 6, 1970. Syndicated.*

**Voices**
**Bruce Wayne/Batman:** Olan Soule; **Dick Grayson/Robin:** Casey Kasem; **Barbara Gordon/Batgirl:** Jane Webb; **Alfred Pennyworth, Wayne's butler:** Olan Soule

## ◎ THE ADVENTURES OF BATMAN AND ROBIN
The caped crusader and his loyal crimefighting partner battle their famous archenemies—the Riddler, the Joker, Two-Face, Catwoman and many others—in this relabeled Saturday morning (and later weekday afternoon) version of *Batman: The Animated Series*, which aired on FOX Network beginning in 1994. (Complete voice credits are under *Batman: The Animated Series*.) *A Warner Bros. Television Animation Production. Color. Half-hour. Premiered on FOX: September 10, 1994–September 5, 1997.*

## ◎ THE ADVENTURES OF BLINKY BILL
Based on a series of books written by Dorothy Wall, this half-hour series from famed Australian animator Yoram Gross follows the far-reaching adventures of a mischievous koala bear who relies on his imagination to help his furry friends Down Under rebuild their Australian Bush community after it's ruined by construction. *A Yoram Gross Film Studio E.M.TV/PTY Ltd. Production. Color. Half-hour. Premiered: September 24, 1994. Syndicated.*

**Voices**
Robyn Moore, Keith Scott

## ◎ THE ADVENTURES OF CHICO AND GUAPO
Follows the gritty *Beavis & Butt-Head*-type escapades of two catastrophic janitors-turned-interns, the slick Puerto Rican named Chico and smart-mouthed Dominican named Guapo, who try making it in the music business—no matter what it takes—at a Manhattan recording studio, Angelo Productions, in this half-hour series for cable's MTV2. Cocreated by Orlando Jones and writers P.J. Pesce and Paul D'Acri and based on the recurring nightly animated segment "The Adventures of Chico and Guapo," which aired on Jones's *The Orlando Jones Show* on FX, the offbeat cartoon series with its sexual innuendo, simulated sex acts and

social commentary—part of the network's *Sic 'Em Fridays* adult programming block—was meant to court viewers of subversive and edgy toons, much like Cartoon Network's highly successful *Adult Swim* late-night animation block. Joining them in their comical misadventures in this original series for MTV2 were recording studio owner, Mr. Angelo (whose full name was Frank C. Angelo); music producer extraordinaire, Hank Holiday; sassy Latina receptionist, Concepcion Rodriguez; and Chico's cousin and "beat master," Cezar. The series debuted on MTV2 in June 2006 and initially ran for eight weeks.

Pesce and D'Acri, who also voiced several characters in the series, devised the characters while living together in New York in the summer of 1983. As Pesce recalled in a newspaper interview, ". . . we started getting a feel for all sorts of voices and characters in New York City. We would act out whole scenes, for hours, [as] these two Hispanic guys, and that became the basis for Chico and Guapo." Previously, the pair made various attempts to produce a series based on the characters, including a sitcom and puppet-animated series using marionettes, à la television's *Thunderbirds*, before teaching themselves the art of Flash animation in 1999 and creating a cartoon pilot that was rejected until Jones took an interest in the project. "We created a bunch of new characters for Orlando to play," notes Pesce, "and he was amazing. It brought the stuff to a whole new level." *An MTV Production. Color. Half-hour. Premiered on MTV2: June 10, 2006–July 29, 2006.*

**Voices**
**Chico Bustello:** Paul D'Acri; **Guapo Martinez:** P.J. Pesce; **Frank C. Angelo:** P.J. Pesce, Michael Donovan; **Concepcion Rodriguez:** Orlando Jones; **Cezar:** Paul D'Acri, José Pou; **Hank Holiday:** Orlando Jones, Lee Tockar

## ◎ THE ADVENTURES OF DON COYOTE AND SANCHO PANDA
Hanna-Barbera coproduced this first-run, half-hour animated series of calamitous 17th- and 18th-century adventures about a gangly coyote knight-errant and his paunchy panda sidekick who fight on the side of truth, justice and innocence (aided by Coyote's noble steed, Rosinante, and Sancho's dyed-in-in-the-horsehair cynic donkey, Dapple). The series was first broadcast in Europe in 1989, based on Miguel Cervantes's original literary classic *Don Quixote*. *A Hanna-Barbera Production in association with RAI (Radiotelevisione Italiana Raiuno). Color. Half-Hour. Premiered: September 23, 1990 (The Fantastic World of the Hanna-Barbera). Syndicated. Rebroadcast on CAR: September 5, 1994.*

**Voices**
**Don Coyote/Dapple:** Frank Welker; **Sancho Panda:** Don Messick; **Rosinante:** Brad Gilbert

## ◎ THE ADVENTURES OF GULLIVER
The tiny folks of Lilliput hold captive the giant, Gulliver, who saves the city and people from destruction. In return they help him find his missing father and buried treasure, and overcome the foul deeds of the evil Captain Leech in this animated adaptation of the Jonathan Swift tale. *A Hanna-Barbera Production. Color. Half-hour. Premiered on ABC: September 14, 1968–September 5, 1970.*

**Voices**
**Gary Gulliver:** Jerry Dexter; **Thomas Gulliver/Captain Leech/ King Pomp:** John Stephenson; **Flirtacia:** Jenny Tyler; **Eger/Glum:** Don Messick; **Tagg:** Herb Vigran; **Bunko:** Allan Melvin

# ◉ THE ADVENTURES OF HOPPITY HOOPER

Naive, lovable frog Hoppity Hooper (originally slated to be called Hippity Hooper, but that was deemed too similar to the name of Warner Bros.' own hopping kangaroo, Hippity Hopper) and associates, Professor Waldo Wigglesworth, a fast-thinking fox, and Fillmore, a dim witted but good-natured bear—travel across the country to explore get-rich schemes in this cartoon series created by Jay Ward, the father of such cartoon favorites as Rocky and Bullwinkle, Dudley Do-Right and Crusader Rabbit.

The comical trio was featured in two episodes of four-part cliffhanging adventures each week, along with episodes of three other components: "Fractured Fairytales" (repeated from *Rocky and His Friends*), which spoofed beloved fairy tales; "Mr. Know-It-All," with Bullwinkle Moose offering solutions to common everyday problems (first seen on *The Bullwinkle Show*); and "Commander McBragg," a boastful, bushy-browed retired naval commander who tells tall tales about his career, which premiered on *Tennessee Tuxedo and His Tales*. The program later contained reruns of "Peabody's Improbable History," hosted by intelligent beagle Peabody and his brainy adopted son, Sherman, who transport themselves back in time to visit historical events through the power of their WABAC machine.

In the fall of 1965, after the first 26 episodes aired on ABC, they were reedited and repackaged for syndication under the title of *Uncle Waldo*. With the network series still on the air, the syndicated version featured only two other recurring segments besides the Hoppity Hooper reruns: "Fractured Fairytales" and "Peabody's Improbable History," the latter repeated from *Rocky and His Friends*. (See series entry for further information.) *A Hooper Production in association with Jay Ward Productions/Leonardo Television. Color. Half-hour. Premiered on ABC: September 12, 1964–September 2, 1967. Syndicated.*

### Voices
**Hoppity Hooper:** Chris Allen; **Professor Waldo Wigglesworth:** Hans Conried; **Fillmore, the bear:** Bill Scott; **Narrator:** Paul Frees; **Narrator, "Fractured Fairytales":** Edward Everett Horton; **Commander McBragg:** Kenny Delmar; **Bullwinkle Moose:** Bill Scott

# ◉ THE ADVENTURES OF HYPERMAN

Befriended by teenage genius Emma C. Squared, who helps him out in his weekly battles while teaching various science lessons along the way, Hyperman, an intergalactic secret agent superhero, along with his faithful dog, Studd Puppy, are assigned to stop badguy Entrobe (and his sidekick Kidd Chaos) from destroying Earth in this comedy/educational series that aired on CBS during the 1994–95 season. *A Hyperion Animation/Illumina Studios/IBM Production. Premiered on CBS: October 14, 1995–August 10, 1996.*

### Voices
**Hyperman:** Steve Mackall; **Entrobe:** Frank Welker; **Emma C. Squared:** Tamera Mowry; **Studd Puppy:** Kevin McDonald; **Kidd Chaos/Comptroller:** Maurice LaMarche; **Hyberboss:** Mark Petrakis; **Narrators:** Neil Ross, Mark Petrakis; **E. Brian Small:** Justin John Ross; **Brittany Bright:** Mayim Bialik

# ◉ THE ADVENTURES OF JIMMY NEUTRON: BOY GENIUS

A 10-year-old boy genius, Jimmy Neutron (whose full name is Jimmy Isaac Neutron, in homage to famed scientist Isaac Newton), invents amazing gadgets meant to improve the quality of everyday life in Retroville, Texas, with his devoted robotic dog, Goddard, and his eclectic friends, Carl, Sheen and primary adversary, Cindy Vortex, who thinks girls are infinitely smarter than boys, and family, including his bumbling car salesman dad, Hugh, and fastidious mother, Judy, but even his high-tech ideas miss every now and then with hilarious results.

Beginning as an award-winning 40-second CGI-animated short subject animated by John A. Davis and Keith Alcorn of Texas-based DNA Productions (with the character originally named Johnny Quasar), Nickelodeon commissioned a pilot for a weekly series based on the Johnny Quasar character, which was originally to be coproduced by Steve Odenkerk's O Entertainment in 1995, but production stalled until 1997. Instead of airing the so-called 83-minute pilot, hoping to capitalize at the box office like they did with 1999's *Rugrats: The Movie*, Nickelodeon instead released the original telefilm through Paramount Pictures as a G-rated full-length theatrical feature, entitled *Jimmy Neutron: Boy Genius* (2001), which pulled in an eye-popping $80 million in domestic ticket revenue and was nominated for an Academy Award for best animated feature. To promote the movie, Nickelodeon aired eight Jimmy Neutron cartoon shorts, beginning with "Cookie Time."

After officially commencing production of a half-hour series in July and August 2002, with the first new episode being "When Pants Attack," Nickelodeon sneak previewed the new computer-animated series before its premiere that September. It became the highest-rated animated series in the network's history. Featuring mostly two 11-minute cartoons per show, with a few exceptions, Jimmy Neutron and friends became one of Nickelodeon's most successful cartoon franchises, starring in 59 half-hours as well as nine prime-time specials, including "Make Room for Daddy-O" (2003) Father's Day special, "Operation Rescue Jet Fusion" (2003); "Nightmare in Retroville" (2003) Halloween special; "Holly Jolly Jimmy" (2003) Christmas special; "Love Potion #976/J" (2004) Valentine's Day special; "Attack of the Twonkies" (2004); "Win, Lose and Kaboom" (2004); "League of the Villains" (2005); "My Big Fat Spy Wedding" (2005); and three hour-long crossover specials with his friend Timmy Turner, "The Jimmy Timmy Power Hour" (2004); "The Jimmy Timmy Power Hour 2: When Nerds Collide" (2006); and "The Jimmy Timmy Power Hour 3: The Jerkinators" (2006). Reruns of the series were shown on Nickelodeon's sister network, Nicktoons, beginning in January 2003. *A DNA Productions/O Entertainment/Nickelodeon Production. Color. Half-Hour. Premiered on NICK: July 20, 2002 (preview); August 5, 2002 (preview); September 6, 2002. Rebroadcast on NICKT: January 12, 2003–    .*

### Voices
**James Isaac "Jimmy" Neutron:** Debi Derryberry; **Hugh Beaumont Neutron, his father:** Mark DeCarlo; **Judy Neutron, his mother:** Megan Cavanagh; **Cynthia Aurora "Cindy" Vortex:** Carolyn Lawrence; **Miss Winifred Fowl:** Andrea Martin; **Goddard/Wendell:** Frank Welker; **Liberty Danielle "Libby" Folfax:** Crystal Scales; **Carlton Ulysses Wheezer:** Rob Paulsen; **Juarerra Estevez:** Jeffrey Garcia; **Nick Dean:** Candi Milo

# ◉ THE ADVENTURES OF JONNY QUEST

One of the most nostalgically popular animated television series of the 1960s, *The Adventures of Jonny Quest* was developed by artist Doug Wildey for Hanna-Barbera Productions. The 26-episode series—the first cartoon series ever to depict realistic human characters in an action adventure format—recounted the adventures of 11-year-old Jonny and his brilliant scientist father, Dr. Benton Quest (voiced by Don Messick in 20 of the series' original episodes). Accompanied by bodyguard-tutor Roger "Race" Bannon, a mysterious Indian boy named Hadji and fearless bulldog Bandit, they embark on a global expedition that becomes more fantastic with each stop. The series premiered on ABC in September of 1964 (the opening episode was "The Mystery of the Lizard Men") and, surprisingly, lasted only one full season. In 1967 the series was dusted off and rebroadcast on CBS for three full seasons, then again on NBC in 1972 and 1979 (the latter as part of *Godzilla and the Super 90*).

In 1986 Hanna-Barbera revived this animated classic and produced 13 all-new half-hour episodes, packaged for weekend syndication as part of *The Funtastic World of Hanna-Barbera* series. Of the original main cast, only Don Messick returned to voice Dr. Benton Quest and Bandit.

Both series were rebroadcast on Cartoon Network beginning in October of 1992. The characters were again revived in all-new animated adventures in 1996 under the title of *The Real Adventures of Jonny Quest*. (See entry for details.) Preceding the series were two made-for-TV movies reintroducing the character to viewers: *Jonny's Golden Quest* (1993), produced exclusively for USA Network, and *Jonny Quest Vs. The Cyber Insects* (1995), which premiered on TNT.

*A Hanna-Barbera Production. Color. Half-hour. Premiered on ABC: September 18, 1964–September 9, 1965 (switched nights December 31, 1964). Rebroadcast on CBS: September 6, 1967–September 5, 1970. Rebroadcast on ABC: September 13, 1970–September 2, 1972; NBC: November 4, 1978–September 1, 1979 (as part of Godzilla and the Super 90): September 7, 1979–November 3, 1979; April 12, 1980–September 6, 1981. Rebroadcast on CAR: October 1, 1992–October 30, 1992 (weekdays); November 10, 1992–December 5, 1992 (weekdays); January 4, 1993–September 17, 1993 (weekdays); January 3, 1994–June 2, 1995; September 4, 1995–(weekdays, Saturdays). Premiere (new series): September 1986 (as part of The Funtastic World of Hanna-Barbera). Syndicated. Rebroadcast on TNT: 1992. Rebroadcast on CAR: November 2, 1992–November 9, 1992; December 6, 1992–January 3, 1993; January 3, 1994–May 1996; 1997–2000. Rebroadcast on BOOM: April 1, 2000–.*

**Voices**
**Dr. Benton Quest:** Don Messick, John Stephenson; **Jonny Quest:** Tim Matthieson, Scott Menville (1986); **Roger "Race" Bannon:** Mike Road, Sonny Granville Van Dusen (1986); **Hadji, Indian companion:** Danny Bravo, Rob Paulsen (1986); **Bandit, their dog:** Don Messick; **Dr. Zin/Others:** Vic Perrin; **Jezebel Jade:** Cathy Lewis

## ◎ THE ADVENTURES OF LARIAT SAM

Written especially for *The Captain Kangaroo Show*, this preschooler series cast honest but friendly cowboy Lariat Sam and his poetry-reading horse, Tippytoes (known as the "Wonder Horse"), in 13 offbeat stories—presented in three parts—about the Old West. Sam's recurring nemesis: Badlands Meeney. The series was created by Robert Keeshan's company, Robert Keeshan Associates. (Keeshan is best known to viewers as Captain Kangaroo). The cartoons were later packaged for syndication. *A Terrytoons/CBS Films, Inc., Robert Keeshan Associates Productions. Black-and-white. Color. Five minutes. Half-hour. Premiered on CBS: September 10, 1962–August 27, 1965. Syndicated.*

**Voices**
**Lariat Sam/Tippytoes, his horse:** Dayton Allen

## ◎ THE ADVENTURES OF PADDINGTON BEAR

After stowing away on a ship out of "darkest Peru," the ever-curious, dignified and helpful little bear, Paddington Brown, sporting his spiffy blue duffel coat and stuffed suitcase and with a ferocious love of marmalade sandwiches, finds adventure in the strange new land of Paddington Station, making his home with the Brown family and getting himself in and out of all sorts of sticky situations, in this third television cartoon series—and first since Hanna-Barbera's 1989 *Paddington Bear*, part of the syndicated *Funtastic World of Hanna-Barbera*—based on Michael Bond's best-selling children's book series that has sold more than 25 million copies worldwide.

Coproduced by Canada's CINAR, Busy Bear Productions and Protecrea, this charming, witty and colorfully animated series originally began in 1997, featured three cartoon adventures per half-hour and bowed on American television following the February 1999 launch of HBO's offspring channel, HBO Family, a new 24-hour commercial-free channel dedicated exclusively to family programming. The series premiered with several other original programs, a mix of animated and preschool programs from producers like CINAR, Curious Pictures, Nelvana, S4C and HIT Entertainment including *George and Martha*, *Anthony Ant* and *A Little Curious*. Twenty half-hours of this popular children's series were produced. As of March 2007, the series continued to rerun twice daily at 9:30 A.M. and 2:00 P.M., seven days a week, during HBO Family's preschool programming block. *A CINAR/Busy Bear Productions/Protecrea Production. Color. Half-hour. Premiered on HBO FAM: February 1, 1999.*

**Voices**
**Paddington Brown:** Jonathan Kydd; **Mr. Brown:** Jon Glover; **Mrs. Brown:** Moir Leslie; **Henry Brown:** John Hernandez; **Isabelle Brown:** Meriam Stover; **Mr. Curry:** Nigel Lambert; **Mr. Grubber:** Cyril Shaps; **Mrs. Bird:** Eve Karpf; **Judy:** Jade Williams; **Narrator:** Michael Hordern

## ◎ THE ADVENTURES OF POW POW

The stories of a young Indian boy (based on Indian folklore and related fables) were recounted in this limited--animated, 26-episode series first telecast on *Captain Kangaroo* in 1957. In 1958 the program was syndicated to local stations nationwide. *A Sam Singer/Tempetoons/Screen Gems Production. Black-and-white. Five minutes. Half-hour. Premiered on CBS: 1957. Syndicated: 1958.*

## ◎ THE ADVENTURES OF RAGGEDY ANN AND ANDY

Secretly coming to life in Marcella's playroom, Raggedy Ann and brother Andy and their friends—Raggedy Cat, Raggedy Dog, Grouchy Bear, the Camel with the Wrinkled Knees and others—are hurled into a world where anything is possible: dragons, perriwonks, fairies and even the presence of evil. Based on Johnny Gruelle's famed children's story, *Raggedy Ann and Andy*. *A CBS Animation Production. Color. Half-hour. Premiered on CBS: September 17, 1988–September 1, 1990.*

**Voices**
**Raggedy Ann:** Christina Lange; **Raggedy Andy:** Josh Rodine; **Marcella:** Tracy Rowe; **Grouchy Bear:** Charlie Adler; **Raggedy Cat:** Kath Soucie; **Raggedy Dog:** Dana Hill; **Camel:** Ken Mars; **Sunny Bunny:** Katie Leigh

## ◎ ADVENTURES OF SONIC THE HEDGEHOG

Programmed for daily syndication, this 65-episode companion series to the ABC network series, *Sonic the Hedgehog* followed the trials and tribulations of the popular video-game star as he tries to save the planet Mobrius from his favorite enemy, Dr. Robotnik. The series debuted 12 days before the premiere of the ABC series. For nearly three seasons, the program was rebroadcast on cable's Toon Disney, along with the series' half-hour holiday special, *Sonic Christ-*

mas Blast, which aired two years after the series' original run. A DIC Enterprises Production in association with Sega of America, Inc. and Bohbot Entertainment. Color. Half-hour. Premiered: September 6, 1993. Syndicated. Rebroadcast on USA: September 4, 1995–1997. Rebroadcast on DIS: April 7, 1998–August 30, 2002.

*Voices*
**Sonic the Hedgehog:** Jaleel White; **Tails:** Christopher Welch; **Dr. Robotnik:** Long John Baldry; **Scratch:** Phil Hayes; **Grounder:** Gary Chalk

### ◉ THE ADVENTURES OF TEDDY RUXPIN

Flying in a wonderous airship, Teddy Ruxpin, Newton Gimmick (an eccentric genius inventor) and Grubby (a valiant octopede) try to uncover the true purpose of a series of long-lost ancient crystals in half-hour adventures that bring them face to face with the evil overlords, M.A.V.O. (Monsters and Villains Organization), whose sole purpose is to rule the Land of Grundo. The series, based on the popular interactive toy of the mid-1980s, originally premiered as a five-part syndicated series in 1986. Sixty-five episodes were produced for daily syndication in 1987. A DIC Enterprises/Alchemy II, Inc./Worlds of Wonder Production. Color. Half-hour. Premiered: 1986 (five-part series); September 1987 (syndicated series). Syndicated.

*Voices*
**Teddy Ruxpin:** Phil Barron; **Gimmick:** John Stocker; **Grubby:** Wili Ryan; **Tweeg:** John Koensgen; **L. B. Prince Arin:** Robert Bauxthall; **Leota:** Holly Larocque; **Aruzia:** Abby Hagyard; **Wooly What's It:** Pierre Paquette

### ◉ THE ADVENTURES OF THE GALAXY RANGERS

In 2086, to keep peace in the universe, the World Federation forms an organization called BETA (Bureau of Extra-Terrestrial Affairs), led by Commander Joseph Walsh, who heads a special team of crimefighters—Zachary Fox, Doc Hartford, Niko and Goose—to protect mankind from alien enemies in outer space. A Gaylord Production in association with Transcom Media and ITF Enterprises. Color. Half-hour. Premiered: September 15, 1986 (five-episode pilot). Premiered: September 14, 1987–1988 (series). Syndicated.

*Voices*

**THE GALAXY RANGERS: Zachary Fox:** Jerry Orbach; **Doc Hartford:** Hubert Kelly; **Niko:** Laura Dean; **Goose:** Doug Preis

**OTHERS: Commander Joseph Walsh/Lazarus Slade/Captain Kidd/Wildfire Cody/King Spartos:** Earl Hammond; **Buzzwang:** Sandy Marshall; **Mogel the Space Sorcerer/The General/ Nimrod/Jackie Subtract/Bubblehead the Memory Bird:** Doug Preis; **Queen of the Crown/The Kiwi Kids:** Corinne Orr; **Zozo/Squeegie/GV/Little Zach Foxx/Brappo:** Bob Bottone; **Waldo/Geezi the Pedulont/Q-Ball/Larry/Scarecrow/Kilbane/ Crown Agent:** Henry Mandell; **Maya/Annie Oh/Mistwalker:** Maia Danzinger; **Macross:** Ray Owen; **Aliza Foxx/Jessica Foxx:** Laura Dean

### ◉ THE ADVENTURES OF THE LITTLE KOALA

Roobear, a koala bear, experiences various adventures through which he learns the importance of life, parents and friends and the world around him. The 26-episode series made its American television debut on Nickelodeon in 1987, airing weekdays. A CINAR Films/Tohokushinsha Film Production. Color. Half-hour. Premiered on NICK: June 1, 1987–April 2, 1993.

*Voices*
**Betty Koala:** Cleo Paskal; **Laura Koala:** Morgan Hallet; **Roobear Koala:** Steven Bednarski; **Mommy Koala:** Jane Woods; **Papa Koala/ Dr. Nose:** Walter Massey; **Miss Lewis/Pamie Penguin:** Bronwen Mantel; **Colt Kangaroo:** Rob Roy; **Duckbill Platypus:** Arthur Gross; **Horsey Kangaroo:** Dean Hagopian; **Kiwi:** Phillip Pretten; **Mr. Mayor/Walter Kangaroo:** A.J. Henderson; **Mimi Rabbit:** Barbara Pogemiller; **Nick Penguin:** Ian Finlay; **Weather:** Richard Dumont

### ◉ THE ADVENTURES OF THE LITTLE PRINCE

Based on the tiny planet of B-612, the Little Prince, an extraordinarily small boy, travels to Earth and other planets, where he makes new friends and helps solve their problems in this series originally produced for French television in 1979, then syndicated in the United States in 1981 over ABC-owned and operated stations. Jameson Brewer, who scripted the Walt Disney classic Fantasia, wrote and produced the series. A Jambre/Gallerie International Films Production. Color. Half-hour. Premiered: September 1982. Syndicated. Rebroadcast on NICK: 1985.

*Voices*
**Little Prince:** Julie McWhirter Dees, Katie Leigh; **Other Voices:** Walker Edmiston, Bob Ridgely, Janet Waldo, Pamela Ziolowski

*An extraordinary small boy travels to Earth and other planets where he makes friends and helps solve their problems in the syndicated favorite* The Adventures of the Little Prince. © Jambre/Gallerie International Films

## ◎ THE ADVENTURES OF T-REX

Five stand-up comic Tyrannosaurus brothers (Buck, Bubba, Bugsy, Bruno and Bernie) transform into the crimefighting superhero group "T-REX" and become heroes when they save Rep City from a sophisticated underground mob, headed by the sinster "Big Boss' Graves." This 52-episode series premiered in syndication in 1992. *A Gunther-Wahl/Kitty Film Creativite et Developpment/All American Communications Production. Color. Half hour. Premiered: September 1992. Syndicated.*

### Voices
Kathleen Barr, Michael Beattie, Gary Chalk, Jennifer Chopping, Ian Corlett, Michael Dobson, Kevin Hayes, Phil Hayes, Janyce Jaud, Allesandro Juliani, Annabel Kershaw, Scott McNeil, Robert O. Smith, Venus Terzo, Dale Wilson

## ◎ AEON FLUX

MTV premiered this cartoon spinoff of the network's cutting-edge anthology series *Liquid Television* four years after its original network debut. The weekly half-hour series continued the exploits of the dangerously sexy, futuristic female "terror agent" (from Colossal Pictures' creator Peter Chung). Due to the unique graphic design and adult subject matter, a viewer disclaimer was required after the series was expanded to a regular half-hour format. After only 10 half-hour episodes were produced, the series producer, Peter Chung, and MTV parted company, and the program has continued in reruns since 1996. *A Colossal Pictures/MTV Production. Color. Half-hour. Premiered on MTV: August 1995.*

### Voices
**Aeon Flux:** Denis Poirier; **Trevor Goodchild:** John Rafter Lee

## ◎ ALF

That wonderful, wise-cracking alien Alf relives his pre-Earth days on the planet Melmac—in this 26-episode half-hour animated series, based on the hit NBC comedy series of the same name. Premiering on NBC in 1987, the series was so successful that it was expanded to 60 minutes in length during its second season run. Added to the show was a new weekly feature: "Alf Tales," offbeat retellings of classic fairy tales, which was spun off into its own series. *An Alien Production in association with DIC Enterprises and Saban Productions. Color. Half-hour. Premiered on NBC: September 26, 1987–September 21, 1989. Rebroadcast on FAM: 1990.*

### Voices
**Alf:** Paul Fusco; **Sgt. Staff/Cantfayl:** Len Carlson; **Flo:** Peggy Mahon; **Augie/Rhoda:** Pauline Gillis; **Stella:** Ellen-Ray Hennessey; **Skip:** Rob Cowan; **Larson Petty/Bob:** Thick Wilson; **Curtis:** Michael Fantini; **Harry:** Stephen McMulkin; **Sloop:** Dan Hennessey

## ◎ ALF TALES

Alf and friends star in irreverent versions of classic children's fairy tales—Robin Hood, Sleeping Beauty, Cinderella, Jack and the Beanstalk, among others—in 21 original adaptations originally broadcast on NBC's animated *Alf* series. *An Alien Production in association with DIC Enterprises. Color. Half-hour. Premiered on NBC: September 16, 1988–August 25, 1990. Rebroadcast on FAM: 1990.*

### Voices
**Alf:** Paul Fusco; **Flo:** Peggy Mahon; **Augie/Rhoda:** Paulina Gillis; **Stella:** Ellen-Ray Hennessey; **Skip:** Rob Cowan; **Larson Petty/Bob:** Thick Wilson; **Sloop:** Dan Hennessey

## ◎ ALIENATORS: EVOLUTION CONTINUES

Led by biology professor Ira Kane and geology professor Harry Block, an unlikely foursome, including a young firefighter (Wayne Green) and a disciplined military officer (Lieutenant Lucy Mai), try to defeat extraterrestrials that are rapidly growing from meteor-carried organisms into menacing creatures that threaten to destroy all life on Earth in this half-hour animated series, spun-off from the live-action science fiction comedy feature *Evolution* (2001) from *Ghostbusters* director Ivan Reitman. The 26-episode series joined FOX network's Saturday morning cartoon block in September 2001 and aired until May 2002. *A DreamWorks SKG/Dentsu Inc./Montecito Pictures Company/DIC/Columbia TriStar Television Production. Color. Half-hour. Premiered on FOX: September 22, 2001–May 18, 2002.*

### Voices
**Dr. Ira Kane:** Kirby Morrow; **Wayne Green:** Andrew Francis; **Professor Harry Phineas Block:** Cusse Mankuma; **Lt. Lucy Mai:** Akiko Morrison; **General Woodman:** John Payne; **Other Voices:** Mark Acheson, Alvin Sanders

## ◎ ALL DOGS GO TO HEAVEN

Lovable German shepherd Charlie B. Barkin and pal dachsund Itchy Itchiford are sent back to Earth as guardian angels to perform acts of goodness in this 20-episode half-hour syndicated series based on the animated feature film series, originally created by animator Don Bluth. Dom DeLuise, a cast member in both movies (as the voice of Itchy), and Charles Nelson Reilly (as Killer), who starred in the first *All Dogs Go to Heaven* (1989) movie, reprised their roles for the television series, as did Ernest Borgnine (Carface), Sheena Easton (Sasha) and Bebe Neuwirth (Annabelle), each of whom starred in the 1996 sequel. *An MGM Animation Production in association with Claster Television. Color. Half-hour. Premiered: September 21, 1996. Syndicated. Rebroadcast on FOX FAM: July 31, 1998–February 26, 2000. Rebroadcast on TDIS: September 6, 2006–October 16, 2006.*

### Voices
**Charlie B. Barkin:** Steven Weber; **Itchy:** Dom DeLuise; **Carface:** Ernest Borgnine; **Killer:** Charles Nelson Reilly; **Sasha:** Sheena Easton; **Annabelle/Belladonna:** Bebe Neuwirth

## ◎ ALL GROWN UP!

By popular demand, following Nickelodeon's airing of 2001's prime-time 10th anniversary special, *Rugrats: All Growed Up*, which was the network's highest-rated program ever, the famed television toddlers returned to star in all-new adventures—now 10 years later—with Tommy, Chuckie, Angelica, Susie and company dealing with a host of preteen and teenage problems.

Production of the series commenced in September 2002, after sneak previewing the program on Saturday, April 12, 2003, at 9:30 P.M. (ET) after the Kids' Choice Awards with the first episode, "Coup DeVille." In late November of that year Nickelodeon began regularly airing the half-hour series featuring 13 first-season episodes and attracting more than 3.2 million viewers—or more than a third of all kid-aged cable television watchers in the United States. Added to the cast and becoming integral parts of the storylines each were Susie and Angelica's best friend, Harold (who is secretly in love with Angelica); Angelica's main rival, Savannah; Chuckie's new best friend, Nicole Boscarelli; and former wrestler-turned school principal, Estes "Slambang" Pangborn.

In March 2004, with the program proving so popular, CBS began airing the children's series on its Saturday-morning *Nick on CBS* program block until September of 2004. Starring in 55 half-hour episodes during its six seasons, the challenged cartoon 'tweens also co-starred in three hour-long specials: *Interview with a Campfire* (2004); *Dude, Where's My Horse?* (2005); and *R.V. Having Fun Yet?* (2006). With its last original episode broadcast in November 2006, the series ended its run on Nickelodeon in early 2007. *A Klasky Csupo/Viacom Production. Color. Half-hour. Premiered on NICK: April 12, 2003 (sneak preview). Premiered on NICK: November 29, 2003–early 2007 (series). Premiered on CBS: March 14, 2004–September 9, 2004.*

**Voices**
**Tommy Pickles:** E. G. Daily; **Chuckie Finster Jr.:** Christine Cavanaugh; **Angelica C. Pickles:** Cheryl Chase; **Phil/Lil DeVille:** Kath Soucie; **Dil Pickles:** Tara Strong; **Susie Carmichael:** Cree Summer; **Kimi Watanabe-Finster:** Dione Quan; **Harold:** Pat Musick; **Savannah:** Shayna Fox; **Estes "Slambang" Pangborn:** Clancy Brown; **Nicole Boscarelli:** Lizzie Murray; **Grandpa Pickles:** Joe Alaskey

### ◎ ALL-NEW DENNIS THE MENACE
Six years after the successful debut of the first-run syndicated series *Dennis The Menace*, CBS commissioned this all-new, half-hour animated series starring the mischievous hellraiser from artist Hank Ketcham's long-running syndicated comic-strip. The character more closely mirrors the 1960s live-action sitcom role of child star Jay North. *A DIC Enterprises Production in association with General Mills. Color. Half-hour. Premiered on CBS: September 11, 1993–August 10, 1994.*

**Voices**
**Dennis Mitchell:** Adam Wylie; **Mr. Wilson:** Greg Burson; **Henry Mitchell, Dennis's father/Ruff:** Dan Gilvezan; **Alice Mitchell, Dennis's mother:** Ana Mathias; **Mrs. Wilson:** June Foray; **Margaret/Peebee:** Jeannie Elias; **Joey:** Katie Leigh

### ◎ THE ALL-NEW EWOKS
The fuzzy little creatures of *Star Wars* fame appear in all-new adventures on the distant forest moon of Endor, led by young scout Wicket, in this new package of 21 episodes broadcast on ABC in 1986. The series ran for only one season. *A Lucasfilm Production in association with Nelvana Limited, Hanho Heung-Up and Mi-Hahn Productions. Color. Half-hour. Premiered on ABC: November 8, 1986–September 5, 1987.*

**Voices**
**Wicket:** Denny Delk; **Teebo:** Jim Cranna; **Princess Kneesa:** Jeanne Reynolds; **Latara:** Sue Murphy; **Shodu:** Esther Scott; **Logray:** Rick Cimino

### ◎ THE ALL-NEW GUMBY
The famous "green man" returned in these all-new, first-run syndicated episodes produced by the character's creator, Art Clokey. The program intermixed episodes from the original cult series with new original stories.

Dal McKennon, the original voice of Gumby, trained several actors through his company, Dalmac Productions, to alternate as the character's voice in this series revival. Creator Art Clokey reprised the role of Pokey (he also voiced Prickle), while wife Gloria lent her vocal talent to the character, Goo.

Initially, the series premiered in 80 television markets nationwide and received airplay on stations in Australia and Europe. In 1998, 10 years after its first telecast in syndication, the sophisticated stop-motion animated series was rebroadcast on Cartoon Network, along with seven other animated programs owned by Warner Bros., two of them previously canceled by Kids' WB!, including *Batman,*

*Famous green man Gumby and pal Pokey from a promotional still for* The All-New Gumby *series.* © *Premavision*

*Road Rovers, Wayneheod, Alvin and the Chipmunks, Beetlejuice, The Fantastic Voyages of Sinbad* and the entire package of *Super Friends. An Art Clokey Productions/Premavision Production in association with Lorimar and later Warner Bros. Color. Half-hour. Premiered: 1988. Syndicated. Rebroadcast on CAR: 1998.*

**Voices**
**Gumby/Professor Cap:** Dalmac Productions; **Pokey/Prickle:** Art Clokey; **Goo:** Gloria Clokey

### ◎ THE ALL-NEW PINK PANTHER SHOW
The never-discouraged feline starred in this series of new cartoons made for television, including cartoons of a new character: Crazylegs Crane, a mixture of Red Skelton's Klem Kadiddlehopper and Edgar Bergen's Mortimer Snerd, joined by his smarter son Crane Jr. and Dragonfly. The 1978 series lasted one season on ABC. *A DePatie-Freleng Enterprises Production. Color. Half-hour. Premiered on ABC: September 9, 1978–September 1, 1979.*

**Voices**
**Crazylegs Crane:** Larry D. Mann; **Crane Jr./Dragonfly:** Frank Welker

### ◎ THE ALL-NEW POPEYE HOUR
In this third television series featuring the famed spinach-gulping sailor, Popeye picks up where he left off, defending his love for his girlfriend, Olive Oyl, by battling the bullying, girl-stealing Bluto, in adventures that were less violent than the theatrical cartoon shorts originally produced by Max Fleischer.

Jack Mercer, the veteran salty voice of Popeye, wrote many of the cartoon scripts for the show, which featured several other familiar characters: hamburger-munching Wimpy; Pappy, Popeye's father; and Popeye's four nephews.

The program contained three segments in the 1978–79 season: "The Adventures of Popeye," following the continuing exploits of Popeye and Bluto; "Dinky Dog," the misadventures of the world's largest dog; and "Popeye's Treasure Hunt," tracing Popeye and Olive Oyl's search for buried treasure, foiled by the ever-scheming Bluto. For the 1979–80 season, a fourth segment was added to the show: "Popeye's Sports Parade," featuring Popeye in various sports competitions. Thirty-second spots, known as "Popeye Health and Safety Tips," were featured on the show during each season. *A Hanna-Barbera Production in association with King Features Syndicate. Color. One hour. Premiered on CBS: September 9, 1978–September 5, 1981.*

*Voices*

**POPEYE: Popeye:** Jack Mercer; **Olive Oyl, his girlfriend/Sea Hag:** Marilyn Schreffler; **Bluto, Popeye's nemesis:** Allan Melvin; **Wimpy, Popeye's friend:** Daws Butler

**DINKY DOG: Dinky:** Frank Welker; **Uncle Dudley, Dinky's owner:** Frank Nelson; **Sandy, his niece:** Jackie Joseph; **Monica, his niece:** Julie Bennett

## THE ALL-NEW POUND PUPPIES

In the fall of 1987, following the success of 1986's *Pound Puppies*, ABC returned with 20 new episodes of this Saturday-morning favorite about adorable puppies who live in a pound waiting to be adopted. *A Hanna-Barbera Production. Color. Half-hour. Premiered on ABC: September 26, 1987–September 3, 1988.*

*Voices*

**Nose Marie:** Ruth Buzzi; **Cooler:** Dan Gilvezan; **Holly:** Ami Foster; **Katrina Stoneheart:** Pat Carroll; **Brattina Stoneheart:** Adrienne Alexander; **Cat Gut/Nabbit:** Frank Welker; **Bright Eyes:** Nancy Cartwright; **Millie Trueblood:** June Lockhart; **Whopper:** B.J. Ward; **Howler:** Bobby Morse

## THE ALL-NEW SCOOBY AND SCRAPPY-DOO SHOW

Cowardly great Dane Scooby-Doo and his feisty pint-size nephew Scrappy-Doo brave ghosts, goblins and ghouls to crack a series of mysteries in all-new comedy adventures. Daphne, who starred in the original Scooby-Doo cartoons, rejoined the cast as a reporter for a teen magazine investigating mysteries. The series was broadcast in combination with *The Puppy's Further Adventures.* (See entry for information.) *A Hanna-Barbera Production. Color. Half-hour. Premiered on ABC: September 10, 1983–September 1, 1984 (Puppy's Further Adventures/The All-New Scooby and Scrappy-Doo Show). Rebroadcast on CAR: November 22, 1994–December 9, 1994 (weekdays); December 19, 1994–December 20, 1994; August 16, 1997– (Saturdays, Sundays).*

*Voices*

**Scooby-Doo/Scrappy-Doo:** Don Messick; **Shaggy Rogers:** Casey Kasem; **Daphne Blake:** Heather North

## THE ALL-NEW SUPER FRIENDS HOUR

Even though Hanna-Barbera's first superheroes cartoon series failed, the amazing popularity of TV's *Wonder Woman* and *The Six Million Dollar Man* spurred network interest in reviving the old *Super Friends* program. This 1977 version was a huge ratings success for ABC. Four additional comic-book characters joined the Justice League in these adventures. *A Hanna-Barbera Production in association with DC Publications. Color. One hour. Premiered on ABC: September 10, 1977–September 2, 1978.*

*Voices*

**Narrators:** Bill Woodson, Bob Lloyd; **Wonder Woman:** Shannon Farnon; **Superman:** Danny Dark; **Aquaman:** Norman Alden; **Batman:** Olan Soule; **Robin:** Casey Kasem; **Zan:** Mike Bell; **Jayna:** Liberty Williams

## ALL-STAR LAFF-A-LYMPICS

In the spring of 1986, ABC replaced Hanna-Barbera's *The 13 Ghosts of Scooby-Doo* with this half-hour retitled version of H-B's popular Saturday-morning Olympic track-and-field competition spoof, *Scooby's All-Star Laff-a-Lympics* (1977–79), repeating episodes of the latter. (See *Scooby's All-Star Laff-a-Lympics* for voice credits.) *A Hanna-Barbera Production. Color. Half-hour. Rebroadcast on ABC: March 1, 1986–September 6, 1986. Rebroadcast on USA: 1989–1992. Rebroadcast on CAR: Summer 1996, Summer 2000. Rebroadcast on BOOM: May 1, 2000–.*

## ALVIN AND THE CHIPMUNKS

Alvin, Theodore, Simon and manager David Seville returned in this series of all-new adventures produced by Ross Bagdasarian's son, Ross Jr., who took over the family business in 1977. Adventures dealt with more contemporary and modern issues and introduced the Chipmunks' female companions, the Chipettes (Jeanette, Brittany and Eleanor). In 1988 the series was retitled *The Chipmunks*, and episodes from the series' first four seasons, including several new half-hour shows, were offered for syndication. The series was later rebroadcast on FOX Network and Nickelodeon. *A Bagdasarian Production in association with DIC Enterprises. Color. Half-hour. Premiered on NBC: September 17, 1983–September 1, 1990. Syndicated: 1988 (under the title The Chipmunks). Rebroadcast on FOX: September 14, 1992–September 1993. Rebroadcast on NICK: October 3, 1994–June 30, 1995.*

*Voices*

**Alvin/Simon/David Seville:** Ross Bagdasarian Jr.; **Theodore/Jeanette/Brittany/Eleanor:** Janice Karman; **Miss Miller:** Dodie Goodman

## THE ALVIN SHOW

Popular recording stars the Chipmunks (Alvin, Theodore and Simon) and their writer-manager, David Seville, starred in this weekly half-hour cartoon series that premiered in prime-time opposite TV's *Wagon Train.* (In 1960 ABC had introduced two prime-time cartoon programs, *Bugs Bunny* and *The Flintstones*; CBS followed suit in 1961 with the Chipmunks.)

The series combined three Chipmunk episodes every week, two of which were sing-along segments built around their songs, and another sequence featuring "The Adventures of Clyde Crashcup," a wacky inventor who took credit for inventing everything, accompanied by his whispering, bald-domed assistant Leonardo.

Songwriter Ross Bagdasarian, who adopted the pseudonym David Seville in real life, created and supplied the voice of all four characters: Alvin, the egotistical, girl-loving leader; Theodore, the faithful, giggling follower; Simon, the intelligent, bespectacled bookworm always dragged into trouble by his brothers; and David Seville, the Chipmunks' peacemaking manager whose temper was known to explode following Alvin's excessive mischief ("Aaaalll-viiinn!").

In 1958, after Bagdasarian first employed a recording technique of speeding up the voices (voices recorded at a slow speed then played back twice as fast) to record his first hit record, "Witch Doctor," the Chipmunks were born. Using this technique, he introduced the squirrely foursome that same year with their first record, "The Chipmunk Song," which sold more than 5 million copies within seven weeks of its release.

Bagdasarian deserves no credit for giving the group its name, however. His children, Carol, Ross Jr. and Adam, are the ones responsible for doing so. After hearing sound recordings, they told their father the voices sounded like chipmunks to them. (Until then he had planned to make the characters rabbits or butterflies.)

As for the characters' individual names, Bagdasarian reportedly named them after Liberty Records executives Al (Alvin) Bennett and Si (Simon) Warnoker and recording engineer Ted (Theodore) Keep. Liberty was the exclusive recording label for the Chipmunks songs.

The following season, CBS moved the 26-episode series to Saturday morning. It lasted in reruns before the network canceled the show in 1965. The series remained on television in syndication through the end of the summer of 1966, even though only one season of cartoons was made. NBC brought back the series in 1979 when the characters experienced a resurgence in popularity, appealing to a whole new generation of children. In the spring of 1994 the series resurfaced again, this time weekdays on Nickelodeon. *A Format Films/Bagdasarian Film Corp. Production. Color. Half-hour. Premiered on CBS: October 14, 1961–September 5, 1962. Rebroadcast on CBS: September 12, 1962–September 18, 1966. Rebroadcast on NBC: February 17, 1979–September 1, 1979 (broadcast under the title* Alvin and the Chipmunks*). Rebroadcast on NICK: March 7, 1994–December 31, 1995.*

*Voices*
**Alvin/Theordore/Simon/David Seville:** Ross Bagdasarian; **Clyde Crashcup:** Shepard Menken; **Daisy Belle/Others:** June Foray; **Mrs. Frumpington:** Lee Patrick; **Dragon:** Joe Besser; **Additional Voices:** Paul Frees, Bill Lee, Johnny Mann, William Sanford, Reg Dennis

### ◉ AMAZIN' ADVENTURES
Seven individual animated series initially made up this two-hour syndicated weekend cartoon block, first offered to independent television stations by television syndicator Bohbot Entertainment in 1992. The first block, known as "Amazin' Adventures I," featured animated series from producers DIC Entertainment and Saban Entertainment, namely *Double Dragon, King Arthur and the Knights of Justice, The Hurricanes, Mighty Max, Saban's Around the World in Eighty Dreams, Saban's Gulliver's Travels* and *The Wizard of Oz,* broadcast on more than 143 stations. Bohbot introduced a second block of weekend programming in 1994, dubbed "Amazin' Adventures II," which included DIC Entertainment's *Gadget Boy and Heather, Street Sharks* and *Ultraforce,* Ruby-Spears Productions' *Mega Man* and *SKYSURFER* Strike Force and New Frontier Entertainment's *Princess Gwenevere and the Jewel Riders. A DIC Enterprises/Saban Entertainment Production in association with Bohbot Entertainment. Color. Two hours. Syndicated: September 7, 1992.*

### ◉ THE AMAZING CHAN AND THE CHAN CLAN
Fictional Chinese detective Charlie Chan, aided by his 10 children, combine comedy and adventure in crime investigations in 16 half-hour episodes that aired for two seasons on CBS. Chan was voiced by actor Keye Luke, who portrayed Charlie Chan's number-one son in several Charlie Chan films of the 1930s and later the wise monk Master Po on TV's *Kung Fu. A Hanna-Barbera Production in association with Leisure Concepts, Incorporated. Color. Half-hour. Premiered on CBS: September 9, 1972–September 22, 1974. Rebroadcast on CAR: December 6, 1992; March 14, 1993 (part of Boomerang, 1972); April 10, 1994– (Sundays). Rebroadcast on BOOM: June 3, 2000–.*

*Voices*
**Charlie Chan:** Keye Luke; **Henry:** Bob Ito; **Stanley:** Stephen Wong, Lennie Weinrib; **Suzie:** Virginia Ann Lee, Cherylene Lee; **Alan:** Brian Tochi; **Anne:** Leslie Kumamota, Jodie Foster; **Tom:** Michael Takamoto, John Gunn; **Flip:** Jay Jay Jue, Gene Andrusco; **Nancy:** Beverly Kushida; **Mimi:** Leslie Juwai, Cherylene Lee; **Scooter:** Robin Toma, Michael Morgan; **Chu-Chu, the dog:** Don Messick

### ◉ THE AMAZING THREE
First released in Japan as "W 3"—meaning "Wonder Three"—this Japanese-made series was edited and dubbed by Joe Oriolo Productions for syndication in America. It involved three outer-space aliens sent to Earth by the Galactic Congress to determine whether the "warlike planet" should be destroyed in order to preserve universal peace. In disguise, the trio—Bonnie (a rabbit), Ronnie (a horse) and Zero (a duck with a Beatle haircut)—are aided in their fight against evil by a young Earthling, Kenny Carter. Japanese cartoon legend Osamu Tezuka, the father of *Astro Boy,* created and produced the series. *A Mushi/Erika Production. Color. Half-hour. Premiered: September 1967. Syndicated.*

*Voices*
Jack Curtis, Jack Grimes, Corinne Orr

### ◉ AMERICAN DAD!
Intense, conservative CIA agent Stan Smith's work spills into his daily personal life as he constantly remains on alert to terrorist activity while going to great extremes to protect his family, especially his doting wife, Francine, his ultra-liberal daughter, Hayley, and her geeky brother, Steve, who is nearing puberty, in this outrageously funny animated sitcom. Continuing its tradition of offering animated prime-time family comedies on Sunday nights, FOX commissioned this new animated series as a mid-season replacement from *Family Guy* creator Seth MacFarlane, premiering the pilot on a weeknight in early February 2005 before launching the prime-time series that May on Sundays with the first episode entitled "Threat Levels."

Produced by 20th Century Fox Television with McFarlane, Mike Barker and Matt Weitzman as executive producers, only six half-hour regular series episodes were broadcast through mid-June of that year, with 16 additional first season episodes produced through mid-May of 2006. On September 10, 2006, the series returned for a second season with 22 additional half-hours. Meanwhile, beginning in May 2005, the cartoon comedy found a new audience of viewers in reruns on Cartoon Network's late-night *Adult Swim* programming block. *A 20th Century Fox Television/Atlantic Creative Production. Color. Half-hour. Premiered on FOX: February 6, 2005 (pilot). Premiered on FOX: May 1, 2005 (series). Rebroadcast on CAR ("Adult Swim"): May 12, 2005–April 24, 2006.*

*Voices*
**Stan Smith/Roger:** Seth MacFarlane; **Francine:** Wendy Schaal; **Hayley:** Rachel MacFarlane; **Steve:** Scott Grimes; **Klaus:** Dee Bradley Baker

### ◉ AMERICAN DRAGON: JAKE LONG
Cool anime-inspired, original action cartoon series about an average 13-year-old American-Asian boy, and descendant of ancient dragons with mystical powers, whose duty is to protect magical creatures secretly living among the residents of New York, who include his family—mother, father, sister, dragon master grandfather, and 600-year-old talking dog, Fu Dog—and his skateboarding friends, Spud and Trixie. Conceived by Jeff Goode, creator of the popular MTV series *Undressed,* Disney Channel initially ordered 24 episodes for the 30-minute series, which premiered in January 2005. In November 2005, Tia Carrere guest starred in an episode as the voice of Yan Yan, a magical hairless Chinese cat. *A Walt Disney Television Animation Production. Color. Half-hour. Premiered on DIS: January 21, 2005.*

*Voices*

**Jake Long:** Dante Basco; **Jake's Father:** Jeff Bennett; **Jake's Mother:** Lauren Tom; **Lao Shi, Jake's Grandfather:** Keone Young; **Haley Long, Jake's sister:** Amy Bruckner; **Fu Dog:** John DiMaggio; **Spud:** Charlie Finn; **Trixie:** Miss Kittie; **Rose/Huntsgirl:** Mae Whitman; **Professor Rotwood:** Paul Rugg

## ◎ AMERICAN HEROES AND LEGENDS

From the producer of *Storybook Classics* and *We All Have Tales,* never-before-told true folktale legends—from Annie Oakley to Moby Dick, celebrating the ethnic and regional diversity of the United States—were re-created in this 15-episode half-hour series that originally debuted on Showtime in October 1992. Stories were narrated by such big-name celebrities as Keith Carradine, Danny Glover, John Candy, Sissy Spacek, Nicholas Cage and others. *A Rabbit Ears Video Production. Color. Half-hour. Premiered on SHO: October 8, 1992.*

## ◎ AMIGO AND FRIENDS

A friend from across the border, Spanish-speaking Amigo (actually a cartoon version of popular Mexican film comedian Cantinflas) takes children on educational and entertaining adventures, from pyramids, to Shakespeare, to electricity, to life on the moon in this half-hour syndicated series produced between 1980 and 1982. Hanna-Barbera Productions and Diamex S.A. coproduced the 52 episodes of this series, redubbed in English and syndicated in the United States under the title of *Amigo and Friends*. Later the original package was resyndicated under its original title, *Cantiflas,* in a bilingual format dubbed in both English and Spanish. *A Televisa, S.A. Production in association with Hanna-Barbera Productions. Color. Half-hour. Premiered: 1980–82. Syndicated.*

*Voices*

**Amigo:** Don Messick; **Narrator:** John Stephenson

## ◎ ANATOLE

Delightful tale of an aristocratic mouse and cheese-tester for the world-famous Duval Cheese Factory and his six charming children—the oldest, Paul and Paulette; the naturally artitistic Claude and Claudette; and rambunctious youngest siblings, Georges and Georgette—and his adventures on the streets of Paris in a multi-cultural world in this half-hour animated series aimed at teaching young viewers the importance of diversity, based on the Caldecott Award-winning children's book series by Eve Titus and illustrated by Paul Galdone. Produced by Canada's Nelvana Limited and France's Alphanim studios, the 26-episode series premiered Saturday mornings on CBS, beginning in October 1998 and ending in September 2000, and was rebroadcast on Disney Channel from 2001 to 2004. *A Scottish Television Enterprises/Nelvana Limited/Alphanim/Valentine Productions s.a.r.l./YTV Production. Color. Half-hour. Premiered on CBS: October 3, 1998–September 9, 2000. Rebroadcast on DIS: 2001–2004.*

*Voices*

**Anatole:** Oliver L'Ecuyer; **Gaston/Mr. Mole:** William Colgate; **Doucette:** Jill Frappier; **Paul:** Joe Dinicol; **Paulette:** Alison Pill; **Claude:** Jamie Haydon-Devlin; **Claudette:** Annick Obonsawin; **Georges:** Cole Caplan; **Georgette:** Sarah Rosen Fruitman; **Pamplemouse:** John Stocker; **Edgar the Rat/Others:** Paul Haddad; **Other Voices:** Robert Tinkler

## ◎ ANGELA ANACONDA

Two-dimensional computer and cut-out animated series about an underachieving and underappreciated freckle-faced, eccentric eight-year-old named Angela who dreams of triumphing over her smarter school rivals, her friends Gina, Gordy, Johnny and her faithful dog, King. Originally created by Joanna Ferrone and Disney's *Pepper Ann* creator Susan Rose as a series of cartoon shorts for Nickelodeon's cartoon anthology series, *KaBlam!* the character was turned into a weekly half-hour series for FOX Family Channel in October 1999 and grouped with Saturday morning newcomers, including *The Kids from Room 202* and *Weird-Ohs.* *An Honest Art Inc./DECODE Entertainment Inc./C.O.R.E. Digital Pictures/Teletoon Canada/Family Channel Production. Color. Half-hour. Premiered on FOX FAM/ABC FAM: October 9, 1999–February 24, 2002.*

*Voices*

**Angela Anaconda:** Susan Rose; **Gordy Rhinehart:** Edward Glen; **Gina Lash:** Bryn McCauley; **Johnny Abatti:** Ali Mukaddam; **Nanette Manoir:** Ruby Smith-Merovitz; **Mrs. Brinks:** Richard Binsley; **Stu/Ray Wu:** Jonathan Malen; **Jimmy Jamal:** Kevin Duhaney; **Uncle Nicky:** Robert Tinkler

## ◎ ANGELINA BALLERINA

Young Angelina Mouseling, who hails from Chipping Cheddar in 1920s London, aspires to become the greatest ballerina in Mouseland in this charming and witty half-hour animated series, based on the popular children's books by Katherine Holabird and Helen Craigs. Produced by Grand Slamm Children's Films for HIT Entertainment, Oscar-winning actress Judi Dench provided the voice of Angelina's friend and ballet teacher, Miss Lilly, for the series. Making its U.S. television debut on PBS, the show also aired on CiTV in the United Kingdom, ABC in Australia, and other networks worldwide. Along with each animated episode, each half-hour featured a live-action segment of students from the Royal Academy of Dance. In the spring of 2004, the original children's program began re-airing as part of PBS's new digital cable channel and video-on-demand service (VOD), PBS Kids Sprout. *A GSCFilms/HIT Entertainment PLC Production. Color. Half-hour. Premiered on PBS: May 10, 2002–June 7, 2003. Rebroadcast on PBS Kids Sprout (VOD): April 4, 2005–. Rebroadcast on PBS Kids Sprout (digital cable): September 26, 2005–.*

*Voices*

**Miss Lilly:** Judi Dench; **Angelina Mouseling/Mrs. Hodgepodge:** Finty Williams; **Alice/Henry/Sammy/Priscilla Pinkpaws:** Jo Wyatt; **Mrs. Matilda Mouseling/Penelope Pinkpaws:** Jonell Elliot; **Mr. Mouseling/Grandpa:** Keith Wickham; **Grandma:** Adrienne Posta

## ◎ ANGRY BEAVERS

Riled and accident-prone Daggett and devil-may-care Norbert, a pair of dam-building brother beavers, try to make it in the big world in this Emmy-nominated half-hour series, from the producers of the *Edith Ann* specials, for Nickelodeon. Sixty-three episodes (two 11-minute cartoons per half hour) aired over five seasons. *A Gunther-Wahl Production. Color. Half-hour. Premiered on NICK: October 7, 1996–November 11, 2001.*

*Voices*

**Norbert:** Nick Bakay; **Daggett:** Richard Horwitz; **Barry the Bear:** John Garry; **Truckee:** Mark Klastorin; **Tree-flower:** Cynthia Mann; **Bing:** Victor Wilson; **Scientist #1:** Ed Winter

## ◎ ANIMANIA

In the tradition of MTV's "Liquid Television," this short-lived half-hour anthology series, also on MTV, mixed live-action and stop-motion animated films. The series opener featured "Slow Bob in the Lower Dimensions." *An MTV Production. Color. Half-hour. Premiered on MTV: December 22, 1991–December 28, 1991.*

## ◎ ANIMANIACS
(See STEVEN SPIELBERG PRESENTS ANIMANIACS.)

## ◎ ANIMATED HERO CLASSICS
The stories of historical figures who made significant contributions to society—including Christopher Columbus, George Washington, Abraham Lincoln, Thomas Edison, Benjamin Franklin and Florence Nightingale—are told in this weekly half-hour HBO series, created by former Disney director Richard Rich, whose credits include *The Swan Princess* and *The Fox and the Hound*. *A Warner-Nest Entertainment/Rich Animation Studios Production. Color. Half-hour. Premiered on HBO: March 1, 1997–April 2, 1999.*

## ◎ ANIMATED TALES OF THE WORLD
Representing the world's largest co-production involving 22 different broadcast networks, this ambitious anthology series featured popular folk tales from 26 countries, offering lessons for young viewers in a 13-episode animated series. Produced by the creators of HBO's *Shakespeare: The Animated Tales* and *Animated Epics* series, each half-hour broadcast featured two 15-minute stories representing two countries and combining a variety of innovative animation styles, including cel and puppet animation. In the United States, the innovative series premiered on HBO Family beginning Wednesday, September 5, 2001, from 8:30 to 9:30 P.M., with two new editions per month as part of its evening program block. In 2002, the series took home two prime-time Emmy Awards, one for outstanding individual achievement in animation for production designer Andrev Zolotukhin for the episode, "John Henry, The Steel Driving Man" and another for outstanding voice-over performance for the narration by Peter Macon of the same episode. *A S4C Production. Color. Half-hour. Premiered on HBO FAM: September 5, 2001.*

### Voices
**Narrator:** Peter Macon; **Other Voices:** Brian Cox, Shirley Henderson, Russel Hunter, Forbes Masson, John Rampage, Ann-Louise Ross, Rory O'Donoghue

## ◎ ANIMATOONS
Thirty-one well-known fairy tales and original children's stories made up this educational and entertaining half-hour series aimed at encouraging development of verbal skills, vocabulary and creative expression in children. Stories included "Peter and the Wolf," "Goldilocks and the Three Bears" and "Ali Baba and the Forty Thieves." *An Animatoons Production in association with Language Arts Films/Radio and Television Packagers. Color. Half-hour. Premiered: 1967. Syndicated.*

### Voices
**Narrator:** Nancy Berg

## ◎ ANNE OF GREEN GABLES: THE ANIMATED SERIES
Further animated adventures of a chatty, adopted freckle-faced, red-headed 11-year-old girl named Anne Shirley who discovers a whole new world and life in stories dealing with preteen issues while retaining the spirit and tone of the acclaimed children's book *Anne of Green Gables* on which it was based. The 26-episode, half-hour series—and the second of two cartoon series adaptations, with the first made for Japanese television in 1979—pro-

duced in Australia and featuring an all-Canadian voice cast, debuted simultaneously on Canada's TV Ontario and the United States' PBS network in September 2001. *An Annemation Productions/Sullivan Entertainment Production. Color. Half-hour. Premiered on PBS: September 2, 2001–March 1, 2002.*

### Voices
**Anne Shirley:** Bryn McAuley; **Matthew Cuthbert:** Wayne Robson; **Marilee Cuthbert:** Patricia Gage; **Diana Barry:** Emily Hampshire; **Gilbert Blythe:** Ali Mukaddam; **Minnie May Barry/Ruby Gillis:** Mami Koyama; **Dalene Irvine:** Felicity King; **Linda Sorensen:** Hetty King; **Kylie Fairlie:** Felix King; **Herself (Q&A Segment):** Haleigh Sheehan

## ◎ ANTHONY ANT
In the fast-paced, bustling underground metropolis of Antville, young Anthony Ant and his hip, street-smart friends, Kevin ("Mr. Cook") Ant, Alexi Ant, Ruby Red Ant, Terry Termite and Billy Bedbug, find amazing adventures below and above ground in this British-produced television cartoon series. The 13-episode, half-hour program debuted on American television on the same launch date—February 1, 1999—as HBO's new spin-off channel, HBO Family, a 24-hour commercial-free family programming network. Other new animated series premiering on the network included *George and Martha* and *The Adventures of Paddington Bear*. *A HIT Entertainment PLC/PASI Animation Group of the Philippines/Nelvana Ltd. Production. Color. Half-hour. Premiered on HBO FAM: February 1, 1999–April 11, 1999.*

### Voices
**Anthony Ant/Arnold, Anthony's Dad/Buzz, Count Mosquito's Nephew:** Alan Marriott; **Ruby/Anne, Anthony's Mom:** April Ford; **Billy Bedbug/Witch Weevil/Nate, Count Mosquito's Nephew:** Adrienne Posta; **Terry Termite/Kevin "Mr. Book" Ant:** Dan Russell; **Count Mosquito/Grandpa (Colonel):** Bob Saker; **Alexi:** Melanie Hudson

## ◎ AQUAMAN
Born in Atlantis, Aquaman, who rules the Seven Seas and water creatures through telepathic brain waves, protects his kingdom from intruders and possible destruction in this half-hour series, which repeated episodes from the CBS Saturday-morning series *The Superman/Aquaman Hour*. (See entry for details.) The series featured 36 seven-minute Aquaman adventures—one each week—and 18 "Guest Superheroes" adventures featuring such comic-book stars as the Teen Titans, Flash, Hawkman, Green Lantern and Atom. *A Filmation Associates/National Periodicals Production. Color. Half-hour. Premiered on CBS: September 14, 1968–September 7, 1969.*

### Voices
**Aquaman:** Ted Knight; **Aqualad:** Jerry Dexter; **Mera:** Diana Maddox

## ◎ AQUA TEEN HUNGER FORCE
Sarcastic and surreal adventures of a trio of human-sized food products—the goateed, condescending and practical bag of French fries and self-appointed leader, Frylock; the sadistic, lazy, crumpled Master Shake; and gentle, caring ball of hamburger meat, Meatward—headquartered out of the above-ground swimming pool of their New Jersey next-door neighbor, Carl, who solve crimes between coming up with a series of "get-rich" schemes on the side in this weekly 15-minute series for Cartoon Network's *Adult Swim*.

One of four original series produced by Atlanta-based Williams Street (*Sealab 2021*, *The Brak Show* and *Harvey Birdman, Attorney at Law*) for the Cartoon Network's *Adult Swim* late-night programming block, the characters were originally created for an episode entitled "Baffler Meal" (a spoof of McDonald's Happy Meal) of Cartoon Network's *Space Ghost: Coast to Coast*, featuring prototypical versions of the fast-food fighting superheroes, which did not air until several years later, after it was retooled and retitled, "Kentucky Nightmare." In the meantime, on December 30, 2000, the pilot episode of *Aqua Teen Hunger Force*—called "Rabbot"—bowed on *Adult Swim*, with the network ordering a full first season of episodes that began airing in September 2001. In 2003, the absurd comedy adventure series was greenlighted for 26 additional episodes.

Written and directed by Dave Willis and Matt Maiellaro, the series, which has aired Sunday nights on *Adult Swim*, began its fourth season in early December 2005 with that season's final original episodes airing the following December. With more new episodes planned for a fifth season to air in 2007, that April the characters starred in their first big-screen feature, the appropriately titled, *Aqua Teen Hunger Force Movie Film for Theaters*, released to theaters nationwide. A Williams Street Production. Color. Fifteen minutes. Premiered on CAR: December 30, 2000 ("pilot"). Premiered on CAR: September 9, 2001.

*Voices*
**Master Shake/Various Others:** Dana Snyder; **Meatwad/Carl/ Various Others:** Dave Willis; **Frylock/Various Others:** Carey Means; **Dr. Weird/Steve:** C. Martin Croker; **Flargin:** Scott Hilley; **Oglethorpe/Merle the Blonde Leprechaun:** Andy Merrill; **Mothmonsterman:** H. Jon Benjamin; **Err:** Matt Maiellaro; **Vegetable Man:** Don Kennedy; **Emory:** Mike Schatz; **Drippy:** Todd Field; **MC Pee Pants:** Christ Ward; **Happy Tim Harry:** David Cross; **Major Shake:** Matt Harrigan; **The www.yzzzerd.com:** Todd Hanson; **Romulox:** Todd Barry; **Wedding DJ:** George Lowe; **Oog:** Jon Glaser; Travis: Brooks Braselman; **Himself:** Ned Hastings; **Wayne the Brain:** Seth MacFarlane; **"Willy Nelson":** Tom Scharplin; **The Voice:** Isaac Hayes III; **The Wisdom Cube:** Jon Schnepp; **The Real Wisdom Cube:** Brian Posehn; **DP/Skeeter:** Patton Oswalt; **Hillbilly Turkatron:** Barry Mills; **Themselves:** Glen Danzig, Ned Hastings, Seth Green

## ⊚ THE ARCHIE COMEDY HOUR

In response to first-season ratings success of *The Archie Show*, CBS brought back creator Bob Montana's *Archie* comic-book characters in this expanded hour-long version of *The Archie Show*, (see the latter for voice credits) featuring musical numbers and further adventures of the gang. Included was "Sabrina, the Teenage Witch," whose popularity later spawned a spin-off series of her own. The show lasted one season in this new format. In the fall of 1970, the show returned as the half-hour, *Archie's Funhouse*. (See entry for further details.) A Filmation Associates Production. Color. One hour. Premiered on CBS: September 13, 1969–September 5, 1970. Rebroadcast on FAM: Fall 1993–94. Rebroadcast on ODY: April 1999–early 2000.

## ⊚ ARCHIE'S BANG-SHANG LALAPALOOZA SHOW

Archie and his regular cohorts, Jughead, Betty, Veronica, and Reggie, share the blame as they encounter new situations in the city of Riverdale in this shortened and retitled version of *The New Archie/Sabrina Hour*. The program also featured Sabrina, the Teenage Witch. Two new characters were added to the series: an Hispanic student named Carlos (voiced by José Flores) and Ophelia

(voiced by Treva Frazce.) (See *The New Archie/Sabrina Hour* for voice credits.) A Fils-Cartoons/Filmation Associates Production. Color. Half-hour. Premiered on NBC: November 26, 1977–January 28, 1978.

## ⊚ ARCHIE'S FUNHOUSE FEATURING THE GIANT JUKE BOX

Assisted by a Giant Juke Box, Archie and the gang play favorite dance numbers and perform sketches in a music-comedy-variety show format that mixed live footage of a studio audience composed of children responding to the skits, jokes and other blackout comedy sketches (some written by former *Rowan and Martin's Laugh-In* writers Jack Mendelsohn and Jim Mulligan) in this half-hour retitled version of CBS's *The Archie Comedy Hour*. (See voice credits for *The Archie Show*.) A Filmation Associates Production. Color. Half-hour. Premiered on CBS: September 12, 1970–September 4, 1971. Rebroadcast on FAM: Fall 1993–94. Rebroadcast on ODY: April 1999–early 2000.

## ⊚ THE ARCHIE SHOW

Perennial students Archie, Jughead, Betty, Reggie, Veronica and Sabrina cause scholastic havoc in the classrooms of Riverdale High School. Based on the *Archie* comic book by Bob Montana, the show comprised two 10-minute skits and a dance-of-the-week selection. A Filmation Associates Production. Color. Half-hour. Premiered on CBS: September 14, 1968–September 6, 1969. Rebroadcast on FAM: Fall 1993–94. Rebroadcast on ODY: April 1999–early 2000.

*Voices*
**Archie Andrews:** Dallas McKennon; **Jughead Jones:** Howard Morris; **Betty Cooper/Veronica Lodge:** Jane Webb; **Reggie Mantle:** John Erwin; **Sabrina, the Teenage Witch:** Jane Webb; **Big Moose/Pops/Dilton Doily/Hot Dog Jr.:** Howard Morris; **Big Ethel/Miss Grundy/Aunt Hilda/Aunt Zelda/Hagatha:** Jane Webb; **Hexter/Irwin/Dad:** John Erwin; **Hot Dog Jr./Chili Dog/ Harvey/Spencer:** Don Messick; **Mr. Weatherbee/Salem/Mr. Andrews/Mr. Lodge/Coach Cleats/Chuck Clayton:** Dallas McKennon

## ⊚ ARCHIE'S TV FUNNIES

Following *Archie's Funhouse*, CBS added this half-hour series to its 1971 fall Saturday-morning cartoon show lineup. This time Archie and his gang produce their own weekly television show featuring their favorite comic-strip stars, in addition to appearing in 16 new madcap adventures of their own.

Nine popular comic strips were adapted for the "TV Funnies" portion of the program: "Dick Tracy," "Broom Hilda," "Moon Mullins," "Emmy Lou," "The Gumps," "The Dropouts," "Smokey Stover," "Nancy and Sluggo" and the "Captain and the Kids." The Archie episodes were later repeated in 1973's *Everything's Archie* series. Meanwhile, "The Captain and the Kids," "Alley Oop," "Nancy and Sluggo" and "Broom Hilda" were resurrected on NBC's *Fabulous Funnies*. A Filmation Associates Production. Color. Half-hour. Premiered on CBS: September 11, 1971–September 1, 1973. Rebroadcast on FAM: Fall 1993–94. Rebroadcast on ODY: April 1999–early 2000.

*Voices*
**Archie Andrews:** Dallas McKennon; **Jughead Jones:** Howard Morris; **Betty Cooper:** Jane Webb; **Veronica Lodge:** Jane Webb; **Reggie Mantle:** John Erwin; **Big Moose:** Howard Morris; **Big Ethel:** Jane Webb; **Carlos:** Jose Flores; **Mr. Weatherbee:** Dallas McKennon; **Miss Grundy:** Jane Webb

**TV FUNNIES: Captain Katzenjammer:** Dallas McKennon; **Hans Katzenjammer:** Dallas McKennon; **Fritz Katzenjammer:** Howard Morris; **Kayo/Chief/Sam Ketchum/Pat Patton/B.O. Plenty:** Dallas McKennon; **Inspector/Sluggo/Sandy/Moon Mullins:** Howard Morris; **Mama/Miss Della/Fritzi Ritz/Grave Gertie:** Jane Webb; **Dick Tracey/Alvin/Smokey Stover:** John Erwin; **Nancy:** Jayne Hamil; **Broom Hilda/Sluggo/Oola:** June Foray; **King Guzzle:** Alan Oppenheimer; **Alley Oop:** Bob Holt

## ⊚ ARCHIE'S WEIRD MYSTERIES

After solving a high school science experiment that goes awry, Archie, now editor of the Riverdale High School newspaper, and his fellow staff members, Jughead, Veronica, Betty, Reggie and Dilto, turn to investigating weird and unexplainable paranormal mysteries in this latest reincarnation of the popular Archie Comics franchise that aired on PAX network from October 1999 to February 2000. Combining elements of FOX's highly rated live-action paranormal series, *The X-Files*, and Hanna-Barbera's *Scooby Doo, Where Are You!* the series re-aired in syndication, beginning in 2001. In 2002, the famed *Archie* comic-book characters starred in a 90-minute animated special, *The Archies in Jug Man*, as part of Nickelodeon's *DIC's Incredible Movie Toons* series. A DIC Enterprises Production. Color. Half-hour. Premiered September 1, 2003 on PAX: October 2, 1999–February 21, 2000. Rebroadcast on PAX: 2002–03. Syndicated.

*Voices*
**Archie Andrews:** Andrew Rannells; **Jughead Jones:** Chris Lundquist; **Veronica Lodge:** Camille Schmidt; **Betty Cooper:** Daniella Young; **Reggie Mantle:** Paul Sosso; **Dilton Doiley:** Ben Beck; **Mr. Weatherbee:** Tony Wike; **Mr. Lodge:** John Michael Lee; **Pop Tate:** Ryle Smith; **Dr. Beaumont/Smithers:** Jerry Longe

## ⊚ AROUND THE WORLD IN EIGHTY DAYS

Based on Jules Vernes's novel of the same name, millionaire Phileas Fogg embarks on a voyage around the world to prove himself worthy of marrying Lord Maze's niece, Belinda, and to win a wager made by Maze against his chances of fulfilling the trip. The 16-episode half-hour series lasted only one season NBC. An Air Programs International Production. Color. Half-hour. Premiered on NBC: September 9, 1972–September 1, 1973. Rebroadcast on CAR: December 6, 1992 (part of Boomerang, 1972). Syndicated.

*Voices*
**Phileas Fogg:** Alistair Duncan; **Jean Passepartout:** Ross Higgins; **Mister Fix:** Max Obinstein

## ⊚ ARTHUR

An eight-year-old boy with the head of an aardvark confronts and solves a series of big problems—from training a puppy to encountering a mean bully—in this half-hour series for PBS, based on a bedtime story by author Marc Brown. Premiering in October of 1996, the half-hour series became an instant hit with children, attracting more than 9 million viewers by March of 1997. Focusing on typical childhood problems of growing up in each broadcast, from schoolyard bullies to classroom cliques, the bespectacled aardvark was joined by a bevy of colorful friends: the tomboyish Francine Frensky; the enthusiastic gourmand Alan "The Brain" Powers; the wealthy girl with a heart of gold, Muffy Crosswire; and geography expert and world traveler, Sue Ellen Armstrong. Other friends getting into the act included the talented, soft-spoken musician, Fern Walters; the bullying Binky Barnes; the shy moose, George Nordgren; the psychic fourth-grader, Prunella; the cat-girl, Jenna Morgan; and Arthur's lovable pet dog, Pal.

Two years after winning a 1998 Daytime Emmy Award for outstanding children's series, Arthur made his first appearance in prime time in November 2000 with his first half-hour special in time for the holidays, *Arthur's Perfect Christmas*. In September 2002, he returned with a second prime-time special, the hour-long *Arthur: It's Only Rock 'n' Roll*, a parody of the Beatles 1964 live-action feature, *A Hard Day's Night*. In November 2005, Arthur, joined by his pal Buster Bunny, cohosted a third special, the two-hour *Arthur and Buster's Thanksgiving Spectacular*.

Becoming PBS's most recognizable daytime character and mascot for its celebrated *Bookworm Bunch* children's programming block, in the fall of 2005 the series joined PBS Kids Go! an afternoon program block that included *Maya & Miguel*, *Postcards from Buster* and *Cyberchase*, which became a separate channel in the fall of 2006. In May 2006, the series marked its 10th season with the airing of 10 new episodes, with 136 episodes produced during its 10-season run. That August, PBS broadcast the first-ever *Arthur* movie, the fully CGI-animated full-length feature, *Arthur's Missing Pal*. The G-rated film was released on DVD four days after its television premiere. A *CINAR Production in association with WGBH Educational Foundation. Color. Half-hour. Premiered on PBS: October 7, 1996–November 15, 1996; October 20, 1997–April 17, 1998; November 16, 1998–January 1, 1999; October 4, 1999–October 18, 1999; September 25, 2000–November 27, 2000; September 24, 2001–November 26, 2001; October 8, 2002–November 29, 2002; September 15, 2002–December 26, 2003; December 27, 2004–April 8, 2005; May 15, 2006–May 26, 2006.*

*Voices*
**Arthur Timothy Read:** Michael Yarmush (1996–2001), Justin Bradley (2001–02), Mark Rendall (2002– ); **Dora Winifred "D.W." Read:** Michael Caloz (1996–99), Oliver Grainger (1999–2003), Jason Szimmer (2003– ); **Binky/David "Dad" Read:** Bruce Dinsmore; **Jane "Mom" Read:** Sonja Ball; **Buster Baxty:** Danny Brochu; **Francine Alice Frensky:** Jodi Resther; **Mary Alice "Muffy" Crosswire:** Melissa Altro; **Alan "The Brain" Powers:** Luke Reid (1996–2000), Stephen Crowder (2000–02), Alex Hood (2002– ); **Mr. Ratburn:** Arthur Holden; **Prunella:** Tammy Kaslov; **Sue Ellen Armstrong:** Patricia Rodriguez; **Principal Herbert Haney:** Walter Massey; **Grandma Thora Read:** Joanne Noyes; **Grandpa Dave/Ed Crosswire:** A.J. Henderson; **Mrs. Sarah MacGrady:** Bronwen Mantel; **Fern Walters:** Holly G. Frankel; **Paige Turner:** Kate Hutchinson; **Nadine:** Hayley Reynolds; **George Nordgren:** Mitchell David; **Baby Kate Read:** Tracy Braunstein; **Marie-Helen:** Jessica Kardos; **Emily:** Vanessa Lengies; **Nemo the Cat:** Greg Kramer; **Pal the Dog:** Simon Peacock

## ⊚ ARTHUR AND THE SQUARE KNIGHTS OF THE ROUND TABLE

In Camelot King Arthur's legendary square knights "protect" the royal crown of England in this British-made half-hour cartoon sendup produced for syndication. *An Air Programs International Production. Color. Half-hour. Premiered: 1968. Syndicated.*

## ⊚ ASSY MCGEE

Assy McGee is no ordinary cop. A toothpick-chomping vigilante police sniper who visually looks like a giant ass, along with his "good cop" partner, Detective Don Sanchez, he still manages to the get the job done taking whatever action is needed using his bolt-action SKS assault weapon and his handy toothpick to stop scumbag criminals in their tracks in this new comedy series parodying gritty detective characters in films like *Dirty Harry* and

*Cobra* for Cartoon Network. Produced by Carl Adams, H. Jon Benjamin and Matt Harrigan of Boston, Massachusetts' Soup-2Nuts, 10 episodes of the Sunday night series premiered on Cartoon Network's *Adult Swim* animation block. A *Soup2Nuts Production. Color. Fifteen minutes. Premiered on CAR: November 26, 2006.*

**Voices**
**Assy McGee/Greg, the Chief/Detective Don Sanchez:** Larry Murphy; **Abigail Morion:** Jen Cohn; **Art Critic:** H. Jon Benjamin; **Actor:** Patrick Borelli

### ⊚ AS TOLD BY GINGER

Middle-school to high-school exploits of a young teenage misfit, Ginger Foutley, and her best friends, Dodie, Macie and Darren, in the fictional Connecticut suburb of Sheltered Shrubs in this half-hour animated series, created by co-executive producer Emily Kapnek and produced by Klasky Csupo (creators of TV's *Rugrats*) for Nickleodeon. In September 1999, a series pilot entitled "Ginger the Girl" was produced but never aired. A year later, in October 2000, the series debuted in prime time on Nickleodeon, airing on Wednesdays. In January 2001, the 49-episode series was moved to Sunday nights, where it remained for the duration of its network run on Nickleodeon to its final season in November 2004. Beginning in September 2002, the series aired simultaneously on Nickleodeon and Saturday mornings on CBS as part of Nick Jr.'s cartoon block for the network until January 2003.

During the series' original network run, three made-for-TV movies based on the series were produced: *Summer of Camp Caprice* (2001); *Far from Home* (2003); *No Turning Back* (2004); and one direct-to-DVD production, *The Wedding Frame.* In addition, the characters headlined three half-hour holiday specials during the series' successful network run: for Halloween, *I Spy a Witch* (2001); for Christmas, *The Even Steven Holiday Special* (2001); and for Thanksgiving, *Ten Chairs* (2004). In 2005, the three-time Emmy-nominated series was also chosen best cartoon at Nickleodeon Netherlands' Kids Choice Awards. That same year, Nickelodeon sporadically re-aired the series, including a January 2 broadcast of "Blizzard Conditions"; a March 27, Easter Sunday showing of "The Easter Ham"; a May 8 broadcast of "Mommy Nearest" as part of a Mother's Day marathon; and rebroadcasts of two holiday specials including *I Spy a Witch* on October 30 and *The Even Steven Holiday Special* on Christmas Day.

In 2006, Nickelodeon started rebroadcasting the series weekday mornings, and then Sunday nights before replacing it with TeenNick programming. A *Klasky Csupo Production. Color. Half-hour. Premiered on NICK: October 25, 2000–November 24, 2004. Premiered on CBS: September 14, 2002–January 25, 2003. Rebroadcast on NICK: October 25, 2000–June 27, 2004. Rebroadcast on NICKT: May 4, 2002–.*

**Voices**
**Ginger Foutley:** Melissa Disney (2000–02), Shayna Fox (2002–04); **Carl Foutley:** Jeannie Elias; **Lois Foutley:** Laraine Newman; **Dedre Hortense "Dodie" Bishop:** Aspen Miller; **Marcie Lightfoot:** Jackie Harris; **Darren Patterson:** Kenny Blank; **Robert Joseph "Hoodsey" Bishop:** Tress MacNeille; **Courtney Gripling:** Liz Georges; **Miranda Kilgallen:** Cree Summer; **Blake Gripling:** Kath Soucie; **Winston:** John Kassir; **Chet Zipper:** Hope Levy; **Mrs. Gordon:** Kathleen Freeman (2000–03); **Mrs. Zorski:** Elizabeth Halpern; **Noelle Sussman:** Emily Kapnek; **Dr. Dave:** David Jeremiah

### ⊚ ASTRO BOY (1963)

Based on one of Japan's most popular comic-strip and cartoon characters—known as Tetsuan-Atoma (the Mighty Atom)—this pint-size android was brought to America by NBC Films, which syndicated the English-dubbed series in 1963. Like the original series, Astro Boy—his Americanized name—was a modern-looking crime fighter created by Dr. Boynton (Dr. Tenma in the Japanese version) of the Institute of Science, who sells the mechanical boy to a circus as a side-show attraction. Rescued by kindly Dr. Elefun (formerly Dr. Ochanomizu), Astro Boy uses his remarkable powers to defend justice and fight the galaxy's most fiendish villains: Phoenix Bird, Sphinx, Long Joan Floater, Crooked Fink, the Mist Men and Zero, the invisible. In all, 104 action-packed episodes were broadcast in the United States. A *Mushi Production. Black-and-white. Color. Half-hour. Premiered: September 7, 1963–1966. Syndicated.*

**Voices**
**Astro Boy/Astro Girl:** Billie Lou Watt; **Dr. Elefun:** Ray Owens; **Mr. Pompus:** Gilbert Mack; **Others:** Peter Fernandez

### ⊚ ASTRO BOY (2004)

All-new series based on the classic anime property following the adventures of the reluctant atomic-powered boy robot superhero Astro Boy, built by renowned scientist Dr. Tenma in the image of his dead son and rediscovered years later by the new head of the Ministry of Science, Dr. O'Shay, who reactivates the powerful robot to use his super abilities, including his jet rocket feet and arms, to fly at super fast speeds and protect the innocent in Metro City, a "retro-futuristic" city inhabited by humans and robots alike. Based on the classic manga and original 1962 cartoon series—the first Japanese program imported to the United States and one of the top-rated syndicated series of its time—created by pioneer Japanese animator Tezuka Osamu, this modern remake, originally produced in 2003, debuted Saturday mornings on the WB Television Network's Kids' WB! in January 2004 (with 26 half-hour episodes ordered for the first season) and two months later on Cartoon Network's Monday-through-Friday *Toonami* action-adventure programming block. Unfortunately, the series never found a permanent home, hopping back and forth between both networks before it was eventually cancelled due to low ratings. A *Tezuka Productions/Sony Pictures Television Production. Color. Half-hour. Premiered on the WB (Kids' WB!): January 17, 2004–June 19, 2004. Premiered on CAR: March 8, 2004–Summer 2004.*

**Voices**
**Astro Boy/Kennedy:** Candi Milo; **Dr. Nagamiya Tenma:** Dorian Harewood; **Dr. O'Shay/Skunk/Blue Knight/Wally Kisagari/Katari/Harley/Kato/Others:** Wally Wingert; **Detective Tawashi:** Bill Farmer; **Pluto:** David Rasner; **Yuko:** Faith Salie; **Daichi/Atlas:** Faith Salie; **Nora:** Jennifer Darling; **Mechanic:** Jonathan Todd Ross; **Alejo:** Lara Jill Miller; **Matthew:** Maile Flanagan; **Abercrombie:** Sandy Martin; **Zoran:** Susan Blu; **Other Voices:** David Wittenberg, Gregg Berger

### ⊚ THE ASTRONUT SHOW

First seen in an episode of *Deputy Dawg* and in several theatrical cartoons from 1964 to 1965, Astronut, a friendly alien, was featured in his own half-hour series, combining theatrical cartoon shorts and new six-minute episodes, for syndication. In the late 1960s the program contained the following components: "Hashimoto," "Sidney" and "Luno, the Flying Horse," each stars of their own theatrical film series. In the 1970s Viacom, the program's distributor, reprogrammed the series with supporting episodes from

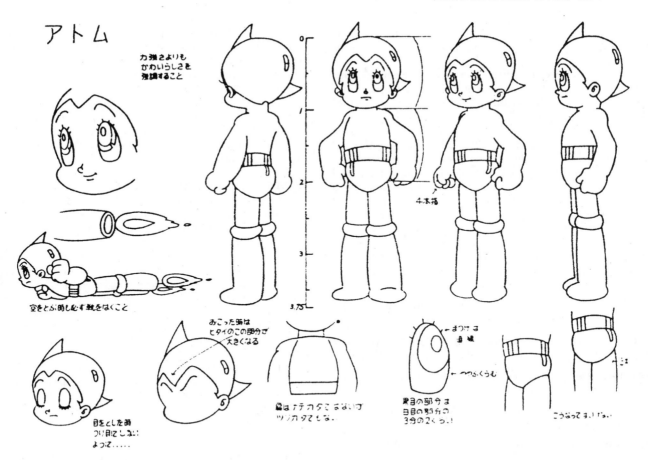

アトム

Model sheet for the popular Japanese cartoon series Astro Boy.

other Terry-Toons' favorites: "Sad Cat," "Possible Possum" and "James Hound."

A *Terry-Toons/CBS Films Production. Color. Half-hour. Premiered: August 23, 1965. Syndicated.*

**Voices**

**Astronut:** Dayton Allen, Lionel Wilson, Bob McFadden; **Oscar Mild, his friend/Sad Cat/Gadmouse/Impressario/Letimore/Fenimore:** Bob McFadden; **Hashimoto/Hanako, his wife/Yuriko/Saburo:** John Myhers; **Sidney, the Elephant:** Lionel Wilson, Dayton Allen; **Stanley the Lion/Cleo the Giraffe/James Hound:** Dayton Allen; **Possible Possum/Billy Bear/Owlawishua Owl/Macon Mouse:** Lionel Wilson

## ◎ A.T.O.M.

Recruited by a top industrialist, Mr. Janus Lee, and equipped with the most advanced gadgets and hottest vehicles ever created for A.T.O.M. (Alpha Teens On Machines), five rebellious teenage test pilots—Axel, Hawk, Shark, King and Lioness—cross paths with the sinister criminal mastermind, Mr. Paine, with past and future worlds colliding, putting them to the test while forging friendships and breaking a few rules along the way in one amazing adventure after another. This futuristic half-hour, French-animated adventure series bowed with 26 episodes, including an hour-long two-part premiere entitled "A Paine by Any Other Name," on the popular *Jetix* action/adventure block on Toon Disney at 8 P.M. and ABC Family, where it was broadcast until August 2006, including a special final weekend marathon featuring two

episodes, "Remote Control" and "Showdown," marking the departure of the *Jetix* block from cable network's regular schedule. A *SIP Animation/Jetix Europe Production. Color. Half-hour. Premiered on TDIS: January 30, 2006. Premiered on ABC FAM: January 30, 2006–August 31, 2006.*

**Voices**

**Axel Manning/Sebastian Manning/Tilian:** James Arnold Taylor; **Zack "Hawk" Hawkes/Stingfly/Cannonball Brothers:** Charlie Schlatter; **Ollie "Shark" Sharker/Rayza:** Brian Donovan; **Crey "King" Kingston/Wrecka:** Alois Hooge; **Cat "Lioness" Leone/Firekat:** Alli Mauzey; **Janus Lee/Marcel "Spydah" Roger/Garrett:** Tom Kenny; **Albert "Flesh"/Vinnie "Mass" Rossi:** Bill Fagerbakke; **Samantha "Magness" Paine:** Kari Wahlgren; **Edge/Icarus:** Jeff Bennett; **Buffy:** Susan Egan; **Dr. Rachelle Logan:** Erin Fitzgerald; **Colonel Richter/Optical/D-Zel:** Jess Harnell; **Eel/Fender:** Maurice LaMarche; **Dr. Nimbus/Bonez:** Pete Sepenuk; **Terrance Yao:** James Sie; **Laura:** Isabella Way

## ◎ THE ATOM ANT/SECRET SQUIRREL SHOW

Essentially two half-hour programs combined, "The Atom Ant/Secret Squirrel Show" was a one-hour block of cartoons comprised of two main stars and their supporting regulars. Each show featured Atom Ant, an invincible superhero ant able to lift ten times his body weight who relentlessly defends law and order, in two six-minute action adventures, followed by one episode each of "The

Hillbilly Bears," the rustic adventures of an idiotic backwoods family, and "Precious Pupp," a troublesome, snickering hound who fools his kindly millionaire owner (Granny Sweet) into thinking he's faithful, obedient and "precious."

Trench-coated Secret Squirrel, a parody of Ian Fleming's James Bond, was the series' other main star, featured in six-minute adventures. Along with his partner Morocco Mole (who sounded like Peter Lorre), the ever-clever squirrel encountered danger in assignments throughout the world. The cartoon components for this half of the show were "Squiddly Diddly," a star-struck squid who hoped to break into show business, and "Winsome Witch," a good-natured witch who used her evil sorcery to perform good deeds. Each appeared in one six-minute cartoon, sandwiched between the adventures of Secret Squirrel. To promote the new Saturday-morning series, NBC broadcast a special hour-long preview on September 12, 1965, entitled *The World of Secret Squirrel and Atom Ant. A Hanna-Barbera Production. Color. One hour. Premiered on NBC: October 2, 1965–December 31, 1966. Rebroadcast on NBC: September 9, 1967–September 7, 1968.*

*Voices*
**Atom Ant:** Howard Morris, Don Messick; **Secret Squirrel:** Mel Blanc; **Morocco Mole:** Paul Frees

**THE HILLBILLY BEARS: Paw Rugg:** Henry Corden; **Maw Rugg/Floral Rugg:** Jean VanderPyl; **Shag Rugg:** Don Messick

**PRECIOUS PUPP: Precious Pupp:** Don Messick; **Granny Sweet:** Janet Waldo

**SQUIDDLY DIDDLY: Squiddly Diddly:** Paul Frees; **Chief Winchley:** John Stephenson

**WINSOME WITCH: Winsome Witch:** Jean VanderPyl

## ⊚ THE ATOM ANT SHOW
Endowed by super powers, a tiny ant is transformed into the world's mightiest insect superhero in this Hanna-Barbera favorite. Other cartoons featured were "Precious Pupp" and "Hillbilly Bears." The series was first broadcast in combination with the adventures of Secret Squirrel as *The Atom Ant/Secret Squirrel Show*. In January 1967 the two were separated and given their own shows, only to be rejoined again in the original format in September of that year. (See *The Atom Ant/Secret Squirrel Show* for details.) *A Hanna-Barbera Production. Color. Half-hour. Premiered on NBC: January 7, 1967–September 2, 1967. Rebroadcast on CAR: September 20, 1993–December 31, 1993 (weekdays); March 5, 1994–September 3, 1994 (Saturdays); September 11, 1994–September 3, 1995 (Sundays, Wednesdays); –July 10, 2004. Rebroadcast on BOOM: April 1, 2000–.*

## ⊚ ATOMIC BETTY
Assisted by her alien pilot, Sparky, and robot, X-5, an unassuming girl who lives in Canada doubles as the superpowered Galactic Guardian and Defender of the Cosmos, Atomic Betty, and battles the galaxy's evil Supreme Overlord, Maximus I.Q., in this Flash-animated series—produced by Atomic Cartoons, Breakthrough Films, and TeleImages Kids—that aired on Canada's Teletoon network and the United States' Cartoon Network. The internationally popular, 52-episode series was telecast for two seasons, including an hour-long 2005 Christmas special, *Atomic Betty: The No-L-9*, followed by new episodes produced for a third season in October 2006. *An Atomic Cartoons/Breakthrough Films/TeleImages Kids Production. Color. Half hour. Premiered on CAR: September 17, 2004–January 1, 2006.*

*Voices*
**Betty/Atomic Betty/Timmy the Droid:** Taija Isen; **Betty's Dad:** Patrick McKenna; **Betty's Mother:** Kristina Nicoll; **Beatrixo, Betty's Grandma:** Jayne Eastwood; **Admiral DeGill:** Adrian Truss; **Robot X-5:** Bruce Hunter; **Sparky:** Rick Miller; **Supreme Overlord Maximus I.Q.:** Colin Fox; **Minimus P.U./Spindly Tam Kanushu:** Len Carlson; **Chip Osbourne/Dalton Osbourne:** Michael D'Ascenzo; **Noah Parker:** Laurie Elliott; **Duncan Payne:** Peter Oldring; **Penelope Lang/Sarah:** Catherine Disher; **Megan:** Stephanie Morganstern; **Dylan/Atomic Roger/Dodger/Mr. Peterson:** Dwayne Hill

## ⊚ ATTACK OF THE KILLER TOMATOES
Nefarious, angry (not mad) scientist Dr. Putrid T. Gangreen and his crazed, beach-hunk assistant Igor, armed with every variation on the common garden tomato that perverted science can produce, try to conquer the little town of San Zucchini and make the world safe for plant life. Opposing their evil designs are Chad Finletter, a dynamic teenage pizza-delivery boy; his uncle Wilbur; the lovely Tara (part girl/part tomato) and their "dog," F.T., in this weekly half-hour animated series based on the 1979 cult horror classic. John Astin, who played the character of Dr. Putrid T. Gangreen in the original full-length feature (and the sequel), reprised his character. The series was the first fully computer-generated cartoon series for FOX Network. *A Marvel/Four Square Production in association with Akom Productions/FOX Children's Network Productions. Color. Half-hour. Premiered on FOX: September 8, 1990–September 12, 1992. Rebroadcast on FOX: September 19, 1992–October 26, 1996. Rebroadcast on FOX FAM: August 23, 1998–January 10, 1999.*

*Voices*
**Dr. Putrid T. Gangreen:** John Astin; **Chad:** Chris Guzek; **Tara:** Kath Soucie; **Whitley White:** Neil Ross; **Wilbur Finletter:** Thom Bray; **Igor:** Cam Clarke; **F.T.:** S. Scott Bullock; **Zoltan:** Maurice LaMarche

## ⊚ AVATAR: THE LAST AIRBENDER
In an ancient world divided into four nations—the Water Tribes, the Earth Kingdom, the Fire Nation and the Air Nomads—where men and women, known as "benders," are born with the amazing ability to manipulate their native element by using the power of martial arts and elemental magic, the Water Tribe rescues a mysterious 12-year-old boy, Aang, who turns out to be not only the last Airbender but also the long-lost Avatar in this half-hour animated action-adventure series.

Production of each episode cost $1 million and took nine to 10 months to complete. Nickelodeon premiered the first 20 episodes of this unique comic adventure ("Book One: Water") beginning in February 2005. Created by Bryan Konietzko and Mike DiMartino, the series combined rich animation and martial arts choreography.

During the 2005–06 season, Nick debuted three hour-long prime-time specials based on the top-rated series, *The Fury of Aang, The Boy in the Iceberg* and the first-season finale, *The Siege of the North*, and made two more specials in 2006: *Secret of the Fire Nation* and the fifth special and second-season finale, *The Guru/ The Crossroads to Destiny.*

On March 17, 2006, the action-packed anime series kicked off its second season, titled "Book Two: Earth," featuring 20 new chapters with an all-new episode, "The Avatar State," with the Earth Kingdom general wanting to use Aang's alter-ego, the mighty Avatar, as a weapon against the evil Fire Nation. In the meantime, due to the series' enormous success, Nickelodeon commissioned 20 more episodes for the program's third season.

*A Nickelodeon Studios Production. Color. Half-hour. Premiered on NICK: February 21, 2005.*

### Voices

**Avatar Roku:** James Garrett; **Katara:** Mae Whitman; **Uncle Iroh:** Makato Iwamasto; **Prince Zuko:** Dante Basco; **Sokka:** Jack DeSena; **Appa/Momo/Others:** Dee Bradley Baker; **Aang:** Zack Tyler Eisen; **Gran Gran:** Melendy Britt; **Princess Yue:** Johanna Braddy; **Master Pakku:** Victor Brandt; **Chief Arnook:** Jon Polto; **Hahn:** Ben Diskin; **Koh:** Erik Dellums; **Fire Lord Ozai:** Mark Hamill; **Toph:** Jessie Flower; **Wan Shi Tong:** Hector Elizondo; **Professor Zei:** Raphael Sharge; **War Minister:** Kristoffer Tabori; **General Sung:** Barry Dennen; **Bureaucrat:** Karen Maruyama; **Than:** Brian Tochi; **Ying:** Kim Mai Guest; **Smellerbee:** Nika Futterman; **Jet:** Crawford Wilson; **Master Yu:** Sab Shimono; **Colonel Mongke:** Malachi Throne; **Xin Fu:** Marc Graue; **Sha-Mo:** Bill Bolender; **Fung:** Peter Jessop; **Ghashiun:** Paul McKinney; **Ty Lee:** Olivia Hack; **General H: Cricket:** Jim Meskimen; **Hakoda:** Andre Sogliuzzo; **Long Feng:** Clancy Brown; **Master:** Sab Shimono; **Guru Pathik:** Brian George; **Bato:** Richard McGonagle; **Earth King:** Phil LaMarr; **Xin Fu:** Marc Graue

### ⊚ AVENGERS

The world's most incredible superheroes—Ant-Man, Scarlet Witch, Falcon, Hawkeye, Tigra, Wasp, and Wonder Man—fight evil forces around the world that threaten its very existence, everything from the robotic Ultron to the extraterrestrial-like The Zodiac, in this half-hour animated series based on the popular Marvel Comics series created in 1963. The series, which begun airing on FOX's Saturday-morning cartoon block in October 1999 as a two-part episode and was produced by Marvel Entertainment and Saban Entertainment for 20th Century Fox Television, was commissioned by FOX, along with the comic book-inspired, *Spider Man Unlimited*, in hopes of emulating the success of the popular 1999 cartoon series, *Batman Beyond*. FOX cancelled the series in April 2000, with scripts written for a second season that would have featured guest appearances by the founding Avenger, Thor and the X-Men, reuniting the Toronto-based cast from the mid-90s cartoon series. *A Marvel Entertainment/Saban Entertainment Production in association with 20th Century Fox Television. Color. Half-hour. Premiered on FOX: October 30, 1999–April 1, 2000.*

### Voices

**Dr. Hank Pym/Ant-Man:** Rod Wilson; **Wanda Maximoff/Scarlet Witch:** Stravroula Logothettis; **Sam Wilson/Falcon:** Martin Roach; **Clint Barton/Hawkeye:** Tony Daniels; **Greer Nelson/Tigra:** Lenore Zann; **Janet Van Dyne/Wasp:** Linda Ballentine; **Simon Williams/Wonder Man:** Harnish McEwan; **Vision:** Ron Ruben; **Raymond Sikorsky:** Ray Landry; **Jarvis:** Graham Harley; **The Computer:** Caroly Larson; **Ultron:** John Stocker; **Captain America:** Dan Chameroy; **Sub-Mariner:** Raoul Trujillo; **Iron Man:** Francis Diakowsky

### ⊚ BABAR

That playful pachyderm who has delighted generations of young readers stars in this 65-episode half-hour series broadcast on HBO following its original debut on Canada's CBC-TV. Flashbacks depict the mythical world of Babar, recounting personal conflicts that arise when, as a little boy, he tries to juggle growing up along with handling grown-up responsibilities. Laurent de Brunoff, the son of Babar's creator, Jean de Brunoff, authorized the series, which won an Ace Award (1989) for outstanding programming achievement. Besides airing on HBO, the beloved children's series was also telecast on HBO's sister channel, HBO Family, from November 1997 to March 2004, becoming part of its daily morning and afternoon program block of popular animated programs, including *A Little Curious, Happily Ever After: Fairy Tales for Every Child, The Little Lulu Show, Rainbow Fish* and *The Adventures of Tintin*. In the fall of 2006, the program became part of a Saturday children's programming block, qubo, broadcast on NBC and the Spanish-language network, Telemundo, and repeated on Fridays on the ION network (formerly PAX-TV). *A Nelvana Production in association with The Clifford Ross Company and the CBC. Color. Half-hour. Premiered on HBO: April 9, 1989–September 1993. Rebroadcast on FAM: September 12, 1993–December 23, 1994. Rebroadcast on HBO FAM: November 1, 1997–March 31, 2004. Rebroadcast on HBO: January 4, 1999–December 23, 2000. Rebroadcast on NBC/TM: September 9, 2006–. Rebroadcast on ION: September 15, 2006–.*

### Voices

**Adult Babar:** Gordon Pinsent; **Young Babar:** Gavin Magrath; **Queen Celeste:** Dawn Greehaigh; **Young Celeste:** Tara Charendoff; **Pompadour:** Stephen Ouimette; **Cornelius:** Chris Wiggins; **Basil:** John Stocker; **The Old Lady:** Elizabeth Hanna; **Rataxes:** Alan Stewart-Coates; **Lady Rataxes:** Corinne Koslo; **Lisa Yamanaka:** Flora; **Pom:** Bobby Becker; **Alexander:** Amos Crawford

### ⊚ BABY BLUES

Cartoon series adaptation of the popular King Features syndicated comic strip of the same name by Jerry Scott and Rick Kirkman, following the urban parenting exploits of a young married couple, Darryl and Wanda MacPherson, and their infant daughter, Zoe, and their not-so-quiet neighbors that aired in prime time on the WB Television Network. Although the series posted better ratings than the WB's other prime time animated series, *Mission Hill* and *The Oblongs*, the network canceled the cartoon comedy after airing only seven of the first season's original 13 episodes. Reportedly, before canceling the program, the WB Television Network ordered 13 additional episodes with plans to bring it back for a second season, beginning in the summer of 2001. Two years after its demise, Cartoon Network picked up the series and aired the final six episodes during the late-night hours on its *Adult Swim* programming block. *A Split the Difference Production in association with Warner Bros. Television. Color. Half-hour. Premiered on WB: July 28, 2000–September 15, 2000. Premiered on CAR: January 6, 2002–March 10, 2002 (Adult Swim).*

### Voices

**Darryl MacPherson/Jack/Others:** Mike O'Malley; **Carl Bitterman/Others:** Joel Murray; **Rodney Bitterman/Megan Bitterman/Others:** Kath Soucie; **Melinda Bitterman/Others:** Arabella Field; **Bizzy the Babysitter/Others:** Nicole Sullivan; **Rex/Others:** Phil LaMarr; **Baby Midge/Zoe:** Elizabeth Daily; **Wanda MacPherson/Maggie Wisowski:** Julia Sweeney; **Additional Voices:** Shari Albert, David Boreanaz, Dan Cortese, Jim Cummings, Ron Fassler, Philip Baker Hall, Alice Hirson, Maurice LaMarche, Wendy Racquel Robinson, Robert Romanus, John Stephenson, George Takei, Fred Tatasciore, Steven Weber

### ⊚ THE BABY HUEY SHOW

The daffy, diapered, 250-pound baby duckling with the strength of Superman made famous in a string of 1950s Paramount theatrical cartoons (again voiced by Syd Raymond), returns in 13 all-new syndicated adventures, packaged with classic Harvey cartoons, including Casper the Friendly Ghost, Buzzy the Crow, Herman and Katnip and Little Audrey. *A Harvey Entertainment Production in association with Claster Television. Color. Half-hour. Premiered: September 17, 1994. Syndicated.*

**Voice**
**Baby Huey:** Syd Raymond

## ◎ BABY LOONEY TUNES

Laugh-packed nursery adventures of Bugs Bunny, Lola Bunny, Daffy Duck, Petunia Pig, Sylvester, Tweety and the Tazmanian Devil as toddlers, raised by Tweety's sweet human caretaker, Granny (until the second season when they were parented by Granny's nephew, Floyd), cast in life-learning situations about friendship and cooperation, including two-minute sing-a-longs between each episode, told in two-part stories. The 53-episode, half-hour series, comprised of three segments per show, simultaneously debuted in first-run syndication and on Cartoon Network in September 2002.

In spring of 2005, 13 new episodes of the series were produced for syndication. That July, the program began re-airing weeknights on Cartoon Network's sister channel, Boomerang, and that August it joined Cartoon Network's new weekday morning *Tickle-U* preschool block for children ages 2–5, including such cartoon series as *Krypto the Superdog* and *Teenage Mutant Ninja Turtles* (2003). *A Warner Bros. Animation Production. Color. Half-hour. Premiered on CAR: September 16, 2002–April 20, 2005. Syndicated: September 3, 2002. Rebroadcast on BOOM: July 4, 2005–. Rebroadcast on CAR: July 4, 2005–.*

**Voices**
**Granny:** June Foray; **Baby Taz:** Ian James Corlett; **Baby Sylvester:** Terry Klassen; **Baby Lola Bunny:** Britt McKillip; **Baby Bugs/Baby Daffy/Baby Tweety:** Sam Vincent; **Baby Petunia:** Chiara Zanni; **Melissa Duck:** Janyce Jaud; **Floyd:** Brian Drummond; **Additional Voices:** Bailey Devlin, Mariko Kage, Ellen Kennedy

## ◎ BACK TO THE FUTURE

Marty McFly, the time-traveling teenager from the highly successful *Back to the Future* movie trilogy series (played by Michael J. Fox), embarks on all-new adventures in this animated CBS Saturday-morning spinoff. Only three stars from the *Back to the Future* films reprised their roles for the series: Christopher Lloyd as Doc, the eccentric inventor (who appeared in live-action educational wraparounds); Thomas F. Wilson as Biff, the peabrained bully who gives Marty trouble; and Mary Steenburgen, back as Clara, Doc's wife. The series was later rebroadcast on the Sci-Fi Channel and FOX Network. *An Amblin/Wang Film Production. Color. Half-hour. Premiered on CBS: September 4, 1991–August 14, 1993. Rebroadcast on SCI: October 1, 1994–June 28, 1996. Rebroadcast on FOX: March 22, 2003–August 30, 2003.*

**Cast (live action)**
**Doc:** Christopher Lloyd; **The Science Guy:** Bill Nye

**Voices**
**Doc:** Dan Castellaneta; **Marty:** David Kaufman; **Biff:** Thomas F. Wilson; **Jules:** Josh Weiner; **Verne:** Troy Davidson; **Einstein:** Danny Mann; **Clara:** Mary Steenburgen

## ◎ THE BACKYARDIGANS

Five colorful, high-spirited, dance-happy preschool friends, Tyrone, Tasha, Uniqua, Pablo and Austin, who sway to a variety of musical sounds from mambo to smoky jazz in a matter of minutes, use their imaginations to transform their backyard into a series of amazing, epic, whimsical adventures in this CG- and 3-D-animated half-hour series created by Janice Burgess for CBS and Nick Jr. Burgess

joined Nick Jr. in 1995 as a production executive for the award-winning series *Blue's Clues* and *Little Bill*. Each episode is comprised of four original songs and set to a specific musical with the dance steps of the characters recreated in animation and choreographed by former Alvin Ailey Dance School director Beth Bogush.

A joint production of Canadian animation studio, Nelvana Limited, and Nick Jr., the rich, lushly animated series, featuring original music by Evan Lurie of the Lounge Lizards and Douglas Weiselman, originally aired on Nick Jr.'s Saturday morning program block on CBS from October 2004 to September 2006. In November 2004, the series began airing weekdays on Nick Jr., which, in 2005, also aired two half-hour specials, based on the series: *Mission to Mars* and *Race to the Tower of Power*. In April 2006, Nick Jr. ordered 20 new episodes of the popular preschool series for the fall 2006 schedule. *A Nelvana Limited/Nickelodeon Production. Color. Half-hour. Premiered on CBS: October 11, 2004–September 2006. Premiered on NICK JR.: November 22, 2004–.*

**Voices**
**Tyrone:** Reginald Davis Jr.; **Tasha:** Naelee Rae; **Uniqua:** LeShawn Jeffries; **Pablo:** Sean Curley; **Austin:** Jonah Bobo, **Tyrone singing:** Corwin C. Tuggles; **Tasha singing:** Kristen Danielle Klabunde; **Uniqua singing:** Jamia Simone Nash; **Pablo singing:** Zach Tyler; **Austin singing:** Thomas Sharkey

## ◎ B.A.D. (BUREAU OF ALIEN DECTECTORS)

When aliens invade Earth, a special resistance task force of seasoned military professionals and townspeople—including two determined teenagers, Zach Trainer and Amanda Burke—seek to protect the world from supernatural encounters in this 13-episode action/adventure series, for UPN. *A Saban Entertainment Production. Color. Half-hour. Premiered on UPN: September 8, 1996–September 20, 1997.*

**Voices**
**Ben Parker:** Michael McConnohie; **Additional Voices:** Bree Anderson, Reuben Daniels, Sammy Lane, Walter Rego, Peter Spellos, Tyrone Week

## ◎ BAD DOG

Animated version of the popular screensaver character created in the late 1990s who, despite every attempt to make his human owners happy, has a knack for messing things up in the worst possible way in this half-hour series—and one of several new cartoon programs—to air on the newly named FOX Family Channel (formerly The Family Channel) in August 1998. On July 18, FOX Family Channel's sister network, FOX, previewed the series with a half-hour Saturday morning special presentation. After becoming the ABC Family in July 2001, when the network was sold to ABC, the series remained on the air until January 2002. *A Cine-Groupe/Storyopolous/Saban Entertainment Production. Color. Half-hour. Premiered on FOX: July 18, 1998 (special presentation). Premiered on FOX FAM/ABC FAM: August 15, 1998–January 11, 2002.*

**Voices**
**Vic Potanski:** Harvey Atkin; **Other Voices:** Sheila McCarthy, Tracey Moore, John Stocker

## ◎ BAGGY PANTS AND NITWITS

Friz Freleng, who created the pantominic Pink Panther, co-produced this half-hour Saturday-morning series with partner David H.

DePatie, which premiered on NBC and lasted one season. Featured were: "Baggy Pants," the adventures of a Chaplinesque cat in silent comedy routines, and "The Nitwits," the misadventures of Tyrone and Gladys (characters created by comedians Arte Johnson and Ruth Buzzi on TV's *Rowan and Martin's Laugh-In* and reprised by them for this series), a comic pair of crimefighting superheroes. A *DePatie-Freleng Enterprises Production. Color. Half-hour. Premiered on NBC: September 10, 1977–October 28, 1978.*

**Voices**
**Tyrone:** Arte Johnson; **Gladys, his wife:** Ruth Buzzi

## ◎ BAGPUSS

Acclaimed stop-motion animated children's series, originally broadcast on BBC in 1974 and in 1998 voted the network's "Best Kiddie Program of All Time," featuring the delightful adventures of a candy cane–striped magical cat, Bagpuss, and his friends—a carved wooden book end, Professor Yaffle; a wicker chair rag doll, Madeleine Remnant; a banjo-playing toad, Gabriel Croaker; and the Mechanical Mouse Organ mice—who come to life in a small London toy shop run by a young girl, Emily (played by Emily Firmin, the daughter of the show's writer-creator, Peter Firmin), who introduced each week's story in live-action. Produced by the British animation studio, Smallfilms, the 13-episode, half-hour series was syndicated in the United States between 1983 and 1986. A *Smallfilms Production. Color. Half-hour. Premiered 1983–1986. Syndicated.*

**Cast (live action)**
**Emily:** Emily Firmin

**Voices**
**Bagpuss/Narrator/Mice/Professor Augustus Barclay Yaffle:** Oliver Postgate; **Gabriel Croaker:** John Faulkner; **Madeleine Remnant:** Sandra Kerr

## ◎ BAILEY'S COMETS

Comet members Barnaby, Bunny, Wheelie, Sarge and Pudge skate against 17 roller-derby teams in a continuing race around the world in search of $1 million in buried treasure, told in two 10-minute adventures each week. Created by Joe Ruby and Ken Spears, the series lasted four months into the first Saturday-morning season. It was shifted to Sunday mornings, then canceled. A *DePatie-Freleng Enterprises Production. Color. Half-hour. Premiered on CBS: September 9, 1973–August 31, 1975.*

**Voices**
**Barnaby Bailey:** Carl Esser; **Pudge:** Frank Welker; **Wheelie:** Jim Begg; **Candy:** Karen Smith; **Bunny:** Sarah Kennedy; **Sarge:** Kathi Gori; **Dude:** Robert Holt; **Dooter Roo:** Daws Butler; **Gabby/Henry Jekyll-Hyde:** Don Messick

## ◎ BANANAMAN

After consuming his daily ration of bananas, unassuming, mild-mannered Eric Wimp becomes the unstoppable crimefighting superhero Bananaman in this British-produced half-hour animated series based on a character created for Britain's *Nutty Comics* in 1980. The series debuted in the United States on Nickelodeon. A *101 Production. Color. Half-hour. Premiered on NICK: October 7, 1985–August 31, 1987.*

**Voices**
**Bananaman/General Blight:** Graeme Garden; **Eric/Crow/Chief O'Reilly/Henry the Nurk/Dr. Gloom/The Weatherman:** Bill Oddie; **Fiona/Samantha/Mother Nurk:** Jill Shilling; **Narrator/King Zorg of the Nurks/Aunty/Appleman:** Tim Brooke-Taylor

## ◎ THE BANANA SPLITS ADVENTURE HOUR

Live actors in animal suits—known as the Banana Splits (Fleegle, Drooper, Bingo and Snorky)—hosted this hour-long format composed of their own misadventures, a live-action adventure series "Danger Island," and four cartoon segments: "The Three Musketeers," "The Arabian Knights," "Hillbilly Bears" and "The Micro Venture." The program marked Hanna-Barbera's first live-action/animation show for television. (For voice credits to the "Hillbilly Bears," see *The Atom Ant/Secret Squirrel Show.*) A *Hanna-Barbera Production. Color. One hour. Premiered on NBC: September 7, 1968–September 5, 1970. Rebroadcast on CAR: September 20, 1993–April 29, 1994 (weekdays); December 5, 1994–June 2, 1995 (weekdays); June 5, 1995–September 1, 1995 (part of hour-long block with The Cattanooga Cats). Rebroadcast on BOOM: May 1, 2000–.*

**Voices**
**Fleegle, the dog:** Paul Winchell; **Drooper, the lion:** Allan Melvin; **Bingo, the gorilla:** Daws Butler; **Snorky, the elephant:** Don Messick

**THE THREE MUSKETEERS: D'Artagnan:** Bruce Watson; **Porthos:** Barney Phillips; **Aramis:** Don Messick; **Athos:** Jonathan Harris; **Toulie*:** Teddy Eccles; **The Queen/Lady Constance:** Julie Bennett

**THE ARABIAN KNIGHTS: Bez:** Henry Corden; **Evil Vangore:** Paul Frees; **Raseem:** Frank Gerstle; **Princess Nida:** Shari Lewis; **Prince Turhan:** Jay North; **Fariik:** John Stephenson

**THE MICRO VENTURE: Professor Carter:** Don Messick; **Jill Carter:** Patsy Garrett; **Mike Carter:** Tommy Cook

**DANGER ISLAND: Professor Irwin Hayden:** Frank Aletter; **Leslie Hayden:** Ronnie Troup; **Link Simmons:** Michael Vincent; **Morgan, the castaway:** Rockne Tarkington; **Chongo:** Kahana; **Mu-Tan:** Victor Eberg; **Chu:** Rodrigo Arrendondo

## ◎ BARBAPAPA

Reminiscent of *The Smurfs*, this Netherlands-produced, half-hour series, following the adventures of a family of troll-like creatures known as the Barbapapas, was offered in syndication in 1977 but was not broadcast in the United States until 1981, when the series was picked up by LBS Communications, a U.S. television syndicator that earlier had syndicated another Dutch import, *Dr. Snuggles*. A *Polyscope (Netherlands)/LBS Communications Production. Color. Half-hour. Premiered: 1981. Syndicated.*

**Voices**
**Storyteller:** Allen Swift; **Other Voices:** Ann Costello, Alexander Marshall

## ◎ THE BARKLEYS

An outspoken, opinionated canine bus driver, Arnie Barkley (copied after TV's Archie Bunker) clashes with his progressive family over timeworn socially related topics in this half-hour Saturday-morning series inspired by the success of the CBS sitcom, *All in the Family*. The series debuted on rival network NBC, with 13 original episodes. It lasted two seasons. A *DePatie-Freleng Enterprises*

---

* The character Toulie was misspelled as "Tooly" in episode titles of this series.

*Production. Color. Half-hour. Premiered on NBC: September 9, 1972–September 1, 1973.*

**Voices**
**Arnie Barkley:** Henry Corden; **Agnes, his wife:** Joan Gerber; **Terri, Barkley's daughter:** Julie McWhirter; **Chester, the eldest son:** Steve Lewis; **Roger, the youngest son:** Gene Andrusco

### ◉ BARNYARD COMMANDOS
Planned as a regular series, this short-lived, four-episode cartoon miniseries featured the ongoing battle between two fiercely competitive animal armies: the pigs (whose code name was P.O.R.K.S.: Platoon of Rebel Killers) versus the sheep (known as the R.A.M.S.: Rebel Army of Military Sheep) in this *Teenage Mutant Ninja Turtles* knock-off from the same producers. The series premiered in first-run syndication on Labor Day weekend of 1990. *A Murikami-Wolf-Swenson Production in association with those Characters From Cleveland and Sachs-Finley. Color. Half-hour. Syndicated: September 4, 1990–September 7, 1990.*

**Voices**
Scott Bullock, Thom Bray, Pat Fraley, Paul Kreppel, John Mariano, Bob Ridgely, Lennie Weinrib, Danny Wells

### ◉ BATFINK
Called into action on a private hotline by the Chief of Police, this pointy-eared crimefighter with wings of steel and his Super Sonic Sonar foils ruthless criminals, mobsters and all-around bad guys with the help of his Japanese assistant Karate in this animated parody of comic-book superhero Batman. The 100-episode series, consisting of 5 five-minute cartoons per each half-hour program, was created by former Fleischer animator Hal Seeger, who originated TV's *Milton the Monster*. Cartoon Network's sister network Boomerang began rebroadcasting the series in 2006. *A Hal Seeger Production. Color. Half-hour. Premiered: Fall 1967. Syndicated. Rebroadcast on BOOM: September 16, 2006–.*

**Voices**
**Batfink/Hugo A Go Go/Various Others:** Frank Buxton; **Karate/The Chief/Various Others:** Len Maxwell

### ◉ THE BATMAN
Now in his mid-20s and in his third year of establishing himself as the famed Caped Crusader, billionaire bachelor Bruce Wayne balances his public persona and responsibilities as a crime-fighting superhero, using his amazing physical prowess, combined with experimental high-tech Bat-gadgets and an amped-up Batmobile, to rid Gotham City of its villainous perpetrators in this spin-off of the DC Comics comic-book series, "The Batman Strikes!"

Along with his fabled partner, Robin, and occasionally Batgirl, the dynamic duo faced a regular rogues' gallery of villains in this combined 2-D cel- and computer-animated half-hour series, including their famed arch-rivals the Catwoman, Joker, Mr. Freeze, Penguin and Riddler, as well as several new forces of evil—among them Black Mask, Clayface, the Everywhere Man, Harley Quinn and Killer Moth—to torment them and save their beloved Gotham City during its first four seasons.

Produced by Warner Bros. Television Animation and executive produced by Sander Schwartz and Alan Burnett, the half-hour series bowed Saturday mornings at 10:30 A.M. (ET) on Kids' WB!—with episodes initially replayed on Friday afternoons and then Monday through Friday afternoons—in September 2004. For kids ages six to 11, 39 half-hour episodes of the high-adventure series were ordered for the first season with major toy tie-ins licensed to Mattel.

In the fall of 2006, the program, along with two others, *Xiaolin Showdown* and *Lunatics Unleashed,* moved to the newly renamed CW Network (formerly the WB) as part of its Kids' WB! Saturday-morning cartoon lineup. That same year, the series won two Daytime Emmy Awards, for outstanding achievement in sound editing and outstanding special class animated program. Beginning in April 2005 the series joined Cartoon Network's famed *Toonami* action block in reruns. The Edge from multi-Grammy Award-winning sensation U2 performed the series' theme song. *A Warner Bros. Television Animation Production. Color. Half-hour. Premiered on Kids WB!: September 11, 2004. Rebroadcast on CAR: April 2, 2005–December 23, 2006.*

**Voices**
**Bruce Wayne/Batman:** Rino Romano; **Alfred Pennyworth:** Alastair Duncan; **Dick Grayson/Robin:** Evan Sabara; **Chief Angel Rojas:** Edward James Olmos, Jesse Corti; **Detective Ellen Yin:** Ming-Na; **Rupert Thorne:** Victor Brandt; **Mayor:** Adam West; **Commissioner James Gordon:** Mitch Pileggi; **Barbara Gordon/Batgirl:** Danielle Judovits; **The Joker:** Kevin Michael Richardson; **Catwoman:** Gina Gershon; **The Penguin:** Tom Kenny; **Mr. Freeze:** Clancy Brown; **Clayface/Detective Steven Harris:** Steve Harris; **Firefly:** Jason Marsden; **The Ventriloquist/Scarface:** Dan Castellaneta; **Man-Bat:** Peter MacNicol; **Cluemaster:** Glenn Shadix; **Bane:** Joaquim de Almeida, Ron Perlman, Clancy Brown; **The Riddler:** Robert Englund; **Professor Hugo Strange:** Frank Gorshin, Richard Green; **Ragdoll/D.A.V.E./Killer Moth:** Jeff Bennett; **Spellbinder:** Michael Massee; **Killer Croc:** Ron Perlman; **Solomon Grundy:** Kevin Grevioux; **Poison Ivy:** Piera Coppola; **Gearhead:** Will Friedle; **Maxie Zeua:** Phil LaMarr; **Cosmo Krank/Toymaker:** Patton Oswalt; **Prank:** Michael Reisz; **Temblor:** Jim Cummings; **Lucious Fox:** Louis Gossett Jr.; **Tony Zucco:** Mark Hamill; **Black Mask:** James Remar; **Number One:** Diedrich Bader; **Everywhere Man:** Brandon Routh; **Hynden Walch:** Harley Quinn; **Clayface:** Wallace Langham

### ◉ BATMAN AND THE SUPER SEVEN
NBC broadcast this hour-long compendium of previous episodes of Filmation's *The New Adventures of Batman,* originally aired on CBS in 1977, and four components ("Isis and the Freedom Force," "Microwoman and Super Stretch," "Web Woman" and "Manta and Moray") first broadcast on the 1978 CBS series *Tarzan and the Super Seven.* (See *The New Adventures of Batman* and *Tarzan and the Super Seven* for details and voice credits.) *A Filmation Associates Production. Color. One hour. Premiered on NBC: September 27, 1980–September 5, 1981.*

### ◉ BATMAN BEYOND
Far into a future with crime at an all-time high after having retired his cowl and cape as Gotham City's most famous crime-fighter, Batman, an elderly Bruce Wayne (voiced by Kevin Conroy), passes the mantel to a high school teenager named Terry McGinnis, who learns of Wayne's long-concealed secret identity and emerges as the new, high-tech-oriented Dark Knight, complete with rocket boots and cloaks, while juggling school and his life as a superhero, to avenge the murder of his father in this spin-off from Warner Bros. Television Animation's *The New Adventures of Batman.*

Debuting in prime time on the WB Television Network in January 1999 as a two-hour made-for-TV movie, this latest adaptation of the popular DC Comics character preceded the highly-rated weekly, half-hour series comprised of 52 episodes that aired through mid-December 2001. Nominated for 11 Daytime Emmy Awards, winning twice in 2001 for outstanding special class animated program and outstanding achievement in music direction and composition, the comic book-inspired adventures were subsequently rebroadcast for two years on Turner Broadcasting's Cartoon Network. The half-hour action/adventure series also spawned a direct-to-video movie, *Batman Beyond: The Return of the Joker* (2000), and a spin-off television cartoon series, *The Zeta Project*. A *Warner Bros. Television Animation Production. Color. Half-hour. Premiered on WB: January 10, 1999 (TV movie "preview"). Premiered on WB: January 16, 1999–December 18, 2001(series). Rebroadcast on CAR: October 1, 2001–February 28, 2003.*

*Voices*

**Terrence McGinnis/Batman:** Will Friedle; **Bruce Wayne:** Kevin Conroy; **Commissioner Barbara Gordon:** Angie Harmon (2000–01), Stockard Channing (1999–2000); **Chelsea Cunningham:** Yvette Lowenstein, Rachel Leigh Cook; **Spellbinder:** Jon Cypher; **Miss Winston:** Mari Devon; **Blade:** Melissa Disney; **Mrs. Mary McGinnis:** Teri Garr; **Nelson Nash:** Seth Green; **Derek Powers/Blight:** Sherman Howard; **Inque:** Shannon Kenny; **Mr. Walker/The King:** George Lazenby; **Matthew McGinnis:** Ryan O'Donahue; **Max Gibson:** Cree Summer; **Dana Tan:** Lauren Tom; **Mr. Freeze/Victor Fries:** Michael Ansara; **Freon/Mary Michaels:** Laura San Giacomo; **Magma/Dr. Mike Morgan:** Robert Davi; **Walter Shreeve/Shrink:** Chris Mulkey; **Ten/Melanie Walker:** Olivia d'Abo; **Jared Tate:** Dorian Harewood; **Paxton Powers:** Cary Elwes; **Ramond:** Ice-T; **Tony Mayzha/Earth Mover:** Stephen Collins; **Richard Vance:** Stacy Keach; **Mad Stan:** Henry Rollins; **Bombshell:** Kate Jackson; **Mutro Botho:** Tim Curry; **Sam Young:** Paul Winfield; **Ian Peek:** Michael McKean; **Ma Mayhem:** Kathleen Freeman; **Zeto:** Gary Cole; **Dr. Peter Corso:** Ed Begley Jr.; **Simon Harper:** Tristan Rogers; **Howard Lewis/Payback:** Bill Fagerbakke; **Dr. Stanton:** Mitch Pileggi; **Kenny:** Adam Wylie; **April:** Daphne Zuniga; **Sable Thorpe:** Gabrielle Carteris; **Paxton Powers:** Parker Stevenson; **Makeba:** T'Keyah "Crystal" Keymah; **Charlie "Big Gime" Bigelow:** Stephen Baldwin, Clancy Brown; **Richard Armacost:** Robert Patrick; **Gordon:** Charles Kimbrough; **R's Al Ghul:** David Warner; **Aquagirl:** Jodi Benson; **Micron:** Wayne Brady; **Barda:** Farrah Forke; **Superman:** Christopher McDonald; **Warhawk:** Peter Onotari; **Dr. Chides:** Xander Berkeley; **Zita Zee:** Diedrich Bader Chelsea

## ◎ THE BATMAN/SUPERMAN HOUR

Well-known comic-book heroes Superman and Batman appear in separate segments of this Saturday-morning series. Three action-filled Superman episodes, repeated from *The New Adventures of Superman* (1966–1967), were packaged with one new 12-minute adventure of Batman and Robin (17 brand-new cartoons were produced exclusively for the program) on each half-hour broadcast. (Episodes of the latter were rebroadcast as part of *The Adventures of Batman*.) A *Filmation Associates Production. Color. One hour. Premiered on CBS: September 14, 1968–September 6, 1969.*

*Voices*

**Clark Kent/Superman:** Bud Collyer; **Lois Lane:** Joan Alexander; **Narrator:** Jackson Beck; **Bruce Wayne/Batman:** Olan Soule; **Dick Grayson/Robin:** Casey Kasem; **Alfred Pennyworth:** Olan Soule

## ◎ THE BATMAN/TARZAN ADVENTURE HOUR

This hour-long fantasy/action series combined new adventures of famed caped crusaders Batman and Robin from 1977's *The New Adventures of Batman and Robin* and eight new episodes of Tarzan, mixed with reruns from his half-hour series, *Tarzan, Lord of the Jungle. A Filmation Associates Production. Color. One hour. Premiered on CBS: September 10, 1977–September 2, 1978.*

*Voices*

**Tarzan:** Robert Ridgely; **Batman:** Adam West; **Robin:** Burt Ward; **Bat-Mite:** Lennie Weinrib

## ◎ BATMAN: THE ANIMATED SERIES

DC Comics caped-crusader Batman, whose alter ego is millionaire playboy Bruce Wayne, continues his mission to squelch evildoers of Gotham City, joined by his crimebusting counterparts Robin (alias Dick Grayson) and Batgirl (alias Barbara Gordon), in this dark and often humorous version of the classic comic-book superhero. The 85-episode half-hour series debuted on FOX Network with a special Sunday-night premiere in September 1992, before airing the following day in its Monday-through-Friday weekday afternoon slot. The series was the number-one-rated afternoon show in its time slot.

In an effort to boost ratings of its Saturday-morning lineup, FOX simultaneously aired the series on Saturdays and (for five months beginning in December 1992) Sunday nights opposite CBS's *60 Minutes* and included episodes such as "I Am the Night," "Dreams of Darkness" and "Christmas with the Joker." To officially launch the 1992–93 television season, FOX aired eight new episodes of the Saturday-morning series starring the famed Caped Crusader and Boy Wonder as part of a special "Batman Premiere Week" from September 5 to September 12, beginning with "The Cat and the Claw, Part I." That same week, on September 6, a special series preview also bowed in prime time, entitled *On Leather Wings*. From January through March 1993, nine additional episodes were aired in prime time: "If You're So Smart, Why Aren't You Rich?"; "The Laughing Fish"; "It's Never Too Late"; "The Mechanic"; "Joker's Favor"; "Robin's Reckoning, Part I"; "Robin's Reckoning, Part II"; "The Strange Secret of Bruce Wayne"; "What Is Reality?"; and "Perchance to Dream."

During the 1994–95 season on Fox, the show was retitled *The Adventures of Batman and Robin*, featuring new episodes, plus previously aired ones from *Batman: The Animated Series*. In 1997 the characters jumped to the WB Television Network to costar in *The New Batman/Superman Adventures*.

Inspired by the success of the television show, Warner Bros. produced a feature-length movie, *Batman: Mask of the Phantasm*, which was released to movie theaters in 1993. The film originally was produced as a direct-to-video production. A sequel, *Batman: Sub-Zero*, was released direct to video in 1998.

On July 4, 2005, Boomerang, Cartoon Network's classic cartoon spin-off network, started re-airing episodes of the famed crimefighting superhero opposite 1996's *Superman: The Animated Series*. On Saturday, August 20, of that year, Boomerang featured the powerful masked hero in a five-hour marathon from 8 P.M. to 1 A.M., and on the following night featured a five-hour marathon of episodes from *Superman: The Animated Series*. Both programs continued airing nightly on Boomerang's late-night two-hour *Boomeraction* block, before finishing their run weekday mornings in August 2006. A *Warner Bros. Television Production. Color. Half-hour. Premiered on FOX: September 6, 1992 (Sunday-night premiere); September 7, 1992–September 10, 1993; September 13, 1993–September 2, 1994. Rebroadcast on CAR: March 2, 1998–December 13, 2003. Rebroadcast on BOOM: July 4, 2005–August 30, 2006.*

*Voices*

**Batman/Bruce Wayne:** Kevin Conroy; **Batgirl/Barbara Gordon:** Melissa Gilbert; **Alfred Pennyworth:** Clive Revill, Efrem Zimbalist Jr.; **Robin/Dick Grayson:** Loren Lester; **Mayor Hamilton:** Lloyd Bochner; **Commissioner Jim Gordon:** Bob Hastings; **Detective Harvey Bullock/Harry Fox:** Bobby Costanzo; **Dr. Leslie Thompkins:** Diana Muldaur; **Summer Gleason:** Mari Devon; **Lucius Fox:** Brock Peters; **The Joker/Other Villains:** Mark Hamill; **Catwoman/Selena Kyle:** Adrienne Barbeau; **The Penguin/Oswald Cobblepot:** Paul Williams; **The Mad Hatter:** Roddy McDowall; **Mr. Freeze:** Michael Ansara; **The Riddler:** John Glover; **District Attorney Dent/Two Face:** Richard Moll; **Poison Ivy/Pamela Isley:** Diane Pershing

## ◉ BATTLE B-DAMAN

Yamato Delgado was raised by cats from the time he was five years old. In a game of marbles, a sport used since ancient times as a way to resolve conflicts, young Yamato uses the most powerful B-Daman marble shooter, the Cobalt Blue, to fend off members of the evil Shadow Alliance in the B-Daman tournament to become B-Daman champion in this Japanese anime series—and Japanese manga—created by Eiji Inuki and first shown in Japanese television in January 1997. Produced by the Japanese studio d-rights, which was also behind another popular anime series called *Beyblade*, the English-dubbed version premiered in the United States in April 2005 on the weekend *Jetix* action/adventure block on ABC Family, thereafter airing weekend mornings on Toon Disney and later became part of its Sunday evening block. Hasbro produced a marble shooting game based on the series, as well as trading card games and toy action figures that more launched in the fall of 2005. A *d-rights/Takara/Nippon Animedia/TV Tokyo/Howling Cat Enterprises/Hasbro Production. Color. Half-hour. Premiered on ABC FAM: April 2, 2005–November 6, 2005. Premiered on TDIS: April 3, 2005–November 5, 2005. Rebroadcast on ABC FAM: June 13, 2005–November 4, 2005. Rebroadcast on CAR: January 6, 2006–June 2, 2006.*

### Voices

**Yamato Delgado/Joshua:** Brian Beacock; **Gray Michael:** Dave Wittenberg; **Terry McScotty:** Mary Elizabeth McGlynn (Episodes 1–6), Barbara Goodson (Episodes 7–   ); **Bull Borgnine:** Mona Marshall; **Enjyu:** Steve Staley; **Wen Yong-Fa:** Brad McDonald; **Li Yong-Fa/Monkey Don:** Derek Stephen Prince; **Armada:** Paul St. Peter, George C. Cole; **Marda B:** Paul St. Peter; **Mie Delgado/Ms. Karat:** Philece Sampler; **Ababa:** Michael Sorich, Steven Blume; **Vinnie V.:** Michael Sorich; **Berkhart/Sigma:** Yuri Lowenthal; **Berkhart Brothers:** Brianne Siddall; **Cain McDonnell/Meowmigos:** Steven Blum; **Joe/Biarce:** Doug Erholtz; **Sly:** Jamieson Price; **Asado:** Colleen O'Shaughnessey; **Marilyn:** Michelle Ruff; **B-DaMage:** Mari Devon, Jane Alan; **The Big Cheese:** R. Martin Klein; **Battle Crow:** Steve Kramer

## ◉ BATTLE OF THE PLANETS

G-Force, a superhuman watchdog squad—Jason, Tiny, Princess and Keyop—commanded by their daring leader, Mark Venture, defend Earth's galaxy from the ever-villainous Zoltar, the ruler of the dying planet Spectra, who aims to conquer the galaxy in this futuristic space-age adventure series. The first major Japanese import hit since 1967's *Speed Racer*, the program was produced by Tatsunko Productions, which also produced the latter. First televised in Japan from 1972 to 1974 under the title *Gatchamans*, the program was retitled and dubbed by producer Sandy Frank, who acquired the property for syndication in the United States. Eighty-five episodes (out of 100 episodes originally produced) were syndicated to independent television stations in 1978. Following its American premiere, the series was rebroadcast on WTBS as G-Force. Beginning Friday, April 23,

2004, the landmark series began airing at 9:00 A.M. on Cartoon Network's Boomerang. That Sunday, in celebration of the 25th anniversary of its U.S. debut, Boomerang rolled out an all-day special edition of the network's *Boomeraction* block, showcasing newly remastered versions of the first 16 half-hour episodes of the acclaimed fantasy-adventure series and airing the additional 69 episodes on Sundays at 9 A.M., 5 P.M. and 1 A.M. A *Tatsunko Production. Color. Half-hour. Syndicated: September 1, 1978–1982. Rebroadcast on BOOM: April 23, 2004–September 26, 2004.*

### Voices

**7-Zark-7/Keyop:** Alan Young; **Zoltar:** Keye Luke; **Mark Venture:** Casey Kasem; **Princess:** Janet Waldo; **Jason:** Ronnie Schell; **Tiny/Dr. Anderson:** Alan Dinehart

## ◉ BATTLETECH

Far into the future, Major Adam Steiner and his team of his high-tech, freedom-fighting warriors battle genetically engineered soldiers (led by the ruthless Star Colonel, Nikolai Malthius), who have invaded Earth for no good purpose in this computer-generated half-hour cartoon series adaptation of the popular virtual reality and role-playing game. A *Saban Entertainment Production. Color. Half-hour. Premiered: September 12, 1994. Syndicated.*

### Voices

**Col. Miles "Hawk" Hawkins:** Peter Spellos; **Other Voices:** Doug Stone

*Major Adam Steiner and his freedom fighters battle genetically engineered soldiers to save their families who live on a distant planet in the state-of-the-art, computer-animated series Battletech. © Saban Entertainment*

## THE BEAGLES

Canine rock-and-roll duo, Stringer and Tubby (called "The Beagles") croon their way in and out of trouble in this timely cartoon parody of Liverpool's Fab Four, The Beatles. Featuring five-minute serialized adventures, the program was produced by the creators of TV's *Underdog* and *Tennessee Tuxedo*. A Total Television Production. Color. Half-hour. Premiered on CBS: September 10, 1966–September 2, 1967. Rebroadcast on ABC: September 9, 1967–September 7, 1968.

**Voices**
Stringer: Sandy Becker; **Tubby/Scotty:** Allen Swift; **Narrator:** Kenny Delmar

## BEANY & CECIL (1962)

Created by Bob Clampett, formerly an animator for Warner Bros. the high-seas adventures of Cecil (the seasick serpent) and his friends Beany Boy and Captain Huffenpuff (Beany's uncle) began as a daily 15-minute puppet show first broadcast in 1949 on Los Angeles television station KTLA Channel 5. The show became so popular locally that Paramount Television picked up the series and offered it nationwide in 1950. It won three Emmy Awards during its run and became a particular favorite of many adults during its long run, including such surprising notables as Lionel Barrymore, Jimmy Stewart, Albert Einstein and Joan Crawford. (Groucho Marx, who was a fan of the puppet version, once told Clampett that "'Time for Beany' is the only kid's show adult enough for my daughter Melinda to watch.")

The puppet series inspired a short-lived cartoon series produced in 1959 by Elliot Hyman of Associated Artists Productions (the films were distributed to foreign countries only, including Australia, Canada and Europe, by Associated Artists' parent company, United Artists) and ultimately a weekly animated series that debuted on ABC in 1962. Sponsored by Mattel Toy Company, the show was first billed as *Matty's Funnies with Beany & Cecil*. (After three months the program's title was appropriately shortened to *Beany & Cecil*.) Each week, sailing on the *Leakin' Lena*, Beany and company encountered a host of unusual characters, such as Homer the Baseball Playing Octopuss, Careless the Mexican Hareless, Tear-a-Long the Dotted Lion, the Terrible Three-Headed Threep and the most dastardly Dishonest John ("Nya-hah-hah!"), a series regular, in 78 high-sea adventures (including the five theatrically produced cartoon shorts, such as "Beany and Cecil Meet Billy the Squid").

Clampett admittedly drew from various influences to create each character. Captain Huffenpuff was based on a Baron Munchausen–type teller of tall tales. (Originally Clampett considered naming him Captain Hornblower.) Cecil was inspired out of a 1920s' silent feature Clampett remembered as a child called *Lost World*, featuring prehistoric dinosaurs. Beany was reminiscent of the precocious Charlie McCarthy, one of Clampett's personal favorites. And Dishonest John was patterned, in part, after one of Clampett's previous bosses at Warner Bros. whom he and his fellow animators affectionately called "Dirty Dalton."

Jim MacGeorge lent his voice for Beany and Captain Huffenpuff, while Irv Shoemaker spoke for Cecil and Dishonest John. (Stan Freberg and Daws Butler did the voices during the first few years of the puppet show.)

Like many cartoons from this era, Beany and Cecil ran into censorship problems with the network. "It was rather ridiculous what the network would censor," Clampett once recalled. "In one cartoon, I had Dishonest John packaging the moon as cheese and bringing it back to Earth to sell it. On the package, I had the word 'Krafty' and ABC was afraid the Kraft Cheese Company would sue them."

One element of the series Clampett and his peers initially underestimated was the popularity of the trademark propellor cap worn by Beany. Prior to his death in 1984, Clampett recalled: "The funny thing about that is, when I first put the propellor on Beany's cap nearly everyone I showed the sketches to said, 'That would be funny for a one time use, but it will never wear well.' Their feelings were so unanimous that, for a short time, I switched to another type of cap before using my own intuition and going back to the propellor cap."

Following its prime-time run on ABC, the series remained on the network until 1968. The cartoons were then syndicated the following year by ABC Films. In the fall of 1989, the series was resyndicated in the United States, where it had been absent from the airwaves for more than a decade. (The series continued to be shown overseas, where it still plays in many markets.) In markets where the show premiered—Baltimore, Chicago, Houston, Dallas, Tampa, San Francisco and Boston—the program scored high ratings and refueled interest in the series nationwide.

A Bob Clampett Production. Color. Half-hour. Premiered on ABC: January 1962–December 1968. Syndicated: 1968–76; 1989.

**Voices**
Captain Huffenpuff/Beany Boy: Jim MacGeorge; **Cecil, the seasick serpent/Dishonest John:** Irv Shoemaker

## BEANY & CECIL (1988)

In the fall of 1988, Bob Clampett's Beany and Cecil characters were featured in this short-lived series revival, this time poking fun at 1980s' culture and themes. ABC canceled the Saturday-morning series after only five episodes. The series was produced and directed by animator John Kricfalusi, who went on to create the Nickelodeon megahit, *The Ren and Stimpy Show*. Actor Billy West, who provided the voice of Cecil the Sea-Sick Serpent, also served as the voice of Stimpy. A Bob Clampett Production in association with DIC Enterprises. Color. Half-hour. Premiered on ABC: September 10, 1988–October 8, 1988.

**Voices**
Beany Boy: Mark Laurence Hildreth; **Cecil the Sea-Sick Serpent:** Billy West; **Captain Huffenpuff:** Jim MacGeorge; **Dishonest John:** Maurice LaMarche

## BEAST MACHINES: TRANSFORMERS

Fugitives in their own world and perhaps facing the greatest challenge of their lives after being ruthlessly hunted by Megatron's new breed of Transformers, the Vehicons, the Maximals—Optimus, Cheetor, Black Arachnia and Rattrap—battle Megatron and his mindless army of drones to retake control of their home planet of Cybertron in this popular science fiction action/adventure series. A sequel to the 1996 syndicated series *Beast Wars: Transformers* and third since Marvel/Sunbow's original 1984 *Transformers* series, this 26-episode, CGI-animated half-hour knockoff, coproduced by Mainframe Entertainment and BLT, which also produced the 1996 series, was the first animated adaptation to premiere on a major television network instead of first-run syndication. Debuting in the fall of 2001 on FOX, the program enjoyed a successful two-year Saturday morning run, spawning the 2001 spin-off, *Transformers: Robots in Disguise*, also on FOX. A *Mainframe Entertainment/BLT/Alliance Communications/YTV/Transformer/Clastertelevision Production*. Color. Half-hour. Premiered on FOX: September 18, 1999–January 20, 2001.

*Voices*
**Botanica:** Kathleen Barr; **Thrust:** Jim Byrnes; **Optimus Primal:** Gary Chalk; **Cheetor:** Ian James Corlett; **Tankorr/Obsidian:** Paul Dobson; **Strika:** Patricia Drake; **Jetstorm:** Brian Drummond; **Diagnostics Drone:** Christopher Gaze; **Nightscream:** Alessandro Julianni; **Megatron/Noble/Mainframe:** David Kaye; **Rattrap/Waspinator/Silverbolt:** Scott McNeil; **Rhinox-Tankorr:** Richard Newman; **Predacon Computer/Oracle:** Elizabeth Carol Savenkoff; **Black Arachnia:** Venus Terzo

### ◎ BEAST WARS: TRANSFORMERS
The heroic Maximals, animals transformed into robots, hope to stop the evil Predacons from controlling a powerful energy source and conquering the galaxy in this 3-D, computer-animated series, based on the popular action figures. *A Mainframe Entertainment/ BLT/Alliance Communications/YTV/Transformer/Clastertelevision Production. Color. Half-hour. Premiered: September 16, 1996–Fall 1999. Syndicated. Rebroadcast on FOX: Fall 1999–Spring 2000. Rebroadcast on G4: January 2, 2006–mid-2006.*

*Voices*
**Scorponok:** Donald Brown; **Inferno:** Jim Byrnes; **Optimus Primael:** Gary Chalk; **Cheetor/Sentinel:** Ian Corlett; **Megatron:** David Kaye; **Tigatron:** Blue Mankuma; **Dinobot/Rattrap/Silverbolt/Waspinator:** Scott McNeil; **Rhinox:** Richard Newman; **Airazor:** Pauline Newstone; **Terrorsaur:** Doug Parker; **Predacon Ship Computer:** Elizabeth Carol Savenkoff; **Blackarachnia:** Venus Terzo; **Tarantulas:** Alec Willows

### ◎ THE BEATLES
Throughout the 1960s, these mop-headed musicians (better known as John, Paul, George and Ringo) dominated the musical scene like no other group. Their music landed them atop national record charts and on several major television shows, including *The Ed Sullivan Show,* wowing teenagers throughout America in the process. The group's success also inspired a weekly animated cartoon series.

Produced in 1965, the series came about through the efforts of producer Al Brodax at King Features after he was approached by an ABC executive with the idea of producing "a Beatles cartoon." Famous toymaker A.C. Gilmer, who envisioned a merchandising goldmine, financed the series.

Premiering on ABC on Saturday, September 25, 1965 at 10:30 A.M., the show was an instant ratings hit. It racked up a 13 score (or 52 share), then unheard of in daytime television. Each half-hour show consisted of two sing alongs, emceed by the Beatles. (Lyrics were flashed on the screen so viewers could join in.) The first episodes that aired were "I Want to Hold Your Hand" and "A Hard Day's Night."

Besides two weekly cartoons, the Beatles show was famous for its clever bridges between episodes and commercials. These included dry, comic vignettes, such as Ringo buying a newspaper from a street vendor and getting hit by a car, only to complain afterward "There's not a word in here [in the paper] about me accident!"

The voices of the Beatles' cartoon look-alikes were supplied by two voice actors, Paul Frees (John and George) and Lance Percival (Paul and Ringo). Animation was sent overseas (TVC of London, which produced the Beatles cult feature, *The Yellow Submarine,* and Astransa, an Australian company, did the bulk of the animation), and scripts were turned out rather easily since episodes were based on popular Beatles songs.

"It took about four weeks to animate each film and I enjoyed it immensely," recalled Chris Cuddington, a series animator. "The characters were easy to draw, and the stories were simple and uncomplicated."

*Paul, George and John enjoy Ringo's appearance on television in* The Beatles *cartoon series, featuring actual recordings of the famed Liverpool musicians. © King Features Entertainment*

Following the first season's success, Brodax considered producing four Beatles prime-time animated specials. But plans to produce them and several other musical-based cartoon series—animated versions of Herman's Hermits and Freddie and the Dreamers—never materialized.

The Beatles remained on ABC for three more years, the last season consisting of repeats from the previous three seasons. The series lost ground during its second season after it was slated opposite CBS's *Space Ghost,* part of a powerful Saturday-morning lineup that included *Frankenstein Jr. and the Impossibles, Mighty Mouse* and *The Mighty Heroes.* (*Space Ghost* won the time slot with a 9.6, a 44 share, while the Beatles slid into second with 7.6, a 36 share.)

In the fall of 1968, the series was moved to Sunday mornings, where it remained until its final broadcast in 1969. Sixteen years later the musical cartoon series returned in reruns on MTV. *A King Features Production. Color. Half-hour. Premiered on ABC: September 25, 1965–April 20, 1969. Syndicated. Rebroadcast on MTV: 1985.*

*Voices*
**John Lennon/George Harrison:** Paul Frees; **Paul McCartney/Ringo Starr:** Lance Percival

### ◎ BEAVIS AND BUTT-HEAD
Originally featured as stars of the cartoon short "Frog Baseball" (in which they were called Bobby and Billy), part of MTV's *Liquid Television* series in 1992, this idiotic, repulsive pair of hard-rock music fans—blond Beavis, the one in a Metallica T-shirt, and dark-haired Butt-Head, traditionally dressed in an AC/DC T-shirt—starred in this long-running half-hour series, which quickly became MTV's highest rated show. Each half-hour program consisted of two cartoon adventures with these suburban misfits amusing themselves by watching bad TV shows, working at the local "Burger World" (and creating chaos at the drive-up window) or attending enriching events such as the "All-Star Monster Tractor Trashathon."

Originally slated to premiere in March 1993, production problems delayed the series, so only two complete programs were aired that month. In May of 1993 MTV "officially" premiered the series in prime time, airing the program Monday through Thursday night. Fierce criticism of the show erupted five months later after an episode prompted an Ohio mother to charge that a "Beavis" episode caused her five-year-old son to start a fire that killed his two-year-old sister. The network subsequently moved the series out of prime time to a late-night slot. Soon producers developed *Beavis and Butt-Head* episodes "more suitable for prime time."

Daria Morgendorffer, the only female friend of Beavis and Butt-Head, debuted that first season. (In March of 1997 she was given her own animated series.) Other series regulars added were: Mr. Buzzcut, the boys' ex-marine gym and hygiene teacher; Tom Anderson, B&B's tormented neighbor; Principal McKicker, the boys' high school principal; and Stewart and Mr. Stevenson, Stewart's dad.

During the series' original run, the characters were spun off into a series of annual "Butt-Bowl" specials that aired during Super Bowl halftimes, beginning in January of 1994. They also appeared on two Christmas specials, in 1994 and 1995 respectively.

In December of 1996 the boys took on Hollywood in their feature film debut, *Beavis and Butt-Head Do America*.

The movie was launched with a pre-release MTV special, *Beavis and Butt-Head Do America: An MTV Movie Special*. After producing 196 episodes, the series concluded its original network run on November 28, 1997 with the finale, "Beavis and Butt-Head Are Dead," only to return on the network in reruns with the promise of future specials. The show's final original broadcast was followed by a "live" special, *Beavis and Butt-Head Do Thanksgiving with Kurt Loder* (an MTV news anchor). Beginning in June 2006, MTV's sister network, MTV2, reran this original MTV animated series on its *Sic'Em Friday* block of "outrageous" programs, which included such animated fare as *The Adventures of Chico and Guapo*, *Celebrity Deathmatch* and *Where My Dogs At? An MTV Networks Production. Color. Half-hour. Premiered on MTV: March 1993; (official "premiere"): May 17, 1993–November 28, 1997. Rebroadcast on MTV: November 29, 1997. Rebroadcast on MTV2: June 10, 2006–.*

### Voices

**Beavis/Butt-Head/Tom Anderson/David van Dreesen/Bradley Buzzcut/Principal McVicker:** Mike Judge; **Cassandra/Daria/Lolitta/Tanqueray/Heather/Jennifer:** Tracy Grandstaff; **Mr. Graham:** Guy; **Todd:** Rottilio Michieli; **Stewart:** Adam Welch

## ⊚ BEETHOVEN

The blubbery St. Bernard, immortalized in two comedy films, returns with the family in tow in weekly half-hour misadventures based on the popular movie series. *A Universal Cartoon Studios/Northern Lights Entertainment/Hyun Young Animation Studios Production. Color. Half-hour. Premiered on CBS: September 17, 1994–September 2, 1995.*

### Voices

**George Newton:** Dean Jones; **Alice Newton/Ginger:** Tress Mac-Neille; **Ryce Newton:** Nicholle Tom; **Ted Newton:** J. D. Daniels; **Emily Newton:** Kath Soucie; **Beethoven:** Joel Murray; **Sparky:** Joe Pantoliano; **Caesar:** Bill Fagerbakke; **Killer the Poodle:** Hank Azaria; **Roger/Other Voices:** Justin Shenkarow; **Additional Voices:** Rene Auberjonois, Gregg Berger, Mark Campbell, Dan Castellanetta, Christine Cavanagh, Brian Cummings, E. G. Daily, Stephen Destefano, Paul Dooley, David Doyle, Brian George, Jess Harnell, Bill Henderson, Dana Hill, Tony Jay, Maurice LaMarche, Scott Menville, Art Metrano, Tim Meil, John Schuck, Pamela Segall, Francesca Marie Smith

## ⊚ BEETLEJUICE

Based on the characters from director Tim Burton's hit movie of the same name, this weekly animated series tells the story of an eccentric con artist and his relationship with a 12-year-old Earth girl (Lydia Deetz) that centers around the surrealistic adventures in the Neitherworld, the place where Beetlejuice resides. The series was an instant hit with young viewers on ABC following its debut in the fall of 1989. Series regulars included Doomie the Cat, a reckless auto with a penchant for chasing cars. In 1991, the series jumped to FOX Network's weekday lineup, featuring 65 new episodes that included spoofs of popular motion pictures and fairy tales. (The original series continued in reruns on ABC.) Beginning in 1994, the series was repeated on Nickelodeon. *A Warner Bros./Nelvana Production in association with The Geffen Film Company and Tim Burton, Inc. Color. Half-hour. Premiered on ABC: September 9, 1989–September 5, 1992. Rebroadcast on FOX: November 1991–September 1993. Rebroadcast on NICK: April 4, 1994–March 31, 1998. Rebroadcast on CAR: 1998–2000.*

### Voices

**Beetlejuice:** Stephen Ouimette; **Lydia Deetz:** Alyson Court; **Charles Deetz, Lydia's father:** Roger Dunn; **Delia Deetz, Lydia's mother:** Elizabeth Hanna

## ⊚ BELLE AND SEBASTIAN

Produced in Japan, this 30-minute series tells the story of a abandoned young boy (Sebastian), who makes friends with a lonely big white dog, Belle. The two experience high adventure and the special bonds of friendship in this touching adaptation of the successful children's book series by author Cecile Aubrey. *An MK Company and Visual 80 Production in association with Toho Company, Ltd. Color. Half-hour. Premiered on NICK: June 1984–1990.*

## ⊚ BEN 10

After stumbling upon a mysterious but powerful device called the Omnitrix, 10-year-old Ben Tennyson transforms himself into an alien superhero for 10 minutes at a pop and uses his awesome powers to fight evil forces while still finding time to have fun in this animated series for Cartoon Network. In December 2005, the series pilot entitled "And Then There Were Ten" premiered during a "sneak peek" of Cartoon Network's Saturday morning lineup, with its second episode, "Washington B.C.," shown as a special during the network's Friday block before becoming a weekly series in January. That May, the second season kicked off with four nights of new episodes in prime time, including the season opener in which Grandpa Max's ex-partner, Phil the plumber, rips off the ultra-super-dangerous Null Voice Projector. In December of that year, Ben and company starred in their first-ever holiday special, *Merry Christmas. A Cartoon Network Studios Production. Color. Half-hour. Premiered on CAR: December 27, 2005 (pilot). Premiered on CAR: January 13, 2006–May 29, 2006 (1st season); May 30, 2006–December 2, 2006 (2nd season).*

### Voices

**Ben Tennyson/Upgrade:** Tara Strong; **Grey Matter:** Richard Horvitz; **Heatblast/Ghostfreak:** Steven Jay Blum; **Diamondhead/KXLRB/Wildvine:** Jim Ward; **Ripjaw/Cannon Bolt:** Fred Tatasciore; **Gwen Tennyson:** Meagan Smith; **Grandpa Max Tennyson:** Paul Eiding; **Fourarms:** Richard McGonagle; **Stinkfly/Wildmutt:** Dee Bradley Baker

## ⊚ THE BERENSTAIN BEARS (1985)

Beartown, a tiny hamlet whose economy is based solely on honey, is home to the Bear Family: Papa Q. Bear; Mama; Brother and Sister Bear; Grizzly and Gran, grandparents; and the hilarious incompetent group of ne'er-do-wells, chief among them Raffish Ralph and Weasel McGreed, whose antics always seem to throw a monkey wrench into the Bear Family's best-laid plans. This CBS Saturday-morning series adapted the beloved children's book characters created by Stan and Jan Berenstain. Previously the characters starred in five half-hour animated specials for

NBC. *A Southern Star Production. Color. Half-hour. Premiered on CBS: September 14, 1985–September 5, 1987. Syndicated: September 7, 2003 (DIC Kids Network block).*

**Voices**
**Mama:** Ruth Buzzi; **Papa Q. Bear:** Brian Cummings; **Sister:** Christine Lange; **Brother:** David Mendenhall; **Raffish Ralph:** Frank Welker

### ◎ THE BERENSTAIN BEARS (2003)

The fun-loving bears of Jan and Stan Berenstain's best-selling children's books return in this second animated series adaptation following the adventures of the furry family, led by Papa Q. Bear and Mama Bear, with Sister and Brother Bear learning many important life-shaping lessons about love, loyalty and working together while overcoming numerous obstacles and challenges. For children ages two to seven, Canadian animation giant Nelvana coproduced this delightful, educational and entertaining half-hour preschool series, featuring two 15-minute adventures per half-hour it made its debut on PBS Kids' weekday program block in January 2003. Initially, PBS ended one 15-minute adventure daily with another 15-minute cartoon from the companion series, *Seven Little Monsters*, until the series was slotted for a full half-hour, starting in mid-September 2003 when the first 30 episodes began airing and continued through mid-October of that year. PBS then began rebroadcasting the series at the end of October and rolled out the next five new episodes from April 5 to April 9, 2004, and the last five from September 6 to September 10, 2004. In April 2005, the show joined the new PBS Kids Sprout digital cable channel and video-on-demand service, providing original PBS Kids programming for preschoolers. The beloved children's program was produced 18 years after the first Saturday-morning series, *The Berenstain Bears*, which aired for two seasons on CBS. Award-winning country artist Lee Ann Womack provided the vocals for the series' theme song. *A Nelvana Limited/Agogo Entertainment/Berenstain Enterprises Inc. Production. Color. Half-hour. Premiered on PBS Kids: January 6, 2003–September 4, 2004 (with Seven Little Monsters). Premiered on PBS Kids: September 15, 2003–September 10, 2004 (series). Rebroadcast on PBS: October 27, 2003–. Rebroadcast on PBS Kids Sprout (VOD): April 4, 2005–. Rebroadcast on PBS Kids Sprout (digital cable): September 26, 2005–.*

**Voices**
**Papa Q. Bear:** Ben Campbell; **Mama Bear:** Camilla Scott; **Brother Bear:** Michael Cera; **Sister Bear:** Tajja Isen; **Gran:** Corinne Conley; **Lizzy Bruin:** Amanda Soha; **Cousin Fred:** Marc McMulkin; **Furdy Factual:** Mark Rendall; **Cub:** Jake Scott; **TooTall:** Gage Knox; **Skuzz:** Patrick Salvagna

### ◎ THE BEST OF SCOOBY-DOO

Classic episodes of the cowardly canine detective Scooby-Doo and his companions, Fred, Shaggy, Daphne and Velma, were rebroadcast in this best-of format for Saturday-morning television. The show combined previously broadcast episodes from past Scooby-Doo programs—from 1969's *Scooby-Doo, Where Are You?* and from 1976's *The Scooby-Doo/Dynomutt Hour.* (See programs for complete voice credits.) The series lasted one full season on ABC. *A Hanna-Barbera Production. Color. Half-hour. Premiered on ABC: September 10, 1983–September 1, 1984.*

### ◎ THE BETTY BOOP SHOW

National Television Associates (NTA), which earlier had acquired the rights to Betty Boop, tried to rekindle interest in the "Boop-Boop-a-Doop" girl by distributing color-painted prints of Max Fleischer's original theatrical cartoons in half-hour packages. (The master negatives were sent overseas to Korea where they were meticulously hand-colored.) *A Max Fleischer Production distributed by NTA. Color. Half-hour. Premiered: Fall 1971. Syndicated.*

**Voices**
**Betty Boop:** Mae Questel

### ◎ BEVERLY HILLS TEENS

This series centers around the lives, loves and longings of a group of typical, fun-loving American teenagers, who just happen to be fabulously wealthy. *A DIC Enterprises Production. Color. Half-hour. Premiered: September 19, 1987–1998. Syndicated.*

**Voices**
**Buck/Wilshire:** Michael Beattie; **Pierce Thorndyke:** Stephen McMulkin; **Shanelle Spencer:** Michelle St. John; **Tara/Jett:** Karen Bernstein; **Jillian/Bianca/Blaise:** Tracy Moore; **Switchboard:** Joanna Schellenberg; **Fifi:** Linda Sorensen; **Nikki Darling:** Corrine Koslo; **Gig/Dad:** Mark Saunders; **Larke/Dog:** Mary Long; **Troy:** Jonathan Potts; **Radley/Guitar:** Hadley Kay

### ◎ BEYBLADE

Armed with blades possessing the amazing strength of Bit Beasts, a team of globetrotting Bladebreakers—13-year-old Tyson Granger and fellow teammates Kai Hiwatari, Max Tate and Ray Kon—try to become the world's best beybladers, with help from the team's resident computer whiz, Kenny, in this intense and exciting half-hour action/adventure anime series imported from Japan. The first two seasons and first third of the third season premiered on ABC Family, becoming part of the network's weekday and weekend *Jetix* action-adventure anime block in September 2002 (becoming the highest rated series that season among boys ages six to 11 on Saturdays), with the remaining episodes of the third season debuting on Toon Disney's *Jetix* action/adventure block in May 2004. In September 2006, the series remained part of Toon Disney's Sunday *Jetix* anime block, including favorites such as *Mon Colle Knights, Shinzo, Daigunder* and *Digimon. A d-rights/Yomiko Advertising Inc./Aoki Takao/BB2 Project/TV Tokyo/Nelvana Production. Color. Half-hour. Premiered on ABC FAM: July 6, 2002–June 12, 2005. Rebroadcast on TDIS: May 14, 2004–.*

**Voices**
**Tyson:** Marlowe Gardiner-Heslin; **Kenny:** Alex Hodd; **Ray:** Daniel DeSanto; **Kai:** David Reale; **Max:** Gage Knox; **Brad Best:** Mark Dailey; **A.J. Toper:** Eric Woolfe; **Dizzi:** Julie Lemieux; **Grandpa:** George Buza, **Mr. Dickenson:** William Colgate; **Cenotaph:** Robert Tinkler; **Max:** Ai Orikasa, **Mr. Tate, Max's Dad:** John Stocker; **Jim/Daichi:** Mary Long; **Gideon/Jin of the Gale/Hiro:** Len Carlson; **Johnny:** Joanne Vannicola; **Oliver/Judy/Antonio/Frankie/Salima:** Susan Roman

### ◎ BIG BAG

Six animated "shorties" ("Samuel and Nina," "Koki," "Slim Pig," "Tobias Totz and His Lion," "Troubles the Cat" and "William's Wish Wellingtons"), plus short music videos make up this hour-long live-action/animated preschool series, hosted by several new Muppet characters (Chelli, Bag and their sock-puppet friends Lyle and Argyle) from Children's Television Workshop (producers of *Cro*), produced for Cartoon Network. *A Children's Television Workshop Production. Color. One hour. Premiered on CAR: June 2, 1996.*

### ◎ BIGFOOT AND THE MUSCLE MACHINES

Serialized adventures told in nine episodes of a powerful group of land vehicles, headed by their appointed leader Yank Justice and including Bigfoot and Orange Blossom, that help a young couple trying to escape from the clutches of the nefarious Mr. Big in this animated miniseries that premiered in syndication in October 1985 as part of Marvel Productions' Super Sunday weekend programming block. According to Marvel Productions' official production records, a five-part, 14-episode series including two additional three-episode blocks (Part 4 and Part 5), was originally planned but then canceled. As reported by Marvel, the completed nine episodes were offered for syndication as a feature-length special entitled *Bigfoot–The Movie*, although no confirmation has been made that the special ever actually aired. *A Marvel Productions Ltd./Sunbow Entertainment Production. Color. Half-hour. Premiered: October 6, 1985. Syndicated.*

### Voices

**Close McCall:** Wally Burr; **Arthur Ravenscroft/Mr. Big:** Peter Cullen; **Yank Justice:** Lance LeGault; **Red/Redder/Jennifer:** Susan Blu; **Professor D:** Vince Howard; **Adrian Ravenscroft/ Ernie Slye:** Chris Latta; **Ravenscroft's Chauffeur:** Neil Ross; **Other Voices:** John Stephenson, Linda Gary, Dick Gautier, Frank Welker, Charlie Adler, Michael Bell, Bill Callaway, Nancy Cartwright, Fred Collins, Brad Crandel, Ed Gilbert, Stanley Ralph Ross, Richard Sanders, Susan Silo, Pat Fraley, Jerry Houser

### ◎ BIGFOOT PRESENTS: METEOR AND THE MIGHTY MONSTER TRUCKS

Small monster trucks, Little Tow and his best friend Meteor of Crushington Park, learn valuable lessons about resiliency, sportsmanship and the rough and tumble physical world of monster truck competition, while overcoming obstacles and accomplishing incredible things. Created by producers David Snyder and Bill Gross of Brandissimo! and codeveloped and produced with Endgame Entertainment, the series premiered a week apart on both Discovery Kids and The Learning Channel (TLC). After its premiere, the series aired weekday mornings during the *Ready Set Learn!* preschool block on Discovery Kids and TLC. In 2007, the program was nominated for a daytime Emmy Award for outstanding special class animated program. *A Meteor the Monster Truck Company LLC/Brandissimo!/Endgame Entertainment Production. Color. Half-hour. Premiered on DSCK: September 25, 2006. Premiered on TLC: October 2, 2006.*

### Voices

**Meteor:** Cameron Ansell; **Jose:** Mitchell Eisner; **Ponytail:** Tajja Isen; **Sarge:** Dan Petronijevic; **Junkboy:** Cliff Saunders; **Amby:** Laurie Elliott; **Sinker:** Linda Ballantyne; **Hook:** Joanne Vannicola; **Race Announcer:** Brad Adamson; **Big Wheelie:** Martin Roach

### ◎ BIG GUY AND RUSTY THE BOY ROBOT

A gigantic 12-foot metallic robot called the BGY-11 (also known as Big Guy), originally created to defend America from alien invasions and then suddenly decommissioned, is reactivated and partnered—under the guidance of pilot Lt. Dwayne Hunter (voiced by Tom Hanks's brother, Jim Hanks)—with an artificially intelligent but inexperienced advanced child robot called Rusty to learn the ways of combat in this science fiction animated series, based on the large-format comic-book series from Dark Horse Comics by Frank Miller and Geof Darrow, published in 1996. First broadcast on FOX's Saturday-morning program block in September 1999, the series was abruptly canceled due to poor ratings after airing only six episodes that October. FOX replaced it and Saban Entertainment's futuristic Spider-Man series, *Spider-Man Unlimited*, with *Saban's The Avengers*, and added time slots of Bohbot Kids Network's *Monster Rancher* and Toei Animation Co.'s *Digimon: Digital Monsters*.

In January 2001, FOX revived the series, adding it to its weekday afternoon lineup, and later to its Saturday morning programming until the end of August. In 2002, the series resurfaced on the ABC Family Channel in reruns. *A Dark Horse Entertainment/Sony Pictures Family Entertainment Production. Color. Half-hour. Premiered on FOX FAM: September 18, 1999–October 23, 1999. Rebroadcast on FOX FAM: July 6, 2002–July 21, 2002. Premiered on ABC FAM: February 15, 2001–March 2, 2001. Rebroadcast on ABC FAM: July 27, 2002–September 1, 2002.*

### Voices

**Rusty/Jo:** Pamela Segall; **Big Guy:** Jonathan David Cook; **Dwayne Hunter:** Jim Hanks; **Dr. Erika Slate:** Gabrielle Carteris; **Dr. Axel Donovan:** Stephen Root; **Jenny the Monkey:** Kathy Kinney; **General Thorton:** R. Lee Ermey; **Garth:** Kevin Michael Richardson; **Mack:** M. Emmet Walsh; **Additional Voices:** Stan Freberg, Clancy Brown, Steve Edwards, Dean Haglund, Maurce LaMarche, Tim Curry, Jeremy Suarez, Maurra Tierney, Ron Perlman, Nick Jameson, Nora Dunn, Dee Bradley Baker, John DeLancie, John Garry, Jennifer Hale, Justin Jon Ross, Cam Clarke, Mary Kay Bergman, Jim Piddock, Kevin Schon, Helen Kalafatic, Brian Doyle Murray, Nancy Cartwright

### ◎ THE BIG O

In futuristic Paradigm City, where an event has erased people's memories, millionaire playboy and expert negotiator, Roger Smith, assisted by his giant robot, The Big O, and android, Dorothy, fights

*An expert negotiator and giant robot ward off foreign invaders intent on destroying Earth in The Big O. © Sunrise. All rights reserved.*

foreign invaders intent on destroying the city in this English-dubbed, Japanese-produced anime series. The first 13 episodes were broadcast on Japanese television beginning in October 1999 and subsequently canceled due to poor ratings. On April 2, 2001, the dubbed series debuted on Cartoon Network's *Toonami* anime block—and subsequently was moved to the network's *Adult Swim* late-night programming block instead—airing edited versions of all 13 episodes from the series' first season. Beginning on August 3, 2003, the science fiction action-adventure series returned for a second season on *Adult Swim* with 13 new episodes. As a result of declining ratings and other market factors, the network canceled the series, with its final U.S. episode airing that November. In October 2006, Cartoon Network began re-airing the series weekdays at 5:00 A.M., followed by the 1960s anime cult classic, *Gigantor*. *A Sunrise Inc./ZRO Limited Production in association with Bandai Visual. Color. Half-hour. Premiered on CAR: April 2, 2001–November 2, 2003. Rebroadcast on CAR: October 31, 2006–.*

**Voices**
**Roger Smith:** David Lucas, Steven Jay Blum; **R. Dorothy Wainwright:** Lia Sargent; **Beck Gold:** Robert Wickes; **Norman Burg:** Ethan Murray, Alan Oppenheimer; **Major Dastun:** James Lyon, Peter Lurie; **Big Ear:** James Lyon, Jamieson K. Price; **Patricia Lovejoy/Angel:** Wendee Lee; **Alan Gabriel:** Crispin Freeman; **Alex Rosewater:** Alfred Thor, Michael Forest; **Gordon Rosewater:** William Knight; **Michael Seebach (Schwarzwald):** Michael McConnohie; **Other Voices:** Richard Barnes, Robert Axelrod, Chuck Farley, Elliott Reynolds

### ◎ THE BIG WORLD OF LITTLE ADAM

The fantastic future of space exploration is seen through the eyes of Little Adam and his big brother Wilbur in this half-hour series consisting of 110 action-packed five-minute episodes. Fred Ladd, the American producer of TV's *Speed Racer* and others, produced the series. John Megna, the voice of Little Adam, is actress Connie Stevens's brother. *A Little Adam Production Inc. Color. Half-hour. Premiered: 1965. Syndicated.*

**Voices**
**Little Adam:** John Megna; **Wilbur, his brother:** Craig Seckler

*A look into the fantastic future of space adventure is vividly told through the eyes of two boys in the action-packed series* The Big World of Little Adam. © *Little Adam Productions Inc.* (COURTESY: FRED LADD)

### ◎ BIKER MICE FROM MARS

Trying to mirror the success of CBS's *Teenage Mutant Ninja Turtles*, this half-hour, syndicated fantasy series follows the adventures of three space-cycling Martian mice (Modo, Throttle and Vinnie), each victims of a terrible lab experiment, who wage an interplanetary revolt against a team of revolutionaries who plan to own the galaxy, and the evil scientist (Dr. Karbunkle) who made them into the mutants they are. *A Marvel Production in association with Brentwood TV Funnies and New World Family Filmworks. Color. Half-hour. Premiered: September 1993–1995 (rebroadcast in 1995 as part of "Marvel Action Hour"). Syndicated.*

**Voices**
**Modo:** Dorian Harewood; **Throttle:** Rob Paulsen; **Vinnie:** Ian Ziering; **Charlie:** Leeza Miller-McGee; **Lawrence Limburger:** Morgan Sheppard; **Dr. Karbunkle:** Susan Silo; **Sweet Georgie Brown:** Jess Harnell; **Grease Pit:** Brad Garrett

### ◎ BILL & TED'S EXCELLENT ADVENTURES

Rockin', southern California teens Bill and Ted of the two-man rock band "Wyld Stalyns" zoom through the annals of history—from ancient Rome to Mozart's Vienna—with the help of their phone-booth time machine and extremely "cool" guide Rufus in this half-hour, animated spin-off of the 1989 hit movie, featuring Alex Winter (Bill), Keanu Reeves (Ted) and George Carlin (Rufus) reprising their movie roles. The series premiered on CBS in 1990 with 13 original episodes. It joined FOX Network's Saturday-morning lineup in 1991, where it completed its run with a season of new episodes, minus the original cast. *A Hanna-Barbera Production in association with Nelson Entertainment and Orion Television. Color. Half-hour. Premiered on CBS: September 1990–August 31, 1991. Premiered on FOX: September 14, 1991–September 5, 1992.*

**Voices**
**Bill:** Alex Winter (1990–91); **Ted:** Keanu Reeves (1990–91); **Rufus:** George Carlin (1990–91); **Mr. Preston, Bill's father:** Dave Madden; **Missy, Bill's stepmom:** Vicki Juditz; **Mr. Logan, Ted's father:** Peter Renaday; **Deacon, Ted's younger brother:** Danny Cooksey

### ◎ THE BIONIC SIX

The Bennett family employ their bionic talents to combat the evil Dr. Scarab and his minions whose goal is to use science for their own selfish motives. This half-hour fantasy/adventure series was originally produced for first-run syndication in 1987. The series resurfaced on the Sci-Fi Channel (in reruns).

*A TMS Production in association with MCA/Universal. Color. Half-hour. Premiered: April 19, 1987–November 16, 1987. Rebroadcast on SCI: January 2, 1995–August 29, 1997. Syndicated.*

**Voices**
**J.D. Bennett:** Norman Bernard; **Helen Bennett:** Carol Bilger; **Meg Bennett:** Bobbi Block; **Jack Bennett:** John Stephenson; **Eric Bennett:** Hal Rayle; **Bunji Bennett:** Brian Tochi; **Madam O:** Jennifer Darling; **Dr. Scarab:** Jim MacGeorge; **F.L.U.F.F.I.:** Neil Ross; **Klunk:** John Stephen-son; **Glove/Mechanic/Chopper:** Frank Welker

### ◎ BIRDMAN AND THE GALAXY TRIO

Three winged superheroes—Birdman, assistant Birdboy and eagle companion Avenger—encounter world forces under the command of Falcon 7. The other half of the superhero talent, billed on the same show, was the Galaxy Trio. Stories depict the adventures of the spaceship *Condor 1* and its principal pilots, Vapor Man, Galaxy Girl and Meteor Man, who all possess superhuman strength. In wake of programming changes from hard-action fantasy cartoons to tamer comedy programs, NBC canceled the series midway into its second season, along two others: *Samson and Goliath* and *Super President And Spy Shadow*, resulting in a loss of $750,000 by the network. *Birdman and the Galaxy Trio* was one of NBC's higher-rated cartoon shows. *A Hanna-Barbera Production. Color. Half-hour. Premiered on NBC: September 9, 1967–September 14, 1968. Rebroadcast on NBC: September 1968–December 28, 1968. Rebroadcast on CAR: October 1, 1992–April 2, 1993 (weekdays); April 3, 1993–January 1, 1994 (Saturdays); January 9, 1994–April 3, 1994 (Sundays); March 4, 1994 (Super Adventure Saturdays); July 29, 1995–2000. Rebroadcast on BOOM: August 12, 2000–.*

**Voices**
**The Birdman: Ray Randall/Birdman:** Keith Andes; **Birdboy:** Dick Beals; **Falcon 7:** Don Messick

**The Galaxy Trio: Vapor Man:** Don Messick; **Galaxy Girl:** Virginia Eiler; **Meteor Man:** Ted Gassidy

### ◎ BIRDZ
In the community of Birdland, a fine-feathered, 10-year-old bird, Eddie Storkowitz, who aspires to become the next "Steven Spielbird," copes with fulfilling his dreams and ambitions and typical preteen anxieties and challenges, with a little help from his eccentric family and support only from his schoolteacher, Miss Finch, in this half-hour Saturday-morning series produced by Canada's Nelvana Limited for CBS. Created and directed by Larry Jacobs of TV's animated *Beetlejuice* and *The Magic School Bus* fame, this Tex Avery-style show was one of several series CBS added to its to fall 1998 Saturday morning lineup, lasting only one season. *A Nelvana Limited Production. Color. Half-hour. Premiered on CBS: October 8, 1998–September 26, 1999.*

**Voices**
**Eddie Storkowitz:** Susan Roman; **Steffy Storkowitz:** Stephanie Morganstern; **Abby Storkowitz:** Alison Sealy-Smith; **Betty Storkowitz:** Sally Cahill; **Morty Storkowitz:** David Huband; **Tommy Turkey:** Adam Reid; **Miss Finch, Eddie's schoolteacher:** Jill Frappier; **Mr. Pip:** Len Carlson; **Officer Pigeon:** Chris Wiggins; **Olivia Owl:** Karen Bernstein; **Mr. Nuthatch:** Richard Binsley; **Gregory Woodpecker:** Rick Jones; **Sleepy the Bat:** Julie Lemieux; **Spring:** Ruby Smith-Merovitz

### ◎ THE BISKITTS
A group of pint-size pups—only a doggie-biscuit tall—named caretakers of the royal treasure following the death of Biskitt Island's good wise king thwart the ongoing efforts of King Max, despot of the rundown kingdom of Lower Suburbia, to steal the treasure along with mangy dogs, Fang and Snarl, and his inept jester, Shecky, in 14 half-hour shows produced for CBS. The series was later rebroadcast on USA Network's *Cartoon Express*. *A Hanna-Barbera Production. Color. Half-hour. Premiered on CBS: September 17, 1983–September 1, 1984. Rebroadcast on CBS: May 30, 1985–September 7, 1985. Rebroadcast on USA: March 3, 1989–March 29, 1991.*

**Voices**
**Waggs:** Darryl Hickman; **Lady:** B.J. Ward; **Scat:** Dick Beals; **Sweets:** Kathleen Helppie; **Spinner/Bump/Flip:** Bob Holt; **Shecky:** Kip King; **Shiner:** Jerry Houser; **Scatch/Fang/Dog Foot:** Peter Cullen; **King Max/Fetch/Snarl:** Kenneth Mars; **Wiggle:** Jennifer Darling; **Downer:** Henry Gibson; **Mooch:** Marshall Efron

### ◎ BLACKSTAR
Astronaut John Blackstar, an intergalactic soldier of fortune, is drawn through a black hole into an alternate universe. There he uses a mystical Power Star to undertake fantastic adventures to the planet Sagar and battle the Overlord of the Underworld, aided by the beautiful sorceress Mara. *A Filmation Associates Production. Half-hour. Color. Premiered on CBS: September 12, 1981–August 20, 1983.*

**Voices**
**John Blackstar:** George DiCenzo; **Balkar/Terra/Klone:** Pat Pinney; **Gossamear/Burble/Rif:** Frank Welker; **Carpo/Overlord:** Alan Oppenheimer; **Mara:** Linda Gary

### ◎ BLASTER'S UNIVERSE
Joined by a silver-toned earthling girl named G.C., who is actually an alien, and her pet M.E.L. (Mechanically Enhanced Lapdog), an impetuous 12-year-old boy named Max Blaster from the Midwest who loves science and space uses logic and creativity to outsmart intergalactic outlaws in the year 2222 while saving the universe in this half-hour series based on the popular series of educational CD-ROMs of the same name. The 13-episode series aired Saturday mornings on CBS beginning in October 1998. *A Nelvana Limited Production. Color. Half-hour. Premiered on CBS: October 2, 1998–September 9, 2000.*

**Voices**
**Max Blaster:** Jonathan Wilson; **G.C.:** Maryke Hendrikse; **M.E.L.:** Juan Chioran

### ◎ BLAZING DRAGONS
Set in Camelhot, gallant and generous dragons King Allfire and his members of the Square Table—Sir Galahot, Queen Griddle and Sir Burnevere—battle greedy humans for gemstones, rescue damsels in distress and generally make the world a better place in which to live in this cartoon-series spoof of King Arthur and the Knights of the Round Table, based on characters created by Monty Python's Terry Jones. *A Nelvana Enterprises/Ellipse Animation Production. Color. Half-hour. Premiered: September 9, 1996. Syndicated. Rebroadcast on TDIS: September 7, 1998–August 29, 2002.*

**Voices**
**King Allfire:** Aron Tager; **Queen Griddle:** Steve Sutcliffe; **Sir Blaze/Minstrel:** Richard Binsley; **Sir Loungealot/Count Geoffrey:** Juan Chioran; **Evil Knight #1:** Cedric Smith; **Evil Knight #2/Sir Burnevere:** John Stocker; **Evil Knight #3:** Dan Hennessey; **Flicker:** Edward Glen; **Flame:** Stephanie Morgenstern; **Cinder/Clinker:** Richard Waugh

### ◎ BLEACH
After his family comes under attack by the malevolent lost soul Hollow, Ichigo Kurosaki, a 15-year-old teen who was born with the ability to see ghosts, becomes a Soul Reaper and dedicates himself to defending the innocent while rendering peace for the tortured poltergeists of the spirit world with the help of fellow Soul Reaper Rukia in this anime action series from famed manga artist Tite Kubo. First shown on Japan's TV Tokyo in October 2004, the English-dubbed version was broadcast in the United States on Cartoon Network *Adult Swim* program block beginning in September 2006. *A TV Tokyo/Studio Perrot/VIZ Media/*

*Studiopolis Production. Color. Half-hour. Premiered on CAR: September 9, 2006.*

**Voices**
**Ichigo Kurosaki:** Johnny Yong Bosch; **Rukia Kuchiki:** Michelle Ruff; **Orihime Inoue:** Stephanie Sheh; **Yasutora "Chad" Sado:** Jamieson Price; **Kisuke Urahara:** Michael Lindsay; **Uryu Ishida:** Derek Stephen Prince; **Renji Abarai:** Wally Wingert

### ◎ BLOOD +

Bitten by a blood-sucking vampire called Chiropteran, and suffering from memory loss, adopted high school senior Saya Otonashi discovers she is the only one with the power to defeat the dreaded Chiropterans in this anime series—first shown in Japan in October 2005 and on Animax and other terrestrial networks—based on the best-selling anime film, *Blood the Last Vampire* (2000). Redubbed in English, the action/adventure series debuted on Cartoon Network in March 2007 after the final broadcast of fellow anime series *Trinity Blood. A Production I.G./Aniplex/Sony Pictures Television International Production. Color. Half-hour. Premiered on CAR: March 10, 2007.*

**Voices**
**Saya Otonashi:** Kari Wahlgren; **Mao:** Olivia Hack; **Riku:** Kamali Minter; **David:** Christopher Nissley; **Solomon:** Dave Wittenberg; **George:** Wally Wingert; **Kai Miyagusuku:** Benjamin Diskin; **Julia:** Abby Craden; **Hagi/Van Argeno:** Crispin Freeman

### ◎ BLUE GENDER

Cryogenically frozen after being diagnosed with a terminal disease, Yuji Kaido awakens more than 20 years later in the year 2031 when Earth has been taken over by alien bugs—known as "Blue"—and joins forces with other surviving humans who are transported to the space station Second Earth to recover the human genes and defeat these menacing creatures. Imported from Japan, the futuristic 26-episode, half-hour science fiction anime series aired in the United States as part of Cartoon Network's late-night *Adult Swim* anime block in 2003. *A Toshiba EMI/AIC/FUNimation Production. Color. Half-hour. Premiered on CAR: August 4, 2003–September 16, 2003.*

**Voices**
**Yuji Kaido:** Eric Vale; **Marlene Angel:** Laura Bailey; **Joey/Heald:** John Burgmeier; **Amick Hendat:** Yonemoto Chizu; **Dice Quaid:** Dameon Clarke; **Sergeant Robert Bradley/Seno Miyagi/Takashi:** Kyle Hebert; **Seamus Han:** Chuck Huber; **Su/Lu/Flower Girl:** Meredith McCoy; **Alicia:** Lisa Ortiz; **Starza:** Sheree Rifkin; **Rick:** Sean Schemmel; **Commander:** James Fields; **Scott:** Chad Cline; **Gernreich:** Ned Record; **Mink:** Megan Woodall; **Doug Vreiss:** Bradford Jackson; **Chairman Victor:** Brice Armstrong; **Other Voices:** Chris Carson, Clint Ford, Sonny Strait

### ◎ BLUE'S CLUES

A live-action host (Steve) and his animated blue puppy (Blue) help kids follow visual clues to solve a puzzle in this play-a-long, educational live-action/animated daytime series for preschoolers.

Since its debut on Nickelodeon's daytime schedule in September 1996, this progressive, cutting-edge half-hour children's series was telecast for six consecutive seasons, with 50 original episodes, through mid-May 2004. Besides airing daily on Nickelodeon's Nick Jr. preschool programming block, the educational series, which won countless accolades and industry awards and honors, including a 2002 Peabody Award, was also broadcast on Nickelodeon's commercial-free children's network, Noggin, starting in January 1999, and for six seasons on CBS's weekend-morning *Nick Jr. on CBS* cartoon block from September 2000 to September 2006. That year, marking its 10th season on the air, the series returned to Nickelodeon with a 12-minute behind-the-scenes documentary, *Behind the Clues: 10 Years with Blue,* and an hour-long prime-time special, *Meet Blue's Baby Brother,* in which Blue's brother was revealed as the multi-colored puppy, Sprinkles.

In 2002, Steve Burns, who played the series' original host, Steve, left the series with his character supposedly enrolling in college and his younger brother, Joe, moving in to take care of his adorable canine companion, Blue. He was replaced by Donovan Patten as Steve's young brother, Joe, who began hosting the series that year. Some episodes featured both Joe and Steve (or at times, only Steve's voice).

In January 2007, Nickleodeon spun-off the wildly popular puppet segment, "Blue's Room," first introduced in the 2004 *Blue's Clues* episode, "The Legend of the Blue Puppy," into its own weekly animated half-hour children's series to air on its preschool channel, Nick Jr. *A Nickelodeon Production. Color. Half-hour. Premiered on NICK: September 9, 1996. Rebroadcast on CBS: September 16, 2000–September 2006. Rebroadcast on NOG: January 31, 1999–.*

**Cast (live action)**
**Steve:** Steven Burns (1996–2001); **Joe:** Donovan Patten (2001–)

**Voices**
**Blue:** Traci Paige; **Mr. Salt:** Nick Balaban; **Mailbox:** Seth O'Hickory; **Tickery Tock:** Kathryn Avery, Kelly Nigh; **Paprika:** Jenna Marie Castle, Corinne Hoffman; **Side Table Drawer:** LaNae Allen; **Mrs. Pepper:** Penny Jewkes, Spencer Kayden; **Slippery Soap:** Cody Ross Pitts, Patrick Van Wagenen; **Shovel:** Jonathan Press; **Pail:** Julia Weatherell

### ◎ BLUE SEED

Aided by her guardian and protector, Mamoru Kusanagi, 15-year-old teen Momiji Fujimiya, a descendant of the mythical Princess Kushinada, fights the angry god Aragami to save Japan in this mythological animated series, based on the ancient Japanese tale of the god Susanoo and the eight-headed monster Orochi no Orochi and first seen on TV Tokyo from October 1994 to March 1995. Beginning in November 1999, the original 26 episodes aired in the United States on the Encore Action Channel as part of the Starz! premium cable networks through January 2000. The English-dubbed, half-hour program sporadically re-aired on Encore Action four times from July 2000 to October 2003, while also re-airing, with two episodes a week, on Encore WAM!, from August 2002 to July 2003. *An Ashi Productions Co. Inc/Production I.G./ADV Films Production. Color. Half-hour. Premiered on EACTN: November 6, 1999–January 29, 2000. Rebroadcast on EACTN: July 1, 2000–August 30, 2000; March 3, 2001–April 28, 2001; May 5, 2002–June 29, 2002; August 2, 2003–October 1, 2003. Rebroadcast on EWAM: August 2, 2002–August 31, 2002; June 2, 2003–July 8, 2003.*

**Voices**
**Kome Sawaguchi:** Tiffany Grant; **Sakura Yamazaki:** Allison Keith; **Mamoru Kusanagi:** Jason Lee; **Momiji Fujimiya/Kaede Kunikida:** Amanda Winn Lee; **Daitetsu Kunikida:** Rob Mungle; **Ryoko Takeuchi:** Marcy Rae; **Yoshiki Yaegashi:** Kurt Stoll; **Akiko/Grandma:** Carol Amerson; **Prime Minister:** Rick Peeples

## ◎ BOB AND MARGARET

First seen in the Academy Award-winning cartoon short "Bob's Birthday," this animated sitcom follows the trials and tribulations of a happily married couple Bob and Margaret Fish and their two dogs William and Elizabeth who live in London (during the first two seasons, with the third and fourth seasons based in Canada), where Bob owns a dental practice and Margaret is a practicing chiropodist. Created by award-winning animators David Fine and Alison Snowden (also the voice of Margaret), the half-hour series first aired in Canada on the Global Network and then in the United States on Comedy Central from June 1998 to December 2001.

Episodes of the series were repeated on Showtime, which began airing all 52 episodes, including the second 26-half-hours, never-before-seen in the United States (and with the characters living in Toronto), in the summer of 2002. (The program also reportedly was rebroadcast on HBO's sister channel, HBO Comedy, but HBO's programming department has no record of the show ever airing on that network.) Adam Hamilton provided the voice of Bob during the first two seasons, with Brian George, featured in many episodes of TV's *Seinfeld*, assuming the role beginning in 2001. Fine and Snowden served as consultants on the series, which was produced by Canada's Nelvana Limited. *A Nelvana Limited/Comedy Partners/Silver Light Production. Color. Half-hour. Premiered on COM: June 22, 1998–December 25, 2001. Rebroadcast on SHO: Summer 2002.*

### Voices
**Bob Fish:** Andy Hamilton, Brian George; **Margaret:** Alison Snowden; **Cookie Fish/Joyce:** Jayne Eastwood; **Trevor:** Dwayne Hill; **Melvin Fish:** Wayne Robson; **Guinivere:** Tracey Hoyt; **Additional Voices:** Peter Baynham, Steve Brody, Steve Coogan, Trevor Cooper, Chris Emmett, Sarah Hadland, Doon Mackichan, Ron Pardo, Adrian Truss

## ◎ BOBBY'S WORLD

Comedian Howie Mandel created the character of this half-hour animated series, debuting on FOX Network, in which his highly imaginative preschool alter ego, four-year-old Bobby, presents his point of view of the world and family life through a series of day-dreams. Each episode opens and closes with live-action wrap-arounds of the comedian talking about the show and at times talking to his animated self. Situations usually revolve around Bobby's home life—with his stubborn father, his sympathetic mother, his taunting older brother Derek and his whiny sister Kelly, and next-door neighbors, including his best friend, Jackie, and his sheepdog, Roger—often confronting some sort of dilemma. One series milestone included was the season-long pregnancy of Bobby's mother, resulting in a guest-appearance by Paul Anka, in a blend of live-action and animation, serenading the cartoon mother-to-be in the episode in which she gave birth with his composition "(You're) Having My Baby."

Airing Saturday mornings and weekday afternoons, the series' last original episode was broadcast in February of 1998. After airing eight seasons on FOX, the series was rebroadcast for nearly three seasons on Fox Family Channel and remained popular in syndication in 65 countries around the world. *A Film Roman Production in association with Alevy Productions and FOX Children's Television Network. Color. Half-hour. Premiered on FOX: September 8, 1990–February 23, 1998. Rebroadcast on FOX FAM: August 17, 1998–May 24, 2001. Syndicated.*

### Voices
**Bobby Generic/Howie:** Howie Mandel; **Martha:** Gayle Matthius; **Uncle Ted:** Tino Insana; **Kelly:** Charity James; **Derek:** Benny Grant, Pam Segall; **Roger:** Danny Mann, Frank Welker; **Aunt Ruth:** Susan Tolsky; **Jackie:** Debi Derryberry; **Captain Squash:** Gary Owens

## ◎ BOBOBO-BO BO-BOBO

Offbeat saga of a golden afro-haired, muscle-bound hero with remarkable power (Bobobo), trained to "hear the voices of the hair," and his sidekicks, Beauty and Captain Don Patch, who is out to save the kingdom of Bald Empire (Magarita in the original Japanese series) from the evil tyrant, Baldy Bald 4th, and his Hair Posse who are bent on taking the hair of its citizenry to make everyone bald and prove Baldy Bald's authority over his people in this Japanese-imported action/comedy anime series, based on the popular manga by Yoshio Sawai, that aired as part of Cartoon Network's successful *Toonami* action animation block. In January 2007, Cartoon Network renewed the successful series for a second season. *A Toei Animation/TV Asahi/phuuz entertainment inc./Illumitoon Entertainment/Westlake Entertainment Inc. Production. Color. Half-hour. Premiered on CAR: October 8, 2005.*

### Voices
**Bobobo-bo Bo-Bobo/Insurmountable Wall Man:** Richard Epcar; **Young Bobobo-bo Bo-Bobo/Boogerball Player:** Mona Marshall; **Bobobo-bo Bo-Bobo's Dad/Chocolate Munchie/Doll Man/Haou/June 7th/Puppet Lad:** Michael Sorich; **Gasser:** Brad MacDonald; **Dengaku Man:** Brian Beacock; **Torpedo Girl:** Melodee M. Spevack; **Jelly Juggler:** Taylor Henry; **Beauty:** Vicky Green; **Heppokomaru:** Naomi Shindoh; **Torpedo Girl:** Melodee Spevack; **Don Patch/Lomax:** Kirk Thorton; **Hatenko/Indus Guy/Sonic:** Jeff Nimoy; **Softon/Additional Voices:** Joe Ochman; **Suzu:** Kate Levine; **OVER/Kittypoo/Pana:** Liam O'Brien; **Captain Battleship/Gunkan:** Paul St. Peter; **Chuunosuke:** Brian Beacock; **Otto:** Dan Lorge; **Maitel/Mesopotamian Guy:** Dan Woren; **Giga/Radio Man/T-500:** David Lodge; **Nightmare:** Doug Erholtz; **Geha the Gale/Hagen/Yellow River Guy:** Ezra Weisz; **MAX Kyokawa:** Joe Ochman; **Halekulani:** Joey Capps; **Killalino/Tarashi:** John Smallberries; **Denbo:** Kate Higgins; **Cathy/Stock Market Voice:** Michelle Ruff; **Botan/Infinite Shoot/Katsu/King Nosehair/The Bad Bard:** Richard Cansino; **Garbel of Manicuria:** Roger Rose; **Gasser's Neckbelt/Gechappi/Lead Battleship Special Forces Member:** Steve Kramer; **Mean Green Soup Alien:** Taylor Henry; **Mother Spoon:** Wendee Lee; **Megafan/Rice:** Yuri Lowenthal; **Young Captain Battleship/Other Voices:** Barbara Goodson; **Narrator/Captain Ishida:** Michael McConnohie; **Other Voices:** Stephanie Sheh, Tom Fahn

## ◎ BOB THE BUILDER

Replete with his hardhat and construction boots, chubby-faced Bob the Builder and his lovable crew of machines—Scoop the scooper, Muck the dump truck, Lofty the crane, Dizzy the cement mixer and Roley the steam roller—and friends, including his cat Pilchard and wacky scarecrow Spud, overcome problems while learning many important lessons about loyalty, friendship and other basic values and working together on jobs assigned to them by Bob's business partner, Wendy, in this imaginative, stop-motion animated educational series for preschool audiences. First telecast in the United Kingdom on BBC2 in April 1999, this enjoyable half-hour series debuted in the United States on Nickelodeon's Nick Jr. weekday preschool programming block in January 2001. During the 2001–02 television season, the series also aired Saturday mornings on CBS as part of Nick's *Nick Jr. on CBS* program block.

In January 2001, Nickelodeon's all-cartoon channel, Nicktoons, picked up the series, re-airing it through September 2004.

In January 2005, HIT Entertainment produced a spin-off series, *Bob the Builder: Project Build It*, which began airing on PBS's PBS Kids preschool block, preceded by 13 existing, never-before-aired episodes of its predecessor. That same year, the original award-winning series re-aired as part of PBS's new video-on-demand (VOD) and digital cable television channel, PBS Kids Sprout. *A HIT Entertainment/HOT Animation/BBC2 Production. Color. Half-hour. Premiered on NICK JR.: January 13, 2001–September 22, 2004. Premiered on CBS: September 15, 2001–September 7, 2002. Rebroadcast on PBS Kids Sprout (VOD): April 4, 2004–. Rebroadcast on PBS Kids Sprout (digital cable): September 26, 2005–.*

**Voices**
**Bob/Lofty/Farmer Pickles:** Neil Morrissey; **Wendy, the Office Clerk/Dizzy/Mrs. Potts:** Kate Harbour; **Scoop/Muck/Roley/Travis/Spud:** Rob Rackstraw

## ◎ BOB THE BUILDER: PROJECT BUILD IT

The popular children's television build-it-buddy returns in this series of new adventures, picking up where the original series left off, with Bob (uttering such memorable catchphrases as "Reduce! . . . Re-use! . . . Recycle! . . .") and his construction team facing new problems and new challenges while undertaking a unique building job: to construct a new, ecologically friendly town from scratch, one brick and one tile at a time. First airing in the United Kingdom on the BBC in May 2005, the half-hour educational series, offering 75 10-minute cartoons and introducing the new character of Packer premiered on PBS Kids' weekday preschool programming block in September 2006. In concert with unveiling the new series, PBS broadcast 13 existing and unaired episodes of the first *Bob the Builder* series, followed by new first season episodes of the spin-off series. Leading preschool children's entertainment company HIT Entertainment produced the series, as well as two specials based on the character, the half-hour *Bob's Big Plan* (2005), listed as a regular episode in PBS's programming records although the producers' inventory shows otherwise, and the hour-long *Snowed Under: The Bobblesberg Winter Games* (2005). *A HIT Entertainment Limited/HOT Animation/Keith Chapman Production. Color. Half-hour. Premiered on PBS Kids: January 1, 2005.*

**Voices**
**Bob the Builder:** Greg Proops; **Robert, Bob's Dad:** Richard Briers; **Bob's Mum:** June Whitfield; **Spud:** Rob Rackstraw; **Scrambler:** Rupert Dugas; **Dizzy:** Kate Harbour

## ◎ BONKERS!

Bonkers D. Bobcat, formerly of the Disney CBS Saturday-morning series *Raw Toonage*, starred in this 65-episode half-hour animated series that captured his manic missions to protect Tinseltown as a member of the Tinseltown Police Force. His well-meaning efforts end in disaster, thwarting the attempts of his mismatched human partner (Sergeant Lucky Piquel) to get promoted. Debuting on Disney Channel in 1993, the series was also syndicated that September as part of The Disney Afternoon two-hour block, replacing *Chip 'n' Dale's Rescue Rangers*. *A Walt Disney Television Animation Production. Color. Half-hour. Premiered on DIS: February 1993–September 1993. Syndicated: September 6, 1993–September 10, 1995.*

**Voices**
**Bonkers/Sergeant Lucky Piquel:** Jim Cummings

## ◎ BOO!

A distinctive patchwork creature with a star-shaped topknot named Boo and his friends Laughing Duck, Sleeping Bear and Growling Tiger play a game akin to "hide and seek" ("Where's Boo?"), introducing children to new environments, new words and new characters in this interactive animated edu-tainment series produced in 2002 and first shown as part of the CBeebies daily children's programming block on the United Kingdom's BBC2 in 2003. The first animated program produced by Britain's Tell-Tale Productions, creators of the hugely popular *Tweenies*, this 3-D CGI-animated program featured a mix of '70s-styled funk and rhythm and blues music and songs and narrated adventures and debuted in the United States in January 2007 as part of a four-hour block of children's programming on the all-new digital television channel, qubo, seen on the ION network (originally PAX-TV). Oddly, prior to the series' arrival in the United States, in December 2006 Boo and company were featured in a half-hour holiday special, *Boo! Christmas Special*, that aired on ION. *A Tell-Tale Productions Ltd. Production. Color. Half-hour. Premiered on Q: January 8, 2007.*

## ◎ THE BOONDOCKS

Racially charged offshoot of Aaron McGruder's popular newspaper strip carried in more than 350 newspapers, known for its subversive humor and sociopolitical sentiments; about the adventures of kid brothers—budding 10-year-old revolutionary Huey Freeman and his eight-year-old thug-in-training brother Riley—who unhappily deal with life after moving to the big city of Chicago with their retired, cantankerous old-school granddad, Robert Jebediah Freeman. Featured in the series were other supporting characters, including the interracial couple Thomas and Sara Dubois and their 10-year-old biracial daughter, Jazmine; Huey's best friends and classmates, Cindy McPhearson and Michael Caesar; and the mentally-challenged neighborhood handyman, Uncle Ruckus.

After talks with HBO, Showtime and MTV failed and FOX rejected the pilot, Cartoon Network premiered the show on its late-night *Adult Swim* animation block in October 2005. The series came under fire from various social groups after using the "N" word 18 times in its debut episode. Nevertheless, the program's premiere pulled in a hefty 2.3 million viewers, and more than a million 18 to 34-year-old viewers its second week.

The controversial cartoon show also drew fire from Rev. Al Sharpton who criticized the "Return of the King" episode for portraying the famed civil rights leader, Martin Luther King, as emerging from a coma and using the N-word in a speech. Despite the controversy surrounding the series, Cartoon Network renewed the edgy animated series for a second season, ordering 20 new episodes, to air in late 2006. *A Sony Pictures Television Production. Color. Half-hour. Premiered on CAR: October 2, 2005 (Adult Swim)–.*

**Voices**
**Huey/Riley Freeman:** Regina King; **Cindy McPhearson:** Daveigh Chase; **Timmy:** Daryl Sabara; **Jazmine Dubois:** Gabby Soleil; **Thomas Dubois:** Cedric Yarbrough; **Sarah Dubois:** Jill Talley; **Robert Jebediah "Grandad" Freeman:** John Witherspoon; **Uncle Ruckus:** Gary Anthony Williams

## ◎ BOTS MASTER

Set in the year 2015, a child prodigy, Ziv Zulaner, develops futuristic 3A manual-labor robots—known as "bots"—for the Robot Megafact Corporation, but the corporation's evil Lewis Paradim plans to build his own version in order to take over the world in this half-hour syndicated series. *A Nuoptix/Avid Arad/Creativite et Developpement Production in association with All American Television. Color. Half-hour. Premiered: 1993. Syndicated.*

*Voices*

**Ziv "ZZ" Zulander:** Mark Hildreth; **Blitzy Zulander:** Crystaleen O'Bray; **Toolzz/Bogie:** Stefano Giulianetti; **GeneSix/Cook:** Michael Donovan; **Jammerzz:** Cusse Mankuma; **Dr. Hiss/Other Voices:** Ian James Corlett; **Sir Lewis Leon Paradim:** Dale Wilson; **Lady Frenzy:** Janyse Jaud; **Additional Voices:** Richard Cox, Kim Restell

## ◎ BOZO THE CLOWN

Frizzy redhaired clown Bozo, former comic-strip favorite and Capitol Records star, found new avenues via syndicated television when Larry Harmon produced this series of 156 five-minute color cartoons featuring Bozo and his circus pal Butchy Boy. The series has remained in continuous syndication since its premiere in 1959. *A Larry Harmon/Ticktin/Jayark Films Production. Color. Half-hour. Syndicated: 1959.*

*Voices*

**Bozo the Clown/Butchy Boy:** Larry Harmon

*Additional Voices*

Paul Frees

## ◎ BRACEFACE

Calamitous adventures of a 14-year-old, Sharon Spitz (voiced by actress Alicia Silverstone of filmdom's *Clueless* fame), whose metal braces cause more than their share of mayhem while she deals with the problems of adolescence and adapting to life at Mary Pickford Junior High. Along for the ride are her mother and brothers, Adam and Josh; her friends, Maria and Alyson; her would-be boyfriend, Alden; born-to-be-dork, Conner Mackenzie; and archnemesis and most popular girl at school, Nina. Storylines progressed to entering high school.

After premiering in June 2001 on FOX Family Channel's weekend programming block, the half-hour cartoon series, which garnered the network's highest-ever ratings, returned for two more seasons under the newly named ABC Family owned by Disney. The joint Canadian-American production was then rebroadcast weekdays, Monday through Saturday, on the Disney Channel. *A Nelvana/Jade Animation (Shenzen) Company Production. Color. Half-hour. Premiered on FOX FAM/ABC FAM: June 2, 2001–May 31, 2003. Rebroadcast on DIS: May 2, 2004–September 1, 2005.*

*Voices*

**Sharon Spitz:** Alicia Silverstone, Stacey DePass; **Adam Spitz:** Dan Petronijevic; **Alden Jones:** Vincent Corazza; **Conner Mackenzie:** Peter Oldring; **Josh Spitz:** Michael Cera; **Maria Wong:** Marnie McPhail; **Mom:** Tamara Bernier; **Nina Harper:** Katie Griffin; **Marvin:** Jordan Allison; **Dion:** Raoul Bhaneja; **Dylan:** Alexander Conti; **Dentist:** Dwayne Hill

## ◎ THE BRADY KIDS

Re-creating their roles from TV's *The Brady Bunch*, Greg, Peter, Bobby, Marcia, Janice and Cindy were featured in this animated spinoff focusing on the kids' problems as independent-minded young adults. Joining the wholesome youngsters were Ping and Pong. Chinese-speaking twin pandas, and Marlon, a magical black mynah bird. The Brady characters were voiced by members of the original television series cast.

The series pilot, *Jungle Bungle* (retitled *The Brady Kids on Mysterious Island* and broadcast as a feature-length cartoon on *The ABC Saturday Superstar Movie* series), was broadcast as the series opener in 1972. The half-hour cartoon series ran for two seasons on ABC, producing 22 episodes (including the two-part pilot).

Original cast members Maureen McCormick, Barry Williams and Christopher Knight did not reprise their characters for the second season. Their voices were supplied by voice actors Erika Scheimer, Lane Scheimer and Keith Allen. *A Filmation Associates Production. Color. Half-hour. Premiered on ABC: September 16, 1972–August 31, 1974.*

*Voices*

**Marcia Brady:** Maureen McCormick, Erika Scheimer; **Greg Brady:** Barry Williams, Lane Scheimer; **Janice Brady:** Eve Plumb; **Peter Brady:** Chistopher Knight, Keith Allen; **Cindy Brady:** Susan Olsen; **Bobby Brady:** Michael Lookin-land; **Marlon the Magic Bird/Ping/Pong:** Larry Storch; **Babs:** Jane Webb; **Moptop:** "Lassie"

## ◎ THE BRAK SHOW

Comical suburban adventures of the fanged, demented space-age teenager, Brak—first popularized as the evil masked space pirate in Hanna-Barbera's classic 1960s cartoon series, *Space Ghost and Dino Boy*—who lives on a distant planet with his alien mother and Cuban father in a beautiful suburb reminiscent of an American suburb, circa 1959, and his encounters with his foul-mouth friend, Zorak, and giant robot neighbor, Thundercleese, in this animated series spin-off for Cartoon Network's *Adult Swim* animation block for grown-ups. Written and produced by *Space Ghost: Coast to Coast* writer/producers Jim Fortier and Pete Smith, who spun off *The Brak Show* from characters that appeared in recurring roles, the new series actually debuted on December 21, 2000, as a one-shot special called *Leave It to Brak: Mr. Bawk Ba Gawk*, on *Adult Swim*.

In September 2001, Cartoon Network made the television sitcom spoof a regular weekly series on *Adult Swim*, with nine episodes produced that season. The following April, the series returned with 11 new episodes, and was renewed for a third season (its last) beginning in October 2003 with 13 additional episodes. The final broadcast included a three-hour New Year's Eve special entitled *New Year's Eve at Brak's House*, with Brak joined by the human-sized mantis, Zorak and other colorful *Adult Swim* characters and new episodes of *Aqua Teen Hunger Force, Harvey Birdman, Attorney at Law, Sealab 2021, Space Ghost: Coast to Coast* and others. To appease the show's loyal fans, in October 2006 Cartoon Network announced plans to produce new installments of the series for Internet viewing on its Web-based, *Adult Swim Fix. A Williams Street/Wild Hare Studios/Turner Production. Color. Fifteen minutes. Premiered on CAR: December 21, 2000 (special). Premiered on CAR: September 2, 2001–December 31, 2003 (series).*

*Voices*

**Voldemar H. "Brak" Guerta:** Andry Merill; **Zorak:** C. Martin Croker; **Brak's Dad:** George Lowe; **Brak's Mom:** Marsha Crenshaw (2001–02), Joanna Daniel (2002); **Thundercleese:** Carey Means; **Fuzzy/Braktonics Keyboardist:** Eddie Horst; **The Brakettes:** Alfreda Gerald

## ◎ BRAND SPANKING NEW! DOUG

Bristle-topped Doug Funnie, the heartwarming, parent-pleasing, likable 12-year-old with his trademark green sweater vest and brown shorts (from Nickelodeon's hit series *Doug*), enters seventh grade at a newly built middle school in Bluffington and deals with a whole new set of trials and tribulations, including his mom's pregnancy and the arrival of a new addition to the Funnie family, in this all-new weekly half-hour animated series. Cast in new situations are regulars from the old series: Doug's best friend, Skeeter Valentine; Tony; the elusive girl of his dreams, Patti Mayonnaise; big, bad bully Roger Klotz and Porkchop, the dog. ABC initially ordered 13 episodes, including a prime-time holiday special, *Doug's Secret Christmas* for the series first season in 1996. The program was so successful that the network expanded the show to one hour.

Retitled *Disney's Doug* in 1998, the show ran for three more seasons on ABC, and in syndication on UPN-owned stations. Episodes were then rerun on Toon Disney. *A Jumbo Pictures Production. Color. Half-hour. One hour. Premiered on ABC: September 7, 1996–October 26, 1996 (half-hour version); November 2, 1996 (one-hour version)–September 8, 2001. Rebroadcast on UPN/Syndicated: August 31, 1998–October 7, 2000. Rebroadcast on TDIS: August 3, 2001–October 31, 2004.*

**Voices**
**Doug Funnie:** Thomas McHugh; **Judy Funnie/Theda Funnie/Connie Benge:** Becca Lish; **Misquito Valentine/Ned Valentine/Mr. Dink:** Fred Newman; **Roger Klotz:** Chris Phillips; **Bebe Bluff:** Alice Playten; **Patti Mayonnaise:** Constance Shulman

## ◎ BRANDY & MR. WHISKERS

After dropping out of an airplane and landing smack dab in the middle of the Amazon rain forest, a spoiled pooch named Brandy and an impetuous eccentric rabbit named Mr. Whiskers overcome their numerous differences to survive in the jungle while forging new friendships with an ensemble of offbeat jungle characters—an over-analytical boa, Lola; the feuding twin toucan sisters, Cheryl and Meryl; the clumsy river otter, Ed; the villainous and self-dubbed dictator of the Amazon, Gaspar and jungle diva, Margo—in this animated "buddy comedy" for Disney Channel. Premiering with a four-show marathon consisting of two episodes each per half-hour, the regular weekday children's series aired at 2 P.M. on the Disney Channel beginning in August 2004 with 21 half-hours and 42 first-season episodes produced in 2003. Disney Channel renewed the program for a second season with 18 additional half-hours, which were telecast from February to August 2006. (Forty-two half-hours were planned but due to declining ratings production of the series was halted.) In January 2006, episodes were subsequently rerun on Disney Channel's sister network, Toon Disney, as part of a five-hour jungle-themed marathon with six episodes, including a special airing of Disney's direct-to-DVD sequel, *Lion King 1½. A Walt Disney Television Animation Production. Color. Half-hour. Premiered on TDIS: August 21, 2004–August 25, 2006. Rebroadcast on TDIS: January 16, 2006.*

**Voices**
**Brandy Harrington:** Kaley Cuoco; **Mr. Whiskers:** Charlie Adler; **Lola Boa:** Alanna Ubach; **Cheryl/Meryl:** Sherri Shepherd; **Ed:** Tom Kenny; **Margo:** Jennifer Hale; **Gaspar Le Gecko:** André Sogliuzzo

## ◎ B.R.A.T.S OF THE LOST NEBULA

Dispatched by their parents to live on the Lost Nebula when an alien army attacks their home planet, a young brother-and-sister duo, Zadam and Triply, forge a mighty alliance with three homeless youths (Ryle, Lavana and Duncan)—called the *Barts of the Lost Nebula*—to battle the same world-destroying forces that attacked their homeland, The Shock, in this 13-episode, half-hour puppet- and computer-animated sci-fi/adventure series produced by *Muppets* creator Jim Henson's son Brian Henson for the WB Television Network's Kids' WB! Only the first three episodes of the series aired in the United States, while the remaining 10 episodes were broadcast on Canada's YTV network. *A Henson Productions/DECODE Entertainment/Wandering Monkey Production. Color. Half-hour. Premiered on the WB (Kids' WB!): October 10, 1998–October 24, 1998.*

**Voices**
**Zadam:** Kirby Morrow; **Triply:** Annick Obonsawin; **Ryle:** Evan Sabba; **Lavana:** Deborah Odell; **Duncan:** Glen Cross; **Additional Voices:** Bill Barretta, Matt Ficner, John Kennedy, Trish Leeper, Jim Rankin, Gordon Robertson, Jeff Sweeney, Mak Wilson

## ◎ BRATZ

Incredibly popular CGI-animated series, based on the successful fashion doll line that has sold more than 100 million dolls since its debut in June 2001 and became a huge hit with preteens, featuring the exciting and glamorous high school adventures of four sassy teenage girls—Yasmin, Cloe, Sasha and Jade—from socially and economically diverse backgrounds with a "passion for fashion" who report the latest scoops for their hip teen magazine. Licensed by leading consumer entertainment products company, MGA Entertainment, and produced by Mike Young Productions, the half-hour series aired as part of 4Kids Entertainment's *4Kids TV* Saturday-morning programming block on FOX, beginning September 2005, with other shows for girls ages six to 12, including *The Winx Club, Mew Mew Power* and *Magical DoReMi*. In the fall of 2006, the series returned for a second season of all-new episodes. *A 4Kids Entertainment/Mike Young/MGA Entertainment Production. Color. Half-hour. Premiered on FOX: September 10, 2005.*

**Voices**
**Yasmin:** Dionne Quan; **Cloe:** Olivia Hack; **Sasha:** Tia Mowry; **Jade:** Soleil Moon Frye; **Burdine:** Wendie Malick; **Kirstee:** Kaley Cuoco; **Kaycee:** Lacey Chabert; **Cameron:** Charlie Schlatter; **Dylan:** Ogie Banks; **Byron Powell:** Greg Ellis

## ◎ BRAVESTARR

Combining the best of the Old West and of the space-age future, this western fantasy/adventure takes place on the distant planet of New Texas in the 24th century. Horse-riding lawman Marshal Bravestarr draws on his super powers to fight for the cause of justice where evil lurks, aided by his Equestroid talking horse, Thirty-Thirty, in this daily series of 65 half-hour programs produced for syndication. Other characters featured in this high-energy action/adventure included Judge B.J., the female magistrate of New Texas, and pint-size alien lawman, Deputy Fuss. *A Filmation Production. Color. Half-hour. Premiered: September 1987–September 1988. Syndicated.*

**Voices**
**Scuzz/Deputy Fuss:** Charlie Adler; **Judge B.J.:** Susan Blu; **Marshal Bravestarr:** Pat Fraley; **Thirty-Thirty/Shaman:** Ed Gilbert

## ◎ THE BROTHERS FLUB

Under the supervision of their green alien dispatcher Ms. Boomdeyay (voiced by actress Charlotte Rae of TV's *Facts of Life*), brothers Fraz and Guapo, a pair of bickering couriers who work for the package delivery company RetroGrade A travel throughout the universe to make important deliveries, including everything from a recipient's unlucky bowling ball to an unruly 600-pound pet, in this half-hour comedy series for Nickelodeon. This joint German-U.S. coproduction, originally planned to air on Nickelodeon in the fall of 1998, instead aired weekend afternoons beginning in January 1999, with the premiere episode "Bad Judgement Day." With 20 episodes originally produced for the series, only 13 half-hours were actually telecast on Nickelodeon until the following January. Many well-known celebrities, including Jerry Lewis, Weird Al Yankovic and Adam West, made guest voice appearances. *A Sunbow Entertainment/Ravenburger Film + TV Production. Color. Half-hour. Premiered on NICK: January 17, 1999–January 8, 2000.*

**Voices**
**Donna:** Christine Cavanaugh; **Judy Hen:** Marsha Clark; **Ms. Tarara Boomdeyay:** Charlotte Rae; **Bob:** Tommy Widmer; **Other Voices:** Nick Bakay, Tim Curry, Richard Steven Horvitz, Jerry Stroka, Charlie Adler, Nancy Cartwright, Jerry Lewis, Weird Al Yankovic, Adam West, R. Lee Ermey

### ⊚ THE BROTHERS GRUNT

Originally developed as characters for MTV network I.D.'s by creator Danny Antonucci (of "Lupo the Butcher" fame), six gross-looking, bug-eyed brothers (Perry, Frank, Tony, Bing, Dean and Sammy), who love cheese, wear bermuda shorts, knee-high black socks and wingtips and communicate only by grunting and twitching, escape from a local monastery and set out on a series of slapstick adventures in this 65-episode half-hour animated series, which premiered on MTV in August of 1994. Each animated half-hour featured three seven-minute cartoons per broadcast. The series lasted one season. *An a.k.a. Cartoon, Inc. Production in association with MTV. Color. Half-hour. Premiered on MTV: August 15, 1994–August 14, 1995.*

**Voices**
**Perryl/Frank/Tony/Bing/Dean/Sammy/various:** Doug Parker; **Various Others:** Jennifer Wilson

### ⊚ BRUNO THE KID

Bruce Willis (known in some circles as "Bruno") co-created and lent his voice to this bespectacled, 11-year-old computer whiz kid with the bulbous head, whose computer-generated superspy alter ego gets him recruited by Globe, an international law-enforcement agency (who assigns Globe operative Jarlsburg to work with him) into the high-stakes world of international espionage. This 36-episode half-hour syndicated adventure series was produced in association with Willis's company, Flying Heart Inc. *A Film Roman Production in association with Flying Heart, Inc. Color. Half-hour. Premiered: September 23, 1996. Syndicated.*

**Voices**
**Bruno the Kid:** Bruce Willis; **Jarlsburg:** Tony Jay; **Leecy Davidson:** Jennifer Hale; **Grace:** Kath Soucie; **Howard:** John Bower; **Lazlo Gigahertz:** Tim Curry; **Booby Vicious:** Matt Frewer; **Harris:** Mark Hamill; **Globe Member 1:** Earl Boen; **Globe Member 2:** Mark Hamill; **Globe Member 3:** Kath Soucie; **Von Trapp:** Kenneth Mars; **Koos Koos:** Frank Welker; **General Armando Castrato:** Bronson Pinchot; **Mr. X:** Paul Edig; **Professor Wisenstein:** Ben Stein; **Di Archer:** Dawnn Lewis

### ⊚ BUCKY AND PEPITO

This early animated series dealt with the adventures of Bucky, a young boy with a wild imagination and the spirit of an explorer, and his best friend, Pepito, the inventor. *A Sam Singer Production. Half-hour. Black-and-white. Premiered: 1959. Syndicated.*

**Voices**
**Bucky Pepito:** Dallas McKennon

### ⊚ BUCKY O'HARE AND THE TOAD WARS

Based on the graphic novel *Echo of Futurepast*, illustrated by Michael Golden, this series followed the misadventures of fearless S.P.A.C.E. (Sentient Protoplasm Against Colonial Encroachment) Captain Bucky O'Hare and his animal cohorts—Deadeye Duck, Bruiser, the gorilla, and Blinky, the adolescent android—who battle evil outer-space amphibians from the planet Genus. *An Abrams Gentile/Sunbow Entertainment/Claster/ Marvel Production in association with Continuity Comics and IDDH. Color. Half-hour. Premiered: September 1991. Syndicated.*

**Voices**
**Bucky O'Hare:** Doug Parker; **Deadeye Duck/Frax:** Scott McNeil: **Bruiser, the Gorilla/ Bruce:** Dale Wilson; **A1C Blinky/Frix:** Terry Klassen; **A1 Negator/Commander Dogstar:** Gary Chalk; **Toad Air Marshal:** Long John Baldry; **Willy DuWitt:** Shane Meier; **Pilot Jenny/Mimi LaFleur:** Margot Pinvidic; **Komplex/Toadborg:** Richard Newman; **Additional Voices:** Jay Brazeau, Simon Kendall, Sam Khouth, Jason Michas, David Steele

### ⊚ BUDGIE THE LITTLE HELICOPTER

The series chronicles the adventures of a high-flying friendly copter and his friends who constantly get into mischief, based on four children's books by Sarah Ferguson, the Duchess of York. Debuting first in overseas syndication in 1994 (becoming a hit in England), one year later the series premiered in the United States on FOX Network's revamped weekday preschool series, *Fox Cubhouse*. Episodes were shown in combination with the serialized adventures of a new animated series, *Magic Adventures of Mumfie*. The duchess got the idea for Budgie in 1987 while practicing for her helicopter pilot's license. *A Fred Wolf Studios/Sleepy Kids Company/ HTV/Dublin Production in association with Westinghouse Broadcasting. Color. Half-hour. Premiered on FOX: October 19, 1995–August 15, 1996.*

### ⊚ BUFORD AND THE GALLOPING GHOST

This half-hour mystery series was composed of two weekly cartoon segments—"The Buford Files," following the exploits of Buford the bloodhound and two teenagers solving crimes; and "The Galloping Ghost," the misadventures of Nugget Nose, a ghost of an Old West prospector who haunts a dude ranch—which originally aired as part of ABC's 90-minute series *Yogi's Space Race* in 1978. (See *Yogi's Space Race* for voice credits.) *A Hanna-Barbera Production. Color. Half-hour. Premiered on NBC: February 3, 1979– September 1, 1979. Rebroadcast on CAR: September 11, 1994 (Sundays).*

### ⊚ THE BUGS BUNNY AND TWEETY SHOW

Bugs Bunny, Tweety and Sylvester star in this program containing classic Warner Bros. cartoons. Added to ABC's Saturday morning schedule in 1986, the half-hour series continued to air weekly for 14 seasons until September 2000. *A Warner Bros. Production. Color. Half-hour. Premiered on ABC: September 13, 1986–September 2, 2000.*

**Voices**
Mel Blanc

### ⊚ THE BUGS BUNNY/LOONEY TUNES COMEDY HOUR

Hour-long anthology of cartoon adventures featuring Bugs Bunny, the Road Runner, Daffy Duck, Foghorn Leghorn, Sylvester the Cat and Pepe Le Pew. The series' debut on ABC marked the end of the rascally rabbit's long association with CBS, where *The Bugs Bunny/Road Runner Hour* has remained a staple of Saturday-morning television since its premiere in 1968. *A Warner Bros. Production. Color. One hour. Premiered on ABC: September 7, 1985–September 6, 1986.*

**Voices**
Mel Blanc

## ◎ THE BUGS BUNNY/ROAD RUNNER HOUR

Bugs Bunny and the Road Runner and Coyote combined to become one of the most popular Saturday-morning vehicles when reruns of their old cartoons were broadcast for the first time on CBS in September 1968. The pairing of these Warner Bros. superstars resulted in consistently high ratings for its time period throughout its 17-year run on CBS. The format was changed only once: In April 1976 the program was aired simultaneously on Tuesday nights in primetime under the title of *The Bugs Bunny/ Road Runner Show*. By November 1977 the series was expanded to 90 minutes, remaining in this mode through the beginning of the 1981–82 season, when it returned to one hour, the length it stayed, ending its reign on CBS in September 1985. *A Warner Bros. Production. Color. One hour. Ninety minutes. Premiered on CBS: September 14, 1968–September 4, 1971. Rebroadcast on CBS: September 6, 1975–November 1977 (as The Bugs Bunny/Road Runner Hour); April 1972–June 1976 (as The Bugs Bunny/Road Runner Show); November 1977–September 1981 (as The Bugs Bunny/Road Runner Show); September 12, 1981–September 7, 1985.*

## ◎ THE BUGS BUNNY SHOW

Like its rival CBS, which brought *The Flintstones* to prime time, ABC premiered this package of Warner Bros. cartoons starring "the screwy rabbit" and his friends (Elmer Fudd, Yosemite Sam, Tweety and Sylvester the Cat, and the Road Runner), which contained significant amounts of new animated material specially made for television. The program remained in prime time for two seasons before it was moved to Saturday mornings, where it dominated kiddie-show ratings in its time slot for more than 20 years. *A Warner Bros. Production. Color. Half-hour. Premiered on ABC: October 11, 1960–September 25, 1962. Rebroadcast on ABC: April 1962–September 1968. Rebroadcast on CBS: September 11, 1971–September 1, 1973. Rebroadcast on ABC: September 8, 1973–August 30, 1975.*

### Voices

Mel Blanc, Arthur Q. Bryan, Daws Butler, June Foray, Julie Bennett, Stan Freberg, Billy Bletcher, Bea Benadaret

## ◎ THE BUGS N' DAFFY SHOW

Continuing to program classic animated shorts from Warner Bros. past, the WB Television Network aired this package of *Looney Tunes* and *Merrie Melodies* shorts (formerly titled *That's Warner Bros.!*), retitling the series and featuring legendary Warner Bros. toonsters Bugs Bunny and Daffy Duck as the stars of the show. This half-hour series debuted on the Kids' WB! lineup in 1996. A second season began in September 1997 and the WB Television Network dropped the series from its weekday schedule for the 1998–99 season. *A Warner Bros. Production. Color. Half-hour. Premiered on WB(Kids' WB!): August 26, 1996–September 1998.*

### Voices

Mel Blanc (primary voice)

## ◎ THE BULLWINKLE SHOW

With new components added, this program was basically a retitled version of the *Rocky and His Friends* series, previously broadcast on ABC from 1959 to 1961. Again, Rocky, the flying squirrel, and Bullwinkle, the moose, tangle with the nefarious Mr. Big, a midget with grandiose ideas, and his two Russian agents, Boris Badenov and Natasha Fatale, in two cliffhanging episodes.

Other holdovers from the former series were "Aesop and Son," "Fractured Fairy Tales" (which alternated each week with "Aesop and Son"), "Peabody's Improbable History" and "Mr. Know-It-All." (For episode titles of each see *Rocky and His Friends*.) Two new segments were added to the show: "Dudley Do-Right of the Mounties" (which rotated every week with "Aesop and Son"), repackaged later as *The Dudley Do-Right Show*, and "Bullwinkle's Corner," short, nonsensical poetry readings by the famed cartoon moose.

In 1981, after eight years off network television, the series returned for a brief run on NBC, then 10 years later for a short run in prime time on CBS as part of the network's Wednesday-night anthology series "Toon Night." Nickelodeon then picked up the series, repeating it on weeknights (under the title of *Bullwinkle's Moose-A-Rama*) from 1992 to 1996. After its final year on Nick, the program returned in reruns on Cartoon Network and Boomerang as *The Rocky and Bullwinkle Show*.

In 2006, the series, under the name *Bullwinkle and Friends*, joined the children's programming lineup of the Black Family Channel (formerly the MBC Network), first daily and then on Saturdays along with *King Leonardo and His Short Subjects*. *A Jay Ward Production in association with Producers Associates for Television. Color. Half-hour. Premiered on NBC: September 24, 1961–September 15, 1963. Rebroadcast on NBC: September 21, 1963–September 5, 1964. Rebroadcast on ABC: September 20, 1964–September 2, 1973. Rebroadcast on NBC: September 12, 1981–July 24, 1982. Rebroadcast on CBS: May 29, 1991–June 12, 1991. Rebroadcast on NICK: August 3, 1992–May 31, 1996 (as Bullwinkle's Moose-A-Rama). Rebroadcast on CAR: June 3, 1996–October 5, 1996 (weekdays); March 2, 1998–March 3, 2002. Rebroadcast on BOOM: July 1, 2002–April 17, 2005. Rebroadcast on BFC: 2006.*

### Voices

**Bullwinkle:** Bill Scott; **Rocky/Natasha Fatale/Nell, Dudley's girlfriend:** June Foray; **Boris Badenov/Inspector Fenwick:** Paul Frees; **Aesop:** Charles Ruggles; **Peabody/Dudley Do-Right:** Bill Scott; **Sherman:** Walter Tetley; **Snidely Whiplash:** Hans Conried; **Narrators:** William Conrad ("Bullwinkle"), Edward Everett Horton; ("Fractured Fairy Tales"), Charles Ruggles ("Aesop and Son")

## ◎ BUMP IN THE NIGHT

Friendly, 10-inch creature Mr. Bumpy—who lives under the bed of a 10-year-old boy and has a penchant for eating socks and car keys—and his playmates wreak all sorts of havoc when they come to life at night in this weekly Saturday-morning series that combined stop-motion animation, live action and computer-animated inserts. ABC, which premiered the series in the fall of 1994 and had ownership interest in the program, took the unusual step of commissioning two years' worth of episodes before the series even debuted. Disney's takeover of Capital Cities/ABC spelled an end for the program. It was canceled in 1996 and later rebroadcast on Toon Disney.

*A Danger/Greengrass Production. Color. Half-hour. Premiered on ABC: September 10, 1994–August 31, 1996. Rebroadcast on ABC: September 1996–August 31, 1998. Rebroadcast on TDIS: April 18, 1998–April 1, 2001.*

### Voices

**Mr. Bumpy/Destructo/Closet Monster:** Jim Cummings; **Bumpsted:** Burke Moses; **Squishington:** Rob Paulsen; **Molly Coddle:** Gail Matthius; **Little Sister:** Anndi McAfee; **The Boy:** Scott McAfee; **Germ Girl:** Elizabeth Daily (as E.G. Daily); **Gloog:** Jeff Bennett; **Additional Voices:** Sheryl Bernstein, Emma Blackwell

## ◎ A BUNCH OF MUNSCH

Canadian humorist Robert Munsch's award-winning, wonderfully wacky children's tales (illustrated by Michael Martchenko) were adapted for this series of Canadian-produced half-hour animated specials, usually featuring two stories about young heroes and imaginary problems in each 30-minute program, often accompanied by original songs. The first Munsch special, "Thomas' Snowsuit and Fifty Below Zero," premiered on Canada's CTV. In the United States, the specials debuted on Showtime on December 17, 1991 and was added to Showtime's fall 1992 lineup, opposite *American Heroes and Legends*, as part of the network's hour-long block of kiddie-oriented programming. The series opener was "The Paper Bag Princess," about a feisty heroine who tilts a rappin', fire-breathing dragon. Additional half-hours included: "Pigs and David's Father," "Something Good and Mortimer," "Murmel, Murmel, Murmel and the Boy in the Drawer," "The Fire Station and Angela's Surprise" and "Blackberry Subway Jam" and "Moira's Birthday." *A CINAR Film Production in association with CTV. Color. Half-hour. Premiered on SHO: December 17, 1991.*

### Voices

Julian Bailey, Sonja Ball, Rick Jones, Gordon Masten, Michael O'Reilly, Anik Matern, Liz MacRae, Mark Hellman, Lianne Picard-Poirier, Matthew Barrot, Tia Caroleo, Jesse Gryn, Lisa Hull, Kaya Scott, Vlasta Vrana, Carlysle Miller, Haley Reynolds, Gabriel Taraboulsy, Michael Rudder, Bronwen Mantel, Carlyle Miller, Terrence Scammell, Kathleen Fee, Harry Standjofsky, Thor Bishopric, Patricia Rodriguez, Norman Groulx, Jory Steinberg, Christian Tessier, Amy Fulco, Eramelinda Boquer, Tamar Kozlov, Richard Dumont, George Morris, Jacob D. Tierney, June Wallack, Andrew Bauer-Gabor, Holly Frankel-Gauthier, A.J. Henderson, Shayne Olszynko-Gryn, Jane Woods

## ◎ THE BUSY WORLD OF RICHARD SCARRY

Set in the happy accident-prone burg of Busytown, this weekly half-hour series, based on the popular Scarry storybooks, followed the exploits of funny animal characters Huckle Cat, Lowly Worm and Grouchy Mr. Gronkle. The internationally coproduced series—a cooperative venture between Cinar France Animation in Canada, Paramount Pictures and the British Broadcasting Corporation, Showtime Networks and the Family Channel—aired Wednesday nights on Showtime, beginning in March of 1994.

The series was brought back with all-new episodes in the fall of that year. In the summer of 1995, while episodes continued to air on Showtime, the series began airing weekdays (in reruns) on Nickelodeon. *A CINAR France Animation/France Co-Production in association with Paramount Pictures/Beta Films/British Broadcasting Corp./Showtime Networks/The Family Channel/Canada's Family Network/Canal J/France 3/Crayon Animation. Color. Half-hour. Premiered on SHO: March 9, 1994. Rebroadcast on NICK: July 3, 1995–May 2000 (weekdays).*

*Celebrated children's book author Richard Scarry's popular storybooks following the adventures of Huckle Cat, Lowly Worm and grouchy Mr. Gronkle were the basis for the weekly half-hour series* The Busy World of Richard Scarry. © *CINAR Films. All rights reserved.*

*Voices*
Keith Knight, Sonja Ball, Phillip Williams, John Stocker, Peter Wildman, Don Dickinson, Paul Haddad, Len Carlson, Judy Marshak, Cathy Gallant, Tara Meyer, Jeremy Ratchford, Keith Hampshire

## ◎ BUTCH CASSIDY AND THE SUN DANCE KIDS

U.S. government agents work undercover as the rock group Butch Cassidy and the Sun Dance Kids, consisting of teenagers Butch, Merilee, Harvey and Stephanie. Stories depicted the World Wide Talent agency team and its dog, Elvis, engaged in dangerous, global spy adventures represented in 13 half-hour programs. *A Hanna-Barbera Production. Color. Half-hour. Premiered on NBC: September 8, 1973–August 31, 1974.*

*Voices*
**Butch:** Chip Hand; **Merilee:** Judi Strangis; **Harvey:** Micky Dolenz; **Stephanie (Steffy):** Tina Holland; **Elvis:** Frank Welker; **Mr. Socrates:** John Stephenson

## ◎ BUTT-UGLY MARTIANS

In the year 2053, an evil Martian emperor's (Bog) plans to conquer the planet are thwarted by three teenage space jockeys—B-Bop-A-Luna, 2-T Fru-T and Do-Wah Diddy—and their robotic pet, Dog, in this futuristic, CGI-animated, British-American series first broadcast on British television in January 2001 and then in the United States on Nickelodeon in November of that year. The 26-episode series ended its run on Nick in April 2002, and was then rebroadcast on Nickelodeon's offspring channel, Nicktoons. *A Just Group/Mike Young Productions/DCDC Studios/Polygram/Universal Production. Color. Half-hour. Premiered on NICK: November 9, 2001–April 7, 2002. Rebroadcast on NICKT: 2002–.*

*Voices*
**Cedric:** Olgie Banks; **Dr. Damage/Emperor Bog/Dr. Brady Hackshaw:** S. Scott Bullock; **Do-Wah Diddy:** Jess Harnell; **2-T Fru-T/Mike/Ronald/Dark Comet:** Rob Paulsen; **B-Bop-A-Luna:** Charlie Schlatter; **Angela/Shaboom-Shaboom:** Kath Soucie; **Stoat Muldoon:** Robert Stack

## ◎ THE BUZZ ON MAGGIE

Inspired antics (told from her point of view) of a creative, expressive 'tween fly named Maggie, in the booming fly metropolis of Stickyfeet, with her brothers Aldrin and Pupert and her best friend Rayna, who lives her life with exuberance whether it's handling her daily routine or other challenges she faces, inevitably creating an undesirable outcome she never counts on in this animated children's series for the Disney Channel.

Produced by Walt Disney Television Animation and executive produced by Laura Perkins Brittain (of Disney Channel's *That's So Raven* sitcom fame), the half-hour daily, Flash-animated cartoon series, created by Dave Polsky and directed by David Wasson (creator of Cartoon Network's *Time Squad*), bowed on the Disney Channel in June 2005 with 21 half-hour programs consisting of two episodes per show and lasting only one season. Episodes were then rebroadcast daily. *A Walt Disney Television Animation/Bardel Entertainment/Future Thought Production. Color. Half-hour. Premiered on DIS: June 17, 2005.*

*Voices*
**Maggie:** Jessica Dicicco; **Aldrin, her older brother:** David Kaufman; **Pupert, her younger brother:** Thom Advoc; **Rayna Cartflight, her best friend:** Cree Summer; **Dawn Swatworthy, Aldrin's girlfriend:** Tara Strong; **Frieda Pesky/Principal Peststrip:** Susan Tolsky; **Chauncey Pesky:** Brian Doyle-Murray; **Principal Peststrip:** Susan Tolsky; **Laura:** Jodi Benson; **George:** Patrick Warburton; **Mr. Bugspit:** Curtis Armstrong; **Eugene/Wendell:** Billy West; **Lacey Ladybug:** Laraine Brewer; **Other Voices:** Dee Bradley Baker, Tom Kenny

## ◎ CADILLACS & DINOSAURS

Set in the 26th century, right after a global meltdown of epic proportions, dinosaurs roam Earth and classic cars race a group of underground woolly mammoths (known as The Mechanics), while two survivors, Jack Tenrac and Hannah Dundee, search for ways to make it in the "Xenozoic" era in this Saturday-morning cartoon adaptation of the popular comic book by writer/artist Mark Schultz. Developed by Steven E. de Souza, writer of such big-screen action hits as *Die Hard* and *Commando*, the action/adventures series premiered on CBS.

*A Nelvana Entertainment/Galaxy Films/deSouza Production. Color. Half-hour. Premiered on CBS: September 18, 1993–March 11, 1994.*

*Voices*
**Jack:** David Keeley; **Hannah:** Susan Roman; **Mustapha:** Bruce Tubbe; **Scharnhorst:** Dawn Greenhaigh; **Hammer:** Tedd Dillon; **Wrench:** Colin O'Meara; **Vice:** Frank Pellegrino; **Kirgo:** David Fox; **Grith/Hobbs:** Don Francks; **Dahlgren:** Kristina Nicoll; **Toulouse:** Philip Williams; **Mikla:** Lenora Zann; **Noe:** Don Dickinson

## ◎ CAILLOU (A.K.A. CAILLOU AND FRIENDS)

Displaying an amazing curiosity and wonder for his age, Caillou, a balding, four-year-old boy, finds a world of adventure around him with his friends, exploring thought-provoking subjects focused on the social and emotional growth of young children in this live-action/animated series. Based on the popular children's books first published in 1987 by Les Editions Chouette, this half-hour children's series was the second adaptation of the character following the 65-episode cartoon series—produced by Canada's CINAR (later renamed Cookie Jar Animation)—that premiered in late 1997 in Canada and other markets worldwide, except in the United States, which began airing this 40-episode version (a mix of five-minute cartoon episodes, puppets, music and live-action segments with children, puppets and music) on PBS stations. In 2003, 16 brand-new 30-minute adventures were added before the show, available in both French and English versions, it went on hiatus for three seasons, until it returned in 2006 with brand-new episodes that aired weekdays on PBS Kids. A year earlier, the popular children's program began re-airing on PBS's new digital cable channel and video-demand-service (VOD), PBS Kids Sprout. *A CINAR/Cookie Jar Production. Half-hour. Premiered on PBS: September 4, 2000–September 24, 2003; April 12, 2006 (new episodes). Rebroadcast on PBS Kids Sprout (VOD): April 4, 2005–. Rebroadcast on PBS Kids Sprout (digital cable): September 26, 2005–.*

*Voices*
**Caillou:** Jaclyn Linetsky; **Caillou's Mom:** Jennifer Seguin; **Caillou's Dad:** Pat Fry; **Rosie/Clementine:** Brigid Tierney; **Gilbert Felinieus:** Bob Stutt; **Rexy:** Pier Kohl; **Teddy:** Matt Ficner; **Deidi:** Tim Gosley; **Storyteller:** Marlee Shapiro; **Leo:** Jonathan Koensgen; **Julie:** Holly Gauthier-Frankel

## ◎ THE CALIFORNIA RAISINS

In this 13 episode Saturday-morning series spinoff that aired on CBS, Will Vinton's "Claymation" stars, noted for their Motown-style singing, take viewers on a "Magical Mystery Tour" from a penthouse above their recording studio, accompanied by their hapless show-biz manager. The Raisins were introduced in 1987, in a series of popular commercials for California raisin growers. A *Murakami-Wolf-Swenson Films Production. Color. Half-hour. Premiered on CBS: September 16, 1989–September 8, 1990.*

**Voices**
Cam Clarke, Dorian Harewood, Jim Cummings, Brian Mitchell, Cree Summer, Rebecca Summers, Gailee Heideman, Michelle Marianna, Todd Tolces, Brian Cummings

## ◎ CALVIN AND THE COLONEL

Loosely patterned after their long-running radio series *Amos 'n' Andy*, Freeman Gosden and Charles Correll created this animated series featuring the comedy mishaps of two Southern backwoods animals—the shrewd fox, Colonel Montgomery J. Klaxon, and his dimwitted, cigar-smoking bear friend, Calvin Burnside. The series premiered in prime time on ABC on October 3, 1961, opposite the CBS hit comedy series *Dobie Gillis*. The program faltered so ABC yanked the show from its nighttime slot and returned it to the airwaves in January 1962, adding it to the network's Saturday-morning lineup to finish out the season. A *Kayro Production. Color. Half-hour. Premiered on ABC: October 3, 1961–October 31, 1961; January 27, 1962–September 22, 1962. Syndicated.*

**Voices**
**Colonel Montgomery J. Klaxon:** Freeman Gosden; **Maggie Belle Klaxon, his wife:** Virginia Gregg; **Calvin Burnside:** Charles Correll; **Sister Sue:** Beatrice Kay; **Gladys:** Gloria Blondell; **Oliver Wendell Clutch, lawyer:** Paul Frees

## ◎ CAMP CANDY

A group of smart-mouthed kids spend summer under the supervision of their camp director, John Candy, the head counselor, head cook and head handyman of Camp Candy, who helps make camp life a special experience for everyone. This half-hour animated series, composed of 39 episodes, ran for two seasons on NBC. The program was honored with the Humanitas Award for the 1991 episode "Wish Upon a Fish." The series entered daily syndication in 1992, after its network run. Providing additional voices on the program were Eugene Levy, Andrea Martin and Dave Thomas, formerly costars with Candy NBC's *SCTV* series. A *DIC Enterprises Frostback/Saban Production. Color. Half-hour. Premiered on NBC: September 2, 1989–September 7, 1991. Syndicated: 1992. Rebroadcast on FOX FAM: August 17, 1998–May 25, 2001.*

**Voices**
**John:** John Candy; **Binky:** Tony Ail; **Rex de Forest:** Lewis Arquette; **Nurse Molly:** Valri Bromfield; **Iggy:** Tom Davidson; **Robin:** Danielle Fernandes, Cree Summer Francks; **Vanessa:** Willow Johnson; **Botch:** Brian George; **Chester:** Danny Mann; **Duncan:** Gary MacPherson; **Rick:** Andrew Seebaran; **Alex:** Chiara Zanni

## ◎ CAMP LAZLO

While summering at that special place, Camp Kidney, in rustic cabins bearing the name of every kind of bean and surrounded by the serene Pimpleback Mountains, an energetic Bean Scout Brazilian monkey named Lazlo and his two best friends, the wise, neurotic elephant, Raj, and smart albino pygmy rhino, Clam, create havoc for their Scoutmaster moose, Alongquin C. Lumpus, in wacky Boy Scout-type adventures in this original series created by Joe Murray (of Nickelodeon's *Rocko's Modern Life* fame). Initially broadcast Friday nights in prime time on Cartoon Network in

July–September 2005, the network ordered 26 half-hours, with 13 of them comprised of two 11-minute episodes except for two episodes, that aired during each of the next two seasons through June 2006. On July 4, the series kicked off its third season with 11 new half-hours, airing Monday through Friday nights, which was to include the series' first prime time special, the *Camp Lazlo Thanksgiving Special*, in 2006 but it never aired.

Lending their voices as the animal characters on the series were Carlos Alazraqui, Tom Kenny (alias *SpongeBob SquarePants*) and Doug Lawrence (credited as Mr. Lawrence), who did considerable voice work on *Rocko's Modern Life*, along with veteran voice Jeff Bennett, first-timer Steve Little, Broadway actress Jodi Benson and Kenny's wife, Jill Talley.

During its original network run, the series was honored with an Emmy nomination for the episode "Hello Dolly/Overcooked Beans," and three Pulcinella Awards for best TV series, best series for children and best character by Cartoons on the Bay in Positano, Italy. A *Cartoon Network Studios Production. Color. Half-hour. Premiered on CAR: July 8, 2005–September 16, 2005 (1st season), October 1, 2005–June 29, 2006 (2nd season); July 4, 2006–November 1, 2006 (3rd season).*

**Voices**
**Lazlo/Clam/Chef Mcmuesli:** Carlos Alazraqui; **Raj/Samson/Commander Hoo Ha/Various Campers:** Jeff Bennett; **Algonquin C. Lumpus/Slinkman/Various Campers:** Tom Kenny; **Edward/Dave/Ping Pong/Nurse Leslie:** Mr. Lawrence; **Patsy Smiles/Jane Doe/Almondine:** Jodi Benson; **Nina Neckerly/Gretchen/Miss Mucus:** Jill Talley; **Chip/Skip/The Lemmings/Various Campers:** Steve Little

## ◎ CANTIFLAS

This series of 52 six-minute cartoons, produced in Mexico by Hanna-Barbera and Diamex S.A., featured the popular Mexican film comedian in entertaining and educational adventures. (See *Amigo and Friends* for details.) First syndicated in America in 1980 under the umbrella title *Amigo and Friends*, the half-hour series featured four cartoon episodes each half-hour, redubbed in English. The package was later resyndicated under the *Cantiflas* title in a bilingual format. A *Hanna-Barbera/Diamex S.A./Televisa S.A. Production. Color. Half-hour. Premiered: 1980–1982. Syndicated.*

**Voices**
**Cantiflas (a.k.a. Amigo):** Don Messick; **Narrator:** John Stephenson

## ◎ CAPITOL CRITTERS

Max, a young field mouse from Nebraska (voiced by Neil Patrick of TV's *Doogie Howser*), moves into the critter-cluttered basement of the White House with his new family of friends—Berkley, a hippie mouse; Trixie, a wise cockroach; Jammet, a combat veteran squirrel; and Mugger, a lab rat survivor—in this short-lived half-hour animated series that poked fun at politics and life in the nation's capital. ABC premiered the series on Tuesday night, January 25, 1992, with a "sneak preview." (The series normally aired on Saturday nights.) Producer Steven Bocho (of *Hill Street Blues* and *St. Elsewhere* fame) and Nat Mauldin, son of Pulitzer Prize–winning cartoonist Bill Mauldin, co-created the series, which never caught on with viewers. A *Steven Bocho Production in association with Hanna-Barbera Productions. Color. Half-hour. Premiered on ABC: January 28, 1992 (sneak preview); January 31, 1992–March 14, 1992. Rebroadcast on CAR: November 11, 1995–December 29, 1996 (Saturdays, Sundays).*

*Voices*

**Max:** Neil Patrick Harris; **Muggle:** Bobcat Goldthwait; **Moze:** Dorian Harewood; **Berkeley:** Jennifer Darling; **Trixie:** Patti Deutsch; **Presidential Felines:** Frank Welker

## ◎ CAPTAIN CAVEMAN AND THE TEEN ANGELS

The idea of three luscious nubile sleuths named "Charlie's Angels" in teasing one-hour TV dramas uncorked several parodies and late-night variety-show spoofs. This animated knock off featured a primitive supersleuth caveman and his three Teen Angels (Dee Dee, Brenda and Taffy) in tame but clever half-hour mysteries. Episodes originally aired as part of *Scooby's All-Star Laff-A-Lympics* and *Scooby's All-Stars* and were repeated in this half-hour series. (It replaced ABC's *Spider-Woman*.) During the 1980–81 season, Captain Caveman returned in new adventures on *The Flintstones Comedy Show*, which was broadcast on NBC. In 1989 the series was shown in reruns on USA Network's *Cartoon Express*. (See *Scooby's All-Star Laff-A-Lympics* for voice credits.) A *Hanna-Barbera Production. Color. Half-hour. Premiered on ABC: March 8, 1980–June 21, 1980. Rebroadcast on USA: February 20, 1989–March 19, 1991. Rebroadcast on BOOM: February 28, 2001–.*

## ◎ CAPTAIN FATHOM

Filmed in "Superanivision," this 1966 animated series, whose pilot was filmed four years earlier, follows the adventures of a submarine captain and his battle against evil in this underwater counterpart of Cambria Studios' *Clutch Cargo* and *Space Angel* series. The series was produced in the same limited illustrative art style and also using the famed "Syncro-Vox" process in which live-action footage of the actors' mouths were superimposed on the cartoon characters' faces. The series consisted of 195 five-minute serialized color adventures that had no story titles but were numbered in order of production. First offered for local syndication in 1966, episodes from the series were shown along with various other cartoons and short subjects as part of the syndicated afternoon kiddie show *Capt. 'n Sailor Bird*, hosted in cartoon wraparounds by a talking parrot, distributed by Sterling Films.

A *Cambria Studios Production. Black-and-white. Color. Half-hour. Premiered 1966. Syndicated.*

*Voices*

**Captain Fathom:** Warren Tufts; **Other Voices:** Margaret Kerry, Hal Smith, Tom Brown, Ned LeFebvre

## ◎ CAPTAIN HARLOCK AND THE QUEEN OF 1,000 YEARS

The aging queen and members of a nomadic planet, Millenia, plan to invade Earth and claim it as their new homeland. Earth's only hope against this alien threat is Captain Harlock, head of an interstellar space galleon, who protects and defends his home planet. A *Toei Co. Ltd./Ziv International Harmony Gold Production. Color. Half-hour. Premiered: September 1985. Syndicated.*

## ◎ CAPTAIN INVENTORY

Various network-run series from Hanna-Barbera's cartoon library were redistributed to television via syndication for local programming. The program rotated adventures from the following: *Birdman and the Galaxy Trio, The Fantastic Four, Frankenstein Jr. and the Impossibles, Herculoids, Moby Dick and the Mighty Mightor, Shazzan!* and *The Space Ghost and Dino Boy*. (See individual series for details.) A *Hanna-Barbera Production. Color. Half-hour. Premiered: 1973. Syndicated.*

## ◎ CAPTAIN N AND THE ADVENTURES OF THE SUPER MARIO BROS. 3

Combining two of its most popular franchises, NBC premiered this hourlong Saturday-morning show in the fall of 1991, featuring half-hour reruns of *Captain N: The Game Master* (one per show) and two new 10-minute *Super Mario Bros. 3* cartoons that lasted for one season. Each program was offered as individual half-hours for syndication with the *Super Mario Bros. 3* show airing only on USA Network from 1991 to 1995 and the former hour show re-airing on the Family Channel from 1992 to 1994. (For voice credits, see *Captain N: Game Master* and *Super Mario Bros. Super Show!*). A *DIC Enterprises Production in association with Nintendo America Incorporated and Ulacom. Color. Half-hour. Premiered on NBC: September 8, 1990–September 7, 1991. Rebroadcast on FAM: 1992–1994. Rebroadcast on USA: September 1991–Summer 1995 (as Super Mario Bros. 3 only).*

## ◎ CAPTAIN N AND THE NEW SUPER MARIO WORLD

Returning for a third season was this retitled half-hour digest menagerie featuring reruns and 10 new 10-minute cartoons (one per show) of the video game–inspired, *Captain N*, and 13 new *Super Mario World* (one per half-hour), including cartoons based on another well-known Nintendo character "Gameboy" that lasted one season and then was rebroadcast on the Family Channel. A *DIC Enterprises Production in association with Nintendo America Incorporated and Ulacom. Color. Half-hour. Premiered on NBC: September 14, 1991–July 25, 1992. Rebroadcast on FAM: 1992–1994.*

*Voices*

**CAPTAIN N: Kevin Keene/Captain N/Narrator:** Matt Hill; **King Hippo:** Gary Chalk; **Dr. Wiley:** Ian James Corlett; **Eggplant Wizard:** Mike Donovan; **Kid Icarus:** Alessandro Juliani; **Simon Belmont:** Andrew Kavadas; **MegaMan:** Doug Parker; **Princess Lana:** Venus Terzo; **Duke:** Tomm Wright; **Mother Brain:** Levi Stubbs Jr.

**SUPER MARIO WORLD: Mario:** Walker Boone; **Luigi:** Tony Rosato; **King Koopa:** Harvey Atkin; **Kootie Pie Koopa:** Paulina Gillis; **Big Mouth Koopa:** Dan Hennessey; **Bully Koopa:** Gordan Masten; **Cheatsy Koopa:** James Rankin; **KookyVon Koopa:** Michael Stark; **Hip and Hop Koopa:** Tara Charendoff; **Princess Toadstool:** Tracey Moore; **Yoshi:** Andrew Sabiston; **Oogtar/Toad:** John Stocker

## ◎ CAPTAIN N: THE GAME MASTER

Keven Keene, a young Nintendo gamestar, is "sucked" into his TV set and becomes Captain N, the ultimate hero who saves Videoland from the evil machinations of Mother Brain and her host of video villains, including King Hippo and the Eggplant Wizard. Along with his loyal dog, Duke, Kevin pulls together the disorganized heroes of Videoland—Simon Belmont, Mega Man and Kid Icarus—to become The N-Team, charged with keeping Princess Lana in power and holding the forces of evil at bay. The 1989 series, broadcast on NBC, was based on the phenomenally successful Nintendo game Captain N: The Game Master. The series returned for a second season in 1990 and was made part of a 60-minute block known as *Captain N: The Adventures of the Super Mario Bros. 3.* Captain N and the Super Mario Brothers were featured in half-hour shows back to back, with three other Nintendo properties—Zelda, Gameboy and Link—in animated adventures. In 1991 the program block returned for a third and final season on NBC, retitled *Captain N and the New Super Mario World.* The series was canceled a year later after NBC stopped producing cartoons for Saturday morning. The series was syndicated to television nationwide in 1992 under the name of *Captain N and the Video Game Masters*. A *DIC Enterprises Production in association with Nintendo of*

America, Inc. Color. Half-hour. Premiered on NBC: September 9, 1989–September 1, 1990. Premiered on NBC (as Captain N and the Adventures of the Super Mario Brothers 3): September 8, 1990–September 7, 1991. Premiered on NBC (as Captain N and the New Super Mario World): September 14, 1991–July 25, 1992. Syndicated: Fall 1992. Rebroadcast on WGN/FAM: Early 1990s.

### Voices

**CAPTAIN N: Kevin Keene/Captain N:** Matt Hill; **King Hippo:** Gary Chalk; **Dr. Wiley:** Ian James Corlett; **Eggplant Wizard:** Mike Donovan; **Kid Icarus:** Alessandro Juliani; **Simon Belmont:** Andrew Kavadas; **MegaMan:** Doug Parker; **Princess Lana:** Venus Terzo; **Duke:** Tomm Wright; **Mother Brain:** Levi Stubbs Jr.; **Narrator:** Matt Hill

**SUPER MARIO BROS. 3: Mario:** Walker Boone; **Luigi:** Tony Rosato; **Princess Toadstool:** Tracey Moore; **Toad:** John Stocker; **Koopa:** Harvey Atkin; **Cheatsy:** James Rankin; **Kooky:** Michael Stark; **Kootie Pie:** Paulina Gillis; **Big Mouth:** Gordon Masten; **Bully:** Dan Hennessey; **Hip:** Stuart Stone; **Hop:** Tara Charendof

### ⊚ CAPTAIN PLANET AND THE PLANETEERS

The world's first environmental superhero (originally to be voiced by actor Tom Cruise) and his heroic quintet—Kwame (Earth), Linka (Wind), Ma-Ti (Heart), Gi (Water) and Wheeler (Fire)—each bestowed with special powers, team up to rid the world of eco-villains (Hoggish Greedly, Verminous Skumm, Duke Nukem, Sly Sludge, Dr. Blight and others) who are polluting and plundering Earth's resources in this long-running weekly animated series, based on an original idea by media mogul Ted Turner, founder of superstation WTBS and the Turner networks.

Simultaneously premiering on TBS and 223 independent stations in the fall of 1990, the series (which opened with the episode "A Hero for Earth") was developed in close collaboration with Burbank, California–based cartoon studio DIC Enterprises, which produced the series for the first three seasons until 1993. Production was taken over by Hanna-Barbera beginning with the 1994–95 season, the show's fourth and final season of original episodes (retitled The New Adventures of Captain Planet). Following the show's 1990 debut, the series became a showcase for Hollywood's environmental activism. Many major Hollywood stars lent their voices to the series (including Elizabeth Taylor, who played Donna, the mother of a young boy—voiced by Doogie Howser's Neil Patrick Harris—who tested positive for HIV, a switch from the series' usually eco-conscious story lines), all working for scale, and each episode focused on different environmental concerns. In 1995 the series was rebroadcast on Cartoon Network.

On April 23, 2005, the groundbreaking, environmentally themed series returned to the airwaves on Cartoon Network's classic cartoons network, Boomerang. On April 22 of the following year, in honor of Earth Day, Boomerang treated U.S. television audiences to an exclusive presentation of the program's never-before-seen 13 half-hour episodes from the sixth and final season as part of a special two-hour marathon. A DIC Entertainment/Hanna-Barbera Cartoons/TBS Production. Color. Half-hour. Premiered on TBS and Syndication: September 10, 1990. Rebroadcast on CAR: March 25, 1995 (episode "Tears in the Hood," part of "Stop the Violence Week"); September 5, 1995–(weekdays). Rebroadcast on BOOM: April 23, 2005–. Syndicated: July 10, 2005.

### Voices

**Captain Planet:** David Coburn; **Kwame:** Levar Burton; **Wheeler:** Joey Dedio; **Gi:** Janice Kawaye; **Ma-Ti:** Scott Menville; **Linka:**
Kath Soucie; **Sushi the Monkey/Lead Suit:** Frank Welker; **Gaia:** Whoopi Goldberg, Margot Kidder

**POLLUTING PERPETRATORS: Hoggish Greedly:** Ed Asner; **Hoggish Greedly Jr.:** Charlie Schlater; **Dr. Blight:** Meg Ryan, Mary Kay Bergman; **Argos Bleak:** S. Scott Bullock; **Looten Plunder:** James Coburn; **Jane Goodair:** Phyllis Diller; **Commander Clash:** Louis Gossett Jr.; **MAL:** Tim Curry, David Rappaport; **Verminous Skumm:** Jeff Goldblum, Maurice LaMarche; **Rigger:** John Ratzenberger; **Sly Sludge:** Martin Sheen; **Zarm:** Sting, David Warner; **Duke Nukem:** Dean Stockwell, Maurice LaMarche; **Ooze:** Cam Clarke

### ⊚ CAPTAIN SIMIAN AND THE SPACE MONKEYS

A lost-in-space NASA astro-chimp named Charlie (supposedly one of the original chimpanzee astronauts back in the Sputnik era) is captured by a group of fed-up superintelligent aliens who turn him into the new defender of the universe. Joined by an intelligent all-primate space crew, he sets out to conquer the once-powerful Lord Nebula and his minions who want to take over the universe in this 26-episode half-hour science-fiction cartoon series, made for first-run syndication. Voice regulars included Babylon 5's Jerry Doyle as Captain Simian and Star Trek's Michael Dorn as the

A lost-in-space astro chimp heads a team of outer space primates who protect the universe in Captain Simian and the Space Monkeys. © Hallmark Entertainment/Monkeyshine Productions

archvillian Nebula. *A Monkeyshine/Hallmark Entertainment Production in association with Epoc Ink/Toon Us In. Color. Half-hour. Premiered: September 2, 1996. Syndicated.*

*Voices*
**Captain Simian:** Jerry Doyle; **Gor:** James Avery; **Spider:** Dom Irrera; **Splittzy:** Maurice LaMarche; **Shao Lin:** Karen Maruyama; **Rhesus 2:** Malcolm McDowell; **Apax:** Frank Welker; **Orbitron:** Jeff Bennett; **Nebula:** Michael Dorn; **The " ":** Oliver Muirhead

## ⊚ CARDCAPTORS

After accidentally setting loose the world's most powerful magic cards called Clow Cards, each of which possesses fantastical forces of nature, 10-year-old fourth-grader Sakura Kinomoto and her mysterious classmate, Li, set out to find and capture the destructive cards before they unleash their fury on an unsuspecting world and to head off a major global disaster in the making in this English-dubbed imported version of the popular Japanese anime series, *Card Captor Sakura.* Coproduced by Canada's Nelvana studios, the magical half-hour adventure series premiered on Saturday, July 17, 2000, on Kids' WB! Airing Saturday mornings at 9:30 A.M. (ET), the show featured 38 of the Japanese series' original 70 episodes redubbed in English. Reruns of the series were aired on the Cartoon Network. *A Madhouse Productions/CLAMP/Kodansha Ltd./Nelvana Limited/NHK Enterprises 21/NEP 21/Sogo Vision/Ocean Group Production. Color. Half-hour. Premiered on Kids' WB!: June 17, 2000–December 14, 2001. Rebroadcast on CAR: June 4, 2001–September 21, 2001.*

*Voices*
**Sakura Avalon:** Carly McKillip; **Li Showron:** Rhys Huber; **Lil Showron #2:** Jordon Killik; **Keroberos:** Matt Hill, Richard Newman; **Madison Taylor:** Maggie Blue O'Hara; **Tori Avalon:** Tony Sampson; **Julian Star:** Sam Vincent; **Aiden Avalon/Mr. Terada:** Brian Drummond; **Layla MacKenzie:** Linda Rae; **Nikki:** Kelly Sheridan; **Chelsea:** Jocelyne Lowen; **Natasha:** Janyse Jaud; **Ruby:** Sarah Lafleur; **Sakura's Dad:** Kirby Morrow; **Eli Moon:** Bill Switzer

## ⊚ THE CARE BEARS (1985)

The lovable bears of Care-A-Lot come down to Earth in their cloud mobiles to help children with their problems. Along with the Care Bear Cousins, who live in the Forest of Feelings, the Care Bears make the world a happier place with their motto of caring and sharing. First series to be based on the popular children's book characters. *A DIC Enterprises Production. Color. Half-hour. Premiered: September 14, 1985–86. Syndicated. Rebroadcast on DIS: 1990–97. Rebroadcast on TDIS: April 17, 1998–September 1, 2002.*

*Voices*
**Tenderheart Bear:** Billie Mae Richards; **Friend Bear:** Eva Almos; **Grumpy Bear:** Bobby Dermie; **Birthday Bear:** Melleny Brown; **Bedtime Bear:** Laurie Waller Benson; **Love A Lot Bear:** Linda Sorenson; **Wish Bear:** Janet Lane Green; **Good Luck Bear:** Dan Hennessy; **Share Bear:** Patrice Black; **Champ Bear:** Terry Sears

*Care Bear Cousins*
**Brave Heart Lion/Loyal Heart Dog:** Dan Hennessy; **Gentle Heart Lamb:** Luba Goy; **Swift Heart Rabbit:** Eva Almos; **Bright Heart Raccoon:** Jim Henshaw; **Lotsa Heart Elephant:** Luba Goy; **Playful Heart Monkey:** Marla Lukovsky; **Proud Heart Cat:** Louise Vallance; **Cozy Heart Penguin/Treat Heart Pig:** Pauline Penny

## ⊚ CARE BEARS (1988)

Tenderheart, Grumpy, Cheer, Champ, Grams Bear, Hugs and Tugs are but a few of the cuddly characters of Care-A-Lot, a place where feelings of "caring" are expressed by symbols on the tummies of the bears in this syndication version of the hit ABC Saturday-morning series, *The Care Bears Family.* The series combined old episodes from the former plus additional new episodes. (See *The Care Bears Family* for voice credits.) *A Nelvana Limited Production. Half-hour. Color. Premiered: September 1988. Syndicated. Rebroadcast on DIS: 1990–1997. Rebroadcast on TDIS: September 7, 1998–August 30, 2002.*

## ⊚ THE CARE BEARS FAMILY

Based on the hit motion picture, each of the bears, from the founding fathers to the little cubs, represent an individual human emotion in brand-new adventures of this Canadian-produced Saturday-morning series that aired on ABC beginning in 1986. A total of 27 episodes were produced for the first season. The program was so well received that ABC renewed it for a second season, which combined 10 new episodes with old ones. The series went straight into syndication following the end of its network run under the title *Care Bears.* Canadian animation house Nelvana Enterprises, which produced the series, also produced three feature-length films starring the cuddly characters. *A Nelvana Production. Color. Half-hour. Premiered on ABC: September 13, 1986–September 5, 1987; September 26, 1987–January 23, 1988. Syndicated: 1988–90. Rebroadcast on DIS: 1990–97. Rebroadcast on TDIS: April 17, 1998–September 1, 2002.*

*Voices*
**Grumpy Bear:** Bob Dermie; **Brave Heart Lion/Loyal Heart Dog/Good Luck Bear:** Dan Hennessey; **Mr. Beastley:** John Stocker; **Birthday Bear:** Melleny Brown; **Lotsa Heart Elephant/Gentle Heart Lamb;** Luba Goy; **Tenderheart Bear:** Billie Mae Richards

## ⊚ CARTOON CLASSICS SERIALS

A collection of serialized animated features grouped and sold to more than 100 worldwide television markets in the 1960s. The package included science-fiction thrillers and fairy-tale classics segmented into cliffhanging episodes. The first package of cartoons went on the air in 1958, with additional fully animated stories syndicated in 1960 and 1965. Boxing promoter Bill Cayton, who entered television with his *Greatest Fights of the Century* series, produced the *Cartoon Classics Serials* series. (Cayton later served as boxing manager for heavyweight champion Mike Tyson.) *A Radio and Television Packagers/Banner Films Production. Color. Half-hour. Premiered 1958. Syndicated.*

## ⊚ CARTOON FUN

In the fall of 1965, ABC added this short-lived series to its Saturday-morning lineup. The half-hour program featured a collection of Jay Ward and Total Television characters seen in repeat episodes, among them Hoppity Hooper, Dudley Do-Right, Commander McBragg and Aesop and Son. (See original series entries for voice credits.) *A Producers Associates for Television Production. Color. Half-hour. Premiered on ABC: September 26, 1965–December 19, 1965.*

## ⊚ CARTOON SUSHI

Similar in format to MTV's successful anthology series *Liquid Television,* the network unveiled this fresh and funny collection of four or five animated short films from around the world from its own New York studio as a weekly series in July of 1997. The premiere episode featured John Dilworth's "Dirty Bird." *An MTV Animation Production. Color. Half-hour. Premiered on MTV: July 1997.*

## ⊚ CASPER

The lovable, friendly ghost, who still hates to scare people, has a whole new attitude (except for his revolting uncles) in this contemporary version of the famed theatrical cartoon star, based on the hit 1995 live-action/animated feature produced by Steven Spielberg. The 52-episode half-hour series, produced for Saturday-mornings, debuted on FOX Network as a midseason show in February 1996. The series won its time period every week that it aired and an Emmy during its first season. In the fall of 1997, the show was added to Fox's weekday afternoon schedule. Also known as "The Spooktacular New Adventures of Casper," the series ended its run in January 1998. *A Universal Cartoon Studios Production in association with Harvey Comics Entertainment. Color. Half-hour. Premiered on FOX: February 24, 1996–August 30, 1997; September 6, 1997–December 28, 1997. Rebroadcast on FOX: September 9, 1997–January 30, 1998 (weekdays).*

*Voices*

**Casper:** Malachie Pearson; **Spooky:** Rob Paulsen; **Kat:** Kath Soucie; **Stinkie/Gorey Narrator:** Joe Alaskey; **Dr. Harvey/Other Voices:** Dan Castellaneta; **Additional Voices:** Jack Angel.

### CASPER AND THE ANGELS

The year is 2179, and Casper the friendly ghost is assigned to help a pair of Space Patrol Officers, Minnie and Maxi, maintain law and order in Space City, tangling with cosmic criminals and solving space emergencies in the process. A new character featured in the series of 26 half-hour adventures (composed of two 11-minute cartoons per show) was the ghostly Hairy Scary, who provided comic relief. *A Hanna-Barbera Production. Color. Half-hour. Premiered on NBC: September 22, 1979–May 3, 1980. Rebroadcast on CAR: March 18, 1995–March 19, 1995 (Look What We Found!); December 1995 (70s Super Explosion)–1996. Rebroadcast on BOOM: June 4, 2001–.*

*Voices*

**Casper:** Julie McWhirter; **Hairy Scary, his assistant/Harry Scary/Commander:** John Stephenson; **Officer Minni:** Laurel Page; **Officer Maxie:** Diane McCannon

### CASPER THE FRIENDLY GHOST AND COMPANY

Repackaged version of previously exhibited Paramount Pictures cartoons—retitled "Harveytoons" in the early 1960s—starring Casper the Friendly Ghost, Baby Huey, Little Audrey and Herman and Katnip. The package was resyndicated in 1991 as *Casper and Friends* by Harvey Comics Entertainment. *A Paramount Cartoon Studios Production for Harvey Films. Color. Half-hour. Premiered: 1974, 1991. Syndicated.*

### CATDOG

Comical adventures of conjoined twins—the debonair, wise Cat and overly optimistic Dog—who live in a house shaped partly like a fish and bone and find fun and trouble being attached, and are joined by Nearburg residents Winslow Mouse and the scummy Greasers Gang (Cliff, Shriek and Lube). Created by Peter Hannan, the half-hour comedy series, featuring two 15-minute episodes per show, aired for two seasons on Nickelodeon. Yielding 66 half-hours during three seasons, on Thanksgiving Day 2000 the rollicking pair were also featured in a made-for-TV movie special, *CatDog Movie: CatDog and the Great Parent Mystery. A Peter Hannan Productions/Studio B/Viacom International Production. Color. Half-hour. Premiered on NICK: April 4, 1998. Rebroadcast on NICKT: May 1, 2002–.*

*Voices*

**Cat:** Jim Cummings; **Dog/Cliff:** Tom Kenny; **Winslow T. Oddfellow/Lube:** Carlos Alzraqui; **Shriek Dubois:** Maria Bamford; **Lola Caricola:** Nika Frost; **Dunglap/Mervis:** John Kassir; **Eddie the**

**Squirrel:** Dwight Schultz; **Rancid Rabbit/Mr. Sunshine/Randolph:** Billy West, Pete Zarustica

### CATSCRATCH

After their owner Mrs. Edna Cramdilly suddenly dies leaving them her mansion and her entire fortune, her manic millionaire kitty heirs, brothers Mr. Bilk, Gordon and Waffle, live a life of adventure, often with disastrous results, in this half-hour comedy cartoon series from creator and executive producer Doug TenNapel for Nickelodeon. With 19 original episodes broadcast over two seasons through mid-October 2006, in February 2007, Nick also aired the series' half-hour special, *Spindango Fundulation. A Nicktoons Production. Color. Half-hour. Premiered on NICK: July 9, 2005–.*

*Voices*

**Mr. Blik:** Wayne Knight; **Gordon/Randall:** Rob Paulsen; **Waffle:** Kevin McDonald; **Human Kimberly:** Liliana Mumy; **Hovis:** Maurice LaMarche; **The Chumpy Chumps:** John DiMaggio; **Bootsy:** Richard McGonagle; **Mitchell the Mammoth:** Jess Harnell; **Other Voices:** Frank Welker

### THE CATTANOOGA CATS

This all-animated series featured a feline rock group (Cheesie, Kitty Jo, Scoots, Groove and Country), who not only starred in segments of their own but also hosted the cartoon-filled show.

Cartoon segments were: "It's the Wolf," the madcap adventures of an overzealous wolf (Mildew) whose meal plans are based on snatching one elusive lamb named Lambsy; "Around the World in 79 Days," the globe-trotting adventures of Phineas Fogg Jr., who travels around the world with two teenage friends (Jenny and Happy) in 79 days instead of 80; and "Autocat and Motormouse," a cat and mouse who beat each other at a different game: race car competitions.

Following the first season, the program was reduced to a half-hour. *A Hanna-Barbera Production. Color. One hour. Half-hour. Premiered on ABC: September 6, 1969–September 5, 1970. Rebroadcast on ABC: September 12, 1970–September 5, 1971 (half hour). Rebroadcast on CAR: December 5, 1994–September 1, 1995 (weekdays). Rebroadcast on BOOM: May 13, 2000–November 3, 2007.*

*Voices*

**Cheesie/Kitty Jo:** Julie Bennett; **Scoots:** Jim Begg; **Groove:** Casey Kasem; **Country:** Bill Callaway; **Mildew, the wolf:** Paul Lynde; **Lambsy/Crumdon:** Daws Butler; **Bristle Hound, Lamby's protector/Bumbler:** Allan Melvin; **Phineas Fogg, Jr.:** Bruce Watson; **Jenny Trent:** Janet Waldo; **Happy/Smerky:** Don Messick; **Autocat:** Marty Ingels; **Motormouse:** Dick Curtis

### CAVE KIDS ADVENTURES

The Flintstones characters Pebbles and Bamm-Bamm appear as prehistoric preschoolers, along with babysitter Dino, in imaginative, lesson-teaching adventures in this half-hour animated series, produced for first-run syndication. *A Hanna-Barbera Production. Color. Half-hour. Premiered: 1996. Syndicated.*

*Voices*

**Pebbles:** Aria Noelle Curzon; **Bamm-Bamm:** Christine Cavanaugh; **Baby Pebbles:** Taylor Gunther; **Singing Bamm-Bamm:** E.G. Daily; **Dino:** Frank Welker

### C.B. BEARS

Three bruin investigators (Hustle, Bump and Boogie) travel in a rigged-up garbage truck (equipped with C.B. and closed-circuit TV) to solve mysteries and strange encounters. The three clumsy bears were lead-ins to five other cartoon regulars: "Shake, Rattle and Roll," the misadventures of three ghostly innkeepers in need of a rest; "Undercover Elephant," starring a bumbling secret agent in "Mission Impossible"–type situations; "Heyyy, It's the King," an animalized parody of Henry Winkler's "Fonzie" (now a smart-alecky lion) from TV's *Happy Days*; "Blast Off Buzzard," a Road Runner and Coyote re-creation casting a nonspeaking buzzard (Blast-Off) and snake (Crazylegs) in the title roles; and "Posse Impossible," the mishaps of three clumsy cowboys in the Old West. *A Hanna-Barbera Production. Color. One hour. Premiered on NBC: September 10, 1977–June 17, 1978. Rebroadcast on CAR: July 5, 1995–May 22, 2004. Rebroadcast on BOOM: January 5, 2002–July 17, 2004.*

*Voices*

**C.B. Bears: Hustle:** Daws Butler; **Bump:** Henry Corden; **Boogie:** Chuck McCann; **Charlie:** Susan Davis

**Shake, Rattle & Roll: Shake:** Paul Winchell; **Rattle:** Lennie Weinrib; **Roll:** Joe E. Ross; **Sidney Merciless:** Alan Oppenheimer

**Undercover Elephant: Undercover Elephant:** Daws Butler; **Loud Mouse:** Bob Hastings; **Chief:** Michael Bell

**Heyyy, It's the King: The King/Yukayuka:** Lennie Weinrib; **Skids:** Marvin Kaplan; **Big H:** Sheldon Allman; **Sheena:** Ginny McSwain; **Clyde the Ape:** Don Messick

**Posse Impossible: Sheriff:** Bill Woodson; **Stick/Duke:** Daws Butler; **Blubber:** Chuck McCann

## ◎ C-BEAR AND JAMAL

Jamal, a 10-year-old boy from south-central Los Angeles, embarks on his journey through adolescence, guided every step of the way by C-Bear, his toy teddy bear (voiced by rapper Tone Loc; also the series' executive producer) who possesses magical powers and teaches Jamal valuable lessons, in this 13-episode half-hour animated series for the Fox Network. Despite its being the highest-rated show in its time slot, Fox canceled the critically acclaimed series prior to its decision to merge with powerhouse cartoon giant Saban Entertainment to supply more of its own programming in house. *A Film Roman Production in association with Taurus Films and Plus One Animation. Color. Half-hour. Premiered on FOX: September 7, 1996–April 3, 1998.*

*Voices*

**Jamal:** Arthur Reggie III; **C-Bear:** Tone Loc; **Hawthorne:** George Wallace; **Grandma:** Dawnn Lewis; **Grandpa:** Darryl Sivad; **Maya:** Kim Fields Freeman; **Big Chill/Kwame:** Aires Spears; **Chipster:** Jeannie Elias; **Kim:** Margaret Cho; **Javier:** Paul Rodriguez; **Sooner:** Danny Mann; **Guest Voices:** Debbie Allen, Jamie Foxx

## ◎ CBS STORYBREAK

Bob Keeshan, of *Captain Kangaroo* fame, hosted this weekly anthology series of half-hour animated films based on popular children's stories. The series, produced by several independent studios, debuted on CBS (the same network on which Keeshan had starred in the long-running children's series) in 1985. CBS broadcast the program—in consecutive years until 1991, when it was replaced by *Inspector Gadget* in the network's fall Saturday-morning lineup. The 26-episode series returned to CBS's Saturday-morning schedule in 1993, combining new half-hour episodes with previously broadcast material. The network dropped the series the following season. In January 1998 the series returned as a midseason replacement in reruns. *A CBS Television Production. Color. Half-hour. Premiered on CBS: March 30, 1985–January 1,*

*1986; September 18, 1993–September 3, 1994. Rebroadcast on CBS: January 3, 1987–October 26, 1991; September 17, 1994–August 19, 1995; January 3, 1998.*

## ◎ CELEBRITY DEATHMATCH

The world's best-known celebrities from film, television, music and politics square off in battle, with play-by-play commentary by announcers Johnny Gomez and Nick Diamond with legendary referee Mills Lane presiding over the action in the ring in this half-hour animated wrestling parody for MTV. Created by Eric Fogel, the clay-animated program originated in a three-minute pilot broadcast in late 1997 on MTV's *Cartoon Sushi* anthology series that resulted in the half-hour MTV Super Bowl half-time special that aired on January 25, 1998, before going weekly in May of that year. Airing for four seasons, the 75-episode series also enjoyed a brief three-month run on the UPN network.

In an attempt to court viewers of subversive and edgy 'toons, much like the Cartoon Network's highly successful *Adult Swim* cartoon block, MTV revived this popular clay-rendered blood-sport series (also called *New Celebrity Deathmatch: Bigger & Better Than Ever*), pitting more famous celebrities in the wrestling ring, for its sister-channel, MTV2. Beginning production in 2005, Canada's Cuppa Coffee Studios produced this latest reincarnation. Premiering in June 2006 as part of the network's *Sic'emation* block with an all-new voice cast and new look, the series' fifth season kick-off episode, which paired Bam Margera doing a double bout against Tony Hawk and Don Vito and was followed by the ultimate catfight with Paris Hilton taking on rival diva Nicole Richie; it attracted more than 2.5 million viewers, becoming MTV2's highest-rated season premiere ever. Of the show's original cast, only Johnny, Nick and Mills Lane returned but were voiced by new actors. (Lane suffered a stroke in 2002 requiring a replacement to voice his character.) On February 9, 2007, the show returned for its sixth season overall, featuring celebrities Kristin Cavallari and Mischa Barton in competition. *A MTV Animation/MGM Television/Cuppa Coffee Animation Production. Color. Half-hour. Premiered on MTV: May 14, 1998–October 20, 2002. Premiered on UPN: January 12, 2001–March 13, 2001. Premiered on MTV2: June 10, 2006–.*

*Voices*

**Johnny Gomez:** Maurice Schlafer (1998–2002), Jim Thorton (2006–   ); **Nick Diamond:** Len Maxwell (1998–2002), Chris Edgerly (2006–   ); **Mills Lane:** Himself, Chris Edgerly (2006–   ); **Stacey Cornbread:** Mz. L; **"Stone Cold" Steve Austin:** Himself; **Nicky Jr.:** Brendan Miller; **Debbie Matenopoulos:** Herself; **Tally Wong:** Masasa; **Don Vito:** John DiMaggio; **Bam Margera:** Scott Menville; **Paris Hilton:** Tara Strong; **Nicole Richie:** Kristina Anapau; **Additional Voices:** Andre, Lauren Ashe, Emily Blau, Wendy S. Beber, George Benager, Dan Blank, Mae Bono, Steven Brinberg, Lisa Collins, Jim Conroy, Billy Cranne, Cricket, Tommy C., D.J. Dan, Darnithead, Scott Dikkora, Seamus Dodd, Michael DuClos, Lauren Echo, Jesse Falcon, Colin Favor, Colt 40, Nick Fenske, Natalie Fingerbutte, Eric Fogel, Mick Foley, Juliet McKuen Foster, Mike Gnu, Kim Howard, Jeff Kagan, The Kidd, Grego Korin, Buck Lee, Lobozzo, Jake Luce, Cha MacLeod, Donna Maxon, Molly Mulholland, Rich Orlow, Bethany Owen, Sophie Perera, Kate Rados, Scott Rayow, Scottie Ray, Teri Richardson, Jonathan Roumie, Jill Schackner, Ann Scobie, Adam Sietz, Edward Staudenmayer, Jimmy St. Cleve, Al Saurez, Topper, Maurice Tyson, David Wills, Thom Zelenka

## ◎ THE CENTURIONS

Computer scientist Crystal Kane and her top-secret team of computer-operated warriors, called Centurions, try saving the world

*Computer-operated warriors try to save the world from destruction in the action/adventure series* The Centurions. *© Ruby-Spears Enterprises*

from destruction at the hands of Doctor Terror's Doom Drones in this first-run action/adventure series. A *Ruby-Spears Enterprises Production. Color. Half-hour. Premiered: 1985. Syndicated. Rebroadcast on CAR: October 1, 1992–April 9, 1993 (weekdays); April 10, 1993–October 1, 1994 (Saturdays); October 3, 1994–September 1, 1995 (weekdays, Sundays, Saturdays); August 5, 1996–May 3, 1997 (weekdays). Rebroadcast on BOOM: April 2, 2000–April 8, 2001; July 1, 2001–May 2002.*

### Voices

**Ace McCloud:** Neil Ross; **Jake Rockwell:** Vince Edwards; **Max Ray/Dr. Wu:** Pat Fraley; **Crystal Kane:** Diane Pershing; **Rex Charger:** Bob Ridgely; **John Thunder:** Michael Bell; **Doc Terror:** Ron Feinberg; **Hacker:** Edmund Gilbert; **Amber:** Jennifer Darling

## ◎ CHALKZONE

Endowed with a magical piece of chalk, a normal-looking elementary school student, Rudy Tabootie (voiced by E.G. Daily, the voice of Tommy Pickles on TV's *Rugrats*) is transported into an alternate dimension, the ChalkZone, in which anything he draws or erases comes to life. He is joined in his adventures by Snap and his classmate Penny in this half-hour fantasy/adventure series for Nickelodeon. First produced as a four-minute short, called "Rudy's First Adventure," seen on Nick's *Oh Yeah! Cartoons* anthology series in October 1998, the program was given a brief trial-run in early 2000 after the series pilot debuted in December 1999, but production delays put off its "official" premiere until March 22, 2002. Beginning in February 2003, the 35-episode series also aired Saturday mornings on CBS as part of the network's *Nick Jr. on CBS* programming block, before being canceled in December 2004. A soundtrack album entitled "In the Zone" also was produced based on the series. Since 2004, the series has been rebroadcast on Nickelodeon and Nicktoons networks. A *Frederator Inc.*

*Production in association with Viacom International. Color. Half-hour. Premiered on NICK: March 22, 2002 (half-hour pilot telecast on December 31, 1999). Premiered on CBS: February 1, 2003–December 9, 2004. Rebroadcast on NICK: since 2004. Rebroadcast on NICKT: November 13, 2006–.*

### Voices

**Rudy Tabootie:** E.G. Daily; **Snap/Reggie Bullnerd/Blocky:** Candi Milo; **Penny Sanchez:** Hynden Walch; **Mildred Tabootie:** Miriam Flynn; **Joe Tabootie:** Jess Harnell; **Mr. Horace T. Wilter, Rudy's teacher:** Robert Cait; **Biclops:** Rodger Bumpass; **Queen Rapsheeba:** Cree Summer; **Spy Fly:** Tress MacNeille; **Skrawl:** Jim Cummings; **The Craniacs:** Rob Paulsen; **Additional Voices:** Jeff Bennett, Tim Curry, Pat Fraley, Daran Norris, Buck Owens, Kevin Michael Richardson, Russi Taylor, Frank Welker, Susan D. Williams

## ◎ CHALLENGE OF THE GOBOTS

Earth becomes the battleground in a titanic interplanetary struggle between good and evil when a distant, scientifically advanced world erupts in war. On the high-tech planet GoBotron, the noble Guardian GoBots—a race of robots able to transform into vehicles—pursue the evil Renegade GoBots who scheme to enslave Earth and exploit its resources to conquer GoBotron and the galaxy in this first-run, 65-episode series based on the famed action-figure toys. The series was later rerun on USA Network's *Cartoon Express*. A *Hanna-Barbera Production in association with the Tonka Corporation. Color. Half-hour. Premiered: September 8, 1984–1986. Syndicated. Rebroadcast on USA: February 17, 1989–March 28, 1991. Rebroadcast on SCI: late 1980s–early 1990s.*

### Voices

**Leader-1:** Lou Richards; **Turbo:** Arthur Burghardt; **Scooter:** Frank Welker; **Cy-Kill:** Bernard Erhard; **Cop-Tur:** Bob Holt; **Crasher:** Marilyn Lightstone; **Matt Hunter:** Morgan Paull; **A.J. Foster:** Leslie Speights; **Nick Burns:** Sparky Marcus; **Dr. Braxis:** Rene Auberjonois; **General Newcastle:** Brock Peters

## ◎ CHALLENGE OF THE SUPER FRIENDS

Evil forces unite to annihilate those guardians of humanity—Superman, Batman and Robin, Wonder Woman, Aquaman and other comic-book superheroes of the Hall of Justice—who are forced to use all their superpowers to combat the wicked Legion of Doom, composed of well-known DC comic book villains Lex Luthor, Braniac, Bizarro, Toyman, The Riddler, and others. The 16-episode series was the third collection of DC comic superheroes transformed into a weekly animated series, following 1973's "Super Friends" and 1977's *All-New Super Friends,* on ABC. A *Hanna-Barbera Production. Color. Half-hour. Premiered on ABC: September 8, 1978–September 15, 1979.*

### Voices

**Narrator:** Bill Woodson

**SUPER FRIENDS: Superman:** Danny Dark; **Batman:** Olan Soule; **Robin/Computer:** Casey Kasem; **Wonder Woman:** Shannon Farnon; **Aquaman:** Bill Callaway; **Zan/Gleek:** Mike Bell; **Jayna:** Liberty Williams; **Black Vulcan:** Buster Jones; **Samurai/Flash/Hawkman:** Jack Angel; **Apache Chief/Green Lantern:** Mike Rye

**LEGION OF DOOM: Luthor:** Stanley Jones; **Brainiac/Black Manta:** Ted Cassidy; **Toyman:** Frank Welker; **Giganta:** Ruth Forman; **Cheeta:** Marlene Aragon; **Riddler:** Mike Bell; **Captain Cold:** Dick Ryal; **Sinestro:** Vic Perrin; **Scarecrow:** Don Messick; **Bizarro:** Bill Callaway; **Solomon Grundy:** Jimmy Weldon; **Grodd the Gorilla:** Stanley Ross

## ◎ CHANNEL UMPTEE-3

Producer Norman Lear (of *All In The Family* fame) dreamed up the concept of this half-hour Saturday-morning series centering on the exploits of a secret TV station (located in "the white space between channels"), established by a small band of wildly enthusiastic television pirates (a seven-foot hyperactive ostrich named Ogden; his best friend and real-life mole, Holey Moley; and resident genius/introverted sluggish snail, Sheldon S. Cargo), who drive around in an "Umptee-3" news van broadcasting stuff "too cool, too weird and too wonderful" for regular television. *An Act II/Enchante-George/Columbia TriStar TV Animation Production. Color. Half-hour. Premiered on the WB (Kids WB!): October 25, 1997–February 20, 1998.*

*Voices*
**Stickley Ricketts:** Jonathan Harris; **Ed:** Neil Ross; **Bud:** Gregg Berger; **Ogden:** Rob Paulsen; **Sheldon:** David Paymer; **Pandora:** Alice Ghostley; **Professor Relevant:** Greg Burson; **Polly:** Susan Silo

## ◎ CHARLIE AND LOLA

Cut-out and collage-style animated preschool series following amazing exploits and travels to fantastic worlds using the imaginations of a kind and patient older brother, Charlie, who also narrates the program, and his younger, feistier, inquisitive and independent sister, Lola, based on series of children's picture books by Lauren Child, who also served as an associate producer on the series originally produced by Britain's Tiger Aspect Productions for the BBC's sister children's channel, the CBBC.

In March 2005, the 52-episode, weekday preschool series debuted in America on Disney Channel's *Playhouse Disney* daytime block, instantly becoming a hit with adults and young viewers with its imaginative stories and eye-catching design. In December 2006, the brother-and-sister pair starred in their first half-hour holiday special, *How Many More Minutes Until Christmas?* Child's first Charlie and Lola book, *I Will Never Not Ever Eat a Tomato* (2001), was awarded the prestigious Kate Greenaway Medal. *A Tiger Aspect Production. Color. Half-hour. Premiered on DIS: March 1, 2005–.*

*Voices*
**Charlie Summer:** Jethro Lundie-Brown (Season 1); Daniel Mayers (Season 2); **Lola Summer:** Massie Cowell, Clementine Cowell (Season 2); **Marv Lowe:** Ryan Harris (uncredited); **Lotta:** Morgan Gayle; **Soren Lorenson:** Stanley Street; **Morten Lowe, Marv's little brother:** Macauley Keeper

## ◎ THE CHARLIE BROWN AND SNOOPY SHOW

Charles Schulz's beloved comic-strip characters come to life in animated vignettes focusing on school, sports and, of course, Snoopy in this half-hour series consisting of three separate stories based on the comic strip. Debuting on CBS in September of 1983, the series aired for three consecutive seasons. (The first two seasons were comprised mostly of original episodes.) The series—as well as practically the entire catalog of *Peanuts* programs—was rebroadcast weekdays on The Disney Channel, beginning in October of 1993.

In 1998, the former CBS Saturday-morning series joined the roster of programs aired on Nickelodeon under the conglomeration known as "You're on Nickelodeon, Charlie Brown," which reran the series five to six days a week, mixed with previous *Peanuts* non-holiday network specials and CBS's *This Is America, Charlie Brown* miniseries after buying the rights to 58 shows overall. On February 13, 2000, when *Peanuts* creator Charles M. Schulz died, Nick aired a few specials in his honor. A week later, all of the programs from the package started airing only on Sundays, and sporadically after that until August of that year. Beginning in January 2004, Nickelodeon's sister channel, Nicktoons, started airing the same mix of specials and *The Charlie Brown and Snoopy Show* seven days a week until that April when Nickelodeon's broadcast rights to the entire package expired. *A Lee Mendelson–Bill Melendez Production in association with Charles M. Schulz Creative Associates and United Feature Syndicate. Color. Half-hour. Premiered on CBS: September 17, 1983–August 16, 1986. Rebroadcast on DIS: October 4, 1993; Rebroadcast on NICK: January 23, 1998–February 13, 2000 (five to six days a week); February 20, 2000–May 5, 2000 (Sundays); May 12, 2000–August 21, 2000 (sporadic broadcasts). Rebroadcast on NICKT: January 5, 2004–April 30, 2004.*

*Voices*
**Charlie Brown:** Brad Kesten, Brett Johnson; **Linus:** Jeremy Schoenberg; **Lucy:** Angela Lee, Heather Stoneman; **Schroeder:** Kevin Brando, Danny Colby; **Peppermint Patty:** Victoria Hodges, Gini Holtzman; **Marcie:** Michael Dockery, Keri Holtzman; **Rerun:** Jason Muller (Mendelson); **Frieda:** Mary Tunnell; **Little Girl:** Dana Ferguson; **Franklin:** Carl Steven; **Singer (theme song):** Desiree Goyette; **Singer:** Joseph Chemay; **Singer:** Joey Harrison Scarbury

## ◎ CHIPMUNKS GO TO THE MOVIES

Alvin, Theodore and Simon and the Chipettes (Brittany, Janette and Eleanor), along with record manager David Seville, spoof blockbuster movies of the era—including *Batman* (retitled *Batmunk*) and *Honey, I Shrunk the Kids* (renamed *Funny We Shrunk the Adults*)—in this short-lived, half-hour animated series for NBC. Interspersed throughout the season were reruns of previous *Alvin* episodes. *A Bagdasarian Production in association with Ruby-Spears Productions. Color. Half-hour. Premiered on NBC: September 8, 1990–September 7, 1991.*

*Voices*
**Alvin/Simon/Dave Seville:** Ross Bagdasarian Jr.; **Theodore/Brittany/Janette/Eleanor:** Janice Bagdasarian; **Ms. Miller:** Dody Goodman

## ◎ CHIP 'N DALE RESCUE RANGERS

Following the enormous success of its number-one-rated daily animated series *DuckTales*, Walt Disney introduced this first-run, half-hour syndicated animated companion featuring chipmunk favorites Chip 'n Dale in cliffhanger stories filled with mystery and intrigue, Indiana Jones–style. The fast-talking, ever-squabbling pair are heads of a small eccentric group of animal characters who solve cases that lead to bigger crimes with far-reaching consequences. Chip 'n' Dale's team of investigators: Monterey Jack, a raucous, back-slapping musclemouse who is Dale's right hand; Zipper the fly; Gadget, a consummate inventor who doubles as Chip and Dale's romantic interest; and Sewer Al, a six-and-a-half-foot-long cajun alligator who acts as the enforcer. After enjoying a one season run on Disney Channel in 1988–89, the 65-episode series was syndicated as part of the *Disney Afternoon* two-hour block in September 1989. *A Walt Disney Television Animation Production. Color. Half-hour. Premiered on DIS: August 27, 1988–September 1989. Syndicated: September 11, 1989–September 3, 1993. Rebroadcast on DIS: December 1, 1997–April 15, 2000. Rebroadcast on TDIS: April 18, 1998–.*

*Voices:*
**Dale/Zipper:** Corey Burton; **Monterey Jack:** Peter Collins (early episodes); **Fat Cat/Monterey Jack:** Jim Cummings (later episodes); **Chip/Gadget:** Tress MacNeille; **Flash the Wonder Dog/Donald Drake:** Rob Paulsen

## ◉ CHUCK NORRIS' KARATE KOMMANDOS

Action film star Chuck Norris supplied his own voice in this short-lived, five-part syndicated series in which the former karate champ encounters worldly villains, including Super Ninja and an evil empire known as Vulture. A *Ruby-Spears Enterprises Production. Color. Half-hour. Premiered: September 1986. Syndicated. Rebroadcast on CAR: April 23–24, 1994 (under one-hour* Look What We Found!).

*Voices*

**Chuck Norris:** Himself; **Tabe, Ninja Henchman:** Robert Ito; **Too-Much:** Mona Marshall; **Kimo:** Key Luke; **Reed:** Sam Fontana; **Pepper:** Kathy Garver; **The Claw:** Bill Martin; **Super Ninja:** Keone Young; **The President:** Alan Oppenheimer

## ◉ CLASS OF 3000

Famed hip-hop star André 3000 (alias André Benjamin) of the Grammy-winning musical group OutKast cocreated and lent his voice to this series following the adventures of an internationally famous pop star, Sunny Bridges, who gives up everything to become a music teacher and teach a group of musically gifted prodigies at Atlanta's Westley School of Performing Arts. Benjamin also wrote and performed the series' soundtrack, including new songs as part of a music video for each episode, for the half-hour prime-time series that premiered on Cartoon Network in November 2006.

On Friday, October 27, 2006, a week before making its world television premiere with a one-hour special, Cartoon Network aired a prime-time half-hour live-action "mockumentary" called *Sunny Bridges from Bankhead to Buckhead* chronicling the life of the fictional superstar, including interviews with the character's fans and celebrity friends. Twelve half-hour episodes were produced for the first season by Cartoon Network in conjunction with Tom Lynch Co. and André Benjamin's production company, Moxie Turtle, with Benjamin and Lynch serving as executive producers and Benjamin providing voices and musical direction for the show. Others lending voices for the series includes Tionne "T-Boz" Watkins, lead singer of TLC, and veteran voice actors Tom Kenny (*SpongeBob SquarePants, Camp Lazlo*), Crystal Scales (*Static Shock, The Adventures of Jimmy Neutron*), Jennifer Hale (*Samurai Jack, The Powerpuff Girls*), Janice Kawaye (*Hi Hi Puffy Ami Yumi*) and Jeff Glen Bennett (*Johnny Bravo, Camp Lazlo*). A *Cartoon Network Studios/Tom Lynch/Moxie Production. Color. Half-hour. Premiered on CAR: November 3, 2006 (one-hour special). Premiered on CAR: November 10, 2006–January 26, 2007 (series).*

*Voices*

**André 3000:** Sunny Bridges; **Li'l D:** Small Fire; **Tamika Jones:** Crystal Scales; **Kam Chin/Kim Chin:** Janice Kawaye; **Philly Phil:** Phil LaMarr; **Edward "Eddie" Phillip James Lawrence III:** Tom Kenny; **Madison Spaghettini Papadopoulos:** Jennifer Hale

## ◉ CLERKS

Further animated adventures centering on the comical exploits of the Quick Stop and RST Video clerks, Dante Hicks and Randal Graves, and their resident drug-dealing partners Jay and Silent Bob, first popularized in the hit 1994 live-action comedy feature of the same name by director Kevin Smith, satirizing pop culture and film, television and sports icons who whine about their miserable lives. Added to the supporting cast were the villainous, rich gay psychopath, Leonardo Leonardo, based on actor Alan Rickman (*Dogma, Die Hard, Galaxy Quest*), who originally voiced the character until the network executives axed him in favor of Alec Baldwin; and the show's only black character, Lando, who appeared in the third episode. Other episodes featured cameo voice appearances by many famous stars, including NBA standout

Charles Barkley and others. ABC commissioned six episodes of the short-lived series—which originally was to debut after the Super Bowl but its broadcast date was pushed back—until it premiered in prime time on May 31, 2000.

After airing for only two weeks, ABC dumped the series due to poor ratings, despite having four more episodes to air. Debuting with 5.2 million viewers its first week, the show slipped to 4.1 million viewers by its second week. (ABC also reportedly decided to yank the series after advertisers balked at its edgy humor.) Smith offered to buy the series from ABC and edit the episodes into a feature-length movie but tabled that idea and instead released all six episodes on video and DVD the following year. In December 2002, the series resurfaced on cable's Comedy Central with a one-time-only six-episode marathon beginning at 9 A.M., including the four half-hour episodes that never aired on ABC. In February 2003, the series, along with the animated *Dilbert*, began airing Sunday nights, replacing two other rebroadcast series, *Gary & Mike* and *Undergrads*. A *Walt Disney Television Animation Production in association with View Askew Productions/Miramax/Touchstone. Color. Half-hour. Premiered on ABC: May 31, 2000–June 7, 2000. Rebroadcast on COM: December 22, 2002 (six-episode marathon); February 3, 2003–October 19, 2003.*

*Voices*

**Dante Hicks:** Brian O'Halloran; **Randal Graves:** Jeff Anderson; **Silent Bob:** Kevin Smith; **Jay:** Jason Mewes; **Leonardo Leonardo:** Alan Rickman, Alec Baldwin

## ◉ CLIFFORD'S PUPPY DAYS

All-new animated puppyhood adventures of the popular big red dog exploring his exciting surroundings in a new setting, the big city (unlike Birdwell Island where its predecessor took place), with his young owner Emily Elizabeth, showing that however small he can make really big things happen, in this spin-off of the successful PBS cartoon series, *Clifford the Big Red Dog*. The first two episodes of this half-hour children's series premiered Labor Day, September 1, 2003, as part of the PBS Kids' *Pet-Tacular*, broadcast on most PBS stations. Thirty-nine half-hours, containing two cartoons per show, were originally broadcast on PBS Kids' preschool programming block through February 2006, with episodes of the series continuing to be rebroadcast. Among the big-name celebrities to join the cast were Henry Winkler as the voice of Norville and Lara Jill Miller as Clifford. A *Scholastic Entertainment Production. Color. Half-hour. Premiered on PBS Kids: September 1, 2003.*

*Voices*

**Clifford the Puppy:** Lara Jill Miller; **Emily Elizabeth Howard/ Mrs. Caroline Howard/Evan's Mother:** Grey DeLisle; **Mark Howard/Crafts Shop Clerk/Nina's Father/Speckle:** Cam Clarke; **Daffodil the Rabbit:** Kath Soucie; **Nina:** Masiela Lusha; **Flo the Cat/Vanessa:** LaTonya Holmes; **Zo the Cat/End Narrator:** Ogie Banks; **Jorge the Dachshund/Gruff the Dog/Mr. Pit-Bull/Choo-Choo/Mr. Sardisky:** Jess Harnell; **Shun:** Lauren Tom; **Norville:** Henry Winkler; **Nina's Mother:** Candi Milo

## ◉ CLIFFORD THE BIG RED DOG

Joined by his human owner, Emily Elizabeth, and his dog pals, Cleo and T-Bone, 20-foot-tall Clifford the Big Red Dog (voiced by the late John Ritter) learns many life-affirming lessons about the importance of acceptance, community and resolving differences in a series of animated adventures aimed at younger audiences. Consisting of two animated stories in each half-hour revolving around the "Speckle Story" read by Emily to her favorite dog companion, this 30-minute educational children's series, which also featured one promotional spot of the characters during each telecast, debuted on PBS Kids in September 2000, with new episodes rolled out in blocks during its near-three-season run. New episodes aired from September 4–26, 2000 (#101–#117); January 16–30, 2001 (#118–#122, #124–#130); February 14, 2001 (#123); October 3, 2001, to December 4, 2001 (#131–#140), February 14–25, 2002 (#201–#208); September 18, 2002, to November 20, 2002 (#209–#218); and February 17–25, 2003 (#219–#225).

Starring television icon John Ritter of TV's *Three's Company* and *8 Simple Rules for Dating My Teenage Daughter* as the voice of Clifford, with the final-seven episodes shown in February 2003, the successful 65-episode, daytime children's series spawned a full-length animated feature, *Clifford's Really Big Movie* (2004), and 25-episode prequel, *Clifford's Puppy Days*, which aired Wednesdays in *Clifford the Big Red Dog's* original time slot on PBS beginning in 2003. Episodes of the series were rerun from January 2001 to the day after the last episode premiered in late February 2003. *A Scholastic Entertainment Production. Color. Half-hour. Premiered on PBS: September 4, 2000–February 25, 2003. Rebroadcast on PBS Kids: January 31, 2001–February 26, 2003.*

*Voices*
**Clifford the Big Red Dog:** John Ritter; **Emily Elizabeth Howard:** Grey DeLisle; **Cleo:** Cree Summer; **T-Bone:** Kel Mitchell; **Samuel:** T.C. Carson; **Vaz:** Ulysses Cuadra; **Charley:** Gary Gray; **Jetta Handover:** Kath Soucie; **Machiavelli/Mark Howard:** Cam Clarke; **Additional Voices:** Erika Alexander, Carol Bachyrita, Earl Boen, Maria Canals, Gabrielle Carteris, Debi Derryberry, Michael Dorn, Mark Hamill, Tyisha Hampton, Nick Jameson, Simbi Khali, Clyde Kusatsu, Edie McClurg, Haunani Minn, Phil Morris, Frankie Muniz, Tony Plana, Charlie Schlatter, Cynthia Songe, Kenan Thompson, Marcelo Tubert, Frank Welker, Henry Winkler

### ◎ CLONE HIGH U.S.A.

At an alternative high school populated entirely by clones of famous historic figures—Abraham Lincoln, Cleopatra, Gandhi, George Washington Carver, JFK and Joan of Arc—originally to be used by the U.S. military in battle, a scurrilous principal, Cinnamon J. Scudworth, has other plans: to staff an amusement park, called "Cloney Island," with them in this half-hour animated series, created and produced by Phil Lord and Christopher Miller who also wrote and helped voice the series.

With its storyboarding and principal production design done by Canadian animation studio, Nelvana, the series was first broadcast from 2001 to 2002 and rebroadcast on Canada's Teletoon from February 2002 to November 2003. Beginning in January 2003, it aired Monday nights in prime time in the United States on MTV. Unfortunately, the provocative series stirred up a storm of controversy with Indian viewers over its offensive portrayal of a Ritalin, junk-food-obsessed Gandhi. Poor ratings resulted in its removal from the network's prime-time rotation. *A Nelvana International Ltd./MTV Networks Inc. Production. Color. Half-hour. Premiered MTV: January 20, 2003–February 10, 2003.*

*Voices*
**Abe Lincoln/Narrator:** Will Forte; **Gandhi/Various Others:** Michael McDonald; **Joan of Arc/Various Others:** Nicole Sullivan; **Cleopatra/Various Others:** Christa Miller Lawrence; **JFK/Mr. Butlerton [Mr. B]/Various Others:** Christopher R. Miller; **George Washington Carver/Toots/Wally:** Donald Adeosun Faison; **Caesar/Gandhi's Dad:** Neil Flynn; **Principal Cinnamon J. Scudworth:** Phil Lord

### ◎ CLUE CLUB

This series followed the adventures of four professional teenage detectives—Pepper, Larry, Dotty and D.D.—who collect clues to unsolvable crimes in the same manner as celebrated London sleuth Sherlock Holmes, with the assistance of two cowardly dogs, Woofer and Wimper. This 16-episode half-hour Saturday-morning series premiered on CBS in 1976 and was briefly retitled *Woofer and Wimper, Dog Detectives* in 1978. *A Hanna-Barbera Production. Color. Half-hour. Premiered on CBS: August 14, 1976–September 3, 1977. Rebroadcast on CBS: September 10, 1978–September 2, 1979. Rebroadcast on CAR: April 10, 1994 (Sundays)–1997. Rebroadcast on BOOM: July 1, 2000–.*

*Voices*
**Larry:** David Joliffe; **D.D.:** Bob Hastings; **Pepper:** Patricia Stich; **Dotty:** Tara Talboy; **Woofer:** Paul Winchell; **Wimper:** Jim MacGeorge; **Sheriff Bagley:** John Stephenson

### ◎ CLUTCH CARGO

Established author Clutch Cargo travels the globe in search of adventure with his constant companions Swampy, Spinner and dog Paddlefoot. Piloting his plane anywhere a friend needs help, Clutch uses only his wits to defeat the villains. Created by one-time cartoonist Clark Haas, these five-minute, 130-episode serialized adventures combined limited animation and a live-action process called Synchro-Vox, invented by Ed Gillette and first used for "talking animal" commercials in the 1950s. This economical but unsophisticated method superimposed the human lips of voice actors over the mouths of their animated counterparts, the only parts of the characters that moved. Twenty-six half-hour shows, each consisting of five 5-minute episodes, were produced for the low-budget series between 1957 and 1960. In 1990 the series was

EXCITING'
CLIFF HANGIN'
COLORFUL

**CLUTCH CARGO**

*T-V's First Comic Strip*

*Clutch Cargo and his pals Spinner and Paddlefoot as seen in Cambria Studios' so-called T-V's First Comic Strip, the animated adventures of Clutch Cargo. © Cambria Studios*

colorized and shown for the first time in nearly three decades on The Comedy Channel. *A Cambria Production. Black-and-white and color. Half-hour. Premiered: March 9, 1959–1961. Syndicated. Rebroadcast on COMEDY: 1990.*

**Voices**
**Clutch Cargo:** Richard Cotting; **Spinner/Paddlefoot:** Margaret Kerry; **Swampy:** Hal Smith

## ◉ COCONUT FRED'S FRUIT SALAD ISLAND

On the carefree, tiny tropical island paradise and silliest spot on the Seven Seas, Fruit Salad Island, best known for its three S's—"sun, surf and sleeping"—Fred, a zany, big-hearted, energetic and eternally optimistic coconut, shows a special ability to turn everything he imagines into reality, undeterred by problems he encounters, in a series of wild, wacky and imaginary adventures with his fruity island cohorts Bingo Cherry, Slip and Slide the "country" banana brothers, Mr. Greenrind the watermelon, Wedgie the lemon and Bunga Berry the wild strawberry. In September 2005 the Flash-animated, Saturday morning comedy/adventure series, designed for kids ages six to 11, was launched with 13 half-hours comprised of two episodes per show on the WB Television Network's Kids' WB! Despite being nominated for two Daytime Emmy Awards for outstanding special class animated program and outstanding achievement in sound editing, the show was canceled after only one season and was replaced on the Kids' WB! schedule in June of 2006 by the animated series *Spider Riders. A Warner Bros. Animation Production. Color. Half-hour. Premiered on the WB Kids' WB!: September 17, 2005–July 1, 2006.*

**Voices**
**Coconut Fred:** Rob Paulsen; **Bingo Cherry:** Tracey Moore; **Mr. Greenrind:** Michael Donovan; **Slip D'Peel/Slide D'Peel:** Eric Bauza; **Bunga Berry:** David Kaye; **Wedgie:** Matthew Charles

## ◉ CODE LYOKO

After uncovering a mysterious parallel universe, a virtual world called LYOKO, a group of ordinary students—Yumi, Ulrich, Odd and Jeremie—become action heroes with special powers as they fight what regular people can't see and travel farther than anyone thought possible to save the planet from a supercomputer that threatens its very existence in this half-hour adventure series.

Characterized by its distinctive blend of traditional 2-D cel and 3-D CGI animation and originally produced in 2003 for French television, the 26-episode, weekday series aired on Cartoon Network beginning in April 2004. The popular program was renewed for two more seasons, featuring an additional 52 first-run half-hour adventures that aired through October 2006. Episodes from the series were subsequently rebroadcast. During the second season, producers added an additional territory, new monsters and several futuristic vehicles. *An Antefilms Studio/MoonScoop Distribution/France 3/Canal J Production. Color. Half-hour. Premiered CAR: April 19, 2004–October 23, 2006. Rebroadcast on CAR: October 26, 2006–   .*

**Voices**
**Elizabeth "Sissy" Delmas/Dorothy/Mrs. Hertz:** Jodie Forrest; **Jim Morales/Herb Pichon:** David Gaasman; **Odd Della Robia/Nicholas Poliakoff:** Matthew Geczy; **X.A.N.A.:** Virtual Jimmy; **Yumi Ishiyama/Milly Solovieff:** Mirabelle Kirkland; **Aelita Hopper/Jeremie Belpost:** Sharon Mann; **Ulrich Stern:** Barbara Scaff; **Principal Jean-Pierre Delmas:** Allan Wenger

## ◉ CODENAME: KIDS NEXT DOOR

Operating out of their treehouse hideaway, five heroic 10-year-olds, all with code names ending in numbers, form a worldwide secret organization called the Kids Next Door whose missions are to free all children from the tyrannical control of adults and teenagers, from going to bed early and having to do homework, in this animated series created by Tom Warburton and produced by San Francisco's Curious Pictures.

In 2002 Cartoon Network ordered production of a full-fledged series after the series' original pilot, "No P in the OOL," was the top vote-getter in its 1999 viewer poll of cartoon shorts broadcast that year. In the pilot, the characters originally were called "The Kids Who Lived Next Door," which was subsequently shortened. In December 2002 the series bowed with its first episode, "Op G.R.O.W.U.P.," featuring two episodes per half-hour with a few exceptions that season. From May to July 2004, the popular kids' series was replayed Saturday mornings on Kids' WB!

Becoming one of Cartoon Network's most-watched original series for six consecutive seasons with 78 episodes, the weekly half-hour series resulted in a few spin-offs. To help celebrate the holiday season, in December 2005 the secret agent kids starred in their first holiday special, *Operation N.A.U.G.H.T.Y.* In March 2006 Cartoon Network announced plans to roll out a brace of TV-movies based on several popular series, including *Codename: Kids Next Door, Foster's Home for Imaginary Friends* and *Teen Titans.* That August the covert kid operatives were featured in their first made-for-TV movie, *Operation Z.E.R.O.,* which was released on DVD shortly after its original broadcast. *A Curious Pictures/Cartoon Network Production. Color. Half-hour. Premiered on CAR: December 6, 2002. Rebroadcast on the WB (Kids' WB!): May 15, 2004–July 3, 2004.*

**Voices**
**Nigel "Numbuh 1" Uno/Hoagie Pennywhistle "Numbuh 2" Gilligan Jr:** Ben Diskin; **Kuki "Numbuh 3" Sanban:** Lauren Tom; **Wally "Numbuh 4" Beatles/Toilenator:** Dee Bradley Baker; **Abigail "Numbuh 5" Lincoln:** Cree Summer; **Mr. Boss:** Jeff Bennett; **Crazy Old Cat Lady:** Grey DeLisle; **Mrs. Thompson:** Jennifer Hale; **Stickybeard:** Mark Hamill; **Chad Dickson:** Jason Harris; **Chester:** Tom Kenny;
**Count Spankulot:** Daran Norris; **Mushi Sanban:** Tara Strong; **Bus Driver:** Frank Welker

## ◉ COLONEL BLEEP

A universe light-years away is the setting for action and adventure in which Colonel Bleep and his Space Deputies, Scratch the Caveman and Squeek the Puppet, battle Doctor Destructo, master criminal of the universe, in this late 1950s' color series produced by Soundac Studios of Miami, Florida. The series consisted of 104 six-minute episodes, shown in a half-hour block (four episodes per show) in syndication beginning in 1957. Originally the series was packaged as part of a franchised children's series *Uncle Bill's TV Club,* broadcast on independent television stations and hosted by local on-air personalities. *A Robert H. Ullman. Inc/Soundac Color Production. Color. Half-hour. Premiered: 1957. Syndicated.*

**Voices**
**Narrator:** Noel Taylor

## ◉ THE COMIC STRIP

Produced in the manner of "Funtastic World of Hanna-Barbera" and "Super Sunday," this two-hour series was a marathon of first-run cartoons featuring several stars in one episodic adventure each week: "Karate Kat," a klutzy karate expert who heads a detective agency (obviously inspired by the popularity of the *The Karate Kid* feature film series); "The Street Frogs," streetwise frogs who encounter comedy and adventure; "The Mini-Monsters," the antics of two brat youngsters and their summer camp monster pals, Dracky, Franklyn, Mumm-O, Blank-O, and Wolfie; and "Tigersharks," an intrepid group of explorers and their underwater adventures. A *Rankin-Bass Production. Color. Two hours. Premiered: September 1987. Syndicated.*

*Voices*

**KARATE KAT:** Earl Hammond, Maggie Jakobson, Larry Kenney, Robert McFadden, Gerrianne Raphael

**MINI-MONSTERS:** Josh Blake, Jim Brownold, Danielle DuClos, Seth Green, Maggie Jakobson, Robert McFadden, Jim Meskimen, Peter Newman

**STREET FROGS:** Donald Acree, Gary V. Brown, Carmen De Lavallade, Robert McFadden, Gordy Owens, Ron Taylor, Tanya Willoughby, Daniel Wooten

**TIGERSHARKS:** Camille Banora, Jim Brownold, Earl Hammond, Larry Kenney, Robert McFadden, Jim Meskimen, Peter Newman

## ◎ COMMITTED

As implied by its title, this animated adaptation of Michael Fry's popular comic strip focuses on the everyday craziness of career woman and housewife Liz Larsen and her frazzled modern middle-class family as she juggles her commitments—her job, her husband Joe and her three children, Tracy, Zelda, and Nicholas—through a sea of challenges mixed with moments of joy, love and satisfaction without self-destructing.

Produced by Canada's Nelvana animation studio, this home-grown cartoon comedy series, featuring an all-Canadian voice cast—including TV's *SCTV* alumni Catherine O'Hara, Eugene Levy and Andrea Martin as Liz and Joe Larsen and Liz's mother, Frances, respectively, and former *NewsRadio* regular Dave Foley as their pet, Bob the Dog—was first shown in Canada on the CTV network before debuting a year later in the United States on cable's Women's Entertainment (WE) Network. (Originally the series was set to launch on FOX Family Channel, but plans were scuttled after the network was bought by ABC.) Airing Sundays at 10:00 P.M. and hoping to attract adult viewers, 13 half-hour episodes were broadcast during the series' network run. A *Nelvana Limited/Philippine Animators Group Inc. Production. Color. Half-hour. Premiered on WE Network: October 6, 2002.*

*Voices*

**Liz Larsen:** Catherine O'Hara; **Joe Larsen:** Eugene Levy; **Frances Wilder:** Andrea Martin; **Tracy Larsen:** Annick Obonsawin; **Zelda Larsen:** Charlotte Arnold; **Nicholas Larsen:** Cole Caplan; **Bob the Dog:** Dave Foley; **Additional Voices:** Len Carlson, Greg Spottiswood

## ◎ THE COMPLETELY MENTAL MISADVENTURES OF ED GRIMLEY

Comedian Martin Short teamed up with Hanna-Barbera Productions to produce this half-hour Saturday-morning show based on his famed *Saturday Night Live* character, Ed Grimley, a sweetly nerdy guy who lives in a funky Victorian apartment with a goldfish named Moby and a clever rat named Sheldon. Plot lines include his encounters with the ever-cranky Mr. Freebus, Ed's landlord; Miss Malone, his gorgeous down-the-hall neighbor; the Truly Remarkable Gustav Brothers, identical twins who look nothing alike; and Ed's favorite television program, Count Floyd and his "Really Scaaary Stories Show." A *Hanna-Barbera Production. Color. Half-hour. Premiered on NBC: September 10, 1988–September 2, 1989. Rebroadcast on CAR: October 4, 1992–April 4, 1993*

(Sundays); *February 6, 1994–October 2, 1995 (Sundays, Saturdays); December 18, 1995–December 22, 1995; December 26, 1995–December 29, 1995; January 6, 1996–June 23, 1997. Rebroadcast on BOOM: July 1, 2002–.*

*Voices*

**Ed Grimley:** Martin Short; **Count Floyd:** Joe Flaherty; **Miss Malone:** Catherine O'Hara; **Mr. Freebus:** Jonathan Winters; **Mrs. Freebus:** Andrea Martin; **Sheldon:** Frank Welker

*The Gustav Brothers*
**Roger:** Jonathan Winters; **Wendell:** Danny Cooksey

## ◎ CONAN AND THE YOUNG WARRIORS

Preteen adventures of the young barbarian warrior and his friends (known as the Barbarian Kids, each of whom is gifted with supernatural powers) who try to rid the world of an evil sorceress, who has turned the family of one of Conan's friends into wolves, and return the family to normal in this short-lived Saturday-morning series, spun-off from 1992's popular syndicated *Conan the Adventurer* cartoon series and based on the blockbuster movie franchise of the early 1980s and comic-book series. Produced by Burbank, California, animation powerhouse, DIC Entertainment, the half-hour fantasy-adventure series premiered as a mid-season replacement on CBS's Saturday morning schedule, lasting only 13 episodes before it was canceled. A *DIC Entertainment/JetLag Productions/Sunbow Entertainment Production in association with Conan Properties. Color. Half-hour. Premiered on CBS: March 5, 1994–August 27, 1994.*

*Voices*

Kathleen Barr, Jim Byrnes, Michael Dobson, Michael Donovan, Phil Hayes, Mark Hildreth, Kelly Sheridan, Louise Vallance, Chiara Zanni

## ◎ CONAN THE ADVENTURER

Enslaved by the evil warlock who turned his family into stone, young musclebound barbarian warrior Conan (a character created for *Weird Tales* magazine by Robert E. Howard in 1932 and later played by Arnold Schwarzenegger in the *Conan* feature-film series of the early 1980s) manages to escape. He embarks on a fearless mission to save the people of his ancient land and to restore his family to their former selves in this half-hour syndicated series. The program—which tried to live up to adventures of the books and movies—debuted in weekly syndication in September 1992 and ran for 13 weeks. In 1993 the program went into daily syndication, with 52 new and original episodes. A *Graz Entertainment/Jet Lag Productions/Sunbow Entertainment Production in association with Conan Properties. Color. Half-hour. Premiered: September 12, 1992. Syndicated: 1993.*

*Voices*

Kathleen Barr, Michael Beattie, Jim Burnes, Gary Chalk, Mike Donovan, John Pyper Ferguson, Janyce Jaud, Scott McNeil, Richard Newman, Doug Parker, Alec Willows

## ◎ CONNIE THE COW

Educational preschool animated series following the experiences of a restless, curious calf, Connie, who lives on a farm with her nurturing mother, Mollie, and her strong, yet calm and reassuring father bull, Bill, and her other animal friends, Patch the puppy, Wally the bird and Grouch the fox, who pokes her nose into everything with comical results. Created by Josep Viciana and produced by Spain's Neptuno Films in association with TV-Loonland, Nickelodeon acquired the 52-episode weekday, 2-D cel-animated series, combined with 3-D computer-generated imagery and

40 educational fillers, to debut on its sister, commercial-free children's channel, Noggin, in September 2003. In June 2006 to honor dads on Father's Day, Noggin aired themed episodes of the series along with other programs from its preschool lineup, including such popular shows as *Franklin*, *Little Bear* and *Miffy and Friends*. For the program's third season, Modern Publishing released sticker and coloring books in the United States to tie-in with the series. *A Neptuno Films/AAC-Kids/TV-Loonland/Alliance Atlantis Production. Color. Half-hour. Premiered on NOG: September 8, 2003.*

*Voices*
**Connie:** Ayesha Gabrielle Mendham; **MollieBrenda/Donna/ Maddie/Sheila/Mama Nigel/Sandy/Timmy/Wilt 2/Woodpecker:** Sara Davidson; **Bill/Patch/Wally/Grouch/Ant 1/Claud/Hedgy/ Henry/Narrator/Title/Tom:** Alex Warner; **Ant 2/Bernie/Butterfly 3/Butterfly 4/Bubble/Cheryl/Clouds/Dodger/Finny/ George/John/Norbert/Scratcher/Sergeant/Stan/Todd/ Trebor/ Worm 3:** Richard Leggott; **Baby Nigel/Sheep:** Dani; **Bella/ Chicks/Daisy/Edith/Little Woodpeckers/Nibble/Pearl/Pip:** Lucy Beckwith; **Bat/Clumsy/Fast Feather/Larry/Nosy:** James Reed; **Beau/Clara/Maury:** Sara Davidson, Sue Flack; **Crick/Petal/ Sheila:** Lucy Beckwith, Sara Davidson; **Flap/Giles/Max/Snooze:** James Reed, Richard Leggot; **Herbie:** Richard Leggott, Lucy Beckwith; **Maxim/Pinto/William:** Richard Leggott, James Reed, Alex Warner; **Paddy:** Sara Davidson, Alex Warner; **Ronny:** Richard Leggott, Sara Davidson, Sue Flack; **Simon:** Alex Warner, Richard Leggott; **Sticky:** James Reed, Lucy Beckwith

## ◎ COOL MCCOOL

Bumbling detective McCool was created by cartoonist Bob Kane, the co-creator of Batman, in the vein of Maxwell Smart, agent 86, who stumbled his way to the solution of crimes in this popular NBC Saturday morning series. McCool was featured in two short adventures each week, along with one episode in between of Keystone Kops–like adventures of Harry McCool, Cool's father, who chases down thieves and other no-goods with the help of two klutzy policemen, Tom and Dick. Twenty half-hour programs were produced in all, each originally telecast in 1966–67 on NBC. The series lasted two more seasons (in reruns) before it was canceled. *A Cavalier/King Features Production. Color. Half-hour. Premiered on NBC: September 10, 1966–August 31, 1969.*

*Voices*
**Cool McCool:** Bob McFadden; **Number One, his boss/Riggs, a scientific genius:** Chuck McCann; **Friday, Number One's secretary:** Carol Corbett

## ◎ C.O.P.S.

Former FBI special agent Baldwin P. Vess tries eradicating organized crime in Empire City with the help of his C.O.P.S. crimefighting force, each member a master of a special skill and dedicated to the cause of justice, in this popular 65-episode half-hour series made for syndication. In the spring of 1993, the series returned as a Saturday-morning network show (retitled *Cyber C.O.P.S.*) on CBS, repeating episodes from the original series.

After CBS canceled the series, it reaired on USA Network's *Cartoon Express*. *A DIC Enterprises Production. Color. Half-hour. Premiered: September 1988–89. Syndicated. Rebroadcast on CBS: March 27, 1993–September 4, 1993. Rebroadcast on USA: January 2, 1995–March 29, 1995.*

*Voices*
**Bulletproof Vess:** Ken Ryan; **Longram:** John Stocker; **The Big Boss/Mace:** Len Carlson; **Badvibes:** Ron Rubin; **Buttons McBoomBoom/Bowzer:** Nick Nichols; **Berserko:** Paul De La Rosa; **Rock Krusher:** Brent Titcomb; **Squeeky:** Marvin Goldhar; **Turbo Tu-Tone:** Dan Hennessy; **Nightshade:** Jane Schoettle; **Bullseye:** Peter Keleghan; **Highway/Barricade:** Ray James; **Hardtop:** Darren Baker; **Mainframe:** Mary Long; **Whitney Morgan:** Jeri Craden; **Mirage:** Liz Hanna; **Ms. Demeanor:** Paulina Gillis

## ◎ CORDUROY

First made popular in a series of live-action specials produced in the 1970s for Canadian television, a young corduroy overall-clad bear with a penchant for mischief experiences the sights and sounds of big city life from a child's point of view with his seven-year-old African-American friend, Lisa, in this animated series for PBS, based on acclaimed author Don Freeman's popular children's books, *Corduroy* and *A Pocket for Corduroy*, celebrating diversity. Beginning in September 2000, the 13-episode children's program was broadcast in the United States on PBS Kids' *Bookworm Bunch* weekend block of cartoon series produced by Canada's Nelvana Limited. *A Lin Oliver/Nelvana Limited/Studio B Production. Color. Half-hour. Premiered on PBS Kids: September 30, 2000–December 2, 2000.*

*Voices*
Todd Schick, Paul Dobson, Jake Goldshie

## ◎ CORNEIL & BERNIE

Chaotic misadventures of an irritable genius talking dog named Corneil, who, unbeknownst to his bizarre owner and so-called "dog sitter" Bernie Barges, speaks fluent English and become best friends after helping his owner out of numerous predicaments. Named *Watch My Chops* in the United Kingdom after Corneil's popular catchphrase, the hit English-dubbed French-animated half-hour comedy series, created and produced by acclaimed global animation studio Millimages aired every night of the week and weekend afternoons on Nicktoons beginning in February 2004. *A Millimages Production. Color. Half-hour. Premiered on NICKT: February 21, 2004.*

*Voices*
**Corneil:** Keith Wickham; **Bernie Barges:** Ben Small; **Other Voices:** Dian Perry, Dan Russell

## ◎ COUNT DUCKULA

Unlike most vampires whose thirst for blood knows no earthly limits, Count Duckula is a reluctant vampire with a hankering for show business who, instead of blood, sucks on broccoli sandwiches. His Castle Duckula and its occupants—Igor, Nanny and Dr. Von Goosewing—are transported anywhere in the world on command, where they experience many madcap adventures. *A Cosgrove-Hall Production in association with Thames Television. Color. Half-hour. Premiered on NICK: February 6, 1988–December 26, 1993.*

*Voices*
**Count Duckula:** David Jason; **Igor:** Jack May; **Nanny:** Brian Trueman; **Von Goosewing:** Jimmy Hibbert; **Narrator:** Barry Clayton

*Additional Voice*
Ruby Wax

## ◎ THE COUNT OF MONTE CRISTO

Those who pervert justice for their own ends are the targets of the Count of Monte Cristo and his two friends, Rico and Jacopo. Cristo has one consuming passion—to see injustice of any sort uncovered and denounced. Halas and Batchelor, once the largest animation film production studio in Europe, produced this cartoon import in 1974. *A Halas and Batchelor/R.A.I. Production. Color. Half-hour. Premiered: 1974. Syndicated.*

*Voices*
George Roubicek, Jeremy Wilkin, Bernard Spear, Peter Hawkins, Miriam Margoyles, Jean England, David de Keyser

### ◎ THE COUNTRY MOUSE AND CITY MOUSE ADVENTURES

Two feisty mice cousins—folksy Emily and dapper urbanite Alexander—travel the globe in this weekly half-hour series, based on characters from Aesop's Fables and presented by *Reader's Digest*. Premiered Sunday mornings on HBO in March of 1998. A *CINAR France Animation/Canada/France Production. Color. Half-hour. Premiered on HBO: March 1, 1998–December 2000. Rebroadcast on HBO FAM: March 6, 1998–November 19, 2004.*

*Voices*
**Emily:** Julie Burroughs; **Alexander:** Terrence Scammel; **No Tail No Good:** Rick Jones

### ◎ COURAGEOUS CAT AND MINUTE MOUSE

Comic-book artist Bob Kane, who created TV's *Cool McCool*, parodied his own creation of caped crusaders Batman and Robin in this first-run half-hour series of 100 five-minute cartoons that featured a crimefighting cat and mouse who fight for truth, justice and self-protection in Empire City (a take-off of Gotham City in the Batman series). Relying on a multipurpose Catgun and Catmobile, Courageous Cat and Minute encounter such villains as the Frog (his real name is "Chauncey" and he is patterned after movie tough guy Edward G. Robinson), his assistant Harry the Gorilla, Rodney Rodent, Black Cat, Professor Noodle Stroodle and Professor Shaggy Dog. A *Sam Singer/Trans-Artist Production. Color. Half-hour. Premiered: September 1960. Syndicated.*

*Voices*
**Courageous Cat/Minute Mouse:** Bob McFadden

### ◎ COW AND CHICKEN

Based on the Emmy-nominated cartoon short created by David Feiss for Hanna-Barbera and Cartoon Network's *World Premiere Toons* series. This half-hour series continues the outrageous antics of a surreal pair of siblings, big brother Chicken (all of 460 pounds) and little sister Cow, whose American dream lifestyle—a nice house with a white picket fence and loving human parents—usually turns fowl, thanks to pugnacious Chicken's attitude, which requires his little sister to bail him out. Premiering in July of 1997, the program consists of three seven-minute shorts, two featuring the series stars and a third entitled "I Am Weasel," the fabulous exploits of the internationally famous I. M. Weasel (voiced by Michael Dorn, a.k.a. Commander Worf on TV's *Star Trek: The Next Generation*) and his insanely jealous, mentally challenged archrival, I.R. Baboon. A *Hanna-Barbera Production. Color. Half-hour. Premiered on CAR: July 22, 1997–July 24, 1999.*

*Voices*
**Cow/Chicken/Red Guy:** Charles Adler; **Mom:** Candi Milo; **Dad:** Dee Bradley Baker; **Flem:** Howard Morris; **Earl:** Dan Castellaneta; **I.M. Weasel:** Michael Dorn; **I.R. Baboon:** Charles Adler

### ◎ COWBOY BEBOP

Adventures of planet-hopping bounty hunter Spike Spiegel, a man with a long, dark past who tries living on his bounties with the help of his partners (Bebop starship owner Jet Black; con-artist Faye Valentine; super-genius Ed; and his Welsh-corgi dog, Ein) in this animated action/drama anime series first broadcast on Japan's TV Tokyo in the summer of 1998 and then on the U.S.' Cartoon Network late-night *Adult Swim* programming block in 2001. The success of the 26-episode series spawned production of a full-length animated feature, *Cowboy Bebop: Knockin' on Heaven*, released to theaters in Japan in September 2001 under the alternate title, *Cowboy Bebop: The Movie,* and later premiered on Cartoon Network. A *Sunrise Inc./ZRO Limited Productions/Bandai Visual Production. Color. Half-hour. Premiered on CAR: September 2, 2001–November 25, 2001.*

*Voices*
**Jet Black:** Beau Billingslea; **Spike Siegel:** Steven Jay Blum; **Edward Wong Hau Pepelu Tirvursky IV:** Melissa Fahn; **Fay Valentine:** Wendee Lee; **Julia:** Melissa Williamson; **Miles:** Jonathan Charles; **McIntyre:** Steve Areno; **Dr. Londez:** Robert Axelrod; **Domino Walker:** Frederick Bloggs; **Stella:** Emily Brown; **Sally Yung:** Angie Callas; **Vicious:** George C. Cole; **Fad:** Toller Cranston; **Preview Narrator:** Jackson Daniels; **Coffee:** Nicole Edward; **Bob:** Jack Emmet; **Muriel:** Rebecca Forstadt; **V.T.:** Sonja S. Fox; **Mao:** W.T. Hatch; **Meifa:** Patricia Ja Lee; **Van:** Gully Jimson; **Gordon:** James Lyon; **Wen:** Mona Marshall; **Herman:** Gary Michaels; **Katrina:** Katia Morales; **Morgan:** James Penrod; **Lin:** Derek Stephen Prince; **Elisa:** Debbie DeRosa; **Abdul:** Joe Romersa; **Judy:** Lia Sargent; **Udai:** Gil Starberry; **Asimov:** Sparky Thorton; **Shin:** Bo Williams

### ◎ THE CRAMP TWINS

Pandemonium ensues when this pair of 10-year-old, polar-opposite twin boys Wayne and Lucien Cramp, who have nothing in common, take their sibling rivalry to new highs and lows in this imported Saturday-morning cartoon series that aired on FOX. Produced by TV-Loonland Animation and based on two graphic novels by Brian Wood, the half-hour comedy series, designed for children ages seven to 12, followed the offbeat shenanigans of Wayne, whose favorite pastimes include fighting, collecting strange stuff and stuffing his face with candy, and Lucien, a practicing vegetarian who likes studying, knitting and saving the world.

Originally a top-rated show in the United Kingdom on both the Cartoon Network and BBC1, the series, which was nominated in 2002 for the British Academy Children's Film and Television Award (BAFTA), was sold to more than 100 stations worldwide, including the United States on FOX's *FOX Box* Saturday-morning programming block along with 4Kids Entertainment's popular anime series *Kirby: Right Back at Ya!* and *Ultimate Muscle: The Kinnikuman Legacy.* The series also re-aired on America's Cartoon Network. A *CanWest Global/Cartoon Network Europe/TV-Loonland Animation/Sunbow Entertainment/4Kids Entertainment/British Broadcasting Corporation/FOX Box/YTV Production. Color. Half-hour. Premiered on FOX: February 1, 2003–January 14, 2005. Rebroadcast on CAR: June 14, 2004–April 3, 2005.*

*Voices*
**Wayne Cramp:** Tom Kenny; **Lucien Cramp:** Kath Soucie; **Tony Parsons/Seth Parsons, Tony's Dad:** Terry Klassen; **Wendy Winkle:** Jayne Peterson; **Mr. Winkle:** Colin Murdock; **Mrs. Winkle/Hilary Hissy/Lily Parsons, Tony's Mom:** Cathy Weseluck; **Mari Phelps:** Tabitha St. Germain; **Dorothy Cramp, the Cramp Twins' Mom:** Nicole Oliver; **Horace Cramp, the Cramp Twins' Dad:** Ian James Corlett; **Dirty Joe Muldoon:** Lee Tockar; **Marsha:** Ellen Kennedy; **Tandy:** Iris Quinn; **Mr. Pretty:** Jay Brazeau (2004– ); **Trailer:** Max Bolinger; **Bouncy Bob:** Dwight Schultz; **Kid #1:** Benjamin B. Smith; **Additional Voices:** Andrew Francis, Peter Kelamis, Jason Michas, Paula Newstone

### ◎ CRASHBOX! CRASHBOX!

Interactive live-action/animated game show for kids ages eight to 12 featuring fast-paced games about history, math, spelling, grammar, culture and vocabulary, mixing in 20 different styles, including stop-motion, cel animation, mixed media, claymation and cutout animation. Produced for HBO Family by Canada's Cuppa Coffee Animation, its first long-form series, each program included seven to eight two-to-five-minute educational games, from "Haunted House Party" to "Captain Bones" to "Dirty Pictures" to "Radio Scramble," hosted by comedian Jerry Stiller. Debuting in January 1999, 31 episodes of the popular weekday series aired until November 2004, after which time the series went into reruns. *A Cuppa Coffee Animation/Planet Grande Pictures Production. Color. Half-hour. Premiered on HBO FAM: January 6, 1999–November 1, 2004. Rebroadcast on HBO FAM: November 2004–.*

**Voices:**
**Host:** Jerry Stiller; **Revolting Slob:** Michael McShane; **Revolting Slob (Polite Voice):** Edie McClurg; **Poop or Scoop Announcer:** Danny Wells; **Haunted House Party Guests:** Carlos Alazaqui; **Dora Smarmy:** Mari Weiss; **Captain Bob/Sketch Pad:** Greg Eagles; **Verity:** Maggie Baird; **Riddlesnake Raj:** Veena Bidasha

### ◎ CREEPY CRAWLERS
In an experiment gone wrong, Chris Carter, a typical teenager, accidentally creates this entourage of kindly crustaceans with special powers (called "The Creepy Crawler Goopmandoes") who end up warring with a bunch of evil goopsters, the Crime Grimes, created by the demented magician Professor Guggengrime, in this 23-episode weekly half-hour fantasy/adventure series, which debuted in first-run syndication in 1994. The show ran two seasons and was later rebroadcast on the Family Channel. *A Saban Entertainment Production. Color. Half-hour. Premiered: September 12, 1994–96. Syndicated. Rebroadcast on FOX FAM: 2000–01.*

**Voices**
Jimmy Flanders, Steve Bulen, Stanley Gurd Jr., Johnny Lamb, Melody Lee, Anthony Mordy, Reed Waxman, Tyrone Work, O. R. Yarbles

### ◎ THE CRITIC
Pudgy, bald and unmerciful New York film critic Jay Sherman (described as "balder than Siskel and fatter than Ebert"), who is divorced, hated by his ex-wife and barely tolerated by his adoptive parents, is host of his own weekly cable television show, *Coming Attractions.* He reviews (and parodies) popular movies while constantly struggling to find happiness in his personal life in this half-hour, prime-time animated series from former *Simpsons* producers Mike Reiss and Al Jean and executive producer James L. Brooks, who developed the concept in March 1992 and initially toyed with making the series a live-action sitcom. Premiering on ABC in January of 1994, the series produced respectable ratings but was yanked after only six episodes had aired. (ABC planned to air the remaining seven episodes later that season.) In June 1994 the series slipped back on the air on ABC but was not renewed. FOX Network picked up the series for the 1994–95 season, ordering new episodes. Comedian Jon Lovitz, of *Saturday Night Live* fame, provided the voice of Jay Sherman. In December of 1995, Comedy Central added the program (in reruns) to its Sunday-night schedule opposite the new hit series *Dr. Katz, Professional Therapist. A Gracie Films/Film Roman Production in association with Columbia Pictures Television. Color. Half-hour. Premiered on ABC: January 26, 1994– March 1994; June 1, 1994–July 20, 1994; Premiered on FOX: March 5, 1995–July 30, 1995. Rebroadcast on COM: December 3, 1995.*

**Voices**
**Jay Sherman/Other Voices:** Jon Lovitz; **Margo:** Nancy Cartwright; **Marty Sherman/Other Voices:** Christine Cavanagh; **Franklin Sherman, Jay's father/Other Voices:** Gerritt Graham;

*An inquiring Cro-Magnon boy, Cro, enlists a highly intelligent mammoth, Phil, and a bumbling pair of Neanderthals in the acclaimed educational cartoon series* Cro.

**Eleanor Sherman, Jay's mother:** Judith Ivey, Kath Soucie; **Doris, Makeup Woman:** Doris Grau; **Vlada/Other Voices:** Nick Jameson; **Jeremy Hawke/Other Voices:** Maurice LaMarche; **Duke/Other Voices:** Charles Napier; **Penny Thompkins:** Russi Taylor; **Alice Tompkins:** Park Overall

### ◎ CRO
When a hip Woolly Mammoth named Phil defrosts in the 20th century, he spins tales about the good ol' days back in the Ice Age, entertaining and informing his modern-day friends Mike and Dr. C about the marvels of science and technology. He switches back and forth between the present and his adventures in the past with Cro, a canny orphaned Cro-Magnon boy, in this 21-episode educational half-hour animated series inspired by the book *The Way Things Work.* The series—aimed to teach children ages six to 11 that science can be fun—was produced by Children's Television Workshop, the people behind PBS's Emmy Award–winning children's series *Sesame Street.* It marked CTW's first animation production for television. *A Children's Television Workshop/Film Roman Production. Color. Half-hour. Premiered on ABC: September 18, 1993–July 15, 1995.*

**Voices**
**Phil:** Jim Cummings; **Dr. C:** April Ortiz; **Mike:** Jussie Smollett; **Cro:** Max Cassella

**THE WOOLLY MAMMOTHS: Ivana:** Laurie O'Brien; **Esmeralda:** Tress MacNeille; **Earle:** Frank Welker; **Mojo/Steamer:** Charlie Adler; **Pakka:** Candi Milo

**THE NEANDERTHALS: Nandy:** Ruth Buzzi; **Ogg:** Jim Cummings; **Gogg/Bobb:** Frank Welker

**THE CREATURES: Selene:** Jane Singer; **Big Red:** Charlie Adler; **Murray:** Jim Cummings

### ◎ CRUSADER RABBIT
Rocky and Bullwinkle creator Jay Ward and Alexander Anderson, the nephew of cartoon producer Paul Terry, originated the long-eared rabbit, Crusader, and pal Ragland ("Rags") T. Tiger in 1948, one year before the characters were "test-marketed" as what historians call the "first cartoon serial" and "first limited animation series"

made for television. Ward and Alexander first placed the characters in a film presentation called *The Comic Strips of Television*, along with two other features, "Hamhock Jones" and "Dudley Do-Right."

For many years it was commonly believed the show was syndicated in 1949. Research proves that the series actually was test-marketed the year before it aired nationally. (Unlike syndication, it was sold on a city-to-city basis, premiering in different cities on different dates due to the method of distribution.) The first Los Angeles air date was found to be Tuesday, August 1, 1950.

Jerry Fairbanks, a contract film supplier, was executive producer of the 1949–51 series, which the network turned down. The program aired during the 1950–51 season on NBC-owned and operated stations in several markets. Initially, 130 five-minute cliff hanging episodes were produced.

In 1957 television producer Shull Bonsall, owner of TV Spots, produced a new color series that was similar in nature to the original program. This time the series was syndicated and appeared on several NBC affiliate stations. *A Television Arts/Jerry Fairbanks Production/Creston Studios Production. Black-and-white. Color. Premiered: Fall 1949 test-marketed. Syndicated. 1950, Fall 1957 (new series).*

**Voices**
**Crusader Rabbit:** Lucille Bliss, Ge Ge Pearson; **Ragland T. Tiger:** Vern Louden; **Dudley Nightshade:** Russ Coughlan; **Narrator:** Roy Whaley

## ◎ CUBIX: ROBOTS FOR EVERYONE

In Bubbletown, a futuristic place where people either love robots (called "botties") or hate them, 13-year-old Connor quickly becomes friends with a robot he repairs named Cubix, and with his friends Chip, Mong and Abby and their companion robots Cerebix, Maximus and Dom-Dom, battles the evil villain Dr. K, who plans to use his army of vicious robots to conquer the world in this CGI-animated half-hour series, which first debuted in the United Kingdom on BBC1 and then in the United States on Kids' WB! in August 2001.

Based on the popular PlayStation game and Korean comic book, the sci-fi/adventure program, produced by 4Kids Entertainment along with the anime series *Yu-Gi-Oh!* for Kids' WB! lasted two seasons through May 2003 before it was picked up by FOX, which rebroadcast the series Saturday mornings from September 2003 to June 2004. In 2002, the British Academy of Film and Television Arts nominated the series for the best international production team award. *A Cinepix Inc./4Kids Entertainment/YTV Production. Color. Half-hour. Premiered on Kids WB!: August 11, 2001–March 16, 2002; March 15, 2003–May 10, 2003. Rebroadcast on FOX: September 6, 2003–June 12, 2004.*

**Voices**
**Dr. K:** Maddie Blaustein; **Connor:** Andrew Rannells; **Cubix:** Scottie Ray; **Chip:** Amy Birnbaum; **Mong/Cerebix:** Jimmy Zoppi; **Abby/Pestixide:** Veronica Taylor; **Maximus:** Frank Frankson; **Raska:** Megan Hollingshead; **Charles:** Ted Lewis; **Dondon/Raska:** Eric Stuart; **Raska (Season 2):** Megan Hollingshead; **Professor Nemo:** Dan Green

## ◎ CURIOUS GEORGE (1989)

Enchanting escapades of a precocious monkey and his resourceful master (the Man in the Yellow Hat) based on the popular children's books by H.A. and Margaret Ray. This Canadian-produced series of five-minute cartoon adventures was produced between 1979 and 1982 and was first shown in America on Nickelodeon in 1984. The cartoons were made a regular feature of the Nickelodeon series *Pinwheel* in 1985 and were later broadcast as a daily half-hour series of their own. In 1989 the entertaining series joined the popular Disney Channel series *Lunch Box* and, more recently, the network's weekday morning anthology series *Circle Time*. *A Lafferty, Harwood and Partners/Milktrain Production. Color. Half-hour. Premiered on NICK: 1984. Rebroadcast on DIS: 1989.*

**Voices**
**Narrator:** Jack Duffy

## ◎ CURIOUS GEORGE (2006)

An updated, animated version of the classic children's book character created by Margret and H.A. Rey, rendered in brightly colored, 2-D animation and geared toward children ages three to five, combining new and old stories. The curious little monkey introduces preschoolers to concepts in math, science and engineering in each episode. Narrated by Academy Award-nominated actor William H. Macy, the series, containing two animated stories with an educational component, followed the successful full-length animated feature of the same name released in February 2006, which grossed nearly $60 million.

Premiering on PBS stations in September 2006, the popular children's series' opening episode was "Curious George Flies a Kite," followed by "From Scratch," in which the clever monkey tries to prove a cat is innocent from scratching up booths in a restaurant. During its inaugural season, the weekday series was part of PBS's acclaimed *Ready Set Learn!* program block with the live-action preschool program *It's a Big, Big World*, with the series first-season episodes airing until mid-January 2007. *An Imagine Entertainment/WGBH-TV/Universal Studios Family Production. Color. Half-hour. Premiered on PBS Kids: September 4, 2006.*

**Voices**
**Narrator:** William H. Macy; **Ted/Man in the Yellow Hat:** Jeff Bennett; **George:** Frank Welker

## ◎ CYBERCHASE

Three extraordinary kids—Matt, the leader; Jackie, the resident fashion guru; and Inez, the ever-inquisitive one—collectively called the Cybersquad, initiate a series of exciting missions in cyberspace with the help of Dr. Marbles and Digit, the Motherboard's faithful aides, and using their brawn and math skills to overpower the dastardly Hacker's plans to become the overlord of cyberspace in this half-hour educational cartoon series for PBS Kids. Premiering in January 2002, the popular comedy/adventure series has remained continuously on the air with new episodes for five consecutive seasons. In 2006 the program became part of *PBS Kids Go!*, an afternoon program block that included *Maya & Miguel*, *Postcards from Buster* and *Arthur*, which became a separate digital channel in the fall of 2006. *A Thirteen-WNET New York/Nelvana International Production. Color. Half-hour. Premiered on PBS Kids: January 21, 2002.*

**Voices**
**The Hacker:** Christopher Lloyd; **Digit:** Gilbert Gottfried; **Matt:** Jacqueline Pilon; **Jackie:** Novie Edwards; **Inez:** Annick Obonsawin; **Buzz:** Len Carlson; **Delete:** Rob Tinkler; **Dr. Marbles:** Richard Binsley; **Motherboard:** Kristina Nicholl

## ◎ CYBER C.O.P.S.

(See C.OP.S.)

## ◎ CYBERSIX

High school biology teacher Lucas Amato's life quickly changes after he sees a man disappear before his eyes and finds a capsule of glowing green liquid that he keeps until the beauteous Cybersix seeks its return, warning him his life will be in peril otherwise, in this joint Japanese and Canadian production based on the popular Japanese comic book series. The 13-episode fantasy series aired Saturday mornings on FOX Network beginning in August 2000. A *T.M.S. Productions/TV Tokyo/NOA/The Ocean Group Production. Color. Half-hour. Premiered on FOX: August 19, 2000–November 4, 2000.*

**Voices**
**Lucas Amato:** Michael Dobson; **Jose:** Alex Doduk; **Julian:** Andrew Francis; **Lori/Grizelda/Elaine:** Janyse Jaud; **Von Reichter:** Terry Klassen; **Cybersix/Adrian Seidelman:** Cathy Weseluck; **Yashimoto:** Brian Drummon; **Terra:** L. Harvey Gold; **Akiko:** Chantal Strand

## ◎ CYBORG 009
Possessing the strength of 100 men, a part-human, part-robotic soldier, the former juvenile deliquent Joe Shinamura, now known as Cyborg 009, with his team of eight uniquely endowed, outcast cyborgs rebels against the evil Black Ghost and his army of perfect soldier robots to save the world from his diabolical plan in this Japanese-imported anime series based on the manga by Shotaro Ishinomori. The third animated television series based on the character, following two previous weekly series shown in Japan in 1966 and 1979, this 2001 English-dubbed production, featuring 26 half-hour episodes, premiered on Cartoon Network in June 2003 as part of the network's weekend-night *Toonami* action program block. *An Ishinomori Productions/TV Tokyo Production. Color. Half-hour. Premiered on CAR: June 30, 2003–November 1, 2004.*

**Voices**
**Joe Shimamura/Cyborg 009:** Joshua Seth; **Francoise Arnoul/Cyborg 003:** Midge Mayes, Dorothy Melendrez; **Jet Link/Cyborg 002:** Kirk Thorton; **Ivan Wisky/Cyborg 001:** R. Martin Klein; **Heinrich Albert/Cyborg 004:** Jim Taggert; **G-Junior/Cyborg 005:** Beau Billingslea; **Dr. Isaac Gilmore:** Sy Prescott; **Chang Changku/Cyborg 006:** Steve Kramer; **Great Britain/Cyborg 007:** Michael Sorich; **Pyunma/Cyborg 008:** Mario L. Patrenella; **Professor Kazumi:** Mike Reynolds; **Rosa:** Jane Allen; **Cyborg 0013/Commander Farej:** Steven Blum; **Jean-Paul/Young G.B./Apollo:** Richard Hayworth; **Black Ghost/Black Ghost Commander:** Richard Epcar; **Hera:** Sonja S. Fox; **Cyborg 0012:** Melora Harte; **Cynthia:** Julie Maddalena; **Captain Zanbarusu:** Jake Martin; **Cynthia's Father:** Michael MacConnohie; **Black Ghost Aide:** Jeff Nimoy; **Helicopter Reporter:** Tony Oliver; **Minotaur:** Bob Papenbrook; **Hilda/Artemis:** Lia Sargent; **Black Ghost Thug:** Gil Starberry; **Black Ghost Thug/Dr. Baruku:** Dave Wittenberg; **Mr. Yasu:** Dan Woren

## ◎ CYBORG BIG "X"
Akira, a young refugee, is changed into a cyborg by Nazi renegade scientists, who place his brain in the body of a powerful robot. As Cyborg Big "X," he uses a special magnetic pen as his sole weapon to do battle with those who could use science for nefarious ends. Created by Osamu Tezuka, the originator of *Astro Boy*, the half-hour science-fiction series was adapted from Tezuka's comic strip, *Big X*. The series, telecast in Japan in 1964, was broadcast in the United States three years later. *A Global/Transglobal Production. Color. Half-hour. Premiered: Fall 1967. Syndicated.*

## ◎ DA BOOM CREW
Four thrill-seeking orphans become space heroes following an accidental power surge and they are transported into the video game world they created in this four-episode hip-hop, science fiction animated series from the creators of *The Proud Family* and *Dave the Barbarian* that aired briefly Saturday mornings on the WB Television Network's Kids' WB! *A BFC Berliner Film Companie/Jambalaya Studio Production. Color. Half-hour. Premiered on the WB (Kids' WB!): September 11, 2004–October 2, 2004.*

**Voices**
**Nate:** Jascha Washington; **Helok:** Morris Day; **Jerome:** Jerome Benton; **Rickie:** Melanie Tonello; **Jubei:** Mitchell Eisner; **Justin:** Jordan Francis

## ◎ THE DAFFY AND SPEEDY SHOW
Daffy Duck and Speedy Gonzales starred in this half-hour Saturday-morning series for NBC, composed of previously released Warner Bros. theatrical cartoons. Lasting only one season, the comical cartoon pair jumped to rival network CBS the following season to headline the short-lived hour-long series *The Daffy and Speedy/Sylvester and Tweety Show*. *A Warner Bros. Television Production. Color. Half-hour. Premiered on NBC: September 12, 1981–September 4, 1982.*

**Voices**
Mel Blanc (primary voice)

## ◎ THE DAFFY AND SPEEDY/SYLVESTER AND TWEETY SHOW
CBS aired this hour-long collection of Warner Bros. theatrical cartoons starring Daffy Duck, Speedy Gonzales and Sylvester and Tweety on the 1981–82 Saturday-morning schedule as the lead-in show to the popular *Bugs Bunny/Road Runner Hour*, amounting to a solid two-hour cartoon block of classic Warner Bros. cartoons. The network pulled the show about a month after its debut. *A Warner Bros. Television Production. Color. One hour. Premiered on CBS: September 18, 1982–October 23, 1982.*

**Voices**
Mel Blanc (primary voice)

## ◎ THE DAFFY DUCK SHOW (1978)
For years the wacky, malicious Daffy Duck pleaded with Bugs Bunny for his own TV show. His ardent efforts were finally rewarded when NBC and the Warner Bros. cartoon department packaged a series starring the slurred-talking duck and a host of other Warner characters—Pepe Le Pew, Speedy Gonzales and Foghorn Leghorn—from old theatrical one-reelers. The show consisted of vintage Warner Bros. and DePatie-Freleng cartoons produced during the 1950s and 1960s. *A Warner Bros. Production. Color. Half-hour. Premiered on NBC: November 4, 1978–September 1981.*

**Voices**
**Daffy Duck/Pepe Le Pew/Speedy Gonzales/Foghorn Leg-horn:** Mel Blanc

## ◎ THE DAFFY DUCK SHOW (1996)
The WB Television Network added this cartoon anthology series to its Saturday-morning Kids' WB lineup in late 1996 to replace the low-rated superhero cartoon series *Freakazoid!* Featuring a new animated opening of Daffy Duck as a "jammin'" duck, the series showcased each half-hour two Daffy Duck cartoons bookended with one cartoon starring other Warner Bros. cartoon luminaries—Elmer Fudd, Tweety and Sylvester or Foghorn Leghorn—and a brief segment called "Hip Clip," featuring excerpts from existing Warner Bros. cartoons. *A Warner Bros. Production. Color. Half-hour. Premiered on WB: 1996.*

*Voices*
Mel Blanc (primary voice)

## ◎ DAIGUNDER
Known as the mighty Daigunder, a young boy named Akira Ake-bono and his team of talking robots—Bullion, Eagle Arrow, Dri-mog, Despector, Tirhorn, Ryugu and Diagu—battle for supremacy against a group of highly skilled robotic foes in tournaments in pursuit of the highly coveted Titan Belt in this futuristic, kid-friendly series, first seen on Japanese television in 2002 and based on Hasbro's high-tech spinning top toys.

Originally produced by NAS for Japan's TV Tokyo, this immensely popular 39-episode science fiction adventure anime series joined cable's ABC Family, airing Saturday and Sunday mornings, to anchor the network's anime offerings, replacing the poorly rated *Tokyo Pig* cartoon series, in September 2003. Return-ing for a second season, the series aired on both ABC Family's weekday and weekend anime block, joined by *Digimon* and *Mebabots*, which were broadcast only on weekends. The program returned in reruns as part of an all-new Jetix program block lineup in June 2006 until ABC Family dropped the popular cartoon block, with Toon Disney picking up the series, along with *Mon Colle Knights, Beyblade, Shinzo* and *Digimon*, to add to its Sunday anime-packed *Jetix* block in September 2006. *An Aeon Inc./NAS/ Nippon Animation/Sensation Animation Production. Color. Half-hour. Premiered on ABC FAM: September 13, 2003–December 28, 2003. Rebroadcast on ABC FAM: June 10, 2006–August 31, 2006. Rebroadcast on TDIS: September 3, 2006–.*

*Voices*
**Akira Akebono:** Barbara Goodson; **Eagle Arrow:** Richard Epcar; **Despector:** Steve Kramer; **Tri-Horn:** Walter Lang; **First Tourna-ment Announcer:** Dave Mallow; **Heruka:** Lara Jill Miller; **Bulion:** Bob Pappenbrook; **Boneres:** Paul Schrier; **Ryugu:** Joshua Seth; **Daigu/Daigunder:** Michael Sorich; **Ginzan:** Tom Wyner; **Bone Rex:** Paul Schrier; **Other Voices:** Michael McConnohie

## ◎ DA MOB
Three friends—Rooster, Tom and JT—form an ultimate hip-hop band and do anything to land a record deal and hit the big time in this joint German-Swedish-British 14-episode half-hour animated comedy series that aired weekends on ABC Family. *A Happy Life/ Quintus Animation/Millimages/TV-Loonland Production. Color. Half-hour. Premiered on ABC FAM: November 3, 2001–March 30, 2002.*

*Voices*
**Rooster/Tom:** Jamie Kennedy; **JT:** Stuart Stone; **Maurice:** Neil Ross, Stephen Fry; **Tupac:** Dame Lee; **Sir Hamsta Booty:** Phil LaMarr; **Tara Byron:** Tara Strong; **Tara's Boyfriend:** Adam Law-son; **Wanda:** Iona Morris; **Twins:** Natasha Slayton; **Melanie Spores:** Kelli Garner; **Other Voices:** Amy Lyndon, Natasha Slayton

## ◎ DAN DARE, PILOT OF THE FUTURE
Joined by his partner Digby and the beautiful Professor Peabody, noble Space Fleet chief pilot Dan Dare defends the universe from the likes of the evil green-headed Mekon in this new computer-animated television series based on the original British science-fic-tion comic strip created by illustrator Frank Hampson. Featuring 13 two-part adventures and the voices of Robbie Coltrane, Tim Curry and Charles Dance as space villains, this $20 million, CGI-animated half-hour science fiction fantasy series produced in 2001 and taking 16 months to make aired in the United States on VOOM's Animania HD. *A Foundation Imaging Production. Color. Half-hour. Premiered on ANI: January 2004.*

*Voices*
**Dan Dare:** Greg Ellis; **Hank Hogan:** Chris Cox; **Professor Joce-lyn Peabody:** Carole Ruggier; **Mekon:** Rob Paulsen; **Other Voices:** Robbie Coltraine, Tim Curry, Charles Dance

## ◎ DANGERMOUSE
The British Secret Service's most dashing rodent safeguards the lives of everyone who values justice and liberty, waging war against the forces of evil—usually in the form of Baron Silas Greenback. This British import came from the makers of the hit series *Count Duckula*, and DangerMouse first appeared in several episodes of that program before he was given his own series. Each program varied, containing either one complete story or two episodes (the latter varied in length) per half-hour broadcast. On September 28, 1981, the 65-episode series premiered on the United Kingdom's ITV Network. It wasn't syndicated in this country until three years later on Nickelodeon. *A Cosgrove Hall Production in association with Thames Television. Color. Half-hour. Premiered on NICK: June 4, 1984–May 31, 1987. Rebroadcast on NICK JR.: September 30, 1991–October 2, 1994. Syndicated: 1984.*

*Voices*
**DangerMouse/Colonel K/Nero/Narrator:** David Jason; **Penfold, his faithful assistant:** Terry Scott; **Baron Silas Greenback:** Edward Kelsey; **Stiletto, Greenback's henchman:** Brian Trueman

## ◎ DANNY PHANTOM
After an experiment at his father Jack Fenton's lab accidentally transforms him into a half-human, half-ghost teen, Danny Phan-tom (alias Danny Fenton) battles supernatural beings while also attending high school and maintaining his life with his family and friends, in this half-hour science-fiction fantasy series created for Nickelodeon by Butch Harman, creator of TV's *The Fairly OddParents*. Becoming one of Nickelodeon's most-watched origi-nal cartoon series, Danny starred in 20 first-season episodes, including his first hour-long prime time animated special based on the hit cartoon series *Reign Storm*, which aired in late July 2005. Renewed for a second season, Nickelodeon commissioned 17 new episodes, including a second hour-long prime time special,

*Debonair British secret service agent DangerMouse and his faithful assistant Penfold find trouble brewing in Cosgrove-Hall's immensely popular animated adventure series DangerMouse. © Cosgrove-Hall Productions. All rights reserved.*

*The Ultimate Enemy*, which aired that September, and a half-hour Christmas special, *Fright Before Christmas*, broadcast that December. In 2006 the ghost-hunting teen superhero was back for a third season, with 16 brand-new episodes and two additional specials that season—the one-hour *Reality Trip* in June and the half-hour *Urban Jungle* in October. *A Nicktoons/Billinfold/Nelvana Production. Color. Half-hour. Premiered on NICK: April 3, 2004.*

### Voices

**Danny Fenton/Phantom/Walla:** David Kaufman; **Maddie Fenton, Danny's mom/Lunch Lady Ghost Empress She-Wolf/Walla:** Kath Soucie; **Jack Fenton, Danny's dad/The Box Ghost/Kid Walla/ Auto Jack/Stuffed Animal #1/Geek Danny/Nicolai Technus:** Rob Paulsen; **Jazz Fenton/Nerd Girl/Walla:** Collen O'Shaughnessey; **Tucker Foley:** Rickey D'Shon Collins; **Paulina/Stuffed Animal #2:** Maria Canals; **Vice-Principal Lancer:** Ron Perlman; **Samantha "Sam" Manson/Police Dispatcher:** Grey DeLisle; **Dash Baxter/Jeremy/Operative O:** Scott Bullock; **Qwan:** Dat Phan, James Sie; **Skulker:** Kevin Michael Richardson; **Mikey/Nathan/Lance Thunder/News Reporter Operative K/Generic TV Reporter/ Scarlet Samarai/Nerds Irving/Observant #1/Guy:** Dee Bradley Baker; **Kwan:** James Sie; **Ember/Penelope Spectra/Tiffany Snow/ Baby Danny/Lydia/Walla/Ember—Nasty Burger Employee:** Tara Strong; **Klemper/Box Store Owner/Dash Baxter:** S. Scott Bullock; **Pam:** Laraine Newman; **Samantha "Sam" Manson:** Grey DeLisle; **Vlad Plasmius:** Martin Mull; **Valerie Grey:** Cree Summer; **Damon:** Phil Morris; **Poindexter:** Peter MacNicol; **Pariah Dark:** Brian Cox; **Fright Knight:** Michael Dorn; **Clockwork:** David Carradine; **Fright Knight:** Michael Dorn; **Daman/Observant #2:** Phil Morris; **Vlad Masters:** Martin Mull; **Dark Danny:** Eric Roberts; **Ghost Writer:** Will Arnett; **Walker:** James Arnold Taylor; **Bertrand:** Jim Ward; **Young Blood:** Taylor Lautner; **Maurice Foley/Old Man/Nerd:** Phil LaMarr; **Freakshow:** Jon Cryer

### ⊚ DARIA

The ultimate "whatever" girl, this dour 16-year-old teen hipster (Daria Morgendorffer), who's almost too smart for her own good, provides observations of the absurdities of life—in high school, with her classmates and as a teenager growing up in the 1990s—in this half-hour weekly spinoff of MTV's immensely popular *Beavis & Butt-Head*. The *My So-Called Life*–styled series—MTV's first full-length animated sitcom—debuted with 13 half-hour episodes, airing regularly on Monday nights on the music cable network in early 1997. In *Beavis & Butt-Head*, Daria was well known to fans as the sardonic "smart kid" who hung around the boys because she found their stupidity entertaining. (In all of her seasons on the show, she was a favorite character of viewers.) For her own series, she moved to a new town, Lawndale, with her stressed-out career-fixated parents, Helen and Jake, and her relentlessly cute and popular younger sister, Quinn. The series was developed by Glenn Eichler and Susie Lewis Lynn, who is also one of the show's producers. *An MTV Animation Production. Color. Half-hour. Premiered on MTV: March 3, 1997–January 21, 2002. Rebroadcast on NOG: July 3, 2002–June 3, 2006.*

### Voices

**Daria Morgendorffer:** Tracey Grandstaff; **Quinn/Helen Morgendorffer/Jane Lane:** Wendy Hoopes; **Jake Morgendorffer:** Julian Rebolledo; **Trent Lane:** Alvero J. Gonzalez; **Kevin Thompson/ Mr. DeMartino/Mr. O'Neill:** Marc Thompson; **Brittany Taylor:** Lisa Collins

### ⊚ DARKSTALKERS

Originated in video arcades in the summer of 1994 to rave reviews (later released as CD-ROM video game) and following the path of other arcade-inspired cartoon series, this 13-episode half-hour syndicated series from the producers of TV's *X-Men* and *The Tick* featured 10 classic supernatural characters done with a 1990s' sensibility and touch of humor à la the animated *Ghostbusters*. *A Graz Entertainment/Capcom Production. Color. Half-hour. Premiered: September 1, 1996. Syndicated.*

### Voices

**Lord Demitri:** Michael Donovan; **Donovan:** Gary Chalk; **Lord Raptor:** Scott McNeill; **Felicia:** Cree Summer, Janyse Jaud; **Morrigan:** Kathleen Barr, Saffron Henderrson; **Harry Grimoire:** Bill Switzer; **Victor/Ship's Computer:** Ian James; **Harry Grimoire:** Kyle Labine; **Jonathan Talbaine:** Lee Tockar; **Pyron:** Tony Jay

### ⊚ DARKWING DUCK

His true identity known only to his best friend, Launchpad McQuack, Drake Mallard (alias Darkwing Duck), an adoptive father, ace avenger and crimebuster extraordinare, balances parenting his precocious nine-year-old daughter Gosalyn with saving the world. He is the shadowy guardian who protects the city of St. Canard from dangerous and despicable delinquents in this half-hour spinoff of the Disney series *DuckTales*. The popular 91-episode comedy/adventure series (originally titled *Double-O Duck*) premiered on The Disney Channel in April of 1991. It aired through September of that year before being added to ABC's fall lineup, running concurrently on the network (with 13 new episodes produced exclusively for ABC and not seen in syndication) and in syndication as anchor of the two-hour weekday cartoon block the *Disney Afternoon*. Nominated for a daytime Emmy Award in 1993, the program replaced Disney's *Adventures of the Gummi Bears*. The animated opener of the syndicated version debuted on the same day as the ABC series as a two-hour Disney special—combined with a look at the new season of *The Mickey Mouse Club*—before airing in its usual Monday-through-Friday time slot.

From 1998 to 2004, reruns aired on Toon Disney with series rebroadcast only once since then in a two-hour block. *A Walt Disney Television Animation Production. Color. Half-hour. Premiered on DIS: April 6, 1991. Premiered on ABC: September 7, 1991–September 4, 1993. Syndicated: September 7, 1991–September 1, 1995. Rebroadcast on TDIS: April 18, 1998–December 25, 2004; January 19, 2007 (two-hour block).*

### Voices

**Darkwing Duck (a.k.a. Drake Mallard)/Negaduck/Moliarty/ Cousin Globby:** Jim Cummings; **Gizmo Duck:** Hamilton Camp; **Gosalyn Mallard:** Cathy Cavadini, Christine Cavanaugh; **J. Gander Hooter:** Danny Mann; **Launchpad McQuack:** Terry McGovern; **Steelbeak:** Rob Paulsen; **Honker Muddlefoot:** Katie Leigh; **Herb Muddlefoot:** Jim Cummings; **Binkie Muddlefoot:** Susan Tolsky; **Tank Muddlefoot:** Dana Hill; **Bushroot:** Tino Insana; **Agent Gryslikoff:** Ron Feinberg; **Megavolt:** Dan Castellaneta; **Morgana Macawber/Aunt Nasty:** Kath Soucie; **Tuskerninni:** Kenneth Mars; **Meraculo Macawber:** Frank Welker

### ⊚ DASTARDLY AND MUTTLEY IN THEIR FLYING MACHINES

Villainous Dick Dastardly, his fumbling henchdog Muttley, and an entourage of World War I flying aces pursue American courier Yankee Doodle Pigeon (who was voiceless) to intercept top-secret information in this offbeat show with bad guys as the series' title characters. Featured each week were two Dastardly and Muttley adventures and four Dick Dastardly Blackouts billed as "Wing Dings." The series theme song, "Stop That Pigeon," was written by Bill Hanna and Hoyt Curtin. *A Hanna-Barbera Production. Color.*

*Half-hour. Premiered on CBS: September 13, 1969–September 3, 1971. Rebroadcast on CAR: April 23, 1995 (Super Chunk). Rebroadcast on BOOM: May 13, 2000–.*

**Voices**
**Dick Dastardly/The General:** Paul Winchell; **Muttley/Yankee Doodle Pigeon/Klunk/Zilly:** Don Messick

## ⊚ DAVEY AND GOLIATH

Long-running 15-minute religious series conceived by Art Clokey, creator of *Gumby and Pokey*, tracing the saga of young Davey Hansen and his talking dog, Goliath, who solve everyday problems while relating the word of God in an entertaining and less preachy fashion. Like *Gumby*, the series of 64 adventures was filmed in pixillation, a stop-motion photography process.

Funded by the Lutheran Council of Churches and produced between 1959 and 1960, the series was first nationally syndicated in January 1961. (Initial experimental efforts were conducted the year before.) Not only was the series a huge success in the United States, it subsequently was dubbed in Portuguese and Spanish. Six half-hour specials were also produced featuring the same cast of characters ("To the Rescue," "Happy Easter," "School . . . Who Needs It?" "Halloween Who-Dun-It," "Christmas Lost and Found," and "New Year Promise").

Production of the series ended when funding from the church foundation ran out. The program is still seen in many television markets today, without five of the series' original episodes, which were removed from circulation for various reasons ("On the Line," "Polka Dot Tie," "Ten Little Indians," "Man of the House" and "The Gang").

In 2004, an all-new stop-motion animated special and first *Davey and Goliath* production in 30 years, *Davey and Goliath's Snowboard Christmas*, was produced for the Hallmark Channel. A *Clokey Production. Color. Half-hour. Premiered: January 1961. Syndicated.*

**Voices**
**Davey Hansen:** Norma McMillan, Nancy Wible; **Goliath:** Hal Smith; **Other Voices:** Richard Beals

*Davey Hansen and his talking dog, Goliath, are flanked by Davey's father in a scene from the long-running religious series, Davey and Goliath. © Clokey Productions*

*A daring team of superheroes battles the evil Ming the Merciless in the futuristic fantasy/adventure series* Defenders of the Earth. *© King Features Entertainment* (COURTESY: MARVEL PRODUCTIONS)

## ⊚ DEFENDERS OF THE EARTH

The year is A.D. 2015. The human race is about to fall under the control of the evil Ming the Merciless, famous intergalactic villain from the planet Mongo. A team of the universe's most adventurous, powerful, superheroes—Flash Gordon, The Phantom, Mandrake the Magician and Lothar—who join forces to overtake Ming with the help of their descendants: Rick Gordon, Flash's scientific genius son; Jedda Walker, the Phantom's mysterious daughter; L.J. (Lothar Junior), the streetwise son of Lother; Kshin, a 10-year-old orphaned Oriental boy; and Zuffy, a cute and cuddly ball of alien fur.

Originally produced in 1985, the series aired one year later in first-run syndication. In 1992 the Sci-Fi Channel began rebroadcasting the series as part of its two-hour cartoon program block *Cartoon Quest. A Marvel Production in association with King Features Entertainment. Color. Half-hour. Premiered: September 8, 1986. Syndicated. Rebroadcast on SCI: September 25, 1992–September 22, 1995.*

**Voices**
William Callaway, Adam Carl, Ron Feinberg, Buster Jones, Loren Lester, Sarah Partridge, Diane Pershing, Peter Renaday, Lou Richards, Peter Mark Richman, Dion Williams

## ⊚ DENNIS THE MENACE

Comic-strip artist Hank Ketcham's popular newspaper strip inspired this first-run, 78-episode half-hour animated series starring the All-American handful, Dennis, whose zest for life spells trouble for his neighbor, Mr. Wilson. First syndicated in 1985, the series also aired on CBS in 1988, featuring all-new episodes. The series was later rebroadcast on USA Network's *Cartoon Express. A DIC Enterprises Production. Color. Half-hour. Premiered: September 1985. Syndicated. Premiered on CBS: January 2, 1988– September 10, 1988. Rebroadcast on USA: July 7, 1996–March 23, 1997. Rebroadcast on FOX FAM: August 1998–May 1999. Rebroadcast on CAR: July 2, 2001–October 12, 2001. Rebroadcast on BFC: October 3, 2005–December 30, 2005. Rebroadcast on BOOM: January 15, 2007–.*

**Voices**
**Dennis Mitchell:** Brennan Thicke; **Alice Mitchell, his mother:** Louise Vallance, Marilyn Lightstone; **Henry Mitchell, his father:** Brian George, Maurice LaMarche; **Mr. Wilson:** Phil Hartman, Maurice LaMarche; **Martha, his wife:** Marilyn Lightstone; **Joey, Dennis's friend/Margaret, Dennis's friend/Tommy:** Jeanine Elias; **Dick/Jim:** Hark Sound; **Ruff:** Phil Hartman

## ◉ DENVER, THE LAST DINOSAUR

The series follows the adventures of fun-loving dinosaur, Denver, and his group of ingenious young friends, Wally, Jeremy, Shades and Mario, who bring him into the mainstream of the 20th century in contemporary situations. Following its debut, the program captured the number-one spot for viewers, aged two to 11, beating all other kids' shows, including *DuckTales, Teenage Mutant Ninja Turtles* and *The Jetsons.* In 1991 the series was rebroadcast on USA Network's weekday cartoon block *Cartoon Express. A World Events/Calico Productions presentation. Color. Half-hour. Premiered on KTTV-Ch. 11, Los Angeles, April 29, 1988. Syndicated. Rebroadcast on USA: October 18, 1991–September 10, 1995.*

**Voices**
**Wally/Jeremy:** Adam Carl; **Mario/Shades:** Cam Clarke; **Morton Fizzback/Professor Funt:** Brian Cummings; **Denver the Last Dinosaur:** Pat Fraley; **Chet/Motley:** Rob Paulsen; **Heather/Casey:** Kath Soucie

## ◉ DEPUTY DAWG

A not-so-bright Southern lawman, Deputy Dawg, fumbles his way to maintaining law and order in Mississippi, hounded by a pack of pranksters. His best friends and worst enemies are other animals from the South: Vincent "Vince" Van Gopher, Ty Coon the Racoon, Muskie the Muskrat and Pig Newton. In October 1960 the pot-bellied sheriff debuted in over 47 television markets, sponsored by W.H. Lay Potato Chips. The success of the character inspired Terrytoons to release several of the made-for-television cartoons theatrically in 1962. Seven years later Deputy Dawg premiered on NBC in a new vehicle, *The Deputy Dawg Show.* The series repeated episodes from the original series and featured two additional segments composed of previously released theatrical cartoons: *Gandy Goose* and *Terry-Toon Classics.*

A *Terrytoons/CBS Films, Inc., Production. Color. Half hour. Syndicated: October 1960 (Deputy Dawg). Premiered on NBC: September 11, 1971–September 2, 1972 (The Deputy Dawg Show).*

**Voices**
**Deputy Dawg/Vincent Van Gopher/Ty Coon/The Sheriff:** Dayton Allen

## ◉ DETENTION

Eight mischievous Benedict Arnold Middle School students— including their brainy leader Shareena; the alien-seeking Emmitt; the strange and energetic Gug; the comic fanatic Jim; the yo-yo wielding Duncan Bubble; and scheming twins Orangejella and Lemonjella—wind up in detention while driving their teacher crazy in this half-hour comedy series broadcast Saturday mornings and weekday afternoons on Kids' WB! *A Warner Bros. Television Animation Production. Color. Half-hour. Premiered on Kids' WB!: September 11, 1999–August 31, 2001.*

**Voices**
**Gug:** Carlos Alazraqui; **Mr. Fletcher/Duncan's Yo-Yo:** Bob Doucette; **Jim Kim:** Roger Eschbacher; **Shelley Kelley:** Pamelyn Ferdin; **Miss Eugenia P. Kisskillya:** Kathleen Freeman; **Patsy Wickett:** Mary Gross; **Lemonjella LaBelle:** Tia Mowry; **Shareena Wickert/Orangella LaBelle:** Tara Strong; **Emmitt Roswell:** Billy West

## ◉ DEVLIN

Star circus attractions, daredevil stunt motorcyclist Ernie Devlin and his orphaned sister and brother—Sandy and Tod—use their skills to help circus animals and others in this half-hour Saturday-morning series, which also featured a weekly safety tip for young viewers. *A Hanna-Barbera Production. Color. Half-hour. Premiered on ABC: September 11, 1974–February 15, 1976. Rebroadcast on BOOM: June 24, 2000–December 18, 2004.*

**Voices**
**Ernie Devlin:** Mike Bell; **Tod Devlin:** Micky Dolenz; **Sandy Devlin:** Michele Robinson; **Hank:** Norman Alden

## ◉ DEXTER'S LABORATORY

A squat, bespectacled, neurotic kid genius with a pouf of bright-red hair creates fantastic inventions in his huge bedroom laboratory despite the pesky intolerance of his ditsy big sister Dee Dee in this computer-generated animated half-hour series produced exclusively for the Cartoon Network. The character was the first "breakout" star of Hanna-Barbera's *World Premiere Toons* series, which had premiered a year earlier on the Cartoon Network featuring the cartoon short "Dexter," produced by then 26-year-old Russian-born filmmaker Genndy Tartakovsky. The film won Tartakovsky both an Emmy nomination in 1995 (and again in 1996 for the series) and a contract from the network to develop "Dexter" into a series. Starring in 52 all-new half-hours, each program includes two *Dexter Laboratory* shorts and a third related segment, either "Dial M for Monkey," about a superpowered, crimefighting primate who sets out to save the world when Dexter isn't looking (1996–97 season), or "Justice Friends," which follows a group of superheroes challenged more by the problems of living together than the evil forces that threaten the world (1997–98 season).

In December 1999, Dexter and company were featured in their first and only hour-long special based on the popular weekly, "Ego Trip." The following season, Christine Cavanaugh, the voice of Dexter, was honored with an Annie Award for "Outstanding Individual Achievement." Following the 1997–1998 season, the series went on hiatus while previously aired episodes remained in reruns. In 2001, production of a 26 new half-hours commenced for the 2001–02 and 2002–03 seasons. Nominated for four Emmy Awards overall, Cartoon Network canceled the show in November 2003. In January 2006, Cartoon Network's sister channel, Boomerang, picked up the series and began reairing it. *A Hanna-Barbera Cartoon Network Production. Color. Half-hour. Premiered on CAR: April 28, 1996–November 20, 2003. Rebroadcast on BOOM: January 16, 2006–.*

*A boy genius who creates fantastic inventions in his bedroom laboratory cooks up all sorts of adventures in the Emmy-nominated series Dexter's Laboratory. © Hanna-Barbera Productions* (COURTESY: CARTOON NETWORK)

**Voices**

**DEXTER: Dexter:** Christine Cavanagh; **Dee Dee:** Allison Moore, Kat Cressida; **Mom:** Kath Soucie; **Dad:** Jeff Bennett

**DIAL M FOR MONKEY: Monkey:** Frank Welker

**JUSTICE FRIENDS: The Infraggable Krunk:** Frank Welker; **Major Glory:** Rob Paulsen; **Valhallen/Living Bullet:** Tom Kenny

## ◎ D.I.C.E.

Part of the intergalactic organization, D.I.C.E. (DNA Integrated Cybernetic Enterprises), which responds to emergencies throughout the Sarbylon galaxy, a special unit of highly trained kids called D.I.C.E. F-99, uses transforming dinosaur vehicles called Dinobreakers to come to the rescue when problems arise in the Sarbylion galaxy in this riveting computer-animated anime series originally made for U.S. television that debuted on Cartoon Network—which acquired all 26 episodes of the series—in January 2005 with the premiere episode "S.O.S. from Planet Saffaron." *A Bandai Entertainment/Xebec/Studio Galapagos Production. Color. Half-hour. Premiered on CAR: January 22, 2005–March 24, 2005.*

**Voices**

**Jet Siegel:** Jeffery Watson; **Puffy Angel:** Caitlyne Medreck; **Chao Lee:** Lucus Gilbertson; **Sam N' Dool:** Zoe Slusar; **Robert Clapice:** Brendan Hunter; **Tak Carter:** Scott Roberts; **Marcia Rizarov:** Carol Anne Day; **Clo-Zan:** Howard Cole; **Captain Sid/Phantom**

**Knight:** Jonathan Love; **Captain Spike:** Mark Gathar; **Smil:** Dave Pettitt; **Mok:** Jennifer Bain

## ◎ THE DICK AND PAULA CELEBRITY SPECIAL

Celebrity talk-show hosts Dick and Paula feature assorted well-known and historic figures, from Charles Darwin to Lewis and Clark, as guests to talk about their work in this animated comedy series for the FX cable network. Television broadcaster Tom Snyder's company coproduced this "Squigglevision" computer-animated series—a technique that caused the edges of characters to constantly vibrate—with Soup2Nuts, producers of the hit Comedy Central cartoon series *Dr. Katz, Professional Therapist, Home Movies* and *Science Court*. Every episode was written using a method known as "retroscripting," whereby actors were given basic outlines and improvised the dialogue that was later melded into a coherent script. Never catching on with audiences, FX quickly canceled the series after broadcasting less than a dozen episodes. *A Tom Snyder/Soup2Nuts Production. Color. Half-hour. Premiered on FX: July 20, 1999–September 21, 1999.*

**Voices**

**Dick:** Richard Snee; **Paula:** Paula Plum; **Other Voices:** H. Jon Benjamin, Jonathan Katz, Andy Kindler, Tom Leopold, Jen Schulman, Bill Braudis

## ◎ THE DICK TRACY SHOW

Originally titled *The Adventures of Dick Tracy*, the famed comic-strip hero battles the world's most ruthless criminals (Flattop, B.B. Eyes, Pruneface, Mumbles, the Brow, Oodles, the Mole, Sketch Paree, Cheapskate Gunsmoke, Itchy and Stooge Viller) with the questionable help of his diminutive-brained team of law enforcers—Hemlock Holmes, Jo Jitsu, Heap O'Calory, Go Go Gomez, and The Retouchables—in this series of 130 five-minute episodes first syndicated in 1961. Four episodes were shown on the program, each telling a complete story.

Chester Gould, Dick Tracy's creator, developed the series format and supervised the initial episode. In an interview, he later admitted that he disliked the series. "We were catering to very small fry and I think we would have been smarter to have taken a more serious view of the thing and played it more or less straight," he said.

Beginning in 2004 the series was rebroadcast weekdays on VOOM's Animania HD opposite reruns of *Felix the Cat, Mister Magoo* and *The Pink Panther. A UPA Production. Color. Half-hour. Premiered: September 1961. Syndicated. Rebroadcast on ANI: 2004.*

**Voices**

**Dick Tracy:** Everett Sloane; **Other Voices:** Mel Blanc, Benny Rubin, Paul Frees, Jerry Hausner, Johnny Coons, June Foray, Joan Gardner

## ◎ DIC'S INCREDIBLE MOVIE TOONS

Weekly showcase featuring made-for-TV and direct-to-video feature-length animated specials, many based on franchised characters that originally starred in popular animated series produced by Burbank, California, animation powerhouse DIC Entertainment, including *Dennis the Menace, Inspector Gadget, Madeline, Sabrina the Teenage Witch,* and other properties from the DIC library, plus original stories and tales inspired from classic literature such as *The Time Machine* (called *Time Kid*), *The Lost World* (retitled *Dinosaur Island*) and *The Mark of Zorro* (renamed *The Amazing Zorro*). Spin-off specials included the series' premiere episode *Sabrina: Friends Forever* followed by *Dennis the Menace: Cruise Control, The*

*Archies: Jug Man, Madeline: My Fair Madeline* and *Inspector Gadget's Last Case: Claw's Revenge.* Also featured during the first season were such animated movies as *The Groove Squad, A Christmas Carol* (originally produced as a direct-to-video production in 1997), *Globehunters: An Around the World in 80 Days Adventure,* and *20,000 Leagues under the Sea.*

Premiering in the United States in October 2002, the animated movie showcase aired Sundays as part of Nickelodeon's weekend series *Nickelodeon Sunday Movie Toons.* Lasting only one season, specials originally aired through December 2002. DIC Entertainment's official records show only 13 specials being produced for the series, although reportedly more adaptations of literature—including, *Annie, Ben Hur, Black Beauty, Thor* and *The Wizard of Oz*—were to have aired in 2003 under the series banner; DIC Entertainment's official records show otherwise, with only 13 specials produced for a single season. The series was broadcast on the Disney Channel as part of a four-year deal in key overseas markets—France, Germany, Italy, Southeast Asia, the United Kingdom, Ireland, Australia, New Zealand, Spain, Portugal, the Middle East and Scandinavia on the Disney Channel. (For additional information, see individual entries under "Animated Television Specials.") A *DIC Enterprises Production. Color. Ninety minutes. Premiered on NICK: October 6, 2002–December 29, 2002.*

## ◉ DIGIMON: DIGITAL MONSTERS

During summer camp, after a horrendous earthquake strikes, seven young kids (Tai, Izzy, Matt, T.K., Sora, Mimi and Joe) are sucked into an alternate realm—a digital world—where they befriend powerful Digital Monsters (Digiwolve, Warp Digiwolve, Mega Digiwolve, DNA Digiwolve, Armor Digiwolve and others) who help them on their perilous journey to get home while saving Earth and the DigiWorld from mass destruction in this English-dubbed Japanese cartoon series, produced in 1999 by Toei Animation and based on the enormously successful *Digimon* franchise. In August 1999, the half-hour anime series, retitled *Digimon: Digital Monsters,* premiered on FOX's Saturday-morning program block, and on FOX Family (subsequently renamed ABC Family after ABC bought the network in 2001) with 54 episodes during its first season. An additional 101 episodes aired during the next two seasons, with the series concluding its run on FOX in September 2002. That fall, the series was syndicated nationally through August 2003 and began re-airing the following February on Toon Disney's daily Jetix program block. A *Toei Co. Ltd./Fuji TV/ Yomimuri Advertising/Saban Entertainment/Sensation Animation Production. Color. Half-hour. Premiered on FOX: August 14, 1999–September 2002. Rebroadcast FOX FAM/ABC FAM: August 14, 1999–December 8, 2001. Syndicated: September 29, 2002–August 29, 2003. Rebroadcast on TDIS: February 14, 2004–.*

### Voices
**DemiDevimon:** Derek Stephen Prince; **Patamon:** Laura Sumer; **Gekomon:** Dave Mallow; **Yamaki:** Steven Jay Blum; **Androman:** Michael Sorich; **Myotismon:** Richard Epcar; **Gomamon:** R. Martin Klein; **Izzy Izumi:** Mona Marshall; **Sheba Izumi, Izzy's Mother:** Jane Alan; **WarGreymon:** Lex Lang; **Centarumon:** Bob Papenbrook; **Cherubimon:** George C. Cole; **Lillymon:** Dorothy Elias-Fahn; **Pamela Hida:** May Elizabeth McGlynn; **Crusadermon:** Melodee Spevack

## ◉ DILBERT

Comical adventures of the cubicle-dwelling Dilbert (voiced by Daniel Stern) as he survives his daily trials and tribulations at work for the huge soulless corporation, Path-E-Tech, among an idiotic pointy-haired boss, hostile coworkers and his malevolent dog, Dogbert, in this half-hour animated comedy series, based on cartoonist Scott Adams' popular syndicated comic strip. Produced for UPN's prime-time schedule, the nighttime series aired Mondays beginning in January 1999. Despite generating the lowest ratings of any program that season, the network renewed the series for a second season, shifting it to Tuesday nights opposite ABC's highly-rated *Buffy the Vampire Slayer.* In August 2000, not surprisingly, UPN canceled the series, which enjoyed new life in reruns for two seasons on Comedy Central beginning in February 2003. The show's main theme song was lifted from the movie, *Forbidden Zone* (1980), and composed by famed movie composer Danny Elfman. An *Idbox/United Media/ Columbia TriStar Production. Color. Half-hour. Premiered on UPN: January 25, 1999–August 15, 2000. Rebroadcast on COM: February 2, 2003–May 7, 2005.*

### Voices
**Dilbert:** Daniel Stern; **Dogbert:** Chris Elliott; **Wally:** Gordon Hunt; **Alice:** Kathy Griffin; **Pointy-Haired Boss:** Larry Miller; **Dilmom:** Jackie Hoffman; **Rathbert/Asok:** Tom Kenny; **Carol/Other Voices:** Tress MacNeille; **Loud Howard:** Jim Wise; **Marketing Guy:** Gary Kroeger; **Marketing Guy:** Billy West; **Garbage Man/Bob the Dinosaur:** Maurice LaMarche; **Catbert:** Jason Alexander

## ◉ DINK, THE LITTLE DINOSAUR

At a time when Earth was scorched by volcanoes, showered by meteor storms and shaken by giant earthquakes and where survival was an everyday adventure, Dink, a self-assured, sometimes scheming brontosaurus, rallies his group of friends around him in a never-ending quest for fun, adventure and discovery in this original half-hour animated adventure series, which debuted on CBS in 1989. The series lasted two seasons featuring two cartoon episodes each half hour. The second season included a new addition: "Factasaurus," fun facts about dinosaurs. A *Ruby-Spears Enterprises Production. Color. Half-hour. Premiered on CBS: September 2, 1989–August 24, 1991. Rebroadcast on CAR: October 4, 1992–April 10, 1994 (Sundays); September 11, 1994– 1998 (Sundays).*

### Voices
**Dink:** R.J. Williams; **Amber, the lively corythosaurs:** Andee McAfee; **Shyler, the bashful edaphosaurus:** Ben Granger; **Flapper, the boastful pterodon:** S. Scott Bullock; **Scat, the nervous compsognathus/Crusty, an old sea turtle:** Frank Welker

*Main model for the Ruby-Spears Enterprises popular Saturday-morning series* Dink, The Little Dinosaur. © *Ruby-Spears Enterprises. All rights reserved.*

## ◎ DINOBABIES

A family of dinosaurs act out famous fairy tales and children's stories presenting a strong pro-literacy message in this wholesome half-hour animated series, created by animator Fred Wolf, whose company (formerly known as Murakami-Wolf-Swenson) produced the hit cartoon series *Teenage Mutant Ninja Turtles*. The series was first sold to foreign television markets in 1994, where it enjoyed great success. Wolf had great difficulty selling the series to American broadcasters. It wasn't until the fall of 1996 that the program was syndicated in this country by Westinghouse Broadcasting International. *A Fred Wolf Films/Shanghai Morning Sun Production in association with Westinghouse Broadcasting International. Color. Half-hour. Premiered: 1996. Syndicated.*

**Voices**
**Franklin:** Sarah Strange; **Others:** Sam Khouth, Andrea Libman, Kathleen Barr, Matt Hill, Scott McNeil

## ◎ DINOSAUCERS

To save the quake-racked planet Reptilon from destruction, the Dinosaucers, the planet's only inhabitants, come to Earth, where they enlist the help of four youngsters, to find the secret that will save their own world and keep them safe from the depredation of their brutal enemies, the Tyrannos. This futuristic half-hour action/adventure series, syndicated in 1987, was reshown on The Family Channel beginning in 1989, then four years later on USA Network's *Cartoon Express*. *A DIC Enterprises Production in association with Michael Maliani Productions. Color. Half-hour. Premiered: September 14, 1987–88. Syndicated. Rebroadcast on FAM: 1989–91. Rebroadcast on USA: March 29, 1993–September 3, 1995.*

**Voices**
**Bonehead/Bronto-Thunder:** Marvin Goldhar; **Genghis 'Rex'/Plesio:** Dan Hennessey; **Quackpot/Allo:** Len Carlson; **Steggy:** Ray Kahnert; **Brachio:** Don McManus; **Tricero:** Rob Cowan; **Ichthyo:** Thick Wilson; **Terrible Dactyl/Ankylo:** John Stocker; **Dimetro:** Chris Wiggins; **Styraco:** Gordon Masten; **Sara:** Barbara Redpath; **Paul:** Richard Yearwood; **Ryan:** Simon Reynolds; **David:** Leslie Toth

## ◎ DINOZAURS

Awakened from their 65-million-year slumber, 12-year-old Kaito and his friend Rena help the DinoZaurs defeat the mighty Drago-Zaurs, who plan to steal the Earth's life force, and save the planet, in this action-packed science fiction anime series, based on the best-selling DinoZones action figure toys and video games. Produced by Japan's Sunrise animation studios, producers of such popular anime fare as *Cowboy Behop* and *Escaflowne*, this 26-episode series, blending traditional 2-D cel animation for the human characters and 3-D computer animation for the Dino-warriors, was added to FOX's weekday afternoon lineup in August 2000 before joining the network's Saturday morning anime block three weeks after its debut. By November, the half-hour series was dumped from FOX's Saturday schedule, and from weekdays by that December, returning briefly in reruns on the network's afternoon docket in January 2001. Of the series' 26 episodes, only 20 were broadcast on FOX. *A Sunrise/Bandai/Saban Entertainment Production. Color. Half-hour. Premiered on FOX: July 28, 2000–December 1, 2000. Rebroadcast on FOX: January 2001.*

**Voices**
**Woolly Mammoth:** Beau Billingslea; **Drago Wing:** Steven Jay Blum; **Taki:** Doug Erholtz; **Ronnie/Emily:** Wendee Lee; **Rick:** Michael Lindsay; **Gigano Dragon:** Bob Pannebrook; **Rena:** Philece Sampler; **Dragozaur Army Forces:** Michael Sorich; **Kaito:** Jason Spisak; **Dino Tyranno:** Kim Strauss; **Dino Kenty/Leon:** James Arnold Taylor; **Dino Brachio:** Tom Wyner; **Dino Ptera:** Lenore Zann; **Drago Ceratops:** David Lodge; **Dino Styraco/Drago Tyran:** Richard Epcar; **Dino Centro/Dino Pachy:** Wally Wingert; **Additional Voices:** Bob Joles, Catherine Battistone, Jason Barson, Joey Camen, Peter Lurie, Scott Weil, Tony Pope

## ◎ DIPSY DOODLE

To tie in with the country's Bicentennial celebration, this hour-long, mostly live-action educational children's show, produced in Cleveland and briefly syndicated in December of 1974 was named after the animated country bumpkin whose supposed heritage linked him to the original Yankee Doodle. *A WJW-TV/SFM/General Foods Production. Color. One hour. Premiered: 1974. Syndicated.*

## ◎ DISNEY/PIXAR'S BUZZ LIGHTYEAR OF STAR COMMAND

The infamous action-toy hero Buzz Lightyear and his Star Command cadets battle to maintain justice while protecting the universe against the threats of Evil Emperor Zurg in this animated series spin-off from Disney and Pixar's direct-to-video release, *Buzz Lightyear of Star Command: The Adventure Begins*. Based on the character made famous in Disney and Pixar's pair of blockbuster computer-animated features *Toy Story* and *Toy Story 2*, this half-hour science fiction/fantasy series picked up where *The Adventure Begins* ended, casting Buzz and his space-age cohorts in 65 episodes first shown in syndication as part of Disney's weekday cartoon block on UPN stations in early October 2000, with 13 episodes also airing Saturday mornings on ABC.

Unlike the famed CGI-animated Pixar features, this first-run syndicated and network series was largely cel-animated with only its opening credits produced in computer animation. Actor Patrick Warburton, who played the character "Puddy" on the hit television sitcom *Seinfeld*, replaced comedian Tim Allen as the voice of Buzz. Rounding out the voice cast were *MADTV* star Nicole Sullivan as Mira Nova, comedian Wayne Knight as Emperor Zurg, comedian Larry Miller as XR and actor/comedian Stephen Furst as Booster. Subsequently, following its network and syndicated run, the series was rebroadcast on Disney Channel and Toon Disney. *A Walt Disney Television Animation Production. Color. Half-hour. Premiered on ABC: October 14, 2000–September 8, 2001. Syndicated/Rebroadcast on UPN: October 2, 2000–August 29, 2003. Rebroadcast on DIS: June 5, 2006–. Rebroadcast on TDIS: June 16, 2002–.*

**Voices**
**Buzz Lightyear:** Patrick Warburton; **Princess Mira Nova:** Nicole Sullivan; **XR:** Neil Flynn, Larry Miller; **Booster Sinclair Munchaper:** Stephen Furst; **Evil Emperor Zurg:** Wayne Knight; **Commander Nebula:** Adam Carolla; **NOS-4-A2:** Craig Ferguson; **XL:** Bocat Goldthwait; **The President:** Roz Ryan; **Dr. Ozma Furbanna:** Linda Hamilton; **Agent Z-Warp Darkmaster:** Diedrich Bader; **Opening Narrator:** Gary Owens

## ◎ DISNEY'S ADVENTURES IN WONDERLAND

Helping kids improve vocabulary and language skills, the denizens of the fantasy world of Lewis Carroll's *Through the Looking Glass*— Alice (played by Elisabeth Harnois), the Mad Hatter, the Red Queen, Tweedle Dum and Tweedle Dee (in live action)—engage in playful wordplay and introduce stories told through the magic of "Claymation" in this weekday live-action/animated series that premiered on Disney Channel in 1992. Will Vinton, of California

Raisins fame, produced 40 animated clay-on-glass episodes for the series, which was later syndicated. *A Betty Productions in association with Disney Channel and Will Vinton Productions. Color. Half-hour. Premiered on DIS: March 23, 1992. Syndicated: September 6, 1993–September 10, 1995.*

### Cast (live action)

**Alice:** Elisabeth Harnois; **March Hare:** Reece Holland; **Red Queen:** Armelia McQueen; **White Rabbit:** Patrick Richwood; **Mad Hatter:** John Robert Hoffman; **Tweedle Dee:** Harry Waters Jr.; **Tweedle Dum:** Robert Barry Fleming; **Caterpillar:** Wesley Mann; **Cheshire Cat:** Richard Kuhlman; **Dormouse:** John Lovelady

## ◎ DISNEY'S ADVENTURES OF THE GUMMI BEARS

Zummi, Gruffi, Grammi, Cubbi, Sunni and Tummi Gummi find themselves in enchanting escapades as they face new foes and find new friends in the mythical forests of Gummi Glen. From encounters with menacing giants and ogres, to the excitement of discovering lost treasure, the Gummies join together for a captivating series of intriguing and whimsical adventure in this Saturday-morning series produced by Walt Disney Television Animation. NBC broadcast the first four seasons beginning in September 1985. The show moved to ABC in September 1989, when it merged with *The New Adventures of Winnie the Pooh* for its fifth season. The program combined half-hour and 15-minute episodes. In 1990 the series joined the *Disney Afternoon* two-hour daily cartoon block in syndication (in reruns) opposite *DuckTales, Chip 'n' Dale's Rescue Rangers* and *Tale Spin* and was rerun on Disney Channel from 1991 to 1996. *A Walt Disney Television Animation Production. Color. Half-hour. Premiered on NBC: September 14, 1985–September 2, 1989. Rebroadcast on ABC: September 9, 1989–September 1, 1990 (as Disney's Gummi Bears/Winnie the Pooh Hour) (as part of Disney Afternoon). Rebroadcast on DIS: 1991–1996.*

### Voices

**Cavin:** Christian Jacobs, Brett Johnson, David Faustino, R.J. Williams; **Chummi Gummi:** Jim Cummings; **Sunni Gummi:** Katie Leigh; **Tummi Gummi:** Lorenzo Music; **Augustus "Gusto" Gummi:** Rob Paulsen; **Zummi Gummi:** Paul Winchell; Jim Cummings; **Gruffi Gummi:** Bill Scott, Corey Burton; **Cubbi Gummi:** Noelle North; **Grammi Gummi:** June Foray; **Gusto Gummi:** Rob Paulsen; **Toadie:** Bill Scott, Corey Burton, Michael Rye; **Giggalin:** Corey Burton; **Clutch:** Paul Winchell, Corey Burton; **Sir Tuxford:** Bill Scott, Hamilton Camp, Roger C. Carmel, Townsend Coleman, Gino Conforti, Peter Cullen, Brian Cummings, Chuck McCann; **Artie Deco/Chillbeard Sr.:** Townsend Coleman, Gino Conforti, Peter Cullen, Brian Cummings; **Knight of Gumadoon:** Townsend Coleman, Gino Conforti, Peter Cullen, Brian Cummings, David Faustino, Alan Oppenheimer; **Angelo Davini/Ogre:** Bill Scott; **Zorlock:** Lennie Weinrib; **Ditto the Boggle/Mervyns/ Mother Griffin:** Frank Welker; **Zummi Gummi/Toadie/Slumber Sprite/Giggalin/Tuck (1987–1989):** Paul Winchell; **King Gregor/Duke Igthorn/Sir Gowan:** Michael Rye; **Sir Paunch:** Allan Melvin, Howard Morris; **Sir Thornberry:** Barry Dennen, Aeryk Egan, Walker Edmiston; **Princess Calla:** Noelle North; **Princess Marie:** Hal Smith, Kath Soucie; **Malsinger/Troll/Horse/ Nip:** Michael Rye; **Unwin/Gad/Zook/King Carpie/Knight:** Will Ryan; **Ogre:** Will Ryan, Michael Rye; **Trina/Aquarianne:** Pat Parris; **Mobile Tree:** June Foray, Noelle North, Katie Leigh; **Giant, with the Wishing Stone/Dom:** Linda Gary; **Gordo of Ghent:** Ed Gilbert, Dana Hill, Bob Holt; **Tadpole:** Chuck McCann; **Bubble Dragon:** Lorenzo Music; **The Most Peaceful Dragon in the World/Counselor Woodale:** June Foray; **Lady Bane/Great Oak/ Marzipan/Mother:** Tress MacNeille; **Zorlock:** Andre Stojka, Les Tremayne, Lennie Weinrib

## ◎ DISNEY'S ALADDIN

Aladdin, Princess Jasmine and their pals Genie, Iago (no longer a bad parrot) and Abu (the friendly monkey) embark on all-new adventures, set in the ancient land of Agrabah, in this half-hour series based on the popular 1992 animated movie. All of the original characters from the movie and subsequent video sequel, *The Return of Jafar*, returned, with the exception of Jafar, who died (for a second time) in the video. A new group of villains were created for the series, including the bearded bandit Abis Mal (voiced by *Seinfeld*'s Jason Alexander), the feline Mirage (whose voice was supplied by Bebe Neuwirth of *Cheers*), barbarian Runter (voiced by Michael Jeter of *Evening Shade*) and his wife, Brawnhilda (brought to life by actress/comedienne Carol Kane).

Premiering weekdays in syndication and Saturdays on CBS in September 1994, CBS commissioned 13 shows for its Saturday-morning lineup (each different from the syndication version), while 65 episodes aired in syndication as part of the *Disney Afternoon* cartoon block. The series finished third in the overall syndication ratings behind the live-action *Mighty Morphin Power Rangers* and Steven Spielberg's *Animaniacs* during its successful first season. (The show was also nominated for an Emmy as outstanding animated children's program.) CBS picked up the series for a second season in 1995, airing eight first-run episodes, while the program continued to air in syndication. In the winter of 1997, previously aired network episodes began airing on Disney Channel.

Most of the original actors who provided the voices in the movie reprised their roles in the series: Scott Weinger (of TV's *Full House*) as Aladdin, Linda Larkin as Jasmine, and Gilbert Gottfried as Iago. Dan Castellaneta (the voice of Homer Simpson) replaced Robin Williams as the wisecracking Genie, his second stint in the role counting the home video sequel *The Return of Jafar*, which Williams also refused to voice. *A Walt Disney Television Animation Production. Color. Half-hour. Premiered on DIS: February 6, 1994; Premiered on CBS: September 17, 1994–August 24, 1996. Syndicated: September 5, 1994–August 29, 1997 (part of Disney Afternoon). Rebroadcast on DIS: December 21, 1997–June 15, 2000. Rebroadcast on TDIS: April 18, 1998–.*

### Voices

**Aladdin:** Scott Weinger; **Jasmine:** Linda Larkin, Deb LaCusta, Kay Kuter, Janice Kawaye, John Kassir; **Genie:** Dan Castellaneta; **Iago:** Gilbert Gottfried; **Abu/Faisal/Rajah/Xerxes:** Frank Welker; **The Sultan of Agrabah:** Sheryl Bernstein, Val Bettin; **Abis Mal/al-Bhatros:** Jason Alexander; **Mirage:** Bebe Neuwirth; **Runter:** Michael Jeter; **Brawnhilda:** Carol Kane; **Akbar/ Amal al-Kateeb/Dominus Trask/Farouk/Hamar/Mad Sultan/ Rasoul/Wazou:** Jim Cummings; **Mozenrath:** Susan Blu, Jonathan Brandis

## ◎ DISNEY'S FILLMORE!

Schoolyard justice prevails as a pair of crime-stopping teens—Cornelius Fillmore, a quick-witted, reformed seventh-grader and his partner, Ingrid Third—stop crime in their tracks, from stolen scooters to smuggled tartar sauce, while making X Middle School, in a Minnesota suburb, a safer place for students in this animated series loosely based on popular cop shows of the 1970s, including TV's *The Mod Squad*. Created by executive producer Scott M. Gimple (*Disney's Pepper Ann, Mrs. Munger's Class*) and produced by Walt Disney Television Animation, the series was rebroadcast on ABC's *ABC Kids* program block beginning in the fall of 2002, and subsequently was rebroadcast on Toon Disney, which rebroadcast the series in its entirety, including all previously unaired episodes after Disney canceled the program in 2003, and ABC Family. *A Walt Disney Television Production. Color. Half-hour. Premiered on ABC: September 14, 2002–January 23, 2004. Rebroadcast on ABC FAM: 2004. Rebroadcast on TDIS: February 17, 2003; September 2, 2003–June 4, 2006.*

*Voices*
**Cornelius Fillmore:** Orlando Brown; **Ingrid Third:** Tara Strong; **Junior Commissioner Vallego:** Horatio Sanz; **Principal Dawn S. Folsom:** Wendie Malick; **Vice Principal Raycliff:** Jeff Probst; **Frankie:** Lukas Behnken; **Jean:** Shanie Calahan; **Julian:** Josh Peck; **Mr. Gaiser:** Kurtwood Smith; **O'Farrell:** Kyle Sullivan; **Joseph Anza:** Danny Tamberelli; **Karen Tehama:** Lauren Tom; **Danny O'Farrell:** Kyle Sullivan; **Tommy:** Josh Uhler; **Robin:** Mae Whitman; **Announcer:** Don LaFontaine

## ◎ DISNEY'S GUMMI BEARS/WINNIE THE POOH HOUR

In 1989 Disney's Gummi Bears, which ran for four successful seasons on NBC, moved to rival network ABC and merged with *The New Adventures of Winnie the Pooh* in all-new episodes in this fantasy/adventure hour for Saturday-morning television. (See *Disney's Adventures of the Gummi Bears* and *The New Adventures of Winnie the Pooh* for voice credits.) *A Walt Disney Television Animation Production in association with Buena Vista. Color. One hour. Premiered on ABC: September 9, 1989–September 1, 1990.*

## ◎ DISNEY'S HERCULES

Mythical strongman Hercules adapts to his life as a teenage hero-in-training by attending Prometheus Academy, a special high school where he learns his craft, while dealing with the usual teenager peer pressure with his girlfriend, Meg (short for Megara), his free-spirited friend, Icarus, his future-seeing friend, Cassandra, and his teacher Philoctetes ("Phil"), as he battles his evil uncle, Hades (voiced by James Woods), ruler of the Underworld, in this animated series based on Disney's 1997 full-length animated feature. Produced by Walt Disney Television Animation, beginning in late August 1998, the 65-episode series aired both in first-run syndication and Saturday mornings on ABC. Thereafter, the program has become a popular mainstay in reruns on Toon Disney. *A Walt Disney Television Production. Color. Half-hour. Premiered on Syndicated/UPN: August 31, 1998–November 16, 1999. Premiered on ABC: September 12, 1998–September 18, 1999. Rebroadcast on TDIS: September 4, 2000–.*

*Voices*
**Hercules:** Tate Donovan; **Icarus:** French Stewart; **Cassandra:** Sandra Bernhard; **Hades:** James Woods; **Pain:** Bobcat Goldthwait; **Panic:** Matt Frewer; **Hermes:** Paul Shaffer; **Adonis:** Diedrich Bader; **Bob the Narrator:** Robert Stack; **Orpheus:** Rob Paulsen; **Philoctetes:** Robert Constanzo; **Meg:** Susan Egan; **Zeus:** Rip Torn; **Hera:** Samantha Eggar; **Alcmene:** Barbara Barrie; **Apollo:** Keith David; **Ares:** Jay Thomas; **Clion:** Gilbert Gottfried; **Athena:** Jane Leeves; **Prometheus:** Carl Reiner; **Artemis:** Reba McEntire; **Poseidon:** Jason Alexander; **Terpsichore:** LaChanze; **Thespis:** Kathy Najimy; **Syrinx:** Annie Potts; **Thalia:** Roz Ryan; **Calliope:** Lillias White; **Melepomene:** Cheryl Freeman; **Clio:** Vaneese Thomas; **Callista:** Lacey Chabert; **Medusa:** Jennifer Love Hewitt; **Aphrodite:** Lisa Kudrow; **Daedalus:** David Hyde Pierce; **Jealousy:** Jon Favreau; **Miss Cassiopeia:** Alice Ghostley; **Numericles:** Stephen Tobolowsky; **Calculus:** Kevin West; **Hippocrates:** Mandy

Patinkin; **Gaia:** Kerri Kenney; **Atropos:** Paddi Edwards; **Clotho:** Tress MacNeille; **Lachos:** Carole Shelley; **Achilles:** Dom Irrera; **Fear:** David Cross; **Hippolyte:** Jane Curtin; **Bacchus:** Dom DeLuise; **Hecate:** Peri Gilpin; **The Winged Wolves:** Jon Cryer; **Cupid:** Tom Arnold; **Jason:** William Shatner; **Medea:** Rebecca Gayheart; **Morpheus:** Jonathan Katz; **Circe:** Idena Menzel; **Paris:** Cary Elwes; **Castor:** Nick Stahl; **Pollux:** Rider Strong; **Helen of Troy:** Jodi Benson; **Galatea:** Jennifer Aniston; **Echidna:** Kathie Lee Gifford; **Andromeda:** Sararh Michelle Gellar; **Parenthesis:** Eric Idle; **King Midas:** Eugene Levy; **Marigold:** Tia Carrere; **Minotaur:** Michael Dorn; **Theseus:** Eric Stoltz; **Triton:** Chris Elliott; **Triton Jr.:** Jesse Spencer; **Loki:** Vince Vaughn; **The Gryphon:** Merv Griffin; **Phil's Mother:** Estelle Harris; **Pegasus:** Frank Welker; **Electra:** Joey Lauren Adams; **Princess Jasmin:** Linda Larkin; **Aladdin:** Scott Weinger; **Jafar:** Jonathan Freeman; **Nemesis:** Linda Hamilton; **Odysseus:** Steven Weber

## ◎ DISNEY'S HOUSE OF MOUSE

Mickey Mouse emceed this weekly roundup of classic Disney cartoon shorts from the 1930s, 1940s and 1950s, as well as newly produced cartoon subjects from within the lavish, upscale and trendy nightclub he owns and operates, billed as "The Tooniest Place on Earth," seen in wraparounds with his *House of Mouse* staff: greeter Donald Duck, reservationist Daisy Duck, waiter Goofy, mascot Pluto, technician Horace Horsecollar and valet driver Max Goof. Comprised of 52 episodes, the half-hour animated series, produced by Walt Disney Television, made its television debut on ABC, where it aired as part of the network's *One Saturday Morning* cartoon block from January 2001 to late August 2002. Subsequently, the series became a popular fixture in reruns on the Disney Channel and Toon Disney. *A Walt Disney Television Production. Color. Half-hour. Premiered on ABC: January 13, 2001–August 30, 2002. Rebroadcast on DIS: September 9, 2002–February 2006. Rebroadcast on TDIS: June 20, 2003–February 23, 2007.*

*Voices*
**Mickey Mouse:** Wayne Allwine; **Donald Duck/Huey/Dewey/Louie:** Tony Anselmo; **Daisy Duck:** Diane Michelle, Tress MacNeille; **Minnie Mouse/Clara Cluck:** Russi Taylor; **Goofy/Pluto/Pete:** Bill Farmer; **Professor Ludwig Von Drake:** Corey Burton; **Pegleg Pete/Other Voices:** Jim Cummings; **Clarabelle Cow/Other Voices:** April Winchell; **Max Goof:** Jason Marsden; **Gus Goose/Other Voices:** Frank Welker; **Chip 'n' Dale:** Tress MacNeille

## ◎ DISNEY'S LITTLE EINSTEINS

Four adventuresome kids—Leo, Annie, Quincy and June, along with their intelligent, transformable space/air/watercraft, Rocket—solve problems and help new friends they meet along the way in this half-hour animated preschool series produced for Disney Channel's *Playhouse Disney* weekday preschool block. Created by Eric Weiner of *Dora the Explorer* fame, the characters originated in a direct-to-video movie, *Our Huge Adventure*, produced and released in August 2005, before becoming a weekly television series in October of that year on the Disney Channel and in Japan on TV Tokyo. Coproduced by Curious Pictures and the Baby Einstein Company, famous works of art and classical music are incorporated in each episode, and moments to encourage young viewers to pat their legs, gesture or sing along help the Einsteins succeed in their missions. Two half-hour holiday specials aired during the series' first season, *A Little Einsteins' Halloween* and *The Christmas Wish*. On January 8, 2006, a new round of episodes of the popular series also bowed in prime time on *Playhouse Disney*. *A Curious*

*Pictures/Baby Einstein Company Production. Color. Half-hour. Premiered on DIS: October 9, 2005–    .*

**Voices**
**Leo:** Jesse Schwartz; **Annie:** Natalia Wojcik; **Quincy:** Aiden Pompey; **June:** Erica Huang

## ◎ DISNEY'S LLOYD IN SPACE

While living on the talking Intrepidville Space Station with the ship's captain, his mother Nora, and his psychic younger sister Francine, an extraterrestrial teenage boy named Lloyd Nebulon encounters the usual problems and growing pains of being a teenager while attending Luna Vista School with his best friends and classmates—the "brains" of the group, Douglas; the purple, food-loving Cyclops, Kurt; and the ginger-haired perpetual schemer and only human classmate, Eddie—in this futuristic animated fantasy/comedy series, cocreated by Joe Ansolabehere and Paul Germain, creators of TV's animated *Disney's Recess*. With characters designed by Eric Keyes and the pilot cowritten by Ansolabehere, Germain and Mark Drop, the 39-episode half-hour series joined ABC's *One Saturday Morning* lineup in February 2001. Airing only two seasons, the first-run series was rebroadcast thereafter on Disney's all-cartoon cable network, Toon Disney. On October 22, 2006, Toon Disney aired a Halloween episode of the series, completing its network run. *A Walt Disney Television Animation/Phil & Joe Productions Production. Color. Half-hour. Premiered on ABC: February 3, 2001–September 7, 2002. Rebroadcast on TDIS: March 5, 2001–October 22, 2006.*

**Voices**
**Lloyd Nebulon:** Courtland Mead; **Captain Nora Nebulon:** April Winchelle; **Francine Nebulon:** Nicolette Little; **Kurt Blobberts:** Bill Fagerbakke; **Douglas:** Pamele Hayden; **Eddie R. Horton:** Justin Shenkarow; **Station:** Brian George; **Miss Bolt:** Tress MacNeille; **Officer Frank Horton:** Clancy Brown; **Mylaar:** Michelle Horn; **Larry:** Eddie Deezen; **Prince Harvulian "Boomer" Standervault:** Diedrich Bader; **Additional Voices:** Ben Stein, Gregg Berger, Erik Von Detten, Tony Jay, Chris Marquette, Anndi McAfee, Justin Jon Ross, John Rubano, Francesca Marie Smith, Tara Strong

## ◎ DISNEY'S MICKEY MOUSE WORKS

Umbrella title for weekly half-hour series featuring all-new Disney cartoon shorts of various lengths starring Mickey Mouse, Donald Duck, Daisy Duck, Goofy, Minnie Mouse, Pluto and others. Using the same look, design and coloring of the characters and original sound effects of the classic Disney shorts produced during Hollywood's golden age, Mickey and his friends were joined each week by other recognizable supporting characters, including Chip 'n' Dale, Clarabelle Cow, Horace Horsecollar, Huey, Dewey and Louie, Humphrey the Bear, Ludwig Von Drake, Ranger J. Aubudon Woodlore and Scrooge McDuck. First broadcast Saturday mornings on ABC in May 1999, the half-hour series was replaced by a new original animated program starring Mickey and company on ABC, *Disney's House of Mouse. A Walt Disney Television Production. Color. Half-hour. Premiered on ABC: May 1, 1999–January 6, 2001.*

**Voices**
**Mickey Mouse:** Wayne Allwine; **Donald Duck/Huey/Dewey/Louie:** Tony Anselmo; **Daisy Duck:** Diane Michelle, Tress MacNeille; **Minnie Mouse:** Russi Taylor; **Goofy/Pluto/Pete:** Bill Farmer; **Professor Ludwig Von Drake/Chief O'Hara/Ranger J. Aubudon Woodlore/Narrator/Other Voices:** Corey Burton; **Chip 'n' Dale:** Tress MacNeille; **Humphrey Bear/Zeke/Other Voices:** Jim Cummings; **Scrooge McDuck:** Alan Young; **Mortimer Mouse:** Maurice LaMarche; **Clarabelle Cow:** April Winchell; **Additional Voices:** Jeff Bennett, John Cleese, Brad Garrett, Eric Idle, Penn Jillette, Tony Jay, Clyde Kusatsu, Kath Soucie, Frank Welker, Jane Withers

## ◎ DISNEY'S 101 DALMATIANS: THE SERIES

Walt Disney Television Animation produced this half-hour cartoon series based on the successful live-action feature and the classic 1961 Disney animated feature of the same name. Premiering in weekday syndication first, then on ABC and airing concurrently in the fall of 1997, the series featured two nine-minute cartoons each half hour: "101 Dalmatians," exploring the lives of Lucky, Rolly, Cadpig and the other polka-dot pups as they grow up on a farm in London, and "The Bark Brigade," following the adventures of the dalmations parents, Pongo and Perdita, as they thwart the plans of the evil Cruella de Vil. Sandwiched between them each week were a series of one- to three-minute comic bits, skits and parodies called "Dalmatian Spots."

The syndicated version aired six days a week featuring 52 episodes; the ABC Saturday-morning series exclusively broadcast an additional 13 episodes not seen in syndication. Jim Jinkins and David Campbell of Jumbo Pictures, Inc. (the team who created *Doug* and *Brand Spanking New! Doug*) helped develop the concept of the new series along with executive producers Roberts Gannaway and Tony Craig (executive producers of *The Lion King's Timon and Pumbaa*) of Walt Disney Television Animation. *A Walt Disney Television Animation/Jumbo Pictures Inc. Production. Color. Half-hour. Premiered: September 1, 1997–August 28, 1998 (syndicated); ABC: September 13, 1997–September 4, 1999. Rebroadcast on TDIS: September 7, 1998–March 9, 2007.*

**Voices**
**Lucky:** Pam Segall, Debi Mae West; **Rolly/Cadpig/Anita Dearly:** Kath Soucie; **Spot:** Tara Charendoff; **Cruella de Vil:** April Winchell; **Horace:** David Lander; **Jasper:** Michael McKean; **Scorch:** Frank Welker; **Roger Dearly:** Jeff Bennett; **Nanny:** Charlotte Rae; **Pongo:** Kevin Schon; **Perdy (Perdita):** Pam Dawber

## ◎ DISNEY'S PEPPER ANN

A spunky, eccentric, opinionated and fiercely independent 12-year-old redhead experiences the trials and tribulations of adolescence—with her reactions to situations seen in vivid fantasies—in this half-hour series based on the childhood memories of the show's creator and executive producer Sue Rose (whose character bears a striking resemblance to her creator). The show debuted in the fall of 1997 as part of ABC's two-hour floating cartoon block *One Saturday Morning*, featuring *Brand Spanking New Doug* and *Disney's Recess*.

In the fall of 2001, Toon Disney, Disney's 24-hour all-animation basic cable network, added the series to its schedule, premiering on Labor Day weekend. The show joined a lineup of critically acclaimed children's series that included fellow ABC *One Saturday Morning* alumni and *Disney's Doug* (formerly *Brand Spanking New! Doug*) and preschool favorite, *Rupert*. The program likewise aired daily on the Disney Channel. In February 2007, more than two years after being pulled from Toon Disney, the show returned to the network's cartoon lineup. *A Walt Disney Television Animation Production. Color. Half-hour. Premiered on ABC: September 13, 1997–November 18, 2000. Syndicated/Rebroadcast on UPN: February 12, 2000–September 2, 2001. Rebroadcast on DIS: September 3, 2001–September 8, 2002. Rebroadcast on TDIS: September 3, 2001–October 29, 2004; February 23, 2007–.*

**Voices**
**Pepper Ann:** Kathleen Wilhoite; **Trinket:** Jenna Von Oy; **Moose:** Pamela Segall; **Nicky:** Clea Lewis; **Nicky's Mum:** Kath Soucie; **Lydia:** April Winchell

## DISNEY'S QUACK PACK

Grown-up teens Huey, Dewey and Louie live with their famous uncle Donald, now a cameraman for a popular TV newsmagazine. Along with his longtime love-duck Daisy, a brash and courageous TV reporter with the same show, Donald and his nephews go on assignment and encounter action, adventure and trouble around the globe in this first-run half-hour series/spinoff to *DuckTales*. It premiered in the fall of 1996 as part of the weekday cartoon block *The Disney Afternoon*. The series working title was *Duck Daze*.

Following its run in syndication, reruns were shown on the Disney Channel and Toon Disney. A *Walt Disney Television Animation Production. Color. Half-hour. Premiered: September 3, 1996–August 29, 1997. Syndicated. Rebroadcast on DIS: September 17, 1998–July 21, 1999. Rebroadcast on TDIS: September 7, 1998–October 31, 2004.*

**Voices**
**Donald Duck:** Tony Anselmo; **Huey Duck:** Jeannie Elias; **Dewey Duck:** Pamela Segall; **Louie Duck:** Elizabeth Daily; **Gwumpki:** Pat Fraley; **Moltoc:** Tim Curry; **Kent Powers:** Roger Rose

## DISNEY'S RAW TOONAGE

(See RAW TOONAGE.)

## DISNEY'S RECESS

An enterprising group of fourth-grade kids—four boys (Vince, Mikey, T.J. and Gus) and two girls (Gretchen and Ashley)—run into trouble during breaks at school whenever those domineering sixth graders are around, in this half-hour Saturday-morning cartoon from executive producers and the co-creators of *Rugrats*, Paul Germaine and Joe Ansolabehere. The series premiered on ABC in the fall . . .

One month after premiering on cable's Disney Channel, this Walt Disney Television Animation-produced, 52-episode, half-hour series, featuring two 15-minute episodes per half-hour, also debuted on ABC's inaugural season of its floating two-hour block *One Saturday Morning* (and subsequent replacement, *ABC Kids*) in September 1997. Added to the network's Saturday-morning schedule along with newcomers *Pepper Ann* and *Brand Spanking New! Doug*, this popular weekly series spawned two direct-to-video releases and a full-length animated feature, *Recess: School's Out* (2001), and also aired daily and weekends on UPN-owned stations from 1999 to 2003.

After ABC canceled the series in 2001, reruns of the program aired weekdays for nearly six seasons on cable's Toon Disney. Two years later, Disney produced two more direct-to-video movies based on the series, *Taking the Fifth Grade* and *Recess: All Growed Down*. A *Walt Disney Television Animation Production. Color. Half-hour. Premiered on DIS: August 31, 1997–July 21, 2005. Premiered on ABC: September 13, 1997–November 21, 2001. Rebroadcast on UPN/Syndication: September 5, 1999–August 29, 2003. Rebroadcast on TDIS: July 20, 2001–January 14, 2007.*

**Voices**
**Vince LaSalle:** Rickey D'Shon Collins; **Mikey Blumberg:** Jason Davis; **T.J. Detweiler:** Ross Malinger (1997–99), Andrew Lawrence (1999–    ); **Gus Griswald:** Courtland Mead; **Gretchen Grundler:** Ashley Johnson; **Ashley Funicello Spinelli:** Pamela Segall; **Miss Alordayne Grotke:** April Beasley; **Principal Prickley:** Dabney Coleman; **Randall Weems/Digger Dave:** Ryan O'Donohue; **King Bob:** Toran Caudell; **Digger Sam:** Klee Bragger; **Miss Muriel P. Finster:** Apri Winchell; **Lieutenant Griswald:** Sam McMurray; **Ashley "Ashley A" Armbruster:** Anndi McAfee; **King Bob:** Toran Caudell; **Upside-Down Girl:** Francess Smith; **Ashley "Ashley Q." Quinlan:** Rachel Crane; **Ashley "Ashley T." Tomossian:** Camille Winbush; **Mikey's Singing Voice:** Robert Goulet; **Erwin Lawson:** Erik von Detten; **Flo Spinelli:** Katey Sagal; **Kristen Kurst:** Mayim Bialik

## DISNEY'S TEACHER'S PET

Spot, a talking dog who acts like a boy, follows his young human owner, Leonard Helperman, to school one day and likes it so much spot decides to enroll in his master's class at Fala D. Roosevelt Elementary and obtain an education with his classmates (who are unaware of his true identity) in this animated comedy series created by Gary Baseman (whose character Spot was inspired by his real-life dog, Hubcaps) and directed by Timothy Björklund. First shown on ABC's *One Saturday Morning* lineup beginning in September 2000, the half-hour series enjoyed a successful two-season run before it was canceled. Nearly one month after its original premiere, the program was rebroadcast on Disney Channel through mid-July 2001, and then on Disney's all-cartoon cable network, Toon Disney. In 2004, Disney released a full-length animated feature based on the series. A *Walt Disney Television Production. Color. Half-hour. Premiered on ABC: September 9, 2000–September 7, 2002. Rebroadcast on DIS: September 29, 2000–July 17, 2001. Rebroadcast on TDIS: October 6, 2000–August 19, 2006.*

**Voices**
**Leonard Amadeus Helperman:** Shaun Fleming; **Spot Helperman/Scott Leadready:** Nathan Lane (2000–01), Kevin Schon (2001–02); **Ian Wasalooskey:** Rob Paulsen; **Mary Lou Moira Angela Darling Helperman:** Debra Jo Rupp; **Principal Stickler:** Wallace Shawn; **Mr. Jolly:** David Ogden Stiers; **Pretty Boy:** Jerry Stiller; **Leslie:** Mae Whitman; **Additional Voices:** Cree Summer

## DISNEY'S THE LEGEND OF TARZAN

Following the death of Tarzan's foster father, Kerchak, the vine-swinging ape man adjusts to his life as the new leader of the apes and as a man married to the former ecologist Jane Porter in this series of new weekly adventures spun-off from Disney's critically acclaimed animated feature *Tarzan* (1999). With a supporting cast featuring Jane's father, Professor Archimedes Q. Porter; the elephant Tantor; wisecracking female ape, Terk; and new characters, including the trading post operator, Renard Dumont, and henchmen, Hugo and Hooft, this 39-episode sequel, originally to air as Toon Disney's first original animated series, instead debuted on UPN's *One Too* weekend-morning cartoon lineup, and in daily syndication by UPN to local stations throughout the country. Following its run on ABC and in first-run syndication, the series joined the programming lineup of cable's Toon Disney, which rebroadcast it in its entirety. A *Walt Disney TV Animation Production. Color. Half-hour. Premiered on UPN/Syndication: September 3, 2001–August 31, 2003. Rebroadcast on TDIS: August 31, 2003–    .*

**Voices**
**Tarzan:** Michael T. Weiss; **Jane:** Olivia d'Abo; **Professor Archimedes Q. Porter:** Jeff Bennett; **Kala:** Susan Blakesleee; **Tantor/Lieutenant Colonel Staquait:** Jim Cummings; **Mungo:**

Jason Marsden; **Manu:** Frank Welker; **Terk:** April Winchell; **Flynt:** Erik von Detten; **Renard Dumont:** Rene Auberjonois; **Hugo:** Dave Thomas; **Hooft:** Joe Flaherty; **Samuel T. Philander:** Craig Ferguson; **Queen Lah:** Diahann Carroll; **Jabarti:** Taylor Dempsey; **Dr. Robin Doyle:** Sheena Easton; **Chief Keewazi:** James Avery; **Basuli:** Phil LaMarr; **Jamila:** Cindy Wilson; **Baruti:** Fred Willard

### ◎ DISNEY'S THE LITTLE MERMAID

Beautiful young "mer-teen" Ariel leaves the sea for life in the human world, enjoying occasional underwater adventures with King Triton and her pals (including Sebastian, the calypso-singing crab), sometimes in the form of spectacular musical numbers, in this half-hour Saturday-morning series, billed as the "prequel" to the blockbuster Disney animated feature on which the series was based. CBS launched the series with a Friday night prime-time special, "A Whale of a Tale," which debuted the night before its Saturday-morning introduction. Jodie Benson, Sam Wright and Kenneth Mars reprised their vocal roles from the movie.

In October of 1995, reruns of the series began airing weekdays on Disney Channel and later on Toon Disney. *A Walt Disney Television Animation Production. Color. Half-hour. Premiered on ABC: September 12, 1992–September 2, 1995. Rebroadcast on DIS: October 2, 1995 (weekdays); December 1, 1997–September 14, 2002; September 10, 2006– . Rebroadcast on TDIS: April 18, 1998–January 14, 2007.*

#### Voices
**Ariel:** Jodi Benson; **Sebastian:** Samuel E. Wright; **Ursula:** Pat Carroll; **Urchin:** Danny Cooksey; **Flounder:** Edan Gross; **Scuttle:** Maurice LaMarche; **King Triton:** Kenneth Mars

### ◎ DISNEY'S THE WEEKENDERS

After the final school bell rings every Friday, four typical teens—the sarcastic but good-hearted Tino Tonitini (who also narrates the show); the pretty tomboy Lor MacQuarrie; the handsome, athletic (and only boy in the group) Carver Descartes; and the highly cultured Tish Katsufrakus—make the most of their short-lived freedom, trying to have as much fun as any teen possibly can on the weekends with advice from Tino's mother when things go wrong in this half-hour animated series, created by well-known animator and improv comic Doug Langdale.

From February 2000 to September 2001 the series aired as part of Disney's *One Saturday Morning* cartoon block. In June 2001 it began re-airing on the Disney Channel, and that fall it was part of Disney's syndicated *One Too* block on UPN stations, through September 2002. In August of that year Disney Channel's sister station Toon Disney started rerunning the series. Then in February 2004 the network premiered new episodes of the series, along with fellow Disney cartoon series *Disney's Lloyd in Space*, airing through August 2006, with episodes repeating until that December, when the program completed its network run. Comedian Wayne Brady wrote and performed the show's opening theme song. *A Walt Disney Television Animation Production. Color. Half-hour. Premiered on ABC: February 26, 2000–September 7, 2001. Syndicated/Rebroadcast on UPN: September 8, 2001–September 7, 2002. Rebroadcast on DIS: June 3, 2001–September 5, 2003. Premiered on TDIS: August 25, 2002–December 21, 2006; February 29, 2004–August 25, 2006 (new episodes).*

#### Voices
**Tino Tontini/Colby:** Jason Marsden; **Carver Descartes:** Phil LaMarr; **Petra "Tish" Katsufrakus Ruby:** Kath Soucie; **Lor MacQuarrie:** Grey DeLisle; **Tino's Mom:** Lisa Kaplan; **Carver's Mom:** Cree Summer; **Thomson Oberman:** Robbie Rist; **Mr. Katsufrakus Pizza Guy/Mr. MacQuarrie:** Jeff Bennett; **Kandi:** Tara Strong; **Gina:** Kristen Kreuk; **Tish's Mom:** Kerri Kenny; **Frances/Bree:** Julianne Buescher

### ◎ D'MYNA LEAGUES

A promising and enthusiastic rookie shortstop and teenage myna bird named Ebbet, leads an odd team of misfit anthropomorphic birds—including reliable second baseman Nikki Tinker; egotistical third sacker Reggie Stainback; mighty slugging first baseman Horatio Powell; and crusty manager and catcher Rip Hickory—who play ball for an independent minor-league team called the Mynaville Mynas in this weekly half-hour series, originally broadcast on Canada's CTV network in 2000. Produced by Vancouver-based animation studio, Studio B, and based on the works of author W.P. Kinsella (who penned the acclaimed novel *Shoeless Joe*, which inspired the smash-hit live-action feature *Field of Dreams* [1989] starring Kevin Costner), the 2-D animated show featured 3-D digital backgrounds and aired Saturday mornings in the United States on the WB Television Network's Kids' WB! beginning in September 2003. In 2004, the baseball-themed series was offered in syndication. *A MSH-Aston Entertainment/Studio B/Sony Pictures International/Columbia/TriStar Production. Color. Half-hour. Premiered on the WB (Kids' WB!): September 6, 2003. Syndicated: 2004.*

#### Voices
**Ebbet:** Mat Hill; **Nikki:** Tabitha St. Germain; **Flamingo Kid/Schlitzy:** Michael Dobson; **Lucinda:** Teryl Rothery; **Divinity Plunkett:** Kathleen Barr; **Paully/Bart:** Ian James Corlett; **Other Voices:** Jim Byrnes, June Foray, David Kaye

### ◎ DR. KATZ, PROFESSIONAL THERAPIST

Based on the stand-up acts of Jonathan Katz, Dom Irerra and Laura Kightlinger, a droll psychiatrist deals with his 23-year-old unemployed slacker son (Ben), who dreams of wealth and freedom but is too lazy to find a real job, in between counseling his neurotic patients and spending his free time at the local bar ("Jacky's 33") with his friends Stan and Julie. This half-hour animated series airing Sunday nights on Comedy Central premiered in May of 1995.

Unlike traditional cartoon series in which episodes are scripted and voice tracks are then recorded, the stand-up routines of Katz and other artists were recorded prior to animating and scripting each half-hour program, then scripted with the improvisational dialogue set to animation through a computer-animation process dubbed "Squigglevision" (so named because of the constant zigzagging around the edges of the characters to give the impression of movement). Well-known comedians and stand-up comics lent their voices as "patients" in each episode, including: Bob Newhart Al Franken (of *Saturday Night Live* fame), Rodney Dangerfield, Richard Lewis, Ray Romano (of *Everyone Loves Raymond*), Rita Rudner and Garry Shandling.

In 1995 the series won an Emmy for outstanding performance in an animated program (Jonathan Katz) and was Comedy Central's second-highest rated original series. *A Popular Arts Entertainment/Tom Snyder Production in association with HBO Downtown Productions. Color. Half-hour. Premiered on COM: May 28, 1995–December 24, 1999.*

#### Voices
**Dr. Katz:** Jonathan Katz; **Ben:** H. Jon Benjamin; **Laura, the receptionist:** Laura Silverman; **Stanley:** Will Le Bow; **Julie:** Julianne Shapiro

## DR. SNUGGLES

Peter Ustinov is the voice of Dr. Snuggles, a good-natured veterinarian who travels anywhere via his pogo stick to care for animals. Ustinov supplied the voice of several other characters in the series as well. A KidPix Production. Color. Half-hour. Premiered: September 12, 1981. Syndicated.

*Voices*
**Dr. Snuggles:** Peter Ustinov

## DO DO—THE KID FROM OUTER SPACE

This British-made 78-episode color half-hour series, imitated popular Japanese imports, featuring the adventures of Do Do and his pet Company, aliens from the atomic planet Hydro, who come to Earth to help a noted scientist, Professor Fingers, perform research on many scientific mysteries left unresolved. The series was telecast on several NBC-owned and operated stations from 1966 through 1970. A Halas and Batchelor Production. Color. Half-hour. Premiered: August 23, 1965. Syndicated.

## DOG CITY

Brian Henson, son of the late Muppets creator Jim Henson, was executive producer of this half-hour, film noir–style live-action/animated detective series following the comical exploits of hardboiled dog detective Ace Heart, Ace's artist creator, a muppet dog named Eliot Shag and their canine friends (Eddie, Bugsy, Frisky, Bruiser and Kitty), who solve mysteries—often by resorting to supernatural means—to make the streets of Dog City safe again. The series was based on a live-action sketch that appeared on NBC's The Jim Henson Hour in 1989. A Jim Henson/Nelvana Production. Color. Half-hour. Premiered on FOX: September 19, 1992–January 28, 1995.

*Voices*
**Ace Heart:** Ron White; **Chief Rosie O'Gravy:** Elizabeth Hanna; **Bugsy:** John Stocker; **Frisky:** James Rankin; **Bruiser:** Howard Jerome; **Kitty:** Paulina Gillis; **Mad Dog:** Stephen Quimette

*Muppet Performers*
**Eliot Shag:** Kevin Clash; **Colleen:** Fran Brill; **Artie:** Joey Mazzarino; **Bruno:** Brian Meehl

## DONKEY KONG COUNTRY

On the exotic tropical island of Congo Bongo, brutish strong-ape Donkey Kong and his sidekick Diddy Kong try to stop the evil King Caroo from stealing the powerful orb, the Crystal Coconut, and assuming control of the island, while the luscious Candy Kong often sidetracks the big ape, in this French-produced computer-animated half-hour series based on the popular Nintendo video game and first shown on French television under the title of La Planète Donkey Kong in September 1996. Dubbed in English, the 40-episode fantasy/adventure series aired Saturday mornings for two seasons on FOX Family Channel beginning in August 1998 and re-aired on FOX. Coincidentally, on December 19, 1998, as part of a crossover promotion of the FOX Family Channel series, FOX aired special presentations of two back-to-back episodes on its Saturday morning schedule: "Raiders of the Lost Banana" and "Buried Treasure." A Medialab/France 2/Le Studio Canal+/Valor 4/WIC Entertainment/Nelvana Production. Color. Half-hour. Premiered on FOX FAM: August 15, 1998–July 2000. Premiered on FOX: July 17, 1999–September 11, 1999.

*Voices*
**Donkey Kong:** Richard Yearwood; **Diddy Kong:** Andrew Sabiston; **Candy Kong:** Joy Tanner; **King K. Rool:** Ben Campbell; **Dixie Kong:** Louise Vallance; **Krusha:** Ron Rubin (Season 1), Frank Welker (Season 2); **Klump:** Len Carlson (Season 1), Neil Ross (Season 2); **Eddie the Mean Old Yeti:** Adrian Truss; **Cranky Kong:** Aaron Tager; **Bluster Kong:** Donald Burda; **Funky Kong:** Damon D'Oliveira; **Inka Dinka Doo:** Rick Jones; **Kritter:** Lawrence Bayne

## DORA THE EXPLORER

An adorable seven-year-old Latina girl wearing mismatched clothes embarks on a series of exciting and educational computer-based adventures with her red-booted monkey friend Boots, her talking Backpack, her singing Map, the ever-sneaky Swiper the fox, her bilingual cousin Diego Marquez and others—in this half-hour children's series co-created by Chris Gifford, Valerie Walsh and Eric Weiner for Nickelodeon's Nick Jr.

Debuting on Nickelodeon's Nick Jr. weekday programming block in August 2000, this highly-rated preschool series offered television's first strong Latina preschool role model for young viewers. After setting a new premiere ratings record on Nick Jr. that August, with an average of 1.1 million viewers daily, Nickelodeon renewed the popular bilingual animated adventure series by ordering 26 new episodes for the following season. Not only was Dora the Explorer an instant success on Nick Jr., but it was also largely embraced by audiences on CBS's Saturday morning Nick Jr. on CBS program block. Remaining Nickelodeon's most watched daytime series, in November 2001 the kids cabler ordered 13 more episodes to air in the first quarter of 2002 and a third season in 2003.

Since 2000 the pint-sized delight and her friends have starred in a brace of top-rated one-hour daytime specials that bowed on Nick Jr. and also aired on Nickelodeon's commercial-free children's programming network, Noggin: Dora the Explorer Mother's Day Special (2002), Dora the Explorer's Christmas Special (2002), Dora's Super Silly Siesta (2004), Dora's Fairytale Adventure (2004), Dora's the Pirate Adventure (2005), Dora's Dance to the Rescue (2005) and Dora's World Adventure (2006).

Airing Monday through Friday at 11:00 A.M. (ET) through the 2006–07 season, Dora continued to maintain the top spot among all preschool programming on commercial television, outranking all broadcast and cable programs in its time period. Syndicated in 125 countries and translated into 24 languages around the world, the 11–time Daytime Emmy Award-nominated children's series spawned a spin-off show in 2005, Go, Diego, Go!, featuring the adventures of Dora's nature expert cousin, Diego. In April 2003, weekday afternoon reruns of the immensely popular children's series began on Nickelodeon's sister network, Noggin. A Nickelodeon/Viacom International Production. Color. Half-hour. Premiered on NICK: August 14, 2000. Premiered on CBS: September 16, 2000–September 25, 2006. Rebroadcast on NOG: April 7, 2003–.

*Voices*
**Dora Jones:** Kathleen Herles; **Boots:** Harrison Chad; **Backpack:** Sasha Tora; **The Map/Swiper/Fiesta Trio:** Marc Weiner; **Benny the Bull:** Paul Iacono, Jake Burbage; **Ricardo:** Jason Thorton; **Tico:** Jose Zelava, Muhammed Cunningham; **Isa:** Ashley Fleming; **Diego Marquez:** Felipe Dieppa, Jake T. Austin; **Papi:** Esai Morales

## DOUBLE DRAGON

Trained from infancy in martial arts and steeped in the nonviolent Code of the Dragon, Billy Lee undergoes his greatest challenge when, along with Marian, a dedicated policewoman, he battles to stop the Shadow Warriors and meets his long lost identical twin brother in this half-hour syndicated fantasy/adventure series first broadcast in 1993 as part of the weekend anthology series *Amazin' Adventures*. In 1996, following its run in syndication, the series was rebroadcast on USA Network's *Cartoon Express*. A *DIC Enterprises/Bohbot Production. Color. Half-hour. Premiered: 1993. Syndicated. Rebroadcast on USA: September 22, 1996–September 12, 1998.*

*Voices*

**Billy Lee/Shadow Warrior/Jawbreaker:** Mike Donovan; **Jimmy Lee/Shadow Boss/Sickle:** Scott McNeil; **Shadowmaster:** Jim Byrnes; **Trigger Happy:** Terry Klassen; **Vortex:** Ian James Corlett; **Blaster/Countdown:** Alvin Sanders; **Wild Willy/Chopper/ Kona:** Gary Chalk; **Oldest Dragon:** French Tichner; **Marian Martin:** Cathy Weseluck; **Michael:** Wezley Morris; **Abobo:** Blu Mankuma

## ◎ DOUG

A painfully average 11-year-old kid (Doug Funnie), who spends half his time thinking about popular Patty Mayonnaise and the other half avoiding school bully Roger Klotz, muddles through tough childhood experiences, such as getting a bad haircut or learning to dance for the first time, which he carefully details in a diary each night, in this Emmy-nominated half-hour animated series created by Jim Jinkins. Each episode charted the delightful misadventures of the likable lad, learning another valuable lesson about growing up. A cast of regulars included best friend Skeeter Valentine, vice principal Lamar Bone and teacher Mrs. Wingo. Jinkins got the idea for *Doug* one night in 1985 while sitting in his New York loft. First he tried to sell the idea as a greeting card line, then as a children's book, but he had no takers.

Premiering in August 1991 on Nickelodeon, as part of a 90-minute Sunday-morning cartoon block that included *The Ren & Stimpy Show* and *Rugrats*, the show slowly built a loyal following. It didn't really become a ratings hit until the original 52 episodes ceased production in 1994 and Nickelodeon started airing reruns along with *Rugrats*, Monday through Friday. (*Rugrats* became Nick's highest-rated show; *Doug* ranked a close second.)

During the character's network run, in 1993 Nickelodeon cast Doug in his first prime-time animated special, *Doug's Halloween Adventure*, in which Doug and Skeeter go to an amusement park for the opening of "the scariest ride ever made." That same year, Doug was also featured in a second half-hour holiday special, *Doug's Christmas Story.*

Beginning in October 1994, Nickelodeon continued retelevising old episodes of the series. In the fall of 1996 Doug returned as a seventh grader (and back from summer vacation) in 13 new episodes in *Brand Spanking New! Doug* (retitled *Disney's Doug* in 1998) for ABC. (See entry for further details.) In January 1999 the popular children's program was repeated weekday afternoons on Nickelodeon's commercial-free children's network, Noggin, until March 2003. Starting in September 2001 Toon Disney rebroadcast the series until 2004 while Nick's sister network, Nicktoons, also rebroadcast the series from May 2002 to October 2004. A *Jumbo Pictures/Ellipse Animation Production in association with Nickelodeon. Color. Half-hour. Premiered on NICK: August 11, 1991–August 8, 1992; August 15, 1992–September 19, 1993; September 26, 1993–October 1, 1994. Rebroadcast on NICK: October 1994. Rebroadcast on NOG: October 31, 1999–March 31, 2002. Rebroadcast on TDIS: September 3, 2001–October 31, 2004. Rebroadcast on NICKT: May 1, 2002–October 30, 2005.*

*Voices*

**Doug Funnie:** Billy West; **Judy Funnie:** Becca Lish; **Patty Mayonnaise:** Constance Shulman; **Bud Dink/Skeeter Valentine:** Fred Newman; **Beebe:** Alice Playten; **Lamar Bone:** Doug Preis; **Mayor White:** Greg Lee

## ◎ DRAGON BALL

Youthful adventures of Goku, a boy in search of mystical orbs, which grant any wish when they are joined together, and the origin of the famed Z-Fighters in this prequel of sorts to the phenomenally successful Japanese-imported anime series, *Dragon Ball Z*, packaged by Saban Entertainment and broadcast in the United States on Cartoon Network. The half-hour collection of episodes began airing in August 2001, preceded by reruns of the series' English-dubbed forerunner, *Dragon Ball Z*, and followed by a third new series in 2003, *Dragon Ball GT*, also on Cartoon Network. A *Toei/Seagull/FUNimation/Ocean Group/Saban Entertainment/Sensation Animation Production. Color. Half-hour. Premiered on CAR: August 20, 2001–April 15, 2004.*

## ◎ DRAGON BALL GT

With the fate of Earth in the balance, Goku and his friends, Trunks and Pan, must recover the Black Star dragon balls, scattered across the galaxy, to save the planet from destruction in this sequel to the popular anime series, *Dragon Ball Z*. The new half-hour series, broadcast weekday afternoons in the United States on Cartoon Network's *Toonami* action-adventure programming block beginning in November 2003 along with anime favorites *Gundam Force* and *Samurai Jack*, was first shown on Fuji television in 1996, one week after the final episode of its predecessor, *Dragon Ball Z*, aired. Sixty-six episodes of the English-language version, produced by FUNimation and Saban Entertainment in association with Japan's Toei Animation, were broadcast on Cartoon Network until April 2005. Producing the English-language version for Cartoon Network was FUNimation. A *Toei/Seagull/FUNimation/Ocean Group/Saban Entertainment/Sensation Animation Production. Color. Half-hour. Premiered on CAR: November 7, 2003–April 16, 2005.*

*Voices*

**Son Goku:** Stephanie Nadolny, Sean Schemmel; **Pan:** Elise Baughman; **Trunks:** Eric Vale; **Gill/Krillin:** Sonny Strait; **Dob:** Sean Teague; **Vegeta/Mr. Popo/Piccolo/Black Smoke Shenlong/ Syn/Omega Shenron/Dragon God/Eternal Dragon/Shenron:** Christopher Sabat; **Bulma:** Tiffany Vollmer; **Bulla:** Pariski Fahhri; **Son Goten:** Robert McCollum; **Son Goham:** Kyle Hebert; **Videl:** Lucy Small; **Chi-Chi:** Cynthia Cranz; **Android 18/Marron:** Meredith McCoy; **Dende:** Justin Cook; **Pilaf/Shigeru Nakhara/ Super Jinzo 'ningen #17:** Chuck Huber; **Shu/Rage Shenron:** Chris Cason; **Mai:** Julie Franklin; **Hercule:** Chris Rager; **Majin Buu:** Josh Martin; **Master Roshi/Turtle Hermit/Baby:** Mike McFarland; **Kibitokai/Elder Kai/Dr. Gero:** Kent Williams; **Sogoro:** Brice Armstrong; **Shusugoro/Ken Yamaguchi:** John Burgmeier; **Dr. Myuu:** Duncan Brannan; **General Rilldo:** Andrew Chandler; **Frieza:** Linda Young; **Cell:** Dameon Clarke; **King Kai:** Sean Schemmel; **Shenron:** Bradford Jackson; **Eis Shenron:** Jerry Jewel; **Oceanus Shenron:** Steve Sanders; **Naturon Shenron:** Christopher Bevins; **Princess Oto:** Laura Bailey; **Narrator:** Andrew Chandler

## ◎ DRAGON BALL Z

Adapted from the phenomenally successful Japanese cartoon. Goku, a rolypoly boy who came to Earth as an infant with powers far beyond those of mortal men to destroy the planet now is mankind's last, best hope to fend off supervillains from his native planet. Their aim: to find the crystal Dragon Balls that will enable them to conquer the universe. This half-hour mystical adventure series was produced for first-run syndication and later rebroadcast on the WB and Cartoon Network. A *Toei Animation/FUNimation/ Saban Entertainment Production. Color. Half-hour. Premiered: September 7, 1996. Rebroadcast on WB: July–August 1998. Syndicated. Rebroadcast on CAR: August 31, 1998–December 29, 2006.*

*Voices*
Don Brown, Ted Cole, Paul Dobson, Brian Drummond, Andrew Francis, Paulina Gillis, Jason Gray Stanford, Doc Harris, Saltron Henderson, Mark Hildreth, Terry Klassen, Lalainia Lindjberg, Scott McNeil, Laara Nadiq, Pauline Newstone, Doug Parker, Jane Perry, Ward Perry, Alvin Sanders, Matt Smith, Jerry Todd, Dave "Squatch" Ward, Cathy Weseluck, Alec Willows

## ◎ DRAGON BOOSTER

In a classic struggle of good versus evil, an average teenage stable boy, Artha Penn, plunges into an incredible adventure and becomes the mythical hero, Dragon Booster, and is charged with riding the legendary dragon, Beuacephalis ("Beau" for short), and uniting humans and dragons to save the world from war in this popular CGI-animated half-hour series broadcast Saturday mornings on ABC Family. Conceived by the Story Hat, with animation produced by Vancouver-based 3-D animation studio, Nerd Corps Entertainment, the 39-episode, high-octane adventure series aired on the *Jetix* action program block on ABC Family (premiering with the two-part episode, "The Choosing") and Toon Disney, where the series is currently still airing. *A DIC Entertainment/Nerd Corps Entertainment/FUNimation Studios/Alliance Atlantis Comunications Production. Color. Half-hour. Premiered on ABC FAM: October 23, 2004–August 20, 2006. Premiered on TDIS: October 25, 2004.*

*Voices*
**Artha Penn/Dragon Booster:** Matt Hill; **Lance Penn/Marianis/ Dragon City News Reporter:** Kathleen Barr; **Parmon Sean/Khatah/Tannis:** Lee Tockar; **Kitt Wonn/Spynn:** Lenore Zann; **Connor Penn/Mortis:** Gary Chalk; **Word Paynn/Original Dragon Booster/Drakkus:** Mark Oliver; **Moordryd Paynn/Wulph/Captain Faier:** Trevor Devall; **Cain:** Scott McNeil; **Propheci/Reepyr:** Michael Kopsa; **Pyrrah/Sentrus:** Nicole Oliver; **Phistus:** Andrew Francis; **Race Marshall Budge:** Richard Newman; **Dorsall/Stewardd/Vociferous:** Sam Vincent; **Kawake:** Brian Drummond; **Armeggaddon:** Gerard Plunkett; **Rivett:** Jonathan Holmes; **Additional Voices:** Michael Donovan, Brent Miller

## ◎ DRAGON FLYZ

Set in the 41st-century city of Airlandis, three heroic brothers and their valiant sister, allied with their mighty dragons, fight against the evil Dread Wing to keep their beloved city floating free. This futuristic, 26-episode half-hour fantasy series premiered in syndication nationwide in the fall of 1996. *An Abrams Gentile Entertainment/Gaumont Multimedia Production. Color. Half-hour. Premiered: September 14, 1996. Syndicated.*

*Voices*
T.J. Benjamin, Saul Bernstein, Thomas Cannizzaro, Donna Daley, Jonathan Kahn, Don Mayo, James Michael, K.C. Noel

## ◎ DRAGON HUNTERS

Two for-hire dragonslayers—the brawny sword expert Lian-Chu and brainy but cowardly Gwizdo—with the aid of their pet dragon, Hector, venture from town to town to rid each place of Borkbacks, Genegenes, Duratonums and various other fire-breathing dragons that are terrorizing the medieval world in this futuristic French-imported animated action-adventure series—originally called *Chasseurs de Dragons*—initially picked up by Cartoon Network to

help bolster its Saturday-morning cartoon lineup. A few weeks after its January 2006 premiere, the series was removed from Cartoon Network's Saturday-morning lineup, with six episodes airing until mid-February, until reappearing that September with four new episodes until October 2006. *A Futurikon Production. Color. Half-hour. Premiered on CAR: January 14, 2006–October 14, 2006.*

*Voices*
**Lian-Chu:** Hary Standjofski; **Gwizdo/Hector:** Rick Jones; **Zaza:** Annie Bovaird; **Jennyline:** Sonja Ball

## ◎ DRAGON'S LAIR

In King Ethelred's kingdom, one knight outshines them all—Dirk the Daring. He performs great deeds and protects the kingdom and his beautiful Princess Daphne from creepy villains and a fiery dragon in this half-hour ABC Saturday-morning series. After its network run ended, the series was subsequently aired on USA Network's *Cartoon Express* then on Cartoon Network. *A Ruby-Spears Enterprise Production. Color. Half-hour. Premiered on ABC: September 8, 1984–April 27, 1985. Rebroadcast on USA: April 30, 1989–March 19, 1992. Rebroadcast on CAR: September 17, 1994–September 18, 1994 (Look What We Found!). Rebroadcast on BOOM: June 30, 2002–.*

*Voices*
**Dirk the Daring:** Bob Sarlatte; **Princess Daphne:** Ellen Gerstell; **King Ethelred:** Fred Travalena; **Timothy:** Michael Mish; **Cinge:** Arthur Burghardt; **Bertram:** Peter Cullen; **Storyteller:** Clive Revill; **Assorted Voices:** Marilyn Schreffler

## ◎ DRAGON TALES

Six-year-old Emmy and her four-year-old brother, Max, find fun and adventure in Dragonland, a magical universe where they overcome all kinds of obstacles with the help of their new dragon friends Cassie, Ord, Zak and Wheezie, and their teacher, Quetzal. This half-hour animated fantasy series was co-created by the late Nina Elias-Bamberger of Sesame Workshop (best known for creating such popular children's shows as *Tiny Planets*) and adapted from the work of artist and retired educator Ron Rodecker who created the characters for the hit television series based on his experiences working with children.

Divided into two 12-minute cartoons linked to sing-a-longs, the top-rated show—whose starring characters were Hispanic—illustrated the importance of diversity and accepting other's differences and handling rejection, as well as how to cope with many other challenges on a day-to-day basis when working together with others. Debuting in September 1999 on PBS Kids, with five new episodes airing the first week and new episodes rolled out in batches of five thereafter, the weekday series' original 96 episodes were broadcast until April 2005. Thereafter, the show aired in reruns on PBS's digital cable television channel and video-on-demand (VOD) service, PBS Kids Sprout. *A Columbia TriStar/Sony Pictures Family Entertainment/CTV/Children's Television (Sesame) Workshop Production. Color. Half-hour. Premiered on PBS Kids: September 6, 1999–April 28, 2005. Rebroadcast on PBS Kids: September 12, 1999–April 11, 2005. Rebroadcast on PBS Kids Sprout (VOD): April 4, 2005– . Rebroadcast on PBS Kids Sprout (digital cable): September 26, 2005–.*

*Voices*
**Emmy:** Andrea Libman; **Max:** Danny McKinnon; **Ord:** Shirley Millner, Ty Olsson; **Cassie:** Chantal Strand; **Zak:** Jason Michas; **Wheezie:** Kathleen Barr; **Quetzal:** Eli Gabay; **Enrique:** Aida Ortega

## DRAGON WARRIOR

Prompted by the success of the Nintendo video-game series *Dragon Quest*, this Japanese animated series emulated its sword-and-sorcery format. Thirteen serialized half-hour episodes present the adventures of a dragon-slaying 16-year-old teen (Abel), who must rescue his childhood friend (Tiala) from the evil monster Baramos and save mankind from the deadly fury of the Great Dragon. *A Saban Entertainment Production. Color. Half-hour. Premiered: September 22, 1990. Syndicated.*

### Voices

Long John Baldry, Jay Brazeau, Jim Byrnes, Gary Chalk, Marcy Goldberg, Sam Kouth, Shelley Lefler, Duff McDonald, Richard Newman

## DRAK PACK

Drak, Frankie and Howler, teenage descendants of the famed monsters Dracula, Frankenstein and the Werewolf, atone for the sins of their ancestors by using their special powers for the good of mankind. Their main adversary: the world's worst villain, Dr. Dred, and his O.G.R.E. group (the Organization Of Generally Rotten Endeavors). *A Hanna-Barbera Production. Color. Half-hour. Premiered on CBS: September 6, 1980–September 12, 1982.*

### Voices

**Drak Jr.:** Jerry Dexter; **Frankie/Howler:** Bill Callaway; **Big D:** Alan Oppenheimer; **Dr. Dred:** Hans Conried; **Vampira:** Julie McWhirter; **Mummy Man:** Chuck McCann; **Toad/Fly:** Don Messick

## DRAWING POWER

In this live-action/animated series, Pop, a white-haired chief animator, and his assistants, Lenny and Kari, dream up educational cartoon messages in a small animation studio, leading into one of several cartoon segments featured each week, namely: "The Book Report," "Bus Stop," "Pet Peeves," "Professor Rutabaga," "Superperson U" and "What Do You Do, Dad (Mom)?" The half-hour program was by the producers of the award-winning children's series *Schoolhouse Rock*. *A Newhall-Yohe Production. Color. Half-hour. Premiered on NBC: October 11, 1980–May 16, 1981.*

### Cast

**Pop:** Bob Kaliban; **Lenny:** Lenny Schultz; **Kari:** Kari Page

## DRAWN TOGETHER

When eight castoffs—each a parody of recognizable cartoon, comic book and video game characters—are forced to live together in the same house, trouble ensues with the farting, copulating cartoon roomies, in this animated reality show spoof of MTV's *The Real World*, created by Dave Jeser and Matt Silverstein for cable television's Comedy Central. Produced by Glendale, California-based Rough Draft Studios, with most of the animation produced overseas at its facilities in Korea, this traditional ink-and-paint animated half-hour comedy series—described as television's "first animated reality show"—made its debut on Comedy Central on October 27, 2004 with the first episode entitled "Hot Tub." Altogether, eight episodes were produced for the first season through December of that year.

Heading the show's unusual cast are the chauvinistic, perverted *Superman*-inspired superhero, Captain Hero; a pampered, righteous princess, Princess Ariel (a parody of Disney's Ariel from *The Little Mermaid* and Belle from *Beauty and the Beast*); a homicidal *Pokemon*-type character blessed with supernatural powers, Ling-Ling; and a sassy, promiscuous black musician, Foxxy Love (a takeoff on Valerie Brown from TV's *Josie and the Pussycats*). Others include a sex-starved party animal, Spanky Ham (a satire of Internet Flash cartoon characters); a token gay video game-inspired hero, Xandir P. Wifflebottom; an out-of-shape sex symbol, Toot Braunstein (based on Max Fleischer's Betty Boop); and a wacky children's show character, Wooldoor Sockbat (modeled after TV's *SpongeBob SquarePants* and Stimpy of TV's *The Ren & Stimpy Show*).

In 2005, the popular adult-humored series was renewed for a second season with the network ordering 14 additional episodes that began airing that October. In January 2006, the series returned for a third season. *A Rough Draft Studios Production. Color. Half-hour. Premiered on COM: October 27, 2004.*

### Voices

**Captain Hero:** Jess Harnell; **Wooldoor Sockbat:** James Arnold Taylor; **Ling-Ling:** Abbey McBride; **Foxxy Love:** Cree Summer; **Xandir P. Whifflebottom:** Jack Plotnick; **Spanky Ham:** Adam Carolla; **Princess Clara/Toot:** Tara Strong; **Buckie Bucks:** Chris Edgerly; **Blue Ball:** Jim Ward

## DROIDS: THE ADVENTURES OF R2D2 AND C3PO

The robotic droids from the *Star Wars* film series return in this series of half-hour animated adventures produced for ABC in 1985..Produced in association with Lucasfilm, the company *Star Wars* creator George Lucas, the series was repackaged with another ABC/Lucas animated series, *The Ewoks*, as the hour-long *The Ewoks and Star Wars Droids Adventure Hour*, which aired on the network in 1986. (See series entry for voice credits and details.) *A Lucasfilm Production in association with Nelvana Limited, Hanho Heung-Up and Mi-Hahn Productions. Color. Half-hour. Premiered on ABC: September 7, 1985–February 22, 1986. Rebroadcast on SCI: March 29, 1993–June 30, 1997 (part of* Cartoon Quest *and Animation Station).*

## DROOPY, MASTER DETECTIVE

Dour-faced basset hound and MGM cartoon star Droopy and his look-alike son Dripple match wits with the most comical crooks of all time in all-new half-hour animated adventures, spun off from Fox's *Tom and Jerry Kids*, on which the two characters were originally featured. The new series combined 13 previously broadcast cartoons with 13 new seven-minute episodes. Two Droopy cartoons were featured on each show, along with one new episode of new adventures of Tex Avery's nuttier-than-a-fruitcake Screwball Squirrel (better known as Screwy Squirrel), who makes life miserable for a public park attendant named Dweeble. Hanna-Barbera cofounder Joe Barbera, who worked at MGM with Avery, served as one of the series' producers. *A Hanna-Barbera Production in association with Turner Entertainment. Color. Half-hour. Premiered on FOX: October 2, 1993–August 12, 1994.*

### Voices

**Droopy:** Don Messick; **Dripple/Lightening Bolt the Super Squirrel:** Charlie Adler; **Miss Vavoom:** Theresa Ganzel; **McWolf:** Frank Welker; **The Yolker:** Pat Fraley

## DUCK DODGERS

Thawed out from his 21st-century spaceship 351 years after he was accidentally frozen, Duck Dodgers (alias Daffy Duck) is appointed captain of a new spaceship with a new galactic crew—including eager space cadet, Porky Pig—after scheming and lying to the head of Earth's Defensive Protectorate, Dr. I-Q High, that his services are needed to fight the planet's mortal enemy, the confident Martian Commander X-2 (alias Marvin Martian), in this half-hour animated series inspired by Chuck Jones's cult classic 1953 cartoon short, *Duck Dodgers in the 24 1/2th Century.*

Featuring many other well-known *Looney Tunes* characters, from Yosemite Sam as a Star Trek-like Klingon, K'chutha Sa'am, to Elmer Fudd as a parasitic alien, "The Fudd," and pop culture references as well as visual and thematic elements from popular *Looney Tunes* theatrical cartoon shorts, the 39-episode series, featuring two 15-minute cartoons per half-hour, debuted on Cartoon Network in August 2003. In 2004, ASIFA-Hollywood recognized the series with four Annie Award nominations for outstanding achievement in an animated television production produced for children, music in an animated television production, production design in an animated television production, and voice acting in an animated television production. Lasting three seasons, the series was canceled in 2005, and rebroadcast thereafter on Cartoon Network's offspring channel, Boomerang. *A Warner Bros. TV Animation Production. Color. Half-hour. Premiered on CAR: August 25, 2003–November 11, 2005. Rebroadcast on BOOM: September 12, 2005– .*

### Voices
**Duck Dodgers/Martian Commander X-2, Marvin Martian:** Joe Alaskey; **Porky Pig, Eager Young Space Cadet:** Bob Bergen; **Dr. I.Q. High:** Richard McGonagle; **Martian Queen:** Tia Carrere; **Martian Centurian Robots:** Michael Dorn; **Captain Star Johnson:** John O'Hurley; **Hal Jordan/Green Lantern:** Kevin Smith

## ◎ DUCKMAN

A politically incorrect, out-of-step family man and duck detective with an offbeat family and peculiar blend of animal and human friends—his shrewish sister-in-law, Bernice; his Sgt. Friday–like sidekick, Cornfed; his duckdude son, Ajax; his two-headed sons, Charles and Mambo; his perpetually flatulent Grandmama; and his irritatingly sweet assistants, Fluffy and Uranus—experiences the joys and frustrations of life in the 1990s in this adult-oriented cartoon series from creator, illustrator and underground cartoonist Everett Peck (and from the makers of *The Simpsons*). In early 1991 the series pilot was developed. Production began in November of that year, with Howard E. Baker directing and Frank Zappa providing some of the musical compositions for the program. (The late rock artist also contributed his library of music, which was used in many episodes.) The series debuted in April 1992 at the MIP-TV International Television Convention in Cannes, France before USA Network commissioned it as a weekly prime-time series.

Premiering in March of 1994, the series attracted a million viewers each week. *Duckman* went on to become USA's signature show, nominated twice (in 1996 and 1997) for an Emmy Award for outstanding animated program and named winner of a CableAce Award for best animated program. Jason Alexander (best known as George Costanza on TV's *Seinfeld*) supplies the voice of Duckman. *A Klasky Csupo/Reno and Osborn Production in association with Paramount Television. Color. Half-hour. Premiered on USA: March 5, 1994–September 6, 1997. Rebroadcast on COM: January 2, 2000–.*

### Voices
**Duckman:** Jason Alexander; **Bernice:** Nancy Travis; **Ajax:** Dweezil Zappa; **Charles:** Dana Hill (1994–96, Pat Musick (1996– ); **Mambo:** E. G. Daily; **Bernice:** Nancy Travis; **Fluffy/Uranus:** Pat Musick

## ◎ DUCKTALES

The first daily animated television series from Walt Disney Studios originally intended as a one-hour network series, *DuckTales* was the studio's answer to the highly popular live-action feature films *Raiders of the Lost Ark* and *Romancing the Stone.* It focused on the daring exploits of that cantankerous canard, Scrooge McDuck, Donald Duck's uncle and the world's richest tightwad. Scrooge is joined by a collection of familiar friends and relatives, including Donald's nephews, Huey, Dewey and Louie, in adventures mixed with fowl play and risky undertakings in the far reaches of the world. The 65 episode series premiered in syndication in September of 1987 as a two-hour special (in most markets), entitled *DuckTales: Treasure of the Golden Suns.*

New characters introduced on the show included Launchpad McQuack, a soldier of outrageous fortune; Mrs. Beakley, the governess to Scrooge's grandnephews; Webbigail ("Webby") Vanderduck, Mrs. Beakley's pesky granddaughter; Doofus, Launchpad's greatest fan and biggest hindrance; and a quartet of masked heavies called the Beagle Boys. Other newly created characters included Duckworth, Fenton Crackshell and Bubba Duck.

In 1988 a second two-hour afternoon special was produced, *DuckTales: Time Is Money,* followed by a third in 1989, *Super DuckTales,* which premiered on NBC's *Magical World of Disney.* A year later the characters starred in their only full-length animated feature, *DuckTales the Movie: Treasure of the Lost Lamp.*

That same year, following its initial run in syndication, the series joined Disney studio's two-hour, syndicated *Disney Afternoon* cartoon block. The fun-filled adventure series was subsequently rebroadcast on Disney Channel and its sister channel, Toon Disney. *A Walt Disney Television Animation Production. Color. Half-hour. Premiered: September 11, 1987–September 4, 1992. Syndicated. Rebroadcast on DIS: September 3, 1999–November 2001. Rebroadcast on TDIS: September 3, 1999–October 31, 2004; February 9, 2007–.*

### Voices
**Uncle Scrooge McDuck:** Alan Young; **Launchpad McQuack:** Jim McGeorge, Terence McGovern; **Huey/Dewey/Louie/Webbigail Vanderduck:** Russi Taylor; **Doofus:** Brian Cummings; **Gyro Gearloose/Flintheart Glomgold:** Hal Smith; **Fenton Crackshell:** Hamilton Camp; **Duckworth:** Chuck McCann; **Magica de Spell/Ma Beagle:** June Foray; **Mrs. Beakley:** Joan Gerber; **Bubba Duck:** Christopher Weeks, Frank Welker; **Ludwig Von Drake:** Steve Bulen, Corey Burton; **Donald Duck:** Tony Anselmo

## ◎ DUDLEY DO-RIGHT AND HIS FRIENDS

(See THE DUDLEY DO-RIGHT SHOW.)

## ◎ THE DUDLEY DO-RIGHT SHOW

First introduced on 1961's *Bullwinkle Show,* inept Royal Canadian Mountie Dudley Do-Right returned along with girlfriend Nell, Inspector Fenwick and Snidely Whiplash for more madcap fun in this weekly half-hour series for Saturday-morning television. The program repeated adventures previously seen on *The Bullwinkle Show,* in addition to previous segments that debuted on *Rocky and His Friends.* "Aesop and Son," "Fractured Fairy Tales" and "Peabody's Improbable History." (For voice credits, see *Rocky and His Friends* and *The Bullwinkle Show.*) The series was later retitled and syndicated as *Dudley Do-Right and His Friends. A Jay Ward Production with Producers Associates for Television. Color. Half-hour. Premiered on ABC: April 27, 1969–September 6, 1970.*

### Voices
**Dudley Do-Right:** Bill Scott; **Nell Fenwick:** June Foray; **Inspector Ray K. Fenwick/Narrator:** Paul Frees; **Snidely Whiplash:** Hans Conried

## ⊚ DUEL MASTERS

Young Shobu Kirifuda masters playing the card game "Duel Masters" and bringing the cards' creatures to life by using the legendary martial art called "Kaijudo," aiming to become a Kaijudo champion like his father in this popular anime series based on the manga by Shigenobu Matsumoto. Acquiring all 26 episodes of the English-language version, Cartoon Network premiered the series with a three-episode preview on its highly rated *Toonami* block. The series officially premiered in March of 2004 on the network's *Toonami* spin-off block, the Saturday Video Entertainment System. Subsequently, the program was moved to *Toonami*'s Saturday evening block. Two additional seasons of brand-new episodes followed, starting in March 2005. A *Shogakukan Productions Co. Ltd./Plastic Cow/Elastic Media Corp./Howling Cat Productions. Color. Half-hour. Premiered on CAR: February 27, 2004 (preview). Premiered on CAR: March 13, 2004 (series).*

*Voices*
**Shobu Kirifuda:** Joshua Seth, Liam O'Brien; **Rekuta:** Alex Gold, Sterling R., Brianne Siddall; **Knight/Shori Kirifuda:** Brahan Lee; **Boy George:** Tim Diamond, Joey Lotsko, Brian Beacock; **Jimera:** David Jeremiah, Charlie Cooke, Philece Sampler; **Mai Kirifuda:** Cindy Alexander, Wendee Lee; **Mimi:** Janice Lee, Colleen O'Shaugnessey; **Aiken:** Brian Beacock; **Kokujoh:** Terrence Stone, Steven Jay Blum; **Dr. Root/Multi-Card Monty:** Derek Stephen Prince; **Hakuoh:** Doug Erholtz; **Knight:** Kirk Thorton; **Your Mama:** Michelle Ruff; **Sho/Extreme Bucket Man:** Steven Jay Blum; **Prince Eugene the Mean:** Bob Papenbrook. **Rikuda's Father/Tohru:** Cam Clarke; **Saiyuki:** Dee Dee Green, Peggy O'Neal; **Prince Irving the Terrible:** Jamieson Price; **Kintaro:** Jay Max, R. Martin Klein; **Rekuta's father:** Joe Ochman; **Benny Haha:** Kerrigan Mahan, Michael Sorich; **Mikuni:** Udel R. Deet, Paul St. Peter; **Johnny Coolburns:** Paul St. Peter; **Fritz:** Richard Steven Horvitz; **Robbie Rotten:** Yuri Lowenthal

## ⊚ THE DUKES

The hilarious folks of Hazzard County compete in an around-the-world race in this action adventure series based on the tremendously successful prime-time series *The Dukes of Hazzard*. This time greedy little Boss Hogg and dopey Sheriff Rosco scheme to foreclose the mortgage on the Dukes. This causes Bo, Luke and Daisy to race the trusty General Lee, the hottest supercharged car ever, to raise money for the poor folks in Hazzard County and pay off the mortgage. The animated program features the voices of the stars of the live-action network series.

The animated series debuted as a midseason replacement on CBS in 1982. CBS renewed the program for a second season but cancelled the show after it was on the air for only a month. A *Hanna-Barbera Production. Color. Half-hour. Premiered on CBS: February 5, 1983–November 5, 1983.*

*Voices*
**Boss Hogg:** Sorrell Booke; **Bo Duke:** John Schneider; **Luke Duke:** Tom Wopat; **Daisy Duke:** Catherine Bach; **Vance Duke:** Christopher Mayer; **Uncle Jesse:** Denver Pyle; **Sheriff Rosco Coltrane:** James Best; **Flash/Smokey/General Lee:** Frank Welker

## ⊚ DUMB AND DUMBER: THE ANIMATED SERIES

Capitalizing on the success of the 1994 feature film, classic dumbsters Harry and Lloyd (portrayed by comedian Jim Carrey and actor Jeff Daniels in the film) spend most of their time looking for jobs—and losing them soon after they are hired—in this Saturday-morning half-hour cartoon series. A *Hanna-Barbera Cartoons Production in association with New Line Television. Color. Half-hour. Premiered on ABC: September 1995–July 24, 1996.*

*Voices*
**Lloyd:** Matt Frewer; **Harry:** Bill Fagerbakke; **Weenie:** Tom Kenny; **Dymbster:** Bronson Pinchot; **Waitress:** Kath Soucie

## ⊚ DUMB BUNNIES

Living in the wooded community of Bunnyville, a family of mentally and physically challenged rabbits—Poppa Dumb Bunny, Momma Dumb Bunny and Baby Dumb Bunny—work together to overcome their problems when their plans go amuck in this Australian and Canadian coproduction, based on author Dav Pilkey's popular children's books. The 26-episode half-hour animated comedy series, which was also released as a series of theatrical shorts in Europe, premiered in the United States on CBS, along with a package of cartoons produced by Canadian animation studio, Nelvana. A *Yoram Gross-EM.TV/Village Roadshow/Nelvana Ltd. Production. Color. Half-hour. Premiered on CBS: October 3, 1998–September 26, 1999.*

*Voices*
**Poppa Dumb Bunny:** Rob Smith; **Momma Dumb Bunny:** Catherine Gallant; **Baby Dumb Bunny:** Dustin Lauzon; **Bill Uppity:** Dwayne Hill; **Sue Uppity:** Linda Kash; **Prissy Uppity:** Rebecca Brenner; **Snow Bunny:** Neil Crone; **Mr. Grudge:** Louis Del Grande; **King:** Adrian Egan; **Mayor:** Ellen Ray Hennessy; **Officer Moodie:** Jeff Knight; **Margaret:** Julie Lemieux; **Billy:** Ben Cook; **Professor Bunsen:** Keith Knight; **Buff:** Michael Lampert; **Ghost/Ned:** Ron Pardo; **Dr. P. Bunny:** Bruce Pirrie; **Mr. Barker:** Wayne Robson; **Momma Hare/Maudin:** Carolyn Scott; **Sly Fox:** Norm Spencer; **Fussbunny:** Sean Sullivan; **Sir Edmund Nerdy:** Ian Thomas; **Baby Hare:** Joshua Tucci; **Dr. Burner:** Jamie Watson; **Tumtee:** Jonathan Wilson; **Narrator:** Peter Wildman

## ⊚ DUNGEONS AND DRAGONS

Based on the popular fantasy game, this 26 episode half-hour series traces the adventures of six children (Sheila, Hank, Eric, Diana, Presto and Bobby) who pile into an amusement park ride only to find themselves on the most mysterious and terrifying ride of all: a trip through time into the realm of dungeons and dragons.

In April 2006, the animated adaptation of TSR's popular 1980s role-playing game returned to television on Toon Disney, which began rebroadcasting the fantasy cartoon series on its *Jetix* cartoon block. A *Marvel Production in association with Dungeons & Dragons Entertainment Group, a division of TSR Incorporated. Color. Half-hour. Premiered on CBS: September 17, 1983–August 30, 1986. Rebroadcast on CBS: June 20, 1987–September 5, 1987. Rebroadcast on FOX: April 29, 2000–October 5, 2000. Rebroadcast on DIS: April 7, 2006– .*

*Voices*
**Hank:** Willie Aames; **Eric:** Donny Most; **Sheila:** Katie Leigh; **Diana:** Toni Gayle Smith; **Presto:** Adam Rich; **Bobby:** Ted Field III; **Dungeon Master:** Sidney Miller; **Venger:** Peter Cullen

## ⊚ DYNOMUTT, DOG WONDER

In the summer of 1978, ABC repeated the adventures of this caped, crusading bionic dog and his faithful leader, the Blue Falcon, who were introduced in tandem on *The Scooby Doo/Dynomutt Hour* in 1976. Created by Joe Ruby and Ken Spears, who formed their own animation studio, Ruby-Spears Enterprises, Dynomutt's voice and mannerisms were patterned after Ed Norton (Art Carney) of *The Honeymooners*.

Before being given its own half-hour time slot that summer, Dynomutt reappeared that season in four two-part broadcasts as part of *Scooby's All-Star Laff-A-Lympics*. (The cartoons were retitled "The Blue Falcon and Dynomutt.") In the fall of 1980, Dynomutt surfaced again briefly as costar of *The Godzilla/Dynomutt Hour with the Funky Phantom* on NBC.

In the spring of 1989 the series began reairing on USA Network's weekday cartoon block *Cartoon Express*, until the fall of 1991. It has since been rebroadcast on Cartoon Network. (For Dynomutt voice credits, see *The Scooby-Doo/Dynomutt Hour*.) *A Hanna-Barbera Production. Color. Half-hour. Premiered on ABC: June 3, 1978–September 2, 1978. Rebroadcast on USA: April 2, 1989–October 25, 1991. Rebroadcast on CAR: October 3, 1992–January 1, 1994 (weekends); January 8, 1994–April 3, 1994 (Saturdays, Sundays); April 9, 1994–September 4, 1994 (Saturdays, Sundays); September 10, 1994–October 15, 1994 (Saturdays); October 17, 1994–September 1, 1995 (with Mighty Man & Yukk); 1996; March 1998; February 1999. Rebroadcast on BOOM: June 16, 2000–.*

## ◎ EARTHWORM JIM

An extraterrestrial supersuit transforms this slimy, spineless 98-gram weakling into a musclebound defender of Earth, the cosmos and everything in between. Every villain wants to nab the supersuit for himself in this 21 episode half-hour cartoon series, based on the popular video game of the same name. *A Universal Cartoon Studios/Akom Production Company/Flextech PLC/Shiny Entertainment Production. Color. Half-hour. Premiered on WB: September 9, 1995–October 12, 1996.*

### Voices

**Earthworm Jim:** Dan Castellaneta; **Queen Slug-for-a-Butt:** Andrea Martin; **Peter Puppy/Narrator:** Jeff Bennett; **Princess What's-Her-Name:** Kath Soucie; **Professor Monkey-for-a-Head:** Charles Adler; **Evil the Cat:** Edward Hibbert; **Snott/Henchrat:** Jon Kassir; **Psy-Crow/Bob, the Killer Goldfish:** Jim Cummings

## ◎ ED, EDD N EDDY

Led by the supposed "brains" of the trio, Eddy, three dorky, pubescent teenagers (including Eddy's foolish partners, Ed and Edd)—collectively called "the Eds"—unleash a series of half-baked schemes in an effort to con their peers for cash to buy their favorite treat, jawbreakers, in their suburban, cul-de-sac neighborhood of Peach Creek Estates, with disastrous results, in this half-hour comedy series—and longest-running animated series—produced for Cartoon Network.

Joined in their off-the-wall adventures by their neighborhood friends, including the more grown-up girl-next-door, Nazz, and her nitwit skateboarding fiend younger brother, Jimmy, *Ed, Edd N Eddy* debuted in prime time on November 16, 1998, at 8:00 P.M., and became the first non-in-house produced series to join the network's daily *Cartoon Cartoon* programming block. Created by acclaimed animator Danny Antonucci, creator of *Lupo the Butcher* and director of Vancouver-based a.k.a. Cartoon Inc., the rapid-paced, mostly hand-drawn and traditional cel-animated comedy series—drawn in the derivative of the jarring style of "Squigglevision," a process popularized in the Comedy Central cartoon series, *Dr. Katz, Professional Therapist*—featured two comedy adventures a week following the madcap exploits of this infantile trio.

During the series' impressive run, Cartoon Network treated the program's millions of devoted fans to three prime-time holiday specials during Christmas, Valentine's Day and Halloween, namely:

*Ed, Edd N Eddy's Jingle Jingle Jangle* (2004); *Ed, Edd N Eddy's Hanky Panky Hullabaloo* (2005); and *Ed, Edd N Eddy's Boo-Haw-Haw* (2005) for Halloween. In 2007, following the production of 64 episodes over five seasons, the series returned for a sixth season, including a 90-minute made-for-TV movie. *An a.k.a. Cartoon Inc. Production. Color. Half-hour. Premiered on CAR: November 16, 1998.*

### Voices

**Ed:** Matt Hill; **Edd "Double D":** Samuel Vincent; **Eddy:** Tony Sampson; **Jimmy:** Keenan Christenson; **Nazz:** Tabitha St. Germain (1999–2000), Erin Fitzgerald (2000–2001, 2003–   ); **Jonny:** Buck (David Paul Grove); **Sarah/Lee Kanker:** Janyse Jaud; **May Kanker:** Erin Fitzgerald (1999–2001, 2003–   ), Jenn Forgie (2003–   ); **Marie Kanker/Kevin:** Kathleen Barr; **Rolf:** Peter Kelamis

## ◎ EDGAR & ELLEN

Mischief and mayhem results when slightly twisted, gothic 12-year-old twins Edgar and Ellen, who live in a creepy 13-story mansion, disrupt the once idyllic town of Nod's Limbs in which they live as they wreak havoc on its goody-two-shoes townspeople with their weird and wacky pranks that often backfire in this half-hour animated series, featuring the characters made famous in the Simon & Schuster children's book series. Beginning in the fall of 2006, the characters, previously seen in 12 two-minute shorts aired daily on Nicktoons starting on October 1, 2005 and as hosts of the network's second annual 48-hour *Scare-a-Thon*, were featured in three half-hour specials celebrating back to school (*Accept No Substitutes*), Halloween (*Trick or Twins*) and the Winter Olympics (*Cold Medalists*), with three more in 2007 on Valentine's Day (*Crushed*), April Fool's Day (*Nobody's Fool*) and during Summer Vacation (*Frog Day of Summer*), with the April Fool's special leading to the slated debut of the television series on the Nicktoons Network in October 2007.

Aimed at viewers ages eight to 12, each half-hour is a blend of animated segments of various lengths, plus kid-driven content inspired by ideas submitted by actual kids online, influencing 10 percent of every show's content, a first for a network series. Besides airing on Nicktoons Network in the United States, the *Edgar & Ellen* series, produced by State Farm Productions, was broadcast by Nickelodeon channels in Australia, Denmark, Finland, Holland, Italy, Norway, Sweden, and on Nickelodeon in the United Kingdom. First announced at the 2006 MIPCOM in Cannes, France, the deal called for 26 episodes to be produced for the first season, along with six half-hour specials. *A Star Farm Productions LLC/Bardel Entertainment Production in association with Nickelodeon and YTV. Color. Two minutes. Half-hour. Premiered on NICKT: October 1, 2005 (two minute shorts). Premiered on NICKT: September 6, 2006 (first of six half-hour specials).*

## ◎ EEK! AND THE TERRIBLE THUNDERLIZARDS

The ever-neurotic cat returned for two more seasons in this half-hour cartoon combo mixing *Eek! The Cat* cartoons and 15-minute serialized adventures (one segment per week) of "The Terrible Thunderlizards," a trio of New Age dinosaurs—Day Z. Cutter, Doc and Bo "Diddly" Squat—from 135 million years ago. Due to creative disagreements between network executives at FOX (which aired the series) and series creator Savage Steve Holland, the program's scheduled September 1993 premiere date was postponed until November of that year. *A FOX Children's Network Production in association with Savage Studios and Nelvana Entertainment. Color. Half-hour. Premiered on FOX: November 20, 1993–September 2, 1995.*

*Voices*
**Eek! The Cat:** Bill Kopp

## ⊚ EEK!STRAVAGANZA

Beginning with the fall 1995 season, this new *Eek! The Cat* series became a showcase for new animated series, airing Saturday mornings and weekday afternoons. The season marked the debut of "Klutter," the mischievous adventures of an ambulatory pile of junk from under a bed, produced by Savage Steve Holland (who co-created and produced *Eek! The Cat*), which alternated with new episodes of "The Terrible Thunder Lizards." *A FOX Children's Network Production in association with Savage Studios and Nelvana Entertainment. Color. Half-hour. Premiered on FOX: September 9, 1995–September 5, 1997.*

*Voices*
Bill Kopp, Charlie Adler, Kurtwood Smith, Elinor Donahue, Dan Castellaneta, John Kassir, Cam Clarke, Jason Priestly, Jaid Barrymore, Savage Steve Holland, Curtis Armstrong, E.G. Daily, Gary Owens, Brad Garrett, Corey Feldman, Tawny Kitaen, Karen Haber, Anita Dangler

## ⊚ EEK! THE CAT

The slapstick antics of a fat, nontalking, neurotic cat—whose good deeds always run astray (and whose life with a suburban family that includes two awful kids isn't much better—was the subject of this weekly 13-episode half-hour animated series. Introduced on FOX Network in September of 1992, it was based on the character created by animator Bill Kopp and director Savage Steve Holland. Featured in two other weekly series on the network—*Eek! And the Terrible Thunderlizards* and *Eek!Stravaganza*—the character also starred in a 1993 prime-time Christmas special, *Eek! The Cat Christmas. A FOX Children's Network Production in association with Savage Studios and Nelvana Entertainment. Color. Half-hour. Premiered on FOX: September 11, 1992–November 13, 1993.*

*Voices*
**Eek! The Cat:** Bill Kopp; **Annabelle:** Tawny Kitaen

## ⊚ EIGHTH MAN

Comic-strip adaptation of Japanese bionic crimefighter reborn from the body of a murdered police detective found by Professor Genius, who transforms him into super-robot, Tobor, the Eighth Man. Resuming the chase for his own killers, Tobor's true identity is known only to Chief Fumblethumbs of the Metropolitan International Police, for whom he helps fight crime in the city. Along the way he encounters such notorious villains as the Armored Man, Dr. Demon, and the Light That Burned, as well as the criminal organization Intercrime. First telecast on Japanese television, the 52 episode half-hour animated series was dubbed in English by Joe Oriolo Productions, producers of TV's *Felix the Cat. A TCJ Animation Center/ABC Films Production. Color. Half-hour. Premiered: September 7, 1965. Syndicated.*

## ⊚ ELLEN'S ACRES

Amazing adventures of five-year-old Ellen, involving her feather duster, her radial tire and the Emerald Acres Hotel, the rural hotel her father and mother own. Ellen, with little else to do and no other kids her age to play with, entertains herself with her vivid imagination and adventures she creates. Airing Mondays at 9:30 A.M. the 20-episode children's series, comprised of two episodes per show, debuted on Cartoon Network. *An Animation Collective Production. Color. Half-hour. Premiered on CAR: January 8, 2007.*

*Voices*
**Ellen:** Emily Currao; **Ellen's Dad:** Marc Thompson; **Ellen's Mom:** Evelyn Lanto; **Connie:** Vibe Jones; **Cooter:** Michael Alston Baley; **Other Voices:** Wayne Grayson, Sean Schemmel

## ⊚ ELLIOT MOOSE

Entertaining preschool series starring Elliot, a young moose, and his colorful cast of friends who play games, sing songs, tell stories and embark on a series of imaginary adventures aimed at teaching kids early lessons in life, produced by Canada's Nelvana and first broadcast in the United States on PBS.

Based on author Andrea Beck's popular 1998 children's book, *Elliot's Emergency*, the live-action/animated series was also written by Beck, consisting of two animated segments each half-hour, and was part of PBS Kids' three-hour, Saturday programming block called *Bookworm Bunch*, featuring seven different segments, all based on popular children's books. Bracketed around live-action wraparounds set in a child's playroom in Elliot's house with costumed actors portraying Elliot and his friends—the industrious beaver, Beaverton; the stuffed teddy bear, Paisley; the playful monkey, Socks; the wise king of the jungle lion, Lionel; the villainous mouse professor, Professor Mousiarty, and the smart aardvark, Amy—whose adventures ran the gamut, including retellings of well-known fairy tales, mysteries and adventures, plus such genres as westerns and science fiction. In December 2000, PBS canceled the series along with another *Bookworm Bunch* component, *Corduroy*. Six years after its final U.S. broadcast on PBS, the delightful kids' series returned to television as part of a four-hour programming block featuring other animated series that had previously aired on other networks, on the all-new digital television network, qubo, distributed on the ION network (originally PAX-TV). *An Ontario TV/Nelvana Production. Color. Half-hour. Premiered on PBS: September 30, 2000–December 2, 2000. Rebroadcast on Q: January 8, 2007–.*

## ⊚ ELOISE: THE ANIMATED SERIES

Residing in New York City's Plaza Hotel with her British nanny and her pets Weeine the pug and Skipperdee the turtle, a precocious, impressionable young girl named Eloise wreaks havoc for the hotel staff in this animated series adaptation of the best-selling *Eloise at the Plaza* children's book series from the 1950s, written by Kay Thompson and illustrated by Hillary Knight. Directed by Wes Archer of TV's *The Simpsons* and *King of the Hill* fame and capturing the visual style and color scheme of the popular children's books, the 13-episode half-hour animated series—aired in two parts and originally entitled *Me, Eloise*—premiered in prime time on Sunday, October 8, 2006, on the premium-pay channel, Starz! Kids & Family.

In addition to the weekly series, featuring the voice talents of two-time Oscar nominee Lynn Redgrave, Tim Curry, Matthew Lillard, Curtis Armstrong and Mary Matilyn Mouser as Eloise, several animated specials were created by its producers, Film Roman and Handmade Films. Walt Disney Television subsequently bought the rights to the series' 13 half-hour episodes to air on both the Family Channel in Canada and Disney Channel in the United States in 2007. *A Film Roman/Handmade Films Production. Color. Half-hour. Premiered on STZK&F: October 8, 2006.*

*Voices*
**Eloise:** Mary Matilyn Mouser; **Nanny:** Lynn Redgrave; **Mr. Salamone:** Tim Curry; **Mrs. Thorton:** Kathleen Gati; **Additional Voices:** Curtis Armstrong, Matthew Lillard

## ◎ EL TIGRE: THE ADVENTURES OF MANNY RIVERA

A well-meaning Latino teenager named Manny Rivera and his conflicted superhero alter-ego, El Tigre, have a difficult time understanding the difference between right and wrong, especially when he is joined by his best friend, Frida Suarez, and her band, the Atomic Sombreros (who easily persuade him to make poor choices), in this animated comedy adventure series for Nickelodeon.

Actually created by a daring duo of Mexican immigrant animators and real-life married couple Jorge R. Guiterrez (a 2000 CalArts graduate with a master's in experimental animation who previously toiled as an animator on PBS Kids' *Maya & Miguel* and Kids' WB!'s *Mucha Lucha*) and Sandra Equihua (who studied graphic design and illustration in Mexico), this colorful half-hour animated series—written mostly in English except for some occasional Los Angeles-inspired catchphrases like "Ay Cahuenga!"—trounced the July 1999 record high of Nickelodeon's long-time ratings champ, *SpongeBob SquarePants*, attracting 3.42 million viewers during its Saturday-morning premiere on Nickelodeon and Nicktoons with back-to-back episodes in March 2007. Featuring music by Shawn Patterson and a clever mix of action and humor, 13 half-hour adventures aired during the first season. *A Nickelodeon Studios Production. Color. Half-hour. Premiered on NICK/NICKT: March 3, 2007.*

### Voices
**Manny Rivera/El Tigre:** Alanna Ubach; **Frida Suarez:** Grey DeLisle; **Rodolfo Rivera/White Pantera:** Eric Bauza; **Grandpapi Rivera/Puma Loco/El Tarantula:** Carlos Alazraqui; **Mano Negra:** Charlie Adler; **Sergio/Senor Siniestro:** Jeff Bennett; **El Oso/General Chaputza:** John DiMaggio; **Zoe Aves/Black Cevero/Ms. Chichita/Teacher:** Candi Milo; **Diego/Dr. Chipolte Jr.:** Richard Horvitz; **Titanium Titan:** Rene Mujica; **Sartana of the Dead:** Susan Silo; **Officer Emiliano Suarez:** Daran Norris; **Maria Rivera:** April Stewart

## ◎ EMERGENCY + FOUR

In this cartoon spinoff from the long-running NBC live-action adventure series *Emergency*, four youngsters (Sally, Matt, Jason, and Randy) help Los Angeles County paramedics rescue endangered citizens from burning buildings and other perils in 26 half-hour adventures. The series was first telecast on NBC's Saturday-morning schedule in 1973–74, then rebroadcast in its entirety for two more seasons until it was cancelled in September of 1976, the same year the live-action series ended its network run.

Kevin Tighe and Randolph Mantooth, stars of the original *Emergency*, voiced the animated version of their characters. *A Fred Calvert/Mark VII Production in association with Universal Television. Color. Half-hour. Premiered on NBC: September 8, 1973–September 4, 1976.*

### Voices
**Roy DeSoto:** Kevin Tighe; **John Gage:** Randolph Mantooth; **Sally:** Sarah Kennedy; **Matt:** David Joliffe; **Jason:** Donald Fullilove; **Randy:** Peter Haas

## ◎ THE EMPEROR'S NEW SCHOOL

Follow-up series to Disney's full-length animated mythical send-up *The Emperor's New Groove*, with the Incan emperor-to-be Kuzco as a spoiled teenager who must pass all his classes at the Kuzco Academy before assuming his rightful place as his country's new emperor; produced for four platforms: Disney Channel, Disney Channel on Demand, Toon Disney and ABC's ABC Kids programming block.

In January 2006, the feature film spin-off debuted first on Disney Channel on Demand, a subscription video-on-demand service available to cable subscribers, followed by individual premieres on Toon Disney in its normal 3 P.M. time slot, Disney Channel in a special time slot, 7:30 P.M., thereafter in its regular time period on Friday and Saturdays at 5 P.M. and, finally, ABC Kids in its normal Saturday 9:30 A.M. time slot. Duplicating the visual and character design of the movie, the half-hour, 2-D animated series retained all four main characters from the popular cartoon feature with three original actors reprising their roles, including Eartha Kitt as the evil sorceress, Yzma; Patrick Warburton as her numbskull sidekick, Kronk; and Wendie Malick as Pacha's loving wife, Chica. J.P. Manoux (as he did previously on the Disney Channel series *House of Mouse*) assumed the voice role of the young emperor hopeful, Kuzco, replacing comedian David Spade, who had originally voiced the character. Actor Fred Tatasciore, best known as the voice of Rijaws on the animated series *Ben 10*, was hired to voice Kuzco's best friend Pacha (instead of John Goodman) and Jessica De Cicco provided the voice of a new character, Malina, a headstrong cheerleader and one of Kuzco's best friends. *A Walt Disney Television Animation Production. Color. Half-hour. Premiered on DIS (VOD): January 20, 2006. Premiered on DIS: January 27, 2006. Premiered on ABC Kids: January 28, 2006. Premiered on TDIS: January 20, 2006.*

### Voices
**Kuzco:** J.P. Manoux; **Malina:** Jessica De Cicco; **Pacha:** Fred Tatasciore; **Chicha:** Wendie Malick; **Tipo:** Shane Baumel; **Yzma:** Eartha Kitt; **Kronk Pepikrankenitz:** Patrick Warburton; **Mr. Molegauco:** Curstis Armstrong; **Bucky:** Bob Bergen; **The Royal Record Keeper:** Rip Taylor

## ◎ ENCHANTED TALES

Some of the world's most beloved literary classics ("Snow White," "Peter Rabbit," *Treasure Island*, "Hercules," among others), backed by three original songs and fully orchestrated scores featuring the music of Beethoven, Mozart, Tchaikovsky and others, are brought to life in this award-winning hour-long anthology series produced for first-run syndication. *A Sony Wonder Production. Color. One hour. Premiered: September 20, 1997. Syndicated.*

## ◎ ENIGMA

Agatha Cherry, a highly ambitious high school student who dreams of becoming a professional ballerina, is instantly transformed into a caped-and-masked superhero whenever she wears a pair of magic dancing shoes in this half-hour series originally produced for French television in the late 1990s. The 26-episode French-German-Spanish coproduction aired weekends and weekday mornings on FOX Family Channel. *A D'Ocon Films/Marathon/M6/Millesime Production. Color. Half-hour. Premiered on FOX FAM: August 22, 1998–June 16, 1999.*

### Voices
Jonnell Elliott, Gary Martin

## ◎ ERKY PERKY

Two lazy, bickering, not-so-bright bugs named Erky and Perky, who live the high life in a hot dog stand, end up being taken into a regular home where they try making it in a scarier world and meet a family of dysfunctional insects. First shown on Australian television and YTV Canada where it was top rated, this Canadian-Australian coproduction aired in the United States on VOOM's Animania HD beginning in 2006. The 13-episode series aired Saturdays and Sundays at 12:30 P.M. (ET) as part of Animania

HD's *Big Wide Action Show* programming block. *An Ambience Entertainment/CCI Entertainment Ltd. Production. Color. Half-hour. Premiered on ANI: September 23, 2006.*

## ⊚ ESCAFLOWNE

Fantasy adventure of a psychic teenage girl (Hitomi Kanzaki), whose vision of battling a dragon turns real when she and the swordsman in her dream (Van) are suddenly thrust into the mysterious planetary world of Gaea, where they come under attack by the evil Zaibach empire as they try unlocking the secrets within a suit of armor called Escaflowne in this English-dubbed Japanese animated series, first seen on Japan's TV Tokyo network in 1996 and aired on FOX network in the United States four years later. Directed by Kazuki Akane, the first 11 episodes of the 26-episode series aired on FOX Kids' Saturday-morning lineup, but were significantly modified and edited from their original versions, resulting in criticism from devoted fans of the series. FOX canceled the series that October. *A Sunrise/TV Tokyo/Bandai/The Ocean Group Production. Color. Half-hour. Premiered on FOX: August 19, 2000–October 14, 2000.*

### Voices
**Van Fanel:** Kirby Morrow; **Hitomi Kanzaki:** Kelly Sheridan; **Allen Schezar/Amano:** Brian Drummond; **Merle:** Jocelyn Loewen; **Dilandu Albantu:** Saffron Henderson; **Folken:** Paul Dobson; **Emperor Dornkirk:** Richard Newman; **The Mole Man/Pyle:** Terry Klassen; **Princess Milerna:** Venus Terzo; **Dryden Fassa:** Ward Perry; **Balgus:** Don Brown; **Varie:** Lisa Ann Beley; **Site Leader:** Ted Cole; **Gaddes/Dryden/Bronze General/Adelfos/Plactu/Gaou:** Michael Dobson; **Prince Chid:** Alex Doduk; **Elysse Aston:** Ellen Kennedy; **King Aston/Jajuka:** Scott McNeil; **Naria:** Nicole Oliver; **Duke Fried:** Dale Wilson; **Other Voices:** Rice Honeywell

## ⊚ EUREKA SEVEN

A bored-out-of-his-mind, extreme sport, hover-board-loving 14-year-old Renton Thurston's life is transformed when he meets a mysterious, beautiful female pilot named Eureka after fulfilling his long-time dream of joining the renegade crew of Gekkostate and its world-renown lifter and leader, Holland, in this anime action series first shown in Japan in April 2005 and redubbed and broadcast Saturdays in the United States on Cartoon Network's late-night *Adult Swim* programming block. *A Bang Zoom! Entertainment/Bandai Entertainment Production. Color. Half-hour. Premiered on CAR: April 15, 2005.*

### Voices
**Renton Thurston:** Yuri Lowenthal (Episodes 1–13), Johnny Yong Bosch; **Eureka:** Stephanie Sheh; **Holland:** Crispin Feeman; **Anemone:** Kari Wahlgren; **Braya:** Michael Forest; **Jurgens:** Michael McConnohie; **Ken-Goh:** Bob Papenbrook, Kyle Herbert (Episode 29).

## ⊚ EVERYTHING'S ARCHIE

The fifth in a series of *Archie* comic-strip series, this entry featured repeat episodes of the previous network shows (*The Archie Show, The Archie Comedy Hour, Archie's Funhouse,* and *Archie's TV Funnies*) combined with new animated wraparounds of the cast. (See *The Archies* for voice credits.)

*A Filmation Associates Production. Color. Half-hour. Premiered on CBS: September 8, 1973–January 26, 1974. Rebroadcast on FAM: Fall 1993–94. Rebroadcast on ODY: April 1999–early 2000.*

## ⊚ EVIL CON CARNE

With the help of his henchmen General Skarr and Major Doctor Ghastley, a madly insane millionaire terrorist's brain is attached to a dim-witted bear named Boskov, and his disembodied stomach carries out his plans for world domination in this spin-off from Cartoon Network's *Grim & Evil*. Created by Maxwell Atoms, the character was first featured in a 2000 pilot and special, opposite a second cartoon component, "The Adventures of Billy and Mandy," that aired in August 2001 and then ran weekly for two seasons on the Cartoon Network's late-night *Adult Swim* cartoon block before each were broken into their own series. Featuring three cartoons (and later two) per half-hour, the 17-episode series premiered in mid-July 2003 and aired until the following October. *A Rough Draft Studios Inc. Production. Color. Half-hour. Premiered on CAR: July 11, 2003–October 22, 2004.*

### Voices
**Hector Con Carne:** Phil LaMarr; **Major Dr. Ghastly:** Grey DeLisle; **General Skarr:** Armin Shimerman; **Boskov:** Frank Welker; **Cod Commando:** Maxwell Adams; **Destructicus Con Carne:** Rino Romano; **Estroy:** Maurice LaMarche

## ⊚ THE EWOKS

The furry, feathered, gnomish clan from George Lucas's *Star Wars* film series star in all-new, animated adventures as fierce defenders of the planet Endor in this ABC Saturday-morning series. The program premiered in September 1985, only to later be combined with its animated counterpart, *Droids: The Adventures of R2D2 and C3PO,* as the hour-long fantasy adventure *The Ewoks and Star Wars Droids Adventure Hour.* (See entry for further details). The series was later reaired on the Sci-Fi Channel's *Cartoon Quest* program block. *A Lucasfilm Production in association with Nelvana Limited, Hanho Heung-Up and Mi-Hahn Productions. Color. Half-hour. Premiered on ABC: September 7, 1985–February 22, 1986. Rebroadcast on SCI: April 16, 1993–May 26, 1997.*

## ⊚ THE EWOKS AND STAR WARS DROIDS ADVENTURE HOUR

The enchantment of George Lucas's box-office sensation *Star Wars* was spun off into this Saturday-morning series, combining two half-hour series of new adventures of those lovable droids, R2-D2 and C3PO, as well as those cuddly creatures, the Ewoks, in this hour-long science-fiction fantasy series.

In *Ewoks,* the furry tribe of peace-loving characters, now the Endorian equivalents of teenagers, enjoy new encounters on the distant forest moon of Endor with friends Princess Kneesa and the mischevious Latara. Young Ewoks scout Wicket leads the pack as they journey through their fantastic world.

The second half, *Droids: The Adventures of R2-D2 and C3PO,* recounts the years between the rise of the Empire and the beginning of the "Star Wars" in animated stories with a liberal comic touch, always told from the droids' point of view.

The series' components each began as separate half-hour shows, debuting on ABC's Saturday-morning schedule in September of 1985. Both shows were combined and broadcast under the new title, *The Ewoks and Star Wars Droids Adventure Hour* beginning in March of 1986. *A Lucasfilm Production in association with Nelvana Limited, Hanho Heung-Up and Mi-Hahn Productions. Color. One hour. Premiered on ABC: March 1, 1986–November 1, 1986.*

### Voices
**THE EWOKS: Wicket:** Jim Henshaw; **Widdle, Wicket's brother:** John Stocker; **Weechee, Wicket's oldest brother:** Greg Swanson; **Teebo:** Eric Peterson; **Paploo:** Paul Chato; **Deej:** Richard Donat; **Shodu:** Nonnie Griffin; **Winda/Baby Nippet:** Leanne Coppen; **Princess Kneesaa:** Cree Summer Francks;

**Latara:** Taborah Johnson; **Logray, the medicine man:** Doug Chamberlain; **Chief Chirpa/Lumat:** George Buza; **Aunt Bozzie/Aunt Zephee:** Pam Hyatt; **Malani:** Alyson Court; **Baby Wiley:** Michael Fantini; **Ashma:** Paulina Gillis; **Chukah-Trok:** Don McManus; **Erphram Warrick:** Antony Parr; **Kaink:** Pauline Rennie; **Mring-Mring (Gupin):** Ron James; **Ubel:** Hadley Kay; **Punt:** Rob Cowan; **Morag:** Jackie Burroughs; **Singing Maiden:** Glori Gage; **Bondo:** Don McManus; **Trebla:** Alan Fawcett; **Jinda Boy:** Greg Swanson; **Rock Wizard:** Desmond Ellis; **Mooth/Hoom/Dulok Scout:** John Stocker; **Zut:** Joe Matheson; **Dobah:** Diane Polley; **Nahkee:** George Buza; **Hoona:** Myra Fried; **King Corneesh/Trome #1:** Dan Hennessey; **Urgah:** Melleny Brown; **Dulok Shaman:** Don Francks; **Shaman's Nephew:** Hadley Kay; **Murgoob:** Eric Peterson; **Trome #2:** Marvin Goldhar; **Trome #3:** Peter Blais

**DROIDS: R2-D2:** (electronic); **C3PO:** Anthony Daniels; **C3PO (guide track):** Graham Haley

**THE TRIGON ONE (EPISODES 1–4): Thall Joben:** Andrew Sabiston; **Jord Dusat:** Dan Hennessey; **Kea Moll:** Lesleh Donaldson, Terri Hawkes; **Tig Fromm:** Maurice Godin; **Sise Fromm:** Michael Kirby; **Vlix/Clones/Sleazy Guard:** Marvin Goldhar; **Demma Moll:** Toby Tarnow; **Boba Fett:** George Buza, Ken Pogue; **BL-17:** Graham Haley; **Proto 1:** Long John Baldry; **Zebulon Dak:** Donny Burns; **Mercenary Droid:** Dan Hennessey

**MON JULPA (EPISODES 5–8, 13): Jann Tosh:** Milah Cheylov; **Jessica Meade:** Taborah Johnson; **Uncle Gundy:** Dan Hennessey; **Kleb Zellock:** Donny Burns; **Mon Julpa/Kez-lban:** Michael Lefebvre; **Kybo Ren:** Don Francks; **Jyn Obah/IG-88/Auctioneer/Miner:** Don McManus; **Sollag/Zatec-Cha/Grej/Miner:** John Stocker; **Vinga/Yorpo:** Dan Hennessey; **Doodnik:** George Buza; **Lord Toda:** Graeme Campbell; **Princess Gerin:** Cree Summer Francks; **Coby Toda:** Jamie Dick, Christopher Young; **Captain Stroon:** Chris Wiggins; **Mr. Slarm:** J. Gordon Masten

**THE ADVENTURES OF MUNGO BAOBAB (EPISODES 9–12): Mungo Baobab:** Winston Reckert, Barry Greene; **Admiral Screed:** Graeme Campbell; **Governor Koong:** Don Francks; **Gaff/Krox:** Rob Cowan; **Auren Yomm:** Jan Austin; **Nilz Yomm/Noop:** Peter MacNeill; **Old Ogger:** Eric Peterson; **Lin-D/Galley Master:** John Stocker; **Bun-Dingo/Announcer at the Games:** Michael Kirby; **Bola Yomm:** Pam Hyatt

## ◎ EXO-SQUAD

In an oppressed, futuristic setting, genetic mutants called Neosapiens and their sinister leader, Phaeton, have taken over Earth (and Venus and Mars), and it's up to the human resistance force (comprised of men and women), Exosquad, to free the solar system from the clutches of Phaeton and his loyalists in the first weekly half-hour animated series from Universal Cartoon Studios. The 52-episode series debuted in first-run syndication in 1993, then returned for a second season in 1994 as part of the *Universal Adventure Hour*, opposite the animated thriller *Monster Force*. Following its syndicated run, USA Network added the series to its Saturday morning action/adventure lineup in 1995, along with the animated *Wild C.A.T.S. A Universal Cartoon Studios Production in association with MCA Television. Color. Half-hour. Premiered: September 1993. Syndicated. Rebroadcast on USA: September 26, 1995.*

*Voices*
**Lieutenant J.T. Marsh:** Robby Benson

## ◎ EXTREME DINOSAURS

Four of the toughest, smartest and coolest dinos from 65 million years ago reappear on Earth to settle an old score with a gang of marauding raptors bent on turning the planet into a hot, steamy raptor paradise in this half-hour syndicated action/adventure series, produced by DIC Entertainment. *A DIC Entertainment Production. Color. Half-hour. Premiered: September 1, 1997. Syndicated.*

*Voices*
**T-Bone:** Scott McNeil; **Bad Rap:** Gary Chalk; **Haxx:** Lee Tokar; **Stegz:** Sam Kouth; **Spike:** Cusse Mankuma; **Bullzeye:** Jason Gray Stanford; **Spittor:** Terry Klassen; **Chedra:** Louise Vallance; **Hardrock:** Blu Mankuma; **Dr. Becky Scarwell:** Marcy Goldberg

## ◎ EXTREME GHOSTBUSTERS

When a new generation of spirits appear on the scene, original ghostbuster Egon Spengler emerges from his reclusive lifestyle to lead a group of four inner-city teens (Roland, Garrett, Eduardo, Kylie) and Slimer! the ghost (now a good ghost) to rid the Big Apple of slime-spewing intruders in this half-hour syndicated cartoon series based on the popular movie series. The 40-episode series premiered Labor Day 1997. The program's working title was *Super Ghostbusters. A Columbia TriStar TV Animation/Adelaide Production. Color. Half-hour. Premiered: September 1, 1997. Syndicated.*

*Voices*
**Egon Spengler:** Maurice LaMarche; **Janine Melnitz:** Pat Musick; **Roland Jackson:** Alfonso Ribeiro; **Kylie Griffin:** Tara Charendoff; **Eduardo Rivera:** Rino Romano; **Garrett Miller:** Jason Marsden; **Slimer!/Mayor McShane:** Billy West

## ◎ THE FABULOUS FUNNIES

Animated vignettes starring comic-strip characters, such as Nancy and Sluggo, Broom Hilda, Alley Oop and the Katzen-jammer Kids. The series featured all-new episodes combined with repeat adventures first shown on *Archie's TV Funnies. A Filmation Associates Production. Color. Half-hour. Premiered on NBC: September 9, 1978–September 1, 1979.*

*Voices*
**Broom Hilda/Sluggo/Oola/Hans and Fritz Katzenjammer:** June Foray; **Nancy:** Jayne Hamil; **Captain Katzenjammer/King Guzzle:** Alan Oppenheimer; **Alley Oop:** Bob Holt

## ◎ THE FAIRLY ODDPARENTS

Tried of being bossed around by his evil babysitter Vicky, 10-year-old—Timmy Turner, an only child, calls upon his Fairy Godparents, Cosmo and Wanda, to grant his every wish; unfortunately, they often go awry in this out-of-this-world cartoon series originally produced for Nickelodeon.

Created by Butch Hartman, who executive produced the series along with Fred Seibert and his company, Frederator Inc., this offbeat fantasy/comedy series first aired on Nickelodeon as a cartoon short in 1998, including 11 episodes altogether, on its popular animated anthology series, *Oh Yeah! Cartoons*. After *Oh Yeah! Cartoons* was canceled in 2001, Nick turned it into a weekly half-hour series on its own right that premiered in late March 2001 opposite *Invader ZIM*.

Following its premiere, this prime-time cartoon series reportedly became Nick's fastest-growing new show and second-most popular series (second only to *SpongeBob SquarePants*), averaging a 6.0/32 audience share and 1.9 million average kid viewers ages two to 11. In 2002, the kids' cabler ordered 20 more episodes for the series' second season as well as 13 episodes of another top-rated property, *Dora the Explorer*.

During production of the series, Nickelodeon commissioned four feature-length made-for-TV movies to air in prime time: *Abra-Catastrophe!* (2003); *Channel Chasers* (2004); *School's Out! Musical* (2005); and *Fairy Idol* (2006). In addition, the characters costarred in three crossover specials, *The Jimmy Timmy Power Hour* (2004); *The Jimmy Timmy Power Hour 2: When Nerds Collide* (2006); and *The Jimmy Timmy Power Hour 3: The Jerkinators* (2006). Series creator Butch Hartman also produced an 11-minute pilot—extended to 30 minutes by adding scenes into the story of Timmy Turner—called *Crash Nebula*, chronicling the adventures of his favorite television star, a Buzz Lightyear space hero, Sprig Speevak, that Nickelodeon aired as a special in the summer of 2004.

After ceasing production of the series in 2005 following completion of 143 episodes over six seasons, two years later Nickelodeon ordered production of 20 more episodes, while plans for a theatrical feature based on the series by Nickelodeon Movies and Paramount Pictures were scrapped. Reruns of the series were also seen on Nickelodeon's offspring channel, Nicktoons. *A Frederator Inc./Nicktoons Production. Color. Half-hour. Premiered on NICK: March 30, 2001–July 21, 2006. Rebroadcast on NICKT: May 11, 2002–   .*

### Voices
**Timmy Turner:** Tara Strong, Mary Bergman (in pilot episode); **Cosmo/Mr. Turner:** Daran Norris; **Wanda/Mrs. Turner:** Susan Blakeslee; **Vicky/Veronica/Tootie:** Grey DeLisle; **A.J. Ibrahim:** Haneef Muhammad; **Chester McBadbat:** Frankie Muniz, Jason Marsden; **A.J.:** Gary Leroi Gray; **Jorgen Von Strangle:** Rodger Bumpass; **Trixie Tang:** Dionne Quan; **Mr. Crocker:** Carlos Alazraqui; **Principal Waxelplax:** Lauren Tom; **Chet Ubetcha:** Jim Ward; **Dr. Bender/Wendall:** Gilbert Gottfried; **Crimson Chin:** Jay Leno; **Cupid:** Tom Kenny; **Mark the Alien:** Rob Paulsen

## ⊚ FAMILY CLASSICS THEATRE
Thirteen hour-long animated specials, based on popular juvenile novels, comprised this series of literary masterpieces converted to animation. Telecast as holiday specials, the films were produced by two animation studios, Australia's Air Programs International and Hanna-Barbera Productions. Titles included: "Tales of Washington Irving," "The Prince and the Pauper," "Robinson Crusoe," "Gulliver's Travels" and others. (See Animated Television Specials for details on each production.) The final season repeated previously shown specials. *An Air Programs International/Hanna-Barbera Production. Color. One hour. Premiered on CBS: November 14, 1971.*

## ⊚ FAMILY CLASSIC TALES
Following the success of *Family Classics Theatre*, CBS aired this series of 11 new animated features for children, packaged as fall holiday specials (see Animated Television Specials for details on each production). *An Air Programs International/Hanna-Barbera Production. Color. One hour. Premiered on CBS: November 15, 1975.*

## ⊚ FAMILY DOG
Originally produced as a half-hour special for Steven Spielberg's ill-fated NBC anthology series *Amazing Stories*, CBS commissioned this half-hour animated spinoff exploring the life of a family's pet dog, which was unleashed in prime time—with two back-to-back episodes—in June of 1993. The long-awaited series from Spielberg and filmmaker Tim Burton encountered numerous creative delays (including a complete production breakdown during which episodes were sent to a Canadian animation house for "fixes") and rising production costs (originally budgeted at $650,000 per episode, costs soared to more than $1 million), only to generate poor ratings. Although 10 episodes were produced, CBS pulled the plug on the series after airing only five of them. *An Amblin Television Production in association with Warner Bros. Television and Universal Television. Color. Half-hour. Premiered on NBC: February 16, 1987 (half-hour special on Amazing Stories). Premiered on CBS: June 23, 1993–July 21, 1993.*

### Voices
**Skip Binford, father:** Martin Mull; **Bev Binford, mother:** Molly Cheek; **Billy Binford, their son:** Zak Huxtable; **Cassie Cole, their daughter:** Cassie Cole; **Dog:** Danny Mann

## ⊚ FAMILY GUY
Peter Griffin is the father of a not-quite-so-average family of middle-class New Englanders, including his loving wife, Lois, who struggles to keep things normal around the house with their children, teen queen Meg, 13-year-old slacker Chris, their diabolically clever youngest child Stewie (who is set to conquer the world) and their brainy dog Brian. Focusing on the everyday trials and tribulations of the Griffin family, this irreverent weekly animated comedy series was created by *American Dad!* creator Seth MacFarlane, who also lent his voice to several characters, including Peter, Brian and Stewie.

Making its debut with "Death Has a Shadow," following Super Bowl XXXIV on January 31, 1999, FOX initially ordered nine episodes of this irreverent cartoon sitcom for its Sunday night prime-time lineup that season. In September 1999, FOX renewed the series for a second season of 26 all-new half-hour episodes, and ordered 22 more for the third season, with the series returning in the summer instead of the fall of 2000. Despite a staunch following, the show produced lackluster ratings, no doubt helped by the fact that FOX shuffled the series around on its prime-time schedule from Sunday to Thursday nights, then to Tuesdays, then to Wednesdays, and finally back to Thursdays.

Canceled in 2002 after less than three years on FOX, the groundbreaking animated comedy hit was resurrected and made U.S. television history by returning to FOX's Sunday night schedule for a second time—and for a fifth season—with 30 brand-new episodes in September 2005, spawned by the remarkably successful DVD sales (more than six million units) of its first four seasons and strong ratings in reruns, routinely making it number one in its time slot, on Cartoon Network's late-night *Adult Swim* program block. Under a unique arrangement, FOX and Cartoon Network shared broadcasting rights to new episodes of the revived series, with Cartoon Network airing them at 11 P.M. (ET) on Thursday and Sunday evenings from June through mid-August 2005. Beginning April 30, 2006, 17 new episodes began airing throughout the year.

For the 2005–06 season, Carol Channing and Phyllis Diller made guest voice appearances, along with Robert Downey Jr. as Lois's institutionalized brother whom she meets for the first time. In late September that year, a direct-to-DVD movie spin-off called *Stewie Griffin: The Untold Story* was released to retail stores, producing an astounding $41 million in retail sales in its first two weeks. In mid-May 2006, the production was aired on FOX as a 90-minute special in three separate half-hour blocks, "Stewie B. Goode," "Banjo Was His Name Oh" and "Stu & Stewie's Excellent Adventure."

In the fall of 2007, with 22 new half-hours produced for the show's seventh season on FOX, Tribune Broadcasting netted the off-net syndication rights to the Emmy Award-winning animated sitcom, with the Griffin family series re-airing in 20 major markets—or 37.8 percent of the United States—on Tribune-owned stations, including WPIX/New York, KTLA/Los Angeles, WGN/Chicago, WPHL/Philadelphia, WLVI/Boston, KDAF/Dallas, WDCW/Washington, KHCW/Houston, KCPQ–KTWB/Seattle, WBZL/Miami, KWGN/Denver, KTXL/Sacramento, KPLR/St. Louis, KWBP/Portland, WXIN–WTTV/Indianapolis, KSWB/San Diego, WTIC–WTXX/Hartford, WXMI/Grand Rapids, WPMT/Harrisburg and WGNO–WNOL/New Orleans. *A Fuzzy Door Productions/Fox Television AnimationProduction. Color. Half-hour. Premiered on FOX: April 6, 1999–April 18, 2002 (originally previewed on January 31, 1999); May 1, 2005. Rebroadcast on CAR: April 20, 2003 (Adult Swim)– . Premiered on CAR: (new episodes): June 12, 2005. Syndicated: Fall 2007.*

**Voices**
**Peter Griffin/Stewie Griffin/Brian Griffin/Glen Quagmire/Tom Tucker:** Seth MacFarlane; **Lois Griffin:** Alex Borstein; **Chris Griffin:** Seth Green; **Megan Griffin:** Lacey Chabert, Mila Kunis; **Cleveland:** Mike Henry; **Janet:** Tara Strong; **Officer Joseph Swanson:** Patrick Warburton; **Diane Simmons:** Lois Alan; **Bonnie:** Jennifer Tilly; **Mr. Weed:** Butch Herman; **Additional Voices:** Lisa Wilbert, Debra Wilson, Patrick Duffy, Rachael MacFarlane, Danny Smith, Phil LaMarr, Nicole Sullivan

## ◎ THE FAMOUS ADVENTURES OF MISTER MAGOO

The myopic Mr. Magoo portrays various literary and historical characters—William Tell, Long John Silver, Don Quixote and others—in this hour-long series that sometimes combined two half-hour stories in one program. The show marked Magoo's first entry into prime time as a regular weekly series. Installments of the series have since been rebroadcast on the Disney Channel. *A UPA Productions of America Production. Color. One hour. Premiered on NBC: September 19, 1964–August 21, 1965. Rebroadcast on DIS.*

**Voices**
**Mr. Magoo:** Jim Backus

## ◎ FANGFACE

Producers Joe Ruby and Ken Spears, formerly top cartoon show creators for Hanna-Barbera, opened shop and animated for ABC their first Saturday-morning kid series under the production company Ruby-Spears. The program dealt with the misadventures of four teenagers—Biff, Kim, Puggsy and Fangs (the latter two reminiscent of Leo Gorcey and Huntz Hall of *Bowery Boys* fame) who fight the forces of evil with the help of Fangs (actually Sherman Fangs-worth), who turns into a werewolf. The ABC Saturday-morning series only lasted one full season, but Fangface returned with a new partner, Fangpuss, in new adventures as part of *The Plastic Man Comedy-Adventure Show* during the 1979–80 season. *A Ruby-Spears Enterprises Production. Color. Half-hour. Premiered on ABC: September 9, 1978–September 8, 1979. Rebroadcast on CAR: July 16, 1994–July 17, 1994 (Look What We Found!); October 3, 1994–December 2, 1994 (weekdays); June 5, 1995–September 1, 1995 (weekdays).*

**Voices**
**Fangface:** Jerry Dexter; **Biff:** Frank Welker; **Puggsy:** Bart Braverman; **Kim:** Susan Blu

## ◎ THE FANTASTIC FOUR (1967)

The superhero team of the Fantastic Four is composed of scientist Reed Richards (Mr. Fantastic), who can stretch his body into various contortions; his wife, Sue (The Invisible Girl); Ben Grimm, alias the Thing, who, once transformed, has the power of 1,000 horses; and Johnny Storm, the Human Torch. Twenty-episode half-hour series aired for two seasons on ABC.

In April 2000, Cartoon Network's 24-hour home of classic cartoons, Boomerang, began airing all 19 half-hour episodes of the original ABC series. A week before the highly touted June 2005 premier of the all-new live-action feature, *The Fantastic Four*, Boomerang presented two prime-time—and television's first-ever—marathons of the series on Saturday, July 2, and Sunday, July 3, from 8 P.M. to midnight. *A Hanna-Barbera Production in association with Marvel Comics Group. Color. Half-hour. Premiered on ABC: September 9, 1967–August 30, 1969. Rebroadcast on ABC: September 7, 1969–August 30, 1970. Rebroadcast on CAR: October 3, 1992–(Saturdays); February 11, 1995 (Super Adventure Saturdays); July 15, 1995 (Power Zone); March 25, 1996–October 5, 1996 (weekdays, Saturdays). Rebroadcast on BOOM: April 9, 2000–.*

**Voices**
**Reed Richards, alias Mr. Fantastic:** Gerald Mohr; **Sue Richards, alias Invisible Girl:** Jo Ann Pflug; **Ben Grimm, alias The Thing/Dr. Doom:** Paul Frees; **Johhny Storm, alias The Human Torch:** Jack Flounder

## ◎ THE FANTASTIC FOUR (1994)

Mr. Fantastic (Reed Richards), the Invisible Girl (Sue Richards), the Human Torch (Johnny Storm) and the Thing (Ben Grimm) battle archenemies Hydro-Man, Madam Medusa, The Wizard and others in this updated version of the famed comic-book superheroes (also known as *Marvel Superheroes Fantastic Four*), part of the hour-long syndicated block, "The Marvel Action Hour." In September 1997, the series aired in syndication as part of the half-hour *Marvel Super-Heroes* rotating with episodes of another popular Marvel cartoon series, *Iron Man*, and then was rebroadcast from September 1998 to September 1999 on UPN as part of the *The Incredible Hulk and Friends*. Beginning in June 2005, the program was rerun on ABC Family and Toon Disney. *A Marvel Films/New World Entertainment Production. Color. Half-hour. Premiered: September 24, 1994. Syndicated. Rebroadcast: September 1997–September 1998 (in syndication as part of Marvel Super-Heroes). Rebroadcast on UPN: September 1998–September 1999 (as part of The Incredible Hulk and Friends). Rebroadcast on ABC FAM/TDIS: June 18, 2005–.*

**Voices**
**Reed Richards, Mr. Fantastic:** Beau Weaver; **Sue Richards, The Invisible Girl:** Lori Alan; **Johnny Storm, The Human Torch:** Quinton Flynn; **Ben Grimm/The Thing:** Chuck McCann; **Alicia Masters:** Pauline Arthur Lomas; **Hydro-Man:** Brad Garrett; **Madam Medusa:** Iona Morris; **The Wizard:** Ron Perlman

## ◎ THE FANTASTIC FOUR (2006)

All-new 2-D and 3-D animated adventures of the famed Marvel Comics crime-fighting superheroes—Mr. Fantastic, the Invisible Woman, the Human Torch and the Thing—as they battle their notorious arch-rival, Dr. Doom, and assorted other dastardly villains in this half-hour series, coproduced by Marvel Studios and the award-winning French animation company Moon-Scoop, producers of the hit Cartoon Network series *Code LYOKO*.

Based on characters originally created by comic-book artists Stan Lee and Jack Lee, the half-hour science-fiction series made its U.S. television debut during Cartoon Network's *Toonami* prime-time cartoon block in September 2006, with the premiere episode, "Doomsday." After its Saturday 8 P.M. debut, the series scored double-digit ratings gains among kids ages six to 11. Cartoon Network ordered 26 half-hour episodes for the series' first season, which also was broadcast by the network in all territories outside of the United States as part of a global broadcasting rights deal with MoonScoop. A *MoonScoop/Marvel Studios/Cartoon Network/M6 Production. Color. Half-hour. Premiered on CAR: September 2, 2006.*

*Voices*
**Reed Richards/Mr. Fantastic:** Hiro Kanagawa; **Susan Storm/Invisible Woman:** Lara Gilchrist; **Johnny Storm/Human Torch:** Christopher Jacot; **Ben Grimm/Thing:** Brian Dobson; **H.E.R.B.I.E.:** Sam Vincent; **Dr. Victor Von Doom/Doom & Mole Man:** Paul Dobson; **Courtney Bonner-Davies:** Laura Drummond; **Alicia Masters:** Sunita Prasad; **Phillip Masters/Puppetmaster:** Alvin Sanders

## ◎ FANTASTIC MAX
Part of *The Funtastic World of Hanna-Barbera,* this half-hour syndicated adventure series follows the earthly and outer-space encounters of a precocious 16-month-old toddler who returns from an unscheduled trip aboard a rocket with a few surprises: an alien friend and a robot babysitter, who make life for Max and his family anything but dull. A *Hanna-Barbera Production. Color. Half-hour. Premiered: September 1988. Syndicated. Rebroadcast on CAR: October 2, 1992–June 25, 1993 (weekdays); September 20, 1993–December 31, 1993 (weekdays); September 6, 1994–September 1, 1995; September 4, 1995 (weekdays, Saturdays).*

*Voices*
**Fantastic Max:** Ben Ryan Ganger; **FX, his pea-green alien friend:** Nancy Cartwright; **A.B. Sitter, his babysitter:** Gregg Berger; **Mom, Max's mother:** Gail Matthius; **Dad, Max's father:** Paul Eiding; **Zoe, his six-year-old sister:** Elisabeth Harnois; **Ben, his five-year-old neighbor:** Benji Gregory

## ◎ FANTASTIC VOYAGE
Trying to save the life of a famous professor who suffers a serious brain injury, a team of government scientists, by means of a special ruby laser, are reduced to the size of a speck and enter the bloodstream in a miniature submarine, beginning a series of incredible adventures, in this 17-episode weekly cartoon series inspired by the 1966 20th Century-Fox feature film of the same name. Debuting on ABC in 1968, the series ran for two seasons before it was finally canceled. The program enjoyed new life in reruns on the Sci-Fi Channel. A *Filmation Associates Production. Color. Half-hour. Premiered on ABC: September 14, 1968–September 5, 1970. Rebroadcast on the SCI: September 27, 1992–September 20, 1996.*

*Voices*
**Scientist Corby Birdwell:** Marvin Miller; **Erica Stone:** Jane Webb; **Commander Jonathan Kidd/Professor Carter:** Ted Knight

## ◎ THE FANTASTIC VOYAGES OF SINBAD THE SAILOR
Guided only by his wits, young seafaring adventurer Sinbad braves the high seas, joined by carefree youth Hakeem and his impressible exotic cat Kulak, as they travel the world in this 26-episode, half-hour cartoon series, which premiered on Cartoon Network. A *WW Productions/Fred Wolf Films/Carrington Production in association with Warner Bros. International Television. Color. Half-hour. Premiered on CAR: February 2, 1998.*

*Voices*
Bob Bergen, Jim Cummings, Melissa Smith Disney, Eric Jacklin, Bob Ridgely, Kath Soucie

## ◎ FAT ALBERT AND THE COSBY KIDS
One of the staples of comedian Bill Cosby's stand-up act in the early 1960s was his childhood recollections of Fat Albert and the gang from North Philadelphia. Real-life situations were cleverly adapted to amusing and educational cartoons by Filmation Studios in this long-running half-hour series that earned an Emmy Award nomination in 1974. Topics covered drug addiction, family conflicts and other social problems.

Bill Cosby voiced several characters in the series besides serving as its host in live-action wraparounds that opened and closed the program and introduced the animated segments.

Four years before the original series aired on Saturday mornings, NBC broadcast a prime-time special *Hey, Hey, Hey, It's Fat Albert,* which was well received by critics and viewers alike. Beginning with the 1979–80 season, the series' name was changed to *The New Fat Albert Show.*

In 1984, under the title of *Fat Albert and the Cosby Kids,* Filmation produced a new crop of 50 half-hour shows combined with old episodes of the original series for first-run syndication. The original series was rerun on NBC beginning in February 1989 and the following September on USA Network. A *Filmation Associates Production. Color. Half-hour. Premiered on CBS: September 9, 1972–September 1, 1979 (as Fat Albert and the Cosby Kids); September 8, 1979–August 25, 1984 (as The New Fat Albert Show). Syndicated: 1984 (as Fat Albert and the Cosby Kids). Rebroadcast on NBC: February 11, 1989–September 2, 1989. Rebroadcast on USA: September 1989–1990. Syndicated.*

*Voices*
**Host:** Bill Cosby; **Fat Albert/Mushmouth/LeroyMudfoot/Dumb Donald/Weird Harold/Brown Hornet:** Gerald Edwards; **Russell/Bucky:** Jan Crawford; **Rudy/Devery:** Eric Suter

## ◎ FATHERHOOD
Based on comedian Bill Cosby's best-selling book of the same name, this prime time animated comedy series—and Nick at Nite's first original animated series—followed the suburban exploits of the Bindlebeep family, headed by Dr. Arthur Bindlebeep, a high school teacher and father of three, as he deals with countless challenges, life lessons and comical confusions of raising his three children—16-year-old Angie, 12-year-old Roy and six-year-old Katherine—with his wife Norma (who manages the campus bookstore) and encounters with his own parents, Lester and Louise.

Debuting on June 20, 2004, at 9 P.M. on Nick At Nite, the combined 2-D/3-D animated, 26-episode series aired regularly in that time slot beginning on June 29 and was rebroadcast Saturdays at 10 P.M. The program marked Cosby's second animated series for Nick, following his popular Daytime Emmy Award-winning Nick Jr. children's series, *Little Bill.* Co-created by Cosby and Charles Kipps, who also executive produced the series, the premiere episode, entitled "It's a Dad, Dad World," featured Dr. Bindlebeep's parents (voiced by Lou Rawls and Ruby Dee) when a health-fanatic father, who is in much better physical shape than his son, gets injured during a game of touch football. Jamie Mitchell, who has produced or directed more than 300 half-hours of television animation, including *Hey Arnold!, Disney's Little Mermaid, Tail Spin* and *DuckTales,* served as the series' supervising producer and director. A *Nick At Nite/Smiley Inc./Toon City/Nickelodeon Network Production. Color. Half-hour. Premiered on NICK: June 20, 2004–November 27, 2005.*

Voices

**Dr. Arthur Bindlebeep:** Blair Underwood; **Norma Bindlebeep:** Sabrina Le Beauf; **Angie Bindlebeep:** Giovonnie Samuels; **Roy Bindlebeep:** Marc John Jeffries; **Katherine Bindlebeep:** Jamai Fisher; **Lester Bindlebeep:** Lou Rawls; **Louise Bindlebeep:** Ruby Dee; **Skye:** Vaneza Leza Pitynski; **Larry Keating:** Daryl Sabara

## ⊚ FATHER OF THE PRIDE

NBC's much-anticipated return to prime-time animation after a four-year hiatus, was produced by Jeffrey Katzenberg and Dream-Works Animation and focused on the lives of the family of white lions—including Larry, the hard-working lion, and Kate, his lioness wife—who were stars of the famed Siegfried & Roy's Las Vegas magic show, and their outlandish mishaps and clashes with their friends and family members. NBC ordered 13 episodes of this CG-animated half-hour family comedy series—and the second CG-animated series for prime time after UPN's *Game Over*—that debuted in August 2004 and was originally conceived as a full-length feature until DreamWorks decided it was more suited as a television series produced in high-end, *Shrek*-style computer animation.

Featuring an all-star voice cast of John Goodman, Danielle Harris, Cheryl Hines, Carl Reiner, Orlando Jones, Julian Holloway and David Herman, the series reportedly cost $1.6 million per episode to produce and nine months to create, mostly due to the high costs associated with farming out the animation to Hong Kong's Imagi Animation Studios. The series' demise was nearly as quick as *Invasion America*, DreamWorks' anime-styled prime time animated drama for the WB Television Network. Debuting to strong ratings, audience viewership declined with each broadcast until NBC pulled the show from the November 2004 sweeps, then canceled it in December after airing the remaining episodes. *A DreamWorks Television Animation SK/Imagi Animation Studios Production. Color. Half-hour. Premiered on NBC: August 31, 2004–December 28, 2004.*

Voices

**Larry:** John Goodman; **Kate:** Cheryl Hines; **Sarmoti:** Carl Reiner; **Snack:** Orlando Jones; **Sierra:** Danielle Harris; **Hunter:** Daryl Sabara; **Siegfried:** Julian Holloway; **Roy:** David Herman; **Foo-Lin:** Lisa Kudrow; **Donkey:** Eddie Murphy; **Emerson:** Danny DeVito; **Blake:** John O'Hurley; **Victoria:** Wendie Malick; **Nelson (Bong Bong):** Andy Richter; **Bernie:** Garry Marshall; **Tommy the Coyote:** David Spade; **Himself:** Kelsey Grammer

## ⊚ FELIX THE CAT

Producer Joe Oriolo, who took over production of the *Felix the Cat* comic strip, produced this series of new color episodes in which Felix sported a new sight gag—his magic bag of tricks. Stories depicted the scheming, bald-domed Professor and his bulldog assistant, Rock Bottom, endeavoring to steal Felix's magic bag to make him powerless. Such attempts failed miserably, with Felix always having the last laugh. Other scripts had Felix babysitting the Professor's nephew, Poindexter, an intellectual junior scientist. Other recurring characters included the Master Cylinder and Vavoom. Episodes were produced between 1958 and 1960 for broadcast. Five cliff-hanging episodes comprised a complete story.

In 2004, the lovable cartoon comedy series began re-airing weekdays on VOOM's Animania HD along with other classic cartoon properties including *The Dick Tracy Show, Mister Magoo* and *The Pink Panther. A Joe Oriolo/Trans-Lux Production. Color. Half-hour. Premiered: January 4, 1960. Syndicated. Rebroadcast on ANI: 2004.*

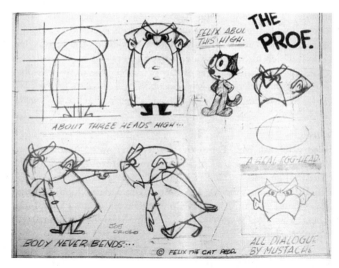

Model sheet for the scheming Professor from TV's original *Felix the Cat* series. © Felix the Cat Productions (COURTESY: JOE ORIOLO PRODUCTIONS)

Voices

**Felix the Cat/The Professor/Poindexter/Rock Bottom/The Master Cylinder/Vavoom:** Jack Mercer

## ⊚ FESTIVAL OF FAMILY CLASSICS

Favorite literary classics for children were adapted into fully animated feature-length cartoons for this first-run syndicated series of 18 hour-long specials (see Animated Television Specials for details on each title) produced by Jules Bass and Arthur Rankin in association with Japan's Mushi Studios, producers of the animated *Astro Boy. A Rankin-Bass Production in association with the Mushi Studios. Color. One hour. Premiered: 1972. Syndicated.*

Voices

Carl Banas, Len Birman, Bernard Cowan, Peg Dixon, Keith Hampshire, Peggi Loder, Donna Miller, Frank Perry, Henry Raymer, Billie Mae Richards, Alfie Scopp, Paul Soles.

## ⊚ FETCH!

Interactive, unscripted part-game, part-reality show, part TV spoof, mixing live-action with animation and an educational and satirical view of America's most popular television genres, starring an unusual animated, potato-shaped dog host named Ruff Ruffman, who tests and challenges six normal kids' problem-solving and science skills every week, with opportunities for viewers to play along online. Created and produced by Boston's WGBH-TV, responsible for award-winning educational children's shows like *Zoom*, and mostly underwritten by the National Science Foundation, the first episode of the 20-episode half-hour series for kids ages six to 10 debuted online on May 22, 2006, a full week before its nationwide Memorial Day television premiere on *PBS Kids' Go!* programming block with a mini-marathon of four "back-to-back" episodes. *A WGBH-TV Production. Color. Half-hour. Premiered on PBS Kids: May 29, 2006.*

Voices

**Ruff Ruffman:** Jim Conroy; **Grandma Ruffman:** Estelle Harris

## ⊚ FIEVEL'S AMERICAN TAILS

Young Fievel Mousekewitz and his 19th-century family—Papa, Mama, Tanya and baby Yasha—journey west to the American frontier and settle in the rugged town of Green River. There Fievel and his pal Tiger set out to tame the Wild West, in this series of continuing escapades based in part on the 1992 sequel *An American Tail: Fievel Goes West*, produced five years after the original 1986 blockbuster *An American Tail*. The series was well received following its debut on CBS in September of 1992 but declining ratings resulted in its cancellation at the end of the season. *An Amblin Entertainment Production in association with Nelvana Enterprises and Universal Television. Color. Half-hour. Premiered on CBS: September 12, 1992–September 11, 1993.*

*Voices*
**Fievel Mousekewitz:** Philip Glasser; **Papa Mousekewitz:** Lloyd Battista; **Tanya Mousekewitz:** Cathy Cavadin; **Tiger:** Dom DeLuise; **Chula the Spider:** Dan Castellaneta; **Cat R. Waul:** Gerrit Graham; **Sweet William:** Kenneth Mars; **Hambone:** Arthur Burghardt; **Jorge:** Carlos Carrasco; **Fernando:** Alex Dent; **Miss Kitty:** Cynthia Ferrer; **Stanley:** Paige Gosney; **Dog:** Danny Mann; **Aunt Sophie:** Patty Parris; **Lorna Holcombe:** Lisa Picotte; **Clint Mousewood:** Hal Rayle; **Jack:** Rolland Thompson

## ⊚ FIGHTING FOODONS

Ten-year-old apprentice chef Chase joins forces with his father and eight-year-old sister Kayla to save the world from a strange and gluttonous confection of food-based monsters, namely the evil King Gorge and his deadly army of tasty minions, Rose Marinade, Clawdia, Cinnamonkey and Grill, in this Japanese-imported, 26-episode half-hour fantasy/adventure anime series, dubbed in English by 4Kids Entertainment and shown in the United States on FOX's Saturday-morning *FOX Box* program block. *A 4Kids Entertainment/Naoto Tsushima/Red Entertainment/Kodansha/Bistro Recipe Project Production. Color. Half-hour. Premiered on FOX: September 14, 2002–August 30, 2003.*

*Voices*
**King "Gorgeous" Gorge:** Michael Alston Bailey; **Chase/Pie Tin:** Tara Jayne; **Oslo:** Adam Blaustein; **Rose Marinade:** Megan Hollingshead; **Frenchy LaToast:** Ted Lewis; **Slice:** Matt Mitler; **Coco:** Lisa Ortiz; **Kayla:** Amy Palani; **Chef Jack/Chef John:** Ed Paul; **Hot Doggone-It:** Mike Pollock; **Fried Ricer/Others:** Andrew Rannells; **Jambalydia:** Kayzie Rogers; **Burnt Meatballs/Cazmacho:** Eric Stuart; **Clawdia/Dia:** Veronica Taylor; **Cinnamonkey:** Jimmy Zoppi; **Grill:** Pete Zarustica; **Chet/Davy Gravy/Juiceman/Rapscallion:** Sean Schemmel; **Narrator:** Scottie Ray; **Other Voices:** Patrick Frankfurt, Jerry Lobozzo, Sean Schemmel, Cathy Weseluck

## ⊚ FILM ROMAN PRESENTS . . . ANIMATED CLASSIC SHOWCASE

This classic collection of Russian animated children's stories, from Han Christian Andersen's "The Ugly Duckling" to an Indian folk adventure entitled "The Golden Antelope" (a Cannes Film Festival award winner), were redubbed in English, mixed with stereo music and effects tracks, and syndicated worldwide in the fall of 1993 as part of a coventure between American cartoon producer Film Roman and Russia's Films by Jove, owned by former Russian actor Oleg Vidov, his wife Joan Borsten and their associate Sonja Konbrandt, which had acquired the rights to distribute the 1,200-title cartoon film library of Soyuzmultifilm Studios. Initially a package of 12 one-hour specials were produced for syndication. *A Film Roman/Films by Jove Production. Color. One hour. Premiered: Fall 1993. Syndicated.*

## ⊚ FIREHOUSE TALES

Fun, adventure and laughter follow as three fresh-off-the-assembly-line, pint-sized fire trucks—Red, a happy little red truck; Crabby, an often unhappy yellow truck; and Petrol, a courageous, Scottish orange truck—attend firefighting school to learn everything they can and practice daily, while also handling actual emergencies, to become big-time firefighters in this original animated series produced by Warner Bros. Animation for the Cartoon Network. Filmed in stop-motion animation much like the award-winning *Thomas the Tank Engine* children's series, this half-hour preschool program, which emphasized that everyone can become a hero whether their fire engine is painted red or chipped, was launched in August 2005 as part of the Cartoon Network's *Tickle-U* two-hour weekday preschool programming block—airing Monday through Friday in the 9:00–11:00 A.M. time slot, including such shows as *Gerald McBoing Boing* and *Gordon the Garden Gnome*. *A Warner Bros. Animation Production. Color. Half-hour. Premiered on CAR: August 22, 2005–September 1, 2006.*

*Voices*
**Red:** Jesse Moss; **Crabby the Fire Truck/Crabby the Pumper Truck:** Richard Ian Cox; **Bubba the Bulldozer:** Blu Mankuma; **Chief the Fire Truck:** Ron Halder; **Mayor Precious Primly:** Ellen Kennedy; **Snootie Tootie/Tech the Mechanic:** Colin Murdock; **Spinner the Chopper:** David Kaye; **Tug the Fire Boat:** Michael Dobson; **Wiser the Fire Truck:** French Tickner

*Additional Voices*
Kathleen Barr, Gary Chalk, Trevor Devall, Paul Dobson, Matt Hill, Terry Klassen, Britt McKillip, Scott McNeil, Tabitha St. Germain, Cathy Weseluck, Dale Wilson

## ⊚ FISH POLICE

Fish City's top underwater cop, Inspector Gil (voiced by John Ritter), unravels a series of murders and mysteries—joined by a kooky cast of characters: Chief Abalone, Gil's growly boss; Catfish, master of disguise; Tad, the police gofer; Sandy, Gil's "living" badge; Crabby, the Cabdriver, and Pearl, the waitress—in this half-hour comedy/mysteries series parody of 1940s' detective movies, based on a comic-book series by Steve Moncuse. The brainchild of Hanna-Barbera head David Kirschner, the series was its first prime-time animated series since 1972's *Wait Till Your Father Gets Home* and was the second cartoon series to debut in prime-time in a month, following ABC's *Capitol Critters*. CBS ordered only six episodes of *Fish Police*, and dropped the series after three episodes. *A Hanna-Barbera Production. Color. Half-hour. Premiered on CBS: February 28, 1992–March 13, 1992.*

*Voices*
**Inspector Gil:** John Ritter; **Chief Abalone:** Edward Asner; **Catfish:** Robert Guillaume; **Tad:** Charlie Schlatter; **Crabby:** Buddy Hackett; **Pearl:** Megan Mullally; **Goldie:** Georgia Brown; **Mayor Cod:** Jonathan Winters; **Sharkster:** Tim Curry; **Calmari:** Hector Elizondo; **Mussels Marinara/Doc Croaker:** Frank Welker; **Angel:** JoBeth Willams

## ⊚ FLASH GORDON

Joined by friends Dale Arden and Dr. Hans Zarkov, a teenage Flash Gordon unites a rebel underground to tumble the dynasty of the evil emperor Ming the Merciless on the planet Mongo in this updated, first-run weekly cartoon version of artist/writer Alex Raymond's famed outer-space comic strip but with a dash of 1990s' technology. The series debuted in 1996 with 26 half-hour episodes. *A Hearst Entertainment/Lacewood Productions/Audiovisuel Dupuis-Carrere Television/France 3 Production. Color. Half-hour. Premiered: September 14, 1996. Syndicated.*

### Voices
**Alex "Flash" Gordon:** Toby Proctor; **Dale Arden:** Lena Doig; **Dr. Hans Zarkov:** Paul Shaffer; **Other Voices:** Lawrence Bayne, Lorne Kennedy, Julie Lemieux, Andy Marshall, Tyrone Benskin, Rob Cohen, Shirley Douglas, Tracy Hoyt, Ray Landry, Marjorie Malpass

## ◎ THE FLINTSTONE KIDS

The original members of *The Flintstones* cast are seen as 10-year-old children in this 1986-produced Saturday-morning series for ABC in which Fred, Barney, Wilma and Betty, together with their dinosaur "pup" Dino, get in and out of scrapes in the familiar surroundings of Bedrock. Complementing the characters is a rich assortment of supporting cast, including Rocky Ratrock, the neighborhood bully; Dreamchip Gemstone, the classic poor little rich girl; Philo Quartz, a budding private detective; and Nate Slate, who will grow up to be Bedrock's biggest businessman.

Three additional segments appeared on the program: "Captain Caveman and Son," exploits of the world's first superhero and his chip-off-the-old-block offspring, Cavey Jr.; "Dino's Dilemmas," demonstrating perils of prehistoric dogdom; and "Flintstone Funnies," a fantasy-adventure segment in which Fred, Barney, Wilma and Betty let their imaginations lead them into exciting adventures.

The series ran for two full seasons on ABC. The program was rebroadcast on ABC from January to May of 1990 and packaged for syndication as part of Hanna-Barbera's *The Funtastic World of Hanna-Barbera* weekend syndicated series. *A Hanna-Barbera Production. Color. One hour. Premiered on ABC: September 13, 1986–October 22, 1988. Syndicated: 1990 (as part of* The Funtastic World of Hanna-Barbera*). Rebroadcast on ABC: January 6, 1990–May 26, 1990. Rebroadcast on CAR: July 4, 1994–June 2, 1995 (weekdays); September 4, 1995–September 29, 1995 (weekdays); December 18, 1995–December 22, 1995; December 26, 1995–December 29, 1995; March 25, 1996 (weekdays).*

### Voices
**Freddy:** Lennie Weinrib; Scott Menville; **Barney:** Hamilton Camp; **Wilma:** Julie Dees; Elizabeth Lyn Fraser; **Betty:** B.J. Ward; **Dino:** Mel Blanc; **Ed Flintstone, Fred's father:** Henry Corden; **Edna Flintstone, Fred's mother:** Henry Corden; **Robert Rubble, Barney's dad:** Mel Blanc; **Doris Slaghoople:** Jean VanderPyl; **Rocky Ratrock:** Marilyn Schreffler; **Dreamchip Gemstone:** Susan Blu; **Phil Quartz:** Bumper Robinson; **Nate Slate:** Frank Welker; **Flab Slab:** Hamilton Camp; **Miss Rockbottom:** B.J. Ward; **Officer Quartz:** Rene Levant; **Fang:** Frank Welker; **Micky/ Mica:** Julie Dees; **Granite Janet:** Susan Blu; **Tarpit Tommy:** Julie Dees; **Stalagbite:** Frank Welker; **Captain Caveman:** Mel Blanc; **Cavey Jr.:** Charles Adler; **Commissioner:** Lennie Weinrib; **Narrator:** Ken Mars

## ◎ THE FLINTSTONES

The town of Bedrock spelled bedlam when the Flintstones and their neighbors, the Rubbles, got together, formulating what has been probably the most heralded situation-comedy cartoon series and the first "adult" cartoon show for television.

The familiar phrase "Yabba dabba do!" was made famous by blow-hard caveman and father Fred Flintstone. Whenever he tangled with his next-door pal, halfwitted practical joker Barney Rubble, normal modern Stone Age situations always ran amuck.

The main characters, Fred, Barney and wives, Wilma and Betty, were adapted from *The Honeymooners* TV show personalities. Both Fred and Barney bore more than a vague resemblance to Ralph Kramden (Jackie Gleason) and Ed Norton (Art Carney). In the 1-minute and 45-second full-color pilot that sold the series—called *The Flagstones* (the original name of the series)—venerable voice artist Daws Butler did the Voices of both Fred and Barney (later assumed by Alan Reed and Mel Blanc) and June Foray was Betty Rubble. The name of the show was eventually changed to *The Flintstones* because the name sounded too much like the Flagtons, a family in the *Hi and Lois* comic strip.

The show's stars faced their share of physical problems, which almost threatened the future of the series. For a full season after Mel Blanc's near-fatal automobile accident in 1962, the show was taped in his bedroom where he lay in a cast from the neck to his toes. Daws Butler filled in as the voice of Barney for at least two episodes, and research has revealed that Hal Smith, best known as Otis the town drunk on *The Andy Griffith Show*, also filled in for Blanc during his illness. As executive producer Joe Barbera explained, "The easy thing would have been to replace him, but we kept going and it worked. Sometimes we'd have as many as 16 people crowded into his bedroom and we hung a mike in front of him."

Another season Alan Reed (the voice of Fred Flintstone) had a cataract operation but worked up to 20 minutes before his scheduled surgery. He returned to the job in four weeks.

Before Reed's operation, the studio taped his parts in advance and worked around him until he was healthy enough to work again. While he was suffering from cataracts, the scripts were typed in special one-inch letters so that Reed could read his lines.

When the show entered its fourth season, Barbera's other half, Bill Hanna, was quoted as saying "He [Reed] tours the country in a leopard skin—he is Flintstone!" Reed died in 1977.

*The Flintstones*, which premiered on ABC (the premiere episode was "The Flintstone Flyer"), was the first made-for-television cartoon series to air in prime time and formerly the longest running prime-time animated series (a record since broken by *The Simpsons*). The program aired on Fridays nights at 7:30. Sponsored by Winston, Alka-Seltzer, One-A-Day Vitamins and Post Cereals, the series ended its 166-episode prime-time run on ABC in the fall of 1966. The following September rival network NBC began rebroadcasting the series. Since the program's original network run, the series has been repeated on TBS, USA Network's *Cartoon Express*, Cartoon Network (the latter since the first day of its launching in 1992) and most recently Boomerang. *A Hanna-Barbera Production. Color. Half-hour. Premiered on ABC: September 30, 1960–September 2, 1966. Rebroadcast: NBC: January 7, 1967–August 1969; September 6, 1969–September 5, 1970. Rebroadcast on TBS; Rebroadcast on USA: February 27, 1989–April 26, 1992; Rebroadcast on CAR: October 1, 1992–October 2, 2004. Rebroadcast on BOOM: May 6, 2000.*

### Voices
**Fred Flintstone:** Alan Reed; **Barney Rubble:** Mel Blanc, Daws Butler, Hal Smith; **Wilma Flintstone:** Jean VanderPyl; **Betty Rubble:** Bea Benadaret; Gerry Johnson; **Pebbles:** Jean VanderPyl; **Dino, the pet dinosaur:** Chips Spam; **Bamm Bamm, the Rubbles' son:** Don Messick; **Hoppy, Barney's pet dinosaur:** Don Messick; **George Slate, Fred's boss:** John Stephenson; **Mrs. Slaghoople:** Janet Waldo; Verna Felton; **Arnold, the newsboy:** Don Messick; **The Great Gazoo:** Harvey Korman

## ◎ THE FLINTSTONES COMEDY HOUR

Complete episodes of *The Flintstones* that previously had aired on the network in other formats reappeared in this hour-long Saturday-morning series, which featured four new episodes of *Pebbles and Bamm-Bamm*, in combination with 20 episodes originally broadcast on 1971's *Pebbles and Bamm-Bamm*.

Other segments included brief vignettes, comedy gag and dance-of-the-week segments rotated in between the series' main cartoon components. The cartoons were repeated the following season under a new series title, *The Flintstones Show*, then shortened to a half-hour, plus as part of *Pebbles and Bamm-Bamm* and the syndicated *Fred Flintstone and Friends*. A Hanna-Barbera Production. Color. One hour. Half-hour (as The Flintstones Show). Premiered on CBS: September 9, 1972–September 1, 1973. Rebroadcast on CBS: September 8, 1973–January 26, 1974 (as The Flintstones Show).

**Voices**
**Fred Flintstone:** Alan Reed; **Wilma Flintstone:** Jean VanderPyl; **Pebbles Flintstone:** Mickey Stevens, Sally Struthers; **Barney Rubble:** Mel Blanc; **Betty Rubble:** Gay Hartwig; **Bamm-Bamm Rubble:** Jay North; **Sylvester Slate, Fred's boss:** John Stephenson; **Penny:** Mitzi McCall; **Fabian:** Carl Esser; **Wiggy:** Gay Hartwig; **Moonrock/Bronto:** Lennie Weinrib; **Zonk:** Mel Blanc; **Noodles:** John Stephenson; **Stub:** Mel Blanc

## ◉ THE FLINTSTONES COMEDY SHOW

The original cast of Fred, Barney, Wilma and Betty were featured in this new format of rollicking, fun-filled comedy set in the Stone Age town of Bedrock, debuting on NBC in the fall of 1980. The program contained six regular cartoon segments of various lengths each week: "The Flintstone Family Adventures," the further comic misadventures of the Flintstones and Rubble families; "Pebbles, Dino and Bamm-Bamm," with Pebbles, Bamm-Bamm, Dino and his friends at work solving various mysteries; and "Captain Caveman," the screw-up prehistoric superhero who is aided by Wilma and Betty in warding off criminals.

Other series components included "The Bedrock Cops," the zany escapades of the Bedrock Police force, joined by part-time deputies Fred and Barney and their supernatural friend, Shmoo, in fighting crime; "Dino and the Cavemouse," in which the Flintstones' pet dinosaur, Dino, squares off with a wild house mouse in this frantic prehistoric version of "watchdog vs. mouse"; and "The Frankenstones," the misadventures of the Flintstones' new and "unusual" looking neighbors, plus a variety of musical and comedy blackouts featuring the series' prehistoric stars.

Following the series' initial network run, three episodes from the series were rebroadcast on NBC under the title, *The Flintstones Family Adventures Hour* in 1981. A Hanna-Barbera Production. Color. One hour and a half. Premiered on NBC: November 22, 1980–September 5, 1981. Rebroadcast on NBC: October 4, 1981–October 18, 1981 (as The Flintstones Family Adventure Hour).

**Voices**
**Fred Flintstone:** Henry Corden; **Wilma Flintstone, his wife:** Jean VanderPyl; **Barney Rubble, their neighbor:** Mel Blanc; **Betty Rubble, his wife:** Gay Autterson; **Dino:** Mel Blanc; **Pebbles Flintstone:** Russi Taylor; **Bamm-Bamm:** Michael Sheehan; **George Slate, Fred's boss:** John Stephenson; **Lou Granite:** Ken Mars; **Penny:** Mitzi McCall; **Wiggy:** Gay Autterson; **Moonrock:** Lennie Weinrib; **Schleprock:** Don Messick; **Shmoo:** Frank Welker; **Sgt. Boulder:** Lennie Weinrib; **Cave Mouse:** Russi Taylor

**THE FRANKENSTONES: Frank Frankenstone, the hulking father:** Charles Nelson Reilly; **Hidea Frankenstone, his wife:** Ruta Lee; **Atrocia Frankenstone, their kooky daughter:** Zelda Rubinstein; **Freaky Frankenstone, their misfit son:** Paul Reubens; **Rockjaw:** Frank Welker; **Captain Caveman:** Joe Baker

## ◉ FLINT THE TIME DETECTIVE

First seen on Japan's Tokyo TV as *Space-Time Detective Genshi-kun* (*Jiku Tantei Genshi-kun*) in 1998, this English-dubbed anime series follows a fossilized caveboy turned into a giant stone ax, and his father, Rocky, aided by Bureau of Time and Space police officer, Dr. Bernard Goodman, and his twin niece and nephew, Tony and Sara, in their time-traveling pursuit of the evil Dark Lord and his villainess accomplice, PetraFina, for destroying their land and fossilizing them. The American series debuted Saturday mornings on FOX in April 2000 and, after its network run, was rebroadcast on FOX Family Channel (and its successor, ABC Family) from 2000 to 2002. A TV Tokyo/Saban Entertainment Production. Color. Half-hour. Premiered on FOX: April 8, 2000–October 13, 2000. Rebroadcast on FOX FAM/ABC FAM: March 5, 2000–February 7, 2002.

**Voices**
**Flint Hammerhead:** R. Martin Klein; **Rocky Hammerhead:** Bob Papenbrook; **Tony Goodman:** Brian Donovan; **Sarah Goodman:** Tifanie Christun; **Bernard Goodman:** Richard Cansino; **Getalong:** Mona Marshall; **Pterry:** Greg Berg; **Merlock Holmes/Coconaut:** Dave Mallow; **Bindi:** Melissa Fahn; **Jillian Gray:** Mari Devon; **PetraFina Dagmar/Ms. Iknow:** Barbara Goodson; **Dino:** Lex Lang; **Principal Mite:** David Lodge; **The Old Timer:** Kim Strauss; **Dark Lord:** Tom Wyner; **Nascal/Uglinator:** Joe Ochman; **Eldora/Artie:** Melodee Spevack; **Lynx/Ominito:** Michael Sorich; **Elekin:** Derek Stephen Prince

## ◉ FLYING HOUSE

From the producers of *Speed Racer* and *Robotech*, this 1982 half-hour syndicated religious cartoon series (called *Tondera House* in Japan and redubbed in English) premiered in syndication and simultaneously on the Christian Broadcasting Network in 1982. The series covered events of the New Testament and was telecast at the same time as another companion series, *Superbook*. (See entry for details.) A CBN/Tatsunoko Production. Color. Half-hour. Premiered: 1982 (in syndication and on CBN). Syndicated.

**Voices**
Billie Lou Watt, Sonia Owens, Hal Studer, Helen Van Koert, Peter Fernandez, Ray Owens, George Gunneau

## ◉ FLYING RHINO JUNIOR HIGH

Comical misadventures of four flying rhinos—Billy O'Toole, Tammy Tupperman, Ruby Snarkis and her brother Marcus—who try to prevent an underachieving, former straight "A" student, Earl P. Sidebottom (also known as the Phantom), and his pet rat, Ratticus, from transforming their junior high into a fantasy world by transporting students to places and events in history. The half-hour animated fantasy-adventure series premiered on CBS's fall 1998 Saturday-morning schedule with 13 episodes during its first season. Produced by Canada's Nelvana cartoon studios, the series was renewed for a second season, with 13 additional episodes, along with three other Nelvana cartoon series: *Anatole, Franklin* and *Mythic Warriors*. A Flying Rhinoceros/Big Daddy Productions/Nelvana Limited/Neurones France s.a.r.l. Production. Color. Half-hour. Premiered on CBS: October 3, 1998–September 9, 2000.

**Voices**
**The Phantom/Earl P. Sidebottom:** Richard Binsley; **Billy O'Toole:** Ashley Brown; **Ruby Snarkis:** Tracey Moore; **Lydia Lopez:** Cindy Henderson; **Raticus/Rod:** Ron Rubin; **Fred/Johnny:** Edward

Glen; **Mrs. Snodgrass/Edna:** Lindsay Leese; **Principal Mulligan:** Len Carlson; **Flo/Nurse Cutlip:** Catherine Gallant; **Buford/Mr. Needlenose:** Paul Haddad

## ⊚ FONZ AND THE HAPPY DAYS GANG

Inspired by television's hit prime-time comedy series *Happy Days*, this series has Fonzie and the rest of the gang (Richie, Ralph and Fonzie's cut-up dog, Mr. Cool) spread cool fun as they travel via a time machine to every time and place throughout Earth's history. Showing them the way is Cupcake, a young futuristic girl who pilots the craft, which they repaired for her following her unscheduled landing in Milwaukee in the year 1957.

Three original cast members of the popular television sitcom voiced their characters on the 24-episode animated series, which lasted two seasons on ABC. *A Hanna-Barbera Production. Color. Half-hour. Premiered on ABC: November 8, 1980–September 18, 1982.*

*Voices*
**Fonzie:** Henry Winkler; **Richie Cunningham:** Ron Howard; **Ralph Malph:** Don Most; **Mr. Cool:** Frank Welker; **Cupcake:** DeeDee Conn

## ⊚ FOO FOO

Somewhat forgotten British-made series of 32 five-minute cartoons about a transparent man in a pencil-sketch world. Produced by England's most noted animation studio, Halas and Batchelor, the series was animated in the same modernistic style of UPA (United Productions of America), which changed the course of animation through limited animation fare like *Gerald McBoing Boing* and *Mister Magoo. A Halas Batchelor Production. Color. Half-hour. Premiered: 1961. Syndicated.*

## ⊚ FOOFUR

A ragtag gang of canines (Fencer, Rocki, Louis, Annabell, Fritz-Carlos and Annabell) try to make it on their own, led by the lanky, good-natured blue hound dog, Foofur, in this half-hour animated series for NBC, based on the world-famous Belgian comic-book character created by cartoonist Freddy Monnickendam.

*A Hanna-Barbera Production. Color. Half-hour. Premiered on NBC: September 13, 1986–September 3, 1988.*

*Voices*
**Foofur:** Frank Welker; **Rocky:** Christina Lange; **Anna-bell:** Susan Tolsky; **Hazel:** Pat Carroll; **Pepe:** Don Messick; **Chucky:** Allan Melvin; **Dolly:** Susan Blu; **Mel:** David Doyle; **Fencer:** Eugene Williams; **Louis:** Dick Gautier; **Fritz-Carlos:** Jonathan Schmock; **Mrs. Escrow:** Susan Silo; **Sam:** Chick Vennera; **Baby:** Peter Cullen; **Burt:** Bill Callaway; **Harvey:** Michael Bell

## ⊚ FOSTER'S HOME FOR IMAGINARY FRIENDS

Mischievous adventures of shy, sensitive eight-year-old Mac and his perfect imaginary friend and alter-ego, Blooregard Q. Kazoo ("Bloo" for short), who resides at Foster's Home for Imaginary Friends (after convincing its proprietress, Madame Foster, to allow Bloo to join), a home for wayward imaginary friends (Wilt, Eduardo, Coco and Duchess) who have been separated from the kids who invented them, in this half-hour comedy series created by Emmy Award-winning animator Craig McCracken, the creator of *The Powerpuff Girls*. The new animated series made its debut on Cartoon Network on Friday, August 13, 2005, with a 90-minute feature, *House of Bloo's*, with the series then airing in its regular

Friday 7 P.M. time slot a week later, with an encore performance at 10:30 P.M. Series regulars joining in on the hi-jinks include the home's staff— Mr. Herriman, a giant bunny-turned-house administrator and Frankie, Madame Foster's sensible granddaughter. Six weeks after its premiere, becoming the best-received new series on television and topping basic cable ratings among kid audiences during its time period, the network ordered an additional 26 episodes, bringing the series total to 52, to take it through its third and fourth seasons.

On April 28, 2006, Mac and his make-believe Pac Man-looking friend returned with four new episodes Friday nights, airing through May 19. In the season opener, after Mac is recruited to be an imaginary superhero sidekick, Bloo becomes so jealous he teams up with an imaginary supervillain. On Monday, July 17, four new episodes premiered as part of Cartoon Network's summer-long presentation of premieres of popular original series every Monday through Thursday at 7 P.M. Renewed for a fifth season, the hit Emmy Award-winning series enjoyed other programming milestones in 2006, including hosting special segments of *Are You a Cartoon Network Kid?* on Cartoon Network's prime-time summer lineup, and an hour-long, prime-time TV movie, *Good Wilt Hunting*, with new characters that premiered on Thanksgiving as part of a 12-hour marathon with brand-new episodes, also aired every Friday in November in honor of National Adoption month. The summer also marked the launch of a new and free interactive online game, *Foster's Big Fat Awesome House Party*, on Cartoon-Network.com that has attracted more than 2 million registered users since its May 15 launch, with more than 11 million games played. For one month in the summer of 2005, reruns were shown Saturday mornings on the WB Television Network's Kids' WB! *A Cartoon Network Studios Production. Color. Half-hour. Premiered on CAR: August 13, 2004. Rebroadcast on the WB (Kids' WB!): July 9, 2005–August 13, 2005.*

*Voices*
**Mac:** Sean Marquette; **Blooregard "Bloo" Q. Kazoo:** Keith Ferguson; **Wilt:** Phil LaMarr; **Eduardo:** Tom Kenny; **Frances "Frankie" Foster:** Grey DeLisle; **Coco:** Candi Milo; **Mr. Herriman:** Tom Kane; **Terrence:** Tara Strong; **Adam:** Jeff Bennett; **Iwan:** Kevin McDonald; **Foul Larry:** Kevin Michael Richardson

## ⊚ FRAGGLE ROCK

Jim Henson's successful muppet clan, the Fraggles, explore everyday adventures in the fun-loving Fraggle community in this animated spinoff of the popular live-action HBO series. Also known as "Jim Henson's Fraggle Rock," the 24-episode animated half-hour version debuted on NBC in September 1987 and lasted one season. It has since appeared in reruns on Disney Channel from 1992 to 1995. *A Jim Henson Production in association with Marvel Productions. Color. Half-hour. Premiered on NBC: September 12, 1987–September 3, 1988. Rebroadcast on DIS: August 13, 1992–June 14, 1995.*

*Voices*
**Wembley:** Bob Bergen; **Gobo/Architect/Wrench:** Town-send Coleman; **Red/Wingnut:** Barbara Goodson; **Mokey/Cotterpin:** Mona Marshall; **Ma Gorg:** Patti Parris; **Boober/Sprocket/Majory:** Rob Paulsen; **Traveling Matt/Pa Gorg/Flange:** Pat Pinney; **Doc/Philo/Gunge:** John Stephenson; **Storyteller:** Stu Rosen

## ⊚ FRANKENSTEIN JR. AND THE IMPOSSIBLES

The awesomely strong, 30-foot-tall Frankenstein Jr. protects the community and his boy owner, Buzz, from danger. Sharing billing with the mechanical monster were "The Impossibles," a trio of crime-fighting agents—Fluid Man, Multi-Man and Coil Man—posing as a rock-and-roll group. NBC later rebroadcast episodes of *Frankenstein Jr.* as part of a midseason replacement series called *The Space Ghost/Frankenstein Jr. Show.* A *Hanna-Barbera Production. Color. Half-hour. Premiered on CBS: September 10, 1966–September 7, 1968. Rebroadcast on CAR: March 5, 1995–97 (Super Chunk). Rebroadcast on BOOM: April 2, 2000–.*

### Voices

**Frankenstein Jr.:** Ted Cassidy; **Buzz Conroy:** Dick Beals; **Dr. Conroy:** John Stephenson

*The Impossibles*
**Multi-Man/Various Others:** Don Messick; **Fluid Man:** Paul Frees; **Coil Man:** Hal Smith

## ◎ FRANKLIN

Between going to school, playing with his friends and helping his parents, Mr. and Mrs. Turtle, good-hearted Franklin the Turtle learns the importance of honesty and being a turtle of good character while learning about the world around him with his friends Bear, Good, Beaver, Rabbit, Mr. Owl, Badger, Snail and others in this popular preschool series based on author Paulette Bourgeois's acclaimed book series.

Produced by Canada's Nelvana Entertainment and first shown on Canadian television in 1985, this animated series adaptation premiered in the United States in 1997 as part of Nickelodeon's Nick Jr. preschool block with 13 half-hour episodes. Beginning in October of 1998, the program aired briefly Saturday mornings on CBS along with several other Nelvana-produced cartoon shows, only to return for a second run in September 2000, lasting two seasons. In October 1999, Nickelodeon's commercial-free children's programming network, Noggin, picked up the series, continuing to re-air episodes on its weekday schedule.

Producing 65 episodes over six seasons, three made-for-video movies (each debuting on Canada's Family Channel) also aired on Nick Jr. and Noggin: *Franklin and the Green Knight* (1999), *Franklin's Magic Christmas* (2001) and *Back to School with Franklin* (2003). During the program's sixth season, three new voice actors joined the cast, including Cole Caplan replacing Noah Reid as the voice of Franklin; Bryn McAuley as his sister Harriet; and Carolyn Scott as Franklin's replacement teacher Miss Koala. A *Nelvana Limited/Kids Can Press Production. Color. Half-hour. Premiered on NICK: November 3, 1997–July 30, 2004. Premiered on CBS: October 3, 1998–January 2, 1999; September 16, 2000–September 7, 2002. Rebroadcast on NOG: October 4, 1999–.*

### Voices

**Franklin:** Cole Caplan (2003– ); **Harriet, His Sister:** Bryn McAuley; **Mr. Turtle/Great Grandfather Turtle:** Richard Newman; **Mrs. Turtle:** Elizabeth Brown; **Bear:** Luca Perlman; **Beaver:** Leah Cudmore; **Goose:** Olivia Garratt; **Rabbit:** Kyle Fairlie; **Fox:** Gil Filar; **Snail:** Kristen Bone; **Otter:** Sophie Lang; **Coach Porcupine/Mrs. Bear:** Mari Trainor; **Mr. Owl:** James Rankin; **Mr. Bear:** Donald Burda; **Mr. Mole:** William Colgate; **Moose:** Amos Crawley; **Mrs. Moose:** Ellen Ray Hennessy; **Porcupine:** Shari-Ann Ross-Laney; **Badger:** Ruby Smith-Merovitz; **Granny Turtle:** Corinne Conley; **Mrs. Goose:** Catherine Disher; **Skunk:** Annick Obonsawin; **Mr. Fox:** Paul Haddad; **Mrs. Muskrat:** Marcia Bennett; **Constable Raccoon:** Dan Lett; **Mrs. Beaver:** Valerie Boyle; **Mr. Skunk:** Shane McPherson; **Mr. Heron:** Wayne Robson; **Squirrel:** Cole Caplan; **Mrs. Badger:** Coretta Jafelice; **Mr. Groundhog:** Chris Wiggins; **Mr. Beaver:** Adrian Truss; **Mr. Coyote:** Stephen Ouimette; **Jack Rabbit:** Tyrone Savage; **Beatrice:**

Susan Roman; **Miss Koala:** Carolyn Scott; **Narrator:** Janet-Laine Green

## ◎ FRANNY'S FEET

Originally produced overseas where it became an international smash hit, this charming, preschool series follows five-year-old Franny Fanttootsie (voiced by Phoebe McAuley), who, after slipping on different shoes in her grandfather's repair shop, is magically transported each week on educational adventures around the globe. First seen on Canada's CBC network in January 2004 and then Canada's Family Channel the following September, the half-hour series, aimed at teaching children the joys of exploring, made its United States debut on PBS Kids in selected markets in July 2006. The season opener featured Franny learning about dinosaurs while digging for fossils in Canada. A *DECODE Entertainment Production. Color. Half-hour. Premiered on PBS Kids: July 15, 2006.*

### Voices

**Franny:** Phoebe McAuley; **Grandpa:** George Buza; **Lucy:** Katherine Crimi; **Additional Voices:** Mark Rendall, Juan Chioran, Stacey DePass, Annick Obonsawin, Luca Perlman, Susan Roman, Ron Rubin, Rob Tinkler, Jonathan Wilson

## ◎ FRED AND BARNEY MEET THE SHMOO

This 90-minute program was a collection of previously broadcast episodes of *The New Fred and Barney Show* and *The Thing* (originally combined as *Fred and Barney Meet the Thing*), plus repeat episodes from *The New Shmoo*, only serialized into two parts. (See *Fred and Barney Meet the Thing* and *The New Shmoo* for further details.) A *Hanna-Barbera Production. Color. Ninety minutes. Premiered on NBC: December 8, 1979–November 15, 1980.*

## ◎ FRED AND BARNEY MEET THE THING

Hanna-Barbera took prehistoric favorites, Fred Flintstone and Barney Rubble, and paired them with Marvel Comics' The Thing in this hour-long series comprised of new adventures of the Flintstone and Rubble families and separate stories revolving around the exploits of high school student Benjamin Grimm, who changes himself into an orange hulk to fight crime. Episodes of both components were repeated on *Fred and Barney Meet the Shmoo*, a 90-minute trilogy series. A *Hanna-Barbera Production. Color. One hour. Premiered on NBC: September 22, 1979–December 1, 1979.*

### Voices

**FRED AND BARNEY: Fred Flintstone:** Henry Corden; **Wilma Flintstone, his wife:** Jean VanderPyl; **Barney Rubble, their friend:** Mel Blanc; **Betty Rubble, his wife:** Gay Autterson; **Pebbles, Fred's daughter:** Jean VanderPyl; **Bamm-Bamm, Barney's son:** Don Messick; **George Slate, Fred's boss:** John Stephenson; **Dino, Fred's pet dinosaur:** Mel Blanc

**THE THING: Benjy Grimm:** Wayne Norton; **The Thing:** Joe Baker; **Kelly, Benjy's friend:** Noelle North; **Betty, Benjy's friend:** Marilyn Schreffler; **Spike, the bully:** Art Metrano; **Ronald Redford, the rich kid:** John Erwin; **Miss Twilly, the teacher:** Marilyn Schreffler

## ◎ FRED FLINTSTONE AND FRIENDS

In new animated wraparounds, Fred Flintstone (voiced by Henry Corden) hosted this series of Hanna-Barbera cartoons originally broadcast by various networks on Saturday mornings: *The Flintstones Comedy Hour, Goober and the Ghost Chasers, Jeannie, Patridge*

*Family: 2200 A.D., Pebbles and Bamm-Bamm and Yogi's Gang. A Hanna-Barbera Production. Color. Half-hour. Premiered: September 1977. Syndicated.*

## ◎ FREE FOR ALL

Cartoonist Brett Merhar's cult-favorite comic strip comes to this life in this animated adult comedy series, combining "biting satire and harmless slapstick in the tradition of 'South Park'" and following the absurd antics of sudden millionaire and wheeler-dealer Clay Zeeman (voiced by Merhar himself), formerly a dysfunctional deadbeat until he won his lawsuit against a fast-food restaurant, and his best friend, college student Johnny G. Jenkins, plus Clay's pet ferret and former lab research animal, Angus. Joined by a cast of equally offbeat characters, including Johnny's sex-obsessed Grandma; alcoholic dad, Dougie Jenkins; and the woman of his life, Paula, his next-door neighbor, this part 2-D cel, part 3-D digitally animated half-hour series—and first animated series for Showtime—became television's first hi-definition animated half-hour mastered in HDCAM Graphics & Animation. Produced exclusively for Showtime by multi-Emmy Award-winning Film Roman studios, Showtime initially ordered seven episodes of Merhar's quirky series, which lasted only one season. *A Film Roman Production. Color. Half-hour. Premiered on SHO: July 11, 2003–September 1, 2003.*

### Voices
**Clay Zeeman:** Brett Merhar; **Johnny G. Jenkins:** Jonathan Silverman; **Paula:** Juliette Lewis; **Doug Jenkins:** Sam McMurray; **Grandma:** Mitzi McCall; **Mr. Stanky:** John Kozeluh; **Omar:** Jonah Convy; **Angus:** Dee Bradley Baker; **Other Voices:** Grey DeLisle

## ◎ FREE WILLY

Based on the 1993 hit family adventure, youngsters Jesse, Randolph and Marlene and their three-ton orca whale friend Willy (who now talks), joined by sea-lion Lucille and baby dolphin Einstein, engage in environmental and scientific adventures, frequently doing battle with the notorious enviro-villain "The Machine" in this weekly ABC Saturday morning series, which debuted in 1994. One of the movie's producers, Lauren Schuler-Donner, served as the series' executive producer. *A Nelvana Entertainment Production. Color. Half-hour. Premiered on ABC: September 24, 1994–August 31, 1996.*

### Voices
**Jesse:** Zachary Bennett; **Willy:** Paul Haddad; **Marlene:** Rachael Crawford; **Randolph:** Michael Fletcher; **The Machine:** Gary Krawford; **Amphonids:** James Kidnie; **Lucille:** Alyson Court; **Ben Shore:** Geordie Johnson; **Einstein:** Kevin Zegers; **Mr. Naugle:** Neil Crone; **P.R. Frickey:** Andrew Sabiston; **Annie:** Sheila McCarthy; **Glenn:** Ron Lea

## ◎ FRISKY DINGO

The world's most evil villain of all time, Killface, finds destroying Earth by propelling it into the sun isn't going to be easy and becomes "dull" and far too complex, with too many boring details to worry about, including media buys, budgets and marketing, with his arch-rival, Awesome-X (alias billionaire playboy Xander Crews), feeling equally ambivalent about squashing Killface's sinister plan in this 15-minute comedy series created by *Sealab 2021* co-creators Matt Thompson and Adam Reed and produced by Atlanta-based 70–30 Productions for Cartoon Network's *Adult Swim Fix* cartoon block. Airing Monday nights, Cartoon Network committed to 13 first-season episodes of the series that began airing in October 2006. A 70-30 Production. Color. Fifteen minutes. Premiered on CAR: October 16, 2006.

### Voices
**Killface/Xander Crews:** Adam Reed; **Valerie:** Mary Kraft; **Grace Ryan:** Kate Miller; **Taqui'l:** Killer Mike; **Phillip:** Christian Danley; **Sinn:** Kelly Jenrette; **Simon:** Mike Bell

## ◎ FULLMETAL ALCHEMIST

When an experiment goes bad, resulting in the loss of his leg and his brother Alphonse's entire body, 15-year-old master of alchemy, Edward Elric, known as the Fullmetal Alchemist, traps his brother's soul inside a suit of armor and replaces his limbs with mechanical ones. Then the brothers venture out to find the legendary Philosopher's Stone and restore their bodies to normal form. Debuting with 13 first-season episodes, the half-hour series—based on the 20th-century science fiction manga created by Hiromu Arakawa and English version of the popular Japanese series—was one of two new anime properties Cartoon Network acquired along with *Ghost in the Shell: Stand Alone Complex* and began airing in November 2004 during Saturday's late-night *Adult Swim* block of animation for adults ages 18 to 34. Fifty-one half-hours were originally broadcast until March 2006. *An Aniplex/BONES/Mainichi Broadcasting/Square-Enix/ FUNimation Production. Color. Half-hour. Premiered on CAR: November 6, 2004–February 15, 2007.*

### Voices
**Edward Elric:** Vic Mignogna; **Alphonse Elric:** Aaron Dsmuke; **Major Alex Louis Armstrong:** Christopher R. Sabat; **Colonel Roy Mustang:** Travis Willingham; **Lieutenant Riza Hawkeye:** Colleen Clinkenbeard

## ◎ FUNKY COPS

Brothers Ace Anderson and Jack Kowalski, two incompetent police detectives who swap the mean streets for disco beats at night, solve crimes, along with their disco dancing friends, at San Francisco's disco scene in this half-hour Saturday-morning cartoon series spoof of 1970s cop shows originally created for French television and broadcast in the United States on FOX. Aimed at viewers ages eight to 12 FOX acquired 26 half-hours for the first season (including a half-hour Christmas special, entitled "And No Partridge in a Pear Tree," the airing of which could not be confirmed) that premiered in August 2003, and an additional second season of 13 episodes to air in 2004. Introduced during the second season was a new recruit, a talented female officer named Foxy. *An AnteFilms Productions/M6/TPS Cinema/Greenlight Media/4Kids Entertainment Production. Color. Half-hour. Premiered on FOX: August 23, 2003–June 12, 2004.*

### Voices
**Ace Anderson:** Frederick B. Owens; **Jack Kowalski:** Andrew Rannells; **Captain Dobbs:** Richard Yearwood; **Fly:** Barbara Scoff

## ◎ THE FUNKY PHANTOM

Three teenagers, Skip, Augie and April, and their dog Elmo, release the ghost of Jonathan Wellington Muddlemore ("Mudsy" for short), a young patriot during the American Revolutionary War who has been trapped for two centuries inside the grandfather's clock at Muddlemore Mansion, where he had taken refuge from the Redcoats. Along with his cat Boo, Mudsy and his new friends travel the countryside to challenge injustice and uphold the ideals of the Declaration of Independence. Produced by Hanna-Barbera, this 17-episode, half-hour animated series premiered on NBC in 1971 and lasted only one season. Episodes were later rebroadcast as part of the syndicated series *The Fun*

*World of Hanna-Barbera* and *The Godzilla/Dynomutt Show*. A *Hanna-Barbera Production. Color. Half-hour. Premiered on ABC: September 11, 1971–September 1, 1972. Syndicated (part of The Fun World of Hanna-Barbera). Rebroadcast on CAR: December 6, 1992; March 14, 1993 (part of Boomerang, 1972); April 10, 1994–May 26, 1996 (Sundays); 1998–99. Rebroadcast on BOOM: September 2, 2000–.*

*Voices*
**Jonathan (Mudsy) Muddlemore:** Daws Butler; **April Stewart:** Tina Holland; **Skip:** Micky Dolenz; **Augie:** Tommy Cook

## ◎ THE FUNNY COMPANY

As members of the Junior Achievement Club, an enterprising group of neighborhood children take on odd jobs to make money, with mixed results in this educational and entertaining series which included educational wraparounds between each cartoon. *A Funny Company/Ken Snyder Production. Color. Half-hour. Premiered: September 1963. Syndicated.*

*Voices*
**Buzzer Bell/Shrinkin' Violette:** Dick Beals; **Polly Plum:** Robie Lester; **Merry Twitter/Jasper N. Park:** Nancy Wible; **Terry Dactyl:** Ken Snyder; **Dr. Todd Goodheart/Belly Laguna/Dr. Von Upp:** Hal Smith; **The Wisenheimer:** Bud Hiestand; **Broken Feather:** Tom Thomas

## ◎ THE FUNTASTIC WORLD OF HANNA-BARBERA

In 1985 Hanna-Barbera Productions launched this syndicated 90-minute cartoon block broadcast on Saturday and Sunday mornings. It was so successful that it was expanded to two hours of continuous cartoon fare. The package was first comprised of three newly animated half-hour series: *Yogi's Treasure Hunt, The Paw Paws* and *Galtar and the Golden Lance*. In its two-hour form, new weekly adventures of *Jonny Quest* were added to the package.

The series' components changed in the following years. In 1987 the producers added *Sky Commanders* and *The Snorks*, retaining *Yogi's Treasure Hunt* and *Jonny Quest* as the other series regulars. The following season the show consisted of *The Further Adventures of Super Ted, Fantastic Max, The Flintstone Kids* and *Richie Rich*, with *Jonny Quest* and *Galtar and the Golden Lance* being the only returnees. The package was pared down in size for the 1989–90 season. It featured *The Further Adventures of Super Ted, Fantastic Max, Paddington Bear* and *Richie Rich*. Additional series added since 1990 included: *Don Coyote and Sancho Panda, The Midnight Patrol, The Pirates of Dark Water, Swat Kats, Two Stupid Dogs, Yo, Yogi* and *Young Robin Hood* (See individual series entries for further details.) *A Hanna-Barbera Production. Color. Ninety minutes. Two hours. Premiered: September 1985. Syndicated.*

## ◎ FUN WORLD OF HANNA-BARBERA

Off-network series featuring episodes from past Hanna-Barbera shows: *Wacky Races, Dastardly and Muttley, Perils of Penelope Pitstop, The Funky Phantom* and *Amazing Chan and the Chan Clan*. (See individual series for information.) *A Hanna-Barbera Production. Color. Half-hour. Premiered: 1977. Syndicated.*

## ◎ THE FURTHER ADVENTURES OF DR. DOLITTLE

In classic stories loosely based on Hugh Lofting's nine critically acclaimed novels, veterinarian Dr. Dolittle, who commands the animals of the world with his conversational powers, with the help of his 14-year-old assistant, Tommy Stubbins, and his animal friends, attempts to thwart fiendish Sam Scurvy's efforts at world domination, in this half-hour, Saturday-morning cartoon series that debuted on NBC. *A DePatie-Freleng Enterprises Production in association with TCF-TV. Color. Half-hour. Premiered on NBC: September 12, 1970–September 2, 1971. Syndicated.*

*Voices*
**Dr. John Dolittle:** Bob Holt; **Sam Scurvy, the pirate:** Lennie Weinrib; **Tommy Stubbins:** Hal Smith; **Mooncat/Various Animals:** Barbara Towers, Don Messick; **The Grasshoppers:** Ronie Fellon, Colin Julian, Annabell

## ◎ THE FURTHER ADVENTURES OF SUPERTED

A once-discarded teddy bear is brought to life by a spotted alien (Spottyman) who endows the poor teddy with magical powers that turn him into the cuddliest superhero in the universe. Together they battle the evil Texas Pete and his marauding mates, Skeleton and Bulk, in this 13-episode, half-hour fantasy/adventure series, originally broadcast on Sunday mornings on *The Funtastic World of Hanna-Barbera*. *A Hanna-Barbera Production. Color. Half-hour. Premiered: September 1988. Syndicated. Rebroadcast on CAR: December 17, 1994–December 18, 1994 (Look What We Found!).*

*Voices*
**SuperTed:** Danny Cooksey; **Spottyman:** Patrick Fraley; **Texas Pete:** Victor Spinetti; **Skeleton:** Melvyn Hayes; **Bulk:** Marvin Kaplan

## ◎ FUTURAMA

Co-created by *The Simpsons'* creator Matt Groening during that show's 10th season, this futuristic adult cartoon comedy series featured the outlandish misadventures of a cryogenically frozen, young New York pizza delivery guy, Philip J. Fry, who awakens a thousand years later and adapts to a changed, futuristic world with his Cyclops girlfriend, Leela; his often rude alcoholic robot, Bender; his great nephew, Professor Farnsworth, and other planetary shipping company coworkers who help ease his transition into the new times in which he lives. Airing Sundays in

*A once-discarded teddy bear discovers fun and adventure as the cuddliest superhero in the universe in* The Further Adventures of SuperTed. *© Hanna-Barbera Productions*

prime time on FOX, beginning in March 1999, the smartly written, laugh-out-loud half-hour series won six Emmy Awards during its four-season run, including four for outstanding animated program (for programming one hour or less) and two more for outstanding individual achievement in animation in 2000 and 2001. Televised for the final time in August 2003, despite being a hit with critics and a cult favorite with viewers, FOX decided not to renew the series for a fifth season, although it was never officially canceled. In January 2003, Cartoon Network began rerunning the series on *Adult Swim*, its popular late-night program block for grown-ups.

Comedy Central announced plans to air 13 newly produced episodes of the Matt Groening-David X. Cohen former futuristic Fox animated comedy series in 2008, with actors Billy West, Katey Sagal and John DiMaggio reprising their roles. *A Curiosity Company/20th Century Fox Television Production. Color. Half-hour. Premiered on FOX: March 28, 1999–August 10, 2003. Rebroadcast on CAR: January 12, 2003–.*

*Voices*
**Philip J. Fry/ Professor Hubert Farnsworth (a.k.a. The Professor)/Dr. John Zoidberg:** Billy West; **Turanga Leela:** Katey Sagal; **Bender Bending Rodríguez:** John DiMaggio; **Linda the News Anchor:** Tress MacNeille; **Hermes Conrad:** Phil LaMarr; **Morbo:** Maurice LaMarche; **Amy Wong:** Lauren Tom; **Utility Player:** Bryne Offutt; **Animal Voices:** Frank Welker; **LaBarbara Conrad/Other Voices:** Dawnn Lewis; **Cubert:** Kath Soucie; **Abner Doubledeal:** Tom Kenny; **Dwight Conrad:** Bumper Robinson; **Old Man Waterfall:** Phil Hendrie; **The Robot Devil:** Dan Castellaneta; **Dixie:** Pamela Anderson; **Electronic Mother's Day Card:** Nicole St. John; **Walla:** Scott Holst; **Himself:** Al Gore; **Herself:** Nichelle Nichols; **Himself:** Leonard Nimoy; **Herself:** Lucy Liu; **Additional Voices:** David Herman, Susie Geiser

## GADGET BOY AND HEATHER

Armed with an arsenal of high-tech crime-fighting accessories, Inspector Gadget, as a juvenile bionic crimefighter, squashes the villainous Spydra, with some help from his coagent Heather, in this first-run, syndicated series that aired as part of the weekend cartoon block *Amazin' Adventures II*. *A DIC Enterprises Production. Color. Half-hour. Premiered: September 18, 1995 (part of Amazin' Adventures II). Syndicated. Rebroadcast on TDIS: April 18, 1998–January 4, 2002*

*Voices*
**Gadget Boy:** Don Adams; **Agent Heather:** Tara Charendoff; **Spydra:** Louise Vallance

*Other Voices*
Maurice LaMarche

## GADGET BOY'S ADVENTURES IN HISTORY

Juvenile crimefighter Gadget Boy (a younger version of the bionic Inspector Gadget), coagent Heather and the morphing canine G-9 time-travel through history to undo the evil schemes of nefarious Spydra and at the same time "realign" history in this half-hour series produced for The History Channel. The 26-episode series was produced by DIC Entertainment in consultation with the National Education Association. *A DIC Entertainment Production in association with the National Education Association. Color. Half-hour. Premiered on HIS: January 10, 1998.*

*Voices*
**Gadget Boy:** Don Adams; **Boris/Dabble/Stromboli/Mulch/ Humus:** Maurice LaMarche; **Agent Heather:** Tara Charendoff; **Spydra:** Louise Vallance

## GALAXY HIGH SCHOOL

These space-age adventures follow the exploits of Doyle Cleverlobe and Aimee Brightower, the first exchange students from Earth to attend an interstellar high school on the asteroid Flutor. Thirteen half-hour shows which aired on CBS. The series' provocative antidrug episode, "Brain Blaster," was nominated for the prestigious Humanitas Award in 1987. In 1993 the program was brought back (in reruns) on the Sci-Fi Channel, its two-hour *Cartoon Quest* program block. *A TMS Entertainment Production. Color. Half-hour. Premiered on CBS: September 13, 1986–September 5, 1987. Rebroadcast on CBS: January 21, 1988–August 27, 1988; Rebroadcast on SCI: September 18, 1993–June 27, 1996.*

*Voices*
**Doyle Cleverlobe:** Hal Rayle; **Aimee Brightower:** Susan Blu; **Rotten Roland:** Neil Ross; **Beef Bonk:** John Stephenson; **Biddy McBrain/Katrina:** Pat Carroll; **Gilda Gossip/Flat Freddy:** Nancy Cartwright; **Earl Eccchhh:** Guy Christopher; **Ollie Oilslick/Reggie Unicycle:** Gino Conforti; **Booey Bubblehead/Wendy Garbo:** Jennifer Darling; **Coach Frogface/Sludge:** Pat Fraley; **Aimee's Locker/Doyle's Locker:** Henry Gibson; **Milo DeVenus:** David L. Lander; **The Creep:** Danny Mann; **Professor MacGreed/Professor Icenstein/Luigi LaBounci:** Howard Morris

## GALTAR AND THE GOLDEN LANCE

Astride his noble steed Thork, the handsome and fearless warrior Galtar uses sword and sorcery to protect the lovely Princess Goleeta and rescue his planet from the scourge of the evil Tormack, whose minions killed Galtar's parents and destroyed his village, in this 20-episode, half-hour fantasy/adventure that was part of the syndicated weekend series *The Funtastic World of Hanna-Barbera*. The series premiered Sunday mornings in 1985

*Students from Earth attend an interstellar high school on the asteroid Flutor in the animated comedy series* Galaxy High School. *© TMS Entertainment*

and was rerun on Cartoon Network and its sister network Boomerang. A *Hanna-Barbera Production. Color. Half-hour. Premiered: September 1985. Syndicated. Rebroadcast on CAR: October 3, 1992–December 3, 1993 (weekends, weekdays); December 11, 1993–January 1, 1994 (weekends); January 8, 1994–April 3, 1994 (Saturdays, Sundays); April 9, 1994–September 2, 1995 (Saturdays); September 3, 1995–1996. Rebroadcast on BOOM: April 15, 2001–June 4, 2003.*

### Voices
**Galtar:** Lou Richards; **Galeeta:** Mary McDonald Lewis; **Tormack:** Brock Peters; **Ither:** Bob Arbogast; **Krimm:** Barry Dennen; **Otar:** George DiCenzo; **Pandat:** Don Messick; **Rak:** Bob Frank; **Zorn:** David Mendenhall; **Tuk/Thork/Koda:** Frank Welker

## ◎ GARFIELD AND FRIENDS

*Garfield* creator Jim Davis oversaw production of this Saturday-morning series featuring the further exploits of Garfield and his comic comrades, Jon, Odie, Nermal and others, in two short weekly animated adventures, which included "blackouts" (usually "teasers" when preceding the credits), almost exclusively adapted from actual comic strips. As in Davis's popular comic strip, Garfield was portrayed as that fat, lazy, lasagna-loving pet of Jon, a cartoonist. Also part of the family was Odie, a very simpleminded dog. Other regulars included Nermal, the world's cutest kitten, and Liz, a veterinarian/love interest of Jon's. Another weekly series component was the series based on Davis's other strip, *U.S. Acres*, which revolved around the misadventures of Orson the pig and his farm friends, Wade the duck, Roy the rooster, Booker the baby chick, Sheldon, a chick still mostly in the egg and the brother-sister sheep pair, Bo and Lanolin. Each episode was backed by its own original music score.

Garfield was first adapted for television in a brace of prime-time, Emmy-winning and Emmy-nominated specials—*Garfield on the Town* (1983), *Garfield in the Rough* (1984), *Garfield's Halloween Special* (1985) and *Garfield in Paradise* (1985), among others—that aired on CBS. The Saturday-morning series debuted five years after the first special, also on CBS, and was so successful that the program was expanded to a full hour beginning with the 1989 season. In 1993 original network episodes were stripped for daily syndication. The series concluded its original network run in 1995 and was subsequently rerun on Cartoon Network, Nickelodeon, Fox Family Channel and ABC Family, Toon Disney and Boomerang. *A Film Roman Production in association with United Media and Paws, Inc. Color. One-hour. Premiered on CBS: September 17, 1988–October 7, 1995. Syndicated: September 20, 1993. Rebroadcast on CAR: September 4, 1995 (weekdays, Sundays). Rebroadcast on NICK: 1997–1999. Rebroadcast on FOX FAM: September 4, 2001–November 9, 2001. Rebroadcast on ABC FAM: November 12–December 28, 2001. Rebroadcast on TDIS: September 1, 2003–2006. Rebroadcast on BOOM: September 18, 2006–May 27, 2007.*

### Voices
**Garfield:** Lorenzo Music; **Jon/Blinky/Roy:** Thom Huge; **Odie/Orson:** Greg Berger; **Nermal:** Desiree Goyette; **Sheldon/Booker/Bo:** Frank Welker; **Wade:** Howie Morris; **Liz/Lanolin:** Julie Payne; **Cactus Jake:** Pat Buttram; **Doc Boy:** David L. Lander

## ◎ GARGOYLES

Frozen in stone since A.D. 994 following a spell cast upon them by the evil dark-age magician Archmage, a band of winged creatures, once perched atop a Viking fortress, are transported to a New York City skyscraper. There they come alive by night, 1,000 years later (headed by good-guy gargoyles Goliath and Hudson), to protect the city from modern-day barbarians in this first-run syndicated,

65-episode fantasy/adventure series—described as "animation's first dramatic series" —produced by Walt Disney Television Animation. The series was used to launch the *Disney Afternoon's* "Action Friday" two-hour cartoon block in October of 1994, debuting with a five-part story and airing only once a week. On September 4, 1995, the series expanded from weekly airings to a four-days-a-week schedule. In 1998 USA Network began reairing the series weekday mornings. An 80-minute, direct-to-video feature, *Gargoyles the Movie: The Heroes Awaken*, was produced in 1994, edited from the television series. *A Walt Disney Television Animation Production. Color. Half-hour. Premiered: October 24, 1994–August 29, 1997. Syndicated. Rebroadcast on USA: 1998. Rebroadcast on ABC FAM: March 13, 2004–September 11, 2004.*

### Voices
**Goliath:?**Keith David; **Broadway:** Bill Fagerbakke; **Lexington:** Thom Adcox-Hernandez; **Hudson:** Ed Asner; **Brooklyn/Magus/Owen:** Jeff Bennett; **Hakon:** Clancy Brown; **Tom:** J.D. Daniels; **Xanatos:** Jonathan Frakes; **Demona:** Marina Sirtis; **Brendan:** Patrick Fraley; **Commander:** Peter Renaday; **Captain:** Ed Gilbert; **Elisa Maza, police detective:** Salli Richardson; **Princess Katharine:** Kath Soucie; **Bronx:** Frank Welker

## ◎ GARGOYLES: THE GOLIATH CHRONICLES

Now with the secret of their existence exposed, Goliath and his small clan of Gargoyle warriors face a growing antigargoyle faction known as the Quarrymen, who will stop at nothing until the Gargoyles are captured, in this weekly Saturday-morning cartoon series based on 1994's *Gargoyles* animated series for ABC that also re-aired on Disney Channel and Toon Disney. *A Walt Disney Television Animation Production. Color. Half-hour. Premiered on ABC: September 7, 1996–April 12, 1997. Rebroadcast on DIS: September 4, 1998–February 27, 2000. Rebroadcast on TDIS: September 7, 1998–.*

### Voices
**Goliath:** Keith David; **Broadway:** Bill Fagerbakke; **Brooklyn/Owen:** Jeff Bennett; **Lexington:** Thom Adcox-Hernandez; **Hudson:** Edward Asner; **Angela:** Brigitte Bako; **Fox:** Laura San Giacomo; **Bronx:** Frank Welker; **John Castaway:** Scott Cleverdon; **David Xanatos:** Jonathan Frakes; **Margot Yale:** Tress MacNeille; **Elisa Marza:** Salli Richardson; **Matt Bluestone:** Thomas F. Wilson

## ◎ GARY & MIKE

Two surburban twenty-somethings—the asthmatic, hypochondriac Gary Newton, and his grungy, undisciplined dreamer, "best friend from hell" and self-described ladies' man, Mike Bonner—take "the road trip of their lives" across America, encountering everything from a cult in rural Kansas to an appearance on television's *The Jerry Springer Show* in this Claymation and dimensional animated series co-produced by Portland, Oregon's Will Vinton Studios and Big Ticket Television, producer of such syndicated shows as *Judge Judy, Judge Joe Brown*, as well as the UPN sitcom *Moesha*. Executive produced by creators Fax Bahr and Adam Small and Oscar-winners Vinton and Tom Turpin, the half-hour comedy series originally was slated to air on FOX, then debuted as a mid-season replacement on UPN, where it was sneak-previewed on a Thursday night before moving into its regular Friday night time slot. Winner of an Emmy Award for outstanding individual achievement in animation in 2001, the 13-episode series lasted only one season and has been rebroadcast since 2002 on Comedy Central. *A Big Ticket Television/Will Vinton Studios Production. Color. Half-hour. Premiered* on UPN: *January 11, 2001–April 13, 2001. Rebroadcast on COM: November 3, 2002–October 27, 2004.*

**Voices**
**Mike Bonner:** Harland Williams; **Gary Newton:** Christopher Moynihan; **Officer Dick:** Kurtwood Smith; **Cassette Tape Narrator:** Charlton Heston

## ◎ THE GARY COLEMAN SHOW

*Different Strokes* star Gary Coleman is the voice of an apprentice guardian angel (Andy LeBeau) who, on probation in heaven, returns to Earth to solve people's problems. His heavenly superior, Angelica, suffers through his mistakes, while the evil character Hornswoggle tries to create problems for the little angel. The 28-episode half-hour series—which featured two cartoons per half-hour show—was based on the character in the NBC-TV movie, *The Kid with the Broken Halo. A Hanna-Barbera Production in association with Gary Coleman Productions. Color. Half-hour. Premiered on NBC: September 18, 1982–September 10, 1983. Rebroadcast on CAR: February 19, 1994 (under one-hour* Look What We Found!). *Rebroadcast on CAR: February 17, 2006–April 12, 2006.*

**Voices**
**Andy LeBeau:** Gary Coleman; **Angelica:** Jennifer Darling; **Hornswoggle:** Sidney Miller; **Spence:** Calvin Mason; **Tina:** La Shana Dendy; **Bartholomew:** Jerry Houser; **Chris:** Lauren Anders; **Lydia:** Julie McWhirter Dees; **Mack:** Steve Schatzberg; **Haggle:** Jeff Gordon; **Announcer:** Casey Kasem

## ◎ GARY THE RAT

Strange things happen when a successful, high-priced New York attorney (Gary Andrews) is transformed into a six-foot feral rat and tries making it in the real world, despite an appearance that turns off many, including a tenant in his upscale apartment building who hires an exterminator to get rid of him. Part of SpikeTV's adult-oriented cartoon block, *The Strip,* the half-hour comedy series premiered in June 2003 and lasted only one season before it was canceled that December. Emmy award-winning actor Kelsey Grammer of TV's *Frasier* fame co-produced the series through his company, Grammer Productions, besides providing the voice of the title character. *A Grammer Productions/Viacom International Production. Color. Half-hour. Premiered TNN/SPIKE: June 26, 2003–December 11, 2003.*

**Voices**
**Gary Milford Andrews:** Kelsey Grammer; **Johnny Horatio Bugz:** Rob Cullen; **Truman Theodore Pinksdale:** Spencer Garret; **Jackson Buford Harrison:** Billy Gardell; **Gary's Therapist:** Vance DeGeneres; **Boots the Cat:** Susan Savage; **Additional Voices:** Rob Paulsen

## ◎ GENERATION O!

Eight-year-old rock star and lead singer Molly O! yearns to live a more normal life away from the public spotlight of her successful rock group, Generation O!, and the band members—her cousin and bassist Edwina ("Eddie), guitarist Nub and rotund drummer Yo-Yo—and their manager, Colonel Bob; she wants to hang out with her best friend, Chadd, while escaping her pesky brother, Buzz, in this animated cartoon series, based on James Proimos's popular children's book, *Joe's Wish.* Produced in association with DC Comics and Sony Music Entertainment, the half-hour comedy series debuted on the WB Television Network's Kids' WB!'s Saturday-morning schedule in August 2000 and later aired on weekday afternoons. *A TM/DC Comics/Sony Music Entertainment/Columbia*

*TriStar Television Animation Production. Color. Half-hour. Premiered on Kids' WB!: August 26, 2000–March 23, 2001.*

**Voices**
**Molly O!:** Chantal Strand; **Molly O! Singing Voice:** Kay Hanley; **Eddie:** Tabitha St. Germain; **Nub:** Scott McNeil; **Colonel Bob:** Jay Brazeau; **Mrs. O!:** Kathleen Barr; **Mr. O!:** Doug Parker; **Buzz O!:** Matt Hill; **Chadd:** Cathy Weseluck; **Kemp:** Andrew Francis; **Other Voices:** Brian Dobson, Saffron Henderson, Nicole Oliver, Chiarr Zanni

## ◎ GENTLE BEN

Television's favorite bear, who starred in the popular NBC adventure series, returns as a superhero who embarks on many exciting but dangerous adventures. *A Gentle Ben Animation Production. Color. Half-hour. Premiered: 1981. Syndicated.*

## ◎ GEORGE AND MARTHA

Faithful adaptation of author/illustrator James Marshall's series of popular children's books involving the everyday trials and tribulations of two larger-than-life hippos, George and Martha, who do everything together, from roller skating to swimming, in this half-hour educational series teaching the importance of friendship and working together, despite disagreements. Featuring the voices of Nathan Lane (George) and Andrea Martin (Martha), the 26-episode program, co-produced by Canada's Nelvana animation studios and Maurice Sendak's Wild Things Productions, originally aired on HBO's newly launched commercial-free family program network, HBO Family, during its daytime children's program block from 1999 to 2000, which included several other original animated and preschool series: *Anthony Ant, A Little Curious* and *The Adventures of Paddington Bear. A Nelvana Limited/Wild Things Production. Color. Half-hour. Premiered on HBO FAM: April 1, 1999–May 1, 2000.*

**Voices**
**George:** Nathan Lane; **Martha:** Andrea Martin; **Wilde/Eton:** Sean Cullen; **Penny:** Robin Duke; **Frieda:** Kathryn Greenwood; **Anton:** Greg Kramer; **Valerie Chuckles:** Debra McGrath; **Oscar/Bud Chuckles:** Colin Mochrie; **Duke:** Tony Rosato; **Other Voices:** Dwayne Hill

## ◎ GEORGE OF THE JUNGLE

Jay Ward, creator of Rocky and Bullwinkle, produced this animated spoof of Edgar Rice Burrough's famed Tarzan character starring a dimwitted, vine-swinging apeman named George, who protects the jungle and his wife, Ursula (Ward's version of Tarzan's wife, Jane), from the hazardous surroundings of the Imgwee Gwee Valley in Africa. George's main confidant and friend is a purplish gorilla, Ape (whose voice recalls actor Ronald Coleman's), who counsels him whenever he is in trouble. He also calls on his friendly elephant, Shep, whom he thinks is a peanut-loving puppy.

Other cartoon segments featured were: "Super Chicken," the misadventures of simpleminded Henry Cabot Henhouse III, who, after downing his famed Super Sauce, becomes a crimefighting super chicken; and "Tom Slick, Racer," a parody of racecar competition following the exploits of American good ol' boy Tom Slick aided by his girlfriend, Marigold, and his grandmother, Gertie.

The series was the only Jay Ward production ever to lose money (more than $100,000) and went straight into syndication following its network run. In the fall of 1992, the series returned for three-month run on FOX Network, then again in the fall of

1995 on ABC, preceding the summer 1997 release of the live-action feature of the same name starring Brendan Fraser. From the mid to late 1990s, the classic cartoon series also reaired on Cartoon Network. *A Jay Ward Production. Color. Half-hour. Premiered on ABC: September 9, 1967–September 5, 1970. Syndicated. Rebroadcast on FOX: September 19, 1992–October 17, 1992. Rebroadcast on ABC: September 9, 1995–October 21, 1995. Rebroadcast on CAR: October 7, 1995–October 5, 1996 (Saturdays, Sundays, weekdays); January 5, 1997–1998 (Sundays, weekdays).*

### Voices
**George of the Jungle:** Bill Scott; **Ursula, his wife:** June Foray; **Ape/Tom Slick/Gertie Growler:** Bill Scott; **Super Chicken:** Bill Scott; **Fred the lion, his butler:** Paul Frees; **Marigold, Tom Slick's girlfriend/Bella:** June Foray; **Narrator/Dick Two-Lane/Baron Otto Mattic:** Paul Frees; **District Commissioner:** Daws Butler

### ◎ GEORGE SHRINKS
After suddenly waking up one morning and finding out he has shrunk to the size of a mouse, a 10-year-old boy (George Shrinks) handles his daily tasks while overcoming and accepting the limitations of his sudden change in size, with the help of friends and family in this animated adaptation of William Joyce's popular children's book of the same name. Featuring stories covering such topics as biology, botany and ecology, the charming half-hour children's series debuted on PBS Kids' *Bookworm Bunch* program block in September 2000, with 40 episodes airing during the first season. Aimed at children ages five and under, the educational series was rebroadcast on PBS beginning in January 2003 and remained on the air the following September. The program currently airs in syndication. *A Nelvana/Jade Animation (Shenzhen) Company/TVOntario Production. Color. Half-hour. Premiered on PBS: September 30, 2000–December 1, 2001. Rebroadcast on PBS Kids: January 6, 2003–September 10, 2004. Syndicated.*

### Voices
**George:** Tracey Moore; **Dad:** Paul Sullivan; **Mom:** Kathleen Lasky; **Junior:** Robbi Jay Thuet; **Betty:** Bryn McAuley

### ◎ GERALD MCBOING BOING
Follows the playful, mischievous hometown adventures of six-year-old Gerald, who communicates only in sounds and noises—like clanks, beeps and clamors—and can mimic nearly any sound and attracts attention every time he opens his mouth; with his talking friends, Jamie and Jacob, his pet dog, Burp (so-named since he only burps), and his parents with whom he lives in a serene suburb. Based on Dr. Seuss's (alias Ted Geisel) classic children's book character and Oscar-winning UPA theatrical cartoon short, this 14-episode half-hour children's series, featuring two 11-minute episodes per show written in rhyme, aired weekdays beginning in August 2005 as part of Cartoon Network's short-lived weekday preschool block, *Tickle-U*, including a collection of new animated programs, among them *Firehouse Tales, Gordon the Garden Gnome, Harry and his Bucket Full of Dinosaurs, Peppa Pig* and *Yoko! Jakamoto! Toto!* Produced by Canada's Cookie Jar Entertainment and directed by Robin Budd, with the series' music and score composed by Ray Parker and Tom Sczesniak, this updated version lasted only one season, continuing in reruns thereafter, before joining the weekday lineup of Cartoon Network's sister classic cartoon network, Boomerang, at 6:00 A.M. (ET) with Warner Bros. Television Animation's *Krypto the Superdog* in February 2007. *A Cookie Jar Entertainment/Mercury Filmworks Production. Color. Half-hour. Premiered on CAR: August 22, 2005. Rebroadcast on BOOM: February 5, 2007.*

### Voices
**Gerald McBoing Boing's Voice:** Glenn Barna; **Janine:** Sam Weinstein; **Jacob:** Joanne Vannicola; **Gerald's father:** Patrick McKenna; **Gerald's mother:** Linda Ballantyne; **Narrator:** Deann DeGruijter

### ◎ THE GERALD MCBOING BOING SHOW
This festival of UPA cartoons presented regular episodes and one-time features in a swiftly paced half-hour variety show format, hosted by Gerald McBoing Boing, one of UPA's most successful theatrical cartoon stars.

Recurring features on the show included "Meet the Artist," lighthearted stories based on the lives of famous artists; "Meet the Inventor," humorous and instructional stories of the trials and triumphs of the world's greatest inventors; and "The Sleuth's Apprentice," in which the self-confident Sleuth gets all the credit for the mysteries solved by his mild-mannered apprentice.

In addition, the series showcased "The Twirlinger Twins," two energetic little girls with Buster Brown haircuts who sing songs, give recitations and take music lessons; "The Etiquette Series," starring the gentlemanly Mr. Charmley who is so intent on learning proper techniques of etiquette that he frequently overlooks practicing them; and "Dusty of the Circus," the adventures of a young boy who enjoys a special relationship with the animals of his father's circus.

Rounding out the series were such one-time features as "Marvo the Magician," a pompous magician who is outdone by his little bearded assistant; "The Two Magicians," a tiny flutist and a huge tubist whose counterpart includes outrageous practical jokes; "The Last Doubloon," in which a miserly pirate captain is sunk by one doubloon too many; "The Matador and the Troubador," concerning the little brother of a famous matador who confuses bulls with a heel-tapping, flamenco style of fighting; and many others.

The program first aired on CBS in December 1957 and was repeated in 1958. UPA syndicated the package in the late 1960s. In the late 1980s the series was reshown on USA Network under the title *The UPA Cartoon Show. A UPA Production. Color. Half-hour. Premiered on CBS: December 16, 1956–March 10, 1957. Rebroadcast on CBS: May 30, 1958–October 3, 1958. Syndicated. Rebroadcast on USA: Late 1980s.*

### Voices
**Commentator:** Bill Goodwin; **Interpreter of Gerald's sound:** Bill Goodwin

### Other Voices
Marvin Miller

### ◎ THE GET ALONG GANG
Traveling through the countryside in their Clubhouse Caboose, this lovable group of animal friends—Monty, the optimistic, leader moose; Dotty, the superstrong pooch; Woolma, a self-indulgent, cuddly lamb; and Zipper, the supercool cat—lend a helping hand to those in need in this half-hour Saturday-morning series based on a series of popular children's books. *A DIC Enterprises Production in association with Scholastic/Lorimar Productions. Color. Half-hour. Premiered on CBS: September 15, 1984–September 7, 1985. Rebroadcast on CBS: September 14, 1985–August 30, 1986. Rebroadcast on PAX: 1998–1999.*

### Voices
Bettina Bush, Donovan S. Freberg, Timothy Gibbs, Eva Marie Hesse, Georgi Irene, Nick Katt, Robbie Lee, Sherry Lynn, Sparky

Marcus, Scott Menville, Don Messick, Chuck McCann, Frank Welker

## ◎ GET ED

A genetically engineered teen crime-fighter, Ed, with the help of his street-smart team of underground courier friends—Burn, the moto-BMX-riding team leader; Loogie, the wingboard whiz; Dr. Pinch, his make-believe catfish hand puppet; Fizz, the hover-ski loving inventor; and Ol' Skool, their friend and mentor,—battle, Bedlam, the evil bureaucrat who has taken control of Progress City, to save humanity in this futuristic computer-animated action series, created and directed by award-winning director Andy Knight of Disney's direct-to-video sequel *Beauty and the Beast: The Enchanted Christmas*. Featuring high-energy stories, stunts and CG effects, in September 2005 the 3-D animated half-hour series debuted on Toon Disney's Monday through Friday *Jetix* action/adventure programming block and on Saturday and Sunday mornings during the *Jetix* block on the Disney-owned ABC Family. In late August 2006, the series joined other *Jetix* block cartoon series for a final weekend marathon and weekday run on ABC Family, which officially dropped *Jetix* at the end of the month. The program continues to air on Toon Disney. *A Red Rover Studios Production. Color. Half-hour. Premiered on TDIS: September 19, 2005. Rebroadcast on ABC FAM: September 24, 2005–August 31, 2006.*

### Voices
**Ed:** Lyon Smith; **Burn:** L. Dean Ifill; **Deets:** Megan Fahlenbock; **Loogie/Dr. Pinch:** Peter Cugno; **Fizz:** Barley Stocker; **Ol' Skool:** Tony Daniels; **Bedlam:** Jamie Watson; **Crouch:** Antonio Rosato; **Kora:** Jennifer Hale; **DJ Drive:** Heather Bambrick

## ◎ G-FORCE

Short-lived remake of syndicator Sandy Frank's *Battle of the Planets* featuring the same characters as before but with new names and identities. The crew members were now called Ace Goodheart (Mark), Dirk Daring (Jason), Agatha June (Princess), Hootie (Tiny) and Professor Brighthead (Anderson). Even the characters' famous tagline, said when they changed into their battle outfits, was changed from "Transmute!" to "Transform!" Their outer-space archnemesis was renamed Galactor (Zoltar). Only six episodes ever aired on TBS. *A Turner Entertainment Systems Production. Color. Half-hour. Premiered on TBS: September 1986. Rebroadcast on CAR: January 2, 1995–June 28, 1995 (weekdays); September 4, 1995–October 5, 1996 (weekdays, Saturdays); January 9, 2000–March 5, 2000.*

### Voices
**Ace Goodheart, the leader:** Sam Fontana; **Dirk Daring, second in command:** Cameron Clarke; **Professor Brighthead/Hootie:** Jan Rabson; **Agatha June/Pee Wee:** Barbara Goodson; **Galactor:** Bill Capizzi

## ◎ GHOSTBUSTERS

In an effort to capitalize on the Ghostbuster fever spawned by the blockbuster movie, this comedy-adventure series was not based on the Bill Murray–Dan Ackroyd comedy feature but rather a live-action comedy series starring former *F Troop* actors Forrest Tucker and Larry Storch entitled *The Ghost Busters*, which ran on CBS's Saturday-morning schedule in 1975. The animated revival has the same theme: three heroes—two human (Kong and Eddie) and a gorilla (Tracy)—track down ghosts, goblins and gremlins, only this time throughout the universe and back and forth in time. The show featured an all-new voice cast. *A Filmation Studios/Tribune Broadcasting Company Production. Color. Half-hour. Premiered: September 1986. Syndication.*

### Voices
**Eddie Spencer Jr.:** Peter Cullen; **Tracy:** Lou Scheimer; **Jake Kong Jr.:** Patrick Fraley; **Prime Evil:** Alan Oppenheimer; **Futura:** Susan Blu; **Jessica:** Linda Gary; **Jessica's nephew:** Erika Scheimer; **G. B./Haunter:** Erik Gunden

## ◎ GHOST IN THE SHELL: SECOND GIG

Major Kusanagi oversees Japan's Section 9 high-mobility anti-crime unit on a series of new cases, including immigrant uprising and a new terrorist entity that arrives on the scene, in this second season of groundbreaking adventures of the hit anime series *Ghost in the Shell: Stand Alone Complex*. First shown on the Japanese satellite television network, Animax, in January 2004, *Second Gig* aired in the United States on Cartoon Network's late-night *Adult Swim* block. *A Bandai Entertainment/Manga Entertainment/Animaze/ZRO Limit Production. Color. Half-hour. Premiered on CAR: September 17, 2005.*

### Voices
**Major Motoko Kusanagi:** Mary Elizabeth McGlynn; **Chief Daisuke Aramaki/Yousuke Armaki:** William Knight; **Batou:** Richard Epcar; **Togusa:** Crispin Freeman; **Ishiwaka:** Michael McCarty; **Saito:** Dave Wittenberg; **Pazu:** Bob Bucholz; **Boma:** Dean Wein; **Tachikoma:** Sherry Lynn, Rebecca Forstadt, Julie Maddalena, Sandy Fox, Melissa Fahn, Lara Jill Miller, Peggy O'Neal, Bridget Hoffman; **Kubota:** Michael Forest; **Minister of Home Affairs:** Tom Wyner; **Section 9 All-Purpose Female Androids:** Debra Rogers; **Prime Minister Yoko Kayabuki:** Barbara Goodson; **Kazundo Gouda:** John Snyder; **Hideo Kuze:** Kirk Thorton

## ◎ GHOST IN THE SHELL: STAND ALONE COMPLEX

Far into the future, the world's most popular female cyborg, Major Motoko Kusanagi, and her police officers from Section 9 continue to battle criminals in both the real and virtual world, solving everything including the mystery of a defective droid, a runaway high-tech killing machine, and an international murder, in this English-dubbed Japanese anime series—and first of two, followed by *Ghost in the Shell: Second Gig*—based on the cult classic anime feature, *Ghost in the Shell*, and science fiction manga created by Masmume Shirow. A month after Dark Horse Comics published the *Ghost in the Shell 2nd Edition* graphic novel, this stunning Japanese series was the first of two anime cartoon programs Cartoon Network acquired (along with *Fullmetal Alchemist*) and aired during Saturday's highly-rated late-night *Adult Swim* block of animation for adults 18 to 34 beginning in November 2004. That same month, PlayStation2 launched a video game version of the anime series. *A Manga Entertainment/Bandai Entertainment Production. Color. Half-hour. Premiered on CAR: November 6, 2004.*

### Voices
**Major Motoko Kusanagi:** Mary Elizabeth McGlynn; **Chief Daisuke Aramaki:** William Knight; **Batou:** Richard Epcar; **Togusa:** Crispin Freeman; **Ishiwaka:** Michael McCarty; **Saito:** Dave Wittenberg; **Paz:** Robert Bucholz; **Boma:** Dean Wein; **Tachikoma:** Carrie Savage, Julie Maddalena, Peggy O'Neal, Sandy Fox; **Kubota:** Michael Forest; **Prime Minister Kayabuki:** Barbara Goodson; **The Laughing Man:** Steven Blum

## ◎ GIGANTOR

Created by Dr. Sparks, this jet-propelled robot, designed for war but reprogrammed as an agent of peace, battles interplanetary evil with the help of 12-year-old Jimmy Sparks, the doctor's son, who takes over control of the robot after his father's death. In keeping the world free from destruction and despair, Gigantor comes face to face with such world-class villains as Dr. Katsmeow, Danger's Dinosaurs, the Evil Robot Brain, invaders from the planet Magnapus and many others.

Shown on Japanese television from 1963 to 1967, the series rocketed to fame in the United States when the property was acquired and edited for American audiences by Trans-Lux, which distributed many other cartoon favorites, including *Felix the Cat* and *Mighty Mr. Titan*. The program was produced by Fred Ladd (who produced *Astroboy* and *Speed Racer*) and Al Singer. Theme music was by Lou Singer and Gene Raskin.

In the early 1980s an all-new color series, *The New Adventures of Gigantor*, was produced in Japan, where it aired exclusively before debuting in the United States on the Sci-Fi Channel in the fall of 1993. The network briefly considered rerunning the old black-and-white favorite prior to the debut of the new color series but plans to do so never materialized.

Originally created by manga author Mitsuteru Yokoyama, best known for such Japanese creations as *Giant Robo* and *Tetsujin 28*, in late October 2006 Cartoon Network began rerunning the popular 1960s anime series weekdays at 5:30 A.M., preceded by rebroadcasts of another futuristic robot cartoon series, *Big O*. *A TCJ Animation Center Production. Black-and-White. Half-hour. Premiered: January 5, 1966. Syndicated. Rebroadcast on SCI: 1993. Rebroadcast on CAR: February 24, 2003–February 28, 2003; October 31, 2005–February 17, 2006; October 31, 2006–*.

### Voices
Billie Lou Watt, Peter Fernandez, Gilbert Mack, Cliff Owens

*A jet-propelled robot reprogrammed as an agent of peace battles interplanetary evil in the Japanese animated cult favorite* Gigantor. (COURTESY: SCOTT WHEELER PRODUCTIONS)

## ◎ G.I. JOE (1989)

The overall goal of the COBRA special mission force is to master the power of Dragonfire, a natural energy like electricity—only infinitely more powerful—that is found in underground "lakes of fire" in a few locations around the world. Their mission is to tap the most powerful repository of all beneath Sorcerer's Mesa, an American Indian site in New Mexico, in this five-part miniseries based on the adventures of the popular syndicated series of the same name. *A DIC Enterprises Production. Color. Half-hour. Premiered: September 16, 1989. Syndicated. Rebroadcast: 1990–92 (syndication). Rebroadcast on USA: 1992–96.*

### Voices
**Sergeant Slaughter:** Bob Remis; **Rock 'N Roll:** Kevin Conway; **Scoop:** Michael Benyaer; **Cobra Commander:** Chris Latta (later Chris Collins); **Destro/Copperhead/Lowlight/Serpentor/Spirit:** Maurice LaMarche; **Alley Viper:** Jim Byrnes; **Gnawga Hyde/ Rampart:** Ian Corlett; **Lady J:** Suzanne Emmett-Balcom; **Duke:** Ted Harrison; **Hawk:** Gerry Nairne; **Sub Zero:** Don Brown; **Mutt/ Gridiron:** Dale Wilson; **Bullhorn:** David Wills; **Ambush/Night Creeper Leader:** Andrew Koenig; **Stretcher:** Alvin Sanders; **Path Finder/Metal Head:** Gary Chalk; **Salvo:** Brent Chapman; **Stalker:** Lee Jeffrey; **Zarana:** Lisa Corps; **Baroness:** Morgan Lofting

## ◎ G.I. JOE: A REAL AMERICAN HERO (1985)

American television viewers first got a glimpse of the heroic escapades of famed comic-book hero G.I. Joe in television's first animated miniseries, *G.I. Joe: A Real American Hero*, broadcast in syndication for the 1983–84 season. A second five-part syndicated miniseries, *G.I. Joe II*, was produced the following season. In the fall of 1985 *G.I. Joe* became a daily, 90-episode animated half-hour series. It featured the further adventures of America's highly trained mission force who outwit the forces of COBRA, a terrorist organization, led by villains Destro and the Baroness.

Because the G.I. Joe characters were so strongly defined as defenders of right against wrong, the series incorporated 30-second messages, with the characters showing young viewers "dos" and "don'ts" in such areas as safety, health and nutrition.

In 1992, at the end of its syndicated run, USA Network began reairing the entire package of first-run episodes through the fall of 1996. On July 1, 2002 at midnight, as a real treat to two generations of fans, Cartoon Network aired 30 episodes of the Marvel/Sunbow syndicated series as part of a six-week trial, repeating the same episodes several days a week later reduced (to once a week) until the show was dropped in August 2003. *A Marvel Production in association with Sunbow Productions. Color. Half-hour. Premiered: September 12, 1983–September 16, 1983; September 10, 1984–September 14, 1985 (as five-part miniseries). Premiered: September 16, 1985–1990 (series). Syndicated. Rebroadcast on USA: September 14, 1992–September 15, 1996. Rebroadcast on CAR: July 1, 2002–August 2, 2003.*

### Voices
Charlie Adler, Jack Angel, Liz Aubrey, Jackson Beack, Michael Bell, Arthur Burghardt, Corey Burton, Bill Callaway, Peter Cullen, Brian Cummings, Pat Fraley, Hank Garrett, Dick Gautier, Ed Gilbert, Dan Gilvezan, Dave Hall, Zack Hoffman, Kene Holiday, Jerry Houser, Chris Latta, Loren Lester, Mary McDonald Lewis, Chuck McCann, Michael McConnohie, Rob Paulsen, Pat Pinney, Lisa Raggio, Bill Ratner, Hal Rayle, Bob Remus, Neil Ross, Will Ryan, Ted Schwartz, John Stephenson, B.J. Ward, Lee Weaver, Frank Welker, Stan Wojno, Keone Young

## ◉ G.I. JOE: EXTREME

A new hand-picked assault team of dedicated, covert operation agents work round-the-clock as peacekeepers, on military maneuvers, to protect the world from the heavily armed forces of SKAR in this third half-hour series based in part on the popular Hasbro toy. The series debuted in syndication in September of 1995. *A Sunbow Production. Color. Half-hour. Premiered: September 23, 1995–Fall 1997. Syndicated.*

### Voices
**Mayday:** Randall Carpenter; **Stone:** Gary Chalk; **Inferno:** Ian James Corlett; **Sgt. Savage:** Michael Dobson; **Eagle Eye:** Brian Drummon; **Metal Head:** Matt Hill; **Black Dragon:** Terry Klassen; **Mr. Clancy:** Campbell Lane; **Freight/Quick Stryke:** Blu Mankuma; **Rampage:** Colin Murdock; **Iron Klaw:** Richard Newman; **Steel Raven:** Elizabeth Carol Savenkoff; **Harpoon:** Francisco Trujillo; **Wreckage/The President/Red:** Dale Wilson

## ◉ G.I. JOE SIGMA 6

Forced to retaliate after their Arctic headquarters is ambushed and the imprisoned COBRA commander escapes, G.I. Joe team leader Duke suits up with the rest of his special forces unit—Scarlett, Tunnel Rat, Snake Eyes, Heavy Duty and others—now called Sigma 6 and protected by high-tech body suits, to battle their arch-enemy, COBRA, in this 21st-century animated series adaptation of the legendary Hasbro toy action figure, produced more than 40 years after its creation.

Featuring special emphasis on secret agent technology and more stylistic flair than previous animated versions, this high-charged, action-packed Saturday-morning series was shown in half-hour blocks on FOX's *4Kids TV* programming block (formerly *FOX Box*), along with other well-known and popular animated properties, including *The Winx Club, Teenage Mutant Ninja Turtles* and *Sonic X.* Produced by Japanese animation studio, GONZO, and 4Kids Entertainment, the series—which tied in with a new line of Hasbro action-figures and toys—featured 13 episodes during the first season, followed by 13 more in its second season. *A 4Kids Entertainment/GONZO Production. Color. Half-hour. Premiered on FOX: August 27, 2005 (sneak peek). Premiered on FOX: September 10, 2005 (series).*

### Voices
**Duke:** Dave Willis, Frank Frankson; **Scarlett:** Veronica Taylor; **Long Range:** Scottie Ray; **Tunnel Rat/Kamakura:** Mike Sinterniklaas; **Heavy Duty:** David Wills; **Hi-Tech:** Eric Stuart; **Snake Eyes:** Jason Griffith; **Jinx:** Lisa Ortiz; **Kamakura/Spirit:** Marc Thompson; **General Hawk:** Anthony Salemo; **Scott:** Matthew Charles; **Cobra Commander/Destro/Zartan:** Marc Thompson; **Baroness:** Amy Birnbaum; **Storm Shadow:** Ed Paul; **Buzzer:** Wayne Grayson; **Stone:** Dan Green; **Firefly:** Sean Schemmel; **Baroness:** Bella Hudson, Kayzie Rogers; **Matchete/Overkill:** Michael Alston Baley; **Other Voices:** Andrew Pauli, Dana Southern, Erica Schroeder, Jack Quevas, Kelly Davis, Liza Jacqueline, Pete Zarustica, Wendy Gaunt

## ◉ GILLIGAN'S PLANET

Most of the original cast of television's favorite castaways provided their voices for this updated version of the classic network sitcom in which the crew board a powerful rocket ship built by the Professor that launches them off their island and maroons them on a remote planet in outer space. One new addition to the cast: a pet alien adopted by Gilligan named Bumper. *A Filmation Associates Production. Color. Half-hour. Premiered on CBS: September 18, 1982–September 10, 1983.*

### Voices
**Gilligan, the first mate:** Bob Denver; **Jonas Grumby, the skipper:** Alan Hale, Jr.; **Thurston Howell III:** Jim Backus; **Lovey Howell, his wife:** Natalie Schafer; **Ginger Grant, the movie star:** Dawn Wells; **Mary Ann Summers, the clerk:** Dawn Wells; **Roy Hinkley, the professor:** Russell Johnson

## ◉ GIRL STUFF/BOY STUFF

Six young teens—three boys (Ben, Jason and Simon) and three girls (Talia, Hanna and Reanne)—who have been best friends forever learn more about each other while exploring their friendships and the world around them in this Canadian-produced half-hour animated series, first seen in the United States weeknights at 6:00 P.M. on The N in late May 2003. Later moved to 5:30 A.M., the series remained on the air until September 2004. *A DECODE Entertainment/YTV Production. Color. Half-hour. Premiered on the N: May 26, 2003–September 19, 2004.*

### Voices
**Hanna:** Carly Stipanic; **Jason:** Jesse Dubinsky; **Reanne:** Kathyleen Johnston; **Ben:** Brennan Stang; **Talia:** Heidi Emery; **Simon:** Matt Rubel

## ◉ GLO FRIENDS

An influx of soft and cuddly characters entered the mainstream of animated-cartoon fare following the success of *The Smurfs* and *Care Bears.* This series was no exception, featuring friendly, fearless creatures whose magical glow makes them extra appealing not only to children but to the mean Moligans. *A Marvel Production in association with Sunbow Productions. Color. Half-hour. Premiered: September 16, 1986. Syndicated.*

### Voices
Charlie Adler, Michael Bell, Susan Blu, Bettina Bush, Joey Camen, Roger C. Carmel, Nancy Cartwright, Townsend Coleman, Jeanine Elias, Pat Fraley, Ellen Gerstell, Skip Hinnant, Keri Houlihan, Katie Leigh, Sherry Lynn, Mona Marshall, Scott Menville, Sarah Partridge, Hal Rayle, Will Ryan, Susan Silo, Russi Taylor, B.J. Ward, Jill Wayne, Frank Welker

## ◉ GO DIEGO GO!

Wearing a Rescue Pack that can transform into any object and possessing an uncanny ability to communicate with animals, Dora the Explorer's resourceful eight-year-old bilingual cousin, Diego Márquez, embarks on daring animal rescue missions in the rain forests of Latin America with his 11-year-old computer whiz sister, Alicia, employing state-of-the-art gadgets, including his talking camera Click (voiced by Rosie Perez) and a computer, to access vital information about every animal he helps in this animated spin-off of Nickelodeon's highly successful daytime preschool series, *Dora the Explorer.*

Nickelodeon ordered 16 half-hour episodes of this all-new children's series that debuted weekdays on Nick Jr. and Saturday mornings on CBS's *Nick Jr. on CBS* cartoon block in September 2005. That December, the Latino pair starred in their first half-hour holiday special that premiered on Nick Jr. and Noggin, *Diego Saves Christmas.* Continually producing high ratings in its time slot, in December 2006 Nick ordered 20 new episodes for the 2007–08 season. *A Nickelodeon Studios Production. Color. Half-hour. Premiered on NICK JR.: September 6, 2005. Premiered on CBS: September 2005–September 25, 2006.*

### Voices
**Diego Márquez:** Jake T. Austin; **Alicia Márquez:** Constanza Sperakis; **Click:** Rosie Perez

## GOD, THE DEVIL AND BOB

Disgusted by the ways of the world, a Jerry Garcia-like God (voiced by James Garner) plans to destroy the planet unless the Devil can find someone who can prove that all is right in the world. Instead, the Devil finds Bob Alman, a disgusting, porn-watching, alcoholic Detroit autoworker with an attitude who becomes God's "Go-To-Guy" in this short-lived, adult-geared prime-time 'toon for NBC. Created by Matthew Carlson, after premiering in early March 2000, the half-hour comedy series was quickly canceled, due to the pressure from Christian groups unhappy with the series' depiction of religion; only four of the series' 13 original episodes were aired. Conversely, the series played well in other countries, like Brazil and the United Kingdom, which telecast it in its entirety on FOX and BBC2 networks. In the United States, beginning in June 2003, the program was also reshown as part of Trio cable network's *Uncensored Comedy: That's Not Funny* program block comprised of other short-lived comedy programs. A Vanity Logo Productions/Carsey-Warner Company Production. Color. Half-hour. Premiered on NBC: March 9, 2000–March 28, 2000. Rebroadcast on TRIO: June 9, 2003.

### Voices
**God:** James Garner; **The Devil:** Alan Cumming; **Bob Alman:** French Stewart; **Donna Alman:** Laurie Metcalf; **Andy Alman:** Kath Soucie; **Megan Alman:** Nancy Cartwright; **Smeck:** Jeff Doucette

## GODZILLA AND THE SUPER 90

Formerly this series was called *The Godzilla Power Hour*, but the half-hour adventures of *Jonny Quest* were added to boost the show's ratings and the title was therefore changed to reflect the program's newly expanded format.

Godzilla, the show's star, appeared in one segment as a friendly dragon joining forces with a scientist, Carl Rogers, to battle evil. Another segment, "Jana of the Jungle," focused on the adventures of a girl searching for her lost father in the rain forest where she lived as a child. The "Jana of the Jungle" cartoons were later bundled in half-hours and rebroadcast on USA Network's *Cartoon Express*. A Hanna-Barbera Production in association with Toho Co. Ltd. and Benedict Pictures Corporation. Color. Ninety minutes. Premiered on NBC: November 4, 1978–September 1, 1979; September 9, 1978–October 28, 1978 (as The Godzilla Power Hour). Rebroadcast on USA: February 27, 1989–March 22, 1991 (Jana of the Jungle).

### Voices
**Godzilla:** Ted Cassidy; **Capt. Carl Rogers:** Jeff David; **Quinn, Carl's aide:** Brenda Thompson; **Pete, Carl's aide:** Al Eisenmann; **Brock, Pete's friend:** Hilly Hicks; **Godzooky, Godzilla's sidekick:** Don Messick; **Jana of the Jungle:** B.J. Ward; **Montaro:** Ted Cassidy; **Dr. Ben Cooper:** Michael Bell; **Natives:** Ross Martin; **Jonny Quest:** Tim Matthieson; **Dr. Benton Quest, his father:** John Stephenson; **Roger "Race" Bannon:** Mike Road; **Hadji, Indian companion:** Danny Bravo; **Bandit, their dog:** Don Messick

## THE GODZILLA POWER HOUR
(See GODZILLA AND THE SUPER 90.)

## THE GODZILLA SHOW

The favorite prehistoric monster comes alive again in new tales of adventure and suspense saving the day for all mankind in times of natural or supernatural disaster. This was the third series try for Hanna-Barbera, featuring the 400-foot-tall creature. Previously the character starred in the short-lived 1978 NBC series The *Godzilla Power Hour*, which was replaced after only two months by *Godzilla and the Super 90*, an expanded version with the addition of classic *Jonny Quest* episodes to its roster.

In November 1979 NBC combined *Godzilla* with reruns of *The Harlem Globetrotters* retitling the series, *The Godzilla/Globetrotters Adventure Hour*. By September 1980 that series had been replaced by *The Godzilla/Dynomutt Hour with Funky Phantom*. Like the former it featured reruns of previously broadcast Godzilla episodes and of network-run episodes of *Dynomutt, Dog Wonder* and *The Funky Phantom*. Two months after its debut, the program was changed again. Dynomutt and the Funky Phantom were shelved in place of Hanna-Barbera's former network hit *Hong Kong Phooey*, which was paired with Godzilla under the title of *The Godzilla/Hong Kong Phooey Hour*. (See *The Godzilla and the Super 90* and individual series for voice credits and further details.)

A Hanna-Barbera Production in association with Toho Co. Ltd. and Benedict Pictures. Color. Half-hour. Premiered on NBC: September 8, 1979–November 3, 1979; November 10, 1979–September 20, 1980 (as The Godzilla/Globetrotters Adventure Hour), September 27, 1980–November 15, 1980 (as The Godzilla/Dynomutt Hour with the Funky Phantom); November 22, 1980–May 16, 1981 (as The Godzilla/Hong Kong Phooey Hour). Rebroadcast on NBC: May 23, 1981–September 5, 1981 (as The Godzilla Show). Rebroadcast on CAR: December 6, 1993–April 29, 1994 (weekdays); September 5, 1994–September 1, 1995 (weekdays); March 25, 1996–May 30, 1999 (weekdays); 2000.

## GODZILLA: THE SERIES

Accompanied by Godzilla's 180-foot-tall giant reptile sibling, an environmental research team—known as H.E.A.T. (Humanitarian Ecological Analysis Team)—travel in its sophisticated aquatic vessel called the Heat Seeker and is headed by noted biologist Nick Tatapoulous, to battle a new generation of giant monsters who wreak havoc in this sequel to TriStar Pictures' full-length feature *Godzilla* (1998). Picking up where the movie concluded in a two-part premiere, the half-hour animated action-adventure, intended for first-run syndication—and the first animated adaptation since Hanna-Barbera's 1979 Saturday-morning series, *The Godzilla Show* for NBC—aired Saturday mornings in the United States on FOX. Broadcast for two seasons, the series re-aired on FOX Family Channel. An Adelaide Productions/Columbia TriStar (later known as Sony Pictures Entertainment) Production. Color. Half-hour. Premiered on FOX: September 12, 1998–April 29, 2000. Rebroadcast on FOX FAM: 2000–01.

### Voices
**Dr. Nick Tatopoulos:** Ian Ziering; **Dr. Mendel Craven:** Malcolm Danare; **Randy Hernandez:** Rino Romano; **Monique Dupre:** Brigitte Bako; **N.I.G.E.L.** Tom Kenny; **Dr. Elsie Chapman:** Charity James; **Philippe Roache:** Keith Szarbarajka; **Mayor:** Michael Lerner; **Major Tony Hicks:** Kevin Dunn; **Audrey Timmonds:** Paget Brewster; **Victor "Animal" Palotti:** Joe Pantoliano

## GO GO GOPHERS

CBS added this half-hour series to its 1968 fall schedule featuring repeat episodes of *Go Go Gophers*, in which renegade Indians Running Board and Ruffled Feathers match wits with the blustering Colonel Kit Coyote of the U.S. calvary, and "Klondike Kat," the exploits of an idiotic mountie and the elusive cheese-stealing mouse Savoir Faire. Each component was originally featured on CBS's *Underdog* cartoon series. (See *Underdog* for voice credits.) A Total TV Production with Leonardo TV Productions. Color. Half-hour. Premiered on CBS: September 14, 1968–September 6, 1969.

*A gorgeous gadabout uses limitless wealth to pursue adventure with an exotic array of James Bond-like gadgetry in* Goldie Gold and Action Jack. *© Ruby-Spears Enterprises*

## ◎ GOLDIE GOLD AND ACTION JACK

A gorgeous, wealthy 18-year-old, Goldie Gold, publisher of the *Gold Street Journal*, is a female James Bond who embarks on 13 exciting half-hour adventures with her reporter/bodyguard Jack Travis, her editor Sam Gritt and her labrador Nugget to pursue stories and solve madcap capers with the aid of 007-type gadgetry. *A Ruby-Spears Enterprises Production. Color. Half-hour. Premiered on ABC: September 12, 1981–September 18, 1982. Rebroadcast on CAR: January 8, 1994 (Saturdays). Rebroadcast on BOOM: January 5, 2003–March 21, 2004.*

### Voices
**Goldie Gold:** Judy Strangis; **Jack Travis, her reporter:** Sonny Melendrez; **Sam Gritt, her editor:** Booker Bradshaw

## ◎ GOOBER AND THE GHOST CHASERS

Using a similar format to *Scooby Doo, Where Are You?* Hanna-Barbera animated the adventures of reporters Tina, Ted, Gillie and Goober, their dog, who investigate haunted houses and ghoulish mysteries for *Ghost Chasers* magazine. Goober is a meek character who actually becomes invisible when frightened by beasties or ghoulies.

The 17-episode half-hour series spotlighted guest stars throughout the season. The most regular were The Partridge Family in cartoon form. The program was later packaged as part of *Fred Flintstone and Friends* for syndication and again rebroadcast on USA Network's *Cartoon Express*. *A Hanna-Barbera Production. Color. Half-hour. Premiered on ABC: September 8, 1973–August 31, 1975. Rebroadcast on USA: February 28, 1989–March 25, 1991. Rebroadcast on BOOM: February 5, 2001–January 1, 2003.*

### Voices:
**Goober:** Paul Winchell; **Gillie:** Ronnie Schell; **Ted:** Jerry Dexter; **Tina:** Jo Anne Harris

**THE PARTRIDGE FAMILY: Laurie Partridge:** Susan Dey; **Chris Partridge:** Brian Forster; **Tracy Partridge:** Suzanne Crough; **Danny Partridge:** Danny Bonaduce

## ◎ GOOF TROOP

Moving to a neighborhood in the small, quiet town of Spoonerville, beloved bumbler Goofy, now a man of the 1990s, is a single father raising a rather obnoxious 11-year-old son, Max, whose outlook on life is far different from his dad's. His neighbor is Mickey Mouse's old nemesis, Pete—alias Pegleg Pet and Black Pete—now a respectable surbuanite, and son Pegleg Pete Jr.—P.J. for short—who hangs out with Max at the local mall. Conflicts between Goofy and Max and Goofy's attempts to fit into his new neighborhood become the basis of weekly story lines in this first-run, 78-episode half-hour series that debuted on The Disney Channel in April of 1992, in celebration of Goofy's 60th birthday. The series was moved to syndication in September of 1992 as part of the *Disney Afternoon* two-hour cartoon block (preceded by a two-hour special, *Disney's Goof Troop*, to launch the syndicated series); it replaced *Duck Tales*. Thirteen additional episodes of the series were broadcast concurrently on ABC's Saturday-morning schedule that September as well. A half-hour holiday special, *A Goof Troop Christmas*, was also produced. In September of 1996, the program began airing weekdays (in reruns) on The Disney Channel. *A Walt Disney Television Animation Production. Color. Half-hour. Premiered on DIS: April 20, 1992. Premiered on ABC: September 12, 1992–September 11, 1993. Syndicated: September 7, 1992–August 30, 1996. Rebroadcast on DIS: September 2, 1996–2000 (weekdays). Rebroadcast on TDIS: April 1998–late 2004.*

### Voices
**Goofy:** Bill Farmer; **Max:** Dana Hill; **Pete:** Jim Cummings; **P.J.:** Rob Paulsen; **Peg:** April Winchell; **Pistol:** Nancy Cartwright; **Burly Guy/"How-to" Narrator/Melvin/Ring Master/School Dean:** Corey Burton; **Fenton Sludge:** Jay Thomas; **Waffles/Chainsaw:** Frank Welker

## ◎ GORDON THE GARDEN GNOME

Delightful animated series following the genuinely cheerful and optimistic gnome, Gordon, and his daily adventures as a gardener working alongside his many animal friends, including his best friend, Andrew the Worm, and gnome neighbors. Produced by British entertainment giant, Collingwood O'Hare Entertainment, and originally voiced by England's beloved television personality Alan Titchmarsh, this fun-filled, educational, 26-episode half-hour series premiered in August 2005 on Cartoon Network. The daily children's series was part of the network's all-new—albeit short-lived—weekday preschool block, *Tickle-U*, including a collection of new animated programs, including *Firehouse Tales*, *Gerald McBoing Boing*, *Harry and His Bucket Full of Dinosaurs*, *Peppa Pig* and *Yoko! Jakamoko! Toto!* Revoiced by American actors, the weekday children's series was canceled after one season, along with Cartoon Network's entire Tickle-U programming block. *A Collingwood O'Hare Entertainment Ltd. Production in association with Southern Star. Color. Half-hour. Premiered on CAR: August 22, 2005–January 13, 2006.*

## ◎ THE GRIM ADVENTURES OF BILLY & MANDY

Macabre, hilarious half-hour comedy series following an unusual pair of kids—Billy, the easily amused, cartoon and video game-loving, dim-witted boy and Mandy, his wise, unflappable scheming friend—who trick the legendary Grim Reaper into becoming "best friends forever" after beating the famed messenger of death in an otherworldly limbo contest, with the strange trio handling a host of challenges in both the spirit world and the average American town of Endsville.

First shown as a 10-minute pilot in August 2000 during Cartoon Network's *The Big Pick* weekend (when it was voted by viewers the best among three final animated shorts that aired; the others were *Whatever Happened to Robot Jones?* and *Longhair and Doubledome*), the characters were spun-off a year later into their own half-hour special and, finally, into their own full-fledged half-hour series beginning in the summer of 2003.

After starring in 13 first-season episodes and becoming one of Cartoon Network's most popular shows, particularly among boys, the network renewed the series for a second season. In June 2003, the program returned with 10 new episodes of otherworldly animated insanity, including its first starring half-hour special, *Billy & Mandy's Jacked Up Halloween*. Two years later, in December 2005, the characters helped ring in the holidays with their first one-hour prime-time special, *Billy & Mandy Save Christmas*.

With 52 additional episodes airing through March 2007, later that month the characters starred in their first-ever 90-minute TV movie, *Billy & Mandy's Big Boogey Adventure*, released on DVD a few days after its original broadcast. *A Cartoon Network Studios/Castle Creek Production. Color. Half-hour. Premiered on CAR: June 13, 2003.*

*Voices*

**Billy/Harold, Billy's Dad:** Richard Steven Horvitz; **Mandy/Milkshakes:** Grey DeLisle; **Grim Reaper/Sperg:** Greg Eagles; **Irwin/Mandy's Mom:** Vanessa Marshall; **Gladys, Billy's Mom:** Jennifer Hale; **Mindy/Eris:** Rachael MacFarlane; **Irwin's Dad:** Phil LaMarr; **Phil, Mandy's Dad:** Dee Bradley Baker; **Hoss Delgado:** Diedrich Bader; **Nergal:** David Warner (Seasons 1–2), Martin Jarvis (Seasons 2–  ); **Nergal Junior:** Debi Derryberry; **Piff/Jeff the Spider:** Maxwell Atoms; **Pud'n:** Jane Carr; **General Skarr:** Armin Shimerman; **Fred Freburger:** C.H. Greenblatt

### ⊚ GRIM & EVIL

This offbeat, slapstick comedy series was selected from a group of submissions during Cartoon Network's *Big Pick* contest in 2000 and was first produced as a pilot that year. Shown that August on the network's highly touted late-night *Adult Swim* cartoon block, it featured two 2-D animated 12-minute cartoon segments: "The Grim Adventures of Billy and Mandy," following the comical exploits of the dreaded Grim Reaper and his new "best friends," and "Evil Con Carne," which offered the unusual exploits of a criminally insane brain set on conquering the world. Lasting two seasons, besides appearing in a half-hour special in 2001, in the summer of 2003 both segments were produced as standalone half-hour series. *A Rough Draft Studios Inc. Production. Color. Half-hour. Premiered on CAR: August 24, 2001–October 18, 2002.*

*Voices*

**Mandy/Major Dr. Ghastly:** Grey DeLisle; **Grim:** Greg Eagles; **Billy/Harold:** Richard Horvitz; **Gladys:** Jennifer Hale; **Hector Con Carne:** Phil LaMarr; **Bosko the Bear/Cod Commando:** Jesse Corti; **Boskov the Bear:** Frank Welker; **General Skarr:** Armin Shimerman

### ⊚ GRIMM'S FAIRY TALES

Recalling those classic children's stories of the past, this beautifully animated half-hour series is a collection of the world-famous Grimm's Fairy Tales, presenting colorful retellings of such favorite tales as "Hansel and Gretel," "Snow White," "Puss N' Boots" and "Little Red Riding Hood." The series premiered on Nickelodeon's Nick Jr. *A Nippon Animation/Saban Entertainment Production. Color. Half-hour. Premiered on NICK JR.: September 1989.*

### ⊚ THE GROOVIE GOOLIES

Humble Hall residents Count Dracula; Hagatha, his plump wife; Frankie, their son; Bella La Ghostly, the switchboard operator; Sabrina, the teenage witch; Wolfie, the werewolf; Bonapart, the accident-prone skeleton; Mummy, Bonapart's buddy; and others haunt trespassers with practical jokes and ghoulish mischief in this movie-monster spoof produced for Saturday-morning television. The characters were originally introduced on 1970's *Sabrina and the Groovie Goolies* series on CBS, before they were resurrected by the network in their own weekly series in 1971. The series ran one full season on CBS and was later repeated on ABC during the 1975–76 season, replacing *Uncle Croc's Block*. *A Filmation Associates Production. Color. Half-hour. Premiered on CBS: September 12, 1971–September 3, 1972. Rebroadcast on ABC: October 25, 1975– September 5, 1976.*

*Voices*

**Frankie/Wolfie/Mummy/Ghouland:** Howard Morris; **Hagatha/ Aunt Hilda/Aunt Zelda/Bella La Ghostly/Broomhilda/Sabrina:** Jane Webb; **Count "Drac"/Ratzo:** Larry Storch; **Bonapart/Dr. Jekyll-Hyde/Batzo/Hauntleroy:** Larry Mann

### ⊚ GROOVIE GOOLIES AND FRIENDS

Like Hanna-Barbera, Filmation Studios packaged for worldwide syndication their own collection of previous cartoon hits: *Groovie Goolies, The Adventures of Waldo Kitty, Lassie's Rescue Rangers, The New Adventures of Gilligan, My Favorite Martian,* and 18 half-hour combinations of *M.U.S.H., Fraidy Cat* and *Wacky and Packy*. (See individual cartoon components for series information.) *A Filmation Associates Production. Color. Half-hour. Premiered: September 1978. Syndicated.*

### ⊚ GROWING UP CREEPIE

Raised by a family of insects—Caroleena, her praying mantis mom; Vinnie, her mosquito dad; and Gnat and Pauly, her two brothers, living in the creepy Dweezold Mansion, Creepie, an orphan teenage girl, struggles to adjust to middle school and to keep secret her family upbringing, in this latest addition to Discovery Kids' *Real Toons* lineup—co-produced by Discovery Kids, DAG and The Story Hat, LLC—that debuted in September 2006. *A Discovery Kids/DAG Entertainment/The Story Hat LLC Production. Color. Half-hour. Premiered on DSCK: September 4, 2006.*

*Voices*

**Creepie/Melanie:** Athena Karkanis; **Caroleena/Mrs. Monsteratte:** Julie Lemieux; **Vinnie:** Dwayne Hill; **Gnat:** Steve Vallance; **Pauly:** David Berni; **Harry Helby:** Scott McCord; **Dr. Pappas:** Juan Chiovan; **Chris-Alice Hollyruler:** Leah Cudmore; **Budge (Beauregard Bentley II):** Richard Yearwood; **Carla:** Stephanie Anne Mills

### ⊚ GRUNT AND PUNT

A cartoon pig and boar review NFL plays of the week in this live-action/animated series of Saturday-morning specials first aired on FOX. Debuting in October 1994 in place of FOX's animated children's series, *Where on Earth Is Carmen Sandiego?*, the series— also known as *The Grunt and Punt Show*—aired monthly for four consecutive months through mid-January 1995 and later aired in syndication. Former Nickelodeon *Nicktoons* cartoon block creative consultant Howard Hoffman created the characters, which were designed by Academy Award–nominated animator and *Courage the Cowardly Dog* creator John R. Dilworth. *A Jumbo Pictures/Indigo Entertainment/NFL Films Production. Color. Half-hour. Premiered on FOX: October 29, 1994; November 26, 1994; December 17, 1994; January 28, 1995. Syndicated.*

### ⊚ THE GUMBY SHOW

The adventures of this lovable green clay figure and his pet horse, Pokey, first appeared as a Saturday-morning kids' show on NBC in

1957. Created by Art Clokey (also the creator of TV's *Davey and Goliath*), the stop-action animated series was spun off from *Howdy Doody*, on whose program Gumby was first introduced in 1956. Adventures were filmed via the process of pixillation—filming several frames at a time, moving the characters slightly, and then shooting more frames to achieve continuous motion.

Originally Bob Nicholson, best known for his portrayal of Clarabell and Cornelius Cobb on *Howdy Doody*, hosted the NBC program as the character Scotty McKee, later comedian Pinky Lee was host.

The full-color six-minute, two- and three-part adventures that made up the half-hour series were produced under the direction of superb stop-motion filmmaker Raymond Peck and offered for syndication in late 1959, mostly to NBC affiliates. A new syndicated package was offered to independent television stations in 1966. (In all, 130 *Gumby* episodes were produced.) The original series was rebroadcast on Disney Channel in 1983, and, in 1988, creator Art Clokey produced a brand-new, daily 65-episode half-hour series of adventures, *All-New Gumby*, for syndication. (See series entry for details.) Nickelodeon reaired the old series weekdays for three seasons beginning in 1994 as did Cartoon Network from 1998 to 2001. *An Art Clokey Production. Color. Half-hour. Premiered on NBC: March 16, 1957–November 16, 1957. Syndicated: 1959, 1966. Rebroadcast on DIS: 1983. Rebroadcast on NICK: June 6, 1994–May 31, 1997. Rebroadcast on CAR: 1998–2001 (as Gumby Adventure).*

**Voices**
**Gumby:** Art Clokey, Dallas McKennon; **Pokey:** Art Clokey

## ◎ GUNDAM SEED

With a cosmic war raging between Earth and the colonies, including the Earth Alliance and the Zodiac Alliance of Freedom Treaty (ZAFT), young Kira Yamato leads the fearless Strike Gundam force to fight his sinister old enemy Athrun Zala and ZAFT, who have stolen four prototype Gundams for evil purposes. Licensed for North American broadcast and redubbed in English by Bandai Entertainment, the futuristic 50-episode half-hour science fiction action series—also known as *Mobile Suit Gundam SEED*—debuted in the United States on Cartoon Network's highly rated Saturday night *Toonami* block in April 2004, followed that May by 20 new episodes of its anime counterpart, *Dragonball GT*. *A Sunrise/Bandai Visual Production. Color. Half-hour. Premiered on CAR: April 17, 2004.*

**Voices**
**Kira Yamato:** Matt Hill; **Lacus Clyne:** Chantal Strand; **Athrun Zala:** Samuel Vincent; **Muruta Azrael:** Andrew Francis; **Miriallia Haw:** Anna Cummer; **Sai Argyle:** Bill Switzer; **Dearka Elsman:** Bradd Swaile; **Romero Pal:** Brendan Van Wijk; **Martin DaCosta:** Brian Dobson; **Nicol Amalfi:** Gabe Khouth; **Kuzzey Buskirk:** Keith Miller; **Murrue Ramius:** Lisa Ann Beley; **Rau Le Creuset:** Mark Oliver; **Jackie Tonomura:** Matt Smith; **Yzak Joule:** Michael Adamthwaite; **Arnold Neuman:** Philip Pacaud; **Tolle Koening:** Richard Cox; **Natarle Badgiruel:** Sarah Johns; **Dalida Lolaha Chandra II:** Simon Hayama; **Flay Allster:** Tabitha St. Germain; **Crot Buer:** Ted Cole; **Mu La Flaga:** Trevor Devall; **Cagalli Yula Athha:** Vanessa Morley

## ◎ .HACK/SIGN

In the year 2010, five years after the great network crash of 2005 and the release of "The World," the first multiplayer online role playing game, after online entertainment had been largely prohibited, an introverted young boy, Tsukasa, found alive inside the popular video game and unable to return to the real world, is pursued by the evil

Ginkan and the Scarlet Knights in this popular anime series. First shown in Japan on TV Tokyo in 2002, this weekly, 25-episode half-hour fantasy action/adventure series was redubbed in English and exclusively broadcast in the United States by Cartoon Network on weekends in its original widescreen format. *A Project.hack/TV Tokyo/Bandai Entertainment/PCB Production. Color. Half-hour. Premiered on CAR: February 1, 2003–March 1, 2004.*

**Voices**
**Tsukasa:** Brianne Siddall; **Mimiru:** Amanda Winn Lee; **Sora:** Dave Wittenberg; **Subaru:** Kim Mai Guest; **BT:** Donna Rawlins; **Bear:** Paul Mercier; **Crim:** Lex Lang; **Morganna:** Valerie Arem; **A-20:** Sandy Fox; **Silver Knight:** Doug Rye

## ◎ HAMMERMAN

Rap singer M.C. Hammer, who changed his name simply to Hammer, starred in this weekly half-hour animated series as a mild-mannered children's recreation center employee who, upon donning a pair of "magic dancing shoes," turns into a fleet-footed, urban crime-fighting superhero. *A DIC Enterprises Production in association with Bustin' Productions. Color. Half-hour. Premiered on ABC: September 9, 1991–September 5, 1992.*

**Voices**
**Hammer/Stanley Kirk Burrell:** Hammer

## ◎ HAMTARO

An outsized, wide-eyed, big-eared, round-faced and small-limbed hamster, Hamtaro, sneaks out when his 10-year-old owner, Laura, and her parents are away, embarking on a series of challenging adventures with his underground pals, the Ham-Ham gang. Based on author Ritusko Kawai's top-selling illustrated children's storybooks and first introduced to Japanese television audiences in July 2000, it became one of TV Tokyo's highest-rated programs; this English-language adaptation of the popular Japanese anime series, *Tottoko Hamtaro*, joined Cartoon Network's Monday-through-Friday schedule in the summer of 2002. Fast becoming one of Japan's hottest children's television programs to air continuously on Cartoon Network, the show's U.S. premiere was tied with the launch of a major merchandising campaign by Hasbro that included assorted licensed dolls, toys and games. In 2003 and 2004, the insatiably curious hamster and his hamster friends co-starred in three specials: the one-hour *Hamtaro Birthday Special* and half-hour *Ham-Ham Halloween!* and the hour-long *Ham-Ham Games*, which aired in August 2004 as part of a three-hour "Saturday Block Party" marathon on Cartoon Network and was the series' final broadcast. *A Shogakukan Music & Digital Entertainment/R Kawai/SMDE/TV Tokyo/Ocean Group/ShoPro Entertainment Production. Color. Half-hour. Premiered on CAR: June 3, 2002–August 21, 2004.*

**Voices**
**Hamtaro:** Chiara Zanni; **Laura:** Carly McKillip; **Boss:** Ted Cole; **Bijou:** Chantal Strand; **Maxwell:** Brad Swaile; **Dexter/Forrest Haruna, Laura's father:** Sam Vincent; **Mr. Yoshi:** Scott McNeil; **Elder Ham:** Dave "Squatch" Ward; **Elder Ham:** Donald Brown; **Kana Iwata:** Daniella Evangelista; **Kaitlin Endo:** Pauline Newstone; **Stan:** Noel Fisher; **Sabu:** Richard Ian Cox; **Bijou:** Chantal Strand; **Sandy:** Brittney Wilson; **Cappy:** Tabitha St. Germain; **Howdy:** Paul Dobson; **Jingle:** Terry Klassen; **Travis:** Matthew Smith; **Dylan:** Michael Donovan; **Oxnard:** Saffron Henderson; **Panda:** Jillian Michaels; **Pashmina:** Jocelyne Loewen; **Laura Haruna:** Moneca Stori; **Pepper/Penelope/Marion Haruna, Laura's mother:** Cathy Weseluck; **Laura's Grandfather:** Richard Newman; **Cindy Iwata, Kana's mother:** Ellen Kennedy; **Conrad**

Iwata, Kana's father: Trevor Devall; **Grandma Willow:** Kathy Morse; **Rosie:** Alexandra Carter; **Mrs. Charlotte Yoshi:** Venus Terzo; **Other Voices:** Sharon Alexander, Michael Coleman, Annette Ducharine, Brian Drummond, Matt Hill, Kelly Sheridan, Ellen Kennedy

## ◎ THE HANNA-BARBERA NEW CARTOON SERIES

In the fall of 1962, following the success of its previous syndicated series, Hanna-Barbera introduced this trilogy of original cartoon programming featuring a new stable of stars: "Wally Gator," a "swinging gator from the swamp" who refuses to be confined to his home in the zoo; "Lippy the Lion," a blustering, bragging lion who gets into multiple messes with his buddy, a sorrowful hyena, Hardy Har Har; and "Touché Turtle," a well-meaning but inept swashbuckling turtle who goes on a series of avenging adventures with his dog, Dum Dum, to right the wrongs of the world.

Each series component contained 52 episodes and was produced for flexible programming, allowing stations to use each series together in longer time periods or scheduled separately in their own half-hour time slots. (See *Lippy the Lion, Touche Turtle* and *Wally Gator* for voice credits.) *A Hanna-Barbera Production. Color. Half-hour. Premiered: September 1962. Syndicated.*

## ◎ HANNA-BARBERA'S WORLD OF SUPER ADVENTURE

This syndicated package of superhero cartoons was first produced for Saturday morning, including *The Fantastic Four, Frankenstein Jr. and the Impossibles, Space Ghost, Herculoids, Shazzan, Moby Dick and the Mighty Mightor* and *Birdman and the Galaxy Trio.* (See individual series for further details.) *A Hanna-Barbera Production. Color. Half-hour. Premiered: September 1980. Syndicated. Rebroadcast on CAR: September 20, 1993.*

## ◎ HAPPILY EVER AFTER: FAIRY TALES FROM EVERY CHILD

This music-filled, once-upon-a-time, half-hour children's series offered new interpretations of classic nursery rhymes and fairy tales, each relating the perspective of different cultural backgrounds. Premiering Sunday nights on HBO in March of 1995, the series opened with a 90-minute episode (normally each show ran a half-hour) featuring three new versions of old favorites, including an African American visualization of "Jack and the Beanstalk," starring Tone Loc as the voice of The Giant (he also sings a rhythm-and-blues song called "Living Large"), a Chinese interpretation of "Little Red Riding Hood" and a Latino variation of "Hansel and Gretel" (featuring Rosie Perez and Cheech Marin).

Other first season episodes included an Asian-styled telling of Hans Christian Andersen's "The Emperor's New Clothes" (including among its cast George Takei of TV's original *Star Trek*), a Jamaican slant on the yarn "Rumplestiltskin" featuring the voices of Robert Townsend, Denzel Washington and Jasmine Guy, among others.

Twenty-six-episodes were produced between 1995 and 1997, including a half-hour prime-time special *Mother Goose: A Rappin' and Rhymin' Special*, featuring a star-studded cast. Robert Guillaume, appearing in live-action wraparounds, served as the series' host. *A Hyperion Animation Production. Color. Half-hour. Premiered on HBO: March 26, 1995; April 13, 1997. Rebroadcast on HBO FAM: December 26, 1996–February 12, 2001.*

## ◎ HAPPY NESS: THE SECRET OF LOCH

From the depths of Scotland's most famous lake, sea creatures Happy Ness, Lovely Ness, Kind Ness, Bright Ness and Silly Ness to name just a few, do their best to change the world into a wonderful place (not without some resistance from some bad "Nessies") after they are discovered by the McCoy kids, who join them in their musical adventures through Happy Land in this part-fable, part-fantasy series produced for first-run syndication. *An Abrams Gentile Entertainment/Creativite & Development/ AB Production. Color. Half-hour. Premiered: September 9, 1995. Syndicated.*

**Voices**
John Brewster, Dan Conroy, Donna Daley, Eddie Korbich Jr., Connor Matthews, Kathryn Zaremba

## ◎ THE HARDY BOYS

Teenage sleuths Frank and Joe Hardy double as rock-and-roll musicians on a world tour as they solve crimes and play some popular music (music was performed by a live band called, appropriately enough, The Hardy Boys) in this updated version of Franklin W. Dixon's long-running series of children's detective novels. *A Filmation Studios Production in association with 20th Century Fox. Color. Half-hour. Premiered on ABC: September 6, 1969– September 4, 1971.*

**Voices**
**Frank Hardy/Chubby Morton:** Dallas McKennon; **Joe Hardy/ Pete Jones/Fenton Hardy:** Byron Kane; **Wanda Kay Breckenridge/Gertrude Hardy:** Jane Webb

## ◎ THE HARLEM GLOBETROTTERS

Famed basketball illusionists Meadowlark Lemon, Curly, Gip, Bobby Joe and Geese perform benefits and defeat evil around the world with the help of their basketball finesse in this popular 21-episode half-hour Saturday-morning entry that was a popular fixture on CBS for three consecutive seasons.

In February 1978, NBC repeated the series as part of the two-hour cartoon extravaganza *Go Go Globetrotters*, which featured several other Hanna-Barbera favorites, including *The C.B. Bears* and *The Herculoids*. All-new adventures of the internationally acclaimed "Wizards of the Court" were produced in 1979 under the new title of *The Super Globetrotters*. (See series entry for details.) *A Hanna-Barbera Production. Color. Half-hour. Premiered on CBS: September 12, 1970–September 2, 1972. Rebroadcast on CBS: September 10, 1972–May 20, 1973. Rebroadcast on NBC: February 4, 1978–September 2, 1978 (as part of Go Go Globetrotters).*

**Voices**
**Meadowlark Lemon:** Scatman Crothers; **Freddie "Curly" Neal:** Stu Gilliam; **Gip:** Richard Elkins; **Bobby Joe Mason:** Eddie "Rochester" Anderson; **Geese:** Johnny Williams; **Pablo:** Robert Do Qui; **Granny:** Nancy Wible; **Dribbles, the dog:** (no voice)

## ◎ HAROLD AND THE PURPLE CRAYON

Charming pantomime adventures of a curious four-year-old, Harold—made famous in a series of popular children's books by Crockett Johnson in the 1950s and 1960s—who escapes to a whole new world he creates with the power of his magical crayon. Winner of a 2002 Emmy Award for best title design, the half-hour children's series, narrated by actress Sharon Stone, debuted on HBO's sister channel, HBO Family, in January 2002 and has continued to air in reruns since its original network run. *A Sony Pictures Family Entertainment Production. Color. Half-hour. Premiered* on HBO FAM: *January 5, 2002–April 4, 2002. Rebroadcast on HBO FAM: Rebroadcast April 2002–*.

**Voices**
**Narrator:** Sharon Stone; **Harold:** Connor Matheus

## ⊚ HARRY AND HIS BUCKET FULL OF ADVENTURES

Harry stumbles upon a dusty, old blue bucket in the attic that contains six toy dinosaurs. He is a five-year-old boy with a wild imagination. As he jumps into the bucket, the dinosaurs become real and he is transported to their special world, Dino-World, on a series of high adventures with his new best friends; Taury, the tough-guy Tyrannosaurus rex; Trike, the naïve and agreeable Triceratops; Pterence, the eager and young pterodactyl; Patsy, the kind and patient Apatosaurus; Sid, the scholarly Scelidosaurus; and Steggy, the nervous, absent-minded Stegosaurus. His grandmother, Nana, and his best friend, Charlotte, join him in his fantasy world come to life. This half-hour series, which teaches children the power of imagination and the importance of friendship, was adapted from the popular children's books by Ian Whybrow. First telecast in August 2005 on Cartoon Network's new weekday preschool block, Tickle-U, becoming one of the network's highest-rated preschool programs, the 52-episode series was canceled after one season along with the block's other series, which included *Firehouse Tales, Gerald McBoing Boing, Gordon the Garden Gnome, Peppa Pig* and *Yoko! Jakamoko! Toto! A CCI Entertainment/Collingwood O'Hare Entertainment Ltd. Production in association with Rocket Fund and Silver Fox Films. Color. Half-hour. Premiered on CAR: August 22, 2005.*

**Voices**
**Harry:** Andrew Chambers; **Taury:** Jamie Wilson; **Trike:** Ron Rubin; **Pterence:** Andrew Sabiston; **Patsy:** Stacey Depass; **Sid:** Juan Chioran; **Steggy:** Jonathan Wilson

## ⊚ HARVEY BIRDMAN, ATTORNEY AT LAW

Developing bad knees and a bad attitude, the aging winged superhero-turned pinstriped and gabardine-suited lawyer, Harvey Birdman (of Hanna-Barbera's cult-classic 1960s cartoon show *Birdman and the Galaxy Trio*), still wears his tights and cowl beneath his expensive suit and is aided by his purple eagle sidekick, Avenger, as he defends famous Hanna-Barbera cartoon luminaries—Dr. Benton Quest, Doggie Daddy and Auggie Daddy, Fred Flintstone, Grape Ape, the Jetsons, Secret Squirrel, Shaggy, Scooby-Doo, Speedy Buggy and others—in assorted copyright law, criminal defense and civil litigation cases under the paranoid, watchful eye of his partner Phil Ken Sebben at a prestigious law firm in this half-hour series for Cartoon Network.

Originally created by Michael Ouwelee and Erik Richter based on characters created by William Hanna and Joseph Barbera and produced by J.J. Sedelmaier and Williams Street Productions, an 11-minute pilot special, *Bannon Custody Battle*, debuted in December 2000 on the Cartoon Network's late-night *Adult Swim* programming block. The weekly 15-minute comedy series followed a second special in September 2001, *Very Personally Injury*, before Cartoon Network commissioned six first-season episodes and added it as a regular weekly series on *Adult Swim* in 2002. A new studio, Allied Arts and Science, replaced J.J. Sedelmaier and Williams Street Productions as its producer, beginning with the second special. Becoming a central component of Sunday evenings on *Adult Swim*'s rotating "The Lab" block featuring *Aqua Teen Hunger Force, The Brak Show* and *Sealab 2021*, the offbeat attorney-at-law series was renewed for three more seasons, produc-

ing a total of 39 15-minute episodes through March 2007 that continue to air on *Adult Swim. An Allied Arts and Science/J.J. Sedelmaier Productions/Williams Street/Turner Production. Color. Fifteen minutes. Premiered on CAR: July 7, 2002.*

**Voices**
**Harvey Birdman/Judge Hiram Mightor:** Gary Cole; **Myron Reducto Esq./Phil Ken Sebben/The Eagle of Truth:** Stephen Colbert; **Peanut:** Thomas Allen; **Mentok the Mindtaker:** John Michael Higgins; **X the Eliminator:** Peter MacNicol; **Avenger:** Erik Richter, Adam Lawson; **Peter Potamus:** Joe Alaskey (first voice), Chris Edgerly (second voice); **DVD/Mr. Finkerton/The Funky Phantom/Augie Doggie/Captain Caveman/Fancy Fancy:** Chris Edgerly; **Gigi:** Debi Mae West; **Azul Falcone/Stan Freezoid/ Apache Chief/Fred Flintstone/Yogi Bear/Der Spuzmacher/Inch High/Speed Buggy/Doggie Daddy/Droopy/Quick Draw McGraw/ Benny the Ball/Dum Dum/Shazzan/Atom Ant:** Maurice LaMarche; **Evelyn Spyro/Throckthorton:** Michael McKean; **Vulturo/Dr. Benton Quest/Ding-A-Ling Wolf:** Neil Ross; **Black Vulcan/Hong Kong Phooey:** Phil LaMarr; **The Bear:** Matt Peccini; **Birdgirl:** Paget Brewster

## ⊚ HBO STORYBOOK MUSICALS

Well-known Hollywood celebrities narrated and provided their voices for this half-hour series of cartoon musical specials, based on popular children's stories, fables and songs and produced for HBO by four independent animation houses. Oscar and Emmy award-winning watercolor-animation specialist Michael Sporn launched the series in 1987 with his Oscar-winning short *Lyle, Lyle Crocodile: The Musical: The House on 88th St.*, which made its world television premiere on HBO as a half-hour special. Sporn's effort was followed a year later by DIC Entertainment's Emmy-nominated special *Madeline*, based on the popular children's book character.

Sporn's New York–based company, Michael Sporn Animation, produced six more half-hours for this anthology showcase. In 1989 he brought to television screens *The Story of the Dancing Frog*, based on Quentin Blake's book, followed by the 1990 adaptation of Hans Christian Anderson's *The Red Shoes*. He also produced *Mike Mulligan and His Steam Shovel* (1990); *Ira Sleeps Over* (1991), adapted from Bernard Weber's book; *A Child's Garden of Verses* (1992), based on the classic Robert Louis Stevenson story; and *The Country Mouse and the City Mouse: A Christmas Tale* (1993).

In 1991 Carol Burnett lent her voice to *The Tale of Peter Rabbit*, the only series entry produced by cartoon studio independent Hare Bear Productions. In the fall of that year, Canadian animation house CINAR Films debuted five half-hours from its *The Real Story of . . .* series, featuring adaptations of popular nursery rhymes and children's tales, beginning with *The Ice Queen Mittens*, starring the voice of Hollywood screen legend Lauren Bacall. Other half-hour installments from CINAR's *The Real Story of . . .* series to premiere under this showcase included: *Spider Junior High* (1991), featuring pop superstar Patti LaBelle and *Cosby* TV star Malcolm-Jamal Warner; *The Runaway Teapot* (1991), with rock star Julian Lennon as one of the voices; *The Rise and Fall of Humpty Dumpy* (1991), costarring Oscar-winning actress Glenda Jackson and rocker Huey Lewis; and *Happy Birthday to You* (1992).

Since its original debut, the popular musical series has been rebroadcast Monday, Wednesday and Friday mornings on HBO's sister channel, HBO Family. *A Michael Sporn Animation/DIC Entertainment/CINAR Films/Hare Bear Production. Color. Half-hour. Premiered on HBO: November 18, 1987–December 8, 1993. Rebroadcast on HBO FAM: 1994–.*

## THE HEATHCLIFF AND DINGBAT SHOW

That tough, orange-striped cat of comic-strip fame costars in this Saturday-morning series in which he typically takes great delight in annoying anyone he encounters in 27 episodic adventures. The program's second segment, "Dingbat and the Creeps," followed the misadventures of a vampire dog (whose vocal characterization is reminiscent of Curly Howard of the Three Stooges), a skeleton and a pumpkin who help people in trouble. The series—the first of three "Heathcliff" cartoon series produced in succession—aired one full season on ABC. *A Ruby-Spears Enterprises Production. Color. Half-hour. Premiered on ABC: October 4, 1980–September 18, 1981. Rebroadcast on CAR: September 6, 1994–December 9, 1994 (weekdays): June 5, 1995–September 1, 1995 (weekdays): December 18, 1995–December 22, 1995; December 26, 1995–December 29, 1995. Rebroadcast on BOOM: April 5, 2002–.*

*Voices*

**HEATHCLIFF:** Heathcliff: Mel Blanc; **Mr. Schultz/Iggy/Spike/Muggsy:** Mel Blanc; **Milkman:** Mel Blanc; **Clem/Digby/Dogsnatcher:** Henry Corden; **Sonja:** Julie McWhirter, Marilyn Schreffler; **Crazy Shirley/Sonja/Grandma/Marcy:** June Foray

**DINGBAT AND THE CREEPS:** Dingbat: Frank Welker; **Nobody, the pumpkin:** Don Messick; **Sparerib, the skeleton:** Don Messick

## THE HEATHCLIFF AND MARMADUKE SHOW

In this series the scruffy tomcat shared the spotlight with that imposing and lovable great Dane, Marmaduke (star of Brad Anderson's popular syndicated comic strip), who was featured in separate six-minute adventures, getting himself into all kinds of mischief without meaning to. Meanwhile, Heathcliff picks up where he left off by triumphing over his adversaries—Spike, the neighborhood bulldog; the garbage collector; the fish store owner; and the chef of the local restaurant. "Dingbat and the Creeps" also returned as an alternating segment in the series, and two 30-second teasers were added: "Marmaduke's Riddles" and "Marmaduke's Doggone Funnies." *A Ruby-Spears Enterprises Production. Color. Half-hour. Premiered on ABC: September 12, 1981–September 18, 1982. Rebroadcast on BOOM: January 17, 2005–.*

*Voices*

**HEATHCLIFF:** Heathcliff: Mel Blanc; **Mr. Schultz/Iggy/Mugsy:** Mel Blanc; **Spike, the bulldog:** Mel Blanc; **Clem/Digby:** Henry Corden; **Dogcatcher:** Henry Corden; **Crazy Shirley/Sonja/Grandma/Marcy:** June Foray;

**DINGBAT AND THE CREEPS:** Dingbat: Frank Welker; **Nobody, the pumpkin:** Don Messick; **Sparerib, the skeleton:** Don Messick; **Marmaduke, the Great Dane:** Paul Winchell; **Phil Winslow, his owner:** Paul Winchell; **Dottie Winslow, his wife:** Russi Taylor; **Barbie Winslow, their daughter:** Russi Taylor; **Barbie's sister:** Marilyn Schreffler; **Billy Winslow, their son:** Russi Taylor; **Missy:** Russi Taylor; **Mr. Snyder/Mr. Post:** Don Messick

## HEATHCLIFF AND THE CATILLAC CATS

Crafty cat Heathcliff of comic-strip fame terrorizes the neighborhood with little regard for anyone for himself in this half-hour comedy series, divided into two 15-minute segments. The second half features the lively and imaginative escapades of The Catillac Cats (Hector, Wordsworth and Mungo), led by boss-cat Riff Raff, whose get-rich-quick schemes and search for the ultimate meal keep them embroiled in trouble one episode after another. The latter were billed on screen as "Cats & Company." Heathcliff also appeared in daily 30-second prosocial segments educating young viewers on the dos and don'ts of proper pet care. The 65-episode series—the third and final in a series of *Heathcliff* cartoon series—was produced for first-run syndication in 1984. Previous segments from the television series were combined with new wraparound footage to produce the first and only full-length Heathcliff animated feature, 1986's *Heathcliff: The Movie. A DIC Enterprises Production in association with LBS Communications and McNaught Syndicated. Color. Half-hour. Premiered: September 15, 1984–87. Syndicated 1989–93. Rebroadcast on NICK: 1989–93. Rebroadcast on FAM: October 2, 1994–February 16, 1996. Rebroadcast on FOX FAM: August 1998; June 1999–July 1999.*

*Voices*

**Heathcliff:** Mel Blanc; **Cleo/Iggy:** Donna Christle; **Spike/Muggsy/Knuckles:** Derek McGrath; **Grandma:** Ted Ziegler; **Sonja:** Marilyn Lightstone; **Bush/Raul:** Danny Wells; **Milkman:** Stanley Jones; **Fish Market Owner:** Danny Mann;

**THE CATILLAC CATS:** Riff Raff/Wordsworth: Stanley Jones; **Mungo:** Ted Ziegler; **Hector:** Danny Mann; **Cleo:** Donna Christie; **Leroy, the junkyard dog:** Ted Ziegler

## HEAVY GEAR: THE ANIMATED SERIES

Armed with their own multi-ton war machines and huge armor (called "Gears"), two dueling teams, the Shadow Dragons, headed by a novice Gear pilot, Marcus Rover, and the Northern Vanguard Justice, led by veteran commander, Major Drake Alexander Wallis III, battle for the Heavy Gear Championship on the planet Terra Nova in this futuristic, 3-D CGI-animated series, based on the amazing and popular role-playing tactical game created by Pierre Ouellette for Dream Pod 9 in 1994. Coproduced by Adelaide Productions and Canada's Mainframe Entertainment (*Reboot, The Transformers*) for Sony Pictures Family Entertainment, the 40-episode, half-hour series was broadcast in first-run syndication worldwide and Saturday mornings on the WB Television Network's Kids' WB! beginning in the fall of 2001. *An Adelaide/Mainframe Entertainment/Sony Pictures Family Entertainment Production. Color. Half-hour. Premiered on the WB (Kids' WB!): September 22, 2001–March 30, 2002. Syndicated.*

*Voices*

**Major Drake Alexander Wallis III:** Charles Shaughnessy; **Colonel Magnilda Rykka:** Sarah Douglas; **Lieutenant Jan Augusta:** Michael Chiklis; **Sergeant Gunther Groonz:** Nicholas Guest; **Marcus Rover:** Lukas Haas; **Sonja Briggs:** Vanessa L. Williams; **Dirx:** David DeLuise; **Rank:** Greg Ellis; **Zerve:** Clancy Brown; **Sebastian:** Ed Hopkins; **Greco:** Tom Kane; **Von "Boom Boom" Maddox:** Jim Wise; **Kusunoki Tachi:** Clyde Kusatsu; **Serge Garpenlov:** Keith Szarabajka; **Yoji Kirakowa:** Karen Maruyama

## THE HECKLE AND JECKLE CARTOON SHOW

The two conniving, talking magpies of motion-picture fame host a collection of other theatrically released Terrytoon cartoons (Little Roquefort, Gandy Goose, Dinky Duck, and "Terry-Toon Classics," including several starring the Terry Bears) and their own misadventures. In 1977 Heckle and Jeckle were cast in a new CBS series entitled *The New Adventures of Mighty Mouse and Heckle and Jeckle. A Terrytoons/CBS Films, Inc., Production. Color. Half-hour. Premiered on CBS: October 14, 1956–September 1957. Rebroadcast on CBS: September 1965–September 3, 1966. Rebroadcast on NBC: September 6, 1969–September 7, 1971. Syndicated.*

*Voices*

**Heckle:** Dayton Allen, Roy Halee; **Jeckle:** Dayton Allen, Roy Halee; **Little Roquefort/Percy the Cat:** Tom Morrison; **Gandy Goose/Sourpuss:** Arthur Kay; **Terry Bears:** Roy Halee, Philip A. Scheib, Doug Moye, **Dinky Duck:** (no voice)

## ⊚ THE HECTOR HEATHCOTE SHOW

A time machine enables a scientist (Hector Heathcote) to rewrite history by transporting him back to famous events in this half-hour Saturday-morning series that featured 39 recycled cartoons originally produced for theaters, plus 32 new cartoon shorts made exclusively for television, including "Hashimoto" and "Sidney the Elephant." (See Animated Theatrical Cartoon Series section entries for details.) *A Terrytoons/CBS Films, Inc., Production. Color. Half-hour. Premiered on NBC: October 5, 1963–September 25, 1965.*

*Voices*

**Hector Heathcote/Hashimoto/Mrs. Hashimoto/Yuriko/Saburo:** John Myhers; **Sidney the Elephant:** Lionel Wilson, Dayton Allen; **Stanley the Lion/Cleo the Giraffe:** Dayton Allen

## ⊚ HELLO KITTY AND FRIENDS

Second incarnation featuring 13 adventures of the popular Japanese anime characters—young kitten, Kitty, and her identical twin sister, Mimmy—with a mix of "Fairy Tale Fantasy" adaptations using animation produced as early as 1991 (including "Hello Kitty in Cinderella," "Hello Kitty in Snow White," "Pekkle in the Adventures of Sinbad" and "Keroppi in Robin Hood"; later released on DVD and VHS by ADV Films. Reports have been published claiming CBS aired the series in 1991, but no records confirm this fact. Redubbed in English, in September 1998, Toon Disney began airing the weekday series until 2002. The series was followed by a third spin-off in 2000, *Hello Kitty's Paradise*, broadcast on cable's FOX Family Channel. *A Sanrio Enterprises/Optimum Productions/ADV Films/Kaleidoscope Entertainment Inc. Production. Color. Half-hour. Premiered on TDIS: September 9, 1998–April 21, 2002.*

*Voices*

**Hello Kitty:** Karen Bernstein; **Pekkle:** Susan Roman; **Narrator:** Mary Long; **Other Voices:** Catherine Gallant, Elizabeth Hanna, Gina Clayton, Gordon Masten, Hadley Kay, Harvey Atkin, Jeff Lumby, Jennifer Griffon, Tracey Hoyt, John Stocker, Julie Lemieux, Kathleen Laskey, Naz Edwards, Ron Rubin, Tony Daniels, Tracey Hoyt

## ⊚ HELLO KITTY'S FURRY TALE THEATER

Delightfully entertaining series of two weekly 15-minute fairy tales, loosely adapted and contemporized, staged by this animal theater group—Hello Kitty (the star) and friends Tuxedo Sam, Chip and My Melody—who take different roles from story to story, match wits with series villains Catnip and Grinder. The 26-episode series was based on the popular furry animal doll. *A DIC Enterprises Production in association with MGM/UA Television. Color. Half-hour. Premiered on CBS: September 19, 1987–September 3, 1988.*

*Voices*

**Hello Kitty:** Tara Charendoff; **Tuxedo Sam:** Sean Roberge; **Chip:** Noam Zylberman; **My Melody:** Maron Bennett; **Grandpa Kitty:** Carl Banas; **Grandma Kitty/Mama Kitty:** Elizabeth Hanna; **Papa Kitty:** Len Carlson; **Catnip:** Cree Summer Francks; **Grinder:** Greg Morton; **Fangora:** Denise Pidgeon

*Hello Kitty and friends Tuxedo Sam, Chip and My Melody in a scene from the CBS Saturday-morning series* Hello Kitty's Furry Tale Theater. *© MGM/UA Television Productions. Certain characters © Sanrio Co. Ltd.* (COURTESY: DIC ENTERPRISES)

## ⊚ HELLO KITTY'S PARADISE

Average kindergartener Hello Kitty and her furry twin sister, Mimmy, enjoy a series of imaginary adventures over the rainbow or around their London home where they live with their parents, George and Mary White, learning social skills from the importance of good manners to good hygiene, in this third series based on the popular toy doll by LJN Toys and Sanrio Company. First shown on Japanese television from 1993 to 1994, the 16-episode series, following its predecessor, *Hello Kitty and Friends*, was seen Saturday mornings in the United States on FOX Family Channel. *A Sanrio Enterprises Production. Color. Half-hour. Premiered on FOX FAM: March 4, 2000–September 9, 2000.*

*Voices*

**Hello Kitty:** Melisa Fahn; **Mimmy:** Laura Summer; **Mama:** Jennifer Darling; **Papa:** Tony Pope; **Mimmy:** Laura Summer; **Lacey the Raccoon:** Sandy Fox

## ⊚ H.E.L.P.!

Lessons on safety and first aid are the premise of this series of educational one-minute fillers (the title is short for Dr. Henry's Emergency Lessons for People), prescreened by a team of respected educators and broadcast through ABC's 1979–80 Saturday-morning schedule. The series was awarded a 1980 Emmy for outstanding children's informational/instructional programming—short format. *An 8 Films/Dahlia/Phil Kimmelman Production. Color. One minute. Premiered on ABC: 1979–80.*

## ⊚ HELP! IT'S THE HAIR BAIR BUNCH!

Wonderland Zoo's three wild bear tenants—Hair, Square and Bubi—campaign for better living conditions in Cave Block #9 in this 1971 CBS series (originally titled, *The Yo Yo Bears.* From 1974 to 1979 the series was syndicated; then later it rebroadcast on USA Network's "Cartoon Express" and on Cartoon Network and Boomerang. *A Hanna-Barbera Production. Color. Half-hour. Premiered on CBS: September 11, 1971–September 2, 1972. Rebroadcast on CBS: September 1973–August 31, 1974. Syndicated: 1974–79. Rebroadcast on USA Network: February 19, 1989–November 7, 1991. Rebroadcast on CAR: January 3, 1994–June 3, 1994 (week-*

days); June 5, 1995–September 1, 1995 (weekdays); September 6, 1995– (Wednesdays). Rebroadcast on BOOM: May 2, 2000–.

**Voices**
**Hair Bear:** Daws Butler; **Bubi Bear:** Paul Winchell; **Square Bear:** Bill Callaway; **Eustace P. Peevly, zoo curator:** John Stephenson; **Botch, Peevly's assistant:** Joe E. Ross

### ⊚ HE-MAN AND THE MASTERS OF THE UNIVERSE (1983)

Residing on the planet Eternia, He-Man (Prince Adam) and She-Ra (Princess Adora) clash with the forces of evil—namely the villainous Skeletor—in this action-adventure series based on the popular Mattel toy line, produced for first-run syndication in 1983. Six years later, the series was rebroadcast on USA Network's *Cartoon Express. A Filmation Associates Production in association with Mattel Inc. and Group W. Color. Half-hour. Premiered: September 1983. Syndicated. Rebroadcast on USA: September 18, 1989–August 14, 1990.*

**Voices**
**Prince Adam/He-Man/Ram-Man:** John Erwin; **Princess Adora/She-Ra:** Melendy Britt; **Skeletor/Marman/Beast Man:** Alan Oppenheimer; **Queen/Evil-Lyn/Sorceress/Teela:** Linda Gary; **Orko/King:** Lou Scheimer; **Battlecat/Gringer/Man-At-Arms:** Erik Gunden

### ⊚ HE-MAN AND THE MASTERS OF THE UNIVERSE (2002)

In the distant future, the fate of his beloved Eternia rests in the hands of her most powerful guardian, He-Man (alias Prince Adam), who uses his mighty powers and takes his allies into battle to defend the universe against his famed arch-nemesis Skeletor and his Evil Warrior henchmen. This lavishly produced and richly animated revival and third adaptation—the first since DIC Enterprises's 1990 syndicated series, *The New Adventures of He-Man*—of the popular toy action figure rolled onto television screens in late August of 2002 on the Cartoon Network with two feature-length 90-minute episodes airing one week apart. Thirty-nine brand-new half-hour episodes, co-produced by Mike Young Productions, featured serialized adventures of He-Man battling Skeletor and his henchmen. Canceled in 2004 after only two seasons due to declining ratings, that same year the series won a Daytime Emmy Award for outstanding achievement in sound editing—live action and animation. Actor Gary Chalk, who voiced He-Man in the early 1990s in the syndicated *The New Adventures of He-Man* series, provided the voice of Man-at-Arms in this latest incarnation. Beginning in January 2006, the series was rebroadcast weekday mornings on Boomerang until that April. *A He-Man/Mike Young Production. Color. Half-hour. Premiered on CAR: August 16, 2002–March 6, 2004. Rebroadcast on BOOM: January 23, 2006–April 22, 2006.*

**Voices**
**He-Man/Prince Adam:** Cam Clarke; **Teela:** Lisa Ann Beley; **Queen Marlena/The Sorceress of Castle Grayskull:** Nicole Oliver; **King Randor/Count Marzo/Robot/Tung Lashor:** Michael Donovan; **Keldor-Skeletor/Buzz-Off:** Brian Dobson; **Duncan/Man-at-Arms/Whiplash:** Gary Chalk; **Mekaneck/Orko:** Gabe Khouth; **Evil-Lyn:** Kathleen Barr; **Man-E-Faces/Snake Face/Trap-Jaw/Tri-Klops/Lord Carnivus:** Paul Dobson; **Beast Man/Clawful/Mer-Man/Ram Man/Stratos/Kobra Khan:** Scott McNeil; **Skeletor/Keldor/Buzz-Off/Webstor/King Hiss/Sssqueeze/Ceratus:** Brian Dobson; **Fisto/Chadzar:** Mark Acheson; **Evilseed:** Don

Brown; **Odiphus/Stinkor/Tuvar (Two of Two-Bad)/Belzar:** Brian Drummond; **Baddhra (Badd of Two-Bad):** Mark Gibbon; **Kulatuk Priest:** Campbell Lane; **Hordak:** Colin Murdock; **General Rattlor/Lord Dactys/The Faceless One/Azdar:** Richard Newman; **Sy-Klone/Moss Man:** John Payne

### ⊚ HENRY'S CAT

Australian-born animator Bob Godfrey (best known for his 1961 cartoon short, "Do-It-Yourself Cartoon Kit") singlehandedly produced this cut-out animated half-hour series of 10-minute cartoons involving a misfit cat named Henry who, along with his many back-alley animal friends, fantasizes about hilarious adventures, spoofing everything from Tarzan to Sherlock Holmes. The series aired on Showtime. Henry's cartoon adventures were repackaged and released on home video, with comedian Dom DeLuise redubbing the narration (supplied by creator Bob Godfrey in the television series). *A Bob Godfrey Films Ltd. Production. Color. Half-hour. Premiered on SHO: 1990.*

**Voices**
Bob Godfrey

### ⊚ THE HERCULOIDS

Futuristic animals Zok the laser dragon, Tundro the rhinoceros, Gloop and Gleep the friendly blobs, Igoo the rock-ape and Dorno, a young boy, strive to save Zandor, their benevolent king, and the primitive planet Amzot from alien invaders in this 18-episode, half-hour fantasy/adventure series (two episodes per show), originally produced for CBS in 1967. Nine years after its network run, the series was repackaged as part of NBC's *Go Go Globetrotters*. In 1981 "The Herculoids" returned in new adventures in NBC's *Space Stars. A Hanna-Barbera Production. Color. Half-hour. Premiered on CBS: September 9, 1967–September 6, 1969. Rebroadcast on NBC: February 4, 1978–September 2, 1978 (part of Go Go Globetrotters). Rebroadcast on CAR: November 8, 1992 (part of Boomerang, 1968); February 7, 1993 (part of Boomerang, 1967); 1993–2000. Rebroadcast on BOOM: July 9, 2000–.*

**Voices**
**Zandor/Zok:** Mike Road; **Tara:** Virginia Gregg; **Dorno:** Ted Eccles; **Gloop/Gleep/Zok:** Don Messick; **Igoo:** Mike Road

### ⊚ HERE COMES THE GRUMP

Young American lad Terry and his dog, Bib, strive to save Princess Dawn from the evil Grump, who has put her under the Curse of Gloom in this half-hour animated fantasy series that debuted on NBC in 1969. The 17-episode series was produced by legendary animator Friz Freleng and partner David H. DePatie for their company, DePatie-Freleng Enterprises. The program later reaired on the Sci-Fi Channel's *Cartoon Quest. A DePatie-Freleng Enterprises Mirisch Production. Color. Half-hour. Premiered on NBC: September 6, 1969–September 4, 1971. Rebroadcast on SCI: September 18, 1993–September 17, 1994.*

**Voices**
**Princess Dawn:** Stefanianna Christopherson; **Terry, the little boy:** Jay North; **The Grump:** Rip Taylor

### ⊚ HEROES ON HOT WHEELS

Moonlighting as race-car drivers, a well-trained team of space scientists and explorers (known as the Shadow Jets), led by the ever-handsome Michael Valiant, prefer the fast action of the speedway in this half-hour adventure series produced for French television two years before its American television debut on The Family Channel in 1991. The weekday series was the second based on Mattel Toys "Hot Wheels" toy car line. (The first: 1969's, *Hot Wheels*, ABC.) *A LaCinq/C & D/Lucky World Productions in association with Mattel. Color. Half-hour. Premiered on FAM: September 16, 1991–August 28, 1992.*

*Voices*

Ian James Corlett, Mike Donovan, Scott McNeil, Venus Terzo, Dale Wilson

## ◎ HEY ARNOLD!

Set in the wilds of the big city, this series—described by creator Craig Barlett (the brother-in-law of *Simpsons* creator Matt Groening) as a "kind of Charlie Brown for the '90s—follows the quirky, philosophical nine-year-old Arnold, a boy with two bristly tufts of blond hair. Arnold lives in a boardinghouse run by his grandparents and inhabited by refugees as he braves the trials and tribulations of childhood and city life. In an unusual step, the series used real children to voice the characters.

Produced under Nickelodeon's "Nicktoons" banner and by the network's Games Animation division, the series, featuring two segments per show, premiered midseason in 1996. In December of 1996, the characters were spun off into their prime-time animated special, *Hey Arnold! The Christmas Show*. Two years later, Arnold and his friends starred in their second half-hour special, *Arnold's Thanksgiving*. Among a mix of regular series episodes were five more half-hour programs that aired on Nick: *Arnold's Valentine* (1997); *Arnold's Halloween* (1997); *Parents Day* (2000); *April Fools Day* (2002); and *Married* (2002), plus the hour-long finale, *The Journal* (2002). In 2002, Nickelodeon produced a feature-length film based on the series and released to theaters, *Hey Arnold! The Movie*. Beginning that May, the popular kids' series was rebroadcast daily on Nickelodeon's spin-off network, Nicktoons. *A Games Animation Production in association with Snee-osh, Inc. Color. Half-hour. Premiered on CBS: September 14, 2002. Premiered on NICK: October 7, 1996–June 8, 2004. Rebroadcast on NICKT: May 1, 2002–.*

*Voices*

**Arnold:** Phillip Van Dyke, Toran Caudell; **Gerald Johnson:** Jamil W. Smith; **Hegla G. Pataki/Sheena/Gloria:** Francesca Smith; **Grandpa/Various Others:** Dan Castellaneta; **Grandma/ Miss Slovak:** Tress MacNeille; **Harold Berman:** Justin Shenkarow; **Sid:** Sam Gifaldi; **Phoebe Heyerdahl:** Anndi McAfee; **Stinky:** Christopher Walberg; **Big Bob Pataki:** Maurice LaMarche; **Miriam Pataki/Mrs. Vitello:** Kath Soucie; **Eugene Horowitz:** Ben Diskin, Christopher Castile; **Olga:** Nika; **Rhonda Wellington Lloyd:** Olivia Hack; **Nadine:** Lauren Robinson; **Kyo Heyerdahl:** George Takei; **Reba Heyerdahl:** Jean Smart; **Ruth P. McDougal:** Lacey Chabert; **Brainy:** Craig Bart-lett; **Jamie O. Johanssen:** Ben Aaron Hoag; **Martin Johanssen:** Rick Fitts; **Ernie Potts:** Dom Irrera; **Oskar Kokoshka:** Steve Viksten; **Mr. Hyunh:** Baoan Coleman; **Marty Green:** James Keane; **Mr. Simmons:** Dan Butler; **Mary Scheer:** Suzie Kokoshka; **Brooke Lloyd:** Lori Alan

## ◎ HEY MONIE!

Originally launched in 2000 on the Oxygen Network as a series of interstitial segments on the half-hour animated anthology series, *X-Chromosone*, and after cultivating a tremendous following of viewers, the Oxygen Network and Black Entertainment Television network both commissioned 13 episodes of a full-blown, Flash-animated half-hour series geared for adults in 2003.

Produced by Soup2Nuts Productions, it followed the outrageous single life of an intense, highly driven African-American advertising executive, Simone ("Monie"), and her crazy best friend and roommate, Yvette. Featuring the voices of Second City comedy troupers and actual best friends Angela V. Shelton and France Callier, the former Second City comedy troupers made their vocal characterizations and "girl talk" sound authentic by improvising their dialogue as it was being recorded. Oxygen and BET co-financed and shared broadcasting rights to the adult cartoon series, with BET telecasting it first in the spring of 2003 and posting the third highest debut of the season. *A Soup2Nuts Production. Color. Half-hour. Premiered on BET: April 15, 2003. Premiered on OXY: June 1, 2003–October 4, 2003.*

*Voices*

**Simone:** Angela V. Shelton; **Yvette:** France Callier; **Chad:** Brendon Small; **Bill:** Bill Braudis; **Other Voices:** Bill Brown, Melissa Bardin Galsky, Dwayne Perkins, Sam Seder

## ◎ HIGGLYTOWN HEROES

Four worldly and wise Weebles-shaped pals (Wayne, Eubie, Twinkle and Kip) and their friend Fran the squirrel explore the city of Higglytown and its many different vocations, learning valuable lessons about teamwork, problem-solving and friendship from real community heroes—from fire fighters to snow plow operators (often voiced by guest celebrities)—in this entertaining and educational cartoon series meant to encourage young viewers to get more involved in making the world a better place. The half-hour 3-D/2-D animated weekday series debuted Sunday, September 12, 2004, with a special prime-time presentation on the Disney Channel before joining the network's weekday morning *Playhouse Disney* block. Renewed for a second season, beginning in January 2006, the popular preschool program bowed with a tune-filled animated episode featuring the voice of choreographer and actress Debbie Allen. Celebrity guest stars who have voiced the series include Sean Astin (*Lord of the Rings* trilogy), John Astin (*The Addams Family*), Tim Curry (*The Wild Thornberrys*), Anne Heche (*Wag the Dog*), Katey Sagal (*Futurama*), Sharon Stone (*Catwoman*), soap star Susan Lucci and recording artists Trace Adkins and Lance Bass among others. The band, They Might Be Giants, performs the show's theme song. *A Wild Brain Company Production. Color. Half-hour. Premiered on DIS: September 12, 2004.*

*Voices*

**Wayne:** Frankie Ryan Manriquez; **Eubie:** Taylor Masamitsu; **Twinkle:** Liliana Mumy; **Kip:** Rory Thost; **Fran:** Edie McClurg

## ◎ HIGHLANDER: THE ANIMATED SERIES

The Highlander wages war against immortal enemies as he defends survivors of the Great Catastrophe from Kortan, who claims sovereign power over Earth, in this French-produced 40-episode animated series based on the popular film and television series. The made-for-television series aired concurrently in syndication and on USA Network beginning in September 1994. *A Nelvana Entertainment/Gaumont Multimedia Production. Color. Half-hour. Premiered on USA: September 18, 1994.*

## ◎ HI HI PUFFY AMIYUMI

Two polar opposites but cool, talented and trend-setting pop stars—the peppy, positive and resourceful Ami and hard-rocking, no-nonsense cynic Yumi—travel from gig to gig with their well-meaning but rather "square" manager, Kaz, or just hang out in their hometown of Tokyo in this Japanese-American animated series, also featuring live-action segments of the real Puffy AmiYumi performing their J-pop hits, which aired on Cartoon Network. After airing during Cartoon Network's popular *Fridays* primetime block of animated comedies, one of Japan's biggest pop music acts returned with nine new episodes in late August 2005. To help ring in 2005, on New Year's Eve 2004, the J-pop sensations cohosted the *Hi Hi Puffy AmiYumi New Year's Eve Special*, beginning at 7 P.M., including a message from them in concert plus episodes of Cartoon Network favorites *Atomic Betty, Codename: Kids Next Door* and *Foster's Home for Imaginary Friends* and a premiere episode of *Hi Hi Puffy AmiYumi*. The extravaganza was followed by a four-hour *Hi Hi Puffy AmiYumi* marathon at midnight. Thirty-nine half-hour programs, featuring three segments per show, were produced, with 34 airing in the United States. *A Renegade Animation Production. Color. Half-hour. Premiered on CAR: November 19, 2004–September 23, 2006.*

*Voices*
**Ami/Janice/Tekirai:** Janice Kawaye; **Yumi/Jang Keng/Squirrel/ Timmy:** Grey DeLisle; **Kaz Harada, their manager/El Diablo:** Keone Young; **Harmony:** Sandy Fox; **Julie/Little Girl:** Tara Strong; **Safety McPrudent:** Ben Stein; **Wacky Wally:** Phil LaMarr; **Yumi's Opera Voice:** Karen Hartman; **Other Voices:** Corey Burton, Nathan Carlson, Kim Mai Guest, Katie Leigh, Diane Michelle, Rob Paulsen, Will Ryan

## ◎ HOLIDAY CLASSICS
Between 1988 and 1991 Rabbit Ears Video produced this enchanting and well-illustrated series of holiday half-hour specials, as told by well-known celebrities, for the home video market and also broadcast on cable networks, such as Showtime and The Family Channel. Productions include *The Gingham Dog and The Calico Cat, The Night Before Christmas, The Tailor of Gloucester, The Savior Is Born* and *The Legend of Sleepy Hollow*. (See individual entries in Animated Television Specials section for further details.) *A Rabbit Ears Video Production. Color. Half-hour. Premiered on SHO: 1989–91; Premiered on FAM: 1992.*

## ◎ HOME MOVIES
Living with his divorced mother (Paula) and adopted baby sister (Josie), eight-year-old filmmaker Brendon Small—named after the same person who created, wrote and voiced the character—produces short films with his best friends, Jason and Melissa, in his spare time after school with entertaining results in this weekly half-hour animated prime-time series for UPN. Featuring many voice actors from Comedy Central's hit cartoon series *Dr. Katz, Professional Therapist*, including Jonathan Katz, H. Jon Benjamin and Melissa Bardin Galsky, the series also costarred comedienne Paula Poundstone as the voice of Brendon's mom during the first season until she was replaced by Janine Ditullo for the show's second season.

Coproduced by Soup2Nuts and Tom Snyder Productions, plots of each episode were outlined—or "retroscripted"—with improvised dialogue to create more realistic conversations. After airing for two seasons on UPN, Cartoon Network picked up the series, rebroadcasting it for three seasons. *A Burns & Burn/Soup2Nuts-Tom Snyder Production. Color. Half-hour. Premiered on UPN: April 26, 1999–May 24, 1999. Rebroadcast on CAR: September 2, 2001–April 4, 2004.*

*Voices*
**Paula Small:** Paula Poundstone, Janine Ditullo; **Brendon Small:** Brendon Small; **Josie Small:** Loren Bouchard; **Coach John McGuirk/Jason Penopolis:** H. Jon Benjamin; **Melissa Robbins:**

Melissa Bardin Galsky; **Erik:** Jonathan Katz; **Mr. Lynch:** Ron Lynch

## ◎ HONEYBEE HUTCH
After being separated from his mother, a brave little bee begins a long and arduous search for his real mother and makes countless friends—and a few foes—along the way as he gets into one predicament after another in this heartwarming, 65-episode, half-hour series based on an original story. *A Tatsumoko/Saban Entertainment Production. Color. Half-hour. Premiered: Fall 1996. Syndicated.*

*Voices*
**Hutch:** Joshua Seth; **Haley:** Heidi Lenhart; **Honeybee Queen:** Edie Mirman; **Narrator:** Mari Devon; **Hutch's Mother:** Melodee Spevack; **Other Voices:** Dorothy Fahn, Dave Mallow, Eugene Rubenzer

## ◎ HONEY HONEY
First telecast in Japan as *The Wonderful Adventures of Honey Honey* from October 1981 through May 1982, this 29-episode half-hour animated series was about a young female moppet who enjoys performing good deeds. The inspirational series was rebroadcast in the United States on CBN. *A Toei Studios/MIC Modern Programs International Production. Color. Half-hour. Premiered on CBN: 1984–1988.*

## ◎ HONG KONG PHOOEY
The crime-fighting karate expert, Hong Kong Phooey, alias Penrod Pooch, a meek police station janitor, maintains justice through his martial-arts abilities (which he learned in a correspondence course) and kayos his opponents in the process. His means of transportation: the "Phooeymobile." Premiering on ABC in 1974, the 16-episode half-hour series ran for two consecutive seasons. After the series' initial run on ABC, the character was reprised on *The Godzilla/Hong Kong Phooey Hour*. (See entry for details.) In 1989 the series joined USA Network's weekday *Cartoon Express* lineup (in reruns), and was later broadcast on the Cartoon Network and Boomerang. *A Hanna-Barbera Production. Color. Half-hour. Premiered on ABC: September 7, 1974–September 4, 1976. Rebroadcast on NBC: February 4, 1978–September 2, 1978; November 22, 1980–May 15, 1981 (part of* The Godzilla/Hong Kong Phooey Hour*); May 1981–September 5, 1981 (as Hong Kong Phooey). Rebroadcast on USA: May 1, 1989–March 27, 1992. Rebroadcast on CAR: October 2, 1994–May 26, 1996 (Sundays); February 17, 1997–2000 (Monday–Thursday late night). Rebroadcast on BOOM: April 7, 2000–    .*

*Voices*
**Penrod Pooch/Hong Kong Phooey:** Scatman Crothers **Sergeant Flint:** Joe E. Ross; **Rosemary, the switchboard operator:** Kathy Gori; **Spot, Phooey's surly cat:** Don Messick

## ◎ HORRIBLE HISTORIES
Two kids, Stitch and Mo, are sent back in time in a series of hilarious historical adventures in which they match wits with their nerdy nemesis Darren Dongle in this half-hour cartoon series, based on the best-selling books. Largely shown overseas, including ABC Australia and in the United Kingdom, the half-hour comedy adventure program, produced by Mike Young Productions in 2001, debuted on VOOM's Animania HD Network in 2006. *A Mike Young Production. Color. Half-hour. Premiered on ANI: 2006.*

*Voices*
**Stitch/Narrator:** Billy West; **Mo:** Cree Summer; **Darren Dongle:** Jess Harnell

## ◎ HORSELAND

Set in the greatest-ever stable, called the Horseland ranch, a young group of horse-loving kids ride and raise horses and other animals that talk to each and enter their equine friends in riding competitions. Based on the online virtual game and Web community, with more than 2 million registered users, the half-hour, CGI- and traditional cel-animated Saturday morning series, featuring action/adventure storylines dealing with the relationships of the five girls and two boys and their cooperation, compassion and honesty with each other and their beloved thoroughbreds, was part of CBS's new branded three-hour programming block, *KOL Secret Slumber Party on CBS. A DIC Entertainment Production. Color. Half-hour. Premiered on CBS: September 16, 2006.*

*Voices*
Daria Dorian, Emily Hernandez, Bianca Heyward, David Kalis, Jerry Longe, Stephen Shelton, Laura Marr, Vincent Michael, Marissa Shea, Aleyah Smith, Michelle Zacharia

## ◎ HOT WHEELS

Created and produced by Ken Snyder, of TV's *Roger Ramjet* fame, this was the first series created by Anamorphic computer animation. It starred Jack Wheeler, organizer of a young auto racers' club, who battles antagonists in racing competitions. The series was the first cartoon show to offer safety tips and information tidbits on weather, the physical principles of flight and the hazards of smoking.

Stories depicted club members Janet Martin, Skip Frasier, Bud Stuart, Mickey Barnes, Ardeth Pratt and Kip Chogi explaining to children the dangers of auto racing while engaged in reckless race car competition. The show's theme song was written and performed by Mike Curb and the Curbstones; the characters of Mickey and Kip were voiced by well-known comedian Albert Brooks. *A Pantomime Pictures/Ken Snyder Production in association with Mattel Toys. Color. Half-hour. Premiered on ABC: September 6, 1969–September 4, 1971.*

*Voices*
**Jack Wheeler/Doc Warren:** Bob Arbogast; **Janice Martin:** Melinda Casey; **Mickey Barnes/Kip Chogi:** Albert Brooks; **Ardeth Pratt:** Susan Davis; **Tank Mallory/Dexter Carter:** Casey Kasem; **Mother O'Hare:** Nora Marlowe; **Mike Wheeler:** Michael Rye

## ◎ HOT WHEELS HIGHWAY 35: WORLD RACE

Recruited along with a handful of world-famous racers, former teenage surfer Vert Wheeler drives for five racecar teams (Wave Rippers, Scorchers, Street Breed, Dune Ratz and Road Beasts) as he races cool-looking, uncommonly powerful vehicles created by scientist Dr. Peter Tezla through dangerous, surreal courses, from challenging desert to urban environments, with one mission in mind: to capture the Wheel of Power, "the greatest source of energy the world has ever known!"

Produced in celebration of the 35th anniversary Mattel's popular Hot Wheels collectibles, this five-part series of half-hour specials premiered on Cartoon Network in July 2003. In December 2003, the entire five-part series was edited into a 110-minute feature and released on DVD by Family Home Entertainment. In 2005 the series spawned a successful series of four hour-long sequels entitled *AcceleRacers. A Mainframe Entertainment/Mattel Inc. Production. Color. Half-hour. Premiered on CAR: July 12, 2003–August 2, 2003.*

*Voices*
**Dr. Peter Tezla:** Michael Donovan; **Vert Wheeler:** Andrew Francis; **Kurt Wylde:** Brian Drummond; **Markie Wylde:** Will Sanderson; **Taro Kitano:** Kevin Ohtsji; **Lani Tam:** Venus Terzo; **Gig:** Kasper Michaels; **Gelorum:** Kathleen Barr; **Other Voices:** Scott McNeil, Cusse Mankuma, John Payne II

## ◎ THE HOUNDCATS

Government intelligence agents Dingdog, Puttypuss, Mussel Mutt, Stutz and Rhubarb undertake impossible missions in the Wild West. The 13-episode comedy/adventure series was a spoof of TV's *Mission Impossible* with cats and dogs as members of the task force. (Unlike the stars of the long-running network series, these characters become hysterical when the recorded voice tells them the message will self-destruct in five seconds.) The series bowed on CBS in 1972 and lasted one season. *A DePatie-Freleng Enterprises Production. Color. Half-hour. Premiered on NBC: September 9, 1972–September 1, 1973.*

*Voices*
**Stutz, the group's leader:** Daws Butler; **Mussel Mutt, the ex-weightlifter dog:** Aldo Ray; **Rhubarb, the inventor:** Arte Johnson; **Puttypuss, cat of thousand faces:** Joe Besser; **Dingdog, the stuntman:** Stu Gilliam

## ◎ THE HUCKLEBERRY HOUND SHOW

The noble-hearted, slow-talking, Southern-accented bloodhound, Huckleberry Hound, starred and hosted his own series, sponsored by Kellogg's Cereals and syndicated by Screen Gems, the television arm of Columbia Pictures. The program made its debut in 1958 and, one year later, became the first animated cartoon to be awarded an Emmy by the Television Academy. By the fall of 1960 an estimated 16 million Americans and foreign viewers were watching the droopy-eyed bloodhound who starred in 57 six-minute cartoons (one per show) over the course of four seasons.

The series' two companion cartoons on the show (one episode per show) were "Pixie and Dixie" (in 57 episodes of their own), who are perpetually tormented by Mr. Jinks, a beatnik cat; and "Yogi Bear" (in 35 episodes), who pilfers picnic baskets from vacationers at lovely Jellystone National Park. In 1960 "Hokey Wolf" (in 28 episodes) was substituted for Yogi Bear, who starred in his own series the following season. Later, during the show's syndication run, "Yakky Doodle" was pulled from *The Yogi Bear Show* to replace Pixie and Dixie on the show. Episodes of *Huckleberry Hound* were later recycled as part of 1967's *Yogi and His Friends.*

The off-network version of the series *Huckleberry Hound and Friends* was rebroadcast on USA Network, from 1989 to 1991, and the original series was reshown on Cartoon Network and later Boomerang. *A Hanna-Barbera Production. Color. Half-hour. Premiered: October 2, 1958. Syndicated. Rebroadcast on USA: February 17, 1989–September 10, 1992. Rebroadcast on CAR: January 9, 1993–January 1, 1994 (Saturdays); January 10, 1993 (part of Boomerang, 1963); January 3, 1994–February 25, 1994 (weekdays, Saturdays); February 26, 1994–April 2, 1994 (Saturdays); April 9, 1994 (Saturdays, Sundays); August 11, 1995–2000. Rebroadcast on BOOM: April 2, 2000–.*

*Voices*
**Huckleberry Hound:** Daws Butler; **Pixie:** Don Messick; **Dixie/Mr. Jinks, the cat:** Daws Butler; **Yogi Bear:** Daws Butler; **Boo Boo, his cub companion:** Don Messick; **Ranger John Smith:** Don Messick; **Hokey Wolf:** Daws Butler; **Ding-a-Ling, the fox:** Doug Young

*Huckleberry Hound (center) stands as master of ceremonies in* The Huckleberry Hound Show, *featuring Jinx the cat (far left), Pixie and Dixie (left), Boo Boo and Yogi Bear (right). © Hanna-Barbera Productions*

## ◉ HULK HOGAN'S ROCK 'N' WRESTLING!

One of wrestling's most outrageous stars inspired this animated sendup of the popular spectator sport, lending his name but not his voice to this 39-episode animated series, which premiered on CBS in September of 1985. Backed by a strong rock music soundtrack, the show featured stories about the wild and outrageous personalities of the high-contact sport as well as battles between opponents on the wrestling mats. Interspersed through each hour-long program were live-action comedy sketch wraparounds starring the famous World Wrestling Federation champion and fellow wrestler "Mene" Gene Okerlund. The series was later repackaged in 30-minute versions for syndication and, in 1994, joined USA Network's *Cartoon Express*. *A DIC Animation City Production in association with Titan Sports and WWF. Color. One hour. Premiered CBS: September 14, 1985–September 5, 1987. Syndicated. Rebroadcast on WGN: 1993–94. Rebroadcast on USA: September 18, 1994–March 19, 1995.*

### Cast (live action)
**Hulk Hogan:** Himself; **Gene Okerlund:** Himself;

### Voices
**Hulk Hogan:** Brad Garrett; **Capt. Lou Albano:** George DiCenzo; **Junkyard Dog:** James Avery; **Andre the Giant:** Ronald A. Feinberg; **Moolah/Richter:** Jodi Carlisle; **Volkoff:** Ronald Gans; **Roddy:** Charlie Adler; **The Iron Sheik:** Aron Kincaid; **Big John Studd:** Chuck Licini; **Mr. Fuji:** Ernest Harada; **Tino Santana:** Joey Pento; **Superfly Snuka:** Lewis Arquette; **Mean Gene:** Neil Ross; **Hillbilly Jim:** Pat Fraley

## ◉ THE HURRICANES

Inheriting her father's multicutural World Soccer League team, high school–age Amanda Carey turns this team of underachievers into world champions by beating the archrival Gorgons in this globe-trotting half-hour adventure series, which aired in syndication in 1993 as part of the weekend cartoon block *Amazin' Adventures I*. Each episode featured live-action cameos of well-known soccer players delivering prosocial messages. ESPN originally announced plans to rebroadcast the series in the fall of 1994–it was to become the "first" toon series to air on the all-sports network—but the network later abandoned such plans. *A DIC Enterprises/Siriol Productions/Scottish Television Enterprises Production in association with Bohbot Entertainment. Color. Half-hour. Premiered: September 12, 1993 (part of* Amazin' Adventures *I). Syndicated.*

### Voices
Andrew Airlie, Carol Alexander, Kathleen Barr, Michael Benyaer, Gary Chalk, Candus Churchill, Ian James Corlett, Roger Crossly, Chris Gaze, Colin Heath, Stuart Hepburn, Carl Hibbert, Mark Hildreth, Chris Humphreys, Christina Lippa, Scott McNeil, Wezley Morris, Alvin Sanders, Louise Vallance, Peter Williams, Jeannie Zahni, Chiara Zanni

## ◉ I AM THE GREATEST: THE ADVENTURES OF MUHAMMAD ALI

Former heavyweight boxing champ Muhammad Ali supplied his own voice for this 13-episode animated series for NBC that blended comedy, adventure and mystery in situations shaped around Ali's heroics. Joining him in his encounters are his niece and nephew, Nicky and Damon, and his public relations agent, Frank Bannister. Failing to deliver a knockout blow in the ratings, the series was canceled at mid-season. *A Farmhouse Films/Fred Calvert Production. Color. Half-hour. Premiered on NBC: September 10, 1977–January 28, 1978. Rebroadcast on NBC: February 11, 1978–September 2, 1978.*

### Voices
**Muhammad Ali:** Himself; **Nicky, his niece:** Patrice Carmichael; **Damon, his nephew:** Casey Carmichael; **Frank Bannister:** Himself

## ◎ IGPX: IMMORTAL GRAND PRIX

In the year 2049 an amateur, minor-league champion crew of pilots, Team Satomi led by Jean-Michel, overcomes impossible odds as it competes for the championship against ruthless teams of high-speed, high-tech fighting machines in the world's most popular sport and the sport's most exalted form of competition, a mix of racing, martial arts and high technology called the Immortal Grand Prix.

Premiering on Saturday, November 5, 2005, at 10 P.M. (EST) with 13 episodes for its first season, the traditional and CGI-animated futuristic series, co-produced by Cartoon Network and renowned Japanese animation studio, Production I.G., and Bandai Entertainment, marked the first original series produced for Cartoon Network's *Toonami* action programming block that first brought anime television to the United States, including such series as *Dragonball Z*, *The Big O* and *Yu Yu Hakusho*. Previously, in September 2003, Cartoon Network partnered with Production I. G. to produce a prequel of five five-minute episodes of the series that aired for five consecutive days as part of the network's acclaimed *Toonami* "Total Immersion Event" that year.

Voicing the series were such well-known actors as Haley Joel Osment (*Forrest Gump, Sixth Sense*) as the voice of leading character, Takeshi Jin; Michelle Rodriguez (*The Fast and the Furious*) as the Team Satomi pilot, Liz Ricarro; and Mark Hamill and Lance Henriksen lending their voices to key characters. Beginning on May 20, 2006, each returned for a second season to voice a fresh batch of 13 new episodes with the newly crowned champions of the Immortal Grand Prix's IG-1 facing formidable new competitors and foes. *A Cartoon Network Studios/Production I. G./Bandai Entertainment Production. Color. Half-hour. Premiered on CAR: September 15, 2003–September 19, 2003 ("Total Immersion Event"). Premiered on CAR: November 5, 2005–August 25, 2006.*

### Voices

**TEAM SATOMI: Takeshi Jin:** Haley Joel Osment; **Amy Stapleton:** Hynden Walch; **Liz Ricarro:** Michelle Rodriguez; **Michiru Satomi:** Kari Wahlgren; **Mark Ramsey:** Kirk Thorton; **Andrei Rublev:** Lance Henriksen; **Jesse Martin:** Julie Maddalena

**TEAM VELSHTEIN: Alex Cunningham Hume ("The Ghost"):** Steven Jay Blum; **Jan Michael:** Dave Wittenberg; **Dew:** Lex Lang; **Coach Sir Hamgra:** Kim Strauss

**TEAM SLEDGE MAMA: Yamma:** Mark Hamill; **Timma:** Dave Wittenberg; **Dimma:** Andre Ware; **River Marque:** Steve Staley

**TEAM BLACK EGG:** Ricardo Montazio (Forward), Grant McKain (Midfielder) and Glass Jones (Defender)

**TEAM EDGERAID: Bjorn Johannsen:** Crispin Freeman; **Sola:** Wendee Lee; **Frank Bullit:** Dave Wittenberg; **Bella DeMarco:** Stephanie Sheh

**TEAM SKYLARK: Fantine Valjean:** Karen Strassman; **Elisa Doolittle:** Michelle Ruff; **Jessica Darlin:** Kate Higgins

**TEAM WHITE SNOW: Zanak Strauss:** Doug Erholt; **Judy Ballasteros:** Megan Hollingshead; **Max Erlich:** Mela Lee
  **Benjamin Bright, IGPX Announcer:** Tom Kenny

## ◎ INCH HIGH PRIVATE EYE

The Finkerton Detective Agency puts its best man on the case: the world's smallest private eye, Inch High, who is fashioned after Maxwell Smart, agent 86, of TV's *Get Smart*. The thumbnail-size detective relies on various weapons and disguises to capture criminals. His best friend in the world is his dog, Braveheart. The 13-episode series aired one full season on NBC. *A Hanna-Barbera Production. Color. Half-hour. Premiered on NBC: September 8, 1973–August 31, 1974. Rebroadcast on USA: 1989–92. Rebroadcast on CAR: July 9, 1995–May 26, 1996 (Sundays); November 17, 1996–January 24, 2004. Rebroadcast on BOOM; June 8, 2000–.*

### Voices

**Inch High:** Lennie Weinrib; **Lorie, his niece:** Kathy Gori; **Gator, his aide:** Bob Luttrell; **Mr. Finkerton, his boss:** John Stephenson; **Mrs. Finkerton:** Jean VanderPyl; **Braveheart, Inch High's dog:** Don Messick

## ◎ THE INCREDIBLE CRASH DUMMIES

Living up to their motto, "We Crash Because We Care," to make the world a safer place, "one crash at a time," crash dummies Crash, Splice, Crunch and Gyro perform amazing crashes and stunts in this series of fast-paced, tongue-in-cheek, one-minute animated segments, or interstitials, based on the public service announcement characters for safe driving created in the early 1990s; began airing on Saturday mornings on Fox in February 2004. Produced by New York-based Animation Collective, a producer of children's programming for television, home video and the Internet, in association with 4Kids Entertainment, this series was televised between commercials as part of FOX's four-hour *4Kids TV* programming block through the fall of 2005, when it was replaced by interstitials starring the Teenage Mutant Ninja Turtles. Following the series debut in 2004, a new line of Incredible Crash Dummies-branded merchandise, including toys, apparel, accessories, stationery, bags and backpacks for children, hit retail stores throughout the United States. The series marked the characters' second appearance in animated form following the 1992 half-hour television special, *The Incredible Crash Dummies*. *An Animation Collective/4Kids Entertainment Production. Color. One minute. Premiered on FOX: February 1, 2004.*

### Voices

**Crash:** Dan Green; **Splice:** Andrew Rannells; **Crunch:** Eric Stuart; **Gyro:** Stuart Zagnit; **Whiskers the Cat:** Bill Kopp; **Fido the Dog:** Traci Paige Johnson

## ◎ THE INCREDIBLE HULK (1984)

NBC added this series, featuring the hulking Marvel superhero, to its Saturday-morning cartoon roster late in the 1984–85 season. The program repeated episodes that first aired on *The Incredible Hulk/Amazing Spider-Man Hour*. *A Marvel Production. Color. Half-hour. Premiered on NBC: December 15, 1984–September 7, 1985.*

### Voices

Michael Bell, Susan Blu, Bill Callaway, Hamilton Camp, Victoria Carroll, Hans Conreid, Robert Cruz, Jerry Dexter, George DiCenzo, Alan Dinehart, Walker Edmiston, Michael Evans, Al Fann, Ron Feinberg, Elliott Field, June Foray, Pat Fraley, Kathy Garver, Dan Gilvezan, John Hayner, Bob Holt, Michael Horton, Stan Jones, Sally Julian, Stan Lee, Anne Lockhart, Keye Luke, Dennis Marks, Allan Melvin, Shepard Menken, Vic Perrin, Bob Ridgely, Neilson Ross, Stanley Ralph Ross, Michael Rye, Marilyn Schreffler, John Stephenson, Janet Waldo, B.J. Ward, Frank Welker, William Woodson, Alan Young

## ◎ THE INCREDIBLE HULK (1996)

Dr. Bruce Banner, also known as the menacing green-skinned goliath the Incredible Hulk, struggles to conquer the inner beast who comes out whenever his emotions rage in this new half-hour animated version based on the Marvel Comics series. Actor Lou Ferrigno, who played the pea-green gargantuan in the 1970s live-action television series, reprised the character in this cartoon version. (Ferrigno, who suffers from a hearing disability, never spoke in the live-action series but did so in the animated series.) The series bowed Sunday mornings on the UPN Network in the fall of 1996. A *Marvel Films/New World Entertainment Production in association with UPN Kids. Color. Half-hour. Premiered on UPN: September 8, 1996–98. Rebroadcast on UPN: September 20, 1998–September 12, 1999 (as The Incredible Hulk and Friends).*

**Voices**
**The Incredible Hulk:** Lou Ferrigno; **Robert Bruce Banner:** Neal McDonough; **Gabriel Jones:** Thom Barry; **Rick Jones:** Luke Perry; **Betty Ross/Sister Rose Erak:** Genie Francis; **She-Hulk/Jennifer Walters:** Lisa Zane; **General Thaddeus "Thunderbolt" Ross:** John Vernon; **Major Glenn Talbot/Abomination/ZZZAX/Samuel Laroquette/Judge:** Kevin Schon; **Doctor Leonard Samson:** Shadoe Stevens; **Leader:** Matt Frewer; **Gargoyle:** Mark Hamill; **Ogress:** Kathy Ireland

## ◉ THE INCREDIBLE HULK/AMAZING SPIDER-MAN HOUR

New episodes of the Incredible Hulk were added to this hour-long fantasy series and combined with previously broadcast episodes of the popular Saturday-morning series *Spider-Man and His Amazing Friends. A Marvel Production. Color. One-hour. Premiered on NBC: September 19, 1982–September 8, 1984.*

**Voices**
Jack Angel, Michael Bell, Lee Briley, Bill Boyett, Cory Burton, Susan Blu, Wally Burr, Bill Callaway, Hamilton Camp, Victoria Carroll, Phil Clarke, Hans Conreid, Rege Cordic, Henry Corden, Brad Crandall, Robert Cruz, Peter Cullen, Brian Cummings, Jeff David, Jack DeLeon, Jerry Dexter, George DiCenzo, Alan Dinehart, Walker Edmiston, Michael Evans, Al Fann, Ron Feinberg, Elliot Field, June Foray, Pat Fraley, Brian Fuld, Kathy Garver, Linda Gary, Dan Gilvezan, John Haymer, Bob Holt, Michael Horton, Ralph James, Lynn Johnson, Stanley Jones, Sally Julian, Lee Lampson, Stan Lee, Anne Lockhart, Morgan Lofting, Keye Luke, Dennis Marks, Mona Marshall, John Mayer, Alan Melvin, Shepard Menken, Don Messick, Vic Perrin, Tony Pope, Richard Ramos, Bob Ridgely, Neilson Ross, Gene Ross, Stanley Ralph Ross, Michael Rye, Marilyn Schreffler, John Stephenson, Ted Schwartz, Gary Seger, Michael Sheehan, Andre Stojka, Janet Waldo, B.J. Ward, Frank Welker, Paul Winchell, William Woodson, Alan Young

## ◉ THE INCREDIBLE HULK AND FRIENDS

Half-hour program block featuring 21 episodes of UPN's *The Incredible Hulk* from the 1996–97 television season with repeat episodes of *Fantastic Four* and *Iron Man* from the syndicated *Marvel Action Hour*, with these components alternating weekly; aired on UPN Kids' Sunday program block, beginning in September 1998. (For cast and production credits, see *The Incredible Hulk* and *Marvel Action Hour.*) A *Marvel Films/N4ew World Entertainment Production. Color. Half-hour. Premiered on UPN: September 20, 1998–September 12, 1999.*

## ◉ THE INHUMANOIDS

A group of ancient subhuman monsters from the center of Earth escape their fiery dwellings to wreak havoc and destruction. Only the Earth Corps, a team of brilliant human scientists, can combat the creatures in this eight-episode series, first aired in a trial run

(in two episodes) on Marvel's "Super Sunday" weekend cartoon block in January of 1986. The series went weekly in September of that year. A *Marvel Production in association with ClasterTelevision and LBS. Color. Half-hour. Premiered: September 21, 1986–Fall 1987. Syndicated.*

**Voices**
Michael Bell, William Callaway, Fred Collins, Brad Crandel, Dick Gautier, Ed Gilbert, Chris Latta, Neil Ross, Stanley Ralph Ross, Richard Sanders, Susan Silo, John Stephenson

## ◉ INSPECTOR GADGET

Don Adams, formerly TV's Maxwell Smart, agent 86, voiced this bumbling Inspector Clouseau type, originally based in a small provincial town as a local police officer, who becomes the first gadget-ized and bionic inspector working for Interpol. With the intelligent help of his young niece, Penny, and faithful, long-suffering dog, Brain, Gadget always manages to vanquish his enemies and come out victorious. The series made its debut in first-run syndication in September 1983. New episodes were produced in 1985, and, two years later, while still in syndication, the series was rebroadcast on Nickelodeon, beginning in the fall. In 1991 CBS rebroadcast the series Saturday mornings. Episodes of the series also popped up on the Family Channel weekend cartoon block *Fun Town*. The series was also rerun on the network's successors, Fox Family Channel and ABC Family. The series was the first syndicated property of its producer, DIC Enterprises. A *DIC Enterprises Production in association with Field Communications Corp./Fr3/Nelvana/LBS/TMS/Cuckoo's Nest. Color. Half-hour. Premiered: September 10, 1983–September 6, 1986. Syndicated. Rebroadcast on NICK: August 31, 1987–September 13, 1991. Rebroadcast on NICK: September 16, 1996–March 4, 2000. Rebroadcast on CBS: September 14, 1991–September 5, 1992. Syndicated: 1991–1992. Rebroadcast on FAM (as part of Fun Town): September 14, 1992–September 1, 1995. Rebroadcast on FOX FAM: September 3, 2001–November 9, 2001. Rebroadcast on ABC FAM: November 12, 2001–December 28, 2001.*

**Voices**
**Inspector Gadget:** Don Adams; **Penny, his niece:** Mona Marshall, Cree Summer Francks, Holly Berger; **Brain, his dog:** Frank Welker; **Chief Quimby:** Maurice LaMarche; **Capeman:** Townsend Coleman; **Dr. Claw/Madcat:** Frank Welker

*Bumbling Inspector Gadget looks as though he has bumbled his last in the popular syndicated cartoon series* Inspector Gadget. © *DIC Animation City* (COURTESY: DIC ENTERPRISES)

## ◎ INSPECTOR GADGET'S FIELD TRIP

Combining animation with live-action footage, bionic crime-buster Inspector Gadget plays host, tour guide and history teacher as he visits the most colorful, interesting and historical sights throughout the world—places like London, Rome, the NASA Space Center and the Great Wall of China—uncovering colorful facts, quirks and interesting legends and lore, in this half-hour educational series, broadcast on The History Channel in 1996. A DIC Enterprises Production. Color. Half-hour. Premiered on HIS: November 3, 1996.

**Voices**
**Inspector Gadget:** Don Adams

## ◎ INUYASHA

Transported through an ancient well on her way from school in feudal Japan and suddenly surrounded by monsters and magic, a young girl, Higurashi Kagome, teams up with the half-demon InuYasha to recover the shards of a shattered magical gem that possesses supernatural power before it ends up in enemy hands. Originally aired Saturdays at midnight, with weekday reruns at 12:30 A.M. on Cartoon Network's late-night *Adult Swim* block, this English-language version of the popular Japanese anime series debuted in late August 2002. Four feature-length direct-to-DVD movies, previously produced and released in Japan, also debuted on *Adult Swim: InuYasha: Affections Touching across Time* (2005); *InuYasha: The Castle beyond the Looking Glass* (2005); *InuYasha: Swords of an Honorable Ruler* (2006); and *InuYasha: Fire on the Mystic Island* (2006). After the series finale in late October 2006, the program was telecast twice a day Monday through Thursday on *Adult Swim*, showing eight episodes weekly. A Yomimuri TV/ Bandai Visual/Sunrise Inc. Production. Color. Half-hour. Premiered on CAR: August 31, 2002–October 27, 2006. Rebroadcast on CAR: January 1, 2007–.

**Voices**
**Higurashi Kagome:** Moneca Stori; **InuYasha:** Richard Cox; **Kohaku:** Alex Doduk; **Rin:** Brenna O'Briend; **Sessho-maru:** David Kaye; **Jaken:** Don Brown; **Shippo:** Jillian Michaels; **Sango:** Kelly Sheridan; **Miroku:** Kirby Morrow; **Myonga/Naraku:** Paul Dobson; **Kiga:** Scott McNeil; **Kikyo:** Willow Johnson; **Gatenmaru:** Adam Henderson; **InuYasha's Mom:** Alaina Burnett; **Mushin:** Alec Willows, **Momiji:** Alexandra Carter; **Toran:** Alison Matthew; **Hakkaku:** Alistair Abell; **Manten:** Alvin Sanders; **Hiten/Tsuyu's Lord:** Andrew Francis; **Serina:** Anna Cummer; **Nobunaga:** Brad Swaile; **Muso/Shouga:** Brian Dobson; **Juromaru/ Kageromaru/Renkotsu:** Brian Drummond; **Suzuna:** Brittany Wilson; **Ayumi/Bunza/Fake Princess/Flesh-Eating Mask/Hakudoushi/Kagome's Mom/Urasue:** Cathy Weseluck; **Asuka/Mayu:** Chantal Strand; **Hakudoshi/The Infant/Yura of the Hair:** Chiara Zanni; **Orochidayu/Royakan/Sango's Father/Water God:** Colin Murdock

## ◎ INVADER ZIM

A cult hit in its post-Nick life on MTV's sister channel, MTV2. Banished from his planet, a tiny green alien named ZIM descends to Earth with plans to conquer the planet and prove to his planet's leaders that he is worthy of becoming a member of its elite Invader force that wreaks havoc on the universe in wickedly original and quirky science fiction comedy series from well-known comic-book artist Jhonen Vasquez (of *Johnny the Homicidal Maniac* and *SQUEE!* fame). First broadcast in March 2001 on Nickelodeon along with another cartoon newcomer, *The Fairy OddParents*, the series' strange humor and dark, cynical style made it a cult favorite with older viewers, but not with the network's core demographic, two-to 11-year-olds. Poor ratings and high production costs forced Nickelodeon to cancel the series after only one and a half seasons. In its post-NICK life, the series has reaired on Nicktoons and MTV2 as part of their *Sic'emation* cartoon block. A Frederator Inc./Nicktoons Production in association with Viacom International. Color. Half-hour. Premiered on NICK: March 30, 2001–October 13, 2002. Rebroadcast on NICKT: May 4, 2002–. Rebroadcast on MTV2: June 10, 2006–.

**Voices**
**Invader ZIM:** Richard Steven Horvitz;; **GIR:** Rosearik Rikki Simons; **Dib:** Andy Berman; **Gaz:** Melissa Fahn; **Professor Membrane:** Rodger Bumpass, **Miss Bitters:** Lucille Bliss; **Almighty Tallest Red:** Wally Wingert; **Almighty Tallest Purple:** Kevin McDonald; **Additional Voices:** Mr. Scolex (alias Jhonen Vasquez).

## ◎ INVASION AMERICA

When his alien emperor father (Tyrusian) and human mother (Rita) end up missing, their 17-year-old son David finds out who his friends and enemies really are while trying to stop both his worlds—alien and human—from going to war in this weekly half-hour science fiction-series produced for primetime television, created by Oscar-winning producer/director Steven Spielberg and coproduced by Harve Bennett of TV's *Star Trek* series. Combining Korean-produced traditional 2-D cel and DreamWorks's 3-D computer animation (with 12,000 to 13,000 frames alone in the first episode), the series, consisting of 13 half-hour episodes broadcast as five hour-long episodes and a 90-minute finale, was broadcast over a six-week period, beginning in June 1998. Despite featuring a stellar voice cast—including Lorenzo Lamas, Kristy McNichol, Leonard Nimoy and Robert Urich—the series didn't produce strong enough ratings to be held over. Consequently, the WB Television Network yanked the series from its primetime schedule and then added it in the fall to its Kids' WB! Saturday morning lineup, where the show's original episodes were re-edited and rebroadcast in half-hours. A DreamWorks Television Animation/ Warner Bros. Production. Color. Half-hour. Premiered on WB: June 8, 1998–July 6, 1998. Rebroadcast on Kids' WB!: September 19, 1998–October 24, 1998.

**Voices**
**David Carter:** Mikey Kelley; **Cale Oosha:** Lorenzo Lamas; **The Dragit:** Tony Jay; **Rafe:** Edward Albert; **Rita Carter/Sonia:** Kath Soucie; **General Konrad:** Leonard Nimoy; **Simon:** Thom Adcox; **Philip Stark:** Greg Eagles; **Angie Romar:** Kristy McNichol; **Doc:** Ronny Cox; **Major Lomack:** Jim Cummings; **General Gordon:** James B. Sikking; **Jim Bailey:** Rider Strong

## ◎ IRON MAN

After sustaining a severe chest injury from an exploding land mine in Vietnam, millionaire businessman Tony Stark went on to become this flying superhero, wearing an armored suit to keep his damaged heart beating while battling the war-related archenemy, the Mandarin, in a series of comic books created by Stan Lee (with the assistance of artist Don Heck) in 1963. Stark, as Iron Man, first flew onto television screens in 1966 in the Grantray-Lawrence animated series *The Marvel Superheroes*. In 1994 Marvel Films produced the first series featuring the famed Marvel Superhero in a starring role, aired as part of the hour-long syndicated block, *The Marvel Action Hour*. Joined in some episodes by the ForceWorks Team, Iron Man once again encounters his old foe, the Mandarin, and his evil team of villains in 26 episodes (including four two-parters) broadcast over two seasons beginning in

1994. *A Marvel Films/New World Entertainment Production. Color. Half-hour. Premiered: September 24, 1994–September 1996. Syndicated. Rebroadcast: 1997–98 (in syndication as part of* Marvel Super-Heroes*). Rebroadcast on UPN:. September 20, 1998–September 12, 1999 (as part of* The Incredible Hulk and Friends*).*

**Voices**
**Iron Man/Tony Stark:** Robert Hays; **Julia Carpenter:** Casey Defranco; **War Machine/Jim Rhodes:** Dorian Harewood; **The Madarin:** Ed Gilbert; **Madam Maque:** Lisa Zane; **Dreadknight:** Neil Dickson; **Blizzard:** Chuck McCann; **Modok:** Jim Cummings; **Justin Hammer:** Tony Steedman; **Hypnotia:** Linda Huldahl; **Fin Fang Foom:** Neil Ross

## ◎ I SPY

With their friends Duck and Wheeler, Spyler and his energetic cat, CeCe, embark on fun and adventure in an imaginary world in this engaging and educational clay- and CGI-animated, interactive preschool children's series encouraging young viewers' participation and imaginations, produced by Scholastic Entertainment, producers of TV's *Clifford the Big Red Dog, Goosebumps* and *The Magic School Bus.* Winner of a 2003 Daytime Emmy Award for best individual achievement in animation, the 26-episode series, complemented by eclectic musical arrangements and inspired by Scholastic's best-selling picture-riddle books, aired in the United States on HBO's sister channel, HBO Family. Each half-hour featured two cartoons adventures. *A Scholastic Entertainment Production. Color. Half-hour. Premiered on HBO FAM: December 14 2002–September 21, 2003. Rebroadcast on HBO FAM: September 2003–February 12, 2007.*

**Voices**
**Spyler:** Tara Jayne: **CeCe:** Ellen Lee; **Duck:** Cindy Creekmore; **Other Voices:** Big A1

## ◎ IT'S ITSY BITSY TIME

Twice-daily anthology children's series, initially presented in one one-hour and two half-hour blocks, offering an assortment of cartoon shorts produced by British and European animation studios, broadcast commercial-free in the United States on FOX Family Channel. A winner of the 2000 Parent's Choice Award, among the cartoons featured were animated shorts by U.K. animation giant, Cosgrove-Hall ("Animal Shelf," "Tom & Vicky," "64 Zoo Lane," "Charley and Mimmo") and episodes of other FOX Family Channel cartoon series, including *Budgie the Little Helicopter. An Itsy Bitsy Entertainment Co. Production. Color. One hour. Half-hour. Premiered on FOX FAM: September 6, 1999–August 30, 2002.*

## ◎ IT'S PUNKY BREWSTER

Based on the prime-time live-action comedy hit of 1984 to 1986, NBC commissioned this animated series version. The 42-episode half-hour series experienced even greater success as a Saturday morning vehicle Punky's special friend, Glomer, transports Punky and her friends to the four corners of Earth in the blink of an eye. *A Ruby-Spears Enterprises Production. Color. Half-hour. Premiered on NBC: September 14, 1985–August 22, 1987. Rebroadcast on NBC: November 12, 1988–September 2, 1989.*

**Voices**
**Punky Brewster:** Soleil-Moon Frye; **Cherie:** Cherie Johnson; **Margaux:** Ami Foster; **Allen Anderson:** Casey Ellison; **Henry Warnimont:** Georges Gaynes; **Glomer:** Frank Welker

## ◎ IT'S THE MR. HELL SHOW

Outlandish adult animated comedy series featuring the exploits of a stylishly dressed nighttime talk-show host, a Satan-esque Mr. Hell, complete with devilish horns, who makes a mockery of his guests with his wicked sense of humor in his own adventures, introducing a series of separate cartoon segments starring a cast of recurring notables, including Serge the Seal of Death, Josh the Reincarnation Guy, the Victorian lady Detective, Tommy Tomorrow the Prophet, and others. First shown on Canadian television in 2000, the half-hour, British-Canadian coproduced adult comedy series, featuring British comedy legend and television host Bob Monkhouse as the voice of Mr. Hell, then bowed in the United Kingdom (as *Aaagh! It's the Mr. Hell Show*) on the BBC in October 2001. Lasting one season, the program subsequently premiered in the United States on Showtime in March 2002. Monkhouse died on December 29, 2003, following a two-year bout with cancer. *A Peafur/Sextant Entertainment/Mr. Hell/BBC Production. Color. Half-hour. Premiered SHO: March 3, 2002.*

**Voices**
**Mr. Hell:** Bob Monkhouse; **Josh the Reincarnation Guy:** Jeff "Swampy" Marsh; **Other Voices:** Paul Dobson, Michael Dobson, Grahame Andrews, Philip Maurice Hayes, Ellie King, Scott McNeil, Pauline Newstone, Gerard Plunkett, Tabitha St. Germain

## ◎ THE ITSY BITSY SPIDER

Originally produced as a 1992 theatrical cartoon short, this wise-guy, four-eyed, spindly-legged troublemaker, whose best friends are a little girl (Leslie) and her young friend (George), tries to keep one step ahead of the Exterminator (a musclebound karate champ who is befriended by the girl's piano teacher/mother) in this half-hour animated spinoff. USA Network commissioned this slapstick-filled Saturday morning series in 1993, the year the network added first-run cartoon series to its regular lineup. (The series aired in tandem with the new animated series *Problem Child.*) In 1995 following its original run, the series was rebroadcast and moved to Sunday-mornings. Frank Welker, who portrayed Itsy in the seven-minute theatrical cartoon short, returned to provide the voice of the title character in the show.

*A Hyperion Animation Production in association with Paramount Television. Color. Half-hour. Premiered on USA: October 31, 1993–September 15, 1996.*

**Voices**
**Itsy/Langston:** Frank Welker; **Adrienne Facts:** Charlotte Rae; **The Exterminator:** Matt Frewer; **Leslie:** Francesca Marie Smith; **George:** Jonathan Taylor Thomas

## ◎ JABBERJAW

Capitalizing on the movie *Jaws,* Hanna-Barbera created the lovable but stupid white shark Jabberjaw, who sounds like Curly Howard of The Three Stooges. He serves as mascot for four teenagers (Clam-Head, Bubbles, Shelly and Biff) and their rock group, The Neptunes, living in an underwater civilization in A.D. 2021. Created by cartoon veterans Joe Ruby and Ken Spears, the 16-episode series bowed on ABC in 1976. *A Hanna-Barbera Production. Color. Half-hour. Premiered on ABC: September 11, 1976–September 3, 1977. Rebroadcast on ABC: September 11, 1977–September 3, 1978. Rebroadcast on USA: 1989–92. Rebroadcast on CAR: (beginning) April 10, 1994 (Sundays); October 19, 1997–May 23, 2004. Rebroadcast on BOOM: May 1, 2000–.*

**Voices**
**Jabberjaw:** Frank Welker; **Clam-Head:** Barry Gordon; **Bubbles:** Julie McWhirter; **Shelly:** Pat Paris; **Biff:** Tommy Cook

**Other Voices**
Don Messick

## ◎ JACKIE CHAN ADVENTURES

Action-packed adventures of the famed martial arts film star as an unassuming amateur archaeologist enlisted by a secret law enforcement organization who, with the help of his family—his niece, Jade, his cantankerous uncle, and his friend, Captain Black—fights to stop a criminal group from obtaining magical artifacts to release an evil spirit and rule the world. Part of the Kids' WB! Saturday-morning lineup, it finished third against all competition among males ages nine to fourteen during the 2003–04 season. This long-running 95-episode half-hour series, which combined cartoon adventures with a live-action segment ("Hey Jackie" starring Chan himself), aired for five seasons from September 2000 to September 2006, and was shown simultaneously on Cartoon Network. Nominated in 2000 and 2001 for four Daytime Emmy Awards for outstanding achievement in sound editing, outstanding achievement in sound mixing and outstanding performer in an animated program, the series was subsequently rebroadcast on Toon Disney's Monday through Friday *Jetix* action programming block. *An Adelaide/JC Group/Blue Train/Sony Entertainment Production. Color. Half-hour. Premiered on the WB (Kids' WB!): September 9, 2000–July 8, 2005. Rebroadcast on CAR: September 14, 2001–September 16, 2006. Rebroadcast on TDIS: September 5, 2006– .*

**Cast (live-action) ("Hey Jackie" Segment)**
**Jackie Chan:** Himself

**Voices**
**Jackie Chan/Shendu/Chow:** James Sie; **Jade Chan:** Stacie Chan; **Tohru:** Noah Nelson; **Uncle Chan:** Shab Shimono; **Mama Tohru:** Amy Hill; **Capt. Augustus Black/Ratso:** Clancy Brown; **Valmont:** Julian Sands (2000–01), Greg Ellis (2001– ); **Finn:** Adam Baldwin; **Hak Foo:** Jim Cummings; **Additional Voices:** John DiMaggio, Miguel Ferrer, CCH Pounder

## ◎ THE JACKSON 5IVE

Jackie, Marion, Jermaine, Tito and Michael, as then-members of Motown's popular rock group The Jackson 5ive, star in real-life situations that spotlight their comedic lifestyles, happenings and misadventures in cartoon form. The 23-episode half-hour cartoon series originally aired on ABC from 1971 to 1973. It returned to the airwaves via daily syndication in the mid-1980s and briefly again in 1996 on Saturday mornings on VH1. *A Halas and Batchelor Production for Rankin-Bass Productions and Motown. Color. Half-hour. Premiered on ABC: September 11, 1971–September 1, 1973. Syndicated. Rebroadcast on VH1: September 7, 1996–October 12, 1996.*

**Voices**
**Jackie:** Sigmund Jackson; **Tito:** Toriano Jackson; **Jermaine:** Jermaine Jackson; **David:** Marion Jackson; **Michael:** Michael Jackson

## ◎ JACOB TWO-TWO

Nicknamed Two-Two since he often has to repeat himself, a good-hearted, high-spirited boy named Jacob, the youngest and smallest of five children, finds a way to be heard when he lands in the middle of action and adventure with his friends, from foiling the plots of international spies to exposing the evil ways of the cafeteria lady, in this half-hour animated series based on Canadian author Mordecai Richler's popular children's book trilogy. Produced by Canada's Nelvana studios, the delightfully entertaining half-hour series, originally broadcast on Canada's YTV beginning in 2003, premiered in the United States on NBC's *qubo* program block in September 2006, along with such animated fare as *Babar*, *Jane and the Dragon* and *VeggieTales*, targeting children ages two to 11. The program block simultaneously aired weekends on ION (PAX) network and Spanish-language channel Telemundo. *A Nelvana Limited//9 Story Entertainment Production. Color. Half-hour. Premiered on NBC/TM: September 9, 2006–. Premiered on ION: September 15, 2006–.*

**Voices**
**Jacob Two-Two:** Billy Rosenberg; **Noah/Agent O'Toole:** Marc McMulkin; **Emma/Intrepid Shapiro:** Kaitlin Howell; **Daniel:** Jeff Berg; **Marfa:** Jocelyn Barth; **Morty:** Harvey Atkin; **Florence:** Janet-Laine Green; **Renee:** Julie Lemieux; **Buford Orville Gayword Pugh:** Kristopher Clark; **Principal Greedyguts:** Dwayne Hill; **Miss Sour Pickle:** Fiona Reird; **Leo Louise:** Howard Jerome

## ◎ JAKERS! THE ADVENTURES OF PIGGLEY WINKS

Set in two settings and time periods, Grandpa Piggley Winks recalls tales of his remarkable childhood as a spunky eight-year-old pig with his best friends Dannan the Duck and Ferny the Bull on Raloo Farm in rural Ireland in the 1950s, for his three rambunctious city-dwelling grandpigs in his home in the United States. Brooklyn-born Wiley the Sheep (voiced by comedy legend Mel Brooks) freely offers advice to his all-too-sheepish flock in this storybook-CGI-animated preschool series.

Soccer great Cobi Jones (captain of the Los Angeles Galaxy) hosts the series and is featured in three-minute live-action epilogues called "Jakers! Live and Learn" before each animated episode. The half-hour series debuted to rave reviews on September 7, 2003, on PBS Kids' program block, with stories teaching important lessons for children ages four to seven. Beginning in September 2005, the Daytime Emmy Award-winning children's series began airing Monday through Friday, with PBS ordering 12 new episodes and a total of 40 episodes since the fall of 2003. For the series' third season Joan Rivers (as the voice of Wiley's sheep-date wife Shirley) as well as author-educator Frank McCourt as Mr. McHoof joined the cast. Storylines were increasingly devoted to exploring intergenerational relationships, a popular component with adult and young viewers of the series.

By the spring of 2005, the award-winning children's series was also rebroadcast on PBS's new digital cable channel and video-on-demand service (VOD), PBS Kids Sprout, featuring a mix of programming for preschool viewers. In 2006, the series won a Daytime Emmy Award for outstanding achievement in production color design and was one of only five PBS Kids shows to garner multiple Daytime Emmy nominations that year. Previously, the series was awarded two 2004 Daytime Emmys, a Parents Choice Award and a Prix Jeunesse for best preschool website. *A Mike Young/Entara Ltd. Production. Color. Half-hour. Premiered on PBS Kids: September 7, 2003. Rebroadcast on PBS Kids Sprout (VOD): April 4, 2005–. Rebroadcast on PBS Kids Sprout (digital cable): September 26, 2005–.*

**Voices**
**Piggley Winks:** Peadar Lamb; **Young Piggley Winks:** Maile Flanagan; **Annie Winks:** Russi Taylor; **Dannan O'Mallard:** Tara Strong; **Mr. Hornsby:** Charles Adler; **Seamus:** Nika Futterman; **Meggie:** Melissa Disney; **Hector MacBadger:** Pamela Adlon; **Wiley the Sheep:** Mel Brooks; **Holly:** Mauri Bernstein; **Miss Nanny:** Susan Silo; **Shirley:** Joan Rivers; **Mr. McHoof:** Frank McCourt

**Live Action**
**Himself:** Cobi Jones

## JAMES BOND JR.

The 17-year-old nephew of the famed fictional British supersleuth encounters saboteurs, criminals and other bad guys—mostly linked to the enemy organization S.C.U.M. (Saboteurs and Criminals United in Mayhem)—employing high-tech gadgetry and acts of derring-do in this first-run half-hour adventure series spin-off of Ian Fleming's internationally known literary character and popular film series. *A Mac.B., Inc./Murikami-Wolf-Swenson Production in association with Claster and MGM/United Artists Television. Color. Half-hour. Premiered: September 16, 1991–93. Syndicated. Rebroadcast on CAR: January 2, 1995–96 (weekdays).*

### Voices

Jeff Bennett, Corey Burton, Julian Holloway, Mona Marshall, Brian Mitchell, Jean Rabson, Susan Silo, Simon Templeman, Aride Talent, Eddie Barth, Cheryl Bernstein, Susan Blu, Susan Boyd, Hamilton Camp, Jennifer Darling, Mari Devon, Jane Downs, Paul Eiding, Jeannie Elias, Pat Fraley, Linda Gary, Ellen Gerstell, Ed Gilbert, Rebecca Gilchrest, Michael Gough, Gaille Heidemann, Vicki Juditz, Matt N. Miller, Pat Musick, Allan Oppenheimer, Samantha Paris, Tony Pope, Bob Ridgely, Maggie Roswell, Kath Soucie, B.J. Ward, Jill Wayne

## JANA OF THE JUNGLE

(See GODZILLA AND THE SUPER 90.)

## JANE AND THE DRAGON

Set in medieval times, Jane, a 13-year-old lady-in-waiting, becomes a brave apprentice knight after befriending a 300-year-old, talking, fire-breathing dragon she keeps in her backyard that accompanies her on her adventures in this CGI-animated comedy/adventure series targeting girls ages six to 11 and based on the popular children's book series by writer/illustrator Martin Baynton; co-produced by Canada's Nelvana Limited and New Zealand's WETA Workshop. Directed by Mike Fallows, the half-hour series, first shown on Canada's YTV and Australia's ABC networks, debuted in the United States on Saturday, September 9, 2006, on NBC and Telemundo as part of a syndicated weekend program block—including such animated series as *Babar, Jacob Two-Two, Dragon* and *VeggieTales*—called *qubo*. The *qubo* block re-aired on ION (formerly PAX) beginning Friday, September 15, 2006. Voice characterizations by Canadian actors were recorded in Canada at Nelvana's studios with physical performances of the characters performed by a team of five actors. The series was animated using motion-capture technology by WETA Workshop's studios in New Zealand. *A Nelvana Limited/WETA Workshop Production. Color. Half-hour. Premiered on NBC/TM: September 9, 2006. Premiered on ION: September 15, 2006.*

### Voices

**Jane:** Taija Isen; **Dragon:** Adrian Truss; **Jester:** Mark Rendal; **Smithy:** Alex House; **Pepper:** Sunday Muse; **Rake:** Will Seatle Bowes; **Gunther:** Noah Reid; **Magnus:** Clive Walton; **King Caradoc:** Juan Chioran; **Prince Cuthbert:** Cameron Ansell; **Princess Lavina:** Isabel De Carteret; **Sir Theodore:** Aron Tager; **Sir Ivan:** Ben Campbell

## JANOSCH'S DREAM WORLD

Based on the works of award-winning German author/illustrator Horst Eckert (whose pen name was Janosch), this half-hour anthology series, first released on home video in the United States in the early 1990s and produced between 1988 and 1990, featured a series of heartwarming and entertaining cartoon fables animated by Germany's WDR studios. The series made its American television debut on Nickelodeon in 1993. *A CINAR Film/WDG Cologne Production. Color. Half-hour. Premiered on NICK: December 6, 1993–June 10, 1994.*

### Voices

Dean Hagopian, Terry Haig, Harry Hill, Terrence Labrosse Ross, Elizabeth MacRae, Howard Ryshpan, Sam Stone, Jane Woods

## JAYCE AND THE WHEELED WARRIORS

Jayce, the son of a famous scientist, and his space-age crew known as the Lightning League—Herc, a mercenary pilot; Gillian, a wise wizard; Flora, a half-plant/half-human girl; and Oon, a mechanical squire/slave—travel the universe in search of his father to reunite the root of a plant that can prevent Saw Boss and his evil plant followers, the Monster Minds, from taking over the universe. The 65-episode series, based on the popular toy line, was produced for first-run syndication and was later rebroadcast on USA Network's *Cartoon Express. A DIC Audiovisuel Production in association with WWP Productions/ICC Canada-France TV/SFM. Color. Half-hour. Premiered: September 16, 1985–Summer 1987. Syndicated. Rebroadcast on USA: June 5, 1994–September 1995.*

### Voices

**Jayce:** Darin Baker; **Audric, Jayce's father:** Dan Hennessey; **Flora:** Valerie Politis; **Oon:** Luba Goy; **Gillian:** Charles Joliffe; **Herc Stormsailer:** Len Carlson; **Saw Boss:** Giulio Kukurugya; **Monster Minds:** Dan Hennessey, Len Carlson, John Stocker; **Ko Kruiser/Sawtrooper:** Dan Hennessey; **Terror Tank:** Len Carlson; **Gun Grinner:** John Stocker

## JAY JAY THE JET PLANE

A perky and playful six-year-old jet plane's curious nature results in a series of electrifying adventures at Tarrytown Airport, where his imagination takes flight with his airplane friends in this popular, educational, CGI 3-D animated series, first produced as a home video series presenting life lessons for preschool children on science and nature. Mixing fantasy, humor, memorable songs and live-action traffic controller character, Brenda Blue, in each story, the beloved 40-episode half-hour series, created by Deborah and David Michel, originally debuted on the Learning Channel in November 1998 and three years later joined the PBS Kids' weekday program block, featuring both new and old episodes with new episodes produced in 2001 and 2005. In April 2005, the popular children's series joined a slate of PBS Kids shows rebroadcast as part of the network's new digital cable channel and video-on-demand (VOD) service, PBS Kids Sprout. Since its debut in 1998, the multiple award-winning series from PorchLight Entertainment has been seen by 80 percent of all U.S. television households weekly and in 60 countries around the world. *A PorchLight Entertainment/Modern Cartoons Ltd./Knightscove Entertainment Production. Color. Half-hour. Premiered TLC: November 2, 1998–December 29, 2000. Premiered on PBS Kids: June 11, 2001. Rebroadcast on PBS Kids Sprout (VOD): April 4, 2005–. Rebroadcast on PBS Kids Sprout (digital cable): September 26, 2005–.*

### Cast (live-action)

**Brenda Blue:** Eva Whittle

### Voices

**Jay Jay:** Mary Kay Bergman; **Other Voices:** Chuck Morgan, Gina Ribini

## JEANNIE

In this cartoon spin-off of TV's *I Dream of Jeannie*, Center City High School teenager Corry Anders discovers a magic lamp containing a lady genie and her bumbling apprentice, Babu. They become his grateful servants and use their magical powers to help him out of trouble in this top-rated 16-episode cartoon series for CBS. Actor Mark Hamill, of *Star Wars*, provided the voice of Corry. *A Hanna-Barbera Production in association with Screen Gems. Color. Half-hour. Premiered on CBS: September 9, 1973–August 30, 1975.*

**Voices**
**Jeannie:** Julie McWhirter; **Babu:** Joe Besser; **Corry Anders:** Mark Hamill; **Henry Glopp, Corry's friend:** Bob Hastings; **Mrs. Anders, Corry's mother:** Janet Waldo

## ◎ JELLABIES
Six cuddly, colorful characters who live in a world made of jelly— Strum, who plays the saxophone; Bouncy, who makes his home in a bumper car; Denny, a boat dwelling jellaby; Pepper, who lives in a tree house; and twins Amber and Coal, who live in hot-air balloons—are joined by Duffy the green Dragon to sing, dance and spread joy and laughter while making rainbows in this half-hour children's series. Britain's first CGI-animated television series, it was first broadcast in the United Kingdom and Europe as *Jellikins*. Narrated by British actor-comedian Rik Mayall and featuring original songs performed by Sherrie Ashton, the fantasy/adventure series aired weekdays in the United States opposite the live-action children's program *The Wiggles* on FOX Family Channel. *A GMTV/ITV/Winchester/Optical Image Ltd. Production. Color. Half-hour. Premiered on FOX FAM: September 6, 1999–December 26, 2000.*

**Voices**
**Narrator:** Rik Mayall; **Singer:** Sherrie Ashton

## ◎ JEM
Jerrica Benton, a beautiful, ambitious and brilliant music executive and founder of a home for teenage runaways has a double identity: Through a magical transformation, she becomes JEM, a glamorous rock star who wages outrageous battles of the bands. First introduced in 1985 as a separate half-hour series, part of Marvel's *Super Sunday* weekend cartoon block, it was so popular with viewers that producers offered the series by itself in weekly syndication in 1986. Three years later, the program reaired on USA Network's *Cartoon Express*. *A Marvel Production in association with Sunbow Production. Color. Half-hour. Premiered: August 3, 1986–Fall 1989 (originally syndicated in 1985 as component of* Super Sunday*). Syndicated. Rebroadcast on USA: September 18, 1989–August 8, 1993.*

**Voices**
Charlie Adler, Tammy Amerson, Patricia Albrecht, Marlene Aragon, Allison Argo, Ellen Bernfield, Bobbi Block, Cathianne Blore, Sue Blue, Jan Britain, Anne Bryant, Wally Burr, Angela Cappelli, Kim Carlson, T.K. Carter, Cathy Cavadini, Linda Dangcil, Louise Dorsey, Walker Edmiston, Laurie Faso, Ed Gilbert, Dan Gilvezan, Diva Grey, Desiree Goyette, Lani Groves, Michael Horton, Ford Kinder, Jeff Kinder, Clyde Kusatu, Kathi Marcuccio, Cindy McGee, Ullanda McCulloug, Samantha Newark, Noelle North, Britta Phillips, Neil Ross, Jack Roth, Michael Sheehan, Hazel Shermet, Tony St. James, Terri Textor, Florence Warner, Valerie Wilson, Keone Young

## ◎ THE JETSONS
Hanna-Barbera's space-age answer to its prehistoric blockbuster *The Flintstones* brought the Jetson family of the 21st century into living rooms in 1963 on ABC. For a one-season show, the program—for which only 24 half-hour episodes were produced—remains immensely popular among viewers today. (Its debut episode was "Rosie the Robot.")

Stories depict the prospects of living in a futuristic society and showcase George Jetson, employee of Spacely Space Age Sprockets; his lovely, practical wife, Jane; his teeny-bopping daughter, Judy; and his inventive son, Elroy. They have the luxury of computer-operated housing facilities, a robot maid named Rosie and compact flying vehicles that fold into the size of a briefcase.

In 1984 Hanna-Barbera produced a new series of half-hour episodes (41 for the first season) for first-run syndication, which were voiced by most of the original cast. One new character was added: a pet alien named Orbity (voiced by Frank Welker). The new series was stripped for daily syndication and combined with episodes from the original 1962 series. In 1987 the syndicated series went back into production, producing 10 more half-hour installments, followed by a two-hour TV movie that same year, *The Jetsons Meet the Flintstones*. A year later the space-age family returned in an animated special, *Rockin' with Judy Jetson*. Members of the original cast were reassembled again to lend their voices to the full-length animated feature *Jetsons: The Movie*, released in 1990. Reruns of the original series have since aired on Cartoon Network and Boomerang. *A Hanna-Barbera Production. Color. Half-hour. Premiered on ABC: September 23, 1962–September 8, 1963. Rebroadcast on ABC: September 21, 1963–April 18, 1964. Rebroadcast on CBS: September 4, 1965–September 5, 1966. Rebroadcast on NBC: October 2, 1965–September 2, 1967; September 10, 1966–September 7, 1967. Rebroadcast on CBS: September 13, 1969–September 4, 1971; Rebroadcast on NBC: September 11, 1971–September 4, 1976; February 3, 1979–September 5, 1981. Rebroadcast on ABC: September 18, 1982–April 2, 1983. Premiered (new series): September 1984–90. Rebroadcast on CAR: October 1, 1992–September 1, 1995; March 4, 1996–October 3, 2004 (weekdays). Syndicated. Rebroadcast on TBS/TNT: 1992–95. Rebroadcast on BOOM: April 1, 2000–.*

**Voices**
**George Jetson:** George O'Hanlon; **Jane Jetson:** Penny Singleton; **Judy Jetson:** Janet Waldo; **Elroy Jetson:** Daws Butler; **Cosmo C. Spacely, George's boss:** Mel Blanc; **Astro, the family dog:** Don Messick; **Rosie, the robot maid:** Jean VanderPyl; **Henry Orbit, janitor:** Howard Morris; **Cogswell, owner of Cogswell: Cogs:** Daws Butler; **Uniblab:** Don Messick; **Orbity:** Frank Welker (1984)

## ◎ JIM AND JUDY IN TELELAND
The various adventures of two children are related in this highly imaginative limited-animated adventure show first produced in 1949–50, combining cut-out animation and animation cels to create each story. The two characters, who began and closed each episode framed inside a television, encountered a host of unbelievable characters along the way—spies, pirates, giant insects and others—in this syndicated series, which is believed to have been aired in weekly, five-minute time slots. Fifty-two five-minute, cliffhanging episodes were produced initially. The series was reissued in 1959 under the title of *Bob and Betty in Adventureland*. *A Television Screen/Film Flash, Inc. Production. Black-and-white. Five minutes. Premiered: 1953. Syndicated.*

**Voices**
**Jim:** Merrill Jolls; **Judy:** Honey McKenzie

## ◎ JIM HENSON'S MUPPETS, BABIES AND MONSTERS
In September 1985, in response to the huge ratings success of Jim Henson and Marvel Productions' Saturday-morning animated children's series, *Muppet Babies*, CBS expanded the Emmy Award-

winning program to 90 minutes and added a new live-action, half-hour segment to the animated Muppet Babies each week: "Little Muppet Monster," featuring live-action characters who produced their own imaginary television show. The new, improved version lasted only one season and was trimmed down to an hour under its former title for the new fall season in 1986. *A Jim Henson Productions/Marvel Production. Color. One-hour. Premiered on CBS: September 14, 1985–September 6, 1986.*

*Voices*
**Kermit/Beaker:** Frank Welker; **Animal:** Howie Mandel, Dave Coulier; **Skeeter:** Howie Mandel, Frank Welker; **Bunsen:** Dave Coulier; **Fozzie/Scooter:** Greg Berg; **Rowlf:** Katie Leigh; **Piggy:** Laurie O'Brien; **Gonzo:** Russi Taylor; **Nannie:** Barbara Billingsley; **Other Voices:** Peter Cullen

## ◉ JOHNNY BRAVO

This series follows the one-track, never-ending obsession (and perpetual failure) with women of this blond, buff-chested, karate-chopping free spirit who believes he is a gift from God to women of Earth, loves his mother and tolerates his next-door neighbor Suzy all at the same time. Created by 26-year-old independent animator Van Partible (who derived the character's name from the classic television series *The Brady Bunch* in the episode entitled "Adios, Johnny Bravo"), *Johnny Bravo* was the third breakout series from Hanna-Barbera that originated as a cartoon short on the Cartoon Network's *World Premiere Toons* series. In July of 1997

*This biceps-bulging, karate-chopping free spirit believes he is a gift from God to the women of Earth in the animated comedy series* Johnny Bravo *(if only he knew!). © Hanna-Barbera Productions* (COURTESY: CARTOON NETWORK)

the character debuted in 13 half-hour programs, each including three seven-minute cartoons, some of which featured animated versions of such celebrities as Farrah Fawcett, Adam West, Donny Osmond and Scooby-Doo (each of whom appeared as special "celebrity guests"). Many other big-name celebrities also lent their voices in future episodes, including Jessica Biel, Alec Baldwin, "Weird Al" Yankovic, Luke Perry, Gary Owens as the Blue Falcon, Dionne Warwick, Mick Jagger, Richard Simmons, Mr. T., Mark Hamill, Shaquille O'Neal and Donny Osmond.

With storylines set in his fictional hometown of Aron City, Johnny was joined in each comical episode by a stellar supporting cast of characters, including his "flower power" mother, Bunny (voiced by Brenda Vaccaro); his annoying red-haired eight-year-old neighbor, Little Suzy; the local genius science geek Carl Chryniszzswics; and father figure, chili restaurant owner, Pops. Amassing 65 episodes in four seasons, the Elvis Presley sound-alike also starred in three half-hour primetime specials, all during the 2003–04 television season, on Cartoon Network: *Johnny Bravo Christmas* (2003), *It's Valentine's Day, Johnny Bravo* (2003) and *Johnny Bravo Goes to Hollywood* (2004). In September 2005, the series aired for the last time on Cartoon Network. *A Hanna-Barbera/Cartoon Network Production. Color. Half-hour. Premiered on CAR: July 1, 1997–September 23, 2005.*

*Voices*
**Johnny Bravo:** Dwayne Johnson (2003–2005), Jeff Bennett; **Bunny "Mama" Bravo:** Brenda Vaccaro; **Little Suzy:** Mae Whitman; **Carl:** Micky Dolenz (1997–99); **Carlos "Carl" Chrysniszzswics:** Tom Kenny; **Pops:** Larry Drake

## ◉ JOHNNY CYPHER IN DIMENSION ZERO

Brilliant Earth scientist Johnny Cypher finds that he has superhuman powers enabling him to travel through the dimensions of inner space and combat sinister forces. This half-hour series of four six-minute adventures, some of them cliffhangers (adding up to 130 episodes in all), was produced by Joe Oriolo, who also produced television's *Felix the Cat* series. *A Seven Arts Production in association with Joe Oriolo Films. Color. Half-hour. Premiered: February 1967. Syndicated.*

*Voices*
**Johnny Cypher:** Paul Hecht; **Zena, his female assistant:** Corinne Orr; **Rhom, galactic being/Other voices:** Gene Allen

## ◉ JOHNNY TEST

Out-of-this-world adventures of a fearless 10-year-old, Johnny—who unwittingly plays test subject to a series of scientific experiments by his supergenius twin-sister scientists, Susan and Mary—and his genetically engineered super-dog, Dukey, who travel back in time and fight evil villains along the way, in this 2-D animated half-hour action/comedy series for kids ages six to 11 created by Scott Fellows, creator/executive producer of the witty live-action Nickelodeon comedy series, *Ned's Declassified School Survival Guide,* and writer for Nick's *The Fairly OddParents.* In September 2005, the series was launched on the WB Television Network's Kids' WB! Saturday morning lineup with 13 first-season episodes. Renewed for a second season, new episodes debuted in the fall of 2006 on the newly christened CW Network. *A Cookie Jar Entertainment Production. Color. Half-hour. Premiered on the WB (Kids' WB!): September 17, 2005. Premiered on CW ("Kids' WB!"): September 23, 2006– .*

*Voices*
**Johnny Test:** James Arnold Taylor; **Johnny's Dad:** Ian James Corlett; **Johnny's Mom:** Kathleen Barr; **Susan Test/Mary Test:**

Brittney Wilson; **Davis:** Lucy Davis; **Dukey:** Jeff Woodlock; **Additional Voices:** Zachery McKay, Tom Kenny, Candi Milo

## ☺ JOJO'S CIRCUS

Colorful stop-motion animated Big Top adventures of an inquisitive six-year-old girl clown and daughter of famous circus clowns who learns valuable everyday lessons about social behavior, motor skills, nutrition and safety while exploring the world in and around Circus Town with her friends, Skeebo, Croaky, Trina and her pet, Goliath the Lion. Created and produced by Jim Jinkins and David Campbell, the half-hour musical-comedy series, featuring games and songs and inviting viewers to participate, premiered weekday mornings on the Disney Channel's *Playhouse Disney* programming block in the fall of 2003. A *Cartoon Cola-Cartoon Pizza/Cuppa Coffee Production. Color. Half-hour. Premiered on DIS ("Playhouse Disney"): September 28, 2003.*

### Voices

**JoJo Tickle:** Madeleine Martin; **Goliath the Lion:** Robert Smith; **Skeebo Seltzer:** Austin Di Iulio, Keeler Sandaus; **Croaky Frogini:** Diana Peressini; **Trina Tightrope:** Tajja Isen; **Mr. Tickle:** David Sparrow, Noah Weisberg; **Peaches Tickle:** Marnie McPhail, Shannon Perreault; **Mrs. Kersplatski:** Jayne Eastwood

## ☺ JOKEBOOK

Twenty to 25 individually styled animated jokes selected from among a wide assortment of foreign and student films, award-winning cartoon shorts and original concepts highlight this colorful fantasy showcase of entertaining animation from throughout the world. Segments ranged from 20 seconds to three minutes each.

Marty Murphy, a cartoonist for various national magazines, including *Playboy*, was a consultant on the series. Frank Ridgeway, syndicated cartoonist for hundreds of newspapers, and Jack Bonestell, cartoonist for national magazines, also contributed their unique styles to the show.

Some of the films shown included the Oscar-winning animated short subjects, "Crunch Bird" and "The Fly," which took best animated short film honors at the Academy Awards. The show's theme song was sung by comedian Scatman Crothers. A *Hanna-Barbera Production. Color. Half-hour. Premiered on NBC: April 23, 1982–May 7, 1982.*

### Voices

Henry Corden, Bob Hastings, Joan Gerber, Joyce Jameson, Don Messick, Sidney Miller, Robert Allen Ogle, Ronnie Schell, Marilyn Schreffler, Hal Smith, John Stephenson, Janet Waldo, Lennie Weinrib, Frank Welker

## ☺ JOSIE AND THE PUSSYCATS

Based on characters created by Dan DeCarlo for the *Archie* comicbook series. Music promoter Alexander Cabot manages an all-girl rock group, the Pussycats, led by the ambitious Josie, whose desire to be the center of attention often results in a blow to his ego. The singing on the show was performed by Cathy Douglas, Patricia Holloway and Cherie Moore (short for Cheryl Ann Stopylmore), who is now better known as Cheryl Ladd. The character of Alexandra Cabot was voiced by Sherry Alberoni, a former Mouseketeer. Musical numbers for the series were composed and arranged by Danny Janssen, Bob Ingeman and Art Mogell under the corporate name of LAla Productions. Sixteen songs were derived from the series and were released on the album of the same name for Capitol Records in 1970. The 16-episode series originally debuted on CBS in 1970 and lasted two full seasons. (It returned in reruns in 1975 as well.) A space-age spinoff was produced in 1972, *Josie*

*and the Pussycats in Outer Space.* Since its original CBS Network run, the program was rebroadcast on Cartoon Network and its offspring, Boomerang. A *Hanna-Barbera and Radio Comics, Inc. Production. Color. Half-hour. Premiered on CBS: September 12, 1970–September 2, 1972. Rebroadcast on CBS: September 6, 1975–September 4, 1976. Rebroadcast on CAR: December 6, 1992 (part of Boomerang, 1972); January 9, 1993 (Josie and the Pussycats Marathon); February 1, 1993–October 1, 1993; January 11, 1993–April 29, 1994 (weekdays); June 6, 1994–June 2, 1995 (weekdays); November 6, 1995–November 25, 1996 (weekdays); 1997–2000. Rebroadcast on BOOM: April 4, 2000–.*

### Voices

**Josie:** Janet Waldo; **Melody, the dimwitted blond drummer:** Jackie Joseph; **Valerie, the guitarist:** Barbara Pariot; **Alan:** Jerry Dexter; **Alexandra Cabot III:** Casey Kasem; **Alexandra Cabot, his sister:** Sherry Alberoni; **Alexandra Cabot, his sister:** Sherry Alberoni; **Sebastian, their pet cat:** Don Messick

## ☺ JOSIE AND THE PUSSYCATS IN OUTER SPACE

The Pussycats (Josie, Melody and Valerie) and company are accidentally launched into outer space when they become trapped in a NASA space capsule. Joined by their manager, Alexander; his sister, Alexandra; Alan; and a new member, Bleep the space mascot, the three teenage girls explore the vast regions of the universe in this 16-episode series spinoff of 1970's *Josie and the Pussycats.* In 1994 Cartoon Network began rerunning the series, initially airing four episodes back to back that July on the 25th anniversary of the Apollo 11 moon landing. Since then the program has reaired on Boomerang. A *Hanna-Barbera and Radio Comics Inc. Production. Color. Half-hour. Premiered on CBS: September 9, 1972–August 31, 1974. Rebroadcast on CAR: July 20, 1994 (25th Anniversary of the Moon Landing with Josie in Outer Space); November 6, 1995–November 25, 1996 (weekdays); 1997–2000. Rebroadcast on BOOM: April 25, 2000–.*

### Voices

**Josie:** Janet Waldo; **Melody:** Jackie Joseph; **Valerie:** Barbara Pariot; **Alan:** Jerry Dexter; **Alexander Cabot III:** Casey Kasem; **Alexandra Cabot:** Sherry Alberoni; **Sebastian, their cat:** Don Messick; **Bleep, the space mascot:** Don Messick; **Group Vocalists:** Cathy Douglas, Patricia Holloway, Cherie Moore

## ☺ JOT

Spiritual and moral lessons are conveyed in this popular syndicated series following the adventures of a happy anthropomorphic white dot, named Little JOT, who encounters problematic situations and learns a valuable lesson. Thirteen four-and-a-half-minute episodes were initially produced by the Southern Baptist Radio-Television Commission and first broadcast on the Dallas-based children's show *Peppermint Place*, which was syndicated to independent television stations in the 1980s and 1990s. A second series of episodes was produced and broadcast in many foreign countries, including Australia, Japan and several western European nations, as well as on a number of independent and religious stations. A *Southern Baptist Radio-Television Commission Production. Color. Half-hour. Premiered: 1965–70. Syndicated.*

## ☺ JOURNEY TO THE CENTRE OF THE EARTH

A Scottish geologist, Professor Oliver Lindenbrook, and his intrepid party of fellow explorers—faithful guide Lars and student Alec McEwen—journey to Earth's core, only to discover an enemy in their midst—the evil Count Saccnusson, who wants to establish his own subterranean empire—in this 17-episode half-hour cartoon series, inspired by the 1959 20th Century–Fox feature (based on Jules Verne's classic 1864 science-fiction novel, *Voyage au Centre de la Terre*). Certain creative liberties were taken with the characters in this animated version. Among them: Lindenbrook's loyal guide Lars was actually named Hans in the book and in the movie; their bitter enemy Count Saccnusson was formerly known as "Count Sakknussem." Ted Knight, who later played the newsman Ted Baxter on *The Mary Tyler Moore Show*, doubled as the voice of Professor Lindenbrook and the Count. The series was a popular fixture (in reruns) on the Sci-Fi Channel's *Cartoon Quest* programming block. A *Filmation Associates Production. Color. Half-hour. Premiered on ABC: September 9, 1967–August 30, 1969. Rebroadcast on SCI: September 18, 1993–July 31, 1996.*

### Voices
**Professor Lindenbrook/Count Saccnusson:** Ted Knight; Cindy Lindenbrook: Jane Webb; **Alec McEwen/Lar/Torg:** Pat Harrington Jr.

## ◉ JUMANJI—THE ANIMATED SERIES
Reality and fantasy blend together with frightening results, when young Peter and Judy Sheperd play an accursed board game "Jumanji" in their Aunt Nora's house. The game sucks them into a world bristling with action-packed scrapes and hair-raising experiences, where they are aided by a 26-year Jumanji captive, Alan Parrish, a bearded nature boy in a loincloth (voiced by *Coach's* Bill Fagerbakke), in this weekly, Saturday-morning cartoon series based on the hit 1995 feature starring Robin Williams. The show premiered Sunday mornings on the UPN Network in the fall of 1996. An *Adelaide/Interscope/Titler Films/Columbia-Tristar Children's Television Production. Color. Half-hour. Premiered on UPN: September 8, 1996–August 28, 1999. Rebroadcast on SCI: October 4, 1999–February 18, 2000.*

### Voices
**Peter Sheperd:** Ashley Johnson; **Judy Sheperd:** Debi Derryberry; **Alan Parrish:** Bill Fagerbakke; **Aunt Nora:** Melanie Chartoff; **Officer Carl Bentley/Tribal Bob:** Richard Allen; **Van Pelt:** Sherman Howard; **Professor Heinrich Ibsen:** William Sanderson; **Professor J.H. Slick (a.k.a: Trader Slick):** Tim Curry; **Rock:** Pamela Segall; **Brute/Manjis:** Billy West; **Dead-Eye/Manjis:** Kevin Schon; **Fang/Manjis:** Danny Mann

## ◉ JUNGLE BEAT
It's a jungle out there as an ensemble cast of animals—including Giraffe, Monkey, Bee and Tortoise—prove with hilarious results in this non-dialogue, first animated series from Zimbabwean production company Sunrise Media. Airing daily at 6:00 A.M. (ET), the half-hour children's series, comprised of 13 five-minute episodes, debuted in the United States on VOOM's Animania HD network along with the interactive animated series *PicMe* and aired weekdays along with classic television cartoon properties like *The Dick Tracy Show*, *Felix the Cat*, *Mister Magoo* and *The Pink Panther*. A *Sunrise Media/Monster Distributes Production. Color. Half-hour. Premiered on ANI: April 15, 2006.*

## ◉ JUNGLE CUBS
In this prequel to Walt Disney's 1967 animated feature *The Jungle Book*, the film's beloved characters Bagheera the panther, Baloo the bear, Kaa the snake, Shere Khan the tiger and Prince Louie experience all-new adventures as mischievous youngsters as they learn the laws of life in the jungle and the importance of friend-

ships in this 22-episode half-hour syndicated series, rebroadcast in 1997 on the Disney Channel until 2000 and on Toon Disney since 1998. A *Walt Disney Television Animation/Wang Film Production. Color. Half-hour. Premiered: October 5, 1996. Syndicated. Rebroadcast on DIS: December 1, 1997–September 3, 2000. Rebroadcast on TDIS: September 7, 1998–.*

### Voices
Jim Cummings, Jason Marsden, Rob Paulsen, Pamela Segall, Adam Wylie

## ◉ JUSTICE LEAGUE
Seven of the world's most formidable superheroes—Batman, Superman, Wonder Woman, Flash, Green Lantern, Hawkgirl and Martian Manhunter—team up to battle forces of evil, including such fabled foes as Lex Luthor and the Joker, in the Warner Bros. Television Animation-produced 'toon based on DC Comics' popular *Justice League of America* comic-book series and spin-off comic-book characters.

Debuting on Cartoon Network in November 2001 with the three-part episode, "Secret Origins," this half-hour science fiction-fantasy/adventure series featured 26 episodes during its first season that (other than its premiere) aired in two parts. The premiere of this dark, broody, multipart storyline version of Hanna-Barbera's original ABC Saturday-morning *Super Friends* franchise, which aired from 1973 to 1980, and latest rendition of *Justice League* characters since Filmation's 1967 *Superman/Aquaman Hour of Adventure* series, set a record on Cartoon Network among adults ages 18 to 34 with 775,000 viewers, which has since been broken by *The Family Guy*.

During the 2003–04 season, an additional 26 two-part episodes aired three times on Saturday and were stripped Monday through Friday as well, with new episodes airing Saturdays at 10 P.M. (ET). Included was an hour-long, two-part special, *A League of Their Own*, airing on consecutive Saturdays, and half-hour holiday special, *Comfort & Joy*. As reported in a 2003 issue of *Variety*, new episodes of *Justice League* brought in more than 1.9 million total viewers each week. In October 2003, the show's ratings soared 18 percent among kids ages six to 11 and 42 percent among adults ages 18 to 194 from the previous season, attracting 613,000 and 624,000 viewers respectively.

On Saturday, May 29, 2004, the high-flying action series concluded its run with a 90-minute feature-length finale, "Starcrossed," with the famed Justice Leaguers returning that July in a new series, *Justice League Unlimited*, for three additional seasons on Cartoon Network. (See *Justice League Unlimited* for additional information.) In 2002, the series' theme song by Lolita Rimanis was nominated for a Daytime Emmy Award. By April 2006, the program was relaunched in reruns late at night on Cartoon Network's classic cartoons sister network, Boomerang. A *Warner Bros. Television Animation Production. Color. Half-hour. Premiered on CAR: November 19, 2001–May 29, 2004. Rebroadcast on BOOM: April 23, 2006–.*

### Voices
**Batman/Bruce Wayne:** Kevin Conroy; **Superman/Clark Kent/Kal-El:** George Newbern; **Green Lantern/John Stewart:** John LaMarr; **Wonder Woman/Diana Prince:** Susan Eisenberg; **Hawkgirl/Shayera Hol:** Maria Canals; **Martian Manhunter/J'onn J'onnz:** Carl Lumbly; **The Flash/Wally West:** Michael Rosenbaum; **Braniac:** Corey Burton; **Richie "Gear" Foley:** P Jason Marsden; **Hotstreak:** Danny Cooksey; **Puff:** Kimberly Brooks; **Carmen Dillo:** Jason Marsden; **Virgil "Static" Hawkins:** Phil LaMarr; **The Joker/Solomon Grundy:** Mark Hamill; **Lex Luthor:** Clancy Brown; **Star Sap-

phire/Carol Ferris: Olivia d'Abo; **UltraHumanire:** Ian Buchanan;
**Faust:** Robert Englund; **Mongul:** Eric Roberts

## ◎ JUSTICE LEAGUE UNLIMITED

After airing for two seasons under the name of *Justice League*,
Superman, Batman and company were nearly canceled until the
Cartoon Network agreed to produce more episodes, but only after
the superhero team's roster was expanded from seven members to
include a stable of lesser-known DC Comics superheroes, including
Captain Atom, Booster Gold, B'wana Beast, Green Arrow, Hawk
& Dove, Huntress, Mister Miracle, Mr. Terrific, Shining Knight,
Stargirl, Supergirl, Vigilante and Zantanna. Produced by Warner
Bros. Television Animation, this half-hour action-adventure series
premiered in primetime on Cartoon Network on Saturday, July 31,
2004, at 8:30 P.M. In this latest incarnation, the original Justice
League assemblage (billed as "the world's greatest superheroes"),
including Batman, Superman, Flash, Green Lantern, Wonder
Woman, Martian Manhunter and Hawkgirl, expand the size of
their group of superheroes aboard their orbiting space station,
Watchtower, to thwart alien invasions, global conspiracies and
arch-villains such as Lex Luthor, Solomon Grundy and Mongul.

After five successful action-packed seasons, the series ended its
network run with a two-episode finale, airing Saturday May 6 and
Saturday May 13, during Cartoon Network's *Toonami* action-
adventure block. In the series finale, the powerful Justice Leaguers
battle to save the world in what was described as "the biggest face-
off of the year between good and evil . . ." *A Warner Bros. Television Animation Production. Color. Half-hour. Premiered on CAR:
July 31, 2004–May 13, 2006. Rebroadcast on CAR: May 20,
2006–October 14, 2006.*

### Voices
**Superman/Clark Kent:** George Newberry; **Batman/Bruce Wayne:**
Kevin Conroy; **The Flash/Wally West:** Michael Rosenbaum;
**Green Lantern/John Stewart:** Phil LaMarr; **Wonder Woman/
Diana Prince:** Susan Eisenberg; **The Martian Manhunter/J'onn
J'onzz:** Carl Lumbly; **Hawkgirl/Shayera Holl:** Maria Canals; **Hal
Jordan/Jonah Hex:** Adam Baldwin; **Aquaman:** Scott Rummell;
**The Atom:** John C. McGinley; **Black Canary:** Morena Baccarin;
**Booster Gold:** Tom Everett Scott; **B'wana Beast:** Peter Onorati;
**Captain Atom:** George Eads, Chris Cox; **Captain Marvel:** Shane
Haboucha (Billy Batson), Jerry O'Connell (Captain Marvel);
**Doctor Fate:** Oded Fehr; **The Elongated Man:** Jeremy Piven;
**Green Arrow:** Kin Shriner; **Hawkman:** James Remar; **The Hunt-
ress:** Amy Acker; **Mister Miracle:** Joan Gruffold; **Orion:** Ron
Perlman; **The Question:** Jeffrey Combs; **Supergirl:** Nicholle Tom;
**Vigilante:** Nathan Fillion; **Vixen:** Gina Torres; **Wildcat:** Dennis
Farina; **Amanda Waller:** C.C.H. Ponder; **General Wade Eiling:**
J.K. Simmons; **Professor Emil Hamilton:** Robert Foxworth; **Lois
Lane:** Dana Delany; **Bat Lash:** Ben Browder; **El Diablo:** Nestor
Carbonell; **Ares:** Michael York; **Atomic Skull:** Lex Lang; **Bra-
niac:** Corey Burton; **Captain Boomerang:** Donal Gibson; **Captain
Cold:** Lex Lang; **The Cheetah:** Sheryl Lee Ralph; **Circe:** Rachel
York; **Darksend:** Michael Ironside; **Doomsday:** Michael Jai
White; **Felix Faust:** Robert Englund; **The Gentleman Ghost:**
Robin Atkin Downes; **Gorilla Grodd:** Powers Boothe; **Kalibak:**
Michael Dorn; **Lex Luthor:** Clancy Brown; **Lord Hades:** John
Rhys-Davies; **Mirror Master:** Alexis Denisof; **Mongul:** Eric Rob-
erts; **Morgaine Le Fey:** Olivia d'Abo; **The Shade:** Stephen
McHattie; **Solomon Grundy:** Mark Hamill; **Tala:** Juliet Landau

## ◎ KABLAM!

Hosted by the squiggly, unnerving and warped preadolescent computer-animated pair, Henry and June (as in controversial author

Henry Miller and his wife), this comic book come-to-life cartoon
anthology series, billed as "TV's first animated sketch comedy
series," showcased various forms of animation, including paper-cut
and clay-animated cartoon shorts and character-based stories on
Friday and Saturday nights on Nickelodeon. The off-kilter series
premiered on Nick in October of 1996, opening with a pair of segments that served as weekly anchors: "Action League Now!,"
filmed in "Chuck-I-Mation" (a combination of stop-motion puppetry and "chucking" of the characters), featuring Barbie-like
action figures who tell warped crime-fighting stories and whose
archnemesis is the car-crushing Stinky, and "Sniz & Fondue," the
cel-animated wiggy adventures of a pair of outrageous cartoon cats
and their pals. Other recurring *KaBlam!* segments included the
paper-cut animation, "Life with Loopy," about a young girl with an
overactive imagination, and "The Offbeats." *A Nickelodeon Production. Color. Half-hour. Premiered on NICK: October 11, 1996–
May 27, 2000. Rebroadcast on NICKT: May 1, 2002–July 1,
2006.*

### Voices
**June:** Julia McIllvane; **Henry:** Noah Segan

## ◎ KAPPA MIKEY

First-ever American-produced anime television series, drawn in
the same frenetic style as Japanese anime, featuring struggling
actor Mikey Simon as the character Kappa Mikey. Simon later
rose to fame as Japan's biggest anime star of all time as the star of
the hit Japanese television series *LilyMu*. First broadcast in February 2006 on Nickelodeon's all-cartoon network, Nicktoons, the
hilarious Kappa Mikey—described as a "show within a show" and
written like a live-action sitcom—debuted to critical acclaim and
become an instant hit with viewers. In May 2006, the entire first
season was broadcast on all of Nick's international channels in
Asia, the United Kingdom and Spain.

Drawn in a Pop Graphic style combining the best of American and Japanese animation styles, the 52-episode, Flash-animated comedy series, known for making countless pop-culture
references throughout each episode, was created and produced by
Larry Schwarz of New York's largest animation studio Animation
Collective. In August 2006, the series also began airing on Nickelodeon in the 11 A.M. time slot as a lead-in for the network's
new series, *Shuriken School*, with all-new episodes (unaired on
Nicktoons) airing Sundays in the same time slot while still airing
on Friday, Saturday and Sunday nights on Nicktoons. That
December, Mikey starred in the Charles Dickens *A Christmas
Carol*-inspired Nicktoons half-hour holiday special, *A Mikey
Christmas*. DefSTAR Records recording artists Beat Crusaders
created and performed the series' theme song. In 2006, episodes
of the series were re-aired on MTV's *Sic'emation* animation
block, featuring new and original animated series and reruns of
others. *An Animation Collective Production. Color. Half-hour.
Premiered on NICKT: February 18, 2006. Rebroadcast on MTV2:
June 10, 2006.*

### Voices
**Mikey Simon:** Michael Sinterniklaas; **Mitsuki:** Evelyn Lanto;
**Lily:** Annice Moriarty; **Gonard:** Sean Schemmel; **Guano:** Gary
Mack; **Ozu:** Stephen Overley; **Yes Man:** Jesse Adams

## ◎ KAPUT AND ZÖSKY

Two space tyrants—Kaput, the short, hot-tempered one sporting a
Mohawk, and Zösky, the tall, thin, ever-cunning partner—travel
the universe in their makeshift spacecraft to conquer and control
planets on which they land, managing to barely escape when their

plans go awry in this half-hour cartoon comedy based on French cartoonist Lewis Trondheim's popular comic book. Featuring a mostly Canadian voice cast, the French-animated series—also known as *Kaput and Zösky: The Ultimate Obliterators* (2002)—was first broadcast late at night on Nickelodeon beginning in March 2004, and also aired on Canada's Teletoon network. Thereafter, Nick's sister network, Nicktoons, rebroadcast the space-age comedy series. A *Tooncan/France 3/Teletoon/Animation Collective Production. Color. Half-hour. Premiered on NICK: March 7, 2004–December 31, 2006. Rebroadcast on NICKT: February 18, 2006–.*

**Voices**
**Kaput:** Rick Jones; **Zösky:** Mark Camacho; **Regis/White Blood Cells/Other Voices:** John Stocker; **Katherine:** Helen King

### ◎ THE KARATE KID

The popular motion picture starring Ralph Macchio and Pat Morita inspired this animated adaptation about the continuing adventures of Daniel and Mr. Miyagi, with stories stressing positive values. The 13-episode Saturday-morning series lasted only one full season on NBC. A *DIC Enterprises Production in association with Jerry Weintraub Productions/Columbia Pictures Television. Color. Half-hour. Premiered on NBC: September 9, 1989–September 1, 1990. Syndicated.*

**Voices**
**Daniel:** Joe Dedio; **Miyagi Yakuga:** Robert Ito; **Taki:** Janice Kawaye

### ◎ KATIE AND ORBIE

This fully animated, half-hour syndicated series follows the entertaining adventures of a bright, curious five-year-old girl, Katie, and her best friend, a pint-size, red-speckled, inquisitive reptilian alien, Orbie, who crash-lands in a pumpkin patch and is adopted by Katie's parents. This half-hour Canadian-produced cartoon series aired on PBS stations from 1995 to 1996. Based on a series of popular children's books by internationally syndicated cartoonist Ben Wicks, the series, featuring three seven-minute cartoons per half-hour program, was written by Wicks's daughter Susan and narrated by actor Leslie Nielsen (of *Naked Gun* fame). In the fall of 1997 The Disney Channel began rerunning the series fives days a week. A *Lacewood Television Production in association with Baton Broadcasting Inc./North Texas Public Broadcasting Inc./Worldwide Sports & Entertainment Inc./La Chaine De TV Ontario/Rogers Telefund/The Ontario Film Development Corp./Motion Picture Guarantors Ltd. Color. Half-hour. Premiered on PBS: 1995–1996. Rebroadcast on DIS: December 1, 1997–December 31, 1999.*

**Voices**
**Narrator:** Leslie Nielsen

### ◎ KENNY THE SHARK

Fish-out-of-water tale of 10-year-old Kat and her cool, 8-foot-long, 1,500-pound pet shark, Kenny, who, after giving up his oceanic existence, learns to adapt to life in the suburbs with Kat and her family, including her understanding parents, Grace and Peter, baby brother, Karl, and Kat's best friend, Oscar. Original episodes of the 26-episode, half-hour series aired Saturday mornings on NBC and on Discovery Kids from November 2003 to February 2005. The series has since been rebroadcast on Discovery Kids. A *Phase 4 Production. Color. Half-hour. Premiered on NBC/DSCK: November 1, 2003–September 25, 2004; October 2, 2004–February 19, 2005. Rebroadcast on DSCK: February 26, 2005–.*

**Voices**
**Kenny the Shark:** Jim Conroy; **Kat:** Kelli Rabke; **Grace:** Karen Culp; **Peter:** Russell Horton; **Oscar:** Alexander King; **Burton Plushtoy III:** Oliver Wyman; **Marty:** Rob Bartlett; **Ellie:** Amy Loye

### ◎ KEWPIES

The Kewpies and their peaceful community of Kewp Valley are threatened by the evil Countess who wants to steal their magical powers in this half-hour fantasy series based on the Kewpie doll characters first drawn by illustrator Rose O'Neill in 1909. The series aired weekends in syndication beginning in the fall of 1997. A *Sachs Family Entertainment Production. Color. Half-hour. Premiered: September 20, 1997.*

### ◎ KIDD VIDEO

Zapped into the fourth dimension, four talented teenage rock musicians (Kidd, Ash, Whiz and Carla) visit the wacky world of the Flip Side, a bright, airy, upbeat, nonthreatening environment except for the diabolical Master Blaster of Bad Vibes. With the dubious help of The Copy Cats (Fat Cat, Cool Kitty and She-Lion), Master Blaster tries to steal the famed musical group's sound. The live-action/animated program was further highlighted by Top 40 hits, each of which was inventively animated. NBC aired the series' original 128 episodes over two consecutive seasons beginning in 1984. The series continued in reruns on NBC through April of 1987 and ended its network run on CBS (in reruns) the following season. In 1989 the series was syndicated under the name of *Wolf Rock Power Hour* with reruns producer DIC Enterprises Wolf Rock TV. A *DIC Enterprises Production in association with Saban Productions. Color. Half-hour. Premiered on NBC: September 15, 1984–April 4, 1987. Rebroadcast on CBS: September 19, 1987–December 26, 1987. Syndicated: 1989–90 (as Wolf Rock Power Hour). Rebroadcast on WGN: 1992.*

**Voices**
**Kidd Video, the group's leader:** Bryan Scott; **Ash:** Steve Alterman; **Whiz:** Robbie Rist; **Carla:** Gabrielle Bennett; **Glitter, Kidd Video's friend:** Cathy Cavadini; **Master Blaster:** Peter Renaday

**THE COPY CATS: Fat Cat:** Marshall Efron; **She-Lion:** Susan Silo; **Cool Kitty:** Robert Towers

### ◎ KIDEO TV

This 90-minute spectacle packaged three animated series for first-run syndication, designed for weekend programming on independent television stations. Initially the series was comprised of reruns of the half-hour network series *The Get Along Gang*; new half-hour adventures of *Popples*, based on the series of dolls and toys created by American Greeting Cards' "Those Characters from Cleveland" division; and *Ulysses 31*, an imported Japanese series following the exploits of the famed Homeric traveler into the 31st century. The latter lasted only 13 weeks and ultimately was replaced in 1987 by *Rainbow Brite*, a half-hour series that was followed by a brace of 1984 and 1985 animated specials, based on characters originally created by Hallmark in 1983. (See individual series entries for further details.) A *DIC Enterprises Production in association with Mattel Toys/Those Characters From Cleveland/Hallmark Cards. Color. Ninety minutes. Premiered: September 1986. Syndicated.*

### ◎ KID KAPERS

One of the first cartoon shows on network weekend television, this 15-minute series consisted of early black-and-white cartoons made for the theaters. Though the content is not known, it is believed the films included Ub Iwerks's *Flip the Frog* and *Willie Whopper* or Paul Terry's silent *Aesop's Fables. An ABC Television Presentation. Black-and-white. Fifteen minutes. Premiered on ABC: October 26, 1952–January 30, 1953.*

### ◉ KID NOTORIOUS

Short-lived Hollywood parody following the bizarre adventures of the notorious playboy movie producer, Robert Evans (playing himself), and his beloved cat, Puss Puss; his long suffering butler, English, maid Tollie Mae and sidekick neighbor Slash (the guitarist of Guns 'N Roses fame), loosely based on Evans's autobiography of the same name. Directed by Pete Michels, the half-hour series debuted on Comedy Central, with its original episodes airing for nine weeks from October 2003 to December 2003 and subsequently rebroadcast for nearly two more seasons. *An Adam & Adams/Brett Morgen Production. Color. Half-hour. Premiered on COM: October 22, 2003–December 16, 2003. Rebroadcast on COM: December 2003–November 28, 2005.*

*Voices*

**Robert Evans/Kid Notorious:** Robert Evans; **English, his butler:** Alan Selka; **Tollie Mae:** Niecy Nash; **Slash:** Slash; **Sharon Stone:** Jeannie Elias; **Donald Rumsfeld:** Billy West; **Additional Voices:** Dave Herman, Toby Huss

### ◉ KID 'N' PLAY

Rappers Christopher "Kid" Reid and Christopher "Play" Martin—best known as the two-man rap music group Kid 'n Play—starred in this short-lived half-hour live-action/animated series in which they played themselves (in live-action wraparounds and rap videos only). The show follows the experiences of two aspiring teen rappers and their neighborhood friends as they get into all sorts of crazy adventures while pursuing their dream of becoming recording stars. The series featured live-action segments in which the famed rappers made fun of themselves, sandwiched between urban animated adventures—involving them, their manager Herbie, Kid's sister Terry and their friends—often conveying prosocial lessons. *A Marvel/Saban Entertainment Production in association with Chriss Cross Inc. and Gordy de Passe Productions. Color. Half-hour. Premiered on NBC: September 8, 1990–September 7, 1991.*

*Voices*

**Kid:** Christopher Hooks; **Play:** Brian Mitchell; **Lela:** Dawn Lewis; **Marika/Downtown:** Cree Summer Francks; **B.B.:** Rain Pryor; **Pitbull:** J.D. Hall; **Wiz/Hurbie:** Martin Lawrence; **Hairy:** Danny Mann; **Jazzy/Acorn:** Tommy Davidson; **Old Blue:** Dorian Harewood

### ◉ KID POWER

The Rainbow Club, a worldwide organization of kids from all cultural and ethnic backgrounds, struggles to save the environment and change the world in a positive manner through teamwork, friendship and sharing. Based on cartoonist Morrie Turner's well-known comic strip, *Wee Pals*, the 17-episode series premiered on ABC in 1972, the same year as CBS's *Fat Albert and the Cosby Kids. A Rankin-Bass/Videocraft Production. Color. Half-hour. Premiered on ABC: September 16, 1972–September 1, 1974.*

*Voices*

**Wellington:** Charles Kennedy Jr.; **Oliver:** Jay Silverheels Jr.; **Nipper:** John Gardiner; **Jerry:** Allan Melvin; **Connie:** Carey Wong; **Ralph:** Gary Shapiro; **Sybil:** Michele Johnson; **Diz:** Jeff Thomas; **Albert:** Greg Thomas

*A worldwide organization of kids struggles to save the environment in the Saturday-morning series Kid Power. © Rankin-Bass Productions*

### ◉ THE KIDS FROM ROOM 402

Classroom exploits of a group of eccentric nine-year-olds at Harding Elementary School who have a propensity to create trouble for their teacher, Miss Graves, in this animated adaptation of the popular children's book by mother-and-son authors Betty and Michael Paraskevas. First broadcast in Canada on Teletoon, the half-hour comedy series—including two supporting characters patterned after legendary film comedians Joe Besser (Principal Besser) and Zasu Pitts (Nurse Pitts)—premiered in the United States in October 1999 on FOX Family Channel's 90-minute weekend cartoon block that included *Angela Anaconda* and *Weird-Ohs. A Cine-Groupe/Storyopolis/Paraskevas Production. Color. Half-hour. Premiered on FOX FAM: October 9, 1999–Fall 2002.*

*Voices*

**Melanie:** Debi Derryberry; **Nancy:** Mindy Cohn; **Miss Graves:** April Winchell; **Sanjay/Penny:** Tara Charendoff; **Polly/Mary/Ellen/Don:** Colleen O'Shaughnessy; **Gabrielle:** Olivia Hack; **Mrs. McCoy:** Edie McClurg; **Freddie Fay:** Bryon McClure; **Arthur Kenneth Venderwall:** Chris Marquette; **Vinny:** Andrew Lawrence; **Jesse McCoy:** Spencer Klein; **Principal Besser:** Rodger Bumpass; **Nurse Pitts:** Lori Alan; **Jordan:** Lauren Tom

### ◉ THE KID SUPER POWER HOUR WITH SHAZAM

Musical-live action segments of a funky rock group were used to introduce two weekly cartoon adventure series in this hour-long NBC Saturday-morning series: "Hero High," a training school for superheroes, and "Shazam," the exploits of three superheroes—Billy Batson (Shazam), Mary Freeman (Mary Marvel) and Freddy Freeman (Captain Marvel Jr.)—as they battle sinister forces of evil, among them, Sivana and Mr. Mind. *A Filmation Associates Production in association with DC Comics. Color. One hour. Premiered on NBC: September 12, 1981–September 11, 1982.*

*Voices*

**HERO HIGH: Captain California:** Christopher Hensel; **Gorgeous Gal:** Becky Perle; **Dirty Trixie:** Mayo McCaslin; **Misty Magic:** Jere Fields; **Rex Ruthless:** John Berwick; **Weatherman:** John Greenleaf; **Punk Rock:** John Venocour; **Mr. Sampson:** Alan Oppenheimer; **Miss Grimm:** Erika Scheimer.

**SHAZAM!: Billy Batson/Shazam:** Burr Middleton; **Mary Freeman/Mary Marvel:** Dawn Jeffery; **Freddie Freeman/Captain Marvel Jr.:** Barry Gordon; **Tawny/Uncle Dudley/Dr. Sivana:**

Alan Oppenheimer; **Sterling Morris:** Lou Scheimer; **Narrator:** Norm Prescott

## ◎ KIKAIDER

A humanoid robot—reminiscent of Ozamu Tezuka's cult-classic, "Astro Boy"—built by an evil scientist's assistant, Dr. Komjoyi, and one of three Kikaider robots originally to be used as part of his boss's (Dr. Gill) evil plan to conquer the world, turns into a hero, defending the good doctor and his family from Gill's sinister army of androids in this first animated adaptation of the famed Japanese manga superhero created by Shotaro Ishinomori. Following two previous live-action series produced in Japan, this 13-episode anime series, produced and first shown in Japan in 2001, was recast and revoiced in English and shown in the United States on Cartoon Network's *Adult Swim* programming block in 2003. *An Ishimon Pro. Inc./SME Visual/Bandai Entertainment Production. Color. Half-hour. Premiered on CAR: June 9, 2003–November 6, 2003.*

### Voices
**Jirio/Kikaider:** David Wittenberg; **Mitsuko Komyoji:** Lia Sargent; **Masaru Komyoji:** Barbara Goodson; **Dr. Komyoji:** Christopher Carroll; **Professor Gill:** Michael Gregory; **Hanpei Hattori:** Kirk Thorton; **Etsuko Sarutobi:** Melissa Fahn; **Saburo/Hakaider:** David Lucas; **Carmine Spider:** Richard Cansino; **Etsuko Sappirai:** Melissa Charles; **Orange Ant:** Bob Papenbrook

## ◎ KIMBA THE WHITE LION

White lion cub Kimba and his friends (Dan'l Baboon, Samson, Pauley Cracker, King Speckle Rex and others) patrol the jungle in order to keep peace in Africa 4,000 years ago in this half-hour syndicated series, originally produced in 1965 by Osamu Tezuka's Mushi Studios in Japan. The Americanized version of the series premiered in the United States in September 1966, distributed by NBC's syndication division, NBC Films. A total of 52 half-hour stories were produced, followed by a sequel, the 26-episode *Leo the Lion*, which, produced in 1966, did not debut on American television until 1984 on the Christian Broadcasting Network. *A Mushi Studios Production in association with NBC Films. Color. Half-hour.*

*Kimba, the lovable white lion cub who patrols the jungle in Africa to keep the peace, fights back in a scene from the popular Japanese action-adventure series* Kimba the White Lion. (COURTESY: NBC)

*Premiered: September 21, 1966–69. Rebroadcast: 1971–October 1978; 1998–. Syndicated.*

### Voices
**Kimba, the White Lion:** Billie Lou Watt

## ◎ KIMBOO

Set in London, a young African boy, joined by his sidekick parrot, returns to his roots and tells stories about Africa in this British-produced half-hour Saturday-morning series, which aired on Black Entertainment Television. Premiering in 1991, the Parents Choice award-winning program incorporated live-action wraparounds of the show's host introducing that week's animated adventure. Unfortunately, little is known about this production. Network records from the period during which this series was broadcast are skimpy, even as far as the name of company that produced these cartoons. *A Black Entertainment Television Production. Color. Half-hour. Premiered on BET: 1991–92.*

## ◎ KIM POSSIBLE

Joined by her smart-alecky partner, Ron Stoppable, and his scene-stealing mole rat, Rufus, red-haired teenage crimefighter and Middleton High School cheerleading squad captain Kim Possible travels the globe to stop crime, rescue others in need and battle some of the world's greatest supervillains while returning home in time to complete her homework for school the next day and deal with various family issues in between in this popular action/adventure cartoon series.

Created by executive producers Mark McCorkle and Bob Schooley, with Oscar-nominated animator Chris Bailey serving as a director and executive producer, this Walt Disney Television Animation-produced series bowed in prime time on cable's Disney Channel in July 2002 with "Crush" (nominated for a prime-time Emmy Award the following year), and joined ABC's Saturday-morning *One Saturday Morning* programming block in September of that year.

In the fall of 2003, the highly rated series returned in the 11:00 A.M. time slot preceding an hour-long block of *Power Rangers Ninja Storm* on ABC's newly crowned *ABC Kids* programming block (replacing *One Saturday Morning*), featuring two new Disney series: the animated *Lilo & Stitch: The Series*, a spin-off of the highly successful full-length feature, and Disney Channel's hit live-action sitcom, *That's So Raven*.

Nominated for nine Daytime Emmy Awards in 2003, 2004 and 2005, winning once in 2005 for outstanding achievement in sound mixing–live action and animation, the production included two feature-length movie specials to air in prime-time on the Disney Channel, including *Kim Possible: A Sitch in Time* (2003) and *Kim Possible Movie: So the Drama* (2005).

In February 2005, the series ceased production after producing 65 episodes over three seasons until the Disney Channel renewed the program for a fourth season, with new episodes premiering in February 2007. In April 2005, reruns of the Emmy Award-winning series began airing on Disney's all-cartoon channel, Toon Disney. *A Walt Disney TV Animation Production. Color. Half-hour. Premiered on DIS: June 7, 2002. Premiered on ABC: September 14, 2002; February 10, 2007 (new episodes). Rebroadcast on TDIS: April 11, 2005.*

### Voices
**Kim Possible:** Christy Carlson Romano; **Bonnie Rockwaller:** Kirsten Storms; **Ron Stoppable:** Will Friedle; **Rufus:** Nancy Cartwright; **Dr. Dad Possible:** Gary Cole; **Dr. Mom Possible:** Jean Smart; **Wade:** Tahj Mowry; **Josh Mankey:** A.J. Trauth; **Monique:**

Raven-Simone; **Brick:** Rider Strong; **Sheego:** Nicole Sullivan; **Dr. Drakken:** John DiMaggio; **Jim and Tim Possible:** Shaun Fleming; **Senor Senior Sr.:** Ricardo Montalban; **Senor Senior Jr.:** Nester Carbonell

## KING ARTHUR AND THE KNIGHTS OF JUSTICE

King Arthur and the Knights of the Round Table are given a new twist in this half-hour animated series, part of the syndicated Sunday-morning cartoon block *Amazin' Adventures.* The real King Arthur has been banished and the powerful Merlin the Magician decides to find a suitable replacement, bringing back a 1990s college quarterback (named Arthur King) and his entire New York Knights football team, to the Middle Ages to save Camelot. The 1992 series debuted on 143 stations in first-run syndication. *A Golden Films/Le Centre Nationale de la Cinematographie Production in association with Bohbot Entertainment. Color. Half-hour. Premiered: September 7, 1992 (part of Amazin' Adventures I). Syndicated.*

### Voices
Kathleen Barr, Michael Beattie, Jim Byrnes, Gary Chalk, Michael Donovan, Lee Jeffrey, Willow Johnson, Andrew Kabadas, Scott McNeil, Venus Terzo, Mark Wilbreth

## KING FEATURES TRILOGY

Designed for flexible programming, this 150-episode half-hour cartoon trilogy featured three comic-strip favorites (in 50 cartoons each) adapted for television: "Beetle Bailey," a numbskull private whose mishaps at Camp Swampy unnerve his less-than-understanding superior, Sgt. Snorkel; "Snuffy Smith," the comic adventures of the moonshining mountain man, his wife, Louisa, and nephew, Jughaid (joined occasionally in guest appearances by hayseed farmer Barney Google), who are constantly at odds with their feuding foe, Clem Cutplug; and "Krazy Kat," the further adventures of the lovable feline and friends Offisa Pup and Ignatz the Mouse.

Al Brodax served as executive producer of the series. The "Beetle Bailey" and "Snuffy Smith" cartoons were directed by Paramount/Famous Studios veteran Seymour Kneitel, while famed Czechoslovakian animator Gene Deitch handled directorial duties for "Krazy Kat."

Although the films were completed in 1962, the series did not make it onto the airwaves until 1963. Prior to the series television run, Paramount released 11 cartoons from the package as theatrical cartoon shorts under the umbrella title of *Comic Kings.* (See Animated Theatrical Cartoon Series entry for details.) *A Paramount Cartoon Studios/King Features Production. Color. Half-hour. Premiered: August 26, 1963, KTLA-TV, Ch. 5., Los Angeles. Syndicated.*

### Voices
**Private Beetle Bailey/General Halftrack:** Howard Morris; **Sergeant Snorkel:** Allan Melvin; **Cookie, Beetle's girlfriend:** June Foray; **Krazy Kat:** Penny Phillips; **Ignatz Mouse/Offissa Pup:** Paul Frees; **Snuffy Smith:** Paul Frees; **Barney Google:** Allan Melvin; **Loweezy:** Penny Phillips

## THE KING KONG SHOW

American scientist Professor Bond establishes a top research center on the remote island of Mondo in the Java Sea. His son Bobby becomes friends with the legendary 60-foot jungle beast King Kong, whom the professor feels may be helpful in his research. Instead, the professor, daughter Susan and Bobby battle the dia-

bolical Dr. Who, an evil scientist who plans to capture Kong for sinister designs.

Other cartoons included the adventures of a U.S. government agent, "Tom of T.H.U.M.B." (Tiny Humans Underground Military Bureau), and his Oriental assistant, Swinging Jack. The program originally debuted in prime time with a one-hour preview special featuring two half-hour episodes. (See Animated Television Specials for detail.)

The 24-episode Saturday-morning series—which premiered on ABC in September of 1966—was heralded as the "first" network cartoon series made in Japan expressly for American television. *A Rankin-Bass Production with Videocraft International. Color. Half-hour. Premiered on ABC: September 10, 1966–August 31, 1969.*

## KING LEONARDO AND HIS SHORT SUBJECTS

King Leonardo, the ruler of Bongo Congo, and his loyal skunk companion Odie Cologne (whose principal foes are Itchy Brother and Biggie Rat) headlined this popular Saturday-morning entry. Also featured were the adventures of "Tooter Turtle," a mild-mannered turtle who is transported back in time through feats of legerdemain performed by his friend Mr. Wizard, and "The Hunter," a bumbling bloodhound detective who, under the command of Officer Flim Flanagan, is outwitted by a wily con-artist, the Fox. Sponsored by General Mills, the series also included an additional component: the adventures of Twinkles the Elephant, who wiggles out of difficulties using his magic trunk, produced as tie-ins to General Mills breakfast cereals and narrated by George S. Irving. (The latter was edited from television prints later offered for syndication.) Originally created to fill a Saturday-morning time slot on NBC left vacant by the cancellation of Hanna-Barbera's *Ruffy and Reddy, King Leonardo and His Short Subjects* debuted on NBC in 1960 and lasted three seasons. The series was later syndicated under the title of *King and Odie.*

In 2006, the series was rediscovered when it began re-airing (only on Saturday mornings) along with repeats of Jay Ward's *Bullwinkle and Friends* (originally known as *The Bullwinkle Show*) on Black Family Channel. *A Leonardo TV Production with Total TV Productions and Producers Associates of Television. Color. Half-hour. Premiered on NBC: October 15, 1960–September 28, 1963. Syndicated (as King and Odie). Rebroadcast on BFC: 2006.*

### Voices
**King Leonardo/Odie Cologne/Biggie Rat/Itchy Brother:** Jackson Beck; **Mr. Tooter:** Allen Swift; **Mr. Wizard:** Frank Milano; **The Hunter:** Kenny Delmar; **The Fox:** Ben Stone

## KING OF THE HILL

In the fictitious suburb of Arlen, Texas, a beer-drinking, car-fixing, mind-your-own-business propane salesman, Hank Hill, and his dysfunctional blue-collar, middle-class family (wife Peggy, 12-year-old son Bobby and niece Luanne), neighbors (Dale and Nancy Gribble) and friends (divorced army sergeant Bill Dauterive and ladies' man Boomhauer) poke fun at life in the slow lane and the world of pickups, trailers and supermarket busybodies in this half-hour animated series, created by *Beavis and Butt-Head* creator Mike Judge and former *Simpsons* producer Greg Daniels. (His first-ever prime-time network series, Judge came up with the idea in 1995, thinking up the name Hank Hill at the last minute before heading to the pitch meeting with FOX Network executives.)

Brought in as a midseason replacement, the series premiered on the FOX Network in January of 1997 as a lead-in to *The Simpsons*, winning its time slot 10 of 11 weeks and becoming the second-highest-rated new show of the 1997 season, trailing only NBC's *Suddenly Susan*. The series ended up pumping new life into *The Simpsons*, whose ratings had dropped significantly due to the loss of the hit sitcom *Married . . . With Children* as its lead-in. In 1997 the program earned its first Emmy Award nomination for outstanding animated children's program. Since then, the Sunday night cartoon comedy was nominated four more times for primetime Emmy Awards—in 1998, 1999, 2001 and 2002—in the same category, winning the coveted trophy once in 1999, besides earning a total of 33 nominations for various other industry awards.

On May 14, 2006, the popular Fox comedy series marked a major milestone with the airing of its 200th episode, "Edu-macating Lucky," featuring Tom Petty as a guest voice, which was originally intended as the finale for its 10th and final season. After considering the show's devoted 5.4 million viewers and its amazing popularity in syndication, in January 2007 FOX re-upped the show for an 11th season, much to the surprise of co-creator Mike Judge (also the voice of Hank). As Judge told *USA Today*, "I felt good about where I thought it was ending, so it was a little weird to come back. But we started looking at the story ideas we had, and we had some good stuff worth doing." By "good stuff," Judge meant previously unexplored topics such as a big-footed Peggy buying shoes where drag queens shop; Hank and Peggy's son, Bobby, leading protests because it makes him more desirable to girls; and Peggy getting a real estate license.

Throughout the program's history, an electric group of guest stars, including Trace Adkins, Ed Asner, Mac David, Johnny Depp, Carl Reiner, Ben Stiller, Betty White, Reese Witherspoon and Tammy Wynette, have provided their voices in supporting roles.

*A Judgmental Films/Deedle-Dee/3 Art Entertainment/Film Roman Production in association with 20th Century Fox Television. Color. Half-hour. Premiered on FOX: January 12, 1997. Syndicated.*

**Voices**
**Hank Hill/Boomhauer/Dooley:** Mike Judge; **Peggy Hill:** Kathy Najimy; **Bobby Hill:** Pamela Segall; **Luanne Platter/Joseph Gribble:** Brittany Murphy; **Dale Gribble:** Johnny Hardwick; **Didi Hill/Nancy Gribble:** Ashley Gardner; **Bill Dauterive:** Stephen Root; **Eustis:** David Herman; **Kahn "Connie" Souphanousinphone Jr.:** Lauren Tom; **Joseph Gribble:** Breckin Meyer; **John Redcorn:** Jonathan Joss; **Principal Moss:** Dennis Burkley; **Maddy Platter:** Joanna Gleason; **Big Jim:** Phil Hendrie

### ◉ KIPPER

Interactive, wildly imaginative adventures of adorable puppy Kipper and his friends, Tiger the dog, Pig and Pig's cousin, Arnold, in this animated adaptation of author Mick Inpen's popular children's book first shown on British television in 1998. Winner of a British BAFTA award for best children's animation, the half-hour children's series was exported to America in 1999 where its debut on Nickelodeon's Nick Jr. daytime program block was preceded by much fanfare, including an all-out merchandizing and ad campaign in association with the Subway sandwich chain. Comprised of three episodes per half-hour, the show was added to CBS's *Nick Jr. on CBS* weekend morning program block, including such popular Nick fare as Blue's Clues and *Dora the Explorer*, in September 2000. Thereafter, the series aired as part of the PBS Kids' Sprout digital cable channel and video-on-demand (VOD) service, featuring repeat episodes of some of PBS Kids' most beloved preschool programs, including *Caillou, Bob the Builder* and *Jay Jay the Jet Plane*, along with other children's series not broadcast on PBS stations, such as *Pingu, Big Sister-Little Brother* and *Kipper*. *A Grand Slamm/HIT/Hallmark Production. Color. Half-hour. Premiered on NICK JR.: February 8, 1999–November 23, 2000. Premiered on CBS: September 16, 2000–September 8, 2001. Rebroadcast on PBS Kids' Sprout (VOD): April 4, 2005–. Rebroadcast on PBS Kids Sprout (digital cable): September 26, 2005–.*

**Voices**
**Kipper:** Martin Clunes; **Kipper's Friends:** Chris Lang

### ◉ KIRBY: RIGHT BACK AT YA!

English-dubbed anime fantasy series, first broadcast in Japan in 2001 under the name of *Hoshi no Kabii (Kabii's Star)* and based on the popular Nintendo video game franchise, following the adventures of Kirby, a Warpster knight-in-training who crashlands in the country of Dream Land and who, after inhaling monsters' powers, uses his newfound abilities to battle—with the help of his friends—the greedy King Dedee and his gruesome monsters and save the planet from destruction. Produced by Warpster Inc., founded by Nintendo and HAL Laboratory Inc., and 4Kids Entertainment, the half-hour retitled American version became a consistent performer on FOX's Saturday-morning *FOX Box* programming block, beginning in September 2002. The series was so successful on FOX that in March 2004 the network ordered 48 new episodes for the 2004–05 season, with a total of 104 episodes airing on the network until December 2006. *A Warpstar/4Kids Entertainment/Ninentdo Co. Ltd. Production. Color. Half-hour. Premiered on FOX: September 14, 2002–December 2, 2006.*

**Voices**
**Kirby:** Makiko Ômoto; **Chef Kawasaki:** Maddie Blaustein; **Tiff:** Kerry Williams; **Tuff:** Tara Jayne; **Tokkori:** Kevin Kolack; **Mayor Ken Blustergas:** Mike Pollock; **Meta Knight:** Eric Stuart; **Fololo/Falala:** Veronica Taylor; **King Dedede:** Ed Paul; **Nightmare:** Andrew Rannells; **Dr. Escargon/Escargoon:** Ted Lewis; **Additional Voices:** Kayzie Rogers, Amy Birnbaum, Dan Green, David Lapkin, Ellen Lee, Carol Jacobanis, Sean Schemmel, Jerry Lobozzo

### ◉ KISSYFUR

Kissyfur, an eight-year-old bear cub, along with his circus father, Gus, escape from civilization to begin life anew deep in a swamp populated by other animals—some good, some bad—living simple lives untouched by human influence in this 26-episode half-hour Saturday-morning series. The series aired for two seasons on NBC, though not consecutively. The show was canceled after the 1986–87 season, then brought back with new episodes for the 1988–89 season. The first season's episodes included four 1985 specials that were simply repeated: *Kissyfur: Bear Roots, Kissyfur: The Birds and the Bears, Kissyfur: The Lady Is a Chump* and *Kissyfur: We Are the Swamp*. (See Animated Television Specials entries for details). *An NBC Production in association with DIC Enterprises. Color. Half-hour. Premiered on NBC: September 13, 1986–September 5, 1987; September 10, 1988–August 25, 1990.*

**Voices**
**Kissyfur:** R.J. Williams, Max Meier; **Gus, Kissyfur's father:** Edmund Gilbert; **Beehonie, a rabbit:** Russi Taylor; **Duane, a persnickety pig:** Neilson Ross; **Stuckey, the porcupine:** Stuart M. Rosen; **Toot, a young beaver:** Devon Feldman, Russi Taylor; **Floyd, the alligator:** Stuart M. Rosen; **Jolene, the alligator:** Terrence McGovern; **Miss Emmy Lou, the schoolmarm:** Russi Taylor; **Cackle Sister/Bessie:** Russi Taylor; **Lenny/Charles:** Lennie

Weinrib; **Uncle Shelby/Howie/Claudette:** Frank Welker; **Ralph:** Susan Silo

## KLUTTER

Unable to have a real family pet because their newspaper-editor father is allergic to everything from dogs to pet rocks, siblings Ryan and Wade zap a pile of junk under their bunk bed, bringing to life this homemade exuberant creature who wreaks domestic havoc in a series of six half-hour cartoons that aired as a component of Saturday morning's *Eek! Stravaganza* series on FOX Network in the fall of 1995.

*A Film Roman/Savage Studios Ltd. Production in association with FOX Network Children's Productions. Color. Half-hour. Premiered on FOX: September 9, 1995–September 5, 1997.*

### Voices

**Ryan Heap:** Cam Clark; **Wade Heap:** Savage Steven Holland; **Sandee Heap:** Sandy Fox; **Andrea Heap:** Kathy Ireland; **John Heap:** David Silverman; **Klutter:** Kirk Thatcher; **Vanna:** Halle Standford; **Mel, Vann's dad:** Dan Castellaneta; **Nel, Vann's mom:** Amy Heckerling; **Kopp:** Kirk Thatcher

## KNIGHTS OF THE ZODIAC

Headed by the bronze knight, Seiya, five warriors, each a member of the Knights of the Zodiac, use their amazing martial arts skills and mystical powers tied to the sign of the Zodiac to battle the dreaded Black Knights in this English-language version of the popular futuristic Japanese anime adventure series, *Saint Seiya*, which originally aired on Japanese television beginning in 1986 and was broadcast in the United States under a new title. Re-edited for American television, the half-hour series aired on Saturday nights for two seasons on Cartoon Network. *A Toei Animation Co. Ltd./Kaleidoscope Entertainment Inc./A.D. Vision/ DIC Entertainment Production. Color. Half-hour. Premiered on CAR: August 30, 2003–November 5, 2005.*

### Voices

Jeff Berg, Shane Bland, George Buza, Bill Colgate, Drew Coombs, Neil Crone, Stacy Depass, Katie Griffin, Tim Hamaguchi, Bill Houston, Tracey Hoyt, Ayumi Izuka, Julie Lemieux, Scott McCord, Mark McMulkin, Annick Obansawin, Andrew Pifko, Martin Roach, Rob Tinkler, Dan Warry Smith, Rob Smith, Stewart Stone, Maurice Dean Wint

## THE KOALA BROTHERS

Cuddly brother koalas, Frank and Buster, take off in their cool yellow two-seater airplane to help a colorful cast of friends in the Australian Outback in this half-hour educational children's series created by United Kingdom's Famous Flying Films and produced by Spellbound Entertainment. Combining plasticine, clay and traditional stop-motion animation, this 57-episode, half-hour puppet-animated series, also shown on United Kingdom and Australia television, debuted in the United States as part of the Disney Channel's *Playhouse Disney* weekday morning program block for preschool age children. In 2005, the Disney Channel also premiered a 30-minute Christmas special starring the pair, entitled *The Koala Brothers Outback Christmas*. *A Famous Flying Films/Spellbound Entertainment Production in association with the British Broadcasting Corporation and Momentum Pictures. Color. Half-hour. Premiered on DIS: October 1, 2003–September 4, 2007. Rebroadcast on DIS: September 2007–.*

### Voices

**Narrator:** Jonathan Coleman; **Frank/Archie/Sammy:** Keith Wickham; **Other Voices:** Lucinda Cowden, Rob Rackstraw, Janet James

## KONG: THE ANIMATED SERIES

The gigantic ape made famous in the classic black-and-white RKO movie of the 1930s is back as a genetically engineered clone created by a brilliant young scientist, Lorna Jenkins, using the ape's original DNA and a small amount of human DNA of her grandson (Jason Jenkins) whom she returns to the prehistoric island where, 18 years later, he battles gigantic prehistoric creatures and monstrous mutants to make the world safe again, in this animated fantasy/adventure series, which was broadcast on FOX's *FOX Kids* Saturday-morning program block. The 13-episode series lasted one season and was rebroadcast beginning in September 2005 on Toon Disney's *Jetix* Saturday and Sunday action program block as a prelude to Peter Jackson's mega-budget *King Kong* remake. That same year, a feature-length animated movie, *King Kong of Atlantis*, based on the series, was also released on DVD and world-premiered on Toon Disney. *A D'Ocon Films/Bohbot Kids Network Production. Color. Half-hour. Premiered on FOX: May 26, 2001–August 25, 2001. Rebroadcast on TDIS: September 19, 2005–.*

### Voices

**Jason Jenkins/Frazetti:** Kirby Morrow; **Eric "Tann" Tanenbaum IV/Omar:** Scott McNeil; **Dr. Lorna Jenkins:** Daphne Goldrick; **Professor Ramon De La Porta:** David Kaye; **Lua:** Saffron Henderson; **Tiger Lucy:** Nicole Oliver; **Chiros:** Paul Dobson; **Harpy:** Pauline Newstone

## KRYPTO THE SUPERDOG

Comedic canine adventures of Superman's fully grown, faithful superdog companion, Krypto (who is armed with an amazing array of superhero powers), whose rocket ship (built by Superman's father) malfunctions and crash-lands on Earth. Krypto battles evil forces that threaten the safety and well-being of the residents and animals of Metropolis with the help of his young human friend, Kevin Whitney in this preschool animated series from Warner Bros. Television Animation and DC Comics. Executive produced by Sander Schwarz and produced by Linda Steiner and Paul Dini, the half-hour series, developed in collaboration with the Child Development Advisory Board, focused on helping preschoolers develop a sense of humor while showing humor as a means to develop friendships, learning and better self-esteem. In March 2005, the 72-episode series, containing two 11-minute episodes per half-hour, was first broadcast with a two-part premiere episode, "Krypto's Scrypto," before airing Monday through Friday mornings beginning in April and then that August as Cartoon Network's first announced series for its new *Tickle U* weekday preschool programming block. After the network aborted its preschool programming in September 2006, the high-flying adventurers joined the CW Network's Kids' WB! Saturday morning lineup, re-airing episodes from its original run on the Cartoon Network. Beginning in February 2007, the series joined Boomerang's weekday morning lineup with the updated animated children's series *Gerald McBoing Boing*, formerly aired on Cartoon Network's *Tickle-U* preschool block. *A Warner Bros. Television Animation Production. Color. Half-hour. Premiered on CAR: March 25, 2005 (two-part premiere); April 4, 2005–May 5, 2006 (series). Rebroadcast on CW (Kids' WB!): September 23, 2006–. Rebroadcast on BOOM: February 5, 2007–.*

### Voices

**Krypto the Superdog:** Samuel Vincent; **Streaky the Supercat:** Brian Drummond; **Kevin Whitney:** Alberto Ghisi; **Melanie Whitney/Andrea:** Tabitha St. Germain; **Ace the Bat-Hound:** Scott McNeil.

**THE DOG STAR PATROL: Brainy Barker:** Ellen Kennedy; **Mammoth Mutt:** Kelly Sheridan; **Bull Dog:** Michael Dobson; **Paw**

Pooch: Dale Wilson; **Tail Terrier:** Peter Kelamis; **Trusky Husky:** Terry Klassen; **Hot Dog:** Trevor Devall; **Drooly:** Ty Olsson

## ⊚ THE KWICKY KOALA SHOW

Cartoon legend Tex Avery developed this series—his last animated production—starring a sweet and superspeedy koala bear, reminiscent of his character Droopy, who becomes entangled in numerous misadventures with the wily but hapless Wilford Wolf. The program featured three additional weekly cartoon segments: "Crazy Claws," a whirlwind wildcat whose snappy one-liners are his only defense against the schemes of Rawhide Clyde; "Dirty Dawg," the con-artist canine of the garbage dump, joined by alley mate Ratso the rodent; and "The Bungle Brothers," two beagles (George and Joey) trying desperately to break into show business, seen in three one-minute segments per show. Avery, whose comedic visual gags created a new dimension in cartoons, worked his last two years of his life at Hanna-Barbera Productions until his death in 1980. The series was later rebroadcast on Cartoon Network. *A Hanna-Barbera Production. Color. Half-hour. Premiered on CBS: September 12, 1981–September 11, 1982. Rebroadcast on CAR: October 2, 1992–January 1, 1993 (weekdays); January 10, 1993–September 19, 1993 (Sundays).*

### Voices
**Kwicky Koala:** Robert Allen Ogle; **Wilfred Wolf:** John Stephenson; **Dirty Dawg:** Frank Welker; **Ratso:** Marshall Efron; **Crazy Claws:** Jim MacGeorge; **Rawhide Clyde:** Robert Allen Ogle;

Bristletooth: Peter Cullen; **Ranger Rangerfield:** Michael Bell; **George:** Michael Bell; **Joey:** Allen Melvin

## ⊚ LADY LOVELYLOCKS AND THE PIXIETAILS

Set in the mystical Land of Lovelylocks, this action/adventure fairy tale centers on the life of a young ruler who learns the lessons of life and the ways of the world, joined by her worthy aides, The Pixietails (Pixiebeauty, Pixiesparkle and Pixieshine), while struggling against the evil workings of Duchess Ravenwaves, who seeks to take over her realm. The 20-episode first-run syndicated series was developed by American Greetings Cards' "Those Characters from Cleveland" division, the same people who introduced *Care Bears.* *A DIC Enterprises Production in association with Those Characters from Cleveland, Mattel and CBS. Color. Half-hour. Premiered: September 1987. Syndicated.*

### Voices
**Lady Lovelylocks:** Tony St. Vincent; **Duchess Ravenwaves:** Louise Vallance; **Maiden Fairhair/Snags:** Jeanine Elias; **Lady Curlycrown:** Louise Vallance; **Comb Gnome, the nasty gnome:** Danny Mann; **Strongheart/Prince (as dog):** Danny Mann; **Shining Glory/Hairbell/Tanglet:** Brian George

### *The Pixietails*
**Pixiesparkle:** Tony St. Vincent; **Pixiebeauty:** Jeanine Elias; **Pixieshine:** Brian George

*A sweet, super-fast koala bear becomes entangled in wildly funny misadventures with the wily but hapless Wilford Wolf in Hanna-Barbera's Saturday-morning comedy series* The Kwicky Koala Show, *the last animated production developed by cartoon legend Tex Avery. © Hanna-Barbera Productions. All rights reserved.*

## ⊚ THE LAND BEFORE TIME

Dinosaurs Littlefoot, Cera, Ducky, Petrie, Spike and Chomper, stars of the popular Universal Studios animated feature and direct-to-video series, star in this series of new adventures in the Great Valley and the Mysterious Beyond. In March 2007, the all-new adventures combining traditional 2-D animation with 3-D backgrounds and featuring many of the film and direct-to-video franchise's most memorable characters, debuted weekday mornings on Cartoon Network. Based on Universal's billion-dollar property and one of the most successful feature-length children's home entertainment franchises in history, 26 half-hour episodes bowed during the first season, with episodes of the series subsequently distributed on DVD by Universal. *A Universal Studios Home Entertainment Family Production. Color. Half-hour. Premiered on CAR: March 5, 2007.*

**Voices**
**Littlefoot:** Cody Arens; **Cera:** Anndi McAfee; **Ducky:** Aria Noelle Curzon; **Petrie:** Jeff Bennett; **Spike/Ruby's Father/Thud:** Rob Paulsen; **Chomper:** Max Burkholder; **Red Claw/Screech:** Peter Sepenuk; **Ruby/Tricia:** Meghan Strange; **Tria:** Jessica Gee; **Ruby's Mother:** Nika Futterman

## ⊚ LASSIE'S RESCUE RANGERS

Jack Wrather's famed TV collie roams the Rocky Mountains under the guidance of the Turner family who, along with Lassie and the forest animals, organize a "Forest Force" rescue team in this half-hour Saturday-morning series, originally broadcast on ABC in 1973.

Production teams from Filmation and Rankin-Bass were behind the weekly series, which borrowed artwork and characters previously seen on the 1972 ABC Saturday Superstar Movie *Lassie and the Spirit of Thunder Mountain.* Stories depicted Lassie and the group's attempts to save the already damaged environment. Actor Ted Knight, (a.k.a. anchorman Ted Baxter on TV's *The Mary Tyler Moore Show*) provided the voice of Ben Turner, the patriarch of the Turner family and head of the Forest Force, and was also the series' narrator. Two other series characters were voiced by three of the offspring of director Hal Sutherland and producer Lou Scheimer. *A Filmation Studios/Production in association with Wrather Productions. Color. Half-hour. Premiered on ABC: September 8, 1973–August 31, 1974. Rebroadcast on ABC: September 8, 1974–August 31, 1975.*

**Voices**
**Narrator:** Ted Knight; **Lassie:** Herself; **Ben Turner:** Ted Knight; **Laura Turner:** Jane Webb; **Jackie Turner:** Lane Scheimer, Keith Sutherland; **Susan Turner:** Erika Scheimer; **Ben Turner Jr./Gene Fox:** Hal Harvey

## ⊚ LAUREL AND HARDY

Temperamental Oliver Hardy (the rotund one) always found himself in "another fine mess" when he and his whining, dimwitted friend, thin Stan Laurel, got together. This basic premise became the recurring theme of a cartoon version of the comic pair, coproduced by Larry Harmon, creator of Bozo the Clown, and Hanna-Barbera Productions, which also produced a series of Abbott and Costello cartoons. With both comedians deceased, the voices of Stan and Ollie were re-created by Harmon and voice-artist Jim MacGeorge. The series, consisting of 130 five-minute color cartoons, debuted in syndication one year after Stan Laurel's death in the fall of 1966. *A Hanna-Barbera Production for Wolper Productions and Larry Harmon Pictures. Color. Half-hour. Premiere: 1966. Syndicated.*

**Voices**
**Stan Laurel:** Larry Harmon; **Oliver Hardy:** Jim MacGeorge; **Other Voices:** Paul Frees, Don Messick

## ⊚ LAVERNE AND SHIRLEY IN THE ARMY

Prime time's hit characters Laverne DeFazio and Shirley Feeny from the popular sitcom *Laverne and Shirley* become privates in the army, where all efforts to instill some military discipline into these two goof-ups fail. *A Hanna-Barbera Production in association with Paramount Pictures Corporation. Laverne and Shirley © 1981 Paramount Pictures Corporation. All material besides Laverne and Shirley © 1981 Hanna-Barbera Productions Inc. Color. Half-hour. Premiered on ABC: October 10, 1981–September 18, 1982.*

**Voices**
**Laverne:** Penny Marshall; **Shirley:** Cindy Williams; **Sgt. Turnbuckle:** Ken Mars; **Squealy, his pet pig:** Ron Palillo

## ⊚ LAVERNE AND SHIRLEY WITH THE FONZ

Laverne and Shirley's adventures in the army continue, this time with the ever-cool Fonz (voiced by actor Henry Winkler, who played the character in the popular sitcom *Happy Days*), now a chief mechanic for the army's motor pool. Fonzie and his sidekick dog, Mr. Cool, add to the laughs and the messed-up missions in this half-hour comedy/adventure that premiered as part of the hour-long block *The Mork and Mindy/Laverne and Shirley/Fonz Hour* on ABC in 1982. The network programmed the series back to back with Ruby-Spears's half-hour animated *Mork and Mindy* series. Repeated were episodes from 1981's *Laverne and Shirley in the Army*, in addition to all-new episodes with the Fonz (voiced by Henry Winkler). Citing contract problems, Cindy Williams, the original Shirley in the live-action comedy series and the animated spinoff, was replaced by actress Lynn Marie Stewart. (See *The Mork and Mindy/Laverne and Shirley/Fonz Hour* for voice credits.) *A Hanna-Barbera Production in association with Paramount Pictures Corporation. Color. Half-hour. Premiered on ABC: September 25, 1982–September 3, 1983.*

## ⊚ LAZER TAG ACADEMY

Thirteen-year-old Jamie Jaren returns to the present from the world of the future and, with the help of two young ancestors and the family's special powers, stops the villainous time-traveler Silas Mayhem from changing the course of history in this short-lived Saturday-morning science-fiction series, originally produced for NBC. Redubbed *Lazer Patrol*, the series was rebroadcast for three seasons on the Sci-Fi Channel's *Cartoon Quest* programming block. *A Ruby-Spears Enterprises Production in association with Alchemy II/Worlds of Wonder Inc. Color. Half-hour. Premiered on NBC: September 13, 1986–August 22, 1987. Rebroadcast on SCI: September 18, 1993–September 10, 1996.*

**Voices**
**Jamie Jaren:** Noelle Harling; **Draxon Drear:** Booker Bradshaw; **Beth Jaren:** Christina McGregor; **Tom Jaren:** Billy Jacoby; **Nicky Jaren:** R.J. Williams; **Andrew Jaren/Skugg:** Frank Welker; **Genna Jaren:** Tress MacNeille; **Professor Olanga:** Sid McCoy; **Charlie/Skugg:** Pat Fraley; **Other Voices:** Susan Blu

## ⊚ THE LEGEND OF CALAMITY JANE

Wild West's Calamity Jane rides again in search of truth and justice using her wits and her whip to aid the downtrodden, while encountering other shoot-'em-up legends along the way—Wyatt Earp, Doc Holliday, Wild Bill Hickok and Buffalo Bill Cody—in this short-lived animated adventure series produced for the WB Television Network. Premiering in September of 1997, the series lasted only three weeks before the network dropped it. Film actress Jennifer Jason Leigh was to have provided the voice of Calamity Jane. Barbara Scaff, an American actress living in Paris, instead took her place. A *Contre-Allze/ Gangster/Canal+/Warner Brothers Television Animation Production. Color. Half-hour. Premiered on WB: September 13, 1997–September 27, 1997.*

*Voices*

**Calamity Jane:** Barbara Scaff; **Wild Bill Hickok:** Clancy Brown; **Joe Presto:** Frank Welker; **Lonely Sue:** Miriam Flynn; **Quanna Parker:** Michael Horse; **Captain John O'Rourke:** Tim Matheson; **Bill Doolin:** Mark Rolston

## ◉ THE LEGEND OF PRINCE VALIANT

Called to Camelot by King Arthur, Prince Valiant is joined by a peasant (Arn) and the blacksmith's daughter (Rowanne) in their quest to become Knights of the Round Table, beset by trouble along the way, in this half-hour adventure series and first original cartoon series for The Family Channel. Originally scheduled to debut in January 1992, network executives, after viewing some of the finished episodes and pleased by the results, moved up the series premiere to September 1991. The series aired Tuesday nights in prime time, and 26 episodes were produced for the first season. Entering its second season in the fall of 1992, the series returned on Friday nights. New adventures explored issues of triumph and failure, love and hate, family honor and friendship as the hero, Prince Valiant, comes of age.

In 1993, returning a third season, 39 additional episodes were produced and the series was shifted to a Monday-through-Friday time slot. In 1994 the series aired (in reruns) Saturday mornings. Two feature-length compilations, based on the series, were also produced for the network: 1991's *Prince Valiant: The Voyage of Camelot* and 1992's *Prince Valiant: Knight of the Round Table.*

Actors Mark Hamill (star of the Oscar-winning *Star Wars* trilogy), Noel Harrison (son of legendary actor Sir Rex Harrison), Fred Savage (of TV's *Wonder Years*) and Harry Hamlin (from NBC's Emmy Award–winning series *L.A. Law*) were among celebrity guest voices to be featured in episodes of the series. A *Hearst Entertainment/IDDH Groupe Bruno Rene Huchez/Polyphonfilm und Fernsehen GmbH/Sei Young Studios Production in association with King Features and The Family Channel. Color. Half-hour. Premiered on FAM: September 3, 1991–May 10, 1992; October 10, 1993–May 13, 1994.*

*Voices*

**Prince Valiant:** Robby Benson; **Arn:** Michael Horton; **King Arthur:** Efrem Zimbalist Jr.; **Guinevere:** Samantha Eggar; **Merlin the Magician:** Alan Oppenheimer; **Sir Gawain:** Tim Curry; **Rowanne:** Noelle North

## ◉ LEGEND OF THE DRAGON

Ang Leung is chosen as the new dragon master and guardian of the ancient Temple of Dragons. His fraternal twin sister, Ling, decides to join the dark side as the Shadow Dragon rather than support him in this animated action-adventure series. Produced by the Bohbot Kids Network for the *Jetix* programming block, the half-hour action adventure series debuted in August 2006 as a special presentation on ABC Family with a two-part, one-hour "sneak peak" episode entitled "Trial by Fire." After ABC Family's final airing of the *Jetix* block in late August 2006, the program began airing weekday mornings that October on Toon Disney. Produced and created by Rick Ungar and written and developed by Sean

Catherine Derek, 24 additional half-hour episodes aired during the first season, followed by 13 additional episodes thereafter. A *BKN Production. Color. Half-hour. Premiered on ABC FAM: August 14, 2006 (sneak peek). Premiered on TDIS October 2, 2006.*

*Voices*

**Ling/Shadow Dragon/Cobra:** Larissa Murray; **Ang/Golden Dragon:** Alan Marriot; **Xuan Chi:** Mark Silk; **Master Chin/ Chow/Dog Guardian Wang Lee:** Dan Russell; **Beingal/Ming/Rat Guardian:** Lucy Porter

## ◉ THE LEGEND OF WHITE FANG: THE ANIMATED SERIES

HBO kicked off the 1994–95 season with two original animated series, each airing on Saturday mornings. First up was this 26-part action/adventure series, based on the Klondike adventures of author Jack London's part-wolf, part-husky hero who was befriended by a 12-year-old girl (Wendy Scott) during the Gold Rush days of the 1890s. Each episode promoted concerns for the environment and offered lessons in life with morals that young viewers could understand easily. Produced by Canadian animation giant CINAR Films, the half-hour series preceded another CINAR-owned property, *The Real Story of. . .,* a series. A *CINAR Films/Crayon Animation/France Animation Production. Color. Half-hour. Premiered on HBO: January 1, 1994.*

*Voices*

**White Fang:** Mark Hellman; **Wendy Scott:** Patricia Rodriguez; **Beauty Smith:** Michael Rudder; **Matt Laberge:** Rick Jones; **Sgt. Oakes:** Pierre Lenoir; **Alex de Laslo/Weedon Scott:** Terrence Scammel; **Raven Moon:** Neil Shee

## ◉ THE LEGEND OF ZELDA

Based on the celebrated Nintendo video game, this fantasy/ adventure series stars a 15-year-old adventurer (Link) and a princess of the same age (Zelda), who fight monsters, ghosts and icky creatures while trying to save the kingdom of Hyrule from the dark depredations of the evil wizard Ganon. The series debuted in syndication in 1989 as part of the *Super Mario Brothers Super Show!* Episodes were later repeated on another Nintendo-inspired animated series, 1990's *Captain N and the Super Mario Brothers 3,* produced for NBC, and as part of the syndicated package, *Captain N and the Video Game Masters.* (See *Super Mario Brothers Show* for voice credits.) A *DIC Enterprises Production in association with Nintendo of America Incorporated. Color. Half-hour. Premiered: September 1989. Syndicated.*

## ◉ LEGION OF SUPER HEROES

One thousand years in the future, an unlikely team of teenage superheroes—Lightning Lad, Saturn Girl, Brainiac 5, Phantom Girl, Bouncing Boy and Timber Wolf—goes back in time to recruit the legendary Man of Steel, Superman, to protect the newly formed United Planets from evil forces, including futuristic supervillains, the Fatal Five, in the 31st century in this fast-paced, action-packed hour fantasy/adventure series, combining humor and high-stakes heroics, inspired by the DC Comics series. Produced by Warner Bros. Television Animation, the new series premiered along with two others—*Shaggy and Scooby-Doo Get a Clue!* and *Tom and Jerry Tales*—as part of the CW Network's fall 2006 Kids' WB! Saturday-morning lineup, featuring former WB Television Network leftovers *Xiaolin Showdown, Lunatics Unleashed* and *The Batman.* A *Warner Bros. Television Animation Production. Color. Half-hour. Premiered on CW (Kids' WB!): September 23, 2006.*

*Voices*
**Lightning Lad:** Andy Miller; **Saturn Girl/Triplicate Girl:** Kari Wahlgren; **Brainiac 5:** Adam Wylie; **Phantom Girl:** Heather Hogan; **Bouncing Boy:** Michael Cornaccia; **Timber Wolf:** Shawn Harrison; **Superman:** Yuri Lowenthal

## ⊚ LEO THE LION

This sequel to NBC's *Kimba, the White Lion* was created by Kimba's originator, Osamu Tezuka, and originally produced in 1966. Unlike the first series, however, the character was not called Kimba—he was named Leo instead—and he was cast as an adult and the father of two cubs, who rule the jungle with him and his mate, Kitty. Only 26 episodes were made in the series, which was originally broadcast on Japanese television. In 1984, 18 years after it was originally produced, the series made its American television debut on CBN (Christian Broadcasting Network). *A Mushi/Sonic International Production. Color. Half-hour. Premiered on CBN: June 1984.*

## ⊚ LIBERTY'S KIDS

A group of teens—including British loyalist Sarah Phillips and Yankee newspaper apprentice James Hiller—become embroiled in clashes of ideology emphasizing the diversity of early America and the people behind the nation's birth from the signing of the Constitution to the Boston Tea Party in this animated children's series set during the American Revolution for seven- to 12-year-old viewers. Produced by DIC Entertainment, the 40-episode series lasted two full seasons on PBS Kids' program block from September 2002 to August 2004. Following its network run, the series was syndicated to network-owned affiliates and independent stations to fulfill mandated FCC requirements to broadcast educational and informational programs. Providing the voices of historical figures were Walter Cronkite (Benjamin Franklin), Sylvester Stallone (Paul Revere), Ben Stiller (Thomas Jefferson), Billy Crystal (John Adams) and Arnold Schwarzenegger (Baron Von Steuben), among others. *A Melusine/Hong Ying Universe Co. Ltd./DIC Entertainment Production. Color. Half-hour. Premiered on PBS Kids: September 2, 2002–August 13, 2004. Syndicated.*

*Voices*
**Sarah Phillips:** Reo Jones; **James Hiller:** Chris Lundquist; **Henri Richard Maurice Dutoit LeFebvre:** Kathleen Barr; **Moses:** D. Kevin Williams; **Abigail Adams:** Annette Irving; **James Madison:** Warren Buffet; **Joseph Plumb Martin:** Aaron Carter; **Benjamin Franklin:** Walter Cronkite; **Patrick Henry:** Michael Douglas; **Gov. Galvez:** Don Francisco; **Deborah Sampson:** Whoopi Goldberg; **Benedict Arnold:** Dustin Hoffman; **Elizabeth Freeman:** Yolanda King; **John Paul Jones:** Liam Neeson; **Baron Von Steuben:** Arnold Schwarzenegger; **Colonel Clark:** General H. Norman Schwarzkopf; **Paul Revere:** Sylvester Stallone; **Thomas Jefferson:** Ben Stiller; **Admiral Lord Howe:** Michael York; **John Adams:** Billy Crystal; **King George III:** Charles Shaughnessy; **Elizabeth Freeman:** Yolanda King

## ⊚ THE LIFE & TIMES OF JUNIPER LEE

Juniper Lee acts like most 11-year-old girls. She serves on her school's yearbook staff, has after-school activities, takes guitar lessons and enjoys hobbies in her spare time, besides also being responsible for a very big secret: She fights the forces of mischief and chaos wherever they lurk, from unruly six-foot leprechauns to troublemaking gnomes, while still managing to maintain a somewhat normal home life with her parents, her grandmother Ah-Mah (Jasmine), her brothers Dennis and Ray Ray, their pug Monroe and her best friends Jody and Ophelia, in this half-hour fantasy/adventure series produced by Cartoon Network Studios. Created by comic book auteur, former *The Real World* cast member and executive producer Judd Winick, every episode featured an array of characters from both the real and fantastical worlds with only Juniper's fearless eight-year-old brother sidekick, Ray Ray, sharing some of her magical gifts and Ah-Man providing wise counsel when needed. Bowing on Cartoon Network in May 2005 with 13 first-season episodes, the program was so well received that Cartoon Network ordered 13 additional half-hours for the second season, including a half-hour Easter special, *June's Egg-cellent Adventure: Juniper Lee Meets the Easter Bunny,* that began airing every Sunday night in October 2005. A second season of new episodes began airing every Sunday night in November 2005. In August 2006, 13 more half-hour adventures were introduced for the series' third season. *A Cartoon Network Studios Production. Color. Half-hour. Premiered on CAR: May 30, 2005.*

*Voices*
**Juniper Lee:** Lara Jill Miller; **Ah-Mah Jasmine Lee:** Amy Hill; **Monroe Connery Boyd Carlyle McGregor Scott Lee V/Michael Lee:** Carlos Alazaqui; **Ray Ray Lee:** Kath Soucie; **Dennis:** Alexander Polinsky; **Jody Irwin:** Colleen O'Shaughnessey; **Ophelia Ramirez/Ms. Gomez/Barbara:** Candi Milo; **Beatrice:** Tara Strong; **Marcus Conner:** Phil LaMarr; **William:** Martin Jarvis

## ⊚ LIFE'S A BITCH

First telecast in February 2000 as three 15-minute cartoons under the title of "Bitchy Bits" on Oxygen Network's popular cartoon anthology series, *X-Chromosone,* this half-hour version followed the comical adventures of Midge McCracken, an unhappy but successful 30-something, Internet dating entrepreneur, and her offbeat friends Yolanda and Troy as they help each other through all kinds of unpleasant situations, unapologetically speaking their minds, no matter the consequences.

Based on the award-winning American cartoonist Roberta Gregory's underground comic book, *Naughty Bits,* this prime-time, weekly animated comedy series, starring the voices of Mo Collins (*MADTV*) as Midge, Khandi Alexander (*CSI Miami*) as Yolanda and Elaine Stritch as Mom (with cameo performances by Quincy Jones, Dr. Drew Pinsky and others), officially debuted on Oxygen in October 2003 and aired until the following spring. *A Cinemania/Oxygen Media Production. Color. Half-hour. Premiered on OXY: October 17, 2003–March 1, 2004.*

*Voices*
**Midge McCracken:** Mo Collins; **Yolanda:** Khandi Alexander; **Mom:** Elaine Stritch

## ⊚ LIFE WITH LOUIE

Eight-year-old Louie experiences the various trials and joys of growing up with his middle-class family while observing an adult world from a child's perspective in this weekly half-hour series based on the routines of stand-up comic Louie Anderson. Introduced to viewers in the fall of 1995 on FOX Network, the series was preceded by a fully animated half-hour Christmas special, *Life with Louie: A Christmas Surprise for Mrs. Stillman,* which aired in December of 1994, also on FOX. The special was FOX's highest-rated, non-*Simpsons* animated show of the season. In June 1995, FOX premiered a second half-hour special in primetime, *Dad Gets Fired. A Hyperion Animation Hassan Entertainment/FOX Children's Network Production. Color. Half-hour. Premiered on FOX: September 9, 1995–September 10, 1999. Rebroadcast on FOX FAM: June 23, 1999–December 3, 2006.*

*Voices*

**Little Louie/Andy Anderson, his father/Narrator:** Louie Anderson; **Ora Anderson, Louie's mother:** Edie McClurg; **Tommy Anderson:** Miko Hughes; **Mike Grunewald/Glenn Glenn:** Justin Shenkarow; **Jeannie Harper:** Debi Derryberry; **Grandma:** Mary Wickes; **Other Voices:** Joe Alaskey, Olivia Hack

### ◎ LILO & STITCH: THE SERIES

Lovable alien castoff Stitch (originally known as Dr. Jumba Jookiba's "Experiment 626") makes his permanent home in Hawaii with Lilo and her extended family, including big sister Nani, their friend David, social worker Cobra Bubbles, and Stitch's alien uncle and aunt, Jumba and Pleakley—as he and Lilo track down many of Dr. Jumba's 625 other destructively equipped experiments, accidentally landed on the island, to change them from bad to good in this weekly half-hour series spin-off of the popular Disney animated feature, *Lilo & Stitch* (2002), and direct-to-video sequel, *Stitch! The Movie* (2003). Produced by Walt Disney Television Animation and originally entitled *Stitch! The Series*, the 65-episode series, also known as *The Adventures of Lilo & Stitch*, aired Saturday mornings at 8:00 A.M. on ABC's ABC Kids cartoon block, followed by *Disney's Recess* and *Disney's Fillmore!* The series was also rebroadcast on the Disney Channel and Toon Disney. *A Walt Disney Television Animation Production. Color. Half-hour. Premiered on ABC: September 20, 2003–July 29, 2006. Rebroadcast on DIS: October 12, 2003–. Rebroadcast on TDIS: January 16, 2006–.*

*Voices*

**Lilo:** Daveigh Chase; **Stitch:** Chris Sanders, Michael Yingling; **Nani:** Tia Carrere; **Pleakley:** Kevin McDonald; **Dr. Jumba Jookiba:** David Ogden Stiers; **Captain Ganta:** Kevin Michael Richardson; **Baron Jacques von Hamsterveil:** Jeff Bennett; **Mertle Edmonds:** Liliana Mumy; **Keoni Jameson:** Shaun Flemming; **Experiment #625:** Rob Paulsen; **Additional Voices:** Tress MacNeille, Frank Welker, Dee Bradley Baker, Jason Marsden, Will Friedle, Jason Scott Lee, Nancy Cartwright, April Winchell, Amy Hill, Jillian Henry, Susan Yezzi, E.G. Daily, Kath Soucie, Billy West, Matt Hill, Jason Scott Lee, Glenn Shadix, Dave Foley, Bruce McCullough, Scott Thompson, "Weird Al" Yankovich, Carlos Alazraqui, Bobcat Goldthwait, Bryan Cranston, Tom Kenny, Tara Strong, Grey DeLisle, Tommy Widmer, Regis Philbin.

### ◎ LINUS THE LIONHEARTED

Three major stars—Jonathan Winters, Sterling Holloway, Carl Reiner—and Sheldon Leonard lent their voices to characters derived from the boxes of Post cereals (produced by General Mills) and brought to life in this weekly Saturday-morning series. The 26-episode series—which debuted on CBS in 1964—revolved around the adventures of Linus the Lionhearted, the frail, docile ruler of the kingdom of animals in Africa, who first appeared on the boxes of Crispy Critters. His costars, Lovable Truly, the postman, and So-Hi, a small Chinese boy, were used to sell Alphabets and Sugar Crinkles. A third character, Sugar Bear, became famous on boxes of Post Cereal's Sugar Crisp.

Not everyone bowed to Linus's command, however. His not-so-loyal subjects–also the custodians of the royal cornfields—were Rory Raccoon, Sascha Grouse, Dinny Kangaroo and Billie Bird. Linus, Sugar Bear, Lovable Truly, Rory Raccoon and So-Hi appeared weekly in their own adventures, with the entire cast spotlighted in episodes termed "The Company." *An Ed Graham/ Format Films Production in association with General Foods. Color. Half-hour. Premiered on CBS: September 26, 1964–September 3, 1966. Rebroadcast on ABC: September 25, 1966–September 7, 1969. Syndicated.*

*Voices*

**Linus:** Sheldon Leonard; **Lovable Truly:** Sterling Holloway; **So-Hi:** Jonathan Winters; **Sugar Bear:** Sterling Holloway; **Billie Bird:** Ed Graham; **Sascha Grouse/Dinny Kangaroo/Rory Raccoon:** Carl Reiner; **The Japanese Giant:** Jonathan Winters

### ◎ THE LIONHEARTS

Inheriting the job once held by his famed father, Leo Sr., Leo Lionheart (voiced by actor William H. Macy) works as Metro-Goldwyn-Mayer's famed movie mascot and deals with the everyday goings-on of his life as the father, husband and provider for his family, including wife Lana and their three children, daughters Kate and Judy and son Spencer—all named after iconic MGM screen stars Lana Turner, Katharine Hepburn, Judy Garland and Spencer Tracy—in this half-hour animated comedy series produced by MGM Animation for syndication, airing weekend mornings beginning in the fall of 1998. *A Metro-Goldwyn-Mayer Animation Production in association with Claster Television and MGM Television. Production. Color. Half-hour. Syndicated: September 19, 1998.*

*Voices*

**Leo Lionheart:** William H. Macy; **Lana Lionheart:** Peri Gilpin; **Kate Lionheart:** Natasha Slayton; **Spencer Lionheart:** Cameron Finley; **Judy Lionheart:** Nicolette Little; **Hank:** Jeffrey Tambor; **Dorothy:** Betty White; **Leo Sr.:** Harve Presnell; **The Director:** Joe Pantoliano; **Freddy:** Wallace Shawn

### ◎ THE LION KING'S TIMON AND PUMBAA

The popular meercat-warthog comedy duo, who coined the "hakuna matata" credo (which means "no worries") in the 1994 box-office hit *The Lion King*, experience all-new adventures as they travel the globe—to Antarctica, the Swiss Alps, the Mayan ruins and beyond—in this weekly, half-hour cartoon series adaptation. Joining them were other characters from the movie in their own segments: Rafiki, the sagelike baboon; the hyenas; and the sneaky henchman Scar. Also featured in episodic adventures were several new characters: the Vulture Police; Timon's meercat cousin, Fred; and an obnoxious, multipurposed foil named Quint. Nathan Lane and Ernie Sabella reprised their roles as Timon and Pumbaa in the series. (Lane shared time with Quinton Flynn, also as the voice of Timon.) In December of 1997, previously broadcast episodes began rerunning on The Disney Channel and its sister cable network, Toon Disney, in April 1998. *A Walt Disney Television Animation Production. Color. Half-hour. Premiered: September 8, 1995–August 25, 1997 (syndicated); CBS: September 16, 1995–March 29, 1997. Rebroadcast on DIS: December 1, 1997–June 15, 2000; June 5, 2006–. Rebroadcast on TDIS: April 1, 1998–.*

*Voices*

**Timon:** Nathan Lane, Quinton Flynn; **Pumbaa:** Ernie Sabella; **Pumbaa Jr.:** Nancy Cartwright; **Rafiki:** Robert Guillaume; **Quint:** Corey Burtion; **Fred:** S. Scott Bullock; **Vulture Police:** Townsend Coleman, Brian Cummings

### ◎ LIPPY THE LION

Hanna-Barbera, who created the likes of Huckleberry Hound and Yogi Bear, produced this first-run syndicated series of outlandish jungle misadventures, pairing a con-artist lion (Lippy) with a sorrowful but pessimistic hyena (Hardy Har Har). The series' 52 five-minute cartoons were offered to local stations as part of a trilogy called *The Hanna-Barbera New Cartoon Series*, featuring two other cartoon adventures, *Touché Turtle* and *Wally Gator*. Although the films were sold to television stations as a package, the cartoons often were programmed independently of each other in their own half-hour time slots. *A Hanna-Barbera Production. Color. Half-hour. Premiered: September 3, 1962. Syndicated.*

**Voices**
**Lippy:** Daws Butler; **Hardy Har Har:** Mel Blanc

## ◎ LIQUID TELEVISION

First produced as interstitial programming—a brace of animated logos and bumpers inserted between rock videos and other programs—MTV inaugurated this expanded, half-hour showcase and the music cable network's first animated variety series, combining cutting-edge animation, over-the-edge graphics and stories from beyond the fringe. Each episode featured a fluid blend of original and acquired animation, animated versions of underground comics, stories featuring live actors in action settings and short films of any description, packaged in collaboration with Britain's BBC and produced by Prudence Fenton, who produced award-winning station I.D.'s for the popular music cable network. Although animation production values varied on each program, the series became one of the tube's finer animation showcases.

Premiering in June of 1991, the first half-hour included Bardal Animation Coloring House's "Lea Press-on Limbs," directed by Chris Miller; "Art School Girls of Doom" (directed by El Noyes; written by Dan Leo; produced by Mark Reusch); "Ms. Lidia's Makeover" (directed by and written by Gordon Clark); "Invisible Hands" (written and designed by Richard Sala); and Mike McKenna and Bob Sabiston's "Grinning Evil Death."

During the first season, serialized segments included: "Aeon Flux" (later adapted into a series of its own), chronicling the adventures of a female secret agent extraordinare; "Stick Figure Theatre," bringing to life scenes from classic movies and television shows; and "Winter Steele," the story of a tough motorcycle babe in search of action. In September of 1992, for the series' second season, new serialized segments were added, namely: "Dog Boy," the misadventures of a boy with a dog's heart; "The Adventures of Thomas and Nardo," the story of a talking, walking insect-eating tenement building; and "Billy & Bobby," the tale of two normal all-American boys gone haywire.

That September "Frog Baseball," an animated short created by Mike Judge featuring two suburban misfits named Bobby and Billy (Beavis and Butt-Head in their original form), debuted. Shortly thereafter, Judge signed a 65 episode contract with MTV to create a Beavis & Butt-Head series.

In 1993 the series was nominated for a daytime Emmy Award for outstanding animated program. *A Colossal Pictures/BBC/MTV Production. Color. Half-hour. Premiered on MTV: June 6, 1991' 1993. Rebroadcast on MTV: 1995–1996.*

## ◎ LITTL'BITS

A pack of fun-loving, adventuruous inch-tall elves—Snoozabit, Lillabit, Williebit and Snagglebit—maintain peace, love and harmony in the Foothill Forest while coping in a world designed for humans in this 26-episode half-hour series, first released in Japan, then redubbed in English on Nickelodeon. *A Tatsunoko Productions Co. Ltd./Saban Entertainment Production. Color. Half-hour. Premiered on NICK: May 1, 1991–April 30, 1995.*

**Voices**
Arthur Grosser, Dean Hagopian, A.J. Henderson, Arthur Holden, Rick Jones, Liz MacRae, Walter Massey, Anik Matern, Terrence Scammel, Jane Woods

## ◎ LITTLE BILL

Comedian Bill Cosby created this animated preschool series told from the viewpoint of the Glover family's youngest son, an inquisitive, imaginative five-year-old, Bill Glover Jr., affectionately called "Little Bill," who learns many valuable lessons while exploring the daily ordinary and extraordinary events of a child. Joined by his housing inspector father, Bill; his photographer mother, Brenda; his two older siblings, April and Bobby; and Brenda's grandmother, Alice the Great, the stories emphasized how kids can make a difference and the importance of family, high self-esteem and strong social skills. The series featured actress Phylicia Rashad, who played Cosby's wife in the hit NBC sitcom, *The Cosby Show*, as the voice of his wife, Brenda, with Gregory Hines providing the voice as her husband and Little Bill's father, Big Bill. Actress Ruby Dee, who also appeared on *The Cosby Show*, voiced the character Alice the Great.

Nominated six times for Daytime Emmy Awards, winning twice in 2003 for outstanding performer in an animated program (Gregory Hines) and in 2004 for outstanding animated program, the series premiered on Nickelodeon in November 1999 and then joined CBS's Saturday morning roster in September 2000 as part of the *Nick Jr. on CBS* program block until September 2002. The following August, the 47 episodes returned on CBS, continuing to air on Saturday mornings until March 2004. The series was subsequently rebroadcast on CBS from September 2004 to September 2006. *A Viacom International Production. Color. Half-hour. Premiered on NICK: November 28, 1999. Premiered on CBS: September 16, 2000–September 7, 2002; August 2, 2003–March 2004. Rebroadcast on CBS: September 16, 2004–September 2006.*

**Voices**
**Little Bill:** Xavier Pritchett; **Big Bill:** Gregory Hines; **Brenda:** Phylicia Rashad; **April:** Monique Beasley; **Bobby:** Devon Malik Beckford, Tyler James Williams (2000); **Alice the Great:** Ruby Dee; **Andrew:** Zach Tyler Eisen; **Fuchsia:** Kianna Underwood; **Kiku:** Eunice Cho; **Dorado:** Vincent Canoles; **Miss Murray:** Ayo Haynes (1999–2000), Melanie Nicholls-King (2001); **Coach Maya:** Robin Reid

## ◎ LITTLE CLOWNS OF HAPPYTOWN

The inhabitants of a small fantasy town (called Itty Bitty City) are all born clowns and their goal in life is to spread the message that "happiness is good for you" in this weekly half-hour series, originally broadcast on ABC. *An ABC Entertainment Production in association with Marvel Productions and Murakami-Wolf-Swenson Films. Color. Half-hour. Premiered on ABC: September 26, 1987–July 16, 1988. Rebroadcast on FAM: 1989–1990.*

**Voices**
Charlie Adler, Sue Blu, Danny Cooksey, Pat Fraley, Ellen Gerstell, Howard Morris, Ron Palillo, Josh Rodine, Frank Welker

## ◎ A LITTLE CURIOUS

Featuring clay, cel and 3-D CGI-animated films and live-action segments, an ensemble of characters based on everyday objects—Bob the Ball, Doris the Door, Mr. String, Pad & Pencil and others—teach young viewers basic learning and cognitive concepts in this first daily, half-hour children's series created by Steve Oakes and John Hoffman, exclusively for HBO Family. Produced by New York-based Curious Pictures, this mixed-media preschool series debuted with the launching of HBO's 24-hour family programming channel in February 1999, featuring a variety of other original animated programming weekday mornings for children, including *Anthony Ant, George and Martha* and *The Adventures of*

*Paddington Bear. A Curious Pictures Production. Color. Half-hour. Premiered on HBO Family: February 1, 1999–April 16, 2000. Rebroadcast on HBO FAM: January 26, 2004–February 26, 2007.*

**Voices**
**Bob the Ball:** Cameron Bowen; **Mop/Mary Jane:** Amanda Kaplan

## ◎ LITTLE DRACULA

Unlike his famous Transylvanian father, young Drac prefers to sink his teeth into rock 'n' roll and surfing, with his bizarre family, friends and foes, in this half-hour, six-part miniseries adapted from the popular British children's book character of the same name. In September 1991 the series aired five of its six episodes—"The Curse of the Ghastly Minimum Wage," "Little D's First Bite," "Little D's Surprise," "Bite Before Christmas" and "Little D Goes Hawaiian"—for one week on FOX network. The sixth installment was broadcast on Halloween, "Little D's Halloween." In late September 1999, nearly eight years after its FOX debut, four existing but never-before-aired episodes were broadcast in succession on the same day on FOX Family Channel. *A Hahn Productions/Island Animation Production. Color. Half-hour. Premiered on FOX: September 3, 1991–September 7, 1991; October 31, 1991. Premiered on FOX: September 30, 1999. Rebroadcast on FOX FAM: October 19, 1999–October 31, 2000.*

**Voices**
**Little Dracula:** Edan Gross; **Big Dracula:** Joe Flaherty; **Mrs. Dracula/Millicent:** Kath Soucie; **Werebunny:** Joey Camen; **Garlic Man:** Brian Cummings; **Deadwood:** Melvyn Hayes; **No Eyes/Twin-Beaks:** Danny Mann; **Maggot:** Neil Ross, **Hannah the Barbarian:** Fran Ryan; **Igor/Granny:** Jonathan Winters

## ◎ THE LITTLE LULU SHOW

Tracey Ullman initially lent her voice as the girl in the signature red dress and corkscrew curls who proves that girls are just as good as boys in all-new, half-hour animated adventures, based on stories from the original 1935 comic strip. Each half-hour program featured three "Lulutoons," reuniting Lulu with characters from the comic strip: sailor-capped Tubby Tompkins; buck-toothed Annie; whiny little Alvin and the rest of the ageless crew. Given a six-week test run on HBO on Sunday nights in October 1995, the series was renewed for a full second season, featuring 20 brand-new episodes and a new actor playing the part of Lulu, that premiered in May 1997. Tracey Ullman left the series after the first six episodes. Voice actress Jane Woods assumed the role thereafter.

Canada's CINAR Films, which produced the program, also sold the rights to the series in 87 territories internationally that same year. In 1998, HBO bought the U.S. rights to the popular CINAR series, plus two other animated programs set to debut that fall, besides renewing Lulu for a third season. Fifty-two half-hour episodes aired during the series' original three-season run through May 1999. Thereafter, the series was rebroadcast on both HBO and its sister channel, HBO Family, until November 2004. *A CINAR Production in association with Western Publishing Company/Loonland Animation/HBO/CTV Television Network. Color. Half-hour. Premiered on HBO: October 22, 1995–May 21, 1999. Rebroadcast on HBO: May 1999–November 21, 2000. Rebroadcast on HBO FAM: January 1, 1997–November 21, 2004.*

**Voices**
**Little Lulu:** Tracey Ullman (episodes 1–6), Jane Woods (episodes 7–26); **Tubby:** Bruce Dinsmore; **Annie:** Michael Caloz; **Alvin:** Ajay Fry; **Iggie:** Jane Woods; **Willie:** Andrew Henry; **Mrs. Mop-**pet: Pauline Little; **Wilbur:** Jacob B. Tierney; **Gloria:** Angelina Bolvin

## ◎ LITTLE MERMAID

(See DISNEY'S THE LITTLE MERMAID; SABAN'S ADVENTURE OF THE LITTLE MERMAID FANTASY.)

## ◎ THE LITTLE RASCALS/RICHIE RICH SHOW

The classic fun and humor of the *Our Gang* short-subject series is recaptured in this animated comedy/mystery series, featuring Spanky, Alfalfa, Darla, Buckwheat and their dog Pete, in new episodes combined with episodes originally broadcast on 1982's *The Pac-Man/Little Rascals/Richie Rich Show.* From their funky treehouse, they plan new schemes and plots that send their adversaries into submission in hilarious fashion. The series was paired with all-new episodes (including reruns from the previous show) of the world's richest youngster, Richie Rich. *A Hanna-Barbera Production in association with King Features Entertainment. Color. Half-hour. Premiered on ABC: September 10, 1983–September 1, 1984.*

**Voices**
**THE LITTLE RASCALS: Spanky:** Scott Menville; **Alfalfa/Porky/Woim:** Julie McWhirter Dees; **Darla:** Patty Maloney; **Buckwheat:** Shavar Ross; **Butch/Waldo:** B.J. Ward; **Pete, the dog/Police Officer Ed:** Peter Cullen.

**RICHIE RICH: Richie Rich:** Sparky Marcus; **George Rich, his father:** Stanley Jones; **Mrs. Rich, his mother:** Joan Gerber; **Dollar, Richie's dog:** Frank Welker; **Gloria, Richie's girlfriend:** Nancy Cartwright; **Freckles, Richie's friend:** Christian Hoff; **Irona, the Rich's maid:** Joan Gerber; **Cadbury, the Rich's butler:** Stanley Jones; **Professor Keenbean:** Bill Callaway; **Reggie Van Goh:** Dick Beals

## ◎ LITTLE ROBOTS

Abandoned at a New Jersey junkyard on a large scrap heap of metal, an optimistic band of small robots—Tiny, Stripy, Sporty, Spotty, Stretchy, Noisy and the Sparky Twins—use the scraps of metals around them to build their own magical place to live—including homes, trees, clouds and, for good measure, the sun and the moon—finding fun and laughter along the way in this stop-motion, animated, educational preschool series produced by Britain's award-winning animation house Cosgrove Hall Films and Create TV and Film Limited. Featuring the voice talents of British comedians Lenny Henry, Martin Clunes, Morwenna Banks, Emma Chambers, Su Pollard and Hayley Carmichael, this animated adaptation of Mike Brownlow's eponymous book, originally produced in 2003 for United Kingdom television's CBeebies and BBC2, premiered in the United States in August 2005 as part of Cartoon Network's short-lived weekday preschool block, *Tickle-U,* including a collection of new animated programs, among them, *Firehouse Tales, Gerald McBoing Boing, Gordon the Garden Gnome, Harry and His Bucket Full of Dinosaurs, Peppa Pig* and *Yoko! Jakamoko! Toto! A Cosgrove Hall Films/Create TV and Film Ltd. Production. Color. Half-hour. Premiered on CAR: August 22, 2005.*

**Voices**
**Tiny:** Hayley Carmichael; **Stripy:** Martine Clunes; **Sporty:** Lenny Henry; **Spotty:** Emma Chambers; **Stretchy:** Jimmy Hibbert; **Noisy:** Su Pollard; **Sparky Twins:** Mel Giedroyc, Sue Perkins; **Rusty:** Morwenna Banks

## ⊚ LITTLE ROSEY

Emmy award–winning comedienne Roseanne Arnold created this half-hour animated series (and served as executive producer with then-husband Tom Arnold) featuring her as a 10-year-old teen who finds adventure in fantasy and real life with her family and friends—her sister Tess, her brother Tater and her best friend, Buddy. Arnold did not supply the voice of her own character in the series (it was provided by actress Kathleen Laskey), which premiered on ABC in 1991, home of her long-running comedy series, *Roseanne*. The comedienne was known to have clashed with network executives over series content—reportedly over their wanting her to "put more boys" into the show, which Arnold adamantly resisted (believing it would result in an increase in violence in each show). Arnold got back at the network for its interference when she financed and produced with Tom Arnold a follow-up half-hour, prime-time animated special, *The Rosey and Buddy Show*, in which network executives were portrayed to look as if they cared only about "money and not children." Strangely, the special aired on ABC. A *Little Rosey Production in association with Nelvana Enterprises. Color. Half-hour. Premiered on ABC: September 8, 1990–August 13, 1991.*

**Voices**

**Little Rosey:** Kathleen Laskey; **Buddy:** Noam Zylberman; **Tess:** Pauline Gillis; **Nanny/Tater:** Lisa Yamanaka; **Mom:** Judy Marshak; **Dad:** Tony Daniels; **Jeffrey/Matthew:** Stephen Bednarski

## ⊚ THE LITTLES

These tiny, near-human creatures, who live behind the walls of people's houses, are discovered by a normal-size young boy (Henry Bigg), the son of a globetrotting scientist, who joins them in many of their adventures in this half-hour series, adapted from John Peterson's popular Scholastic children's book series. Produced two years after the success of another cartoon series about tiny people, NBC's *The Smurfs*, the series enjoyed a successful three-season run on ABC. *An ABC Entertainment/DIC Enterprises/Tetsuo Katayama Production. Color. Half-hour. Premiered on ABC: September 10, 1983–September 6, 1986. Rebroadcast on FAM: September 18, 1989–September 10, 1993. Rebroadcast on TDIS: April 17, 1998–September 2, 2002. Syndicated: September 6, 2003.*

**Voices**

**Henry Bigg, the young boy:** Jimmy E. Keegan; **George Bigg/Dinky:** Robert David Hall; **Mrs. Bigg:** Laurel Page; **Tom Little:** Donavan Freberg; **Lucy Little:** Bettina Bush; **Grandpa:** Alvy Moore; **Ashley:** B.J. Ward; **Slick:** Patrick Fraley

## ⊚ LITTLE SHOP

Inspired by the 1986 musical film remake of Roger Corman's classic 1961 black comedy, *Little Shop of Horrors*, this half-hour animated series was a toned-down musical spinoff featuring the comical exploits of the primary characters from both movies: Mushnick, the deviled florist; his nerdy assistant Seymour; Seymour's girlfriend Audrey; and even the talking, people-eating plant Audrey, but differently cast from previous efforts. In the cartoon series of offbeat adventures, Seymour and Audrey are teenagers (with Seymour raising the carnivorous talking plant); Mushnick plays Audrey's father; and Audrey Junior loves to sing rap instead of craving live flesh. Debuting on FOX Network in 1991, the series was subsequently rebroadcast on the Sci-Fi Channel's Cartoon Quest. *A Marvel Films/Saban Entertainment Production. Color. Half-hour. Premiered on FOX: September 7, 1991–September 5, 1992. Rebroadcast on SCI: September 18, 1993–September 10, 1996.*

**Voices**

Harvey Atkins, David Huban, Tamar Lee, Roland "Buddy" Lewis, Marlo Vola

**Singing Voices**

**Junior Rap:** Terry McGee; **Seymour:** Jana Lexxa; **Audrey:** Jennie Kwan; **Paine:** Mark Ryan Martin; **Mushnick:** Michael Rawls

## ⊚ LITTLEST PET SHOP

A group of cantankerous pets (from Stu the sheepdog to Chloe the cat), mysteriously reduced to teeny-weeny size, experience a series of madcap adventures after they are sold to unwitting pet shop customers by the store's eccentric owner/operator Elwood Funk, only to keep sneaking back to his "Littlest Pet Shop," in this 40-episode half-hour syndicated series, coproduced by U.S.-based Sunbow Entertainment in 1995. *A Sunbow Production in association with Claster Television. Color. Half-hour. Premiered: (week of) September 11, 1995. Syndicated.*

**Voices**

**Viv:** Lynda Boyd; **Sarge:** Gary Chalk; **Chloe:** Babs Chula; **Squeaks:** Tel Cole; **Elwood:** Ian James Corlett; **Stu:** Mike Donovan; **Delilah:** Shirley Milliner; **Rookie:** Sarah Strange; **Chet:** Lee Tockar

## ⊚ LITTLE WIZARDS

Aided by three tiny helpers, Boo, Winkle and Gump, a young boy-prince, Prince Dexter, seeks to regain his kingdom from his powerful uncle, King Renwick, in this magical half-hour fantasy/adventure series, first telecast on ABC. *A Marvel Production in association with Janson and Menville Productions. Color. Half-hour. Premiered on ABC: September 26, 1987–September 3, 1988.*

**Voices**

Charlie Adler, Joey Camen, Peter Cullen, Katie Leigh, Danny Mann, Scott Menville, Amber Souza, Frank Welker

## ⊚ LOLA & VIRGINIA

Two 12-year-old girls with completely opposite life-styles—the down-to-earth Lola and cross-town snooty neighbor Virginia—clash over their friends, the clothes they wear and, naturally, boys. First shown on Nickelodeon Asia in March 2006, the Flash-animated half-hour comedy, based on an original concept by Icon Animation creative director and founding partner Myriam Ballesteros and comprised of 52 12-minute episodes, premiered in the United States on VOOM's Animania HD network, where it aired regularly Saturday and Sunday afternoons. *An Icon Animation/Millimages/France 3/TV Catalnya/ETB Production. Color. Half-hour. Premiered on ANI: October 14, 2006.*

## ⊚ LONE RANGER

The noted avenger of evil and upholder of justice, also known as the Masked Man, and his faithful Indian companion, Tonto, battle villainous cowboys, cutthroats and ruthless land barons of the Old West in this 26-episode half-hour series that aired weekly on CBS. The series was the first animated version of the popular radio and television series character, originally created for radio in 1933 by George W. Trendle and Fran Striker for Trendle's Detroit radio station WXYZ. The Saturday-morning series, featuring three brief adventures per episode, premiered opposite ABC's *The Beatles* in 1966. The series was canceled three years later. In 1980 Filmation produced a new series of cartoons as part of its *The Tarzan/Lone Ranger Adventure Hour*, also for CBS. *A Lone Ranger Production in*

*Noted upholder of justice the Lone Ranger and faithful companion Tonto get ready for trouble in a scene from the* Lone Ranger *cartoon series.*
© *Lone Ranger Productions*

association with the Jack Wrather Corporation. Color. Half-hour. Premiered on CBS: September 10, 1966–September 6, 1969.

**Voices**
**Lone Ranger:** Michael Rye; **Tonto:** Shepard Menken: **Etcetera:** Marvin Miller, Hans Conried; **Warlock:** Marvin Miller; **Tiny Tom:** Richard Beals; **Black Widow:** Agnes Moorehead

### ⊚ LONG AGO & FAR AWAY

Hosted by actor James Earl Jones, this weekly dramatic series captured the magic of storytelling for children as well as adults, featuring mostly award-winning animated and some live-action films from around the world, usually as half-hour specials. Many of the programs were based on classic children's books, folktales and fairy tales, with others adapted from original screenplays. Produced by WGBH Boston and presented in partnership with the International Reading Association for Library Service to Children, the series aired Saturday nights on PBS stations beginning in 1989, providing an alternative to traditional commercial cartoon fare shown on the most cable networks.

Opening the first season, which lasted 16 weeks, was *The Pied Piper of Hamelin*, based on the famous poem by Robert Browning and produced by England's preeminent puppet animation studio, Cosgrove Hall Productions. Other first-season specials included *The Reluctant Dragon*, also by Cosgrove Hall; *Abel's Island* by award-winning New York animator Michael Sporn; *The Happy Circus*, an episodic half-hour of French clay animation; *Hungarian Folk Tales*, produced by MTV Enterprises, Hungary; *The Talking Parcel*, a two-part tale based on the book by Gerald Durell; *The Wind in the Willows*, the only two-hour special in the series, based on Kenneth Grahame's book; and *Svatohor*, an animated Russian folktale featuring sophisticated puppet animation of the time.

In 1990 the series returned for a second season, reduced to 13 weeks. The season featured more animated films from England, France, Hungary and the United States and one live-action film from Sweden. Kicking off the season was the haunting animated version of *Beauty and the Beast*, narrated by actress Mia Farrow.

PBS renewed the series for a third season in 1991, increasing the show to 24 weeks of original films. Launching the series' third season was the special two-part premiere of *The Fool of the World*

*and the Flying Ship*, a fanciful adaptation of a classic Russian folktale using groundbreaking animation with "lifelike puppets," made in conjunction with England's Cosgrove Hall Productions. Included among that season's other productions was the Emmy-nominated animator Michael Sporn's adaptation of an old Hans Christian Andersen story, *The Emperor's New Clothes*, narrated by Regis Philbin and Peggy Cass. Sporn also produced the heartwarming musical *Jazztime Tale*, the story of of an interracial friendship between two girls set in Harlem in 1919, which also aired that season. Producer Joshua Greene for Lightyear Entertainment brought to television screens *Merlin and the Dragons*, following two previous memorable installments of the *Long Ago & Far Away* series: *Beauty and the Beast* and *Noah's Ark*.

For the series' fourth and final season in 1992–93, 26 half-hour programs and one 90-minute special were offered, mostly reruns from past seasons with the exception of three new programs: Michael Sporn's *Nightingale*, yet another adaptation of a story by Hans Christian Andersen, veteran animator John Matthews *Mouse Soup*, based on a book by the award-winning children's author/illustrator Arnold Lobel (and featuring the voice of comedian Buddy Hackett); and a second special from Sporn, *The Talking Eggs*, adapted from a Creole folktale and narrated by actor Danny Glover.

Funding for the series was provided by General Cinema Corporation/The Neiman Marcus Group, the National Endowment for the Humanities, The Arthur Vining Davis Foundations and others. WGBH Boston's Sandy Cohen produced the award-winning series, with Carol Greenwald serving as project director and series editor. (For a complete listing of individual shows from each season, see Animated Television Specials section for details.) *A WGBH Boston Production for PBS. Color. Half-hour (mostly). Premiered on PBS: January 28, 1989–May 13, 1990; September 8, 1990–December 1, 1990; October 5, 1991–March 14, 1992; September 6, 1992–February 28, 1993.*

### ⊚ LOONATICS UNLEASHED

Set 700 years in the future, six descendants of Warner Bros.' famed *Looney Tunes* characters—Ace Bunny (Bugs Bunny), Lexi Bunny (Lola Bunny), Danger Duck (Daffy Duck), Tech E. Coyote (Wile E. Coyote), Rev. Runner (Road Runner) and Slam Tasmanian (Tasmanian Devil)—form a team of uniquely skilled and super-powered superheroes who defend Acmetropolis from some of the world's most dastardly villains with their own special skills and strengths in this anime-inspired designed action-comedy series. Joining the WB Television Network's Kids' WB! Saturday-morning lineup in the fall of 2005, 13 episodes of the series were produced during the first season. In September 2006, the program returned with six brand-new episodes, along with two other series, *Xiaolin Showdown* and *The Batman*, on the newly renamed CW Network. For the second season, new descendant characters included Ophiuchus Sam (Yosemite Sam), Sylth Vester, (Sylvester the Cat), The Royal Tweetums (Tweety Bird) and Melvin the Martian (Marvin the Martian). *A Warner Bros. Television Animation Production. Color. Half-hour. Premiered on the WB (Kids' WB!): September 11, 2005–.*

**Voices**
**Ace Bunny:** Charlie Schlatter; **Lexi Bunny:** Jessica Di Cicco; **Danger Duck:** Jason Marsden; **Slam Tasmanian/Tech E. Coyote/Trick Daley:** Kevin Michael Richardson; **Rev Runner/Gorlop:** Rob Paulsen; **Dr. Fidel Chroniker/Colonel Trench:** Jeff Bennett; **Zodavia/Misty Breeze/Harriet "Ma" Runner/Sagittarius Stomper/Sagittarius Stomper's Mom:** Candi Milo; **Mr. Leghorn:** Bill Farmer; **Ophiuchus Sam/Pierre LePew:** Maurice LaMarche; **The**

**Royal Tweetums/Sylth Vester:** Joe Alaskey; **Queen Grannicus:** Candi Milo (normal voice), Kevin Michael Richardson (disguised voice); **Ralph "Pa" Runner:** Daran Norris; **Rip Runner:** Mikey Kelley; **Gunnar the Conqueror:** Tom Kenny; **Professor Zane:** Jeff Bennett; **Fuz-Z:** Steven Blum; **Black Velvet:** Vivica A. Fox; **Weathervane:** Kaley Cuoco; **Dr. Dare:** Simon Templeman; **Ringmaster:** Tim Curry; **Otto the Odd:** Dee Bradley Baker; **Massive:** Michael Clarke Duncan; **Drake Sypher:** Phil LaMarr; **Time Skip:** David Faustino; **Mallory "Mastermind" Casey:** Florence Henderson; **Optimatus:** Charlie Adler; **General Deuce:** Khary Payton; **Adolpho:** Mark Hamill

## ◎ LOONEY TUNES

In 1955, in both New York (WABD-TV) and Los Angeles (KTLA-TV), Warner Bros.' library of pre-1948 *Looney Tunes*, a calvacade of the studio's most memorable cartoon stars (Bosko, Buddy, Daffy Duck, Porky Pig and others), made their television premiere. (Initially the films were seen on weekdays with local personalities hosting the show.) At first, the studio released 190 cartoons under the series name to television. Prints of each film were black-and-white. It wasn't until 1969, when television stations across the country demanded color, that Warner Bros. struck color prints of those films that were originally produced in that form. In 1960 Warner added post-1948 color *Looney Tunes* to the package for syndication. Portions of the syndicated package (mostly post-1960 cartoons, black-and-white shorts and "colorized" Porky Pig cartoons from the 1930s) began airing afternoons on Nickelodeon in 1988. The half-hour broadcasts (replete with the opening logo: "Looney Tunes on Nickelodeon") usually featured three to four cartoons, including at least one black-and-white oldie starring Bosko, Buddy and Porky Pig. The *Looney Tunes* show was later added to Nick at Nite's lineup of classic television shows aimed at adults, where it was well received by viewers.

Meanwhile, in 1997, Turner-owned cable networks Cartoon Network, TBS and TNT all began showing Looney Tunes cartoons that originally aired on Kids' WB!'s *The Bugs 'N Daffy Show* and *That's Warner Bros.!* cartoon anthology series. After becoming the longest-running animated series in Nickelodeon's history, in October 1999 cartoons previously seen on Nick began airing on Cartoon Network, becoming part of its daily hour-long showcase of classic cartoons, the *ACME Hour* (also featuring Tom and Jerry and the Pink Panther) which was launched in April 1998. The final package of post-1948 Warner Bros. *Looney Tunes* and *Merrie Melodies*, formerly part of ABC's *Bugs Bunny and Tweety Show*, began airing as part of the mix on Cartoon Network in July 2001. After Cartoon Network dropped the *ACME Hour* in September 2002, three years later the program, including Warner Bros.' *Looney Tunes* and *Merrie Melodies*, found a new home, airing daily on Cartoon Network's classic cartoons channel, Boomerang. *A Warner Bros. Production. Black-and-white. Color. Half-hour. Premiered: April 11, 1955. Rebroadcast on NICK: September 12, 1998–1999. CAR: 1997–September 1, 2002. Rebroadcast on TBS/TNT: 1997. Rebroadcast on BOOM: December 1, 2005–.*

## ◎ LUNCH BOX

Aimed at younger viewers, this daily half-hour series broadcast on the Disney Channel beginning in 1989 was comprised of live action and cartoon shorts, including such favorites as "Curious George," "Paddington Bear" and "Rupert," as well as many cartoons never before shown in America. *An Alfred Bestall/Siriol Studios (Cardiff)/Kingroll Films Production (and various others). Color. Half-hour. Premiered on DIS: July 1, 1989–1993. Rebroadcast: 1993–December 23, 1994.*

## ◎ LUPIN THE 3RD

Thanks to intricate planning and numerous disguises, the world's most accomplished and cunning thief, Arsene Lupin, aided by his surly gunman, Jigen, and mute martial arts expert, Goemon, eludes police and others set on catching him as he steals exotic treasure around the globe in this cartoon series inspired by the manga created by Kazuhiko Kato in 1967. Debuting in January 2003, the English-dubbed, half-hour comic spy caper joined two other action-adventure additions on Cartoon Network's late-night *Adult Swim* roster, *Reign: The Conqueror* and *Trigun*. *A Tokyo Movie Shinsha/Nippon Television Network/Monkey Punch/Pioneer Entertainment Production. Color. Half-hour. Premiered on CAR: January 13, 2003–March 9, 2006.*

*Voices*
**Arsene Lupin III:** Antonio Oliver; **Inspector Koichi Zenigata:** Jake Martin; **Goemon Ishiwaka:** Walter Lang; **Daisuke Jigen:** Richard Epcar; **Diana:** Cynthia Cranz; **Other Voices:** Dorothy Melendrez, Ivan Buckley, Joe Romersa, Kirk Thorton, Philece Sampler, Steven Jay Blum

## ◎ MACRON I

In the year A.D. 2545, a teleportation experiment goes wrong and test pilot David Jance is rocketed through the center of the galaxy into another universe, where he is caught in a life-and-death struggle against the tyrannical armies of GRIP, led by the villainous Dark Star. The good forces of both universes combine and form Marcon 1 to defeat Dark Star's army in this first-run action-packed adventure series, backed by the latest Top-40 rock tunes. Rock group Duran Duran performed the series' theme song, "Reflex." *A Saban Entertainment Production in association with Tamerlaine Publishing and Orbis. Color. Half-hour. Premiered: September 1985. Syndicated.*

*Voices*
Angeria Rigamonti, Bill Laver, Christopher Eric, Octavia Beaumont, Tamara Shawn, Rich Ellis, Susan Ling, Oliver Miller

## ◎ MADELINE

The first weekly animated series based on a series of popular children's books by critically acclaimed author Ludwig Bemelmans, this series followed the adventures of the precocious and engaging French smallfry and her equally petite friends (Chloe, Nicole and Danielle), set in a boarding school in Paris. The award-winning series, backed by original songs and played against lovely Parisian backgrounds painted in a unique homage to artistic impressionism (and narrated by actor Christopher Plummer), debuted on The Family Channel in 1993, as part of a Sunday-night programming block for kids that featured the animated series *Babar* (in reruns) and a new live-action series, *Baby Races*.

*Madeline* produced solid enough ratings that the network renewed it for a second season in 1994, featuring new episodes. The weekly series, which won a CableAce Award for outstanding children's series, followed by a brace of prime-time animated specials, the first produced for the *HBO Storybook Musical* series in 1988 (simply entitled *Madeline*), then five new specials (*Madeline's Christmas, Madeline and the Bad Hat, Madeline's Rescue, Madeline and the Gypsies* and *Madeline in London*), each originally broadcast on The Family Channel in 1990 and 1991. Madeline's voice, provided by Marsha Moreau in the animated specials, was performed by Tracey-Lee Smythe in the series.

In 1995 the series moved to ABC, with 13 new episodes, entitled *The New Adventures of Madeline*. (See individual entry for details.) The Family Channel series was rebroadcast on Disney Channel beginning in the fall of 1997.

Rebroadcast on the Disney Channel until early September 2005, the popular cartoon adaptation was rebroadcast on CBS in the fall of 2006 as part of its new three-hour Saturday children's programming block (that some CBS affiliates aired on Saturday and Sunday in 90-minute blocks instead), *KOL Secret Slumber Party on CBS*, along with *Sabrina: The Animated Series and Horseland Princess Natasha*, among others. *A DIC Enterprises Production in association with The Family Channel. Color. Half-hour. Premiered on FAM: September 12, 1993–September 1995. Rebroadcast on DIS: December 1, 1997–September 3, 2005. Rebroadcast CBS: September 16, 2006–.*

**Voices**
**Madeline:** Tracey-Lee Smyth; **Miss Clavel/Genevieve:** Louise Vallance; **Narrator:** Christopher Plummer

### ◎ MADISON'S ADVENTURES—GROWING UP WILD

A cartoon cat introduces youngsters to exotic locales and wild animals in their natural habitats through a myriad of real-life video clips in this live-action/animated educational series for children, which aired in first-run syndication and was later rebroadcast on the Learning Channel and Animal Planet. *A BBC/Lionheart Television/Wildvision Entertainment/Time-Life Video/Kookanooga Toons Production. Color. Half-hour. Premiered: September 10, 1994. Syndicated. Rebroadcast on TLC: December 24, 1996–August 14, 1998. Rebroadcast on AP: October 1, 1996–September 1999.*

### ◎ MAD JACK THE PIRATE

Zany high-sea adventures of a cowardly, blundering pirate named Mad Jack and his comical sidekick rat, Snuk, in their unsuccessful quest to discover buried treasure after setting sail in their ship, the *Sea Chicken*, in this short-lived, 13-episode Saturday morning cartoon series, featuring two cartoon segments per half-hour, created by Bill Kopp (also the voice of Mad Jack) for FOX. *A Bill Kopp/Fox Arts Animation Studios/Saban Entertainment Production. Color. Half-hour. Premiered on FOX: September 12, 1998–May 1, 1999; May 8, 1999–June 26, 1999 (combined with "Secret Files of the Spy Dog").*

**Voices**
**Mad Jack:** Bill Kopp; **Snuk:** Billy West; **Flash Dashing:** Jess Harnell; **Darsh the Dragon:** Brad Garrett; **Fuzzy:** Cam Clarke; **Magic Pink Fairy:** Sandy Fox; **Other Voices:** Jocelyn Blue

### ◎ THE MAD SCIENTIST TOON CLUB

Wacky scientist Doctor Pi performs conducts outrageous experiments and lessons for the benefit of young children in this live-action, hour-long syndicated series (offered as two half-hours to stations as well), which featured two regular cartoon components: "The Wacky World of Tic and Tac," the wild comical adventures of a bird and a hippo done in pantomine, and "Eggzavier the Eggasaurus," a good Samaritan dinosaur whose fluttery voice was like that of comedian Ed Wynn. The 1993 syndicated series followed the success of other live-action educational programs, *Beakman's World* and *Bill Nye the Science Guy. A Saban Entertainment Production. Color. One hour. Premiered: 1993. Syndicated.*

**Cast** (*live action*)
**Doctor Pi:** Michael Sorich

**Voices**
Mikey Godzilla, Dave Molen, Steve Norton, Wendy Swan

### ◎ MAGGIE AND THE FEROCIOUS BEAST

Maggie, a precocious five-year-old girl, imagines her own fantasy world, Nowhere Land, where she explores with her favorite stuffed toys come-to-life, Hamilton Hocks and the Ferocious Beast, in this entertaining and educational half-hour series based on the children's books by Betty and Michael Paraskevas. Directed by Jamie Whitney and produced by Canada's Nelvana studios, the series, incorporating lessons about politeness, teamwork and proper behavior, debuted in the United States on Nickelodeon's Nick Jr. weekday program block, and was rebroadcast weeknights at 5:00 P.M. on the commercial-free children's program network, Noggin. *A Nelvana Limited/Paraskevas Productions Production. Color. Half-hour. Premiered on NICK JR.: June 5, 2000–April 25, 2004. Rebroadcast on NOG: April 7, 2003–.*

**Voices**
**Maggie:** Kristen Bone; **Beast:** Stephen Ouimette; **Hamilton:** Michael Caruana

### ◎ MAGIC ADVENTURES OF MUMFIE

A little white elephant in a pink rain coat with a big heart, who lives alone, travels to help other creatures overcome life's curious obstacles in this series of serialized, song-filled half-hour adventures (also known as *Britt Alcroft's Magic Adventures of Mumfie*) broadcast Tuesday mornings on the FOX Network's revamped preschooler series *FOX Cubhouse*, beginning in the fall of 1995. The series, from the co-creator of the hit PBS children's series *Shining Time Station*, made its American television debut on the kiddie-oriented program, which also included the cartoon adventures of *Budgie the Little Helicopter. A Britt Alcroft Production. Color. Half-hour. Premiered on FOX: September 12, 1995–January 3, 1997. Rebroadcast on FOXFAM/ABC FAM: August 17, 1998– November 2001.*

**Voices**
**Mumfie/Other Characters:** Patric Breen

### ◎ MAGICAL DOREMI

Three young aspiring witches, third grader Dorie Goodwyn and her best friends, Reanne and Mirabelle, use music to fulfill the eight required steps of their apprenticeship to become full-fledged witches and experience remarkable adventures as a result. This half-hour English-language version of the popular Japanese cartoon show *Ojamajo Doremi* was added to FOX's four-hour *4Kids TV* programming block in August 2005, airing alongside such popular animated series as *Teenage Mutant Ninja Turtles, One Piece, The Winx Club, Shaman King* and *Sonic X*. Of the original 26 episodes, all but three aired during the series' first season. *An Aeon Inc./ Kodansha/Pierrot/Tokyu AgencyTV Aichi/We've Inc./4Kids Entertainmen/GONZO Production. Color. Half-hour. Premiered on FOX: August 13, 2005.*

**Voices**
**Dorie Goodwyn:** Amy Palant; **Reanne Griffith:** Rebecca Soler; **Mirabelle Haywood:** Annice Moriarty; **Caitlyn Goodwyn:** Liza Jacqueline; **Ellie Craft/Drana:** Jessica Calvello; **Patina:** Lisa Ortiz; **Lorelei:** Andi Whaley; **Miss Cooper:** Kate Roland; **Miss Shannon/Todd:** Kayzie Rogers; **Simon/Mirabelle's Dad:** Sean Schemmel; **Stewart:** Mike Sinterniklaas; **Dorie's Mom:** Bella Hudson; **Dorie's Dad:** Dan Green; **Conya:** Mollie Weaver; **Vice-Principal Shoople:** Eric Stuart; **Queen Lumina:** Carol Jacobanis; **Oliver/ Reanne's Father:** Tom Wayland; **Reanne's Mother:** Kerry Williams; **Amaretta:** Kelly Ray; **Belinda Higgins:** Amanda Brown; **Stacey:** Veronica Taylor; **Lee Goodwyn, Dorie's Brother:** Chris-

topher C. Adams; **Reanne's Brother:** Jason Anthony Griffith; **Dennis Haywood, Mirabelle's Brother:** Wayne Grayson; **Boris the Wizard:** Mike Pollock; **Duke the Wizard:** Ed Paul; **Reuskin the Wizard:** Ted Lewis

## ◎ THE MAGICAL PRINCESS GIGI

Lighthearted fantasy about the Princess from the Kingdom of Fairyland, who comes to earth as a 12-year-old mortal, but with the powers of a Fairy Princess, to do good deeds. This five-part fantasy/adventure series was reedited from the Japanese animated feature *Magic Princess Miki Momo*. The title of this Japanese import was released as *The Magical World of Gigi* in some countries. An Ashi/Harmony Gold Production. Color. Half-hour. Premiered: 1985. Syndicated.

### Voices
Reva West, Lisa Paulette, Sal Russo, Abe Hurt, Betty Gustavson, Ryan O'Flannigan, Anita Pia, Sam Jones

## ◎ THE MAGICIAN

Talented magician Ace Cooper uses his impressive magical powers, illusionary skills and vast resources of props, along with his girlfriend Mona and accomplices Angel, Zina, Vega, Freidricks and Duc Paparazzo, to fight global crime in this French-imported half-hour animated series produced by Gaumont Multimedia, first shown on French television in 1997 and broadcast in the United States on FOX. Joining FOX's Saturday morning lineup in late February 1999 as a mid-season replacement (taking the slot formerly held by the live-action series *Mystic Knights of Mir Ta Nog*), only 26 of the series' original 52 half-hour episodes were broadcast. By June, the series simultaneously aired weekday afternoons on FOX, remaining there even after FOX removed it from its Saturday morning schedule. A Gaumont Multimedia/France 3/France 2/Pro Sieben Production. Color. Half-hour. Premiered on FOX: February 27, 1999–September 10, 1999.

### Voices
**Ace Cooper/The Magician:** Michael Donovan; **Cosmo/Sonnyboy:** Rob Paulsen; **BlackJack/Derek Vega:** Charles Napier; **Mona/Angel:** Kath Soucie; **Duc Paparazzo:** Billy West

## ◎ THE MAGILLA GORILLA SHOW

The anxious, bewildered owner of Mr. Pebbles Pet Shop in Los Angeles, California, makes futile bids to sell or even give away his permanent animal resident, an amiable and fun-loving gorilla named Magilla, who by nature stumbles into all sorts of fantastic and unbelievable incidents. His best friend is a little neighborhood girl called Ogee.

The gorilla made his entrance into syndicated television in January 1964 (telecast in 151 markets), as the star of this three-segment cartoon series, made up of six-minute cartoons. The two original components of the show were "Punkin Puss and Mush Mouse," a pair of hillbilly cats who engage in a nonstop feud like those of the Hatfields and the McCoys, and "Richochet Rabbit," a fast-paced rabbit sheriff who chases all dirty-deeders out of town with the aide of his deputy, Droop-A-Long Coyote.

In January of 1965 "Richochet Rabbit," which moved over to the syndicated *Peter Potamus and His Magic Flying Baloon* series, was replaced by "Breezly and Sneezly," which had originated on the latter. The series followed the misadventures of a foolish polar bear (Breezly) and clear-minded arctic seal (Sneezly) who spend most of their time trying to infiltrate an Alaskan army base, Camp Frostbite, headed by the commander Colonel Fusby.

In January of 1966, both *The Magilla Gorilla Show* and "Peter Potamus" (now billed as *The Peter Potamus Show*) began airing on ABC's Saturday morning lineup while the original series continued in syndication. New episodes of each component were added during the series' original syndication and network run through September of 1967. Sponsor: Ideal Toys.

USA Network rebroadcast the off-network version of the series, *Magilla Gorilla and Friends*, for three years beginning in 1989. Five years later the original series began airing (in reruns) on Cartoon Network and even later on Boomerang. A Hanna-Barbera Production in association with Ideal Toys and Screen Gems. Color. Half-hour. Premiered: January 14, 1964. Syndicated. Rebroadcast on ABC: January 1, 1966–September 2, 1967. Rebroadcast on USA: April 3, 1989–January 16, 1992. Rebroadcast on CAR: January 10, 1993–May 1, 1993 (Sundays); May 15, 1993–January 2, 1994. Rebroadcast on BOOM: April 1, 2000–.

### Voices
**Magilla Gorilla:** Allan Melvin; **Mr. Peebles:** Howard Morris; **Ogee:** Jean VanderPyl; **Punkin Puss:** Allan Melvin; **Mush Mouse:** Howard Morris; **Richochet Rabbit/Various Others:** Don Messick; **Deputy Droopalong:** Mel Blanc; **Breezly:** Howard Morris; **Sneezly:** Mel Blanc; **Colonel Fusby:** John Stephenson

## ◎ MAISY

A young mouse named Maisy and her friends, Charlie Crocodile, Tallulah the Baby Chicken, Cyril Squirrel and Eddie Elephant (who communicate in their own language by making animal sounds), partake in a little innocent mischief while never straying far from Maisy's mother's wishes and always doing the honorable thing in the end in this animated children's series adapted from the popular picture-book series by British author/illustrator Lucy Cousins and developed for Nickelodeon's Nick Jr. daytime program block for preschool-age viewers. Brian Green narrated this American version (with Neil Morrissey doing the narration for the British series), which aired weekdays on Nick Jr. beginning in February 1999. Following its original network run, the series jumped to Noggin, where existing episodes were rebroadcast starting in January 2001. A King Rollo Film/Polygram Visual Programming Production. Color. Half-hour. Premiered on NICK JR.: February 11, 1999–November 2, 2000. Rebroadcast on NOG: January 29, 2001–.

### Voices
**Narrator:** Brian Green; **The Umbilical Brothers:** David Collins, Shane Dundas

## ◎ MAKE WAY FOR NODDY

Britain's legendary little wooden boy, Noddy—who lives in the magical place of Toyland with his friends, Big Ears the rabbit and Tessie Bear—returns in all-new half-hour adventures. They continually make mistakes in a puzzling and complex world but overcome them by learning the importance of patience, responsibility, teamwork, respect and confidence in this third adaptation following the popular 1990s children's series, *Noddy*, combining original stop-action shorts produced by Brian Cosgrove and Mark Hall with live-action stories, which aired in the United States on PBS. Produced between 2001 and 2004 and first shown on Britain's Five network in 12-minute increments as part of the *Milkshake* program, this latest computer-animated version of author Enid Blyton's famed children's book character, co-produced by United Kingdom's Chorion and the United States' SD Entertainment, debuted in the United States on PBS's 24-hour digital preschool television network, PBS Kids Sprout, in October 2005. The daytime preschool program aired in combination with 100 new two-minute interstitials, entitled *Say It with Noddy*, in which Noddy (voiced by a different actor than in the half-hour series) learns new words and phrases of different languages from French to Russian with his best friend, Whizz, and music videos anchored by a live host. In September 2006, the program returned with 20 new half-hour episodes. *A Chorion Ltd./SD Entertainment Production. Color. Half-hour. Premiered on PBS Kids' Sprout (VOD): April 2005. Premiered on PBS Kids' Sprout (digital television nework): October 26, 2005– .*

### Voices

**Noddy (in "Say It with Noddy" interstitials):** Alberto Ghisi; **Noddy (half-hour series):** David Kaye; **Big Ears:** Michael Dobson; **Mr. Plod:** Richard Newman; **Tessie Bear:** Britt McKillip; **Other Voices:** Kathleen Barr, Cathy Weseluck, Ian James Corlett, Chantal Strand

## ◎ MAPLE TOWN

Led by Mrs. Raccoon, the cuddy characters of Maple Town (Bobby Bear, Patty Rabbit, Danny Dog, Mayor Lion, Funny Fox, Kevin Cat, Penny Pig, Susie Squirrel and the entire Beaver family: Bernard, Bitty and Bucky) defend their wholesome community from the town's only criminal, Wilde Wolf, in this half-hour live-action/animated series, based on Tonka Toys' bestselling toy line. Lasting only three weeks in syndication following its 1987 debut, the series featured a live-action host, Mrs. Maple (played by Janice Adams) to inform young viewers on the lesson learned that day. *A Saban/Maltese Companies Production in association with Toei Animation/Tonka Toys/Orbis. Color. Half-hour. Premiered: Fall 1987. Syndicated.*

### Cast (live action)
**Mrs. Maple:** Janice Adams

### Voices

Tracey Alexander, Jeff Iwai, Wayne Kerr, Bebe Linet, Heidi Lenhart, Lou Pitt, Alice Smith, Jon Zahler

## ◎ MARINE BOY

Campy series imported from Japan ("It's Marine Boy, brave and free, fighting evil beneath the sea. . . .") about a daring aquaboy, the son of aquatic scientist Dr. Mariner, who dedicates himself to preserving the world, most notably beneath the sea, for all mankind. Drawing oxygen from Oxygum, life-sustaining oxygen in gum form, he keeps the world safe as a member of the Ocean Patrol, an international defense organization headed by his father. With shipmates Bulton, Piper and pet dolphin Splasher (named "Whity" in the Japanese version), Marine Boy takes to the watery depths in their P-1 submarine to battle the Patrol's main foes—Captain Kidd, Count Shark and Dr. Slime—using special gear (a bulletproof wet suit, propeller boots and an electric/sonic boomerang) to emerge victorious. Stripped for Monday-through-Friday syndication in 1966, the series was the second Japanese import to be produced in color (NBC's *Kimba the White Lion* was the first), and three of the series' 78 episodes (numbers 42, 55 and 57) never aired in the United States. Japanese series name: *Kaitai Shonen Marine. A Japan Telecartoons//K. Fujita Associates/Seven Arts Production. Color. Half-hour. Premiered: October, 1966. Syndicated.*

### Voices

**Marine Boy/Neptina/Cli Cli:** Corinne Orr; **Dr. Mariner/Various Villains:** Jack Curtis; **Bulton:** Peter Fernandez; **Piper:** Jack Grimes; **Splasher, Marine Boy's dolphin:** Jack Grimes; **Dr. Fumble/Commander:** Jack Grimes

## ◎ MARSUPILAMI

This former Belgian comic-book sensation—a hyperactive cheetah with the world's largest tail—and his brawny, nontalking gorilla pal Maurice starred in this half-hour Saturday-morning cartoon series for CBS, comprised of weekly adventures originally seen the previous season on Disney's anthology cartoon series *Raw Toonage*, also on CBS. Also repeated from the latter, as weekly components, were: "Shnookums & Meat," the comical exploits of a battling dog and cat; and "Sebastian," adventures of the Calypso-singing crab and costar of the hit Disney animated feature *The Little Mermaid. A Walt Disney Television Animation Production. Color. Half-hour. Premiered on CBS: September 18, 1993–August 27, 1994. Rebroadcast on TDIS: April 18, 1998–January 6, 2002.*

### Voices

**Marsupilami:** Steve Mackall; **Stuie/Groom:** Charlie Adler, Rene Auberjonois, Sheryl Bernstein, Dan Castellaneta; **Maurice/Norman:** Jim Cummings; **Norman's Aunt:** E.G. Daily, J.D. Daniels, Debi Derryberry, June Foray; **Eduardo:** Brad Garrett, Bill Kopp, Steve Landesberg; **Woman:** Tress MacNeille; **Shnookums:** Danny Mann; Jason Marsden; **Meat:** Andi McAfee, Kathy McAuley, Michael Pace, Malachi Pearson, Hal Rayle, Ronnie Schell, Susan Tolsky, Darryl Tookes, Marcia Wallace, Frank Welker; **Sebastian:** Ken Williams; April Winchell; Samuel E. Wright

## ◎ MARTIN MYSTERY

A pair of mismatched teens named Martin and Diana, with completely opposite personalities, investigate the strangest paranormal enigmas and the slimiest creatures from beyond in this fantasy/adventure series created by Vincent Chalvon-Demersay and David Michel, directed by Stephanie Berry and co-produced by Marathon Animation (Paris, France), makers of *Team Galaxy* and *Totally Spies*. First shown in 2003 on Canada's YTV and in 2004 on Disney Channel Asia, this hilarious 65-episode half-hour series, partially based on the Italian comic *Martin Mystère*, with animation resembling the style of Japanese anime, debuted in the United States weekday afternoons on Discovery Kids Channel. In October 2005, as part of a Halloween week "Ghastly Ghost" event, Discovery Kids aired all-new episodes in prime time, opposite the live-action reality show *Ghost Trackers*, reportedly featuring "real-life ghost stories" from both series. Beginning in May 2005, Nickelodeon's sister network, Nicktoons, rebroadcast the cartoon comedy. *A Marathon Animation Productions Production in association with YTV/RAI/M6/Merchandising M l nchen GMBH. Color. Half-hour. Premiered on DISCK: September 2005. Rebroadcast on NICKT: May 16, 2005–.*

### Voices

**Martin Mystery/Billy:** Samuel Vincent; **Diana Lombard:** Kelly Sheridan; **MOM/Various Others:** Teryl Rothery; **Java:** Dale Wilson; **Other Voices:** Kathleen Barr, Tabitha St. Germain, Matt Hill, Michael Donovan, Cathy Weseluck, Brian Dobson

## ◎ THE MARVEL ACTION HOUR

See THE FANTASTIC FOUR (1994) and IRON MAN.

## ◎ THE MARVEL ACTION UNIVERSE

Spider-Man is among a cast of superhero characters featured in the this 90-minute animated action/adventure series adapted from comic books, for television, which originally aired in syndication in 1988. The series was made up of 24 Spider-Man episodes origi-nally aired on 1981's *Spider-Man and His Amazing Friends* (NBC), plus two other weekly components: "Dino Riders," the adventures of 20th-century robot dinosaurs back in prehistoric times (in 11 episodes), and "RoboCop," about a lawkeeping policeman-turned-indestructible cyborg (Alex Murphy), based on the popular 1985 live-action feature. A cartoon version of the comic-book series *X-Men* was originally planned as a regular segment of the series, but only one episode was featured, "Pryde of the X-Men," a 1989 pilot that aired during the series' syndicated run. *A Marvel Pro-duction in association with Orion Pictures and New World Entertain-ment. Color. One hour and a half. Premiered: October 2, 1988. Syndicated.*

*Voices*
Charlie Adler, Michael Bell, Robert Bockstael, Earl Bowen, Bar-bara Budd, Wally Burr, Len Carlson, Andi Chapman, Cam Clar-kee, Joe Colligen, Peter Cullen, Shawn Donahue, Pat Fraley, Ronald Gans, Dan Gilvezan, Rex Hagon, Dan Hennessy, Ron James, Gordon Matson, Greg Morton, Noelle North, Allen Oppenheimer, Patrick Pinney, Susan Roman, Neil Ross, Susan Silo, Kath Soucie, John Stephenson, Alexander Stoddart, Alan Stewart-Coates, Chris Ward, Frank Welker

## ◎ MARVEL SUPER HEROES
Half-hour series rotating reruns of episodes of two popular Marvel cartoon series, 1994's *The Fantastic Four* and *Iron Man*, repackaged for syndication in 1997. (See individual series for voice credits). *A Marvel Films/New World Enterprises Production. Color. Half-hour. Premiered: 1997–1998. Syndicated.*

## ◎ MARVEL SUPER HEROES
Five famous Marvel comic-book characters—Incredible Hulk, Iron Man, Sub-Mariner, The Mighty Thor and Captain Amer-ica—starred in this half-hour children's series, consisting of 195 six-minute cartoons, based on the long-running comic-book adventures. Budgeted at around $6,000 each, the cartoons were animated in the style of comic-book panels, with the characters appearing in a series of still poses. (Only their lips moved.) The series was produced by Steven Krantz of Krantz Films and Bob Lawrence of Grantray-Lawrence Animation, a company created in 1954 in association with longtime studio animators Grant Sim-mons and Ray Patterson. (The company was founded chiefly to produce advertising cartoons.) The names of the actors who voiced the characters in the series remain unknown. *A Grantray-Lawrence Animation/Paramount/ARP/Krantz Films Production. Color. Half-hour. Premiered: 1966–1968. Syndicated.*

## ◎ MARVIN THE TAP-DANCING HORSE
Marvin, a gentle, fun-loving, tap-dancing horse, and his carnival traveling friends—Stripes the Tiger, Elizabeth the Emotional Pig and Diamonds the Elephant—overcome various problems while working together and learning some valuable lessons along the way in this animated children's series, written by Michael and Betty Paraskevas and based on their popular children's book, pub-lished in 1999. First broadcast in the fall of 2000 on PBS Kids' weekend-morning *Bookworm Bunch* program block for the pre-school set, the popular children's series, featuring two 12-minute cartoon adventures, was last broadcast on Labor Day weekend, September 3–4, 2004. In January 2007, the program returned to the airwaves in reruns as part of a four-hour program block on the all-new 24-hour digital television network, qubo, carried by ION network and its affiliate stations nationwide. *A Paraskevas/Tele-*

*toon/Nelvana Limited Production. Color. Half-hour. Premiered on PBS: September 30, 2000–September 4, 2004. Rebroadcast on Q: January 8, 2007–.*

*Voices*
**Marvin:** Ron Pardo; **Eddy Largo:** Marlowe Windsor-Menard; **Jack:** Dwayne Hill; **Elizabeth the Emotional Pig:** Sheila McCar-thy; **Diamonds the Elephant:** Fiona Reid

## ◎ MARY-KATE AND ASHLEY IN ACTION!
Grown-up twin superstars Mary-Kate and Ashley Olsen provided their voices as a pair of globe-trotting undercover spies sent on secret missions by their boss Bennington (voiced by Sean Con-nery's son, Jason), using an arsenal of high-tech gadgetry to thwart evil-doers and save the planet in this action-packed half-hour animated series that debuted on both ABC and ABC Family in the fall of 2001. (Coincidentally, ABC Family, when it was known as FOX Family Channel, aired the duo's live-action mystery series, *The Amazing Adventures of Mary-Kate and Ashley*, from June 1999 to February 2002.) Produced by Burbank's DIC Entertainment and the Olsens' DualStar Productions, the 26-episode, Saturday morn-ing series (also spun-off into a series of "Super Teen Agent" chil-dren's books published by Harper Entertainment), featuring live-action wraparounds of the famed twins introducing each new cartoon adventure, was canceled after one season due to poor rat-ings, with the program airing the longest on ABC Family. In September 2002, Toon Disney subsequently began re-airing the series. *A Dual/Star/DIC Entertainment Production. Color. Half-hour. Premiered on ABC: October 20, 2001–August 3, 2002. Premiered on ABC FAM: October 20, 2001. Rebroadcast on TDIS: September 7, 2002–.*

*Voices*
**Special Agent Misty:** Mary-Kate Olsen; **Special Agent Amber:** Ashley Olsen; **Clive Hedgemorton-Smythe:** Michael Richard Dobson; **Q.U.I.N.C.E.:** Brendan Beiser; **Rodney Choy:** Terry Chen; **Bennington:** Jason Connery; **Oliver Dickens:** Chris Gray; **Bernice Shaw/Dr. Sandy:** Kim Hawthorne; **Ivan Quintero:** Michael Monroe Heyward; **Romy Bates:** Maggie O'Hara; **Capital D:** Sam Vincent; **Renee LaRouge:** Lenore Zann; **Kyle:** Mike Coleman; **Monique:** Moneca Stori; **Flee:** Kristie Marsden; **Addi-tional Voices:** Jamie Alexander

## ◎ M.A.S.K.
Led by Matt Tracker, the Mobile Armored Strike Kommand (M. A.S.K.) is a secret organization that fights crime in an unusual fashion. By donning specially charged masks, participants gain extraordinary powers to undermine the villainous forces of V. E.N.O.M. (Vicious Evil Network of Mayhem), in their insidious plot for world control. Joining Tracker in *Mission Impossible*–type missions are his team of special agents: master of disguise specialist Buddy Hawkes; kung fu expert Gloria Baker; computer whiz Alex Sector; technical wizards Bruce Sato; weapons specialist Monk McLean; and special vehicle drivers Dusty Hayes (driver of "Gator") and Brad Turner (behind the wheel of "Condor"). Pro-duced for first-run syndication in 1985, the series was close-cap-tioned for the hearing impaired. *A DIC Enterprises Production in association with Kenner-Parker Toys/Canada-France Co./ICC/LBS. Color. Half-hour. Premiered: September 30, 1985–88. Syndicated.*

*Voices*
**Matt Tracker:** Doug Stone; **Alex Sector/Floyd Malloy/Miles Mayhem:** Brendon McKane; **Jacques Lafleur/Nevada Rushmore:** Brendon McKane; **Brad/Calhoun Burns/T-Bob:** Graem McK-enna; **Buddy Hawkes/Ace Riker/Sly Rax:** Mark Halloran; **Gloria**

*Commandeering a secret strike force, Matt Tracke and his team of special agents don specially charged masks that give them special powers in DIC Enterprises' M.A.S.K. © Kenner Products, a division of Kenner Parker Toys* (COURTESY: DIC ENTERPRISES)

**Baker/Vanessa Warfield:** Sharon Noble; **Scott, Matt Tracker's son:** Brennan Thicke; **Nash Gorey/Dusty Hayes/Bruno Shepard:** Doug Stone; **Boris Bushkin/Max Mayhem:** Doug Stone; **Lester Sludge/Jimmy Rashad:** Brian George

## ◎ THE MASK

Wearing an ancient "mask" that possesses special powers, reticent Stanley Ipkiss is converted into a cartoonish master of mayhem who spins, contorts, flattens and twists his way through the crime-infested streets of his own Edge City with the help of Milo the Wonder Dog and a variety of characters in this weekly half-hour cartoon series based on the 1994 blockbuster feature film starring Jim Carrey (who did not lend his voice for this animated spinoff) and featuring many characters from it. Ipkiss's alter ego puts his powers to good use encountering his share of sleazy super-villains: an archetypical madman scientist named Pretorius and a toxic balloonatik named Kablam. The 24-episode series aired for two seasons on CBS beginning in 1995 (a month before the debut of the network's new fall lineup) and was rebroadcast for four months on FOX Family Channel in 1999. *A Sunbow Entertainment Production in association with New Line Television and Film Roman, Inc. Color. Half-hour. Premiered on CBS: August 12, 1995–March 29, 1997. Syndicated: September 3, 1996. Rebroadcast on FOX FAM: June 22, 1999–October 8, 1999.*

### Voices
**Stanley Ipkiss/The Mask:** Rob Paulsen; **Doyle/Lars:** Jim Cummings; **Pretorius:** Tim Curry; **Mrs. Peenan:** Tress MacNeille; **Mrs. Francis Forthwright:** Mary McDonald-Lewis; **Lieutenant Kellaway:** Neil Ross; **Mayor Tilton:** Kevin Richardson; **Peggy Brandt:** Heidi Shannon; **Charlie Schumacher:** Mark Taylor; **Milo/Pepe/Baby Forthwright:** Frank Welker

## ◎ MATTY'S FUNDAY FUNNIES

Mattel Toys sponsored this repackaged version of former Paramount Famous Studios cartoons—Casper the Friendly Ghost, Herman and Katnip, Little Audrey, Baby Huey and other minor characters from the studio's *Noveltoons* series (Buzzy the Crow, Owly the Owl, Finny the Goldfish, etc.)—which originally premiered on late Sunday afternoons on ABC. The films, renamed *Harveytoons* (after Harvey Publishing Company, which purchased the rights to the old cartoons), were presented in combination with two weekly hosts, a young boy, Matty, and his Sisterbelle, who introduced each cartoon adventure.

Instantly successful with young audiences, the program was moved to prime time in 1960, airing one hour before *The Flintstones*. In 1962 the network overhauled the series by replacing the *Harveytoons'* with the cartoon adventures of *Beany and Cecil*, an animated version of Bob Clampett's syndicated puppet show. In April 1962, when ABC decided to drop the series' cartoon hosts, the program was simply named *Beany and Cecil*. The riotious adventures of Beany, Cecil, Captain Huffenpuff and Dishonest John were given their own Saturday-morning time slot in January 1963, after the *Matty's Funday Funnies* series concluded its network run. *A Harvey Films and Bob Clampett Production for ABC. Black-and-white. Color. Premiered on ABC: October 11, 1959–December 29, 1962.*

## ◎ MAURICE SENDAK'S LITTLE BEAR

Based on the popular children's books illustrated by Maurice Sendak and written by Else Holmelund Minarik, this enchanting daily half-hour series revolves around the sweet adventures (imaginary or real) of a bear cub as he learns to take his steps and understand the world and how it works, with the help of his parents and pals, told from a child's point of view. Premiering on Nickelodeon's Nick Jr. preschool daytime block in November 1995, the program (also simply known as "Little Bear") was part of the network's $30 million commitment to produce new, original programming for this time period.

Staying true to the book series, the Little Bear was joined in each episode by a cast of supporting animal characters, including a duck and a cat and his beloved Mother Bear, Father Bear and, on occasion, Grand Bears, offering words of wisdom and guidance throughout his many adventures.

For the series, Sendak, who illustrated the book series in the late 1950s, served as story editor and consulted on the look of the characters with the series' producers, Nelvana, a Canadian animation house. *A Nelvana Entertainment/John B. Carls Production in association with Nickelodeon. Color. Half-hour. Premiered on NICK: November 6, 1995. Rebroadcast on CBS: September 16, 2000–September 8, 2001. Rebroadcast on NOG: September 10, 2001–.*

### Voices
**Little Bear:** Kristin Fairlie; **Mother Bear:** Janet-Laine Green; **Father Bear:** Dan Hennessey; **Owl:** Amos Crawley; **Duck:** Tracey Ryan; **Hen:** Elizabeth Hanna; **Cat:** Andrew Sabiston; **Emily:** Jennifer Martini; **Mitzi:** Ashley Taylor; **Grandmother Bear:** Diane D'Aquila; **Grandfather Bear** Sean McCann

## ◎ MAX, THE 2000 YEAR OLD MOUSE

Producer Steve Krantz created Max, a lovable little mouse who takes viewers back through the most exciting world events of the past 2,000 years. The educational cartoon series combined film clips and still pictures to tell each story, hosted at the beginning and the end by the program's mouse historian. Memorable moments include Columbus discovering America, the *Mayflower* voyage and others. For trivia buffs, the theme music for the program was later heard on Siskel and Ebert's movie-review series, *Sneak Previews*, for PBS. *A Krantz Animation/Quality Entertainment/ARP Production. Color. Half-hour. Premiered: 1969. Syndicated.*

## ◎ MAX & RUBY

Polar opposite brother and sister bunnies, the mischievous three-year-old Max and his precise, well-organized sister, Ruby, learn to get along while remaining true to themselves in a series of daily adventures involving their neighbor's grandmother and other adults in this popular daytime series based on the popular children's book series by Rosemary Wells. Produced for television's preschool set, with stories in the ffirst series adapted from books, storylines celebrated, in Wells's own words, "the relationship between Ruby and her younger brother, Max, and the universal nature of sibling relationships," with the two bunnies never deciding on the same thing and their plans always causing hilarious results. First broadcast on Nickelodeon's Nick Jr. preschool block in October 2002, this superbly animated children's show debuted with 15 first-season half-hour programs containing three episodes per show, followed by 11 more half-hours produced for the second season. Among the series adventures was the holiday episode, "Max's Christmas." In August 2004, the series began re-airing on Nickelodeon's commercial-free children's programming network, Noggin. *A Nelvana Production. Color. Half-hour. Premiered on NICK JR.: October 21, 2002–. Rebroadcast on NOG: August 16, 2004–.*

**Voices**
**Max:** Billy Rosenberg; **Ruby:** Katie Griffin; **Louise:** Julie Lemieux; **Grandma Rosalina:** Kay Hawtrey

## ◎ MAXIE'S WORLD

One of the most popular students at Surfside High School, Maxie, a tall, pretty young girl and straight-A student, is the center of a series of adventures shaped around her Malibu-bred schoolmates, the loves of her life and her outside interests, including her own local weekly television show, in this 32-episode series that aired in first-run syndication in 1989. Episodes from two other animated series, *Beverly Hills Teens* and *It's Punky Brewster*, rotated on a daily basis with first-run *Maxie* episodes during the series' syndicated run. *A DIC Enterprises Production in association with Claster Television. Color. Half-hour. Premiered: September, 1989. Syndicated.*

**Voices**
**Maxie:** Loretta Jafelice; **Rob:** Simon Reynolds; **Carly:** Tara Charendoff; **Ashley:** Susan Roman; **Simone:** Suzanne Coy; **Jeri:** Nadine Rabinovitch; **Ferdie:** Yannick Bisson; **Mushroom:** Geoff Kahnert; **Mr. Garcia:** John Stocker

## ◎ MAYA & MIGUEL

Joined by their family, diverse neighborhood friends and relatives, a pair of 10-year-old Latino twins, Maya and Miguel Santos, learn how to leave their stamp on the vibrant world around them in a series of educational adventures. With episodes stressing "a positive attitude toward knowing and learning more than one language," the popular educational series was partially funded by a Ready to Learn cooperative pact with the U.S. Department of Education. Joining PBS Kids' afternoon program lineup in October 2004, the program was renewed for a second season in 2005, with new episodes airing on *PBS Kids Go!*, an afternoon program block that included *Postcards from Buster, Cyberchase* and *Arthur*, which became a separate channel in the fall of 2006.

The week of September 25, 2006, coinciding with National Deaf Awareness Week, the animated multicultural favorite made its second season debut in an episode with Tino befriending a deaf boy, broadcast with open captions and repeated daily during the week. That same year, the series earned an Emmy nomination for outstanding achievement in music direction and composition. *A Scholastic Entertainment Production in association with PBS. Half-hour. Color. Premiered on PBS Kids: October 1, 2004–(Season 1); September 25, 2005–(Season 2).*

**Voices**
Candi Milo, Erik Estrada, Lucy Liu, Carlos Ponce, Elizabeth Pena

## ◎ MAYA THE BEE

Maya, a friendly little female bee, protects her other bug friends—including best friends Willie the bee and Flip, a musical grasshopper—from their natural predators in stories that relate the importance of sharing, loving and friendship in this half-hour series based on Waldemar Bonsals's *The Adventures of Maya the Bee.* Originally produced in Austria in 1982 and 1989, the 55-episode series made its American television debut in 1990 on Nickelodeon. *An Apollo Film of Vienna/Zuge Elzo/Saban International. Color. Half-hour. Premiered on NICK: January 1, 1990–December 31, 1992.*

**Voices**
**Maya:** Pauline Little; **Willi:** Richard Dumont; **Flip:** R.J. Henderson; **Grimelda:** Anna MacCormack; **Cassandra:** Jane Woods

## ◎ MEATBALLS AND SPAGHETTI

Rock musicians Meatballs and Spaghetti, his mod singer-wife, turned animated cartoon stars along with Clyde, Meatball's sidekick, and Woofer, Spaghetti's loyal dog, appear in a variety of misadventures featuring original songs performed by the famous rock group in this short-lived Saturday-morning series, originally aired on CBS. *A Marvel Production in association with InterMedia Entertainment. Color. Half-hour. Premiered on CBS: September 18, 1982–September 10, 1983.*

**Voices**
Jack Angel, Wally Burr, Phillip Clarke, Peter Cullen, Ronald Gans, Barry Gordon, David Hall, Sally Julian, Morgan Lofting, Ron Masak, Bill Ratner, Ronnie Schell, Marilyn Schreffler, Hal Smith, Frank Welker, Paul Winchell

## ◎ MEDABOTS

Dreaming of becoming a top-ranked mediafighter, 10-year-old Ikki Tenrio fulfills his lifelong dream when he uses his own artificially intelligent secondhand robot, Metabee, to robattle their opponents, despite their inexperience, to determine the champion in this futuristic series set in the year 2122. Premiering on the FOX Kids Network in September 2001, the half-hour anime fantasy/adventure series, based on the popular computer game of the same name, was the network's highest rated program of its new shows that season. The program was subsequently rebroadcast on cable's ABC Family, beginning in September 2002, as part of its new seven days a week action-adventure anime lineup, including such animated shows as *Beyblade* and *Tokyo Pig. A Nelvana Limited/Medarot Company/Bee Train/NAS/Kodansha/TV Tokyo Production. Color. Half-hour. Premiered on FOX: September 8, 2001–September 7, 2002. Rebroadcast on ABC: September 9, 2002–May 18, 2003.*

**Voices**
**Ikki Tenrio:** Samantha Reynolds; **Mr. Referee:** Dennis Akiyama; **Samantha:** Julie Lemieux, Shannon Perreault; **Metabee:** Joseph Motiki; **Dr. Meta-Evil/Hobson/Samurai:** Len Carlson; **Roks/Eddie:** Mark Dailey; **Sloan/Digimole:** Darren Frost; **Rokusho:** Dan Green; **Shrimplips Limpowitz:** Paul Haddad; **Squidguts:** Terry McGurrin; **Spyke/Seaslug/Cyandog/Krosserdog:** Robert Tinkler; **Koji Karakuchi:** Joanne Vannicola; **Erika:** Lisa Yamanaka; **Additional Voices:** Susan Laney Dalton, Ashley Taylor, Jamie Watson

## ⊚ MEGA BABIES

Three messy babies, Meg, Derrik and Buck, who suddenly acquire super powers after being struck by lightning, use their super strength to protect Earth from monsters and aliens in their town in this 26-episode, half-hour series with "... a 'Rugrats' spin with a little gross-out humor" that aired weekly on FOX Family Channel for two years, beginning in January 1999. A *Lionsgate/Cine-Groupe/Landmark Entertainment/Sony Wonder Production. Color. Half-hour. Premiered on FOX FAM: January 5, 1999–April 30, 2001.*

**Voices**
**Meg:** Jaclyn Linetsky; **Buck:** Sonja Ball; **Nurse Lazlo:** Bronwen Mantel; **Grizzy/Various Others:** Dean Hagopian; **Other Voices:** Lora Teasdale

## ⊚ MEGA MAN

A 21st-Century superrobot and his robot dog, Rush, match wits with a dialobical scientist's evil robotic creations in this half-tour animated series based on the best-selling Nintendo and Sega video game, produced for first-run syndication as part of Bohbot Entertainment's weekend cartoon block, *Amazin' Adventures II.* A *Ruby-Spears Production in association with Bohbot/Summit Media Group. Color. Half-hour. Premiered: September 17, 1994 (part of Amazin' Adventures II). Syndicated. Rebroadcast on FOX FAM/ABC FAM: July 18, 1999–August 27, 2001.*

**Voices**
**Mega Man/Rush:** Ian Corlett; **Dr. Wily/Proto Man:** Scott McNeil; **Guts Man:** Garry Chalk; **Roll:** Robyn Ross; **Dr. Light:** Jim Byrnes; **Cut Man:** Terry Klassen

## ⊚ MEGAMAN NT WARRIOR

In the year 200X with the Cyber Revolution underway, talented fifth-grader Lan Hikari, as his NetNavi and alter-ego, the blue-suited, virus-fighting, virtual superhero MegaMan, team up with his friends, using a host of high-tech gadgetry, to battle evil Net crime organizations—Grave, Nebula and World Three—that plan to wreak havoc on the world in this futuristic animated adventure series, based jointly on the popular CAPCOM *MegaMan* video-game series and the successful Shogakukan Corocoro comic-book line. The English-dubbed, Japanese animation series earned impressive ratings on Kids' WB! where it was rated the most popular series among viewers ages nine to 14 in May 2004. In the United States, 103 half-hour episodes were on the WB Television Network during the series' three-season run. A *NAS/Shogakukan Productions Co. Ltd./TV Tokyo/Xebec/ShoPro Entertainment/The Ocean Group Production. Color. Half-hour. Premiered on Kids' WB!: May 17, 2003–December 9, 2005.*

**Voices**
**Lan Hikari:** Alex Doduk, Brad Swaile; **MegaMan:** Andrew Francis; **Maylu Sakurai:** Brittney Wilson; **Dex Oyama:** Tony Sampson; **Yai Ayano:** Jocelyne Loewen; **Tory Froid:** Reece Thompson; **Glide:** Ted Cole; **Miyu Kuroi:** Anna Cummer; **Mr. Match:** Trevor Devall; **Yahoot:** Ron Halder; **Ms. Mari:** Janyse Jaud; **ProtoMan:** David Kaye; **GutsMan:** Scott McNeil; **Count Zap:** Colin Murdock; **Maysa:** Richard Newman; **Sal:** Kelly Sheridan; **Maddy:** Tabitha St. Germain; **Mr. Higsby:** Lee Tockar; **NumberMan/IceMan:** Samuel Vincent; **Roll:** Lenore Zann

## ⊚ MEGAS XLR

High-flying intergalatic adventures of Coop Cooplowski, a 20-something slacker and lower of fast cars, punk rock, video games and wrestling, who, after stumbling upon a sophisticated 80-foot-tall fighting robot—known as M.E.G.A.S. (Mecha Earth Guard Attack System)—at a local dump, turns it into a souped-up cruising machine and is joined by the robot's original architect, an ace pilot, Kiva, and Coop's wisecracking friend, Jamie, to ward off out-of-this-world bad guys who want to destroy him and his advanced piece of machinery. Co-created and executive produced by George Kristic and Jody Schaeffer who worked on the Emmy-nominated cartoon series, *MTV Downtown,* the original seven-minute pilot—produced by Low Brow Studios and entitled *Low Brow*—bowed on Cartoon Network's "Cartoon Cartoon Weekend" in August 2002. Retitled *Megas XLR,* 26 half-hours were created of this combined 2-D cel- and 3-D GGI-animated action-comedy series fusing Japanese anime with Western storytelling and humor (originally announced to premiere in December 2003) that bowed on the network's top-rated *Toonami* action-adventure anime block in May 2004 and lasted one season. Kristic and Schaeffer imagined the concept for the series after playing with video games. As Schaeffer recalled in an interview, "We said, 'Wouldn't it be cool if we made a cartoon about a guy that used his video game experience to pilot a giant robot?" A *Cartoon Network/Low Brow Studios Production. Color. Half-hour. Premiered on CAR: August 23, 2002 (pilot). Premiered on CAR: May 1, 2004–April 26, 2005 (series).*

**Voices**
**Coop Cooplowski:** David DeLuise; **Commander Kiva Andrew:** Wendee Lee; **Jamie:** Steven Jay Blum; **Goat:** Scot Rienecker; **Gorrath:** Clancy Brown; **Glorft Commander:** Kevin Michael Richardson; **Little Tommy:** Sean Marquette; **Ally:** Julie Nathanson; **Darklos:** Tia Carrere; **Galaxa:** Janice Kawaye; **Gina:** Rachael MacFarlane; **Lunar Captain:** Richard McGonagle; **Magnanimous:** Bruce Campbell; **Skippy:** Frankie Ryan Manriquez; **Other Voices:** Tom Kenny

## ⊚ MEL-O-TOONS

This full-color series of six-minute cartoons were based on popular 45 rpm children's records, some featuring famous legends, fairy tales and literary works as story lines (with narration provided by famous announcers, including Don Wilson of TV's *The Jack Benny Show*). The 104-episode series included adaptations of the works of author Thorton Burgess, of "Peter Cottontail" and "Paddy Beaver" fame. A *New World Productions/United Artists Television Production. Color. Half-hour. Premiered: 1960. Syndicated.*

## ⊚ MEN IN BLACK: THE SERIES

A team of sharply dressed, unflappable government agents (Jay and Kay), replete with conservative black suits, skinny ties and sunglasses, who cruise the streets of New York City, are assigned to keep aliens in line in this half-hour animated series closely patterned after the hit live-action feature starring Tommy Lee Jones and Will Smith and produced for the WB Television Network. An *Amblin Entertainment/Columbia TriStar/Adelaide Production. Color. Half-hour. Premiered on WB: October 11, 1997–July 14, 2001.*

**Voices**
**Jay:** Keith Diamond; **Kay:** Ed O'Ross; **Zed:** Charles Napier, Gregg Berger; **Elle:** Jennifer Lien; **Twin/Worm:** Pat Pinney; **Twin/Worm:** Pat Fraley; **Buzzard:** Sherman Howard

## ⊚ METALOCALYPSE

One of the world's most famous Norwegian heavy metal bands—featuring the incredibly talented Nathan Explosion, William

Murderface Skwisgaar Swigelf, Toki Wartooth and Pickles—causes a path of destruction and murder wherever it goes. Featuring guest appearances by renowned musicians like Kirk Hammett and James Hetfield of Metallica, the 15-minute comedy series, part of Cartoon Network's *Adult Swim* program block, was co-created and executive produced by Brendon Small (best known as Brendon Small on the *Home Movies* animated series) and Tommy Blacha. Originally entitled *Death Clock Metalocalypse*, this heavy-metal music series debuted with 20 first-season episodes. *A Timouse Inc. Production. Color. Fifteen minutes. Premiered on CAR: August 4, 2006.*

### Voices

**Nathan Explosion/Pickles/Skwisgaar Skwigelf/Charles Ofdensen/Others:** Brendon Small; **William Murderface/Toki Wartooth/Dr. Rockso/Others:** Tommy Blacha; **Senator Stampingston/Jean-Pierre/Mr. Selatcia/Others:** Mark Hamill; **General Crozier/Cardinal Ravenwood/Others:** Victor Brandt

### ◎ METRIC MARVELS

This entertaining and educational series of 150-second bumpers, starring Meter Man, Wonder Gram, Liter Leader and Super Celcius conveying the wonders of the metric system to young viewers, was first broadcast on NBC's Saturday-morning schedule, between the network's animated cartoon programming, in the fall of 1978. Producing the series was Newall-Yohe, which had produced other instructional interstitial series: NBC's *H.E.L.P.* and ABC's *Schoolhouse Rock. A Newall-Yohe Production. Color. One second. Premiered on NBC: Fall 1978–Fall 1979.*

### ◎ MEW MEW POWER

During her date with a boy she has a huge crush on, 13-year-old Zoey Hanson gets more than she bargained for when she is accidentally zapped by a mysterious ray that fuses her DNA with that of an endangered wildcat, then sprouts the ears and tail of her newfound species while possessing super powers. Joining four other uniquely endowed girls with the genes of other rare animals as members of the top-secret Mew Project, they use their special powers to protect Earth from an alien invasion in this Japanese-imported anime series based on the popular selling manga.

Redubbed in English, the half-hour fantasy/adventure series was added to FOX's four-hour 4Kids TV programming block in mid-February 2005, airing along with such popular animated series as *Teenage Mutant Ninja Turtles, One Piece, The Winx Club, Shaman King* and *Sonic X.* Of the original 26 episodes, all but three aired during the series' first season. *An Aeon Inc./Kodansha/Pierrot/Tokyu AgencyTV Aichi/We've Inc./4Kids Entertainmen/GONZO Production. Color. Half-hour. Premiered on FOX: February 19, 2005–November 12, 2005.*

### Voices

**Zoey Hanson/Zoey's Mother:** Amanda Brown; **Corina Bucksworth:** Andi Whaley; **Bridget Verdant:** Bella Hudson; **Kiki Benjamin:** Kether Donahue; **Renee Roberts:** Mollie Weaver; **Wesley J. Coolridge III/Cyniclons Dren:** Andrew Rannells; **Mimi:** Caroline Lawson; **Cynicilons Tarb:** Jimmy Toppi; **Cyniclons Sardon:** Pete Zarustica; **Mark:** Scottie Ray; **Elliot Grant:** Sean Schemmel; **Meghan:** Sharon Feingold; **R2000/Mini Mew:** Tom Wayland; **Zoey's Father:** Jim Malone; **Ian:** Frank Frankson; **Marco:** Marc Thompson; **Maria Rivera:** Rita Rivera; **Ms. Rosbe:** Veronica Taylor; **Chrys:** Carol Jacobanis; **Additional Voices:** Amy Palant, Kerry Williams, Lisa Ortiz, Matthew Charles, Rachael Lillis

### ◎ MGM CARTOONS

First syndicated in 1960, this series offered for the first time Metro-Goldwyn-Mayer's pre-1948 animated films to television stations for local programming. The package included such studio cartoon favorites as *Tom and Jerry, Barney Bear, Screwy Squirrel, George and Junior, Bosko* (not the Warner Bros. version), *Captain and the Kids* and *Happy Harmonies.* (See individual series in Theatrical Sound Cartoon Series for details.)

After acquiring Metro-Goldwyn-Mayer studios in 1986, the studio's massive 3,330 title pre-1986 film library became the property of Turner Entertainment (now owned by Warner Bros.). The MGM cartoons began airing in subsequent years on Turner's TBS, TNT and Turner Classic Movies cable, networks (also as part of its popular anthology series *Cartoon Alley*), as well as on the Cartoon Network and Boomerang, where the classic shorts were shown as part of both networks' weekday cartoon showcase the ACME Hour.

*A Metro-Goldwyn Mayer Production. Black-and-white. Color. Premiered: September 1960. Syndicated. Rebroadcast on TBS: 1986–Fall 1998. Rebroadcast on TNT: 1988–Fall 1998. Rebroadcast on TCM: 1994–. Rebroadcast on CAR: April 1, 1998–September 1, 2003 (ACME Hour). Rebroadcast on BOOM: December 1, 2005 (ACME Hour)–.*

### ◎ MICKEY MOUSE CLUBHOUSE

Animated series revival for the Disney Channel starring Mickey Mouse and friends Minnie Mouse, Donald Duck, Daisy Duck, Goofy and others with the characters produced for the first time in CG animation. Originally premiering in prime time in May 2006, the half-hour preschool series became part of the network's *Playhouse Disney* weekend block, airing in the 9:00 to 9:30 A.M. timeslot. Featuring numerous guest stars (including such Disney cartoon icons as Ludwig Von Drake, Chip 'n' Dale, Clarabelle Cow, Willie the Giant and others), episodes combined cognitive, social and creative learning to stimulate problem solving among young children. Mickey and his pals previously co-starred in two other series for television: *Disney's Mickey Mouse Works* (1999–2001) and *Disney's House of Mouse* (2001–03). *A Walt Disney Television Animation Production. Color. Half-hour. Premiered on DIS: May 5, 2006.*

### Voices

**Mickey Mouse:** Wayne Allwine; **Minnie Mouse:** Russi Taylor; **Goofy/Pluto:** Bill Farmer; **Donald Duck:** Tony Anselmo; **Daisy Duck/Chip 'n' Dale/Baby Red Bird/Mrs. Claus:** Tress MacNeille; **Mouskatools Toodles:** John Jackson; **Professor Ludwig Von Drake:** Corey Burton; **Clarabelle Cow:** April Winchell; **Black Pete/Butch the Bulldog:** Jim Cummings; **Willie the Giant:** Will Ryan; **Mr. Pettybone/Baby Bear:** Frank Welker; **Boo Boo Chicken:** Emily Dickinson; **Pac-a-Derm:** Kevin Rose; **Bella/Sheep:** George Campbell; **Baby Sheep/The Elephant Birthday:** Bob Stutt; **Santa Claus:** Dee Bradley Baker

### ◎ THE MIDNIGHT PATROL: ADVENTURES IN THE DREAM ZONE

In a series of dream-making adventures, four young friends (Carter, Nick, Rosie and Keiko), accompanied by the sarcastic springer spaniel Pottsworth and a toy dinosaur named Murphy, meet in their dreams every night—becoming the superpowered "Midnight Patrol"—to protect the peaceful slumber of those in "The Dream Zone" and to conquer the villainous Nightmare Prince and his henchmen, who are constantly trying to turn a pleasant night's sleep into a terrifying nightmare. Lending a hand to the heroic foursome is their mentor, the Grand Dozer, the ever-snoozing sovereign of "The Dream Zone" (the name of the place to which they report), along with his assistant, Sebastian, and the irascible Greystone Giant. The 1990 half-hour fantasy/adventure series aired Sunday mornings as part of *The Funtastic World of Hanna-Barbera*. *A Hanna-Barbera Production in association with the Sleepy Kid Co. Ltd. Color. Half-hour. Premiered: 1990 (as part of* The Funtastic World of Hanna-Barbera) *Syndicated. Rebroadcast on CAR: November 19, 1994–November 20, 1994 (Look What We Found!).*

**Voices**
**Carter:** George Lemore; **Rosie:** Elisabeth Harnois; **Nick:** Whitby Hertford; **Keiko:** Janice Kamaye; **Pottsworth, Carter's dog:** Clive Revill; **Grand Dozer:** Hamilton Camp; **Sebastian:** Michael Bell; **The Greystone Giant:** Kenneth Mars; **Nightmare Prince:** Rob Paulsen

## ◎ MIFFY AND FRIENDS

Sporting her cute blue sweater, adorable Miffy the rabbit learns about colors, numbers, songs and shapes through the eyes of a four-year-old while having fun with her friends Farmer John, Boris and Barbara Bear, Poppy Pig, Snuffy and many others. Launched in the spring of 2003 on Nickelodeon's commercial-free preschool network, Noggin, the popular stop-motion animated, half-hour daytime series aired weekdays at 7:00 A.M. (ET) and was based on renowned Dutch artist Dick Bruna's award-winning children's book series; it has consistently ranked as one of the network's top-performing shows since its debut. *A Mercis Media BV and Palm Plus BV/Big Tent Entertainment Production. Color. Half-hour. Premiered on NOG: April 7, 2003–.*

**Voices**
**Narrator:** Cyd Vandenberg

## ◎ MIGHTY DUCKS: THE ANIMATED SERIES

Transported to Earth from a parallel universe though a space-time vortex, the Mighty Ducks, now an intergalactic hockey team of superpowered half human, half mallards, get trapped on Earth, turning a defunct hockey rink into their headquarters. They decide to save the planet from their archenemy, the dastardly warlord Draconus, in this half-hour animated series based on the live-action feature-film series. The series premiered simultaneously in syndication and in prime time on ABC on September 6, 1996. Regular episodes aired concurrently as part of ABC's Saturday-morning lineup the following day and in syndication beginning the following Monday as part of the *Disney Afternoon* syndicated two-hour block, which also featured *Darkwing Duck, Gargoyles, Disney's Aladdin, The Lion King's Timon and Pumbaa* and *Disney's Quack Pack*. Voice regulars included actors Jim Belushi, Tim Curry, Dennis Franz and television sports commentator Roy Firestone. Episodes were subsequently rerun on the Disney Channel and Toon Disney. *A Walt Disney Television Animation Production. Color. Half-hour. Premiered on ABC/Syndication: September 6, 1996. Premiered on ABC: September 7, 1996–August 30, 1997. Rebroadcast on DIS: December 1, 1997–September 3, 2005. Rebroadcast on TDIS: September 7, 1998–October 31, 2004; March 2, 2007–.*

**Voices**
Charles Adler, James Belushi, Jeff Bennett, Clancy Brown, Corey Burton, Tim Curry, Roy Firestone, Dennis Franz

## ◎ THE MIGHTY HERCULES

Mythological Greek hero Hercules, beautiful maiden Helena, wholesome satyr Tweet and their half-human horse, Newton, tra-verse the plush Learien Valley of ancient Greece thwarting the machinations of the villainous, blue-hooded Daedelus in this 1963 syndicated series comprised of 130 five-minute, full-color adventures. Produced by Joe Oriolo (who produced and directed 1960's *Felix the Cat* series). The series' theme song, "The Mighty Hercules," was written by Johnny Nash. *An Oriolo Studios/Adventure Cartoons for Television Production in association with Trans-Lux. Color. Half-hour. Premiered: September 1963. Syndicated.*

**Voices**
**Hercules:** Jerry Bascombe; **Helena:** Helene Nickerson; **Newton/Tewt/Daedelus:** Jimmy Tapp

## ◎ THE MIGHTY HEROES

Animator Ralph Bakshi (of *Fritz the Cat* fame), as supervising director of *Terry-Toons*, devised this half-hour series for television following the exploits of a strange quintet of crimefighters—Diaper Man, Cuckoo Man, Rope Man, Strong Man and Tornado Man (each with a large "H" emblazoned on his costume)—who use their wit and muscle to champion the likes of such archcriminals as The Ghost Monster, The Enlarger, The Frog, The Scarecrow, The Shrinker, The Shocker and The Toy Man in this half-hour comedy series produced for CBS in 1966. Of the series' 25 episodes, 10 were released as theatrical cartoons in 1969–70. *A Terrytoons/CBS Films, Inc., Production. Color. Half-hour. Premiered on CBS: October 29, 1966–September 2, 1967.*

**Voices**
**The Mighty Heroes:** Herschel Benardi, Lionel Wilson

## ◎ MIGHTY MAX

Putting on his skull-shape cap, a precocious 11-year-old teen, left at home by his single working mother, travels through time and space with his talking-bird guide, Virgil, and his giant defender, Norman, doing everything in his power to avoid being captured by the villainous Skullmaster in this half-hour syndicated series, part of the weekend series *Amazin' Adventures*, and based on the popular pocket toy of the same name. One of the top-ranked action/adventure programs for kids ages 6 to 11, the series expanded to five days a week starting in September 1994. In 1996 the series reaired on USA Network. *A Film Roman/Bohbot Production in association with Bluebird Canal and DA. Color. Half-hour. Premiered: 1993 (part of Amazin' Adventures) Syndicated. Rebroadcast on USA: September 22, 1996–September 12, 1998.*

**Voices**
**Max:** Rob Paulsen; **Virgil:** Tony Jay; **Norman:** Richard Moll; **Skullmaster:** Tim Curry; **Max's mother:** Tress MacNeille

## ◎ MIGHTY MR. TITAN

This superrobot who fights crime was featured in a series of three-and-a-half-minute color cartoons, produced by Richard H. Ullman, producer of TV's *Colonel Bleep*. Issued to television by syndicator Trans-Lux, which distributed TV's *Felix the Cat* and *The Mighty Hercules*, the series appeared on television screens in 1965, following the popularity of robotic cartoons such as *Gigantor*, which were captivating moppet-head youngsters in every city in America. *A Mister Titan/Trans-Lux Presentation. Color. Half-hour. Syndicated: 1965.*

## ◎ THE MIGHTY MOUSE PLAYHOUSE

Brawny superhero Mighty Mouse, Terry-Toons' most popular character, was the star of this pioneer cartoon show seen regularly on Saturday mornings beginning in 1955. The phenomenal success of the program paved the way for other cartoon studios to follow with their own fully animated series. (In 1957 Hanna-Barbera challenged Mighty Mouse with its long-running *Ruff and Reddy* series.) In addition to impacting the cartoon industry, the series revived the career of the supermouse. The program remained a staple of network television through 1966.

A year later Viacom, which had purchased the Terry-Toons (the name was not subsequently hyphenated) library from CBS (the network initially paid a staggering $3.5 million, for Paul Terry's entire library of films), packaged *The Mighty Mouse Show*. In its original format, the series contained one or two Mighty Mouse adventures plus other *Terry-Toons* featuring an assortment of Paul Terry's creations. Under the syndicated version, two series joined the package: "Luno," the time-traveling adventures of Tim and his flying white stallion, and "The Mighty Heroes," featuring a group of clumsy crime-fighting superheroes (Diaper Man, Cuckoo Man, Rope Man, Strong Man and Tornado Man). Episodes from both series received theatrical distribution as well.

Mighty Mouse later appeared in two series revivals, *The New Adventures of Mighty Mouse and Heckle and Jeckle*, produced by Filmation, and *Mighty Mouse: The New Adventures*. The latter was produced by animator Ralph Bakshi, who, incidentally, began his career working at Terry-Toons. *A Terrytoons/CBS Films, Inc., Production. Color. Half-hour. Premiered on CBS: December 10, 1955–October 2, 1966. Syndicated: 1967.*

### Voices

**Mighty Mouse:** Tom Morrison; **The Mighty Heroes:** Lionel Wilson, Herschel Bernardi; **Luno, the Wonder Horse/Tim:** Bob McFadden

## ⊚ MIGHTY MOUSE: THE NEW ADVENTURES

Tracing back to his origins as ordinary Mike the Mouse, the legendary Terry-Toons star forges onward to his status as life-and-limb-saving superhero in new cartoon adventures (three per show) in this half-hour Saturday-morning series cowritten and directed by animator Ralph Bakshi. Bakshi radically overhauled the crime-fighting mouse in this updated version, giving him the new alter ego of Mike Mouse, an assembly-line worker at Pearl Pureheart's factory. Featured in episodes were old *Terry-Toons* favorites, including Deputy Dawg, Gandy Goose and Oil Can Harry. While a major hit with adult viewers, the series failed to ignite much interest from the 2-to-11 crowd and was canceled after two seasons. *A Ralph Bakshi Animation Production. Color. Half-hour. Premiered on CBS: September 19, 1987–September 2, 1989.*

### Voice

Dana Hill, Patrick Pinney, Maggie Roswell, Beau Weaver

## ⊚ THE MIGHTY ORBOTS

In the 23rd century, robots have reached an advanced stage of sophistication. Five unique but friendly robots (Bo, Boo, Bort, Crunch and Ohno), called "orbots" (and developed by scientist Rob Simmons of Galactic Patrol), come together to form a single, incredible crime-fighting force to thwart the efforts of the villainous cyborg Umbra, ruler of the Shadow Star, who plans to destroy Earth, in this 13-episode half-hour fantasy/adventure series, produced for ABC. *A TMS Entertainment and MGM/UA Entertainment Company/Intermedia Production. Color. Half-hour. Premiered on ABC: September 8, 1984–August 31, 1985.*

### Voices

**Bo:** Sherry Alberoni; **Boo:** Julie Bennett; **Bort:** Bill Martin; **Crunch/Rondu:** Don Messick; **Ohno:** Noelle North; **Robert Simmons:** Barry Gordon; **Dia:** Jennifer Darling; **Umbra/Tor:** Bill Martin; **Returns:** Robert Ridgely; **Narrator:** Gary Owens

## ⊚ MIGRAINE BOY

A young boy whose constant headache gives him a different perspective of life berates his friends and plays with his dog, Tylenol, in this half-hour series that aired briefly on MTV, based on the comic strip created by Greg Fiering. The series sprang from a series of 12 30-second interstitials originally produced for MTV in 1996. *An MTV Animation Production. Color. Half-hour. Premiered on MTV: 1997.*

## ⊚ MIKE, LU AND OG

Hopelessly marooned on the small tropical island of Albonquetine, a smart-alecky Manhattan foreign exchange student, Mike (short for Micheline); a haughty and arrogant island princess, Lu; and her native cousin/inventor whiz, Og, mix with the native islanders, learning their customs while teaching them about American culture. Spun-off from the original cartoon short created, written and directed by Chuck Swenson (creative producer of TV's *Rugrats*), Mikhail Aldashin and Mikhail Shindel, which premiered in May 1999 on Cartoon Network's *Cartoons Cartoon Fridays* block, this weekly half-hour series aired for two seasons, featuring two cartoon episodes per half-hour, until August 2000. In June 2006, the internationally produced series—using storyboards created by Moscow's premiere independent animation studio, Pilot Studio, scripts and final storyboards by Venice, California's Kinofilm and parts of the production completed by facilities in Korea—began reairing daily following reruns of *Dexter's Laboratory* on Cartoon Network's sister channel, Boomerang. *A Kinofilm Studios/Pilot Studio Production. Color. Half-hour. Premiered on CAR: May 7, 1999 (What-A-Cartoon! Show); November 12, 1999–August 18, 2000. Rebroadcast on BOOM: June 6, 2006–.*

### Voices

**Micheline Ann "Mike" Mavinski:** Nika Frost; **Lulu "Lu":** Nancy Cartwright; **Og:** Dee Bradley Baker; **Wendel:** S. Scott Bullock; **Old Queeks:** Corey Burton; **Alfred:** Martin Rayner; **Margery:** Kath Soucie; **Captain:** Brian George

## ⊚ MIKHAIL BARYSHNIKOV'S STORIES FROM MY CHILDHOOD

Unique showcase of award-winning animated fairy tales by Russia's renowned animation studio, Soyuzmultifilm Studios, produced in collaboration with Hollywood's Film Roman and Russia's Films by Jove, founded by ex-Soviet actor Oleg Vidow and his wife; repackaged (from the syndicated series, *Film Roman Presents . . . Animated Classic Showcase*) and redubbed in English by such well-known celebrities as Jim Belushi, Kirsten Dunst, Charlton Heston and others in half-hour edited versions of such Russian animated features as *Beauty and the Beast, A Tale of the Crimson Flower, The Snow Queen, The Petal, Pinocchio and the Golden Key*, among others. Hosted by world-famous ballet star Mikhail Baryshnikov, the program aired on PBS stations beginning in 1996 and also on the Bravo cable network. *A Soyuzmultifilm/Films by Jove/Film Roman Production. Color. Half-hour. Premiered on PBS: 1996–98. Rebroadcast on BRAVO.*

### Cast (live-action)

**Host:** Mikhail Baryshnikov

### Voices

Jim Belushi, Timothy Dalton, Kirsten Dunst, Charlton Heston, Laura San Giacomo, Harvey Fierstein, Bill Murray, Kathleen Turner

## ⊚ MINORITEAM

Five unusually empowered, racially diverse superheroes—El Jefe, the sombero-wearing, leaf blower-propelled Mexican oil tycoon; Nonstop, the giant turban-topped, magic carpet-flying Arabian convenience store clerk; Fasto, a green-masked African American known for his lightning fast speed; and Jewcano, the racially-oppressed, muscle-bound Jewish Moses look-a-like who spews boiling lava; and Dr. Wang, the Chinese paraplegic and "human calculator" team leader—fight the evil forces of discrimination, including White Shadow and his stable of lackeys Corporate Ladder, The Standardized Test and Racist Frankenstein, in this animated comedy series for Cartoon Network.

Premiering as a 15-minute animated special entitled "Operation Blackout" on Cartoon Network's late-night *Adult Swim* program block in November 2005, the network commissioned a 20-episode weekly series that followed, airing from March 19 to July 24, 2006. The special, as well as the series, were the brainchild of a trio of '60s and '70s-era Marvel superhero comics fans—writer/actor/director Adam de la Peña, whose TV credits include *Jimmy Kimmel Live* and *I'm With Busey* among others, Peter Girardi and Todd James—who had worked together on the absurd Comedy Central hit, *Crank Yankers*. *A Cartoon Network Studios Production. Color. Fifteen minutes. Premiered on CAR: November 6, 2005 (pilot)). Premiered on CAR: March 19, 2006 (series).*

### Voices
**Jewcano:** Enn Reitel; **El Jefe:** Nick Puga; **Dr. Wang/Corporate Ladder:** Dana Snyder; **Fasto:** Rodney Saulsberry; **Nonstop:** Keith Lal; **Racist Frankenstein:** Adam De La Pena

## ⊚ THE MILTON THE MONSTER SHOW

By mixing the ingredients of the hillbilly Gomer Pyle and the gothic Frankenstein, the Hal Seeger animators produced one lovable character, Milton the Monster. Milton resides with his goblin companions atop Horrible Hill in the city of Transylvania where they brew trouble for their visitors.

Milton shared the spotlight with five other cartoon characters, each featured in their own episodes, in this ABC Saturday-morning series that premiered in the fall of 1965. They included: "Fearless Fly," a tiny superhero insect who battles sinister bug villains; "Penny Penguin," a precocious child whose good deeds often backfire; "Muggy Doo," a sly, fast-talking fox who cons his way out of predicaments; "Stuffy Durma," a hobo who inherits a fortune but reverts back to living the simple pleasures of his former lifestyle; and "Flukey Luke," a private-eye cowpoke who, aided by his faithful Irish Indian companion Two Feathers, thwarts the efforts of the evil Spider Webb.

On the day after Thanksgiving in 1966, ABC ran cartoons from its Saturday-morning lineup in place of its regular daytime schedule, and "Fearless Fly" was given a 15-minute slot of its own.

Jack Mercer, the voice of Popeye, cowrote the production with Kin Platt. Cartoon veteran James "Shamus" Culhane was one of the series' directors. *A Hal Seeger Production. Color. Half-hour. Premiered on ABC: October 9, 1965–September 8, 1968. Syndicated.*

### Voices

**MILTON THE MONSTER: Milton the Monster:** Bob McFadden; **Professor Weirdo:** Dayton Allen; **Count Kook:** Larry Best;

**FEARLESS FLY: Fearless Fly:** Dayton Ilen; **Florrie Fly:** Bev Arnold

**PENNY PENGUIN: Penny Penguin:** Bev Arnold; **Chester, Penny's dad:** Dayton Allen; **Beulah, Penny's mom:** Hettie Galen

**STUFFY DURMA: Stuffy Durma/Bradley Brinkley:** Dayton Allen

**MUGGY DOO: Muggy Doo:** Larry Best;

**FLUKEY LUKE: Flukey Luke:** Dayton Allen; **Two Feathers:** Larry Best

## ⊚ MISSION HILL

Life suddenly changes for 24-year-old Andy French, a lazy, wannabe cartoonist, when his dorky, high school senior brother, Kevin, moves into his hip Mission Hill loft apartment, caring most about his sexual exploits with women. Andy deals with that and the unusual goings on of his other equally dysfunctional friends, including his girlfriend, Gwen, and his squabbling gay neighbors, Gus and Wally. Created by former *The Simpsons* executive producers Bill Oakley and Josh Weinstein and designed by Lauren MacMullan (who later directed episodes of *The Simpsons*), the WB Television Network first optioned this half-hour comedy series in 1997; originally called *The Downtowners* (then retitled due to MTV's similarly sounding titled cartoon series, *MTV Downtown*); it premiered two years later in primetime and aired only six of the original 13 episodes before being put on hiatus due to poor ratings. In the summer of 2000, the WB put the series back on the air, finally canceling it after airing four more episodes. Since its cancellation, the show has attained a cult status in reruns as part of Cartoon Network's *Adult Swim* late-night program block and on TBS's *Too Funny to Sleep* block.

Winning wide acclaim for its unique stylistic design, in particular its use of bright neon colors and mix of "modern animation and traditional 'cartoonish' drawings," the series is more popular in foreign markets, including Australia, eastern Europe, Latin America, Spain and New Zealand. Cake performed the series' theme song, an upbeat, tempo version of "Italian Leather Sofa." *A Film Roman/Bill Oakley-Josh Weinstein Production. Color. Half-hour. Premiered on WB: September 21, 1999–October 8, 1999; June 25, 2000–July 16, 2000. Rebroadcast on CAR: May 19, 2002–July 6, 2006. Rebroadcast on TBS: 2005.*

### Voices

**Andy French:** Wallace Langham; **Posey Tyler/Natalie Leibowitz-Hernandez:** Vicki Lewis; **Jim Kuback:** Brian Posehn; **Kevin French:** Scott Menville; **Gus/Mr. French/Stogie:** Nick Jameson; **Wally:** Tom Kenny; **Carlos Hernandez-Leibowitz:** Herbert Siguenza; **Gwen:** Jane Wiedlin; **Mrs. French:** Tress MacNeille

## ⊚ MISSION: MAGIC

By drawing a mystical circle on her blackboard, Miss Tickle, a high-school teacher, magically transports her and her prize pupils Carol, Franklin, Harvey, Kim, Socks and her pet cat Tut-Tut back in time to the lands of fantasy in this half-hour series, originally produced for ABC. Recording star Rick Springfield, who plays a troubleshooter, sang his own songs on each program. *A Filmation Associates Production. Color. Half-hour. Premiered on ABC: September 1973–August 31, 1974.*

### Voices

**Rick Springfield:** himself; **Miss Tickle, teacher:** Erika Scheimer; **Carl/Kim:** Lola Fisher; **Vickie/Franklin:** Lane Scheimer; **Harvey/Socks/Mr. Samuels/Tolamy/Tut-Tut:** Howard Morris

## ⊚ MISS SPIDER'S SUNNY PATCH FRIENDS

Delightful spiderific adventures for preschool-age children of Miss Spider, the kind arachnid, Holley, her bespectacled mate, and her Starburst-colored web of siblings and friends and their encounters with other bugs, including the evil Spiderus and the world around them as they learn to appreciate their differences in this half-hour children's series based on David Kirk's best-selling children's book series of the same name. Preceded by an hour-long special produced by Canada's Nelvana studios for Nickelodeon in 2003, this 3-D animated series, which included the half-hour holiday-themed episode, "Hum Bug"/"Dashing Through the Snow," was added to Nickelodeon's Nick Jr. morning preschool program block in the fall of 2004. Actress Kristen Davis (TV's *Sex and the City*) signed on to voice Miss Spider, replacing Brooke Shields who originally voiced the character in the special, while Robert Smith assumed the role of Holley, previously voiced by actor/comedian Rick Moranis. Actor Tony Jay, the voice of Spiderus, was nominated for a 2006 Emmy Award for outstanding performer in an animated program. Three additional half-hour specials—*Froggy Day in Sunny Patch* (also known as *Secret Frog*), *The Big Green Bug* and *Be Good to Bugs . . . And Frogs*, with only *Froggy Day* actually airing on Nick Jr., and one hour-long made-for-TV movie, *The Prince, The Princess and the Bee*—were also produced. After its successful run on Nick Jr., the series was rerun weekdays in the 2:30 to 3:00 P.M. time slot on Noggin beginning in April 2003. *A Nelvana Limited/Absolute Digital/Callaway Arts & Entertainment Production. Color. Half-hour. Premiered on NICK JR.: September 13, 2004. Rebroadcast on NOG: November 22, 2004–.*

### Voices
**Miss Spider:** Kristen Davis; **Holley Spider:** Robert Smith; **Spiderus:** Tony Jay; **Squirt:** Scott Beaudin; **Bounce:** Julie Lemieux; **Shimmer:** Rebecca Brenner; **Dragon:** Mitchell Eisner; **Snowdrop:** Alexandra Lai; **Pansy:** Aaryn Doyle; **Spinner:** Austin Di Iulio; **Wiggle:** Marc Donato; **Betty Beetle:** Patricia Gage; **Mr. Mantis:** Wayne Robson; **Stinky:** Scott McCord; **Eunice Earwig:** Carar Pifko; **Gus:** Peter Oldring; **Beetrice:** Catherine Gallant; **Gus:** Peter Oldring; **Ned:** Jonathan Wilson; **Ted:** Philip Williams; **Felix:** Richard Binsley; **Eddy:** Ezra Perlman; **Lil Sis:** Tajja Isen

## ⊚ MISTER BOGUS

A rambunctious but affable 12-inch gremlin, who resides with a typical American family, decides to change his ways—wearing all sorts of disguises—in a series of harmless escapades presented in this half-hour, syndicated series (also known as "The Mister Bogus Show")—that mixed standard and clay animation—from the same producers as the 1990 syndicated series *Widget, The World Watcher*. *A YC Alligator Films/Zodiac/Calico Entertainment Production. Color. Half-hour. Premiered: Fall 1991. Syndicated.*

### Voices
**Mister Bogus:** Cam Clarke

## ⊚ MISTER MAGOO

The myopic, often irritable Mr. (Quincy) Magoo, played by actor Jim Backus, was given new life in this first-run series of 130 five-minute misadventures, produced for television between 1960 and 1962, featuring several of his relatives, including his beatnik nephew, Waldo, and his English nephew, Prezley. The Magoo adventures actually began on film as a theatrical cartoon series in 1949. Because of his renewed popularity, he was later featured in several prime-time specials (*Mister Magoo's Christmas Carol* and *Uncle Sam Magoo*) and his own prime-time show, *The Famous Adventures of Mister Magoo*, in which he portrayed different historical and literary characters in American history. His nearsighted persona was again revived by DePatie-Freleng's *What's New, Mister Magoo?*, which debuted on CBS in 1977. Episodes from the latter and the 1960's series were bundled together, along with other UPA cartoons (from *The Gerald McBoing Boing Show*), in 1989 under the title of *Mister Magoo & Friends*, broadcast on USA Network's *Cartoon Express*.

Beginning in 2004, the series was rebroadcast weekdays on VOOM's Animania HD along with other classic cartoon properties including *The Dick Tracy Show, Felix the Cat* and *The Pink Panther*. *A UPA Production. Color. Half-hour. Premiered: November 7, 1960. Syndicated. Rebroadcast on USA: September 18, 1989–September 16, 1990. Rebroadcast on BOOM; October 7, 2003–February 18, 2005. Rebroadcast on ANI: 2004–.*

### Voices
**Mr. Magoo:** Jim Backus; **Prezley:** Daws Butler, Paul Frees, Jerry Hausner; **Waldo:** Jerry Hausner, Daws Butler; **Millie, Waldo's girlfriend:** Julie Bennett; **Mother Magoo:** Jim Backus; **Tycoon Magoo:** Paul Frees; **Hamlet:** Richard Crenna

## ⊚ MR. MEN

Smiling Mr. Happy, clumsy Mr. Bump, dizzy Miss Scatterhorn and a cast of 40 other characters created by Roger Hargraves are featured in this collection of animated shorts designed to educate children about personality traits and emotions. A hit in Europe for more than two decades, the half-hour series, complete with live-action wraparounds starring The Mr. Men Players, premiered in syndication in 1997. *A Marina/Mr. Film/France 3/Mr. Showbiz Production in association with Breakthrough Films and Television Inc./Telegenic Programs/Lacey Entertainment/The Summit Media Group. Color. Half-hour. Premiered: September 15, 1997. Syndicated.*

### Cast (live action)
**THE MR. MEN PLAYERS:** Catherine Fitch, Peter Keleghan, Marguerite, Pigott, Cliff Saunders, Sean Sullivan

### Voices
Len Carlson, Alyson Court, Neil Crone, Catherine Disher, Judy Marshak, Ron Rubin

## ⊚ MISTER T

Tough guy Mr. T, of TV's *The A-Team* fame, plays coach to a multiracial team of American teenage gymnasts (Robin, Kim, Spike, Woody and Jeff) who travel the world to competitions and wind up pursuing and capturing criminals in various locales in this weekly half-hour cartoon series that aired on NBC in 1983. Bracketed around each of the series' 30 episodes were live-action closings of Mr. T delivering a valuable moral lesson to young viewers. The series was rebroadcast on USA Network's Cartoon Express, Cartoon Network and Boomerang. *A Ruby-Spears Enterprises Production. Color. Half-hour. Premiered on NBC: September 17, 1983–September 6, 1986. Rebroadcast on USA: February 21, 1989–March 26, 1992; Rebroadcast on CAR: March 19, 1994–March 20, 1994 (Look What We Found!); June 17, 1995–June 18, 1995 (Look What We Found!); June 1995–96. Rebroadcast on BOOM: May 22, 2006–.*

### Voices
**Mr. T:** himself; **Robin:** Amy Linker; **Kim:** Siu Ming Carson; **Spike:** Teddy S. Field III; **Woody:** Phillip LaMarr; **Jeff:** Shawn Lieber; **Miss Bisby:** Takayo Fisher

## ◎ MOBILE FIGHTER G GUNDAM

Led by the Neo's reluctant fighter, Domon Kasshu, Gundams from every country fight in the prestigious "Gundam Fight" tournament until only one is left standing, with the winning nation obtaining sovereignty rights over the other in this 15-episode science fiction cartoon series that aired on Cartoon Network's top-rated Toonami action/adventure block. The series was the third overall to premiere in the United States based on the popular 1979 Japanese cartoon series. A *Sunrise/Nagoya TV/Sotsu/Bandai Entertainment Production. Color. Half-hour.* Premiered on CAR: August 5, 2002–03.

*Voices*

**Cas:** Kae Araki; **Janet Smith/Gina Rodriguez:** Colleen Blackmore; **Allenby Bearsley:** Carol Anne Day; **Schwarz Brude:** Matt Embry; **Past Domon Kasshu:** Matthew Erikson; **Domon Kasshu:** Mark Gatha; **Natasha:** Onalea Gilbertson; **Cha:** Scott Hendrickson; **Rain Mikamura:** Jennifer Holder; **Argo Gulskii:** Stephen Holgate; **Commander Urubi:** Dave Kelly; **Hans:** Masami Kikuchi; **Michelo Chariot:** Jonathan Lover; **Seitt:** Ryan Luhning; **Black Joker:** Yuko Mizutani; **Stalker:** Steve Olson; **Master Asia:** Dave Pettit; **Chibodee Crocket:** Roger Rhodes; **Sophia/Cecile:** Katie Rowan; **Marie Louise/Young Gina/Ming:** Chris Simms; **Sai Sachi:** Zoe Slusar; **Bunny:** Mariette Sluyter; **Hoi:** Jeffrey Watson; **Saishi Sai:** Yamaguchi Kappei

## ◎ MOBILE SUIT GUNDAM

Following a massive intergalactic war involving every space colony and lunar settlement, and resulting in the discovery of the Earth Federation's latest weaponry of destruction, the Gundam, a crew of Zeon refugee soldiers attempt to change the history of the year-old war in this animated science fiction series, first shown in Japan in 1979 and in the United States in 2001 on Cartoon Network. The half-hour series debuted in July 2001, more than a year after the premiere of a later version, *Mobile Suit Gundam Wing.* Two additional half-hour series followed, both airing on Cartoon Network: *Mobile Fighter G Gundam* and *SD Gundam Force.* A *Nippon Sunrise/Nagoya TV/Sotsu/Ocean Group/Bandai Entertainment Production. Color. Half-hour.* Premiered on CAR: July 23, 2001–September 12, 2001; January 1, 2002. Rebroadcast on CAR: June 8, 2002–June 29, 2002; August 3, 2002–January 11, 2003.

*Voices*

**Amuro Ray:** Brad Swaile; **Ma Kube:** Michael Benyaer; **Captain Poallo:** Don Brown; **Sayla Mass/Artesia Zeon Daikun:** Alaina Burnett; **Commandant Wakkein/Gene:** Ted Cole; **Kai Shiden:** Richard Ian Cox; **General Reville:** Michael Dobson; **Garma Zabi/Flanagan Boone:** Brian Drummond; **Lala Sun:** Willow Johnson; **Char Aznable/Caspar Zeon Daikun:** David Kaye; **Frau Bow:** Carly McKillip; **Teniente Reed:** Scott McNeil; **Slegger Rowe:** Bill Mondy; **Hayato Kobayashi:** Matt Smith; **Woody Malden:** Kirby Morrow; **Ranba Ral:** John Payne; **Kycillia Zabi:** Michelle Porter; **Degwin Zabi:** Eric Schneider; **Miharu Ratokie:** Kelly Sheridan; **Dozle Zabi:** French Tickner; **Mirai Yashima:** Cathy Weseluck; **Crowley Hamon:** Lenore Zann; **Manilda:** Sylvia Zaradic; **Narrator:** Ross Douglas

## ◎ MOBILE SUIT GUNDAM WING

Replete with highly advanced mobile suits, called Gundams, five young pilots—Heero Yuy, Duo Maxwell, Trowa Barton, Quatre Rabera Winner and Chang Wufei—band together to destroy the Organization of the Zodiac, headed by five rogue scientists who have turned evil. Revoiced in English, this futuristic imported series, loosely based on the 1979 Japanese television series created by Hajime Yatate and Yoshiyuki Tomino, was the second of four animated renditions of the *Gundam Wing* franchise to air on Cartoon

Network's Toonami block. The others included the first, *Mobile Suit Gundam,* followed by *Mobile Fighter G Gundam* and *SD Gundam Force.* A *Sunrise/Sotsu/Bandai Entertainment Production. Color. Half-hour.* Premiered on CAR: March 6, 2000–May 11, 2001.

*Voices*

**Heero Yuy:** Mark Hildreth; **Duo Maxwell:** Scott McNeil; **Trowa Barton:** Kirby Morrow; **Zechs Merquise/Milliardo Peacecraft:** Brian Drummond; **Treize Khushrenada:** David Kaye; **Relena Darlian:** Lisa Ann Beley; **Quatre Raberba Winner:** Brad Swaile; **Chang Wufei:** Ted Cole; **Lucrezia Noin:** Saffron Henderson; **Lady Une:** Enuka Vanessa Okuma; **Narrator:** Campbell Lane

## ◎ MOBY DICK AND THE MIGHTY MIGHTOR

Hanna-Barbera produced this half-hour, Saturday-morning action/adventure series for CBS in 1967, which combined two cartoon segments: "Moby Dick," an updated version of Herman Melville's classic literary tale in which the famous Great White Whale protects a pair of marooned youngsters, Tom and Tub, and their seal friend Scooby, in dangerous seafaring adventures, and 18 episodes (one per show) of "The Mighty Mightor," starring a young prehistoric boy, Tor, who draws his strength from his magic club, becoming a masked superhuman guardian of the jungle accompanied by his dinosaur/dragon companion, Tog. Thirty-six "Moby Dick" (two per show) and 18 "The Mighty Mightor" (one per show) cartoons were produced for the weekly series, which concluded its run on CBS in 1969. A *Hanna-Barbera Production. Color. Half-hour.* Premiered on CBS: September 9, 1967–September 6, 1969. Rebroadcast on CAR: February 7, 1993 (part of Boomerang, 1967); February 18, 1995–97 ("Mighty Mightor," part of Super Adventure Saturdays). Rebroadcast on BOOM: November 11, 2000–April 24, 2004.

*Voices*

**MOBY DICK: Tom:** Bobby Resnick; **Tub:** Barry Balkin; **Scooby, their pet seal:** Don Messick;

**MIGHTY MIGHTOR: Mightor:** Paul Stewart; **Tor:** Bobby Diamond; **Sheera:** Patsy Garrett; **Pondo/Ork/Tog/Rollo:** John Stephenson; **Li'l Rok:** Norma McMillan

## ◎ MONCHHICHIS

A tribe of highly developed monkeylife creatures protect their treetop society in this colorful fantasy tale of good and evil. Looking out for the loving creatures in the kindly wizard Wizzar, who often conjures up powerful spells to save them from the evil grasp of the Grumplins of Grumplor, led by the horrible Horrg, in this half-hour fantasy series first telecast on ABC in 1983. Rebroadcast on USA Network's *Cartoon Express.* A *Hanna-Barbera Production in association with Mattel, Inc. Color. Half-hour.* Premiered on ABC: September 10, 1983–September 1, 1984. Rebroadcast on USA: March 26, 1989–October 17, 1991.

*Voices*

**Moncho:** Bobby Morse; **Kyla:** Laurel Page; **Tootoo:** Ellen Gerstell; **Patchitt:** Frank Welker; **Thumkii:** Hank Saroyan; **Horrg:** Sidney Miller; **Wizzar:** Frank Nelson; **Snogs:** Bob Arbogast; **Shreeker/Snitchitt/Gonker:** Peter Cullen; **Yabbott/Fasit/Scumgor:** Laurie Faso

## ◎ MON COLLE KNIGHTS

Determined to protect six magical items that will bring monsters of a dimensional world (called Mon World) and humans together to live in universal peace, Professor Hiragi, a noted scientist, his daughter, Rockna, and her boyfriend, dubbed Mon Colle Knights, fight to stop the nefarious Prince Eccentro and his mighty minions from ruining their plans and using the items for their evil purposes to rule both worlds, in this half-hour anime series, based on the popular Japanese trading card game. The English-language version was shown in America on FOX, where it premiered in July 2001 with a one-hour special before being added to the network's Saturday morning schedule in mid-November. Unfortunately, the series finale was never aired since FOX canceled the series in early September 2002. In September 2006, four years after its premiere on FOX, the series returned on Toon Disney to co-anchor the all-anime Sunday *Jetix* cartoon block along with such anime favorites as *Beyblade, Shinzo, Daigunder* and *Digimon. A Studio Deen/Saban Entertainment Production. Color. Half-hour. Premiered on FOX: November 24, 2001–September 7, 2002. Rebroadcast on TDIS: September 3, 2006– .*

*Voices*
**Mondo Ooya:** Derek Stephen Prince; **Rockna:** Brianne Siddall; **Professor Hiragi:** Jamieson Price; **Prince Eccentro:** Joe Ochman; **Batch/Ms. Naomi Loon/Lovestar:** Wendee Lee; **Gluko:** Dina Sherman; **Kahimi:** Tifanie Christun; **Luke:** Kevin Hoolihan; **Impy:** R. Martin Klein; **Grabiolis/Redda:** Daran Norris; **Beginner:** Philece Sampler; **Tenaka:** Michael Sorich; **Fire Angel/ Winged Warrior:** Melodee Spevack

## ◉ MONKEY MAGIC

Using his amazing power, an ambitious leader of a clan of monkeys, Kongo (formerly Stone Monkey), battles the evil Dearth Void, ruler of the Dark Side of the Universe, for supremacy in this redubbed half-hour Japanese anime series, known in Japan as *Saiyuki* (a cult-classic live-action TV series produced in the late 1970s in Japan) or *Journey to the West,* the classic Chinese novel on which it was based. Combining traditional 2-D cel animation for the characters and 3-D computer animation for the backgrounds, the 13-episode half-hour fantasy/adventure series was syndicated in the United States beginning in September 1998. *A Bandai Entertainment Production. Color. Half-hour. Premiered: September 20, 1998. Syndicated.*

*Voices*
**Kongo/Sarge:** Samuel Vincent; **Prince Nata:** Andrew Francis; **Fania/Blossom:** Kathleen Barr; **Batty/Admiral Dopuck/Boady/ Slimelord/West General:** Michael Dobson; **Dearth Void/Master/ North General/Subodye:** Paul Dobson; **Lord Refang/Milesight/ Guardian/South General:** Scott McNeil; **Jade Emperor/East General:** Ward Perry; **Biedy:** Brian Drummond; **Empress Dowager:** Cathy Weseluck; **Bandit/Emperor:** Don Brown; **Redchimp/ Sansoh:** Richard Ian Cox; **Runlay:** Rochelle Greenwood; **Beedy:** Ted Cole; **Lao Tzu/Minister Fuchin, Sonicmate/Wowzer:** Terry Klassen

## ◉ MONSTER ALLERGY

Aided by his classmate and new kid on the block in Oldmill Village, Elena Potato, and his talking cat and mentor, Timothy-Moth, an allergic 10-year-old, Zick Barrymore (originally called Ezekiel Zick in the comic-book series), who has an eye for the supernatural and a sixth sense that enables him to see invisible supernatural ghosts and monsters that walk among the living, hopes to harness his powers and become a monster tamer like his missing dad, in this animated fantasy-adventure based on the international best-selling comic-book. Produced by Italy's Rainbow S.r.l., all 26 episodes of the frightfully entertaining half-hour anime comedy series were jointly acquired by Kids' WB! and Cartoon Network, making their U.S. television debut on the Kids' WB! Saturday-morning schedule

in November 2006, with three other brand-new series from Warner Bros. Animation: *Legion of Super Heroes, Shaggy & Scooby-Doo Get a Clue!* and *Tom and Jerry Tales. A Rainbow S.r.l. Production. Color. Half-hour. Premiered on Kids WB!: November 25, 2006.*

*Voices*
**Zick Barrymore:** Holly Gauthier-Frankel; **Elena Potato:** Annie Bovaird; **Timothy-Moth:** Michael Perron; **Bombo:** Rick Jones; **Magnacat:** Al Gouem; **Synakutz Bu:** Gordon Masten

## ◉ MONSTER FORCE

A cadre of supernatural-stalking, college-age bounty hunters battle to save mankind from a marauding band of monsters that include Dracula, Bela the Werewolf, HoTep the Mummy and the Creature from the Black Lagoon in this half-hour syndicated series, based on popular Universal Studio's film monsters and animated by the studio's cartoon division. *A Universal Cartoons Studio L & P Animation/Lacewood Production. Color. Half-hour. Premiered: September 12, 1994. Syndicated.*

*Voices*
**Dr. Reed Crawley:** Lawrence Bayne; **Luke Talbot, the Wolfman:** Paul Haddad; **Shelley Frank:** Caroly Larson; **Tripp Hansen:** Philip Akin; **Lance McGruder:** David Hewlett; **Frankenstein Monster:** Howard Jerome; **Dracula:** Robert Bockstael; **Bela/Niles Lupon:** Rob Cowan; **Other Voices:** Ray Landry

## ◉ MONSTER MANIA

When his aunt mysteriously vanishes after spending the night at her spooky mansion, 10-year-old Brian McKenzie meets his first monster—clumsy, big-hearted Boo Marang—who jumps from a bed post and whisks the young boy off of Monster Mania, a land of crazy monsters (located in dark closests everywhere). He helps the monsters battle the evil Osh and a variety of other monsters, in this weekly, 26-episode half-hour fantasy/adventure series made for first-run syndication. *A Kookanooga Toons Production in association with Action Media Group and Hallmark Entertainment. Color. Half-hour. Premiered: (week of) September 11, 1995. Syndicated.*

*Voices*
**Brian/Jamm/Creature Key:** Jeannie Elias; **Olive/Coin #1:** Miriam Flynn; **Stan/Limo:** Mark Taylor; **Boo/Sootybush/Bus:** Jim Cummings; **Gertie/Fudge/Taxi:** Tress MacNeille; **Nougat/Droolblossom/Underwood:** Frank Welker; **Osh/Bellylint/Doorman:** Mark Hamill

## ◉ MONSTER RANCHER

While playing his favorite video game, Genki, an 11-year-old "Monster Rancher" contest winner, is suddenly transported into the game's surrealistic world where—joined by the orphaned Holly, and other creatures who inhabit it, including Golem, Hare, Moochi, Suezo and Tiger—he tries to stop the evil Moo the Monster from taking control.

Based on the popular Sony PlayStation video game, this weekly half-hour anime series premiered in syndication and on cable's Sci-Fi Channel in August 1999. Broadcast on Sci-Fi until 2000, the FOX network added the show to its Saturday-morning FOX Kids schedule in November 1999, where it aired twice, once after *Power Rangers Lost Galaxy* at 8:30 A.M. and then after *Xyber 9: New Dawn* at 9:30 A.M., before it was canceled in March 2001. In the meantime, in September 2000, the series began reairing on FOX Family Channel through the following October. *A TMS Entertainment/Ocean Group/Bobhot Production. Color. Half-hour. Premiered on SCI: August 30, 1999–2000. Syndicated: August 30, 1999. Rebroadcast on FOX: November 6, 1999–March*

A remarkable young boy discovers there really are monsters living in the world—in his bedroom—in the half-hour syndicated series Monster Mania. © Kookanooga Toons Ltd.

9, 2001. Rebroadcast on FOX FAM: September 16, 2000–October 4, 2001.

*Voices*

**Weed/Little Mew:** Paul Dobson; **Tiger of the Wind/Ebony:** Brian Drummond (1999–2001); **Genki:** Andrew Francis (1999–2001), Doc Harris (2001), Saffron Henderson (2001); **Moochi/Pixie:** Janyse Jaud; **Mono the Monolith:** David Kaye; **Suezo/Captain Black Dino/Grey Wolf:** Scott McNeil; **Golem/Moo:** Richard Newman; **Holly:** Maggie O'Hara; **Game Narrator/Red Tiger/Big Blue/Slave:** Ward Perry; **Hare:** Samuel Vincent; **Other Voices:** Michael Dobson, Cathy Weseluck

### ◎ MORAL OREL

Eleven-year-old Orel Puppington consistently misinterprets the beliefs of his Protestant Christian faith and "the Lord's wishes," doing many things that are against his religion—from smoking pot to trying euthanasia—in this politically incorrect cartoon comedy series created by *Late Night With Conan O'Brien*, *Mr. Show* and *TV Funhouse* writer Dino Stamatopoulos for Cartoon Network. Following the premiere of the 15-minute pilot, "The Best Christmas Ever" as a holiday special on Cartoon Network's late-night Adult Swim block, the program joined the Adult Swim roster in January 2006.

Joining Orel in his riotous misadventures were his parents, Clay and Bloberta; his school coach, Stopframe; Reverend Putty; and his younger brother, Shapey. Stamatopoulos has said in interviews that the series, though its animation visually resembles that of the popular 1960s religious cartoon series

favorite, *Davey and Goliath*, it was not meant as a parody of the latter but instead designed as a send-up of a *Leave It to Beaver*–like 1950s family comedy, which was originally to star Iggy Pop. Instead, the concept evolved into an animated property with Cartoon Network commissioning 10 first-season episodes, including the pilot special. Since growing in popularity, the series returned for a second season in November 2006 with 20 new 15-minute episodes. A *Moral Oral/Shadow Machine Films/Williams Street Production. Color. Fifteen minutes. Premiered on CAR: December 13, 2005 (special). Premiered on CAR: January 23, 2006 (series).*

*Voices*

**Orel:** Carolyn Lawrence; **Clay Puppington/Doughy/Various Others:** Scott Adsit; **Bloberta Puppington/Nurse Bendy/Nurse Blinkless/Miss Sculptham/Tommy:** Britta Phillips; **Shapey Puppington/Block Posabule:** Tigger Stamatopoulos; **Coach Stopframe/Officer Papermouth/Principal Fakey/Miss Censordoll:** Jay Johnston; **Reverend Putty:** William Salyers; **Billy Figurelli/Various Others:** Dino Stamatopolous

### ◎ MORK AND MINDY/LAVERNE AND SHIRLEY/FONZ HOUR

Shazbot! the spaced-out spaceman from the planet Ork and friend Mindy, played by Robin Williams and Pam Dawber in the hit prime-time television series that aired on ABC from 1978 to 1982, reprised their roles in these animated adventures in which Mork enrolls at Mt. Mount High, upon orders from his planet's superior, Orson, to learn more about the experiences of Earthlings during adolescence. Airing on ABC in September of 1982, the half-hour comedy cartoon series was half of the hour-long cartoon block known as the *Mork and Mindy/Laverne and Shirley/Fonz Hour*, sharing the spotlight with another new animated series, "Laverne and Shirley with the Fonz." (See individual entry for details.) Hanna-Barbera and Ruby-Spears Enterprises coproduced the "Mork and Mindy" series, while Hanna-Barbera served as sole producer of the "Laverne and Shirley/Fonz" series, the second such animated adaptation of producer Garry Marshall's popular TV sitcom, following 1981's *Laverne and Shirley in the Army*, also produced by Hanna-Barbera. A *Hanna-Barbera/Ruby Spears Enterprises Production in*

Comedian Robin Williams lent his voice as the spaced-out spaceman Mork in ABC's Saturday-morning spin-off comedy cartoon block Mork and Mindy/Laverne and Shirley/Fonz Hour, based on the network's hit live-action sitcoms. © Hanna-Barbera Productions/Ruby-Spears Enterprises. All rights reserved.

*association with Paramount Television. Color. Half-hour. Premiered on ABC: September 25, 1982–September 3, 1983.*

**Voices**

**MORK AND MINDY: Mork:** Robin Williams; **Mindy:** Pam Dawber; **Doing, Mork's pet:** Frank Welker; **Fred McConnell, Mindy's father:** Conrad Janis; **Mr. Caruthers, the principal:** Stanley Jones; **Orson, Mork's superior:** Ralph James; **Eugene, Mork's friend:** Shavar Ross; **Hamilton, Mork's friend:** Mark Taylor

**LAVERNE AND SHIRLEY/FONZ: Laverne:** Penny Marshall; **Shirley:** Lynn Marie Stewart; **Sgt. Turnbuckle:** Ken Mars; **Squealy:** Ron Palillo; **Fonz:** Henry Winkler; **Mr. Cool:** Frank Welker

## ◎ MORTAL KOMBAT: DEFENDERS OF THE REALM

This series was based on the highly successful "Mortal Kombat" franchise, including the popular arcade and video games. A group of "chosen warriors"—a ninja (voiced by Luke Perry), a former riot cop (Ron Perlman) and a special-forces officer (Olivia d'Abo)—band together, forming the Outer World Investigation Agency, to battle the forces of the dreaded Emperor Shao Khan and threats to the Mortal Kombat universe in this half-hour series that premiered in 1996 on USA Network's weekend *Cartoon Express*. *A Film Roman Production in association with Threshold Entertainment. Color. Half-hour. Premiered on USA: September 21, 1996.*

**Voices**
**Sub-Zero:** Luke Perry; **Stryker:** Ron Perlman; **Sonya Blade:** Olivia d'Abo; **Liu Kang:** Brian Tochi; **Rayden:** Clancy Brown; **Princess Kitana:** Cree Summer; **Jax:** Dorian Harewood; **Nightwolf:** Todd Thawley

## ◎ MOST IMPORTANT PERSON

Originally seen daily on *Captain Kangaroo*, this educational series aimed at preschoolers starred Mike, a baseball-capped boy, and Nicola, a pigtailed black girl, who present a variety of subjects relating the importance of physical and mental health. The films were subsequently syndicated as a half-hour series. *A Sutherland Learning Associates Production in association with H.E.W. and Viacom. Color. Half-hour (syndication). Premiered on CBS: April 3, 1972–May 18, 1973 (on Captain Kangaroo).*

## ◎ MOTHER GOOSE AND GRIMM

Those obnoxious and appealing characters from Pulitzer Prize–winning political cartoonist Mike Peters's comic strip—namely the grannyish Mother Goose and the ever-cynical Grimmy the dog—are paired in a series of offbeat adventures, joined by an equal cast of misfits, in this half-hour Saturday-morning series for CBS. The series, which enjoyed a two-season run, was retitled *Grimmy* for the 1992 season. *A Lee Mendelsohn/Film Roman Production in association with Grimmy, Inc. Tribune Media and MGM-UA Television. Color. Half-hour. Premiered on CBS: September 14, 1991–March 13, 1993.*

**Voices**
Gregg Berger, Charlie Brill, Greg Burton, Mitzi McCall

## ◎ MOTORMOUSE AND AUTOCAT

Sportscar maniac Autocat tries everything possible to beat his speedy archrival, Motormouse, in outlandish contests in this half-hour series for Saturday-morning television. The program, which aired on ABC in 1970, featured repeated episodes of the freewheeling cat and mouse and "It's the Wolf," both originally seen for the first time on 1969's *The Cattanooga Cats*. (See *The Catta-*

*nooga Cats for voice events.) A Hanna-Barbera Production. Color. Half-hour. Premiered on ABC: September 12, 1970–September 4, 1971.*

## ◎ THE MOUSE AND THE MONSTER

In the story of the unlikeliest pals, a big-hearted, manic rodent, Chesbro, and his half-brained, good-natured, hulking blue monster companion, Mo, operate on the fringe of utter madness as they stay on the run from Mo's evil creator, the mad Dr. Wackerstein and his haughty highbrow bride, Olga, in this wacky half-hour cartoon series produced for the UPN Network. Created by Jerry Leibowitz, an accomplished graphic artist, painter and print cartoonist who founded the first all-comics newspaper, *L.A. Funnies* in 1983, *The Mouse and the Monster* was born out of Leibowitz's "longing for some of the great non-superhero cartoons of the past, particularly those of Jay Ward ('Rocky and Bullwinkle') and Bob Clampett ('Beany & Cecil')." The series premiered in the fall of 1996 Sunday mornings on UPN. *A Saban Entertainment Production. Color. Half-hour. Premiered on UPN: September 8, 1996. Rebroadcast on FOX FAM: September 19, 1998–December 27, 1998.*

## ◎ MTV DOWNTOWN

Created by former *Beavis and Butt-Head* animator Chris Prynoski, this short-lived series followed the urban life adventures of a multicultural group of New York City teens—brother-and-sister Alex and Chaka Henson and their friends Jen, Fruity, Goat, Matt, Mecca and Serena—based on interviews with actual people. Nominated for an Emmy Award for outstanding animated program, the 13-episode, half-hour program, which debuted on MTV in the summer of 1999, lasted only one season. *An MTV Animation Production. Color. Half-hour. Premiered on MTV: August 3, 1999–November 8, 1999.*

**Voices**
**Alex Henson:** Gregory Gillmore; **Chaka Henson:** Leyora Zuberman; **Jen:** Tammy Lang; **Serena:** Phoebe Summerquash; **Mecca:** Aurora Lucia-Levey; **Goat:** Scot Rienecker; **Fruity:** Marco H. Rodriguez; **Matt:** Hector Fontanez; **Virginia Capers:** Delia Bonner; **Additional Voices:** Wayne Barker, Ralph Buckley, MM Capper, Mike DeSeve, Susannah Jo Maurer, Guy Maxtone-Graham, Clem Peckerwood, Lynn Richardson, Aunt Rose, Paul Savior, Sean Seagrave, A.F. Toney

## ◎ MTV ODDITIES

In December of 1994, MTV launched this weekly animated series featuring strange characters in unusual worlds and situations. The series kicked off with six episodes of "The Head," the story of an Everyman named Jim and his symbiotic relationship with an alien, created by artist-animator Eric Fogel. In April of 1995, the series returned for a second season, opening with another six-episode commitment of "The Maxx," the adventures of a man who travels between two worlds, based on the Image comic book created by Sam Keith. The series launched its third and final episode in February of the following year with seven new episodes of "The Head" (told in individual half-hour adventures.) *An MTV Animation Production. Color. Half-hour. Premiered on MTV: December 19, 1994–March 5, 1996.*

**Voices**

**THE HEAD:** Eric Fogel, John Andrews, Gordon Barnett, Patricia Bibby, Jason Candler, Bill Chesley, Ted Gannon, Russ Hexter, Tad Hills, Melanie Holtzman, Chris Johnson, Mike Judge, John

Lynn, Susie Lewis Lynn, Clem Peckerwood, Mike Ruschak, Paul Williams, Yon Hong Zhong

**THE MAXX: The Maxx:** Michael Haley; **Julie Winters/Gloriee:** Glynnis Talken; **Sara James:** Amy Danles; **Sara's Mom:** Patty Wynne-Hughs; **Mr. Gone:** Barry Stigler; **Tommy/Isz:** David Valera; **Sgt. Ocono:** Tony Fucile; **Other Voices:** James Dean Conklin, Scott Curtis, Molly McLucas, David Thomas, Chris Vanzo

## ◎ ¡MUCHA LUCHA!

Set in the town of Lucha Libra, three mascaritas—Rikochet, the descendant of a famous family of wrestlers; Buena Girl the world's foremost expert on the "Code of Masked Wrestling"; and the short-tempered, undisciplined The Flea—complete with colorful masks and costumes and their own signature moves developed while studying as students at a world-famous wrestling school, put their wrestling prowess to good use to protect the weak and help others for the sake of "Honor, Family, Tradition and Doughnuts" in this over-the-top, half-hour Saturday-morning cartoon comedy/adventure series—and first Flash-animated series—for the WB Television Network's Kids' WB!

Creators Lili Chin and Eddie Mort of FWAK! Animation in Sydney, Australia, first produced the cartoon series as Flash cartoons, using Macromedia Flash software, for the Internet before Warner Bros. bought the property in 2001 to broadcast on its WB Television Network beginning in August 2002. During the 2003–04 season, Warner Bros.' "fastest mouse in all of Mexico," Speedy Gonzales, made a special guest appearance on the show's November 8 broadcast that also included the debut of the series' first half-hour holiday special, *The Match Before Christmas*. In March 2004, Cartoon Network began replaying episodes of the masked wrestling comedy/action series every Friday at 8:30 and 10:30 P.M. as part of its weekly showcase of animated comedies. The 52-episode series completed its network run in February 2005. *A Warner Bros. Television Animation Production. Color. Half-hour. Premiered on the WB (Kids' WB!): August 17, 2002–May 28, 2005. Rebroadcast on CAR: March 5, 2004–.*

### Voices
**Buena Girl:** Jessica Di Cicco (speaking vocals), Kimberly Brooks (rapping vocals), Samuel Vincent (singing vocals); **The Flea:** Grey DeLisle (speaking vocals), Cree Summer (rapping vocals), Candi Milo (singing vocals); **Rikochet:** Alana Ubach, Kathleen Barr (speaking vocals), Carlos Alazraqui (rapping vocals), Jason Marsden (singing vocals); **Snow Pea:** Grey DeLisle; **Cindy Slam:** Carlos Alazraqui, Tom Kenny; **Mr. Midcarda:** Jason Marden; **Headmistress/Mama:** Candi Milo; **El Rey:** Daran Norris, Michael Donovan; **Megawatt:** Michael Donovan; **Masked Dog:** Frank Welker; **Timmy of a Thousand Masks:** Matt Hill; **Carlton Cold Jones/El Loco Mosquito:** Lee Tockar; **Rikochet's Aubelito:** Terry Klassen; **Prima-Donna:** Kathleen Barr; **El Haystack Grande:** Gary Chalk; **Potato Potata Jr.:** Cusse Munkuma; **Dragonfly:** Janyse Jaud; **Kid Wombat:** James Arnold Taylor; **Mr. Spongy's Spongecake:** Scott McNeil

## ◎ MUMMIES ALIVE!

After a 3,000-year slumber, a group of Egyptian mummies come back to life in modern-day San Francisco to protect a 12-year-old boy who embodies the spirit of an Egyptian pharaoh and who holds the secret to eternal life in this 52-episode half-hour syndicated series created by film producer Ivan Reitman (of *Ghostbusters* fame). *A DIC Entertainment/Ivan Reitman Production. Color. Half-hour. Premiered: September 15, 1997–99. Syndicated. Rebroadcast on SCI: September 30, 1999–August 24, 2000. Rebroadcast: 2003– (in syndication).*

### Voices
**Rath:** Scott McNeil; **Nefertina:** Cree Summer; **Presley:** Bill Switzer; **Ja-Kal:** Dale Wilson; **Armon:** Graeme Kingston; **Scarab:** Gerald Plunkett; **Heka:** Pauline Newstone; **Amanda/Khati:** Louise Vallance

## ◎ THE MUMMY: THE ANIMATED SERIES

In order to rule the world, Imhotep, the resurrected and still corrupt mummy High Priest, aided by Colin Weasler, his lackey assistant, must snatch the powerful Manacle of Osiris worn on the wrist of curious 11-year-old Alex O'Connell who is traveling the globe with this archaeologist parents in this animated spin-off designed to capitalize on the success of Universal Studios' blockbuster, special effects-laden, live-action *Mummy* feature films, set a year after the movie *The Mummy Returns* (2001).

Originally set to debut on the WB Television Network's Kids' WB! Saturday-morning schedule on September 14, 2001, following the horrific terrorist attacks of 9/11, the series instead premiered two weeks later. The series remained on air until mid-May when it was put on hiatus and replaced by the series, *Phantom Investigators*. Over a two-week period, episodes aired again on Kids' WB! in September 2002 before the network ordered a second season of new episodes under a revamped version entitled *The Mummy: Secrets of the Madjai*, which premiered in February 2003. While the quality was an improvement over the show's first season, the show failed to excite young viewers and the WB subsequently canceled the series after its final broadcast in early August 2003. Reruns of the show were later shown on the *Jetix* program block on Toon Disney, where it was replaced with *Digimon* on Tuesdays and Thursdays and *Shinzo* on Saturdays and Sundays. *A Universal Studios/Sun Woo Entertainment Production. Color. Half-hour. Premiered on the WB (Kids' WB!): September 29, 2001–May 18, 2002; September 14, 2002–September 28, 2002; February 21, 2003–August 5, 2003. Rebroadcast on TDIS: October 3, 2006–March 4, 2007.*

### Voices
**Alex O'Connell:** Chris Marquette; **Imhotep:** Jim Cummings; **Evy O'Connell:** Grey DeLisle; **Rick O'Connell:** John Schneider; **Jonathan Carnahan:** Tom Kenny; **Colin Weasler:** Michael Reisz; **Ardeth Bey:** Nicholas Guest

## ◎ MUPPET BABIES

These "babies" are animated versions of creator Jim Henson's familiar Muppet characters as small children who never actually leave their home yet through their imaginations go anywhere, do anything and be anyone they choose. Henson was executive producer of this long-running series, which premiered on CBS in 1984 as a half-hour series and during the course of its run was expanded to one hour and later 90 minutes. During the 1985–86 season the series was renamed *Jim Henson's Muppet Babies And Monsters* and expanded to 90 minutes (see entry for details). In 1989, the series' sixth season on CBS, 65 episodes from previous seasons were packaged for syndication. The same package and later episodes were rebroadcast weekdays on the FOX Children's Network beginning in the fall of 1991. Nickelodeon added the series, in reruns, to its daily Nick Jr. schedule in 1992. *A Marvel Production in association with Henson Associates and Akom Productions. Color. Half-hour. One hour. Ninety minutes. Premiered on CBS: September 15, 1984–September 7, 1985 (half hour); September 14, 1985–September 6, 1986 (90 minutes); September 13, 1986–September 12, 1987 (one hour); September 19, 1987–September 3, 1988 (90 minutes); September 10, 1988–September 9, 1989 (one hour); September 16, 1989–September 8, 1990 (one hour); September*

14, 1991–September 7, 1992. *Rebroadcast on FOX: September 2, 1991–September 4, 1992. Rebroadcast on NICK: September 28, 1992–98. Syndicated: 1989. Rebroadcast on ODY: April 1999–Fall 2000.*

**Voices**
Kermit/Beaker: Frank Welker; **Animal:** Howie Mandel, Dave Coulier; **Skeeter:** Howie Mandel, Frank Welker; **Bean Bunny/ Statler/Waldorf/Bunsen:** Dave Coulier; **Fozzie/Scooter:** Greg Berg; **Rowlf:** Katie Leigh; **Piggy:** Laurie O'Brien; **Gonzo:** Russi Taylor; **Nanny:** Barbara Billingsley

### ◎ MUTANT LEAGUE

Playing like the Mighty Ducks, the Bad News Bears and the New York Mets rolled into one mutated mess, the once-hapless Midway Monsters, after drafting the greatest rookie prospect—the incomparable Bones Justice—finally become a team to reckon with in the anything-goes-style-of-play Mutant League. A cartoon parody of professional sports based on the series of video games from Electronic Arts and produced for first-run syndication. *A Franklin-Watterman Production in association with Claster Television. Color. Half-hour. Premiered: September 17, 1994. Syndicated.*

**Voices**
Bones Justice: Roman Foster; **Zalgor Prigg/Spewter:** Jim Hirbie; **Razor Kidd:** Rich Buchlloyd; **KT Blayer/Kang/Mo:** Mark Fleisher; **Eleanor McWhimple:** Kati Starr; **Bob Babble/George McWhimple/Jukka:** Robert Brousseau

### ◎ MY DAD THE ROCK STAR

Internationally famous hard rock KISS star Gene Simmons created this half-hour comedy following the adventures of Willy Zilla, the 12-year-old son of a seven-foot-tall flamboyant billionaire musician, Rock Zilla, who semi-retires and moves his family to a new home in the sleepy suburb of Silent Springs. Produced by Canada's Nelvana studios, the half-hour series debuted in the United States on Nickelodeon's Nicktoons with 26 first-season episodes. *A Nelvana Production. Color. Half-hour. Premiered on NICKT: February 7, 2005.*

**Voices**
Willy Zilla: Joanne Vannicola; **Rock Zilla:** Lawrence Zayne; **Crystal Zilla, Willy's mother:** Kathleen Laskey; **Serenity Zilla, Willy's sister:** Stephanie Mills; **Alyssa, Willy's best friend:** Sara Gadon; **Quincy:** Martin Villafana; **Shunk:** Don Francks

### ◎ MY FAVORITE MARTIANS

A Martian crash-lands in the vicinity of the Los Angeles freeway and is discovered by writer Tim O'Hara. Convincing O'Hara that revealing his true identity would cause worldwide panic, the alien assumes the identity of Tim's Uncle Martin and they become roommates. O'Hara (now joined by a teenage niece named Katy) must guard the well-being not only of Uncle Martin but also of his other space friend, Andromeda (or "Andy"), in this cartoon spin-off of the TV hit *My Favorite Martian,* which starred Ray Walston and Bill Bixby. (Neither actor supplied his voice for this animated version.) The animated series featured some of the same supporting characters from the famous science-fiction sitcom, including Tim O'Hara's scatterbrained landlady Lorelei Brown and suspicious police detective Bill Brennan (recast with an equally snoopy son, Brad, and pet chimpanzee, Chump), none voiced by the original actor. *A Filmation Associates/Jack Chertok Production. Color. Half-hour. Premiered on CBS: September 8, 1973–August 30, 1975.*

**Voices**
Martin O'Hara (Uncle Martin): Jonathan Harris; **Tim O'Hara:** Howard Morris; **Andromeda (Andy):** Lane Scheimer; **Katy O'Hara, Tim's niece/Lorelei Brown, Tim's landlady:** Jane Webb; **Bill Brennan, security officer:** Howard Morris; **Brad Brennan, his son:** Lane Scheimer; **Tiny/Crumbs/Chump/Okey:** Howard Morris; **Jan/Coral/Miss Casserole:** Jane Webb

### ◎ MY GYM PARTNER'S A MONKEY

A clerical mistake in the spelling of his last name results in 12-year-old Adam Lyon (misspelled "Lion") being sent to Chester Darwin Middle School for zoo animals instead of Charles Arthur Middle School for humans, where he adjusts to his new environment and strange practices of his classmate and new best friend whom he meets in gym class, a hyperactive, adventurous spider monkey named Jake. Written and created by Timothy Cahill and Julie McNally Cahill and produced by Cartoon Network Studios, this half-hour comedy series, featuring an all-animal supporting cast, including Ingrid Giraffe, Lupe Toucan and a bull shark school bully, Tyson, premiered in December 2005 with a sneak peek of the pilot episode, featuring two cartoon shorts, "Inoculation Day" and "Animal Day." Regular airings of the series began in February 2006 when the series moved to a new nighttime slot at 9 P.M. On May 26, 2006, the network slated a six-episode marathon of previously aired riotous adventures along with a new episode of Jake and Ingrid wanting to go with Adam to the school dance. Through 2006, 51 episodes were produced, with Jake and company starring in a feature-length 90-minute made-for-TV movie in January 2007 entitled *The Big Field Trip. A Cartoon Network Studios Production. Color. Half-hour. Premiered on CAR: December 26, 2005 ("sneak preview"); February 20, 2006 (series).*

**Voices**
Adam: Nika Futterman; **Jake:** Tom Kenny; **Additional Voices:** Grey DeLisle, Maurice LaMarche, Phil LaMarr, Rick Gomez, Brian Doyle-Murray, Cree Summer

### ◎ MY LIFE AS A TEENAGE ROBOT

Even robots want to have fun as a 16-year-old super-powered, super-sensitive, six-foot-tall female android XJ-9 (also known as Jenny), created by a mom-and-dad team of mad scientists, proves when she decides to attend high school to be like other teens her age and hang out at the mall with her friends, Brad and Tuck, instead of protecting Earth from disaster and outerwordly villains as she was designed to do. Based on Rob Renzetti's cartoon short *My Neighbor Is a Teenage Robot* for Nickelodeon's *Oh Yeah! Cartoons* anthology series, this weekly half-hour science fiction comedy series, comprised of two cartoon shorts each half-hour, was first broadcast on Nickelodeon in August 2003. Two years later, in August 2005, a feature-length made-for-TV movie entitled *Escape from Cluster Prime* (based on the series) was produced for Nickelodeon and nominated for a 2006 Emmy Award for outstanding animated program (for programming one hour or less). *A Frederator Inc./Nicktoons Production. Color. One-hour. Premiered on NICK: August 1, 2003.*

**Voices**
Jenny: Janice Kawaye; **Brad:** Chad Doreck; **Sheldon Lee/Don Prima:** Quinton Flynn; **Tuck:** Audrey Wasilewski; **Mrs. Wakeman/Jantrice/Ptreza:** Candi Milo; **Mezmer:** Victor Brandt; **Tiff Krust:** Cree Summer; **Brit Krust:** Moira Quirk; **Queen Vexus:** Eartha Kitt; **Additional Voices:** Grey DeLisle, Ogie Banks III, Jason Marsden, Neil Ross, Kevin Michael Richardson, Tom Kenny, Carlos Alazraqui, Bob Joles, Billy West, Daran Norris, Pat Pinney, Wally Wingert, Nick Jameson, Aaron Anthony Tamasta, Tony

Masa, Kath Soucie, John Kassir, Jocelyn Blue, Roger Rose, S. Scott Bullock, Steven Jay Blum, Michael Gough, Bruce Campbell

### ⊚ MY LITTLE PONY 'N FRIENDS

Pastel-colored, talking ponies that possess magical powers help three children—the only people on Earth to know of the existence of the fairy-tale region called Ponyland—overcome the villainy of the evil Stratadons in this first-run fantasy adventure series produced in 1986 and based on Hasbro Toys' "My Little Pony" toy line. Featured on each 30-minute program were two seven-minute "My Little Pony" adventures along with one seven-minute segment of "The Glo Friends," "Potato Head Kids" or "Moondreamers," which alternated as the series' third cartoon segment. Some episodes originated from the 1985 "pilot" TV special, *My Little Pony: Escape from Catrina*. The series spawned the 90-minute theatrical feature, *My Little Pony: The Movie*, also released in 1986. A *Marvel Production in association with Sunbow-Wildstar/Starwild/Hasbro-Claster. Color. Half-hour. Premiered: September 15, 1986–1990. Syndicated. Rebroadcast on DIS: 1992–95.*

### Voices

Charlie Adler, Michael Bell, Sue Blue, Bettina, Nancy Cartwright, Peter Cullen, Jeanine Elias, Ian Freid, Linda Gary, Susie Garbo, Ellen Gerstell, Melanie Gaffin, Scott Grimes, Skip Hinnant, Keri Houlihan, Christina Lang, Jody Lambert, Katie Leigh, Sherry Lynn, Kellie Martin, Ken Mars, Ann Marie McEvoy, David Mendenhall, Scott Menville, Brecken Meyer, Laura Mooney, Sarah Partridge, Andrew Potter, Russi Taylor, B.J. Ward, Jill Wayne, Frank Welker; Bunny Andrews, William Callaway, Adam Carl, Phillip Clarke, Danny Cooksey, Peter Cullen, Jennifer Darling, Marshall Efron, Pat Fraley, Elizabeth Lyn Fraser, Liz Georges, Robert Ito, Renae Jacobs, Robin Kaufman, Danny Mann, Tress MacNeille, Terry McGovern, Michael Mish, Clive Revill, Stu Rosen, Neil Ross, Ken Sansom, Rick Segal, Judy Strangis, Lennie Weinrib, Charlie Wolfe, Ted Zeigler

### ⊚ MY LITTLE PONY TALES

The "My Little Pony" characters featured in the popular syndicated series *My Little Pony 'N Friends* starred in this new half-hour series (minus the The Glo-Friends, Moondreamers and Potato Head Kids characters) in newly filmed adventures, combined with repeated episodes, for Disney Channel. A *Graz Entertainment/ Wildstar/Starwild/Sunbow Pro-duction. Color. Half-hour. Premiered on DIS: February 28, 1993. Rebroadcast on DIS: April 1, 1996–May 28, 1997.*

### Voices

Briggata Dau, Laura Harris, Willow Johnson, Lalainia Lindbherg, Shane Meier, Maggie O'Hara, Kate Robbins, Tony Sampson, Kelly Sheridan, Brad Swaile, Venus Terzo, Chiara Zanni

### ⊚ MY PET MONSTER

Whimsical tale of a young boy (Max) who longs for a best friend and finds one in the form of a furry stuffed animal who is transformed into a lovable six-foot monster in this series from the creators of TV's *Care Bears*, which bowed on ABC. A *Nelvana Limited/Those Characters From Cleveland/Telefilm Canada Production. Color. Half-hour. Premiered on ABC: September 12, 1987–September 3, 1988.*

### Voices

**Max:** Sunny Bensen Thrasher; **Chuckie:** Stuart Stone; **Monster:** Jeff McGibbon; **Jill:** Alyson Court; **Beastur:** Dan Hennessey; **Mr. Hinkle:** Colin Fox; **Princess:** Tracey Moore; **Ame:** Tara Charandoff

*A young boy named Max (left) finds a best friend in the form of a furry stuffed animal transformed into a six-foot monster in* My Pet Monster. *© Nelvana Limited*

### ⊚ MYSTERIOUS CITIES OF GOLD

Led by young Esteban, the children of the Sun search for the cities of gold, crossing unchartered territory and discovering the unknown in this 39-episode, half-hour adventure series that aired daily on Nickelodeon, beginning in 1986, opposite *Belle and Sebastian* and *DangerMouse*.

All episodes of the series were untitled, and voices are uncredited. *An MK Company Production. Color. Half-hour. Premiered on NICK: June 30, 1986–June 29, 1990.*

### ⊚ MYTHIC WARRIORS: GUARDIANS OF THE LEGEND

Teenager Hermes narrates this modern retelling of some of the greatest heroic stories of all time, featuring the mythical gods of Mount Olympus, based on the best-selling Children's Choice award-winning paperback series by Laura Geringer and illustrated by Peter Bolinger, and produced as a half-hour Saturday morning action/adventure series for CBS. Enjoying a two-season run with 13 episodes per season, the action-packed cartoon show was originally set to debut in September 1998, but its premiere had to be pushed to November as a result of animation production problems. A *Nelvana Limited/Marathon/Hong Guang Animation (Su Zhou) Co. Ltd./France 3 Production. Color. Half-hour. Premiered on CBS: November 7, 1998–September 9, 2000.*

### Voices

**Hermes/Narrator:** James Blendick; **Hercules:** Lawrence Bayne; **Antonius:** Juan Chioran; **Castor:** Rod Wilson; **Pollux:** Paul Essiembre; **Andromeda:** Caroly Larson; **Perseus:** Robin Dunne; **Cassiopeia:** Shannon Lawson; **Hera:** Janet-Lane Green; **Ulysses:** Roger Honeywell; **Medusa:** Jennifer Dale; **Jason:** David Orth; **Chiron:** Ron Lea; **Hades:** Norm Spencer; **Persephone:** Lenore Zann; **Apollo:** Jesse Collins; **Zeus:** Gary Krawford; **Daedalus/King Midas:** Ben Campbell; **Icarus:** Amos Crawley; **Athena:** Lally Cadeau; **Circe:** Torri Higginson; **Atalanta:** Natalie Brown; **Aphrodite:** Wendy Lands; **Prometheus:** Jonathan Potts; **Pandora:** Terri Hawkes; **Bellerophon:** Greg Spottswood; **Theseus:** Paul Haddad; **Penelope:** Julie Lemieux; **Cadmus:** Philip De Wilde; **Europa:** Reagan Pasternak; **Medea:** Sally Chaill; **Damon:** Jeremy Harris; **Pythias:** Lyon Smith; **Actaeon:** Michael Hall; **Phaeton:** Rob Stefaniuk; **Androcles:** Robert Tinkler

## ◎ NARUTO

Feared and detested by the villagers of the hidden leaf village of Konoha, Naruto Uzumaki, a young and hardworking but clumsy and rebellious ninja-in-training, must learn to conceal his special powers and inner demon in order to become a respected master ninja in his village in this international sensation, first shown on Japanese television in 2002 and for the first time in English on Cartoon Network's highly rated *Toonami* Saturday prime time action block in September 2005. Making its U.S. debut on September 10 at 9 P.M., the half-hour animé series, which already had a tremendous underground following in the U.S. on DVD, was the first of 52 episodes Cartoon Network acquired, based on the popular manga series created by Masahi Kishimoto.

Quickly becoming a phenomenon on U.S. television, with impressive double-digit ratings since its premiere, to ring in 2006 Cartoon Network celebrated New Year's Eve 2005 with an eight-hour marathon, featuring 17 consecutive episodes and a new episode, beginning at 2:30 P.M. (EST). The show's second season kicked off on Saturday, April 16, 2006, with a recap of the first 25 episodes, with new half-hours airing directly after them on Saturday nights. Since its first-season debut, the series has become one of *Toonami's* highest-rated programs, delivering a 20 percent increase in ratings among boys ages nine to 14; 15 percent among kids ages six to 11; and 33 percent among kids ages nine to 14 overall. Beginning June 12, 2006, while continuing to air Saturday nights on *Toonami*, the hit Japanese series joined Cartoon Network's prime-time weekday strip, airing Monday through Thursdays at 9 P.M. *A Studio Pierrot/Viz Media/STUDIOPOLIS/ShoPro Entertainment Production. Color. Half-hour. Premiered on CAR: September 10, 2005.*

### Voices

**Naruto Uzumaki:** Maile Flanagan; **Zabuza Momochi:** Steven Jay Blum; **Asuma Sarutobi:** Doug Erholtz; **Iruka:** Quinton Flynn; **Ebisu:** Crispin Freeman; **Shikamaru Nara:** Tom Gibis; **Sakura Haruno:** Kate Higgins; **Third Hokage:** Steve Kramer; **Sasuke:** Yuri Lowenthal; **Ino Yamanaka/Konohamaru:** Colleen O'Shaughnessey; **Mizuki:** Michael Reisz; **Chouji Akimichi:** Robbie Rist; **Tsunade:** Cindy Robinson; **Hinata Hyuuga:** Stephanie Sheh; **Gatou:** Fred Tatasciore; **Tazuna:** Kirk Thorton; **Kakashi Hatake:** Dave Wittenberg

## ◎ NASCAR RACERS

Spawned by the success of the two-hour movie special that aired on FOX in 1999, featuring three half-hour episodes, good guy racers Team Fastex (Megan Fassler, Steve Sharp, Mark McCutchen and Carlos Rey) burn up the race track in their ultra-high-tech, souped-up race cars to defeat their evil nemesis, Team Rexcor (Lyle Owens, Hondo Hines, Diesel Spitz and Zorina) in high-speed, futuristic competition in Motor City in this Saturday-morning cartoon series spin-off. Launched with merchandise tie-ins that included a companion Hasbro video game, the half-hour series debuted on FOX in February 2000 and was simultaneously broadcast on FOX's sister cable network, FOX Family Channel. Lasting three seasons on FOX, 20 half-hour adventures were produced with the series airing both weekends and weekday afternoons. In the second season, several new characters were added, including Redline, Tanker, Grim Repo and Octane. After its first run, the series reaired sporadically in its entirety on the newly christened ABC Family (formerly FOX Family Channel) from September 2002 through August 2006. *A Saban Entertainment/Saban International Production. Color. Half-hour. Premiered on FOX: February 5, 2000–August 12, 2000; October 20, 2000–March 23, 2002. Premiered on FOX FAM: February 5, 2000–December 23, 2000; October 28, 2000–March 24, 2001. Rebroadcast on ABC FAM: September 14, 2002–August 27, 2006.*

### Voices

**Megan "Spitfire" Fassler:** Kathleen Barr; **Mark "Charger" McCutchen:** Ian James Corlett; **Steve "Flyer" Sharp:** Roger R. Cross; **Miles McCutchen:** Andrew Francis; **Garner Rexton:** Ron Halder; **Redline:** Kirby Morrow; **Specks:** Richard Newman; **Carlos "Stunts" Rey:** Rino Romano; **Duck Dunaka/Mike Hauger:** Dale Wilson

## ◎ NBC COMICS

In 1950 NBC made broadcast history with this series of newspaper-strip adventures that featured strip-art panels filmed sequentially in exciting three-minute adventures comprising this 15-minute program, becoming the first made-for-TV network cartoon program. Actually syndicated in 1949 as *Tele-Comics*, the black-and-white series originally presented serialized adventures of "Brother Goose," "Joey and Jug," "Rick Rack Secret Agent" and "Su Lah."

When NBC picked up the series, four new characters were added appearing in stories of their own. They were: "Danny March," hired by the mayor as his personal detective to stop crime; "Kid Champion," a boxing story about a youth (Eddie Hale) who refuses to talk about his past; "Space Barton," who blasts off to Mars in a rocketship built by Professor Dinehart, an astronomer, and his brother Jackie; and "Johnny and Mr. Do-Right," the exploits of a young boy and his dog.

Once the program finished its network run, it was again syndicated under the title of *Tele-Comics*. The cartoons were never titled. *A Vallee Video Production. Black-and-white. Fifteen minutes. Syndicated: 1949 (as Tele-Comics). Premiered on NBC: September 18, 1950–March 30, 1951 (as NBC Comics).*

### Voices

Bob Bruce, Pat McGeeham, Howard McNear, Lurene Tuttle

## ◎ NED'S NEWT

A hyperactive boy's self-made superhero is a 500-pound pet salamander named Newton, created by overfeeding him, who shrinks down to four inches at the most inopportune time, usually when trouble strikes, in this half-hour comedy series airing Saturday mornings on FOX Network. *A Nelvana Entertainment/TMO-Loonland Film GmbH Production. Color. Half-hour. Premiered on FOX: February 7, 1998–December 31, 1999.*

### Voices

**Ned Flemkin:** Tracey Moore; **Newton:** Harland Williams, Ron Pardo; **Sharon Flemkin/Ned's Mom:** Carolyn Scott; **Eric Flemkin/Ned's Dad:** Peter Keleghan; **Linda Bliss:** Tracey Ryan; **Renfrew/Doogle Pluck:** Colin O'Meara; **The Usual Guy:** Jim Millington

## ◎ NELVANAMATION

Totonto-based Nelvana Entertainment, producers of the hit *Care Bears* motion picture and television series, produced this popular anthology series of six half-hour animated specials—*A Cosmic Christmas* (1977), *The Devil and Daniel Mouse* (1978), *Romie-O and Julie-8* (1979), *Intergalactic Thanksgiving* (1979), *Easter Fever* (1980) and *Take Me Up to the Ballgame* (1980)—broadcast in syndication beginning in 1977. (See individual titles under Animated Television Specials for further details.) *A Nelvana/CBC Production for Viacom Television. Color. Half-hour. Premiered: 1977–90. Syndicated.*

## ⊚ THE NEVERENDING STORY

Bastian Balthazar travels to the magical world of Fantasia to renew fond friendships and confront formidable foes in adventures that take him across curious landscapes, including the Goab Desert of Colors, the floating metropolis of the Silver City, the desolate Swamps of Sadness, the darkest corners of Spook City and the uncharted depths in the Sea of Mist, in this half-hour animated children's series based on Michael Ende's bestselling classic novel, which aired Saturday mornings on HBO. *A Nelvana Limited/CineVox Filmproduktion GmbH & Co. TV KG/Ellipse Animation/The Family Channel, Canada/Pro Sieben, Germany/Canal France/Channel 4 and Nickelodeon, UK Production. Color. Half-hour. Premiered on HBO: December 2, 1995–January 25, 1997. Rebroadcast on HBO FAM: December 11, 1996–August 22, 2005.*

### Voices

**Bastian:** Christopher Bell; **Barktroll:** Richard Binsley; **Barney:** Geoffrey Barnes; **Laroe Head:** Colin Fox; **Falkor:** Howard Jerome; **Engywook:** Wayne Robson

## ⊚ THE NEW ADVENTURES OF BATMAN

The Caped Crusader and Boy Wonder face new dangers in these half-hour animated segments voiced by TV's original Batman and Robin, actors Adam West and Burt Ward. They are joined in their crime-fighting adventures by Batgirl and their prankish mascot, Bat-Mite, in 16 action-packed episodes broadcast Saturday mornings on CBS in 1977. Episodes from the series were later repeated on *The Batman/Tarzan Adventure Hour, Tarzan and the Super 7,* and *Batman and the Super 7.* (See individual series for details.) *A Filmation Associates Production. Color. Half-hour. Premiered on CBS: February 10, 1977–September 10, 1977.*

### Voices

**Bruce Wayne/Batman:** Adam West; **Dick Grayson/Robin:** Burt Ward; **Barbara Gordon/Batgirl:** Melendy Britt; **Bat-Mite:** Lennie Weinrib, Lou Scheimer

## ⊚ THE NEW ADVENTURES OF CAPTAIN PLANET

(See CAPTAIN PLANET AND THE PLANETEERS.)

## ⊚ THE NEW ADVENTURES OF FLASH GORDON

Originally brought to the screen by actor Buster Crabbe in a favorite movie matinee serial by Universal Pictures in 1936, this animated re-creation of Alex Raymond's science-fiction epic follows the universe-zapping exploits of pilot Flash Gordon, Dale Arden and Dr. Zarkov as they brave the dangers of the planet Mongo, ruled by the evil dictator Ming the Merciless, now joined by an equally merciless daughter named Aura. The 16-episode series—featuring other regulars such as the kindly Prince Barin and Queen Fria and lionlike Thun—was produced for NBC's Saturday-morning lineup in 1979 by Filmation studios, producers of TV's *The Archies, Fat Albert, Gilligan's Planet* and others. NBC canceled the series in 1980, and episodes were reedited into a two-hour feature film, *Flash Gordon: The Greatest Adventure of All,* released theatrically in Europe and broadcast as a special on NBC in August of 1982. (See entry in Animated Television Specials for details.) In 1992 the series began rerairing on the Sci-Fi Channel's *Cartoon Quest. A Filmation Associates Production in association with King Features. Color. Half-hour. Premiered on NBC: September 22, 1979–September 20, 1980. Rebroadcast on SCI: September 27, 1992–June 24, 1995.*

### Voices

**Flash Gordon/Prince Barin:** Robert Ridgely; **Ming the Merciless/Dr. Zarkov:** Alan Oppenheimer; **Aura/Fria:** Melendy Britt; **Dale:** Diane Pershing; **Thun/Voltan:** Allan Melvin, Ted Cassidy; **Gremlin:** Lou Scheimer

## ⊚ THE NEW ADVENTURES OF GIGANTOR

Young Jimmy Sparks and his jet-propelled robot again keep the world safe from destruction and despair while conquering old foes in this full-color update of the 1960s black-and-white classic. Originally produced for Japanese television in the early 1980s, the series premiered in its own time slot on the Sci-Fi Channel in 1993 and also aired as part of the network's two-hour cartoon program block (on a rotating basis), Cartoon Quest (later called Animation Station). *A Tokyo Movie Shinsha Company Production. Color. Half-hour. Premiered on SCI: September 9, 1993–June 30, 1997.*

### Voices

**Barbara Goodson:** Jimmy Sparks; **Bob Brilliant/Other Voices:** Doug Stone; **Inspector Blooper/Other Voices:** Tom Wyner

## ⊚ THE NEW ADVENTURES OF GILLIGAN

This series featured tales of the faithful charter ship S.S. *Minnow* and five dissimilar passengers who embark on a pleasure cruise and are shipwrecked on a deserted uncharted isle where they must learn survival techniques. Based on the popular TV series, this animated version starred five of the original cast members: Alan Hale, Bob Denver, Jim Backus, Natalie Schager and Russell Johnson. (Dawn Wells, who played Mary Ann, demurred.) In this animated version, Gilligan was given the first name of Willy and an adopted pet monkey named Snubby. The 24-episode series was broadcast three consecutive seasons. *A Filmation Associates Production. Color. Half-hour. Premiered on ABC: September 7, 1974–September 4, 1977. Syndicated.*

### Voices

**Willy Gilligan, bumbling first mate:** Bob Denver; **Jonas Grumby, the skipper:** Alan Hale; **Thurston Howell III, millionaire:** Jim Backus; **Lovey Howell, the millionaire's wife:** Natalie Schafer; **Roy Hinkley, the professor:** Russell Johnson; **Ginger Grant, movie actress:** Jane Webb; **Mary Ann Summers, clerk:** Jane Edwards; **Snubby:** Lou Scheimer

## ⊚ THE NEW ADVENTURES OF HE-MAN

Traveling through time from Castle Grayskull to the Triax solar system, He-Man (alias Prince Adam) and his friends defend the planet Primus from the evil deeds of Skeletor in this all-new, 65-episode animated series produced for first-run syndication. The series—the second cartoon series to be based on the He-Man character—debuted as a five-part miniseries in September 1990 before becoming a weekly series. *A Jetlag Productions/DIC Enterprises Production in association with Mattel Inc. and Parafrance Communication. Color. Half-hour. Premiered: September 17, 1990–91 (as five-part miniseries). Syndicated.*

### Voices

**He-Man/President Pell/Alcon/Sgt. Krone/Andros/Gross/Artilla:** Gary Chalk; **Skeletor/Sagitar:** Campbell Lane; **Gepple/Optikk/Quake/Kayo/Viser/Hydron/Werban:** Don Brown; **Mara/The Sorceress:** Venus Terzo; **Drissi:** Tracy Eisner; **Flipshot/Krex/B.H./Captain Zang:** Scott McNeil; **Caz:** Mark Hildreth; **Wall Street/Meldoc/Hoove/Prince Adam:** Doug Parker; **Flogg/Tuskador:** Alvin Sanders; **Gleep/Slushead/Karatti/Staghorn/Spinwit:** Ted Cole; **Sebrian:** Anthony Holland; **General Nifel:** Mike Donovan

### THE NEW ADVENTURES OF HUCK FINN

Mark Twain's immortal characters Huck Finn, Tom Sawyer and Becky Thatcher, fleeing Injun Joe, are engulfed in a whirling sea in this live-action/animated series with superimposed animated backgrounds. The 20-episode series lasted only one season on NBC. A Hanna-Barbera Production. Color. Half-hour. Premiered on NBC: September 15, 1968–September 7, 1969. Rebroadcast on BOOM: October 20, 2001–December 28, 2004.

**Cast (live action)**
**Huck Finn:** Michael Shea; **Tom Sawyer:** Kevin Schultz; **Becky Thatcher:** Lu Ann Haslam; **Injun Joe:** Ted Cassidy; **Mrs. Thatcher\*:** Dorothy Tennant; **Aunt Polly\*:** Anne Bellamy

**Voices**
Daws Butler, Bill Beckly, Julie Bennett, Danny Bravo, Ted Cassidy, Henry corden, Dennis Day, Ted DeCorsia, Bernard Fox, Paul Frees, Jack Kruschen, Charles Lane, Keye Luke, Dayton Lummis, Don Messick, Marvin Miller, John Myhers, Jay Novello, Vic Perrin, Mike Road, Abraham Sofaer, Joe Sirola, Hal Smith, Paul Stewart, Janet Waldo, Peggy Webber, Than Wyenn

### THE NEW ADVENTURES OF MADELINE

In this Saturday-morning series narrated by actor Christopher Plummer), which premiered on ABC in 1995, the French pixie schoolgirl and her boarding school classmates, each dressed in identical yellow uniforms and white gloves, cavort around Paris, experiencing new whimsical adventures (including trading pranks with Madeline's best friend, Pepito, at a nearby boys' school). The "new" half-hour series was the offspring of the highly successful animated series *Madeline*, which aired on The Family Channel beginning in 1993 and was based on the stories by children's author Ludwig Bemelman. The producers moved the series to ABC in 1995, producing 13 new episodes. After it failed to draw young viewers (and landed at the bottom of the Saturday-morning rating heap), ABC dropped the series that October, replacing it with reruns of *The New Adventures of Winnie the Pooh*, which originally aired on ABC from 1988 to 1993. Despite the show's poor ratings, it was nominated for a daytime Emmy in 1996 for outstanding animated children's program.

In April 1998, reruns began airing on Toon Disney, and on the Disney Channel in October 2000. A DIC Entertainment Production. Color. Half-hour. Premiered on ABC: September 9, 1995–October 21, 1995. Rebroadcast on TDIS: April 18, 1998–September 11, 2005; January 15, 2007–. Rebroadcast on DIS: October 29, 2000–August 25, 2005.

**Voices**
**Madeline:** Tracey-Lee Smyth; **Miss Clavel/Genevieve:** Louise Vallance; **Chloe:** Vanessa King; **Danielle:** Kelly Sheridan; **Nicole:** Kristin Fairlie; **Pepito:** A.J. Bond; **Narrator:** Christopher Plummer

### THE NEW ADVENTURES OF MIGHTY MOUSE AND HECKLE AND JECKLE

Two of Terry-Toons' most famous characters from the 1940s and 1950s returned in new animated adventures in this series revival, which was first broadcast on CBS in an hour-long format in 1979, then trimmed to a half-hour for its second and final season. In these updated stories, Heckle and Jeckle still find ways to get into trouble, while Mighty Mouse defends mice everywhere and pro-

tects his girlfriend, Pearl Pureheart, from the evil clutches of his archenemy, Oil Can Harry, and his sidekick, Swifty. Two Mighty Mouse cartoons were featured on the show in serialized form, plus one self-contained adventure, along with two short Heckle and Jeckle adventures. Mighty Mouse also appeared in 30-second environmental bulletins cautioning youngsters on wasting resources and littering. Another series component was "Quackula," a vampire mallard who terrorizes his landlord and others. A Filmation Associates Production. Color. One hour. Half-hour. Premiered on CBS: September 8, 1979–August 30, 1980. Rebroadcast on CBS: September 6, 1980–September 12, 1982.

**Voices**
**Mighty Mouse:** Alan Oppenheimer; **Pearl Pureheart, his girlfriend:** Diane Pershing; **Oil Can Harry, the villain:** Alan Oppenheimer; **Heckle/Jeckle/Quackula:** Frank Welker; **Theodore H. Bear:** Norm Prescott

### THE NEW ADVENTURES OF PINOCCHIO

Wooden boy Pinocchio and his creator/mentor Geppetto are featured in 130 modernized five-minute adventures—actually "chapters" that formed a series of five-chapter 25-minute episodes—in this half-hour color series, based on Carlo Collodi's world-renowned characters. The naive puppet is exposed to contemporary subjects, such as beatniks and greedy movie producers. Filmed in the stop-motion animation technique called "Animagic" (a laborious single-frame process using puppetlike figures to animate a complete story), the series was produced by Arthur Rankin Jr. and Jules Bass, heads of Canada's Videocrafts International (later renamed Rankin-Bass Productions), who produced many perennial holiday specials, including *Rudolph the Red-Nosed Reindeer* and *Jack Frost*. Initially the series aired in syndication from 1960 to 1961 on local TV afternoon kiddie shows, hosted by a local on-air personality, before stations ran the show by itself. A Videocraft International Production. Color. Half-hour. Syndicated: 1960–1961.

**Voices**
**Geppetto:** Larry Mann; **Foxy Q. Fibble:** Stan Francis; **Other Voices:** Joan Fowler, Jack Mather, Paul Kligman, Claude Ray

### THE NEW ADVENTURES OF SPEED RACER

Speed Racer, his perky girlfriend, Trixie, best friend Sparky, Speed's brother Spridle, the mischievous monkey Chim Chim and Pops Racer return in this modified, half-hour syndicated version of the 1967 original. Speed Racer travels through time from tropical jungles to futuristic sites in the souped-up Special Formula Mach 5. MTV began airing the 52 episodes of the original *Speed Racer* series prior to the arrival of the new short-lived syndicated version. A Fred Wolf Films/Speed Racer Entertainment/ Murikami-Wolf-Swenson/Group W Production. Color. Half-hour. Premiered: 1993. Syndicated.

### THE NEW ADVENTURES OF SUPERMAN

Mild-mannered *Daily Planet* reporter Clark Kent, alias Superman, whose only weakness is kryptonite, frustrates criminal activities in Metropolis and elsewhere in the first Saturday-morning cartoon series ever produced by Filmation studios. Added to CBS's Saturday morning lineup in 1966, the series—brought on by CBS program executive Fred Silverman to compete with ABC's highly successful *The Beatles* cartoon series—scored the highest ratings shares in the history of Saturday-morning network television at that time. The weekly half-hour series was comprised of two six-

---

\* This character appeared only in the series' first episode.

minute "Superman" cartoons, sandwiched between one six-minute episode of "The Adventures of Superboy," chronicling Superman's youth in the town of Smallville, U.S.A., and featuring Krypto, Superboy's superdog. The series was one of six superhero cartoon programs scheduled back to back on Saturday mornings when it first premiered. Adventures later aired as part of *The Superman/Aquaman Hour* and *The Batman/Superman Hour*. (See individual entries for details.) CBS rebroadcast the series in its entirety during the 1969–70 season before it was canceled. *A Filmation Associates Production. Color. Half-hour. Premiered on CBS: September 10, 1966–September 2, 1967. Rebroadcast on CBS: September 13, 1969–September 5, 1970.*

**Voices**

**Clark Kent/Superman:** Bud Collyer; **Lois Lane:** Joan Alexander; **Superboy:** Bob Hastings; **Narrator:** Jackson Beck

#### ◎ THE NEW ADVENTURES OF TINTIN

The globe-trotting, 16-year-old Belgian journalist, who works for an unnamed newspaper, and his faithful fox terrier, Snowy, invaded U.S. television in this Indiana Jones-styled, fast-moving, 'round-the-world adventure series—with Tintin in hot pursuit of a story—based on 10 of 24 comic books by Tintin creator Herge (pen name of the late Belgian artist Georges Remi), a European favorite among children and young adults since 1929. The Canadian produced series premiered on HBO in 1991, producing high ratings. *An Nelvana Entertainment/Ellipse Animation Production. Color. Half-hour. Premiered on HBO: December 19, 1991–December 29, 2000.*

**Voices**

**Tintin:** Colin O'Meara; **Haddock:** David Fox; **Calculus:** Wayne Robson; **Thompson:** John Stocker; **Thomson:** Dan Hennessey; **Snowy:** Susan Roman; **Castafiore:** Maureen Forrester; **Nestor:** Vernon Chapman

#### ◎ THE NEW ADVENTURES OF VOLTRON

(See VOLTRON: DEFENDER OF THE UNIVERSE.)

#### ◎ THE NEW ADVENTURES OF WINNIE THE POOH

The unforgettably charming characters of A.A. Milne's "Pooh" stories, who live in the imagination of young Christopher Robin, come to life in these joyful escapades filled with laughter and whimsy. The program marked the first time that a classic Disney character was seen on Saturday-morning television. The series was in production for over a year before its network premiere, producing 25 half-hours for the first season (most Saturday morning shows average between 13 and 17 in a single season), which consisted of either two 11-minute episodes or one 22-minute story. Prior to its network run, the series enjoyed a brief run on the Disney Channel in 1988.

In the fall of 1989, the series was merged with *Disney's Adventures of the Gummi Bears* in all-new episodes in a new one-hour show called *Disney's Gummi Bears/Winnie the Pooh Hour*. (See series entry for details.) The following season *The New Adventures of Winnie Pooh* returned, back as a half-hour series, on ABC, featuring new episodes along with old ones. The well-received series was winner of two Emmy Awards in the outstanding animated program category. *A Walt Disney Television Animation Production. Color. Half-hour. Premiered on DIS: 1988. Rebroadcast on ABC: September 10, 1988–September 2, 1989; September 7, 1990–September 4, 1993.*

**Voices**

**Winnie the Pooh:** Jim Cummings; **Christopher Robin:** Tim Hoskins; **Tigger:** Paul Winchell, Jim Cummings; **Eeyore:** Peter Cullen, Stan Ross; **Piglet:** John Fiedler; **Rabbit:** Ken Samson; **Gopher:** Jackie Gonneau, Michael Gough; **Roo:** Chuck McCann, Nicholas Melody; **Kanga:** Laura Mooney, Nicholas Omana, Patty Parris **Owl:** Hal Smith

#### ◎ THE NEW ARCHIES

The classic characters of Riverdale High—Archie, Jughead, Reggie, Betty and Veronica—meet new challenges with limitless imagination, dream big dreams and create havoc, this time as a group of nine-year-olds, with friendship always prevailing in spite of their efforts to outdo one another in 26 classic adventures. The series debuted on NBC in 1987 and ran for two seasons. *A DIC Enterprises Production in association with Saban Productions. Color. Half-hour. Premiered on NBC: September 12, 1987–September 3, 1988. Rebroadcast on NBC: November 12, 1988–February 4, 1989. Rebroadcast on FAM: 1992–93. Rebroadcast on TDIS: April 1998–September 1, 2003.*

**Voices**

**Archie:** J. Michael Roncetti; **Eugene:** Colin Waterman; **Jughead:** Michael Fantini; **Amani:** Karen Burthwright; **Reggie:** Sunny Bensen Thrasher; **Betty:** Lisa Coristine; **Veronica:** Allyson Court; **Big Ethel:** Jazzman Lausanne; **Coach:** Greg Swanson; **Miss Grundy:** Linda Sorensen; **Mr. Weatherbee:** Marvin Goldhar

#### ◎ THE NEW ARCHIE/SABRINA HOUR

Taking two of its most prized properties, Filmation Studios produced this hour-long comedy series combining 13 previously broadcast episodes of Archie and the Riverdale High School gang from *The Archie Comedy Hour* and of Sabrina, the teenage witch from 1971's *Sabrina, the Teenage Witch* series, plus another animated segment called "Surprise Package."

In November 1977, following poor ratings, NBC yanked the series off the air and put in its place a new, improved version, *Archie's Bang-Shang Lalapalooza Show*. Unfortunately, the show fared no better than the former series since it was opposite CBS's 90-minute version of *The Bugs Bunny/Road Runner Show*, which dominated its time slot. (See *The Archie Comedy Hour* and *Sabrina, the Teenage Witch* for voice credits.) *A Filmation Associatess Production. Color. Half-hour. Premiered on CBS: September 10, 1977–November 5, 1977.*

#### ◎ THE NEW BATMAN/SUPERMAN ADVENTURES

The famed comic-book superheroes shared the spotlight in this hour-long series for the WB Television Network's Kids' WB! featuring all-new cartoon adventures. In the new Batman adventures, Bruce Wayne (alias Batman) adopts 13-year-old waif Tim Drake, who becomes the new Robin, joined by Batgirl and occasionally the old Robin (now known as Nightwing) as they fight crime in Gotham City. The Superman adventures followed the Man of Steel's attempt to foil some formidable old adversaries—Lex Luthor, Mr. Mxyzptlk, Braniac, to name a few. *A Warner Bros. Television Animation Production. Color. One hour. Premiered on the WB (Kids' WB!): September 13, 1997–September 8, 2000.*

**Voices**

**Clark Kent/Superman/Bizarro:** Tim Daly; **Lois Lane:** Dana Delany; **Perry White:** George Dzundza; **Jimmy Olsen:** David Kaufman; **Jonathan Kent:** Mike Farrell; **Martha Kent:** Shelley Fabares; **Jor-El:** Christopher McDonald; **Lauren Tom:** Angela

Chen; **Prof. Hamilton:** Victor Brandt; **Brainiac:** Corey Burton; **Corben/Metallo:** Malcolm McDowell; **Darkseid:** Michael Ironside; **Lana Lang:** Joely Fisher, Kelly Schmidt; **Lex Luthor:** Clancy Brown; **Livewire:** Lori Petty; **Mercy Graves:** Lisa Edelstein; **Rudy/The Parasite:** Jim Belushi, Brion James; **Bruno Mannheim:** Bruce Weitz; **Bibbo:** Brad Garrett; **Supergirl:** Nicholle Tom; **The Toyman:** Bud Cort; **Sqweek:** David L. Lander; **Gnaww:** Don Harvey; **Mr. Mxyzptlk:** Gilbert Gottfried; **Dan Turpin:** Joseph Bologna; **Maggie Sawyer:** Joanna Cassidy

## ◎ THE NEW CASPER CARTOON SHOW

First appearing in his own theatrical cartoon series in the 1940s and 1950s for Paramount's Famous Studios, this friendly ghost, who frightened away those he hoped would be his friends, was the star of this half-hour program for Saturday mornings featuring all-new seven-minute Casper cartoons (including supporting cast members Nightmare the Galloping Ghost, Wendy the Good Little Witch and the Ghostly Trio) as well as several Paramount/Famous theatrical cartoons originally released to theaters between 1959 and 1962. Twenty-six half-hour programs were made, each consisting of three cartoons. Airing six seasons on ABC, the series was briefly retitled *The New Adventures of Casper* before ending its network run and entering syndication. Animator Seymour Kneitel, who directed most of the Paramount Casper theatrical cartoons, directed the series. *A Harvey Films Production in association with Famous Studios. Color. Half-hour. Premiered on ABC: October 5, 1963–January 30, 1970.*

*Voices*
**Casper:** Ginny Tyler

## ◎ THE NEW FANTASTIC FOUR

Three transformable humans—the stretchable Mr. Fantastic; his wife, Sue (also known as the Invisible Girl); and the rocklike being The Thing—are joined by a wise-cracking computer, HER-B (Humanoid Electronic Robot "B" model), in 13 half-hour adventures based on the Fantastic Four comic-book series in which they encounter weird machines and villains. *A DePatie-Freleng Production in association with Marvel Comics Group. Color. Half-hour. Premiered on NBC: September 9, 1978–September 1, 1979.*

*Voices*
**Mr. Fantastic:** Mike Road; **Invisible Girl:** Ginny Tyler; **The Thing:** Ted Cassidy; **HER-B the robot:** Frank Welker; **Dr. Doom:** John Stephenson

## ◎ THE NEW FRED AND BARNEY SHOW

America's favorite prehistoric families, the Flintstones and the Rubbles, returned in this half-hour program for Saturday mornings that included 13 original *Flintstones* episodes redubbed for broadcast. Pebbles and Bamm-Bamm were back in the fold as well, but as infants. Henry Corden had assumed the voice of Fred Flintstone, replacing Alan Reed, who died in 1977. The series was later rebroadcast on USA Network's Cartoon Express programming block. *A Hanna-Barbera Production. Color. Half-hour. Premiered on NBC: February 3, 1979–September 15, 1979. Rebroadcast on USA: March 13, 1989–April 21, 1992.*

*Voices*
**Fred Flintstone:** Henry Corden; **Wilma Flintstone, his wife:** Jean VanderPyl; **Barney Rubble, their neighbor:** Mel Blanc; **Betty Rubble, his wife:** Gay Autterson; **Pebbles:** Jean VanderPyl; **Bamm-Bamm:** Don Messick; **George Slate, Fred's boss:** John Stephenson

## ◎ NEW KIDS ON THE BLOCK

The New Kids on the Block (Donnie Wahlberg, Jordan Knight, Joe McIntyre and Danny Wood), the 1990's rhythm 'n' blues teen-singing sensations, starred in this weekly animated series that combined MTV-like, live concert footage segues with animated adventures (voiced by other actors) in which the Kids go on a tour and try to have fun like normal kids and still make it to each concert on time. Each half-hour animated story was punctuated by their popular music. *A DIC Enterprises Production in association with Big Step/Dick Scott Enterprises. Color. Half-hour. Premiered on ABC: September 8, 1990–August 31, 1991. Rebroadcast on DIS: 1992.*

*Cast (live action)*
**Donnie Wahlberg:** Himself; **Joe McIntyre:** Himself; **Danny Wood:** Himself; **Jordan Knight:** Himself; **Jonathan Knight:** Himself

*Voices*
**Donnie Wahlberg:** David Coburn; **Joe McIntyre:** Scott Menville; **Danny Wood:** Brian Mitchell; **Jordan Knight:** Loren Lester; **Jonathan Knight:** Matt Mixer; **Dick Scott, their manager:** Dave Fennoy; **Bizcut, their bodyguard:** J.D. Hall; **Nikko, Jonathan's dog:** David Coburn

## ◎ THE NEW PINK PANTHER SHOW

The happy-go-lucky cat and his pantomimic ways provided the entertainment in this half-hour children's series for NBC consisting of *Pink Panther*, *The Inspector* and *The Ant and the Aardvark* cartoons, each originally released as theatrical cartoon shorts. (See individual entries in Theatrical Sound Cartoon Series section for details.) Additional network shows followed, among them *The Pink Panther Laugh and a Half Hour and a Half Show*, *Think Pink Panther!* and *The All-New Pink Panther Show*. *A DePatie-Freleng Enterprises Production. Color. Half-hour. Premiered on NBC: September 11, 1971–September 4, 1976.*

## ◎ THE NEW SCOOBY AND SCRAPPY-DOO SHOW

Huge, lumbering Great Dane Scooby-Doo acts his way out of scary situations—doing almost any daring act for a Scooby snack—with the help of his pal Shaggy, fiesty nephew Scrappy-Doo and Daphne (who returns to the series), whose predicaments as an investigative reporter propel the foursome into trouble in a 12th season of 13 new half-hours with two episodes broadcast on ABC. *A Hanna-Barbera Production. Color. Half-hour. Premiered on ABC: January 21, 1984–September 1, 1984. Syndicated. Rebroadcast on USA: September 1989–September 1994. Rebroadcast on TBS/TNT: Fall 1994–98. Rebroadcast on CAR: Fall 1994–.*

## ◎ THE NEW SCOOBY-DOO MOVIES

This one-hour cartoon format starred the bashful canine and his pals who are joined weekly by celebrity guests, such as the Three Stooges, Phyllis Diller, Don Knotts, Jonathan Winters, Laurel and Hardy, the Addams Family and Sonny and Cher, all in animated form. The series premiered on CBS in September of 1972 with the opening episode, "The Ghastly Ghost Town," featuring animated characterizations of the Three Stooges.

Sixteen original shows were produced for the 1972–73 season. Featured were an entertaining collection of movies, including two comedy movies with Don Knotts: "Guess Who's Coming to Dinner?" and "The Spooky Fog"; three Scooby-Doo mystery movies: "The Dynamic Scooby-Doo Affair," "Scooby Doo Meets Laurel and Hardy" and "Scooby-Doo Meets the Addams Family," as well as Phyllis Diller as a guest voice in "A Good Medium Is Rare,"

Sandy Duncan in "Sandy Duncan's Jekyll and Hydes" and even Sonny and Cher, as themselves, in "The Secret of the Shark Island." Other first season stories included: "The Frickert Fracas" (with Jonathan Winters), "The Phantom of the Country Music Hall" (with country singer/actor Jerry Reed), "The Ghostly Creep from the Deep" (with the Harlem Globetrotters), "Ghost of the Red Baron" (featuring the second appearance of the Three Stooges), "The Loch Ness Mess," "The Haunted Horseman In Hagglethorn Hall" (starring Davey Jones of The Monkees) and "The Caped Crusader Caper" (with Batman and Robin).

ABC renewed the series for a second season but produced only eight new hour-long installments for the 1973–74 season, combined with repeat episodes from the first season. The stories featured mostly Hanna-Barbera cartoon characters and a few celebrities in their own comedy movies. Comedian Tim Conway, of *McHale's Navy* fame, was the featured voice in "The Spirited Spooked Sports Show." Don Adams, agent 86 from TV's *Get Smart*, starred in "The Exterminator." Singer Cass Elliot of the Momas and the Poppas was an unlikely guest voice in "The Haunted Candy Factory."

The five remaining comedy movies for that season all featured Hanna-Barbera characters in starring roles: "The Haunted Showboat" (with Josie and the Pussycats), "Mystery of Haunted Island" (with the Harlem Globetrotters from *The Harlem Globetrotters* series), "Scooby-Doo Meets Jeannie" (with Jeannie and Babu from Hanna-Barbera's animated *Jeannie* series), "The Weird Winds of Winona" (with Speedy Buggy) and "Scooby-Doo Meets Dick Van Dyke."

ABC canceled the series following the second season. Subsequently, after being offered in syndication, the show was rerun on USA Network, TBS and TNT and later Cartoon Network. Beginning on Saturday, June 3, 2000, at 11 A.M., Cartoon Network's Boomerang rebroadcast episodes of the classic cartoon series until October 2005. *A Hanna-Barbera Production. Color. One hour. Premiered on CBS: September 9, 1972–August 31, 1974. Syndicated: 1980s. Rebroadcast on USA: 1989–Fall 1994. Rebroadcast on TBS/TNT: Fall 1994–98. Rebroadcast on CAR: December 26, 1994–December 30, 1994; February 28, 1995–September 3, 1995 (Tuesdays, Thursdays, Sundays); October 23, 1995–October 27, 1995; October 12, 1996–October 11, 1997 (Saturdays); October 13, 1997 (weekdays). Rebroadcast on BOOM: June 3, 2000–October 29, 2005.*

**Voices**
**Scooby-Doo:** Don Messick; **Freddy:** Frank Welker; **Daphne:** Heather North; **Shaggy:** Casey Kasem; **Velma:** Nicole Jaffe

### ⓔ THE NEW SCOOBY-DOO MYSTERIES

Scooby-Doo, Scrappy-Doo, Shaggy and Daphne uncover clues to a series of new mysteries in this half-hour program (and 13th season of Scooby-Doo programs overall) produced for Saturday-morning television. Former cast members Freddy Jones and Velma Dinkley made guest star appearances in several episodes, though they were not series regulars. The season opener was a two-part celebration of Scooby's 15th birthday and a retrospective of his life. Besides reairing the series, the two-part episode "The Nutcracker Scoob" was rebroadcast on USA Network in 1991 as a Christmas special. Reruns later aired on Cartoon Network and Boomerang. *A Hanna-Barbera Production. Color. Half-hour. Premiered on ABC: September 9, 1984–August 31, 1985. Rebroadcast on USA: 1989–Fall 1994. Rebroadcast on TBS/TNT: Fall 1994–98. Rebroadcast on CAR: December 21, 1994–December 23, 1994; August 16, 1997 (Saturdays, Sundays). Rebroadcast on BOOM: December 3, 2001–. Syndicated.*

*Al Capp's lovable comic-strip character shows the comical side of his psychic character in the Saturday morning series* The New Shmoo. *© Hanna-Barbera Productions*

**Voices**
**Scooby-Doo/Scrappy-Doo:** Don Messick; **Freddy Jones:** Frank Welker; **Shaggy Rogers:** Casey Kasem; **Daphne Blake:** Heather North; **Velma Dace Dinkley:** Maria Frumkin

### ⓔ THE NEW SHMOO

Al Capp's lovable and trusting comic-strip character uses its ability to change into virtually anything to help three young reporters—Mickey, Nita and Billy Joe—who work for "Mighty Mysteries Comics" and investigate cases of psychic phenomena in this NBC Saturday-morning series. Within three months of its debut in 1979, the series was retooled into the 90-minute extravaganza, *Fred and Barney Meet the Shmoo*, featuring repeat episodes from two previously broadcast Hanna-Barbera cartoon shows: 1979's *The New Fred and Barney Show* and *The Thing*, of Marvel Comics' fame (from 1979's *Fred and Barney Meet the Thing*), both of which originally aired on NBC. *A Hanna-Barbera Production. Color. Half-hour. Premiered on NBC: September 22, 1979–December 1, 1979.*

**Voices**
**Shmoo:** Frank Welker; **Nita:** Dolores Cantu-Primo; **Billy Joe:** Chuck McCann; **Mickey:** Bill Idelson

### ⓔ NEW TALES FROM THE CRYPTKEEPER

Popular comic-book ghoul the Cryptkeeper returns to host this second animated anthology series featuring more hair-raising spooky tales, spun off from the 1990s Saturday-morning cartoon series for ABC, *Tales from the Cryptkeeper*. Produced five years later, the weekly spin-off picked up where the original ABC series left off, with more morality-based tales emphasizing stronger values for children. Canadian animation studio Nelvana, which produced the ABC series, was contracted to produce 13 new half-hour episodes for the new series—at a reported cost of more than $400,000 per episode—that joined the CBS fall Saturday morning schedule in October 1999. John Kassir, the voice of the Cryptkeeper in the original ABC cartoon series, returned to voice the character for the new series. *An EC/Tales from the Crypt Holdings Inc./Nelvana Production. Color. Half-hour. Premiered on CBS: October 2, 1999–September 9, 2000.*

**Voices**
**Cryptkeeper:** John Kassir; **Vaultkeeper:** Dan Hennessey

## ◎ THE NEW THREE STOOGES

Moe Howard, Larry Fine and Curly-Joe DeRita (the fourth comedian to play the "third Stooge" in the long-running comedy act) starred in this series, which combined live-action wraparounds and animated segments to tell one complete story. The cartoons reflected the Stooges' style and humor yet in a less violent manner. Only 40 live-action openings and endings were filmed for this series. (The live segments were rotated throughout the package's 156 cartoon episodes.) Dick Brown, who produced such animated favorites as *Clutch Cargo* and *Space Angel*, produced the series in association with Normandy III Productions (the Stooges' own company, named after their producer/agent, Norman Maurer). *A Cambria Studios Production in association with Normandy/Heritage III. Color. Half-hour. Premiered: December 20, 1965. Syndicated.*

### Cast (live action)
**Moe:** Moe Howard; **Larry:** Larry Fine; **Curly-Joe:** Joe DeRita

### Other Actors
Emil Sitka, Peggy Brown/Margaret Kerry, Emil Sitka, Harold Brauer, Jeffrey Maurer (later Jeffrey Scott), Cary Brown, Tina Brown, Eileen Brown, Ned Lefebvre

**Voices**
**The Three Stooges:** Themselves

## ◎ NIGHTMARE NED

Ned Needlemeyer, a sensitive, solitary eight-year-old boy, who has a rather banal existence—at home, at school and with his family—finds adventure when he drifts off into dreamland, entering a world filled with a host of nutty nocturnal visitors and other nightmarish events, in this half-hour cartoon series, which debuted on ABC.

Brad Garrett, best known for his later work on CBS's long-running hit sitcom *Everybody Loves Raymond*, provided the voice of the character's dad. *A Walt Disney Television Animation Production. Color. Half-hour. Premiered on ABC: April 19, 1997–August 30, 1997.*

**Voices**
**Ned Needlemeyer:** Courtland Mead; **Dad Needlemeyer:** Brad Garrett; **Mom Needlemeyer:** Victoria Jackson.

## ◎ NODDY

Stop-motion animated adventures of a little wooden boy, Noddy, and his friends, including Big Ears the rabbit, who reside in the cozy confines of Toyland's finest toy store; based on Britain's legendary children's book series by Enid Blyton published from 1949 to 1963 and first produced as a series of animated shorts in 1975 by British animators Brian Cosgrove and Mark Hall through their company, Stop Frame Productions. This 65-episode half-hour

series, along with one-hour Christmas special entitled *Anything Can Happen at Christmas* (that premiered on select PBS stations in December 1998), was redubbed using Canadian actors to overcome difficulties with British dialects, with live-action segments featuring the goings-on of three child actors within the toy store bracketed around each animated adventure. Replacing the popular PBS cartoon series *The Magic School Bus*, the series bowed on U.S. PBS stations nationwide in August 1998 and aired until September 2002. In 2000, the program was nominated for a Daytime Emmy Award for outstanding achievement in costume design/styling. In 2005, a brand-new computer-animated series entitled *Make Way for Noddy*, including 100 new two-minute foreign language instructional interstitials (entitled *Say It with Noddy*), debuted on PBS's all-new 24-hour digital preschool channel, PBS Kids Sprout. *A BBC Children's International/BBC Worldwide America/TV Ontario/CBC/Cosgrove-Hall/Catalyst/Enid Blyton Production. Color. Half-hour. Premiered on PBS: October 4, 1998–September 13, 2002.*

### Cast (live-action)
**Noah:** Sean McCann; **Kate:** Katie Boland; **Truman:** Max Morrow; **Daniel Johnson (D.J.):** Kyle Kassardjian; **Aunt Agatha Flugelschmidt:** Jayne Eastwood; **Mrs. Skittles:** Teryl Rothbery; **Noah Tomtem, Kate's Grandpa:** Sean McCann; **Bud Topper:** Neil Crone; **Carl Spiffy:** Dan Redican; **Boobull:** Gil Filar; **Island Princess:** Alyson Court; **Truman Tomten:** Max Morrow

**Voices**
**Noddy:** Denise Bryer; **Gertie Gator:** Taborah Johnson

## ◎ THE NOOZLES

Twelve-year-old Sandy discovers that Blinky, her favorite stuffed animal, actually becomes a live koala whenever she rubs noses with him. Together they journey magically throughout the universe in search of fun and excitement in this 26-episode half-hour series that debuted weekday afternoons on Nickelodeon Nick Jr.'s in 1988. *A Saban International Services Production in association with Fuji Eight Company. Color. Half-hour. Premiered on NICK: November 8, 1988–April 2, 1993.*

## ◎ THE NUTTY SQUIRRELS

Television's forerunners to Ross Bagdasarian's *Alvin and the Chipmunks*, this animated series boasted the exploits of another recording group, The Nutty Squirrels, who beat Alvin, Theodore, Simon and David Seville to television screens by one full year. Established jazzman Don Elliot and TV composer Alexander "Sascha" Burland made up this musical twosome, which recorded their own speeded-up songs, featuring Chipmunk-like voices for Hanover-Signature records (of which comedian Steve Allen was part owner). The pair's first song, "Uh-Oh!" recorded as a single, ranked number 14 in the "Hit Parade" for the week of December 28, 1959, nearly one year after the Chipmunks' "Chipmunk Song" made the same list. Transfilm-Wilde, which specialized in producing animated television commercials, brought the rights to the Nutty Squirrel characters and produced this half-hour series, consisting of 100 five-minute "Nutty Squirrel" cartoons that premiered in syndication in the fall of 1960. *A Transfilm/Wilde Production. Color. Half-hour. Syndicated: Fall 1960.*

## ◎ OBAN STAR-RACERS

Set in the year 2082, Earth's fastest racing team—including rebellious teenager Molly and her teammates Rick Thunderbolt, Jordan, Stan and Koji—competes in the the Greatest Race of Oban, enjoying a series of thrilling galactic adventures in this French/

*Twelve-year-old Sandy brings her favorite stuffed koala bear, Blinky, to life by rubbing noses in the Nickelodeon cartoon series* Noozles. © Saban International. All rights reserved.

Japanese-produced English-dubbed animated series created by Savin Yeatman-Eiffel. The half-hour series aired with an hour-long premiere on Monday, June 5, 2006, during the *Jetix* action/adventure block on Toon Disney at 8:30 P.M., with encore airings on Friday, June 9 at 8:00 P.M. and Saturday, June 10 at 10:30 A.M. on ABC Family. Thereafter, episodes aired in regular time slots during *Jetix* on Toon Disney, Mondays at 8 P.M., and Saturdays at 10:30 A.M. on ABC Family. In late August 2006, ABC Family held a final weekend marathon that included the network premiere of a new episode entitled "Make Way," subsequently ending the *Jetix* block by the end of the month in favor of live-action programming. *A Sav! The World Production. Color. Half-hour. Premiered on TDIS: June 5, 2006. Premiered on ABC FAM: June 10, 2006–August 31, 2006.*

**Voices**
**Molly:** Chiara Zanni; **Jordan:** Sam Vincent; **Koji:** Alessandro Juliani; **Stan:** Dexter Bell; **Prince Aikka:** Kirby Morrow; **Rick:** Michael Dobson; **Avatar:** Paul Dobson; **Don Wei:** Ron Halder

### ◉ THE OBLONGS

Unusual antics abound in the life of this atypical Hill Valley family—the loving, limbless, perpetually happy-go-lucky patriarch, Bob Oblong (voiced by comedian Will Ferrell of *Saturday Night Live*), and his adoring, alcohol- and tobacco-addicted wife Pickles and their four children, the conjoined twins, Biff and Chip, their four-year-old daughter, Beth, and youngest son, Milo—each with a variety of strange physical and emotional abnormalities caused by living near a toxic industrial waste site in this animated series loosely adapted from characters in Angus Oblong's graphic novel, *Creepy Susie and 13 Other Tragic Tales for Troubled Children*, who also created the series.

Produced by Jobsite Productions and Mohawk Productions, the WB Television Network programmed this off-kilter half-hour comedy series—apparently its answer to FOX's, and television's, longest-running sitcom, *The Simpsons*—in prime time on Sunday nights opposite FOX's popular sitcom, *Malcolm in the Middle*. Premiering in April 2001, viewers didn't embrace the program or its concept of a dysfunctional nuclear family. The series was canceled six weeks later after airing only eight of its original 13 episodes. In August 2002, the program enjoyed a second life in reruns on Cartoon Network's late-night *Adult Swim* cartoon block and also reaired on TBS beginning in 2005. *An Oblong/Film Roman/Jobsite/Warner Bros. Production. Color. Half-hour. Premiered on WB: April 1, 2001–May 20, 2001. Rebroadcast on CAR: August 4, 2002–December 16, 2006. Rebroadcast on TBS: 2005.*

**Voices**
**Bob Oblong:** Will Ferrell; **Pickles Oblong:** Jean Smart; **Biff Oblong:** Randy Sklar; **Chip Oblong:** Jason Sklar; **Milo:** Pamela Segall Adlon; **Beth Oblong/Susie/Mikey:** Jeanne Elias; **Helga Fugley:** Lea DeLaria; **Peggy/Pristine Klimer/Debbie Klimer:** Becky Thyre; **George Klimer/James/Anita Bider:** Billy West

### ◉ O CANADA

One of the world's top producers of innovative animation, the National Film Board of Canada produced this weekly anthology of outstanding Canadian-animated shorts from the 1950s to the present, many of them Oscar winners and nominees and representing all styles of animation. The series opener featured the Oscar-winning cartoon short, "Bob's Birthday," about a dentist who is none too happy about turning 40. The half-hour series premiered on Cartoon Network.

*A National Film Board of Canada Production. Color. Half-hour. Premiered on CAR: January 8, 1997.*

### ◉ THE ODDBALL COUPLE

Adapted from Neil Simon's Broadway and Hollywood film hit and long-running TV series, which mismatched sloppy Oscar Madison and fastidious Felix Unger, this animated spin-off casts the perfectionist cat Spiffy (Unger) and the troublesome dog Fleabag (Madison) in equally funny situations as reporters at large in 16 half-hour episodes, produced for this Saturday-morning series, which originally aired on ABC. *A DePatie-Freleng Enterprises Production. Color. Half-hour. Premiered on ABC: September 6, 1975–September 3, 1977.*

**Voices**
**Spiffy:** Frank Nelson; **Fleabag:** Paul Winchell; **Goldie, the secretary:** Joan Gerber

### ◉ OFF TO SEE THE WIZARD

Legendary animators Chuck Jones and Abe Levitow produced and directed animated buffers and wraparounds featuring familiar characters from the 1939 MGM classic *The Wizard of Oz* as "hosts" of this hour-long prime-time series. The series served as an umbrella for 26 live-action properties, including first-run specials and television series pilots. Debuting on ABC in 1967, opposite CBS's *The Wild Wild West* and NBC's *Tarzan*, the Friday-night series lost the ratings battle and was canceled. *An MGM Television Production. Color. One hour. Premiered on ABC: September 8, 1967–September 20, 1968.*

## ◎ O'GRADY

Quirky adventures of four self-absorbed high school teenagers—Kevin, Abby, Beth and Harold—in the not-so-normal town of O'Grady, examining their daily trials and tribulations in dealing with friendships, boy-girl relationships, school activities and, above all else, "weirdness," an inexplicable phenomenon that afflicts the townspeople in strange ways, in this animated comedy series billed as a cross between *Friends* and *The Twilight Zone*—the first original animated series: for the digital cable network, The N. Debuted in July 2004, a second season of episodes began airing in March 2006.

Scripted with characters mimicking the real-life conversation style of typical teens, using slang phrases like "omigod," "totally" and others, Massachusetts-based Soup2Nuts animation studios, known for its work on such popular series as *Dr. Katz, Professional Therapist* and *Home Movies*, produced and animated this light-hearted half-hour comedy created by Tom Snyder and Carl Adams, whose style visually resembled its predecessors. Conan O'Brien and *Saturday Night Live*'s Amy Poehler lent their voices as a star-crossed couple—Chip, a gangly, red-haired lifeguard and Wendy a concession stand worker—caught up in the town's ongoing "weirdness" in the second season's opening episode, "Frenched." Other guest stars in the six-episode season included *Arrested Development*'s Will Arnett and David Cross, *Saturday Night Live*'s Rachel Dratch, *The Daily Show*'s Rob Corddry and comedian Sam Seder, with Kelly Osbourne singing the show's theme song. A *Soup2Nuts Production. Color. Half-hour. Premiered on The N: July 30, 2004–May 13, 2005; March 3, 2006–April 24, 2006.*

### Voices
**Kevin:** H. Jon Benjamin; **Abby:** Melissa Bardin Galsky; **Beth:** Holly Schlesinger; **Harold:** Patrice O'Neal

## ◎ OH YEAH! CARTOONS

After forming and heading his own animation studio, Frederator Inc., former Hanna-Barbera CEO Fred Seibert created the concept for this proposed animated anthology series that became Nickelodeon's runner-up to Cartoon Network's acclaimed *World Premiere Toons*, and its eventual successor, *What a Cartoon!*

Premiering on Nickelodeon in July 1998, the half-hour series, offering the work of 17 animators, turned into one of television's biggest development deals. During its first season, the series introduced 39 seven-minute cartoons packaged into 13 half-hour episodes, and 99 seven-minute cartoons with 54 characters altogether during its three-season run. Besides introducing many pilot episodes of proposed animated series, the ambitious production resulted in three cartoons being spun-off into their own dedicated half-hour three-season runs: *Rudy and Snap*, adapted into *Chalk-Zone*; *The Fairly OddParents* and *My Life as a Teenage Robot*, formerly known as *My Neighbor Is a Teenage Robot*. For the show's second season in 1999, Kenan Thompson of the popular Nickelodeon live-action children's series *Kenan and Kel* served as the show's host. A *Frederator Inc. Production. Color. Half-hour. Premiered on NICK: July 19, 1998–June 1, 2001. Rebroadcast on NICKT: May 2002–.*

## ◎ ONCE UPON A TIME . . . THE AMERICAS

The fabulous story of the American continent—the first Americans, the pioneer explorers, England and the 13 colonies, Cortez and the Aztec Indians, the Inca Empire and others—is chronicled in this historical half-hour series that debuted on The History Channel. The series was the first of three *Once Upon a Time . . .* anthology series originally produced for French television. A *Procidis Production. Color. Half-hour. Premiered on HIS: January 7, 1995.*

## ◎ ONCE UPON A TIME . . . THE DISCOVERERS

The stories of the great inventions and the illustrious sages who revolutionized the world, from yesterday's famed elders Aristotle, Archimedes, Ptolemy and Hero to modern-day discoverers Leonardo da Vinci, Alexander Graham Bell, Thomas Edison and Albert Einstein, are presented in this well-animated 26 episode half-hour historical series—the second of three—first produced for French television by producer Albert Barille. The series premiered in the United States on The History Channel. A *Procidis Production. Color. Half-hour. Premiered on HIS: April 8, 1995.*

## ◎ ONCE UPON A TIME . . . MAN

The primary focus of this French-produced historical half-hour cartoon series, originally made for French television, is the history of man from his earliest origins. It is on the members of one family (led by Peter, an ordinary man, and his beautiful wife, Pierrette) in different historical settings facing the problems of everyday existence. This third and final edition of French producer Albert Barille's *Once Upon a Time . . .* historical series debuted in the United States on The History Channel in 1996. A *Procidis Production. Color. Half-hour. Premiered on HIS: January 6, 1996.*

## ◎ ONE PIECE

Long dreaming of becoming the greatest pirate in the world, young Monkey D. Luffy, endowed with rubber-like stretching powers, and his crew of skilled fighters, Roronoa Zolo, Nami and Usopp, set out to recover an infamous piece of lost treasure—"Once Piece"—that once belonged to the now-executed pirate king, Gold Roger, so Monkey can become the so-called King of the Pirates, in this Japanese-imported anime series, based on the fourth-highest-selling manga in Japanese history and Japan's most popular and third-best-selling Shōnen Jump title.

Premiering in the United States in the fall of 2004 in the 9:30 A.M. time slot with the episode "I'm Gonna Be King of the Pirates!" the half-hour fantasy/adventure series, redubbed in English by 4Kids Entertainment, joined FOX's Saturday-morning *FOX Box* four-hour children's programming block that became known as the 4Kids TV in January 2005 and included such popular animated series as *Teenage Mutant Ninja Turtles, Winx Club, Mew Mew Power, Shaman King, Sonic X* and *The Incredible Crash Dummies*. Forty-eight action-packed adventures were broadcast through August 2005, with an additional 36 new episodes airing through March 2007. In April 2005, Cartoon Network added the popular anime series in reruns to its Saturday night *Toonami* action/anime block with 18 new episodes, beginning with *The Mermen*, debuting back-to-back at 10 P.M. and 10:30 P.M. in April 2005. A *Toei Animation/Fuji TV/4Kids Entertainment Production. Color. Half-hour. Premiered on FOX: September 18, 2004. Premiered on CAR: April 23, 2005.*

### Voices
**Monkey D. Luffy:** Erica Schroeder; **Roronoa Zolo:** Dan Green; **Nami:** Kerry Williams; **Usopp:** Jason Griffith; **Koby:** Kayzie Rogers; **Kid Luffy:** Tara Jayne; **Merry:** Ted Lewis, **Pepper:** Pete Zarustica; **Nico Robin/Ms. Sunday:** Veronica Taylor; **Helmeppo:** Sean Schemmel; **Don Kreig:** Marc Thompson; **Sanji:** David Moo; **Narrator:** Eric Stuart; **Additional Voices:** Frederick B. Owens

## ◎ OSCAR'S ORCHESTRA

British animator Tony Collingwood teamed up with actor/comedian Dudley Moore to develop this series about a young music impressario (Oscar) who, with the help of instruments that come to life, presents examples of classical music by the world's legendary composers, including Bach, Mozart, Beethoven, Tchaikovsky, Brahms and many others, interwoven into each week's adventure. Based on an original idea by Jan Younghusband, the series, originally produced in 1996, was first syndicated in the United States in 1997. *A Warner Music Vision and Europe Images/Tony Collingwood/Rubberneck Television Production in association with Lacey Entertainment and The Summit Media Group. Color. Half-hour. Premiered: September 13, 1997. Syndicated.*

**Voices**
**Oscar:** Dudley Moore; **Thadius Vent/Tank:** Colin McFarlane; **Rebecca:** Elly Fairman; **Mr. Crotchet:** Michael Kilgarriff; **Lucius:** Murray Melvin; **Narrator:** David DeKyser; **Eric:** Eric Meyers; **Monty:** John Baddeley; **Trevor/Lewis:** Steven Lander; **Goodtooth:** Sean Barrett; **Sylvia:** Eve Karpf

## ◎ THE OSMONDS

Featuring the voices of the famed brother singing group, the Osmonds and their talking dog, Fugi, embark on a worldwide tour as goodwill ambassadors. This weekly half-hour Saturday-morning series produced for ABC took them to a different country each week. Only 17 half-hour adventures were produced, each originally telecast during the show's first season in 1972–73. The series was canceled in September of 1974. *A Rankin-Bass Production. Color. Half-hour. Premiered on ABC: September 9, 1972–September 1, 1974.*

**Voices**
**Allen Osmond:** Himself; **Jay Osmond:** Himself; **Jimmy Osmond:** Himself; **Donny Osmond:** Himself; **Merrill Osmond:** Himself; **Wayne Osmond:** Himself; **Fugi, the dog:** Paul Frees

## ◎ OSWALD

A large whimsical blue octopus, Oswald, is joined by his apartment-dwelling friends—Henry the penguin, Katrina the baby caterpillar, Madame Butterfly, and his pet dachshund, Weenie—as they embark on exciting adventures in the Big City in this animated children's series, based on characters created by author Dan Yaccarin and coproduced by Nickelodeon and United Kingdom's HIT Entertainment for Nickelodeon's Nick Jr. and CBS's *Nick Jr. on CBS* Saturday-morning cartoon block. First broadcast on Nickelodeon in August 2001 and on CBS that September, 26 episodes were produced, including the first-season holiday-themed episode, "Catrina's First Snow"/"The Snow Festival," which was canceled after one season. Since April 2003 scheduled weekday afternoons at 4:30 P.M. (ET), the children's series has reaired on the commercial-free children's program network, Noggin. *An HIT Entertainment/PLC/Nicktoons Production. Color. Half-hour. Premiered on NICK: August 20, 2001–September 19, 2003. Premiered on CBS: September 15, 2001–September 7, 2002. Rebroadcast on NOG: April 7, 2003– .*

**Voices**
**Oswald:** Fred Savage; **Henry:** David Lander; **Weenie/Katrina:** Debi Derryberry; **Daisy:** Crystal Scales; **Madame Butterfly/Cactus Polly:** Laraine Newman; **Johnny Snowman:** Mel Winkler; **The Egg Twins: Eggbert:** Daran Norris, **Leo:** J. Grant Albrecht; **Pongo:** Richard King; **Sammy Starfish:** Tony Orlando; **Steve Tree:** Fred Stoller; **Andy:** Eddie Deezen; **Bingette Bunny:** Kathy Najimy; **Other Voices:** Mac Davis, Michael McKean

## ◎ OUTLAW STAR

Aboard their highly advanced, faster-than-light prototype spacecraft, renamed *Outlaw Star*, and picking up more crew members along the way, a pair of space outlaws, Gene Starwind and hacker partner Jim Hawking, joined by their onboard android, Melfina, battle space pirates in their quest to locate the Galactic Leyline in this futuristic cartoon series loosely based on the Japanese manga by Takehiko Ito. Edited and redubbed in English by Bandai Entertainment and ZRO Limit Productions, the 26-episode half-hour anime series aired in the United States on Cartoon Network. *A ZRO Limit/Animaze/Sunrise Inc./Sotsu Agency/Bandai Entertainment Inc. Production. Color. Half-hour. Premiered on CAR: July 16, 2000–February 1, 2001. Rebroadcast on CAR: July 16, 2001–October 9, 2001; December 3, 2001–January 11, 2005.*

**Voices**
**Gene Starwind:** Robert Wicks; **Melfina:** Ruby Marlowe, Emily Brown; **Gilliam:** G. Gordon Baer; **James "Jim" Hawking:** Ian Hawk; **Twilight Suzuka/Kei Pirate:** Wendee Lee; **Lady Aisha Clanclan:** Zn; **Fred Lou:** Michael McConnohie; **Henry Williams:** Steve Cannon; **Swanzo:** Chip Nickey; **Tao Master:** Mike D'Gord; **Hilda:** Melissa Williamson; **Horace:** Simon Isaacson; **Iris:** Reba West; **Lord Hazanka:** Abe Lasser; **Gwynn Con:** Ethan Murray; **Clyde Murterdale:** Sparky Thornton; **Narrator:** Beau Billingslea

## ◎ OZZY & DRIX

Further adventures of the problem-solving white blood cell cop, Osmosis "Ozzy" Jones, and his partner Drix, the over-the-counter cold pill, as they fight to maintain order and the health and vitality of the body of 13-year-old teen, Hector Cruz, in which they live, in this animated series inspired by the characters in Warner Bros.'s live-action/animated full-length feature *Osmosis Jones* (2001). The half-hour comedy/adventure joined the WB Television Network's Kids' WB! Saturday-morning lineup in September 2002, becoming a popular mainstay for two seasons. In June 2004, the WB added the program to its weekday afternoon schedule, where it aired until its final broadcast that July. In October of that year, Cartoon Network began airing the inventive half-hour series on weekday nights.

During the 2003–04 season, *Ozzy & Drix* ranked as the number-one broadcast series in its 9:30 A.M. time slot with kids ages two to 11 and ages six to 11, and ranked second with boys ages two to 11. The buddy-cop comedy also placed second overall among boys ages six to 11, tying with Nickelodeon's *The Fairly OddParents.* The Warner Bros. Television Animation-produced series likewise earned three Daytime Emmy Award nominations, including two in 2003 for outstanding achievement in sound editing–live action and animation and outstanding special class animated program, and one in 2004 for outstanding special class animated program. *A Warner Bros. Television Animation Production. Color. Half-hour. Premiered on the WB (Kids' WB!): September 14, 2002–July 5, 2004. Rebroadcast on CAR: October 2004– .*

**Voices**
**Osmosis "Ozzy" Jones:** Phil LaMarr; **Drix:** Jeff Bennett; **Mayor Spryman:** Alanna Ubach; **Police Chief Gluteus:** Jim Cummings; **Maria Amino:** Tasia Valenza; **Ellen Patella:** Vivica Fox; **Hector Cruz:** Justin Crowden

## ◎ THE PAC-MAN/LITTLE RASCALS/RICHIE RICH SHOW

The popular video game character starred in this hour-long series that featured more episodes of Pakky, in combination with new premiere episodes of "The Little Rascals" and new episodes of *Richie Rich.* The series aired back to back with the first season run of *The Pac-Man Show* on ABC in 1982 and lasted one full season. In 1983 ABC brought the series back but split its components—

*Pac Man and The Little Rascals/Richie Rich Show*—into two separate time slots. *A Hanna-Barbera Production. Color. One hour. Premiered on ABC: September 5, 1982–September 3, 1983.*

**Voices**

**PAC-MAN:** Pac-Man: Marty Ingels; **Ms. Pepper Pac-Man:** Barbara Minkus; **Baby Pac:** Russi Taylor; **Chomp Chomp:** Frank Welker; **Sour Puss:** Peter Cullen; **Mezmaron:** Alan Lurie; **Clyde Monster:** Neilson Ross; **Blinky/Pinky Monsters:** Chuck McCann; **Inky Monster:** Barry Gordon

**THE LITTLE RASCALS:** Spanky: Scott Menville; **Alfalfa/Porky/Woim:** Julie McWhirter Dees; **Darla:** Patt Maloney; **Buckwheat:** Shavar Ross; **Butch/Waldo:** B.J. Ward; **Officer Ed/Pete the Pup:** Peter Cullen

**RICHIE RICH:** Richie Rich: Sparky Marcus; **Mrs. Rich/Irona:** Joan Gerber; **Reggie Van Goh:** Dick Beals; **Professor Keenbean:** Bill Callaway; **Gloria:** Nancy Cartwright; **Mr. Rich/Cadbury:** Stanley Jones; **Dollar:** Frank Welker

## ◎ THE PAC-MAN/RUBIK THE AMAZING CUBE HOUR

Pac-Man, Ms. Pac, Baby Pac and the rest of the Pac-Land gang returned in all-new adventures in this hour-long fantasy/adventure series that provided equal time to its costar, Rubik, the Amazing Cube, which made its Saturday-morning television debut. Rubik is discovered by a young boy (Carlos), who brings the colorful cube to life—after he aligns all the cube's sides—and sets out on a magical adventure tour along with his brother and sister, Renaldo and Lisa. (The series was rebroadcast in the spring of 1985 as a mid season replacement.) Hanna-Barbera Productions (Pac-Man) and Ruby-Spears Enterprises (Rubik) coproduced the series. *A Hanna-Barbera and Ruby-Spears Enterprises Production. Color. One hour. Premiered on ABC: September 10, 1983–September 1, 1984.*

**Voices**

**Pac-Man:** Marty Ingels; **Ms. Pac:** Barbara Minkus; **Baby Pac:** Russi Taylor; **Super-Pac:** Lorenzo Music; **Pac-Junior:** Darryl Hickman; **Chomp Chomp:** Frank Welker; **Sour Puss:** Peter Cullen; **Mezmaron:** Alan Lurie; **Sue Monster:** Susan Silo; **Inky Monster:** Barry Gordon; **Clyde Monster:** Neilson Ross; **Rubik:** Ron Palillo; **Carlos:** Michael Saucedo; **Renaldo, his brother:** Michael Bell; **Lisa, his sister:** Jennifer Fajardo; **Ruby Rodriguez:** Michael Bell; **Marla Rodriguez:** Angela Moya

## ◎ THE PAC-MAN SHOW

The immensely popular video game character starred in this half-hour series, along with his wife, Ms. Pac, a peppery liberated lady; the energetic Baby Pac; Chomp Chomp, a lovable dog; and Sour Puss, their sly cat, in fantasy adventures that took place in Pac-Land, a pretty pastel world composed of brightly glowing dots. Their perfect world had one enemy, however: the ever-sinister Mezmaron, who tried to rob the Power Pellet Forest of the power pellets Pac-Land thrives on. (His attempts were always bungled by his comical ghost monsters, Inky, Blinky, Pinky, Clyde and Sue.)

In 1983 the series was rebroadcast in combination with Ruby-Spears Enterprises' *Rubik The Amazing Cube* as *The Pac-Man/Rubik/The Amazing Cube Hour.* Several new characters were added during the second season to the Pac-Man cartoons: Pac-Junior, Pac-Man's fast-talking, free-wheeling cousin, and Super-Pac, a vain and powerful superhero. *A Hanna-Barbera Production. Color. Half-hour. Premiered on ABC: September 25, 1982–September 3,* 1983. *Rebroadcast on ABC: September 10, 1983–September 1, 1984 (as The Pac-Man/Rubik/The Amazing Cube Hour). Rebroadcast on USA: February 26, 1989–March 20, 1992. Rebroadcast on CAR: February 18, 1995–February 19, 1995 (Look What We Found!).*

**Voices**

**Pac-Man:** Marty Ingels; **Ms. Pac:** Barbara Minkus; **Baby Pac:** Russi Taylor; **Super-Pac:** Lorenzo Music; **Pac-Junior:** Darryl Hickman; **Chomp Chomp:** Frank Welker; **Sour Puss:** Peter Cullen; **Mezmaron:** Alan Lurie; **Sue Monster:** Susan Silo; **Inky Monster:** Barry Gordon; **Blinky/Pinky Monsters:** Chuck McCann; **Clyde Monster:** Neilson Ross

## ◎ PADDINGTON BEAR (1981)

Author Michael Bond's childlike honeybear who can talk was cast in this short-lived series produced by London's preeminent model animation studio, FilmFair Animation, for public television based on chapters from Bond's popular children's books, including his first, *A Bear Called Paddington.* Oscar-winning entertainer Joel Grey introduced each program, featuring five vignettes that blends stop-action animation of a stuffed bear and flat, cut-out figures to tell each story. Between 1985 and 1986, three additional half-hour specials were also produced: "Paddington's Birthday Bonanza," "Paddington Goes to the Movies" and "Paddington Goes to School." Each aired on The Disney Channel. *A FilmFair Animation/Paddington & Co. Ltd. Production. Color. Half-hour. Premiered on PBS: April 13, 1981–May 18, 1981.*

**Voices**
**Narrator/Others:** Michael Hordern

## ◎ PADDINGTON BEAR (1989)

The Brown family discovered a lost little bear at London's Paddington Station, whom they named Paddington and raised as their child in this half-hour animated adaptation of the storybook favorite. The program was broadcast on Sunday mornings as part of *The Funtastic World of Hanna-Barbera. A Hanna-Barbera Production. Color. Half-hour. Premiered: September 1989.*

**Voices**

**Paddington Bear:** Charlie Adler; **Mr. Brown:** John Standing; **Mrs. Brown:** B.J. Ward; **Jonathan Brown, their son:** Cody Everett; **Judy Brown, their daughter:** Katie Johnson; **Mrs. Bird, their housekeeper:** Georgia Brown; **David Russell, the Browns' cousin:** R.J. Williams; **Mr. Gruber, an antique dealer:** Hamilton Camp; **Mr. Curry, the Browns' neighbor:** Tim Curry

## ◎ PANDAMONIUM

Three talking panda bears (Algernon, Chesty and Timothy) and their teenage human friends (Peter Darrow and his sister, Peggy) embarked to find the lost pieces of the magical, mystical Pyramid of Power in this 13-episode half-hour fantasy/adventure series, co-created by Fred Silverman, who also served as one of the series' executive producers. The series originally aired on CBS. *A Marvel Production in association with InterMedia Entertainment. Color. Half-hour. Premiered on CBS: September 18, 1982–September 10, 1985.*

**Voices**

**Algernon:** Walker Edmiston; **Chesty:** Jesse White; **Timothy:** Cliff Norton; **Peter Darrow:** Neilson Ross; **Peggy, his sister:** Katie Leigh; **Amanda Panda:** Julie McWhirter Dees; **Moondraggor:** William Woodson

## ◎ PAPA BEAVER'S STORY TIME

These half-hour weekday series cartoon re-creations of clever fables and wondrous children's stories of French author Pere Castor recounted tales of sacrifice, bravery and redemption. They debuted on Nickelodeon's Nick daytime preschool block in 1995. *An M5 Production. Color. Half-hour. Premiered on NICK: May 18, 1995–December 31, 1997.*

### Voices
**Papa Beaver:** Walter Massey; **Granddaughter:** Pauline Little; **Grandson:** Teddy Lee Dillon; **Other Voices:** Rick Jones, Bruce Dinsmote, Kathleen Fee

## ◎ PARTRIDGE FAMILY: 2200 A.D.

Widow Connie Partridge led an interplanetary rock-and-roll group comprised of family members Keith, Laurie, Danny, Tracy and Chris in futuristic adventures on Earth and in outer space, performing their music to new audiences of every kind—alien and otherwise. A spin-off of the popular TV sitcom *The Partridge Family,* the program featured the voices of the original cast members (except Shirley Jones and David Cassidy) and reprised one of the group's most famous songs in each show. The series' 16 half-hour episodes originally aired on CBS in 1974–75 and were later syndicated as part of 1977's *Fred Flintstone and Friends. A Hanna-Barbera Production. Color. Half-hour. Premiered on CBS: September 7, 1974–March 8, 1975. Syndicated: 1977.*

### Voices
**Connie Partridge:** Joan Gerber; **Keith Partridge:** Chuck McClendon; **Laurie Partridge:** Susan Dey; **Danny Partridge:** Danny Bonaduce; **Christopher Partridge:** Brian Forster; **Tracy Partridge:** Suzanne Crough; **Reuben Kinkaid:** David Madden; **Marion:** Julie McWhirter; **Veenie:** Frank Welker

## ◎ THE PAW PAWS

The muffled patter of small tom-toms was the only clue to the whereabouts of the Paw Paws, a tribe of tiny, tenderhearted bearlets who inhabited the enchanted forest where past, present and future are blended in this half-hour fantasy/adventure series offered as part of weekend syndie package, *The Funtastic World of Hanna-Barbera* in 1985. But all was not rosy for Princess Paw Paw and her tribe, for across the river Dark Paw and his evil tribe, the Meanos, lay waiting for their next chance to conquer the peace-loving Paw Paws. The series was rebroadcast on USA Network's Cartoon Express and Cartoon Network. *A Hanna-Barbera Production. Color. Half-hour. Premiered: September 1985. Syndicated. Rebroadcast on USA: September 18, 1989–March 20, 1992. Rebroadcast on CAR: October 2, 1992–April 2, 1993 (weekdays); July 4, 1993–September 17, 1993 (Sundays); January 5, 1994–June 2, 1995–(weekdays); September 4, 1995–96 (weekdays).*

### Voices
**Princess Paw Paw:** Susan Blu; **Brave Paw:** Thom Pinto; **Mighty Paw:** Bob Ridgely; **Laughing Paw:** Stanley Stoddart; **Wise Paw:** John Ingle; **Trembly Paw:** Howard Morris; **Pupooch:** Don Messick; **Dark Paw:** Stanley Ralph Ross; **Bumble Paw:** Frank Welker; **Aunt Pruney:** Ruth Buzzi

## ◎ PB&J OTTER

Three young sibling otters (seven-year-old Peanut, his five-year-old sister Jelly and baby sister Butter) enjoy life on their customized houseboat on Lake Hoohaw, frolicking with their neighbors—families of raccoons, ducks and beavers—in this half-hour animated series created by animator Jim Jinkins (the father of *Doug*) for Disney Channel. *A Siriol Animation Ltd., Cardiff Production for S4C, Wales. Color. Half-hour. Premiered on DIS: March 14, 1998–April 8, 2005.*

### Voices
**Baby Butter Otter:** Gina Maria Tortorici; **Jelly Otter:** Jenell Brook Slack; **Peanut Otter:** Adam Rose; **Opal Otter:** Gwen Shepherd; **Ernest Otter/Murchy Beaver/Cap'n Crane/Walter Raccoon:** Chris Phillips; **Cody Pennes (Pinch Raccoon/Scootch):** Cody Pennes; **Wanda Raccoon/Shirley Duck/Georgina Snooty:** Corinne Orr; **Flick Duck/Edouard Snooty/Ootsie & Bootsie Snooty:** Eddie Korbich; **Mayor Jeff:** Bruce Bayley Johnson; **Mrs. Crane:** Jackie Hoffman; **Aunt Nanner:** Nancy Giles

## ◎ PEBBLES AND BAMM-BAMM

Barney Rubble's muscular son, Bamm-Bamm, and Fred Flintstone's gorgeous daughter, Pebbles, are young adults experiencing the tribulations of teenagers—dating, finding work and earning money—but in a prehistoric setting in this weekly 16-episode Saturday-morning cartoon series, produced for CBS.

Sally Struthers, of TV's *All in the Family* fame, was the voice of Pebbles. (She was replaced by Mickey Stevens when the character was reprised in new adventures on *The Flintstones Comedy Hour.*) Episodes later appeared on the syndicated *Fred Flintstone and Friends* in the late 1970s and in the late 1980s and 1990s were rebroadcast on USA Network's *Cartoon Express* and Cartoon Network. In May 2000 the series began airing on Boomerang. *A Hanna-Barbera Production. Color. Half-hour. Premiered on CBS: September 11, 1971–September 2, 1972. Rebroadcast on CBS: May 1973–September 1973; February 1974–September 1974; March 8, 1975–September 4, 1976. Rebroadcast on USA: March 31, 1989–May 25, 1992. Rebroadcast CAR: February 1, 1993–February 7, 1993 (including Pebbles and Bamm-Bamm Marathon); January 2, 1995–June 19, 2004 (weekdays). Rebroadcast on BOOM: May 27, 2000–.*

### Voices
**Pebbles Flintstone:** Sally Struthers; **Bamm-Bamm Rubble:** Jay North; **Moonrock:** Lennie Weinrib; **Penny:** Mitzi McCall; **Wiggy/Cindy:** Gay Hartwig; **Fabian:** Carl Esser

## ◎ PECOLA

Whether he's trying to help a postal carrier win an award or the town's fire department, a curious but hyperactive penguin named Pecola causes mischief—with good intentions, of course—in the quiet, off-kilter port of Cube Town, where everything is literally "square," including the residents, in this colorful CGI-animated children's series. Airing weekday mornings on Cartoon Network at 10:00 A.M. beginning in May 2003, the 26-episode, half-hour series, first shown on Fuji television in April 1998, was produced by Canada's Nelvana animation studios—the third production from its state-of-the-art 3-D facility in Toronto—for $5.5 million, with sales of licensed merchandise topping $68.5 million through 2003 in Japan alone. Broadcast in 30 countries, the series won second prize at the Vancouver Effects and Animation Festival (VEAF) in Canada and Special Distinction at the 2001 Annecy International Animated Film Festival in France.

Beginning in January 2007, the former Cartoon Network series was rebroadcast on the qubo's all-new 24-hour digital television network four-hour programming block, including other returning Nelvana-animated cartoon series like *Elliot Moose, Marvin the Tap-Dancing Horse* and *Rupert,* beamed on the ION network (formerly PAX-TV). *A Milkycartoon Ltd./*

*Yomiko Advertising/Nelvana Production. Color. Half-hour. Premiered on CAR: May 5, 2003–January 1, 2004. Rebroadcast on Q: January 8, 2007–.*

**Voices**
**Pecola:** Austin Di Iulio; **Robbie Rabbit:** Michael Cara; **Officer Kumada:** Len Carlson; **Aunty:** Jill Frappier; **Dark Pecola:** Ray Waters; **Hillary:** Tracy Hoyt, Jennifer Thompson; **Mr. Goat:** William Colgate; **Additional Voices:** Jason Alexander, Stephanie Beard, Richard Binsley, Donald Burda, George Buza, Neil Crone, Jake Goldsbie, Keith Hampshire, Julie Lemieux, David Marx

## ◉ PEEP AND THE BIG WIDE WORLD

A curious newly hatched baby chick named Peep and his adventurous fine-feathered friends—the young robin, Chirp, and the oldest of the three, Quack the duck, who live in a big park (also known to them as the "big wide world")—explore such childhood experiences as discovering their shadows and being afraid that the world is falling, along with the wonder and mystery of simple science and math concepts with a humorous touch in this colorfully animated half-hour educational series based on the National Film Board of Canada cartoon short by Academy Award-winning producer Kai Pindal, who created the show and served as creative producer.

Narrated by actress Joan Cusack, this innovative, interactive preschool offering, featuring two animated segments and a two-minute live-action segment demonstrating ideas discussed in the show, was produced by Boston's public broadcasting station, WGBH, and Toronto's 9 Story Entertainment for the Learning Channel's *Ready Set Learn!* 6:00 to 9:00 A.M. weekday program block, premiering in April 2004 with 26 half-hours. The program also aired weekdays, twice daily, on Discovery Kids. Nominated for three Daytime Emmy Awards, including twice in 2005 and 2006 for outstanding children's animated program and winning once for outstanding performer in an animated program (Joan Cusack), in November 2005 the popular preschool series returned on TLC and Discovery Kids for a second season of new episodes dealing with Quack's decision to save a piece of bread for a rainy day, only to learn an important lesson about how food can go bad. *A WGBH/9 Story Entertainment/Discovery Kids/TV Ontario/Alliance Atlantis Communications Production. Color. Half-hour. Premiered TLC: April 12, 2004–September 31, 2005; November 14, 2005. Premiered on DSCK: April 14, 2004–September 23, 2005; November 14, 2005. Rebroadcast on TLC: October 3, 2005–November 11, 2005. Rebroadcast on DSCK: September 26, 2005–November 11, 2005.*

**Voices**
**Narrator:** Joan Cusack; **Peep:** Scott Beaudin; **Chirp:** Amanda Soha; **Quack:** Jamie Watson

## ◉ PEPPA PIG

Colorfully animated adventures dealing with the lovable antics of cheeky but pushy little pink piglet, Peppa, who enjoys life to the fullest between romping in the garden, playing dress-up and swaddling in the mud with joy, sometimes to the consternation of her little brother George, her pleasant but oftentimes frustrated mother, Mummy Pig, and her sometimes grumpy father, Daddy Pig, with whom she lives. Produced by England's Astley Baker Davies Ltd. in association with the Contender Group, this half-hour animated children's series, made up of 52 five-minute episodes, bowed on Cartoon Network in August 2005. Winner of a 2005 British Academy of Film and Television Arts (BAFTA) preschool children's animation award, the British imported, Flash-animated series was a component of Cartoon Network's newly launched weekday preschool block, *Tickle-U*, which included such popular children's programs as *Firehouse Tales, Gerald McBoing Boing, Gordon the Garden Gnome, Harry and his Bucket Full of Dinosaurs* and *Yoko! Jakamoko! Toto!* After its initial season, the popular children's series remained on the air in reruns. *An Astley Baker Davies Ltd./Contender Entertainment Group Production. Color. Half-hour. Premiered on CAR: August 22, 2005–.*

## ◉ PERFECT HAIR FOREVER

Mentored by his wise, gray-bearded, balding Uncle Grandfather and Rod, the Anime God, young Gerald Bald Z overcomes his untimely baldness by traveling to strange and mystic lands in search of "perfect hair," thwarted every step of the way by Coiffio, the evil Controller of Cats, and his mighty minions, including Catman, Model Robot and the Astronomic Cat, in this half-hour comedy series for Cartoon Network.

Based on the November 2004 cartoon pilot first telecast on Cartoon Network's after-hours *Adult Swim* animation block, this absurdly funny CGI-animated 15-minute series, mirroring the same humor and style of Cartoon Network's *Space Ghost Coast to Coast, Aqua Teen Hunger Force* and *Sealab 2021*, bowed on *Adult Swim* in the fall of 2005 in the 12:45 A.M. time slot with six first-season episodes, along with two other new series, *Squidbillies* and *12 Oz. Mouse*. Added to the mix each week was an odd assortment of supporting characters, among them, Action Hotdog, Norman Douglas (formerly Inappropriately Comedy Tree), the King of All Animals, and Twist (also known as Terry). In October 2006, 16 brand-new episodes were ordered that aired exclusively on the *Adult Swim Fix* website in the second quarter of 2007. *A Williams Street Production. Color. Half-hour. Premiered on CAR: November 7, 2004 (pilot); November 20, 2005 (series).*

**Voices**
**Gerald Bald Z:** Kim Manning; **Coffio/Uncle Grandfather/Catman:** Dave Willis; **Comedy Tree:** Nick Ingkatanuwat; **Twisty:** H. Jon Benjamin; **Sherman the Giraffe:** MF Doom

## ◉ THE PERILS OF PENELOPE PITSTOP

In this spoof of the famed silent movie serial *The Perils of Pauline*, lovely heroine race driver Penelope Pitstop (formerly of Hanna-Barbera's *The Wacky Races*) is imperiled by the Hooded Claw (alias Sylvester Sneekly), who seeks to get rid of her in order to acquire her inheritance. Penelope is protected by her legal guardians, a bevy of buffoons known as the Ant Hill Mob, who also appeared in *The Wacky Races*. (Their car's name was changed from "The Bulletproof Bomb" to "Chug-A-Boom.") The 17-episode half-hour series bowed on CBS in 1969, featuring an entertaining ensemble of voice actors, including veterans Mel Blanc and Don Messick, comedian Paul Lynde (from TV's original *Hollywood Squares*) and former *Rowan and Martin's Laugh-In* announcer Gary Owens. Episodes were later syndicated as part of *The Fun World of Hanna-Barbera* and reshown on Cartoon Network and Boomerang. *A Hanna-Barbera Production. Color. Half-hour. Premiered on CBS: September 13, 1969–September 5, 1971. Syndicated: 1977. Rebroadcast on CAR: June 28, 1993–October 1993 (weekdays); June 6, 1994–September 2, 1994 (weekdays); June 5, 1995–October 1, 1995 (weekdays, Sundays); March 25, 1996–June 27, 1997 (weekdays). Rebroadcast on BOOM: May 13, 2000–.*

**Voices**
**Narrator:** Gary Owens; **Penelope Pitstop:** Janet Waldo; **Sylvester Sneekly/The Hooded/Claw:** Paul Lynde; **Bully Brothers/Yak Yak:** Mel Blanc; **Clyde/Softly:** Paul Winchell; **Zippy/Dum Dum/Snoozy/Pockets/Narrator:** Don Messick; **Chug-A-Boom:** Mel Blanc

## PET ALIEN

A group of goofy aliens—Dinko, Gumpers, Flip, Swanky, and Scruffy—turn a rather normal taffy-eating, video game-loving 12-year-old boy's (Tommy) life upside down after taking up residence in his DeSpray Bay lighthouse hideaway, doing everything they can to fit in on Earth with his help, in this 3-D CGI-animated fantasy/adventure series—bearing physical gags reminiscent of legendary Warner Bros. and MGM screwball animator Tex Avery and the outrageous humor of Nickelodeon's *SpongeBob SquarePants*—for Cartoon Network. Coproduced by Mike Young Productions and MoonScoop and based on an intellectual property by Jeff Muncy of John Doze Studios, the clever 26-episode half-hour series—aimed at kids ages six to 11—premiered Sunday morning, January 23, 2005, on Cartoon Network with the first episode, "I Was a Teenage Bearded Boy," and regularly aired thereafter in its 10:00 A.M. time slot. In 2006, actress Jess Harnell, the voice of Gumpers and Swanky, was nominated for a Daytime Emmy Award for outstanding performer in an animated program for her work on the series. A *Mike Young/Antefilm/TF1 France/Crest/Telegael/Taffy Entertainment Production. Color. Half-hour. Premiered on CAR: January 23, 2005.*

### Voices
**Tommy Cadle/Clinton:** Charlie Schlatter; **Dinko/Flip:** Charles Adler; **Gumpers/Swanky:** Jess Harnell; **Gabby/Tommy's Mom/Melba:** Candi Milo

## PETER PAN & THE PIRATES

Bad pirates (including the bone-chilling scourge of the seven seas, Captain Hook), magical Indians and mythical beasts and the world of flying urchin Peter Pan and friends, Tinker Bell, Wendy and Tiger Lily, come to life in this daily half-hour cartoon series (also known as *Fox's Peter Pan & the Pirates*), inspired by British author James M. Barrie's novel *Peter and Wendy.* Originally to be called "The Never Told Tales of Peter Pan," this stunning animated series was commissioned by FOX prior to the theatrical release of Steven Spielberg's full-length live-action feature *Hook.* It experienced declining ratings in its daily time slot and, in an effort to improve its rating status, was moved to the network's Saturday-morning schedule in January 1991, only to be pulled from the lineup permanently that September. Six years later, the series was rebroadcast on FOX Family Channels. A *Southern Star/TMS Entertainment Production in association with FOX Children's Network Productions. Color. Half-hour. Premiered on FOX: September 8, 1990–September 11, 1992. Rebroadcast on FOX FAM: August 30, 1998–February 28, 1999.*

### Voices
**Peter Pan:** Jason Marsden; **Tinker Bell:** Debi Derryberry; **Wendy:** Christina Lange; **John:** Jack Lynch; **Michael:** Whitby Hertford; **Tiger Lily:** Cree Summer; **Captain Hook:** Tim Curry; **Alf Mason:** Tony Jay; **Billy Jukes:** Eugene Williams; **Cookson:** Jack Angel; **Curly:** Josh Wiener; **Great Big Little Panther:** Michael Wise; **Hard-to-Hit:** Aaron Lohr; **Mullins:** Jack Angel; **Nibs:** Adam Carl; **Slightly:** Scott Menville; **Smee:** Ed Gilbert; **Starkey:** David Shaughnessy; **Tootles:** Chris Allport; **Twin #1:** Michael Bacall; **Twin #2:** Aaron Lohr

### Additional Voices
Linda Gary

## PETER POTAMUS AND HIS MAGIC FLYING BALLOON

Umbrella title for Hanna-Barbera's sixth syndicated series, whose main star was a purple hippo, Peter Potamus (whose voice sounded like comedian Joe E. Brown), and his sidekick, So So the monkey, who travel back in time and make history in the process.

Other series regulars were: "Breezly and Sneezly," the misadventures of a goofy polar bear and smart arctic seal who first debuted on *The Magilla Gorilla Show*; and "Yippee, Yappee and Yahooey," tracing the madcap attempts of three palace guard dogs to serve the king. Two years after its debut, the show was rebroadcast on ABC and again in syndication as *The Magilla Gorilla/Peter Potamus Show. A Hanna-Barbera Production. Color. Half-hour. Premiered: September 16, 1964. Syndicated.*

### Voices
**Peter Potamus:** Hal Smith; **So So:** Don Messick; **Breezly:** Howard Morris; **Sneezly:** Mel Blanc; **Colonel:** John Stephenson; **Yippee:** Doug Young; **Yappee:** Hal Smith; **Yahooey:** Daws Butler; **The King:** Hal Smith

## THE PETER POTAMUS SHOW

Network version of the syndicated series that first appeared on television screens nationwide in 1964 under the title *Peter Potamus and His Magic Flying Balloon.* ABC picked up the series and added the program to its Saturday-morning children's lineup in 1966. The cartoon components from the former series remained intact (see entry for voice credits and further details), combining new episodes with cartoons that aired previously in syndication. A *Hanna-Barbera Production. Color. Half-hour. Premiered on ABC: January 2, 1966–December 24, 1967.*

## PHANTOM INVESTIGATORS

Four 12-year-old junior high school students—Kira, a telepathic hip-hop amateur D.J.; Jericho, a cool, smart telekinetic Casey, a nerdish shape-shifter, and Daemona Prune, a regular girl-next-door—operate their own detective agency and investigate and solve paranormal phenomena in this stop-motion, cut-out animated series that aired on the WB Television Network Kids' WB! The half-hour Saturday morning series—and first television series produced by San Francisco animation studio, (W)holesome Products—was originally telecast Saturday mornings and weekday afternoons on the WB but was canceled five weeks after its debut in May 2002. Seven of the series' original 13 episodes went unaired. A *(W)holesome Products Inc./Sony Pictures Family Entertainment Production. Color. Half-hour. Premiered on the WB (Kids' WB!): May 25, 2002–June 29, 2002.*

### Voices
**Kira:** Amber Ross; **Casey:** Andrew Decker; **Daemona's Mom/Others:** Jessica Gee; **Daemona's Dad/Others:** Dave Mallow; **Other Voices:** Kasha Kropinski, Steve Marvel, Courtney Vineys

## PHANTOM 2040

The series is set in a future on the brink of environmental disaster. Kit Walker Jr., a college student who is heir to the 500-year legacy of the Phantom, assumes the famed superhero's identity—known down the ages as "the ghost who walks"—to battle a corrupt corporation that plans to destroy Earth's ecosystem in this 33-episode half-hour series stripped for weekend syndication. A *Hearst Entertainment, MINOS S. A.1 France 18 Production in association with King Features. Color. Half-hour. Premiered: September 18, 1994–September 1996. Syndicated.*

### Voices
**Phantom/Kit Walker Jr.:** Scott Valentine; **Rebecca Madison:** Margot Kidder; **Guran:** J.D. Hall; **Graft:** Ron Perlman; **Maxwell Madison:** Jeff Bennett; **Vain Gloria:** Deborah Harry; **Dr. Jax:** Mark Hamill

## ☺ PIC ME

Award-winning interactive animated series created by John Rice where children literally star in their own personalized cartoon with stories about themselves. Commissioned by RTE, the series featured only a few first-season episodes until an additional 52 episodes were ordered after the broadcast rights to the series were sold to Animania HD in the United States, Nickelodeon United Kingdom, KIKA Germany, Teletoon France and Medialink in the Middle East. Awarded the Grand Prix award and the Digital storytelling award at the Digital Media Awards, the popular program aired alongside such classic cartoon series as *The Dick Tracy Show, Felix the Cat, Mister Magoo* and *The Pink Panther* on VOOM's high-definition channel, Animania. *A JAM Media/Monster Distributes Production. Color. Half-hour. Premiered on ANI: April 1, 2006–   .*

## ☺ PIGGSBURG PIGS!

In a town entirely populated by pigs, those big-time porkers the Bacon Brothers (Bo, Portley and Pighead) go up against Piggsburg's notorious villain, Rembrandt Proupork, in a series of madcap adventures in this short-lived half-hour series that aired on FOX Network. Premiering in the fall of 1990, the series went up against stiff competition during its network debut: It was scheduled opposite CBS's hit animated series, *Teenage Mutant Ninja Turtles.* FOX pulled the program from its Saturday-morning lineup in the spring of 1991, replacing it with the live-action series *Swamp Thing.* The program finished its network run, twice returning to replace the latter, albeit briefly, in reruns. Only 13 half-hour episodes were produced. The show's original working title was *Pig Out. A Ruby-Spears Production in association with the Fred Silverman Company/Sy Fischer Company/FOX Children's Network Productions. Color. Half-hour. Premiered on FOX: September 13, 1990–April 13, 1991; May 25, 1991–June 29, 1991; August 10, 1991–August 31, 1991.*

**Voices**
Robert Cait, Tara Charandoff, David Huband, Keith Knight, Jonathan Potts, Susan Roman, Ron Rubin, Norman Spencer, Greg Spottiswood, John Stocker, Peter Wildman, Harvey Atkin, Len Carlson, Don Francks, Catherine Gallant, Rex Hagon, Elizabeth Hanna, Robert Bockstael, Dan Hennessey, Gordon Masten, Allen Stewart-Coates

## ☺ PILOT CANDIDATE

On Zion, the last planet inhabited solely by humans, five young pilots commandeer five gigantic fighting robots, the Goddesses, defending mankind against the invasion of a vicious alien species determined to destroy the last remaining human colony. Adapted from Yukiru Sugisaki's post-apocalyptic manga, *Megami Kouhosei,* this English-dubbed weekly half-hour anime series, combining traditional cel and 3-D computer animation and featuring 12 episodic adventures, bowed on Cartoon Network in 2002. *A XEBEC/Megami Kuhosei Productions/Bandai/Sunrise Production. Color. Half-hour. Premiered on CAR: February 23, 2002–August 17, 2002.*

**Voices**
**Zero Enna:** Joshua Seth; **Kizna Towryk:** Georgette Rose; **Hiead Gner:** John Burnley; **Azuma Hijikata:** Richard Cansino; **Gaeras Elidd:** Matthew Robert Dunn; **Ikhny Allecto:** Jessica Gee; **Teela Zain Elmes:** Melora Harte; **Clay Cliff Fortran:** Jim Taggert; **Luz Sawamura:** Peter Toll; **Azuma Hijikata:** Richard Hayworth

## ☺ THE PINK PANTHER

Legendary Warner Bros. animator and Pink Panther creator Friz Freleng served as a creative consultant, along with David H. DePatie, who coproduced with Freleng several previous Pink Panther animated television series on this newly produced half-hour syndicated series in which the suave, shrewd cat talked (voiced by Matt Frewer, of TV's *Max Headroom* and *Doctor, Doctor* fame).

Premiering in the fall of 1993, the series' new adventures combined the same visual humor and slapstick gags as previously made cartoons and featured lesser-known DePatie-Freleng theatrical cartoon characters in supporting roles, including the Ant and the Aardvark (voiced by John Byner) and The Dogfather (voiced by Joe Piscopo) as well as several new characters: Voodoo Man (voiced by Dan Castellaneta), Manly Man (voiced by Jess Harnell), among others.

Fifty-two new and original episodes were filmed for the series, which returned for a second season in 1994, comprised of reruns. One episode, "Driving Mr. Pink," was released as a theatrical short in 1995. It first aired as a syndicated television episode in 1994 combined with two other first-run episodes, "Dazed and Confused" and "Three Pink Porkers." The short opened jointly with Don Bluth's full-length animated feature. *The Pebble and the Penguin. An MGM Animation Production in association with Claster Television. Color. Half-hour. Premiered: 1993: Syndicated.*

**Voices**
**Pink Panther:** Matt Frewer; **The Ant and the Aardvark:** John Byner; **The Dogfather/Puggs:** Joe Piscopo; **Inspector Clouseau:** Brian George; **Voodoo Man:** Dan Castellaneta; **Many Man:** Jess Harnell; **The Parrot:** Charles Nelson Reilly; **The Boss:** Wallace Shawn; **Grandmother/The Witch:** Ruth Buzzi

## ☺ PINK PANTHER AND SONS

The Pink Panther is the father of three sons, Pinky, Panky, and Punkin, in all-new misadventures that test his skills at fatherhood in managing the terrorsome trio. As in previous films, the witty panther conveys his message via pantomime in this half-hour series comprised of 26 cartoon adventures (two per show) originally broadcast on NBC in 1984. *A DePatie-Freleng Enterprises Production in association with Hanna-Barbera Productions. Color. Half-hour. Premiered on NBC: September 15, 1984–September 7, 1985. Rebroadcast on ABC: March 1, 1986–September 6, 1986.*

**Voices**
**Pinky:** Billy Bowles; **Panky/Punkin:** B.J. Ward; **Chatta:** Sherry Lynn; **Howl:** Marshall Efron; **Anney/Liona:** Jeanine Elias; **Finko/Rocko:** Frank Welker; **Bowlhead:** Gregg Berger; **Buckethead:** Sonny Melendrez; **Murfel:** Shane McCabe

## ☺ THE PINK PANTHER LAUGH AND A 1/2-HOUR AND A 1/2

Following the success of NBC's long-running *The New Pink Panther Show,* DePatie-Freleng Enterprises produced this 90-minute version featuring a myriad of old and new cartoon favorites: *The Pink Panther, The Inspector, The Ant and the Aardvark, The Texas Toads* (formerly *The Tijuana Toads,* Poncho and Toro, who were redubbed by actors Don Diamond and Tom Holland for television) and *Misterjaws.* (See individual entries in Theatrical Sound Cartoon Series for complete details.) *A DePatie-Freleng Enterprises Production. Color. Ninety minutes. Premiered on NBC: September 11, 1976–September 3, 1977.*

## ☺ THE PINK PANTHER MEETS THE ANT AND THE AARDVARK

Following the ratings success of *The Pink Panther Show,* NBC ordered this follow-up half-hour series featuring Pink Panther and

*The Ant and the Aardvark* cartoons (see individual entry in Theatrical Animated Cartoon Series section for details), originally produced as cartoon shorts for theaters. The series was as successful as its predecessor, garnering high ratings. A *DePatie-Freleng Enterprises Production. Color. Half-Hour. Premiered on NBC: September 12, 1970–September 11, 1971.*

## ◎ THE PINK PANTHER SHOW

Two madcap adventures of the Academy Award-winning mute feline were presented each week in this half-hour series, hosted by Lenny Schultz and featuring the comical exploits of Paul and Mary Ritts puppets. Backed by Henry Mancini's popular theme song, the series' episodes were comprised of cartoons from the theatrical cartoon series made in the 1960s.

Other segments included *The Inspector,* featuring cartoon shorts originally released to theaters between 1965 and 1969. The program was the first of several Saturday-morning series starring the unflappable feline, followed by 1970's *The Pink Panther Meets the Ant and the Aardvark,* 1971's *The New Pink Panther Show,* 1976's *The Pink Panther Laugh and a Half-Hour and a Half Show,* 1978's *Think Pink Panther!* 1978's *The All-New Pink Panther Show* and 1984's *Pink Panther and Sons.* A *DePatie-Freleng Enterprises Production. Color. Half-hour. Premiered on NBC: September 6, 1969–September 5, 1970.*

## ◎ PINKY & THE BRAIN

(See STEVEN SPIELBERG PRESENTS PINKY & THE BRAIN.)

## ◎ PINKY DINKY DOO

Pinky Dinky, a precocious, pink-haired seven-year-old with a rich imagination, known for wearing a big wedge of cheese to school, and whose brain expands greatly in size when she has a great big idea, happily tells made-up stories with big words to her little brother, Tyler, and her pet, Mr. Guinea Pig, as she solves kid-sized problems in this entertaining and educational children's series, coproduced by Sesame Workshop and based on Random House's successful 14-book children's series by author and illustrator Jim Jinkins (*Doug, PB&J Otter, JoJo's Circus*). Using Flash animation over photo collage backgrounds, each week the 26-episode, half-hour cartoon series (with two cartoons per show)—aimed at preschool audiences and Noggin's first original series dedicated to enhancing early literacy—explores literacy through storytelling and interactive game-play. Simultaneously premiering on both Noggin and its sister network, Nick Jr., in April 2006, the series aired regularly weekday mornings and afternoons on Noggin thereafter. Included among its first season inventory of shows was the holiday episode, "Pinky's Wintery Dintery Doo." A *Sesame Workshop/Cartoon Pizza Production. Color. Half-hour. Premiered on NOG: April 10, 2006. Premiered on NICK JR.: April 10, 2006.*

**Voices**
**Pinky:** India Ennenga; **Mommy Dinky Doo:** Heather Dolly; **Nicholas Bisquit:** Justin Riordan

## ◎ PINKY, ELMYRA & THE BRAIN

Revamped version of Warner Bros. Animation's highly successful series, *Pinky & the Brain,* featuring the famed Acme Lab genetically engineered mice setting up shop in costar Elmyra Duff's house with Pinky and the Brain still trying to take over the world, in this half-hour series, coproduced by Steven Spielberg's Amblin Entertainment. Also known as *Steven Spielberg Presents Pinky, Elmyra & the Brain,* the weekly Saturday-morning version, offering 13 half-hour adventures, aired on the WB Television Network for one season and then as part of the WB's *The Cat & Birdy Warnertoonie Pinky Brainy Big Cartoonie Show* from January to August 2000. An *Amblin Entertainment/WB Television Animation Production. Color. Half-hour. Premiered on the WB's (Kids' WB!): September 9, 1998–January 9, 1999; January 16, 2000–August 31, 2000 (as part of the WB's "The Cat & Birdy Warnertoonie Pinky Brainy Big Cartoonie Show").*

**Voices**
**Pinky:** Rob Paulsen; **The Brain:** Maurice LaMarche; **Elmyra:** Cree Summer; **Rudy Mookich:** Nancy Cartwright

## ◎ PIPPI LONGSTOCKING

Known for her amazing super-strength, Pippi Longstocking, the likeable, free-spirited, pig-tailed, freckle-faced heroine—and famed daughter of Captain Longstocking—returns after having sailed the Seven Seas, seven times no less, to handle every conceivable obstacle put in her path while living on her own with her characteristically good humor in her first animated series for television, based on noted author Astrid Lindgren's classic children's books.

A spin-off of the largely unsuccessful 1997 full-length animated feature, *Pippi Longstocking,* this 26-episode half-hour series, coproduced by Canada's Nelvana (which also coproduced and released the previous feature), marked the second time the character had appeared in animated form, following previous adaptations that had included more than 40 live-action films and television programs. First shown in the United States on HBO in the summer of 1998, HBO continued airing the series in reruns through 2001. Actress Melissa Altro, the voice of Pippi in the ill-fated cartoon feature, reprised the role for the series. A *Nelvana Limited/Svensk Filmindustri/TFC Trickompany Filmproduktion GmbH/Taurus Film Production. Color. Half-hour. Premiered on HBO: July 4, 1998–September 1, 1999. Rebroadcast on HBO: September 1999–2001.*

**Voices**
**Pippi Longstocking:** Melissa Altro; **Mr. Nilsson:** Richard Binsley; **Tommy Settergren:** Noah Reed; **Anika Settergren:** Olivia Garrett; **Captain Efraim Longstocking:** Benedict Campbell; **Mr. Settergren:** Ray Landry; **Mrs. Settergren:** Karen Bernstein; **Mr. Eriksson:** William Colgate; **Puppet:** John McGrath; **Mrs. Prysselius:** Catherine O'Hara, Jill Frappier; **Thunder-Karlsson:** Len Carlson; **Bloom:** Wayne Robson; **Constable King:** Rick Jones; **Constable Klang:** Philip Williams; **Fridolf:** Chris Wiggins

## ◎ PIRATES OF DARK WATER

First produced as a 1991 five-part animated miniseries (simply called *Dark Water*) that bowed on FOX network, chronicling the noble quest to save a dying alien planet, this weekly half-hour sword-and-sorcery series revolved around the continuing plight of the planet Mer and the Kingdom of Octopon, in danger of becoming ruled by the evil forces of Dark Water, a highly intelligent, dictatorial liquid entity determined to take over the planet. Saving the day are a determined young Prince, a fussy sidekick, a dashing pirate rogue and a highly independent woman who come to the rescue. Premiering as a series and renamed *Pirates of Dark Water* on ABC in the fall of 1992, the program was part of the weekend syndicated extravaganza *Funtastic World of Hanna-Barbera.* A *Hanna-Barbera Production in association with Fils-Cartoons, Inc. and Tama Production Co. Color. Half-hour. Premiered on FOX: February 25, 1991 ("The Quest"); February 26, 1991 ("Dishonor"); February 27, 1991 ("The Breakup"); February 28, 1991 ("Betrayal"); March 1, 1991 ("Victory"). Premiered on ABC: September 7, 1991–September 5, 1992. Rebroadcast: 1992 (as*

*a weekly series, part of* Funtastic World of Hanna-Barbera*).
Rebroadcast on CAR: January 3, 1991–April 1, 1994 (weekdays);
June 6, 1994–September 2, 1994 (weekdays); January 5, 1995–June
2, 1995 (weekdays); March 25, 1996–May 3, 1997 (weekdays,
Sundays); 1999; March 2, 2003–mid 2003. Rebroadcast on BOOM:
April 2, 2000–.*

*Voices*

**Konk:** Tim Curry; **Mantus:** Peter Cullen; **Tula:** Jodi Benson; **Nidder:** Frank Welker; **Ren:** George Newbern; **Bloth:** Brock Peters; **Queen:** Jessica Walter; **Ioz:** Hector Elizondo; **Skorian:** Jim Cummings; **Lugg Brother #1:** Earl Boen; **Kangent:** Rene Auberjonois; **Garen:** Paul Williams; **Additional Voices:** Michael Bell, Hamilton Camp, Darleen Carr, Philip L. Clarke, Regis Cordic, Keene Curtis, Barry Dennen, Paul Eiding, Harlan Ellison, Richard Erdman, Linda Gary, Richard Gautier, Ellen Geer, Ed Gilbert, Stacy Keach Sr., Paul Lukather, Allan Lurie, Tress MacNeille, Kenneth Mars, Nan Martin, Julie McWhirter, Candi Milo, Dan O'Herlihy, Phil Proctor, Jim Rabson, John Rhys-Davies, Neil Ross, Michael Rye, Pepe Serna, Mark Silverman, Andre Stojka, Les Tremayne, B.J. Ward

## ◎ THE PJS

Satirical comedy following the ups and downs of a hot-tempered, vulgar, big city chief housing superintendent named Thurgood Stubbs (voiced by Eddie Murphy), who lives in Detroit's Hilton-Jacobs Project with his devoted wife, Muriel, and a bizarre multiethnic cast of tenants who drive him crazy. Produced in the stop-motion process known as "Foamation," the three-time Emmy-winning, clay-animated half-hour comedy series, cocreated by Eddie Murphy, Larry Wilmore and Steve Tompkins, was originally broadcast in prime time on FOX in January 1999, where it was canceled after a single season. The season included the series' half-hour holiday special, *The PJs Christmas Special: "How the Super Stoled Christmas."* In October 2000, the series moved to the WB Television Network. As a result of the laborious clay animation process, producing a single episode often took more than two months.

Emmy Award-winning Portland-based Will Vinton Studios of TV's *The California Raisins* fame coproduced the weekly 41-episode series with Imagine Entertainment and Eddie Murphy in association with Touchstone Television, which distributed the series. Actor Phil Morris, the son of TV's *Mission Impossible* star Greg Morris, substituted for Eddie Murphy as the voice of Stubbs in several episodes. After its departure from the WB Television Network, reruns of the series, including three previously unaired episodes, were shown beginning in June 2003 on Trio network under the program block called *Uncensored Comedy: That's Not Funny,* featuring rebroadcasts of short-lived series that originally aired on television's Big Three networks, ABC, CBS and NBC. *An Eddie Murphy/Imagine Television/Will Vinton Studios/Touchstone Television Production. Color. Half-hour. Premiered on FOX: January 10, 1999–September 5, 2000. Premiered on WB: October 8, 2000–June 17, 2001. Rebroadcast on TRIO: June 9, 2003–.*

*Voices*

**Thurgood Stubbs:** Eddie Murphy, Phil Morris; **Muriel Stubbs:** Loretta Devine; **Mrs. Avery:** Ja'net DuBois; **Calvin Banks:** Crystal Scales; **Juicy Hudson:** Michele Morgan; **Jimmy Ho:** Michael Paul Chan; **Bebe Ho:** Jenifer Lewis; **Walter:** Marc Wilmore; **Tarnell:** James Black; **Smokey:** Shawn Michael Howard; **Ms. Mambo Garcelle (Haiti Lady):** Cheryl Francis Harrington; **Mr. Sanchez:** Pepe Serna; **Sharique:** Wanda Christine; **Papa Hudson/Rasta Man:** Kevin Michael Richardson; **Smokey:** Shawn Michael Howard; **Tarnell:** James Black; **HUD Woman:** Cassi Davis

## ◎ THE PLASTIC MAN/BABY PLAS SUPER COMEDY

As if one superhero in the family wasn't enough, Plastic Man and wife, Penny, give birth to a son, Plastic Baby (Baby Plas for short), who possesses the same fantastic attributes as his famous elastic father, in a series of all-new misadventures for ABC. The series, composed of 13 "Plastic Family" and "Baby Plas" cartoons (one per show) and a series of 30-second consumer tips by Plastic Man himself, was the follow-up series of the two-hour extravaganza *The Plastic Man Comedy-Adventure Show,* which also aired on ABC. In 1993 the series resurfaced in reruns on Cartoon Network. *A Ruby-Spears Production. Color. Half-hour. Premiered on ABC: October 4, 1980–September 5, 1981. Rebroadcast on CAR: June 28, 1993–September 17, 1993 (weekdays); May 2, 1994–September 2, 1994 (weekdays); January 5, 1995 (weekdays); February 25, 1995 (Super Adventure Saturdays); July 22, 1995 (Power Zone).*

*Voices*

**Plastic Man:** Michael Bell; **Penny, his wife:** Melendy Britt; **Baby Plas, their son:** Michael Bell; **Chief:** Melendy Britt; **Hula Hula:** Joe Baker

## ◎ THE PLASTIC MAN COMEDY-ADVENTURE SHOW

Spawned by the success of competing studios' superhero cartoons, Ruby-Spears Enterprises adapted a comic-book super-crimefighter of their own: Plastic Man, whose elasticity enables him to stretch like a rubber band and twist his body into different shapes. Aided by friends Penny and Hula-Hula (whose voice is similar to comedian Lou Costello's), the moldable superhero comes to the rescue wherever evil lurks. The series, which bowed on ABC in 1979 in a two-hour format (three months following its debut the show was shortened to 90 minutes), featured three additional cartoon components on each program: "Mighty Man and Yukk," the adventures of a thimble-size superhero (Mighty) and the ugliest dog in the world (Yukk); "Fangface and Fangpuss," the exploits of a teenage werewolf and his equally wolfy cousin; and "Rickey Rocket," in which four teenagers (Comso, Splashdown, Sunstroke and Venus) with a makeshift rocket head a space detective agency. The series was the first of two programs to star the DC Comics superhero, followed by *The Plastic Man/Baby Plas Super Comedy. A Ruby-Spears Enterprises Production. Color. Two hours. One hour and a half. Premiered on ABC: September 22, 1979–September 27, 1980 (two-hour format until December 1979). Rebroadcast on CBS: November 12, 1983–February 4, 1984. Rebroadcast on CAR: 1993–95.*

*Voices*

**PLASTIC MAN: Plastic Man:** Michael Bell; **Chief/Penny:** Melendy Britt; **Hula Hula:** Joe Baker;

**MIGHTY MAN AND YUKK: Mighty Man/Brandon Brewster:** Peter Cullen; **Yukk:** Frank Welker; **Mayor:** John Stephenson

**FANGFACE AND FANGPUSS: Fangface/Fangpuss:** Frank Welker; **Kim, their friend:** Susan Blu; **Biff, their friend:** Jerry Dexter; **Puggsy, their friend:** Bart Braverman

**RICKETY ROCKET: Rickey Rocket:** Al Fann; **Cosmo:** Bobby Ellerbee; **Splashdown:** Johnny Brown; **Sunstroke:** John Anthony Bailey; **Venus:** Dee Timberlake

## ◎ PLAYBOY'S DARK JUSTICE

Set in futuristic Metro City in the year 2120, sultry girl reporter-turned crime fighter, Justina, uses her martial arts skills and vast array of high-tech gadgets, weapons and vehicles to stay one step ahead of police as she battles the city's bizarre villains in a post-apocalyptic world in this first animated series produced for cable's premium pay Playboy TV channel. Coproduced by adult film-maker Michael Ninn (who also directed the series) and soft-core porn star Jane Hamilton, also known as Veronica Hart and billed as Jane Hart for the voice of Justina, the 26-episode, 3-D computer-animated half-hour fantasy series—described as "a parody of the superhero/crime fighting genre"—premiered on Saturday, September 3, 2000, at 10:30 P.M. (ET), with the airing of its first two episodes. Thereafter, according to Playboy TV's official programming records, six more first-run episodes began airing weekly on October 15, 2000, through mid-November. The network's programming department has no record of the airdates of the series' additional 20 episodes. *A Hope Ranch LLC/Playboy Production. Color. Half-hour. Premiered on PLYBY: September 3, 2000–November 19, 2000.*

**Voices**
**Justina:** Jane Hamilton (billed as Jane Hart); **Other Voices:** Julia Ashton, Tina Tyler, Julia Ann, Anthony Crane

### ◉ THE PLUCKY DUCK SHOW
Adolescent Daffy Duck look-alike Plucky Duck, the splentic, frenetic costar of Steven Spielberg's popular *Tiny Toon Adventures* cartoon series, hosted this 1991 Saturday-morning entry, comprised solely of repeat episodes from *Tiny Toon Adventures.* Following a three-month run, the series was changed back to *Tiny Toon Adventures,* offering more repeat adventures. *A Spielberg/Warner Brothers Television Animation Production. Color. Half-hour. Premiered on FOX: September 19, 1992–November 7, 1992.*

**Voices**
**Plucky Duck:** Joe Alaskey

### ◉ POCKET DRAGON ADVENTURES
Outside the Wizard's house where they live, six pocket-sized, fun-loving, mischievous, cookie-eating dragons (including Filbert, the oldest and most responsible; the brainy Specs; the inventive Scribbles; Zoom-Zoom, the hopeful flier; Cuddles, the sleepwalking, hero wannabe; and the youngest, Binky—find mystery and adventure and fantastic creatures along the way in this animated adaptation of the popular UbiSoft video game. Produced by Burbank, California's DIC Entertainment and offered in first-run syndication as part of the Bohbot Kids Network, this half-hour series, comprised of 52 cartoon adventures, bowed on American television in the fall of 1998. *A DIC Entertainment/D'Ocon Film/WolfMill Entertainment/Bohbot Entertainment Production. Color. Half-hour. Premiered: September 7, 1998. Syndicated.*

**Voices**
**Filbert:** Ian James Corlett; **Zoom-Zoom:** Jason Gray Stanford; **Specs:** Samuel Vincent; **Scribbles:** Kathleen Barr; **Binky:** Tabitha St. Germain; **Sparkles:** Robert O. Smith; **Cuddles:** Terry Klassen, Venus Terzo; **Wizard:** Christopher Gaze; **Princess Betty Bye Bell:** Saffron Henderson; **Other Voices:** Gary Chalk, Long John Baldry, Lee Tockar, Dave Ward, French Tickner, Jessy Moss, Michael Dobson, Jay Brazeau, Alec Willows, Dale Wilson, Don Brown, Doug Parker, Mark Oliver, Russel Roberts, Richard Newman, Bill Reiter

### ◉ POKÉMON
On the day of his 10th birthday, a *Pokémon* card-trading boy, Ash Ketchum (Satoshi in the original Japanese series), travels the globe with Misty and Brock, his best friends and so-called Poké-mon trainers, and Pikachu, their personal pocket monster, to be crowned Pokémon Master of the world by beating his long-time nemesis Gary Oak. First shown in Japan in 1997 as *Poketto Monsuta* and dubbed in English, this half-hour fantasy adventure series, based on the phenomenally successful Nintendo Game Boy video games, premiered in the United States in first-run syndication in September 1998, quickly becoming television's highest rated and most-watched syndicated cartoon series.

Enjoying a tremendous built-in audience of kid and teenage *Pokémon* video gamers and card collectors, in February 1999 the WB Television Network added the top-rated children's series to its Saturday morning Kids' WB! lineup and shortly thereafter weekdays as well, where it regularly beat out its competition every week. The stunning success of the series spawned telecasts of four 90-minute movie specials of the franchise's theatrical features, *Mewtwo Strikes Back* (*Pokémon the First Movie*); *The Power of One* (*Pokémon the Movie 2000*); *Spell of the Unown* (*Pokémon 3 The Movie: Spell of the Unown*); *Latios and Latias* (*Pokémon Heroes*); plus an additional 90-minute special, *Celebi: Voice of Forest.*

In November 2003, the series entered its sixth season on Kids' WB! as *Pokémon Advanced Challenge,* featuring all-new episodes costarring popular *Pokémon Ruby* and *Pokémon Sapphire* video game characters. Fifty new episodes were offered for the show's seventh season, bringing the overall series total to 364 available episodes. By June of 2006, the *Pokémon* cartoon franchise found a new permanent home at Cartoon Network, which broadcast two other incarnations, *Pokémon Chronicles* and *Pokémon: Battle Frontier.* In July 2006, Cartoon Network's classic cartoons sister channel, Boomerang, began reairing the first season of the smash hit anime series until that October. *A TV Tokyo/Softix/Shogakukan Production Co. (ShoPro)/J P Kikachu/Nintendo/CREATURES/GameFreak/4Kids Entertainment Production in association with Summit Media Group. Color. Half-hour. Premiered: September 7, 1998–September 10, 1999; Syndicated. Premiered on the WB (Kids' WB!): February 13, 1999–October 25, 2003. Premiered on CAR: November 4, 2002. Rebroadcast on BOOM: July 31, 2006–October 9, 2006.*

**Voices**
**Ash Ketchum/Delia/May:** Veronica Taylor; **Misty/Jessie:** Rachel Lillis; **Brock/James/Kadabra/Charizard/Magmar/Hypno/Squirtle/Wartortle/Gastly/Scythe r:** Eric Stuart; **Meowth/Growlithe/Abra/Corphish:** Adam Blaustein; **Gary Oak:** Matthew Mitler; **Pikachu:** Ikue Ohtani; **Professor Samuel Oak:** Stan Hart; **Tracey:** Ted Lewis; **Cassidy/Lapras/Chikorita/Bayleef/Squirtle/Blastoise/Pidgeotto/Hitmonchan/Zubat:** Lisa Ortiz; **Arbok/Hitmonlee/Mr. Mime/Marril/Victreebell/Farfetch'd/Onix:** Kayzie Rogers; **Ratata/Grimer/Muk/Shellder/Quagsire/Spearow/Snubble:** Jimmy Zoppie; **Carmander/Hitmonlee/Psyduck/Dewgong/Geodue/Golduck:** Michael Haigney; **Nurse Joy/Officer Jenny:** Megan Hollingshead; **Other Voices:** Rikako Aikawa, Carlos Alazraqui, Mandy Bonhomme, Ken Gates, Meguki Hayashibara, Tatsuyuki Ishimori, Unsho Ishizuka, Tara Jayne, Satomi Koorogi, Lobozzo, Rika Matsumoto, Shinichio Miki, Chinami Nishimura, Annie Pondel, Nathan Price, Rei Takano, Nicholas James Tate, Jack Taylor, Yuji Ueda

### ◉ POKÉMON: ADVANCED CHALLENGE
The saga of the highly popular anime series continues with Ash Ketchum and Pikachu traveling to the mysterious Hoenn Region. There they find adventure with more than 100 Pokémon and, with two new friends, Ash forms a whole new team of Pokémon, learning the new rules of competition, adapting to new tools and technologies and facing new challenges. First aired on Japanese

television from 2002 to 2003, this sixth season of *Pokémon*, featuring all-new episodes showcasing new characters and perennial favorites from the popular *Pokémon Ruby* and *Pokémon Sapphire* video games, opened with a two-episode ("Get the Show on the Road" and "A Ruin with a View") "sneak preview" during the 2003–04 season on the WB Television Network's Kids' WB! in March 2003. That November, episodes of the series regularly began airing Saturday mornings at 10:00 A.M. In June 2004, a 90-minute special, *Jirachi Wish Maker*, also debuted on WB Television Network's Kids' WB! In May 2006, the program and its follow-up series, *Pokémon Advanced Battle*, starting airing as part of the *Miguzi* block on Cartoon Network, while its sister network, Boomerang, reaired the series from July to October of that year. A *TV Tokyo/Shogakukan Production Co./Oriental Light and Magic/4Kids Entertainment/Viz Media Production. Color. Half-hour. Premiered on the WB (Kids' WB!): November 1, 2003–September 4, 2004. Rebroadcast on CAR: May 15, 2006–. Rebroadcast on BOOM: July 31, 2006–October 20, 2006.*

*Voices*
**Ash Ketchum:** Veronica Taylor, Sarah Natochenny (Episode #145); **Pikachu:** Ikue Ohtani; **Brock/James/Team Magma Member:** Eric Stuart; **Meowth:** Addie Blaustein; **Harley:** Andrew Rannels; **Jessie:** Rachael Lillis

### ⊚ POKÉMON: BATTLE FRONTIER

After leaving the strange territory of Hoenn, Ash Ketchum, Pikachu and their friends travel back to the Kanto region where they face their biggest adventure yet by competing in the Battle Frontier competition and battling powerful opponents in this English-dubbed version (dubbed by Pokémon USA instead of 4Kids Entertainment, whose contract to license the series in the United States had expired) of the iconic animated series. Bowing on American television in September 2006, this ninth season of the phenomenally successful *Pokémon* animated series aired exclusively Saturday mornings on Cartoon Network. It debuted with the premiere special, *Pokémon Mystery Dungeon: Team Go-Getters Out of the Gate!*, the second special overall in the *Pokémon* series, followed by a third later that season, *The Mastermind of Mirage Pokémon*. Previously, on June 3 of that year, Cartoon Network also premiered the never-before-seen *Pokémon* series in the United States, *Pokémon Chronicles*, during its acclaimed *Toonami* action block. Voice actor Sarah Natochenny took over as the voice of Ash Ketchum in the series. A *TV Tokyo/Shogakukan Production Co./Oriental Light and Magic/Pokémon USA/Viz Media Production. Color. Half-hour. Premiered on CAR: September 8, 2006.*

*Voices*
**Ash Kethcum/Medicham/Baby Kangaskhan:** Sarah Natochenny; **Pikachu:** Ikue Ohtani; **Brock:** Bill Rogers; **Meowth/James/Gengar:** Jimmy Zoppi; **Jessie/May/Chikorita:** Michaelle Knotz; **Max/Mime Jr./Squirtle/Wobbuffet:** Kayzie Rogers; **Narrator:** Ken Gates

### ⊚ POKÉMON CHRONICLES

Not part of the continuing *Pokémon* saga, this half-hour collection featured mini-stories revolving around old and new characters—Pikachu, Misty, Butch, Cassidy, and others—and their adventures when not accompanying the protagonist Ash Ketchum on his journeys. Previously aired in Japan, Britain and Latin America but never-before-seen in the United States, the all-new, 22-episode version of the hit animated series, featuring the stories of the unsung heroes and villains from the *Pokémon* universe, joined Cartoon Network's top-rated Saturday night *Toonami* action-anime block in June 2006 with the premiere

three-episode story, "The Legend of Thunder." In September, Cartoon Network debuted a new 90-minute special starring Ash and company entitled *Lucario and the Mystery of Mew*. That December, Pikachu and company starred in a half-hour holiday special, *Pikachu's Winter Vacation*, featuring two back-to-back episodes, "Christmas Night" and "Kanga Game," which also aired on Cartoon Network. A *TV Tokyo/Shogakukan Production Co./4Kids Entertainment Production. Color. Half-hour. Premiered on CAR: June 3, 2006.*

*Voices*
**Pikachu:** Ikue Ohtani; **Meowth:** Maddie Blaustein; **Cassidy:** Andi Whaley; **James/Brock/Professor Sebastian/Butch:** Eric Stuart; **Professor Nanba:** Jhonen Vasquez; **Gary Oak:** Matt Mitler; **Lily/Office Jenny:** Megan Hollingshead; **Misty/Jessie/Violet:** Rachael Lillis; **Togepi:** Satomi Koorogi; **Jimmy:** Sean Schemmel; **Professor Oak:** Stan Hart; **Richie:** Tara Jayne; **Butch/Tracey:** Ted Lewis; **Marina:** Vanessa Yardley; **Sakura/Casey:** Kerry Williams; **Nurse Joy:** Lisa Ortiz; **Narrator:** Mike Pollock; **Vincent:** Wayne Grayson; **Eugene:** Dan Green; **Daisy:** Lisa Ortiz; **Nurse Joy:** Bella Hudson; **Narrator:** Mike Pollock

### ⊚ POLE POSITION

A stunt-racing and daredevil family team puts on thrilling automotive acrobatics at the Pole Position Stunt Show, run by Dan Darret and his two sisters, Tess and Daisy, after their parents disappear in an unexplained explosion during a stunt race. The kids carry on their parents' work, along with pet Kuma and two computerized cars, Roadie and Wheels, using the cutting-edge technology of their high-tech vehicles to fight crime in this 13-episode half-hour Saturday-morning series, based on the popular video arcade game of the same name. A *DIC Enterprise/Namco Ltd./2B5 Production. Color. Half-hour. Premiered on CBS: September 15, 1984–August 30, 1986. Rebroadcast on FAM: 1989–91.*

*Voices*
**Dan Darret:** David Coburn; **Tess, his sister:** Lisa Lindgren; **Daisy, his sister:** Kaleena Kiff; **Dr. Zachary, their uncle:** Jack Angel; **Wheels:** Mel Franklyn; **Roadie:** Daryl Hickman; **Kuma:** Marilyn Schreffler; **Teacher:** Helen Minniear

### ⊚ POLICE ACADEMY: THE SERIES

Those wacky defenders of law and order (Mahoney, Jones, Hightower, Zed, Captain Harris and others), known for their hijinks in a series of live-action feature-length action/comedies, return to the beat in this first-run, daily half-hour series as they attempt to keep the peace while using the most outrageous crime-prevention methods ever seen. Syndicated in 1988, voice work for the series was recorded in Canada. A *Ruby-Spears Enterprise Warner Bros. Production. Color. Half-hour. Premiered: September 1988. Syndicated.*

*Voices*
**Mahoney:** Ron Rubin; **Hightower:** Charles Gray, Greg Morton; **Hooks/Callahan:** Denise Pidgeon; **Jones:** Greg Morton; **Zed/Tackleberry:** Dan Hennessey; **Sweetchuck/Professor:** Howard Morris; **Proctor:** Greg Swanson; **Lassard:** Gary Krawford; **Harris:** Len Carlson; **House:** Dorian Joe Clark

### ⊚ POOCHINI

An adopted dog, who lived a life of luxury until his wealthy owner died and the dog wound up at the pound, tries adapting to his new life-style with his new owners, the Whites, an average American family in this half-hour comedy series, cocreated by Dave Thomas and Dave March. Comprised of three cartoons per half-hour, the series aired Saturday mornings on the WB Television Network's Kids' WB! and in first-run syndication, beginning in the fall of 2002. *A Wild Brain/EM-TV Production. Color. Half-hour. Premiered on the WB (Kids' WB!)/Syndicated: September 7, 2002.*

**Voices**
**Poochini/Walter White/Mr. Garvey/Lockjaw:** Billy West; **Billy White/Knucklehead/Bunk:** Dee Bradley Baker; **Wendy White:** Leslie Carrara; **Dirt:** Maurice LaMarche

## ◎ THE POPEYE AND OLIVE SHOW

In this Saturday-morning series of all-new adventures based on Edgar Segar's popular comic-strip creations, Popeye and Olive shared top billing. This comedy/adventure show consisted of three weekly segments—one ensemble series, "The Popeye Show," which starred Popeye, Olive and old favorites Bluto and Wimpy, in 24 cartoon shorts, plus two additional series of short cartoons (16 episodes each): "Private Olive Oyl," in which Popeye's string-bean girlfriend stars as a clumsy army private; and "Prehistoric Popeye," with the muscleman sailor trying to contend with caveman situations before the availability of spinach cans. (The films were mixed in with other modern-day adventures.) Since its original network run, the series was rebroadcast on The Family Channel. *A Hanna-Barbera Production in association with King Features Entertainment. Color. Half-hour. Premiered on CBS: September 12, 1981–November 27, 1982. Rebroadcast on FAM: September 15, 1990–September 29, 1996.*

**Voices**
**Popeye:** Jack Mercer; **Olive Oyl:** Marilyn Schreffler; **Bluto:** Allan Melvin; **Wimpy:** Daws Butler; **Sgt. Bertha Blast, Olive's sergeant:** Jo Anne Worley; **Alice the Goon:** Marilyn Schreffler; **Colonel Crumb:** Hal Smith

*Seafaring sailor Popeye starred in a new made-for-television series of episodic adventures in the 1960s. © King Features Entertainment*

## ◎ POPEYE AND SON

Updated adventures of strongman sailor Popeye and spindly girlfriend Olive Oyl who, now married and living in a ramshackle beach house, find they have their hands full with son, Popeye Jr. a feisty, rugged nine-year-old who's a real chip off the old block, except that he hates spinach. Old rival Bluto returns to make trouble, with his own son, Tank, who is more "like father, like son" than Popeye Jr. is to his famous fighting father. The 26-episode Saturday-morning series premiered on CBS in 1987, featured two 11-minute cartoon adventures each week. The series was later run on USA Network's *Cartoon Express* and on The Family Channel. *A Hanna-Barbera Production. Color. Half-hour. Premiered on CBS: September 19, 1987–September 10, 1988. Rebroadcast on USA: September 29, 1989–September 16, 1990. Rebroadcast on FAM: September 4, 1994–December 31, 1995.*

**Voices**
**Popeye:** Maurice LaMarche; **Olive Oyl:** Marilyn Schreffler; **Popeye Jr.:** Josh Rodine; **Bluto:** Allan Melvin; **Lizzie, Bluto's wife:** Marilyn Schreffler; **Tank, their son:** David Markus; **Woody, Junior's friend:** Nancy Cartwright; **Polly, Junior's friend:** Penina Segall; **Dee Dee, Junior's friend:** Kaleena Kiff; **Rad:** B.J. Ward; **Puggy:** Marilyn Schreffler; **Wimpy:** Allan Melvin; **Eugene the Jeep:** Don Messick

## ◎ POPEYE THE SAILOR

The King Features syndicate, which owns the rights to Popeye, produced this new made-for-television series of 210 six-minute episodic adventures reprising the adversarial relationship of spinach-gobbling sailor Popeye and seafaring bully Brutus (whose name was changed to Bluto in the Max Fleischer cartoons), as they continue to battle over the affections of fickle Olive Oyl. The rest of the supporting cast from the original Max Fleischer cartoon shorts were also featured, including Wimpy, Swee'pea, Sea Hag and Eugene the Jeep.

The series, sold to local stations based on two "pilot" cartoons, "Hits and Missiles" and "Barbecue for Two," was produced by Al Brodax for King Features within a two-year period and premiered in syndication in 1960. Five different independent studios were used to animate the series. Jack Kinney Studios produced the pilot "Barbecue for Two" and animated most of the series (101 cartoon shorts in all). Paramount Cartoon Studios produced theatrical "Popeye" cartoon shorts up until 1957 and handled animation for 63 films, including the pilot "Hits and Missiles." Other studios engaged to animate the series were producer William L. Snyder's Rembrandt Films (producers of the Oscar-winning short "Munro"), which produced 28 new "Popeye" cartoons in association with Britain's Halas and Batchelor and Czech cartoon director Gene Deitch's studio in Prague. Larry Harmon Productions, which created and produced TV's *Bozo the Clown*, handled production of 18 cartoons, while Gerald Ray's TV Spots, an all-purpose animation factory, produced 10 vehicles for the series. *A King Features Production in association with Larry Harmon Productions/Paramount Cartoon Studios/Jack Kinney Studios/Gene Deitch Studios/Rembrandt Films, TV Spots/Halas and Batchelor. Color. Half-hour. Premiered: 1960. Syndicated.*

**Voices**
**Popeye:** Jack Mercer; **Brutus:** Jackson Beck; **Olive Oyl:** Mae Questel; **J. Wellington Wimpy:** Charles Lawrence, Jack Mercer; **Swee'pea/Sea Hag/Eugene the Jeep:** Mae Questel; **Rough House:** Jack Mercer

## ◉ POPEYE THE SAILOR

One of several early series repackaging old films for television, this series was comprised of the six-minute "Popeye the Sailor" cartoons produced between 1933 and 1954 by Paramount Pictures. In many television markets, the cartoons were screened for young viewers in programs hosted by local television celebrities. (See entry in Theatrical Sound Cartoon Series for listing of films.) Famous Studios and Paramount Pictures produced 125 theatrical cartoon shorts until 1957. Paramount ultimately sold the entire Popeye backlist to Associated Artists Productions (AAP), which syndicated the package of films to television. Subsequently, AAP was sold to United Artists, which later merged with Metro-Goldwyn-Mayer, and the Popeye film library became the property of Turner Entertainment following Ted Turner's purchase of MGM in 1986. Turner sold off MGM's production end two years later but retained its vast film holdings. As a result, the former MGM films ended up airing on Turner-owned cable networks TBS and then TNT, beginning in the 1980s, and in the 1990s on Cartoon Network and Turner Classic Movies and later on Cartoon Network's sister network, Boomerang. On Cartoon Network, the cartoon shorts were often shown on the popular weekday anthology series *ACME Hour*, which was canceled in 2002 but re-emerged three years later on Boomerang. In 2001, for the first time since their original theatrical releases, Cartoon Network also aired the Fleischer and Famous Studios Popeye cartoons, unaltered, complete and uncut in both black-and-white and color, under the title of *The Popeye Show*. A Max Fleischer/Famous Studios Production in association with Paramount Pictures. Black-and-white. Color. Half-hour. Premiered: September 10, 1956. Syndicated. Rebroadcast on TBS: 1986–Fall 1998. Rebroadcast on TNT: 1988–Fall 1998. Rebroadcast on TCM: 1994–. Rebroadcast on CAR: April 1, 1998–September 1, 2002 ("ACME Hour"). Rebroadcast on CAR: 2001 ("The Popeye Show"). Rebroadcast on BOOM: December 1, 2005 ("ACME Hour")–.

### Voices

**Popeye:** William Costello, Jack Mercer; **Olive Oyl:** Mae Questel; **Bluto:** Gus Wickie, Pinto Colvig, William Pennell; **J. Wellington Wimpy:** Jack Mercer, Lou Fleischer, Frank Matalone; **Swee'pea:** Mae Questel; **Poodpeck Pappy/Pupeye/Peepeye/Pipeye:** Jack Mercer; **Shorty:** Arnold Stang

## ◉ POPPLES

Able to produce just about anything they need—from a trampoline to a pair of skates—these furry little creatures live in a world scaled for adults with their human friends, Bonnie and Billy and always come up with creative solutions to any obstacles in their way. A DIC Enterprises Production. Color. Half-hour. Premiered: September 13, 1986–June 27, 1987. Syndicated.

### Voices

**Bonnie/Billy/Mike:** Valrie Bromfield; **Potato Chip:** Donna Christie; **Penny:** Jeannie Elias; **Punkster/Putter:** Danny Mann; **Pan Cake:** Sharon Noble; **Party/Punkity/Prize/Puffball:** Louise Vallance; **Puzzle:** Maurice LaMarche; **Other Voices:** Len Carlson, Diane Fabian, Dan Hennessey, Hadley Kaye, Jazmin Lausanne, Barbara Redpath, Pauline Rennie, Linda Sorenson, Noam Zylberman

**THE POPPLES:** **Potato Chip:** Donna Christie; **Penny:** Jeanine Elias; **Punkster/Putter:** Danny Mann, **Pancake:** Sharon Noble; **Party/Punkity/Prize/Puffball:** Louise Vallance; **Puzzle:** Maurice LaMarche

*Furry little creatures bring fun and excitement wherever they go in DIC Enterprises' Popples. © American Greetings Corp. (COURTESY: DIC ENTERPRISES)*

## ◉ POP-UPS

Paul Klein produced this series of 12 one-minute education fillers, aimed at encouraging reading among young viewers, that were broadcast sporadically as part of NBC's Saturday-morning schedule in 1971. An Educational Solutions Production. Color. One minute. Premiered on NBC: January 23, 1971–August 28, 1971.

## ◉ THE PORKY PIG SHOW

P-P-Porky Pig was the host of his own Saturday-morning series, featuring the cartoons of "Daffy Duck," "Bugs Bunny," "Sylvester and Tweety," "Foghorn Leghorn" and "Pepe Le Pew." In 1971, four years after its network run, the series was syndicated to television under the title *Porky Pig and His Friends*. (See series' entries in Theatrical Sound Cartoon Series for complete details.) A Warner Bros. Production. Color. Half-hour. Premiered on ABC: September 20, 1964–September 2, 1967.

### Voices

**Porky Pig:** Mel Blanc

## ◉ POSTCARDS FROM BUSTER

Live-action/animated spin-off from the 2003 episode of the Emmy Award-winning animated series, *Arthur*, following the adventures (which he narrates) of the famed aardvark's eight-year-old rabbit bestfriend, Buster, and his divorced pilot father, Bo Baxter, who flies a rock group on a North American tour, with Buster recording the amazing people, places and discoveries on his video camera (given to him by his mom, Bitzi) via first-person video postcards he sends to his friends in his hometown of Elwood City. Promoting cultural understanding and literacy, language and communication skills, the half-hour children's series, coproduced by WGBH Boston, Marc Brown Studios and Canadian animation giant, CINAR Animation (now called Cookie Jar Entertainment), and funded in part by a Ready To Learn cooperative agreement with the U.S. Department of Education, the 42-episode children's series, first aired on October 11, 2004, on *PBS Kids GO!* weekday program block. A CINAR Animation/WGBH Boston/Marc Brown Studios Production. Color. Half-hour. Premiered on PBS Kids: October 11, 2004.

### Voices

**Arthur Read:** Cameron Ansell; **David Read, Arthur's Father/Binky Barnes:** Bruce Dinsmore; **Jane Read, Arthur's Mother:** Sonja Ball; **Buster Baxter:** Daniel Brochu; **Bitzi Baxter:** Ellen

David; **Bo Baxter:** Marcel Jeannin; **Holy G. Frankel:** Fern Walters; **Mora of Los Viajeros:** Elizabeth Diaga (2004–05), Stephanie Martin (2005–  ); **Carlos of Los Viajeros:** Norman Groulx; **Muffy Crosswire:** Melissa Altro; **Ed Crosswire:** A.J. Henderson; **Mr. Rathburn:** Arthur Holden; **Sue Ellen Armstrong:** Jessica Kardos; **Francine Frensky:** Jodie Resther; **Dora Winfred "D.W." Read:** Jason Szimmer; **Alan "The Brain" Powers:** Alex Wood

### ◉ POUND PUPPIES

Inspired by the hit toy from Tonka Corporation, this half-hour adventures series centered on the exploits of 11-year-old Holly and her merry band of canine friends who live in the Wagga Wagga Pound and do everything they can to find happy homes for deserving dogs, despite the efforts of Katrina and Brattina. The series was preceded by a 1985 hour-long syndicated animated special, *Pound Puppies,* which aired on ABC. The 13-episode series debuted Saturday mornings on ABC, in September of 1986. In 1987 a second series followed: *All-New Pound Puppies.* The original series was later rebroadcast on Disney Channel and Cartoon Network. *A Hanna-Barbera Production. Color. Half-hour. Premiered: October 1985 (special). Premiered on ABC: September 13, 1986–September 5, 1987. Rebroadcast on DIS: 1991. Rebroadcast on CAR: April 5, 1993–June 3, 1994 (weekdays); September 4, 1995–1997 (weekdays).*

**Voices**
**Cooler, the leader:** Dan Gilvezan; **Bright Eyes:** Nancy Cartwright; **Howler:** Bobby Morse; **Whopper:** B.J. Ward; **Nose Marie:** Ruth Buzzi; **Holly, their 11-year-old friend:** Ami Foster; **Katrina Stoneheart:** Pat Carroll; **Brattina Stoneheart, her sister:** Adrienne Alexander; **Nabbit/Cat Gut:** Frank Welker

### ◉ THE POWERPUFF GIRLS

After combining "sugar, spice and everything nice" during a laboratory experiment to create the "perfect girl," Professor Utoniun mistakenly includes "Chemical X" as part of his potion and accidentally creates three cute superpowered girls who fight the forces of evil—the butt-kicking Bubbles, the brassy Buttercup and the take-charge Blossom—in this original animated series created by animator Craig McCracken for Cartoon Network.

McCracken originated the popular superheroines in a 1992 cartoon short he produced called *The Whoopass Girls! In a Sticky Situation,* which played at the Spike and Mike's Sick and Twisted Festival of Animation in 1994. In 1995, Cartoon Network subsequently commissioned him to write, produce and direct a series of additional cartoon shorts. retitled *The Powerpuff Girls,* which premiered on Cartoon Network's *World Premiere Toons* anthology series, with their first appearance entitled "Meat Fuzzy Lumkins."

Three years later, in 1998, production commenced on a regular weekly cartoon series that debuted later that year, enjoying the highest-rated premiere in Cartoon Network history and regularly ranking as the network's highest-rated series largely with boys and girls as well as with teens and adults. Named one of *TV Guide's* "Top 10 New Kids Shows" after its debut, the dueling crimefighters starred in an amazing 80 cartoon adventures over six seasons, amassing their share of industry honors, including five prime time Emmy Award nominations, winning in 2000 and 2005 for outstanding individual achievement in animation.

In 2002, Cartoon Network anticipated the characters' success would translate to the box office and starred the trio in their only theatrical cartoon feature, *The Powerpuff Girls Movie* (2002). Budgeted at $25 million, the film grossed a disappointing $11 million in domestic ticket revenue and was a financial flop. Meanwhile, in May of that year, the powerful trio began reairing Saturday mornings on the WB Television Network's Kids' WB!

Beginning in late February 2003, dubbed and edited 22-minute episodes of the popular superheroines were shown exclusively for one year on terrestrial television in China through China Central Television Station (CCTV) and were viewed by nearly 90 percent of the nation's 1.3 billion people. That May, Cartoon Network debuted the famous threesome's animated movie, *The Powerpuffs Girls Movie* (2002), followed by an all-new, hour-long, direct-to-video holiday special in December entitled *'Twas the Fright before Christmas,* released on DVD that October by Warner Home Video.

During the series' impressive run, the characters' burgeoning popularity created a frenzy of licensed apparel and other merchandise that topped more than $1 billion in retail sales. In January 2004, the superpowered sisters starred in a new batch of episodes that premiered Friday night in prime time. *A Hanna-Barbera/Cartoon Network Production. Color. Half-hour. Premiered on CAR: November 18, 1998–March 1, 2005. Rebroadcast on the WB (Kids' WB!): May 25, 2002–July 20, 2002.*

**Voices**
**Blossom:** Cathy Cavadine; **Buttercup:** E. G. Daily; **Bubbles:** Tara Strong; **Professor Utonium:** Tom Kane; **Princess Morbucks/Ms. Keane:** Jennifer Hale; **Mayor:** Tom Kenny

### ◉ PREHISTORIC PLANET

Comedian Ben Stiller narrated this kid-friendly, state-of-the-art, digitally-animated series, featuring footage first seen in two hugely successful prime-time specials, *Walking with Dinosaurs* and *Walking with Prehistoric Beasts,* coproduced by the Discovery Channel and the BBC. Airing Saturday mornings on NBC and Discovery Kids, on which the show simultaneously premiered in October 2002, this educational half-hour series was comprised of ingeniously scripted and produced "dino-dramas" featuring animated recreations of amazing lumbering giants that once roamed the Earth, including the Brachiosaurus, the Diplodocous, the Ornithocheirus, the Stegosaurus and many others. Actor Christian Slater later replaced Stiller as the series' narrator. *A Stone House Productions/BBC/Discovery Kids Production. Color. Half-hour. Premiered on NBC: October 5, 2002–September 2003. Premiered on DSCK: October 5, 2002–September 2003. Rebroadcast on DSCK: September 2003–.*

**Voices**
**Narrator:** Ben Stiller, Christian Slater

### ◉ PRINCE PLANET

Sent to Earth by the Galactic Council to see if the planet is fit to join the Galactic Union of Worlds, Prince Planet, a member of the Universal Peace Corps, takes on a new identity once on Earth (Bobby). Using his awesome powers, whose source is a generator on the planet Radion, he battles criminal conspirators and other sinister beings who plan to take over the world. Corps members Hadji and Dynamo join Prince Planet in the fight. The 52-episode half-hour series was among a handful of many Japanese-made cartoons syndicated in the United States in the 1960s. *A TCJ Animation Center (Eiken Studios) Production in association with American-International. Color. Half-hour. Premiered: September 1966. Syndicated.*

**Voices**
**Prince Planet:** Bobbie Byers; **Dan Dynamo:** Mark Harris; **Ajababa:** Kurt Nagel; **Warlock:** Arnie Warren; **Krag:** Frank Schuller; **Diana Worthy:** Sandy Warshaw; **Pop Worthy:** Jeff Gillen

## PRINCESS GWENEVERE AND THE JEWEL RIDERS

The Princess and two heroic teenage girls, who "ride the wild magic," try to recover Merlin's crown jewels of the kingdom in this half-hour fantasy/adventure series broadcast as part of the syndicated weekend block *Amazin' Adventures II*. Debuting in 1995 with the two-part episode "Jewel Quest," 26 half-hours were produced of the series, which aired for two seasons in first-run syndication. A *New Frontier Entertainment/Bohbot Production*. *Color. Half-hour. Premiered: September 9, 1995–January 10, 1997 (part of Amazin' Adventures II). Syndicated.*

### Voices

**Princess Gwenevere:** Kerri Butler; **Other Voices:** Deborah Allison, John Beach, Laura Dean, Peter Fernandez, Jean Louisa Kelly, Henry Mandell, Corinne Orr

## PRINCESS NATASHA

Originally developed by founder and CEO Larry Schwarz of Animation Collective as a flagship web series with 20 original cartoons developed for America Online's children's service, AOL Kids, and its first online animated cartoon to migrate to network television, this half-hour animated counterpart featured the adventures of a foreign exchange student and secret agent, Princess Natasha of Zoravia, who thwarts her evil Uncle Lubek's plan to assume control of her beloved country between playing on the varsity basketball team and developing a huge crush on her host family's older son, Greg O'Brien. Produced for television by New York independent studio, Animation Collective, the half-hour Flash-animated series debuted on Cartoon Network. In the fall of 2006, CBS picked up the series to reair as part of its new Saturday (and Sunday on some CBS affiliates, which broke it into two 90-minute blocks) three-hour programming block, *KOL Secret Slumber Party on CBS*. An *Animation Collective Production. Color. Half-hour, Premiered on CAR: May 1, 2004. Rebroadcast on CBS: September 16, 2006–.*

## PROBLEM CHILD

Junior Healy, a "bad boy"–adopted junior high teen, makes big problems for his parents, his teachers (with help from his co-conspirator/classmate, Cyndi) and the world at large, thanks to his insatiable curiosity and hyperactive imagination, in this weekly half-hour series adaptation based on the popular film series. The program was broadcast opposite *The Itsy Bitsy Spider* cartoon series as part of USA Network's Sunday-morning Cartoon Express beginning in 1993. A *D'Ocon Film/Universal Cartoon Studios Production. Color. Half-hour. Premiered on USA: October 31, 1993–September 15, 1996.*

### Voices

**Peabody:** Gilbert Gottfried; **Junior Healy:** Ben Diskin; **Cyndi:** E.G. Daily; **Big Ben Healy:** Jonathan Harris; **Yoji/Murph:** John Kassir; **Little Ben Healy:** Mark Taylor; **Betsy/Ross:** Nancy Cartwright; **Spencer:** Cree Summer; **Miss Hill:** Iona Morris

## PROJECT G.E.E.K.E.R.

The plans of a rich industrialist (Mr. Moloch) to conquer the world with the help of an artificially created "humanoid" (G.e.e.K.e.R.), a skinny, drooling dork in a jumpsuit who possesses unlimited powers but doesn't know how to use them, are foiled when his prized creation is stolen by streetwise thief Lady Macbeth and her highly intelligent 10-foot dinosaur named Noah, who help G.e.e.K.e.R. fight the ruthless corporate conglomerate that would exploit his powers in this half-hour fantasy series created by Douglas TenNapel and Doug Landgale. A *Columbia-TriStar Children's Television Production. Color. Half-hour. Premiered on CBS: September 14, 1996–August 30, 1997.*

### Voices

**G.e.e.K.e.R.:** Billy West; **Dr. Maston/Jake Dragonn:** Charles Adler; **Moloch/Will Dragonn:** Jim Cummings; **Lady Macbeth (Becky):** Cree Summer; **Noah:** Brad Garrett

## PROSTARS

The world's greatest sports superstars—Wayne Gretzky, Bo Jackson and Michael Jordan—teamed up to save the globe from ecological disasters, armed with an arsenal of high-tech gadgetry, in this action-packed half-hour series of globe-trotting adventures preceded by live-action wraparounds of the famous sports figures to introduce each week's cartoon. DIC Enterprises, which produced the series, originally developed the idea in 1990 for ESPN (then under the name of *All-Stars*), but ESPN opted not to produce the series. The series instead premiered on NBC in the fall of 1991 and was later rebroadcast on the Family Channel. A *DIC Enterprises Production in association with Reteitalia, S.P.A. and Telecinco. Color. Half-hour. Premiered on NBC: September 14, 1991–July 25, 1992. Rebroadcast on FAM: September 5, 1992–March 27, 1994.*

### Cast (live action)

**Bo Jackson:** Himself; **Wayne Gretsky:** Himself; **Michael Jordan:** Himself

### Voices

**Wayne Gretzky:** Townsend Coleman; **Bo Jackson:** Dave Fennoy; **Michael Jordan:** Dorian Harewood; **Mama:** Susan Silo; **Denise:** Diana Barrows

## THE PROUD FAMILY

Pubescent 14-year-old Penny Proud tackles the all-important 'tween years of her life and living with her crazy family—Oscar, her over-protective dad; Trudy, loving mom; and siblings, her sister BeBe and younger brother CeCe—and her wild friends, while dealing with situations vital to kids her age (such as trying out for cheerleading) in this animated cartoon sitcom featuring a mostly black cast.

Created by Bruce Smith (*Space Jams, Tarzan*), who coexecutive produced the series along with Ralph Farquhar, Tom Wilhite and Willard Carroll, through his own Jambalaya Studios, this half-hour comedy series, originally produced as a pilot for possible airing on Nickelodeon, premiered on the Disney Channel in the fall of 2001 and was added to ABC's *One Saturday Morning* lineup the following August.

A favorite of young viewers, the 52-episode series returned for a second season on ABC's newly christened *ABC Kids* programming block in September 2003, airing at 9:30 A.M., following *Disney's Fillmore!* and two new series: Disney's animated *Lilo & Stitch: The Series* and the Disney Channel's top-rated live-action sitcom *That's So Raven.*

Numerous well-known African-American figures from the areas of film, television and music lent their voices in guest roles, including David Alan Grier, Robert Guillaume, Mo'Nique, Al Roker, Cicely Tyson, Luther Vandross and Vanessa L. Williams. In September 2004, Disney's all-cartoon network, Toon Disney, began rebroadcasting the series. A *Jambalaya Studios/Disney Enterprises Production. Color. Half-hour. Premiered on DIS: September 15, 2001. Premiered on ABC: August 30, 2002. Rebroadcast on TDIS: September 6, 2004–.*

**Voices**
Penny Proud: Kyla Pratt; Oscar Proud: Tommy Davidson; Trudy Proud: Paula Jai Parker; Suga Mama Proud: Jo Marie Payton; BeBe and CeCe Proud/Puff the Dog: Tara Strong; Bobby Proud: Cedric the Entertainer; Dijonay Jones: Karen Malina White; Sticky Webb: Orlando Brown; Zoey Howzer: Soleil Moon Frye; Michael Collins: Phil LaMarr; Felix Boulevardez: Carlos Mencia; Sunset Boulevardez: Maria Canals; Papi: Alvaro Guittierez; LaCienega Boulevardez: Alisa Reyes; Nubia Gross: Raquel Lee; Wizard Kelly/Lil' Wiz: Aries Spears; Boonnetta Proud: Mo'Nique; Ray Ray Proud Sr.: Anthony Anderson; Dr. Vincent Parker: Robert Guillaume; Mrs. Maureen Parker: Cicely Tyson; Reuben Parker: David Alan Grier; Leslie Parker: Wendy Raquel Robinson; Diana Parker: Sheryl Lee Ralph; Chanel Parker: Solange Knowles; Ray Ray Proud Jr.: Jamal Mixon; Herself: Mariah Carey; Herself: Alicia Keys; Johnny Lovely: Pablo Santos; Agatha Ordinario: Erica Rivera; Omar/Dr. Payne: Kevin Michael Richardson; Himself: Al Roker; Chester the Duck: Frank Welker; Debra Williams: Vanessa L. Williams; Lisa Raye: LisaRaye McCoy; Fifteen "15" Cent: Omarion; Sista Spice: Jenifer Lewis; Michael Collins: Luther Vandross; Peabo: Cree Summer; Smart Baby/Red-Nosed Baby: Ron Glass

## ⊚ PUCCA

Amidst living in the opulent and crazy Sooga Village and with its quirky residents—including Ring Ring, the jealous Beijing Opera singer and Abyo, the Bruce Lee wanna-be,—Pucca, the young, feisty and mischievous daughter of a Chinese restaurant owner, has one purpose in life: to win the heart of the long-suffering Garu, by using either her girlish charms or martial arts in this international cartoon hit, created by VOOZ Co. Ltd. and animated by Studio B of Vancouver, Canada, for Toon Disney's *Jetix* comedy/action/adventure programming block. Twenty-four half-hours comprised of three cartoon episodes were produced for the first season. A cult favorite in Korea and throughout Asia, the character was introduced as the cheeky, eponymous star of a popular online e-card service developed by VOOZ in 2000. The show's second season featured more globetrotting adventures and time-travel plots set in such exotic locales as London and Rio. A *Studio B/VOOZ Co. Ltd. Production/Buena Vista Television. Color. Half-hour. Premiered on TDIS: September 18, 2006–    .*

**Voices**
Pucca: Tabitha St. Germain; Master Soo: Richard Newman; Garu: Brian Drummond; Abyo: Lee Tockar; Chief (Jing Jing): Shannon Chan-Kent; Linguini: Dale Wilson; Ching: Chantal Strand; Santa: French Tickner; Uncle Dumpling: Brian Dobson; Ho: Michael Dobson

## ⊚ A PUP NAMED SCOOBY-DOO

Scooby-Doo, the world's favorite chicken-hearted canine, returns as a cute but clumsy puppy along with kid versions of friends Shaggy, Daphne, Velma and Freddy as they solve kid-size mysteries and encounter ghouls, ghosts and goblins in this 27-episode half-hour series for Saturday mornings. The Emmy award–winning series originally aired for three seasons from 1988 to 1991—marking the 15th, 16th and 17th seasons of Scooby-Doo shows on Saturday-morning television—on ABC. Thirteen brand-new episodes were produced for the first season, eight for the second season and only six for the third season packaged with repeats. ABC then rebroadcast the series for one more season. Reruns later aired on Cartoon Network and its sister network, Boomerang. *A Hanna-Barbera Production. Color. Half-hour. Premiered on ABC: September 10, 1988–August 31, 1991. Rebroadcast on ABC: September 12, 1992–September 4, 1993. Rebroadcast on CAR: April 4, 1994 (weekdays, Sundays); February 26, 1995 (Super Chunk); October 13, 1997 (weekdays, Saturdays). Rebrodcast on BOOM: June 7, 2002–.*

**Voices**
Scooby Doo: Don Messick; Shaggy Rogers: Casey Kasem; Velma Dace Dinkley: Christina Lange; Daphne Blake: Kellie Martin; Freddy Jones: Carl Stevens; Red Herring: Scott Menville

## ⊚ THE PUPPY'S FURTHER ADVENTURES

Joined by his girlfriend, Dolly, and three delightful canine friends, Petey the Pup embarks on a worldwide search for his lost family in this second Saturday-morning series based on several successful *ABC Weekend Specials*, including 1978's *The Puppy Who Wanted a Boy*, which first introduced the character to television audiences. Ten half-hour episodes were produced for the fall of 1983, airing ahead of Hanna-Barbera's *The All-New Scooby and Scrappy-Doo Show* on ABC. *A Ruby-Spears Enterprises Production. Color. Half-hour. Premiered on ABC: September 10, 1983–November 10, 1984. Rebroadcast on ABC: January 21, 1984–September 1, 1984.*

**Voices**
Petey the Pup: Billy Jacoby; Dolly: Nancy McKeon; Duke/Dash: Michael Bell; Lucky: Peter Cullen; Tommy: Tony O'Dell; Glyder: Josh Rodine; Mother: Janet Waldo; Father: John Stephenson

## ⊚ THE PUPPY'S GREAT ADVENTURES

Marking the character's third animated series, Petey the Pup, formerly of 1982's *The Scooby & Scrappy-Doo/Puppy Hour* and 1983's *The Puppy's Further Adventures*, returned in a handful of new episodes in this half-hour weekly series for ABC. The series was the least successful of the three, losing the rating battles against NBC's *Snorks* and CBS's *Shirt Tales*, both produced by Hanna-Barbera. *A Ruby-Spears Enterprises/Hanna-Barbera Production. Color. Half-hour. Premiered on ABC: September 8, 1984–November 10, 1984. Rebroadcast on CBS: September 13, 1986–November 8, 1986.*

**Voices**
Petey the Pup: Billy Jacoby; Dolly: Nancy McKeon; Duke/Dash: Michael Bell; Lucky: Peter Cullen; Tommy: Tony O'Dell; Glyder: Josh Rodine; Mother: Janet Waldo; Father: John Stephenson

## ⊚ Q.T. HUSH

This satirical "who-dun-it?" series spotlighted the adventures of a private eye, Q.T. Hush, and his "private-nose" bloodhound, Shamus, who combine forces to solve baffling crimes and mysteries. Hush succeeded in jailing criminals by transforming himself into a shadow named Quincy, who operated independently in tracking down clues in this half-hour series, comprised of 100 five-minute cliff-hanging adventures (10 segments constituted a complete story), produced for first-run syndication. *An Animation Associates M & A Alexander/NTA Production. Color. Half-hour. Premiered: September 24, 1960. Syndicated.*

**Voices**
Q.T. Hush: Dallas McKennon

## ⊚ QUACK ATTACK

Daily anthology series, airing since 1992 on The Disney Channel, showcasing classic Disney animated cartoon shorts representing 60 years of work by studio animators. *A Walt Disney Company Production. Color. Half-hour. Premiered on DIS: 1992.*

*U.S. Marshall Quick Draw McGraw and sidekick Baba Looey are joined by series stars Blabber, Doggie Daddy, Augie Doggie, and Snooper from Hanna-Barbera's Quick Draw McGraw series. © Hanna-Barbera Productions*

## ◎ QUICK DRAW MCGRAW

Law and order are the name of the game as U.S. Marshall Quick Draw McGraw and his Mexican burro sidekick, Baba Looey, corral cutthroats and other villains in untypical cowboy-hero fashion. (Quick habitually ignores his pal's advice and strides resolutely into catastrophe.) Additional plot lines feature Quick as notorious crime fighter El Kabong, a klutzy takeoff of Disney's popular *Zorro* television series, and his own romantic entanglements with a frustrated filly named Sagebrush Sal. Snuffles, a "dog-biskit" loving dog, was another recurring character in the series. (Once rewarded, he gently floated in midair, symbolizing his ecstasy.)

McGraw's cartoon adventures were the main ingredient of this popular, 45-episode syndicated series, sponsored by Kellogg's and first syndicated in 1959. The program marked Hanna-Barbera's second syndicated series effort made especially for the children's market. It featured two other series regulars: "Snooper and Blabber," a cat (Super Snooper) and mouse (Blabber Mouse) pair of crime investigators who, operating out of the Super Snooper Detective Agency, flush out the city's most-wanted criminals; and "Augie Doggy and Doggie Daddy," starring the ever-affectionate father dog, Daddy (who sounds like Jimmy Durante) and his canine son, Augie, who get caught up in various misadventures.

The program was later rebroadcast on CBS as part of its Saturday-morning lineup in 1963 before returning to syndication and was aired on USA Network. Ted Turner's Cartoon Network began airing the series in 1994 and packaged episodes from the show as

part of a 1995 weeklong prime-time showcase, "Prime Quick Draw McGraw," hosted by popular hosts Haas and Little Joe, daytime stars of Cartoon Network's "High Noon Toons." In April 2000 the series began reairing on Cartoon Network's classic cartoons channel, Boomerang. *A Hanna-Barbera Production in association with screen Gems. Color. Half-hour. Premiered: September 29, 1959. Syndicated. Rebroadcast on CBS: September 28, 1963–September 3, 1966. Rebroadcast on USA: 1989–92. Rebroadcast on CAR: September 11, 1994–June 28, 1995 (Sundays, Wednesdays); February 26, 1995 (Super Chunk); July 24, 1995–June 28, 1995 (Prime Quick Draw McGraw); October 13, 1997– (weekdays). Rebroadcast on BOOM: April 1, 2000–.*

**Voices**
**Quick Draw McGraw/Baba Looey/Injun Joe/Snuffles:** Daws Butler; **Sagebrush Sal:** Julie Bennett; **Snooper/Blabber/Augie Doggie:** Daws Butler; **Doggie Daddy:** Doug Young

***Other Voices***
Don Messick

## ◎ THE RACCOONS

Bert Raccoon is just about the best friend anyone could wish for. He's funny, brave, friendly and slightly crazy. He lives with his good friends Ralph and Melissa in a Raccoondominium. Together they run the forest newspaper, the *Evergreen Standard*. However, Bert is usually more interested in playing detective or flying a hang glider than in writing his news column in this half-hour series, originally created by Kevin Gillis for Canadian television. The series debuted on the Canadian CBC TV network in the late 1970s and premiered in the United States on the Disney Channel in 1985. Previously the characters appeared in several successful animated specials, among them *The Christmas Raccoons* and *The Raccoons on Ice*. A Gillis-Wiseman Production in association with Atkinson Film-ARTS/CBC. Color. Half-hour. Premiered on DIS: October 1985–1992.

**Voices**
**Bert Raccoon:** Len Carlson; **Ralph Raccoon:** Bob Dermer; **Melissa Raccoon:** Linda Feige, Susan Roman; **Schaeffer:** Carl Banas; **Cyril Sneer/Snag:** Michael Magee; **Cedric Sneer:** Marvin Goldhar; **Dan the Ranger:** Murray Cruchley; **Julie:** Vanessa Lindores; **Tommy:** Noam Zylberman; **Bear:** Bob Dermer; **Sophia/Broo:** Sharon Lewis; **Pig One:** Nick Nichols; **Pig #2/Pig #3:** Len Carlson; **Narrator:** Geoffrey Winter

## ◉ RAINBOW BRITE

Rainbow Brite, a courageous young girl with a special rainbow-making belt, travels the world by rainbow roads to spread happiness and hope to those in need and to chase away unhappiness in the form of the miserable and mean Murky and Lurky, who do what they can to take Rainbow's power away. Rainbow is joined in her adventures by her faithful horse, Starlite, and her best friend, Twink. This half-hour series was part of the 90-minute syndicated cartoon block "Kideo TV." (See entry for details.) The characters previously appeared in a brace of half-hour animated specials: *Rainbow Brite: The Peril of the Pits* (1984), *Rainbow Brite: The Mighty Monstermunk Menace* (1984) and *Rainbow Brite: The Beginning of Rainbowland* (1985). A DIC Enterprises Production in association with Hallmark Cards. Color. Half-hour. Premiered: 1986. Syndicated.

**Voices**
**Rainbow Brite:** Bettina Nash; **Starlite, her horse:** Andre Stojka; **Twink, her best friend:** Robbie Lee; **Murky/Monstromurk/Narrator:** Peter Cullen; **Lurky/Buddy/Evil Force:** Pat Fraley; **Brian:** Scott Menville; **Indigo/Violet/Lala/Sprites:** Robbie Lee; **Red/Patty/Canary:** Mona Marshall; **Moonglow/Tickled Pink:** Ronda Aldrich

## ◉ RAINBOW FISH

Rainbow Fish, the colorful male fish with his distinctive shiny scales and his water-faring friends—including female companion Sea Filly, Salmontha, and others made famous in Mark Pfister's beloved children's book—come to the small screen in this series of adventures in which they learn many valuable lessons about friendship, sharing, tolerance and perseverance. Produced by DECODE Entertainment in association with Sony Wonder, this 26-part, half-hour series targeting boys and girls ages four to seven made its debut in the United States on HBO in February 2000. It followed a successful series of animated videos released in Canada in 1997. A DECODE Entertainment/United Media/Sony Wonder Production. Color. Half-hour. Premiered on HBO FAM: February 19, 2000–April 10, 2000. Rebroadcast on HBO FAM: April 2000–February 24, 2007.

**Voices**
**Rainbow Fish:** Rhys Huber; **Salmontha/Girly Girl:** Erin Fitzgerald

## ◉ RAMBO

Rambo, the leader of the specially trained team, the Force of Freedom, and fellow agents Kat, Turbo, Nomad, Sgt. Havoc and Mad Dog, are unofficially assigned by the U.S. government to accomplish seemingly impossible missions—their target: the diabolical organization, S.A.V.A.G.E., led by the sinister General Warhawk—in this

*A decorated Vietnam war veteran turned freedom fighter leads a team of specially trained agents in Ruby-Spears's* Rambo. *© Ruby-Spears Enterprises/Anabasis Investments*

first-run adventure series based on the character played by Sylvester Stallone in the top-grossing action-adventure film series. First syndicated in April of 1986 as a five-part miniseries entitled "The Invasion," in which General Warhawk plans to take over a Third World country for a permanent home base, the program returned as daily series, with 65 original episodes, in the fall of that year. A Ruby-Spears Enterprises Production in association with Carolco International/Worldvision. Color. Half-hour. Premiered: April 14, 1986–April 18, 1986 (five-part miniseries); September 15, 1986–87 (series). Syndicated.

**Voices**
**Rambo:** Neil Ross; **Colonel Trautman:** Alan Oppenheimer; **Kat:** Mona Marshall; **Turbo:** James Avery; **Nomad:** Edmund Gilbert; **General Warhawk:** Michael Ansara; **Gripper:** Lennie Weinrib; **Sgt. Havoc:** Peter Cullen; **Mad Dog:** Frank Welker; **Black Dragon:** Robert Ito

## ◉ RAVE MASTER

Following a 50-year-old epic battle between the forces of light and darkness that resulted in the explosion of the light's previous Rave Stones throughout the world, a new Rave Master named Haru Glory embarks on the heroic journey of a lifetime to find the legendary stones that will give him amazing power, while joining forces with a girl named Elie and a lovable creature named Plue to defeat the evil Shadow Stones. The English version of this popular anime series began airing on Cartoon Network in June 2004 with 26 half-hour episodes. A Studio DEEN/RAVE Production Committee/TBS Production. Color. Half-hour. Premiered on CAR: June 4, 2004–September 25, 2005.

**Voices**
**Haru Glory:** Yuri Lowenthal; **Elie:** Michelle Ruff; **Plue:** Mona Marshall; **Sieg Hart:** Crispin Freeman; **Hedara Musica:** Doug Erholtz; **Let:** Doug Stone; **Griff:** Tom Kenny; **King:** Peter Lurie; **Solasido:** Ping Wu; **La Grace:** Joe Ochman; **Gunnert:** R. Martin Klein; **Berial:** Kirk Thorton; **Mikan/Rub:** Bob Glouberman; **Hebi:** Nicholas Guest; **Real Admiral/Big Guard:** David Lodge; **Narrator/Shiba:** Alan Shearman

## ◉ RAW TOONAGE

This kiddie-oriented, fully animated half-hour series (a sort of animated *Saturday Night Live* for kids), hosted by a different guest host each week, served as a showcase for a pair of new 'toons featured in their own segments each week: "Bonkers," the madcap adventures of misfit Bonkers T. Bobcat (an unemployed cartoon star) who tries to make it as a delivery boy, and "Marsupilami," based on the Franco-Belgain comic-book character of a quick-witted cheetah who gets out of a series of jams thanks to his tail (which happens to be the world's longest). The series ran for one full season on CBS; thereafter, "Bonkers" and "Marsupilami" were spun off into their own half-hour series. *A Walt Disney Television Animation Production. Color. Half-hour. Premiered on CBS: September 19, 1992–September 4, 1993.*

*Voices*
**Jitters A. Dog:** Jack Angel, Rene Auberjonois, Jeff Bennett; **Grumbles the Grizzly:** Gregg Berger, Scott Bullock, Rodger Bumpass; **Ludwig Von Drake:** Corey Burton; **Fawn Deer:** Jody Carlisle, Nancy Cartwright; **Gosalyn Mallard:** Christine Cavanaugh; **Bonkers D. Bobcat/Norman/Don Karnage/Roderick Lizzard:** Brian Cummings; **Goofy:** Bill Farmer; **Norman's Aunt:** David Fenoy, June Foray; **Marsupilami:** Pat Fraley, Teresa Ganzel, Maurice LaMarche, Katie Leigh, Steve Mackall; **Launchpad McQuack:** Tress MacNeille, Gail Matthius, Terry McGovern; **Badly Animated Man:** Rita Moreno, Gary Owens; **Maurice:** Rob Paulsen, Joe Piscopo, Hal Rayle, Kath Soucie, Russi Taylor, Dave Thomas, Marcia Wallace, B.J. Ward, Frank Welker; **Sebastian:** Samuel E. Wright; **Scrooge McDuck:** Alan Young

### ⊚ THE REAL ADVENTURES OF JONNY QUEST

Originally called *Jonny Quest: The New Adventures*, this series brought Jonny, Hadji, Bandit, Dr. Benton Quest, Race Bannon and the rest of the crew back from the 1960's cartoon series, this time caught in dangers in the real world and in virtual reality, armed with an array of high-tech gadgets. For this series of 65 new half-hour adventures, the characters were radically revamped and featured an *NYPD Blue*–style theme song and a virtual reality segment called "Questworld." Jonny, now 13, was made more muscular than his punky former self. Race Bannon suddenly went from being a dashing bachelor to a father with a daughter, Jessie, supplying some conflict in the story lines. Johnny's barking dog Bandit was cut form the original cast and was not featured in the new series.

In an attempt to overcome the limited viewership of Cartoon Network, then beamed into only 12 million homes, Turner Broadcasting System simultaneously premiered the series on TNT and TBS. The series premiered in late August of 1996, airing for 21 consecutive weeks on all three networks. The show's debut came three months after a 24 Farewell Marathon of Hanna-Barbera's original *Adventures of Jonny Quest*. Unfortunately, this latest rendition produced dismal ratings and only 52 episodes were aired. Cartoon Network continued running the series on its Toonami program block until September 1999 and in other time slots until December 2002. The action-adventure series was also rebroadcast on FOX's Saturday-morning FOX Kids' block from November 1999 to May 2000. *A Hanna-Barbera Production. Color. Half-hour. Premiered on CAR/TBS/TNT: August 26, 1996–April 16, 1997. Rebroadcast on CAR: April 23, 1997–September 24, 1999 (Toonami); September 1999–December 14, 2002. Rebroadcast on FOX: November 22, 1999–May 26, 2000.*

*Voice*
**Jonny Quest:** J.D. Roth, Quinton Flynn; **Dr. Benton Quest:** George Segal, John de Lancie; **Hadji:** Michael Benyaer, Rob Paulsen; **Bandit:** Frank Welker; **Race Bannon:** Robert Patrick, Robert Foxworth; **Jessie Bannon:** Jesse Douglas, Jennifer Hale;

**Williams Messenger:** Dee Bradley Baker, Michael Benyaer; **Ezekiel Rage:** Michael Bell; **Dr. Forbes:** Earl Boen; **Dr. Karel:** Dean Jones; **Dr. Vedder:** Jim Meskimen; **Iris the Computer:** B.J. Ward

### ⊚ THE REAL GHOSTBUSTERS

To avoid confusion with Filmation's *Ghostbusters* series based on the popular 1975 live-action series, the producers of this series, adapted from the hit motion picture, changed the title of their program to make sure that audiences knew the difference. In this animated update, those three misfits who singlehandedly saved New York from supernatural destruction are up to their same old tricks, keeping the city safe from demons, curses, spooks and every other off-the-wall weirdness known (and unknown) to mortal man. Premiering on ABC in 1986, the series entered daily syndication, with all-new episodes, in 1987.

Comedian Arsenio Hall was the voice of Peter Venkman and Winston Zeddmore for the 1986–87 season. He was replaced the next season by voice artists Lorenzo Music (as Venkman) and Edward L. Jones (as Zeddmore). Ray Parker Jr.'s original hit song is featured as the program's theme. In 1988, after two successful seasons on the network, ABC commissioned a third season of shows under the new title of *Slimer! The Real Ghostbusters*. The concept was reprised in the 1997 syndicated series *Extreme Ghostbusters*, featuring mostly an all-new cast of characters.

USA Network rebroadcast the original series for two years as part of its cartoon program block *Cartoon Express* beginning in 1992. The series was then rerun on Fox Family Channel beginning in August 1998. *A DIC Enterprises Production. Color. Half-hour. Premiered on ABC: September 13, 1986–September 3, 1988. Syndicated: September 14, 1987–September 4, 1992. Rebroadcast on USA: September 18, 1992–September 4, 1994. Rebroadcast on FOX FAM: August 14, 1998–October 8, 1999.*

*Voices*
**Peter Venkman:** Arsenio Hall, Lorenzo Music; **Winston Zeddmore:** Arsenio Hall, Edward L. Jones; **Egon Spengler:** Maurice LaMarche; **Janine Melnitz:** Laura Summer, Kath Soucie; **Ray Stantz:** Frank Welker; **Slimer:** Frank Welker

### ⊚ THE REAL STORY OF . . .

Thirteen famous nursery rhymes and classic children's tales, including Humpty Dumpty and others, are brought to life by a cast of well-known motion picture stars and recording artists, many of whom narrate each story and provide other voices, in this series of half-hour specials (repackaged versions of episodes from a 1990 Canadian television cartoon series called *Favorite Songs*) that premiered on HBO on New Year's Day 1994. The series opened with the half-hour adaptation of "Baa Baa Black Sheep," featuring the voices of Robert Stack and Shelley Long. It was preceded each Saturday morning by another animated series, *The Legend of White Fang* (by the same producer).

Subsequent specials included "Au Clair de la Lune," featuring Milton Berle as the Prince of Darkness; "Frere Jacques," with Stevie Nicks as the Wizard Owl; "Happy Birthday to You," costarring Roger Daltrey and Ed Asner; "Here Comes the Bride," featuring Carol Kane as Margaret Mouse; and "Humpty Dumpty," featuring the voices of Huey Lewis and Oscar-winning actress Glenda Jackson.

Other series titles included: "I'm a Little Teapot," starring Julian Lennon, son of former Beatle John Lennon; "Itsy Bitsy Spider," with voices by Malcolm Jamal-Warner and Patti LaBelle; "O Christmas Tree," costarring John Ritter and Deborah Harry; "Rain, Rain, Go Away," featuring Joe Piscopo and Robin Leach (of TV's *Lifestyles of the Rich and Famous* fame); "Sur le Pont D'Avignon," voiced by Robert Guillaume; "Three Little Kittens," starring Lauren Bacall as the character Freezelda; and "Twinkle Twinkle Little Star," costarring Martin Short and *Wheel of Fortune*'s Vanna White. (See individual entries under Animated Television Specials for further details.)

Some entries in the series—"Rain, Rain Go Away" (retitled, "The Prince's Rain"), "Humpty Dumpty" (instead called, "The Rise and Fall of Humpty Dumpty"), "I'm A Little Teapot" (renamed "The Runaway Teapot"), "Itsy Bitsy Spider" (retitled, "Spider Junior High") and "Three Little Kittens" (renamed, "The Ice Queen's Mittens")—originally debuted in 1991 as part of the HBO cartoon anthology series, *HBO Storybook Musicals*. (See individual entries in Animated Television Specials for further details.) *A CINAR Films Production in association with France Animation. Western Publishing Company/CTV Television. Color. Half-hour. Premiered on HBO: January 1, 1994.*

## ◉ REBOOT

Daring to defy evil, Bob, the heroic digital denizen of a personal computer, battles an evil virus named MegaByte and sister strain Hexadecimal from taking control of the computer metropolis of Mainframe. In so doing he protects his friends Dot Matrix, her brother Enzo and thousands of friendly bionomes from this vicious plague in the first all-computer-generated animated series produced for network television. It took the series' producers three years—and many backers—to bring the innovative 23-episode show, which premiered on ABC in the fall of 1994 (with opening episode "The Tearing"), to the air. In 1996, Disney's takeover of Capital Cities/ABC, resulted in the show's cancellation, despite high ratings. That fall Claster Television, a well-known syndicator, repackaged episodes from both seasons and sold the series to 105 independent stations, airing in daytime syndication through September of 1997. A third season of new *ReBoot* cartoons aired for the first time on U.S. television on Cartoon Network followed by rebroadcasts of the original episodes from the first two seasons. *A BLT/Alliance Communications/Mainframe Entertainment Production in association with Claster Television. Color. Half-hour. Premiered on ABC: September 10, 1994–September 2, 1995; September 9, 1995–July 20, 1996. Syndicated: September 16, 1996–September 12, 1997. Premiered/Rebroadcast on CAR: March 15, 1999–December 28, 2001.*

### Voices
**Bob:** Michael Benyaer, Ian James Corlett; **Dot:** Kathleen Barr; **Young Andraia:** Andrea Libman; **Young Enzo:** Jesse Moss, Matthew Sinclair; **Grown Andraia:** Sharon Alexander; **Grown Enzo:** Paul Spencer Dobson; **Megabyte:** Tony Jay; **Hexadecimal:** Shirley Miller; **Slash-2:** Scott McNeil; **Mouse:** Louise Vallance; **Mike the TV/Phong/Cecil:** Michael Donovan; **Hack:** Gary Chalk

## ◉ THE RED PLANET

Jim and P.J., a brother and sister, are sent to the frightening Lowell Academy, far from home and their parents, on a beautiful but dangerous colony planet where they come of age in this three-part miniseries aired on consecutive Saturday mornings on the FOX Network and based on the novel of the same name. The series was an Environmental Award winner. *A Gunther-Wahl/FOX Children's Network Production. Color. Half-hour. Premiered on FOX: May 14, 1994 (part 1); May 21, 1994 (part 2); May 28, 1994 (part 3). Rebroadcast on FOX: January 7, 1995 (part 1); January 14, 1995 (part 2); January 21, 1995 (part 3); May 4, 1996 (part 1); May 11 (part 2); May 18, 1996 (part 3).*

## ◉ REDWALL

An adopted young mouse named Matthias, along with his friends Cornflower the dormouse, Basil the hare, Constance the badger and the Sparra warriors, saves the besieged Abby, a once peaceful place to live, from the ravages of evil Cluny the Scourge who intends to destroy it in this animated adaptation of author Brian Jacques's series of 12 award-winning children's books. Coproduced by Nelvana Limited of Canada and Alphanim of France, this half-hour fantasy series, first shown on Canada's TeleToon network and on the U.S. PBS Kids' weekend-morning lineup beginning in April 2001 with 13 episodes, featured original artwork, used as models for the animators and painted by acclaimed artist Fangom (a.k.a. Chris Baker), who created the cover art for the British editions, with music performed by the Czechoslovak State Orchestra. A second season of 13 half-hours also aired. *A Nelvana Limited/Alphanim/France 2/France 3/Centre National de la Cinematographic/Molitor Productions Ltd./CTV/United Productions Inc./Teletoon Production. Color. Half-hour. Premiered on PBS: April 1, 2001.*

### Voices
**Matthias Mouse:** Tyrone Savage; **Cornflower Fieldmouse:** Alison Pill, Melissa McIntyre; **Constance Badger:** Janet Wright; **Basil Stag Hare:** Richard Binsley; **Cluny the Scourge:** Diego Matamoros; **Father Abbott:** Chris Wiggins; **Laterose:** Lindsay Connell; **Myrtle:** Alyson Court; **Martin the Warrior:** Amos Crawley; **Slagar:** Tim Curry; **Mrs. Churchmouse/Winifred/Sparra:** Catherine Disher; **Cynthia Vole/Tess Churchmouse:** Sarah Gadon; **Vitch:** Jake Goldsbie; **Sela:** Julie Lemieux; **Warbreak:** Tracey Moore; **Felldoh/Jube:** Ali Muikaddam; **Jess/Rosyqueen:** Susan Roman; **Mattimeo:** Michael Seater; **Abbot Mordalfus:** John Stocker

## ◉ REIGN: THE CONQUEROR

Macedonia's legendary king and the world's most powerful warrior, Alexander the Great, rises to power and triumphs in battle over his enemies in this 21st-century telling with a science fiction twist, produced and designed by Peter Chung of MTV's *Aeon Flux* fame.

First telecast on Hong Kong television in August 1997 as *Alexander Senki* and released in America on home video four years later, this Japanese-imported anime series joined Cartoon Network's *Adult Swim* lineup in February 2003. *An Alexander Committee/Kadokawa/Madhouse/MediaFactory/KBS/Samsung/TokyoPop/MXX Entertainment/TBS Production. Color. Half-hour. Premiered on CAR: February 10, 2003–January 1, 2004.*

### Voices
**Alexander:** Andy Philpot; **Philip/Antipater:** John DiMaggio; **Olympia:** Julia Demita; **Aristotle:** John Lee; **Parmenion:** Michael Scott Ryan; **Attalas:** Dwight Schultz; **Cletus/Hephaestion:** John Demita; **Ptolemy:** Matt McKenzie; **Philotas:** Alex Fernandez; **Narrator:** Jimmy Silver

## ◉ THE RELUCTANT DRAGON AND MR. TOAD

Based on characters and stories in British author Kenneth Grahame's novel *The Wind in Willows*, the kind-hearted, fire-breathing reluctant dragon of Willowmarsh Village, protected by the bumbling knight Sr. Malcolm, and fun-loving gadabout Mr. Toad, master of Toad Hall, were featured in this 17-episode half-hour series, which premiered on ABC in 1970 opposite CBS's *Bugs Bunny/Road Runner Hour* and NBC's *The Heckle and Jeckle Cartoon Show*. *A Rankin-Bass Production. Color. Half-hour. Premiered on ABC: September 12, 1970–September 17, 1972.*

### Voices
Paul Soles, Donna Miller, Claude Rae, Carl Banas

## ◉ REN & STIMPY ADULT PARTY CARTOON

Best known for their flatulence jokes and gross-out humor, Ren, a scrawny, big-eyed asthmatic chihuahua, and Stimpy, his fat, bulbous-nosed cat accomplice return in all-new half-hour adventures intended for adult audiences.

Preceded three days earlier by the premiere of a half-hour special called *Man's Best Friend* (actually a formerly produced yet unaired episode from the original Nickelodeon series, (which the network banned due to its violent and sadistic content), this new half-hour comedy series by *Ren & Stimpy* creator John Kricfalusi, featuring more adult themes and situations than its predecessor, debuted in June 2003 on Spike TV's (formerly TNN)—which billed itself as "The Network for Men"—adult-oriented cartoon block, *The Strip*, along with Kelsey Grammer's animated comedy, *Gary the Rat*, ex-siren Pamela Anderson's fantasy/adventure series, *Stripperella,* and digitally remastered reruns of Kricfalusi's original *The Ren & Stimpy Show* (subtitled "Digitally Re-mastered Classics"). Producing mixed results, the offensive content of the series' five new episodes (that reportedly used plots developed for the original Nickelodeon series), including its premiere with Ren and Stimpy making their gay relationship "official," turned off advertisers and was removed from the schedule in early October of that year and subsequently canceled. In its absence, the classic *The Ren & Stimpy Show* continued airing Tuesday through Saturday at 2:00 A.M. until early July 2004. *A Spumco Production. Color. Half-hour. Premiered on TNN/SPIKE: June 26, 2003–October 2, 2003.*

**Voices**
**Ren Hoek/Dr. Mr. Horse:** John Kricfalusi; **Stimpson J. "Stimpy" Cat:** Eric Bauza; **Fire Chief:** Ralph Bakshi; **Chief's Date:** Cheryl Chase; **Frog:** Tony Hay; **Woman:** Diane Robin; **Narrator:** Vincent Waller

## ◎ THE REN & STIMPY SHOW
Created by John Kricfalusi, this long-running, cynical, wacked-out twist on traditional cartoon teams like Tom and Jerry, featuring a scrawny, asthmatic chihuahua and his obese, dimwitted, tube-sucking feline sidekick in outlandish situations, replete with bad-taste humor, be-bop background music and unhappy endings, was an instant hit with college-age viewers (ages 18–24) following its premiere on Nickelodeon in 1991. Spawning a brace of licensed toys and other merchandise, the series quickly attained cult status with viewers and went on to become a successful franchise for the network.

Kricfalusi, formerly an animation director for Ralph Bakshi's *Mighty Mouse: The New Adventures*, created the characters years ago as office doodles and had tried to sell CBS, ABC and NBC on making the series, diluting the idea by surrounding the characters with a bunch of kids in a show called *Your Gang*. Neither network jumped at the idea. Animation veteran Vanessa Coffey, whom Nickelodeon hired to develop the network's first animated cartoon lineup, saw the potential in Kricfalusi's characters that the major networks had missed.

The series debuted as part of a 90-minute, Sunday-morning cartoon block on Nickelodeon in August 1991 along with *Doug* and *Rugrats*. Six programs were produced for the 1991 season at costs of up $400,000 per episode (almost twice as much as the average Saturday-morning network cartoon series), each comprised of two 11-minute episodes and occasional commercial "parodies." The series was initially broadcast on Sunday mornings on Nickelodeon and was given an 11-week run on MTV, airing Saturday nights, at the end of that year. It proved to be a such a rating success that Nickelodeon renewed the program for a second season and moved it to Saturday evenings in August 1992.

Kricfalusi was busy at work on 13 new half-hour episodes for the 1992–93 season when creative differences, mostly over story content, erupted between him and network executives and his failure to produce new episodes on time resulted in his ouster that September. (The network was forced to repeat the previous six original

episodes because of such delays.) Reportedly, the network rejected at least two episodes because they were "inappropriate and offensive." By the time of his dismissal, Kricfalusi had completed portions of new episodes for the show's third season. Series producer Bob Camp, whom the network had retained, salvaged the shows, bridging them with new animation produced by the network-owned Games Animation division, producers of another Nickelodeon cartoon series, *Rocko's Modern Life*. From 1993 through 1995, the series returned with all-new episodes and was nominated twice for Emmy Awards for outstanding animated program.

From July 2000 to 2001, Nickelodeon rebroadcast the series, with the all-music network VH1 then rerunning the series (as *Ren & Stimpy Rocks*) for two seasons, until Nicktoons began rebroadcasting it under the title of *Ren & Stimpy Extra* two years afterward. In June 2003, digitally remastered reruns of the comedy series, called *The Ren & Stimpy Show: Digitally Remastered Classics*, aired on cable's Spike TV during its adult-oriented *The Strip* cartoon block, including the all-new *Ren & Stimpy Adult Party Cartoon*, Kelsey Grammer's animated comedy series, *Gary the Rat*, and Pamela Anderson's fantasy cartoon series, *Stripperella*. While the new series left the airwaves a month after its premiere, the original Nickelodeon classic cartoon series continued airing Tuesday through Saturday on Spike TV until early July 2004. *A Spumco Company/Games Animation Production. Color. Half-hour. Premiered on NIK: August 11, 1991–August 8, 1992; August 15, 1992–September 9, 1993; September 26, 1993–October 1, 1994; October 8, 1994–September 1995. Rebroadcast on MTV: December 28, 1991–March 7, 1992. Rebroadcast on NICK: September 1995–September 1, 1998. Rebroadcast on NICK: July 3, 2000–01. Rebroadcast on VH1: 2001–03 as Ren & Stimpy Rocks). Rebroadcast on NICKT: 2002–    (as Ren & Stimpy Extra).*

**Voices**
**Ren Hoek:** John Kricfalusi, Bob Camp, Billy West; **Stimpson J. "Stimpy" Cat:** Billy West; **Powered Toast Man:** Gary Owens; **George Liquor:** Michael Pataki; **Singers:** Randy Creenshaw, Edan Gross, Lesa O'Donovan, Churlie Brissette

## ◎ THE REPLACEMENTS
After answering an ad in a comic book for Fleemco Replacement People, two orphaned siblings, Todd and Riley, order themselves a replacement family, including new parents—Agent K, a British super-spy, and Dick Daring, a renowned stuntman, as their new mom and dad—and a superintelligent, highly sarcastic talking spy car, C.A.R.T.E.R. (voiced by David McCallum), with the power to replace any adult in their lives thanks to the mysterious agency in this original animated series for Disney Channel, created by famed children's author/illustrator Dan Santat (*The Guild of Geniuses*) and executive produced by Jack Thomas (*The Fairly OddParents*). Following a three-part crossover special of Disney Channel sitcoms, *That's So Raven*, *The Suite Life of Zack and Cody*, and *Hannah Montana* (called *That's So Suite Life of Hannah Montana*), Disney Channel debuted the series with a "sneak peak," featuring two 11-minute cartoon episodes entitled "Todd Strikes Out" and "The Jerky Girls," which drew 4.4 million viewers. The series itself debuted one day apart on both the Disney Channel and ABC's Saturday-morning *ABC Kids* program block in September 2006. *A Walt Disney Television Animation Production. Color. Half-hour. Premiered on DIS: September 8, 2006. Premiered on ABC Kids: September 9, 2006.*

**Voices**
**Todd:** Nancy Cartwright; **Riley:** Grey DeLisle; **Agent K:** Kath Soucie; **Dick Daring:** Daran Norris; **C.A.R.:** David McCallum; **Conrad Fleem:** Jeff Bennett

## ◎ RESCUE HEROES

A dedicated, elite rescue team of multiethnic emergency response professionals, including motorcyclist Jake Justice, ex-fire chief William "Billy" Blazes, firewoman Wendy Watters, and noted geologist Richmond "Rocky" Canyon, combine teamwork with their firefighting and police skills and other special talents and are called upon to protect the world from disasters in this half-hour Saturday-morning series originally aired on CBS. Emphasizing core values, including teamwork, health and safety, in each episode, the series was canceled by the network after airing its original 13 episodes. In mid-2001, a year and a half after its demise, the action/adventure series was resurrected with 25 new episodes and under a new title, *Rescue Heroes: Global Response Team*, on Kids' WB! *A Nelvana Limited/Fisher-Price Production. Color. Half-hour. Premiered on CBS: October 9, 1999–January 29, 2000.*

*Voices*

**Jake Justice:** Martin Roach, Panou (Pilot); **Billy Blazes:** Norm Spencer; **Richmond "Rocky" Canyon:** Joe Motiki; **Wendy Watters:** Lenore Zann; **Warren Watters:** John Bourgeois; **Tyler:** Marc Donato; **Roger Houston:** Christopher Earle; **Gil Gripper:** Paul Essiembre; **Cliff Hanger:** Adrian Hough; **Ariel Flyer:** Deborah Odell; **Jack Hammer:** Rod Wilson; **Coach:** Dwayne Hill; **Additional Voices:** Michael Daingerfield, Tony Daniels, Daniel DeSanto, Maryke Hendrikse, Elana Shilling

## ◎ RESCUE HEROES: GLOBAL RESPONSE TEAM

Returning adventures of the heroic emergency response squad, previously seen in the CBS Saturday-morning cartoon series, *Rescue Heroes*, who employ firefighting, police and rescue skills to save the planet from terrific tragedies. Featuring two stories per episode, in the summer of 2001 the highly charged action series joined the WB Television Network's Kids' WB! Saturday-morning lineup. Airing for two seasons, including weekly as part of the WB's Monday through Friday schedule, the series was tremendously popular with young viewers, especially following the terrorist attack of September 11, 2001. *A Nelvana Ltd./Fisher-Price Production. Color. Half-hour. Premiered on the WB (Kids' WB!): July 21, 2001–December 31, 2003. Rebroadcast on CAR: June 14, 2004–October 1, 2004.*

*Voices*

**Jake Justice:** Martin Roach, Panou (Pilot); **Billy Blazes:** Norm Spencer; **Richmond "Rocky" Canyon:** Joe Motiki; **Wendy Watters:** Lenore Zann; **Warren Watters:** John Bourgeois; **Tyler:** Marc Donato; **Roger Houston:** Christopher Earle; **Gil Gripper:** Paul Essiembre; **Cliff Hanger:** Adrian Hough; **Ariel Flyer:** Lisa Messinger; **Jack Hammer:** Rod Wilson; **Coach:** Dwayne Hill; **Additional Voices:** Michael Daingerfield, Tony Daniels, Daniel DeSanto, Maryke Hendrikse, Elana Shilling

## ◎ RETURN OF THE PLANET OF THE APES

In the year A.D. 3180, on the futuristic planet Earth, a society of apes rule and humans (a trio of displaced space travelers: Bill Hudson, Judy Franklin and Jeff Carter) are slaves. This 13-episode Saturday-morning series was based on the popular *Planet of the Apes* film series and novel by Pierre Boule and produced for NBC in 1975. Between 1992 and 1994 it was rebroadcast on the Sci-Fi Channel's *Cartoon Quest* (also in its own time slot). *A DePatie-Freleng Enterprises Production in association with 20th Century Fox. Color. Half-hour. Premiered on NBC: September 6, 1975–September 4, 1976. Rebroadcast on SCI: September 27, 1992–June 25, 1994.*

*Voices*

**Bill Hudson/Dr. Zaius:** Richard Blackburn; **Jeff Carter:** Austin Stoker; **Judy Franklin/Nova:** Claudette Nevins; **Cornelius:** Edwin Mills; **Zira:** Philipa Harris; **General Urko:** Henry Corden

## ◎ RICHIE RICH (1986)

In January 1986 CBS added this half-hour series recycling 13 adventures of the wealthy blonde kid, his dedicated butler, Cadbury, and his faithful dog, Dollar, that originally premiered as part of ABC's hourlong Saturday-morning series, *The Richie Rich/Scooby-Doo Hour*. The network reran the program until August and again from November to December of that year. Later the series was rebroadcast on Cartoon Network and Boomerang. (See THE RICHIE RICH/SCOOBY-DOO HOUR for voice credits.) *A Hanna-Barbera Production in association with Harvey Comics. Color. Half-hour. Rebroadcast on CBS: January 11, 1986–August 30, 1986; November 15, 1986–December 27, 1986. Rebroadcast on CAR: January 4, 1993–June 3, 1994; January 2, 1995–June 2, 1995; September 4, 1995–1998 (weekdays). Rebroadcast on BOOM: May 4, 2000–.*

## ◎ RICHIE RICH (1996)

Retaining the authenticity of the famed Harvey comic-book character, Richie Rich ("the richest kid in the world") starred in this half-hour syndicated series, made up of 13 *Richie Rich* comedy-mystery cartoon adventures and selected cartoons from the classic Harvey film library. Updated for today's audiences, series regulars included Professor Keenbean, Cadbury, Dollar, Gloria Glad, Reggie Van Dough, Chef Pierre, Bascomb, Mayda Munny, Freckles, Pee Wee and Tiny. Reruns aired on FOX Family Channel in 1998. *A Film Roman Production in association with Harvey Entertainment. Color. Half-hour. Premiered: September 21, 1996–Fall 1997. Syndicated. Rebroadcast on FOX FAM: 1998.*

*Voices*

**Richie Rich/Irona:** Katie Leigh; **Regina Rich:** Susan Silo; **Richard Rich Sr./Professor Keenbean/Chef Pierre:** Rene Auberjonois; **Cadbury/Bascomb:** Martin Jarvis; **Dollar:** Pat Fraley; **Gloria Glad/Reggie Van Dough/Freckles/Tiny:** Jeannie Elias

## ◎ THE RICHIE RICH/SCOOBY-DOO HOUR

This hour-long Saturday morning series combined new adventures of Richie Rich, a lucky kid with a $100,000 weekly allowance, who uses his wealth for good causes, and 39 new seven-and-a-half-minute episodes (three per show) of Scooby-Doo and his crazy cousin, who previously appeared in 1979's *Scooby and Scrappy-Doo*. Richie Rich was based on the popular comic-book character owned by Harvey Comics.

In the Scooby and Scrappy-Doo adventures, only Shaggy remained from the original cast. Freddy, Daphne and Velma were dropped as well as the mystery format, which had run its course. The new cartoons marked another cast change: Don Messick took over as the voice of Scrappy-Doo (originally voiced by Lennie Weinrib on 1979's *Scooby and Scrappy-Doo*). In addition, for the first time, rather than build plots about crooks in disguise as ghosts and goblins, the ghosts and monsters in the new episodes were real, and Shaggy, Scooby and Scrappy "splatted" them in the end.

Alternating with the misadventures of Scooby-Doo and Scrappy-Doo were several short comical vignettes starring Richie Rich, each running three minutes, seven minutes and 30 seconds long. (No new 30-second spots were produced for the second season). During its second season in September 1981, the program was retitled *The Richie Rich/Scooby-Doo Show—and Scrappy, Too!* featuring eight new half hours of Richie Rich cartoons.

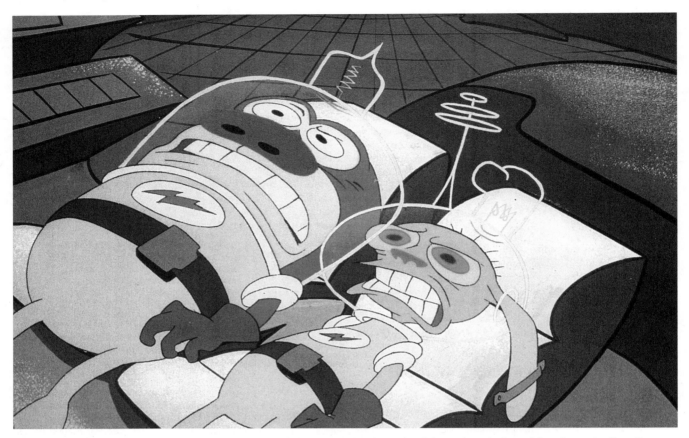

*Bulbous-nosed Cornish Rex cat Ren and his scrawny asthmatic chihuahua hound pal Stimpy feel the accelerated effects of the g-forces after blastoff in a scene from "Space Madness" from twice Emmy-nominated Nickelodeon series* Ren and Stimpy. *© Viacom International. All rights reserved.*

In the fall of 1982, Richie Rich was paired again with Hanna-Barbera's cartoon version of the Our Gang kids in *The Little Rascals/Richie Rich Show*, in all-new episodes, which ran through the 1983 season. In 1988 the program was repackaged and rebroadcast in syndication as part of *The Funtastic World of Hanna-Barbera.* Five years later it was rebroadcast on Cartoon Network. *A Hanna-Barbera Production in association with Harvey Comics. Color. One hour. Premiered on ABC: November 8, 1980–August 30, 1982.*

**Voices**
**Richie Rich:** Sparky Marcus; **Freckles, Richie's friend:** Christian Hoff; **Gloria, Richie's girlfriend:** Nancy Cart-wright; **Reggie Van Dough, Richie's friend:** Dick Beals; **George Rich, Richie's father:** Stan Jones; **Mrs. Rich, Richie's mother:** Joan Gerber; **Cadbury, the Riches' butler:** Stan Jones; **Irona, the Riches' maid:** Joan Gerber; **Dollar, the Riches' dog:** Frank Welker; **Professor Keenbean:** Bill Callaway; **Scooby-Doo:** Don Messick; **Scrappy-Doo:** Don Messick; **Shaggy:** Casey Kasem; **Velma:** Pat Stevens, Maria Frumkin; **Freddy:** Frank Welker; **Daphne:** Heather North

**◎ RICK MORANIS IN GRAVEDALE HIGH**
A high school teacher's unorthodox methods land him a job in the scariest school in town, Gravedale High, built in the heart of a creepy cemetery, with coffins for lockers and monsters for students—each a teenage version of popular monsters: Vinnie Stoker, the world's hippest teenage vampire; Reggie Moonshroud, the resident werewolf; Medusa ("Duzer"), a snake-headed Madonna wannabe; Frankentyke, the school prankster; Gill Waterman, a surfing swamp creature; Cleofatra, a rotund teenage mummy; Sid, the invis-

ible kid; Blanche, a Southern belle zombie; and J.P. Ghostly the III—in this half-hour cartoon series for NBC. The series featured the voices of Rick Moranis, Shari Belafonte, Tim Curry, television talk-show host Ricki Lake and comedian Jonathan Winters. *A Hanna-Barbera Production in association with NBC. Color. Half-hour. Premiered on NBC: September 8, 1990–September 7, 1991.*

**Voices**
**Max Schneider:** Rick Moranis; **Vinnie Stoker:** Roger Rose; **Reggie Moonshroud:** Barry Gordon; **Medusa ("Duzer"):** Kimmy Robertson; **Frankentyke/J.P. Ghostly:** Frank Welker; **Gill Waterman:** Jackie Earl Haley; **Cleofatra:** Ricki Lake; **Sid:** Maurice LaMarche; **Blanche:** Shari Belafonte; **Miss Dirge:** Eileen Brennan; **Miss Webner:** Sandra Gould; **Boneyard:** Brock Peters; **Mr. Tutner:** Tim Curry; **Coach Cadaver:** Jonathan Winters; **Crone:** Georgia Brown

**◎ RING RAIDERS**
Led by Ring Commander Victor Vector, a group of heroic aviators from all eras of flight—past, present and future—defend the world. Their enemy: the most sinister airborne threat ever known, the evil pilots of the Skull Squadron. The *Top Gun*–style battles and adventures in this five-part daily miniseries were first introduced as a two-hour special. *A DIC Enterprises Production in association with Those Characters from Cleveland/Bohbot. Color. Half-hour. Premiered: September 11, 1989. Syndicated.*

**Voices**
**Victor Vector, commander:** Dan Gilvezan; **Joe Thundercloud:** Efrain Figueroa; **Hubbub:** Stuart Goetz; **Cub Jones:** Ike Eisen-

*A group of heroic aviators from all eras of flight, led by Commander Victor Vector, defend the world from the most sinister airborne threat ever known in* Ring Raiders. © *Those Characters From Cleveland*
(COURTESY: DIC ENTERPRISES)

mann; **Kirchov:** Gregory Martin; **Mako:** Jack Angel; **Jenny Gail:** Chris Anthony; **Max Miles:** Roscoe Lee Browne; **Scorch:** Rodger Bumpass; **Yasu Yakamura:** Townsend Coleman; **Baron Voin Clawdeitz:** Chuck McCann; **Siren:** Susan Silo

### ◎ THE RIPPING FRIENDS

With their mission to "rip" or conquer anything that stands in the path of freedom and justice, a young muscle-headed four-some, who intensely train by day to become the world's most powerful superheroes, use their amazing physical prowess, strength, ability and inventiveness to fight crime in this offbeat animated comedy series created, written and produced by famed *Ren & Stimpy* creator John Kricfalusi for FOX. Launched in the fall of 2000 as a component of FOX's *FOX Box* Saturday-morning program block, the 13-episode half-hour series, casting the brawny crimefighters in comical misadventures, was canceled after one season due to poor ratings. In early October 2002, eight months after airing on FOX, the series moved to Cartoon Network where it became a Sunday night fixture on the popular late-night *Adult Swim* programming block until May 2004. A *Spumco Production. Color. Half-hour. Premiered on FOX: September 22, 2001–January 26, 2002. Rebroadcast on CAR: October 6, 2002–May 9, 2004.*

**Voices**
**Crag:** Harvey Atkin, Mark Daley; **Chuck:** Michael Kerr; **Rip:** Mike McDonald; **Slab:** Mermie Mandeair; **He-Mom:** Miriam McDonald; **Future Cat:** Eric Bauza; **Rip's Shorts:** Dwayne Hill; **Citricet:** John Kricfalusi; **Jimmy the Idiot Boy:** Phil LaMarr; **Other Voices:** Ron Pardo, Frenchy McFarlane

### ◎ ROAD ROVERS

Following their master's signal, regular run-of-the-mill kennel dogs spring into action as courageous crime-fighting superhounds to protect and defend all that's good in the galaxy in this 13-episode half-hour action/adventure series, first aired Saturday mornings on the WB Television Network in 1996 and then rebroadcast for two seasons on Cartoon Network. A *Warner Bros. Television Animation Production. Color. Half-hour. Premiered on WB: September 7, 1996–February 23, 1997. Rebroadcast on CAR: March 7, 1998–June 30, 2000.*

**Voices**
**Hunter:** Jess Harnell; **Colleen:** Tress MacNeille; **Exile:** Kevin Richardson; **Blitz:** Jeff Bennett; **Shag:** Frank Welker; **The Master:** Joseph Campanella; **General Parvo:** Jim Cummings; **The Groomer:** Sheena Easton

### ◎ THE ROAD RUNNER SHOW

The predictable antics of foxy, fleet-footed Road Runner and his constant pursuer Wile E. Coyote were repackaged for television, with theatrical cartoons from the Warner Bros. library produced between 1949 and 1966 added to spice up the proceedings. Warner characters featured in the series were Daffy Duck, Foghorn Leghorn, Porky Pig and others. The Road Runner/Coyote cartoons were subsequently paired with reruns of Bugs Bunny cartoons as *The Bugs Bunny/Road Runner Hour,* which premiered on CBS in 1968. A *Warner Bros. Production. Color. Half-hour. Premiered on CBS: September 10, 1966–September 7, 1968. Rebroadcast on ABC: September 11, 1971–September 2, 1972.*

**Voices**
Mel Blanc

### ◎ ROBOCOP: ALPHA COMMANDO

In the year 2030, reactivated by the eccentric scientist, Dr. Cornelius Neumeier after a five-year absence, the robotic crime-fighting RoboCop, with his skeptical partner Special Agent Nancy Miner of the federal government's high-tech Alpha Division, battles evil forces around the globe in this animated spin-off—and second animated series incarnation since Marvel Animation's *RoboCop: The Animated Series* in 1988—of Orion Films' highly successful R-rated, live-action, futuristic feature film series. Produced by MGM Animation, the weekly half-hour series, which was the studio's last animated series, was syndicated to television stations nationwide in September 1998. Besides using many of the same writers who worked on Marvel Animation's Saturday-morning series for FOX, characters Cornelius Neumeier and Nancy Miner (who replaced Officer Ann Lewis in the live-action movies) were named after real life *RoboCop* creators Edward Neumeier and Michael Miner. An *MGM Animation/Summit Media Production. Color. Half-hour. Premiered: September 7, 1998–February 1, 1999. Syndicated.*

**Voices**
**RoboCop:** David Sobolov; **Richie:** Andrew Francis; **Cornelius Neumeier:** Dean Haglund; **Jennifer:** Janyse Jaud; **Alpha Prime:** Campbell Lane; **Sergeant Reed:** Blu Mankuma; **Special Agent Nancy Miner:** Akiko Morrison; **Additional Voices:** Doug Parker, Don Brown, Gary Chalk, Ian James Corlett, Michael Dobson, Paul Dobson, Saffron Henderson, David Kaye, Terry Klassen, Lalainia Lindbjerg, Scott McNeil, Richard Newman, Teryl Rothery, Alvin Sanders, French Tickner, Dave "Squatch" Ward, Cathy Weseluck, Alec Willows, Dale Wilson

### ◎ ROBOTBOY

Originally designed as a weapon capable of wiping out entire armies, a cyborg named Robotboy is sent into hiding by its creator (world-renowned scientist Professor Moshimo) and learns how to act and behave like a real boy with the help of a trio of flesh-and-blood friends, ten-year-old Tommy Turnbull and his two friends, Gus and Lola, who keep him safe from the hands of the diabolical Dr. Kamizaki. Created and designed by Jan Van Rijsselberge, this half-hour science fiction series, first broadcast on French television in October 2005 and then on Cartoon Network United Kingdom that November, premiered in the United States on Cartoon Network as part of a "sneak peek" preview week of the network's new

Saturday morning lineup. *A Cartoon Network Studios/Alphanim/ Luxanimation Production. Color. Half-hour. Premiered on CAR: January 14, 2006.*

*Voices*
**Tommy Turnbull/Dr. Kamizaki:** Charlie Schlatter; **Robotboy:** Tara Strong; **Gus/Constantine:** Jason Davis

## ◎ ROBOT CHICKEN
Popular stop-motion animated sketch comedy series, whose name was inspired by the name of a dish at a Chinese restaurant frequented by the show's creators Seth Green and Matthew Senreich, parodying the worlds of pop culture and celebrity using action figures, dolls, toys and clay-animated objects.

Airing late-night on Cartoon Network's highly watched *Adult Swim* cartoon block starting in February 2005, in its first season this top-rated animated series averaged a robust 870,000 adult viewers ages 18 to 34, nearly doubling *Adult Swim's* total-day average in this all-important audience demographic. The series, which aired Sundays and Thursdays, premiered to 732,000 adults and peaked in the week of June 26, 2005, with 1.1 million viewers in that same category.

In 2005, Cartoon Network ordered 20 new episodes of the hit stop-motion satire that premiered that spring. *A Stoopid Monkey/ Sony Pictures Digital/ShadowMachine Films Production. Color. Fifteen minutes. Premiered on CAR: February 20, 2005.*

*Voices*
Seth Green, Dan Milano, Dax Shepard, Matthew Senreich, Mike Henry, Tom Root, Breckin Meyer, Chad Morgan, Adam Talbott

## ◎ ROBOTECH
When Earth is invaded by a fleet of giant alien spaceships capable of destroying the entire planet in a split second, the only hope for survival lies in Robotech Defense Force, led by Captain Gloval and his troop of newly trained cadets, which protects the planet from destruction in this 85 episode half-hour series produced for first-run syndication in 1985. Eight years after its initial run in syndication, the series was rebroadcast on the Sci-Fi Channel's *Cartoon Quest* (and in its own time slot) and later on Cartoon Network. *A Tatsunoko Production/Harmony Gold U.S.A. Production in association with ZIV International. Robotech is a registered trademark owned and licensed by Harmony Gold U.S.A. Color. Half-hour. Syndicated: March 4, 1985–1986. Rebroadcast on SCI: September 13, 1993–April 30, 1994. Rebroadcast on CAR: January 1998–October 1998; July 19, 1999–January 2, 2000. Rebroadcast on ANIME: July 27, 2004–.*

*Voices*
Greg Snow, Reba West, Jonathan Alexsander, Drew Thomas, Deanna Morris, Thomas Wyner, Brittany Harlow, Donn Warner, Axel Roberts, Tony Oliver, A. Gregory, Noelle McGraph, Sandra Snow, Guy Garrett, Jimmy Flinders, Anthony Wayne, Eddie Frierson, Leonad Pike, Aline Leslie, Shirley Roberts, Wendee Swan, Larry Abraham, Sam Fontana, Penny Sweet, Mary Cobb, Celena Banas, Chelsea Victoria

## ◎ ROCKET POWER
Four extreme sport obsessed kids—Otto Rocket, his sister Reggie, and their friends Twister and Sam—go where the action is to compete with Reggie's dad and their business partner, Tito Makani, to help them keep things in perspective and, above all else, maintain their friendships. Created by Arlene Klasky, the half-hour action/adventure, featuring two episodes per show, premiered on Nickelodeon in August 1999. Sixty episodes were produced during the show's three seasons. In February 2002, the characters were spun-off into their first 90-minute special, *Race Across the Island.* That summer, they returned in an hour-long special, *The Big Day.* In May 2002, the series began airing on weekends on Nick's sister channel, Nicktoons, before airing weekdays instead beginning in September 2003. Original episode aired on Nickelodeon until August 2002 and were rebroadcast for two more seasons. In July 2003, Ray, Reggie, Otto and company starred in their second 90-minute special, *Reggie's Big (Beach) Break,* and that December in their first-ever holiday special and the show's first 30-minute episode, *A Rocket X-Mas.* The following summer, they appeared in their third 90-minute special, *Island of Menehune. A Klasky Csupo/Viacom International Production. Color. Half-hour. Premiered on NICK: August 16, 1999–August 2, 2004. Premiered on NICKT: May 6, 2002. Rebroadcast NICK: August 5, 2002–July 30, 2004.*

*Voices*
**Ray "Raymundo" Rocket:** John Kassir; **Regina "Reggie" Rocket/ Dani Rocket:** Shayna Fox; **Oswald "Otto" Rocket:** Joseph Anton; **Tito Makami Jr.:** Ray Bumatai; **Noelani:** Kim Mai Guest; **Lars "Twister" Rodriguez:** Gilbert Leal Jr., Lombardo Boyar; **Sammy "The Squid" Dullard:** Gary Leroi Gray, Sean Marquette; **Trish/Sherry:** Lauren Tom; **Maurice "Twister" Rodriguez:** Gilbert Leal Jr.; **Sammy "The Squid" Dullard:** Gary Leroi Gray; **Eddie "Prince of the Netherworld" Valentine:** Jordan Warkol

## ◎ ROCKET ROBIN HOOD AND HIS MERRY SPACEMEN
The year is 3000. Headquartered on the floating solar-powered asteroid Sherwood Forest, intergalactic crimefighter Rocket Robin Hood and his Merry Spacemen—Will Scarlet, Little John, Alan A. Dale, Jiles and Friar Tuck—team up to battle the universe's top villain, the wicked Sheriff of N.O.T.T., in this half-hour series comprised of 156 five-minute episodes first syndicated in 1967. Veteran animator James "Shamus" Culhane produced and directed the series in cooperation with Steve Krantz, executive producer of *Marvel Superheroes. A Trillium/Steve Krantz Production. Color. Half-hour. Premiered: Fall 1967. Syndicated.*

*Voices*
Carl Banas, Ed McNamara, Chris Wiggins, Bernard Cowan, Len Birman, Paul Kligman, Gillie Fenwick, John Scott

## ◎ ROCKO'S MODERN LIFE
Loosely based on creator Joe Murray's outrageous theatrical cartoon "My Dog Zero," a newly arrived pint-size Australian wallaby, joined by his menagerie of household pets (Heffer the cow and his brain-dead Spunky the dog), finds small-town life difficult. Zero is thrown into situations that incessantly threaten his existence, in the first Nickelodeon-created cartoon series of Games Animation, the network's owned-and-operated cartoon division. Premiering in the fall of 1993 with 13 original episodes, the weekly half-hour series mirrored the same gross-out humor as the network's cult favorite, *The Ren & Stimpy Show,* becoming an instant ratings hit. The show's success prompted Nickelodeon to order 26 new episodes for the 1994–95 season. Beginning in late May 1994, the series was rebroadcast for several weeks on MTV, as part of an experiment to reach a wider audience. The character of Rocko originated in Murray's comic strip *Zak and Travis,* the adventures of Zak, a chubby little man with girls on his mind, and Travis (Rocko). *A Games Animation Production. Color. Half-hour. Premiered on NICK: September 18, 1993–November 1, 1996. Rebroadcast on MTV: May 1994. Rebroadcast on NICKT: May 1, 2002–.*

*Voices*
**Rocko:** Carlos Alazraqui; **Heffer Wolfe:** Tom Kenny; **Filbert Turtle:** Doug Lawrence; **The Bigheads:** Charlie Adler; **Dr. Hutchinson:** Linda Wallem

## ◎ ROCKY AND HIS FRIENDS

The flying squirrel Rocky and simple-minded, bristle-haired Bullwinkle Moose (whose voice was reminiscent of Red Skelton's punch-drunk fighter character, Willie Lump-Lump) battle the evil Mr. Big, a midget underworld gangster who hires sinister Boris Badenov and the fetching agent Natasha Fatale to foil the duo's activities in cliff-hanging, serialized adventures (narrated by actor William Conrad) that first premiered on ABC in 1959.

Other cartoon segments included "Fractured Fairytales," "Aesop and Son," "Peabody's Improbable History," and "Mr. Know It All."

In 1961, following its ABC network run, NBC broadcast a new, expanded edition of the series, retitled *The Bullwinkle Show.* (See entry for information.)

The series was the second all-new cartoon show to air on network television, created by Jay Ward and Alex Anderson (whose uncle was Paul Terry, the man behind *Terry-Toons*, and with whom he served as an apprentice at his New York Terry-Toons studios). Anderson teamed up with Ward to form Television Arts Productions, based in Berkeley, California, to produce cartoon ideas. Among the characters they created were Crusader Rabbit (and his sidekick, Rags the Tiger) and what became the nucleus of "Rocky and Bullwinkle": Rocket J. Squirrel, Bullwinkle and Dudley Do-Right (of these concepts, only "Crusader" Rabbit was sold to television as a syndicated series in 1949).

Several of the series' writers would go on to later glories: Allan Burns to *The Mary Tyler Moore Show*, Lloyd Turner to *All in the Family*, and Chris Hayward to *Barney Miller*. *A Jay Ward Production. Color. Half-hour. Premiered on ABC: September 29, 1959–September 3, 1961.*

*Voices*
**Rocky, the flying squirrel:** June Foray; **Bullwinkle Moose:** Bill Scott; **Boris Badenov:** Paul Frees; **Natasha Fatale:** June Foray; **Narrator:** William Conrad; **Aesop:** Charles Ruggles; **Aesop's**

*Rocky and His Friends, starring Rocky the flying squirrel, his friend Bullwinkle Moose, and villains Natasha and Boris, marked the second all-cartoon show to air on network television. The series was created by Jay Ward, who also created* Crusader Rabbit. *© Jay Ward Productions*

**Son:** Daws Butler; **Narrator:** Charles Ruggles; **Mr. Peabody:** Bill Scott; **Sherman, his adopted son:** Walter Tetley; **Narrator ("Fractured Fairytales"):** Edward Everett Horton

## ◎ ROD ROCKET

Entertaining and educational space adventures in serial form of Rod Rocket, his sidekick Joey, his sister Casey, and their friend Professor Argus. The half-hour series of five-minute cartoons was the first fully animated series produced by Jiro Enterprises. *A Jiro Enterprises/Victor Corp. Production in association with Paramount Televisionn. Color. Half-hour. Premiered: 1963. Syndicated.*

*Voices*
**Professor Argus:** Hal Smith; **Rod Rocket/Joey:** Sam Edwards; **Cassie:** Pat Blake

## ◎ ROGER RAMJET

The terms "daredevil," "flying fool" and "all-round good guy" fittingly describe American Eagle Squadron antihero scientist Roger Ramjet (voiced by famed radio/television personality Gary Owens). A proton energy pill gives Roger the power of 20 atom bombs for a period of 20 seconds. He battles the evil Noodle Romanoff from N.A.S.T.Y., Jacqueline Hyde, Henry Cabbage Patch, Lance Crossfire, the Solenoid Robots, General G.I. Brassbottom, Clara Finork, Lotta Love, the Height Brothers (Cronk, Horse and Gezundt) and other baddies.

Of course, Roger himself has quite a staff of good-doers on the flying squadron: Yank, Doodle, Dan and Dee.

The show avoided violent confrontations and undue violence by inserting the appropriate title cards "Whack!" "Thunk!" "Hurt!" "Pain!" and "Ouch!" The same technique was later employed on TV's *Batman* series.

In 1996, following a resurgence of interest in the series (which previously was issued on home video), Cartoon Network began reairing the series. *A Snyder–Koren/Pantaomime Pictures/CBS Films Production. Color. Half-hour. Premiered: September, 1965. Syndicated. Rebroadcast on CAR: June 1, 1996–October 5, 1996 (Saturdays); July 23, 1997–1998 (Saturdays).*

*Voices*
**Roger Ramjet:** Gary Owens; **Yank/Dan:** Dick Beals; **Doodle/Noodles Romanoff:** Gene Moss; **Dee/Lotta Love:** Joan Gerber; **General G.I. Brassbottom/Ma Ramjet:** Bob Arbogast; **Lance Crossfire/Red Dog:** Paul Shively; **The Announcer:** Dave Ketchum

## ◎ ROLIE POLIE OLIE

Colorful adventures of a loving, traditional robotic family, featuring hairless, glassy-eyed six-year-old Olie, his sister Zowie, their parents Mr. and Mrs. Polie, Grandpa Pappy and their pet dog Spot, who live in a teapot-shaped house, complete with fruit-striped appliances, in the high-tech town of Polieville, created by acclaimed children's author Willam Joyce (also the creator of TV's *George Shrinks*), who based the series on his childhood and his own idealized version of 1950s American suburban life—a cross between TV's *Leave It to Beaver* and *The Matrix* and *Blade Runner* movies.

Coproduced by Ontario, Canada's Nelvana Enterprises, Metal Hurlant Productions and Sparx, the 3-D, computer-animated series—and first fully computer-generated television series for preschoolers—premiered in the United States on Disney Channel in January 1998. The five-time nominated, Daytime Emmy Award-winning show (for outstanding special class animated program) aired weekdays on Disney Channel until 2001 and spawned two direct-to-DVD movies, *The Great Defender of Fun* and *The Baby-Bot*

*Chase.* The series' original episodes were broadcast on Disney Channel until 2006. *A Nelvana Limited/Metal Hurlant Productions/Spars/Canada-France Coproductions Production. Color. Half-hour. Premiered on DIS: October 4, 1998–September 15, 2006.*

**Voices**
**Olie:** Cole Caplan; **Zowie:** Kristen Bone; **Pappy:** Len Carlson; **Mr. Polie:** Adrian Truss; **Mrs. Polie:** Catherine Disher; **Spot:** Robert Smith; **Billy Bevel:** Joshua Tucci;; **Little Gizmo:** Michael Cera

## ⊚ ROMAN HOLIDAYS
Forum Construction Company engineer Gus Holiday, his wife, Laurie, and their children, Precocia and Happius, struggle with 20th-century lifestyles in Rome, A.D. 63 in this 13-episode half-hour series originally produced for NBC. The series was later broadcast on Cartoon Network and Boomerang. *A Hanna Barbera Production. Color. Half-hour. Premiered on NBC: September 9, 1972–September 1, 1973. Rebroadcast on CAR: January 14, 1994–January 15, 1994 (Look What We Found!); July 9, 1995– Sundays). Rebroadcast on BOOM: June 3, 2000–October 22, 2002.*

**Voices**
**Gus Holiday:** Dave Willock; **Laurie, his wife:** Shirley Mitchell; **Precocia, their daughter:** Pamelyn Ferdin; **Happius (Happy), their son:** Stanley Livingston; **Mr. Evictus, the landlord:** Dom DeLuise; **Mr. Tycoonius, Holiday's boss:** Hal Smith; **Brutus, the family lion:** Daws Butler; **Groovia, Happy's girlfriend:** Judy Strangis; **Herman, Gus's friend:** Hal Peary; **Henrietta, his wife:** Janet Waldo

## ⊚ RONIN WARRIORS
Five young men (Ryo, Cye, Sage, Rowen and Kento), each gifted with mystical, superpowered samurai armor, fight an otherworldly invasion from the dark dimension known as the "Phantom World," headed by the evil warlord Arago, in this phenomenally popular Japanese series originally produced in 1989 as *Samurai Troopers.* Redubbed in English (with most of the characters renamed as well), the series was imported to the United States by Graz Entertainment under the title *Ronin Warriors,* premiering in first-run syndication in the summer of 1995. The 39-episode series was subsequently reaired on Sci-Fi Channel's *Animation Station* and Cartoon Network. *A Sunrise Inc./Graz Entertainment Production. Color. Half-hour. Premiered: June 26, 1995. Syndicated. Rebroadcast on SCI: June 30, 1996–December 31, 1996. Rebroadcast on CAR: September 27, 1999–May 6, 2000; November 13, 2000–March 8, 2001.*

**Voices**
**Ryo of the Wildfire:** Matt Hill; **Narrator:** David Kaye; **Kento of Hardrock:** Jason Gray-Stanford; **Anubis/Dara/Lord Sabre-Stryke:** Paul Dobson; **Talpa:** Mira Mina; **Rowen of Strata/Sekhmet/Badamon:** Ward Perry; **Yuli:** Christopher Turner; **Sage of the Halo/Cye of the Torrent:** Michael Donovan; **Other Voices:** Peter Wilds, Teryl Rothery, Mathew Smith, Richard Newman, Lalania Lindbjerg, Jane Perry

## ⊚ ROSWELL CONSPIRACIES: ALIENS, MYTHS AND LEGENDS
Led by ex-bounty hunter Nick Logan, an organization of covert operatives called the Global Alliance, Detective Detail, hunt down aliens who have assimilated themselves among Earth's humans—disguised as mythical creatures, from werewolves to vampires—posing a threat to mankind in this animated science fiction series, originally broadcast in syndication as part of the BKN (Bohbot Kids Network) cartoon programming block and on cable's Sci-Fi Channel in 1999. In the spring of 2001, after com-

pleting its network and syndication run, FOX rebroadcast the 40-episode half-hour series Saturday mornings and weekday afternoons through May of that year. *A Bohbot Production. Color. Half-hour. Premiered on SCI: August 27, 1999–November 26, 1999. Syndicated: August 28, 1999–June 3, 2000. Rebroadcast on FOX: April 7, 2001–May 27, 2001.*

**Voices**
**Nick Logan:** Scott McNeil; **Sh'lainn Blaze:** Janyse Jaud; **Nema Perrera:** Saffron Henderson; **Simon "Fitz" Fitzpatrick:** Peter Kelamis; **Queen Mab:** Saffron Henderson; **Hanek:** Dale Wilson; **Other Voices:** Lee Tockar, Richard Newman, Alex Zahara

## ⊚ ROTTEN RALPH
A mischievous, rule-breaking red cat with a "Bart Simpson attitude" Ralph tends to do something bad before he can be good and can't help being rotten, but he is loved unconditionally, despite his naughtiness, by his owner and best friend Sarah, even as he creates havoc for her and her parents in this stop-motion, clay-animated series based on the popular Harper Collins children's book series by author Jack Gantos and illustrator Nicole Rubel. Produced by the United Kingdom's Cosgrove-Hall, producers of such classic animated television shows as *Count Duckula* and *DangerMouse,* this half-hour comedy series, comprised of 22 10-minute cartoons and two half-hour specials originally shown on BBC1 in 1998 and then repackaged as 13 half-hours, aired Saturdays in the United States on FOX Family Channel (later renamed ABC Family). *A Cosgrove-Hall Production/Italtoons Corporation/Tooncan Productions/BBC Worldwide/Pearson TV Production. Color. Half-hour. Premiered on FOX FAM/ABC FAM: August 2, 1999–April 25, 2001.*

**Voices**
**Rotten Ralph:** Rick Jones; **Sarah:** Brigid Tierney; **Mom:** Sonja Ball; **Dad:** Mark Camacho; **Other Voices:** Jennifer Seguin, Terrence Scammel

## ⊚ ROUGHNECKS: STARSHIP TROOPER CHRONICLES
An elite mobile infantry unit known as Razak's Roughnecks, including three heroic servicemen (the newly recruited Private Juan "Johnny" Rico, Private Isabelle "Dizzy" Flores and Lieutenant Carmen Ibanez), races against time to defeat a sect of highly advanced, gigantic alien insect invaders who plan to destroy all of humanity in this animated science fiction action/adventure series based on the novel, "Starships Troopers" (1959), by famed science fiction writer Robert Heinlein, and the live-action film, *Starship Troopers* (1997), adapted from the same work, the weekly, half-hour CGI-animated series premiered in syndication Monday through Fridays and on cable's Sci-Fi Channel in August 1999. Forty episodes were planned for the series, but only 36 were completed. After its debut on the Sci-Fi Channel, episodes aired sporadically on the network until the following August. *An Adelaide Productions/Sony Pictures Family Entertainment/Bohbot Entertainment Production. Color. Half-hour. Premiered on SCI/Syndicated: August 30, 1999–August 24, 2000.*

**Voices**
**Private Juan "Johnny" Rico:** Rino Romano; **General Redwing:** Irene Bedard; **Private Isabelle "Dizzy" Flores:** E. G. Daily; **Sergeant Francis Brutto:** David DeLuise; **Corporal Jeff Gossard:** Bill Fagerbakke; **Major Sander Barcalow:** Nicholas Guest; **Lieutenant Jean Razak:** Jamie Haines; **Lieutenant Carmen Ibanez:** Tish Hicks; **Corporal Richard "Doc" LaCroix:** James Horan; **Robert Higgins:** Alexander Polinsky; **T'Phai:** Steve Staley; **Carl Jenkins:** Rider Strong

## ◎ RUBBADUBBERS

A colorful group of bath toys finds their imaginations taking them from their ordinary bathroom on incredible journeys, including fantastic islands of toothbrush trees, bath-rack sailing ships and spongy desert islands, in this high-spirited, animated preschool series that premiered on Nick Jr. in the fall of 2003. Produced and developed by HOT Animation, makers of HIT Entertainment's *Bob the Builder*, episodes focused on inspiring children to "believe they can be anything they want to be," featuring an ensemble cast of characters—including Tubb the Frog, the "leader of the bath"; Finbar the toy shark; Splosby the starfish-shaped sponge; Terence the crocodile-shaped bubble bath bottle; Winona the squeaky toy whale; Reg the battery-operated robot; and Amelia the flying submarine. In 2003 Simon & Schuster's children's publishing imprint, Simon Spotlight, and Scholastic published a line of books based on the half-hour, 20-episode animated preschool series. A *HOT Animation/HIT Entertainment Production. Color. Half-hour. Premiered on NICK JR.: September 15, 2003–January 1, 2004.*

**Voices**
**Tubb/Terence/Reg:** John Gordon Sinclair; **Finbar:** Sean Hughes; **Amelia/Splosby/Winona:** Maria Darling

## ◎ RUBIK THE AMAZING CUBE

The famous multicolored cube that frustrated consumers in their attempts to figure it out and his human companions, the Rodriguez children—Carlos, Lisa and Renaldo—were featured in this half-hour series of magical adventures, originally produced as part of 1983's *The Pac-Man/Rubik the Amazing Cube Hour*. The original hour-long cartoon block lasted one full season on ABC, with the "Rubik the Amazing Cube" portion repeated as a half-hour show of its own in April of 1985. (See *The Pac-Man/Rubik the Amazing Cube Hour* for voice credits.) A *Ruby-Spears Enterprises Production. Color. Half-hour. Premiered on ABC: September 10, 1983–September 1, 1984 (as part of The Pac-Man/Rubik The Amazing Cube Hour). Rebroadcast on ABC: April 4, 1985–August 31, 1985 as (Rubik the Amazing Cube).*

## ◎ RUDE DOG AND THE DWEEBS

Rude Dog is a cool, "Fonzie-like" dog who drives a pink 1956 Cadillac. The Dweebs are his equally cool gang of canines. Together they spell problems of every kind in this stylized animated series (in two cartoons per show) featuring a whole new color palette for Saturday-morning animation: "hot pinks and neon." CBS canceled the series in December of 1989, replacing it with *Dungeons and Dragons*. The network brought back the series for a summer run in 1990. A *Marvel Production in association with Akom Productions, Ltd./Sun Sportswear. Color. Half-hour. Premiered on CBS: September 16, 1989–December 9, 1989. Rebroadcast on CBS: June 17, 1990–September 8, 1990.*

**Voices**
**Rude Dog:** Rob Paulsen; **Barney:** Dave Coulier; **Winston/Herman:** Peter Cullen; **Satch:** Jim Cummings; **Kibble/Gloria:** Ellen Gerstell; **Tweek:** Hank Saroyan; **Reggie:** Mendi Segal; **Caboose/Rot/Seymour:** Frank Welker

## ◎ THE RUFF AND REDDY SHOW

Telecast in black-and-white until 1959, Hanna-Barbera created this pioneering made-for-television cartoon series that featured the adventures of a talking dog and cat team, Ruff and Reddy, battling sinister forces of evil (Captain Greedy, Scary Harry Safari,

*A talking dog and cat battle evil forces in Hanna-Barbera's pioneering made-for-television cartoon series* The Ruff and Reddy Show, *first broadcast on NBC in 1957. © Hanna-Barbera Productions.*

Killer and Diller and others) in serialized stories that were presented in 10 or more six-minute installments in the fashion of Jay Ward's *Crusader Rabbit*. The original half-hour series, which debuted on NBC, featured *Ruff and Reddy* cartoons as wraparounds bookended with a package of Columbia Pictures theatrical cartoons (*Color Rhapsodies, Fox and the Crow* and *Li'l Abner*) originally released to theaters. Televised live from WNBC, New York, the NBC program was hosted by Jimmy Blaine from 1957 to 1960, when it was canceled and replaced by *King Leonardo and His Short Subjects*. Bob Cottle succeeded Blaine as host from 1962 to 1964, when the series returned to NBC. In all, 156 five-minute *Ruff and Reddy* cartoons were produced, with production ending in 1960. Episodes were rebroadcast on the later NBC series and via syndication in 1964. In 1998, Cartoon Network reran the series. Then, beginning in April 2000, the series was rebroadcast on Cartoon Network's classic cartoons network, Boomerang. A *Hanna-Barbera Production. Black-and-white. Color. Half-hour. Premiered on NBC: December 14, 1957–October 8, 1960; September 29, 1962–September 26, 1964. Syndicated: 1964. Rebroadcast on CAR: 1998. Rebroadcast on BOOM: April 8, 2000–January 11, 2004.*

**Voices**
**Ruff/Professor Gizmo/Ubble-Ubble/Others:** Don Messick; **Reddy/Other Voices:** Daws Butler

## ◎ RUGRATS

The floor-level antics of a group of young toddlers—one-year-old Tommy Pickles and other diaper-clad tots (his one-toothed friend Chuckie, his bossy cousin Angelica and double-trouble infant twins Phil and Lil)—are seen from their viewpoint in this offbeat and funny half-hour cartoon series (in two 11-minute episodes) from the producers of *The Simpsons*.

Premiering on Nickelodeon in August 1991 as part of a 90-minute Sunday morning cartoon block that included "Doug," *The Ren & Stimpy Show* and *Rugrats*, the series was a late bloomer and became more successful in reruns than during its original network run. Producers tried to broaden its appeal, introducing some news characters during the 1993–94 season, namely an African American family—a little girl named Susie and her parents, Randy and Lily—but it did little to help the show's ratings. During that season the series' first half-hour prime-time special, *Rugrats: Hollyween*, premiered. In 1995 a second half-hour special, *A Rugrats Passover*, bowed on Nick.

Production ended on the Emmy-nominated series in 1994 after 65 episodes. In 1995 Nickelodeon moved the show from weekends to weekdays (in reruns), where it became the network's top-rated show. Surprised by the series' sudden success, the network ordered 13 new episodes (marking the first time Nickelodeon ever went back to a producer and ordered more than 65 episodes for an animated series), which began airing in May of 1997 with the premiere of *Rugrats Mother's Day Special*. The program was the first new episode since 1996's *Rugrats the Santa Experience* special.) In the spring of 1998, the gang starred in yet another prime-time special, *Rugrats Vacation*. A Klasky Csupo, Inc. Production. Color. Half-hour. Premiered on NICK: August 11, 1991–August 8, 1992; August 15, 1992–September 19, 1993; September 26, 1993–October 1, 1994; October 8, 1994–September 30, 1995; May 6, 1997–November 5, 2006. Rebroadcast on NICK: 1995–1997. Premiered on CBS: February 1, 2003–July 26, 2003. Rebroadcast on NICKT: May 1, 2002–.

**Voices**
Tommy Pickles: E. G. Daily; **Chuckie:** Christine Cavanagh; **Angelica:** Cheryl Chase; **Phil/Lil/Betty Pickles, Drew's wife:** Kath Soucie; **Charlotte:** Tress MacNeille; **Stu Pickles, Tommy's dad:** Jack Riley; **Didi Pickles, Tommy's mom:** Melanie Chartoff; **Drew Pickles, Stu's brother/Charles Sr., Chuckie's dad:** Michael Bell; **Grandpa Pickles:** David Doyle; **Susie:** Cree Summer; **Randy, Susie's dad:** Ron Glass; **Lily, Susie's mom:** Lisa Dinkins; **Dr. Lucy Carmichael:** Cheryl Carter; **Suzie Carmichael:** Cree Summer; **Lipschitz Hotline:** Tony Jay

### ◎ RUPERT (1989)
Famed British cartoonist Alfred Bestell produced this limited-animated series of cartoon vignettes featuring the adventures of the bold little bear and his friends from Nutwood Village from Mary Tourtel's famous comic-strip series of the same name. Bestell, who had taken over drawing the comic strip for Tourtel in 1935 due to her failing eyesight, produced an earlier *Rupert* series consisting of stop-motion puppet shorts in the 1970s. His limited-animated series was broadcast in the United States on the Disney Channel's *Lunch Box* series beginning in 1989. An Alfred Bestell Production. Color. Half-hour (part of the Disney Channel series Lunch Box). Premiered on DIS: July 1989–1993.

### ◎ RUPERT (1993)
The lovable and well-meaning little bear with a nose for excitement joined by his parents and trusted old friend, The Professor embarks on round-the-world adventures, to Africa, Asia, Europe and elsewhere, in this second series based on Mary Tourtel's long-running British comic-strip character. Produced by Toronto-based Nelvana Enterprises and Ellipse Animation, the half-hour cartoon series originally premiered on the Canadian cable service YTV in 1992. The series made its American television debut on The Family Channel (opposite reruns of *Babar*, another Nelvana-produced series) in 1993. The following fall the series joined Nickelodeon's Nick Jr. daily preschool programming block. The Nelvana studios property was subsequently rebroadcast on CBS for half a season before joining Toon Disney's weekday lineup two years later.

Beginning in January 2007, the popular children's series was rebroadcast on the qubo's all-new 24-hour, digital television network, four-hour programming block, along with other Nelvana-produced cartoon series, including *Elliot Moose and Marvin the Tap-Dancing Horse*, carried by the ION network (formerly PAX-TV) and its many affiliate stations nationwide. A Nelvana Enterprises/Ellipse Animation Production in association with TVS and YTV. Color. Half-hour. Premiered on FAM: September 6, 1993. Rebroadcast on NICK JR: September 1994–1999. Rebroadcast on CBS: January 9, 1999–September 26, 1999. Rebroadcast on TDIS: September 4, 2001–August 30, 2002. Rebroadcast on Q: January 8, 2007–.

**Voices**
Rupert: Ben Sandford; **Bill Badger:** Torquil Campbell; **Pong Ping:** Oscar Hsu; **Pudgy Pig:** Hadley Kay; **Mr. Bear:** Guy Bannerman; **Mrs. Bear:** Lally Cadeau; **Algy Pig:** Keith White; **The Professor:** Colin Fox; **Tiger Lady:** Stephanie Morgenstern; **Sage of Um:** Wayne Robson

### ◎ RURONI KENSHIN: WANDERING SAMURAI
Wielding his legendary reverse-blade sword, a young Samurai master named Ruroni Kenshin bands together with the young orphan Kaoru Kamiya; the powerful mercenary Sansosuke Sagara; the young pupil Yahiko Myojin; and doctor Megumi Takami, seeking redemption and honor as he battles the oppressors of the weak in the name of freedom and justice in this popular Japanese anime series originally known as *Samurai X*.

Adapted from the popular manga by Nobuhito Watsuki, this weekly half-hour fantasy action/adventure series was re-edited (removing graphic violence, profanity and nudity from the original Japanese version) and redubbed in English with its 95 episodes shown in the United States on Cartoon Network. A Fuji Television Networks Inc./SPE Visual Works/Studio Gallop/ Anime Works/A.D. Vision/BangZoom Entertainment Production. Color. Half-hour. Premiered on CAR: March 17, 2003–January 1, 2006.

**Voices**
Jane Alan, Steven Jay Blum, Rebecca Davis, Elyse Floyd, Richard Hayworth, Walter Lang, Wendee Lee, Dorothy Melendrez, Derek Stephen Prince, Michelle Ruff, Kirk Thorton, J. Shannon Weaver, Melissa Williamson

### ◎ SABAN'S ADVENTURES OF OLIVER TWIST
Set in Victorian London, adorable and adventurous mutt Oliver embarks on numerous adventures as he and streetwise scamp the Artful Dodger explore London Town from top to bottom, only to get into trouble and learn a lesson or two along the way in this weekly, 26-episode syndicated series inspired by Charles Dickens's classic novel. A Saban Entertainment Production. Color. Half-hour. Premiered: September 9, 1996. Syndicated. Rebroadcast on FAM: 1998–2001.

**Voices**
Oliver Twist: Mona Marshall; **Charlie Bates:** Tony Pope; **Other Voices:** Eugene Rubenezer

### ◎ SABAN'S ADVENTURES OF PINOCCHIO
Lovable wooden puppet Pinocchio experiences the trials and joys in his unrelenting quest to become human as he encounters Benny the Mouse, Jack the Fox, Willie the Weasel and the evil Puppetmaster Sneeroff in adventures that carry strong educational messages. This updated, half-hour cartoon series is an adaptation of

the classic children's stories by Italian author Collodi (whose real name was Carlo Lorenzini). The 52-episode series made its American television morning debut on HBO in July of 1992, paired weekday mornings with reruns of the hit cartoon series *Babar*, as part of the "HBO for Kids" program block. *A Tatsunoko/Saban Entertainment/Orbis Production. Color. Half-hour. Premiered on HBO: July 1, 1992–May 18, 1994.*

## SABAN'S ADVENTURES OF THE LITTLE MERMAID FANTASY

No relation to Disney's 1989 classic animated feature and television series spinoff, this half-hour syndicated series tells the story of the Little Mermaid and her earthly friend, the young and noble Prince Justin, as they travel through their wondrous worlds above and below the sea and battle the powers of an evil sea witch, who tries again and again to keep them separated forever. In this syndicated 26-episode series based on the Hans Christian Andersen classic. *A Saban Entertainment Production. Color. Half-hour. Premiered: Fall 1991. Syndicated.*

**Voices**
**Marina the Mermaid/Hedwig:** Sonja Ball; **Prince Justin:** Thor Bishopric; **Dudhlee:** Ian Finley; **Ridley:** Arthur Holden; **Chauncy:** Gordon Masten; **Winnie:** Annik Matern; **Anselm:** Aaron Tiger; **Narrator:** Jane Woods

## SABAN'S AROUND THE WORLD IN EIGHTY DREAMS

Carlos, a seasoned, robust sailor, and his three adopted children, A.J., Koki and Marianne, head out into countless escapades around the world to authenticate Carlos's remarkable stories of his past in this 26-episode half-hour series, part of the syndicated Sunday-morning programming block *Amazin' Adventures*. The series premiered in September 1992, along with three other new cartoon series: *King Arthur and the Knights of Justice, Saban's Gulliver's Travels* and *The Wizard of Oz*. *A Saban Entertainment Production in association with Antenna 2/MBC/Silvio Brulsconi Communications/Telecino. Color. Half-hour. Premiered: September 7, 1992. Syndicated.*

**Voices**
**Carlos:** Mark Camacho; **Oscar/Grandma Tadpole:** Rick Jones; **Koki:** Pauline Little; **A.J.:** Sonja Ball; **Marianne:** Patricia Rodriguez

## SABAN'S EAGLE RIDERS

In the not-too-distant future, faced with an alien invasion, an elite team of five teenage freedom fighters—Hunter (code name: "Hawk"), the team leader; Flash ("Falcon"), a cyborg and master strategist; Kelly ("Dove"), skilled at hand-to-hand combat; Ollie ("Owl"), the team's wise-cracking navigator; and Mickey ("Merlin"), the smallest, youngest member—under the direction of brilliant scientist Dr. Thadeaus Keane of the Global Security Council, emerge from their underwater refuge and bravely battle outer space archenemies Galaxor and Cybercon to save the planet from total domination in this half-hour fantasy/adventure series that debuted in first-run syndication in 1996. *A Saban Entertainment/Tatsunoko Production. Color. Half-hour. Premiered: September 1, 1996. Syndicated.*

**Voices**
**Auto:** Dena Burton; **Hunter Harris:** Richard Cansino; **Dr. Aikens:** Lara Cody; **Joe Thax:** Bryan Cranston; **Mallanox:** R. Martin Klein; **Kelly Jenar:** Heidi Lenhart; **Dr. Keane:** Greg O'Neill; **Ollie Keeawani:** Paul Schrier; **Cyberon:** Peter Spellos

## SABAN'S GULLIVER'S TRAVELS

A seafaring cabin boy and his sister venture to distant and wondrous lands in this modified version of Jonathan Swift's famed 17th-century novel. The series aired as a component of the Sunday morning syndicated cartoon block *Amazin' Adventures*. *A Saban Entertainment Production in association with Antenna 2/MBC/Silvio Brulsconi Communications/Telecino. Color. Half-hour. Premiered: September 7, 1992. Syndicated (as part of* Amazin' Adventures*).*

**Voices**
**Gulliver:** Terence Scammel; **Rafael:** Danny Brochu; **Folia:** Jessalyn Gilsig; **Fosla:** Sonja Ball; **Flim:** A.J. Henderson

## SABAN'S THE WHY WHY? FAMILY

Centered around the inquisitive Baby Victor, who has an insatiable appetite for information, an eccentric family—a Mr. Fix-it–type father, Max; a nature expert mother, Vanilla; and a "hip" grandma, Eartha—try to answer questions from their ever-curious son and grandson about the scientific origins of everything from genetics to internal combustion in this 26-episode half-hour "edutoonment" series aimed at school-age children produced for first-run syndication. *A Saban Entertainment Production. Color. Half-hour. Premiered: September 9, 1996. Syndicated. Rebroadcst on FOX FAM: August 22, 1998–November 2, 2000.*

**Voices**
Stanley Gurd Jr., Heidi Lenhart, Derek Patrick, Mendi Segal, Jamie Simone, Gengha Studebacker

## SABER RIDER AND THE STAR SHERIFFS

In this out-of-this-world futuristic fantasy with a western twist, Saber Rider, the dashing leader of the Star Sheriffs unit, maintains peace and unity for the settlers of the new frontier by defending against the ghostly "Outrider" foes, mysterious vapor beings who have perfected the technique of "dimension jumping."

The program was the first animated strip to incorporate interactive technology, a revolutionary new concept that enables viewers to participate with the program by using specially designed toys. *A World Events Production. Color. Half-hour. Premiered: September 1987–1989. Syndicated.*

**Voices**
Townsend Coleman, Peter Cullen, Pat Fraley, Pat Musick, Rob Paulsen, Jack Angel, Michael Bell, Brian Cummings, Diane Pershing, Hal Smith, Alison Argo, Ardt Burghardt, Tress MacNeille, Neil Ross, B. J. Ward, Len Weinrib

## SABRINA, SUPERWITCH

In attempt to bolster its sagging ratings, NBC repeated 13 episodes of *Sabrina, the Teenage Witch*, giving the program a new title, as a last-ditch effort to bring some excitement to its Saturday-morning cartoon lineup. (Initially the program was titled *The New Archie/Sabrina Hour*.) Unfortunately, the program failed to cast a spell over its audience and was pulled two months after its debut. The original *Sabrina* was first broadcast on rival network, CBS, in 1971. (See *Sabrina, the Teenage Witch* for voice credits.) *A Filmation Associates Production. Color. Half-hour. Premiered on NBC: November 26, 1977–January 28, 1978.*

## SABRINA AND THE GROOVIE GOOLIES

One year after her debut on *The Archie Comedy Hour*, Sabrina, a teenage sorceress, was coupled with The Groovie Goolies, a group of strange monsters (see *The Groovie Goolies*), in this hour-long series of new animated misadventures and humorous vignettes. Sabrina was so well received that she was given her own series,

*Saber Rider, the dashing leader of the Star Sheriffs, maintains peace and unity for the settlers of a new futuristic frontier in the syndicated series* Saber Rider and the Star Sheriffs. © *World Events Productions*

*Sabrina, the Teenage Witch,* on CBS. *A Filmation Associates Production. Color. One hour. Premiered on CBS: September 12, 1970–September 4, 1971.*

**Voices**
**Sabrina, the Teenage Witch:** Jane Webb; **Hot Dog Jr./Chili Dog/Harvey/Spencer:** Don Messick; **The Groovie Goolies:** Jane Web, Howard Morris, **Larry Storch, Larry D. Mann**

## ◎ SABRINA'S SECRET LIFE

The famed *Archie Comics* and television character icon returns in a new series of adventures as a 14-year-old high school student (with her friends Chloe moving away and Gem Stone enrolling in a private school in the area) while attending Greendale High School as a freshman. Joined by her best friends, Maritza and Nicole, Sabrina contends with her powers becoming stronger as she deals with her school rival and arch-nemesis teen witch, Cassandra, and her full-blown crush on her friend Harvey Kinkle. This spin-off of 1999's *Sabrina: The Animated Series* follows the plot and characters introduced in the television movie special *Sabrina: Friends Forever* (broadcast on Nicklelodeon's *DIC's Incredible Movie Toons* series) and debuted in November 2003 as part of the three-hour DIC Kids' Network syndicated block, with 26 half-hour episodes. *A DIC Entertainment Production. Color. Half-hour. Premiered: November 10, 2003. Syndicated.*

**Voices**
**Sabrina Spellman:** Britt McKillip; **Salem Saberhagen:** Maurice LaMarche; **Cassandra:** Tifanie Christun; **Aunt Zelda:** Jane Mortifee; **Aunt Hilda:** Moneca Stori; **Harvey Kinkle:** Bill Switzer; **Maritza:** Vanessa Tomasino

## ◎ SABRINA: THE ANIMATED SERIES

Living with her teenage witch aunts, Hilda and Zelda, her beloved mortal uncle, Quigley, and her mischievous, sarcastic cat, Salem, big-hearted, skinny but spunky 12-year-old Sabrina Spellman—half-human and half-witch—learns how to use her powers while wreaking havoc with her hilarious miscast spells in this prequel to the hit live-action ABC comedy series, *Sabrina, The Teenage Witch,* starring Melissa Joan Hart and based on the *Archie* comic-book character. Featuring a supporting cast—including her naïve friend, Harvey, the bratty spoiled rich girl, Gem Stone, and her spaced out friend, Pi—this weekly, half-hour fantasy comedy series debuted in syndication in September 1999 as part of UPN's weekday Disney *One Too* afternoon block, and also aired on ABC's *One Saturday Morning* block and Sunday mornings on UPN. Sixty-five original half-hour episodes were produced, along with a two-hour made-for-TV movie spin-off in October 2002 as the premiere installment of *DIC's Incredible Movie Toons* anthology series on Nickelodeon.

With the original series subsequently re-airing on the Disney Channel and Toon Disney, in 2003 the popular cartoon series spawned a second incarnation, *Sabrina's Secret Life.* In the fall of 2006, CBS rebroadcast the former series Saturday mornings as part of its *KOL Secret Slumber Party on CBS,* a three-hour weekend programming block. Melissa Joan Hart, who played Sabrina in the popular live-action ABC sitcom, signed on to provide the voices of Hilda and Zelda, with costar Nick Bakay reprising his role as the voice of Salem the cat. Hart's sister, Emily, took over as the voice of Sabrina. *A DIC Entertainment/Harbreak Film/Savage Studios/Pearson Television International Production. Color. Half-hour. Premiered: September 6, 1999. Syndicated. Premiered on ABC: September 11, 1999–October 13, 2001. Premiered on UPN: September 12, 1999–September 3, 2001. Rebroadcast on DIS: September 9, 2002–October 10, 2003. Rebroadcast on TDIS: September 2, 2002–August 29, 2004. Rebroadcast on CBS: September 16, 2006 ("KOL Secret Slumber Party").*

**Voices**
**Sabrina Spellman:** Emily Hart; **Hilda Spellman/Zelda Spellman:** Melissa Joan Hart; **Salem Saberhagen:** Nick Bakay; **Harvey Kinkle:** Bill Switzer; **Gemini Stone:** Chantal Strand; **Uncle Quigley:** Jay Brazeau; **Spookie Jar:** David Sobolov; **Chloe:** Cree Summer

## ◎ SABRINA, THE TEENAGE WITCH

A 15-year-old apprentice witch works her sorcery on friends Archie Andrews, Jughead, Veronica Lodge, Reggie Mantle, Riverdale High School principal Mr. Weatherbee and teacher Miss Grundy in this fantasy/comedy series inspired by the success of TV's *Bewitched.* The series ran for three successful seasons on CBS.

Sabrina originally debuted as a recurring character on 1969's *The Archie Comedy Hour.* The fast-thinking witch was later combined with *The Groovie Goolies* in a one-hour time slot under the series of *Sabrina and the Groovie Goolies,* broadcast on CBS in 1970. (The program was later edited into a half-hour for syndication.) *A Filmation Associates Production. Color. Half-hour. Premiered on CBS: September 11, 1971–August 31, 1974. Syndicated.*

**Voices**
**Sabrina:** Jane Webb

## ☺ SAGWA, THE CHINESE SIAMESE CAT

High-spirited exploits of a curious, energetic young Siamese cat named Sagwa who explores the world of ancient China, with her siblings and friend Fu-Fu, as they learn many valuable lessons about the people and its culture. Based on the popular children's book by renowned author Amy Tan (*The Joy Luck Club*), this half-hour children's series for the five to eight-year-old set, featuring two 11-minute adventures and a live-action segment focused on China's children and culture today, was coproduced by Sesame Workshop, creator of TV's *Sesame Street* and *Dragon-Tales*, and CineGroupe, producer of *The Kids from Room 402*, for PBS. Beginning in April 2005, the educational program was among a slate of PBS preschool programs that were rebroadcast as part of PBS's new digital cable channel and video-on-demand (VOD) service, PBS Kids Sprout. *A Sagwa Inc. Production/if/X/ CineGroupe Production. Color. Half-hour. Premiered on PBS: September 3, 2001–February 7, 2003. Rebroadcast on PBS Kids Sprout (VOD): April 4, 2005–. Rebroadcast on PBS Kids Sprout (digital cable): September 26, 2005–.*

*Voices*

**Sagwa:** Holly G. Frankel; **Fu-Fu:** Rick Jones; **Dongwa:** Oliver Grainger; **Sheegwa:** Jesse Vinet; **Baba Wim Bao Miao:** Arthur Holden; **Mama Shao Fun Miao:** Ellen David; **Yeh-Yeh:** Neil Shee; **Nai-Nai:** Sonja Ball; **Magistrate:** Hiro Kanagawa; **Tai-Tai:** Khaira Ledeyo; **Ba-Do:** Kathy Tsoi; **Luk-Do:** Leanne Adachi; **Huang-Do:** Rose Yee; **Cook:** Raugi Yu; **Reader:** Russell Yuen

## ☺ SAILOR MOON

Given awesome powers from mysterious feline Guardians, five ordinary high-schoolers—Sailor Moon (earthly name: Serena), Sailor Mars (Raye), Sailor Mercury (Amy), Sailor Jupiter (Lita) and Sailor Venus (Mina)—are transformed into glamorous and empowered fighters to battle the evil Queen Beryl (ruler of the Negaverse), whose goal is to accumulate enough "life energy" to release an explosive energy force that would destroy the world. This popular first-run action/adventure series was broadcast in syndication in 1995. The series, dubbed in English, was an American version of the runaway hit on Japan's TV Asahi called *Pretty Soldier Sailor Moon*. One week prior to its debut, FOX aired a half-hour series preview special entitled *Sailor Moon: The Return of Sailor Moon*. The beloved anime sensation was rebroadcast on USA Network from 1997 to 1998, Cartoon Network for four seasons from 1998 to 2002 and briefly on the WB Television Network's Kids' WB! in September 2001. *A DIC Entertainment Production. Color. Half-hour. Premiered on FOX September 2, 1995 (special). Premiered: September 11, 1995 (series). Syndicated. Rebroadcast on USA: June 9, 1997–March 1998. Rebroadcast on CAR: June 1, 1998–July 5, 2002. Rebroadcast on Kids' WB: September 3, 2001–September 14, 2001.*

*Voices*

**Sailor Moon/Serena:** Tracey Moore, Terri Hawkes; **Sailor Mercury/Amy:** Karen Bernstein; **Sailor Mars/Raye:** Katie Griffin, Emilie Barlow; **Sailor Jupiter/Lita:** Susan Roman; **Sailor Venus/Mina:** Stephanie Morgenstern; **Sailor Pluto/Luna:** Jill Frappier, Sabrina Grdevich; **Tuxedo Mask/Darien:** Jonathon Potts, Toby Proctor, Rino Romano, Vince Corazza; **Queen Beryl:** Naz Edwards; **Zoycite (a.k.a. Cinnabar)/Emerald:** Kirsten Bishop; **Malachite (a.k.a Kunczite):** Dennis Akiyama; **Jedite (a.k.a Emery)/Wiseman/Jordan:** Tony Daniels; **Neflite (a.k.a Mica):** Kevin Lund; **Luna:** Jill Frappier; **Artemis:** Ron Rubin; **Melvin (a.k.a. Umino):** Roland Parliament; **Molly (a.k.a. Naru)/Catsy:** Mary Long; **Sammy:** Julie Lemieux; **Andrew:** Colin O'Meara; **Miss Haruna:** Nadine Rabinovitch; **Rini:** Tracey Hoyt; **Alan:** Vince Corazza; **Chad:** Steven Bednarski; **Moonlight Knight:** Toby Proctor; **Metallia/Negaforce:** Maria Vacratsis; **Rubeus:** Robert Tinker; **Tree of Life:** Liz Hannah; **Catsy:** Alice Poon; **Birdie:** Kathleen Laskey; **Avery:** Jennifer Griffiths; **Prisma:** Norma Dell'Agnese; **Grandpa:** David Fraser; **Serena's Dad:** David Huband

## ☺ SAILOR MOON R

After two space aliens travel to Earth from a faraway galaxy disguised as regular students, Sailor Moon and the senshi battle the wicked time-traveling Black Moon family (Dimando, Esmeraude, Rubeus, Sapphire, Wiseman and others) while learning that Rini is the daughter of the future ruler of Earth in this second installment of the Sailor Moon franchise from Japan.

This English-language version of the original Japanese favorite—split into two parts—was first telecast in America in first-run syndication in September 1995, featuring 42 half-hour episodes (excluding one episode from the original Japanese version). Starting in June 1998, the popular fantasy/adventure series was replayed on Cartoon Network. *A Toei Animation/Kodansha/DIC Production. Color. Half-hour. Premiered: September 11, 1995. Syndicated. Rebroadcast on CAR: June 1, 1998–.*

*Voices*

**Sailor Moon/Serena:** Terri Hawkes; **Sailor Mars/Raye:** Katie Griffin, Emilie Barlow; **Sailor Mercury/Amy:** Karen Bernstein; **Sailor Jupiter/Lita:** Susan Roman; **Sailor Venus/Mina:** Stephanie Morgenstern; **Darien/Tuxedo Mask:** Rino Romano, Toby Proctor, Vince Corazza; **Luna/Luna Ball/Queen Beryl:** Jill Frappier; **Artemis:** Ron Rubin; **Ikuko/Serena's Mother:** Barbara Radecki; **Serena's Dad:** David Hubard; **Andrew:** Colin O'Meara; **Grandpa Hino:** David Fraser; **Avery:** Jennifer Griffiths; **Sammy:** Julie Lemieux; **Birdie:** Kathy Laskey; **Emerald:** Kirsten Bishop; **Wicked Lady:** Liz Brown; **Doom Tree:** Liz Hannah; **Prince Sapphire:** Lyon Smith; **Patricia Haruna:** Nadine Rabinovitch; **Prisma:** Norma Dell'Agnese; **Prince Diamond:** Robert Bockstael; **Rubeus:** Robert Tinkler; **Chad:** Steven Bednarski; **Rini:** Tracey Hoyt; **Alan Granger:** Vince Corazza; **Catsy:** Alice Poon, Mary Long; **Molly:** Mary Long; **Chessmaster/Melvin:** Roland Parliament; **Anne Granger/Luna Ball/Sailor Pluto/Trista Meiou:** Sabrina Grdevich

## ☺ SAILOR MOON S

In this third installment and sequel to 1995's *Sailor Moon R*, Sailor Moon and her fellow heroines battle a new cast of villains—Professor Tomoe, Kaori Knight, Mistress 9 and Pharoah 90, known as the Death Busters—whose single goal is to rule the world by mining energy from the pure heart crystals of innocent victims unless Sailor Moon and company can intercede. The half-hour, English-dubbed series aired on Cartoon Network, which also broadcast the full-length theatrical feature, *Sailor Moon S, The Movie: Hearts on Ice* in 2001. *A Toei Animation/Kodansha/Clowerway/Pioneer Entertainment L.P. Production. Color. Half-hour. Premiered on CAR: June 12, 2000–August 1, 2000.*

*Voices*

**Sailor Moon/Serena:** Linda Ballantyne; **Sailor Mercury/Amy:** Liza Balkan; **Sailor Mars/Raye:** Katie Griffin; **Sailor Jupiter/Lita:** Susan Roman; **Sailor Venus/Mina:** Emilie Barlow; **Sailor Uranus/Amara Tenoh:** Sarah LeFleur; **Sailor Neptune/Michelle Kaiou:** Barbara Radecki; **Sailor Saturn/Professor Hotaru Tomoe:** Jennifer Gould; **Sailor Mini-Moon/Rini:** Stephanie Beard; **Sailor Pluto/Trista Meioh:** Susan Aceron; **Tuxedo Mask/Darien:** Vince

Corazza; **Luna:** Jill Frappier; **Artemis:** Ron Rubin; **Mimet:** Catherine Disher; **Grandpa Hino:** David Fraser; **Dr. Souichi Tomoe:** Jeff Lumby; **Andrew:** Joel Feeney; **Kaori Knight:** Kirsten Bishop; **Eugeal:** Loretta Jafelice; **Molly:** Mary Long; **Melvin:** Roland Parliament; **Chad:** Steven Bednarski; **Mistress 9:** Susan Aceron

### ◎ SAILOR MOON SUPER S

In this fourth chapter of the continuing saga, Sailor Moon and her sensei battle the villainous Dead Moon Circus, consisting of the Amazon Trio, the Amazoness Quartet, Nehelenia and Zirconia, who plot to—what else?—take over the world unless they are stopped. A year after completing its original network run, Cartoon Network premiered the third theatrical feature in the series (also dubbed in English), first released in Japan in 1995, *Sailor Moon Super S, The Movie: Black Dream Hole. A Toei Animation/Kodansha/Clowerway/Pioneer Entertainment L.P. Production. Color. Half-hour. Premiered on CAR: September 26, 2000–November 16, 2000.*

*Voices*
**Sailor Moon/Serena:** Linda Ballantyne; **Sailor Mercury/Amy:** Liza Balkan; **Sailor Mars/Raye:** Katie Griffin; **Sailor Jupiter/Lita:** Susan Roman; **Sailor Venus/Mina:** Emilie Barlow; **Sailor Mini-Moon/Rini:** Stephanie Beard; **Tuxedo Mask/Darien:** Vince Corazza; **Luna:** Jill Frappier; **Artemis:** Ron Rubin; **Diana/Eugeal:** Loretta Jafelice, Naomi Emmerson; Ikuko Tsukino, **Serena's mom:** Barbara Radecki; **Grandpa Hino:** David Fraser; **Hawk's-eye:** Benji Plener; **Fisheye:** Deborah Drakeford; **Tiger's-eye:** Jason Barr; **Sammy Tsukino:** Julie Lemieux; **Queen Nehellenia:** Lisa Dalbello; **Eugeal: Junjun/Miharu/Molly:** Mary Long; **Pegasus/Helios:** Robert Bockstael; **Melvin:** Roland Parliament; **Chad:** Steve Bednarski; **Elizabeth:** Susan Aceron; **Melanie:** Tanya Donato; **Dentist:** Tony Daniels

### ◎ SALTY'S LIGHTHOUSE

Educational preschooler series following the adventures of five-year-old Salty, who plays elaborate make-believe games and dress-up in a lighthouse with his seaside friends (Ocho the octopus, Claude the hermit crab and others), combining traditional cel animated wraparounds of Salty and his pals with model animated and live-action segments to tell each story. The series airs weekdays on the Learning Channel. *A Bank Street/GMTV/Ealing Animation/Sony Wonder/Sunbow Entertainment Production in association with The learning Channel. Color. Half-hour. Premiered on TLC: March 30, 1998.*

*Voices*
**Salty:** Rhys Huber; **Ocho/Aunt Chovie:** Kathleen Barr; **Other Voices:** Ian James Corlett, Scott McNeil, Janyce Jaud, Andrea Libman, French Tickner, Lenore Zann

### ◎ SAM AND MAX: FREELANCE POLICE

A pair of crime-solving pets—a gregarious dog and manic rabbit—team up as freelance police officers to solve bizarre mysteries, aided by the Geek, a teenage braniac who invents devices and vehicles to help them out in this half-hour Saturday morning series based on the cult comic book by Steve Purcell for the FOX Network. *A Nelvana Production. Color. Half-hour. Premiered on FOX: October 4, 1997–July 4, 1998. Rebroadcast on FOX: July 6, 1998–September 11, 1998 ("Cartoon Cabana" cartoon block).*

*Voices*
**Sam:** Harvey Atkin; **Max:** Robert Tinkler; **The Geek:** Tracey Moore

### ◎ SAMMY

Film and television comedian David Spade, best known for his work on NBC's *Saturday Night Live* and *Just Shoot Me*, created this semi-autobiographical animated comedy series following the exploits of standup comic Jamie Blake and his deadbeat dad Sammy who suddenly wants a piece of the pie after his son achieves fame and fortune as the star of the fictional sitcom, *Hey, Rebecca*. Loosely based on his real-life experiences, Spade's first prime-time animation venture fared poorly. Of the 10 episodes that were produced, only two episodes aired before NBC canceled the series. Spade provides the voices of both characters. Following its cancelation, except for airings of holiday cartoon specials, NBC took a hiatus from producing prime-time animation until 2004 when it debuted the much-ballyhooed DreamWorks CG-animated series *Father of the Pride*, about the lives of the white lions and star attraction in the Las Vegas show of famed illusionists Siegfried and Roy. *A Brad Grey Television/Desert Rat Productions/NBC Production. Color. Half-hour. Premiered on NBC: August 8, 2000–August 15, 2000.*

*Voices*
**Sammy Blake/Jamie Blake:** David Spade; **Todd Blake:** Harland Williams; **Gary Blake:** Bob Odenkirk; **Mark Jacobs:** Andy Dick; **Kathy Kelly:** Maura Tierney; **Marie:** Julia Sweeney; **Steve:** Jeffrey Tambor; **Lola:** Olivia Hack; **Emily Blake:** Janeane Garofalo

### ◎ SAMSON AND GOLIATH

Loosely based on the classic biblical tale, a young boy (Samson) and his pet dog (Goliath) are transformed into superhumans—in a colossal man and golden, ruffled-haired lion—by rubbing two gold bracelets together (and declaring "I need Samson Power!") in order to battle despotic fiends and beastly creatures in this 26-episode half-hour adventure series that originally aired on NBC. Debuting in September of 1967, the show was originally called *Samson and Goliath*. On April 6, 1968 the show was retitled *Young Samson*, perhaps in an effort to differentiate itself from Art Clokey's syndicated Christian stop-motion animated series *Davey and Goliath*. Reruns later aired on USA Network in syndication and on Boomerang. *A Hanna-Barbera Production. Color. Half-hour. Premiered on NBC: September 9, 1967–March 1968 (as Samson and Goliath); April 6, 1968–August 31, 1968 (as Young Samson). Rebroadcast on USA: February 20, 1989–March 26, 1991 (with Space Kidettes). Syndicated. Rebroadcast on BOOM: September 2, 2001–.*

*Voices*
**Samson:** Tim Matthieson

### ◎ SAMURAI CHAMPLOO

During ancient Japan's so-called Edo era, fate brings together two powerful samurai warriors, Mugen and Jin, and a 15-year-old girl named Fuu who convinces them to embark on a journey to find the mysterious samurai that smells like sunflowers in this modern, hip-hop anime series combining action, adventure and comedy. Originally broadcast in 2004 on Fuji television in Japan, Geneon Entertainment produced this 20-episode, English-translated version, based on the manga by its creator Shinichiro Watanabe that aired late Saturday nights on Cartoon Network's *Adult Swim* block. *A Fuji TV/Manglobe Inc./Shimoigusa Champloos/Bandai Entertainment/ Bang! Zoom! Entertainment/Madman Entertainment/Geneon Entertainment Production. Color. Half-hour. Premiered on CAR: May 14, 2005–March 18, 2006. Rebroadcast on CAR: March 25, 2006–.*

*Voices*
**Mugen:** Steven Jay Blum; **Jin:** Kirk Thorton; **Fuu:** Kari Wahlgren

## ◎ SAMURAI JACK

From Emmy Award-winning animation genius Genndy Tartakovsky, creator of TV's popular *Dexter's Laboratory, The Powerpuff Girls* and *Star Wars: Clone Wars*, comes this entertaining and serious saga of an ancient magic samurai sword-wielding warrior, stuck in the future due to a curse put upon him by the nefarious shape-shifting wizard, Aku, who uses his wits and mastery to battle Aku and his robot enemies (who "bleed" only oil in battle scenes) and save the world, while finding an open portal to take him back home. Basing its look on a unique combination of cinematic and comic-book styles and loosely inspired by Frank Miller's best-selling graphic novel, *Ronin*, this brilliantly animated half-hour adventure series, featuring little dialogue and mostly action-driven stories, aired for four seasons on Cartoon Network from August 2001 to September 2004. The show's final broadcast featured four episodes airing during Saturday night's *Toonami* action/anime block with a special presentation of all 20 chapters of Tartakovsky's *Star Wars: Clone Wars* epic microseries. Originally Cartoon Network ordered 52 half-hour episodes during the series' four-season run, with some episodes airing after the show was canceled, as a special or in reruns.

Overall, the show earned three Emmy Award nominations for outstanding animated program, winning once in 2004. Series animators Wes Bane, Derrik Steinhagen, Dan Krall, Scott Willis and Bryan Andrews were also each awarded an Emmy for outstanding individual achievement in animation for their artistic work on the series. *A Cartoon Network Animation Production. Color. Half-hour. Premiered on CAR: August 7, 2001–September 25, 2004.*

### Voices
**Samurai Jack/Mad Jack:** Phil LaMarr; **Aku:** Makoto Iwamatsu; **Bounty Hunter Brotok:** Brian George; **Demongo:** Kevin Michael Richardson; **Monkey-man:** Jeff Bennett; **The Scotsman:** John Di Maggio

## ◎ SAMURAI PIZZA CATS

Using their pizza parlor as headquarters, these young samurai crime-fighters (Speedy Cerviche, Guido Anchovi and Polly Esther) protect the myopic Princess Violet and the city from the force of the evil Big Cheese, head of the Little Tokyo Big Business Association, who plans to force residents into buying anything his slimy vendors have to sell in this action-packed half-hour series made for first-run syndication. *A Saban Entertainment/Tatsunoko Production. Color. Half-hour. Premiered: September 9, 1996. Syndicated.*

### Voices
**Polly Esther/Mama-san/Carla Crow/Empress Fredia:** Sonja Ball; **Spritz T. Cat/Bucky Road Runner:** Mark Camacho; **Lucille/Princess Violet/Lucinda:** Susan Glover; **Seymour "Big" Cheese:** Dean Hargrove; **"Big" Al Dente/General Catton:** A.J. Henderson; **Speedy/Bad Bird/Meozwzma/Mojo Rojo:** Rick Jones; **Francine Manx/Junior/Abigail:** Pauline Little; **Guru Lou/Crow Magnon:** Walter Massey; **Wally/The Professor:** Michael O'Reilly; **Guido/Narrator/Jeff Atrick/Emperor Fred/Bat Cat:** Terrence Scammel

## ◎ SAMURAI 7

After a small village in feudal Japan is terrorized by samurai sword-wielding bandits who raid their crops, the down-on-their luck villagers are facing starvation, and hire their own brave, master swordsmen (led by the young priestess Kirara) to defend them in this English-dubbed Japanese-imported series, based on Akira Kurosawa's classic film epic, *The Seven Samurai*.

Produced in high definition at a cost of $300,000 per episode (nearly twice the cost of an average non-hi-def series), the anime series—already a huge success on home video in the United States—premiered nationally on VOOM's Animania HD on Wednesday, March 1, 2006, at 9:00 P.M. (EST) as part of the channel's new Wednesday *Animayhem* block. Conversely, the International Film Channel (IFC) began airing the half-hour series on Sunday, April 1, at 10:30 P.M. (EST) in conjunction with its popular *Samurai Saturday* movie stand, a weekly presentation of classic Asian martial-arts movies. The season finale on IFC aired on September 30, 2006. *A FUNimation Entertainment/GONZO Digimation/Rainbow Media Production. Color. Half-hour. Premiered on ANI: March 1, 2006– . Premiered on IFC: April 1, 2006–September 30, 2006.*

### Voices
**Gorobei Katayama:** Bob Carter; **Kikuchiyo:** Christopher R. Sabat; **Shichiroji:** Duncan Brannan; **Heihachi Hayashida:** Greg Ayres; **Kambei Shimada:** R. Bruce Elliott; **Katsushiro Okamoto:** Sean Michael Teague; **Kyuzo:** Sonny Strait; **Ukyo:** Anthony Bowling; **Kirara Mikumari:** Colleen Clinkenbeard; **Rikichi:** J. Michael Tatum; **Komachi Mikumari:** Lucy Christian; **Tortoise-Express Rider:** Alison Retzloff; **Troupe Girl B:** Amber Cotton; **Village Elder:** Andrew Haskett; **Gonzo:** Andy Mullins; **Amanushi:** Anthony Bowling; **Ayamaro:** Barry Yandell; **Prime Minister:** Bill Flynn; **Syusai:** Brett Weaver; **Masamune:** Brice Armstrong; **Troupe Girl C/Uma:** Brina Palencia; **Honoka:** Carrie Savage; **Farmer Gosaku:** Christopher Bevins; **The Royal Envoy:** Chuck Huber; **Sanae:** Clarine Harp; **Hie:** Elise Baughman; **Farmer Yohei:** Grant James; **Yukino:** Gwendolyn Lau; **Messenger:** Jeremy Inman; **Hyogo:** Jerry Jewell; **Kanzo:** John Burgmeier; **Setsu (Matriarch):** Juli Erickson; **Troupe Girl:** Kate Borneman; **Hanaole:** Kent Williams; **Farmer Mosuke:** Kyle Hebert; **Mizuki:** Laura Bailey; **Farmer Manzo:** Mark Stoddard; **Sobei:** Michael Sinterniklaas; **Shino:** Monica Rial; **Tessai:** Robert McCollum; **Tanomo, Nobuseri Leader:** Scott McNeil; **Genzo:** Sean Schemmel; **Shika:** Stephanie Young; **Okara:** Zarah Litte

### Additional Voices
Adrian Cook, Alison Retzloff, Andrew Haskett, Andy Mullins, Barry Yandell, Bill Townsley, Brad Jackson, Chris Cason, Chris Rager, Chuck Huber, Dana Schultes, Daniel Katsük, Dave Trosko, Doug Burks, Ed Blaylock, Egg Nebula, Greg Dulcie, Jakie Cabe, Jamie Marchi, Jay Moses, Jay S. Jones, Jeff Johnson, Jeremy Inman, Jerry Russell, Jerry Zumwalt, Jim Johnson, John Burgmeier, Jonathan C. Osborne, Josh Martin, Juli Erickson, Justin Cook, Kevin M. Connolly, Lane Pianta, Lauren Goode, Leah Clark, Linda Young, Maria Vu, Mark Lancaster, Mark Orvik, Markus Lloyd, Matthew Thompkins, Melinda Wood Allen, Mike McFarland, Phillip Wilburn, Robert Colin, Steven Morris, Troy Williams, Will Helms, Z. Charles Bolton

## ◎ SANTO BUGITO

Creator Arlen Klasky, cofounder of Klasky Csupo (original producers of *The Simpsons*), got the idea for this half-hour Saturday-morning cartoon series from her own children who, like most kids, were alternately grossed out and fascinated by bugs. Billed as the "world's first Tex-Mex cartoon," this Latin music–driven cartoon series deals with an all-insect cast who live life to the fullest in a Tex-Mex border town of 64 million insects, led by Paco and Carmen De La Antchez, the free-spirited proprietors of Santo Bugito's Cocina, a popular eatery where all the locals hang out. Premiering on CBS in 1995, the series was the first Saturday-morning effort from independent animation giant Klasky Csupo and featured music by Mark Mothersbaugh, formerly of DEVO. *A Klasky Csupo*

*Production. Color. Half-hour. Premiered on CBS: September 16, 1995–August 17, 1996.*

**Voices**
**Carmen De La Antchez:** Marabina Jaimes; **Paco De La Antchez:** Tony Plana; **Eaton Woode:** Charlie Adler; **Ralph:** George Kennedy; **Clem:** William Sanderson; **Burt:** Michael Stanton; **Amelia:** Joan Van Ark; **Carmen:** Marabina Jaimes; **Lencho:** Cheech Marin; **Rosa:** Candi Milo; **Mr. Mothmeyer:** Henry Gibson; **The Professor:** David Paymer

### ◎ SATURDAY SUPERCADE

Five segments made up this hour-long series of video game–inspired cartoons that ran for two seasons on CBS. The first season lineup featured: "Donkey Kong," about a gorilla who escapes from the circus and keeps on the run to avoid captivity; "Donkey Kong Jr.," the misadventures of Donkey Kong Jr. and his friend, Bones, in search of Kong's missing father; "Frogger," the story of a frog and his companions (Fanny Frog and Shelly the Turtle) as reporters for the *Swamp Gazette*; "Piffall," the exploits of a treasure hunter, his niece and their cowardly pet who travel the world to unearth lost treasures; and "Q*bert," a teenager who battles the evil Coilee Snake and his accomplices (Viper, Ugh and Wrong Way) with the help of his girlfriend, Q*tee.

"Frogger" and "Pitfall Harry" aired only during the first season. For the second season, they were replaced by two new video game–derived segments: "Space Ace," a handsome, gallant space hero with his lovely partner, Kimberly, who protects the heavens from the evil doings of Commander Borf, who plots to rule the universe; and "Kangaroo," the misadventures of three youngsters, Joey, Katy and Sidney, who run into all sorts of problems at the local zoo. *A Ruby-Spears Enterprises Production. Color. One hour. Premiered on CBS: September 17, 1983–August 24, 1985.*

**Voices**

**DONKEY KONG: Donkey Kong:** Soupy Sales; **Pauline:** Judy Strangis; **Mario:** Peter Cullen

**DONKEY KONG JR.: Donkey Kong Jr.:** Frank Welker; **Bones, his friend:** Bart Braverman

**FROGGER: Frogger:** Bob Sarlatte; **Fanny:** B.J. Ward; **Shellshock:** Marvin Kaplan; **Tex:** Ted Field, Sr.; **Mac:** Alan Dinehart

**PITFALL: Pitfall Harry:** Bob Ridgely; **Rhonda:** Noelle North; **Quickclaw:** Ken Mars

**Q*BERT: Q*bert:** Billy Bowles; **Q*tee/Q*val:** Robbie Lee; **Q*bertha/Q*Mom/Viper:** Julie Dees; **Q*bit:** Dick Beals; **Q*mungus/Q*ball/Q*Dad/Coilee Snake/Ugg/Wrongway/Sam Slick:** Frank Welker

**SPACE ACE: Space Ace:** Jim Piper; **Kimberly:** Nancy Cartwright; **Dexter:** Sparky Marcus; **Space Marshall Vaughn:** Peter Renaday; **Commander Borf:** Arthur Burghardt

**KANGAROO: Katy:** Mea Martineau; **Joey:** David Mendenhall; **Mr. Friendly:** Arthur Burghardt; **Sidney:** Marvin Kaplan; **Monkey Biz Gang:** Frank Welker, Pat Fraley

### ◎ THE SAVAGE DRAGON

In futuristic Chicago, the Chicago Police Department's top cop—the half-reptile, half-human Dragon—helps to overcome a generation of superpowered perversions known as Superfreaks who grip the city in a villainous stranglehold. This 13-episode half-hour cartoon series was based on the bestselling comic book created by Erik Larsen. The series premiered on USA Network's Saturday-morning Cartoon Express in the fall of 1995. *A Lacewood Produc-tion in association with Studio B Productions/Universal Cartoon Studio/P3 Entertainment. Color. Half-hour. Premiered on USA: October 21, 1995–July 26, 1998.*

**Voices**
**The Savage Dragon:** Jim Cunnings, Rene Auberjonois, Jeff Bennett; **Other Voices:** Paul Eiding, Jennifer Hale, Mark Hamill, Dorian Harewood, Tony Jay, Danny Mann, Rob Paulsen, Robert Picardo, Neil Ross, Kath Soucie, Mercelo Tubert, Frank Welker

### ◎ THE SAVE-UMS!

Monitoring the sky, land, sea and even outer space from their compound by the sea, Save-Ums Central, a small but powerful new breed of super action heroes races to help others and respond to emergencies through collaborative problem-solving, critical thinking and creative use of technology in this fast-paced 3-D computer-animated children's series. Commissioned by The Learning Channel (TLC) and Discovery Kids and produced by Canada's DECODE Entertainment, 26 fantastical adventures debuted on Discovery Kids and TLC's weekday preschool program block in February 2003. In June 2004, 13 additional half-hour episodes of the educational preschool favorite were produced. *A DECODE Entertainment/CBC/Discovery Kids/Dan Clark Co./C.O.R.E. Toons Production. Color. Half-hour. Premiered on TLC/DSCK: February 24, 2003.*

**Voices**
**Noodle:** Mark Rendall; **Ka Chung:** Mitchell Eisner; **Jazzi:** Tajja Isen; **Foo:** Aaryn Doyle; **Custard:** Jordan Francis; **B.B. Jammies:** Connor Price

### ◎ SCARY SCOOBY FUNNIES

Scooby Doo, his feisty dog cousin Scrappy-Doo and their goofy adult companion, Shaggy, undo baffling mysteries in this hour-long mystery/adventure show featuring episodes repeated from *The Richie Rich/Scooby-Doo Hour*. The series was shown opposite *The New Scooby-Doo Mysteries* on ABC. *A Hanna-Barbera Production. Half-hour. Premiered on ABC: October 13, 1984–August 31, 1985.*

### ◎ SCHOLASTIC'S THE MAGIC SCHOOL BUS

Lily Tomlin is the voice of Ms. Frizzle, a schoolteacher who takes a group of elementary school students on unusual field trips that turn into fantastic voyages. With the help of her magic school bus, which can literally go anywhere and be anything, they explore space, the Arctic, the human body and the principles of science in this, and PBS's first fully animated series, based on the bestselling children's books by Joanna Cole and illustrator Bruce Degen.

Various celebrity guest stars, including Carol Channing and Tyne Daly (as Dr. Tonelli), hopped aboard the souped-up yellow bus in episodic adventures. Produced by Scholastic Productions in association with Canadian-based Nelvana Limited, the fun-filled entertainment and educational half-hour series premiered on PBS in September of 1994. On September 10, 1994, the show's debut was preceded by a Saturday-morning "sneak preview" special "Inside Ralphie" on FOX and PBS affiliates. The program spawned two prime-time animated specials: *A Magic School Bus Halloween* (1995) and *The Magic School Bus Holiday Family Special* (1996), featuring Dolly Parton as celebrity guest voice. The animated series' hip theme song was written by Peter Lurye and performed by rock 'n' roll legend Little Richard. *Fraggle Rock* cocreator Jocelyn Stevenson was the series head writer. In 1995 Tomlin won a daytime Emmy Award for outstanding performer in an animated program. *A Scholastic Production in association with Nelvana Limited. Color. Half-hour. Premiered on PBS: September 10, 1994 (sneak preview); September 11, 1994 (premiere). Premiered on FOX: September 10, 1994 (sneak preview special).*

## Voices

**Ms. Valerie Frizzle/Institute Inhabitant:** Lily Tomlin; **Producer:** Malcolm-Jamal Warner; **Ralphael "Ralphie" Tennelli:** Stuart Stone; **Arnold Perlstein:** Danny Tamberelli; **Dorothy Ann:** Tara Meyer; **Wanda Li:** Lisa Yamanaka; **Carlos Ramon:** Daniel DeSanto; **Keesha Franklin:** Erica Luttrell; **Timothy:** Andre Ottley-Lorant

## ◎ A SCHOOLHOUSE ROCK

The brainchild of advertising executive David McCall, this long-running, award-winning educational series was developed in conjunction with ABC children's television head Michael Eisner (now chairman of the board of the Walt Disney Company) and Warner Bros. cartoon legend Chuck Jones. Beginning as a series of 90- to 180-second musical multiplication films called "Multiplication Rock" shown six times weekly during and between the network's Saturday-morning cartoon shows, 13 problem-solving films were produced for the 1972–73 season, covering such topics as "Zero, My Hero" and "Naughty Number Nine."

Different variations evolved in ensuing seasons to educate young viewers: "Grammar Rock" (1973), info-snippets designed to help children with grammar; "American Rock" (1974), a series of patriotic informational bites; "Bicentennial Rock" (1976), chronicling important historical moments in our nation's 200-year heritage (and begun two years before the bicenntial celebration); "Science Rock" (1978–79), dealing with scentific issues; "Body Rock (1979), a three-episode series covering the importance of good health; and "Scooter Computer and Mr. Chips" (1980s), to aid children in understanding computers and related technology.

The four-time Emmy Award–winning series, consisting of 41 episodes, went off the air in September of 1985, only to return with brand-new episodic vignettes (including new episodes of "Grammar Rock ) on ABC in October 1993. The new animated films were designed by Tom Yohe Jr., son of *Schoolhouse Rock 's* original executive producer. *A Newall/Yohe-Scholastic Rock, Inc. Production. Color. Half-hour. Premiered on ABC: January 6, 1973– September 1985; October 1993–May 24, 1996.*

## ◎ SCIENCE COURT

Using a courtroom as the teaching ground, a judge (voiced by stand-up comedienne Paula Poundstone) presides over cases in which attorney Doug Savage and court adversary Alison Kremel present evidence trying to prove basic scientific principles and theories, from evaporation to gravity, in order to win in this educational comedy series. It was created by Bill Braudis (who provides the voice of attorney Doug Savage) and famed radio/television personality Tom Snyder, cocreator and executive producer of Comedy Central's *Dr. Katz, Professional Therapist. A Tom Snyder Production. Color. Half-hour. Premiered on ABC: September 13, 1997.*

## Voices

**Judge Stone:** Paula Poundstone; **Doug Savage:** Bill Braudis; **Alison Krempel:** Paula Plum

## ◎ SCOOBY AND SCRAPPY-DOO

Back for an eighth season, the mystery-solving Great Dane, Scooby-Doo, and pals Fred, Shaggy, Daphne and Velma returned to the trail of mystery in this new 16-episode half-hour series, featuring a new addition: Scooby's overly zealous little nephew, Scrappy-Doo, who instigates all the trouble for the gang.

The series marked the final appearance of Fred, Daphne and Velma, who departed after the series' network run. (In 1983, only Daphne returned in the recurring role of a reporter for a teen magazine investigating mysteries on ABC's *The All-New Scooby and*

*Scrappy-Doo Show.* Former series regulars Freddy Jones and Velma Dinkley reappeared in guest-starring roles on 1984's *The New Scooby-Doo Mysteries).* In 1980–81, 39 new seven-and-a-half-minute episodes were featured in *The Richie Rich/Scooby-Doo Show Hour,* also on ABC. In January 1984 Scooby and Scrappy-Doo returned in a newly titled series of cartoon reruns *The New Scooby and Scrappy-Doo Show.* The popular mystery series enjoyed a rebirth in reruns on Cartoon Network and its sister channel, Boomerang. *A Hanna-Barbera Production. Color. Half-hour. Premiered on ABC: September 22, 1979–November 1, 1980. Rebroadcast on ABC: 1984 (as The New Scooby and Scrappy-Doo Show). Rebroadcast on CAR: April 14, 1997 (weekdays). Rebroadcast on BOOM: February 26, 2001–.*

## Voices

**Scooby-Doo:** Don Messick; **Scrappy-Doo:** Lennie Weinrib; **Freddy Jones:** Frank Welker; **Shaggy Rogers:** Casey Kasem; **Daphne Blake:** Heather Storm; **Velma Dace Dinkley:** Maria Frumkin (replaced Patricia Stevens)

## ◎ THE SCOOBY & SCRAPPY-DOO/PUPPY HOUR

Scooby-Doo, the lovable canine afraid of his own shadow, and his fearless little nephew, Scrappy-Doo, comically extricate themselves from fantastic predicaments in this hour-long series for Saturday morning in 1982 that featured as its second half "The Puppy's New Adventures," the warmhearted tale of Petey the puppy and his human friend, Dolly, and canine buddies Duke, Dash and Lucky as they search for Petey's lost family. The characters were first introduced in a series of "ABC Weekend Specials" beginning with *The Puppy Who Wanted a Boy,* produced between 1978 and 1981 by Ruby-Spears Productions. Coproduced by Hanna-Barbera Productions ("Scooby and Scrappy-Doo") and Ruby-Spears Enterprises ("The Puppy's New Adventures"), the series, featuring three "Scooby and Scrappy-Doo" cartoons and one half-hour adventure of Petey the Puppy, aired in its full hour format for one season on ABC.

The Scooby and Scrappy-Doo cartoons featured a new addition: Scooby's Wild West cousin, Yabba-Doo, who helped Scrappy maintain law and order in separate show segments. Other weekly segments had Scooby, Scrappy and Shaggy eneountering new mysteries in various locales while vacationing.

In the fall of 1983, a second series of new cartoons was produced, *The Puppy's Further Adventures,* which ran as the lead-in to Hanna-Barbera's *The All-New Scooby and Scrappy-Doo Show.* A third and final Petey the Pup series was produced in 1984, *The Puppy's Great Adventures. A Hanna-Barbera/Ruby-Spears Production. Color. One hour. Premiered on ABC: September 25, 1982–January 1, 1983. Rebroadcast on ABC: January 8, 1983–September 3, 1983 (as The Scooby-Doo/Puppy Hour).*

## Voices

**Scooby-Doo/Scrappy-Doo/Yabba-Doo:** Don Messick; **Freddy Jones:** Frank Welker; **Shaggy Rogers:** Casey Kasem; **Daphne Blake:** Heather North; **Velma Dace Dinkley:** Patricia Stevens; **Deputy Dusty:** Frank Welker; **Petey the Pup:** Billy Jacoby; **Dolly:** Nancy McKeon; **Duke/Dash:** Michael Bell; **Tommy:** Tony O'Dell; **Lucky:** Peter Cullen

## ◎ SCOOBY-DOO, WHERE ARE YOU!

A cowardly great Dane, Scooby-Doo, and his four teenage partners–Freddy, Daphne, Velma and Shaggy–tour the country in their "Mystery Machine" van in search of the supernatural. The title of the program was a takeoff on the classic television comedy series *Car 54 Where Are You?* Following its inital three-season run on CBS, the network rebroadcast the series twice—in 1974–75 and 1975–76—

before it switched to ABC in 1978 with 16 brand-new episodes under the title of *The Scooby-Doo Show*. The series was rerun on ABC in 1984 under its former title. During the 1978 repeat season, ABC also aired a new series on the same day, *Scooby's All-Stars*, featuring all-new episodes. In the fall of 1981 ABC rebroadcast 25 episodes from the series under the retitled *Scooby-Doo Classics*, which also featured 24 episodes from 1976's *Scooby-Doo/Dynomutt Hour*. (Episodes also were repeated on two other series: 1977's *Scooby's All-Star Laff-a-Lympics* and 1983's *The Best of Scooby-Doo*.) ABC broadcast the series when Hanna-Barbera's *Laverne and Shirley in the Army* animated series was delayed. The series subsequently aired in reruns on TBS, USA Network's *Cartoon Express* and Cartoon Network. By May 2000, Boomerang, Cartoon Network's classic cartoons network, began re-running this cult classic daily at 11 A.M. A Hanna-Barbera Production. Color. Half-hour. *Premiered on CBS: September 13, 1969–September 2, 1972. Premiered on ABC: September 8, 1978—November 4, 1978 (as The Scooby-Doo Show). Rebroadcast on CBS: September 1974–August 1975; September 1975–August 1976. Rebroadcast on ABC: October 6, 1984–October 13, 1984. Rebroadcast on USA: September 1989–September 11, 1994. Rebroadcast on TBS/TNT: Fall 1994–98. Rebroadcast on CAR: November 28, 1994–September 1, 1995; January 1, 1996–. Rebroadcast on BOOM: May 20, 2000–.*

#### Voices
**Scooby-Doo:** Don Messick; **Freddy Jones:** Frank Welker; **Shaggy Rogers:** Casey Kasem; **Daphne Blake:** Stefanianna Christopherson, Heather North, Velma Dace Dinkley, Nichole Jaffe

## ◎ SCOOBY-DOO CLASSICS
Fred, Shaggy, Daphne, Velma, Scooby-Doo and Scooby's courageous nephew Scrappy solve unsolvable mysteries in this half-hour Saturday-morning series featuring repeat episodes from previously broadcast series from 1969's *Scooby-Doo, Where Are You!* and from 1976's *Scooby-Doo/Dynomutt Hour*. (See both entries for voice credits.) A Hanna-Barbera Production. Color. Half-hour. *Premiered on ABC: September 1981–September 19, 1982; 1983–1984.*

## ◎ THE SCOOBY-DOO/DYNOMUTT HOUR
Canine detective Scooby-Doo and the superhero dog wonder Dynomutt share the spotlight in this one-hour show as each stars in his own half-hour cartoon adventures. The bionic Dynomutt, whose voice recalls Art Carney's, teams up with big-city crime fighter the Blue Falcon to uphold law and order, while Scooby Doo and the gang (Freddy, Daphne, Shaggy and Velma) try cracking unusual mysteries (known as *The Scooby-Doo Show*). Joining Scooby and his friends was a new character: Scooby-Dum, Scooby-Doo's country cousin reminiscent of Edgar Bergen's Mortimer Snerd), and the female Scooby-Dee, who appeared in "The Chiller Diller Movie Thriller," a Scooby-Doo segment from the series. A Hanna-Barbera Production. Color. One hour. *Premiered on ABC: September 11, 1976–November 1976; December 1976–September 3, 1977 (as The Scooby-Doo/Dynomutt Show).*

#### Voices
**Scooby-Doo:** Don Messick; **Freddy Jones/Dynomutt, dog wonder:** Frank Welker; **Daphne Blake:** Heather North; **Shaggy Rogers:** Casey Kasem; **Velma Dace Dinkley:** Nichole Jaffe; **Scooby-Dum:** Daws Butler; **Scooby-Dee:** Julie McWhirter; **The Blue Falcon:** Gary Owens

## ◎ THE SCOOBY-DOO SHOW
Following the successful two-season run of *The New Scooby-Doo Movies* on CBS, the Scooby-Doo franchise jumped to ABC in September 1976 with this revamped version of 1969's *Scooby-Doo, Where Are You!* as one half of *The Scooby-Doo-Dynomutt Hour*, and in September 1977 was featured in eight new episodes and reruns as part the hour-long *Scooby's All-Star Laff-a-Lympics*, also on ABC. In September 1978, the show was given its own half-hour run with nine new episodes on ABC until that November when it joined ABC's 90-minute *Scooby's All-Star Laff-a-Lympics*, airing seven new unaired episodes and reruns of show's 1978–79 episodes. In the fall of 1980, the show was repackaged for first-run syndication featuring 16 episodes from 1978–79 season of ABC's *Scooby-Doo, Where Are You!*; 16 Scooby-Doo episodes from the 1976–77 season of *The Scooby-Doo/Dynomutt Hour*, and eight Scooby-Doo episodes from the 1977–1978 season of *Scooby's All-Star Laff-a-Lympics* (40 episodes total). Reruns aired on USA Network, TBS, TNT, Cartoon Network and Boomerang. (See individual series for voice credits.) A Hanna-Barbera Production. Color. Half-hour. *Premiered on ABC: September 11, 1976–November 1976; December (as part of The Scooby-Doo/Dynomutt Hour); December 1976–September 3, 1977 (as part of The Scooby-Doo/Dynomutt Show). Premiered on ABC: September 10, 1977–September 2, 1978 (as part of Scooby's All-Star Laff-a-Lympics). Premiered on ABC: September 9, 1978–November 4, 1978 (as The Scooby-Doo Show). Premiered on ABC: November 11, 1978–September 8, 1979 (as part of Scooby's All-Stars). Syndicated: 1980 (as The Scooby-Doo Show). Rebroadcast on USA: Fall 1989–Fall 1994. Rebroadcast: Fall 1994–98 on TBS/TNT. Rebroadcast on CAR: Fall 1994–. Rebroadcast on BOOM: July 1, 2000–.*

#### Voices
**Scooby-Doo:** Don Messick; **Freddy Jones:** Frank Welker; **Daphne Blake:** Heather North; **Shaggy Rogers:** Casey Kasem; **Velma Dace Dinkley:** Patricia Stevens

## ◎ SCOOBY'S ALL-STAR LAFF-A-LYMPICS
More than 45 of Hanna-Barbera's favorite cartoon characters participate in track and field competition, spoofing ABC's *Wide World of Sports*, in this two-hour Saturday-morning series, the first in network history. Assigned to different teams—the Really Rottens, the Scooby Doobys and the Yogi Yahooeys—the winner of each event earns the prestigious Laff-a-Lympics gold medallion. Snagglepuss and Mildew Wolf serve as the play-by-play announcers.

Other program segments were: "Captain Caveman and the Teen Angels," "Dynomutt, Dog Wonder" (featured in four new two-part episodes under the title of "The Blue Falcon and Dynomutt," plus reruns of old episodes) and "Scooby-Doo." The 1977–78 season combined eight new episodes and reruns of *The Scooby-Doo Show*. Renewed for a second season in 1979, the program was shortened to 90 minutes and re-titled, *Scooby's All Stars*. In its new format, *Laff-a-Lympics* aired 16 new episodes of *The Scooby-Doo Show*, including seven previously unaired and nine that originally premiered that September through November on ABC when *The Scooby-Doo Show* was given its own half-hour time slot, along with new episodes of "Captain Caveman and the Teen Angels" and new episodes of *Laff-a-Lympics*. Beginning in June 1980, ABC rebroadcast *Laff-a-Lympics* as the hourlong *Scooby's Laff-a-Lympics*, and briefly again in 1986 in a half-hour format as *All-Star Laff-a-Lympics* before it was cancelled. The program later reaired on USA Network, Cartoon Network and Boomerang.

Following the 1977–78 season, the program returned for a second season under the title of *Scooby's All-Stars*. The series aired a total of three seasons, concluding its network run as *Scooby's Laff-a-Lympics*, a shortened one-hour version comprised of repeat episodes, later rebroadcast on USA Network's *Cartoon Express* and on Cartoon Network.

On Monday, May 1, 2000, the classic Hanna-Barbera sports spoof series began reairing daily at 11 A.M. on Cartoon Network's sister classic cartoons network, Boomerang. From August 13 to 15, 2004, in tribute to the Athens 2004 Olympic Summer Games, the network held a three-day, 72-hour weekend marathon of the former Saturday morning series, which last aired on Boomerang in February 2006. A Hanna-Barbera Production. Color. Two hours. Ninety minutes. One hour. Half-hour. Premiered on ABC: September 10, 1977–September 2, 1978 (as Scooby's All-Star Laff-a-Lympics). Premiered on ABC: September 9, 1978–September 8, 1979 (as Scooby's All-Stars). Rebroadcast on ABC: June 21, 1980–November 1, 1980 (as Scooby's Laff-a-Lympics). Rebroadcast on ABC: March 1986–September 6, 1986 (as All-Star Laff-a-Lympics with reruns of episodes from Scooby's All-Star Laff-a-Lympics from 1977–79). Rebroadcast on ABC: March 1, 1986–September 6, 1986 (as All-Star Laff-a-Lympics). Syndicated. Rebroadcast on USA: May 2, 1989–October 17, 1991. Rebroadcast on CAR: October 3, 1994–November 25, 1996; Summer 1996; Summer 2000. Rebroadcast on BOOM: May 1, 2000–February 24, 2006.

### Voices

**ANNOUNCERS: Snagglepuss:** Daws Butler; **Mildew Wolf:** John Stephenson

**THE YOGI YAHOOEYS: Yogi Bear/Huckleberry Hound/Hokey Wolf/Snooper/Blabber/Wally Gator/Quick Draw McGraw/Augie-Doggie/Dixie/Jinks:** Daws Butler; **Doggie Daddy:** John Stephen-son; **Boo Boo/Pixie:** Don Messick; **Grape Ape:** Bob Holt; **Yakky Doodle:** Frank Welker; **Cindy Bear:** Julie Bennett

**THE SCOOBY-DOOBYS: Scooby-Doo:** Don Messick; **Scooby-Dum:** Daws Butler; **Shaggy:** Casey Kasem; **Hong Kong Phooey:** Scatman Crothers; **Jeannie:** Julie McWhirter; **Babu:** Joe Besser; **Dynomutt/Tinker:** Frank Welker; **Blue Falcon:** Gary Owens; **Captain Caveman/Speed Buggy:** Mel Blanc; **Brenda Chance:** Marilyn Schreffler; **Dee Dee Sykes:** Vernee Watson; **Taffy Dare:** Laurel Page

**THE REALLY ROTTENS: Mumbly/Dastardly Dalton/Mr. Creepley:** Don Messick; **Daisy Mayhem:** Marilyn Schreffler; **Sooey Pig/Magic Rabbit:** Frank Welker; **Dread Baron/The Great Fondoo:** John Stephenson; **Orful Octopus/Dinky Dalton:** Bob Holt; **Dirty Dalton:** Daws Butler; **Mrs. Creepley:** Laurel Page

### @ SCOOBY'S MYSTERY FUNHOUSE

Canine detective Scooby-Doo and pals Shaggy and Scrappy-Doo starred in this half-hour collection of classic ghostbusting tales and mysteries originally broadcast on *The Scooby and Scrappy-Doo/Puppy Hour, The New Scooby and Scrappy-Doo Show, Scary Scooby Funnies* and others. (See programs for voice credits.) A Hanna-Barbera Production. Color. Half-hour. Premiered on ABC: September 7, 1985–March 1986.

### @ SD GUNDAM FORCE

In the once-serene Neotopia, humans and robots band together, with Captain Gundam and his top-secret Gundam Force fearlessly fighting evil invaders from another out-of-this-world dimension, the Dark Axis, in this imported Japanese action/adventure series. In 2003, Cartoon Network acquired 26 episodes of the English-dubbed series—and fourth in a succession of *Gundam Wing* animated programs—that made its U.S. debut that September and aired Monday through Friday as part of the network's acclaimed afternoon action/adventure block, *Toonami*, including popular favorites *Dragonball Z, Justice League* and *Yu Yu Hakusho*. A Bandai/Sunrise/Sotsu/Frame-

works/Asahi Productions/Cartoon Network Production. Color. Half-hour. Premiered on CAR: September 1, 2003–March 4, 2004.

### Voices

**Shute:** Deborah Sale Butler; **Captain Gundam/Grappler/Fen/Zalu:** Doug Erholz; **Chief Hero/Mark Destroyer Dom:** Scott Jasper; **Commander Sazabi/Asharamaru/Red Zaku/Grey Doga/Prio/Young Train:** Dominic Joseph; **Zapper/Kao Lin/Entengo:** Danny Katiana; **Knight Alex:** Masami Kikuchi; **Knight Z Gundam:** Tsujitani Kouji; **Bakunetsumaru:** Yello Lollicups; **Sayla:** Michelle Ruff; **Keiko:** Kate Savage; **Zero/Bell Wood:** Aliki Theopilopoulos

### @ SEABERT

Together with human friends Tommy and Aura, Seabert, a lovable seal, travels the globe, by land and by sea, protecting his fellow animals in this 26-episode half-hour animated series produced by Belgian-based Sepp International (coproducers of *The Smurfs*) that debuted on HBO. A Sepp International Production. Color. Half-hour. Premiered on HBO: April 5, 1987–June 30, 1988.

### Voices

Diana Ellington, Melissa Freeman, Ron Knight, Bruce Robertson, Morgan Upton

### @ SEALAB 2020

Earth, A.D. 2020. Dr. Paul Williams leads an underwater expedition to study living conditions while searching for scientific solutions in a domed experimental city operated by 250 inhabitants. Williams is unexpectedly joined on his expedition by Captain Mike Murphy, his niece and nephew, Sallie and Bobby, and radio dispatcher Sparks, who were rescued by three Sealab aquanauts (Hal, Ed and Gail) when their ship ran into trouble. The 13-week half-hour series debuted on NBC in 1972. A Hanna-Barbera Production. Color. Half-hour. Premiered on NBC: September 9, 1972–September 1, 1973. Rebroadcast on CAR: December 6, 1992; March 14, 1993 (part of Boomerang, 1972).

### Voices

**Dr. Paul Williams:** Ross Martin; **Captain Mike Murphy:** John Stephenson; **Bobby Murphy:** Josh Albee; **Sallie Murphy:** Pamelyn Ferdin; **Sparks:** Bill Callaway; **Hal:** Jerry Dexter; **Gail:** Ann Jillian; **Ed:** Ron Pinckard; **Mrs. Thomas:** Olga James; **Jamie:** Gary Shapiro; **Other Voices:** Don Messick

### @ SEALAB 2021

Crazy captain Hazel "Hank" Murphy commands a perverse but lovable multinational crew of men and women scientists dedicated to exploring and underwater colonization from their remarkable high-tech undersea laboratory in this update of Hanna-Barbera's classic 1970s cartoon series, *Sealab 2020*, set one year after the original.

Originally developed and telecast in December 2000 as three different pilot specials—"Radio Free Sealab," "Happycake" and "I, Robot"—at various early-morning time slots on Cartoon Network, this weekly half-hour comedy/adventure series doled out deep-sea laughs following its debut in early September 2001 with 13 first-season episodes. The quirky comedy series drew critical attention, airing Sunday evenings on *Adult Swim'* midnight to 1 A.M. (*The Lab*) block opposite other offbeat 15-minute cartoon comedy shows, including *Aqua Teen Hunger Force, The Brak Show* and *Harvey Birdman, Attorney at Law.* Enjoying a remarkable four-season run with 39 additional episodes, the series' underwater exploits aired through the 2004–05 season. A 70-30 Productions/Williams Street Production. Color. Half-hour. Premiered on CAR: December

21, 2000; December 30, 2000 (pilots); September 2, 2001–August 25, 2005 (series). Rebroadcast on CAR: September 1, 2005–.

*Voices*
**Captain Hazel "Hank" Murphy:** Harry Goz; **Captain Bellerophon "Tornado" Shanks:** Michael Goz; **Debbie DuPree:** Kate Miller; **Derek "Stormy" Waters:** Ellis Henican; **Doctor Quentin Q. Quinn:** Brett Butler; **Jodene Sparks:** Bill Lobley; **Behop Cola Machine:** Adam Reed; **Sharko:** Matt Thompson; **Marco Rodrigo Diaz de Vivar Gabriel Garcia Marquez:** Erik Estrada; **Hesh Hipplewhite:** Chris Ward; **Himself:** John J. Miller; **Black Debbie:** Angela Gibbs; **Big Brain:** Dave Willis; **Health Inspector:** Christian Danley; **Himself:** Christopher Reid; **Access Tonight Reporter:** Tiffany Morgan

### ◎ SECRET FILES OF THE SPYDOG

Employed by a secret organization dedicated to keeping mankind safe from "really bad stuff," SpyDogs—three normal-looking domestic dogs led by high-ranking mutt, Ralph, and accompanied by his sexy pink terrier partner, Mitzy, and SpyDog-in-training, Scribble—sniff out trouble wherever it may be in this animated comedy series featuring the voices of Mickey Dolenz of *The Monkees* as Ralph and Scribble and Adam West of TV's *Batman* fame as their organizational leader, Dog Zero. Thirteen half-hours, featuring two cartoon episodes per show, aired Saturday mornings on FOX. A Saban Entertainment Production. Color. Half-hour. Premiered on FOX: September 12, 1998–September 11, 1999.

*Voices*
**Ralph/Scribble:** Micky Dolenz; **Dog Zero:** Adam West; **Mitzy/Mitzy's Owner:** Mary Kay Bergman; **Ayanna:** Dawnn Lewis; **Erin/Rosie:** Tress MacNeille; **Noofle/Chukchi:** Billy West; **Angus/Bitochki/Dahg Chow:** Jim Ward; **Catastrophe/Von Rabie:** Jim Cummings; **Sir William/Frank:** Jess Harnell; **Stahl:** Michael Donovan; **Collar Communicator Voice:** Kath Soucie; **Space Slug:** Maurice LaMarche; **Oatz Cautere:** Ami Dolenz; **Other Voices:** Ben Stein, Charles Adler

### ◎ THE SECRET LIVES OF WALDO KITTY

Based on James Thurber's story, "The Secret Life of Walter Mitty," the series stars cowardly Waldo, a daydreaming cat who imagines himself as the roughriding savior Lone Kitty, the superhero Cat Man and others, fighting swaggering bulldog Tyrone for the honor of his pussycat girlfriend, Felicia, in 13 cartoon adventures. Introduced each week with live-action footage of Waldo, feline friend Felicia and bullying Tyrone, the series was originally produced for NBC in 1975 and lasted only one season. A Filmation Associates Production. Color. Half-hour. Premiered on NBC: September 6, 1975–September 4, 1976.

*Voices*
**Waldo Kitty/Wetzel/Lone Kitty/Catman/Catzan/Robin Cat/Captain Herc:** Howard Morris; **Felicia/Pronto/-Sparrow/-Lt. O-Hoo-Ha:** Jane Webb; **Tyrone/Mr. Crock/Ping/Brennan Hench Dog/Dr. Moans:** Allan Melvin

### ◎ THE SECRET SHOW

Special agents Victor Volt and Anita Knight, agents for the top-secret agency U.Z.Z., protect the world against the evil forces of T.H.E.M., run by its boss, Changed Daily, and are joined in their missions by the insane scientist, Professor Professor, to save the world. Commissioned by the BBC and produced entirely by the United Kingdom's independent studio, Collingwood O'Hare Entertainment (producers of the BAFTA-winning series, *Yoko!*

*Jakamoto! Toto!*), this 26-episode madcap comedy series bowed in the United States on Nicktoons in January 2007 with the pilot episode, "Lucky Leo," featuring Stephen Fry as the voice of the guest villain, after premiering in 2006 on Britain's CBBC network. A Collingwood O'Hare Entertainment Production. Color. Half-hour. Premiered on NICKT: January 20, 2007.

*Voices*
**Victor Volt:** Alan Marriott; **Anita Knight:** Kate Harbour; **Professor Professor:** Rob Rackstraw; **Ray:** Martin Hyder; **Changed Daily:** Keith Wickham

### ◎ THE SECRET SQUIRREL SHOW

Packaged for two seasons as part of the hour-long *The Atom Ant/Secret Squirrel Show*, the buck-toothed squirrel private investigator and the supporting elements— Squiddly Diddly" and "Winsome Witch —from his half of the original network series were given their own half-hour show in 1967, repeating episodes from the 1965–66 series, which premiered on the same network. The program concluded its network run the way it began, again paired with Atom Ant and company as *The Atom Ant/Secret Squirrel Show* in September 1967. (See entry for voice credits.) In the early 1990s, the show began rerunning on Cartoon Network and in 2000 on Boomerang. A Hanna-Barbera Production. Color. Half-hour. Premiered on NBC: January 1967–September 2, 1967. Rebroadcast on CAR: September 20, 1993–December 31, 1993 (weekdays); February 28, 1994–September 3, 1994 (weekdays, Saturdays); September 11, 1994–September 3, 1995 (Sundays, Wednesdays). Rebroadcast on BOOM: April 1, 2000–.

### ◎ SECTAURS

On the distant planet, Symbion, a group of telepathically bonded warriors join with their insect companions in the ultimate battle of survival in this first-run, half-hour miniseries comprised of five episodic adventures. A Ruby-Spears Enterprises Production. Color. Half-hour. Premiered: September 1985. Syndicated.

*Voices*
**Dargon/Dragonflyer:** Dan Gilvezan; **Pinsor/Battle Beetle:** Peter Renaday; **Mantor/Skito/Toxid:** Peter Cullen; **Zak/Bitaur:** Laurie Faso; **Spidrax/Spiderflyer:** Arthur Burghardt; **Skulk/Trancula/Raplor:** Frank Welker; **Waspax/Wingid:** Neil Ross

### ◎ SEVEN LITTLE MONSTERS

Seven monsters—who aren't little but are actually each 10 feet tall and endowed with a special quality (one can fly, another can twist off his head)—who all live under the same roof with their mother embark on a series of hilarious day-to-day adventures, from going to school and to doing their chores to bickering like most families and learning the importance of working together as a family. Adapted from world-renowned author/illustrator Maurice Sendak's best-selling children's book series, the animated preschool series, produced by Canada's Nelvana and Treehouse Television, originated as a 15-minute component of PBS's popular *Bookworm Bunch* weekend program block in late September 2000. In January 2003, all-new 15-minute episodes, paired with 15-minute episodes of a second Nelvana-Treehouse coproduction *The Berenstain Bears*, were broadcast as a daily half-hour series on PBS Kids. A Treehouse Television/Nelvana Production. Color. Half-hour. Premiered on PBS Kids: September 30, 2000 (15 minutes). Premiered on PBS: January 6, 2003–September 4, 2004 (half-hour).

*Voices*
**Four/Five/Seven:** Sean Cullen; **Three:** Dwayne Hill; **Mom:** Debra McGrath; **Two:** Colin Mochrie; **Six:** Michele Scarabelli; **One:** Joanne Vanicola

## ◎ SHAGGY AND SCOOBY-DOO GET A CLUE!

Taking up residence in their Uncle Albert's bling'd-out mansion, quivering teen sleuth Shaggy teams up with his lovable Great Dane, Scooby-Doo, who transforms himself into everything from a flying canine superhero to a giant magnet thanks to his nano-technology-infused Scooby Snacks, toward off evil in this series of new half-hour mysteries. The program was one of three new cartoon series added to the CW Network's Kids' WB! *Too Big for Your TV* fall 2006 Saturday-morning programming block, including *Tom and Jerry Tales* and *Legion of Super Heroes*, along with three returning favorites from the former WB! network, *Xiaolin Showdown*, *Lunatics Unleashed* and *The Batman*. *A Warner Bros. Television Animation Production. Color. Half-hour. Premiered on the CW Kids' WB!: September 23, 2006.*

*Voices*
**Scooby-Doo:** Frank Welker; **Shaggy Rogers:** Scott Menville; **Robi:** Jim Meskimen; **Dr. Phineus Phibes:** Jeff Bennett

## ◎ SHAKESPEARE: THE ANIMATED TALES

William Shakespeare's literary classics— *A Midsummer Night's Dream, Twelfth Night, Hamlet, Romeo and Juliet, Macbeth* and others—are brought to life in this first-ever animated series based on his work. Hosted by Robin Williams, the monthly half-hour condensations—using three different styles: stop-action puppetry, cel animation and painting on glass plates, done at the Soyuzmultifilm Studios in Moscow, debuted on HBO in 1992. Animated by studio artists in Armenia and Russia as well as in Cardiff, Wales, six half-hour episodes were produced the first year, costing around $850,000 each. Character voices were provided by members of Britain's National Theatre and Royal Shakespeare Company. *A Soyuzmultifilms/HIT Communications (U.K.) Production in association with Christmas Films/s4C Channel 4 Wales/HIT Entertainment PLC/HBO/Fujisankie/Dave Edwards Studios. Color. Half-hour. Premiered on HBO: November 15, 1992.*

*Cast (live-action)*
**Host:** Robin Williams

*Voices*
Daniel Massey, Menna Tussler, Members of the Royal Shakespeare Company.

## ◎ SHAMAN KING

Thrilling adventure series about a young man's quest to become Shaman King after competing in a competition that takes place every 500 years; based on the anime series and manga series by Hiroyuki Takei that first aired on Japan's TV Tokyo. Licensed in 2001 by 4Kids Entertainment, this English-dubbed version began airing on FOX's FOX Box (later renamed 4Kids TV) Saturday-morning cartoon block in September 2003 with 64 episodes available for broadcast. *A Tokyo/NAS/XEBEC/4Kids Entertainment Production. Color. Half-hour. Premiered on FOX: August 30, 2003–September 3, 2005.*

*Voices*
**Anna:** Tara Jayne; **Amidamaru/Rio:** Sean Schemmel; **Yoh Asakura/Zeke Asakura:** Sebastian Arcelus; **Mortimer "Morty" Oyamada:** Peter Zurustica; **Pinka:** Rachael Lillis; **Trey Racer:** Jonathan Todd Ross, Michael Sinterniklaas; **Len Tao:** Andy Rannells; **Li Pai Long/Silva:** Dan Green; **Jun Tao:** Lisa Ortiz; **Haro Haro/Faust VIII:** Sam Regal; **En Tao/Basil:** Marc Thompson; **Marco:** Eric Stuart; **Mikihisa Asakura:** Ted Lewis; **Lysberg Diethel:** Bella Hudson; **Tamara "Tammy:** Veronica Taylor; **Mortimer "Morty:** Pete Zarustica; **Sharona:** Megan Hollingshead; **Elly:** Kerry Williams; **Millie:** Amy Palant

## ◎ SHAZZAN!

Twins Chuck and Nancy find a broken ancient ring inscribed with the word "Shazzan!" that, joined together, transports them back to the age of the Arabian Nights. The leader of the group, Shazzan, a 60-foot genie, guards the children by working his wizardry on evildoers in this 26-episode half-hour fantasy/adventure series that bowed on CBS in 1967. In the 1990s, the series reaired on Cartoon Network and later Boomerang. *A Hanna-Barbera Production. Color. Half-hour. Premiered on CBS: September 9, 1967–September 6, 1969. Rebroadcast on CAR: November 8, 1992 (part of Boomerang, 1968); February 7, 1993 (part of Boomerang, 1967); August 5, 1995. Rebroadcast on BOOM: April 29, 2000.*

*Voices*
**Shazzan:** Barney Phillips; **Nancy:** Janet Waldo; **Chuck:** Jerry Dexter; **Kaboobie, the flying camel:** Don Messick

## ◎ SHEEP IN THE BIG CITY

After living on a small country farm and being chosen to fuel a new sheep-powered ray gun, a runaway sheep escapes to the Big City to hide from General Specific and his Top Secret Military Organization, finding romance, adventure, problems and plenty of unwelcome characters (including his love interest, Swanky the Poodle, and Swanky's sheep-loathing owner, Lady Richington) in this animated comedy series originally broadcast on Cartoon Network.

Created by Mo Willems, who also served as executive producer, this half-hour program actually originated as a 15-minute pilot called "In the Baa-inning" that aired in early November 2000 on Cartoon Network's *Adult Swim* block. In mid-November, the 27-episode series, featuring two episodes per 30-minute broadcast, officially joined the *Adult Swim* lineup. Becoming Cartoon Network's ninth original animated series, the program remained on the air until April 2003. *A Curious Pictures/Cartoon Network Production. Color. Half-hour. Premiered CAR: November 4, 2000 (pilot). Premiered on CAR: November 17, 2000—April 6, 2003 (series).*

*Voices*
**Sheep/General Specific/Ranting Swede:** Kevin Seal; **Farmer John/Private Public:** James Godwin; **Narrator/Ben Plotz:** Ken Schatz; **Angry Scientist:** Mo Willems; **Lady Richington:** Stephanie D'Abruzzo; **Wonderful Boy:** Christine Walters; **Other Voices:** Ruth Buzzi, Bradley Glenn

## ◎ SHELLEY DUVALL'S BEDTIME STORIES

Shelley Duvall, the force behind cable TV's *Faerie Tale Theatre* and *Tall Tales & Legends*, produced and cowrote this live-action/animated series presenting contemporary bedtime stories based on famous children's stories and narrated by big-name stars, including Robin Williams, Jean Stapleton, Tatum O'Neal, Billy Crystal, among others. The series opener featured two tales: "Elbert's Bad Word," about a boy who hears a bad word and uses it (read by Ringo Starr), and "Weird Parents," about a youngster who is totally embarrassed by her mom and dad (voiced by Bette Midler). Two or three segments made up each half-hour show to encourage children to read and write. In Christmas 1994 Duvall produced a holiday special version of "The Christmas Witch" (read by Angela Lansbury). (See Animated Television Specials for details.) *A Think Entertainment/MCA Family Entertainment/Universal Cartoon Studios Production. Color. Half-hour. Premiered on SHO: April 21, 1992.*

## ◎ SHE-RA: PRINCESS OF POWER

He-Man's twin sister, Adora, transformed by her magic swords into She-Ra, defender of the Crystal Castle, battles the evil forces of Hordak in this 65-episode companion series to *He-Man and the*

*Masters of the Universe* produced for first-run syndication in 1985 and later rebroadcast on USA Network's *Cartoon Express*. A *Filmation Studios Production in association with Mattel Toys and Group W. Color. Half-hour. Premiered: September 23, 1985–January 1988. Syndicated. Rebroadcast on USA: February 28, 1989–July 10, 1989.*

**Voices**
**Princess Adora/She-Ra/Madama Raxx/Frosta:** Melendy Britt; **Hordak:** George DiCenzo; **Castaspella/Glimmer/Shadow Weaver/ Catra; Linda Gary; Broom/He-Man:** John Erwin; **Skeletor:** Alan Oppenheimer; **Kowl/Mantella/Leech:** Erik Gundin; **Imp:** Erika Scheimer; **Light-rope/Sprint/Swiftwind/Horde Soldiers/Loo-Kee:** Lou Scheimer

## ◉ SHERLOCK HOLMES IN THE 22ND CENTURY

Brought back to life in 22nd-century New London, former consulting detective Sherlock Holmes join forces with a robotic Dr. Watson and female New Scotland Yard inspector Beth Lestrade and the Baker Street Irregulars to battle an evil clone of Dr. Moriarty who is on a rampage in this futuristic cartoon adaptation of Arthur Conan Doyle's classic literary character. Jointly produced by Burbank, California's DIC Enterprises and Scottish Television, the 25-episode half-hour series was first telecast Saturday mornings and weekday afternoons on FOX. After its cancellation in 2000, the WB Television Network planned to offer the series on its weekday-morning schedule but demurred after network cutbacks forced it to change course. Instead, in the spring of 2001, Tribune Entertainment offered the Emmy-nominated series in syndication. *A DIC Entertainment/Scottish Television Enterprises/Tribune Entertainment Production. Color. Half-hour. Premiered on FOX: September 18, 1999–February 21, 2000. Syndicated: March 31, 2001.*

**Voices**
**Sherlock Holmes:** Jason Gray Stanford; **Dr. John Watson:** John Payne; **Inspector Beth Lestrade:** Akiko Morison; **Deidre:** Jennifer Copping; **Professor James Moriarty:** Richard Newman; **Martin Fenwick:** Ian James Corlett; **Chief Inspector Charles Greyson:** William Samples; **Newscaster:** Jo Beates; **Wiggins:** Viv Leacock

## ◉ SHINZO

After a race of genetic beings called the Enterrans (originally created to fight a deadly virus) destroys mankind, one survivor named Yakumo, the daughter of a famous scientist, teams up with three Enterrans—Mushra, Sago and Kutal—to make peace with the creatures that have taken over Earth and restore the human race in this Japanese animated series, first shown on Japanese television in February 2000 and then in the United States, dubbed in English, on ABC Family. Retitled *Shinzo* (formerly *Mashuranbo*), the half-hour anime series aired twice weekly during its first season until August 2002, with its second season bowing on the *Jetix* action/ adventure anime program block on both ABC Family and Toon Disney, beginning in January 2005. In late August 2005, ABC Family discontinued the *Jetix* cartoon block it shared with Toon Disney in favor of live-action programming. That September, Toon Disney carried over several programs, with *Shinzo* becoming part of its Sunday anime lineup. *A Toei/BVS Entertainment/Saban Production. Color. Half-hour. Premiered on ABC FAM: December 17, 2001–January 16, 2002; July 6, 2002–August 31, 2002 (1st season); January 2005–September 2005 (2nd season). Premiered on TDIS: January 2005–August 31, 2005. Rebroadcast on TDIS: September 3, 2005–.*

**Voices**
**Sago:** Steven Jay Blum; **Mushra:** Tom Gibis, Michael Sorich; **Ruspyn:** Wendee Lee; **Yakumo:** Mary Elizabeth McGlynn, Peggy

O'Neal; **Kutal:** Bob Pappenbrook; **Eillis:** Tom Wyner; **Other Voices:** Tom Fahn, David Rogers, Stephen Apostolina, Steve Kramer, Tom Wyner

## ◉ THE SHIRT TALES

Lovable little animals, wearing message-bearing T-shirts, help others in need around the world after receiving holographic messages of distress on their sophisticated wristwatch communicators in this weekly Saturday-morning series based on the Hallmark greeting card character. The series was produced by NBC as Saturday-morning competition to CBS's *Sylvester and Tweety/Daffy and Speedy* and ABC's *The Pac-Man/Little Rascals/Richie Rich Show* in 1982. The series' second season featured a new cast member: Kip Kangaroo, a trusting, loving character with powerful hindquarters. After its two-season run on NBC, the series was rerun on CBS, USA Network's *Cartoon Express* and Cartoon Network. *A Hanna-Barbera Production. Color. Half-hour. Premiered on NBC: September 18, 1982–September 8, 1984. Rebroadcast on CBS: September 15, 1984–May 23, 1985. Rebroadcast on USA: April 2, 1989–March 23, 1992. Rebroadcast on CAR: October 1, 1992–September 17, 1993 (weekdays); January 3, 1994–September 2, 1994 (weekdays); January 5, 1994–June 2, 1995 (weekdays); September 4, 1995–1996 (weekdays). Rebroadcast on BOOM: April 5, 2002.*

**Voices**
**TYG Tiger:** Steve Schatzberg; **Pammy Panda:** Pat Parris; **Digger Mole:** Bob Ogle; **Bogey Orangutan:** Fred Traval-ena; **Rick Raccoon:** Ronnie Schell; **Kip Kangaroo:** Nancy Cartwright; **Mr. Dinkel:** Herb Vigram

## ◉ THE SHNOOKUMS & MEAT FUNNY CARTOON SHOW

Previously featured in two previously unsuccessful series, *Raw Toonage* and *Marsupilami*, this battling off-the-wall cat-and-dog team were cast as the title stars of this series used to launch "Manic Monday," a retooled version of Disney studio's the *Disney Afternoon* two-hour weekday cartoon block in January 1995. The program ran once a week and lasted only one season. *A Walt Disney Television Animation Production. Color. Half-hour. Premiered: January 2, 1995–August 28, 1995. Syndicated.*

**Voices**
**Shnookums:** Danny Mann, Jason Marsden; **Meat:** Frank Welker; **Chafe:** Charlie Adler; **Pith Possum/Tex Tinstar:** Jeff Bennett; **Ian/Krusty Rustnuckle:** Corey Burton; **Narrator (Tex Tinstar):** Jim Cummings; **Commissioner Stress/Wrongo:** Brad Garrett; **Floyd the Rattler/Lieutenant Tension:** Jess Harnell; **Husband:** Bill Kopp, Steve Mackall; **Wife:** Tress MacNeille; **Doris Deer:** April Winchell; **Obediah/The Wonder Raccoon:** Patric Zimmerman

## ◉ SHURIKEN SCHOOL

As first-year students at the acclaimed martial arts academy, Shuriken School, 10-year-old Eizan Kaburagi and his two best friends and classmates—wealthy New York native Jimmy B. and hard-working Okuni Dohan, who lives in a nearby fishing village—find adventure studying and applying the legendary art of Ninjitsu—including levitation, vanishing, flying through the air and employing disguises— against the kids from their rival school, Katana, in this quirky, 2-D Flash-animated comedy for Nickelodeon. Produced by French animation studio Xilam Animation, the 12-episode, half-hour series, combining action, adventure, humor and, of course, martial arts, joined Nickelodeon's Sunday morning cartoon lineup, airing at 11:30 A.M. (ET), in mid-August 2006. *A Xilam Animation/Zinkia Entertainment Production. Color. Half-hour. Premiered on NICK: August 20, 2006. Rebroadcast on NICKT: September 9, 2006–.*

*Voices*
**Eizan Kaburagi:** Nathan Kress; **Jimmy B.:** Kimberly Brooks; **Okuni:** Jessica Dicicco; **Naginata:** Maurice LaMarche; **Principal of Katana:** Charlie Adler

## ◎ SIEGFRIED & ROY: MASTERS OF THE IMPOSSIBLE

World-renowned magicians Siegfried and Roy (voiced by other actors) starred in this short-lived four-part miniseries—that never took off as a daily or weekly series—as a pair of muscular do-gooders who battle the villainous Loki and his evil group the Titans, accompanied by legendary mythological character Rumplestiltskin. Coproduced by Burbank, California-based DIC Entertainment, the series was originally telecast in four parts: "In the Beginning," "Kingdom of Gold," "Monsters of the Mind" and "The Realm of Endland."

Contrary to the *Las Vegas Review-Journal*'s official Siegfried and Roy timeline reporting that the series premiered in 1993, most records indicate that the series actually debuted in September 1995 under the title *The Legend of Sarmoti: Siegfried & Roy*. From February 19 to 22, 1996, the four-part miniseries, retitled *Siegfried & Roy: Masters of the Impossible*, aired on consecutive mornings on FOX, followed by an 80-minute feature-length compilation of all four episodes edited together and released on August 20, 1996, by 20th Century Home Video. *A DIC Entertainment/L. P./Irving Feld and Kenneth Feld Productions Inc. Production. Color. Half-hour. Premiered: September 1995. Syndicated. Rebroadcast on FOX: February 19, 1996 ("In the Beginning"); February 20, 1996 ("Kingdom of Gold"); February 21, 1996 ("Monsters of the Mind"); February 22, 1996 ("The Realm of Endland").*

*Voices*
**Siegfried:** Andrew Hawkes; **Roy:** Jeff Bennett; **Loki:** Charles Adler; **Rumplestiltskin:** Barry Peal; **Additional Voices:** Jim Cummings, Samantha Eggar, Brad Garrett, Dorian Harewood, Billie Hayes, Tony Jay, Maurice LaMarche, Iona Morris, Kevin Michael Richardson, Neil Ross, Susan Silo, Kath Soucie, Brenda Vaccaro, David Warner

## ◎ SILVERHAWKS

Music-driven animated series featuring metallic-looking characters–known as The Silverhawks–led by Commander Stargazer, who fight extraterrestrial gangsters and villains, including Mon Star and his Mob. This series was a follow-up to the Rankin-Bass first-run cartoon series *ThunderCats. A Rankin-Bass Production in association with Telepictures. Color. Half-hour. Syndicated: September 8, 1986–Fall 1987. Rebroadcast on CAR: September 2000–March 2, 2001.*

*Voices*
Larry Kenney, Robert McFadden, Earl Hammond, Maggie Jakobson, Peter Newman, Adolph Newman, Adolph Caesar, Doug Preis

## ◎ SILVER SURFER

This flashy-looking Marvel Comics superhero (created by Stan Lee and Jack Kirby) roams the galaxy on his flying board in search of his long-lost home, Zenn-La, and the love of his life, Shalla-Bal, battling evil wherever he finds it in this half-hour series produced for the FOX Network. The 13-episode series debuted in February 1998 with the three-part series opener, "The Origin of Silver Surfer. *A FOX Kids Network/Saban International/Marvel Entertainment Group Production. Color. Half-hour. Premiered on FOX: February 7, 1998–May 30, 1998.*

*Voices*
**Norrin Radd-Silver Surfer:** Paul Essiembre; **Shalla-Bal:** Camilla Scott; **Uatu the Watcher:** Colin Fox; **Master of Zenn-La:** Aron Tager; **Galactus:** James Blendick; **Thanos:** Gary Krawford

## ◎ SILVERWING

Coming-of-age tale of the life of Shade Silverwing, a bat banished from ever seeing the sun again after an infamous battle centuries earlier between birds and beasts; he dares to break the law in search of his father and creates serious consequences for the rest of the colony. Vancouver-based animation studio Bardel Entertainment produced the heart-pumping action/adventure series—first launched in the fall of 2003 on Canada's Teletoon network and based on the international best-selling trilogy of the same name by Ken Oppel. Three feature-length 72-minute television movies were produced in addition to this 13-episode half-hour series: *A Glimpse of the Sun, Towers of Fire* and *Redemption*, which also debuted in the United States on Toon Disney. *A Bardel Entertainment Production. Color. Half-hour. Premiered on TDIS: June 5, 2006 (series).*

*Voices*
**Shade Silverwing:** Bill Switzer; **Breeze:** Louise Vallance; **Goth:** Michael Dobson; **Chinook:** Matt Hill; **Ursa:** Candus Churchill; **Frieda:** Pam Hyatt; **Throbb/Brutus/Zephyr:** Richard Newman; **Luger/Romulus:** Lee Tockar; **Mercury/Scirocco:** Ian James Corlett; **Marina:** Sharon Alexander

## ◎ THE SIMPSONS

Cartoonist Matt Groening (*Life in Hell*) created this outlandish series based on the adventures of an exuberantly blue-collar family who are just about everything that most television families are not—crude, loud, obnoxious and sloppily dressed characters, with bizarre hairdos and severe overbites. The characters were originally featured in brief segments on FOX Network's *The Tracy Ullman Show* before the network spotlighted them in their own weekly series. From the series inception in 1989, independent cartoon studio Klasky Csupo animated each episode through the 1991–92 season. Film Roman, producers of TV's *Garfield and Friends*, took over production of the series in March of 1992, in time for the 1992–93 season.

Within months of its premiere in January 1990, the show jumped into Nielsen's Top Fifteen, an extraordinary accomplishment for FOX, which at the time reached only four-fifths of America's television viewing public. That same year, the prime-time comedy hit won its first of several Emmy awards for outstanding animated program, and would again win television's highest industry honor in 1991, 1995, 1997, 1998, 2000, 2001 and 2003, and be nominated five more times in 1996, 1999, 2002, 2004 and 2005 in the same category. Additionally, the series' stellar voice cast walked off with prime-time Emmys over the years as well, including Dan Castellaneta (the voice of Homer Simpson); Julie Kavner (the voice of Marge Simpson); Nancy Cartwright (the voice of Bart Simpson); and Yeardley Smith (the voice of Lisa Simpson), for outstanding voice-over performance.

During the series' long and illustrious network run, a long list of notable celebrities have lent their voices in guest appearances, including Tony Bennett, Dustin Hoffman, Michael Jackson, Larry King and Leonard Nimoy. The series also has spawned its share of prime-time specials, including *The Simpsons Christmas Special* (1989) and *The Simpsons Halloween Special: Tree House of Horror*, the first in a series of annual Halloween shows.

With the airing of the series' 167th episode (called "The Itchy & Scratch & Poochie Show") on February 9, 1997, the Emmy-winning series dethroned *The Flintstones* (which aired 166 episodes

*Cartoonist Matt Groening's outlandish blue-collar family from the longest running prime-time cartoon series in history,* The Simpsons. © FOX Network.

in prime time from 1960 to 1966) as the longest-running prime-time animation series.

Seen in most territories around the world with more than 40 million viewers (including syndicated reruns of the show's first 100 episodes beginning in September 1994), the intelligently written and subversively humorous series has generated an estimated $2 billion in revenue. The show's phenomenal success also resulted in an explosion of merchandise the world over, from beach towels to best-selling books written by *The Simpsons'* creator Matt Groening, including *The Simpsons: A Complete Guide to Our Favorite Family* (HarperCollins, 1998), plus a platinum-recording called *The Simpsons Sing the Blues* (Geffen, 1991) that spawned two music videos ("Do the Bartman" and "Deep, Deep Trouble") and another best-selling CD, *Songs in the Key of Springfield*, distributed by Rhino Records in the spring of 1997.

FOX picked up the series for two more seasons, guaranteeing that it will air at least through the 2007–08 season. For the program's 18th season in 2006, Natalie Portman, Kiefer Sutherland and Dr. Phil were among the featured celebrity voices. The premiere episode, "The Mook, the Chef, His Wife and His Homer," costarred HBO's *Sopranos* veterans Michel Imperioli and Joe Pantoliano with Joe Mantegna reprising his role as Springfield's mob boss. On May 20, 2007, the show reached yet another milestone, broadcasting its landmark 400th episode, followed by the summer release of *The Simpsons Movie*, the first—and long-awaited—full-length animated feature based on the series, produced by 20th Century Fox, Gracie Films and Film Roman and directed by longtime *Simpsons* producer David Silverman. *A Gracie Films/Klasky Csupo/Film Roman Production in association with 20th Century Fox Television. Color. Half-hour. Premiered on FOX: January 14, 1990. Syndicated: September 1994.*

**Voices**
**Homer J. Simpson/Abraham J. Simpson (Grandpa)/Herschel Krustofsky ("Krusty the Clown")/Barney Gumble:** Dan Castellaneta; **Marjorie (Marge) Simpson/Patty Bouvier/Selma Bouvier/Jacqueline Bouvier:** Julie Kavner; **Bartholomew (Bart) Jo-Jo Simpson/Nelson Muntz/Rod Flanders/Todd Flanders/Ralph Wiggum:** Nancy Cartwright; **Lisa Maria Simpson:** Yeardley Smith; **Maggie Simpson (pacifier sucking):** Matt Groenig; **Maggie Simpson (speaking, one show only):** Elizabeth Taylor; **Apu Nahasapeemapetilon/Moe Szyslak/Police Chief Clancy Wiggun/Comic Book Guy/Dr. Nick Riviera:** Hank Azaria; **Charles Montgomery Burns/Waylon Smithers/Ned Flanders/Seymour Skinner/Otto Mann:** Harry Shearer; **Charles Montgomery Burns/Moe Szyslak (first two seasons):** Christopher Collins; **Lunchlady Doris:** Doris Grau; **Lionel Hutz/Troy McClure:** Phil Hartman; **Milhouse van Houten/Janey Powell/Jimbo Jones/Dolph:** Pamela Hayden; **Agnes Skinner/Ms. Albright/Mrs. Glick:** Tress MacNeille; **Maude Flanders/Luanne van Houten/Helen Lovejoy/Miss Elizabeth Hoover:** Maggie Roswell; **Bleeding Gums Murphy:** Ron Taylor; **Martin Prince/Uter/Sherri/Terri/Lewis Wendell:** Russi Taylor; **Mrs. Krabappel:** Marcia Wallace

## SINBAD JR.

Originally called *The Adventures of Sinbad, Jr.*, the cartoons star the son of the famed sea adventurer, Sinbad, who becomes superhuman whenever he draws power from a magic belt. He is assisted in his high-sea adventures by his first mate, Salty, the parrot in this half-hour series, comprised of 100 five-minute cartoon adventures, first syndicated in 1965. The first series of Sinbad cartoons were produced by Sam Singer in 1965. Hanna-Barbera took over production of the series the following season. *A Hanna-Barbera Sam Singer and Production in association with American International Pictures. Sinbad is a trademark of American International Pictures. Color. Half-hour. Premiered: Fall 1965. Syndicated.*

### Voices
Sinbad: Tim Matthieson; **Salty:** Mel Blanc

## SITTING DUCKS

Whimsical and wacky adventures of the mismatched duo of Bill (a duck) and Aldo (an alligator) and their friends (Bill's Ducktown neighbors, Ed, Olly and Waddle and Aldo's gator friends in neighboring Swampwood) who are more interested in having Bill and his duck pals for dinner than becoming friends with them in this half-hour series that aired Monday through Friday mornings on Cartoon Network. Joining the network's weekday lineup along with another new series called *Pecola*, the CGI-animated, 26-episode series (inspired by Michael Bedard's world-famous series of airbrushed paintings, posters and books) aired for two seasons from May 2003 to February 2004. By January 2007, the series was back on the air as part of a four-hour programming block of animated fare on the all-new 24-hour digital television network, qubo, broadcast nationwide on the ION network (previously known as PAX-TV). *A Sitting Ducks Productions/Krislin Company/Creative Capers Entertainment/Universal Studios Inc. Production. Color. Half-hour. Premiered on CAR: May 6, 2003–February 28, 2004. Rebroadcast on Q: January 8, 2007.*

### Voices
Bill/Cecil: Ian James Corlett; **Aldo the Alligator:** Dave "Squatch" Ward; **Arnold the Alligator:** Scott McNeil; **Waddle:** Jay Brazeau; **Drill Sergeant Duck:** Cathy Weseluck; **Jerry the Parrot:** Garry Chalk; **Additional Voices:** Alec Willows, Paul Dobson, Lee Tockar, Pauline Newstone

## 64 ZOO LANE

With the help of Georgina the Giraffe on whose neck she slides down to escape from her bedroom window every night, a young blonde girl named Lucy, who lives next door to the local zoo, joins her animal friends—Boris the Bear, Giggle and Tickles the Monkeys, Harriet the Hippo, and Nelson the Elephant—who tell exciting tales that help Lucy get a cozy night's sleep in this half-hour children's series first telecast in the United Kingdom on the BBC. Each episode of this intelligently written, picture-book-quality animated series, created by award-winning director An Vrombaut and produced by Britain's Millimages and Zoo Lane Productions Ltd., stressed the use of language and vocabulary and recurring social themes, including the importance of friendships and helping others. In June 2001, the series was first shown in the United States in 11-minute segments as part of FOX Family Channel's *It's Itsy Bitsy Time*. Later repackaged as 52 half-hours combining two episodes, the series, which won a Pulcinella Award for best children's series, was rebroadcast on the commercial-free children's network, Noggin. Actress Ciara Johnson provided the voice of Lucy in the British version, with other British actors voicing her animal friends. *A Millimages/Zoo Lane Productions Ltd.*

*Production. Color. Half-hour. Premiered on ABC FAM: June 4, 2001–March 23, 2002. Rebroadcast on NOG: January 3, 2005–    .*

## THE SKATEBIRDS

Live-action stars Scooter the Penguin, Satchel the Pelican, Knock Knock the Woodpecker and Scat Cat host this series comprised of wraparounds, comedy skits and animated cartoons, such as "Woofer and Wimper, Dog Detectives" (formerly of *The Clue Club*); "The Robonic Stooges," featuring Moe, Larry and Curly as bionic crimefighters; "Wonder Wheels," which pairs two high school journalists and a heroic motorcycle in remarkable adventures; and the film serial "Mystery Island." First broadcast on CBS in 1977, the show was canceled after only four months on the air because of poor ratings. It was replaced by *Speed Buggy* and "The Robonic Stooges" (retitled *The Three Robonic Stooges*). (The cartoon trio received better ratings in *The Skatebirds* than any other segment.) In September 1979 *The Skatebirds* returned to CBS on Sunday mornings, where it completed its network run. *A Hanna-Barbera Production. Color. Half-hour. Premiered on CBS: September 10, 1977–January 21, 1978. Rebroadcast on CBS: September 1979–August 1980; September 1980–January 25, 1981. Rebroadcast on CAR: July 5, 1995–(Wednesdays).*

### Voices
Scooter: Don Messick; **Satchel:** Bob Holt; **Knock Knock:** Lennie Weinrib; **Scat Cat:** Scatman Crothers

**WOOFER AND WIMPER: Larry:** David Joliffe; **D.D.:** Bob Hastings; **Pepper:** Patricia Smith; **Dotty:** Tara Talboy; **Woofer:** Paul Winchell; **Wimper:** Jim MacGeorge; **Sheriff Bagley:** John Stephenson

**THE ROBONIC STOOGES: Moe:** Paul Winchell; **Larry:** Joe Baker; **Curly:** Frank Welker; **Triple-Zero:** Ross Martin

**WONDER WHEELS: Willie Sheeler:** Micky Dolenz; **Dooley Lawrence:** Susan Davis

### Cast

**MYSTERY ISLAND: Chuck Kelly:** Stephen Parr; **Sue Corwin:** Lynn Marie Johnston; **Sandy Corwin:** Larry Volk; **Dr. Strange:** Michael Kermoyan; **P.A.U.P.S. (voice):** Frank Welker

## SKELETON WARRIORS

Featuring high-tech, computer-generated effects, the very human Skeleton Hunters, led by Prince Justin Lightstar and his royal family, defend themselves from Baron Dark and his army of Skeleton Warriors to reunite two halves of the Lightstar Stone and rescue the world from eternal night in this futuristic, mythic fantasy/ adventure series created by Garry Goddard. *A Landmark/Graz Entertainment Production. Color. Half-hour. Premiered on CBS: September 17, 1994–September 2, 1995.*

### Voices
Jeff Bennett, Earl Boen, Nathan Carlson, Philip L. Clarke, Michael Corbett, Jim Cummings, Paul Eiding, Jeannie Elias, Linda Gary, Michael Gough, Jennifer Hale, Tony Jay, Danny Mann, Richard Molinare, Valery Pappas, Jan Rabson, Kevin Michael Richardson, Rodney Saulsberry, Kevin Schon

## SKY COMMANDERS

The Sky Commanders, a motley crew of renegade soldiers, battle a world-class villain, the evil General Plague, who is bent on world destruction, in the late 21st century, when technology comes face to face with a perilous new wilderness in this first-run half-hour adventure series based on the popular toy line by Kenner Toys. The program aired on Sunday mornings on *The Funtastic World of Hanna-Barbera* and later in reruns on Cartoon Network. *A Hanna-Barbera Production in association with Kenner Toys. Color. Half-hour. Premiered: July 5, 1987–88. Syndicated. Rebroadcast on CAR: January 21, 1995 (Super Adventures); July 8, 1995 (Power Zone) 1996; September 9, 2001–June 23, 2002. Rebroadcast on BOOM: Fall 2003–January 18, 2005.*

**Voices**

**General Mike Summit, the Sky Commanders leader:** Bob Ridgely; **Cutter Kling, crew member:** William Windom; **R.J. Scott, crew member:** Darryl Hickman; **Books Baxter, crew member:** Richard Doyle; **Jim Stryker, crew member:** Dorian Harewood; **Spider Reilly, crew member:** Triston Rogers; **Kodiak Crane, crew member:** Soon-Teck Oh; **Red McCullough, crew member:** Lauren Tewes; **General Plague:** Bernard Erhard; **Mordax:** Dick Gautier; **Raider Rath:** Paul Eiding; **Kreeg:** Charlie Adler; **Dr. Erica Slade:** B.J. Ward

## ◎ SKY DANCERS

Five young dance students are appointed the guardians of the Sky Swirl Stone that safeguards Wingdom from the cyclonic villain Sky Clone in this 26-episode half-hour fantasy/adventure series based on the popular Galoob toy line. The 26 half-hour episode series premiered in syndication in the fall of 1996. *An Abrams Gentile Entertainment/Gaumont Multimedia Production. Color. Half-hour. Premiered: September 9, 1996. Syndicated.*

**Voices**

T.J. Benjamin, Andrea Burns, Thomas Cannizaro, Donna Daley, Jonathan Khan, Ciarrai Ni Mhaiile, James Michael, K.C. Noel

## ◎ SKYHAWKS

A former air force colonel, widower Mike Wilson; his children, Steve and Caroline; his World War I flying ace father, Pappy; and Pappy's foster children, Baron Hughes and Little Cindy, head a daredevil air transport rescue service that saves troubled charter planes, helicopter pilots and test pilots. Sponsored by Mattel Toys, the 17-episode series debuted on ABC in 1969, opposite CBS's *The Archies* and NBC's *The Banana Splits.* Despite such stiff competition, the series returned for a second season in 1970, comprised entirely of repeat episodes. *A Ken Snyder/Pantomime Pictures Production. Color. Half-hour. Premiered on ABC: September 6, 1969–September 4, 1971.*

**Voices**

**Captain Mike Wilson:** Michael Rye; **Steve Wilson, his son/Joe Conway:** Casey Kasem; **Caroline Wilson, his daughter:** Iris Rainer; **Pappy Wilson, Mike's father/Baron Hughes, Pappy's foster child:** Dick Curtis; **Cynthia "Mugs" Hughes:** Melinda Casey; **Maggie McNalley:** Joan Gerber; **Buck Devlin:** Bob Arbogast

## ◎ SKYLAND

In the year 2251, a heroic pair of siblings—Mahad, a rebellious 17-year-old teen, and Lena, his 12-year-old sister—try to overtake the Sphere, a ruthless government that is controlling the world's precious water supply. What is left of Earth (shattered in an explosion called Skyland) is headed by Oslo, a power-hungry dictator who now orbits the planet in this futuristic motion picture capture imagery animated series. Coproduced by Toronto's 9 Story Entertainment and Paris' Method Films, this half-hour space-traveling action/adventure was previewed on television networks worldwide in November 2005 (Australia's ABC, Canada's Teletoon, France's France 2, United Kingdom's CITV and the U.S. Nicktoons Network). In July 2006, Nicktoons re-aired the show's one-hour pilot,

before officially launching the weekly series in January 2007 with 13 half-hour episodes. *A Canada-France/Story 9 Entertainment/DQ Entertainment Ltd./Method films/Luxanimation/France 2/Canal J. Production. Color. Half-hour. Premiered on NICKT: November 26, 2005 (preview). Premiered on NICKT: January 20, 2007 (series). Rebroadcast on NICKT: July 2, 2006 (pilot).*

**Voices**

**Mahad:** Tim Hamaguchi; **Lena:** Phoebe McAuley; **Oslo:** Juan Chioran; **Mila:** Alex Belcourt; **Vector:** William Colgate; **Aran Cortes:** Jack Langedijk; **Cheng:** Cameron Ansell; **Dahlia:** Alyson Court; **Diwan:** Athena Karkanis; **Wayan:** Milton Barnes

## ◎ SKYSURFER STRIKE FORCE

A pedestrian-looking bunch are magically transformed into imposing crimefighters who battle evil on antigravity "skyboards" (a cross between Jet Skis and skateboards) in this futuristic sci-fi cartoon series produced for first-run syndication. The series premiered in the fall of 1995 as part of the weekend syndicated block, *Amazin' Adventures II. A Ruby-Spears/Ashi/Bobhot Production. Color. Half-hour. Premiered: September 24, 1995 (part of Amazin' Adventures II). Syndicated.*

**Voices**

**Skysurfer/Jack, Noxious:** Mike Donovan, David Kaye; **Crazy Stunts/Mickey, Chronozoid/Replicon:** Paul Dobson; **Soar Loser/Brad:** Ward Perry; **Lazerette (formerly Darklight), Myko:** Vernus Terzo; **Sliced Ice/Kim, Cerena:** Jansyse Jaud; **Five Eyes/Grenader (formerly X-Ploder)/Garland/Foster:** Richard Newman; **Air Enforcer/Nathan (Nate)/Cybron/Wyland:** Alvin Sanders; **Zachariah Easel (formerly Pablo Palet)/Hagedorn/Adam:** Terry Klassen

## ◎ SLIMER! AND THE REAL GHOSTBUSTERS

Those ghostbusting idiots of the 1984 box-office sensation return for more mysteries and mishaps, joined by their tag-along mascot, Slimer! in this half-hour comedy/mystery series that originally aired on ABC (retitled after a two—season run as *The Real Ghostbusters* on the same network). The show was expanded to a full hour for the first season (1988–89), featuring 42 new *Slimer! and the Real Ghostbusters* cartoons, plus several new preteen characters. The character of Peter Venkman, formerly voiced by comedian Arsenio Hall and Lorenzo Music (the voice of Garfield the Cat) in the previous Saturday-morning series, was now voiced by Dave

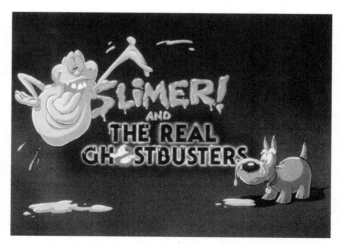

*Title card from the popular ABC Saturday-morning series* Slimer! and the Real Ghostbusters. © *Columbia Pictures Television, a division of CPT Holdings Inc. All rigns reserved.* (COURTESY: DIC ENTERPRISES)

Coulier. ABC renewed the series for the 1989–90 season and the program was reduced to a half hour, divided into two 15-minute adventures each week. Among the season's broadcasts was the premiere of the prime-time Halloween special *Slimer! And The Real Ghostbusters: The Halloween Door.* ABC canceled the series after four seasons. It was later rebroadcast on USA Network's *Cartoon Express. A DIC Enterprises Production in association with Columbia Pictures Television. Color. One hour. Half-hour. Premiered on ABC: September 10, 1988–September 7, 1992. Rebroadcast on USA: September 18, 1992–September 4, 1994. Syndicated.*

**Voices**

**Slimer: Rafael:** Charlie Adler; **Professor Dweeb:** Jeff Altman; **Mrs. Van Huego:** Fay De Witt; **Chilly Cooper:** Cree Summer Francks; **Linguini/Bud:** Danny Mann; **Rudy:** Jeff Marder; **Morris Grout:** Alan Oppenheimer; **Slimer:** Frank Welker

**The Real Ghostbusters: Peter Venkman:** Dave Coulier; **Ray Stantz/Slimer:** Frank Welker; **Egon Spengler:** Maurice LaMarche; **Winston Zeddmore:** Edward L. (Buster) Jones; **Janine Melnitz:** Kath Soucie; **Catherine:** April Hong; **Jason:** Katie Leigh; **Donald:** Danny McMurphy

## ◎ THE SMOKEY BEAR SHOW

The National Forest Fires Commission folk hero and spokesbear, "Only you can prevent forest fires," stars in this animated series, as both a bear and cub, in which he protects the forests and its creatures from fire. The 17-episode series, which debuted on ABC in 1969, fared poorly in the ratings, running third each week behind CBS's *The Bugs Bunny/Road Runner Hour* and NBC's *The Heckle and Jeckle Cartoon Show.* Even though the program was not a ratings blockbuster, ABC reran it for a second season before canceling it. *A Rankin-Bass Production. Color. Half-hour. Premiered on ABC: September 13, 1969–September 5, 1970. Rebroadcast on ABC: September 13, 1970–September 12, 1971.*

**Voices**
**Smokey the Bear:** Jackson Weaver

## ◎ THE SMURFS

In a tucked away village populated by little blue people who are only three apples tall and make their homes in mushrooms, Papa Smurf, a wise old magician, guides the rest of his hyperactive crew—Brainy, Vanity, Hefty, Clumsy, Jokey, Greedy, Lazy, Handy, Grouchy, Harmony and Smurfette, the only female Smurf— through their unfriendly encounters with the inept wizard Gargamel and his henchcat Azrael, who want to rid of the world of these happy blue busybodies.

French artist Pierre "Peyo" Culliford created these enchanting characters (called "Schtroumpf" in Flemish) in a Belgian comic strip in 1957, long before they appeared in this Emmy Award-winning series, which following its premiere in 1981—was the highest rated Saturday-morning show in eight years and the highest for an NBC animated series since 1970.

In 1982 NBC expanded the show to an unprecedented 90 minutes. Two new human characters joined the fun that season in cartoon adventures of their own: Johan, a young squire in the swashbuckling Errol Flynn mold, and Peewit, his comical sidekick. That same year *The Smurfs* won its first Emmy as Outstanding Children's Entertainment Series, the first of many awards for the series.

During the 1983–84 season, the series welcomed the arrival of Baby Smurf, and by the 1985–86 season it featured a tiny foursome of Smurf kids: the Smurflings (Nat, Slouchy, Snappy and Sassette,

the second female). The following season two new characters, Grandpa Smurf (voiced by comedian Jonathan Winters) and Scruple, were introduced. In 1983 Hanna-Barbera, the series' producers, broke new ground by introducing the first deaf character in an animated series: Laconia, the mute wood elf who used sign language to communicate.

The Smurfs' format returned to one hour in the 1983–84 season. In the 1989–90 season, the Smurfs left Smurf Village and became involved in events and key periods in world history, from the prehistoric days to ancient Egypt.

The series (retitled *The Smurfs' Adventures*) enjoyed long life in syndication as well, beginning in 1986, while the network series continued to win its time slot. In 1989 the program was revived in reruns on USA Network's Cartoon Express, then again in 1993 on Cartoon Network. In January 2005, this long-running, and one of the most successful animated series in television history, returned to American television when Burbank's DIC Entertainment acquired 26 half-hour episodes of the hit Hanna-Barbera series to re-air as part of its syndicated DIC Kids' Network three-hour programming block provided to stations with children's programming to meet "core" FCC requirements. *A Hanna-Barbera Production in association with Sepp International, S.A. Color. One hour. Ninety minutes. Premiered on NBC: September 12, 1981–September 1, 1990. Syndicated 1986–90. Rebroadcast on USA: April 12, 1989– September 12, 1993. Rebroadcast on CAR: October 1993–September 2, 1994 (weekdays); September 5, 1994–June 2, 1995 (weekdays, Sundays); June 30, 1997– (weekdays). Rebroadcast on BOOM: April 3, 2000–December 29, 2000; April 19, 2001–May 4, 2001; June 4, 2001–November 2, 2001; January 7, 2002–March 28, 2002; April 17, 2003–. Rebroadcast on DIC Kids Network: January 3, 2005– September 2005.*

**Voices**

**Gargamel:** Paul Winchell; **Azrael/Papa Smurf:** Don Messick; **Brainy Smurf:** Danny Goldman; **Clumsy/Painter Smurf:** Bill Callaway; **Hefty/Poet/Peewit Smurf/Clockwork Smurf:** Frank Welker; **Jokey Smurf:** June Foray; **Smurfette:** Lucille Bliss; **Vanity Smurf/ Hominbus:** Alan Oppenheimer; **Greedy Smurf/Harmony Smurf:** Hamilton Camp; **Lazy Smurf/Handy Smurf/Grouchy Smurf/ Johan:** Michael Bell; **King:** Bob Holt; **Dame Barbara:** Linda Gary; **Tailor:** Kip King; **Sloppy:** Marshall Efron; **Farmer/Scaredy:** Alan Young; **Baby Smurf:** Julie Dees; **Grandpa Smurf:** Jonathan Winters; **Scruple:** Brenda Vaccaro; **Nanny Smurf:** Susan Blu

**The Smurflings: Snappy:** Pat Musick; **Nat:** Charlie Adler; **Sassette:** Julie Dees; **Puppy:** Frank Welker; **Slouchy:** Noelle North; **Narrator:** Paul Kirby, Kris Stevens

## ◎ SNIP SNAP

A stop-motion animated series from English cartoon studio Halas and Batchelor featuring the exploits of a dog (Snap) cut out of paper and a pair of scissors (Snip), presented in 18 episodes. Originally broadcast in Britain under the title *Snip the Magic Scissors* (for which 26-episodes were produced), the series was syndicated in America in 1961 along with another H-B cartoon program, *Foo Foo. A Halas and Batchelor/Interstate Production. Color. Half-hour. Syndicated: 1961.*

## ◎ THE SNORKS

Deep under the sea in the mystical underwater world of Snorkland lives a society: tiny, adorable, snorkel-headed creatures who enjoy remarkable adventures with high school student Allstar and his girlfriend, Casey. Created by Freddy Monnickendam, the Snorks first gained popularity as Belgian comic-book characters. The series premiered on NBC in 1984 with 26 first-run episodes (two per half-hour program) with an additional 20 episodes for the 1985–86 season. An additional 62 (including 22 half-hours) episodes were filmed before the series finished its NBC run and entered daily syndication in 1989. The first-run syndicated series combined the new episodes with previously produced ones. A year later *The Snorks* were repackaged for syndication as part of Hanna-Barbera's weekend cartoon block, *The Funtastic World of Hanna-Barbera*. The original series was rebroadcast on USA Network's *Cartoon Express* and then in 1992 on Cartoon Network, airing weekdays. In April 2000, the former Saturday-morning network series joined the weekday afternoon lineup of Cartoon Network's sister channel, Boomerang, in reruns. *A Hanna-Barbera/Sepp, S.A. Production. Color. Half-hour. Premiered on NBC: September 15, 1984–September 6, 1986. Syndicated: September 14, 1987–September 25, 1988 (part of The Funtastic World of Hanna-Barbera in 1990). Rebroadcast on USA: October 23, 1989–August 28, 1991. Rebroadcast on CAR: October 2, 1992–December 31, 1993 (weekdays); January 3, 1994–September 2, 1994 (weekdays); January 5, 1994–June 2, 1995 (weekdays); September 4, 1995–1999 (weekdays). Rebroadcast on BOOM: April 3, 2000–.*

### Voices
**Allstar/Elder #4:** Michael Bell; **Tooter/Occy:** Frank Welker; **Dimmy:** Brian Cummings; **Governor Wetworth:** Frank Nelson; **Junior Wetworth:** Barry Gordon; **Casey:** B.J. Ward; **Mrs. Wetworth:** Joan Gardner; **Daffney:** Nancy Cartwright; **Mrs. Seaworthy:** Edie McClurg; **Galeo:** Clive Revill; **Elders 1, 2 & 3:** Peter Cullen; **Baby Smallstar:** Gail Matthius; **Willie:** Fredricka Weber; **Mr. Seaworthy:** Bob Holt; **Auntie Marina:** Mitzi McCall; **Mrs. Kelp:** Joan Gerber; **Mr. Kelp:** Bob Ridgely

### ◎ SONIC THE HEDGEHOG
Sonic the Hedgehog (voiced by Jaleel White of TV's *Family Matters*) encounters famed archenemy Dr. Robotnik as he attempts to free the people of the planet Morbius in this 26-episode half-hour network series version of the bestselling 1991 Sega Genesis video game. The series premiered on ABC on September 18, 1993, five days after the debut of a second 65-episode syndicated series, *Adventures of Sonic the Hedgehog*. (See entry for details.) Two different versions of the show were produced for ABC and syndication, the latter of which ran six days a week. It marked the first time since the premiere of *Slimer! and the Real Ghostbusters* that a character had debuted in syndication and on a network at same time. *A DIC Animation City/Bohbot Production in association with Sega of America, Inc. Color. Half-hour. Premiered on ABC: September 18, 1993–June 10, 1995. Rebroadcast on USA: 1995–97.*

### Voices
**Sonic the Hedgehog:** Jaleel White; **Tails:** Bradley Pierce; **Dr. Robotnik:** Jim Cummings; **Antoine:** Rob Paulsen; **Rotor:** Mark Ballou; **Snively:** Charlie Adler; **Princess Sally:** Kath Soucie; **Bunnie:** Christine Cavanaugh

### ◎ SONIC UNDERGROUND
As the popular rock group, Sonic Underground, Sonic and his two siblings, Sonic his sister, and Manic his brother, tangle with Sonic's age-old enemy Dr. Robotnik and his Swat Bots, who are determined to prevent the hedgehogs from fulfilling the prophecy of defeating him and bringing peace to the planet in this third animated series based on the popular Nintendo video game character. Produced in 1999, the 40-episode, half-hour series, following 1993's syndicated *Adventures of Sonic the Hedgehog* and ABC Saturday morning series *Sonic the Hedgehog*, aired weekday mornings

on cable's Sci-Fi Channel and in first-run syndication on UPN stations beginning in August of that year. Four years later, the character returned to star in a fourth series for FOX, *Sonic X. A DIC Entertainment/Sega/Bohbot Production. Color. Half-hour. Premiered on SCI: August 30, 1999–October 21, 1999. Premiered on UPN/Syndication: August 30, 1999.*

### Voices
**Sonic/Manic/Sonia:** Jaleel White; **Dr. Ivo Robotnick:** Gary Chalk; **Sleet:** Maurice LaMarche; **Dingo:** Peter Wilds; **Cyrus/Knuckles:** Ian James Corlett; **Queen Aleana:** Gail Webster; **Trevor:** Matt Hill; **Bartalby:** Phil Hayes; **Sonic's Singing Voice:** Samuel Vincent; **Manic's Singing Voice:** Tyley Ross; **Other Voices:** Kathleen Barr, Terry Klassen, Frank Welker

### ◎ SONIC X
Racing against the clock, Sonic and his friends Amy, Knuckles, Tails and others join forces with a 12-year-old boy named Christopher to collect the powerful seven Chaos Emeralds before the evil Dr. Eggman can do so and thus take over the new planet they inhabit in this fourth animated version of the best-selling Sega video game character. A joint venture between Japan's Tokyo Movie Shinsha (TMS) Entertainment, VIZ Media and FUNimation, the half-hour fantasy action/adventure, produced in Japan and redubbed in English by 4Kids Entertainment, aired Saturday mornings on FOX's *FOX Box* cartoon block (renamed *4Kids TV* in 2005) with 78 action-packed episodes. *A TMS Entertainment/Akios/Sonic Productions Production. Color. Half-hour. Premiered on FOX: September 6, 2003–May 6, 2006.*

### Voices
**Sonic:** Jason Anthony Griffith; **Rouge the Bat:** Kathleen Delaney; **Sam Speed:** Frank Frankson; **Knuckles the Echidna:** Dan Green; **Cream:** Rebecca Honig; **Danny:** Rachael Lillis; **Miles "Tails" Prower:** Amy Palant; **Helen/Cosmo:** Amy Birnbaum; **Christopher Thorndyke:** Suzanne Goldish; **Dr. Eggman/Ella:** Mike Pollock; **Amy Rose/The President's Secretary:** Lisa Ortiz; **Cream the Rabbit:** Rebecca Honig; **Decoe/Bokkun/Mr. Stewart/Narrator:** Andrew Rannells; **Bocoe/Mr. Tanaka:** Darren Dunstan; **Topaz:** Kayzie Rogers; **Chuck Thorndyke:** Jerry Lobozzo; **Dark Oak/Red Pine:** Jonathan Todd Ross; **Pale Bay Leaf:** Jim Napalitano; **Black Narcissus:** Sean Schemmel; **Yellow Zelkova/Nelson Thorndyke/President:** Ted Lewis; **Lindsay Thorndyke:** Jennifer Blood; **Danny:** Rachael Lillis; **Frances:** Kerrie Williams; **Other Voices:** Jock Quevas, Nappy, Karen Neill, Ed Paul, Jimmy Zoppi

### ◎ SOUTH PARK
Four foul-mouthed third graders—Kyle, Kenny, Cartman and Stan—in the eerie Colorado town of South Park experience all sorts of strange, unexplainable and weird phenomena, including alien abductions, in this offbeat comedy series done in "paper-cut" animation. The series was based on a crudely animated short, *Jesus vs. Frosty,* featuring prototypes of South Park characters Kenny (known as Cartman) and Kyle, produced in 1992 by series creators Trey Parker and Matt Stone as students at the University of Colorado. Three years later, Parker and Stone produced a second short film called *Jesus vs. Santa,* for Brian Garden, a Hollywood Foxlab executive who commissioned them to make it and sent it out as a video Christmas card to friends in the industry. The popularity of the video led to the pair creating a weekly series, written, directed, edited and also voiced by them.

Since its premiere in August 1997, the off-the-wall comedy series has racked up 158 episodes over 11 seasons. On September 19, 2005, previously broadcast episodes of the raunchy cartoon series were offered in syndication, with some of the more offensive material edited from several episodes. Despite often producing its share of controversy over the show's provocative material, the Comedy Central series has been nominated six times for a prime-time Emmy Award—in 1998, 2000, 2002, 2004, 2005 and 2006—for outstanding animated program, winning once in 2005 for the episode "Best Friends Forever," and in 2006 it won a Peabody Award, becoming only the third Comedy Central program to win such an honor.

In July 1999, Parker and Stone took *South Park* to the big screen, producing the full-length animated feature *South Park: Bigger Longer & Uncut*, produced by Paramount Pictures and nominated for an Academy Award for best original song for "Blame Canada," one of 12 songs written by Trey Parker and Marc Shaiman. The NC-17-rated flick hauled in an impressive $23 million opening weekend, and more than $52 million in ticket sales in the United States alone.

Isaac Hayes, the voice of the Chef and a practicing Scientologist, quit the series after voicing 138 episodes a week before the start of the 10th season in a public spat with the show and its creators, saying he could no longer stomach its take on religion. In November 2005, producers Matt Stone and Trey Parker mocked Tom Cruise and the Church of Scientology in an episode entitled "Trapped in the Closet," which was nominated for an Emmy Award. (The episode was scheduled to repeat in March 2006 but didn't make it into the repeat rotation on Comedy Central. In response, creators Matt Stone and Trey Parker threatened to sever ties with the network and its parent company, Viacom. The pair and the network patched up their differences. The controversial episode re-aired on July 19, and they produced a new seven-episode run of *South Park*, premiering in October of that year.)

After leaving the series, Stone and Parker skewered Hayes and his former character in the 10th season opener, editing together voice tracks of Hayes's dialogue and turning his character into a raving pedophile, with the *South Park* boys taking him to strip clubs to try to "save" him. *A Comedy Partners/Celluloid Studios/Braniff Production. Color. Half-hour. Premiered on COM: August 13, 1997–February 25, 1998; April 1, 1998–January 20, 1999; April 7, 1999–January 12, 2000; April 5, 2000–December 20, 2000; June 20, 2001–December 12, 2001; March 6, 2002–December 11, 2002; March 19, 2003–December 17, 2003; March 17, 2004–December 15, 2004; March 9, 2005–December 7, 2005; March 22, 2006–November 15, 2006; March 7, 2007–    . Syndicated: September 19, 2005.*

**Voices**
**Stan Marsh/Eric Cartman/Mr. Garrison/Officer Barbrady/Various Others:** Trey Parker; **Kyle Broflovski/Kenny McCormick/Pip/Jesus/Jimbo Marsh/Various Others:** Matthew Stone; **Chef:** Isaac Hayes; **Sheena:** Jeanie Adler; **Bebe Stevens:** Jennifer Howell; **Token Williams:** Adrien Beard; **Liane Cartman:** April Stewart; **Mr. Slave:** John "Nancy" Hansen; **Ike Broflovski:** Kyle McCulloch, Dimitri Mendoza, Jessie Howell; **Filmore Anderson:** Nico Agnone; **Mr. Wyland:** Bruce Howell; **Towelie:** Vernon Chatman; **Paris Hilton:** Jessica Makinson; **Chris:** Dian Bachar; **Live Action Woman:** Pam Brady; **Miss Information:** Dee Dee Green; **Biggie Smalls:** Eldridge "El Hud" Hudson; **Sister Anne:** Anne Garefino; **Jay Leno:** Himself; **The Frizzie:** Tom Vogt; **Missionary:** Michael Ann Young; **Additional Voices:** Mona Marshall, Eliza Schneider; Mary Kay Bergman, Gracie Lazar, Milan Agnone, Toddy Walters, Spencer Lacey, Toby Morton, Dante Alexander, Rochelle Leffler, Eric Stough, Dakota Sky, Kief Davidson

### ◎ SPACE ANGEL

This classic animated series follows the intergalactic adventures of Scott McCloud—code name: "Space Angel"—a one-man Marine Corps for the Earth Bureau of Investigation who, working in utmost secrecy, tackles assignments involving the security of the solar system. McCloud's crew aboard the superspaceship *Starduster* includes Taurus, an expert pilot and mechanic; Crystal, a specialist in electronics and astronavigation; and Professor Mace, head of base station Evening Star, who make up the bureau's Interplanetary Space Force. Produced by the creators of *Clutch Cargo* and *Captain Fathom*, these serialized science-fiction stories were strung together in 52 weekly half-hour programs. Former National Comics artist Alexander Toth served as art director for the series, which was created by Dik Darley and Dick Brown. Like *Clutch Cargo*, films featured the Synchro-Vox process, superimposed human lips speaking over the mouths of the characters. *A Cambria Studios/T.V. Comics Production. Color. Half-hour. Premiered: February 6, 1962. Syndicated.*

**Voices**
**Scott McCloud/Space Angel:** Ned Lefebvre, Jim Chandler; **Other Voices:** Margaret Kerry, Hal Smith

### ◎ SPACECATS

A highly evolved team of space exploring cats (under the rule of D.O.R.C.: Disembodied Omnipotent Ruler of Cats) from the planet Triglyceride 7, led by Captain Catgut and his assistants, Tom, Scratch and Sniff, battle larger-than-life villains on Earth in this live-action/puppet/animated series from producers Paul Fusco and Bernie Brillstein, who produced the hit live-action sitcom *Alf*. *A Paul Fusco/Marvel Production. Color. Half-hour. Premiered on NBC: September 14, 1991–July 25, 1992.*

**Voices**
Charles Nelson Reilly (D.O.R.C.), Jack Angel, Gregg Berger, Sheryl Bernstein, Susan Blu, Hamilton Camp, Cam Clarke, Townsend Coleman, Jennifer Darling, Walker Edmiston, Jeannie Elias, John Erwin, Lea Floden, Pat Fraley, Paul Fusco, Brad Garrett, Barry Gordon, Pat Musick, Rob Paulsen, Jan Rabson, Hal Rayle, Bob Ridgely, Maggie Roswell, Susan Silo, Kath Soucie, John Stephenson, Lennie Weinrib

### ◎ SPACE GHOST AND DINO BOY

A black-hooded interplanetary crimefighter who draws powers from his magic belt, Space Ghost (voiced by former *Rowan and Martin's Laugh-in* announcer Gary Owens) counters evil forces assisted by two teenage wards, Jan and Jace, and their pet space monkey, Blip. The companion cartoon in this series revolved around the adventures of young boy (Tod) who is left in prehistoric times following a time-warp experiment that kills his father. (He earns the name "Dino Boy" by riding on a brown-spotted brontosaurus named Bronty.) A caveman (Ugh) saves the boy and the pair become inseparable.

First run on CBS in 1966, slated opposite ABC's *The Beatles* and NBC's *Space Kidettes*, *Space Ghost and Dino Boy* featured 42 "Space Ghost" adventures per show and 18 "Dino Boy" cartoons during its two-season run on the network. In 1976 NBC purchased the show and combined repeat episodes with another Hanna-Barbera property, *Frankenstein Jr. and the Impossibles*, packaging them together as *The Space Ghost/Frankenstein Jr. Show* to replace the struggling live-action series *Land of the Lost*.

The character was revived five years later (reprised by Gary Owens) in all-new episodes as part of 1981's *Space Stars* for NBC. In April of 1994 the original series was aired again as a three-hour marathon on the Cartoon Network preceding the debut of the network's first late-night talk show, *Space Ghost Coast to Coast*. Reruns continued on Cartoon Network through the late 1990s and again beginning in 2000 on Boomerang. *A Hanna-Barbera*

*Production. Color. Half-hour. Premiered on CBS: September 10, 1966–September 7, 1968. Rebroadcast on NBC: November 27, 1976–September 3, 1977 (as The Space Ghost/Frankenstein Jr. Show). Rebroadcast on CAR: February 7, 1993 (part of Boomerang, 1967); April 15, 1994 (Space Ghost Mini-Marathon); May 2, 1994–July 1, 1994 (weekdays); September 5, 1994–September 30, 1994 (weekdays); March 25, 1996–June 2, 1996 (weekdays); January 1997–2000; February 23, 2002–June 2004 (Fridays, Saturdays). Rebroadcast on BOOM: April 1, 2000– .*

**Voices**
**Space Ghost:** Gary Owens; **Jan:** Ginny Tyler; **Jace:** Tim Matthieson; **Dino Boy (Tod):** Johnny Carson (not the talk-show host); **Ugh:** Mike Road; **Bronty:** Don Messick

### ◎ SPACE GHOST COAST TO COAST

The Cartoon Network's first original toon, this surprise cult hit features the black-hooded interplanetary superhero as host of this bizarre, hour-long late-night talk show from outer space (cohosted by archenemies Moltar and Zorak, enslaved as unwilling members of Space Ghost's late-night crew) featuring live-action celebrity interviews. Debuting in April of 1994, the series premiered as a weekly 15-minute talk show airing Friday nights. (Guests on the show's premiere were Susan Powter, Kevin Meaney and the Bee Gees). Celebrities who appeared in series episodes include Catherine Bach, Fran Drescher, Ashley Judd, Donny Osmond, and even the cast of *Gilligan's Island* (Bob Denver, Dawn Wells and Russell Johnson).

Footage from the original 1960s Saturday-morning cartoon series was reedited and composited over a live-action miniature set to create what producers called "the first cartoon talk show." In the beginning, the network hired actors to conduct the off-screen interviews of special guests, with George Lowe (the voice of Space Ghost), rerecording the questions in the studio. Each question-and-answer interview was videotaped, and the video image of that particular celeb was inserted into the finished cartoon—in this case, projected on a suspended TV screen on the miniature set, with the animated Space Ghost appearing to interact like a normal TV talk-show host.

In July of 1997, 24 new episodes began airing on the network. Guests included Billy Mumy, Peter Fonda, and Mark Hamil. *A Hanna-Barbera/Cartoon Network/Ghost Planet Industries/Big Deal Cartoons/DESIGNefx Production. Color. One hour. Premiered on CAR: April 15, 1994–July 11, 1997; July 18, 1997 (new episodes).*

**Voices**
**Space Ghost:** George Lowe; **Moltar/Zorak:** C. Martin Croker

### ◎ THE SPACE GHOST/FRANKENSTEIN JR. SHOW

As a replacement for the poorly rated *Land of the Lost* live-action series, NBC tried to bolster ratings of that time slot with this half-hour compendium of two Hanna-Barbera favorites who starred in their own successful network series. (See *Space Ghost and Dino Boy* and *Frankenstein Jr. and the Impossibles* for voice credits and details.) *A Hanna-Barbera Production. Color. Half-hour. Premiered on NBC: November 27, 1976–September 3, 1977.*

### ◎ SPACE GOOFS

In this cutting-edge animated series that premiered on FOX Network, five alien monsters who crash on Earth find refuge in an abandoned house and do anything they can to keep the house from being rented, including scaring away prospective tenants. Originally the 26-episode series was called *Home to Rent. A Gaumont Multimedia/Pro (Sieben)/France3/Saban Production. Color.*

*Half-hour. Premiered on FOX: September 6, 1997–September 11, 1999.*

**Voices**
**Candy:** Charlie Adler; **Etno:** Maurice Lamarche; **Bud Buddiovec/Stereo:** Jeff Bennett; **Gorgious:** Danny Mann; **Other Voices:** Michael Stealy

### ◎ SPACE KIDETTES

Accompanied by their comical pet dog, Pup Star, a group of junior space rangers explore the cosmos from their space-capsule clubhouse and battle with creatures and enemies in outer space. In this 20-episode half-hour fantasy/adventure series originally broadcast on NBC in 1966, the kiddettes' main antagonist was Captain Sky Hook (a parody of Captain Hook in *Peter Pan*), the meanest pirate in the universe. Episodes from the series were rerun as part of *The Go-Go Gophers* on CBS in 1968 and even later in syndication on *Young Samson*. (The latter was rebroadcast in its entirety on USA Network's *Cartoon Express*.) Voice cast regulars included Chris Allen, the voice of Jay Ward's Hoppity Hooper, and Lucille Bliss, best known as the voice of Crusader Rabbit. *A Hanna-Barbera Production. Half-hour. Premiered on NBC: September 10, 1966–September 2, 1967. Rebroadcast on USA: February 20, 1989–March 26, 1991. Rebroadcast on BOOM: September 2, 2001– .*

**Voices**
**Scooter:** Chris Allen; **Snoopy:** Lucille Bliss; **Jennie:** Janet Waldo; **Count Down/Pup Star:** Don Messick; **Captain Sky Hook/Static:** Daws Butler

### ◎ SPACE STARS

Average space citizens and superpowered heroes tackle jet-age problems and cosmic evil in five suspenseful and humorous segments. In "Teen Force," three superteenagers (Kid Comet, Moleculad and Elektra) fight for freedom in the tradition of Robin Hood and his merry men. In "Astro and the Space Mutts," a trio of interstellar police officers—the Jetsons' family pet Astro and two clumsy canines, Cosmo and Dipper—fight crime directed by their police boss, Space Ace. In "Space Stars Finale," "Space Stars" are pitted against a collection of galactic rogues and rascals. The remaining two weekly segments were "Herculoids" and "Space Ghost," back in all-new episodes produced for television. The hour-long series debuted on NBC in 1981 as a lead-in for another NBC animated series, *Spider-Man and His Amazing Friends*.

In 1989 the program's "Teen Force" cartoons were rebroadcast on USA Network's *Cartoon Express. A Hanna-Barbera Productions. Color. One hour. Premiered on NBC: September 12, 1981–September 11, 1982. Rebroadcast on USA: May 31, 1989–January 2, 1992 (Teen Force).*

**Voices**

**TEEN FORCE: Elektra:** B.J. Ward; **Moleculad:** David Hubbard; **Kid Comet:** Darryl Hickman; **Plutem/Glax:** Mike Winslow; **Uglor, the terrible:** Allan Lurie; **Narrator:** Keene Curtis

**ASTRO AND THE SPACE MUTTS: Astro:** Don Messick; **Cosmo:** Frank Welker; **Dipper:** Lennie Weinrib; **Space Ace:** Mike Bell

**HERCULOIDS: Zandor/Tundro/Zok/Igoo:** Mike Road; **Tara:** Virginia Gregg; **Dorno:** Sparky Marcus; **Gloop/Gleep:** Don Messick; **Narrator:** Keene Curtis

**SPACE GHOST: Space Ghost:** Gary Owens; **Jan:** Alexandra Stewart; **Jace:** Steve Spears; **Blip:** Frank Welker; **Narrator:** Keene Curtis

*In the distant future, courageous Captain Nemo and his bold crew battle the evil Phantom Warriors in the three-dimensional animated series* Space Strikers. © *Saban Entertainment*

## ⓢ SPACE STRIKERS

In this futuristic, 3-D animated version of the Jules Verne classic *20,000 Leagues Under the Sea*, a pumped-up heroic Captain Nemo (now captain of his own starship) and his bold *Nautilus* crew battle the half-human, half-robot Master Phantom and his evil Phantom Warriors, who have conquered the planet Earth and plan to harvest the Planet's valuable resources. This 26-episode action/adventure series, aired Sunday mornings on the UPN network, featuring state-of-the-art computer-generated 3-D action sequences, beginning in 1995. A *Saban Entertainment Production. Color. Half-hour. Premiered on UPN: September 10, 1995–September 7, 1996.*

## ⓢ SPARTAKUS AND THE SUN BENEATH SEA

Living deep in the center of Earth are the Arcadians, a primitive civilization whose lives depend on the power of their sun, Terra. When this once-reliable source fails, they create a beautiful messenger—Arkanna—to send above for help. The foreign-produced, 52-episode series, with theme song performed by the teen rock group Menudo, made its American television on Nickelodeon in 1986. A *RMC Audio Visual/Monte Carlo Bon Bon/DR Movie/France 3/Multidub/International/Saban Production. Color. Half-hour. Premiered on NICK: October 11, 1986–July 28, 1991.*

## ⓢ SPEED BUGGY

Teenagers Debbie, Tinker and Mark and chugging auto partner Speed Buggy travel throughout the country and to foreign locales finding mystery and adventure, with Speedy always saving the day in 16 first-run episodes originally produced for CBS in 1973. Over 10 years, the series aired on two different networks, and Speed Buggy made guest appearances on the popular ABC series *Scooby's All-Star Laff-A-Lympics*. It was later rebroadcast on cable's Cartoon Network and Boomerang. A *Hanna-Barbera Production. Color. Half-hour. Premiered on CBS: September 8, 1973–August 30, 1975. Rebroadcast on ABC: September 6, 1975–September 4, 1976. Rebroadcast on NBC: November 27, 1976–September 3, 1977. Rebroadcast on CBS: January 28, 1978–September 2, 1978. Rebroadcast on CBS: September 18, 1982–September 3, 1983. Rebroadcast on CAR: July 9, 1995–May 26, 1996 (Sundays). Rebroadcast on BOOM: June 5, 2000.*

### Voices
**Speed Buggy:** Mel Blanc; **Debbie:** Arlene Golonka; **Tinker:** Phil Luther Jr.; **Mark:** Mike Bell; **Other Voices:** Don Messick

## ⓢ SPEED RACER

Adventure-loving hero, Speed Racer, a young race-car enthusiast, speeds around the world to fight the forces of evil in his super-charged Mach 5 race car. Speed's efforts are supported by his girlfriend, Trixie, kid brother, Spridal, and pet monkey, Chim Chim. The 52-episode series was unquestionably one of the most popular Japanese-made cartoon programs to air on American television. In 1993, the series was rebroadcast on MTV preceding the fall debut of brand-new adventures, entitled *The New Adventures of Speed Racer*, produced for first-run syndication. (See entry for further details.) The Cartoon Network reaired the series beginning in 1996 for almost three years. In November 2003, the classic auto racing series returned in reruns on Speed Channel, airing Monday through Friday at 6 P.M., Saturday and Sunday mornings, beginning at 7 A.M. and late night Friday with encore performances from midnight to 2 A.M. A *Tatsunoko Production. Color. Half-hour. Premiered: September 23, 1967. Syndicated. Rebroadcast on MTV: 1993–94. Rebroadcast on CAR: February 18, 1996 (Sundays); March 4, 1996– (weekdays);*

*Adventure-loving Speed Racer (center), kid brother Spridal, pet monkey Chim Chim and girlfriend Trixie stand in front of their Mach 5 race car, ready for action, in the Japanese cartoon favorite* Speed Racer. *Tatsunoko Productions*

*July 1996–99. Rebroadcast on SPEED: November 17, 2003–04. Rebroadcast on NICK G: 2004.*

**Voices**
**Speed Racer:** Jack Grimes; **Trixie, Speed's girlfriend/Spridal, Speed's brother/Mrs. Racer, Speed's mother:** Corinne Orr; **Racer X, Speed's older brother/Pops Racer, Speed's father:** Jack Curtis

## ◉ SPEED RACER X
With his father Pops equipping the famed Mach 5 race car with a more powerful engine, teenage race driver Speed Racer enters the world-class Grand Prix determined to become the best Grand Prix driver of all and win the race in honor of his late brother, Rex, who died while test driving his father's new high-speed engine in competition. Debuting on Nickelodeon in August 2002, the half-hour series, produced in Japan and redubbed by English-speaking actors, was broadcast Sunday afternoons as part of the network's *SLAM!* program block through May 2003. It marked the third animated rendition of the character, following 1993's syndicated series *The New Adventures of Speed Racer*, and second remake of the original 1960s cartoon show, *Speed Racer. A DIC Enterprises/Speed Racer Entertainment/Tatsunoko Production. Color. Half-hour. Premiered on NICK: August 25, 2002–May 11, 2003.*

**Voices**
**Speed Racer:** David Lelyveld; **Spridal/Trixie:** Chris Chaney; **Pops Racer:** Jackson Daniels; **Sparky:** Joshua Seth; **Mom Racer:** Michelle Ruff

## ◉ SPICY CITY
Veteran animator Ralph Bakshi (*Fritz the Cat, Cool World*) created and produced this late-night, six-part adult animated series—and second HBO Animation adult cartoon series—set in a surreal, retrofuturistic urban landscape. Written in the style of the pulp magazines of the 1930s and 1940s and tied together by the continuing character Raven, the proprietor of a social club (voiced by singer/actress Michelle Phillips), the series is set in a city where nothing is ever what it seems and where everything has a price. Each half-hour episode covered such genres as science fiction, horror and noir. The series debuted in July of 1997 with the opening episode "Love Is a Download" (written by Bakshi's son, Preston). *A Ralph Bakshi/HBO Animation Production. Color. Half-hour. Premiered on HBO: July 11, 1997–August 22, 1997.*

**Voices**
**Raven:** Michelle Phillips; **Other Voices:** James Keane, Barry Stigler, Mary Mara, John Hostetter, Vince Melocchi, Letitia Hicks, Matt K. Miller, Andy Philpot, Alex Fernandez, Cecilia Noel, Ralph Bakshi, James Hanes, Carlos Ferro, Charlie Adler, Pamela Tyson, Tuesday Knight, Darrell Kunitomi, Grace Zandarski, James Asher, Tasia Valenza, Tony Amendola, Julia De Mita, Rick Najera, Lewis Arquette, Jennifer Darling, E.G. Daily, Matthew Flint, Joey Carmen, Michael Yama, Marnie Mosiman, Brendan O'Brien, Brock Peters, Dave Fennoy, Danny Mann

## ◉ SPIDER-MAN (1967)
College student Peter Parker, reporter for the *New York Daily Bugle*, takes on underground syndicates and other criminals as famed superhero Spider-Man. He encounters such formidable foes as the Phantom from Space, The Sorcerer, One-Eyed Idol, Blotto, Scorpion and others in this 52-episode half-hour series based on Stan Lee's *The Amazing Spider-Man* comic-book adventures. Airing on ABC beginning in 1967, the series enjoyed a successful three-season run before entering daily syndication.

Executive producers were Robert L. Lawrence and Ralph Bakshi (uncredited), who also served as story supervisor. Cosmo Anzilotti was assistant director while Martin Taras served as one of the principal animators. Like Bakshi, Anzilotti and Taras were former Terry-Toon animators. *A Grantray-Lawrence Animation and Krantz Animation Production in association with Marvel Comics. Color. Half-hour. Premiered on ABC: September 9, 1967–August 30, 1969. Rebroadcast on ABC: March 22, 1970–September 6, 1970. Syndicated. Rebroadcast on ABC FAM: May 25, 2002–July 3, 2004.*

**Voices**
**Peter Parker/Spider-Man:** Bernard Cowan, Paul Soles; **Betty Brant, a reporter:** Peg Dixon; **J. Jonah Jameson, the editor:** Paul Kligman

## ◉ SPIDER-MAN AND HIS AMAZING FRIENDS
A small suburban town is the setting for this comedy-adventure series about the world's most popular superhero, alias Peter Parker, a shy, 18-year-old science major, who teams up with two superhuman teenagers, Angelica Jones (Firestar—the Girl of Fire) and Bobby Drake (Iceman), in the name of peace and justice. Episodes were later repeated on *The Incredible Hulk/Amazing Spider-Man Hour.* (See series entry for information.) In 1984 NBC split the program up and Spider-Man returned for one final bow in his own time slot.

In May 2002, cable's ABC Family began replaying the series at different times over the course of four seasons, including a two-week run, its last, in May 2006. Nearly two years earlier, Toon Disney had added the comic-inspired program to its roster, airing it until Memorial Day weekend in 2006, including a three-hour marathon on May 27, a few months before the show's 25th anniversary, feting Spidey and the gang. *A Marvel Production. Color. Half-hour. Premiered on NBC: September 12, 1981–September 10, 1983. Rebroadcast on NBC: September 15, 1984–September 6, 1986. Rebroadcast on ABC FAM: May 26, 2002–May 31, 2006. Rebroadcast on TDIS: November 1, 2004–May 31, 2006.*

**Voices**
**Peter Parker/Spider-Man:** Dan Gilvezan; **Angelica Jones/Firestar/Sally/Storm:** Kathy Garber; **Bobby Drake/Iceman/Flash Thompson/Ms. Lion/Blockbuster/Angelica's Father/Francis Byte/Videoman/Wolf-Thing/Matt Murdock:** Frank Welker; **Aunt May:** June Foray; **Narrator:** Dick Tufeld (Season 1), Stan Lee (Seasons 2 & 3); **Additional Voices:** Michael Ansara, Michael Bell, Bob Bergen, Susan Blu, Bill Callaway, Hans Conried, Peter Cullen, Jerry Dexter, George DiCenzo, Alan Dinehart, Walker Edmiston, Michael Evans, Pat Fraley, Al Fann, Dan Gilvezan, John Haymer, Stanley Jones, Sally Julian, Chris Latta, Annie Lockhart, Keye Luke, Dennis Marks, William H. Marshall, Alan Melvin, Shepard Menkin, Robert Ridgley, Neil Ross, Michael Rye, Marilyn Schreffler, John Stephenson, Janet Waldo, William Woodson, Alan Young

## ◉ SPIDER-MAN: THE ANIMATED SERIES
Pop culture's most enduring web-slinging comic-book superhero (alias Peter Parker) battles classic foes the Kingpin, the Scorpion, Mysterio, the Rhino, Dr. Octopus, the Vulture, the Green Goblin and the Lizard, and an array of formidable new supervillains—Hydro-Man, Venom, Morbius the Living Vampire and the Shocker—with his superhuman strength, wall-clinging ability and "spider sense" in and around New York City in this new series of 65 half-hour adventures. Story lines placed greater emphasis on Parker's romances and experiences with friends at college than did previous animated attempts. The first episode, entitled, *Night of the*

*Lizard*, debuted in November of 1994 as a half-hour Saturday-morning special, with weekly airings beginning in early February of 1995. That June, FOX brought the series to prime time by airing a half-hour Sunday night special, *Day of the Chameleon*, opposite the all-new *X-Men* cartoon special, *Weapon X, Lies and Video Tape*. The program's last original Saturday-morning episode was a two-part finale, ending in early February of 1998. It was one of Fox Network's highest-rated animated programs. From 1998 to 1999, the action-charged series was also rebroadcast on UPN-owned stations and in syndication. FOX Family Channel and its successor, ABC Family, subsequently re-aired the series as well as FOX network, from August 1999 to February 2006. *A Marvel/New World Entertainment/Saban Entertainment/Graz Entertainment Production. Color. Half-hour. Premiered on FOX: February 4, 1995–September 26, 1999. Rebroadcast on UPN/Syndicated: September 14, 1998–September 11, 1999. Rebroadcast on FOX FAM: August 16, 1998–July 26, 2000. Rebroadcast on FOX: June 25, 2001–August 25, 2001. Rebroadcast on ABC FAM: June 16, 2001–February 28, 2006.*

*Voices*
**Peter Parker/Spider-Man:** Christopher Daniel Barnes; **Mary Jane Parker:** Sara Ballantine; **Spider-Carnage/Ben Reilly:** Christopher Daniel Barnes; **J. Jonah Jameson:** Ed Asner; **Aunt May:** Linda Gary; **Deborah Whitman:** Liz Georges; **Dr. Curt Connors/The Lizard:** Joseph Campanella; **Eddie Brock/Venom:** Hank Azaria; **Felicia Thompson/Black Cat:** Jennifer Hale; **Flash Thompson:** Patrick Laborteaux; **Harry Osborn/Green Goblin:** Gary Imhoff; **Herman Shultz/Shocker:** Jim Cummings; **Liz Osborn:** Marla Rubinoff; **Mac McGargon/Scorpion:** Martin Landau; **Mariah Crawford/Calypso:** Susan Beaubian; **Norman Osborn/Green Goblin:** Neil Ross; **Otto Octavius/Dr. Octopus:** Efrem Zimbalist Jr.; **Wilson Fisk/The Kingpin:** Roscoe Lee Browne; **Alistair Smythe:** Maxwell Caulfield; **Joe "Robbie" Robertson:** Rodney Saulsberry; **Detective Terri Lee:** Dawnn Lewis

## ◉ SPIDER-MAN: THE NEW ANIMATED SERIES (2003)
Bitten by a radioactive spider and sprouting spider-like super powers, humble New York *Daily Bugle* newspaper photographer and computer web designer Peter Parker becomes the heroic superhero Spider-Man, using his newfound abilities to fight crime and assorted supervillains, besides finding time for his personal life with his girlfriend, Mary Jane, in this entirely computer-animated rendition of the classic Marvel Comics character.

Produced by Canada's Mainframe Entertainment, the half-hour series (also known as *Spider-Man: The Animated Series*), using bright lively colors and a nearly realistic neon-lit city set in the future, featured the web-spinning superhero in new adventures that picked up from the story of the blockbuster, live-action feature *Spider-Man* (2002), starring Tobey Maguire. Neil Patrick Harris (of TV's *Doogie Howser M.D.*) was cast as the voice of the title character, with Lisa Loeb as Mary Jane and Ian Ziering as Harry Osborn. Originally broadcast in prime time on MTV beginning in July 2003, the half-hour comic-book adaptation, featuring 13 episodes, aired until mid-September of that year. *A Mainframe Entertainment/CTDT Family Entertainment/Marvel Studios/Columbia TriStar-Sony Pictures Television/MTV Production. Color. Half-hour. Premiered on MTV: July 11, 2003–September 12, 2003.*

*Voices*
**Peter Parker/Spider-Man:** Neil Patrick Harris; **Mary Jane:** Lisa Loeb; **Harry Osborn:** Ian Ziering; **Indy Daimonji:** Angelle Brooks; **Agent Mosely:** Keith David; **Wilson Fisk/The Kingpin:** Michael Clarke Duncan; **Max Dillon/Electro:** Ethan Embry;

**Cheyenne Tate/Talon:** Eve; **Shikata:** Gina Gershon; **Silver Sable:** Virginia Madsen; **Billy Connors:** Christian Maguire; **Dr. Curt Connors/The Lizard:** Rob Zombie

## ◉ SPIDER-MAN UNLIMITED
When arch-villains Venom and Carnage hijack a Terran space shuttle crew launched into space above Counter-Earth, the famed Marvel Comics web-slinging superhero Spider-Man (alias Peter Parker) attempts to rescue them, but instead is drawn into battling the planet's tyrannical ruler the High Evolutionary and his old enemies Venom and Carnage, who are set on global domination in this action-adventure spin-off of 1994's *Spider-Man: The Animated Series*.

Unfortunately, the series faced some tough Saturday-morning competition opposite the Kids' WB!'s *Pokemon*, which overshadowed it in the weekly ratings. Unable to muster up better ratings, nearly a month after its debut, FOX removed the series, along with Columbia/TriStar Television's *Big Guy and Rusty the Boy Robot*, from its FOX Kids' Saturday-morning lineup, replacing them with Saban Entertainment's *The Avengers*, and added time slots for BKN's (Bohbot Kids Network) *Monster Rancher* and Toei Animation Co.'s *Digimon: Digital Monsters*. In December 2000, FOX resumed airing the program, but broadcast only the first 13 episodes, including the series' season-ending cliffhanger. As it was, the series was not renewed for a second season, even though Saban had already produced—but not animated—six episodes. Meanwhile, beginning in October 1999, the series was subsequently rebroadcast in three installments on cable's FOX Family Channel (renamed ABC Family in November 2001). *A Marvel Productions Ltd./Saban Entertainment/New World Entertainment Production. Color. Half-hour. Premiered on FOX: October 2, 1999–October 31, 1999; December 23, 2000–April 28, 2001. Rebroadcast on FOX FAM: October 2, 1999–May 31, 2001. Rebroadcast on ABC FAM: May 26, 2002–July 18, 2004.*

*Voices*
**Spider-Man/Peter Parker/The Goblin:** Rino Romano; **John Jameson:** John Payne; **Karen O'Malley:** Kimberly Hawthorne; **Daniel Bromley:** Christopher Gaze; **Dr. Naoko Yamada-Jones:** Akiko Morison; **Shayne Yamada-Jones:** Rhys Huber; **Lady Vermin of the Next-Men/Mary Jane Watson:** Jennifer Hale; **J. Jonah Jameson/High Evolutionary:** Richard Newman; **Carnage/Cletus Kasady:** Michael Donovan; **Lord Tyger:** David Sobolov; **Lady Ursula:** Tasha Simms; **Sir Ram:** Ron Halder; **Venom/Eddie Brock:** Brian Drummond; **Nick Fury:** Mark Gibbon

## ◉ SPIDER RIDERS
Wishing to do more than be indoors, even at school, young Hunter Steele's life changes for good when, after falling into the Inner World and overcoming his fear of spiders, he joins a team of consummate warriors known as the Spider Riders to defend their land from the evil Invectids, in this 52-episode half-hour series—geared for boys ages six to 12—from award-winning Japanese director Koichi Mashimo, and adapted from the book *Spider Riders—Shards of the Oracle* by Emmy award-winning writers Ted Anasti and Patsy Cameron-Anasti.

On June 17, 2006, the action-packed adventure series, coproduced by Canada's Cookie Jar Entertainment and Japanese animation studio Bee Train, producers of the popular cult favorite *hack. SIGN*, premiered on the CW Network's Kids' WB! Saturday-morning block, with an hour-long block of episodes broadcast the following Saturday, June 24, followed by a two-hour, four-episode marathon on July 1 before moving into its regular 10:30 A.M. time slot on July 8. *A Cookie Jar Entertainment, Inc./Yomiko Production. Color. Half-hour. Premiered on the CW (Kids' WB!): June 17, 2006.*

*Voices*

**RIDERS: Narrator:** Ron Pardo; **Hunter Steele:** Julie Lemieux; **Corona:** Stacey DePass; **Prince Lumen:** Cameron Ansell; **Princess Sparkle:** Melanie Tonello; **Igneous:** Tim Hamaguchi; **Magma:** Lyon Smith

**SPIDERS: Shadow:** Joseph Motiki; **Venus:** Caroly Larson

**INVECTID: Mantid:** Lawrence Bayne; **Buguese:** Jack Langedijk; **Grasshop:** Carman Melville; **Beerain:** Ellen-Ray Hennessey

## ◎ SPIDER-WOMAN

*Justice* magazine editor-publisher Jessica Drew spins herself into Spider-Woman to fight evil and nab supernatural foes, among them Tomand, ruler of the Realm of Darkness; the Great Magini; and The Fly. This half-hour adventure series was based on a character created by Stan Lee, creator of Marvel Comics' *The Amazing Spider-Man. A De Patie-Freleng Enterprises Production in association with Marvel Comics Group. Color. Half-hour. Premiered on ABC: September 22, 1979–March 1, 1980.*

*Voices*

**Jessica Drew/Spider-Woman:** Joan Van Ark; **Jeff Hunt, Jessica's photographer:** Bruce Miller; **Billy Drew, Jessica's nephew:** Bryan Scott; **Police Chief:** Lou Krugman; **Detective Miller:** Larry Carroll; **Announcer:** Dick Tufield

## ◎ THE SPIRAL ZONE

An international super force known as the 5 Zone Riders, headed by Commander Dirk Courage and joined by multiracial agents Max, Katarina, Razorback, Tank and Hiro, unite to battle their archrival, Overlord, a renegade scientist and his band of evil villains, the Black Widows, to preserve peace and freedom on Earth. This first-run daily syndicated series featured 65 original half-hour episodes. *An Atlantic-Kushner Locke Production in association with The Maltese Companies and Orbis. Color. Half-hour. Premiered: September 21, 1987–88. Syndicated.*

*Voices*

**Dirk Courage:** Dan Gilvezan; **Max:** Hal Rayle; **McFarland/Reaper:** Denny Delk; **Dr. Lawrence/Razorback:** Frank Welker; **Hiro:** Michael Bell; **Duchess Dire/Katerina/Mommy:** Mona Marshall; **Overlord/Tank/Bandit:** Neil Ross

## ◎ SPIRIT OF FREEDOM

To celebrate America's Bicentennial, legendary animator Shamus Culhane produced this series of three-minute animated vignettes tracing the nation's heritage. *A Shamus Culhane Production. Color. Three minutes. Syndicated: 1975.*

## ◎ SPONGEBOB SQUAREPANTS

Set in the undersea city of Bikini Bottom, a bright yellow, child-like, squeaky-clean, square sponge named SpongeBob SquarePants (who flips Krabbie Patties by day as a fry cook at the famed Krusty Krab fast-food eatery) cavorts with his underwater pals—the dim-witted Patrick Star; the oxygen-supported squirrel, Sandy Cheeks; the ill-tempered Squidward Tentacles, not to mention his boss, Krusty Krab himself—in this top-rated, long-running prime-time cartoon series.

Created by former Nickelodeon animator and creative director (*Rocko's Modern Life*) Stephen Hillenburg, the half-hour comedy series—originally called *SpongeBoy*—premiered on Nickelodeon's Saturday morning schedule in July 1999. Becoming an overnight sensation with viewers, especially after Nick shifted the series to weeknights two years later, the silly saltwater adventures attracted more than 2 million children, age two to 11, and more than 60 million viewers monthly. Avid viewers of the program included many well-known celebrities, among them, Jennifer Love Hewitt, Sigourney Weaver, Rob Lowe, Bruce Willis, Ellen DeGeneres and Jerry Lewis. In recognition of the program's success, the series has been honored with numerous awards, including a 2002 Television Critics Association award for best children's program and two Emmy Award nominations in 2003 and 2004 for outstanding animated program.

Yielding 80 episodes during its first four seasons, with Nick ordering 20 more for the 2006–07 season, Hillenburg's little under-the-sea sitcom consistently ranked among the most-watched weekly cable programs in the United States, including 12 half-hour animated specials that also aired on Nickelodeon: *Scaredy Pants/I Was a Teenage Gary* (1999); *Valentine's Day/The Paper* (2000); *Fools in April/Neptune Spatula* (2000); *Christmas Who?* (2000); *Shanghaiied (Your Wish Special)* (2001); *SpongeBob's House Party* (2002); *The Sponge Who Could Fly (The Lost Episode Special)* (2003); *SpongeBob BC (Before Comedy)* (2004); *and Have You Seen This Snail (Where's Gary?)* (2005), which officially kicked off the 2005–06 season of 20 new episodes, including two news specials, *Best Day Ever* (2006) and *Dunces and Dragons (Lost in Time)* (2006).

Besides becoming one of Nickelodeon's most licensed properties and producing merchandise featuring the famed Bikini Bottom residents, in November 2004 SpongeBob and company also starred in their first full-length animated feature, *The SpongeBob SquarePants Movie* (2004), with the $30 million film taking more than $85 million in revenue in the United States and more than $137 million worldwide.

Upon the conclusion of the 2004–05 season, Hillenburg bowed out of the series, and Nickelodeon continued to produce the program without him. In February 2006, a new series episode produced the program's highest ratings in five years. *A United Plankton Pictures Inc./Viacom Production. Color. Half-hour. Premiered on NICK: July 17, 1999. Rebroadcast on NICKT: May 1, 2002– .*

*Voices*

**SpongeBob SquarePants/Gary/Mr. SquarePants/Narrator:** Tom Kenny; **Mr. Eugene H. Krabs:** Clancy Brown; **Patrick Star:** Bill Fagerbakke; **Sandy Cheeks:** Carolyn Lawrence; **Squidward Tentacles:** Rodger Bumpass; **Plankton/Larry the Lobster/Other Voices:** Mr. Lawrence; **Pearl Krabs:** Lori Alan

## ◎ SPORT BILLY

A mascot of major international sports federations is sent to Earth to maintain goodwill and fair play for all those who are involved in sports. Aided by his female companion, Lilly, and pet dog, Willy, Billy crusades to keep the world of sports on the right track. *A Filmation Associates Production. Color. Half-hour. Premiered: June 1982. Syndicated. Premiered on NBC: July 31, 1982–September 11, 1982.*

*Voices*

**Sport Billy:** Lane Scheimer; **Sport Lilly/Queen Vanda:** Joyce Bulifant; **Willie/Sporticus XI:** Frank Welker

## ◎ SPUNKY AND TADPOLE

This series of investigative cliffhangers features the lanky lad Spunky and friend Tadpole, a real-life teddy bear, in 150 exciting five-minute adventures and tall tales first syndicated in 1958. In most markets the cartoons were shown on existing children's programs hosted by television station celebrities as well as independently in half-hour time slots. Ten episodes comprised one complete story. Hanna-Barbera voice legend Don Messick provided the voice

*A bright young lad and his teddy bear experience exciting adventures and tall tales in* Spunky and Tadpole. © *Beverly Film Corporation*

of Tadpole and most of the series' supporting characters. *A Beverly Hills Corporation TV Cinema Sales/Guild Films Production. Black-and-white. Color. Premiered: September 6, 1958. Syndicated.*

**Voices**
**Spunky:** Joan Gardner; **Tadpole:** Don Messick, Ed Janis

## ◎ SPY GROOVE

A pair of sophisticated secret agents, Agent 1 and Agent 2, wearing the latest name-brand fashions and brandishing the latest high-tech gadgets, find adventure and espionage traveling to exotic locales on top-secret missions in this adult-humor comedy series for MTV. Thirteen episodes of the series were completed for broadcast. *A MTV Animation Production. Color. Half-hour. Premiered on MTV: June 26, 2000–August 3, 2000.*

**Voices**
**Agent #1/Madre Blanco/Xappo Xerxes/Mr. Fish/Corey Haim:** Michael Gans; **Agent #2/Rock Debrie/Julio Blanco/Xippo Xerxes/Tommy Hilfiger:** Richard Register; **Mac:** Jessica Shaw; **Helena Troy:** Fuschia; **Narrator Carlo Fabrini:** Dean Elliott; **General/Hector Blanco:** Kevin Thomsen; **The Contessa:** Garet Scott; **Bunny von Schnickle:** Maggie Gans; **Jo Melekelikimaka:** Robyn Weiss

## ◎ SQUIDBILLIES

Led by ex-con Early Cuyler who tries reconciling with his son, Rusty, a modern-day family of poor inbred squids stranded in the rural North Georgia mountains lives in true redneck fashion, quickly adapting to the locals' reckless ways of drinking, feuding, fighting and fornicating in this series created by *Aqua Teen Hunger Force* cocreator David Willis and *The Brak Show* cocreator Jim Fortier.

This weekly series was one of three new programs, created by Atlanta-based Williams Street and added to Cartoon Network's *Adult Swim* late-night lineup in November 2005, opposite *Perfect Hair Forever* and *12 Oz. Mouse*. The concept of the CGI-animated, half-hour series was first announced in 2004, with the pilot heavily promoted and originally set to premiere that November on *Adult Swim*. With the script for the pilot undergoing numerous rewrites and producers not sold on the finished product, the pilot was subsequently scrapped and Cartoon Network aired another Williams Street-produced pilot called *Squidbillies* in its place. In 2004, footage of the show was previewed at San Diego's ComiCon and Atlanta's

Dragon Con to mixed results, with a rough cut of the pilot airing on the Cartoon Network in April 2005 during *Adult Swim*. On Sunday, October 16, 2005, the series premiered at midnight with its first episode, entitled "This Show Is Called Squidbillies," with 20 episodes ordered for the first season. *A Williams Street Production. Color. Half-hour. Premiered on CAR: October 16, 2005.*

**Voices**
**Early Cuyler:** Danny "Unknown Hinson" Baker; **Russell "Rusty" Cuyler:** Daniel McDevitt; **Granny:** Dana Snyder; **Lil:** Patricia French; **Sheriff:** Charlies Napier (Episodes 1–9), Bobby F. Ellerbee; **Dan Halen:** Todd Hanson; **Reverend:** Scott Hilley; **Clerk:** Pete Smith; **Narrator:** Dave Willis

## ◎ SQUIGGLEVISION

This revamped follow-up version to ABC's Saturday-morning series *Science Court* combined science, comedy and the courtroom to educate young viewers. The weekly half-hour spin-off featured three educational segments, one of which was "Science Court," along with two new components: "See You Later, Estimator," offering math lessons by Professor Parsons, and "Fizz and Martha's Last Word," highlighting the word-of-the-day. Like its predecessor, the new series was coproduced by noted radio and television broadcaster Tom Snyder, who created the limited-animation method called "Squigglevision," which imposes a constant zigzag movement of squiggly black lines on the characters' mouths and bodies and is the technique for which the series was named. The Saturday-morning program ran for two seasons. *A Tom Snyder Productions/Burns & Burns Production. Color. Half-hour. Premiered on ABC: September 12, 1998–September 2, 2000.*

**Voices**
**Judge Stone:** Paula Poundstone; **Doug Savage:** Bill Braudis; **Alison Krempel:** Paula Plum; **Professor Parsons:** H. Jon Benjamin; **Stenographer Fred:** Fred Stoller; **Other Voices:** Jennifer Schulman

## ◎ SQUIRREL BOY

*Duckman* creator Everett Peck (who also served as executive producer) returned to television with this series of wacky neighborhood misadventures of 10-year-old Andy and his brainy furry "pest" friend, Rodney, a mischievous, know-it-all squirrel, accompanied by Rodney's squirrel pal, Leon (voiced by Tom Kenny, the voice of Nickelodeon's *SpongeBob SquarePants*). Debuting in May 2006 on Cartoon Network as a half-hour Summer Preview Special featuring two episodes, "Line in the Sandwich" and "Tree for Two," the 13-episode half-hour comedy series began airing weeknights at 7 P.M. in July of that year. That December, the series switched to airing Monday through Thursdays at 9:30 P.M. Also tapped to voice the series were Richard Horvitz (*Invader ZIM*) as Rodney J. Squirrel, Pamela S. Adlon (Disney's *Teacher's Pet*) as Andy Johnson and Kurtwood Smith (*That '70s Show*) as Andy's father. *A Cartoon Network Studios Production. Color. Half-hour. Premiered on CAR: May 29, 2006 (special); July 14, 2006 (series).*

**Voices**
**Andy Johnson:** Pamela Adlon; **Rodney J. Squirrel:** Richard Steven Horvitz; **Mr. Johnson:** Kurtwood Smith; **Mrs. Johnson:** Nancy Sullivan; **Leon:** Tom Kenny; **Salty Mike:** Carlos Alazraqui; **Kyle:** Billy West; **Oscar:** Jason Spisak; **Archie the Rabbit:** Charles Shaughnessy

## ◎ STANLEY

Aided by his conversations with his pet goldfish Dennis, his best friend and confidant, a highly imaginative, creative boy named Stanley, who lives with his loving and supportive parents and his older brother, learns many important lessons by observing how his favorite animals handle similar situations and then applying what he has learned to his life, bolstering his self-confidence and personal growth in this popular, interactive preschool series. Featuring two 15-minute segments per half-hour, the program dealt with a variety of issues facing preschool-age children, from handling growth and rules to working with others. Developed and coproduced by Jim Jinkins and David Campbell through their new independent company, Cartoon Pizza, and based on famed British author Andrew Griff's popular children's book series, the 65-episode series became one of the highest rated preschool programs for the Disney Channel's *Playhouse Disney* program block. Actor Charles Shaughnessy, the voice of Dennis, won an Emmy Award in 2002 for his performance in the series. *A Jumbo Pictures/Cartoon Cola/Cartoon Pizza/Walt Disney Television Animation Production. Color. Half-hour. Premiered on DIS: September 15, 2001–June 12, 2005; May 2, 2006.*

**Voices**
**Stanley:** Jessica D. Stone; **Dennis:** Charles Shaughnessy; **Mimi/Marcy:** Khylan Jones; **Dad:** David Landsberg; **Harry:** Rene Mujica; **Lionel:** Shawn Pyfrom; **Elsie:** Hynden; **Ms. Diaz:** Candi Milo; **Mom:** Ari Myers; **Lester:** Philece Sampler

## ◎ STARBLAZERS

Actually Japan's *Space Battleship Yamato* series dubbed into English, this adventure series—set in the year 2199—chronicles the story of a group of patriots, known as Star Force, whose mission is to save Earth from an enemy space fleet. Heading the Star Force fleet is Captain Avatar, whose crew includes Cadet Derek Wildstar, the second-in-command; Nova, Wildstar's girlfriend and the team's radar operator; Cadet Mark Venture, chief of operations; IQ-9, a robot (nicknamed "Tin-Wit" for his good sense of humor); Sandor, the chief mechanic; and Dr. Sane, the team's physician. First offered in U.S. syndication in 1979, the series was comprised of 26 original *Space Battleship Yamato* episodes, previously aired on Japanese television, plus a group of 26 new half-hours produced in 1977. The combined 52 episodes were packaged together and syndicated to selected major markets by Claster Television, which originally considered retitling the series *Star Force.* In 1984 the series returned with 25 new episodes. *An Office Academy/Sunwagon Production in association with Claster Television and Westchester Films Inc. Star Blazers is a registered trademark of Westchester Films Inc. Color. Half-hour. Premiered: September 10, 1979–80; September 8, 1984–85. Syndicated.*

## ◎ STARCOM: THE US SPACE FORCE

A peacekeeping force in a planetary community uses ultra-sophisticated vehicles and state-of-the-art technology to combat the sinister Emperor Dark and his Shadow Force of evil warriors and robot drones in this first-run syndicated series that debuted in 1987. Lasting only 13 weeks in syndication, the series was repeated on the Family Channel beginning in 1993. *A DIC Enterprises Production in association with Coca-Cola Television. Color. Half-hour. Premiered: September 20, 1987–September 1988. Syndicated. Rebroadcast 1989–91 on FAM: September 19, 1993–94.*

**Voices**
**Dash:** Rob Cowan; **Crowbar/Torvak:** Robert Cait; **Slim:** Phil Aikin; **Kelsey:** Susan Roman; **Vondar:** Marvin Goldhar; **Malvanna:** Elva May Hoover; **Col. Brickley:** Don Francks; **Klag:** Dan Hennessey; **Romak:** Louis DiBianco

## ◎ STARGATE INFINITY

Stargate Command Major Gus Bonner and his four young Air Force Academy pilots fight to clear their commander's good name (after he is wrongfully found guilty of treason for a crime he did not commit) in order to return to Earth while they guard a strange, mysterious alien who holds the key to the secrets of Stargate and find a new portal to take them back home in this futuristic animated action/adventure series set three decades after the popular live-action feature film and Showtime television series. Coproduced by DIC Entertainment and MGM in association with 4Kids Entertainment, this 26-episode, Saturday-morning science fiction fantasy series aired for one season on FOX and was subsequently syndicated as part of a package with other DIC cartoon shows. *A DIC Entertainment/MGM/4Kids Entertainment Production. Color. Half-hour. Premiered on FOX: September 14, 2002–March 15, 2003. Syndicated.*

**Voices**
**Major Gus Bonner:** Dale Wilson; **Draga:** Kathleen Barr; **R.J. Harrison:** Mark Hildreth; **Pahk'kal:** Mackenzie Gray; **Seattle Montoya:** Bettina Busch; **Other Voices:** Mark Archeson, Jim Byrnes, Tifanie Christian, Gus Gould, Ron Halder, Kimberly Hawthorne, Blue Mankuma, Cusse Mankuma, Moneca Stori, Lee Tockar, Cathy Weseluck

## ◎ STAR TREK

The indomitable Captain James T. Kirk; his pointy-eared science officer Spock; chief engineer Scotty; Dr. Leonard McCoy; and the crew of the U.S.S. *Enterprise* probe outer space, where they encounter intelligent aliens and new civilizations and battle sophisticated forces of evil in this half-hour animated version that premiered on NBC in 1973. The cartoon spinoff from the cult live-action series earned an Emmy Award in 1975 (for the episode "Yesteryear"), with the stars of the original voicing their own characters. (The character of Ensign Paval Chekov, played by actor Walter Koenig, did not appear on the animated series.) Two new characters were added to this animated version: Arrex, a three-legged alien, and M'Ress, a feline being. Budgeted at $75,000 per episode, the 22-episode series ran for two seasons on NBC. The series was later rebroadcast on Nickelodeon, Sci-Fi Channel's *Cartoon Quest* and TV Land. *A Filmation Studios Production in association with Norway/Paramount Pictures Television. Color. Half-hour. Premiered on NBC: September 8, 1973–August 30, 1975. Rebroadcast on NICK: May 31, 1986–August 5, 1989. Rebroadcast on SCI: September 27, 1992–March 26, 1994. Rebroadcast on TV Land: 1999.*

**Voices**
**Capt. James T. Kirk:** William Shatner; **Science Officer Spock:** Leonard Nimoy; **Dr. Leonard McCoy:** DeForest Kelley; **Chief Engineer Montgomery Scott:** James Doohan; **Nurse Christine Chapel:** Majel Barrett; **Lieutenant Sulu:** George Takei; **Arrex:** James Doohan; **M'Ress:** Majel Barrett

## ◎ STAR WARS: CLONE WARS

Brilliantly animated continuing saga, set between the live-action *Star Wars* prequels, *Star Wars—Episode II: Attack of the Clones* (2002) and *Star Wars—Episode III: Revenge of the Sith* (2005), of young Anakin Skywalker's rise to power during the epic Clone Wars and the battle of the valiant Jedi Knights and the republic's Clone Army against a new band of evil separatists; of Anakin's would-be assassin, the Dark Jedi Asajj Ventress, and Yoda's dangerous rescue of fellow Jedis, Barris Offee and Luminara Unduli, joined by Padme Amidala, C-3PO and R2-D2—as told in 25 two- to three-minute "chapters" in this science-fiction microseries made for the Cartoon Network by Emmy award-winning animator Genndy Tartakovsky (*The Powerpuff Girls, Samurai Jack*) in partnership with *Star Wars* creator George Lucas's studio, Lucasfilm. The first 10 chapters debuted weekdays at 8 P.M. ET, November 7–21, 2003, followed by the March 26–April 8, 2004, premiere of chapters 11–20 with subsequent episodes airing weeknights and a Friday and Saturday marathon. Receiving a prime-time Emmy Award for outstanding animated program (for more than one hour) in 2004, five new 12-minute chapters, setting the stage for the May 19 release of the feature-length theatrical prequel, *Star Wars–Episode III: Revenge of the Sith*, aired nightly at 7 P.M. from Monday, March 21 to Friday, March 25, 2005. On Saturday, March 26, all five chapters were repeated back-to-back. Since then, Lucas produced an all-new CG-animated feature film, *Star Wars: The Clone Wars*, to premiere in August 2008, followed by the television debut of a new series in the fall. *A Cartoon Network Studios/Lucasfilm Production. Color. Three minutes. Premiered on CAR: November 7, 2003–March 25, 2005.*

*Voices*

**THE REPUBLIC: Anakin Skywalker:** Mat Lucas; **Obi-Wan Kenobi:** James Arnold Taylor; **Yoda:** Tom Kane; **Mace Windu:** T.C. Carson; **Ki-Adi-Mundi/Daakman Barrek:** Daran Norris; **K'Kruhk:** Kevin Michael Richardson; **Luminara Unduli:** Cree Summer; **Barris Offee:** Tatyana Yassukovich; **Padmé Amidala/ Shaak Ti:** Grey DeLisle; **Captain Typho:** André Sogliuzzo; **Chancellor Palpatine:** Nick Jameson; **C-3PO:** Anthony Daniels

**THE CONFEDERACY OF INDEPENDENT SYSTEMS: Count Dooku/San Hill:** Corey Burton; **General Grievous:** John DiMaggio (Chapter 20), Richard McGonagle (Chapters 21–25); **Asaji Ventress:** Grey DeLisle; **Durge:** Daran Norris

### ⊚ STATIC SHOCK

After being exposed to a gas that gives him electromagnetic superpowers, fast-thinking Dakota teen Virgil Hawkins, as the urban superhero Static, tries making a difference in the community by fighting crime and other problems confronting kids, from peer pressure to gangs, aided by best friend Richie in this animated series based on the popular comic book series by cocreator Dwayne McDuffie, who retained creative control over the series' plot and characterization and also wrote some of the episodes.

Premiering September 26, 2000, the science fiction action-adventure Saturday-morning series produced high ratings, featuring 52 action-packed episodes during its four-season run on the WB Television Network's Kids' WB! Besides regularly including other characters from the comic book in the animated series, many other DC Comics superheroes, including Batman and Green Lantern, appeared in various episodes along with many real-life guest stars, such as NBA basketball great Shaquille O'Neal and popular recording artist Lil' Romero, who performed the show's theme song in its final two seasons. Nominated for two awards, including three Emmys in 2003 and 2004 (winning twice for outstanding achievement in music direction and composition), the series was rebroadcast on Cartoon Network as part of its *Miguzi* program block beginning in September 2004. *A DC Comics/Warner Bros. Television Animation Production. Color. Half-hour. Premiered on the WB (Kids' WB!): September 26, 2000–August 21, 2004. Rebroadcast on CAR: September 27, 2004–.*

*Voices*

**Virgil Ovid Hawkins/Static Shock:** Phil LaMarr; **Robert Hawkins:** Kevin Michael Richardson; **Sharon Hawkins:** Michelle Morgan; **Trina Jessup:** Sheryl Lee Ralph; **Richard "Richie" Osgood Foley/Gear:** Jason Marsden; **Adam Evans/ Rubberband Man:** Kadeem Hardison; **Shenice Vale/She-Bang:** Rosslynn Taylor Jordan; **Anansi the Spider:** Carl Lumbly; **Morris Grant/Soul Power:** Brock Peters; **Phillip Rollins/Sparky:** Rodney Saulsberry

### ⊚ STEVEN SPIELBERG PRESENTS ANIMANIACS

Created in the 1930s but considered so wild that they were locked in the Warner Bros. studio water tower, three zany offspring—brothers Yakko and Wakko and their sister Dot—are finally set free, running amok at the studio every day and creating havoc in this half-hour comedy/musical series originally produced for FOX Network. The successor to Steven Spielberg's *Tiny Toon Adventures*, the series featured two to three cartoon shorts a day starring the three Warner siblings, Rita and Runt (a cat and dog who live at the studio), the Goodfeathers (three pigeons), Slappy Squirrel (an old-time sassy female brought out of retirement) and the studio CEO, guard, nurse and psychologist.

Spielberg helped create the characters and added his input between directing the blockbuster hit movie *Jurassic Park*, and the NBC live-action series *seaQuest DSV*, reading every script and approving every cartoon before it aired. Sixty-five episodes were initially ordered for the series, which premiered on FOX Network in September 1993. The series moved to the WB Television Network in 1995, where 13 new episodes were ordered to kick off new kids' fall lineup. In January 1997, Cartoon Network aired the series in a two-hour time slot for four consecutive Friday night prime-time showings along with *Freakazoid!*, *Pinky & the Brain* and *Superman* and continuing airing the program until August 2001. Nickelodeon then bought the rights to the series, rebroadcasting it for nearly four years on Nick and Nicktoons. The show was honored with three Emmy Awards for outstanding animated program during its original run.

In the spring of 1994, the crazy nutsos (Yakko, Wakko and Dot) starred in their first and—to date—only theatrical cartoon short, "I'm Mad." (See Theatrical Cartoon Series section for details.) The short, about the travails of taking the bickering siblings on a car trip, made its television debut on November 12, 1994 on FOX's Saturday edition of the series. *A Warner Bros. Television Animation Production. Color. Half-hour. Premiered on FOX: September 20, 1993–September 13, 1995. Rebroadcast on the WB: September 9, 1995–May 9, 1998. Rebroadcast on CAR: January 24, 1997–August 24, 2001. Rebroadcast on NICK: September 3, 2001–02. Rebroadcast on NICKT: May 1, 2002–May 15, 2005.*

*Voices*

**Yakko Warner/Pinky/Dr. Otto Scratchansniff:** Rob Paulsen; **Wakko Warner:** Jess Harnell; **Dot Warner/Hello Nurse/Marita Hippo:** Tress MacNeille; **Bobby Pigeon:** John Marino; **Pesto Pigeon:** Chick Vennera; **The Brain/Squit Pigeon:** Maurice LaMarche; **Ralph the Guard/The C.E.O./Buttons/Runt/Flavio Hippo/Chicken Boo:** Frank Welker; **Slappy Squirrel:** Sherri Stoner; **Skippy:** Nathan Ruegger; **Rita:** Bernadette Peters; **Mindy:** Nancy Cartwright; **Minerva Mink:** Julie Brown; **Newt:** Arte Johnson; **Albert Einstein:** Paul Rugg; **Narrator:** Jim Cummings, Tom Bodett; **Sid the Squid:** Jack Burns; **Katie Kaboom:** Laura Mooney; **Katie's Mom:** Mary Gross; **Beanie the Bison:** Avery Schreiber

### ⊚ STEVEN SPIELBERG PRESENTS FREAKAZOID!

In this comic take on the superhero genre, computer geek Dexter Douglas is an easygoing teenager who, while surfing the Internet, gets sucked into his computer and comes as out as the costumed, uncontrollable, unpredictable high-strung superhero, Freakazoid! in this series of offbeat and witty half-hour action adventures developed and produced by Steven Spielberg in association with Warner Bros. television animation. The series—which the producers treated like a series of half-hour "pilots"—premiered on the WB Television Network in September 1995 and was the centerpiece of the network's Kids WB Saturday lineup, which included *Steven*

*Spielberg Presents Pinky & the Brain, The Sylvester and Tweety Mysteries* and *Earthworm Jim.*

Produced in association with six different animation houses, the series, featuring 24 half-hours, lasted one full season and part of a second season before it was canceled due to low ratings. Originally the series was to be produced as a straight superhero action/adventure series with comedic overtones, as first conceived by animator Bruce Timm, but Spielberg nixed the idea, wanting instead a show that topped *Animaniacs.* Reruns were shown on Cartoon Network. *A Warner Bros. Television Animation Production. Color. Half-hour. Premiered on the WB (Kids' WB!): September 9, 1995–November 29, 1996. Rebroadcast on CAR: January 31, 1997–March 28, 2003.*

**Voices**
**Freakazoid!:** Paul Rugg; **Announcer:** Joe Leahy; **Sgt. Mike Cosgrove:** Ed Asner; **Dexter Douglas:** David Kaufman; **Debbie Douglas:** Tress MacNeille; **Douglas Douglas:** John P. McCann; **Duncan Douglas:** Googy Gress; **Steph:** Tracy Rowe; **The Lobe:** David Warner; **Lord Bravery/Cave Guy/Candle Jack/The Huntsman:** Jeff Bennet; **Fan Boy:** Stephen Furst; **Armondo Guittierez:** Ricardo Montalban; **Longhorn:** Maurice LaMarche; **Foamy the Freakadog:** Frank Welker

## ⦿ STEVEN SPIELBERG PRESENTS PINKY & THE BRAIN

Two lab mice—one the genuis (The Brain), the other insane (Pinky)—who live at Acme Labs plan to take over the world in order to prove their mousey worth in this half-hour animated spinoff of Warner Bros. *Animaniacs.* Featuring three seven-minute cartoons each half-hour, the series premiered on the WB Television Network in September of 1995 and was so successful that it was moved to a prime-time, Sunday-night time slot that same season. Produced that year was the pair's first and only prime-time special, *A Pinky and the Brain Christmas,* which won an Emmy Award for outstanding animated program. In the 1996–97 season, the series began offering full-length stories instead of a brace of cartoon shorts in each half-hour. Sixty-five episodes alone were produced through the 1996–97 season, with 40 new episodes filmed for the 1997–98 season, when the show aired weekdays and Saturday nights. *A Warner Bros. Television Animation Production. Color. Half-hour. Premiered on the WB: September 9, 1995–September 3, 1999. Rebroadcast on CAR: February 7, 1997.*

**Voices**
**Pinky:** Rob Paulsen; **The Brain:** Maurice LaMarche

## ⦿ STEVEN SPIELBERG PRESENTS TINY TOON ADVENTURES

Rambunctious adolescent versions of beloved Warner Bros. characters—Buster Bunny (Bugs), Plucky Duck (Daffy), Hampton (Porky), Dizzy Devil (Tazmanian Devil)—run wild as they attend Acme University in this next generation of classic Looney Tunes, which featured recurring characters such as Pinky and the Brain (who were subsequently spun off into their own series), Slappy Squirrel, Mindy and Buttons and Rita and Runt.

Premiering on 135 stations in September of 1990, the syndicated series was a gigantic hit for Warner Bros. Cartoons, which produced the series in association with filmmaker Steven Spielberg, who helped develop characters and stories and critiqued each show before it was finished. (Spielberg himself appeared, in animated form, in the 1991 episode "Buster and Babs Go Hawaiian.") Aiming for a higher quality than its industry competitors, the series used more animation cels (single-frame drawings) than other Saturday-morning or syndicated cartoon series: 25 per frame versus the standard 12.

Initially 65 episodes were produced for the series (which earned two Emmys for outstanding animated program). Thirteen more were produced for the 1991–92 season (as was the CBS prime-time special *Tiny Toon Adventures: The Looney Beginning*), and 22 more for the start of the 1992–93 season, when the series joined FOX Network's FOX Kids lineup in September 1993. The characters starred in a brace of FOX prime-time animated specials as well: *It's a Wonderful Tiny Toons Christmas* (1992), *How I Spent My Vacation* (1993), *Tiny Toons Spring Break Special* (1994) and the Emmy-nominated hour-long, *Tiny Toons' Night Ghoulery* (1995), which pokes fun at horror anthology TV series like *Night Gallery* and *The Twilight Zone.* In 1995, the series opened its third season on the WB Television Network's new Kids' WB! weekday afternoon program block with 13 new episodes. An additional 18 original episodes were produced thereafter over the next few seasons and the Kids' WB! continued to air the series until cancelling it in 1998 (the last new *Animaniacs* episode aired that November). Meanwhile, in 1995, all 100 *Tiny Toon Adventures* began reairing weekdays on Nickelodeon until September 1997. In 1999, Cartoon Network began rebroadcasting the series until 2001 before returning to Nickelodeon from 2002 to 2004 and then airing on Nick's sister channel, Nicktoons. *Premiered: September 14, 1990–September 1992. Syndicated. Premiered on FOX: September 14, 1992 (part of The Plucky Ducky Show September 19, 1992–November 24, 1992)–September 8, 1995. Premiered on the WB (Kids WB!): September 9, 1995–September 8, 1998. Rebroadcast on NICK: September 15, 1995–September 1997; 2002–04. Rebroadcast on CAR: 1999–2001. Rebroadcast on NICKT: 2004–05 (weekdays).*

**Voices**
**Buster Bunny:** Charlie Adler; **Babs Bunny:** Tress MacNeille; **Plucky Duck:** Joe Alaskey; **Hamton J. Pig:** Don Messick; **Montana Max:** Danny Cooksey; **Elmyra Duff:** Cree Summer; **Dizzy Devil:** Maurice LaMarche; **Shirley the Loon:** Gail Matthius; **Sweetie:** Candi Milo; **Blink/Arnold/Fowlmouth:** Rob Paulsen; **Fifi Le Fume/Sneezer:** Kath Soucie; **Furrball/Calamity Coyote/Gogo/Dodo/Little Beeper:** Frank Welker

## ⦿ STICKIN' AROUND

These segments began as a series of one-minute interstitial adventures of imaginary stick figures from the mind of eight-year-old Stacy Stickler and her best friend, Bradley, used to punctuate CBS's 1994–95 Saturday-morning lineup. Created by Robin Steele (of MTV's *Stick Figure Theatre* fame) and Brianne Leary, the segments were expanded to a full half-hour series airing on the Fox Network. Premiering in the fall of 1997, the series, animated to resemble a self-created coloring book, with stick figures drawn against a background of crayon, paste and photocollage, revolved around heartfelt commentaries of growing up in the 1990s, as only kids can tell it. *A Nelvana Limited/Ellipse Animation/Prima TV, Italy Production. Color. Half-hour. Premiered on CBS: September 1994 (interstitials). Premiered on FOX: September 26, 1997–November 29, 1997 (series). Rebroadcast on FAM/FOX FAM: 1998–1999.*

**Voices**
**Stacy:** Ashley Taylor; **Bradley:** Ashley Brown; **Stella:** Catherine Disher; **Stanley:** Phillip Williams; **Lance:** Andrew Craig; **Russell:** Amos Crawley; **Polly:** Marianna Galati; **Mr. Doddler:** Nicholas Rice

## ⦿ THE STONE PROTECTORS

Five teenage rock band musicians (Cornelius, Clifford, Angus, Maxwell and Chester), transformed into superpowered, troll-like creatures by powerful gemstones try to save the planet Mythrandi from the evil warlords Zok and Zinc, in this half-hour series produced for syndication. *A Graz Entertainment Production in association with Ace Novelty Co. Inc./Fantasy, Ltd./Liu Concept Design and Associates. Color. Half-hour. Premiered: 1993. Syndicated.*

**Voices**
Don Brown, Ted Cole, Scott McNeil, Cathy Weseluck, Rob Morton, Jim Byrnes, Ian Corlett, John Tench, Terry Klassen, Louise Vallance, Cam Lane

### ◎ STOP THE SMOGGIES!
A moppet-headed bunch of happy little heroes known as the Suntots find their picturesque coral island is threatened by pollution with the arrival of the garbage-strewing villainous trio—the "Smoggies"—in this groundbreaking 52-episode half-hour series created and directed by Oscar nominee Gerry Potterton. A top-rated show in Canada, both in French- and English-language versions, and in the United Kingdom, the series was sold to more than 40 territories worldwide and earned favorable reviews for its imaginative scripts, environmental content and liquid animation techniques. The first animation production to deal with the environment, the series premiered in the United States via nationwide syndication in 1991 and was subsequently rebroadcast on HBO. *A CINAR/Initial Groupe Production. An Initial Audiovisual/CINAR Films/Antenne 2 Production. Color. Half-hour. Premiered: September 8, 1991. Syndicated. Rebroadcast on HBO: June 24, 1994.*

**Voices**
Teddy Lee Dillon, Brian Dooley, Richard Dumont, Karen Marginson, Walter Massey, Stephanie Morgenstern, Joan Orenstein, Harvey Berger, Pier Paquette

### ◎ STORYBOOK CLASSICS
Well-known motion picture, stage and television personalities narrated this stunning collection of 13 half-hour specials (not 18 as erroneously reported elsewhere) adapted from classic children's stories, produced for home video, then broadcast on Showtime between 1989 and 1991.

Rabbit Ears Video (producers of *American Heroes & Legends, Holiday Classics* and *We All Have Tales* series) produced this series revisiting the worlds of master storytellers such as Rudyard Kipling, Beatrix Potter and Hans Christian Andersen. Each episode was backed by musical scores and animated by a different illustrator. The series included such award-winning specials as "Red Riding Hood and Goldilocks," "The Ugly Duckling," "The Tale of Peter Rabbit and the Tale of Mr. Jeremy Fisher," "The Three Billy Goats Gruff and The Three Little Pigs." "The Fisherman and His Wife," "The Velveteen Rabbit," "How the Leopard Got His Spots," "The Emperor and the Nightingale," "Thumbelina," "The Emperor's New Clothes," "How the Rhinoceros Got His Skin/How the Camel Got His Hump," "The Elephant's Child" and "The Steadfast Tin Soldier."

Celebrity narrators included Danny Glover, Jodie Foster, Jack Nicholson, Jeremy Irons, Kelly McGillis, Holly Hunter, Meg Ryan, Meryl Streep and John Gielgud. (See individual entries in Animated Television Specials section for more details.) *A Rabbit Ears Video Production. Color. Half-hour. Premiered on Showtime: 1989–1991.*

### ◎ STORY TIME
Series of engagingly animated on-air and online interstitials or short one-minute segments, using a storytelling format with celebrities reading stories to help develop language and critical thinking skills and fire up the imaginations of young viewers ages three to seven. Programmed between other animated fare on the commercial-free children's network, Noggin, each episode featured familiar fairy tales with additional sequels told in "chapters," narrated by children in animated form, including *Jack and the Beanstalk, The Three Little Pigs* and others. The daily series premiered on Noggin in early April 2003 and aired for nearly four full seasons. *A Noggin Presentation. Color. One minute. Premiered on NOG: April 9, 2003–January 10, 2007.*

### ◎ STRAWBERRY SHORTCAKE: THE SERIES
Based on the top-selling girl's brand created by American Greetings, the impish Strawberry Shortcake returns with her good friends Orange Blossom, Ginger Snap, Angel Cake and Huckleberry Pie in exciting new adventures in and around the magical world of Strawberryland in this traditionally animated half-hour series—and second incarnation of the characters after a series of animated specials in the 1980s—that premiered Saturday mornings on FOX in 2003 and was syndicated three years later. In addition to the weekly series, in 2003 HBO aired a trio of brand-new hour-long animated specials featuring the good-hearted and lovable characters: *Meet Strawberry Shortcake, Get Well Adventure* and *Berry, Merry Christmas;* a few other direct-to-video specials were made but never aired. *A DIC Entertainment Production. Color. Half-hour. Premiered on FOX: March 29, 2003. Syndicated: January 2, 2006.*

**Voices**
**Strawberry Shortcake:** Sarah Heinke; **Orange Blossom:** Dejare Barfield; **Huckleberry:** Daniel Canfield; **Pupcake/Pet Sounds:** Nils Haaland; **Honey Pie Pony:** Hannah Koslosky; **Custard the Cat:** Sarah Koslosky; **Apple Dumplin':** Katie Labosky; **Ginger Snap:** Samantha Triba; **Angel Cake:** Rachel Ware

### ◎ STREET FIGHTER
Based on the fastest-selling video game in history of the same name. Former UN Forces leader Colonel Guile and his team of martial-arts street fighters (Chun Lii, Dee Jay. T. Hawk, Ken and Ryu) do battle with a secret criminal organization—the big, bad Bison and his no-good gang, Shadowru—in this half-hour action/adventure series that premiered on USA Network's Saturday morning *Cartoon Express. A Manga Entertainment Capcom U.S.A. Production in association with Graz Entertainment/USA Network. Color. Half-hour. Premiered on USA: October 21, 1995–July 26, 1998.*

**Voices (main cast)**
Kathleen Barr, Lisa Ann Beley, Paul Dobson, Michael Donovan, Tong Lung, Scott McNeil, Richard Newman, John Payne, Donna Yamamoto

### ◎ STREET SHARKS
Accidentally transformed into monstrous half shark, half humans during an illegal experiment that used an untested DNA genetic formula, four crimefighting brothers join forces to protect the world from the disastrous designs the evil scientist plans to unleash in this 13-episode, half-hour action/adventure series based on top-selling action figures. Introduced as a three-part miniseries in first-run syndication in the spring of 1994, the program went weekly in the fall of 1995 as part of the weekend cartoon block, *Amazin' Adventures II.* In 1996 the series was added to ABC's Saturday morning lineup (in reruns) for a brief run (it was replaced by Disney's *Mighty Ducks: The Animated Series*) while the original syndicated series reaired on USA Network. *A Surge Entertainment/StreetWise Designs/DIC Entertainment/Bohbot Production. Color. Half-hour. Premiered: (week of) September 4, 1995 (part of Amazin' Adventures II). Syndicated. Rebroadcast on ABC: September 14, 1996–October 26, 1996. Rebroadcast on USA: September 22, 1996.*

*Voices*
**Dr. Piranoid:** J. Michael Lee; **Slammu/Slobster/Killamari:** D. Kevin Williams; **Streex:** Andy Rannells; **Slash:** Terry Berner; **Lena:** Pam Carter; **Bends:** Jim Hoggatt; **Guy in the Sky:** Tony Wike

## STRESSED ERIC

Follows the chaotic trials and tribulations of Eric Feeble, a middle-class divorced father of two who lives in America (in London in the original British version) and is literally stressed out by his family—precocious, allergic daughter, Claire; nerdish son, Brian; and psychopathic ex-wife, Liz—his coworkers, and everything else in between in this animated comedy series, first shown on the United Kingdom's BBC2 in early 1998.

Produced by Hollywood's Klasky Csupo in association with Absolutely Productions and becoming its first animated series marketed outside the United States, the widely acclaimed series, which critics overseas touted as Britain's answer to *The Simpsons*, aired in the United States that summer after NBC bought the broadcasting rights to the series. In the U.S. version, actor Hank Azaria was hired to revoice the character Eric. Becoming NBC's first prime-time cartoon series broadcast since Hanna-Barbera Productions' 1982 show *Joke Book*, the program unfortunately produced lukewarm ratings and was unceremoniously yanked after only four episodes. *An Absolutely Productions/Klasky Csupo/Novanim Animation and Digital Services Production. Color. Half-hour. Premiered on NBC: August 12, 1998–August 26, 1998.*

*Voices*
**Eric Feeble:** Hank Azaria; **Claire Feeble/Heather Perfect:** Morwenna Banks; **Maria/Allison:** Doon McKichan; **Liz:** Rebecca Front; **Ray Perfect:** Xander Armstrong; **Mrs. Perfect:** Alison Steadman; **Paul Power (P.P.):** Geoff McGivern; **Doc:** Paul Shearer

## STRIPPERELLA

An exotic dancer by day for the popular strip club Tenderloins, by night Erotica Jones (voiced by Pamela Anderson) is the superhero Stripperella (also known as Agent 69), who, working for the secret agency FUGG with Chief Stroganoff and his technicians, Hal and Bernard, fights crime in this half-hour adult cartoon fantasy/adventure series created by legendary Marvel Comics artist Stan Lee and produced by his company, POW! Entertainment. Rated TV-MA for adult content, including adult situations and nudity, the program premiered on Spike TV as part of *The Strip*, a two-hour prime-time block of adult-oriented cartoon programming aimed at mature male viewers in the spring of 2003 and lasted only one season. *A POW! Entertainment/Viacom International Production. Color. Half-hour. Premiered on TNN/Spike TV: June 26, 2003–April 1, 2004.*

*Voices*
**Erotica Jones/Stripperella:** Pamela Anderson; **Giselle/Various Others:** Jill Talley; **Special Agent 14/Various Others:** Tom Kenny; **Chief Stroganoff/Leonard/Various Others:** Maurice LaMarche; **Persephone Cliché:** Sirena Irwin; **Clifton/Various Others:** Jon Cryer; **Cheapo:** Jon Lovitz

## STROKER & HOOP

Comical misadventures of a bumbling private eye named Stroker, who still hasn't mastered lock-picking, car-hood sliding or preventing his gun from falling out of his waistband when bending over, and his self-proclaimed "master of disguise" partner Hoop, who, together with their misbehaving talking AMC Pacer hatchback C.A.R.R., do their best to solve crimes in this Flash-animated "buddy cop" comedy series spoof of television detective shows like *Starsky and Hutch*. Bowing in August 2005 on Cartoon Network's *Adult Swim* with the pilot episode "C.A.R.R. Trouble" (a.k.a. "Feeling Dirty"), the weekly series regularly aired at midnight, with produced 13 episodes altogether for the first season. Created by Casper Kelly and Jeff Olsen and produced by Atlanta's Williams Street Productions, the detective show parody was canceled in February 2006 because of high production costs and lasted only one season. *A Williams Street Productoins. Color. Half-hour. Premiered on CAR: August 1, 2005 (pilot). Premiered on CAR: August 28, 2005–February 2006 (series).*

*Voices*
**Stroker:** Jon Glaser; **Hoop:** Paul Christie; **C.A.R.R.:** Timothy Levitch

## STUART LITTLE

Separated by species but joined by brotherhood, the world's most beloved talking mouse Stuart and his human brother George embark on a series of fun, entertaining and life-changing escapades, including his parents Mr. and Mrs. Little and Snowbell the cat, in this animated television series adaptation of the successful full-length feature film produced in 1999 and loosely based on humorist E.B. White's classic novella, *Stuart Little*. Produced by Red Wagon Productions, Sony Pictures Television and Columbia TirStar Television, this 13-episode, half-hour animated incarnation lasted one season on the digital cable channel HBO Family, beginning in the spring of 2003. *A Red Wagon Productions/Sony Pictures/Columbia TriStar Production. Color. Half-hour. Premiered on HBO FAM: March 1, 2003–May 24, 2003. Rebroadcast on HBO FAM: May 2003–February 21, 2007.*

*Voices*
**Stuart Little:** David Kaufman; **Mr. Frederick Little:** Hugh Laurie; **George Little:** Myles Jeffrey; **Eleanor Little/Martha:** Jennifer Hale; **Snowbell:** Kevin Schon; **Rick Ruckus:** Matthew Kaminsky; **Tiger:** Michael Chiklis

*Other Voices*
Dee Bradley Baker, Quinton Flynn, Kathy Najimy, André Sogliuzzo

## STUNT DAWGS

The wildest bunch of world-class Hollywood stuntmen and stuntwomen (Crash, Splatter, Sizzle and Lucky), who double as crime-fighters, save the world from the wicked Stunt Scabs, a band of villainous Tinseltown athletes, in this 40-episode half-hour syndicated series, inspired by director Hal Needman's 1980 comedy *Hooper* starring Burt Reynolds. The series premiered in first-run syndication.

*A Rainforest Entertainment Production for Claster Television. Color. Half-hour. Premiered: September 28, 1992. Syndicated.*

*Voices*
**Needham/Whizkid:** Neil Crone; **Fungus:** John Stocker; **Splatter/Crash/Velda:** Greg Morton; **Lucky/Skiddd:** Greg Swanson; **Airball/Slyme:** Ron Rubin; **Badyear/Half-a-Mind:** Harvey Atkin; **Sizzle:** Lenore Zann; **Nina Newscaster:** Barbara Budd

## SUNDAY PANTS

Half-hour animated variety show featuring a fast-moving collection of hilarious "freshly pressed and fabric-softened" animated shorts produced in a variety of animation styles—traditional hand-drawn, Flash, CGI and others—and occasionally voiced by celebrity by animators from around the world, as well as rock-and-roll videos by the Slacks. The half-hour block aired in prime time on Sunday nights on Cartoon Network, beginning October 2, 2005.

Creators, writers and directors whose work was featured included Monkmus, Lance Taylor (Facelift Enterprises, Inc.); Lincoln Pierce (Global Mechanic); Tim McKeon and Adam Pava (Cartoon Network Studios); Andy Fielding (Red Kite Animation); Andy Merrill, Craig "Sven" Gordon and Stuart Hill (Cartoon Network); and many others. *A Cartoon Network Studios/Facelift Enterprises, Inc/Global Mechanic/Red Kite Animation/6 Point Harness/Kachew!/ Curious Pictures/Soup2Nuts/Acme Filmworks/Primal Screen/Josh Koppel Productions/Cosgrove Hall Films Limited/ Canal+France/Teletoon France/BRB Internacional S.A./Noodlesoup/ Curious Pictures/Spazzco Animation Production. Color. Half-hour. Premiered on CAR: October 2, 2005.*

## ◎ SUPER BOOK

This Japanese-produced retelling of stories from the Bible, redubbed in English, was first syndicated in 1982 by the Christian Broadcasting Network (which also broadcast the series simultaneously). Animated by Tatsunoko Studios, the producers of *Speed Racer*, the program, which originally aired on Japanese television, was the first nationally broadcast religious cartoon series since 1960's *Davey and Goliath*, featuring 26 original episodes. *Flying House*, a companion animated series also produced by Tatsunoko Studios, also aired in 1992 in syndication and on the Christian Broadcasting Network. (See entry for details.) *A CBN/Tatsunoko Production. Color. Half-hour. Premiered: 1992 (in syndication and on CBN). Syndicated.*

### Voices
Bill Mack, Ray Owens, Sonia Owens, Helene Van Koert, Billie Lou Watt

## ◎ SUPER DAVE

Super Dave Osborne, the world's most inept stuntman (and alter ego of comedian Bob Einstein) is joined by his Asian sidekick, Fuji, as he battles incredible villains, including his semi-bionic archenemy, Slash Hazard, in this live-action/animated series for FOX Network, inspired by Einstein's 1980–85 Showtime live-action series, *Super Dave*. The klutzy stuntman appeared in live-action wraparounds in each program. Preliminary objections from a prominent Asian American psychologist—that the characterization of sidekick Fuji was demeaning to Asian Americans—led to the character's being revised. *A DIC Enterprises/Blye-Einstein/Rete-italia Ltd. Production. Color. Half-hour. Premiered on FOX: September 12, 1992–August 28, 1993. Rebroadcast on FAM: June 11, 1994–September 24, 1994.*

### Voices
**Super Dave:** Bob Einstein; **Fuji:** Art Irizawa

## ◎ SUPER DUPER SUMOS

A trio of unassuming, larger-than-life teenage sumo wrestlers Booma, Kimo and Mamoo, use their immense physical prowess and strength, not to mention a few impressive wrestling moves, to thwart the evil Ms. Mister and her BAD Inc. monsters from destroying Generic City in this animated action/adventure comedy series created by Kevin O'Donnell. First shown on Canada's YTV and then on the United Kingdom's BBC1, the 25-episode, half-hour program, coproduced by DIC Entertainment, was imported to the United States where it aired on Nickelodeon from 2002 to 2003 before it was syndicated under the new title *Super Duper Sumo Wrestlers*. Game Boy Advance and PlayStation both released video games based on the series in 2003 and 2004, respectively. *A DIC Entertainment/Ameko Entertainment Company/Digital eMotion Production. Color. Half-hour. Premiered on NICK: April 7, 2002–February 2, 2003. Syndicated (as Super Duper Sumo Wrestlers).*

### Voices
**Booma:** Matt Hill; **Kimo:** Ben Hur; **Mamoo:** Cusse Mankuma; **Wisdom Sam:** Richard Newman; **Prima:** Chantal Strand; **Ms. Mister:** Deborah DeMille; **Genghis Fangus/Billy Swift:** Michael Richard Dobson; **Dr. Stinger:** Peter Kelemis; **Additional Voices:** Kathleen Barr, Ian James Corlett, Brenda Crichlow, Gail Fabrey, Jason Michas, Brent Miller, Shirley Millner, Colin Murdock

## ◎ SUPER FRIENDS

Justice League superheroes Batman, Robin, Superman, Wonder Woman and Aquaman, along with three new members, Marvin, Wendy and Wonder Dog, are called to fight supernatural creatures and other powerful forces in this second assemblage of famed crime-fighters from the pages of DC Comics (the first was *The Superman/Aquaman Hour of Adventure*, in which the "Justice League" superheroes appeared), produced as a weekly Saturday-morning series for ABC in 1975. Sixteen half-hours were produced.

Four spin-off series followed: *The All-New Super Friends Hour* (1977), *Challenge of the Super Friends* (1978), *The World's Greatest Super Friends*(1979) and *The Super Friends Hour* (1980), each with new characters added and each produced for ABC. *A Hanna-Barbera Production in association with DC Publications. Color. One-hour. Premiered on ABC: September 8, 1973–August 30, 1975. Rebroadcast on ABC: February 7, 1976–September 3, 1977. Rebroadcast on CAR: June 3, 1996–late 1999 (weekdays). Rebroadcast on BOOM: April 2, 2000–.*

### Voices
**Narrator:** Ted Knight; **Superman:** Danny Dark; **Batman:** Olan Soule; **Robin:** Casey Kasem; **Aquaman:** Norman Alden; **Wonder Woman/Wendy:** Sherry Alberoni; **Marvin/Wonder Dog:** Frank Welker

## ◎ SUPER FRIENDS HOUR

Incorporating newly animated safety tips, this hour-long Saturday-morning series, which aired on ABC in 1980, is a retread of 1977's *All-New Super Friends Hour*, also for ABC, featuring repeat episodes from the latter. (See show entry for voice credits and details.) *A Hanna-Barbera Production in association with DC Publications. Color. One hour. Premiered on ABC: October 4, 1980–September 3, 1983.*

## ◎ SUPER FRIENDS: THE LEGENDARY SUPER POWERS SHOW

Comic-book superheroes Wonder Woman, Batman and Robin take on evil forces with help from several new superhuman characters in this 16-episode half-hour fantasy/adventure series, which originally aired on ABC. *A Hanna-Barbera Production. Color. Half-hour. Premiered on ABC: September 8, 1984–August 31, 1985.*

### Voices
**Superman:** Danny Dark; **Wonder Woman:** B.J. Ward; **Batman:** Adam West; **Robin:** Casey Kasem; **Firestorm:** Mark Taylor; **Cyborg:** Ernie Hudson; **Darkseid/Kalibak:** Frank Welker; **Desaad:** Rene Auberjonois

## ◎ THE SUPER GLOBETROTTERS

The Harlem Globetrotters, America's funniest basketball team, are transformed from terrific basketball players to superheroes (Multi-Man, Sphere Man, Gismo Man, Spaghetti Man and Fluid Man), and use their athletic abilities to fight crime throughout the universe. The series was the third animated version of the internationally known hoopsters. The first was 1971's *The Harlem Globetrotters* for CBS, followed by *Go Go Globetrotters*, comprised of reruns from the latter, for NBC. The superhero format lasted three months before the series was paired with Hanna-Barbera's *Godzilla Power Hour* as *The Godzilla/Globetrotters Adventure Hour*. A *Hanna-Barbera Production. Color. Half-hour. Premiered on NBC: September 22, 1979–December 1, 1979. Rebroadcast on NBC: November 10, 1979–September 20, 1980 (as The Godzilla/Globetrotters Adventure Hour). Rebroadcast on CAR: August 20, 1994–August 21, 1994 (Look What We Found!); July 5, 1995– (Wednesdays).*

*Voices*

**Curley Neal (Sphere Man):** Stu Gilliams; **Geese Ausbie (Multi-Man):** John Williams; **Sweet Lou Dunbar (Gismo Man):** Adam Wade; **Nate Branch (Fluid Man):** Scatman Crothers; **Twiggy Sander (Spaghetti Man):** Buster Jones; **Crime Globe:** Frank Welker; **Announcer:** Mike Rye

#### ◉ SUPERMAN

The famed Man of Steel—newspaper reporter Clark Kent of the *Daily Planet* in disguise—keeps the streets of Metropolis safe from the likes of such notorious criminals as Lex Luthor, the Master Shadow and Cybron in this Saturday-morning cartoon series revival of the popular comic-book character, originally broadcast on CBS in 1988. In addition to featuring 13 new adventures of the fabled crimefighter, the series also contained a second segment, "Superman Family Album," tracing Superman's youth in 13 separate episodes. *A Ruby-Spears Enterprises Production in association with DC Comics. Color. Half-hour. Premiered on CBS: September 17, 1988–September 12, 1989*

*Voices*

**Superman/Clark Kent:** Beau Weaver; **Lois Lane:** Ginny McSwain; **Jimmy Olsen:** Mark Taylor; **Perry White:** Stanley Ralph Ross; **Lex Luthor:** Michael Bell; **Jessica Morganberry:** Lynn Marie Stewart; **Ma Kent:** Tress MacNeille; **Pa Kent:** Alan Oppenheimer

#### ◉ THE SUPERMAN/AQUAMAN HOUR OF ADVENTURE

One year after the debut of his Saturday-morning series, Superman, the Man of Steel, returned in this hour-long fantasy/adventure series that featured the leader of the lost continent of Atlantis, Aquaman, as its costar. Aided by his young sidekick Aqualad, and wife, Mera, Aquaman made the transition to animated cartoon beginning with new episodes produced especially for this series.

Six seven-minute cartoons were rotated during each broadcast. Two episodes each of Superman and Aquaman were shown, along with two episodes of "Superboy" (repeated from *The New Adventures of Superman*), which alternated with "Guest Star" cartoons that marked the cartoon debut of The Atom, Flash, The Green Lantern, Hawkman and Hawkgirl, the Teen Titans and the Justice League of America, each successful comic-book superheroes. (The cartoons were rebroadcast as part of the syndicated *Aquaman* series). *A Filmation Studios Ducouny/National Periodicals Production. Color. One hour. Premiered on CBS: September 9, 1967–September 7, 1968.*

*Voices*

**SUPERMAN AND SUPERBOY: Clark Kent/Superman:** Bud Collyer; **Lois Lane:** Joan Alexander; **Perry White/Superboy Narrator:** Ted Knight; **Superboy:** Bob Hastings; **Lana Lane:** Janet Waldo; **Superman Narrator:** Jackson Beck; **Other Voices:** Jack Grimes, Julie Bennett, Janet Waldo, Cliff Owens

**AQUAMAN: Aquaman:** Marvin Miller; **Imp/Tusky/Narrator:** Ted Knight; **Aqualad:** Jerry Dexter; **Mera:** Diana Maddox

**THE ATOM/FLASH/THE GREEN LANTERN/HAWKMAN AND HAWKGIRL/TEEN TITANS AND THE JUSTICE LEAGUE: The Atom/Speedy:** Pat Harrington Jr.; **The Flash:** Cliff Owens; **Kid Flash:** Tommy Cook; **Green Lantern:** Gerald Mohr; **Hawkman:** Gilbert Mack; **Wonder Girl:** Julie Bennett; **Kyro/Guardian of the Universe:** Paul Frees

#### ◉ THE SUPERMAN-BATMAN ADVENTURES

Half-hour syndicated package featuring 130 cartoon episodes of the Caped Crusader and the Man of Steel culled from several popular Saturday-morning cartoon series, originally produced by Filmation and Hanna-Barbera and broadcast on USA Network. *A Hanna-Barbera/Filmation Production in association with Warner Bros. Television International. Color. Half-hour. Rebroadcast on USA: 1996–98. Rebroadcast on CAR: October 1998–2000. Rebroadcast on BOOM: July 31, 2000–.*

#### ◉ SUPERMAN: THE ANIMATED SERIES

The Man of Steel, alias mild-mannered reporter Clark Kent, defends his native Metropolis from classic comic-book villains Braniac, Lex Luthor, Parasite, the Toyman and a whole new gang of baddies, among them Superman's evil clone, Bizarro, in this new half-hour series of adventures based on the popular DC Comics series. The usual cast of characters from the comic book are featured: *Daily Planet* editor Perry White, reporter Lois Lane and pal Jimmy Olsen, as well as a new character: Angela Chen, star gossip columnist and host of the *Metropolis Today* TV show. Airing Saturday mornings on the Kids' WB! block on the WB Television Network, the series originally premiered in September 1996 as a 90-minute prime-time special. On the Fourth of July, 2005, Cartoon Network's classic cartoon channel, Boomerang, began rerunning episodes of the high-flying superhero along with 1992's *Batman: The Animated Series*. On Saturday, August 20, 2005, Boomerang spotlighted the famed Man of Steel with a four-hour marathon airing from 8 P.M. to 1 A.M., with a second five-hour marathon on Sunday night of episodes of fellow DC Comics superhero Batman, from *Batman: The Animated Series*. Meanwhile, the so-called "titans in tights" aired nightly back-to-back on Boomerang's two-hour *Boomeraction* block from 11 P.M. to 1 A.M., ending its run weekday mornings in August 2006. *A Warner Bros. Television Animation Production in association with DC Comics. Color. Half-hour. Premiered on the WB (Kids' WB!): September 6, 1996 (special). Premiered on WB: September 6, 1997 (series)–February 12, 2000. Rebroadcast on CAR: February 14, 1997. Rebroadcast on BOOM: July 4, 2005–August 30, 2006.*

*Voices*

**Superman/Clark Kent:** Tim Daly; **Lois Lane:** Dana Delany; **Perry White:** George Dzundza; **Jimmy Olsen:** David Kaufman; **Jonathan Kent:** Mike Farrell; **Martha Kent:** Shelley Fabares; **Jor-El:** Christopher McDonald; **Angela Chen:** Lauren Tom; **Braniac:** Corey Burton; **Corben:** Malcolm McDowell; **Darkseid:** Michael Ironside; **Lana Lang:** Joely Fisher; **Lex Luther:** Clancy Brown; **Live Wire:** Lori Petty; **Mercy Graves:** Lisa Edelstein; **Rudy/The Parasite:** Jim Belushi

#### ◉ SUPER MARIO ALL-STARS

Repackaged series of 39 episodes from NBC's popular Saturday-morning series *Super Mario Bros. Super Show!* and *Super Mario World* (part of *Captain N and the New Super Mario World*), airing in syndication and on the Family Channel and USA Network. (See individual series for voice credits.) *A DIC Enterprises Production in association with Nintendo America Incorporated. Color. Half-hour.*

*Premiered: 1993–94. Syndicated. Rebroadcast on FAM: 1994–96. Rebroadcast on USA: January 13, 1997–June 6, 1997.*

## ◎ SUPER MARIO BROS. SUPER SHOW!

World-famous brothers Mario and Luigi play two misfit plumbers from the Italian section of Brooklyn who suddenly find themselves flushed through a Warp Zone to the exciting and everchanging Mushroom Kingdom. There they set out to rescue the perky Princess Toadstool and her factotum Toad from the dastardly King Koopa and his laughable Nintendo minions. This popular half-hour syndicated series was based on the popular Nintendo video games. Each program included the cartoon adventures of the Super Mario Bros. and the fantasy/adventure series The Legend of Zelda (see individual entry for details), sandwiched between Club Mario, a series of live-action wraparound segments featuring Mario and Luigi (played by Captain Lou Albano and Danny Wells, respectively), resident scientist Dr. Know It All and a menagerie of other characters. New episodes (two per show) were repackaged with reruns of half-hour episodes of *Captain N* as part of the NBC network series *Captain N and the Super Mario Bros. 3* (1990–91). Thirteen new *Super Mario World* cartoons were produced for a third season as the half-hour series, called *Captain N and the Super Mario World* (1991–92), also on NBC (see individual series for details). *A DIC Enterprises Production in association with Nintendo America Incorporated and Ulacom. Half-hour. Premiered: September 4, 1989–September 5, 1991. Syndicated. Rebroadcast on FAM: September 9, 1991–September 2, 1994.*

*Voices*

**Super Mario Brothers: Mario:** Lou Albano; **Luigi:** Danny Wells; **King Koopa/Mushroom Mayor/Tryclyde/Sniffet:** Harvey Atkin; **Toad/Mouser/Troopa/Beezo/Flurry:** John Stocker; **Princess Toadstool/Shyguy:** Jeanine Elias

**The Legend of Zelda: Zelda:** Cyndy Preston; **Link:** Jonathan Potts; **Harkinian:** Colin Fox; **Triforce of Wisdom:** Elizabeth Hanna; **Moblin:** Len Carlson

**Club Mario (live-action cast): Mario:** Captain Lou Albano; **Luigi:** Danny Wells; **Tammy Treehuger:** Victoria Delany; **Tommy Treehugger** Chris Coombs; **Evil Eric:** Michael Anthony Rawlins; **Dr. Know It All:** Kurt Weldon; **The Big Kid:** James Rose; **The Band:** James Abbott; **Princess Centauri:** Shanta Kahn

## ◎ SUPER POWERS TEAM: GALACTIC GUARDIANS

An alliance of the world's greatest superheroes (Superman, Wonder Woman, Batman, Robin, Firestorm and Cyborg) work to help mankind resist the incursions of Darkseid, the "Godfather" of intergalactic crime, as they battle injustices on Earth and through the vast reaches of space in this half-hour fantasy/adventure series—under a new title following 1984's season-long telecast of Saturday morning's *Super Friends: The Legendary Super Powers Hour*—originally produced for ABC. The series ran a distant second in the ratings to the powerhouse NBC series *The Smurfs* and was canceled after only one season. *A Hanna-Barbera Production in association with DC Publications. Color. Half-hour. Premiered on ABC: September 7, 1985–September 30, 1986.*

*Voices*

**Superman:** Danny Dark; **Wonder Woman:** B.J. Ward; **Batman:** Adam West; **Robin:** Casey Kasem; **Firestorm:** Mark Taylor; **Cyborg:** Ernie Hudson; **Darkseid/Kalibak:** Frank Welker; **Desaad:** Rene Auberjonois

## ◎ SUPER PRESIDENT AND SPY SHADOW

U.S. President James Norcross inherits supernatural powers, turning into a crimefighter (becoming "Super President"), when a cosmic storm showers him with potent chemical particles. He uses his powers to combat cunning criminals in the nation's capital in the main part of this half-hour animated series, originally broadcast on NBC. The series' second supporting segment was "Spy Shadow," the adventures of private eye Richard Vance and his independently functioning shadow hot on the case. *A DePatie-Freleng Enterprises Production. Color. Half-hour. Premiered on NBC: September 16, 1967–September 14, 1968.*

*Voices*

**President James Norcross:** Paul Frees; **Richard Vance:** Daws Butler; **Other Voices:** Ted Knight, June Foray, Paul Frees, Shep Menken, Don Menken, Don Messick, Lorrie Scott, Mark Scot

## ◎ SUPER ROBOT MONKEY TEAM HYPER FORCE GO!

Transformed into a brave fighter, Chris, a resourceful young teenage boy, leads a scrappy band of high-tech, superhero, robotic monkey warriors as they battle to save the city of Shuggazoom from the evil cosmic villain, Skeleton King, who wants to turn the futuristic planet into an evil empire in this anime-style action series (combining Western humor and Japanese pop anime) coproduced by Walt Disney Television animation.

Created by Ciro Nieli, who coproduced the highly successful animated *Teen Titans* series, this quirky, fast-paced, futuristic half-hour science fiction/fantasy series for kids ages six to 12 debuted with 14 half-hour episodes on the *Jetix* program blocks on ABC Family and Toon Disney in September 2004. Disney renewed the breakout-hit series for three additional seasons, ordering 11 episodes for the second season, 15 more for the third and 13 for its fourth and final season. In late August 2006, ABC Family discontinued the Jetix program block, resulting in the cancelation of the series. In February 2006, the animated monkeys were feted with their own special Super Bowl marathon. Later that month, Toon Disney aired a two-part special of the series creator's favorite episodes "Wormhole" and "Belly of the Beast" presented in widescreen format. *A Walt Disney Studios Production. Color. Half-hour. Premiered on ABC FAM: September 18, 2004–August 31, 2006. Premiered on TDIS: September 18, 2004.*

*Voices*

**Antauri:** Kevin Michael Richardson; **Chiro:** Greg Cipes; **Gibson:** Tom Kenny; **Nova:** Kari Wahlgren; **Otto:** Clancy Brown; **Sprx:** Corey Feldman; **The Skeleton King:** Mark Hamill; **Mandarin:** James Hong; **Jinmay:** Ashley Johnson; **Velma:** Hynden Walch; **Scrapperton:** Eric Idle; **Dr. Maezno:** Dee Bradley Baker; **Gyrus Krinkle:** Jeffrey Combs; **Aurora Six:** Meredith Salenger; **Super Quasier:** Keone Young; **Skurg:** Wil Wheaton; **Thingy:** Frank Welker

## ◎ THE SUPER SIX

Under the organization name of Super Service, Inc., a funky group of superheroes, whose names coincide with their superpowers (Granite Man, Super Scuba, Elevator Man, Magnet Man and Captain Wammy), employ their special powers to fight crime in this weekly half-hour Saturday morning series originally broadcast on NBC in 1966. (A sixth superhero, Super Stretch, was either renamed or dropped from the series and no other information could be found regarding his appearance on the show.) Programmed opposite CBS's ratings champ *The Mighty Mouse Playhouse*, the series offered 21 "Super Six" episodes, bracketed between two supporting segments: "Super Bwoing," a guitar-strumming daredevil, and "The Brothers Matzoriley" (Weft, Wong and Wight), a three-headed brother act occupying one body (who first appeared as the villains in the first "Inspector" cartoon, "The Great DeGaulle Stone Operation").

The series was rerun for two consecutive seasons from 1967 to 1969. This was DePatie-Freleng Enterprises' first production for Saturday-morning television. *A DePatie-Freleng Enterprises/Mirisch-Rich Production. Color. Half-hour. Premiered on NBC: September 10, 1966–September 6, 1969.*

**Voices**
**Magnet Man:** Daws Butler; **Elevator Man:** Paul Stewart; **Super Scuba:** Arte Johnson; **Granite Man:** Lyn Johnson; **Captain Zammo:** Paul Frees; **Super Bwoing:** Charles Smith; **Other Voices:** Pat Carroll, June Foray, Joan Gerber, Diana Maddox

**THE BROTHERS MATZORILEY: Weft/Wong:** Paul Frees; **Wight:** Daws Butler

## ◎ SUPER SUNDAY

The short, cliff-hanging serial, once a popular staple of Saturday-morning movie matinees, was revived in this syndicated, animated series comprised of three separate weekly half-hour series—*Robotix, Bigfoot and the Muscle Machines* and *JEM*—programmed for weekend syndication in 1985. Produced by Marvel Productions, the series was the studio's first attempt at weekend block programming.

The series' first component, *Robotix*, presented in 15 action-packed episodes, followed the confrontations between two human-oid forces on the planet Skalorr. It acted as a lead-in to another serialized component, *Bigfoot and the Muscle Machines*, told in nine episodes, which dealt with a group of powerful land vehicles that assist a young couple in their attempt to escape the evil Mr. Big. The third component in the mix was the nonserialized *JEM*, the adventures of a beautiful young music executive who doubles as a glamorous rock star. The latter was replaced in January of 1986 by the serialized *Inhumanoids* (only two episodes aired), tracing the exploits of a courageous team of scientists who fight side by side with friendly creatures known as Mutroes against vicious monsters who plan to destroy civilization and the world. The series remained in syndication through the fall of 1986. *A Marvel/Sunbow/Claster Television Production. Color. Ninety minutes. Premiered: October 6, 1985. Syndicated.*

**Voices**
Charlie Adler, Michael Bell, Susan Blu, Bill Callaway, Nancy Cartwright, Fred Collins, Brad Crandel, Peter Cullen, Linda Gary, Dick Gautier, Ed Gilbert, Chris Latta, Neil Ross, Stanley Ralph Ross, Richard Sanders, Susan Silo, John Stephenson, Frank Welker

## ◎ SWAMP THING

This seven-foot-tall, slimy-green, superpowered creature from the Louisiana swamplands, first created in a 1972 DC comic by Len Wein and Berni Wrightston, is given a new twist in this half-hour animated series. Dr. Alec Holland (alias Swamp Thing) discovers a plant-growing formula in his high-tech Tree Lab that could end world hunger and must prevent it from falling into evil hands. CBS premiered this five-part miniseries in September 1990; originally planned as a weekly series, CBS elected not to pick up its option. Episodes included "The Un-Men Unleashed," To Live Forever," "Falling Red Star," "Legend of the Lost Cavern," and "Experiment in Terror." On Halloween 1990 FOX rebroadcast the first installment, "The Un-Men Unleashed," as a half-hour Saturday-morning special. FOX rebroadcast the other four episodes in the series in

April 1991, replacing the ill-fated *Piggsburg Pigs*. In July 1991, FOX brought the series back (in reruns), again replacing *Piggsburg Pigs* in its time slot, this time re-airing all five episodes in succession. The Disney Channel later reran the series as well. *A DIC Enterprises/Batfilm Production. Color. Half-hour. Premiered on CBS: September 1990. Rebroadcast on FOX: October 31, 1990 ("The Un-Men Unleashed"); April 20, 1991 ("To Live Forever"); April 27, 1991 ("Falling Red Star"); May 4, 1991 ("Legend on the Lost Cavern"); May 11, 1991 ("Experiment in Terror"); July 6, 1991; July 13, 1991; July 20, 1991; July 27, 1991; August 30, 1991.*

**Voices**
**Dr. Alex Holland/Swamp Thing:** Len Carlson; **Dr. Anton Arcane:** Don Francks; **Abby, Dr. Areane's Niece:** Paulina Gillis; **Bayou Jack:** Phillip Atkin; **Tomahawk:** Harvey Atkin; **J.T.:** Richard Yearwood; **Delbert:** Jonathan Potts; **Dr. Deemo:** Errol Slue; **Weed Killer:** Joe Matteson; **Skin Man:** Gordon Masten

## ◎ SWAT KATS: THE RADICAL SQUADRON

Jake Clawson and Chance Furlong, auto mechanics by day, transform into T-Bone and Raxor, crime fighting SWAT Kats by night, to keep the peace in Megakat City (entirely populated by humanized cats), in their high-tech, land-air-sea vehicle. This first-run half-hour series was syndicated as part of the *Funtastic World of Hanna* and also broadcast on superstation WTBS beginning in 1993. In the fall of 1994 the series debuted on The Cartoon Network with all-new episodes. *Premiered: September 11, 1993–February 16, 1995. Syndicated. Premiered on TBS: September 11, 1993–January 1995. Premiered on CAR: September 10, 1994 (new episodes). Rebroadcast on CAR: August 7, 1995–September 1, 1995; September 4, 1995–2000 (weekdays, Saturdays); February 13, 2006–February 20, 2006. Rebroadcast on BOOM: April 19, 2000–.*

**Voices**
Charlie Adler, Frank Birney, Earl Boen, Keene Curtis, Jim Cummings, Linda Gary, Edmund Gilbert, Barry Gordon, Tress MacNeille, Gary Owens, Frank Welker

## ◎ SWISS FAMILY ROBINSON

A shipwrecked family with three children make a new life as castaways on a deserted island in this animated adaptation of Jonathan David Wyss's classic novel. The half-hour series was originally produced for Japanese television in 1989 and debuted in the United States on The Family Channel that same year. *A Nippon Animation/PMT Production. Color. Half-hour. Premiered on FAM: September 8, 1989–August 30, 1992.*

**Voices**
**Ernest:** Jeremy Platt; **Becca:** Reba West; **Fritz:** R. Dwight; **Jack:** Grace Michaels; **Anna:** Wendee Swann

## ◎ THE SYLVANIAN FAMILIES

Young children are transported in time to a warm, wonderful and whimsical forest where they become as tiny as the wee bears, rabbits, raccoons, mice, beavers and foxes, sidestepping trouble by banding together to solve their problems. Based on the popular children's toy line, the 26-episode half-hour series was produced for first-run syndication in 1987. *A DIC Enterprises Claster Television Production. Color. Half-hour. Premiered: September 1987. Syndicated. Rebroadcast on PAX: September 6, 1998–September 1999.*

**Voices**
**The Woodkeeper:** Frank Proctor; **Packbat/Papa Herb Wildwood:** Len Carlson; **Gatorpossum/Grandpa Smokey Wildwood:** John Stocker; **Mama Honeysuckle Evergreen:** Jeri Craden; **Papa**

Ernest Evergreen: Thick Wilson; Grandma Primrose Evergreen: Ellen Ray Hennessey; Ashley Evergreen: Pauline Gillis; Preston Evergreen: Michael Fantini; Rusty Wildwood: Noam Zylberman; Holly Wildwood: Catherine Gallant; Papa Slick Slydale: Brian Belfry; Mama Velvetter Slydale/Grandma Flora Wildwood/Mama Ginger Wildwood: Diane Fabian; Buster Slydale: Jeremiah McCann; Scarlette Slydale: Lisa Coristine

## ◎ SYLVESTER & TWEETY

Half-hour anthology series comprised of previously released Warner Bros. theatrical cartoons directed by legendary Warner Bros. animators Friz Freleng, Chuck Jones and Robert McKimson, repackaged as a Saturday-morning network show. *A Warner Bros. Production. Color. Half-hour. Premiered on CBS: September 11, 1976–September 3, 1977.*

**Voices**
Mel Blanc, June Foray

## ◎ THE SYLVESTER & TWEETY MYSTERIES

The slurred-voiced pussycat and foxy canary travel the globe with Granny, now a Jessica Fletcher–like detective who investigates strange mysteries and bizarre events, joined by the ever-dutiful Hector the Bulldog (Tweety's guardian, who keeps Sylvester in his place) in this new half-hour series—and the first all-new "puddytat" cartoons in 30 years—premiering on the WB Television Network's Kids' WB! Saturday lineup in 1995. Producers tried to recapture the look and feel of legendary Warner Bros. animator Friz Freleng's original Sylvester and Tweety shorts in 53 half-hour episodes. Supertalented voice artist June Foray reprised her role as Granny for the series. Cartoon Network picked up the series in 2002 and aired the last original episodes, "The Tail End" and "This Is the End" that December. *A Warner Bros. Television Animation Production. Color. Half-hour. Premiered on the WB: September 9, 1995–February 5, 2000; September 4, 2000–March 2, 2001. (Also seen as a component of WB's "The Cat & Birdy Warnertoonie Pinky Brainy Big Cartoonie Show," January 16, 1999–August 31, 2000.) Rebroadcast on CAR: October 14, 2002–.*

**Voices**
Sylvester/Tweety/Charlie Dog/Announcer: Joe Alaskey; Granny: June Foray; Hector: Frank Welker

## ◎ TABALUGA

In order to save his kingdom of Greenland, Tabaluga, a young green dragon (and last surviving dragon of his kind) and the crown prince, seek to recover a magical pendant once owned by his father that possesses great power. They battle a bunch of eco-villains, including the evil ice king Arktos and nefarious sand-spirit Humsin in this Australian-German coproduction produced by Australia's Yoram Gross Films, which produced three animated series based on the character—26 episodes per season—in 1994, 1999 and 2001.

The first, 15-minute series, featuring the mythical character, bowed on American television in 1998 on FOX Family Channel as part of the network's 9:00 A.M. to noon preschool program block *The Captain's Treasure House.* Hosted by members of *The All-New Captain Kangaroo,* an update of the classic CBS (1955–1984) and PBS (1984–93) children's series originally hosted by Bob Keeshan, with John McDonough as the new "Captain," the block included such preschool fare as Britt Alcroft Productions' *The Magic Adventures of Mumfie* and *Shining Time Station* with Thomas the Tank Engine. In early November 1999, a second series of 26 half-hour episodes was shown on FOX Family Channel until the following August. *A Yoram*

*Gross/EM.TV Production in association with ZDF. Color. Half-hour. Premiered on FAM: August 15, 1998 (The All-New Captain Kangaroo). Premiered on FOX FAM: November 1, 1999–August 10, 2000.*

**Voices**
Keith Scott, Robyn Moore, Jamie Oxenbould, Rufus Beck

## ◎ TALES FROM THE CRYPTKEEPER

Spun off from the popular HBO live-action series and full-length features (both based on the *Tales from the Crypt* comic book), this animated horror anthology series served up scary tales hosted by the show's wise-cracking, gruesome host, the Cryptkeeper. Premiering on ABC in the fall of 1993, this Saturday-morning series cost an estimated $400,000 per episode to produce. *A Nelvana Enterprises/EC Production in association with Tales from The Crypt Holdings, Inc. Color. Half-hour. Premiered on ABC: September 18, 1993–July 15, 1995.*

**Voices**
Cryptkeeper: John Kassir; Vaultkeeper; Dan Hennessey

## ◎ TALES OF LITTLE WOMEN

Four young Massachusetts sisters (Meg, Amy, Jo and Beth March), characters from Louisa May Alcott's 19th-century novel, are left temporarily fatherless during the American Civil War in this half-hour, weekly animated adaptation produced for Japanese and North American television markets. The series bowed on HBO. *A Toei Animation/Harmony Gold Production. Color. Half-hour. Premiered on HBO: July 3, 1988–December 1990.*

## ◎ TALES OF THE WIZARD OF OZ

L. Frank Baum's "Oz" stories were brought to life in this limited-animated series starring Dorothy, Tin Man, Scarecrow and the Cowardly Lion in all-new animated adventures that patterned the cartoon personalities after the MGM classic stars: Judy Garland, Ray Bolger, Jack Haley and Bert Lahr. The program, consisting of 130 five-minute episodes, was produced by Arthur Rankin Jr. and Jules Bass, of *Rudolph, The Red-Nosed Reindeer* and *Frosty the Snowman* fame. *A Rankin-Bass/Videocrafts International/Crawley Films Production. Color. Half-hour. Premiered: September 1, 1961. Syndicated.*

**Voices**
Stan Francis, Alfie Scopp, Carl Banas, Larry Mann, Susan Conway

## ◎ TALE SPIN

Baloo the Bear, now a devil-may-care ace cargo pilot in the tropical seaport of Cape Suzette, and his young feisty cub friend, Kit Cloudkicker, find mystery, intrigue and humor in high-flying adventures as they do battle with a menacing band of pirates in this half-hour animated series produced as part of the weekday syndicated *Disney Afternoon* cartoon block. Reuniting Baloo and characters Louie the Ape (featured as a music-loving nightclub owner) and Shere Khan from the 1967 Disney animated favorite *The Jungle Book,* the program featured several new characters: Baloo's boss, Rebecca Cunningham, who provides the cargo company's down-to-earth business sense; her five-year-old daughter, Molly; and Wildcat, the company's whiz mechanic. Produced as a companion to Disney's *DuckTales* and *Chip 'n' Dale Rescue Rangers,* also parts of the cartoon block, the 65-episode series marked the first time the classic Disney television animation had been combined with state-of-the-art computer animation.

After its run in syndication, the popular daytime show re-aired on Disney Channel and Toon Disney. *A Walt Disney Television Animation*

Production. Color. Half-hour. Premiered on DIS: September 8, 1990–September 9, 1990. Premiered: September 10, 1990–September 2, 1994. Syndicated. Rebroadcast on DIS: September 5, 1994–April 15, 2000. Rebroadcast on TDIS: April 18, 1998–January 29, 2006; December 1, 2006–.

**Voices**
**Baloo the Bear:** Ed Gilbert; **Kit Cloudkicker:** R.J. Williams; **Rebecca Cunningham:** Sally Struthers; **Molly Cunningham:** Janna Michaels; **Wildcat:** Patrick Fraley; **King Louie/Don Karnage:** Jim Cummings; **Shere Khan:** Tony Jay; **Dumptruck:** Chuck McCann; **Maddog:** Charlie Adler; **Dunder:** Lorenzo Music; **Spigot:** Michael Gough

### ⊚ TAMA AND FRIENDS

Tama, a sweet, curious kitten, and her dog and cat friends Chopin, Momo, Pimmy, Rockney and Tiggle embark on a series of misadventures as seen from the lovable cat's viewpoint in this imported Japanese animated series, redubbed in English and broadcast in the United States in first-run syndication. Joined by their human friends, including Tama's owner Casey, her friend Amy and their mothers, this family-friendly series originated in Japan around 1983 as an original video animated (OVA) series, topped off by a 43-minute cartoon in 1993 celebrating the characters' 10th anniversary. That year, six additional three-minute cartoons were released, with 51 half-episodes, including one full-length episode for its finale, broadcast in Japan by MBS and TBS (Tokyo Broadcast Network) the following year. In 2001 4Kids Entertainment produced 26 English-dubbed episodes, 13 of which aired in first-run syndication in the United States. Veronica Taylor, best known as the voice of Ash Ketchum in the animated Pokémon series, provided the voice of Tama's owner, Amy, in the series. A Lacey Entertainment/4Kids Entertainment/Taj Studios, Inc. Summit Media Production. Color. Half-hour. Premiered: September 15, 2001. Syndicated.

**Voices**
**Tama:** Jimmy Zoppi; **Chopin:** Lisa Ortiz; **Bengbu:** Rachael Little; **Momo:** Jerry Lobozzo; **Pimmy:** Kayzie Rogers; **Rockney:** Eric Stuart; **Wocket:** Vincent J. Thomas Baker; **Casey, Tama's owner:** Don Green; **Casey's Mom:** Tara Jayne; **Amy:** Veronica Taylor; **Other Voices:** Andrew Rannels, Cathy We$luck, Kerry Williams

### ⊚ TARO, GIANT OF THE JUNGLE

Gifted with a secret power drawn from a radioactive tree, Taro, a jungle-born man, safeguards the jungle in this half-hour action/adventure series from Japan. A Global Production. Color. Half-hour. Premiered: 1969. Syndicated.

### ⊚ TARZAN AND THE SUPER SEVEN

The famous vine-swinging hero Tarzan expanded his horizons in this 90-minute show produced for CBS in 1978, in which he traveled to wherever his interests could best help others. The program mixed eight new episodes with old episodes from Tarzan, Lord of the Jungle, originally broadcast on CBS during the 1976–77 season, along with new episodes of seven weekly components: Batman and Robin, (in all-new episodes) Web Woman, Isis and the Freedom Force, Microwoman and Super Stretch, Web Woman, Manta and Moray and Jason of Star Command, a live-action series that ran only during the first season and was spun off into its own half-hour series. In 1980 the "Super Seven" components reaired as the Batman and the Super Seven series. A Filmation Associates Production. Color. Ninety minutes. Premiered on CBS: September 9, 1978–August 30, 1980.

**Voices**
**Tarzan:** Robert Ridgely; **Batman:** Adam West; **Robin:** Burt Ward; **Bat Mite:** Lennie Weinrib

Gifted jungle man Taro maintains peace in the jungle in the Japanese animated action/adventure series Taro, Giant of the Jungle. © Global Productions

**Voices**

**ISIS AND THE FREEDOM FORCE:** **Isis:** Diane Pershing; **Hercules:** Bob Dennison; **Merlin/Sinbad/Super Samurai:** Michael Bell

**MICROWOMAN AND SUPER STRETCH:** **Microwoman:** Kim Hamilton; **Super Stretch:** Ty Henderson

**WEB WOMAN:** **Kelly Webster:** Linda Gary; **Spinner:** Lou Scheimer

**MANTA AND MORAY:** **Manta:** Joe Stern; **Moray:** Joan Van Ark

**JASON OF STAR COMMAND (LIVE-ACTION CAST):** **Jason:** Craig Littler; **The Commander:** James Doohan, John Russell; **Professor E.J. Parsafoot:** Charlie Dell; **Nicole Davidoff:** Susan O'Hanlon; **Dragos:** Sid Haig; **Voice of Twiki:** Larry Storch; **Peepo the Robot:** Himself.

### ⊚ TARZAN/LONE RANGER/ZORRO ADVENTURE HOUR

Zorro, the caped freedom fighter of early California, and famed masked man the Lone Ranger join Tarzan, the jungle lord, in separate adventures full of intrigue and cliff-hanging excitement. The series marked the first appearance of Zorro in animated form. Episodes of Tarzan were repeated from the previously broadcast network series Tarzan, Lord of the Jungle.

A Filmation Associates Production. Color. One hour. Premiered on CBS: September 12, 1981–September 11, 1982.

**Voices**

**TARZAN:** **Tarzan:** Robert Ridgely

**LONE RANGER:** **The Lone Ranger/Opening Announcer:** J. Darnoc [William Conrad]; **Tonto:** Ivan Naranjo

**ZORRO:** **Don Diego/Zorro:** Henry Darrow; **Maria:** Christine Avila; **Sergeant Gonzales:** Don Diamond; **Captain Ramon:** Eric Mason; **Amigo/Miguel:** Julie Medina; **Frey Gaspar:** East Carlo; **Lucia:** Socorro Valdez; **Don Alejandro/Governor General:** Carlos Rivas

### ⊚ TARZAN LORD OF THE JUNGLE

Edgar Rice Burroughs's comic-strip and movie character displays his legendary ability to swing by jungle vines and repulse attackers and evil game hunters in this animated version of the famed jungle champion of justice. The 16-episode series premiered on CBS in 1976. A *Filmation Associates Production. Color. Half-hour. Premiered on CBS: September 11, 1976–September 3, 1977. Rebroadcast on CBS: February 11, 1984–September 8, 1984.*

**Voices**
**Tarzan:** Robert Ridgely; **N'Kima:** Lou Scheimer; **Other Voices:** Linda Gary, Joan Gerber, Ted Cassidy, Barry Gordon, Allan Oppenheimer, Jane Webb

### ◉ TAZ-MANIA

In this toned-down version of the classic Looney Tunes character, Tazmanian Devil (now simply known as Taz) is a whirling dervish from Down Under (Australia, in other words), working as a hotel bellhop and sparking his share of outrageous escapades involving members of his extended family—his dad, Hugh; his mother, Jean; and his "Valley girl-ish" sister, Molly—and many other friends in this half-hour Saturday-morning cartoon series produced for the FOX Network. On September 1, 1991, six days before bowing on FOX's Saturday morning schedule, the network broadcast a half-hour prime-time series preview special featuring two episodes "Like Father Like Son" and "Frights of Passage." A *Warner Bros. Television Animation Production. Color. Half-hour. Premiered on FOX: September 1, 1991 (series preview). Premiered on FOX: September 7, 1991–September 6, 1996 (series). Rebroadcast on CAR/TBS/TNT: September 9, 1996–September 5, 1999.*

**Voices**
**Taz/Bushwhacker Bob/Buddy Boar/Wendel T. Wolf:** Jim Cummings; **Jean:** Miriam Flynn; **Mr. Thickley:** Dan Castellaneta; **Molly Tasmanian Devil:** Kellie Martin; **Bull Gator:** John Astin; **Willie Wombat:** Phil Proctor; **Hugh:** Maurice LaMarche; **Constance:** Rosalyn Landor; **Didgeri Dingo III/Axle Dog the Turtle:** Rob Paulsen; **Jake:** Debi Derryberry; **Didgeri Dingo:** Kevin Thudeau; **Other Voices:** Edward Paulsen

### ◉ TEAM GALAXY

A trio of outrageous Galaxy High School students—Josh, Brett and Yoko—rigorously train to become Space Marshals while balancing the trials and tribulations of regular teenagers in this fast-paced, high-flying, anime-inspired adventure series. Produced by France's Marathon Animation and revoiced in English, the traditional 2-D animated series, combining elements of computer animation as well, aired Saturday mornings on Cartoon Network with 21 half-hour episodes produced for the first season. A *Marathon Animation Production. Color. Half-hour. Premiered on CAR: September 9, 2006–*

**Voices**
**Josh:** Kirby Morrow; **Brett:** Tabitha St. Germain; **Yoko:** Katie Griffin; **Principal Kirkpatrick:** Brian Dobson

### ◉ TEAMO SUPREMO

Three superhero kids—Captain Crandall, Skate Lad and Rope Girl—battle to save the planet from supervillains, including the evil Blitz and shape-changing femme fatale, Madame Snake, in this half-hour animated series produced by Walt Disney Television Animation. Premiering on ABC's *One Saturday Morning* block in January 2002, the half-hour, 39-episode series remained on the air until September, after which it began airing on Toon Disney, including most of the series' second season. Through the spring of 2003, half of the third series aired on ABC's *ABC Kids* block; by September it had been replaced by Disney's *Lilo & Stitch: The Series.* The series' remaining episodes premiered on Toon Disney. A *Walt Disney Television Animation Production. Color. Half-hour.*

*Premiered on ABC: January 19, 2002–September 14, 2002. Premiered on TDIS: March 15, 2002–August 27, 2006.*

**Voices**
**Crandall/Captain Crandall:** Spencer Breslin; **Brenda/Rope Girl, Hector/Skate Lad:** Alanna Ubach; **Governor Kevin:** Martin Mull; **Paulsen:** Fred Willard; **Chief:** Brian Doyle-Murray, Joe Alaskey; **Crandall's Mom:** Julia Sweeney; **Jean, Crandall's Sister:** Rachel Crane; **Hypnotheria:** April Winchell; **Laser Pirate:** Tim Curry; **Birthday Bandit:** Mark Hamill; **Hippy Chick:** Shelly Bennett; **Other Voices:** Jeff Bennett, Jess Harnell

### ◉ TEENAGE MUTANT NINJA TURTLES (1987)

Crime fighting comes into a new age when a band of feisty, fun-loving, sewer-dwelling, pizza-eating turtles (Michaelangelo, Leonardo, Donatello and Raphael), masters of the fine art of ninja, battle underground criminals and assorted villains using their quick-footed fighting skills to overcome evil in this half-hour syndicated and Saturday-morning favorite. First aired as a miniseries in December 1987, the series went weekly via syndication in October 1988, then daily in 1989, capturing an astounding 73 percent of the market share. Impressed by the series' syndicated success, CBS commissioned new episodes and expanded the program to one hour, adding the show to its fall 1990 Saturday morning lineup, while the first-run half-hour series still aired in daily syndication. (CBS launched its version with a Friday-night prime-time special, "The Cuff Link Capers." A second special, "Planet of the Turtletoids," aired a year later. CBS's *Teenage Mutant Ninja Turtles* not only won its time slot but became the highest-rated show on Saturday-morning television, amassing 185 episodes during its successful six-season run, which ended in 1996. In the fall of 1993, USA Network began rerunning the series on a daily basis. A *Murakami-Wolf-Swenson/Fred Wolf Films Production in association with Mirage Studios. Color. Half-hour. Premiered: December 14, 1987–December 18, 1987 (miniseries). Premiered: October 1, 1988–August 27, 1993. Syndicated. Premiered on CBS: September 8, 1990–September 1997. Rebroadcast on USA: September 20, 1993–September 1998.*

**Voices**
**Michaelangelo:** Townsend Coleman; **Leonardo:** Cam Clarke; **Donatello:** Barry Gordon; **Raphael:** Rob Paulsen; **Shredder:** James Avery; **Krang:** Pat Fraley; **April O'Neil:** Renae Jacobs; **Splinter:** Peter Renaday; **Irma:** Jennifer Darling

### ◉ TEENAGE MUTANT NINJA TURTLES (2003)

Continuing battles of cult-hero martial arts turtles—Leonardo, Raphael, Michaelangelo and Donatello—in all-new irreverent battles of the sewer-dwelling favorites against ruthless gangs, lowlife crooks, deranged cyborgs and others in this half-hour animated revival for FOX network. Produced by 4Kids Entertainment in association with the characters' license holders, Mirage Licensing, the series became a powerhouse ratings success on FOX's Saturday-morning *FOX Box* (now called *4Kids TV*) program block, beginning in February 2003. With Mirage Studios asserting more creative control over the outcome, the characters had a darker and edgier feel in the way they were drawn that was closer to its original comic roots than in the first, 1987 Saturday-morning series. Featuring more complex plotlines, but with lighthearted moments, the well-crafted series was a popular fixture on FOX for four consecutive seasons, with 104 episodes airing altogether, and also on Cartoon Network.

For its fifth season, starting on July 29, 2006, the series was overhauled and retitled *Teenage Mutant Ninja Turtles–Fast Forward,* with the half-shelled heroes redesigned with new costumes

*The Teenage Mutant Ninja Turtles in a scene from their long-running CBS Saturday morning series. Characters © Mirage Studios Inc., exclusively licensed by Surge Licensing.* (COURTESY: MURAKAMI-WOLF SWENSON)

and equipped with energy-powered weapons, and recast into the future with their wise teacher, Splinter, ending up in Manhattan in the year 2015 where they encounter new allies and powerful new enemies, including genetically enhanced versions of themselves. *A Mirage Licensing/4Kids Entertainment Production. Color. Half-hour. Premiered on FOX: February 8, 2003–July 2006. Premiered on CAR: December 29, 2003–June 4, 2006.*

*Voices*
**Leonardo:** Michael Sinterniklaas; **Raphael:** Wayne Grayson; **Michaelangelo:** Frank Frankson; **Donatello:** Sam Regal; **Splinter:** Darren Dunstan; **The Shredder:** Scottie Ray; **April O'Neal:** Veronica Taylor; **Casey Jones:** Marc Thompson; **Baxter Stockman:** Scott Williams; **Hun:** Greg Carey; **Harry/Quarry:** Eric Stuart; **Karai:** Karen Neil; **Constable Biggles/Sh'Okanabo:** Sean Schemmel

## ◉ TEENAGE MUTANT NINJA TURTLES— FAST FORWARD

Having lived a sheltered, happy life underground for so many years, Splinter and his sons leave the sewer behind and find themselves transported 100 years into the future, to New York City circa 2015, where, joined by Turtles Leonardo, Raphael, Michelangelo and Donatello, they embark on a whole new series of adventures living above ground with humans. Shelving the idea of producing a fifth season of the popular updated FOX series that began in 2003, this all-new series featured 26 original animated comedy adventures and was launched on the *4Kids TV* block on FOX in September 2006, with 15 episodes airing through March 2007's release of the advanced CGI-animated feature film *Teenage Mutant Ninja Turtles* (2007). *A 4Kids Entertainment Production. Color. Half-hour. Premiered on FOX: July 29, 2006.*

*Voices*
**Michaelangelo:** Frank Frankson; **Leonardo:** Michael Sinterniklaas; **Raphael:** Wayne Grayson; **Donatello:** Sam Riegel; **Splinter:** Darren Dunstan; **Shredder:** Scottie Ray

## ◉ TEEN TITANS

In a future ripe with intergalactic unrest and interplanetary battles, a new young breed of superheroes—Robin, Starfire, Raven, Cyborg, and Beast Boy—who reside in their large T-shaped Titan Tower, unite to protect Earth from their arch-nemesis Slade and his mighty minions in this stylishly animated series of high-flying adventures based on DC Comics' *The New Teen Titans* comic-book series created in 1980 by Marv Wolfman and George Perez.

The final episode of the 13-episode first season was recorded by the end of January 2003, and the long-awaited action/adventure series was slated to bow on the Kids' WB in May 2003, with the first episode, "Final Exam." However, the series premiere was pushed off to August and November. Instead the show debuted on Cartoon Network on Saturday, July 19, at 9 P.M., airing thereafter in this same time slot. The series was then previewed on the Kids' WB! in November but reportedly did poorly in the ratings. Nonetheless, that December, for an entire week, the Kids' WB officially began airing new episodes of the series.

During the series' first season, Cartoon Network's telecasts earned double- and triple-digit ratings gains among kids six to 11 and two to 11, and it was the most-watched network premiere ever with boys ages six to 11. Replays on Sunday evenings also ranked as the network's most-watched program in its time period with the same age groups for boys and girls. After airing for five successful seasons, the 65-episode series was canceled.

In March 2006, Cartoon Network announced plans to roll out a brace of TV-movies based on the popular series, including *Codename: Kids Next Door*, *Foster's Home for Imaginary Friends* and *Teen Titans*, resulting in production of the feature-length *Teen Titans: Trouble in Tokyo*. *A Warner Bros. Cartoons Production. Color. Half-hour. Premiered on CAR: July 19, 2003. Premiered on the WB (Kids' WB!): December 8–12, 2003 (series).*

*Voices*
**Robin:** Scott Menville; **Beast Boy:** Greg Cipes; **Starfire/Blackfire:** Hynden Walch; **Raven:** Tara Strong; **Cyborg:** Khary Payton; **Tramm:** Dave Coulier. **Aqualad:** Wil Wheaton; **Slade, the Terminator:** Ron Perlman; **Jinx and Gizmo:** Clancy Brown, Tom Kenny, Rino Romano, Lauren Tom; **Mammoth:** Kevin Michael Richardson; **Hive's Headmistress:** Andrea Romano

## ◉ TEEN WOLF

Scott Howard, an average teenager, has a secret known only to his best friends, Styles and Boof: He turns into a werewolf (so does his father Harold, sister Lupe and Grandma) in this weekly Saturday-morning series based on the 1985 hit comedy starring Michael J. Fox. Actor James Hampton (Scott's dad in the original movie) was the only cast member from the film to lend his voice to the series. *A Southern Star/Hanna-Barbera Australia/Kushner-Locke Company/Clubhouse Pictures/Atlantic Entertainment Group Production. Color. Half-hour. Premiered on CBS: September 13, 1986–August 27, 1988. Rebroadcast on CBS: October 29, 1988–September 2, 1989.*

*Voices*
**Scott Howard/Teen Wolf:** Townsend Coleman; **Boof:** Jeannie Elias; **Grandma/Mrs. Sesslick:** June Foray; **Grandpa:** Stacy Keach Sr.; **Harold:** James Hampton; **Stiles:** Donny Most; **Mick:** Craig Schaffer; **Chuck:** Will Ryan

## ◉ TEKNOMAN

In the year 2087 an evil intergalactic warlord named Darkon invades Earth. It is up to a young man who possesses a powerful crystal and can transform himself into an unstoppable crime fighting machine and his team of superagents to save the planet from destruction in this half-hour action/adventure series that originally aired in the United States on the UPN Network's fall 1995 Saturday lineup. *A Saban Entertainment Production. Color. Half-hour. Premiered on UPN: September 10, 1995.*

## ◉ TELE-COMICS

Regarded as one of the first cartoon series ever produced for television (along with the serialized, cliff-hanging adventures of *Cru-*

sader *Rabbit*) this half-hour syndicated series, using comic-strip panel illustrations and animation effects, featured four serialized stories: "Brother Goose," "Joey and Jug," "Rick Rack Street Agent" and "Su Lah." Receiving limited television airplay in 1949, NBC optioned the property in 1950 and repackaged (and retitled) the program as *NBC Comics*. The new series, comprised of three-minute vignettes, made broadcast history as the first made-for-TV network cartoon program. Following the conclusion of its run on NBC, the series reverted to its original title and was telecast on live-action children's programs throughout the United States. (See *NBC Comics* entry for further details.) *A Vallee Video Production. Black-and-white. Fifteen minutes. Premiered: 1949. Syndicated.*

### ◎ TENCHI MUYO!

An average-looking high school teen (Tenchi Masaki) fights off the affections of a condemned beauteous female space pirate (Ryoko) and her mystical army of beauties seeking refuge at his serene mountaintop home, while employing his newfound powers, including a magical sword, to battle for the hand of an outer space princess in this half-hour anime series based on Kajishma Masaki's cult-classic manga of the same name.

Originally produced in Japan in 1995 as *Tenchi Universe* and re-edited, retitled and redubbed in English five years later as *Tenchi Muyo!*, this 26-episode fantasy/adventure series made its U.S. television debut in July 2000 on Cartoon Network's *Toonami* action-adventure block in the 7:00 P.M. time slot, where it aired for two seasons. *A Geneon Entertainment/Pioneer Entertainment Production. Color. Half-hour. Premiered on CAR: July 3, 2000–May 18, 2002.*

*Voices*
**Tenchi Maaki:** Matthew K. Miller; **Ryoko Hakabi:** Petrea Burchard; **Ayeka Jurai:** Jennifer Darling; **Sasami Jurai/Kiyone Makabi/Tsuami:** Sherry Lynn; **Mihoshi Kurumitsu:** Rebecca Forstadt, Ellen Gerstel; **Washu Hakubi:** K.T. Vogt; **Katsunito/Nobuyuki:** Jay Hopper; **Ryo-Ohki:** Debi Deryberry

### ◎ TENKO AND THE GUARDIANS OF THE MAGIC

In a mix of live-action and animation, real-life illusionist Princess Tenko uses her special powers as a magician to entertain audiences while scouting the globe with her band of crime-fighting Guardians (Hawk, Bolt, Steel and Ali) to recover lost magical jewels before they fall into the wrong hands in this 26-episode half-hour fantasy/adventure series made for first-run syndication. *A Saban Entertainment/Tour de Force International Production. Color. Half-hour. Premiered: (week of) September 11, 1995. Syndicated.*

*Voices*
**Princes Tenko:** Mary Kay Bergman; **Other Voices:** Thomas Lee, Webster King, Robbie Mathews, Michelle Alberts, Sofia Coleman, Derek Patrick, Gloria Bell, Michael Sorich, Pearl Sutton

*Live-Action Cast*
**Princess Tenko:** Herself

### ◎ TENNESSEE TUXEDO AND HIS TALES

Wisecracking penguin Tennessee Tuxedo (voiced by Don Adams) and walrus Chumley undertake to change the living conditions of the denizens of Megalopolis Zoo. When insoluble situations arise, the pair visit their educator friend, answer man Phineas J. Whoopie, who tackles their problems scientifically and practically. Other recurring characters were Yak, a long-horned steer, and Baldy, a bald American eagle, who portrayed Tennessee's and Chumley's friends.

*Tennessee Tuxedo tells pal Chumley to hang on in a scene from the 1960s television favorite* Tennessee Tuxedo and His Tales. *© Leonardo-TTV*

Also featured were supporting segments of "The King and Odie," "The Hunter" and "Tooter Turtle," each repeated from the NBC series, *King Leonardo and His Short Subjects*. The program later added a new segment, seen first on this program, called "The World of Commander McBragg," the tall-tale adventures of a long-winded ex-naval commander with a fantastic imagination. The segment was later repeated on *The Hoppity Hooper Show* and *Underdog*.

Introduced on CBS in 1963, the series, following its initial three-season run, was rebroadcast on ABC during the 1966–67 and 1967–68 seasons (the latter billed as *The Beagles and Tennessee Tuxedo*). *A Leonardo TV Production with Total TV Productions. Color. Half-hour. Premiered on CBS: September 28, 1963–September 3, 1966. Rebroadcast on ABC: September 10, 1966–December 17, 1966.*

*Voices*
**Tennessee Tuxedo:** Don Adams; **Chumley:** Bradley Bolke; **Professor Phineas J. Whoopie:** Larry Storch; **Yak/Baldy/The Hunter/Commander McBragg:** Kenny Delmar; **King Leonardo/Biggy Brat:** Jackson Beck; **Odie Cologne/Itchy Brother/Tooter Turtle:** Allan Swift; **Mr. Wizard:** Frank Milano; **The Fox:** Ben Stone; **Other Voices:** Jackson Beck, Ben Stone, Allen Swift, Delo States, Norman Rose, Mort Marshall, George Irving

### ◎ TESTAMENT: THE BIBLE IN ANIMATION

The time-tested stories of the Old Testament, scripted and designed based on theological opinions from Jewish, Protestant, Catholic and Muslim experts, are presented in this half-hour series from the producers of *Shakespeare: The Animated Tales*. First premiering overseas in the Welsh language on S4C and in English on BBC 2 in autumn of 1996, the series debuted in the United States on HBO in January 1997, shown every Monday night. That year the series was awarded an Emmy for outstanding individual achievement in animation. *A BBC Wales/S4C/Cartwyn Cymru (Cardiff)/Christmas Films (Moscow) Production. Half-hour. Color. Premiered on HBO: January 6, 1997–January 1, 1998.*

*Voices*
**Noah:** Joss Ackland; **God:** David Burke; **David:** Paul McGann; **Other Voices:** Hannah Gordon, Ciaran Hinds, Anton Lesser, Ian McNeice, Clive Russell, David Schofield, Ivor Roberts

### ◎ THAT'S WARNER BROS.!

One hundred eighty-five classic *Looney Tunes* and *Merrie Melodies* cartoon shorts, culled from the Warner Bros. cartoon library, were repackaged under this weekday offering, telecast on the WB

Television Network's Kids' WB! lineup in 1995. Each half-hour broadcast included three cartoons and a short recurring segment called "Hip Clip," featuring excerpts reedited from existing cartoons. (Most cartoons were previously broadcast on Nickelodeon's *Looney Tunes* program.) In 1996 the program was overhauled and changed to *The Bugs n' Daffy Show*, featuring a new animated opening of Daffy and Bugs singing the show's theme song. *A Warner Bros. Production. Color. Half-hour. Premiered on the WB (Kids' WB!): September 18, 1995–August 23, 1996.*

**Voices**
Mel Blanc (primary voice)

## ◉ THESE ARE THE DAYS
In the fashion of TV's dramatic series *The Waltons*, this series chronicled the trials and tribulations of the turn-of-the-century Day family, led by Martha, a widow; her children, Ben, Cathy and Danny; and their grandfather, Jeff Day, owner and proprietor of Day General Store, in their hometown of Elmsville. This weekly Saturday-morning series composed of 16 half-hour episodes, first aired on ABC in 1974. *A Hanna-Barbera Production. Color. Half-hour. Premiered on ABC: September 7, 1974–September 5, 1976. Rebroadcast on CAR: June 28, 1993–September 17, 1993 (weekdays).*

**Voices**
**Martha Day:** June Lockhart; **Kay Day:** Pamelyn Ferdin; **Danny Day:** Jack E. Haley; **Grandpa Day:** Henry Jones; **Ben Day:** Andrew Parks; **Homer:** Frank Cady

## ◉ THINK PINK PANTHER!
The Pink Panther returned to NBC's Saturday-morning lineup with this fourth and final series entry for the network. The program repeated episodes of the nonspeaking feline star, "Misterjaws, Supershark" and "The Texas Toads." Each was previously featured in *The Pink Panther Laugh and a Half Hour and a Half Show. A De Patie-Freleng Enterprises Production. Color. Premiered on NBC: February 4, 1978–September 2, 1978.*

**Voices**
**Misterjaws:** Arte Johnson; **Catfish, his friend:** Arnold Stang; **Fatso:** Don Diamond; **Banjo:** Tom Holland

## ◉ THE 13 GHOSTS OF SCOOBY-DOO
In his 16th year on television, Scooby-Doo reteams with Shaggy, Daphne, Scrappy-Doo and a new sidekick, Flim Flam, a nine-year-old con man, as they track down the 13 worst ghosts, goblins and monsters in spine-tingling new adventures, narrated by famed movie macabre artist Vincent Price (called Vincent Van Ghoul). In 1986 the ABC Saturday-morning series was replaced by reruns of March *All-Star Laff-A-Lympics*. Later the proram was rerun on Cartoon Network and Boomerang. *A Hanna-Barbera Production. Color. Half-hour. Premiered on ABC: September 7, 1985–February 22, 1986. Rebroadcast on CAR: December 12, 1994–December 16, 1994. Rebroadcast on BOOM: December 10, 2001–December 31, 2005. Rebroadcast on USA: Fall 1989–Fall 1994. Rebroadcast on TBS/TNT: Fall 1994–98. Syndicated.*

**Voices**
**Scooby-Doo/Scrappy-Doo:** Don Messick; **Shaggy Rogers:** Casey Kasem; **Daphne Blake:** Heather North; **Flim Flam:** Susan Blu; **Vincent Van Ghoul:** Vincent Price; **Weerd:** Artie Johnson; **Bogel:** Howard Morris

## ◉ THIS IS AMERICA, CHARLIE BROWN
Charlie Brown and the gang (Lucy, Linus, Snoopy, Schroeder, Sally and Peppermint Patty) revisit important events in American history in this weekly CBS cartoon miniseries comprised of eight half-hour stories. Series components included: "The *Mayflower* Voyagers," "The Birth of the Constitution," "The NASA Space Station," "The Wright Brothers at Kitty Hawk," "The Building of the Transcontinental Railroad," "The Great Inventors," "The Smithsonian and the Presidency" and "The Music and Heroes of America." The series was repeated on CBS in its entirety in the summer of 1990 and rebroadcast on Nickelodeon from 1998–2000.

*A Lee Mendelson-Bill Melendez Production in association with Charles M. Schulz Creative Organization and United Features Syndicate. Color. Half-hour. Premiered on CBS: October 21, 1988; November 11, 1988; February 10, 1989; March 10, 1989; April 19, 1989; May 23, 1989; May 30, 1990; July 25, 1990. Beginning in 1998, the historical cartoon series was rebroadcast in its entirety on Nickelodeon. Rebroadcast on NICK: ("The Birth of the Constitution") February 2, 1998; February 20, 1998; March 31, 1998; April 28, 1998; May 28, 1998; July 13, 1998; July 27, 1998; August 12, 1998; September 13, 1998; October 26, 1998; November 2, 1998; November 16, 1998; November 30, 1998; March 31, 1999; May 22, 1999; June 14, 1999; June 28, 1999; August 28, 1999; April 1, 2000; ("The Building of the Transcontinental Railroad") February 8, 1998; February 26, 1998; April 8, 1998; May 10, 1998; June 12, 1998; July 13, 1998; August 16, 1998; September 7, 1998; November 17, 1998; December 26, 1998; April 10, 1999; May 28, 1999; July 5, 1999; July 19, 1999; July 23, 1999; October 24, 1999; ("The Great Inventors") March 1, 1998; April 2, 1998; May 6, 1998; June 5, 1998; June 8, 1998; June 22, 1998; July 21, 1998; August 3, 1998; August 17, 1998; August 31, 1998; December 21, 1998; January 24, 1999; April 16, 1999; June 4, 1999; September 6, 1999; September 20, 1999; October 30, 1999; July 3, 2000; July 17, 2000; ("The Mayflower Voyagers") February 1, 1998; February 18, 1998; March 22, 1998; April 22, 1998; May 25, 1998; June 26, 1998; July 6, 1998; July 20, 1998; August 30, 1998; October 19, 1998; November 22, 1998; November 25, 1998; March 1, 1999; March 15, 1999; May 6, 1999; June 21, 1999; August 21, 1999; January 22, 2000; ("The Music and Heroes of America") February 12, 1998; March 15, 1998; April 17, 1998; May 17, 1998; June 17, 1998; August 2, 1998; September 3, 1998; September 14, 1998; September 28, 1998; December 23, 1998; April 9, 1999; May 23, 1999; July 17, 1999; October 14, 1999; November 6, 1999; ("The NASA Space Station") February 6, 1998; February 24, 1998; April 3, 1998; May 11, 1998; May 25, 1998; June 26, 1998; July 25, 1998; August 10, 1998; September 10, 1998; November 16, 1998; December 24, 1998; January 23, 1999; April 5, 1999; April 15, 1999; April 19, 1999; June 7, 1999; August 4, 1999; November 27, 1999; ("The Smithsonian and the Presidency") February 16, 1998; March 20, 1998; May 3, 1998; June 2, 1998; July 5, 1998; August 10, 1998; August 24, 1998; September 24, 1998; October 21, 1998; December 28, 1998; April 11, 1999; May 29, 1999; June 7, 1999; June 21, 1999; August 20, 1999; October 31, 1999; August 21, 2000; ("The Wright Brothers at Kitty Hawk") February 22, 1998; April 1, 1998; May 7, 1998; June 1, 1998; June 9, 1998; June 15, 1998; June 29, 1998; July 27, 1998; August 19, 1998; September 20, 1998; November 9, 1998; November 23, 1998; January 11, 1999; January 25, 1999; April 17, 1999; June 5, 1999; August 2, 1999; August 16, 1999; August 29, 1999; January 10, 2000; January 24, 2000.*

**Voices**
**Charlie Brown:** Erin Chase, Jason Rifle; **Lucy:** Ami Foster, Eric Gayle; **Linus:** Jeremy Miller, Brandon Stewart; **Sally Brown:** Christina Lange, Brittany Thorton; **Peppermint Patty:** Jason Mendelson; **Schroeder:** Curtis Anderson; **Marcie:** Keri Houlihan,

Marie Lynn Wise, Tani Taylor Powers; **Franklin:** Hakeen Abdul Samad, Grant Gelt

## ◎ THE 3 FRIENDS AND JERRY SHOW

New kid in town, Jerry, who isn't accepted by his classmates, does everything possible to be liked by a gang of three 10-year-old boys, Frank, Thomas and Eric, known as "The 3 Friends," in this animated series, originally created by Magnus Carlsson and produced by Happy Life and TV-Loonland studios for Swedish television. The series aired in the United States on FOX Family Channel from August 1998 to February 2000. *A Happy Life/TV-Loonland/ HIT Entertainment Production. Color. Half-hour. Premiered on FOX FAM: August 23, 1998–February 25, 2000.*

### Voices

**Frank:** Trey Parker; **Thomas:** Jeff Bennett; **Eric:** Mark Camacho; **Jerry:** Tara Strong; **Jerry's Dad:** Billy West; **Principal:** Scott McNeil; **Narrator:** John Leguizamo; **Additional Voices:** Ian James Corlett, Andrea Libman, Doug Rand

## ◎ THE THREE ROBONIC STOOGES

Originally introduced as a weekly component of CBS's live-action cartoon show *The Skatebirds*, this series of 32 five-minute cartoons was so well received (it drew the best ratings in *The Skateboards*) that CBS decided to give the series (formerly known as "The Robonic Stooges") its own Saturday-morning time slot in 1978 as a midseason replacement. Norman Maurer, a former Three Stooges producer and son-in-law of Moe Howard, wrote the series which cast the boys as bionic-limbed superstooges. Repeated was another supporting cartoon segment, "Woofer and Wimper, Dog Detectives." In 1979, the series was moved to Sunday mornings until concluding its broadcasts two years later. (See *The Skatebirds* for voice credits.) *A Hanna-Barbera Production in association with Norman Maurer Productions. Color. Half-hour. Premiered on CBS: January 28, 1978–September 6, 1981.*

## ◎ 3-SOUTH

Absurd comical misadventures of longtime friends Sanford and Del and their roommate, Joe, encountering life as college freshmen at Barder College in this short-lived animated series, created by *Family Guy* writer Mark Hentemann (also the voice of Joe) for MTV and first and only series to date produced for the popular cable network by Warner Bros. Animation. Of the 13 produced episodes, only 11 aired. *An MTV Animation/Warner Bros. Animation Production. Color. Half-hour. Premiered on MTV: November 7, 2002–January 16, 2003.*

### Voices

**Sanford Reilly:** Brian Dunkleman; **Del Swanson/Todd Wolfschmidtmansternowitz:** Brian Poselin; **Joe Tait/Ed Bickel:** Mark Hentemann; **Other Voices:** Dean Earheart, Jeffrey Tambor

## ◎ THUNDARR THE BARBARIAN

When a new world evolves unlike the one before, savagery, sorcery and evil beings now rule the universe. One man battles these evil elements: Thundarr, a slave who frees himself and tries to bring justice back into the world by taking on the evil elements that prevail in this half-hour Saturday-morning series, first broadcast on ABC. Premiering in 1980, the 21 episode series was a ratings hit on ABC airing two seasons and was rerun on NBC for one season. After reairing on USA Network in the 1980s, the series has since been broadcast on Cartoon Network and Boomerang. *A Ruby-Spears Enterprises Production. Color. Half-hour. Premiered on ABC: October 4, 1980–September 12, 1982. Rebroadcast on NBC: April 9, 1983–September 8, 1984. Rebroadcast on USA: 1980s.*

*Rebroadcast on CAR: October 3, 1992–April 4, 1993 (Sundays); April 5, 1993–September 17, 1993 (weekdays); January 8, 1994– April 3, 1994 (Saturdays, Sundays); April 9, 1994–September 3, 1994 (Saturdays); September 5, 1994–October 5, 1996 (weekdays, Saturdays). Rebroadcast on BOOM: April 11, 2000–    .*

### Voices

**Thundarr the Barbarian:** Bob Ridgely; **Princess Ariel, his aide:** Nellie Bellflower; **Ookla, his aide:** Henry Corden

## ◎ THUNDERBIRDS: 2086

The heroes of this futuristic series are members of International Rescue, an elite corps of daredevil cadets, who fly fantastic fleets of supersonic vehicles as they protect the world from man-made and natural disasters. *An ITC Entertainment Production. Color. Half-hour. Premiered on SHO: 1983–1986. Syndicated: September 1986.*

### Voices

Joan Audiberti, Paollo Audiberti, Earl Hammond, Ira Lewis, Keith Mandell, Alexander Marshall, Terry Van Tell

## ◎ THUNDERCATS

Originally action-figure toys, this quintet of muscular heroes (Lion-O, Tygra, Panthro, Cheetara, Jaga and Pumrya) battles the sinister Mutants with good always triumphing over evil in these 65 half-hour episodes, produced for first-run syndication. The program was introduced via a one-hour special entitled *ThunderCats*, in January 1985, prior to the distribution of 65 half-hour episodes in the fall. In 1986 a two-hour special was made, *ThunderCats Ho!* which was reedited into a five-part adventure for the weekday strip. *A Rankin-Bass Production. Color. Half-hour. Premiered: January 1985 (one-hour special). Premiered: Sept 11, 1985–90 (series). Syndicated. Rebroadcast on CAR: March 17, 1997–May 29, 1998; August 31, 1998–October 1998, January 25, 1999–March 12, 1999; July 19, 1999–February 27, 2000; March 27, 2000–May 4, 2001; December 31, 2001–February 22, 2002; April 15–May 31, 2002.*

### Voices

**Lion-O-Jackalman:** Larry Kenney; **Snarf/S-S-Slithe:** Robert McFadden; **Cheetara/Wilykit:** Lynne Lipton; **Panthro:** Earle Hyman; **Wilykat/Monkian/Ben-Gali/Tygra:** Peter Newman; **Mumm-Ra/Vultureman/Jaga:** Earl Hammond; **Pumyra:** Gerianne Raphael; **Other Voices:** Doug Preis

## ◎ THE TICK

Replete with tight-fitting tights, this clumsy, 400-pound blue bug of cult comic-book fame sets out to save The City from villainy with the help of his partner/ex-accountant, Arthur, who dons a moth costume, in this satirical half-hour series based on the hit comic book by cartoonist Ben Edlund (who contributed many of the scripts, storyboards and models for the series). It debuted on the FOX Network in 1994. In September of 1966 Comedy Central picked up the series, airing brand-new episodes, even while FOX Network continued to air the show, through 1997. During the holidays of the 1995–96 television season, FOX aired the series' only half-hour, *The Tick Loves Santa!* first on Saturday morning and then in prime time. *An Akom/Graz Entertainment/Sunbow Production. Color. Half-hour. Premiered on FOX: September 10, 1994–September 25, 1997; Premiered on COM: September 22, 1996–March 23, 1997. Rebroadcast on TDIS: June 13, 2005–.*

### Voices

**The Tick:** Townsend Coleman; **Arthur:** Micky Dolenz (1994–95); Rob Paulsen (1995–96); **Speak/Sewer Urchin:** Jess Harnell; **Die Fledermaus:** Cam Clarke; **Mr. Mental/Multiple Santa:** Jim Cummings; **Taft:** Dorian Harewood; **The Deadly Bulb/Mr.**

Smartypants/Thrakorzog: Maurice LaMarche; **American Maid:** Kay Lenz; **Dot:** Kimmy Robertson; **Jungle Janet:** Susan Silo; **Carmelita Vatos:** Jennifer Hale; **Breadmaster:** Martin Jarvis; **Chairface Chippendale:** Tony Jay

## TIMELESS TALES FROM HALLMARK

Hanna-Barbera in association with Hallmark Entertainment produced this 1990 series of educational cartoon adaptations, originally made available on home video and laser disc, featuring half-hour editions of eight popular children's stories: "The Elves and the Shoemaker," "The Emperor's New Clothes," "Puss in Boots," "Rapunzel," "Rumpelstiltzkin," "The Steadfast Tin Soldier," "Thumbelina" and "The Ugly Duckling." Hosted by award-winning singer Olivia Newton John (who appears in live action), each episode offered Earth-saving environmental messages for children. In December of 1991 USA Network aired the series for one week. *A Hanna-Barbera/Hallmark Entertainment Production. Color. Half-hour. Premiered on USA: December 16, 1991–December 20, 1991. Rebroadcast on CAR: August 14, 1994; April 16, 1995.*

### Cast (live action)
**Host:** Olivia Newton-John

## TIME SQUAD

A hapless trio of time cops journeys back in time to prevent important moments in history from unraveling and turning out differently than they happened, from famed cotton gin inventor Eli Whitney creating flesh-eating robots to well-known composer Beethoven taking up professional wrestling, in this animated comedy series created by David Wasson for Cartoon Network. The 26-episode comedy series, offering two cartoon adventures per half-hour, lasted two seasons through November 2003, thereafter continuing to air in reruns for two more seasons. *A Cartoon Network Studios Production. Color. Half-hour. Premiered on CAR: June 8, 2001–September 23, 2005.*

### Voices
**Beauregard "Buck" Tuddrussel:** Rob Paulsen; **Lawrence "Larry" 3000:** Mark Hamill; **Otto Osworth:** Pamela Segall; **Shiela Sternwell:** Mari Weiss; **J.T. Laser:** Jim Wise; **Sister Thornley:** Dee Dee Rescher; **George Washington:** Michael Gough; **Butcher:** David Wasson; **Alfred Nobel:** John Kassir; **Eli Whitney:** Tom Kenny; **Blackbeard:** Roger Rose; **Comic:** Carlos Alazraqui; **Horses:** Frank Welker; **Announcer:** Daran Norris

## TIMON AND PUMBAA
(See THE LION KING'S TIMON AND PUMBAA.)

## TIMOTHY GOES TO SCHOOL

Timothy, a smart, young raccoon, and his kindergarten classmates—Nora, the boisterous mouse; Fritz, the curious badger; Lilly, the forgetful fox; and Yoko, the violin-playing cat—learn the importance of being on their best behavior and keeping a positive attitude in school while learning about the world around them in this delightful half-hour animated series, based on acclaimed British author/illustrator Rosemary Wells's children's books. Premiering on September 30, 2000, 26 original episodes of the half-hour children's cartoon series aired weekdays on PBS Kids as part of a three-hour *Bookworm Bunch* weekend program block, along with *George Shrinks, Corduroy, Elliot Moose, Marvin the Tap-Dancing Horse* and *Seven Little Monsters.* The series remained as part of a revised two-hour *Bookworm Bunch* block until Labor Day weekend 2004. The program has since aired weekday mornings on the Learning Channel (TLC) and Discov-

ery Kids. *A Nelvana Limited/Animation Services Hong Kong Ltd. Production. Color. Half-hour. Premiered on PBS Kids: September 30, 2000–September 20, 2001; Rebroadcast on PBS Kids: September 27, 2001–September 4, 2004. Rebroadcast on TLC/DSCK: September 2004–.*

### Voices
**Timothy:** Austin Diiulio; **Mrs. Jenkins:** Fiona Reid; **Yoko:** Lisa Yamanaka; **Doris:** Tracy Ryan; **Nora:** Alyson Court; **Fritz:** Laurie Elliott; **Lilly:** Mag Ruffman; **Charles:** Max Morrow; **Grace:** Linda Kash; **Claude:** Joanne Vannicola; **Henry:** Jamie Walson

## TIN TIN

A European comic-strip favorite, young teenager reporter Tin Tin and his faithful dog, Snowy, engage in rough adventures and mysterious quests in this animated adaptation of Belgian cartoonist Herge's creation. Produced in France and Belgium from 1961 through 1966, the series was first syndicated in the United States by National Television Associates (NTA) in 1962 and again by Tele-Features in 1971. The company of "Bozo" creator Larry Harmon, Larry Harmon Productions, did the American voice dubbing for the series. (Harmon himself did the voice of Tintin, although he went uncredited, while voice impressario Paul Frees lent his voice to other characters.) In 1991 a new series, *The New Adventures of Tintin*, was produced, airing on HBO. *A Tele-Hatchette/Belvision Production in association with National Television Associates (NTA) and Tele-Features. Black-and-white. Color. Premiered: 1962, 1971. Syndicated.*

### Voices (U.S. version)
**Tintin:** Larry Harmon; **Other Voices:** Paul Frees

## TINY PLANETS (A.K.A. BING AND BONG'S TINY PLANETS)

From the icy environs of their home planet in the heart of the Tiny Universe, two curious furry inhabitants, Bing, the larger, older abominable snowman, and Bong, his younger, smaller six-legged sidekick, speak through actions in pantomime and spend their time exploring nearby planets in the solar system (thanks to their fluffy white couch that launches them into space), including the mysteries of light, color, sound, technology, self and nature while solving problems and having fun at the same time. Coproduced by the United States' Sesame Workshop and the United Kingdom's Pepper Ghost Productions, this interactive series of 65 five-minute adventures, much like several other edu-tainment shows, *Rolie Polie Olie, Blues Clues* and *Oswald,* was aimed at encouraging children ages three to six to be explorers while stimulating their sense of discovery.

Originally conceived in 2000 as a preschool series to be shown on PBS by the late Nina Elias-Bamberger of Sesame Workshop, responsible for developing *Dragon Tales* and several other children's series, the show instead premiered in the United Kingdom, where it won a British Academy of Film and Television Arts (BAFTA) Award in 2001, before airing in the United States on the commercial-free children's program network, Noggin, in the spring of 2002 as a series of interstitials between the network's other half-hour children's programs. Nominated as best new property by *License! Magazine* at that year's New York Licensing Show, the fast-paced, animated interstitial series, which also had been sold to 73 other countries, was so well received that by October 2003 it was expanded to a half-hour and Noggin awarded it its own weekday morning time slot. *A Sesame Workshop/Pepper's Ghost Productions Production. Color. Half-hour. Premiered on NOG: April 1, 2002–January 10, 2007 (interstitials). Premiered on NOG: October 13, 2003–April 4, 2006 (series).*

## ◎ TINY TOON ADVENTURES

(See STEVEN SPIELBERG PRESENTS TINY TOON ADVENTURES.)

## ◎ TOAD PATROL

A group of young toadlets struggles to survive a perilous journey through the Great Forest after missing the migration to Toad Hollow and becoming trapped, making many new friends along the way and learning the importance of friendship, cooperation and hard work. The 26-episode, Canadian-produced fantasy/adventure series, based on the concept of *Toad Tunnels* created by George Sarson (who also created the series), aired for two seasons in the United States on Toon Disney beginning in 2002. *A Toadbag Productions/AKOM Productions/VISION Entertainment/Universal Pictures International Production. Color. Half-hour. Premiered on TDIS: September 3, 2002–September 5, 2004.*

*Voices*

**Mistle Toad:** Long John Baldry; **Panther Cap/Beauty Stem:** Sonja Ball; **Hera/The Outsider:** Kate Hurman; **Erebus/Digger/Puff Ball:** Rick Jones; **Daphne:** Ann K. Leger; **Oyster:** Bryn McAuley; **Slippery Jack:** Brady Moffatt; **Elf Cup:** Nancy Nelson; **Earth Star:** Michael O'Reilly; **Fur Foot:** Terrence Scammell; **Shaggy Mane:** Neil Shee

## ◎ TODD MCFARLANE'S SPAWN

The first project of HBO Animation, a new production division created to develop original animated programming for HBO and explore the largely untapped field of adult-oriented animation, *Todd McFarlane's Spawn* is the story of CIA operative Al Simmons, who cuts a deal with the devil for a second chance on Earth. He returns to the living world five years later as a soldier of evil with incredible powers in this half-hour series adaptation of McFarlane's hit comic book. McFarlane also served as executive producer of the series. The late-night, visually striking, cutting-edge animated series debuted in May of 1997 with the season opener "Burning Visions." *A Madhouse Ltd./D.R. Movie/HBO Animation/Ko-Ko Entertainment/Todd McFarlane Entertainment Production. Color. Half-hour. Premiered: May 23, 1997–May 28, 1999.*

*Voices*

**Spawn:** Keith David; **Cogliostro:** Richard Dysart; **Clown:** Michael Nicolosi; **Wanda Blake:** Dominique Jennings; **Terry Fitzgerald:** Victor Love; **Cyan:** Kath Soucie; **Sam Burke/Tony Twist:** James Keane; **Twitch Williams:** Michael McShane; **Jason Wynn:** John Rafter Lee; **Senator Scott McMillan/Billy Kincaid:** Ronny Cox

## ◎ TODDWORLD

Quirky but charming preschool series featuring an artistic, offbeat six-year-old boy named Todd with a highly active imagination, along with his friends Pickle, Dot, Sophie, his dog Otto and cat Mitzi and a wide assortment of vibrantly colored animals, in uplifting stories dealing with common social challenges of a young child's life and offering reassuring messages about acceptance, tolerance and the importance of self-confidence along with the prevailing message that "It's okay to be different," based on Todd Parr's best-selling collection of children's books.

Produced by the Woodland Hills, California-based award-winning Mike Young Productions animation studios, the 52-episode, 2-D Crayola color-animated half-hour fantasy/adventure series, comprised of two 11-minute episodes, aired five days a week on the Learning Channel's *Ready Set Learn!* commercial-free preschool programming block and two times a day, five days a week on the Discovery Kids channel beginning in November 2004. *A Mike Young Productions/L&G Creative Resources/Discovery Kids Production. Color. Half-hour. Premiered on TLC/DISC Kids: November 1, 2004.*

*Voices*

**Todd:** Ryan Hirakida; **Pickle:** Peter Kelamis; **Stella:** Maggie Blue O'Hara; **Sophie:** Chantal Strand; **Benny the Dog:** Doron Bell; **Mitzi the Cat:** Shirley Millner

## ◎ TOKYO PIG

Adventures of a young boy named Spencer, whose drawings in his magic diary come to life, leaving him with one of its characters, a pig named Sunny, who becomes his pet in this anime series first seen on Japan's TV Tokyo in July 1997 under the title of *Super Pig*. Dubbed in English with American actors, the half-hour fantasy/adventure series premiered in the United States on ABC Family in September 2002 as part of its weekend action-adventure anime block, along with rebroadcasts of the popular animated series *Beyblade* and *Medabots*. The 61-episode series aired on the cable network until the following May. *A Miramax Television/SME Visual Works Inc. Production. Color. Half-hour. Premiered on ABC FAM: September 14, 2002–May 18, 2003.*

*Voices*

**Spencer Weinberg-Takahama:** Joshua Seth; **Sunny Pig:** Mika Kanai; **Mom:** Dorothy Elias-Fahn; **Dad:** Wally Wingert; **Dizzy Lizzy:** Colleen O'Shaughnessey; **The Weather Lady:** Diane Michelle; **Angus/Wigstaff:** Jason Spisak; **Tiffany Van Hootenberg/Sweater Girl:** Brianne Siddall; **Ms. Spelt:** Wendee Lee; **The Principal:** Neil Kaplain

## ◎ THE TOM AND JERRY COMEDY SHOW

The popular cartoon cat-and-mouse team, joined by MGM counterparts Barney Bear, Droopy the Dog and his nemesis the Wolf (renamed "Slick"), father-and-son canines Spike and Tyke, and Jerry's nephew Tuffy starred in all-new escapades in this half-hour Saturday-morning series for CBS. As in the Oscar-winning MGM theatrical cartoon series, Tom and Jerry never talked in these new cartoon adventures, which were considerably toned down versions of their slapstick antics. The series marked the first appearance of Droopy since the end of his original MGM theatrical cartoon series in 1957 and the only appearance of Barney Bear since 1954. Other characters were modified. The Spike the bulldog characters from the MGM Tom and Jerry and Droopy cartoon series were combined into one character and sported a Jimmy Durante accent. Droopy opened each program and appeared between each cartoon literally "painting" the entire setting with one stroke of a large brush.

Only 16 half-hour programs, each consisting of two seven-and-a-half minute Tom and Jerry episodes and one seven-and-a-half-minute episode of Droopy and the others, were produced for the series, which premiered on CBS in September 1980. Venerable voice artist Frank Welker provided the voices of the other supporting characters (except during the 1980 industry strike, when producer Lou Scheimer filled in to provide all the voices). *A Filmation Production in association with MGM-TV. Color. Half-hour. Premiered on CBS: September 6, 1980–September 4, 1982.*

*Voices*

Frank Welker, Lou Scheimer

## ◎ THE TOM AND JERRY/GRAPE APE SHOW

Bill Hanna and Joe Barbera, the co-creators of this famous cat-and-mouse team, produced this less violent series revival for their studio, Hanna-Barbera Productions, featuring the cautious cat and mischievous mouse in brand-new misadventures, part of this hour-long spectacle first broadcast on ABC in 1975. The show's costar was Grape Ape, a 30-foot purple ape (an oversize version of Magilla Gorilla), and his fast-talking canine associate, Beagle, who engaged in fast-paced comedy capers of their own. In 1976 the series returned as *The Tom and Jerry/Grape Ape/Mumbly Show*. (See entry for details.) *A Hanna-Barbera Production in association with Metro-Goldwyn-Mayer. Color. One hour. Premiered on ABC: September 6, 1975–September 4, 1976.*

*Voices*
**Grape Ape:** Bob Holt; **Beagle:** Marty Ingels

## THE TOM AND JERRY/GRAPE APE/ MUMBLY SHOW

The popular cat-and-mouse team from MGM's cartoon heydays headlined this repackaged hour-long series. It featured their own misadventures plus those of the purple primate, Grape Ape, from 1975–76's *The Tom and Jerry/Grape Ape Show*, combined with new episodes of the investigating dog, Mumbly, who tracks down criminals with the help of his assistant, Schnooker. In December 1976 Grape Ape was removed from the cast and the show was shortened to a half-hour under the title of *The Tom and Jerry/Mumbly Show*. *A Hanna-Barbera Production. Color. One hour. Premiered on ABC: September 11, 1976–November 27, 1976; December 4, 1976–September 3, 1977 (as The Tom and Jerry/Mumbly Show).*

*Voices*
**Grape Ape:** Bob Holt; **Beagle, his canine associate:** Marty Ingels; **Mumbly:** Don Messick; **Schooker:** John Stephenson

## TOM AND JERRY KIDS

Inspired by the original Tom and Jerry MGM cartoon shorts created by legendary animators William Hanna and Joseph Barbera, the classic nontalking cat-and-mouse team are back for more rousing animated escapades. This time they square off as kids in a half-hour Saturday-morning cartoon series that premiered on FOX Network in the fall of 1990. Each half-hour program featured two seven-minute Tom and Jerry cartoons, along with one adventure (alternating each week) of MGM cartoon star Droopy the dog (teamed with his look-alike son, Dripple, as they try to outfox the villainous McWolf); father-and-son canines Spike and Tyke: and Tex Avery–style cartoons starring several new characters: Wild Mouse, Slow Poke Antonio, The Mouse Scouts and the Gator Brothers. (Droopy and Dripple were later spun off into their own weekly series, 1993's *Droopy, Master Detective*.) The series debuted as weekly in September 1990 and performed so well in its time slot that FOX expanded it to weekdays in 1992, with 39 new episodes. The show later reappeared in reruns on Cartoon Network and Boomerang. *A Hanna-Barbera Production in association with Turner Entertainment. Color. Half-hour. Premiered on FOX: September 8, 1990–October 2, 1993 (weekly); September 14, 1992–August 12, 1994 (daily). Rebroadcast on CAR: September 4, 1995 (weekdays, Sundays): October 13, 1997 (weekdays). Rebroadcast on BOOM: April 2, 2001–.*

*Voices*
**Droopy:** Don Messick; **Dripple:** Charlie Adler; **McWolf:** Frank Welker; **Spike:** Dick Gautier; **Tyke:** Patric Zimmerman

## THE TOM AND JERRY SHOW

MGM's top cartoon stars in the 1940s and 1950s, the nontalking Tom the cat and Jerry the mouse made their way to television in this half-hour program broadcast on CBS between 1965 and 1972. The series repackaged many of the original theatrical films starring the destructive duo plus other MGM cartoon favorites such as Barney Bear and Droopy. MGM later retitled the series *Tom and Jerry and Friends* for syndication. *A Metro-Goldwyn-Mayer Production. Color. Half-hour. Premiered on CBS: September 25, 1965–September 17, 1972.*

*Voices*
**Barney Bear:** Billy Bletcher, Paul Frees; **Droopy:** Bill Thompson, Don Messick, Daws Butler; **Spike, the bulldog:** Bill Thompson, Daws Butler

## TOM AND JERRY TALES

First made-for-TV series of new, original adventures and first television cartoon series in more than 13 years to star MGM's famed Oscar-winning cat-and-mouse team—Tom the scheming cat and Jerry his prankster mouse rival—in 39 all-new slapstick cartoon episodes. Emulating the style, spirit and over-the-top mayhem of Metro-Goldwyn-Mayer's popular theatrical cartoons, the half-hour series was born out of the success of a series of previously produced direct-to-video releases starring the iconic superstars, including *The Magic Ring, Blast Off to Mars, The Fast and Furry* and *Shiver Me Whiskers,* many of which also were shown on television. Produced by Warner Bros. Television Animation, Tom and Jerry cocreator and animation pioneer Joe Barbera coexecutive produced the series with veteran Warner Bros. producer Steven Schwartz.

Debuting in September 2006 from 8:30 to 9:30 A.M., the comedy series was one of three new animated programs—including *Shaggy and Scooby-Doo Get a Clue!* and *Legion of Super Heroes*—that made up the Kids' WB! fall 2006 Saturday-morning lineup on the newly christened the CW Network (formerly the WB!), along with three leftovers from the former the WB! Network (*Xiaolin Showdown, Lunatics Unleashed* and *The Batman*). Some familiar MGM cartoon characters also appeared in a few episodes, including the beloved sad-sack bloodhound Droopy and Tom's notorious bulldog rival, Butch. *A Warner Bros. Television Animation Production. Color. Half-hour. Premiered on the CW (Kids' WB!): September 23, 2006.*

*Voices*
**Tom:** Don Brown; **Jerry:** Samuel Vincent; **Spike:** Michael Donovan

## THE TOMFOOLERY SHOW

Patterned after NBC's comedy-variety series *Rowan and Martin's Laugh-In* but aimed at children, this half-hour series consisted of riddles, stories, limmericks and jokes based on the characters and events portrayed by Edward Lear in *The Nonsense Books.* Premiering in 1970 on NBC, the purpose of the 17-episode series was to entertain and enlighten young viewers on elements of children's literature. *A Halas and Batchelor Production for Rankin-Bass Productions. Color. Half-hour. Premiered on NBC: September 12, 1970–September 4, 1971.*

*Voices*
Peter Hawkins, Bernard Spear, The Maury Laws Singers

## TOM GOES TO THE MAYOR

Things run amuck when the mayor of the eccentric small town of Jefferton endorses a bunch of crackpot ideas suggested to him by Tom Peters, a new resident and would-be entrepreneur/civic do-gooder in this animated late-night offering, mixing 3-D graphics, pencil line drawings and live-action, in 15-minute episodes (and a few 17-minute episodes that were produced), which aired during Cartoon Network's *Adult Swim* program block beginning in November 2004.

Written and produced by creators Tim Heidecker and Eric Wareheim, who also provided the voices for two of the show's main characters, the program—called "one of the weirdest series on television"—was originally produced as a web cartoon in 2002 that also was shown at numerous independent film festivals. Comedian Bob Odenkirk enjoyed the original short film so much (and provided the voice of the mayor) that he helped develop it into a 15-minute series after signing on as an executive producer and selling the idea to Cartoon Network in 2003. Soon becoming a cult hit, the show was picked up for a second season, starting Sunday, June 4, with six new episodes airing weekly. Featured in the new episodes were several celebrity guest voices, including Gary Busey, Judd Hirsch, Sean Hayes, Janeane Garofalo, Robert Loggia and Sir Mix-a-Lot. Other series guest stars included David Cross, Michael Ian Black and Edward Herrmann. The quirky series lasted 30 episodes before production was finally halted in September 2006. *A Cartoon Network Studios Production. Color. Fifteen minutes. Premiered on CAR: November 14, 2004–September 25, 2006.*

### Voices

**Tom Peters/Jan Skylar/Various Others:** Tim Heidecker; **The Mayor/Wayne Skylar/Various Others:** Eric Wareheim; **Renee the Receptionist/Joy Peters:** Stephanie Courtney; **City Council Members:** Craig Anton, Ron Lynch; **Additional Voices:** Bob Odenkirk

### ☺ TOM TERRIFIC

The world's smallest superhero, this curly-haired boy derived his superpowers from his funnel hat, which enabled him to assume any shape or figure and become anything he wanted—a bird, a rock or a locomotive—to apprehend culprits with the help of his reluctant, droopy-eyed canine, Mighty Manfred the Wonder Dog. His and Manfred's main nemesis was the infamous Crabby Appleton, who was "rotten to the core."

Each story lasted five episodes and was initially presented as a daily cliffhanger on *The Captain Kangaroo Show,* Monday through Friday, beginning in 1957. Foreign cartoon producer Gene Deitch created *Tom Terrific* in late 1956 along with his fellow artists at Terrytoons, one year after the studio was sold to CBS. (It became a division of CBS Films.) The package of films remained on *Captain Kangaroo* at least until 1965. Following its serialization on *Captain Kangaroo,* the episodes were edited into 26 half-hour adventures and syndicated nationwide. *A Terrytoons Production in association with CBS Films. Black-and-white. Half-hour. Premiered on CBS: June 10, 1957–Late 1960s. Syndicated.*

### Voices

**Tom Terrific/Mighty Manfred:** Lionel Wilson

### ☺ TOONSYLVANIA

This ghoulishly funny Saturday-morning cartoon parody of the Frankenstein legend focuses on the oddball antics of hunchbacked lab assistant Igor and his lumbering monster sidekick Phil, who answer to Dr. Vic Frankenstein, an overbearing scientist residing in a castle above the TransFernando Valley. Steven Spielberg (overseeing the first animated series for his co-owned company DreamWorks) and Bill Kopp (the voice of *Eek! The Cat*) are executive producers of the half-hour series, which debuted on FOX Network. *A DreamWorks SKG Production. Color. Half-hour. Premiered on FOX: February 7, 1998–December 21, 1998.*

### Voices

**Igor:** Wayne Knight; **Phil Wilder:** Brad Garrett; **Dr. Vic Frankenstein:** David Warner; **Melissa Screetch:** Nancy Cartwright; **Fred/Newark/The Professor:** Billy West; **Stiffany/Miss Mann/Mother Screetch:** Valery Pappas; **Ace Deuce:** Tom Kenny; **General Mills:**

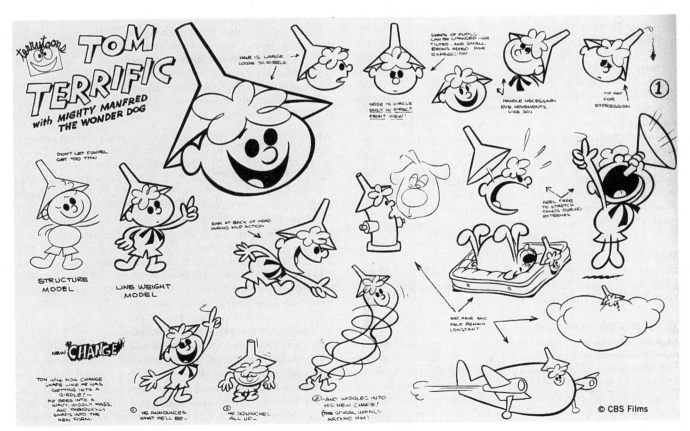

*Original model sheet for the popular cliffhanger adventure series* Tom Terrific, *seen Monday through Friday on CBS's The Captain Kangaroo Show.* © Terrytoons CBS Films. All rights reserved.

Jim Cummings; **Dedgar Deadman:** Matt Frewer; **Other Voices:** Charlie Adler, Jocelyn Blues, Jess Harnell

## ◎ TOP CAT

Near the outskirts of the 13th Precinct police station in New York City, Top Cat—T.C. for short—is a sly con artist and leader of a pack of Broadway alley cats (Choo-Choo, Benny the Ball, Spook, Fancy-Fancy and The Brain), who do everything possible to out-swindle and outsmart the cop on the beat, Officer Dibble, in madcap situations. The series debuted in prime time—becoming Hanna-Barbera's second prime-time cartoon series, following *The Flintstones*—in September of 1961. All 31 episodes originally aired in prime time. Following the series' prime-time run, they were rebroadcast Saturday mornings on ABC in 1962 and on NBC from 1965 to 1968. In 1992 the series began reairing on the Cartoon Network. *A Hanna-Barbera Production. Color. Half-hour. Premiered on ABC: September 27, 1961–September 26, 1962. Rebroadcast on ABC: October 6, 1962–March 30, 1963; NBC: April 3, 1965–May 10, 1969. Syndicated: 1969–92. Rebroadcast on USA: 1989–92. Rebroadcast on CAR: October 1, 1992–April 2, 1993 (weekdays); January 10, 1993 (part of Boomerang, 1963); June 28, 1993–September 17, 1993 (weekdays); January 3, 1994 (weekdays); September 4, 1995–2000 (weekdays). Rebroadcast on BOOM: April 1, 2000–.*

### Voices
**Top Cat (T.C.):** Arnold Stang; **Choo Choo:** Marvin Kaplan; **Benny the Ball:** Maurice Gosfield; **Spook/The Brain:** Leo de Lyon; **Goldie:** Jean VanderPyl; **Fancy Fancy/Pierre:** John Stephenson; **Office Dibble:** Allen Jenkins

## ◎ TOTALLY SPIES

A trio of ordinary high school girls—Sam, Clover and Alex—land their own dream house in Beverly Hills and become undercover secret agents for the World Organization of Human Protection (W.O.O.H.P.). They fight international crime with assorted cool high-tech gadgets supplied to them by their boss, Jerry—from titanium drilled-heel boots to anti-gravity propulsion rings—while balancing their day-to-day responsibilities of shopping at the mall or studying for exams in this stylish animated cartoon confection by France's Marathon Animation studios. Bearing a distinctive visual style reminiscent of Hanna-Barbera's *Josie and the Pussycats* and Japanese anime, the half-hour action/adventure series was first broadcast in the United States on ABC Family from November 2001 to September 2002. In April 2006, Cartoon Network acquired all 50 episodes of the series to rebroadcast. *A TFI/Marathon Animation Production. Color. Half-hour. Premiered on ABC FAM: November 3, 2001–September 13, 2002. Rebroadcast on CAR: July 7, 2003–April 4, 2006.*

### Voices
**Clover:** Andrea Baker; **Alex:** Katie Leigh; **Sam:** Jennifer Hale; **Jerry:** Jess Harnell; **Additional Voices:** Geoffrey Blake, Katie Griffin, Maurice La Marche, Adrian Truss

## ◎ TOUCHÉ TURTLE

Brandishing his trusty sword, knightly Touché Turtle and his simpleminded assistant, Dum Dum, heroically save queens, maidens and other people in distress in a series of 52 five-minute cartoon adventures that were first distributed to television stations in 1962 as part of a trilogy series called *The Hanna-Barbera New Cartoon Series.* Along with the series' two other components—"Wally Gator" and "Lippy the Lion"—stations programmed the cartoons back to back, in separate time slots or as elements of popular daytime children's programs. One of the Touché Turtle cartoons

offered in the package was actually produced in 1960, two years before the character appeared in this series. The episode was called "Whale of a Tale." Bill Thompson, who created the voice of MGM's sorrowful basset hound Droopy, supplied the voice of Touché Turtle. *A Hanna-Barbera Production. Color. Half-hour. Premiered: September 3, 1962. Syndicated.*

### Voices
**Touché Turtle:** Bill Thompson; **Dum Dum:** Alan Reed; **Other Voices:** Daws Butler, Don Messick

## ◎ TOXIC CRUSADERS

Hideously deformed creatures of superhuman size fight for the good of their hometown, the only unpolluted town in the country, in this half-hour series based on the popular live-action *Toxic Avenger* films of the mid-1980s and early 1990s. First test marketed as a five-part miniseries in syndication in January of 1991, the program went weekly in the fall of that year. Only 13 episodes were broadcast. *A Murikami-Wolf-Swenson/Sachs Family Entertainment Production in association with Troma Films. Color. Half-hour. Premiered: January 1991 (as five-part miniseries). Premiered: Fall 1991 (as weekly series). Syndicated.*

### Voices
Gregg Berger, Susan Blu, Paul Eiding, Chuck McCann, Rodger Bumpass, Rad Rayle, Susan Silo, Kath Soucie, Ed Gilbert, Patric Zimmerman, Michael J. Pollard

## ◎ TRANSFORMERS

The Autobots, residents of the planet Zobitron, try to stop the Decepticons, deadly robots who want to control the universe in this futuristic battle of good over evil. This half-hour series, first syndicated in 1984, was based on the popular Hasbro toy line. The original series became the longest-running cartoon program (in reruns) on Sci-Fi Channel's *Cartoon Quest* (and its later own time slot). *A Marvel/Sunbow/Claster Television Production in association with Hasbro Inc. Color. Half-hour. Premiered: September 17, 1984–November 1987. Syndicated. Rebroadcast on SCI: September 25, 1992–August 28, 1997.*

### Voices
**Astro Train:** Jack Angel; **Prowler/Scrapper/Swoop/Junkion:** Michael Bell; **Grimlock:** Gregg Berger; **Arcee:** Susan Blu; **Devastator:** Arthur Burghardt; **Spike/Brawn/Shockwave:** Corey Burton; **Cyclonus:** Roger C. Carmel; **Optimus Prime/Ironhide:** Peter Cullen; **Jazz:** Scatman Crothers; **Dirge:** Brad Davis; **Inferno:** Walker Edmiston; **Perceptor:** Paul Eiding; **Blitzwing:** Ed Gilbert; **Bumblebee:** Dan Gilvezan; **Blaster:** Buster Jones; **Scourge:** Stan Jones; **Cliffjumper:** Casey Kasem; **Star Scream/Cobra Commander:** Chris Latta; **Daniel:** David Mendenhall; **Gears:** Don Messick; **Blurr:** John Moschitta; **Hot Road/Rodimus:** Judd Nelson; **Shrapnel:** Hal Rayle; **Kickback:** Clive Revill; **Bone Crusher/Hook/Springer/Slag:** Neil Ross; **Soundwave/Megatron/Galatron/Rumble/Frenzy/Wheelie:** Frank Welker

## ◎ TRANSFORMERS: ARMADA

In the year 2010, after discovering the existence of the Mini-Cons, much smaller Transformers robots who awaken from a centuries-old deep freeze on Earth, the Autobot and Decepticons battle to win the allegiance of these newly discovered powerful robots while the fate of Earth and the universe hangs in the balance in this sixth adaptation of the famed Hasbro toy franchise. Featuring returning favorites Megatron and Optimus Prime, this cel-animated, half-hour science fiction/fantasy adventure series, produced in Japan and redubbed in English, debuted on U.S. television in late August

2002 as a 90-minute movie special consisting of three half-hour episodes ("First Encounter," "Metamorphosis" and "Base"), followed by the Friday premiere of the regular series a week later. Less violent than its predecessors and played mostly for laughs, the 52-episode series ran two seasons on cable's Cartoon Network. *An Aeon Inc./Dangun Pictures/Hangzhou Feilong Donghua/MSJ/Sabella-Dern Entertainment/Hasbro/Cartoon Network Production. Color. Half-hour. Premiered on CAR: August 23, 2002 (special). Premiered on CAR: August 30, 2002–June 11, 2004 (series).*

### Voices

**Rad:** Kirby Morrow; **Carlos:** Matt Hill; **Alexis:** Tabitha St. Germain; **Billy:** Andrew Francis; **Fred:** Tony Sampson; **Optimus Prime:** Gary Chalk; **Hotshot:** Brent Miller; **Red Alert:** Brian Dobson; **Demolisher:** Alvin Sanders; **Cyclonus:** Donald Brown; **Thrust:** Scott McNeil; **Smokescreen:** Dale Wilson; **Narrator:** Jim Conrad

## ◎ TRANSFORMERS: CYBERTRON

While criss-crossing the universe in search of the Cyber Planet Keys, the Transformers and their leader Optimus Prime and descendant line of robots the Autobots, along with the planet of Cybertron itself, face a greater threat to their survival than ever before with the warring Decepticons hot on their trail. Based on Hasbro's Transformers toyline, this all-new CGI-animated, English-language follow-up to *Transformers: Armada* and *Transformers: Energon* first aired in July 2005 on Cartoon Network. Fourteen of the series' regular 52-episode series aired Saturdays on Cartoon Network's Toonami action anime block and later weekday mornings as well, until that September when the show moved to the WB Television Network's Kids' WB! Monday to Friday with old and new episodes before airing on G4 in 2006. The series returned with new episodes on Cartoon Network on Saturday March 11, 2007 at 7 P.M. (ET) on *Toonami. A Takara/Hasbro Production. Color. Half-hour. Premiered on CAR: July 2, 2005; March 11, 2007 (new episodes). Premiered on Kids' WB!: September 19, 2005–January 2006. Premiered on G4: July 23, 2006–December 31, 2006.*

### Voices

**Optimus Prime:** Gary Chalk; **Thundercracker/Undermine:** Mark Oliver; **Crumplezone:** Mark Acheson; **Red Alert/Clocker:** Brian Dobson; **Dr. Suzuki:** Tabitha St. Germain; **Ransack:** Louis Chirillo; **Vector Prime:** Richard Newman; **Scattershot:** Richard Ian Cox; **Hot Shot:** Kirby Morrow; **Scourge:** Trevor Devall

## ◎ TRANSFORMERS: ENERGON

With the evil Unicron aiming to steal Earth's single energy source, Energon, to put him back in power, Optimus Prime mobilizes the small Autobots force, creating larger, more powerful robots to stop the Decepticons and Unicron in their tracks. This latest CG-animated installment of the legendary toy action figures joined Cartoon Network's Saturday night lineup of action/adventure programming, including *Cyborg 009, Justice League* and *Samurai Jack*, in January 2004 at 7:30 P.M. *A TV Tokyo/ACTAS, Inc./A-CAT/NAS/Takara/We've Inc./Voicebox Productions/Hasbro Production. Color. Half-hour. Premiered on CAR: January 31, 2004–June 17, 2005.*

### Voices

**Kicker:** Brad Swaile; **Optimus Prime:** Gary Chalk; **Demolishor:** Alvin Sanders; **Scorponok:** Colin Murdock; **Cyclonus/Mischa's father/Snowcat:** Don Broan; **Tidal Wave/Mirage:** Doug Parker; **Mischa:** Ellen Kennedy; **Rad:** Kirby Morrow; **Carlos:** Matt Hill; **Starscream's Ghost:** Michael Dobson; **Dr. Jones:** Ron Halder; **Jetfire/Strongarm:** Scott McNeil; **Alexis:** Tabitha St. Germain; **Alpha Q:** Trevor Devall; **Prowl:** Alistair Abell; **Shockblast/Sixshot:** Brian Drummond; **Megatron/Galvatron:** David Kaye;

**Cliffjumper:** Doron Bell Jr.; **Bulkhead:** French Tickner; **Narrator:** Mark Acheson; **Other Voices:** Michael Daingerfield, Nicole Oliver, Paul Dobson, Ron Halder, Samuel Vincent, Sharon Alexander, Terry Klassen, Ty Olsson, Ward Perry

## ◎ TRANSFORMERS: GENERATION II

This second-generation *Transformers* cartoon series was produced for syndication in 1992, featuring episodes from the original 1984 series, modified with computer-enhanced bumpers and segues. The voice cast is the same as in the original series. *A Sunbow/Claster Television Production. Color. Half-hour. Premiered: 1992–94. Syndicated.*

## ◎ TRANSFORMERS: ROBOTS IN DISGUISE

Koji (Yuuki in the Japanese original), the son of noted scientist Professor Onishi who is kidnapped by evil transforming robots, teams up with the heroic Cybertron forces, led by the transformable Optimus Prime, to rescue his famed father and defend Earth against the evil Gigatron and his henchmen. Based on the popular Transformers toy line, this retitled English-language version (first telecast in Japan under the name of *Transformers: Car Robots*) was broadcast Saturday mornings on FOX as "filler" while production commenced on the next cartoon series in the franchise, *Transformers: Armada*. In 2000, due to financial problems, only 39 of the planned 52 half-hour episodes were produced and completed for broadcast. *A Saban Entertainment/NAS/Dong Woo Animation/Studio Gallop/TV Tokyo/Hasbro Production. Color. Half-hour. Premiered on FOX: September 8, 2001–September 7, 2002.*

### Voices

**Koji:** Jason Spisak; **Dr. Onishi:** Kirk Thorton; **Optimus Prime/Ro-Tor:** Neil Kaplan; **X-Brawn:** Bob Joles; **Prowl:** Wankus; **Sideburn/Mirage:** Wally Wingert; **Skid-Z/Rollbar:** Michael Linsday; **Tow-Line:** Lex Lang; **Ultra Magnus:** Kim Strauss; **R.E.V., Cerebros/Fortress Maximus:** Steve Kramer; **Railspike:** Mike Reynolds; **Rapid Run:** Keith Diamond; **Midnight Express/Railracer:** David Lodge; **Hot Shot/Ironhide:** Michael McConnohie; **Crosswise:** Dan Woren; **Dark Scream/W.A.R.S.:** Steven Blum; **Wedge/Landfill:** Michael Reisz; **Heavy Load/Jenny:** Colleen O'Shaughnessey; **Hightower:** Keith Anthony; **Grimlock:** Tom Wyner; **T-Ai:** Sandy Fox; **Dorie Dutton:** Tifanie Christian; **Slapper:** Peter Lurie; **Gas Skunk:** Jerry DeCapua; **Megatron/Galvatron/Omega Prime:** Daniel Riordan; **Sky-Byte:** Peter Spellos; **Movor:** Robert Axelrod; **Mega Octane/Ruination:** Bob Papenbrook; **Kelly:** Philece Sampler; **Carl:** Joshua Seth; **Scourge:** Barry Stigler; **Grimlock:** Tom Wyner

## ◎ TRANZOR Z

The evil Dr. Demon and his army of powerful robot beasts try to take control of the world but encounter a protector of peace more powerful than all of them combined: Tranzor Z, a superrobot ("the mightiest of machines") created by the great Dr. Wells, in this Japanese-animated series made for first-run syndication. *A Toei Animation 3B Productions/T.E.N. Production. Color. Half-hour. Premiered: September, 1984–85. Syndicated.*

### Voices

Gregg Berger, Mona Marshall, Paul Ross, Willard Jenkins, Robert A. Gaston, James Hodson, William Lloyd Davis

## ◎ TRIGUN

On a distant deserted planet, the universe's most ruthless, heartless gunfighter, Vash the Stampede (with a $60 billion reward for his capture), is just the opposite of his press clippings: a pacifist at heart who isn't a bad guy at all and who defends the weak and helpless, becoming a hero, despite acting like an idiot, in this futuristic space western. Redubbed and imported from Japan, the series, first shown on Japanese television under the name of *Toraigan* in 1998, made its U.S. television debut on Cartoon Network in March 2003. Adapted from the popular Japanese manga created by Yasuhiro Nightow in 1995, the half-hour series joined Cartoon Network's late-night *Adult Swim* roster, along with two other action-adventure series *Lupin the Third* and *Reign: The Conqueror*. A *Tokuma Shoten/Madhouse Animation/Victor Company of Japan Ltd./Pioneer Entertainment Production. Color. Half-hour. Premiered on CAR: March 31, 2003–August 5, 2006.*

*Voices*
**Vash the Stampede:** Johnny Yong Bosch; **Meryl Strife:** Dorothy Melendrez; **Milly Thompson:** Lia Sargent; **Rem Sevarem:** Ruby Marlowe; **Nicholas D. Wolfwood:** Bo Williams; **Legato Bluesummers:** Richard Hayworth

## ◎ TRINITY BLOOD

In a world where the war between the vampires, the dark forces of evil, and the humans continues in earnest, the Vatican counters with a special operations group called the Ax, led by priest Peter Abel Nightroad and overseen by Cardinal Catherina, to defend all of humanity from these evil beings. Based on the epic serial novels of Sunao Yoshida, the new anime series aired Saturdays at midnight on Cartoon Network's *Adult Swim* animation block, following another new anime series entry *Bleach*. A *Gonzo/Madhouse Studios/FUNimation Production. Color. Half-hour. Premiered on CAR: September 9, 2006.*

*Voices*
**Peter Abel Nightroad:** Troy Baker; **Archbishop Alfonso D'Este:** John Swasey; **Cardinal Catherina Sforza:** Lydia Mackey; **Cardinal Francesco di Medici:** John Gremillion; **Esther Blanchett:** Colleen Clinkenbeard; **Hugue de Watteau:** John Bergmeier; **Kate Scott:** Gwendolyn Lao; **Leon Garcia de Asturias:** Phil Parsons; **Mistress Noelle Bor:** Christine Auten; **Pope Allessandro XVIII:** Greg Ayres; **Professor William Walter Wordsmouth:** Jason Douglas; **Tres Iqus:** Christopher Sabat; **Vaclay Havel:** Chuck Huber; **Narrator:** R. Bruce Elliott

## ◎ TRIPPING THE RIFT

Adult-humored science-fiction spoof, based on filmmakers Chris Moeller and Chuck Austen's award-winning Internet film short of the same name, following the intergalactic adventures of Chode McBlob (voiced by Stephen Root of *Dodgeball* and *Office Space* fame), the horny, purple and rotund captain of a smuggling spacecraft, *The Free Enterprise,* and his warped crew who embark on a series of raucous adventures in space, encountering a strange galaxy of characters and grotesque situations modeled after film and television's *Star Trek* franchise. Produced in Canada, the edgy, CGI-animated, 26-episode half-hour comedy series aired in prime time over two seasons on Sci-Fi Channel, beginning in March 2004, as well as on various outlets internationally. Providing voices for the show's supporting characters were Maurice LaMarche (*Pinky and the Brain*) as Gus, Chode's sexually confused robot slave, and Gina Gershon in the first season as Six the sexy cyborg; Carmen Electra assumed the role afterward. A third season of 13 new episodes was produced for Canada's Teletoon network. A *CinéGroupe Production. Color. Half-hour. Premiered on SCI: March 1, 2004–October 19, 2005.*

*Voices*
**Chode McBlob:** Stephen Root; **Six:** Gina Gershon, Carmen Electra; **T'nuk:** Gayle Garfinkle; **Whip:** Rick Jones; **Gus:** Maurice LaMarche; **Spaceship Bob:** John Melendez; **Darph Bobo:** Chris Moeller

## ◎ THE TROLLKINS

A mini-civilization of wee playful folks with purple, blue and green faces find modern living possible by fashioning 20th-century devices out of glow worms, spider threads and other natural wonders in the magical community of Trolltown. This weekly Saturday-morning series was originally broadcast on CBS. A *Hanna-Barbera Production. Color. Half-hour. Premiered on CBS: September 12, 1981–September 4, 1982. Rebroadcast on CAR: June 6, 1993–April 3, 1994 (Sundays); September 11, 1994 (Sundays). Rebroadcast on BOOM: June 15, 2002–December 7, 2002.*

*Voices*
**Sheriff Pudge Trollsom:** Allan Oppenheimer; **Pixlee Trollsom/DepuTroll Dolly Durkle:** Jennifer Darling; **Blitz Plumkin:** Steve Spears; **Flooky/Bogg/Top Troll:** Frank Welker; **Grubb Trollmaine:** Michael Bell; **Depu Troll Flake:** Marshall Efron; **Mayor Lumpkin:** Paul Winchell; **Afid:** Hank Saroyan; **Slug:** Bill Callaway

## ◎ TROLLZ

Together, five colorful wild-haired teenage girls and "Best Friends for Life" (BFFL)—Amethyst, Ruby, Sapphire, Topaz and Onyx—combine to make "The Power of 5" as they hang out after school dealing with the usual teen issues such as boys, money, shopping, homework and casting magical spells in Trollzopolis in this animated series, featuring stylized and contemporary versions of the Troll dolls first made popular in the 1950s. Produced by Burbank, California's DIC Entertainment, the series debuted in the United States on Toon Disney with 27 half-hour adventures in September 2005. Coinciding with the series launch in America was a first wave of merchandise based on the show's characters that rolled out on retail shelves in July in time for the back-to-school rush. A *DIC Entertainment Production. Color. Half-hour. Premiered on TDIS: September 23, 2005.*

*Voices*
**Amethyst Van Der Troll:** Britt McKillip; **Ruby Trollman:** Chiara Zanni; **Sapphire Trollzawa:** Alexander Carter; **Topaz Trollhopper:** Leah Juel; **Onyx Von Trollenberg:** Anna Van Hooft; **Alabaster:** Samuel Vincent; **Rock:** Matt Hill; **Coal:** Jesse Moss; **Simon:** Reese Thompson; **Mr. Trollheimer:** Jason Connery

## ◎ TURBO TEEN

A top-secret government experiment goes awry when a high school journalism student, Bret Matthews, accidentally crashes his sports car through the walls of the test laboratory and is struck by a ray from a machine that causes him to become one with his car. As a result of this freak accident, Matthews is able to transform himself into a car whenever his temperature rises. He then uses his unique ability to solve mysteries and fight crime, assisted by his friends Pattie and Alex, who share his secret. The 12-episode half-hour series premiered on ABC in 1984 and was later rebroadcast on USA Network's *Cartoon Express* and on Cartoon Network. A *Ruby-Spears Enterprises Production. Color. Half-hour. Premiered on ABC: September 8, 1984–August 31, 1985. Rebroadcast on USA: May 5, 1989–March 4, 1992; Rebroadcast on CAR: October 16, 1994–October 17, 1994 (Look What We Found!).*

*Voices*
**Brett Matthews:** Michael Mish; **Pattie, his girlfriend:** Pamela Hayden; **Alex, his friend:** T.K. Carter; **Eddie:** Pat Fraley; **Flip/Rusty:** Frank Welker; **Other Voices:** Clive Revill

## ◉ TUTENSTEIN

Brought back among the living after being struck by lightning, a 3,000-year-old mummy of a boy pharaoh schemes to assume his place as the supreme leader of the world with the help of a hip, 21st-century Egyptology-loving 12-year-old named Cleo, and his faithful, talking cat-servant Luxor in this weekly half-hour animated series based on an idea by Canadian artist Jay Stephens. The recipient of numerous awards and nominations, including a 2004 Daytime Emmy for outstanding special class animated program and the Parents Choice Seal of Approval, the two-time Emmy-nominated series, produced by PorchLight Entertainment, debuted on NBC and Discovery Kids (which provided programming for NBC's Saturday-morning schedule) in November 2003 with 13 episodes its first season. Thirteen additional episodes were produced for the second season, with 11 more new episodes ordered for its third season. Renowned Egyptologist Dr. Peter Lacovara worked as a consultant on the series to authenticate the program's Egyptian content. *A PorchLight Entertainment/Discovery Kids Production. Color. Half-hour. Premiered on NBC/DSCK: November 1, 2003–August 28, 2004; September 4, 2004–September 2, 2005; September 9, 2006.*

### Voices

Marcus Muldoon, Loren Manda, Baen Mosquito, Joseph Samuels, Anne Hawkins, Pryde Ballard, Vince del Castillo, John Harrison, Marisa Michel, Lex Lang, Jeannie Elias

## ◉ 12 OZ. MOUSE

Crudely drawn, alcoholic Mouse "Fitz" Fitzgerald performs a series of odd jobs so he can buy himself another beer in this series created by Matt Maiellaro, cocreator of TV's *Aqua Teen Hunger Force, The Brak Show* and *Space Ghost: Coast to Coast,* and produced by Williams Street for Cartoon Network's *Adult Swim* programming block. In June 2005, the pilot episode entitled "Hired" originally aired on *Adult Swim* before the show because a regular series in the *Adult Swim* lineup that October, joined by two new series that premiered that fall: *Squidbillies* and *Perfect Hair Forever.* On New Year's Eve of that year, Cartoon Network aired a "12 Oz. New Year Marathon," rebroadcasting the first season's six episodes and premiering the seventh unfinished episode "Adventure Mouse." In September 2006, the program returned for a second and final season on *Adult Swim,* concluding its run that December with 20 episodes. *A Williams Street Production. Color. Half-hour. Premiered on CAR: June 19, 2005 (pilot). Premiered on CAR: October 16, 2005–January 1, 2006; September 25, 2006–December 18, 2006 (series).*

### Voices

**Mouse "Fitz" Fitzgerald:** Matt Maiellaro; **Liquor:** Matt Harrigan; **Eye:** Nick Ingkatanuwat; **Shark:** Adam Reed; **Siren Lady:** Bonnie Rosmarin; **Rectangle:** Kurt Soccolich; **Talent Scout:** Matt Thompson; **The Policeman:** Nick Weidenfeld; **Rhoda:** Dave Willis

## ◉ TWINKLE, THE DREAM BEING

Set on the planet Possible, this magical, stellar-shaped intergalactic genie helps turn the dreams of his girlfriend, Jedda, and friends the Oogies into reality. Only the wretched sorceress Miss Diva Weed is bent on stopping the twinkling dreamster and making all the denizens of the planet subservient to her needs in this 26-episode half-hour fantasy/adventure series produced for syndication. *A Sei Young/MBC/Calico/Zodiac Entertainment Production. Color. Half-hour. Premiered: 1993. Syndicated.*

### Voices

**Twinkle:** Tress MacNeille; **Other Voices:** Pat Fraley, Russi Taylor, Cam Clarke.

## ◉ THE TWISTED TALES OF FELIX THE CAT

In the fall of 1994 the feisty feline of film and television fame was reintroduced to young viewers in a series of 50 five-second bumpers that aired Saturday mornings on CBS, resulting in production of this half-hour network series (originally to be called *The New Adventures of Felix the Cat*) reported to have been the most expensive cartoon series ever produced by Film Roman studios. Retaining the retro look of creator Otto Messmer's original Felix, the series premiered in the fall of 1995, also on CBS, featuring three cartoon shorts and occasional live-action or computer-animated segments. In all, 58 cartoons were produced during the series' two-season run. *A Film Roman Production in association with Felix the Cat Productions. Color. Half-hour. Premiered on CBS: September 16, 1995–August 23, 1997.*

### Voices

**Felix the Cat:** Thom Adcox Hernandez, Charlie Adler; **Poindexter:** Cam Clarke; **Rosco:** Phil Hayes; **Sheba Bepoporeba:** Cree Summer; **Other Voices:** Susan Silo, Patrick Fraley, Jennifer Hale, Jess Harnell, Janna Levinstein, Townsend Coleman, Kevin Schon

## ◉ 2 STUPID DOGS

This breakout Hanna-Barbera cartoon series marked a distinct departure from the studio's past television cartoons, producing a series that was much more in step with 1990s' cartoon fare, such as *The Ren & Stimpy Show,* in which the series' main stars—a pair of dogs, one smart (Little Dog), one dumb (Big Dog)—end up in disastrous situations marked by outrageous gags and toilet humor. Each half-hour program was comprised of two seven-minute "2 Stupid Dogs" cartoons and featured another series component: "Super Secret Squirrel," a retooled version of Hanna-Barbera's mid-1960s cartoon character Secret Squirrel, back with gibbering assistant Morocco Mole, in brand-new adventures (one per show). The series premiered simultaneously in syndication and on TBS in September of 1993. The series was later rerun on Cartoon Network and Boomerang. *A Hanna-Barbera Turner Program Services Production. Color. Half-hour. Premiered: September 1993. Syndicated. Premiered on TBS: September 12, 1993. Rebroadcast on CAR: September 10, 1994–October 2, 1995; August 18, 1995–2000 ("Super Chunk"). Syndicated. Rebroadcast on BOOM: April 6, 2005–.*

### Voices

**2 Stupid Dogs: Big Dog:** Brad Garrett; **Little Dog:** Mark Schiff; **Hollywood:** Brian Cummings; **Principal Schneider/Announcer:** Gary Owens

**Super Secret Squirrel: Secret Squirrel:** Jess Harnell; **Morocco Mole:** Jim Cummings; **Chief:** Tony Jay

## ◉ ULTIMATE BOOK OF SPELLS

Creating some controversy for its striking resemblance to J.K. Rowling's best-selling *Harry Potter* book series, three highly gifted students who attend a school of wizardry—Cassy, a third-year junior witch; Gus, a part-elf second-year junior wizard; and Verne, a logical kid who has difficulties mastering the art of magic—undertake an exciting underground journey to the center of the Earth to defeat the evil wizard Zarlac with the help of their magical talking book U.B.O.S. (Ultimate Book of Spells). First telecast on Canada's YTV network, the fantasy adventure series, comprised of 26 half-hour episodes, aired in the United States on the Disney Channel. *A BKN International Production. Color. Half-hour. Premiered on DIS: September 3, 2002–August 29, 2003.*

*Voices*

**Cassandra "Cassy" X:** Janyse Jaud; **U.B.O.S.:** Ron Halder; **Verne:** Cathy Weseluck; **Other Voices:** Jim Byrnes, Patricia Drake, Saffron Henderson, Kirby Morrow, Pauline Newstone, Nicole Oliver, Blu Mankuma

### ◎ ULTIMATE MUSCLE: THE KINNIKUMAN LEGACY

Accidentally displaced as the prince of his home planet, a bulging biceped superhero wrestler named Kid Muscle (the son of the legendary King Muscle) competes in the ultimate intergalactic wrestling tournament to prove his princely heritage, taking on the diabolical dMp to save the planet, in this Japanese anime series first broadcast on Japan's TV Tokyo in 2002. Revoiced in English with an all-American cast, the half-hour series, also known as *Kinnikuman Nisei* in Japan and produced by 4Kids Entertainment, premiered on U.S. television in September 2002 on FOX's Saturday-morning *FOX Box* program block. The 77-episode series aired for two seasons, becoming more popular with American audiences than in its own country. A *Toei Company Ltd./FUNimation/4Kids Entertainment Production. Color. Half-hour. Premiered on FOX: September 14, 2002–May 22, 2004.*

*Voices*

**Kid Muscle/Mantaro Kinnikuman/Ramen Man/Tyrannoclaw/Mars/Eskara/Baron Maximillion:** Marc Thompson; **Dik Dik Van Dik/Mac Metaphor/Suguru Kinnikuman/King Muscle/Adversarious/Dial BolicGeronimo/Sgt. Kinnikuman/Hanzo/The Protector/Jagg-Ed:** Eric Stuart; **Belinda/Bibinda Muscle/Frau Essen/Jeager Supporter:** Veronica Taylor; **Road Rage:** Sebastian Arcelus; **Checkmate/Jeager/Brocken, Jr./Ricardo/Mr. French/Mr. Dispenser/Gyro-Man/Dazz-Ling/Buffaloman:** Wayne Grayson; **Wally Tusket/Comrade Turbinski/Lord Flash/Warsman/Buster Crab:** Madeleine Blaustein; **Terry "The Grand" Kenyon/Forkolossus/Sly Scraper/D-Struction/Skullduggery:** Frank Frankson; **Vance McMadd/Minch/Chijimi-Man/Herr Essen/Jeager Supporter:** Darren Dunstan; **Robin Mask/Buffalo Man/Hydrozoa/Pumpinator/El Niño:** Dan Green; **Trixie/Photo Pat:** Megan Hollingshead; **Kevin Mask/Doc Nakano/Cranky Doodle Craw Daddy/Terryman/Barrier-Free Man/Niles/King Kastle/Ninja Ned/Monsieur Cheeks:** Ted Lewis; **Roxanne:** Lisa Ortiz; **Meat:** Mike Pollock; **Kiki:** Kerry Williams; **Additional Voices:** Andrew Rannells

### ◎ ULTRAFORCE

With the mysterious appearance of hundreds of "Ultras"—ordinary humans suddenly bestowed with extraordinary powers used for pure evil—a team of superhero Ultras (Prime, Prototype, Ghoul, Contrary and Topaz) is born. It is led by reluctant hero Hardcase to combat the evils of notorious archenemies Rune, Lord Pumpkin, Sludge and others and settle mass confusion on Earth in this action-packed, half-hour sci fi/adventure series based on the popular comic book of the same name. Premiering in September of 1995, the series was originally part of the syndicated *Amazin' Adventures II* two-hour weekend cartoon block. In 1996 USA Network began reairing the series. A *DIC Entertainment/Malibu Comics/Bohbot Entertainment Production. Premiered: October 15, 1995–December 31, 1995 (part of Amazin' Adventures II). Syndicated. Rebroadcast on USA: September 22, 1996–September 12, 1998.*

*Voices*

**Hardcase:** Rod Wilson; **Topaz:** Catherine Disher

### ◎ ULYSSES 31

Originally produced for television in 1981 but unable to find a suitable buyer, this Japanese imported series debuted five years later as a regular component of the 90-minute syndicated spectacular *Kideo TV*, airing only for 13 weeks before it was dropped from the series. The futuristic series, set in the 31st century, followed the exploits of Ulysses. (See *Kideo TV* for details.) An *Osmond International/DIC Enterprises Production. Color. Half-hour. Premiered: September 13, 1986–87 (part of Kideo TV).*

### ◎ UNCLE CROCK'S BLOCK

Charles Nelson Reilly, in live segments, hosted this 1975 ABC series spoof of local children shows presenting skits and jokes along with his buffoonish assistant, Mr. Rabbit Ears. (He also occasionally engaged in some lighthearted bickering with his program's director, Basil Bitterbottom, played by Jonathan Harris.) Between shticks, Reilly introduced several animated cartoons to round out the program. They were: "Fraidy Cat," a cowardly cat who is haunted by his eight ghostly selves; "M*U*S*H*," a satirical takeoff of the television sitcom M*A*S*H; and "Wacky and Packy," a pair of Stone Age characters who become misplaced—in New York, of all places—and learn to deal with modern civilization. A *Filmation Associates Production. Color. One hour. Premiered on ABC: September 6, 1975–February 14, 1976.*

*Cast*

**Uncle Croc:** Charles Nelson Reilly; **Mr. Rabbit Ears:** Alfie Wise; **Basil Bitterbottom:** Jonathan Harris

*Voices*

**FRAIDY CAT: Fraidy Cat/Tinker/Dog/Mouse/Hokey:** Alan Oppenheimer; **Tonka/Wizard/Captain Kitt/Sir Walter Cat/Winston:** Lennie Weinrib

**M*U*S*H: Bullseye/Tricky John/Sonar/Hilda:** Robert Ridgely; **Sideburns/Coldlips/Colonel Flake/General Upheaval:** Ken Mars

**WACKY AND PACKY: Wacky/Packy:** Allan Melvin

### ◎ UNCLE WALDO

In 1965 this syndicated series, a retitled version of *The Adventures of Hoppity Hooper*, first appeared. The show was designed for weekday programming. Two episodes of "Hoppity Hooper" were featured daily, along with one episode each of "Fractured Fairytales" and "Peabody's Improbable History." (See *The Adventures of Hoppity Hooper* for voice information and further details.) A *Jay Ward Production. Color. Half-hour. Premiered: 1965.*

### ◎ UNDERDOG

From his guise of humble, lovable canine Shoeshine Boy, superhero Underdog (voiced by *Mr. Peppers'* TV series star *Wally Cox*) emerges to overpower criminals in Washington, D.C., in this half-hour comedy series, first introduced on NBC in 1964. His main enemies: mad scientist Simon Bar Sinister and underworld boss Riff Raff.

Two adventures were featured each week, along with repeat episodes of several rotating components: "The Hunter," which was first seen on *King Leonardo and His Short Subjects* and "The World of Commander McBragg," which first appeared on *Tennessee Tuxedo and His Tales.*

In the fall of 1966, after the series' initial run on NBC, the program was restructured and moved to CBS. (It replaced *Tennessee Tuxedo and His Tales.*) The original components were replaced by

"Go Go Gophers," the comical exploits of Running Board and Ruffled Feathers, a pair of renegade, buck-toothed gopher Indians, who are rebuffed by Colonel Kit Coyote, a blustering Teddy Roosevelt type, in their continuous scheme to seize the U.S. fort near Gopher Gulch; and "Klondike Kat," the hilarious adventures of a dumb mountie and his hot pursuit of the cheese-stealing mouse, Savior Faire. In 1968 CBS repeated episodes of both components in a half-hour series titled *Go Go Gophers*. That same year NBC began rebroadcasting the *Underdog* series, which lasted three more seasons. In the 1990s and 2000s, the classic cartoon series reaired on Cartoon Network and Boomerang. *A Total TV Production with Leonardo TV Productions. Color. Half-hour. Premiered on NBC: October 3, 1964–September 3, 1966; CBS: September 10, 1966–September 2, 1967. Rebroadcast on NBC: September 7, 1968–September 1, 1973; Rebroadcast on CAR: July 6, 1996–October 5, 1996 (Saturdays, Sundays). Rebroadcast on BOOM: July 1, 2001–May 21, 2004.*

**Voices**
**Underdog:** Wally Cox; **Sweet Polly Purebred, reporter:** Norma McMillan; **The Hunter/Colonel Kit Coyote:** Kenny Delmar; **Ruffled Feathers/Sergeant Okey Homa:** Sandy Becker; **Running Board/Narrator:** George S. Irving; **Commander McBragg:** Kenny Delmar

### ◎ UNDERGRADS
Six undergraduate college freshmen—Nitz, the so-called everyman, Rocko, the frat boy; Cal, the regular ladies man; Gimpy, the campus nerd; Jessie, the tomboy; and Kimmy, the classic ditz—do everything possible to maintain their longtime friendships while struggling to survive their first year in college at different campuses. Created by Pete Williams, who at age 19 dropped out of college to create the series (and also did most of the voices), the 13-episode half-hour series was originally broadcast in the United States on MTV in 2001 and became a cult favorite in reruns on Comedy Central beginning in 2002. *A Click Productions/DECODE Entertainment/MTV Production. Color. Half-hour. Premiered on MTV: April 22, 2001–February 2, 2003. Rebroadcast on COM: November 3, 2002–September 19, 2004.*

**Voices**
**Parker "Nitz" Walsh/Justin "Gimpy" Taylan/Cal Evans/Rocky Gambiani:** Pete Williams; **Kimmy Burton:** Susan Dalton; **Jessie:** Jene Yeo; **Additional Voices:** Yannick Bisson, Josh A. Cagan

### ◎ THE UPA CARTOON SHOW
This series is a repackaged version of *The Gerald McBoing Boing Show*, which was first shown on CBS in December 1956. The program was repeated in 1957 and then syndicated in the late 1960s (under the title of *UPA Cartoon Parade*) by United Productions of America (UPA). In 1989 the series was packaged as part of the *Mr. Magoo and Friends* show and broadcast on USA Network.

Hosted by Gerald McBoing Boing, the series features cartoon segments starring The Twirlinger Twins, Dusty of the Circus, among others, as well as 130 five-minute Mr. Magoo cartoons produced in the 1960s and episodes from *What's New Mr. Magoo?* produced in 1977 by DePatie-Freleng Enterprises in association with UPA. (See *The Gerald McBoing Boing Show* for voice credit information.) *A UPA Production. Color. Half-hour. Syndicated. Rebroadcast on USA: September 18, 1989–September 16, 1990 (as part of Mister Magoo and Friends).*

### ◎ THE U.S. OF ARCHIE
In this half-hour Saturday morning series composed of 16 original episodes, timed to coincide with the country's Bicentennial, Archie, Jughead and Veronica re-create the accomplishments of America's forefathers. It was a major ratings failure for CBS. By mid-season, the program was moved to Sunday mornings, where it completed its network run. *A Filmation Associates Production. Color. Half-hour. Premiered on CBS: September 7, 1974–September 5, 1976. Rebroadcast on FAM: Fall 1993–94. Rebroadcast on ODY: April 1999–2000.*

**Voices**
John Erwin, Dal McKennon, Howard Morris, Jane Webb

### ◎ VALLEY OF THE DINOSAURS
A modern-day family gets caught up in a whirlpool while exploring an unchartered river in the Amazon and is transported back in time to the world of prehistoric animals and cave people in this 16-episode half-hour fantasy/adventure series first broadcast on CBS. *A Hanna-Barbera Production. Color. Half-hour. Premiered on CBS: September 7, 1974–September 4, 1976. Rebroadcast on CAR: June 28, 1993–September 17, 1993 (weekdays); May 2, 1994–September 2, 1994 (weekdays); June 5, 1995–September 1, 1995 (weekdays). Rebroadcast on BOOM: April 9, 2000–January 16, 2005.*

**Voices**
**John Butler, the father:** Mike Road; **Kim Butler, his wife:** Shannon Farnon; **Katie Butler, their daughter:** Margene Fudenna; **Greg Butler, their son:** Jackie Earle Haley; **Gorak, the prehistoric father:** Alan Oppenheimer; **Gera, his wife:** Joan Gardner; **Tana, their daughter:** Melanie Baker; **Lock:** Stacy Bertheau

**Other Voices**
Andrew Parks

### ◎ VAN-PIRES
Four scrapyard vans and cars (under the leadership of Tracula) that acquire human traits following a meteor crash plan to sap Earth of all its natural gases in order to fulfill their gluttonous appetites, unless four teenagers (known as The Motor-Vaters) who know of their plan can stop them in this weekly live-action/computer-animated adventure series made for Saturday-morning television. *An Abrams Gentile Entertainment/MSH Entertainment/Animation Factory Production. Color. Half-hour. Premiered: September 13, 1997. Syndicated.*

**Cast (live action)**
**Snap:** Garlikayi Mutambirwa; **Rev:** Melissa Marsala; **Nuke:** Marc Schwarz; **Axle:** Jason Hayes

**Voices**
James Michael, Jonathan Kahn, Max Grace, Donna Daley, Bruce Jay, Billy Boy, Don Mayo

### ◎ THE VENTURE BROS.
Comical exploits of high-pitched, dim-witted identical twins, Hank and Dean Venture, born six minutes apart, who enjoy thrilling adventures—and speak and act like they are from the 1960s. With their world-renowned scientist father Dr. Venture and their faithful bodyguard Brock Samson, they come face-to-face with megalomaniacs, zombies and suspicious ninjas in this animated takeoff of Hanna-Barbera's cult favorite 1960s series *Jonny Quest* and popular pulp novel favorites *The Hardy Boys*. First broadcast as a special on Cartoon Network's late-night *Adult Swim* program block in February 2003, following its success the network commissioned this popular series of 15-minute adventures that regularly began airing on *Adult Swim* in August 2004. With 13 episodes broadcast that season, a holiday special entitled *A Very Venture Christmas* was also produced and aired that December. A second

season of 14 new episodes began in June 2006, including one two-part episode "Showdown at Cremation Creek." A *Noodlesoup Productions. Color. Fifteen minutes. Premiered on CAR: August 7, 2004.*

**Voices**
**Hank Venture:** Christopher McCulloch; **Dean Venture:** Michael Sinterniklaas; **Dr. Thaddeus S. "Rusty" Venture:** James Urbaniak; **Brock Samson:** Patrick Warburton

## ◎ VIDEO POWER

Established video arcade game stars Kuros, Kwirk, Big Foot and Max Force (properties of the Acclaim and Williams Electronics video companies) appeared in cartoon sequences that made up this live-action/animated series, hosted by video-game junkie Johnny Arcade (played by Stivi Paskoski). The daily half-hour series was a hodgepodge of live-action bits, film clips and animated segments, largely appealing to younger viewers. The series aired for two seasons in syndication, beginning in 1990. (For the final season, the show was all live action.) A *Saban Entertainment/Acclaim/Bohbot Production. Color. Half-hour. Premiered: 1990. Syndicated.*

**Cast (live action)**
**Johnny Arcade:** Stivi Paskoski

**Voices**
Mike Donovan, Lee Jeffrey, Terry Klassen, Jason Michas, Richard Newman, John Novak, Dale Wilson

## ◎ VIEWTIFUL JOE

Quirky Japanese anime import, originally broadcast Saturdays on Japan's Tokyo TV from October 2004 to September 2005, based on the popular video game of the same name developed by Capcom, featuring a heroic wisecracker who, upon being transformed into a red-suited superhero (and granted his superpowers by his action-flick movie idol Captain Blue), battles celluloid monsters in Movie Land in search of his girlfriend Silvia. Redubbed with American voice actors, the stylish half-hour action-adventure series premiered on Kids' WB! at 11:30 A.M. as part of its fall 2005 Saturday-morning block. The network ordered 26 episodes of the highly anticipated series from Geneon Entertainment, which produced the series for American television audiences. On September 2, 2006, the WB—now called the CW Network—dropped the series, replacing it with Warner Bros. Television Animation's *The Batman* series. A *Geneon Entertainment/Kids WB! Production. Color. Half-hour. Premiered on the CW (Kids' WB!): November 5, 2005–August 26, 2006.*

**Voices**
**Joe/Viewtiful Joe:** Jeff Nimoy; **Junior/Captain Blue Jr.:** Kate Levine; **Silvia/Go-Go Silvia:** Philece Sampler; **Captain Blue (Ep. 1–21):** Bob Papenbrook; **Captain Blue (Ep. 23–  ):** Paul St. Peter; **Sprocket:** Wendee Lee; **Charles the Third/Biankes:** Terrence Stone; **Joe Cooker:** Hulk Davidson; **Alastor/Gran Bruce:** Ross Lawrence; **Fire Leo:** Crispin Freeman; **Rotten Jack:** Kirk Thorton; **Holly:** Kari Wahlgren; **Koko/Thomas/Jim:** Mona Marshall

## ◎ VISIONAIRIES: KNIGHTS OF THE MAGIC LIGHT

On the planet Prysmos, the age of technology has come to an end and a new age of magic has begun under the great wizard, Merklyn, who transforms knights into warriors with spectacular capabilities. Calling themselves The Spectral Knights, they protect the citizens from the evil forces of the Darkling Lords in this first-run half-hour series first syndicated in 1987. Based on the Hasbro action

toy figures, the 13-week series was originally planned to be part of a cartoon combo known as *The Air Raiders/Visionaries Shows*. Only the latter was produced. A *Marvel/Sunbow TMS Entertainment Production in association with Hasbro and Claster Television. Visionairies are trademarks of Hasbro, all rights reserved. Color. Half-hour. Premiered: September 21, 1987. Syndicated.*

**Voices**
**SPECTRAL KNIGHTS: Leoric:** Neil Ross; **Ectar/Lexor:** Michael McConnohie; **Cyrotek:** Bernard Erhard; **Witterquick/Bearer of Knowledge:** Jim Cummings; **Arzon/Wisdom Owl:** Hal Rayle; **Feryl:** Beau Weaver; **Galadria:** Susan Blu

**DARKLING LORDS: Darkstorm/Cravex:** Chris Latta; **Mortredd:** Jonathan Harris; **Cindarr:** Peter Cullen; **Reekon:** Roscoe Lee Browne; **Virulina:** Jennifer Darling; **Narrator:** Malachi Throne; **Other Voices:** Ellen Gerstel

## ◎ VIVA PINATA

A party-going cast of piñata friends—the classic superstar Hudson Horstatchio; the ever-nervous Fergy Fudgehog; the keenly observant Paulie Pretztail; and the practically perfect Franklin Fizzybear—discover mystery and adventure on the uncharted exotic Pinata Island in this half-hour series produced by 4Kids Entertainment. The fun-filled 3-D CGI-animated television series featured 26 half-hour episodes during its premiere in the fall of 2006 on 4Kids TV's programming block on FOX. The off-the-wall Saturday-morning comedy series returned in 2007 for a second season with an additional 26 half-hour adventures. The series' September 2006 launch served as a springboard for a new licensed Microsoft Xbox 360 video game and other merchandise by Playmate Toys and American Greetings. A *Bardel Entertainment/4Kids Entertainment Production. Color. Half-hour. Premiered on FOX: September 9, 2006.*

**Voices**
**Hudson Horstachio:** Dan Green; **Fergy Fudgehog:** David Wills; **Paulie Pretztail:** Brian Maillard; **Franklin Fizzybear:** Marc Thompson; **Teddington Twingersnaps:** Jamie McGonnigal

## ◎ VOLTRON: DEFENDER OF THE UNIVERSE

Set in the 25th century, a team of young, dauntless space explorers seek and recover five fierce robot lions who unite to form "Voltron," the most incredible robot warrior ever. Once united, the Voltron force protects the planet Arus and neighboring galaxies and establishes peace in the universe in this daily syndicated series, which originated as a 90-minute special in 1983. The half-hour series was distributed to 76 markets a year later and subsequently was rebroadcast on USA Network's *Cartoon Express*. In 1997 the series was resyndicated under the title, *The New Adventures of Voltron*, while episodes of the original series aired weekdays on Cartoon Network. A *World Events Production. Color. Half-hour. Syndicated: September 10, 1984–86; September 13–14, 1997–Fall 1998. Rebroadcast on USA: September 16, 1991–June 27, 1993; Rebroadcast on CAR: March 17, 1997–January 1998; May 1998–October 1998; July 19, 1999–February 27, 2000; November 14, 2006–July 19, 2007 (Adult Swim).*

**Voices**
Jack Angel, Michael Bell, Peter Cullen, Tress MacNeille, Neil Ross, B.J. Ward, Lennie Weinrib

## ◎ VOLTRON: THE THIRD DIMENSION

Five years after their destruction of the nefarious Fleet of Doom, the legendary Voltron force—Keith, Lance, Pidge, Hunk and Allura—reunites to battle a new threat to the universe: a powerful

*The most incredible robot warrior ever made protects the planet Arus and neighboring galaxies from intruders in the popular syndicated series* Voltron: Defender of the Universe. *© World Events Productions*

band of space pirates, led by the dastardly cyborg, Lotor (voiced by actor Tim Curry), who has formed a deadly alliance with the famed mistress of dark magic, Haggar, in this syndicated, animated science-fiction adventure series spun-off from a 1984 predecessor, *Voltron: Defender of the Universe.*

Winner of a 1999 Daytime Emmy Award for outstanding sound editing–special class, this spectacular CGI-animated series—and first entire CGI-animated series produced by U.S-based studio, Netter Digital—was planned as a sequel to the cel-animated series *Voltron: Defender of the Universe,* which aired in syndication in the mid-1980s and again in the late 1990s, retitled as *The New Adventures of Voltron.* Bearing little connection to the previous rendition, this 26-episode, half-hour series, coproduced by Mike Young Productions in association with Japan's Toei Animation, bowed in first-run syndication in September 1998. In May 2000, almost two years after its premiere, the series was canceled. Shortly thereafter its producer, Netter Digital, closed its doors due to bankruptcy. In the fall of 2006, the series resurfaced in reruns on VOOM's high-definition channel Animania. *A Toei Co. Ltd./Mike Young Productions/Netter Digital Entertainment/World Events Production. Color. Half-hour. Premiered: September 12, 1998–Fall 2000. Syndicated. Rebroadcast on ANI: 2006.*

**Voices**
**Lotor/King Alfor:** Tim Curry; **Zarkon/Hunk:** Kevin Michael Richardson; **Princess Allura/Hagar:** B.J. Ward; **Pidge:** Billy West; **Lance/Coran:** Michael Bell; **Keith/Amalgamus:** Neil Ross; **Queepueg:** Clancy Brown; **Lafitte:** Tress MacNeille

## ◉ VOR-TECH

Two antagonistic brothers compete to turn humans into powerful machines as a result of technology in this half-hour science-fiction/fantasy series that premiered in 1996 as part of the weekend cartoon strip "Power Block," featuring the newly animated *All Dogs Go to Heaven* and first-run animated adventures of *Richie Rich. A Universal Cartoon Studios Kenner/Mediatoon Production. Color. Half-hour. Premiered: September 16, 1996. Syndicated.*

**Voices**
**Hardfire:** Ian James Corlett; **Damian Roarke:** David Sobolov; **Miranda Ortiz:** Venus Terzo

## ◉ THE VOYAGES OF DR. DOLITTLE

With his helpers Tommy and Maggie, the world's most famous doctor sets sail around the world to exotic lands and meets, among others, the Monkey King, the Whiskered Rat and Pushmi-Pullyu, the two-headed creature. In this adaptation of Hugh Lofting's classic tale, the good doctor and his patients converse in animal talk. *A Knack Television Production in association with 20th Century Fox Television. Color. Half-hour. Premiered: 1984. Syndicated.*

**Voices**
**Dr. Dolittle:** John Stephenson; **Tommy Stubbins:** B.J. Ward; **Maggie Thompson:** Jeanine Elias; **Other Voices:** Stanley Jones, William Callaway, Ralph James, Jerry Dexter, Linda Gary

## ◉ VYTOR, THE STARFIRE CHAMPION

This program highlights the adventures of the teenage hero, Vytor, and his female costar, Skyla, who work together to recapture the Starfire Orb, the world's most powerful energy source, and create peace and unity in the world. The program aired via syndication as a one-week miniseries in 1989. *A World Events/ Calico Productions presentation. Half-hour. Color. Premiered: January 1989. Syndicated.*

**Voices**
**Vytor:** Michael Horton; **Skyla/Lyria:** Liz Georges; **Myzor/Eldor:** Peter Cullen; **Targil:** Neil Ross; **Baboose:** Allison Argo; **Windchaser/Mutoids:** Patrick Fraley

*The world's most famous talking animals doctor sails to exotic lands in new half-hour animated adventures in* The Voyages of Dr. Doolittle, *based on Hugh Lofting's classic novels. © Knack Television. All rights reserved.*

## ◎ WACKY RACES

Zany race-car drivers and their equally daffy turbine-driven contraptions enter international competitions, with the single goal of winning the coveted title "the World's Wackiest Racer." Their efforts are endangered by the devious activities of evildoer Dick Dastardly and his snickering dog, Muttley.

Competitors include Pat Pending, Rufus Ruffcut, Sawtooth, Penelope Pitstop, The Slag Brothers (Rock and Gravel), the Ant Hill Mob, the Red Max, the Gruesome Twosome, Luke and Blubber Bear.

Hanna-Barbera produced this weekly Saturday-morning series, first offered on CBS in 1968. Thirteen original half-hour episodes were produced, each airing that first season, then rebroadcast in their entirety the following season, before the series was canceled. *A Hanna-Barbera Production. Color. Half-hour. Premiered on CBS: September 14, 1968–September 5, 1970. Rebroadcast on CAR: October 3, 1992–February 26, 1994 (Saturdays); May 7, 1994–September 3, 1994 (Saturdays); June 5, 1995–October 1, 1995 (weekdays); March 25, 1996–June 27, 1997 (weekdays). Rebroadcast on BOOM: April 5, 2000–.*

*Voices*
**Dick Dastardly/Private Meekly:** Paul Winchell; **Penelope Pitstop:** Janet Waldo; **Red Max/Rufus Ruffcut/Rock and Gravel Slag/Peter Perfect/The Sarge/Big Gruesome:** Daws Butler; **Rock/Muttley Sawtooth/Ring-A-Ding/Little Gruesome/Professor Pat Pending:** Don Messick; **Luke and Blubber Bear/General:** John Stephenson; **The Ant Hill Mob:** Mel Blanc; **Narrator:** Dave Willock

## ◎ THE WACKY WORLD OF TEX AVERY

The side-splitting, fast-paced, gag-filled style of cartoons, replete with squash-and-stretch animation, pioneered by the late legendary Warner Bros. and MGM animator Tex Avery who died in 1980 is emulated in this daily half-hour syndicated series in which Avery, as a rubber-bodied, in-your-face cartoon cowboy, serves as the host. Produced by DIC Entertainment (which bought the rights to Avery's name from his daughter), the program features seven all-new characters, one-upping their adversaries, in six-minute cartoon shorts, ranging from prehistoric inventor Einstone to pesky Freddy the Fly. Available in 65 half-hours or a package of 197 six-minute shorts for flexible programming. DIC's president Andy Heyward (who worked with Avery at Hanna-Barbera until his death) spearheaded the concept and also served as the series executive producer. The series' working title was *Tex Avery Theater. A DIC Entertainment Telecima SA/Milimetros/Les Studios Tex SARL/General Mills Production. Color. Half-hour. Premiered: September 1, 1997. Syndicated.*

*Voices*
**Tex Avery/Freddie The Fly/Sagebrush Kid:** Billy West; **Dan The Man:** Alec Willows; **Maurice:** Terry Klassen; **Mooch/Mr. Squab/Narrator:** Maurice LeMarche; **Khannie:** Cree Summer; **Chastity Knott:** Kathleen Barr; **Pompeii Pete/Einstone:** Ian James Corlett; **Amanda Banshee:** Scott McNeil; **Ghengia:** Lee Tockar; **Power Pooch:** Phil Hayes; **Mrs. Squab:** Jane Montifee

## ◎ WAIT TILL YOUR FATHER GETS HOME

Cast in the mold of TV's long-running *All in the Family*, this wildly funny first-run syndicated series illustrated the generation gap between an old-fashioned father (Harry Boyle, president of Boyle Restaurant Supply Company) and his modern-day children (Chet, Alice and Jamie), who have difficulty accepting their father's time-worn methods and philosophies of life. Broadcast between 1972 and 1974, the 48-episode series appeared in prime time (Hanna-Barbera's first prime-time cartoon series since 1970's *Where's Huddles?*) in many major markets, including five owned and operated NBC affiliates across the United States. In the 1990s, this popular family show was rerun on Cartoon Network and again in 2006 on Boomerang. *A Hanna-Barbera Production. Color. Half-hour. Premiered: September 12, 1972. Syndicated. Rebroadcast on CAR: October 4, 1992–May 2, 1993 (Sundays); May 16, 1993–April 3, 1994 (Sundays); April 4, 1994–July 2, 1995 (weekdays, Sundays); July 5, 1995–March 11, 1997 (Wednesdays); March 17, 1997 (Mondays–Thursdays). Rebroadcast on BOOM: September 18, 2006–.*

*Voices*
**Harry Boyle:** Tom Bosley; **Irma Boyle, his wife:** Joan Gerber; **Alice Boyle, the daughter:** Kristina Holland; **Chet Boyle, the son:** David Hayward; **Jamie Boyle, the youngest son:** Jackie Haley; **Ralph, their neighbor:** Jack Burns

## ◎ WAKE, RATTLE AND ROLL

In the basement of his family home, a computer-loving teenager (Sam Baxter) enjoys watching cartoons on his talking robot (D.E.C.K.S.), made from old VCR parts. Along with his magician-grandfather (Grandpa Quirk), older sister (Debbie) and young female friend (K.C.), he hosts this live-action/animated series that introduced two all-new weekly cartoon series: "Fender Bender 500," a series of race-car adventures starring Hanna-Barbera favorites Yogi Bear, Huckleberry Hound, Top Cat, Dastardly and Muttley, and "Monster Tails," the offbeat adventures of the pets of Hollywood's most famous movie monsters, left behind in a creepy castle. Created by Hanna-Barbera president and chief executive officer David Kirschner (co-executive producer with Steven Spielberg of *An American Tail*), the daily half-hour series—the first children's program designed specifically for morning weekday time periods since *Captain Kangaroo*—premiered in syndication on 90 stations in September 1990. A year later it was rebroadcast on The Disney Channel under the new title of *Jump, Rattle and Roll. A Hanna-Barbera Production in association with Four Point Entertainment. Color. Half-hour. Premiered: September 17, 1990. Syndicated. Rebroadcast on DIS: 1991 (as Jump, Rattle and Roll).*

*Cast (live action)*
**Sam:** R.J. Williams; **K.C.:** Ebonie Smith; **Debbie Detector:** Terri Ivens; **Grandpa Quirk:** Avery Schreiber; **D.E.C.K.S.:** Tim Lawrence; **Voice of D.E.C.K.S.:** Rob Paulsen

*Voices*

**FENDER BENDER 500: Yogi Bear:** Greg Burson; **Top Cat:** Arnold Stang; **Choo Choo:** Marvin Kaplan; **Dick Dastardly:** Paul Winchell; **Muttley:** Don Messick; **Announcer:** Shadoe Stevens

**MONSTER TAILS:** Charlie Adler, Tim Curry, Dick Gautier, Pat Musick, Frank Welker, Jonathan Winters

## ◎ WALLY GATOR

Giddy alligator Wally, who speaks like comedian Ed Wynn, yearns for freedom from the confines of his zoo cage in 52 five-minute cartoon adventures first offered to television stations as a component of *The Hanna-Barbera New Cartoon Series*, also featuring *Touché Turtle* and *Lippy the Lion* in their own individual series. Local television programmers broadcast the cartoons in consecutive or individual time slots and as part of daily children's programs hosted by local television personalities. *A Hanna-Barbera Production. Color. Half-hour. Premiered: September 3, 1962. Syndicated. Rebroadcast on USA; 1989–92. Rebroadcast on CAR 1992–2000. Rebroadcast on BOOM: April 11, 2000.*

*Voices*
**Wally Gator:** Daws Butler; **Mr. Twiddles, his friend:** Don Messick

## ◎ WALTER MELON

In the fashion of James Thurber's classic daydreamer, Walter Mitty, Walter Melon is a jolly, big-nosed, middle-aged man who achieves the impossible as a superhero-for-hire (joined by his partner, Bitterbug) by helping others in distress and fighting bad guys wherever they lurk in this parody of comic-book superheroes and pop-culture television and movie characters from *Star Trek, Jurassic Park, The Terminator, Star Wars* and other sources. Originally produced for French television under the title *Achille Talon*, this English-dubbed version, adapted from the popular French comic strip, aired in the United States for two seasons on FOX Family Channel. On August 8, 1998, in an effort to cross-promote the series, FOX Family Channel's sister network, FOX, aired a half-hour Saturday-morning preview special featuring two episodes: "The Far Flower Rangers" and "The Mark of Zorro." *A Saban France Production. Color. Half-hour. Premiered on FOX: August 8, 1998 (special presentation). Premiered on FOX FAM: August 16, 1998–July 11, 1999 (series).*

*Voices*
David Kaye, Michael McConnohie, Mary Kay Bergman, Dave Mallow

## ◎ WARNER BROS. HISTERIA!

An oddball ensemble cast of characters—Father Time, Lucky Bob, Lydia Karaoke, Miss Information, Mr. Smartypants, Aka Pella, Froggo, Fetch and Big Fat Baby—revisit and spoof well-known personalities, noted figures, and major events and periods in American and world history and culture, from Julius Caesar and Abraham Lincoln to the Civil War and the Boston Tea Party, in this off-the-wall slapstick comedy series, created by Tom Ruegger (creator of such hit Warner Bros. cartoon shows as *Animaniacs, Pinky & the Brain* and *Tiny Toon Adventures*) for Warner Bros. Television Animation.

Developed in response to the FCC's 1997 mandate calling for networks to produce more educational programming, this half-hour series was designed to both entertain and educate viewers. Unfortunately, the concept never fully caught on. Producing low ratings, the show was canceled after two seasons, spending its first season on the Kids' WB! Saturday-morning schedule and then being relegated to early weekday mornings in the fall of 1999, where it completed its run. *A Warner Bros. Television Animation Production. Color. Half-hour. Premiered on Kids' WB!: September 19, 1998–August 30, 2001.*

*Voices*
**Father Time/Fetch:** Frank Welker; **Aka Pella:** Cree Summer; **Miss Information/Charity Bazaar:** Laraine Newman; **Cho-Cho/Pepper Mills:** Tress MacNeille; **Lucky Bob/Napoleon:** Jeff Bennett; **Lydia Karaoke/Statue of Liberty:** Nora Dunn; **Mr. Smartypants:** Rob Paulsen; **Froggo:** Nathan Ruegger; **Loud Kiddington:** Cody Ruegger; **Big Fat Baby:** Luke Ruegger; **Other Voices:** Tony Attaway, Julie Bernstein, Steve Bernstein, Jess Harnell, Cindy Henerson, Maurice LaMarche, Elizabeth Lamers, Jane Marsden, Don Novello, Don Pardo, Paul Rugg, Fred Travalena, Billy West, James Wickline

## ◎ WAR PLANETS

Led by the ignoble miner Graveheart, four warring planets (Rock, Ice, Fire and Bone) that robbed each other of their natural resources in the past join forces to ward off their mutual enemy the Beast Planet in this half-hour science-fiction cartoon series, loosely based on the popular Shadow Raiders toy line and produced by Canada's Mainframe Entertainment for syndication in 1998. *A Mainframe Entertainment/Alliance Atlantis Communications/Summit Media Group Production. Color. Half-hour. Premiered: September 19, 1998. Syndicated.*

*Voices*
**Graveheart:** Paul Dobson; **Jade:** Enuka Okuma; **Pelvus:** Scott McNeil; **Lord Mantle:** Blu Mankuma; **Grand Vizier:** Jim Byrnes; **Prince Pyrus:** Matt Hill; **Lady Zera:** Tegan Moss; **King Cryos:** Mark Oliver; **Emperor Femur:** Gary Chalk; **Tekla:** Donna Yamamoto; **Lamprey:** Tasha Simms; **Voxx:** UK; **Blokk:** Alec Willows; **Jewelia:** Janyse Jaud; **Zuma:** Ellen Kennedy

## ◎ WAYNEHEAD

Comic actor and talk-show host Daymon Wayans (of TV's *Living Color* fame) created this half-hour animated series about the adventures of Damey Wayne, a resilient 10-year-old with a physical disability growing up in Manhattan and with his close-knit family and friends, based on real-life experiences. *A Warner Bros. Television Animation Production. Color. Half-hour. Premiered on the WB (Kids' WB!): October 19, 1996–May 17, 1997. Rebroadcast on CAR: March 7, 1998–October 1, 2000.*

*Voices*
**Damey Wayne:** Orlando Brown; **Mom:** Kim Wayans; **Dad:** John Witherspoon; **Kevin:** Gary Coleman; **Aki/Roz/Shavonne:** T'Keyah "Crystal" Keymah; **Marvin:** Tico Wells; **Mo Money Jr.:** Jamil Smith; **Toof:** Shawn Wayans; **Blue:** Marlon Wayans; **Tripod:** Frank Welker; **Monique:** James Altuner

## ◎ WE ALL HAVE TALES

This follow-up batch of heartwarming animated children's series from the producers of the award-winning *Storybook Classics* series aired sporadically on Showtime beginning in 1991. Told in a "storybook-animation format," 13 stories were initially adapted for television, including the Japanese tale "The Boy Who Drew Cats"; the classic fable "King Midas and the Golden Touch"; the African folktale "Kai and the Kola Nuts"; and many others. Each program was narrated by famous celebrities, including William Hurt, Michael Caine, Ben Kingsley and Whoopi Goldberg. Comedian Robin Williams narrated the series opener, "Flying Ship." The series' original 13 episodes were broadcast over a two-year period, with new episodes airing in early 1994. Susan Sarandon and Michael Palin were among the new crop of celebrity narrators to lend their voices to the new half-hour editions. *A Rabbit Ears Video Production. Color. Half-hour. Premiered on SHO: April 9, 1991.*

## ◎ WEIRD-OHS

Off-the-beaten path of Route 66 in the town of Weirdsville, where cars rule the road and racing is a way in life, two hot-rod-loving teens, Digger Eddie and Portia, coexist with a group of talking automobiles, the Chassis Family, and their fellow residents, Leaky Boat Louie and Slingrave Curvette, in this innovative, squash-and-stretch CGI-animated series, first broadcast on Canada's YTV network. Produced by Canada's Mainframe Entertainment (the makers of *Reboot* and *Beast Machines*), this 13-episode series made its U.S. television debut in October 1999 on Fox Family Channel as part of the network's cartoon block that included *Angela Anaconda* and *The Kids in Room 402. A Weird Ohs/Mainframe Entertainment Inc./DECODE Entertainment Production. Color. Half-hour. Premiered on FOX FAM: October 9, 1999–February 19, 2000.*

*Voices*
**Digger/Mama-B Chassis:** Kathleen Barr; **Portia:** Tabitha St. Germain; **Eddie:** Cusse Mankuma; **Daddy-O Chassis/Davey/Killer McBash:** Scott McNeil; **Uncle Huey:** Gary Chalk; **Leaky Boat Louie:** Mark Atchison; **Wade, Baby Chassis:** Ian James Corlett; **Slingrave Curvette:** Elizabeth Carol Savenkoff

## ◎ WHAT A CARTOON! SHOW

(See WORLD PREMIERE TOONS.)

## ◎ WHAT-A-MESS

A royal-born, incredibly grubby puppy, Prince Amir of Kinjan (affectionately dubbed What-A-Mess because of his tousled appearance), tackles everyday mysteries of life, determined to be every bit as brave and heroic as his royal Afghan ancestors, in this 26-episode half-hour Saturday-morning cartoon series based on a character created by British TV personality Frank Muir. The gangly accident-prone puppy was first introduced in a series of interstitials produced for ABC in 1994. *A DIC Entertainment/Link Entertainment Production. Color. Half-hour. Premiered on ABC: September 1994 (interstitials). Premiered on ABC: September 16, 1995–August 31, 1996 (series). Rebroadcast on TDIS: April 20, 1998–September 1, 2002.*

*Voices*
**What-A-Mess:** Ryan O'Donohue; **Felicia:** Jo Ann Harris Belson; **Trash:** Joe Nipote; **Frank:** Frank Muir; **Duchess:** Charity James; **Mother:** Miriam Flynn; **Father:** Michael Bell; **Daughter:** Debi Derryberry; **Son:** Adam Hendershott

## ◎ WHATEVER HAPPENED TO ROBOT JONES?

Three feet, eight inches tall, weighing 500 pounds and with a 9,468 mega-volt memory, Robot Jones is no ordinary teenager but spunky experimental prototype adapting to his retro-1980s life with humans, where robots have become a vital cog of society—from robo-bartenders to mechanical butlers—while surviving adolescence with his friends Sock, Mitch, Cubey, and the girl of his life Shannon, in this futuristic animated series produced for Cartoon Network.

Created by Greg Miller, this half-hour comedy cartoon series, featuring two stories per show, was commissioned by Cartoon Network after the series pilot aired in 2000 among other cartoon shorts and pilots as part of CAR's "Big Pick" viewers' poll, which *The Grim Adventures of Billy & Mandy* subsequently won. In July 2002, nearly two years after the pilot's premiere, the series debuted in prime time with six first-season episodes. Production began on a second season of seven more episodes, all of which aired, before the series was canceled in February 2004. In 2005, episodes were sporadically rebroadcast on Cartoon Network, along with other previously aired Cartoon Network series including *Courage the Cowardly Dog* and *Cow and Chicken*. *A Cartoon Network Studios Production. Color. Half-hour. Premiered on CAR: August 25, 2000 (pilot). Premiered on CAR: July 19, 2002–February 1, 2004. Rebroadcast on CAR: September 13, 2005–August 14, 2006.*

*Voices*
**Robot Jones (Bobby Block):** Himself; **Mom Unit/Shannon Westaberg/Connie:** Grey DeLisle; **Robot Dad:** Maurice LaMarche; **Timothy "Socks" Martin/Dan:** Kyle Sullivan; **Cubey:** Myles Jeffrey; **Lenny Yogman:** Josh Peck; **Principal Madman:** Jeff Bennett; **Mr. Uerkraut:** Dee Bradley Baker; **Tim Baines/Little Kevin:** Jonathan Osser; **Mr. McMcmc:** Rip Taylor; **Other Voices:** Greg Cipes, Austin Farmer, Gary LeRoi Gray, Josh Peck, Kath Soucie, Austin Stout

## ◎ WHAT'S NEW, MISTER MAGOO?

The nearsighted, Academy Award–winning Mr. Magoo is joined by an equally myopic canine companion, McBarker, in further adventures marked by mistaken-identity gags and other improbable situations reminiscent of earlier productions featuring the querulous and sometimes irritable character. The half-hour Saturday-morning series debuted on CBS in 1977 in 13 half-hours, composed of 26 new cartoon adventures (two per show). Episodes from the series were packaged together with the original 1960s' series under the title of *Mister Magoo & Friends*, rebroadcast on USA Network's *Cartoon Express* from 1989 to 1990. *A DePatie-Freleng Enterprises Production in association with UPA Productions. Color. Half-hour. Premiered on CBS: September 10, 1977–September 9, 1979. Rebroadcast on USA: September 18, 1989–September 16, 1990.*

*Voices*
**Mr. Magoo:** Jim Backus; **McBarker, his bulldog:** Robert Ogle; **Waldo:** Frank Welker

## ◎ WHAT'S NEW, SCOOBY-DOO?

Latest spin-off of Hanna-Barbera's popular Saturday-morning teen mystery series, *Scooby-Doo, Where Are You!*, retaining the original mystery-solving element of teenage detectives—Fred, Shaggy, Daphne, Velma, and their Great Dane companion, Scooby—caught in the middle of a bunch of new creepy capers having to catch assorted masked bad guys in this updated "whodunit," originally produced for the WB Television Network's Kids' WB! Saturday-morning programming block in 2002.

Noticeable changes were made to bring the comedy/adventure series into the 21st century, such as incorporating the use of modern technology in episodes, including laptops, PDAs, mobile communicators and GPS systems and character makeovers (and the removal of Fred's famous ascot). Besides featuring new-age music and new sound effects (except for Casey Kasem returning as the voice of Shaggy), the series featured a new supporting voice cast, with Frank Welker taking over as the voice of Scooby; Grey DeLisle as Daphne; and Mindy Cohn (of TV's *Facts of Life*) as Velma. Fourteen episodes were broadcast during the first season, with 29 additional episodes produced thereafter. (14 for the second season, 13 for the third and only two for the final season combined with repeats). Reruns of the modern animated "whodunit" were shown weekdays on Cartoon Network beginning in March 2003. On Halloween day, October 31, 2005, the newest award-winning Scooby-Doo mystery-comedy series joined Boomerang's weekday lineup in reruns, concluding a six-day, 144-hour marathon (or so-called "Scooberang") featuring all the Scooby-Doo television series (from 1969's original *Scooby-Doo, Where Are You!* to 1988's *A Pup Named Scooby-Doo*), television movies and three direct-to-DVD animated specials starting that Wednesday at midnight. *A Hanna-Barbera/Warner Bros. Animation Production. Color. Half-hour. Premiered on the WB (Kids' WB!): September 14, 2002–July 21, 2006. Rebroadcast on CAR: March 28, 2003–. Rebroadcast on BOOM: October 31, 2005–.*

*Voices*
**Scooby-Doo/Fred Jones:** Frank Welker; **Velma Dace Dinkley:** Mindy Cohn; **Shaggy Rogers:** Casey Kasem; **Daphne Blake:** Grey DeLisle

## ◎ WHAT'S WITH ANDY?

Considering himself "the world's greatest prankster," Andy Larkin, a hyperactive teenager, stages elaborate stunts and practical jokes on everybody in the town of East Gackle where he lives, including his sister Jen and town bullies Peter and Andrew, with the help of his best friend Danny, while trying to impress a young girl named Lori Mackney in this Canadian-produced series, based on Australian children's author Andy Griffiths's *Just* books and originally made for Canada's Teletoon network. First made as an interactive Flash movie voiced by other actors, and a promotional piece for FOX Kids, the half-hour comedy series, featuring crudely pencil-drawn animation called "Doodlevision," was first broadcast weekday mornings in the United States on ABC Family from September 2001 until April 2002. Afterward, the series re-aired briefly weekdays on Toon Disney in early 2005. *A Cine-Groupe/Teletoon Production. Color. Half-hour. Premiered on ABC FAM: September 22, 2001–April 16, 2002. Rebroadcast on TDIS: January 18, 2005–June 2, 2005.*

*Voices*
**Andy Larkin:** Ian James Corlett; **Danny:** Bumper Robinson, Daniel Brochu; **Jen:** Jenna von Oÿ, Jessica Kardos; **Lori:** Colleen O'Shaughnessey, Jaclyn Linetsky; **Dad:** Dee Bradley Baker, Arthur Holden; **Mom/Terri/Mrs. Weebles:** Cathy Cavadini, Susan Glover; **Lik:** Danny Cooksey, Mark Hauser; **Leech:** Scott Parken, Craig Francis; **Craig:** Matt Holland; **Additional Voices:** E.G. Daily, Holly G. Frankel, Kath Soucie

## ◎ WHEELIE AND THE CHOPPER BUNCH

The world's greatest stunt-racing car, Wheelie, a souped-up Volkswagen, takes on the Chopper Bunch motorcycle gang, whose leader tries to win the affections of the "bug" girlfriend, Rota Ree, in situations that involve other rotary-engined characters with distinct personalities in this 1974 Saturday-morning series, first broadcast on NBC. Hanna-Barbera produced 13 half-hour episodes of the series, which lasted only one season. It was later rebroadcast on USA Network's *Cartoon Express*, Cartoon Network and Boomerang. *A Hanna-Barbera Production. Color. Half-hour. Premiered on NBC: September 7, 1974–August 30, 1975. Rebroadcast on USA: May 16, 1989–March 28, 1991. Rebroadcast on CAR: July 5, 1995 (Wednesdays). Rebroadcast on BOOM: June 24, 2000–December 11, 2003.*

*Voices*
**Wheelie/Chopper:** Frank Welker; **Rota Ree:** Judy Strangis; **Scrambles:** Don Messick; **Revs:** Paul Winchell; **High Riser:** Lennie Weinrib; **Other voices:** Rolinda Wolk

## ◎ WHERE ON EARTH IS CARMEN SANDIEGO?

The world's greatest thief is on the loose and it's up to two young detectives to find her. The only complication is that they and the thief they are chasing exist inside a computer game and must depend on their human "player" to provide them with essential information in this educational half-hour mystery series, which challenges young viewers to figure out the weekly crimes. Based on the best CD-ROM game (which has sold more than 4 million units since 1985), the series premiered on FOX Network in 1993.

Burbank-based DIC Entertainment developed and produced the series, which was in the development stage for three years at CBS. Finally, DIC president Andy Heyward sold the series to FOX. The series has earned three daytime Emmy nominations for outstanding animated program, winning the award for the 1994–95 season. *A DIC Entertainment Production. Color. Half-hour. Premiered on FOX: February 5, 1994–October 31, 1996; March 30, 1998–April 1, 1998. Rebroadcast on FOX FAM: August 22, 1998–March 28, 2000. Rebroadcast on PAX: 1999.*

*Voices*
**Carmen:** Rita Moreno; **The Chief:** Rodger Bumpass; **Ivy:** Jennifer Hale; **Zack:** Scott Menville; **The Players:** Asi Lang, Joanie Pleasant, Jeffrey Tucker, Justin Shenkarow

## ◎ WHERE'S HUDDLES?

Originally a prime-time summer replacement for CBS's *The Glen Campbell Goodtime Hour*, the weekly half-hour show revolves around a fumbling football quarterback, Ed Huddles, and his next-door neighbor, team center Bubba McCoy, who are members of the Rhinos, a disorganized pro team that Huddles somehow manages to lead to victory. Given a test run in the summer of 1970, the series was supposed to jump into a permanent nighttime slot in January of 1971, but CBS decided otherwise when the series faltered in the ratings. Instead, the series' original 10 episodes were rebroadcast the following summer. Series regulars include Hanna-Barbera stock players Alan Reed (Mad Dog), Mel Blanc (Bubbs) and Jean VanderPyl (Marge Huddles), best known as Fred, Barney and Wilma on *The Flintstones*, as well as comedian Paul Lynde (a regular on the popular TV game show *Hollywood Squares*), former Duke Ellington orchestra singer/vocalist Herb Jeffries and actress Marie Wilson in her final role before her death in 1972.

In 1989 the series enjoyed a brief run (in reruns) on USA Network's *Cartoon Express* and again returned to the air in 1995 on Cartoon Network and in 2001 on Boomerang. *A Hanna-Barbera Production. Color. Half-hour. Premiered on CBS: July 1, 1970–September 10, 1970. Rebroadcast on CBS: July 1971–September 5, 1971. Rebroadcast on USA: March 1, 1989–March 21, 1989. Rebroadcast on CAR: December 1995. Rebroadcast on BOOM: September 12, 2001–November 13, 2004.*

*Voices*
**Ed Huddles:** Cliff Norton; **Bubba McCoy:** Mel Blanc; **Marge Huddles, Ed's wife:** Marie Wilson, Jean VanderPyl; **Claude Pertwee, perfectionist neighbor:** Paul Lynde; **Mad Dog Mahoney, Rhinos' coach:** Alan Reed; **Freight Train:** Herb Jeffries; **Fumbles/Beverly:** Don Messick; **Sports Announcer:** Dick Enberg

## ◎ WHERE'S MY DOGS AT?

Two stray canines, Buddy a beagle and Wolfie a large bulldog, voiced by comedian Jeffrey Ross and *Saturday Night Live* alum Tracy Morgan, hang out—and lampoon—real-life, A-list Hollywood celebrities and pop culture icons in this half-hour series, cocreated by Ross and Aaron Matthew Lee, that premiered on MTV's spin-off channel, MTV2, as part of its *Sic'emation* program block to court viewers of subversive and edgy toons (akin to Cartoon Network's highly successful *Adult Swim*). The network came under fire for the series' degrading depiction of black women after its July 1, 2006, airing of the first season episode "Wolfie Loves Snoop Dogg," which had the famous rap star walking into a pet store with two bikini-clad women on leashes who squatted on all fours to defecate on the floor. Even though the program carried a TV-PG rating advising parents some material might be unsuitable for children under 14, critics slammed the network for showing "poor judgment" by airing the weekly series on Saturday mornings when many young children could be watching. Initially ordering eight episodes of the series, the show drew a cumulative audience of 17.2 million viewers during its first-season run. *A MTV Production. Color. Half-hour. Premiered on MTV2: June 10, 2006–July 29, 2006.*

*Voices*
**Buddy:** Jeffrey Ross; **Wolfie:** Tracy Morgan; **Dog Catcher/Various Others:** John Di Maggio; **50 Cent/Jay-Z/Various Others:** Dean

Edwards; **Rexia/Tom Cruise/Courtney Love/Various Others:** Jeff Richards; **Britney Spears/Various Others:** Lauren Tom; **Paris Hilton/Various Others:** Jackie Harris; **Bruce Willis/Various Others:** Colin Mahan; **Additional Voices:** Aaron Matthew Lee, Greg Eagles

## ⊚ WHERE'S WALDO?

The bespectacled young man with the striped turtleneck sweater and ski cap, featured in the bestselling picture-puzzle book created by British artist Martin Handford, starred in this half-hour network series adaptation. Waldo, his girlfriend, Wilma, and pet dog, Woof, embarked on globetrotting adventures, sometimes to help others, presented in two weekly cartoons (called "Waldo Minutes") in which the action was freeze-framed to give young viewers time to find clues to the mystery. *A DIC Enterprises/Waldo Film Company Production. Color. Half-hour. Premiered on CBS: September 14, 1991–September 7, 1992.*

**Voices**
Townsend Coleman, Jim Cummings, Julian Holloway, Dave Workman, Joe Alaskey, Jack Angel, Jeff Bennett, Gregg Berger, Susan Blu, Carol Channing, Cam Clarke, Brian Cummings, Jennifer Darling, Jeanne Elias, Pat Fraley, Maurice LaMarche, Mary McDonald Lewis, Michele Mariana, John Mariano, Chuck McCann, Pat Musick, Alan Oppenheimer, Rob Paulsen, Jan Robson, Roger Rose, Susan Silo, Frank Welker

## ⊚ WIDGET, THE WORLD WATCHER

An awesome, tiny flying extraterrestial with chameleonlike powers becomes the hero of the day, with the help of three young humans—eight-year-old Brian, his 16-year-old sister, Christine, and their older brother, Kevin—when he solves some of Earth's most pressing environmental and endangered species problems in this half-hour animated series syndicated in 1990. Initially produced as a weekly series, the program began airing daily in 1991. The program lasted five seasons and was rebroadcast until 1997. Peter Keefe, creator of the syndicated animated favorite *Denver, The Last Dinosaur*, created the series. *A Kroyer Films/Zodiac Entertainment/Calico Creations Production in association with Dinosaur Productions. Color. Half-hour. Premiered: September 29, 1990. Syndicated.*

**Voices**
**Widget:** Russi Taylor; **Mega Brain/Elder #1:** Jim Cummings; **Brian/Christine:** Kath Soucie; **Kevin:** Dana Hill; **Elder #2:** Tress MacNeille

## ⊚ WILDC.A.T.S.

Two prehistoric alien races—the superheroic, good-guy C.A.T.S. (Covert Action Team) and the ever-evil Daemonites battle for galactic domination in this half-hour cartoon series based on Jim Lee's widely popular comic book. The series originally debuted on CBS and was rerun on USA Network's Cartoon Express block. *A Nelvana Entertainment Production. Color. Half-hour. Premiered on CBS: September 17, 1994–September 2, 1995. Rebroadcast on USA: September 17, 1995–96.*

**Voices**
**Dockwell:** Dennis Akiyama; **Zealot:** Roscoe Handford; **Void:** Janet-Laine Green; **Voodoo:** Ruth Marshall; **Marlowe:** Sean McCann; **Warblade:** Dean McDermott; **Maul:** Paul Mota; **Grifter:** Colin O'Meara; **Spartan:** Rod Wilson; **Helspont:** Maurice Dean Wint

## ⊚ WILDFIRE

This 13-episode half-hour adventure series, originally broadcast on CBS in 1986, tells the story of Princess Sara of the planet Dar-Shan who, as an infant, is spirited away from the clutches of an evil sorceress, Diabolyn, by the mystically powerful stallion Wildfire. Wildfire carries the baby princess to the safety of the mortal world where, now grown up, she reunites with the great stallion to defeat Diabolyn and rescue Dar-Shan for the forces of goodness. She is joined by a motley band of companions (Dorin, Brutus and Alvinar) who help her on every step of her perilous quest. Grammy Award–winning composer Jimmy Webb created the series' music. *A Hanna-Barbera Production. Color. Half-hour. Premiered on CBS: September 13, 1986–September 5, 1987. Rebroadcast on CAR: April 15, 1995–April 16, 1995 (Look What We Found!).*

**Voices**
**Princess Sara:** Georgi Irene; **Wildfire, the stallion:** John Vernon; **Dorin, a young boy:** Bobby Jacoby; **Brutus, his clumsy horse:** Susan Blu; **Alvinar, a loyal farmer:** Rene Auberjoinois; **John, Sara's father:** David Ackroyd; **Ellen, John's best friend:** Lilly Moon; **Diabolyn, wicked sorceress:** Jessica Walter; **Dweedle, her hapless servant:** Billy Barty; **Mrs. Ashworth:** Vicky Carroll

## ⊚ THE WILD THORNBERRYS

Eliza, an amazing young girl with an ability to talk to animals, journeys around the world in an RV with her famous television-documentary (à la Discovery Channel) hosts, her parents Nigel (voiced by actor Tim Curry, who also narrates the series) and Marianne Thornberry, filming wildlife documentaries covering rare and little-known species. Joining them in their world travels are their oldest daughter Debbie, who yearns for the trappings of her suburban life back home; Donnie, their highly curious four-year-old adopted son; and Darwin, their "Swiss cheese" crunchies-loving chimpanzee friend.

Cocreated by Arlene Klasky, Gabor Csupo and Steve Pepoon and produced by Klasky Csupo, producers of Nickelodeon's smash-hit series *The Rugrats*, this animated documentary series spoof premiered in September 1998 in prime time on Nickelodeon, becoming the first Nick cartoon series to exclusively feature entire 30-minute stories, with 20 first-season episodes.

Premiering in September 1998 on Nickelodeon's prime-time lineup, the half-hour series was so successful that it spawned a slate of made-for-TV specials on Nick: their first 90-minute telefilm *The Origin of Donnie* (2001); one-hour special *Sir Nigel* (2003); and full-length animated feature spin-off *The Wild Thornberrys Movie* (2002). Encompassing five seasons and 83 regular episodes altogether, the popular children's series aired not only on Nickelodeon but also in reruns on Saturday mornings on CBS as part of the Nickelodeon-produced *Nick Jr.* on CBS programming block from September 2002 to March 2004. In April 2003, Nickelodeon aired the last original episode "Look Who's Squawking." The series' last actual episode, "Eliza Unplugged," was set to air in June 2004, but Nickelodeon aired an episode of *The Fairly Odd-Parents* instead. Since May 2002, the series has rerun weekday mornings on Nicktoons. *A Klasky Csupo/Viacom International Production. Color. Half-hour. Premiered on NICK: September 1, 1998. Rebroadcast on CBS: September 14, 2002–March 2004. Rebroadcast on NICKT: May 1, 2002–.*

**Voices**
**Eliza Thornberry:** Lacey Chabert; **Debbie Thornberry:** Danielle Harris; **Donnie Thornberry:** Flea; **Nigel Thornberry/Colonel Thornberry:** Tim Curry; **Marianne Thornberry:** Jodi Carlisle; **Darwin the Chimp:** Tom Kane; **Kip O'Donnell:** Keith Szarabajka; **Neil Beidermann:** Jerry Sroka; **Cordelia Thornberry:** Lynn Redgrave; **Grandma Sophie:** Betty White

## WILD WEST C.O.W.-BOYS OF MOO MESA

In this weekly half-hour take-off of the Old West, a group of bovine cowboys led by Marshall Moe Montana and his deputies Tenderfoot, Dakota Dude and Cowlorado Kid, uphold the "Code of the West" (the meaning of the acronym, "C.O.W.-Boys") and protect the friendly residents of Cow Town from a pair of power-hungry, corrupt gangs bent on making trouble. *A Gunther-Wahl/Ruby-Spears/RC Bee/Greengrass Production in association with King World Productions. Color. Half-hour. Premiered on ABC: September 13, 1992–September 11, 1993; September 18, 1993–August 27, 1994. Rebroadcast on TDIS: April 20, 1998–March 30, 2001.*

### Voices

1992–93 and 1993–94 episodes: Troy Davidson, Pat Fraley, Bill Farmer, Michael Horse, Neil Ross. 1992–93 episodes: Robby Benson, Tim Curry, Michael Gough, Michael Greer, Kath Soucie, Sally Struthers, Russi Taylor. 1993–94 episodes: Charlie Adler, Jack Angel, Michael Bell, Corey Burton, Ruth Buzzi, Jodi Carlisle, Jim Cummings, David Doyle, Brad Garrett, Ellen Gerstell, Mark Hamill, Dorian Harewood, Kate Mulgrew, Rob Paulsen, Stu Rosen.

## WILL THE REAL JERRY LEWIS PLEASE SIT DOWN?

Comedian Jerry Lewis created this half-hour series for ABC in 1970 in which his animated self, a bumbling janitor for the Odd Job Employment Agency, becomes a last-minute substitute and is reluctantly given several temporary assignments by the agency's owner, Mr. Blunderbuss. Lewis did not voice his own character in the series (David L. Lander, a.k.a. Squiggy on TV's *Laverne and Shirley*, provided the voice characterization), but he did contribute to several stories based on his roles in features including *The Caddy* (1958) and *The Errand Boy* (1962). Other series regulars included his girlfriend, Rhonda; his sister, Geraldine; and Spot, her pet frog. *A Filmation Associates Production. Color. Half-hour. Premiered on ABC: September 12, 1970–September 2, 1972.*

### Voices

**Jerry Lewis:** David L. Lander; **Geraldine Lewis/Rhonda:** Jane Webb; **Mr. Blunderbuss/Ralph Rotten Lewis/Won Ton Son/Professor Lewis/Hong Kong Lewis/Uncle Seadog:** Howard Morris

## WING COMMANDER ACADEMY

This original half-hour cartoon series, spun off from the popular CD-ROM interactive game, features a team of futuristic rocket jockeys who earn their wings. Produced for USA Network, it features the voices of Mark Hamill, Tom Wilson, Malcolm McDowell and Dana Delany. *A Universal Cartoon Studios/Electronic Arts/Origin Systems Production. Color. Half-hour. Premiered on USA: September 21, 1996–July 26, 1998.*

### Voices

**Christopher "Maverick" Blair:** Mark Hamill; **Commodore Geoffrey Tolwyn:** Malcolm McDowell; **Todd "Maniac" Marshall:** Thomas F. Wilson; **Gwen "Archer" Bowman:** Dana Delany; **Alien:** Michael Dorn

## WINKY DINK AND YOU

Children were given the chance to participate and solve problems in this unique series, featuring the adventures of Winky, a little boy, and his dog, Woofer. By attaching a transparent sheet to the television screen, kids were able to assist their cartoon friends in escaping from danger by drawing outlets and other imaginary pathways on the sheet with ordinary crayons. The program originally aired on CBS between 1953 and 1957, hosted by Jack Barry, who co-created the series with Dan Enright. (Barry and Enright later gained prominence as producers of such top-rated game shows as *The Joker's Wild*.) CBS Films syndicated the old black-and-white series through the mid-1960s before it was given a color revival in 1969. *An Ariel Productions in association with Barry-Enright/W.J. Seidler Productions. Color. Half-hour. Premiered on CBS: October 10, 1953–April 27, 1957. Premiered: 1969. Syndicated.*

### Voices

**Winky Dink:** Mae Questel; **Woofer:** Dayton Allen

## THE WINX CLUB

Set in the far reaches of the universe, six smart, sassy, stylish and magically gifted teenaged fairies (the fiery red-headed Bloom; the blonde-haired Fairy of the Sun and the Moon, Stella; the pigtailed, tomboy Musa; the shy but friendly Fairy of Nature, Flora; the intelligent Fairy of Technology, Tecna; and curly haired, athletic and adventuresome Fairy of Fluids, Layla) attend the Alfea School for Faeries—the oldest and most prestigious fairy school—employ their amazing magical powers to defeat evil witches who threaten the Realm of Magix in a battle of good versus evil. Part of 4Kids Entertainment's television program block, the 26-episode comedy/adventure series, created by Igninio Straffi and produced by Italy's Rainbow S.p.A., premiered on FOX's *FOX Box* Saturday-morning schedule in June 2004. In May 2005, the action-packed series joined Cartoon Network's *Miguzi* Monday through Friday afternoon adventure block, featuring such series as *Teen Titans, Justice League* and *Megas XLR*. *A Rainbow S.p.A./4Kids Entertainment Production. Color. Half-hour. Premiered on FOX: June 19, 2004–September 11, 2004; September 18, 2004–September 30, 2006. Rebroadcast on CAR: May 16, 2005–.*

### Voices

**Bloom:** Liza Jacqueline; **Prince Sky:** Frank Frankson; **Stella:** Amy Birnbaum; **Flora:** Kerry Williams; **Icy/Musa/Digit/Mitzi:** Lisa Ortiz; **Tecna:** Dani Schaffel, Dana Southern; **Layla:** Vasthy Mompoint; **Darcy:** Caren Manuel; **Stormy:** Suzy Myers; **Daphne:** Bella Hudson; **Professor Faragonda/Lucy/Dextia/Amaryl:** Rachael Lillis; **Professor Griselda:** Sebastian Arcelus; **Mike:** Stuart Zagnit; **Brandon:** Dan Green; **Professor Griffin:** Carol Jacobanis; **Lord Darkar/Codatorta:** Matt Hoverman; **Knut:** Marc Thompson; **WizGiz:** Oliver Wyman; **Incidentals:** Suzanne Goldish; **Saladin:** David Brimmer; **Riven:** Michael Sinterniklaas; **Livy:** Natasha Malinsky; **Mirta:** Amy Palant; **Lockette:** Andi Whaley; **Narsisia:** Sara Paxton

## WISHKID STARRING MACAULAY CULKIN

*Home Alone* film star Macaulay Culkin plays a young kid, named Nick McClary, whose magic baseball glove grants him his every wish, in this half-hour cartoon series telecast on NBC. Culkin, who provided the voice of his character, also appeared at the beginning of each episode in a live-action segment. The series, which lasted one full season on NBC, was rebroadcast Saturday mornings on the Family Channel from 1992 to 1994, becoming a top-rated cartoon series on the network. In January 1994, DIC announced signing an exclusive agreement with the Family Channel to produce 52 all-new episodes that began airing that September and were packaged with the original 13 half-hours DIC produced for NBC. *Wishkid* was later rebroadcast for four seasons on Toon Disney. *Premiered on NBC: September 14, 1991–September 7, 1992. Rebroadcast on FAM: 1992–94. Premiered on FAM: September 5, 1994–Fall 1996 (new episodes). Rebroadcast on TDIS: April 18, 1998–September 2, 2002.*

**Voices**
Macaulay Culkin, Quinn Culkin, Paul de la Rosa, Paul Haddad, Marilyn Lightstone, Judy Marshak, Andrew Sabiston, Stuart Stone, James Rankin, Harvey Atkin, Tara Charendoff, Joe Matheson, Benji Plener, Catherine Gallant, Susan Roman, Greg Swanson

## ◎ W.I.T.C.H.

Possessing elemental superpowers, five trendy, heroic schoolgirls, Will (the Heart of Handrakhar), Irma (Water), Taranee (Fire), Cornelia (Earth) and Hay Lin (Air), chosen as the Guardians to protect two universes separated by good and evil, harness their awesome powers to battle out-of-this world villains, including the ruthless Prince Phobos, in this action/fantasy series based on Disney's popular comic book.

Coproduced by Jetix Concept Animation, Walt Disney Television Animation and French production company SIP Animation, along with German and French broadcasters Super RTL and France 3, the half-hour series, aimed at viewers ages six to 12, aired on the *Jetix* branded action programming block on December 19, 2004, with an hour-long preview on both Toon Disney and ABC Family. Thereafter, *W.I.T.C.H.* premiered in its regular timeslots on Saturday, January 15 as part of *Jetix* on ABC Family (9:30 A.M.) and on Monday, January 17, 2005, on Toon Disney (8:30 P.M.). The first season consisted of 26 half-hours, with a second season of 12 new episodes in which the teenage superheroes battled a different bunch of evildoers, premiering during *Jetix* on Monday, June 5, 2006, on Toon Disney and Saturday, June 10, on ABC Family. When ABC Family dropped its *Jetix* block in late August 2006, following a weekend marathon, Toon Disney continued airing the series.

In the meantime, the program also aired on the Jetix Europe programming block on BBC2 and CBBC in the United Kingdom, and in several other countries as well, including Canada. *A Jetix Concept Animation/Walt Disney Television Animation/SIP Animation/Super RTL/France 3 Production. Color. Half-hour. Premiered on TDIS/ABC FAM: December 19, 2004 (sneak preview). Premiered on ABC FAM: January 15, 2005–June 4, 2006 (1st season); June 10, 2006–August 31, 2006 (2nd season). Premiered on TDIS: January 17, 2005–June 1, 2006 (1st season); June 5, 2006–December 23, 2006 (2nd season).*

**Voices**
**Wilhelmina "Will" Vandom:** Kelly Stables; **Irma Lair:** Candi Milo; **Miss Kittie:** Taranee Cook; **Cornelia Hale:** Christel Khalil; **Hay Lin:** Liza Del Mundo, Laura Pelerins; **Cedric/Adam:** Dee Bradley Baker; **Caleb/Clubber:** Greg Cipes; **Blunk:** Steven Jay Blum; **Phobos/Guard:** Mitchel Whitfield; **Grandma Yan Lin/ Susan:** Lauren Tom; **Christopher:** Toby Linz; **Vathek:** Lloyd Sherr; **Uriah:** Byrne Offutt

## ◎ THE WIZARD OF OZ

Spirited Kansas farm girl Dorothy and her spunky terrier, Toto, are summoned back to Oz to help her friends (the tenderhearted Tin Man, the resourceful Scarecrow and the timid Cowardly Lion) where the Wicked Witch of the West and her evil winged monkeys have taken over the Emerald City. There Dorothy struggles to learn the most valuable lesson of all: to believe in yourself. This half-hour animated series adaptation was loosely based on the 1939 MGM feature-film classic. Featuring story line variations and memorable music from the original movie, the series debuted on ABC in the fall of 1990. The characterizations and voices of the Scarecrow, the Tin Man, the Cowardly Lion, the Wizard and the Wicked Witch of the West—even the Munchkins—were all drawn and based on the characters in MGM's 1939 film version,

except for Dorothy, who was redesigned to look more like Disney's Little Mermaid (not actress Judy Garland). The 26-episode series lasted one season on ABC and was rerun in syndication as part of the weekend cartoon block, *Amazin' Adventures. A DIC Enterprises/Bohbot Production in association with Turner Entertainment. Color. Half-hour. Premiered on ABC: September 8, 1990–September 6, 1991. Syndicated: 1992 (part of* Amazin' Adventures). *Rebroadcast on TDIS: April 18, 1998–September 1, 2002.*

**Voices**
**Dorothy:** Liz Georges; **Scarecrow:** David Lodge; **Tin Man:** Hal Rayle; **Cowardly Lion:** Charlie Adler; **Wizard:** Alan Oppenheimer; **Toto/Truckle:** Frank Welker; **Wicked Witch:** Tress MacNeille; **Glinda The Good Witch:** B.J. Ward; **Munchkin Mayor:** Susan Silo

## ◎ WOLF'S RAIN

In a post-apocalyptic future wherein wolves (thought to be extinct for nearly one hundred years) resurface as mystical creatures disguised as humans, one lone wolf named Kiba, in the company of other wolves (the young Toboe; the street-smart Hige; and the disillusioned warrior, Tsume) hunt down the scent of Lunar Flower that they believe will lead them to paradise. Instead, the source of the scent is from another world, the mysterious Cheza, known as the Flower Maiden, who ends up getting kidnapped with Kiba journeying to find her. Originally produced in 2003, this English-dubbed, 30-episode anime series aired weekdays on Cartoon Network. *An Astasu DK/Bandai Visual/BONES/ Fuji TV/Bandai Entertainment/Animaze/ZRO Limit Production. Color. Half-hour. Premiered on CAR: April 24, 2004–March 9, 2005.*

**Voices**
**Kiba:** Johnny Yong Bosch; **Toboe:** Mona Marshall; **Hige:** Joshua Seth; **Tsume:** Crispin Freeman; **Cheza:** Sherry Lynn; **Darcia:** Steven Jay Blum; **Hubb Lebowski:** Robert Wicks; **Quent Yaiden:** Tom Wyner

## ◎ WOLF ROCK TV

Famous radio disc jockey Wolfman Jack (alias Bob Smith) hires three teenagers, Sarah, Ricky and Sunny, to run his rock-and-roll television station. Along with their pet bird, Bopper, they keep the station manager, Mr. Morris, on the edge of his seat worrying about the next broadcast in this half-hour comedy series, first broadcast on ABC in 1984. The eight-episode series, produced in association with Dick Clark, was rerun in syndication, combined with another DIC Enterprises music-video series, *Kidd Video*, under the title of *Wolf Rock Power Hour. A DIC Enterprises Production in association with Dick Clark Productions. Color. Half-hour. Premiered on ABC: September 8, 1984–September 13, 1984. Syndicated: 1989–90 (as* Wolf Rock Power Hour).

**Voices**
**Wolfman Jack:** Himself; **Sarah:** Siu Ming Carson; **Sunny:** Noelle North; **Bopper:** Frank Welker; **Mr. Morris:** Jason Bernard; **Ricardo:** Robert Vega

## ◎ THE WONDERFUL STORIES OF PROFESSOR KITZEL

Historic and cultural events are related by Professor Kitzel, an electronic wizard, combining film clips, commentary and animation in this half-hour educational series produced by veteran animator James "Shamus" Culhane. The series, which was originally produced for classroom instruction, was syndicated between 1972 and 1976. A MG *Animation Production in association with Worldvision.* Color. Half-hour. *Premiered: 1972. Syndicated.*

## ☺ THE WONDERFUL WIZARD OF OZ

The land of Oz is revisited in this half-hour animated series of adventures featuring Dorothy, the Scarecrow, the Tin Man, the Cowardly Lion and all the favorite Oz characters (Ozma, the Gnome King, Jack Pumpkinhead and General Ginger). The 26-episode series, first broadcast in Canada in 1987, then in the United States on HBO three years later, was narrated by actress Margot Kidder of *Superman* film fame. *A CINAR Films Production. Color. Half-hour. Premiered on HBO: May 6, 1990–June 30, 1992.*

### Voices

**Dorothy:** Morgan Hallett; **Tinman:** George Morris; **The Lion:** Neil Shee; **The Scarecrow:** Richard Dumont; **Narrator:** Margot Kidder

## ☺ WONDER PETS!

Globe-trotting adventures of three funny, heroic, operetta-singing classroom pets—Linny the Guinea Pig, Ming-Ming Duckling and Tuck the Turtle—who save the world and endangered animals in this 22-episode preschool series (comprised of two cartoons per half-hour), produced for Nick Jr. and Noggin's spring 2006 weekday morning program blocks, using photo-puppetry animation, a style of animation created specifically for the show. Written like mini-operas, including original scores penned by Broadway and pop composers and accompanied by full orchestras, every episode of the popular series encouraged the importance of teamwork and problem solving.

Since debuting in March 2006, the program has been sold to 67 countries throughout the world, including 49 in South America and the Caribbean, three in Europe and 15 in Asia and the Pacific. Becoming one of the three top-ranked preschool series in all commercial television, Nick Jr. renewed the beloved daytime series for a second season in June 2006. That December, the fun-loving trio starred in their very own half-hour holiday special *The Wonder Pets Save the Reindeer. A Little Airplane Productions, Inc. Production. Color. Half-hour. Premiered on NICK JR./NOG: March 3, 2006.*

### Voices

**Linny the Guinea Pig:** Sofie Zamchick; **Ming-Ming Duckling:** Danica Lee; **Tuck the Turtle:** Teala Dunn; **Jazz Mouse:** Matthew Black; **Mamma Cow:** Emlyn Elisabeth Morinelli

## ☺ WOODY WOODPECKER AND HIS FRIENDS

Cartoon favorite Woody Woodpecker appeared in this syndicated series of popular cartoon shorts, combined with additional episodes of creator Walter Lantz's "Inspector Willoughby," "Chilly Willy," "Maw and Paw," "The Beary Family," and others in this half-hour weekday program for first-run syndication. In 1995 Woody joined USA Network's *Cartoon Express* in reruns and in 1997 on Cartoon Network. *A Walter Lantz Production. Color. Half-hour. Premiered: 1958–1966, 1972. Syndicated. Rebroadcast on USA: May 29, 1995–February 26, 1996; Rebroadcast on CAR: June 23, 1997–December 26, 1997.*

## ☺ THE WOODY WOODPECKER SHOW (1957)

Walter Lantz's high-strung woodpecker, whose staccato laugh ("Ha-ha-ha-ha-ha!") was his trademark, headlined this series of theatrical one-reelers starring himself and other characters from Lantz's studio, namely Oswald the Rabbit, Wally Walrus, Andy Panda and Chilly Willy. The series was first broadcast on ABC in 1957. Creator Walter Lantz initially hosted the program in live-action wrap-arounds, introducing the cartoons. In 1970, the series shifted to NBC, which broadcast 26 additional half hours of episodes from Lantz's post-1948 cartoon classics, including "Foolish Fables," "Chilly Willy," "Inspector Willoughby," "Maw and Paw," "The Beary Family" and "Doc." The program was later syndicated, with additional episodes, as *Woody Woodpecker and Friends. A Walter Lantz Production in association with MCA and Kellogg's. Black-and-white. Color. Premiered on ABC: October 3, 1957–September 25, 1958; Premiered on NBC: September 1970–September 1971 (new episodes). Rebroadcast on NBC: September 1971–September 1972; September 1976–September 3, 1977. Syndicated.*

### Voices

**Woody Woodpecker:** Mel Blanc, Ben Hardaway, Grace Stafford; **Andy Panda:** Bernice Hansen, Sarah Berner, Walter Tetley; **Wally Walrus:** Hans Conried, Paul Frees; **Buzz Buzzard/Hickory/Dickory/Inspector Willoughby:** Dal McKennon; **Maw and Paw:** Grace Stafford, Paul Frees; **Chilly Willy/Smedley/Windy/Gabby Gator:** Daws Butler; **Space Mouse:** Johnny Coons; **Doc:** Paul Frees; **The Beary Family:** Paul Frees, Grace Stafford

## ☺ THE WOODY WOODPECKER SHOW (1999)

Latest reincarnation of the high-strung woodpecker, best known for his trademark staccato laugh, "Ha-ha-ha-ha-ha!" heard in the

*Three heroic classroom pets—Linny the Guinea Pig, Tuck the Turtle and Ming-Ming Duckling—travel the globe to rescue other animals in need in the popular Nick Jr. preschool series* Wonder Pets! © *Little Airplane Productions. All rights reserved.*

longest-running theatrical short-cartoon series, originally created and produced by legendary animator Walter Lantz. This 1999 knockoff (also known as *The All New Woody Woodpecker Show* and *The New Woody Woodpecker Show*) sported a newly modified Woody in 40 new animated cartoons—three seven-minute cartoons per half-hour—that premiered on FOX Kids block. Emmy-nominated producer-director Bob Jaques of *The Ren & Stimpy Show* fame produced and directed the Saturday-morning series, written by former *Ren & Stiimpy* and *Tiny Toons* writer Jim Gomez under the Universal Cartoon Studios banner. Veteran voice artist Billy West took over as the voice of Woody in the series, whose supporting voice cast included long-time voice artist Tress MacNeille, Mark Hamill of *Star Wars* and Nika Futterman of NBC's *Suddenly Susan*. The series was pulled from FOX's Saturday morning schedule after only four months, but returned in September 2001 with all-new episodes and several well-known Lantz characters in the mix, including Woody's niece and nephews Splinter and Knothead, Andy Panda and others. After a brief three-week return on FOX's afternoon weekend schedule, the show was back on Saturday mornings in May 2002, concluding its network run by September. *A Universal Cartoon Studios Production. Color. Half-hour. Premiered on FOX Kids: May 8, 1999–September 11, 1999; September 17, 2001–October 6, 2001; May 25, 2002–September 7, 2002.*

### Voices

**Woody Woodpecker/Wally Walrus:** Billy West; **Buzz Buzzard:** Mark Hamill, Jim Cummings; **Splinter:** Tress MacNeille, Nika Futterman; **Knothead:** E.G. Daily; **Winnie Woodpecker:** B.J. Ward; **Ms. Meany:** Andrea Martin; **Papa Panda:** Rip Taylor

## ◎ THE WORLD OF DAVID THE GNOME

Based on the world-famous children's books *The Gnomes* and *The Secret of the Gnomes* by Rien Poortvliet and Wil Huygen, this half-hour series narrates the life and circumstances of a Gnome family, including their enemies, the Trolls. The 26-episode series, which aired weekdays on Nickelodeon's Nick Jr. program block beginning in 1988 and was later rebroadcast on The Learning Channel, is narrated by actor Christopher Plummer. *A CINAR Films Production in association with Miramax Films and B.R.B. Internacional, S. A. Color. Half-hour. Premiered on NICK JR.: January 4, 1988. Rebroadcast on TLC: September 30, 1996–March 23, 1998.*

### Voices

**David, the father:** Tom Bosley; **Lisa, the mother:** Jane Woods; **Holler:** A.J. Henderson; **Susan:** Barbera Pogemiller; **King:** Richard Dumont; **Pit:** Adrian Knight; **Pat:** Rob Roy; **Pot:** Marc Denis; **Narrator:** Christopher Plummer

## ◎ THE WORLD OF PETER RABBIT AND FRIENDS

This series of six half-hour specials is based on nine of Beatrix Potter's popular Peter Rabbit storybooks in celebration of the popular character's 100th anniversary. Mischievous young Peter, the bad boy of the cabbage patch, creates trouble for his doting mother, his siblings—Flopsy, Mopsy and Cottontail—and other woodland creatures.

The Emmy Award–nominated British series made its American television debut on The Family Channel in March 1993 (the premiere episode: "The Tale of Peter Rabbit and Benjamin Bunny"), marking the first time that Potter's work was adapted as an animated series. Subsequent episodes—"The Tale of Samuel Whiskers," "The Tailor of Gloucester," "The Tale of Pigling Bland," "The Tale of Tom Kitten and Jemina Puddleduck" and "The Tale of Mrs. Tiggly-Winkle and Mr. Jeremy Fisher"—were broadcast in the summer, fall and winter of that year. Each episode opened with a beautiful live-action sequence, filmed in Potter's home, featuring Niamh Cusack as young Beatrix Potter, shown writing and painting, to introduce each story. The series was the most expensive animation project ever undertaken in the United Kingdom—costing an estimated $11 million to produce. *A TVC London Production for Frederick Warner and Company/BBC in association with Pony Canyon Inc. and Fuji Television Inc. Color. Half-hour. Premiered on FAM: March 29, 1993–November 13, 1995 (original broadcasts). Rebroadcast on FAM: April 4, 1993–December 19, 1997.*

### Cast (live action)
**Beatrix Potter:** Niamh Cusack

### Voices

Niamh Cusack, Derek Jacobi, Prunella Scales, Rory Carry, Andrew Clitherne, Alan Bowe, Mary Jane Bowe, Jenny Moore, Rosemary Leach, Patricia Routledge, Sue Pollard, Dinsdale Landen, Enn Reitel, Selma Cadell, June Whitfield, Richard Wilson, June Watson, Sara Woolcock, Moir Lesley

## ◎ WORLD PREMIERE TOONS

Re-creating cartoons the way they were supposed to be made in the 1930s and 1940s—short, fast and furious—this 10-minute weekly series showcased the largest outpouring of original cartoon shorts in 50 years. The series debuted in February of 1995 under the title *World Premiere Toon-In*, as part of a half-hour simulcast on Cartoon Network, TBS and TNT, hosted by Space Ghost, followed by the animated feature showcase *Mr. Spim's Cartoon Theatre*. The program was the brainchild of Hanna-Barbera president Fred Seibert and Cartoon Network president Betty Cohen, who developed the idea after contemplating one day the fate of "funny cartoons." The result was the initial production of 48 cutting-edge animated shorts produced and directed by well-known and independent animators, including Bill Hanna, Joe Barbera, Pat Ventura, Jerry Reynolds, Craig McCracken, Van Partible, Eugene Mattos, Meinert Hansen, Don Jurwich, Jerry Eisenberg, Butch Hartman and Jon and Chris McClenahan.

"Dexter's Laboratory" (by Tartakovsky), about a boy genius in pursuit of scientific greatness, debuted on the series opener (and was later spun off into its own series), followed by many other first-timers: "Short Orders" starring Yuckie Duck (directed by Ventura), the frenetic goings-on of a duck waiter in a chic restaurant; The PowerPuff Girls in "Meat Fuzzy Lumkins," the superhero adventures of barely-out-of-diapers crimefighting kindergarteners Blossom, Buttercup and Bubbles (directed by McCracker, who called them "Whoopass Girls" in a previous cartoon short that he produced and directed); "Stay Out" (directed by Barbera), the first of a proposed series starring the Flintstones' Dino; and "Johnny Bravo," about a womanizing, pompadour-wearing rocker out to win the affection of an attractive zookeeper (directed by Partible), also later turned into an animated series of its own.

Other new 'toons to debut included Slegehammer O'Possum in "Out and About" (directed by Ventura), about a dog who meets trouble in the form of a malevolent possum; "Look Out Below" (by Ventura), a new George and Junior cartoon (an updated version of Tex Avery's buffoonish bears) in which they confront a belligerent, hammer-wielding pigeon; and William Hanna's "Hard Luck Duck," the misadventures of a duck chased by a Cajun fox.

Also spotlighted on the show were animated "one shots," such as "Shake and Flick" (by Mattos), about a timid dog (Shake), who shudders at the sight of a terminator flea (Flick); "The Adventures of Captain Buzz Cheeply" (by Hansen), about a comical superhero who vows to rescue his friend after he takes care of his laundry; "Rat in a Hot Tin Can" (by Reynolds), the story of a skid-row denizen who happens to be a rat (O. Ratz) and his pet fly (David D. Fly), featuring the voices of Harvey Korman and Marvin Kaplan; "Short Pfuse" (by Hartman), in which a land shark (Phish) and a Scottish tabby cat (Chip) have the misfortune of working on a bomb squad; "Drip Dry Drips" (by the McClenahans), about two down-on-their-luck fat cats (Louie and Elmo) who undertake their latest "get-rich" scheme; and "Yoink of the Yukon" (by Jurwich and Eisenberg), about a grizzly fed up with hunters who steals uniforms off the wrong people—the Royal Canadian Mounties.

Subsequent broadcasts introduced other first-timers: "Mina and the Count," directed by Rob Renzetti; "Cow and Chicken," created by David Feiss (later spun off into a series of its own on the network); and the world television premiere of the 1996 Oscar-nominated animated short "The Chicken from Outer Space," about a cowardly dog named Courage who battles with a beady-eyed chicken from outer space, written and directed by John R. Dilworth. In late April of 1996 the series name was changed to *What a Cartoon! Show*, airing three times a week. The show mixed repeats with new animated shorts.

In April 1996, the popular anthology series continued but under the new name, *What a Cartoon! Show*. Many animated shorts that aired on this weekly amalgamation were spun-off into their own weekly series, including *Dexter's Laboratory*, *Johnny Bravo* and *Cow and Chicken*. The same would later happen for three others: *The Powerpuff Girls*, *Courage the Cowardly Dog* and *Mike, Lu & Og*. In 1997, Cartoon Network again renamed the property, as *Cartoons Cartoons*, now featuring previous *World Premiere Toons* shorts and newly produced shorts broadcast during prime time. By the summer of 1999, this popular melding of animation was turned into *Cartoons Cartoon Fridays*, serving as bumpers to an entire night of animated programming. In 2000, Cartoon Network added a new component to *Cartoons Cartoon Fridays*, *Premieres Premieres*, showcasing new animated shorts each week, and then launched a weekend-long marathon of original cartoon shorts that summer entitled *The Big Pick*, giving viewers the opportunity to vote on their favorite cartoon shorts to be produced as new series. Two animated series picked as winners based on their cartoon shorts in the first and second marathons were *The Grim Adventures of Billy & Mandy* and *Codename: Kids Next Door*. In September 2005, Cartoon Network relaunched the program as *The Cartoon Cartoon Show*. *A Hanna-Barbera Cartoons/Cartoon Network Production. Color. Ten minutes. Premiered on CAR: February 20, 1995 (as half-hour World Premiere Toon-In); April 28, 1996 (as What a Cartoon! Show). Premiered on CAR: April 28, 1996 (as What A Cartoon! Show). Premiered on CAR: 1997 (as Cartoons Cartoons). Premiered on CAR: Summer 1999 (as Cartoons Cartoon Fridays). Premiered on CAR: September 2005 (as The Cartoon Cartoon Show).*

## ◎ THE WORLD'S GREATEST SUPER FRIENDS

The success of Hanna-Barbera's 1978 superheroes series *The All-New Super Friends* spurred network interest in another show based on the comic-book stories of the Justice League. The new series, comprised of eight half-hour episodes, featured, as did the earlier one, such popular superheroes as Superman and Wonder Woman in animated form. *A Hanna-Barbera Production. Color. One hour. Premiered on ABC: September 22, 1979–September 27, 1980.*

### Voices

**Wonder Woman:** Shannon Farnon; **Superman:** Danny Dark; **Batman:** Olan Soule; **Robin:** Casey Kasem; **Aquaman:** Bill Callaway; **Zan/Gleek:** Mike Bell; **Jayna:** Liberty Williams; **Narrator:** Bill Woodson

## ◎ WOWSER

A large white sheepdog named Wowser acts as a guinea pig of sorts to try out a series of strange inventions created by his eccentric master, Professor Dinghy, in this half-hour series coproduced in Europe and Japan in 1988. The series was broadcast daily for 12 months in the United States on The Family Channel, beginning in September of 1989. *A Telecable Benelux/Saban Entertainment Production. Color. Half-hour. Premiered on FAM: September 4, 1989–September 14, 1990. Rebroadcast on FOX FAM: September 9, 1998–September 2, 1999 (Morning Scramble).*

## ◎ WOW! WOW! WUBBZY!

Animated preschool series following the whimsical adventures of a curious little guy named Wubbzy who solves everyday kid problems and predicaments using cooperation, creativity and humor, with help and advice from his two friends Walden and Widget, in the mythical, surreal city of Wuzzelburg. The 26-episode half-hour Flash-animated preschool comedy series—featuring two 10-minute adventures per half-hour followed by an original music video—became the first-ever preschool series to premiere as a video podcast before making its television debut on Nick Jr. and its sister network, Noggin, with two back-to-back episodes. The series regularly aired weekdays on Nick Jr. Series creator Bob Boyle accomplished the impossible with the simultaneous debuts of two of his creations on separate networks: *Wow! Wow! Wubbzy!* on Nick Jr. and *Yin Yang Yo!* on Toon Disney. Originally offering the concept to Random Books as a potential children's book series, Boyle had previously been turned down by Nick Jr. after pitching the idea for the series, which they later greenlighted. The series' first season included the premiere of the half-hour holiday special, "The Snow Shoo Shoo." *A Bolder Media for Boys and Girls Production in association with IDT Entertainment/Film Roman. Color. Half-hour. Premiered on NICK JR./NOG: August 21, 2006.*

### Voices

**Wubbzy:** Grey DeLisle; **Walden:** Carlos Alazaqui; **Widget:** Lara Jill Miller

## ◎ WULIN WARRIORS: LEGEND OF THE SEVEN ARTS

Inventive anime action show spoofing traditional action series in which hand puppets meet kung-fu movies, featuring a trio of karate-chopping warriors (Lone Sword, Scar and Phoenix) who are trained in swordsmanship and martial arts by Sensei Oracle at his mountaintop academy and then embark on an improbable journey in search of a mightier power, the Seven Stars, to save the world from an evil ninja and his minions. Described as *Crouching Tiger, Hidden Dragon* with a teen attitude, this half-hour series—a blend of action, comedy, hand-puppetry and martial arts—premiered on Saturday, January 4, 2005, at 8:00 P.M. on Cartoon Network's popular Saturday-night action block, *Toonami*.

Produced by New York's Animation Collective and distributed by Broadway Video, the program was a dubbed English-language version of the popular Taiwan television puppet show, *Pili*. Thirteen episodes were produced but only two aired, since the series was canceled following poor ratings and viewer complaints over some of the show's inappropriate content. *An Animation Collective/Broadway Video Production. Color. Half-hour. Premiered on CAR: February 4, 2006–February 11, 2006.*

## ◎ THE WUZZLES

The Wuzzles (Bumblelion, Eleroo, Hoppotamus, Moosel, Rhinokey and Butterbear) are two creatures in one (i.e., a duck/fox, a pig/chicken, etc.) who live on the island of Wuz. The furry creatures never leave the island, so they never encounter any being that is not born by Wuzzle convention, nor are they even aware of other such beings in this 13-episode fantasy/adventure series originally produced for CBS in 1985. Following its CBS run, the Saturday-morning series was rebroadcast on ABC for one full season and immediately thereafter on Disney Channel and later on Toon Disney. A *Walt Disney Television Animation Production. Color. Half-hour. Premiered on CBS: September 14, 1985–September 6, 1986. Rebroadcast on ABC: September 13, 1986–September 5, 1987; Rebroadcast on DIS: 1987; September 9, 1996–December 29, 1996. Rebroadcast on TDIS: September 5, 1998–January 6, 2002.*

*Voices*
**Bumblelion/Flizard:** Gregg Berger, Brian Cummings; **Eleroo/Girafbra:** Henry Gibson; **Hoppopotamus:** Frank Welker, Jo Anne Worley; **Moosel/Brat:** Will Ryan, Bill Scott; **Rhinokey/Croc/Pack-Cat:** Alan Oppenheimer; **Butterbear:** Kathleen Helppie; **Mrs. Pedigree:** Steve Kramer, Tress MacNeille; **Narrator:** Stan Freberg

## ◎ X-CHROMOSOME

Weekly anthology series, featuring 14 female-oriented animated shorts, first telecast on the Oxygen Network in February 2000 and aimed at the network's predominantly female viewers. Besides offering one-shot cartoon subjects, the breakthrough series also featured recurring animated segments, including real-life sex columnist Amy Sohne's "Avenue Amy"; Corky Quackenbush's clay-animated film parodies "Corky Q.'s Chick Flicks"; Paul and Sandra Fierlinger's "Drawn From Life"; Allee Willis's "Fat Girl"; plus two others that were spun-off into half-hour series of their own, "Bitchy Bits," adapted from award-winning cartoonist Roberta Gregory's comic book and *Life's a Bitch*, starring the voices of Second City comediennes Angela V. Shelton and France Callier. *An Oxygen Network Production. Color. Half-hour. Premiered on OXY: February 5, 2000–August 10, 2002.*

## ◎ XIAOLIN SHOWDOWN

Omi, a young, gifted Xiaolin temple monk-in-training, and his fellow trainees—J-pop hipster girl Kimiko; flashy, street-smart Brazilian Raimundo; and Texas Kung Fu cowboy Clay—engage in extreme martial arts-styled showdowns in their quest to uncover and protect the sacred Shen Gong Wu artifacts, which hold the key to supernatural martial arts powers that can control good and evil in the world, from their annoying genius nemesis Jack Spicer and his robot army. This *Powerpuff Girls*-style, cel- and computer-animated series was based on the ancient, mythical Xiaolin martial arts and created and produced by Christy Hui for the WB Television Network.

Joining the WB Television Network's Kids' WB! Saturday-morning cartoon lineup in November 2003, this Warner Bros. Television Animation-produced mystical, high-adventure cartoon series, along with two others (*Loonatics Unleashed* and *The Batman*), moved to the renamed CW Network in the fall of 2006. A *Warner Bros. Television Animation Production. Color. Half-hour. Premiered on the WB (Kids' WB!): November 1, 2003.*

*Voices*
**Omi:** Tara Strong; **Kimiko:** Grey DeLisle; **Raimundo:** Tom Kenny; **Clay:** Jeff Bennett; **Master Fung:** René Auberjonois; **Dojo:** Wayne Knight; **Wuya:** Susan Silo; **Jack Spicer:** Danny Cooksey

## ◎ X-MEN

With a telephatic therapist on their side (Professor Charlers Xavier), these crimefighting mutants (Cyclops, Wolverine, Jubilee, Storm, Rogue, Gambit, the Beast and Jean Grey), each bestowed with superhuman abilities, band together to fight for self-respect and overcome their enemies (Apocalypse, Magneto, Mr. Sinister, the Sentinels, Juggernaut, Proteus and others) in this half-hour Saturday-morning series, based on one of the largest-selling comic-book lines in history from Marvel Comics, Three years after producing a pilot "Pryde of the X-Men" that aired in syndication, the weekly half-hour adventure series debuted on the FOX Network in October 1992; it missed its original premiere date due to production delays. Finishing as the number-one rated show with children after only six weeks on the air, according to A.C. Nielsen, the success of *X-Men* not only bolstered FOX's ratings position on Saturday morning with young viewers but contributed to the erosion of kid viewers for ABC and CBS, the only major networks that still aired animated cartoons on Saturday. Beginning in 2004, the series was rebroadcast on Toon Disney. A *Marvel Films/Saban Entertainment/Graz Entertainment Production. Color. Half-hour. Premiered: 1989 (half-hour pilot as part of Marvel Action Universe). Syndicated. Premiered on FOX: October 24, 1992–September 20, 1997. Rebroadcast on FOX: September 27, 1997–January 24, 1998. Rebroadcast on UPN/Syndicated: September 14, 1998–September 5, 1999. Rebroadcast on FOX: July 17, 2000–January 29, 2001. Rebroadcast on TDIS: September 26, 2004–February 19, 2006.*

*Voices*
**Scott Summers/Cyclops:** Norm Spencer; **Logan/Wolverine:** Cal Dodd; **Ororo Munroe/Storm:** Alison Sealy-Smith, Iona Morris; **Gambit:** Chris Potter; **Jean Grey:** Catherine Disher; **Hank McCoy/The Beast:** George Buza; **Rogue:** Lenore Zann; **Jubilation Lee/Jubilee:** Alyson Court; **Professor Charles Xavier:** Cedric Smith

## ◎ X-MEN EVOLUTION

Youthful teenage mutants Cyclops, Jean Grey, Rogue, Nightcrawler, Shadowcat and a new character named Spike attend Xavier's Institute for the Gifted where they learn how to harness and manage their amazing powers and put them to good use while battling evil in a world that fears and hates them, in this weekly, half-hour science fiction fantasy series loosely based on the cult-classic Marvel comic-book series. Featuring fan favorites Wolverine, Storm, Professor X and many others, this weekly half-hour series was produced after the blockbuster, *X-Men* full-length, live-action feature in 2000 and targeted younger audiences; it became a popular component on the WB Television Network's Kids' WB! Saturday-morning block beginning that November. Winner of two Daytime Emmy Awards in 2001 and 2003 (for outstanding achievement in sound mixing and outstanding achievement in sound editing), the four-time Emmy-nominated series ran for four seasons, with 52 action-packed adventures, until November 2003. The popular daytime series was the second animated incarnation of the Marvel Comics characters since FOX's long-running 1992 cartoon series *X-Men*. A *Film Roman Productions/Marvel Enterprises Productions Inc. Production. Color. Half-hour. Premiered on the WB (Kids' WB!): November 4, 2000–November 15, 2003. Rebroadcast on CAR: April 5, 2003–November 9, 2003.*

*Voices*
**Cyclops/Scott:** Kirby Morrow; **Jean Grey:** Venus Terzo; **Nightcrawler/Kurt:** Brad Swaile; **Shadowcat/Kitty Pryde:** Blue O'Hara; **Rogue:** Megan Black; **Spyke/Evan:** Neil Denis; **Wolverine/Logan:** Scott McNeil; **Professor X/Charles Xavier:** David Kaye; **Storm/Ororo:** Kristen Williamson; **Fred/Blob:** Michael Dobson; **Quicksilver/Pietro:** Richard Cox; **Avalanche/Lance:** Christopher Grey; **Toad/Todd:** Noel Fisher; **Mystique/Darkholme:** Colleen Wheeler;

**Magneto:** Christopher Judge; **Sabertooth:** Michael Donovan; **Colossus:** Michael Adamthwaite; **Nick Fury:** Jim Byrnes; **Amara/Magma:** Alexander Carter; **Sunspot:** Michael Coleman; **Bobby/Iceman:** Andrew Francis; **Angel/Archangel:** Mark Hildreth; **Alan/Havok:** Matt Hill; **Callisto:** Saffron Henderson; **Jamie/Multiple:** David A. Kaye; **Destiny:** Ellen Kennedy; **Hank/Beast:** Michael Kopsa; **Jason/Mastermind:** Campbell Lane; **Tabitha:** Megan Leitch; **X23:** Andrea Libman; **Wanda/Scarlet Witch:** Kelly Sheridan; **Principal Kelly:** Dale Wilson; **Jubilee:** Chiara Zanni

### ◎ THE X'S

A family of world-class, oddball, undercover super-spies—the ultra-confident Mr. X; the mercurial, over-the-top Mrs. X; bratty Truman; and practical teen Tuesday—act and live like regular suburbanites in their super-secret, high-tech equipped spy house, Home Base, but thwart evil-doers bent on destroying them and the world, led by Glowface, the maniacal leader of the terrible agency of evil, S.N.A.F.U., in this hilarious half-hour series, comprised of two super-adventures, for Nickelodeon. First broadcast on November 25, 2005, with three back-to-back episodes (including the premiere episode "Photo Ops") and then airing Fridays at 8:30 P.M. on Nickelodeon, this cloak-and-dagger comedy series, created by Annie Award-winner Carlos Ramos (*Oh Yeah! Cartoons*), featured Patrick Warburton (*Seinfeld*'s Puddy) and Wendie Mack (*Just Shoot Me*) as the voices of the parents. In June 2006 the world-class spies starred in a feature-length TV movie special *Truman X: Super Villain*, which aired as part of Nick's "Summer Movies" promotion. *A Nickelodeon Studios Production. Color. Half-hour. Premiered on NICK: November 25, 2005–. Rebroadcast on NICKT: April 3, 2006–.*

*Voices*

**Mr. X (Aaron Truman Extreme Sr.):** Patrick Warburton; **Mrs. X (Andrea Martha Cohen Extreme):** Wendie Malick; **Tuesday X (Tabbatha Tuesday Extreme):** Lynsey Bartilson; **Truman X (Aaron Truman Extreme Jr.):** Jansen Panettiere; **Homebase:** Stephen Root; **Glowface (Arthur Emmons):** Chris Hardwick; **Lorenzo Suave:** Tom Kane; **Sasquatch:** "Macho Man" Randy Savage; **Brandon Emmons:** Jason Schwartzman; **Copperhead:** Tom Kenny

### ◎ XYBER 9: NEW DAWN

Protected by the powerful Xyber 9 super-computer, a young orphan named Jack fights intergalactic evil and the evil underworld ruler Machestro in his quest to become king and save civilization in this futuristic, CGI-animated series. Airing between *Digimon: Digital Monsters* and *Monster Rancher* from 9:00 to 9:30 A.M., this weekly science fiction/fantasy series—touted by its producers as "*Star Wars* meets *Mad Max*"—premiered with a two-part, one-hour special ("New Acquaintances" and "Enter Ikira") Saturday mornings on FOX Kids Network in September 1999, and was canceled three months later with only 10 of its original 13 episodes airing.

Beginning in September 1999, the same 10 first-season episodes were rebroadcast in their entirety on Toon Disney's *Jetix* action/adventure block. Starting in February 2007, the network premiered three unaired first-season episodes ("Ground Zero," "The Astral Hand, Part I" and "The Astral Hand, Part II"), followed by nine second-season episodes, including the three-part series finale "Eye of Darkness" in late March and early April 2007. *A Saban Entertainment/Bokabi Productions Production. Color. Half-hour. Premiered on FOX: September 5, 1999–December 4, 1999. Rebroadcast on TDIS: September 25, 1999 (one-hour special). Octo-* ber 2, 1999–December 4, 1999 (series). Premiered on TDIS: February 24, 2007–April 8, 2007.

*Voices*

**Xyber 9:** Rene Auberjonois; **Jack:** Jason Marsden; **King Renard:** Tim Curry; **Mick:** Quinton Flynn; **Anakonda:** Nika Frost; **Lord Machestro:** Tony Jay; **Princess Rozalyn/Ana:** Jolie Jenkins; **Willy:** Rodney Saulsberry; **Ikira:** Christopher Marquette; **Other Voices:** Obba Babatundé, Phil Buckman, Victor Brandt, David Jeremiah, Tom Kane, Neil Ross, Tom Strauss, Keith Szarabajka, Jim Ward, Frank Welker

### ◎ YAKKITY YAK

An attention-starved yak seeking to hit the big time as a standup comedian (so serious that he hires his own agent) settles for being a class clown and a sports team mascot while attending Onion Falls High with his two best friends, Keo, who lives next door, and Lemony, in this short-lived cartoon series for Nickelodeon. Supporting Yakkity in his quest for stardom are his dad and mother; his grandmother, Granny Yak; his agent, Mr. Trilobyte; and his eccentric science teacher—and boarder at Yakkity's house—Professor Crazyhair.

Created by Mark Garvas, the half-hour comedy series (known for its slogan "It's Just Plain Stupid") premiered on Sunday, November 9, 2003, on Nickelodeon with four episodes as part of a two-hour afternoon block. Canceled a month after its debut due to poor ratings, only 13 half-hour shows—consisting of 26 11-minute episodes—were broadcast on Nickelodeon, with three unaired episodes seen on Canadian television. The full 52-episode series was shown on Australia's Network Ten and on Nicktoons in England, while reruns have been shown in the United States on Nicktoons since May 2004. *A Studio B Productions/Kapow Pictures/Nickelodeon Production. Color. Half-hour. Premiered on NICK: November 9, 2003–December 11, 2003. Rebroadcast on NICKT: May 28, 2004–.*

*Voices*

**Yakkity Yak:** Lee Tockar; **Keo:** Brian Drummond; **Granny Yak:** Pam Hyatt; **Lemony:** Andrea Libman; **Mr. Highpants/Rondo Jr.:** Ian James Corlett; **Keo's Dad:** Michael Dangerfield; **Mr. Trilobyte:** Jason Schombing; **Professor Crazyhair:** Scott McNeil; **Penelope:** Tabitha St. Germain; **Wanda:** Brenda Crichlow

### ◎ YING YANG YO!

In a world of chaos and disarray, two polar opposite brother-and-sister rabbits—Ying, the smart, sassy pink female and Yang, the video-game, motorcycle-loving blue male—who train to become Woof Foo Knights under the tutelage of Yo, a grumpy old martial arts master, and panda, try to save the world from Carl the Evil Cockroach Wizard who plans to plunge the world into eternal darkness in this animated series, produced by Burbank's Walt Disney Television and Toronto's George Elliott Animation, and created, directed and executive produced by Bob Boyle, the cocreator of Nickelodeon's runaway hit *The Fairly OddParents*.

Viewers were given their first glimpse of the Flash-animated show when it debuted on the Web, starting July 10, before being broadcast on television in the United States, Europe, the Middle East and Latin America. Aimed at young viewers ages six to 11 the 26-episode half-hour series was sneak previewed during a final *Jetix* block marathon on ABC Family, followed by a Labor Day weekend marathon, September 2–4, 2006, on Toon Disney before airing weeknights during *Jetix*, becoming the action-oriented block's first full-fledged comedy series. *A Walt Disney Television Anima-*

*tion/George Elliott Animation Production. Color. Half-hour. Premiered on ABC FAM: August 26, 2006–August 31, 2006. Premiered on TDIS: September 4, 2006–.*

**Voices**
Tony Daniels, Megan Fahlenbock, Dwayne Hill, Kathleen Laskey, Stephanie Morgenstern, Scott McCord, Damon Papadopoulos, Martin Roach, Jamie Watson, Jonathon Wilson

## ◉ YO, YOGI!

Yogi Bear, Boo Boo, Cindy Bear, Snagglepuss and Huckleberry Hound starred as crimebusting teens (each redesigned by Hanna-Barbera animators in the same vein as *A Pup Named Scooby-Doo*) who hang out at the Jellystone Mall and whose principal trouble-makers are "retro" versions of Dastardly and Muttley in this half-hour Saturday-morning cartoon series that debuted on NBC in the fall of 1991. Starting with the January 25, 1992 broadcast, the series went entirely to 3-D (requiring special 3-D glasses offered inside Kellogg's Rice Krispies boxes) for 13 consecutive episodes, becoming the first TV show to be produced with 3-D effects in nearly every episode. NBC dumped the series—as well as all animated cartoons—from its fall 1992 Saturday-morning lineup, in favor of live-action programs. In the fall of 1992 the series was repeated in syndication on *The Funtastic World of Hanna-Barbera*. *A Hanna-Barbera Production. Color. Half-hour. Premiered on NBC: September 14, 1991–January 18, 1992; January 25, 1992–April 18, 1992 (in 3-D); April 25, 1992–July 25, 1992. Syndicated: 1992 (part of* The Funtastic World of Hanna-Barbera*).*

**Voices**
**Yogi Bear/Quick Draw McGraw/Snagglepuss:** Greg Burson; **Boo Boo/Atom Ant/Muttley:** Don Messick; **Huckleberry Hound:** Greg Berg; **Hokey Wolf:** Matt Hurwitz; **Top Cat:** Arte Johnson; **Magilla Gorilla:** Allan Melvin; **Dick Dastardly/Hardy Har Har/Super Snooper:** Rob Paulsen; **Baba Looey:** Henry Polic II; **Morocco Mole:** Neil Ross; **Blabber Mouse:** Hal Smith; **Cindy Bear/Secret Squirrel:** Kath Soucie; **"Diamond" Doggie Daddy/Mr. Jinks:** John Stephenson; **Peter Potamus:** Frank Welker; **Augie Doggie/Dixie:** Patric Zimmerman

## ◉ YOGI AND HIS FRIENDS

The picnic-basket–stealing Yogi and best friend, Boo Boo, enjoyed new life in syndication via this half-hour series of old Hanna-Barbera favorites, costarring Hokey Wolf, Huckleberry Hound, Pixie and Dixie, Snagglepuss and Yakky Doodle. *A Hanna-Barbera Production. Color. Half-hour. Premiered: 1967. Rebroadcast on CAR: February 27, 1995–June 28, 1995 (weekdays).*

## ◉ YOGI BEAR

In 1988, Hanna-Barbera resurrected its favorite picnic basket–stealing bear Yogi, casting him and his able companion, Boo Boo, in 65 all-new adventures (three per show), in a half-hour program (also known as *The New Yogi Bear Show*) for first-run syndication. Years later, the program was rebroadcast on Cartoon Network's Boomerang network. *A Hanna-Barbera Production. Color. Half-hour. Premiered: September 12, 1988–89. Syndicated. Rebroadcast on BOOM: December 22, 2000–.*

**Voices**
**Yogi Bear:** Gregg Burson; **Boo Boo/Ranger Smith:** Don Messick

## ◉ THE YOGI BEAR SHOW

After making his debut on *The Huckleberry Hound Show* in 1958, shrewd Yogi ("Smarter than the average bear") and his shy sidekick, Boo Boo, quickly rose to stardom and were given their own half-hour series two years later, sponsored by Kellogg's Cereals and syndicated by Screen Gems, a subsidiary of Columbia Pictures. The program contained madcap adventures of the picnic-stealing bars (one per show) who cause trouble for vacationers at Jellystone Park, plus individual episodes of two other Hanna-Barbera favorites: Snagglepuss, the calamity-stricken lion ("Exit stage left . . .") and Yakky Doodle, a dwarf duckling protected by his friend, Chopper the bulldog (who affectionately calls Yakky "little fella").

The series was kicked off in syndication in 1961 with 27 new Yogi Bear cartoons produced between 1960 and 1961, including 24 Snagglepuss and 24 Yakky Doodle cartoon shorts (one each per show), packaged as 30-minute programs. New episodes of each character were added to the mix, produced between 1961 and 1962, for broadcast, and the series remained in syndication through 1963.

From 1989 to 1992, the program was rebroadcast on USA Network, then again from 1991 to 1992 on Nickelodeon as *Nickelodeon's Most Wanted: Yogi Bear*, before joining Cartoon Network, in reruns from 1992 to 2000, and its offspring classic cartoon network, Boomerang, in April 2000. *A Hanna-Barbera Production in association with Screen Gems. Color. Half-hour. Premiered: January 30, 1961–September 1963. Syndicated. Rebroadcast on USA: 1989–92. Rebroadcast on NICK: 1991–92. Rebroadcast on CAR: September 20, 1993–January 7, 1994 (weekdays, Saturdays); January 9, 1994–October 2, 1994 (weekdays, weekends); May 5, 1997–2000 (weekdays). Rebroadcast on BOOM: April 2, 2000–.*

**Voices**
**YOGI BEAR: Yogi Bear:** Daws Butler; **Boo Boo/Ranger Smith:** Don Messick; **Cindy Bear:** Julie Bennett

**SNAGGLEPUSS: Snagglepuss/Major Minor:** Daws Butler

**YAKKY DOODLE: Yakky Doodle:** Jimmy Weldon; **Chopper:** Vance Colvig; **Fibber Fox:** Daws Butler

## ◉ YOGI'S GALAXY GOOF-UPS

When NBC shuffled its Saturday-morning cartoon lineup in November 1978, *The Galaxy Goof-Ups* series, formerly segmented on *Yogi's Space Race*, was given its own half-hour, Saturday-morning time slot and a new title in which the series' original 13 episodes were rebroadcast. The cast of characters—Yogi Bear, Huckleberry Hound, Scarebear and Quack-Up—inter-galactic army officers under the astute command of Captain Snerdley, find more time for disco dancing than protecting the universe. (For voice credits see *Yogi's Space Race*.) *A Hanna-Barbera Production. Color. Half-hour. Premiered on NBC: November 4, 1978–January 27, 1979. Rebroadcast on USA: 1989–92. Rebroadcast on CAR: September 20, 1993–December 31, 1993 (weekdays under Yogi's Spin-Offs). Rebroadcast on BOOM: December 20, 2000–.*

## ◉ YOGI'S GANG

Yogi Bear, Boo Boo, Snagglepuss, Wally Gator and a host other cartoon pals traverse the world in a flying ark, battling environmental pollution and other hazards along the way, in this weekly Saturday-morning series produced for ABC in 1973. The series featured 17 half-hour episodes, broadcast during the 1973–74 season (then rebroadcast the following season), including a two-part episode "Yogi's Ark Lark". *A Hanna-Barbera Production. Color. Half-hour. Premiered on ABC: September 8, 1973–August 30, 1975. Rebroadcast on USA: 1989–92. Rebroadcast on CAR: September 20, 1993–December 31, 1993 (weekdays under Yogi's Spin-Offs). Rebroadcast on BOOM: June 10, 2000–.*

**Voices**
Yogi Bear/Huckleberry Hound/Snagglepuss/Quick Draw McGraw/Augie Doggie/Wally Gator/Peter Potamus: Daws Butler; **Boo Boo/Touché Turtle/Squiddly Diddly/Ranger Smith/ Atom Ant/So-So:** Don Messick; **Paw Rugg:** Henry Corden; **Doggie Daddy:** John Stephenson; **Magilla Gorilla:** Allan Melvin; **Secret Squirrel:** Mel Blanc

## YOGI'S SPACE RACE

The science-fiction classic *Star Wars* inspired this animated spoof teaming the irrepressible Yogi Bear and his pals in a space race to different galactic planetoids. Along the way they battle space guardian Captain Good, Clean Cat (alias Phantom Phink) and Sinister Sludge, who try to prevent Yogi and friends from crossing the finish line in this half-hour comedy/science-fiction series broadcast Saturday mornings on NBC.

Yogi's TV return was minus his longtime cherubic cub partner, Boo Boo, who had starred in early television adventures. Instead, Hanna-Barbera's animators created a new sidekick, Scarebear (voiced by former Three Stooges member Joe Besser) for the "Space Race" and "The Galaxy Goof-Ups" segments.

In November 1978 NBC gave "The Galaxy Goof-Ups" its own half-hour time slot after shuffling the Saturday-morning kidvid network lineup. It was the most popular segment of the entire *Space Race* show, featuring Yogi Bear, Scarebear, Huckleberry Hound and Quack-Up (a modern version of Daffy Duck) as purveyors of justice—under the command of Captain Snerdley (a Joe Flynn prototype)—who find more time for disco dancing than completing missions.

Other weekly segments of *Yogi's Space Race* were: "The Buford Files," a crime-solving dog and his teenage companions, Woody and Cindy Mae; and "Galloping Ghost," the adventures of a wild and woolly cowboy ghost, Nugget Nose. A *Hanna-Barbera Productions. Color. Ninety minutes. Premiered on NBC: September 9, 1978–March 3, 1979. Rebroadcast on USA: 1989–92. Rebroadcast on TNT: 1992–93. Rebroadcast on CAR: September 20, 1993–December 31, 1993 (weekdays under Yogi's Spin-Offs). Rebroadcast on BOOM: June 10, 2000–.*

**Voices**
Yogi Bear/Huckleberry Hound: Daws Butler; **Scarebear:** Joe Besser; **Quack-Up:** Mel Blanc; **Captain Snerdley:** John Stephehenson; **Jabberjaw/Buford, dog detective/Nugget Nose:** Frank Welker; **Woody:** Dave Landsburg; **Cindy Mae/Rita:** Pat Parris; **Sheriff:** Henry Corden; **Goofer McGee, his deputy:** Roger Peltz; **Wendy:** Marilyn Schreffler; **Mr. Fuddy:** Hal Peary

## YOGI'S TREASURE HUNT

Yogi Bear captains a crew of classic Hanna-Barbera characters (Ranger Smith, Boo Boo, Top Cat, Huckleberry Hound, Super Snooper, Blabbermouse, Snagglepuss, Augie Doggie and Doggie Daddy), who set sail aboard the magical S.S. Jelly Roger in search of treasures, which they donate to charitable causes. Episodes were produced for first-run syndication as part of *The Funtastic World of Hanna-Barbera*, then later rebroadcast on USA Network's Cartoon Express, on Cartoon Network and on Boomerang. A *Hanna-Barbera Production. Color. Half-hour. Premiered: September 1985. Syndicated. Rebroadcast on USA: September 18, 1989–September 10, 1992. Rebroadcast on CAR: October 1, 1992–January 9, 1993 (weekdays); June 28, 1993–September 18, 1993 (weekdays, Saturdays); October 31, 1994–99 (weekdays). Rebroadcast on BOOM: December 21, 2000–.*

**Voices**
Yogi Bear/Huckleburry Hound/Quick Draw McGraw/Snooper/ Blabbermouse/Augie Doggie/Snagglepuss: Daws Butler; **Boo**

*Yogi Bear and his cartoon pals set forth in search of riches and adventure in Yogi's Treasure Hunt. © Hanna-Barbera Productions*

**Boo/Ranger Smith/Muttley:** Don Messick; **Top Cat:** Arnold Stang; **Doggie Daddy:** John Stephenson; **Dastardly:** Paul Winchell

## YOKO! JAKAMOKO! TOTO!

A colorful trio—Yoko the independent-minded bird of paradise; Jakamoko the steady but slow armadillo; and Toto the cheeky monkey—learn about each other's foibles while working through their problems during one eventful journey after another. Based on an animated short that premiered in America in 2003 at the New York Children's Film Festival, this 52-episode half-hour series, featuring two cartoon adventures per show, aired as part of Cartoon Network's short-lived weekday preschool block *Tickle-U*, featuring *Firehouse Tales, Gerald McBoing Boing, Gordon the Garden Gnome, Harry and His Bucket Full of Dinosaurs,* and *Peppa Pig* as well as other children's cartoon series. A *Collingwood O'Hare/ HIT Entertainment Production. Color. Half-hour. Premiered on CAR: August 22, 2005–March 17, 2006.*

**Voices**
Yoko the Bird of Paradise: Alex Kelly; **Jakamoko the Armadillo:** Gary Martin; **Toto the Monkey:** Rob Rackstraw

## YOUNG ROBIN HOOD

This preteen and teen version of Robin Hood and His Merrie Men (including Will Scarlet and "Brother" Tuck) and other well-known fictional characters (such as Maid Marian and Prince John) from legendary Sherwood Forest, in half-hour animated adventures tracing the origin of the Robin Hood legend was originally produced in Canada and France in 1989 and syndicated in the United States two years later (part of the weekend cartoon block *The Funtastic World of Hanna-Barbera*). Following the path of previous Hanna-Barbera "retro" cartoon series (*Flintstone Kids* and *A Pup Named Scooby-Doo*) of established properties, the series introduced several new characters—Mathilda, Marian's nurse/ escort; Hagalah, a kindly sorceress and Robin Hood's surrogate mother; Gilbert of Griswold, assistant to the Sheriff of Nottingham; and Gertrude, Gilbert's jealous sister—in order to create additional subplots and story lines for each program. In 1994 the series was rebroadcast on Cartoon Network. A *Hanna-Barbera/*

*Cinar/France Animation/Antennae 2 Production in association with Crayon Animation/France Animation/Fils-Cartoons. Color. Half-hour. Premiered: September 1991–1992 (part of The Funtastic World of Hanna-Barbera). Syndicated. Rebroadcast on CAR: October 2, 1994 (Sundays). Rebroadcast on BOOM: June 30, 2002–June 14, 2004.*

*Voices*

**Robin Hood:** Thor Bishopric; **Will Scarlet:** Sonja Ball; **Mathilda:** Kathleen Fee; **Gertrude of Griswold:** Jessalyn Gilsig; **Maid Marian:** Anik Matern; **Sheriff of Nottingham:** A.J. Henderson; **Hagalah:** Bronwen Mantel; **Alan-A-Dale:** Michael O'Reilly; **Prince John:** Michael Rudder; **Little John:** Terrence Scammell; **Brother Truck:** Harry Standjofsky

## ◉ THE YOUNG SENTINELS

Three young teenagers, who represent different races of the world, use their superhuman powers to frustrate evil on planet Earth in this weekly science-fiction/adventure series first broadcast on NBC in 1977. The 13-episode series was moved to a different time slot at midseason and subsequently retitled *Space Sentinels*. *A Filmation Associates Production. Color. Half-hour. Premiered on NBC: September 10, 1977–September 2, 1978.*

*Voices*

**Hercules/Sentinel One:** George DiCenzo; **Astrea:** Dee Timberlake; **Mercury:** Evan Kim; **M.O.:** Ross Hagen

## ◉ YU-GI-OH!: CAPSULE MONSTERS

Yugi and his friends go on a much-needed vacation, thanks to Joey who wins a trip for four to an exotic island destination. After their plane crashes, they meet noted archeologist Dr. Alex Brisbane, only to be suddenly transported into the portal world of Capsule Monsters in this 12-episode action-packed adventure series. Unlike the entire Yu-Gi-Oh series and its predecessor, 2005's *Yu-Gi-Oh!: Grand Championship/Dawn of the Duel* that aired on the WB Television Network's Kids' WB!, this sixth incarnation aired Saturday mornings on FOX. *A Yoshihiro Tagashi/Sheuisha/Fuji TV/Studio Pierot/U.S. Manga Corp./FUNimation Production. Color. Half-hour. Premiered on FOX: September 9, 2006.*

*Voices*

**Yugi Mutou/Yami Yugi:** Dan Green; **Joey Wheeler:** Wayne Grayson; **Tea Gardner:** Amy Birnbaum; **Tristan Taylor:** Frank Frankson; **Solomon Moto:** Maddie Blaustein; **Dr. Alex Brisbane/Alexander the Great:** Pete Zarustica

## ◉ YU-GI-OH!: ENTER THE SHADOW REALM

While playing his favorite card game come-to-life, "Duel Masters," Yugi has to escape from the virtual world or his friends will be stuck forever in the Shadow Realm in this top-rated successor to the WB Television Network's Kids' WB! (and one of television's hottest cartoon series) *Yu-Gi-Oh!: King of Games*. Beginning the series' third season overall in November 2003, this 46-episode anime adventure sequel, revoiced in English by 4Kids Entertainment, aired Saturday mornings for one full season, followed by the franchise's popular fourth installment, *Yu-Gi-Oh! Waking the Dragons*. *A Studio Gallop/NAS/TV Tokyo/4Kids Entertainment Production. Color. Half-hour. Premiered on the WB (Kids' WB!): November 1, 2003–September 4, 2004.*

*Voices*

**Yugi Mutou/Yami Yugi:** Dan Green; **Joey Wheeler/Shadi/Dartz:** Wayne Grayson; **Tea Gardner:** Army Birnbaum; **Seto Kaiba/Guardian Seto:** Eric Stuart; **Mokuba Kaiba:** Tara Jayne; **Serenity**

**Wheeler:** Lisa Ortiz; **Duke Devlin/Rafael/Valon:** Marc Thompson; **Noah Kaiba/Leon von Schroeder:** Andrew Rannells; **Marik Ishtar/Yami Marik:** Jonathan T. Ross; **Fuguta:** Eric Stuart; **Roland:** Wayne Grayson

## ◉ YU-GI-OH!: GRAND CHAMPIONSHIP/ DAWN OF THE DUEL

Following the battle with Dartz, Yugi and his friends compete against duelists from all over the world in a new tournament, the Grand Championship, to become champion of the world, with the villainous duelist Zigfried Von Schroeder attempting to undermine the event. Airing under the title of *Yu-Gi-Oh!: Grand Championship* during the first part of the season, then as *Yu-Gi-Oh!: Dawn of the Duel* during the second half, this fifth season of the hugely successful imported Japanese cartoon series aired Saturday mornings on the WB Television Network's Kids' WB! during the 2005–06 season. After the merger between the WB and UPN created the all-new CW network in September 2006, *Yu-Gi-Oh!* joined FOX's Saturday-morning *FOX Box* program block with an all-new 12-episode series *Yu-Gi-Oh!: Capsule Monsters*. *A Yoshihiro Tagashi/Sheuisha/Fuji TV/Studio Pierot/U.S. Manga Corp./FUNimation Production. Color. Half-hour. Premiered on the WB (Kids' WB!): August 27, 2005–September 2, 2006.*

*Voices*

**Yugi Mutou/Yami Yugi:** Dan Green; **Joey Wheeler/Shadi/Dartz:** Wayne Grayson; **Tea Gardner:** Army Birnbaum; **Seto Kaiba/Guardian Seto:** Eric Stuart; **Mokuba Kaiba:** Caroline Lawson; **Duke Devlin/Rafael/Valon:** Marc Thompson; **Professor Arthur Hawkins/Zorc the Dark One:** Mike Pollock; **Zigfried von Schroeder/Guardian Aknadin:** Pete Zarustica; **Noah Kaiba/Leon von Schroeder:** Andrew Rannells; **Rebecca Hawkins:** Kerry Williams; **Roland:** Wayne Grayson; **Tristan Taylor:** Frank Frankson

## ◉ YU-GI-OH! GX

Living at a prestigious and highly competitive duel academy, where books and computers have been supplanted by Duel Disks and Monster Cards, an entirely new generation of young students, led by the highly gifted Jaden Yuki, train to become the next "King of Games" in this all-new series of animated adventures. The half-hour anime series, featuring 104 episodes during its first two seasons, premiered exclusively on Cartoon Network in October 2005 as part of its Monday-through-Friday afternoon action-adventure block, *Miguzi*. *A NAS/TV Tokyo/Studio Gallop/4Kids Entertainment/FUNimation Production. Color. Half-hour. Premiered on CAR: October 10, 2005–.*

*Voices*

**Jaden Yuki:** Pete Capella; **Syrus Truesdale:** Wayne Grayson; **Zane Truesdale:** Scottie Ray; **Alexis Rhodes:** Priscilla Everett; **Bastion Misawa:** Eric Stuart; **Chazz Princeton:** Anthony Salerno; **Dr. Vellian Crowler:** Sean Schemmel

## ◉ YU-GI-OH!: KING OF THE GAMES

As his powerful alter-ego "Game King," a smaller than average high school student named Yugi morphs into a mighty hero who defeats monsters in his favorite card game in this English-language version adapted from the enormously popular game, Japanese anime and manga franchise created by Kazuki Takahashi. In partnership with Warner Bros., 4Kids Entertainment, which obtained the U.S. merchandising and television rights to the hit Japanese anime series, produced this dubbed version under the new title, *Yu-Gi-Oh!: King of the Games*, for the WB Television Network's

Kids WB! Bowing on the Kids' WB! in September 2001, the half-hour fantasy/adventure series became an instant hit with young viewers—becoming the number-one-ranked program with boys ages six to 11, tweens ages nine to 14 and male tweens ages nine to 14, as well as the number-one broadcast series among boys ages two to 11. Due to the program's remarkable success, the WB Television Network also began airing the 97-episode series during its Monday-through-Friday afternoon cartoon block, and slated a spin-off series (*Yu-Gi-Oh!: Enter the Shadow Realm*), that began airing in the fall of 2003. *A Studio Gallop/NAS/TV Tokyo/4Kids Entertainment Production. Color. Half-hour. Premiered on the WB (Kids' WB!): September 29, 2001–November 9, 2002 (1st season); November 16, 2002–November 1, 2003 (2nd season).*

*Voices*

**Yugi Mutou/Yami Yugi:** Dan Green; **Joey Wheeler/Shadi/Dartz:** Wayne Grayson; **Tea Gardner:** Army Birnbaum; **Mai Valentine:** Megan Hollingshead; **Maximillian Pegasus:** Darren Dunstan; **Seto Kaiba/Guardian Seto:** Eric Stuart; **Mokuba Kaiba:** Tara Jayne; **Solomon Muto/Shimon Muran:** Maddie Blaustein; **Tristan Taylor:** Sam Regal (Episodes 1–10), Frank Frankson (Episodes 11– ); **Ryo Bakura/Yami Bakura/Bandit Keith/Alister/Thief Bakura:** Ted Lewis; **Serenity Wheeler:** Lisa Ortiz; **Weevil Underwood:** Jimmy Zoppi; **Professor Arthur Hawkins/Zorc the Dark One:** Mike Pollock; **Kisara:** Veronica Taylor; **Duke Devlin/Rafael/Valon:** Marc Thompson; **Ishizu Ishtar/Guardian Isis:** Kayzie Rogers; **Noah Kaiba/Leon von Schroeder:** Andrew Rannells; **Odio Ishtar/Guardian Shada:** Michael Alston Baley

## ◎ YU-GI-OH!: WAKING THE DRAGON

After the conclusion of the Battle City Finals, three Egyptian god cards are stolen, a terrifying new villain rears its ugly head and real monsters appear around the world for Yugi and his friends to battle in this fourth-season successor to 2003's *Yu-Gi-Oh!: Enter the Shadow Realm* on the WB Television Network's Kids' WB! Premiering in September 2004, the newly titled half-hour series featured 40 new episodes of the popular Japanese anime series. *A Studio Gallop/NAS/TV Tokyo/4Kids Entertainment Production. Color. Half-hour. Premiered on the WB (Kids' WB!): September 11, 2004–May 28, 2005.*

*Voices*

**Yugi Mutou/Yami Yugi:** Dan Green; **Joey Wheeler/Shadi/Dartz:** Wayne Grayson; **Tea Gardner:** Army Birnbaum; **Mai Valentine:** Megan Hollingshead; **Maximillian Pegasus:** Darren Dunstan; **Seto Kaiba/Guardian Seto:** Eric Stuart; **Mokuba Kaiba:** Tara Jayne; **Ryo Bakura/Yami Bakura/Bandit Keith/Alister/Thief Bakura:** Ted Lewis; **Weevil Underwood:** Jimmy Zoppi; **Professor Arthur Hawkins/Zorc the Dark One:** Mike Pollock; **Kisara:** Veronica Taylor; **Duke Devlin/Rafael/Valon:** Marc Thompson; **Solomon Muto/Shimon Muran:** Maddie Blaustein; **Rex Raptor:** Sebastian Arcelus; **Tristan Taylor:** Frank Frankson; **Roland:** Wayne Grayson

## ◎ YU YU HAKUSHO: GHOST FILES

Returning to Earth from the afterlife after making the noblest of sacrifices to save a child's life, a 14-year-old rebel named Yusuke Urameshi uses his newfound supernatural powers when he joins forces with a motley crew of former rivals (Kuwabara, Kurama and Hiei) to battle criminals caught between the spirit and the real world. This popular half-hour anime series from Japan, created by Yoshihiro Togashi, was added to Cartoon Network's top-rated *Toonami* afternoon action-adventure programming block, airing weekdays at 6:00 P.M. beginning in March 2003. Togashi is married to Naoko Takeuchi, the creator of the anime hit *Sailor Moon*. A

*Yoshihiro Tagashi/Sheuisha/Fuji TV/Studio Pieriot/U.S. Manga Corp./ FUNimation Production. Color. Half-hour. Premiered on CAR: February 23, 2002–March 31, 2006.*

*Voices*

**Yusuke Ukimura:** Justin Cook; **Kazuma Kuwahura:** Christopher R. Sabat; **Botan:** Cynthia Cranz; **Jaganshi Hiei:** Chuck Huber; **Youko Kurama/Shuichi Minamino:** John Burgmeier; **Koenma:** Sean Trague; **Narrator:** Kent Williams; **Atsuko Urameshi:** Meredith McCoy; **Genkai:** Linda Young; **Shizuru:** Kasey Buckley; **Yukima:** Jessica Dismuke; **Kayko:** Laura Bailey; **Other Voices:** Eric Vale

## ◎ ZATCH BELL!

To become the mamodo king over all of Earth's demons, the good-hearted Zatch Bell is faced with his toughest battle: to conquer all of mamodo king-wannabes. With the help of his friend Kiyo, the two become a powerful force in this classic good-versus-evil action anime series. Adapted from the popular manga series by Makoto Raiku and the Toei Animation anime series, Cartoon Network acquired this English-dubbed version, premiering Saturdays at 8:30 P.M. during the network's *Toonami* cartoon block in March 2005. A *Toei Animation/VIZ Media Production. Color. Half-hour. Premiered on CAR: March 1, 2005.*

*Voices*

**Zatch Bell:** Debi Derryberry; **Kiyo:** Jason Spisak; **Brago:** Wally Wingert; **Kanchome:** Richard Horvitz; **Kiddo:** Brianne Sidall; **Dr. Riddles:** Quinton Flynn; **Sherry:** Saffron Henderson; **Suzie:** Colleen O'Shaughnessey; **Li-Ein:** Gwendoline Yeo; **Iwajima/Kane/Wonrei/Others:** Crispin Freeman

## ◎ ZAZOO U

Created by children's author and illustrator Shane DeRolf, this half-hour animated series follows the misadventures of an offbeat, fanciful and diverse menagerie of Americanimals, led by the cool, unflappable Boink, who attend an exceptionally zany institute of higher knowledge where anything can happen. Airing briefly on FOX Network, episodes followed the school day of the series' characters through a series of short, funny and hip vignettes and feature transitions by rappers Rawld-O and Buck, rocking commentary by Boink and his bandmate—gross-out king Grizzle, a razorback hog with a ravenous appetite; Tess, the tough but sweet tomboy; and Bully, the gentle, giant, music-loving "moolly wammouth"—plus at least one poem reading per half-hour. *A Film Roman Production in association with Wang Film Productions/Cuckoo West Studios/FOX Children's Productions. Color. Half-hour. Premiered on FOX: September 8, 1990–January 19, 1991; February 2, 1991–August 31, 1991.*

*Voices*

**Boink:** Michael Horton; **Grizzle:** Jerry Houser; **Logan/Chomper:** Neil Ross; **Ms. Devine:** Tress MacNeille; **Seymour:** Lee Thomas; **Bully:** Brian Cummings; **Rawld-O/Buck/Poem Reader:** Dorian Harewood; **Tess:** Susan Silo; **Rarf:** Danny Mann; **Dr. Russell:** Stu Rosen

## ◎ THE ZETA PROJECT

In the year 2040, a team of National Security Agency agents, led by Agent Bennett, chases down a runaway government robot, Infiltration Unit Zeta, programmed and equipped to destroy and to assume the identity of others, while a 15-year-old street orphan named Rosalie ("Ro") Rowen helps find its creator in order to earn the robot his freedom in this futuristic animated science-fiction spin-off from the WB's *Batman Beyond*. First broadcast Saturday mornings on the WB Television Network's Kids' WB! in January 2001, the 26-episode series, created by Robert Goodman and featuring the voice of Diedrich Bader (of TV's *The Drew Carey Show*) as Zeta, aired for two seasons until it was canceled in August 2002. *A Warner Bros. TV Animation Production. Color. Half-hour. Premiered on the WB (Kids' WB!): January 27, 2001–May 18, 2002; July 13, 2002–August 10, 2002.*

**Voices**
**Zeta/Zee:** Diedrich Bader; **Agent Rush:** Dominique Jennings; **Young Zee:** Scott Marquette, Eli Marienthal; **Rosalie "Ro" Rowen:** Julie Nathanson; **Agent West:** Michael Rosenbaum; **Agent James Bennett:** Kurtwood Smith; **Agent Lee:** Lauren Tom; **Bucky Buenventura:** Ulises Cuadra

### ◎ ZOIDS: CHAOTIC CENTURY

A 17-year-old Republican orphan named Van Flyheight, and Fiona, his female companion, learn about their past while becoming engulfed in the beginning of an epic war on the futuristic planet Zi between two nations, the Empire and the Republic—a war that they try to prevent. The first of five anime series—and four overall—based on the popular Japanese mecha toy models—to air in the United States, this 34-episode half-hour series premiered on Cartoon Network in February 2002. The popular science fiction adaptation was followed by four others: *Zoids: Guardian Force* (with episodes combined with its sequel, *Zoids: Chaotic Century* in April 2002); *Zoids: New Century Zero*; *Zoids: Fuzors*. *A Shogakukan Productions Co. Ltd./Xebec/The Ocean Group/Geneon Entertainment/Viz Media Production. Color. Half-hour. Premiered on CAR: February 18, 2002 (with episodes of "Zoids: Guardian Force" beginning April 5, 2002.)*

**Voices**
**Van Flyheight:** Matthew Erikson; **Fiona:** Carol-Anne Day; **Moonbay:** Onalea Gilbertson; **Irvine:** Mark Gatha; **Raven:** Scott Henrickson; **Gunther Prozen:** Dave Kelly; **Karl Lichen Schubaltz:** Jonathan Love; **Doctor D/Dr. Rosso/Zeke:** Dave Pettit; **Viola:** Meredith Taylor-Parry; **Lieutenant O'Connell:** C. Adam Leigh; **Alina:** Colleen Blackmore; **Maria:** Jennifer Holder; **Marienne/Rosa:** Katie Rowan; **Captain Rob Herman:** Kurtis Sanheim; **Metlenick:** Stephen Holgate; **Colonel Krueger:** Steve Olson; **Phantom:** Tom Edwards

### ◎ ZOIDS: FUZORS

Years later with their battles now moving to the coliseum, R.D. and the Mach Storm team face much more powerful Zoids enemies with enhanced speed and power in this final installment of four half-hour science fiction series to air in the United States on Cartoon Network. *A Voicebox Productions/TOMY/East Japan Marketing & Communications/ShoPro/Hasbro Production. Color. Half-hour. Premiered on CAR: October 4, 2003–February 14, 2004.*

**Voices**
**R.D.:** Brad Swaile; **Sweet:** Nicole Bouna; **Hop:** Russell Roberts; **Sigma:** Ted Cole; **Crime Boss/Leader:** Alec Willows; **Burton:** Alessandro Juliani; **Rastami:** Andrew Kavadas; **Dr. Wolfgang Pierce/Helmut:** Brian Dobson; **Blake/Mark:** Brian Drummond; **Amy/Chiara:** Chiara Zanni; **Deed:** Cusse Mankuma; **Haldo/Mr. Pendergrass:** Dale Wilson; **Matt:** Danny McKinnon; **Vulcan:** Doug Parker; **Tracy:** Jocelyn Loewen; **Announcer:** John Lampinen; **Keefe:** Louis Chirillo; **Bartender/Jean Holiday/Rattle:** Matt Hill; **Bone/Dan:** Michael Dobson; **Angeli/Sarah Slam:** Nicole Oliver; **Marvis:** Paul Dobson; **Gummie/Michael:** Phil Hayes; **Malloy:** Samuel Vincent; **Rastani Sr./Serge/TV Announcer:** Scott McNeil; **Ciao/Female Announcer/Julie/Sandra/Storekeeper:** Tabitha St. Germain; **Jackie:** Ted Cole; **Billy/Dispatch/Fence/Miguel/Nathan:** Terry Klassen; **Rotten Roger:** Trevor Devall; **Gilbert the Impaler/Watts:** Ward Perry

### ◎ ZOIDS: GUARDIAN FORCE

Set four years after the events of *Zoids: Chaotic Century*, an elite multinational peacekeeping force, called the Guardian Force, featuring highly trained soldiers from the Helic Republic and Guylos Empire militaries, thwart the evil efforts of terrorists, dissidents and militant groups that rise up against them. The English-dubbed, 33-episode half-hour series began airing on Cartoon Network in April 2002 with episodes of its predecessor, *Zoids: Chaotic Century*. The series was the third of four adaptations of the famous Japanese mecha toy model series to air in the United States. *A Shogakukan Productions Co. Ltd./Xebec/The Ocean Group/Geneon Entertainment/Viz Media Production. Color. Half-hour. Premiered on CAR: April 5, 2002 (with episodes of "Zoids: Chaotic Century").*

**Voices**
**Van Flyheight:** Matthew Erikson; **Fiona:** Carol-Anne Day; **Moonbay:** Onalea Gilbertson; **Irvine:** Mark Gatha; **Raven:** Scott Henrickson; **Gunther Prozen:** Dave Kelly; **Karl Lichen Schubaltz:** Jonathan Love; **Doctor D/Dr. Rosso/Zeke:** Dave Pettit; **Reese:** Mariette Sluyter; **Viola:** Meredith Taylor-Parry; **Lieutenant Thomas Shubaltz:** Ryan Luhning; **Lieutenant O'Connell:** C. Adam Leigh; **Alina:** Colleen Blackmore; **Maria:** Jennifer Holder; **Marienne/Rosa:** Katie Rowan; **Captain Rob Herman:** Kurtis Sanheim; **Hiltz:** Scott Roberts; **Metlenick:** Stephen Holgate; **Colonel Krueger:** Steve Olson; **Phantom:** Tom Edwards

### ◎ ZOIDS: NEW CENTURY ZERO

On the far-flung planet of Zi, the honorable Bit Cloud and Liger Zero of the Blitz Team use Zoids as their personal weapons to compete in a no-holds-barred, coliseum-style tournament against the no-good Backdraft Group, including the Champ Team, the Fluegels Team and the Zebers Team, in this third half-hour series based on the popular mechanical-model kits by TOMY. The 26-episode science fiction adventure program aired on Cartoon Network. *A Voicebox Productions/TOMY/East Japan Marketing & Communications/ShoPro/Hasbro Production. Color. Half-hour. Premiered on CAR: October 22, 2001–September 20, 2003.*

**Voices**
**Bit Cloud:** Richard Ian Cox; **Leena Toros:** Kelly Sheridan; **Brad Hunter:** Samuel Vincent; **Jamie Hemeros:** Bill Switzer; **Steve Toros:** Ron Halder; **Oscar Hemeros/Jack Cisco:** Brian Drummond; **Dr. Laon:** Michael Dobson; **Harry Champ:** Brad Swaile; **Naomi Fluegel:** Saffron Henderson; **Leon Toros:** Ted Cole; **Mary Champ:** Lisa Ann Beley; **Vega Obscura:** Alex Doduk; **Sarah:** Ellen Kennedy; **Pierce:** Alaina Burnett; **Major Polta/Captain Stigma Stoeller:** Scott McNeil; **Captain Sanders:** Matt Smith; **Altail:** Don Brown

### ◎ ZORAN, SPACE BOY

Accompanied by his pet Space Squirrel, Zoran, a superhero from outer space, travels to Earth looking for his sister only to find action and adventure in this 96-episode, Japanese cartoon import for first-run syndication. *A TCJ Eiken/Global Production. Color. Half-hour. Premiered: 1966. Syndicated.*

### ◎ ZORRO

A legendary figure with all the zest and zeal of a 1990s hero, Zorro, an unmatched horseman and master of sword and whip (whose true identity, as Don Diego de la Vega, is a secret to all but his faithful companions Isabella and Bernardo), unnerves his opponents—notably the Spanish military force, headed by its cruel and ruthless commandant, Capitan Montecero, and aided by his overweight second-in-command, Sergeant Garcia—in his never-ending fight against injustices in this 26-episode half-hour series produced for weekend syndication. A *Fred Wolf Films, Dublin Production in association with Warner Bros. Productions, Warner Bros. International Television, Harvest Entertainment, Carring Productions International and Zorro Productions, Inc. Color. Half-hour. Premiered: (weekend of) September 20, 1997. Syndicated.*

**Voices**
**Diego/Zorro:** Michael Gough; **Isabella:** Jeannie Elias; **Capitan Montecero:** Earl Boen; **Sergeant Garcia:** Tony Pope; **Don Alejandro:** Pat Fraley

## ◎ THE ZULA PATROL

A group of aliens—stalwart Captain Bula; absent-minded, fun-loving scientist Professor Multo; space pilot Zeeter; the amazing space pet Gorga; and twin flying scouts Wizzy and Wigg—travel the galaxies to save the universe from intergalactic danger while teaching children facts about science and astronomy through wacky, fun-filled space-age adventures in this educational half-hour series created and executive produced by Deborah Manchester and Beth Hubbard and written by the multiple Emmy-nominated writing team of Cydne Clark and Steve Granat (*Disney's Doug, 101 Dalmatians, Dennis the Menace*). Produced by the Hatchery LLC, this imaginative and entertaining 26-episode 3-D CGI-animated preschool series (ages four and up) bowed Saturday morning on PBS affiliates nationwide in the fall of 2005. A *MarVista Entertainment/The Hatchery LLC Production. Color. Half-hour. Premiered on PBS Kids: Fall 2005.*

**Voices**
**Captain Bula/Professor Multo:** Cam Clarke

@ @ @ @ @

# AWARDS AND HONORS

@ @ @ @ @

## ACADEMY AWARDS

The Academy of Motion Picture Arts and Science first began recognizing animated cartoons in its annual Oscars derby in the 1931–32 season. Initially the films were nominated under one category—best short subject—along with live-action comedy and novelty short subjects. (The category underwent several changes throughout its history and is now called best short films.) Over the years animated films have garnered nominations in other major categories, including best musical score, best song and many others.

The following is a complete listing of the winners and runners-up in the respective categories for each year. Winners are preceded by an asterisk.

### 1931–32
*Flowers and Trees*, Walt Disney
Mickey's Orphans, Walt Disney
It's Got Me Again, Warner Bros.

### 1932–33
Building a Building, Walt Disney
The Merry Old Soul, Walter Lantz
*The Three Little Pigs*, Walt Disney

### 1934
Holiday Land, Charles Mintz/Columbia
Jolly Little Elves, Walter Lantz
*The Tortoise and the Hare*, Walt Disney

### 1935
The Calico Dragon, MGM
*Three Orphan Kittens*, Walt Disney
Who Killed Cock Robin? Walt Disney

### 1936
*Country Cousin*, Walt Disney
Old Mill Pond, MGM
Sinbad the Sailor, Max Fleischer

### 1937
Educated Fish, Max Fleischer

The Little Match Girl, Charles Mintz/Columbia
*The Old Mill*, Walt Disney

### 1938
Brave Little Tailor, Walt Disney
Mother Goose Goes Hollywood, Walt Disney
*Ferdinand the Bull*, Walt Disney
Good Scouts, Walt Disney
Hunky and Spunky, Max Fleischer

### 1939
Detouring America, Warner Bros.
Peace on Earth, MGM
The Pointer, Walt Disney
*The Ugly Duckling*, Walt Disney

### 1940
*Milky Way*, MGM
Puss Gets the Boot, MGM
A Wild Hare, Warner Bros.
**Best Original Score:** *Pinocchio* (Leigh Harline, Paul J. Smith, Ned Washington)
**Best Song:** "When You Wish Upon A Star" from *Pinocchio* (Leigh Harline, Ned Washington) ·

### 1941
Boogie Woogie Bugle Boy of Company B, Walter Lantz
Hiawatha's Rabbit Hunt, Warner Bros.
How War Came, Columbia
*Lend a Paw*, Walt Disney
The Night Before Christmas, MGM
Rhapsody in Rivets, Warner Bros.
The Rookie Bear, MGM
Rhythm in the Ranks, George Pal Puppetoon
Superman No. 1, Max Fleischer
Truant Officer Donald, Walt Disney
**Best Scoring of a Musical Picture:** *Dumbo* (Frank Churchill, Oliver Wallace)
**Best Song:** "Baby Mine" from *Dumbo* (Frank Churchill, Ned Washington)

*Special Award: Walt Disney, William Garity, John N.A. Hawkins, and the RCA Manufacturing Company for their outstanding contribution in the advancement of sound in motion pictures through the production of *Fantasia* (certificate)

*Special Award: Leopold Stokowski and his associates for their innovative achievement in the creation of a new form of visualized music in *Fantasia*

*Irving Thalberg National Award for Consistent High-Quality Production: Walt Disney

### 1942

*All Out for V*, Terry-Toons
*The Blitz Wolf*, MGM
**The Fuehrer's Face*, Walt Disney
*Juke Box Jamboree*, Walter Lantz
*Pigs in a Polka*, Warner Brothers
*Tulips Shall Grow*, George Pal Puppetoons
**Best Documentary:** *The New Spirit* (Donald Duck), Walt Disney
**Best Documentary:** *The Grain That Built a Hemisphere*, Walt Disney
**Best Song:** "Love Is a Song" from *Bambi* (Frank Churchill, Larry Morey), Walt Disney
**Best Score:** *Bambi* (Frank Churchill, Edward Plumb), Walt Disney
**Best Sound Recording:** *Bambi* (C.O. Slyfield), Walt Disney

### 1943

*The Dizzy Acrobat*, Walter Lantz
*The Five Hundred Hats of Bartholomew Cubbins*, George Pal Puppetoon
*Greetings Bait*, Warner Bros.
*Imagination*, Columbia
*Reason and Emotion*, Walt Disney
**Yankee Doodle Mouse*, MGM
**Best Song:** "Saludos Amigos" from *Saludos Amigos* (Charles Wolcott, Ned Washington), Walt Disney
**Best Sound Recording:** *Saludos Amigos* (C.O. Slyfield), Walt Disney
**Best Scoring of a Musical Picture:** *Saludos Amigos* (Edward H. Plumb, Paul J. Smith, Charles Wolcott), Walt Disney
**Best Scoring of a Dramatic or Comedy Picture:** *Victory Through Air Power* (Edward H. Plumb, Paul J. Smith, Oliver G. Wallace), Walt Disney
**Special Award:** George Pal for the development of novel methods and technique in the production of short subjects known as *Puppetoons* (Plaque)

### 1944

*And to Think I Saw It on Mulberry Street*, George Pal Puppetoon
*The Dog, Cat and Canary*, Columbia
*Fish Fry*, Walter Lantz
*How to Play Football*, Walt Disney
**Mouse Trouble*, MGM
*My Boy, Johnny*, Terry-Toons
*Swooner Crooner*, Warner Bros.

### 1945

*Donald's Crime*, Walt Disney
*Jasper and the Beanstalk*, George Pal Puppetoons
*Life with Feathers*, Warner Brothers
*Mighty Mouse in Gypsy Life*, Terry-Toons
*The Poet & Peasant*, Walter Lantz
**Quiet Please*, MGM
*Rippling Romance*, Columbia
**Best Scoring of a Musical Picture:** *The Three Caballeros* (Edward H. Plumb, Paul J. Smith, Charles Wolcott), Walt Disney

**Best Sound Recording:** *The Three Caballeros* (C.O. Slyfield), Walt Disney
**Best Picture:** *Anchors Aweigh*, MGM (has animated sequence with Jerry Mouse)
**Best Song:** "I Fall in Love Too Easily" from *Anchors Aweigh* (Jules Styne, Sammy Cahn), MGM
**Best Scoring of a Musical Picture:** *Anchors Aweigh* (Georgie Stoll), MGM

### 1946

**The Cat Concerto*, MGM
*Chopin's Musical Moments*, Walter Lantz
*John Henry and the Inky Doo*, George Pal Puppetoons
*Squatter's Rights*, Walt Disney
*Walky Talky Hawky*, Warner Bros.
**Special Scientific or Technical Award:** Arthur F. Blinn, Robert O. Cook, C.O. Slyfield and the Walt Disney Studio Sound Department for the design and development of an audio finder and track viewer for checking location noise in sound tracks (certificate)

### 1947

*Chip 'an' Dale*, Walt Disney
*Dr. Jekyll and Mr. Mouse*, MGM
*Pluto's Blue Note*, Walt Disney
*Tubby the Tuba*, George Pal Puppetoon
**Tweetie Pie*, Warner Bros.
**Best Scoring of a Musical Picture:** *Song of the South* (Daniele Amfitheatrof, Paul J. Smith, Charles Wolcott), Walt Disney
**Best Song:** "Zip-A-Dee-Doo-Dah" from *Song of the South* (Allie Wrubel, Ray Gilbert), Walt Disney
**Special Award:** James Baskette for his able and heartwarming characterizations of Uncle Remus, friend and storyteller to the children of the world (statuette)

### 1948

**The Little Orphan*, MGM
*Mickey and the Seal*, Walt Disney
*Mouse Wreckers*, Warner Bros.
*Robin Hoodlum*, UPA
*Tea for Two Hundred*, Walt Disney
**Best Two-Reel Subject:** *Seal Island*, Walt Disney
**Best Song:** "The Woody Woodpecker Song" from *Wet Blanket Policy* (Ramey Idriss, George Tibbles), Walter Lantz

### 1949

**For Scent-Imental Reasons*, Warner Bros.
*Hatch Up Your Troubles*, MGM
*The Magic Fluke*, UPA
*Toy Tinkers*, Walt Disney
**Best Song:** "Lavender Blue" from *So Dear to My Heart* (Eliot Daniel, Larry Morey), Walt Disney (has animated sequence)
**Special Award:** Bobby Driscoll as the outstanding juvenile actor of 1949 for *So Dear to My Heart*, Walt Disney (miniature statuette)
**Best Documentary Short:** *So Much for So Little* (cartoon), Warner Bros.

### 1950

**Gerald McBoing Boing*, UPA
*Jerry's Cousin*, MGM
*Trouble Indemnity*, UPA
**Best Scoring of a Musical Picture:** *Cinderella* (Oliver Wallace, Paul J. Smith), Walt Disney
**Best Song:** "Bibbidy-Bobbidy-Boo" from *Cinderella* (Mack David, Al Hoffman, Jerry Livingston), Walt Disney

**1951**

Lambert, the Sheepish Lion, Walt Disney
Rooty Toot Toot, UPA
*Two Mouseketeers, MGM
**Best Scoring of a Musical Picture:** Alice in Wonderland (Oliver Wallace), Walt Disney

**1952**

*Johann Mouse, MGM
Little Johnny Jet, MGM
Madeline, UPA
Pink and Blue Blues, UPA
Romance of Transportation, National Film Board of Canada
**Best One-Reel Subject:** Neighbors, National Film Board of Canada/Norman McLaren
**\*Best Documentary Short:** Neighbors, National Film Board of Canada/Norman McLaren

**1953**

Christopher Crumpet, UPA
From A to Z-Z-Z-Z, Warner Bros.
Rugged Bear, Walt Disney
The Tell-Tale Heart, UPA
*Toot, Whistle, Plunk and Boom, Walt Disney
**Best Two-Reel Subject:** Ben and Me, Walt Disney

**1954**

Crazy Mixed-Up Pup, Walter Lantz
Pigs Is Pigs, Walt Disney
Sandy Claws, Warner Bros.
Touché, Pussy Cat!, MGM
*When Magoo Flew, UPA

**1955**

Good Will to Men, MGM
The Legend of Rockabye Point, Walter Lantz
No Hunting, Walt Disney
*Speedy Gonzales, Warner Bros.

**1956**

Gerald McBoing! Boing! on Planet Moo, UPA
The Jaywalker, UPA
*Magoo's Puddle Jumper, UPA
**Best Documentary Short:** Man in Space, Walt Disney

**1957**

*Birds Anonymous, Warner Bros.
One Droopy Knight, MGM
Tabasco Road, Warner Bros.
Trees and Jamaica Daddy, UPA
The Truth About Mother Goose, Walt Disney

**1958**

*Knighty Knight Bugs, Warner Bros.
Paul Bunyan, Walt Disney
Sidney's Family Tree, Terry-Toons

**1959**

Mexicali Shmoes, Warner Bros.
*Moonbird, Storyboard, Inc.
Noah's Ark, Walt Disney
The Violinist, Pintoff Productions
**Best Documentary Short:** Donald in Mathemagic Land, Walt Disney
**\*Special Scientific or Technical Award:** Ub Iwerks of Walt Disney Productions for the design of an improved optical printer for special effects and matte shots

**1960**

Goliath II, Walt Disney
High Note, Warner Bros.
Mouse and Garden, Warner Bros.
*Munro, Rembrandt Films (released by Paramount)
A Place in the Sun, George K. Arthur-Go Pictures, Inc.

**1961**

Aquamania, Walt Disney
Beep Prepared, Warner Bros.
*Ersatz (The Substitute), Zagreb Film
Nelly's Folly, Warner Bros.
The Pied Piper of Guadalupe, Warner Bros.

**1962**

*The Hole, Storyboard, Inc.
Icarus Montgolfier Wright, Format Films
Now Hear This, Warner Bros.
Self Defense—for Cowards, Rembrandt Films
Symposium on Popular Songs, Walt Disney

**1963**

Automania 2000, Halas and Batchelor Productions
*The Critic, Pintoff-Crossbow Productions
The Game, Zagreb Film
My Financial Career, National Film Board of Canada
Pianissimo, Cinema 16
**Best Scoring of Music—Adaptation or Treatment:** The Sword in the Stone (George Bruns), Walt Disney

**1964**

Christmas Cracker, National Film Board of Canada
How to Avoid Friendship, Rembrandt Films
Nudnik No. 2, Rembrandt Films
*The Pink Phink, DePatie-Freleng

**1965**

Clay or the Origin of Species, Eliot Noyes
*The Dot and the Line, MGM
The Thieving Magpie, Giulio Gianini-Emanuele Luzzati

**1966**

The Drag, National Film Board of Canada
*Herb Alpert and the Tijuana Brass Double Feature, Hubley Studio (released by Paramount)
The Pink Blueprint, DePatie-Freleng

**1967**

*The Box, Murakami-Wolf Films
Hypothese Beta, Films Orzeaux
What on Earth! National Film Board of Canada

**1968**

The House That Jack Built, National Film Board of Canada
The Magic Pear Tree, Murakami-Wolf Productions
Windy Day, Hubley Studio (released by Paramount)
*Winnie the Pooh and the Blustery Day, Walt Disney

**1969**

*It's Tough to Be a Bird, Walt Disney
Of Men and Demons, Hubley Studio (released by Paramount)
Walking, National Film Board of Canada

**1970**

The Further Adventures of Uncle Sam: Part Two, The Haboush Company
*Is It Always Right to Be Right? Stephen Bosustow Productions
The Shepherd, Cameron Guess and Associates

**Best Original Song Score:** A Boy Named Charlie Brown (music by Rod McKuen and John Scott Trotter; lyrics by Rod McKuen, Bill Melendez and Al Shean; adapted by Vince Guaraldi)

### 1971

*The Crunch Bird, Maxwell-Petok-Petrovich Productions
Evolution, National Film Board of Canada
The Selfish Giant, Potterton Productions

### 1972

*The Christmas Carol, Richard Williams
Kama Sutra Rides Again, Bob Godfrey Films
Tup Tup, Zagreb Film

### 1973

*Frank Film, Frank Mouris
The Legend of John Henry, Stephen Bosustow-Pyramid Film Production
Pulcinella, Luzzati-Gianini
**Best Song:** "Love" from Robin Hood (music by George Bruns; lyrics by Floyd Huddleston), Walt Disney

### 1974

*Closed Mondays, Lighthouse Productions
The Family That Dwelt Apart, National Film Board of Canada
Hunger, National Film Board of Canada
Voyage to Next, Hubley Studio
Winnie the Pooh and Tigger Too, Walt Disney

### 1975

*Great, British Lion Films, Ltd.
Kick Me, Swarthe Productions
Monsieur Pointu, National Film Board of Canada
Sisyphus, Hungarofilms

### 1976

Dedalo, Cineteam Realizzazioni
*Leisure, Film Australia
The Street, National Film Board of Canada

### 1977

The Bead Game, National Film Board of Canada
The Doonesbury Special, Hubley Studio
Jimmy the C, Motionpicker Productions
*Sand Castle, National Film Board of Canada

### 1978

Oh My Darling, Nico Crama Productions "Rip Van Winkle," Will Vinton/Billy Budd
*Special Delivery, National Board of Canada
**Honorary Award:** Walter Lantz, for bringing joy and laughter to every part of the world through his unique animated motion pictures (statuette)

### 1979

Dream Doll, Godfrey Films/Zagreb Films/Halas and Batchelor
*Every Child, National Film Board of Canada
It's So Nice to Have a Wolf Around the House, AR&T Productions for Learning Corporation of America

### 1980

All Nothing, National Film Board of Canada
*The Fly, Pannonia Film
History of the World in Three Minutes, Michael Mills Productions, Ltd.

### 1981

*Crac, Societ Radio-Canada
The Creation, Will Vinton Productions

The Tender Tale of Cinderella Penguin, National Film Board of Canada

### 1982

The Great Cognito, Will Vinton Productions
The Snowman, Snowman Enterprises, Ltd.
*Tango, Film Polski

### 1983

Mickey's Christmas Carol, Walt Disney Productions
Sound of Sunshine—Sound of Rain, Hallinan Plus
*Sundae in New York, Motionpicker Productions

### 1984

*Charade, Sheridan College
Doctor Desoto, Sporn Animation
Paradise, National Film Board of Canada

### 1985

*Anna & Bella, The Netherlands
The Big Snit, National Film Board of Canada
Second Class Mail, National Film & Television School

### 1986

The Frog, the Dog and the Devil, New Zealand National Film Unit
*A Greek Tragedy, CineTe pvba
Luxo Jr., Pixar Productions
**Best Song:** Somewhere Out There (An American Tail, Universal; music by James Horner and Barry Mann, lyrics by Cynthia Well)

### 1987

George and Rosemary, National Film Board of Canada
*The Man Who Planted Trees, Societe Radio-Canada
Your Face, Bill Plympton

### 1988

The Cat Came Back, National Film Board of Canada
Technological Threat, Kroyer Films, Inc.
*Tin Toy, Pixar

### 1989

*Balance, A Lauenstein Production
The Cow, The "Pilot" Co-op Animated Film Studio with VPTO Videofilm
The Hill Farm, National Film & Television School
**Best Original Song:** "Kiss the Girl" (The Little Mermaid, Walt Disney; music by Alan Menken; lyrics by Howard Ashman)
**\*Best Original Song:** "Under the Sea" (The Little Mermaid, Walt Disney; music and lyrics by Alan Menken and Howard Ashman)

### 1990

A Grand Day Out, National Film & Television School
*Creature Comforts, Aardman Animations Ltd. Production
Grasshoppers (Cavallette), Bruno Bozetto Productions

### 1991

Blackfly, National Film Board of Canada
*Manipulation, Tandem Films Production
Strings, National Film Board of Canada
**Best Picture:** Beauty and the Beast, Walt Disney
**Best Original Song:** "Belle" (Beauty and the Beast, Walt Disney; music and lyrics by Alan Menken and Howard Ashman)
**Best Original Song:** "Be Our Guest" (Beauty and the Beast, Walt Disney; music and lyrics by Alan Menken and Howard Ashman)

**\*Best Original Song:** "Beauty and the Beast" (*Beauty and the Beast*, Walt Disney; music and lyrics by Alan Menken and Howard Ashman)

**Best Sound:** *Beauty and the Beast*, Walt Disney (David J. Hudson, Doc Kane, Mel Metcalfe and Terry Porter)

*1992*

*Adam*, Aardman Animations Ltd. Production

*\*Mona Lisa Descending a Staircase*, Joan C. Gratz Production

*Reci, Reci, Reci . . . (Words, Words, Words)*, Kratky Film Production

*Screen Play*, Bare Boards Film Production

*The Sandman*, Batty Berry Mackinson Production

**Best Original Song:** "Friend Like Me" (*Aladdin*, Walt Disney; music and lyrics by Alan Menken and Howard Ashman)

**\*Best Original Song:** "A Whole New World" (*Aladdin*, Walt Disney, music and lyrics by Alan Menken and Howard Ashman)

**Best Sound:** *Aladdin*, Walt Disney (David J. Hudson, Doc Kane, Mel Metcalfe, Terry Porter)

**Best Sound Effects Editing:** *Aladdin*, Walt Disney (Mark Mangini)

*1993*

*Blindscape*, National Film & Television School

*Small Talk*, Bob Godfrey Films

*The Mighty River*, Canadian Broadcasting Corporation/Societe Radio-Canada Production

*\*The Wrong Trousers*, Aardman Animations Ltd. Production

*1994*

*\*Bob's Birthday*, Snowden Fine Animation "The Big Story," Spitting Image Production

*The Janitor*, Vanessa Schwartz Production

*The Monk and the Fish*, Folimage Valence Production

*Triangle*, Gingco Ltd. Production

**\*Best Original Score:** *The Lion King*, Walt Disney (music and lyrics by Elton John and Tim Rice)

**Best Original Song:** "Hakuna Matata" (*The Lion King*, Walt Disney; music and lyrics by Elton John and Tim Rice)

**Best Original Song:** "Circle of Life" (*The Lion King*, Walt Disney; music and lyrics by Elton John and Tim Rice)

**\*Best Original Song:** "Can You Feel the Love Tonight" (*The Lion King*, Walt Disney; music and lyrics by Elton John and Tim Rice)

*1995*

*\*A Close Shave*, Aardman Animations Ltd. Production

*Gagarin*, Second Frog Animation Group Production

*Runaway Brain*, Walt Disney Pictures Production

*The Chicken from Outer Space*, Stretch Films/Hanna-Barbera/Cartoon Network Production

*The End*, Alias/Wavefront Production

**Best Original Music or Comedy Score:** *Toy Story*, Walt Disney (music and lyrics by Randy Newman)

**Best Original Song:** "You've Got a Friend in Me" (*Toy Story*, Walt Disney; music and lyrics by Randy Newman)

**Best Screenplay (Written Directly for the Screen):** *Toy Story*, Walt Disney (Joel Cohen, Peter Docter, John Lasseter, Joe Ranft, Alec Sokolow, Andrew Stanton, Joss Whedon)

**\*Special Achievement Award:** John Lasseter, *Toy Story*, Walt Disney

*1996*

*Canhead*, Timothy Hittle Production

*La Salla*, National Film Board of Canada

*\*Quest*, Thomas Stellmach Animation Production

*Wat's Pig*, Aardman Animations Ltd. Production

**Best Original Musical or Comedy Score:** *The Hunchback of Notre Dame*, Walt Disney (music by Alan Menken and lyrics by Stephen Scwartz).

**Best Original Musical or Comedy Score:** *James and the Giant Peach*, Walt Disney (music and lyrics by Randy Newman).

*1997*

*Famous Fred*, TVC London Production

*\*Geri's Game*, Pixar Animation Production

*La Vielle Dame et Les Pigeons (The Old Lady and the Pigeons)*, Production Pascal Blais

*The Mermaid*, Film Company DAGO/Alexander Pictures Production

*Redux Riding Hood*, Walt Disney Television Animation Production

**Best Song:** "Go the Distance" (*Hercules*, Walt Disney; music by Alan Menken and lyrics by David Zippel)

**Best Song:** "Journey to the Past" (*Anastasia*, 20th Century-Fox; music and lyrics by Diane Warren)

**Best Original Musical or Comedy Score:** *Anastasia*, 20th Century-Fox (music by Stephen Flaherty and lyrics by Lynn Ahrens)

*1998*

*\*Bunny*, Blue Sky Studios

*The Canterbury Tales*, 54C-BBC Wales/HBO

*Jolly Roger*, Astley Baker-Silver Bird for Channel 4

*More*, Bad Clams Productions/Swell Productions/Flemington Productions

*When Life Departs*, A. Film Productions

**Best Original Musical or Comedy Score:** *A Bug's Life*, Buena Vista Pictures (music and lyrics by Randy Newman)

**Best Original Musical or Comedy Score:** *Mulan*, Walt Disney (music by Matthew Wilder and Jerry Goldsmith; lyrics by David Zipple)

**Best Original Musical or Comedy Score:** *The Prince of Egypt*, Dreamworks (music and lyrics by Stephen Schwartz and Hans Zimmer)

**Best Original Song:** "The Prayer" (*Quest for Camelot*, Warner Bros.; music and lyrics by Carol Bayer Sager, David Foster, Tony Renis and Alberto Testa)

**Best Original Song:** "When You Believe" (*The Prince of Egypt*, Dreamworks; music and lyrics by Stephen Schwartz)

*1999*

*Humdrum*, Aardman Animations Limited

*My Grandmother Ironed The King's Shirts*, National Film Board of Canada/Studio Magica a.s.

*\*The Old Man and the Sea*, Productions Pascal Blais/Imagica Corp./Dentsu Tech./NHK Enterprise 21/Panorama Studio of Yaroslavl

*3 Misses*, CinéTé Film

*When the Day Breaks*, National Film Board of Canada

**Best Song:** \*"You'll Be in My Heart" (*Tarzan*, Walt Disney Pictures; music by Phil Collins)

**Best Song:** "Blame Canada" (*South Park: Bigger Longer & Uncut*, Paramount Pictures/Warner Bros.; music and lyrics by Marc Shaiman)

**Best Song:** "When She Loved Me" (*Toy Story 2*, Buena Vista; music and lyrics by Randy Newman)

*2000*

*\*Father and Daughter*, Cinete Filmproductie bv/Cloudrunner Ltd.

*The Periwig Maker*, Ideal Standard Film

*Rejected*, Bitter Films
**Best Song:** "My Funny Friend and Me" (*The Emperor's New Groove*, Walt Disney Pictures; music by Sting and lyrics by David Hartley)

## 2001

*Fifty Percent Grey*, Zanita Films
\*For the Birds, Pixar Animation
*Give Up Yer Aul Sins*, Irish Film Board/Radio Telefis Eireann/Arts Council/Brown Bag Films
*Strange Invaders*, National Film Board of Canada
*Stubble Trouble*, Calabash Animation
**Best Animated Feature:**
\*Shrek, DreamWorks SKG
*Jimmy Neutron: Boy Genius*, Paramount Pictures
*Monsters, Inc.*, Buena Vista
**Best Effects, Sound Effects Editing:** *Monsters, Inc.*, Buena Vista, Gary Rydstrom, Michael Silvers
**Best Screenplay (Based on Material Previously Produced or Published): Shrek,** DreamWorks SKG, Ted Elliott, Terry Rossio, Joe Stillman, Roger S.H. Schulman
**Best Song:** \*"If I Didn't Have You" (*Monsters, Inc.*, Buena Vista; music and lyrics by Randy Newman)
**Best Original Score:** *Monsters, Inc.*, Buena Vista (music and lyrics by Randy Newman)

## 2002

*The Cathedral*, Platige Image
\*The ChubbChubbs!, Sony Pictures Imageworks
*Das Rad*, Filmakademie Baden-Württemberg GmbH
*Mike's New Car*, Pixar Animation Studios
*Mr. Head*, Yamamura Animation
**Best Animated Feature:**
\*Spirited Away, Buena Vista
*Ice Age*, 20th Century Fox
*Lilo & Stitch*, Buena Vista
*Spirit: Stallion of the Cimarron*, Buena Vista
*Treasure Planet*, Buena Vista
**Best Song:** "Father and Daughter" (*The Wild Thornberrys Movie*, Paramount Pictures/Nickelodeon Movies; music and lyrics by Paul Simon)

## 2003

*Boundin'*, Pixar Animation Studios
*Destino*, Walt Disney Pictures
*Gone Nutty*, Blue Sky Studios
\*Harvie Krumpet, Melodrama Pictures
*Nibbles*, Acme Filmworks
**Best Animated Feature:**
\*Finding Nemo, Buena Vista
*Brother Bear*, Buena Vista
*The Triplets of Belleville*, Sony Pictures Classics
**Best Original Score:** *Finding Nemo*, Buena Vista; music and lyrics by Thomas Newman
**Best Screenplay (Written Directly for the Screen):** *Finding Nemo*, Buena Vista; screenplay/story by Andrew Stanton and screenplay by Bob Peterson and David Reynolds
**Best Song:** "Belleville Rendez-Vous," *The Triplets of Belleville*, Sony Pictures Classics; music by Benoit Charets and lyrics by Sylvain Chomet
**Best Sound Editing:** *Finding Nemo*, Buena Vista, Gary Rydstrom, Michael Silvers

## 2004

*Birthday Boy*, Australian Film, Television and Radio School
*Gopher Broke*, Blur Studio
*Guard Dog*, Bill Plympton
*Lorenzo*, Walt Disney Pictures
\*Ryan, National Film Board of Canada/Copper Heart Entertainment
**Best Animated Feature:**
\*The Incredibles, Buena Vista
*Shark Tale*, DreamWorks SKG
*Shrek 2*, DreamWorks SKG
**Best Song:** "Believe," *The Polar Express*, DreamWorks SKG; music and lyrics by Glen Ballard and Alan Silvestri
**Best Song:** "Accidentally in Love," *Shrek 2*, DreamWorks SKG; music/lyrics by Adam Duritz, music by Jim Bogios, David Immergluck, Matthew Malley and David Bryson, and lyrics by Dan Vickrey
**Best Sound:** *The Incredibles*, Buena Vista, Randy Thom, Gary Rizzo, Doc Kane
**Best Sound:** *The Polar Express*, DreamWorks SKG, William B. Kaplan, Randy Thom, Tom Johnson, Dennis S. Sands
**Best Sound Editing:** \*The Incredibles, Buena Vista, Michael Silvers, Randy Thom
**Best Sound Editing:** *The Polar Express*, Buena Vista, Randy Thom, Dennis Leonard

## 2005

*Badgered*, National Film and Television School
\*The Moon and the Son: An Imagined Conversation, John Canemaker Production
*The Mysterious Geographic Explorations of Jasper Morello*, 3D Films
*9*, Shane Acker Production
*One Man Band*, Pixar Animation Studios
**Best Animated Feature:**
*Wallace & Gromit: The Curse of the Were-Rabbit*, DreamWorks Animation SKG
*Howl's Moving Castle*, Buena Vista
*Corpse Bride*, Warner Bros.

## 2006

\*The Daniest Poet, National Film Board of Canada
*Lifted*, Buena Vista
*The Little Matchgirl*, Buena Vista
*Maestro*, SzimplaFilm
*No Time For Nuts*, 20th Century Fox
**Best Animated Feature:**
*Cars*, Buena Vista
\*Happy Feet, Warner Bros.
*Monster House*, Sony Pictures Releasing
**Best Song:** "Our Town," *Cars*, Buena Vista, music and lyrics by Randy Newman

## EMMY AWARDS

In 1949, following the formation of the National Academy of Television Arts and Sciences, the annual presentation of the Emmy Awards was born. Local and national awards shows were organized to honor local television station programming and prime-time entertainment programming that aired on the three major networks. The awards presentation ceremony became an annual event in 1957. Animated cartoons have been the recipients of Emmys throughout the history of the awards. A complete listing of Emmy-nominated cartoon series and prime-time animated specials follows. Winners are preceded by an asterisk.

## 1959–60

**Outstanding Achievement in the Field of Children's Programming:**

*Huckleberry Hound* (Syndicated)
*Quick Draw McGraw* (Syndicated)

### 1960–61
**Outstanding Achievement in the Field of Children's Programming:**
*Huckleberry Hound* (Syndicated)

### 1965–66
**Outstanding Children's Program:**
*\*A Charlie Brown Christmas* (CBS)

### 1966–67
**Outstanding Children's Program:**
*\*Jack and the Beanstalk* (NBC)
*Charlie Brown's All-Stars* (CBS)
*It's the Great Pumpkin, Charlie Brown* (CBS)

### 1973–74
**Outstanding Children's Special:**
*A Charlie Brown Thanksgiving* (CBS)

### 1974–75
**Outstanding Children's Special:**
*\*Yes, Virginia There Is a Santa Claus* (CBS)
*Be My Valentine, Charlie Brown* (CBS)
*Dr. Seuss' the Hoober-Bloob Highway* (CBS)
*It's the Easter Beagle, Charlie Brown* (CBS)
**Outstanding Entertainment Children's Series:**
*\*Star Trek* (NBC)
*The Pink Panther* (NBC)

### 1975–76
**Outstanding Children's Special:**
*\*You're a Good Sport, Charlie Brown* (CBS)
**Outstanding Informational Children's Special:**
*\*Happy Anniversary, Charlie Brown* (CBS)

### 1976–77
**Outstanding Children's Special:**
*It's Arbor Day, Charlie Brown* (CBS)
*The Little Drummer Boy, Book II* (NBC)

### 1977–78
**Outstanding Children's Special:**
*\*Halloween Is Grinch Night* (ABC)
*A Connecticut Yankee in King Arthur's Court* (CBS)
*The Fat Albert Christmas Special* (CBS)

### 1978–79
**Outstanding Animated Program:**
*\*The Lion, the Witch and the Wardrobe* (CBS)
*You're the Greatest, Charlie Brown* (CBS)
*Happy Birthday, Charlie Brown* (CBS)

### 1979–80
**Outstanding Animated Program:**
*\*Carlton Your Doorman* (CBS)
*Dr. Seuss' Pontoffel Rock, Where Are You?* (ABC)
*Pink Panther in Olym-Pinks* (ABC)
*She's a Good Skate, Charlie Brown* (CBS)

### 1980–81
**Outstanding Children's Program:**
*Paddington Bear* (PBS)
**Outstanding Animated Program:**
*\*Life Is a Circus, Charlie Brown* (CBS)
*Bugs Bunny: All American Hero* (CBS)
*Faeries* (CBS)

*Gnomes* (CBS)
*It's Magic, Charlie Brown* (CBS)

### 1981–82
**Outstanding Animated Program:**
*\*The Grinch Grinches the Cat in the Hat* (ABC)
*A Charlie Brown Celebration* (CBS)
*The Smurf Springtime Special* (NBC)
*Smurfs* (NBC)
*Someday You'll Find Her, Charlie Brown* (CBS)

### 1982–83
**Outstanding Animated Program:**
*\*Ziggy's Gift* (CBS)
*Here Comes Garfield* (CBS)
*Is This Goodbye, Charlie Brown?* (CBS)
*The Smurfs Christmas Special* (NBC)
*What Have We Learned, Charlie Brown?* (CBS)

### 1983–84
**Outstanding Animated Program:**
*\*Garfield on the Town* (CBS)
*A Disney Christmas Gift* (NBC)
*It's Flashbeagle, Charlie Brown* (CBS)
*The Smurfic Games* (NBC)

### 1984–85
**Outstanding Animated Program (Daytime):**
*\*Jim Henson's Muppet Babies* (CBS)
*Alvin and the Chipmunks* (NBC)
*Fat Albert and the Cosby Kids* (Syndicated)
*Smurfs* (NBC)
**Outstanding Animated Program (Nighttime):**
*\*Garfield in the Rough* (CBS)
*Donald Duck's 50th Birthday* (CBS)
*Snoopy's Getting Married* (CBS)

### 1985–86
**Outstanding Animated Program (Daytime):**
*\*Jim Henson's Muppet Babies* (CBS)
*CBS Storybreak* (CBS)
*The Charlie Brown and Snoopy Show* (CBS)
*Fat Albert and the Cosby Kids* (Syndicated)
*The Smurfs* (NBC)
**Outstanding Animated Program (Nighttime):**
*\*Garfield's Halloween Special* (CBS)
*Garfield in Paradise* (CBS)

### 1987–87
**Outstanding Animated Program (Daytime):**
*\*Jim Henson's Muppet Babies* (CBS)
*Alvin and the Chipmunks* (NBC)
*Disney's Adventures Of The Gummi Bears* (NBC)
*Punky Brewster* (NBC)
*The Smurfs* (NBC)
**Outstanding Animated Program (Nighttime):**
*\*Cathy* (CBS)
*Garfield Goes Hollywood* (CBS)

### 1987–88
**Outstanding Animated Program (Daytime):**
*\*Jim Henson's Muppet Babies* (CBS)
*Alvin and the Chipmunks* (NBC)
*CBS Storybreak* (CBS)
*Disney's DuckTales* (Syndicated)
*The Smurfs* (NBC)
**Outstanding Animated Program (Nighttime):**

*A Claymation Christmas Celebration (CBS)
Brave Little Toaster (Disney)
A Garfield Christmas Special (CBS)

### 1988–89
**Outstanding Animated Program (Daytime):**
*The New Adventures of Winnie the Pooh (ABC)
DuckTales (Syndicated)
Jim Henson's Muppet Babies (CBS)
A Pup Named Scooby-Doo (ABC)
The Smurfs (NBC)
**Outstanding Animated Program—For Programming More Than One Hour (Nighttime):**
*Disney's DuckTales: Super DuckTales (NBC)
**Outstanding Animated Program—For Programming Less Than One Hour (Nighttime):**
*Garfield: Babes and Bullets (CBS)
Abel's Island (PBS)
Garfield: His Nine Lives (CBS)
Madeline (HBO)
Meet the Raisins (CBS)

### 1989–90
**Outstanding Animated Program (Daytime):**
*The New Adventures of Winnie the Pooh (ABC)
*Beetlejuice (ABC)
**Outstanding Animated Program—One Hour or Less (Nighttime):**
*The Simpsons (Fox)
Garfield's Feline Fantasies (CBS)
Garfield's Thanksgiving (CBS)
Why, Charlie Brown, Why? (CBS)
The Simpsons Christmas Special (FOX)

### 1990–91
**Outstanding Animated Program (Daytime):**
Bobby's World (Fox)
Captain Planet and the Planeteers (TBS)
Garfield and Friends (CBS)
Slimer! and the Real Ghostbusters (ABC)
*Tiny Toon Adventures (Syndicated)
**Outstanding Animated Program—One Hour or Less (Nighttime):**
Garfield Gets a Life (CBS)
*The Simpsons (FOX)
Tiny Toon Adventures: The Looney Beginning (CBS)
Will Vinton's Claymation Comedy of Horrors (CBS)

### 1991–92
**Outstanding Animated Program (Daytime):**
Darkwing Duck (ABC/Syndicated)
Doug (Nickelodeon)
The New Adventures of Winnie the Pooh (ABC)
*Rugrats (Nickelodeon)
Tiny Toon Adventures (Syndicated)
**Outstanding Animated Program—One Hour or Less (Nighttime):**
A Claymation Easter (CBS)
The Ren & Stimpy Show (Nickelodeon)
Shelly Duvall's Bedtime Stories (Showtime)
*The Simpsons (FOX)

### 1991–92
**Outstanding Achievement in Animation:**
*Will Vinton's Claymation Comedy of Horrors (CBS), Teresa Drilling, Animator; Jeff Mulcaster, Animator

### 1992–93
**Outstanding Animated Program (Daytime):**
*Tiny Toon Adventures (Syndicated)
Batman: The Animated Series (FOX)
Disney's Darkwing Duck (ABC)
Doug (Nickelodeon)
Rugrats (Nickelodeon)
**Outstanding Animated Program—One Hour or Less (Nighttime):**
*Batman: The Animated Series (FOX)
Inspector Gadget Saves Christmas (NBC)
Liquid Television (MTV)
The Ren & Stimpy Show (Nickelodeon)
The World of Peter Rabbit and Friends: The Tale of Peter Rabbit and Benjamin Bunny (The Family Channel)

### 1992–93
**Outstanding Achievement in Animation:**
*A Claymation Easter (CBS), John Ashlee Pratt, Principal Animator

### 1993–94
**Outstanding Animated Program (Daytime):**
*Rugrats (Nickelodeon)
Batman: The Animated Series (FOX)
The Halloween Tree (Syndicated)
Rugrats (Nickelodeon)
Animaniacs (FOX)
**Outstanding Animated Program—One Hour or Less (Nighttime):**
Duckman (USA)
Flintstones Family Christmas (ABC)
The Ren & Stimpy Show (Nickelodeon)
*The Roman City (PBS)
The Town Santa Forgot (NBC)

### 1993–94
**Outstanding Achievement in Animation:**
*Shakespeare: The Animated Tales (HBO), Natalia Demidova, Production Designer; Peter Kotor, Production Designer
*Shakespeare: The Animated Tales (HBO), Sergei Glagolev, Animator; Demitri Norosyolov, Animator

### 1994–95
**Outstanding Animated Program (Daytime):**
*Where on Earth Is Carmen Sandiego? (FOX)
Animaniacs (FOX)
Disney's Aladdin (CBS)
Disney's the Little Mermaid (CBS)
Rugrats (Nickelodeon)
**Outstanding Animated Program—One Hour or Less (Nighttime):**
Dexter's Laboratory in "Changes" (Cartoon Network)
Dr. Seuss' Daisy-Head Mayzie (TNT)
A Rugrats Passover (Nickelodeon)
*The Simpsons (FOX)
Steven Spielberg Presents Tiny Toons Night Ghoulery (FOX)

### 1994–95
**Outstanding Performer in an Animated Program:**
Tim Skullmaster, Mighty Max (Syndicated)
*Lily Tomlin, Scholastic's The Magic School Bus (PBS)
Roscoe Lee Browne, Spider-Man: The Animated Series (FOX)
Rita Moreno, Where on Earth Is Carmen Sandiego? (FOX)
Ruby Dee, Whitewash (HBO)

### 1995–96
**Outstanding Animated Program (Daytime):**

*Animaniacs* (WB Television Network)
*The New Adventures of Madeline* (ABC)
*Scholastic's The Magic School Bus* (PBS)
*Where on Earth Is Carmen Sandiego?* (FOX)
**Outstanding Animated Program—One Hour or Less (Nighttime):**
*Cow and Chicken* in "No Smoking" (Cartoon Network)
*Dexter's Laboratory* (Cartoon Network)
*Duckman* (USA)
\**A Pinky & the Brain Christmas Special* (WB)
*The Simpsons* (FOX)

**1995–96**
**Outstanding Achievement in Animation:**
\**Shakespeare: The Animated Tales* (HBO), Natasha Dabizha, *Animator*
**Outstanding Performer in an Animated Program:**
\**Nathan Lane, *The Lion King's Timon and Pumbaa* (CBS/Syndicated)
Ernie Sabella, *The Lion King's Timon and Pumbaa* (CBS/Syndicated)
Lily Tomlin, *Scholastic's The Magic School Bus* (PBS)
Ed Asner, *Spider-Man: The Animated Series* (FOX)
Rita Moreno, *Where on Earth Is Carmen Sandiego?* (FOX)

**1996–97**
**Outstanding Children's Animated Program (Daytime):**
\**Stephen Spielberg Presents Animaniacs* (WB Television Network)
*Pinky & The Brain* (WB Television Network)
*Scholastic's The Magic School Bus* (PBS)
*Schoolhouse Rock* (ABC)
*Where on Earth Is Carmen Sandiego?* (FOX)

**1996–97**
**Outstanding Children's Animated Program (Special Class):**
\**Freakazoid* (WB)
*The New Adventures of Madeline* (FAM)
*Superman* (WB)
**Outstanding Performer in an Animated Program:**
Dennis Franz, *Disney's Mighty Ducks* (ABC)
\**Louie Anderson, *Life with Louie* (FOX)
Lily Tomlin, *Scholastic's The Magic School Bus* (PBS)
Rob Paulsen, *Steven Spielberg Presents Pinky & the Brain* (WB)
Rita Moreno, *Where on Earth Is Carmen Sandiego?* (FOX)
**Outstanding Achievement in Animation:**
*Boo to You Too! Winnie the Pooh* (CBS), Phil Weinstein, *Storyboard Artist*
*Testament: The Bible in Animation* (HBO), Gary Hurst, *Production Designer*
*The Willows in Winter* (The Family Channel), Loraine Marshall, *Color Director*
**Outstanding Animated Program—One Hour or Less (Nighttime):**
*Dexter's Laboratory* (Cartoon Network)
*Duckman* (USA)
*King of the Hill* (FOX)
*Rugrats* (Nickelodeon)
\**The Simpsons* (FOX)
*The Willows in Winter* (The Family Channel)

**1997–98**
**Outstanding Children's Animated Program (Daytime):**
\**Arthur* (PBS)
*Disney's 101 Dalmations: The Series* (ABC)
*Scholastic's The Magical School Bus* (PBS)

*Steven Spielberg Presents Animaniacs* (WB)
*Steven Spielberg Presents Pinky & The Brain* (WB)
**Outstanding Children's Animated Program (Special Class):**
*Genie's Great Minds* (ABC)
*The Sylvester & Tweety Mysteries* (WB)
*The Wacky World of Tex Avery* (Syndicated)
\**The New Batman/Superman Adventures* (WB)
**Outstanding Performer in an Animated Program:**
Robin Williams, *Genie's Great Minds* (ABC)
\**Louie Anderson, *Life with Louie* (FOX)
Lily Tomlin, *Scholastic's The Magic School Bus* (PBS)
Maurice LaMarche, *Steven Spielberg Presents Pinky & the Brain* (WB)
Rob Paulsen, *Steven Spielberg Presents Pinky & the Brain* (WB)
**Outstanding Achievement in Animation:**
\**The Lion King's Timon and Pumbaa* (CBS), Kexx Singleton, *Color Director*
\**The Magic Pearl,* (ABC), Barbara Schade, *Background Artist*

**1998–99**
**Outstanding Children's Animated Program (Daytime):**
\**Arthur* (PBS)
*Steven Spielberg Presents Pinky, Elmyra & the Brain* (WB)
*Disney's Doug* (ABC)
*Steven Spielberg Presents Animaniacs* (WB)
*Disney's 101 Dalmations: The Series* (ABC)
**Outstanding Children's Animated Program (Special Class):**
*How Things Work* (ABC)
*Life with Louie* (FOX)
*The New Batman/Superman Adventures* (WB)
*Rolie Polie Olie* (Disney Channel)
\**Steven Spielberg Presents Pinky and the Brain* (WB)
**Outstanding Performer in an Animated Program:**
Dom DeLuise, *All Dogs Go to Heaven* (FOX)
Ernest Borgnine, *All Dogs Go to Heaven* (FOX)
Louie Anderson, *Life with Louie* (FOX)
Jeffrey Tambor, *Lionhearts* (Syndicated)
\**Rob Paulsen, *Steven Spielberg Presents Pinky and the Brain* (WB)
**Outstanding Achievement in Animation**
\**Spawn* (HBO), Eric Radomski, *Production Designer*
**Outstanding Animated Program (For Programming One Hour or Less) (Nighttime):**
*Cow and Chicken* (Cartoon Network)
*Dexter's Laboratory* (Cartoon Network)
*King of the Hill* (FOX)
*South Park* (Comedy Central)
\**The Simpsons* (FOX)

**1999–2000**
**Outstanding Children's Animated Program (Daytime):**
*Arthur* (PBS)
*Disney's Doug* (ABC)
*Maurice Sendak's Little Bear* (Nickelodeon)
*The New Batman/Superman Adventures* (WB)
\**Steven Spielberg Presents Pinky, Elmyra and the Brain* (WB)
**Outstanding Children's Animated Program (Special Class):**
*Angela Anaconda* (FOX Family Channel)
*Batman Beyond* (WB)
*Disney's Mickey MouseWorks* (ABC)
*The Sylvester & Tweety Mysteries* (WB)
\**Rolie Polie Olie* (Disney Channel)
**Outstanding Performer in an Animated Program:**
French Stewart, *Disney's Hercules* (ABC)
\**James Woods, *Disney's Hercules* (ABC)

Pam Grier, *Happily Ever After: Fairy Talles for Every Child: "The Empress' Nightingale"*

Robert Guillaume, *Happily Ever After: Fairy Tales for Every Child: "The Empress' Nightingale"*

**Outstanding Children's Program (Nighttime):**
*Winnie the Pooh Thanksgiving* (ABC)
*Nick News Special Edition: The Clinton Crisis* (Nickelodeon)
*Rosie O'Donnell's Kids Are Punny* (HBO)
*Rugrats* (Nickelodeon)
*\*The Truth about Drinking: The Teen Files* (Syndicated)

**Outstanding Animated Program (For Programming More Than One Hour):**
*Our Friend, Martin* (STARZ!)
*\*Todd McFarlane's Spawn* (HBO)

**Outstanding Animated Program (For Programming One Hour or Less):**
*Futurama* (FOX)
*\*King of the Hill* (FOX)
*The PJs* (FOX)
*The Powerpuff Girls* (Cartoon Network)
*The Simpsons* (FOX)

**Outstanding Achievement in Animation:**
*\*Animated Epics: The Canterbury Tales: Leaving London—The Wife of Bath Tales* (HBO), Joanna Quinn, *Animator*
*\*Animated Epics: The Canterbury Tales: Leaving London—The Wife of Bath Tales* (HBO), Joanna Quinn, *Production Design*
*\*Animated Epics: The Canterbury Tales: Leaving London—The Wife of Bath Tales* (HBO), Ashley Potter, *Background Artist*
*\*Animated Epics: The Canterbury Tales: Leaving London—The Wife of Bath Tales* (HBO), Les Mills, *Color Direction*

## 2000–01
**Outstanding Children's Animated Program (Daytime):**
*\*Arthur* (PBS)
*Clifford the Big Red Dog* (PBS)
*Dragon Tales* (PBS)
*Madeline* (Disney Channel)
*The Wild Thornberrys* (Nickelodeon)

**Outstanding Children's Animated Program (Special Class):**
*Angela Anaconda* (FOX Family Channel)
*\*Batman Beyond* (WB)
*Disney/Pixar's Buzz Lightyear of Star Command* (ABC)
*Roughnecks: The Starship Trooper Chronicles* (Syndicated)
*Sherlock Holmes in the 22nd Century* (FOX Kids)

**Outstanding Performer in an Animated Program:**
Kel Mitchell, *Cifford the Big Red Dog* (PBS)
Cree Summer, *Clifford the Big Red Dog* (PBS)
John Ritter, *Clifford the Big Red Dog* (PBS)
*Nathan Lane, *Disney's Teacher's Pet* (ABC)
Ruby Dee, *Little Bill* (Nickelodeon)

**Outstanding Children's Program (Nighttime):**
*Disney's Young Musicians Symphony Orchestra In Concept* (Disney Channel)
*\*Goodnight Moon and Other Sleepytime Tales* (HBO)
*Here's to You Charlie Brown: 50 Great Years!* (CBS)
*\*The Color of Friendship* (Disney Channel)

**Outstanding Animated Program (For Programming More Than One Hour):**
*Olive, The Other Reindeer* (FOX)
*\*Walking with Dinosaurs* (Discovery Channel)

**Outstanding Animated Program (For Programming One Hour or Less):**
*Family Guy* (FOX)
*MTV Downtown* (MTV)

*South Park* (Comedy Central)
*The Powerpuff Girls* (Cartoon Network)
*\*The Simpsons* (FOX)

**Outstanding Achievement in Animation:**
*Futurama* (FOX), Bari Kumar, *Color Stylist*
*Goodnight Moon and Other Sleepytime Tales* (HBO), Maciek Albrecht, *Production Designer*
*The PJs* (FOX), Nelson Lowry, *Art Director*
*The Powerpuff Girls* (Cartoon Network), Don Shank, *Art Director*

## 2001–02
**Outstanding Children's Animated Program (Daytime):**
*Arthur* (PBS)
*Dragon Tales* (PBS)
*\*Madeline* (Disney Channel)
*Clifford the Big Red Dog* (PBS)
*Dora the Explorer* (Nickelodeon)

**Outstanding Special Class Children's Animated Program:**
*Batman Beyond* (WB)
*\*Disney's Teacher's Pet* (ABC)
*Disney's the Legend of Tarzan* (Syndicated)
*Little Bill* (Nickelodeon)

**Outstanding Performer in an Animated Program:**
Alicia Silverstone, *Braceface* (ABC Family)
Kel Mitchell, *Clifford the Big Red Dog* (PBS)
John Ritter, *Clifford the Big Red Dog* (PBS
Stacie Chan, *Jackie Chan Adventures* (WB)
*Charles Shaugnessy, *Stanley* (Disney Channel)

**Outstanding Children's Program ((Nighttime):**
*King Gimp* (HBO)
*Nick News with Linda Ellerbee* (Nickelodeon)
*Peter Pan Starring Cathy Rigby* (A&E)
*Rugrats* (Nickelodeon)
*\*The Teen Files: Surviving High School* (UPN)

**Outstanding Animated Program (For Programming More Than One Hour):**
*\*Allosaurus: A Walking with Dinosaurs Special* (Discovery Channel)

**Outstanding Animated Program (For Programming One Hour or Less):**
*As Told by Ginger* (Nickelodeon)
*Futurama* (FOX)
*King of the Hill* (FOX)
*The Powerpuff Girls* (Cartoon Network)
*\*The Simpsons* (FOX)

**Outstanding Achievement in Animation:**
*\*Futurama* (FOX), Rodney Clouden, *Storyboard Artist*
*\*Gary And Mike* (UPN), Curt Enderle, *Art Director*
*\*Gary And Mike* (UPN), Brad Schiff, *Lead Animator*
*\*Invader ZIM* (Nickelodeon), Kyle Menke, *Storyboard Artist*

## 2002–03
**Outstanding Children's Animated Program (Daytime):**
*Arthur* (PBS)
*Clifford the Big Red Dog* (PBS)
*Dora the Explorer* (Nickelodeon)
*Dragon Tales* (PBS)
*\*Rugrats* (Nickelodeon)

**Outstanding Special Class Children's Animated Program:**
*Ozzy & Drix* (Kids' WB!)
*Rolie Polie Olie* (Disney Channel)
*\*Disney's Teacher's Pet* (ABC)
*My Fair Madeline* (Nickelodeon)

**Outstanding Performer in an Animated Program:**

John Ritter, *Clifford the Big Red Dog* (PBS)
Walter Cronkite, *Liberty's Kids* (PBS)
Ruby Dee, *Little Bill* (Nickelodeon)
*Gregory Hines, *Little Bill* (Nickelodeon)
Mindy Cohn, *What's New, Scooby-Doo?* (Kids' WB!)
**Outstanding Children's Program (Nighttime):**
*Nick News Special Edition: Faces of Hope: The Kids* (Nickelodeon)
*Nick News with Linda Ellerbee* (Nickelodeon)
*Rugrats* (Nickelodeon)
*SpongeBob SquarePants* (Nicklelodeon)
*The Making of "A Charlie Brown Christmas"* (ABC)
**Outstanding Animated Program (For Programming More Than One Hour):**
*Trilogy (Samurai Jack)* (Cartoon Network)
*Walking with Prehistoric Beasts* (Discovery Channel)
*When Dinosaurs Roamed America* (Discovery Channel)
**Outstanding Animated Program (For Programming One Hour or Less):**
*As Told by Ginger* (Nickelodeon)
*Futurama* (FOX)
*King of the Hill* (FOX)
*South Park* (Comedy Central)
*The Simpsons* (FOX)
**Outstanding Achievement In Animation:**
*Animated Tales of the World* (HBO), Andrey Zolotoukhine, *Production Designer*
*'Twas the Night* (HBO), Maciek Albrecht, *Production Designer*
*'Twas the Night* (HBO), Maciek Albrecht, *Animator*

## 2003–04
**Outstanding Children's Animated Program (Daytime):**
*Disney's Kim Possible* (Disney Channel)
*Dora the Explorer* (Nickelodeon)
*Little Bill* (Nickelodeon)
*Rugrats* (Nickelodeon)
**Outstanding Special Class Children's Animated Program:**
*Disney's Fillmore!* (ABC)
*Duck Dodgers* (Cartoon Network)
*Ozzy & Drix* (WB)
*Rolie Polie Olie* (Disney Channel)
*Static Shock* (Kids' WB!)
*Tutenstein* (NBC)
**Outstanding Performer in an Animated Program:**
John Ritter, *Clifford the Big Red Dog* (PBS)
Henry Winkler, *Clifford's Puppy Days* (PBS)
Nancy Cartwright, *Kim Possible* Disney Channel)
*Joe Alaskey, *Duck Dodgers* (Cartoon Network)
Walter Cronkite, *Liberty's Kids* (PBS)
**Outstanding Animated Program (For Programming More Than One Hour) (Nighttime):**
*Chased by Dinosaurs* (Discovery Channel)
**Outstanding Animated Program (For Programming One Hour or Less):**
*As Told by Ginger* (Nickelodeon)
*Disney's Kim Possible* (Disney Channel)
*Futurama* (FOX)
*SpongeBob SquarePants* (Nickelodeon)
*The Simpsons* (FOX)
**Outstanding Achievement in Animation:**
*Samurai Jack* (Cartoon Network), Dan Krall, *Layout Artist*
*Samurai Jack* (Cartoon Network), Scott Wills, *Art Director*
*Through a Child's Eyes: September 11, 2001* (HBO), Maciek Albrecht, *Animator*

## 2004–05
**Outstanding Children's Animated Program (Daytime):**
*Arthur* (PBS)
*Dora the Explorer* (Nickelodeon)
*Kim Possible* (Disney Channel)
*Peep and the Big Wide World* (TLC)
*ToddWorld* (TLC)
**Outstanding Special Class Children's Animated Program:**
*The Batman* (Kids' WB!)
*Duck Dodgers* (Cartoon Network)
*Rolie Polie Olie* (Disney Channel)
**Outstanding Performer in an Animated Program:**
Mel Brooks, *Jakers! The Adventures of Piggley Winks* (PBS)
Christy Carlson Romano, *Kim Possible* (Disney Channel)
Joan Cusack, *Peep and the Big Wide World* (TLC)
Kevin Michael Richardson, *The Batman* (Kids' WB!)
*Henry Winkler, *Clifford's Puppy Days* (PBS)
**Outstanding Children's Program (Nighttime):**
*Happy to Be Nappy and Other Stories of Me* (HBO)
*Lizzie McGuire* (Disney Channel)
*Nick News Special Edition—Courage to Live: Kids* (Nickelodeon)
*Nick News Special Edition—There's No Place Like Home* (Nickelodeon)
*Sesame Street Presents "The Street We Live On"* (PBS)
**Outstanding Animated Program (For Programming More Than One Hour):**
*Star Wars: Clone Wars* (Cartoon Network)
*The Powerpuff Girls: Twas the Fight before Christmas* (Cartoon Network)
**Outstanding Animated Program (For Programming One Hour or Less):**
*Futurama* (FOX)
*Samurai Jack* (Cartoon Network)
*South Park* (Comedy Central)
*SpongeBob SquarePants* (Nickelodeon)
*The Simpsons* (FOX)
**Outstanding Achievement in Animation:**
*My Life As a Teenage Robot* (Nickelodeon), Seonna Hong, *Background Stylist*

## 2005–06
**Outstanding Children's Animated Program (Daytime):**
*Arthur* (PBS)
*Baby Looney Tunes* (Cartoon Network)
*Dora the Explorer* (Nickelodeon)
*Jakers! The Adventures of Piggley Winks* (PBS)
*Peep and the Big Wide World* (Discovery Kids)
*ToddWorld* (Discovery Kids)
**Outstanding Children's Animated Program:**
*The Batman* (Kids WB!)
*Coconut Fred's Fruit Salad Island!* (Kids' WB!)
*The Save-Ums!* (Discovery Kids)
*Tutenstein* (NBC)
**Outstanding Performer in an Animated Program:**
*Maile Flanagan, *Jakers! The Adventures of Piggley Winks* (PBS)
Russi Taylor, *Jakers! The Adventures of Piggley Winks* (PBS)
Tara Strong, *Jakers! The Adventures of Piggley Winks* (PBS)
Tony Jay, *Miss Spüder's Sunny Patch Friends* (Nickelodeon)
Jess Harnell, *Pet Alien* (Cartoon Network)
**Outstanding Children's Program (Nighttime):**
*Classical Baby* (HBO)
*Nick News with Linda Ellerbee: Never Again? From the Holocaust to Sudan* (Nickelodeon)
*Pride* (A&E)

*That's So Raven* (Disney Channel)
*Zoey 101* (Nickelodeon)
**Outstanding Animated Program (For Programming More Than One Hour):**
*Dragons: A Fantasy Made Real* (Animal Planet)
*\*Star Wars Clone Wars Vol. 2 (Chapters 21–25)* (Cartoon Network)
**Outstanding Animated Program (For Programming One Hour or Less):**
*Family Guy* (FOX)
*Samurai Jack* (Cartoon Network)
*\*South Park* (Comedy Central)
*SpongeBob SquarePants* (Nickelodeon)
*The Simpsons* (FOX)
**Outstanding Achievement in Animation:**
*\*Classical Baby* (HBO), Barbara Wierzchowska, *Animator (Bear Hugs)*
*\*Foster's Home for Imaginary Friends* (Cartoon Network), Craig McCracken, *Character Design*
*\*Foster's Home for Imaginary Friends* (Cartoon Network), Mike Moon, *Art Direction*
*\*Foster's Home for Imaginary Friends* (Cartoon Network), Ed Baker, *Storyboard Artist*
*\*Samurai Jack* (Cartoon Network), Bryan Andrews, *Storyboard Artist*
*\*Star Wars Clone Wars Vol. 2 (Chapters 21–25)* (Cartoon Network), Justin Thompson, *Background Supervisor*
*\*The Fairly OddParents* (Nickelodeon), Gordon Hammond, *Character Designer*
*\*The Powerpuff Girls* (Cartoon Network), Frederick Gardner, *Background Designer*

## 2006–07
**Outstanding Children's Animated Program (Daytime):**
*Arthur* (PBS)
*Baby Looney Tunes* (Cartoon Network)
*Dora the Explorer* (Nickelodeon)
*Jakers! The Adventures of Piggley Winks* (PBS)
*Peep and the Big Wide World* (Discovery Kids)
*ToddWorld* (Discovery Kids)
**Outstanding Animated Program (Special Class):**

*The Batman* (Kids WB!)
*Coconut Fred's Fruit Salad Island!* (Kids WB!)
*Save-Ums!* (Discovery Kids)
*Tutenstein* (NBC)
**Outstanding Performer in an Animated Program:**
*\*Maile Flanagan, *Jakers! The Adventures of Piggley Winks* (PBS)
Russi Taylor, *Jakers! The Adventures of Piggley Winks* (PBS)
Tara Strong, *Jakers! The Adventures of Piggley Winks* (PBS)
Tony Jay, *Miss Spider's Sunny Patch Friends* (Nickelodeon)
Jess Harnell, *Pet Alien* (Cartoon Network)
**Outstanding Children's Program (Nighttime):**
*Classical Baby 2* (HBO)
*\*High School Musical* (Disney)
*\*I Have Tourette's But Tourette's Doesn't Have Me* (HBO)
*Nick News with Linda Ellerbee: Do Something! Caring for the Kids of Katrina* (Nickelodeon)
**Outstanding Animated Program (For Programming More Than One Hour):**
*\*Before the Dinosaurs* (Discovery Channel)
*Escape from Cluster Prime* (Nickelodeon)
**Outstanding Animated Program (For Programming One Hour or Less):**
*Camp Lazlo* (Cartoon Network)
*Family Guy* (FOX)
*Foster's Home for Imaginary Friends* (Cartoon Network)
*South Park* (Comedy Central)
*\*The Simpsons* (FOX)
**Outstanding Achievement in Animation:**
*\*Classical Baby 2* (HBO), Jarek Szyszko, *Animator for* "The Hippo Dance"
*\*Escape from Cluster Prime* (Nickelodeon), Bryan Arnett, *Character Design*
*\*Foster's Home for Imaginary Friends* (Cartoon Network), Shannon Tindle, *Character Designer*
*\*Robot Chicken* (Cartoon Network), Sarah E. Meyer, *Animator*
*\*The Grim Adventures of Billy & Mandy* (Cartoon Network), Mike Diederich, *Storyboard Artist*
*\*The Life and Times of Juniper Lee* (Cartoon Network), Frederick Gardner, *Background Key Designer*

# MILESTONES OF ANIMATION

Major milestones in animation history since its inception.

**1899:** Arthur Melbourne produces the stop-motion public service announcement, *Matches: An Appeal*, featuring stop-motion images of moving matches.

**1900:** Animation pioneer James Stuart Blackton debuts "The Enchanted Drawings," with his stop-motion chalk drawings.

**1905:** Spanish animator Segundo de Chomon's *The Electric Hotel* premieres, bringing to life a myriad of stop-motion objects.

**1908:** Pioneer French animator Emile Cohl employs cutout animation and other techniques in his acclaimed film *Fantasmagorie*.

**1914:** Cartoonist-turned-animator Winsor McCay (as part of his vaudeville act) unveils the first animated film—and the industry's first real cartoon star—*Gertie the Dinosaur*.

**1914–15:** John Randolph Bray and Earl Hurd create the first patented system of animation—transforming drawings onto celluloid sheets—with a registration system to keep images in place.

**1915:** Cartoon pioneer Max Fleischer patents his famed Rotoscope process.

**1915:** Special effects animator Willis O'Brien creates his first stop-motion film *The Dinosaur and the Missing Link*. He will later direct the revolutionary stop-motion animation for *The Lost World* (1925) and the original *King Kong* (1933).

**1917:** Italian artist Quirino Christiani produces what may have been the first animated feature, *El Apostol*, which may have been animated or a series of non-animated drawings—no print of the film exists.

**1918:** Winsor McCay produces, directs and animates the first serious animated reenactment of an historical event, *The Sinking of the Lusitania*.

**1920:** Bray Pictures Corporation produces the first color cartoon, *The Debut of Thomas Cat*, using the primitive two-color Brewster Color process.

**1921:** Legendary animator Walt Disney animates his first "Newman Laugh-O-Gram"—and first film—sold to theater chain owner Frank L. Newman.

**1921:** German filmmaker Walther Ruttman produces the first abstract film, "Light Play, Opus I," accompanying the 13-minute film on the cello.

**1923:** Oskar Fischinger's *Wax Experiments* is given its first public showing in Germany.

**1924:** Max and Dave Fleischer produce the first sound cartoon, "Mother Pin a Rose on Me," for its *Song Car-Tunes* series, using the Lee DeForest Phonofilm sound process.

**1926:** German animator Lotte Reiniger animates the first—and fully verified—full-length animated feature, *Adventures of Prince Achmed*, using her silhouette technique. The film premieres in Berlin.

**1927:** Oskar Fischinger screens his acclaimed *R-1, A Form Play* using five 35 millimeter movie projectors and a slide projector.

**1928:** Walt Disney directs the first synchronized talking sound cartoon, *Steamboat Willie*.

**1930:** NBC's experimental TV station features toy filmdom's greatest silent cartoon star, Felix the Cat, in a series of test broadcasts.

**1932:** French filmmaker Berthold Bartosch produces the first animated film dealing with serious social issues, *L'Idea*.

**1932:** Walt Disney produces the first cartoon using three-strip Technicolor, the *Silly Symphony*, "Flowers and Trees."

**1933:** Disney's beloved *Silly Symphony* cartoon "Three Little Pigs" shows the possibilities of personality animation by featuring cartoon characters with different personalities.

**1933:** Alexandre Alexeieff and Claire Parker produce the first film using pinscreen animation, "Night on Bald Mountain."

**1933:** Lillian Friedman becomes the first woman animator in the United States, for Max Fleischer Studios.

**1934:** Max Fleischer successfully uses table-top animation to create the illusion of depth in the Betty Boop color cartoon "Poor Cinderella," while Ub Iwerks and Walt Disney achieve a greater three-dimensional effect using the famed multiplane animation technique in Iwerks's Willie Whopper cartoon "The Cave Man" (1934) and Disney's *Silly Symphony* cartoon "The Old Mill" (1937).

**1937:** Walt Disney releases the first commercially successful full-length animated feature in America, *Snow White and the Seven Dwarfs*.

**1937:** Animators for New York's Fleischer Studio stage the industry's first major strike.

**1938:** Former Disney animator Chad Grothkopf produces the first animated show for a network, NBC, the eight-minute, black-and-white cartoon, "Willie the Worm," that debuts on 50 television sets that April.

**1940:** Disney uses the first multichannel stereo system, known as "Fantasound," in six theaters for the animated classic *Fantasia*.

**1941:** Felix the Cat creator Otto Messmer animates the world's first television commercials for Botany Ties, shown on NBC-TV in New York until 1949.

**1941:** Walt Disney animators launch the costliest labor strike in industry history.

**1950:** Television's first limited animated cartoon, *Crusader Rabbit*, created by Alex Anderson and produced by Jay Ward, airs on television in Los Angeles.

**1953:** Walt Disney, Walter Lantz and Famous Studios produce America's first 3-D theatrical cartoons, Disney's "Melody" and "Working for Peanuts" starring Donald Duck, Lantz's "Hypnotic Hick" with Woody Woodpecker, and Famous's "The Ace of Space" featuring the spinach-gulping sailor Popeye.

**1956:** Television's first half-hour network cartoon show featuring new animation expressly made for television, *The Gerald McBoing Boing Show*, debuts on CBS.

**1957:** Bill Hanna and Joe Barbera introduce their first animated television series, *The Ruff and Reddy Show*, using their system of limited animation.

**1958:** The first completely new half-hour cartoon series, *The Huckleberry Hound Show*, premieres in syndication, featuring episodes with Huckleberry Hound, Yogi Bear and Pixie and Dixie.

**1959:** Jay Ward's beloved animated series, *Rocky and His Friends*, becomes television's first animated series to be animated abroad, in Mexico.

**1960:** Hanna-Barbera's prehistoric comedy series, *The Flintstones*, becomes television's first prime-time animated series.

**1960:** Disney is the first to use a Xerox process to ink cels in the theatrical cartoon show *Goliath II*, and, a year later produces the first feature to use the process, *101 Dalamatians*.

**1961:** Parental groups protest the violence in animated kids' cartoons like UPA's *The Dick Tracy Show*, with a growing protest over similar violence displayed in later cartoon shows, including Hanna-Barbera's *The Adventures of Jonny Quest* and *The Fantastic Four*.

**1961:** Japanese animation is introduced in America with great success in the imported animated features *Magic Boy*, *Panda and the Magic Serpent*, and *Alakazam the Great* and Osamu Tezuka's syndicated TV favorite, *Astro Boy*, in 1963.

**1962:** UPA's "Mister Magoo's Christmas Carol" becomes the first made-for-TV animated special and first animated TV special on NBC.

**1964:** Disney's *Mary Poppins* becomes the first feature to use a sodium loss process to produce special effects mattes.

**1969:** The Federal Trade Commission pulls *Linus, the Lionhearted* off the air, citing in its decision that television commercial characters could not star in television programs.

**1972:** Ralph Bakshi produces the first X-rated animated feature in America, *Fritz the Cat*.

**1981:** Television's animated adventure *Strawberry Shortcake in the Big Apple City*, becomes the first "modern" animated half-hour advertisement for a popular toy line.

**1984:** Robert Abel & Associates produces television's first commercial for the Canned Food Information Council, "Sexy Robot," using computer-generated 3-D character animation.

**1985:** The first made-for-TV cartoon series stripped for five days a week in syndication, *He-Man and the Masters of the Universe*, airs across the country.

**1986:** Don Bluth produces the first successful independently produced feature, *An American Tail*.

**1986:** John Lasseter directs the widely distributed computer-animated short *Luxo Jr.*

**1987:** The first direct-to-video cartoon features, *G.I. Joe the Movie* and *Through the Looking Glass*, are released.

**1988:** Disney produces the landmark live-action/animated feature, *Who Framed Roger Rabbit*, restoring the industry's vitality at the box office and resulting in a boom in animation.

**1990:** FOX debuts *The Simpsons*, the first prime-time animated series since Hanna-Barbera's *Wait 'Till Your Father Gets Home*.

**1990:** Walt Disney's *Rescuers Down Under* becomes the first cartoon feature to use computerized ink instead of hand-inked cels.

**1991:** Nickelodeon premieres the first original cartoon shows, *Rugrats, Doug* and *The Ren & Stimpy Show*, made for basic cable.

**1992:** Independent animator Bill Plympton produces the first widely successful feature produced, directed and animated by a single person, *The Tune*.

**1992:** Television's first 24-hour animation network Cartoon Network, is launched.

**1994:** Walt Disney's *The Lion King* becomes the industry's first property to top a billion dollars in revenue.

**1995:** Pixar Animation produces the first all-computer-animated full-length feature, *Toy Story*.

**1999:** Paramount Pictures' feature-length spin-off, *South Park: Bigger, Longer and Uncut*, is awarded the industry's first NC-17 rating.

**1999:** *Pokémon the First Movie: Mewto Strikes Back* becomes the most successful foreign-made animated feature in American movie history.

**1999:** John R. Dilworth's *Courage, the Cowardly Dog* becomes the first animated television program shown in HDTV besides conventional formats.

**2000:** Disney produces the first animated feature released in 70 millimeter to IMAX theaters, *Fantasia/2000*.

**2001:** *Final Fantasy: The Spirits Within*, inspired by the best-selling series of video games, becomes the first photo-realistic, computer-generated feature film to be released.

**2002:** DreamWorks' blockbuster computer-animated feature, *Shrek* (2001), becomes the first film to win an Academy Award for best animated feature, a category introduced this year.

**2002:** Legendary Japanese animator Hayo Miyazaki's *Spirited Away* becomes the highest grossing Japanese movie of all time, and also was the first anime feature film receive an Academy Award for best animated feature a year later.

**2003:** Pixar Animation and Walt Disney's *Finding Nemo* tops Disney's *The Lion King* as the highest grossing animated film with $339,714,978 and $864,624, 978 in box-office revenue worldwide.

**2003:** Disney announces plans to discontinue producing traditionally hand-drawn animated features, with the release of *Home on the Range* becoming its last 2-D animated film, and will switch to producing 3-D full CGI animated films popularized by Pixar thereafter.

**2004:** DreamWorks' animated sequel, *Shrek 2*, bypasses Pixar's *Finding Nemo* (2003) with the biggest opening ever for an animated feature and goes on to become the highest-grossing animated film of all time, with total domestic revenues of $441,226,247, and $919.8 million worldwide.

**2005:** Paramount Pictures acquires DreamWorks SKG studio, co-founded in 1994 by Steven Spielberg, Jeffrey Katzenberg, and David Geffen, for $1.6 billion, marking the studio's demise after producing some of the most critically acclaimed and financially successful films during its 11-year existence.

**2006:** Following a 12-year co-financing and distribution partnership, the Walt Disney Company buys Pixar Animation Studios Inc. for $7.4 billion in stock, concluding their previous deal in June 2006 after Pixar's completion of the computer-animated adventure, *Cars* (2006).

# SELECTED BIBLIOGRAPHY

Adamson, Joe. *Tex Avery: King of Cartoons*. New York: Popular Film Library, 1975.

———. *The Walter Lantz Story*. New York: Putnam, 1985.

Bakshi, Ralph. *The Animated Art of Ralph Bakshi*. Norfolk, Va.: Donning Company Publishers, 1989.

Beck, Jerry. *The Animated Movie Guide*. Chicago: Chicago Review Press, 2005.

Beck, Jerry, and Friedwald, Will. *Looney Tunes and Merrie Melodies: A Complete Illustrated Guide to the Warner Bros. Cartoons*. New York: Henry Holt, 1989.

Blanc, Mel, and Bashe, Phillip. *That's Not All Folks!: My Life in the Golden Age of Cartoons and Radio*. New York: Warner Books, 1988.

Brooks, Tim, and Marsh, Earle. *The Complete Guide to Prime Time Network TV Shows: 1946–Present*. New York: Ballantine Books, 1988.

Cabarga, Leslie. *The Fleischer Story*. New York: DaCapo Press, 1988.

Canemaker, John. *Felix: The Twisted Tale of the World's Most Famous Cat*. New York: Pantheon Books, 1991.

———. *Winsor McCay: His Life & Art*. New York: Abbeville Press, 1987.

Crafton, Donald. *Before Mickey: The Animated Film 1898–1928*. Cambridge, Mass.: MIT Press, 1982.

Culhane, Shamus. *Animation from Script to Screen*. New York: St. Martin's Press, 1990.

———. *Talking Animals and Other People*. New York: St. Martin's Press, 1986.

Edera, Bruno. *Full Length Animated Feature Films*. New York: Hastings House, 1977.

Erickson, Hal. *Television Cartoon Shows, Second Edition. 1949–2003*. Jefferson, N.C.: McFarland & Company, 2005.

Fischer, Stuart. *Kids' TV: The First 25 Years*. New York: Facts On File, 1983.

Gifford, Denis. *American Animated Films: The Silent Era, 1897–1929*. New York: McFarland & Company, 1990.

Grant, John. *Walt Disney's Encyclopedia of Animated Characters*. New York: Harper & Row, 1987.

Grossman, Gary H. *Saturday Morning TV*. New York: Arlington House, 1987.

Jones, Chuck. *Chuck Amuck: The Life & Times of an Animated Cartoonist*. New York: Farrar Straus & Giroux, 1989.

Lenburg, Jeff. *The Great Cartoon Directors*. Jefferson, N.C.: McFarland & Company, 1983.

Maltin, Leonard. *Of Mice and Magic*. New York: McGraw-Hill, 1980.

McNeil, Alex. *Total Television: A Comprehensive Guide to Programming from 1948 to 1980*. New York: Penguin, 1980.

Peary, Danny, and Peary, Gerald. *The American Animated Cartoon: A Critical Anthology*. New York: E.P. Dutton, 1980.

Schneider, Steve. *That's All Folks!: The Art of Warner Bros. Animation*. New York: Henry Holt, 1988.

Sennett, Ted. *The Art of Hanna-Barbera: Fifty Years of Creativity*. New York: Viking, 1989.

Terrace, Vincent. *Encyclopedia of Television Series, Pilots and Specials: 1937–1973*. New York: New York Zoetrope.

———. *Encyclopedia of Television Series, Pilots and Specials: 1974–1984*. New York: New York Zoetrope.

Woolery, George. *Children's Television: The First Thirty-Five Years, 1946–1981*. (Part I: Animated Cartoon Series.) Metuchen, N.J.: Scarecrow Press, 1983.

# INDEX

Boldface numbers indicate major treatment of a topic; *italic* numbers indicate illustrations.